CARSWELL

Constitutional Law of Canada

2021 Student Edition

PETER W. HOGG
(Founding author)

Former Professor Emeritus, Osgoode Hall Law School
York University, Toronto

Former Scholar in Residence,
Blake, Cassels & Graydon, LLP,
Toronto

WADE K. WRIGHT
(As of 2021)

Faculty of Law
Western University, London

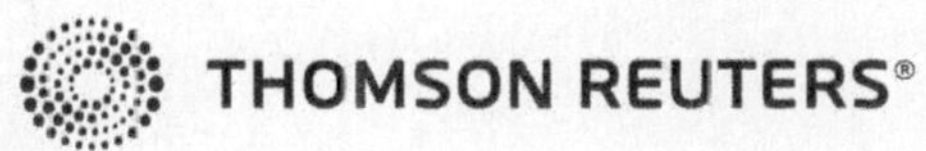

Mat #42869586

A cataloguing record for this publication is available from Library and Archives Canada

ISBN 978-1-7319-0805-6
ISSN 1914-1262

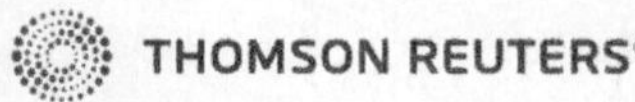

THOMSON REUTERS CANADA, A DIVISION OF THOMSON REUTERS CANADA LIMITED

One Corporate Plaza
2075 Kennedy Road
Toronto, ON
M1T 3V4

Customer Support
1-416-609-3800 (Toronto & International)
1-800-387-5164 (Toll Free Canada & U.S.)
Fax 1-416-298-5082 (Toronto)
Fax 1-877-750-9041 (Toll Free Canada Only)
E-mail CustomerSupport.LegalTaxCanada@TR.com

In Memory of Peter W. Hogg CC, QC, FRSC

With great sadness, we mark the passing of Peter W. Hogg, a pillar in the legal community and leading authority on Canadian constitutional law. He was Scholar-in-Residence at Blakes for many years, providing advice and counsel to government, served as counsel for the Government of Canada in several prominent cases, including the Same-Sex Marriage Reference in 2004. We greatly cherish our five decades' long association with Peter as author of Constitutional Law of Canada. Peter's great warmth and intelligence will be missed.

Preface to the Student Edition, 2021

This student edition is an abridgement of the two-volume loose-leaf edition of *Constitutional Law of Canada*, the fifth edition of which was completed by Peter Hogg in the spring of 2007. The abridgement contains the text of the loose-leaf edition (which includes changes made since 2007, including my first update as the new author), but with the omission of 25 of the 60 chapters. The idea is to produce a book that is suitable for student use. The soft cover and the smaller size make the book less expensive, and it is also less bulky to carry around.

The 35 chapters that have been retained in this student edition are those that Peter (and now I) judged mostly likely to be useful to students. They have been retained in full, without any alteration from the loose-leaf edition, including to the chapter numbering. In the case of the omitted 25 chapters, a student who wishes to consult those chapters will need to go to the full loose-leaf edition of the book, which is available in print and electronically. In the student editions up to and including the 2020 Student Edition, the titles of the omitted 25 chapters were listed in the table of contents, and the titles and contents of these chapters were also listed at the appropriate place in the book. Unfortunately, this is no longer possible for technical reasons. For the sake of convenience, here is a list of the titles of the omitted 25 chapters:

Part I: Basic Concepts
- Chapter 10: The Crown
- Chapter 11: Treaties
- Chapter 13: Extraterritorial Competence

Part II: Distribution of Powers
- Chapter 19: Criminal Justice
- Chapter 23: Companies
- Chapter 24: Financial Institutions
- Chapter 25: Bankruptcy and Insolvency
- Chapter 26: Citizenship
- Chapter 27: The Family
- Chapter 29: Public Property
- Chapter 30: Natural Resources
- Chapter 31: Taxation
- Chapter 33: Social Security

Part III: Civil Liberties
- Chapter 46: Mobility
- Chapter 48: Unreasonable Search or Seizure
- Chapter 49: Arbitrary Detention or Imprisonment
- Chapter 50: Rights on Arrest or Detention
- Chapter 51: Rights on Being Charged
- Chapter 52: Trial within Reasonable Time
- Chapter 53: Cruel and Unusual Punishment
- Chapter 54: Self-incrimination
- Chapter 57: Education

Part IV: Practice
- Chapter 58: Effect of Unconstitutional Law
- Chapter 59: Procedure
- Chapter 60: Proof

Toronto
Wade K. Wright
June 2021

Preface to the Fifth Edition

This is the preface for my first update as the new author of *Constitutional Law of Canada*. This preface is intended to be read together with the original preface to the fifth edition of *Constitutional Law of Canada* prepared by Peter Hogg. It does not repeat, but rather supplements, the information contained in that preface about the content and organization of the book.

It was a great honour to be asked to assume authorship of *Constitutional Law of Canada* in 2020. The book has been the "go-to" resource for judges, scholars, lawyers and law students about the constitutional law of Canada for decades. The book is cited frequently by the courts, including the Supreme Court of Canada. I purchased my first copy of the book (in student edition) as a law student at Osgoode Hall Law School in 2001 and have always had a well-used copy on my shelf since then. Over the years, I had the good fortune to play a small role in the preparation of the book, when Peter asked for my comments on discrete passages. I cherish the conversations I had with Peter about the book, especially now.

It is a particular honour for me to be stepping into Peter's shoes as the new author of *Constitutional Law of Canada*. These are very big shoes to fill indeed. Since Peter's death in February 2020, I have had various conversations with others about him. One phrase came up repeatedly in these conversations – a "legal giant." Peter was indeed a legal giant, including of constitutional law, the subject of this book. However, he was also kind, humble and supportive. He was a wonderful mentor and friend to me (and countless others) over the years. And so, while I am honoured to be assuming authorship of such an important book, I am particularly honoured to be assuming authorship *from and for Peter*.

One thing that I pondered a great deal when I agreed to assume authorship of *Constitutional Law of Canada* was what approach I should take to my new role. On the one hand, it did not seem appropriate to me to adopt a highly interventionist approach, deleting or revising any passages of text with which I might disagree; after all, one of the many things that I and others have valued about the book is Peter's incisive analyses of and opinions about constitutional cases and controversies. In any case, given the length and scope of the book, this interventionist approach would not have been realistic, at least for this first update. On the other hand, it also did not seem appropriate to me to adopt a highly non-interventionist approach, by refraining from providing my own views, even when they might differ from Peter's views. And knowing Peter as I did, I know he would have disapproved of such an approach in any case. I had the good fortune to collaborate with Peter on various publications over the years, and he always made it abundantly clear to me that he valued my views, especially when they differed from his own. I have therefore decided to adopt an approach that charts a middle ground between these two competing approaches.

Here is what this middle-ground approach means in practice. First, in passages that I have not revised, I have retained Peter's opinions, including his practice of using the first person to identify his opinions. As a result, where the first person is used in the book ("in my view", etc.), the opinion being provided remains Peter's opinion, and not necessarily my own opinion.

Second, in those passages that I have revised significantly in this first update, I have not used the first person, so that it will be clear that the opinions expressed elsewhere in the book in the first person are Peter's. In addition, in these significantly revised passages, if Peter provided an analysis or opinion with which I disagree, I have made this clear in the text, often in a footnote.

Third, as a general rule, where a case is discussed that was released after 2019, it is safe to assume that any analysis of, and opinions expressed about, the case are mine (and not Peter's).

This is admittedly an imperfect solution. Under this approach, it may not always be easy to identify which passages I have significantly revised, and even when it is possible to do so, it may not be easy to distinguish those situations where Peter had not expressed an opinion on a particular topic from those situations where he had expressed an opinion on a particular topic that is reflected in the revised text. However, these challenges are inherent, it seems to me, in a book passed between authors in this way, and for now at least, this seems like the best approach to adopt, in order to avoid weighing the book down with footnotes addressing these matters.

Peter updated *Constitutional Law of Canada* every year between 2007 (the year this fifth edition was first released) and 2019 (the year of his last update). (His practice of updating the book on a yearly basis began in 1992, with the release of the third edition.) These yearly updates kept the book largely up to date. However, as Peter acknowledged in his preface to the fifth edition, since the yearly updates may often involve a piecemeal approach to revision, at a certain point, a more significant rewriting of some parts of the book may become appropriate, even if only to streamline the text. For my first update, I have updated certain terminology used throughout the book. I have further updates to terminology planned for future updates as well. In addition, for my first update, I have rewritten some passages of the book. Future updates to the book will involve more significant rewrites of portions and aspects of the book.

In 2021, Thomson Reuters, the publisher of *Constitutional Law of Canada*, decided to introduce a new version of the book, which will allow it to be offered in new electronic formats. This has necessitated various formatting changes to the book, including to the headings, footnotes, and cross-references. The book may look – and to some extent read – differently to seasoned readers, but the hope is that the book will be more easily accessible to a wider audience.

I have received assistance from various individuals in planning for, and preparing, this first update. I benefitted greatly from conversations with Jamie Cameron and Bruce Ryder (both former professors of mine, and colleagues of Peter's, at Osgoode Hall Law School) about my role as the new author of Constitutional Law of Canada. Various individuals also provided helpful feedback on parts of my first update. They are Benjamin Berger, Lauren Gillingham, Alex Irwin, Noura Karazivan, Asha Kaushal, Julie Murray, Alex Penny, Akis Psygkas, Christopher Sherrin and Allison Thornton (a former research assistant, collaborator and Blakes colleague of Peter's and mine). Erika Chamberlain (the Dean of my home faculty, the Faculty of Law at Western University) and Andrew Botterell (the Associate Dean (Research and Graduate Studies) of my home faculty) also provided encouragement and other support, including help with arranging research assistance. Several excellent research assistants helped me prepare this first update. They are Raffi Dergalstanian, Brooklyn Hallam, Ainsley Leguard and Rahul Sapra.

I would like to acknowledge the financial support of Blake, Cassels & Graydon LLP (where Peter was the Scholar in Residence, and I articled and was a lawyer), which has generously offered to support my work on future updates through its summer and articling student programs.

I would also like to acknowledge the Hogg family (particularly David and Anne) for their encouragement and support as I have taken on this project. I hope I do them (and Peter) proud.

Above all, I would like to thank my family – and in particular my wonderful husband, Alex Irwin – for their unflinching love, support and encouragement.

This update is dedicated to Alex. I prepared this first update under the shadow of the COVID-19 pandemic, during a period when we were largely isolated and working together at home. Alex lived this update right alongside me, in a variety of ways. I could not have done it without him.

Toronto
Wade K. Wright
June 2021

This is the fifth edition of *Constitutional Law of Canada*.

The first edition of the book was published in 1977. This was before the Charter of Rights, which was adopted in 1982, and the first edition ran to what now seems the meagre length of 548 pages. The second edition was published in 1985. This was after the Charter of Rights, but only three Charter cases had been decided by the Supreme Court of Canada at the time of writing. Nonetheless, the second edition, at 988 pages, was nearly double the size of the first. After 1985, the Charter cases, along with some Aboriginal rights cases and of course some distribution of powers cases, produced a steady stream of nearly 40 constitutional cases per year. (At the time of writing, this has slowed down to about 30 per year.) The third edition, published in 1992, swelled to 1478 pages. The effort of producing such a large work caused me to yield to the longstanding suggestion of Carswell that the book should be published in loose-leaf format so that it could be supplemented annually. That way, subscribers to the loose-leaf version would have a book that never got too badly out of date. So the third edition was published in loose-leaf format as well as in the normal bound version. That was also done with the fourth edition (1584 pages), published in 1997. In addition, Carswell publishes annually an abridged version of the loose-leaf edition in soft cover for students.

Ten years have elapsed since the publication of the fourth edition. Although the annual supplements have provided piecemeal updates, it is time for a complete rewriting. That is the reason for the fifth edition. In this rewriting, I have introduced three new chapters (26 Citizenship, 32 Health, and 33 Social Security). The chapters (after 26), the sections of chapters and the footnotes have been renumbered. Textbook references in the footnotes have been brought up to the latest edition, and a variety of ways of citing articles has been made consistent. Some chapters have seen major revisions, and I have virtually rewritten the chapter on Equality (now 55) to take account of the revolution in doctrine wrought by the Supreme Court of Canada. Throughout the book, wherever I judged that pre-2006 developments had not been adequately covered in the annual supplements (or had been overlooked), I have remedied the fault. In the result, hardly a page of the previous edition (as supplemented to 2005) has escaped some alteration.

The fifth edition, like its predecessor, is arranged in four parts. Part I, Basic Concepts, consists of 14 chapters, which cover the sources of Canadian constitutional law, the constitutional history of Canada, the status and amendment of the Constitution of Canada, the theory of federalism and judicial review, and the structures of Canadian government. Part II, Distribution of Powers, consists of 19 chapters, which cover the federal distribution of powers, including each of the principal legislative powers and the doctrines and techniques of judicial review on federal grounds. These two parts comprise volume 1 of the loose-leaf version. Part III, Civil Liberties, consists of 24 chapters, which cover the protection of civil liberties, with emphasis on the Charter of Rights. Part IV, Practice, consists of three chapters, which cover the effect of an unconstitutional law and the practice and procedure of constitutional litigation. Parts Ill and IV comprise volume 2 of the loose-leaf version. With the earlier editions, the publishers were able to keep the hard cover version down to a single volume. However, the steady growth of the book, which has taken the fifth edition to 2062 pages, has caused us to bow to the inevitable: the hard cover version of the fifth edition is now in two volumes. The abridged student edition in soft cover can still be accommodated in a single volume.

The book is about the law of Canada and makes no claim to be a comparative study. However, there are many references to the constitutional law of the United Kingdom, New Zealand, Australia and the United States. The American Bill of Rights is included as an appendix. The International Covenant on Civil and Political Rights is also included as an appendix, and some reference is made to that instrument and other international human rights instruments and their jurisprudential exegesis.

I have tried to be sparing in citation, concentrating on the leading cases and commentaries. Decisions below the level of the Supreme Court of Canada and the secondary literature are cited only if they are especially interesting or important. I never forget the admonition of Dixon C.J. in the High Court of Australia that "not everything that appears in the law reports" is the law (*White v. The Queen* (1962) 107 C.L.R. 174, 175). There is accordingly much criticism of judicial reasoning, but always with a view to the recognition and application of sound principle. Others will not always agree with my "sound principle", but I have tried to be frank in identifying my own opinions so that they can be appropriately discounted by the reader. I appeared as counsel in some of the cases discussed in the text. Wherever there is extensive discussion of any of those cases, I have disclosed my involvement in a footnote, just in case my objectivity has been impaired by my role as counsel.

I was a professor at the Osgoode Hall Law School of York University from 1970 to 2003, the last five years as Dean. That is where most of the writing has been done over the years, and I could not have wished for a happier or more supportive environment for a scholar and a teacher. I was able to continue both writing and teaching even during my term as Dean. Since 2003, I have been the Scholar in Residence at Blake, Cassels & Graydon LLP, an ill-defined position that enables me to combine some practice with academic work. That is where the fifth edition has been prepared. I have had a long relationship with the firm, having spent periods of leave there before I became Dean, and I am profoundly grateful for their longstanding support for my academic work. As well as a stimulating and happy collegial environment, the firm has a well-stocked and well-staffed library, and all the facilities and services needed to write a book in ideal conditions. I will only single out two people at the firm for special thanks. One is the Chair of the firm, Jim Christie, who called me during my last year as Dean and was no doubt surprised at the alacrity with which I accepted his invitation to become the firm's Scholar in Residence after my retirement from the University. The other is my assistant, Madeline Rumble, whose secretarial work is a constant support, and who is responsible for the accuracy and completeness of the manuscript of the fifth edition, as well as some of the research.

A series of able student research assistants helped me with research for the fifth edition or helped me to prepare the annual supplements to the fourth edition which are now largely incorporated into the fifth edition. They are Allison Bushell (now Thornton), Daniel Brothman, Peninah Brickman, Rachel Li Wai Suen, Hooman Tabesh, Cara Zwibel, Gail Henderson, Tara Rivers and Shashu Clacken (who did the bibliographic work on all the footnotes). Sujit Chaudhry, Faculty of Law, University of Toronto, read and commented on one of my new chapters. Blakes lawyers who helped me by discussing recent cases or difficult issues are too numerous to name; those who read and commented on portions of the manuscript include the aforementioned Allison Thornton, Wade Wright and Leena Grover. The path to publication was a smooth one, thanks to the efficiency of Julia Gulej, Ken Mathies, Debbie Bowen and their colleagues at Carswell. Above all, I thank my wife, Frances Hogg, who has the happy knack of tolerating my obsessive work habits and at the same time helping me keep a nice balance in my life.

Toronto
Peter W. Hogg

Table of Contents

PART I. BASIC CONCEPTS

CHAPTER 1. SOURCES

I. DEFINITION OF CONSTITUTIONAL LAW

§ 1:1 Definition of constitutional law

II. CONSTITUTION ACT, 1867

§ 1:2 Constitution Act, 1867

III. CONSTITUTION ACT, 1982

§ 1:3 Constitution Act, 1982

IV. CONSTITUTION OF CANADA

§ 1:4 Constitution of Canada

V. IMPERIAL STATUTES

§ 1:5 Imperial statutes

VI. CANADIAN STATUTES

§ 1:6 Canadian statutes

VII. PARLIAMENTARY PRIVILEGE

§ 1:7 Parliamentary privilege

VIII. CASE LAW

§ 1:8 Case law

IX. PREROGATIVE

§ 1:9 Prerogative

X. CONVENTIONS

§ 1:10 Definition of conventions
§ 1:11 Conventions in the courts

§ 1:12 Convention and usage
§ 1:13 Convention and agreement
§ 1:14 Convention and law
§ 1:15 Convention and policy

CHAPTER 2. RECEPTION

I. RULES OF RECEPTION

§ 2:1 Rules of reception

II. SETTLED COLONIES

§ 2:2 Date of reception
§ 2:3 Exclusion of unsuitable laws
§ 2:4 Amendment of received laws

III. CONQUERED COLONIES

§ 2:5 General rules of reception
§ 2:6 Ontario and Quebec

IV. CONFEDERATION

§ 2:7 Confederation

V. ADMISSION OF NEW PROVINCES AND TERRITORIES

§ 2:8 Section 146 of the B.N.A. Act
§ 2:9 Territories and prairie provinces
§ 2:10 British Columbia
§ 2:11 Prince Edward Island
§ 2:12 Newfoundland

VI. IMPERIAL STATUTES

§ 2:13 Imperial statutes

CHAPTER 3. INDEPENDENCE

I. BONDS OF EMPIRE

§ 3:1 Bonds of Empire

II. COLONIAL LAWS VALIDITY ACT, 1865

§ 3:2 Colonial Laws Validity Act, 1865

III. STATUTE OF WESTMINSTER, 1831

§ 3:3 Statute of Westminster, 1931

IV. CANADA ACT, 1982

§ 3:4 Canada Act 1982

V. PATRIATION OF THE CONSTITUTION

§ 3:5 Definition of patriation
§ 3:6 Canada Act 1982
§ 3:7 Autochthony
§ 3:8 Termination of imperial authority
§ 3:9 Autonomy

CHAPTER 4. AMENDMENT

I. HISTORY OF AMENDMENT

§ 4:1 Imperial amendment
§ 4:2 The search for a domestic amending procedure
§ 4:3 The failure to accommodate Quebec

II. PART V OF THE CONSTITUTION ACT, 1982

§ 4:4 Summary of Part V
§ 4:5 Comparison with Australia and United States
§ 4:6 Constitution of Canada
§ 4:7 Charter of Rights

III. GENERAL AMENDING PROCEDURE (S. 38)

§ 4:8 Section 38(1)
§ 4:9 Proclamation
§ 4:10 Initiation
§ 4:11 Opting out
§ 4:12 Compensation for opting out
§ 4:13 Revocation of assent or dissent
§ 4:14 Section 42
§ 4:15 "Regional veto" statute

IV. UNANIMITY PROCEDURE

§ 4:16 Unanimity procedure (s. 41)

V. SOME-BUT-NOT-ALL-PROVINCES PROCEDURE

§ 4:17 Some-but-not-all-provinces procedure (s. 43)

VI. FEDERAL PARLIAMENT ALONE

§ 4:18 Federal Parliament alone (s. 44)

VII. PROVINCIAL LEGISLATURE ALONE

§ 4:19 Provincial Legislature alone (s. 45)

VIII. FUTURE AMENDMENTS

§ 4:20 Forces of change
§ 4:21 Division of powers
§ 4:22 Central institutions
§ 4:23 Criticism of amending procedures

CHAPTER 5. FEDERALISM

I. DISTRIBUTION OF GOVERNMENTAL POWER

§ 5:1 Federalism
§ 5:2 Confederation
§ 5:3 Legislative union
§ 5:4 Special status
§ 5:5 Dominion and provinces
§ 5:6 Regions
§ 5:7 Subsidiarity

II. REASONS FOR FEDERALISM

§ 5:8 Reasons for federalism

III. FEDERALISM IN CANADA

§ 5:9 The terms of the Constitution
§ 5:10 Early federal dominance
§ 5:11 Judicial interpretation of the distribution of powers
§ 5:12 Federal-provincial financial arrangements
§ 5:13 Disallowance
§ 5:14 Appointment of Lieutenant Governors
§ 5:15 Appointment of judges
§ 5:16 Educational appeals
§ 5:17 Declaratory power
§ 5:18 Conclusion

IV. SUPREMACY OF THE CONSTITUTION

§ 5:19 Supremacy of the Constitution

V. ROLE OF THE COURTS

§ 5:20 Development of judicial review
§ 5:21 Limitations of judicial review
§ 5:22 Alternatives to judicial review

VI. AMENDING POWER

§ 5:23 Amending power

VII. SECESSION

§ 5:24 The power to secede

§ 5:25 Secession by amendment
§ 5:26 Secession by unilateral act

VIII. COOPERATIVE FEDERALISM

§ 5:27 Cooperative federalism

CHAPTER 6. FINANCIAL ARRANGEMENTS

I. CONFEDERATION ARRANGEMENTS

§ 6:1 Confederation arrangements

II. DEVELOPMENT OF DIRECT TAXATION

§ 6:2 Development of direct taxation

III. TAX RENTAL AGREEMENTS: 1941-1962

§ 6:3 Tax rental agreements: 1941–1962

IV. TAX COLLECTION AGREEMENTS: 1962-PRESENT

§ 6:4 Tax collection agreements: 1962-present

V. TAX ABATEMENTS

§ 6:5 Tax abatements

VI. EQUALIZATION PAYMENTS

§ 6:6 Equalization payments

VII. CONDITIONAL FEDERAL GRANTS

§ 6:7 Conditional federal grants

VIII. SPENDING POWER

§ 6:8 Federal power
§ 6:9 Provincial power

IX. CONCLUSIONS

§ 6:10 Conclusions

CHAPTER 7. COURTS

I. PROVINCIAL COURTS

§ 7:1 Establishment of provincial courts
§ 7:2 Appointment and payment of provincial judges
§ 7:3 Tenure of provincial judges: s. 99
§ 7:4 Tenure of provincial judges: s. 11(d)

§ 7:5 Inferior courts
§ 7:6 Court Martial
§ 7:7 Jury
§ 7:8 Inferior courts of civil jurisdiction
§ 7:9 Administrative tribunals

II. FEDERAL COURTS

§ 7:10 Supreme Court of Canada
§ 7:11 Federal Court of Canada
§ 7:12 Tax Court of Canada
§ 7:13 Territorial courts
§ 7:14 Appointment, payment and tenure of federal judges

III. IMPLICATIONS OF CONSTITUTION'S JUDICATURE SECTIONS

§ 7:15 Separation of powers
§ 7:16 Inferior courts
§ 7:17 County or district courts
§ 7:18 Superior courts
§ 7:19 Administrative tribunals
§ 7:20 Privative clauses

CHAPTER 8. SUPREME COURT OF CANADA

I. IN GENERAL

§ 8:1 Establishment of Court
§ 8:2 Abolition of Privy Council appeals
§ 8:3 Composition of Court
§ 8:4 Appointment of judges

II. APPELLATE JURISDICTION

§ 8:5 Constitutional basis of jurisdiction
§ 8:6 Civil appeals
§ 8:7 Criminal appeals

III. REFERENCE JURISDICTION

§ 8:8 Federal references
§ 8:9 Provincial references
§ 8:10 Constitutional basis
§ 8:11 Advisory character
§ 8:12 Proof of facts

IV. PRECEDENT; REFORM OF COURT

§ 8:13 Precedent
§ 8:14 Reform of Court

CHAPTER 9. RESPONSIBLE GOVERNMENT

I. RESPONSIBLE GOVERNMENT

§ 9:1 Definition of responsible government
§ 9:2 History of responsible government
§ 9:3 Law and convention

II. THE EXECUTIVE BRANCH

§ 9:4 The ministry
§ 9:5 The cabinet and the Privy Council
§ 9:6 The Prime Minister
§ 9:7 Ministerial responsibility

III. THE LEGISLATIVE BRANCH

§ 9:8 The Parliament
§ 9:9 The House of Commons
§ 9:10 The Senate
§ 9:11 The Governor General
§ 9:12 The cabinet

IV. DEFEAT OF THE GOVERNMENT

§ 9:13 Withdrawal of confidence
§ 9:14 Dissolution of Parliament
§ 9:15 Resignation or dismissal

V. THE GOVERNOR GENERAL'S PERSONAL PREROGATIVES

§ 9:16 The principle
§ 9:17 Appointment of Prime Minister
§ 9:18 Dismissal of Prime Minister
§ 9:19 Dissolution of Parliament
§ 9:20 Fixed election dates
§ 9:21 Prorogation of Parliament
§ 9:22 Appointments to Senate and bench
§ 9:23 The justification for a formal head of state
§ 9:24 The monarchy

CHAPTER 12. PARLIAMENTARY SOVEREIGNTY

I. SOVEREIGNTY IN THE UNITED KINGDOM

§ 12:1 Sovereignty in the United Kingdom

II. SOVEREIGNTY IN CANADA

§ 12:2 Federalism

§ 12:3 Charter of Rights
§ 12:4 Constitutional amendment
§ 12:5 Extraterritorial competence
§ 12:6 Delegation
§ 12:7 Retroactive legislation
§ 12:8 Wisdom or policy of legislation

III. SELF-IMPOSED RESTRAINTS ON LEGISLATIVE POWER

§ 12:9 Substance of future laws
§ 12:10 Manner and form of future laws

CHAPTER 14. DELEGATION

I. POWER OF DELEGATION

§ 14:1 Introduction to delegation
§ 14:2 United Kingdom Parliament
§ 14:3 Provincial Legislatures
§ 14:4 Federal Parliament

II. LIMITATIONS IMPOSED BY CONSTITUTION

§ 14:5 Delegation of legislative power
§ 14:6 Delegation of judicial power
§ 14:7 Classification of laws
§ 14:8 Office of Lieutenant Governor or Governor General
§ 14:9 Requirement of a Legislature or Parliament

III. FEDERAL INTER-DELEGATION

§ 14:10 Legislative inter-delegation
§ 14:11 Administrative inter-delegation

IV. REFERENTIAL LEGISLATION

§ 14:12 Incorporation by reference
§ 14:13 Anticipatory incorporation by reference
§ 14:14 Independent validity of incorporated law

V. CONDITIONAL LEGISLATION

§ 14:15 Conditions as delegations
§ 14:16 Conditions as administrative inter-delegations
§ 14:17 Conditions as legislative inter-delegations

VI. DELEGATION BY ACQUIESCENCE

§ 14:18 Delegation by acquiescence

VII. CONCLUSIONS ON FEDERAL INTER-DELEGATION

§ 14:19 Conclusions on federal inter-delegation

PART II. DISTRIBUTION OF POWER

CHAPTER 15. JUDICIAL REVIEW ON FEDERAL GROUNDS

I. SCOPE OF CHAPTER

§ 15:1 Scope of chapter

II. PRIORITY BETWEEN FEDERAL AND CHARTER GROUNDS

§ 15:2 Priority between federal and Charter grounds

III. PROCEDURE AND REASONING OF JUDICIAL REVIEW

§ 15:3 Procedure of judicial review
§ 15:4 Reasoning of judicial review

IV. CHARACTERIZATION OF LAWS

§ 15:5 "Matter"
§ 15:6 Singling out
§ 15:7 Double aspect
§ 15:8 Purpose
§ 15:9 Effect
§ 15:10 Efficacy
§ 15:11 Colourability
§ 15:12 Criteria of choice
§ 15:13 Presumption of constitutionality

V. SEVERANCE; READING DOWN

§ 15:14 Severance
§ 15:15 Reading down

VI. INTERJURISDICTIONAL IMMUNITY

§ 15:16 Definition of interjurisdictional immunity
§ 15:17 Federally-incorporated companies
§ 15:18 Federally-regulated undertakings
§ 15:19 Other federal matters
§ 15:20 Rationale of interjurisdictional immunity
§ 15:21 Provincial subjects

VII. INTERPRETATION OF CONSTITUTION

§ 15:22 Relevance
§ 15:23 Exclusiveness
§ 15:24 Ancillary power

§ 15:25 Concurrency
§ 15:26 Exhaustiveness
§ 15:27 Progressive interpretation
§ 15:28 Unwritten constitutional principles
§ 15:29 Legislative history
§ 15:30 Precedent

CHAPTER 16. PARAMOUNTCY

I. PROBLEM OF INCONSISTENCY

§ 16:1 Problem of inconsistency

II. DEFINITION OF INCONSISTENCY

§ 16:2 Definition of inconsistency

III. EXPRESS CONTRADICTION

§ 16:3 Impossibility of dual compliance
§ 16:4 Frustration of federal purpose

IV. NEGATIVE IMPLICATION

§ 16:5 Covering the field
§ 16:6 Express extension of paramountcy

V. OVERLAP AND DUPLICATION

§ 16:7 Constitutional significance
§ 16:8 Double criminal liability
§ 16:9 Double civil liability

VI. EFFECT OF INCONSISTENCY

§ 16:10 Effect of inconsistency

CHAPTER 17. PEACE, ORDER, AND GOOD GOVERNMENT

I. RESIDUARY NATURE OF POWER

§ 17:1 Residuary nature of power

II. THE "GAP" BRANCH

§ 17:2 The "gap" branch

III. THE "NATIONAL CONCERN" BRANCH

§ 17:3 History of national concern
§ 17:4 Definition of national concern

§ 17:5 Distinctness
§ 17:6 Newness

IV. THE "EMERGENCY" BRANCH

§ 17:7 The non-emergency cases
§ 17:8 War
§ 17:9 Apprehended insurrection
§ 17:10 Inflation
§ 17:11 Temporary character of law

V. RELATIONSHIP BETWEEN NATIONAL CONCERN AND EMERGENCY

§ 17:12 Relationship between national concern and emergency

CHAPTER 18. CRIMINAL LAW

I. DISTRIBUTION OF POWERS

§ 18:1 Distribution of powers

II. DEFINITION OF CRIMINAL LAW

§ 18:2 Definition of criminal law

III. FOOD AND DRUGS

§ 18:3 Food and drug standards
§ 18:4 Illicit drugs
§ 18:5 Tobacco

IV. HEALTH

§ 18:6 Health

V. ENVIRONMENTAL PROTECTION

§ 18:7 Environmental protection

VI. ABORTION

§ 18:8 Abortion

VII. ASSISTED HUMAN REPRODUCTION

§ 18:9 Assisted human reproduction

VIII. GENETIC DISCRIMINATION

§ 18:10 Genetic Discrimination

IX. COMPETITION LAW

§ 18:11 Competition law

X. SUNDAY OBSERVANCE LAW

§ 18:12 Federal power
§ 18:13 Provincial power

XI. GUN CONTROL

§ 18:14 Gun control

XII. PREVENTION OF CRIME

§ 18:15 Prevention in general
§ 18:16 Young offenders

XIII. CRIMINAL LAW AND CIVIL REMEDY

§ 18:17 Federal power generally to create civil remedies
§ 18:18 Criminal law power to create civil remedies

XIV. CRIMINAL LAW AND REGULATORY AUTHORITY

§ 18:19 Criminal law and regulatory authority

XV. PROVINCIAL POWER TO ENACT PENAL LAWS

§ 18:20 Provincial power to enact penal laws

CHAPTER 20. TRADE AND COMMERCE

I. RELATIONSHIP TO PROPERTY AND CIVIL RIGHTS

§ 20:1 Relationship to property and civil rights

II. INTERPROVINCIAL OR INTERNATIONAL TRADE AND COMMERCE

§ 20:2 In the Privy Council
§ 20:3 In the Supreme Court of Canada

III. GENERAL TRADE AND COMMERCE

§ 20:4 General trade and commerce

IV. SPECIFIC TOPICS

§ 20:5 Specific topics

CHAPTER 21. PROPERTY AND CIVIL RIGHTS

I. IN GENERAL

§ 21:1 Importance of property and civil rights
§ 21:2 History of property and civil rights

§ 21:3 Civil liberties
§ 21:4 Local or private matters

II. INSURANCE

§ 21:5 Reasons for regulation
§ 21:6 Provincial power
§ 21:7 Federal power

III. BUSINESS IN GENERAL

§ 21:8 Business in general

IV. PROFESSIONS AND TRADES

§ 21:9 Professions and trades

V. LABOUR RELATIONS

§ 21:10 Provincial power
§ 21:11 Federal power

VI. MARKETING

§ 21:12 Reasons for regulation
§ 21:13 Federal power
§ 21:14 Provincial power

VII. SECURITIES REGULATION

§ 21:15 Provincial power
§ 21:16 Federal power

VIII. PROPERTY

§ 21:17 General
§ 21:18 Foreign ownership
§ 21:19 Heritage property

IX. DEBT ADJUSTMENT

§ 21:20 Debt adjustment

X. CONSUMER PROTECTION

§ 21:21 Consumer protection

XI. EXTRATERRITORIAL COMPETENCE

§ 21:22 Extraterritorial competence

CHAPTER 22. TRANSPORTATION AND COMMUNICATION

I. DISTRIBUTION OF POWER

§ 22:1 Distribution of power

II. WORKS AND UNDERTAKINGS

§ 22:2 Works and undertakings

III. TRANSPORTATION AND COMMUNICATION

§ 22:3 Transportation and communication

IV. CONNECTION WITH ANOTHER PROVINCE

§ 22:4 Connection with another province

V. UNDIVIDED JURISDICTION

§ 22:5 Undivided jurisdiction

VI. CONTINUOUS AND REGULAR SERVICE

§ 22:6 Continuous and regular service

VII. RELATED UNDERTAKINGS

§ 22:7 Common ownership
§ 22:8 Common management
§ 22:9 Dependency

VIII. WORKS FOR THE GENERAL ADVANTAGE OF CANADA

§ 22:10 Works for the general advantage of Canada

IX. TRANSPORTATION BY LAND

§ 22:11 Transportation by land

X. TRANSPORTATION BY WATER

§ 22:12 Transportation by water

XI. TRANSPORTATION BY AIR

§ 22:13 Basis of legislative jurisdiction
§ 22:14 Intraprovincial aeronautics
§ 22:15 Provincial jurisdiction

XII. COMMUNICATION BY RADIO

§ 22:16 Basis of legislative jurisdiction

§ 22:17 Intraprovincial broadcasting
§ 22:18 Content regulation

XIII. COMMUNICATION BY TELEVISION

§ 22:19 Broadcast television
§ 22:20 Cable television
§ 22:21 Pay television

XIV. COMMUNICATION BY TELEPHONE

§ 22:22 Communication by telephone

XV. COMMUNICATION BY OTHER MEANS

§ 22:23 Film
§ 22:24 Theatre
§ 22:25 Literature

CHAPTER 28. ABORIGINAL PEOPLES

I. FEDERAL LEGISLATIVE POWER

§ 28:1 Section 91(24)
§ 28:2 Indians
§ 28:3 Lands reserved for the Indians
§ 28:4 Canadian Bill of Rights
§ 28:5 Charter of Rights
§ 28:6 Treaties

II. PROVINCIAL LEGISLATIVE POWER

§ 28:7 Application of provincial laws
§ 28:8 First exception: singling out
§ 28:9 Second exception: Indianness
§ 28:10 Third exception: paramountcy
§ 28:11 Fourth exception: Natural Resources Agreements
§ 28:12 Fifth exception: section 35

III. SECTION 88 OF THE INDIAN ACT

§ 28:13 Text of s. 88
§ 28:14 Laws of general application
§ 28:15 Paramountcy exception
§ 28:16 Treaty exception

IV. NATURAL RESOURCES AGREEMENTS

§ 28:17 Natural resources agreements

V. ABORIGINAL RIGHTS

§ 28:18 Recognition of aboriginal rights

§ 28:19 Definition of aboriginal rights
§ 28:20 Aboriginal self-government
§ 28:21 Aboriginal title
§ 28:22 Extinguishment of Aboriginal rights

VI. TREATY RIGHTS

§ 28:23 Introduction
§ 28:24 History
§ 28:25 Definition of treaty
§ 28:26 Interpretation of treaty rights
§ 28:27 Extinguishment of treaty rights

VII. THE NEED FOR CONSTITUTIONAL PROTECTION

§ 28:28 The need for constitutional protection

VIII. SECTION 35

§ 28:29 Text of s. 35
§ 28:30 Outside Charter of Rights
§ 28:31 "Aboriginal peoples of Canada"
§ 28:32 "Aboriginal and treaty rights"
§ 28:33 "Existing"
§ 28:34 "Recognized and affirmed"
§ 28:35 Application to treaty rights
§ 28:36 Application to extinguishment
§ 28:37 Application to provincial laws
§ 28:38 Duty to consult Aboriginal people
§ 28:39 Jurisdiction of the provincial courts
§ 28:40 Remedies for breach of s. 35

IX. SECTION 25

§ 28:41 Section 25

X. SECTION 35.1

§ 28:42 Section 35.1

XI. CHARLOTTETOWN ACCORD

§ 28:43 Charlottetown Accord

CHAPTER 32. HEALTH

I. PROVINCIAL POWER OVER HEALTH

§ 32:1 Provincial power over health

II. FEDERAL POWER OVER HEALTH

§ 32:2 Federal power over health

III. CANADA HEALTH ACT

§ 32:3 Canada Health Act

IV. UNIVERSALITY OF PUBLIC HEALTH CARE

§ 32:4 Universality of public health care

V. COMPREHENSIVENESS OF PUBLIC HEALTH CARE

§ 32:5 Comprehensiveness of public health care

VI. ACCESSIBILITY OF PUBLIC HEALTH CARE

§ 32:6 Accessibility of public health care

PART III. CIVIL LIBERTIES

CHAPTER 34. CIVIL LIBERTIES

I. DEFINITIONS OF CIVIL LIBERTIES

§ 34:1 Definition of civil liberties

II. COMMON LAW

§ 34:2 Common law

III. STATUTE

§ 34:3 Human rights codes
§ 34:4 Statutory bills of rights

IV. CONSTITUTION ACT, 1867

§ 34:5 Express guarantees
§ 34:6 Distribution of powers
§ 34:7 Implied bill of rights

V. CONSTITUTION ACT, 1982

§ 34:8 Constitution Act, 1982

CHAPTER 35. CANADIAN BILL OF RIGHTS

I. HISTORY OF BILL OF RIGHTS

§ 35:1 History of Bill of Rights

II. APPLICATION TO FEDERAL LAWS

§ 35:2 Application to federal laws

III. EFFECT OF INCONSISTENT STATUTES

§ 35:3 Meaning of s. 2
§ 35:4 Effect on earlier statutes
§ 35:5 Effect on later statutes
§ 35:6 Conclusions

IV. CONTENTS OF BILL OF RIGHTS

§ 35:7 Contents of Bill of Rights

V. JUDICIAL INTERPRETATION

§ 35:8 Judicial interpretation

VI. SCRUTINY BY MINISTER OF JUSTICE

§ 35:9 Scrutiny by Minister of Justice

CHAPTER 36. CHARTER OF RIGHTS

I. IN GENERAL

§ 36:1 History of Charter
§ 36:2 Protection of civil liberties
§ 36:3 Enhancement of national unity

II. EXPANSION OF JUDICIAL REVIEW

§ 36:4 New grounds of review
§ 36:5 Vagueness of concepts
§ 36:6 Role of s. 1
§ 36:7 Role of s. 33

III. DIALOGUE WITH LEGISLATIVE BRANCH

§ 36:8 The idea of dialogue
§ 36:9 Second look cases
§ 36:10 Remedial discretion
§ 36:11 Dialogue within government

IV. POLITICAL QUESTIONS

§ 36:12 Political questions

V. CHARACTERIZATION OF LAWS

§ 36:13 Comparison with federalism review
§ 36:14 Purpose or effect
§ 36:15 Trivial effects
§ 36:16 Severance
§ 36:17 Reading down

VI. INTERPRETATION OF CHARTER

§ 36:18 Progressive interpretation
§ 36:19 Generous interpretation
§ 36:20 Purposive interpretation
§ 36:21 Process as purpose
§ 36:22 Hierarchy of rights
§ 36:23 Conflict between rights
§ 36:24 English-French discrepancies
§ 36:25 Interpretation of exceptions

VII. SOURCES OF INTERPRETATION

§ 36:26 Pre-Charter cases
§ 36:27 American cases
§ 36:28 International sources
§ 36:29 Legislative history

VIII. PRIORITY BETWEEN FEDERAL AND CHARTER GROUNDS

§ 36:30 Priority between federal and Charter grounds

IX. COMMENCEMENT OF CHARTER

§ 36:31 Commencement of Charter

X. UNDECLARED RIGHTS

§ 36:32 Undeclared rights

CHAPTER 37. APPLICATION OF CHARTER

I. BENEFIT OF RIGHTS

§ 37:1 The issue
§ 37:2 Everyone, anyone, any person
§ 37:3 Individual
§ 37:4 Citizen
§ 37:5 Permanent resident

II. BURDEN OF RIGHTS

§ 37:6 Both levels of government
§ 37:7 Parliament or Legislature
§ 37:8 Statutory authority
§ 37:9 Amending procedures
§ 37:10 Government
§ 37:11 Courts
§ 37:12 Common law
§ 37:13 Private action

§ 37:14 Extraterritorial application

III. WAIVER OF RIGHTS

§ 37:15 Definition of waiver
§ 37:16 Rationale of waiver
§ 37:17 Waiver of presumption of innocence
§ 37:18 Waiver of right to silence
§ 37:19 Waiver of unreasonable search and seizure
§ 37:20 Waiver of right to counsel
§ 37:21 Waiver of speedy trial
§ 37:22 Waiver of right to jury
§ 37:23 Waiver of right to interpreter
§ 37:24 Waiver by contract

CHAPTER 38. LIMITATION OF RIGHTS

I. OVERVIEW OF S. 1

§ 38:1 Introduction to s. 1
§ 38:2 Rationale of s. 1
§ 38:3 Relationship between s. 1 and rights

II. BURDEN OF PROOF

§ 38:4 Burden of proof

III. PRESUMPTION OF CONSTITUTIONALITY

§ 38:5 Presumption of constitutionality

IV. LIMITS

§ 38:6 Limits

V. PRESCRIBED BY LAW

§ 38:7 Definition of prescribed by law
§ 38:8 Discretion
§ 38:9 Vagueness

VI. REASONABLE AND DEMONSTRABLY JUSTIFIED

§ 38:10 Introduction
§ 38:11 Oakes test

VII. SUFFICIENTLY IMPORTANT OBJECTIVE

§ 38:12 Identification of objective
§ 38:13 Importance of objective
§ 38:14 Quebec's distinct society
§ 38:15 Inadmissible objectives

§ 38:16 Shifting objectives
§ 38:17 Cost

VIII. RATIONAL CONNECTION

§ 38:18 Definition
§ 38:19 Causation

IX. LEAST DRASTIC MEANS

§ 38:20 Minimum impairment
§ 38:21 Margin of appreciation

X. PROPORTIONATE EFFECT; APPLICATION TO EQUALITY RIGHTS

§ 38:22 Proportionate effect
§ 38:23 Application to equality rights

XI. APPLICATION TO QUALIFIED RIGHTS

§ 38:24 Scope of s. 1
§ 38:25 Section 7
§ 38:26 Section 8
§ 38:27 Section 9
§ 38:28 Section 11
§ 38:29 Section 12
§ 38:30 Section 23

XII. APPLICATION TO COMMON LAW

§ 38:31 Application to common law

XIII. APPLICATION TO DISCRETIONARY DECISIONS

§ 38:32 Application to discretionary decisions
§ 38:33 Emergency measures

CHAPTER 39. OVERRIDE OF RIGHTS

I. SECTION 33

§ 39:1 Section 33

II. HISTORY OF S. 33

§ 39:2 History of s. 33

III. RIGHTS THAT MAY BE OVERRIDDEN

§ 39:3 Rights that may be overridden

IV. FIVE-YEAR LIMIT

§ 39:4 Five-year limit

V. SPECIFICITY OF DECLARATION

§ 39:5 Specificity of declaration

VI. RETROACTIVE EFFECT

§ 39:6 Retroactive effect

VII. JUDICIAL REVIEW

§ 39:7 Judicial review

VIII. EVALUATION OF S. 33

§ 39:8 Evaluation of s. 33

CHAPTER 40. ENFORCEMENT OF RIGHTS

I. SUPREMACY CLAUSE

§ 40:1 Section 52(1)
§ 40:2 Section 24(1) compared
§ 40:3 Nullification
§ 40:4 Temporary validity
§ 40:5 Severance
§ 40:6 Reading in
§ 40:7 Reading down
§ 40:8 Constitutional exemption
§ 40:9 Reconstruction
§ 40:10 Limitation of actions

II. REMEDY CLAUSE

§ 40:11 Section 24(1)
§ 40:12 Applicable to Charter only
§ 40:13 Non-exclusive remedy
§ 40:14 Standing
§ 40:15 Apprehended infringements
§ 40:16 Court of competent jurisdiction
§ 40:17 Range of remedies
§ 40:18 Declaration
§ 40:19 Damages
§ 40:20 Costs
§ 40:21 Exclusion of evidence
§ 40:22 Remedies outside s. 24(1)
§ 40:23 Supervision of court orders
§ 40:24 Appeals
§ 40:25 Limitation of actions

III. ADMINISTRATIVE TRIBUNALS

§ 40:26 With power to decide questions of law

§ 40:27 Without power to decide questions of law
§ 40:28 Preliminary inquiry judge
§ 40:29 Provincial court judge

IV. SCRUTINY BY MINISTER OF JUSTICE

§ 40:30 Scrutiny by Minister of Justice

V. LEGISLATIVE ENFORCEMENT

§ 40:31 Legislative enforcement

CHAPTER 41. EXCLUSION OF EVIDENCE

I. SCOPE OF CHAPTER

§ 41:1 Scope of chapter

II. ORIGIN OF S. 24(2)

§ 41:2 Origin of s. 24(2)

III. TEXT OF S. 24(2)

§ 41:3 Text of s. 24(2)

IV. CAUSATION

§ 41:4 Causation

V. BURDEN OF PROOF

§ 41:5 Burden of proof

VI. REASONABLE PERSON TEST

§ 41:6 Reasonable person test

VII. DEFINITION OF DISREPUTE

§ 41:7 Definition of disrepute

VIII. NATURE OF EVIDENCE

§ 41:8 Nature of evidence

IX. NATURE OF OFFICIAL CONDUCT

§ 41:9 Deliberate violations
§ 41:10 Extenuating circumstances
§ 41:11 Good faith

X. NATURE OF CHARTER BREACH

§ 41:12 Nature of Charter breach

XI. EFFECT OF EXCLUDING EVIDENCE

§ 41:13 Effect of excluding evidence

XII. CONCLUSION

§ 41:14 Conclusion

CHAPTER 42. RELIGION

I. DISTRIBUTION OF POWERS

§ 42:1 Distribution of powers

II. SECTION 2(A) OF THE CHARTER

§ 42:2 Section 2(a) of the Charter

III. FREEDOM OF CONSCIENCE

§ 42:3 Freedom of conscience

IV. FREEDOM OF RELIGION

§ 42:4 Freedom of religion

V. SUNDAY OBSERVANCE

§ 42:5 Sunday observance

VI. OTHER RELIGIOUS PRACTICES

§ 42:6 Other religious practices

VII. WAIVER OF RELIGIOUS PRACTICE

§ 42:7 Waiver of religious practice

VIII. RELIGION IN PUBLIC SCHOOLS

§ 42:8 Religion in public schools

IX. DENOMINATIONAL SCHOOLS

§ 42:9 Denominational schools

X. RELIGION IN PUBLIC BODIES OTHER THAN SCHOOLS

§ 42:10 Religion in public bodies other than schools

XI. RELIGIOUS MARRIAGE

§ 42:11 Religious marriage

CHAPTER 43. EXPRESSION

I. DISTRIBUTION OF POWERS

§ 43:1 Classification of laws
§ 43:2 Political speech
§ 43:3 Provincial power
§ 43:4 Federal power

II. SECTION 2(B) OF THE CHARTER

§ 43:5 Section 2(b) of the Charter

III. COMPARISON WITH FIRST AMENDMENT

§ 43:6 Comparison with first amendment

IV. REASONS FOR PROTECTING EXPRESSION

§ 43:7 Reasons for protecting expression

V. MEANING OF EXPRESSION

§ 43:8 Definition of expression
§ 43:9 Criminal expression
§ 43:10 Violence
§ 43:11 Content neutrality

VI. WAYS OF LIMITING EXPRESSION

§ 43:12 Prior restraint
§ 43:13 Border control
§ 43:14 Penal prohibition
§ 43:15 Civil prohibition
§ 43:16 Forced expression
§ 43:17 Language requirement
§ 43:18 Search of press premises
§ 43:19 Disclosure of journalists' sources
§ 43:20 Time, manner and place

VII. COMMERCIAL EXPRESSION

§ 43:21 Protection of commercial expression
§ 43:22 Language requirements
§ 43:23 Advertising restrictions
§ 43:24 Signs
§ 43:25 Prostitution

VIII. PICKETING; HATE PROPAGANDA; DEFAMATION

§ 43:26 Picketing
§ 43:27 Hate propaganda

§ 43:28 Defamation

IX. PORNOGRAPHY

§ 43:29 Pornography

X. ACCESS TO PUBLIC PROPERTY

§ 43:30 Access to public property

XI. ACCESS TO COURTS

§ 43:31 Fair trial concerns
§ 43:32 Restrictions on reporting
§ 43:33 Restrictions on access

XII. ACCESS TO LEGISLATIVE ASSEMBLY

§ 43:34 Generally

XIII. CONTEMPT OF COURT; PUBLIC SERVICE; MANDATORY LETTERS OF REFERENCE

§ 43:35 Contempt of court
§ 43:36 Public service
§ 43:37 Mandatory letters of reference

XIV. ELECTION EXPENDITURES; VOTING

§ 43:38 Election expenditures
§ 43:39 Voting

XV. ACCESS TO GOVERNMENT; ACCESS TO GOVERNMENT DOCUMENTS

§ 43:40 Access to government
§ 43:41 Access to government documents

CHAPTER 44. ASSEMBLY AND ASSOCIATION

I. DISTRIBUTION OF POWERS

§ 44:1 Distribution of powers

II. FREEDOM OF ASSEMBLY

§ 44:2 Freedom of assembly

III. FREEDOM OF ASSOCIATION

§ 44:3 Section 2(d) of Charter
§ 44:4 Formation of association
§ 44:5 Purpose of association

§ 44:6 Exercise of constitutional rights
§ 44:7 Exercise of non-constitutional rights
§ 44:8 Freedom not to associate

CHAPTER 45. VOTING

I. VOTING

§ 45:1 Pre-Charter law
§ 45:2 Section 3 of Charter
§ 45:3 One person, one vote
§ 45:4 Regulation of elections
§ 45:5 Contested elections

II. CANDIDACY

§ 45:6 Candidacy

III. DURATION OF LEGISLATIVE BODIES

§ 45:7 Duration of legislative bodies

IV. ANNUAL SITTINGS OF LEGISLATIVE BODIES

§ 45:8 Annual sittings of legislative bodies

CHAPTER 47. FUNDAMENTAL JUSTICE

I. DISTRIBUTION OF POWERS OVER LEGAL RIGHTS

§ 47:1 Distribution of powers over legal rights

II. SECTION 7 OF CHARTER

§ 47:2 Section 7 of Charter

III. APPLICATION OF S. 1

§ 47:3 Application of s. 1

IV. BENEFIT OF S. 7

§ 47:4 Corporations
§ 47:5 Immigrants
§ 47:6 Foetus

V. BURDEN OF S. 7

§ 47:7 Burden of s. 7

VI. LIFE

§ 47:8 Life

VII. LIBERTY

§ 47:9 Physical liberty
§ 47:10 Economic liberty
§ 47:11 Political liberty

VIII. SECURITY OF THE PERSON

§ 47:12 Security of the person

IX. PROPERTY

§ 47:13 Property

X. FUNDAMENTAL JUSTICE

§ 47:14 Procedure and substance
§ 47:15 Definition of fundamental justice

XI. ABSOLUTE AND STRICT LIABILITY

§ 47:16 Categories of offences
§ 47:17 Absolute liability offences
§ 47:18 Strict liability offences

XII. MURDER

§ 47:19 Murder

XIII. UNFORESEEN CONSEQUENCES

§ 47:20 Unforeseen Consequences

XIV. INVOLUNTARY ACTS

§ 47:21 Automatism
§ 47:22 Duress
§ 47:23 Intoxication

XV. OVERBROAD LAWS

§ 47:24 Overbroad laws

XVI. DISPROPORTIONATE LAWS

§ 47:25 Disproportionate laws

XVII. ARBITRARY LAWS

§ 47:26 Arbitrary laws

XVIII. VAGUE LAWS

§ 47:27 Void for vagueness

§ 47:28 Standard of precision
§ 47:29 Application to other Charter rights

XIX. WRONG LAWS

§ 47:30 Wrong laws

XX. RIGHT TO SILENCE

§ 47:31 Right to silence

XXI. FAIR TRIAL

§ 47:32 The right to a fair trial
§ 47:33 Full answer and defence
§ 47:34 Pre-trial disclosure by the Crown
§ 47:35 Pre-trial disclosure by third parties
§ 47:36 Preservation of evidence
§ 47:37 Statutory limits on pre-trial disclosure

XXII. FAIR ADMINISTRATIVE PROCEDURES

§ 47:38 Fair administrative procedures

CHAPTER 55. EQUALITY

I. IN GENERAL

§ 55:1 Distribution of powers
§ 55:2 Canadian Bill of Rights
§ 55:3 American Bill of Rights
§ 55:4 Section 15 of Charter

II. APPLICATION OF S. 15

§ 55:5 Individual
§ 55:6 "Law" in s. 15
§ 55:7 Private action

III. EQUALITY

§ 55:8 Four equalities of s. 15
§ 55:9 Absolute equality
§ 55:10 Aristotle's definition
§ 55:11 Similarly situated
§ 55:12 Formal and substantive equality
§ 55:13 Reasonable classification
§ 55:14 Valid federal objective
§ 55:15 Early applications of s. 15

IV. DISCRIMINATION

§ 55:16 Discrimination

V. LISTED OR ANALOGOUS GROUNDS

§ 55:17 Requirement of a listed or analogous ground
§ 55:18 Addition of analogous grounds

VI. HUMAN DIGNITY

§ 55:19 Ambiguity in Andrews
§ 55:20 Impairment of human dignity
§ 55:21 The factor of correspondence
§ 55:22 Discrimination without human dignity

VII. DISADVANTAGE

§ 55:23 Selection of comparator group
§ 55:24 Requirement of disadvantage
§ 55:25 Objective and subjective disadvantage
§ 55:26 Human dignity and disadvantage
§ 55:27 Group disadvantage

VIII. DIRECT AND INDIRECT DISCRIMINATION

§ 55:28 Substantive equality
§ 55:29 Unintended discrimination
§ 55:30 Reasonable accommodation

IX. JUSTIFICATION UNDER S. 1; AFFIRMATIVE ACTION

§ 55:31 Justification under s. 1
§ 55:32 Affirmative action

X. DISCRIMINATION PERMITTED BY CONSTITUTION

§ 55:33 Age in ss. 23, 29, 99
§ 55:34 Race in s. 91(24)
§ 55:35 Religion in s. 93
§ 55:36 Province of residence in ss. 91, 92
§ 55:37 Citizenship in s. 6
§ 55:38 Language in ss. 16-23

XI. RACE; RELIGION

§ 55:39 Race
§ 55:40 Religion

XII. SEX

§ 55:41 Direct discrimination
§ 55:42 Systemic discrimination
§ 55:43 Section 28

XIII. OTHER GROUNDS OF DISCRIMINATION

§ 55:44 Age

§ 55:45 Mental or physical disability
§ 55:46 Citizenship
§ 55:47 Marital status
§ 55:48 Sexual orientation
§ 55:49 Place of residence
§ 55:50 Occupation

CHAPTER 56. LANGUAGE

I. LANGUAGE IN CANADA

§ 56:1 Language in Canada

II. DISTRIBUTION OF POWERS OVER LANGUAGE

§ 56:2 Distribution of powers over language

III. LANGUAGE OF CONSTITUTION

§ 56:3 Language of Constitution

IV. LANGUAGE OF STATUTES

§ 56:4 Constitutional requirements
§ 56:5 Quebec's Charter of the French Language
§ 56:6 Manitoba's Official Language Act
§ 56:7 Incorporation by reference
§ 56:8 Delegated legislation

V. LANGUAGE OF COURTS

§ 56:9 Constitutional requirements
§ 56:10 Definition of courts
§ 56:11 Language of process
§ 56:12 Language of proceedings
§ 56:13 Right to interpreter

VI. LANGUAGE OF GOVERNMENT

§ 56:14 Section 16 of Charter
§ 56:15 Section 20 of Charter

VII. LANGUAGE OF COMMERCE

§ 56:16 Language of commerce

VIII. LANGUAGE OF EDUCATION

§ 56:17 Section 93 of Constitution Act, 1867
§ 56:18 Mackell case
§ 56:19 Section 23 of the Charter
§ 56:20 Mother tongue of parent

§ 56:21 Language of instruction of parent in Canada
§ 56:22 Language of instruction of child in Canada
§ 56:23 Where numbers warrant
§ 56:24 Denominational schools
§ 56:25 Supervision of remedial orders

APPENDICES

Appendix A. Constitution Act, 1867
Appendix B. Canada Act 1982
Appendix C. Constitution Act, 1982
Appendix D. Canadian Bill of Rights
Appendix E. American Bill of Rights
Appendix F. International Covenant on Civil and Political Rights
Appendix G. Optional Protocol to International Covenant on Civil and Political Rights

Bibliography

Table of Cases

Index

Part I

BASIC CONCEPTS

Chapter 1

Sources

I. DEFINITION OF CONSTITUTIONAL LAW

§ 1:1 Definition of constitutional law

II. CONSTITUTION ACT, 1867

§ 1:2 Constitution Act, 1867

III. CONSTITUTION ACT, 1982

§ 1:3 Constitution Act, 1982

IV. CONSTITUTION OF CANADA

§ 1:4 Constitution of Canada

V. IMPERIAL STATUTES

§ 1:5 Imperial statutes

VI. CANADIAN STATUTES

§ 1:6 Canadian statutes

VII. PARLIAMENTARY PRIVILEGE

§ 1:7 Parliamentary privilege

VIII. CASE LAW

§ 1:8 Case law

IX. PREROGATIVE

§ 1:9 Prerogative

X. CONVENTIONS

§ 1:10 Definition of conventions
§ 1:11 Conventions in the courts

§ 1:12 Convention and usage
§ 1:13 Convention and agreement
§ 1:14 Convention and law
§ 1:15 Convention and policy

I. DEFINITION OF CONSTITUTIONAL LAW

§ 1:1 Definition of constitutional law

Constitutional law is the law prescribing the exercise of power by the organs of a State. It explains which organs can exercise legislative power (making new laws), executive power (implementing the laws) and judicial power (adjudicating disputes), and what the limitations on those powers are. In a federal state, the allocation of governmental powers (legislative, executive and judicial) among central and regional (state or provincial) authorities is a basic concern. The rules of federalism are especially significant in Canada because they protect the cultural, linguistic and regional diversity of the nation. Civil liberties are also part of constitutional law, because civil liberties may be created by the rules that limit the exercise of governmental power over individuals. A constitution has been described as "a mirror reflecting the national soul":[1] it must recognize and protect the values of a nation.

The word "constitutionalism" is sometimes used to convey the idea of a government that is limited by law.[2] Often the phrase "rule of law" is used to convey the same idea.[3] These terms describe a society in which government officials must act in accordance with the law. For this to be a reality, remedies must be available to citizens when officials act outside the law. This in turn requires an independent judiciary and an independent legal profession. In Canada, the rule of law reaches up into the Parliament of Canada and the Legislatures of the provinces, each of which must stay within the powers allocated to that level of government by the constitution, and each of which must respect the civil liberties guaranteed by the constitution. Laws enacted in breach of the constitution may be challenged in the courts by citizens, and the laws will be

---

[Section 1:1]

[1]Cheffins and Tucker, The Constitutional Process in Canada (2nd ed., 1976), 4. For an elegant analysis of the Constitution of Canada and how it reflects "two constitutional logics", one accommodating the particular, local communities who joined together (or were present) in 1867, and the other giving effect to the universal principles of governance that were adopted in 1982, see B. L. Berger, "Children of two logics: A way into Canadian constitutional culture" (2013) 11 Int. J. of Con. Law 319.

[2]W. Waluchow, "Constitutionalism" (2002) in Stanford Encyclopedia of Philosophy, online at http://plato.stanford.edu/entries/constitutionalism.

[3]Canadian-focussed contributions to the vast literature on the rule of law include W.J. Newman, "The Principles of the Rule of Law and Parliamentary Sovereignty in Constitutional Theory and Litigation" (2005) 16 Nat. J. Con. Law 175; D. Dyzenhaus, "The Logic of the Rule of Law: Lessons from Willis" (2005) 55 U. Toronto L.J. 691; P.W. Hogg and C.R. Zwibel, "The Rule of Law in the Supreme Court of Canada" (2005) 55 U. Toronto L.J. 715. See also ch. 15, Judicial Review on Federal Grounds, under heading § 15:28, "Unwritten constitutional principles".

struck down by the courts. Actions by government departments, public agencies, officials and the police must also stay within the limits laid down by the constitution and by the law contained in statutes and common law (judge-made law). Illegal actions by public officials may be challenged in the courts by citizens, and will be remedied by the courts. A society governed by law is obviously the foundation of personal liberty. Less obviously, perhaps, it is also the foundation of economic development, since investment will not take place in a country where private rights are not respected.[4]

In the rest of this introductory chapter, I describe the various sources of constitutional law in Canada. Constitutional law is one of the few legal subjects in which statutes enacted by Parliament or the provincial Legislatures are not principal sources of the law.[5] The only statutes that are central to the subject are the Constitution Act, 1867 and the Constitution Act, 1982, which are enactments of the Parliament of the United Kingdom passed for the purpose of creating the federal nation of Canada (in 1867) and making some important changes to the 1867 scheme (in 1982). Canada's history as a British colony explains why these "foreign" interventions have remained fundamental to Canada's constitutional law; this will be pursued in the next two chapters.[6]

II. CONSTITUTION ACT, 1867

§ 1:2 Constitution Act, 1867

In most countries, the bulk of the constitutional law is contained in a single constitutional document, which can be and usually is described as "the Constitution". In most cases, this document came into being after the gaining of independence, or after a revolution, or after a war, and was intended to symbolize and legitimize a new regime of law. In the United States, for example, the constitutional document of 1787 (and its amendments) is the Constitution.[1] It was adopted after the American colonists had won their independence from Britain by war. Naturally, the brilliant men who framed that document borrowed from their British traditions, as well as from other sources. But they wanted a document that would be complete in itself, for the previous constitutional rules had been irrevocably repudiated, and the new document was to be the foundation stone of the new nation. Accordingly, they set out the es-

---

[4]M. Olson, Power and Prosperity (Basic Books, 2000); H. De Soto, The Mystery of Capital (Basic Books, 2000).

[5]I was driven to reflect on this feature of constitutional law by J. Waldron, The Dignity of Legislation (1999), which justly criticizes the neglect of legislation in jurisprudence (legal theory).

[6]Chapters 2, Reception, and 3, Independence.

[Section 1:2]

[1]The document was adopted by a constitutional convention that met in Philadelphia in 1787. It was subject to ratification by the states, and was effective when the ninth state, New Hampshire, ratified it in 1788. The new government was organized in 1789.

sentials of the entire scheme of government—legislative, executive and judicial—in one impressive document.

In Canada (as in the United Kingdom), there is no single document comparable to the Constitution of the United States, and the word "Constitution"[2] accordingly lacks a definite meaning.[3] The closest approximation to such a document is the British North America Act, 1867,[4] which was renamed the Constitution Act, 1867 in 1982.[5] The B.N.A. Act (as I shall continue to call it in historical contexts) created the new Dominion of Canada by uniting three of the colonies of British North America and by providing the framework for the admission of all the other British North American colonies and territories.[6] The B.N.A. Act established the rules of federalism, that is, the rules that allocate governmental power between the central institutions (especially the federal Parliament) and the provincial institutions (especially the provincial Legislatures). But the B.N.A. Act did not mark any break with the colonial past. Independence from the United Kingdom was not desired or even contemplated for the future. The new Dominion, although enjoying a considerable degree of self-government, remained a British colony. In fact, of course, after 1867, there was an evolution to full independence, but it was a gradual process continuing well into the twentieth century.[7]

The B.N.A. Act did not follow the model of the Constitution of the United States in codifying all of the new nation's constitutional rules. On the contrary, the B.N.A. Act did no more than was necessary to accomplish confederation. The reason was stated in the preamble to the Act: the new nation was to have "a Constitution similar in principle to that of the United Kingdom". Apart from the changes needed to establish the new federation, the British North Americans wanted the old rules to continue in both form and substance exactly as before. After 1867, therefore, much of Canada's constitutional law continued to be found in a variety of sources outside the B.N.A. Act. Indeed, as will be

---

[2]For discussion of the meaning of "constitution", see Wheare, Modern Constitutions (2nd ed., 1966), 2–4; M.S.R. Palmer, "Using Constitutional Realism to Identify the *Complete* Constitution: Lessons from an Unwritten Constitution" (2006) 54 Am. J. Comp. Law 587; M.S.R. Palmer, "What is New Zealand's constitution and who interprets it? Constitutional realism and the importance of public office holders" (2006) 17 Public Law Review 133.

[3]There is a definition of "Constitution of Canada" in s. 52(2) of the Constitution Act, 1982. This definition applies when that term is used in the Constitution Act, 1982: see § 1:4, "Constitution of Canada".

[4]The Constitution Act, 1867 (U.K.) 30 & 31 Vict., c. 3, is reproduced in R.S.C. 1985, Appendix II, No. 5. All the other instruments of the Constitution of Canada, as defined in s. 52(2) of the Constitution Act, 1982, are in the same Appendix II, along with some other instruments of constitutional interest. Department of Justice, Canada, A Consolidation of the Constitution Acts, 1867 to 1982 (1989) is a convenient consolidation of the Constitution Acts. Part of this consolidation is printed with permission as an appendix to this book.

[5]Constitution Act, 1982, s. 53(2).

[6]The history of confederation is related in ch. 2, Reception, under heading, § 2:7, "Confederation".

[7]See ch. 3, Independence, under heading § 3:1, "Bonds of Empire".

elaborated later in this chapter, some of the most important rules were not matters of law at all, but were simply "conventions" which were unenforceable in the courts.

The best-known example of the colonists' reliance on the old regime is the absence of any general amending clause in the B.N.A. Act. We do not have definite information as to the reasons for this omission, because on this point (as on many others) there is no record of any discussion at the conferences in Charlottetown, Quebec and London which preceded the passage of the Act. But two facts may be assumed with confidence. First, the framers of the B.N.A. Act could not have overlooked such a vital matter: they were far too intelligent and pragmatic to imagine that they had drafted a document which would never require amendment, and they were very familiar with the United States' Constitution which of course contained an amending clause. Secondly, the framers must have known that the absence of an amending clause would mean that amendments would have to be enacted by the imperial Parliament. The conclusion is inescapable that the Canadian framers of the B.N.A. Act were content for the imperial Parliament to play a part in the process of amending the new Constitution.[8] Because of the absence of an amending clause in the B.N.A. Act, the imperial Parliament enacted amendments to the Act until 1982, when the Constitution Act, 1982 (itself an imperial statute) finally supplied amending procedures which could be operated entirely within Canada.[9]

Another gap in the B.N.A. Act concerns the office of Governor General. The Act, by s. 9, vests general executive authority for Canada in "the Queen", and confers several specific powers on a "Governor General". But the office of Governor General is nowhere created by the Act and no rules are provided for the appointment or tenure of that officer. The reason for this gap was the assumption that the office would be created and filled in the same way as colonial governorships had always been created and filled, that is, by the Queen acting on the advice of the British Colonial Secretary. The office of Governor General has never been formalized in an amendment to the B.N.A. Act. The office is still constituted by the royal prerogative,[10] and appointments are still made by the Queen, although, needless to say, she now acts on the advice of her Canadian ministers.[11]

The system of responsible (or cabinet) government, which had been achieved before confederation by the uniting colonies,[12] is another gap in the B.N.A. Act. It was intended in 1867 that this system would apply to

[8]See also, Livingston, Federalism and Constitutional Change (1956), 19–21; Mallory, The Structure of Canadian Government (rev. ed., 1984), 420; Forsey, Freedom and Order (1974), 229.

[9]The history of the search for a domestic amending formula is related in ch. 4, Amendment, under heading § 4:2 "The search for a domestic amending procedure".

[10]Letters Patent constituting the office of Governor General of Canada, 1947, R.S.C. 1985, Appendix II, No. 31.

[11]See ch. 9, Responsible Government.

[12]The history of the development of responsible government is related in ch. 9,

the new federal government, but it never seems to have occurred to anyone to write the rules of the system into the B.N.A. Act, and so there is no mention of the Prime Minister, or of the cabinet, or of the dependence of the cabinet on the support of a majority in the House of Commons: the composition of the actual executive authority and its relationship to the legislative authority were left in the form of unwritten conventions—as in the United Kingdom. That is still their status today.[13]

Nor did the Canadians write into their B.N.A. Act a new supreme court on the model of the Supreme Court of the United States. The B.N.A. Act, by s. 101, gave authority for such a court to be established, but it did not actually establish it. The reason was simple. The framers were accustomed to look to the Judicial Committee of the Privy Council in England as the final appellate authority for British North America (and other colonies), and they were content to leave the appellate authority in those same safe British hands. This was regarded as so natural and obvious—like responsible government—that the Judicial Committee of the Privy Council is not mentioned anywhere in the B.N.A. Act. When the Supreme Court of Canada was established in 1875, it was established by an ordinary federal statute,[14] and the right of appeal to the Privy Council was retained; the abolition of Privy Council appeals did not occur finally until 1949.[15] It is still the case that the existence, composition and jurisdiction of the Supreme Court of Canada depend at least in part upon an ordinary federal statute.[16]

The Canadian framers of the B.N.A. Act even eschewed the alluring American precedent of a bill of rights, and instead left the civil liberties of Canadians to be protected by the moderation of their legislative bodies and the rules of the common law—as in the United Kingdom.[17] When in 1960 Canada adopted the Canadian Bill of Rights,[18] it was enacted as a federal statute, not as an amendment to the B.N.A. Act, and it was made applicable only to federal laws. The Constitution Act, 1982 finally

---

Responsible Government. For discussion of whether changes to (aspects of) the Letters Patent may nonetheless still require a formal constitutional amendment, see ch. 4, Amendment, under heading § 4:6, "Constitution of Canada".

[13]Responsible government is the subject of ch. 9.

[14]The history of the Supreme Court of Canada is related in ch. 8, Supreme Court of Canada.

[15]See ch. 8, Supreme Court of Canada, under heading § 8:2, "Abolition of Privy Council Appeals".

[16]Supreme Court Act, R.S.C. 1985, c. S-26. The qualification is included in the sentence in the text because the effect of the Supreme Court of Canada's decision in *Re Supreme Court Act, ss. 5 and 6*, [2014] 1 S.C.R. 433 was to add some of the provisions of the Supreme Court Act to the Constitution of Canada. For fuller discussion, see § 1:4, "Constitution of Canada"; see also ch. 4, Amendment, under heading § 4:6, "Constitution of Canada".

[17]The uniquely Canadian issues of language rights and denominational-school rights could not be evaded in 1867 and were dealt with in ss. 93 and 133 of the B.N.A. Act.

[18]Canadian Bill of Rights, R.S.C. 1985, Appendix III. The Canadian Bill of Rights is set out in an appendix to this book. It is the subject of ch. 35.

added to Canada's constitutional law a bill of rights—the Canadian Charter of Rights and Freedoms—which is entrenched (that is, alterable only by the process of constitutional amendment) and applicable to provincial as well as federal laws.

III. CONSTITUTION ACT, 1982

§ 1:3 Constitution Act, 1982

As the foregoing account shows, the constitutional settlement of 1982 made some important repairs to Canada's constitutional law: a domestic amending formula was adopted; the authority over Canada of the United Kingdom (imperial) Parliament was terminated; and the Charter of Rights was adopted. But in terms of the accessibility and comprehensibility of Canada's constitutional law very little was accomplished. The leading instrument of the 1982 settlement was the Canada Act 1982,[1] a short statute of the United Kingdom Parliament, which terminated the authority over Canada of the United Kingdom Parliament. Schedule B of the Canada Act 1982 was the Constitution Act, 1982,[2] which contains the Charter of Rights, the amending formula and the other changes to Canada's constitutional law. Neither the Canada Act 1982 nor the Constitution Act, 1982 purports to be a codification or even consolidation of Canada's constitutional law. In fact, the two 1982 statutes are not even integrated into earlier constitutional instruments. The Canada Act 1982 consists of only four short sections,[3] none of which purports to be an amendment of the B.N.A. Act. The Constitution Act, 1982 is longer—60 sections—and it makes a few amendments to the B.N.A. Act,[4] but for the most part it too is a self-sufficient instrument. In a sense, the two 1982 statutes worsen the formal state of Canada's constitutional law, because they add two more statutes to the variety of sources which existed before.

The Constitution Act, 1982 does do two things which are intended to effect some modernization and rationalization of Canada's constitutional law. First, the name of the B.N.A. Act is changed to the Constitution Act, 1867.[5] This change seems to me to smack of re-writing history, and inevitably leads to confusion with the Constitution Act, 1982, which, as related above, is not technically an amendment to the B.N.A. Act (Constitution Act, 1867). Since 1982, to avoid ambiguity, the dates of the two instruments always have to be used.

[Section 1:3]

[1]U.K. Stats. 1982, c. 11. The Canada Act 1982 is set out in an appendix to this book.

[2]The Constitution Act, 1982 is set out in an appendix to this book.

[3]Section 1 incorporates the Constitution Act, 1982 as Schedule B to the Canada Act 1982. Section 2 terminates the authority over Canada of the United Kingdom Parliament. Section 3 incorporates a French version as Schedule A. Section 4 gives the short title.

[4]Constitution Act, 1982, ss. 50, 51, 53 and schedule, item 1.

[5]Constitution Act, 1982, s. 53(2). The later B.N.A. Acts (amending the 1867 Act) are similarly changed to Constitution Acts.

A second rationalization attempted by the Constitution Act, 1982 is the provision for the first time of a definition of the phrase "Constitution of Canada". That definition is discussed in the next section of this chapter.

IV. CONSTITUTION OF CANADA

§ 1:4 Constitution of Canada

The phrase "Constitution of Canada" is defined in s. 52(2) of the Constitution Act, 1982,[1] as follows:

52.(2) The Constitution of Canada includes

(a) the Canada Act 1982, including this Act;

(b) the Acts and orders referred to in the schedule; and

(c) any amendment to any Act or order referred to in paragraph (a) or (b).

The definition of the Constitution of Canada includes three categories of instruments. The first category (paragraph (a)) is the Canada Act 1982, which includes the Constitution Act, 1982 (being Schedule B of the Canada Act 1982). The second category (paragraph (b)) is a list of 30 Acts and orders in the schedule to the Constitution Act, 1982. This list includes the Constitution Act, 1867 and its amendments, the orders in council and statutes admitting or creating new provinces or altering boundaries,[2] and the Statute of Westminster.[3] The third category (paragraph (c)) comprises the amendments which may in the future be made to any of the instruments in the first two categories.[4] At the time of writing (2012), there have been 11 such amendments.[5]

[Section 1:4]

[1]See W.J. Newman, "Defining the 'Constitution of Canada' since 1982" (2003) 22 Supreme Court L.R. (2d) 423.

[2]The admission or creation of new provinces after 1867 is described in ch. 2, Reception, under heading §§ 2:8 to 2:12, "Admission of new provinces and territories". In *Hogan v. Nfld.* (2000), 183 D.L.R. (4th) 225 (Nfld. C.A.), it was held that the Terms of Union of Newfoundland with Canada were part of the Constitution of Canada, because, although not listed in the schedule to the Constitution Act, 1982, the Terms of Union were confirmed by, given the force of law by, and set out in the schedule to, the Newfoundland Act, an imperial statute which is listed (as item 21) in the schedule to the Constitution Act, 1982; they were "part of the Newfoundland Act by reference" (para. 44). A contrary conclusion in *Hogan* would have led to the startling conclusion that the Terms of Union were unamendable.

[3]The Statute of Westminster is described in ch. 3, Independence, under heading § 3:3, "Statute of Westminster, 1931".

[4]Section 52(2) does not contemplate a future addition to the Constitution that does not take the form of an amendment to the instruments already forming part of the Constitution of Canada. Suppose, for example, it was decided to entrench the letters patent constituting the office of Governor General, and the amending procedure of s. 41 of the Constitution Act, 1982 was operated to accomplish that result. This would be a freestanding addition to the Constitution that is not caught by the existing definition (at least not explicitly). It would be necessary to amend the definition by adding a reference

to the new instrument. The Meech Lake Accord of 1987, now lapsed, proposed to remedy this defect in s. 52(2) by adding a new paragraph: "(d) any other amendment to the Constitution of Canada".

[5]The amendments are as follows:

(1) Constitution Amendment Proclamation, 1983, R.S.C. 1985, Appendix II, No. 46, amending s. 25(b), and adding ss. 35(3), 35(4), 35.1, 37.1 and 54.1 to the Constitution Act, 1982. This amendment was adopted by the Parliament and nine Legislatures (all except Quebec) under s. 38 of the Constitution Act, 1982.

(2) Constitution Act, 1985 (Representation), R.S.C. 1985, Appendix II, No. 47, repealing and replacing s. 51 of the Constitution Act, 1867. This was enacted by the Parliament of Canada alone, acting under s. 44 of the Constitution Act, 1982.

(3) Constitution Amendment, 1987 (Newfoundland Act), Can. Stat. Instruments, SI 88-11, amending the Newfoundland Act with respect to denominational school rights. This amendment was adopted by the Parliament of Canada and Legislature of Newfoundland, acting under s. 43 of the Constitution Act, 1982.

(4) Constitution Amendment Proclamation, 1993 (New Brunswick Act), Can. Stat. Instruments, SI 93-54, adding s. 16.1 to the Charter of Rights to give English and French linguistic communities "equality of status and equal rights and privileges." This amendment was adopted by the Parliament of Canada and the Legislature of New Brunswick, acting under s. 43 of the Constitution Act, 1982.

(5) Constitution Amendment Proclamation, 1993 (Prince Edward Island), Can. Stat. Instruments, SI 94-50, amending the Schedule to the P.E.I. Terms of Union to provide that a fixed crossing may substitute for a steam (ferry) service. This amendment was adopted by the Parliament of Canada and the Legislative Assembly of P.E.I., acting under s. 43 of the Constitution Act, 1982.

(6) Constitution Amendment Proclamation, 1997 (Newfoundland Act), Can. Stat. Instruments, SI 97-55, amending the Newfoundland Act with respect to religious education. This amendment was adopted by the Parliament of Canada and the Legislative Assembly of Newfoundland, acting under ss. 43 and 47 of the Constitution Act, 1982, allowing Parliament to proclaim an amendment to the Constitution without a resolution from the Senate.

(7) Constitution Amendment Proclamation, 1997 (Quebec), Can. Stat. Instruments, SI 97-141, amending s. 93 of the Constitution Act, 1867, so that the provisions regarding the special protection of denominational schools do not apply to Quebec. This amendment was adopted by the Parliament of Canada and the National Assembly of Quebec, acting under s. 43 of the Constitution Act, 1982.

(8) Constitution Amendment Proclamation, 1998 (Newfoundland Act), Can. Stat. Instruments, SI 98-25, amending the Newfoundland Act with respect to religious education. This amendment (which repealed the 1997 amendment, item (6), above), was adopted by the Parliament of Canada and the House of Assembly of Newfoundland, acting under s. 43 of the Constitution Act, 1982.

(9) Constitution Act, 1999 (Nunavut), S.C. 1998, c. 15, Pt. II, providing for representation for the new territory of Nunavut in the Senate and House of Commons. This was enacted by the Parliament of Canada alone, acting under s. 44 of the Constitution Act, 1982.

(10) Constitution Amendment, 2001 (Newfoundland and Labrador), Can. Stat. Instruments SI 2002-117, amending the Newfoundland Act by changing the name of the province to "Province of Newfoundland and Labrador". This was enacted by the Parliament of Canada and the House of Assembly of Newfoundland, acting under s. 43 of the Constitution Act, 1982.

The Charter of Rights is part of the Constitution of Canada because it is Part I of the Constitution Act, 1982, which is Schedule B of the Canada Act 1982, which is expressly named in s. 52(2). Among the rights that the Charter guarantees is "freedom of association" (s. 2(d)). In the *Health Services Bargaining* case (2007),[6] the Supreme Court of Canada held that this guarantee protected a trade union's right to collective bargaining, not merely the process of collective bargaining, but the fruits of past collective bargaining, namely, the collective agreement entered into by the union, on behalf of its members, with the employer. British Columbia enacted a statute to weaken the job-protection provisions (seniority, layoffs, bumping and contracting out) of the collective agreements between hospitals and their unionized health care workers. The goal was to help the hospitals operate more efficiently and rein in their labour costs. In the past it had always been assumed that a statute was superior in force to a collective agreement, and would prevail over a collective agreement in the case of conflict. However, the Court held that the statute was invalid as a breach of freedom of association. The curious result of the decision is that a collective agreement negotiated between a union and an employer is now superior to a statute.[7] It has the same status as if it were part of the Charter of Rights itself, that is, part of the Constitution of Canada.[8]

The definition of the "Constitution of Canada" in s. 52(2) is introduced by the word "includes". In general, in Canadian statutes, the word "includes" indicates that the definition is not exhaustive. The word "means" is customary for an exhaustive definition. In *New Brunswick Broadcasting Co. v. Nova Scotia* (1993),[9] a majority of the Supreme

---

(11) Fair Representation Act, S.C. 2011, c. 26, replacing s. 51(1) of the Constitution Act, 1867. This was enacted by the Parliament of Canada alone, acting under s. 44 of the Constitution Act, 1982.

[6]*Health Services and Support—Facilities Subsector Bargaining Assn. v. B.C.*, [2007] 2 S.C.R. 391.

[7]The parties to a collective agreement privately negotiate a compromise of their own interests without regard for wider public interests. There is nothing wrong with that, but in areas like health care and education (for example) wider public interests are involved. That is why, in principle, a statute enacted by the Legislature ought to prevail over a collective agreement. The Legislature represents all of the people of the province, it debates the issues in public, and it is ultimately accountable to the people through the electoral process. See R.E. Charney, "The Contract Clause Comes to Canada: The British Columbia *Health Services* Case and the Sanctity of Collective Agreements" (2007) 23 Nat. J. Con. Law 65. In my view, if there is to be constitutional protection for the collective bargaining process (as the Court has now decided), it ought to stop short of constitutional protection for the collective agreement.

[8]Charter rights differ from other provisions of the Constitution in that Charter rights are, by virtue of s. 1 of the Charter, subject to reasonable limits prescribed by law. Collective agreements could therefore be amended by a statute that satisfied the standards stipulated by the Supreme Court of Canada for s. 1 justification: ch. 38, Limitation of Rights. In this case, however, the majority of the Court held that the statute was not saved by s. 1.

[9]*New Brunswick Broadcasting Co. v. Nova Scotia*, [1993] 1 S.C.R. 319. The majority opinion was written by McLachlin J., with whom La Forest, L'Heureux-Dubé,

Court of Canada held that the definition in s. 52(2) is not exhaustive.[10] The Court held that the unwritten doctrine of parliamentary privilege should be included in the definition, although s. 52(2) makes no mention of parliamentary privilege. The inclusion of parliamentary privilege was said to be implied by the reference in the preamble of the Constitution Act, 1867 to "a constitution similar in principle to that of the United Kingdom". As Sopinka J. commented in a separate opinion,[11] this vague phrase is a frail foundation for the addition of new elements to the definition of the "Constitution of Canada" in s. 52(2). Moreover, the Court's decision means that the definition is capable of judicial expansion by virtue of implications from other parts of the Constitution. This raised the possibility of further additions, which destroys the certainty apparently afforded by the list of 30 instruments that is scheduled to s. 52(2).

The Court in *New Brunswick Broadcasting* did not add a new *document* to the scheduled list referred to in s. 52(2). What the Court added was the unwritten doctrine of parliamentary privilege. This was a surprising decision in that the definition in s. 52(2) is expressed solely in terms of written instruments, which seemed to presuppose that the Constitution of Canada was confined to written instruments.[12] Could the Court also add additional written instruments to the scheduled list of Acts and orders? Obviously, this could not be ruled out in view of the Court's holding that the definition in s. 52(2) is not exhaustive.[13] But, considering the specificity of the scheduled list of Acts and orders, and the grave consequences (namely, supremacy and entrenchment, described later in this section) of the inclusion of other instruments, a court should exercise great caution when invited to make additions[14] to the 30 instruments in the schedule.[15] Truly compelling reasons are

---

Gonthier and Iacobucci JJ. agreed. Lamer C.J. and Sopinka J., who each wrote a concurring opinion, and Cory J., who wrote a dissenting opinion, did not need to rule, and did not rule, on the question whether the definition of the Constitution of Canada was exhaustive, and, if not, whether it included parliamentary privilege.

[10]See also *Re Senate Reform*, [2014] 1 S.C.R. 704, 2014 SCC 32, para. 24.

[11]*New Brunswick Broadcasting Co. v. N.S*, [1993] 1 S.C.R. 319, 396.

[12]But see ch. 15, Judicial Review on Federal Grounds, under heading § 15:28, "Unwritten constitutional principles".

[13]In *B.C. v. Can. (Vancouver Island Ry.)*, [1994] 2 S.C.R. 41, Iacobucci J., for the Supreme Court, left open the "possibility that documents not listed in s. 52(2) might yet be considered constitutional in certain contexts" (at 94). The effect of the Court's decision in *Re Supreme Court Act, ss. 5 and 6*, [2014] 1 S.C.R. 433 was to add some of the provisions of the Supreme Court Act – which is not explicitly included in s. 52(2) – to the Constitution of Canada. The *Supreme Court Reference* is discussed more fully later in this section: see also ch. 4, Amendment, under heading § 4:6, "Constitution of Canada".

[14]A possible function for the word "includes" would be to catch future constitutional amendments that are missed by para, (c) of s. 52(2): see § 1:4 note 4, above. The argument for treating the definition as exhaustive is very powerful with respect to instruments that existed in 1982.

[15]Monahan et al., Constitutional Law (5th ed., 2017), 191–193, approves of the "flexibility" afforded to the courts in adding new elements to the definition, including statutes in existence in 1982 that could have been and were not listed in the schedule,

needed to treat the scheduled list as other than exhaustive.[16] It is important to note that the scheduled list omits many instruments of importance. For example, the definition omits the pre-1867 instruments which governed the territory now forming part of Ontario and Quebec: the Royal Proclamation of 1763,[17] the Quebec Act of 1774, the Constitutional Act of 1791 and the Union Act of 1840.[18] Also omitted are the pre-1867 instruments which are still the constitutions of Nova Scotia (1749), Prince Edward Island (1769), New Brunswick (1784), Newfoundland (1832) and British Columbia (1866).[19] Nor does the definition include the Letters Patent of 1947,[20] which constitute the office of Governor General, or the Supreme Court Act,[21] which establishes the Supreme Court of Canada, or the Canadian Bill of Rights,[22] which remains in force notwithstanding the adoption of the Charter of Rights.

Among the many important statutes of a constitutional character that are not included in the schedule to the Constitution Act, 1982 is the Act of Settlement, 1701 (U.K.), which is an imperial statute enacted by the Parliament of the United Kingdom with application not only to the United Kingdom but also to its dominions, including Canada. The Act was part of the revolution settlement enacted on the accession to the English throne of William and Mary that followed the turbulent reigns of the Stuart kings. The Act, among other things, settled one of the succession issues that was a source of conflict in the seventeenth century. The Act provided that a Roman Catholic, or a person married to a Roman Catholic, may not succeed to the Crown of England. In *O'Donohue v. Canada* (2003),[23] an application was brought to the Superior Court of Justice in Ontario seeking a declaration that these provisions of the Act

---

for example, the Supreme Court Act. The disadvantage of this flexibility is that statutes making changes to the Supreme Court of Canada, the powers of the Governor General or Lieutenant Governor, or official languages legislation (to give three examples) are now all vulnerable to constitutional attack on the ground that a constitutional amendment should have been used for the change.

[16]So held in *Re Dixon* (1986), 31 D.L.R. (4th) 546, 556-557 (B.C.S.C.) (Constitution of B.C. not included); *MacLean v. A.G.N.S.* (1987), 35 D.L.R. (4th) 306 (N.S.S.C.) (Constitution of N.S. not included).

[17]However, the Royal Proclamation of 1763 is identified in s. 25 of the Charter of Rights, which provides that "[t]he guarantee in this Charter of certain rights and freedoms shall not be construed so as to abrogate or derogate from . . . (a) any rights or freedoms that have been recognized by the Royal Proclamation of October 7, 1763; . . .".

[18]These instruments are described in ch. 2, Reception.

[19]These instruments are also described in ch. 2, Reception.

[20]R.S.C. 1985, Appendix II, No. 31. For discussion of whether changes to (aspects of) the Letters Patent may nonetheless still require a formal constitutional amendment, see ch. 4, Amendment, under heading § 4:6, "Constitution of Canada".

[21]R.S.C. 1985, c. S-26. But see § 1:4 notes 33-38, discussing *Re Supreme Court Act, ss. 5 and 6*, [2014] 1 S.C.R. 433; and see also ch. 4, Amendment, under heading § 4:6, "Constitution of Canada".

[22]R.S.C. 1985, Appendix III.

[23]*O'Donohue v. Canada* (2003), 109 C.R.R. (2d) 1 (Ont. S.C.J.), affd. (2005) 137 A.C.W.S. (3d) 1131 (Ont. C.A.); folld. *Teskey v. Can.* (2014), 377 D.L.R. (4th) 39 (Ont. C.A.).

discriminated on the basis of religion and were of no force or effect in Canada by virtue of the equality guarantee in s. 15 of the Charter of Rights. Rouleau J. struck out the application on the basis that the rules of succession in the Act of Settlement could not be challenged under the Charter. Pointing to the reference in the preamble to the Constitution Act, 1867 to a federal union "under the Crown of the United Kingdom", he said that it is a basic principle underlying the Constitution of Canada that Canada is a constitutional monarchy that is united under and shares the monarch of the United Kingdom. It follows from this, he said, that the rules of succession "must be shared and be in symmetry with those of the United Kingdom".[24] Following the *New Brunswick Broadcasting* case, he said that the Charter could not be used to challenge the rules of succession in the Act of Settlement because "[i]f the courts were free to review and declare inoperative certain parts of the rules of succession, Canada could break symmetry with Great Britain, and could conceivably recognize a different monarch than does Great Britain".[25] This would not only be "contrary to settled intention", it would bring about a fundamental change in the office of the Queen, without satisfying the requirements of a constitutional amendment.[26] Rouleau J.'s decision was affirmed by the Ontario Court of Appeal.

It is possible to read *O'Donohue* in two different ways. First, it can be read to hold that the provisions relating to the rules of succession in the Act of Settlement are implicitly part of the Constitution of Canada.[27] Second, it can be read to hold that it is not the provisions relating to the rules of succession, but rather the principles underlying the rules of succession that are implicitly part of the Constitution of Canada. In *Motard v. Canada* (2019),[28] the Quebec Court of Appeal took the second view – that it is not the provisions relating to the rules of succession, but rather the principles underlying the rules of succession (in particular, the principle of symmetry with the monarch of the United Kingdom) that are implicitly part of the Constitution of Canada. In that case, it was argued that the federal Parliament had acted unconstitutionally in

---

[24] *O'Donohue v. Canada* (2003), 109 C.R.R. (2d) 1 (Ont. S.C.J.), affd. (2005) 137 A.C.W.S. (3d) 1131 (Ont. C.A.), para. 27.

[25] *O'Donohue v. Canada* (2003), 109 C.R.R. (2d) 1 (Ont. S.C.J.), affd. (2005) 137 A.C.W.S. (3d) 1131 (Ont. C.A.), para. 29.

[26] *O'Donohue v. Canada* (2003), 109 C.R.R. (2d) 1 (Ont. S.C.J.), affd. (2005) 137 A.C.W.S. (3d) 1131 (Ont. C.A.), para. 29, 33.

[27] This is how one of the co-authors of this book (Peter Hogg) appeared to read Rouleau J.'s reasons. In an earlier iteration of this section of this chapter, he indicated that Rouleau J. had concluded that "although the Act of Settlement was not scheduled to the Constitution Act, 1982, the impugned provisions of the Act were nonetheless part of the Constitution of Canada". He also indicated that, in an even earlier iteration of this section of this chapter, he had "interpreted the *O'Donohue* decision as taking the radical step of adding an unscheduled statute to the Constitution of Canada", and that he had come to "think that is incorrect" – that Rouleau J.'s opinion "is restricted to the provisions relating to the rules of succession".

[28] *Motard v. Canada*, 2019 QCCA 1826 (Que. C.A.), leave to appeal to the S.C.C. denied April 23, 2020. Rancourt J.A. wrote the opinion of the three-judge panel of the Court (which included then Kasirer J.A.).

enacting the Succession to the Throne Act, 2013[29] without pursuing a constitutional amendment. The Act assented to changes that the United Kingdom Parliament made to the rules of succession to eliminate discriminatory requirements relating to sex and religion, changes that removed part (but not all) of the discriminatory religious requirement challenged in *O'Donohue*.[30] The conclusion that the provisions relating to the rules of succession were not part of the Constitution of Canada was important, because it followed from it that the Act could be enacted without pursuing a constitutional amendment. After all, if it is the principle of symmetry that is part of the Constitution of Canada and not the provisions relating to the rules of succession, no constitutional amendment was required because the Act did not purport to change the principle of symmetry. Indeed, the Act actually *confirmed* the principle of symmetry, by affirming that Canada is content that its monarch will continue to be the same person that is the monarch of the United Kingdom.[31]

In an earlier version of this book, I interpreted the *O'Donohue* decision as taking the radical step of adding an unscheduled statute to the Constitution of Canada. However, I now think that is incorrect. Rouleau J. is careful not to go that far. His opinion is restricted to the *rules of succession* in the Act of Settlement: "These rules of succession, and the requirement that they be the same as those of Great Britain, are necessary to the proper functioning of our constitutional monarchy and, therefore, the rules are not subject to Charter scrutiny."[32] At bottom, the decision is about changing the definition of "the Queen" in the Constitution Act, 1867, which is what would have occurred if the Charter of Rights were to be held to require that Canada adopt rules of succession out of harmony with the United Kingdom (and the other Commonwealth realms).[33]

Another important statute of a constitutional character that, as noted earlier, is not included in the schedule to the Constitution Act, 1982 is the Supreme Court Act,[34] which is a statute of the Parliament of Canada enacted under s. 101 of the Constitution Act, 1867 (the power to estab-

[29]S.C. 2013, c. 6

[30]The changes were made by the Succession to the Crown Act 2013 (U.K.), c. 20. The UK Act repealed the rule of male preference primogeniture (which gave the monarch's eldest legitimate *son* priority of succession to the throne, even if the monarch's eldest legitimate child was a daughter), and the rule that a person married to a Roman Catholic may not succeed to the throne. It did not repeal the rule that a Roman Catholic may not succeed to the throne.

[31]This is a requirement of convention, not of strict law: see further, ch. 9, Responsible Government, under heading § 9:3, "Law and convention"; see also P.W. Hogg, "Succession to the Throne" (2014) 33 Nat. J. Con. Law 83.

[32]*O'Donohue v. The Queen* (2003), 109 C.R.R. (2d) 1 (Ont. S.C.J.), affd. (2005) 137 A.C.W.S. (3d) 1131 (Ont. C.A.); folld. *Teskey v. Can.* (2014), 377 D.L.R. (4th) 39 (Ont. C.A.)., paras. 37.

[33]For elaboration of this point, see P.W. Hogg, "Succession to the Throne" (2014) 33 Nat. J. Con. Law 83.

[34]R.S.C. 1985, c. S-26.

lish "a general court of appeal for Canada"). Although the Constitution Act, 1982 did not amend s. 101 and did not add the Supreme Court Act to the schedule of constitutional instruments, the Constitution Act, 1982 did make two references to the Court in Part V, which is the part that provides the amending procedures for the Constitution of Canada. Section 41(d) lists "the composition of the Supreme Court of Canada" as one of the items that require the unanimity procedure for its amendment, and s. 42(1)(d) lists ("subject to para. 41(d)") "the Supreme Court of Canada" as one of the items that require the seven-fifty procedure for its amendment.[35] The view I took in earlier versions of this book was that, until the Court was expressly entrenched in the Constitution of Canada (as was in fact proposed in the unsuccessful Meech Lake (1987) and Charlottetown (1992) Accords), these provisions were ineffective ("empty vessels") because ss. 41 and 42 applied only to amendments of the "Constitution of Canada" and the Supreme Court Act was not part of the Constitution of Canada. In the *Supreme Court Reference* (2014),[36] the Supreme Court had to decide whether Parliament could unilaterally enact a small change to the qualifications for appointment to the Court from Quebec (former as well as current members of the bar). On the empty vessels theory, the answer would have been yes. The Court held that the answer was no. According to the Court, the implication to be drawn from the references to the Court in Part V, reinforced by the importance of the Court's "position within the architecture of the Constitution",[37] was that the provisions of the Supreme Court Act dealing with the composition of the Court should be treated as part of the Constitution of Canada requiring the unanimity procedure for their amendment as stipulated by s. 41(d).[38] Therefore, Parliament alone could not change those provisions. And, the Court added, the provisions of the Supreme Court Act dealing with "the other essential features" of the Court should also be treated as part of the Constitution of Canada requiring the seven-fifty procedure for their amendment as stipulated by s. 42(1)(d).[39] The effect of this decision is to add some of the provisions of the Supreme Court Act to the Constitution of Canada.

The definition of the "Constitution of Canada" in s. 52(2) is needed to give content to the supremacy clause and the entrenchment clause of the Constitution Act, 1982. The supremacy clause is s. 52(1), which provides as follows:

---

[35] Chapter 4, Amendment, under headings § 4:14, "Section 42", and § 4:16, "Unanimity procedure".

[36] *Re Supreme Court Act, ss. 5 and 6*, [2014] 1 S.C.R. 433, 2014 SCC 21.

[37] *Re Supreme Court Act, ss. 5 and 6*, [2014] 1 S.C.R. 433, 2014 SCC 21, para. 87.

[38] *Re Supreme Court Act, ss. 5 and 6*, [2014] 1 S.C.R. 433, 2014 SCC 21, paras. 75, 91. These provisions were identified as ss. 4(1) (nine judges), 5 (who may be appointed) and 6 (three judges from Quebec).

[39] *Re Supreme Court Act, ss. 5 and 6*, [2014] 1 S.C.R. 433, 2014 SCC 21, paras. 75, 90, 94. These provisions were not specifically identified, although the Court said (para. 94) that: "These essential features include, at the very least, the Court's jurisdiction as the final general court of appeal for Canada, including in matters of constitutional interpretation, and its independence."

> 52.(1) The Constitution of Canada is the supreme law of Canada, and any law that is inconsistent with the provisions of the Constitution is, to the extent of the inconsistency, of no force or effect.

This gives priority to the "Constitution of Canada" where it is inconsistent with other laws.[40] This supremacy clause obviously calls for a definition of the Constitution of Canada because that is the thing to which supremacy is accorded.

The entrenchment clause is s. 52(3), which provides as follows:

> 52.(3) Amendments to the Constitution of Canada shall be made only in accordance with the authority contained in the Constitution of Canada.

The effect of s. 52(3) is to entrench the "Constitution of Canada": it cannot be amended by ordinary legislative action, but only by the special amending procedures laid down by Part V of the Constitution Act, 1982.[41] This entrenchment clause obviously calls for a definition of the Constitution of Canada that is entrenched.

The definition of the Constitution of Canada in s. 52(2) is vital to the application of the supremacy clause and the entrenchment clause. But it will probably have little effect on the use of the term "constitution" in other contexts. That term will continue to take its colour from its context, sometimes meaning the definition in s. 52(2), sometimes including the whole of Canada's constitutional law, and sometimes meaning only the Constitution Act, 1867 or only the Constitution Act, 1982, or both the last two instruments. Canada's gradual evolution from colony to nation has denied it any single comprehensive constitutional document.

In the light of history it is perfectly understandable why Canada lacks a document which contains ringing declarations of national purpose and independence, and which is intended to state all of the most important constitutional rules. Some Canadians feel that the lack of such a document is a reproach to Canada's nationhood. But this kind of thinking, while clad in the garb of Canadian nationalism, is probably at bottom a desire to copy the United States; and the idea that a new constitution could somehow be manufactured which would be more Canadian, more legitimate and more inspiring is unhistorical and naive. The one real disadvantage of the absence of a comprehensive constitutional document is that the rules of the Constitution are not readily accessible to non-lawyers. The Constitution Act, 1867 and the Constitution Act, 1982 (especially the latter) are rather detailed lawyers' instruments, lacking in elegance and brevity and not always easy to understand. And, as emphasized above, they do not by any means include all of the rules of Canadian constitutional law. These rules have to be hunted down in a variety of places. In the following sections of this chapter, I shall briefly survey those various sources.

---

[40] The supremacy clause is discussed in ch. 5, Federalism, under heading § 5:19, "Supremacy of the Constitution", and in ch. 40, Enforcement of Rights, under heading §§ 40:1 to 40:10, "Supremacy clause".

[41] The amending procedures of Part V are discussed in ch. 4, Amendment. Within Part V, two sections, namely, ss. 44 and 45, do authorize certain categories of amendments by ordinary legislative action, but all other categories require a special, more difficult procedure.

V. IMPERIAL STATUTES

§ 1:5 Imperial statutes

The Constitution Act, 1867 and the Constitution Act, 1982 are both imperial statutes, that is to say, statutes enacted for Canada by the United Kingdom Parliament in its role as imperial Parliament.[1] These two statutes are within the definition of the "Constitution of Canada" in s. 52(2) of the Constitution Act, 1982, and they are the two most important elements of the Constitution of Canada. Also within the definition are 17 other imperial statutes, mostly amendments to the Constitution Act, 1867, and four orders in council made under the authority of s. 146 of the Constitution Act, 1867, admitting to Canada the federal territories and the provinces of British Columbia and Prince Edward Island.

As the next two chapters of this book will explain, imperial statutes that are not part of the "Constitution of Canada"[2] no longer have any special status in Canada. They are not supreme over the statutes enacted by Parliament or the Legislatures, and like any other statute they are subject to amendment or repeal by Parliament or by the Legislatures of the provinces, depending on which level of government has authority over the subject matter of the particular imperial statute. For those imperial statutes that are part of the Constitution of Canada, they are supreme over other laws and can be amended or repealed only in accordance with the amending procedures of Part V of the Constitution of Canada.

VI. CANADIAN STATUTES

§ 1:6 Canadian statutes

The definition of the "Constitution of Canada" in s. 52(2) of the Constitution Act, 1982 includes eight Canadian statutes. Three of these created the provinces of Manitoba, Alberta and Saskatchewan. These statutes were enacted under the power to create provinces out of federal territories, which was granted to the federal Parliament by the Constitution Act, 1871.[1] The other five Canadian statutes were amendments to the Constitution Act, 1867. These statutes were enacted under limited

[Section 1:5]

[1]See ch. 2, Reception, under heading § 2:13, "Imperial statutes".

[2]Generally speaking, only those imperial statutes listed in the schedule to the Constitution Act, 1982 are part of the Constitution of Canada, but it has been held that the principles underlying the rules of succession to the throne are part of the Constitution of Canada, even though the rules themselves are contained in an unlisted imperial statute: see further the text beginning at § 1:4 note 22, above.

[Section 1:6]

[1]See ch. 2, Reception, under heading § 2:9, "Territories and prairie provinces".

powers of amendment granted to the federal Parliament by the Constitution Act, 1867 (including an amendment in 1949).[2]

The eight Canadian statutes forming part of the Constitution of Canada were of course enacted by the federal Parliament in the ordinary way. However, their inclusion in the definition of the "Constitution of Canada" means that they are now supreme over other federal statutes by virtue of s. 52(1) of the Constitution Act, 1982, and are entrenched (unalterable except by use of the amending procedures) by virtue of s. 52(3) of the Constitution Act, 1982.

There are other Canadian statutes, which, although not included in the definition of the "Constitution of Canada", are constitutional in the sense that they establish or regulate some of the important institutions of the country. The Canadian Bill of Rights of 1960,[3] which purports to limit the powers of the federal Parliament,[4] is the clearest example of such a statute. The statute that created the Supreme Court of Canada in 1875[5] is also in this category, and the statute that created the Federal Court of Canada in 1971[6] has a claim to be included as well. One might also include federal statutes upon such basic matters as the franchise and citizenship. In each province, too, there are statutes that establish the system of courts, that provide for elections to the Legislature and that regulate the proceedings of the Legislature; these statutes are clearly constitutional in character. As well, Saskatchewan, Alberta and Quebec have each enacted a Bill of Rights.[7] Of course, statutes that are not included in the definition of the Constitution of Canada may be repealed or amended by the ordinary legislative process.

VII. PARLIAMENTARY PRIVILEGE

§ 1:7 Parliamentary privilege

The federal Houses of Parliament and the provincial legislative assemblies possess a set of powers and privileges that are "necessary to their capacity to function as legislative bodies".[1] These powers and rights are known collectively as "parliamentary privilege".[2] In *New Brunswick Broadcasting Co. v. Nova Scotia* (1993),[3] the Supreme Court of Canada held that the Nova Scotia legislative assembly could ban the televising

[2]See ch. 4, Amendment, under heading § 4:18, "Federal Parliament alone (s. 44)".

[3]R.S.C. 1985, Appendix III.

[4]See ch. 35, Canadian Bill of Rights.

[5]See ch. 8, Supreme Court of Canada.

[6]See ch. 7, Courts, under heading § 7:11, "Federal Court of Canada".

[7]See ch. 34, Civil Liberties, under heading § 34:4, "Statutory bills of rights".

[Section 1:7]

[1]*New Brunswick Broadcasting Co. v. N.S.*, [1993] 1 S.C.R. 319, 381 per McLachlin J. for the majority.

[2]See W.J. Newman, "Parliamentary Privilege, the Canadian Constitution and the Courts" (2008) 39 Ottawa L. Rev. 573.

[3]*New Brunswick Broadcasting Co. v. Nova Scotia*, [1993] 1 S.C.R. 319. The major-

of its proceedings, because the power to exclude "strangers" from the legislative chamber was part of the assembly's parliamentary privilege.[4] Parliamentary privilege also includes: freedom of speech in debate during legislative proceedings, including legal immunity for things said during debate;[5] exclusive control of the proceedings of the legislative assembly, as well as the control of publication of debates and proceedings;[6] the privilege of members of a legislative assembly not to testify in court proceedings while Parliament or the Legislature is in session;[7] and the authority to discipline members and non-members for interference with the discharge of legislative functions.[8]

In *Canada v. Vaid* (2005),[9] it was argued that the privileges of the Parliament of Canada included the management of all the employees of the Senate and the House of Commons (the legislative branch). The issue was sparked by a complaint to the Canadian Human Rights Commission by the chauffeur of the Speaker of the House. The chauffeur alleged that he had been constructively dismissed on grounds that were forbidden by the Canadian Human Rights Act. The House of Commons and the Speaker took the position that the hiring and firing of all House employees were "internal affairs" of Parliament that were not subject to review by any tribunal or court or other body external to Parliament. The Supreme Court of Canada rejected this position. The Court held that such a sweeping claim of parliamentary privilege failed the test of necessity. Exclusive and unreviewable jurisdiction over all House employees was not necessary for the functioning of the House of Commons as a deliberative body. The management of some employees (whom the Court did not identify) was undoubtedly necessary to protect the deliberative functions of the House, and would be covered by parliamentary privilege. But the privilege did not extend to the majority of the House's employees (2,377 in number), who staffed the restaurant, the library, public information, repair and maintenance, parking and traffic

---

ity opinion was written by McLachlin J., with the concurrence of La Forest, L' Heureux-Dubé, Gonthier and Iacobucci JJ. Separate concurring opinions were written by Lamer C.J. and Sopinka J. Cory J. dissented.

[4]See similarly, *Payson v. Hubert* (1904), 34 S.C.R. 400; *Can. v. Vaid*, [2005] 1 S.C.R. 667, para. 29(10); *Chagnon v. Syndicat de la fonction publique et parapublique du Québec*, [2018] 2 S.C.R. 687, para. 31.

[5]*Janssen-Ortho v. Amgen Can.* (2005), 256 D.L.R. (4th) 407, paras. 73-78 (Ont. C.A.); *Canada v. Vaid*, [2005] 1 S.C.R. 667, para. 29(10) (citing, among others, *Prebble v. Television New Zealand Ltd.*, [1995] 1 A.C. 321 (P.C.); *Hamilton v. Al Fayed*, [2000] 2 All E.R. 224 (H.L.)) *Chagnon v. Syndicat de la fonction publique et parapublique du Québec*, [2018] 2 S.C.R. 687, para. 31.

[6]*New Brunswick Broadcasting Co. v. Nova Scotia*, [1993] 1 S.C.R. 319, 385 per McLachlin J.; *Canada v. Vaid*, [2005] 1 S.C.R. 667, para. 29(10); *Chagnon v. Syndicat de la fonction publique et parapublique du Québec*, [2018] 2 S.C.R. 687, para. 31.

[7]*Telezone v. Can.* (2004), 69 O.R. (3d) 161 (C.A.); *Canada v. Vaid*, [2005] 1 S.C.R. 667, para. 29(10).

[8]*Harvey v. N.B.*, [1996] 2 S.C.R. 876; *Canada v. Vaid*, [2005] 1 S.C.R. 667, para. 29(10); *Chagnon v. Syndicat de la fonction publique et parapublique du Québec*, [2018] 2 S.C.R. 687, para. 31.

[9]*Canada v. Vaid*, [2005] 1 S.C.R. 667. Binnie J. wrote the opinion of the Court.

control, and performed manifold other functions that were only indirectly connected to the legislative proceedings in the House. The Speaker's chauffeur was in this latter category. His dismissal was not an unreviewable matter of parliamentary privilege.

The issue in *Vaid* re-emerged in *Chagnon v. Syndicat de la function publique et parapublique du Québec* (2018).[10] In this case, the President (the Speaker) of the National Assembly of Québec dismissed three security guards for using the Assembly's cameras to spy on the guest rooms of a nearby hotel. The security guards' union challenged their dismissals by filing grievances with a labour arbitrator. In response, the President argued that the dismissal decisions were a matter of parliamentary privilege, and were therefore unreviewable by the labour arbitrator (and the courts). The President invoked two parliamentary privileges in support of this argument. As in *Vaid*, the President argued that the dismissal decisions were protected by a parliamentary privilege to manage employees. However, unlike in *Vaid*, the President also argued that the dismissal decisions were protected by the parliamentary privilege to exclude "strangers", not because the security guards were strangers themselves to the Assembly, but because they were tasked with assisting the Assembly with excluding strangers. Karakatsanis J., who wrote for the majority of the Court, rejected both arguments. Beginning with the first argument, Karakatsanis J. said that, while the Court had acknowledged in *Vaid* that parliamentary privilege "no doubt . . . attaches to the House's relations with some of its employees",[11] it had not actually gone so far as to recognize "the existence of any form of privilege over the management of employees",[12] and that it did not need to recognize such a parliamentary privilege in this case either, because even if it did exist "the management of the security guards – including their dismissals – would fall beyond the scope of any such privilege".[13] The security guards assisted the Assembly in maintaining the security necessary to allow the Assembly to perform its constitutional functions as a deliberative body, but the President had failed to establish that the external "enforcement of basic employment and labour protections for the security guards" would impede the Assembly's ability to perform its constitutional functions.[14] As for the second argument, Karakatsanis J. noted that it was well accepted that there is a parliamentary privilege

---

[10] *Chagnon v. Syndicat de la function publique et parapublique du Québec*, [2018] 2 S.C.R. 687. Justice Karakatsanis wrote the opinion for the majority of the Court, which was joined by Wagner C.J. and Abella, Moldaver, Gascon and Martin JJ. Rowe J. wrote a concurring decision. Côté and Brown JJ. wrote a joint dissenting opinion.

[11] *Chagnon v. Syndicat de la function publique et parapublique du Québec*, [2018] 2 S.C.R. 687, para. 35, citing *Can. v. Vaid*, [2005] 1 S.C.R. 667, para. 75.

[12] *Chagnon v. Syndicat de la function publique et parapublique du Québec*, [2018] 2 S.C.R. 687.

[13] *Chagnon v. Syndicat de la function publique et parapublique du Québec*, [2018] 2 S.C.R. 687, para. 36.

[14] *Chagnon v. Syndicat de la function publique et parapublique du Québec*, [2018] 2 S.C.R. 687, para. 44. Karakatsanis J. acknowledged that "it may be necessary . . . for the President to have the absolute right to oversee certain *functions* exercised by a given

to exclude strangers, but said that the President's dismissal decisions did not fall within the scope of this established parliamentary privilege. It was not necessary for the dismissals of employees – like the security guards – who assist the Assembly with excluding strangers to "be immune from external review for the Assembly to be able to discharge its legislative mandate".[15] As a result, like the dismissal in *Vaid*, the dismissals of the security guards were not an unreviewable matter of parliamentary privilege.[16]

Parliamentary privilege could be regarded as a branch of the common law in that it is not contained in any statute or other written instrument, and it is the courts who determine its existence and extent. In the *New Brunswick Broadcasting* case, for example, the Supreme Court of Canada asked itself whether the power to exclude strangers from the legislative chamber was necessary for the proper functioning of Nova Scotia's legislative assembly. Only after the Court had satisfied itself that the answer was yes did the Court uphold the existence of the power. In this respect, parliamentary privilege is like the royal prerogative, which is also circumscribed by the decisions of the courts.[17] However, in the *New Brunswick Broadcasting* case, the majority of the Supreme Court of Canada attributed two peculiar characteristics to parliamentary privilege that distinguish it from the royal prerogative and from other branches of the common law.

The first peculiar characteristic of parliamentary privilege, according to *New Brunswick Broadcasting*, is that parliamentary privilege is part of the "Constitution of Canada". This aspect of the decision has already been explained and criticized.[18] The second peculiar characteristic, according to *New Brunswick Broadcasting*, is that the powers authorized by parliamentary privilege are not subject to the Charter of Rights. In that case, for example, the majority of the Court, having determined that the legislative assembly had a parliamentary-privilege power to exclude strangers from the legislative chamber, did not need to consider, and did not consider, whether the assembly's denial of access to the television media was a breach of the freedom of the press guaranteed by s. 2(b) of the Charter. This immunity from the Charter distinguishes parliamentary privilege from the royal prerogative and other common law powers of government; all other common law powers must be

group of employees or certain *aspects* of their employment relationship", but that this does not "necessarily require the recognition of a broad privilege over their management": *Chagnon v. Syndicat de la function publique et parapublique du Québec*, [2018] 2 S.C.R. 687, para. 45 (emphasis in original).

[15] *Chagnon v. Syndicat de la function publique et parapublique du Québec*, [2018] 2 S.C.R. 687, paras. 55-56.

[16] Côté and Brown JJ., writing jointly in dissent, would have held that the President's dismissal decisions were an unreviewable matter of parliamentary privilege, on the basis that the tasks of the security guards fell "within a sphere of activity that is necessary to the proper functioning of the Assembly, namely security" (para. 131).

[17] See § 1:9, "Prerogative".

[18] § 1:4, "Constitution of Canada".

exercised in conformity with the Charter of Rights.[19] The immunity from the Charter also distinguishes parliamentary privilege from other powers conferred by the Constitution of Canada on the federal Parliament and the provincial Legislatures; all the other powers of these legislative bodies must be exercised in conformity with the Charter of Rights.[20]

The powers and privileges of a provincial legislative assembly have been held to be alterable by a statute enacted by the provincial Legislature, on the basis that the powers and privileges are part of the "constitution of the province".[21] Since 1982, the power of each provincial Legislature over the constitution of the province is to be found in s. 45 of the Constitution Act, 1982. (The federal Parliament would possess a similar power over the powers and privileges of each of the two Houses of Parliament under s. 44 of the Constitution Act, 1982, which confers power over "the Senate and House of Commons".) It is not clear whether the decision in *New Brunswick Broadcasting*, by holding that the powers and privileges of provincial legislative assemblies are part of the Constitution of Canada, has deprived the provincial Legislatures of the power to amend the powers and privileges of their legislative assemblies. Sopinka J., in his separate opinion in *New Brunswick Broadcasting*,[22] expressed the opinion, obiter, that this was the result of the majority's decision, describing it as "a high price . . . to pay in order to escape the Charter". It is possible, however, that the powers and privileges of a provincial legislative assembly would remain part of the constitution of the province, and therefore amendable under s. 45, even if they are also part of the Constitution of Canada.[23]

The ruling in *New Brunswick Broadcasting* established the special constitutional status of parliamentary privilege, where the privilege was "inherent" in the creation of a provincial Legislature. Unlike the provincial Legislatures, Parliament has the power, conferred by s. 18 of the Constitution Act, 1867, to enact laws defining the privileges of the Senate and House of Commons. Parliament has exercised this power by enacting a law defining the privileges of the Senate and House of Commons as being those possessed in 1867 by the House of Commons in the United Kingdom.[24] The federal privileges are therefore ascertained by reference to the law and custom of the House of Commons at

[19]See ch. 37, Application of Charter, under heading § 37:12, "Common law".

[20]See ch. 37, Application of Charter, under heading § 37:7, "Parliament or Legislature", where this part of the *New Brunswick Broadcasting* decision is criticized.

[21]*Fielding v. Thomas*, [1896] A.C. 600.

[22]*New Brunswick Broadcasting Co. v. Nova Scotia*, [1993] 1 S.C.R. 319, 396; Lamer C.J. (at p. 352) expresses a similar view.

[23]In *Chagnon v. Syndicat de la fonction publique et parapublique du Québec*, [2018] 2 S.C.R. 687, Rowe J. said in a concurring opinion that "s. 45 of the Constitution Act, 1982, as did s. 92(1) before it, includes the power to enact laws in relation to the privileges of a provincial legislature" (para. 62). The question whether s. 45 of the Constitution Act, 1982 extends to amendments of the Constitution of Canada is discussed in ch. 4, Amendment, under heading § 4:19, "Provincial Legislature alone".

[24]Parliament of Canada Act, R.S.C. 1985, c. P-1, s. 4.

Westminster. If the existence and scope of a privilege at Westminster is established, then it exists in Ottawa as well without the need for inquiry into its necessity.[25]

Since parliamentary privilege at the federal level is legislated, the question arises whether it enjoys the special constitutional status that attaches to inherent privilege. In *New Brunswick Broadcasting*,[26] Lamer C.J., in a separate concurring opinion, said that "legislated" privilege would lack the constitutional status of "inherent" privilege. His reasoning was that all other legislative powers conferred by the Constitution Act, 1867 are subject to the Charter of Rights, and therefore the laws of Parliament in relation to parliamentary privilege, like any other laws, should be subject to Charter review. This point seems unanswerable. Moreover, the other opinions, including the principal majority opinion of McLachlin C.J., did not dispute the point. McLachlin C.J.'s reasoning was rather carefully limited to "inherent" privilege.[27] However, in *Vaid*,[28] Binnie J. for the Court said that "the logic" of the majority opinion "points away from such a conclusion", and "the point must now be taken as settled". This dictum was obiter, but it was obviously carefully considered. It seems, therefore, that there is no difference in constitutional status between legislated privilege and inherent privilege. Both are exempt from the Charter of Rights.

VIII. CASE LAW

§ 1:8 Case law

The courts have the task of interpreting the Constitution Acts and the other constitutional statutes. Their decisions constitute precedents for later cases so that a body of judge-made or decisional law, usually called case law, develops in areas where there has been litigation. While the courts' role is simply one of interpretation, the cumulative effect of a series of precedents will constitute an important elaboration or even modification of the original text. In particular, the provisions of the Constitution Act, 1867 that distribute legislative power between the central Parliament and the provincial Legislatures are now overlaid by such an accumulation of cases that it would be unthinkable to attempt to ascertain the relevant rules by recourse to the Act alone. The Charter of Rights (Part I of the Constitution Act, 1982) has also attracted a vast case law despite its much shorter life. Obviously, the case law that interprets the Constitution Acts and the other constitutional statutes is also constitutional law.

As part of the process of "interpretation", the Supreme Court of Can-

---

[25]*Canada v. Vaid*, [2005] 1 S.C.R. 667, para. 37 per Binnie J. for the Court. Binnie J. went on to note (still in para. 37) that provincial privilege, lacking the underpinning of s. 18 of the Constitution Act, 1867, would normally have to meet the necessity test.

[26]*New Brunswick Broadcasting Co. v. N.S.*, [1993] 1 S.C.R. 319, 364.

[27]*New Brunswick Broadcasting Co. v. N.S.*, [1993] 1 S.C.R. 319, 393-394 (answering constitutional question by reference to "inherent" privilege).

[28]*Canada v. Vaid*, [2005] 1 S.C.R. 667, para. 33.

ada has not hesitated to find "unwritten" principles that "underlie" the text of the Constitution Act, 1867 and the Constitution Act, 1982.[1] We have already noticed the Court's use of the doctrine of parliamentary privilege, which is nowhere mentioned in the two Acts, to exempt the actions of legislative assemblies from the Charter of Rights.[2] In *Re Remuneration of Judges* (1997),[3] the majority of the Supreme Court of Canada asserted that there was an unwritten principle of judicial independence in the Constitution of Canada that could have the effect of invalidating statutes that reduced judicial salaries. La Forest J., in dissent, expressed his objection to the limiting of the powers of legislatures "without recourse to express textual authority".[4] In the *Secession Reference* (1998),[5] the Supreme Court of Canada invoked unwritten principles of democracy, federalism, constitutionalism and the protection of minorities to hold that, if a province were to decide in a referendum that it wanted to secede from Canada, the federal government and the other provinces would come under a legal duty to enter into negotiations to accomplish the secession.[6] These cases illustrate the active and creative role that the modern Supreme Court of Canada has carved out for itself.[7] The cases carry the Constitution of Canada way beyond the literal language of its text and way beyond the intentions of the framers. They raise the concern (expressed by La Forest J.) that the Court is trespassing into fields more properly left to the legislative and executive branches of government. This is a theme that cannot be fully explored here. It runs throughout this book.[8] For present purposes, the point is that case law is an exceedingly important source of constitutional law.

In addition, some of the common law, that is to say, case law which is independent of any statute or constitution, could be characterized as constitutional law. For example, the Crown (meaning the executive government) retains a few vestigial prerogative powers, which spring not from statute, but from the common law; the prerogative is discussed in the next section of this chapter. It is also the courts which have developed many of the rules concerning the liability of the Crown and

---

[Section 1:8]

[1]See ch. 15, Judicial Review on Federal Grounds, under heading § 15:28, "Unwritten constitutional principles".

[2]§ 1:7, "Parliamentary privilege".

[3]*Re Remuneration of Judges*, [1997] 3 S.C.R. 3.

[4]*Re Remuneration of Judges*, [1997] 3 S.C.R. 3, para. 316. This issue is more fully examined in ch. 7, Courts, under heading § 7:8, "Inferior courts of civil jurisdiction".

[5]*Re Secession of Quebec*, [1998] 2 S.C.R. 217.

[6]*Re Secession of Quebec*, [1998] 2 S.C.R. 217, para. 88. This issue is more fully examined in ch. 5, Federalism, under heading § 5:24, "The power to secede".

[7]See also ch. 34, Civil Liberties, under heading § 34:7, "Implied bill of rights" (importation of civil liberties guarantees); ch. 47, Fundamental Justice, under heading § 47:15, "Definition of fundamental justice" (residuary theory of s. 7).

[8]Among many cross-references, note in particular, ch. 5, Federalism, under heading §§ 5:20 to 5:22, "Role of the courts", and ch. 36, Charter of Rights, under heading §§ 36:4 to 36:7, "Expansion of judicial review".

its employees.[9] The courts have also made much of the law concerning civil liberties by establishing rules to limit the powers of government officials and administrative agencies, and procedures to enable private individuals to seek judicial review of administrative action.[10] The common law can always be changed by statute. In almost every field that initially developed purely as common law, there has been considerable statutory intervention, modifying the judge-made rules. That is true of the examples given, but much of the law is still case law.

IX. PREROGATIVE

§ 1:9 Prerogative

The royal prerogative[1] consists of the powers and privileges accorded by the common law to the Crown. Dicey described it as "the residue of discretionary or arbitrary authority, which at any given time is left in the hands of the Crown".[2] The prerogative is a branch of the common law, because it is the decisions of the courts which have determined its existence and extent.[3]

The term prerogative should be confined to powers or privileges that are unique to the Crown. Powers or privileges enjoyed equally with private persons are not, strictly speaking, part of the prerogative. For example, the Crown has the power to acquire and dispose of property, and to enter into contracts, but these are not prerogative powers, because they are possessed by everyone. Sometimes, the term prerogative is used loosely, in a wider sense, as encompassing all the powers of the Crown that flow from the common law.[4] Although this usage is histori-

---

[9]See ch. 10, The Crown.

[10]See ch. 34, Civil Liberties, under heading § 34:2 "Common law".

[Section 1:9]

[1]See D.W. Mundell, "Legal Nature of Federal and Provincial Executive Governments" (1960) 2 Osgoode Hall L.J. 56; Cheffins and Tucker, The Constitutional Process in Canada (2nd ed., 1976), ch. 4; C.R. Munro, Studies in Constitutional Law (Butterworths, London, 2nd ed., 1999), ch. 8; Evatt, The Royal Prerogative (1987); E.G. MacDonald, A Contemporary Analysis of the Prerogative (LL.M. thesis, Osgoode Hall Law School, York University, 1988); de Smith and Brazier, Constitutional and Administrative Law (8th ed., 1998), ch. 6; Sunkin and Payne (eds.), The Nature of the Crown (1999); Hogg, Monahan and Wright, Liability of the Crown (4th ed., 2011), sec. 1.5(b).

[2]Dicey, Law of the Constitution (10th ed., 1965), 424, but see discussion at § 1:9 note 18.

[3]*Case of Proclamations* (1611), 12 Co. Rep. 74, 77 E.R. 1352 (K.B.), holding that "the King hath no prerogative, but that which the law of the land allows him".

[4]Dicey, Law of the Constitution (10th ed., 1965), 455, said that "every act which the executive government can lawfully do without the authority of an Act of Parliament is done by virtue of the prerogative". For criticism of this usage, see D.W. Mundell, "Legal Nature of Federal and Provincial Executive Governments" (1960) 2 Osgoode Hall L.J. 56, 58–59; C.R. Munro, Studies in Constitutional Law (Butterworths, London, 2nd ed., 1999), 159–160.

cally inaccurate,[5] it has become increasingly common. Nothing practical now turns on the distinction between the Crown's "true prerogative" powers and the Crown's natural-person powers, because the exercise of both kinds of powers is reviewable by the courts.[6]

In the next chapter, we shall see that the Crown possessed certain prerogative legislative powers over British colonies. The King, acting without the concurrence of Parliament, had the power to create the office of Governor, executive council, legislative assembly and courts for a colony. In the case of a conquered colony (as opposed to a settled colony), the King possessed a general power of legislation but only until such time as the colony was granted its own legislative assembly.[7] These powers are of mainly historical interest for Canada today; but the constitutions of Nova Scotia, New Brunswick and Prince Edward Island still consist of prerogative instruments,[8] and the office of Governor General still depends upon a prerogative instrument.[9]

Apart from the power over the colonies, the courts held that there was no prerogative power to legislate: only the Parliament could make new laws.[10] The Bill of Rights of 1688 denied the prerogative powers to "suspend" a law for a period of time, or to "dispense" with a law in a particular case.[11] The Bill of Rights of 1688 also affirmed that only Parliament could levy taxes.[12] And the courts established that only Parliament could authorize the expenditure of public funds.[13] The courts also held that there was no prerogative power to administer justice: only the courts could adjudicate disputes according to law.[14] These decisions confined the prerogative to executive governmental powers. And within this area the prerogative was further limited by the doctrine that most executive action which infringed the liberty of the subject required the

---

[5]W. Blackstone, Commentaries (1765), vol. 1, 239, says that: "It assumes in its etymology (from *prae* and *rogo)* something that is required or demanded before, or in preference to, all others".

[6]See § 1:9 notes 23-30, below.

[7]See ch. 2, Reception.

[8]See ch. 2, Reception, under heading § 2:4, "Amendment of received laws".

[9]Letters Patent constituting the office of Governor General of Canada, 1947, R.S.C. 1985, Appendix II, No. 31.

[10]*Case of Proclamations* (1611), 12 Co. Rep. 74, 77 E.R. 1352 (K.B.) (King by proclamation could not prohibit new buildings in London).

[11]de Smith and Brazier, Constitutional and Administrative Law (8th ed., 1998), 73–74; and see ch. 34, Civil Liberties, under heading § 34:2, "Common law".

[12]*Bowles v. Bank of England*, [1913] 1 Ch. 57 (resolution of parliamentary committee, approved by House of Commons, cannot levy a tax).

[13]*Auckland Harbour Bd. v. The King*, [1924] A.C. 318 (P.C., N.Z.) (money spent by government without legislative appropriation is recoverable by government); E. Campbell, "Parliamentary Appropriations" (1971) 4 Adelaide L.R. 145.

[14]*Prohibition del Roy* (1607), 12 Co. Rep. 63, 77 E.R. 1342 ("The King in his own person cannot adjudge any case, either criminal . . . or betwixt party and party").

authority of a statute.[15] Moreover, the prerogative could be abolished or limited by statute,[16] and, once a statute had occupied the ground formerly occupied by the prerogative, the Crown had to comply with the terms of the statute.[17] All of these rules, and especially the last (displacement by statute), have had the effect of shrinking the prerogative powers[18] of the Crown down to a very narrow compass. The conduct of foreign affairs, including the making of treaties[19] and the declaring of war, continues to be a prerogative power in Canada. So are the appointment of the Prime Minister (by the Governor General) and other ministers (by the Governor General on the advice of the Prime Minister),[20] the issue of

---

[15] *Entick v. Carrington* (1765), 19 St. Tr. 1030, 95 E.R. 807 (K.B.) (no prerogative power of search and seizure). An exception was that property could be taken or destroyed in time of war, although the prerogative power was accompanied by an obligation to pay compensation: *Burmah Oil Co. v. Lord Advocate*, [1965] A.C. 75 (H.L.) (Crown ordered to pay compensation for oil installations in Burma destroyed during second world war).

[16] Any bill diminishing the Crown's prerogative should receive "royal consent" signified by the Governor General at some stage in the bill's consideration in either one of the two Houses. Royal consent is not to be confused with "royal assent", which of course is the final stage in the enactment of every bill. Royal consent is helpfully explained by the Speaker of the Senate in "Speaker's Ruling: Bill C-232 and the Royal Consent", Senate of Canada, March 21, 2011 (holding that royal consent was not needed for a statute that did not affect any Crown prerogative). This requirement is one of internal parliamentary procedure only. In a case where royal consent was required, and was not obtained, if the bill went through all stages of enactment, including royal assent, the statute would be validly enacted. On the conferral of royal assent, "the question of royal consent becomes moot": Speaker's Ruling: Bill C-232 and the Royal Consent", Senate of Canada, March 21, 2011, 4.

[17] *A.G. v. De Keyser's Royal Hotel*, [1920] A.C. 508 (H.L.) (Crown ordered to satisfy statutory requirement of compensation for building occupied in time of war). Compare *Barton v. Cth. of Aust.* (1974), 131 C.L.R. 477 (extradition under prerogative upheld; not displaced by statute); *R. v. Home Secretary; Ex parte Northumbria Police Authority*, [1989] Q.B. 26 (C.A.) (prerogative power to supply riot equipment to police not displaced by statute); *Ross River Dena Council Band v. Can.*, [2002] 2 S.C.R. 816, para. 58 (prerogative power to create Indian reserves "limited" but not "ousted" by statute); *Can. v. Khadr*, [2010] 1 S.C.R. 44, para. 35 (prerogative power over foreign affairs not displaced by statute).

[18] As well as prerogative powers, there are a number of prerogative privileges or immunities, which give to the Crown immunities from some kinds of legal proceedings, priority in the payment of debts, etc. This miscellaneous class of prerogatives, which is ignored in Dicey's definition accompanying Dicey, § 1:9 note 2, above, has also been reduced by statute, but some of it lingers on. The part concerned with the liability of the Crown to legal proceedings is discussed in ch. 10, The Crown.

[19] *Turp v. Can.* (2012), 415 F.T.R. 192 (F.C.) (prerogative power to withdraw from Kyoto Accord, despite parliamentary implementation of treaty).

[20] *Guergis v. Novak* (2012), 112 O.R. (3d) 118 (S.C.J.), paras. 10–15 (affirming existence of prerogative power to dismiss minister at pleasure without judicial review). The plaintiff was also unsuccessful in challenging her dismissal from the government caucus; the Court held that the P.M. had that power too, although its source was parliamentary privilege, not Crown prerogative: *Guergis v. Novak* (2012), 112 O.R. (3d) 118 (S.C.J.), paras. 16–22. On appeal under the same name, these rulings were affirmed without discussion: (2013) 116 O.R. (3d) 280 (C.A.).

passports, the creation of Indian reserves,[21] and the conferring of honours such as Queen's Counsel.[22] But most governmental power in Canada[23] is exercised under statutory, not prerogative power.

It used to be asserted that the exercise of prerogative powers was not subject to judicial review.[24] The assertion is belied by the many cases in which the exercise or purported exercise of prerogative powers has been reviewed by the courts. The courts will determine whether a prerogative power that is asserted by the Crown does in fact exist,[25] and, if it does exist, what are its limits and whether any restrictions on the power have been complied with.[26] The courts will also determine whether a prerogative power has been displaced by statute.[27] The courts will also require, not only that prerogative powers be exercised in conformity with the Charter of Rights[28] and other constitutional norms,[29] but also that administrative-law norms such as the duty of fairness be observed.[30]

---

[21]*Ross River Dena Council Band v. Can.*, [2002] 2 S.C.R. 816.

[22]*Black v. Chrétien* (2001), 54 O.R. (3d) 215 (C.A.).

[23]Canada being a federal state, the prerogative powers had to be distributed between the federal government (the Crown in right of Canada) and the provincial governments (the Crown in right of each province). The Constitution Act, 1867 was silent on the point. The courts held that the prerogative powers followed the comparable legislative powers: see ch. 9, Responsible Government, under heading § 9:3, "Law and Convention".

[24]de Smith and Brazier, Constitutional and Administrative Law (8th ed., 1998), 136–137, rejecting the assertion.

[25]The leading cases are cited in § 1:9 notes 10-15, above.

[26]*Burmah Oil Co. v. Lord Advocate*, [1965] A.C. 75 (H.L.) (prerogative power accompanied by a duty to pay compensation). Compare judicial review of claims to withhold evidence by virtue of Crown privilege: ch. 10, The Crown, under heading §§ 10:6 to 10:9, "Crown privilege".

[27]See § 1:9 note 17, above.

[28]*Operation Dismantle v. The Queen*, [1985] 1 S.C.R. 441 (weapon testing under prerogative upheld, but prerogative power in principle subject to Charter); *Can. v. Kamel*, [2009] 4 F.C.R. 449 (F.C.A.) (refusal of passport upheld under s. 1 of Charter); *Abdelrazik v. Can.*, [2010] 1 F.C.R. 267 (F.C.) (refusal of passport struck down for breach of Charter); *Can. v. Khadr*, [2010] 1 S.C.R. 44 (declaration of breach of Charter issued even though remedial action might involve exercise of prerogative power over foreign affairs).

[29]*Air Can. v. B.C.*, [1986] 2 S.C.R. 539 (mandamus issued to overrule denial of royal fiat for proceedings against Crown to recover unconstitutional taxes).

[30]*R. v. Criminal Injuries Comp. Bd.; Ex parte Lain*, [1967] 2 Q.B. 864 (certiorari issued for error of law on face of record by board established under prerogative); *Council of Civil Service Unions v. Minr. for Civil Service*, [1985] 1 A.C. 374 (H.L.) (remedy denied, but prerogative control of civil service held in principle to be subject to duty of fairness); *R. v. Foreign Secretary; Ex parte Everett*, [1989] Q.B. 811 (C.A.) (remedy denied, but refusal of passport under prerogative held to be subject to duty of fairness); *R. v. Secretary of State; Ex parte Bentley*, [1994] Q.B. 349 (Div. Ct.) (ministerial refusal to exercise prerogative of mercy struck down on ground that all alternatives had not been considered); *Black v. Chrétien* (2001), 54 O.R. (3d) 215 (C.A.) (remedy for denial of honour denied, but prerogative powers affecting individual rights held to be reviewable).

The courts will also determine whether a prerogative power has been properly delegated.[31]

Before the development of responsible government, the prerogative powers of the Crown were exercised by the reigning monarch in accordance with his or her own discretion. Such powers could not survive the growth of democratic ideals, for the monarch was not (and still is not) an elected official. In most countries, the acceptance of democratic ideals led to the abolition of the monarchy: all executive and legislative powers were then conferred on elected officials. In the United Kingdom, the acceptance of democratic ideals led to the system of responsible government, under which the King (or Queen) continued as head of state, and retained many of his powers, but he exercised those powers only on the "advice" of (meaning at the direction of) his ministers. The ministers were the leaders of the party commanding a majority in the elected House of Commons. In this way, the requirements of democracy were satisfied without giving up the forms of monarchical government.

Responsible government had not been extended to the colonies by 1776. Indeed, it was not established in the United Kingdom itself until the nineteenth century. For the 13 American colonies that declared their independence in 1776, the democratic answer to rule by an absentee King and his appointed governors was independence under a republican form of government. For the loyal British North American colonies that remained in the Empire until after responsible government was established in the United Kingdom, the solution turned out to be the gradual extension of responsible government to each colony. At first just the colonial governor, but later the King or Queen as well, was to act on the advice of the ministers who enjoyed the confidence of the local representative assembly. At first various matters of imperial concern (for example, treaty-making) were excluded from responsible government and reserved for British decision, but eventually local responsible government extended to everything. The story of the extension of responsible government to British North America, and the working out of the full implications of that idea, is the story of Canada's achievement of independence.[32]

An extraordinary feature of the system of responsible government is that its rules are largely not legal rules in the sense of being enforceable in the courts.[33] They are primarily conventions. The exercise of the Crown's prerogative powers in this context is thus regulated largely by

---

[31] *Ross River Dena Council Band v. Can.*, [2002] 2 S.C.R. 816, paras. 63–64 (Governor in Council would "normally" exercise prerogative power to create Indian reserves, but duly authorized agent of the Crown could also do so; no agent had authority to do so in this case).

[32] The history of responsible government is related in ch. 9, Responsible Government.

[33] But see *R. (Miller) v. The Prime Minister*, [2019] UKSC 41, 3 W.L.R. 589, in which the Supreme Court of the United Kingdom held that Prime Minister Boris Johnson's advice to the Queen to prorogue Parliament was justiciable, and also unlawful, rendering the prorogation itself also unlawful. This extraordinary case is discussed in greater detail in ch. 9, Responsible Government, under heading § 9:21, "Prorogation of Parliament".

conventions, not laws.[34] Conventions are the topic of the next section of this chapter.

X. CONVENTIONS

§ 1:10 Definition of conventions

Conventions are rules of the constitution that are not enforced by the law courts.[1] Because they are not enforced by the law courts, they are best regarded as non-legal rules, but because they do in fact regulate the working of the constitution, they are an important concern of the constitutional lawyer. What conventions do is to prescribe the way in which legal powers shall be exercised. Some conventions have the effect of transferring effective power from the legal holder to another official or institution. Other conventions limit an apparently broad legal power, or even prescribe that a legal power shall not be exercised at all.

Consider the following examples. (1) The Constitution Act, 1867, and many Canadian statutes, confer extensive powers on the Governor General or on the Governor General in Council, but a convention stipulates that the Governor General will exercise those powers only in accordance with the advice of the cabinet or in some cases the Prime Minister.[2] (2) The Constitution Act, 1867 makes the Queen, or the Governor General, an essential party to all federal legislation (s. 17), and it expressly confers upon the Queen and the Governor General the power to withhold the royal assent from a bill that has been enacted by the two Houses of Parliament (s. 55), but a convention stipulates that the royal assent shall never be withheld.[3]

Each of these two conventions is discussed later in this book, and many other examples will be encountered as well. The two that have been described are two of the most fundamental rules of the Canadian Constitution. Yet, like all conventions, they are not enforceable in the

---

[34]The Queen in the United Kingdom, and her representatives elsewhere in the Commonwealth, retain a few "personal prerogatives", namely, powers which are exercised at the personal discretion of the Queen (or Governor General or Lieutenant Governor). These powers are needed for the situation where there is no ministry that commands the confidence of the elected assembly. They are discussed in ch. 9, Responsible Government, under heading §§ 9:16 to 9:24, "The Governor General's personal prerogatives".

[Section 1:10]

[1]The best-known of the abundant writings on conventions are Dicey, The Law of the Constitution (10th ed., 1965), chs. 14, 15; Jennings, The Law and the Constitution (5th ed., 1959), ch. 3; Wheare, Modern Constitutions (2nd ed., 1966), ch. 8; Marshall, Constitutional Conventions (1986); de Smith and Brazier, Constitutional and Administrative Law (6th ed., 1989), 28–47. A recent Canadian study is Heard, Canadian Constitutional Conventions (1991). Conventions are also discussed in Tremblay, Droit Constitutionnel— Principes (2nd ed., 2000), 19–30; W.J. Newman, "Of Dissolution, Prorogation, and Constitutional Law, Principle and Convention: Maintaining Fundamental Distinctions during a Parliamentary Crisis" (2009) 27 Nat. J. Con. Law 217.

[2]See ch. 9, Responsible Government.

[3]See ch. 9, Responsible Government, under heading §§ 9:8 to 9:12, "The legislative branch".

courts. If the Governor General exercised one of his powers without (or in violation of) ministerial advice, the courts would not deny validity to his act. If the Governor General withheld his assent to a bill enacted by both Houses of Parliament, the courts would deny the force of law to the bill, and they would not issue an injunction or other legal remedy to force the Governor General to give his assent. None of these things has ever happened, because conventions are in fact nearly always obeyed by the officials whose conduct they regulate.

In the parliamentary democracies of the United Kingdom, Canada, Australia and New Zealand, conventions play a very important role in the constitutional arrangements because they govern the rules of responsible government which have the effect of transferring political power from an unelected Queen (or King) or Governor General to the elected Prime Minister. But these are not the only conventions, and it seems likely that conventions exist in all government systems, even those like the United States where the term "convention" is not part of the usual political, let alone constitutional, discourse. For example, the Constitution of the United States provides (article II, section 1(3)) that the President is to be chosen by "electors" appointed by the state legislatures, and George Washington, the first President, was in fact chosen by independent electors. But the unwritten rule (clearly a convention) soon developed that the electors of each state have no discretion in the matter: they must vote for the candidate who won the popular vote in their state in the general election for President. It would be unthinkable for an elector to ignore the unwritten rule because the rule gives effect to the democratic idea that the President should be chosen by popular vote.[4]

If a convention is disobeyed by an official, then it is common, especially in the United Kingdom, to describe the official's act or omission as "unconstitutional". But this use of the term unconstitutional must be carefully distinguished from the case where a legal rule of the constitution has been disobeyed. Where unconstitutionality springs from a breach of law, the purported act is normally a nullity and there is a remedy available in the courts.[5] But where "unconstitutionality" springs merely from a breach of convention, no breach of the law has occurred and no legal remedy will be available.[6]

---

[4]This example, and many others, are described by Gerard N. Magliocca, "The Anti-Partisan Principle" (2014), Indiana University, Robert H. McKinney School of Law, Legal Studies Research Paper No. 2014-27.

[5]In some cases of breach of a constitutional law, there is no remedy, for example, because the legal rule is held to be non-justiciable, or because the legal rule is held to be directory only and not mandatory, or because no individual is sufficiently affected by the breach of the legal rule to have "standing" to seek a judicial remedy, or because there is no appropriate remedy. But these are unusual cases.

[6]In *Re Resolution to Amend the Constitution*, [1981] 1 S.C.R. 753, 909, the Court distinguished between these two senses of the word unconstitutional, and held that breach of a convention did not cause invalidity or give rise to any remedy. Other cases where courts have explicitly refused to enforce a convention are *Re Disallowance and*

§ 1:11 Conventions in the courts

Although a convention will not be enforced by the courts, the existence of a convention has been recognized by the courts. For example, the courts have taken notice of the conventions of responsible government, which make a Minister accountable to Parliament, as a consideration in deciding to give a broad rather than a narrow interpretation to a statute conferring power on a Minister.[1] In these cases, and in other cases in which the existence of a convention has been recognized,[2] the existence of the convention was relevant to the disposition of a legal issue, usually the interpretation of either a statute or a written constitution.

In the *Patriation Reference* (1981),[3] the Supreme Court of Canada was asked on a reference whether there was a convention requiring that the consent of the provinces be obtained before the federal government requested the United Kingdom Parliament to enact an amendment to the Constitution of Canada that would affect the powers of the provinces. The Court was also asked whether there was a legal requirement of provincial consent. The questions had been referred to the courts by three of the eight provinces that were opposed to Prime Minister Trudeau's proposals for a constitutional settlement to patriate the constitution and obtain an amending procedure and a charter of rights.[4] The Supreme Court of Canada obviously had to decide the legal question, and it did so by holding that there was no legal requirement of provincial consent to the constitutional proposals. But the Court went on to decide the convention question as well. A majority of the Court held that there was a convention, and that the convention required the federal government to obtain a "substantial degree" or "substantial measure" of provincial consent[5] before requesting the requisite legislation from the United Kingdom.[6]

Reservation of Provincial Legislation, [1938] S.C.R. 71; *Currie v. MacDonald* (1949), 29 Nfld. & P.E.I.R. 294 (Nfld. C.A.); *Madzimbamuto v. Lardner-Burke*, [1969] 1 A.C. 645 (P.C., So. Rhodesia).

[Section 1:11]

[1]E.g., *Liversidge v. Anderson*, [1942] A.C. 206 (H.L.); *Carltona v. Commrs. of Works*, [1943] 2 All E.R. 560 (C.A.); compare *A.-G. Que. v. Blaikie* (No. 2) [1981] 1 S.C.R. 312, 320 (Acts include regulations in view of conventions linking government with Legislature).

[2]Other cases are cited in *Re Resolution to Amend the Constitution*, [1981] 1 S.C.R. 753, 775–784, 885. Add to these *OPSEU v. Ont.*, [1987] 2 S.C.R. 2, 44–45 (convention of political neutrality of Crown servants recognized).

[3]*Re Resolution to Amend the Constitution*, [1981] 1 S.C.R. 753.

[4]The history of this constitutional settlement is related in ch. 4, Amendment.

[5]*Re Resolution to Amend the Constitution*, [1981] 1 S.C.R. 753, 905.

[6]Four opinions were written, none attributed to an individual judge. On the legal question, there was a majority opinion, signed by Laskin C.J., Dickson, Beetz, Estey, McIntyre, Chouinard and Lamer JJ., and a dissenting opinion, signed by Martland and Ritchie JJ. On the convention question, there was a majority opinion, signed by Martland, Ritchie, Dickson, Beetz, Chouinard and Lamer JJ., and a dissenting opinion

The decision in the *Patriation Reference* did not, strictly speaking, enforce a convention. Indeed, as related above, the Court specifically held that there was no legal obligation upon the federal government to obtain the consent of the provinces. Nonetheless, as a matter of practical politics, the decision made it impossible for the federal government to proceed with its constitutional proposals without a "substantial degree" of provincial consent. After the decision, Prime Minister Trudeau and the Premiers met again to try and reach the agreement which had hitherto eluded them, and on November 5, 1981 they did in fact reach agreement on the constitutional settlement which became the Canada Act 1982 and the Constitution Act, 1982.

The Supreme Court of Canada in the *Patriation Reference* had said that the convention required a "substantial degree" of provincial consent to amendments as far-reaching as those proposed by Prime Minister Trudeau. After the agreement of November 5, 1981, doubt remained as to whether this rule had been satisfied. The agreement included nine of the ten provinces, but did not include Quebec, the only predominantly French-speaking province and one that (at that time) included over 25 per cent of Canada's population. Was the consent of Quebec necessary as part of a "substantial degree" of provincial consent? Quebec referred this question to its Court of Appeal for answer. By the time the question reached the Supreme Court of Canada, the Canada Act 1982 had actually been enacted by the United Kingdom Parliament. Not only was the question solely about a convention, but the issue was moot even in a political sense. Nonetheless, in the *Quebec Veto Reference* (1982),[7] the Supreme Court of Canada answered the question, deciding that Quebec's consent was not necessary to make up the requisite "substantial degree" of provincial consent. By this decision the Court destroyed the spectre of an "unconstitutional constitution"![8]

The convention questions in the *Patriation Reference* and *Quebec Veto Reference* raised no legal issues, and the answers could not lead to any legal consequences. Was the Supreme Court of Canada wrong to answer the questions? The Court pointed out that courts had in previous cases recognized the existence of conventions,[9] but, as mentioned earlier, in the previous cases the existence of the convention had been relevant to the disposition of a legal issue. That was not true in the *Patriation Reference*, where the answer to the convention question had no bearing on the answer to the legal question; nor was it true in the *Quebec Veto Reference*, where no legal question was asked. The Court also pointed out that the convention questions had been referred to the Court for an-

---

signed by Laskin C.J., Estey and McIntyre JJ.

[7]*Re Objection by Que. to Resolution to Amend the Constitution*, [1982] 2 S.C.R. 793.

[8]Of course, if the decision had been otherwise, the Canada Act 1982 and the Constitution Act, 1982 would still have been valid; they would have been unconstitutional only in the conventional sense; see § 1:10 note 6, above.

[9]*Re Resolution to Amend the Constitution*, [1981] 1 S.C.R. 753, 885.

swers,[10] but the Court has in the past often asserted (and exercised) a discretion not to answer questions referred to it that are unsuitable for judicial determination.[11] The issue really comes down to the question whether the convention questions were suitable for judicial determination. The only possible effect of answering the convention question in the *Patriation Reference* was to influence the outcome of the political negotiations over the 1981-82 constitutional settlement.[12] The answer to the convention question strengthened the hands of the provinces in that negotiation, and is probably the reason why the provinces were able to secure the insertion of the override clause in the Charter of Rights and the substitution of the opting-out amending formula—the two major concessions made by the federal government to achieve the agreement of November 5, 1981. In my view, the Court, which is not an elected body, and which is not politically accountable for its actions, should have confined itself to answering the legal question, and should not have gone beyond the legal question to exert any further influence over the negotiations.[13]

§ 1:12 Convention and usage

Conventions are often distinguished from "usages": a convention is a rule which is regarded as obligatory by the officials to whom it applies; a usage is not a rule, but merely a governmental practice which is ordinarily followed, although it is not regarded as obligatory. An example of a usage is the practice of appointing to the position of Chief Justice of Canada the person who is the senior puisne judge of the Supreme Court of Canada at the time of the vacancy.[1] This practice has been observed many times, but it is probable that the Prime Minister (who by convention makes the recommendation to the Governor General who by law makes the appointment) does not feel obliged to follow the practice, for

[10] *Re Resolution to Amend the Constitution*, [1981] 1 S.C.R. 753, 884.

[11] The discretion not to answer questions posed on a reference is described in ch. 8, Supreme Court of Canada, under heading §§ 8:8 to 8:12, "Reference jurisdiction".

[12] In the *Re Resolution to Amend the Constitution*, [1981] 1 S.C.R. 753, 884, even this effect was missing, since the amendments had been enacted. The Supreme Court of Canada (at pp. 805–806) gave two reasons for answering the question: (1) the Quebec Court of Appeal had answered it, and (2) "it appears desirable that the constitutional question be answered in order to dispel any doubt over it". It may be noted that the Court is rarely so deferential to the lower court, or so intolerant of doubt on questions that need not be decided.

[13] This position is argued, and other criticisms made of the *Patriation Reference*, in P.W. Hogg, Comment (1982) 60 Can. Bar Rev. 307.

[Section 1:12]

[1] Another example of a usage is the practice of appointing three judges to the Supreme Court of Canada from Ontario. This practice was consistently followed until 1978 when Spence J. (from Ontario) retired and was replaced by McIntyre J. (from British Columbia). In 1982, when Martland J. (from Alberta) retired, he was replaced by Wilson J. (from Ontario), and Ontario's usual complement of three members was restored.

it has been departed from in recent appointments,[2] those of Chief Justice Laskin in 1973 and Chief Justice Dickson in 1984, neither of whom was the senior puisne judge at the time of his appointment. The practice was resumed with the appointment of Chief Justice Lamer in 1990, but was again departed from with the appointment of McLachlin C.J. in 2000 and of Wagner C.J. in 2017.[3]

A usage may develop into a convention. If a practice is invariably followed over a long period of time, it may come to be generally regarded as obligatory and thereby cease to be merely a usage. The resulting convention may be called a custom. This process of evolution from usage to convention (or custom) is the way in which most conventions have been established. It should be noticed, however, that very little turns on the question whether a practice is a usage or a convention, because a convention is as unenforceable as a usage. The most that can be said is that there is a stronger moral obligation to follow a convention than a usage, and that departure from convention may be criticized more severely than departure from usage.

Before the *Patriation Reference* (1981),[4] it was generally assumed that there was no judicial procedure for adjudicating a dispute about whether a particular practice was a convention or a usage. Since no legal consequence could flow from the answer, the issue appeared to be non-justiciable. In the *Patriation Reference*, however, as we have seen, the Supreme Court of Canada undertook, for the first time in any common law jurisdiction, to adjudicate such a dispute. The issue was whether the past practice of securing provincial consents to constitutional amendments affecting provincial powers was a usage (as the federal government and two provinces argued) or a convention (as eight provinces argued). In order to resolve the dispute, the Court looked at three questions: (1) what were the precedents? (2) what were the beliefs of the actors in the precedents? and (3) what was the reason for the practice?[5] With respect to the precedents, the Court surveyed the history of constitutional amendment in Canada and concluded that there had been an invariable practice of obtaining provincial consents to amendments

[2]Another departure occurred on the appointment of Anglin C.J. in 1924.

[3]It may be that this practice of appointing the senior puisne judge has been (or is being) overtaken by another practice, one that incorporates aspects of the old practice – namely, alternating the Chief Justiceship between the senior Quebec and senior non-Quebec puisne judge. For example, although McLachlin C.J. was not the most senior puisne judge when she was appointed Chief Justice in 2000 (L'Heureux-Dubé and Gonthier JJ., both from Quebec, were more senior), she was the most senior non-Quebec puisne judge, appointed to replace Lamer C.J., who was from Quebec. Similarly, although Wagner C.J. was not the most senior puisne judge when he was appointed Chief Justice in 2017 (Abella, Moldaver and Karakatsanis JJ., all from Ontario, were more senior), he was the most senior Quebec puisne judge, appointed to replace McLachlin C.J., who was from British Columbia (originally Alberta).

[4]*Re Resolution to Amend the Constitution*, [1981] 1 S.C.R. 753.

[5]The three questions were taken from Jennings, The Law and the Constitution (5th ed., 1959), 136. The discussion of the questions is to be found in *Re Resolution to Amend the Constitution*, [1981] 1 S.C.R. 753, 888–909.

that made a change in legislative powers. With respect to the beliefs of the actors, the Court concluded from statements in a federal white paper and by federal ministers that the actors on the federal side felt bound to obtain provincial consents to such amendments. With respect to the reason for the practice, the Court found it in a "federal principle" which condemned any modification of provincial powers "by the unilateral action of the federal authorities".[6] The Court accordingly concluded that there was a convention.

Having decided that there was a convention, the Court had to decide what the convention was. As noted earlier, the Court decided that the convention required a "substantial degree" or "substantial measure" of provincial consent, but that it was not necessary to decide exactly what the requisite degree was.[7] It was enough to decide that the constitutional proposals, which at that time enjoyed the support of only Ontario and New Brunswick, did not have "a sufficient measure of provincial agreement".[8] This part of the Court's decision was rather unsatisfactory, not only because it was an implausible reading of the history of constitutional amendment,[9] but also because it was so vague.

The vagueness of the "substantial degree" rule quickly led to further litigation. After the agreement of November 5, 1981, in which the federal government obtained the consents of nine out of ten provinces to a modified constitutional settlement, Quebec returned to the Supreme Court of Canada with a new reference, the *Quebec Veto Reference* (1982),[10] which asked whether the convention of a "substantial degree" of provincial consent required the consent of Quebec. With respect to the precedents, it was clear that Quebec's consent had always been required in the past. With respect to the reason for the practice, it could be found in a principle of "duality", which implied special protection of the powers of the only predominantly French-speaking province. But the Supreme Court of Canada concentrated its attention on the beliefs of the actors, finding that a Quebec veto had never been articulated by any of the actors in the precedents (although it had never been denied either). In the Court's view, "a convention could not have remained wholly inarticulate, except perhaps at the inchoate stage when it has not yet been accepted as a binding rule".[11] The Court accordingly held that there was no requirement of Quebec's consent: the nine predominantly English-

---

[6] *Re Resolution to Amend the Constitution*, [1981] 1 S.C.R. 753, 905–906.

[7] *Re Resolution to Amend the Constitution*, [1981] 1 S.C.R. 753, 905.

[8] *Re Resolution to Amend the Constitution*, [1981] 1 S.C.R. 753, 905.

[9] In my comment (1982) 60 Can. Bar Rev. 307, I argue that the history was consistent with either a convention of unanimity (contended for by seven provinces) or no convention at all (contended for by the federal government and two provinces), but not the substantial degree rule (contended for by only one province).

[10] *Re Objection by Que. to Resolution to Amend the Constitution*, [1982] 2 S.C.R. 793.

[11] *Re Objection by Que. to Resolution to Amend the Constitution*, [1982] 2 S.C.R. 793, 817. This point seems dubious. There is undoubtedly a convention that the Queen or Governor General or Lieutenant Governor will not withhold the royal assent from bills which have been passed by the appropriate legislative chambers, but I am not aware

speaking provinces comprised a "substantial degree" of provincial consent, which satisfied the convention.

§ 1:13 Convention and agreement

As noticed above, most conventions have developed from a long history of past practice, which has eventually attracted a sense of obligation or normative character. But this process of evolution from usage to convention (or custom) is not the only way in which a convention may be established. If all the relevant officials agree to adopt a certain rule of constitutional conduct, then that rule may immediately come to be regarded as obligatory.[1] The resulting convention could hardly at the beginning be described as a custom. For example, in 1930 the Prime Ministers of the self-governing dominions of the Commonwealth agreed that thenceforth the King (or Queen) would appoint the Governor General of a dominion solely on the advice of the government of the dominion.[2] They also agreed that thenceforth the imperial Parliament would not enact a law for any of the dominions except at the request and with the consent of the dominion.[3] These agreements established conventions. It should be noticed too that conventions established by agreement will normally be written down by the officials concerned in precise and authoritative terms. Conventions are not necessarily unwritten rules, although conventions established by custom are rarely written down in terms that are accepted as precise and authoritative.[4]

---

that any Queen or King or Governor General or Lieutenant Governor has ever explicitly acknowledged the obligation. The convention is well understood although tacit. For further criticism of the decision, see A. Petter, "The Quebec Veto Reference" (1984), 6 Supreme Court L.R. 387.

[Section 1:13]

[1]Latham, The Law and the Commonwealth (1949), 610, makes the point that "in domestic affairs agreement rarely, if ever, creates constitutional convention, because the usual parties namely, ministers, members of Parliament, the Houses of Parliament, and the King have no moral authority to bind their successors by mere agreement apart from precedent. But in Commonwealth relations it has long been recognized that the agreement of the executive government of a member binds its successors, because it would be derogatory to its autonomy if other members, in order to ascertain their rights and obligations in relation to it, were compelled to examine its internal affairs". It may perhaps be noticed that the problem of "moral authority to bind their successors" exists in Commonwealth relations too, but agreements to create conventions of Commonwealth relations have been made and observed.

[2]See ch. 9, Responsible Government, under heading § 9:3, "Law and Convention".

[3]See ch. 3, Independence, under heading § 3:3, "Statute of Westminster, 1931". This convention accorded with prior usage and may even have been established before the agreement in 1930, but the agreement settled its status as a convention.

[4]The distinction between written and unwritten rules is hard to draw and is rarely useful. For example, even conventions established by custom are written down in textbooks on government or constitutional law, and such accounts are of persuasive authority in determining the existence or scope of a particular convention. Note also the *Re Objection by Que. to Resolution to Amend the Constitution*, [1982] 2 S.C.R. 793 holding that no convention had been established, because the claimed rule had never been

§ 1:14 Convention and law

A convention could be transformed into law by being enacted as a statute.[1] A convention would also be transformed into law if it were enforced by the courts. If a court gave a remedy for a breach of convention, for example, by ordering an unwilling Governor General to give his or her assent to a bill enacted by both Houses of Parliament, then we would have to change our language and say that the Governor General was under a legal obligation to assent, and not merely a conventional obligation. In that event, a convention would have been transformed into a rule of common law.

In the *Patriation Reference* (1981),[2] it was argued by the provinces that the convention requiring provincial consents to constitutional amendments had "crystallized" into law, so that there was a legal obligation to obtain provincial consents. But it was not clear how this process had occurred, and there seemed to be no precedents of crystallization. The Court rejected the argument in terms which suggested that a convention could never be transformed into a rule of common law. Their lordships pointed out that a convention develops through precedents established by political officials, while the common law develops through precedents established by the courts.[3] One of the opinions even disapproved my statement in an earlier edition of this book that a judicial decision could have the effect of transforming a convention into a legal rule.[4] But, with respect, the statement is true by definition. If a court did enforce a convention (and admittedly no court has ever done so), the convention would be transformed into a legal rule, because the rule would no longer be unenforceable in the courts, and that is the only characteristic which distinguishes a convention from a legal rule.

Since conventions are not legally enforceable, one may well ask: why are they obeyed? The primary reason is that breach of a convention would result in serious political repercussions, and eventually in changes in the law. An attempt by a Governor General to act without advice or to refuse assent to a bill would quickly be followed by his dismissal, and would lead to an irresistible demand to enact a statute embodying the terms of the convention. Similar kinds of grave political consequences would flow from breach of the other conventions, for example, the refusal of the Queen to appoint as Governor General the person recommended by the Canadian government, or the refusal by the Prime Minister to resign after losing his majority in the House of Commons.

---

articulated.

[Section 1:14]

[1]Legislation implementing a conventional rule, in this case the convention of public service neutrality, makes the rule subject to the Charter of Rights: *Osborne v. Can.*, [1991] 2 S.C.R. 69 (restrictions on political activity by public servants held unconstitutional).

[2]*Re Resolution to Amend the Constitution*, [1981] 1 S.C.R. 753.

[3]*Re Resolution to Amend the Constitution*, [1981] 1 S.C.R. 753, 774–775.

[4]*Re Resolution to Amend the Constitution*, [1981] 1 S.C.R. 753, 856.

Law and convention are "closely interlocked", as the examples given show; the conventions "do not exist in a legal vacuum".[5] They regulate the way in which legal powers shall be exercised, and they therefore presuppose the existence of the legal powers. Their purpose is "to ensure that the legal framework of the constitution will be operated in accordance with the prevailing constitutional values or principles of the period".[6] They bring outdated legal powers into conformity with current notions of government. Each convention takes a legal power that would be intolerable if it were actually exercised as written, and makes it tolerable. If the convention did not exist, the legal power would have to be changed. It would be intolerable to Canadians if the Queen or Governor General were actually to exercise significant governmental powers. Such powers would be inconsistent with representative democracy. But the legal powers can continue to exist, so long as they are invariably exercised in conformity with the conventions that assure democratic control of the powers. Thus, the conventions allow the law to adapt to changing political realities without the necessity for formal amendment.

Not only do conventions presuppose the existence of law, much law presupposes the existence of conventions. The Constitution Act, 1867 was drafted the way it was because the framers knew that the extensive powers vested in the Queen and Governor General would be exercised in accordance with the conventions of responsible government, that is to say, under the advice (meaning direction) of the cabinet or in some cases the Prime Minister. Modern statutes continue this strange practice of ignoring the Prime Minister (or provincial Premier) and his cabinet. They always grant powers to the Governor General in Council[7] (or the Lieutenant Governor in Council) when they intend to grant powers to the cabinet. The numerous statutes that do this are of course enacted in the certain knowledge that the conventions of responsible government will shift the effective power into the hands of the elected ministry where it belongs.

While much law is enacted in the shadow of established conventions which will govern the way the law is implemented, it is not normally plausible to regard the enactment of a statute as also creating a brand-new convention, especially one that is inconsistent with the text of the statute. That difficult argument was made in *Conacher v. Canada* (2010),[8] which was an action for a declaration that Prime Minister Harper had acted in violation of a constitutional convention in advising the Governor General to dissolve Parliament for an election on a date that was a year earlier than the date stipulated in the fixed-election-

---

[5]de Smith and Brazier, Constitutional and Administrative Law (6th ed., 1989), 36–37.

[6]*Re Resolution to Amend the Constitution*, [1981] 1 S.C.R. 753, 880.

[7]The actual phrase that is used in modern statutes is "the Governor in Council", which omits the word "General".

[8]*Conacher v. Canada* (2010), 320 D.L.R. (4th) 530 (F.C.A.). The opinion of the Court was written by Stratas J.A.

date legislation. (The legislation had been recently enacted by Parliament at the initiative of Mr Harper's government.) It was argued that the Hansard debates made clear that the intent of the legislation was to restrict the calling of elections to the statutory date, except in the case where the Prime Minister had lost the confidence of the House. What the legislation said was that: "Nothing in this section [establishing the fixed dates] affects the powers of the Governor General, including the power to dissolve Parliament at the Governor General's discretion." This unqualified language could not be interpreted as including the suggested restriction. And so the applicant argued that the Hansard debates had established a convention embodying the suggested restriction. The Hansard debates were of course debates about the establishment of a new statute, not (at least in any explicit way) about the establishment of a new convention, let alone a convention that significantly narrowed the application of the statute. The only relevant precedent was the election that was under challenge, which contradicted the suggested convention and made clear that the relevant actors, the Prime Minister and Governor General, did not believe in the existence of any such convention. Therefore, the existence of the convention was not established.[9]

§ 1:15 Convention and policy

In two cases,[1] the Supreme Court of Canada was faced with an argument by public school supporters that provincial education statutes violated a constitutional convention. The objection to the statutes was that they restricted the traditional autonomy of the public school boards by imposing increased central governmental control over them. The argument, if successful, would not have invalidated the statutes, because a convention cannot override a statute, but the proponents presumably believed that a favourable ruling would help them to secure a political remedy, namely, the repeal or amendment of the statutes. The Court held in both cases that no convention restricted the policy or substance of what could be enacted by the provincial Legislature in exercise of its power to make laws in relation to education. (The power is in s. 93 of the Constitution Act, 1867.) Conventions affected only the structure of governmental power, not the policies to which governmental power was addressed. Iacobucci J. for the Court said that the fact that "the province has used a particular design [of public school system] for an extended period of time reflects consistency in public policy. It does not

---

[9]The decision is criticized by A. Heard, "*Conacher* Missed the Mark on Constitutional Conventions and Fixed Election Dates" (2010) 19 Constitutional Forum 21, and supported by R.E. Hawkins, "The Fixed-Date Election Law: Constitutional Convention or Conventional Politics?" (2010) 19 Constitutional Forum 33.

[Section 1:15]

[1]*Public School Boards' Assn. of Alta. v. Alta.*, [2000] 2 S.C.R. 409, paras. 38–42; *Ont. English Catholic Teachers' Assn. v. Ont.*, [2001] 1 S.C.R. 470, paras. 63–66.

announce the arrival of a new principle of responsible government".[2]

---

[2] *Ont. English Catholic Teachers' Assn. v. Ont.*, [2001] 1 S.C.R. 470, para. 65.

Chapter 2

Reception

I. RULES OF RECEPTION

§ 2:1 Rules of reception

II. SETTLED COLONIES

§ 2:2 Date of reception
§ 2:3 Exclusion of unsuitable laws
§ 2:4 Amendment of received laws

III. CONQUERED COLONIES

§ 2:5 General rules of reception
§ 2:6 Ontario and Quebec

IV. CONFEDERATION

§ 2:7 Confederation

V. ADMISSION OF NEW PROVINCES AND TERRITORIES

§ 2:8 Section 146 of the B.N.A. Act
§ 2:9 Territories and prairie provinces
§ 2:10 British Columbia
§ 2:11 Prince Edward Island
§ 2:12 Newfoundland

VI. IMPERIAL STATUTES

§ 2:13 Imperial statutes

I. RULES OF RECEPTION

§ 2:1 Rules of reception

How did Canada acquire its legal systems? The answer is that they were received from the former imperial power, the United Kingdom, and, to a much lesser extent, France, during the colonial period. This chapter explains how "reception"[1] occurred in British North America, and traces the process up to the present time.

[Section 2:1]

[1]The process is usually described as "reception", although "adoption", "migration"

Since British North America was eventually entirely colonized by the United Kingdom, we must look to the English common law of colonization for the basic rules of reception. The common law distinguished between a colony acquired by the United Kingdom by settlement and a colony acquired by conquest. In the case of a colony acquired by settlement, the settlers brought with them English law, and this became the initial law of the colony. In the case of a colony acquired by conquest, the law of the conquered people continued in force, except to the extent necessary to establish and operate the governmental institutions of British colonial rule. A colony acquired by cession (that is, by transfer from another country) was treated as acquired by conquest.

In British North America, the two rules of reception were not as useful as they might appear. In the first place, they were often applied in disregard of the existence of the aboriginal peoples, who were in possession of much of British North America before the arrival of Europeans. Their presence, supported by their considerable military capability, explains the survival of aboriginal customary law in parts of British North America.[2] It is clear that all aboriginal customary law did not disappear at the time of European settlement, as the rule of reception for a settled British colony might imply.[3] The account which follows will not pursue the complex issue of the survival of aboriginal customary law,[4] but will simply attempt to trace the reception of English and French law into British North America.

The reception of English and French law into British North America is by no means a straightforward story. In view of early French claims to large areas of British North America, it is not always clear whether a particular territory should be treated as having been acquired by the United Kingdom by settlement or by conquest (or cession). As we shall see, outside the territory now included in Ontario and Quebec (which

---

and "introduction" are also occasionally used. For accounts of the process, see H.D. Anger and J.D. Honsberger, Law of Real Property (Canada Law Book, 2nd ed., 1985), ch. 3; W.R. Jackett, "Foundations of Canadian Law in History and Theory" in Lang (ed.), Contemporary Problems of Public Law in Canada (1968), 3; Laskin, The British Tradition in Canadian Law (1969), 3–10; Lederman, Continuing Canadian Constitutional Dilemmas (1981), ch. 4; E.G. Brown, "British Statutes in the Emergent Nations of North America: 1606–1949" (1963) 7 Am. J. Legal History 95; J.E. Cote, "The Reception of English Law" (1977) 15 Alta. L. Rev. 29.

[2] *Connolly v. Woolrich* (1867), 11 L.C. Jur. 197 (Que. S.C.); affd. (1869) 17 R.J.R.Q. 266 (Que. Q.B.).

[3] The Supreme Court of Canada has held that those aboriginal "practices, customs and traditions" that were central to the distinctive culture of aboriginal societies prior to contact with Europeans, and that continued after contact, and that were not specifically extinguished, not only survived the reception of English or French law, but since 1982 have been protected as aboriginal rights under s. 35 of the Constitution Act, 1982: *R. v. Van der Peet*, [1996] 2 S.C.R. 507, paras. 28–43 per Lamer C.J. for majority; *R. v. Côté*, [1996] 3 S.C.R. 139, paras. 42–54. The recognition of aboriginal rights is discussed in ch. 28, Aboriginal Peoples, under heading §§ 28:18 to 28:22, "Aboriginal rights".

[4] The Eurocentric assumptions of international law and the domestic law of reception are questioned in B. Slattery, "Aboriginal Sovereignty and Imperial Claims" (1991) 29 Osgoode Hall L.J. 1. See also ch. 28, Aboriginal Peoples.

was indisputably acquired by either conquest or cession), the tendency of the courts was to prefer the "settled" classification. The settled classification entailed the automatic reception of English, not French law, a result that was congenial to the English population. In the case of the three maritime provinces, which as a matter of historical fact were acquired by cession from France, the possibility of the survival of French law seems never to have been seriously considered. The reception of English law into these provinces has often been explained on the patently false basis that they were "settled" colonies.[5] Settlement and conquest were not the only ways in which English and French laws were received in British North America. Adoption was a third way. The colonial Legislature could enact a statute adopting the laws of England as of a certain date. This would occur, either because the colony was not content with the body of law received by settlement or conquest, or because the date of reception was open to dispute. We shall see that reception of English laws in Ontario, the four western provinces and the two federal territories now depends upon adoption. A fourth mode of reception was imposition by the imperial power. We shall see that the King (exercising a prerogative power to legislate for a conquered colony) or the imperial Parliament could impose upon a colony the laws of England as of a

[5]The leading case, *Uniacke v. Dickson* (1848), 2 N.S.R. 287 (S.C. N.S.), establishes that English law was received in Nova Scotia as of 1758, when the first legislative assembly was held. This decision proceeded from the premise that Nova Scotia was a settled colony. In fact, Nova Scotia (excepting Cape Breton Island) was ceded from France to Britain by the Treaty of Utrecht in 1713. (Some of New Brunswick may have been included—the boundaries are not clear.) Nova Scotia was therefore a conquered colony, but after a British colonial government was constituted by appointment of a governor in 1749, and especially after the expulsion of the French settlers in the 1750's, the colony came to be treated as settled. Cape Breton Island, Prince Edward Island and New Brunswick (to the extent that it had not been ceded in 1713) were ceded from France to Britain by the Treaty of Paris in 1763, and were annexed to Nova Scotia in 1763. The effect of annexation would be to receive Nova Scotia's law which was English law as of 1758. This would continue to be the received law in Prince Edward Island after it was separated from Nova Scotia in 1769 and held its first legislative assembly in 1773. There does not seem to be a clear-cut decision in favour of 1758 for Prince Edward Island and commentators do not all agree on 1758: see H.D. Anger and J.D. Honsberger, Law of Real Property (Canada Law Book, 2nd ed., 1985), ch. 3; W.R. Jackett, "Foundations of Canadian Law in History and Theory" in Lang (ed.), Contemporary Problems of Public Law in Canada (1968), 3; Laskin, The British Tradition in Canadian Law (1969), 3-10; Lederman, Continuing Canadian Constitutional Dilemmas (1981), ch. 4; E.G. Brown, "British Statutes in the Emergent Nations of North America: 1606-1949" (1963) 7 Am. J. Legal History 95; J.E. Cote, "The Reception of English Law" (1977) 15 Alta. L. Rev. 29. The same date 1758 should also be the reception date of New Brunswick, which was separated from Nova Scotia in 1784 and held its first legislative assembly in 1786. However, the New Brunswick courts have held that 1660 is the reception date of New Brunswick, on the idiosyncratic basis that the Restoration of the Stuart Kings (Charles II) should be treated as the reception date for all North American colonies: *Scott v. Scott* (1970), 15 D.L.R. (3d) 374 (N.B.A.D.) (Abolition of Old Tenures Act, 1660 (Eng.), enacted after Restoration of Charles II, not in force in N.B.); and see D.J. Bell's two comments (1979) 28 U.N.B.L.J. 195; (1980) 29 U.N.B.L.J. 157. The constitutions of the maritime provinces are described, with references, in J.E. Read, "The Early Provincial Constitutions" (1948) 26 Can. Bar Rev. 621. See also N. Wiseman, "Clarifying Provincial Constitutions" (1996) 6 Nat. J. Con. Law 269.

certain date. We shall see that this occurred by royal proclamation in Quebec in 1763, although the pre-conquest French law was restored, this time by imperial statute, in 1774.

II. SETTLED COLONIES

§ 2:2 Date of reception

When an uninhabited territory was settled by British subjects, the rule of the common law was that the first settlers were deemed to have imported English law[1] with them. In the absence of any competing legal system, English law followed British subjects and filled the legal void in the new territory. The importation was deemed to have occurred on the date of the first settlement of the colony, but in practice settlement was a gradual process and the date of the first settlement was unknown or disputable. The courts which later had to identify the rules of English law which had been received selected the date of "the institution of a local legislature in the colony" as the date of reception.[2] For example, Newfoundland, which had been settled (contrary to official British policy) for centuries, was deemed to have received English law in 1832 when the first legislative assembly was held.[3] The same principle probably yields dates of reception for Nova Scotia, New Brunswick and Prince Edward Island, on the dubious basis that they were settled (rather than conquered) colonies.[4] The dates of reception thus derived are quite artificial and are really cut-off dates, marking the end of a period of continuous reception, rather than a single event.

The law that was imported into a settled colony was the entire body of English law—statute law as well as common law—except to the extent that the law was unsuitable to the circumstances of the colony (an exception that will be discussed later). So far as statute law was concerned, the date of reception was important. If a statute was in force in England at the date of reception, then (unless it was unsuitable to the colony) it was imported to the colony. Its subsequent repeal in England would have no effect on its continued operation within the colony. By the same token, a statute enacted in England after the date of reception would not come into force in the colony. For example, Nova Scotia, with its reception date of 1758,[5] received the Statute of Uses, 1536 and the Statute of Frauds, 1677 (which established basic rules of property and

[Section 2:2]

[1]After the union of England and Scotland in 1707, when the United Kingdom of Great Britain was created, with two systems of private law, English and Scottish, equal in status, the law that automatically followed citizens of Great Britain to new colonies was English, not Scottish, law: Latham, The Law and the Commonwealth (1949), 517. See also § 2:13 note 3, below on the definition of the term "United Kingdom".

[2]*Young v. Blaikie* (1822), 1 Nfld. L.R. 277, 283 (S.C. Nfld.), settling the date for Newfoundland.

[3]*Young v. Blaikie* (1822), 1 Nfld. L.R. 277, 283 (S.C. Nfld.).

[4]See § 2:1 note 5 and accompanying text.

[5]See § 2:1 note 5.

contract law), but Nova Scotia did not receive the Divorce and Matrimonial Causes Act, 1857 (which introduced divorce). By contrast, Manitoba, Saskatchewan and Alberta, with an adopted reception date of 1870,[6] did receive the English law of divorce.

So far as common law[7] was concerned, the date of reception was not important. In colonial times, the common law was conceived of as a comprehensive body of doctrine, which was uniform throughout the British Empire, and which could provide a rule for any situation. The changes in the common law which in fact occurred as the courts fashioned new rules for new situations were regarded as merely the elaboration of pre-existing doctrine. This theory would have been hard to maintain if the common law had developed differently in different jurisdictions, but the Privy Council, as the final court of appeal for all British colonies, preserved the uniformity of the common law, not only throughout British North America but throughout the British Empire.[8] If different rules developed in different jurisdictions, one of those rules would eventually be declared to be the correct rule by either the Privy Council or the House of Lords and all common law jurisdictions would loyally accept the verdict of their lordships.[9]

In practice, the reception of common law was a continuous process, as

[6]See § 2:9, "Territories and prairie provinces". The rules regarding the significance of the date of reception were the same regardless of whether the date was fixed by settlement or by legislative adoption.

[7]By common law, I include all judge-made law, including the doctrines of equity. The problem of reception of equity in Upper Canada (now Ontario) (a conquered colony with a statutory reception of English law: see § 2:6, "Ontario and Quebec") stemmed, not from different rules of reception, but from the absence until 1837 of a court with equitable jurisdiction: see J.E. Cote, "The Reception of English Law" (1977) 15 Alta. L. Rev. 29, 57–59.

[8]There was no mechanism to resolve differences between the House of Lords (with jurisdiction within the United Kingdom) and the Privy Council (with jurisdiction over overseas territories), because they were co-ordinate courts. But such differences (although not unknown) were rare because the same law lords sat on both courts. As well, the Privy Council acknowledged the position of the House of Lords as "the supreme tribunal to settle English law": *Robins v. National Trust Co.*, [1927] A.C. 515, 519; in that case, the Privy Council said that colonial courts were bound to follow the House of Lords; the further implication was that the Privy Council itself would defer to the House of Lords.

[9]The myth of the monolithic common law was not able to persist in the United States, where most issues of common law could not be appealed beyond the highest court of the state, so that permanent differences in the common law rules inevitably developed from state to state. Within the Commonwealth the same development is now occurring. Many jurisdictions have abolished appeals to the Privy Council and recognize their own highest court as able to depart from Privy Council or House of Lords precedents: see G. Bale, "Casting off the Mooring Ropes of Binding Precedent" (1980) 58 Can. Bar Rev. 255 (discussing rulings by the Supreme Court of Canada and High Court of Australia to that effect). Even in a jurisdiction which has retained the appeal to the Privy Council, the Privy Council has now accepted that the common law need not be the same as the common law of England: *Australian Consolidated Press v. Uren*, [1969] 1 A.C. 590 (P.C., on appeal from Australia, refusing to follow *Rookes v. Barnard*, [1964] A.C. 1129 (H.L.), allowing punitive damages for libel). Australia has since abolished appeals to the Privy Council, as have Canada and New Zealand: ch. 8, Supreme Court of Canada, under

the courts of each colonial jurisdiction absorbed without question developments in the common law of England as "declared" by the Privy Council and House of Lords. It was unusual for a colonial court to pay any attention to the date of reception of common law (as opposed to statute law).[10] Under the theory of a single, monolithic body of common law, it was only the fact of reception that mattered, not the date.[11]

§ 2:3 Exclusion of unsuitable laws

The English laws which were received by a settled colony did not include those laws that were not suited to the circumstances of the colony. It was for a court of the colony, when adjudicating a dispute to which a rule of English law appeared relevant, to determine whether that rule was suited to the circumstances of the colony. If the court found it to be unsuitable, then the law was deemed never to have been received by the colony. In fact, colonial courts rarely found a rule of common law to be unsuitable, although they frequently rejected a statutory rule on that ground.[1] This vague doctrine of unsuitability introduced even more uncertainty into the already hazardous tasks in each colony of determining the date of reception (which was not always free from doubt) and of determining exactly which English laws were in force on that date (which was often difficult to determine given the unsystematic English statute book).

In *Conseil scolaire francophone de la Colombie-Britannique v. British Columbia* (2013),[2] the issue was whether an English Act of 1731, which required that proceedings in court be in the English language, had been received in British Columbia. The 1731 Act had been enacted before B.C.'s date of reception, which is 1858,[3] but the main issue was whether the 1731 Act was unsuited to the circumstances of the colony. The applicant, a French-language school board, which was suing the province of B.C., applied to put in evidence documents in French without English translations. The Supreme Court of Canada held that the French-language documents were inadmissible by virtue of the 1731 Act. The applicant argued that the applicability of the 1731 Act should be assessed as of the time when the facts of its case arose rather than as of the date of reception. The Court unanimously rejected that argument. If

heading § 8:2, "Abolition of Privy Council appeals".

[10]An exception is *Kungl v. Schiefer*, [1962] S.C.R. 443, 448 (no action for alienation of affections recognized by English law at the date of reception for Ontario, namely, 1792); but compare *Fleming v. Atkinson*, [1959] S.C.R. 513 (recognition of new common law duty to prevent domestic animals straying onto highway).

[11]Lederman, Continuing Canadian Constitutional Dilemmas (1981), 68.

[Section 2:3]

[1]The case-law is discussed by J.E. Cote, "The Reception of English Law" (1977) 15 Alta. L. Rev. 29, 62–81.

[2]*Conseil scolaire francophone de la Colombie-Britannique v. British Columbia*, [2013] 2 S.C.R. 774, 2013 SCC 42. Wagner J. wrote the opinion for the majority of four. Karakatsanis J., with LeBel and Abella JJ., wrote a dissenting opinon.

[3]§ 2:10, "British Columbia".

the suitability of the law had to be reassessed every time a party attempted to rely on the law, this "would be to introduce an unacceptable level of uncertainty into the law and to impose significant and unnecessary burdens on litigants".[4] The suitability of the law was to be assessed once and for all as of the date of reception.[5] Nor was the test of suitability a strict one. The purpose of reception was to avoid a vacuum of law in the receiving province, and it was not necessary to show that each received law was "necessary" for the receiving province in the sense that the mischief intended to be remedied in England existed as well in the province. It was true that in 1858 the circumstances of the province bore no resemblance to those of England, but the government of the province did function in English, and immigration into the province was coming largely from the English-speaking United States (as a result of the gold rush). Nothing in the circumstances of the province at the date of reception would have made unsuitable a law requiring court proceedings to be conducted in English. As the next section of this chapter explains, the province's Legislature had the power to repeal or amend any unwanted received law. The majority of the Court held that the province had not repealed or amended the Act of 1731.[6] Therefore the Act of 1731 was in force in the province.

§ 2:4 Amendment of received laws

The received laws of a settled colony could of course be altered by legislation. The legislation required to provide the institutions of government for the colony—a governor, a council, an assembly and courts—could be enacted by the King alone. Although the common law denied to the King (outside Parliament) any power to legislate for England,[1] it did accept a "prerogative" (common law) power to grant the institutions of government to a colony.[2] This explains why the constitutions of Nova Scotia, New Brunswick and Prince Edward Island consist, not of imperial statutes, but of prerogative instruments, namely, royal proclamations and commissions and instructions to colonial governors.[3] However, the King's prerogative power to legislate for a settled colony did not

---

[4] *Conseil scolaire francophone de la Colombie-Britannique v. British Columbia*, [2013] 2 S.C.R. 774, 2013 SCC 42, para. 35 per Wagner J. for the majority.

[5] *Conseil scolaire francophone de la Colombie-Britannique v. British Columbia*, [2013] 2 S.C.R. 774, 2013 SCC 42, paras. 37–40 per Wagner J., 78 per Karakatsanis J.

[6] So held by Wagner J. for the majority: para. 54. Karakatsanis J.'s dissenting opinion left open the possibility that the 1731 Act had been implicitly modified by later laws. However, the basis of her dissent was her interpretation of the 1731 Act as not precluding the exercise of the B.C. court's inherent jurisdiction to admit into evidence without translation French language documents prepared independently of the litigation.

[Section 2:4]

[1] *Case of Proclamations* (1611), 12 Co. Rep. 74, 77 E.R. 1352.

[2] With respect to a conquered colony, this power existed as well, but went well beyond into a general power to legislate for the colony: see following text.

[3] See J.E. Read, "The Early Provincial Constitutions" (1948) 26 Can. Bar Rev. 621,

extend beyond the provision of the institutions of government. The English law which the settlers brought with them included the rule that the King had no general power of legislation. Any other changes in the received law of the colony could only be enacted by the imperial Parliament or (once it was established) the colonial legislative assembly.[4]

III. CONQUERED COLONIES

§ 2:5 General rules of reception

When a colony was acquired by British conquest (or cession), as opposed to settlement, the rule of the common law was that the law of the conquered people continued in force in the colony, except in matters involving the relationship between the conquered people and the new British sovereign. The effect of this rule was that the pre-existing private law (including criminal law) of the colony continued in force, while the public law of the colony (establishing British governmental institutions) was replaced by English law.

The received laws of a conquered colony could of course be altered by legislation. Obviously, legislation for the colony could be enacted by the imperial Parliament. In the case of a conquered colony, legislation could also be enacted by the King alone. This prerogative power extended beyond the provision of governmental institutions (which could be provided by the King alone even in settled colonies),[1] and was a general legislative power. However, the prerogative power of legislation terminated as soon as a conquered colony was granted its own legislative assembly. Thereafter, the law of the colony could not be altered by the King alone, but only by either the imperial Parliament or the colonial assembly. This temporal limitation on the prerogative was established by *Campbell v. Hall* (1774).[2] That case concerned the colony of Grenada, which had been acquired by conquest from France. The King issued a proclamation which granted an assembly to the colony. Then he issued another proclamation which purported to impose an export tax on the residents of the colony. The Court of Queen's Bench in England held that the tax

---

where the constitutions are described and full references given. See also § 2:1 note 4, above, for the principal historical dates. Newfoundland is exceptional in that its constitution has a statutory basis: Newfoundland Act, 1832 (U.K.), 2 & 3 Wm. IV, c. 78 (authorizing establishment of assembly), but this statute is very brief and the substance of the constitution is contained in four prerogative instruments of 1832: the Governor's Commission, the Governor's Instructions, a Despatch accompanying the Commission and Instructions, and the Proclamation for an election to the assembly. These instruments are reproduced in the Consolidated Stats. Nfld. (3rd series, 1916), vol. I, Appendix, pp. 3, 13, 33, 41.

[4]The received law must be contrasted with the imperial statutes in force in a colony *ex proprio vigore*, which could not be altered by the colonial legislative assembly, although they could of course be altered by the imperial Parliament: see § 2:13, "Imperial statutes".

[Section 2:5]

[1]See text accompanying § 2:4 note 2, above.

[2]*Campbell v. Hall* (1774), 1 Cowp. 204, 98 E.R. 1045.

was invalid. The prior grant of the assembly had terminated the King's prerogative power to legislate. Had the two proclamations been issued in the reverse order, so that the tax had been imposed before the assembly was granted, the tax would have been valid.

§ 2:6 Ontario and Quebec

The territory now comprising Ontario and Quebec was part of the French colony of New France. After the British victory on the Plains of Abraham in 1759, the whole of New France was ceded to Great Britain by France in the Treaty of Paris, 1763. New France was thus acquired by conquest. The Royal Proclamation of 1763,[1] an exercise of the King's prerogative power, provided for the government of "Quebec", which was a defined part of the valley of the St. Lawrence River—the area in fact settled by the French. This proclamation (at least by implication), reinforced by an ordinance of the first British governor, imposed English law on the colony,[2] thereby excluding the pre-existing French civil law, and changing the common law rule that the pre-conquest French civil law should continue as the private law of the conquered colony.

The Quebec Act, 1774,[3] by s. 8, restored the pre-conquest French civil law as the law of Quebec. Section 8 provided that "in all matters relative to property and civil rights, resort shall be had to the laws of Canada for the decision of the same". In this provision, the phrase "laws of Canada" meant the French-derived civil law which prevailed before the conquest. By s. 11 of the Act, English criminal law was continued in force, apparently because the French law at that time was particularly harsh.[4] The Quebec Act, 1774 was not a prerogative instrument like the Royal Proclamation of 1763. The prerogative authority of the King had terminated with the pledge of an assembly in the Royal Proclamation.[5] The Quebec Act, and the subsequent constitutional provisions for what is now Ontario and Quebec, had to take the form of an imperial statute.

The Quebec Act, 1774 differed from the Royal Proclamation of 1763 in two other respects that are relevant to the present account. First, the definition of the colony of Quebec was much wider in the Quebec Act, so that the colony encompassed much of what is now Ontario as well as Quebec. Secondly, the Quebec Act made no provision for an elected

---

[Section 2:6]

[1]The Royal Proclamation, 1763 (U.K.), R.S.C. 1985, Appendix II, No. 1.

[2]There was some doubt as to the efficacy of the imposition of English law: see B. Slattery, "The Land Rights of Indigenous Canadian Peoples as Affected by the Crown's Acquisition of Territories" (D. Phil, thesis, Oxford University, 1979), 206.

[3]Quebec Act, 1774 (U.K.), R.S.C. 1985, Appendix II, No. 2.

[4]See M.L. Friedland, A Century of Criminal Justice (Carswell, 1984), 49; Edwards, "The Advent of English (Not French) Criminal Law and Procedure into Canada" (1984) 26 Crim. Law Q. 464.

[5]*Campbell v. Hall* (1774), 1 Cowp. 204, 98 E.R. 1045, was a decision based on the same Royal Proclamation of 1763, which made provision for the constitutions of Grenada, East Florida and West Florida, as well as Quebec.

assembly. (The assembly authorized by the Royal Proclamation had never met.) The lack of an assembly became a source of grievance, especially after the immigration of English-speaking United Empire Loyalists following the American revolution. Many of the loyalists settled in the St. Lawrence valley, west of the French-speaking settlements, in what is now Ontario.

The Constitutional Act, 1791[6] separated the English and the French by dividing Quebec into two provinces, a predominantly English-speaking Upper Canada and a predominantly French-speaking Lower Canada, separated by the present boundary between Ontario and Quebec. The Act satisfied loyalist demands for an assembly by providing an elected assembly for each province. Section 33 of the Act provided that the laws of the former province of Quebec were to continue in force in both Upper and Lower Canada until altered by the assemblies of those provinces. This meant, of course, so far as private law was concerned, the French civil law. This was satisfactory to the province of Lower Canada, which made no general change in this received body of law. The continuance of French civil law did not, however, suit the Upper Canadians, and the first Act enacted by the Legislature of Upper Canada provided that "in all matters of controversy relative to property and civil rights, resort shall be had to the laws of England as the rule for the decision of the same".[7] This was an adoption of English laws as of 1792, and it established 1792 as the date of reception of English law for what is now Ontario.

The elected assemblies constituted by the Constitutional Act, 1791 were in chronic conflict with the British governors and their appointed executive councils. In 1837, the inability of the popular assembly to control the executive led to armed rebellions in both provinces, and the appointment of Lord Durham to find a solution. The Durham Report (1839) recommended the institution of responsible government, a recommendation which was rejected at the time by the British government, but which was accepted within a decade when it became clear that it was the only viable solution to the conflict within the colonies.[8]

Lord Durham did not want to entrust a French majority with responsible government. In order to destroy French nationalism and to hasten what Lord Durham saw as the inevitable assimilation of the French-speaking Canadians into the English-speaking majority, Lord Durham recommended the union of the two Canadas. The Union Act, 1840[9] implemented this recommendation. The two provinces were fused into the united province of Canada with a single Legislature. The elected

---

[6]The Constitutional Act, 1791 (U.K.), R.S.C. 1985, Appendix II, No. 3.

[7]Stats. Upp. Can. 1792 (32 Geo. III), c. 1, s. 1. The phrase "property and civil rights" had also appeared, it will be recalled, in the Quebec Act, 1774 (U.K.), s. 8. The phrase was carried forward to s. 91(13) of the British North America Act, 1867: see ch. 21, Property and Civil Rights, under heading § 21:2 "History of property and civil rights".

[8]The history of the development of responsible government is related in ch. 9, Responsible Government, under heading § 9:2 "History".

[9]The Union Act, 1840 (U.K.), R.S.C. 1985, Appendix II, No. 4.

assembly included equal numbers of representatives from Upper Canada (now called Canada West) and Lower Canada (now called Canada East), despite the smaller population of Upper Canada. The motive was to ensure an English-speaking majority in the united assembly. Ironically, the population of Upper Canada quickly outgrew the population of Lower Canada, so that under-representation in the assembly became a grievance in Upper Canada. The achievement of representation by population became a major incentive for Upper Canadians to support a confederation scheme in which there would be representation by population in the lower house of the national Parliament.

The Union Act, 1840 did not change the two legal systems now so inappropriately united. Section 46 provided that all laws in force in Upper Canada and Lower Canada at the time of the union were to remain in force in the two parts of the united province of Canada. English law thus continued as the basis of the private law of Canada West, and French law continued as the basis of the private law of Canada East. The single Legislature of the united province had the power to change these bodies of law, of course, but it did not do so except in occasional and interstitial ways. Often, too, statutes enacted by the Legislature were applicable only to either Canada West or Canada East. Thus, the period of union, which lasted until confederation in 1867, did not disturb the essential differences between the English-derived laws of the predominantly English-speaking Canada West and the French-derived laws of the predominantly French-speaking Canada East.

IV. CONFEDERATION

§ 2:7 Confederation

The confederation of the colonies of British North America received its major impetus from the political difficulties in the united province of Canada. For English-speaking Canada West, now more populous than Canada East, it offered representation by population in the new national Parliament, as well as a separate provincial Legislature. For French-speaking Canada East, it offered a separate provincial Legislature controlled by a French majority, with authority over education, culture, and most private law. More generally, confederation offered the prospect of greater military strength to resist the power of the United States, then engaged in civil war and on the union side hostile to English Canada. It also offered the economic advantages of a common market and the increased wealth to undertake large public projects, especially the building of a railway to link the Canadas with the ice-free ports of the maritimes, and the opening and settlement of the west.

The British North America Act, 1867[1] gave effect to the confederation scheme settled at conferences in Charlottetown (1864), Quebec City

---

[Section 2:7]

[1]The British North America Act, 1867 (U.K.), R.S.C. 1985, Appendix II, No. 5; renamed the Constitution Act, 1867 by the Constitution Act, 1982, s. 53(2).

(1864) and London, England (1867).[2] It united the provinces of Canada, Nova Scotia and New Brunswick into a single "Dominion" under the name of Canada. It established a bi-cameral national Parliament with representation by population in the elected lower house—the House of Commons, and representation by region in the appointed upper house—the Senate. It established a common market, and allocated important economic powers to the new federal Parliament: over trade and commerce, transportation and communication, banking, currency, customs and excise and other forms of taxation; criminal law also became a federal responsibility, as did marriage and divorce. The provincial Legislatures were given other powers, notably, over "property and civil rights", municipal institutions, education and the administration of justice.[3] Nova Scotia and New Brunswick retained their existing Legislatures and other institutions of government. The province of Canada was divided into two new provinces, Ontario (the old Canada West, formerly Upper Canada) and Quebec (the old Canada East, formerly Lower Canada). The Act accordingly established a Legislature and other institutions of government for each of Ontario and Quebec.[4]

At confederation, what happened to the legal systems, with their various reception dates and differing laws, in the uniting provinces? The answer is that they remained unchanged. Section 129 of the British North America Act continued in force the laws existing at the time of union in the united province of Canada and in Nova Scotia and New Brunswick. After confederation, these laws could be altered by either the new federal Parliament (acting within its limited powers) or a provincial Legislature (acting within its limited powers).[5]

The effect of s. 129 was to avoid a vacuum of law. With respect to matters within provincial legislative authority, each province retained its existing body of laws.[6] That body of laws had five sources: (1) the laws "received" from England or (in the case of Quebec) France by virtue of the rules discussed earlier in this chapter; (2) laws enacted for the province under the royal prerogative; (3) statute law enacted for the province

[2]Browne, Documents on the Confederation of British North America (1969) and Ajzenstat (ed.), Canada's Founding Debates (1999) are the best collections of source materials.

[3]The list of federal powers is mainly in s. 91 of the Act; the provincial list is mainly in s. 92.

[4]On the constitution of Quebec, see J.-Y. Morin, "Pour une nouvelle Constitution du Québec" (1985) 30 McGill L.J. 171.

[5]The imperial Parliament (which had enacted the B.N.A. Act) also retained legislative power over Canada: see § 2:13, "Imperial statutes".

[6]The boundaries of Quebec in 1898, and of Ontario, Quebec and Manitoba in 1912, were extended to include parts of the Northwest Territories, which of course had a different reception date than Ontario and Quebec and different laws than Ontario, Quebec or Manitoba. It has always been assumed that the effect of these annexations was to extend the laws of each province into the territory annexed to that province: J.E. Cote, "The Reception of English Law" (1977) 15 Alta. L. Rev. 29, 52. The statutes (which are silent on the reception point) are S.C. 1898, c. 3 (Quebec); S.C. 1912, c. 32 (Manitoba); S.C. 1912, c. 40 (Ontario); S.C. 1912, c. 45 (Quebec).

by the imperial Parliament; (4) judicial developments in the common law (or civil law) since the date of reception; and (5) statute law enacted by the predecessor colonial Legislature.[7] With respect to matters within federal legislative authority, there was no single body of law in 1867; such matters were regulated by a part of each of the five kinds of pre-confederation laws which were continued in force by s. 129. Gradually, of course, after 1867 the federal Parliament enacted statutes on the matters coming within its authority,[8] and thereby supplanted the diverse pre-confederation laws with a body of statute law which was usually uniform across the country.[9]

V. ADMISSION OF NEW PROVINCES AND TERRITORIES

§ 2:8 Section 146 of the B.N.A. Act

The British North America Act, by s. 146, contemplated the admission to Canada of the rest of British North America. In the case of the three remaining colonies, namely, British Columbia, Prince Edward Island and Newfoundland, s. 146 provided that each could be admitted by imperial order in council at the request of the Legislature of the colony. In the case of the territories of Rupert's Land and the North-western Territory, s. 146 provided that each could be admitted by imperial order in council at the request of the Parliament of Canada.

§ 2:9 Territories and prairie provinces

From the Rocky Mountains eastward into what is now northern Ontario and northern Quebec[1] lay the huge territories of Rupert's Land and the North-western Territory. In 1870, the procedure established by

---

[7]For example, the civil code of Quebec was for 128 years after confederation the Civil Code of Lower Canada, Stats. Prov. Can. 1865, c. 41, which was replaced by the Civil Code of Québec, S.Q. 1991, c. 64, proclaimed in force on January 1, 1994. Of course, those portions of the Civil Code of Lower Canada that deal with subjects that were assigned to the federal Parliament by the Constitution Act, 1867, for example, marriage, interest, insolvency, bills of exchange and maritime law, remain in force to the extent that they have not been replaced since 1867 by federal statute law: R.A. Macdonald, "Encoding Canadian Civil Law" in Mélanges Paul-André Crépeau (Yvon Blais, Quebec, 2006), 579.

[8]There is no constitutional requirement that the federal Parliament (or a provincial Legislature for that matter) actually exercise its authority. In the area of divorce (a federal responsibility under s. 91(26)), the federal Parliament was very tardy indeed, not enacting a Canada-wide statute until 1968. Before then the law differed from province to province, depending upon the state of the law initially received in that province. In some provinces, where reception yielded no divorce law, a territorially-limited federal statute was enacted to fill the vacuum: see, e.g., Divorce Act (Ontario), S.C. 1930, c. 14. See generally ch. 27, The Family, under heading § 27:5, "Divorce".

[9]There is no constitutional requirement that federal laws be uniform across the country, and there are many examples of territorially-limited federal statutes: see, e.g., Divorce Act (Ontario), S.C. 1930, c. 14. See generally ch. 27, The Family, under heading 27:5, "Divorce", below.

[Section 2:9]

[1]In 1898 and 1912 the parts of the Northwest Territories lying north of Ontario,

s. 146 was employed to admit these territories to Canada.[2] On admission, they did not become provinces; they became federal territories, entirely subject to the authority of the federal Parliament.[3]

In 1870, immediately following the admission of the territories, the federal Parliament by statute created the province of Manitoba out of part of Rupert's Land.[4] What was left of Rupert's Land and the North-western Territory was renamed the Northwest Territories.[5] In 1898, in response to the influx of population caused by the gold rush, the Yukon Territory was carved out of the Northwest Territories and formed into a separate territory.[6] In 1993, Nunavut was carved out of the Northwest Territories and formed into a separate territory.[7] In 1905, the provinces of Alberta[8] and Saskatchewan[9] were created out of the Northwest Territories. As in the case of Manitoba, the provinces of Alberta and Saskatchewan were created by federal statute. The constitutions of Manitoba, Alberta and Saskatchewan thus take the curious form of a federal statute.

In the absence of legislation, the date of reception of English law into Rupert's Land and the North-western Territory and therefore into Manitoba, Alberta, Saskatchewan, the Northwest Territories, the Yukon Territory and Nunavut would be quite unclear. Happily, the reception date for these three provinces and three territories has been fixed by statute as 1870.[10] When the Yukon Territory was created in 1898, when Alberta and Saskatchewan were created in 1905, and when Nunavut

---

Quebec and Manitoba were annexed to those provinces: § 2:1 note 6, above.

[2]Rupert's Land and North-Western Territory Order, 1870 (U.K.), R.S.C. 1985, Appendix II, No. 9. This did not cover all British territories in the north; the remaining (Arctic) territories were admitted by the Adjacent Territories Order, 1880 (U.K.), R.S.C. 1985, Appendix II, No. 14.

[3]British North America Act, 1871 (U.K.) (now renamed the Constitution Act, 1871), R.S.C. 1985, Appendix II, No. 11, s. 4; and see next note.

[4]Manitoba Act, 1870 (Can.), R.S.C. 1985, Appendix II, No. 8. The power of the federal Parliament to create provinces out of federal territories was not expressly conferred by the British North America Act, 1867. The power was granted retroactively (and the Manitoba Act confirmed) by ss. 2 and 5 of the British North America Act, 1871 (since renamed the Constitution Act, 1871). The same Act, by s. 4, conferred upon the federal Parliament full legislative authority over the federal territories.

[5]Manitoba Act, 1870, s. 35.

[6]Yukon Territory Act, 1898 (Can.); see now Yukon Act, S.C. 2002, c. 7.

[7]Nunavut Act, S.C. 1993, c. 28. The Northwest Territories continues to be governed by the Northwest Territories Act, R.S.C. 1985, c. N-27.

[8]Alberta Act, 1905 (Can.), R.S.C. 1985, Appendix II, No. 20.

[9]Saskatchewan Act, 1905 (Can.), R.S.C. 1985, Appendix II, No. 21.

[10]After Manitoba was created, the provincial Legislature enacted the reception date of July 15, 1870: Queen's Bench Act, S.M. 1874, c. 12, s. 5. This law could only apply to matters within provincial jurisdiction, and so it was supplemented by a federal statute fixing the same date: Manitoba Supplementary Provision Act, S.C. 1888, c. 33, s. 4. The same date was provided for the Northwest Territories, including what later became the Yukon Territory, and the provinces of Alberta and Saskatchewan: North-West Territories Amendment Act, S.C. 1886, c. 25, s. 3. This federal statute had been preceded by a territorial ordinance two years earlier fixing the same date: An Ordinance Respecting Prop-

was created in 1993, their constituent statutes preserved the reception date of 1870 by expressly continuing in force the laws in existence at the time of their creation.

§ 2:10 British Columbia

The province of British Columbia is the product of the fusion of two settled colonies, namely, Vancouver's Island and British Columbia (formerly New Caledonia).[1] Vancouver's Island was constituted by imperial statute in 1849,[2] and granted an assembly which first met in 1856. British Columbia, the mainland of present-day British Columbia, was constituted by imperial statute in 1858,[3] but no assembly was granted, the governor alone being authorized to make laws. The governor, by proclamation, stipulated 1858 as the date of reception of English laws. In 1866, the two colonies were amalgamated by imperial statute;[4] the new colony was called British Columbia. Legislative power over the enlarged colony was exercised by a Legislative Council composed of a majority of appointed members and a minority of elected members.[5] The Legislative Council, by ordinance, stipulated 1858 as the date of reception of English laws for the entire colony.[6]

British Columbia was admitted to Canada in 1871 by imperial order in council,[7] made at the request of its Legislative Council, which was the procedure provided by s. 146 of the British North America Act. The Terms of Union said nothing about the continuance in force of existing laws, but term 10 provided that the provisions of the British North America Act were to be applicable to British Columbia in the same way as they were applicable to the other provinces "as if the colony of British Columbia had been one of the provinces originally united by this Act". Term 10 made s. 129 of the B.N.A. Act applicable to British Columbia,

---

erty and Civil Rights, O.N.W.T. 1884, c. 26, s. 1. Saskatchewan has re-enacted the reception date of 1870 and repealed s. 11 of the North-West Territories Act "to the extent that it applies to matters within the legislative jurisdiction of Saskatchewan": Queen's Bench Amendment Act, 2010, S.S. 2010, c. 28, adding s. 51.2 to the Queen's Bench Act, 1998. The purpose was to make the reception date more accessible to modern readers.

[Section 2:10]

[1]See J.E. Read, "The Early Provincial Constitutions" (1948) 26 Can. Bar Rev. 621, 634–635; Lederman, Continuing Canadian Constitutional Dilemmas (1981), 73–74; J.E. Cote, "The Reception of English Law" (1977) 15 Alta. L. Rev. 29, 91–92; C. Sharman, "The Strange Case of a Provincial Constitution: The British Columbia Constitution Act" (1984) 17 Can. J. Pol. Sci. 87.

[2]Administration of Justice in Vancouver's Island Act, 1849 (U.K.), 12 & 13 Vict., c. 48.

[3]Government of British Columbia Act, 1858 (U.K.), 21 & 22 Vict., c. 99.

[4]British Columbia Act, 1866 (U.K.), 29 & 30 Vict., c. 67. All the constitutional documents (pre-confederation and post-confederation) relating to Vancouver Island and British Columbia are collected in R.S.B.C. 1979, vol. 7 (Appendices).

[5]The people of Vancouver Island thereby lost their elected assembly.

[6]The English Law Ordinance, 1867, S.B.C. 1867, c. 7.

[7]British Columbia Terms of Union, 1871 (U.K.), R.S.C. 1985, Appendix II, No. 10.

and thus continued in force the laws existing in British Columbia at the time of its admission. The reception date of 1858 was thus preserved.[8]

British Columbia at the time of its admission in 1871 was unlike any of the other provinces in that its Legislature still consisted of a Legislative Council with a majority of appointed members, and it had not achieved responsible government. These disabilities were mentioned in term 14 of the Terms of Union, and their early elimination was contemplated. In 1871, British Columbia acquired a fully elected Legislature,[9] and, in 1872, the province achieved responsible government.[10]

§ 2:11 Prince Edward Island

Prince Edward Island was ceded from France to Britain by the Treaty of Paris in 1763, and was then annexed to Nova Scotia. It was separated from Nova Scotia and constituted as a separate colony in 1769.[1] It held its first legislative assembly in 1773. By virtue of the annexation to Nova Scotia in 1763, Prince Edward Island probably acquired the same reception date as Nova Scotia's, that is, 1758.[2]

Prince Edward Island, although a participant in the pre-confederation discussions in 1864 at Charlottetown (obviously) and Quebec City, did not become one of the original uniting provinces. The Island was not admitted to Canada until 1873. The instrument of admission was an imperial order in council,[3] made at the request of the Island's Legislature, which was the procedure provided by s. 146 of the B.N.A. Act. As in the case of British Columbia, the Terms of Union incorporated the provisions of the B.N.A. Act, including s. 129, and thus continued in force the laws existing in Prince Edward Island at the time of its admission.

---

[8]B.C. has codified the common law rule and confirmed the reception date of 1858: Law and Equity Act, R.S.B.C. 1996, c. 253, s. 2; and see *Conseil scolaire francophone de la Colombie-Britannique v. B.C.*, [2013] 2 S.C.R. 774, 2013 SCC 42 (holding that English Act of 1731 was received in the province).

[9]The Legislative Council replaced itself with a fully elective Legislative Assembly: Constitution Act, 1871 (B.C.), 34 Vict., c. 147. The history of electoral representation in B.C. is related in *Re Dixon* (1986), 31 D.L.R. (4th) 546, 552–553 (B.C.S.C.).

[10]After union, the Lieutenant Governor, on instructions from the federal government that appointed him, appointed a responsible ministry: Saywell, The Office of Lieutenant-Governor (1957), 79–87.

[Section 2:11]

[1]The Constitution consisted of two prerogative instruments of 1769, namely, the Commission and Instructions to the Governor: J.E. Read, "The Early Provincial Constitutions" (1948) 26 Can. Bar Rev. 621, 630 supplies references.

[2]See § 2:1 note 5, above.

[3]Prince Edward Island Terms of Union, 1873 (U.K.), R.S.C. 1985, Appendix II, No. 12.

§ 2:12 Newfoundland

We have already noted that Newfoundland was a settled colony, and that its date of reception had been judicially fixed at 1832 when its first assembly was held.[1] It achieved responsible government in 1855.[2]

Newfoundland did not join confederation in 1867. It continued as a separate colony into the twentieth century, and indeed began to progress on the same path to independence that Canada, Australia and New Zealand followed. Like Canada, Australia and New Zealand, Newfoundland was described as a "Dominion" in the Balfour declaration of 1926 and in the Statute of Westminster of 1931.[3] But the depression so injured Newfoundland's economy that it was unable to pay its debts. In 1933, the Newfoundland Legislature formally requested the United Kingdom to suspend Newfoundland's constitution until Newfoundland became self-supporting again, and to replace the Legislature and other institutions of responsible government with a "Commission of Government". This request was implemented by an imperial statute,[4] and from 1934 Newfoundland was governed by a Commission of Government consisting of a Governor and a six-member Commission, all appointed by the United Kingdom Government. The Commission of Government exercised all legislative and executive power until 1949. In that year, Newfoundland was admitted to Canada.

Newfoundland's admission to Canada was effected by an imperial statute,[5] which followed two referenda in Newfoundland, the second of which had approved union with Canada by a narrow majority.[6] The procedure for the admission of new provinces in s. 146 of the B.N.A. Act,

---

[Section 2:12]

[1]*Young v. Blaikie* (1822), 1 Nfld. L.R. 277, 283 (S.C. Nfld.).

[2]G.E. Gunn, The Political History of Newfoundland 1832–1864 (U. Toronto P., 1966), ch. 9.

[3]See ch. 3, Independence, under heading § 3:3, "Statute of Westminster, 1931". Unlike the other dominions, however, Newfoundland had not signed the Treaty of Versailles separately from the United Kingdom; had never joined the League of Nations; and entrusted all of her external relations to the United Kingdom. Although the Statute of Westminster included Newfoundland in the definition of "Dominion", Newfoundland never adopted the operative provisions of the Statute. The Statute did not become operative within Newfoundland until union with Canada, by virtue of term 48 of the Terms of Union: British North America Act, 1949 (U.K.) (since renamed the Newfoundland Act), R.S.C. 1985, Appendix II, No. 32. The Terms of Union are a schedule to the Act.

[4]Newfoundland Act, 1933 (U.K.), 24 Geo. V, c. 2.

[5]British North America Act, 1949 (U.K.) (since renamed the Newfoundland Act), R.S.C. 1985, Appendix II, No. 32. The Terms of Union are a schedule to the Act.

[6]The 1949 statute (previous note) was, in my opinion, a breach of convention by the United Kingdom, because union with Canada had never been requested by the Newfoundland Legislature: see ch. 3, Independence, under heading § 3:3, "Statute of Westminster, 1931". The Newfoundland Act, 1933 (U.K.), which instituted the Commission of Government, did not contemplate anything other than the restoration of responsible government to a separate Newfoundland. Fidelity to the original request for the Commission of Government required simply that the pre-1934 Legislature and responsible government be restored. The Legislature would then have been free to

which had been used for the admission of British Columbia and Prince Edward Island, could not be used for Newfoundland, because s. 146 required that admission be requested by the Legislature of the province seeking admission, and in 1949 Newfoundland lacked a Legislature. The Terms of Union restored Newfoundland's Legislature and other institutions of responsible government (which it needed to function as a province), by providing (in Term 7) that "the Constitution of Newfoundland as it existed prior to the sixteenth day of February, 1934 [when the Commission of Government had taken over], is revived at the date of Union".

As with the other provinces, Newfoundland's admission did not break the continuity of its laws. Term 18 of the Terms of Union continued in force the laws existing in Newfoundland at the time of admission. The reception date of 1832 was unaffected.

VI. IMPERIAL STATUTES

§ 2:13 Imperial statutes

In the account so far, frequent reference has been made to imperial statutes. The instruments which mark the constitutional history of British North America include many imperial statutes: for example, the constitutions of several of the provinces, including the sequence of constitutions of what is now Ontario and Quebec, and, of course, the British North America Act, 1867 and most of its amendments.[1] As well as these constitutional instruments, many other imperial statutes were in force in colonial British North America, and a considerable number are in force in Canada today.[2]

From the earliest colonial times the Parliament at Westminster had the power not only to make laws for the United Kingdom,[3] but also to make laws for the overseas territories of the British Empire. In perform-

---

explore the question of confederation and, if desired, take the steps contemplated by s. 146 of the B.N.A. Act to achieve it. The validity of the 1949 statute was challenged on the basis of this breach of convention, but the Newfoundland courts held that the convention did not affect the legal authority of the United Kingdom Parliament to legislate as it pleased for Newfoundland: *Currie v. MacDonald* (1948), 29 Nfld. & P.E.I.R. 314 (Nfld. S.C.); affd. (1949) 29 Nfld. & P.E.I.R. 294 (Nfld. C.A.).

[Section 2:13]

[1]Even the Canada Act 1982 and its schedule, the Constitution Act, 1982, is an imperial statute, that is, an enactment of the Parliament of the United Kingdom that is intended to regulate the affairs of a territory outside the United Kingdom, in this case, Canada.

[2]There are perhaps one hundred currently in force in Canada: Ward, Dawson's The Government of Canada (6th ed., 1987), 296.

[3]The United Kingdom now means the United Kingdom of Great Britain and Northern Ireland. It is in fact the union of four countries: England, Wales, Scotland and Northern Ireland. England annexed Wales in 1284 and Wales was fully integrated into English government and law in 1536, so much so that in most legal contexts the term England is taken to include Wales. In 1707 England (that is, England and Wales) united with Scotland and formed the United Kingdom of Great Britain (usually simply called Great Britain) under a single United Kingdom Parliament but retaining partially sepa-

ing the latter function it was known as the imperial Parliament and its enactments were known as imperial statutes. An imperial statute applied in a colony, neither by virtue of the reception of English laws, nor by the adoption of the colonial legislature, but by the imperial statute's own force (ex proprio vigore).

In force in any colony there would be two classes of statute, both enacted by the Parliament of the United Kingdom. The first class consisted of those domestic statutes of the United Kingdom which were in force in England at the colony's reception date. These statutes had been enacted to regulate affairs within the United Kingdom, and had never been intended to apply outside the United Kingdom. Nevertheless, they became part of the law of a colony if they happened to be in force in England at the date upon which English laws were received into the colony.[4] This body of "received" statute law (like the common law) could be freely amended by the colonial legislature (within any limits imposed upon its authority). The only function of received law was to ensure that there was no vacuum of law in the colony. Received law was not a mechanism of imperial control over the colony and raised no question of independence from the imperial power.

The second class of statutes of the Parliament at Westminster that would be in force in a colony consisted of the imperial statutes in force ex proprio vigore. Those statutes had been passed to regulate the affairs of the colony or colonies to which they applied. They became law in the colony by their own terms, whether or not they were also in force in England (some were and some were not), and whether or not they were enacted before the date upon which the colony received English laws. Imperial statutes, unlike received statute law or common law, could not be amended by the colonial legislature.[5] Imperial statutes were a means by which the imperial power could impose its will on the colony. Once enacted, an imperial statute constituted a restriction on the power of the colonial legislature, a restriction which could be removed only by the imperial Parliament.[6] So long as a British territory included among its laws some that it was powerless to change, and so long as it remained

---

rate English and Scottish judicial and legal systems. In 1801 Great Britain (that is, England, Wales and Scotland) united with Ireland to form the United Kingdom of Great Britain and Ireland. There followed a succession of constitutional arrangements for Ireland which culminated in the creation in 1922 of a new "dominion", the Irish Free State (after 1937, Eire, and since 1949, the Republic of Ireland, no longer a member of the Commonwealth). Six northern counties remained in the United Kingdom, which thenceforth meant the United Kingdom of Great Britain and Northern Ireland. For a brief constitutional history of the United Kingdom, see C.R. Munro, Studies in Constitutional Law (Butterworths, London, 2nd ed., 1999), ch. 2; de Smith and Brazier, Constitutional and Administrative Law (8th ed., 1998), 48–57.

[4]The only exception was for those statutes judicially determined to be unsuitable to conditions in the colony: § 2:3, "Exclusion of unsuitable laws".

[5]An exception was the occasional imperial statute that expressly authorized its own amendment by the colonial Legislature. Parts of the British North America Act, 1867 could be amended within Canada for that reason.

[6]The identification of the imperial statutes in force in a particular colony was exceedingly important. The Colonial Laws Validity Act, 1865 (U.K.), which is described

vulnerable to future laws that it did not desire, that territory was a colony: its subservience to the imperial power was inconsistent with the independence that characterizes a sovereign state. The next chapter will relate how Canada gradually became free from the imperial power of the Parliament at Westminster, and thereby shed its colonial status.

---

in the next chapter, provided a rule of identification: an imperial statute was in force in a colony only if the statute, by its own terms, was applicable to the colony "by express words or necessary intendment". This rule is less than crystal clear, but it was a big improvement over the confusion that prevailed before 1865.

Chapter 3

Independence

I. BONDS OF EMPIRE

§ 3:1 Bonds of Empire

II. COLONIAL LAWS VALIDITY ACT, 1865

§ 3:2 Colonial Laws Validity Act, 1865

III. STATUTE OF WESTMINSTER, 1831

§ 3:3 Statute of Westminster, 1931

IV. CANADA ACT, 1982

§ 3:4 Canada Act 1982

V. PATRIATION OF THE CONSTITUTION

§ 3:5 Definition of patriation
§ 3:6 Canada Act 1982
§ 3:7 Autochthony
§ 3:8 Termination of imperial authority
§ 3:9 Autonomy

I. BONDS OF EMPIRE

§ 3:1 Bonds of Empire

The previous chapter, entitled Reception, has described the confederation of the colonies of British North America that took place in 1867.[1] But confederation must not be confused with independence. The British North America Act, while it created a new Dominion under the name of Canada, did not create an independent country. The federating provinces were all British colonies, although they had achieved responsible government[2] and a large measure of self-government in local affairs. The new federation also became a British colony,[3] subordinate to the

[Section 3:1]

[1]Chapter 2, Reception, under heading § 2:7, "Confederation".

[2]Ch. 8, Responsible Government.

[3]The term colony does not seem entirely appropriate for territories, such as Canada, Australia and New Zealand, which had achieved a considerable degree of self-government, and in the early 1900s the term "dominion" became usual to distinguish the

United Kingdom in international affairs, and subject to important imperial limitations in local affairs: the power of the imperial Parliament to enact statutes extending to Canada;[4] the powers of reservation and disallowance, which in effect allowed the British government to invalidate Canadian statutes;[5] the British appointment of Canada's Governor General;[6] the Canadian incapacity to enact any statute repugnant to an imperial statute extending to Canada;[7] the supposed incapacity to legislate with extraterritorial effect;[8] the supposed incapacity to change the succession to the throne or the royal style and titles;[9] and the right to ap-

---

more advanced colonies from the more dependent ones. However, even the dominions did not achieve full independence from the United Kingdom until well into the twentieth century: see § 3:1 note 11, below. For the dominions that remained in the Commonwealth, that is, Canada, Australia and New Zealand, and for other independent states within the Commonwealth, the term "Member of the Commonwealth" has become the preferred description. The history of the word "dominion" is related in ch. 5, Federalism, under heading § 5:5, "Dominion and provinces".

[4]See ch. 2, Reception, under heading § 2:13, "Imperial statutes".

[5]These powers are contained in ss. 55, 56 and 57 of the B.N.A. Act (Constitution Act, 1867). In the imperial conference of 1930 (§ 3:3 note 3, and accompanying text, below) it was agreed that the power of disallowance would not be exercised by the United Kingdom government, and that the power of reservation would not be exercised under United Kingdom instructions by the Governor General of Canada. The powers have accordingly fallen into disuse; and even before 1930 this was arguably the case. Reservation had occurred 21 times between 1867 and 1878, but had never occurred after 1878 (when the royal instructions were changed); of the 21 bills reserved, six were denied the royal assent: Bourinot, Parliamentary Procedure and Practice (2nd ed., 1892), 648–650. Disallowance had occurred only once (in 1873): Mallory, The Structure of Canadian Government (rev. ed. 1984), 17, 23. Under s. 90 of the B.N.A. Act, provincial legislation is subject to powers of reservation and disallowance, but the power of disallowance is exercisable not by the United Kingdom government but by the Canadian federal government and so no issue of Canadian independence is thereby raised. Reservation and disallowance of provincial statutes is discussed in ch. 5, Federalism, under heading § 5:13, "Disallowance".

[6]The B.N.A. Act (Constitution Act, 1867) is silent on the appointment and tenure of the Governor General, and these matters were initially determined by the United Kingdom government, technically, the Queen, acting on the advice of her ministers in the United Kingdom. Since the imperial conference of 1930, however, it has been accepted that the appointment must always be made on the advice of the Canadian federal government, and it is the Canadian government that decides upon the term of office: see ch. 9, Responsible Government, under heading § 9:3, "Law and Convention".

[7]This incapacity and its removal is discussed later in this chapter.

[8]See ch. 13, Extraterritorial Competence.

[9]At the imperial conference of 1930, it was agreed that changes to the succession to the throne or the royal style and titles would be made by the U.K. only with the assent of the other Commonwealth realms. The convention was articulated in the preamble to the Statute of Westminster (Imp.), which stipulated that "it would be in accord with the established constitutional position of all the members of the Commonwealth in relation to one another that any alteration of the law touching the Succession to the Throne or the Royal Style and Titles shall hereafter require the assent as well of the Parliaments of all the Dominions as of the Parliament of the United Kingdom". Canada has not in fact enacted its own law respecting succession to the throne or the royal style and titles. On succession to the throne, Canada simply recognizes the U.K. law as governing succession to the throne of Canada: see Succession to the Throne Act, S.C. 1937, c. 16 (as-

peal from Canadian courts to the Privy Council.[10] As the footnotes have indicated, these colonial limitations have now disappeared, by convention if not by law, as the British Empire has evolved into the Commonwealth, and the colonies have evolved into independent states within the Commonwealth. It is outside the scope of this book to describe all of the details of Canada's evolution to statehood.[11] However, the history of the status within Canada of imperial statutes is relevant to an understanding of the current foundation of much of Canada's constitutional law.

II. COLONIAL LAWS VALIDITY ACT, 1865

§ 3:2 Colonial Laws Validity Act, 1865

In the previous chapter, entitled Reception, we noticed the dual capacity of the Parliament at Westminster, which functioned (1) as a Parlia-

---

senting to the U.K.'s enactment of the change in succession caused by the abdication of Edward VIII); Succession to the Throne Act, 2013, S.C. 2013, c. 6 (assenting to the U.K.'s enactment of changes in succession to eliminate elements of sexual and religious discrimination); Canada could, of course, choose to diverge from the rules of succession of the U.K., but this would involve an amendment to the definition of the Queen (as the same person as the Queen of the U.K.) that is implicit in the Constitution Act, 1867, which would probably require a constitutional amendment to the "office of the Queen" (Constitution Act, 1982, s. 41(a), requiring unanimous consent of the provinces): P.W. Hogg, "Succession to the Throne" (2014) 33 Nat. J. Con. Law 83; see also *Motard v. Can.*, 2019 QCCA 1826 (Que. C.A.), leave to appeal to the S.C.C. denied April 23, 2020 (no constitutional amendment needed for the Succession to the Throne Act, 2013; discussed further in ch. 1, Sources, under heading § 1:4, "Constitution of Canada"). On the royal style and titles, Canada simply recognizes the proclamation of the monarch, issued under a prerogative power, establishing her or his royal style and titles for Canada: see Royal Style and Titles Act, S.C.1952-53, c. 9; Royal Style and Titles Act, S.C. 1947, c. 72. Canada could choose to enact the royal style and titles for the monarch of Canada; that would displace the prerogative; it. For a discussion of whether this might also be an amendment to the Constitution of Canada, requiring the unanimous consent of the provinces, see ch. 4, Amendment, under heading § 4:6, "Constitution of Canada".

[10] This appeal and its abolition are discussed in ch. 8, Supreme Court of Canada, under heading § 8:2, "Abolition of Privy Council appeals".

[11] The important developments include: separate signature to the Treaty of Versailles, 1919; separate membership of the League of Nations, 1919; recognition of equal status in the Balfour declaration, 1926; acquisition of increased legal capacity by virtue of the Statute of Westminster, 1931; assumption of responsibility for external affairs, including treaty-making; separate declarations of war against Germany and Japan, 1939 and 1941; and membership of the United Nations, 1945. In *Re Offshore Mineral Rights of B.C.*, [1967] S.C.R. 792, 816, the Supreme Court of Canada said that:

> There can be no doubt Canada has become a sovereign state. Its sovereignty was acquired in the period between its separate signature to the Treaty of Versailles in 1919 and the Statute of Westminster, 1931.

See generally, Kennedy, The Constitution of Canada 1534–1937 (2nd ed., 1938), esp. chs. 21, 25, 28; Laskin, Canadian Constitutional Law (5th ed. 1986, by Finkelstein), 65–70; Stanley, A Short History of the Canadian Constitution (1969), ch. 7; Wheare, The Constitutional Structure of the Commonwealth (1960); F.R. Scott, "The End of Dominion Status" (1945) 23 Can. Bar Rev. 725; I.C. Rand, "Some Aspects of Canadian Constitutionalism" (1960) 38 Can. Bar Rev. 135; Oliver, The Constitution of Independence (2005).

ment for the United Kingdom, and (2) as a Parliament for the overseas territories of the British Empire.[1] In performing the latter function, it was known as the imperial Parliament, and its enactments were known as imperial statutes. The British North America Act was, as we have seen, an imperial statute. The significance of this fact can be understood only in the light of some history.

In the previous chapter, we also noticed the distinction between (1) "received" statutes (and common law), which applied in a colony by virtue of settlement, conquest or adoption, and (2) imperial statutes, which applied in a colony by virtue of their own force.[2] The distinction was important in colonial times, because received statutes and common law could be amended by the colonial legislature, but imperial statutes could not be. The Colonial Laws Validity Act, 1865[3] defined an imperial statute as an "Act of Parliament [i.e., of the Parliament at Westminster] extending to the colony", and provided that an Act of Parliament was deemed to extend to the colony only if it was made applicable to the colony "by the express words or necessary intendment" of the statute itself. The Colonial Laws Validity Act went on to provide that colonial laws were void if they were "repugnant" to an imperial statute (as defined), but were not void if they were repugnant to a received statute or rule of common law. The Colonial Laws Validity Act was intended to remove doubts as to the capacity of colonial legislatures to enact laws that were inconsistent with English law. By narrowly defining the class of imperial statutes, and thereby confining the doctrine of repugnancy, the Act was intended to extend rather than restrict the powers of the colonial legislatures. Nevertheless, the Act did leave the colonial legislatures powerless to alter any imperial statute which by its own terms applied to the colony. If the colony wished to alter or repeal such an imperial statute it had to persuade the imperial Parliament to enact the required law.

The B.N.A. Act was enacted in 1867, two years after the Colonial Laws Validity Act. Section 129 of the B.N.A. Act continued in force pre-confederation laws that were in force in the uniting provinces, and it gave to the federal Parliament or provincial Legislatures (depending upon which was competent) the power to repeal, abolish or alter such pre-confederation laws. However, s. 129 excluded from the power of repeal, abolition or alteration such laws "as are enacted by or exist under Acts of the Parliament of Great Britain or of the Parliament of the United Kingdom of Great Britain and Ireland". This exclusion made

[Section 3:2]

[1] Chapter 2, Reception, under heading § 2:13, "Imperial statutes".

[2] Chapter 2, Reception, under heading § 2:13, "Imperial statutes".

[3] 28 & 29 Vict., c. 63 (U.K.). For history, see Wheare, The Statute of Westminster and Dominion Status (5th ed., 1953), 74–79.

clear that the power conferred by s. 129 was subject to the restriction defined by the Colonial Laws Validity Act.[4]

III. STATUTE OF WESTMINSTER, 1831

§ 3:3 Statute of Westminster, 1931

In 1926, two events made the Canadian government anxious to escape from the sovereignty of the imperial Parliament, and to secure equality of status as between the dominions and the United Kingdom. One event was the King-Byng dispute, which is related later in this book,[1] and which was treated by Prime Minister Mackenzie King as an issue of Canadian independence. The other event was the decision in *Nadan v. The King* (1926),[2] in which the Privy Council struck down a federal statute of 1888 (the statute purported to abolish appeals to the Privy Council in criminal cases), on the ground that the statute exceeded Canadian legislative power by its extraterritorial effect and its inconsistency with two imperial statutes.

The concerns of Canada and some of the other dominions[3] led to the "imperial conferences" (conferences of the Prime Ministers of the United Kingdom and the self-governing dominions) of 1926 and 1930, which grappled with the task of removing the remaining vestiges of colonial status from the dominions.[4] The conference of 1926 adopted the "Balfour Declaration" (named after the chairman of the drafting committee):[5]

> They [the United Kingdom and the dominions] are autonomous communities within the British Empire, equal in status, in no way subordinate one to another in any aspect of their domestic or external affairs, although

---

[4]Section 129's exclusion is in broad terms which would literally be apt to deny Canadian power to amend or repeal British statutes received by settlement, conquest or adoption, as well as those protected by the Colonial Laws Validity Act. However, it seems likely that s. 129 was intended to be no wider than the Colonial Laws Validity Act's definition of imperial statutes "extending to the colony": Laskin, Canadian Constitutional Law (5th ed., 1986, by Finkelstein), 66. The restriction on repealing or amending pre-confederation statutes was removed by the Statute of Westminster: see following text.

[Section 3:3]

[1]See ch. 9, Responsible Government, under heading § 9:19, "Dissolution of Parliament".

[2]*Nadan v. The King*, [1926] A.C. 482.

[3]Another cause of concern was created by the Chanak crisis of 1922, when Britain almost went to war with Turkey, and made a last-minute appeal to the dominions for assistance. The crisis passed, but the dominions became concerned about Britain involving them in European wars, and wanted formal recognition of their autonomous status.

[4]The dominions represented at the imperial conferences of 1926 and 1930 were Canada, Australia, New Zealand, Newfoundland, South Africa and the Irish Free State. (Newfoundland has since become a province of Canada. South Africa and the Irish Free State, which is now the Republic of Ireland, later left the Commonwealth. South Africa has since returned to the Commonwealth.) The records of the conferences are in Ollivier, Colonial and Imperial Conferences (1954), vol. 3, 137–344; there are also extracts in Dawson, The Development of Dominion Status 1900–1936 (1965), 329–350, 394–411.

[5]Ollivier, Colonial and Imperial Conferences (1954), vol. 3, 146; Dawson, The Development of Dominion Status 1900–1936 (1965), 331.

> united by a common allegiance to the Crown, and freely associated as members of the British Commonwealth of Nations.

The declaration was important, because it accepted the principle that the dominions were equal in status to the United Kingdom. However, the measures required to implement this principle were left to the conference of 1930.

The most difficult issue of equality concerned the power over the dominions of the imperial Parliament. How could that power be limited? The imperial conference of 1930 adopted a "convention"[6] that "no law hereafter made by the Parliament of the United Kingdom shall extend to any dominion otherwise than at the request and with the consent of that dominion"; the conference also recommended the enactment by the imperial Parliament of the Statute of Westminster.[7] The Statute of Westminster, 1931[8] was enacted by the imperial Parliament in pursuance of that recommendation: the Statute recited the convention in its preamble, and it provided, by s. 4, that hereafter no statute of the United Kingdom would extend to a dominion "unless it is expressly declared in that Act that the dominion has requested, and consented to, the enactment thereof. Notice how s. 4 of the Statute and the convention reinforce each other. Neither Statute nor convention purports to destroy the power of the imperial Parliament to enact statutes applying to the dominions; on the contrary, each expressly recognizes and preserves that power. But the convention defines the occasions when the power is to be exercised (only when the dominion concerned has requested and consented to its exercise), and the Statute defines how the power is to be exercised (only by including in the statute an express declaration that the dominion has requested and consented to the measure).[9]

The limitation of the power of the imperial Parliament, which was the object of the convention and s. 4, was not the only reform needed to eliminate the subjection of the dominions to imperial statutes. It was also necessary to increase the powers of the dominion legislatures so that the dominions could amend or repeal the imperial statutes which did apply to them. To that end, the Statute of Westminster, by s. 2(1), repealed the Colonial Laws Validity Act in its application to the dominions, and, by s. 2(2), granted to each dominion the power to repeal or amend imperial statutes which were part of the law of the dominion. Section 2(2) also stated that no dominion statute should be void for

---

[6]See ch. 1, Sources, under heading § 1:10, "Conventions".

[7]See Latham, The Law and the Commonwealth (1949); Marshall, Parliamentary Sovereignty and the Commonwealth (1957), ch. 6; Wheare, The Statute of Westminster and Dominion Status (5th ed., 1953); Wheare, The Constitutional Structure of the Commonwealth (1960).

[8]R.S.C. 1985, Appendix II, No. 27.

[9]The efficacy of these attempts to limit imperial legislative power has been much debated in the books cited in 3:3 note 7, above, and in the periodical literature. Fortunately, as the Privy Council once observed, disregard by the imperial Parliament of either the convention or s. 4 "is theory and has no relation to realities": *British Coal Corp. v. The King*, [1935] A.C. 500, 520.

repugnancy to any existing or future imperial statute. Section 7(2) made clear that s. 2 applied to Canada's provincial Legislatures as well as to Canada's federal Parliament, but that each Legislature and the Parliament could only enact laws within their own competence under the B.N.A. Act. The power of amendment or repeal extended to future as well as existing imperial statutes.[10]

Section 7(1) of the Statute of Westminster provided that "nothing in this Act shall be deemed to apply to the repeal, amendment, or alteration of the British North America Acts, 1867 to 1930, or to any order, rule or regulation made thereunder". This provision was inserted because the Canadian delegates to the imperial conferences feared that without such a provision the Canadian Parliament and Legislatures would have gained the power to alter the B.N.A. Act by ordinary statute. In a unitary state, such as the United Kingdom, the power to alter the constitution by ordinary statute is not necessarily objectionable, but in a federal state it is essential that at least the distribution of powers between federal Parliament and provincial Legislatures be unalterable by either Parliament or a Legislature acting on its own. Before the Statute of Westminster, the supremacy of the B.N.A. Act was derived from the fact that it was an imperial statute protected from alteration by the Colonial Laws Validity Act.[11] Therefore, when it was proposed to destroy the protected status of imperial statutes generally, Canada insisted on the exemption of its constituent statute.[12] That was the reason for s. 7 of the Statute of Westminster.[13]

---

[10]Section 129 of the B.N.A. Act, which continues in force the pre-confederation laws in the confederating provinces, and gives power to the competent Canadian legislative body to repeal or amend those laws, expressly excludes from the power of repeal or amendment those laws contained in imperial statutes. (One problem with this provision was referred to in § 3:3 note 4.) In A Consolidation of the Constitution Acts, 1867–1982 (2001), the Department of Justice correctly asserts in a footnote to s. 129 that the restriction on repealing or amending pre-confederation imperial statutes "was removed by the Statute of Westminster".

[11]N. Siebrasse, "The Doctrinal Origin of Judicial Review and the Colonial Laws Validity Act" (1993) 1 Review of Const. Studies 75, says that this statement is wrong, because judges based judicial review more often on a doctrine of excess of power than on repugnancy, although he acknowledges (at p. 92) that the distinction between the two rationales of judicial review may be "so fine as to be invisible". On the competing rationales of judicial review, see ch. 5, Federalism, under heading § 5:20, "Development of judicial review".

[12]See also ss. 8 and 9 exempting the constituent statutes of Australia and New Zealand. Australia, as a federal state, had the same problem as Canada. Although Australia had a domestic amending formula from the beginning (Constitution of Australia, s. 128), it did not want the amending formula to be bypassed by the Commonwealth Parliament acting unilaterally under the Statute of Westminster. New Zealand, as a unitary state, did not need the exemption, and the Parliament of New Zealand (which already had the power to amend much of its constituent statute in 1931) acquired the power "to alter, suspend or repeal" its constituent statute in 1947: New Zealand Constitution (Amendment) Act, 1947 (U.K.), 11 Geo. VI, c. 4.

[13]Wheare, Constitutional Structure of the Commonwealth (1960), 61. The question whether s. 7(1) was necessary in any event is considered in ch. 5, Federalism, under

IV. CANADA ACT, 1982

§ 3:4 Canada Act 1982

The final stage in the history of imperial statutes in Canada came with the passage of one last imperial statute, the Canada Act 1982 (which included, as Schedule B, the Constitution Act, 1982).

The Canada Act 1982 repealed s. 7(1) of the Statute of Westminster,[1] which was the provision that exempted the B.N.A. Act and its amendments from the liberating effect of the rest of the Statute of Westminster. However, this does not mean that the B.N.A. Act (Constitution Act, 1867) and its amendments are now vulnerable to ordinary legislative change just like other imperial statutes. The supremacy of the "Constitution of Canada", a defined phrase which includes the Constitution Act, 1867 and its amendments,[2] is maintained by s. 52(1) of the Constitution Act, 1982. Section 52(1) provides:

> The Constitution of Canada is the supreme law of Canada, and any law that is inconsistent with the provisions of the Constitution is, to the extent of the inconsistency, of no force or effect.

This provision serves exactly the same function as s. 7(1) of the Statute of Westminster formerly served. Section 7(1) preserved the doctrine of repugnancy expressed in the Colonial Laws Validity Act in its application to the B.N.A. Act and its amendments. Now s. 52(1) directly enacts a similar doctrine of repugnancy or inconsistency.[3] By virtue of s. 52(1), the Constitution of Canada is superior to all other laws in force in Canada, whatever their origin: federal statutes, provincial statutes, pre-confederation statutes, received statutes, imperial statutes and common law; all of these laws must yield to inconsistent provisions of the Constitution of Canada. Section 52(1) provides an explicit basis for judicial review of legislation in Canada, for, whenever a court finds that a law is inconsistent with the Constitution of Canada, the court must hold that law to be invalid ("of no force or effect").

With respect to future imperial statutes, it will be recalled that s. 4 of the Statute of Westminster had expressly preserved the authority over the dominions of the United Kingdom Parliament. The Canada Act 1982 repealed s. 4 of the Statute of Westminster[4] and, by s. 2, formally terminated the authority over Canada of the United Kingdom

---

heading § 5:20, "Development of judicial review".

[Section 3:4]

[1]Constitution Act, 1982, s. 53(1) and schedule, item 17.

[2]See ch. 1, Sources, under heading § 1:4, "Constitution of Canada".

[3]*Re Manitoba Language Rights*, [1985] 1 S.C.R. 721, 746 (recognizing that s. 52(1) has replaced the Colonial Laws Validity Act as the foundation of judicial review). The validity of s. 52(1) itself is analyzed in my article, "Supremacy of the Charter" (1983), 61 Can. Bar Rev. 69.

[4]Constitution Act, 1982, s. 53(1) and schedule, item 17.

Parliament.[5] The efficacy of this abdication of authority by the United Kingdom Parliament is discussed later in this chapter.[6] For the moment, it is sufficient to explain why such a provision could not have been enacted in the Statute of Westminster in 1931, but could be enacted in 1982.

There were two reasons why the Statute of Westminster did not terminate the authority of the United Kingdom Parliament over the dominions. The first reason was a theoretical one. In 1931, it was widely believed by constitutional lawyers that an attempt by the United Kingdom Parliament to terminate its authority over the dominions would be legally ineffective, on the basis that a sovereign Parliament could not abdicate any part of its sovereignty. Now, the more widely held belief is that an abdication of power over a former dominion or colony would be legally effective.[7]

In the case of Canada, there was in 1931 a second, more practical reason for the preservation of the legislative authority over the dominions of the United Kingdom Parliament, and that was the fact that the B.N.A. Act lacked any general procedure for its amendment within Canada. So long as that disability existed, the power over Canada of the United Kingdom Parliament had to be preserved, for that Parliament was the only body with legal authority to amend the B.N.A. Act. That disability was eliminated in 1982 by Part V of the Constitution Act, 1982, which provides procedures for the amendment of all parts of the Constitution of Canada without recourse to the United Kingdom. The adoption of these Canadian amending procedures rendered the continuing power of the United Kingdom Parliament unnecessary.[8]

Thus, in 1982, there was no longer any theoretical or practical justification for the continuing authority over Canada of the United Kingdom (imperial) Parliament. Indeed, the existence of the power was an affront to Canadian nationalism, and its abolition could be regarded as a "patriation" of the Canadian Constitution. It is to that idea that the final section of this chapter is addressed.

V. PATRIATION OF THE CONSTITUTION

§ 3:5 Definition of patriation

The "patriation" of the Constitution means bringing it home to Canada.[1] The term "patriation" is a uniquely Canadian coinage, derived from the verb "repatriate" meaning "to restore to one's own country". As

[5]Australia and New Zealand subsequently adopted a similar provision: Australia Act 1986 (U.K.), 1986, c. 2, s. 1; Constitution Act 1986 (N.Z.), s. 15(2).

[6]§ 3:8, "Termination of imperial authority".

[7]§ 3:8, "Termination of imperial authority".

[8]Amendment of the Constitution of Canada is the topic of ch. 4.

[Section 3:5]

[1]This section of the book is adapted from my article, "Patriation of the Canadian Constitution" (1983), 8 Queen's L.J. 123. On the history of patriation, see G. Rémillard,

the B.N.A. Act has never been a Canadian Act, it cannot be *restored* to Canada; patriation conveys the idea of our Constitution *becoming* a Canadian instrument. There is no one accepted definition of what patriation involves. Several possible meanings are analyzed in the text that follows.

Patriation has not usually been regarded as entailing the abolition of the monarchy. Canada's link with the United Kingdom through recognition of the same Queen has of course been preserved. For practical purposes, however, the Queen's role for Canada is primarily as a ceremonial head of the Commonwealth, the Commonwealth being an informal association of countries that were formerly members of the old British Empire.[2]

§ 3:6 Canada Act 1982

The Canada Act 1982 and its Schedule B, the Constitution Act, 1982, were enacted by the United Kingdom Parliament on March 29, 1982, when they received the royal assent. The Canada Act 1982 came into force as Canadian law immediately. The Constitution Act, 1982, by virtue of s. 58, did not come into force until "a day to be fixed by proclamation". That proclamation was issued by the Queen, who came to Canada for that purpose, at a ceremony in Ottawa on April 17, 1982; and the proclamation fixed April 17, 1982 as the day upon which the Constitution Act, 1982 was to come into force. Did these events accomplish the "patriation" of Canada's Constitution?

At first blush, it does not seem plausible to regard the enactment of the Canada Act 1982 and the Constitution Act, 1982 as a patriation of the Canadian Constitution. Their enactment added two more imperial statutes to the series that existed before.[1] Since 1982, more, not less, of Canada's Constitution is to be found in the statute book of the United Kingdom.

Nor have any formal steps been taken to give the Canada Act 1982 or the Constitution Act, 1982, or any of the other constitutional instruments enacted in the United Kingdom, some form of Canadian imprimatur. It is true that the two 1982 statutes were requested by a joint resolution of the two Houses of the Canadian Parliament;[2] but that has been true of every statute enacted for Canada by the United

---

"Historique du rapatriement" (1984) 25 Cahiers de Droit (Laval) 15; G. Rémillard, Le Fédéralisme Canadien, vol. 2 (1985); B.L. Strayer, Canada's Constitutional Revolution (2013), chs. 1–9. For analysis, see P. Oliver, "The 1982 Patriation of the Canadian Constitution: Reflections on Continuity and Change" (1994) 28 Revue Juridique Themis 875; P. Oliver, "Canada, Quebec and Constitutional Amendment" (1999) 49 U. Toronto L.J. 519, 552–575; Oliver, The Constitution of Independence (2005), chs. 11–14.

[2]On the abolition of the monarchy, see ch. 9, Responsible Government, under heading § 9:24, "The monarchy".

[Section 3:6]

[1]The schedule to the Constitution Act, 1982 lists 22 United Kingdom statutes and orders in council as included in the "Constitution of Canada".

[2]The resolution was passed by the House of Commons on December 2, 1981 and by

Kingdom Parliament since 1895,[3] and so it cannot be regarded as a new development, let alone as a patriation. It is also true that the terms of the joint resolution were agreed to by nine of the ten provincial Premiers at a meeting in Ottawa on November 5, 1981; but five previous statutes enacted for Canada by the United Kingdom Parliament were preceded by the unanimous agreement of the provincial Premiers, and so there is nothing of special note in that fact.[4] The enactment of the 1982 statutes has not been followed by ratification, either by Canadian legislative bodies or by popular referendum.

If the Constitution has been patriated—brought home to Canada—that event has obviously not occurred in the physical world. It must have occurred in a metaphysical world stocked with the ideas of constitutional lawyers. It is to that world that we must now turn our attention.

§ 3:7 Autochthony

One possible meaning of patriation could be the securing of constitutional autochthony. Autochthony[1] requires that a constitution be indigenous, deriving its authority solely from events within Canada. The Constitution of the United States is, of course, autochthonous, because its only claim to authority springs from within the United States: the American revolution had broken the chain of legal authority which in the colonial period had linked the American assemblies to the imperial Parliament. But in Canada no such revolution (or break in legal continuity) occurred—and certainly not in 1982. The legal force of the Canada Act 1982 and the Constitution Act, 1982, like other United Kingdom statutes extending to Canada, depends upon the power over Canada of the United Kingdom Parliament. These instruments have an external rather than a local root.[2]

If patriation means the securing of constitutional autochthony, I conclude that it has not been achieved.

---

the Senate on December 8, 1981.

[3]See ch. 4, Amendment, under heading §§ 4:1 to 4:3, "History of amendment".

[4]See ch. 4, Amendment, under heading §§ 4:1 to 4:3, "History of amendment".

[Section 3:7]

[1]I am using the term in the sense employed by Wheare, Constitutional Structure of the Commonwealth (1960), ch. 4. The term is neither very clear nor very useful, as Marshall, Constitutional Theory (1971), 57–64, demonstrates. Indeed, the requirement of a break in legal continuity, which is assumed in my text, may be disputed. It may be said that every independent country has a local "root" to its legal system, since it is the fundamental rules of validity and change laid down by the local courts which at bottom determine which laws are to be accepted as valid: see B. Slattery, "The Independence of Canada" (1983), 5 Supreme Court L.R. 369.

[2]The Committee on the Constitution of the Canadian Bar Association, *Towards a New Canada* (1978), 6 recommended that patriation be accomplished by action taken within Canada which constituted "a break with the established legal order". Other proposals for patriation have never gone that far.

§ 3:8 Termination of imperial authority

A second possible meaning of patriation could be the termination of the authority over Canada of the United Kingdom Parliament. Geoffrey Marshall has pointed out that the concern with autochthony (in the sense just described) involves a confusion between the continuity of new institutions with the old system, on the one hand, and the *subordination* of the new institutions to the old, on the other.[1] A break in continuity does not necessarily mean that British legislative authority no longer extends to the new institutions, and, if it still does so extend, then nothing important has been accomplished by the achievement of a "local root" to the new constitution. Marshall puts it this way:[2]

> The fundamental question raised by an assertion of "autochthony" is whether a legally effective abdication of British legislative authority has been made by the United Kingdom. If it has, further local operations, proclamations, and breaches of continuity are superfluous. If it has not, they are ineffective.

On this view, which seems sound, the question we should be asking is whether a legally effective termination[3] of British legislative authority has occurred.

The Canada Act 1982 contains an express abdication of British legislative authority over Canada. Section 2 provides as follows:

> No Act of the Parliament of the United Kingdom passed after the Constitution Act, 1982 comes into force shall extend to Canada as part of its law.

Has this provision accomplished the patriation of the Canadian constitution? On the argument accepted so far, the answer must be yes—if s. 2 is legally effective.

Under the traditional view of parliamentary sovereignty, s. 2 cannot be legally effective. The traditional view holds that a sovereign parliament cannot limit its own sovereignty.[4] In other words, s. 2 cannot be legally effective, because the United Kingdom Parliament could at any

---

[Section 3:8]

[1] Marshall, Constitutional Theory (1971), 63.

[2] Marshall, Constitutional Theory (1971), 61. He is using the word "autochthony" in this passage in a broader sense than I have been using it in the text. He is really using it as equivalent to patriation.

[3] Marshall uses the word "abdication", which is too narrow and perhaps even begs the question under consideration, since it implies the necessity of a voluntary surrender of authority by the United Kingdom Parliament. No such voluntary surrender occurred in respect of the thirteen American colonies, and yet after the revolutionary war the authority of the United Kingdom Parliament over the former colonies had obviously terminated. Even in the case of Canada (and other Commonwealth countries) it is arguable that the termination of British authority depends more on their accession to independence than on an "abdication" by the United Kingdom Parliament. This point is developed later in this section of the text.

[4] de Smith and Brazier, Constitutional and Administrative Law (8th ed., 1998), ch. 4.

time in the future repeal s. 2 and reassert its authority over Canada. This traditional view was generally accepted by constitutional lawyers before the second world war, and their refusal to acknowledge the efficacy of an abdication of power is one reason why the Statute of Westminster, 1931 contained no such provision.[5] But the better view, which is now more widely accepted, is that, whatever view British courts would take,[6] the courts of the former colony would not accept a reversal of independence: "Freedom, once conferred, cannot be revoked".[7] If the United Kingdom Parliament did purport to repeal s. 2 of the Canada Act 1982, and enact a law purporting to extend to Canada, it is inconceivable that the Supreme Court of Canada would accept the resuscitated power and uphold the new law. Without doubt, the Canadian court would hold that the unwanted law had the same status in Canada as a law enacted for Canada by Portugal, and that is, no status at all: the law would be a nullity in Canada.[8]

If I am right that a law enacted for Canada after 1982 by the United Kingdom Parliament would be treated by Canadian courts as a nullity, does this establish that s. 2 of the Canada Act 1982 is a legally effective provision? The answer to this question is not necessarily yes. It can be plausibly argued that it is not s. 2 but the fact of Canadian independence which has terminated the United Kingdom's authority to enact laws for Canada. This is the view taken by S.A. de Smith in analyzing the situation of Mauritius, whose independence statute contained a provision similar to s. 2 of the Canada Act 1982. de Smith says that "the achievement of independence should in itself be understood as having liberated the legal order of Mauritius from its hierarchical subordination to that of the United Kingdom, so that the omnicompetence of the United Kingdom Parliament ceased to prevail in the local legal system".[9] If this view is correct, then the United Kingdom Parliament had lost much of its authority over Canada before 1982: what it retained was only what was necessary to fill the gaps in Canadian domestic legislative power.[10] Now that the new amending procedures contained in Part V of the Constitution Act, 1982 leave no gaps in Canadian domestic

[5]Wheare, Constitutional Structure of the Commonwealth (1960), 25.

[6]A court in the United Kingdom would decline to hold invalid any statute duly enacted (in the correct "manner and form") by the United Kingdom Parliament: *Manuel v. A.-G.*, [1982] 3 W.L.R. 821 (Eng. C.A.) (upholding validity of Canada Act 1982). But the question at issue is not the attitude of the courts in the United Kingdom, for they have no power to enforce their rulings in an independent country, but the attitude of the courts in the country to which the law purports to extend.

[7]*Ndlwana v. Hofmeyr*, [1937] A.D. 229, 237; and see de Smith and Brazier, Constitutional and Administrative Law (8th ed., 1998), 80–81.

[8]This would also have been the result before 1982 in respect of United Kingdom statutes enacted for Canada without any request or consent by Canada. Any other result would involve a denial of Canada's status as an independent country. See P.W. Hogg, Comment (1982) 60 Can. Bar Rev. 307, 330.

[9]de Smith and Brazier, Constitutional and Administrative Law (8th ed., 1998), 81.

[10]It must be noted that this view is not easy to reconcile with obiter dicta in *Re Resolution to Amend the Constitution of Canada*, [1981] 1 S.C.R. 753, 790, 794, 797, 799,

legislative power, the authority over Canada of the United Kingdom Parliament has shrunk to nothing.

On this analysis, s. 2 of the Canada Act 1982 is not the reason for the termination of the authority over Canada of the United Kingdom Parliament. Canadian courts would now deny the existence of that authority, whether or not s. 2 of the Canada Act 1982 existed. That is the view of Brian Slattery, who says:[11]

> What residual power Westminster retained after independence stemmed from the absence of any corresponding local power. There is no longer any sphere in which Canada cannot act, and so Westminster's role automatically expires. What can be done in Canada cannot be done elsewhere if Canada is fully sovereign.

The inevitable conclusion from this line of reasoning is that s. 2 of the Canada Act 1982 is redundant.[12] It is not the reason for the termination of the authority over Canada of the United Kingdom Parliament, and therefore s. 2 does not accomplish the patriation of the Canadian Constitution.

§ 3:9 Autonomy

W.R. Lederman has suggested a third definition of patriation. He argued in 1967 that bringing the Constitution home meant "to make into law a set of amending procedures that can be carried out in Canada entirely by Canadian governments, legislative bodies, or electorates, act-

801, which suggested that there had been no diminution of the legal authority over Canada of the United Kingdom Parliament since colonial times. It is because of these dicta that this part of my text is expressed tentatively.

[11] B. Slattery "The Independence of Canada" (1983), 5 Supreme Court L.R. 369, 403.

[12] B. Slattery "The Independence of Canada" (1983), 5 Supreme Court L.R. 369, 403. Contra, Marshall, Constitutional Conventions (1984), 207–209; P. Oliver, "Canada, Quebec, and Constitutional Amendment" (1999) 49 U. Toronto L.J. 519, 565–570; Oliver, The Constitution of Independence (2005), 348. Marshall and Oliver both argue from the position that the authority over Canada of the U.K. Parliament had not been diminished before 1982 (as the dicta in *Re Resolution to Amend the Constitution*, [1981] 1 S.C.R. 753 assert). They then argue that the traditional view of the "continuing" sovereignty of the Parliament at Westminster should be modified to a "self-embracing" sovereignty, which accepts that the sovereign can limit its own sovereignty. On this basis, s. 2 can be seen as valid and effective, and the constitutional independence of Canada (like that of Australia and New Zealand) depends solely on the actions of the Parliament at Westminster. Needless to say, this is a coherent explanation of Canada's constitutional independence. The reason why I adhere to the alternative "independence" explanation in the text is because I cannot accept that, if in 1981 (before 1982) the Parliament at Westminster had enacted a law for Canada without any request or consent from Canada, the Supreme Court of Canada would have held the law to be valid and applicable in Canada. I know that holding is implied by the dicta in *Re Resolution to Amend the Constitution*, [1981] 1 S.C.R. 753. I just do not believe that, if the hypothetical situation had actually arisen, the Court would have upheld the "imperial" law as a valid law of Canada. Marshall, Oliver and I end up in the same place with respect to post-1982 laws of the Parliament at Westminster. They cannot apply to Canada.

ing severally or in combinations of some kind".[1] There is no doubt that the Constitution Act, 1982 has satisfied that definition of patriation. Section 52(2) defines the "Constitution of Canada", and s. 52(3) provides that amendments to the Constitution of Canada "shall be made only in accordance with the authority contained in the Constitution of Canada". The phrase "the authority contained in the Constitution of Canada" is a reference to the amending procedures established by Part V of the Constitution Act, 1982. These procedures fulfil Lederman's definition because they can be carried out entirely in Canada.[2]

Lederman's definition of patriation has been described as "autonomy", a condition that is achieved when "all processes for operating constitutional change are locally operated".[3] But if the United Kingdom Parliament retains some authority over Canada, then Canada is still subject to the thrall, however theoretical, of the old imperial power. The achievement of an "autonomy" which could be overridden at any time by the United Kingdom hardly seems worth describing as a patriation. Once again we are driven back to Marshall's test: has there been a legally effective termination of British legislative power over Canada?

The principal consequence of Canada's achievement of autonomy, that is, the adoption of domestic amending procedures, is that Canada will never again request the United Kingdom to pass a law amending the Canadian Constitution (or making any other change in the law of Canada). In practice, this means of course that the United Kingdom Parliament will never again pass a law purporting to extend to Canada. But does the United Kingdom Parliament retain the legal power to enact a law extending to Canada? I think not. The achievement of autonomy, by eliminating the necessity for any continuing role for the United Kingdom Parliament in Canada's law-making process, has made Canada's legal system technically self-sufficient—perfectly independent of the United Kingdom.[4] If the United Kingdom Parliament were to do the unthinkable after 1982 and pass a law purporting to extend to Can-

[Section 3:9]

[1]W.R. Lederman, "The Process of Constitutional Amendment for Canada" (1967), 12 McGill L.J. 371, 377; reprinted in Lederman, Continuing Canadian Constitutional Dilemmas (1981), 85.

[2]It is important to notice that the definition of the Constitution of Canada, which includes the list of instruments in the schedule to the Constitution Act, 1982, includes all of the British North America Acts (renamed Constitution Acts). By virtue of s. 7(1) of the Statute of Westminster, "the British North America Acts, 1867 to 1930" were before 1982 protected from amendment by legislative bodies in Canada. Since 1982 the position is that every law in force in Canada, whatever its source and whatever its name, can be amended by one of the three following Canadian procedures: (1) the Canadian Parliament, or (2) a provincial Legislature, or (3) one of the procedures stipulated by Part V of the Constitution Act, 1982.

[3]Marshall, Constitutional Theory (1977), 58; see also Wheare, Constitutional Structure of the Commonwealth (1960), 58.

[4]In a non-technical sense, Canada has been independent of the United Kingdom at least since 1931, because the conventions agreed to at the imperial conferences of 1926 and 1930 ensured that the residual powers over Canada of the United Kingdom Parlia-

ada, and if such a law were challenged in the courts in Canada (as it obviously would be), the courts in Canada would ask whether such a law was authorized by the rules of the Canadian legal system. The only conceivable answer to that question would be no: Canada's legal system does not recognize the right of the United Kingdom (or Portugal or any other foreign country) to enact laws binding in Canada. Thus the achievement of autonomy has terminated the authority over Canada of the United Kingdom Parliament.[5] In that important sense, the patriation of the Canadian Constitution has been achieved.

---

ment and Government would be exercised only in accordance with the wishes of Canada.

[5]See § 3:8 note 11, and accompanying text, above.

Chapter 4

Amendment

I. HISTORY OF AMENDMENT

§ 4:1 Imperial amendment
§ 4:2 The search for a domestic amending procedure
§ 4:3 The failure to accommodate Quebec

II. PART V OF THE CONSTITUTION ACT, 1982

§ 4:4 Summary of Part V
§ 4:5 Comparison with Australia and United States
§ 4:6 Constitution of Canada
§ 4:7 Charter of Rights

III. GENERAL AMENDING PROCEDURE (S. 38)

§ 4:8 Section 38(1)
§ 4:9 Proclamation
§ 4:10 Initiation
§ 4:11 Opting out
§ 4:12 Compensation for opting out
§ 4:13 Revocation of assent or dissent
§ 4:14 Section 42
§ 4:15 "Regional veto" statute

IV. UNANIMITY PROCEDURE

§ 4:16 Unanimity procedure (s. 41)

V. SOME-BUT-NOT-ALL-PROVINCES PROCEDURE

§ 4:17 Some-but-not-all-provinces procedure (s. 43)

VI. FEDERAL PARLIAMENT ALONE

§ 4:18 Federal Parliament alone (s. 44)

VII. PROVINCIAL LEGISLATURE ALONE

§ 4:19 Provincial Legislature alone (s. 45)

VIII. FUTURE AMENDMENTS

§ 4:20 Forces of change
§ 4:21 Division of powers

§ 4:22 Central institutions
§ 4:23 Criticism of amending procedures

I. HISTORY OF AMENDMENT

§ 4:1 Imperial amendment

The British North America Act, 1867 (now the Constitution Act, 1867) differed from the constitutions of the United States and Australia (and other federal countries) in that it contained no general provision for its own amendment.[1] The reason for this omission[2] was that the framers were content for amendments to be made in the same way as the B.N.A. Act itself—by the imperial Parliament.[3] Until 1982, that was Canada's amending procedure: amendments to the B.N.A. Act had to be enacted by the United Kingdom (imperial) Parliament. In 1931, when the Statute of Westminster conferred upon Canada (and the other dominions) the power to repeal or amend imperial statutes applying to Canada, the B.N.A. Act and its amendments were excluded from the new power at Canada's insistence. This was done so that the B.N.A. Act could not be amended by an ordinary statute of either the federal Parliament or a provincial Legislature.[4] The idea was, and still is, that a constitution should be more difficult to amend than an Income Tax Act.

After the Statute of Westminster, while other imperial statutes had lost their protected status, the B.N.A. Act could still be amended only by the United Kingdom Parliament. This did not mean, however, that the amending process was outside the control of Canadians. At the imperial conference of 1930 (the same conference that recommended the enactment of the Statute of Westminster), it was agreed by the Prime Ministers of the United Kingdom and all the dominions that the United Kingdom Parliament would not enact any statute applying to a dominion except at the request and with the consent of that dominion.[5] This agreement, which reflected already longstanding practice, created a constitu-

---

[Section 4:1]

[1]For accounts of Canada's amending process before 1982, see Gérin-Lajoie, Constitutional Amendment in Canada (1950); Livingston, Federalism and Constitutional Change (1956), ch. 2; Favreau, The Amendment of the Constitution of Canada (1965); Lalonde and Basford, The Canadian Constitution and Constitutional Amendment (1978); Lederman, Continuing Canadian Constitutional Dilemmas (1981), chs. 5, 6; Monahan, Constitutional Law (2nd ed., 2002), ch. 5.

[2]There were some limited domestic powers of amendment, of which the most important were contained in s. 91(1) (power in the federal Parliament to amend a narrowly-defined "Constitution of Canada") and s. 92(1) (power in each provincial Legislature to amend the "constitution of the province"). These provisions were both repealed by the Constitution Act, 1982. They have their counterparts within Part V of the Constitution Act, 1982, namely, ss. 44 and 45, discussed later in this chapter.

[3]See ch. 1, Sources, under heading § 1:2, "Constitution Act, 1867".

[4]See ch. 3, Independence, under heading § 3:3, "Statute of Westminster, 1931".

[5]See ch. 3, Independence, under heading § 3:3, "Statute of Westminster, 1931".

tional convention.[6] The convention meant that the United Kingdom Parliament would not enact an amendment to the B.N.A. Act (or any other law applying to Canada) except at the request and with the consent of Canada.

The convention did not stipulate which governmental bodies in Canada should make the request for, and give the consent to, proposed amendments to the B.N.A. Act. However, long before 1930, the practice had developed of requesting amendments by a "joint address" of the Canadian House of Commons and the Canadian Senate. The joint address consisted of a resolution which requested the United Kingdom government to lay before the United Kingdom Parliament a bill to accomplish the desired amendment; the text of the bill was always included in the resolution. After the resolution was passed by the two Houses of Parliament, it was sent to the United Kingdom government for introduction in the United Kingdom Parliament, and enactment. This procedure became established in 1895 and was employed for every amendment to the B.N.A. Act which was enacted by the United Kingdom Parliament after that date.

What was the role of the provinces in the amending process which has just been described? Before the decision of the Supreme Court of Canada in the *Patriation Reference* (1981),[7] the position was unclear. There had been no consistent practice by the federal government of obtaining the consent of the provinces before requesting an amendment, although unanimous provincial consent had been obtained for all amendments directly affecting provincial powers.[8] When Prime Minister Trudeau proposed the amendments which ultimately (and after substantial change) became the Canada Act 1982 and the Constitution Act, 1982, he asserted that, if provincial consent could not be obtained, the federal government would proceed unilaterally to request the enactment of the amendments by the United Kingdom Parliament. The proposed amendments, including as they did a Charter of Rights and an amending formula, had a substantial direct effect on the powers of the provinces. Three provinces directed references to their Courts of Appeal, asking (1) whether there was a requirement of law that provincial consents be obtained, and (2) whether there was a requirement of convention that provincial consents be obtained. On appeal from a variety of answers in

---

[6]See ch. 1, Sources, under heading § 1:10, "Conventions".

[7]*Re Resolution to Amend the Constitution*, [1981] 1 S.C.R. 753.

[8]Favreau, The Amendment of the Constitution of Canada (1965), lists 22 amendments, and this list was reproduced by the Supreme Court of Canada in *Re Upper House*, [1980] 1 S.C.R. 54, 60 and no less than three times in *Re Resolution to Amend the Constitution*, [1981] 1 S.C.R. 753, 826, 859, 888. Of the 22 amendments, only five—in 1931, 1940, 1951, 1960 and 1964—were preceded by the unanimous consent of the provinces. However, these five included the three amendments—in 1940, 1951 and 1964—which had altered the distribution of legislative powers between the two levels of government; and they also included the Statute of Westminster, 1931, which was not literally an amendment to the B.N.A. Act, but which added to the powers of both levels of government. Of the other 17 amendments, none was preceded by unanimous provincial consent, and most were not preceded by provincial consultation.

the three Courts of Appeal, the Supreme Court of Canada in the *Patriation Reference* (1981)[9] held that the consent of the provinces to the proposed amendments was not required "as a matter of law", but that a "substantial degree" of provincial consent was required "as a matter of convention".[10] After this decision, agreement was reached on November 5, 1981 between the Prime Minister and nine of the ten provincial Premiers[11] on an altered version of the amendments.[12] This agreed-upon version was passed as a joint address by both Houses of the federal Parliament,[13] was sent to London, and was enacted by the United Kingdom Parliament as the Canada Act 1982,[14] which included, as Schedule B, the Constitution Act, 1982.[15]

The Constitution Act, 1982, by Part V, introduces into the Canadian Constitution a set of amending procedures which enable the B.N.A. Act (now renamed the Constitution Act, 1867) and its amendments to be amended within Canada without recourse to the United Kingdom Parliament. The role of the United Kingdom Parliament in Canada's amendment process is thus eliminated, and the Canada Act 1982 formally terminates the authority of the United Kingdom Parliament over Canada.[16] The roles of the federal and provincial governments in the amendment process are now defined in precise statutory language.

---

[9]*Re Resolution to Amend the Constitution*, [1981] 1 S.C.R. 753. I have discussed this decision more fully in a comment in (1982) 60 Can. Bar Rev. 307.

[10]As to the meaning of a "convention", see ch. 1, Sources, under heading § 1:10, "Conventions".

[11]The Premier of Quebec was the sole dissenter. This raised the question whether the conventional rule of a "substantial degree" of provincial consent had to include Quebec. On a reference of the question by Quebec, the Quebec Court of Appeal and, on appeal, the Supreme Court of Canada, in the *Que. Veto Reference*, answered no: *Re Objection by Que. to Resolution to Amend the Constitution*, [1982] 2 S.C.R. 793.

[12]The history of the 1982 amendments is analyzed by (among many others) McWhinney, Canada and the Constitution 1979-1982 (1982); Banting and Simeon (eds.), And No One Cheered (1983); Romanow, Whyte, Leeson, Canada . . . Notwithstanding (1984); Weiler and Elliot (eds.), Litigating the Values of a Nation (1986), Part I; Pelletier, La modification constitutionnelle au Canada (1996). The documentary sources are collected in Bayefsky, Canada's Constitution Act, 1982 and Amendments: A Documentary History (1989), 2 vols.

[13]The resolution was passed by the House of Commons on December 2, 1981 and by the Senate on December 8, 1981.

[14]Canada Act 1982 (U.K.), 1982, c. 11. The foregoing is the correct citation: see Banks, Comment (1983) 61 Can. Bar Rev. 499.

[15]The reason for two Acts seems to have been to separate the provisions relating to the United Kingdom Parliament (in the Canada Act 1982) from the provisions relating to Canadian institutions (in the Constitution Act, 1982). The Canada Act 1982 came into force on March 29, 1982, when it received the royal assent. The Constitution Act, 1982, being a schedule to the Canada Act 1982, also became law at the same time; but under s. 58 its coming into force was postponed until "a day to be fixed by proclamation". The proclamation fixed April 17, 1982 as the in-force date: The Canada Gazette, Part III, p. 33 (21 September, 1982).

[16]See ch. 3, Independence, under heading § 3:5, "Patriation of the Constitution".

The vague and unsatisfactory rules[17] laid down by the Supreme Court of Canada in the *Patriation Reference* have accordingly been supplanted and have no current relevance. The new procedures in Part V of the Constitution Act, 1982 constitute a complete code of legal (as opposed to conventional) rules which enable all parts of the "Constitution of Canada" to be amended. Those rules are described later in this chapter.

§ 4:2 The search for a domestic amending procedure

The Constitution Act, 1982 was the culmination of a search for a domestic amending procedure which started in 1927.[1] The federal Minister of Justice had placed the issue on the agenda of the dominion-provincial conference of 1927. He was influenced by the Balfour declaration of 1926, in which Canada had been recognized as the equal of the United Kingdom.[2] Equality plainly called for the elimination of the role of the United Kingdom Parliament in Canada's amendment process. But that could not be accomplished until a new domestic amending procedure had been enacted into Canada's Constitution. Until November 5, 1981, agreement on a domestic procedure had eluded Canada's political leaders. And even the 1981 agreement, as related above, did not include Quebec.

Agreement had nearly been reached on two earlier occasions. In 1964, the Fulton-Favreau formula was agreed to by all provinces except Quebec. It was almost an agreement not to agree, because it required the unanimous consent of the federal Parliament and all provincial Legislatures for most significant amendments. Even so, Quebec did not agree to it, and it was not proceeded with.[3] Then in 1970, the Victoria Charter formula was agreed to by the Prime Minister and all Premiers, but the agreement was subject to ratification by each provincial government, and Quebec decided not to ratify it.[4] For most amendments the Victoria Charter formula required the consent of the federal Parliament and a complex distribution of provinces: (1) any province that has had at any time 25 per cent of the population of Canada; (2) at least two of the Atlantic provinces; and (3) at least two of the Western provinces that have a combined population of at least 50 per cent of the population of all the Western provinces. Category (1) insured a permanent veto for

---

[17]They were vague in their stipulation of a "substantial degree" of provincial consent. They were unsatisfactory in that this requirement was one of convention only; the provinces had no legal protection from changes to the Constitution initiated unilaterally by the federal Parliament, a situation inconsistent with principles of federalism.

[Section 4:2]

[1]The history from 1964 to 1982 is related by an insider in B.L. Strayer, Canada's Constitutional Revolution (2013), chs. 2–9.

[2]See ch. 3, Independence, under heading § 3:3, "Statute of Westminster, 1931".

[3]Forsey, Freedom and Order (1974), 235–237.

[4]All of the other provinces either did ratify it or would have done so if Quebec's refusal had not made the issue moot. Quebec was the only dissenter.

Quebec (as well as Ontario). Even so, Quebec did not agree to it, and it was not proceeded with.[5]

It will be noticed that both the Fulton-Favreau formula and the Victoria Charter formula gave a veto to Quebec. Moreover, in 1964 and 1971, it was clear that all participants understood that Quebec had to be a party to whatever agreement was reached, because the sole dissent of Quebec was sufficient to abort both of these previous projects. When Prime Minister Trudeau tabled the constitutional proposals which evolved into the Constitution Act, 1982, the amending formula which he proposed was essentially the Victoria Charter formula. Eight provinces now opposed that formula,[6] and proposed an alternative "Vancouver formula". The Vancouver formula required for most amendments the agreement of the federal Parliament and two-thirds of the provincial Legislatures representing 50 per cent of the population of all the provinces. This formula did not give any province a veto; and it was formally proposed in a much-publicized eight-province accord which repeatedly affirmed the "equality" of the provinces.[7] Premier Levesque of Quebec was one of the eight signatories to that document: for the first time Quebec had formally abandoned its claim to a special status involving (at the minimum) a veto over constitutional amendments.[8]

The agreement of November 5, 1981 was achieved when the Prime Minister and his two provincial allies, the Premiers of Ontario and New Brunswick, gave up their support for the Victoria Charter formula and accepted instead a modified Vancouver formula.[9] Seven of the eight dissenting provincial Premiers, on their part, agreed to accept a modified Charter of Rights.[10] Premier Levesque did not agree with the compromise, and even found the new amending formula unacceptable, despite his earlier agreement to the very similar Vancouver formula.[11]

Once again, as in 1964 and 1971, there was an agreement on an amending formula which included all Premiers, except the Premier of Quebec. But this time the absence of Quebec from the agreement did not stop the process. The Prime Minister was determined to press on with the proposal despite the incomplete agreement, and the Supreme Court of Canada had ruled in the *Patriation Reference* that the consent of

[5]Forsey, Freedom and Order (1974), 237–238.

[6]Seven of these provinces had agreed to it as part of the Victoria Charter in 1971.

[7]Constitutional Accord, April 16, 1981. The text of the Accord appeared in all newspapers of that evening or the next morning.

[8]The veto was replaced with an opting-out provision, which was available to any province. Opting out is discussed in § 4:11, "Opting out".

[9]The only change was the elimination of a provision for payment of compensation to an opting-out province. However, after November 5, 1981, in an unsuccessful effort to secure Quebec's agreement, a right to compensation was restored for opting-out of amendments relating to "education or other cultural matters". This is now in s. 40 of the Constitution Act, 1982, and is discussed in § 4:10, "Compensation for opting out".

[10]The major change in the Charter of Rights was the introduction of the override clause, now s. 33 of the Constitution Act, 1982, discussed in ch. 39, Override of Rights.

[11]See § 4:2 note 9, above.

Quebec (or any other province) was not required by law, and was probably not required by convention either.[12] The federal-provincial agreement of November 5, 1981, supplemented by four changes agreed to later,[13] was accordingly embodied in a resolution for a joint address which passed both Houses of the federal Parliament in December 1981,[14] and was then transmitted to London. The Canada Act 1982 was enacted by the United Kingdom Parliament on March 29, 1982. When the Constitution Act, 1982 came into force on April 17, 1982,[15] Canada had at last acquired domestic amending procedures.[16] Those procedures are analyzed in a later section of this chapter.

§ 4:3 The failure to accommodate Quebec

The Constitution Act, 1982 was a major achievement, curing several longstanding defects in the Constitution of Canada. As well as the adoption of domestic amending procedures (ss. 38–49), a Charter of Rights was adopted (ss. 1–34), aboriginal rights were recognized (s. 35), equalization was guaranteed (s. 36), provincial powers over natural resources were extended (ss. 50–51), and the Constitution of Canada was defined and given supremacy over other laws (s. 52). But the Constitution Act, 1982 failed to accomplish one of the goals of constitutional

[12]Quebec had directed one of the three references to the Court on the amendment proposals, and it had not copied the questions submitted by Manitoba and Newfoundland (the other two provinces that had directed references). Instead, it drafted questions of its own, but none of its questions asked for a ruling on the question whether Quebec had a veto. The Supreme Court of Canada in the *Patriation Reference (Re Resolution to Amend the Constitution*, [1981] 1 S.C.R. 753) accordingly did not address itself to that issue, simply providing the vague ruling that a "substantial degree" of provincial consent was required by convention. After the federal-provincial agreement of November 5, 1981, Quebec directed a second reference to the Court of Appeal asking whether Quebec's consent was necessary, by convention, as a pre-condition to the passage of the proposed amendments. Both the Quebec Court of Appeal and the Supreme Court of Canada answered no: *Re Objection by Que. to Resolution to Amend the Constitution*, [1982] 2 S.C.R. 793.

[13]The four new elements were (1) an aboriginal rights clause (s. 35), (2) the removal of the sexual equality clause (s. 28) from the override power (s. 33), (3) compensation for opting out of amendments relating to education or culture (s. 40), and (4) limitation of minority language educational rights in Quebec (s. 59).

[14]It is an interesting commentary on "executive federalism" that of the nine Premiers who signed the agreement of November 5, 1981 only one bothered to submit it to the Legislature for approval. It was approved by the Alberta Legislature on November 10, 1981, and it was disapproved by the Quebec National Assembly on December 1, 1981.

[15]See § 4:1 note 15, above.

[16]For references to the literature on the history of the 1982 settlement, see McWhinney, Canada and the Constitution 1979-1982 (1982); Banting and Simeon (eds.), And No One Cheered (1983); Romanow, White, Leeson, Canada . . . Notwithstanding (1984); Weiler and Elliot (eds.), Litigating the Values of a Nation (1986), Part I; Pelletier, La modification constitutionnelle au Canada (1996); Bayefsky, Canada's Constitution Act, 1982 and Amendments: A Documentary History (1989), 2 vols.

reform, and that was the better accommodation of Quebec within the Canadian federation.[1]

The Premier of Quebec had been the sole dissenter to the federal-provincial meeting of November 5, 1981; the Quebec National Assembly had passed a resolution condemning the constitutional settlement that had been agreed upon;[2] and Quebec had even sought relief in the courts, though without success.[3] Nor were Quebec's concerns without substance. The new amending procedures denied a veto to Quebec, something that in the past had always been recognized in practice. The new Charter of Rights restricted the powers of the provincial Legislatures, and in particular limited the capacity of the Quebec National Assembly to implement French-language policy.[4] Thus, the outcome of the constitutional changes of 1982 was a diminution of Quebec's powers and a profound sense of grievance in the province.

In assessing the gravity of Quebec's alienation from the constitutional changes of 1982, it is important to cast one's mind back to Quebec's referendum on sovereignty-association, which was held by the Parti Québécois government on May 20, 1980.[5] The referendum was defeated by a popular vote of 59.5 per cent to 40.5 per cent. In the referendum campaign, the federalist forces promised that a "no" to sovereignty-association was not a vote for the status quo, and the defeat of the referendum would be followed by constitutional change to better accommodate Quebec's aspirations. The defeat of the referendum was in fact immediately followed by a series of federal-provincial conferences in the summer and early fall of 1980, but these conferences failed to yield agreement on the specifics of constitutional change. On October 6, 1980, despite the absence of a federal-provincial agreement, Prime Minister Trudeau introduced in the House of Commons a resolution calling for the set of constitutional amendments that, after substantial alteration, became the Canada Act 1982 and the Constitution Act, 1982. For the reasons explained in the previous paragraph, these 1982 changes did not fulfil the promises made during the 1980 referendum campaign in Quebec.

Quebec was of course legally bound by the Constitution Act, 1982, because the Act had been adopted into law by the correct constitutional procedures. However, the government of Quebec thereafter refused to participate in constitutional changes that involved the new amending

[Section 4:3]

[1]See P. Oliver, "Canada, Quebec, and Constitutional Amendment" (1999) 49 U. Toronto L.J. 519.

[2]See § 4:2 note 14, above.

[3]See § 4:2 note 12, above.

[4]This concern was shown to be justified by the later decisions of the Supreme Court of Canada in *A.G. Que. v. Que. Protestant School Bds.*, [1984] 2 S.C.R. 66 (striking down Quebec's restrictions on admission to English-language schools) and *Ford v. Que.*, [1988] 2 S.C.R. 712 (striking down Quebec's prohibition of English-language commercial signs).

[5]See ch. 5, Federalism, under heading §§ 5:24 to 5:26, "Secession".

procedures. And the government "opted out" of the new Charter of Rights to the maximum extent possible under s. 33 by introducing a "notwithstanding clause" into each of its existing statutes, and into every newly-enacted statute.[6] In these ways, the point was made that the Constitution Act, 1982 lacked political legitimacy in the province of Quebec.

In 1984, Prime Minister Trudeau resigned, and, after an election later in the year, the Progressive Conservative government of Prime Minister Mulroney took office. One of the new government's policies was to achieve a reconciliation with Quebec. In 1985, an election was held in Quebec, and the Parti Québécois government was defeated. The new Liberal government of Premier Bourassa moved to seek a reconciliation with the rest of Canada. The government announced five conditions that were required for Quebec's acceptance of the Constitution Act, 1982. These were: (1) the recognition of Quebec as a distinct society; (2) a greater role in immigration; (3) a provincial role in appointments to the Supreme Court of Canada; (4) limitations on the federal spending power; and (5) a veto for Quebec on constitutional amendments.

The Prime Minister and the other provincial Premiers agreed to negotiate on Quebec's five conditions. The outcome of those negotiations was the Meech Lake Constitutional Accord of 1987[7] which was an agreement entered into by all eleven first ministers on a set of amendments, essentially giving effect to Quebec's five conditions. This seemed at the time to be an immensely important development, reconciling the government of Quebec to the Constitution Act, 1982. However, in order to become law, the Accord had to be ratified by resolutions of the Senate and House of Commons and of the legislative assembly of every province.[8] It was ratified by the Senate and House of Commons[9] and by eight of the ten provinces, but it was not ratified by all ten provinces.[10] The Accord therefore lapsed.

---

[6]See ch. 39, Override of Rights, under heading § 39:2, "History of s. 33".

[7]The Meech Lake Constitutional Accord was made at Meech Lake, Quebec, on April 30, 1987. The actual constitutional text was settled at a second First Ministers' Conference in the Langevin Block, Ottawa, on June 3, 1987. The text, with explanatory commentary, is set out in Hogg, Meech Lake Constitutional Accord Annotated (1988). See also Schwartz, Fathoming Meech Lake (1987); Forest (ed.), L'adhésion du Québec à l'Accord du Lac Meech (1988); Swinton and Rogerson (eds.), Competing Constitutional Visions: The Meech Lake Accord (1988); Behiels (ed.), The Meech Lake Primer (1989); Monahan, Meech Lake: The Inside Story (1991). Many other books, articles and committee reports were also published on the Accord.

[8]The unanimity procedure of s. 41 of the Constitution Act, 1982 was applicable, because the Accord included provisions relating to the composition of the Supreme Court of Canada (s. 41(d)) and a change in the amending procedures (s. 41(e)).

[9]The Senate actually refused to ratify it, but was overridden by the House of Commons under s. 47 of the Constitution Act, 1982.

[10]The government of New Brunswick changed in 1987 before ratification, and the Liberal government of Premier McKenna refused to ratify. The same thing happened in Manitoba in 1988 and the new Progressive Conservative government of Premier Filmon refused to ratify. The government of Newfoundland changed in 1989 after ratification, and the new Liberal government of Premier Wells acted under s. 46(2) of the Constitution Act, 1982 to revoke the previous ratification. In an attempt to bring the dissenters

In 1991, the process was resumed, but with an even more ambitious goal—to cure everybody's constitutional discontents as well as Quebec's. After a prolonged period of public consultation and discussion, in 1992 the eleven first ministers reached an agreement at Charlottetown, Prince Edward Island. The Charlottetown Accord[11] included all the elements of the Meech Lake Accord, and much else besides,[12] including provision for an elected Senate and for aboriginal self-government. In a radical break with past practice, the first ministers agreed to submit the Accord to a national referendum[13] before proceeding to the legislative ratifications that were required by the Constitution's amending procedures.[14] The referendum was held on October 26, 1992, and decisively lost. The Accord was rejected by a national majority of 54.4 per cent to 44.6 per cent; the no side prevailed in six of the ten provinces, including Quebec.[15] The referendum result spelled the end of the Charlottetown Accord, which

on board, a companion accord was agreed to by the First Ministers in Ottawa on June 6, 1990, which proposed some changes to the original Accord. This was followed by New Brunswick's ratification, but the legislative assemblies of Manitoba and Newfoundland adjourned without bringing the issue to a vote by June 23, 1990. Section 39(2) of the Constitution Act, 1982 caused the process to lapse on that date, which was three years from the date of the first legislative ratification, which had been by Quebec on June 23, 1987.

[11]The Charlottetown Accord was made on August 28, 1992. It was an agreement of the eleven first ministers, the two territorial leaders and the leaders of the four national aboriginal organizations. The Accord was not in the form of a legal text, but a Draft Legal Text, prepared by officials, was issued on October 9, 1992. The text of the Accord and the Draft Legal Text is set out in the appendices to McRoberts and Monahan (eds.), *The Charlottetown Accord, the Referendum and the Future of Canada* (U. Toronto Press, 1993).

[12]The provisions designed to appeal to Quebec included not only the five elements of the Meech Lake Accord, but also a perpetual guarantee for Quebec of 25 per cent of the seats in the House of Commons, a double-majority requirement for Senate passage of bills "that materially affect French language or culture", restrictions on the federal spending power and an explicit grant to the provinces of exclusive jurisdiction over culture in the province. The rest of the Accord was designed to appeal to western Canada (the Senate), aboriginal peoples (aboriginal self-government) and many other constituencies that sought constitutional recognition (an omnibus "Canada clause" and a "social and economic charter").

[13]The referendum was a national one, held under the authority of federal law, every where except in Quebec, where the referendum was a provincial one, held under the authority of provincial law. Although, technically, there were two referendums, they were held at the same time on the same question and the results were amalgamated into national figures.

[14]The unanimity procedure of s. 41 of the Constitution Act, 1982 was applicable, for the same reasons that made s. 41 applicable to the Meech Lake Accord: The unanimity procedure of s. 41 of the Constitution Act, 1982 was applicable, because the Accord included provisions relating to the composition of the Supreme Court of Canada (s. 41(d)) and a change in the amending procedures (s. 41(e)).

[15]The question to which the voters answered no was as follows:

> Do you agree that the Constitution of Canada should be renewed on the basis of the agreement reached on August 28, 1992?

It was understood that the referendum would have to have to pass in every province because no provincial Legislature would be willing to pass a resolution ratifying a proposal that had been rejected by that province's voters.

never even started on the process of legislative ratification. The referendum result, following as it did the failure of the Meech Lake Accord, also brought to an end the search for a constitutional accommodation with Quebec. Not only had all the political actors become weary of the long constitutional process, it had become clear that it was impossible to design a package of amendments that could command popular support in all regions of the country.[16]

The failure of the Meech Lake and Charlottetown Accords to accomplish any constitutional change led to a resurgence in the popular support for the separatist movement in Quebec. In the federal election of 1993, which was won by the Liberal Party under Prime Minister Chretien, the separatist Bloc Québécois party took 52 of Quebec's 75 seats and actually became the official opposition in the federal Parliament. In Quebec's provincial election of 1994 the Liberals were defeated and the Parti Québécois, now under Premier Parizeau, once again formed the provincial government. The Parti Québécois had promised to hold a referendum on sovereignty if they were elected, and on October 30, 1995 they did so.[17] This time, the referendum did not propose merely a mandate to negotiate sovereignty-association (the 1980 question) but outright sovereignty, although the sovereignty was to be declared only after Quebec had "made a formal offer to Canada for a new economic and political partnership". Despite the stronger question, the referendum nearly passed. It was defeated by 50.6 per cent to 49.4 per cent. After the referendum vote, Premier Parizeau resigned, and was replaced by Premier Bouchard, who announced that, after the next Quebec election, if his government was re-elected, another referendum on sovereignty would be held.

The federal government of Prime Minister Chretien reacted to the shock of the close vote in the referendum and to the prospect of another referendum with two measures. One was a resolution of the House of Commons that recognized Quebec as a "distinct society" and promised to be "guided by that reality".[18] The second was the regional veto statute,[19] which was enacted by the federal Parliament, and which purported to give a veto over future constitutional changes to Quebec (as well as to

[16]Although the vote in Quebec was similar to the vote in the rest of Canada, the reasons that caused the no vote were quite different. Outside Quebec, there was a widespread sentiment that Quebec had been given too much, while inside Quebec there was a widespread sentiment that Quebec had not been given enough!

[17]See ch. 5, Federalism, under heading §§ 5:24 to 5:26, "Secession".

[18]*House of Commons Debates* (29 November 1995) at 16971 (text of resolution); (11 December 1995) at 17536 (passage of resolution). However, eleven years later, under the Conservative government of Prime Minister Harper, the House of Commons went a good step further in passing, by the remarkable vote of 265 to 16, a resolution "That this House recognize that the Québécois form a nation within a united Canada": *House of Commons Debates* (22 November 2006) at 5197 (text of resolution); (27 November 2006) at 5412 (passage of resolution).

[19]S.C. 1996, c. 1. The Act does not have an official short title; the long title is An Act respecting constitutional amendments. The Act is discussed in § 4:15, "Regional veto statute".

Ontario, British Columbia, a majority of Prairie provinces and a majority of Atlantic provinces). Neither of these measures was a constitutional amendment, and there was little general support for them. Both measures were criticized by the provincial premiers (who had not been consulted) and both were opposed by the Bloc Quebecois, with the majority of seats in Quebec, and the Reform Party, with the majority of seats in the Western provinces. As measures to accommodate Quebec, they were modest—to say the least.[20]

II. PART V OF THE CONSTITUTION ACT, 1982

§ 4:4 Summary of Part V

Part V of the Constitution Act, 1982 is headed "Procedure for Amending Constitution of Canada". It provides five different amending procedures:[1]

(1) A general amending procedure (s. 38), for amendments not otherwise provided for (as well as for amendments listed in s. 42), requiring the assents of the federal Parliament and two-thirds of the provinces representing 50 per cent of the population;

(2) A unanimity procedure (s. 41), for five defined kinds of amendments, requiring the assents of the federal Parliament and all of the provinces;

(3) A some-but-not-all-provinces procedure (s. 43), for amendment of provisions not applying to all provinces, requiring the assents of the federal Parliament and only those provinces affected;

(4) The federal Parliament alone (s. 44) has power to amend provisions relating to the federal executive and Houses of Parliament; and

---

[20]More robust initiatives to counter separatism were later taken by the federal government of Prime Minister Chrétien when it directed a reference to the Supreme Court of Canada for a ruling as to whether a unilateral secession by a province was authorized by the Constitution of Canada. The Court's negative answer came in *Re Secession of Quebec*, [1998] 2 S.C.R. 217. This decision was followed by the enactment of the Clarity Act, S.C. 2000, c. 26, requiring a clear majority on a clear question in any future referendum as a precondition to negotiations by the federal government. These initiatives are discussed in ch. 5, Federalism, under heading §§ 5:24 to 5:26, "Secession".

[Section 4:4]

[1]The amending procedures are analyzed by R.I. Cheffins, "The Constitution Act, 1982 and the Amending Formula" (1982) 4 Supreme Court L.R. 43; S.A. Scott, "Pussycat, Pussycat or Patriation and the New Constitutional Amendment Processes" (1982) 20 U. West. Ont. L. Rev. 247; S.A. Scott, "The Canadian Constitutional Amendment Process" (1982) 45 Law & Contemp. Problems 249; J.P. Meekison, "The Amending Formula" (1983) 8 Queen's L.J. 99; W.R. Lederman, "Canadian Constitutional Amending Procedures, 1867–1982" (1984) 32 Am. Jo. Comp. Law 339; Beaudoin, La Constitution du Canada (1990), ch. 6; Pelletier, La modification constitutionnelle au Canada (1996); Hurley, Amending Canada's Constitution: History, Processes, Problems and Prospects (1996); Monahan, Constitutional Law (2nd ed., 2002), ch. 6; W.J. Newman, "Living with the Amending Procedures: Prospects for Future Constitutional Reform in Canada" (2007) 37 Supreme Court L.R. (2d) 383.

(5) Each provincial Legislature alone (s. 45) has power to amend "the constitution of the province".

Each of these procedures will be considered in turn in later sections of this chapter.

§ 4:5 Comparison with Australia and United States

Before turning to the detail and complexity of Canada's new amending procedures, it is interesting to contrast the simpler amending procedures of Australia and the United States. In the case of Australia, s. 128 of the Constitution requires approval by a simple majority in both Houses of the federal Parliament, followed by a popular referendum in which the amendment is approved by a "double majority" of votes: (1) a national majority, and (2) a state majority in a majority of states (that is, four of the six states).[1] In the case of the United States, Article V of the Constitution requires approval by a two-thirds majority in both Houses of the federal Congress followed by ratification by the Legislatures of three-quarters of the states (or, alternatively, at the discretion of the Congress, by constitutional conventions in three-quarters of the states—a method that has been used only once).[2]

§ 4:6 Constitution of Canada

The "Constitution of Canada" is defined in s. 52(2) of the Constitution

[Section 4:5]

[1]The text of s. 128 of the Constitution of Australia is as follows:

> 128. This Constitution shall not be altered except in the following manner:
>
> The proposed law for the alteration thereof must be passed by an absolute majority of each House of the Parliament, and not less than two nor more than six months after its passage through both Houses the proposed law shall be submitted in each State and Territory to the electors qualified to vote for the election of members of the House of Representatives
>
> . . .
>
> And if in a majority of the States a majority of the electors voting approve the proposed law, and if a majority of all the electors voting also approve the proposed law, it shall be presented to the Governor-General for the Queen's assent . . .

On the Australian experience with s. 128, see G. Moens and J. Trone, Lumb and Moens' The Constitution of the Commonwealth of Australia Annotated (Butterworths, Australia, 6th ed., 2001), ch. 8; P.J. Hanks, Constitutional Law in Australia (Butterworths, Australia, 2nd ed., 1996), 99–102. As of 2006, only eight of 44 proposals have carried.

[2]The text of Article V of the Constitution of the United States is as follows:

> The Congress, whenever two thirds of both Houses shall deem it necessary, shall propose amendments to this Constitution, or, on the application of the legislatures of two thirds of the several States, shall call a convention for proposing amendments, which in either case, shall be valid to all intents and purposes, as part of this Constitution when ratified by the legislatures of three fourths of the several States, or by conventions in three fourths thereof, as the one or the other mode of ratification may be proposed by the Congress;

On the American experience with Article V, see J.E. Nowak and R.D. Rotunda, Constitutional Law (West, 7th ed., 2004), Appendix B. See also D.A. Strauss, "The Irrelevance of Constitutional Amendments" (2001) 114 Harv. L. Rev. 1457 (arguing that constitutional amendments have not been important sources of constitutional change in the United States).

Act, 1982.[1] The amending procedures of Part V of the Constitution Act, 1982 apply to amendments to the Constitution of Canada, as defined.[2] The amending procedures are not required for the amendment of statutes or instruments that are not part of the Constitution of Canada; anything that is not part of the Constitution of Canada can be amended by the ordinary action of the competent legislative body.

Section 41(a) of the Constitution Act, 1982 requires the unanimity procedure for amendments to the Constitution of Canada relating to "the office of the Queen, the Governor General and the Lieutenant Governor of the province". To the extent that these topics are provided for in documents that are explicitly included in the definition of the Constitution of Canada in s. 52(2), they are clearly entrenched by the strict rule of unanimity.[3] But the definition of the Constitution of Canada does not explicitly include various documents that also relate to these topics, like the Letters Patent of 1947 (which establishes and confers powers and duties on the office of the Governor General),[4] the Royal Style and Titles Act[5] and the Governor General's Act.[6] For this reason, there is a strong argument[7] that these documents are freely amendable by the federal Parliament using the ordinary legislative process.[8] And yet, since the Supreme Court of Canada has now seen fit to hold that the constitutional amending procedures can still apply to documents that are not explicitly included in the definition of the Constitution of Canada,[9] amendments to these (and other similar) documents have now become vulnerable to constitutional attack on the ground that the una-

[Section 4:6]

[1]The definition is discussed in ch. 1, Sources, under heading § 1:4, "Constitution of Canada".

[2]An exception is the fifth procedure of s. 45 (provincial Legislature alone), which applies to amendments to "the constitution of the province".

[3]These topics are addressed in, for example, ss. 9-17, 54-68 and 90 of the Constitution Act, 1867. This list is not intended to be exhaustive.

[4]Letters Patent constituting the office of Governor General of Canada, 1947, R.S.C. 1985, Appendix II, No. 31.

[5]R.S.C. 1985, c. R-12.

[6]R.S.C. 1985, c. G-9.

[7]This argument was advanced by one of the co-authors of this book (Peter Hogg) in earlier iterations of this section.

[8]The Governor General's Act has in fact been amended several times using the ordinary legislative process, with the most recent amendments being in 2012: Jobs, Growth and Long-term Prosperity Act, S.C. 2012, c. 19. The procedure for royal assent to bills was also amended in 2002 to provide for royal assent to be signified by written declaration (as an alternative to the customary procedure in Parliament assembled); this was also done by the ordinary legislative process: Royal Assent Act, S.C. 2002, c. 15.

[9]See *Re Supreme Court Act, ss. 5 and 6*, [2014] 1 S.C.R. 433, discussed later in this section, in the text accompanying § 4:7 notes 20-23, below. For criticism of the Court's addition of documents to the Constitution of Canada that were not explicitly listed in 1982, see ch. 1, Sources, under heading 1:4, "Constitution of Canada".

nimity procedure (or one of the constitutional amending procedures) should have been used.[10]

The definition of the Constitution of Canada in s. 52(2) also does not explicitly include the federal Official Languages Act.[11] For this reason, even though "the use of the English or French language" is one of the topics listed in s. 41 as engaging the unanimity procedure, there is again a strong argument that the Act is freely amendable by the federal Parliament using the ordinary legislative process.[12] And yet, for the same reason referred to in the previous paragraph, amendments to the Act have become vulnerable to constitutional attack on the ground that the unanimity procedure (or one of the constitutional amending procedures) should have been used.[13]

The Supreme Court Act[14] is not among the instruments listed in the schedule to the Constitution Act, 1982 as comprising the Constitution of Canada, which is something of a puzzle because the amending procedures of the Constitution Act, 1982 make two explicit references to the Court: s. 42(1)(d) lists "the Supreme Court of Canada" as one of the items requiring the general (seven-fifty) amending procedure; and s. 41(d) lists "the composition of the Supreme Court of Canada" as one of the items requiring the unanimity amending procedure. The probable explanation is that the intention of the 1982 framers was to put the main features of the Court into the Constitution of Canada, although this remained unfinished business after the 1982 patriation; it was in fact proposed in the Meech Lake Accord of 1987[15] and (after the Meech Lake Accord failed to achieve the required number of ratifications) in the Charlottetown Accord of 1992[16] (which was defeated in a referendum and never proceeded to ratification). As long as the Court was not in the Constitution of Canada, the natural assumption would be that changes to the Supreme Court Act could still be enacted in the ordinary way by Parliament in the exercise of its power to create a "general court of ap-

[10]The argument that amendments to these documents are subject to constitutional attack on this basis is developed further in M. Bédard and P. Lagassé (eds.), *The Crown and Parliament in Canada* (2015), ch. 8 (by P. Lagassé & P. Baud) (discussing, among other things, the Letters Patent of 1947 and various federal statutes, including the Seals Act, Royal Style and Titles Act, Governor General's Act, Oath of Allegiance Act and Lieutenant Governors Superannuation Act); and P. Monahan et al., *Constitutional Law* (5th ed., 2017), 208-209 (discussing the Letters Patent of 1947). For a case where an argument along these lines was rejected, see *Motard v. Can.*, 2019 QCCA 1826 (Que. C.A.), leave to appeal to the S.C.C. denied April 23, 2020 (no constitutional amendment needed for the Succession to the Throne Act, 2013); discussed further in ch. 1, Sources, under heading 1:4, "Constitution of Canada".

[11]R.S.C. 1985, c. 31 (4th Supp.).

[12]This argument was advanced by one of the co-authors of this book (Peter Hogg) in earlier iterations of this section.

[13]Some of the provisions of the Act have already been constitutionalized in ss. 16-20 of the Charter, which are discussed in ch. 52, Language.

[14]R.S.C. 1985, c. S-26.

[15]See § 4:3 note 7, above.

[16]See § 4:3 note 11, above.

peal for Canada" under s. 101 of the Constitution Act, 1867. Section 101 is the provision that authorized the creation of the Supreme Court in 1875 and the many changes to the Court's composition and jurisdiction since then.[17] Section 101 had been left unchanged in 1982 (and the changes to s. 101 proposed at Meech Lake and Charlottetown had never been adopted). On the assumption that s. 101 remained intact, Parliament in 1987 followed the normal legislative process to enact amendments to various sections of the Supreme Court Act,[18] amendments that have (so far) never been challenged.

In 2013, Parliament again followed the normal legislative process to enact an amendment to the Supreme Court Act; the new s. 6.1 purported to make former members of the bar of Quebec eligible to fill the three places reserved for judges from Quebec.[19] (Current members of the bar of Quebec were expressly eligible under s. 6 of the Act.) This time, the amendment to the Act was challenged, and, in the *Supreme Court Reference* (2014),[20] the Supreme Court held that the amendment was unconstitutional. In a surprising ruling, the Court held that the provisions of the Act dealing with "the composition of the Supreme Court of Canada"[21] had somehow migrated into the Constitution of Canada and could now only be changed by a constitutional amendment under the unanimity procedure stipulated by s. 41(d). The Court added that the provisions of the Act dealing with "the other essential features of the Court" had also migrated into the Constitution of Canada and could now only be changed by a constitutional amendment under the general (seven-fifty) procedure stipulated by s. 42(1)(d).[22] What about s. 101 of the Constitution Act, 1867, which had always been interpreted as conferring on Parliament plenary power in relation to the Court? Not any more, according to the Court: all that s. 101 now authorized were "routine amendments necessary for the continued maintenance of the Supreme Court", and then "only if those amendments do not change the

---

[17] Chapter 8, Supreme Court of Canada.

[18] S.C. 1987, c. 42 (dealing with delivery of judgment otherwise than in open court, signature to opinion by absent judge, grant or denial of leave to appeal without oral hearing, time periods for appeals). These are in practice significant matters, but perhaps they could be characterized as "routine amendments necessary for the continued maintenance of the Supreme Court" (see text accompanying § 4:7 note 23).

[19] S.C. 2013, c. 40, s. 472.

[20] *Re Supreme Court Act, ss. 5 and 6*, [2014] 1 S.C.R. 433, 2014 SCC 21.

[21] The Court (para. 91) identified these as ss. 4(1) (nine judges), 5 (eligibility for appointment) and 6 (three judges from Quebec and their eligibility for appointment).

[22] Section 42(1)(d) says nothing about "essential features", but the Court held (para. 94) that s. 42(1)(d) applied "to the essential features of the Court rather than to all of the provisions of the Supreme Court Act". The Court did not identify the provisions of the Act that deal with "essential features", contenting itself with saying (para. 94): "These essential features include, at the very least, the Court's jurisdiction as the final general court of appeal for Canada, including in matters of constitutional interpretation, and its independence."

constitutionally protected features of the Court".[23] This decision does not change the express stipulations in Part V of the Constitution Act, 1982 that the amending procedures are required only for changes to the "Constitution of Canada", but the Court's willingness to add bits and pieces of the unscheduled Supreme Court Act to the Constitution of Canada could obviously extend to other important statutes, and does mean that the definition of the "Constitution of Canada" in s. 52(2) of the Constitution Act, 1982 is no longer a certain guide as to what is and is not in the Constitution of Canada.

§ 4:7 Charter of Rights

Must constitutional amendments conform to the Charter of Rights?

The Charter of Rights is itself part of the Constitution of Canada, and can be amended by the general (seven-fifty) amending procedure. It is therefore obvious that neither the general amending procedure (s. 38), nor the unanimity amending procedure (s. 41) can be constrained by the Charter of Rights. This conclusion is reinforced by s. 32 of the Charter of Rights, which makes the Charter applicable to the Parliament of Canada and the Legislatures of each province, but which makes no reference to the combinations of legislative resolutions that are required to operate three of the five amending procedures. It seems clear, therefore, that the Charter of Rights does not apply to the general amending procedure (s. 38), the unanimity procedure (s. 41), or the some-but-not-all-provinces procedure (s. 43).[1]

Under s. 44 of the Constitution Act, 1982, the Parliament of Canada alone has the power to enact amendments to the Constitution of Canada in relation to the federal executive and Houses of Parliament, and, under s. 45, each provincial Legislature alone has the power to enact amendments to "the constitution of the province". There is no reason why these two categories of legislation should be exempt from the Charter of Rights, and of course they are caught by the literal words of s. 32 of the Charter. Therefore, it has been held that provincial laws respecting electoral districts[2] and qualifications of candidates for election,[3] although constituting amendments to the constitution of the province, are subject to the Charter of Rights.

---

[23]*Re Supreme Court Act, ss. 5 and 6*, [2014] 1 S.C.R. 433, 2014 SCC 21, para. 101.

[Section 4:7]

[1]*Penikett v. Can.* (1987), 45 D.L.R. (4th) 108 (Y.T.C.A.); *Sibbeston v. Can.* (1988), 48 D.L.R. (4th) 691 (N.T.C.A.). Both cases held that the amendments comprising the (subsequently lapsed) Meech Lake Constitutional Accord, § 4:3 note 7, above, could not be challenged for breach of the Charter of Rights. Accord, *Hogan v. Nfld.* (2000), 183 D.L.R. (4th) 225, para. 88 (Nfld. C.A.) (Charter of Rights inapplicable to amendment under s. 43, because amendment was not "the sole exercise of any of the legislative or governmental bodies named in s. 32").

[2]*Re Provincial Electoral Boundaries (Sask.)*, [1991] 2 S.C.R. 158, 179.

[3]*MacLean v. A.G.N.S.* (1987), 35 D.L.R. (4th) 306 (N.S.S.C.).

III. GENERAL AMENDING PROCEDURE (S. 38)

§ 4:8 Section 38(1)

As related above, Part V of the Constitution Act, 1982 provides for five amending procedures. The general procedure, which applies when none of the four more specific procedures (in ss. 41, 43, 44 and 45) is applicable,[1] is stipulated by s. 38(1), which provides as follows:

> **38.**(1) An amendment to the Constitution of Canada may be made by proclamation issued by the Governor General under the Great Seal of Canada where so authorized by
>
> (a) resolutions of the Senate and House of Commons; and
>
> (b) resolutions of the legislative assemblies of at least two-thirds of the provinces that have, in the aggregate, according to the then latest general census, at least fifty per cent of the population of all the provinces.

Section 38(1) requires that an amendment to the "Constitution of Canada"[2] be authorized by (a) resolutions of both Houses of the federal Parliament,[3] and (b) resolutions of the legislative assemblies[4] of at least two-thirds of the provinces, provided that they represent at least 50 per cent of the population of all the provinces. The two-thirds requirement means that at least seven of the ten provinces must agree to an amendment. Seven provinces would inevitably include at least one of the four western provinces and at least one of the four Atlantic provinces. The 50 per cent population requirement means that the agreeing provinces must include at least one of Ontario or Quebec, since the combined population of Ontario (14.7 million) and Quebec (8.5 million) is more than 50 per cent of the population of Canada (38 million). However, no single province has a constitutionally-entrenched veto over amendments.[5]

The general amending procedure is often called the seven-fifty

---

[Section 4:8]

[1]So held in *Re Senate Reform*, [2014] 1 S.C.R. 704, 2014 SCC 32, para. 75.

[2]See § 4:6, "Constitution of Canada".

[3]The Senate can be overridden by the House of Commons under s. 47. This was done in the case of the Meech Lake Constitutional Accord of 1987, and also in the Constitution Amendment Proclamation, 1997 (Newfoundland Act): ch. 1, Sources.

[4]Section 38(1) does not stipulate any procedural requirements for the passage of a resolution of the House of Commons, the Senate or the legislative assembly of a province. It would therefore be the rules of the particular legislative chamber that would determine the quorum and other procedures. But s. 38(2) calls for a resolution "supported by a majority of the members" (as opposed to a majority of those present and voting) where the proposed amendment "derogates from the legislative powers, the proprietary rights or any other rights or privileges of the legislature or government of a province". (This is the same class of amendments in respect of which opting-out is available under s. 38(3).) Section 38(2) is a safeguard against a hasty decision by a poorly attended legislative chamber.

[5]By virtue of the regional veto statute, S.C. 1996, c. 1, four provinces (Ontario, Quebec, British Columbia and Alberta) now have an indirect veto over constitutional amendments which come under s. 38(1): see § 4:15, "Regional veto statute".

formula, because of its requirements of seven provinces and 50 per cent of the population. Since 1982, it has been successfully operated once.[6]

§ 4:9 Proclamation

Once the authority for an amendment has been provided by the requisite number of resolutions of assent, s. 38(1) provides that the formal act of amendment is accomplished by a "proclamation issued by the Governor General under the Great Seal of Canada". Section 39 imposes time limits on the issue of this proclamation. Under s. 39(1), the proclamation is not to be issued until a full year has elapsed from the adoption of "the resolution initiating the amendment procedure",[1] unless before then all provinces have adopted resolutions of assent or dissent.[2] The purpose of this rule is to give each legislative assembly time to consider each proposal.[3] Under s. 39(2), the proclamation is not to be issued after three years have elapsed from the adoption of the resolution initiating the amendment procedure. The purpose of this rule is to prevent a proposed amendment from limping along for many years, gradually picking up assents, and eventually coming into force without ever having had widespread support.

§ 4:10 Initiation

The procedures for amendment "may be initiated either by the Senate or the House of Commons or by the legislative assembly of a province" (s. 46(1)). In other words, the amending procedure can start in any of the legislative chambers that have the power to authorize an amendment.

§ 4:11 Opting out

"Opting out" is permitted by s. 38(3) in respect of any amendment "that derogates from the legislative powers, the proprietary rights or any other rights or privileges of the legislature or government of a

---

[6]Chapter 1, Sources, under heading § 1:4, "Constitution of Canada".

[Section 4:9]

[1]This phrase is not defined, but it must mean the first of the authorizing resolutions to be passed under s. 38(1); see also the discussion of initiation in the following text.

[2]Section 48 provides that the "Queen's Privy Council for Canada" (i.e., by convention, the cabinet) shall "advise" (i.e., direct) the Governor General to issue a proclamation "forthwith on the adoption of the resolutions required for an amendment . . .". The word "forthwith" appears to contradict s. 39(1)'s requirement of a one-year delay. Section 48 must obviously be read as subject to the more specific requirement of s. 39(1).

[3]This is particularly important with respect to proposals that would derogate from the powers, rights or privileges of the provinces. The one-year delay ensures that opting out under s. 38(3) (discussed in the following text), which is available only "prior to the issue of the proclamation", cannot be defeated by the speedy manoeuvering of those governments that desire an amendment.

province".[1] Section 38(3) permits the legislative assembly of a province to pass a resolution of dissent to an amendment of the kind described, and then the amendment "shall not have effect in [that] province".[2] Section 38(3) is not a unanimity requirement or a veto, because it does not permit a single province to block an amendment that is wanted by the federal government and seven provinces representing 50 per cent of the population. All that s. 38(3) does is to enable any province to opt out of an amendment that derogates from that province's powers, rights or privileges, and that is unacceptable to it. A maximum of three provinces could opt out of an amendment: if there were more than three dissenting provinces, the amendment would not have the support of two-thirds of the provinces and would therefore be defeated.

The operation of opting out may be illustrated by an example. Take the following hypothetical case:

> An amendment is proposed by the federal government to add to the list of exclusive federal powers "the regulation of product standards", a matter now within the exclusive provincial authority over property and civil rights in the province.[3] The proposed amendment is authorized by resolutions supported by a majority of the members of the Senate, the House of Commons and seven of the ten legislative assemblies, all except Quebec, Alberta and Newfoundland. The Quebec Legislature passes the resolution of dissent contemplated by s. 38(3). The Alberta and Newfoundland Legislatures do nothing. One year after the resolution initiating the amending procedure (see s. 39(1)) the Governor General issues the proclamation required by s. 38(1).

In this example, the amendment has been validly enacted, because the amendment has been authorized by resolutions of the Senate, the House of Commons and the legislative assemblies of two-thirds of the provinces (seven out of ten) having 50 per cent of the population of all the provinces. Therefore, the federal Parliament has acquired its new legislative power, and that power has effect not only in the provinces which agreed to the amendment, but also in Alberta and Newfoundland, which did not. In nine provinces, the provincial Legislatures would have lost their authority over the regulation of product standards. However, the amendment is one that derogates from the legislative powers of the provinces, and Quebec has passed a resolution of dissent under s. 38(3). Therefore the new federal power does not have effect in Quebec. In Quebec, the regulation of product standards remains within the authority of the Quebec Legislature. If the federal Parliament decides to

---

[Section 4:11]

[1]Note also the procedural requirements for resolutions authorizing amendments of this kind: see § 4:8 note 4, above.

[2]An example of a constitutional amendment from which opting out is not available is "an institutional reform" making a change in the tenure of senators. This may have an impact on provincial interests, but it "does not affect the legislative powers, property rights, or any other rights or privileges of the legislature or government of a province.": *Re Senate Reform*, [2014] 1 S.C.R. 704, 2014 SCC 32, para. 83.

[3]*Labatt Breweries v. A.-G. Can.*, [1980] 1 S.C.R. 914.

exercise its new power of passing a law regulating product standards, the members of parliament and senators from Quebec will be allowed to vote on the bill (and may have to do so to preserve the government's majority),[4] but once the bill has been enacted into law the law will not apply in Quebec.

A resolution of dissent under s. 38(3) must be passed "prior to the issue of the proclamation to which the amendment relates" (s. 38(3)). In the example just discussed, neither Alberta nor Newfoundland could opt out of the amendment after the issue of the proclamation. However, if a resolution of dissent has been passed prior to the issue of the proclamation, it can be revoked "at any time before or after the issue of the proclamation" (s. 38(4)). In the example just discussed, Quebec can opt into the amendment at any time that its legislative assembly has a change of mind. A resolution of assent, on the other hand, may be revoked only before the issue of the proclamation (s. 46(2)). In the example just discussed, Ontario (or any of the other assenting provinces), having passed a resolution of assent prior to the issue of the proclamation, could not after the issue of the proclamation revoke its assent and thereby destroy the amendment.

§ 4:12 Compensation for opting out

Section 40 provides as follows:

> 40. Where an amendment is made under subsection 38(1) that transfers provincial legislative powers relating to education or other cultural matters from provincial legislatures to Parliament, Canada shall provide reasonable compensation to any province to which the amendment does not apply.

Section 40 imposes upon the federal government the obligation to provide "reasonable compensation" to any province that has opted out of an amendment that transfers "provincial legislative powers relating to education or other cultural matters" from the provincial Legislatures to the federal Parliament. The purpose of this obligation is to ensure that a province is not pressured by financial considerations into abandoning jurisdiction over educational or cultural matters. For example, if an amendment transferring legislative authority over universities from the provincial Legislatures to the federal Parliament could obtain the requisite two-thirds provincial support, in the absence of s. 40 there would be a powerful incentive on non-agreeing provinces not to opt out, because opting out would involve bearing a substantial expense (the cost of running the universities) from which other provincial governments would be freed by the amendment. With s. 40 in the Constitution Act, 1982, a province is freed from financial considerations in deciding whether or not to opt out of the amendment.

Amendments that do not relate to education or cultural matters do not carry any constitutional right to compensation for opting out. Take the example given earlier of an amendment transferring legislative

[4]This strange result has in the past been viewed as a grave defect in the idea of "special status" for one or more provinces: see heading § 4:21, "Division of powers".

authority over "the regulation of product standards" from the provincial Legislatures to the federal Parliament. If a province opted out of this amendment, it would have to continue to bear the cost of regulating product standards, a cost which in other provinces would now be borne by the federal government. It is in fact quite likely that the opting-out province would be successful in negotiating compensation (either in the form of extra tax room or a cash grant) for this extra burden,[1] but it could not invoke any constitutional right to compensation.

It will be recalled that the Vancouver formula, which was the first version of the present amending procedures, provided a right to compensation for opting out of all amendments. This part of the Vancouver formula was dropped in the federal-provincial agreement of November 5, 1981. Section 40 is a compromise between universal compensation and no compensation; it singles out education and culture because of their special significance to Quebec. Section 40 was agreed to by the Prime Minister and the nine Premiers of the English-speaking provinces after the agreement of November 5, 1981 in an attempt to make the amending formula more attractive to Quebec. However, the inclusion of s. 40 did not soften Quebec's opposition to the amending formula.[2]

§ 4:13 Revocation of assent or dissent

A resolution of assent may be revoked only before the issue of the proclamation authorized by the resolution (s. 46(2)). A revocation of assent after the issue of the proclamation cannot be permitted, because that would render every amendment permanently vulnerable to abrogation by the action of a single province or a few provinces.

A resolution of dissent (an opting-out resolution), on the other hand, may be revoked at any time, before or after the issue of the proclamation (s. 38(4)). A revocation of dissent after the issue of the proclamation is not objectionable, because it simply has the effect of extending to the opted-out province an amendment which is already applicable to the other provinces. Indeed, the checkerboard effect of opting out is so obviously undesirable that no obstacle should be raised to an opted-out province which, perhaps after a change of government, has now decided to opt in.

§ 4:14 Section 42

The point has already been made that the general amending procedure (the seven-fifty formula) is the correct one for the residual class of

---

[Section 4:12]

[1]See ch. 12, Financial Arrangements.

[2]See § 4:2 note 9, above. Both the unsuccessful Meech Lake Accord of 1987, (see § 4:3 note 7, above), and the unsuccessful Charlottetown Accord of 1992, (see § 4:3 note 11, above), would have amended s. 40 so that the right to compensation would apply to all transfers of provincial legislative powers, not just those relating to education or other cultural matters.

amendments which are not covered by the more specific procedures of ss. 41, 43, 44 and 45. In addition, s. 42 requires that the general amending procedure be used for six defined classes of amendments to the Constitution of Canada. Section 42 provides as follows:

42.(1) An amendment to the Constitution of Canada in relation to the following matters may be made only in accordance with subsection 38(1):

(a) the principle of proportionate representation of the provinces in the House of Commons prescribed by the Constitution of Canada;

(b) the powers of the Senate and the method of selecting Senators;

(c) the number of members by which a province is entitled to be represented in the Senate and the residence qualifications of Senators;

(d) subject to paragraph 41(d), the Supreme Court of Canada;

(e) the extension of existing provinces into the territories; and

(f) notwithstanding any other law or practice, the establishment of new provinces.

(2) Subsections 38(2) to (4) do not apply in respect of amendments in relation to matters referred to in subsection (1).

Section 42(1) lists six matters in respect of which an amendment to the Constitution of Canada may be made only in accordance with the general amending procedure of s. 38(1) (two-thirds provinces with 50 per cent population). Like ss. 38 and 41, s. 42 applies only to amendments to the "Constitution of Canada".[1]

Paragraph (a) of s. 42(1) refers to "the principle of proportionate representation of the provinces in the House of Commons". The principle of proportionate representation in the House of Commons was an essential element of the confederation scheme of 1867.[2] However, the principle has never been applied rigidly, and in 1915[3] the "Senate floor" of s. 51A was introduced into the Constitution Act, 1867, which guaranteed to each province a minimum number of Commons seats equal to the number of the province's Senate seats. The purpose was to limit the decline in representation of the maritime provinces that was caused by the relative decline in their populations. In 1985, the Representation Act, 1985, repealed and replaced s. 51 of the Constitution Act, 1867, which is the provision that provides for a readjustment of representation in the House of Commons every ten years, following a census, and provides the formula for that readjustment. The new s. 51 included a grandfather clause, which guaranteed that provinces with declining populations would not lose any seats on a readjustment. The effect of this clause was to further compromise the principle of representation by population. In *Campbell v. Canada* (1988),[4] it was held that a provision

[Section 4:14]

[1]See § 4:6, "Constitution of Canada".

[2]See ch. 2, Reception, under heading § 2:7, "Confederation".

[3]Constitution Act, 1915, R.S.C. 1985, Appendix II, No. 23.

[4]*Campbell v. Canada* (1988), 49 D.L.R. (4th) 321 (B.C.C.A.).

to protect the representation of declining provinces should not be regarded as offending "the principle" of proportionate representation, and did not require a seven-fifty amendment under s. 42(1)(a). The Act was to be characterized as a law in relation to the House of Commons; and it was a valid exercise of the federal Parliament's unilateral amending power under s. 44.

Paragraph (b) of s. 42(1) refers to "the powers of the Senate and the method of selecting Senators", and paragraph (c) refers to "the number of members by which a province is entitled to be represented in the Senate and the residence qualifications of Senators". These are all matters that (at least in theory) have significance to the provinces as well as to the central government. The effect of paragraphs (b) and (c) is to withdraw these matters from the federal Parliament's unilateral amending power over "the Senate" in s. 44, and to require that any amendment be adopted by the seven-fifty formula of s. 38. In the *Senate Reform Reference* (2014),[5] the Supreme Court of Canada was asked (among other questions) whether Parliament could provide for "consultative elections" to the Senate as part of the process of appointment (which is by the Governor General advised by the Prime Minister). The Court answered no. This would be an amendment in relation to "the method of selecting Senators" which was a matter listed in paragraph (b) of s. 42(1) and withdrawn from Parliament's unilateral power under s. 44. The Court was also asked whether Parliament could impose "term limits" on senators to substitute a fixed term of years for the existing tenure to age 75. Term limits are not among the matters listed in paragraphs (b) and (c), which would appear to leave them to Parliament's power in s. 44. But the Court answered no to this question too. The Court held that, in addition to the matters listed in paragraphs (b) and (c), which are *expressly* withdrawn from Parliament's power in s. 44, any other "changes that engage the provinces in the Senate" were *impliedly* withdrawn from Parliament's power in s. 44.[6] The introduction of term limits would reduce the independence of senators, and that was a change that would engage the interests of the provinces. Therefore, term limits could not be enacted by Parliament; they would require a seven-fifty amendment under s. 38, which is the procedure when none of the more specific procedures is applicable.

Paragraph (d) of s. 42(1) refers to the Supreme Court of Canada in all aspects other than its composition (which is specifically listed in s. 41(d)—the unanimity amendment procedure). The reference to the Supreme Court of Canada is puzzling, because, unlike the other matters listed in s. 42(1), the Supreme Court of Canada is nowhere provided for in the Constitution of Canada. The Court is constituted by the Supreme Court Act, and the Supreme Court Act is a federal statute that is not one of the instruments forming part of the Constitution of Canada. It would seem to follow that, since s. 42 applies only to amendments to the "Constitution of Canada", Parliament, acting under s. 101 of the Consti-

[5] *Re Senate Reform*, [2014] 1 S.C.R. 704, 2014 SCC 32.

[6] *Re Senate Reform*, [2014] 1 S.C.R. 704, 2014 SCC 32, para. 75.

tution Act, 1867, still has the power to amend the Supreme Court Act. However, as has been explained, in the *Supreme Court Reference* (2014),[7] the Supreme Court held that the provisions of the Supreme Court Act dealing with "the essential features of the Court" had mysteriously migrated into the Constitution of Canada and could be amended only by the general (seven-fifty) amending procedure stipulated by s. 42(1)(d).[8] Section 42(1)(d) says nothing about "essential features", but the Court made clear that the migration did not include all of the provisions of the Supreme Court Act, just those dealing with the Court's essential features.[9] The Court did not identify the provisions of the Act that had made the migration, although it said: "These essential features include, at the very least, the Court's jurisdiction as the final general court of appeal for Canada, including in matters of constitutional interpretation, and its independence."[10] The Court must have intended this description to cover a great deal of the Act, because the Court added that Parliament's unilateral power under s. 101 was now reduced to "routine amendments necessary for the continued maintenance of the Supreme Court", and then "only if those amendments do not change the constitutionally protected features of the Court".[11]

Paragraph (e) of s. 42(1) refers to the extension of existing provinces into the territories, and paragraph (f) to the establishment of new provinces. It is probably wrong to treat these paragraphs as requiring the seven-fifty formula for the extension of existing provinces or the establishment of new provinces. The Constitution Act, 1871, by s. 2, authorizes the federal Parliament to establish new provinces in federal territories, and, by s. 3, authorizes the federal Parliament, with the consent of a province, to extend the boundaries of a province. These provisions were not repealed or amended in 1982, and can still be operated without any change in the Constitution of Canada. The effect of paras, (e) and (f) of s. 42(1) is to protect ss. 2 and 3 of the Constitution Act, 1871 from repeal or amendment, except by the seven-fifty formula.[12]

Section 42(2) prohibits any province from opting out of amendments

---

[7]*Re Supreme Court Act, ss. 5 and 6*, [2014] 1 S.C.R. 433, 2014 SCC 21; for fuller description, see § 4:6, "Constitution of Canada".

[8]The decision concerned a purported amendment to a provision dealing with the "composition" of the Court, which the Court held could only be amended under the unanimity procedure stipulated by s. 41(d). However, the discussion of s. 42(1)(d) and s. 101 was probably not obiter dicta, since the migration theory was an unprecedented judicial initiative that really demanded a fuller explanation than one limited to composition.

[9]*Re Supreme Court Act, ss. 5 and 6*, [2014] 1 S.C.R. 433, 2014 SCC 21, para. 94.

[10]*Re Supreme Court Act, ss. 5 and 6*, [2014] 1 S.C.R. 433, 2014 SCC 21, pata. 94.

[11]*Re Supreme Court Act, ss. 5 and 6*, [2014] 1 S.C.R. 433, 2014 SCC 21, para. 101.

[12]In the 2nd edition of this book (1985), at p. 63, I took the position that ss. 2 and 3 of the Constitution Act, 1871 should be regarded as impliedly repealed by s. 42(1) (e) and (f). I now think that that position gives insufficient weight to the fact that s. 42(1) is directed only to amendments of the Constitution of Canada, and the extension of provinces and the establishment of new provinces requires no amendment of the Constitution of Canada. The position is not totally clear, however, especially having regard to the obscure notwithstanding clause in s. 42(1)(f). Other constitutional issues that would

coming within s. 42. Thus, Quebec could not opt out of, let alone block, an amendment to the House of Commons or Supreme Court of Canada coming within s. 42(1), if the amendment was approved by the federal Parliament and seven provinces representing 50 per cent of the population. This illustrates the inferior protection provided to Quebec by the opting-out provision (even if accompanied by full compensation) in comparison with a veto over constitutional amendments.[13]

§ 4:15 "Regional veto" statute

The general (seven-fifty) amending formula of s. 38 does not give any province a veto over constitutional amendments. It will be recalled that this was a conscious choice in 1982, when the Vancouver formula, which was based on the equality of the provinces, was preferred over the Victoria Charter formula, which was based on a system of regional vetoes (with Quebec as one of the required regions).[1] The fact that the seven-fifty formula does not give Quebec a veto has been occasionally advanced as a criticism of the Constitution Act, 1982. (However, it should be recalled that Premier Levesque of Quebec was one of the eight provincial premiers that had urged the adoption of the Vancouver formula, and persuaded Prime Minister Trudeau to shift his support away from the Victoria Charter formula.)[2] The Meech Lake and Charlottetown Accords had not proposed a reversion to the Victoria Charter formula: they had proposed a widening of the categories of amendments for which the unanimity procedure (a veto for all provinces) was required, and an extension of the right to compensation for opting out of amendments.[3]

After the narrow defeat of Quebec's 1995 referendum on sovereignty, the federal Parliament enacted a statute to ensure that Quebec would in future have a veto over most constitutional amendments. However, instead of revisiting the measures proposed in the Meech Lake and Charlottetown Accords, or conferring a veto on Quebec alone, the statute

---

need to be resolved on the establishment of a new province are: representation in the Senate; representation in the House of Commons; and (perhaps) a modification of the amending formula.

[13]Quebec would have obtained a veto under the Victoria Charter formula, which was abandoned in 1982 for the current formula: § 4:2 notes 6-11, above. The unsuccessful Meech Lake Accord, § 4:3 note 7, above, would have moved the s. 42 list (of matters relating to the structure and central institutions of federalism) into s. 41, thereby requiring unanimity for their amendment and giving a veto to Quebec (and every other province).

[Section 4:15]

[1]See § 4:2, "The search for a domestic amending procedure".

[2]The formula as enacted differed slightly from the Vancouver proposal, in particular, by limiting the entitlement to compensation for opting out: see § 4:12, "Compensation for opting out".

[3]See § 4:16 note 21, below.

went back to the regional veto idea of the Victoria formula. The regional veto statute[4] provides as follows:

> No Minister of the Crown shall propose a motion for a resolution to authorize an amendment to the Constitution of Canada, other than an amendment in respect of which the legislative assembly of a province may exercise a veto under section 41 or 43 of the *Constitution Act, 1982* or may express its dissent under subsection 38(3) of that Act, unless the amendment has first been consented to by a majority of the provinces that includes
>
> (a) Ontario;
> (b) Quebec;
> (c) British Columbia;
> (d) two or more of the Atlantic provinces that have, according to the then latest general census, combined populations of at least fifty per cent of the population of all the Atlantic provinces; and
> (e) two or more of the Prairie provinces that have, according to the then latest census, combined populations of at least fifty per cent of the population of all the Prairie provinces.

The purpose of the statute is to import new conditions into the general (seven-fifty) formula for amending the Constitution of Canada. On top of the *constitutional* requirement of support by seven provinces representing 50 per cent of the population, the statute imposes the new *statutory* requirement that the seven agreeing provinces must include the five "regions" stipulated in the Act, namely, Ontario, Quebec, British Columbia, two Atlantic provinces and two Prairie provinces.[5]

The statute accomplishes its purpose indirectly. A direct alteration of the procedures for amending the Constitution could only be accomplished by constitutional amendment. As is explained in the next section of this chapter, an amendment of the amending procedures is one of the matters that requires the unanimous consent of Parliament and the provincial legislatures pursuant to s. 41(e) of the Constitution Act, 1982. So this Act purports to control only the action of Ministers of the Crown, who must refrain from proposing that Parliament adopt a resolution for a constitutional amendment unless the requirements of the statute have first been met.[6] Under the general (seven-fifty) procedure, resolutions of

---

[4]S.C. 1996, c. 1. The Act does not have an official short title. Its long title is "An Act respecting constitutional amendments".

[5]The statutory regions differ from those in the Victoria Charter in two respects. First, British Columbia was not recognized as a separate region in the Victoria Charter, which required the assent of two of the "Western provinces" having a combined population of 50 per cent of all the Western provinces. By treating British Columbia as a separate region, the statute effectively grants Alberta a veto too, since its population exceeds that of the combined populations of Saskatchewan and Manitoba, the other Prairie provinces. Secondly, there was no requirement in the Victoria Charter that the two Atlantic provinces had to represent 50 per cent of the populations of all the Atlantic provinces. Under the Victoria Charter, any two Atlantic provinces would do.

[6]The power of Parliament to enact such a statute probably comes from the peace, order, and good government power (see ch. 17, Peace, Order and Good Government), or possibly s. 44 of the Constitution Act, 1982 (see § 4:18, "Federal Parliament alone (s. 44)").

assent must be passed by both Houses of Parliament (unless the Senate has been by-passed under s. 47). The statute does not prohibit someone other than a Minister of the Crown from introducing a resolution for a constitutional amendment that lacks the regional support required by the statute, and it does not prohibit the Houses of Parliament from passing such a resolution.[7] But the political reality is that a resolution on a matter as important as amending the Constitution of Canada would be unlikely to pass if it had not been initiated by the government of the day, that is, by a Minister of the Crown. By binding Ministers of the Crown to its provisions, this statute effectively adds its own conditions to the general procedure for amending the Constitution. This means that all five of the "regions" defined by the statute must have given their consent to a proposed constitutional amendment before a Minister of the Crown is permitted to introduce a resolution of approval into either of the Houses of Parliament. The regions thereby obtain a veto by proxy. Of course, since the veto is statutory only, it could be repealed or amended by Parliament at any time in the future.

The regional veto statute only applies to amendments that are to follow the general (seven-fifty) amending procedure of s. 38, and that do not afford a dissenting province the constitutional right to "opt out". Amendments that require unanimity under s. 41, or that must be ratified by some-but-not-all provinces under s. 43, are expressly excluded. Amendments that come within the exclusive jurisdiction of the federal Parliament under s. 44 are excluded by implication, since s. 44 speaks of amendment by "laws" rather than by "resolutions". And amendments that are competent to the provinces alone under s. 45 are not affected by the statute, because they require no action by the Parliament of Canada.

The regional veto statute was hastily conceived and implemented after the Quebec sovereignty referendum of 1995. It was designed to achieve through federal legislation what the failed Meech and Charlottetown Accords had been unable to achieve through constitutional amendment, namely, a greater role for Quebec over future amendments of the Constitution. At the same time, a resolution recognizing Quebec as a "distinct society" was passed by the House of Commons—another matter that the Meech and Charlottetown Accords would have put into the Constitution. Even by the standard of accommodating the concerns of Quebec, the regional veto statute was probably an unwise initiative, because it makes the Constitution even more difficult to amend, and further reduces the faint hope of genuine constitutional change. For example, before the Act was enacted, the seven-fifty procedure[8] would have enabled a distinct society clause to be put into the Constitution

[7]A statute that purported to restrict the discretion of the Houses of Parliament to pass future resolutions for constitutional amendments would be constitutionally suspect: see ch. 12, Parliamentary Sovereignty, under heading §§ 12:9 to 12:10, "Self-imposed restraints on legislative power".

[8]It is possible that a distinct society clause could be put into the Constitution under s. 43, that is, with the consent of only Quebec and the federal Parliament, but the conventional wisdom is that the seven-fifty formula is required.

without the assents of British Columbia or Alberta, where opposition to this element of the Meech Lake and Charlottetown Accords was most intense. The Act would now require the assents of both those provinces, since British Columbia is recognized as a region and Alberta has more than 50 per cent of the population of the Prairie provinces.

IV. UNANIMITY PROCEDURE

§ 4:16 Unanimity procedure (s. 41)

Section 41 of the Constitution Act, 1982 provides as follows:

> **41.** An amendment to the Constitution of Canada in relation to the following matters may be made by proclamation issued by the Governor General under the Great Seal of Canada only where authorized by resolutions of the Senate and House of Commons and of the legislative assembly of each province:
>
> (a) the office of the Queen, the Governor General and the Lieutenant Governor of a province;
>
> (b) the right of a province to a number of members in the House of Commons not less than the number of Senators by which the province is entitled to be represented at the time this Part comes into force;
>
> (c) subject to section 43, the use of the English or the French language;
>
> (d) the composition of the Supreme Court of Canada; and
>
> (e) an amendment to this Part.

Section 41 lists five matters in respect of which an amendment to the Constitution of Canada[1] requires the unanimous support of the provinces, as opposed to the two-thirds majority called for by the general amending procedure of s. 38(1). In respect of these matters, each province has a veto over amendments. The five listed topics are specially entrenched because they are deemed to be matters of national significance which should not be altered over the objection of even one province.

Paragraph (a)—"the office of the Queen, the Governor General and the Lieutenant Governor of a province"— has the effect of entrenching those provisions of the Constitution of Canada that deal with the monarchy and its representatives in Canada. If this topic were not listed in s. 41, it would be arguable that changes could be made for Canada by the federal Parliament alone under s. 44, and for a province by the provincial Legislature alone under s. 45. As noted earlier in this chapter,[2] the definition of the Constitution of Canada does not explicitly include various documents – like the Letters Patent of 1947 (which establishes and confers powers and duties on the office of Governor General),[3] the Royal

[Section 4:16]

[1]See § 4:6, "Constitution of Canada".

[2]Section 4:6, "Constitution of Canada".

[3]Letters Patent constituting the office of Governor General of Canada, 1947, R.S.C. 1985, Appendix II, No. 31.

Style and Titles Act[4] and the Governor General's Act[5] – that relate to "the office of the Queen, the Governor General and the Lieutenant Governor of a province". As a result, there is a strong argument[6] that these documents are freely amendable by the federal Parliament using the ordinary legislative process.[7] And yet, because the Supreme Court of Canada has now taken it upon itself to hold (in the *Supreme Court Reference*, which is discussed later in this section)[8] that the constitutional amending procedures can apply to documents that are not explicitly included in the definition of the Constitution of Canada, amendments to these documents have now become vulnerable to constitutional challenge on the ground that the unanimity procedure (or one of the constitutional amending procedures) should have been utilized.[9]

Paragraph (b) of s. 41 entrenches the right of the least populous provinces to a minimum number of members in the House of Commons, thereby modifying the relentless application of representation by population. This provision, called the "Senate floor", was established, to limit the declining representation of the maritime provinces,[10] by the British North America Act, 1915,[11] which added a new s. 51A to the B.N.A. Act (now the Constitution Act, 1867). If s. 51A were not protected by s. 41, it would be arguable that it could be repealed or amended by the federal Parliament alone under s. 44.

Paragraph (c) of s. 41 entrenches those provisions of the Constitution of Canada that make provision for "the use of the English or French language".[12] As noted earlier in this chapter,[13] the definition of the Constitution of Canada does not explicitly include the federal Official Lan-

---

[4]R.S.C. 1985, c. R-12.

[5]R.S.C. 1985, c. G-9.

[6]This argument was advanced by one of the co-authors of this book (Peter Hogg) in earlier iterations of this section.

[7]As noted earlier, there have been amendments to some of these documents using the ordinary legislative process: see § 4:6 note 8, above.

[8]Text accompanying § 4:16 notes 18-20; see also sec. 4:6, "Constitution of Canada", text accompanying § 4:6 notes 20-23, above.

[9]For a case where an argument along these lines was rejected, see *Motard v. Can.*, 2019 QCCA 1826 (Que. C.A.), leave to appeal to the S.C.C. denied April 23, 2020 (no constitutional amendment needed for the Succession to the Throne Act, 2013); discussed further in ch. 1, Sources, under heading 1:4, "Constitution of Canada".

[10]Ward, Dawson's The Government of Canada (6th ed., 1987), 89–90; *Campbell v. Can.* (1988), 49 D.L.R. (4th) 321, 324-327 (B.C.C.A.). At the present time, this provision benefits Prince Edward Island and New Brunswick.

[11]Constitution Act, 1915, R.S.C. 1985, Appendix II, No. 23.

[12]There are provisions of the Constitution of Canada in relation to the use of the English or French language in s. 133 of the Constitution Act, 1867, s. 23 of the Manitoba Act, 1870, and ss. 16 to 23 and 55 to 57 of the Constitution Act, 1982. However, not all of these provisions are caught by paragraph (c) of s. 41. Paragraph (c) is expressly subject to s. 43, which provides for the some-but-not-all-provinces procedure (discussed next). Section 43(b) covers those language provisions that apply to one or more but not all provinces and that relate to the use of the English or French language within a province. Many of the language provisions are in this category, and, once they are subtracted, the unanimity requirement of s. 41(c) applies only to s. 133 of the Constitution Act, 1867

guages Act.[14] As a result, even though the Act relates to "the use of the English or French language", there is a strong argument that the Act is freely amendable by the federal Parliament using the ordinary legislative process.[15] And yet, for the same reason referred to in the discussion of paragraph (a),[16] amendments to the Act have now become vulnerable to constitutional attack on the ground that the unanimity procedure (or one of the constitutional amending procedures) should have been used.[17]

Paragraph (d) of s. 41 entrenches "the composition of the Supreme Court of Canada". The law relating to the composition of the Supreme Court of Canada is contained in the Supreme Court Act, which is an ordinary statute enacted by Parliament and not one of the instruments scheduled to the Constitution Act, 1982 as comprising the Constitution of Canada. The Supreme Court Act of 1875 and its many subsequent amendments were enacted under the power conferred on Parliament by s. 101 of the Constitution Act, 1867, which authorizes the establishment of a "general court of appeal for Canada". So long as the Court was not part of the Constitution of Canada, could its composition still be changed by the ordinary legislative process of s. 101? Parliament thought so, and in 2013 it passed an amendment to the Supreme Court Act purporting to add a new s. 6.1 to the Act which made former members of the bar of Quebec eligible for appointment to the Court to fill the three places reserved for judges from Quebec. (Current members of the bar of Quebec were expressly eligible by s. 6.) The government then appointed a judge of the Federal Court of Appeal who was a former member of the bar of Quebec to fill one of the Quebec places on the Supreme Court. In the *Supreme Court Reference* (2014),[18] the Supreme Court held that the new s. 6.1 was unconstitutional and the appointment was unauthorized. The Court held that the provisions of the Supreme Court Act dealing with the composition of the Court, namely, ss. 4(1) (nine judges), 5 (who may be appointed), and 6 (three judges from Quebec), including the details of eligibility for appointment, had mysteriously migrated into the Constitution of Canada, and could now only be amended by the unanimity

---

in its application to federal institutions (but not Quebec institutions) and ss. 16(1), 16(3), 17(1), 18(1), 19(1), 20(1), 21, 22, 23 and 55 to 57 of the Constitution Act, 1982.

[13]Section 4:6, "Constitution of Canada".

[14]R.S.C. 1985, c. 31 (4th Supp.).

[15]This argument was advanced by one of the co-authors of this book (Peter Hogg) in earlier iterations of this section.

[16]Text accompanying § 4:16 note 1, above.

[17]Some of the provisions of the Act have already been constitutionalized in ss. 16-20 of the Charter, which are discussed in ch. 52, Language.

[18]*Re Supreme Court Act, ss. 5 and 6*, [2014] 1 S.C.R. 433, 2014 SCC 21. McLachlin C.J. and LeBel, Abella, Cromwell, Karakatsanis and Wagner JJ. wrote the opinion of the majority. Moldaver J. dissented; in his view, the existing s. 6 of the Act authorized the appointment of former members of the bar; he did not go on to decide the constitutional question, although he expressed qualified agreement with the majority on that question. For fuller description of the decision, see § 4:6, "Constitution of Canada".

amending procedure prescribed by s. 41(d).[19] The Court added that the provisions of the Act dealing with the "other essential features" of the Court had also migrated into the Constitution of Canada, and could also be changed only by constitutional amendment, although the general (seven-fifty) procedure prescribed by s. 42(1)(d) was the process for the other essential features.[20]

Paragraph (e) provides that any amendment to the amending procedures themselves ("this Part" being Part V of the Constitution Act, 1982) can only be effected by the unanimity procedure of s. 41. Section 49 of the Constitution Act, 1982 also stipulates that the amending procedures must be reviewed at a constitutional conference to be held within 15 years of April 17, 1982 (when the Constitution Act, 1982 came into force). This provision expired in 1997 without any alteration of the amending formula, a result which is not surprising in view of the unanimity requirement.[21]

Paragraph (e) of s. 41 was applied in the *Senate Reform Reference* (2014).[22] One of the questions put to the Supreme Court in the *Reference* concerned the amending procedure that would be applicable to the abolition of the Senate. At first blush, the answer to the question seemed obvious: since the abolition of the Senate was not one of the five matters reserved for unanimity by s. 41, would it not come within the general (seven-fifty) amending procedure of s. 38? What the Court held was that the unanimity procedure would be the applicable one. The Court pointed out that Part V of the Constitution Act, 1982 gave the Senate a role in all the amending procedures except for the unilateral provincial procedure over "amendments to the constitution of the province" in s. 45. While the Senate could only delay most categories of amendments (s. 47), its abolition "would render this mechanism of review inoperative and effectively change the dynamics of the constitutional amendment process. The constitutional structure of Part V as a whole would be

[19] *Re Supreme Court Act, ss. 5 and 6*, [2014] 1 S.C.R. 433, 2014 SCC 21, paras. 75, 91. Moldaver J., who dissented, did not directly address the constitutional question, but he expressed doubt that the details of eligibility for appointment were included in the composition of the Court: *Re Supreme Court Act, ss. 5 and 6*, [2014] 1 S.C.R. 433, 2014 SCC 21, para. 115.

[20] *Re Supreme Court Act, ss. 5 and 6*, [2014] 1 S.C.R. 433, 2014 SCC 21, paras. 75, 90, 94. Section 42 of the Constitution Act, 1982 is discussed in § 4:14.

[21] Proposals for changing the amending procedures were part of the unsuccessful Meech Lake Accord of 1987, (see § 4:3 note 7, above), and the unsuccessful Charlottetown Accord of 1992, (see § 4:3 note 11, above). Each would have effected two changes: (1) the expansion of the right to compensation for opting out in s. 40, so that it was no longer limited to education or other cultural matters; and (2) the expansion of the unanimity procedure of s. 41, so that it included the matters listed in s. 42 as well. Parliament effected an indirect *statutory* alteration of the general (seven-fifty) amending procedures by its passage of a 1996 Act; see § 4:15, "Regional veto statute". However, there was no *constitutional* change to the amending formulas before the April 1997 deadline. According to Prime Minister Chretien, the obligation to reconsider the amending procedures was "discharged" after a brief discussion at a June 21, 1996 First Ministers' Conference: *The [Toronto] Globe and Mail* (22 June 1996).

[22] *Re Senate Reform*, [2014] 1 S.C.R. 704, 2014 SCC 32.

fundamentally altered."[23] The Court concluded that the abolition of the Senate should be regarded as an amendment to Part V that, by virtue of s. 41(e), required the unanimity procedure.

An amendment made under the unanimity procedure of s. 41 is brought into force by a proclamation of the Governor General. However, the time-limits prescribed by s. 39 for the issue of the proclamation apply only to amendments made under the general (seven-fifty) procedure. It is easy to see why an amendment under the unanimity procedure should be able to be proclaimed in force without waiting for a minimum period of one year to elapse: since all legislative bodies have approved, there is no point in delay. It is not, however, easy to see why the maximum period of three years does not apply to amendments covered by the unanimity procedure; yet the three-year time limit of s. 39(2) is expressly applicable only to amendments under s. 38(1)—the general procedure. This means that the process of legislative ratification of an amendment covered by s. 41—the unanimity procedure—is subject to no time limit. If it takes more than three years to secure all the required approvals, the amendment can still be proclaimed into law.

The Meech Lake Accord of 1987[24] raised an interesting point of interpretation regarding the three-year time-limit. The Accord was a package of related amendments, some of which were subject to the seven-fifty procedure, and others of which (dealing with the Supreme Court of Canada and the amending procedures) were subject to the unanimity procedure. In order to bring the entire package into force, obviously the unanimity procedure had to be employed. Did this mean that no time-limit applied to the ratification of the Accord? Probably, the answer to that question was no: the existence within the package of seven-fifty amendments required that the time-limit be adhered to. Certainly, that was the view that was generally held, and the Accord was treated as having lapsed when two provincial legislative assemblies were still debating the Accord at the expiry of three years from the date of the initiating resolution.

V. SOME-BUT-NOT-ALL-PROVINCES PROCEDURE

§ 4:17 Some-but-not-all-provinces procedure (s. 43)

Section 43 of the Constitution Act, 1982 provides as follows:

> **43.** An amendment to the Constitution of Canada in relation to any provision that applies to one or more, but not all, provinces, including
> (a) any alteration to boundaries between provinces, and
> (b) any amendment to any provision that relates to the use of the English or the French language within a province,
>
> may be made by proclamation issued by the Governor General under the Great Seal of Canada only where so authorized by resolutions of the

[23] *Re Senate Reform*, [2014] 1 S.C.R. 704, 2014 SCC 32, para. 107.

[24] See § 4:3 note 7, above.

Senate and House of Commons and of the legislative assembly of each province to which the amendment applies.

There are provisions of the Constitution of Canada[1] which apply to one or more, but not all, provinces. For example, s. 93 of the Constitution Act, 1867 (education) applies to only six of the ten provinces; a similar but separate provision in each of the Manitoba Act, Alberta Act, Saskatchewan Act and Newfoundland Act (all included in the Constitution of Canada) applies to each of the other four provinces.[2] Section 94 of the Constitution Act, 1867 (uniformity of laws) does not apply to Quebec. Section 97 of the Constitution Act, 1867 (qualifications of judges) does not apply to Quebec; s. 98 (on the same topic) applies only to Quebec. A number of language provisions apply only to Quebec or Manitoba or New Brunswick.[3] For the amendment of provisions of this kind, s. 43 requires authorizing resolutions of only those provinces to which the amendment applies (as well as the Senate and House of Commons).[4] The obvious intent is to make such provisions somewhat easier to amend, but the ease of amendment will depend upon the number of provinces involved. In the case of s. 97 of the Constitution Act, 1867, which is applicable to all provinces except Quebec, s. 43 would seem to require authorizing resolutions from all nine of the provinces to which it applies— a procedure that is more onerous than the seven-fifty requirement of s. 38.

Newfoundland's substitute for s. 93 of the Constitution Act, 1867 (education) is Term 17 of the Terms of Union of Newfoundland with Canada, a provision that is part of (in the form of a schedule) the Newfoundland Act, which is part of the Constitution of Canada. Term 17 in its original form granted power over education to the Legislature of the province, but also guaranteed the public funding of denominational schools. Term 17 has been amended no less than three times, in each case employing s. 43's bilateral procedure of resolutions by the Legislative Assembly of Newfoundland and both Houses of the Parliament of Canada. The last of the three amendments removed the guarantees of public funding of denominational schools. This radical change had been approved by a referendum in the province in which 72 per cent of the

[Section 4:17]

[1]See § 4:6, "Constitution of Canada".

[2]To be more precise, s. 93 continues to apply to Alberta and Saskatchewan, but with major change. By an amendment of 1997 (made under s. 43, upheld in *Potter v. Que.*, [2001] R.J.Q. 2823 (Que. C.A.)), this is now true of Quebec as well. Section 93 does not apply at all to Manitoba and Newfoundland. Newfoundland's substitute provision has been amended (under s. 43) three times (the third time attracting an unsuccessful court challenge, *Hogan v. Newfoundland* (2000), 183 D.L.R. (4th) 225 (Nfld. C.A.).)

[3]Section 133 of the Constitution Act, 1867 applies only to Quebec (and the federal government), and s. 23 of the Manitoba Act applies only to Manitoba, and ss. 16(2), 17(2), 18(2), 19(2) and 20(2) of the Constitution Act, 1982 apply only to New Brunswick.

[4]The procedure has been used seven times since 1982: see ch. 1, Sources, under heading § 1:4 "Constitution of Canada".

population voted in favour. In *Hogan v. Newfoundland* (2000),[5] the validity of the amendment was challenged in court by supporters of Roman Catholic denominational schools. They argued that s. 43 could not be the correct procedure for the amendment, because the constitutional rights of a minority should not be able to be overridden by the majority. The Newfoundland Court of Appeal rejected the argument, holding that the amending procedure of s. 43 was the applicable one. Term 17 was a provision that applied only to Newfoundland, and it was therefore amendable under s. 43.[6] The "inescapable fact" was that the amending procedure of the Constitution "entrusts minority rights to the majority".[7] The process of amendment was, however, more difficult than the enactment of a simple statute. In the case of constitutional provisions that could be amended under s. 43, the increased difficulty consisted in the requirement that the resolution had to pass at the federal as well as the provincial level. It was the more elaborate procedure that constituted the protection for minority rights, and no additional step, such as the consent of those particularly affected, was required.[8]

As *Hogan* decides, s. 43 expressly applies to a provision of the Constitution of Canada which applies to only one province.[9] The Constitution Act, 1867, which, it will be recalled, created Ontario and Quebec out of the old united province of Canada, contains a set of provisions (ss. 69 to 87) which are essentially the constitutions of those two provinces. Section 88 arguably incorporates by reference the pre-confederation constitutions of Nova Scotia and New Brunswick. The Constitution Act, 1867 is part of the Constitution of Canada, and therefore these provisions are part of the Constitution of Canada. As well, the instruments admitting or creating the remaining six provinces are part of the Constitution of Canada. Section 43, read by itself, seems to insist that any part of the constitution of a province that is to be found within the Constitution of Canada may be amended only by the procedure stipulated by s. 43; that procedure includes resolutions by the Senate and House of Commons. This is a strange result, because there is no good reason for any involvement by the federal Parliament in a province's decision to make some change in those provisions governing its Legislature, its ex-

[5]*Hogan v. Newfoundland* (2000), 183 D.L.R. (4th) 225 (Nfld. C.A.).

[6]The position would have been different if the amendment had altered a provision of the Charter of Rights; in that case, s. 38 would have been the applicable procedure. Even in that case, however, there is no provision specifically requiring the consent or even consultation of the minority affected. Moreover, as the Court pointed out in *Hogan v. Newfoundland* (2000), 183 D.L.R. (4th) 225 (Nfld. C.A.), para. 75, if s. 38 were the appropriate procedure (which was one of the submissions of the plaintiffs), then the Terms of Union could have been amended without the consent of even Newfoundland!

[7]*Hogan v. Newfoundland* (2000), 183 D.L.R. (4th) 225 (Nfld. C.A.), para. 125.

[8]Accord, *Potter v. Que.*, [2001] R.J.Q. 2823 (Que. C.A.) (upholding amendment under s. 43 to remove protection of denominational school rights in Quebec).

[9]E.g., *Re Senate Reform*, [2014] 1 S.C.R. 704, 2014 SCC 32, para. 93 (s. 23(6) of the Constitution Act, 1867, which stipulates the qualifications of senators from Quebec, could be repealed under s. 43 by resolutions of the two federal Houses and the legislative assembly of Quebec).

ecutive or its courts, simply because the provisions happen to be within an instrument which is part of the Constitution of Canada.

Before the coming into force of the Constitution Act, 1982, a province was free to amend any part of the constitution of the province, including those parts provided for in the Constitution Act, 1867, without any federal involvement. Section 92(1) of the Constitution Act, 1867 authorized the Legislature of each province, by ordinary legislation, to amend the constitution of the province, "notwithstanding anything in this Act [the Constitution Act, 1867]". Section 92(1) has been repealed by the Constitution Act, 1982, and replaced by s. 45 of the Constitution Act, 1982, but s. 45 does not expressly authorize amendments to the Constitution of Canada. Section 43, on the other hand, does expressly authorize amendments to provisions of the Constitution of Canada that apply to only one province. One way of reconciling s. 43 with s. 45 would be to read s. 43 as applying to an amendment of a provision applying to a single province when that provision is contained in one of the instruments which comprise the Constitution of Canada, and to read s. 45 as applying to an amendment of the "constitution of the province" only when the provision to be amended is not to be found in any of the instruments comprising the Constitution of Canada. Nevertheless, I argue in the commentary to s. 45 (below) that s. 45 should be read as extending to the amendment of those provisions of the Constitution of Canada which can also be characterized as part of the constitution of the province. If this is correct, then s. 43 would be necessary to amend provisions of the Constitution of Canada which apply to only one province only if the provisions could not be characterized as part of the constitution of the province.[10]

VI. FEDERAL PARLIAMENT ALONE

§ 4:18 Federal Parliament alone (s. 44)

Section 44 of the Constitution Act, 1982 provides as follows:

> **44.** Subject to sections 41 and 42, Parliament may exclusively make laws amending the Constitution of Canada in relation to the executive government of Canada or the Senate and House of Commons.

Section 44 authorizes the federal Parliament, by ordinary legislation, to amend those parts of the Constitution of Canada[1] which relate to "the executive government of Canada or the Senate and House of Commons". Section 44 is subject to ss. 41 and 42 and those two sections entrench some aspects of the executive government of Canada, the Senate and House of Commons. The matters listed in s. 41 (which include the office

[10]For example, even before 1982 it was held that language rights applicable to a single province are not part of the constitution of the province, because that would render them vulnerable to ordinary legislative change: *A.G. Que. v. Blaikie*, [1979] 2 S.C.R. 1016; *A.G. Man. v. Forest*, [1979] 2 S.C.R. 1032. Now, of course, s. 43(b) makes that explicit.

[Section 4:18]

[1]See § 4:6, "Constitution of Canada".

of the Queen and the Governor General and the minimum provincial representation in the House of Commons) can be amended only with the unanimous consent of the provinces. The matters listed in s. 42 (which include some of the rules regarding the Senate and House of Commons) can be amended only by the general (seven-fifty) amending procedure of s. 38(1), which requires the consent of two-thirds of the provinces having at least 50 per cent of the population.[2]

Section 44 replaced s. 91(1) of the Constitution Act, 1867.[3] Section 91(1) was repealed by the Constitution Act, 1982. Section 91(1) conferred on the federal Parliament the power to amend the "Constitution of Canada". That phrase was then undefined;[4] it was however given a very narrow meaning by the Supreme Court of Canada,[5] and it was subject to important exceptions which were expressed in s. 91(1) itself. The result is that the scope of s. 44 is similar to the scope of the old s. 91(1).[6] The procedure has been successfully used three times since 1982.[7]

The scope of the power to amend the Constitution of Canada in relation to "the Senate" that is conferred on Parliament by s. 44 was the subject of the *Senate Reform Reference* (2014).[8] In the *Reference*, the federal government asked the Supreme Court (among other things) whether Parliament had the power to impose "term limits" on the tenure of senators. This proposal would require an amendment of s. 29 of the Constitution Act, 1867, under which a senator (no matter how young on appointment) holds his or her place until age 75. Parliament's power under s. 44 is expressly subject to ss. 41 and 42. Section 41 (the unanimity procedure) has five paragraphs, none of which refers to amendments

---

[2]With respect to proportionate representation in the House of Commons, see *Campbell v. Canada* (1988), 49 D.L.R. (4th) 321 (B.C.C.A.).

[3]The text of s. 91(1) was as follows:

> The amendment from time to time of the Constitution of Canada, except as regards matters coming within the classes of subjects by this Act assigned exclusively to the Legislatures of the provinces, or as regards rights or privileges by this or any other Constitutional Act granted or secured to the Legislature or the Government of a province, or to any class of persons with respect to schools or as regards the use of the English or the French language or as regards the requirements that there shall be a session of the Parliament of Canada at least once each year, and that no House of Commons shall continue for more than five years from the day of the return of the Writs for choosing the House: provided, however, that a House of Commons may in time of real or apprehended war, invasion or insurrection be continued by the Parliament of Canada if such continuation is not opposed by the votes of more than one-third of the members of such House.

[4]It was defined for the first time in s. 52(2) of the Constitution Act, 1982.

[5]*Re Upper House*, [1980] 1 S.C.R. 54 (holding that s. 91(1) did not authorize the abolition or alteration of the Senate). For criticism of the decision, and analysis of the history and scope of s. 91(1) generally, see P.W. Hogg, Comment (1980) 58 Can. Bar Rev. 631.

[6]In order to make the comparison, s. 44 must be read with s. 4 (restricting the extension of the House of Commons) and s. 41(c) (requiring unanimity for amendments relating to language).

[7]See ch. 1, Sources, under heading § 1:4, "Constitution of Canada".

[8]*Re Senate Reform*, [2014] 1 S.C.R. 704, 2014 SCC 32. The opinion of the unanimous Court was attributed to "the Court".

in relation to the Senate.[9] Section 42 (the seven-fifty procedure) has six paragraphs, two of which refer to amendments in relation to the Senate: s. 42(1)(b) refers to "the powers of the Senate and the method of selecting Senators";[10] s. 42(1)(c) refers to "the number of members by which a province is entitled to be represented in the Senate and the residence qualifications of Senators". These are the only express exceptions to Parliament's s. 44 power over the Senate; the exceptions cover important aspects of the Senate; they have obviously been carefully drafted in some detail; and they do not include term limits. The ineluctable conclusion surely is that Parliament has the power to impose term limits on senators, and it was so argued by the Attorney General of Canada. The Court condemned this argument as "a narrow textual approach to this issue".[11] The Court held that, in addition to the matters *expressly* excluded from s. 44, any other "changes that engage the interests of the provinces"[12] are *impliedly* excluded from s. 44. Any reduction in the independence of the Senate, the Court held, would engage the interests of the provinces. Any kind of fixed term for senators, even if non-renewable and even if lengthy, would reduce the independence of the Senate. Fixed terms "imply a finite time in office and necessarily offer a lesser degree of protection from the potential consequences of freely speaking one's mind on the legislative proposals of the House of Commons". Therefore, Parliament had no power to impose term limits on senators.

What was left of Parliament's power, expressly conferred by 44, to amend the Constitution of Canada in relation to the Senate? The Court held that, after excluding measures that engage the interests of the provinces, what was left was "measures that maintain or change the

[9]The Court held, however, in response to one of the questions put to it, that the unanimity procedure would apply to a proposal to abolish the Senate on the basis that the abolition of the Senate would constitute an amendment to Part V (the amending procedures), which is in the unanimity list as s. 41(e): *Re Senate Reform*, [2014] 1 S.C.R. 704, 2014 SCC 32, para. 110.

[10]The Court held, in response to another of the questions put to it, that a proposal for "consultative elections" of nominees for appointment to the Senate would be an amendment in relation to "the method of selecting Senators", which was caught by s. 42(1)(b) and therefore withdrawn from Parliament's power under s. 44. The Court added that consultative elections would in any case be a constitutional change that engaged provincial interests, and (like term limits, discussed in following text) would be invalid on that ground as well: *Re Senate Reform*, [2014] 1 S.C.R. 704, 2014 SCC 32, para. 67.

[11]*Re Senate Reform*, [2014] 1 S.C.R. 704, 2014 SCC 32, para. 73. See also the earlier comment by the Court (para. 64) that: "The words employed in Part V are guides to identifying the aspects of our system of government that form part of the protected content of the Constitution." This suggests a unique interpretative approach to Part V. The words employed in other parts of the Constitution, for example, to define the federal division of legislative powers or the Charter of Rights, have always been assumed to be controlling; they have never been described as mere "guides".

[12]This phrase, which recurs throughout the opinion, is never defined. A longer form of the phrase is "a change that engages the interests of the provinces *as stakeholders in Canada's constitutional design*": *Re Senate Reform*, [2014] 1 S.C.R. 704, 2014 SCC 32, para. 82 (emphasis added); the emphasized words can be interpreted as covering almost any change in the confederation arrangements, whether or not the change has any actual effect on the provinces.

Senate without altering its fundamental nature and role".[13] The Court's decision, that the introduction of a term limit that was non-renewable and lengthy would engage the interests of the provinces and would alter the Senate's fundamental nature and role, makes clear that the scope of s. 44 is now narrow indeed. However, in response to another question posed on the *Reference*, the Court held that s. 44 did extend to the repeal of the property qualifications of senators: s. 23 of the Constitution Act, 1867 requires that senators must own real property worth $4,000 in the province from which they are appointed and have a personal net worth (all assets minus all liabilities) of at least $4,000.[14] The repeal of these requirements would not "engage the interests of the provinces" and would not "affect the fundamental nature and role of the Senate".[15] Parliament had the power to enact that amendment under s. 44.

VII. PROVINCIAL LEGISLATURE ALONE

§ 4:19 Provincial Legislature alone (s. 45)

Section 45 of the Constitution Act, 1982 provides as follows:

> **45.** Subject to section 41, the legislature of each province may exclusively make laws amending the constitution of the province.

Section 45 authorizes each provincial Legislature, by ordinary legislation, to amend the "constitution of the province". Section 45 is subject to s. 41, which by paragraph (a) requires that an amendment relating to the office of the Lieutenant Governor be made only with the unanimous consent of all the provinces. Section 45 differs from ss. 38, 41, 42, 43 and 44 in that s. 45 makes no reference to the "Constitution of Canada", a term which is defined in s. 52(2) of the Constitution Act, 1982. Instead, s. 45 refers to the "constitution of the province", which is not defined anywhere in the Constitution Act, 1982.

Section 45 replaced s. 92(1) of the Constitution Act, 1867.[1] Section 92(1) was repealed by the Constitution Act, 1982. Section 92(1) conferred on each provincial Legislature the power to amend the "constitution of

---

[13] *Re Senate Reform*, [2014] 1 S.C.R. 704, 2014 SCC 32, para. 75.

[14] With respect to the real property qualification, there was a complication in the case of Quebec, where senators are appointed from 24 "electoral divisions", and must either hold real property in the electoral divisions from which they are appointed or reside in those divisions: Constitution Act, 1867, ss. 22, 23(6). Because of this "special arrangement" for Quebec, the repeal of the real property qualification of senators from Quebec would require a resolution of the Legislative assembly of Quebec under s. 43 of the Constitution Act, 1982: *Re Senate Reform*, [2014] 1 S.C.R. 704, 2014 SCC 32, para. 93. In the case of all other senators, the repeal of the real property qualification could be enacted by Parliament alone under s. 44: *Re Senate Reform*, [2014] 1 S.C.R. 704, 2014 SCC 32, para. 94.

[15] *Re Senate Reform*, [2014] 1 S.C.R. 704, 2014 SCC 32, paras. 88–90, 94.

[Section 4:19]

[1] The text of s. 92(1) was as follows:

> The amendment from time to time, notwithstanding anything in this Act, of the constitution of the province, except as regards the office of Lieutenant Governor.

the province". Subject to the doubt expressed in the next paragraph, the case-law under s. 92(1)[2] should continue to be relevant under s. 45.[3] Interpreting s. 92(1), the Supreme Court of Canada has said that a law is an amendment to the constitution of the province if "it bears on the operation of an organ of government of the province".[4] This definition embraces laws respecting the abolition of a province's Legislative Council (upper house),[5] the public service of the province,[6] the powers and privileges of the legislative assembly,[7] and the term of the legislative assembly.[8] The amending power of the province also extends to s. 53 of the Constitution Act, 1867, which requires that taxes be levied only by the Legislature.[9] Some laws are expressly or impliedly withdrawn from the amending power of the province. The office of Lieutenant Governor was expressly exempted from 92(1),[10] and is also expressly exempted from s. 45.[11] The constitutional guarantees of language rights were held to be implicitly withdrawn from the provincial amending power in s. 92(1),[12] and are now explicitly withdrawn from s. 45.[13] It has been suggested as well that s. 92(1) would not authorize "a profound constitutional upheaval by the introduction of political institutions foreign to and incompatible with the Canadian system".[14]

The scope of s. 45 is somewhat obscured by s. 43 (the some-but-not-all-

---

[2]See Forsey, Freedom and Order (1974), 205–207, 227; McConnell, Commentary on the B.N.A. Act (1977), 245–248; M.A. Banks, "Defining 'Constitution of the province' " (1986) 31 McGill L.J. 466; N. Wiseman, "Clarifying Provincial Constitutions" (1996) 6 Nat. J. Con. Law 269; W.J. Newman, "Defining the 'Constitution of Canada' since 1982" (2003) 22 Supreme Court L.R. (2d) 423, 437–457.

[3]*OPSEU v. Ont.*, [1987] 2 S.C.R, 2, 33, per Beetz J. ("It may well be thought that the coming into force of the amending procedure has not altered the power of the province to amend its own constitution but I refrain from expressing any view on the matter").

[4]*OPSEU v. Ont.*, [1987] 2 S.C.R, 2, 40.

[5]W.J. Newman, "Defining the 'Constitution of Canada' since 1982" (2003) 22 Supreme Court L.R. (2d) 423, 442–443.

[6]W.J. Newman, "Defining the 'Constitution of Canada' since 1982" (2003) 22 Supreme Court L.R. (2d) 423, 442-443.

[7]*Fielding v. Thomas*, [1896] A.C. 600.

[8]*R. ex rel. Tolfree v. Clark*, [1943] O.R. 501 (C.A.), but note that since 1982 there has been an express limitation to five years in s. 3 of the Charter of Rights.

[9]*Re Eurig Estate*, [1998] 2 S.C.R. 565, para. 35.

[10]This exception defeated the regime of direct democracy in *Re Initiative and Referendum Act*, [1919] A.C. 935, although it was successfully circumvented in *R. v. Nat Bell Liquors*, [1922] 2 A.C. 128. These cases are discussed in ch. 14, Delegation, § 14:8, "Office of Lieutenant Governor or Governor General", and § 14:9, "Requirement of a Legislature or Parliament".

[11]Section 45 is expressly subject to s. 41, which requires the unanimity procedure for amendments to the Constitution of Canada in relation to "the office of . . . the Lieutenant Governor of a province".

[12]See § 4:17 note 10 above.

[13]Sections 41(c), 43(b).

[14]*OPSEU v. Ont.*, [1987] 2 S.C.R. 2, 47, citing *Re Initiative and Referendum Act*, [1919] A.C. 935.

provinces procedure). As noted in the commentary to s. 43,[15] s. 43 explicitly authorizes an amendment to any provision of the Constitution of Canada which applies to a single province, and most of the important rules of each province's constitution are contained in instruments which form part of the Constitution of Canada.[16] But s. 43 requires the concurrence of the Senate and House of Commons for its amendments. The question is whether s. 45, which does not require the concurrence of the Senate and House of Commons, can be employed to amend those provisions of a province's constitution that are contained in instruments forming part of the Constitution of Canada. A negative answer to this question would mean that s. 45 was for no good reason much narrower than the old provincial amending power under s. 92(1), which extended to provisions of those instruments which are now called the "Constitution of Canada".[17] Indeed, a negative answer would leave s. 45 with very little work to do. The affirmative answer seems the more plausible one, leaving s. 43 to apply to only those provisions of the Constitution of Canada which, although applicable to only one province, do not come within the phrase the "constitution of the province".[18]

VIII. FUTURE AMENDMENTS

§ 4:20 Forces of change

The movement for constitutional reform which led to the constitutional amendments of 1982, and which will lead to continuing efforts to adopt other amendments to the Constitution, is powered by a number of forces.[1]

---

[15] § 4:17, "Some-but-not-all-provinces procedure (s. 43)".

[16] The origins and sources of the constitutions of the provinces are described in ch. 2, Reception.

[17] For example, Quebec has amended s. 71 of the Constitution Act, 1867 by abolishing its upper house: Legislative Council of Quebec Act, S.Q. 1968, c. 9; and Ontario and Quebec have amended s. 85 of the Constitution Act, 1867 by extending the term of each legislative assembly from four years to five: Legislative Assembly Act, R.S.O. 1980, c. 235, s. 3; Legislature Act, R.S.Q. 1977, c. L-1, s. 31. The Ontario extension of term was upheld in *R. ex rel. Tolfree v. Clark*, [1943] O.R. 501 (C.A.).

[18] Accord, *Re Eurig Estate*, [1998] 2 S.C.R. 565, paras. 35–36 per Major J. for majority (province has power under s. 45 to amend s. 53 of the Constitution Act, 1867, although it must do so expressly); Binnie J. concurring and Bastarache J. dissenting did not need to address point. In *Chagnon v. Syndicat de la fonction publique et parapublique du Québec*, [2018] 2 S.C.R. 687, Rowe J. said in a concurring opinion that "s. 45 of the Constitution Act, 1982, as did s. 92(1) before it, includes the power to enact laws in relation to the privileges of a provincial legislature" (para. 62). Contra, *New Brunswick Broadcasting Co. v. Nova Scotia*, [1993] 1 S.C.R. 319, 352 per Lamer C.J. obiter, 396 per Sopinka J. obiter, assuming that if parliamentary privilege were part of the "Constitution of Canada", as held by the majority, the provincial Legislature would have lost the power to amend it.

[Section 4:20]

[1] This section of the chapter draws to some extent on my article, "The Theory and Practice of Constitutional Reform" (1981) 3 Alta. L. Rev. 335; see also K.M. Lysyk, "Reshaping Canadian Federalism" (1979) 13 U.B.C. L. Rev. 1; P.C. Weiler, "Confederation Discontents and Constitutional Reform" (1979) 29 U. Toronto L.J. 253; The Task

First and foremost is French-Canadian nationalism.[2] French Canadians are a minority in the nation as a whole, but a majority in the province of Quebec. Their distinctive language and culture, nurtured by the memory of the conquest by the English and the constant danger of assimilation, has made them anxious to be masters in their own house. This inevitably leads to demands for greater power in the provincial Legislature in Quebec City—the Legislature that is controlled by a French-Canadian majority.

The extreme form of French-Canadian nationalism would be satisfied only by a separate nation in the territory of Quebec. On May 20, 1980, Quebecers voted in a referendum on a proposal to give to the government of Quebec a mandate to negotiate a sovereignty-association agreement with Canada. This proposal, which of course was far from a proposal of outright separation, was defeated by a majority of 59.5 per cent to 40.5 per cent.[3] However, the promises of constitutional change which were made by the "no" forces during the referendum campaign created a moral obligation to take steps to better accommodate Quebec's aspirations. Unfortunately, the constitutional amendments of 1982, which were the culmination of the process which followed the referendum, did not accomplish that goal; indeed, they reduced the powers of Quebec's National Assembly; and Quebec was the only province that did not agree to the amendments. Even more unfortunately, the Meech Lake Accord of 1987, which was a set of amendments that would have reconciled Quebec to the Constitution of Canada, fell two provinces short of the unanimous ratification that was required for its passage.[4] The Charlottetown Accord of 1992 was another set of amendments with the same purpose; this Accord was agreed to by all first ministers, but was rejected in a national referendum, and never proceeded to legislative ratification.[5] The failure to accommodate the concerns of Quebecers in the Constitution of Canada led to a second Quebec referendum, on October 30, 1995.[6] That referendum proposed the negotiation of a "new economic and political partnership" between Canada and a sovereign Quebec, but it went beyond the 1980 referendum in authorizing the Quebec National Assembly to make a unilateral declaration of independence if negotiations should prove fruitless. The referendum was defeated again, but this time the vote was very close: 50.6 per cent for "no" and 49.4 per cent for "yes". After the close result, the Parti

---

Force on Canadian Unity, *A Future Together* (1979).

[2]For the recent history of Quebec within confederation, see McWhinney, Quebec and the Constitution 1960–1978 (1979); McWhinney, Canada and the Constitution 1979–1982 (1982); K. McRoberts, Quebec: Social Change and Political Crisis (Oxford, 3rd ed., 1988); Tremblay, La Reforme de la Constitution au Canada (1995).

[3]See ch. 5, Federalism, under heading §§ 5:24 to 5:26, "Secession".

[4]See § 4:3, "The failure to accommodate Quebec".

[5]See § 4:3, "The failure to accommodate Quebec".

[6]The Quebec sovereignty referendum of October 30, 1995 is discussed in more detail in § 4:3, "The failure to accommodate Quebec", and in ch. 5, Federalism, under heading §§ 5:24 to 5:26, "Secession".

Quebecois government announced that it would try again, but the government did not call another referendum before losing power in the provincial election of 2003. However, it is obvious that there is a need to better accommodate the concerns of Quebecers, and this must be one of the priorities of any future constitutional change.

A second force of constitutional change is western regionalism. This is based, not on a distinctive language or culture, but on the distinctive economic base of the four western provinces. Their economies depend upon the primary production of grain, wood, metals, oil, gas and other minerals. Because the bulk of Canada's population is concentrated in Ontario and Quebec, federal policies have tended to favour the manufacturing industries and consumers of central Canada.[7] This tendency has been reflected in the tariffs that protect domestic manufacturing, in transportation policies, and for a time in federal control of the price of oil and gas. Two responses by western Canadians have inevitably been invoked. One is to seek to reduce the power of the federal government, which they cannot control, and to enhance the powers of the provincial governments, which they can control. The other response is to seek to make central institutions, that is, the institutions of the federal government, more responsive to regional interests. The latter idea is discussed later in this chapter. The 1982 amendments conferred some increase in provincial powers over natural resources,[8] but did nothing about central institutions.

A third force of constitutional change is the demand by the Indigenous peoples of Canada—the First Nations, Inuit and Métis peoples—for entrenchment of their traditional rights. The Indigenous peoples were successful in securing several provisions in the Constitution Act, 1982, including a guarantee of "existing aboriginal and treaty rights" (s. 35) and a commitment to further constitutional discussions (s. 37).[9] The settlement of their land claims is, of course, the overwhelming remaining problem, but they also seek entrenchment of an explicit right to self-government and a right to participate in the process of constitutional amendment, at least where aboriginal rights could be affected.[10] The Charlottetown Accord of 1992[11] would have recognized that Indigenous peoples have an inherent right of self-government within Canada, and would have required Indigenous consent to future amendments of constitutional provisions referring to Indigenous peoples. The defeat of

---

[7]There is a school of thought which holds that the west has been disadvantaged by free market forces rather than by federal policies: Smiley, Canada in Question (3rd. ed., 1980), 180 briefly summarizes the arguments. I am agnostic on this issue, but I believe that the text accurately reports widespread western perceptions, which are all that are relevant for present purposes.

[8]Constitution Act, 1867, s. 92A was added in 1982.

[9]These provisions were amended again in 1983: Constitution Amendment Proclamation, 1983, R.S.C. 1985, Appendix II, No. 46.

[10]For analysis of the constitutional provisions respecting aboriginal peoples, see ch. 28, Aboriginal Peoples.

[11]See § 4:3 note 11, above.

the Accord in a national referendum blocked these proposals. It is obvious that there is also a need to better accommodate the concerns of Indigenous peoples, and this must be another priority of any future constitutional change.

A fourth force of constitutional change has been Canadian nationalism, the constitutional dimension of which was addressed to the removal of the vestiges of the colonial relationship between Canada and the United Kingdom, the former imperial power. At the minimum, this required the "patriation" of the Constitution,[12] and (so that the constitution can be amended without recourse to the United Kingdom) the adoption of domestic amending procedures. The 1982 amendments accomplished these changes, although, as noted earlier, there may have to be an alteration in the amending procedures to meet Quebec's objections to them.[13] The patriation process did not touch the position of the Queen, who continues to be Canada's formal head of state, or Canada's membership of the Commonwealth of Nations (successor to the British Empire and later the British Commonwealth).

A fifth force of constitutional change is the civil libertarian impulse to entrench a Charter of Rights in the Constitution. This was accomplished by the 1982 amendments, although an override provision had to be inserted to secure the agreement of seven provincial governments. Quebec has never agreed to the Charter of Rights, although of course the Charter is legally binding on the province. In the Meech Lake Accord of 1987,[14] Quebec did not insist upon changes to the Charter, but only that the Constitution include a declaration that Quebec was a "distinct society". The legal effect of this declaration was not entirely clear, but it would probably have helped Quebec to sustain against Charter challenge those laws that were designed to protect the French language and culture. The "distinct society" clause turned out to be the most controversial element of the Accord. The Accord did not receive the requisite level of provincial legislative approval and it lapsed in 1990. In the Charlottetown Accord of 1992,[15] the same issue was revived, and another "distinct society" clause was proposed for inclusion in the Constitution. The Charlottetown Accord was rejected in a national referendum held in 1992, which caused it to lapse.[16]

Sixthly, there will be a continuing need for amendments, not neces-

---

[12]See ch. 3, Independence, under heading § 3:5, "Patriation of the Constitution".

[13]The Meech Lake Accord of 1987, § 4:3 note 7, above, which has now lapsed, included an agreement to increase the number of matters that were subject to the unanimity procedure, and to extend the right to compensation for opting out of amendments.

[14]See § 4:3 note 7, above.

[15]See § 4:3 note 11, above.

[16]After the 1995 referendum on Quebec sovereignty was defeated by a very narrow margin, the House of Commons passed a resolution which declared that it recognized Quebec as a distinct society, and would be "guided by this reality": *House of Commons Debates* (29 November 1995) at 16971 (text of resolution); *House of Commons Debates* (11 December 1995) at 17536 (passage of resolution). This resolution did not meet Quebec's previous requests, which were for *constitutional* recognition of its distinctness. Eleven years later, under the Conservative government of Prime Minister Harper, the

sarily sponsored by interest-groups falling within any of the above five categories, but which are perceived as necessary to repair gaps in the existing constitutional provisions, to alter judicial interpretations that are unacceptable, or to give effect to values that were not recognized at the time of confederation. Examples from the past of this miscellaneous category are the amendments to confer powers over unemployment insurance[17] and old age pensions[18] on the federal Parliament, and the amendment imposing a retiring age on superior-court judges.[19]

§ 4:21 Division of powers

As noted earlier, the most obvious way to redress the grievances of French Canadians and western Canadians is to reduce the powers of the federal Parliament, which they do not control, and to increase the powers of the provincial Legislatures, which they do control.

The 1982 amendments made only one change in the division of powers between the two levels of government,[1] and that was an increase in the provincial power over natural resources.[2] This went some distance to meet western objections to two decisions of the Supreme Court of Canada which had narrowly defined the provincial powers to tax natural resources and to control the production and price of natural resources.[3]

Other changes in the division of powers which have been actively considered in recent years include: transferring to the provinces some aspects of control over communications, especially cable television; transferring marriage and divorce to the provinces; transferring fisheries and offshore resources to the provinces; transferring the residuary power to the provinces, and narrowly defining the federal power over the peace, order, and good government of Canada; limiting or abolishing the federal declaratory power; and limiting the federal spending power.

House of Commons went further, passing a resolution by a vote of 265 to 16 "That this House recognize that the Québécois form a nation within a united Canada": *House of Commons Debates* (22 November 2006) at 5197 (text of resolution); *House of Commons Debates* (27 November 2006) at 5412 (passage of resolution). The 1995 referendum and these two resolutions are discussed in § 4:3, "The failure to accommodate Quebec".

[17]Section 91(2A), conferring power over unemployment insurance, was added by the Constitution Act, 1940 (U.K.), R.S.C. 1985, Appendix II, No. 28. It abrogated the decision in *A.G. Can. v. A.G. Ont.* (Unemployment Insurance) [1937] A.C. 355.

[18]Section 94A, conferring power over old age pensions, was added by the British North America Act, 1951 (U.K.),R.S.C. 1985,Appendix II, No. 35, and was expanded to include supplementary benefits by the Constitution Act, 1964 (U.K.), R.S.C. 1985, Appendix II, No. 38.

[19]Section 99(2), imposing a retirement age for superior-court judges, was added by the Constitution Act, 1960 (U.K.), R.S.C. 1985, Appendix II, No. 37.

[Section 4:21]

[1]The Charter of Rights does not fall into this category, since it imposed limitations on the legislative powers of both levels of government and did not augment the powers of either level of government.

[2]This is now Constitution Act, 1867, s. 92A.

[3]*Can. Industrial Gas and Oil v. Sask.*, [1978] 2 S.C.R. 545; *Central Can. Potash Co. v. Sask.*, [1979] 1 S.C.R. 42.

On the federal side of the ledger, a case can be made for the enlargement of certain federal powers to facilitate effective national economic policies in areas where federal power is lacking or unclear or available only in an emergency, for example, foreign ownership, securities regulation and wage and price controls.[4] None of these changes was seriously proposed as part of the 1982 constitutional settlement.

The experience of federal-provincial negotiations shows that it is very difficult to secure agreement on changes in the division of powers. The overall thrust of most reform proposals has been in the direction of decentralization of powers. But the federal government naturally resists decentralization; and it is true that the Canadian provinces are already more powerful, in both legislative and fiscal terms, than are the American or Australian states in relation to their central governments. Moreover, the provinces differ so greatly in their size and wealth and aspirations that they do not agree on what new responsibilities they should assume and what they should give up.[5] The smaller provinces, in particular, cannot easily make common cause with the larger provinces: the smaller provinces are heavily dependent on federal funding to maintain the standard of living of their residents, are also dependent upon federal policies for protection from the unintended adverse effects of the policies of other provinces (for example, energy prices), and they lack the capacity to substantially increase their own responsibilities. It is only realistic to acknowledge that a substantial alteration in the division of powers between the federal and provincial governments is neither practicable nor desirable.

§ 4:22 Central institutions

A different approach to constitutional change concentrates on reforming the institutions of the federal government so that regional attitudes and interests are more effectively represented within those institutions. The theory is that the more effectively these attitudes and interests are represented within the central institutions the wider is the range of powers that may be conferred on central institutions. If French Canadians and western Canadians could be confident that their interests would be fairly accommodated in the development of federal policies, then, so the argument goes, they would have less reason to demand that

---

[4]Arguments for reform in a wide range of areas are to be found in the studies collected in Beck and Bernier (eds.), Canada and the New Constitution (1983), vols. 1 and 2.

[5]"Special status", under which one or more provinces could have different powers than the others, is a possible answer to the differing aspirations and capacities of the provinces. However, special status raises difficult questions about the role in the central institutions, especially the federal Parliament, of the representatives of the province or provinces with special status. It seems wrong that they should participate in decisions which in their province are a provincial responsibility. Yet their participation may be necessary to retain a government majority. Opting out, under the present amendment procedures, will lead to special status for the opted-out province (or provinces) and to the same difficulty regarding the role of its representatives in central institutions: see § 4:11, "Opting out"; § 5:4, "Special status".

powers be transferred from federal institutions to provincial institutions. Thus, the reform of central institutions becomes an alternative to decentralization of powers as a means of redressing regional grievances. This approach to constitutional change has been dubbed "intrastate federalism" by political scientists in contrast to "interstate federalism", which involves the decentralization of powers.[1]

The most popular application of intrastate federalism by constitutional reformers has been to the Senate, the upper house of the federal Parliament. One idea, modelled on West Germany's upper house (the Bundesrat), is to convert the Senate into a "House of the Provinces" with members appointed by provincial governments. This would then become the means by which provincial governments could exercise a direct influence over federal policies. Another idea is to convert the Senate into an elected house, with equal representation from each province. The "Triple-E" Senate (equal, elected, effective) would operate, so it is claimed, to defend provincial interests in the formation of federal legislative policy. These ideas are discussed later in this book.[2]

The second most popular application of intrastate federalism has been to the Supreme Court of Canada, where attention has been directed to the introduction of a provincial role in the appointment of judges; to rules ensuring that the judges are drawn from all regions of the country; and to the restructuring of the Court to provide a special constitutional Court, or panel of the present Court, to decide constitutional cases. These ideas are discussed later in this book.[3]

Intrastate federalism does not stop with the Senate and Supreme Court of Canada. Smiley's study of the topic also addresses the House of Commons, the cabinet, the federal civil service, federal regulatory agencies and the political parties.[4] These institutions must also respond to the French, multicultural, aboriginal and regional interests. For the most part, however, changes in these institutions do not call for constitutional amendments.

§ 4:23 Criticism of amending procedures

This chapter should not be permitted to end on a note that suggests flexibility and responsiveness on the part of the new amending procedures. It will be difficult to secure any amendment to the Constitution, because of the high level of agreement required by the general

---

[Section 4:22]

[1]Smiley, "Central Institutions" in Beck and Bernier (eds.), Canada and the New Constitution (1983), vol. 1, 19.

[2]See ch. 9, Responsible Government, under heading § 9:10, "The Senate".

[3]Chapter 8, Supreme Court of Canada, under heading § 8:14, "Reform of Court".

[4]Smiley, "Central Institutions" in Beck and Bernier (eds.), Canada and the New Constitution (1983), vol. 1, 19.

amending procedure.[1] Eight governments out of eleven is a group which is hard to assemble on anything, and, where opting out is available, there will be a strong impulse to proceed only when the assent of all governments is assured, since the "checkerboard constitution" which would develop through opting out would impose such severe strains on central institutions[2] that is likely to be unacceptable to the federal government and at least undesirable to most provincial governments.

The unanimity rule is even more difficult to operate. The Meech Lake Accord did achieve unanimous agreement at two First Ministers' Conferences held in 1987. However, over the next three years, provincial elections caused three changes of government before the process of ratification by all legislative assemblies was complete, and in each case the new government refused to respect the agreement of its predecessor. In the end, the Accord lapsed, because two of the newly-constituted legislative assemblies had not ratified it when the three-year time-limit for ratifications expired.[3] Unanimity was achieved a second time when the Charlottetown Accord was agreed to at a First Ministers' Conference in 1992. However, the first ministers agreed to put the Accord to a national referendum, with the understanding that it would need to be approved by eleven majorities, namely, a national majority and a majority in every one of the ten provinces. The referendum was held in 1992, and the voters rejected the Accord by a national majority, and by majorities in six provinces. The Accord, therefore, never started on the process of legislative ratification.[4]

The requirement of resolutions of assent by the Houses of Parliament and the legislative assemblies of the provinces dates only from 1982. Before 1982, an agreement by the first ministers was regarded as a sufficient manifestation of federal-provincial approval to enable an amendment to be transmitted to the United Kingdom for enactment.[5] Since 1982, any such executive agreement has to be ratified by the various legislative bodies. This adds a new hazard to the process, because it means that whatever agreement is achieved by first ministers must be maintained throughout the period of ratification. The three-year maximum period for ratification is far too long. In the case of the Meech Lake Accord, it allowed the process to drift on while elections were held and governments changed. A period of one year, or even six months, would surely be ample for legislative review of a constitutional proposal.

The requirement of legislative ratifications ensures that there is a

---

[Section 4:23]

[1]There has been one amendment under the general amending procedure: Constitution Amendment Proclamation, 1983, R.S.C. 1985, Appendix II, No. 46, adding new provisions respecting aboriginal peoples. The details are described in §§ 28:1 et seq., Aboriginal Peoples.

[2]See § 4:21 note 5 above.

[3]The story is told in more detail in § 4:3, "The failure to accommodate Quebec".

[4]§ 4:3, "The failure to accommodate Quebec".

[5]Strayer, The Patriation and Legitimacy of the Canadian Constitution (1982), 3–13.

public process to review any constitutional proposal. It was that public process that caused the destruction of the Meech Lake Accord. Ironically, it was a common complaint that the process was not public enough. What was lacking was a process of public scrutiny *before* the first ministers achieved their agreement. Whether this would have salvaged the Accord, or simply destroyed it earlier, cannot be known now.

In the case of the Charlottetown Accord, the agreement of the first ministers was preceded by an extraordinarily widespread public consultation. This started with a set of proposals for constitutional reform that was tabled in the federal Parliament by the federal government on September 24, 1991.[6] These proposals were referred to a Special Joint Committee of the House of Commons and the Senate, which received 3,000 submissions and listened to 700 individuals, and which produced a lengthy report on February 28, 1992.[7] During the same period all provinces and territories also established legislative committees to publicly examine the federal proposals. A series of five televised national conferences on the constitutional proposals was held between January and March of 1992. Starting in March, the federal and provincial governments, joined by the two territorial governments and the four aboriginal organizations, began multilateral discussions to reach an agreement. Those discussions culminated in a First Ministers' Conference at Charlottetown where the Charlottetown Accord was agreed to on August 28, 1992. Never in the history of Canada (and perhaps anywhere else) had there been such a thorough public consultation in preparation for a set of constitutional amendments. The first ministers decided to seek the definitive popular seal of approval for the Accord by putting it to a national referendum. A national referendum campaign followed in which the yes side (to approve the Accord) enjoyed the well-financed support of the federal government, all ten provincial governments, both territorial governments, most of the opposition leaders, all four aboriginal organizations, most business and labour organizations and most media editors and commentators. Despite this support (and all the earlier consultations), when the vote was held on October 26, 1992, it produced a decisive defeat for the yes side. The Accord was rejected by a majority of 54.4 per cent to 44.6 per cent. The process of legislative ratifications, which would have followed a yes vote, was never started.

The defeat of the Charlottetown Accord shows that no amount of public consultation guarantees the success of proposals to amend the Constitution. However, it is probably safe to assume that an absence of public consultation does guarantee failure. There is no escape from the conclusion that the Constitution's requirement of legislative ratifications of the text of any amendment must be supplemented by ample opportunities for public participation before the text has been settled. The Charlottetown process indicates some of the ways in which those op-

---

[6]Government of Canada, Shaping Canada's Future Together: Proposals (1991).

[7]*Report of the Special Joint Committee on a Renewed Canada* (Beaudoin-Dobbie Report) (Government of Canada, 1992).

portunities can be structured. The hearings of the special joint committee and the five national conferences were particularly valuable vehicles for criticism of the proposals and for new ideas.

Whatever provision is made for public participation in the existing amending procedures, at some stage in the process of amendment there has to be an agreement of the first ministers. This is because they control their legislative bodies,[8] and it is highly unlikely that any significant number of legislative assents could be obtained for a constitutional proposal that had not first been agreed to by the first ministers. Unfortunately, obtaining an agreement from the first ministers inevitably turns into a process of bargaining, which excludes popular involvement at the crucial moment, and which leaves no assurance that any given position has been accepted or rejected on the merits. Moreover, the Prime Minister and Premiers are unlikely to agree to any significant restructuring of governmental institutions, since it is to the existing institutions that they owe their positions and powers.[9]

During the pre-1982 constitutional negotiations I argued[10] (without the slightest effect, needless to say) that one mode of constitutional amendment—not the only mode, but one mode—should be some form of "initiative and referendum",[11] under which a proposal for a constitutional amendment could be initiated by petition signed by a stipulated (fairly large) number of voters, and could be adopted by a referendum that obtained majorities in each region of the country.[12] The availability of an initiative and referendum procedure would place ultimate control over the amending power in the hands of the people, instead of the political elites. Note that governments would not be excluded from the initiative and referendum procedure. They could, and no doubt would, campaign

[8]See ch. 9, Responsible Government.

[9]Accord, R.I. Cheffins, "The Constitution Act, 1982 and the Amending Formula" (1982) 4 Supreme Court L.R. 43.

[10]Hogg, "The Theory and Practice of Constitutional Reform" (1981) 3 Alta. L. Rev. 335, 348–351.

[11]For discussion of initiative and referendum as a law-making process, as it was adopted in Alberta and Manitoba early this century, see ch. 14, Delegation, § 14:8, "Office of Lieutenant Governor or Governor General", and § 14:9, "Requirement of a Legislature or Parliament". Australia and Switzerland use referenda as their amending procedures. In Australia, however, the referendum can only be initiated by the federal Parliament, while in Switzerland it can be initiated either by the federal Assembly or by popular initiative. Australia's amending procedure is set out in heading § 4:5, "Comparison with Australia and United States". Switzerland's amending procedure is described in Government of Canada, *The Canadian Constitution and Constitutional Amendment* (1978), 4–5.

[12]The requirement of regional majorities is necessary to avoid results like those of the national referendums on prohibition in 1898 and on conscription of 1942. In each case, the referendum was carried by an English-speaking majority despite French-speaking opposition. The only other national referendum that has ever been held was on the Charlottetown Accord in 1992; in that case, where the referendum was lost, Quebec was not isolated: the vote in Quebec was similar to that in the nation as a whole.

for or against a particular proposal.[13] But the campaign would have to be addressed to the merits of the particular proposal. Support or opposition could no longer be simply a bargaining ploy, because that would not persuade the voters. Nor could radical proposals for change in the institutions of government be stifled or blocked by the existing institutions.

---

[13]This is what happens in Australia, where, although state legislatures play no role in the amending process, state governments will often campaign against an amendment proposal that is supported by the federal government. Any fear that the resources of the federal government would enable it to win any referendum is not borne out by the Australian experience. In Australia, since federation in 1900, 44 proposed amendments have been put to referenda. In each instance the proposal was supported by the federal government (which must initiate the process). Only eight of the proposals have carried by the requisite "double majority" (a majority of all those voting and a majority of those voting in each of a majority of states): see heading § 4:5, "Comparison with Australia and United States".

Chapter 5

Federalism

I. DISTRIBUTION OF GOVERNMENTAL POWER

§ 5:1 Federalism
§ 5:2 Confederation
§ 5:3 Legislative union
§ 5:4 Special status
§ 5:5 Dominion and provinces
§ 5:6 Regions
§ 5:7 Subsidiarity

II. REASONS FOR FEDERALISM

§ 5:8 Reasons for federalism

III. FEDERALISM IN CANADA

§ 5:9 The terms of the Constitution
§ 5:10 Early federal dominance
§ 5:11 Judicial interpretation of the distribution of powers
§ 5:12 Federal-provincial financial arrangements
§ 5:13 Disallowance
§ 5:14 Appointment of Lieutenant Governors
§ 5:15 Appointment of judges
§ 5:16 Educational appeals
§ 5:17 Declaratory power
§ 5:18 Conclusion

IV. SUPREMACY OF THE CONSTITUTION

§ 5:19 Supremacy of the Constitution

V. ROLE OF THE COURTS

§ 5:20 Development of judicial review
§ 5:21 Limitations of judicial review
§ 5:22 Alternatives to judicial review

VI. AMENDING POWER

§ 5:23 Amending power

VII. SECESSION

§ 5:24 The power to secede

§ 5:25 Secession by amendment
§ 5:26 Secession by unilateral act

VIII. COOPERATIVE FEDERALISM

§ 5:27 Cooperative federalism

I. DISTRIBUTION OF GOVERNMENTAL POWER

§ 5:1 Federalism

Canada is a federal state, or a federation. Other familiar examples of federal states are the United States of America and Australia.[1] The United Kingdom and New Zealand, by contrast, are unitary states. What is a federal state? How does it differ from a unitary state?

In a federal state, governmental power is distributed between a central (or national or federal) authority and several regional (or provincial or state) authorities, in such a way that every individual in the state is subject to the laws of two authorities, the central authority and a regional authority. For example, anyone in Ontario is subject to the laws of the Parliament of Canada (the central authority) and the Legislature of Ontario (the regional authority). The central authority and the regional authorities are "coordinate", that is to say, neither is subordinate to the other. The powers of the Legislature of Ontario are not granted by the Parliament of Canada, and they cannot be taken away, altered or controlled by the Parliament of Canada. And the Legislature of Ontario, even acting in concert with all the other provincial Legislatures, is likewise incompetent to take away, alter or control the powers of the Parliament of Canada.

In a unitary state, governmental power is vested in one national authority. There are, of course, local or municipal governments with law-making power over their local territories. But these local authorities differ from the provinces or states of a federation in that the local authorities are subordinate to the national authority. The powers of a city, borough or county are granted to it by the national legislature, and may be taken away, altered or controlled at any time by the national legislature; in fact, this happens quite often when local government is reorganized. This is also the position of local or municipal governments within a federal state. They are subordinate to a regional authority, for example, the city of Montreal to the province of Quebec.

In a federal state, it is common to speak of two "levels" of government. The metaphor is apt in that the power of the central authority extends throughout the country, and is in that sense "higher" than the power of each regional authority, which is confined to its region. Moreover, in most federations, in the event of inconsistency between a federal law and a provincial or state law, it is the federal or national law which

---

[Section 5:1]

[1]There are many other federations: see R.L. Watts, Comparing Federal Systems (2nd ed., 1999).

prevails.[2] But to speak of the central authority as a "higher level" of government must not carry the implication that the regional authorities are legally subordinate to the centre; on the contrary, they are coordinate or equal in status with the centre.

The notion of equality which is conveyed by the word "coordinate" does not necessarily imply equality of wealth, status or actual power. The tiny province of Prince Edward Island is not equal to the province of Ontario in that sense;[3] nor is any province equal to the federal government in that sense. Within every federation some regions are wealthier and more powerful than others, and the central authority is wealthier and more powerful than any of the regions. At different periods of a federal nation's history, the balance of power between the centre and the regions shifts. We shall see in the next chapter that during the second world war, for example, the needs of national power led to enormous accretions in the wealth and power of the federal governments of Canada, Australia and the United States. Since then the balance of power has tended to shift back towards the regions, although this tendency has been less marked in Australia and the United States than it has been in Canada.

Depending upon the actual balance of power between the centre and the regions, federal states may be placed on a "spectrum" running from a point that is close to disintegration into separate countries to a point that is close to the centralized power of a unitary state or an empire.[4] With the growth of central power in the principal federations the question whether a state is still truly "federal" depends upon whether there is still "an area of guaranteed autonomy for each unit of the system".[5] It is this legal guarantee of autonomy to each of the regional authorities, however disparate in size and wealth they may be, which justifies the description of them as coordinate with the central authority. If in a once-federal country the area of guaranteed autonomy of the regions were attenuated to the point of triviality, then we would probably want to deny the term "federal" to the country. But it could not plausibly be argued that the growth of central power in Canada, or in Australia or the United States, has reached that point of substantial equivalence to a unitary state.

K.C. Wheare defined "the federal principle" as "the method of dividing powers so that the general and regional governments are each, within a

---

[2]While federal or national law prevails in the event of such a conflict in most federations, this is not true of all federations: see e.g. Constitution of the Republic of Iraq, 2005, Articles 115, 121.

[3]There are also some minor differences in the legal position of the provinces: see § 5:4, "Special status".

[4]Livingston, Federalism and Constitutional Change (1956), 4; W.H. Riker, Federalism: Origin, Operation, Significance (Little, Brown, Boston, 1964), 5. Riker argues that the degree of centralization in any federal state may be measured by the degree of centralization in the organization of the political parties.

[5]G. Sawer, Modern Federalism (Watts, London, 1969), 27; W.H. Riker, Federalism: Origin, Operation, Significance (Little, Brown, Boston, 1964), 6.

sphere, co-ordinate and independent".[6] This definition has been criticized as unduly stressing the separate and distinct spheres of the central and regional authorities.[7] Other writers have contributed alternative definitions which emphasize the "interdependence" of central and regional authorities in a federal state,[8] or the "diversification" of the society within the federal state,[9] or the existence within the state of distinctive groups with common objectives,[10] or the constitutionally-entrenched incorporation of regional units in its decision-making procedures,[11] or the existence of "specific communities bound together under a common legal framework that has been adopted by covenant".[12] These writers have all contributed insights to the nature of federal states, but they have so eroded the concept of federalism that it has become too vague to be useful.

In fact, however, there are very important differences in the constitutional law and governmental practices between "federal" states such as Canada, Australia and the United States on the one hand, and "unitary" states such as the United Kingdom and New Zealand on the other. There are a set of distinctive issues concerning the distribution of legislative power, the distribution of executive power and the administration of justice that have to be resolved in each of the federal states, and that are unimportant or non-existent in the unitary states; and these distinctive issues all relate to the fact that in a federal state the citizen is subject to two levels of government which are, to some degree at least, legally and politically independent of each other. It is true that in many spheres the central and regional powers overlap and that where they come into conflict the central power prevails. It is also true that financial arrangements between the central and regional governments have extended the powers of the financially dominant central authority deeply into spheres once reserved for the regions. And it is also true that the extent of modern governmental involvement in social and economic matters has produced policies which require constant interaction between each government, and in some cases the cooperative action of more than

[6]Wheare, Federal Government (4th ed., 1963), 10; compare Dicey, The Law of the Constitution (10th ed., 1965), 140, whose definition has obviously influenced Wheare's. For similar definitions, see W.H. Riker, Federalism: Origin, Operation, Significance (Little, Brown, Boston, 1964), 11; G. Sawer, Australian Federalism in the Courts (Melbourne U.P., 1967), 1; Smiley, The Federal Condition in Canada (1987), 2; J.-F. Gaudreault-DesBiens in Calvo-Garcia and Felstiner (eds.), Federalism (2004), 129.

[7]Birch, Federalism, Finance and Social Legislation (1955), 306.

[8]M.J.C. Vile, The Structure of American Federalism (Oxford, 1961), 198–199.

[9]Livingston, Federalism and Constitutional Change (1956), 4.

[10]C.J. Friedrich, Man and His Government (McGraw-Hill, New York, 1963), 594–595.

[11]P.T. King, Federalism and Federation (Johns Hopkins U.P., 1982), 77. Tremblay, Droit Constitutionnel-Principes (2nd ed., 2000), 192–193.

[12]N. Aroney, "Formation, Representation and Amendment in Federal Constitutions" (2006) 54 Am. J. Comp. Law 277, 316. In the same article, he agrees that the division of powers is one element of federal constitutionalism, but that it needs to be supplemented by elements of formation, representation and amendment.

one government. So far as Canada is concerned these points will be amply demonstrated in succeeding chapters.

Perhaps Wheare did not sufficiently stress the elements of interdependence of central and regional authorities, but they are not inconsistent with his definition of federalism. If in a nation paramount central power completely overlapped regional power, then that nation would not be federal on his definition. The same conclusion would follow if the financial arrangements of a nation subjected the regions totally to central control.[13] It is only where overlapping of power is incomplete, or the scope of central control is limited, that we have a federal system. In that case there are two levels of government which are "within a sphere" coordinate and independent. That is true of Canada, Australia and the United States, and it is untrue of the United Kingdom[14] and New Zealand.

§ 5:2 Confederation

Canada is often described as a "confederation", and the process of union which culminated in 1867 is often described as "confederation". Outside Canada the term confederation is usually used to mean a loose association of states in which the central government is subordinate to the states.[1] In a confederation in the technical sense the central government is the delegate of the states or provinces; its powers are delegated to it by the states or provinces, who retain the right to resume the delegated powers if they wish. It was a "confederation" that was established by the American colonies by the Articles of Confederation of 1777, because under that arrangement the central government was merely the delegate of the states. After the revolutionary war, the final constitution which was adopted by the United States in 1787 made the federal government independent of the states and coordinate with them.

In Canada, the union of the provinces, like the 1787 union of the United States, established a central government which was in no sense the delegate of the provinces. It was independent of the provinces and coordinate with them. Indeed, as we shall see later in this chapter, to the extent that the provinces and the central government are not coordinate, it is the provinces that are subordinate to the central government—the opposite of confederation. During the discussions of union in British North America before 1867, the terms union, federation and confederation were not used in any consistent or precise sense; and the term confederation has now become an accepted term for the Canadian

---

[13]Wheare might prefer to say in this case that the "constitution" was still federal, but the "government" was unitary.

[14]The United Kingdom has created elected assemblies for Wales, Scotland and Northern Ireland, but the assemblies remain subordinate to the Parliament at Westminster: Government of Wales Act 2006 (U.K.), c. 32; Scotland Act 1998 (U.K.), c. 46; Northern Ireland Act 1998 (U.K.), c. 47.

[Section 5:2]

[1]Wheare, Federal Government (4th ed., 1963), 32.

union of provinces. There is no point in cavilling about this use of the word: for Canada, usage has made it correct.[2]

§ 5:3 Legislative union

The closest possible kind of union is a "legislative union", in which the united states or provinces form a new unitary state which incorporates the former units and subjects them to the authority of a single central legislature. The United Kingdom is a legislative union of England, Wales, Scotland and Northern Ireland. The Parliament at Westminster has full authority to legislate for all four regions.[1]

At the time of the union of the British North American colonies there was a good deal of sentiment in favour of a legislative union. John A. Macdonald wanted a legislative union, as did many people in Upper Canada (which became Ontario). But they had to settle for a federation because Lower Canada (which became Quebec) and the maritime provinces of New Brunswick, Nova Scotia and Prince Edward Island would not have agreed to a legislative union. Lower Canada feared that if it joined in a legislative union, its French language, culture and institutions and its Roman Catholic religion would be threatened by the English-speaking Protestant majority; the maritime provinces also feared for their local traditions and institutions. On the other hand, union would provide the military strength needed for security, and the economic strength needed for prosperity. The compromise between these conflicting impulses was a federation, providing the unity necessary for military and economic strength, while allowing diversity of language, culture, religion and local institutions.[2] Even so, the maritime provinces were reluctant to join, and Prince Edward Island did not do so until 1873.[3]

---

[2]For extended discussion of the term confederation, see Kennedy, The Constitution of Canada 1534–1937 (2nd ed., 1938), 401–404.

[Section 5:3]

[1]The organization of a country with regional authorities that are subordinate to the centre is often described as "devolution". Within Canada, the government of the three territories is based on devolution of power from the federal Parliament; the territorial Legislatures have powers nearly as extensive as those of provincial Legislatures, but they remain subordinate to the federal Parliament: Northwest Territories Act, R.S.C. 1985, c. N-27; Nunavut Act, S.C. 1993, c. 28; Yukon Act, S.C. 2002, c. 7. Within the United Kingdom, there has been a devolution of power to elected assemblies for Wales, Scotland and Northern Ireland, but the assemblies remain subordinate to the Parliament at Westminster: § 5:1 note 14 above.

[2]W.H. Riker, Federalism: Origin, Operation, Significance (Little, Brown, Boston, 1964), 5, (1964), ch. 2, argues that a similar set of conditions prevailed at the origin of every modern federal system.

[3]Lower Canada had a special reason to support the federation. Since 1840 (as Canada East) it had been united with Upper Canada (Canada West) in the united province of Canada, and so federation offered more not less autonomy for French-speaking Canada. The maritime provinces had never been united and were reluctant to yield some of their autonomy: see generally Creighton, The Road to Confederation (1964).

§ 5:4 Special status

As noted earlier, the provinces are not equal in wealth, status or actual power. Nor is their constitutional situation exactly equal. A number of the provisions of the Constitution apply to only one or only some of the provinces.[1] And the terms upon which each province was admitted usually included unique terms[2] which operate as legally enforceable provisions applicable only to that province.[3]

While the provinces are not perfectly equal, the differences are not so marked as to justify the description "special status" for any province. "Special status" is the term[4] which has been applied to proposals for constitutional change under which one province (most likely, Quebec) would possess larger powers than the other provinces.[5] This could arise under the new amending procedures if Quebec (or any other province) opted out of a constitutional amendment transferring a provincial power to the federal Parliament. As noted in the discussion of opting out,[6] special status for one or a few provinces would impose severe strains on central institutions, and especially the federal Parliament. If the Parliament had authority to regulate a matter, say, product standards (to use my earlier example), everywhere except in Quebec, the members of parliament and senators from Quebec would presumably be permitted to vote on a bill regulating product standards, and they might have to do so in order to preserve a governmental majority, but the bill when enacted would not apply in Quebec. This problem has never been solved by political scientists, and it means that special status is a viable

[Section 5:4]

[1]For example, Constitution Act, 1867, ss. 93 (denominational schools), 94 (uniformity of laws), 133 (language); Constitution Act, 1982, ss. 6(4) (affirmative action), 16(2), 17(2), 18(2), 19(2), 20(2), 59 (language).

[2]For example, the denominational schools guarantees in s. 20 of the Manitoba Act, 1870, s. 17 of the Alberta Act, s. 17 of the Saskatchewan Act and s. 17 of the Terms of Union of Newfoundland; the language guarantee in s. 23 of the Manitoba Act, 1870; and provisions regarding the natural resources of Manitoba, Alberta and Saskatchewan enacted by the Constitution Act, 1930.

[3]*The Queen (Can.) v. The Queen (P.E.I.)*, [1978] 1 F.C. 533 (C.A.) (enforcing terms of union promising ferry service); *Jack v. The Queen*, [1980] 1 S.C.R. 294 (interpreting term of union regarding policy towards Indians); *Moosehunter v. The Queen*, [1981] 1 S.C.R. 282 (enforcing term of natural resources agreement guaranteeing Indian hunting rights); *B.C. v. Can.*, [1994] 2 S.C.R. 41 (interpreting term of union promising construction of railway).

[4]The term has a pejorative connotation. The more neutral term is "asymmetry", but there are undoubtedly serious limits of politics and law to the asymmetry that can be tolerated within a federation, and very few federations provide examples of significant and permanent constitutional asymmetry (or special status) for their constituent units. The overwhelming pattern of federal constitutions is uniformity of powers for the constituent units. See Watts, Comparing Federal Systems (2nd ed., 1999), ch. 6.

[5]"Special status", under which Quebec would remain within Canada, must be distinguished from "sovereignty-association", under which Quebec would secede from Canada and would retain only an economic association with (the rest of) Canada: see §§ 5:24 to 5:26, "Secession".

[6]See ch. 4, Amendment, under heading § 4:11, "Opting out".

constitutional arrangement only up to a point. Of course, Quebec already enjoys a de facto special status, as the only province that has opted out of the Canada Pension Plan and the Hospital Insurance Plan (and some other national shared-cost programmes).[7] But these arrangements do not give to Quebec any special *constitutional* powers: the other nine provinces continue to possess the same powers as Quebec over pensions and hospital insurance, and they could if they chose follow an independent course like Quebec.

The Meech Lake Constitutional Accord of 1987[8] was a failed attempt to reconcile Quebec to the terms of the Constitution Act, 1982, by which the province was legally bound, but to which it had never given its assent. The Accord made provision for (1) the recognition of Quebec as a distinct society, (2) a provincial role in immigration, (3) a provincial role in appointments to the Supreme Court of Canada, (4) a limitation of the federal spending power and (5) a veto for Quebec over some kinds of constitutional amendments. Although these five points were sought by Quebec alone, the Accord was carefully drafted to avoid making special provision for Quebec, and the new provincial powers were conferred on all provinces, not just Quebec. This even included the veto over constitutional amendments, which took the form of a unanimity requirement, conferring a veto on all provinces.

The one point that would not yield to the ingenious avoidance of special provision for Quebec[9] was the recognition of Quebec as a "distinct society". In my opinion, even this provision could not plausibly be regarded as creating a special status for Quebec, in that it was an interpretative provision only. It did not directly confer any new powers on the province, and, if its interpretative role did lead to some expansion of Quebec's powers, that expansion was bound to be minor—well within the range of variation in provincial powers that is now to be found within the Constitution of Canada. Nevertheless, there was much public debate about the undesirability of special status for Quebec, and the distinct society clause was the major objection that led to the failure by two provinces to ratify the Accord, which caused the Accord to lapse.[10]

In 1995, the House of Commons, reacting to the close result in the sovereignty referendum that Quebec had held that year, passed a reso-

---

[7]See ch. 6, Financial Arrangements.

[8]See ch. 4, Amendment, under heading § 4:3, "The failure to accommodate Quebec".

[9]To be strictly accurate, the Accord also guaranteed that three of the judges of the Supreme Court of Canada would come from Quebec. This provision, although singling out Quebec for special treatment, was not controversial, because it constitutionalized a longstanding statutory requirement.

[10]The "distinct society" clause was also part of the unsuccessful Charlottetown Accord of 1992: see ch. 4, Amendment, under heading § 4:3 "The failure to accommodate Quebec". The Accord also repeated the guarantee that three judges of the Supreme Court of Canada would come from Quebec (see previous note). The Accord contained a new guarantee that Quebec's representation in the House of Commons would never fall below 25 per cent. This special provision for Quebec (along with the distinct society clause) seems to have been an important factor in the defeat of the Accord in the western provinces.

lution declaring that the House recognized Quebec as a "distinct society", and would be "guided by this reality".[11] This is not a constitutional amendment (it is not even a statute), and so it does not confer any special constitutional status on Quebec. Even so, the resolution was opposed (because it went too far) by the Reform Party, with most of the seats in the western provinces, and (because it did not go far enough) by the Bloc Quebecois, with most of the seats in Quebec.

Eleven years later, in 2006, under the Conservative government of Prime Minister Harper, the House of Commons went a good deal further, passing a resolution "That this House recognize that the Québécois form a nation within a united Canada".[12] Unlike the 1995 resolution, this resolution passed overwhelmingly, by a vote of 265 to 16 – with support from not only the governing Conservatives, which had the majority of the seats in the western provinces,[13] but also the Bloc Québécois, which had the majority of the seats in Quebec. Even so, this is also not a constitutional amendment (or even a statute), and so it does not confer any special constitutional status on Quebec.

§ 5:5 Dominion and provinces

In a federal state it is necessary to find suitable vocabulary to describe (1) the regional authorities, (2) the central authority, and (3) the nation as a whole. The first issue is rarely a problem. In Canada the regions are known as provinces, while in Australia and the United States they are known as states; and of course each province or state has a proper name of its own. It is, however, difficult to find a description for the central authority which is both accurate and dignified, and which at the same time distinguishes the central government apparatus from the nation as a whole. In Canada the terminological problem has not been satisfactorily resolved.

The British North America Act, 1867, by s. 3, created "one Dominion under the name of Canada". After 1867, the country was usually described officially as "the Dominion of Canada." When it was desired to distinguish the central government authority from the provinces, the central authority was called "the Dominion".

The term "dominion" gained currency outside Canada in the early 1900s to denote the self-governing countries of the British Empire. Canada, Australia, New Zealand and South Africa by then enjoyed a substantial measure of self-government, and it did not seem appropriate to describe them as colonies. In order to distinguish them from the more dependent territories of the Empire, they came to be called dominions.

---

[11] *House of Commons Debates* (29 November 1995) at 16971 (text of resolution); *House of Commons Debates* (11 December 1995) at 17536 (passage of resolution).

[12] *House of Commons Debates* (22 November 2006) at 5197 (text of resolution); *House of Commons Debates* (27 November 2006) at 5412 (passage of resolution).

[13] Granted, many Conservative MPs did express reservations about the motion, and were also threatened with expulsion from the Conservative caucus if they did not support it.

But terminology changed to meet changing facts and perceptions. The British Empire became the British Commonwealth and, later on, simply the Commonwealth. And after the second world war the term dominion became unfashionable. It was thought to carry a colonial connotation, and so, outside Canada, the term dominion has generally been superseded by the term "member of the Commonwealth" as a description of the self-governing countries of the Commonwealth.[1]

In Canada, the objections to the use of the word dominion were especially significant, since the word appeared as part of the official name of the country. In fact, however, s. 3 of the B.N.A. Act, although it used the word Dominion, did not actually name the country "the Dominion of Canada" but simply "Canada". In the 1930s, the federal government decided to switch the official name of the country from the Dominion of Canada to Canada. The substitution has been made in Acts of Parliament, for example, and efforts have been made to discontinue the use of the word Dominion wherever else it used to occur. Dominion-provincial conferences have since 1950 become federal-provincial conferences; the Dominion Bureau of Statistics has become Statistics Canada; and so on.

Most writers on constitutional law and government have continued to make discreet use of the term "Dominion", because it is convenient to have a name to distinguish the central authority from the provinces. It is of course possible to speak of the federal government or the national government, but these terms are not normally apt to include the legislative branch of government, and so clarity often requires that one use another term— the federal (or national) Parliament—when legislative power is in issue. The only proper noun which would replace Dominion is "Canada", but this causes ambiguity, since the central governmental authority is not the same as the nation as a whole. If one says that "Canada has the power to regulate aeronautics", it is not clear whether the statement means that the power to regulate aeronautics is one of the powers of the federal Parliament (which is a proposition about the distribution of legislative powers within the federal system), or whether the statement means that the power to regulate aeronautics exists somewhere in the country (which does not involve a proposition about the distribution of powers in the federal system).[2] The statement that "the Dominion has the power to regulate aeronautics" would in most contexts be an unambiguous statement about the distribution of legislative power within the federal system.

A related point of nomenclature concerns the names of the Canadian legislative bodies. These are all "parliaments" in the sense that each is modelled on the United Kingdom Parliament at Westminster. But the

---

[Section 5:5]

[1]Wheare, The Constitutional Structure of the Commonwealth (1960), 14–16.

[2]The Constitution Act, 1867 is itself guilty of this ambiguity. While "Canada" usually means the nation as a whole, e.g., in ss. 3, 4, 5, 16, 22, in several places the word means the central governmental authority, e.g., in s. 101 (federal jurisdiction over "laws of Canada") and ss. 108, 111, 117, 119, 120, 125 (the public property provisions).

Canadian practice is to confine the term "Parliament" to the federal Parliament, and to use the term "Legislature" to describe each provincial parliament. This is the usage in the Constitution Acts, and it is almost invariable in Canadian constitutional writing.

§ 5:6 Regions

The term "region" has no precise meaning in Canadian political discourse,[1] but the idea of region has been influential in several contexts.

Membership of the Senate of Canada[2] does not follow the American and Australian pattern of equal representation of each state. The numbers of the Canadian Senate are drawn equally from regions, which the Act describes as "divisions". Originally, three divisions were recognized, namely, Ontario, Quebec and the three maritime provinces, and each division was represented by 24 senators. In 1915, the four western provinces were recognized as a fourth division, also represented by 24 senators. In recent times, the regional logic has been compromised. On the admission of Newfoundland in 1949, the province was not included in the maritime division, but was allocated an additional six senators. And in 1975, the Yukon and Northwest Territories were given one senator each, also outside the existing divisions, but perhaps constituting a recognition of the North as a region. In 1999, the third territory, Nunavut (created in 1993) was also given a senator.

Membership of the Supreme Court of Canada[3] has also been based on a regional idea. The Supreme Court Act requires that three of the nine judges be appointed from Quebec. This legal requirement has been supplemented by a practice of appointing three judges from Ontario, two judges from the four western provinces,[4] and one judge from the four Atlantic provinces.

The Victoria Charter amending formula, which was almost agreed to in 1970,[5] called for the agreement of provinces on a regional basis. An amendment would have required the consent of the federal Parliament and (1) any province that had at any time 25 per cent of the population of Canada (that is, Ontario and Quebec), (2) at least two of the four Atlantic provinces, and (3) at least two of the four western provinces having a combined population of at least 50 per cent of the population of all the western provinces. In 1981, a variant of the Victoria Charter

---

[Section 5:6]

[1]See Smiley, The Federal Condition in Canada (1987), 22–23.

[2]The composition of the Senate is governed by s. 22 of the Constitution Act, 1867. The Senate is discussed in ch. 9, Responsible Government, under heading § 9:10, "The Senate".

[3]See ch. 8, Supreme Court of Canada, under heading § 8:3, "Composition of Court".

[4]Since 1978, one of the two western judges has been drawn from British Columbia, which may constitute a recognition that B.C. is a region separate from the prairies.

[5]See ch. 4, Amendment, under heading § 4:2, "The search for a domestic amending procedure".

formula was rejected by the first ministers in favour of the seven-fifty formula that is now embodied in s. 38 of the Constitution Act, 1982.[6]

The seven-fifty formula of s. 38 rejects the idea of regions in favour of the equality of the provinces. An amendment requires the consent of the federal Parliament and two-thirds of the provinces (that is, seven provinces) having a combined population of 50 per cent of the population of all the provinces. In fact, this formula does indirectly impose some regional requirements in that seven provinces will always include at least one western province and at least one Atlantic province, and 50 per cent of the population will always include either Ontario or Quebec, because the other eight provinces have less than 50 per cent of the population. What the seven-fifty formula avoids, however, is the explicit recognition of regions, which is particularly distasteful to the wealthy provinces of British Columbia (unless it is recognized as a region by itself) and Alberta (which dislikes being simply lumped in with the western provinces).

A "regional veto statute" passed by the federal Parliament in 1996, however, has the indirect effect of incorporating regions into the seven-fifty formula.[7] While the statute cannot properly be considered part of the constitutional amending formula, as it is an ordinary statute rather than a constitutional amendment, the statute does purport to prevent a Minister of the Crown from introducing any resolution authorizing an amendment into the House of Commons without prior consent by the Legislatures of:

(a) Ontario;
(b) Quebec;
(c) British Columbia;
(d) two or more of the Atlantic provinces representing at least fifty per cent of the population of the Atlantic provinces; and
(e) two or more of the Prairie provinces representing at least fifty per cent of the population of the Prairie provinces.

Practically speaking, since a resolution on a matter as significant as the amendment of the Constitution of Canada can only pass in the House of Commons with the support of the government of the day, this statute superimposes a requirement of regional consent on the seven-fifty formula.

The regions contemplated by the statute are similar to those which would have been created under the Victoria Charter formula. There are two differences, however. First, under the regional veto statute, British Columbia is a separate region which was not the case under the Victoria Charter. Secondly, under the regional veto statute, the two or more Atlantic provinces which support the amendment must represent at least fifty per cent of the population of the Atlantic provinces; under the

[6]See ch. 4, Amendment, under heading §§ 4:8 to 4:15, "General amending procedure (s. 38)".

[7]S.C. 1996, c. 1. For further discussion, see ch. 4, Amendment, under heading § 4:15, "Regional veto statute".

Victoria charter, any two Atlantic provinces would suffice. By giving indirect vetos to the four most populous provinces,[8] the regional veto statute compromises the equality of the provinces envisioned in the seven-fifty formula. The idea behind the statute was, of course, to give Quebec a greater influence over future amendments of the Constitution.[9]

§ 5:7 Subsidiarity

Subsidiarity is a principle of social organization that prescribes that decisions affecting individuals should, as far as reasonably possible, be made by the level of government closest to the individuals affected.[1] The principle has been adopted in the European Community as a guideline for the division of responsibilities between the Community institutions in Brussels and the national institutions of the member states. In Canada, the principle has rarely been invoked in political discourse, but it does offer some useful ways of thinking about the Constitution of Canada.

One of the primary goals of confederation in 1867[2] was to preserve a considerable degree of autonomy for the four original provinces. It was critical to the acceptance of the plan by French Canadians that the Legislature of the new province of Quebec, in which French speakers would be in a majority, be invested with enough powers to safeguard the French language, culture and civil law tradition. New Brunswick and Nova Scotia had existing Legislatures and had enjoyed responsible government since 1848. They wanted their Legislatures to continue to regulate much of the daily life of the people as they had before confederation. The British North America Act, 1867 accordingly invested the provincial Legislatures with authority over such matters as property and civil rights, the courts and the police, municipal institutions, hospitals and education. This was consistent with the principle of subsidiarity.

Another of the primary goals of confederation was to provide the uniting provinces with the collective benefits of an economic union, greater financial strength and an increased capacity for defence. To these ends, the British North America Act, 1867 invested the federal Parliament with authority over such matters as customs and excise, interprovincial and international trade and commerce, banking and currency, all forms of taxation and national defence. This was consistent with the principle of subsidiarity. The catalogue of federal powers does include some that

---

[8]The consent of the Legislatures of Ontario, Quebec and British Columbia are expressly required. The consent of the Alberta Legislature is also required because Alberta has more than fifty per cent of the population of the Prairie provinces.

[9]See ch. 4, Amendment, under heading § 4:3, "The failure to accommodate Quebec".

[Section 5:7]

[1]See P.W. Hogg "Subsidiarity and the Division of Powers in Canada" (1993) 3 N.J.C.L. 341; and see the other articles in the symposium on subsidiarity of which that article is one contribution: (1993) 3 N.J.C.L. 301–427.

[2]See ch. 2, Reception, under heading § 2:7, "Confederation".

one might expect to find in the provincial list, for example, the criminal law, penitentiaries and marriage and divorce. These were powers that could have been exercised at the provincial level, but, for various reasons particular to the situation of the colonies in 1867, were entrusted to the federal level, contrary to the principle of subsidiarity.

Despite some departures, the division of powers in the British North America Act, 1867 did generally adhere to what we would now describe as the principle of subsidiarity. The principle was reinforced by the decisions of the courts in the early years of confederation, which established rules that continue to set the pattern of government in modern Canada. The provincial power over property and civil rights was given a broad interpretation, so that it now includes not only the private law of property, contract and torts, but also most of commercial law, consumer law, environmental law, labour law, health law and social-services law.[3] The result is that the laws that impact most directly on individuals are for the most part provincial. The early decisions tended to interpret the principal federal powers narrowly, but since the second world war the Supreme Court of Canada has generally accepted the idea that, where matters take on a national dimension, they can be regulated by the federal Parliament under its powers over peace, order, and good government,[4] trade and commerce[5] and transportation and communication.[6] This is the corollary to subsidiary, namely, that those matters that cannot be effectively regulated at the provincial level should be the responsibility of the more distant federal level of government.

The idea of subsidiarity was invoked by the Supreme Court of Canada in *114957 Canada v. Hudson* (2001)[7] as a prelude to deciding that a "general welfare" power in Quebec's municipal legislation authorized a municipality to pass a by-law severely restricting the use of pesticides in the municipality, and that the by-law was not displaced by provincial and federal legislation also dealing with pesticides. The Court held that the local decision, which was to impose more stringent standards on pesticide use in the local area, should be respected. L'Heureux-Dube J. for the majority of the Court pointed out that "matters of governance are often examined through the lens of subsidiarity", which she described as "a proposition that law-making and implementation are often best achieved at a level of government that is not only effective, but also closest to the citizens affected and thus most responsive to their needs . . . ."[8]

---

[3]See ch. 21, Property and Civil Rights.

[4]See ch. 17, Peace, Order, and Good Government.

[5]See ch. 20, Trade and Commerce.

[6]See ch. 22, Transportation and Communication.

[7]*114957 Canada v. Hudson*, [2001] 2 S.C.R. 241, para. 3. The concurring opinion of LeBel J. is to the same effect, but makes no mention of subsidiarity.

[8]See also *Can. Western Bank v. Alta.*, [2007] 2 S.C.R. 3, para. 45 (interjurisdictional immunity, by limiting provincial but not federal power, undermines "the principles of subsidiarity").

In *Re Assisted Human Reproduction Act* (2010),[9] the issue was whether Parliament had authority under the criminal law power to regulate, by licensing and other regulatory measures, assisted human reproduction. Some of the provisions of the Act were absolute prohibitions (for example, of the sale and purchase of human embryos), and these were conceded to be valid exercises of the criminal law power. For LeBel and Deschamps JJ., writing for two others, the more detailed regulatory measures could not be upheld as ancillary to the absolute prohibitions. They commented that, if there was any doubt about this result, "this is where the principle of subsidiarity could apply, not as an independent basis for the distribution of legislative powers, but as an interpretive principle", which would indicate that the regulation of assisted human reproduction be connected with "the provinces' jurisdiction over local matters, not with the criminal law power".[10] McLachlin C.J., writing for three others, would have upheld the Act in its entirety under the criminal law power. She pointed out that "subsidiarity does not override the division of powers in the Constitution Act, 1867"; and she said that "the criminal law power may be invoked where there is a legitimate public health evil, and the exercise of this power is not restricted by concerns of subsidiarity".[11] Cromwell J., the ninth judge, who wrote a short opinion agreeing in result with most of the LeBel-Deschamps opinion, said nothing about subsidiarity.

II. REASONS FOR FEDERALISM

§ 5:8 Reasons for federalism

The genesis of the federal system in Canada was a political compromise between proponents of unity (who would have preferred a legislative union) and proponents of diversity (who were unwilling to submerge the separate identities of their provinces). Probably, a tension of this sort lies at the origin of all federal systems. But it should not be assumed that federalism is just a second-best alternative to a legislative union. The federal form of government has some distinctive advantages.[1]

In a country that covers a large area,[2] and includes diverse regions, there may be advantages of efficiency and accountability in dividing the powers of government so that a national government is responsible for

[9] *Re Assisted Human Reproduction Act*, [2010] 3 S.C.R. 457.

[10] *Re Assisted Human Reproduction Act*, [2010] 3 S.C.R. 457, para. 273.

[11] *Re Assisted Human Reproduction Act*, [2010] 3 S.C.R. 457, para. 72.

[Section 5:8]

[1] A well-known account of the political merits of federalism is in J.B. Bryce, The American Commonwealth (1897), ch. 29. For modern Canadian discussions, see Smiley, The Federal Condition in Canada (1987), 15–22; Smith, Federalism and the Constitution of Canada (2010).

[2] Federalism is also a convenient device for developing a new and large country, allowing the gradual expansion of settlement to be accompanied by local governments that are suitable to the needs of each new region. This is one of the "merits of the federal system" offered in J.B. Bryce, The American Commonwealth (1897), 248.

matters of national importance and provincial or state governments are responsible for matters of local importance. There would inevitably be diseconomies of scale if all governmental decision-making was centralized in one unwieldy bureaucracy. And a more decentralized form of government can be expected to be able to identify and give effect to different preferences and interests in different parts of the country.

A related point is that a province or state, being more homogeneous than the nation as a whole, will occasionally adopt policies that are too innovative or radical to be acceptable to the nation as a whole. In this way, a province or state may serve as a "social laboratory" in which new kinds of legislative programmes can be "tested".[3] If a new programme does not work out, the nation as a whole has not been placed at risk. If the programme works well, it will be copied by other provinces or states, and perhaps (if the Constitution permits) by the federal government. One can observe this kind of development in Canada with respect to social credit (which started in Alberta in 1935 and never took hold), medicare (which started in Saskatchewan in 1961 and became a national programme in 1968), family property regimes (which now exist in all provinces) and no-fault automobile insurance (which now exists in several provinces).

An entirely different argument in favour of federalism is that the division of governmental power inherent in a federal system operates to preclude an excessive concentration of power and thus as a check against tyranny.[4] The other side of that argument is that "federal government means weak government", because the dispersal of power makes it hard to enact and implement new public policies, especially radical policies.[5] In the right conditions, however, as we have noticed,[6] change can be initiated by a province or state, and later adopted more widely.

---

[3]*New State Ice Co. v. Liebmann* (1932), 285 U.S. 262, 311 per Brandeis J. ("It is one of the happy incidents of the federal system that a single courageous state may, if its citizens choose, serve as a laboratory; and try novel social and economic experiments without risk to the rest of the country.") See also Trudeau, Federalism and the French Canadians (1968), 124–150.

[4]See P.-J. Proudhon, The Principle of Federation (1863) (trans, by R. Vernon, U. Toronto Press, 1979), who extols federalism as the best possible compromise between liberty and authority; A. Hamilton, J. Madison and J.J. Jay, *The Federalist* papers (1787–1788) (New American Library, New York, 1961), esp. Nos. 10, 51 by Madison, arguing that federalism is a protection for minorities (especially property-owning minorities) against the rule of the majority.

[5]Dicey, The Law of the Constitution (10th ed., 1965), 171; Smiley, The Federal Condition in Canada (1987), 19–22.

[6]See § 5:8 note 3 above.

III. FEDERALISM IN CANADA

§ 5:9 The terms of the Constitution

What is Canada's position on the "spectrum"[1] of federal states? There are many indications that the framers of the B.N.A. Act planned a strong central government. The Act gives the provinces only enumerated powers to make laws, giving the residue of power to the federal Parliament.[2] This was a departure from the American precedent[3] where residuary power had been left with the states. (When the Australian colonies united in 1900 they followed the American precedent.)[4] And the list of specified heads of federal power included several topics left to the states in the United States (and, later, in Australia). Thus, the Canadian federal Parliament was given, by s. 91(2), the power to regulate "trade and commerce" without qualification, while the United States Congress had been given the more limited power to regulate "commerce with foreign nations and among the several states and with the Indian tribes".[5] Banking (s. 91(15)), marriage and divorce (s. 91(26)), the criminal law (s. 91(27)) and penitentiaries (s. 91(28)) were other topics allocated to the federal Parliament in Canada, but reserved to the states in the United States.[6] Even more significantly, the federal government was envisaged as fiscally dominant. The federal Parliament was given, by s. 91(3), the power to levy indirect as well as direct taxes while the provinces were confined, by s. 92(2), to direct taxes; in the 1860s, the indirect taxes of customs and excise accounted for 80 per cent of the uniting colonies' revenues, and so a system of federal grants to the prov-

[Section 5:9]

[1]Text accompanying § 5:1 note 4, above.

[2]See ch. 17, Peace, Order and Good Government, under heading § 17:1, "Residuary nature of power".

[3]Lord Haldane seemed to think that this departure made Canada not truly federal: *A.-G. Aust. v. Colonial Sugar Refining Co.*, [1914] A.C. 237, 252–254; criticized by Kennedy, The Constitution of Canada 1534–1937 (2nd ed., 1938), 408–412; Wheare, Federal Government (4th ed., 1963), 12.

[4]Watts, Comparing Federal Systems (2nd ed., 1999), 39, argues that it is the history of federation that explains the location of the residual power. "In most federations, especially those created by a process of aggregating previously separate units, the residual power has been assigned to the unit governments." He offers the United States and Australia as examples. But "where devolution from a more centralized unitary regime characterized the process of federal formation, the residual powers were left with the federal government." He offers Canada as an example.

[5]United States Constitution, art. 1, s. 8(3). Ironically, the qualified language of the U.S. "commerce clause" has been given almost unlimited scope in the courts, while the unqualified language of the Canadian trade and commerce power has been severely restricted in the courts: see ch. 20, Trade and Commerce.

[6]Australia's later federal list borrowed banking and marriage and divorce, but not the criminal law or penitentiaries.

inces was established from the beginning in recognition that the provinces' tax-raising capacity would not be adequate for their needs.[7]

Not only did the B.N.A. Act's distribution of powers contemplate a more centralized system than that of the United States— the only useful federal precedent in existence in 1867,[8] in several respects, the provinces were actually made subordinate to the centre, in violation of the principle that in a federal state the regions should be coordinate with the centre. First, by s. 90 the federal government was given the power to disallow (i.e., invalidate) provincial statutes. Secondly, by s. 58, the federal government was given the power to appoint the Lieutenant Governor of each province (and, by s. 92(1), the provinces were denied the power to alter that part of their constitutions). Thirdly, by s. 96, the federal government was given the power to appoint the judges of the superior, district and county courts of each province. Fourthly, by s. 93, the federal government was given the power to determine appeals from provincial decisions affecting minority educational rights, and the federal Parliament was given the power to enforce a decision on appeal by the enactment of "remedial laws". Fifthly, by ss. 91(29) and 92(10)(c), the federal Parliament was given the power unilaterally to bring local works within exclusive federal legislative jurisdiction simply by declaring them to be "for the general advantage of Canada". None of these five matters is to be found among the federal powers in the earlier Constitution of the United States or in the later Constitution of Australia.

Wheare was so impressed by the elements of provincial subordination in the Constitution of Canada that he refused to describe it as federal; he preferred to say that "Canada has a quasi-federal constitution".[9] This judgment is fully justified by a literal reading of the terms of the Constitution. However, the subsequent development of case law, convention and practice has virtually eliminated the elements of provincial subordination in the Constitution.

§ 5:10 Early federal dominance

In the early years of confederation, the relationship between the new national government and the provinces was if anything understated by the term quasi-federal; it was more akin to a colonial relationship. The national government, with the bulk of the governmental revenues and most of the ablest politicians, exercised a control over the provinces not

[7]Nowadays, of course, the "direct" taxation of personal and corporate income is the most lucrative source of governmental revenue; and the prohibition on "indirect" taxation has proved easy to circumvent. But these accretions in provincial fiscal capacity have still left the federal government fiscally dominant. This is related in detail in the next chapter, ch. 6, Financial Arrangements.

[8]The only other federal constitution in existence in 1867 was that of Switzerland, but its small geographic size, and different social and political environment made it a dubious precedent in comparison with the United States: see Birch, Federalism, Finance and Social Legislation (1955), xiv.

[9]Wheare, Federal Government (4th ed., 1963), 19, although he conceded (at p. 20) that the Constitution was "predominantly federal in practice".

at all unlike that of an imperial government over its colonies.[1] Over the years, however, there has been a steady growth in the power and importance of the provinces.[2] If we re-examine the centralizing features of the Constitution of Canada in the light of the current body of case law, convention and practice, it is clear that Canada now has a federal Constitution on Wheare's definition, or any other reasonable definition, and indeed one that is less centralized than that of either the United States or Australia.

§ 5:11 Judicial interpretation of the distribution of powers

The Judicial Committee of the Privy Council was the final court of appeal for Canada in constitutional cases until appeals were abolished in 1949. Two figures dominated the course of decision in Canadian constitutional cases: Lord Watson, who was a law lord (and thus a member of the Privy Council) from 1880 to 1899,[1] and Lord Haldane, who was a law lord from 1911 to 1928.[2] They believed strongly in provincial rights, and they established precedents that elevated the provinces to coordinate status with the Dominion,[3] and gave a narrow interpretation to the principal federal powers (the residuary power and the trade and commerce power) and a wide interpretation to the principal provincial power (over property and civil rights in the province).[4] The decisions of the Privy Council—the "wicked stepfathers of confederation", as Forsey called them— were much criticized in English Canada[5] (although not in French Canada)[6] for their provincial bias.

In retrospect, the decisions of the Privy Council can be seen as consis-

---

[Section 5:10]

[1]See J.R. Mallory in Crepeau and Macpherson (eds.), The Future of Canadian Federalism (1965), 3.

[2]See ch. 6, Financial Arrangements.

[Section 5:11]

[1]On Lord Watson, see Haldane's eulogy of Watson (1899) 11 Juridical Review 278; F.M. Greenwood, "Lord Watson, Institutional Self-interest, and the Decentralization of Canadian Federalism in the 1890s" (1974) 9 U.B.C.L. Rev. 244; S. Wexler, "The Urge to Idealize: Viscount Haldane and the Constitution of Canada" (1984) 29 McGill L.J. 608; Saywell, The Lawmakers: Judicial Power and the Shaping of Canadian Federalism (2002), ch. 6.

[2]On Lord Haldane, see R.F.V. Heuston, Lives of the Lord Chancellors 1885-1940 (Oxford, 1964), 185–240; J. Robinson, "Lord Haldane and the B.N.A. Act" (1970) 20 U. Toronto L.J. 55; S. Wexler, "The Urge to Idealize: Viscount Haldane and the Constitution of Canada" (1984) 29 McGill L.J. 608; Saywell, The Lawmakers: Judicial Power and the Shaping of Canadian Federalism (2002), ch. 7.

[3]*Hodge v. The Queen* (1883), 9 App. Cas. 117 (provincial legislative powers as plenary and ample as imperial Parliament); *Liquidators of the Maritime Bank v. Receiver General of N.B.*, [1892] A.C. 437 (provincial executive powers match legislative powers).

[4]For a full account see F.R. Scott, "Centralization and Decentralization in Canadian Federalism" (1951) 29 Can. Bar Rev. 1095; see also ch. 17, ch. 20, and ch. 21.

[5]E.g., O'Connor Report (Senate of Canada, 1939); B. Laskin, "Peace, Order and Good Government Re-Examined" (1947) 25 Can. Bar Rev. 1054; F.R. Scott, "Centralization and Decentralization in Canadian Federalism" (1951) 29 Can. Bar Rev. 1095.

tent with other tendencies in Canada towards a less centralized federal system than that of the United States or Australia.[7] Recent appraisals of the work of the Privy Council have tended to recognize this, and have been much less critical.[8] Judicial interpretation since the abolition of appeals has permitted some growth of federal power, and this may well continue. However, it is unlikely that there will be any wholesale rejection of Privy Council decisions: the main lines of judicial interpretation are probably irreversible.[9] For present purposes, the point is that the distribution of powers in the Constitution of Canada is much less favourable to the federal power than would be suggested merely by comparing the text with that of the American or Australian Constitutions.

§ 5:12 Federal-provincial financial arrangements

The fiscal dominance of the federal government which was established by the B.N.A. Act in 1867 has continued, but since the second world war there has been a substantial shift in power back to the provinces; and

---

[6]E.g., Tremblay Report (Quebec, 1956); L.-P. Pigeon, "The Meaning of Provincial Autonomy" (1951) 29 Can. Bar Rev. 1126; J. Beetz in Crepeau and Macpherson, The Future of Canadian Federalism (1965), 113. Tremblay, *Les compétences legislatives au Canada* (1967), although Tremblay concedes (at p. 47) that "les intentions des péres de la fédération . . . étaient de créer un régime fortement centralisé".

[7]See ch. 6, Financial Arrangements, under heading § 6:10, "Conclusions". McWhinney, Judicial Review (4th ed., 1969), 25–27, 70–71, argues that the Privy Council interpretations were consistent with the dominant political viewpoint in Canada at the time; he notes that from 1896 onwards, when the Privy Council rendered its pro-provincial decisions, Canada was mostly dominated by the Liberal Party, which depended upon the French Canadians for its parliamentary majority far more than the Conservative Party. Trudeau, Federalism and the French Canadians (1968), 198, says that "if the law lords had not leaned in that [provincial] direction, Quebec separation might not be a threat today; it might be an accomplished fact." Gilbert, Australian and Canadian Federalism 1867–1984 (1986) finds that Australian decisions tended to favour central power, while Canadian decisions tended to favour provincial power. Comparisons with the United States would produce the same, although more marked, divergence in trends of interpretation: on the commerce power, see Smith, The Commerce Power in Canada and the United States (1963).

[8]The definitive study is A.C. Cairns, "The Judicial Committee and its Critics" (1971) 4 Can. J. Pol. Sci. 301. See also Browne, The Judicial Committee and the British North America Act (1967); Cheffins and Tucker, The Constitutional Process in Canada (2nd ed., 1976), 105–110; W.R. Lederman, "Unity and Diversity in Canadian Federalism" (1975) 53 Can. Bar Rev. 597; F. Vaughan, "Critics of the Judicial Committee of the Privy Council" (1986) 19 Can. J. Poli. Sci. 495. Contra, Saywell, The Lawmakers: Judicial Power and the Shaping of Canadian Federalism (2002), who is unrelenting in his criticism of the work of the Privy Council.

[9]See the studies of the decisions of the Supreme Court of Canada since 1949 by P.C. Weiler, "The Supreme Court and Canadian Federalism" (1973) 23 U. Toronto L.J. 307; P.W. Hogg, "Is the Supreme Court of Canada Biased in Constitutional Cases?" (1979) 57 Can. Bar Rev. 721; Monahan, Politics and the Constitution (1987); Swinton, The Supreme Court and Canadian Federalism (1990); J. Leclair, "The Supreme Court of Canada's Understanding of Federalism: Efficiency at the Expense of Diversity" (2003) 28 Queen's L.J. 411; P.W. Hogg and W.K. Wright, "Canadian Federalism, the Privy Council and the Supreme Court: Reflections on the Debate about Canadian Federalism" (2005) 38 U.B.C. L. Rev. 331.

the present federal-provincial financial arrangements give the Canadian provinces more financial autonomy than is enjoyed by the states of the United States or Australia.[1] The financial arrangements are the subject of the next chapter.

§ 5:13 Disallowance

The federal power to disallow provincial statutes[1] was frequently exercised by the dominant federal government in the early years of confederation. Its use today would provoke intense resentment on the part of the provinces. If the federal objection to a provincial statute is that it is ultra vires or inconsistent with a federal law, the province may fairly insist that a court is the appropriate forum to determine the issue. If the federal objection to a provincial statute is that it is unwise, then the province may fairly reply that its voters should be left to determine the wisdom of the policies of the government which they have elected. In my view, the provincial case is unimpeachable: the modern development of ideas of judicial review and democratic responsibility has left no room for the exercise of the federal power of disallowance. This view has not been espoused in so many words by the federal government, but I think it may be safely assumed to be the prevailing official federal sentiment,[2] since the power of disallowance has not been exercised since 1943.[3] The

---

[Section 5:12]

[1]See ch. 6, Financial Arrangements, under heading § 6:10, "Conclusions".

[Section 5:13]

[1]Constitution Act, 1867, s. 90. This is not to be confused with the imperial power to disallow federal statutes: ch. 3, Independence, under heading § 3:1, "Bonds of Empire".

[2]Note, however, that in 1975 the Prime Minister suggested the possibility of using the power of disallowance over provincial laws where "their effect cuts directly across the operation of federal law or creates serious disorder particularly beyond the boundaries of the province enacting them": Letter from Prime Minister Trudeau tabled in House of Commons, July 21, 1975, *Sessional Papers* No. 301-5/185.

[3]For the history of federal disallowance of provincial legislation, see La Forest, Disallowance and Reservation of Provincial Legislation (1965); see also Saywell, The Office of Lieutenant-Governor (1957), ch. 8; Forsey, Freedom and Order (1974), 177–191; L. Wilson, "Disallowance: The Threat to Western Canada" (1975) 39 Sask. L. Rev. 156; R.C. Vipond, "Alternative Pasts, Legal Liberalism and the Demise of the Disallowance Power" (1990) 39 U.N.B.L.J. 126. In *Re Powers of Disallowance and Reservation*, [1938] S.C.R. 71, the Supreme Court of Canada held that the power of disallowance was "still a subsisting power". In *Re Resolution to Amend the Constitution*, [1981] 1 S.C.R. 753, 802, the Court said, obiter, that "reservation and disallowance of provincial legislation, although in law still open, have, to all intents and purposes, fallen into disuse." In *The Queen v. Beauregard*, [1986] 2 S.C.R. 56, 72, the Court said, obiter, that the disallowance power has fallen into "disuse". Some commentators would still support its occasional use, especially to protect civil liberties: e.g., Mallory, The Structure of Canadian Government (1984 rev. ed.), 369–370; Forsey, Freedom and Order (1974), 167–171; while others argue that it is now (by convention) obsolete: e.g., Trudeau, Federalism and the French Canadians (1968), 149; Cheffins and Tucker, The Constitutional Process in Canada (2nd ed., 1976), 86, 123; Laskin, The British Tradition in Canadian Law (1969), 122 says that the power is "dormant, if not entirely dead." Dawson, The Government of Canada (6th

Charlottetown Accord of 1992[4] would have repealed the power of disallowance, but the defeat of that set of constitutional amendments has left the power in the Constitution.

§ 5:14 Appointment of Lieutenant Governors

The federal power to appoint Lieutenant Governors is another apparent breach of the federal principle. This power is regularly exercised by the federal government,[1] but once an appointment is made the Lieutenant Governor is in no sense the agent of the federal government:[2] he or she is obliged by the conventions of responsible government to act on the advice of the provincial cabinet.[3] The Lieutenant Governor does have power under s. 90 of the Constitution Act, 1867 to withhold the royal assent from a bill enacted by the provincial legislative assembly, and to "reserve" the bill for consideration by the federal government. But the power of reservation is as obsolete as the power of disallowance, and for the same reasons; the federal government would never today instruct a Lieutenant Governor to reserve a provincial bill. There have been occasional reservations in modern times, but they have been "almost wholly frivolous and acutely embarrassing to the federal government".[4]

§ 5:15 Appointment of judges

The federal power under s. 96 of the Constitution Act, 1867 to appoint the judges of the higher provincial courts is exercised by the federal cabinet whenever a superior, district or county court judgeship has to be filled.[1] Moreover, some federal governments have been wont to treat the power as one of patronage, and to give preference to supporters of the

---

ed., 1987 by Ward), 226, says that "some of the main reasons that might have been adduced to activate the disallowance power before 1982 seem to have been largely dissipated by the Charter . . .".

[4]See ch. 4, Amendment, under heading § 4:3, "The failure to accommodate Quebec".

[Section 5:14]

[1]See ch. 9, Responsible Government, under heading § 9:3, "Law and convention".

[2]See ch. 9, Responsible Government, under heading § 9:3, "Law and convention".

[3]The Lieutenant Governor also has certain "reserve powers" which are not exercised on the advice of the provincial cabinet. These powers are designed to bridge the situation where no government enjoys the confidence of the legislative assembly. The reserve powers would be exercised upon the Lieutenant Governor's personal discretion and not upon instructions from the federal government; if the federal government were asked for advice, it would undoubtedly refuse the request. The reserve powers are discussed in ch. 9, Responsible Government, under heading §§ 9:16 to 9:24, "The Governor General's personal prerogatives".

[4]Mallory, The Structure of Canadian Government (1984 rev. ed.), 371.

[Section 5:15]

[1]See ch. 7, Courts. Actually, as that chapter shows, the more important "unitary" feature of the administration of justice in Canada consists in the fact that provincial courts decide cases arising under federal as well as provincial laws, and their decisions are subject to appeal to the central general court of appeal, the Supreme Court of Canada.

party in power in Ottawa (which is often not the party in power in the provincial capital). But the tradition of judicial independence is so strong that it has never been seriously claimed that the federally-appointed provincial judges would tend to favour the federal interest in disputes coming before them. In any event, cases involving important federal-provincial issues, for example, a challenge to the constitutionality of a statute, are usually appealed out of the provincial courts.

Before 1949, the final court of appeal was the Privy Council, whose members were appointed by the United Kingdom government. Since 1949, the final court of appeal has been the Supreme Court of Canada, which is a federal court created by a federal statute, whose judges are appointed and paid by the federal government. One of the contributions of French Canadian commentary has been to point out that the final court of appeal should not have its composition, and indeed its very existence, depend upon one government and Parliament. It is of course not seriously suggested that Ottawa would ever abolish the Court, take away the judges' tenure, attempt to influence its appointees, or "pack" the Court with centralists; but it is suggested that justice in federal-provincial controversies would be better seen to be done if the Court were entrenched in the constitution, and if the provinces had a role in appointing the judges. These ideas are pursued in the later chapter on the Supreme Court of Canada.[2]

§ 5:16 Educational appeals

The federal power under s. 93 of the Constitution Act, 1867 to enact remedial laws to correct provincial incursions on minority educational rights[1] has never been exercised, and has in practice become "obsolete".[2] It was almost exercised in 1896, when a Conservative government introduced in the federal Parliament a remedial bill to solve the Manitoba school question. But before the bill could be passed the government was defeated in an election fought on that issue. The new Liberal government of Prime Minister Laurier persuaded Manitoba itself to rectify the situation, which it did by statute in 1897.[3] Federal power under s. 93 has not been used (or seriously threatened) since 1896.

§ 5:17 Declaratory power

The federal Parliament's power under s. 92(10)(c) to bring a local work within federal jurisdiction by declaring it to be "for the general advantage of Canada" was frequently used in the past, mainly in respect

---

[2]Chapter 8, Supreme Court of Canada, under heading § 8:14, "Reform of Court".

[Section 5:16]

[1]Compare Constitution of the United States, thirteenth amendment, fourteenth amendment, fifteenth amendment, conferring upon the Congress the power to "enforce" those three amendments.

[2]Dawson, The Government of Canada (6th ed., 1987 by Ward), 306.

[3]See Schmeiser, Civil Liberties in Canada (1964), 158–166.

of local railways. It has been used only sparingly in recent years.[1] The Charlottetown Accord of 1992[2] would have amended s. 92(10)(c) to make the declaratory power subject to the consent of the Legislature of the province in which the declared work was located. The defeat of the Accord has left the power in its original, unilateral condition.

§ 5:18 Conclusion

It is fair to conclude that the unitary elements of the Canadian Constitution are quite unimportant in relation to the federal elements, and that the Canadian Constitution is federal under any reasonable definition of that term.

IV. SUPREMACY OF THE CONSTITUTION

§ 5:19 Supremacy of the Constitution

The essential characteristic of a federal constitution, as we have seen, is the distribution of governmental power between coordinate central and regional authorities. This requires a constitution which defines the powers vested in the central and regional authorities. The constitution (or at least this part of it) must be in writing, because such a vital matter could not be left to unwritten understandings.[1] The constitution must be "supreme", meaning that it must be binding on, and unalterable by, each of the central and regional authorities.[2] If either could unilaterally change the distribution of powers, then the authorities would not be coordinate: supreme power would lie with the authority having the power to change the constitution. The same idea is sometimes expressed by saying that a federal constitution must be "rigid" (or "entrenched"). The term "rigid" does not imply that it cannot be amended— for all federal constitutions contain provision for amendment—but it does imply that the power-distributing parts of the constitution cannot be amended by ordinary legislative action: a special, and more difficult, process is required for amendment.

In most unitary states, the constitution is also rigid and in writing, but it does not have to be. In the United Kingdom or New Zealand, for example, the constitution is "flexible", meaning that any part of it can be altered by ordinary legislative action. Much of the constitution of each country is not in writing; and those parts that are in writing are alterable by the ordinary legislative process.

[Section 5:17]

[1]See ch. 22, Transportation and Communication, under heading § 22:10, "Works for the general advantage of Canada".

[2]See ch. 4, Amendment, under heading § 4:3, "The failure to accommodate Quebec".

[Section 5:19]

[1]Wheare, Federal Government (4th ed., 1963), 54; Dicey, The Law of the Constitution (10th ed., 1965), 146.

[2]Wheare, Federal Government (4th ed., 1963), 54; Dicey, The Law of the Constitution (10th ed., 1965), 144.

In Canada, the powers of the Dominion and the provinces are defined in the Constitution Acts, 1867 to 1982, which are part of the "Constitution of Canada".[3] As explained in Chapter 4, Amendment, neither the federal Parliament nor a provincial legislature has the power to alter unilaterally the provisions of the Constitution of Canada: the amending procedures of Part V of the Constitution Act, 1982 must be used for that purpose.[4] For most amendments, Part V requires the assents of the two Houses of the federal Parliament and two-thirds of the provincial legislative assemblies representing 50 per cent of the population of all the provinces. This entrenchment of the Constitution of Canada makes it "rigid". As well, s. 52(1) of the Constitution Act, 1982 expressly affirms the supremacy over all other laws of the Constitution of Canada.[5]

V. ROLE OF THE COURTS

§ 5:20 Development of judicial review

We have seen that a distribution of legislative power among independent and coordinate authorities entails the supremacy of a written constitution. It has another consequence too. The provisions of a constitution distributing legislative power will be couched in general language which cannot possibly be free from doubt or ambiguity. And so there will be disputes as to whether or not a particular legislative body has the power to enact a particular statute. Any federal system therefore has to have a machinery for settling disputes about the distribution of legislative power. Neither the Constitution of the United States nor the Constitution of Canada expressly provides a machinery for settling disputes about the distribution of legislative power, and there is controversy as to what the framers of each constitution intended.[1]

In *Marbury v. Madison* (1803),[2] the Supreme Court of the United States, in an opinion delivered by Marshall C.J., took upon itself the power to settle disputes about the distribution of legislative power. The Court reached the momentous decision that an Act of Congress was invalid as unconstitutional. The Act in question purported to give to the Supreme Court of the United States the jurisdiction to issue writs of mandamus against federal courts and officials. The Court held that this

---

[3]The term is defined in s. 52(2) of the Constitution Act, 1982. The definition is discussed in ch. 1, Sources, under heading § 1:4, "Constitution of Canada".

[4]Within Part V, ss. 44 and 45 are exceptional in that they authorize limited kinds of amendment by the federal Parliament alone and the provincial Legislature alone, but ss. 44 and 45 do not extend to any of the power-distributing provisions of the Constitution of Canada.

[5]Section 52(1) is discussed in ch. 3, Independence, under heading § 3:4, "Canada Act 1982".

[Section 5:20]

[1]Strayer, The Canadian Constitution and the Courts (3rd ed., 1988), ch. 1; J. Smith, "The Origins of Judicial Review in Canada" (1983) 16 Can. J. Pol. Sci. 115. The later Australian constitution appears to envisage judicial review: G. Sawer, Australian Federalism in the Courts (Melbourne U.P., 1967), 76.

[2]*Marbury v. Madison* (1803), 5 U.S. (1 Cranch) 137.

power was original jurisdiction and not appellate jurisdiction. But the Constitution stated that with certain specified exceptions the Supreme Court was to have only appellate jurisdiction. The Supreme Court's decision that the statute was invalid was based on very simple reasoning. (The question, the Court said, was "happily, not of an intricacy proportioned to its interest".) The Court said that its duty was to say what the law was. But here there were two inconsistent laws, the Constitution and the statute. It was therefore necessary to decide which one was in truth the law. The Court held that in a conflict between the Constitution and a statute, the Constitution should prevail, because it was superior to the statute. "The people", who had established the Constitution, had "supreme" authority; they could seldom act; and they intended the Constitution to be permanent. After *Marbury v. Madison*, it became accepted in the United States (though not immediately by the executive branch of the government) that the courts did have the role of settling disputes as to the distribution of powers under the Constitution, and therefore that the courts had the power to declare invalid the acts of a democratically elected legislature.

The Privy Council (as the ultimate court of appeal for Canada) and the provincial courts, in the years immediately after 1867, assumed the right to review the validity of legislation enacted by the Canadian legislative bodies. They used an argument similar to the one that had been accepted in *Marbury v. Madison*, although the Canadian rationale was "based more on imperialism than on constitutionalism".[3] If a statute was inconsistent with the B.N.A. Act, then the B.N.A. Act had to prevail, because it was an imperial statute. Imperial statutes extending to Canada had overriding force because the Colonial Laws Validity Act provided that colonial legislation repugnant to an imperial statute extending to the colony was invalid.[4] After the Supreme Court of Canada was established in 1875, it naturally assumed the same power.[5] Since 1982, of course, the doctrine of re-pugnancy defined by the Colonial Laws Validity Act has been replaced by the supremacy clause in s. 52(1) of the Constitution Act, 1982.[6] Section 52(1) stipulates that the "Constitution of Canada"[7] is "the supreme law of Canada", and that "any law that is inconsistent with the provisions of the Constitution is, to the extent of the inconsistency, of no force or effect". Section 52(1) is the current basis of judicial review in Canada.[8]

The Constitution Act, 1982 also broadened the scope of judicial review

---

[3]Russell, The Judiciary in Canada (1987), 93.

[4]See ch. 3, Independence, under heading § 3:2, "Colonial Laws Validity Act, 1865".

[5]Strayer, The Canadian Constitution and the Courts (3rd ed., 1988), ch. 1.

[6]See ch. 3, Independence, under heading § 3:3, "Canada Act 1982".

[7]This term is defined in s. 52(2) of the Constitution Act, 1982.

[8]This point is disputable. It could be argued that judicial review does not now depend on s. 52(1), and did not before 1982 depend on the Colonial Laws Validity Act. The argument is that judicial review depends, not on a doctrine of inconsistency or repugnancy, but on a doctrine of ultra vires. (N. Siebrasse, "The Doctrinal Origin of Judicial Review and the Colonial Laws Validity Act" (1993) 1 Review of Const. Studies

by adding a Charter of Rights to the Constitution of Canada. A Charter of Rights is not essential to a federal system, of course, but when it exists it adds an additional set of provisions limiting the powers of legislative bodies. Those additional limits then give rise to judicial review in the same way as the limits created by the distribution-of-powers provisions. In the United States, judicial review under the Bill of Rights has become much more frequent than judicial review under the distribution-of-powers provisions of the Constitution. In Canada, the experience with the Charter of Rights since 1982 has been the same: many more laws are reviewed on Charter grounds than on federalism grounds.

Within the existing institutional structure in Canada (and the United States and Australia) some degree of judicial review is inevitable.[9] It is true that the courts could have developed a quite different doctrine from that of *Marbury v. Madison* by holding that each legislative body is the interpreter of its own powers. But this would only have reduced judicial review.[10] It would not have eliminated it, because eventually the courts would have had to decide which of two inconsistent laws enacted by two different law-making bodies within the federation was valid. Even if this were the only task of the courts, it would be a very important and difficult one. There would be the problem (which arises now in fields of concurrent jurisdiction) of deciding when laws were inconsistent. Then there would be the problem of deciding which of two inconsistent laws should prevail. The latter task might involve interpreting the constitution in much the same way as occurs now. (If the courts simply accorded paramountcy to federal legislation, as they do now, then the Parliament

---

75, says that the ultra vires rationale was more commonly advanced by judges in the early Canadian judicial review cases.) What is important about a constitution is, not that it is a supreme law, but that it limits the powers of legislative bodies. An attempt by a legislative body to act outside its powers is void because it is ultra vires. This argument is made in Wheare, The Constitutional Structure of the Commonwealth (1960), ch. 3. The argument suggests that s. 52(1) is not necessary to support judicial review. But the argument presupposes that it is possible to identify the provisions that limit the powers of legislative bodies. Even on the ultra vires rationale, s. 52(1) would serve the function of identifying all of the "Constitution of Canada" as constituting a set of limits on the powers of Canadian legislative bodies, since s. 52(1) declares that a law that is inconsistent with any provision of the Constitution of Canada is "of no force or effect". Thus, the difference between the inconsistency theory and the ultra vires theory now lacks practical importance for Canada, although, as Wheare shows, before 1982 in Canada and elsewhere in the Commonwealth the point was not wholly academic. It was treated in more length in the first edition of this book (1977) at pp. 43–45.

[9]Accord, H. Kelsen, General Theory of Law and State (Harvard U.P., 1946), 268.

[10]It would, however, have eliminated judicial review of legislation under the bill of rights, and thereby rendered the bill of rights powerless in the face of contradictory legislation, except to the extent that the bill of rights confers enforcement power on some body other than a court. Congressional enforcement is authorized by the thirteenth, fourteenth and fifteenth amendments of the Constitution of the United States, but judicial review has overwhelmingly dominated enforcement. In Canada, the federal Parliament and provincial legislatures can enact legislation that implements and enforces the provisions of the Charter of Rights, but only to the extent that the legislation otherwise falls within their jurisdiction; this is because the Charter expressly provides that "Nothing in this Charter extends the legislative powers of any body or authority" (s. 31).

would be legally able to take over the entire legislative field.) The fact is that disputes as to the distribution of legislative power are inevitable within a federation, and the body that is usually given the power to resolve these disputes is the courts.[11] "The need for a final, independent judicial arbiter of disputes over federal-provincial jurisdiction is implicit in a federal system."[12]

In a unitary state, the courts may also have the power to declare legislation invalid. This will be so in any unitary state that has adopted a rigid constitution. But in the United Kingdom and New Zealand the courts do not have this power. Setting aside the case where the Parliament has failed to follow the correct procedure (or manner and form) of legislation,[13] any law enacted by the United Kingdom or New Zealand Parliament will be held valid in the courts, even if it amends the constitution.[14] This is just another way of saying that the constitutions of the United Kingdom and New Zealand are flexible.

§ 5:21 Limitations of judicial review

In a federal state such as Canada, where legislative powers are distributed between a central legislative body (the federal Parliament) and regional legislative bodies (the provincial Legislatures), one function of judicial review is to enforce the distribution-of-powers rules (the rules of federalism). The courts often have to determine whether a particular statute comes within the powers conferred by the Constitution on the legislative body that enacted the statute: if the statute is judicially determined to be outside the powers conferred upon the enacting body, then the statute is ultra vires and for that reason invalid. As well, a con-

[11]Weiler, In the Last Resort (1974), ch. 6, argues that the courts should allow each legislative body to be the interpreter of its own powers, but he still concedes two functions to the courts: (1) resolving clashes between inconsistent laws (the point mentioned in the text), and (2) enforcing a prohibition on provincial laws discriminating against extra-provincial persons or products. He also leaves open the possibility of judicial review under a bill of rights. Weiler's argument is criticized in Swinton, The Supreme Court and Canadian Federalism (1990), ch. 2. See also D. Greschner, "The Supreme Court, Federalism and Metaphors of Moderation" (2000) 79 Can. Bar Rev. 47 (arguing for judicial restraint in federalism cases); A. W. MacKay, "The Supreme Court of Canada and Federalism: Does\Should Anyone Care Anymore" (2001) 80 Can. Bar Rev. 241 (welcoming a more active role for judicial review).

[12]*Re Supreme Court Act, ss. 5 and 6*, [2014] 1 S.C.R. 433, 2014 SCC 21, para. 83.

[13]See ch. 12, Parliamentary Sovereignty, under heading § 12:10, "Manner and form of future laws".

[14]Even the United Kingdom's Human Rights Act 1998, c. 42, which enacts into domestic law the terms of the European Convention on Human Rights, does not directly override inconsistent legislation, although the Act authorizes a court to make a "declaration of incompatibility" where U.K. legislation is found to be inconsistent with the Convention (s. 4(4)), and the Act authorizes a Minister of the Crown to "make amendments to the legislation as he considers necessary to remove the incompatibility" (s. 10(2)). The devolution of power to elected assemblies for Wales, Scotland and Northern Ireland creates only subordinate bodies and does not limit the powers of the Parliament at Westminster: Government of Wales Act 2006 (U.K.), c. 32; Scotland Act 1998 (U.K.), c. 46; Northern Ireland Act 1998 (U.K.), c. 47.

stitution, such as that of Canada, will contain some restrictions on legislative power which serve to protect civil libertarian values, or at any rate values other than the federal distribution of powers. Even before the adoption of the Charter of Rights in 1982, the Constitution of Canada contained various restrictions on legislative power,[1] and since 1982 the Charter of Rights has imposed a new set of restrictions on legislative power. A second function of judicial review is to enforce the Charter restrictions and the other non-federal restrictions. The courts often have to decide whether a statute violates a constitutional prohibition, for example, by unjustifiably abridging freedom of expression: if the statute is judicially determined to violate the prohibition, then the statute is ultra vires[2] and for that reason invalid.

Whether judicial review takes place on distribution-of-powers (or federalism) grounds or on Charter grounds, it appears to be a normal judicial task, since it involves the interpretation of an authoritative text, the Constitution of Canada. This task is similar to the interpretation of a statute, a will or a contract, for example. Indeed, the Constitution, like a statute, a will or a contract, often provides a clear answer to the questions it addresses, which in the case of the Constitution are questions about the extent of governmental power. It is perfectly clear, for example, that the provincial Legislatures possess the power to regulate the disposition of property on death, and that the federal Parliament lacks this power.[3] It is equally clear that both the federal Parliament and the provincial Legislatures lack the power to prohibit criticism of the government.[4] No court has ever decided either of these points, and no court is likely to be called upon to do so: they are clear from the text of the Constitution. To these and many other constitutional questions, lawyers can and do give confident answers without recourse to the courts.[5]

The questions that come before the courts are those which are difficult or doubtful, and certainly there is no lack of these. The language of the Constitution is for the most part broad and vague. The rules that distribute the whole range of legislative power occupy only a few pages of text, as does the Charter of Rights. The scope of potential governmental activity that the rules address is so enormous that many problems will

---

[Section 5:21]

[1]E.g., Constitution Act, 1867, s. 93 (denominational schools), ss. 96-100 (judiciary), s. 125 (intergovernmental taxation), s. 133 (language). There are many judicial decisions striking down laws for breach of each of these prohibitions.

[2]Some constitutional lawyers would reserve the term ultra vires for breach of the distribution-of-powers rules, but I think it is better to regard the Charter and other prohibitions as additional restrictions on the powers of the legislative bodies.

[3]The governing rule is the allocation to the provincial Legislatures of "property and civil rights in the province" by s. 92(13) of the Constitution Act, 1867.

[4]The governing rule is the guarantee of "freedom of . . . expression" in s. 2(b) of the Charter of Rights.

[5]Imagine how often lawyers have been asked by their clients, "Is there any way I can challenge this statute?", and have replied, "No".

inevitably be overlooked by the framers of the text. Moreover, the passage of time produces social and economic change which throws up new problems which could not possibly have been foreseen by the framers of the text. For these reasons, the court probably has to apply a larger discretionary judgment to its constitutional decisions than it does to its decisions in other fields of the law. That is why Hughes C.J. of the United States Supreme Court made his celebrated remark that: "We are under a Constitution, but the Constitution is what the judges say it is".[6]

The judges upon whom the large task of judicial review rests are not well suited to the policy-making which is inevitably involved. Their mandate to make decisions differs from that of other public officials in that judges are not accountable to any electorate or to any government for their decisions; on the contrary, they occupy a uniquely protected place in the system of government, which is designed to guarantee their independence from political or other influences.[7] Their background is not broadly representative of the population: they are recruited exclusively from the small class of successful, middle-aged lawyers; they do not necessarily have much knowledge of or experience in public affairs, and after appointment they are expected to remain aloof from most public issues. The resources available to the judges are limited by the practice and procedure of an Anglo-Canadian court: they are obliged to decide cases on the basis of the limited information presented to them in court; they have no power to initiate inquiries or research, no staff of investigators or researchers, and of course no power to enact a law in substitution for one declared invalid.

These limitations of mandate, background, information and power led Sir Owen Dixon, the great Chief Justice of the High Court of Australia, to say that "there is no other safe guide to judicial decisions in great conflicts than a strict and complete legalism".[8] But a "strict and complete legalism" cannot be an answer to the exercise of choice by judges in their decision-making. In those cases which find their way to the higher appellate courts, there are always competing plausible interpretations of the constitutional text and its case-law exegesis. The judges cannot escape making a choice, and the choice cannot be wholly explained by the pre-existing state of the law. It is undeniable that, as Oliver Wendell Holmes said long ago, a judicial decision may "depend on a judgment or intuition more subtle than any articulate major premise".[9]

Holmes' famous comment was made in dissent in *Lochner v. New York* (1905),[10] a case in which the Supreme Court of the United States struck down a state statute forbidding employment in a bakery for more than

---

[6]Quoted, E.S. Corwin, The Constitution and What it Means Today (Princeton U.P., 14th ed., 1978), xiii. Hughes was Governor of New York when he made the remark.

[7]See ch. 7, Courts, under heading § 7:3, "Tenure of provincial judges".

[8]The statement was made on his appointment as Chief Justice: (1952) 85 C.L.R. xiv.

[9]*Lochner v. New York* (1905), 198 U.S. 45, 76.

[10]See *Lochner v. New York* (1905), 198 U.S. 45.

60 hours per week or 10 hours per day. This law, the majority held, deprived the employer of his "liberty" of contract without "due process of law" in violation of the fourteenth amendment. Holmes J. pointed out in his dissenting opinion that this legal argument (substantive due process) masked an economic theory which had been rejected by the legislature. But the majority's ruling was applied in 159 later Supreme Court decisions, in which attempts by states to fix maximum working hours, minimum wages and maximum prices, and to prohibit anti-union activity, were held to be unconstitutional on similar grounds.[11] *Lochner* and the other substantive due process cases of that era were not overruled until 1937.[12]

The High Court of Australia—Dixon C.J.'s own court—is open to the charge that, under the cloak of "a strict and complete legalism", it was influenced by laissez faire economic theories. It blocked the major peacetime initiatives of the federal Labour government that was in office from 1941 to 1949: federal legislation to provide medical security, to regulate state banking, and to nationalize the airlines and banks was held to be unconstitutional.[13] J.R. Mallory reaches a similar conclusion about the decisions of the Canadian courts in striking down legislation enacted by the Western provinces during the depression and drought of the 1930s to relieve their farmers of the burden of debt.[14] Another Canadian example is the line of seminal decisions of the Privy Council giving a provincial cast to the British North America Act's distribution-of-powers provisions. It is widely accepted that these decisions must be explained in part by conceptions of federalism held by Lords Watson and Haldane, the dominant members of the Privy Council between 1880 and 1928.[15]

There can be no doubt that judicial review permits, indeed requires, non-elected judges to make decisions of great political significance.[16] Yet Canada's adoption of the Charter of Rights in 1982 was a conscious deci-

---

[11] W.B. Lockhart, The American Constitution (West, 8th ed., 1996), 228.

[12] *West Coast Hotel v. Parrish* (1937), 300 U.S. 379.

[13] B. Galligan, Politics of the High Court (U. Queensland, P. 1987).

[14] Mallory, Social Credit and the Federal Power (1954), esp. ch. 6.

[15] See § 5:11, "Judicial interpretation of the distribution of powers".

[16] I avoid the term "political decision", because I do not acknowledge that judges make political decisions similar to those made by politicians. To me, the element of political choice in a judicial decision is reduced to a very narrow compass by the substantive constraints of the language of the constitutional text and decided cases, and by the procedural constraints of the litigation process. A much wider choice of outcomes and reasoning is open to politicians. There is a vast American literature on the question whether and to what extent judicial decisions can be distinguished from political decisions. A seminal article is H. Wechsler, "Towards Neutral Principles of Constitutional Law" (1959) 73 Harv. L. Rev. 1, which probably exaggerates the neutrality of the process. The literature has reached avalanche proportions in recent years. Important books include A.M. Bickel, The Least Dangerous Branch (Yale U.P., 1962); R. Berger, Government by Judiciary (1977); R.M. Dworkin, Taking Rights Seriously (Duckworth, London, 1978); J.H. Ely, Democracy and Distrust (Harvard U.P., 1980); J.H. Choper, Judicial Review and the National Political Process (U. Chicago P., 1980); M.J. Perry, The Constitution, the Courts and Human Rights (Yale U.P., 1982); P. Bobbitt, Constitutional Fate (Oxford, 1982). Canadian contributions include Weiler, In the Last Resort (1974); Monahan,

sion to increase the scope of judicial review. It is hard to say whether public acceptance of judicial review flows from a belief in the myth of "a strict and complete legalism", or whether people really are content that some political choices be made by judges. It seems to me, however, that the judges' lack of democratic accountability, coupled with the limitations inherent in the adversarial judicial process, dictates that the appropriate posture for the courts in distribution of powers (or federalism) cases is one of restraint: the legislative decision should be overridden only where its invalidity is clear.[17] There should be, in other words, a presumption of constitutionality. In this way a proper respect is paid to the legislators, and the danger of covert (albeit unconscious) imposition of judicial policy preferences is minimized.

§ 5:22 Alternatives to judicial review

It is inevitable that the role of "umpire" in a federal system will attract criticism, and criticism of the courts has sometimes led to suggestions that we take away from them the task of judicial review. The difficulty is that some other and better way of resolving federalism disputes has to be found. It is already true in Canada that federal-provincial conferences of various kinds now settle many of the problems of divided jurisdiction which would otherwise reach the courts. This tendency, which is discussed later in this chapter, and in more detail in the next chapter on federal-provincial financial arrangements, could be consummated by a constitutional amendment removing federalism disputes from the jurisdiction of the courts and remitting them for solution to direct negotiations between the interested governments.[1] But the danger of this proposal is that it might leave minority regional and cultural interests, and civil liberties, insufficiently protected from the acts of powerful majorities.

A quite different proposal for reform involves the establishment outside the ordinary courts of a specialized tribunal for constitutional

---

Politics and the Constitution (1987); Swinton, The Supreme Court and Canadian Federalism (1990); Mandel, The Charter of Rights and the Legalization of Politics in Canada (1994); Hutchinson, Waiting for Coraf: A Critique of Law and Rights (1995); Bakan, Just Words: Constitutional Rights and Social Wrongs (1997); Morton and Knopff, The Charter Revolution and the Court Party (2000); Howe and Russell (eds.), Judicial Power and Canadian Democracy (2001).

[17] This argument is pursued in the later chapter on Judicial Review on Federal Grounds: see ch. 15, under heading § 15:12, "Criteria of choice", and (i), "Presumption of constitutionality". In Charter cases, however, where the constitutional contest is not between two levels of government, but between government and individual, and where the s. 33 override is available, the argument for judicial restraint is weaker; and in any event the language of s. 1 of the Charter is not consistent with judicial restraint. The scope of judicial review in Charter cases is examined in ch. 36, Charter of Rights, under heading §§ 36:4 to 36:7, "Expansion of judicial review", and ch. 38, Limitation of Rights, under heading § 38:5, "Presumption of constitutionality".

[Section 5:22]

[1] This is Weiler's argument: Weiler, *In the Last Resort* (1974), ch. 6. As pointed out, however, this does not wholly eliminate the necessity for judicial review.

disputes, which could include non-lawyers as well as lawyers, and which could be consciously composed so as to reflect different cultural and regional interests within Canada.[2] A less radical but similar proposal is to divide the Supreme Court of Canada into specialized divisions—a common law division, a civil law division and a constitutional law division; each division would be composed in such a way as to ensure maximum expertise in its own field of law, the constitutional division reflecting the different regional and cultural interests within the country.[3] But a specially-composed constitutional court or division would probably become an activist tribunal, assuming the role of giving positive direction to our constitutional law. In my view, the better posture of a court in federalism cases is one of restraint, endeavouring as far as possible to uphold the laws enacted by the elected legislative bodies.[4] Moreover, it is very difficult, and probably unwise, to isolate constitutional issues for determination by a special court or division, when they usually arise in practice in a factual setting which also raises issues of statutory interpretation, common law and (in Quebec) civil law. Indeed, when constitutional issues have been decided in isolation from their factual setting, as they sometimes are now on constitutional references, most observers agree that the resulting opinions have often been too broad and abstract.[5] On the whole, there is much to be said in favour of the present system of judicial review by a court of general appellate jurisdiction.[6]

VI. AMENDING POWER

§ 5:23 Amending power

Every nation requires the power to amend its constitution. In a unitary state with a flexible constitution, amendment is easy, requiring only an ordinary statute enacted by the state's single central legislative body. In a state with a rigid constitution, the process of amendment is by definition more difficult than the ordinary legislative process. We have already noticed that a federal state always has at least a partially rigid constitution, because it is essential that at least the power-distributing parts of the constitution be protected from change by the

[2]J.-Y. Morin, "A Constitutional Court for Canada" (1965) 43 Can. Bar Rev. 545; J.-Y. Morin, "Le Québec et l'arbitrage constitutionnel" (1967) 45 Can. Bar Rev. 608.

[3]E. McWhinney, in The Confederation Challenge (Ontario Advisory Committee on Confederation, 1967), 89; A.S. Abel, "The Role of the Supreme Court in Private Law Cases" (1965) 4 Alta. L.R. 39 argues for a similar result by removing from the Supreme Court's jurisdiction all private law cases in fields of provincial legislative authority; to like effect is P. Russell, "The Jurisdiction of the Supreme Court of Canada" (1968) 6 Osgoode Hall L.J. 1.

[4]§ 5:21 note 17 and accompanying text, above.

[5]See ch. 8, Supreme Court of Canada, under heading §§ 8:8 to 8:12, "Reference jurisdiction".

[6]The case is well argued by G.E. Le Dain, "Concerning the Proposed Constitutional and Civil Law Specialization at the Supreme Court Level" (1967) 2 Revue Juridique Thémis 107.

unilateral action of either the central or regional legislative bodies. It is therefore a feature of the federal constitutions of the United States, Australia and Canada that the amending process includes procedures designed to ensure that any amendment enjoys the support, not only of the federal legislative body (which is of course elected by all the people), but of some of the regional legislatures or governments or electorates as well.[1] Amendment is the topic of Chapter 4 of this book.

VII. SECESSION

§ 5:24 The power to secede

There is no reason in principle why a federal constitution should not give a power of secession to its provinces or states.[1] In the United States, there was a long controversy as to the existence of such a power which was only settled by the civil war of 1861-1865. After the war was over, the Supreme Court of the United States declared that "the Constitution, in all its provisions, looks to an indestructible union, composed of indestructible states".[2] In Australia, the preamble to the Constitution describes the union as "indissoluble". In Canada, there is neither judicial decision nor explicit text to the same effect, but the absence of any provisions in the Constitution authorizing secession makes clear that no unilateral secession is possible.

The question whether a province has the power to secede from the Canadian federation[3] became an issue after the election in Quebec in 1976 of the Parti Quebecois. The Parti Quebecois government held a referendum on May 20, 1980, asking the voters whether they would give to the government of Quebec a mandate to negotiate a "sovereignty-association" agreement with the government of Canada. Sovereignty-association was

[Section 5:23]

[1]Livingston, Federalism and Constitutional Change (1956) is a comparative study of the amending process in federal constitutions.

[Section 5:24]

[1]Wheare, Federal Government (4th ed., 1963), 85–87. P.J. Monahan, M.J. Bryant, N.C. Coté, "Coming to Terms with Plan B: Ten Principles Governing Secession" (C.D. Howe Institute, 1996), reviews the constitutions of 89 states; of the 89, seven permit secession, 60 are silent on the issue, and 22 forbid secession. Of the seven that permit secession, none allow a unilateral declaration of independence, and none allow the seceding territory to set the question or conduct the referendum.

[2]*Texas v. White* (1868), 74 U.S. (7 Wall.) 700, 725.

[3]For a selection of the voluminous Canadian literature on secession, see Brossard, L'accession à la souveraineté et le cas du Québec (2nd ed., 1995); D. Matas, "Can Quebec Separate?" (1975) 21 McGill L.J. 387; N. Finkelstein and G. Vegh, "The Separation of Quebec and the Constitution of Canada" (York University Centre for Public Law and Public Policy, 1992); Grand Council of the Crees, Sovereign Injustice (study by Paul Joffe, 1995); Young, The Secession of Quebec and the Future of Canada (rev. ed., 1998); P.J. Monahan, "Cooler Heads Shall Prevail: Assessing the Costs and Consequences of Quebec Separation" (C.D. Howe Institute, 1995); P.J. Monahan, M.J. Bryant, N.C. Coté, "Coming to Terms with Plan B: Ten Principles Governing Secession" (C.D. Howe Institute, 1996); P.W. Hogg, "Principles Governing the Secession of Quebec" (1997) 8 Nat. J. Con. Law 19 (part of symposium on topic taking up entire volume of journal).

a compromise between outright separation and continuance as a province of Canada. Sovereignty-association did involve the secession of Quebec (hence "sovereignty"), but it also involved an "economic association" between the new sovereign state of Quebec and (the rest of) Canada (hence "association").[4] This proposal was rejected by the Quebec voters by a majority of 59.5 per cent to 40.5 per cent.

The defeat of the 1980 referendum was followed by constitutional discussions, one purpose of which was to act on the grievances that contributed to nationalist sentiment in Quebec. Unfortunately, the Constitution Act, 1982, which emerged from this process, did not achieve the goal of an accommodation with Quebec, and Quebec was the only province that did not agree to the terms of the Constitution Act, 1982. After changes of government in Ottawa and Quebec City, Quebec did join an agreement that would have enabled it to give its approval to the Constitution Act, 1982. The Meech Lake Accord of 1987[5] seemed to provide an answer to the question, "what does Quebec want?", but unfortunately the Accord did not achieve the ratification by all provincial Legislatures that was necessary for it to come into force. The failure of the Accord led to another attempt to find an accommodation with Quebec, and this was achieved by first ministers in the Charlottetown Accord of 1992,[6] to which the Premier of Quebec was a party. Unfortunately, that Accord was also never implemented, because it was defeated in a national referendum held in 1992.

After the failures of the Meech Lake and Charlottetown Accords, the Parti Quebecois won the Quebec election of 1994 with the mandate to hold another referendum on sovereignty. The referendum was held on October 30, 1995, and it asked the voters whether "Quebec should become sovereign, after having made a formal offer to Canada for a new economic and political partnership . . . ".[7] The referendum was defeated by the narrow margin of 50.6 per cent to 49.4 per cent. Although the

---

[4]The full text in English of the question was as follows:

The Government of Quebec has made public its proposal to negotiate a new agreement with the rest of Canada, based on the equality of nations; this agreement would enable Quebec to acquire the exclusive power to make its laws, administer its taxes and establish relations abroad in other words, sovereignty and at the same time, to maintain with Canada an economic association including a common currency; any change in political status resulting from these negotiations will be submitted to the people through a referendum; on these terms, do you agree to give the government of Quebec the mandate to negotiate the proposed agreement between Quebec and Canada? Yes/No.

[5]See ch. 4, Amendment, under heading § 4:3, "The failure to accommodate Quebec".

[6]See ch. 4, Amendment, under heading § 4:3, "The failure to accommodate Quebec".

[7]The full text in English of the question was:

Do you agree that Quebec should become sovereign, after having made a formal offer to Canada for a new economic and political partnership, within the scope of the bill respecting the future of Quebec and of the agreement signed on June 12, 1995?

The "bill respecting the future of Quebec" was tabled in the Quebec National Assembly on September 7, 1995 as Bill 1, but was not to be enacted until after an affirmative vote in the referendum; it therefore was never enacted. This Bill purported to set out some of the arrangements for sovereignty, including assertions that Quebec's boundaries would remain the same (s. 10), that Quebec citizenship could be held concurrently question held out to voters the prospect of a continuing "economic and political partnership" with Canada, the question was stronger than the 1980 question for two reasons. First, whereas the 1980 referendum had merely sought a mandate to negotiate sovereignty-association with Canada, the terms of the 1995 referendum made clear that sovereignty was going to be declared regardless of whether Canada accepted the offer of partnership. The voters had to contemplate the possibility of sovereignty without association. Secondly, whereas the 1980 referendum question was explicit that a second referendum would be held to approve the outcome of the sovereignty-association negotiations, the terms of the 1995 referendum made clear that the Quebec National Assembly was empowered to proclaim Quebec as a sovereign state as soon as the partnership negotiations were completed or as soon as the partnership negotiations were judged to be fruitless.[8] In neither case was there to be a second referendum to enable the people to pass judgment on the actual arrangements for the separation of the province.

The 1995 referendum proceeded on the assumption that a unilateral declaration of independence would be legally effective to remove Quebec, with its present boundaries, from Canada, without the need for any amendment of the Constitution of Canada and regardless of whether the terms of separation were agreed to by Canada. This extraordinary claim was not challenged by the federal government of Prime Minister Chretien before or during the referendum campaign. The claim was challenged by a private citizen, Guy Bertrand, who obtained a declaration from the Quebec Superior Court that Quebec had no power to proclaim itself independent in disregard of the amending procedures of the Constitution.[9] However, the Court refused to issue an injunction to prohibit the holding of the referendum, and the referendum proceeded as scheduled, yielding the narrow "No" majority that has already been described. The Attorney General of Canada had refused to participate in the *Bertrand* proceedings, leaving to a private citizen the role of protecting the territorial integrity of the nation.[10]

Eventually, after nearly losing the referendum, and facing the pros-

---

with Canadian citizenship (s. 13), that Quebec's currency would remain the Canadian dollar (s. 14), and that Quebec would continue to be a party to the North American Free Trade Agreement (s. 15). The "agreement signed on June 12, 1995" was an agreement between the leaders of Quebec's three separatist parties: the Bloc Québécois, the Parti Québécois, and the Action democratique du Quebec. That agreement was scheduled to Bill 1 and it set out the terms of the "new economic and political partnership" that would be proposed to Canada following an affirmative vote. The terms included the creation of supra-national institutions in which Quebec would be equally represented with Canada and would have the power to veto Canadian policies in a wide range of economic and political matters.

[8]Bill 1, previous note, s. 26.

[9]*Bertrand v. Que.* (1995), 127 D.L.R. (4th) 408 (Que. S.C.).

[10]*Bertrand v. Que.* (1995), 127 D.L.R. (4th) 408 (Que. S.C.) had been decided in an interlocutory proceeding before trial. After the referendum, the Attorney General of Quebec moved to have the action dismissed, not merely on the ground that it was moot (the referendum having been held), but also on the ground that the court had no jurisdiction to rule on Quebec secession. This latter ground finally drew the Attorney General

pect that another referendum on secession would eventually be held in Quebec,[11] the federal government did come to appreciate the merit of securing a legal ruling on the validity of a unilateral declaration of independence. The *Secession Reference* (1998)[12] was a reference by the federal government to the Supreme Court of Canada, in which the Court was asked whether Quebec could secede unilaterally from Canada. Three questions were put to the Court.[13] The first asked what was the position under the Constitution of Canada, to which the Court replied that unilateral secession was not permitted. The second question asked what was the position under international law, to which the Court gave the same answer. The third question, which asked what was the position if the Constitution of Canada and international law were in conflict, did not have to be answered.[14]

The Supreme Court of Canada in the *Secession Reference* held that the secession from Canada of a province could not be undertaken in defiance of the terms of the Constitution of Canada. The principle of the rule of law or constitutionalism required that a government, even one mandated by a popular majority in a referendum, must still obey the rules of the Constitution. A secession would require an amendment of the Constitution of Canada, and would have to be accomplished in accordance with the Constitution's amending procedures. The Court had not been asked to determine which of the amending procedures was the correct one, and it expressly refrained from doing so.[15] However, the Court did state that the procedure would involve the participation of the federal government and the other provinces. It followed that Quebec's secession would need to be negotiated with the federal government and the other provinces, and could not be accomplished unilaterally. This

---

of Canada into the case to argue that secession had to proceed in accordance with the rule of law, and the court had jurisdiction to determine what were the applicable rules. The motion to dismiss was denied: *Bertrand v. Que.* (1996), 138 D.L.R. (4th) 481 (Que. S.C.). The Attorney General of Quebec then withdrew from the proceedings, announcing that "the only judge and the only jury that can decide the future of the people of Quebec are Quebecers themselves": The Globe and Mail, September 5, 1996, p. A1. The Government of Canada, seeking a speedier resolution of the issues, then directed the reference that is described in the text.

[11]After the defeat of the Yes side in the 1995 referendum, Premier Parizeau resigned as leader of the Parti Québécois and Premier of Quebec, and was replaced by Premier Bouchard, who immediately announced that another referendum would be held, but not until after the next provincial election.

[12]*Re Secession of Quebec*, [1998] 2 S.C.R. 217. The unanimous judgment was delivered by "the Court".

[13]The government of Quebec refused to participate in the reference, but the Court appointed a counsel from Quebec to be an amicus curiae (friend of the court), and the amicus argued the case in opposition to the federal government.

[14]The Court held (paras. 111–138) that the right of self-determination in international law did not authorize a unilateral secession except in the case of a people under colonial rule or foreign occupation or perhaps some analogous form of domination, none of which applied to Quebec. Otherwise, international law would require compliance with the domestic constitutional law of the host state. Therefore, there was no difference between the requirements of international law and those of domestic constitutional law.

[15]*Re Secession of Quebec*, [1998] 2 S.C.R. 217, para. 105.

was straightforward constitutional law (although it had always been denied by the Parti Quebecois government of Premier Bouchard), but the Court did not stop there. The Court said that a referendum in Quebec that yielded a "clear" majority on a "clear" question in favour of secession, while ineffective by itself to accomplish a secession, "would confer legitimacy on demands for secession" and "would give rise to a reciprocal obligation on all parties to Confederation to negotiate constitutional changes to respond to that desire".[16]

This obligation to negotiate the terms of secession was an entirely new idea in the constitutional law of Canada. The Court found it to be a corollary of the fundamental, but unwritten, constitutional principles of "democracy" and "federalism".[17] The actual negotiations had to proceed in accordance with the same two principles of democracy and federalism, along with the equally fundamental principles of "constitutionalism and the rule of law, and the protection of minorities". The way in which these vague principles would govern negotiations was not made clear, but they seemed to add up, in the view of the Court, to an obligation on each side to negotiate in good faith. The Court acknowledged that the complications of a secession were such that "even negotiations carried out in conformity with the underlying constitutional principles could reach an impasse", but the Court reaffirmed that the Constitution required an amendment, which required a negotiated agreement, and the Court refused to "speculate" as to what would transpire if an agreement were not achieved.[18]

What would happen if one side refused to negotiate or did not do so in good faith? Or, to put the same question in different words, how is the constitutional obligation to negotiate to be enforced? The Court acknowledged that "where there are legal rights there are remedies", but went on to suggest that in these circumstances the only remedies might be "political". (The Court did not explain why the obligation to negotiate was a legal one if it were subject to no legal sanction.) The Court said that it "has no supervisory role over the political aspects of negotiations". These political aspects included the question whether the referendum had yielded "a clear majority on a clear question" (which is the fact that gives rise to the obligation to negotiate) and the question whether the different parties were negotiating in good faith (that is, adopting negotiating positions that were in accord with the underlying constitutional principles).[19] What were the "political" sanctions for a failure to negotiate or to negotiate in good faith? The Court did not say, except to note that any such failure might have "important ramifications

[16] *Re Secession of Quebec*, [1998] 2 S.C.R. 217, para. 88.

[17] See ch. 15, Judicial Review on Federal Grounds, under heading § 15:28, "Unwritten constitutional principles".

[18] *Re Secession of Quebec*, [1998] 2 S.C.R. 217, para. 97.

[19] *Re Secession of Quebec*, [1998] 2 S.C.R. 217, paras. 97–102.

at the international level", undermining the defaulting government's legitimacy in the eyes of the international community.[20]

The Court did not close its eyes to the possibility that a de facto secession might take place without the required agreement or the required amendment. Such a secession would be unconstitutional. However, an unconstitutional secession could become successful if the seceding government achieved effective control of a territory and recognition by the international community. In that case, the constitutional law of Canada would eventually have to recognize the reality. This was the principle of effectiveness (the Court coined the word "effectivity"). In that way, a unilateral secession might ultimately become the successful root of a new state. The principle of effectiveness, which was only briefly discussed by the Court,[21] but which could become of great importance in the event of a failure of negotiations, is discussed more fully later in this chapter.[22]

The immediate sequel to the *Secession Reference* was the enactment by Parliament of the Clarity Act,[23] which picks up on the Court's insistence that it would be for the political actors, not the Court, to determine whether a referendum had yielded a clear majority on a clear question. Section 1 of the Act provides that, if a province proposes a referendum on secession, the House of Commons is to consider the proposed question and determine whether the question is "clear". Whether a question is clear depends on whether, in the opinion of the House of Commons, "the question would result in a clear expression of the will of the population of a province on whether the province should cease to be part of Canada and become an independent state". The Act stipulates in advance that a question is not clear if it "merely focuses on a mandate to negotiate", or if it "envisages economic or political arrangements with Canada that obscure a direct expression of the will of the population of that province on whether the province should cease to be part of Canada". (Note that neither the 1980 question nor the 1995 question

[20] *Re Secession of Quebec*, [1998] 2 S.C.R. 217, para. 103.

[21] *Re Secession of Quebec*, [1998] 2 S.C.R. 217, paras. 106–108 (constitutional law), 140–146 (international law).

[22] § 5:26, "Secession by unilateral act".

[23] An Act to give effect to the requirement for clarity as set out in the opinion of the Supreme Court of Canada in the Quebec Secession Reference, S.C. 2000, c. 26. The Act does not have an official short title. For commentary on the Act, see P.J. Monahan, Doing the Rules (C.D. Howe Institute Commentary, 2000). The Parti Québécois Government of Quebec countered the federal Act with its own Act (also lacking a short title), An Act respecting the exercise of the fundamental rights and prerogatives of the Quebec people and the Quebec State, S.Q. 2000, c. 46, which asserts, among other things, that the Quebec people have the right "to determine alone" the legal status of Quebec (s. 3); and that the winning option in a referendum for that purpose is "fifty per cent of the valid votes cast plus one" (s. 4). Although the assertions are perhaps open to more than one interpretation, each appears to be inconsistent with the rulings in the *Secession Reference*.

would qualify as clear under the Act.)[24] If the question is determined not to be clear, then the Government of Canada is prohibited by the Act from entering into negotiations for secession following a referendum based on that question. Needless to say, the Act does not (and constitutionally could not) prohibit a province from holding a referendum on an unclear question, and indeed the Government of Quebec might wish to consult the people on new political or economic arrangements (for example), but a referendum on an unclear question could not become the basis for the secession of the province (as opposed to some new constitutional or administrative structure).

Section 2 of the Clarity Act provides that, if a question is clear, and if a referendum on that question gains a majority of votes in favour of the secessionist option, the House of Commons is to consider the result and determine whether the majority is "clear". The Act does not define when a majority is clear. It leaves the issue for determination by the House of Commons, requiring that the House of Commons take into account the size of the majority, the percentage of eligible voters who voted, and "any other matters or circumstances it considers to be relevant". A definite rule as to the required size of the majority would have been clearer, for example, a requirement of a two-thirds majority of those voting or a majority of all those eligible to vote. The theory of the Act, no doubt, is that a definite rule would be too crude an instrument, and it is better for the House of Commons to make a judgment in all the circumstances of a particular referendum as to whether the majority was large enough and sufficiently inclusive of minorities to form a stable basis for a new state. If the judgment of the House of Commons is that the majority in favour of secession is not clear, then the Government of Canada is prohibited by the Act from entering into negotiations for secession.

Section 3 of the Clarity Act "recognizes" that, under the Constitution of Canada, there is no right of unilateral secession, and that an amendment of the Constitution of Canada would be required for a province to secede from Canada. It is odd to find propositions of constitutional law articulated in a statute, but there may be some point in enacting the obvious. It is worth remembering that, until the clear rulings of the *Secession Reference*, these propositions were vehemently and routinely denied by the Government of Quebec, and that, before and during the 1995 referendum campaign, the Government of Canada was too timid to assert these basic safeguards of the integrity of the nation. Section 3 goes on to provide that, even if a question is clear and the majority is clear, no Minister of the Crown is to propose a constitutional amendment to effect the secession of the province unless "the Government of Canada has addressed, in its negotiations, the terms of secession that

[24]Contrast the question put to the people of Scotland in a secession referendum on September 18, 2014: "Do you agree that Scotland should be an independent country?". Not only was this question free of the wordy obfuscations of the Quebec referenda of 1980 and 1995 (§ 5:24 notes 4 and 7), it had been settled by agreement of the governments of the United Kingdom and Scotland. In the vote, the "no" side prevailed by 55 percent to 45 per cent.

are relevant in the circumstances, including the division of assets and liabilities, any changes to the borders of the province, the rights, interests and territorial claims of the Aboriginal peoples of Canada, and the protection of minority rights".

The *Secession Reference* and the Clarity Act make clear that a constitutional amendment is needed for the secession of a province, and they set some useful ground rules for the consultation of the Quebec population, and for the initiation of negotiations leading to the required constitutional amendment. By the same token, they acknowledge that Canada is divisible, and that a clearly expressed will to secede would have to be respected by the rest of the country, at least to the point of good-faith negotiation of the terms of secession.

§ 5:25 Secession by amendment

The Supreme Court of Canada in the *Secession Reference*[1] affirmed the obvious proposition that the secession of a province could be accomplished by amendment of the Constitution of Canada. However, it is not clear which of the five different amending procedures is the correct one.[2] It is clear that a secession amendment could not be enacted by the province desiring to secede, relying on s. 45 of the Constitution Act, 1982 (which allows for amendment by the provincial Legislature alone), because secession would not be simply an amendment of the "constitution of the province". It would have myriad effects on the constitution of the rest of the country by reducing the number of provinces, reducing the territory, reducing the population, reducing federal public property, reducing the membership of the Senate, House of Commons and Supreme Court of Canada, and requiring new arrangements with respect to (among many other things) shared use of the St. Lawrence Seaway, land access from the western portion of the country to the eastern portion, division of the national debt, boundary adjustments, citizenship, mobility and immigration, trade, currency, aboriginal and treaty rights, language rights, and so on. It is also clear that a secession amendment could not be enacted by the federal Parliament alone under s. 44 of the Constitution Act, 1982 or by the "some-but-not-all-provinces procedure" of s. 43.

The question is whether a secession could be accomplished under the general amending procedure of s. 38 of the Constitution Act, 1982 (which is the seven-fifty formula, requiring the assents of both houses of the federal Parliament and of the legislative assemblies of two-thirds of the provinces representing 50 per cent of the population), or whether it would require the unanimity procedure of s. 41 (which requires the assents of both houses of the federal Parliament and of the legislative assemblies of all of the provinces). The argument for the general amending procedure of s. 38 is that s. 38 covers all matters not specifically provided

[Section 5:25]

[1] *Re Secession of Quebec*, [1998] 2 S.C.R. 217.

[2] The amending procedures are described in ch. 4, Amendment.

for elsewhere in the amending procedures, and secession is not provided for anywhere else. The argument for the unanimity procedure of s. 41 is that secession would have an indirect impact on the matters specified in s. 41, and it would be anomalous if secession (the most radical amendment of all) could be accomplished more easily than some other classes of amendments. Academic commentators are divided on this difficult question.[3] The Supreme Court of Canada was not asked to provide a ruling on the issue in the *Secession Reference* and the Court did not express any view. The issue will have to be resolved if secession ever becomes a reality, and another reference back to the Court will be needed in order to obtain an answer that is authoritative.

The important element that the Supreme Court of Canada added to the amending procedures in its opinion in the *Secession Reference* was the existence of an obligation on the part of all parties to the amending procedures to use their best efforts to negotiate an agreed-upon amendment in the event that the people of Quebec voted to secede by a clear majority on a clear question. Without this ruling, it is by no means obvious that the federal government and the other provinces would be prepared to negotiate the break-up of their country. In the United States, the attempt by the southern states to secede in 1861 was opposed by the federal government and crushed by war. In Canada and Australia, more cautious attempts to secede by Nova Scotia in 1868 and by Western Australia in 1934 were successfully opposed by the federal government.[4] While the secession of the southern states of the United States was complicated by the slavery issue, there is no doubt that the secessionist movements in the southern United States, Nova Scotia and Western Australia enjoyed the support of a majority of the people in those regions.[5] Yet this fact was not regarded as sufficient to justify federal cooperation or even acquiescence. If the Supreme Court's new rule had

[3]My tentative view is that the general amending procedure is the correct one, a view that is shared by Brun and Tremblay, Droit constitutionnel (4th ed., 2002), 245 and J. Woehrling, "Les aspects juridiques d'une éventuelle sécession du Québec" (1995) 74 Can. Bar Rev. 293, 310–313. The majority of commentators line up behind the unanimity procedure, e.g., N. Finkelstein and G. Vegh, "The Separation of Quebec and the Constitution of Canada" (York University Centre for Public Law and Public Policy, 1992), 6–8; P.J. Monahan, "Cooler Heads Shall Prevail: Assessing the Costs and Consequences of Quebec Separation" (C.D. Howe Institute, 1995), 8; Young, The Secession of Quebec and the Future of Canada (rev. ed., 1998), 247; Monahan, Constitutional Law (2nd ed., 2002), 200, 218.

[4]In 1868, Nova Scotia petitioned the imperial Parliament for an amendment allowing Nova Scotia to secede from Canada. Like all requests for amendments which did not come from the federal government, the petition was denied. In 1934, Western Australia requested an imperial amendment to the Australian Constitution allowing it to secede from the Commonwealth. A select committee of Lords and Commons decided that the request should not be considered because it had not come from the federal government (which was opposed): *Report to consider the petition of the State of Western Australia* (House of Commons, Parliamentary Papers, 1934–35, vol. 6). The precedents of Nova Scotia and Western Australia are examined by Brossard, L'accession à la souveraineté et le cas du Québec (2nd ed., 1995), 275–281; D. Matas, "Can Quebec Separate?" (1975) 21 McGill L.J. 387, 392.

[5]In Nova Scotia, nearly two-thirds of the voters had signed a petition in favour of

applied to these earlier precedents, the Confederacy, Nova Scotia and Western Australia would presumably have become new nation states. There is no historical basis for the proposition that a referendum[6] in the province that desires to secede should impose an obligation of negotiation on the other parties[7] to the amending procedures. However, this is now the law of Canada.

§ 5:26 Secession by unilateral act

The Supreme Court of Canada in the *Secession Reference* (1998)[1] held that Quebec had no right to secede unilaterally from Canada, even if secession was approved by a clear majority of people in Quebec voting in a referendum on a clear question. However, the referendum would give rise to a constitutional obligation on the part of the federal government and the other provinces to negotiate in good faith with Quebec with a view to producing an agreed-upon amendment to the Constitution of Canada. In an ideal world, an amendment would be agreed upon, and the secession of the province would be accomplished in compliance with the Constitution. In the real world, there is a serious risk that the participants, even working in the shadow of the constitutional obligation, would be unable to reach an agreement on the issue. What would happen then? The Supreme Court of Canada acknowledged this possibility, but refused to speculate on what would happen then.[2] However, the Court did recognize the possibility of a unilateral declaration of independence by Quebec, and the Court pointed out that a de facto secession could eventually become successful by virtue of the principle of effectiveness ("effectivity", as the Court described it). The principle of effectiveness would eventually confer legality on a de facto secession by Quebec after Quebec achieved effective control of its territory to the exclusion of the federal government.[3]

A unilateral secession would, of course, be illegal because it would be unauthorized by the existing rules of constitutional law. But such a

---

secession; in Western Australia nearly two-thirds of the voters had voted for secession in a referendum: D. Matas, "Can Quebec Separate?" (1975) 21 McGill L.J. 387, 402.

[6]A referendum was the basis for the admission of Newfoundland to confederation in 1949. The admission was accomplished by imperial amendment of the Constitution, but the request for the amendment was preceded by a referendum in Newfoundland in which a majority of votes cast favoured entry. However, the referendum was employed in that case only because Newfoundland had no Legislature in 1949 and the procedure for admission stipulated by s. 146 of the Constitution (addresses by the Parliament of Canada and Legislature of Newfoundland) had to be modified.

[7]The special position of the Aboriginal people in Quebec, to whom the federal government owes a fiduciary duty, is the subject of a massive study, *Sovereign Injustice* (1995), which was prepared by Paul Joffe, and commissioned and published by the Grand Council of the Crees; it is a wide-ranging, scholarly examination of the domestic and international law on secession.

[Section 5:26]

[1]*Re Secession of Quebec*, [1998] 2 S.C.R. 217.

[2]*Re Secession of Quebec*, [1998] 2 S.C.R. 217, para. 97.

[3]*Re Secession of Quebec*, [1998] 2 S.C.R. 217, para. 106.

break in legal continuity may equally be regarded as a revolution, and it is a demonstrable fact that a successful revolution eventually becomes the foundation of a new and entirely legitimate legal order. The legal efficacy of a successful revolution is demonstrated by the fact that many countries whose regimes are universally recognized as lawful have had breaks in legal continuity at some time in their history. The United States springs most readily to mind: the declaration of independence in 1776, the adoption of state constitutions by each of the rebelling colonies after 1776, the adoption of the articles of confederation in 1777 and their replacement by the present federal constitution in 1787 were all unauthorized by any existing rules of constitutional law. Even the United Kingdom has had breaks in legal continuity: in 1649, when Charles I was executed and the Commonwealth was established under Cromwell; in 1660, when the Stuarts were restored to the throne; and in 1689, when William and Mary assumed the throne under the Bill of Rights.[4]

In assessing the legality of a regime established by revolution—meaning any break in legal continuity—the issue for the courts is simply whether or not the revolution has been successful. As de Smith says, "legal theorists have no option but to accommodate their concepts to the facts of political life".[5] In *Madzimbamuto v. Lardner-Burke* (1969),[6] the Privy Council had to decide whether validity should be accorded to the acts of the legislature and government of Southern Rhodesia after the "unilateral declaration of independence" (U.D.I.) from Britain in 1965. Their lordships held that the post-U.D.I. acts were not valid, because it could not be said "with certainty" that the break-away government was in effective control of the territory which it claimed the right to govern. Their lordships pointed out that Britain was still claiming to be the lawful government and was taking steps to regain control. In a later case, the Appellate Division of the High Court of Rhodesia decided that, having regard to developments since the decision of *Madzimbamuto*, it could "now predict with certainty that sanctions will not succeed in their objective of overthrowing the present government and of restoring the British government to the control of the government of Rhodesia".[7] The Court accordingly held that the existing Rhodesian government was the legal government, and the post-U.D.I. constitution was the only valid constitution.[8]

---

[4]Jennings, The Law and the Constitution (5th ed., 1959), 159; de Smith and Brazier, Constitutional and Administrative Law (8th ed., 1998), 70.

[5]de Smith and Brazier, Constitutional and Administrative Law (8th ed., 1998), 71.

[6]*Madzimbamuto v. Lardner-Burke*, [1969] 1 A.C. 645.

[7]*R. v. Ndhlovu*, [1968] 4 S.A.L.R. 515, 532. The decision was never appealed to the Privy Council, probably because the Rhodesian government did not recognize the authority of the Privy Council (the government was not represented before the Privy Council in *Madzimbamuto)* and an appeal would have been futile.

[8]Subsequent events suggested that this conclusion was premature. Guerilla war led the break-away government to seek a constitutional settlement with the United

In *Republic of Fiji v. Prasad* (2001),[9] a military-supported Interim Government, which had assumed power following a coup d'etat against an elected parliamentary government, had purported to abrogate the 1997 constitution of Fiji. The Interim Government had put in place a process to develop a new constitution that would be more favourable to the interests of indigenous Fijians (as opposed to Indo-Fijians, the other principal community). Mr Prasad, a citizen of Fiji (of the Indo-Fijian community), brought an action for a declaration that the 1997 constitution was still in force as the supreme law of Fiji. A judge of the High Court of Fiji granted the declaration. The Interim Government, instead of ignoring the decision in normal revolutionary fashion, appealed the decision to the Court of Appeal of Fiji.[10] The Court of Appeal affirmed the decision of the trial judge. The Court acknowledged that the Interim Government was securely in control of the government, but noted that the elected pre-coup government was ready, willing and able to resume power, and several court proceedings (as well as Mr Prasad's) had been brought to reestablish the former government. As well, although the nation was peaceful, affidavit evidence showed widespread unhappiness with the coup and a desire for the restoration of normal parliamentary government. In these circumstances, the effectiveness of the new regime was not established, and the pre-coup constitution had not been abrogated. This decision brought an end to the coup, because it was accepted by the Interim Government, which made way for the restoration of parliamentary government under the 1997 constitution.[11]

Applying the same analysis to the hypothetical case of a unilateral declaration of independence by Quebec, the issue for the courts would be whether they could predict with certainty that the secession would be successful, that is to say, that federal authority would no longer be exercised in Quebec.[12] Obviously, the application of this criterion would depend a great deal on the attitude of the federal government. As long

---

Kingdom (as well as with the Black majority of Southern Rhodesia). A settlement was agreed upon at a conference in London in 1979, and independence and a new constitution (under which the white minority no longer held power) was granted to the state, now called Zimbabwe, by imperial statute: Zimbabwe Act 1979 (U.K.), c. 60; Zimbabwe Constitution Order 1979 (U.K.), S.I. 1979, No. 1600.

[9]*Republic of Fiji v. Prasad*, [2001] FJCA 1 (Fiji C.A.).

[10]The Court of Appeal comprised judges who were based outside Fiji, two from New Zealand, one from each of Australia, Papua New Guinea and Tonga. All had been sworn in before the coup d'état.

[11]See G. Williams, "The Case that Stopped a Coup: The Rule of Law and Constitutionalism in Fiji" (2001) 1 Oxford U. Cth. L.J. 73. Immediately after the decision, the Interim Government resigned. Rather than reappointing the pre-coup Prime Minister and cabinet, the President of Fiji appointed the Interim Government as a caretaker administration, dissolved Parliament and called a general election under the 1997 constitution.

[12]This would be the issue for the courts *inside* Quebec, and it must be remembered that the courts in Quebec are not federal courts, although the judges of the superior courts are federally appointed. Presumably, the Supreme Court of Canada, although a federal court, would decide issues arising on appeal from Quebec as if it were a Quebec court. The issue would be different for courts outside Quebec, whether Canadian or

as it asserted its continuing authority over Quebec in areas of federal jurisdiction, it would be difficult for the courts to characterize the secession as successful. Notice that a mere likelihood of success would not justify the courts in "changing sides", for that would have the perverse effect of rendering illegal any efforts by the federal government to assert its authority, which would tend to implicate the courts in the political struggle.[13] The courts would have to uphold the pre-existing law of the federation until it was certain that it had been effectively replaced.[14] Only after the federal government had expressly or im pliedly abandoned its authority over Quebec (and there was no significant insurgency within Quebec), would the courts pronounce the separatist regime lawful.[15]

---

foreign; they would not exercise their own judgment as to the efficacy of the separatist regime, but would ascertain the attitude of their own government and act upon it as correct: *Carl Zeiss Stiftung v. Rayner and Keeler (No. 2)*, [1967] 1 A.C. 853; contrast *R. v. Ndhlovu*, [1968] 4 S.A.L.R. 515, 532 with *Adams v. Adams*, [1971] P. 188 (P.D.A. Div.); if the separatist government were unrecognized, then its acts would be treated as invalid, although it is possible that effect could be given to some acts under the principle of necessity: [1967] 1 A.C. 853, 954; H.R. Hahlo, "The Privy Council and the Gentle Revolution" (1970) 16 McGill L.J. 92, 97–101; P.W. Hogg, "Necessity in a Constitutional Crisis" (1989) 15 Monash U.L. Rev. 253.

[13] *Madzimbamuto v. Lardner-Burke*, [1969] 1 A.C. 645, 725. The argument by H.R. Hahlo, "The Privy Council and the Gentle Revolution" (1970) 16 McGill L.J. 92, 101–104, that the judges of the break-away country "have no choice but to obey [the revolutionary government's] decrees", apparently without regard for the question whether the revolution has been successful, seems objectionable in principle since it involves disregarding existing law in favour of the acts of a temporary usurper; it is also inconsistent with the decision in *Madzimbamuto*, in which, it must be remembered, the Privy Council was sitting as a Rhodesian court: [1969] 1 A.C. 645, 724.

[14] The doctrine of *effectiveness* (discussed in the text) recognizes a revolution in the radical sense that it causes the displacement of the constitution and its replacement by a new constitutional structure. There is also a doctrine of *necessity* that recognizes a revolution in the limited sense of upholding the legality of acts that were unauthorized by the constitution in order to preserve order and avoid chaos. The doctrine of necessity will uphold some acts of a usurping regime whose authority has not been established by the doctrine of effectiveness. The doctrine of necessity was applied by the Supreme Court of the United States after the civil war to some of the internal acts performed by the confederate states during their unsuccessful secession: see, e.g., *Texas v. White* (1868), 7 Wall. (74 U.S.) 700, 733; *Horn v. Lockhart* (1873), 17 Wall. (84 U.S.) 570, 580; *Baldy v. Hunter* (1898), 64 Davis (171 U.S.) 388, 400, 491. It was applied by Lord Pearce in dissent in *Madzimbamuto v. Lardner-Burke*, [1969] 1 A.C. 645, but Lord Reid for the majority, without rejecting the principle, held it inapplicable to Southern Rhodesia on the ground that the United Kingdom had enacted a regime of law for the colony which left "no legal vacuum": *Madzimbamuto v. Lardner-Burke*, [1969] 1 A.C. 645, 729. The doctrine of necessity was applied by the Court of Appeal of Fiji in *Republic of Fiji v. Prasad*, [2001] FJCA 1 (Fiji C.A.), to uphold most of the decisions of the illegal Interim Government while it was in control of the government: for discussion, see G. Williams, "The Case that Stopped a Coup: The Rule of Law and Constitutionalism in Fiji" (2001) 1 Oxford U. Cth. L.J. 73. See also ch. 58, Effect of Unconstitutional Law, under heading § 58:8, "Wholesale invalidation of laws".

[15] See Brossard, L'accession à la souveraineté et le cas du Québec (2nd ed., 1995), 309; D. Matas, "Can Quebec Separate?" (1975) 21 McGill L.J. 387, 393–395.

VIII. COOPERATIVE FEDERALISM

§ 5:27 Cooperative federalism

The formal structure of the Constitution carries a suggestion of eleven legislative bodies each confined to its own jurisdiction, and each acting independently of the others. In some fields, that is exactly what happens.[1] However, in many fields, effective policies require the joint, or at least complementary, action of more than one legislative body. Particularly is this so where humanitarian and egalitarian sentiments have called for nation-wide minimum standards of health, education, income maintenance and other public services, most of which are within the territorially-limited jurisdiction of the provinces.

The formal structure of the Constitution also carries a suggestion of eleven separate fiscal systems, with each province levying taxes to raise the revenue it needs for its legislative policies, and the federal government doing the same. But if this were in fact the case the poorer provinces would be forced to provide much lower standards of public services, and much less economic opportunity, for their residents. In order to counter Canada's disparities in regional wealth, the richer regions have to help the poorer regions. To some extent they have always done so, but the current redistribution of governmental revenue through shared-cost programmes and equalization grants is on an unprecedented scale of size and complexity.

No federal nation could survive and flourish through war and peace, depression and inflation—to say nothing of shifting popular values—without the means of adapting its constitution to change. But the formal institutions lack the capacity to respond. Major change does not come through the courts: judicial interpretation accomplishes only incremental changes in the Constitution, and the changes do not necessarily reflect the needs of the day. Nor does change typically occur through the amending process. The amending procedures of the Constitution Act, 1982 require such broad consensus for most amendments that they cannot be a regular form of adaptation.

The related demands of interdependence of governmental policies, equalization of regional disparities, and constitutional adaptation have combined to produce what is generally described as "cooperative federalism".[2] The essence of cooperative federalism is a network of relationships between the executives of the central and regional

---

[Section 5:27]

[1]There is a school of thought that holds that competition between governments is more typical than cooperation, and more desirable, because competing governments are more likely to provide people with the policies they prefer: Royal Commission on the Economic Union and Development Prospects for Canada, *Report* (Macdonald Report) (1985) Supplementary Statement by Albert Breton, vol. 3, 486–526; Smiley, The Federal Condition in Canada (1987), 94–97. This model of "competitive federalism" is close to the idea of provinces as "social laboratories": see heading § 5:8, "Reasons for federalism".

[2]Lederman, Continuing Canadian Constitutional Dilemmas (1981), ch. 17; Smiley, The Federal Condition in Canada (1987), ch. 4.

governments. Through these relationships mechanisms are developed, especially fiscal mechanisms, which allow a continuous redistribution of powers and resources without recourse to the courts or the amending process.[3] These relationships are also the means by which consultations occur on the many issues of interest to both federal and provincial governments. The area where cooperative federalism has been most dominant is in the federal-provincial financial arrangements. Changes in the financial arrangements have naturally altered the balance of powers within the federation. Yet the federal-provincial financial arrangements since the second world war have been worked out by the executives of the various governments, at first almost at the dictation of the federal government, latterly by intergovernmental negotiation leading to genuine agreements. The recent history of federal-provincial financial relations, and their enormous impact on the distribution of power within Canada, is the subject of the next chapter, Financial Arrangements. In that chapter, it will be explained how the taxing sources in Canada are shared between the federal and provincial governments, how federal intervention has secured nation-wide plans of health, education and welfare—matters within provincial jurisdiction, and how the richer regions of the country transfer wealth to the poorer regions. These arrangements are of course the fruits of cooperation between governments, and they in turn require that intergovernmental relations continue so that they can be maintained and adapted.

An explicit invocation of cooperative federalism was made in 2018 in a federal-provincial proposal for a national securities regulator, a project

[3]This description of "cooperative federalism" was approved as a "descriptive concept" in *Que. v. Can. (Firearms Sequel)*, [2015] 1 S.C.R. 693, 2015 SCC 14, para. 17, but the Court went on to point out that the term has also been used to describe a constitutional principle the effect of which is to encourage the dual operation of federal and provincial legislation by restricting the doctrines of interjurisdictional immunity and paramountcy so as to avoid "unnecessary constraints on provincial legislative action." In this case, the federal government had decided to repeal the "long gun" registry which had been established by a previous government. Quebec requested the data that had been collected in Quebec in order to facilitate the establishment of a provincial registry. The federal government not only refused the request, but amended the repealing bill by inserting a provision requiring the destruction of the data "as soon as feasible"! The bill was enacted with the destruction provision, and Quebec challenged the constitutionality of the destruction provision, arguing that Parliament had breached its duty of cooperative federalism by enacting a law designed to impede another level of government from exercising its powers. The majority of the Court rejected the argument. The principle of cooperative federalism did not "limit the scope of legislative authority" or "impose a positive obligation to facilitate cooperation where the constitutional division of powers authorizes unilateral action" (para. 20). The dissenting minority would however have struck down the destruction provision on grounds of cooperative federalism. For discussion of the constitutional principle of cooperative federalism, see three related articles by W.K. Wright, "Facilitating Intergovernmental Dialogue: Judicial Review of the Division of Powers in the Supreme Court of Canada" (2010) 51 Sup. Ct. L. Rev. (2d) 612; "The Political Safeguards of Canadian Federalism: The Intergovernmental Safeguards" (2016) 36 Nat. J. Con. Law 1; "Courts as Facilitators of Intergovernmental Dialogue: Cooperative Federalism and Judicial Review" (2016) 72 Sup. Ct. L. Rev. (2d) 365.

that in the past had been stymied by constitutional issues.[4] In *Re Pan-Canadian Securities Regulation* (2018),[5] what was proposed was a "cooperative securities regulator", which would have two components: (1) a uniform provincial securities act, which would be broadly similar to existing provincial securities acts, and which would be enacted by all provinces participating in the cooperative system;[6] and (2) a federal act aimed at preventing and managing "systemic risk", establishing criminal offences relating to securities markets, and creating a national securities regulator. Aside from the federal power over systemic risk, the national securities regulator would derive its regulatory powers by delegation from the provinces in their uniform securities acts; the national securities regulator would become the sole regulator in the participating provinces. As is explained elsewhere in this book,[7] the Supreme Court upheld the constitutionality of the proposal for a cooperative securities regulator.

The proposed cooperative securities regulator referred to in the previous paragraph was the product of an intergovernmental agreement entered into by the federal government and several provincial and territorial governments.[8] Intergovernmental agreements often result from particular instances of cooperative federalism.[9] These intergovernmental agreements might involve the federal government and one or more provincial and/or territorial governments, or only provincial and/or territorial governments.[10] An obvious question that arises is whether these intergovernmental agreements are legally binding on their signatories.[11] The answer is maybe. Intergovernmental agreements can be "merely

[4]See discussion in ch. 21, Property and civil rights, under heading §§ 21:15 to 21:16, "Securities regulation".

[5]*Re Pan-Canadian Securities Regulation* [2018] 3 S.C.R. 189. The opinion of the nine-judge court was issued by "The Court". The explicit invocation of "cooperative federalism" is in para. 16 and is elaborated in paras. 17–20.

[6]At the time of the litigation (2018), not all provinces were on board, Quebec and Alberta being the most important hold-outs. The agreement between the participating provinces included an undertaking to use their best efforts to persuade the hold-outs to join the cooperative system: 2018 3 S.C.R. 189, 2018 SCC 48, para. 26.

[7]See discussion in ch. 21, Property and civil rights, under heading §§ 21:15 to 21:16, "Securities regulation".

[8]The supporting provincial and territorial governments were Ontario, British Columbia, Saskatchewan, New Brunswick, Prince Edward Island and the Yukon. The two most important provincial holdouts were Quebec and Alberta: see § 5:27 note 6, above.

[9]J. Poirier, C. Saunders & J. Kincaid (eds.), *Intergovernmental Relations in Federal Systems* (2015), ch. 5 (by M.-A. Adams, J. Bergeron and M. Bonnard) (estimating that there are thousands of intergovernmental agreements in Canada (at 154)).

[10]Intergovernmental agreements can also involve municipal and Indigenous governments as well. This paragraph focuses on intergovernmental agreements involving only the federal, provincial and/or territorial governments. Intergovernmental agreements involving Indigenous governments raise their own unique issues, particularly if they rise to the level of a "treaty" under s. 35 of the Constitution Act, 1982: see ch. 28, Aboriginal Peoples.

[11]This paragraph addresses the legal situation of the *parties*. There are particular issues that arise in determining whether intergovernmental agreements create legally

aspirational and political", in which case they are legally non-binding.[12] However, intergovernmental agreements can also be legally binding. Intergovernmental agreements will be legally binding if they are incorporated by legislation.[13] In addition, intergovernmental agreements will also be legally binding on their own terms, like ordinary private law contracts, if they were intended to create legal obligations.[14] However, legislation is required to implement intergovernmental agreements to the extent that they purport to modify federal and/or provincial law.[15] The Supreme Court of Canada has set out various factors to take into account in determining whether an intergovernmental agreement demonstrates an intention to create legal obligations, including the subject matter of the intergovernmental agreement, the language used in it, the mechanism for resolving disputes about it and any relevant subsequent conduct.[16] Applying these factors, the Court held, by way of example, that reciprocal taxation agreements between the federal and British Columbia governments "resemble private law contracts and were intended to create legally binding obligations".[17] Even if an intergovernmental agreement is legally binding, it can be overridden or modified by legislation.[18]

Most intergovernmental relationships depend upon informal arrangements which have no foundation in the Constitution, or in statutes, or in the conventions of parliamentary government. The most visible and important of these arrangements are the "first ministers' conferences",[19] which are federal-provincial conferences of the provincial Premiers and

---

binding obligations for third parties: see *Que. v. Moses*, [2010] 1 S.C.R. 557, para. 86 per LeBel and Deschamps JJ. dissenting. The legal status of intergovernmental agreements is discussed in, among others: N. Bankes, "Co-operative Federalism: Third Parties and Intergovernmental Agreements and Arrangements in Canada and Australia" (1991) 29 Alta. L. Rev. 792; S. A. Kennett, "Hard Law, Soft Law and Diplomacy: The Emerging Paradigm for Intergovernmental Cooperation in Environmental Assessment" (1993) 31 Alta. L. Rev. 644; J.P. Meekison, H. Telford and H. Lazar (eds.), *Canada: The State of the Federation 2002 - Reconsidering the Institutions of Canadian Federalism* (2004), 425-464 (by J. Poirier).

[12]*Can. v. British Columbia Investment Management*, 2019 SCC 63, para. 94.

[13]*Can. v. British Columbia Investment Management*, 2019 SCC 63, para. 93.

[14]*Can. v. British Columbia Investment Management*, 2019 SCC 63, paras. 93-94.

[15]*Can. v. British Columbia Investment Management*, 2019 SCC 63, para. 93, citing *Re Anti-Inflation Act*, [1976] 2 S.C.R. 373, 433; *Re Pan-Canadian Securities Regulation*, [2018] 3 S.C.R. 189, para. 66.

[16]*Can. v. British Columbia Investment Management*, 2019 SCC 63, para. 95.

[17]*Can. v. British Columbia Investment Management*, 2019 SCC 63, paras. 96-102.

[18]*Can. v. British Columbia Investment Management*, 2019 SCC 63, para. 92, citing *Re Canada Assistance Plan (B.C.)*, [1991] 2 S.C.R. 525, 548-49; *Re Pan-Canadian Securities Regulation*, [2018] 3 S.C.R. 189, paras. 62-71. For a fuller explanation of this point, see ch. 12, Parliamentary Sovereignty, under heading §§ 12:9 to 12:10, "Self-imposed restraints on legislative power".

[19]These conferences used to be called dominion-provincial conferences, until the term dominion fell out of favour, as related earlier in this chapter. The conferences were then called federal-provincial conferences, but there are now so many conferences between the federal and provincial governments at levels below that of first minister that

the federal Prime Minister. It is at these conferences that the federal-provincial relationships are settled.[20] Their overweening importance stems primarily from the fact that a Premier or Prime Minister, with his supporting delegation of senior ministers and officials, is normally in a position to make commitments on behalf of his government, including commitments which require legislative action. In a system of responsible government, it is only in an unusual cabinet or parliamentary situation that there is any possibility of a Premier or Prime Minister having a commitment repudiated on his return home from a conference. Thus, the first ministers, when they meet, bring together the totality of executive power and (in practice) legislative power. As well, in Canada the relatively small number of provinces keeps the number of participants at a manageable level which facilitates direct relationships between the governments and ensures that each government has an influence on the result.

The picture of intergovernmental relations does not end at the level of the first ministers. There are several important standing federal-provincial committees of ministers, and nearly every cabinet minister meets with his counterparts in the other governments from time to time. It has been said only half in jest that there are usually more provincial cabinet ministers in Ottawa on any given day than there are federal cabinet ministers. Similarly, there are frequent meetings of permanent government officials from the provincial and federal governments. At any given time, there are over 150 organizations, conferences and committees involved in intergovernmental liaison, indicating the vast array of consultative organisms within the Canadian federation. In addition, of course, there are countless informal contacts among civil servants of all governments.[21]

The dominant role of the executive branch of government in working out intergovernmental relations has led Smiley to characterize the Canadian constitution today as "executive federalism".[22] It certainly must be frustrating for legislators to find that their role is confined to ratifying arrangements worked out elsewhere. But in any country, whether federal or unitary, which has adopted the system of responsible government, the legislative bodies have little real influence in policy-making in any case. The federal Parliament, despite its representation from all parts of the country, is too dominated by cabinet and the party system to be a suitable forum for federal-provincial adjustment; and it does not

---

the first ministers' conferences have had to have a distinctive name. Their history, functions and practices are described in MacKinnon, "First Ministers' Conferences" in Dwivedi (ed.), Public Policy and Administrative Studies (U. of Guelph, 1988), vol. 5, 38.

[20]In practice, the amending procedures are normally initiated by a first ministers' conference, and this reality has been recognized by provision for first ministers' conferences in the Constitution Act, 1982, ss. 37, 37.1, 49.

[21]Smiley, Canada in Question (3rd ed., 1980), 94.

[22]Smiley, The Federal Condition in Canada (1987), 83.

pretend to such a role.[23] It is the elected and permanent officials of the executive branches of the federal and provincial governments who, through "diplomacy", search for cooperative means to accomplish limited social and economic objectives which require the action of more than one government.[24] The next chapter, Financial Arrangements, is almost a case-study of cooperative (or executive) federalism. It includes failures as well as successes, but the process which it describes is undeniably an important feature of Canada's constitutional law.

---

[23]In the United States' Congress the absence of strict party discipline has allowed regional interests to be somewhat better accommodated. This is one reason why there are fewer relations between governments in the United States than in Canada. For more comparisons in the financial area, see ch. 6, Financial Arrangements, under heading § 6:10, "Conclusions".

[24]Simeon, Federal-Provincial Diplomacy (1972) is a study of three cases of federal-provincial negotiations.

Chapter 6

Financial Arrangements

I. CONFEDERATION ARRANGEMENTS

§ 6:1 Confederation arrangements

II. DEVELOPMENT OF DIRECT TAXATION

§ 6:2 Development of direct taxation

III. TAX RENTAL AGREEMENTS: 1941-1962

§ 6:3 Tax rental agreements: 1941–1962

IV. TAX COLLECTION AGREEMENTS: 1962-PRESENT

§ 6:4 Tax collection agreements: 1962-present

V. TAX ABATEMENTS

§ 6:5 Tax abatements

VI. EQUALIZATION PAYMENTS

§ 6:6 Equalization payments

VII. CONDITIONAL FEDERAL GRANTS

§ 6:7 Conditional federal grants

VIII. SPENDING POWER

§ 6:8 Federal power
§ 6:9 Provincial power

IX. CONCLUSIONS

§ 6:10 Conclusions

I. CONFEDERATION ARRANGEMENTS

§ 6:1 Confederation arrangements

At confederation,[1] the immediate and most urgent tasks facing Canada related to the economic development of the isolated pioneer communities which comprised British North America. The building of railways, roads, canals, harbours and bridges to link the provinces with each other and with the rest of the world was the prerequisite of economic development. This task, along with defence, was assigned to the new Dominion; the Dominion also assumed all the debts of the provinces. The functions assigned to the provinces were important too, for example, the administration of justice, municipal institutions, health, education, welfare and local matters; but in 1867, when laissez-faire was the prevailing philosophy of government, these functions were much less costly.

The initial financial arrangements reflected the allocation of functions. The most lucrative sources of revenue were the "indirect" taxes of customs and excise, which accounted for 80 per cent of the revenues of the uniting provinces just before confederation. By s. 122 of the B.N.A. Act "the customs and excise laws of each province" were transferred to the new Dominion, and by s. 91(3)—the power to raise money "by any mode or system of taxation"—the new Dominion received the power to impose any new taxes, direct or indirect, that it saw fit.

The less costly functions of the provinces were matched by the assignment to them of less extensive taxing powers. Section 92(2) conferred the power to impose only "direct" taxes, and s. 92(9) conferred the power to impose licence fees.[2] At the time of confederation, although some municipalities (not provinces) imposed property and income taxes, and all provinces received some revenue from their public property and imposed licence fees of various kinds, these sources of revenue amounted to less than 20 per cent of their revenue. Moreover, there are indications that it was not expected in 1867 that direct taxes on property or income would ever become particularly lucrative, because of their unpopularity. Accordingly, in order to enable the provinces to carry out their functions without the major sources of taxation, the B.N.A. Act provided for payment of annual subsidies by the Dominion to the provinces. These "statutory subsidies", as they are now called, were to comprise a major part of the expected revenues of the provinces. Although expressed by s. 118 of

---

[Section 6:1]

[1]The sources of information on all the federal-provincial financial arrangements are diffuse and sometimes fugitive, and they become out-of-date very quickly. The Federal-Provincial Relations Office of the Department of Finance publishes a list of federal transfers to provinces and territories on its website (www.fin.gc.ca/activity/fedprov-e.html). The Canadian Tax Foundation annually publishes *Finances of the Nation* on its website (www.ctf.ca). These are probably the easiest sources of up-to-date information; they also provide useful accounts of the history of the various arrangements.

[2]The taxing powers in the Constitution, both federal and provincial, including the concepts of "direct" and "indirect" taxes, are discussed in ch. 31, Taxation.

the B.N.A. Act to be "in full settlement of all future demands on Canada", they quickly proved inadequate for provincial needs; and they have been increased and varied in various ways for the original uniting provinces, and upon the entry of new provinces.[3] The statutory subsidies continue to this day. However, they have been dwarfed by other transfer programs discussed later in this chapter.

"Vertical imbalance" is the term that is used to describe the situation in a federation when the revenues of the constituent units are inadequate to fulfil their constitutionally assigned expenditure responsibilities. Canada is not unusual in exhibiting this vertical imbalance. In most federations, the major taxing powers are assigned to the federal government, because they are "closely related to the development of the customs union and more broadly to an effective economic union".[4] And in most federations responsibility for the expensive health, education and welfare programmes is assigned to the constituent units on the basis that they are "best administered on a regional basis where particular regional circumstances can be taken into account".[5] While on the topic of "imbalance", we should note that "horizontal imbalance" is also common in federations; that is the situation where there is variation in the revenue-raising capacities of the constituent units "so that they are not able to provide their citizens with services at the same level on the basis of comparable tax levels".[6] This is a quite different form of imbalance, which in Canada is primarily addressed through federal equalization payments to the poorer provinces; equalization payments are discussed later in this chapter.[7]

II. DEVELOPMENT OF DIRECT TAXATION

§ 6:2 Development of direct taxation

The provinces were gradually driven to the levying of direct taxes. The first provincial personal income tax was levied by British Columbia in 1876, and the second by Prince Edward Island in 1894. They were the only provinces to levy such a tax in the half century after confederation. Between 1923 and 1939 five more provinces followed their example, and the remaining three waited until 1962. In some provinces, municipalities levied income taxes before any provincial tax was enacted. Corporation taxes and corporate income taxes were for most provinces an earlier

[3]The "full settlement" language of s. 118 was accompanied by the omission from the list of federal legislative powers of an express power to make grants to the provinces, something that was initially proposed at the Quebec conference of 1864, but was not adopted by the delegates: Browne, Documents on the Confederation of British North America (1969), 77–79. Section 118 was replaced (but not repealed) by the Constitution Act, 1907 (U.K.), which did not repeat the "full settlement" language; s. 118 was repealed by the Statute Law Revision Act, 1950 (U.K.).

[4]Watts, Comparing Federal Systems (2nd ed., 1999), 46.

[5]Watts, Comparing Federal Systems (2nd ed., 1999), 46.

[6]Watts, Comparing Federal Systems (2nd ed., 1999), 46.

[7]§ 6:6, "Equalization payments".

source of revenue than the personal income tax. All provinces were taxing corporations on the basis of place of business, paid-up capital, and so on, by 1903, and corporate income taxes were general by the 1930s.

Inheritance taxes were another early source of provincial revenue. Ontario imposed a succession duty in 1892 which was quickly copied by all the other provinces.

Meanwhile, the customs and excise taxes did not continue to suffice for the federal government. Federal entry to the field of direct taxation occurred during the first world war with the enactment of the 1916 war profits tax, which was followed in 1917 by the introduction of personal and corporate income taxes. These were regarded as temporary measures only, because it was generally agreed then that the field of direct taxation should be left to the provinces; and indeed federal rates were substantially reduced in the period between the first and second world wars. The Dominion did not "invade" the inheritance tax field until the second world war, levying succession duties in 1941.

In 1937, after the depression and the rejection by the Privy Council of the Bennett New Deal, the Rowell-Sirois Commission was appointed to review the whole financial structure of Canadian government. The situation at that time was chaotic, with federal, provincial and municipal taxes of various kinds, at differing rates, on differing bases, producing a complex burden of taxation which varied greatly from municipality to municipality, and region to region. The Commission proposed that only the Dominion should levy the three standard taxes on personal income, corporate income and inheritances; and it proposed that the Dominion should pay "national adjustment grants" to the poorer provinces. The Rowell-Sirois Report[1] was rejected at the 1941 dominion-provincial conference because of the opposition of Alberta, British Columbia and Ontario, the three provinces which would have received nothing under the proposed system of adjustment grants.

III. TAX RENTAL AGREEMENTS: 1941-1962

§ 6:3 Tax rental agreements: 1941–1962

Only months after the rejection of the Rowell-Sirois Report in January 1941, its recommendation that the provinces withdraw from the three standard tax fields was adopted, but as a temporary measure for the duration of the second world war. The federal government entered into agreements with the provinces under which the provinces abandoned their personal income taxes, corporate income taxes and inheritance taxes. In return, the provinces were to receive unconditional payments to compensate them for the lost revenue. The federal government, now alone in the three most lucrative tax fields, raised its rates of personal and corporate income taxes, and imposed succession duties for the first time. However, in the agreement with each province, the federal govern-

---

[Section 6:2]

[1] Report of the Royal Commission on Dominion Provincial Relations (1940).

ment undertook that at the end of the war it would reduce federal taxes so as to make "room" for the provinces to resume levying the three taxes.

At the end of the war, however, the federal government wished to continue to levy the major taxes in order to finance peacetime reconstruction and to use centralized fiscal policy as a tool of national economic management. In 1947, the federal government persuaded all provinces except Ontario and Quebec to enter into "tax rental agreements", under which the federal government "rented" from each agreeing province the right to levy personal income tax, corporate income tax and succession duty. The agreeing provinces did not levy these taxes, and received grants ("rent") from the federal government to compensate for the foregone revenue. Ontario and Quebec, which did not sign rental agreements, in 1947 reimposed corporate income taxes and succession duties, but not personal income taxes. On the renewal of the agreements in 1952, Ontario joined the system, although it retained the right to levy succession duties. Quebec remained outside the system; and in 1954 it imposed a personal income tax, so that Quebec was then levying all three of the standard taxes.

In 1957, new tax rental agreements were entered into, but with several major changes in favour of the provinces. First, the rental payments were fixed as a percentage of the yield of each tax rented; the use of percentage points ensured that rental payments would rise at the same rate as federal tax collections, and it led the federal government to characterize the 1957 rental agreements as "tax-sharing" arrangements. Secondly, if a province preferred to levy its own tax, instead of renting the tax to the Dominion, then its residents would receive an "abatement" (or reduction) of federal tax of the same percentage as the rental payments; this was designed to leave room for a provincial tax. Eight provinces signed agreements to rent all three taxes. Ontario rented only personal income tax, and levied its own corporate income tax and succession duties. Quebec did not sign a rental agreement at all, and continued to levy all three standard taxes. The federal government accordingly allowed abatements of corporate income tax and succession duties to taxpayers in Ontario and abatements of these taxes and personal income tax to taxpayers in Quebec. Thirdly, the 1957 agreements pro-vided that each province (whether or not it rented its taxes) would receive an "equalization payment" to bring its share of tax rental payments (or the value of its abatements) up to the same per capita figure as the average per capita yield in the two provinces whose yield was highest (at that time, Ontario and British Columbia).

IV. TAX COLLECTION AGREEMENTS: 1962-PRESENT

§ 6:4 Tax collection agreements: 1962-present

The tax rental agreements ended in 1962 and were replaced by the tax collection agreements. Under these agreements the provinces imposed their own income taxes at their own rates. Provided a province used the same tax base as the federal tax base,[1] the federal government would collect the provincial tax on behalf of the province free of charge. In this way taxpayers would only have to file a single return. To give the provinces room to levy their own taxes the federal government agreed to allow abatements (reductions) of corporate and personal income taxes to taxpayers in all provinces. All of the provinces except Quebec signed a collection agreement for personal income taxes, and all provinces except Ontario and Quebec signed a collection agreement for corporate income taxes.[2] Equalization payments continued.

The tax collection agreements continue to the present day. As of 2006, all provinces except Quebec have signed a collection agreement for personal income taxes; and all provinces except Quebec, Ontario and Alberta[3] have signed a collection agreement for corporate income taxes.[4] Quebec's personal income tax is collected by the province, as is the corporate income tax of Quebec, Ontario and Alberta. Equalization payments continue, although, as is related below, they have been substantially modified.

V. TAX ABATEMENTS

§ 6:5 Tax abatements

An "abatement" is a reduction in a federal tax. It is not a "grant", because it does not involve the transfer of funds from the federal treasury to the provincial treasuries. But it is analogous to a grant in that it allows the provinces room to impose their own taxes. As noted, it is the vehicle by which the standard tax fields are shared. It is unconditional in the sense that the provinces are not obliged to levy their own taxes; if they do levy taxes, they are not obliged to do so at the same rate as the

[Section 6:4]

[1]The use of the same tax base is ensured by stipulations in the agreements that provincial rates of personal income tax and corporate income tax must be expressed as a percentage of federally-defined taxable income. Without departing from this general rule, the federal government has agreed to administer some special provincial tax measures which produce some variation in the tax base from province to province.

[2]With respect to succession duty, in 1962 the provinces were given the choice, either of accepting 50 per cent of federal estate tax collections, or of levying their own succession duties in return for their deceaseds' estates receiving an abatement of 50 per cent of federal estate tax. In 1963 the provincial share was raised from 50 per cent to 75 per cent. Only Ontario and Quebec began the five-year period levying their own succession duties (which they had been doing, of course, since 1947), but they were joined by British Columbia in 1963. These arrangements continued until the end of 1971 when the federal Parliament repealed its estate tax. It agreed to collect provincial succession duties for a fee, so long as at least four provinces using the same tax base entered into three-year collection agreements. Six provinces enacted uniform success ion duty statutes and entered into the collection agreement, leaving Alberta as a succession duty haven; British Columbia, Ontario and Quebec continued to collect their own succession duties. Subsequently, however, all provinces repealed their succession duty statutes.

[3]Alberta began collecting its own corporate income tax in 1981.

[4]The three territories levy personal and corporate income taxes, and have entered into collection agreements with the federal government for the taxes.

federal abatement, or to apply funds raised by their taxes for any particular purpose.

In 1972, the federal Income Tax Act was amended to conceal the abatement. Before 1972, a taxpayer would calculate his or her federal "basic" tax; and then he or she would deduct the abatement, which in 1971 was 28 per cent of the basic tax, in order to derive the actual federal tax liability. Then the taxpayer would calculate the provincial tax, which like the abatement consisted of a percentage of the federal basic tax.[1] In 1972, the abatement was concealed from the taxpayer, by the federal government lowering its rates to produce a basic tax figure which was 28 per cent lower than in 1971, and by the provincial governments raising their rates so that their yield (which now had to be expressed as a percentage of the lower basic tax figure) was the same as before. In 1977, when further tax room (or tax "points")[2] was transferred to the provinces, the increased abatement was handled in the same way: federal rates were lowered and provincial rates were raised. It is questionable whether the word "abatement" is apt to describe a reduction in federal tax which takes the form of a lowering of rates. It is becoming increasingly common to describe these adjustments as "tax point transfers" or simply "tax transfers".[3]

Explicit abatements have not entirely disappeared. An explicit abatement is still allowed to corporate taxpayers to leave room for provincial corporate income taxes. And an explicit abatement of personal income tax is still allowed to Quebec taxpayers to compensate them for the foregone federal contributions to shared-cost programmes from which Quebec has opted out.[4]

There are two main sources of tax transfers (implicit and explicit abatements) to the provinces. First, and most important, is the reduction of federal tax which has been allowed to the provinces ever since 1962 in order to leave room for the provinces to impose their own personal and corporate income taxes.

Secondly, a reduction in federal tax is provided as part of the Canada Health Transfer and the Canada Social Transfer programmes. The Canada Health Transfer supports provincial health care. The Canada Social Transfer supports provincial post-secondary education and social programmes. The federal government has supported such programmes since shortly after the second world war, but its contributions once took the exclusive form of conditional cash grants to the universities (in the

[Section 6:5]

[1]See § 6:4 note 1, above.

[2]Tax points are percentage points of federal tax on personal income (the income of individuals) and percentage points of the federally-defined taxable income of corporations: see § 6:4 note 1, above.

[3]For example, the legislation enacting the Canada Health and Social Transfer (which inherits the tax points once allocated for the "established programmes") uses the term "tax transfer": Budget Implementation Act, 1995, S.C. 1995, c. 17.

[4]See § 6:7, "Conditional federal grants".

case of post-secondary education) and to the provinces (in the case of the other programmes). In 1967, when the grants for post-secondary education were made payable to the provinces rather than directly to the universities, a transfer of tax points replaced part of the grants for post-secondary education. In 1977, when post-secondary education and health were grouped together as "established programmes",[5] a transfer of additional tax points replaced part of the federal grants in aid of both purposes.[6] The federal contribution to provincial social programmes came through the Canada Assistance Plan and always took the form of cash grants. In 1996, the Canada Health and Social Transfer was implemented to replace both the Canada Assistance Plan and the established programmes funding. The Canada Health and Social Transfer involved no new tax points transfers, but "inherited" those that were allocated to fund the established programmes. In 2004, the Canada Health and Social Transfer became two separate transfers, the Canada Health Transfer and the Canada Social Transfer. There was no change in the tax points transfers.

The transferred tax points do not provide the full federal contribution to the Canada Health Transfer and the Canada Social Transfer. The balance takes the form of a cash grant. This is vital to a continuing federal influence over health and social assistance, because it is the power to withhold all or part of the grant which is the sanction against non-compliance by a province with federal conditions.[7]

VI. EQUALIZATION PAYMENTS

§ 6:6 Equalization payments

The Rowell-Sirois Report had in 1940 recommended a system of equalization payments called "national adjustment grants", whereby the federal government would make special grants to the poorer provinces. This recommendation was rejected, but in 1957 equalization payments did become an explicit federal expenditure programme for the first time. There was in fact an equalizing element in the federal-provincial fiscal arrangements between 1941 and 1957, because grants were made to the provinces on a per capita basis, which naturally returned a larger share

---

[5]They were described as established programmes in the Act which provided for their funding, namely, the Federal-Provincial Fiscal Arrangements and Federal Post-Secondary Education and Health Contributions Act, R.S.C. 1985, F-8, because they were regarded as having attained such a level of maturity that their continuance by the provinces was assured. Accordingly, in 1977, federal control over the established programmes was considerably loosened. That loosening process continued with the Canada Health and Social Transfer, implemented by amendments to the same Act (now renamed the Federal-Provincial Fiscal Arrangements Act): see § 6:7, "Conditional federal grants".

[6]For historical reasons (it had accepted a form of opting-out from some shared-cost programmes before 1977), Quebec received more tax points and less cash under the established programmes funding arrangements. The same is true for the Canada Health and Social Transfer. Except for this difference in apportionment, Quebec's entitlements were, and are, calculated in the same manner as those for the other provinces.

[7]See § 6:7, "Conditional federal grants".

of revenue to the provinces with lower per capita tax yields. But under the 1957 tax rental (or tax-sharing) agreements, it will be recalled, each agreeing province received as "rent" a percentage share of the actual yield from its residents of the federal personal income tax, the federal corporate income tax and federal succession duties (later estate tax). Needless to say, rental payments varied greatly from the high per capita yields of Ontario and British Columbia down to the low per capita yields of Prince Edward Island and Newfoundland. The equalization payments were calculated to bring each province's rent up to the per capita average of the two highest-yielding provinces (at that time, Ontario and British Columbia). Even Quebec, which did not enter into a rental agreement, was included in the equalization system, and received payments calculated by bringing her hypothetical yield from the provincial percentage of the three federal taxes up to the per capita average of the two highest-yielding provinces.

One defect in the original equalization formula was that it equalized only the yield from the three standard taxes, namely, those on personal income, corporate income and inheritances. However, the equalization base has gradually been broadened to comprise, not only the three standard taxes, but nearly all provincial revenue sources, including sales taxes, gasoline taxes, liquor taxes, payroll taxes, movie admission taxes, race track taxes, motor vehicle registration fees, hospital and medical care insurance premiums, municipal property taxes, lottery profits, and revenues from oil, natural gas, water power and forestry. The result is that most provincial revenues are now equalized.

As the base of equalization has been expanded by the addition of further sources of provincial revenue, the cost of equalization has naturally increased. In 1967, in order to reduce the cost, the standard of equalization (the level to which provincial revenues were to be raised) was lowered from the average per capita yield of the two highest-yielding provinces down to the average per capita yield of all the provinces. Then, in 1973, and for some years thereafter, the price of oil rose so sharply that the revenues of the oil-producing provinces made even the lower national-average standard too expensive. At first, this problem was met by excluding from the equalization base a substantial part of provincial revenues from "non-renewable resources". In 1982, these revenues were restored in full to the base, but the standard of equalization was lowered again, this time to the average per capita yield of five "representative" provinces. The five provinces are British Columbia, Saskatchewan, Manitoba, Ontario and Quebec. The list thus excludes Alberta, which by 1982 had become far and away the largest recipient of revenue from non-renewable resources. The new "representative average" standard (which is still in force at the time of writing in 2006) is therefore not affected by Alberta's huge resource revenues.

The formula for calculating equalization payments[1] does not turn on the actual tax revenues of each province, because rates of tax and definitions of tax bases vary from province to province, depending on each province's discretionary tax policies. Instead, an attempt is made to measure the potential tax revenues of each province, that is, the tax-raising capacity or "fiscal capacity" of each province. This is done by estimating the revenue which each province would receive from a standard tax system with average provincial rates of tax. An estimate is made of the tax base in each province of each provincial source of revenue (amount of personal income, amount of corporate income, volume of retail sales, etc.). A single (national average) rate of tax for each base is then applied to each of the province's tax bases. The total of all these calculations yields the fiscal capacity of the province. The fiscal capacity of each province, divided by its population so as to give a per capita figure, is then compared with the average per capita fiscal capacity of (under the current standard) the five representative provinces. If a province has a higher per capita fiscal capacity than the average of the five representative provinces (a fiscal capacity excess), that province is not entitled to equalization. If a province has a lower per capita fiscal capacity than the average of the five representative provinces (a fiscal capacity deficiency), that province is entitled to equalization; the amount of the equalization grant is the amount of the province's per capita deficiency multiplied by the province's population.

For the fiscal year 2004–05, eight provinces were "have-not" provinces that were entitled to equalization grants.[2] The "have" provinces that were not entitled to equalization grants were Alberta and Ontario. British Columbia's fiscal capacity has fluctuated above and below the equalization standard; it has usually been a have province, but from 2001-02 to 2004-05 it has been a have-not province. There is a wide disparity between the fiscal capacity of the provinces, which means that one percentage point of personal income tax or corporate income tax (for example) yields a much higher per capita figure in the wealthier provinces than it does in the poorer provinces. Alberta enjoys far and away the highest per capita revenues with the lowest "tax effort" (low rates of income tax and no sales tax, for example). It must be emphasized, however, that the have provinces of Alberta and Ontario do not contribute to equalization grants. The grants come entirely from the federal government. That is why the rise in oil prices since 1973 has necessitated a lowering of the equalization standard. Increases in the resource revenues of the producing provinces swell the equalization entitlements of the have-not provinces, but the producing provinces do not contribute to the payments. This has led to suggestions that a portion of provincial

---

[Section 6:6]

[1]The equalization rules have of course always been contained in a federal statute. The current statute is the Federal-Provincial Fiscal Arrangements Act, R.S.C. 1985, c. F-8.

[2]The equalization programme does not apply to the three territories, which receive federal funding under a programme known as Territorial Formula Financing.

resource revenues should be pooled and shared directly among all provinces.[3]

The total amount of equalization payments in 2004–05 was $9.7 billion. The payments are unconditional, so that the receiving provinces are free to spend the money in accordance with their own priorities, which may or may not benefit the poorest residents. It is arguable that this vast sum would be better spent in the form of direct financial assistance to the poorest individuals (or families) in Canada, wherever they lived. Equalization payments swell the size of provincial governments, requiring the poor (and the rich for that matter)[4] in the have-not provinces to accept benefits in the form of enriched provincial public services.[5] However, the Constitution Act, 1982, by s. 36(2), explicitly recognizes "the principle of making equalization payments to ensure that provincial governments have sufficient revenues to provide reasonably comparable levels of public services at reasonably comparable levels of taxation".[6] This provision suggests that equalization payments will continue into the foreseeable future.

The constitutional obligation to make adequate equalization payments to the poorer provinces is probably too vague, and too political, to be justiciable.[7] It is like the "directive principles of state policy" in the Constitution of India, which are statements of economic and social goals that ought to guide governments but which are not enforceable in court.[8] It should be noted, however, that there is room for doubt as to whether the federal government is in compliance with s. 36(2). The lowering of the equalization standard in 1982 to the average of the five representative provinces means that the low-income provinces are not even being brought up to the national average, and of course equalization does not

---

[3]See e.g., T. Courchene, Refinancing the Canadian Confederation (C.D. Howe Research Institute, Montreal, 1979), 39. See also § 6:7 note 9, below. The idea of direct sharing of provincial resource revenues is unlikely to be agreed to by the producing provinces.

[4]Who benefits from equalization depends entirely on the design of the recipient province's public services. It is possible that equalization redistributes income from poor people in have provinces to rich people in have-not provinces.

[5]If benefits were received directly by individuals or families, that would still leave inequality in the value of provincial public services (or burdens of taxation) as between residents of have provinces and residents of have-not provinces. The purpose of equalization is to reduce this inequality.

[6]See A. Nader, "Providing Essential Services: Canada's Constitutional Commitment under Section 36" (1996) 19 Dal. LJ. 306.

[7]For an indication that the courts would be willing to consider a constitutional argument made under s. 36, see *Re Man. Keewatinowi Okimakanak v. Man. Hydro-Electric Bd.* (1992), 91 D.L.R. (4th) 554, 557 (Man. C.A.) (obiter). A. Nader, "Providing Essential Services: Canada's Constitutional Commitment under Section 36" (1996) 19 Dal. LJ. 306, 349, says that "s. 36 is as justiciable as all other provisions of the Constitution Act, 1982." Accord, K. Busby, "Providing Essential Services of Reasonable Quality to All Canadians: Understanding Section 36(1)(c) of the Constitution Act, 1982" (2015) 20 Review of Canadian Studies 191.

[8]See C.C. Aikman, "Fundamental Rights and Directive Principles of State Policy in India" (1987) 17 Viet. U. Wgton. L. Rev. 373.

bring the high-income provinces down. However, the federal government's lack of access to provincial resource revenues make it unrealistic to suppose that equalization could be significantly enriched in the foreseeable future.[9]

None of the provinces that receive equalization payments have ever brought legal proceedings to force the Government of Canada to increase the payments on the ground that the payments are insufficient to ensure reasonably comparable levels of public services at reasonably comparable levels of taxation. But, in *Cape Breton v. Nova Scotia* (2009),[10] the regional municipality of Cape Breton sued the province of Nova Scotia, which is a recipient of equalization payments, for a declaration that the province was breaching a constitutional commitment under s. 36 by failing to distribute its equalization receipts equitably among the regions of the province. Cape Breton was poorer than the other regions of the province and could not afford to provide its residents with services comparable to those of other Nova Scotia municipalities, despite the fact that the province received equalization payments from Ottawa for this very purpose. The municipality sought only a declaration that the province was in breach of s. 36; no specific remedial order was sought, no doubt on the assumption that it would be difficult to persuade a court to redesign the province's funding of municipalities. The proceeding for a declaration was dismissed by the trial court as disclosing no cause of action, and that decision was upheld by the Nova Scotia Court of Appeal. The Supreme Court denied leave to appeal.

In order to understand the decision in *Cape Breton*, it is worth setting out the text of s. 36 of the Constitution Act, 1982. It provides as follows:

> **36.** (1) Without altering the legislative authority of Parliament or of the provincial legislatures, or the rights of any of them with respect to the exercise of their legislative authority, Parliament and the legislatures, together with the government of Canada and the provincial governments, are committed to
>
> (a) promoting equal opportunities for the well-being of Canadians;
>
> (b) furthering economic development to reduce disparity of opportunities; and
>
> (c) providing essential public services of reasonable quality to all Canadians.
>
> (2) Parliament and the government of Canada are committed to the principle of making equalization payments to ensure that provincial

[9] P.A. Cumming, "Equitable Fiscal Federalism: The Problems in respect of Resources Revenue Sharing" in Royal Commission on the Economic Union and Development Prospects for Canada (Macdonald Commission), *Report* (1985), vol. 65, 49–95, arguing that the disparity between have and have-not provinces is now so wide as to constitute a breach of s. 36(2); reporting and supporting the arguments by Courchene and other economists that provincial resource revenues should be shared by the producing provinces; and arguing that s. 36(2) should be amended to impose the obligation of equalization on the provinces as well as the federal government.

[10] *Cape Breton v. Nova Scotia* (2009), 277 N.S.R. (2d) 350 (N.S. C.A.). MacDonald C.J.N.S. wrote the opinion of the three-judge Court.

governments have sufficient revenues to provide reasonably comparable levels of public services at reasonably comparable levels of taxation.

In *Cape Breton*, the municipality argued that s. 36 created justiciable obligations. The Court of Appeal did not reject the argument. MacDonald C.J., who wrote for the Court, took the view that the word "committed" in s. 36 "may indeed, in appropriate circumstances, represent an actionable obligation among the parties to the agreement that is being codified in s. 36".[11] However, subsection (2) of s. 36 imposed its commitment only on "Parliament and the government of Canada" and could not be interpreted as imposing any obligation on the province of Nova Scotia. And subsection (1) of s. 36, while it did impose its commitments on the provinces as well as Canada, did not contain the kind of language that could be interpreted as conferring on an individual or a municipality rights that would be actionable against a province. "The justiciable rights, if any, belong to those [federal and provincial] governments, not to individuals or municipalities."[12] It may be questioned whether it is plausible to read s. 36 as conferring a right of action on the federal government to redress inequalities within a province; certainly, it is hard to imagine the federal government embarking on a proceeding that would intrude so deeply into provincial responsibilities. This all reinforces the point made earlier that s. 36, even if it is justiciable, is no guarantee that equalization payments will find their way to those individuals (or regions) that are most in need.

VII. CONDITIONAL FEDERAL GRANTS

§ 6:7 Conditional federal grants

A conditional grant is a transfer of funds that is made on condition that the grantee use the funds in accordance with the stipulations of the grantor. Within Canada, the federal government has used the device of the conditional grant to establish shared-cost programmes, under which the federal and provincial governments share the cost of a programme within a particular province. In broad terms, the shared-cost programmes were originally established in this way: the federal government decided upon the desirability of a particular programme, for example, the provision of insured hospital services; it worked out the details of the programme; and it proposed the programme as a joint venture to each province, on the basis that the federal government and the provincial government would each bear 50 per cent of the cost of the programme. The programme proposed may have been well down on the province's list of priorities, or a different kind of programme might have been preferable to the province; nevertheless, the federal offer was always very difficult to refuse, because refusal would deny to the province the federal grant. Indeed, refusal of a federal offer to share the costs of a programme would have worn an aspect of taxation without benefit, since the residents of a non-participating province would still

[11] *Cape Breton v. Nova Scotia* (2009), 277 N.S.R. (2d) 350 (N.S. C.A.), para. 65.

[12] *Cape Breton v. Nova Scotia* (2009), 277 N.S.R. (2d) 350 (N.S. C.A.), para. 69.

have had to pay the federal taxes which financed the federal share of the programme in the other provinces. The result was that the provinces usually felt sufficiently tempted by "50-cent dollars" to join the federally-initiated shared-cost programmes.

Since the second world war, at least 100 shared-cost programmes have been established on federal initiative. Some of the programmes were temporary and designed to fulfil a specific objective, such as building the Trans-Canada Highway. Of the continuing programmes, four were much more expensive and important than the others. The post-secondary education programme began in 1951 as a programme of federal grants to universities, and was reformed in 1967 into a programme of grants (and tax transfers) to the provinces to assist in the financing of their universities. The Canada Assistance Plan was created in 1966 to share the cost of various provincial social services and income-support programmes. The hospital insurance programme, under which hospital services were made universally available, began in 1958. The medical care programme, under which doctors' services were made universally available, began in 1968.

Except for university funding (where the federal grants did not match provincial costs), these major programmes began as traditional shared-cost programmes, with the federal government contributing a cash grant equal to half of the costs incurred by the provinces. A gradual transition has since occurred in the way in which they are funded and controlled. In 1977, federal support for post-secondary education and the two health services programmes was amalgamated into one annual transfer, termed "established programmes funding". The basis of the federal contribution (which took the form of a combination of tax points and cash grant) to the established programmes was changed to a formula that was independent of the actual costs of post-secondary education and health care services.[1] In 1996, Canada Assistance Plan transfers (which had continued to be based on actual costs) ended and these transfers, along with the established programmes funding, were replaced with the Canada Health and Social Transfer (CHST). The CHST was the federal contribution to provincial health and social programmes (embracing all four of the original shared-cost programmes) and, like the established programmes before it, the CHST transfers were based on a funding formula that was related to the gross national product and provincial populations, not to provincial spending levels. The cash component of the CHST transfers was still conditional in the sense that it was subject to provincial compliance with federal standards relating to health care programmes and entry to social assistance programmes.[2] However, the direct sharing of costs was eliminated. This meant that provinces had a

---

[Section 6:7]

[1]See § 6:5, "Tax abatements".

[2]Current conditions require provinces to comply with the Canada Health Act (a statute which sets out the federal government's health care policy) and forbid them from setting minimum residency standards for social assistance; the federal government is also obliged not to impose any additional conditions without consulting first with the

greater incentive to control their costs, and the federal government had no interest in controlling or auditing provincial expenditures.[3] In 2004, the CHST was split into two separate transfers, the Canada Health Transfer (for provincial health insurance) and the Canada Social Transfer (for post-secondary education and social services). The funding formula, including the conditional cash contribution, was not changed.

Shared-cost programmes have assured Canadians a high minimum level of some important social services. Without the federal initiative, and the federal sharing of the costs, it is certain that some at least of these services would have come later, at standards which varied from province to province, and not at all in some provinces. But the programmes have effected a substantial shift in the distribution of power within confederation. Since the provinces have traditionally borne half of the cost of most programmes, each province has been committed to substantial expenditures for purposes which have been selected, not by the province which raised the money, but by the federal government. This has locked a substantial portion of provincial budgets outside the normal provincial processes of priority setting and budgetary control. Thus shared-cost programmes have been pursued at the expense of provincial functions for which no federal assistance is available.

The federal government has over the past few decades shown increased sensitivity to the criticism that federal conditional grants amount in substance to federal dictation of provincial spending priorities. In a 1969 working paper it was proposed, not as a definite federal policy but as a suggestion for discussion, that for the future shared-cost programmes should be subject to two requirements. First, a shared-cost programme should be established only after a "broad national consensus in favour of the programme" had been demonstrated to exist, and this would be ascertained by prior submission of a federal proposal to provincial Legislatures. Secondly, "the decision of a provincial Legislature to exercise its constitutional right not to participate in any programme, even given a national consensus, should not result in a fiscal penalty being imposed on the people of the province."[4]

---

provinces: Budget Implementation Act, 1995, S.C. 1995, c. 17. See also S. Choudhry, "Bill 11, The Canada Health Act and the Social Union: The Need for Institutions" (2000) 38 Osgoode Hall L.J. 39.

[3]A source of conflict under the old shared-cost system was the unequal treatment of the provinces. As a cost-cutting measure in 1990, the CAP entitlements of the three then "have"provinces of Alberta, British Columbia, and Ontario (but not of the seven other provinces) were restricted to a five per cent increase per year, and this quickly led to major reductions in the per capita grants to those provinces relative to the other seven. British Columbia unsuccessfully challenged the differential treatment in a reference: *Re Canada Assistance Plan*, [1991] 2 S.C.R. 525. The differential treatment has since been eliminated. The funding of the Canada Social Transfer (and the Canada Health Transfer) is the same per capita for all provinces.

[4]Trudeau, Federal-Provincial Grants and the Spending Power of Parliament (1969), 36.

These two points may probably be regarded as settled federal policy.[5] Certainly, since 1969, there have been no new programmes which have violated these precepts.

Substantial adjustments have also been made to existing programmes to increase provincial autonomy. In 1977, as has already been noted, funding for three of the four most significant shared-cost programmes was folded into "established programmes funding"; and in 1996, the established programmes funding and the Canada Assistance Plan (which was by then the last true shared-cost programme) were replaced by the Canada Health and Social Transfer, which combined all four of the original shared-cost programmes into one annual federal grant. The formulas for calculating the federal contribution to the post-1977 established programmes funding and the post-1996 Canada Health and Social Transfer were made independent of provincial expenditures. In 2004, when the CHST was split into the Canada Health Transfer and the Canada Social Transfer, the funding formula remained the same. Because the federal government no longer shares the actual provincial costs of operating the programmes, the federal government has no interest in the actual level of each province's expenditures on the programmes and no incentive to control or monitor the province's expenditures. Under the established programmes formula, the federal contribution was not just cash, but a combination of cash and tax points, which gave the provinces additional "tax room" to generate their own funding for the programmes.[6] The same tax room was carried forward into the formula for the Canada Health and Social Transfer, and for the Canada Health Transfer and Canada Social Transfer. To the extent that the federal contribution takes the form of tax points, there is a loss of federal influence over the provinces, because tax points cannot in practice be taken back by the federal government. It is the power to withhold the cash portion of the grant that is the only effective federal sanction against provincial noncompliance with federal standards.[7] Provincial concerns were given further recognition by Canada Health and Social Transfer

---

[5]The Meech Lake Accord of 1987 and the Charlottetown Accord of 1992, both of which lapsed (see ch. 4, Amendment, under heading § 4:3 "The failure to accommodate Quebec"), would have added a new s. 106A to the Constitution Act, 1867, which would have obliged the federal government to provide for opting-out with reasonable compensation in any new shared cost programme in an area of exclusive provincial jurisdiction. However, in order to qualify for the constitutional entitlement, the opting-out province would have had to itself carry out a programme which was "consistent with the national objectives". The new s. 106A would have been less tolerant of opting-out arrangements than the policy contemplated by the 1969 working paper. Yet s. 106A proved to be one of the more controversial elements of the Accords, on the basis that it weakened the federal government's ability to establish new shared-cost programmes. In a federal-provincial agreement, the Social Union Framework Agreement of 1999, it was agreed that in any new Canada-wide initiatives respecting health, education, or welfare, provinces will receive their share of federal funding, the only prerequisite being the province's commitment to "agreed Canada-wide objectives and . . . the accountability framework".

[6]See § 6:5, "Tax abatements".

[7]The Budget Implementation Act, 1996, S.C. 1996, c. 18, recognized the risk to federal influence of declining cash contributions by setting a floor of $11 billion per an-

provisions that gave provincial governments a voice in setting future standards: the CHST legislation explicitly contemplated the participation of the provinces in developing "shared principles and objectives . . . with respect to the operation of social programs".[8] This is a declaration that the federal government will in the future no longer set conditions on its funding by unilateral fiat, which is how the conditions were established for the original shared-cost programmes.[9]

Before the terms of provincial participation in the shared-cost programmes were relaxed, provinces could still exercise a degree of autonomy by electing a form of opting-out. In 1959, the first opting-out arrangement was made whereby Quebec was given an increased abatement of corporate income tax in return for assuming the entire financial responsibility for its universities. Similar opting-out provisions were later drafted for other shared-cost programmes. Only Quebec took advantage of those provisions, which carried with them additional tax abatements. When established programmes funding was implemented, those additional abatements became part of that programme and they were incorporated into the Canada Health and Social Transfer when it replaced the established programmes funding. Nothing changed when the CHST was divided into the Canada Health Transfer and the Canada Social Transfer. While the original decision to opt out affects the split between tax points and cash transfers to Quebec, it has otherwise been reduced to an historical footnote.

Quebec also elected to opt out of the Canada Pension Plan. The establishment of this contributory scheme of retirement payments and supplementary benefits was preceded by a period of negotiation with Quebec. The original federal proposal was a "pay-as-you-go" or "non-funded" plan, under which pensions and benefits would be paid out of current contributions. Quebec was determined to have a plan of its own which would be "funded", because this would result in the accumulation of a large investment fund which could be used as a source of capital by the province. The result of the negotiations between the federal and Quebec governments was that Quebec agreed to some modifications of the Quebec plan in order to facilitate the portability of pension rights for employees moving between Quebec and the other provinces, and Quebec added its consent to those of the other provinces to a constitutional amendment to give the federal government the power to include in the Canada plan benefits to survivors and to persons disabled before retire-

---

num on the cash payments to the provinces under the Canada Health and Social Transfer; the payments could not decline below the $11 billion figure. Both the Canada Health Transfer and the Canada Social Transfer have cash floors.

[8]Budget Implementation Act, 1995, S.C. 1995, c. 17.

[9]The Social Union Framework Agreement of 1999 requires that the federal government use conditional grants in a "cooperative manner" with the provinces. Thus, the Agreement provides for a federal duty to consult with the provinces at least one year prior to renewal or alteration of the grants, as well as an obligation to consult with provinces and obtain a majority consensus among the provincial Legislatures before introducing new Canada-wide initiatives to be funded by the federal government.

ment age.[10] The federal government for its part agreed to put its plan on a partially funded basis, and to make the resulting investment fund available as a source of capital to the participating provinces. The federal government also agreed to permit opting out by a province with "a comparable plan". Only Quebec accepted this option. In 1965, two identical plans were enacted, the Canada Pension Plan[11] covering nine provinces, and the Quebec Regime de rentes[12] covering Quebec.

From a provincial perspective, a common flaw in all of these opting-out arrangements is that they have obliged the opting-out province to continue established programmes without significant change or, in the case of new programmes, to establish or continue comparable provincial programmes. Thus the "provincial autonomy" afforded by opting-out provisions has really amounted to nothing more than a transfer of administrative responsibility to the opting-out province. It has not given that province the freedom to divert resources, which would otherwise be committed to a federally initiated programme, into other endeavours. Federal "compensation" to the opting-out province has been just as conditional as the federal contribution to participating provinces. The federal working paper of 1969 suggested (though it is not explicit) that the federal government may be willing to offer a real opting-out choice in future shared-cost proposals.[13] This would have to involve the offer of tax points or a grant of similar value to the federal share of the cost of the programme which would not be tied to the maintenance of the same or a similar programme, but would be available for use by the province in accordance with its own priorities. The trouble with this form of opting out is that it removes any incentive for a province to join the programme. This probably explains why the 1969 suggestion has never been implemented.

VIII. SPENDING POWER

§ 6:8 Federal power

When the federal government makes an unconditional grant to a province, the grant is of course used by the province for its own purposes. This means that funds raised by federal taxes end up being applied to objects which are outside federal legislative authority. When the federal government contributes to a shared-cost programme which lies within

[10]Section 94A of the Constitution Act, 1867, which had been inserted by amendment in 1951, gave to the federal government the power "to make laws in relation to old age pensions in Canada". It was apparently believed by the federal government that this power would not authorize a pension plan which included "supplementary benefits, including survivors' and disability benefits irrespective of age", and so, after all provinces had agreed, in 1964 an amendment was obtained from the United Kingdom Parliament substituting a new s. 94A.

[11]S.C. 1964-65, c. 51.

[12]S.Q. 1964, c. 24.

[13]Trudeau, Federal-Provincial Grants and the Spending Power of Parliament (1969), 36. Compare the constitutional proposals of 1987 and 1992, and the Social Union Framework Agreement of 1999.

the legislative authority of the provinces, the same is true: federal funds are applied to provincial objects. If, in addition, those federal funds are granted on condition that the programme accord with federal stipulations, then those stipulations will effectively regulate the programme even though it lies outside federal legislative authority. In fact, many of the shared-cost programmes do lie outside federal legislative authority, and yet are administered in accordance with federally-imposed stipulations. We have already seen that the sum total of these programmes has amounted to a heavy federal presence in matters which are within provincial legislative responsibility.[1]

Take, for example, Medicare,[2] a programme under which the provinces provide for the delivery of hospital and physicians' services to their residents. There is no doubt that these health care services come exclusively within the legislative competence of the provinces, and the services are delivered in each province under provincial law (each province having enacted its own provincial health care insurance plan). Yet Medicare is seen as a national programme. It was initiated by the federal government, first for hospital services (1961)[3] and then for physicians' services (1968).[4] The federal government makes a contribution to the provinces of cash and tax points to help defray the cost of their health care plans. And the Canada Health Act, a federal Act, stipulates the most important terms of the programme in the form of conditions that must be accepted by the provinces (and enacted into their health care plans) if they are to receive the cash portion of the federal contribution.

What is the constitutional basis for federal grants to the provinces, and for federal involvement in shared-cost programmes that are outside federal legislative competence? The only possible basis is the "spending power" of the federal Parliament, a power which is nowhere explicit in the Constitution Act, 1867, but which must be inferred from the powers to levy taxes (s. 91(3)), to legislate in relation to "public property" (s. 91(1A)), and to appropriate federal funds (s. 106). Plainly the Parliament must have the power to spend the money which its taxes yield, and to dispose of its own property. But of course the issue is whether this spending power authorizes payments for objects which are outside federal legislative competence.

[Section 6:8]

[1]See § 6:7, "Conditional federal grants".

[2]The constitutional basis of health care in Canada is explained in more detail in ch. 32, Health.

[3]The genesis of national hospital insurance goes back to a proposal for postwar reconstruction by the federal government in 1945. The provinces had not been consulted. After discussions with the provinces, the programme started in 1958 with five provinces participating, and became a national programme in 1961 when all provinces came in. See Carter, Canadian Conditional Grants since World War II (1971), 32–34.

[4]National physician insurance became a federal commitment in 1963 (it had been an election promise). The provinces had not been consulted. After discussions with the provinces, it was introduced in 1968. See Carter, Canadian Conditional Grants since World War II (1971), 76.

Some constitutional lawyers, including Pierre Elliott Trudeau (before he assumed high federal office), have argued that the federal spending power is confined to objects within federal legislative competence.[5] The argument is that the general pattern of the distribution of powers in the Constitution Act, 1867 implicitly confines the taxing power of the federal Parliament in s. 91(3) to raising taxes for the legislative objects of the federal Parliament, and for no other objects; that provincial taxing power in s. 92(2) is also so limited; and that the spending powers of federal and provincial governments are also implicitly limited to their own legislative objects.[6]

The political corollary to the narrow view of the spending power is the theory of "fiscal responsibility": each level of government should finance its own expenditures by its own taxation. On this theory, the federal government should levy no more taxes than are necessary to finance its own legislative responsibilities, and each province should be given the taxing sources it needs to finance its legislative responsibilities without federal assistance. What this theory overlooks is the wide disparity of wealth and hence of tax-raising capacity among the provinces.[7] The fact is that unless federal grants are made to the poorer provinces their residents will have to accept either far higher levels of taxation or far lower levels of public services than the residents of the richer provinces. This is of course the reason for equalization payments; and for the "implicit equalization" in federal contributions to shared-cost programmes.[8] The theory, now embodied in s. 36 of the Constitution Act, 1982, is that Canadians in all provinces should receive "reasonably comparable levels of public services at reasonably comparable levels of taxation".

It is true that the framers of the Constitution could hardly have foreseen the rise of the welfare state with its enormous growth in provincial responsibilities. But to interpret the Constitution as impliedly forbidding the richer regions of the country from helping the poorer ones

---

[5]Tremblay Report *(Report of the Royal Commission of Inquiry on Constitutional Problems)* (Quebec, 1956), vol. 2, 217–233; P.-E. Trudeau, "Federal Grants to Universities" (1957) in Federalism and the French Canadians (1968), 79; A. Petter, "Federalism and the Myth of the Federal Spending Power" (1989) 68 Can. Bar Rev. 448.

[6]This view can be supported by the language of the appropriation provisions of the Constitution Act, 1867, distinguishing between "the public service of Canada" (s.102), "the public service" [probably meaning "of Canada"] (s. 106), and "the public service of the province" (s. 126), the argument being that they constitute implied prohibitions on appropriations for purposes outside the legislative power of the appropriating legislative body.

[7]The answer to Professor Trudeau "Federal Grants to Universities" (1957) in Federalism and the French Canadians (1968) was given by Prime Minister Trudeau in a federal working paper: Trudeau, Federal-Provincial Grants and the Spending Power of Parliament (1969), 30.

[8]The per capita formula for federal financing of the shared-cost programmes has two consequences: (1) it redistributes tax revenue from the provinces with high per capita tax yields to the provinces with low per capita tax yields; and (2) it pays a higher proportion of the actual costs in provinces with low costs than in provinces with high costs. Both these effects work to the benefit of the have-not provinces with their lower tax yields and their less costly medical and post-secondary facilities.

is to attribute a narrowness of vision to the framers which is thoroughly at odds with what we know of them. This is indeed the "watertight compartments"[9] view of federalism carried to an extreme. And, while the Constitution is generally silent on the spending power (which is what has led to this debate), let us not forget that it did from the beginning require federal grants to the provinces, including a special grant to the poorest of the original provinces, New Brunswick. We have already discussed the "statutory subsidies" provided for in the B.N.A. Act.[10] For present purposes, the point is that these subsidies (which still continue) would consist of money raised by federal taxation, which would be paid to the provinces and applied by them to provincial objects. Section 36 of the Constitution Act, 1982, expressing a commitment to redressing regional disparities and to making equalization payments, also seems to reinforce by implication a broad interpretation of the spending power.

It seems to me that the better view of the law is that the federal Parliament may spend or lend its funds to any government or institution or individual it chooses, for any purpose it chooses; and that it may attach to any grant or loan any conditions it chooses, including conditions it could not directly legislate. There is a distinction, in my view, between compulsory regulation, which can obviously be accomplished only by legislation enacted within the limits of leg-islative power, and spending or lending or contracting, which either imposes no obligations on the recipient (as in the case of unconditional grants) or obligations which are voluntarily[11] assumed by the recipient (as in the case of a conditional grant, a loan or a commercial contract). There is no compelling reason to confine spending or lending or contracting within the limits of legislative power, because in those functions the government is not purporting to exercise any peculiarly governmental authority over its subjects. And, as I argue in the next section of this chapter, the same reasoning would apply with equal force to the provincial Legislatures, which are free to spend money for any purpose they choose and subject to whatever conditions they choose; for example, a province could make a conditional grant to another province or to the federal government.[12]

---

[9]The metaphor is Lord Atkin's: *A.G. Can. v. A.G. Ont* (Labour Conventions) [1937] A.C. 326, 354.

[10]See § 6:1, "Confederation arrangements".

[11]I appreciate that where there are discrepancies in bargaining power the recipient may not assume obligations "voluntarily" in the broadest sense of that term; but there is a legal distinction between the consensual assumption of an obligation and the compulsory imposition of an obligation. For example, in the realm of contract, a dominant contracting party may be able to secure the acceptance of a standard-form contract; that is still not legislating. Compare *A.-G. B.C. v. E. & N. Ry. Co.*, [1950] A.C. 87, 110 ("Legislation and contract are entirely different methods of creating rights and liabilities and it is essential to keep them distinct").

[12]Sections 91 and 92 of the Constitution Act, 1867 are literally limited to the making of "laws". This is not conclusive in favour of my argument for an unlimited spending power, since spending must be authorized by a legislative appropriation of funds, and of course the funds are raised by taxation. J.-F. Gaudreault-DesBiens in Calvo-Garcia and Felstiner (eds.), Federalism (2004), 104, argues that ss. 91 and 92 should be interpreted

In *Re Canada Assistance Plan* (1991),[13] a constitutional challenge was brought by British Columbia to federal legislation amending the Canada Assistance Plan that would place a five per cent annual cap on the growth of federal contributions to the then three "have" provinces of British Columbia, Alberta and Ontario. Under the Canada Assistance Plan (CAP), the federal government had entered into cost-sharing agreements with these three (and the other seven) provinces, under which the federal government undertook to pay 50 per cent of the costs incurred by the provinces in carrying out provincial welfare programmes that met the conditions stipulated in the CAP legislation. The practical effect of the amending legislation was to modify the federal government's obligations under the agreements. The amending legislation was challenged on a variety of grounds, all of which were rejected by the Supreme Court of Canada.

One of the grounds raised by the intervening province of Manitoba in the *CAP* case came dangerously close to a challenge to the power of the Parliament to make conditional grants to the provinces in a field of provincial jurisdiction.

(The other participating provinces made no such challenge.) Sopinka J. for the unanimous Court said:[14]

> The written argument of the Attorney General of Manitoba was that the legislation "amounts to" regulation of a matter outside federal authority. I disagree. The Agreement under the Plan set up an open-ended cost-sharing scheme, which left it to British Columbia to decide which programmes it would establish and fund. The simple withholding of federal money which had previously been granted to fund a matter within provincial jurisdiction does not amount to the regulation of that matter.

This is a rather clear affirmation both of the Parliament's power to authorize grants to the provinces for use in fields of provincial jurisdiction and the power to impose conditions on the recipient provinces. Provided the Parliament's intervention does not go beyond the granting or withholding of money, there is no unconstitutional trespass on provincial jurisdiction.

This broad interpretation of the federal spending power has been accepted by the federal government, of course, and probably by all provincial governments, despite occasional objections to federal intrusions on provincial autonomy.[15] It is, as noted, the basis of the federal-

as restricting the federal power to make grants to the provinces (p. 104), but he then goes on to argue that the implicit restriction would not limit federal power to make unconditional grants (p. 123) or even conditional grants provided the conditions take the form of "standards" rather than "rules" ("federal diktats to provinces"), a distinction that he acknowledges is "not clear-cut" (pp. 123–125).

[13] *Re Canada Assistance Plan*, [1991] 2 S.C.R. 525. The opinion of the Court was written by Sopinka J. I disclose that I was one of the counsel for the Attorney General of Canada.

[14] *Re Canada Assistance Plan*, [1991] 2 S.C.R. 525, 567.

[15] The Meech Lake Accord of 1987, now lapsed (ch. 4, Amendment, under heading

provincial financial arrangements of the last 30 years.[16] It is also the basis of the myriad of federal grants and loans to private firms or individuals,[17] of the tax expenditure provisions of the Income Tax Act,[18] and of the commercial activities of the federal government.[19] It is supported by the case-law[20] and by most commentators.[21]

---

§ 4:3 "The failure to accommodate Quebec"), proposed an amendment to the Constitution that would have confirmed the federal power to spend in areas of exclusive provincial jurisdiction, and the power to make its spending conditional (in order to establish a shared-cost programme), but would have required that any new national shared-cost programme in an area of exclusive provincial jurisdiction had to permit opting out with reasonable compensation for a province that itself established a programme that was "compatible with the national objectives". The Charlottetown Accord of 1992, also now lapsed (ch. 4, Amendment, under heading § 4:3, "The failure to accommodate Quebec"), repeated the same proposal, and also proposed an amendment that would have obligated the federal government, when requested by the government of a province, to negotiate an agreement to stop federal spending programmes in particular (listed) areas of provincial jurisdiction.

[16] *Re Canada Assistance Plan*, [1991] 2 S.C.R. 525; *Winterhaven Stables v. Can.* (1988), 53 D.L.R. (4th) 413 (Alta. C.A.) (upholding Canada Health Act, Canada Assistance Plan and the Federal-Provincial Fiscal Arrangements legislation); *Que. v. Can.*, [2011] 1 S.C.R. 368, para. 41 (assuming validity of federal payments to provinces under the Canada Assistance Plan); *Eldridge v. B.C.*, [1997] 3 S.C.R. 624, para. 25 (dictum upholding Canada Health Act). Compare *Finlay v. Canada*, [1986] 2 S.C.R. 607 (assuming validity of federal conditions on grants to provinces under Canada Assistance Plan). In the United States, conditional grants to the states have been upheld: *Oklahoma v. U.S. Civil Service Commn.* (1947), 330 U.S. 127 (upholding condition on federal highway grants that state officials not engage in political activities); *South Dakota v. Dole* (1987), 483 U.S. 203 (upholding condition on federal highway grants that state prohibit under-age-21 drinking). In Australia, conditional grants to the states are explicitly authorized by s. 96 of the Constitution.

[17] *Angers v. M.N.R.*, [1957] Ex. C.R. 83 (upholding federal family allowances); *Central Mortgage and Housing Corp. v. Co-op College Residences* (1975), 13 O.R. (2d) 394 (C.A.) (upholding federal loans for student housing); *YMHA Jewish Community Centre v. Brown*, [1989] 1 S.C.R. 1532 (upholding federal job creation programme, involving federal wages subsidy). *Canada Mortgage and Housing Corp. v. Iness* (2004), 70 O.R. (3d) 148 (C.A.) (upholding conditions on federal housing subsidy and holding provincial human rights law inapplicable). Compare *A.G. Can. v. A.G. Ont.* (Unemployment Insurance) [1937] A.C. 355 (refusing to uphold federal unemployment insurance as a spending measure, because it also established a contributory insurance scheme, involving the imposition of duties— to pay premiums—on employers and employees; dicta on extent of spending power at 366–367 per Lord Atkin are equivocal).

[18] The Income Tax Act provides for many exemptions, deductions, credits and other preferences that pursue non-tax policies, e.g., to encourage manufacturing and processing, research and development, pollution control or charitable giving. It has become commonplace to describe these provisions as "tax expenditures", because their economic effect is equivalent to a direct expenditure equal to the tax foregone by the tax preference. The description reflects the interchangeability as policy instruments of direct expenditures and tax expenditures. Constitutional restrictions on the one would presumably apply to the other as well.

[19] See ch. 29, Public Property, under heading § 29:3, "Executive power over public property".

[20] § 6:8 notes 16 and 17, above.

[21] F.R. Scott, "The Constitutional Background of the Taxation Agreements" (1955) 2 McGill L.J. 1, 6–7 ("Making a gift is not the same as making a law."); W.R. Lederman,

In the United States, the spending power of the federal Congress is explicit. It is combined with the taxing power in the first head of power in s. 8 of the Constitution of the United States, which enumerates the powers of Congress. The spending power reads: "The Congress shall have power . . . to pay the debts and provide for the common defence and general welfare of the United States . . .". There was disagreement among the framers as to whether the "general welfare of the United States" was restricted to those aspects of the general welfare coming within the other enumerated heads of federal power (Madison's view) or whether it extended to purposes that would otherwise be outside federal legislative power (Hamilton's view). The Supreme Court of the United States resolved the disagreement by taking the latter (broader) view,[22] and no federal expenditure has ever been struck down on the ground that it did not further the general welfare. Much federal spending takes the form of grants to the states, and it is often conditional; the conditions imposed on the states by Congress may require the states to fulfil requirements that Congress would be powerless to legislate directly.[23] The justification for this broad spending power is the fact that the Congress is not making a coercive law when it imposes a condition on a federal grant; the relationship between the federal and state governments is akin to a contract. The states who accept a federal conditional grant have voluntarily agreed to abide by the condition, and the condition is ultimately implemented by force of state legislative power, not federal legislative power. This is all very similar in doctrine and rationale to the Canadian law of the spending power.

The American Supreme Court has however from time to time suggested a limitation on the spending power that has never been adverted to in the Canadian cases: federal spending legislation cannot "coerce" state participation in federal programs.[24] This limitation was never actually applied until *National Federation of Independent Businesses v.*

"Some Forms and Limitations of Cooperative Federalism" (1967) 45 Can. Bar Rev. 409, 433; J.E. Magnet, "The Constitutional Distribution of Taxation Powers in Canada" (1978) 10 Ottawa L. Rev. 473, 480; La Forest, The Allocation of Taxing Power under the Canadian Constitution (2nd ed., 1981), 51; E.A. Driedger, "The Spending Power" (1981) 7 Queen's L.J. 124, 133–134; Laskin, Canadian Constitutional Law (5th ed., 1986 by Finkelstein), 783–784. Scholars who take issue with the broad interpretation of the federal spending power are A. Petter, "Federalism and the Myth of the Federal Spending Power" (1989) 69 Can. Bar Rev. 34; S. Arrowsmith, "Government Contracts and Public Law" (1990) 10 Legal Studies 231, 236–238; D.W.S. Yudin, "The Federal Spending Power in Canada, Australia and the United States" (2002) 13 Nat. J. Con. Law 437; B. Frédéric, "Addressing the Elephant in the Room: Spending Power in Canada" (2016) 36 Nat. J. Con. Law 287.

[22] *U.S. v. Butler* (1936), 297 U.S. 1, 65–66, is the leading case.

[23] E.g., *South Dakota v. Dole* (1987), 483 U.S. 203, 205–206 (upholding federal highway grants to states conditioned on the state raising the minimum drinking age to 21).

[24] *South Dakota v. Dole* (1987), 483 U.S. 203, 211. The Court held that the inducement was not impermissibly coercive because a failure to accept the grant would involve the loss of only 5 per cent of the state's highway funds, comprising less than half of one per cent of the state's budget.

Sebelius (2012).[25] That case was a constitutional challenge to a health-care reform enacted by Congress that would (among other things) grant additional federal funds to the states for Medicaid (a federal program to enable states to provide health care to needy persons) on condition that the states expanded the class of persons eligible for assistance. The challenge to the federal law did not stem from the condition requiring the states who accepted the new funding to expand their public health-care entitlements; that was clearly valid. But there was also a financial sanction associated with the grant: a state that refused the grant could lose, not only the new Medicaid funding (obviously), but also all of its existing federal Medicaid funding.[26] That sanction, the majority of the Court held, had the effect of imposing a financial penalty on any state that chose not to participate in the expanded program, a penalty that was so large that it would leave the states with no real choice but to join the program. This amounted to coercion, and was unconstitutional. Ginsburg J. dissented, rejecting the notion of coercion on the ground that it entailed "political judgments that defy judicial calculation". However, she concurred with the majority that the legislation could be salvaged by limiting the sanction to the loss of the new Medicaid funding, and on that revised basis the conditional grant was upheld.[27]

§ 6:9 Provincial power

The understandable preoccupation of governments and commentators with the power to disburse from the federal purse has not been matched by an equivalent concern with the extent of the provincial spending power.[1] But the distinction between compulsory regulation, on the one hand, and spending or lending or contracting, on the other, is surely as valid for the provinces as it is for the Dominion.[2] To be sure, the provincial taxing power is expressly limited to "the raising of a revenue for provincial purposes" (s. 92(2)), but Duff C.J. has said that the phrase "for provincial purposes" means only that the revenue raised is "for the

---

[25]*National Federation of Independent Businesses v. Sebelius* (2012), 567 U.S. 519. Roberts C.J. wrote the opinion of the majority.

[26]The Secretary of Health and Human Services, the federal administrator of Medicaid, had authority to withhold in whole or in part federal Medicaid funds from states that failed to comply with the Medicaid legislation as amended from time to time. The Secretary had a discretion, but the Court assumed that the loss of all Medicaid funding would follow from even a partial failure to comply with the federal legislation.

[27]Scalia, Kennedy, Thomas and Alito JJ. dissented, rejecting the salvage remedy on the ground that it would save "a statute Congress did not write".

[Section 6:9]

[1]See La Forest, The Allocation of Taxing Power under the Canadian Constitution (2nd ed., 1981), 60–62; E.A. Driedger, "The Spending Power" (1981) 7 Queen's L.J. 124, 131–132; *Dunbar v. A.G. Sask.* (1984), 11 D.L.R. (4th) 374 (Sask. Q.B.) (upholding provincial appropriation for international aid); *Lovelace v. Ont.*, [2000] 1 S.C.R. 950, para. 111 (upholding provincial programme for Indian communities).

[2]*Valley Rubber Resources v. B.C.* (2002), 219 D.L.R. (4th) 1 (B.C. C.A.) (provincial programme of incentives for recycling valid under spending power; no statutory regulation needed for voluntary programme with no sanctions).

exclusive disposition of the legislature".[3] In addition, there are cases which decide that a province may validly sell its property subject to conditions which would be outside its legislative competence.[4] In fact, the provinces have never recognized any limits on their spending power and have often spent money for purposes outside their legislative competence, for example, by running a commuter train service on interprovincial trackage,[5] by acquiring an airline,[6] by giving international aid,[7] or by paying casino profits to Indian communities.[8]

IX. CONCLUSIONS

§ 6:10 Conclusions

The history of federal-provincial financial arrangements from 1867 to the present is a history of continuous constitutional adaptation to changing circumstances and values. The pendulum has swung several times between federal and provincial power as the balance has been altered by factors impinging on the economy or security of the nation.[1] The depression of the 1930s followed by the second world war led to a great increase in federal power. The depression, as well as nearly bankrupting some provinces, emphasized the importance of national monetary and banking systems as economic tools. The war effort required central direction of the economy, and enormous national resources. The resulting concentration of federal power continued well into the postwar period.

There were a number of reasons why the pendulum did not start to swing back until the mid-1950s. First of all, of course, the growth of federal power had altered the balance of bargaining power to a degree which would take years for the provinces to redress even if they strove single-mindedly to that end. Secondly, the problems of postwar reconstruction were comparable in magnitude to those of the war, and

---

[3]*Re Employment and Social Insurance Act*, [1936] S.C.R. 427, 434 per Duff C.J. dissenting. This makes the phrase "for provincial purposes" virtually meaningless, but the phrase "with provincial objects" in the incorporation power (s. 92(11)) has met a similar fate: see ch. 23, Companies, under heading § 23:3 "Functional limitation". The provincial appropriation power (the provincial equivalent to ss. 102 and 106) is s. 126, which uses the phrase "for the public service of the province". E.A. Driedger, "The Spending Power" (1981) 7 Queen's L.J. 124, 131–132, argues that this phrase (and its variants in ss. 102 and 106) does not import any restrictions on the purposes for which funds may be appropriated.

[4]*Smylie v. The Queen* (1900), 27 O.A.R. 172; *Brooks-Bidlake and Whitall v. A.G. B.C.*, [1923] A.C. 450; and see §§ 29:1 et seq., Public Property, under heading § 29:2, "Legislative power over public property".

[5]*The Queen (Ont.) v. Bd. of Transport Commrs.* (Go-Train) [1968] S.C.R. 118.

[6]*The Queen (Alta.) v. Can. Transport Comm.*, [1978] 1 S.C.R. 61.

[7]*Dunbar v. A.G. Sask.* (1984), 11 D.L.R. (4th) 374 (Sask. Q.B.).

[8]*Lovelace v. Ont.*, [2000] 1 S.C.R. 950.

[Section 6:10]

[1]See Advisory Commission on Intergovernmental Relations, *In Search of Balance—Canada's Intergovernmental Experience* (1971); Bastien, Federalism and Decentralization: Where do we stand? (1981).

the federal government had in fact developed ambitious national policies for the transition to peace and an unprecedented level of prosperity. Thirdly, humanitarian and egalitarian ideals which emphasized governmental responsibility for the provision of minimum standards of income, health, education and welfare to all Canadians could only be fulfilled by action at the national level. Fourthly, the existence of only one taxing authority eliminated much complexity and duplication in collection machinery and in the obligations of taxpayers to file returns, and enabled one national fiscal policy to regulate the economy and stimulate employment. And fifthly, there were administrative and political advantages to the provinces in not having to administer a system of tax collection, and in not having to take responsibility for levying the most painful taxes. These factors all combined to produce a continuation of highly centralized fiscal arrangements well into the 1950s. (Some of the factors are, of course, enduring and will assure the federal government a major fiscal role into the foreseeable future.) In the tax rental agreements of 1947–1962, Ottawa remained the sole taxing authority, and it used the power of the purse to establish conditional grant and shared-cost programmes, which extended federal power deeply into the traditionally provincial domains of housing, highways, health and social welfare; these programmes, and the equalization payments, required Ottawa to raise taxes well in excess of its own legislative requirements.

But there were factors tugging in the opposite direction too, and especially autonomist sentiment in Quebec. Quebec had remained outside the rental system and had refused to join some of the shared-cost programmes, although it had joined some programmes and had accepted massive equalization payments. After the death of Premier Duplessis in 1959, and the election of a Liberal government under Premier Lesage in 1960, Quebec embarked on ambitious policies of social and economic reform, which inevitably brought it into conflict with Ottawa over money (for the policies were costly) and policy (for the policies often duplicated or clashed with federal policies). While the other provinces did not design their policies in the service of cultural integrity, and did not make any such dramatic break with the past, they too by 1960 were becoming increasingly active in social and economic affairs. All of the provinces have grown stronger and more selfconfident, and have recruited able public servants. Until recently, Ontario has been the wealthiest province, with the least to gain from centralized financial arrangements, and it is not surprising that it has never been a full participant in the tax rental or tax collection arrangements. Alberta, now far and away the wealthiest province (on a per capita basis), has withdrawn from the tax collection arrangements with respect to corporate income tax. Alberta is naturally suspicious of centralized financial arrangements, and especially of the proposals which surface periodically for the sharing of oil revenues.

What began to happen in the mid-1950s, and accelerated after 1960, was a swing of the pendulum back towards provincial power. After 1962, the provinces imposed their own taxes at their own rates, and these have steadily increased in relation to federal revenues. On the other hand, the federal government retains the dominant role in setting tax policy, because it is the federal Parliament which legislates the tax base, and all provinces within the collection system have to use the federal base. Equalization grants and other forms of provincial aid are accepted by the provinces, and these require the federal government to continue to raise much more revenue than it needs for strictly federal programmes. However, the federal government has modified many of its programmes to take account of provincial objections. The direct grants to provincial universities have been abandoned and replaced with grants to the provinces for post-secondary education. Shared-cost programmes, once virtually dictated to the provinces by the federal government on a take-it-or-leave-it basis, have become a matter for prior consultation and discussion, and opting-out alternatives have been introduced. Even the cost-sharing aspect, implying federal control of provincial expenditures, has been abandoned with respect to all major programmes in favour of a formula which is independent of actual provincial expenditures, and which includes tax points as well as cash. All these developments have collectively enhanced the provinces' control over their universities, their social programmes and (to a lesser extent) their health care systems.[2]

If the fiscal arrangements in Canada still appear to be loaded in favour of the federal government, comparisons with Australia and the United States are instructive. In Australia,[3] as in Canada, the federal government assumed a monopoly of income taxation during the second world war. In Australia, however, this has continued to the present. The states levy no income taxes, and if any did their residents would not receive any abatement of federal taxes.[4] The states also levy no retail sales taxes or value added taxes. The federal government alone levies a Goods and Services Tax (a value added tax), and all the revenue is granted to the states. The bulk of the states' revenue comes from grants from the federal government. The result is a high degree of uniformity in public services across the country, and a high degree of state dependence upon federal grants for revenue. These arrangements are much more centralized than in either Canada or the United States, reflecting the fact that Australia has only six states, and that they are relatively homogeneous. One could add the further speculation that Australia's relative isolation from European countries has fostered a sense of unity

[2]The Canada Health Act, R.S.C. 1985, c. C-6, which was enacted in 1984, is opposed to the general tendency, because it strengthened the federal conditions on grants to the provinces for insured health services and in particular required (on pain of financial penalty) provincial bans on extra-billing by doctors and user fees by hospitals. These conditions, which have made it very difficult for the provinces to control the cost of their provincial health care plans, apply to grants within the Canadian Health Transfer: see heading § 6:7, "Conditional federal grants".

[3]For comparisons, see Gilbert, Australian and Canadian Federalism 1867–1984 (1986); Cullen, Federalism in Action: the Australian and Canadian Offshore Disputes (1990).

[4]Abatements which varied from state to state would probably be unconstitutional in Australia, because the Constitution by s. 51(2) requires federal taxation to be uniform.

and acceptance of strong central government, especially in comparison with Canada.[5]

The fiscal arrangements of the United States[6] are highly uncoordinated, but the balance of power is nevertheless closer to the centre than it is in Canada. The federal government dominates the income tax field. The states can levy income taxes, and many do; but no federal abatements are available, and high federal rates allow room for only low rates of state tax, usually around five to seven per cent. Federal occupancy of most of the income tax field, coupled with wide acceptance of deficit financing at the federal level, has given overwhelming fiscal supremacy to the federal government. This has not been accompanied by Canadian-style tax-sharing arrangements with the states. The federal government does make conditional (or categorical) grants to states and municipalities, and these account for around 19 per cent of state and local revenue; but it makes few unconditional grants to states or municipalities. There are no equalization payments to allow the poorer states to bring their public services up to national average levels, and there is a wide disparity in state public services.[7] There is a continuing proliferation of different taxes on various bases, at various rates—like the situation in Canada before the second world war.

The relative lack of coordination between the two levels of government in the United States is the product of a number of distinctively American constitutional and cultural factors. For a start, there are practical difficulties in securing any general federal-state agreement on tax-sharing or anything else. There is no forum comparable to Canada's first ministers' conferences where an agreement could be struck between the federal and state governments. The state Governors, unlike provincial Premiers, are rarely in a position to make firm commitments on behalf of their states because, with the separation of executive and legislative branches and the absence of strict party discipline in the state Legislatures, a Governor is rarely in control of his state Legislature. The large number of states in comparison with provinces would in any case make general agreement difficult. (Of course some federal-state adjustment occurs within the federal Congress, which is not controlled by the executive and does not adhere to strict party discipline, and within the federal bureaucracy.) On top of the practical difficulties, Americans seem to be much less willing than Canadians or Australians to compromise the principle of "fiscal responsibility"—the principle that the spending authority should also be the taxing authority.

The uncoordinated situation is, as noted, one of unchallenged federal

---

[5]Gilbert, Australian and Canadian Federalism 1867–1984 (1986), 156–157.

[6]See *In Search of Balance—Canada's Intergovernmental Experience* (Advisory Commission on Intergovernmental Relations, Washington, D.C., 1971). (Updated on Tax Foundation Website.)

[7]The disparity in welfare benefits is roughly four times the disparity between the rich provinces and poor provinces in Canada: *In Search of Balance—Canada's Intergovernmental Experience* (Advisory Commission on Intergovernmental Relations, Washington, D.C., 1971). (Updated on Tax Foundation Website.)

fiscal dominance. This is also reinforced by factors which are lacking in Canada. African-Americans in the United States are not concentrated in any one state, and their political influence has been unsympathetic to states' rights: they have tended to look to Washington for redress of grievances. In Canada, the concern of French Canadians to protect their language and cultural integrity has taken the form of a provincial rights movement, leading to Quebec's continual insistence that it be master in its own house. Moreover, Quebec, with 7.6 million people out of a total of 32 million, is much larger in relation to Canada as a whole than any one state is in relation to the United States as a whole, and Ontario, with 12.5 million, is even larger. The Canadian provinces, or small groups of them, also come much closer to representing distinct economic regions of the country than do the American states, so that the provinces have become the natural advocates of regional interests.

Federalism in Canada, Australia and the United States, like other federal countries, is of necessity "cooperative", because of the high degree of interdependence between the parts of the system, but in the United States cooperation is much less evident than in Australia and Canada. In Canada, the centralized form of federalism which developed during and after the second world war has been replaced by a form of cooperative federalism in which the provinces have sufficient autonomy to influence the outcome of federal provincial relationships. The ideal of cooperative federalism is that each government recognizes its interdependence with the other governments, and is concerned about the repercussions of its actions on the policies of the others. This requires much more than respect for the legislative authority of others; it involves consultation with others before exercising one's own undoubted legislative authority, in order to ensure that one's own actions are as far as possible compatible with the plans of others. In Canada, in the fiscal area, major federal developments have normally been preceded by a period of consultation leading to the agreement of all or most of the provinces. Indeed, fiscal cooperation is now institutionalized in the form of several intergovernmental committees which meet regularly, and do much of the work preparatory to the first ministers' conferences, which will of course continue to make the decisions. Cooperation has become the rule and unilateral initiative the exception.

Chapter 7

Courts

I. PROVINCIAL COURTS

§ 7:1 Establishment of provincial courts
§ 7:2 Appointment and payment of provincial judges
§ 7:3 Tenure of provincial judges: s. 99
§ 7:4 Tenure of provincial judges: s. 11(d)
§ 7:5 Inferior courts
§ 7:6 Court Martial
§ 7:7 Jury
§ 7:8 Inferior courts of civil jurisdiction
§ 7:9 Administrative tribunals

II. FEDERAL COURTS

§ 7:10 Supreme Court of Canada
§ 7:11 Federal Court of Canada
§ 7:12 Tax Court of Canada
§ 7:13 Territorial courts
§ 7:14 Appointment, payment and tenure of federal judges

III. IMPLICATIONS OF CONSTITUTION'S JUDICATURE SECTIONS

§ 7:15 Separation of powers
§ 7:16 Inferior courts
§ 7:17 County or district courts
§ 7:18 Superior courts
§ 7:19 Administrative tribunals
§ 7:20 Privative clauses

I. PROVINCIAL COURTS

§ 7:1 Establishment of provincial courts

The Constitution Act, 1867, by s. 92(14), allocates to the provinces the power to make laws in relation to "the administration of justice in the province".[1] The power expressly includes "the constitution, maintenance, and organization of provincial courts, both of civil and criminal jurisdic-

---

[Section 7:1]

[1]See Russell, The Judiciary in Canada (1987); Beaudoin, La Constitution du Canada (3rd ed., 2004), ch. 4.

tion", and "procedure in civil matters in those courts". The power embraces courts of criminal as well as civil jurisdiction, despite the fact that "the criminal law" is by s. 91(27) allocated to the federal Parliament; but the provincial power does not include criminal procedure, because "procedure in criminal matters" is by s. 91(27) allocated to the federal Parliament along with the substantive criminal law.[2]

At the time of confederation, each of the uniting provinces had its own system of courts modeled on the English courts. The system included a "superior" court or courts with jurisdiction throughout the province, unlimited by subject matter. Below the superior court in all provinces except Quebec were "county" or "district" courts with jurisdiction limited by territory to a local county or district as well as by subject matter. Below the county or district courts were "inferior" courts staffed by magistrates or justices of the peace with jurisdiction over small civil claims and minor criminal offences. All these courts were expressly continued after confederation by s. 129 of the Constitution Act, 1867, and their organization and jurisdiction remained the responsibility of the provinces by virtue of s. 92(14).[3]

The structure of the courts in each province, including those provinces admitted after confederation, did not initially depart radically from the pre-confederation pattern. In each province, despite variations in nomenclature, organization and jurisdiction, it was still possible to identify the three tiers of the judicial system: (1) the "superior" court or courts, which in each province now includes a court of appeal as well as a trial division; (2) the "county" or "district" courts, which did not however exist in Quebec; and (3) the "inferior" courts, which in most provinces are now called "provincial courts".[4] In the 1970s, the idea of "amalgamating" the county and district courts into the superior court became popular among court reformers. What is involved in amalgamation is the abolition of the county and district courts and an increase in the size of the superior court. Amalgamation has now occurred in all of the nine provinces that originally had district or county courts. The intermediate tier of county or district courts no longer exists.

The administration of justice in Canada has important unitary as well as federal characteristics.[5] Of course, as one would expect in a federal country, there is a separate hierarchy of provincial courts in each

[2]The administration of justice in the province includes criminal justice, even though criminal law and procedure is a federal responsibility under s. 91(27). Criminal justice, including investigation of crime, policing, prosecution, punishment and public inquiries, is dealt with in ch. 19, Criminal Justice.

[3]The history is related in Laskin, The British Tradition in Canadian Law (1969), 10–21.

[4]The reason for the adjective "provincial" is that the judges are appointed and paid by the provincial governments. Unfortunately, the change in nomenclature occasionally leads the ill-informed to assume that the superior, district and county courts in each province are "federal" courts. This is incorrect: these courts are also provincial, despite the national elements of the system, and despite federal appointment and payment of the judges, as described in the following text.

[5]This idea is explored in more detail in P.W. Hogg, "Federalism and the Jurisdic-

province. But these courts, whether they were in existence at the time of confederation or were established later under s. 92(14), are not confined to deciding cases arising under provincial laws. The provincial power over the administration of justice in the province enables a province to invest its courts with jurisdiction over the full range of cases, whether the applicable law is federal or provincial or constitutional.[6] Then, there is an appeal from the provincial court of appeal, which stands at the top of each provincial hierarchy, to the Supreme Court of Canada. Although the Supreme Court of Canada is established by federal legislation, it is more of a national than a federal court, because it is a "general court of appeal for Canada", with power to hear appeals from the provincial courts (as well as from the federal courts, which are described later) in all kinds of cases, whether the applicable law is federal or provincial or constitutional.[7] The position of the Supreme Court of Canada, with its plenary jurisdiction, at the top of each provincial hierarchy, has the effect of melding the ten provincial hierarchies into a single national system. The national character of the system is reinforced by the judicature sections of the Constitution Act, 1867, which are described in the next section of this chapter, and which require that the judges of the superior, district and county courts of each province be appointed and paid by the federal government.

The general jurisdiction of the provincial courts means that there is no need for a separate system of federal courts to decide "federal" questions. Nor does the power to decide federal questions have to be specifically granted to the provincial courts by the federal Parliament. On the contrary, if federal law calls for the exercise of adjudication, but is silent as to the forum, the appropriate forum will be the provincial courts.[8] Thus, most disputes involving banking and commercial paper, although governed by federal law, are disposed of by provincial courts because the applicable federal law is silent on the question of

---

tion of Canadian Courts" (1981) 30 U.N.B.L.J. 9. The unitary elements of the system have been recognized in judicial dicta: *R. v. Thomas Fuller Construction*, [1980] 1 S.C.R. 695, 706; *A.-G. Can. v. Law Society of B.C.*, [1982] 2 S.C.R. 307, 327; *Ont. v. Pembina Exploration*, [1989] 1 S.C.R. 206, 215, 217, 225, 226.

[6]*Valin v. Langlois* (1879), 3 S.C.R. 1, 19; *Ont. v. Pembina Exploration*, [1989] 1 S.C.R. 206, 217. The same rule applies to provincial administrative tribunals; if they have been given (expressly or impliedly) the power to decide questions of law, then they must apply all applicable laws, whether provincial, federal or constitutional: *Paul v. B.C.*, [2003] 2 S.C.R. 585, para. 21 (holding that B.C.'s Forest Appeals Commission had power to rule on a claim of aboriginal rights).

[7]The Supreme Court of Canada is the topic of the next chapter.

[8]*Board v. Board*, [1919] A.C. 956 (Supreme Court of Alberta has jurisdiction over divorce); *Ont. v. Pembina Exploration*, [1989] 1 S.C.R. 206 (Small Claims Court of Ontario has jurisdiction over admiralty); *Knox Contracting v. Can.*, [1990] 2 S.C.R. 338, 360 (Court of Queen's Bench of New Brunswick has power to determine issue under Income Tax Act); Laskin, The British Tradition in Canadian Law (1969), 114. In *Kourtessis v. M.N.R.*, [1993] 2 S.C.R. 53, the Court divided on the question whether the power to decide federal questions flowed from an assumed adoption by Parliament of the provincial forum (La Forest J. at 77) or from the plenary provincial power over the administration of justice (Sopinka J. at 105). The latter explanation is the orthodox one and, in my view, the correct one.

adjudication.[9] The federal Parliament does have the power to stipulate the forum of adjudication over matters in relation to which it has legislative competence, and it may stipulate provincial courts or tribunals.[10] This has been done, for example, in the Criminal Code,[11] the Divorce Act[12] and the Young Offenders Act:[13] cases arising under those federal statutes are dealt with in the provincial courts under specific grants of jurisdiction contained in each statute.

It is not uncommon for a provincial court to receive a grant of jurisdiction from both the provincial Legislature and the federal Parliament. In *R. v. Sciascia* (2017),[14] the provincial court of Ontario had been granted jurisdiction to try charges under provincial law by provincial law and to try summary conviction criminal charges by the federal Criminal Code. The accused, following an episode of erratic driving, was charged with the provincial highway traffic offence of failing to stop for the police and the Criminal Code offence of dangerous driving. He was tried and convicted of both offences in a single trial by a provincial court judge. On appeal, he argued that the provincial court judge lacked jurisdiction to conduct a joint trial of the provincial and criminal charges. Moldaver J., writing for the majority of the Supreme Court of Canada, rejected the argument. The judge had jurisdiction over both charges, and at common law had the discretion to conduct a joint trial where a joint trial would be in the interests of justice. The two jurisdiction-granting statutes were silent about joint trials of provincial and criminal offences, but they did not prohibit them. Because the two charges arose out of the same set of facts and there was no prejudice to the accused (who had in fact consented to the joint trial), the interests of justice were better served by a joint trial than two trials where the evidence would largely be duplicated. Moldaver J. concluded that that the trial judge did not err in holding the joint trial of the provincial and criminal charges. He upheld the convictions. Côté J. dissented. In her view, the provincial offences statute should be interpreted as implicitly prohibiting provincial offences to be tried at the same time as the typically more serious crimi-

---

[9]Judicial review of federal administrative tribunals was another example of provincial jurisdiction acquired by silence, but in 1971 that function was vested in the newly-established Federal Court: Federal Court Act, R.S.C. 1985, c. F-7, ss. 18, 28.

[10]*Valin v. Langlois* (1879), 3 S.C.R. 1 (superior court); *Re Vancini* (1904), 34 S.C.R. 621 (police magistrate); *Coughlin v. Ont. Highway Transport Bd.*, [1968] S.C.R. 569 (administrative tribunal); *Papp v. Papp*, [1970] 1 O.R. 331 (Ont. C.A.) (superior court and master thereof); *R. v. Trimarchi* (1987), 63 O.R. (2d) 515 (C.A.) (provincial court); *Re Young Offenders Act*, [1991] 1 S.C.R. 252 (youth court). The federal cause, if civil, will be regulated by the provincially-enacted procedure of the provincial court, although the federal Parliament may, if it chooses, stipulate the procedure to be followed: Laskin, Canadian Constitutional Law (5th ed., 1986 by Finkelstein), 184–188. It has done so in divorce, for example.

[11]R.S.C. 1985, c. C-46, ss. 468, 798.

[12]S.C. 1986, c. 4, s. 3.

[13]R.S.C. 1985, c. Y-1, s. 2.

[14]*R. v. Sciascia*, [2017] 2 S.C.R. 539, 2017 SCC 57. Moldaver J. wrote the opinion of the six-judge majority. Côté J. wrote a dissenting opinion.

nal offences. She would have quashed the convictions and ordered two new trials.

While the Constitution Act, 1867 does not require a separate system of federal courts to decide federal questions, s. 101 does authorize the federal Parliament to establish federal courts "for the better administration of the laws of Canada". This power was exercised in 1875 by the establishment of the Exchequer Court of Canada. Then in 1971 the Exchequer Court was replaced by the Federal Court of Canada. These federal courts constitute an exception to the generally unitary character of the administration of justice in Canada; for since 1875 it has been necessary to bring certain kinds of "federal" cases in a federal court instead of a provincial court. The federal court system is discussed later in this chapter.[15]

§ 7:2 Appointment and payment of provincial judges

Section 92(4) of the Constitution Act, 1867 confers on each province the power to make laws in relation to "the establishment and tenure of provincial offices and the appointment and payment of provincial officers". Under this provision, the province appoints and pays the judges of the "inferior" courts. The province does not appoint and pay the judges of the "superior" courts, or the judges of the "district" or "county" courts (when they used to exist), because the judicature sections of the Constitution Act, 1867 (ss. 96 to 101) provide (among other things) for the appointment and payment of these judges by the federal government.

Section 96 of the Constitution Act, 1867 provides that "the Governor General", that is, the federal government, "shall appoint the judges of the superior, district and county courts in each province". On the face of it, this provision is an anomaly in a federal constitution.[1] Why should the federal government make appointments to the provinces' higher courts?[2] The answer that has become conventional is that s. 96 reinforces judicial independence by insulating the judges from local pressures. But this explanation, although enthusiastically endorsed by the Privy Council,[3] is not particularly convincing. There is no reason to suppose that judges appointed by the provinces would be less competent[4] or indepen-

---

[15]§§ 7:10 to 7:14, "Federal Courts".

[Section 7:2]

[1]Section 96 has no counterpart in the Constitutions of the United States and Australia, where the federal government plays no role in the selection of state judges.

[2]The legislative history is not clear: see B. Laskin, "Municipal Tax Assessment and Section 96" (1955) 33 Can. Bar Rev. 993, 998; Pepin, Les tribunaux administratifs et la constitution (1969), Part I, ch. 1.

[3]*Martineau & Sons v. Montreal*, [1932] A.C. 113, 120; *Toronto v. York*, [1938] A.C. 415, 426.

[4]The provinces would undoubtedly appoint from the same group of senior lawyers as the federal government now appoints from. Considerations of provincial politics would sometimes operate in favour of different individuals, especially where the provincial government was controlled by a different political party than the federal

dent[5] than judges appointed by the federal government. I believe that the reason for s. 96 is to be found in the fact that the provincial courts are courts of general jurisdiction.[6] Since the provincial courts decide questions of federal law as well as provincial law, and questions of constitutional law as well as private law, some federal involvement in their establishment is appropriate.[7]

Associated with s. 96 are several other sections whose purpose is more obvious. Sections 97 and 98 require that the federally-appointed judges of the superior, district and county courts in each province be appointed from the bar of the province. This ensures that the judges are lawyers and that they are versed in the local law.

Section 100 provides that the salaries of the judges of the superior, district and county courts be "fixed and provided by the Parliament of Canada". This section makes clear that the federally-appointed judges are to be paid from the federal treasury, not the provincial treasury. In addition, however, by insisting that the salaries be fixed and provided by the Parliament, s. 100 protects the judiciary from executive power to impair judicial independence by reductions or raises of salary.[8] Of course, in a system of responsible government, the executive can usually rely upon the Parliament to do its bidding, but a government which had decided to tamper improperly with judicial salaries would have to expose its decision to parliamentary debate, and this would raise a storm of protest from the opposition and from the press. Indeed, during the depression of the 1930s, there was much controversy in Canada (and England) as to whether it was proper to reduce judicial salaries by ten per cent (20 per cent in England) by a statute which applied to the entire federal civil service as well. The argument that such a non-discriminatory reduction would threaten judicial independence seems

government, but this would be unlikely to impair the relative quality of appointments.

[5]The formal and informal guarantees of judicial independence, which are discussed in the next section of this chapter, would continue to apply if the s. 96 judges were appointed by the provinces.

[6]This thesis is advanced in P.W. Hogg, "Federalism and the Jurisdiction of Canadian Courts" (1981) 30 U.N.B.L.J. 9, and in N. Duplé's contribution to Beck and Bernier (eds.), *Canada and the New Constitution* (1983), vol. 1, 129.

[7]This rationale is very powerful where there are no federal courts (the situation at confederation), or where the federal courts have very limited jurisdiction (the situation at the establishment of the Exchequer Court in 1875), but its force diminishes as more and more federal questions are removed from the jurisdiction of the provincial courts and vested in the federal courts (as has steadily occurred, especially at the establishment of the Federal Court of Canada in 1971). The establishment of these federal courts is described later in this chapter. However, the provincial courts still decide many issues under federal law, including the trial of all criminal offences, and they retain jurisdiction over constitutional cases—a jurisdiction that cannot be taken away from them: *A.-G. Can. v. Law Society of B.C.*, [1982] 2 S.C.R. 307; *Can. Labour Relations Bd. v. Paul L'Anglais*, [1983] 1 S.C.R. 147.

[8]*Beauregard v. Can.*, [1986] 2 S.C.R. 56, 75 (a condition of judicial independence is that a judge's right to salary or pension should "not be subject to arbitrary interference by the Executive").

fantastic, but it was seriously advanced by constitutional lawyers, judges, government ministers and members of parliament.[9]

The argument that a non-discriminatory reduction of judicial salaries would threaten judicial independence has actually been accepted by the Supreme Court of Canada. In *Re Remuneration of Judges* (1997),[10] the legislation of three provinces, in each case reducing provincial-court judges' salaries by an across-the-board percentage that applied to all persons in the public sector, was struck down as an unconstitutional breach of judicial independence. Because the judges were members of inferior courts, ss. 99 and 100 were not applicable, and the case was decided under s. 11(d) of the Charter of Rights, which is discussed later in this chapter.[11] The Court made clear that the same ruling would apply to the courts covered by ss. 99 and 100.[12] The Court did not raise an absolute bar to reductions in judicial salaries, but any reduction (or freeze or even increase) would have to be preceded by a report of a judicial compensation commission (the composition of which was stipulated by the Court). If the legislation departed from the recommendations of the commission, a "legitimate reason" would have to be articulated for the departure, and that reason would be subject to judicial review on the basis of a standard of rationality. In this case, the legislation of the three provinces had not been preceded by a report of a judicial compensation commission, and so the legislation was invalid. This surprising ruling is more fully discussed later in this chapter.[13]

The result of the judicature sections of the Constitution Act, 1867 is compulsory co-operative federalism. It is for the provinces under s. 92(14) to create all provincial courts, and to determine how many judges are to be appointed. But, with respect to the higher courts, the actual appointments must be made by the federal government (from the bar of the province), and the judges' salaries must be provided by the federal Parliament.[14] The federal appointments are made by the cabinet, with the federal Minister of Justice recommending the names of puisne (ordinary) judges, and the Prime Minister recommending the names of chief justices.[15] Salaries are fixed by the federal Judges Act.[16]

---

[9]The history is related by W.R. Lederman, "The Independence of the Judiciary" (1956) 34 Can. Bar Rev. 769, 789, 1139, 1164.

[10]*Re Remuneration of Judges*, [1997] 3 S.C.R. 3.

[11]§ 7:5, "Inferior courts".

[12]*Re Remuneration of Judges*, [1997] 3 S.C.R. 3, paras. 160–165.

[13]See text accompanying § 7:5 note 8 and § 7:8 note 3, below.

[14]Provincial requests for new judicial appointments are not always granted, and are sometimes granted on condition that reforms in provincial judicial management are carried out: P.H. Russell "Constitutional Reform of the Canadian Judiciary" (1967) 9 Alta. L. Rev. 103, 121.

[15]Russell, The Judiciary in Canada (1987), 112. Before a federal appointment is recommended to the cabinet by the federal Minister of Justice (for puisne judges) or the Prime Minister (for chief justices), there is a vetting process. This vetting process consists of: (1) an expression of interest and eligibility by the candidate; and (2) an assessment and recommendation by an independent Judicial Advisory Committee. Judicial

A reorganization of provincial courts sometimes gives rise to difficult questions as to the location of the required powers. There is a fine line between the reorganization of the provincial courts, which is competent to the province by virtue of s. 92(14), and the appointment of higher-court judges, which is incompetent to the province by virtue of s. 96. A provincial statute authorizing a county court judge to sit in a county other than that for which he was appointed has been held to be valid.[17] But a provincial statute authorizing the Lieutenant Governor to assign superior court judges to a new appellate division of the court and to designate one of them as the Chief Justice has been struck down as a usurpation of the federal power of appointment.[18] It appears that, while the creation of new divisions of the superior court (or even of new superior courts) is competent to the provinces under s. 92(14), any such provincial reorganization must leave to the federal government the function of assigning or designating (appointing) judges to the new divisions or courts,[19] and the reorganization will be inoperative unless and until the federal government acts.[20]

The provisions of the Constitution Act, 1867 which have just been described (ss. 96, 97, 98 and 100) apply only to the higher courts, or, more precisely, to "the superior, district and county courts in each province". They do not apply to the courts below the level of the district and county courts. Some "inferior" courts existed at the time of confederation, and many more have been created since then under the provincial power over the administration of justice (s. 92(14)). For these courts, the Constitution is silent as to the qualifications of the presiding judges (or magistrates or justices of the peace): there is no constitutional requirement that the judges be members of the bar. Nor is there any constitutional requirement of federal appointment: the province makes the appointments and fixes and pays the salaries of the appointees.[21]

§ 7:3 Tenure of provincial judges: s. 99

Section 99 of the Constitution Act, 1867 guarantees the tenure of the judges of the superior courts. The section provides that "the judges of the superior courts shall hold office during good behaviour, but shall be removable by the Governor General on address of the Senate and House of Commons". Section 99, unlike the other judicature sections, applies only to superior courts, and does not extend to district or county courts.

Advisory Committees exist in every province and territory and consist of members drawn from the bench, bar and general public.

[16]R.S.C. 1985, c. J-1.

[17]*Re County Courts of B.C.* (1892), 21 S.C.R. 446.

[18]*A.-G. Ont. v. A.-G. Can.* (Judges) [1925] A.C. 750.

[19]*Scott v. A.-G. Can.*, [1923] 3 W.W.R. 929 (P.C., unreported in A.C.).

[20]See generally, Ontario Law Reform Commission, *Report on Administration of Ontario Courts: Part 1* (1973), 71–81.

[21]The misleading practice of naming the inferior courts "Provincial Courts", as if the higher courts were not provincial courts, has been commented upon in heading § 7:1, "Establishment of provincial courts".

In its original form, s. 99 provided no retirement age. Successive federal governments took the view that s. 99 guaranteed tenure for life, and that the statutory imposition of a mandatory retirement age would be unconstitutional. In 1960, when it was decided to impose a mandatory retirement age, it was accomplished by amendment of the Constitution Act: a new subsection requiring retirement at age 75 was added to s. 99.[1]

The independence of the judiciary is a value which is now deeply rooted in Canada and elsewhere in the common law world. It is inherent in the concept of adjudication, at least as understood in the western world, that the judge must not be an ally or supporter of one of the contending parties.[2] Indeed, John Locke claimed that the adjudication of disputes by neutral judges was the most important benefit of civilization.[3] The independence of the judge from the other branches of government is especially significant, because it provides an assurance that the state will be subjected to the rule of law. If the state could count on the courts to ratify all legislative and executive actions, even if unauthorized by law, the individual would have no protection against tyranny. In England, the Stuart Kings badly impaired the independence of the judiciary by the practice of dismissing judges who rendered decisions unfavourable to them. Accordingly, as part of the revolution settlement on the accession of William and Mary, the English Parliament enacted the Act of Settlement, 1701, which guaranteed the tenure of the judges "during good behaviour", and which provided for their removal "upon the address of both Houses of Parliament". Section 99 of the Constitution Act, 1867 is closely modelled on the Act of Settlement.[4]

The independence of the judiciary has since become such a powerful

---

[Section 7:3]

[1]There has, however, been a statutory retirement age of 75 for judges of the Supreme Court of Canada since 1927: S.C. 1926-27, c. 38, s. 2.

[2]Adjudication by courts is compulsory in that it does not depend upon the consent of the parties. Although the courts cannot themselves enforce their judgments, which has led to the description "the least dangerous branch", their judgments are enforceable, because they are backed by the coercive power of the state. (Arbitration, by contrast, depends upon the consent of the parties, and any relief will be enforceable only if the parties have previously so agreed. Mediation also depends upon the consent of the parties, although the mediator does not reach a decision but helps the parties to find their own solution. See Russell, The Judiciary in Canada (1987), 5.) Since parties that have taken a dispute to court cannot choose their judge, it is essential that they be confident that any judge will be a neutral third party.

[3]Locke, The Second Treatise on Government (Peardon ed., Macmillan, N.Y., 1985), 9–10; quoted Russell, The Judiciary in Canada (1987), 20.

[4]It is likely that s. 99 would preclude actions short of removal that would have the effect of impairing judicial independence. In *MacKeigan v. Hickman*, [1989] 2 S.C.R. 796, the Court held that superior court judges could not be compelled to testify before a provincial commission of inquiry in order to elaborate on their written reasons for judgment; nor could the Chief Justice be compelled to testify as to his reasons for assigning a particular judge to a particular case. The decision was based on the interpretation of Nova Scotia's Public Inquiries Act, but the tenor of the judgments suggests that even an explicit statutory authority for the testimony would have been ineffective, because it

tradition in the United Kingdom and Canada[5] that there may be little point in a fine analysis of the language of the provisions by which it is formally guaranteed. Nevertheless, the meaning of s. 99 of the Constitution Act, 1867 (and the similar language of the Act of Settlement) is not wholly free from doubt. The question is whether s. 99 provides for one mode of removal or two. It could be read as meaning that a judge may be removed only by joint parliamentary address and then only for bad behaviour. But the section could also be read as meaning that a judge may be removed for bad behaviour by the government without the need for a joint parliamentary address, and may in addition be removed for any reason whatsoever (not necessarily involving bad behaviour) by a joint parliamentary address. On principle, the former interpretation is preferable, because it is more apt to secure the independence of the judiciary, which is the purpose of the provision.[6] In fact no Canadian government has ever attempted to by-pass the joint address procedure; and even the joint address procedure has never been carried to a conclusion, though it has been started on several occasions. It is a matter of record therefore that no superior court judge has ever been removed from office.[7]

Section 99 applies only to superior courts. In this, it follows the Act of Settlement. The rationale for the exclusion of inferior courts was that inferior courts would be subject to the superintendence of the superior courts on appeal or judicial review. Section 100, which also plays a role in securing the independence of the judiciary by securing their financial independence, also applies only to superior courts—now that the county and district courts (which are also covered by s. 100) have all been abolished. With respect to the judges of the inferior courts, who are provincially appointed, the Constitution Act, 1867 provides no formal constitutional guarantee of independence. Of course, the powerful tradition of judicial independence would in practice protect them from arbitrary removal, and for most judges this tradition has been reinforced by statutory guarantees of tenure.[8] In 1982, the adoption of the Charter of Rights added another constitutional guarantee of independence for all

---

would have been contrary to s. 99.

[5]Judicial independence is examined in S. Shetreet, *Judges on Trial* (North-Holland, Amsterdam, 1976); W.R. Lederman, "The Independence of the Judiciary" (1956) 34 Can. Bar Rev. 769; Deschenes, Masters in their own House (1981); Russell, The Judiciary in Canada (1987), chs. 4, 7; Friedland, A Place Apart: Judicial Independence and Accountability in Canada (Canadian Judicial Council, 1995).

[6]So held in *Gratton v. Can.*, [1994] 2 F.C. 769 (T.D.), where the scholarly literature is reviewed by Strayer J. He went on to hold that a permanent infirmity (caused by a stroke in that case) would be a breach of good behaviour justifying dismissal under s. 99.

[7]The federal Judges Act, R.S.C. 1985, c. Jl, Part II, establishes a Canadian Judicial Council, which is composed of the Chief Justice of Canada and the Chief Justices of all the superior courts, to inquire into complaints against judges of superior, district or county courts, as a precondition of removal. Several judges have resigned after recommendations by the Canadian Judicial Council that they be removed from office, and several also retired before an inquiry was completed.

[8]The position in the provinces is reviewed in Deschenes, Masters in their own House (1981), 103–124; Russell, The Judiciary in Canada (1987), 178–190; Friedland, A Place Apart: Judicial Independence and Accountability in Canada (Canadian Judicial

judges exercising criminal jurisdiction, which would include judges of inferior courts. That guarantee is in s. 11(d) and it is discussed in the succeeding sections of this chapter. In 1997, in *Re Remuneration of Judges* (1985),[9] the Supreme Court of Canada found an "unwritten" guarantee of independence that protects the judges of all courts no matter what kinds of cases they decide. That finding is discussed in a later section of this chapter.[10]

In the judicial independence cases that are discussed in the succeeding sections of this chapter, it has usually been the employment conditions of the judges that have been in issue. This has led the Supreme Court of Canada to hold that judicial independence requires that the judges have security of tenure, financial security, and administrative freedom from the executive branch of government.[11] However, at least as fundamental as these three points, is adjudicative independence, by which I mean the freedom of the judges to perform their judicial role in an even-handed manner ("without fear or favour"). This comes up in cases where the government is a party, and where rules of procedure or evidence have been enacted that favour the government.

For example, s. 39 of the Canada Evidence Act excludes from court proceedings any documents that are certified by the clerk of the Privy Council as containing information that would reveal cabinet confidences. According to the Act, the certificate is not subject to judicial review: no judge has jurisdiction to inquire into whether a certified document really would reveal a cabinet confidence, and if so whether that fact should outweigh the interest of reaching a just result in the litigation. In *Babcock v. Canada* (2002),[12] the government had withheld 51 documents under this provision. The plaintiffs, who were suing the government and wanted to see the documents (which were all relevant to the cause of action), challenged the validity of s. 39, arguing that it compromised the adjudicative independence of the trial court. The Supreme Court of Canada rejected the challenge. McLachlin C.J. for the unanimous Court held that Parliament had the power to enact laws that "some would consider draconian" so long as no law goes so far as to "fundamentally alter or interfere with the relationship between the courts and the other

---

Council, 1995), 105–113. In all provinces except Prince Edward Island, a guarantee of tenure during good behaviour is supplemented by the establishment of a judicial council—a committee of judges with power to inquire into complaints against judges and make recommendations as a pre-condition to disciplinary action. The size, composition and powers of provincial judicial councils vary from province to province, so that, for example, some provinces include federally-appointed judges on the council (e.g., Ontario), while others select only provincially-appointed judges (e.g., British Columbia). Unlike the federal Canadian Judicial Council, the provincial judicial councils are generally composed of both judges and lawyers, although the ratio varies across the country.

[9] *Re Remuneration of Judges*, [1997] 3 S.C.R. 3.

[10] § 7:8, "Inferior courts of civil jurisdiction".

[11] The leading case is *Valente v. The Queen*, [1985] 2 S.C.R. 673; discussed in text accompanying § 7:5 note 1, below.

[12] *Babcock v. Canada*, [2002] 3 S.C.R. 3.

branches of government".[13] In her view, s. 39 did not go that far. The section was upheld and the documents remained secret.[14]

Emboldened perhaps by McLachlin C.J.'s reference to "draconian" laws (and by similar statutes in the United States),[15] British Columbia enacted the Tobacco Damages and Health Care Costs Recovery Act, which was directed solely at tobacco companies and which created a new cause of action under which the government of the province could sue the companies to recover that part of the province's past and anticipated future health care costs that were attributable to tobacco-related disease. The government had to establish that a tobacco company had committed a wrong (for example, a false or misleading claim about the product) at some time in the past. The Act was retroactive, and all existing limitation periods were retroactively repealed for the purpose of the litigation. The Act went on to enact a presumption that all persons who smoked tobacco would not have been exposed to the product but for the misrepresentation by the company. This presumption was intended to overcome the facts that many persons are unaware of or do not believe false health claims made in the past by tobacco companies, and many persons smoke tobacco in full knowledge of the risks they run. The presumption was rebuttable. Another presumption enacted by the Act was that exposure to tobacco was the cause of disease in a proportion of the population. This presumption was also rebuttable, but the companies were expressly denied access to the health care records of individuals in attempting any rebuttal. The "damages" for this new "tort" were the company's share (based on its share of the market for cigarettes) of all of the health care expenditures that had been incurred by the province for tobacco-related illness since the time of the company's misrepresentation as well as the present value of anticipated future expenditures. No causal link between smoking and any individual's disease had to be established.[16]

On the day that British Columbia's legislation was enacted, the

---

[13]*Babcock v. Canada*, [2002] 3 S.C.R. 3, para 57.

[14]Another adjudicative-independence case is *Re Application under s. 83.28 of the Criminal Code*, [2004] 2 S.C.R. 248, which upheld the "judicial investigative hearing" established for the investigation of terrorism offences. The case is discussed in § 7:5, "Inferior courts", at § 7:5 note 44.

[15]"Recoupment actions", which were authorized by state legislation in the United States to permit the states to recover health-care costs attributed to tobacco-related disease, were settled by the tobacco companies, which agreed with the states to observe certain marketing restrictions and to pay damages to the states. No verdicts were obtained from courts. The only reported constitutional challenge was to the Florida recoupment statute, which differed from the B.C. statute in that it was not limited to tobacco companies and did not reverse the presumptions of causation. The statute was upheld by the Supreme Court of Florida, except for the abolition of limitation periods (invalid) and the exclusion of individual health-care records (invalid): *Agency for Health Care Administration v. Associated Industries of Florida* (1996), 678 So. 2d 1239 (S.C. Fla.).

[16]In *Agency for Health Care Administration v. Associated Industries of Florida* (1996), 678 So. 2d 1239 (S.C.Fla.), Overton J. commented (p. 1256) that the recoupment could have been accomplished by a tax on the harmful product. In Canada, of course, taxes make up most of the price of a package of cigarettes. The B.C. Act is silent on the

government of the province commenced the court proceeding against the tobacco companies that was the sole reason for the legislation. The defendants challenged the legislation as a breach of judicial independence. There was no doubt that the province could have imposed a special tax on the tobacco companies (at least those within the province) to recoup some of its health care costs. Instead of taking that straightforward approach, the province wanted to recover health care costs in the form of a damages judgment issued by a court following the trial of an action in tort. But the tort was created for that one trial, and new rules of procedure and evidence were created for that one trial. The definition of the tort and the new rules of procedure and evidence were designed to ensure that the government would succeed in that trial. By using the trial court of the province in this way, did not the legislation (in the language of *Babcock)* "fundamentally alter or interfere with the relationship between the courts and the other branches of government"? In *British Columbia v. Imperial Tobacco* (2005),[17] the Supreme Court of Canada answered no. Major J. for the Court said that it did not matter if the Act's rules were "unfair or illogical".[18] The Act did not disable the court from independently applying the law, finding the facts and awarding a remedy. "The fact that the Act shifts certain onuses of proof or limits the compellability of information that the appellants assert is relevant does not in any way interfere, in either appearance or fact, with the court's adjudicative role". Judicial independence, he said, "can abide unconventional rules of civil procedure and evidence".[19] The Act was upheld.[20]

Given the extraordinary nature of the British Columbia recoupment statute, it is clear that the Supreme Court sets a high bar indeed for a challenge to judicial independence based on adjudicative independence.[21] This stands in sharp contrast to the Court's readiness to find a breach of judicial independence in any reduction of the salaries or perquisites of judges.[22]

§ 7:4 Tenure of provincial judges: s. 11(d)

The Charter of Rights contains a guarantee of judicial independence in s. 11(d). Section 11(d) grants to "any person charged with an offence" the right:

---

question whether a set-off is available for taxes collected by the province on cigarettes (which would presumably reduce the damages to nil).

[17]*British Columbia v. Imperial Tobacco*, [2005] 2 S.C.R. 473. Major J. wrote the opinion of the Court.

[18]*British Columbia v. Imperial Tobacco*, [2005] 2 S.C.R. 473, para. 49.

[19]*British Columbia v. Imperial Tobacco*, [2005] 2 S.C.R. 473, para. 55.

[20]Challenges based on extra-territoriality and the rule of law were also rejected by the Court.

[21]*B.C. v. Phillip Morris International*, [2018] 2 S.C.R. 595, 2018 SCC 36 (denying to tobacco company access to health care databases).

[22]*Re Remuneration of Judges*, [1997] 3 S.C.R. 3; discussed with other cases following it in § 7:5, "Inferior courts".

to be presumed innocent until proven guilty according to law in a fair and public hearing by an independent and impartial tribunal.

This right to "an independent and impartial tribunal" applies only to courts of criminal jurisdiction, because the right is possessed only by a person "charged with an offence". But the guarantee reaches deeply into the court system, because more than 90 per cent of criminal cases, including most of the cases involving serious indictable offences, are heard by inferior courts, that is, courts with provincially-appointed judges.[1]

§ 7:5 Inferior courts

In *Valente v. The Queen* (1985),[1] the question arose whether the provincially-appointed judges of Ontario's Provincial Court (Criminal Division) were disqualified from performing their functions by reason of s. 11(d). The argument was made that the degree of control over the judges that was possessed by the provincial Attorney General raised a reasonable apprehension that the judges would be biased in favour of the Crown. The argument could not be based on insecure tenure, because the judges had a statutory guarantee of tenure during good behaviour to age 65. But the argument enumerated a host of minor ways in which the judges remained subject to executive power: the judges were appointed by the Attorney General;[2] the Attorney General had discretions to designate a (higher-paid) "senior judge", to authorize leaves of absence, and to authorize paid extra-judicial work; the judges' salaries were fixed by regulation, not statute; and pensions were provided out of the general provincial civil service plan, not a special judges' plan.

The Supreme Court of Canada in *Valente* rejected the challenge to the Provincial Court (Criminal Division)'s jurisdiction. The Supreme Court held that "the essential conditions of judicial independence" were satisfied by the Provincial Court (Criminal Division). What were those conditions? First, the Supreme Court said, was "security of tenure". This did not need to be expressed to be "during good behaviour" (as in s. 99); nor was it necessary that a judge be removable only on an address of the Legislature (as in s. 99). What was required was that a judge be removable "only for cause related to the capacity to perform judicial functions",[3] and that there be a judicial inquiry to determine cause. Second, was "financial security". This did not require that salaries be fixed by

---

[Section 7:4]

[1]P.H. Russell, "Constitutional Reform of the Judicial Branch" (1984) 17 Can. J. Pol. Sci. 227.

[Section 7:5]

[1]*Valente v. The Queen*, [1985] 2 S.C.R. 673. The judgment of the Court was written by Le Dain J.

[2]The powers of the Attorney General were in fact powers vested in the Lieutenant Governor in Council, i.e., by convention, the cabinet, but in practice in matters of this kind the advice of the Attorney General would be decisive.

[3][1985] 2 S.C.R. 673, 697. The Court did find a breach of the security-of-tenure

the Legislature (as in s. 100), but it did require that the right to salary or pension be established by law, even if the law was (as Ontario's was) a regulation rather than a statute. Third and last[4] was "the institutional independence of the tribunal with respect to matters of administration bearing directly on the exercise of its judicial function".[5] This did not preclude involvement by the Attorney General in the administration of the courts, but it did require that the judges control the "assignment of judges, sittings of the court, and court lists".[6] The Court held that Ontario's Provincial Court (Criminal Division) did satisfy all three conditions of independence, and was accordingly capable of trying criminal cases without any breach of s. 11(d) of the Charter.

With respect to *Valente's* second condition of independence, namely, financial security, Le Dain J. for the Court had rejected the argument that the guarantee of judicial independence in s. 11(d) required governments to establish judicial compensation commissions to make recommendations as to judicial salaries.[7] In *Re Remuneration of Judges* (1997),[8] Lamer C.J. for the majority of the Supreme Court of Canada dismissed this ruling as obiter, and decided that s. 11(d) required that each province (and the same requirement would apply to the federal government for the s. 96 judges) must establish a judicial compensation commission to report on the salaries of the judges. The commission's members must not all be appointed by the government, and some must come from the judiciary; they must enjoy some security of tenure; and they must report regularly. Any increase, reduction or freeze of judicial salaries would be unconstitutional if it was not preceded by the report of such a commission. It was not necessary for the report of the commission to be binding on the government, but, if any recommendation was not accepted, the executive or the legislature (whichever sets the salaries) "must be prepared to justify this decision, if necessary in a court of law".[9] The standard of justification was not the full *Oakes* test (required for s. 1 of the Charter), but merely a requirement of "rationality", calling

---

condition in the statutory provision for judges who were reappointed after retirement age to hold office during pleasure. However, the judge who declined jurisdiction in this case did not hold a post-retirement appointment, and in the meantime the statute had been amended to make the continuance in office after retirement dependant on the discretion, not of the Attorney General, but of the chief judge (for ages 65–70) and a judicial council (for ages 70–75). The new provisions created a post-retirement status that was "by no means ideal", but was sufficient for the purpose of s. 11(d).

[4]These three conditions are all associated with the terms of employment of the judges. The courts have also recognized a fourth category, which may be described as "adjudicative independence", which is the freedom of judges to perform their adjudicative role without interference from the other branches of government. These cases are discussed in § 7:3, "Tenure of provincial judges: s. 99".

[5]*Valente v. The Queen*, [1985] 2 S.C.R. 673, 708.

[6]*Valente v. The Queen*, [1985] 2 S.C.R. 673, 709.

[7]*Valente v. The Queen*, [1985] 2 S.C.R. 673, 706.

[8]*Re Remuneration of Judges*, [1997] 3 S.C.R. 3. Lamer C.J. wrote the opinion of the majority; La Forest J. wrote a dissenting opinion.

[9]*Re Remuneration of Judges*, [1997] 3 S.C.R. 3, para 180.

for the articulation of "a legitimate reason for why it has chosen to depart from the recommendation of the commission".[10]

The dire consequences of failure to follow this elaborate procedure were illustrated by the outcome of this case, which was a challenge to the reduction of the salaries of provincial court judges that had been enacted by the Legislatures of Prince Edward Island, Alberta and Manitoba. In each province, the provincial judges' salaries had all been reduced by an across-the-board measure that applied to all other public sector salaries. In each case, the motive was to reduce the province's deficit by reducing its wages liability without excessive layoffs. How any reasonable person could regard this as threatening the independence of the judiciary was never explained by Lamer C.J., who nonetheless repeatedly warned of "the danger" of "political interference through economic manipulation". He acknowledged that an across-the-board measure posed "less of a danger", and that such a measure would be "prima facie rational",[11] but he still held that the three provinces' salary reductions were unconstitutional in their application to the judges, because they had not been preceded by the report of a judicial compensation commission.[12] The likely effect of the decision is to shield judges from general reductions in public sector salaries, because (even where a judicial compensation commission exists) it is time-consuming and complicated to go through the steps that are necessary to make the reductions applicable to the judges.

The unconstitutionality of any reduction in judicial salaries was reinforced and even extended in *Mackin v. New Brunswick* (2002),[13] which was a challenge to legislation enacted in New Brunswick abolishing supernumerary status for provincial court judges. This legislation was enacted in 1995 and had not been preceded by a report of a judicial

---

[10]*Re Remuneration of Judges*, [1997] 3 S.C.R. 3, para. 183. In *Re B.C. Legislative Assembly Resolution on Judicial Compensation* (1998), 160 D.L.R. (4th) 477 (B.C. C.A.), the Legislative Assembly had rejected a judicial compensation commission's recommendation for a pay increase for provincial court judges that in a time of fiscal restraint was far in excess of the pay increases allowed elsewhere in the public sector; the Court held that the legislative response did not satisfy the standard of rationality, and remitted the issue back to the Legislative Assembly for reconsideration.

[11]*Re Remuneration of Judges*, [1997] 3 S.C.R. 3, para. 184.

[12]After the decision, the three provinces returned to the Court to seek a postponement of the requirement of a judicial compensation commission, which the Court granted for one year: *Re Remuneration of Judges (No. 2)*, [1998] 1 S.C.R. 4, para. 18. However, the Court said (para. 20) that the postponement "does not change the retroactivity of the declarations of invalidity made in this case", so the postponement apparently did not cure the invalidity of the pay reductions. The Court also said (para. 8) not to worry about the fact that all decisions in criminal cases rendered by provincial courts in those provinces (and all other provinces without the newly-required judicial compensation commissions) had been rendered by judges who were not independent; the "doctrine of necessity" allowed a disqualified judge to sit where no qualified judge was available, and since *all* judges were disqualified in the non-compliant provinces, their decisions could not be challenged!

[13]*Mackin v. New Brunswick*, [2002] 1 S.C.R. 405. Gonthier J. wrote the opinion of the majority of seven; Binnie J., with the agreement of LeBel J., dissented.

compensation commission for the excellent reason that the Supreme Court of Canada had not announced this requirement until 1997 when the Court decided *Re Remuneration of Judges.* Under "supernumerary status", a judge who qualified for early retirement could elect supernumerary status instead of retiring, and would continue to receive his or her full-time salary in return for carrying out "such judicial duties as may be assigned . . . by the chief judge". The expectation was that the chief judge would assign only about 40 per cent of a normal workload, and the plaintiff Judge Mackin in fact spent his supernumerary winters in Australia. The expectation was not enacted into law, and other judges, including the other plaintiff Judge Rice, were assigned a full-time schedule of cases while on supernumerary status. In any case, workloads varied dramatically from one region of the province to another. The repeal of supernumerary status did not affect the salary of the judges who had elected supernumerary status, but it did require them to assume a full workload (or to retire). The Supreme Court of Canada, by a majority of seven to two, held that the legislation was unconstitutional for failure to follow the procedure stipulated in *Re Remuneration of Judges.* The mere expectation, not guaranteed by law, of less than a full workload during supernumerary status was an economic benefit to provincial court judges. The repeal of supernumerary status deprived them of that benefit, and was therefore equivalent to a reduction in salary. Gonthier J. for the majority acknowledged that the legislation was driven by "a perfectly legitimate purpose" in trying to improve the flexibility and efficiency of the judiciary.[14] He made no attempt to answer Binnie J.'s dissenting assertion that a reasonable and well informed person "would not regard the creation, continuation or ultimate repeal of the discretionary workload benefit associated with supernumerary status as compromising judicial independence".[15] The effect of the majority's decision is that every perquisite of judicial office, however discretionary, is now "wrapped in constitutional protection and beyond legislative recall" except in accordance with the procedure stipulated in *Re Remuneration of Judges.*[16]

After the decision in *Re Remuneration of Judges*, all governments were forced to establish judicial compensation commissions. Predictably (given their composition), the commissions typically recommended much higher increases to the judges than were received by senior civil servants. Predictably, several provincial governments balked at the recommendations. Predictably, the disappointed judges sought judicial review of the government's refusals. Predictably, the courts that had to hear the cases had great difficulty in deciding what level of review was mandated by the Supreme Court's standard of "rationality", and what the remedy should be for a failure by government to meet the standard. Predictably, the decisions on judicial review were appealed on up to the Supreme Court. Eventually, 47 counsel crowded into the Supreme Court

---

[14] *Mackin v. New Brunswick*, [2002] 1 S.C.R. 405, para. 70.

[15] *Mackin v. New Brunswick*, [2002] 1 S.C.R. 405, para. 161.

[16] *Mackin v. New Brunswick*, [2002] 1 S.C.R. 405, para. 94 per Binnie J.

chamber to argue the momentous question of whether provincial court judges in New Brunswick, Ontario, Alberta and Quebec should be paid every penny of the recommendations of the provincial commissions. None of the counsel representing the judges seems to have suggested that the purpose or effect of the actions of the four provincial governments, in granting less than the recommended salary increases, was to impair judicial independence. But that did not matter. In *Provincial Court Judges' Association v. New Brunswick* (2005),[17] often now called "*Bodner*", the Supreme Court of Canada, describing the case as raising "the important question of judicial independence",[18] solemnly reviewed at great length the reasons that had been offered by the four governments for their refusals to follow the recommendations of their commissions. The Court set out three requirements for a reviewing court to take into account in determining whether a government's decision to depart from a commission's recommendation meets the standard of rationality: (1) whether "the government has articulated a legitimate reason for departing from the commission's recommendation"; (2) whether "the government's reasons rely upon a reasonable factual foundation"; and (3) whether, "viewed "globally", the commission process has been respected and its purposes – "preserving judicial independence and depoliticizing the setting of judicial remuneration" – have been achieved.[19] These requirements will no doubt be daunting to a government contemplating the rejection of an extravagant compensation recommendation. But the truly important part of the Court's opinion concerns remedies. If the rationality standard is not met, the appropriate remedy by the reviewing court "will generally be to return the matter to the government for reconsideration"; in particular, the court "should avoid issuing specific orders to make the recommendations binding unless the governing statutory scheme gives them that option".[20] In other words, all that can be achieved on judicial review is a reconsideration by government. Perhaps this will staunch the flow of litigation. The actual decision in the case was to uphold the rationality of the reasons provided by New Brunswick, Ontario and Alberta, and reject the rationality of the reasons provided by Quebec with respect to its municipal judges. In the case of Quebec, however, no order was made granting

[17]*Provincial Court Judges' Association v. New Brunswick*, [2005] 2 S.C.R. 286. The opinion of the Court was attributed to "the Court".

[18]*Provincial Court Judges' Association v. New Brunswick*, [2005] 2 S.C.R. 286, para. 1. In my view, if governments simply use their best judgment, and as a default remedy provide salary increases to judges equivalent to those granted to deputy ministers or other top public sector employees, that is a far better way to set judicial salaries than the elaborate rigmarole of the judicial compensation commissions, and poses no threat whatsoever to judicial independence. The Court's view is that when this happens provincial governments may be "accused of manipulating the courts for their own purposes" (para. 11). The Court fell short of saying that the accusation would sometimes be justified, but they must have thought so in order to make the point.

[19]*Provincial Court Judges' Association v. New Brunswick*, [2005] 2 S.C.R. 286, para. 31.

[20]*Provincial Court Judges' Association v. New Brunswick*, [2005] 2 S.C.R. 286, para. 44.

the recommended increase (31 per cent); the government's reasons (for only granting 8 per cent) were simply sent back for reconsideration.

The provincial cabinets often play an important role in determining whether provincial governments will accept or reject the recommendations of their judicial compensation commissions, even when the legal authority to make a final decision lies elsewhere (for example, in a provincial Legislature). As a result, a party seeking to challenge a provincial government's decision to reject the recommendations of a commission by way of the form of judicial review described in the previous paragraph (often now called *Bodner* review) may request the production of relevant confidential cabinet documents. Can the courts order the production of such cabinet documents as part of a *Bodner* review if a government refuses to provide them, and if so, when? In *British Columbia v. Provincial Court Judges' Association of British Columbia* (2020),[21] the Supreme Court of Canada held that the answer is yes. Karakatsanis J., who wrote for the Court, said that "special considerations arise when the party seeking *Bodner* review asks the government to produce a [cabinet] document" that relates to the recommendations of a commission,[22] but she indicated that this class of cabinet documents, like other cabinet documents, does not enjoy an absolute immunity from production. She set out a three-stage process that a reviewing court should follow in determining whether to order the production of relevant cabinet documents during a *Bodner* review. At the first stage, the party challenging a provincial government's response to a judicial compensation commission's recommendation must provide the reviewing court with some reason to believe that the cabinet document in question may contain evidence showing that the government failed to meet one of the three *Bodner* requirements.[23] At the second stage, if the party is successful at stage one, the cabinet document will then need to be produced to the reviewing court, which will review it in private to determine if it actually contains some evidence showing that the government failed to meet one of the *Bodner* requirements. At the third and final stage, if the reviewing court is satisfied that the cabinet document provides some evidence showing that the provincial government did not meet one of the *Bodner* requirements, the court must then consider whether any other rule of evidence, such as solicitor-client privilege or public interest immunity (also called Crown privilege, as in this book), bars its production.[24] In this case, the Provincial Court Judges' Association of British Columbia – which represented judges that were disappointed by the provincial government's decision to reject the recommendation of the province's Judicial Compensation Commission – sought disclosure of a

[21]*British Columbia v. Provincial Court Judges' Association of British Columbia*, 2020 SCC 20. Karakatsanis J. wrote the opinion of the Court.

[22]*British Columbia v. Provincial Court Judges' Association of British Columbia*, 2020 SCC 20, para. 62.

[23]The relevant requirements are described in the previous paragraph.

[24]For further discussion of Crown privilege, see ch. 10, The Crown, under heading §§ 10:6 to 10:9, "Crown privilege".

submission that was made to the provincial cabinet by the Attorney General after receiving the Commission's recommendation. Karakatsanis J. held that the Association's request failed at the first stage of the analysis, because the Association had not provided any evidence that the submission to cabinet may contain evidence showing that the government did not meet one of the *Bodner* requirements.[25]

A second point that was decided in *Re Remuneration of Judges* was that it would be a breach of judicial independence if "negotiations" took place between the judiciary and the government over the level of judicial remuneration. If negotiations took place, according to Lamer C.J., "the reasonable person might conclude that judges would alter the manner in which they adjudicate cases in order to curry favour with the executive".[26] In my view, this theory is highly implausible. It assumes that there is a real possibility that judges would violate their oath of office and decide cases wrongly (for example, by convicting an innocent person or imposing an unduly harsh penalty) in order to obtain some (highly speculative and likely trivial) advantage at the negotiating table. In any case, as La Forest J. pointed out in dissent, discussions between judges and the government over salaries are not true negotiations, because judicial salaries are not set by agreement: the judges are not unionized and no collective bargaining rules apply; there is not the give and take and compromise that are characteristic of negotiations. All that the judges can do in discussions with government is make representations. "Those representations merely provide information and cannot, as a result, be said to pose a danger to judicial independence."[27]

In *Re Remuneration of Judges*, Lamer C.J. acknowledged that, even after the legislated cutbacks, no one had argued that the salaries of the judges in the three provinces of Prince Edward Island, Alberta and Manitoba fell below "an acceptable minimum level". But, he warned, if salaries were allowed to fall below that minimum (which he did not attempt to define), then that too would be a breach of constitutionally-guaranteed independence. If salaries are too low, "there is always the danger, however speculative, that members of the judiciary could be tempted to adjudicate cases in a particular way in order to secure a higher salary from the executive or the legislature or *to receive benefits from one of the litigants*".[28] In a society where corruption has all but disappeared, this seems implausible to me. It is not made more plausible by Lamer C.J.'s assurances that the guarantee of a minimum salary "is not a device to shield the courts from the effects of deficit reduction",

[25]The Court, per Karakatsanis J., reached the opposite conclusion in a companion case: *N.S. v. Judges of the Provincial Court and Family Court of Nova Scotia*, 2020 SCC 21 (parts of a report of Nova Scotia's Attorney General to the provincial cabinet should be disclosed because there was reason to believe they might help to show that the provincial government did not meet the *Bodner* requirements and there was no rule of evidence that precluded disclosure).

[26]*Re Remuneration of Judges*, [1997] 3 S.C.R. 3, para. 187.

[27]*Re Remuneration of Judges*, [1997] 3 S.C.R. 3, para. 188 per La Forest J.

[28]*Re Remuneration of Judges*, [1997] 3 S.C.R. 3, para. 193 (emphasis added).

and "is not meant for the benefit of the judiciary"; rather, as a means to judicial independence, a minimum salary is "for the benefit of the public".[29]

The judicial-compensation-commission requirement applies to any increase, reduction or freeze of judicial salaries. Does it apply to the initial salaries of the judges on the creation of a new court? That was the issue in *Conférence des juges de paix magistrats du Québec v. Quebec* (2016).[30] Quebec had created a new category of justices of the peace, "Presiding Justices of the Peace" (PJP), who performed very limited "judicial functions".[31] There was no doubt that the constitutional guarantee of independence extended to justices of the peace who performed judicial functions.[32] However, with respect to financial independence, the constituting legislation, enacted in 2004, simply stipulated the salaries of the PJPs, and provided that a judicial compensation commission would be created to review the salaries in 2007. Quebec justified the delay in review on the ground that there was no increase, reduction or freeze of judicial salaries: it was the creation of a new court. Both lower courts agreed. Since this was a case of first impression, it provided an opportunity for the Supreme Court to rein in the cumbersome (and weakly justified) judicial-compensation-commission requirement. Instead, the Court chose to expand the requirement to the creation of a new court. The judicial-compensation-commission review of salaries was required within a "reasonable time" of the creation of the court, and a reasonable time "should be measured in months, not years".[33] The reasons for the urgent review were a concern about "political interference through economic manipulation",[34] and a concern that the salaries might not satisfy the "constitutional minimum to ensure the integrity of the new office".[35] Because no judicial-compensation-commission review occurred between 2004 and 2007, there was a breach of the constitutional guarantee of financial independence and the new PJPs

[29]*Re Remuneration of Judges*, [1997] 3 S.C.R. 3, paras. 193, 196.

[30]*Conférence des juges de paix magistrats du Québec v. Quebec*, [2016] 2 S.C.R. 116, 2016 SCC 39. Karakatsanis, Wagner and Côté JJ. wrote the opinion of the Court.

[31]All that was said about their functions was that (para. 10) "a PJP cannot preside over bail hearings or hear summary conviction proceedings". Nothing was said about what they could do, but presumably the issue of search warrants would be one such function.

[32]So held in *Ell v. Alta.*, [2003] 1 S.C.R. 857; discussed at § 7:5 note 42 below.

[33]*Conférence des juges de paix magistrats du Québec v. Quebec*, [2016] 2 S.C.R. 116, 2016 SCC 39, para. 80.

[34]*Conférence des juges de paix magistrats du Québec v. Quebec*, [2016] 2 S.C.R. 116, 2016 SCC 39, paras. 45, 58, 94. A convoluted hypothetical example was offered in para. 45 bearing no resemblance to the facts of this case.

[35]*Conférence des juges de paix magistrats du Québec v. Quebec*, [2016] 2 S.C.R. 116, 2016 SCC 39, para. 46. The "integrity of the new office" was not explained, and no examples of breaches, not even hypothetical ones, were provided. Of course, Lamer C.J.'s extravagant concern was that, if salaries fell below an undefined minimum, the judges would be tempted to take bribes: § 7:5 note 28, above. Perhaps that is what was meant by the "integrity of the new office".

were unconstitutional for that period. Fortunately, however, "the doctrine of necessity will prevent the reopening of past decisions of [the PJPs] by reason only of their lack of independence".[36]

With respect to *Valente's* third condition of independence, namely, institutional independence in the exercise of the judicial function, the Supreme Court of Canada in *Re Remuneration of Judges* struck down a provision of the Alberta Provincial Court Judges Act that conferred power on the Attorney General to "designate the place at which a judge shall have his residence". According to Lamer C.J., this provision "creates the reasonable apprehension that it could be used to punish judges whose decisions do not favour the government, or alternatively, to favour judges whose decisions benefit the government".[37] No examples were provided of such a power ever having been used for such malign purposes. The Court also struck down an Alberta provision that authorized the Attorney General to "designate the day or days on which the Court shall hold sittings" and a Manitoba decision to close the courts on certain Fridays (as a cost-cutting measure).[38] In these rulings with respect to sittings, the Court did not reach beyond *Valente*, which had stipulated for judicial control over sittings of the Court.

In *R. v. Lippé* (1991),[39] the question arose whether the municipal court judges of Quebec were disqualified from trying criminal cases by s. 11(d). The problem was that the municipal judges were part-time judges, who maintained private law practices when not serving on the bench. It was argued that the judges' continuing relationships with private clients gave them an appearance of bias and were therefore inconsistent with the independence and impartiality required by s. 11(d). The Supreme Court of Canada held that the test for bias under s. 11(d) was the same as in other legal contexts, namely, whether "an informed person, viewing the matter realistically and practically", would have a "reasonable apprehension of bias".[40] The Court determined that 11(d) was not offended, because the judges' oath of office, code of ethics, and the statutory rules of recusement (disqualification) to avoid conflicts of interest, were sufficient to allay any reasonable apprehension that the judges would be biased.[41]

---

[36] *Re Remuneration of Judges*, [1997] 3 S.C.R. 3, para. 106. See ch. 58, Effect of Unconstitutional Law, under heading § 58:7, "Judges by necessity".

[37] *Re Remuneration of Judges*, [1997] 3 S.C.R. 3, para. 266.

[38] *Re Remuneration of Judges*, [1997] 3 S.C.R. 3, paras. 267, 276.

[39] *R. v. Lippé*, [1991] 2 S.C.R. 114. Gonthier J. wrote an opinion with the agreement of three others. Lamer C.J. wrote an opinion with the agreement of two others.

[40] The test was laid down in a pre-Charter case, *Committee for Justice and Liberty v. Nat. Energy Bd.*, [1978] 1 S.C.R. 369, 394; and it has been applied in a variety of contexts, e.g., *R. v. Bain*, [1992] 1 S.C.R. 91; *Nfld. Telephone Co. v. Nfld.*, [1992] 1 S.C.R. 623; *Idziak v. Can.*, [1992] 3 S.C.R. 631; *Ruffo v. Conseil de la Magistrature*, [1995] 4 S.C.R. 267.

[41] For Lamer C.J., there was no issue of independence, because "independent" in s. 11(d) meant only independent from government; the issue was one of impartiality. For Gonthier J. "independent" included independence from private parties, so that the words

In *Ell v. Alberta* (2003),[42] the province of Alberta enacted legislation elevating the qualifications required for justices of the peace. Those existing justices of the peace who did not meet the new qualifications (they now had to be lawyers) were removed from office. They challenged their removal. The justices of the peace were not covered by the express guarantee of independence in s. 99, because they were not superior court judges. Nor were they covered by s. 11(d), because they did not try criminal cases. However, they did perform the judicial functions of presiding over bail hearings and granting search warrants. The Supreme Court of Canada held that these functions were sufficient to bring them within the unwritten principle of judicial independence, so that their security of tenure was constitutionally guaranteed. However, the Court went on to decide that less stringent rules should protect their tenure than the rules that protect judges who perform more important judicial functions. In this case, the legislative judgment to require legal training for justices of the peace was intended to advance the same underlying interests as the principle of judicial independence. The dismissal of justices on that ground "cannot be said to be arbitrary, and does not violate the principle of judicial independence".[43] The Court accordingly upheld the dismissals.

In *Re Application under s. 83.28 of the Criminal Code* (2004),[44] the Supreme Court was invited to hold that a "judicial investigative hearing" was unconstitutional. This hearing was provided for by federal statute, and it called for witnesses to be examined before a judge in order to gather information in relation to a "terrorism offence" (a defined term). It was argued that this provision conferred on the judges a role that was essentially investigatory, giving rise to the perception that the judge was an ally of the executive for the purpose of seeking evidence of crime. This was accepted by LeBel and Fish JJ., who would have declared the hearing provision unconstitutional for violation of the unwritten principle of judicial independence. The majority of the Court disagreed, pointing out that judges routinely play a role in criminal investigations through their authorization of search warrants, DNA warrants and wire taps, where they operate as a restraint on (rather than an ally of) the executive. In the case of the judicial investigative hearings, the judge would play the restraining role of applying the rules of evidence and making sure that the witness was protected from self-incrimination.[45] These functions were judicial, and the hearings did not compromise judicial independence.

"independent" and "impartial" were overlapping requirements, both of which were in issue. Lamer C.J. and Gonthier J. agreed in the result, yielding a unanimous Court.

[42] *Ell v. Alberta*, [2003] 1 S.C.R. 857. Major J. wrote the opinion of the Court.

[43] *Ell v. Alberta*, [2003] 1 S.C.R. 857, para. 37.

[44] *Re Application under s. 83.28 of the Criminal Code*, [2004] 2 S.C.R. 248. Iacobucci and Arbour JJ. wrote the plurality opinion. Bastarache J. wrote a concurring opinion. LeBel and Binnie JJ. wrote dissenting opinions, but Binnie J.'s dissent was not on this issue.

[45] The nature of the witness' right against self-incrimination is discussed in ch. 47, Fundamental Justice, under heading §§ 47:27 to 47:29, "Right to silence".

§ 7:6 Court Martial

In *R. v. Généreux* (1992),[1] the question arose whether a Court Martial, constituted under the federal National Defence Act for the purpose of trying a member of the armed forces for a breach of the military Code of Service Discipline,[2] qualified as "an independent and impartial tribunal" for the purpose of s. 11(d). The Court Martial was presided over by a judge advocate, who was a legally trained officer of the armed forces serving in the legal branch of the forces. The judge advocate had the authority to determine questions of law or of mixed fact and law. The members of the Court Martial were between five and seven regular officers of the armed forces, and, under the direction of the judge advocate as to the applicable law, they had the authority to determine the guilt or innocence of the accused, and to determine the sentence in the event of a guilty verdict. The majority of the Supreme Court of Canada held that this tribunal did not satisfy the three conditions of judicial independence stipulated by the Court in *Valente.* With respect to "security of tenure", the Court noted that the judge advocate and the members of the Court Martial were appointed for a particular trial by their superior officers, and this would give rise to a reasonable apprehension that their careers in the armed forces might be affected by reaching a decision that was displeasing to their superiors. With respect to "financial security", there was a reasonable apprehension that future salary increases of the judge advocate and members might be determined by their superiors on the basis of their decision in the Court Martial. With respect to "institutional independence", there was no real independence from the superior officers who appointed the members and who also appointed the prosecutor. Therefore, the requirements of s. 11(d) were not met,[3] and the statutory provision for the Court Martial was unconstitutional.[4]

In 1991, the Queen's Regulations and Orders for the Canadian Forces (QR&Os) were amended to strengthen the independence of the Court Martial. The changes were not in force at the time of the Court Martial in *Généreux*, but they were referred to with cautious approval by Lamer C.J. throughout his opinion, which left the impression that the s. 11(d) issues had been solved. In *Lauzon v. The Queen* (1998),[5] the Court

[Section 7:6]

[1] *R. v. Généreux*, [1992] 1 S.C.R. 259. The judgment of the majority was written by Lamer C.J. with the agreement of four others. Stevenson J. wrote a concurring opinion with the agreement of two others. L'Heureux-Dubé J. dissented.

[2] The breach was held to be an "offence" so as to make s. 11 applicable.

[3] These breaches of independence were also held not to be necessary for the maintenance of discipline in the armed forces, and therefore to be unjustified under s. 1.

[4] See generally J. Walker, "Military Justice from Oxymoron to Aspiration" (1994) 32 Osgoode Hall L.J. 1.

[5] *Lauzon v. The Queen*, CMAC-415; (1998) 230 N.R. 272 (Ct. Martial Appeal Court); folld. in *Boivin v. The Queen* CMAC-410; (1998) 245 N.R. 341 (Ct. Martial Appeal Court).

Martial Appeal Court[6] held otherwise. In that case, the defendant was a male soldier who was charged with offences stemming from unwanted sexual advances to a female coworker on a military base. He was convicted by a Court Martial, and he appealed on the ground that the Court Martial was not an independent tribunal under s. 11(d). The Court agreed. With respect to security of tenure, under the amended QR&Os, an officer who served as the judge advocate of a Court Martial[7] had to be appointed by the Minister of Defence as a "military trial judge" for a fixed term of two to four years. A fixed term was an improvement on the ad hoc appointment process struck down in *Généreux*, but the fixed term was renewable, and the power of reappointment remained with the Minister of National Defence, which raised the possibility that reappointment might be influenced by whether the judge's decisions had been popular or unpopular with the Department of National Defence.[8] With respect to financial security, the amended QR&Os provided that the pay of a legal officer performing judicial duties is equal to the maximum of the annual range for a legal officer of the same rank. This also did not pass muster because, the Court, following the Supreme Court's then very recent decision in *Re Remuneration of Judges* (1997),[9] pointed out that a reduction in the salary ranges of all the legal officers would have the effect of reducing judicial salaries; judicial salaries had to be protected from this form of equal treatment by some independent, effective and objective mechanism which did not exist in the National Defence Act or the QR&Os. The result in *Lauzon* was to strike down the provisions of the Act and the QR&Os respecting the tenure and financial security of military court judges, with invalidity postponed for one year.[10] The unconstitutional provisions have since been replaced by more robust guarantees.[11]

---

[6]The Court Martial Appeal Court is the civilian court (composed of judges from federal or provincial superior courts) which hears appeals from courts martial.

[7]Court martials are of two kinds. The "General Court Martial", which was the tribunal in issue in *Généreux*, consists of a military judge and a panel of officers, with roles approximating loosely to a judge and jury in the general court system. The "Standing Court Martial", which was the tribunal in issue in *Lauzon*, consists of a military judge sitting alone. For less serious offences, there is a summary trial presided over by a commanding officer who need not be legally trained and who cannot impose a penalty more serious than a 30-day detention.

[8]*Lauzon v. The Queen*, CMAC-415; (1998) 230 N.R. 272 (Ct. Martial Appeal Court). The Minister also had power to remove military trial judges before the end of their term of office on the recommendation of an inquiry committee composed of the Judge Advocate General, the Colonel Commandment of the Legal Branch of the Canadian Forces, and the chief military trial judge.

[9]*Re Remuneration of Judges*, [1997] 3 S.C.R. 3; discussed in text accompanying § 7:5 note 8.

[10]The defendant was not exempted from the postponement of invalidity, and his convictions were, perhaps unnecessarily, also upheld under the doctrine of necessity because the constitutional defect applied to all of the military judges: *Lauzon v. The Queen*, CMAC-415; (1998), 230 N.R. 272 (Ct. Martial Appeal Court), para. 38.

[11]The National Defence Act, s. 165.21, now provides for appointment of military

In *R. v. Cawthorne* (2016),[12] another independence challenge was brought to the military justice system. The National Defence Act grants to the Minister of National Defence the power to appeal from a decision of a Court Martial (which goes to the Court Martial Appeal Court) and from a decision of the Court Martial Appeal Court (which goes to the Supreme Court of Canada). It was argued under ss. 7 and 11(d) that a fair trial required that a prosecutor be independent and be seen to be independent: since the Minister was a member of cabinet, responsible for the control of the Canadian Forces, he was not independent in fact or appearance. The Supreme Court rejected the argument, relying on the established role of the Attorney General, who was also a minister and a member of cabinet. Despite these ministerial responsibilities, the Attorney General had been held to be under a constitutional duty to act independently of partisan concerns when supervising prosecutorial decisions.[13] In the context of military justice, the position of the Minister was comparable to that of the Attorney General. The Attorney General was entitled to a strong presumption that he or she "can and does set aside partisan duties in exercising prosecutorial responsibilities", and there was "no compelling reason to treat the Minister differently in this regard".[14] There was no violation of s. 7's principles of fundamental justice or of s. 11(d)'s requirement of an independent tribunal.

§ 7:7 Jury

Section 11(d) requires a fair hearing of a criminal charge by an "independent and impartial" tribunal. It could not be doubted that a jury selected according to the rules of the Criminal Code would fully satisfy the three requirements stipulated in *Valente* for independence. But in *R. v. Bain* (1992),[1] the jury was successfully attacked as not meeting the requirement of impartiality.[2] The majority of the Supreme Court of Canada held that the Crown's ability to "stand by" up to 48 jurors gave to the prosecution an undue advantage in the composition of the jury. When the power of standby was exercised, the juror had to stand aside

---

judges by the Governor in Council, tenure until age 60, removal before age 60 by the Governor in Council on the recommendation of an independent committee composed of three members of the Court Martial Appeal Court. The QR&Os, ch. 24, now make various provisions for the salaries of military judges that support their independence.

[12] *R. v. Cawthorne*, [2016] 1 S.C.R. 983, 2016 SCC 32. McLachlin C.J. wrote the opinion of the Court.

[13] *R. v. Cawthorne*, [2016] 1 S.C.R. 983, 2016 SCC 32, para. 23, citing *Krieger v. Law Society of Alberta*, [2002] 3 S.C.R. 372, para. 30, and *Miazga v. Kvello Estate*, [2009] 3 S.C.R. 339.

[14] *R. v. Cawthorne*, [2016] 1 S.C.R. 983, 2016 SCC 32, para. 32.

[Section 7:7]

[1] *R. v. Bain*, [1992] 1 S.C.R. 91. The majority opinion was written by Cory J. with the agreement of two others; Stevenson J. wrote a concurring opinion; Gonthier J. wrote a dissenting opinion with the agreement of two others.

[2] The distinction between "independent" and "impartial" is also referred to in § 7:5 note 40, above.

until the entire panel of jurors had been called. Although the juror was not dismissed, and could be called again if the jury was not filled by the time the jury list had been gone through once, in practice the power of standby operated in much the same way as a peremptory challenge, excluding the person from the jury without any showing of cause. Since the accused did not possess the power of stand-by, and only had a limited number of peremptory challenges,[3] the prosecution had a greater influence in the selection process than did the accused. For the minority of the Supreme Court of Canada, this was of no constitutional significance, because the Crown attorney was a public officer, who would be under a duty to use the power of stand-by in order to form an impartial jury, not in order to fashion a jury that would be predisposed to convict the accused. But, for the majority of the Court, the Crown attorney's greater role in the selection of the jury gave rise to a reasonable apprehension that the jury could be biased in favour of the Crown. This appearance of bias, whether or not reflected in fact, was a breach of the requirement of an "impartial" tribunal in s. 11(d).[4]

§ 7:8 Inferior courts of civil jurisdiction

We have noticed that s. 99 of the Constitution Act, 1867 guarantees the independence of the judges of the "superior courts",[1] and that s. 11(d) of the Charter of Rights guarantees the independence of any "tribunal" (whether a superior or inferior court) exercising criminal jurisdiction.[2] Neither of the two constitutional guarantees catches inferior courts of civil jurisdiction. Of course, the judges of an inferior court that exercised criminal as well as civil jurisdiction would have the benefit of s. 11(d), but the judges of a court that exercised only civil jurisdiction, or the members of an administrative tribunal, do not have an explicit constitutional guarantee of independence. In *Re Remuneration of Judges* (1997),[3] Lamer C.J. for the majority of the Court said that there was an "unwritten constitutional principle" of independence. The explicit constitutional guarantees of independence were not exhaustive, but were simply exemplary of "a general principle of judicial indepen-

---

[3]The accused had four, twelve or twenty peremptory challenges, depending on the seriousness of the charge. The Crown had four peremptory challenges, regardless of the seriousness of the charge, as well as the power of stand-by. Both sides had unlimited challenges for cause.

[4]The Court (at 165) permitted Parliament "six months in which to provide new legislation, otherwise the Code provisions will be invalidated to the extent that they permit the impugned inequality". Parliament acted on this instruction, amending the Criminal Code to repeal the Crown's power of stand-by, and to give the Crown the same number of peremptory challenges as the accused: S.C. 1992, c. 41, s. 1, amending s. 634 of the Criminal Code (which was repealed in 2019).

[Section 7:8]

[1]§ 7:3, "Tenure of provincial judges: s. 99".

[2]§ 7:4, "Tenure of provincial judges: s. 11(d)".

[3]*Re Remuneration of Judges*, [1997] 3 S.C.R. 3.

dence that applies to all courts no matter what kind of cases they hear".[4] The unwritten principle found its source in the preamble to the Constitution Act, 1867, which declared that Canada was to have "a constitution similar in principle to that of the United Kingdom". Since judicial independence was a fundamental rule of constitutional democracy in the United Kingdom in 1867, the preamble imports the same rule into Canada's constitution.[5] La Forest J., who dissented in *Re Remuneration of Judges*, pointed out that judicial independence in the United Kingdom dates back to the Act of Settlement of 1701, but that Act never had constitutional force in the United Kingdom in the sense of a restriction on parliamentary sovereignty, and the United Kingdom Parliament retained (and still retains) full power to impair judicial independence should it wish to do so. Moreover, the Act of Settlement guaranteed the independence of only the superior courts, the rationale being that inferior courts and tribunals were subject to judicial review by the superior courts. Section 99 of the Constitution Act, 1867 closely followed the terms of the Act of Settlement, which is why it was limited to the superior courts. La Forest J. commented that "it seems strained to extend the ambit of this protection by reference to a general preambular statement".[6] Lamer C.J. noted this difficulty, but replied that "our Constitution has evolved over time", and since 1867 "judicial independence has grown into a principle that now extends to all courts, not just the superior courts of this country".[7] The new principle had never before been articulated, and La Forest J. expressed concern about the legitimacy of judicial review "when courts attempt to limit the power of legislatures without recourse to express textual authority".[8]

Despite the power of La Forest J.'s criticisms, Lamer C.J.'s opinion attracted the support of five other judges of the seven-judge bench. The assertion of an unwritten principle of judicial independence was an obiter dictum, because the case (which was a challenge to cutbacks in judicial salaries) was decided on the basis of s. 11(d) (the cutbacks were unconstitutional). However, in *Mackin v. New Brunswick* (2002),[9] where the Supreme Court of Canada held that the repeal of supernumerary status for provincial court judges was unconstitutional, the Court was careful to place its decision on the unwritten principle as well as s.

[4] *Re Remuneration of Judges*, [1997] 3 S.C.R. 3, para. 107.

[5] This theory has its analogue in the "implied bill of rights", which some judges have attempted to draw out of the preamble: ch. 34, Civil Liberties, under heading § 34:7, "Implied bill of rights". Another analogue is the residuary theory of s. 7 of the Charter of Rights, under which the apparently precise language of the criminal justice provisions of the Charter of Rights is not determinative, because it is supplemented by a vague "residue" in s. 7: ch. 47, Fundamental Justice, under heading § 47:15, "Definition of fundamental justice". Both these theories allow judges to strike down laws and other official acts that do not offend any of the explicit rules of the Constitution.

[6] *Re Remuneration of Judges*, [1997] 3 S.C.R. 3, para. 322.

[7] *Re Remuneration of Judges*, [1997] 3 S.C.R. 3, para. 106.

[8] *Re Remuneration of Judges*, [1997] 3 S.C.R. 3, para. 316.

[9] *Mackin v. New Brunswick*, [2002] 1 S.C.R. 405. The reliance on the unwritten principle is found in paras. 34, 69–70, 71–72 per Gonthier J. for majority.

11(d). It seems clear, therefore, that all courts, including inferior courts of civil jurisdiction, now enjoy constitutional protection for the independence of their judges.

In *Re Therrien* (2001),[10] a judge of Quebec's provincial (inferior) court challenged his removal from office based on the unwritten constitutional principle. He had been dismissed for cause following a judicial inquiry into his conduct. The procedure complied with Quebec's Courts of Justice Act, which provided for the removal of provincial court judges. However, the former judge argued that the statutory procedure did not comply with the unwritten constitutional principle of independence because the statutory procedure did not include an address of the Legislature (which is the Act of Settlement procedure, adopted for superior courts in Canada by s. 99 of the Constitution Act, 1867). The Supreme Court of Canada rejected the argument. It had been decided in *Valente v. The Queen* (1985)[11] that an address of the Legislature was not required by s. 11(d) of the Charter of Rights for the removal of judges of inferior courts of criminal jurisdiction. It was enough that there was a requirement of cause and a judicial inquiry into the existence of cause. Gonthier J. for the Court in *Therrien* held that it was not practical to have a different standard of independence for judges when they hear civil cases (and are covered by the unwritten constitutional principle) than for when they hear criminal cases (and are covered by s. 11(d)). Therefore, he held, the unwritten constitutional principle should not be regarded as affording greater protection than that guaranteed by s. 11(d). Since Quebec's statutory procedure satisfied the *Valente* standard for s. 11(d), it passed muster under the unwritten constitutional principle as well, and Therrien's objection to his removal from office was unfounded.[12]

§ 7:9 Administrative tribunals

We noticed in the previous section of this chapter that the Supreme Court of Canada in *Re Remuneration of Judges* (1997)[1] found an "unwritten constitutional principle" that guaranteed the independence of all courts. If the unwritten constitutional principle could embrace inferior courts of civil jurisdiction that were left uncovered by s. 99 of the Constitution Act, 1867 (superior courts) and s. 11(d) of the Constitution Act, 1982 (courts of criminal jurisdiction), then could it embrace administrative tribunals as well? Many administrative tribunals perform important adjudicative functions, but few if any of them have protections for their

---

[10] *Re Therrien*, [2001] 2 S.C.R. 3. The opinion of the Court was written by Gonthier J.

[11] *Valente v. The Queen*, [1985] 2 S.C.R. 673; for discussion, see text accompanying § 7:5 note 1, above.

[12] Folld. in *Moreau-Bérubé v. N.B.*, [2002] 1 S.C.R. 249 (upholding dismissal of provincial court judge by provincial Judicial Council).

[Section 7:9]

[1] *Re Remuneration of Judges*, [1997] 3 S.C.R. 3; discussed in text accompanying § 7:5 note 8, above.

independence comparable to those of the courts. To be sure, administrative tribunals are subject to the reviewing authority of the superior courts, which would correct any decisions that were infected by bias, but that is also true of inferior courts and they are certainly covered by the unwritten principle.

In *Ocean Port Hotel v. British Columbia* (2001),[2] the Ocean Port Hotel challenged a decision of the Liquor Appeal Board of British Columbia, which had suspended the liquor licence of the hotel as a penalty for various infractions of the liquor laws. Under British Columbia's licensing statute, the members of the Board were appointed by the Lieutenant Governor in Council (that is the provincial cabinet) and served "at the pleasure of the Lieutenant Governor in Council". The British Columbia Court of Appeal set aside the decision of the Board on the ground that the Board lacked the independence that was appropriate for a tribunal with power to impose penalties. The Supreme Court of Canada reversed. McLachlin C.J., who wrote the opinion of the unanimous Court, refused to extend the unwritten constitutional principle of judicial independence to administrative tribunals. "It is the Legislature or Parliament", she held, "that determines the degree of independence required of tribunal members."[3] Administrative tribunals need not be independent of the executive branch of government, because administrative tribunals are "created precisely for the purpose of implementing government policy", even when "that policy may require them to make quasi-judicial decisions".[4] In this case, the Board was first and foremost a licensing body, and the suspension of the hotel license was an incident of the licensing function. There being no constitutional requirement of independence, the Legislature's judgment as to the appropriate tenure for the members of the Board was not subject to judicial review.

Does *Ocean Port Hotel* provide a definitive "no" answer to the question of whether there is a constitutional requirement of independence for administrative tribunals? Probably not. First of all, the description of administrative tribunals as instruments of government policy, while undoubtedly accurate for most tribunals, does not in this context seem to apply to those tribunals that possess nothing but adjudicatory functions; they are much closer to courts than the Liquor Appeal Board of British Columbia. Secondly, while McLachlin C.J. seemed categorical that the opinion in *Re Remuneration of Judges* applied only to courts,[5] she also stated without elaboration that "tribunals may sometimes attract Charter requirements of independence".[6] Since the unwritten constitutional principle is not a Charter requirement (the Charter being a written instrument), it is not clear what she had in mind in this

---

[2] *Ocean Port Hotel v. British Columbia*, [2001] 2 S.C.R. 781. The opinion of the Court was written by McLachlin C.J.

[3] *Ocean Port Hotel v. British Columbia*, [2001] 2 S.C.R. 781, para. 20.

[4] *Ocean Port Hotel v. British Columbia*, [2001] 2 S.C.R. 781, para. 24.

[5] *Ocean Port Hotel v. British Columbia*, [2001] 2 S.C.R. 781, paras. 28–32.

[6] *Ocean Port Hotel v. British Columbia*, [2001] 2 S.C.R. 781, para. 24.

statement. In any event, the reasoning does leave some room for the Court in a subsequent case to impose independence requirements on an administrative tribunal that is very similar to a court.[7] However, for the general run of administrative tribunals, including those with power to inflict penalties on individuals for breaches of a statute,[8] there is no constitutional requirement of independence from the executive branch of government.[9]

II. FEDERAL COURTS

§ 7:10 Supreme Court of Canada

We have already noticed that the Constitution Act, 1867, by s. 92(14), confers on the provinces the power to establish and maintain provincial courts with jurisdiction encompassing matters arising under both provincial and federal laws. The Act, by s. 101, confers on the federal Parliament a less sweeping power to establish federal courts. Section 101 has two branches: it authorizes the establishment of (1) "a general court of appeal for Canada", and (2) "any additional courts for the better administration of the laws of Canada". Acting under the first branch of ss. 101, the Parliament of Canada in 1875 established the Supreme Court of Canada with civil and criminal appellate jurisdiction throughout Canada.[1] The Supreme Court of Canada is the topic of the next chapter of this book.

§ 7:11 Federal Court of Canada

The second branch of s. 101 of the Constitution Act, 1867, by conferring on the federal Parliament the power to establish "any additional courts for the better administration of the laws of Canada", authorizes the Parliament to establish a system of federal courts to determine cases arising under federal laws.[1] The federal Parliament has generally

---

[7]But see *Bell Canada v. Can. Telephone Employees Assn.*, [2003] 1 S.C.R. 884, para. 29 (unwritten principle of judicial independence inapplicable to Canadian Human Rights Tribunal, although it has no policy function and its only role is adjudicative).

[8]If a penalty, by its magnitude, was a "true penal consequence", then the Charter guarantees of s. 11 would apply, including the requirement of an independent and impartial tribunal: *R. v. Wigglesworth*, [1987] 2 S.C.R. 541, 561; discussed in ch. 51, Rights on Being Charged, under heading § 51:3, "Offence".

[9]R. Ellis, Unjust by Design (2013), 70, 218–228, 233, argues forcefully that the unwritten constitutional requirements of judicial independence should apply to administrative tribunals that exercise judicial functions, including the "adjunct judicial functions exercised by regulatory agencies" (p. 228).

[Section 7:10]

[1]Supreme and Exchequer Courts Act, S.C. 1875, c. 11; see now Supreme Court Act, R.S.C. 1985, c. S-26.

[Section 7:11]

[1]The Parliament could probably even establish courts of criminal jurisdiction, despite their express allocation to the provinces in s. 92(14), because s. 101 is expressed to apply "notwithstanding anything in this Act". Doubt arises from the express exclusion

been content to leave the provincial courts with the jurisdiction to determine federal as well as provincial issues.[2] Until 1875, there were no federal courts at all. In 1875, the federal Parliament established the Exchequer Court of Canada, but gave it a very limited jurisdiction over cases involving the revenue and the Crown in right of Canada. This jurisdiction was gradually increased to cover copyright, trade marks, patents, admiralty, tax, citizenship and a few other matters regulated by federal laws.[3] In 1971, the Exchequer Court was replaced by the Federal Court of Canada.[4] The new Court inherited the jurisdiction of its predecessor, but was also given additional jurisdiction, including the power to review the decisions of federal agencies and officials and the power to entertain claims for relief in respect of aeronautics, interprovincial undertakings and certain kinds of commercial paper. The establishment of the Federal Court, with its broader jurisdiction and more elaborate structure (it has a trial division and an appeal division),[5] is a step in the direction of the dual court system in the United States, a system which leads to multiple litigation and complex jurisdictional disputes.[6]

The power of the federal Parliament to establish federal courts is of course limited by the terms of s. 101 of the Constitution Act, 1867. Section 101 does not authorize the establishment of courts of general jurisdiction akin to the provincial courts. It only authorizes courts "for the better administration of the laws of Canada". This has two important consequences. First, it means that the Federal Court has no inherent jurisdiction; its jurisdiction is confined to those subject matters conferred upon it by the Federal Court Act or other statute.[7] Secondly, it means that the Federal Court can be given jurisdiction over only subject matters governed by "the laws of Canada".

What are "the laws of Canada"? It is well settled that this phrase does not mean all laws in force in Canada whatever their source, but means

---

from s. 91(27) of "the constitution of courts of criminal jurisdiction", and the existence of a notwithstanding clause in s. 91. See Laskin, Canadian Constitutional Law (5th ed., 1986 by Finkelstein), 179. The Federal Courts Act, R.S.C.1985, c. F-7, provides that the Federal Court of Appeal (s. 3) and the Federal Court (s. 4) are superior courts of record "having civil and criminal jurisdiction", but the Act does not go on to confer any criminal jurisdiction on the Courts.

[2]See heading § 7:1, "Establishment of provincial courts".

[3]Supreme and Exchequer Courts Act, S.C. 1875, c. 11; for jurisdiction in 1971, see Exchequer Court Act, R.S.C. 1970, c. E-11.

[4]Federal Court Act, S.C. 1970-71-72, c. 1; now Federal Courts Act, R.S.C. 1985, c. F-7.

[5]The Courts Administration Service Act, S.C. 2002, c. 8, s. 16, amended the Federal Court Act to divide the Federal Court of Canada into two separate courts, the Federal Court of Appeal in place of the Federal Court-Appeal Division, and the Federal Court in place of the Federal Court-Trial Division.

[6]Russell, The Judiciary in Canada (1987), ch. 1, describes the history and functions of the Federal Court of Canada.

[7]*Windsor v. Canadian Transit Co.*, [2016] 2 S.C.R. 617, 2016 SCC 54, para. 33 per Karakatsanis J. for majority. But see N. Lambert, "The Nature of Federal Court Jurisdiction: Statutory or Inherent?" (2010) 123 Can. J. Admin. Law & Practice 145, arguing that jurisdiction, at least for judicial-review purposes, is inherent.

federal laws.[8] The clearest example of a law of Canada is a federal statute, including, of course, a regulation or order made under a federal statute. Much of the subject matter of the jurisdiction of the Federal Court is governed by federal statute law, and this part of the Court's jurisdiction raises no constitutional issue. But some of the subject matter of the Court's jurisdiction is governed by provincial statute law or by the common law,[9] and this part of the Court's jurisdiction does raise a constitutional issue.

Until 1976, there was substantial judicial support for the view that a federal court could be given jurisdiction over any matter in relation to which the federal Parliament had legislative competence, even if that matter was not in fact regulated by federal statute law. On this basis the "laws of Canada" could include a rule of provincial statute law or a rule of the common law (including civil law) if its subject matter was such that the law could have been enacted or adopted by the federal Parliament. However, in *Quebec North Shore Paper Co. v. Canadian Pacific* (1976),[10] the Supreme Court of Canada unexpectedly rejected the test of federal legislative competence. The Court held that the Federal Court had no jurisdiction over an action brought by Canadian Pacific against the Quebec North Shore Paper Co. for breach of a contract to build a marine terminal, which was part of a larger contract for the transportation of newsprint from a paper plant in Quebec to newspaper houses in the United States. The Federal Court Act included an express grant of jurisdiction over the case. The test of federal legislative competence was satisfied, because the Constitution Act, 1867, by ss. 91(29) and 92(10), confers on the federal Parliament legislative competence over the international transportation of goods. But the federal Parliament had not in fact enacted any law governing the contract, and the contract stipulated that it was to be interpreted in accordance with the civil law of Quebec. The Supreme Court of Canada held that the Federal Court could not constitutionally assume jurisdiction over the case

[8]The Constitution Acts, 1867 to 1982 are not "laws of Canada", but the Federal Court does have jurisdiction to determine constitutional issues; like any other court or tribunal, the Federal Court, when called upon in the exercise of its jurisdiction to apply a law (in the case of the Federal Court, it will be a "law of Canada"), is under a duty to determine the constitutional validity of that law when the validity of the law is challenged: *Northern Telecom Can. v. Communications Workers of Can.*, [1983] 1 S.C.R. 733. However, s. 101 does not authorize the federal Parliament to confer on the Federal Court exclusive jurisdiction to determine the constitutionality of federal laws: *A.-G. Can. v. Law Society of B.C.*, [1982] 2 S.C.R. 307; or of federal administrative action: *Can. Labour Relations Bd. v. Paul L'Anglais*, [1983] 1 S.C.R. 147.

[9]The term "common law" is ambiguous, sometimes meaning the English-derived system of judge-made law that we call the common law, and sometimes meaning the background legal system (the droit commun or jus commune, as it is called in the preamble to the Civil Code of Quebec, evidently struggling to avoid the phrase common law). In this context, the latter sense is intended, and the common law includes the civil law in the province of Quebec, as well as the judge-made common law in the other provinces.

[10]*Quebec North Shore Paper Co. v. Canadian Pacific*, [1977] 2 S.C.R. 1054.

because the case was not governed by "applicable and existing federal law".[11]

In *McNamara Construction v. The Queen* (1977),[12] the Supreme Court of Canada held that the Federal Court had no jurisdiction over an action brought by the Crown in right of Canada (the federal Crown) against a builder and an architect, alleging the breach of a contract to build a penitentiary in Alberta. Once again, the Federal Court Act included an express grant of jurisdiction over the case. Once again, the test of federal legislative competence was satisfied, because the Constitution Act, 1867 confers on the federal Parliament legislative competence over the federal Crown (s. 91(1A)) and over penitentiaries (s. 91(28)). But, because the applicable law was the common law, the Supreme Court of Canada held that its new requirement of "applicable and existing federal law" was not satisfied. Therefore, the Federal Court could not constitutionally assume jurisdiction over the case.

The decisions in *Quebec North Shore* and *McNamara Construction* are, in my view, open to serious criticism.[13] First, it seems to me that the test of federal legislative competence, which was well established before 1976,[14] is a perfectly defensible definition of "laws of Canada" in s. 101. Any laws within federal legislative competence could easily be converted into federal laws by the enactment of a federal statute incorporating them by reference (or adopting them) as federal statute law.[15] Since this can be so easily done, it seems to me that laws within federal legislative competence should be regarded as laws of Canada without requiring the referential incorporation.

Secondly, even if one accepts the requirement of "applicable and existing federal law", I can see no reason why the rules of the common law (including civil law) in a field of federal legislative competence should not qualify as "laws of Canada".[16] Indeed, it seems almost unarguable that "because the common law is potentially subject to overriding legisla-

[11]*Quebec North Shore Paper Co. v. Canadian Pacific*, [1977] 2 S.C.R. 1054, 1065–66. The adjectives "applicable" and "existing" seem to be redundant, especially the second of them, but that is the way Laskin C.J. phrased the requirement, and in this technical area it seems wise to repeat the precise language in which the rule has been judicially expressed.

[12]*McNamara Construction v. The Queen*, [1977] 2 S.C.R. 655. The case was decided after *Quebec North Shore*, although reported earlier.

[13]For more detailed criticism, see P.W. Hogg, Comment (1977) 55 Can. Bar Rev. 550; P.W. Hogg, "Federalism and the Jurisdiction of Canadian Courts" (1981) 30 U.N.B.L.J. 9; J.B. Laskin and R.J. Sharpe, "Constricting Federal Court Jurisdiction" (1980) 30 U. Toronto L.J. 283; J.M. Evans, Comment (1981) 59 Can. Bar Rev. 124; S.A. Scott, "Canadian Federal Courts and the Constitutional Limits of their Jurisdiction" (1982) 27 McGill L.J. 137; J.M. Evans and B. Slattery, Comment (1989) 68 Can. Bar Rev. 817; B.A. Crane, "Constitutional Restraints on the Federal Court in relation to Crown Litigation" (1992) 2 N.J.C.L. 1.

[14]It is accepted without question, for example, in the pre-1976 editions of Laskin, Canadian Constitutional Law see 3rd ed., 1969, at p. 817; 4th ed., 1975, at pp. 792–793.

[15]J.M. Evans, Comment (1981) 59 Can. Bar Rev. 124, 151 makes this suggestion.

[16]In *McNamara Construction*, since the federal Parliament could have enacted a

tive power, there is federal common or decisional law and provincial common or decisional law according to the matters respectively distributed to each legislature by the B.N.A. Act".[17] But that is not what the Supreme Court of Canada has decided. According to the Court, the contracts in *Quebec North Shore* and *McNamara Construction*, although subject to overriding federal legislative power, were, as a matter of constitutional law, beyond the jurisdiction of the Federal Court. The same result has been reached with respect to a dispute over a contract to build a federal office building.[18] It is implicit in these decisions that there is no such thing as federal common law.[19] And yet, the Supreme Court has from time to time made obscure reference to the existence of federal common law,[20] and has actually held that some parts of the common law do qualify as federal law. One of these is the contractual liability of the federal Crown,[21] which has the curious consequence that a federal government contract is within Federal Court jurisdiction if the federal Crown is the defendant, but not if the federal Crown is the plaintiff.[22] Although the Court has never offered any criteria for the identification of these little enclaves of federal common law,[23] it may be

---

body of law regarding the construction of the penitentiary, there seems as much reason to describe the common law as federal law as there is to describe it as provincial law. It has a double aspect. Writing before *McNamara Construction*, Laskin, Canadian Constitutional Law (4th ed. rev., 1975), said (at pp. 792–793):

> "Laws of Canada" must also include common law which relates to the matters falling within classes of subjects assigned to the Parliament of Canada.

[17]Laskin, Canadian Constitutional Law (4th ed. rev., 1975), 793. This approach could even be said to be imposed by s. 129 of the Constitution Act, 1867 for common law (as well as for pre-confederation colonial law and received English law): S.A. Scott, "Canadian Federal Courts and the Constitutional Limits of their Jurisdiction" (1982) 27 McGill L.J. 137, 159. Nor (as Scott comments) is it easy to devise another coherent or workable test.

[18]*R. v. Thomas Fuller Construction*, [1980] 1 S.C.R. 695. (The Federal Court did have jurisdiction over the liability of the federal Crown, but not other parties to the contracts.) Compare *Southam v. Can.*, [1990] 3 F.C. 465 (C.A.) (privileges, immunities and powers of the Senate are not laws of Canada).

[19]See *Caisse populaire Desjardins de l'Est de Drummond v. Can.*, [2009] 2 S.C.R. 94, paras. 81, 112 per Deschamps J. dissenting (suggesting that there is no federal common law and citing *Quebec North Shore* and *McNamara Construction* in support).

[20]*Que. North Shore Paper Co. v. CP*, [1977] 2 S.C.R. 1054, 1063, 1065–1066; *McNamara Construction v. The Queen*, [1977] 2 S.C.R. 655, 662–663; *Rhine v. The Queen*, [1980] 2 S.C.R. 442, 447; *Northern Telecom Can. v. Communications Workers of Can.*, [1983] 1 S.C.R. 733, 740; *B.C. v. Provincial Court Judges' Association of British Columbia*, 2020 SCC 20, para. 98.

[21]*R. v. Thomas Fuller Construction*, [1980] 1 S.C.R. 695.

[22]*McNamara Construction v. The Queen*, [1977] 2 S.C.R. 655. Another anomaly is that there is no Federal Court jurisdiction over a tort action against a Crown agent based on direct liability: *Can. Saltfish Corp. v. Rasmussen*, [1986] 2 F.C. 500 (C.A.); but there is jurisdiction if the action is based on vicarious liability: *Briére v. Can. Mtge. & Housing Corp.*, [1986] 2 F.C. 484.

[23]Another area of federal common law is the law of aboriginal title: *Roberts v. Can.*, [1989] 1 S.C.R. 322; *R. v. Côté*, [1996] 3 S.C.R. 139, para. 49; *Nfld. v. Uashaunnuat (Innu*

that the Court has in mind those few common law doctrines that cannot be altered by the provincial Legislatures.[24]

A third criticism of the requirement of "applicable and existing federal law" is that it is exceedingly difficult to apply, often requiring litigation to determine the appropriate forum for cases in which the applicable laws come from a variety of sources.[25] Where a single cause of action is governed partly by federal law and partly by common law, the Supreme Court has in two cases been willing to concede federal jurisdiction.[26] In *Roberts v. Canada* (1989),[27] however, the Court disapproved of a dictum that it is sufficient "if the rights and obligations of the parties are to be determined to some material extent by federal law". In that case, the Court[28] also rejected the doctrine of "pendent jurisdiction", which has been developed by the federal courts of the United States to reduce the fragmentation of litigation between the federal and state court systems.[29] Under the doctrine of pendent jurisdiction, where a federal court has jurisdiction over a particular case, then the court has jurisdiction to determine all of the issues that are derived from the "common nucleus of operative fact," including "state" issues over which the federal court would have no independent jurisdiction. Why this sensible doctrine would be unacceptable to the Supreme Court of Canada is a mystery. It means that there is no clear rule to deal with a cause of action governed by both federal and provincial law. And it means that where there are two causes of action against the same defendant, arising out of the same facts, only the cause of action based on federal law can be tried in the Federal Court; if the second cause of action is based on provincial law, a second proceeding must be brought in a provincial court.[30]

A fourth criticism of the requirement of "applicable and existing

---

of Uashat and of Mani-Utenam), 2020 SCC 4, paras. 118, 135 per Brown and Rowe JJ. dissenting. Compare *Bisaillon v. Keable*, [1983] 2 S.C.R. 60 (police informer rule is a common law rule of criminal law that cannot be altered by the province).

[24]The common law in fields of unexercised federal legislative competence is mainly subject to provincial alteration as well: § 7:11 note 16, above.

[25]Without burdening this book with dozens of citations, I refer the reader to the index to each volume of the Federal Court Reports. That shows that many challenges to federal-court jurisdiction were made on constitutional grounds in the years following the decisions in *Quebec North Shore* and *McNamara Construction*. Before 1976 such cases were rare.

[26]*Rhine v. The Queen*, [1980] 2 S.C.R. 442; *ITO-International Terminal Operators v. Miida Electronics*, [1986] 1 S.C.R. 752.

[27]*Roberts v. Canada*, [1989] 1 S.C.R. 322, 333.

[28]*Roberts v. Canada*, [1989] 1 S.C.R. 322, 344; but compare *ITO-International Terminal Operators v. Miida Electronics*, [1986] 1 S.C.R. 752, 781–782, which seemed to accept the doctrine of pendent jurisdiction.

[29]The Constitution of the United States, art. III, ss. 1, 2, confines the jurisdiction of the federal courts to cases or controversies coming within "the judicial power of the United States", a defined phrase of which a major element is cases arising under "the laws of the United States": see C.A. Wright and M.K. Kane, Law of Federal Courts (West, 6th ed., 2002), chs. 1, 2.

[30]So held in *Que. Ready Mix v. Rocois Construction*, [1989] 1 S.C.R. 695.

federal law" is that the Federal Court cannot dispose of the whole of a controversy when some issues are governed by federal law and some are not. We have noticed that proceedings against a single defendant may have to be split where there is more than one cause of action.[31] Where there is more than one defendant, or a third party, or a counterclaim, it is common to find that the liability of some parties is governed by federal law, and that of others is not. This situation is illustrated by *R. v. Thomas Fuller Construction* (1979).[32] In that case, an action was brought against the federal Crown by a contractor (Foundation) who was constructing a building for the federal government. This action was brought in the Federal Court, and it satisfied the requirements stipulated by the previous cases. The Federal Court Act granted jurisdiction over the cause of action. The Constitution Act, 1867, by s. 91(1A), conferred federal legislative competence over the liability of the federal Crown and over federal public property. And, in this case, the liability of the federal Crown was assumed to be governed by "applicable and existing federal law".[33] The principal action was therefore properly brought in the Federal Court and could in fact be brought in no other court, because federal-court jurisdiction over suits against the federal Crown was exclusive.[34] However, the federal Crown issued a third party notice against a contractor (Fuller) (also working on the same building), in which the Crown claimed indemnity against or contribution towards the Crown's liability to the plaintiff (Foundation). The problem was that the liability of the third party (Fuller) was not based on federal law, but on either (a) the contract between the federal Crown and the third party (Fuller), or (b) Ontario's Negligence Act providing for contribution between joint and concurrent tortfeasors. The Supreme Court of Canada, in a majority opinion written by Pigeon J., held, therefore, that the requirement of "applicable and existing federal law" was not satisfied, and the Federal Court was prohibited by the Constitution from taking jurisdiction over the third party proceeding. The decision in *Fuller Construction* meant that the federal Crown would have to bring a separate action in the Ontario courts in order to recover indemnity or contribution against the third party. A minimum of two lawsuits, and perhaps as many as four lawsuits, would be necessary to settle the rights and liabilities of the three parties.[35]

Fuller Construction is not an unusual case. Multi-party litigation in

---

[31] *Que. Ready Mix v. Rocois Construction*, [1989] 1 S.C.R. 695.

[32] *R. v. Thomas Fuller Construction*, [1980] 1 S.C.R. 695.

[33] Pigeon J. for the majority assumed without discussion that the principal action satisfied all three tests, although (at p. 707) he defined "laws of Canada" as "laws enacted by Parliament", i.e., as excluding the common law; and yet the only applicable law seemed to be the common law. Compare Martland J., dissenting, but not on this point, at pp. 703–704 (federal statute removing procedural bar of fiat was the "law of Canada").

[34] This has since been changed: see text accompanying § 7:11 note 49, below.

[35] Note that Fuller had not been joined as a defendant by the plaintiff (Foundation), presumably because the suit against Fuller would have been outside the jurisdiction of the Federal Court. Foundation would probably want to sue Fuller directly in case the

the Federal Court often has to be fragmented into federal and provincial components.[36] Recognizing this problem, Reed J. of the Federal Court, Trial Division, has held[37] that parties can be joined in the Federal Court when the two claims are "so intertwined that findings of fact with respect to one defendant are intimately bound up with those that would have to be made with respect to the other". This doctrine of intertwining has been rejected by the Federal Court of Appeal,[38] but given cautious approval in an obiter dictum of the Supreme Court of Canada.[39] The doctrine of intertwining, if it becomes established, would be a long step in the direction of the American doctrine of "ancillary jurisdiction", which permits a federal court in the United States, when it has jurisdiction over a particular proceeding, to take jurisdiction over an "ancillary" proceeding of which it could not take cognizance if it were independently presented.[40] Like the doctrine of pendent jurisdiction, mentioned above,[41] the doctrine of ancillary jurisdiction rests on the reasonable assumption that a federal court should have the power to resolve a case in its entirety.[42]

Fuller Construction illustrates the deficiencies of the Supreme Court

---

federal Crown was held not liable; that would require a third action in the courts of Ontario. But, if Fuller was sued in the courts of Ontario, he would not be able to claim contribution or indemnity from the federal Crown except by a fourth action in the Federal Court. Thus, four actions would be needed to fully determine the respective rights and liabilities of the three parties arising out of a single factual situation.

[36]E.g., *Pacific Western Airlines v. The Queen*, [1980] 1 F.C. 86 (C.A.); *Peel v. Can.*, [1989] 2 F.C. 562 (C.A.).

[37]*Marshall v. The Queen*, [1986] 1 F.C. 437, 449. Reed J. is addressing the Court's statutory jurisdiction, but by implication she is also holding that the requirement of applicable and existing federal law is also satisfied.

[38]*Varnam v. Can.*, [1988] 2 F.C. 454 (C.A.).

[39]*Roberts v. Can.*, [1989] 1 S.C.R. 322, 333 ("*Marshall* seems to strike an appropriate balance by requiring the claim or claims against the private litigant to be inextricably linked with those against the Crown.")

[40]See generally C.A. Wright and M.K. Kane, Law of Federal Courts (West, 6th ed., 2002), chs. 1, 2.

[41]§ 7:11 note 29, above, and accompanying text.

[42]It must be conceded that the *Canadian* authorities before *Marshall* provided little support for a doctrine of ancillary jurisdiction. The weight of authority held that the Federal Court could take jurisdiction over a third party notice, counterclaim or codefendant only if the Court would have had jurisdiction if the issue had been presented independently in a separate proceeding. On third party notices, see *The King v. Hume; Consolidated Distilleries v. Consolidated Exporters Corp.*, [1930] S.C.R. 531; *Bank of Montreal v. Royal Bank of Can.*, [1933] S.C.R. 311; *McNamara Construction v. The Queen*, [1977] 2 S.C.R. 654, 664; but compare *Schwella v. The Queen*, [1957] Ex. C.R. 226, where ancillary jurisdiction over a third party notice seems to have been accepted. On counterclaims, see *Bow, McLachlan & Co. v. The Ship "Camosun"*, [1909] A.C. 597; *A.-G. Can. v. Boeing Co.* (1983), 41 O.R. (2d) 777 (C.A.). On codefendants, see *Pacific Western Airlines v. The Queen*, [1980] 1 F.C. 86 (C.A.); but compare *The Ship "Sparrows Point" v. Greater Vancouver Water District*, [1951] S.C.R. 396. However, most of these cases were decided before the decisions in *Quebec North Shore* and *McNamara Construction* made the problems more acute. I would argue that the Supreme Court of Canada should develop a doctrine of ancillary jurisdiction to mitigate the difficulties which it has created in those two decisions.

of Canada's rigid approach to the requirement of "existing and applicable federal law". It also illustrates a deficiency in the Federal Court Act that has now, fortunately, been corrected. Until 1990, the Federal Court Act conferred on the Federal Court *exclusive* jurisdiction over proceedings against the federal Crown. This meant, obviously, that a plaintiff with a cause of action against the federal Crown had no choice but to sue in the Federal Court.[43] However, the Federal Court would normally have no jurisdiction over federal Crown servants,[44] or federal Crown agents,[45] who might also be involved in the dispute; and the Court would normally have no jurisdiction over other co-defendants,[46] third parties,[47] or counterclaims by the Crown.[48] In 1990, the Federal Court Act was amended to make the jurisdiction over proceedings against the Crown concurrent rather than exclusive.[49] Since this amendment, proceedings against the federal Crown can be brought in the appropriate provincial court, which is likely to have jurisdiction over all the other parties as well. If the plaintiff chooses the provincial forum, split proceedings can be avoided.[50]

The 1990 amendment to the Federal Court Act invites the question whether there is any reason to preserve even concurrent Federal Court jurisdiction over proceedings against the federal Crown. The same question could be posed with respect to other parts of the Federal Court's jurisdiction. As noted earlier in this chapter, Canada does not need a dual court system. The provincial courts have general jurisdiction over all causes of action; the judges of the higher courts are federally appointed; and consistency of decisions is guaranteed by the appeal to the Supreme Court of Canada. The existence of a parallel hierarchy of federal courts cannot fail to give rise to wasteful jurisdictional disputes and multiple proceedings. I accordingly regret the expansion of the federal-court system which has occurred in Canada since 1875.[51] But it cannot be denied that the Constitution Act, 1867, by s. 101, authorizes

---

[43]In *Rudolf Wolff & Co. v. Can.*, [1990] 1 S.C.R. 695 and *Dywidag Systems v. Zutphen Bros.*, [1990] 1 S.C.R. 705, it was held that the exclusive jurisdiction of the Federal Court, although admittedly a cause of hardship, delay and unnecessary expense, did not offend s. 15 of the Charter.

[44]*Pacific Western Airlines v. The Queen*, [1980] 1 F.C. 86 (C.A.).

[45]*Can. Saltfish Corp. v. Rasmussen*, [1986] 2 F.C. 500 (C.A.).

[46]*Pacific Western Airlines v. The Queen*, [1980] 1 F.C. 86 (C.A.).

[47]*R. v. Thomas Fuller Construction*, [1980] 1 S.C.R. 695.

[48]Compare *McNamara Construction v. The Queen*, [1977] 2 S.C.R. 655 (proceedings by Crown outside federal jurisdiction).

[49]S.C. 1990, c. 8, amending s. 17 of the Federal Court Act.

[50]If the plaintiff chooses the federal forum, and the Crown wants to make a counterclaim or add a third party, the Attorney General is entitled to a stay of proceedings under s. 50.1 of the Federal Court Act (added in 1990). Although s. 50.1 refers only to the Attorney General, presumably it would also be possible for other parties to obtain a stay on the ground that the Federal Court is the less convenient forum.

[51]The argument that, at least for Canada, federalism does not require the federalizing of the judiciary is made in P.W. Hogg "Federalism and the Jurisdiction of Canadian Courts" (1981) 30 U.N.B.L.J. 9.

the federal Parliament to create a federal-court system, and that the federal Parliament has deliberately chosen to do so. In these circumstances, it seems to me that the Supreme Court of Canada should develop rules which will enable the parallel jurisdictions to operate as smoothly as possible. It must be remembered that the burden of inadequate rules is borne not by governments but by individual litigants who have no means of escape from the uncertainties, expenses, delays, inconsistencies and injustices which are inherent in multiple lawsuits. The Supreme Court of Canada's rejection of the rule of legislative competence as the definition of "laws of Canada", and the Court's refusal to develop rules of ancillary and pendent jurisdiction, have exacerbated the problems of a dual court system.

In *ITO-International Terminal Operators v. Miida Electronics* (1986),[52] the Supreme Court re-articulated the framework for Federal Court jurisdiction as follows:

1. There must be a statutory grant of jurisdiction by the federal Parliament.
2. There must be an existing body of federal law which is essential for the disposition of the case and which nourishes the statutory grant of jurisdiction.
3. The law on which the case is based must be a "law of Canada" as the phrase is used in s. 101 of the Constitution Act, 1867.

In that case, ITO, a stevedoring company, undertook to unload and store a shipment of goods from a seller in Japan to a purchaser in Montreal. ITO unloaded and stored the goods, but they were stolen from ITO's warehouse. The purchaser of the goods sued the seller and ITO for the loss in the Federal Court. Did the Federal Court have jurisdiction over the proceedings? The Supreme Court, by a majority of four to three, held that the three elements of Federal-Court jurisdiction were satisfied: (1) the Federal Court Act itself conferred jurisdiction over claims based on maritime law; (2) this proceeding was governed by Canadian maritime law, which was essential for the disposition of the case and which nourished the statutory grant of jurisdiction; and (3) Canadian maritime law was a "law of Canada" because it had been adopted into Canada by the Federal Court Act and was within the federal power over navigation and shipping in s. 91(10) of the Constitution Act, 1867. Chouinard J. dissented on the basis that the proceeding was not governed by maritime law: it was an action for a tort (delict) committed in Quebec (negligence in the storage of goods), which was governed by the civil law of Quebec, and came within the jurisdiction of the civil courts of Quebec, not the Federal Court.

---

[52] *ITO-International Terminal Operators v. Miida Electronics*, [1986] 1 S.C.R. 752, para 11. McIntyre J. wrote the opinion of the majority. Chouinard J. wrote a partial dissent.

Another divided Supreme Court decided *Windsor v. Canadian Transit Co.* (2016).[53] In that case, the Canadian Transit Co., a company incorporated under federal law, which owned and operated the Canadian half of the Ambassador Bridge connecting Windsor with Detroit, had acquired over 100 residential properties in Windsor with the intention of demolishing them and using the land to facilitate maintenance and expansion of the bridge and its facilities. However, most of the properties had simply been left vacant and allowed to fall into disrepair. The City did not appreciate this blight on one of its neighbourhoods, and, pursuant to its by-laws, issued repair orders against the properties. The company did not comply with the repair orders, claiming that the Ambassador Bridge was a federal international undertaking to which the City's by-laws could not constitutionally apply. The company applied to the Federal Court for declarations supporting its position. The City disputed the jurisdiction of the Federal Court, arguing that only Ontario's superior court had jurisdiction to decide the issue. The Supreme Court, by a majority, sided with the City. Karakatsanis J., who wrote for the majority, applied the three-part *ITO* test: (1) the company's claim was based on constitutional law (the doctrine of interjurisdictional immunity), not on an Act of Parliament, and the Federal Court Act did not confer jurisdiction over such a claim; (2) the governing law was not a federal law ("law of Canada"), but municipal and constitutional law; and (3) no law of Canada was dispositive of the issue. She concluded that the company's application to the Federal Court was "bereft of any possibility of success"; it was "plain and obvious that the Federal Court lacks jurisdiction over the application".[54] Three of the four dissenting judges disagreed on all three points, holding that the company's constituent Act was a federal law; it was applicable to the dispute; and it would be essential to the company's constitutional claim.[55]

§ 7:12 Tax Court of Canada

The Tax Court of Canada[1] was established in 1983, when it replaced an administrative tribunal, the Tax Review Board. The primary jurisdiction of the Tax Court is to hear income tax appeals.

§ 7:13 Territorial courts

For the sake of completeness it should also be mentioned that the

---

[53]*Windsor v. Canadian Transit Co.*, [2016] 2 S.C.R. 617, 2016 SCC 54. Karakatsanis J. wrote the opinion of the five-judge majority. Moldaver and Brown JJ. (with Côté J.) wrote a dissenting opinion. Abella J. wrote a separate dissenting opinion.

[54]*Windsor v. Canadian Transit Co.*, [2016] 2 S.C.R. 617, 2016 SCC 54, para. 72.

[55]*Windsor v. Canadian Transit Co.*, [2016] 2 S.C.R. 617, 2016 SCC 54, para. 118. Abella J. dissented separately, holding that a stay should be issued in the Federal-Court proceedings because the provincial superior court was the preferable venue to resolve the issues.

[Section 7:12]

[1]Tax Court of Canada Act, R.S.C. 1985, c. T-2.

federal Parliament has provided for a system of courts for each of the three federal territories, the Northwest Territories, Yukon and Nunavut.[1] These courts are analogous to provincial courts, but of course they have to be established by the federal Parliament because it has plenary legislative powers over the three territories.[2]

§ 7:14 Appointment, payment and tenure of federal judges

Do the provisions of ss. 96 to 100 of the Constitution Act, 1867, dealing with appointment, payment and tenure of higher court judges, apply to the Supreme Court of Canada, the Federal Court of Appeal, the Federal Court, the Tax Court of Canada and the higher territorial courts?[1] There is no doubt that those courts are "superior courts". However, ss. 96 to 98, concerning appointment, are clearly confined to provincial courts, and s. 100, concerning salaries, should probably be read in the same sense. This reading of the sections is reinforced by the language of s. 101, which gives the federal Parliament power to create federal courts "notwithstanding anything in this Act".[2] In my opinion, therefore, ss. 96 to 100 of the Constitution Act, 1867 do not apply to the federal courts.[3] It follows that the federal Parliament could if it chose confer appointing power on some body other than the Governor General (despite s. 96), it could authorize the appointment of judges who were not members of the bar (despite ss. 97 and 98), and it could leave the judges' salaries to be determined administratively (despite s. 100).[4]

The Parliament has done none of these things. The constituent stat-

---

[Section 7:13]

[1]Northwest Territories Act, R.S.C. 1985, c. N-27, Part II; Yukon Act, S.C. 2002, c. 7, ss. 38–44; Nunavut Act, S.C. 1993, c. 28, ss. 31–36.

[2]Constitution Act, 1871, s. 4.

[Section 7:14]

[1]All these federal courts are expressly declared to be superior courts, although this status was only conferred on the Tax Court of Canada with effect in 2003, 20 years after its creation: S.C. 2002, c. 8, s. 60.

[2]A possible response to this latter point is given in the text accompanying § 7:14 note 8, below.

[3]*R. v. Can. Labour Relations Bd.; Ex parte Federal Elec. Corp.* (1964), 44 D.L.R. (2d) 440, 462-463 (Man. Q.B.) (federal administrative agency); *Papp v. Papp*, [1970] 1 O.R. 331, 339 (C.A.) (Master); *A.-G. Can. v. Canard*, [1976] 1 S.C.R. 170, 176 (federal minister), but compare the more guarded language at 202–203, 210; Laskin, Canadian Constitutional Law (5th ed., 1986 by Finkelstein), 112. Contra, *C.I.B.C. v. Rifou*, [1986] 3 F.C. 486, 491, 493, but Stone J. dissented on this issue at 515 (C.A.); W.R. Lederman "The Independence of the Judiciary" (1956) 34 Can. Bar Rev. 1139, 1176; R. Elliot, Comment (1984) 18 U.B.C.L. Rev. 127. Note, however, that the federal Parliament may not be able to confer a s. 96 function on a *provincially-established* court or tribunal: *McEvoy v. A.-G.N.B.*, [1983] 1 S.C.R. 704; discussed in ch. 19, Criminal Justice, under heading §§ 19:2 to 19:5, "Courts of criminal jurisdiction".

[4]This interpretation does not leave the independence of judges of the federal courts constitutionally unprotected. The Supreme Court of Canada has recognized an "unwritten constitutional principle" of judicial independence, which protects the judges of all courts, no matter what kind of cases they decide: see § 7:8, "Inferior courts of civil juris-

ute of each of the federal courts (including the Tax Court) confers appointing power on the Governor in Council, and requires that an appointee either be a judge of a superior, district or county court in Canada, or be a member of at least ten years' standing of a provincial bar; the salaries of all federal judges are "fixed and provided" by the Judges Act,[5] the same statute that fixes and provides the salaries of the s. 96 judges. The conventions with respect to the mode of appointment of s. 96 judges are also observed in appointing federal judges, that is to say, puisne (ordinary) judges are appointed by the cabinet on the recommendation of the Minister of Justice, and the Chief Justices are appointed by the cabinet on the recommendation of the Prime Minister.[6] However, the point that sections 96, 97, 98 and 100 of the Constitution Act, 1867 do not apply is still important, because it means that the federal Parliament, unlike the provincial Legislatures, is not under any constitutional restraint in assigning jurisdiction to federal administrative tribunals or officials (or to federal inferior courts, if it chose to create some): such bodies may be invested with functions of a kind traditionally exercised by a superior, district or county court if the Parliament so enacts.[7]

What about s. 99, the section giving tenure "during good behaviour"? Successive federal governments have taken the view that s. 99 does not apply to the federal courts. Thus, in 1927, when s. 99's guarantee of tenure was unqualified by the retirement provision which was inserted by amendment in 1960, it was provided by ordinary statute that the judges of the Supreme Court must retire at age 75.[8] And after s. 99 was amended to include a subsection providing for the retirement of superior court judges at age 75, the Federal Court Act initially provided that the judges of the Federal Court must retire at age 70.[9] (The retirement age

diction" (discussing *Re Remuneration of Judges*, [1997] 3 S.C.R. 3). In addition, the Court has also held that changes to certain aspects of the Supreme Court of Canada are subject to the formal constitutional amending procedures in Part V of the Constitution Act, 1982: see ch. 8, Supreme Court of Canada, under heading § 8:1, "Establishment of Court" (discussing *Re Supreme Court Act, ss. 5 and 6*, [2014] 1 S.C.R. 433).

[5]R.S.C. 1985, c. J-1.

[6]Russell, The Judiciary in Canada (1987), 112. Note, however, that there is a special process that applies to appointments to the Supreme Court of Canada: see ch. 8, Supreme Court of Canada, under heading § 8:4, "Appointment of judges".

[7]For the limits on provincial power to do these things, because of implications drawn judicially from s. 96, see §§ 7:15 to 7:20, "Implications of Constitution's judicature sections", below. With respect to the limits on federal power, see § 7:14 notes 2 to 5 and accompanying text, above; but also see the text accompanying § 7:20 notes 18 to 25, below, discussing cases that suggest that the federal Parliament is also constitutionally constrained in its ability to assign jurisdiction to federal administrative tribunals or officials (or federal inferior courts, if it chose to create some).

[8]S.C. 1926-27, c. 38, s. 2.

[9]S.C. 1970-71-72, c. 1, s. 8. This provision was held to be unconstitutional in *Addy v. The Queen*, [1985] 2 F.C. 452 (T.D.), on the basis that s. 99 applied to federal as well as provincial superior courts. The federal government did not appeal, and s. 8 of the Federal Court Act was amended to raise the retirement age to 75: S.C. 1987, c. 21, s. 7.

has since been let out to 75, in line with all other federal judges.)[10] The arguments in favour of the federal government's position would be, no doubt, that (1) the term "superior court" in s. 99 takes its colour from the previous sections which are rather clearly limited to provincial "superior, district or county courts", and (2) the phrase in s. 101, "notwithstanding anything in this Act", exempts all federal courts from other provisions of the Constitution Act, 1867. These arguments are strong, but not conclusive. The term "superior court" in s. 99 could be read as applying to all superior courts in Canada; and the notwithstanding clause in s. 101 is primarily designed to override s. 92(14) (giving to the provinces the exclusive power to legislate for "the administration of justice in the province") and need not be read as overriding provisions such as s. 99 which are not directly inconsistent with s. 101.[11]

Felipa v. Minister of Citizenship and Immigration (2010),[12] was a constitutional challenge to a proceeding in the Federal Court which was presided over by a "deputy judge" who was over 75 years of age. Since the Federal Court is a superior court, it was argued that s. 99(2) of the Constitution Act, 1867, which provides for the mandatory retirement at age 75 of judges of "superior courts", prohibited anyone over 75 from acting as a judge of the Federal Court. The Federal Courts Act, by s. 10, empowers the Chief Justice of the Federal Court to appoint former judges to act as "deputy judges" of the Court. Deputy judges (which do not exist in the provincial superior courts) are temporary judges who are appointed to assist with the workload of the Court. They have all the powers of a full-time Federal Court judge. They are often over the age of 75. Lufty C.J. of the Federal Court rejected the constitutional argument, holding that s. 99(2) was inapplicable to judges of the Federal Court.[13] He held that the term "superior court" in s. 99 was restricted by its context and history to the superior courts of the provinces and was inapplicable to the superior courts created by Parliament under s. 101. And he held that the phrase "notwithstanding anything in this Act" in s. 101 reinforced the restricted interpretation of s. 99. Therefore, s. 99(2) did not impose any upper limit on the age of judges of federal superior courts.[14] This meant, of course, that the constitutional guarantee of independence in s. 99(1) was also inapplicable to judges of federal superior courts, but Lufty C.J. pointed out that the independence of judges who

[10]Previous note.

[11]W.R. Lederman, "The Independence of the Judiciary" (1956) 34 Can. Bar Rev. 769, 789, 1176, argues that s. 99 is applicable to the federal superior court judges. This position is supported by *Addy v. The Queen*, [1985] 2 F.C. 452 (T.D.).

[12]*Felipa v. Minister of Citizenship and Immigration*, 2010 FC 89 (Lufty C.J.).

[13]He also held (para. 135) that the provision for mandatory retirement of judges at age 75 in s. 8(2) of the Federal Courts Act was inapplicable on the ground that deputy judges, although they acted as judges, did not "hold office" as judges.

[14]He refused (paras. 92–98) to follow *Addy v. The Queen*, [1985] 2 F.C. 452 (T.D.).

were not covered by s. 99(1) was constitutionally protected by the unwritten principle of judicial independence.[15]

Lufty C.J.'s decision was overturned on appeal to the Federal Court of Appeal.[16] However, Sharlow and Dawson JJ.A., who wrote for the majority of the Court of Appeal, based their decision on an interpretation of s. 10 of the Federal Courts Act, concluding that, properly interpreted, s. 10 did not empower the Chief Justice of the Federal Court to appoint former judges to act as "deputy judges" of the Federal Court. They expressly declined to decide whether s. 99 of the Constitution Act, 1867 applies to the federal courts.[17] Even so, they did say that they considered it "arguable that section 101 judges are within the scope of sections 96, 99 and 100 insofar as those provisions state the elements of the constitutional guarantees of judicial independence".[18] Stratas J.A. dissented. He said that, properly interpreted, s. 10 of the Act did allow former judges to be appointed as "deputy judges" of the Federal Court. In addition, unlike his colleagues, he went on to consider whether s. 99 applies to the federal courts, agreeing with Lufty C.J.'s conclusion that it does not. Like Lufty C.J., he emphasized that this conclusion did not mean that the independence of judges of the federal courts was constitutionally unprotected; federal court judges, he said, are protected by the unwritten constitutional principle of judicial independence.[19]

III. IMPLICATIONS OF CONSTITUTION'S JUDICATURE SECTIONS

§ 7:15 Separation of powers

There is no general "separation of powers" in the Constitution Act, 1867. The Act does not separate the legislative, executive and judicial functions and insist that each branch of government exercise only "its own" function. As between the legislative and executive branches, any separation of powers would make little sense in a system of responsible government;[1] and it is clearly established that the Act does not call for any such separation.[2] As between the judicial and the two political branches, there is likewise no general separation of powers. Either the Parliament or the Legislatures may by appropriate legislation confer non-judicial functions on the courts and (with one important exception,

---

[15]*Felipa v. Minister of Citizenship and Immigration*, 2010 FC 89, para. 99. This was one reason for refusing to follow *Addy*, which had been decided in 1985 before the unwritten principle was discovered in *Re Remuneration of Judges*, [1997] 3 S.C.R. 3.

[16]*Felipa v. Can.*, [2012] 1 F.C.R. 3 (C.A.). Sharlow and Dawson JJ.A. wrote the opinion for the majority of the three-judge panel of the Court. Stratas J.A. wrote a dissenting opinion.

[17]*Felipa v. Can.*, [2012] 1 F.C.R. 3 (C.A.), para. 76.

[18]*Felipa v. Can.*, [2012] 1 F.C.R. 3 (C.A.), para. 78.

[19]*Felipa v. Can.*, [2012] 1 F.C.R. 3 (C.A.), para. 151.

[Section 7:15]

[1]See ch. 9, Responsible Government, under heading § 9:12, "The Cabinet".

[2]See ch. 14, Delegation, under heading § 14:5, "Delegation of legislative power".

to be discussed) may confer judicial functions on bodies that are not courts.

Each Canadian jurisdiction has conferred non-judicial functions on its courts, by enacting a statute which enables the government to refer a question of law to the courts for an advisory opinion.[3] The rendering of advisory opinions to government is traditionally an "executive" function, performed by the law officers of the government. For that reason, the Supreme Court of the United States and the High Court of Australia have refused to render advisory opinions, reasoning that a separation of powers doctrine in their Constitutions confines the courts to the traditional judicial function of adjudicating upon genuine controversies. But in the *Reference Appeal* (1912),[4] the Privy Council refused to read any such limitation into Canada's Constitution. Their lordships upheld the federal reference statute, apparently as a law in relation to the Supreme Court of Canada (s. 101). In the *Secession Reference* (1998),[5] the Supreme Court of Canada affirmed this ruling, holding that the reference jurisdiction was authorized by s. 101, and that "there is no constitutional bar to this Court's receipt of jurisdiction to undertake such an advisory role". The validity of the provincial reference statutes has never been squarely ruled on, but they are undoubtedly valid as laws in relation to the administration of justice in the province (s. 92(14)).

The conferral of judicial functions on bodies which are not courts is likewise subject to no general prohibition. However, here there is an important qualification to be made. The courts have held that the provincial Legislatures may not confer on a body other than a superior, district or county court judicial functions analogous to those performed by a superior, district or county court.[6] This little separation of powers doctrine has been developed to preclude evasion of the stipulations of ss. 96 to 100 of the Constitution Act, 1867.

If ss. 96 to 100 of the Constitution Act, 1867 were read literally, they could easily be evaded by a province which wanted to assume control of its judicial appointments. The province could increase the jurisdiction of its inferior courts so that they assumed much of the jurisdiction of the higher courts; or the province could vest higher-court jurisdiction in a newly-established tribunal, and call that tribunal an inferior court or an administrative tribunal. It is therefore not surprising that the courts have added a gloss to s. 96 and the associated constitutional provisions.

---

[3] See ch. 8, Supreme Court of Canada, under heading §§ 8:8 to 8:12, "Reference jurisdiction", where authority is provided for the statements in the text.

[4] *A.-G. Ont. v. A.-G. Can.* (Reference Appeal) [1912] A.C. 571.

[5] *Secession Reference*, [1998] 2 S.C.R. 217, para. 15.

[6] There is a strong argument that the federal Parliament is not subject to a similar limitation, at least in relation to *federal* administrative tribunals or officials (or federal inferior courts, if it chose to create some): see § 7:14, "Appointment, payment and tenure of federal judges". However, the Supreme Court of Canada has nonetheless seemingly extended a similar limitation to the federal Parliament as well: see § 7:20 notes 18 to 25, and accompanying text, below.

What they have said is this: if a province invests a tribunal with a jurisdiction of a kind that ought properly to belong to a superior, district or county court, then that tribunal, whatever its official name, is for constitutional purposes a superior, district or county court and must satisfy the requirements of s. 96 and the associated provisions of the Constitution Act, 1867. This means that such a tribunal will be invalidly constituted, unless its members (1) are appointed by the federal government in conformity with s. 96, (2) are drawn from the bar of the province in conformity with ss. 97 and 98, and (3) receive salaries that are fixed and provided by the federal Parliament in conformity with s. 100.

So far the law is clear, and the policy underlying it is comprehensible. But the difficulty lies in the definition of those functions that ought properly to belong to a superior, district or county court. The courts have attempted to fashion a judicially enforceable rule which would separate "s. 96 functions" from other adjudicatory functions. The attempt has not been successful, and it is difficult to predict with confidence how the courts will characterize particular adjudicatory functions. The uncertainty of the law, with its risk of nullification, could be a serious deterrent to the conferral of new adjudicatory functions on inferior courts or administrative tribunals, and a consequent impediment to much new regulatory or social policy. For the most part, the courts have exercised restraint in reviewing the provincial statutes which create new adjudicatory jurisdictions, so that the difficulty has not been as serious as it could have been. However, in the late twentieth century there was a regrettable resurgence of s. 96 litigation: six challenges to the powers of inferior courts or tribunals based on s. 96 succeeded in the Supreme Court of Canada,[7] and these decisions spawned many more challenges. These developments are described in the text that follows.

§ 7:16 Inferior courts

In the *Adoption Reference* (1938),[1] the Supreme Court of Canada had to pass on the validity of four Ontario statutes concerning adoption, neglected children, illegitimate children and deserted wives. This batch of social legislation gave rise to constitutional doubt because each statute conferred a new-jurisdiction upon inferior courts presided over by justices of the peace or magistrates—officials who were appointed by the province. In a long and scholarly opinion written for the whole Court, Duff C.J. upheld the grants of new jurisdiction. He pointed out that s. 96 contemplated the existence of inferior courts whose judges could be appointed and paid by the province, and who need not be drawn from

---

[7] *A.-G. Que. v. Farrah*, [1978] 2 S.C.R. 638; *Re Residential Tenancies Act*, [1981] 1 S.C.R. 714; *Crevier v. A.-G. Que.*, [1981] 2 S.C.R. 220; *Re B.C. Family Relations Act*, [1982] 1 S.C.R. 62; *McEvoy v. A.-G. N.B.*, [1983] 1 S.C.R. 704; *MacMillan Bloedel v. Simpson*, [1995] 4 S.C.R. 725. Since the abolition of Privy Council appeals, two other challenges have also been successful, namely, *A.-G. Ont. v. Victoria Medical Building*, [1960] S.C.R. 32; *Seminary of Chi-coutimi v. A.-G. Que.*, [1973] S.C.R. 681.

[Section 7:16]

[1] *Re Adoption Act*, [1938] S.C.R. 398.

the ranks of the bar. The jurisdiction of these courts was not to be frozen at the limits in existence in 1867. Increases in their jurisdiction, or the establishment of new inferior courts, were within the legislative competence of the provinces. The only qualification to this power was that the new jurisdiction must "broadly conform to a type of jurisdiction generally exercisable by courts of summary conviction rather than the jurisdiction exercised by courts within the purview of s. 96".[2] In this case the provisions for making adoption orders, for enforcing obligations to maintain wives and children, for protecting neglected children and for trying juvenile offenders, were more closely analogous to traditional inferior-court jurisdiction than to higher-court jurisdiction.

In *Re B.C. Family Relations Act* (1982),[3] the Supreme Court of Canada followed the *Adoption Reference* and upheld inferior-court jurisdiction over guardianship and custody, reasoning that, once adoption had been admitted to inferior-court jurisdiction, the lesser orders of guardianship and custody should not be treated differently. However, the Court struck down provisions purporting to confer on an inferior court the power to make orders with respect to the occupancy of (and access to) the family residence. This power was "more conformable to that exercised and exercisable by a s. 96 court", because it involved the adjudication of "proprietary rights" and the granting of relief "akin to injunctive relief".[4]

The test of "broad conformity" or "analogy", while providing a test for the allocation of new forms of jurisdiction, might be thought to prevent increases in traditional inferior-court jurisdiction which have the effect of transferring some higher-court jurisdiction to an inferior court.[5] This is the effect of an increase in the pecuniary limit of inferior-court jurisdiction, for example. But in *Re Quebec Magistrate's Court* (1965),[6] the Supreme Court upheld an increase in the jurisdiction of the Quebec Magistrate's Court from $200 to $500. This was a very modest increase, since the $200 limit dated from the establishment of the court in 1869. The Supreme Court had little trouble in determining that the increase in jurisdiction, "when considered in the light of the current value of the dollar", was constitutional; and the Court made clear that reasonable

---

[2]*Re Adoption Act*, [1938] S.C.R. 398, 421.

[3]*Re B.C. Family Relations Act*, [1982] 1 S.C.R. 62. See also *Ont. v. Pembina Exploration*, [1989] 1 S.C.R. 206 (admiralty jurisdiction was not exercised by superior, district or county courts at confederation); *Re Young Offenders Act*, [1991] 1 S.C.R. 252 (youth court jurisdiction was exercised by inferior courts at confederation).

[4]*Re B.C. Family Relations Act*, [1982] 1 S.C.R. 62, 87–91.

[5]Note the more liberal way in which the test has been framed for administrative tribunals (as opposed to inferior courts) in *Re Residential Tenancies Act*, [1981] 1 S.C.R. 714; discussed at § 7:19 note 4. In particular, the three-step test proposed in that case seems irrelevant to inferior courts, since their functions are nearly always judicial (step (2)), and an inferior court has no different expertise, resources or procedures than a s. 96 court has (step (3)). However, in *Re Young Offenders Act*, [1991] 1 S.C.R. 252, a majority of the Court did apply the three-step test to an inferior court, although La Forest J. took the view that steps (2) and (3) were inapplicable.

[6]*Re Quebec Magistrate's Court*, [1965] S.C.R. 772 (opinion of Fauteux J. for the Court in French), (1965) 55 D.L.R. (2d) 701 (translation).

increases in inferior-court jurisdiction were within the *Adoption Reference* ruling.[7]

Quebec has had less success with another of its increases in inferior-court jurisdiction. In *Seminary of Chicoutimi v. A.-G. Que.* (1972),[8] the Supreme Court of Canada held that a transfer from the Quebec Superior Court to the Provincial Court of the power to quash municipal by-laws on grounds of illegality was unconstitutional. Fauteux C.J., who wrote the opinion for the Court, contented himself with the finding that the quashing of municipal by-laws had since before confederation been within the jurisdiction of s. 96 courts in Quebec. For this reason, without more, he held that the *Adoption Reference* test of "broad conformity" to inferior-court jurisdiction was not satisfied. The power to quash municipal by-laws could only be conferred upon a court which satisfied the stipulations of s. 96 of the Constitution Act, 1867. This reasoning is remarkably sparse. After all, in *Re Quebec Magistrate's Court*, it could have been said with equal truth that jurisdiction over pecuniary claims between $200 and $500 had always been exercised in Quebec by s. 96 courts. If the decline in the value of the dollar since confederation could justify an increase in the pecuniary limit, surely the vast increase in municipal functions and the consequent proliferation of bylaws since confederation might also justify the introduction of a speedier and cheaper means of testing the legality of by-laws. Perhaps in answer to this argument it could be said (although Fauteux C.J. did not say it) that the supervisory jurisdiction of the superior courts over inferior statutory bodies (such as municipalities) is too fundamental a guarantee of government according to law to be entrusted to a court constituted without the constitutional protections of ss. 96 to 100 of the Constitution Act, 1867.[9]

---

[7]After the decision, Quebec rapidly further enlarged the jurisdiction of the Magistrate's Court, which became the Provincial Court and is now called the Court of Québec, from the increased limit of $500 to $1,000 (1965), and then to $3,000 (1969), and then to $6,000 (1979), and then to $10,000 (1982), and then to $15,000 (1984), and then to $30,000 (1995), and then to $70,000 (2002): see Code of Civil Procedure, R.S.Q. 1977, c. C-25, art. 34, as amended. In 2016, a new Code of Civil Procedure came into effect in Quebec, which increased the limit yet again to $85,000: see Code of Civil Procedure, C.Q.L.R. c. C-25.01, art. 35. In 2019, the Quebec Court of Appeal held that the new limit of $85,000 was invalid: *Re Court of Québec*, 2019 QCCA 1492. The Court of Appeal indicated that "in order to respect section 96 of the Constitution Act, 1867, the maximum limit for the civil jurisdiction of the Court of Québec must fall between $55,000 and $70,000": *Re Court of Québec*, 2019 QCCA 1492, para. 188. The Court of Appeal suspended the implementation of its decision for one year, and the Supreme Court of Canada stayed the decision pending the resolution of an appeal. As of the time of writing, the Supreme Court's decision in the appeal had not been released. The Supreme Court's decision will be important, as other provinces have also substantially increased the jurisdiction of their Provincial Courts (although, as the Court of Appeal's decision makes clear (para. 146), none have done so as much as Quebec).

[8]*Seminary of Chicoutimi v. A.-G. Que.*, [1973] S.C.R. 681.

[9]See the subsequent case of *Crevier v. A.-G. Que.*, [1981] 2 S.C.R. 220.

In *McEvoy v. A.-G. N.B.* (1983),[10] the Supreme Court of Canada held that the federal Parliament could not confer jurisdiction over all indictable offences on a provincial inferior court (a proposed "unified criminal court"), because the trial of indictable offences was within superior-court jurisdiction in 1867. Unfortunately, the Court did not indicate any awareness of the fact that the Criminal Code then (and now) conferred on provincial inferior courts jurisdiction over nearly all indictable offences. These jurisdictional provisions, although they have been upheld in earlier cases, are now vulnerable to attack on s. 96 grounds.[11]

In *MacMillan Bloedel v. Simpson* (1995),[12] the Supreme Court of Canada had to review a provision in the federal Young Offenders Act that purported to give the youth court of each province exclusive jurisdiction over "every contempt of court committed by a young person" except where the contempt was committed "in the face" of a court other than the youth court. The accused in *MacMillan Bloedel* was a 16-year-old boy who had disobeyed an injunction that had been issued by the Supreme Court of British Columbia (a superior court) and had therefore acted in contempt of that court. Since the contempt had not been committed "in the face" of the superior court, the Young Offenders Act purported to confer exclusive jurisdiction over the offence on the youth court. But the Supreme Court of Canada, by a majority, held that Parliament was barred from transferring to an inferior court (the youth court) exclusive jurisdiction over contempt committed against a superior court. The majority's reasoning to this result broke new ground. They held that there was a guaranteed core of superior-court jurisdiction which could not be removed from a superior court under any circumstances. The power of a superior court to punish contempts against itself, whether in the face of the court or outside the face of the court, was part of that guaranteed core. Therefore, it was contrary to s. 96 of the Constitution Act, 1867 to give *exclusive* jurisdiction to the youth court over a contempt committed against a superior court.

Before the *MacMillan Bloedel* case, the jurisprudence on the application of s. 96 to inferior courts had proceeded on a different track from the cases dealing with administrative tribunals. That is the reason why the present section of this chapter deals with inferior courts and a later section deals with administrative tribunals. As we shall see in that later section, the Supreme Court of Canada in *Re Residential Tenancies Act* (1981)[13] developed a rule (involving a three-step test) for the validity of a conferral of jurisdiction on administrative tribunals, but did not gener-

---

[10] *McEvoy v. A.-G. N.B.*, [1983] 1 S.C.R. 704.

[11] The prior cases had finessed the s. 96 issue by applying the rule that the federal Parliament was not bound by s. 96. *McEvoy*'s sudden rejection of that rule, and the implications for the present Criminal Code provisions, are discussed in ch. 19, Criminal Justice, under heading §§ 19:2 to 19:5, "Courts of criminal jurisdiction".

[12] *MacMillan Bloedel v. Simpson*, [1995] 4 S.C.R. 725. The majority opinion of Lamer C.J. was concurred in by La Forest, Sopinka, Gonthier and Cory JJ.; the dissenting opinion of McLachlin J. was concurred in by L'Heureux-Dube, Iacobucci and Major JJ.

[13] § 7:19 note 4 and accompanying text, below.

ally use that test in cases involving inferior courts. In the *MacMillan Bloedel* case, both the majority and the minority assumed that the *Residential Tenancies* rule was the appropriate one to test the validity of the jurisdiction of the youth court. All judges applied that rule, and all judges held that the youth court's jurisdiction did not offend s. 96 on the basis of that rule. For the minority, that resolved the issue in favour of the validity of the youth court's jurisdiction over contempt. However, the majority went on to add a new requirement to the rule in *Residential Tenancies*, namely, the requirement that there be no breach of the guaranteed core of superior-court jurisdiction. On the basis of this new requirement, the majority struck down the youth court's exclusive jurisdiction over contempt. Obviously, the rule establishing a guaranteed core of superior-court jurisdiction could be broken by a grant of exclusive jurisdiction to an administrative tribunal as well as to an inferior court. Therefore, a convergence of the inferior-court cases and the administrative-law cases has occurred. The validity of grants of jurisdiction to both inferior courts and administrative tribunals is now to be tested by the same rules: the *Residential Tenancies* rule supplemented by the rule that guarantees a core of superior-court jurisdiction.[14] Both these rules are more fully described in the later section of this chapter headed "Administrative tribunals".[15]

§ 7:17 County or district courts

After confederation, the jurisdiction of county and district courts was steadily increased, to the point that in some provinces it became almost co-extensive with that of the superior courts. The cases so far discussed invite the question of whether the transfer of superior court powers to the district and county courts was constitutionally valid. County and district courts were s. 96 courts so that the federal appointment power would not have been violated by such transfers. But it will be recalled that s. 99 guarantees only the tenure of superior court judges. By analogy with the s. 96 reasoning, could it not be argued that s. 99 was offended when district or county court judges, whose tenure was not constitutionally guaranteed, decided cases which were traditionally decided by superior courts? The expansion of county and district court jurisdiction was never challenged,[1] however, and this question will not

[14] Accord, *R. v. Ahmad*, [2011] 1 S.C.R. 110, paras. 57–65 (applying the rules to uphold a grant of exclusive jurisdiction over disclosure of privileged documents to Federal Court, even though the criminal trial in which the documents were relevant was in the superior court of the province). Note that the jurisdiction taken away from the superior court of the province was vested in the Federal Court, which is itself a *superior* court, although one not covered by s. 96.

[15] § 7:19, "Administrative tribunals".

[Section 7:17]

[1] In *Re Adoption Act*, [1938] S.C.R. 398, 416–417, Duff C.J. asserted, obiter, that increases in district or county court jurisdiction were not constitutionally vulnerable. Compare *A.-G. B.C. v. McKenzie*, [1965] S.C.R. 490, 498–499 (upholding appointment of

be answered as the county and district courts have now been eliminated in all of the provinces which once had them.[2]

§ 7:18 Superior courts

Section 96 and the other judicature provisions of the Constitution Act, 1867 do not impose any constraints on the jurisdiction that can be conferred on a *superior* court. A superior court is, of course, subject to the maximum constitutional protection. Therefore, there is no constitutional objection to the conferral on a superior court of a novel jurisdiction, or a jurisdiction traditionally exercised by inferior courts.[1] Note, however, that, according to the narrow majority in *MacMillan Bloedel v. Simpson* (1995),[2] there are constitutional restrictions on the jurisdiction that can be *withdrawn* from a superior court. No part of an ill-defined "core" of superior-court jurisdiction may be withdrawn from a superior court.[3] Apart from this exception, the nature and scope of superior-court jurisdiction are simply issues of policy to be resolved and enacted by the competent legislative body.[4]

The notion that no part of the "core" of superior-court jurisdiction may be withdrawn from a superior court was accepted and given an unexpectedly robust interpretation in *Trial Lawyers' Association of British Columbia v. British Columbia* (2014).[5] In that case, the Supreme Court held, by a majority, that s. 96 invalidated a rule of the superior court of British Columbia that imposed hearing fees on litigants. The party who set down a case for trial (normally the plaintiff) was required to undertake to pay fees on a sliding scale that increased with the length of the trial and came to $3,500 for a ten-day trial, which was the length of the trial that was the subject of the litigation. The obligation to pay the fees was subject to an exception for a plaintiff who was on public assistance or was "otherwise impoverished". The plaintiff in this case was not on public assistance, but she was a person of modest means and the hearing fee represented a month of her income. The Supreme Court held

---

county court judges as local judges of the superior court, despite lack of independence guarantee for judges); *Re Judicature Amendment Act, 1970 (No. 4)*, [1971] 2 O.R. 521 (C.A.) (same decision). These cases were discussed at more length in the 2nd edition of this book (1985), 154–155.

[2]See § 7:1, "Establishment of provincial courts".

[Section 7:18]

[1]*Re Young Offenders Act*, [1991] 1 S.C.R. 252, 274 (and answer to question 3(b)(ii) of the reference).

[2]*MacMillan Bloedel v. Simpson*, [1995] 4 S.C.R. 725.

[3]*MacMillan Bloedel v. Simpson*, [1995] 4 S.C.R. 725, para. 42. Lamer C.J. even said that a transfer of a core power to another superior court would be unconstitutional.

[4]Even non-judicial functions can be conferred: § 7:15 note 3 and accompanying text, above.

[5]*Trial Lawyers' Association of British Columbia v. British Columbia*, [2014] 3 S.C.R. 31, 2014 SCC 59. McLachlin C.J. wrote the majority opinion for five members of the seven-judge bench. Cromwell J. wrote a concurring opinion. Rothstein J. wrote a dissenting opinion.

that she was not "impoverished", and was therefore not within the express exception to the hearing-fee scheme. However, McLachlin C.J. who wrote for the majority, found that the plaintiff could not afford to pay the fee for her trial and that the hearing-fee scheme had the effect of denying access to the courts to persons of modest means like the plaintiff. The Chief Justice agreed that the province, under its power over "the administration of justice in the province" (s. 92(14)), had the power to levy (or authorize its courts to levy) hearing fees for the purposes of defraying some of the cost of court services, encouraging the efficient use of court resources, and discouraging frivolous resort to the courts. However, this power was limited by s. 96, and s. 96 should be interpreted as prohibiting hearing fees that had the effect of denying some prospective litigants access to the superior courts: measures that deny access to the superior courts "infringe the core jurisdiction of the superior courts".[6] This conclusion was also supported by "the underlying principle of the rule of law."[7] The Chief Justice refused to "read in" a wider exemption from the hearing-fee scheme (as the Court of Appeal had done),[8] and held that the hearing-fee scheme was unconstitutional. Cromwell J. concurred with the majority, but on administrative-law grounds, not commenting on the constitutional ground relied on by the majority. Rothstein J. dissented, describing the majority view as "an overly broad reading" and a "novel reading" of s. 96; his view was that "no aspect of the core jurisdiction of superior courts is removed by legislation that merely places limits on access to superior courts."[9]

§ 7:19 Administrative tribunals

The last 100 years have seen a great increase in the number of administrative tribunals in Canada (and elsewhere), to the point that administrative tribunals undoubtedly decide more cases and probably dispose of more dollars than do the ordinary courts. The cause of this development is the vast increase in social and economic regulation which has occurred in the last 100 years. The novel tasks of adjudication which are entailed by new schemes of regulation have commonly been entrusted to administrative tribunals rather than to the courts. Some of the reasons for this preference can be identified. First is the desire for a specialist body: specially qualified personnel can be appointed to a tribunal, and those who do not start off specially qualified can acquire

---

[6] *Trial Lawyers' Association of British Columbia v. British Columbia*, [2014] 3 S.C.R. 31, 2014 SCC 59, para. 32.

[7] *Trial Lawyers' Association of British Columbia v. British Columbia*, [2014] 3 S.C.R. 31, 2014 SCC 59, para. 64. The rule-of-law reasons are discussed in ch. 15, Judicial Review on Federal Grounds, under heading § 15:28, "Unwritten constitutional principles".

[8] *Trial Lawyers' Association of British Columbia v. British Columbia*, [2014] 3 S.C.R. 31, 2014 SCC 59, para. 66. The reading-in reasons are discussed in ch. 40, Enforcement of Rights, under heading § 40:6, "Reading in".

[9] *Trial Lawyers' Association of British Columbia v. British Columbia*, [2014] 3 S.C.R. 31, 2014 SCC 59, paras. 81, 86, 90.

experience and expertise in the field of regulation (whether it be labour relations, marketing of agricultural products, transportation, broadcasting, liquor licensing, or whatever). Second is the desire for innovation: a tribunal can be given broad discretion to develop the policies and remedies required to implement a new scheme of regulation (such as foreign investment review, control of pay television). Third is the desire for initiative: a tribunal (such as a human rights commission or a securities commission) can be given power to initiate proceedings, to undertake investigations, to do research, and to play an educative and policy-formulating role as well as an adjudicative one. Fourth is the problem of volume: if adjudication is required with great frequency (as in workers' compensation, unemployment insurance, immigration, income tax objections, for example), the tribunal can develop procedures to handle a case-load that would choke the ordinary court system. Fifth is economy: a tribunal can be structured and mandated to be less formal, speedier and less expensive than the ordinary courts (although in many fields the complexity of the issues and the sums at stake preclude this kind of advantage).[1]

When the advantages of administrative adjudication are reviewed, it is easy to see why legislative bodies have chosen to confer many adjudicative functions on administrative tribunals rather than the ordinary courts. But the ordinary courts, through their exegesis of s. 96 and the other judicature sections of the Constitution Act, 1867, have assumed the power to review legislation investing a provincially-established administrative tribunal[2] with adjudicative functions: if those functions ought properly to belong to a superior, district or county court, then the legislation will be unconstitutional.[3] By this means, the courts have erected constitutional barriers to legislative encroachments on their own traditional functions.

The leading case on the impact of s. 96 on the creation of provincial administrative tribunals is the decision of the Supreme Court of Canada

[Section 7:19]

[1]I have attempted to formulate a division of functions between administrative tribunals and courts in P.W. Hogg, "Judicial Review: How Much Do We Need?" (1974) 20 McGill L.J. 157.

[2]There is a strong argument that the federal Parliament is not subject to a similar limitation, at least in relation to *federally-established* administrative tribunals: see § 7:14, "Appointment, payment and tenure of federal judges". However, the Supreme Court of Canada has nonetheless seemingly extended a similar limitation to the federal Parliament as well: see § 7:20 notes 18 to 25, and accompanying text, below.

[3]Unconstitutionality would be avoided, of course, if the tribunal's members (1) are appointed by the federal government in conformity with s. 96, (2) are drawn from the bar of the province in conformity with ss. 97 and 98, and (3) receive salaries which are fixed and provided by the federal Parliament in conformity with s. 100. So far as I am aware, no province has ever attempted to establish a tribunal on these terms, which would normally be inconsistent with the purposes of establishing a tribunal in the first place, and which would in any case have to be agreed to and implemented by the federal government.

in *Re Residential Tenancies Act* (1981).[4] In that case, Dickson J. for the Court suggested a three-step approach to the resolution of a s. 96 challenge to an administrative tribunal's powers.[5] The first step is an historical inquiry into whether the impugned power broadly conforms to a power exercised by a superior, district or county court at confederation. The second step, reached only if the answer to the historical inquiry is yes, is an inquiry into whether the impugned power is a "judicial" power. The third step, reached only if the answer to both the historical inquiry and the judicial inquiry is yes, is an inquiry into whether the power in its institutional setting has changed its character sufficiently to negate the broad conformity with superior, district or county court jurisdiction.

The first step—the historical inquiry—involves an investigation of whether the impugned power was one that was within the powers of a superior, district or county court at confederation. A negative answer to this inquiry will resolve the s. 96 issue in favour of the validity of the power without the necessity to proceed to steps (2) and (3).[6]

For a tribunal's power to be held to be a s. 96 power at confederation, it is clear that the impugned power must have been within the *exclusive* jurisdiction of s. 96 courts at confederation. If there was even concurrent jurisdiction in inferior courts or tribunals at confederation, then this will lead to a negative answer to the historical inquiry.[7] This rule places great weight on the way in which the impugned power is characterized. For example, a tribunal's remedial powers may have been within the exclusive jurisdiction of s. 96 courts at confederation,[8] while its subject-matter jurisdiction was only concurrent. And with respect to subject-matter, jurisdiction can be expressed broadly (e.g., labour relations), which may give rise to concurrent jurisdiction, or narrowly (e.g., unjust dismissal), which may not. In *Sobeys Stores v. Yeomans* (1989),[9] which was a challenge to a reinstatement order made by a labour standards tribunal, Wilson J. for the majority of the Supreme Court of Canada recognized the existence of these choices. She suggested that the Court

---

[4]*Re Residential Tenancies Act*, [1981] 1 S.C.R. 714.

[5]*Re Residential Tenancies Act*, [1981] 1 S.C.R. 714, 734. The three-step test is summarized by Laskin C.J. in *Massey-Ferguson Industries v. Govt. of Sask.*, [1981] 2 S.C.R. 413, 429.

[6]E.g., *Jones v. Edmonton Catholic School Trustees*, [1977] S.C.R. 872 (power of tribunal to resolve assessment disputes was exercised by similar tribunal at Alberta's entry to confederation); *Council of Canadians v. Canada* (2006), 277 D.L.R. (4th) 527 (Ont. C.A.) (power of NAFTA tribunals to resolve disputes arising under international treaty in accordance with international law was not a power exercised by superior, district or county courts at confederation).

[7]*A.-G. Que. v. Grondin*, [1983] 2 S.C.R. 364; *Sobeys Stores v. Yeomans*, [1989] 1 S.C.R. 238; *Re Young Offenders Act*, [1991] 1 S.C.R. 252; *Re Residential Tenancies Act (N.S.)*, [1996] 1 S.C.R. 186.

[8]The character of the remedial powers was the critical issue in *Tomko v. Labour Rels. Bd. (N.S.)*, [1977] 1 S.C.R. 112; *Re Residential Tenancies Act*, [1981] 1 S.C.R. 714; but note *Sobeys Stores v. Yeomans*, [1989] 1 S.C.R. 238, 255 ("It is, in my view, the type of dispute that must guide us and not the particular remedy sought.")

[9]*Sobeys Stores v. Yeomans*, [1989] 1 S.C.R. 238.

should lean in the direction of an affirmative answer to the historical test, that is, a finding that the tribunal's power was within the exclusive powers of a superior, district or county court at confederation, so as to protect the traditional jurisdiction of the s. 96 courts.[10] In that way, the historical inquiry would become a rather low threshold, easily crossed, and the issue of validity would be resolved in steps (2) and (3) of the s. 96 reasoning.

To which jurisdiction, and to which date, is the historical inquiry directed? The ten provinces entered confederation at different times, and the division of jurisdiction between s. 96 courts and inferior courts and tribunals at the time of entry differed from province to province. If the historical inquiry is addressed only to the situation of the province that established the impugned tribunal, then the outcome of the inquiry would not settle the same question for another province. In *Re Residential Tenancies Act* itself, the Court held that certain powers[11] of Ontario's rent tribunal to make orders evicting tenants and to make orders requiring landlords or tenants to comply with the rent control legislation failed all three tests and were accordingly unconstitutional for breach of s. 96. But in *A. G. Que. v. Grondin* (1983),[12] the Supreme Court of Canada upheld essentially similar powers in Quebec's rent tribunal, on the basis that the historical inquiry revealed that in Quebec, unlike Ontario, powers to resolve landlord-tenant disputes, including powers to order specific performance or rescission of the lease, were at the time of confederation possessed by inferior courts as well as superior courts.

The conflicting outcomes of the *Residential Tenancies* and *Grondin* cases made clear that litigation was required to settle the validity of the rent tribunal in each province that had established one.[13] Of course, the same was true for other kinds of tribunals. In *Sobeys Stores v. Yeomans* (1989),[14] a case concerning the power over unjust dismissal of a Nova Scotia labour standards tribunal, Wilson J. for the majority of the Court acknowledged the inconvenience of a single-province historical inquiry, and held that the inquiry "should be expanded somewhat to include examination of the general historical conditions in all four original confederating provinces".[15] Tribunals established in the other six provinces would be subjected to the same test, on the basis that provinces joining confederation after 1867 must be taken to have accepted the

---

[10] *Sobeys Stores v. Yeomans*, [1989] 1 S.C.R. 238, 254. Accord, *Chrysler Can. v. Can.*, [1992] 2 S.C.R. 394, 416 (power to punish for contempt for breach of tribunal's orders within exclusive jurisdiction of s. 96 courts at confederation).

[11] The power to fix rents was not impugned, and could not be impugned: *A.-G. Que. v. Grondin*, [1983] 2 S.C.R. 364, 376–377.

[12] *A.-G. Que. v. Grondin*, [1983] 2 S.C.R. 364.

[13] E.g. *Re Proposed Legislation Concerning Leased Premises* (1978), 89 D.L.R. (3d) 460 (Alta. A.D.) (invalid in Alberta); *Re Pepita and Doukas* (1979), 101 D.L.R. (3d) 577 (B.C.C.A.) (valid in *B.C.); Re Fort Massey Realties* (1982), 132 D.L.R. (3d) 516 (N.S.C.A.) (valid in Nova Scotia).

[14] *Sobeys Stores v. Yeomans*, [1989] 1 S.C.R. 238.

[15] *Sobeys Stores v. Yeomans*, [1989] 1 S.C.R. 238, 265.

1867 arrangements. In this way, there would be national uniformity in the answer to the historical inquiry, although of course different results could emerge from the answer to the second and third steps of the s. 96 inquiry. In *Sobeys Stores* itself, Wilson J. examined the state of the law at confederation in Ontario, Quebec and New Brunswick, as well as Nova Scotia, although it was Nova Scotia that had established the impugned tribunal. Wilson J.'s examination revealed an unexpected infirmity in the four-province test, because it produced a tie: two provinces passed the test, and two failed it! In order to break the tie, she said, it is necessary to look to the position in the United Kingdom in 1867. In the United Kingdom in 1867, she held, power over unjust dismissal was the exclusive preserve of the superior courts. Therefore, the historical test was failed, meaning that an affirmative answer had to be given to the historical test, sending the inquiry on to steps (2) and (3). (The tribunal was saved at step (3) by the institutional setting test.)

Whether the new four-province historical test has become established or not is unclear. In the first place, it means that either *Residential Tenancies* or *Grondin* is wrongly decided, because the only reason given in *Grondin* for the different outcome was that the law of Quebec in 1867 was different from the law of Ontario.[16] In the second place, Wilson J.'s opinion attracted only a bare majority of four of the seven-judge bench. La Forest J., writing for the other three (who concurred in the result), agreed that the inquiry should not be confined to the province that had established the impugned tribunal, but he did not agree that the inquiry should be confined to the four original provinces.[17]

The second step in the s. 96 reasoning—the "judicial" inquiry—involves the notoriously elusive task of characterizing the impugned power as "judicial" (in which case the s. 96 inquiry must proceed) or as "administrative" or "legislative" (in which case the s. 96 inquiry can stop). In *Re Residential Tenancies Act*,[18] Dickson J. suggested that a power was "judicial" if it involved (1) "a private dispute between parties", (2) that must be adjudicated "through the application of a recognized body of rules", and (3) that must be adjudicated "in a manner consistent with fairness and impartiality". He concluded that these characteristics were all present in the powers of the rent tribunal in that case. Of course, in the case of an inferior court (as opposed to an administrative tribunal), the power in question is almost certain to be

[16] *Sobeys Stores v. Yeomans*, [1989] 1 S.C.R. 238, 266 (although not explicitly saying that one must be wrong).

[17] *Sobeys Stores v. Yeomans*, [1989] 1 S.C.R. 238, 289. In *Re Young Offenders Act*, [1991] 1 S.C.R. 252, Lamer C.J. (with two others) and Wilson J. (with one other) applied the four-province test. La Forest J. (with one other) said nothing about which provinces provided the historical comparison. In *Re Residential Tenancies Act (N.S.)*, [1996] 1 S.C.R. 186, 225 (Lamer C.J. with two others), 235 (McLachlin J. with five others on this issue, including La Forest J.), all nine judges seem to accept the four-province test. The 1981 *Residential Tenancies* case was distinguished on the basis that it concerned only the two remedies of compliance orders and eviction orders.

[18] *Re Residential Tenancies Act*, [1981] 1 S.C.R. 714, 735; accord, *Massey-Ferguson Industries v. Govt. of Sask.*, [1981] 2 S.C.R. 413, 429.

classified as judicial, and this step of the inquiry is not significant. Even in the case of an administrative tribunal, where the historical inquiry (the first step) has yielded the answer that the power in question was one that was exercised by a superior court at the time of confederation, in most cases the power will be classified as judicial. But in some cases a power, challenged for breach of s. 96, has been upheld as insufficiently judicial, either for absence of a private dispute between parties,[19] or for absence of a controlling body of rules,[20] or for both reasons.[21]

The third step in the s. 96 reasoning—the "institutional setting" inquiry—involves an examination of the power in its institutional setting to see whether it still broadly conforms to a s. 96 power. This step of the process had been emphasized before *Residential Tenancies* in *Tomko v. Labour Relations Board (Nova Scotia)* (1977),[22] where, in upholding a labour relations board's power to issue a cease and desist order, Laskin C.J. for the majority of the Supreme Court of Canada said that the superficially close analogy with superior-court injunctions was not decisive, because it was necessary to consider not the "detached jurisdiction or power alone", but rather "its setting in the institutional arrangements in which it appears". The Privy Council in the *John East* case (1949)[23] had also decided that the institutional setting of a labour relations regime transformed a power to enforce contracts into a non-s. 96 function. In both *Tomko* and *John East*, the court-like adjudicative function of the labour relations board was ancillary to a broader administrative and policy-making role as administrator of the labour relations legislation. A similar argument carried the day in *Sobeys Stores*,[24] where a labour standards tribunal's power to reinstate employees was upheld as "a necessarily incidental aspect of the broader social policy goal of providing minimum standards of protection for non-unionized employees". In settings other than labour relations, the institutional setting has sustained many other adjudicative functions vested in administrative tribunals.[25]

The institutional setting will not save an adjudicative function which,

[19]*Massey-Ferguson Industries v. Govt. of Sask.*, [1981] 2 S.C.R. 413 (compensation board had self-initiated investigatory function).

[20]*Massey-Ferguson Industries v. Govt. of Sask.*, [1981] 2 S.C.R. 413 (compensation board not limited to legal considerations in fixing compensation); *Capital Regional District v. Concerned Citizens of B.C.*, [1982] 2 S.C.R. 842 (provincial cabinet could affirm or reverse pollution tribunal on basis of policy).

[21]*A.-G. Que. v. Udeco*, [1984] 2 S.C.R. 502 (Minister's power to suspend board of directors not judicial).

[22]*Tomko v. Labour Relations Board (Nova Scotia)*, [1977] 1 S.C.R. 112, 120.

[23]*Labour Rels. Bd. (Sask.) v. John East Ironworks*, [1949] A.C. 134.

[24]*Sobeys Stores v. Yeomans*, [1989] 1 S.C.R. 238, 282.

[25]*Mississauga v. Peel*, [1979] 2 S.C.R. 244 (Ontario Municipal Board's function ancillary to restructuring of municipalities under Board supervision); *Massey-Ferguson Industries v. Govt. of Sask.*, [1981] 2 S.C.R. 413 (compensation board's function part of a public insurance plan); *Capital Regional District v. Concerned Citizens of B.C.*, [1982] 2 S.C.R. 842 (provincial cabinet possessed administrative and regulatory authority as well as adjudicatory authority); *Chrysler Can. v. Can.*, [1992] 2 S.C.R. 394 (Competition

having been held to be a s. 96 function at confederation (step (1)), and having been characterized as judicial (step (2)), is the "sole or central function" of the tribunal.[26] That was the case in *Re Residential Tenancies Act*[27] where the Supreme Court of Canada held that, although the rent tribunal did perform other functions in the administration of Ontario's residential tenancy legislation, the other functions were ancillary to the central function of adjudicating disputes between landlords and tenants.

The institutional setting was also unavailing to save the impugned power in *A.-G. Que. v. Farrah* (1978),[28] where the sole function of the Quebec Transport Tribunal was to sit on appeal from a tribunal of first instance and decide "any question of law"; this was held to be an unconstitutional s. 96 function. That was also the holding in *Crevier v. A.-G. Que.* (1981),[29] where the sole function of the Quebec Professions Tribunal was to sit on appeal from several tribunals of first instance; the Professions Tribunal also had the power to decide questions of law. In both *Farrah* and *Crevier*, a privative clause purported to exclude superior-court review of the appellate tribunal's decisions; that aspect of the cases is discussed in the next section of this chapter. The three concurring opinions in *Farrah* emphasized the exclusion of superior-court review as if it was the unreviewable character of the authority of the Quebec Transport Tribunal that was important. But, in *Crevier*, Laskin C.J. for the Court, as well as holding the privative clause unconstitutional, seemed to hold that the fact that the sole function of the Quebec Professions Tribunal was that of "a general tribunal of appeal" was a fatal flaw by itself.[30]

The three-step approach now favoured by the Supreme Court of Can-

---

Tribunal required power to enforce its orders by punishment for contempt). Cases where the institutional setting has been ignored are *Toronto v. York*, [1938] A.C. 415; *Quance v. Thomas A. Ivey & Sons*, [1950] O.R. 397 (C.A.); *Toronto v. Olympia Edward Recreation Club*, [1955] S.C.R. 454; these cases all concern the Ontario Municipal Board, holding that decisions regarding liability to assessment cannot be made by the Board (and the Act now remits these decisions to the Ontario Court of Appeal); in light of *John East* and the other authorities which rely on the institutional setting test, these cases are probably wrongly decided.

[26] *Re Residential Tenancies Act*, [1981] 1 S.C.R. 714, 736.

[27] *Re Residential Tenancies Act*, [1981] 1 S.C.R. 714, 736.

[28] *A.-G. Que. v. Farrah*, [1978] 2 S.C.R. 638.

[29] *Crevier v. A.-G. Que.*, [1981] 2 S.C.R. 220.

[30] If this is correct, then the decision is not easy to understand. Laskin C.J. acknowledged in *Farrah* (at p. 642) that an administrative tribunal could be given authority to decide questions of law, and could be given appellate authority (extending to questions of law) over another tribunal. He could have added that superior-court jurisdiction over administrative tribunals never (apart from statute) included appellate authority extending to all questions of law, but merely review authority over questions of jurisdiction and (on certiorari) errors of law on the face of the record. It would seem to follow that (apart from the privative clause issue, to be discussed in the next section of the chapter), the powers in *Farrah* and *Crevier* would yield a negative answer to the historical inquiry (step (1)), making it unnecessary to go on to steps (2) and (3). Yet in *Crevier*, Laskin C.J. (at p. 234) quoted with approval, and appeared to rely upon as an

ada is no doubt a sound synthesis of the prior case-law. But it is not satisfactory as constitutional-law doctrine. Each of the three steps is vague and disputable in many situations, and small differences between the provinces in their history or institutional arrangements can spell the difference between the validity and invalidity of apparently similar administrative tribunals. The Supreme Court of Canada's holdings of invalidity in the *Residential Tenancies, Farrah* and *Crevier* cases (as well as the *B.C. Family Relations Act, McEvoy* and *MacMillan Bloedel* cases, discussed in the earlier section of this chapter on inferior courts) cast doubt on the constitutionality of many provincial administrative tribunals (and some inferior courts), encouraged a spate of litigation on this issue, and led to pressure from the provinces for an amendment to s. 96. I think an amendment is the only solution. The courts are unlikely to abandon doctrine which has been built up over a long time; nor are they likely to abandon their concern (which I regard as extravagant) to prevent the erosion of superior-court jurisdiction. To me, the allocation of jurisdiction between different levels of courts and administrative tribunals is primarily a political question, upon which the inevitably self-interested views of the courts should not be unduly influential. An amendment proposal which has been circulated for discussion by the federal Department of Justice would specifically grant to the provinces the power to confer on an administrative tribunal (but not an inferior court) any function within provincial legislative competence (including a s. 96 function), so long as the tribunal's decisions remained subject to superior-court review.[31] This proposal would remove a swamp of uncertainty from our constitutional law, and give to the provinces more security in assigning functions to administrative tribunals.

As was explained in the earlier section of this chapter on inferior courts, the Supreme Court of Canada in *MacMillan Bloedel v. Simpson* (1995)[32] decided that the *Residential Tenancies* three-step rule applies to the conferral of jurisdiction on inferior courts as well as administrative tribunals. The federal Young Offenders Act purported to invest a "youth court", which in British Columbia was an inferior court, with exclusive jurisdiction over the offence of contempt of court[33] when committed by a "young person". The accused, aged 16, was a "young person" within the meaning of the Young Offenders Act, and he was arrested (along with many others) for disobeying an injunction issued by the Supreme Court

independent ground of decision, a dictum in *Re Residential Tenancies Act* that a scheme "is invalid when the adjudicative function is a sole or central function of the tribunal *(Farrah)* so that the tribunal can be said to be operating 'like a s. 96 court'."

[31]The Constitution of Canada: A Suggested Amendment Relating to Provincial Administrative Tribunals (Department of Justice, Ottawa, 1983).

[32]*MacMillan Bloedel v. Simpson*, [1995] 4 S.C.R. 725.

[33]The Act distinguished between contempt in the face of the court and contempt outside the face of the court. The youth court had exclusive jurisdiction over both categories where the contempt was committed against the youth court itself. The youth court had exclusive jurisdiction over only the second category, namely, contempt outside the face of the court, where the contempt was committed against a court other than the youth court.

of British Columbia that prohibited any obstruction of the logging operations of MacMillan Bloedel in an area of old growth forest in Clayoquot Sound on Vancouver Island. He was tried and convicted by the Supreme Court of British Columbia of the offence of contempt of court. He appealed the conviction, relying on the express language of the Young Offenders Act for the proposition that only the youth court possessed the jurisdiction over a contempt of court committed by a young person. The Supreme Court of Canada held that the power to punish for contempt of a superior court was within the exclusive jurisdiction of superior courts at Confederation (step (1)); and that the power was a judicial one (step (2)); but that in the institutional setting of a court with procedures and remedies tailored to the needs of young people (step (3)) the power lost its conformity with superior-court functions.

Because step (3) of the *Residential Tenancies* reasoning was answered in favour of the validity of the power, it followed that the youth court could be invested with jurisdiction over contempt of court. According to the prior case-law, it would make no difference whether the youth court's jurisdiction was exclusive or concurrent. This was the view of McLachlin J., who would have upheld the exclusive jurisdiction of the youth court, and would have held that the young person accused could not be tried by any court other than the youth court. But McLachlin J.'s opinion attracted the support of only three others, and was the dissenting opinion. Lamer C.J., writing with the support of four others (for a bare five-four majority), held that the *Residential Tenancies* tests exhausted the inquiry only when the challenged jurisdiction of the inferior court or tribunal was concurrent with the jurisdiction of the superior court. In his view, whenever *exclusive* jurisdiction was granted by statute to an inferior court or tribunal, it was necessary to ask a further question, which was whether the grant of exclusive jurisdiction took away any part of a superior court's "core" jurisdiction. Lamer C.J. held that the power of a superior court to punish breaches of its own orders through contempt outside the face of the court was part of the core of superior-court jurisdiction. Therefore, although a grant of concurrent jurisdiction could validly be made to the youth court (since the grant satisfied the *Residential Tenancies* third step), a grant of exclusive jurisdiction could not be. The majority of the Court concluded, therefore, that the Supreme Court of British Columbia had not lost its power to punish contempts against itself by young persons, which meant that the accused had been validly tried and convicted.

In my view, the theory that s. 96 guarantees a core of superior-court jurisdiction that cannot under any circumstances be taken away from a superior court is an unfortunate and needless supplement to what is already a complex body of law. First of all, it seems to me to be unwise to introduce even more restrictions on the powers of Parliament and the Legislatures to constitute inferior courts and administrative tribunals. It is true that the doctrine of the core does not preclude the grant of concurrent powers, but concurrent powers lead to forum-shopping and the alternative of resorting to a superior court is likely to conflict with the legislative policy, as it obviously did in the case of the young person accused in *MacMillan Bloedel*, who was tried in an adult court without the protections and remedies of the youth court.[34] Secondly, the new restrictions are intolerably uncertain, because no one knows what is included in the guaranteed core.[35] In *MacMillan Bloedel*, Lamer C.J. acknowledged that he was not able to specify the powers that comprised the core, but he said that it was "unnecessary in this case", because the power to punish for contempt was "obviously" within the core.[36] In other words, only a series of cases going all the way to the Supreme Court of Canada will chart the boundaries of the untouchable core.[37] Thirdly, the policy reason supplied by Lamer C.J. seems exaggerated. He said that "destroying part of the core jurisdiction would be tantamount to abolishing the superior courts of general jurisdiction".[38] But it must be remembered that only those superior-court powers that satisfy the *Residential Tenancies* third step can be vested in an inferior court or tribunal, and any exercise of the powers by the inferior court or tribunal would be reviewable by a superior court: exclusivity does not exclude superior-court review on administrative-law grounds. I find it hard to accept that the doctrine of the core is needed to maintain the institution of the superior court.[39]

§ 7:20 Privative clauses

The decisions of inferior courts and administrative tribunals have for centuries been subject to review by superior courts through the prerogative writs of certiorari, prohibition, mandamus, quo warranto and habeas corpus; and in more recent times by actions for a declaration or

---

[34]The Supreme Court of British Columbia sentenced the accused to 45 days in prison and a fine of $1,000. In my opinion, no youth court would have imposed such a harsh penalty on a 16-year-old boy who was trying to protect the forest.

[35]For examples of other cases applying the doctrine of the core, see § 7:20 note 21, below.

[36]*MacMillan Bloedel*, [1995] 4 S.C.R. 725, para. 38. As to the meaning of the core, Lamer C.J. used other descriptive phrases: "a core or inherent jurisdiction which is integral to their operations" (para. 15); "inherent jurisdiction" (para. 30); "powers which are 'hallmarks of superior courts' " (para. 35); "an essential attribute of superior courts" (para. 40). As to obviousness, it is by no means clear that a superior court must possess the power to punish contempt outside the face of the court. As McLachlin J. pointed out in dissent (paras. 84–88), there is no greater risk of noncompliance if a prosecution for contempt must be brought by the Attorney General in another court, in this case, the youth court.

[37]In *Can. v. Vavilov*, 2019 SCC 65, an important administrative law case, the Supreme Court of Canada acknowledged that jurisdiction is a concept that is difficult to define and apply, and jettisoned "jurisdictional questions" as a separate category of legal question requiring non-deferential correctness review by the courts on judicial review: for further discussion, see the text beginning with § 7:20 note 22, below.

[38]*MacMillan Bloedel*, [1995] 4 S.C.R. 725, para. 37.

[39]The doctrine of the core was trenchantly criticized by McLachlin J. in dissent, who made the points in the text and some others as well, but unaccountably failed to attract the concurrence of more than three of her colleagues. On the other side of the argument, there has been academic support for a guaranteed core of superior-court jurisdiction: see § 7:20 note 14.

injunction; and even more recently in some jurisdictions by special statutory remedies such as an application for judicial review. Judicial review under these various procedures does not involve a full reconsideration of the merits of the decision under review, but it does enable the superior court to review the decision in accordance with standards established by administrative law.[1] To the extent that superior-court review is available, the establishment of a new administrative tribunal does not involve a total exclusion of superior-court jurisdiction.

It is common for legislative bodies, when establishing a new administrative tribunal, to include in the constituent statute a "privative clause", which is a provision purporting to exclude judicial review of the tribunal's decision. Privative clauses come in a variety of fairly standard forms. There is the "finality clause", which declares that the decisions of the tribunal shall be "final" and not subject to review; the "exclusive jurisdiction" clause declares that the tribunal's jurisdiction to decide issues before it is exclusive and unreviewable; the "no-certiorari clause" declares that certiorari and other remedies which would otherwise be available for review purposes are not available to review the tribunal's decision; and one could also include "notice clauses" and "limitation clauses" which exclude review unless prior notice has been given or unless proceedings are brought within a short time. The superior courts have tended to give little effect to privative clauses. This result has traditionally been achieved by statutory interpretation or factoring privative clauses into a broader doctrinal framework, rather than by invocation of any constitutional doctrine. However, the Canadian courts have now developed a cluster of constitutional doctrines with respect to privative clauses, and the end result of that development seems to be a constitutional prohibition on privative clauses that purport to exclude judicial review for jurisdictional error.

There has always been at least one constitutional limit on the efficacy of privative clauses: they are ineffective to exclude a superior-court decision as to the constitutionality of a statute. This to so because the Constitution's distribution of powers and Charter of Rights[2] has been assumed to require implicitly that the courts police the distribution to prevent usurpation by a legislative body of powers that do not belong to

---

[Section 7:20]

[1]Judicial review under the various administrative-law remedies is to be contrasted with an appeal. An appeal is a creature of statute, and depending on the terms of the statute, it can permit an appellate court to review the merits of the decision under appeal. There is no constitutional right to an appeal: *Charkaoui v. Can.*, [2007] 1 S.C.R. 350, para. 136. It is for the competent legislative body to decide whether or not an appeal should be granted from the decision of a tribunal or court and if so on what grounds.

[2]*Okwuobi v. Lester B. Pearson School Bd.*, [2005] 1 S.C.R. 257, para. 45. Indeed, even a direct challenge to a law, bypassing the administrative tribunal, cannot be wholly excluded, for example, where an injunction is sought from a superior court on a matter of urgency: *Okwuobi v. Lester B. Pearson School Bd.*, [2005] 1 S.C.R. 257, paras. 54–55.

it.[3] For similar reasons, where an administrative tribunal is placed in the invidious position of having to decide a constitutional issue, its decision must be subject to review by a superior court on a standard of correctness notwithstanding any privative clause.[4] A common case is where a provincial labour relations board has to decide whether a particular industry is within federal or provincial jurisdiction. Since a provincial Legislature has no power to regulate labour relations in an industry within federal jurisdiction, it cannot authorize a provincial tribunal to determine conclusively whether or not a particular industry is within provincial or federal jurisdiction; otherwise, the tribunal by a wrong decision on the classification of the industry could extend provincial power into the forbidden federal area.[5]

In *A.-G. Can. v. Law Society of B.C.* (1982),[6] the Law Society of British Columbia brought an action in the superior court of British Columbia against the Attorney General of Canada, claiming a declaration that the Combines Investigation Act (now the Competition Act, Canada's antitrust statute) was unconstitutional in its application to the legal profession. It was objected by the Attorney General that this was a matter within the exclusive jurisdiction of the Federal Court, so that the Law Society was suing in the wrong court. It was a difficult question of statutory interpretation as to whether the exclusive jurisdiction of the Federal Court covered an action for a declaration of invalidity. The Supreme Court of Canada, in an opinion written by Estey J., held that it was not necessary to decide the question of statutory interpretation, because the federal Parliament lacked the constitutional authority to invest the Federal Court with exclusive jurisdiction over a case that raised the constitutional validity of a federal statute. This was so because the federal Parliament's power in s. 101 of the Constitution Act, 1867, to create federal courts "for the better administration of the laws of Canada", did not authorize a provision which excluded the provincial superior courts from deciding constitutional questions. Therefore, even if the Federal Court Act purported to confer exclusive jurisdiction on the Federal Court, an action seeking a declaration of the invalidity of a federal statute could be brought in the superior court of any province.

The *Law Society of B.C.* case was taken a step further in *Canada*

---

[3]Laskin, Canadian Constitutional Law (5th ed., 1986 by Finkelstein), 68–69; Strayer, The Canadian Constitution and the Courts (3rd ed., 1988), ch. 3; *Amax Potash v. Govt. of Sask.*, [1977] 2 S.C.R. 576 (Sask. cannot bar recovery by taxpayer of taxes found to be unconstitutional); *Air Canada v. B.C.*, [1986] 2 S.C.R. 539 (B.C. cannot use fiat to bar recovery of unconstitutional taxes).

[4]Chapter 40, Enforcement of Rights, under heading §§ 40:26 to 40:29, "Administrative tribunals".

[5]For examples of these "constitutional jurisdictional facts", see *Can. Labour Relations Bd. v. Paul L'Anglais*, [1983] 1 S.C.R. 147; *Northern Telecom Can. v. Communications Workers of Can.*, [1983] 1 S.C.R. 733; and see Strayer, The Canadian Constitution and the Courts (3rd ed., 1988), 95–96.

[6]*A.-G. Can. v. Law Society of B.C.*, [1982] 2 S.C.R. 307. Folld. in *Can. v. McArthur*, [2010] 3 S.C.R. 626, para. 14 (Federal Court cannot be given jurisdiction over constitutional issues to the exclusion of provincial superior courts).

Labour Relations Board v. Paul L'Anglais (1983),[7] where the Supreme Court of Canada, in an opinion written by Chouinard J., held that the Federal Court could not be invested with exclusive jurisdiction to review the decisions of federal administrative tribunals in those cases where the application for judicial review was made on a constitutional ground. In that case, an employer had applied to the superior court of Quebec to review a decision of the federal labour relations board on the ground that the employment activities in issue (the sale of television commercial time and the production of commercials) fell outside the constitutional authority of the federal Parliament. The Supreme Court of Canada held that, since judicial review was applied for on this constitutional ground, the superior court of Quebec was properly seized of the case. A privative clause in the Canada Labour Relations Act, and an exclusive-jurisdiction clause in the Federal Court Act, both of which purported to exclude review of the board by provincial superior courts, were unconstitutional— but only to the extent that they purported to exclude review that was based on the constitutional limits to the authority of the federal Parliament.

There can be no quarrel with the proposition that a legislative body should not be able to insulate its statutes or its administrative tribunals from judicial review on constitutional grounds. That does indeed seem to be entailed by the federal distribution of powers and the Charter of Rights. But, in both the *Law Society of B.C.* case and the *Paul L'Anglais* case, judicial review had not been eliminated; it remained available, albeit in the Federal Court. It is not easy to see why the federal Parliament should be disabled from shifting the forum of judicial review from the superior courts of the provinces to the Federal Court. The Federal Court is a superior court staffed by judges with the same credentials as the judges of the superior courts of the provinces, and subject to an appeal to the Supreme Court of Canada.[8] Thus, the two decisions, although ostensibly resting on lofty principles of federalism, seem to fit more comfortably into that large category of cases that are really based on hostility to federal-court jurisdiction.[9]

None of these cases decided that superior-court review of administrative tribunals was constitutionally protected where no constitutional issue was involved.[10] That large step was taken in *Crevier v. A.-G. Que.* (1981),[11] where the Supreme Court of Canada struck down a privative clause in a Quebec statute that purported to exclude all judicial review of Quebec's Professions Tribunal. Laskin C.J.'s opinion for the Court acknowledged that a privative clause could constitutionally exclude

---

[7]*Canada Labour Relations Board v. Paul L'Anglais*, [1983] 1 S.C.R. 147.

[8]Compare *Brink's Canada v. CLRB*, [1985] 1 F.C. 898 (T.D.) (privative clause is effective to exclude judicial review by Federal Court, even on constitutional grounds).

[9]§ 7:11 note 51 and accompanying text, above.

[10]In P.W. Hogg, "Is Judicial Review of Administrative Action Guaranteed by the British North America Act?" (1976) 54 Can. Bar Rev. 716, 1 answered my question, no. The Supreme Court of Canada has now held that the answer is yes: see following text.

[11]*Crevier v. A.-G. Que.*, [1981] 2 S.C.R. 220.

review on questions of law not going to the limits of the tribunal's jurisdiction,[12] but, he held, a privative clause could not exclude all judicial review, including review on questions of the limits of the tribunal's jurisdiction.[13] Most of the language of Laskin C.J.'s opinion suggests that the reason for the invalidity of the privative clause was that, by conferring unreviewable authority on the Professions Tribunal, the Quebec Legislature was attempting to constitute the tribunal as a s. 96 court.[14] In other words, it was the grant of unreviewable authority to the tribunal, rather than the taking away of the superior court's power of review,[15] that was unconstitutional. This is not a distinction without a difference, because, if it is the grant of unreviewable authority to the

[12]*Crevier v. A.-G. Que.*, [1981] 2 S.C.R. 220, 235. Subsequent cases have upheld privative clauses that did not exclude review for jurisdictional error: *Capital Regional District v. Concerned Citizens of B.C.*, [1982] 2 S.C.R. 842; *A.-G. Que. v. Grondin*, [1983] 2 S.C.R. 364.

[13]The concept of jurisdictional error is one of the most elusive and susceptible to judicial manipulation in Anglo-Canadian law. Laskin C.J., [1981] 2 S.C.R. 220, at p. 236, invoking a gift of understatement, acknowledged that "there may be differences of opinion as to what are questions of jurisdiction", but he made no attempt to suggest a definition. It is alarming that this concept should now be enshrined in our constitutional law, immune from legislative change. This is a fundamental difficulty with the rule in *Crevier:* see Mullan, "The Uncertain Position of Canada's Administrative Appeal Tribunals" (1982) 14 Ottawa L. Rev. 239. Recognizing these problems, the Supreme Court jettisoned the category of "jurisdictional questions" in the administrative law context in *Can. v. Vavilov*, 2019 SCC 65: for further discussion, see the text beginning with § 7:20 note 22, below.

[14]There is one passage in the opinion, [1981] 2 S.C.R. 220, 236, in which Laskin C.J. describes "review of decisions on questions of jurisdiction" as standing "on the same footing" as review of decisions on questions of "constitutionality". The analogy seems strained to me, since the integrity of the federal system relies upon superior-court determinations of constitutionality, whereas no such issues are at stake when the question is simply the location of final decision-making power (court or tribunal) on issues entirely within provincial legislative competence. Nevertheless, the passage could be read as carrying the suggestion of a guaranteed core of superior-court jurisdiction. Elsewhere in the opinion, however, and indeed even in the passage referred to, Laskin C.J. is at pains always to frame his new rule as applicable to privative clauses protecting "provincial" administrative tribunals. The qualifying adjective would not be necessary if the decision was based on a guaranteed core of superior-court jurisdiction. See Mullan, "The Uncertain Position of Canada's Administrative Appeal Tribunals" (1982) 14 Ottawa L. Rev. 239, 260; and see also next note.

[15]W.R. Lederman, "The Independence of the Judiciary" (1956) 34 Can. Bar Rev. 769 and 1139, at p. 1174, has argued that a guaranteed core of superior-court jurisdiction should be derived from the judicature sections of the Constitution Act, 1867. For similar views, see J.N. Lyon, Comment (1971) 49 Can. Bar Rev. 365; G.E. Le Dain, "Sir Lyman Duff and the Constitution" (1974) 12 Osgoode Hall L.J. 261, 334–336; R. Elliot, Comment (1982) 16 U.B.C.L. Rev. 313. The argument in essence is that judicature provisions in a constitution "are only meaningful as long as judges carry out meaningful tasks": P.H. Russell, "Constitutional Reform of the Canadian Judiciary" (1967) 7 Alta. L. Rev. 103, 108; compare the similar argument with respect to legislative bodies in ch. 14, Delegation, under heading § 14:11 "Administrative inter-delegation". The implication of a guaranteed core of superior-court jurisdiction is that a privative clause is objectionable, not just because it confers unreviewable authority on an administrative tribunal, but because it takes away part of the superior court's guaranteed core of jurisdiction. On this basis, the federal Parliament would be as disabled as the provincial Legislatures

tribunal that is objectionable, then, since s. 96 does not apply to federal courts or tribunals,[16] the rule would not invalidate a privative clause protecting a federal administrative tribunal.[17] However, in *MacMillan Bloedel v. Simpson* (1995),[18] in which a majority of the Supreme Court of Canada committed themselves for the first time to the existence of a guaranteed core of superior-court jurisdiction, Lamer C.J. for the majority cited *Crevier* for the proposition that no part of the core jurisdiction could be taken away from superior courts.[19] This is rather a clear affirmation that a superior court's power of judicial review for jurisdictional error cannot be taken away in any circumstances by either the federal Parliament or a provincial Legislature. Even so, the position was arguably best viewed as unsettled by *MacMillan Bloedel*, since the point was made in obiter, was agreed to by only a bare majority of the Court and is inconsistent with other cases.[20] And yet, in several decisions released after *MacMillan Bloedel*, the Court has appeared to treat as settled that s. 96 prevents both the federal Parliament and the provincial Legislatures from taking away any part of the core jurisdiction of the superior courts.[21]

---

from enacting a privative clause that excluded all provincial superior-court review. The theory of a guaranteed core of jurisdiction is attacked in P.W. Hogg, "Is Judicial Review of Administrative Action Guaranteed by the British North America Act?" (1976) 54 Can. Bar Rev. 716, and is inconsistent with *Pringle v. Fraser*, [1972] S.C.R. 821, *A.-G. Can. v. Canard*, [1976] 1 S.C.R. 170, 202 and *CLRB v. Paul L'Anglais*, [1983] 1 S.C.R. 147, 154. It is, of course, clear that there is no guaranteed core of *inferior-court* jurisdiction: *Re Young Offenders Act*, [1991] 1 S.C.R. 252, 274.

[16]See § 7:14, "Appointment, payment and tenure of federal judges".

[17]In *Pringle v. Fraser*, [1972] S.C.R. 821, the Supreme Court of Canada upheld a federal privative clause precluding review even on jurisdictional grounds of the decisions of the federal Immigration Appeal Board. The provisions of the Federal Court Act, conferring exclusive review power on the Federal Court, also have the effect of taking away the review power of the provincial superior courts, and their validity (except as to questions of constitutionality) has been recognized: *A.-G. Can. v. Canard*, [1976] 1 S.C.R. 170, 202; *CLRB v. Paul L'Anglais*, [1983] 1 S.C.R. 147, 154.

[18]*MacMillan Bloedel v. Simpson*, [1995] 4 S.C.R. 725.

[19]*MacMillan Bloedel v. Simpson*, [1995] 4 S.C.R. 725, para. 35.

[20]§ 7:20 note 17, above.

[21]*Re Remuneration of Judges*, [1997] 3 S.C.R. 3, para. 88 (suggesting "s. 96 restricts not only the legislative competence of provincial legislatures, but of Parliament as well"); *Dunsmuir v. N.B.*, [2008] 1 S.C.R. 190, paras. 31, 52, 159 (ditto); *Trial Lawyers' Association of British Columbia v. B.C.*, [2014] 3 S.C.R. 31, paras. 29-30 (ditto). Compare *Babcock v. Can.*, [2002] 3 S.C.R. 3, paras. 58-61, holding that s. 39 of the Canada Evidence Act, which forbids judicial review of a claim of Crown privilege made in proper form for cabinet documents, does not "invade the core jurisdiction of the superior courts"; *R. v. Ahmad*, [2011] 1 S.C.R. 110, paras. 61-65, holding that s. 38 of the Canada Evidence Act, which vests in the Federal Court exclusive jurisdiction to review claims of Crown privilege on grounds of national security even when the privileged documents are relevant to a criminal trial in provincial superior court, does not have the effect of "removing the core jurisdiction of a s. 96 court to safeguard the fair trial rights of an accused".

However, the Supreme Court's decision in *Canada v. Vavilov* (2019)[22] suggests that the scope of at least some aspects of the protection that s. 96 affords to judicial review in the superior courts should not be regarded as settled. In *Vavilov*, the Court engaged in an important reconsideration of the law relating to substantive review in administrative law. In doing so, the Court took a step that had been hinted at in previous cases, jettisoning "jurisdictional questions" as a separate category of legal question requiring non-deferential correctness review by the courts on judicial review.[23] In taking this step, the Court acknowledged that jurisdiction is a concept that is difficult to define and apply, calling it "inherently 'slippery' ".[24] The Court did not question the *Crevier/MacMillan Bloedel* line of cases. Indeed, citing *Crevier* (but not *MacMillan Bloedel*), the Court affirmed that "because judicial review is protected by s. 96 of the Constitution Act, 1867, legislatures cannot shield administrative decision making from curial scrutiny entirely".[25] However, the Court did not refer to "core jurisdiction" or jurisdictional error in identifying the protection that s. 96 confers on judicial review in the superior courts. In addition, by abandoning jurisdictional questions as a separate category in the administrative law context, and highlighting the difficulties that arise in trying to define and apply the concept of jurisdiction, the Court's decision raises questions about whether jurisdiction will – or *should* – continue to be used as a limiting concept in the s. 96 context as well. If the Court also sidelines jurisdiction in the s. 96 context, but not (as seems quite likely) the idea that s. 96 protects some level of superior court judicial review, it will need to identify some other concept or standard to apply in determining whether legislative schemes have gone too far in "shield[ing] administrative decision making from curial scrutiny".

[22] *Canada v. Vavilov*, 2019 SCC 65. Wagner C.J. and Moldaver, Gascon, Côté, Brown, Rowe and Martin JJ. wrote a joint opinion for the majority of the Court. Abella and Karakatsanis JJ. wrote a joint concurring opinion (which in many respects reads more like a joint dissent).

[23] *Canada v. Vavilov*, 2019 SCC 65, paras. 65-68.

[24] *Canada v. Vavilov*, 2019 SCC 65, para. 66, citing *Can. (CHRC) v. Can.*, [2018] 2 S.C.R. 230, para. 38; *City of Arlington, Texas v. Federal Communications Commission* (2013), 569 U.S. 290, 299.

[25] *Canada v. Vavilov*, 2019 SCC 65, para. 24, citing *Crevier*, along with *Dunsmuir v. N.B.*, [2008] 1 S.C.R. 190, para. 31; *U.E.S., Local 298 v. Bibeault*, [1988] 2 S.C.R. 1048, 1090.

Chapter 8

Supreme Court of Canada

I. IN GENERAL

§ 8:1 Establishment of Court
§ 8:2 Abolition of Privy Council appeals
§ 8:3 Composition of Court
§ 8:4 Appointment of judges

II. APPELLATE JURISDICTION

§ 8:5 Constitutional basis of jurisdiction
§ 8:6 Civil appeals
§ 8:7 Criminal appeals

III. REFERENCE JURISDICTION

§ 8:8 Federal references
§ 8:9 Provincial references
§ 8:10 Constitutional basis
§ 8:11 Advisory character
§ 8:12 Proof of facts

IV. PRECEDENT; REFORM OF COURT

§ 8:13 Precedent
§ 8:14 Reform of Court

I. IN GENERAL

§ 8:1 Establishment of Court

The Supreme Court of Canada[1] was not established at confederation. It was not necessary, because the Judicial Committee of the Privy

[Section 8:1]

[1]For studies of the Supreme Court of Canada, see Brossard, La cour suprême et la constitution (1983); Russell, The Supreme Court of Canada as a Bilingual and Bicultural Institution (1969); Weiler, In the Last Resort (1974); Snell and Vaughan, The Supreme Court of Canada: History of the Institution (1985); Beaudoin (ed.), The Supreme Court of Canada (1986); Canadian Bar Association, Committee on the Supreme Court of Canada, Report (1987); Russell, The Judiciary in Canada (1987), ch. 14; Bushnell, The Captive Court: A Study of the Supreme Court of Canada (1992); Saywell, The Lawmakers: Judicial Power and the Shaping of Canadian Federalism (2002), chs. 10, 11; Songer, The Transformation of the Supreme Court of Canada (2008). The Supreme Court Law Review is an annual journal, established in 1980, which is devoted to the work of the Court.

Council in the United Kingdom served as the final court of appeal from all British colonies, including those of British North America, and that right of appeal continued after confederation. (The abolition of Privy Council appeals is described in the next section of this chapter.) However, the Constitution Act, 1867 did make provision for the later establishment of a Canadian court of appeal. Section 101 authorized the federal Parliament "to provide for the constitution, maintenance, and organization of a general court of appeal for Canada". Acting under this power, in 1875 the federal Parliament, by statute, established the Supreme Court of Canada.[2]

The Supreme Court of Canada's existence, and therefore the details of its composition and jurisdiction, depend upon an ordinary federal statute. As the following text will show, over the years there have been many changes in its composition and jurisdiction, and these have been accomplished by federal statutes. The history demonstrates that, at least before 1982, the Supreme Court Act could be amended, even in radical ways, by the unilateral action of the Parliament of Canada, acting under the power conferred by s. 101 of the Constitution Act, 1867. In 1982, however, s. 101 was supplemented by two references to the Supreme Court in the amending procedures of the Constitution Act, 1982. Section 41(d) lists "the composition of the Supreme Court of Canada" as one of the items that require the unanimity procedure for its amendment, and s. 42(1)(d) lists ("subject to para. 41(d)") "the Supreme Court of Canada" as one of the items that require the seven-fifty procedure for its amendment.[3] The view I took in earlier versions of this book was that these provisions were ineffective ("empty vessels") because ss. 41 and 42 apply only to amendments to the "Constitution of Canada", and the Supreme Court Act is not one of the instruments comprising the Constitution of Canada that are listed in the schedule to the Constitution Act, 1982. I concluded that after 1982 the Court continued to be subject to the unilateral amending power of the federal Parliament.

What was contemplated in 1982 was that the main features of the Court would be expressly entrenched in the Constitution of Canada so as to place it beyond the reach of unilateral federal legislative power. The Meech Lake Accord of 1987 proposed precisely that, including new ss. 101A to 101E of the Constitution Act, 1867, which would have provided for the existence of the Court, its composition, and the appointment, tenure and salary of its judges. After the Meech Lake Accord failed to achieve the necessary levels of legislative ratification, the same provisions (with one addition) were agreed to in the Charlottetown Accord of 1992, which was defeated in a referendum and never proceeded to legislative ratification.[4] If either of these projects had been successful, then the main features of the Court would have been expressly provided

---

[2]Supreme and Exchequer Courts Act, 1875, S.C. 1875, c. 11; see now Supreme Court Act, R.S.C. 1985, c. S-26.

[3]Chapter 4, Amendment, under headings § 4:14, "Section 42", and § 4:16, "Unanimity procedure".

[4]The Meech Lake and Charlottetown Accords are described in ch. 4, Amendment,

for in the Constitution of Canada, and ss. 41(d) and 42(1)(d) would have supplied the applicable amending procedures for the new constitutional provisions.

In the *Supreme Court Reference* (2014),[5] a reference was directed to the Supreme Court to determine whether Nadon J.A., who was a judge of the Federal Court of Appeal from Quebec, was eligible to be appointed to the Supreme Court to fill one of the three places reserved for Quebec by s. 6 of the Supreme Court Act.[6] The Court interpreted s. 6 of the Supreme Court Act as requiring that the three appointments from Quebec must come from current members of the Quebec Court of Appeal, the Quebec Superior Court, or the bar of Quebec. Nadon J.A., as a current member of the Federal Court of Appeal and a *former* member of the bar of Quebec, was ineligible.[7] Anticipating that the Court might reach this decision, Parliament had enacted a new s. 6.1 of the Supreme Court Act declaring that former members of the bar of Quebec were also eligible for appointment under s. 6. This amendment of the Act would have saved the appointment, except that it was successfully challenged on constitutional grounds. The majority of the Court held that the provisions of the Supreme Court Act prescribing the composition of the Court, namely, ss. 4(1) (nine judges), 5 (who may be appointed), and 6 (three judges from Quebec), including the details of eligibility for appointment, were part of the Constitution of Canada, and could be changed only by a constitutional amendment under the unanimity procedure, as prescribed by s. 41(d) of the Constitution Act, 1982.[8] Since the new s. 6.1 had been enacted by Parliament alone, it was unconstitutional, and Nadon J.A. was therefore ineligible for appointment. Moreover, the Court added, changes to "the other essential features of the Court" could be made only by the seven-fifty amending procedure, as prescribed by s. 42(1)(d) of the

---

under heading § 4:3, "The failure to accommodate Quebec". Other proposals for reform of the Court are discussed later in this chapter: § 8:14, "Reform of Court".

[5]*Re Supreme Court Act, ss. 5 and 6*, [2014] 1 S.C.R. 433, 2014 SCC 21. McLachlin C.J. and LeBel, Abella, Cromwell, Karakatsanis and Wagner JJ. wrote the opinion of the majority. Moldaver J. wrote a dissenting opinion.

[6]Section 6 provides: "At least three of the judges shall be appointed from among the judges of the Court of Appeal or of the Superior Court of the province or from among the advocates of that province."

[7]Moldaver J.'s dissenting view was that former members of the bar of Quebec (like Nadon J.A.) were eligible for appointment. He did not need to move on to the constitutional question, but he said in passing (paras. 114–115) that he agreed with the majority that the requirement of three judges from Quebec was now constitutionally entrenched as part of the composition of the Court, but he doubted that the details of eligibility should be regarded as included in the composition of the Court. In *Quebec v. Can.*, [2015] 2 S.C.R. 179, 2015 SCC 22, the Court in a brief oral judgment held that s. 98 of the Constitution Act, 1867, although expressed in similar language to s. 6 of the Supreme Court Act, authorized the appointment of Mainville J.A., a current judge of the Federal Court of Appeal and former member of the bar of Quebec, to the Quebec Court of Appeal. From there, of course, he would be eligible for appointment to the Supreme Court of Canada!

[8]*Re Supreme Court Act, ss. 5 and 6*, [2014] 1 S.C.R. 433, 2014 SCC 21, paras. 75, 91.

Constitution Act, 1982.[9] The power of Parliament to legislate in relation to the Supreme Court Act under s. 101 of the Constitution Act, 1867, was now restricted to "routine amendments necessary for the continued maintenance of the Supreme Court, but only if those amendments do not change the constitutionally protected features of the Court".[10]

The majority of the Court in the *Supreme Court Reference* never really explained the mystery of the migration of parts of the Supreme Court Act into the Constitution of Canada. They recited the "historical evolution" of the Court from its creation in 1875 to "an institution whose continued existence and functioning engaged the interests of both Parliament and the provinces".[11] Of particular importance was the abolition of appeals to the Privy Council which made the Court "the final, independent judicial arbiter of disputes over federal-provincial jurisdiction".[12] But, of course, until 1982, every step in the historical evolution of the Court had been taken by the unilateral action of Parliament acting under s. 101 of the Constitution Act, 1867. And, in 1982, the Supreme Court Act had been left out of the list of instruments comprising the Constitution of Canada. Nevertheless, the majority of the Court in the *Supreme Court Reference* held that the Constitution Act, 1982 "confirmed [the Court's] status as a constitutionally protected institution".[13] The majority rejected my "empty vessels" theory of ss. 41(d) and 42(1)(d). While acknowledging that those provisions were included "in the context of ongoing constitutional negotiations that anticipated future amendments relating to the Supreme Court", they held that "the clear intention was to freeze the status quo in relation to the Court's constitutional role, pending further changes."[14] By this they meant that in 1982 the existing provisions of the Supreme Court Act providing for the "composition" of the Court became part of the Constitution of Canada, and so did the parts of the Act providing for "the other essential features" of the Court.

§ 8:2 Abolition of Privy Council appeals

At confederation, the Judicial Committee of the Privy Council was the final court of appeal from all colonial courts, and to this day it continues

[9] *Re Supreme Court Act, ss. 5 and 6*, [2014] 1 S.C.R. 433, 2014 SCC 21, paras. 75, 90, 94. The closest the Court came to defining "essential features" is in para. 94: "These essential features include, at the very least, the Court's jurisdiction as the final general court of appeal for Canada, including in matters of constitutional interpretation, and its independence."

[10] *Re Supreme Court Act, ss. 5 and 6*, [2014] 1 S.C.R. 433, 2014 SCC 21, para. 101.

[11] *Re Supreme Court Act, ss. 5 and 6*, [2014] 1 S.C.R. 433, 2014 SCC 21, para. 76.

[12] *Re Supreme Court Act, ss. 5 and 6*, [2014] 1 S.C.R. 433, 2014 SCC 21, para. 83.

[13] *Re Supreme Court Act, ss. 5 and 6*, [2014] 1 S.C.R. 433, 2014 SCC 21, para. 88.

[14] *Re Supreme Court Act, ss. 5 and 6*, [2014] 1 S.C.R. 433, 2014 SCC 21, para. 100.

to serve as a Commonwealth court for those members of the Commonwealth that have retained the appeal.[1]

The full Privy Council in the United Kingdom is a large body which now exercises only formal functions.[2] Its members are appointed by the Queen, acting on the advice of the Prime Minister, and they always include (among many others) the senior judges of the United Kingdom. The Judicial Committee is a committee of the Privy Council consisting of those Privy Councillors who are judges. The quorum of the Judicial Committee is three, but most appeals are heard by a bench of five, and these five are usually drawn from the law lords of the House of Lords.[3] Because the Judicial Committee is a committee rather than a court, it does not render a judgment, but merely "advises" the Queen as to the disposition of each appeal. In practice, of course, the "advice" is treated as a binding judgment.[4] The Judicial Committee used to render its advice in the form of a single opinion. The theory was that advice to the Crown should not be divided. This meant that no dissenting opinion was ever written, and there was no disclosure of a dissenting view in the single opinion filed.[5] This practice was abandoned in 1966 (long after the abolition of Canadian appeals); dissenting opinions (but not separate concurring opinions) are now permitted.[6]

The jurisdiction of the Judicial Committee of the Privy Council (hereafter simply the Privy Council) comes partly from the royal prerogative and partly from a series of imperial statutes. The Privy Council's authority over the British North American colonies was continued for Canada by s. 129 of the Constitution Act, 1867. When the Supreme Court of Canada was established by federal statute in 1875, the right to appeal to the Privy Council was in no way impaired. Not only was there an appeal from the Supreme Court to the Privy Council,[7] but the pre-1875 appeals from the provincial courts directly to the Privy Council were

---

[Section 8:2]

[1]The Privy Council in the United Kingdom and its Judicial Committee are described in de Smith and Brazier, Constitutional and Administrative Law (9th ed., 1998), ch. 8.

[2]The Canadian equivalent, the Queen's Privy Council for Canada, is described in ch. 9, Responsible Government, under heading § 9:5, "The cabinet and the Privy Council".

[3]The judicial members of the Privy Council and thus the members of the Judicial Committee include not only the Lords of Appeal in Ordinary (the law lords who sit in the House of Lords), but also the Master of the Rolls and the Lords Justices of Appeal (who sit in the Court of Appeal). As well, a few distinguished Commonwealth judges are appointed, and occasionally sit on appeals.

[4]The advisory character of its decisions may explain why the Judicial Committee never treated its prior decisions as strictly binding precedent, unlike the House of Lords before 1966: see § 8:13, "Precedent".

[5]One of the law lords who sat in *A.-G. Can. v. A.-G. Ont.* (Labour Conventions) [1937] A.C. 326 disclosed in a published, extra-judicial speech that he had dissented in that case: see ch. 11, Treaties, under heading § 11:12, "Evaluation of Labour Conventions case".

[6]Judicial Committee (Dissenting Opinions) Order 1966 (U.K.) (S.I. 1966, No. 1100).

[7]There was controversy about the retention of appeals between the Canadian

preserved; these "per saltum" appeals enabled appellants to bypass the Supreme Court altogether.[8] Laskin C.J. aptly commented that the Supreme Court "was left in the ambiguous position where it could not command appeals to it nor effectively control appeals from it".[9]

The continuance of Privy Council appeals denied the Supreme Court a decisive voice in the development of Canadian law, including constitutional law.[10] As the nation increased in maturity and shed other vestiges of colonial status, it became increasingly unacceptable that the rights of Canadian litigants, and the final say as to Canadian law, should be settled by a court in the United Kingdom. In 1887, the federal Parliament enacted an amendment to the Criminal Code which purported to abolish appeals to the Privy Council in criminal cases. Thirty-eight years later, in *Nadan v. The Queen* (1926),[11] the Privy Council held that the statute was invalid, primarily because it conflicted with two imperial statutes.[12] We have already noticed that this unexpected decision was one factor leading to the imperial conference of 1926, which set afoot an inquiry into how the vestigial inequalities between the United Kingdom on the one hand and the dominions on the other could be removed.[13] After the Statute of Westminster had conferred on the dominions the capacity to repeal or amend imperial statutes, Canada re-enacted the 1888 statute,[14] and as re-enacted it was held to be valid.[15]

In 1939, the federal government introduced a bill to abolish the remaining appeals to the Privy Council, and referred the bill to the Supreme Court of Canada for a decision as to its validity. There was little doubt that s. 101 of the Constitution Act, 1867 authorized the abolition of appeals from the Supreme Court of Canada to the Privy Council: that could fairly be characterized as a law in relation to "a general court of appeal for Canada". But this bill also purported to abolish the per saltum appeals, which lay from the provincial courts directly to the Privy Council. Was this not a matter solely within "the administration

---

government, which would have preferred to abolish them or seriously reduce them, and the British government, which wanted them retained; the British view prevailed: see Strayer, The Canadian Constitution and the Courts (3rd ed., 1988), 25.

[8]"Per saltum" means by a leap or a bound. Per saltum appeals were not exceptional. Nearly half of the constitutional cases decided by the Privy Council were appealed directly from the provincial courts: Russell, The Judiciary in Canada (1987), 336.

[9]"The Role and Function of Final Appellate Courts" (1975) 53 Can. Bar Rev. 459, 461.

[10]Saywell, The Lawmakers: Judicial Power and the Shaping of Canadian Federalism (2002), chs. 2–9, relates the history of Privy Council adjudication in Canadian constitutional cases.

[11]*Nadan v. The Queen*, [1926] A.C. 482.

[12]A subsidiary ground of decision, which was clearly wrong, was that the statute purported to have extraterritorial effect: see ch. 13, Extraterritorial Competence, under heading § 13:2, "Federal Parliament".

[13]See ch. 3, Independence, under heading § 3:3, "Statute of Westminster, 1931".

[14]An Act to amend the Criminal Code, S.C.1933, c. 53, s. 17.

[15]*British Coal Corp. v. The King*, [1935] A.C. 500. The one point for decision was whether the Canadian Parliament could legislate upon the royal prerogative.

of justice in the province" and therefore outside federal competence? In the *Privy Council Appeals Reference* (1947),[16] the Privy Council, affirming the Supreme Court of Canada, held that the bill was within federal competence. The power to establish a general court of appeal for Canada included not only the power to make its jurisdiction ultimate, but also the power "to deny appellate jurisdiction to any other court".[17] After this decision, the bill was enacted,[18] and the new law came into force on December 23, 1949. Cases "commenced" before that date could still be carried to the Privy Council,[19] and the last Canadian appeal was not determined until 1959.[20] But for cases commenced since 1949 there is no longer any appeal to the Privy Council.[21]

§ 8:3 Composition of Court

The Supreme Court of Canada originally comprised six judges, and the Court's statute stipulated that at least two of them had to come from Quebec. In 1927 a seventh judge was added; and in 1949 two more judges were added, bringing the number to its present figure of nine, of whom three must come from Quebec.[1] Since 1949, a pattern of regional representation has been maintained under which three judges come from Quebec (the statutory requirement), three from Ontario (on the

---

[16] *A.-G. Ont. v. A.-G. Can.* (Privy Council Appeals) [1947] A.C. 127.

[17] *A.-G. Ont. v. A.-G. Can.* (Privy Council Appeals) [1947] A.C. 127, 153.

[18] Act to Amend the Supreme Court Act, S.C. 1949 (2nd sess.), c. 37, s. 3.

[19] Act to Amend the Supreme Court Act, S.C. 1949 (2nd sess.), c. 37, s. 7.

[20] *Ponoka-Calmar Oils v. Wakefield*, [1960] A.C. 18.

[21] The Australian Constitution, adopted in 1900, also preserved appeals to the Privy Council, but under s. 74 (and supplementary legislation) questions as to the limits inter se of the constitutional powers of the Commonwealth and states ("inter se questions") can be appealed to the Privy Council only with the leave of the High Court of Australia. Since inter se questions include most constitutional questions, and since the High Court of Australia has (with one exception) always denied leave to appeal inter se questions to the Privy Council, the High Court of Australia has in practice always been the final court of appeal on most constitutional questions. In 1968 appeals from the High Court of Australia to the Privy Council on all remaining questions of constitutional law (that is, questions other than inter se questions) were abolished. Appeals on federal law were also abolished in 1968; appeals on state law were abolished in 1975; and per saltum appeals from state courts were abolished in 1986; no appeals remain. See P.J. Hanks, Constitutional Law in Australia (Butterworths, Sydney, 2001), ch. 1. New Zealand also retained appeals to the Privy Council, and only abolished them in 2003, establishing at the same time a new Supreme Court, above the Court of Appeal. See P. Nevill, "New Zealand: The Privy Council is replaced by a domestic Supreme Court" (2005) 3 Int. J. of Con. Law 115.

[Section 8:3]

[1] The changes in the composition of the Court were enacted in 1927 and 1949 by Parliament in the exercise of its power under s. 101 of the Constitution Act, 1867. Since the decision in *Re Supreme Court Act, ss. 5 and 6*, [2014] 1 S.C.R. 433, 2014 SCC 21, which held that the composition of the Court was entrenched in the Constitution of Canada, the composition can no longer be changed except by a constitutional amendment adopted under the unanimity procedure of s. 41(d) of the Constitution Act, 1982. This decision is described in § 8:1, "Establishment of Court".

basis that Ontario should have the same number of places as Quebec), two from the Western provinces and one from the Atlantic provinces.[2] The Chief Justiceship has usually alternated between French-speaking and English-speaking incumbents.[3]

Since the Court's beginning, five judges have constituted a quorum, and the quorum has not been increased as the membership has risen from six to nine.[4] The most frequent size of panels is seven, although panels of five are not uncommon.[5] The more important cases are usually heard by the full Court. When the full Court does not sit, there is a tendency towards regional or provincial specialization by the inclusion in the panel for a particular case of the judges from the province or region in which the case arose. This is almost invariable in the case of appeals from Quebec. There are however no rules as to the composition of the bench for each case: it lies within the discretion of the Chief Justice.[6]

The Court has never accepted an obligation to announce its decisions in the form of a single opinion containing at least the lowest common denominator of agreement among the majority judges. In that respect it has not followed the practice of the Privy Council, or even of the Supreme Court of the United States, which, while not suppressing separate concurring opinions or dissenting opinions, does attempt to produce an official majority opinion. It used to be common for the Canadian Court to produce a proliferation of opinions, even though the opinion-writers agreed on the result and, in substance, on the reasoning.[7] In recent years, however, it has become more common for only one or two or three judges to write opinions with each of the others simply expressing agree-

---

[2]This regional distribution has been disturbed only once, in 1978, when Spence J. from Ontario retired and was replaced by McIntyre J. from British Columbia. But in 1982, when Martland J. from Alberta retired, he was replaced by Wilson J. from Ontario, thus restoring the traditional regional distribution.

[3]The practice of alternation, which had been followed since 1944, was departed from in 1984, when Dickson C.J. was appointed to succeed Laskin C.J. The practice was resumed in 1990 when Lamer C.J. was appointed to succeed Dickson C.J. and continued in 2000 when McLachlin C.J. was appointed to succeed Lamer C.J. It was also continued in 2017 when Wagner C.J. was appointed to succeed McLachlin C.J.

[4]There is provision in the Supreme Court Act (it is now s. 30) for the appointment of ad hoc judges "where at any time there is not a quorum" of permanent judges available to sit. Twenty-four ad hoc appointments have been made, but none since the increase in the number of judges to nine in 1949 made the quorum easy to achieve: R. Boult, "Ad Hoc Judges of the Supreme Court of Canada" (1978) 26 Chitty's L.J. 289.

[5]L. Hausegger, M. Hennigar and T. Riddell, *Canadian Courts: Law, Politics and Process* (2009), 112.

[6]Apart from the power to preside over the hearings in which he or she participates, the selection of the bench of judges for each case appears to be the principal special power of the Chief Justice of Canada. He or she will also assign the writing of opinions where there are no volunteers. The functioning of the Court is described in Russell, The Judiciary in Canada (1987) 349–354.

[7]E.g., *A.-G. N.S. v. A.-G. Can.* (Nova Scotia Inter-delegation) [1951] S.C.R. 31, where the seven-judge bench produced seven concurring opinions. This kind of proliferation was not unusual at that time.

ment with one of the written opinions.[8] Obviously, there is now some prior consultation and circulation of draft opinions among the judges, and some effort to avoid unnecessary extra opinions. However, an absence of coordination is still occasionally noticeable in that a dissenting opinion will not always directly refer to the language and ideas of the concurring opinion, and vice versa. Once again, the opinions in the Supreme Court of the United States, which are normally careful to address the opposing views of their colleagues, present a more disciplined collegiality.

In *Wewaykum Indian Band v. Canada* (2003),[9] the Court had to consider what to do with an allegation of bias against the Court. After the Court had rendered judgment on an appeal, it had come to light that one of the judges (the one who had written the opinion of the Court) had had a minor involvement with the case as counsel before his appointment. The parties moved to have the Court's judgment set aside on the ground of bias. The Court rejected the motion, holding that no reasonable apprehension of bias was established. The Court went on to offer a description of its decision-making process:[10]

> Each member of the Supreme Court prepares independently for the hearing of appeals. All judges are fully prepared, and no member of the Court is assigned the task to go through the case so as to "brief the rest of the coram before the hearing. After the case is heard, each judge on the coram expresses his or her opinion independently. Discussions take place on who will prepare draft reasons, and whether for the majority or the minority. Draft reasons are then prepared and circulated by one or more judges. These reasons are the fruit of a truly collegial process of revision of successive drafts. In that sense, it can be said that reasons express the individual views of each and every judge who signs them, and the collective effort and opinion of them all.

The Court concluded that, even if the involvement of a single judge had given rise to a reasonable apprehension of bias, the remaining eight judges would remain untainted. For present purposes, it is interesting to note the effort that the Court now puts into producing an agreed-upon opinion.

Although the Court is required to sit in panels of no less than five judges (the quorum), there is no rule requiring that an odd number of judges hear an appeal. The practice of every Chief Justice has been to select an odd number of judges for each panel. Occasionally, however, a death, retirement or illness will reduce a panel to an even number, rais-

---

[8]For a time, multi-author opinions were uncommon – although in some constitutional cases, the Court would issue a single unanimous opinion described as that of "The Court". However, in recent years, multi-author opinions (including opinions by "The Court") have become more common: P. McCormick, " 'By the Court': The Untold Story of a Canadian Judicial Innovation" (2016) 53 Osgoode Hall L.J. 1048, para. 31. The reason for this development is not clear.

[9]*Wewaykum Indian Band v. Canada*, [2003] 2 S.C.R. 259.

[10]*Wewaykum Indian Band v. Canada*, [2003] 2 S.C.R. 259, para. 92. See also B. Wilson, "Decision-making in the Supreme Court" (1986) 36 U. Toronto L.J. 227.

ing the possibility of an evenly divided Court. The rule for an even division is that the judgment of the court below is affirmed, and this has happened several times.[11] In the normal situation, when the panel comprises an odd number of judges, the Court is sometimes evenly split on a particular issue,[12] and occasionally a complex configuration of opinions on various issues makes the actual outcome hard to discern.[13]

§ 8:4 Appointment of judges

The judges of the Court are appointed by the Governor in Council,[1] that is, by the federal cabinet. It is often said that the practices that are followed in the appointment of judges to the superior, district and county courts of the provinces are followed here too, that is, the Chief Justice is appointed on the recommendation of the Prime Minister, and the puisne judges are appointed on the recommendation of the federal Minister of Justice.[2] However, it seems more likely that the Prime Minister is usually involved in the selection of the puisne judges as well as the Chief Justice. That is certainly the case with the process announced by the Prime Minister's office in 2016, which is explained in more detail below: the final decision on the appointment of all nine judges is made by the Prime Minister.

The only fetters imposed by the Supreme Court Act on the appointing power of the federal executive are rules regarding the qualifications of the appointees: each appointee must be either a judge of the superior court of a province, or a lawyer of at least ten years' standing at the bar of a province;[3] and at least three of the nine judges must come from Quebec.[4] There is no requirement that appointments be ratified by the Senate or the House of Commons or a legislative committee. In 2006, the Conservative government of Prime Minister Harper was elected

---

[11]E.g., *Tiny Separate School Trustees v. The Queen*, [1927] S.C.R. 637; J.T. Irvine, "The Case of the Evenly Divided Court" (2001) 64 Sask. L. Rev. 222.

[12]E.g., *Lavoie v. Can.*, [2002] 1 S.C.R. 769 (majority of seven to two that statute breached s. 15 of Charter; even division of four to four on s. 1 justification; but six judges voted to uphold the statute; therefore, it was upheld).

[13]E.g., *RJR-MacDonald v. Can.*, [1995] 3 S.C.R. 199 (four judges voted to strike down the statute; four judges voted to uphold the statute; one judge voted to strike down the statute but keep it in force for one temporary year; last position seems to be the only one that attracts a majority, but Court order was to strike down the statute with immediate effect).

[Section 8:4]

[1]Supreme Court Act, R.S.C. 1985, c. S-26, s. 4. For a thoughtful study, see L.E. Weinrib, "Appointing Judges to the Supreme Court of Canada in the Charter Era: A Study in Institutional Function and Design" in Ontario Law Reform Commission, *Appointing Judges: Philosophy, Politics and Practice* (1991).

[2]See ch. 7, Courts, under heading § 7:2, "Appointment and payment of provincial judges".

[3]Section 5.

[4]Section 6. This is supplemented by the conventions reported in the previous section of this chapter that three judges must come from Ontario, two from the Western provinces and one from the Atlantic provinces.

with a policy of holding public confirmation hearings by a parliamentary committee. There was a vacancy on the Court at the time, and the government's nominee to fill the vacancy, Mr. Justice Rothstein, was interviewed publicly by a parliamentary committee before he was formally appointed. However, this process was not consistently followed by the Harper government.[5]

The Harper government was defeated in the general election of 2015 and replaced by the Liberal government of Prime Minister Justin Trudeau. In 2016, the Prime Minister's office announced a new process for appointments to the Supreme Court.[6] The centrepiece of the new process is a seven-person non-partisan "advisory board" of distinguished people. Persons seeking appointment to the Court, who now have to be "functionally bilingual", have to apply for the position. Applications are then reviewed by the advisory board, which will submit a shortlist of three to five individuals for consideration by the Prime Minister. The Minister of Justice is to consult on the shortlist with the Chief Justice of Canada, relevant provincial or territorial attorneys general, relevant cabinet ministers, opposition Justice critics, and members of the relevant House of Commons and Senate committees. After these consultations, the Minister of Justice will make recommendations to the Prime Minister, who will choose the nominee. The nominee will then take part in a "moderated question and answer session" with members of the relevant House of Commons and Senate committees and representatives of the Bloc Québécois and the Green Party.[7]

The provinces have no role in the selection of judges, although provincial Attorneys General are usually consulted before an appointment is made. Since the Court has to decide constitutional disputes between the federal government and the provinces, it is arguable that the judges should not be appointed just by one side. Indeed, from time to

---

[5]The process was not followed by the Harper government for the appointment of Justice Cromwell (2009), but that did not indicate any change in policy: a dissolution and a prorogation of Parliament caused such delay in convening a parliamentary committee that the Harper government decided to proceed with the appointment without the public interview. The parliamentary-committee process was resumed by the Harper government for the appointments of Justices Moldaver (2011), Karakatsanis (2011), Wagner (2012) and Nadon (2013) (who never served because he was subsequently determined to be ineligible for the appointment: *Re Supreme Court Act, ss. 5 and 6*, [2014] 1 S.C.R. 433, 2014 SCC 21), but the parliamentary-committee process was bypassed again for the appointment (after a long delay) of Nadon's replacement, Justice Gascon (2014), and for the appointment (without any delay) of Justices Côté (2014) and Brown (2015). (The saga of Nadon J.'s invalid appointment and the Supreme Court's 2014 holding (above) that much of the Supreme Court Act has migrated into the "Constitution of Canada" is related and analyzed by H. Cyr, "The Bungling of Justice Nadon's Appointment to the Supreme Court of Canada" (2014) 67 Supreme Court L.R.(2d) 273; and C. Mathen & M. Plaxton, *The Tenth Justice: Judicial Appointments, Marc Nadon and the Supreme Court Act Reference* (2020).)

[6]Office of the Prime Minister, "Prime Minister announces new Supreme Court of Canada Judicial Appointments process", Prime Minister's Office, August 2, 2016.

[7]This process was used by the Justin Trudeau government for the appointment of Justice Rowe in 2016, Justice Martin in 2017 and Justice Kasirer in 2019.

time veiled accusations of a centralist bias are directed at the Court. Studies of the Court (including one commissioned by the separatist Parti Québécois government of Quebec) have found no such bias.[8] Nevertheless, there is support in various reform proposals for incorporating some provincial role in the appointing process. The suggestions for reform of the Court are discussed later in this chapter.[9]

II. APPELLATE JURISDICTION

§ 8:5 Constitutional basis of jurisdiction

The Supreme Court Act, by s. 35, provides that the Court "shall have and exercise an appellate, civil and criminal jurisdiction within and throughout Canada". The breadth of jurisdiction granted by this provision is fully justified by s. 101 of the Constitution Act, 1867, which authorizes the federal Parliament to establish "a general court of appeal for Canada".

The jurisdiction of the Supreme Court of Canada that is contemplated by s. 101 and is conferred by the Supreme Court Act is not a jurisdiction confined to cases arising under federal laws or otherwise coming within some limited area of federal jurisdiction. Now that Privy Council appeals have been abolished, the Supreme Court of Canada stands at the top of the hierarchy not only of federal courts but of provincial courts as well. It hears appeals not only from the Federal Court of Appeal but also from all the provincial courts of appeal, and those appeals may raise questions of constitutional law, federal law or provincial law. The Supreme Court of Canada is thus a powerful unitary element in the court system of Canada, uniting the ten provincial hierarchies of courts into what is essentially a single, national system.[1] Like the Privy Council before it, the Supreme Court of Canada is the final authority on the interpretation of the entire body of Canadian law, whatever its source. Unlike the Privy Council, which was an imperial or (latterly) a Commonwealth court, the Supreme Court of Canada is a federal court in the technical sense that it is established by federal law. But, from the standpoint of its plenary jurisdiction, it is as much a provincial court as a federal court. The fact that a case raises only a question of provincial law does not affect the right of appeal, and a large number of such cases are in fact appealed to and disposed of by the Court.

---

[8] L'Ecuyer, *La Cour supreme du Canada et le partage des competences 1949–1978* (Gouver-nement du Quebec, Ministere des affaires intergouvernementales, 1978); P.W. Hogg, "Is the Supreme Court of Canada Biased in Constitutional Cases?" (1979) 57 Can. Bar Rev. 721; P.H. Russell, "The Supreme Court and Federal-Provincial Relations" (1985) 11 Can. Public Policy 161.

[9] § 8:14, "Reform of Court".

[Section 8:5]

[1] The Supreme Court of Canada takes judicial notice of (accepts without proof) all laws in force in every province (and territory), not just those of the jurisdiction in which the appeal originated. In the Supreme Court of Canada, the laws of provinces other than the province in which the appeal originated are not "foreign" laws, and therefore need not be proved as facts, as they must be in the courts of a province. See ch. 13, Extraterritorial Competence, under heading § 13:5, "Impairment of extraprovincial rights".

In the United States, there is no general court of appeal with jurisdiction over the entire body of the law. The jurisdiction of the Supreme Court of the United States is confined by article III, s. 1, of the Constitution to the "judicial power of the United States". The Constitution, by article III, s. 2, then defines the "judicial power of the United States" as follows:

> The judicial power shall extend to all cases, in law and equity, arising under this constitution, the laws of the United States, and treaties made, or which shall be made, under their authority;—to all cases affecting ambassadors, other public ministers and consuls;—to all cases of admiralty and maritime jurisdiction;—to controversies to which the United States shall be a party; to controversies between two or more states;—between a state and citizens of another state; between citizens of different states; between citizens of the same state claiming lands under the grants of different states, and between a state, or the citizens thereof, and foreign states, citizens or subjects.

The result is that the jurisdiction of the Supreme Court of the United States (and the lower federal courts)[2] cannot go beyond the "cases" and "controversies" coming within the judicial power of the United States. For the most part, these cases and controversies are matters governed by constitutional law or by federal law. When the Supreme Court of the United States (or a lower federal court) does have jurisdiction over a case which is not governed by constitutional law or by federal law, as occurs for example under its "diversity jurisdiction" (controversies between citizens of different states), the Court has decided in *Erie Railroad Co. v. Tompkins* (1938),[3] that it should defer to the law as laid down by the highest court of the state whose law is applicable. Thus, while most issues of state law cannot and do not go beyond the highest court of the state, even those that do reach the Supreme Court of the United States are not decided in accordance with any nation-wide uniform rule. The inevitable consequence is that the common law, or at least that part of it within state jurisdiction, is not necessarily the same in each state, and on many topics divergent rules have in fact developed. For the same reason, a state statute which has been enacted in identical terms in several states could receive a different interpretation in the courts of one state than in the courts of another. The rule in *Erie Railroad Co. v. Tompkins* disables the Supreme Court from imposing uniformity on state law. This rule of restraint could be regarded as entailed by a federal system: the law of the several states is left to each state to develop judicially, just as it is legislatively.

When the Supreme Court of Canada has to determine a question of provincial law, it might perhaps be expected that it would defer to the

[2] In addition to the Supreme Court, the federal courts of the United States consist of a District Court of original jurisdiction for each of 87 "districts" and a Court of Appeals of mainly appellate jurisdiction for each of ten "circuits" and for the District of Columbia. See generally C.A. Wright and M.K. Kane, The Law of Federal Courts (West, 6th ed., 2002).

[3] *Erie Railroad Co. v. Tompkins* (1938), 304 U.S. 64.

decisions of the courts of that province (or at least decide the question as a court of that province would have done). This is not what has happened at all. *Erie Railroad Co. v. Tompkins* has no place in the law or practice of the Supreme Court of Canada. The Supreme Court of Canada always makes its own determination of any question before it, even if it is a question of provincial law, and it does not hesitate to reverse a decision rendered by a provincial court of appeal in a case raising only questions of provincial law. The Supreme Court of Canada does not tolerate divergences in the common law from province to province, or even divergences in the interpretation of similar provincial statutes. Such divergences do develop from time to time, of course, but they are eventually eliminated by the Supreme Court of Canada. The assumption of the Court, which is shared by the Canadian bar, is that, wherever variations can be avoided, Canadian law, whether federal or provincial, should be uniform. Needless to say, each province has a distinctive body of statute law, and Quebec also has a distinctive body of civil law (instead of common law); but the final interpretation of even these unique provincial laws lies with the Supreme Court of Canada.[4] But, apart from distinctive provincial statute law and Quebec's civil law, the law in Canada is generally uniform across the country, and does not differ from province to province.[5]

Albert Abel has argued that the Supreme Court of Canada should follow the lead of the Supreme Court of the United States and adopt a rule of restraint in provincial law cases like the rule in *Erie Railroad Co. v. Tompkins*. He argues that such a rule would make the law more responsive to the differing needs and sentiments of the provinces.[6] This idea has a good deal of merit with respect to the civil law of Quebec with which only the three Quebec members of the Supreme Court of Canada are normally familiar, but with respect to the nine common law provinces it is easy to agree with Gibson that "such a change would result in many more interprovincial legal discrepancies than could be attributed to cultural differences".[7] It must be remembered that whenever a province does desire a different regime of law, it is free to enact a statute. In my opinion, the uniformity of the common law throughout Canada,

---

[4]In the later section of this chapter on leave applications, I point out that the Court will often refuse leave to appeal a decision raising a question of law particular to a single province, but its power to grant the leave and hear the appeal is not in doubt. Appeals in civil law cases from Quebec are quite common, for example. With the great increase in constitutional law cases spawned by the Charter of Rights, the Court now has less time for cases raising issues of provincial law, and it therefore often denies leave to appeal such cases. In this way, Canada is creeping in the direction of *Erie Railroad Co. v. Tompkins*, as the provincial courts of appeal increasingly become the final arbiters of much provincial law.

[5]J. Willis, "Securing the Uniformity of Law in a Federal System—Canada" (1944) 5 U. Toronto L.J. 352.

[6]A.S. Abel, "The Role of the Supreme Court in Private Law Cases" (1965) 4 Alta. L.R. 39; see also Russell, The Supreme Court of Canada as a Bilingual and Bicultural Institution (1969), 218.

[7]D. Gibson, Comment (1966) 44 Can. Bar Rev. 674, 679.

while undoubtedly at variance with an ideal model of federalism, does not really impair provincial autonomy in any practical way. Moreover, the rule of uniformity makes Canada's laws much less complicated than those of the United States, and it allows the highest court (with presumably the best judges) to apply its talents to the development of all Canada's laws, both provincial and federal.

Quebec, with its distinctive civil law, is in a special situation. From the time of confederation to the present, Quebecers have found it hard to understand why a Court comprising a majority of common law judges should have the power to reverse a Quebec court of appeal in a case governed by the civil law; indeed, this concern was an important factor in delaying the establishment of the Supreme Court until 1875.[8] When the Court was established, the statutory provision for Quebec's representation was included to guarantee the membership of some civilian judges. Since 1949, when Quebec's representation was increased from two to three, it has been possible to assemble a quorum of five judges with a majority of civilians. This is now the usual composition of the bench when the Court hears a civil law appeal from Quebec. A bench so composed does not wholly meet the Quebec criticism, because, for example, two common law judges and one civilian could outvote two civilians and reverse a decision reached unanimously in Quebec; but it does offer some protection for the distinctiveness of Quebec's civil law.[9]

If a province would prefer that litigation in a field within provincial jurisdiction be finally disposed of at the level of the provincial court of appeal, it cannot constitutionally give effect to that preference. In *Crown Grain Co. v. Day* (1908),[10] the Privy Council struck down a Manitoba statute that provided that decisions of the Manitoba superior court in mechanics' liens actions were to be "final and binding", and that "no appeal shall lie therefrom". Their lordships held that this provision was inconsistent with the Supreme Court Act, which conferred a right of ap-

[8]There was a substantial body of French Canadian opinion which regarded the Privy Council as better equipped to interpret Quebec's laws than any general Canadian court would be: Russell, The Supreme Court of Canada as a Bilingual and Bicultural Institution (1969), 7–9. The history of "the historical compromise that led to the creation of the Supreme Court" is related in *Re Supreme Court Act, ss. 5 and 6*, [2014] 1 S.C.R. 433, 2014 SCC 21, paras. 46–59.

[9]Russell, The Supreme Court of Canada as a Bilingual and Bicultural Institution (1969), 60–63, and see Russell's ch. 4 for analysis of the influence of the common law judges in the outcome of appeals from Quebec. Russell's data covered the period from 1875 to 1964. D.J. Wheat, "Disposition of Civil Law Appeals by the Supreme Court of Canada" (1980) 1 Supreme Court L.R. 425, studying the period from 1965 to 1978, concluded (at pp. 451–452) that "the common law members of the Court in fact have exercised very little influence over the outcome of civil law appeals". F. Vaughan, "Civil Code Influences on the Supreme Court of Canada, 1875–1980" (1986) 20 Law Society of Upper Canada Gazette 48, reaches a similar conclusion. Of course, as Russell points out (at p. 173), opinions differ on the desirability of common law influences on the civil law. The ideological value of the "purity" of the civil law may be countered by the pragmatic value of critical re-examination of civil law doctrine in the light of ideas from the other system.

[10]*Crown Grain Co. v. Day*, [1908] A.C. 504.

peal to the Supreme Court of Canada from any "final judgment" of the highest court of final resort in a province.[11] Under the rule of federal paramountcy,[12] the Supreme Court Act's grant of a right of appeal prevailed over the Manitoba statute's purported denial of a right of appeal.[13] In *Re Sutherland* (1982),[14] the Manitoba Court of Appeal had to consider a Manitoba statute that purported to make "final" the decisions of the county court in cases relating to recovery of wages. The Manitoba Court of Appeal held that the provision was valid and effective to preclude appeals to the Manitoba Court of Appeal but that it could not be effective to preclude an appeal to the Supreme Court of Canada, and that it should be interpreted as not purporting to oust the jurisdiction of the Supreme Court of Canada. Therefore, the Supreme Court of Canada could still, if it chose, grant leave to appeal from a decision of the county court.[15]

§ 8:6 Civil appeals

In civil matters, before 1975 there was an appeal as of right in cases where the amount in controversy exceeded $ 10,000. This loaded the Court's docket with cases that were unimportant except to the parties. In 1975 this appeal as of right was abolished.[1] Most civil appeals[2] now require leave.[3] This means that the Court has control over its civil docket, allowing it to focus on issues of public legal importance. As a

---

[11]With some modifications that are irrelevant in this context, this provision is still in the current Supreme Court Act, R.S.C. 1985, c. S-26, s. 40.

[12]Paramountcy is the subject of ch. 16.

[13]Under the theory (§ 8:1 note 3, above) that the Supreme Court Act has since 1982 become part of the Constitution of Canada, the provincial statute would today not merely be inoperative by virtue of paramountcy, but would be invalid by virtue of the supremacy clause in s. 52(1) of the Constitution Act, 1982. The possibility that the Charter provides constitutional appeal rights is discussed by D. Gibson, "The Crumbling Pyramid: Constitutional Appeal Rights in Canada" (1989) 38 U.N.B.L.J. 1.

[14]*Re Sutherland* (1982), 134 D.L.R. (3d) 177 (Man. C.A.).

[15]Compare *M & D Farm v. Man. Agricultural Credit Corp.*, [1998] 1 S.C.R. 1074, para. 4 (provincial legislation cannot control what relief can be granted by Supreme Court of Canada).

[Section 8:6]

[1]S.C. 1974-75-76, c. 18, proclaimed in force January 27, 1975.

[2]So far as I can work out, the only exceptions are (1) an appeal from the decision of a provincial court of appeal on a "reference" by the provincial government: Supreme Court Act, s. 36; and (2) an appeal from the decision of the Federal Court of Appeal in the case of a controversy between Canada and a province or between two or more provinces: Federal Court Act, s. 32. In these two cases the appeal lies as of right. In criminal cases, there are still several categories of appeals as of right: see § 8:7 note 3, below.

[3]See B.A. Crane, "Practice Note: Civil Appeals to the Supreme Court of Canada" (1977) 15 Osgoode Hall L.J. 389; S.I. Bushnell, "Leave to Appeal Applications to the Supreme Court of Canada" (1982) 2 Supreme Court L.R. 479; Flemming, Tournament of Appeals: Granting Judicial Review in Canada (2004). Since 1986, each annual issue of the Supreme Court L.R. has included an analysis of leave to appeal applications for the previous year.

result, the Court says that its mandate has become "oriented less to error correction and more to development of jurisprudence".[4]

In the case of appeals from provincial courts of appeal, leave can be granted by the provincial court of appeal itself "where, in the opinion of that court, the question involved in the appeal is one that ought to be submitted to the Supreme Court for decision".[5] The Federal Court of Appeal has an identically expressed power to grant leave to appeal from its own decisions.[6] The existence of these powers to grant leave is anomalous, because the main purpose of requiring leave for appeals is to enable the Supreme Court of Canada itself to control the size and nature of its caseload. This has been recognized by the courts of appeal, which have held that they should grant leave sparingly, doing so only in "obvious" or "special" cases.[7] In practice, the courts of appeal rarely grant leave.[8]

The important power to grant leave is the power possessed by the Supreme Court of Canada itself. It has this power:[9]

> where, with respect to the particular case sought to be appealed, the Supreme Court is of the opinion that any question involved therein is, by reason of its public importance or the importance of any issue of law or any issue of mixed law and fact involved in that question, one that ought to be decided by the Supreme Court or is, for any other reason, of such a nature or significance as to warrant decision by it . . .

Because the Court does not give reasons for the grant or denial of leave to appeal, there is no case law on the kinds of considerations that the Court takes into account in determining applications for leave.[10] Generally speaking, however, the broader the significance of the case, the more likely it is that leave will be granted. Appeals raising constitutional or civil liberties issues are likely to receive leave. Appeals arising out of an important federal statute, or of a provincial statute which has its counterparts in other provinces, or of an important point of common law, or of a will or contract which is a standard form, are more likely to receive leave than appeals arising out of a unique statute or contract or

[4] *R. v. Henry*, [2005] 3 S.C.R. 609, para. 53; *Re Supreme Court of Canada Act, ss. 5 and 6*, [2014] 1 S.C.R. 433, 2014 SCC 21, para. 86.

[5] Supreme Court Act, s. 37.

[6] Federal Court Act, s. 31(1).

[7] *MNR v. Creative Shoes*, [1972] F.C. 1425, 1428 (C.A.); *Jodrey Estate v. Nova Scotia* (1978), 29 N.S.R. (2d) 369, 370 (N.S. A.D.); *Central Computer Services v. Toronto Dominion Bank* (1980), 109 D.L.R. (3d) 660, 662–664 (Man. C.A.); *Campbell v. East-West Packers* (1982), 143 D.L.R. (3d) 136, 137 (Man. C.A.).

[8] B.A. Crane, "Practice Note: Civil Appeals to the Supreme Court of Canada" (1977) 15 Osgoode Hall L.J. 389, 390; S.I. Bushnell, "Leave to Appeal Applications to the Supreme Court of Canada" (1982) 2 Supreme Court L.R. 479, 500.

[9] Supreme Court Act, s. 40(1); Federal Court Act, s. 31(2); the quoted language is identical in each of the two provisions.

[10] The Supreme Court of New Zealand does not give reasons when it grants leave to appeal, but it gives short written reasons in every case when it denies leave to appeal. This is unusual in a final court of appeal.

unusual problem or a fact-dominated case, which may lack the element of "public importance" even if a large sum of money is at stake.[11] Once leave is granted, it can be withdrawn if in the opinion of the Court a supervening event has the effect of denying public importance to the question of law for which appeal was granted.[12] A denial of leave to appeal does not imply that the leave-denying panel of the Supreme Court thought that the lower decision was rightly decided.[13]

On applications for leave to appeal, the practice of the Court used to be to sit in panels of three judges and hear brief oral argument by counsel for the parties. The Supreme Court Act required an oral hearing, and stipulated a quorum of three judges (instead of five).[14] In 1987, the Act was amended to allow applications for leave to appeal in "clear" cases to be determined on the basis of the written material, without an oral hearing.[15] The majority of applications are now disposed of in this way.[16] For applications that are not "clear", the Court can order an oral hearing, in which case the pre-amendment practice is followed. The amendment did not change the quorum requirement, which remains at three, even if no hearing is held.[17] As noted earlier, decisions on applications for leave are rendered without reasons.

§ 8:7 Criminal appeals

Criminal law and procedure is a federal responsibility under s. 91(27) of the Constitution Act, 1867.[1] The federal Criminal Code[2] invests provincial courts with the jurisdiction to try criminal cases, and it makes

---

[11]The criteria for granting leave are discussed in B.A. Crane, "Practice Note: Civil Appeals to the Supreme Court of Canada" (1977) 15 Osgoode Hall L.J. 389, 390–392 and S.I. Bushnell, "Leave to Appeal Applications to the Supreme Court of Canada" (1982) 2 Supreme Court L.R. 479, 510–518.

[12]*Forum des maires de la Péninsule acadienne v. Can.*, [2005] 3 S.C.R. 906 (enactment of statute denied public importance to the legal issue).

[13]*R. v. Côté*, [1978] 1 S.C.R. 8, 16. S.I. Bushnell, "Leave to Appeal Applications to the Supreme Court of Canada" (1982) 2 Supreme Court L.R. 479, 518, comments that "in practice it would seem inevitable that the refusal to grant leave would have the effect of acting as some measure of approval in the eyes of the public and the legal profession".

[14]Supreme Court Act, s. 43; the general rule that five are a quorum is in s. 25.

[15]S.C. 1987, c. 42, substituting a new s. 45 (43 in R.S.C. 1985).

[16]The process followed by the Court is that the applications for leave are examined by the Court's staff lawyers (not the judges' clerks), who prepare summaries along with recommendations as to whether leave should be granted. The summaries are then forwarded to the panels of three judges who are reviewing the applications. The panels decide whether or not to grant leave. The panel decisions are reviewed by the full bench in conference before decisions are announced, but apparently panel decisions are rarely disturbed. See Flemming, Tournament of Appeals: Granting Judicial Review in Canada (2004), 12–16.

[17]Contrast the position in the United States where petitions for certiorari are considered by all Justices, although there is no oral hearing, and a petition is granted on the affirmative votes of four of the nine Justices.

[Section 8:7]

[1]Criminal law is the subject of ch. 18.

provision for appeals from the provincial courts of appeal to the Supreme Court of Canada. In criminal cases there is still an extensive appeal as of right, that is, without leave. Generally speaking, this exists on any "question of law" on which a judge of the provincial court of appeal has dissented.[3] The appeal as of right thus depends upon the existence of a dissenting opinion in the provincial court of appeal. Where there is no such dissenting opinion, an appeal still lies, but only on a "question of law", and only with the leave of the Supreme Court of Canada.[4] Needless to say, there is a body of jurisprudence on what constitutes a "question of law".[5] These provisions (unlike the admittedly vague provisions regarding civil appeals) do not stipulate the grounds upon which leave should be granted or denied, and the Court does not give reasons for a grant or denial of leave, so that there is no case law on the point.[6]

III. REFERENCE JURISDICTION

§ 8:8 Federal references

The Supreme Court Act imposes on the Supreme Court of Canada the function of giving advisory opinions on questions referred to the Court by the federal government. Section 53 provides that "the Governor in Council may refer to the court for hearing and consideration important questions of law or fact"; and, when such a reference is made, "it is the duty of the Court to hear and consider it and to answer each question so referred".

The reference procedure[1] has been used mainly for constitutional questions.[2] It has rarely been used to seek answers to non-constitutional questions, although it is available for that purpose as well. The ques-

---

[2]R.S.C. 1985, c. C-46.

[3]R.S.C. 1985, c. C-46, ss. 691(1)(a), 692(3)(a), 693(1)(a). As well, an appeal as of right is provided for by s. 784(3) (denial of habeas corpus) and s. 691(2) (reversal of verdict of acquittal), even where there is no dissenting opinion in the court of appeal.

[4]R.S.C. 1985, c. C-46, ss. 691(1)(b), 692(3)(b), 693(1)(b).

[5]E.L. Greenspan, *Martin's Annual Criminal Code* (Canada Law Book, Toronto, revised annually), commentary to ss. 691–693.

[6]The Supreme Court Act, s. 43, as amended by S.C. 1987, c. 42, permitting applications for leave to appeal in "clear" cases to be disposed of without an oral hearing, applies to criminal cases as well as to civil cases: *R. v. Chaulk*, [1989] 1 S.C.R. 369.

[Section 8:8]

[1]See Strayer, The Canadian Constitution and the Courts (3rd ed., 1988), ch. 9; J.L. Huffman and M. Saathoff, "Advisory Opinions and Canadian Constitutional Development" (1990) 74 Minn. L. Rev. 1251; C. Mathen, *Courts Without Cases: The Law and Politics of Advisory Opinions* (2019).

[2]Strayer, The Canadian Constitution and the Courts (3rd ed., 1988), 334, reports that from 1867 to 1966, of the 197 constitutional cases reaching the highest available court (the Privy Council until 1949, the Supreme Court of Canada thereafter), 68 or about 35 per cent were references; in the period 1967 to 1986, of the 155 constitutional cases reaching the Supreme Court of Canada, 23 or about 15 per cent were references. He speculates that the relative decline in resort to the reference jurisdiction is explained by the greater ease of private access to the courts through acceptance of the action for a declaratory judgment as a means of constitutional challenge, liberal rules as to standing,

tions referred are usually about the constitutionality of a federal law (or a proposed federal law), but the constitutionality of a provincial law can also be referred, and this has been done from time to time.[3]

The only body[4] that can direct a reference to the Court is the "Governor in Council", which means, by convention, the federal government (cabinet). The reference procedure is therefore a privilege open only to government. A private person cannot direct a reference to the Court. However, the Court has compensated for this inequality by developing liberal rules of standing to allow a private person to bring a declaratory action to challenge the validity of a federal or a provincial law.[5] This procedure does not provide automatic access to the Supreme Court of Canada, but it does provide access to the superior court of the province, and normal rights of appeal are of course available.

§ 8:9 Provincial references

A provincial government has no power to direct a reference to the Supreme Court of Canada. However, each of the ten provinces has enacted legislation permitting the provincial government to direct a reference to the provincial court of appeal.[1] Each provincial law is broadly framed, allowing the constitutionality of federal laws as well as provincial laws to be referred,[2] as well as non-constitutional questions. Following the pattern of the federal legislation, each provincial law confines the power to direct a reference to the provincial government. A provincial reference will secure an advisory opinion from the provincial court of appeal. However, when the provincial court of appeal has

---

legal aid, and more numerous special interest groups able to undertake or support litigation.

[3]E.g., of federal references of provincial statutes, *A.-G. Alta. v. A.-G. Can.* (Bank Taxation) [1939] A.C. 117; *Re Minimum Wage Act* (Sask.) [1948] S.C.R. 248. The constitutionality of such references seems never to have been judicially doubted: Strayer, The Canadian Constitution and the Courts (3rd ed., 1988), 322; for a doubt, see *Gulf Oil Corp. v. Gulf Canada*, [1980] 2 S.C.R. 39.

[4]A second kind of reference, authorized by the Supreme Court Act, s. 56, is the reference of a private bill by the Senate or House of Commons of the federal Parliament. There were some early references by the Senate, but, so far as I can tell, none by the House of Commons: J.L. Huffman and M. Saathoff, "Advisory Opinions and Canadian Constitutional Development" (1990) 74 Minn. L. Rev. 1251, 1257, 1291.

[5]See ch. 59, Procedure, under heading §§ 59:2 to 59:6, "Standing".

[Section 8:9]

[1]See Strayer, The Canadian Constitution and the Courts (3rd ed., 1988), 315–318.

[2]E.g., of provincial references of federal statutes, *A.-G. Ont. v. Can. Temperance Federation*, [1946] A.C. 193; *Re Agricultural Products Marketing Act*, [1978] 2 S.C.R. 1198; *Re Exported Natural Gas Tax*, [1982] 1 S.C.R. 1004; *McEvoy v. A.-G. N.B.*, [1983] 1 S.C.R. 704. In the last case (at pp. 708–709) "the Court" raised a doubt about the constitutionality of provincial references of federal legislation and said that "we expressly refrain from comment on such issue". Considering the broad jurisdiction of the provincial courts to decide federal as well as provincial questions, and the right of appeal to the Supreme Court of Canada, it is hard to see the basis for the Court's doubt. Strayer, The Canadian Constitution and the Courts (3rd ed., 1988), 322, does not regard the point as doubtful.

rendered an opinion on a reference (as opposed to an actual case), there is an appeal as of right to the Supreme Court of Canada.[3] This right to appeal without leave means in effect that the provincial governments enjoy the same privilege as the federal government in being able to secure a ruling from the Supreme Court of Canada on a controverted point.

§ 8:10 Constitutional basis

The rendering of advisory opinions to government is not traditionally a judicial function for two reasons. First, it lacks the adversarial and concrete character of a genuine controversy; and, secondly, it is a function normally undertaken by the executive branch of government, specifically, the Attorney General. In Australia, the High Court of Australia has refused to render advisory opinions, on the ground that it is a non-judicial function.[1] And the Supreme Court of the United States has informally indicated a similar constitutional objection to the function.[2]

It would not have been surprising if the Canadian courts had held that the rendering of advisory opinions by the Supreme Court of Canada was precluded by the Constitution Act's description of the Court in s. 101 as "a general court of appeal for Canada". When the point was litigated up to the Privy Council in the *Reference Appeal* (1912),[3] the reference statute was upheld. Their lordships acknowledged that the function was not a judicial one, and emphasized that "the answers are only advisory and will have no more effect than the opinions of the law officers", but their lordships held nevertheless that the function could be conferred by statute on the Court.[4] This decision is often taken as authority for the proposition that no separation-of-powers doctrine is to be read into the Constitution of Canada.[5] The provincial reference statutes seem never to have been squarely challenged, but have always been accepted as valid, apparently as laws in relation to the administration of justice in the province.[6]

A different kind of constitutional objection to federal (but not

---

[3]Supreme Court Act, s. 36, requiring no leave to appeal.

[Section 8:10]

[1]*Re Judiciary and Navigation Act* (1921), 29 C.L.R. 257.

[2]The refusal to render an advisory opinion is contained in correspondence in 1793 between the President and Secretary of State, on the one hand, and the judges of the Court, on the other. The refusal is undoubtedly consistent with the requirement of a "case" or "controversy" in the definition of the "judicial power of the United States", which limits the jurisdiction of the Supreme Court of the United States, as well as the lower federal courts. Several states authorize advisory opinions, however. See generally Note, "Advisory Opinions on the Constitutionality of Statutes" (1956) 69 Harv. L. Rev. 1302; Tribe, American Constitutional Law (2nd ed., 1988), 73–77.

[3]*A.-G. Ont. v. A.-G. Can.* (Reference Appeal) [1912] A.C. 571.

[4]This holding was reaffirmed in *Re Secession of Quebec*, [1998] 2 S.C.R. 217, para. 15.

[5]See ch. 7, Courts, under heading § 7:15, "Separation of powers".

[6]Strayer, The Canadian Constitution and the Courts (3rd ed., 1988), 139; see the

provincial) references would be based on the fact that they are an exercise of original rather than appellate jurisdiction by the Court. Section 101 of the Constitution Act, 1867 authorizes the establishment of "a general court of appeal for Canada". It will be recalled that in the United States it was the attempt to confer original jurisdiction on the Supreme Court of the United States that led to the celebrated case of *Marbury v. Madison* (1803), in which a federal statute was held unconstitutional for the very first time.[7] Oddly, this objection was never taken to the reference jurisdiction of the Supreme Court of Canada until the *Secession Reference* (1998).[8] In that case, the Court decided that "an appellate court can receive, on an exceptional basis, original jurisdiction not incompatible with its appellate jurisdiction".[9] The federal Parliament therefore had the power to confer some original jurisdiction on a court whose functions were primarily appellate.[10] The reference jurisdiction was valid for that reason.

§ 8:11 Advisory character

In the *Reference Appeal* (1912),[1] as quoted above, the Privy Council held that the Court's answer to a question posed on a reference was "advisory" only and of "no more effect than the opinions of the law officers". It follows that the Court's answer is not binding even on the parties to the reference, and is not of the same precedential weight as an opinion in an actual case. This is certainly the black-letter law. But there do not seem to be any recorded instances where a reference opinion was disregarded by the parties, or where it was not followed by a subsequent court on the ground of its advisory character. In practice, reference opinions are treated in the same way as other judicial opinions.[2]

The Supreme Court Act and the provincial reference statutes impose

---

rest of Strayer's ch. 5 on the constitutionality of references.

[7]*Marbury v. Madison* (1803), 5 U.S. (1 Cranch) 137 is discussed in ch. 5, Federalism, under heading § 5:20, "Development of judicial review". (The Supreme Court of the United States has some original jurisdiction, but only what is expressly authorized by the Constitution.)

[8]*Re Secession of Quebec*, [1998] 2 S.C.R. 217.

[9]*Re Secession of Quebec*, [1998] 2 S.C.R. 217, para. 9.

[10]In *Gulf Oil Corp. v. Gulf Canada*, [1980] 2 S.C.R. 39, the Supreme Court of Canada, over objection, exercised an original jurisdiction to enforce letters rogatory (a request for documents from a foreign court) conferred by the Canada Evidence Act.

[Section 8:11]

[1]*A.-G. Ont. v. A.-G. Can.* (Reference Appeal) [1912] A.C. 571.

[2]*Can. v. Bedford*, [2013] 3 S.C.R. 1101, 2013 SCC 72, para. 40 ("While reference opinions may not be legally binding, in practice they have been followed."). However, the normal panoply of remedies is not available on a reference. In *Re Remuneration of Judges (No. 2)*, [1998] 1 S.C.R. 4, the Court refused to issue a binding declaration on the ground (para. 9) that the case was a reference that could yield only "an advisory opinion and not a judgment". The Court distinguished *Re Manitoba Language Rights*, [1985] 1 S.C.R. 721, where a binding declaration was issued on a reference, on the basis that in that case a remedy was necessary and no other remedy was available. The Court said (para. 10): "The rule of law gave this Court constitutional authority to provide a binding

on the Court a duty to answer reference questions. However, the Court has often asserted and occasionally exercised a discretion not to answer a question posed on a reference.[3] It may exercise that discretion where the question is not yet ripe,[4] or has become moot,[5] or is not a legal question,[6] or is too vague to admit of a satisfactory answer,[7] or is not accompanied by enough information to provide a complete answer.[8]

In the *Same-Sex Marriage Reference* (2004),[9] the Court refused to answer a reference question where none of the usual objections applied. The Court was asked, as a fourth question, whether the opposite-sex requirement for marriage was consistent with the Charter of Rights. The Court answered the first three questions posed to it (which related to Parliament's authority to legalize same-sex marriage, and the impact of the Charter's guarantee of freedom of religion). But the Court refused to answer the fourth question on the ground that it would be "inappropriate".[10] The Court's explanation boiled down to two points. First, since the Government was planning to legalize same-sex marriage by legislative enactment anyway, an answer to the question "serves no legal purpose".[11] This was not quite true, because at the time of the Court's decision there was no guarantee that the proposed legislation (on which a free vote had been promised) would in fact pass. (It was later introduced and did pass.) Second, the Court said that, if it were to

remedy in this unique situation." *Re Manitoba Language Rights* is discussed in ch. 58, Effect of Unconstitutional Law, under heading § 58:8, "Wholesale invalidation of laws".

[3]J. McEvoy, "Separation of Powers and the Reference Power: Is there a Right to Refuse?" (1988) 10 Supreme Court L.R. 429 argues that there is no discretion to refuse to answer a reference question, but he acknowledges the abundant authority to the contrary.

[4]*A.-G. Ont. v. A.-G. Can.* (Local Prohibition) [1896] A.C. 348, 370 (refusing to answer questions that "have not as yet given rise to any real and present controversy" and are therefore "academic rather than judicial"). Query the force of this reasoning given that references often pose questions that are hypothetical in the sense of not yet giving rise to a real dispute: *Re Secession of Quebec*, [1998] 2 S.C.R. 217, para. 25.

[5]*Re Objection by Que. to Resolution to Amend the Constitution*, [1982] 2 S.C.R. 793, 806 (asserting discretion not to answer a question "where the issue has become moot", while deciding to answer the question nonetheless).

[6]*Re Can. Assistance Plan*, [1991] 2 S.C.R. 525, 545 (asserting discretion to refuse to answer a "purely political" question, although the question in the case did have "a sufficient legal component to warrant a decision by a court").

[7]In *McEvoy v. A.-G. N.B.*, [1983] 1 S.C.R. 704, 707–715 where the Court in the end decided to answer a question which it described as suffering from "excessive abstractness", the Court cited four cases in which questions were not answered for lack of specificity. A fifth could be added: *A.-G. B.C. v. A.-G. Can.* (Fishing Rights) [1914] A.C. 153, 162. A sixth case is *Re GST*, [1992] 2 S.C.R. 445, 485–486 (refusing to answer question on grounds that it was "hypothetical" and "the answer given would not be precise or useful").

[8]*Re Secession of Quebec*, [1998] 2 S.C.R. 217, para. 30.

[9]*Re Same-Sex Marriage*, [2004] 3 S.C.R. 698. I disclose that I was counsel for the Attorney General of Canada, arguing that the question should be answered.

[10]*Re Same-Sex Marriage*, [2004] 3 S.C.R. 698, paras. 12, 62.

[11]*Re Same-Sex Marriage*, [2004] 3 S.C.R. 698, para. 65.

answer that the opposite-sex requirement was consistent with the Charter, that would be contrary to lower court decisions that had held the opposite, and upon the faith of which many same-sex marriages had been performed. What is odd about this reason is that it implies that there was no way for the Court to know how it was going to answer the question, despite the fact that the Court had received full written and oral argument on the point. Elsewhere in the opinion, it is strongly implied that the Court believed that the opposite-sex requirement was not consistent with the Charter, and, if the Court were to answer the question in that way, then the jeopardizing of existing marriages would not be a problem. Obviously, the Court did not want to answer the question, but surely not for the reasons provided. I speculate that the reason was a desire by the Court to make Parliament play a role in the legalization of same-sex marriage, so that it could not be claimed that such a controversial project was being entirely driven by judges.

The refusal to answer the fourth question in the *Same-Sex Marriage Reference* is contrary to the Court's general approach to reference questions. As noted in the discussion of conventions in chapter 1,[12] in the reference litigation concerning the constitutional settlement of 1982, the Court was astonishingly liberal in the questions that it elected to answer. While acknowledging its power not to answer, the Court in the *Patriation Reference*[13] and the *Quebec Veto Reference*[14] answered questions about the existence and meaning of constitutional conventions—questions that raised no legal issue and had only political consequences.[15]

Generally speaking, it is my opinion that the Court has not made sufficient use of its discretion not to answer a question posed on a reference. The reference procedure has often presented the Court with a relatively abstract question divorced from the factual setting which would be present in a concrete case. It has been a common and justified complaint that some of the opinions rendered in references have propounded doctrine that was too general and abstract to provide a satisfactory rule. A number of the most important Canadian cases are open to criticism on this ground.[16]

Even when the questions are specific and the factual setting is adequately presented, the lack of a concrete controversy can lead the Court to miss the point of an important question. *Re Agricultural Products Marketing Act* (1978)[17] is an example. The case concerned the validity of a complex scheme for regulating the market in eggs which had been enacted by complementary federal and provincial legislation. A

[12]Chapter 1, Sources, under heading § 1:10, "Conventions".

[13]*Re Resolution to Amend the Constitution*, [1981] 1 S.C.R. 753.

[14]*Re Objection by Que. to Resolution to Amend the Constitution*, [1982] 2 S.C.R. 793. In this case the only question posed was not only non-legal, it was also (as the Court acknowledged at pp. 805–806) "moot" even in a political sense.

[15]Compare *Re Secession of Quebec*, [1998] 2 S.C.R. 217, para. 22 (answering question of international law).

[16]Strayer, The Canadian Constitution and the Courts (3rd ed., 1988), 323–328.

[17]*Re Agricultural Products Marketing Act*, [1978] 2 S.C.R. 1198.

series of specific questions was asked on a reference by the Ontario government. Large quantities of factual information were placed before the Court. Oral argument occupied four days. The Court took six months to write two concurring opinions. But when the opinions are analyzed, they are found to be unclear as to whether or not the levies imposed on egg producers by the federal egg marketing agency were wholly valid. Since this was one of the main points in dispute, which had led the Ontario government to direct the reference in the first place, the opinions were seriously deficient.[18] An action by the federal agency to collect unpaid levies, or a suit by a dissident producer to enjoin their collection, would have yielded a forthright outcome.

A balanced assessment of the reference procedure must acknowledge its utility as a means of securing an answer to a constitutional question. The reference procedure has been used mainly in constitutional cases.[19] This is because it enables a government to obtain an early and (for practical purposes) authoritative ruling on the constitutionality of a legislative programme. Sometimes questions of law are referred in advance of the drafting of legislation; sometimes draft legislation is referred before it is enacted; sometimes a statute is referred shortly after its enactment; often a statute is referred after several private proceedings challenging its constitutionality promise a prolonged period of uncertainty as the litigation slowly works its way up the provincial or federal court system. The reference procedure enables an early resolution of the constitutional doubt.

§ 8:12 Proof of facts

Proof of facts in a reference is peculiarly difficult, because a reference originates in a court that is normally an appellate court: there is no trial, and no other procedure enabling evidence to be adduced. A statement of facts is sometimes included in the "order of reference", which is the document posing the questions that the government wishes the Court to answer. Sometimes, too, affidavits or Brandeis briefs or other material of a factual character are filed informally, or under the direc-

---

[18] I should disclose that I was one of the counsel in the case, and admit the possibility that counsel were at fault in not sufficiently emphasizing the significance of this issue. On the other hand, the majority opinion opened with the astonishing phrase (at p. 1289) "Being pressed for time . . .". Whoever was at fault, such an unsatisfactory outcome could only have been produced by the reference procedure.

[19] Strayer, The Canadian Constitution and the Courts (3rd ed., 1988), 334, reports that from 1867 to 1966, of the 197 constitutional cases reaching the highest available court (the Privy Council until 1949, the Supreme Court of Canada thereafter), 68 or about 35 per cent were references; in the period 1967 to 1986, of the 155 constitutional cases reaching the Supreme Court of Canada, 23 or about 15 per cent were references. He speculates that the relative decline in resort to the reference jurisdiction is explained by the greater ease of private access to the courts through acceptance of the action for a declaratory judgment as a means of constitutional challenge, liberal rules as to standing, legal aid, and more numerous special interest groups able to undertake or support litigation.

tion of the Court. The topic of evidence, including evidence in references, is taken up in Chapter 60, Proof.[1]

IV. PRECEDENT; REFORM OF COURT

§ 8:13 Precedent

Canadian courts accept the doctrine of precedent (or stare decisis),[1] under which the decisions of a court are binding on courts lower in the judicial hierarchy.[2] Before the abolition of appeals to the Privy Council in 1949, the Supreme Court of Canada was lower in the judicial hierarchy and was accordingly bound by decisions[3] of the Privy Council.[4] During that period, the Supreme Court of Canada decided that it was also bound by its own prior decisions.[5] However, after its accession to final appellate status, the Court gradually came to accept that, while it should normally adhere to its prior decisions, it was not absolutely bound to do so; and the Court has often (based on "compelling reasons")[6] explicitly refused to follow a prior decision of its own.[7] Similarly, the Court gradually came to accept that the decisions of the Privy Council should have

---

[Section 8:12]

[1]Chapter 60, Proof, under heading §§ 60:8 to 60:13, "Evidence".

[Section 8:13]

[1]Precedent or stare decisis is not to be confused with res judicata, under which the judgments of a court are permanently binding on the parties to the litigation.

[2]See generally J.D. Murphy and R. Rueter, Stare Decisis in Commonwealth Appellate Courts (Butterworths, Toronto, 1981).

[3]Decisions in reference cases, being advisory only, were not binding. However, as noted § 8:11 note 2, in practice decisions in reference cases have been given the same weight as decisions in other cases.

[4]The rule in *Robins v. National Trust Co.*, [1927] A.C. 515, 519, that the House of Lords was "the supreme tribunal to settle English law", also made the decisions of the House of Lords binding on the Supreme Court of Canada.

[5]*Stuart v. Bank of Montreal* (1909), 41 S.C.R. 516.

[6]*R. v. Henry*, [2005] 3 S.C.R. 609, para. 44.

[7]E.g., *Brant Dairy v. Milk Comm. of Ont.*, [1973] S.C.R. 131, 152–153; *Paquette v. The Queen*, [1977] 2 S.C.R. 189, 197; *McNamara Construction v. The Queen*, [1977] 2 S.C.R. 655, 661; *Keizer v. Hanna*, [1978] 2 S.C.R. 342, 347; *Vetrovec v. The Queen*, [1982] 1 S.C.R. 811, 830; *Min. of Indian Affairs v. Ranville*, [1982] 2 S.C.R. 518, 527; *Argentina v. Mellino*, [1987] 1 S.C.R. 536, 547; *Re Bill 30 (Ont. Separate School Funding)*, [1987] 1 S.C.R. 1148, 1195; *Clark v. CNR*, [1988] 2 S.C.R. 680, 704; *Brooks v. Canada Safeway*, [1989] 1 S.C.R. 1219, 1243–1250; *Central Alta. Dairy Pool v. Alta.*, [1990] 2 S.C.R. 489, para. 51; *R. v. B. (K.G.)*, [1993] 1 S.C.R. 740, paras. 62–72; *R. v. Robinson*, [1996] 1 S.C.R. 683, para. 16; *United States v. Burns*, [2001] 1 S.C.R. 283, paras. 131, 144; *R. v. Henry*, [2005] 3 S.C.R. 609, paras. 43–47; *Health Services and Support—Facilities Subsector Bargaining Assn. v. B.C.*, [2007] 2 S.C.R. 391, para. 36; *Can. v. Craig*, [2012] 2 S.C.R. 489, paras. 24–28; *Can. v. Bedford*, [2013] 3 S.C.R. 1101, 2013 SCC 72, paras. 38–47; *Tsilhqot'in Nation v. B.C.*, [2014] 2 S.C.R. 257, 2014 SCC 44, para. 150; *Mounted Police Assn. v. Can.*, [2015] 1 S.C.R. 3, 2015 SCC 1, para. 127; *Sask. Federation of Labour v. Sask.*, [2015] 1 S.C.R. 245, 2015 SCC 4, para. 32; *Carter v. Can.*, [2015] 1 S.C.R. 331, 2015 SCC 5, paras. 41–47; *R. v. Jordan*, [2016] 1 S.C.R. 631, 2016 SCC 27, para. 45.

no more (and no less) binding force than its own decisions; and the Court has explicitly refused to follow a Privy Council precedent in three constitutional cases.[8]

The practice of other final appellate courts is similar.[9] The House of Lords was exceptional in holding itself to be bound by its own prior decisions,[10] but in 1966 it reversed this self-denying ordinance and assumed the power to refuse to follow its own prior decisions.[11] (The House of Lords was replaced by the Supreme Court of the United Kingdom in 2005;[12] presumably, the Supreme Court will continue the same policy.) The Privy Council, however, never regarded itself as bound by its own prior decisions,[13] although in Canadian constitutional appeals there is no instance of an explicit refusal[14] to follow a prior decision.[15] The Supreme Court of the United States[16] and the High Court of Australia[17] are both free to refuse to follow their own prior decisions.

It is generally accepted that precedent should be adhered to more strictly by courts that are not final. Obviously, they are bound by the de-

[8]The first case is *Re Agricultural Products Marketing Act*, [1978] 2 S.C.R. 1198, 1234, 1291. This is a strong example since (as Laskin C.J. acknowledged at p. 1256) the Privy Council case, *Lower Mainland Dairy Products v. Crystal Dairy*, [1933] A.C. 168, had been followed by the Supreme Court of Canada in *Re Farm Products Marketing Act*, [1957] S.C.R. 198, and the marketing levies successfully challenged in *Re Agricultural Products Marketing Act* had been enacted by the federal Parliament in reliance on the two decisions. Neither judicial re-affirmation nor legislative reliance sufficed to save the Privy Council decision. The second case is *Re Bill 30 (Ont. Separate School Funding)*, [1987] 1 S.C.R. 1148, 1190–1196, overruling *Tiny Roman Catholic Separate School Trustees v. The King*, [1928] A.C. 363. The third case is *Wells v. Newfoundland*, [1999] 3 S.C.R. 199, para. 47, overruling *Reilly v. The King*, [1934] A.C. 176.

[9]G. Bale, "Casting off the Mooring Ropes of Binding Precedent" (1980) 58 Can. Bar Rev. 255.

[10]*London Street Tramways Co. v. London County Council*, [1898] A.C. 375 (H.L.).

[11]*Practice Statement (Judicial Precedent)*, [1966] 1 W.L.R. 1234.

[12]Constitutional Reform Act 2005 (U.K.), c. 4.

[13]*Tooth v. Power*, [1891] A.C. 284, 292 (P.C., Aust).

[14]The Privy Council did occasionally depart from precedent, but never admitted that it was doing so. See for example, the tortuous history of the peace, order, and good government power, ch. 17, where there are several unacknowledged departures from prior precedent. Compare also *Re Regulation and Control of Radio Communication in Can.*, [1932] A.C. 304 with *A.-G. Can. v. A.-G. Ont.* (Labour Conventions) [1937] A.C. 326. The Privy Council did occasionally explicitly dissociate itself from dicta in earlier cases, e.g., *P.A.T.A. v. A.-G. Can.*, [1931] A.C. 310, 326 per Lord Atkin, rejecting Lord Haldane's "domain of criminal jurisprudence" dictum; *A.-G. Ont. v. Can. Temperance Federation*, [1946] A.C. 193, 206 per Viscount Simon, rejecting Lord Haldane's "national binge" explanation of *Russell v. The Queen* (1882), 7 App. Cas. 829.

[15]In *A.-G. Ont. v. Can. Temperance Federation*, [1946] A.C. 193, in which the Privy Council reaffirmed the largely discredited decision in *Russell v. The Queen* (1882), 7 App. Cas. 829 primarily on the ground of its longevity, Viscount Simon said (at p. 206) that "on constitutional questions it must be seldom indeed that the Board would depart from a previous decision which it may be assumed will have been acted on both by government and subjects".

[16]§ 8:13 note 25, below.

[17]§ 8:13 note 26, below.

cisions[18] of courts higher in the same judicial hierarchy.[19] But they are also bound by their own prior decisions except in highly exceptional cases.[20] The mistakes of a court that is not final can be corrected on appeal by the courts above it. The courts of appeal that exist in the provinces and territories and in the federal jurisdiction are not final in that an appeal lies to the Supreme Court of Canada. But in most cases this appeal lies only with leave, and the Supreme Court, rightly concerned to control the size of its docket, refuses leave in the great majority of cases. In order to obtain leave, the appellant must show that the appeal raises an issue of "public importance".[21] It is not a sufficient ground for leave that the decision of an appeal court was wrong. This means that, for practical purposes, the court of appeal is the final court of appeal in its jurisdiction. On this basis, the Court of Appeal for Ontario has decided that it has the same freedom to depart from its previous decisions as the Supreme Court of Canada.[22]

It is arguable that in constitutional cases the Court should be more willing to overrule prior decisions than in other kinds of cases.[23] In non-constitutional cases, there is always a legislative remedy if the doctrine developed by the courts proves to be undesirable: the unwanted doctrine can simply be changed by the competent legislative body. That is not true of constitutional doctrine, which after its establishment by the Court can be altered only by the difficult process of constitutional amendment. It follows that there is a greater need for judicial adaptation of constitutional law to keep the law abreast of new technology and new social and economic needs. There is sound policy in the dictum of Black J. of the Supreme Court of the United States that "the Court has a special responsibility where questions of constitutional law are

---

[18]Since a court has only adjudicative jurisdiction, it is necessary to distinguish between the ratio decidendi (the reasoning that is necessary to the decision), which is binding, and an obiter dictum (a comment that is unnecessary to the decision), which is not binding. For a time an incautious statement by the Supreme Court encouraged the belief that even the Court's obiter dicta were binding on lower courts. This was partially corrected in *R. v. Henry*, [2005] 3 S.C.R. 609, para. 57, by Binnie J. for the Court, who did however assert that, in addition to the ratio decidendi of a precedent case, there is "a wider circle of analysis which is obviously intended for guidance and which should be accepted as authoritative". He did not say whether this assertion was part of the authoritative "wider circle of analysis", but that was probably his intention.

[19]E.g., *Can. v. Craig*, [2012] 2 S.C.R. 489, paras. 18–23 (holding FCA bound to follow decision of SCC, even though SCC agreed with FCA that the prior SCC decision was wrong; only SCC could overrule it; and SCC did overrule it).

[20]The clear case is where the earlier decision was rendered per incuriam, meaning that it over-looked an applicable statute or a binding precedent.

[21]§ 8:6, "Civil appeals".

[22]*David Polowin Real Estate v. Dominion of Canada General Insurance Co.* (2005), 76 O.R. (3d) 161, paras. 126–145 (C.A.). Sharpe J.A. wrote the opinion of the Court.

[23]It is even arguable that res judicata should be relaxed in constitutional litigation between entities in a federation; otherwise res judicata could lead "to just that rigidity in constitutional interpretation which the Court has otherwise successfully avoided in the application of the doctrine of precedent to its previous decisions": *Queensland v. Commonwealth* (1977), 139 C.L.R. 585, 605 (H.C. Aust.) per Stephen J.

involved to review its decisions from time to time and where compelling reasons present themselves to refuse to follow erroneous precedents; otherwise its mistakes in interpreting the Constitution are extremely difficult to alleviate and needlessly so".[24] The Supreme Court of the United States has often refused to follow constitutional precedents where it has found "compelling reasons" to do so,[25] and the High Court of Australia has occasionally done the same.[26] Until the decision in *Bedford*, which is discussed in the next paragraph, the Supreme Court of Canada had never expressly recognized that constitutional precedents are different from other precedents, but the Court has in fact often changed its mind on constitutional doctrine (sometimes without any explicit overruling of the relevant precedents),[27] and has explicitly overruled a disproportionate number of constitutional precedents.[28]

In *Canada v. Bedford* (2013),[29] the Supreme Court decided that three prostitution-related offences in the federal Criminal Code were unconstitutional under s. 7 of the Charter on the ground that they deprived prostitutes of their security of the person in breach of the principles of

---

[24]*Green v. U.S.* (1958), 356 U.S. 165, 195. Accord, *Queensland v. Commonwealth* (1977), 139 C.L.R. 585, 593, 599, 604, 610; Laskin, Canadian Constitutional Law (5th ed., 1986, by Finkelstein), 311–313.

[25]The best-known example is *Brown v. Bd. of Education* (1954), 347 U.S. 483, refusing to follow *Plessy v. Ferguson* (1896), 163 U.S. 537 which laid down the separate-but-equal doctrine which authorized racial segregation in public facilities. Almost as famous is *West Coast Hotel v. Parrish* (1937), 300 U.S. 379, refusing to follow *Lochner v. New York* (1905), 198 U.S. 45 which held that a state law imposing maximum hours of work was an unconstitutional denial of an employer's "liberty" to contract with workers. There are many other examples. A.P. Blaustein and A.H. Field, "Overruling Opinions in the Supreme Court" (1958) 57 Mich. L.J. 151 report 90 overrulings between 1810 and 1956. E.M. Maltz "Some Thoughts on the Death of Stare Decisis in Constitutional Law" [1980] Wisconsin L. Rev. 467 reports 47 overrulings between 1960 and 1979.

[26]The best-known examples are *Amalgamated Society of Engineers v. Adelaide SS. Co.* (1920), 28 C.L.R. 129; *Victoria v. Commonwealth* (Second Uniform Tax Case) (1957) 99 C.L.R. 575; *Commonwealth v. Cigamatic* (1962), 108 C.L.R. 372; *Cole v. Whitfield* (1988), 165 C.L.R. 360. Other examples are given by Aickin J. in *Queensland v. Commonwealth* (1977), 139 C.L.R. 585, 620–631; L. Zines, The High Court and the Constitution (Butterworths, Sydney, 4th ed., 1997), 348–9.

[27]The equality guarantee in s. 15 of the Charter provides the most dramatic example of frequent changes in doctrine; they are described in P.W. Hogg, "What is Equality? The Winding Course of Judicial Interpretation" (2005) 29 Supreme Court L.R. (2d.) 39.

[28]The explicit overrulings referred to earlier included the following constitutional cases: *Paquette v. The Queen*, [1977] 2 S.C.R. 189, 197; *McNamara Construction v. The Queen*, [1977] 2 S.C.R. 655; *Keizer v. Hanna*, [1978] 2 S.C.R. 342, 347; *Argentina v. Mellino*, [1987] 1 S.C.R. 536; *Re Bill 30 (Ont. Separate School Funding)*, [1987] 1 S.C.R. 1148; *Clark v. CNR*, [1988] 2 S.C.R. 680; *R. v. Robinson*, [1996] 1 S.C.R. 683; *United States v. Burns*, [2001] 1 S.C.R. 283; *R. v. Henry*, [2005] 3 S.C.R. 609; *Health Services and Support—Facilities Subsector Bargaining Assn. v. B.C.*, [2007] 2 S.C.R. 391; *Can. v. Bedford*, [2013] 3 S.C.R. 1101, 2013 SCC 72; *Tsilhqot'in Nation v. B.C.*, [2014] 2 S.C.R. 257, 2014 SCC 44; *Mounted Police Assn. v. Can.*, [2015] 1 S.C.R. 3, 2015 SCC 1; *Sask. Federation of Labour v. Sask.*, [2015] 1 S.C.R. 245, 2015 SCC 4; *Carter v. Can.*, [2015] 1 S.C.R. 331, 2015 SCC 5; *R. v. Jordan*, [2016] 1 S.C.R. 631, 2016 SCC 27.

[29]*Canada v. Bedford*, [2013] 3 S.C.R. 1101, 2013 SCC 72. McLachlin C.J. wrote the opinion of the Court.

fundamental justice. Two of the offences (keeping a common bawdy house and communicating in public for the purpose of prostitution) had been challenged under s. 7 and upheld by the Court in the earlier *Prostitution Reference* (1990).[30] The Court in *Bedford* had no difficulty in overruling the earlier case, which had been decided before significant developments in the s. 7 jurisprudence and without the benefit of the evidentiary record in *Bedford*. This case was an unsurprising addition to the line of constitutional cases in which the Court had overruled itself. What was interesting about the case, however, was that the *trial judge* had not regarded herself as bound by the decision in the *Prostitution Reference*, and the Supreme Court chose to comment on what she had done. McLachlin C.J., who wrote for the Court, emphasizing that this was a constitutional case,[31] held that the trial judge was entitled to revisit a matter that had been decided by the Supreme Court "when a new legal issue is raised, or if there is a significant change in the circumstances or evidence".[32]

Although McLachlin C.J. in *Bedford* said that her stated threshold for revisiting a Supreme Court precedent by a lower court was "not an easy one to reach",[33] the requirement of a "new legal issue" or "a significant change in the circumstances or evidence" surely provides ample scope for lower courts to depart from Supreme Court precedent. In the past, the Court had insisted on a much stricter rule of *vertical* stare decisis (lower court faced with decision of Supreme Court) than of *horizontal* stare decisis (Supreme Court faced with decision of its own).[34] For example, in *Canada v. Craig* (2012),[35] the Court had rebuked the Federal Court of Appeal for failing to follow a Supreme Court precedent that the Court of Appeal thought was wrongly decided, even though the Supreme Court agreed that the precedent decision was wrongly decided and went on to affirm the decision of the Court of Appeal. According to *Craig*, the Court of Appeal was bound by the Supreme Court precedent and should have followed it (strict vertical stare decisis), leaving to the Supreme Court to decide whether or not the precedent should be overruled (flexible horizontal stare decisis). In *Bedford*, the Court made no reference to *Craig*, although it had been decided only a year earlier and by a unanimous Court. Presumably, the difference is that *Bedford* was a constitutional case, while *Craig* was not (it was a tax case).

---

[30] *Re s. 193 and 195.1 of Criminal Code* (Prostitution Reference) [1990] 1 S.C.R. 1123.

[31] *Canada v. Bedford*, [2013] 3 S.C.R. 1101, 2013 SCC 72, paras. 42, 43.

[32] *Canada v. Bedford*, [2013] 3 S.C.R. 1101, 2013 SCC 72, para. 44.

[33] *Canada v. Bedford*, [2013] 3 S.C.R. 1101, 2013 SCC 72, para. 44.

[34] See S.T. Kraicer and S.Z. Green, "Bound and Determined? Vertical Stare Decisis Today" [2013] Annual Review of Civil Litigation (Carswell) 111, arguing for a strict rule of vertical stare decisis (even in constitutional cases (pp. 145–147)) and a flexible rule of horizontal stare decisis. Unfortunately, this excellent article came out before the decision of the Supreme Court in *Bedford*, and so the authors do not discuss the Supreme Court decision.

[35] *Can. v. Craig*, [2012] 2 S.C.R. 489.

In *Carter v. Canada* (2015),[36] the Supreme Court decided that the Criminal Code offence of aiding a person to commit suicide was unconstitutional in its application to physician-assisted death in certain conditions. The Court held that the offence was "overbroad", which was a breach of fundamental justice under s. 7 of the Charter. The offence had previously been upheld by the Court in *Rodriguez v. British Columbia* (1993),[37] also applying s. 7 of the Charter, and responding to very similar facts (an adult person of sound mind suffering from a fatal degenerative disease). In *Carter*, as in *Bedford*, the trial judge had refused to follow the earlier decision of the Supreme Court and had struck down the law that had been upheld in the earlier decision. And, as in *Bedford*, the Supreme Court commented on the propriety of her doing that. The Court held that a "new legal issue" was raised because the jurisprudence on s. 7 "had materially advanced since *Rodriguez*."[38] There was also a "significant change" in the evidence because the evidence adduced at the *Carter* trial contradicted the factual findings that had been decisive in *Rodriguez*. This meant that the two conditions stipulated in *Bedford*, either of which would be sufficient to liberate a trial judge from a Supreme-Court precedent, were both satisfied, and the trial judge was justified in refusing to follow *Rodriguez*. The Supreme Court in *Carter* went on to accept the trial judge's findings of fact and affirmed her decision as to the invalidity of the challenged law as if *Rodriguez* did not exist.[39]

In *R. v. Comeau* (2018),[40] the trial judge in the New Brunswick Provincial Court had to decide whether the province's Liquor Control Act imposed a valid restriction on the amount of liquor that could be brought into the province. A decision of the Supreme Court of Canada in *Gold Seal v. Alberta* (1921)[41] had upheld a federal law aimed at assisting "dry" provinces to keep liquor out of their territories; in doing so, the Court had rejected an argument invoking s. 121 of the Constitution Act, 1867.[42] But the provincial judge in *Comeau* declined to follow *Gold Seal* on the ground that it was wrongly decided, and held instead that s. 121

---

[36]*Carter v. Canada*, [2015] 1 S.C.R. 331, 2015 SCC 5. The unanimous opinion was attributed to the Court.

[37]*Rodriguez v. British Columbia*, [1993] 3 S.C.R. 519.

[38]*Carter v. Canada*, [2015] 1 S.C.R. 331, 2015 SCC 5, para. 46.

[39]The Court is supposed to provide a "compelling reason" for a refusal to follow a previous decision of its own, but in this case it never gives any explanation for doing so. The only discussion of precedent is the passage just reported above concerning the propriety of the trial judge refusing to follow the decision. This was also the case in *Sask. Fed. of Labour v. Sask.*, [2015] 1 S.C.R. 245, 2015 SCC 4, para. 32 (trial judge entitled to depart from precedent; no explanation of SCC's own departure).

[40]*R. v. Comeau*, [2018] 1 S.C.R. 342, 2018 SCC 15. The opinion is attributed to "the Court". The substantive issue before the Court is discussed in ch. 20, Trade and Commerce, under heading § 20:3 "In the Supreme Court of Canada".

[41]*Gold Seal v. Alberta* (1921), 62 S.C.R. 424.

[42]Section 121 provides: "All articles of the growth, produce, or manufacture of any one of the provinces shall, from and after the union, be admitted free into each of the other provinces."

invalidated the Liquor Control Act's purported restriction on the amount of liquor that could be brought into the province. The judge's holding that *Gold Seal* was wrongly decided was based on the evidence of an historian who testified as to the legislative history of s. 121 and offered interpretative conclusions from that history. When *Comeau* moved up to the Supreme Court of Canada, the Court held that *Gold Seal* was a binding authority which could not be bypassed by historical evidence. The correct interpretation of s. 121 could not be ceded to an expert; it was the "primary task" of the judge himself. In carrying out that task, the judge was bound by *Gold Seal*. The case was not like *Bedford*[43] and *Carter*,[44] where new evidence had established "a significant evolution in the foundational legislative and social facts"[45] (concerning prostitution and physician-assisted death). In *Comeau*, the evidence was "simply a description of historical information and one expert's assessment of that information," and it "[did] not evince a profound change in social circumstances from the time *Gold Seal* was decided;" it was "not evidence of social change;"[46] and it did not permit the trial judge to "by-pass an existing binding interpretation on the basis of a new understanding of the legislative context and history".[47] It followed that the judge in *Comeau* was bound by the decision of the higher court in *Gold Seal* and was not at liberty to refuse to follow it. Of course, once *Comeau* had reached the Supreme Court of Canada, the point was academic since the Supreme Court *was* at liberty to refuse to follow *Gold Seal*, a previous decision of its own. However, in *Comeau*, the Supreme Court showed no inclination to do that, explaining that in *Gold Seal* "the law did not impede the flow of goods across provincial boundaries as its primary purpose; rather it was part of a larger federal-provincial scheme to facilitate provinces' decisions, as informed by local referendums, to impose temperance to avoid harms associated with alcohol consumption. Therefore the law in *Gold Seal* did not violate s. 121."[48] And the Supreme Court went on to decide that New Brunswick's restriction on the amount of liquor that could be brought into the province also did not violate s. 121.

§ 8:14 Reform of Court

Proposals to reform the Supreme Court of Canada[1] have focused on the idea of making the Court more acceptable to the provinces as an arbiter of federal-provincial constitutional conflict.[2]

---

[43] *Canada v. Bedford*, [2013] 3 S.C.R. 1101, 2013 SCC 72.

[44] *Carter v. Canada*, [2015] 1 S.C.R. 331, 2015 SCC 5.

[45] *R. v. Comeau*, [2018] 1 S.C.R. 342, 2018 SCC 15, para. 31 per "the Court".

[46] *R. v. Comeau*, [2018] 1 S.C.R. 342, 2018 SCC 15, para. 36.

[47] *R. v. Comeau*, [2018] 1 S.C.R. 342, 2018 SCC 15, para. 39.

[48] *R. v. Comeau*, [2018] 1 S.C.R. 342, 2018 SCC 15, para. 115.

[Section 8:14]

[1] This section draws on part of my article "The Theory and Practice of Constitutional

As noted earlier in this chapter,[3] the composition of the Court already reflects to some extent Canada's regional and linguistic differences. The Supreme Court Act stipulates that three of the nine judges must be appointed from Quebec; and, by convention, the remaining judges are appointed as follows: three from Ontario, two from the four Western provinces and one from the four Atlantic provinces. Of course, the nature of the judicial function, as understood in Canada and other countries in which the judiciary is independent, does not allow a judge to "represent" the region from which he or she was appointed in any direct sense, and certainly does not allow the judge to favour the arguments of persons or governments from that region. What regional representation does do, however, is to ensure that there are judges on the Court who are personally familiar with each major region of the country, and who can bring to the decision of a case from that region an understanding of the region's distinctive legal, social and economic character. When the Court does not sit as a full bench, one finds that the judges (or judge) from the region from which each appeal originated are nearly always assigned to that appeal; and that one of those judges will usually write the opinion of the majority.

The regional composition of the Court must enhance the sensitivity and acceptability of its opinions, but the structure of the Court has still attracted some strong criticisms which reveal considerable discontent, especially in Quebec and Western Canada.

The first point of criticism (which has been weakened somewhat by the Court's decision in the *Supreme Court Reference* (2014))[4] is that the Court's existence and jurisdiction are not guaranteed by the Constitution. The Court was created by the Supreme Court Act, which is a federal statute enacted under s. 101 of the Constitution Act, 1867. As related earlier in this chapter,[5] the entrenchment of the Court in the Constitution of Canada was a piece of unfinished business after the patriation project of 1982. The constitutional proposals in the Meech Lake Accord (1987) and the Charlottetown Accord (1992) would each have put the main features of the Court into the Constitution of Canada so as to

---

Reform" (1981) 19 Alta. L. Rev. 335. More comprehensive studies of proposals to reform the Supreme Court of Canada are W.R. Lederman, "Current Proposals for Reform of the Supreme Court of Canada" (1979) 57 Can. Bar Rev. 687; Beck and Bernier (eds.), Canada and the New Constitution (1983), vol. 1, 165 (by J.C. MacPherson); P.H. Russell, "Constitutional Reform of the Judicial Branch" (1984) 17 Can. J. Pol. Sci. 227; W.R. Lederman, "Constitutional Procedure and the Reform of the Supreme Court of Canada" (1985) 26 Cahiers de Droit (Laval) 195; Delperee, "Cour supreme, cour d'arbitrage ou cour constitutionnelle?" (1985) 26 Cahiers de Droit (Laval) 205; Verrelli (ed.), The Democratic Dilemma: Reforming Canada's Supreme Court (2013).

[2] This is one aspect of the application of "intrastate federalism" to central institutions: see ch. 4, Amendment, under heading § 4:22, "Central institutions".

[3] § 8:3, "Composition".

[4] *Re Supreme Court Act, ss. 5 and 6*, [2014] 1 S.C.R. 433, discussed more fully at § 8:15 note 7, below, and in § 8:1, "Establishment of Court", § 8:1 note 5, above.

[5] § 8:1, "Establishment of the Court", at § 8:1 note 4, above.

place them beyond the reach of unilateral federal legislative power.[6] Unfortunately, the Meech Lake Accord did not achieve the required level of legislative ratification, and the Charlottetown Accord was defeated in a referendum and never proceeded to legislative ratification. After these two failed projects, the enthusiasm of Canadian politicians for constitutional reform was replaced by an aversion to the exercise that made it unlikely that the Court would be expressly entrenched in the Constitution of Canada in the foreseeable future. In the *Supreme Court Reference* (2014),[7] the Court itself rode to the rescue, with a heroic decision that there was no need for any exercise of the amending power. The Court held that, in 1982 (unbeknownst to the politicians who prepared and attempted to implement the Meech Lake and Charlottetown Accords), the Court had been *implicitly* entrenched in the Constitution of Canada. The constitutional issue in the case was whether Parliament could enact an amendment to s. 6 of the Supreme Court Act to make judges of the Federal Court from Quebec eligible for appointment to the Supreme Court. The Court held that the amending statute was unconstitutional. The provisions of the Act dealing with the "composition" of the Court[8] should be regarded as having migrated into the Constitution of Canada in 1982, along with the provisions of the Act dealing with "the other essential features of the Court".[9]

The *Reference* case decides that some of the provisions of the Supreme Court Act—those dealing with "composition" and "other essential features" of the Court—are now entrenched in the Constitution of Canada. The Court's decision is remarkable since this outcome mysteriously bypassed the amending procedures that had proved to be so difficult to operate for the Meech Lake and Charlottetown Accords. It is also bad constitutional reform for two reasons. One problem is uncertainty: although the Court identified the sections of the Supreme Court Act that were entrenched under the rubric of "composition", it did not identify the sections of the Act that were entrenched under the rubric of "other essential features". The Court was obviously content for these sections of the Act to be identified (and inserted in the Constitution of Canada) in subsequent litigation. The other problem is rigidity: the framers of constitutional amendments should be careful to avoid including a lot of detail so that incremental change can still be achieved by the ordinary legislative process. But in the *Reference*, having concluded that s. 6 of the Supreme Court Act was a provision dealing with "composition", the Court held that a full-dress constitutional

[6]The goal was also to make a change in the appointing procedures so as to give the provinces a role.

[7]*Re Supreme Court Act, ss. 5 and 6*, [2014] 1 S.C.R. 433, 2014 SCC 21. The decision is more fully described in § 8:1, at § 8:1 note 5, above.

[8]The Court (para. 91) identified these as ss. 4(1) (nine judges), 5 (eligibility for appointment), and 6 (three judges from Quebec and their eligibility for appointment).

[9]The Court did not identify these provisions of the Act, contenting itself with saying (para. 94): "These essential features include, at the very least, the Court's jurisdiction as the final general court of appeal for Canada, including in matters of constitutional interpretation, and its independence."

amendment under the unanimity procedure of s. 41 of the Constitution Act, 1982 was needed to make even a trivial change to the qualifications of judges appointed from Quebec. There is no good reason why an otherwise qualified member of the bar of Quebec should be disqualified from appointment to the Supreme Court simply by accepting an appointment to the Federal Court[10]—but the correction of that anomaly cannot now be enacted by Parliament.[11]

A second criticism of the structure of the Court is that the judges are appointed solely by the federal government. It has often been proposed that the provinces should play a role in the selection of judges to the Court. The principal argument for this proposal is that the Court serves as the "umpire of federalism", and it is inappropriate that the judges should be selected by only one of the contending levels of government. Since 1982, the Court has also been reviewing statutes under the Charter of Rights, and this power also has the potential to limit provincial (as well as federal) powers, which is an additional argument for some provincial influence on the composition of the Court. This could be accomplished by giving each provincial government a direct role in the selection of a judge from that province. For example, the federal government could be required to make its selection from names submitted by the provinces,[12] or selections could be made by a nominating commission comprised of representatives of both levels of government (as well as other interested groups).[13] If the initial selection continued to be made by the federal government alone, a provincial role could still be provided by a process of ratification by a reformed Senate or other legislative body or committee upon which the provinces are represented.[14]

A third point of criticism is that there are too few judges from Quebec

---

[10]This point is implicitly acknowledged by the majority of the Court (paras. 60–61) and is emphasized by Moldaver J. in dissent (paras.144–153). In *Quebec v. Can.*, [2015] 2 S.C.R. 179, 2015 SCC 22, the Court in a brief oral judgment held that s. 98 of the Constitution Act, 1867, although expressed in language similar to s. 6 of the Supreme Court Act, authorized the appointment of Mainville J.A., a current member of the Federal Court of Appeal and a former member of the bar of Quebec, to the Quebec Court of Appeal. From there, of course, he would be eligible for appointment to the Supreme Court of Canada!

[11]Other—admittedly more substantive—changes to eligibility that have been proposed from time to time include a requirement that the judges of the Court be bilingual and a requirement that one of the judges be an aboriginal person: for discussion, see H. Cyr, "The Bungling of Justice Nadon's Appointment to the Supreme Court of Canada" (2014) to be published in the Supreme Court Law Review.

[12]This was the mechanism agreed to in the Meech Lake Accord of 1987, and the Charlottetown Accord of 1992. Neither Accord established a procedure to resolve a deadlock, but the Charlottetown Accord provided for the appointment by the Chief Justice of an "interim judge" where a vacancy had not been filled after 90 days. The Victoria Charter of 1970 would have required agreement between the Attorney General of Canada and the Attorney General of the province, and in the case of a deadlock the choice would be made by a nominating council. None of these provisions was implemented.

[13]Russell, The Supreme Court of Canada as a Bilingual and Bicultural Institution (1969), 130–135.

[14]The model here is article II, s. 2, of the Constitution of the United States, requir-

on the Court. As noted earlier, the present position, mandated by the Supreme Court Act, is that three of the nine judges must come from Quebec. The argument that three are too few depends upon an evaluation of the Court's capacity to decide three classes of cases: (1) those in which the record and argument are in the French language, (2) those raising issues of civil law, and (3) those raising constitutional issues. The argument for increased representation from Quebec is quite strong with respect to the first two classes of case. The judges from Quebec would have a perfect fluency in French and a familiarity with the civil law which the judges from outside Quebec would often lack.

The argument that there should be more judges from Quebec to decide constitutional cases is not as strong. It depends upon the premise that Quebec has a special stake in the outcome of constitutional controversies. With respect to some issues, the premise is correct. Issues of culture, language and communications probably do have a deeper impact in Quebec than elsewhere. But with respect to other issues the premise is incorrect. Issues of resource ownership or control are of much greater interest to the Western provinces and (in the case of offshore resources) coastal provinces than they are to Quebec. Many other issues, for example, those relating to civil liberties, consumer protection or economic development, while they may be important to Quebec, have an equally significant impact in other provinces. It seems, therefore, that for many constitutional issues a larger complement of judges from Quebec would not lead to better informed decision-making, and might even lead to resentment in the under-represented parts of the country. I conclude that the case for larger Quebec representation on the Court should turn on the capacity of the Court to handle French language and civil law cases, rather than on the capacity of the Court to handle constitutional cases.

If it is agreed that there should be more judges from Quebec on the Court, the details of that change are still difficult to work out. Any increase in Quebec's numbers involves either a decrease in the numbers drawn from other regions or an increase in the size of the Court. The former alternative is hard to defend on principle and would obviously meet with resistance. The latter alternative—an increase in the size of the Court—carries risks to the quality of the oral argument before the Court and to the collegiality of the Court, which may lead to more fragmentation and more delay in the Court's decisions.[15]

Finally, in proposals to restructure the Supreme Court of Canada, it has occasionally been suggested that there should be a special

---

ing ratification by the Senate of presidential appointments to the Supreme Court of the United States. For Canada, quite apart from provincial concerns, which have been the cause of proposals to reform the appointing procedure, the idea of a public scrutiny of the qualifications of proposed judges seems to me to be intrinsically sound. For the beginnings of this practice in Canada, see § 8:4, "Appointment of judges".

[15]Note however that there are courts of last resort with more than nine judges, e.g., India, Japan, International Court of Justice. However, they tend to sit in panels rather than as a full court. See McWhinney, Supreme Courts and Judicial Law-Making (1985) 34–41.

constitutional court, or a special constitutional panel of the present Court, to decide constitutional cases. This suggestion has already been discussed in ch. 5, Federalism.[16] One version of this suggestion is premised on a dualist view of Canada, under which constitutional issues should be determined by a tribunal upon which French Canada has an equal voice with English Canada. As noted earlier, this is a dubious proposition having regard to the range and variety of constitutional issues which have as much or more impact on provinces other than Quebec. The dualist view of Canada also fails to reflect the actual composition of the Canadian population, which includes aboriginal people as well as those of neither English nor French heritage, not to mention the immigrants who have come from other parts of the world. To the extent that the proposal for a constitutional court is premised on the desire to assemble a broader range of talented individuals (not necessarily lawyers) to decide constitutional cases, it involves the risk of creating an active policy-making body which is not amenable to any of the processes of democratic accountability. And, as a technical matter, there is good reason not to try to decide constitutional issues in isolation from the other elements of a justiciable controversy, which supply the context and colour and are in my view indispensable to wise constitutional decision-making. My conclusion is that judicial review should continue to be the function of the same Supreme Court of Canada that serves as a general court of appeal for Canada.

[16] § 5:22, "Alternatives to judicial review".

Chapter 9

Responsible Government

I. RESPONSIBLE GOVERNMENT

§ 9:1 Definition of responsible government
§ 9:2 History of responsible government
§ 9:3 Law and convention

II. THE EXECUTIVE BRANCH

§ 9:4 The ministry
§ 9:5 The cabinet and the Privy Council
§ 9:6 The Prime Minister
§ 9:7 Ministerial responsibility

III. THE LEGISLATIVE BRANCH

§ 9:8 The Parliament
§ 9:9 The House of Commons
§ 9:10 The Senate
§ 9:11 The Governor General
§ 9:12 The cabinet

IV. DEFEAT OF THE GOVERNMENT

§ 9:13 Withdrawal of confidence
§ 9:14 Dissolution of Parliament
§ 9:15 Resignation or dismissal

V. THE GOVERNOR GENERAL'S PERSONAL PREROGATIVES

§ 9:16 The principle
§ 9:17 Appointment of Prime Minister
§ 9:18 Dismissal of Prime Minister
§ 9:19 Dissolution of Parliament
§ 9:20 Fixed election dates
§ 9:21 Prorogation of Parliament
§ 9:22 Appointments to Senate and bench
§ 9:23 The justification for a formal head of state
§ 9:24 The monarchy

I. RESPONSIBLE GOVERNMENT

§ 9:1 Definition of responsible government

"Responsible government" (or cabinet or parliamentary government)[1] is the term that is used to describe the system of government that evolved in the United Kingdom and was exported to the British colonies, including those of British North America. In a system of responsible government, there is a "dual executive", consisting of a formal head of state and a political head of state. The *formal* head of state for Canada is the Queen, but she is represented in Canada by the Governor General of Canada and the Lieutenant Governors of the provinces. In Canada, the Queen rarely exercises any power, except for the occasional act on a royal visit. Most of the time, the role of formal head of state is performed nationally by the Governor General and provincially by the Lieutenant Governors. The *political* head of state for Canada is the Prime Minister, who is the leader of the party that commands a majority in the elected House of Commons. In each province, the equivalent of the Prime Minister is the Premier, who is the leader of the party that commands a majority in the elected Legislative Assembly.

The formal head of state retains many functions, of which the most important is the giving of the royal assent to bills that have been enacted by the Houses of Parliament or the provincial Legislatures. But in a system of responsible government the formal head of state must nearly always act under the "advice" (meaning direction) of the political head of state. In this way, the forms of monarchical government are retained, but real power is exercised by the elected politicians who give the advice to the Queen and her representatives. In a democracy, it would of course be unacceptable for real powers of government to be possessed by an unelected official, whether a King, a Queen, a Governor General or a Lieutenant Governor. Responsible government transfers the real power to the elected Prime Minister. The Queen, the Governor General and the Lieutenant Governors, who are not elected officials, do not exercise any personal initiative or discretion in the exercise of the normal powers of government. (There are certain "reserve powers", or "personal prerogatives" which are exercised by the Governor General or Lieutenant Governors under their own personal discretion, but these apply only in exceptional circumstances when the Prime Minister or Premier no lon-

---

[Section 9:1]

[1]See Dawson, The Government of Canada (6th ed., 1987 by Ward), chs. 9, 10; Mallory, The Structure of Canadian Government (rev. ed., 1984), chs. 1–3; de Smith and Brazier, Constitutional and Administrative Law (8th ed., 1998), Part 2; Forsey, Freedom and Order (1974), Parts 1, 2; Cheffins and Johnson, The Revised Canadian Constitution (1986), ch. 6; Beaudoin, La Constitution du Canada (3rd ed., 2004), ch. 2; Aucoin, Jarvis and Turnbull, Democratizing the Constitution: Reforming Responsible Government (2011).

ger commands a majority in the House of Commons or Legislative Assembly.)[2]

The government is "responsible" in the sense that the executive is responsible to the legislative assembly, meaning that the executive must have the confidence of the legislative assembly in order to continue in office. The Prime Minister is the leader of the party that commands a majority in the House of Commons. He must be a member of parliament and he must draw his ministers from the ranks of the members of parliament. The ministers meet together as a cabinet to take important decisions. Because the Prime Minister is the leader of the party that commands a majority in the House of Commons (and the Premier of a province is in the same situation), he can normally control the House of Commons. If he loses control of the House of Commons, then he must either resign to allow the Governor General to appoint a new Prime Minister who can control the House of Commons, or he must advise the Governor General to call an election to form a new House of Commons. This is quite unlike the position of the President of the United States (or the Governor of a state), who is elected for a fixed term of four years, and who remains in office for the entire term regardless of whether the Congress supplies the money and passes the bills that he recommends. In the United States, it is quite common for the President to be of a different party from the majority in the House of Representatives. And, even when they are of the same party, the House of Representatives may still disagree with the President about important issues. That cannot happen in a system of responsible government.

In any legal system, there will be a legislative branch, an executive branch and a judicial branch. Each branch has distinct functions. In Canada, the legislative branch consists of the Parliament of Canada and the Legislatures of the provinces, and these are the only institutions that have the power to supply public money for government and the only institutions that have the power to make new laws. The executive branch, which in Canada consists of the Prime Minister or Premier and his cabinet and the government departments that they head, is restricted to spending the money supplied by the legislative branch and executing the laws enacted by the legislative branch. The judicial branch, consisting of the courts, decides disputes arising under the laws.

It is very important in any system of government for the courts to be independent of the other branches of government, because otherwise they will not be able to render just decisions on issues that affect the other branches of government. For example, in Canada, the Crown (meaning the executive branch) is a litigant before the courts in every criminal prosecution and in many civil cases. Obviously, the courts must be, and must be seen to be, even-handed between Crown and subject. In other words, the judicial power must be separate from the legislative and executive powers. But, in a system of responsible government, the separation of powers does not extend to the legislative and executive

[2]§§ 9:16 to 9:24, "The Governor General's personal prerogatives".

branches of government. While the powers of the legislative and executive branches remain distinct, these two branches do not operate independently of each other. This is because the executive branch is headed by the same persons as lead the majority party in the elected legislative assembly. The executive branch therefore exercises considerable control over the legislative branch. The control is important, because, as this chapter will explain, a loss of control on an important issue (an issue of "confidence") leads to either the resignation of the government or (more commonly) an election. Again, the obvious contrast is the constitution of the United States, which observes a separation between all three branches of government. In the United States, not only are the courts independent of the legislative and executive branches (as in Canada), but the executive branch has no power of control over the legislative branch (unlike Canada).

§ 9:2 History of responsible government

By 1832, the colonies of British North America had achieved representative government,[1] but they had not achieved responsible government. The government of each colony was "representative", because it included a legislative assembly elected by the people of the colony. The assembly had the power to make laws, to raise taxes, and to grant supply (money) to the executive. But colonial government was not "responsible", because the executive was not responsible to the assembly. Executive power was possessed by the British-appointed governor, who was responsible to the Colonial Office of the United Kingdom government, which had appointed him, instructed him, and continued to supervise his work. The governor also received advice from a local executive council whom he appointed, but the members of the executive council in each province were drawn from a wealthy elite who not only lacked the confidence of the assembly but who often actively opposed the policies determined by the assembly. This meant that laws enacted by the assembly would often not be enforced; policies opposed by the assembly would often be implemented; civil servants regarded as unsuitable or incompetent by the assembly would often be appointed; and colonial revenues which did not come from taxes would often be spent for purposes of which the assembly disapproved.

In every colony, there was chronic conflict between the assembly and the governor (and his executive council). In Upper and Lower Canada, these frustrations led to armed rebellions in 1837. After the rebellions, Lord Durham was appointed governor of all the British North American colonies with instructions to report upon the causes of and remedies for

---

[Section 9:2]

[1]British Columbia was an exception. As related in ch. 2, Reception, British Columbia did not acquire a fully elective assembly until 1871. That chapter describes the establishment of assemblies in all the other colonies, the last being Newfoundland in 1832.

the colonial discontent. Lord Durham reported in 1839.[2] He accurately identified the causes of conflict between assembly and executive, and he recommended the institution of responsible government: in Durham's view, the Colonial Office should instruct each governor to appoint to his executive council only persons who enjoyed the confidence of a majority of the assembly. This recommendation simply applied to the colonies the same system that had recently evolved in the United Kingdom to reconcile the powers of the representative Parliament and the hereditary King.[3] In the colonies, however, there was a further complication. How could the governor obey instructions from the Colonial Office in London as well as following the advice of his local executive council? Durham's solution was to distinguish between matters of imperial concern and matters of local concern. The only matters of imperial concern, he submitted, were constitutional arrangements, foreign affairs, external trade, and the disposal of public lands. On these matters, the governor would act on the instructions of the Colonial Office. On all other matters, the governor would act on the advice of his local executive council.

At first, the government of the United Kingdom would not accept Lord Durham's wise recommendation (although it readily accepted his foolish plan for the union of Upper and Lower Canada).[4] But in 1846 a new Colonial Secretary, Earl Grey, did accept the recommendation and instructed the governors along the lines indicated by Lord Durham. In 1848 the new system was put to the test in Nova Scotia, when after a general election the assembly carried a vote of no confidence in the executive council. The council resigned and the governor appointed the leader of the majority party in the assembly to be premier with power to name the other members of the new council—all in accordance with the conventions of responsible government. Changes of government occurred in the same way in the united province of Canada and in New Brunswick also in 1848, in Prince Edward Island in 1851, and in Newfoundland in 1855. Responsible government was thus achieved in those provinces. British Columbia did not achieve responsible government until 1872, a year after its admission to Canada. Manitoba (created in 1870), Alberta

[2]Lord Durham's Report (1839) has been published in an edited version by McClelland and Stewart: G.M. Craig (ed.), Lord Durham's Report (1963).

[3]Lederman, Continuing Canadian Constitutional Dilemmas (1981), 50–51, notes that the thirteen American colonies, forming their new government in 1789 before responsible government had developed in the United Kingdom (the development was not complete until around the time of Lord Durham's report), created a President whose relationship to the Congress was similar to that of George III in relation to the British Parliament. Once a President has been elected, for his four-year term he possesses executive power independent of the Congress. Conflict between the legislative and executive branches is therefore a characteristic of the American Constitution to this day. The Americans thus froze this aspect of the constitutional arrangements of 1789, which in the United Kingdom continued to evolve into a new system of responsible government.

[4]See ch. 2, Reception, under heading § 2:4, "Amendment of received laws".

(created in 1905) and Saskatchewan (also created in 1905) were each granted responsible government at the time of their creation.[5]

§ 9:3 Law and convention

In a system of "responsible government" (or cabinet or parliamentary government, as it may also be called) the formal head of state, whether King or Queen, Governor General or Lieutenant Governor, must always act under the "advice" (meaning direction) of ministers who are members of the legislative branch and who enjoy the confidence of a majority in the elected house of the legislative branch. Responsible government is probably the most important non-federal characteristic of the Canadian Constitution. Yet the rules which govern it are almost entirely "conventional", that is to say, they are not to be found in the ordinary legal sources of statute or decided cases.[1]

As noted in the previous section of this chapter, responsible government had been achieved in each of the uniting colonies at the time of confederation in 1867. The intention to continue the same system after confederation was evidenced by the assertion in the preamble to the Constitution Act, 1867 that Canada was to have "a constitution similar in principle to that of the United Kingdom". Other than this vague reference, however, the Constitution Act is silent on responsible government; it confers powers on the Queen and the Governor General but makes no mention of the Prime Minister or the cabinet. Thus, s. 9 provides that the "executive government" of Canada is vested in "the Queen"; s. 10 contemplates that the Queen's powers may be exercised by a "Governor General"; and s. 11 establishes a "Queen's Privy Council for Canada" whose function is "to aid and advise in the government of Canada" and whose members are to be appointed and removed by the Governor General. The Governor General is also an essential part of the legislative branch in that a "bill" which has been enacted by both Houses of Parliament passes into law (and becomes an "Act" or a "statute") only after the Governor General (or the Queen) has given the royal assent to the bill (ss. 17, 55). In addition, the Governor General is given power to appoint the members of the appointed upper house, the Senate (s. 24), to summon into session the members of the elective lower house, the House of Commons (s. 38), to dissolve the House of Commons (s. 50), to withhold the royal assent from a bill passed by both Houses of Parliament or to "reserve" the bill "for the signification of the Queen's pleasure" (s. 55). The Queen herself has a discretion whether or not to assent to a bill reserved by the Governor General (s. 57), and she has the further power

[5]See Dawson, The Government of Canada (5th ed., 1970), ch. 1 (not in 6th ed.). Some of the history of the provincial governments is also described in ch. 2, Reception.

[Section 9:3]

[1]Conventions and their role in the Constitution are discussed in § 1:10, "Conventions".

to "disallow" (annul) any statute enacted by the Canadian Parliament (s. 56).[2]

In each province, there is a "Lieutenant Governor" and an "Executive Council" with powers similar to those of the Governor General and Privy Council (ss. 58–68, 90). The Lieutenant Governors are appointed by the Governor General in Council (s. 58),[3] and it is the Governor General (rather than the Queen) to whom a Lieutenant Governor reserves a provincial bill; and it is the Governor General in Council (rather than the Queen in Council) in whom is vested the power of disallowance of a provincial statute (s. 90).[4] There are other provisions of the Constitution Act, 1867 which confer specific powers on the Governor General or the Lieutenant Governors. Furthermore, the statute books will reveal that the Canadian Parliament and provincial Legislatures to this day usually confer major powers of government upon the Governor General in Council (often shortened to the "Governor in Council") or the Lieutenant Governor in Council.

The Constitution Act, 1867 also tells us that Canada is a monarchy, that is to say, the formal head of state is "the Queen". The Queen is vested with executive authority over Canada (s. 9), and she is also a formal part of the Parliament of Canada, along with the Senate and House of Commons (s. 17). The Constitution Act, 1867 does not expressly define "the Queen", but the preamble to the Act recites that the uniting provinces are to be "federally united into one Dominion under the Crown of the United Kingdom". That recital makes clear that the Queen or King of Canada is to be the same person as the Queen or King of the

---

[2]Reservation and disallowance of federal statutes have been nullified by convention: see ch. 3, Independence, under heading § 3:1, "Bonds of Empire".

[3]The fact that the Lieutenant Governor is to be appointed by the Governor General (the federal government) led to early controversy as to whether he was a representative of the Crown or of the federal government. The issue was important because if the Lieutenant Governor were not the representative of the Crown then the provincial government would not be entitled to the executive powers and prerogatives of the Crown; all executive powers and prerogatives would rest with the central government, unless specifically delegated to the provinces. In *Liquidators of Maritime Bank v. Receiver General of N.B.*, [1892] A.C. 437, the Privy Council, speaking through Lord Watson, emphatically rejected the view that the Lieutenant Governors (and their provincial governments) were subordinate to the Governor General (and his federal government): "a Lieutenant-Governor, when appointed, is as much the representative of Her Majesty for all purposes of provincial government as the Governor-General himself is for all purposes of Dominion government" (p. 443). It followed that the federal distribution of legislative power entailed a matching distribution of executive powers and prerogatives as well: see also *Bonanza Creek Gold Mining Co. v. The King*, [1916] 1 A.C. 566. In the early years of confederation, the Lieutenant Governors did also fulfil a secondary role as federal officers, but this has fallen into disuse: Hendry, Memorandum on the Office of Lieutenant-Governor of a Province (1955); Saywell, The Office of Lieutenant-Governor (1957), chs. 1, 7. For analysis of the significance of these decisions, see S.M. Birks, "The Survival of the Crown in the Canadian State" (LL.M. thesis, Osgoode Hall Law School, York University, 1980).

[4]Reservation and disallowance of provincial statutes have probably been nullified by convention: see ch. 5, Federalism, under heading § 5:11, "Judicial interpretation of the distribution of powers".

U.K.[5] That person is identified by the law of royal succession of the United Kingdom. When the law of royal succession is changed by the U.K. Parliament, as it was in 1936, when Edward VIII abdicated, and in 2013, when some discriminatory provisions respecting sex and religion were eliminated, the U.K. law automatically takes effect in Canada, not because the U.K. law applies in Canada, but because Canada takes as its monarch whoever is entitled to be monarch of the U.K. Canada has a rule of recognition rather than its own rules of succession. All that Canada needs to do—and this is a requirement of convention, not strict law—is for Parliament to provide its "assent" to the U.K. change.[6] Of course, Canada, as a sovereign country, is free to adopt rules of succession that diverge from those of the U.K., but that unlikely initiative would be a change in the definition of the Queen in the Constitution of Canada and would involve a constitutional amendment.[7]

The Queen has in fact delegated all of her powers over Canada[8] to the Canadian Governor General, except of course for the power to appoint or dismiss the Governor General.[9] Moreover, most powers of government, whether conferred by the Constitution or by ordinary statute, are

---

[5]The Constitution Act, 1867, by s. 2, provided that references to "the Queen" "extend also to the heirs and successors of Her Majesty, Kings and Queens of the United Kingdom". This provision reinforced the preamble with a clear statement that the Queen of Canada was the same person as the Queen of the U.K. Section 2 was repealed by the Statute Law Revision Act, 1893 (U.K.) when the provision was replicated by the Interpretation Act, 1889 (U.K.).

[6]The convention was adopted at the imperial conference of 1930, which had the goal of enhancing the equality of the Dominions with the U.K., and it is recited in a preamble to the Statute of Westminster, 1931 (U.K.), which says that "it would be in accord with the established constitutional position of all the members of the Commonwealth in relation to one another that any alteration of the law touching the Succession to the Throne or the Royal Style and Titles shall hereafter require the assent as well of the Parliaments of all the Dominions as of the Parliament of the United Kingdom". The changes to the law of succession of the U.K. in 1936 and 2013 were accompanied by Canadian statutes providing the "assent" of the Parliament of Canada: Succession to the Throne Act, S.C. 1937, c. 16, s. 1; Succession to the Throne Act, S.C. 2013, c. 6, s. 2. For further detail, see P.W. Hogg, "Succession to the Throne" (2014) 33 Nat. J. Con. Law 83, especially note 14; see also *Motard v. Can.*, 2019 QCCA 1826 (Que. C.A.), leave to appeal to the S.C.C. denied April 23, 2020 (no constitutional amendment needed for the Succession to the Throne Act, 2013; discussed further in ch. 1, Sources, under heading § 1:4, "Constitution of Canada").

[7]Part V of the Constitution Act, 1982 seems to call for the unanimity procedure: s. 41(a) ("the office of the Queen"). That would certainly be the case if Canada decided to abolish the monarchy.

[8]An exception may be the power to appoint additional senators under s. 26 of the Constitution Act, 1867, which by referring to both the Governor General and the Queen perhaps implies a continuing non-delegable role for the Queen, to be exercised however only on the advice of Canadian ministers. When this power was exercised in 1990 (for the first time in Canadian history), a direction from the Queen was in fact obtained: see *Re Appointment of Senators* (1991), 78 D.L.R. (4th) 245 (B.C.C.A.); *Singh v. Can.* (1991), 3 O.R. (3d) 429 (C.A.); *Weir v. Can.* (1991), 84 D.L.R. (4th) 39 (C.A.).

[9]Letters Patent constituting the office of Governor General of Canada (1947), R.S.C. 1985, Appendix II, No. 31, art. II; Mallory, The Structure of Canadian Government (rev. ed., 1984), 21, 37–39. As Mallory explains, a few powers are still in practice

conferred upon the Governor General (or the Governor General in Council) directly. It is therefore simpler, and sufficiently accurate for most purposes, to speak of the Governor General being the formal head of state.[10] He or she is appointed by the Queen, and in colonial times of course the Queen acted on the advice of her British ministers in making the appointment. However, the imperial conference of 1926 declared that the Governor General was not the "representative or agent" of the British government, and the imperial conference of 1930 resolved that thenceforth the Governor General would be appointed by the Queen acting on the advice of the ministers of the dominion concerned.[11] Since 1930, all Canadian Governors General have been selected by the Canadian Prime Minister with the Queen merely formalizing the appointment.[12] It is also the Canadian Prime Minister who determines the Governor General's term of office, and the Canadian Parliament that fixes the salary.[13]

The Governor General does not use any personal initiative or discretion in the exercise of the powers of government that belong to the office,

---

exercised by the Queen, but the delegation is complete so that they could be exercised by the Governor General. Needless to say, those powers which are conferred by the Constitution or by statute upon the Governor General directly do not require any delegation from the Queen for their exercise. Article VIII of the Letters Patent provides that the office devolves upon the Chief Justice of Canada "in the event of the death, incapacity, removal, or absence of Our Governor General out of Canada"; and upon "the senior judge for the time being of the Supreme Court of Canada" in the event of "the death, incapacity, removal or absence out of Canada of Our Chief Justice"; while the powers are vested in the Chief Justice or senior judge, he or she is "to be known as Our Administrator".

[10]Within each province the office of Lieutenant Governor is equivalent to that of Governor General of Canada; to that extent the Letters Patent constituting the office of Governor General of Canada (1947), R.S.C. 1985, Appendix II, No. 31, art. II are misleading in their delegation of "all powers and authorities" to the Governor General. There is no provision in the Constitution Act, 1867 (or elsewhere) for an acting Lieutenant Governor in the event of the death or incapacity of the Lieutenant Governor; this means that government business requiring the imprimatur of the Lieutenant Governor, for example, new statutes and orders in council, has to await the appointment by the federal government of a replacement.

[11]On the imperial conferences of 1926 and 1930, see ch. 3, Independence. No comparable convention has been established with respect to the appointment of Lieutenant Governors. Under s. 58 of the Constitution Act, 1867, such appointments are to be made by the Governor General in Council; this power is exercised on the advice of the federal Prime Minister not the provincial Premier. This means that the appointee will often be a member of the political party in power in Ottawa, and the provincial Premier may not even be consulted, especially if he is not a member of that party: Saywell, The Office of Lieutenant-Governor (1957), ch. 1; MacKinnon, The Government of Prince Edward Island (1951), 144–149; Donnelly, The Government of Manitoba (1963), 115–116; Forsey, Freedom and Order (1914), 161–164. In Australia, the state governors are appointed on the advice of the state governments, not the federal government.

[12]By convention the advice is tendered by the Prime Minister, and the decision is his alone, although no doubt he would usually consult his cabinet: Mallory, The Structure of Canadian Government (rev. ed., 1984), 93. Similarly, by convention it is the Prime Minister who tenders advice as to the appointment of Lieutenant Governors: Saywell, The Office of Lieutenant-Governor (1957), 24.

[13]Constitution Act, 1867, s. 105, confers the power to fix the salary, but the Act is silent with respect to appointment and tenure.

except for certain "reserve powers" or "personal prerogatives", which are exercisable only in exceptional circumstances, and which are discussed later in this chapter.[14] The effect of responsible government is to transfer effective political power to elected officials.

II. THE EXECUTIVE BRANCH

§ 9:4 The ministry

What precisely are the conventions of responsible government? For convenience of exposition, I shall concentrate on Canada's federal government, but the rules are much the same in each of the provinces (and indeed in all those jurisdictions outside Canada whose governments are responsible in the technical sense).[1] Where there is any significant variation in provincial practice, that fact will be noted.

The narrative must start with an exercise by the Governor General of one of the exceptional reserve powers or personal prerogatives. In the formation of a government, it is the Governor General's duty to select the Prime Minister. The Governor General must select a person who can form a government that will enjoy the confidence of the House of Commons. For reasons that will be explained later, the Governor General rarely has any real choice as to whom to appoint: he or she must appoint the parliamentary leader of the political party that has a majority of seats in the House of Commons. But it is still accurate to describe the Governor General's discretion as his or her own, because, unlike nearly all of his or her other decisions, it is not made upon ministerial advice.

When the Prime Minister has been appointed, he selects the other ministers, and advises the Governor General to appoint them. With respect to these appointments, the Governor General reverts to his or her normal non-discretionary role and is obliged by convention to make the appointments advised by the Prime Minister. If the Prime Minister later wishes to make changes in the ministry, as by moving a minister from one portfolio to another, or by appointing a new minister, or by removing a minister, then the Governor General will take whatever action is advised by the Prime Minister, including if necessary the dismissal of a minister who has refused the Prime Minister's request to resign.

It is basic to the system of responsible government that the Prime Minister and all the other ministers be members of Parliament.[2] Occasionally a person who is not a member of Parliament is appointed as a

---

[14]§§ 9:16 to 9:24, "The Governor General's personal prerogatives".

[Section 9:4]

[1]For the provinces, see MacKinnon, The Government of Prince Edward Island (1951); Beck, The Government of Nova Scotia (1957); Saywell, The Office of Lieutenant-Governor (1957); Donnelly, The Government of Manitoba (1963); Schindeler, Responsible Government in Ontario (1969); Bellamy, Pammett, Rowat (eds.), The Provincial Political Systems (1976), esp. ch. 20 (by Saywell).

[2]The responsibility to Parliament of each minister is explained in § 9:7, "Ministerial responsibility". Note that the term "deputy minister" is used in Canada to describe

minister, but then the minister must quickly be elected to the House of Commons or appointed to the Senate. If the minister fails to win election, and is not appointed to the Senate, then he or she must resign (or be dismissed) from the ministry. The usual practice when a non-member of Parliament is appointed to the ministry is that a member of the Prime Minister's political party will be induced to resign from a "safe seat" in Parliament, which will precipitate a by-election in which the newly-appointed minister will be the candidate from the Prime Minister's party.

A ministry lasts as long as the tenure of the Prime Minister. When a Prime Minister dies, resigns or is dismissed, the ministry comes to an end, and a new ministry is formed by his or her successor.[3] A ministry does not come to an end when Parliament is dissolved for an election; that would leave the country without a government. The ministry continues in office and awaits the result of the election. If the election is won by the governing party, there is no interruption in the ministry. If the election is lost by the governing party, the Prime Minister will no longer command a majority in the House of Commons and will resign (or be dismissed by the Governor General).

When a government (ministry) remains in office following a dissolution of Parliament, whether or not the government has lost the confidence of the House of Commons, there is a risk that the government will lose the ensuing election and will not command a majority in the House of Commons of the next Parliament. The period from the dissolution of one Parliament, through the election campaign and the election, until the summoning of the new Parliament, is often a long time: the average is well over four months (144 days) and it has been as long as six months.[4] During this period, the government retains its full panoply of legal powers (statutory, prerogative and common law), and of course it has to continue to govern the country. However, by *convention*,

---

the permanent head of a government department, who is of course a civil servant and not a member of Parliament. In Australia, New Zealand or the United Kingdom any title including the word "minister" would imply a parliamentary appointee.

[3]Although the ministry is dissolved by the death, resignation or dismissal of the Prime Minister, individual ministers, who of course hold their positions by virtue of a commission from the Crown (granted by the Governor General), continue to exercise their functions until the new Prime Minister requests their resignation. No actual resignation is needed; the office is simply at the disposal of the new Prime Minister. If there is no change of government, the new Prime Minister may well want some ministers to remain in office. For those portfolios, no new appointments are necessary. The Prime Minister will simply advise the Governor General of the continuing roles, and the ministers will continue in office under their existing commissions, although they are now in a new ministry under the new Prime Minister. If there is a change of government, the new Prime Minister will normally want to replace all of the ministers in the outgoing ministry. They will, however, continue to exercise their functions until the Governor General, on the advice of the new Prime Minister, commissions new ministers to replace the members of the outgoing ministry, causing the automatic "resignation" of the members of the outgoing ministry.

[4]For details, see C.E.S. Franks, "Parliaments, 1945–2008", Appendix 2 to Canada's Public Policy Forum, Towards Guidelines on Government Formation (Public Policy Forum, Ottawa, 2012), 20–23.

it is expected to behave as a caretaker and to restrain the exercise of its *legal* authority. This "caretaker convention" was clarified in 2008, when the Privy Council Office of the Government of Canada issued guidelines in writing for decisions by federal ministers and senior officials in the federal public service. For the caretaker period,[5] the guidelines stipulate that "in matters of policy, expenditure and appointments", the government should restrict itself "to activity that is: (a) routine, or (b) non-controversial, or (c) urgent and in the public interest, or (d) reversible by a new government without undue cost or disruption, or (e) agreed upon by the Opposition (in those cases where consultation is appropriate)".[6] The Clerk of the Privy Council would be expected to remind the Prime Minister and the senior ranks of the public service of these restrictions during caretaker periods. A similar caretaker convention applies to the governments of the provinces and territories. Like other conventions,[7] the caretaker convention is observed because it is well understood to be the only appropriate behaviour; there is no legal sanction for a breach. But obviously a clear breach would attract severe criticism and be politically damaging to the offending party.

§ 9:5 The cabinet and the Privy Council

When the ministers meet together as a group they constitute the cabinet.[1] The cabinet is not mentioned in the Constitution Act, 1867, although we have already noticed that a body called the Queen's Privy Council for Canada is established by s. 11,[2] The cabinet ministers are all appointed to the Queen's Privy Council for Canada. But the Privy

---

[5]The period starts with the dissolution of Parliament and would end with the beginning of the new Parliament. It could however end earlier. A decisive election outcome in favour of the incumbent government would bring it to an end, as would a decisive election outcome in favour of the Opposition, in which case the caretaker period would end with the resignation of the incumbent government and the commissioning of the new government.

[6]Government of Canada, Guidelines on the Conduct of Ministers, Secretaries of State, Exempt Staff and Public Servants During an Election (Government of Canada, Ottawa, 2008); quoted in Towards Guidelines on Government Formation, § 9:4 note 4 with the explanation that the document had been obtained under Canada's Access to Information Act.

[7]Chapter 1, Sources, under heading § 1:10, "Conventions".

[Section 9:5]

[1]The ministry and the cabinet are not necessarily identical. In the United Kingdom and Australia, for example, not all ministers are members of cabinet. Whether a particular minister is admitted to the cabinet lies in the discretion of the Prime Minister. The usual Canadian practice has been for the Prime Minister to admit all ministers to the cabinet: Dawson, The Government of Canada (6th ed., 1987 by Ward), 196; and this has been the general practice of the provincial Premiers as well.

[2]Canada's Privy Council is of course modelled on the Privy Council in the United Kingdom, which is a body under the formal duty of advising the Queen as to the government of the United Kingdom. The United Kingdom's Privy Council used to have considerable significance for Canada in that its Judicial Committee was the final court of appeal for Canadian law-suits. The appeal to the Judicial Committee was abolished in 1949.

Council includes many other people as well.[3] Appointments to the Privy Council are for life, so that its membership always includes not only the ministers of the government in office, but also all living persons who were ministers in past governments. Moreover, appointments to the Privy Council are often made to persons of distinction as an honour, so that its membership will include such persons as the Duke of Edinburgh, the Prince of Wales, a British Prime Minister, a Canadian High Commissioner, or a provincial Premier; and of course such honorific appointments will be for life. The whole Privy Council would be a body of some one hundred members of widely differing political persuasions. Such a body could not, and does not, conduct the business of government. The whole Privy Council meets very rarely, and then only for ceremonial occasions.[4]

The cabinet, which does meet regularly and frequently, is in most matters the supreme executive authority. (The "reserve powers" remain in the Governor General, and some powers are vested in the Prime Minister; these powers are discussed later.) The cabinet formulates and carries out all executive policies, and it is responsible for the administration of all the departments of government. It constitutes the only active part of the Privy Council, and it exercises the powers of that body. The Governor General does not preside over, or even attend, the meetings of the cabinet.[5] The Prime Minister presides. Where the Constitution or a statute requires that a decision be made by the "Governor General in Council" (and this requirement is very common indeed), there is still no meeting with the Governor General. The cabinet (or a cabinet committee to which routine Privy Council business has been delegated) will make the decision, and send an "order" or "minute" of the decision to the Governor General for signature (which by convention is automatically given).[6] Where a statute requires that a decision be made by a particular minister, then the cabinet will make the decision, and the relevant minister will formally authenticate the decision. Of course a cabinet will be content to delegate many matters to individual ministers, but each minister recognizes the supreme authority of the cabinet should the cabinet seek to exercise it.

---

[3]This is not true in the provinces, where the membership of the executive council and the cabinet is identical.

[4]The last occasion was on April 17, 1982, when the Queen proclaimed into force the Constitution Act, 1982.

[5]In the provinces, too, the Lieutenant Governor never presides over or attends meetings of the cabinet: Saywell, The Office of Lieutenant-Governor (1957), 35–36.

[6]Mallory, The Structure of Canadian Government (rev. ed., 1984), 74–75.

§ 9:6 The Prime Minister

While in most matters the cabinet is the supreme executive authority, the Prime Minister (or provincial Premier)[1] has certain powers which he or she does not need to share with his or her colleagues.[2] Two of these are of great importance. First, there is the power to select the other ministers, and the power to promote, demote or dismiss them at pleasure. (Technically, of course, the Prime Minister only has power to recommend such measures to the Governor General, but the recommendations will invariably be acted upon.) Secondly, the Prime Minister is personally responsible for tendering advice to the Governor General as to when Parliament should be dissolved for an election, and when an elected Parliament should be summoned into session.[3]

Not only are these powers important in their own right, but the Prime Minister's possession of them also ensures that the Prime Minister's voice will be the most influential one within the cabinet. In addition, the Prime Minister enjoys the special authority which derives from having been selected by a political party as its leader, and from having led the party to victory in the previous election. Modern Canadian election campaigns have increasingly emphasized the qualities of the competing leaders, and this practice inevitably strengthens the position within the party of the leader of the victorious party. No doubt the extent of a Prime Minister's personal power varies from government to government, depending upon a number of factors. But in some governments a Prime Minister, who chooses to take on his own initiative, or on the advice of a few ministers, decisions which would traditionally be the preserve of the cabinet, is politically able to do so; and the extent to which the full cabinet plays a role in important decision-making may depend in large measure upon the discretion of the Prime Minister. In this connection it is important to notice that the Prime Minister calls the meetings of cabi-

---

[Section 9:6]

[1] On the office of Prime Minister, see generally Hockin (ed.), Apex of Power (2nd ed., 1977); Savoie, Governing from the Centre: The Concentration of Power in Canadian Politics (1999).

[2] Privy Council minute, P.C. 3374, October 25, 1935 provides:

> the following recommendations are the special prerogative of the prime minister: dissolution and convocation of Parliament: Appointment of—privy councillors; cabinet ministers; lieutenant governors (including leave of absence to same); provincial administrators, speaker of the Senate; Chief Justices of all courts, senators, sub-committees of council; Treasury Board; . . .

Not included in this list is the recommendation to the Queen for appointment of a Governor General, which is another power that, by convention, the Prime Minister may exercise independently of the other ministers.

[3] These important powers are limited by the Constitution Act, 1982, s. 4 of which prescribes a maximum duration for the House of Commons or a provincial legislative assembly of five years, and s. 5 of which requires that there be a sitting of Parliament and of each Legislature at least once every twelve months. See also ss. 50 and 86 of the Constitution Act, 1867.

net, settles the agenda, presides over the meetings, and "defines the consensus"[4] on each topic.

The Prime Minister (or provincial Premier) effectively controls the executive branch of government through his control over ministerial appointments and over the cabinet. But, as will be explained in more detail later in this chapter, the Prime Minister effectively controls the legislative branch as well. In the normal situation of majority government (and assuming a compliant Senate), the Prime Minister's leadership of the majority party in the House of Commons, reinforced by strict party discipline, and sanctioned by his power to dissolve the House for an election, enables him to determine what legislation will be enacted. This latter power is not possessed by the President of the United States (or a state Governor), who is elected for a fixed term independently of the Congress, who does not control either of the Houses of Congress (even if they both happen to be dominated by his own party, which is rarely the case), and who can rely only on moral suasion to influence the Congress's legislative agenda. The Canadian system of responsible government thus leads to a concentration of power in the hands of the Prime Minister that has no counterpart in the presidential system.

§ 9:7 Ministerial responsibility

There is a minister at the head of each of the departments of government. Most of the cabinet ministers have charge of at least one department. There are often one or more "ministers without portfolio" who are members of the cabinet, but who do not have charge of a department. Each minister who does have charge of a department has the administrative duties that go with such an office. In addition, the minister "represents" his or her department in Parliament: the minister pilots the departmental estimates of proposed expenditures through the House, explains and defends the policies and practices of the department, and introduces into Parliament any bills that relate to the work of the department.[1]

A government department is, of course, administered by civil servants, who, in contrast to the minister, are supposed to be politically neutral. The senior civil servant in each department, who in Canada is

---

[4]Votes are not taken at cabinet meetings. When the Prime Minister believes that there has been sufficient discussion of a topic, he will "define a consensus" on the topic. Observers have noted that the "consensus" is often not a consensus and is not even always the majority view: Savoie, Governing from the Centre: The Concentration of Power in Canadian Politics (1999), 85–87. The practice appears to be the same in provincial cabinets, with the Premier defining the consensus.

[Section 9:7]

[1]In addition to one or more departments, a minister will often have a number of Crown corporations and regulatory agencies assigned to his or her ministry. These bodies are outside the departmental structure because they are intended to operate with more autonomy than a government department. However, because they are publicly funded, they have to be subjected to some degree of ministerial control; the mechanisms of that control differ greatly from one body to another.

usually called a "deputy minister", is the link between the minister and the civil servants. The deputy minister acts both as an adviser to the minister and as the senior manager of the department. Of course, the minister is under no obligation to follow the advice of the deputy minister. The deputy minister is within the tradition of civil service neutrality: when the government changes, the deputy minister, like other career civil servants, will usually retain his or her position. However, the deputy minister is not appointed by normal civil service procedures: the appointment is made by order in council on the recommendation of the Prime Minister. The appointment is normally made from within the ranks of the career civil service, and is not treated as political patronage. Nevertheless, it is not unusual for a deputy minister to be replaced when a new government takes office.

One aspect of the political neutrality of civil servants is the convention that they are anonymous in the sense that they should not be criticized personally or otherwise held accountable in Parliament. All the acts of the department are done in the name of the minister, and it is the minister who is responsible to Parliament for those acts. In this context, the word "responsible" is often said to entail two consequences. First, the minister is supposed to explain to Parliament, when asked, the actions of his or her department. This is a real responsibility. During the regular question period, a minister will be frequently called upon by other members of Parliament to answer questions about the work of the department.[2] Secondly, the minister is supposed to resign if a serious case of maladministration occurs within the department. This second aspect of ministerial responsibility is often asserted to exist, but is of much more doubtful strength. In a case of misconduct or serious maladministration by a minister personally, the principle would certainly apply and would require the resignation of the minister. In a case of misconduct or maladministration by a civil servant in the minister's department, a ministerial resignation is quite unlikely to follow in Canada. Accordingly, it may be more realistic (and therefore accurate) to define ministerial responsibility as not including an obligation to resign for merely departmental sins, although such resignations are often called for by the opposition and do occasionally occur.[3]

The notion of the responsibility of individual ministers is related to, but distinct from, the notion of the "collective responsibility" of the cabinet as a whole. All cabinet ministers collectively accept responsibility for cabinet decisions. This means that a cabinet minister is obliged to give public support to any decision reached by the cabinet, even if the

---

[2]Contrast the United States, where the President and his ministers are not members of Congress and do not have to answer questions posed by members of Congress.

[3]There is no personal *legal* responsibility on the part of a minister for torts or crimes committed by civil servants within a minister's department. In tort, vicarious liability for the acts of civil servants attaches to the Crown, which is the employer, not to individual ministers: *Bainbridge v. Postmaster-General*, [1906] 1 K.B. 178 (C.A.) (minister not liable for torts committed by subordinates). In criminal law, there is no general doctrine of vicarious liability: *Bhatnager v. Can.*, [1990] 2 S.C.R. 217 (ministers not liable for contempt of court order of which they were unaware).

minister personally opposed the decision within the cabinet and still disagrees with it. If the minister does decide to express dissent in public, then the minister should resign; and, if the minister does not resign, he or she can expect to be dismissed by the Prime Minister (although the Prime Minister might decide to tolerate the offence). Even after a minister resigns or is dismissed, the obligations of confidentiality and unanimity continue, but the Prime Minister will normally give permission to the minister to publish his or her reasons for resignation.

Collective responsibility implies more than cabinet solidarity. Its most fundamental consequence is that if a cabinet decision is attacked in Parliament the issue is one of confidence in the government. As will be explained later in this chapter, if a government is defeated in the House of Commons[4] on an issue of confidence in the government, then the government must either resign or advise the Governor General to dissolve the House for an election. Consequently, the government will insist that its supporters in the House vote on party lines in favour of the government. Since the government is in office because it commands a majority of the members of the House, it is normally in a position to resist any opposition attack on its policies. The vigour of the doctrine of collective responsibility is what undermines the doctrine of individual responsibility. If a ministerial decision has been approved or ratified by the cabinet, then the individual minister will be protected by collective responsibility. More bluntly, one must acknowledge that if the government does not want a minister to resign, then no matter how clearly the facts would seem to warrant the minister's resignation, there is no way that the opposition can force it to happen.

III. THE LEGISLATIVE BRANCH

§ 9:8 The Parliament

The legislative power of the federal government is vested in the Parliament of Canada, which consists (in the language of s. 17 of the Constitution Act, 1867) "of the Queen, an upper house styled the Senate, and the House of Commons". There are thus three elements which must combine for passage of legislation and the cabinet is not one of them. Nevertheless the cabinet is able to control the legislative process. In order to see why this is so, let us examine separately each element of the process.

§ 9:9 The House of Commons

The House of Commons is a body which is elected on the basis of universal adult suffrage. As such it is representative of most shades of Ca-

[4]The responsibility of the government and of individual ministers is to the elective lower house, and not to the Senate. A defeat in the Senate does not entail resignation or dissolution. This is one reason why only a few cabinet members are drawn from the Senate. Another reason is that a minister who sits in the Senate is not available to answer questions during question period in the House of Commons.

nadian opinion.[1] But the Prime Minister and his cabinet (the government) are in office solely because they have the support of a majority of members in the House of Commons. In normal circumstances this support is unwavering and is available for every measure proposed by the government. Canada's political parties insist upon strict party discipline from their parliamentary members. Party discipline is effective to the point that each member of the government party can nearly always be relied upon to support all government measures. Very rarely does an issue arise which so divides the government party that any members will vote against the government. When that happens the combined votes of the opposition parties and the government defectors may defeat the government.

A more common situation in which the government may lose the support of a majority in the House of Commons is after a close election has given neither of the two major parties a majority in the House of Commons, and the control of the House depends upon one of the major parties being able to secure the cooperation of one of the minor parties. Here the cabinet's control is much more precarious, and the minor party can bring about the defeat of the government whenever it chooses. Sometimes this situation of "minority government" can be stabilized by the major party entering into coalition with the minor party and admitting its leaders to the cabinet. Coalition governments have not been uncommon in the provinces,[2] and in countries outside Canada,[3] but the Canadian federal government's only experience of this kind was the "union government" which was formed during the first world war. Since then, there have been frequent minority governments in which either the Conservative Party or the Liberal Party has had to depend upon the support of a third party,[4] but there does not seem to have been any seri-

---

[Section 9:9]

[1]Note, however, the controversies about the merits of different electoral systems: Irvine, Does Canada Need a New Electoral System? (1979).

[2]E.g., Manitoba in the 1930s and 1940s, British Columbia from 1941 to 1952, Saskatchewan from 1999 to 2002.

[3]In the democracies of western Europe and New Zealand, where elections are held on the basis of proportional representation and many parties contend for office, a majority for one party is highly unusual, coalition governments are normal and provide stable government. Canada (like Italy and Israel) is an outlier in the resistance of its politicians to any sustained form of inter-party cooperation and in its consequent inability to maintain stable minority governments: Russell, Two Cheers for Minority Government (2008), ch. 4; Hazell and Paun (eds.), Making Minority Government Work (2009), ch. 3.

[4]There have been nine federal minority governments: (1) 1921-22, 1923-24 and 1925-26 (King); (2) 1926 (Meighen); (3) 1957-58 and 1962-63 (Diefenbaker); (4) 1963-68 (Pearson); (5) 1972-74 (Trudeau); (6) 1979-80 (Clark); (7) 2004-2005 (Martin); (8) 2006-2011 (Harper); (9) 2019-present (J. Trudeau). Whenever more than two parties are contending for office, there is a risk of minority government, and, since the formation of the Bloc Quebecois in 1991, Canada has had four major parties contending in federal elections. For a thoughtful study of minority government, see Russell, § 9:9 note 3.

ous consideration of coalition.[5] However, even a minority government is able to exercise very substantial control over the legislative process. The minor party is inhibited from voting against the government by the fact that, for reasons given later, a vote against the government is almost certain to force a new general election. An election is always expensive and exhausting and is not to be lightly precipitated, especially as a minor party which has overturned a government without a very good reason is likely to lose votes and seats.[6] On the whole then it is a fair generalization to say that all measures proposed by the cabinet are assured of passage through the House of Commons.

§ 9:10 The Senate

The second element in the legislative process is the Senate.[1] Its members are appointed by the Governor General, which of course means, by convention, the cabinet. The Constitution Act, 1867, by s. 21, provides for a fixed number of senators and, by s. 29, provides that once appointed a senator holds office until age 75. Since each government tends to appoint its own supporters to the Senate, a government which has been in office for a long time will have a majority and sometimes an overwhelming majority of its own party members in the Senate. After a long-standing government loses an election the new government will be faced with a Senate which is still controlled by the opposition party, and it may be a long time before deaths, retirements and resignations enable

---

[5]An exceptional (but, as it turned out, unimportant) event was the entering into of a written agreement dated December 1, 2008 between the leaders of the opposition Liberal Party (77 seats) and New Democratic Party (37 seats), which proposed a coalition government with the leader of the Liberal Party as Prime Minister and cabinet members from both parties. With the support of the Bloc Quebecois (49 seats), which was also promised in writing, they had the votes to bring down the minority Conservative government of Prime Minister Stephen Harper (143 seats). However, their first opportunity to do so was precluded by the proroguing of Parliament on December 4. Within days of Parliament's resumption on January 26, 2009, the erstwhile coalition partners disagreed on whether to support the government's budget and divided on the confidence vote on the budget, allowing the Conservative government to stay in office, and bringing the coalition agreement to an untimely end. The story is told in § 9:20, "Prorogation of Parliament".

[6]Federal governments have only been defeated by a withdrawal of the confidence of the House of Commons eight times since Confederation, namely, 1873 (Macdonald), 1926 (King), 1926 (Meighen), 1963 (Diefenbaker), 1974 (Trudeau), 1979 (Clark), 2005 (Martin) and 2011 (Harper). Minority governments are not always defeated by a loss of confidence in the House of Commons. The Prime Minister of a minority government sometimes requests (and receives) a dissolution before any loss of confidence has occurred, e.g., 1957 (Diefenbaker), 1965 (Pearson), 1968 (Trudeau) and 2008 (Harper).

[Section 9:10]

[1]None of the provinces now has an upper house, although Manitoba, New Brunswick, Nova Scotia, Prince Edward Island and Quebec each used to have one (a Legislative Council) and subsequently abolished it: W.J. Newman, "Defining the 'Constitution of Canada' since 1982" (2003) 22 Supreme Court L.R. (2d) 423, 442–443.

the new government to redress the unhappy balance.[2] Even in this situation, however, the Senate has rarely refused passage of measures proposed by the government.[3] Although the Constitution Act, 1867 gives to the Senate the same powers as the House of Commons (except that, by s. 53, money bills must originate in the House of Commons), it has to be (and usually is) accepted by opposition as well as government senators that the appointive nature of the Senate must necessarily make its role subordinate to the elective House.[4]

The Senate was intended to serve as a protector of regional interests, which is a traditional function of the upper house in federal systems. Its membership was drawn equally from the three original regions (or "divisions", as the Constitution calls them) of Canada, namely, Ontario, Quebec and the maritime provinces. The west later became a fourth

---

[2]The Constitution Act, 1867, by s. 26, authorizes the appointment "at any time" of four or eight additional senators (drawn equally from the four divisions: (1) Ontario; (2) Quebec; (3) the three maritime provinces; and (4) the four western provinces) as a remedy for the obstruction of government measures by the Senate. But the numbers four or eight are too small to redress the substantial imbalances that are common, and so the section has only been used once. That occasion, in 1990, was when the Progressive Conservative government of Prime Minister Mulroney was faced with an opposition majority in the Senate that (after six years of Progressive Conservative government) had been reduced to less than eight. In that rare situation, s. 26 was an effective measure, enabling the government to secure Senate passage of the Goods and Services Tax Bill. The use of s. 26 was unsuccessfully challenged in the courts: *Re Appointment of Senators* (1991), 78 D.L.R. (4th) 245 (B.C.C.A.); *Singh v. Can.* (1991), 3 O.R. (3d) 429 (C.A.); *Weir v. Can.* (1991), 84 D.L.R. (4th) 39 (C.A.).

[3]For figures as to amendments and rejections of bills by the Senate, see MacKay, The Unreformed Senate of Canada (rev. ed., 1963), 199 (Appendix A); Kunz, The Modern Senate of Canada 1925–1963 (1965), 378 (Appendix 1). The pattern of restraint was broken by the Liberal majority in the Senate after the election in 1984 of the Progressive Conservative government of Prime Minister Mulroney. The Senate opposed some major government measures. The Senate refused to ratify the Meech Lake Constitutional Accord in 1987, and had to be overridden by the House of Commons under s. 47 of the Constitution Act, 1982. The Senate actually precipitated the election on Free Trade in 1988 by refusing to enact the government's bill to implement the Free Trade Agreement with the United States. The government won the election, and the Senate then passed the Bill. In the government's second term, the Senate refused to pass the Goods and Services Tax Bill, but by then the Liberal majority had been reduced to the point that the appointment under s. 26 (previous note) of eight additional senators tipped the balance and enabled the Bill to pass just before the GST's planned start-up date of January 1, 1991. In 1991, despite the government's slender majority, the Senate defeated with a tied vote the government's Abortion Bill, which had been passed by the House of Commons, but on a free vote. Throughout this period of activism, senators tended to vote on party lines, regardless of the region or province from which they were appointed.

[4]The Senate of the United States is able to function as a strong upper house, partly because it is an elected body, and also because the President is elected separately from the legislative branch for a fixed term of office: he is not dependent upon a majority in the Congress for his continuance in office. In Australia, where the Senate is also elected but the system is one of responsible government, the Senate's occasional bursts of independence (as in the denials of supply to Prime Minister Whitlam in 1974 and 1975, the latter leading to the Prime Minister's dismissal) have created almost unbearable political tensions. A strong upper house is not compatible with responsible government.

region.[5] The plan was to offset representation by population in the House of Commons with equality of regions in the Senate. The distribution of senators by province is now bizarre. Ontario and Quebec, which have the largest numbers in the House of Commons by virtue of representation by population, also have far and away the most senators (24 each). British Columbia and Alberta, the third and fourth largest provinces have only six each. New Brunswick has ten and tiny Prince Edward Island has four.

The plan to protect regional or provincial interests was fatally flawed from the beginning. A body that is appointed not elected, and appointed by the federal government not the provinces, cannot serve as a protector of regional or provincial interests. Prime Ministers overwhelmingly choose to appoint members of their own (federal) political party. There are strong incentives to make these appointments: they are a source of patronage for loyal supporters of the party, and once appointed the senator will join a party caucus and generally vote on party lines. There do not seem to be any recorded instances of the Senate defeating a bill for the purpose of protecting regional or provincial interests.

Whether it is now feasible to reform the Senate[6] so as to restore the original plan is doubtful. The difficulty is that in a system of responsible government the cabinet is responsible to the House of Commons, not the Senate. If government policy is defeated in the House of Commons, then the government must resign and make way, either for a new government that can command the support of the House of Commons, or for an election that will yield a new House of Commons. An upper house has no obvious place in this scheme of things. That is why, in so many jurisdictions with parliamentary systems, the upper house has been abolished or reduced to impotence. And that is why the assertions of independence by the Australian Senate that led to the dismissal of Prime

[5]The Senate consists of 105 senators: Constitution Act, 1867, s. 22. There are 24 senators from each of four divisions, namely: (1) Ontario; (2) Quebec; (3) the three maritime provinces; and (4) the four western provinces. On Newfoundland's entry to confederation in 1949, six senators were added to represent that province. In 1975 the Yukon and Northwest Territories were each given one senator. In 1993, the third territory, Nunavut, was given one Senator. Under s. 26, the number can be increased by either four or eight senators, drawn equally from the four divisions. This power was exercised in 1990 (for the first time in Canadian history) by the appointment of eight additional senators: § 9:10 note 2, above. This increased the number of senators by eight, but, under s. 27, the increase is temporary only, because after such a s. 26 increase, the first two vacancies in each division cannot be filled.

[6]A federal proposal for reform was held to be outside the competence of the federal Parliament in *Re Upper House*, [1980] 1 S.C.R. 54. Since the adoption of the Constitution Act, 1982, the general (seven-fifty) amending procedure is required for amendments to the Constitution of Canada in relation to "the powers of the Senate and the method of selecting Senators" (s. 42(1)(b)) and "the number of members by which a province is entitled to be represented in the Senate and the residence qualifications of Senators" (s. 42(1)(c)). These matters are withdrawn from s. 44, which grants to Parliament alone power to amend the Constitution of Canada in relation to "the Senate". Two unsuccessful post-1982 attempts to reform the Senate are described below at § 9:10 notes 8 and 10.

Minister Whitlam in 1975 were so bitterly controversial in that country.[7] A powerful upper house could block major government bills (as the Australian Senate did), could refuse to vote supply to the government (as the Australian Senate did), and could eventually bring the government down (as the Australian Senate did). The Australian experience should also provide a warning that a powerful upper house would be more likely to vote on party lines (as the Australian Senate does) than to ignore party discipline in order to protect the interests of regions or provinces.

The Charlottetown Accord of 1992[8] proposed the creation of a new Senate. Its members were to be elected, and each province was to be represented by an equal number of six senators. The new Senate, although elected, was not to be a confidence chamber, so that the defeat of a government in the Senate would not entail the resignation of the government or the dissolution of Parliament. The new Senate was to have no power to block revenue and expenditure bills, merely a 30-day power of delay. In the case of most other bills,[9] defeat or amendment by the Senate would trigger a joint sitting of the Senate and House of Commons, where the fate of the bill would be determined by majority vote. Since the House of Commons would be five times more numerous than the Senate, the government's majority in the House of Commons would normally exceed the opposition's majority in the Senate, in which case the government's bill would be passed at the joint sitting. In these ways, the supremacy of the House of Commons was to be preserved. The defeat of the Charlottetown Accord in the referendum of 1992 spelled the end of this proposal for reform of the Senate, and the much-maligned existing Senate obtained a new lease on life.

The lesson learned by Canadian politicians from the failure of the Charlottetown Accord (1992) (which had followed the failure of the Meech Lake Accord (1987)) was that it was practically impossible to successfully operate the seven-fifty (or unanimity) amending procedure. Conservative Prime Minister Stephen Harper, who was elected in 2006, had a longstanding policy to reform the Senate, but he had to face the reality that much of the Senate was unamendable. The Constitution

---

[7]Of the vast literature on the Australian crisis, reference may be made to G. Sawer, Federation under Strain (Melbourne U.P., Carlton, Vic, 1977); G.J. Evans (ed.), Labor and the Constitution 1972–1975 (Heinemann Educational Australia, Richmond, Vic, 1977); J.R. Kerr, Matters for Judgment (Macmillan, London, 1978) (the Governor General's version); E.G. Whitlam, The Truth of the Matter (Penguin, Vic, 2nd ed., 1983) (the Prime Minister's version); G. Barwick, Sir John Did His Duty (Serendip, Wahroonga, 1983) (the Chief Justice's version).

[8]Chapter 4, Amendment, under heading § 4:3, "The failure to accommodate Quebec".

[9]Bills materially affecting French language or culture were a special category, requiring a "double majority" in the Senate, that is, passage by a majority of French-speaking Senators as well as by an overall majority; the defeat or amendment of such bills by the Senate could not be overcome by a joint sitting. Bills taxing natural resources were another special category, in which defeat or amendment by the Senate could not be overcome by a joint sitting.

Act, 1982, by s. 44, granted to Parliament alone the power to amend the Constitution of Canada in relation to "the Senate", but s. 42(1)(b) and (c) withdrew from this apparently plenary power four important aspects of the Senate: (1) "the powers of the Senate", (2) "the method of selecting Senators", (3) "the number of members by which a province is entitled to be represented in the Senate", and (4) "the residence qualifications of Senators". The four withdrawn matters could be changed only by the seven-fifty procedure. The Prime Minister proposed to introduce "consultative elections" as part of the process of appointment and "term limits" to substitute a fixed term of years for the existing tenure to age 75. The Government directed a reference to the Supreme Court of Canada asking whether each of these proposals was competent to Parliament under s. 44. In the *Senate Reform Reference* (2014),[10] the Court answered no to both questions.

In the case of consultative elections, a preliminary issue was whether this would be an amendment of the Constitution of Canada. It did not involve any change to the text of the Constitution of Canada: s. 24 of the Constitution Act, 1867, which provides for the appointment of senators by the Governor General, would remain unchanged as the formal process of appointment. And, in fact, the province of Alberta had since 1989 had been holding elections to identify nominees to fill vacancies in the province's six Senate places. Some Prime Ministers chose to appoint from the elected pool and others did not.[11] Since the Prime Minister was free to consult as he chose in making appointments, it was hard to see why he could not be required to at least consider the claims of persons chosen by election before recommending appointments to a Governor General. But the Court took the view that the proposal for federal legislation for consultative elections "would amend the Constitution of Canada by changing the Senate's role in our constitutional structure from a complementary legislative body of sober second thought to a legislative body endowed with a popular mandate and democratic legitimacy".[12] In substance, the Court held, the proposal would be a change to "the method of selecting Senators", which is one of the four matters withdrawn from Parliament's legislative power over the Senate. Therefore, Parliament could not enact legislation to provide for consultative elections.

As for term limits, these were not included in the four matters

[10] *Re Senate Reform*, [2014] 1 S.C.R. 704, 2014 SCC 32. The unanimous opinion was given by "the Court". For commentary on the case, see P.W. Hogg, "Senate Reform and the Constitution" (2015) 68 Sup. Ct. L. Rev. (2d) 591; W.J. Newman, "Putting One's Faith in a Higher Power: Supreme Law, the Senate Reform Reference, Legislative Authority and the Amending Procedures" (2015) 34 Nat. J. Con. Law 99.

[11] Alberta had held elections in 1989, 1998, 2004 and 2012 which had produced a list of nominees to fill vacancies. Of these nominees, six were appointed (by Conservative Prime Ministers Mulroney and Harper) and the other nominees were passed over (by Liberal Prime Ministers Chrétien and Martin, who made five appointments from Alberta). The elections had been held under the auspices of provincial legislation; the constitutionality of the legislation and the resulting appointments was never challenged.

[12] *Re Senate Reform*, [2014] 1 S.C.R. 704, 2014 SCC 32, para. 63.

withdrawn from Parliament's legislative power over the Senate. Did it not follow inexorably that term limits could be enacted by Parliament under s. 44? No, held the Court, that would be a "narrow textual approach" to the issue.[13] In addition to the four matters *expressly* withdrawn from Parliament's power over the Senate, any other "changes that engage the interests of the provinces in the Senate" were *impliedly* withdrawn from s. 44![14] Even after taking that huge interpretative leap, there was no obvious basis for concluding that term limits would engage the interests of the provinces. With or without term limits senators appointed by the Prime Minister would normally vote the federal party line with little or no regard for the interests of the provinces. But the Court took the view that any impairment of the supposed independence of the Senate would engage the interests of the provinces. And the Court held that any form of fixed term, whether renewable or non-renewable, and whether short or long, would impair the independence of the Senate. Fixed terms, the Court said "imply a finite time in office and necessarily offer a lesser degree of protection from the potential consequences of freely speaking one's mind on the legislative proposals of the House of Commons".[15] Therefore, Parliament could not enact legislation to replace the current rule of senatorial tenure to age 75 with a fixed term limit.

In Canada, with few exceptions,[16] the Senate has not been a major obstruction to important government policy, even when its majority has been controlled by the opposition. This is so although the Canadian Senate's powers are, in law, as ample as those of the Australian Senate. The restraint by the Canadian Senate is caused by its recognition that, as an appointed body, it has no political mandate to obstruct the elected House of Commons. The Australian Senate, as an elected body, is not subject to the same inhibitions. If the Canadian Senate were reformed, either by making its membership elected or by making its membership appointed by provincial governments, it would naturally want to make more use of its powers. Serious obstruction of the House of Commons could be avoided if limitations were imposed on the powers of a reformed upper house. That was part of the package comprising the Senate proposals of the Charlottetown Accord (described above): the reformed Senate was to be an elected body, with equal representation of the provinces, but one with less power than the House of Commons (the confidence chamber).[17]

---

[13] *Re Senate Reform*, [2014] 1 S.C.R. 704, 2014 SCC 32, para. 73.

[14] *Re Senate Reform*, [2014] 1 S.C.R. 704, 2014 SCC 32, para. 75.

[15] *Re Senate Reform*, [2014] 1 S.C.R. 704, 2014 SCC 32, para. 80.

[16] I assume that the attitude of the Liberal majority in the Senate from 1984 to 1990 was exceptional and anomalous.

[17] Reform of the Senate, like reform of the Supreme Court of Canada, is a central tenet of "intrastate federalism", designed to make central institutions more responsive to the various regions and cultures of the country. Intrastate federalism is discussed in ch. 4, Amendment, under heading § 4:22, "Central institutions".

§ 9:11 The Governor General

The Governor General, who must complete the legislative process by conferring the royal assent[1] on a bill enacted by both Houses of Parliament, plays no discretionary role whatever. It is true that the Constitution Act, 1867, by s. 55, gives the Governor General the power to withhold the royal assent from a bill, and the power to reserve a bill for the signification of the Queen's pleasure; and by s. 56 gives to the Queen the power to disallow a Canadian statute. But the imperial conference of 1930 resolved that the powers of reservation and disallowance must never be exercised.[2] This conference and the full acceptance of responsible government have established a convention that the Governor General must always give the royal assent to a bill which has passed both Houses of Parliament.[3] There is no circumstance which would justify a refusal of assent,[4] or a reservation,[5] or a British disallowance.[6]

[Section 9:11]

[1]*Royal assent*, which is the last stage in the enactment of a bill, is not to be confused with *royal consent*, which is an internal parliamentary procedural requirement for bills that would diminish Crown prerogatives (ch. 1, Sources, under heading § 1:9, "Prerogative"), or *royal recommendation*, which is the requirement imposed by s. 54 of the Constitution Act, 1867 for bills that authorize spending or taxes.

[2]See ch. 3, Independence, under heading § 3:1, "Bonds of Empire".

[3]The Governor General, in this matter as in others, must act on the advice of the Prime Minister who commands a majority in the House of Commons. The Prime Minister is not regarded in parliamentary systems of government as having a veto over legislation, and is under a conventional duty to advise that royal assent be granted to a bill that has passed both Houses of Parliament, even if he disagrees with the bill and voted against it (which can happen on a free vote or in a minority government). There may be some highly unusual circumstance in which the Prime Minister would be justified in advising against the granting of royal assent (a fatal drafting error perhaps), and, in that case, the Governor General would be under a conventional duty to follow the advice and withhold assent. But the withholding of assent against the advice of the Prime Minister would be incompatible with the conventions of responsible government.

[4]There has never been a refusal of assent (as opposed to a reservation) by the Governor General: Mallory, The Structure of Canadian Government (rev. ed., 1984), 241–2; although there have been refusals by the Lieutenant Governors: MacKinnon, The Government of Prince Edward Island (1951), 154–155; Beck, The Government of Nova Scotia (1957), 181–182. Refusals of assent are, however, as MacKinnon comments (p. 164), "clearly incompatible with the principles of responsible government". But note the unusual situation where the Governor General (or Lieutenant Governor) is advised by the Prime Minister (or Premier) to withhold assent: previous note. It is the withholding of assent against advice that is incompatible with the principles of responsible government.

[5]In Australia, where the constitutional conventions of responsible government are essentially the same as in Canada, there have been occasional reservations by the Governor General of bills which have some particular resonance for the Queen and whose personal assent is desired for ceremonial or courtesy reasons: Royal Style and Titles Act 1953 (Cth., No. 32 of 1953); Flags Act 1953 (Cth., No. 1 of 1954); Royal Style and Titles Act 1973 (Cth., No. 114 of 1973). These cases are different from the traditional reservations in that they undoubtedly had the full approval of the government of the day.

[6]By s. 90 provincial legislation is also made subject to reservation and disallow-

§ 9:12 The cabinet

It will now be obvious that in a system of responsible government there is no "separation of powers" between the executive and legislative branches of government. The head of the executive branch, the cabinet, draws its personnel and its power to govern from the legislative branch, the Parliament; and the cabinet controls the Parliament.[1] This contrasts with the presidential form of government in the United States, which was established at a time when the separation of the executive, legislative and judicial powers of government was regarded by influential political theorists as the ideal constitution for the preservation of individual liberty.[2] The President of the United States is not a member of the Congress, nor are the members of his cabinet; he is often not a member of the party with the majority of members in the Congress; and he is never able to exercise control over the Congress.

In Canada, the legislative programme for each session of Parliament is planned by the cabinet, and announced at the beginning of the session in the speech from the throne which is delivered by the Governor General. The speech is written by the Prime Minister. The cabinet determines the order of business in the Parliament, and generally exercises close control over the proceedings. Nearly all bills which are subsequently enacted are "government bills", that is to say, bills which have been approved by cabinet and introduced by one of the ministers. The Constitution Act, 1867, by s. 54, requires that a "money bill" must be introduced in the House of Commons only after it has been "first recommended to that House by message of the Governor General". Needless to say, it is the cabinet which prepares the message, and a minister who transmits the message to the House and introduces the bill. Other bills can be introduced in either House and by any member of Parliament, but the cabinet uses its majority in the House of Commons to ensure that the bulk of the Parliament's time is devoted to consideration of the government's own legislative programme, and, except for "private bills",[3] it is only the measures that have been approved by the cabinet

---

ance, but the power of reservation is in the Lieutenant Governor (instead of the Governor General) and the power of disallowance is in the Governor General (instead of the Queen). It is less clear whether these powers have been effectively nullified by convention: see ch. 5, Federalism, under heading § 5:13 "Disallowance".

[Section 9:12]

[1]There is a famous quotation from Walter Bagehot, The English Constitution (T. Nelson, London, 1872), 14: "A cabinet is a combining committee—a hyphen which joins, a buckle which fastens, the legislative part of the state to the executive part of the state".

[2]See Jennings, The Law and the Constitution (5th ed., 1959), ch. 1 and Appendix 1; de Smith and Brazier, Constitutional and Administrative Law (8th ed., 1998), 17–21. The independence, if not formal separation, of the judicial branch from the executive and legislative branches is, however, still generally regarded as essential to the impartial administration of justice both in the United States and in countries such as Canada which have inherited their non-federal constitutional law from the United Kingdom.

[3]"Private bills", which relate to a particular person or institution, or a particular

and introduced by a minister ("government bills") which stand any real chance of passage.

The control of the Legislature by the executive is not normally something that the courts are concerned with, but it can occasionally be an issue in litigation. In *Wells v. Newfoundland* (1999),[4] the Legislature of Newfoundland enacted a statute that abolished the Public Utilities Board of the province and replaced it with another body. The plaintiff, who was a member of the Board, lost his position as the result of the statute. He had been appointed to the Board under a contract of employment that allowed him to remain in office (during good behaviour) until age 70. He sued the province for breach of contract. The province argued that the contract of employment had been frustrated by the passage of the statute, because the statute had made the continued employment of the plaintiff impossible. The Supreme Court of Canada rejected this argument. Major J., who wrote the opinion of the Court, pointed out that self-induced frustration was not an excuse for nonperformance of a contract. The province could not claim that the contract was frustrated simply because it was the legislative branch that had made performance by the executive branch impossible. The reality was that "the same individuals control both the executive and legislative branches of government".[5] It was therefore "disingenuous for the executive to assert that the legislative enactment of its own agenda constituted a frustrating act beyond its control".[6] The Court ordered the province to pay the plaintiff damages for breach of contract.

IV. DEFEAT OF THE GOVERNMENT

§ 9:13 Withdrawal of confidence

Since the major premise of responsible government is that the cabinet (or "government" or "administration") enjoys the confidence of a majority in the House of Commons, it follows that a cabinet which has lost that confidence cannot indefinitely continue in office. This is the primary meaning of the "collective responsibility" of the cabinet to the House of Commons.

If the House of Commons passes a motion of no confidence in the government, that is the clearest possible evidence that the government has lost the confidence of the House of Commons;[1] but the defeat of the government on any important vote is usually regarded as a withdrawal

---

locality, are enacted by a different and simpler procedure, which does not require government sponsorship, and they are often enacted after introduction by a private member. Private bills should not be confused with "private members' bills", which are bills introduced by private members. They may be either public or private bills, but when they are public bills they stand little chance of passage.

[4]*Wells v. Newfoundland*, [1999] 3 S.C.R. 199.

[5]*Wells v. Newfoundland*, [1999] 3 S.C.R. 199, para. 53.

[6]*Wells v. Newfoundland*, [1999] 3 S.C.R. 199, para. 52.

[Section 9:13]

[1]It was the passage of a motion of no confidence on November 28, 2005 that

of confidence.[2] Where the defeat is on a matter of little importance, the defeat would not need to be treated as a withdrawal of confidence. A more difficult case is where the defeat occurs on a major measure, but is the result of a "snap vote" which catches the government party with some of its supporters inadvertently absent from the House at the time of the vote. A snap vote led to the defeat in the House of Commons of a government measure in 1968, and the Pearson government decided not to treat it as a withdrawal of confidence. The government reinforced its decision and acknowledged the primacy of the House by subsequently securing the passage of a resolution to the effect that the prior defeat was not to be interpreted as a withdrawal of confidence in the government.[3]

§ 9:14 Dissolution of Parliament

When a motion of no confidence is passed or a government measure is defeated in the House of Commons, then, subject to the comments made in the previous paragraph, the House of Commons is deemed to have withdrawn its confidence from the government. There are then only two alternatives: either the government must resign to make way for a new cabinet which will command the confidence of the House, or the House must be dissolved to make way for an election which will produce a new House of Commons.

It is the dissolution of the House of Commons which is the course normally favoured by a Prime Minister whose government has been defeated in the House, and that is the course which the Prime Minister will normally advise the Governor General to take. In the event of a dissolution the Prime Minister and the ministers remain in office, despite the fact that they have lost the confidence of the House of Commons. The period between the dissolution of one House of Commons and the

---

defeated the Liberal government of Prime Minister Martin. This was the first time that such a motion had carried in the House of Commons. All other government defeats (§ 9:9 note 6) have been defeats on a substantive measure (such as a budget bill).

[2]The rule did not used to be so strict. Many British and Canadian governments were defeated in the House of Commons last century without either resigning or advising dissolution. The reason was the looser party discipline and the number of independent members. The strict rule is more appropriate today where party discipline is tight and there are very few or no independent members. But minority government restores some of the fluidity of former times, and it may be sensible and constitutional for a minority government to follow the earlier precedents and revert to a laxer rule as to what amounts to a withdrawal of confidence in the government. This position is cogently argued by Forsey, Freedom and Order (1974), 114–116; and there are precedents accumulating in its favour, e.g., the defeat of the British government on March 10, 1976: (1976) 53 The Parliamentarian 174; the defeat of the Ontario government on June 15, 1976: the Globe and Mail, June 16, 1976 and June 17, 1976. In neither case did the minority government resign.

[3]Dawson, The Government of Canada (6th ed., 1987 by Ward), 145. In the United Kingdom since 1945 there have been several government defeats on "snap votes"; the government has in each case "mustered its full resources and procured a reversal of the vote": de Smith and Brazier, Constitutional and Administrative Law (8th ed., 1998), 195–196.

election of another may be as long as several months, but the government must remain in office and exercise its functions: the country cannot be left without any government at all.[1] The ensuing election may produce a new House of Commons which the government is able to control. If that happens the government will continue in office without a break. Thus, while the Constitution imposes a maximum duration for the House of Commons of five years,[2] there is no maximum duration for any particular government and most Canadian governments have lasted for longer than five years. It is the hope of continuance in office which makes dissolution a more attractive alternative than resignation for the government which has lost the confidence of the House of Commons.

As we shall see later in this chapter, it is probable that the Governor General has a reserve power to refuse to grant a dissolution to a Prime Minister whose government has lost the confidence of the House of Commons, but this has happened only once this century in Canada—in 1926. If a dissolution were refused, the Prime Minister whose government had lost the confidence of the House of Commons would have to resign, or be dismissed by the Governor General; and the resignation or dismissal of a Prime Minister involves the resignation or dismissal of the entire ministry.

§ 9:15 Resignation or dismissal

If a Prime Minister whose government has lost the support of the House of Commons does resign (whether voluntarily or because a dissolution has been refused by the Governor General), or is dismissed from office by the Governor General, then the Governor General would have to find a member of parliament who could become Prime Minister and form a government which would enjoy the confidence of the House. In selecting a new Prime Minister, as we have already noticed, the Governor General is entitled to exercise a personal discretion.[1]

V. THE GOVERNOR GENERAL'S PERSONAL PREROGATIVES

§ 9:16 The principle

The Governor General has certain "personal prerogatives" or "reserve powers" which he or she may exercise upon his or her own personal discretion.[1] Whereas in the exercise of governmental powers generally

---

[Section 9:14]

[1]But note the "caretaker convention", which restrains governmental action during the period following a dissolution: § 9:4, "The ministry".

[2]Constitution Act, 1867, s. 50; Constitution Act, 1982, s. 4.

[Section 9:15]

[1]The narrow scope of the "discretion" is explained in the next section of this chapter.

[Section 9:16]

[1]There are two major studies of the reserve powers: Evatt, The King and His Dominion Governors (2nd ed., 1967) and Forsey, The Royal Power of Dissolution of

the Governor General must act in accordance with the advice of the Prime Minister or cabinet, there are some occasions on which he or she may act without advice, or even contrary to advice.

The definition of those occasions when the Governor General may exercise an independent discretion has caused much constitutional and political debate. But it is submitted that the basic premise of responsible government supplies the answer: so long as the cabinet enjoys the confidence of a majority in the House of Commons, the Governor General is always obliged to follow lawful and constitutional advice which is tendered by the cabinet. But there are occasions, as we have seen, when a government continues in office after it has lost the confidence of the House of Commons, or after the House of Commons has been dissolved. There are also occasions, for example, after a very close election, or after a schism in a political party, where for a period it is difficult to determine whether or not the government does enjoy the confidence of a majority in the House of Commons. In all these situations it is submitted that the Governor General has a discretion to refuse to follow advice which is tendered by the ministry in office.

When a government is in office without the support of the House of Commons, there are the makings of a constitutional crisis: not only can the government not secure the passage of any legislation, it cannot even secure parliamentary approval of supply to meet government expenditures. The crisis can be resolved or averted by a new election or by the resignation or dismissal of the ministry. But the ministry in office, which lacks the support of the House of Commons and which stands to lose most by the resolution of the crisis, is not the fittest group to determine the mode of resolution of the crisis. It is true of course that the Governor General has even less of a political base than the ministry in office, but it is for this very reason that the Governor General may reasonably be trusted to set aside partisan considerations and act impartially in the interests of the country as a whole. In this situation the role of Governor General is somewhat akin to that of a judge—another non-elected official to whom we readily entrust large powers in the expectation that they will be exercised impartially.[2]

Parliament in the British Commonwealth (1943, reprinted with new preface, 1968). See also McWhinney, The Governor General and the Prime Ministers (2005), for an historical and anecdotal account of relationships between the Governor General and the Prime Minister.

[2]In exercising the reserve powers, the Governor General (and a Lieutenant Governor is in the same position) does not act on the "advice" (formal advice) of the Prime Minister (or Premier), but that does not stop the Governor General from consulting the Prime Minister where that is appropriate. Also available for consultation (informal advice) is the Clerk of the Privy Council and his or her officials. It has also become common for the Governor General to consult with lawyers or political scientists who are expert and independent of government. In Australia, there are some precedents of the Governor-General consulting with judges of the High Court of Australia. These have been controversial, and for good reasons: the advice is certainly not a judicial function; judges may be drawn into the fraught politics of a parliamentary crisis; and it is even possible for litigation to follow a parliamentary crisis. For an excellent discussion of

§ 9:17 Appointment of Prime Minister

Perhaps the clearest and least controversial of the Governor General's reserve powers or personal prerogatives is the power to select a Prime Minister.[1] This power has to be exercised whenever a Prime Minister resigns. The resignation of the Prime Minister (unless it is a personal retirement) automatically vacates all ministerial offices, and thus involves the resignation of the entire ministry or government. Resignation may occur, as we have seen, when the House of Commons withdraws its confidence from the government. The more usual case of resignation occurs after an election in which the government party has failed to obtain a majority of the seats in the House of Commons. The theory of responsible government indicates that the Prime Minister would be justified in remaining in office until the House of Commons assembles and votes against the government, but the modern practice (perhaps it is now a convention) is to resign as soon as the election results make clear that the opposition party has gained control of the House of Commons. However, if the election gave no party a clear majority, and it was not clear which major party would attract the support of minor parties or independent members, the Prime Minister would certainly be justified in awaiting a Commons vote.[2]

Once a government has resigned, for whatever reason, the appointment of a new Prime Minister has to be made by the Governor General. This decision is always a personal one in the sense that the Governor General does not act upon ministerial advice. But other conventions of responsible government have now severely limited the discretion that the Governor General really possesses. The Governor General must find the person who has the ability to form a government which will enjoy the support of the House of Commons. The only person with this qualification is the leader of the party which has a majority of seats in the

---

the position in Australia (with some Canadian references as well), see A. Twomey, "Advice to vice-regal officers by crown law officers and others" (2015) 26 Public Law Review 193.

[Section 9:17]

[1]On the selection of provincial Premiers, see Saywell, The Office of Lieutenant-Governor (1957), ch. 4.

[2]Prime Minister St. Laurent resigned after the election of 1957 as soon as the election results showed that his Liberal party had won fewer seats than the Progressive Conservative party, despite the fact that neither party had an absolute majority. He apparently did not want to appear to be clinging to office after an electoral "defeat". But since the election results did not answer the question of who could command the support of a majority in the House of Commons, it seems to me that the Prime Minister would have been fully justified in remaining in office until the parliamentary situation was clear, which might not have been until Parliament met. It turned out, however, that the Progressive Conservative party was able to form a government which lasted for a year so that Prime Minister St. Laurent's resignation could be interpreted as an accurate reading of the parliamentary situation. Prime Minister King had been faced with a similar situation after the election of 1925 in which his Liberal government won fewer seats than the Conservative party. He did not resign, and it turned out that he was able to continue in office for eight months with the support of Progressive, Labour and Independent members.

House of Commons. Moreover, each Canadian party has procedures for selecting its own parliamentary leader. This means that in most cases the Governor General's "choice" is inevitable.

One situation which has occurred and could again is the death or retirement of a Prime Minister in office before his party has selected a successor. In that case, when the government still retains a majority in the House, the death or retirement is personal and the government as a whole does not vacate office.[3] The country does not lack a government, but merely a Prime Minister. How is he or she to be replaced? Canadian political parties do not normally choose a deputy leader or second-in-command at the same time as they select a leader. The cabinet will usually designate a minister to act as Prime Minister during the absence from Ottawa of the Prime Minister, but the Acting Prime Minister is not intended to be the successor to the Prime Minister in the event of the Prime Minister's death or retirement.[4] Before 1896, there were a number of occasions on which a Governor General had to use his own initiative to find a Prime Minister by reason of the death or retirement of the Prime Minister in office.[5] The situation has not recurred since 1896, because every Prime Minister since then has decently refrained from dying or retiring until his party has selected a successor. However, Dawson says that "there is no reason whatever to assume that the power has vanished in the interval".[6] But Dawson is probably wrong on this point. If a Prime Minister did die or retire in office without a successor, it is certain that the government party would want to choose the successor by its own procedures, and would not be content to accept the Governor General's choice. Given this political fact, the Governor General would be obliged to appoint the party's choice, for only the party's choice would be successful in forming a government. The utmost initiative which I can conceive of the Governor General exercising would be the appointment of a caretaker Prime Minister for the period when the party was making its choice; but even in this circumstance it is likely that the party, perhaps by vote of its parliamentary caucus,[7] would also wish to designate the caretaker, and, in the absence of some gross impropriety

[3]The cabinet, which is the creation of the Prime Minister (or Premier), is automatically dissolved by the death or retirement of the Prime Minister, but the ministers, who have been appointed by the Governor General (or Lieutenant Governor), continue to hold their offices and continue in their membership of the Privy Council (or Executive Council): J.R. Mallory, "The Royal Prerogative in Canada: The Selection of Successors to Mr Duplessis and Mr Sauve" (1960) 26 Can. J. Ec. and Pol. Sci. 314, 316. Moreover, there is nothing to stop them from meeting informally (like a cabinet) if they wish to do so before a new Prime Minister has been appointed.

[4]Mallory, The Structure of Canadian Government (rev. ed. 1984), 98–99.

[5]Mallory, The Structure of Canadian Government (rev. ed. 1984), 78–79; Dawson, The Government of Canada (6th ed., 1987 by Ward), 184.

[6]Dawson, The Government of Canada (6th ed., 1987 by Ward), 184.

[7]Strictly speaking, the only person who can "advise" the Governor General (or Lieutenant Governor) is the Prime Minister (or Premier), and there is no such person. However, others can make recommendations. Strictly speaking, a recommendation could not be made by the cabinet, because the cabinet was dissolved by the death or retire-

in the mode of selection, a Governor General would be obliged to defer to the party's wish.[8]

§ 9:18 Dismissal of Prime Minister

The second reserve power of the Governor General is the power to dismiss the Prime Minister. The dismissal (or resignation) of a Prime Minister automatically involves the dismissal (or resignation) of the entire ministry. Thus what is formally a dismissal of a Prime Minister is in substance the dismissal of the ministry or government.

The power of dismissal has been exercised very rarely. In Canada no federal Prime Minister has ever been dismissed, and no provincial Premier has been dismissed since 1905.[1] In the United Kingdom no Prime Minister has been dismissed since 1783.[2]

When does the power of dismissal arise? It is obvious that a Governor General may not dismiss a ministry because he or she believes its policies to be unwise, or because he or she believes it to be incompetent. Those are judgments which in a democracy may be made only by the people or their elected representatives. Could the Governor General dismiss a ministry because he or she believed its policies to be illegal? There is a New South Wales precedent for such a dismissal, but it is soundly criticized by Evatt on the ground that the Governor of New South Wales (or any other head of state) has neither the competence nor the authority to assume to adjudicate a question of law and to provide a remedy for a finding of illegality; questions of illegality are properly jus-

---

ment of the Prime Minister (or Premier). In any event, the practice is for the recommendation to be made by the parliamentary caucus: see next note. A.M. Dodek, "Rediscovering Constitutional Law: Succession upon the Death of the Prime Minister" (2000) 49 U.N.B.L.J. 33 argues that it would be a better practice for the governing party to appoint a Deputy Prime Minister whose duty would not be merely to act in the absence or incapacity of the Prime Minister, but to act on the death or retirement of the Prime Minister (until a new permanent leader had been selected by the governing party). To be sure, this would be a quicker and easier transition, but the practice is otherwise: see § 9:17 note 8, below.

[8]Three Quebec Premiers have died in office: Duplessis in 1959, Sauve in 1960 and Johnson in 1968; in each case the parliamentary caucus of the governing Union Nationale party selected a successor, and presented a "petition" to the Lieutenant Governor asking him to commission the person chosen; the Lieutenant Governor complied. In the last case the Premier so chosen, Premier Bertrand, insisted upon his appointment also being ratified by a subsequent party leadership convention: see Mallory, The Structure of Canadian Government (rev. ed. 1984), 79–80. Although there have been no recent deaths of Premiers, there have been the sudden resignations of Premiers van der Zalm (B.C., 1991), McKenna (N.B., 1997) and Clark (B.C., 1999). In each case, the Lieutenant Governor appointed a successor on the basis of a recommendation of the parliamentary caucus: R.I. Cheffins, "The Royal Prerogative and the Office of Lieutenant Governor" (2000) 23 Can. Parliamentary Review 14, 18–19.

[Section 9:18]

[1]Saywell, The Office of Lieutenant-Governor (1957), ch. 5.

[2]de Smith and Brazier, Constitutional and Administrative Law (8th ed., 1998), 122.

ticiable and remediable in the courts.[3] There is also the Australian federal precedent of the dismissal in 1975 of Prime Minister Whitlam. The Whitlam Labour government had a secure majority in the lower house, but could not obtain supply from the upper house. This dismissal also seems improper since its effect was to install in office a government which the Governor General knew could not command a majority in the lower house. It is true that the Governor General stipulated that the new government should be a "caretaker government" only, which would "make no appointments or dismissals or initiate new policies before a general election is held". But to solve a political crisis by dismissing a government with a majority in the lower house seems to me to be a breach of the conventions of responsible government—a political initiative that is well outside the narrow realm of vice-regal discretion.[4]

My opinion is that the only occasion upon which a Governor General would be justified in dismissing a ministry is when the ministry has lost the support of a majority of the House of Commons. When this happens, as we have already noticed, one of two changes must occur: either the House must be dissolved for an election which will produce a new House, or the ministry must resign to make way for a new ministry which will enjoy the confidence of the existing House. If a Prime Minister who had lost parliamentary support refused to advise dissolution and refused to resign, then the Governor General would have no alternative but to dismiss the Prime Minister and call upon the leader of the opposition to form a government.

A related question is whether a Prime Minister whose advice has been rejected by the Governor General is obliged by convention to resign. It is often assumed that there is such a convention, but this is probably wrong because there does not seem to be a good reason for the convention. The Prime Minister is responsible to the House of Commons, not to the Governor General. The only precedent is the King-Byng dispute of 1926, which is described in the next section of this chapter.[5] In that case, Prime Minister King resigned immediately when Governor General Byng refused his request for a dissolution. That is not a very useful precedent since the Prime Minister's resignation could as easily

[3]Evatt, The King and His Dominion Governors (2nd ed., 1967), chs. 19, 20. See also G. Lindell, "The role of a State Governor in relation to illegality" (2012) 23 Public Law Review (Australia) 268.

[4]The dismissal means that the Australian Senate can force a federal government out of office by denying supply, despite the fact that the government is not responsible to the Senate, and the action would not ordinarily involve the risk of the Senate's own dissolution. The Governor General's correct course, in my view, was to do nothing, and wait for a political resolution of the crisis. For commentary on the crisis, see G. Sawer, Federation under Strain (Melbourne U.P., Carlton, Vic, 1977); G.J. Evans (ed.), Labor and the Constitution 1972-1975 (Heinemann Educational Australia, Richmond, Vic, 1977); J.R. Kerr, Matters for Judgment (Macmillan, London, 1978) (the Governor General's version); E.G. Whitlam, The Truth of the Matter (Penguin, Vic, 2nd ed., 1983) (the Prime Minister's version); G. Barwick, Sir John Did His Duty (Serendip, Wahroonga, 1983) (the Chief Justice's version).

[5]§ 9:19, "Dissolution of Parliament".

be attributed to partisan motives as to the existence of any convention. The Prime Minister had not at that point lost the confidence of the House of Commons, but he wanted to avoid the continuation of a parliamentary debate that was likely to lead to a resolution of censure of his government. As well, he knew that his immediate resignation would create a problem for the Governor General by leaving little time for the Governor General to explore the viability of an alternative government formed by the opposition leader, Mr. Meighen.[6]

§ 9:19 Dissolution of Parliament

The Constitution Act, 1867, by s. 50, provides that a House of Commons "shall continue for five years" unless it is "sooner dissolved by the Governor General". (The Constitution Act, 1982, by s. 4, makes a similar stipulation, which applies to the legislative assemblies of the provinces as well as to the House of Commons.)[1] It has never been the practice of Canadian Prime Ministers to allow the House of Commons to continue until the expiration of the five-year term. The practice has been for the Prime Minister to select what he regards as a propitious time for an election (usually about four years from the last election) and to advise the Governor General to dissolve the House in time for a new election on the selected date.[2] In the normal situation of majority government, the Prime Minister has not lost the confidence of the House, and is simply seeking an earlier renewal of the government's mandate than would be provided by the eventual expiration of the House. (Exactly the same practice has been followed in the provinces, where the Premier has normally advised the Lieutenant Governor to dissolve the legislative assembly in time for an election on a date chosen by the Premier.)

There is only one Canadian precedent of a refusal by the Governor General of a request for a dissolution by a Prime Minister, and that is the famous King-Byng precedent of 1926. In 1926, Prime Minister

---

[6]The same question could have arisen out of the prorogation issue of 2008, which is discussed in § 9:21, "Prorogation of Parliament". Governor General Jean in fact granted Prime Minister Harper's request for a prorogation of Parliament, but, if she had refused the request, there is no reason why the Prime Minister should have felt obliged to resign. He still possessed the confidence of the House, and he could have remained in office (where he would soon have had to face a no-confidence motion in the House of Commons).

[Section 9:19]

[1]Section 4(2) permits an extension beyond five years by a two-thirds majority vote "in time of real or apprehended war, invasion or insurrection". This is of no use for the House of Commons, because s. 50 was not similarly amended at the same time. During the First World War, the House of Commons was in fact extended to a term of 5 years, 10 months and 22 days, the longest Parliament in Canadian history. Section 50 was overcome by a temporary amendment to the British North America Act, 1867, which (pre-1982) required an imperial statute applicable to Canada, namely, the British North America Act, 1916 (U.K.), which was immediately spent and was formally repealed by the Statute Law Revision Act, 1927 (U.K.).

[2]This practice has been criticized, and precipitated a federal fixed election date law (and fixed election date laws in all but one province as well): see § 9:20, "Fixed election dates".

Mackenzie King's minority Liberal government, which had been governing with the support of some of the Progressive, Labour and Independent members,[3] was faced with an opposition motion of censure that was likely to carry (since the government had been defeated on motions to amend and to adjourn). Before the motion of censure was voted on (and certainly before any vote of no-confidence was held), Prime Minister King advised the Governor General, Lord Byng, to dissolve Parliament for an election. Lord Byng took the view that he had a discretion in the matter, by reason of the short time since the previous election (it was 11 months) and the imminence of the vote of censure, and he refused the dissolution.[4] Prime Minister King immediately resigned. Lord Byng then called on the leader of the opposition Conservative Party, Mr Meighen, to form a government. Mr Meighen did so, but within a week his government was defeated, and so he advised Lord Byng to dissolve Parliament. Lord Byng accepted this advice, thereby granting to Mr Meighen the dissolution that he had so recently denied to Mr King. In the ensuing election, Mr King used the incident as an issue of independence from the Empire (represented by Lord Byng), and the Liberals won the election, bringing Mr King back into office. It is clear that Lord Byng's failure to follow Prime Minister King's advice was unwise,[5] but there is no agreement among constitutional writers as to whether it was in violation of a constitutional convention.

Nevertheless, the King-Byng precedent surely carries important les-

---

[3]The exact standings of the parties in the House of Commons were: Liberals, 101; Conservatives, 116; Progressives, 24; and Labour and Independents, 4.

[4]Forsey, The Royal Power of Dissolution in the British Commonwealth (1943, reprinted, 1968), 146–162, takes the view that in some situations refusal of a dissolution would be appropriate, e.g., where a motion of censure is under debate in the House of Commons, or where the last election was very recent. For both these reasons he would support Lord Byng's refusal of a dissolution in 1926 (discussed in the text following) even if Mr. King still had the support of a majority in the House of Commons. For provincial precedents, see Saywell, The Office of Lieutenant-Governor (1957), ch. 6.

[5]The most thorough study of the King-Byng dispute is Forsey's *The Royal Power of Dissolution of Parliament in the British Commonwealth* (1943, reprinted, 1968), chs. 5, 6, and Forsey comes down strongly in support of Lord Byng's action: see previous note. My view that Lord Byng's refusal to dissolve Parliament was at least unwise is based on the fact that Lord Byng and Mr. Meighen must have known that Meighen would have great difficulty in forming a government because of the legal requirement of that time (it was repealed in 1931) that each minister with portfolio had to vacate his seat and seek re-election in a by-election. If Meighen had formed a ministry in the normal way he would have lost about 15 of his supporters in the House. Since he could not afford such a loss (see the voting figures: Forsey, 159), he formed a "temporary ministry" of ministers without portfolio who became "acting ministers" of the departments of government. This device evaded the necessity for ministerial by-elections, but led to a motion in the House of Commons condemning the device which passed by one vote: Forsey, 131-139. While the exact fashion of the Meighen government's downfall was obviously not foreseeable when Byng refused King's request for a dissolution, it was manifest at that time that the formation of a government by Meighen would present "unusual difficulties" (as Forsey, 135, admits). Marshall, *Constitutional Conventions* (1984), 39, suggests that convention authorizes the refusal of a dissolution only if the Governor General can rely on finding a Prime Minister who can form an alternative government; if this is correct, Lord Byng did not observe the convention.

sons for Governor Generals today. The main lesson is that, absent extraordinary circumstances, a request for dissolution from a Prime Minister should be granted. If it is refused, there is a risk that the Prime Minister will resign (as Mr King did)[6] and the Governor General will have to commission a new Prime Minister from within the existing House (as Lord Byng did). If the Governor General cannot be sure that the leader of the opposition can form a reasonably stable government, then there is no alternative to granting the dissolution. If the Governor General does commission the leader of the opposition as Prime Minister (as Lord Byng did), and if the new government falls soon after the old one fell (as Mr Meighen's did), then the Governor General's initial refusal of the dissolution will have created a political crisis in which the legitimacy and neutrality of the Governor General's decisions inevitably become the topic of partisan debate (as happened in 1926). The crisis would not arise if the first request for dissolution had been granted. That is why, apart from the lonely King-Byng precedent, every Canadian Governor General has always granted a request by a Prime Minister for a dissolution, regardless of whether the Prime Minister possessed a secure majority in the House, or had been defeated on an issue of confidence, or who anticipated defeat on an issue of confidence, or who claimed that Parliament had become dysfunctional, or who simply saw some partisan advantage in an election. From the Governor General's point of view, any impulse to say "no" to a request for dissolution is normally overwhelmed by the difficulties that a "no" answer would create.

§ 9:20 Fixed election dates

The Prime Minister's effective power to select the date of the next election (within the five-year constitutional time frame) is often regarded as giving the governing party an advantage in the election. This has led to suggestions that Canada should move to a system of fixed election dates, like those of the United States, in order to strip the Prime Minister of a discretion that may be used for purely partisan purposes. Needless to say, in a system of responsible government, any regime of fixed election dates needs to preserve the discretion of the Governor General to dissolve the House in the event that the government loses the confidence of the House of Commons before the stipulated date. But as long as this discretion is preserved, fixed election dates are not inconsistent with responsible government. In fact, fixed election dates at intervals of four years have now been established by statute for the

[6] I say "a risk", because, in my view, the Prime Minister is not obliged to resign when his advice is rejected: text accompanying § 9:18 notes 5 and 6, above.

federal House of Commons[1] and for nine of the ten provincial legislative assemblies.[2]

The federal fixed-election-date legislation takes the form of an amendment to the Canada Elections Act,[3] introducing a new s. 56.1, which provides as follows:

> **56.1.** (1) Nothing in this section affects the powers of the Governor General, including the power to dissolve Parliament at the Governor General's discretion.
>
> (2) Subject to subsection (1), each general election must be held on the third Monday of October in the fourth calendar year following polling day for the last general election, with the first general election after this section comes into force being held on Monday, October 19, 2009.

Subsection (1) of s. 56.1 preserves the power of the Governor General to dissolve Parliament. As explained, that is necessary in order to permit the conventions of responsible government to function. The continuing importance of the discretionary powers of the Governor General is illustrated by the events that followed the passage of s. 56.1. The legislation was enacted by Parliament on May 3, 2007. It had been introduced by the Conservative Government of Prime Minister Harper, which was a minority government that had been elected on January 22, 2006. Although the government party held less than a majority, the government was never defeated, it survived a series of votes on matters of confidence, and Parliament passed a considerable number of government bills. During the summer adjournment of the House of Commons in 2008, the

[Section 9:20]

[1]An Act to Amend the Canada Elections Act, S.C. 2007, c. 10. This Act is discussed in more detail in the next paragraph of text.

[2]B.C.: Constitution (Fixed Election Dates) Amendment Act, 2001, S.B.C. 2001, s. 36 (amended by Constitution Amendment Act, 2017); Alta.: Election Amendment Act, 2011, S.A. 2011, c. 19; Sask.: The Legislative Assembly and Executive Council (Fixed Election Dates) Amendment Act, 2008, S.S. 2008, c. 6; Man.: The Lobbyists Registration Act and Amendments to The Elections Act, The Elections Finances Act, The Legislative Assembly Act and The Legislative Assembly Management Commission Act, S.M. 2008, c. 43; Ont.: Election Statute Law Amendment Act, 2005, S.O. 2005, c. 35 (revised by Election Statute Law Amendment Act, 2016, S.O. 2016, c. 33); Que.: An Act to amend the Election Act for the purpose of establishing fixed-date elections, C.Q.L.R. 2013, c. 13; N.B.: An Act to Amend the Legislative Assembly Act, R.S.N.B. 2007, c. 57 (amended by Legislative Assembly Act, R.S.N.B. 2014, c. 116); N.S.: No statute; P.E.I.: An Act to Amend the Election Act, S.P.E.I. 2007, c. 29; N.F.L.: An Act to Amend the House of Assembly Act, S.N.L. 2004, c. 44. Two of the territories also have fixed election date laws: Yukon: No statute; N.W.T.: Elections and Plebiscites Act, S.N.W.T. 2006, c. 15; Nunavut: An Act to Provide for a Fixed Election Date, S.Nu. 2014, c. 5.

[3]The Canada Elections Act is enacted under the peace, order, and good government power of Parliament (discussed, ch. 17, Peace, Order and Good Government) and the fixed-election-date amendment is enacted under the same power. A weak argument can be made that it is a law in relation to the House of Commons under s. 44 of the Constitution Act, 1982, but s. 44 applies only to "laws amending the Constitution of Canada" and the Canada Elections Act is not part of the Constitution of Canada. Nor does the fixed-election-date provision conflict with s. 50 of the Constitution Act, 1867 or s. 4 of the Constitution Act, 1982, the provisions that stipulate a *maximum* duration for the House of Commons, and which do form part of the Constitution of Canada.

Prime Minister claimed that the House had become "dysfunctional" and advised the Governor General to dissolve the House for an election on October 14, 2008—a full year earlier than the election date established by his own legislation.[4] The Governor General dissolved the House, the election was held, and it yielded another Conservative minority government.

In *Conacher v. Canada* (2010),[5] Democracy Watch, an organization that promotes democratic ideas, applied to the Federal Court for a declaration that the Prime Minister had contravened the fixed-election-date legislation by advising the Governor General to dissolve the House of Commons for the election of October 14, 2008, which was a year earlier than the election date stipulated in the legislation (October 19, 2009). The applicant argued that the "fixed" election date was "meaningless" if the Prime Minister was free to disregard the legislated date whenever he wanted to call an election at an earlier time. The Federal Court of Appeal refused to grant the declaration. The Court pointed out that subsection (1) of s. 56.1 expressly preserves the power of the Governor General to dissolve Parliament "at the Governor General's discretion". The Court rejected the argument that subsection (1) should be "read down" so that it applied only when the government had lost the confidence of the House. The words of subsection (1) were clear and unqualified by any such restriction—and any such restriction may have required a constitutional amendment since the Governor General's power of dissolution is expressly recognized in s. 50 of the Constitution Act, 1867. The applicant also sought a declaration that the passage of the legislation created a new constitutional convention prohibiting any Prime Minister who had not lost the confidence of the House from advising the Governor General to dissolve Parliament except in accordance with the schedule of dates set by the legislation. This declaration was also refused. There were plenty of statements in Hansard to the effect that the legislation was intended to remove the government's power to call "snap elections" at opportune times. But the only relevant precedent was the election that was under challenge, which contradicted the suggested convention and demonstrated that the relevant actors, namely, the Prime Minister and Governor General, did not believe in any such convention. Therefore, there was no convention supporting the fixed-date regime.[6]

The 2008 election—the one that was unsuccessfully challenged—reset the four-year election clock to the third Monday in October 2012. But the election returned another minority Conservative government, and the government was defeated on a vote of no-confidence on March 25,

[4]In the absence of a fixed election date, there is ample precedent for a Prime Minister of a minority government seeking dissolution before being defeated in the House on an issue of confidence: § 9:9 note 6, above.

[5]*Conacher v. Canada* (2010), 320 D.L.R. (4th) 530 (F.C.A.). The opinion of the Court was written by Stratas J.A.

[6]On conventions and their formation, see ch. 1, Sources, under heading § 1:10, "Conventions".

2011, causing the Prime Minister to advise and the Governor General to grant a dissolution of Parliament leading to an election on May 2, 2011. Once again, Parliament had not survived for the four-year statutory term. Canadian politicians, unlike those of most other countries,[7] seem to be incapable of the cooperation and accommodation that would keep a minority government in office for four years. No minority government has ever lasted that long, and obviously the fixed-date-legislation is not going to change behaviour that seems to be deeply rooted in the Canadian political culture. One is forced to conclude that the fixed-election-date legislation is essentially inoperative during a period of minority government.

The 2011 election reset the election clock to the third Monday in October 2015. The 2011 election broke a long pattern of minority governments, and returned a safe Conservative majority. This did not necessarily mean that the next election would be held on the statutory date. The 2008 election demonstrated that the Prime Minister—at least of a minority government—did not regard himself as morally bound by the statutory date, and the *Conacher* decision decides that no Prime Minister (whether or not with a majority) is legally bound by the statutory date. However, for a Prime Minister with a majority in the House, the statute will exert at least a strong political influence on the date of the next federal election. Prime Minister Harper did in fact call the next election for the statutory date of the third Monday in October 2015. In that election, his Conservative Party was defeated by the Liberal Party: Justin Trudeau became the Prime Minister with a safe majority in the House.

The 2015 election reset the election clock again for the statutory date of the third Monday in October 2019. Prime Minister Trudeau called the next election for the statutory date. The election returned the Liberals to government, and Justin Trudeau remained Prime Minister, but this time with only a minority government. The 2019 election reset the election clock to the statutory date of the third Monday in October 2023. However, taking previous minority governments as a guide, it seems highly unlikely the Liberal government will last for four years.

§ 9:21 Prorogation of Parliament

The Governor General has the power to *prorogue* Parliament,[1] which brings a *session* of Parliament to an end.[2] This is not the same as a dissolution, because prorogation suspends Parliament but does not bring it to an end and therefore does not require the election of a new

[7] The democracies of Western Europe (and New Zealand) elect their popular houses by some variant of proportional representation which almost never gives one party a majority, and yet they mostly have stable governments that last far longer than the two years that is normal in Canada for a minority government.

[Section 9:21]

[1] For a fuller account of what follows, see P.W. Hogg, "Prorogation and the Power of the Governor General" (2009) 27 Nat. J. Con. Law 193.

[2] The Crown's power to prorogue Parliament is a prerogative power, although it is recognized in the Parliament of Canada Act, R.S.C. 1985, c. P-1, s. 3.

Parliament. As well, unlike a dissolution, the proclamation of prorogation stipulates the date when the new session is to start.[3] However, prorogation is not the same as an adjournment, because prorogation terminates the session, causing unenacted bills to lapse and committee business to cease.[4] A new session[5] starts with a speech from the throne which sets out the government's policy proposals for the session. The speech from the throne is prepared by the government, of course, but it is delivered by the Governor General to both Houses of Parliament assembled in the Senate chamber. After the speech from the throne, the House of Commons withdraws to its own chamber, and debates and votes on the speech from the throne. This vote provides the new session's first test of confidence in the government. Assuming the government's speech from the throne is approved by the House of Commons, the government will then proceed to introduce the bills needed to carry out its promised legislative agenda. (If the government wishes to enact any bills that were introduced but not passed in the previous session, the bills have to be reintroduced.) When the government has a majority, a Parliament usually lasts for four years, and there is typically more than one session in the life of the Parliament. When the government has only a minority, a Parliament usually only lasts for about two years and there may be only a single session. Prorogation is part of the normal governmental conduct of parliamentary business, and no Governor General has ever refused the Prime Minister's advice to prorogue Parliament.[6]

In 2008, Governor General Michaëlle Jean was faced with a request for prorogation in unprecedented circumstances.[7] Prime Minister Stephen Harper, who had been in office with a minority government since January 11, 2006, had been re-elected with a Conservative plurality (but not a majority) on October 14, 2008.[8] The first session of Parliament started on November 18, and on November 27 the House of Commons

[3]The practice is to issue two simultaneous proclamations, one to prorogue the session and the other to recall Parliament for the next session. In Alberta, Manitoba, Ontario, Prince Edward Island and Yukon, it is provided by statute that, on prorogation of the Legislature, "it is not necessary" to name a recall date: Legislative Assembly Act, R.S.A. 2000, c. L-9, s. 5; The Legislative Assembly Act, C.C.S.M, c. L110, s. 7; Legislative Assembly Act, R.S.O. 1990, c. L.10, s. 5; Legislative Assembly Act, R.S.P.E.I. 1974, c. L-7, s. 6(3); Legislative Assembly Act, R.S.Y. 2002, c. 136, s. 3.

[4]In New Brunswick and Nova Scotia, it is provided by statute that the Legislative Assembly may by resolution confer upon a committee the power to sit after prorogation of the Legislature: Legislative Assembly Act, R.S.N.B. 1973, c. L-3, s. 9; House of Assembly Act, R.S.N.S. (1992 Supp.), c. 1, s. 36(1).

[5]There has to be a session of Parliament "at least once every twelve months": Constitution Act, 1982, s. 5. This limits the duration of any prorogation.

[6]In 1873, the Governor General, Lord Dufferin, hesitated but finally acceded to Prime Minister John A. Macdonald's request for a prorogation over the summer which had the effect of terminating a parliamentary committee investigation into the Pacific Scandal: Mallory, The Structure of Canadian Government (rev. ed., 1984), 245.

[7]Russell and Sossin (eds.), Parliamentary Democracy in Crisis (2009) is a collection of essays prompted by the incident.

[8]The standings of the parties were as follows: Conservative, 143; Liberal, 77; New

approved the speech from the throne, thereby confirming its confidence in the Harper government. However, on December 1, the leaders of the three opposition parties, the Liberal Party, the New Democratic Party (NDP) and the Bloc Quebecois (BQ) (together representing a majority of the House) announced that they had lost confidence in the Harper government; that they would introduce and pass a vote of no-confidence in the government at the earliest opportunity; that they were prepared to support a Liberal-NDP coalition government[9] led by Liberal leader Stéphane Dion;[10] and that, an election having been held less than two months earlier, they would request the Governor General to commission Mr. Dion as Prime Minister in lieu of Mr. Harper. The first opportunity for the opposition to introduce and pass a vote of no-confidence was an opposition day scheduled for December 8. Mr. Harper's reaction to his likely imminent defeat was to call on the Governor General on December 4 and advise her to prorogue Parliament until January 26, 2009. The Governor General accepted the advice and prorogued Parliament as advised. The prorogation denied the opposition parties their opportunity to bring down the government on December 8.

The proroguing of Parliament after a session of only 16 days in which nothing of importance had been accomplished, and with the effect of averting a vote of no-confidence, was certainly unprecedented. Did Governor General Jean have a discretion to reject the advice of the Prime Minister on December 4?[11] At that time, having secured approval of the speech from the throne, the Prime Minister still possessed the confidence of the House. Normally, the Governor General must follow the advice of a Prime Minister who possesses the confidence of the House. In this case, however, it was public knowledge that the opposition parties were united in their determination to pass a vote of no-confidence on December 8, and the Governor General had been so advised by letters from the opposition leaders that had been made public. There is no doubt that the Governor General has a discretion to refuse the advice of a Prime Minister who has *lost* a vote of no-confidence. Although there are no close precedents,[12] the same discretion must surely be available when the Prime Minister is *about to lose* a vote of no-

---

Democratic Party, 37; and Bloc Quebecois, 49.

[9]If this had come to pass, it would have been only the second coalition federal government, the first being the Borden/Meighen Unionist government of 1917–21.

[10]The leaders of the Liberal Party, Stephane Dion, and the New Democratic Party, Jack Layton, signed a formal agreement dated December 1, 2008 for a coalition government with Mr. Dion as leader and cabinet positions shared by the two parties. The agreement was to last until June 30, 2011. The leader of the Bloc Quebecois, Gilles Duceppe, who was not part of the coalition, agreed in writing to support the coalition government until June 30, 2010.

[11]I disclose that I was the legal adviser to the Governor General in the period up to and including December 4. However, this account is restricted to information in the public domain and does not disclose either the advice that I provided (which is confidential) or the reasons that drove the Governor General's ultimate decision (which I do not know).

[12]The closest precedent is the King-Byng precedent of 1926, described § 9:19. The

confidence. If that were not the case, a Prime Minister could avoid (or at least postpone) a pending vote of no-confidence simply by advising the prorogation of the pesky Parliament. We may safely infer that Governor General Jean believed that she had a discretion, because, when the Prime Minister called on the Governor General on December 4, she took two and a half hours of the Prime Minister's time (with the media stationed all around Rideau Hall for the duration) before he emerged to announce that she had acceded to his request.[13] The majority of commentators have concluded that she did have a discretion to refuse the request for the prorogation because of the impending vote of no-confidence.[14] Of course, she in fact followed the Prime Minister's advice to prorogue Parliament, but it was on the basis of her personal judgment of the course of action that would best comport with the principles of parliamentary government.

Assuming that the Governor General did indeed have a discretion, was she wise to grant the prorogation on December 4, 2008? It interrupted the normal course of Parliament, and denied the opposition an early opportunity to pass judgment on the government.[15] But the prorogation was only for a short period, from December 4, 2008 to January 26, 2009, and the government had promised to consult widely during the period of prorogation and introduce a budget on January 27. The budget would include measures to stimulate the economy, which had

---

Governor General refused the Prime Minister's request for a dissolution (not a prorogation), made at a time when Parliament was debating and would likely pass a resolution of censure of the government. Although the Governor General's actions are controversial, the controversy does not extend to the proposition that the Governor General has a personal discretion to reject the advice of a Prime Minister who is about to lose a vote of censure in the House. That is also the interpretation that is generally placed on the Macdonald-Dufferin precedent of 1873: § 9:21 note 6, above. The Governor General's grant of prorogation in 1873 was not only protested by the Liberal (opposition) members, but by some of the Conservative (government) members as well, all of whom must have believed that that the Governor General had a discretion. For a contrary interpretation of the precedent, see N.A. MacDonald and J.W.J. Bowden, "No Discretion: On Prorogation and the Governor General" (2011) 8 Can. Parliamentary Rev. 7 (arguing that even an imminent loss of confidence does not liberate the Governor General from the binding force of the Prime Minister's advice to prorogue Parliament).

[13]M. Valpy, "G-G made Harper work for prorogue", The Globe and Mail, December 6, 2008, A4. For more background, Russell and Sossin (eds.), Parliamentary Democracy in Crisis (2009), ch. 1 (by M. Valpy).

[14]Russell and Sossin (eds.), Parliamentary Democracy in Crisis (2009), 36, 46 (by C.E.S. Franks), 55 (by A. Heard), 65–66 (by L. Weinrib), 89 (by B. Slattery) 191 (by D.R. Cameron). J. LeClair and J.-F. Gaudreault-Desbiens sit on the fence at 117 ("we are not yet convinced" that the prorogation request was "exceptional enough" to trigger the Governor General's discretion).

[15]Andrew Heard in Russell and Sossin (eds.), Parliamentary Democracy in Crisis (2009), 58–59, takes the view that the Governor General should have refused the prorogation for this reason. He also argues (60) that "the events of December 2008 now provide a clear precedent for any future prime minister to demand that Parliament be suspended whenever he or she feels threatened with defeat". This argument assumes that the Governor General has no discretion to refuse a Prime Minister's "demand" for prorogation. Since she has a discretion, she will be governed by her judgment in the circumstances of the time.

fallen into recession; it was the absence of any such measures that was the reason publicly offered by the opposition for replacing the government. On the resumption of Parliament, therefore, the budget would provide an early opportunity for a confidence vote, and that vote would be informed by the measures proposed in the new budget.

Now consider what would have happened if the Governor General had exercised her discretion to deny the requested prorogation on December 4, 2008. In that event, there would have been a vote of no-confidence in the House of Commons on December 8, and that vote would have passed. This would have left the Governor General with the options of either dissolving Parliament for an election or commissioning an alternative Prime Minister from the existing House of Commons. The option of dissolution was almost unthinkable, since it would involve putting the country through another general election when the previous election had been held only two months earlier. The other option was to commission Mr. Dion as Prime Minister of a Liberal-NDP coalition government. But that option was also unattractive. It was true that Mr. Dion could produce a written coalition agreement. But Mr. Dion, the moving force in forming the coalition, was only an interim leader of the Liberal Party, having resigned after his poor showing in the previous election; he remained as leader only until the Party selected a new leader.[16] Moreover, the coalition agreement had been negotiated in haste and in anger,[17] and was an entirely new departure for the Liberal Party, which in periods of minority government had never before proposed a coalition with the NDP. The coalition did not have the numbers to govern without the support of the BQ's 49 members, which was admittedly promised in writing, but it meant that three parties would have had to stay in line on all confidence issues to avoid defeat at the hands of the Conservatives. On December 4, 2008, the Governor General could hardly predict the disintegration of the coalition that occurred less than two months later (which is about to be described), but it was reasonable for her to conclude that the coalition was likely to be an unstable alternative government.

Parliament did resume on January 26, 2009. The speech from the throne was given on that day.[18] As promised, the budget was introduced

[16]Mr. Dion was in fact replaced by Michael Ignatieff as the leader of the Liberal Party on December 9, 2008. Mr. Ignatieff had been reported by the media to be less than enthusiastic about the coalition agreement, which he had not been involved in negotiating, despite being a leading contender to replace Mr. Dion as leader.

[17]The coalition was spurred by anger at a government proposal to eliminate public funding for political parties, which would have damaged the opposition parties more seriously than the Conservative Party because the opposition parties were less successful in private fund raising. This proposal (and some other provocative proposals) had been withdrawn by the time the coalition was formed, but the anger remained. The remaining major grievance was the failure of the government to bring forward measures to stimulate the economy which had fallen into recession, but on this issue the government had promised to consult and bring forward a new budget on January 27.

[18]The debate on the speech from the throne, which could have led to a confidence vote, was adjourned at the initiative of Mr. Ignatieff, the Liberal leader, so that the budget could be introduced as promised. Clearly, there was a bipartisan understanding

by the government on the next day, January 27. The budget contained major spending initiatives to stimulate the economy—the kinds of measures the opposition had been calling for. By that time the leadership of the Liberal Party had changed—Stéphane Dion had been replaced by Michael Ignatieff—and Liberal enthusiasm for coalition government seemed to have evaporated. When Mr. Ignatieff announced on January 28 that his party would support the budget, his erstwhile coalition partner, the leader of the NDP (Jack Layton), immediately proclaimed the coalition agreement to be terminated. The confidence vote on the budget took place on February 3, and the budget passed with the support of the Liberal Party, over the opposition of the NDP and BQ, leaving the Conservative government in office. The coalition agreement, which on paper had a duration of two and a half years, had lasted less than two months.

The events of January 2009 could not have been anticipated in detail by the Governor General when she granted the prorogation on December 4, 2008, but they make it very difficult to question the soundness of the Governor General's judgment.[19] The continued threat of the no-confidence vote had forced the government to craft a conciliatory budget that could and did gain the confidence of the House. The fragility of the coalition had been demonstrated in the most dramatic way possible by the inability of the coalition parties to maintain a common front on the first policy issue that they faced, namely, the budget. In hindsight, the prorogation seems to have been the wise solution to the difficult choice faced by the Governor General on December 4, 2008.

Prime Minister Harper requested and was granted another controversial prorogation on December 30, 2009, again with much of his legislative program unenacted, and this time with the effect of closing down a parliamentary committee investigating alleged misconduct by Canadian forces in Afghanistan. The committee had demanded the production by the government of documents, and the government had refused to comply. However, on this occasion, the Prime Minister, although leading a minority government, possessed the confidence of the House of Commons, and was not facing a vote of no-confidence in the House. The Governor General was therefore bound by convention to accept his advice.

Another "tactical" (and therefore controversial) prorogation occurred in Ontario on October 18, 2012. Premier Dalton McGuinty requested and was granted a prorogation of the Legislature with the effect of closing down a legislative committee that was pursuing allegations that the Premier and two of his senior ministers had misled the Legislature about the cost of closing two gas plants just before the last election (which had taken place a year earlier). One of the ministers had already been charged with contempt of the Legislature for failure to disclose

---

that confidence would be granted or withheld on the basis the of the budget.

[19]Accord, Russell and Sossin (eds.), Parliamentary Democracy in Crisis (2009), 46 (by C.E.S. Franks), 65–66 (by L. E. Weinrib), 191–194 (by D.R. Cameron). *Contra*, A. Heard in Russell and Sossin (eds.), Parliamentary Democracy in Crisis (2009), 58–59.

documents to the committee, and the committee was considering contempt proceedings against the Premier. On the same day as the prorogation was granted, Premier McGuinty announced his retirement from the Premiership. In this case, the prorogation proclamation did not stipulate the date at which the prorogation would end, and the Premier announced publicly that his (as yet unknown) successor as Premier would decide when to recall the Legislature, thereby leaving the date of recall quite indefinite.[20] However, the Premier, although leading a minority government, possessed the confidence of the Legislature, and was not facing a vote of no-confidence. The Lieutenant Governor was therefore bound to accept his advice. The prorogation in fact lasted for four months. During that time, the Ontario Liberal Party chose a new leader, Kathleen Wynne, who was sworn in as Premier on February 11th, 2013, and, on her advice, the Lieutenant Governor summoned the Legislature back into session on February 19, 2013.

Yet another controversial – and arguably "tactical" – prorogation occurred federally in 2020. On August 18, 2020, Prime Minister Justin Trudeau, who was leading a minority government, requested and was granted a prorogation of Parliament until September 23, 2020 by Governor General Julie Payette. The Prime Minister claimed that the prorogation was necessary to allow for a new throne speech that would lay out the next phase of the federal government's response to the COVID-19 pandemic, which began in early 2020. The previous throne speech, which had been delivered just eight months earlier, had occurred before the onset of, and therefore understandably did not respond to, the pandemic. However, the prorogation came just one day after the Minister of Finance resigned from the federal cabinet. The prorogation also had the effect of closing down several parliamentary committees that were investigating whether the Trudeau government had acted improperly in the early weeks of the pandemic in awarding a contract to administer a large student grant program to the WE Charity. There was a certain irony to the prorogation, as the Prime Minister had criticized, and pledged to avoid, the tactical prorogations of his predecessor. However, when the Prime Minister advised the Governor General to prorogue Parliament, the Prime Minister, although leading a minority government, possessed the confidence of the House of Commons, and was not facing a vote of no-confidence in the House. The Governor General was therefore bound by convention to accept his advice. The new session of Parliament did begin on September 23, 2020 with a new throne speech. The confidence vote on the throne speech took place on October 6, 2020, and the throne speech was approved by a majority of the House, with the support of the NDP, leaving the Trudeau government in power.

It was suggested in an earlier chapter of this book that the exercise of the Crown's prerogative powers relating to the system of responsible government – including the power of prorogation – has been regulated

---

[20]In Ontario, it is not necessary to name a recall date in the instrument of prorogation: see heading § 9:21, "Prorogation of Parliament".

largely by conventions, which are not enforceable in the courts.[21] This state of affairs seems to have been accepted in Canada, as there was little discussion about challenging the "tactical" prorogations referred to in the previous paragraphs in the courts. This may now change in light of the extraordinary decision of the Supreme Court of the United Kingdom in *R. (Miller) v. The Prime Minister* (2019).[22] This appeal had its roots in the 2016 "Brexit" referendum, in which a majority of voters in the United Kingdom supported leaving the European Union (EU). The central issue in the appeal was whether Prime Minister Boris Johnson's advice to the Queen to prorogue Parliament for a five-week period in 2019 (from September 9 to October 14) was unlawful. The Johnson government claimed that this prorogation was necessary to bring what had been a long parliamentary session to an end, and to allow for a new throne speech to be prepared. However, there was a widespread sense that the prorogation was actually aimed at stifling further parliamentary debate about, and preventing parliamentary action to delay or block, Brexit – which at that point in time was set to occur on October 31, 2019. There was a strong argument for dismissing the appeal on the basis that the issue raised was not justiciable in the courts – a view that had been taken by two lower courts in the proceedings.[23] However, in a stunning decision, the Supreme Court (which sat as a full panel of 11) held that the Prime Minister's prorogation advice to the Queen was not only justiciable, but unlawful, and therefore null and of no effect.

The Court said that the appeal raised four issues. The first was whether the lawfulness of the Prime Minister's advice to the Queen to prorogue Parliament was justiciable in the courts. The second issue was what standard should be used to assess the lawfulness of the Prime Minister's prorogation advice to the Queen, if it was justiciable in the courts. The third issue was whether, applying this standard, the Prime Minister's prorogation advice to the Queen was unlawful. The fourth and final issue, if the advice was unlawful, was the remedy that should be granted.

On the first issue (justiciability), the Court said that, since a prerogative power (to prorogue Parliament) was involved, it was important to distinguish between two different types of issues. The first type of issue is the *existence* and *scope* of the particular prerogative power being claimed; the second type of issue is whether the *exercise* of a prerogative power within its scope can be challenged in the courts on some other

[21] Chapter 1, Sources, under heading § 1:9, "Prerogative".

[22] *R. (Miller) v. The Prime Minister*, [2019] UKSC 41, 3 W.L.R. 589. Lady Hale and Lord Reed wrote a joint opinion for the unanimous Court.

[23] *Cherry v. Advocate General for Scotland*, [2019] CSOH 70 (Outer House, Scottish Court of Session); and *R. (Miller) v. The Prime Minister*, [2019] EWHC 2381 (Q.B.). An appeal of the *Cherry* decision was allowed by the Inner House, Scottish Court of Session, which held that the Prime Minister's prorogation advice and the prorogation that followed it were unlawful, and therefore null and of no effect: *Cherry v. Advocate General for Scotland*, [2019] CSIH 49.

basis.[24] The Court said that the first type of issue "undoubtedly lies within the jurisdiction of the courts and is justiciable", whereas the second type of issue "may raise questions of justiciability", depending on the nature and subject matter of the prerogative power involved.[25] The lower courts in this appeal had understood the issue to involve the *exercise* of the prerogative power of prorogation (the second type of issue), raising questions of justiciability. However, the Court said that the issue in the appeal related to the *scope* of the prerogative power of prorogation (the first type of issue), and thus was clearly justiciable.[26]

On the second issue (the standard to apply), the Court said that, since the prerogative powers are "recognised by the common law", they must be "compatible with common law principles", including "the fundamental principles of . . . constitutional law".[27] The Court then went on to identify two constitutional principles that, it said, were relevant to the scope of the prerogative power to prorogue Parliament: parliamentary sovereignty and parliamentary accountability. On the one hand, the Court said, these two constitutional principles suggested the need for *some* legal limit on the scope of the prerogative power to prorogue Parliament. Otherwise, "the executive could, through the use of the prerogative, prevent Parliament from exercising its legislative authority for as long as it pleased", contrary to the principle of parliamentary sovereignty, and could also avoid accountability to Parliament for as long as it pleased, contrary to the principle of parliamentary accountability.[28] On the other hand, the Court said, since the prerogative power to prorogue Parliament clearly existed, these two constitutional principles could not be taken so far as to deny the existence of the power altogether; even though prorogation could impede the ability of Parliament to exercise its legislative authority and to hold the executive to account, it must be consistent with parliamentary sovereignty and parliamentary accountability *in some situations*. The Court then went on to articulate the following standard for the courts to apply in determining the scope of the prorogation power: "a decision to prorogue Parliament (or to advise the monarch to prorogue Parliament) will be unlawful if the prorogation has the effect of frustrating or preventing, without reasonable justification, the ability of Parliament to carry out its constitutional functions as a legislature and as the body responsible for the supervision of the executive".[29]

On the third issue, the Court concluded, applying this standard, that the Prime Minister's advice to the Queen to prorogue Parliament exceeded the scope of the prerogative power, and was therefore unlawful.

---

[24] *R. (Miller) v. The Prime Minister*, [2019] UKSC 41, 3 W.L.R. 589, para. 35.

[25] *R. (Miller) v. The Prime Minister*, [2019] UKSC 41, 3 W.L.R. 589, para. 35, citing *Council of Civil Service Unions v. Minister for the Civil Service*, [1985] A.C. 374 (H.L.).

[26] *R. (Miller) v. The Prime Minister*, [2019] UKSC 41, 3 W.L.R. 589, para. 52.

[27] *R. (Miller) v. The Prime Minister*, [2019] UKSC 41, 3 W.L.R. 589, paras. 38-39.

[28] *R. (Miller) v. The Prime Minister*, [2019] UKSC 41, 3 W.L.R. 589, paras. 41-42, 48.

[29] *R. (Miller) v. The Prime Minister*, [2019] UKSC 41, 3 W.L.R. 589, para. 50.

The Prime Minister's advice to the Queen to prorogue Parliament had the effect of frustrating Parliament's constitutional role in holding the government to account. The prorogation here was five weeks, which "might not matter in some circumstances", but it did matter here, because it prevented Parliament from holding the government to account just when a "fundamental change was due to take place in the Constitution of the United Kingdom" due to Brexit.[30] In addition, no reasonable justification had been offered for the Prime Minister's advice to the Queen to prorogue Parliament for five weeks. The government claimed that it needed this time for the preparation of a new throne speech, but the evidence of a previous Prime Minister – Sir John Major – was that only four to six days was normally required for this task.

On the final issue (remedy), the Court was only asked to issue a declaration that the Prime Minister's advice to the Queen to prorogue Parliament was unlawful, but it decided to go even further. It held that, since the Prime Minister's advice was unlawful, and therefore null and of no effect, the subsequent Order in Council authorizing the prorogation – and by extension, the prorogation itself – were also unlawful, and therefore null and of no effect.[31] It followed from this that Parliament had simply never been prorogued at all. The impact of this was swift. The morning after the Court released its decision, the Speaker of the House of Commons summoned MPs to Westminster and resumed the parliamentary session as if Parliament had never been prorogued.

It is tempting to sympathize with the Court's decision.[32] The Prime Minister did seem to be using the prorogation power "tactically", to avoid parliamentary accountability at a moment of profound significance for the United Kingdom and its constitution. The Court's decision prevented this anti-democratic result. Even so, there are good reasons to question the decision. First, while the Court is clearly right that the power to prorogue Parliament is a prerogative power, it is a prerogative power of a particular kind – namely, one that had, until the Court's decision, been regulated largely by conventions, which are not enforceable in the courts. The Court's decision paid little attention to this fact, or to the impact that it will or could have on the existing conventions relating

[30] *R. (Miller) v. The Prime Minister*, [2019] UKSC 41, 3 W.L.R. 589, para. 57.

[31] In reaching this conclusion, the Court rejected an argument that it was precluded from taking this additional step by the Bill of Rights of 1688, which provides, by article 9, that "Proceedings in Parlyament" [sic] cannot "be impeached or questioned in any Court". The Court said that, while the prorogation took place in Parliament, it is not a proceeding in Parliament, because it is not a decision of either House, but is "imposed upon them from outside": [2019] UKSC 41, 3 W.L.R. 589, para. 68.

[32] For commentary on the decision, some critical, some more positive, see J. Finnis, "The unconstitutionality of the Supreme Court's prorogation judgment" (2019); A. McHarg, "The Supreme Court's Prorogation Judgment: Guardian of the Constitution or Architect of the Constitution?" (2020) 24 Edin. L. Rev. 88; P. Craig, "The Supreme Court, Prorogation and Constitutional Principle" [2020] 1:2 Public Law 248; M. Loughlin, "A note on Craig on *Miller, Cherry*" [2020] 1:2 Public Law 278; S. Tierney, "*R. v. Prime Minister*; *Cherry v. Advocate General of Scotland*" (2019) 40 Scots Law Times 170; M. Elliott, "Constitutional Adjudication and Constitutional Policies in the United Kingdom: The Miller II Case in Legal and Political Context" (2021) 16 Eur. Const. L. Rev. 1.

to the prorogation power.[33] Second, the Court provided little explanation for why the existing legal and political safeguards on the use of the prorogation power were inadequate, beyond suggesting that they provided "scant reassurance".[34] Third, while the Court is right that the cases have drawn a distinction between the existence and scope of a prerogative power (which are justiciable) and its exercise (which may not be justiciable), the standard the Court said should be applied in determining the scope of the prorogation power (particularly the requirement for "reasonable justification")[35] gives a very broad reach to the scope analysis; the result is that "any constraint on the exercise of [the] power can potentially be recast as a limit on its scope".[36] Finally, and notwithstanding the Court's claims to the contrary,[37] the standard the Court said should be applied in determining the scope of the prorogation power will also require the courts to make difficult and politically-charged "questions of judgment – both as to the effects of the prorogation on the exercise of Parliament's functions, and the adequacy and weight of the reasons offered".[38] Given these issues, it is striking that the Court itself did not seem to have complete confidence in – and so seemed inclined to try to downplay – the expanded role it was taking on in the case. In an unusual passage at the outset of its opinion, the Court said that the case was "a 'one off' ", which arose "in circumstances which have never arisen before and are unlikely ever to arise again".[39]

One question that will naturally arise for readers in Canada is whether the courts in Canada will – or should – follow *Miller*. So far, the courts in Canada have been cautious in reviewing decisions involving

---

[33]On the one hand, while the decision claims to "express no view on" whether the Queen was obligated, as a matter of convention, to accept the Prime Minister's advice to prorogue Parliament ([2019] UKSC 41, 3 W.L.R. 589, para. 30), it has been argued that the decision can be read to treat the Prime Minister's advice to the Queen as "legally determinative, not just factually causative", indirectly enforcing a convention to this effect – which of course the courts are not supposed to do: L. Sirota, "Heresy!", Double Aspect Blog (last accessed February 1, 2021). On the other hand, if the Queen was not obligated by convention to accept the Prime Minister's advice, questions then arise about the impact of the Court's decision going forward; should, for example, the Queen now refuse to prorogue Parliament if, in her view, the standard articulated in the Court's decision is not satisfied in some situation?

[34]*R. (Miller) v. The Prime Minister*, [2019] UKSC 41, 3 W.L.R. 589, para. 43.

[35]The full standard is set out in the text accompanying § 9:21 note 32, above.

[36]McHarg, "The Supreme Court's Prorogation Judgment: Guardian of the Constitution or Architect of the Constitution?" (2020) 24 Edin. L. Rev. 88, 93.

[37]See e.g. *R. (Miller) v. The Prime Minister*, [2019] UKSC 41, 3 W.L.R. 589, para. 51, where the Court insisted that the extent to which a prorogation frustrates or prevents Parliament from carrying out its constitutional functions "is a question of fact which presents no greater difficulty than many other questions of fact which are routinely decided by the courts".

[38]McHarg, "The Supreme Court's Prorogation Judgment: Guardian of the Constitution or Architect of the Constitution?" (2020) 24 Edin. L. Rev. 88, 93-94.

[39]*R. (Miller) v. The Prime Minister*, [2019] UKSC 41, 3 W.L.R. 589, para. 1.

the prerogative powers relating to responsible government.[40] In light of the concerns identified in the previous paragraph, it is to be hoped that this caution will continue. It is also worth pointing out that, unlike the United Kingdom, Canada has an entrenched Constitution that imposes an express limit on any prorogation both federally and provincially. This is found in section 5 of the Charter of Rights, which provides that "[t]here shall be a sitting of Parliament and of each legislature at least once every twelve months". A central concern underlying the Court's decision in *Miller* was that Parliament could be prorogued indefinitely. Section 5 dulls the force of this concern in Canada, as a prorogation of more than twelve months would clearly be unconstitutional.[41] Section 5 may appear to set the limit on prorogation too high, but those who would support the importation of *Miller* into Canada for prorogations less than twelve months will need to justify why it would be appropriate for the courts to supplement the clear twelve-month rule set out in s. 5, effectively rewriting the provision, without satisfying the requirements of a formal constitutional amendment.

§ 9:22 Appointments to Senate and bench

The Governor General's power to appoint senators (Constitution Act, 1867, s. 24) and judges (s. 96) is of course exercised on the advice of the cabinet.[1] In 1896, however, after Parliament had been dissolved and after a new election had decisively defeated the incumbent Conservative government of Prime Minister Tupper, the Tupper government advised the Governor General, Lord Aberdeen, to appoint a number of senators and judges. The Governor General refused to make the appointments. The Tupper government accordingly resigned (as it would have had to do anyway because of the election result). The Governor General then invited Mr. Laurier, the leader of the Liberal Party, which had won the election, to form a new government. Mr. Laurier did so, and his government filled the vacancies which the previous government had attempted to fill. The action of the Governor General in this case seems to me to be

---

[40] *Guergis v. Novak* (2012), 112 O.R. (3d) 118 (S.C.J.), affd. (2013) 116 O.R. (3d) 280 (C.A.) (exercise of the prerogative power to dismiss a minister at pleasure not justiciable); *Conacher v. Can.* (2009), 311 D.L.R. (4th) 678 (F.C.), affd. (2010) 320 D.L.R. (4th) 530 (F.C.A) (Prime Minister's advice to the Governor General to dissolve Parliament not justiciable; however, the question of whether the federal fixed-election-date *statute* was respected was justiciable). See also *Black v. Can.* (2001), 54 O.R. (3d) 215 (C.A.) (advice given by the Prime Minister to the Queen about the conferral of honours on Canadian citizens not justiciable).

[41] In the unlikely event there was an attempt to prorogue Parliament or a provincial Legislature for more than 12 months, a court might be asked to intervene to enforce s. 5. In such a case, the argument for judicial review could be grounded in the Charter itself, and unlike in the United Kingdom, the courts would presumably be asked to enforce the clear twelve-month rule in s. 5, rather than engage in the sort of line-drawing exercise contemplated in *Miller*.

[Section 9:22]

[1] To be precise, the appointment of Chief Justices and senators is made on the advice of the Prime Minister alone: see heading § 9:6, "The Prime Minister".

both wise and in accordance with convention. It was quite improper for the Tupper government to attempt to strengthen its support in the Senate and (less obviously) the bench after it had been defeated at the polls. True, the government was still in office, but the Governor General was entitled to recognize that it was not going to have a majority in the newly-elected House of Commons. In this circumstance the Governor General had a discretion to refuse to concur in an important and irrevocable decision which could await the early and inevitable formation of a new government which was bound to enjoy a majority in the House of Commons.[2]

§ 9:23 The justification for a formal head of state

A system of responsible government cannot work without a formal head of state who is possessed of certain reserve powers. While the occasions for the exercise of these powers arise very rarely, the powers are of supreme importance, for they insure against a hiatus in the government of the country or an illegitimate extension of power by a government which has lost its political support. The strength and the weakness of responsible government lie in the executive's dependence on support in the legislature. The strength lies in its provision of an executive which is in accord with the latest expression of the electorate's wishes and which is able to execute its policies. The weakness lies in the absence of clear legal rules as to when governmental power shall be assumed or relinquished and when elections shall be held. In situations where a discredited government is reluctant to relinquish its power, or where parliamentary support is fluid, the head of state is able to resolve the impasse impartially, either through formation of a government, or through an election.

This function of the head of state is unnecessary in a presidential (or gubernatorial) form of government, where the president (or governor) is directly elected for a fixed term and is not dependent upon the support of the legislative branch. The Americans have therefore been able to unite in the one office the formal head of state and the political executive of the nation (or state). The countries which have inherited the British system of responsible government have all had to establish a dual executive in which a formal head of state presides over a government which is actually administered by political officials. While the formal head of state rarely has to exercise the reserve powers, it should not be overlooked that he or she also performs many formal, ceremonial and social functions which are important in the life of the nation.

§ 9:24 The monarchy

While responsible government requires a dual executive, it does not require that the formal head of state be the Queen. This is demonstrated by countries such as India, Ireland, Israel and South Africa,

---

[2]Accord, Mallory, The Structure of Canadian Government (rev. ed. 1984), 83.

which possess responsible government, but no monarchy.[1] Canada could if it chose easily become a republic by the simple device of securing an amendment of the Constitution to make the Gov-ernor General the formal head of state in his or her own right.[2] Many constitutional and statutory powers are in any case conferred directly upon the Governor General or the Governor General in Council, and would need no alteration. Those powers that are expressly conferred on the Queen could easily be amended to substitute the Governor General for the Queen. The personal prerogatives which are nowhere authoritatively defined, but which are exercised by the Governor General under a delegation from the Queen, should probably be explicitly conferred on the Governor General directly, although it could be argued that they are implicit in the position of a head of state in a system of responsible government. Certainly, they would not need to be defined in detail, unless that exercise was regarded as worthwhile in itself.[3] A new mode of appointing the Governor General would have to be worked out, because at present the appointment is made by the Queen. But the Queen makes the appointment on the advice of the Canadian Prime Minister anyway, and so the real power of appointment has already been domesticated. In short, the shift from a monarchy to a republic could be accomplished with practically no disturbance of present constitutional practice. In considering the question whether Canada should make the change, the constitutional considerations may be dismissed as neutral or unimportant; obviously, such matters as tradition, sentiment and ceremony are the important considerations.[4]

[Section 9:24]

[1]Abolition of the monarchy would not entail leaving the Commonwealth. The Queen would no longer be Canada's head of state, and would play no role in the government of Canada, but she would still be recognized by Canada as the head of the Commonwealth and as the symbol of that association. This was the formula which was adopted in 1949 when India decided to become a republic within the Commonwealth; since then, of course, many of the members of the Commonwealth have become republics: Wheare, The Constitutional Structure of the Commonwealth (1960), ch. 7; de Smith and Brazier, Constitutional and Administrative Law (8th ed., 1998), 118; McWhinney, The Governor General and the Prime Ministers (2005), ch. 7.

[2]The Constitution Act, 1982, by s. 41, requires the assents of the federal Parliament and all provinces (unanimity procedure) for an amendment in relation to "the office of the Queen".

[3]Evatt in *The King and His Dominion Governors* (2nd ed., 1967) deplores the uncertainty in the scope of the personal prerogatives and argues that they should be reduced to writing and enacted as a statute. Significantly, however, he does not himself attempt to draft a model statute and that is the hard part. On the question of reducing conventions to writing, see also K.J. Keith, "The Courts and the Conventions of the Constitition" (1967) 16 Int. Comp. L.Q. 542.

[4]For strong support of the monarchy, see MacKinnon, The Crown in Canada (1976). Forsey, Freedom and Order (1974), 21–32, in opposing the "absurd" suggestion that Canada might abolish the monarchy, exaggerates the constitutional problems which would be involved. The Canadian Bar Association's Committee on the Constitution has recommended the replacement of the monarchy with a Canadian Head of State chosen by the House of Commons: *Towards a New Canada* (1978), 34–35. The issue is discussed by

J.D. Whyte, "The Australian Republican Movement and its Implications for Canada" (1993) 4 Constitutional Forum (U. of Alta.) 88.

Chapter 12
Parliamentary Sovereignty

I. SOVEREIGNTY IN THE UNITED KINGDOM

§ 12:1 Sovereignty in the United Kingdom

II. SOVEREIGNTY IN CANADA

§ 12:2 Federalism
§ 12:3 Charter of Rights
§ 12:4 Constitutional amendment
§ 12:5 Extraterritorial competence
§ 12:6 Delegation
§ 12:7 Retroactive legislation
§ 12:8 Wisdom or policy of legislation

III. SELF-IMPOSED RESTRAINTS ON LEGISLATIVE POWER

§ 12:9 Substance of future laws
§ 12:10 Manner and form of future laws

I. SOVEREIGNTY IN THE UNITED KINGDOM

§ 12:1 Sovereignty in the United Kingdom

The "sovereignty" of the United Kingdom Parliament[1] is said by Dicey to be established by the rule that the Parliament has the power "to make or unmake any law whatever".[2] In the United Kingdom, the argument goes, there are no limits to legislative power: there is no fundamental law which cannot be altered by ordinary parliamentary action; there is no constituent instrument which allocates some subject matters of legislation to the Parliament and denies others to it; and there is no bill of rights which denies to the Parliament the power to destroy or curtail civil liberties.[3] Any law, upon any subject matter, is within the Parliament's competence.

The practical consequence of the sovereignty of the United Kingdom

---

[Section 12:1]

[1]The definitive study, covering both history and theory, is J. Goldsworthy, The Sovereignty of Parliament (Oxford, 1999).

[2]Dicey, The Law of the Constitution (10th ed., 1965), 39.

[3]But see the text accompanying § 12:1 notes 9 to 13, below, where the statement in the text is qualified to some degree.

Parliament is that there is no judicial review of legislation: the courts have no power to deny the force of law to any statute enacted by the Parliament.[4] A power of judicial review in England was actually asserted by Coke C.J. in 1610, in his famous statement that "when an Act of Parliament is against the common right and reason, or repugnant, or impossible to be performed, the common law [that is, the courts] will control it, and adjudge such Act to be void".[5] But it seems likely that Coke C.J.'s view was never more than an "empty phrase".[6] Certainly, the asserted power to hold an Act of Parliament void was never actually exercised by an English court. According to de Smith, at least by the time of the Revolution of 1688, "the judges had tacitly accepted a rule of obligation to give effect to every Act of Parliament, no matter how preposterous its content".[7] The safeguards against preposterous legislation were "political and conventional, not strictly legal".[8]

In seventeenth century England, Parliament became accepted as superior to the other two branches of government, namely, the King and the courts. All conflicts between Parliament and the other branches were settled in Parliament's favour. This development was an inevitable outcome of the growth of ideas of democracy. Even the judges could see that Parliament's view of "common right and reason" should be preferred to that of the courts. As the franchise was extended and corrupt election practices were eliminated, it seemed even more obvious that the solemnly legislated decisions of an elected Parliament should prevail over the policy preferences of non-elected judges.

The conventional view is that the unfettered power of the Parliament of the United Kingdom continues to this day.[9] However, the United Kingdom's membership in the European Union, formerly the European Community, was moving it away from the pure model of parliamentary sovereignty.[10] While the United Kingdom is no longer a member of the

---

[4] *Pickin v. British Railways Bd.*, [1974] A.C. 765 (H.L.) (courts lacked jurisdiction to consider whether statute had been procured by fraud).

[5] *Dr. Bonham's Case* (1610), 8 Co. Rep. 113, 118; 77 E.R. 646, 652 (K.B.).

[6] de Smith and Brazier, Constitutional and Administrative Law (8th ed., 1998), 75.

[7] de Smith and Brazier, Constitutional and Administrative Law (8th ed., 1998), 75.

[8] de Smith and Brazier, Constitutional and Administrative Law (8th ed., 1998), 76.

[9] Note the debate about whether Parliament can abdicate its authority over former colonies, as it has purported to do in the Canada Act 1982 and in many other statutes granting independence to former colonies: see Oliver, The Constitution of Independence (2005); and see also ch. 3, Independence, under heading § 3:8, "Termination of imperial authority".

[10] European Community (Union) law was held to take priority over U.K. domestic law; but on the conventional view, this priority did not undermine the sovereignty of the United Kingdom Parliament because it was by virtue of the European Communities Act 1972 (U.K.), c. 68: *R. v. Secretary of State for Transport; Ex parte Factortame*, [1990] 2 A.C. 85 (H.L.); *R. v. Secretary of State for Transport; Ex parte Factortame (No. 2)*, [1991] 1 A.C. 603 (H.L.); European Union Act 2011 (U.K.), c. 12, s. 18. For discussion, see H.W.R. Wade, "Sovereignty—Revolution or Evolution?" (1996) 112 L.Q.R. 569; T.R.S. Allan, "Parliamentary Sovereignty: Law, Politics and Revolution" (1997) 113 L.Q.R. 443;

European Union (it left in January 2020),[11] the enactment into domestic law of the European Convention on Human Rights[12] and the creation of elected assemblies for Wales, Scotland and Northern Ireland[13] are arguably still moving the United Kingdom away from the pure model of parliamentary sovereignty.[14]

New Zealand now provides a purer example of parliamentary sovereignty than the mother of parliaments at Westminster.[15] New Zealand is a unitary state lacking in the complications of nascent federal institutions (like those of Wales, Scotland and Northern Ireland) and unfettered by membership in an evolving international community (as the United Kingdom was while a member of the European Union). It also lacks an entrenched bill of rights, and the statutory New Zealand Bill of Rights Act 1990 explicitly provides that it does not override inconsistent statutes.[16] Dicey would have noted with approval that the

M. Sunkin and S. Payne (eds.), *The Nature of the Crown* (1999), 328-333 (P. Craig); N.W. Barber, "The afterlife of Parliamentary sovereignty" (2011) 9 Int. J. Con. Law 144.

[11]The U.K. formally left the European Union on January 31, 2020, following a "Brexit" referendum in June 2016. This was achieved domestically by the European Union (Withdrawal) Act 2018 (U.K.), c. 16, which repealed the European Communities Act 1972 (U.K.), c. 68 as of "exit day". The European Union (Withdrawal Agreement) Act 2020 (U.K.), c. 1 preserved the effect of the European Communities Act 1972 (U.K.) during a transitionary ("implementation") period and formally incorporated the Withdrawal Agreement with the European Union into domestic law. The transitionary period ended on December 31, 2020.

[12]The Human Rights Act 1998 (U.K.), c. 42 authorizes U.K. courts to make a "declaration of incompatibility" when U.K. legislation is found to breach the Convention; but on the conventional view, this does not undermine the sovereignty of the United Kingdom Parliament because the incompatible legislation continues in force until amended.

[13]On the conventional view, this does not undermine the sovereignty of the United Kingdom Parliament because the elected assemblies are merely subordinate bodies created by statute (Government of Wales Act 1998 (U.K.), c. 38; Scotland Act 1998 (U.K.), c. 46; Northern Ireland Act 1998 (U.K.), c. 47), and the United Kingdom Parliament retains an unimpaired power to legislate for Wales, Scotland and Northern Ireland. Against the conventional view, see Scotland Act 2016 (U.K.), c. 11, especially s. 1 (declaring "that the Scottish Parliament and the Scottish Government are not to be abolished except on the basis of a decision of the people of Scotland voting in a referendum").

[14]There is also obiter dicta in some cases suggesting potential common law limits on parliamentary sovereignty: see, in particular, *R. (Jackson) v. Attorney General*, [2006] 1 A.C. 262 (H.L.), para. 102 per Lord Steyn, paras. 104, 107 per Lord Hope, para. 159 per Baroness Hale; *R. (Privacy International) v. Investigatory Powers Tribunal*, [2019] UKSC 22 (U.K.S.C.), paras. 113, 144 per Lord Carnwath (Lady Hale and Lord Kerr concurring).

[15]Oliver, The Constitution of Independence (2005), 323–328.

[16]Unlike the Human Rights Act of the United Kingdom, the New Zealand Bill of Rights Act does not authorize courts to make a declaration of incompatibility when legislation is found to be inconsistent with the Act. (There is such a procedure for complaints that a law infringes the right to be free from discrimination, but not for any other infringement.) However, the New Zealand Court of Appeal (perhaps taking a leaf out of the U.K. book) has suggested, obiter, that a court would have the power to "indicate" when a statutory provision is inconsistent with the Act: *Moonen v. Film and Literature Board of Review*, [2000] 2 N.Z.L.R. 9, 17 (C.A.); see P. Rishworth et al, The New Zealand Bill of Rights (Oxford U.P., Melbourne, Australia, 2003), 833–837.

New Zealand Parliament is still a body with the power "to make or unmake any law whatever".[17]

II. SOVEREIGNTY IN CANADA

§ 12:2 Federalism

At confederation in 1867, the framers of the British North America Act not only contemplated a continuing colonial relationship between the new Dominion of Canada and the United Kingdom, they sought to model the new Dominion's institutions upon those of the United Kingdom. However, the federal character of Canada forced some fundamental departures from British concepts. Legislative power had to be distributed between the federal Parliament and the provincial Legislatures. This meant that each legislative body was given the power to make laws in relation to certain classes of subjects, and denied the power to make laws in relation to other classes of subjects. Moreover, as we have seen, the courts assumed the power to determine whether or not the Parliament or a Legislature had acted within its powers in enacting a statute, and to declare the statute invalid if it were outside the powers of the enacting body (ultra vires).[1] It followed that there was no legislative body in Canada that was sovereign in the sense of being able to make or unmake any law whatsoever.

While federalism was inconsistent with one omnicompetent Legislature like the United Kingdom Parliament, the idea of parliamentary sovereignty remained an important influence in Canadian constitutional theory.[2] The Constitution Act, 1867 for the most part limited legislative power only to the extent necessary to give effect to the federal principle.[3] Any power withheld from the federal Parliament was possessed by the

---

[17]Commentators have pointed out that it is hard to predict if courts would hold the line if faced with a statute that was fundamentally at odds with basic constitutional principles, although this is unlikely to arise in a democracy like New Zealand: see J. Goldsworthy, "Is Parliament Sovereign? Recent Challenges to the Doctrine of Parliamentary Sovereignty" (2005) 3 N.Z. J. of Public and Int. Law 7 (criticizing various suggestions that the N.Z. Parliament is not sovereign). In Canada, the Supreme Court of Canada has held that there are "unwritten constitutional principles" that are not express but also have the effect of invalidating statutes: see ch. 15, Judicial Review on Federal Grounds, under heading § 15:28, "Unwritten constitutional principles".

[Section 12:2]

[1]The history of judicial review in Canada is related in ch. 5, Federalism, under heading §§ 5:20 to 5:22, "Role of the Courts". As well, until the passage of the Statute of Westminster, 1931, laws enacted by the Canadian Parliament or a provincial Legislature were void to the extent of any repugnancy with any imperial statute extending to Canada: see ch. 3, Independence, under heading § 3:2, "Colonial Laws Validity Act, 1865".

[2]A.F. Bayefsky, "Parliamentary Sovereignty and Human Rights in Canada" (1983) 31 Political Studies 239.

[3]The courts have added some corollaries of their own which they have regarded as entailed by the federal principle, for example, the incapacity to preclude judicial review of the unconstitutionality of a statute (discussed in ch. 7, Courts, under heading § 7:20, "Privative clauses"), the incapacity to delegate powers from one level of government to

provincial Legislatures, and vice versa. If there was room for doubt on this point, the Privy Council scotched it by repeatedly enunciating the principle of exhaustive distribution of legislative powers: "whatever belongs to self-government in Canada belongs either to the Dominion or to the provinces, within the limits of the British North America Act".[4] The federal Parliament and provincial Legislatures, provided they stayed within the limits imposed by the scheme of federalism, received powers as "plenary and ample" as those of the United Kingdom Parliament.[5]

In the *Same-Sex Marriage Reference* (2004),[6] the Supreme Court of Canada upheld a proposed law that would expand the definition of marriage to include same-sex marriage. In opposition to the proposed law, it had been argued that the word "marriage" in Parliament's power over "marriage and divorce" in s. 91(26) did not extend to same-sex unions. Since it was clear that the provinces could not legislate a change in the definition of marriage, the argument meant that only a constitutional amendment would enable the expansion of the definition of marriage. The Supreme Court of Canada reaffirmed "the principle of exhaustiveness", which it described as "an essential characteristic of the federal distribution of powers". A "legislative void is precluded". It followed that "legislative competence over same-sex marriage must be vested in either Parliament or the Legislatures", and the most apt home for the matter was s. 91(26).[7]

§ 12:3 Charter of Rights

After the newly-independent thirteen American colonies formed their union in 1787, they added ten amendments to the new Constitution in 1789, and these first ten amendments became a Bill of Rights which

---

the other (discussed in ch. 14, Delegation, under heading § 14:10, "Legislative interdelegation"), and the incapacity to enact laws that are excessively broad and vague (discussed in ch. 15, Judicial Review on Federal Grounds, under heading § 15:5, "Matter").

[4]*A.-G. Ont. v. A.-G. Can.* (Reference Appeal) [1912] A.C. 571, 581, 583. Accord, *Bank of Toronto v. Lambe* (1887), 12 App. Cas. 575, 587; *Union Colliery Co. v. Bryden*, [1899] A.C. 580, 584–585; *A.-G. Can. v. A.-G. Ont.* (Labour Conventions) [1937] A.C. 326, 353–354; *Murphy v. CPR*, [1958] S.C.R. 626, 643; *Jones v. A.-G. N.B.*, [1975] 2 S.C.R. 182, 195; *Que. v. Can. (Firearms Sequel)*, [2015] 1 S.C.R. 693, 2015 SCC 14, para. 44; Browne, The Judicial Committee and the British North America Act (1967), 33–35. Note however the dictum by Laskin C.J. in *Central Can. Potash v. Govt. of Sask.*, [1979] 1 S.C.R. 42, 75 that "it does not follow [from the principle of exhaustive distribution] that legislation of a province held to be invalid may ipso facto be validly enacted by Parliament in its very terms". In the context of that case, this implies that neither level of government could enact a scheme for the prorationing of potash produced in Saskatchewan—a constitutional hiatus. This must surely be wrong.

[5]*Hodge v. The Queen* (1883), 9 App. Cas. 117, 132.

[6]*Re Same-Sex Marriage*, [2004] 3 S.C.R. 698.

[7]*Re Same-Sex Marriage*, [2004] 3 S.C.R. 698, para. 34. If the word "marriage" had been interpreted as limited to opposite-sex unions, a possible solution to the location of legislative power would have been Parliament's residuary peace, order, and good government power.

could not be altered except by further constitutional amendment.[1] When the loyal British North American colonies united in 1867, they did not copy this radical departure from British tradition. Apart from certain educational[2] and language rights,[3] no Bill of Rights was incorporated into the British North America Act.[4] This meant that the Parliament or a Legislature was not limited in its powers to curtail civil liberties.[5]

The adoption in 1982 of the Canadian Charter of Rights and Freedoms has now imposed upon the federal Parliament and the provincial Legislatures a set of limitations on their powers to curtail civil liberties. The civil liberties protected by the Charter include freedom of religion, expression, assembly and association (s. 2), voting rights (s. 3), mobility rights (s. 6), various procedural and other legal rights (ss. 7–14), the right to equal protection of the laws (ss. 15, 28) and new language rights (ss. 16–23). These protected civil liberties cannot be abridged by either the federal Parliament or a provincial Legislature. Since 1982, therefore, the Parliament and the Legislatures have been subject to two principal sets of constitutional limitations on their powers: (1) the federal limitations, mainly dating from 1867, which are designed to protect federal values; and (2) the Charter limitations, dating from 1982, which are designed to protect civil libertarian values.[6]

Canada's Charter of Rights is similar in principle and in much of its content to the American Bill of Rights. But the idea of parliamentary sovereignty influenced the final form of the Charter, and led to a crucial difference between the two instruments. Section 33 of the Charter, which has no counterpart in the American Bill of Rights, enables the Parliament or a Legislature to "override" most of the provisions of the Charter. This is accomplished by including in a statute an express declaration that the statute is to operate notwithstanding a provision included in s. 2 or ss. 7 to 15 of the Charter.[7] Once this declaration is included, the statute will operate free of the invalidating effect of the Charter provisions specified in the declaration. In this way, the Parliament or a Legislature, provided it is willing to include the express declaration required by the override provision, is able to enact a law that abridges

---

[Section 12:3]

[1]The original Bill of Rights was later supplemented by the thirteenth, fourteenth and fifteenth amendments, adopted after the civil war, and by the nineteenth, twenty-fourth and twenty-sixth amendments, adopted in the twentieth century.

[2]Constitution Act, 1867, s. 93; discussed in ch. 7, Education.

[3]Constitution Act, 1867, s. 133; discussed in ch. 56, Language.

[4]Other restrictions on legislative power of a non-federal character were (and still are) ss. 96–98 (appointment of judiciary), 99 (independence of judiciary), 121 (free movement of goods) and 125 (intergovernmental taxation).

[5]Judicial attempts to find an "implied bill of rights" in the Constitution Act, 1867 are discussed in ch. 34, Civil Liberties, under heading § 34:7, "Implied bill of rights".

[6]Not all limitations on legislative powers fit into these two categories, but these are the main categories.

[7]The override clause is analyzed in detail in ch. 39, Override of Rights. It does not apply to ss. 3–5 (democratic rights), 6 (mobility), 16–23 (language), 28 (sexual equality).

rights guaranteed by s. 2 or ss. 7 to 15 of the Charter. The override provision thus preserves parliamentary supremacy over much of the Charter.

§ 12:4 Constitutional amendment

One power that was always withheld from the federal Parliament and the provincial Legislatures was the power to amend the Constitution itself. That power resided with the United Kingdom Parliament until 1982, and since 1982 has been possessed by the various combinations of legislative bodies stipulated in Part V of the Constitution Act, 1982.[1]

If one thinks of the Part V amending procedures as a third legislative process, then it is now literally true that legislative power in Canada is exhaustively distributed among Canadian institutions. Every law is amenable to repeal or amendment by one of three processes: (1) the federal Parliament has authority over all laws within federal legislative power; (2) the provincial Legislatures have authority over all laws within provincial legislative power; and (3) one of the various amending procedures is available to repeal or amend any law that is outside the competence of both the federal Parliament and the provincial Legislatures. Judicial review of legislation occurs when the courts are called upon to determine whether the correct process was employed to enact a particular law.

§ 12:5 Extraterritorial competence

The extent of the power of the federal Parliament and provincial Legislatures to legislate with extraterritorial effect will be discussed in chapter 13, Extraterritorial Competence.

§ 12:6 Delegation

The extent of the power of the federal Parliament and provincial Legislatures to delegate their powers will be discussed in chapter 14, Delegation.

§ 12:7 Retroactive legislation

The extent of the power of the federal Parliament and provincial Legislatures to enact retroactive legislation will be discussed in chapter 48, Rights on Being Charged.[1]

[Section 12:4]

[1]See ch. 4, Amendment. As is there explained, some provisions of what is now called the Constitution of Canada were before 1982 and still are amendable by the unilateral action of the federal Parliament or a Legislature.

[Section 12:7]

[1]Chapter 51, Rights on Being Charged, under heading § 51:26, "Retroactive offences (s. 11(g))".

§ 12:8 Wisdom or policy of legislation

The idea underlying parliamentary sovereignty is that in a democratic society important public policy choices should be made in the elected legislative assemblies, and not by non-elected judges. It is often said, for example, that the courts have no concern with "the wisdom or expediency or policy" of a statute.[1] This follows from the fact that nearly all potential laws, however foolish or ineffective, are competent to one or the other legislative body. But the courts do have to make policy choices in determining the validity of statutes. Even in a distribution-of-powers case, if the text of the Constitution is not clear and there is no clearly governing prior precedent, the court ends up making a choice between the two levels of government which involves an important element of discretion. In Charter cases, the assessment of whether a law has abridged a guaranteed right, and if so whether the law is a "reasonable" limit on the right, and whether the law can be "demonstrably justified in a free and democratic society", plainly calls upon the courts to make discretionary choices.

As related in the earlier discussion of judicial review,[2] it is likely that the personal predilections of the judges have influenced the course of judicial review in the United States, Australia and Canada. It is hardly surprising to discover that judges are human and are not successful in shedding the baggage of prejudices accumulated before their appointment to the bench. However, there is little doubt that most judges make a conscientious attempt to exclude their personal policy preferences from the process of constitutional adjudication. The facts, the constitutional text, the precedents, the inferences that can reasonably be drawn from the facts, the constitutional text and the precedents, and the implications of the alternative outcomes, are to be assessed in as neutral a fashion as possible. If this counsel of perfection cannot be fully achieved in practice, it is nonetheless the ideal to which a judge must strive. The ideal of professional neutrality is the assumption upon which litigation is conducted; otherwise, why bother with evidence and argument? And the attempt to achieve professional neutrality is what, in a democratic society, justifies the conferral of powers of judicial review on non-elected judges.

III. SELF-IMPOSED RESTRAINTS ON LEGISLATIVE POWER

§ 12:9 Substance of future laws

Not only may the Parliament or a Legislature, acting within its allotted sphere of competence, make any law it chooses, it may repeal any of

---

[Section 12:8]

[1] *A.-G. Ont. v. A.-G. Can.* (Reference Appeal) [1912] A.C. 571, 583; the point has been repeated many times, e.g., by Laskin C.J. in the *Anti-Inflation Reference*, [1976] 2 S.C.R. 373, 424–425.

[2] § 12:2 note 1, above.

its earlier laws.[1] Even if the Parliament or Legislature purported to provide that a particular law was not to be repealed or altered, this provision would not be effective to prevent a future Parliament or Legislature from repealing or amending the "protected" law. The later law, though in conflict with the protecting provision, would unhesitatingly be upheld by the courts.[2] Where two laws of the same legislative body are inconsistent, the general rule is that the later is deemed to impliedly repeal the earlier.[3] In political terms, the rationale of this rule is clear. If a legislative body could bind itself not to do something in the future, then a government could use its parliamentary majority to protect its policies from alteration or repeal. This would lay a dead hand on a government subsequently elected to power in a new election with new issues. In other words, a government while in office could frustrate in advance the policies urged by the opposition.[4]

In *Re Canada Assistance Plan* (1991),[5] a constitutional challenge was made to a federal bill to implement a federal budget proposal that would place a five per cent annual cap on the growth of Canada Assistance Plan transfer payments from the federal government to the three provinces of Alberta, British Columbia and Ontario. (These three provinces were singled out because they were the three wealthiest provinces, as measured by their failure to qualify for equalization payments.) The Canada Assistance Plan (CAP) was a federal statute that authorized cost-sharing agreements to be entered into by the federal government with the provinces, under which the federal government would undertake to pay 50 per cent of the costs incurred by the provinces in the provision of certain stipulated social assistance and welfare programmes. Under this authority, the federal government entered into CAP agreements with all ten provinces. By the terms of both the CAP legislation and each agreement, each agreement could be amended only with the consent of both the federal government and the province. It

---

[Section 12:9]

[1]Exceptions are the Constitutions of Manitoba, Alberta and Saskatchewan. These consist of statutes which were enacted by the federal Parliament under s. 2 of the Constitution Act, 1871, but which cannot be repealed or amended by the federal Parliament, because s. 45 of the Constitution Act, 1982 confers on each provincial Legislature the power to amend "the constitution of the province".

[2]See *Vauxhall Estates v. Liverpool Corp.*, [1932] 1 K.B. 733, 746 (Div. Ct.); *Ellen Street Estates v. Min. of Health*, [1934] 1 K.B. 590, 597 (C.A.).

[3]See ch. 16, Paramountcy, under heading § 16:1, "Problem of inconsistency".

[4]The incapacity of an elected legislative assembly to bind its successors as to the substance of future legislation seems such a fundamental requirement of democracy that one is tempted to suggest that the incapacity must be inherent in all elected assemblies. The principle is certainly accepted in the United States: *Fletcher v. Peck* (1810), 10 U.S. 87, 135 per Marshall J. ("one legislature is competent to repeal any act which a former legislature was competent to pass", a principle that "can never be controverted"); *U.S. v. Winstar Corp.* (1996), 518 U.S. 839, 873 per Souter J. (quoting Marshall J. with approval).

[5]*Re Canada Assistance Plan*, [1991] 2 S.C.R. 525. The unanimous judgment of the Court was written by Sopinka J. I disclose that I was one of the counsel for the Attorney General of Canada.

was argued that the budget proposal, by restricting the federal contributions to less than the agreed-upon 50 per cent share,[6] was in effect a unilateral amendment of the three agreements which had not been made with the consent of the three affected provinces.

While there was no doubt that the federal government was obliged to fulfil its side of the CAP agreements so long as the CAP legislation remained unchanged, the effect of the proposed bill, once it was enacted, would be to amend the CAP legislation and thereby place a statutory limit on the federal government's CAP payments. Following the orthodox theory of parliamentary sovereignty, the Supreme Court of Canada held that Parliament remained free to amend the CAP legislation in this way (or any other way) notwithstanding the cost-sharing agreements with the provinces. The Court also considered an ingenious argument that a doctrine of "legitimate expectations" applied, not to Parliament itself, but to the federal government. The effect of the doctrine, it was argued, was to constrain the Minister of Finance (or any other member of the government) from introducing a bill into Parliament, if the effect of the bill would be to defeat the legitimate expectations of the provinces that had been created by the terms of the CAP agreements. In rejecting this argument, the Court held, in effect, that the doctrine of parliamentary sovereignty flowed upstream from the legislative chamber to protect from judicial review the process of legislative policy-making by cabinet and the preparation and introduction of bills for consideration by Parliament. The Court pointed out that: "A restraint on the Executive in the introduction of legislation is a fetter on the sovereignty of Parliament itself."[7]

Re Canada Assistance Plan illustrates another important consequence of the principle of parliamentary sovereignty: that the federal and provincial governments cannot unilaterally fetter the law-making power of their respective legislatures, including by intergovernmental agreement. The Supreme Court of Canada's decision in *Re Pan-Canadian Securities Regulation* (2018)[8] also illustrates this point. This case involved a cooperative securities scheme proposed by the federal government and several provincial and territorial governments. The proposed cooperative securities scheme included interlocking "draft" federal legislation and "model" provincial legislation, and a new national securities regulator. It also contemplated that a Council of Ministers

[6]Only if the growth in provincial costs exceeded five per cent in a particular year would the federal contribution fall short of the full 50 per cent contribution.

[7]*Re Canada Assistance Plan*, [1991] 2 S.C.R. 525, 560. Strictly speaking, a restraint on the Executive would not preclude the introduction into Parliament of a private member's bill, but the reality of the Canadian legislative process is that only government bills stand any real chance of securing parliamentary time, let alone passage. In fact, the bill in issue had been certified by the Speaker as a money bill, which by virtue of s. 54 of the Constitution Act, 1867, can only be a government bill. Sopinka J. (at p. 560) referred to this fact, but only as a reinforcement of the general proposition that the entire legislative process was immune from review.

[8]*Re Pan-Canadian Securities Regulation*, [2018] 3 S.C.R. 189. The opinion of the nine-judge Court was issued by "the Court".

would be involved in overseeing the overall operation of the cooperative securities scheme, including by playing a role in relation to any amendments to the draft federal and model provincial legislation.[9] These details were set out in an intergovernmental agreement ("Memorandum") entered into by the relevant governments. Quebec directed a reference to its Court of Appeal opposing the cooperative securities scheme. Quebec argued,[10] among other things,[11] that the cooperative securities scheme captured in the Memorandum would be constitutionally invalid because, in effect, it would *prohibit* the Legislatures of the participating provinces from making certain legislative changes without the consent of the Council of Ministers, and also *require* them to make certain legislative changes approved by the Council of Ministers, improperly fettering their law-making power, contrary to the principle of parliamentary sovereignty.

The majority of the Quebec Court of Appeal accepted this argument, but on appeal, the Supreme Court of Canada rejected it, in a unanimous opinion by "the Court". The Court said that, as drafted, the Memorandum did not actually fetter the sovereignty of the participating provincial Legislatures, because it did not purport to prohibit or require any legislative changes. The participating provincial Legislatures remained free to adopt or reject any legislative changes that might be rejected or adopted by the Council of Ministers, in keeping with the principle of parliamentary sovereignty.[12] However, the Court also said that, even if the Memorandum did purport to prohibit or require provincial legislative changes, Quebec's argument could still not succeed for a second reason: that it "rest[ed] on the flawed premise that the executive signatories are *actually capable* of binding [their] legislatures".[13] The Court reaffirmed that the federal and provincial governments cannot unilaterally fetter the law-making power of their respective legislatures, and it said that

---

[9]The Council of Ministers was to comprise the ministers responsible for capital markets regulation in the federal and participating provincial and territorial governments.

[10]Alberta and Manitoba joined Quebec in opposing the cooperative securities scheme.

[11]Quebec also advanced two other arguments against the cooperative securities scheme: 1) that it contemplated an impermissible delegation of law-making powers; and 2) that the draft federal legislation would be invalid if enacted because it would exceed Parliament's trade and commerce power (s. 91(2)). The Supreme Court rejected both of these other arguments as well. The aspect of the Court's decision relating to the trade and commerce power is discussed elsewhere in this book: ch. 20, Trade and Commerce, under heading § 20:4, "General trade and commerce".

[12]In accepting the argument that the provincial Legislatures were improperly fettering their law-making power, the majority of the Quebec Court of Appeal seemed to place some weight on an assumption that the decision-making role of the Council of Ministers had been incorporated by reference into the model provincial legislation: see, in particular, *Renvoi relatif à la réglementation pancanadienne des valeurs mobilières*, 2017 QCCA 756, paras. 74-75. This incorporation by reference assumption was also rejected by the Supreme Court: *Re Pan-Canadian Securities Regulation*, [2018] 3 S.C.R. 189, para. 51.

[13]*Re Pan-Canadian Securities Regulation*, [2018] 3 S.C.R. 189, para. 61 (emphasis in original).

"[w]hen an action of the executive branch appears to clash with the legislature's law-making powers, parliamentary sovereignty can be invoked for the purpose of determining the legal *effect* of the impugned executive action, but not its underlying *validity*".[14] As a result, if "an action of the executive branch" purports to require or prohibit legislative changes, the action will not be "constitutionally invalid", as Quebec argued, "but will quite simply not have the desired effect".[15]

A central assumption underlying Quebec's argument in *Re Pan-Canadian Securities Regulation* – which was accepted by the Court of Appeal, but rejected by the Supreme Court – was that the practical effect of executive branch actions should be taken into account in assessing a claim that the law-making power of the legislative branch has been fettered. The Court's opinion makes it clear that it is legal power, not practical effect, that is important in assessing such claims. And because the executive branch is understood to lack the *legal* power to control the legislative branch by fettering its law-making power, "any de facto control that the executive may be said to have over the legislature is", in this context, "irrelevant" – not "constitutionally cognizable".[16]

While a government cannot fetter the powers of a legislative body by contract, this does not necessarily mean that the other contracting party is without remedy if the legislative body acts in defiance of a contract. In *Wells v. Newfoundland* (1999),[17] the Government of Newfoundland had appointed the plaintiff to the province's Public Utilities Board on the terms that he would hold the office (during good behaviour) until age 70. The Legislature later abolished the Board and replaced it with another body. The plaintiff, whose appointment had disappeared with the Board, sued the province for breach of contract. The Supreme Court of Canada agreed that the Legislature had the right to abolish the Board, and that the plaintiff's appointment could not survive the abolition of the Board. But, although the legislation validly cancelled the plaintiff's office, it did not cancel his right to be compensated for breach of the contract of employment. The Legislature had the power to take that step as well, but "clear and specific language would be required to extinguish existing rights previously conferred on that party".[18] Since the legislation contained no clear and specific language denying the plaintiff compensation for the loss of his contract of employment, he was entitled to damages for breach of contract.[19] The Court also rejected the argument that the plaintiff's contract had been frustrated by the passage of the

[14] *Re Pan-Canadian Securities Regulation*, [2018] 3 S.C.R. 189, para. 62 (emphasis in original).

[15] *Re Pan-Canadian Securities Regulation*, [2018] 3 S.C.R. 189, paras. 62, 67.

[16] *Re Pan-Canadian Securities Regulation*, [2018] 3 S.C.R. 189, para. 69, citing *Can. v. Can.*, [1989] 2 S.C.R. 49, 103.

[17] *Wells v. Newfoundland*, [1999] 3 S.C.R. 199. Major J. wrote the opinion of the Court.

[18] *Wells v. Newfoundland*, [1999] 3 S.C.R. 199, para. 41. See also ch. 29, Public Property, under heading § 29:5, "Expropriation".

[19] Contrast *Authorson v. Can.*, [2003] 2 S.C.R. 40 (Crown's fiduciary duty to pay

legislation. To be sure, the legislation had made the continued appointment of the plaintiff impossible. But Major J. for the Court pointed out that self-induced frustration did not excuse non-performance of a contract. In a system of responsible government, "the same individuals control both the executive and legislative branches of government".[20] It was therefore "disingenuous for the executive to assert that the legislative enactment of its own agenda constitutes a frustrating act beyond its control".[21] The passage of the legislation therefore entitled the plaintiff to damages for breach of contract.[22]

§ 12:10 Manner and form of future laws

While a legislative body is not bound by self-imposed restraints as to the content, substance or policy of its enactments,[1] it is reasonably clear that a legislative body may be bound by self-imposed procedural (or manner and form) restraints on its enactments.[2]

There is of course no doubt as to the binding character of the rules in the Constitution that define the composition of the legislative bodies and the steps required in the legislative process.[3] A bill passed by a provincial legislative assembly which is not presented to the Lieutenant Governor for the royal assent is invalid, because the Lieutenant Governor's assent is part of the legislative process required by the Constitution.[4] A bill passed by Manitoba's Legislature in English only is invalid, because s. 23 of the Manitoba Act, 1870 (which is part of the Constitution of Can-

---

interest on veterans' pension funds extinguished by statute by clear and specific language).

[20] *Wells v. Newfoundland*, [1999] 3 S.C.R. 199, para. 53. See also ch. 9, Responsible Government.

[21] *Wells v. Newfoundland*, [1999] 3 S.C.R. 199, para. 52.

[22] See also *U.S. v. Winstar Corp.* (1996), 518 U.S. 839 (holding that Congress could not be prevented from repealing a law promised by contract, but that the United States was obliged to pay damages for the breach of contract, and could not rely on its own act to excuse performance).

[Section 12:10]

[1] A related issue is whether a legislative body can abdicate its functions or some of them. Even Dicey accepted the legal efficacy of a total abdication: The Law of the Constitution (10th ed., 1965), 68–69; but the efficacy of a partial abdication has been more controversial: see ch. 3, Independence, under heading § 3:8, "Termination of imperial authority".

[2] The courts will not impose additional procedural requirements on legislative bodies: *Authorson v. Can.*, [2003] 2 S.C.R. 40 (Parliament need not provide fair hearing before taking away individual rights; normal parliamentary procedure is all that is required).

[3] W.E. Conklin, "Pickin and its Applicability to Canada" (1975) 25 U. Toronto L.J. 193, 201–204.

[4] *Gallant v. The King*, [1949] 2 D.L.R. 425 (P.E.I. S.C.) (absence of royal assent prevented bill from becoming law, and could not be corrected by subsequent purported royal assent).

ada) requires Manitoba's statutes to be enacted in French as well as English.[5]

The foregoing examples involved provisions of the Constitution. Would the Parliament or a Legislature be bound by *self-imposed* rules as to the "manner and form"[6] in which statutes were to be enacted? The answer, in my view, is yes. The Parliament or a Legislature could re-define itself by changing the nature of the legislative process. To be sure, the Parliament could not unilaterally abolish the Senate or the requirement of the royal assent, and the provincial Legislatures could not affect the office of Lieutenant Governor; but this is because "the office of the Queen, the Governor General and the Lieutenant Governor of a province" and "the powers of the Senate" are expressly included, by Part V of the Constitution Act, 1982 (ss. 41(a), 42(1)(b)), among the topics that can only be altered by a special amending procedure.[7] But five provinces have abolished their upper houses by ordinary legislation, and a province without an upper house could establish one.[8] The Parliament or a Legislature could add other elements to the legislative process, either for all statutes or just for particular kinds of statutes. For example, the federal Parliament could provide that a law to abolish the office of Auditor General must first be approved by a referendum of voters,[9] or a provincial Legislature could provide that a law altering the constituen-

[5]*Re Manitoba Language Rights*, [1985] 1 S.C.R. 721.

[6]The phrase "manner and form" (instead of procedural) has become customary in this branch of the law, because it was used in s. 5 of the Colonial Laws Validity Act, 1865 (U.K.), which authorized colonial legislatures to amend their constitutions, provided that any such amendments were "passed in such manner and form as may from time to time be required by any Act of Parliament . . . in force in the said colony."

[7]As well as these explicit restrictions on legislative alterations to the legislative process, there are some implied limits associated with the Constitution Act, 1867's establishment or recognition of the Governor General, the Lieutenant Governors and representative assemblies: see the discussion of the initiative and referendum cases in ch. 14, Delegation, under heading § 14:8, "Office of Lieutenant Governor or Governor General".

[8]Quebec, Nova Scotia, New Brunswick, Prince Edward Island and Manitoba each abolished their upper houses, as an amendment to "the constitution of the province" under s. 92(1) of the Constitution Act, 1867: for details, see W.J. Newman, "Defining the 'Constitution of Canada' since 1982" (2003) 22 Supreme Court L.R. (2d) 423, 442–443. Section 92(1) was repealed in 1982 and replaced by s. 45 of the Constitution Act, 1982, the similar language of which would confer a similar power. In fact, there is now no province with an upper house. Section 45 could however be used to establish one. In *Re Upper House*, [1980] 1 S.C.R. 54, the Court held that the federal Parliament lacked the power to abolish or substantially alter the Senate. This decision was based on s. 91(1) of the Constitution Act, 1867, which was repealed in 1982 and replaced by s. 44 of the Constitution Act, 1982. Section 44, through its express subjection to s. 42(1)(b) and (c), excludes some powers over the Senate and remits them to the seven-fifty amending procedure. In *Re Senate Reform*, [2014] 1 S.C.R. 704, 2014 SCC 32, para. 110, the Supreme Court held that the abolition of the Senate would involve the unanimity amending procedure, because the abolition of the Senate would constitute an amendment of Part V of the Constitution Act, 1982 (the amending procedures) which is remitted to the unanimity procedure by s. 41(e).

[9]The requirement of a referendum is generally assumed to be a valid manner and form provision, despite the fact that it remits the decision to a body outside the legisla-

cies for elections must be passed by a two-thirds majority in the legislative assembly. These "manner and form" laws, which purport to redefine the legislative body, either generally or for particular purposes, are binding for the future. A law which purported to disregard these hypothetical examples of manner and form laws, for example, by purporting to abolish the office of Auditor General without a prior referendum, or to alter the provincial electoral law by a simple majority, would be held to be invalid by the courts.[10] Thus, while the federal Parliament or a provincial Legislature cannot bind itself as to the substance of future legislation, it can bind itself as to the manner and form of future legislation.

Not all manner and form provisions are legally effective. Take the case of Ontario's Taxpayer Protection Act, 1999,[11] which prohibited any member of the executive council from introducing into the Legislature a bill to impose a new tax without first holding a referendum on the proposal and obtaining the approval of the voters. This was enacted in 1999 when the Legislature was controlled by a Progressive Conservative government. During the 2003 election campaign, Dal-ton McGuinty, the leader of the Liberal Party, publicly signed a promise in writing to respect the Act's requirement of no new taxes without the explicit consent of Ontario voters. After he won the election, however, the new Liberal government levied a new health tax, and did so without a prior referendum. It was done in two steps. As a first step, the government introduced and secured the passage of a bill to amend the Taxpayer Protection Act to create an exception for a health tax that was to be introduced later that session. Then, as soon as the exception had become law, the government introduced and secured the passage of a second bill that levied the health tax. Neither bill was preceded by a referendum. The health tax was challenged in court on the basis that it was not enacted in the correct manner and form because it had not been preceded by the required referendum. Ontario's Superior Court of Justice held in *Canadian Taxpayers Federation v. Ontario* (2004)[12] that the Taxpayer Protection Act was not "an effective manner and form requirement".[13] The requirement of a prior referendum applied to the introduction of a

---

tive assembly; the bypass of representational democracy is presumably justified on the basis that the referendum will be determined by the same people who elected the assembly. But a law that enfranchised only a portion of the electorate by requiring the consent of a small group or a single individual is unlikely to be accepted as a manner and form provision; the veto on legislative change by a person, body or group outside the assembly would be regarded as substantive rather than procedural, for example, the § 47:1 requirement of the approval of a majority of grain producers for a law amending the Wheat Board Act: § 12:10 notes 14 and 40, below.

[10]For other examples, see K.M. Lysyk, Comment (1965) 4 Alta. L. Rev. 154, 156–157; Forsey, Freedom and Order (1974) 227; W.E. Conklin, "Pickin and its Applicability to Canada" (1975) 25 U. Toronto L.J. 193, 204–206; K. Swinton, "Challenging the Validity of an Act of Parliament" (1976) 14 Osgoode Hall L.J. 345, 379.

[11]S.O. 1999, c. 7.

[12]*Canadian Taxpayers Federation v. Ontario* (2004), 73 O.R. (3d) 621 (S.C.J.).

[13]*Canadian Taxpayers Federation v. Ontario* (2004), 73 O.R. (3d) 621 (S.C.J.), para.

bill imposing a new tax, but it did not apply to the introduction of a bill amending (or repealing) the Taxpayer Protection Act itself. Therefore, the first bill, which amended the Act to make an exception for the proposed health tax, did not need a referendum. And, once the exception had been passed into law, the referendum requirement no longer applied to the second bill, which imposed the health tax. It followed that the health tax had been validly enacted notwithstanding the absence of any prior referendum.

What the Ontario health tax case shows is that, in order to be fully effective in law, a manner and form provision must apply to itself (be self-referencing or doubly entrenched). The manner and form provision must not only apply to the protected category of laws (in this case, laws imposing new taxes), it must also apply to laws amending or repealing the manner and form provision itself. Without the self-reference, the manner and form requirement can be evaded by the two-step process that was employed in Ontario.[14] The absence of a self-reference is a significant compromise,[15] obviously, but it does not make the manner and form provision completely futile. The provision is still a political obstacle to the enactment of the protected category of laws. In the Ontario case, the referendum requirement made it harder to raise the new tax. Two separate laws had to be enacted, and the first law constituted a public confession that the legally-required referendum would not be held. The entire project was accompanied by a more intense storm of political criticism than would have been brought on by a new tax if there had been no Taxpayer Protection Act in place.[16]

Assuming that a manner and form requirement applies to itself, so that it is effective to avoid the end run around it that was taken by the Ontario Legislature in the health tax case, the binding nature of a man-

---

50.

[14]The Canadian Wheat Board Act, R.S.C. 1985, c. C-24, s. 47.1 (introduced in 1998) requires an affirmative vote of grain producers to be held before introducing certain amendments to the Act. Query whether that would be a valid manner and form provision, since it provides a veto to an institution outside Parliament (unlike a special majority or quorum) and one that is unrepresentative of the electorate (unlike a referendum): *Can. v. Friends of the Can. Wheat Bd.* (2012), D.L.R. (4th) 163 (F.C.A.), para. 86 per Mainville J.A. for Court (obiter). In any case, s. 47.1 does not restrict its own amendment or repeal: "It does not stop Parliament from enacting . . . legislation that amends or repeals s. 47.1 itself": *Friends of the Can. Wheat Bd. v. Can.* (2008), 373 N.R. 385 (F.C. A.), para. 4 per Sharlow J.A. for Court (obiter).

[15]Of course, the absence of a self-reference could be an inadvertent defect in the provision, but that was not the case in the Ontario example, where it was recognized in the legislative debates of 1999 that the provision could be amended without a prior referendum. The assumption was that this would come at a considerable political cost. It is also possible, of course, that the compromise was intended to avoid raising the constitutional issue of whether a fully effective manner and form provision would be constitutional: see following text.

[16]This brouhaha was so damaging to the new Liberal government that it seemed likely to lose the next election, but the new tax was introduced early in the mandate. Memories fade and new issues supervene, and in 2008 the same Liberal government was re-elected to a new four-year term.

ner and form requirement is not entirely free from doubt. There is still a school of thought that holds that even a manner and form restriction cannot bind a "sovereign" legislature.[17] The effect of this school of thought is to deny to a legislative body the power to change its traditional forms and structures: this would invalidate such things as special-majority rules, the abolition or creation of upper houses, and the addition of referenda to the legislative process.[18] It seems implausible that a legislative body should be disabled from making changes to its present structure and procedures. Moreover, the case-law, while not conclusive, tends to support the validity of self-imposed manner and form requirements.[19]

Even the Mother of Parliaments at Westminster has made changes to the manner and form in which statutes are to be enacted. Traditionally, and still today for most purposes, the Parliament of the United Kingdom consists of the elected House of Commons, the non-elected House of Lords and the monarch (royal assent, however, being an automatic formality). The Parliament Act 1911, which was duly enacted by the Lords as well as the Commons,[20] sought to ensure the primacy of the

---

[17]The classical exposition is Dicey, The Law of the Constitution (10th ed., 1965), ch. 1, and the introduction by E.C.S. Wade, the editor of the 10th ed.; also H.W.R. Wade, "The Basis of Legal Sovereignty" [1955] Camb. L.J. 172. A Canadian contribution to this side of the issue is R. Elliot, "Rethinking Manner and Form" (1991) 29 Osgoode Hall L.J. 215. For a nuanced article that leans in this direction, see J. Lovell, "Legislating against the Grain: Parliamentary Sovereignty and Extra-parliamentary Vetoes" (2008) 24 Nat. J. Con. Law 1. The dominant theory now is that manner and form restrictions are effective: Jennings, The Law and the Constitution (5th ed., 1959), ch. 4; Marshall, Parliamentary Sovereignty and the Commonwealth (1957), passim; Tarnopolsky, The Canadian Bill of Rights (2nd ed., 1975), ch. 3; de Smith and Brazier, Constitutional and Administrative Law (8th ed., 1998), ch. 4. J. Goldsworthy, The Sovereignty of Parliament (Oxford U.P., 1999), 14–16, 259, states the issues, but does not express a firm opinion.

[18]R. Elliot, "Rethinking Manner and Form" (1991) 29 Osgoode Hall L.J. 215, would invalidate manner and form restrictions "in all but the most unusual circumstances"; they could be valid if consistent with "the values of the legal and political culture of the society in question"; but any change in the simple-majority rule would not be valid. Why the simple-majority rule enjoys such extraordinary value, when it is modified for special purposes by most organizations, is not explained.

[19]Outside Canada, the leading cases are *A.-G. N.S.W. v. Trethowan*, [1932] A.C. 526 (P.C., Australia); *Harris v. Min. of Interior*, [1952] 2 S.A.L.R. (A.D.) 428 (S. Africa A.D.); *Bribery Commr. v. Ranasinghe*, [1965] A.C. 172 (P.C., Ceylon). None of these cases unequivocally supports the proposition in the text. *Trethowan* is the only case of a self-imposed manner and form restriction, and it could be explained as resting on s. 5 of the Colonial Laws Validity Act. *Harris* and *Ranasinghe* involved restrictions in the Constitution itself, although the Constitution was as freely amendable as an ordinary statute.

[20]The Parliament Act 1911 was provoked by the implacable opposition of the House of Lords to the initiatives of successive Liberal governments in possession of a majority in the House of Commons. For example, in 1893 the Lords defeated Gladstone's bill to grant Home Rule to Ireland (the centrepiece of the Liberal party platform), and in 1909 they defeated Lloyd George's finance bill (thereby denying supply to the government and forcing a new election). The House of Lords only passed the Parliament Act 1911 after Liberal Prime Minister Asquith made clear that he had secured the agreement of King George V to create enough new Liberal peers to pass the measure should it be defeated

elected House of Commons by providing that a bill[21] could "become an Act of Parliament", without the consent of the Lords, if it were passed by the Commons and rejected by the Lords in three successive sessions of Parliament over a period of not less than two years. In 1949, this procedure was then used to enact (without the consent of the Lords) the Parliament Act 1949, which expanded the power of the Commons by reducing the Lords' delaying power to two sessions and one year. These new manner and form rules were used to bypass the Lords from time to time (including the grant of Home Rule to Ireland in 1914), and were never challenged in court until a Labour government had the effrontery to use its parliamentary majority in the Commons to enact a ban on fox hunting. The Hunting Act 2004 was passed by the Commons and rejected by the Lords in two successive sessions of Parliament over a period of one year, and became law without the consent of the Lords by virtue of the Parliament Acts 1911 and 1949. Supporters of fox hunting brought proceedings for a declaration that the Parliament Act 1949 and therefore the Hunting Act 2004 were invalid, because neither Act had been consented to by the Lords.

In *R. (Jackson) v. Attorney General* (2005),[22] the Appellate Committee of the House of Lords (technically a committee of the House of Lords, but in fact an independent court—the final court of appeal for the United Kingdom) upheld both Acts notwithstanding the absence of consent by the Lords. The nine judges who comprised the Appellate Committee for the appeal wrote nine separate opinions, but were basically agreed upon the reasoning and were unanimous in the result. As Baroness Hale put it:[23] "If Parliament can do anything, there is no reason why Parliament should not decide to redesign itself, either in general or for a particular purpose." That is what Parliament did in 1911. Having done so, "it follows that Parliament can allow its redesigned self further to modify the design". That is what it did in 1949. Having done so, the modified, redesigned Parliament was free to create an Act of Parliament when the conditions stipulated by the 1949 Act were satisfied. That was what it did when it enacted the Hunting Act 2004. That was all that was needed to decide the case, but Baroness Hale (with the approval of Lord Steyn) went one step further:[24]

If the sovereign Parliament can redesign itself downwards, to remove or

---

this time. The threat of the new appointments sufficed to persuade the Lords to pass the measure.

[21]Special provision was made for a "money bill", which could be passed by the House of Commons alone if the House of Lords had not passed it without amendment within one month of it being passed by the House of Commons and sent up to the House of Lords.

[22]*R. (Jackson) v. Attorney General*, [2006] 1 A.C. 262 (H.L.). For comment on the case, see M. Elliott, "Bicameralism, sovereignty and the unwritten constitution" (2007) 5 Int. J. Con. Law 370.

[23]*R. (Jackson) v. Attorney General*, [2006] 1 A.C. 262 (H.L.), paras. 160–161.

[24]*R. (Jackson) v. Attorney General*, [2006] 1 A.C. 262 (H.L.), para. 163. Accord, para. 81 per Lord Steyn. Contra, para. 113 per Lord Hope ("no means whereby . . . it can entrench an Act of Parliament").

> modify the requirement for the consent of the Upper House, it may very well be that it can also redefine itself upwards, to require a particular parliamentary majority or a popular referendum for particular types of measure. In each case, the courts would be respecting the will of the sovereign Parliament as constituted when that will had been expressed. But that is for another day.

With respect, the logic of Baroness Hale's point seems inescapable. If Parliament can validly *reduce* the manner and form requirements for an Act of Parliament, as this case squarely decides, then it could also *increase* the manner and form requirements.[25] In other words, Parliament could bind its successors, not as to the substance of future legislation, but as to the manner and form of future legislation. Parliamentary sovereignty is a self-embracing concept, which permits Parliament to pass laws that change its own procedures. Those laws are binding upon it, and have the effect of limiting its powers.[26]

In Canada, the leading case is *R. v. Mercure* (1988),[27] in which the Supreme Court of Canada held that the Saskatchewan Legislature was bound by a statutory requirement that its statutes be enacted in both English and French. The statutory requirement had been enacted in 1876, before the creation of the province of Saskatchewan, by the Parliament of Canada, exercising its authority over the federal territory that in 1905 became Saskatchewan. Although the bilingual requirement had not been enacted by the Legislature itself, it had been enacted by the Legislature's predecessor, and it could be freely repealed or amended by the Legislature. La Forest J., for the majority of the Court, treated the case as no different from a self-imposed manner and form requirement,[28] and held the requirement to be valid and binding. While the Legislature was free to repeal the bilingual requirement, it could not ignore it, and until the requirement was expressly repealed by the correct manner and

[25] J. Lovell, "Legislating against the Grain: Parliamentary Sovereignty and Extra-parliamentary Vetoes" (2008) 24 Nat. J. Con. Law 1, questions my appeal to symmetry, pointing out that a downward redefinition (making it easier to pass legislation) "results in a situation where a statute enacted in the morning may face repeal in the afternoon", while upward redefinition (making it harder to pass legislation) "promises the more troubling spectacle of Parliament painting itself (and future generations) into a corner with undryable paint".

[26] On one theory of "self-embracing sovereignty", the Parliament of the United Kingdom can abdicate powers over former colonies by granting them independence, something that gives great difficulty to the supporters of traditional "continuing sovereignty", who deny that a sovereign body can limit its own powers. In my view, a special set of considerations bears on the validity of independence statutes.

[27] *R. v. Mercure*, [1988] 1 S.C.R. 234.

[28] *R. v. Mercure*, [1988] 1 S.C.R. 234, 278, approving the view of Jennings, The Law and the Constitution (5th ed., 1959), ch. 4, and me (in the 2nd edition of this book). On the other hand, La Forest J. did say (at pp. 277, 279) that the manner and form restriction was in the Legislature's "constituent instrument". The issue would be unequivocally raised by Ontario's French Language Services Act, R.S.O. 1990, c. F.32, s. 3(2), which provides that: "The Public Bills of the Legislative Assembly introduced after the 1st day of January, 1991 shall be introduced and enacted in both English and French."

form[29] the requirement had to be observed. A statute enacted by the Legislature in English only, in disregard of the bilingual requirement, was accordingly struck down.

In Canadian statutes, it is not uncommon to find "primacy clauses" that purport to declare that the statute containing the clause is supreme over other statutes, future as well as past.[30] Such clauses are intended to defeat the doctrine of implied repeal,[31] under which a later statute would impliedly repeal an inconsistent earlier statute to the extent of the inconsistency. The best-known example is the Canadian Bill of Rights, which is a federal statute, which provides in effect that the Canadian Bill of Rights is supreme over any other federal statute unless in the other statute "it is expressly declared . . . that it shall operate notwithstanding the Canadian Bill of Rights". The Supreme Court of Canada has held that this primacy clause has the effect of rendering inoperative inconsistent statutes that do not contain the notwithstanding clause.[32] The Quebec Charter of Human Rights and Freedoms, which is a Quebec statute, contains a similar clause making the Charter supreme over other statutes "unless such Act expressly states that it applies despite the Charter". The Supreme Court of Canada has held that this is effective also, rendering inoperative a later Quebec statute that purported to derogate from one of the guaranteed rights.[33] Human Rights Codes (anti-discrimination statutes) in several provinces also contain primacy clauses,[34] and these have been held to be effective by the Supreme Court of Canada.[35] Indeed, the Supreme Court of Canada has gone so far as to hold that human rights legislation takes precedence over inconsistent later statutes even without a primacy clause. The Court said that, because "human rights legislation is of a special nature

[29]After the decision, Saskatchewan enacted a statute in both English and French which validated past English-only statutes, and repealed the requirement for the future: The Language Act, S.S. 1988, c. L-6.1. Alberta, which was in the same situation (*R. v. Paquette*, [1990] 2 S.C.R. 1103), enacted in both languages a similar statute: Languages Act, S.A. 1988, c. L-7.5.

[30]As well as the examples given in the text, see the statutes implementing income tax treaties, e.g., Canada-United States Tax Convention Act, S.C. 1984, c. 20, s. 3(2). In *A.-G. Can. v. Public Service Staff Relations Bd.*, [1977] 2 F.C. 663 (C.A.), the Court held that s. 28 of the Federal Court Act, authorizing judicial review of federal agencies "notwithstanding . . . the provisions of any other Act", superseded a privative clause excluding judicial review in the Public Service Staff Relations Act. The privative clause predated s. 28, but Le Dain J. suggested (at p. 671) that s. 28 might well be effective even against future privative clauses.

[31]See ch. 16, Paramountcy, under heading § 16:1, "Problem of inconsistency".

[32]See ch. 33, Canadian Bill of Rights, under heading § 35:3, "Effect on inconsistent statutes".

[33]*Ford v. Quebec*, [1988] 2 S.C.R. 712; *Devine v. Que.*, [1988] 2 S.C.R. 790.

[34]A.F. Bayefsky, "Parliamentary Sovereignty and Human Rights in Canada" (1983) 31 Political Studies 239, 250–252.

[35]*Scowby v. Glendinning*, [1986] 2 S.C.R. 226, 236 (obiter dictum, not referring to the primacy clause in s. 44 of the Saskatchewan Human Rights Code); *Tranchemontagne v. Ont.*, [2006] 1 S.C.R. 513, para. 33 (giving effect to primacy clause in Ontario Code and describing Code as "fundamental, quasi-constitutional law").

and declares public policy regarding matters of general concern", it may not be repealed or amended "save by clear legislative pronouncement".[36]

The theory under which primacy clauses are effective has never been articulated by the Court, but it must rest on the principle that a legislative body may bind itself as to manner and form. The primacy clause binds the legislative body not to repeal or amend the protected legislation, except in the manner and form indicated by the primacy clause. That involves using the formula contemplated by the primacy clause, such as the notwithstanding declaration contemplated by the Canadian Bill of Rights. If no particular formula is provided by the primacy clause, then it must be taken as requiring express words, as opposed to mere implication, for the repeal or amendment of the protected statute.

A statutory provision cannot be a manner and form requirement unless it is unmistakably addressed to the future action of the enacting legislative body. In *Re Canada Assistance Plan* (1991),[37] a case that was examined earlier in this chapter, the Supreme Court of Canada had to consider the effect of a statutory provision that required the consent of the provinces for any amendment to certain cost-sharing agreements between Canada and the provinces. It was argued that this provision implicitly precluded any amendment of federal legislation that would have the effect of limiting the federal government's obligations under the agreements, unless the consent of the provinces had first been obtained. The Court held that the consent requirement was not a manner and form requirement for the simple reason that it expressly applied to amendments to the agreements, not to amendments to the legislation. Since the legislation was silent on the question of the Parliament's power to enact new laws, that power was unimpaired, and could be used to alter the federal government's obligations under the agreements. The Court said that it would require a very clear indication in a statute, especially a non-constitutional statute, before the court would find "an intention of the legislative body to bind itself in the future."[38]

A statutory provision that is unmistakably addressed to the future action of the enacting legislative body may be a manner and form provision. But it is not necessarily so. A statutory provision that looks like a manner and form restriction may be one of four other kinds of laws. First, the statutory provision could be regarded as an attempt to

---

[36]*Winnipeg School Division No. 1 v. Craton*, [1985] 2 S.C.R. 150, 156; *Quebec v. Montreal*, [2000] 1 S.C.R. 665, para. 26. This reasoning is dubious. Much other legislation "declares public policy regarding matters of general concern". Surely, in the absence of a primacy clause, the Court is in no position to create priorities between public policies. Accord, P.J. Monahan and A.J. Petter, "Developments in Constitutional Law" (1987) 9 Supreme Court L.R. 69, 143–150. Compare *MacBain v. Lederman*, [1985] 1 F.C. 856 (C.A.), holding that the Canadian Bill of Rights rendered inoperative a provision of the federal Human Rights Code. The courts thus seem to be recognizing a hierarchy of statutes.

[37]*Re Canada Assistance Plan*, [1991] 2 S.C.R. 525.

[38]*Re Canada Assistance Plan*, [1991] 2 S.C.R. 525, 563.

restrict the substance of future legislation, which is of course ineffective.[39] Secondly, the statutory provision could be regarded as a "directory" procedural requirement; the breach of a directory, as opposed to a mandatory, requirement does not lead to invalidity.[40] Thirdly, the statutory provision could be regarded as a rule of interpretation, which would be displaced by any clear statutory indication to the contrary.[41] Fourthly, the statutory provision could be regarded as an "internal" rule of parliamentary procedure; the breach of such a rule does not invalidate the resulting statute.[42] None of these four kinds of provisions forms the basis for judicial review of legislation. A manner and form provision, on the other hand, does form the basis for judicial review, because if a statute is enacted in disregard of an applicable manner and form provision, the purported statute is a nullity and will be so declared by a court.

---

[39]E.g., an ostensibly procedural requirement which is virtually impossible of fulfilment, such as approval by eighty per cent of the voters in a referendum: see W. Friedmann, "Trethowan's Case" (1950) 24 Aust. L.J. 103, 105–105; Marshall, Parliamentary Sovereignty and the Commonwealth (1957), 41–42; de Smith and Brazier, Constitutional and Administrative Law (8th ed., 1998), 92. In *Re Can. Assistance Plan*, [1991] 2 S.C.R. 525, 564, the Court held that the consent of the provinces could not be a valid manner and form requirement for the federal Parliament, because this would be a restraint of substance rather than procedure. Compare the rule that Parliament may not delegate its legislative powers to the provinces: ch. 14, Delegation, under heading §§ 14:10 to 14:11, "Federal inter-delegation". Similarly, the consent of a majority of producers of grain would not be a valid manner and form requirement because it would provide a veto on parliamentary action to "a small group not forming part of Parliament": *Can. v. Friends of the Can. Wheat Bd.* (2012), 352 D.L.R. (4th) 163 (F.C.A.), para. 86 per Mainville J.A. for the Court (obiter dictum).

[40]E.g., *Simpson v. A.-G.*, [1955] N.Z.L.R. 271 (N.Z. C.A.); *Clayton v. Heffron* (1960), 105 C.L.R. 215 (H.C. Aust.). In *Re Man. Language Rights*, [1985] 1 S.C.R. 721, 740–743, the Court held that s. 23 of the Manitoba Act, 1870, requiring statutes to be enacted in both English and French, was not "directory", but was "mandatory". See J. Evans, "Mandatory and Directory Rules" (1981) 1 Legal Studies 227.

[41]See for example the discussion of the effect of statutory provisions purporting to require the use of express words to bind the Crown: ch. 10, The Crown, under heading § 10:14, "Effect of Interpretation Acts"; see also discussion of the effect of s. 2 of the Canadian Bill of Rights: ch. 35, Canadian Bill of Rights, under heading § 35:3, "Meaning of s. 2".

[42]W.E. Conklin, "Pickin and its Applicability to Canada" (1975) 25 U. Toronto L.J. 193; K. Swinton, "Challenging the Validity of an Act of Parliament" (1976) 14 Osgoode Hall L.J. 345.

Chapter 14

Delegation

I. POWER OF DELEGATION

§ 14:1 Introduction to delegation
§ 14:2 United Kingdom Parliament
§ 14:3 Provincial Legislatures
§ 14:4 Federal Parliament

II. LIMITATIONS IMPOSED BY CONSTITUTION

§ 14:5 Delegation of legislative power
§ 14:6 Delegation of judicial power
§ 14:7 Classification of laws
§ 14:8 Office of Lieutenant Governor or Governor General
§ 14:9 Requirement of a Legislature or Parliament

III. FEDERAL INTER-DELEGATION

§ 14:10 Legislative inter-delegation
§ 14:11 Administrative inter-delegation

IV. REFERENTIAL LEGISLATION

§ 14:12 Incorporation by reference
§ 14:13 Anticipatory incorporation by reference
§ 14:14 Independent validity of incorporated law

V. CONDITIONAL LEGISLATION

§ 14:15 Conditions as delegations
§ 14:16 Conditions as administrative inter-delegations
§ 14:17 Conditions as legislative inter-delegations

VI. DELEGATION BY ACQUIESCENCE

§ 14:18 Delegation by acquiescence

VII. CONCLUSIONS ON FEDERAL INTER-DELEGATION

§ 14:19 Conclusions on federal inter-delegation

I. POWER OF DELEGATION

§ 14:1 Introduction to delegation

It is impossible for the federal Parliament or any provincial Legislature to enact all of the laws that are needed in its jurisdiction for the purpose of government in any given year. When a legislative scheme is established, the Parliament or the Legislature will usually enact the scheme in outline only, and will delegate to a subordinate body the power to make laws on matters of detail. The subordinate body (or delegate) to which this law-making power is delegated is most commonly the Governor in Council or the Lieutenant Governor in Council; each of these bodies is in practice the cabinet of the government concerned.[1] Sometimes a power of law-making is delegated to a single minister, or a public corporation, or a municipality, or a school board, or an administrative agency, or a court. The body of law enacted by these subordinate bodies vastly exceeds in bulk the body of law enacted by the primary legislative bodies.[2]

The legislation of subordinate bodies is called "subordinate legislation" or "delegated legislation"; these terms encompass all laws made by bodies other than Parliament or a Legislature. Some other terms are used to describe particular kinds of subordinate (or delegated) legislation: a "regulation" usually means a law enacted by the Governor in Council or Lieutenant Governor in Council or a minister or agency of the federal or provincial government; a "by-law" usually means a law enacted by a municipality; a "rule" usually means a law enacted by a court or administrative agency to regulate its procedure; and an "order" usually means a direction for a particular case. Terminology is not, however, consistent.

§ 14:2 United Kingdom Parliament

It was settled in England in the seventeenth century that the King had no power to make new laws.[1] Only the elected Parliament had the power to make new laws. But Parliament, as a sovereign body, could enact any law that it chose, and therefore it could enact a law delegating law-making power to the King or to his ministers or to any other official or body.[2]

§ 14:3 Provincial Legislatures

Was this power of delegation inherited by the Parliament and Legislatures of Canada? An argument that the power had not been

[Section 14:1]

[1]See ch. 9, Responsible Government.

[2]For useful accounts of delegation in Canada, see Third Report of the Special Committee on Statutory Instruments (House of Commons, Canada, 1969); Cheffins and Tucker, The Constitutional Process in Canada (2nd ed., 1976), ch. 3.

[Section 14:2]

[1]*Case of Proclamations* (1611)12 Co. Rep. 74, 77 E.R. 1352.

[2]Dramatic examples of delegation are to be found in the three devolution statutes that confer legislative powers on elected assemblies for Wales (Government of Wales Act 2006 (U.K.), c. 32), Scotland (Scotland Act 1998 (U.K.), c. 46) and Northern Ireland (Northern Ireland Act 1998 (U.K.), c. 47).

inherited in Canada was based on the premise that the powers of the Canadian legislative bodies had been delegated to them by the imperial Parliament; since the Canadian legislative bodies were themselves mere delegates, they could not further delegate (or sub-delegate) their powers: delegatus non potest delegare.[1] In *Hodge v. The Queen* (1883),[2] the Privy Council rejected this argument. In that case, the Ontario Legislature had delegated to a Board of License Commissioners the power to make regulations for licensed taverns. The Privy Council held that the delegation was valid. It was erroneous, they held, to regard the powers conferred by the Constitution Act, 1867 on the provincial Legislatures as delegated powers. On the contrary, provincial legislative power was "as plenary and as ample within the limits prescribed by section 92 as the Imperial Parliament in the plenitude of its power possessed and could bestow."[3]

The Privy Council's references to the plenitude and amplitude of colonial legislative power, and of its equivalence to that of the Parliament of the United Kingdom, suggested that there were no limits to the power of delegation. But the power actually delegated in *Hodge*—to license and regulate taverns—hardly called for a decision as to the outer limits of legislative power; and the Privy Council described the power at one point as "an authority ancillary to legislation" and as a "limited discretionary authority".[4] Thus the facts and some of the dicta invited an argument that even plenitude and amplitude may have their limits, and that a sweeping delegation might run into some, as yet unidentified, constitutional obstacle.

It seems clear, however, that sweeping delegations by provincial Legislatures are valid. For example, the conventional kind of natural products marketing statute simply confers on the Lieutenant Governor in Council the power to establish marketing schemes and boards to administer them, and leaves to the discretion of the Lieutenant Governor in Council the question of which products should be regulated, by what board and upon what terms. In *Shannon v. Lower Mainland Dairy Products Board* (1938),[5] the Privy Council was faced with the argument that such a skeletal statute was an invalid delegation of "legislative powers". This argument was rejected by their lordships as "subversive" of provincial legislative power and as inconsistent with the "supremacy" of the provincial Legislatures.[6]

[Section 14:3]

[1]A delegate has no power to delegate. For analysis of this doctrine, see J. Willis, "Delegatus non potest delegare" (1943) 21 Can. Bar Rev. 257.

[2]*Hodge v. The Queen* (1883), 9 App. Cas. 117.

[3]*Hodge v. The Queen* (1883), 9 App. Cas. 117, 132.

[4]*Hodge v. The Queen* (1883), 9 App. Cas. 117, 132.

[5]*Shannon v. Lower Mainland Dairy Products Board*, [1938] A.C. 708.

[6]*Shannon v. Lower Mainland Dairy Products Board*, [1938] A.C. 708, 722, effectively though not explicitly overruling *Credit Foncier Franco-Canadien v. Ross*, [1937]

§ 14:4 Federal Parliament

The Privy Council in *Hodge* did not have to determine the extent of the federal Parliament's power of delegation, but their lordships indicated in a dictum that the federal power was just as "plenary and ample" as that of the provincial Legislatures.[1]

In *Re Gray* (1918),[2] the Supreme Court of Canada had to determine the validity of the delegation of legislative power contained in the War Measures Act, 1914. That Act, passed at the beginning of the first world war, empowered the Governor in Council to proclaim a state of "real or apprehended war, invasion or insurrection", and then "to make from time to time such orders and regulations, as he may by reason of the existence of real or apprehended war, invasion or insurrection, deem necessary or advisable for the security, defence, peace, order and welfare of Canada".[3] In effect, the War Measures Act transferred to the federal cabinet virtually the whole legislative authority of the Parliament for the duration of the war. The Court held that even a delegation as sweeping as this one was valid. However, the four opinions each contained indications that the power of delegation was not absolute, and that an "abdication", "abandonment" or "surrender" of the Parliament's powers would be invalid.[4] But, since none of the majority judges regarded the War Measures Act as an unconstitutional abdication, abandonment or surrender, it is not easy to imagine the kind of delegation that would be unconstitutional. Nor did the judges indicate how their suggested limitation was to be reconciled with the *Hodge* doctrine of plenary and ample power; or, to put the same question in another way, what principle of constitutional law dictated the suggested limitation.[5]

Another sweeping delegation by the federal Parliament, although one that never seems to have been challenged in the courts, is the grant of extensive powers of self-government to the three federal territories. The Northwest Territories Act, the Yukon Act and the Nunavut Act establish a Legislature for each territory, and empower the Legislature to make laws for the government of its territory in relation to a long list of

---

3 D.L.R. 365 (Alta. A.D.).

[Section 14:4]

[1] *Hodge v. The Queen* (1883) 9 App. Cas. 117, 132. See also *A.-G. Can. v. Cain*, [1906] A.C. 542, 547. For application of the *Hodge* doctrine outside Canada, see *R. v. Burah* (1878), 3 App. Cas. 889 (India); *Powell v. Apollo Candle Co.* (1885), 10 App. Cas. 282 (Australia); *Cobb & Co. v. Kropp*, [1967] 1 A.C. 141 (Australia).

[2] *Re Gray* (1918), 57 S.C.R. 150.

[3] The War Measures Act has been upheld as an exercise of the federal Parliament's "peace, order, and good government" power: see ch. 17, Peace, Order and Good Government, under heading § 17:8, "War".

[4] *Re Gray* (1918) 57 S.C.R. 150, 157, 165, 171, 176.

[5] See J. Willis, "Administrative Law and the B.N.A. Act" (1939) 53 Harv. L. Rev. 251; Laskin, Canadian Constitutional Law (5th ed., 1986 by Finkelstein), 42.

subjects roughly corresponding to the list of subjects allocated to the provincial Legislatures by s. 92 of the Constitution Act, 1867.[6]

II. LIMITATIONS IMPOSED BY CONSTITUTION

§ 14:5 Delegation of legislative power

It goes without saying that the Constitution could impose limitations on the power of the Canadian legislative bodies to delegate their powers. What *Hodge, Shannon* and *Gray* establish is that the courts will not readily imply any such limitations. In particular, these cases establish that in Canada there is no requirement that "legislative" and "executive" powers be exercised by separate and independent bodies. A delegation cannot be attacked on the ground that it confers "legislative" power on the executive branch of government.[1]

In the United States, the position is otherwise. There, the separation of powers doctrine which is embedded in the federal and state constitutions has been held to prohibit the delegation by the federal Congress or a state Legislature of any of its "legislative" powers. In practice, however, this has not proved to be a serious restraint on the conferral of law-making powers upon administrative agencies or officials, because the courts have given a very attenuated meaning to legislative powers. So long as the Congress or Legislature limits the scope of its delegate's law-making authority by reference to some "standard", then the grant of power is deemed not to be a forbidden delegation of legislative power. Moreover, the courts have accepted vague phrases such as "just and reasonable rates" or "unfair methods of competition" as adequate standards.[2] But there is always the danger that an exceptionally broad and vague delegation might be classified as a delegation of legislative power; and in fact there are two decisions of the Supreme Court of the United States

---

[6]See Northwest Territories Act, R.S.C. 1985, c. N-27, ss. 9, 16; Yukon Act, S.C. 2002, c. 7, ss. 17–27; Nunavut Act, S.C. 1993, c. 28, ss. 12, 23; for dicta affirming the validity of the delegation, see *Re Gray* (1918), 57 S.C.R. 150, 170. The federal Parliament's power to legislate for the territories comes from the Constitution Act, 1871, s. 4.

[Section 14:5]

[1]There is one case to the contrary, *Credit Foncier Franco-Canadien v. Ross*, [1937] 3 D.L.R. 365 (Alta. A.D.) holding that legislative power may not be delegated, but the case has been effectively overruled by the Privy Council (*Shannon v. Lower Mainland Dairy Products Board*, [1938] A.C. 708) and the Supreme Court of Canada in *Re Criminal Law Amendment Act 1968–69* (Breathalyzer) [1970] S.C.R. 777 (*Re Criminal Law Amendment Act, 1968–69*, [1970] S.C.R. 777), and has never been followed: for discussion, see J. Willis, "Administrative Law and the B.N.A. Act" (1939) 53 Harv. L. Rev. 251, 258; G.S. Rutherford, "Delegation of Legislative Power" (1948) 26 Can. Bar Rev. 533.

[2]E.g., *Whitman v. American Trucking Assns.* (2001), 531 U.S. 457 (upholding delegation by Congress to the Environmental Protection Agency of the power to set air pollution standards that, with "an adequate margin of safety, are requisite to protect the public health").

in which delegations have been held to be unconstitutional on this ground.[3]

The difference between the Canadian and American systems resides not only in the different language of the two constitutional instruments, but in Canada's retention of the British system of responsible government. The close link between the executive and legislative branches which is entailed by the British system is utterly inconsistent with any separation of the executive and legislative functions.[4] In Australia, where responsible government was also retained, but where the federal constitution (although not the state constitutions) follows the American pattern of making a separate distribution of the legislative, executive and judicial powers, the courts have been forced to conclude that the federal Parliament may delegate legislative power to the executive without offending the constitutional limitation.[5]

It is possible that there is one legislative power in Canada that cannot be delegated, and that is the federal Parliament's power to levy taxes. Section 53 of the Constitution Act, 1867 provides that a bill levying a tax must originate in the House of Commons, and s. 54 provides that the House of Commons shall not pass any such bill unless the bill was recommended by message of the Governor General.[6] It is arguable that a delegation of the taxing power is implicitly forbidden by these sections, because a tax levied under a delegated power would not originate in the House of Commons or be recommended by a message of the Governor General.[7]

The argument that the federal taxing power cannot be delegated was made in *Re Agricultural Products Marketing Act* (1978),[8] as part of a constitutional attack on a federal statute that authorized marketing boards to impose levies on farmers. The Supreme Court of Canada held that the levies were not taxes, but administrative charges, and so the Court did not need to determine the issue. However, Pigeon J. for a majority of the Court rejected the argument anyway, on the basis that ss.

---

[3] *Panama Refining Co. v. Ryan* (1935), 293 U.S. 388; *Schechter Poultry Corp. v. U.S.A.* (1935), 295 U.S. 494.

[4] See ch. 9, Responsible Government, under heading § 9:12, "The cabinet". Responsible government is not inconsistent with a separation of the *judicial* function from the two political branches. In Canada the judicature provisions of the Constitution have been construed as imposing limits upon the kinds of bodies which can be invested with some judicial functions: see the next section of this chapter.

[5] *Roche v. Kronheimer* (1921), 29 C.L.R. 329; *Victorian Stevedoring and Gen. Contracting Co. v. Dignan* (1931), 46 C.L.R. 73. With respect to judicial power, however, the separation has been insisted upon: *A.-G. Cwlth. v. The Queen* (Boilermakers) (1957) 95 C.L.R. 529.

[6] Sections 53 and 54 apply to the provinces as well, by virtue of s. 90. Accordingly, exactly the same argument can be made about the existence of provincial capacity to delegate the power to levy taxes.

[7] See Cheffins and Tucker, The Constitutional Process in Canada (2nd ed., 1976), 58; La Forest, The Allocation of Taxing Power under the Canadian Constitution (2nd ed., 1981), 40–41.

[8] *Re Agricultural Products Marketing Act*, [1978] 2 S.C.R. 1198.

53 and 54 could be amended by the federal Parliament,[9] and any inconsistent legislation should be treated as an implicit amendment.[10] This seems an unsatisfactory holding. Surely, the fact that the provisions can be amended by the federal Parliament should not justify their disregard (as opposed to explicit amendment or repeal) by Parliament. Another possible answer to the argument that ss. 53 and 54 prohibit delegation is that ss. 53 and 54 are merely directory provisions addressed to the "internal" procedures of the House of Commons, and (like other such procedures) are not enforceable by the courts. This answer is more plausible, but the presence of ss. 53 and 54 in the Constitution Act, 1867 suggests that they enjoy a higher status than internal parliamentary procedure.

In *Re Eurig Estate* (1998),[11] the Supreme Court of Canada struck down a probate fee imposed by the province of Ontario on the estates of deceased persons. The probate fee was levied by the Lieutenant Governor in Council, acting under a statutory power to impose "fees" in court proceedings. The Court unanimously held that the probate fee had as its main purpose the raising of revenue and was therefore a tax. The Court by a majority then held that the tax was invalid for failure to comply with s. 53 of the Constitution Act, 1867.[12] (The Court did not rely on s. 54, which it interpreted as applying only to the appropriation of taxes, not the imposition of taxes.)[13] Major J., speaking for the majority, held that s. 53 "ensures parliamentary control over, and accountability for taxation" by "requiring any bill that imposes a tax to originate with the legislature", and prohibiting "any body other than the directly elected legislature from imposing a tax on its own accord".[14] Moreover, s. 53 "is a constitutional imperative that is enforceable by the courts".[15] What of the obiter dictum in the *Agricultural Products Marketing* case that any

---

[9]At that time (before 1982) the amendment of ss. 53 and 54 would have been possible under s. 91(1) of the Constitution Act, 1867. That provision has now been repealed and replaced by s. 44 of the Constitution Act, 1982, which would also authorize an amendment of ss. 53 and 54.

[10]*Re Agricultural Products Marketing Act*, [1978] 2 S.C.R. 1198, 1291. Laskin C.J. in a separate concurring opinion discussed the argument (at pp. 1227–1229), but did not reach any conclusions on its force.

[11]*Re Eurig Estate*, [1998] 2 S.C.R. 565. On the issue of the effect of s. 53, the majority opinion of Major J. was disagreed with by both the concurring opinion of Binnie J. (who struck down the tax on administrative-law grounds) and the dissenting opinion of Bastarache J. (who would have upheld the tax). I disclose that I was one of the counsel in the case representing the executor of the Eurig estate.

[12]The application to the provinces is by virtue of s. 90: § 14:5 note 6, above.

[13]*Re Eurig Estate*, [1998] 2 S.C.R. 565, paras. 37, 56.

[14]*Re Eurig Estate*, [1998] 2 S.C.R. 565, paras. 30, 32. Bastarache J., dissenting, took the view that s. 53 was addressed only to the relationships between an upper and lower house; now that no province had a bicameral Legislature, s. 53 had become redundant in its application to the provinces (para. 54). Binnie J., concurring in the result, took a similar view that s. 53 was applicable only to "legislative procedure", and if a taxing measure never took the form of a "bill" s. 53 had no work to do (para. 60).

[15]*Re Eurig Estate*, [1998] 2 S.C.R. 565, para. 34. Accord, *620 Connaught v. Can.*, [2008] 1 S.C.R. 131, paras. 4–6 (but upholding the impost in that case as a regulatory

inconsistent legislation should be upheld as an indirect or implicit amendment of s. 53? Major J. said that the dictum should no longer be followed. It was true that s. 45 of the Constitution Act, 1982 empowered a provincial Legislature to amend the constitution of the province, and it was also true that the requirement of s. 53 was a provision that could be amended under that power, but s. 45 should be interpreted as requiring that any such amendment be direct or express, not merely indirect or implied.[16] The probate fee, being a tax that had not been imposed by the Legislature itself, was therefore invalid.[17]

Does it follow from the *Eurig* case that the taxing power cannot be delegated by Parliament or the Legislature to subordinate bodies like the Governor in Council, the Lieutenant Governor in Council, ministers, agencies or municipalities? Or is the democratic principle satisfied if the Parliament or Legislature enacts a statute delegating the power to tax? Major J. raised this question but refused to decide it. The Ontario Legislature had enacted a statute delegating to the Lieutenant Governor in Council the power to levy "fees" in court proceedings, but it had not delegated the power to levy a tax. "Therefore, whether it could constitutionally do so does not need to be addressed."[18] However, in an earlier passage, he implied that the taxing power could not be delegated, because he said that "my interpretation of s. 53 does not prohibit Parliament or the legislatures from vesting any control over *the details and mechanism of taxation* in statutory delegates such as the Lieutenant Governor in Council".[19] This view that the taxing power (apart from details and mechanism) cannot be delegated, in my opinion, is the better one. Once a taxing power has been delegated, the resulting taxes do in practice escape the democratic accountability that occurs when a bill is introduced in the legislative assembly. Ontario's probate fee, for example, had been increased tenfold since 1950 when the power was vested in the Lieutenant Governor in Council, and the last increase, which was a tripling of the rate in 1992, had been quietly imposed after the government of the province had publicly announced that there would be no further increases in taxation!

In *Ontario English Catholic Teachers' Association v. Ontario* (2001),[20] the question was whether the power to fix the rate of Ontario's property tax for education could be delegated. The property tax was imposed by statute, but the rate was to be fixed by the Minister of Finance. The

---

charge, not a tax); *Confederation des syndicats nationaux v. Canada*, [2008] 3 S.C.R. 511, paras. 81–94 (striking down tax imposed by Governor in Council).

[16] *Re Eurig Estate*, [1998] 2 S.C.R. 565, para. 35.

[17] The province immediately enacted the Estate Administration Tax Act, 1998, to impose a tax at the same rates and on the same base as the probate fee, and made the legislation retroactive to 1950, when the probate fee had first been imposed by the Lieutenant Governor in Council.

[18] *Re Eurig Estate*, [1998] 2 S.C.R. 565, para. 36; see also para. 39.

[19] *Re Eurig Estate*, [1998] 2 S.C.R. 565, para. 30 (emphasis added).

[20] *Ontario English Catholic Teachers' Association v. Ontario*, [2001] 1 S.C.R. 470. Iacobucci J. wrote the opinion of the Court.

Supreme Court of Canada held that the power to fix the rate was an essential element of the power to tax so that a delegation of the power to tax had indeed occurred. And the Court went on to hold that, while only the Legislature could create a new tax, the imposition of the tax could be delegated so long as the delegation was contained in a statute in language that was "express and unambiguous". The "democratic principle" was preserved by the fact that "the legislation expressly delegating the imposition of the tax must be approved by the legislature".[21] In this case, the Minister's power to set the rate of the property tax was contained in the Education Act in express and unambiguous language. The delegation was therefore valid. Was this a case in which only the "details and mechanism" of the property tax were being delegated? Iacobucci J. quoted the passage from *Eurig* in which the phrase appeared,[22] and he pointed out that the setting of the property tax rate "takes place within a detailed statutory framework, setting out the structure of the tax, the tax base, and the principles for its imposition".[23] The better reading of the opinion is that it maintains the restriction on the delegation of taxing power to details and mechanism,[24] although it holds that setting the rate of a tax is one of the "details" that can be delegated.

Another rate-setting case produced a different result in *Confédération des syndicats nationaux v. Canada* (2008).[25] The issue was whether Parliament could delegate the power to set Employment Insurance (EI) premiums. Under the federal Employment Insurance Act, the premiums were normally set by the Employment Commission, an agency created by the Act, under an express statutory power that directed the Commission to set premiums at a level that would provide for the payment of benefits each year and create a reserve to keep premiums stable during downturns in the economic cycle. These premiums were not taxes. They were regulatory charges designed to fund the EI program, and the power to set premium rates was clearly delegated to the Commission. The Act was amended with effect only in 2002, 2003 and 2005 to temporarily move the premium-setting power to the Governor in Council and to suspend the statutory directions linking the setting of premiums to the payment of benefits. The Governor in Council in fact set premiums that were far in excess of anticipated benefit liabilities, creating a huge surplus that was paid into the Consolidated Revenue Fund and used for general government expenditures. A group of Quebec unions brought

---

[21]*Ontario English Catholic Teachers' Association v. Ontario*, [2001] 1 S.C.R. 470, para. 74.

[22]*Ontario English Catholic Teachers' Association v. Ontario*, [2001] 1 S.C.R. 470, para. 71.

[23]*Ontario English Catholic Teachers' Association v. Ontario*, [2001] 1 S.C.R. 470, para. 75.

[24]Accord, *Confédération des syndicats nationaux v. Can.*, [2008] 3 S.C.R. 511, para. 88 per LeBel J. (persuasively criticizing my contrary view in the previous edition of this book).

[25]*Confédération des syndicats nationaux v. Canada*, [2008] 3 S.C.R. 511. LeBel J. wrote the opinion of the Court.

proceedings to attack the validity of this use of EI premiums that had been paid by employers and employees for the purpose of funding the EI program. The Supreme Court of Canada held that, for the three years covered by the amendments, the statutory link between premiums and benefits having been lost, the premiums were no longer regulatory charges, but had been converted into a tax, a kind of payroll tax.[26] The government argued that, even if the premiums were characterized as taxes, they should be upheld because Parliament had the power to impose a payroll tax. But the Court followed *Eurig* to hold that s. 53 of the Constitution Act, 1867 required that taxes be imposed by Parliament, or (in the case of details and mechanism) by a statutorily authorized delegate of Parliament. The delegate for the years 2002, 2003 and 2005 was the Governor in Council, but the only power delegated by the Act was to set "premiums". This was not clear enough to confer a power to set the rate of a "tax", and therefore did not authorize the levy of the premiums which in those three years were really taxes. Therefore, for those three years, the power to set premiums was invalid and the EI premiums were collected without the necessary legislative authorization.[27]

§ 14:6 Delegation of judicial power

The absence of any general separation of powers doctrine in Canada means that there is no general prohibition on the delegation of judicial power to bodies other than courts. However, s. 96 of the Constitution Act, 1867 has been interpreted as implicitly prohibiting the delegation of judicial functions analogous to those performed by a superior, district or county court to a body that is not a superior, district or county court. This prohibition applies to the provincial Legislatures, but not to the federal Parliament, except when the federal Parliament invests a provincial body with judicial functions. The prohibition has been discussed in ch. 7, Courts.[1]

§ 14:7 Classification of laws

The Constitution of Canada, as a federal constitution, distributes legislative powers among the federal Parliament and the provincial

[26]For more discussion, see ch. 31, Taxation, under heading § 31:16, "Regulatory charges", and ch. 33, Social Security, under heading § 33:2, "Unemployment insurance".

[27]The cost and difficulty (or more likely impossibility) of returning the invalid premiums to all the employers and employees who had paid them evidently weighed (silently) on the Court, which suspended the declaration of invalidity for 12 months "to allow the consequences of that invalidity to be rectified" (para. 94). Parliament promptly enacted a retroactive amendment to the Act to restore the required link between the premium-setting power and the benefits for the years 2002, 2003 and 2005, and thereby retroactively validated the premiums: Budget Implementation Act, S.C. 2009, c. 2, ss. 227, 228.

[Section 14:6]

[1]Chapter 7, Courts, under heading §§ 7:15 to 7:20, "Implications of Constitution's judicature sections".

Legislatures. Every law enacted by the Parliament or a Legislature must fall within one of the classes of subjects allocated by the Constitution to the enacting legislative body. Otherwise it is invalid. This is as true of a law effecting a delegation as it is of any other law. The invalidity of a statute which is ultra vires the enacting legislative body will of course destroy any powers which the statute purported to delegate to the government or to an administrative agency.

This is obvious enough, but a more subtle effect of the federal distribution of powers on the power to delegate is possible. It has been suggested in Australia that a particularly broad or vague delegation by the federal Parliament of law-making power could be held invalid on the ground that "the enactment attempting it is not a law with respect to any particular head or heads of legislative power".[1] In Canada, the same idea surfaced in a famous dictum of Rand J. in *Saumur v. Quebec* (1953)[2] as a reason for striking down a municipal by-law that forbade the distribution of literature on the streets of Quebec City without the permission of the chief of police. Because the by-law supplied no standards for the guidance of the chief of police, it was impossible to be sure from its terms whether the by-law was addressed to street regulation of soliciting and littering (in which case it would be valid) or to censorship of the religious and political content of material proposed for distribution (in which case it would be invalid). For Rand J. (none of the other judges took this point), the absence of precision in the drafting of the by-law was by itself a fatal flaw. The relevant passage of his opinion is not easy to summarize, and so I set it out in full:

> Conceding, as in the Alberta Reference, that aspects of the activities of religion and free speech may be affected by provincial legislation, such legislation, as in all other fields, must be sufficiently definite and precise to indicate its subject matter. In our political organization, as in federal structures generally, that is the condition of legislation by any authority within it: the courts must be able from its language and its relevant circumstances, to attribute an enactment to a matter *in relation to which* the legislature acting has been empowered to make laws. That principle inheres in the nature of federalism; otherwise, authority, in broad and general terms, could be conferred which would end the division of powers. Where the language is sufficiently specific and can fairly be interpreted as applying only to matter within the enacting jurisdiction, that attribution will be made; and where the requisite elements are present, there is the rule of severability. But to authorize action which may be related indifferently to a variety of incompatible matters by means of the device of a discretionary licence cannot be brought within either of these mechanisms; and the Court is powerless, under general language that overlaps exclusive jurisdictions, to delineate and preserve valid power in a segregated form. If the purpose is street regulation, taxation, registration or other local object, the language must, with sufficient precision, define the matter and mode of administra-

---

[Section 14:7]

[1] *Victorian Stevedoring and Gen. Contracting Co. v. Dignan* (1931), 46 C.L.R. 73, 101.

[2] *Saumur v. Quebec*, [1953] 2 S.C.R. 299, 333.

tion; and by no expedient which ignores that requirement can constitutional limitations be circumvented.

This seems to be the only suggestion in the Canadian cases that a sweeping delegation might run foul of the federal distribution of powers.[3] In most cases, of course, a law can be attributed to a matter coming within a class of subject, such as banking, even if the law includes a delegation to a subordinate body. And more sweeping delegations, covering laws of various classifications, are not necessarily invalid. Thus, the federal delegations to the Legislatures of the three territories are undoubtedly valid as laws in relation to federal territories.[4] It is possible that other sweeping delegations could be upheld, if federal, as in relation to "the peace, order, and good government of Canada"[5] or "the executive government of Canada";[6] and, if provincial, as in relation to the amendment of "the constitution of the province".[7]

§ 14:8 Office of Lieutenant Governor or Governor General

Before 1982, each provincial Legislature had, under s. 92(1) of the Constitution Act, 1867, the power to amend "the constitution of the province, except as regards the office of Lieutenant Governor". The office of Lieutenant Governor was thus explicitly withdrawn from the provincial power of amendment. Section 92(1) was repealed in 1982 and replaced by s. 45 of the Constitution Act, 1982, which also confers the power to amend "the constitution of the province". While s. 45 itself does not make an exception for the office of Lieutenant Governor, s. 45 is expressly made subject to s. 41 (the unanimity procedure), and s. 41(a) stipulates that an amendment to the Constitution of Canada in relation to "the office of . . . the Lieutenant Governor of a province" may be made only by the unanimity procedure of s. 41.[1] It is probably safe to

---

[3] *N.S. Bd. of Censors v. McNeil*, [1978] 2 S.C.R. 662 presented a similar situation of an absence of standards in a delegation to a censorship board, but the Court "read down" the broad power so that the power excluded censorship of political or religious ideas. The Court sustained the thus-limited power. This approach would have been possible in *Saumur* too. In that case, it could have been said that those exercises of the chief of police's discretion directed to the censorship of political or religious ideas were invalid, while preserving the by-law as a vehicle of street regulation. Since the adoption of the Charter of Rights, there is now, by s. 1, a constitutional requirement of standards in a law that abridges a Charter right: ch. 38, Limitation of Rights, under heading §§ 38:7 to 38:9, "Prescribed by law".

[4] § 14:4 note 6, above.

[5] Constitution Act, 1867, s. 91 (opening words).

[6] Constitution Act, 1982, s. 44.

[7] Constitution Act, 1982, s. 45.

[Section 14:8]

[1] Sections 41 (unanimity procedure) and 45 (provincial Legislature alone), as well as the other amending procedures, are discussed in ch. 4, Amendment.

conclude that the provincial power of amendment under s. 45 is essentially the same as it was under s. 92(1)[2]

The exception of the office of Lieutenant Governor from the provincial power of amendment has been held to limit the provincial power to delegate. The cases defining this limitation arose out of Western Canadian experiments with theories of "direct democracy", in which, through the mechanism of "initiative" and "referendum", the electorate participates directly in the legislative process.

In 1916, Manitoba enacted the Initiative and Referendum Act. This Act allowed the electors (persons with the right to vote) to "initiate" a proposed law through a petition signed by eight per cent of the electors and presented to the Legislative Assembly. If the Legislative Assembly did not enact the proposed law, then the law had to be submitted to the electorate in a "referendum". If the proposed law was approved by a majority of the votes cast in the referendum, then it became law without any action on the part of the Manitoba Legislature. The Act also provided a similar procedure for the repeal of existing laws.

The Initiative and Referendum Act left the Manitoba Legislature intact, and in possession of all its powers. It followed that the normal representative process through the Legislature could still be used to enact statutes and indeed it could be used to repeal or alter the initiative and referendum process. But the grant of power to the electors was quite unlimited and appeared to be as plenary as that of the Legislature, so that, for example, the initiative and referendum process could be employed to repeal or alter the normal representative process through the Legislature. This is, as S.A. Scott has commented, "a highly interesting situation: for, two equally competent legislative processes, each independent of the other, may act disharmoniously, each undoing the work of the other (the last to speak laying down, in principle, the governing law) or even engage in a race to the statute book to alter the constitution of the other, restrict its power, or even abolish it outright."[3]

In *Re Initiative and Referendum Act* (1919),[4] the Privy Council held that the Initiative and Referendum Act had to be regarded as an amendment of the constitution of Manitoba, and that it went beyond the power of amendment conferred by the Constitution Act, 1867. Their lordships held that the exception to s. 92(1) of "the office of Lieutenant Governor" was applicable, because the statute purported to alter the position of the Lieutenant Governor by creating a legislative process in which he played

[2]It should be noted however that s. 41 is confined to amendments to the "Constitution of Canada", while s. 45 is not so confined. It could be argued that a change in the office of the Lieutenant Governor that did not involve any change in the instruments that form part of the Constitution of Canada would not be caught by s. 41 and would accordingly be open to the province, either under s. 45 or under one of the other heads of provincial legislative power.

[3]S.A. Scott, "Constituent Authority and the Canadian Provinces" (1967) 12 McGill L.J. 528, 536.

[4]*Re Initiative and Referendum Act*, [1919] A.C. 935.

no part.[5] Thus their lordships fastened upon what must be the least important feature of the Initiative and Referendum Act to find it invalid. It must be remembered that, under the conventions of responsible government, the Lieutenant Governor's function of giving royal assent to a bill which has passed the representative house of the Legislature is an automatic formality: the Lieutenant Governor of a province (like the Governor General of Canada) has no power of veto akin to that possessed by the President of the United States or the Governor of a state.[6]

Another attempt to bypass the requirement of royal assent led to invalidity in *Re Manitoba Language Rights* (1985).[7] At issue was a Manitoba statute that purported to provide a two-stage procedure for the enactment of laws in both English and French (which is required in Manitoba by s. 23 of the Manitoba Act, 1870). The statute contemplated that a law could be enacted initially in English only, and the French version would be deemed to be enacted by the later deposit with the Clerk of the House of Assembly of a certified translation of the law. The Supreme Court of Canada pointed out that the certified translation, although given the full force of law, would not have received the royal assent. The Court cited the *Initiative and Referendum Reference*, and held that Manitoba's attempt to do away with the royal assent was "an unconstitutional attempt to interfere with the powers of the Lieutenant Governor".[8]

The protected status of the Lieutenant Governor was given a startling application in *Credit Foncier Franco-Canadien v. Ross* (1937),[9] where the Appellate Division of the Supreme Court of Alberta held that a delegation of law-making power to the Lieutenant Governor in Council was invalid as "an interference with the office of the Lieutenant Governor."[10] Harvey C.J. for the Court purported to follow the *Initiative and Referendum Reference*, saying: "This case is different only in that it adds to rather than subtracts from the Lieutenant Governor's functions. That difference in my opinion is of no importance."[11] If this decision were correct, it would destroy most of the delegations on the provincial statute books. In each province, the body to which law-making powers are most frequently delegated by statute is the cabinet, and of course

[5]Compare *R. v. Nat Bell Liquors*, [1922] 2 A.C. 128; discussed, see text accompanying § 14:9 note 6, below.

[6]The power to refuse the royal assent to a bill exists at law, but has been nullified by convention: see ch. 9, Responsible Government, under heading § 9:11, "The Governor General".

[7]*Re Manitoba Language Rights*, [1985] 1 S.C.R. 721.

[8]*Re Manitoba Language Rights*, [1985] 1 S.C.R. 721, 777. The two-stage procedure was held to be unconstitutional on another ground as well, namely, that s. 23 of the Manitoba Act, 1870 implicitly required that the English and French versions of the statute be enacted at the same time: *Re Manitoba Language Rights*, [1985] 1 S.C.R. 721, 776.

[9]*Credit Foncier Franco-Canadien v. Ross*, [1937] 3 D.L.R. 365 (Alta. A.D.).

[10]*Credit Foncier Franco-Canadien v. Ross*, [1937] 3 D.L.R. 365, 368 (Alta. A.D.).

[11]*Credit Foncier Franco-Canadien v. Ross*, [1937] 3 D.L.R. 365, 368 (Alta. A.D.).

the normal drafting technique for that purpose is to delegate the power to "the Lieutenant Governor in Council". It is possible that the Court intended to confine its decision to cases where the Lieutenant Governor in Council had the power to provide exemptions from the Act itself (a power he was given in *Credit Foncier)*, but the Court did not say so. Even so limited, the decision is a most implausible reading of s. 92(1), which did not prohibit all laws with respect to the Lieutenant Governor, but simply prohibited any amendment to the constitution of the province which would affect the office of Lieutenant Governor. Anyway, *Credit Foncier* has been criticized and perhaps overruled; it has never been followed; and many delegations to the Lieutenant Governor in Council have been held or assumed to be valid.[12]

The protection of the office of Lieutenant Governor was before 1982 (under s. 92(1) of the Constitution Act, 1867) and still is (under s. 45 of the Constitution Act, 1982) a limitation on the power of each Legislature to amend "the constitution of the province". The comparable power of the federal Parliament before 1982 was s. 91(1) of the Constitution Act, 1867, which did not include any comparable protection for the office of Governor General. Section 91(1) was repealed in 1982 and replaced by s. 44 of the Constitution Act, 1982, which confers the power to amend the Constitution of Canada in relation to "the executive government of Canada or the Senate and House of Commons". Section 44 (like s. 45) is expressly made subject to s. 41 (the unanimity procedure), and s. 41(a) stipulates that an amendment to the Constitution of Canada in relation to "the office of . . . the Governor General" may be made only by the unanimity procedure of s. 41.[13] The office of Governor General is thus withdrawn from the federal Parliament's amending power, and the ground of decision in the *Initiative and Referendum Reference* would apply to a federal statute establishing a new legislative process that bypassed the Governor General.

§ 14:9 Requirement of a Legislature or Parliament

We have seen that the *Initiative and Referendum Reference* was decided on the basis that there was a constitutional prohibition of a legislative process that bypassed the province's Lieutenant Governor. But a more substantial objection could be made to legislation by initiative and referendum, and that is, that the process bypasses the province's legislative assembly. In the *Initiative and Referendum Reference*, the lower court, the Manitoba Court of Appeal, decided that the regime of direct democracy was bad, not merely because it bypassed the Lieutenant Governor, but also because it invested primary powers of legislation

[12]See *Credit Foncier Franco-Canadien v. Ross*, [1937] 3 D.L.R. 365 (Alta. A.D.).

[13]Sections 41 (unanimity procedure) and 44 (federal Parliament alone), as well as the other amending procedures, are discussed in ch. 4, Amendment.

in a body (the electorate) which was not a "Legislature".[1] In other words, the Constitution contemplated that primary law-making authority could be exercised only by a Legislature, and the term Legislature involved the participation of some form of representative assembly. The Privy Council deliberately refrained from passing upon this ground of decision, but in an obiter dictum they suggested that they agreed with it.[2]

If the initiative and referendum procedure were construed as *delegated* rather than primary law-making power, then it would be immaterial that it were vested in a body other than a "Legislature"; that, after all, is exactly *what Hodge*[3] decided was permissible.[4] The Privy Council in the *Initiative and Referendum Reference* asserted that, while *Hodge* permitted a provincial Legislature to "seek the assistance of subordinate agencies", it did not follow "that [the Legislature] can create and endow with its own capacity a new legislative power not created by the [Constitution] Act to which it owes its own existence".[5] One is prompted to ask, why not? And then to ask, why does the Initiative and Referendum Act fall into the forbidden rather than the permitted category? It could hardly be the unrestricted scope of the power conferred on the electorate, because a delegator always retains the power to restrict or withdraw a grant of unrestricted power to a delegate. It could perhaps be the power of the electorate to alter or abolish the powers of the delegator (the Legislature). Certainly, this is a fundamental power, but it is arguable that it is not a sufficient reason to condemn the entire Initiative and Referendum Act; it would be sufficient to "read down" the Act by deciding that, while an attempt to turn against the Legislature itself would be invalid, other exercises of the power would be valid.

The Privy Council had another opportunity to pass on these fundamen-

---

[Section 14:9]

[1] *Initiative and Referendum Reference* (1916), 27 Man. R. 1 (Man. C.A.); and see S.A. Scott, "Constituent Authority and the Canadian Provinces" (1967) 12 McGill L.J. 528, 552–553 for the relevant passages.

[2] *Re Initiative and Referendum Act*, [1919] A.C. 935, 945. Accord, *OPSEU v. Ont.*, [1987] 2 S.C.R. 2, 47 (obiter dictum denying provincial power to introduce "political institutions foreign to and incompatible with the Canadian system"). The argument that law-making power must be exercised by a Legislature is analogous to one that has been accepted in the United States, where the federal and state constitutions attempt to separate the legislative, executive and judicial powers. There the principle of separation of powers has been invoked for the proposition that "legislative" power may not be delegated to the executive: see *Panama Refining Co. v. Ryan* (1935), 293 U.S. 388; *Schechter Poultry Corp. v. U.S.A.* (1935), 295 U.S. 494.

[3] *Hodge v. The Queen* (1883), 9 App. Cas. 117.

[4] S.A. Scott, "Constituent Authority and the Canadian Provinces" (1967) 12 McGill L.J. 528, 548 says that delegation is also an answer to the by-passing of the Lieutenant Governor. But the federal distribution of powers requires us to classify the Initiative and Referendum Act and find a provincial head of power which supports it. Even if the Act is merely a "delegation", it probably has to be classified as an amendment of the constitution of the province, and the office of Lieutenant Governor is expressly exempted from the power.

[5] *Re Initiative and Referendum Act*, [1919] A.C. 935, 945.

tal questions in *R. v. Nat Bell Liquors* (1922),[6] when it had to decide whether Alberta's Liquor Act of 1916 was valid. The Alberta Legislature in 1913 had enacted the Direct Legislation Act, which established an initiative and referendum procedure. Under the Alberta procedure, where a proposed statute had been initiated by a proportion of electors, and then approved in a referendum of electors, "the said proposed statute shall be enacted by the Legislature at its next session without amendment . . . and . . . shall come into force upon receiving royal assent . . .". The Alberta procedure differed from the Manitoba procedure in its require-ment that the statute be enacted by the Legislature. It will be recalled that the Manitoba procedure bypassed the Legislature altogether. However, the Alberta Act clearly contemplated that, after a referendum had approved a proposed statute, the Legislature was under a duty to enact the statute without amendment; in other words, the Legislature's role was to be formal only.

Alberta's initiative and referendum procedure was employed to enact the Liquor Act of 1916, and Nat Bell Liquors was convicted of an offence under the Liquor Act. On appeal from an application to quash this conviction, the Privy Council held that it was no objection to the validity of the Liquor Act that it had been enacted by the initiative and referendum procedure. They relied upon the fact that the procedure had culminated in passage through the Alberta Legislature, including the giving of royal assent. They concluded: "It is impossible to say that [the Liquor Act] was not an Act of the Legislature and it is none the less a statute because it was the statutory duty of the Legislature to pass it."[7] Their lordships' ready acceptance of the idea that the Direct Legislation Act had imposed a "statutory duty" on the Legislature to enact measures approved by referendum is surely inconsistent with their earlier decision in the Manitoba *Initiative and Referendum Reference*[8] (to which they did not refer, although it was referred to in argument). Once it is accepted that the Legislature's role is formal only, simply to place a rubber stamp on the result of the referendum, then the reasoning which appealed to the Privy Council and Manitoba Court of Appeal in the *Initiative and Referendum Reference* seems applicable again, that is to say, the office of Lieutenant Governor is again impaired, and primary legislative power is again granted away from the Legislature. *R. v. Nat Bell Liquors* can be reconciled with the earlier case only if the referendum were held to be advisory rather than mandatory, that is, if the apparent attempt by the Direct Legislation Act to impose a statutory duty were held to be ineffective. Then, and only then, would the Liquor Act have been a genuine enactment of the Alberta Legislature.[9]

Another difficulty with the decision in *R. v. Nat Bell Liquors* is that it violates a basic rule of parliamentary sovereignty, namely, that a legisla-

---

[6]*R. v. Nat Bell Liquors*, [1922] 2 A.C. 128.

[7]*R. v. Nat Bell Liquors*, [1922] 2 A.C. 128, 134.

[8]*Re Initiative and Referendum Act*, [1919] A.C. 935.

[9]For another (and more charitable) analysis of the *Nat Bell* case, see S.A. Scott, "Constituent Authority and the Canadian Provinces" (1967) 12 McGill L.J. 528, 557–561.

tive body cannot bind itself as to the substance (as opposed to the manner and form) of its future enactments.[10] Alberta's Direct Legislation Act of 1913, as interpreted by the Privy Council, purported to tie the hands of future Legislatures by imposing upon them a duty to enact whatever policies were determined upon by the initiative and referendum process. Such a self-imposed restraint on the discretion of future Legislatures should not have been upheld.

The argument accepted by the Manitoba Court of Appeal in the *Initiative and Referendum Reference*, namely, that the Constitution Act, 1867 contemplates that primary law-making authority be exercised only by the organs that it establishes or recognizes, would seem to apply with the same force to the federal Parliament as to the provincial Legislatures.[11] Indeed, it was applied, as one of the reasons of the Supreme Court of Canada, in the *Upper House Reference* (1979).[12] In deciding that the federal Parliament had no power to abolish the Senate, the Court characterized such a measure as "a transfer by Parliament of all its legislative powers to a new legislative body of which the Senate would not be a member", and the Court cited with approval the reasoning of the Manitoba Court of Appeal in the *Initiative and Referendum Reference.*[13] With respect, this is a rather strained application of the argument. There is little analogy between a regime of direct democracy, which would bypass deliberative assemblies altogether, and the abolition of an upper house, which would leave the elected lower house (and the head of state) in possession of full legislative power. Moreover, such an argument has never been used to prevent a province from abolishing its upper house; and five provinces have in fact abolished their upper houses by ordinary statute, including Quebec, whose upper house was established in the Constitution Act, 1867 itself.[14] In the *Sen-*

[10]See ch. 12, Parliamentary Sovereignty, at heading § 12:9, "Substance of future laws".

[11]There is an obiter dictum in *Re Initiative and Referendum Act*, [1919] A.C. 935, 943, suggesting that the federal Parliament's possession of the "residuary power of legislation" might give it increased power "to set up new legislative bodies".

[12]*Re Upper House*, [1980] 1 S.C.R. 54. The constitutional background to the case is explained, and the reasoning of the decision criticized, in P.W. Hogg, Comment (1980) 58 Can. Bar Rev. 631. The doubt as to the extent of the federal Parliament's power was caused by the breadth and vagueness of s. 91(1) of the Constitution Act, 1867, which was then (before 1982) the federal Parliament's power of unilateral constitutional amendment. Section 91(1) was repealed in 1982 and replaced by s. 44 of the Constitution Act, 1982. Because s. 44 is expressly made subject to s. 42, and because s. 42(1)(b) requires the general amending procedure to be used to alter "the powers of the Senate and the method of selecting Senators", it is now clear without judicial interpretation that the federal Parliament alone cannot abolish the Senate.

[13]*Reference re Legislative Authority of Parliament of Canada*, [1980] 1 S.C.R. 54, 72.

[14]Constitution Act, 1867, s. 71, established the Legislative Council of Quebec. None of the five provincial abolitions of upper houses (detailed in Forsey, *Freedom and Order* (1974), 227) was challenged in the courts, but in *Re Upper House*, [1980] 1 S.C.R. 54, 74, the Supreme Court of Canada referred to them and assumed them to be valid, distinguishing them on grounds that do not touch the present argument.

ate Reform Reference (2014),[15] the Supreme Court was asked to revisit the question of the abolition of the Senate in light of the provisions of Part V of the Constitution Act, 1982 (the amending procedures), which had been adopted after the 1979 decision in the *Upper House Reference.* The Court held that the abolition of the Senate was outside the power of the federal Parliament: the unanimity amending procedure of s. 41 would be required because the abolition of the Senate would constitute an amendment to Part V, which was listed among the unanimity items as s. 41(e). On this question, the Court made no reference to its earlier decision in the *Upper House Reference* and no reference to the *Initiative and Referendum* reasoning.[16]

III. FEDERAL INTER-DELEGATION

§ 14:10 Legislative inter-delegation

Federal "inter-delegation" is the delegation of federal power to the provinces, or of provincial power to the Dominion.[1] In the 1930s and 1940s, federal inter-delegation came to be seen as a device by which the Dominion and the provinces could in effect agree for specific purposes to lend each other needed legislative powers. The result of the Privy Council's interpretation of the Canadian Constitution was that in some fields, most notably that of marketing, neither Parliament nor a Legislature was competent to enact effective measures. The Privy Council conceded that this was so, and exhorted the unfortunate Canadian legislative bodies to "cooperate" to produce effective measures.[2]

Cooperation through inter-delegation was first attempted as a solution to the problem of old age pensions. The federal government wanted to establish a scheme of old age pensions which would be financed by contributions from employers and employees as well as from the federal government and the provinces. This proposal ran into two constitutional difficulties. The first was the Privy Council's decision in the *Unemployment Insurance Reference* (1937),[3] which suggested that any contributory pension scheme would be outside the power of the Dominion, al-

---

[15]*Re Senate Reform*, [2014] 1 S.C.R. 704, 2014 SCC 32, paras. 95–110.

[16]The Court did say (para. 97) that "removing the bicameral form of government" would "fundamentally alter our constitutional architecture", but the rest of the Senate-abolition reasoning was devoted to the text of ss. 41 and 42.

[Section 14:10]

[1]For discussion of federal inter-delegation, see W.R. Lederman, "Some Forms and Limitations of Cooperative Federalism" (1967) 45 Can. Bar Rev. 409; P.C. Weiler, "The Supreme Court and the Law of Canadian Federalism" (1973) 23 U. Toronto L.J. 307, 311–318; G.V. La Forest, "Delegation of Legislative Power in Canada" (1975) 21 McGill L.J. 131; E.A. Driedger, "The Interaction Of Federal and Provincial Laws" (1976) 54 Can. Bar Rev. 695.

[2]*A.-G. B.C. v. A.-G. Can.* (Natural Products Marketing) [1937] A.C. 377, 389.

[3]*A.-G. Can. v. A.-G. Ont.* (Unemployment Insurance) [1937] A.C. 355, which was overcome so far as unemployment insurance was concerned by an amendment to the Constitution Act, 1867 in 1940 adding "unemployment insurance" as s. 91(2A) to the list of federal powers.

though inside the power of the provinces. The second difficulty was that several of the provinces wanted to finance their contribution to the scheme by levying an indirect sales tax, which would be outside the power of the provinces, although inside the power of the Dominion.[4] A suggested solution lay in complementary delegations. The provincial Legislatures would each enact a statute delegating to the federal Parliament the provincial power "to make laws in relation to any matter relating to employment"; and the federal Parliament would enact a statute delegating to the provincial Legislatures the power to levy "a retail sales tax of the nature of indirect taxation". The federal Parliament could then enact the pension scheme, exercising authority delegated to it by the provincial Legislatures; and the provincial Legislatures could then levy the sales taxes, exercising authority delegated to them by the federal Parliament.

Was the proposed inter-delegation constitutional? There is no express power of inter-delegation in the Canadian Constitution,[5] as there is in the Australian Constitution.[6] But since the *Hodge* doctrine allowed the federal Parliament and provincial Legislatures to delegate their powers to subordinate bodies, could they not also delegate their powers to each other? The answer came in the *Nova Scotia Inter-delegation* case (1950).[7] A bill was introduced in the Nova Scotia Legislature to carry out the provincial side of the inter-delegation scheme. The bill was referred to the Supreme Court of Nova Scotia for a decision as to its constitutionality. The Nova Scotia court held that the bill was invalid. On appeal to the Supreme Court of Canada, this decision was affirmed. The reasoning of the two Courts was, essentially, that inter-delegation would disturb the scheme of distribution of powers in the Constitution. The various legislative bodies should not be permitted to agree to alter that scheme in the absence of clear authority in the Constitution itself. There was no express authority, and none should be implied.

This result does seem to follow inexorably from the premise that inter-delegation would involve a change in the distribution of powers effected by the Constitution. But the premise is incorrect. A delegation of power

---

[4]Constitution Act, 1867, ss. 91(3), 92(2); and see ch. 31, Taxation, under heading § 31:12, "Sales taxes".

[5]The Fulton-Favreau amendment proposal (1964) would have inserted a power of inter-delegation in the Constitution. The closest provision actually in the Constitution Act, 1867 is s. 94, which appears to contemplate an irrevocable transfer of legislative power from the Legislatures to the Parliament; as Lederman comments, W.R. Lederman, "Some Forms and Limitations of Cooperative Federalism" (1967) 45 Can. Bar Rev. 409, 421, "perhaps this is one reason why it has never been used".

[6]Constitution of Australia, s. 51(37), authorizing the states to "refer" powers to the federal Parliament, but not vice versa. Of course, in Australia most federal legislative powers are concurrent with the states anyway, so that there is little need for a corresponding federal power of delegation. Section 51(37) has been used only occasionally. For discussion, see G. Moens and J. Trone, Lumb and Moens' The Constitution of the Commonwealth of Australia Annotated (Butterworths, Chatswood, N.S.W., 6th ed., 2001), 174–176; Hanks, Constitutional Law in Australia (1991), 364–365.

[7]*A.-G. N.S. v. A.-G. Can.* (Nova Scotia Inter-delegation) [1951] S.C.R. 31.

does not divest the delegator of its power; nor does it confer a permanent power on the delegate. The delegator has the continuing power to legislate on the same topic concurrently if it chooses, and it can withdraw the delegation at any time. This being so, why not apply the *Hodge* doctrine and concede that legislative power in Canada is sufficiently "plenary and ample" to sustain inter-delegation? The majority judges do not provide a satisfying answer to this line of reasoning. Nor do they explain why, as a matter of policy, Canadian federalism should be denied the flexibility of cooperation through inter-delegation.

Only Rand J. made a brief attempt to grapple with the merits by asserting that the "continued exercise of delegated power" would give rise to "prescriptive claims" to the permanent possession of the power, and "the power of revocation might in fact become no more feasible, practically, than amendment of the Act of 1867 of its own volition by the British Parliament".[8] W.R. Lederman, in an important article in the Canadian Bar Review, agrees, and adds that delegation between the federal Parliament and provincial Legislatures "could seriously confuse the basic political responsibility and accountability of members of the federal Parliament and the federal Cabinet, and too much of this could destroy these federal institutions".[9] There is force in these arguments, but they come very close to an enquiry into the wisdom of legislative policy, and it is doubtful whether they are sufficient to warrant carving an exception out of such basic constitutional principles as the *Hodge* doctrine of plenary and ample power[10] and its associated doctrine that the totality of legislative power is distributed to Canadian legislative bodies.[11]

The immediate benefit sought to be achieved by the Nova Scotia inter-delegation, namely, a contributory old age pension scheme, was a long time in coming. After the *Nova Scotia Inter-delegation* decision, the federal government decided to attempt to achieve the desired result through constitutional amendment. It proposed two constitutional amendments, one to confer on the federal Parliament the power to enact a pension scheme, and the other to confer on the provincial Legislatures the power to levy an indirect sales tax. After a lengthy correspondence with the provincial governments, and several changes in the detail of the proposal, the federal government secured the unanimous consent of the ten provincial governments to the pension amendment. However, the sales tax amendment secured the consent of only eight provincial governments, and the two dissenters were Ontario and Quebec. The federal government went ahead with the pension amendment, but refused to continue its support for the sales tax amendment. In the end, therefore, only one address was submitted to the federal Parliament, and only one amendment was enacted by the Parliament at Westminster,

[8] *A.-G. N.S. v. A.-G. Can.* (Nova Scotia Inter-delegation) [1951] S.C.R. 31, 50.

[9] W.R. Lederman, "Some Forms and Limitations of Cooperative Federalism" (1967) 45 Can. Bar Rev. 409, 426.

[10] *Hodge v. The Queen* (1883), 9 App. Cas. 117, 132.

[11] See ch. 12, Parliamentary Sovereignty.

in 1951.[12] This amendment became s. 94A of the Constitution Act, 1867, giving authority to the federal Parliament to make "laws in relation to old age pensions".[13] This amendment was followed by the federal enactment of the Old Age Security Act, 1951, which provided for payment of an old age pension financed wholly by federal taxation. The Canada Pension Plan, which is a contributory scheme, was not introduced for another fourteen years in 1965 and after another constitutional amendment in 1964 had replaced the 1951 version of s. 94A with a different version.[14] The delays and difficulties in providing for old age pensions do not by themselves establish the desirability of inter-delegation, because they sprang from a variety of causes. But one of those causes was the difficulty of constitutional adaptation by formal amendment of the Constitution. Governments wanted to be able to adapt the Constitution more easily and less permanently. Consequently governments continued to consider the device of inter-delegation, despite the *Nova Scotia Inter-delegation* case.

§ 14:11 Administrative inter-delegation

Two years after *Nova Scotia Inter-delegation*, a slightly different form of inter-delegation came before the courts in *P.E.I. Potato Marketing Board v. Willis* (1952).[1] By the Agricultural Products Marketing Act 1949, the federal Parliament gave power to the Governor General in Council (that is, the federal cabinet) to delegate to *provincial* marketing boards the power to regulate the marketing of agricultural products "outside the province in interprovincial and export trade". Prince Edward Island had earlier enacted a marketing statute which empowered the Lieutenant Governor in Council (that is, the provincial cabinet) to establish schemes to regulate the marketing of agricultural products within the province, and to establish marketing boards to administer such schemes. In 1950, this statute was amended to bring it into line with the federal Act, and in particular to authorize provincial marketing boards, once established by the provincial government, to exercise any powers delegated to them by the federal government. Also in 1950, the government of Prince Edward Island, acting under the authority of the provincial statute, established a scheme for the marketing of potatoes in the province, and established a board of five members, the P.E.I. Potato Marketing Board, to administer the scheme. The federal government, acting under the authority of the federal statute, then delegated to the P.E.I. Potato Marketing Board the authority to regulate the marketing

[12] The pre-1982 amending procedure is described in ch. 4, Amendment.

[13] Added by British North America Act, 1951 (U.K.), R.S.C. 1985, Appendix II, No. 35; for history, see Livingston, Federalism and Constitutional Change (1956), 66–68.

[14] Added by Constitution Act, 1964 (U.K.), R.S.C. 1985, Appendix II, No. 38; for history, see W.R. Lederman, "Some Forms and Limitations of Cooperative Federalism" (1967) 45 Can. Bar Rev. 409, 412.

[Section 14:11]

[1] *P.E.I. Potato Marketing Board v. Willis*, [1952] 2 S.C.R. 392.

of P.E.I. potatoes outside the province in interprovincial and export trade.

The object of the inter-delegation from the federal Parliament to the provincial marketing board was to ensure that the provincial board was possessed of the totality of regulatory power over P.E.I. potatoes. The Privy Council, in striking down earlier marketing schemes,[2] had explained that effective regulation required "cooperation" between Parliament and the Legislatures.[3] Their lordships did not concern themselves with the great difficulties of securing cooperation, nor did they indicate what forms of cooperation would be constitutionally permissible. We have seen that in the *Nova Scotia Inter-delegation* case in 1950 one form of cooperation, namely, *legislative* inter-delegation, was held to be unconstitutional. Here was a second form of cooperation, namely, *administrative* inter-delegation: the delegate (or recipient of the power) was not the provincial Legislature itself, but an administrative agency created by the provincial Legislature.

On the face of it, the argument for validity did not look promising. If the federal Parliament could not delegate federal power to the provincial Legislature, surely by parity of reasoning the federal Parliament could not delegate federal power to a creature of the provincial Legislature. If the provincial Legislature could not itself accept a delegation of federal power, surely it could not create an administrative agency with capacity to accept a delegation of federal power. Nevertheless, in *P.E.I. Potato Marketing Board v. Willis* (1952),[4] the Supreme Court of Canada held that administrative inter-delegation was valid. The federal Parliament could, if it chose, "adopt as its own" a provincial agency and authorize it to exercise federal powers side by side with its provincial powers. And the provincial Legislature could confer on a provincial agency the capacity to accept a delegation of federal powers. Rand J. pointed out that "the Dominion by appropriate words could create a similar Board, composed of the same persons, bearing the same name, and with a similar formal organization, to execute the same Dominion functions".[5] None of the judges explained why the same reasoning had not prevailed in the *Nova Scotia Inter-delegation* case. Why could not the Dominion select the name, the members and the procedures of a provincial Legislature as the recipient of its delegation?[6]

Lederman takes the view that there is a constitutionally significant difference between legislative inter-delegation and administrative inter-delegation. As noted earlier, he supports the *Nova Scotia Inter-delegation* case on the basis that delegation from one legislative body to another could seriously confuse the "basic political responsibility and account-

---

[2]Marketing is discussed in ch. 21, Property and Civil Rights, under heading §§ 21:12 to 21:14, "Marketing".

[3]E.g., *A.-G. B.C. v. A.-G. Can.* (Natural Products Marketing) [1937] A.C. 377, 389.

[4]*P.E.I. Potato Marketing Board v. Willis*, [1952] 2 S.C.R. 392.

[5]*P.E.I. Potato Marketing Board v. Willis*, [1952] 2 S.C.R. 392, 414–415.

[6]See J.B. Ballem, Comment (1952) 30 Can. Bar Rev. 1050, 1057.

ability" for legislative discretion. Delegation to an administrative agency, he argues, does not involve that risk: "Even when regulation-making power is involved for the subordinate delegate body, if that regulation-making power is properly limited, still there is no threat to responsibility for primary legislative discretions under our federal system".[7] A preliminary difficulty with this argument is that a delegation by Parliament to a Legislature (or vice versa) can also be "properly limited", and it is certain that the courts would declare invalid an attempt by the delegate Legislature to enact federal laws outside the scope of the "properly limited" authority. The more fundamental difficulty springs from Lederman's assumption that an administrative inter-delegation must be "properly limited". The cases decided after Lederman's article have shown that the federal Parliament need not enact even the skeleton of a regulatory scheme, but, by combining an administrative inter-delegation[8] with referential legislation (which is the topic of the next section of this chapter), a federal responsibility can be entirely remitted to the discretion of the provincial Legislature.[9]

IV. REFERENTIAL LEGISLATION

§ 14:12 Incorporation by reference

Incorporation by reference is a technique which is occasionally used by legislative bodies, especially where it is desired to enact the same law as another jurisdiction.[1] Instead of repeating in full the desired rules, the drafter may simply incorporate by reference, or adopt, the rules of

---

[7]W.R. Lederman, "Some Forms and Limitations of Cooperative Federalism" (1967) 45 Can. Bar Rev. 409, 427.

[8]Administrative inter-delegations were upheld in *R. v. Wilson* (1980), 119 D.L.R. (3d) 558 (B.C. C.A.) (federal power over young offenders delegated to the provincial Lieutenant Governor in Council); *Peralta v. Ont.*, [1988] 2 S.C.R. 1045 (federal power over fishing delegated to provincial minister); *R. v. S.(S)*, [1990] 2 S.C.R. 254 (federal power over diversion programmes for young offenders delegated to provincial Attorney General); *R. v. Furtney*, [1991] 3 S.C.R. 89 (federal power over gaming delegated to provincial Lieutenant Governor in Council); *Jackson v. Ont.* (2009), 2 Admin. L.R. (5th) 248 (Ont. C.A.) (federal power over fishing delegated to provincial minister).

[9]*Coughlin v. Ont. Highway Transport Bd.*, [1968] S.C.R. 569; *Re Agricultural Products Marketing Act*, [1978] 2 S.C.R. 1198, 1222–1226; *Martin v. Alta.*, [2014] 1 S.C.R. 546, 2014 SCC 25; and see discussion accompanying § 14:13 note 2, below. The constitutional rule is not a prohibition of the inter-delegation of "legislative" power, as the Ontario Court of Appeal wrongly assumed in *Re Peralta* (1985), 49 O.R. (2d) 705 (C.A.); affirmed under name *Peralta v. Ont.*, [1988] 2 S.C.R. 1045. What is prohibited is the inter-delegation of any kind of power, including administrative power, to a primary law-making body—the Parliament or a Legislature. What is permitted is the inter-delegation of any kind of power, including "legislative" power, to a body or official other than a primary law-making body: *R. v. Furtney*, [1991] 3 S.C.R. 89, 104 (upholding federal delegation to Lieutenant Governor in Council, regardless of whether delegated power is "administrative" or "legislative"); *Jackson v. Ont.* (2009), 2 Admin. L.R. (5th) 248 (Ont. C.A.), para. 48 (upholding federal delegation to provincial minister regardless of characterization of delegated power; *Peralta* disapproved on this point).

[Section 14:12]

[1]Where the incorporating legislative body is under an obligation to enact statutes

another jurisdiction. The leading case on the validity of this technique is *A.-G. Ont. v. Scott* (1956),[2] where the Supreme Court of Canada upheld an Ontario statute which provided for the enforcement in Ontario of orders to pay maintenance obtained in England (and some other foreign jurisdictions) by wives who were resident in England against husbands who were resident in Ontario. Section 5(2) of the Ontario statute provided that in proceedings to enforce a foreign maintenance order the husband was entitled "to raise any defence that he might have raised in the original proceedings [in England] had he been a party thereto". In other words, the Ontario Legislature, instead of itself specifying the defences which were available in Ontario to the husband, was accepting whatever defences were specified by the Parliament of the United Kingdom. The Supreme Court of Canada held that this provision was valid. Their lordships denied that there was a delegation involved; all that was involved was the incorporation or adoption of certain English laws into Ontario law.

§ 14:13 Anticipatory incorporation by reference

In *Scott*, the Court recognized, but did not attach particular importance to, the fact that the Ontario statute adopted not only the English rules in existence at the time of the enactment of the Ontario statute, but the English rules in existence from time to time in the future. Yet the "anticipatory" character of the incorporation makes the Ontario statute difficult to distinguish from a delegation. The effect of the Ontario statute is that, whenever the Parliament of the United Kingdom alters the laws of England governing defences to maintenance applications, it also alters the law of Ontario. It is important to notice, however, that even if *Scott* were treated as a case of delegation, the result would not necessarily be wrong. As Laskin pointed out in his casebook, the *Nova Scotia Inter-delegation* case did not say anything about the validity of a delegation to a non-Canadian legislative body. Since such a delegation would not disturb the federal distribution of powers, one might well assume that the *Hodge* doctrine would operate to validate the delegation.[1] The distinction between anticipatory incorporation and delegation would only become significant if it were the enactments of another Canadian legislative body which had been incorporated.

It was not long before the Supreme Court of Canada was confronted with this latter case. Once again, some background may be helpful to appreciate the problem which the various governments were attempting

---

in both official languages, the general rule is that the incorporated instrument must also be in both languages: see ch. 56, Language, under heading § 56:7, "Incorporation by reference".

[2] *A.-G. Ont. v. Scott*, [1956] S.C.R. 137.

[Section 14:13]

[1] Laskin, Canadian Constitutional Law (5th ed., 1986 by Finkelstein), 43. Compare *Coughlin v. Ont. Highway Transport Bd.*, [1968] S.C.R. 569, 584.

to solve. In *A.-G. Ont. v. Winner* (1954),[2] the Privy Council decided that the provinces had no power to regulate motor carrier services which extended beyond the limits of the province. This was an inconvenient decision, because the regulation of motor carriers in Canada, both intraprovincial and interprovincial, was in fact wholly provincial; and the federal government did not have the administrative or physical facilities to assume the task of regulating the interprovincial and international carriers.

The federal government, after conferring with the provinces, decided to avoid the *Winner* decision altogether. In order to do so, it secured the enactment by the federal Parliament of the Motor Vehicle Transport Act. This Act, which was a model of brevity as well as constitutional ingenuity, simply provided that extra-provincial carriers operating in a province had to obtain a licence from the provincial transport board. The provincial transport board, in licensing extra-provincial carriers, was to do so "upon the like terms and conditions and in the like manner as if the extra-provincial undertaking operated in the province were a local undertaking". In this way, the federal Parliament not only delegated the unwanted regulatory power back to the provincial transport boards, but directed them to apply the provincial laws in existence from time to time. This was an administrative inter-delegation coupled with an anticipatory incorporation by reference. Was it valid?

In *Coughlin v. Ontario Highway Transport Board* (1968),[3] a majority of the Supreme Court of Canada, in an opinion written by Cartwright J., held that the federal Motor Vehicle Transport Act was valid. The delegation to the provincial transport boards was valid on the authority of *P.E.I. Potato Marketing Board v. Willis.*[4] The anticipatory incorporation by reference was valid on the authority of *A.-G. Ont. v. Scott.*[5] The latter point involved taking *Scott* at its face value, namely, as authority for the proposition that anticipatory incorporation by reference is not delegation. Only Ritchie J., who (with Martland J.) dissented, attempted to penetrate through the form of the statute to its substance. He pointed out that there would "be no objection to Parliament enacting a statute in which *existing* provincial legislation is incorporated by reference so as to obviate the necessity of re-enacting it verbatim"; but in this case Parliament had "adopted the provisions of the provincial statutes in question as they may be amended from time to time".[6] In Ritchie J.'s view, the result of this so-called adoption was a delegation of the kind condemned in the *Nova Scotia Inter-delegation* case: the federal Parliament had "left the power to exercise control of the licensing of extra-provincial

[2] *A.-G. Ont. v. Winner*, [1954] A.C. 541.

[3] *Coughlin v. Ontario Highway Transport Board*, [1968] S.C.R. 569.

[4] *P.E.I. Potato Marketing Board v. Willis*, [1952] 2 S.C.R. 392.

[5] *A.-G. Ont. v. Scott*, [1956] S.C.R. 137.

[6] *Coughlin v. Ontario Highway Transport Board*, [1968] S.C.R. 569, 582–583.

undertakings to be regulated in such manner as the Province might from time to time determine".[7]

The majority of the Court in *Coughlin* did not attempt to meet Ritchie J.'s argument. They said that the difference between this case and *Nova Scotia Inter-delegation* was "too obvious to require emphasis",[8] but they did not explain what the difference was. Certainly, *Coughlin* enables *Nova Scotia Inter-delegation* to be readily evaded. Instead of the federal Parliament delegating directly to the provincial Legislature (or vice versa), the federal Parliament simply delegates to an agency of the provincial Legislature and directs that agency to apply provincial law.[9] The trading of powers which was condemned in *Nova Scotia Inter-delegation* can easily be accomplished by the *Coughlin* technique.[10] What *Nova Scotia Inter-delegation* said could not be done directly, *Coughlin* now allows to be done indirectly.[11]

§ 14:14 Independent validity of incorporated law

There is nevertheless an important (if not "obvious") difference between *Coughlin* and *Nova Scotia Inter-delegation*. The provincial legislation which was incorporated by reference in *Coughlin* was (or would be in the future) enacted by the provincial Legislature within its competence and for its own purposes, namely, to regulate intraprovincial carriers; the provincial legislation was not created just for the federal purpose of regulating extra provincial carriers. Thus Laskin, in summarizing the result of the decisions, says: "There is no unconstitutional delegation

---

[7]*Coughlin v. Ontario Highway Transport Board*, [1968] S.C.R. 569, 584.

[8]*Coughlin v. Ontario Highway Transport Board*, [1968] S.C.R. 569, 575.

[9]This technique reached its nadir in *Re Agricultural Products Marketing Act*, [1978] 2 S.C.R. 1198, where ten provincial marketing boards (and a federal board) drew powers from both levels of government. Laskin C.J. in a concurring opinion (at pp. 1222–1226) held that the provincial boards could be directed to apply provincial law, or could be given federal authority to make regulations which differed from province to province; there was no "constitutional requirement in the delegation of authority that standards be fixed by Parliament" (p. 1226). Pigeon J.'s short opinion for the majority (he said at p. 1289 that he was "pressed for time") agreed (at p. 1290) with Laskin C.J.'s conclusion on the delegation point, and clearly agreed with the substance of the reasoning. As one of the counsel in the case, I can testify to the impossibility of tracing the lines of responsibility for many of the decisions of the marketing boards back to one level of government or the other. This combination of administrative inter-delegation and anticipatory incorporation by reference has become the model for other national marketing plans, and its validity was reaffirmed in *Federation des producteurs v. Pelland*, [2005] 1 S.C.R. 292.

[10]E.g., Government Employees Compensation Act, R.S.C. 1985, s. 4, which grants to federal government employees entitlement to workers' compensation "at the same rate and under the same conditions as are provided under the law of the province where the employee is usually employed", and delegates to the workers' compensation board of that province the power to determine claims for compensation; in *Martin v. Alta.*, [2014] 1 S.C.R. 546, 2014 SCC 25, it was held that the eligibility to workers' compensation of a federal government employee employed in Alberta was to be determined by the Alberta workers' compensation board, applying Alberta law and policy; denial of eligibility by the board was upheld.

[11]See K. Lysyk, Comment (1969) 47 Can. Bar Rev. 271.

involved where there is no enlargement of the legislative authority of the referred legislature, but rather a borrowing of provisions which are within its competence and which were enacted for its own purposes, and which the referring legislature could have validly spelled out for its own purposes".[1] In effect, what is being insisted upon is that the legislation which is incorporated by reference should have a validity and significance independent of the scheme of delegation.[2] This element was present in *Coughlin*, because the provincial transportation laws were enacted within provincial competence to regulate intraprovincial carriers. This being so, they could also be "borrowed" by the federal Parliament to regulate interprovincial carriers. In *Nova Scotia Inter-delegation*, by contrast, it was contemplated that the legislative bodies to which powers were delegated would each enact laws which would apart from the delegation be outside their competence, and which were solely for the purpose of carrying out the pension plan scheme.

The ratio decidendi of *Nova Scotia Inter-delegation* may also be understood by looking at the case from the standpoint of the primary legislative body that is the *recipient* of the power. What *Nova Scotia Inter-delegation* decides is that the powers of a primary legislative body cannot be enlarged by delegation from another legislative body. The scheme of legislative inter-delegation that was struck down in *Nova Scotia Inter-delegation* contemplated that the federal Parliament and provincial Legislatures would each acquire by delegation the power to do something that was not authorized by ss. 91 and 92 of the Constitution Act, 1867. The schemes that were upheld in *Willis* and *Coughlin* did not contemplate that the Legislature of Prince Edward Island (in *Willis)* or the Legislature of Ontario (in *Coughlin)* would enact a law that went beyond the powers granted by s. 92.[3] The legal test is captured by this question: does the scheme of inter-delegation purport to enlarge the powers of one of the primary legislative bodies? If the answer is yes, the scheme is an invalid legislative inter-delegation (as in *Nova Scotia Inter-delegation)*. If the answer is no, the scheme is a valid administra-

---

[Section 14:14]

[1]Laskin, Canadian Constitutional Law (5th ed., 1986 by Finkelstein), 43; accord, E.A. Driedger, "The Interaction Of Federal and Provincial Laws" (1976) 54 Can. Bar Rev. 695, 709.

[2]Compare the doctrine of "facts of independent significance" which has been recognized by American writers on the law of wills; such facts do not need to satisfy the rules for a valid incorporation by reference: see T.E. Atkinson, Law of Wills (West, 2nd ed., 1953), 394.

[3]Note, however, that in practice if not in theory the federal adoption of provincial law in the federal Motor Vehicle Transport Act (the Act upheld in *Coughlin)* does enlarge the powers of the provincial Legislatures. In *R. v. Smith*, [1972] S.C.R. 359, the Court upheld the Alberta transport board's policy of discriminating between local truckers and extraprovincial truckers. In *National Freight Consultants v. Motor Transport Bd.*, [1980] 2 S.C.R. 621, the Court upheld the Alberta transport board's restriction on a trucking activity in British Columbia. The federal adoption enabled Alberta law to discriminate against interprovincial transportation in *Smith*, and to have extraterritorial effect in *National Freight Consultants.* Query whether these cases are rightly decided.

tive inter-delegation (as in *Willis* and *Coughlin*) or a valid incorporation by reference (as in *Scott* and *Coughlin*).[4]

V. CONDITIONAL LEGISLATION

§ 14:15 Conditions as delegations

There is no doubt that the Parliament or a Legislature may make the application of its legislation conditional on the doing of some act or the happening of some event. It is very common, for example, for a statute to provide that it shall come into force on a date to be fixed by proclamation of the Governor in Council or the Lieutenant Governor in Council. Such a provision is undoubtedly valid as a condition to the operation of the legislation.[1]

In *Siemens v. Manitoba* (2003),[2] Manitoba had enacted the Gaming Control Local Option (VLT) Act, which authorized municipalities to hold a plebiscite to ban video lottery terminals from the municipality. If, in any municipality, such a plebiscite was held, and a ban on video lottery terminals was approved by a majority of the electors, the Act prohibited video lottery gaming in the municipality. The effect of the Act was to make the plebiscite binding, because approval by the electors automatically triggered the prohibition on video lottery gaming. The Act was challenged as an unlawful grant of legislative power to municipal electors. The Supreme Court of Canada held that the Act was valid "conditional legislation". The prohibition of video lottery gaming had been properly enacted by the Legislature, and had been made conditional on the approval by the electors of each municipality. The Court pointed out that Canada had a long history of "local option" legislation, usually related to the sale of alcohol, and there was no doubt of the competence of legislative bodies to make the application of legislation conditional on the approval of municipal electors.[3]

Where the fulfilment of the condition requires the action of some

---

[4]The anticipatory incorporation by reference in s. 88 of the Indian Act, which is discussed in detail in ch. 28, Aboriginal Peoples, under heading §§ 28:13 to 28:16, "Section 88 of the Indian Act", was upheld in *Dick v. The Queen*, [1985] 2 S.C.R. 309. See also *R. v. Francis*, [1988] 1 S.C.R. 1025 (upholding Indian Reserve Traffic Regulation that incorporated provincial traffic laws); *R. v. Furtney*, [1991] 3 S.C.R. 89, 105 (upholding Criminal Code provision that incorporated provincial gaming laws); *Wewaykum Indian Band v. Can.*, [2002] 4 S.C.R. 245, para. 116 (upholding Federal Court Act provision that incorporated provincial limitation statutes). For further examples, see E.A. Driedger, "The Interaction Of Federal and Provincial Laws" (1976) 54 Can. Bar Rev. 695, 708–713 and National Energy Board Act, R.S.C. 1985, c. N-7, s. 114, enacted to overcome *Campbell-Bennett v. Comstock Midwestern*, [1954] S.C.R. 207. With respect to the requirement of bilingual enactment in s. 133 of the Constitution Act, 1867, see ch. 56, Language, under heading § 56:7, "Incorporation by reference".

[Section 14:15]

[1]The most dramatic example of a law which is conditional upon proclamation was the War Measures Act and is now the Emergencies Act, S.C. 1988, c. 29.

[2]*Siemens v. Manitoba*, [2003] 1 S.C.R. 6. Major J. wrote the opinion of the Court.

[3]*Siemens v. Manitoba*, [2003] 1 S.C.R. 6, para. 40. The Canada Temperance Act, which is conditional on local adoption by electors, was upheld in *Russell v. The Queen*

person or body, such as the Governor in Council or Lieutenant Governor in Council, it is obvious that the conditional law also delegates a power to the actor—the power to bring the legislation into force. Sometimes the power delegated in the form of a condition is akin to a power to legislate. In the *Breathalyzer Reference* (1970),[4] a federal statute provided that "this Act or any of the provisions of this Act shall come into force on a day or days to be fixed by proclamation". The Supreme Court of Canada held that this condition enabled the Governor in Council to proclaim in force the part of the Act which provided for the compulsory taking of breath samples from drivers, and to except from the proclamation the part of the Act which stipulated that the suspected driver be provided with a sample. In a case of this kind, the civil libertarian issue must turn on the meaning of the condition in the statute. If the language of the statute authorizes the Governor in Council to proclaim in force the main obligation without the safeguard, then there is the end of the case. The *Hodge* doctrine[5] makes clear that, as a matter of constitutional law, such a delegation of power is within the competence of the Canadian legislative bodies.

§ 14:16 Conditions as administrative inter-delegations

Conditional legislation may raise a constitutional issue where the laws of one level of government are conditional upon the actions of another level of government. Here there is the potential of an argument that the condition is in truth an invalid federal inter-delegation. But the scope which has been allowed to federal inter-delegation by the cases discussed in the preceding sections of this chapter makes clear that even "interjurisdictional conditions" are usually valid. For example, there is no reason to doubt the validity of a federal law which comes into force in each province[1] upon a proclamation by the Lieutenant Governor of the province.[2] This is a delegation of power from the federal Parliament to the executive branch of the provincial government,[3] but the federal inter-delegation cases which have been discussed make clear that the

(1882), 7 App. Cas. 829, 835, where it was described as "conditional legislation", and upheld again in *A. G. Ont. v. Can. Temperance Federation*, [1946] A.C. 193.

[4] *Re Criminal Law Amendment Act, 1968–69*, [1970] S.C.R. 777.

[5] *Hodge v. The Queen* (1883), 9 App. Cas. 117.

[Section 14:16]

[1] A federal law need not be uniformly applicable throughout Canada, but may apply in some provinces and not others: ch. 17, Peace, Order and Good Government, under heading § 17:4, "Definition of national concern".

[2] *Ex parte Kleinys* (1965), 49 D.L.R. (2d) 225 (B.C. S.C.) upheld such a delegation; see also *Re Anti-Inflation Act*, [1976] 2 S.C.R. 373, 431; compare *R. v. Burah* (1878), 3 App. Cas. 889 (India).

[3] *Re Anti-Inflation Act*, [1976] 2 S.C.R. 373, 430–436, while holding that the Anti-Inflation Act could not be brought into force in the provincial public sector by an agreement with the provincial government which was unauthorized by provincial legislation, did not doubt that the federal Parliament could by apt language make its laws applicable in a province subject to a condition to be satisfied by the provincial government.

only delegation which is inadmissible is to the legislative branch of the provincial government— the one struck down in the *Nova Scotia Inter-delegation* case.[4]

§ 14:17 Conditions as legislative inter-delegations

Closer to the forbidden territory marked out by *Nova Scotia Inter-delegation* are the cases where a federal law is conditional upon the existence of a provincial law. In *Gold Seal v. Dominion Express Co.* (1921),[1] the Supreme Court of Canada upheld a federal law which prohibited the importation of liquor into any province where its sale for beverage purposes was prohibited by provincial law. Under this provision, the applicability of the federal law would depend upon whether the provincial Legislature enacted or repealed a liquor prohibition law. But presumably the Court's decision to uphold the federal law could be justified on the same ground as the incorporation by reference in *Coughlin*, that is to say, any such provincial law would have independent validity and significance.[2] The federal law did not purport to enlarge the powers of the provincial Legislatures.[3]

In *Lord's Day Alliance of Canada v. A.-G. B.C.* (1959),[4] however, the Supreme Court of Canada did in my opinion sanction conditional federal legislation which had the effect of enlarging the powers of the provincial Legislatures. The federal Lord's Day Act (like the motor carrier legislation enacted after *Winner)* was enacted to overcome an inconvenient decision of the Privy Council. The decision was *A.-G. Ont. v. Hamilton Street Railway* (1903),[5] in which the Privy Council struck down Ontario's Lord's Day Act, on the basis that the prohibition of work on Sundays was a "criminal law" within exclusive federal jurisdiction under s. 91(27) of the Constitution Act, 1867. Before this decision, it had been widely assumed that Sunday observance was within provincial competence as a matter of "property and civil rights in the province" (s. 92(13)) or as a matter of a "merely local or private nature in the province" (s. 92(16)). Several provinces had Sunday observance statutes, and the Dominion had none. After the decision, the federal Parliament came under pressure to fill the void, and it exercised the jurisdiction thrust upon it with the same ingenuity which characterized the *post-Winner* scheme many years later. The federal Lord's Day Act of 1906 prohibited various activi-

---

[4] *A.-G. N.S. v. A.-G. Can.* (Nova Scotia Inter-delegation) [1951] S.C.R. 31.

[Section 14:17]

[1] *Gold Seal v. Dominion Express Co.* (1921), 62 S.C.R. 424.

[2] § 14:14 note 2 and accompanying text, above.

[3] See also *Siemens v. Man.*, [2003] 1 S.C.R. 6, para. 35 (Criminal Code prohibited gaming except where a lottery scheme had been established by a province; Court upheld under s. 92(13) or s. 92(16) provincial law regulating lotteries that operated to suspend Criminal Code prohibition).

[4] *Lord's Day Alliance of Canada v. A.-G. B.C.*, [1959] S.C.R. 497.

[5] *A.-G. Ont. v. Hamilton Street Railway*, [1903] A.C. 524; on Sunday observance laws, see ch. 18, Criminal Law.

ties on Sunday,[6] but the principal sections each allowed individual provinces to "opt out" of the prohibition if they chose. Thus s. 6 provided: "It is not lawful for any person, on the Lord's Day, *except as provided in any provincial Act or law now or hereafter in force*, to engage in any public game . . . at which any fee is charged . . . for admission . . .".

The opting-out clause, which I have italicized, appeared to be an invitation to the provinces to reassume the jurisdiction which had been denied them in *Hamilton Street Railway*. What was its true effect? Was it an inadmissible delegation to the provincial Legislatures of the federal power to enact criminal law? Or was it something else, which was admissible under the Constitution? In the *Lord's Day Alliance* case, it was necessary to determine the validity of a British Columbia bill which proposed to amend the Vancouver Charter to allow the City of Vancouver by by-law to permit fee-paying spectator sport on Sunday afternoons. The Supreme Court of Canada held unanimously that the proposed provincial statute was valid. In Rand J.'s words, the opting-out clause was "a condition of fact in relation to which Parliament itself has provided a limitation for its own legislative Act."[7]

The description of the opting-out clause in the Lord's Day Act as "a condition"[8] does not eliminate the possibility that it is also an invalid inter-delegation. The question remains: does the provincial law have independent provincial validity and significance? If it does not—if it is merely derivative from the Lord's Day Act—then consistently with *Nova Scotia Inter-delegation* it cannot be effective. The judges of the Supreme Court of Canada were obviously troubled by this question. However, they decided that the law permitting Sunday sport was within provincial competence, either as a law in relation to property and civil rights in the province (s. 92(13)), or as a law in relation to matters of a merely local or private nature in the province (s. 92(16)).

In my view, the Court's classification of the law in *Lord's Day Alliance* cannot be supported. The *Hamilton Street Railway* case decided that a

[6]The basic prohibition was held to be a valid criminal law in *R. v. Big M Drug Mart*, [1985] 1 S.C.R. 295, but was held to be unconstitutional for breach of the Charter of Rights guarantee of freedom of religion.

[7]*Lord's Day Alliance of Canada v. A.-G. B.C.*, [1959] S.C.R. 497, 510; to the same effect, 503 per Kerwin C.J., 511 per Locke J.; see also *Lord's Day Alliance v. A.-G. Man.*, [1925] A.C. 384 (upholding another similar provision of the Lord's Day Act); *R. v. Morgentaler*, [1988] 1 S.C.R. 30 (upholding in question 5 of reference Criminal Code provision for provincial law to permit abortions); J.A. Osborne and C.S. Campbell, "Recent Amendments to Lottery and Gaming Laws" (1988) 26 Osgoode Hall L.J. 19 (discussing Criminal Code provision for provincial law to permit lotteries).

[8]Another way of looking at the opting-out clause is to treat it as a "waiver of paramountcy": see Ontario Law Reform Commission, *Report on Sunday Observance Legislation* (1970), 279. The theory is that there are two inconsistent valid laws, the permissive provincial law and the prohibitory federal law. Apart from the opting-out clause, the federal law would override the provincial law by the doctrine of federal paramountcy. The opting-out clause however avoids this result by waiving paramountcy, and allowing the provincial law to override the federal. There seems no reason to doubt that the federal Parliament can if it chooses waive its paramountcy in a field where concurrent federal and provincial laws are possible.

Sunday observance law was a criminal law, exclusively within federal competence. That unfortunate ruling (which had been reaffirmed by the Supreme Court of Canada in the *Henry Birks* case of 1955)[9] was accepted without reservation by the Court in *Lord's Day Alliance.* If the making of a Sunday observance law is a matter of criminal law outside provincial competence, then the repealing of a Sunday observance law is equally a matter of criminal law outside provincial competence. To be sure, the British Columbia statute did not purport directly to repeal part of the Lord's Day Act, but its sole purpose was to lift from the people of Vancouver the criminal prohibition imposed by the Lord's Day Act. If the criminal prohibition had not existed, no amendment to the Vancouver Charter would have been needed or desired. The amendment had no significance except as a removal of a criminal prohibition. This is outside provincial competence as surely as the imposition of a criminal prohibition.

The conclusion is that *Lord's Day Alliance* is inconsistent with *Nova Scotia Inter-delegation*, because in *Lord's Day Alliance* the federal statute was in effect held to enlarge the powers of the provincial Legislatures.[10]

VI. DELEGATION BY ACQUIESCENCE

§ 14:18 Delegation by acquiescence

What happens if the federal Parliament or a provincial Legislature oversteps its bounds by passing a law that is arguably outside the powers of the enacting body, but the assumption of jurisdiction is congenial to the other level of government, so that the other level of government never challenges the dubious law? If effective, this would be a de facto delegation from the acquiescing level of government to the enacting level of government. The short answer is that this kind of de facto delegation is normally ineffective.

The absence of challenge by the level of government whose powers have been encroached upon does not immunize the dubious law from judicial review. That is because any person potentially affected by a law may bring court proceedings to challenge the constitutional validity of the law. The likelihood is, therefore, that someone who would benefit from the striking down of the law will challenge its validity, and a court will have to review its validity. When that happens, the normal rules of judicial review have to be applied, and acquiescence by both levels of government is not a relevant consideration.[1] Since, as we have seen, an explicit delegation from one level of government to another is not permit-

[9] *Henry Birks & Sons v. Montreal*, [1955] S.C.R. 799.

[10] Accord, K. Lysyk, Comment (1969) 47 Can. Bar Rev. 271, 273; P.C. Weiler, "The Supreme Court and the Law of Canadian Federalism" (1973) 23 U. Toronto L.J. 307, 315; E.A. Driedger, "The Interaction Of Federal and Provincial Laws" (1976) 54 Can. Bar Rev. 695, 707.

[Section 14:18]

[1] A failure by one level of government to legislate to the full limit of its powers does

ted, obviously an implicit one is not permitted either. An early example of this is *Toronto Electric Commissioners v. Snider* (1925),[2] where the Privy Council in 1925 struck down a federal labour relations law that had been in force since 1907. The long period for which the Act had been in force, with the acquiescence of the provinces, did not affect the duty of the court "simply to interpret the British North America Act [the Constitution Act, 1867] and to decide whether the statute in question has been within the competence of the Dominion Parliament under the terms of s. 91 of that Act."[3] The Privy Council held that the regulation of labour relations was a matter within provincial, not federal, jurisdiction,[4] and the Act was accordingly invalid.

All that being said, the modern Supreme Court of Canada has occasionally acknowledged that, when a law has not been challenged by a government, but only by a private party, there is good reason for "bearing in mind the other level of government's position"[5] and being "cautious" before striking down the law.[6] This does not challenge the proposition that there can be no delegation by acquiescence, but it does articulate an understandable attitude of restraint in reviewing laws that are not challenged by (or are actively supported by) the other level of government.

VII. CONCLUSIONS ON FEDERAL INTER-DELEGATION

§ 14:19 Conclusions on federal inter-delegation

The decision in *Nova Scotia Inter-delegation* (1950) denied to the various Canadian legislative bodies the power to delegate their powers to each other. The reasoning to this conclusion was unpersuasive, and the conclusion was unfortunate as a matter of policy, since it denied to the Canadian federation a flexible means of constitutional adaptation. The cases which have been decided since 1950, especially, *Willis* (1952), *Scott* (1956), *Lord's Day Alliance* (1959) and *Coughlin* (1968), have reinstated federal inter-delegation as an important tool of cooperative federalism. Indeed, these cases invite the comment that the Canadian legislative bodies, through administrative inter-delegation, or referential legislation, or conditional legislation, or some mixture of these devices, may now do indirectly what they cannot do directly.

---

not augment the powers of the other level of government: *Union Colliery Co. v. Bryden*, [1899] A.C. 580, 588; ch. 15, Judicial Review on Federal Grounds, under heading § 15:23, "Exclusiveness".

[2]*Toronto Electric Commissioners v. Snider*, [1925] A.C. 394.

[3]*Toronto Electric Commissioners v. Snider*, [1925] A.C. 394, 398 per Viscount Haldane.

[4]Chapter 21, Property and Civil Rights, under heading §§ 21:10 to 21:11, "Labour relations".

[5]*Rothmans, Benson & Hedges v. Sask.*, [2005] 1 S.C.R. 188, para. 26 per Major J. for the Court.

[6]*R. v. Demers*, [2004] 2 S.C.R. 489, para. 28 per Iacobucci and Bastarache JJ. for majority (providing other references as well). For further discussion of this idea, see W.K. Wright, "Courts as Facilitators of Intergovernmental Dialogue: Cooperative Federalism and Judicial Review" (2016) 72 S.C.L.R. (2d) 365.

The only vestige of a prohibition against inter-delegation which now remains is the rule that one legislative body cannot enlarge the powers of another by authorizing the latter to enact laws which would have no significance and validity independent of the delegation. It is arguable that even this rule can no longer stand in the light of *Lord's Day Alliance*, because that case, according to my analysis (but not according to the Court's analysis), did sanction the enlargement by the federal Parliament of a province's legislative powers. However, since the judges in each of the later cases have been careful to acknowledge the continued viability of *Nova Scotia Inter-delegation*, and since no judge has pushed the analysis to the point of questioning the correctness of the decision, it may well be that the Supreme Court would be reluctant to overrule *Nova Scotia Inter-delegation.* Presumably, too, the Court is unlikely to be faced squarely with the issue, since the inter-delegations of the near future are more likely to tread the safe paths formed by the later cases than they are to take the riskier course of direct legislative inter-delegation with its unavoidable challenge to the correctness of *Nova Scotia Inter-delegation.*

Part II

DISTRIBUTION OF POWER

Chapter 15

Judicial Review on Federal Grounds

I. SCOPE OF CHAPTER

§ 15:1 Scope of chapter

II. PRIORITY BETWEEN FEDERAL AND CHARTER GROUNDS

§ 15:2 Priority between federal and Charter grounds

III. PROCEDURE AND REASONING OF JUDICIAL REVIEW

§ 15:3 Procedure of judicial review
§ 15:4 Reasoning of judicial review

IV. CHARACTERIZATION OF LAWS

§ 15:5 "Matter"
§ 15:6 Singling out
§ 15:7 Double aspect
§ 15:8 Purpose
§ 15:9 Effect
§ 15:10 Efficacy
§ 15:11 Colourability
§ 15:12 Criteria of choice
§ 15:13 Presumption of constitutionality

V. SEVERANCE; READING DOWN

§ 15:14 Severance
§ 15:15 Reading down

VI. INTERJURISDICTIONAL IMMUNITY

§ 15:16 Definition of interjurisdictional immunity
§ 15:17 Federally-incorporated companies
§ 15:18 Federally-regulated undertakings
§ 15:19 Other federal matters

§ 15:20 Rationale of interjurisdictional immunity
§ 15:21 Provincial subjects

VII. INTERPRETATION OF CONSTITUTION

§ 15:22 Relevance
§ 15:23 Exclusiveness
§ 15:24 Ancillary power
§ 15:25 Concurrency
§ 15:26 Exhaustiveness
§ 15:27 Progressive interpretation
§ 15:28 Unwritten constitutional principles
§ 15:29 Legislative history
§ 15:30 Precedent

I. SCOPE OF CHAPTER

§ 15:1 Scope of chapter

This chapter is the beginning of Part II of the book, which is devoted to the distribution of powers. Chapter 5, Federalism, has already introduced the principal ideas of a federal constitution. As has been explained, it is the distribution of powers between a central authority (in Canada, the federal Parliament) and regional authorities (in Canada, the provincial Legislatures) that constitutes the essence of a federal constitution. That distribution of powers has to be contained in a written constitution that is binding on the central and regional authorities, and is unalterable by the unilateral action of either of them. Thus the Constitution of Canada (like all other federal constitutions) defines the kinds of laws that may be enacted by the federal Parliament and the kinds of laws that may be enacted by each provincial Legislature. When a question arises whether the federal Parliament or a provincial Legislature has enacted a law that comes within the Constitution's definition of the powers allocated to the enacting body, an authoritative answer to that question can be provided only by the courts. This is the justification for judicial review of legislation, which is the power to determine whether any particular law is valid or invalid. The law is valid (intra vires) if the court finds that the law was enacted within the powers allocated by the Constitution to whichever legislative body enacted the law, and the law is invalid (ultra vires) if the court finds that the law was enacted outside the powers allocated to the enacting body.

The history and rationale of judicial review of legislation in Canada have been examined in chapter 5, Federalism. This chapter will examine the doctrines, the techniques and the language employed by the courts in carrying out their function of judicial review.

The constitutional provisions distributing power between the federal Parliament and the provincial Legislatures are not the only restraints on legislative power in Canada. As has been explained in ch. 12, Parliamentary Sovereignty, there are other kinds of restraints as well, and the most important of these is the Charter of Rights. These other restraints also give rise to judicial review of legislation. However, this chapter, and indeed the whole of Part II of the book, is confined to judicial review on federal grounds (or distribution-of-powers grounds), because a distinctive set of doctrines, techniques and language has accumulated around this branch of judicial review. Judicial review on Charter grounds will be examined separately in chapter 36, Charter of Rights, which is in Part III of the book, Civil Liberties.

II. PRIORITY BETWEEN FEDERAL AND CHARTER GROUNDS

§ 15:2 Priority between federal and Charter grounds

When a law is challenged on both federal and Charter grounds, does the Constitution accord priority to one ground over the other?

It must be conceded that this question has little practical significance, since s. 52 of the Constitution Act, 1982 makes clear that a law that is contrary to any provision of the Constitution of Canada is "of no force or effect". Both the federal distribution of powers and the Charter of Rights are part of the "Constitution of Canada".[1] A successful challenge to a law on the federal ground that the law is outside the authority of the enacting legislative body is attended by the same consequence of invalidity as a successful challenge on the Charter ground that the law contravenes a provision of the Charter of Rights.

Nevertheless, it is, I think, meaningful and accurate to assert that the provisions of the Constitution distributing powers to the federal Parliament and the provincial Legislatures are logically prior to the Charter of Rights. These provisions create the powers that are exercisable by Canadian legislative bodies. It is impossible for a nation to be governed without bodies possessing legislative powers, but it is possible for a nation to be governed without a Charter of Rights. The Charter of Rights assumes the existence of legislative powers, although admittedly it imposes limits on those powers. I conclude that the argument that a law is invalid because it is outside the powers conferred on the enacting body by the federal part of the Constitution is a prior, or more radical, argument than the argument that a law is invalid because it offends a prohibition contained in the Charter of Rights.[2] In other words, in reviewing the validity of a law, the first question is whether the law is

[Section 15:2]

[1]The phrase is defined in s. 52(2); the definition is discussed in ch. 1, Sources, under heading § 1:4, "Constitution of Canada".

[2]Accord, *Westendorp v. The Queen*, [1983] 1 S.C.R. 43, 46 per Laskin C.J. J.D. Whyte, "Developments in Constitutional Law: the 1982–83 Term" (1984) 6 Supreme Court L.R. 49, 55–56 criticizes this dictum on the ground that Canada's constitutional law has never hitherto ranked arguments in order of precedence. A possible answer to Professor Whyte is that Canada's constitutional law has never hitherto had a Charter of Rights, and judicial review has hitherto rarely been faced with two different kinds of invalidating constitutional provisions applicable to a single law.

within the law-making power of the enacting body, and the second question is whether the law is consistent with the Charter of Rights.

This way of comparing the status of the federal part of the Constitution with the Charter of Rights finds support in the language of s. 32(1) of the Charter of Rights. Section 32(1) is the provision that makes the Charter applicable to the federal Parliament and the provincial Legislatures.[3] It provides as follows:

> **32.**(1) This Charter applies
>
> (a) to the Parliament and government of Canada in respect of all matters within the authority of Parliament including all matters relating to the Yukon Territory and Northwest Territories; and
>
> (b) to the legislature and government of each province in respect of matters within the authority of the legislature of each province.

At first reading, the language of s. 32 seems unduly prolix. What is the force of the phrase "in respect of all matters within the authority of" the Parliament or the Legislature? The answer is that the quoted phrase limits the application of the Charter to laws within the distribution-of-powers authority of the Parliament or the Legislature. Thus, the Charter does not apply to a law that is ultra vires on federal grounds; such a law is invalid, of course, but only for breach of the power-distributing provisions of the Constitution; it cannot also be invalid for breach of the Charter. In other words, where there is a distribution-of-powers argument and a Charter argument for the invalidity of a law, the arguments cannot both be successful.

If I am right that a federal ground of judicial review takes priority over a Charter ground, all that this means is that an argument based on a Charter ground should be framed as an alternative, not an addition, to an argument based on a federal ground. The priority of the federal ground does not mean that a court deciding a constitutional case must always dispose of the federal issue before proceeding to the Charter issue. On the contrary, the court can and undoubtedly will do what it has always done in every kind of case, and, that is to decide the case on the ground that seems strongest to the court. Where the opposition to the law is primarily based on a civil libertarian value, and the law is invalid for breach of the Charter of Rights, there is no reason for the court to decide a more tenuous and difficult federalism issue. Even though the federalism issue would be the more fundamental defect were it decided against the law, there is no logical problem in the court deciding the case on the basis of the alternative Charter issue.

There is a well-known line of cases in which laws limiting free expression have been challenged on federal grounds. The challenged laws were: a law imposing on newspapers the obligation to publish a government reply to any criticism of a provincial government, a law restricting the distribution of literature on the streets, a law prohibiting the propagation of "communism or bolshevism", a law subjecting films to

[3]See ch. 37, Application of Charter.

censorship, and a law prohibiting all public assemblies for a short period of time.[4] These cases genuinely raised federal issues, because neither the text of the Constitution nor any underlying federal principle offers a clear or general answer to the question of which level of government has the authority to restrain the fundamental political freedoms. But commentators have been quick to point out that the results of some of the cases seemed to turn more on a judicial concern to protect freedom of speech than on an assessment of the federalism issues at stake. Paul Weiler has argued, for example, that the Supreme Court of Canada in the 1950s used doctrines of federalism as a kind of surreptitious bill of rights, allocating jurisdiction to that level of government that had not exercised it, in order to invalidate a law that the Court really believed should not have been enacted at all.[5] Now that the Charter of Rights is available as a ground of review, a denial of a fundamental political liberty can be frankly acknowledged as a ground of invalidity under s. 2 of the Charter. The difficult federal issue would not then have to be decided. Of course, if the court decided that the law did not violate the Charter, perhaps by virtue of justification under s. 1, then the federal issue would have to be decided: in that event the alternative road could not be by-passed.

Another point in favour of the logical priority of federalism issues over Charter issues is the presence in the Charter of Rights of the power of override. Section 33 of the Charter of Rights enables the Parliament or a Legislature to override most of the provisions of the Charter of Rights by including in a statute a declaration that the statute is to operate notwithstanding the relevant provision of the Charter of Rights.[6] Such a statute is then valid, despite the breach of the Charter of Rights. There is no similar saving provision for a breach of the federal distribution of powers. A law that is invalid for breach of the federal distribution of powers cannot be re-enacted by the enacting Parliament or Legislature (unless the Constitution is first amended).[7] On the other hand, such a law can be enacted by the other level of government: if by virtue of the federal distribution of powers a law is incompetent to the federal Parliament, the law can be enacted by the provincial Legislatures, and vice versa.[8] The limits of the Charter of Rights, by contrast, apply to both the federal Parliament and the provincial Legislatures. Whatever the Charter denies to one level of government is also denied to the other.

---

[4] The cases are described in ch. 43, Expression, under heading §§ 43:1 to 43:4, "Distribution of powers".

[5] P.C. Weiler, "The Supreme Court and the Law of Canadian Federalism" (1973) 23 U. Toronto L.J. 307, 342–352.

[6] See ch. 39, Override of Rights.

[7] An amendment of the federal distribution of powers would involve the cooperative action of Parliament and at least seven provincial Legislatures: see ch. 4, Amendment, under heading §§ 4:8 to 4:15, "General amending procedure (s. 38)".

[8] See ch. 12, Parliamentary Sovereignty, and § 15:26, "Exhaustiveness".

III. PROCEDURE AND REASONING OF JUDICIAL REVIEW

§ 15:3 Procedure of judicial review

The procedural and evidentiary rules respecting judicial review on federal grounds are mostly the same as those respecting judicial review on Charter grounds. They are dealt with in ch. 59, Procedure, and ch. 60, Proof. Those chapters discuss remedies, standing, mootness, ripeness, alternative grounds, notice to Attorneys General, intervention, legislative history and evidence.

§ 15:4 Reasoning of judicial review

In Canada the distribution of legislative power between the federal Parliament and the provincial Legislatures is mainly set out in ss. 91 and 92 of the Constitution Act, 1867.[1] Section 91 lists the kinds of laws that are competent to the federal Parliament; s. 92 lists the kinds of laws that are competent to the provincial Legislatures.[2] Both sections use a distinctive terminology, giving legislative authority in relation to "matters" coming within "classes of subjects". This terminology emphasizes and helps to describe the two steps involved in the process of judicial review:[3] the first step is to identify the "matter" (or pith and substance) of the challenged law; the second step is to assign the matter to one of the "classes of subjects" (or heads of legislative power).[4]Of course, neither of these two steps has any significance by itself. The

[Section 15:4]

[1]Other sections conferring legislative power include ss. 92A (added 1982), 93, 94, 94A (added 1951, revised 1964), 95, 101, 132 of the Constitution Act, 1867; ss. 2, 3, 4 of the Constitution Act, 1871; ss. 2, 3 of the Statute of Westminster, 1931.

[2]Canada's two lists of legislative powers may be contrasted with the Constitutions of the United States and Australia, which list only federal legislative powers, most of which are concurrent with a general, unenumerated state power. This means that the two-step process of judicial review described in the following text is not generally applicable to state laws in the United States and Australia: there are no enumerated classes into which state laws have to be fitted. Judicial review in Australia is compared with judicial review in Canada in Gilbert, Australian and Canadian Federalism 1867-1984 (1986).

[3]On the process of judicial review on federal grounds, see D.W. Mundell, "Tests for Validity of Legislation under the B.N.A. Act" (1954) 32 Can. Bar Rev. 813; B. Laskin, "Tests for Validity of Legislation: What's the 'Matter'?" (1955) 11 U. Toronto L.J. 114; D.W. Mundell, "Tests for Validity of Legislation: A Reply to Professor Laskin" (1955) 33 Can. Bar Rev. 915; W.R. Lederman in Lederman (ed.), The Courts and the Canadian Constitution (1964), 177; W.R. Lederman in Crépeau and Macpherson (eds.), The Future of Canadian Federalism (1965), 91; Browne, The Judicial Committee and the British North America Act (1967), passim; A.S. Abel, "What Peace, Order and Good Government?" (1968) 7 West. Ont. L. Rev. 1; A.S. Abel, "The Neglected Logic of 91 and 92" (1969) 19 U. Toronto L.J. 487; W.R. Lederman, "Unity and Diversity in Canadian Federalism" (1975) 53 Can. Bar Rev. 597.

[4]"What the process of constitutional adjudication involves is a distillation of the 'constitutional value' represented by challenged legislation (the 'matter' in relation to which it is enacted) and its attribution to a head of power (or 'class of subject')": Laskin, Canadian Constitutional Law (5th ed., 1986 by Finkelstein), 242.

challenged statute is characterized (or classified) as in relation to a "matter" (step 1) only to determine whether it is authorized by some head of power in the Constitution. The "classes of subjects" are interpreted (step 2) only to determine which one will accommodate the matter of a particular statute. The process is, in Laskin's words, "an interlocking one, in which the British North America Act and the challenged legislation react on one another and fix each other's meaning".[5] Nevertheless, for purposes of analysis it is necessary to recognize that two steps are involved: the characterization[6] of the challenged law (step 1) and the interpretation of the power-distributing provisions of the Constitution (step 2).

IV. CHARACTERIZATION OF LAWS

§ 15:5 "Matter"

The first step in judicial review is to identify the "matter" of the challenged law.[1] What is the "matter" of a law? Laskin says it is "a distillation of the 'constitutional value' represented by the challenged legislation";[2] Abel says it is "an abstract of the statute's content";[3] Lederman says it is "the true meaning of the challenged law";[4]Mundell says it is the answer to the question, "what in fact does the law do, and why?";[5] Beetz J. says it is "a name" for "the content or subject matter" of the

---

[5]B. Laskin, "Tests for Validity of Legislation: What's the 'Matter'?" (1955) 11 U. Toronto L.J. 114; D.W. Mundell, "Tests for Validity of Legislation: A Reply to Professor Laskin" (1955) 33 Can. Bar Rev. 915; Abel, "The Neglected Logic of 91 and 92" (1969) 19 U. Toronto L.J. 487.

[6]The term characterization or classification is used in two senses in constitutional writing. The sense used in this chapter is the identification of the "matter" (or pith and substance) of a challenged law (step 1). Sometimes, the term is used to refer to the entire process of judicial review, i.e., as including allocation of the matter to a class of subject or head of power (step 2). Both usages are sanctioned by good practice.

[Section 15:5]

[1]The challenged law is usually a single statute. The challenged law can be a regulation or bylaw or other form of delegated legislation, e.g., *A.-G. Man. v. Man. Egg & Poultry Assn.*, [1971] S.C.R. 689. The challenged law can be a statute and a regulation made under the statute, e.g., *R. v. Morgentaler (No. 3)*, [1993] 3 S.C.R. 463, 480, holding that a very general statute and a specific regulation "must be considered together for the purposes of constitutional characterization". The challenged law can take the form of a "legislative scheme" (as it is called in Australia) consisting of several related statutes. The challenged law can be part only of a statute: § 15:14 "Severance". The challenged law can also be "non-statutory", as with the significant aspects of Canadian maritime law that are drawn from precedent and custom: see § 15:5 note 23, below.

[2]§ 15:4 note 4, above.

[3]Abel, "The Neglected Logic of 91 and 92" (1969) 19 U. Toronto L.J. 487, 490.

[4]W.R. Lederman in Lederman (ed.), The Courts and the Canadian Constitution (1964), 186.

[5]D.W. Mundell, "Tests for Validity of Legislation: A Reply to Professor Laskin" (1955) 33 Can. Bar Rev. 915, 928. Gilbert, Australian and Canadian Federalism 1867-1984 (1986), 27, comments that the last two words of this quotation sum up the difference between Canadian and Australian characterization techniques; Australian judges do not ask "and why?".

law;[6] other judges have sometimes said that it is the "leading feature" or "true nature and character" or the "main thrust" of the law, but usually they have described it as "the pith and substance" of the law.[7] The general idea of these and similar formulations is that it is necessary to identify the dominant or most important characteristic of the challenged law.[8]

As emphasized earlier, the sole purpose of identifying the "matter" of a law is to determine whether the law is constitutional or not. In identifying the "matter" of the law, the Courts therefore tend to use concepts that will assist in determining to which head of power the "matter" should be alloccted.[9] For example, if a law were characterized as in relation to the regulation of insurance, then it would be clear that the law was competent only to the provinces because it is settled by precedent that the regulation of insurance is a matter coming within "property and civil rights in the province", which is a provincial class of subject (s. 92(13)). Indeed, sometimes the "matter" of a law will be described in the very language of a class of subject. For example, the federal Bank Act would undoubtedly be characterized as a law in relation to banking, making perfectly clear that it relates to a matter coming within "banking", which is a federal class of subject (s. 91(15)). The point is that the identification of the "matter" of a statute will often effectively settle the question of its validity, leaving the allocation of the matter to a class of subject little more than a formality.[10]

The difficulty in identifying the "matter" of a statute is that many statutes have one feature (or aspect) which comes within a provincial head of power and another which comes within a federal head of power. Clearly, the selection of one or the other feature as the "matter" of the statute will dispose of the case; equally clearly, the court in making its selection will be conscious of the ultimate result which is thereby dictated. Take the case of a provincial statute that imposes a direct tax on banks. One feature of this law is "direct taxation" which comes within

---

[6] *Re Anti-Inflation Act*, [1976] 2 S.C.R. 373, 450.

[7] The phrase "pith and substance" seems to have been first used in this context in *Union Colliery Co. v. Bryden*, [1899] A.C. 580, 587 per Lord Watson.

[8] Pith and substance is not relevant to judicial review on Charter grounds. For that purpose, one identifies the "purpose" and the "effect" of an impugned statute. If either the purpose or the effect of the statute is to abridge a Charter right, then the statute will be invalid, unless it is saved by s. 1: *R. v. Big M Drug Mart*, [1985] 1 S.C.R. 295, 331. See generally ch. 36, Charter of Rights, under heading § 36:12, "Characterization of laws".

[9] Note that a "matter" must be sufficiently specific to come within a class of subject: *Saumur v. Que.*, [1953] 2 S.C.R. 299, 333 per Rand J.; or, if it comes within the national concern branch of the peace, order, and good government power, sufficiently specific to serve as a limited, justiciable restraint on federal power: *Re Anti-Inflation Act*, [1976] 2 S.C.R. 373, 450–459 per Beetz J.; *R. v. Crown Zellerbach*, [1988] 1 S.C.R. 401, 432 per Le Dain J.

[10] Abel, "The Neglected Logic of 91 and 92" (1969) U. Toronto L.J. 487, 490, while not denying that this is what in fact occurs, argues that the courts should discern the "matter" of a statute in disregard of the effect of the characterization on constitutionality.

a provincial class of subject (s. 92(2)); but another feature of the law is banking which comes within a federal class of subject (s. 91(15)). If the law is in relation to direct taxation it is good, but if it is in relation to banking it is bad. How does the court make the crucial choice? Logic offers no solution: the law has both the relevant qualities and there is no logical basis for preferring one over the other. What the courts do in cases of this kind is to make a judgment as to which is the most important feature of the law and to characterize the law by that feature: that dominant feature is the "pith and substance" or "matter" of the law; the other feature is merely incidental, irrelevant for constitutional purposes.[11] In *Bank of Toronto v. Lambe* (1887),[12] the Privy Council upheld a provincial law which imposed a tax on banks. The dominant feature of the law was to raise revenue, and accordingly the "matter" of the law was taxation, not banking. This distinction is commonly expressed by using the phrase "in relation to", which appears in ss. 91 and 92. One would say of the impugned law in *Bank of Toronto v. Lambe* that it was "in relation to" taxation (the matter) and merely "affected" banking.

It is important to recognize that this "pith and substance" doctrine enables one level of government to enact laws with substantial impact on matters outside its jurisdiction. The levy of the tax in *Bank of Toronto v. Lambe* was, after all, a significant exercise of legislative power over the banks; but because the law was characterized as "in relation to" taxation (its pith and substance or matter), it could validly "affect" banking.[13] There are many examples of laws which have been upheld despite their "incidental" impact on matters outside the enacting body's jurisdiction. A provincial law in relation to insurance (provincial matter) may validly restrict or even stop the activities of federally-incorporated companies (federal matter); a provincial law reorganizing municipalities (provincial matter) may validly alter the interest payable on debt owed to out-of-province creditors (federal matter); a federal law in relation to navigation and shipping (federal matter) may validly regulate labour relations in a port (provincial matter); a federal law in relation to the national capital region (federal matter) may validly regulate land use in

[11] W.R. Lederman in Lederman (ed.), The Courts and the Canadian Constitution (1964), 188–189, 195–197.

[12] *Bank of Toronto v. Lambe* (1887), 12 App. Cas. 575.

[13] The same idea as that expressed by the contrasting "in relation to" and "affecting" has been expressed in terms of an "ancillary" doctrine, which is examined later in this chapter. A similar "trenching" doctrine has fallen into disuse: see *Papp v. Papp*, [1970] 1 O.R. 331, 335 per Laskin J.A.; Laskin, Canadian Constitutional Law (5th ed., 1986 by N. Finkelstein), 255; W.R. Lederman in Lederman (ed.), The Courts and the Canadian Constitution (1964), 197. In particular, the theory that laws passed under the peace, order, and good government power had a lesser capacity to "trench upon" provincial classes of subject is no longer accepted, and is contradicted by *Johannesson v. West St. Paul*, [1952] 1 S.C.R. 292 and *Munro v. National Capital Comm.*, [1966] S.C.R. 663.

Ontario and Quebec (provincial matter). These and other well-known cases are footnoted below.[14]

Needless to say, a different result follows if the pith and substance of the challenged law is adjudged to be a matter outside jurisdiction. *Bank of Toronto v. Lambe* may be contrasted with the *Alberta Bank Taxation Reference* (1938),[15] in which the Privy Council struck down an Alberta law which imposed a special tax solely on the banks. Their lordships concluded that the pith and substance of this particular law was to discourage the operation of the banks in Alberta. Its "matter" therefore came within "banking" and the taxing quality of the law was merely incidental. The province's power to tax could not save the law, because its pith and substance was not taxation.[16]

Another case like the *Alberta Bank Taxation Reference* is *Quebec v. Lacombe* (2010),[17] where a municipal by-law in Quebec prohibited the use of lakes as aerodromes. Land use zoning comes within provincial power over property and civil rights, and is typically delegated by provincial Legislatures to municipalities (as was the case here). In the normal course, therefore, a zoning law could have an incidental effect on a matter coming within federal jurisdiction, like aeronautics.[18] In the Supreme Court of Canada, that was the conclusion of two of the judges, who would have held that the by-law was effective to prohibit the use of a lake as an aerodrome for float planes. But the majority of the Court

[14]*Workmen's Comp. Bd. v. CPR*, [1920] A.C. 184 (workmen's compensation; international shipping; extraprovincial rights); *Lymburn v. Mayland*, [1932] A.C. 318 (securities regulation; federal companies); *Ladore v. Bennett*, [1939] A.C. 468 (municipal institutions; property outside province); *Johannesson v. West St. Paul*, [1952] 1 S.C.R. 292 (aeronautics; land use); *Stevedores Reference*, [1955] S.C.R. 529 (navigation and shipping; local labour relations); *A.-G. Ont. v. Barfried Enterprises*, [1963] S.C.R. 570 (unconscionable contracts; interest); *Oil, Chemical and Atomic Wkrs. v. Imperial Oil*, [1963] S.C.R. 584 (labour relations; federal elections); *Munro v. National Capital Comm.*, [1966] S.C.R. 663 (national capital region; land use); *Carnation Co. v. Que. Agricultural Marketing Bd.*, [1968] S.C.R. 238 (local marketing; interprovincial trade); *Walter v. A.-G. Alta.*, [1969] S.C.R. 383 (land use; religion); *Papp v. Papp*, [1970] 1 O.R. 331 (divorce; custody); *Can. Indemnity Co. v. A.-G. B.C.*, [1977] 2 S.C.R. 504 (insurance; trade and commerce; federal companies); *A.-G. Que. v. Kellogg's Co.*, [1978] 2 S.C.R. 211 (advertising for children; television); *Construction Montcalm v. Minimum Wage Comm.*, [1979] 1 S.C.R. 754 (minimum wage; airport); *Four B Manufacturing v. United Garment Workers*, [1980] 1 S.C.R. 1031 (labour relations; Indian reserve); *Consortium Developments v. Sarnia*, [1998] 3 S.C.R. 3 (local government; criminal law); *Re Firearms Act*, [2000] 1 S.C.R. 783 (gun control; criminal law; property); *Kitkatla Band v. B.C.*, [2002] 2 S.C.R. 146 (heritage property; Indian artifacts); *Can. Western Bank v. Alta.*, [2007] 2 S.C.R. 3 (insurance; banking); *Chatterjee v. Ont.*, [2009] 1 S.C.R. 624 (property; criminal law and procedure); *Can. v. PHS Community Services Society*, [2011] 3 S.C.R. 134, paras. 51–52 (criminal law; health services).

[15]*A.-G. Alta. v. A.-G. Can.* (Bank Taxation) [1939] A.C. 117.

[16]For criticism of the decision, see J.R. Mallory, "The Courts and the Sovereignty of the Canadian Parliament" (1944) 10 Can. J. Ec. & Pol. Sci. 165, 171–172.

[17]*Quebec v. Lacombe*, [2010] 2 S.C.R. 453. McLachlin C.J. wrote the opinion of the seven-judge majority. LeBel and Deschamps JJ. wrote dissenting opinions.

[18]Chapter 22, Transportation and Communication, under heading §§ 22:13 to 22:15, "Transportation by air".

held that the pith and substance of the by-law was in relation to aeronautics, not zoning, and the by-law was accordingly struck down because it was outside provincial (and therefore municipal) competence. A companion case was *Quebec v. Canadian Owners and Pilots Association* (2010),[19] where a provincial law prohibited non-agricultural uses of land zoned by the province as an "agricultural zone". Now the majority of the Court agreed that the law was a valid provincial law, because it was in relation to land use or agriculture. In the normal course, therefore, the law could have the incidental effect of prohibiting the use of land in an agricultural zone for a purpose coming within federal jurisdiction, for example, as the location of a branch of a bank. However, the majority of the Court held that the location of aerodromes was part of the essential "core" of the federal power over aeronautics, and the provincial law could not have the effect of impairing that core. Therefore, while the agricultural zoning law was valid for most of its applications, it could not constitutionally apply to the use of land for the landing and taking off of aircraft. This decision was based on the doctrine of interjurisdictional immunity, which is an exception to the general rule that a valid law can have effects on matters within the jurisdiction of the other level of government; the doctrine is discussed later in this chapter.[20]

A pith and substance analysis usually involves all or part of a single legislative enactment (statute, regulation, bylaw or so on) or combination of legislative enactments.[21] How is a court to conduct a pith and substance analysis where a legislative enactment is not involved? This question was addressed by the Supreme Court of Canada in *Desgagnés Transport v. Wärtsilä Canada* (2019).[22] In this case, the Court was asked to consider whether federal law (in particular, Canadian maritime law) or provincial law (in particular, the Civil Code of Quebec) governed a contractual claim relating to defective marine engine parts for an oceangoing ship. A significant component of Canadian maritime law is, as the Court noted, "non-statutory", involving legal principles that are derived from precedent and custom.[23] The Court said that, when non-statutory Canadian maritime law is involved, the pith and substance analysis must be altered. It remains necessary to characterize the "matter" involved, but rather than attempt to characterize the pith and substance of a legislative enactment, "the matter should be characterized by looking at the substantive law at issue and to the particular fact

---

[19]*Quebec v. Canadian Owners and Pilots Association*, [2010] 2 S.C.R. 536. The Court divided on the same lines as in the companion case, *Quebec v. Lacombe*, [2010] 2 S.C.R. 453.

[20]§§ 15:16 to 15:21, "Interjurisdictional immunity".

[21]See further, § 15:5 note 1, above.

[22]*Desgagnés Transport v. Wärtsilä Canada*, 2019 SCC 58. This case is discussed more fully in ch. 22, Transportation and Communication, under heading § 22:12, "Transportation by water".

[23]*Desgagnés Transport v. Wärtsilä Canada*, 2019 SCC 58, para. 18.

situation".[24] In addition, where the case involves a contractual dispute, the focus should be on the contract, "understood in light of the terms [and] the purpose of the contract, and the circumstances in which it was formed".[25] The *Desgagnés* case involved a particular context – Canadian maritime law – but the basic point made by the Court holds true for other contexts as well. Where there is no legislative enactment involved, a court will need to alter its usual approach to the pith and substance doctrine to take this into account.

§ 15:6 Singling out

The *Alberta Bank Taxation Reference* is occasionally read as prohibiting the provincial Legislatures from "singling out" banks or other federal undertakings for special treatment. The same point is occasionally made by the proposition that provincial laws "of general application" may validly apply to banks or other federal undertakings. But in the *Alberta Bank Taxation Reference* the singling out of the banks was only one of the factors which led the Privy Council to characterize the law as in relation to banking. The high rate of tax imposed by the law, and the fact that the law was part of a package of social credit policies inimical to bank credit, were at least equally important. There are a number of cases in which provincial laws have been upheld, notwithstanding that the laws singled out a person or class of persons within federal jurisdiction. For example, in *Bank of Toronto v. Lambe*, the leading case referred to earlier,[1] the taxing statute, although it applied to other corporations as well as banks, did impose a special rate of tax on banks alone; yet the Privy Council did not hesitate to characterize the law as in relation to taxation, not banking. Similarly, a provincial tax levied on a single company which operated an international railway bridge (within federal jurisdiction under s. 92(10)) has been upheld.[2] A provincial electoral law has been upheld notwithstanding that it discriminated against certain aliens and naturalized subjects ("naturalization and aliens" being a federal class of subject (s. 91(25)).[3] A provincial moratorium law has been upheld notwithstanding that it applied only to proceedings against a single federally-incorporated company.[4] A provincial law authorizing compulsory inspection of bank records in civil litigation has been upheld as in relation to civil procedure, notwithstanding that it

---

[24]*Desgagnés Transport v. Wärtsilä Canada*, 2019 SCC 58, para. 33. This approach was approved by six judges. Wagner C.J. and Brown J. wrote a joint concurring opinion, which was joined by Abella J., in which they criticized this approach, and said that the focus should be on characterizing "the claim" (paras. 123, 127).

[25]*Desgagnés Transport v. Wärtsilä Canada*, 2019 SCC 58, para. 34.

[Section 15:6]

[1]*Bank of Toronto v. Lambe* (1887), 12 App. Cas. 575.

[2]*Van Buren Bridge Co. v. Madawaska* (1958), 15 D.L.R. (2d) 763 (N.B. A.D.).

[3]*Cunningham v. Tomey Homma*, [1903] A.C. 151.

[4]*Abitibi Power and Paper Co. v. Montreal Trust Co.*, [1943] A.C. 536.

singled out the banks.[5] A provincial law expropriating the assets of only one of five companies engaged in mining asbestos in the province has been upheld notwithstanding that the company singled out was federally-incorporated.[6]

These cases show that a provincial law need not be of general application to apply validly to undertakings within federal jurisdiction. A law is characterized by its pith and substance (its dominant feature). The singling out of undertakings within federal jurisdiction is not conclusive of pith and substance. Exactly the same principles would apply to federal laws that singled out local works or undertakings or other matters within provincial jurisdiction, although there do not seem to be any illustrative cases.

While a provincial law of special application to undertakings within federal jurisdiction is not necessarily invalid, it is also true that a provincial law of general application is not necessarily valid in its application to undertakings within federal jurisdiction. Normally, as we have seen, a provincial law of general application which is in relation to a provincial matter may validly affect federal matters as well. But the courts have carved out an important exception to this general rule. If the effect of the provincial law would be to impair the status or essential powers of a federally-incorporated company, or to impair a vital part of a federally-regulated enterprise, then the provincial law, although valid in the generality of its applications, will not apply to the federally-incorporated company or federally-regulated enterprise.[7]

§ 15:7 Double aspect

One might well ask why a law which presents both federal and provincial characteristics should not be treated as competent to both the federal Parliament and the provincial Legislatures. At first glance, such a result seems inconsistent with the stipulation in ss. 91 and 92 that each list of classes of subject is assigned "exclusively" to either the Parliament or the Legislatures.[1] But the Privy Council early announced that "subjects which in one aspect and for one purpose fall within s. 92, may in another aspect and for another purpose fall within s. 91".[2] This doctrine has become known as the "double aspect" doctrine; it would perhaps be clearer if it had become known as the "double matter" doctrine, because it acknowledges that some kinds of laws have both a

---

[5] *Sommers v. Sturdy* (1957), 10 D.L.R. (2d) 269 (B.C. C.A.); see also *Gregory Co. v. Imperial Bank*, [1960] C.S. 204 (Que. S.C.); compare *A.-G. Can. v. A.-G. Que.* (Bank Deposits) [1947] A.C. 33.

[6] *Société Asbestos v. Société nationale de l'amiante* (1981), 128 D.L.R. (3d) 405 (Que. C.A.).

[7] See §§ 15:16 to 15:21, "Interjurisdictional immunity".

[Section 15:7]

[1] See § 15:23, "Exclusiveness".

[2] *Hodge v. The Queen* (1883), 9 App. Cas. 117, 130.

federal and a provincial "matter" and are therefore competent to both the Dominion and the provinces.[3]

The courts have not explained when it is appropriate to apply the double aspect doctrine, and when it is necessary to make a choice between the federal and provincial features of a challenged law. Lederman's explanation seems to be the only plausible one: the double aspect doctrine is applicable when "the contrast between the relative importance of the two features is not so sharp".[4] In other words, the double aspect doctrine is the course of judicial restraint. When the court finds that the federal and provincial characteristics of a law are roughly equal in importance, then the conclusion is that laws of that kind may be enacted by either Parliament or a Legislature.

The Supreme Court of Canada has upheld provincial highway traffic offences of driving without due care and attention and failing to remain at the scene of an accident as laws in relation to conduct on the roads, which is a matter coming within provincial power, probably under "property and civil rights in the province" (s. 92(13)); at the same time the Court has upheld very similar federal offences contained in the Criminal Code as laws in relation to the punishment of crime, which is a matter coming within "criminal law", a federal head of power (s. 91(27)).[5] It is clear from these cases that laws prescribing rules of conduct on the roads have a "double aspect", and are therefore competent to both the Parliament and a Legislature.

Securities regulation is another field where some laws have a double aspect. The Supreme Court of Canada has upheld both a provincial and a federal law, each creating an offence of issuing a false prospectus.[6] The Court has also upheld both a provincial and a federal law, each creating

[3]A law can also have a double aspect in that it presents characteristics from more than one class of subject in the same list. For example, provincial regulation of the legal profession has been attributed to both property and civil rights in the province (s. 92(13)) and the administration of justice in the province (s. 92(14)): *Law Society of B.C. v. Mangat*, [2001] 3 S.C.R. 113, paras. 42–46. Since this does not give any legislative authority to the other level of government, it is normally irrelevant. Occasionally it is relevant, as in *Re Exported Natural Gas Tax*, [1982] 1 S.C.R. 1004, 1074 (federal tax on provincial property would escape s. 125 if it were also a trade and commerce measure); *A.-G. Can. v. CN Transportation*, [1983] 2 S.C.R. 206, 279–280 (Dickson J.'s dissenting view, rejected by majority, that federal criminal law could be enforced federally only if it were also a trade and commerce measure).

[4]Lederman, Continuing Canadian Constitutional Dilemmas (1981), 244; this formulation was approved by Dickson J. for the majority in *Multiple Access v. McCutcheon*, [1982] 2 S.C.R. 161, 181 in reaching his conclusion (also at p. 181) that "insider trading provisions have both a securities law and a companies law aspect"; and again by Dickson C.J. for the majority in *Rio Hotel v. N.B.*, [1987] 2 S.C.R. 59, 65 in reaching his conclusion that prohibitions of nude dancing in taverns have both a liquor-licensing and a criminal law aspect.

[5]*O'Grady v. Sparling*, [1960] S.C.R. 804; *Stephens v. The Queen*, [1960] S.C.R. 823; *Mann v. The Queen*, [1966] S.C.R. 238.

[6]*Smith v. The Queen*, [1960] S.C.R. 776.

a civil remedy for insider trading.[7] The provincial power in both cases came from the characterization of the provincial laws as regulating the trade in securities, which is a matter coming within "property and civil rights in the province" (s. 92(13)). The federal power came from the characterization of the federal false prospectus offence as a "criminal law" (s. 91(27)) and the federal insider trading remedy as a corporate law coming within the federal power to incorporate companies (s. 91 opening words). However, when Parliament proposed to enact a comprehensive securities-regulation statute, relying on the trade and commerce power, the Supreme Court refused to recognize a double aspect and held that the proposed statute was an unconstitutional intrusion into property and civil rights.[8]

The double aspect doctrine confers effective concurrency of power over some fields of law,[9] and gives rise to the possibility of conflict between a valid federal law and a valid provincial law. The resolution of such conflicts in favour of the federal law is the function of the doctrine of "federal paramountcy", which is the subject of the next chapter.

§ 15:8 Purpose

The characterization of a law for constitutional purposes is, as we have seen, the identification of the "matter" of the law; the matter is often described as the "pith and substance" of the law, but is perhaps best described as the dominant or most important characteristic of the law.[1] The process of characterization is not a technical, formalistic exercise, confined to the strict legal operation of the impugned law. As we noticed in the earlier discussion of the *Alberta Bank Taxation Reference* (1938),[2] the fact that a provincial law levies a tax (for example) is not decisive of its classification as a taxing measure. The Court will look beyond the direct legal effects to inquire into the social or economic purposes which the statute was enacted to achieve. If the Court concludes that the purpose of the ostensible tax is to regulate or destroy

[7] *Multiple Access v. McCutcheon*, [1982] 2 S.C.R. 161. See generally ch. 21, Property and Civil Rights, under heading §§ 21:15 to 21:16, "Securities regulation".

[8] *Re Securities Act*, [2011] 3 S.C.R. 837.

[9] E.g., insolvency: *A.-G. Ont. v. A.-G. Can.* (Voluntary Assignments) [1894] A.C. 189; *Robinson v. Countrywide Factors*, [1978] 1 S.C.R. 753; temperance: *A.-G. Ont. v. A.-G. Can.* (Local Prohibition) [1896] A.C. 348; interest rates: *A.-G. Ont. v. Barfried Enterprises*, [1963] S.C.R. 570; maintenance of spouses and children and custody of children: *Papp v. Papp*, [1970] 1 O.R. 331 (C.A.); entertainment in taverns: *Rio Hotel v. N.B.*, [1987] 2 S.C.R. 59; gaming: *R. v. Furtney*, [1991] 3 S.C.R. 89; representation before federal administrative tribunals: *Law Society of B.C. v. Mangat*, [2001] 3 S.C.R. 113; professional responsibility by Crown prosecutors: *Krieger v. Law Society of Alberta*, [2002] 3 S.C.R. 372; gaming: *Siemens v. Man.*, [2003] 1 S.C.R. 6, para. 22; sale of marine engine parts: *Desgagnés Transport v. Wärtsilä Canada*, 2019 SCC 58.

[Section 15:8]

[1] See heading § 15:5 "Matter".

[2] *A.-G. Alta. v. A.-G. Can.* (Bank Taxation) [1939] A.C. 117.

the banks, then the law will be characterized as being in relation to banking and will be held to be invalid.[3]

The cases on Sunday closing present an interesting illustration of the importance of legislative purpose in characterization. In *R. v. Big M Drug Mart* (1985),[4] the Supreme Court of Canada, following earlier authority, held that the federal Lord's Day Act, which prohibited various commercial activities on Sundays, was a valid exercise of the federal Parliament's power over criminal law. (The Act was actually struck down for breach of the Charter of Rights.) The criminal character of the Act flowed from its purpose, which was the religious one of "the preservation of the sanctity of the Christian sabbath".[5] The religious purpose could be discovered from the name and history of the Act. The Court acknowledged that if the purpose of the statute had not been religious "but rather the secular goal of enforcing a uniform day of rest from labour", then the Act would have fallen under provincial rather than federal competence.[6] The latter case arrived at the Court's doorstep just one year later. In *R. v. Edwards Books and Art* (1986)[7] the Court held that Ontario's Retail Business Holidays Act, which prohibited retail stores from opening on Sundays, was a valid exercise of the province's power over property and civil rights in the province. (The Act also survived a Charter attack, by virtue of s. 1.) In this case, the Court discovered the secular purpose of the Act—providing a uniform pause day for retail workers—in the legislative history, which consisted of the parliamentary debates and the law reform commission report that preceded the enactment of the Act. The different outcomes in *Big M* and *Edwards Books* turned on the different purposes of the challenged laws: the prohibition of work on Sunday fell within federal or provincial competence depending upon whether the purpose of the prohibition was religious or secular.[8]

In *Ward v. Canada* (2002),[9] the Supreme Court of Canada had to characterize a federal law that prohibited the sale of baby seals. A law regulating the marketing of seals would be within the provincial author-

---

[3]In Australia, the "pith and substance" or purposive approach to characterization has been generally rejected in favour of a more formal approach which looks to the strict legal operation of the law, eschewing consideration of social or economic purposes or effects. This formalistic approach has had the effect of expanding the federal enumerated powers, because it permits a law to control indirectly matters within state jurisdiction, so long as the direct legal effect of the law is attributable to a matter within federal jurisdiction. The approach does not have a similarly expansive effect on state powers, because the states do not have enumerated powers, and state laws rarely require characterization. The differing approaches to characterization in Canada and Australia are analyzed in Gilbert, Australian and Canadian Federalism 1867-1984 (1986); see also G. Sawer, Australian Federation in the Courts (Melbourne U.P., 1967), 109–111.

[4]*R. v. Big M Drug Mart*, [1985] 1 S.C.R. 295.

[5]*R. v. Big M Drug Mart*, [1985] 1 S.C.R. 295, 354.

[6]*R. v. Big M Drug Mart*, [1985] 1 S.C.R. 295, 355.

[7]*R. v. Edwards Books and Art*, [1986] 2 S.C.R. 713.

[8]See generally ch. 18, Criminal Law, under heading § 18:12, "Sunday observance law".

[9]*Ward v. Canada*, [2002] 1 S.C.R. 569.

ity over "property and civil rights in the province" (s. 92(13)). But the Court accepted evidence that the purpose of the law was the indirect one of limiting the killing of baby seals. The Court accordingly held that the pith and substance of the law was the management of the fishery, which came within the federal authority over "sea coast and inland fisheries" (s. 91(12)). The law was therefore upheld.[10]

What is meant by the "purpose" of a statute? An inanimate object such as a statute can have a purpose in the sense of a function, and sometimes a preamble to the statute or a purpose clause will make clear what that purpose is.[11] Sometimes, the courts refer to the "intention" of the statute or of the legislative body that enacted it. This language does no harm as long as it is not taken too literally. A statute cannot have an intention, and a deliberative body such as a legislature is likely to have as many intentions (or purposes) as there are members.[12] As Lederman has said, what is really being sought is "the full or total meaning of the rule", judged "in terms of the consequences of the action called for".[13]

In determining the "purpose" of a statute in this special sense, there is no doubt as to the propriety of reference to the state of law before the statute and the defect in the law (the "mischief") which the statute purports to correct. These may be referred to under ordinary rules of statutory interpretation. Until recently, there was doubt about the propriety of reference to parliamentary debates (Hansard) and other sources of the "legislative history" of the statute. The relevance of legislative history is obvious: it helps to place the statute in its context, gives some explanation of its provisions, and articulates the policy of the government that proposed it. Historically, legislative history was inadmissible in Canada as an aid to the interpretation of an ordinary statute, but this exclusionary rule has been relaxed, with the result that these materials are now generally admissible, and the question instead

[10]See ch. 30, Natural Resources, under heading § 30:27, "Marketing of fish".

[11]In *Abitibi Power and Paper Co. v. Montreal Trust Co.*, [1943] A.C. 536, 548, the Privy Council stated that it would require "cogent grounds" before imputing to the enacting body an object other than the one appearing in the preamble on the face of the legislation. To the same effect, *A.-G. Can. v. Hallet & Carey*, [1952] A.C. 427, 444. Contrast *Re Anti-Inflation Act*, [1976] 2 S.C.R. 373, where the existence of a preamble that made no reference to an emergency did not prevent Laskin C.J. (at p. 422) and Ritchie J. (at p. 438), for the majority, from characterizing the Anti-Inflation Act as an emergency measure. Beetz J., who dissented, emphasized (at pp. 465–467) the text of the preamble. In *A.-G. Can. and Dupond v. Montreal*, [1978] 2 S.C.R. 770, Beetz J. for the majority referred (at p. 795) to the recitals in the preamble to the impugned bylaw, and Laskin C.J. for the minority did so too (at p. 774), in support of their differing characterizations. See also *Chatterjee v. Ont.*, [2009] 1 S.C.R. 624, para. 17 per Binnie J. for the Court ("While the Court is not bound by a purpose clause when considering the constitutional validity of an enactment, a statement of legislative intent is often a useful tool . . .").

[12]For this reason, individual ministers (or other members of the legislature) cannot be compelled to testify as to the purpose of statutes that they introduced (or debated): R.E. Charney, "Evidence in Charter Cases: Expert Evidence and Proving Purpose" (2004) 16 Nat. J. Constitutional Law 1.

[13]Lederman, Continuing Canadian Constitutional Dilemmas (1981), 239.

is typically how much weight to give to them.[14] In any case, the interpretation of a particular provision of a statute is an entirely different process from the characterization of the entire statute for the purposes of judicial review.[15] There seems to be no good reason why legislative history should not be resorted to for the latter purpose, and, despite some earlier authority to the contrary, it is now established that reports of royal commissions and law reform commissions, government policy papers and even parliamentary debates are indeed admissible.[16]

§ 15:9 Effect

In characterizing a statute—identifying its "matter" or "pith and substance"—a court will always consider the effect of the statute, in the sense that the court will consider how the statute changes the rights and liabilities of those who are subject to it. This simply involves understanding the terms of the statute, and that can be accomplished without going beyond the four corners of the statute. But, as we noticed in the previous section of this chapter, the search for pith and substance will not remain within the four corners of the statute if there is reason to believe that the direct legal effects of the statute are directed to the indirect achievement of other purposes.[1] In such a case, said Lord Maugham L.C. in the *Alberta Bank Taxation Reference*, "the Court must take into account any public general knowledge of which the Court would take judicial notice, and may in a proper case require to be informed by evidence as to what the effect of the legislation will be".[2]

In the *Alberta Bank Taxation Reference*,[3] the Privy Council examined the impact on the banks of the tax which Alberta proposed and used the severity of the tax as one of the reasons for concluding that the statute should be characterized as in relation to banking rather than taxation.

---

[14]R. Sullivan, *Sullivan on the Construction of Statutes* (6th ed., 2014), secs. 23.56-23.58. See also e.g. *Rizzo & Rizzo Shoes Ltd. (Re.)*, [1998] 1 S.C.R. 27, para. 35; *C.N. Railway v. Can.*, [2014] 2 S.C.R. 135, para. 47; *British Columbia Human Rights Tribunal v. Schrenk*, [2017] 2 S.C.R. 795, para. 60.

[15]Also to be distinguished, is the use of legislative history for the purpose of interpreting the Constitution Acts, 1867 to 1982: see ch. 60, Proof, under heading §§ 60:1 to 60:7, "Legislative history".

[16]See ch. 60, Proof, under heading §§ 60:1 to 60:7, "Legislative history".

[Section 15:9]

[1]*Kitkatla Band v. B.C.*, [2002] 2 S.C.R. 146, para. 54 per LeBel J. for the Court ("in looking at the effect of the legislation, the Court may consider both its legal effect and its practical effect"); *Que. v. Lacombe*, [2010] 2 S.C.R. 453, para. 20; *Re Securities Act*, [2011] 3 S.C.R. 837, paras. 63-64; *Que. v. Can. (Firearms Sequel)*, [2015] 1 S.C.R. 693, para. 29; *Desgagnés Transport v. Wärtsilä Canada*, 2019 SCC 58, para. 31.

[2]*A.-G. Alta. v. A.-G. Can.* (Bank Taxation) [1939] A.C. 117, 130. See generally ch. 60, Proof, under heading §§ 60:8 to 60:13, "Evidence".

[3]*A.-G. Alta. v. A.-G. Can.* (Bank Taxation) [1939] A.C. 117; see *A.-G. Alta. v. A.-G. Can.* (Bank Taxation) [1939] A.C. 117.

In *Texada Mines v. A.-G. B.C.* (1960),[4] the Supreme Court of Canada examined the effect of a provincial law imposing a tax on iron ore, and concluded that the tax was so heavy as to make it uneconomic to sell the ore outside the province; the Court accordingly characterized the law as in relation to interprovincial trade, a federal head of power (s. 91(2)), rather than as in relation to direct taxation within the province (s. 92(2)). In *Central Canada Potash Co. v. Government of Saskatchewan* (1978),[5] the Court examined the effect of a provincial scheme for the prorationing of potash; finding that nearly all of the province's production was exported, and that the province had abundant reserves, the Court characterized the scheme as in relation to interprovincial and international trade rather than the conservation of a natural resource.[6] Of course, in many cases, evidence as to the likely effect of legislation would not add anything useful to the task of characterization, but would merely bear on the wisdom or efficacy of the statute. In those cases the evidence is not relevant.[7]

There have been cases in which the Court has examined the administration of a statute as an aid to classifying it for constitutional purposes. In *Saumur v. Quebec* (1953),[8] there was a constitutional challenge to a municipal by-law which made it an offence to distribute literature in the streets of Quebec City without having previously obtained the written permission of the chief of police. Such a law could have been passed for the purposes of protecting pedestrian traffic or controlling litter in the city streets, and indeed four judges of the Supreme Court did uphold the law as being in relation to the streets, a perfectly legitimate topic of provincial regulation. But the other five judges—a majority—took note of the way in which the by-law was actually administered. They found that, on an application for permission to distribute literature, the chief of police would examine the contents of the material to be distributed, and would make his decision on the basis of whether he found the contents to be objectionable or not. In other words, the chief of police used the by-law as a vehicle of censorship, and the by-law constituted an effective bar to the dissemination of literature by an unpopular minority group such as the Jehovah's Witnesses, who had brought the action challenging the by-law. On the basis of these findings, the majority classified the by-law as in relation to speech or religion, and held that it was

---

[4]*Texada Mines v. A.-G. B.C.*, [1960] S.C.R. 713.

[5]*Central Canada Potash Co. v. Government of Saskatchewan*, [1979] 1 S.C.R. 42.

[6]In *A.-G. Man. v. Manitoba Egg and Poultry Assn.*, [1971] S.C.R. 689, 704–705, Laskin J. complained about the absence of any "factual underpinning" for a reference of the validity of a provincial egg marketing plan; in particular, the volume of out-of-province eggs in the province's market would have assisted in the characterization of the plan.

[7]*Re Anti-Inflation Act*, [1976] 2 S.C.R. 373, 424–455, rejecting evidence that federal wage and price controls were unlikely to reduce inflation. On the irrelevance of the wisdom or policy of a law, see ch. 12, Parliamentary Sovereignty.

[8]*Saumur v. Quebec*, [1953] 2 S.C.R. 299.

incompetent to the province.[9] Of course, the reason for the by-law's invalidity was not its administration by the chief of police, but the fact that its language was apt to authorize a regime of political and religious censorship; and it is possible that the majority judges would have reached the same result solely on the basis of the language of the by-law. But it is obvious that the judges were influenced by the actual use of the by-law, and it is even more obvious that they regarded the facts as to the actual use of the by-law as relevant and admissible on the question of classification.[10]

§ 15:10 Efficacy

The last two sections of this chapter have made clear that, in characterizing a statute for the purpose of judicial review on federal grounds, it is relevant to look at the purpose of the statute and the effects of the statute. However, that does not mean that the reviewing court should pass judgment on the likely efficacy of the statute. That would breach the longstanding injunction that courts are not concerned with the wisdom or policy of legislation.[1] A reviewing court may well believe that the legislative policy is misguided, but that belief should play no role in classifying the law for constitutional purposes. The classification must be based on the purpose and effects as understood by the legislators.

In *Re Firearms Act* (2000),[2] the question was whether Parliament's gun control legislation should be upheld as criminal law. There was no doubt that the purpose of the legislation was to promote public safety, which was a typically criminal purpose. But those attacking the constitutionality of the legislation argued that the legislation's regime of registration of guns and licensing of owners would be completely useless as a contributor to public safety. Gun control, it was argued, simply burdens law-abiding farmers and hunters with pointless red tape and has no effect on those who use guns for criminal purposes or even those who carelessly misuse guns. The Court was clearly sceptical about these points, because the Court pointed out that restrictions on access to guns

---

[9] Of the five majority judges, only four, namely, Rand, Kellock, Estey, and Locke JJ., held the by-law to be unconstitutional. The fifth member of the majority, Kerwin J., held that it was constitutional, but inapplicable to a religious group such as the Jehovah's Witnesses because it conflicted with the Freedom of Worship Act, a pre-confederation statute which in Kerwin J.'s opinion protected their proselytizing practices.

[10] In *A.-G. B.C. v. McDonald Murphy Lumber*, [1930] A.C. 357, 363, the Privy Council reinforced its conclusion that the challenged provincial tax was an invalid export tax with the fact that the portion of the tax purportedly payable on timber used locally was not actually collected. In *R. v. Hydro-Québec*, [1997] 3 S.C.R. 213, para. 147, the majority of the Court looked at the administration of the Canadian Environmental Protection Act (finding only a small number of toxic substances under regulation) to reinforce the conclusion that it was a criminal law.

[Section 15:10]

[1] Chapter 12, Parliamentary Sovereignty, under heading § 12:8, "Wisdom or policy of legislation".

[2] *Re Firearms Act*, [2000] 1 S.C.R. 783.

could have an effect on the incidence or severity of crime, especially domestic crime, and could reduce suicides and accidents, while a register of firearms would help to trace stolen or lost guns and contribute to the detection of crime. But the conclusive answer to the argument was the institutional one that efficacy was a matter for Parliament and not the Court: "Parliament is the judge of whether a measure is likely to achieve its intended purposes; efficaciousness is not relevant to the Court's division of powers analysis."[3]

The same answer was given by the Supreme Court of Canada in *Ward v. Canada* (2002)[4] to a constitutional challenge to a federal regulation that prohibited the sale of baby seals. A ban on sale was on the face of it within property and civil rights in the province and therefore outside federal power. But the Court upheld the validity of the law under the federal power over fisheries (s. 91(12)) by classifying the law as a measure to protect the resource. The Court accepted the evidence of the Government of Canada that the purpose of the ban on sale was not to regulate the marketing of baby seals but to limit the killing of baby seals by removing the commercial incentive to harvest them. This invited the question of why the Government did not directly prohibit the killing of the animals if that was indeed its purpose. McLachlin C.J. for the Court held that this was an impermissible inquiry into the efficacy of the law: "The purpose of legislation cannot be challenged by proposing an alternate, allegedly better, method for achieving that purpose."[5]

§ 15:11 Colourability

The courts are, of course, concerned with the substance of the legislation to be characterized and not merely its form. The "colourability" doctrine is invoked when a statute bears the formal trappings of a matter within jurisdiction, but in reality is addressed to a matter outside jurisdiction. In the *Alberta Bank Taxation Reference*,[1] for example, the Privy Council held that the legislation, although ostensibly designed as a taxation measure, was in reality directed at banking. Similarly, attempts by the federal Parliament to regulate insurance (a provincial matter) by incorporating provisions into the Criminal Code (criminal law being federal), or by enacting special taxing measures, have been struck down as colourable.[2] A provincial attempt to relieve debtors from the payment of interest (a federal matter) by forgiving part of the principal of the loan has also been condemned as colourable,[3] as has

[3] *Re Firearms Act*, [2000] 1 S.C.R. 783, para. 18; also to the same effect, para. 57.

[4] *Ward v. Canada*, [2002] 1 S.C.R. 569.

[5] *Ward v. Canada*, [2002] 1 S.C.R. 569, para. 26.

[Section 15:11]

[1] *A.-G. Alta. v. A.-G. Can.* (Bank Taxation) [1939] A.C. 117.

[2] *A.-G. Ont. v. Reciprocal Insurers*, [1924] A.C. 328; *Re Insurance Act of Can.*, [1932] A.C. 41.

[3] *A.-G. Sash v. A.-G. Can.* (Sask. Farm Security) [1949] A.C. 110.

been a provincial attempt to prohibit the propagation of communism (speech being a federal matter) by controlling the use of property.[4]

In *Re Upper Churchill Water Rights* (1984),[5] the Supreme Court of Canada struck down a Newfoundland statute that expropriated the assets of a company that generated hydro-electricity at Churchill Falls in Labrador. On the face of it, the statute seemed valid, because it was clear that Newfoundland had the power to expropriate property situated within its borders. But the Court held that the pith and substance of the statute was to deprive the company of the capacity to fulfil a long-term contract to supply power to Hydro-Quebec at below-market rates. The nullification of this contract was outside the power of Newfoundland, because the contract created rights in Quebec. The statute made no mention of the power contract or of any rights outside the province, and was thus "cloaked in the proper constitutional form".[6] The statute was nevertheless held to be invalid as "a colourable attempt to interfere with the power contract".[7]

In *R. v. Morgentaler (No. 3)* (1993),[8] the Supreme Court of Canada struck down a Nova Scotia statute that required "designated" medical procedures to be performed in a hospital. The designation had been accomplished by a regulation, which listed nine medical procedures, of which the fourth was abortion. The statute declared that its purpose was "to prohibit the privatization of the provision of certain medical services in order to maintain a single high-quality health-care delivery system for all Nova Scotians". On the face of it, the statute seemed to be a health measure, which would be within the constitutional power of the province. The Supreme Court of Canada, in a unanimous opinion by Sopinka J., pointed to uncontradicted testimony that the stimulus for the statute came from a proposal by Dr. Henry Morgentaler to establish an abortion clinic in the province, and the Court quoted extensively from the legislative history of the statute to show the legislators' preoccupation with stopping the establishment of the Morgentaler clinic. None of this was literally inconsistent with the stated purpose of the legislation. Nor did the Court attempt to resolve "the intractable dispute between the parties as to whether this legislation will in fact restrict access to abortion in Nova Scotia".[9] Nevertheless, the Court held that the statute and regulation "were aimed primarily at suppressing the perceived harm or evil of abortion clinics", and that they were properly characterized as invalid criminal laws.[10] The Court struck down the statute and regulation in their entirety, despite the fact that eight of the nine designated hospital procedures had nothing to do with abortion. By this holding,

---

[4] *Switzman v. Elbling*, [1957] S.C.R. 285.

[5] *Re Upper Churchill Water Rights*, [1984] 1 S.C.R. 297.

[6] *Re Upper Churchill Water Rights*, [1984] 1 S.C.R. 297, 332.

[7] *Re Upper Churchill Water Rights*, [1984] 1 S.C.R. 297, 333.

[8] *R. v. Morgentaler (No. 3)*, [1993] 3 S.C.R. 463.

[9] *R. v. Morgentaler (No. 3)*, [1993] 3 S.C.R. 463, 515.

[10] *R. v. Morgentaler (No. 3)*, [1993] 3 S.C.R. 463, 512.

the Court made clear that it regarded the designation of the eight non-abortion procedures as a smokescreen to conceal from a reviewing court the true purpose of the legislation. This is a remarkable application of the colourability doctrine.[11]

In these colourability cases there is a very fine line between adjudication on policy and adjudication on validity. Indeed, the adjective "colourable" carries a strong connotation of judicial disapproval, if not of the policy of the statute, at least of the means by which the legislative body sought to carry out the policy. Such disapproval is entirely out of place, serving only to cast doubt on the neutrality of judicial review. The colourability doctrine can and should be stated without impugning the legislative branch: it simply means that "form is not controlling in the determination of essential character".[12]

The colourability doctrine applies the maxim that a legislative body cannot do indirectly what it cannot do directly. However, as is suggested by the paucity of citations in this section of the chapter, arguments of colourability are rarely successful. Often, a legislative body will find a way to do indirectly what it cannot do directly. For example, the federal Parliament cannot regulate the delivery of health care in the provinces, but it can transfer cash and tax points to only those provinces whose health care plans comply with federal standards of universality, accessibility and mobility.[13] Neither the federal Parliament nor the provincial Legislatures can delegate powers to each other, but each can delegate powers to agencies created by the other.[14] A provincial Legislature cannot regulate television programmes or advertising, but it can prohibit certain kinds of advertising in all media, and the prohibition will be valid and effective as a bar to television advertising.[15] A provincial Legislature cannot levy a sales tax on the vendor of a good, because such a tax would be indirect, but the Legislature can impose on the vendor an obligation to collect a tax that is formally levied on the consumer of the good.[16]

§ 15:12 Criteria of choice

The characterization of a statute is often decisive of its validity, and the Court will obviously be aware of that fact. The choice between competing characteristics of the statute, in order to identify the most important one as the "matter", may be nothing less than a choice between validity or invalidity. What are the criteria of importance that

[11]Sopinka J. (at 496) denied that he was applying the colourability doctrine. This is one of those occasions where the text-writer must rely on what the Court has done rather than on what the Court says it has done!

[12]A.S. Abel, "The Neglected Logic of 91 and 92" (1969) 19 U. Toronto L.J. 487, 494.

[13]See ch. 6, Financial Arrangements, under heading § 6:8, "Spending power".

[14]See ch. 14, Delegation, under heading §§ 14:10 to 14:11, "Federal inter-delegation".

[15]*Irwin Toy v. Quebec*, [1989] 1 S.C.R. 927, 953 (expressly rejecting colourability argument).

[16]See ch. 31, Taxation, under heading § 31:12, "Sales taxes".

will control or at least guide this crucial choice? No doubt, full understanding of the legislative scheme, informed by relevant extrinsic material, will often reveal one dominant statutory policy to which other features are subordinate. No doubt, too, judicial decisions on similar kinds of statutes will often provide some guide. But in the hardest cases the choice is not compelled by either the nature of the statute or the prior judicial decisions. The choice is inevitably one of policy.

The policy choice that lies at the base of a characterization decision is bound to be related to the ultimate consequence of the choice which is, I am assuming, the validity or invalidity of the statute. The choice must be guided by a concept of federalism. Is this the kind of law that should be enacted at the federal or the provincial level?[1] The reasoning at this point should not be affected by judicial approval or disapproval of the particular statute in issue; nor by the political situation which provided the controversy, let alone the political allegiances of the contending parties. The only "political" values which may be accepted as legitimate to judicial review are those that have a constitutional dimension to them, that is, values that may reasonably be asserted to be enduring considerations in the allocation of power between the two levels of government.[2]

There would be little dispute as to some of the considerations that it is legitimate for a judge to take account of in resolving an issue of characterization. The allocations of power that are explicit in the Constitution are suggestive of the kinds of new laws that should be allocated to each level of government. The caselaw that elaborates the constitutional text offers other suggestions and analogies. But there are many other values to be drawn from history, political science, economics and sociology, which are arguably inherent in Canada's federal system, but which are much more controversial. Simeon[3] has suggested the three values of community, efficiency and democracy as criteria that are helpful to an appraisal of the allocation of power in a federal system. But, as he acknowledges, there is room for much argument as to the existence and relative weight of these values. Conceptions of community, namely, whether Canada or a particular province is the primary community to which the citizen should feel allegiance, are subject to reasonable disagreement, especially between many English-speaking Canadians and

[Section 15:12]

[1]Lederman, Continuing Canadian Constitutional Dilemmas (1981), 241.

[2]This seems to me to be the thesis of H. Wechsler, "Toward Neutral Principles of Constitutional Law" (1959) 73 Harv. L. Rev. 1, but his use of the word "neutral" was unfortunate, since it implied a value-free process of reasoning which Wechsler did not intend. His article was an attempt to defend the legitimacy of judicial review by emphasizing the rational side of adjudication, in contrast to the legal realists, who viewed adjudication as a policy choice by (unelected, unaccountable and unrepresentative) judges. The debate continues to this day between the "interpretivist" and "noninterpretivist" constitutional theorists. For a balanced view, acknowledging both the constraining function of legal texts, principles and rules, and the role of values, see J.O. Newman, "Between Legal Realism and Neutral Principles" (1984) 72 Calif. L. Rev. 200.

[3]R.E. Simeon, "Criteria for Choice in Federal Systems" (1983) 8 Queen's L.J. 131.

many French-speaking Quebecers. Conceptions of efficiency, namely, whether a particular governmental power is exercised most efficiently by the federal government or by a province, are also subject to reasonable disagreement, with varying weight being given, on the one hand, to economies of scale, national economic policies, nationwide mobility of resources, and uniform access to rights, resources and opportunities by all citizens and, on the other hand, to local diversity and experimentation and smaller bureaucracies. Conceptions of democracy, namely, whether the federal government or a provincial government is more responsive and accountable to the people and more protective of minorities, are also subject to reasonable disagreement.[4]

One cannot say that a judge is wrong to take account of these kinds of considerations. How else is the judge to reach a decision as to the appropriate characterization of a statute, where conventional legal sources fail to supply the answer? But, in assessing these kinds of criteria, the judge has little to provide guidance and may tend to assume that his or her personal preferences are widely shared if not impliedly embodied in the Constitution. In that sense, judicial review can never be wholly neutral, wholly divorced from the predilections of the judges. This is one reason why in federalism cases judicial restraint should be a governing precept.[5] In other words, where the choice between competing characterizations is not clear, the choice which will support the legislation is normally to be preferred.

§ 15:13 Presumption of constitutionality

Judicial restraint in determining the validity of statutes may be expressed in terms of a "presumption of constitutionality".[1] Such a term transfers from the law of evidence the idea that a burden of demonstration lies upon those who would challenge the validity of a statute which has emerged from the democratic process. The presumption of constitutionality carries three legal consequences. One is the point made in the previous section of the chapter: in choosing between competing, plausible characterizations of a law, the court should normally choose that one that would support the validity of the law.[2] Secondly, where the validity of a law requires a finding of fact (for example, the existence of an emergency), that finding of fact need not be proved strictly by the govern-

---

[4]See generally P.J. Monahan, "At Doctrine's Twilight: The Structure of Canadian Federalism" (1984) 34 U. Toronto L.J. 47; Swinton, The Supreme Courtaud Canadian Federalism (1990), chs. 5–7.

[5]Fuller reasons are offered in ch. 5, Federalism, under heading §§ 5:20 to 5:22, "Role of the courts".

[Section 15:13]

[1]*N.S. Bd. of Censors v. McNeil*, [1978] 2 S.C.R. 662, 687–688; J.E. Magnet, "The Presumption of Constitutionality" (1980) 18 Osgoode Hall L.J. 87; Strayer, The Canadian Constitution and the Courts (3rd ed., 1988), 251–254; Charles, Cromwell and Jobson, Evidence and the Charter of Rights and Freedoms (1989), 35–47.

[2]*Re Firearms Act*, [2000] 1 S.C.R. 783, para. 25; *Siemens v. Man.*, [2003] 1 S.C.R. 6, para. 33.

ment; it is enough that there be a "rational basis" for the finding.[3] Thirdly, where a law is open to both a narrow and a wide interpretation, and under the wide interpretation the law's application would extend beyond the powers of the enacting legislative body, the court should "read down" the law so as to confine it to those applications that are within the power of the enacting legislative body.[4] These three doctrines have the effect of reducing interference by unelected judges with the affairs of the elected legislative branch of government. Where a law is challenged on Charter grounds, as opposed to federal grounds, there is no presumption of constitutionality, except for the third doctrine, "reading down", which also applies in Charter cases. Other than the reading down doctrine, determinations of law and fact in Charter cases are subject to their own set of rules, and those rules are not compatible with a presumption of constitutionality.[5]

V. SEVERANCE; READING DOWN

§ 15:14 Severance

A statute, however complex, is usually the elaboration of a single legislative plan or scheme. The leading feature of that plan or scheme will be the pith and substance (or the matter) of the entire statute. For constitutional purposes the statute is one law, and it will stand or fall as a whole when its validity is questioned.[1] Occasionally, however, it is possible to say that part only of a statute is invalid, and the balance of the statute would be valid if it stood alone. Of course, the balance does not stand alone; and the question arises whether the court should "sever" the bad part, thereby preserving the good part, or whether the court should declare the entire statute to be bad. The rule which the courts have developed is that severance is inappropriate when the remaining good part "is so inextricably bound up with the part declared invalid that what remains cannot independently survive"; in that event, it may be assumed that the legislative body would not have enacted the remain-

---

[3]See ch. 60, Proof, under heading § 60:13, "Standard of proof".

[4]See § 15:15, "Reading down", later in this chapter.

[5]See ch. 38, Limitation of rights, under heading § 38:5 "Presumption of constitutionality".

[Section 15:14]

[1]A "legislative scheme" (as it is called in Australia) exists when a single policy is embodied in more than one statute. In that case, the courts will examine the entire scheme in order to characterize any one statute, and a holding of invalidity will affect all parts of the scheme (the opposite result to severance), e.g., *A.-G. Ont. v. Reciprocal Insurers*, [1924] A.C. 328; *Re Insurance Act of Canada*, [1932] A.C. 41; *Re Alberta Statutes*, [1938] S.C.R. 100; affirmed with respect to one statute only in *A.-G. Alta. v. A.-G. Can.* (Bank Taxation) [1939] A.C. 117; *Texada Mines v. A.-G. B.C.*, [1960] S.C.R. 713. This mode of reasoning has not been applied to schemes involving complementary legislation by both levels of government: see ch. 14, Delegation, under heading §§ 14:10 to 14:11, "Federal inter-delegation". For a comparative study of legislative schemes in Australia and Canada, see Gilbert, Australian and Canadian Federalism 1867-1984 (1986), chs. 6, 7.

ing part by itself.[2] On the other hand, where the two parts can exist independently of each other, so that it is plausible to regard them as two laws with two different "matters", then severance is appropriate, because it may be assumed that the legislative body would have enacted one even if it had been advised that it could not enact the other.[3]

The Privy Council and the Supreme Court of Canada have both been difficult to persuade that severance is appropriate. They have usually struck down the entire statute once an adverse conclusion has been reached as to the constitutionality of part. When one considers the large number of cases in which statutes have been held to be unconstitutional, the few cases in which severance has been ordered emphasize how rarely the occasion for its use has been held to arise.[4] Statutes have mostly been held to stand or fall in their entirety, often without any reference to the possibility of severance. Although the courts have not expressed themselves in these terms, there appears to be a presumption that a statute embodies a single statutory scheme of which all the parts are interdependent. In other words, there seems to be a presumption against severance.

A "severance clause" is a section of a statute that provides that, if any part of the statute is judicially held to be unconstitutional, the remainder of the Act is to continue to be effective. At the very least, such a clause should reverse the presumption against severance: instead of the presumption that the various parts of the statute are interdependent and inseverable, the presumption should be that the parts are independent and severable. This is the way severance clauses work in the United States and Australia, where they seem to have been more common than they are in Canada.[5] To give some effect to a severance clause seems sound, since the clause indicates the legislative intent with respect to severance, and the courts have always claimed that the inquiry into severability is an inquiry into legislative intent.[6] However, in what seems to be the only Canadian case dealing with a statute containing a sever-

---

[2]*A.-G. Alta. v. A.-G. Can.* (Alta. Bill of Rights) [1947] A.C. 503, 518.

[3]Lederman, Continuing Canadian Constitutional Dilemmas (1981), 247–248; Strayer, The Canadian Constitution and the Courts (3rd ed., 1988), 301–303.

[4]Severance was ordered in *Toronto v. York*, [1938] A.C. 415; *Roy v. Plourde*, [1943] S.C.R. 262; *Re s. 5(a) of the Dairy Industry Act* (Margarine) [1949] S.C.R. 1 (the appeal to the Privy Council did not include this issue); *Can. Federation of Agriculture v. A.-G. Que.*, [1951] 1 A.C. 179); *MacDonald v. Vapor Can.*, [1977] 2 S.C.R. 134; *N.S. Bd. of Censors v. McNeil*, [1978] 2 S.C.R. 662; *Re Agricultural Products Marketing Act*, [1978] 2 S.C.R. 1198; *Regional Municipality of Peel v. McKenzie*, [1982] 2 S.C.R. 9. Severance was explicitly refused in *Re Initiative and Referendum Act*, [1919] A.C. 935, 944; *A.-G. Can. v. A.-G. Ont.* (Unemployment Insurance) [1937] A.C. 355, 367; *A.-G. Man. v. A.-G. Can.* (Natural Products Marketing) [1937] A.C. 377, 388–389; *A.-G. Alta. v. A.-G. Can.* (Alta. Bill of Rights) [1947] A.C. 503, 518.

[5]For the United States, see *Carter v. Carter Coal Co.* (1936), 298 U.S. 238, 312–313, 321–322. For Australia, see *Bank of N.S.W. v. Commonwealth* (State Banking) (1948) 76 C.L.R. 1, 368–372.

[6]To attribute an intention to a deliberative body is artificial enough; when the intention is predicated on a hypothetical situation, the usefulness of the attribution may well be questioned. However, the courts have used this mode of reasoning, and it does

ance clause, the Privy Council refused to sever the unconstitutional portion of the statute from the rest. Their lordships applied the usual rule regarding severance, and seemed to assume that the severance clause (to which their lordships referred) made no difference.[7]

Severance is far more common in Charter cases than in federalism cases. Although the same test is applied, it is highly unusual to find that an entire statute is struck down under the Charter of Rights. Charter review is not based on the pith and substance of a law, but on the question whether either the "purpose" or the "effect" of the law abridges a Charter right.[8] Under this test, it is usually only a single section or a few sections of a statute[9] that abridge a Charter right, and it is usually beyond argument that the rest of the statute can independently survive. For example, it could hardly be argued that the invalidity of the search and seizure power of the Competition Act[10] entailed the striking down of the entire Act, or that the invalidity of the felony-murder rule[11] entailed the striking down of the entire Criminal Code.

There seems to be only a few cases in the Supreme Court of Canada where the entire statute was struck down. The first (and for some time only) case was *R. v. Big M Drug Mart* (1985),[12] which held that the Lord's Day Act was wholly bad.[13] In most other cases the offending provision has been severed from the rest of the statute, usually without argument or discussion.[14] It seems reasonable to conclude that the presumption against severance in federalism cases has been replaced in Charter cases by a presumption in favour of severance. Severance is an

---

convey the sense that severance is an issue closely analogous to statutory interpretation.

[7]*A.-G. B.C. v. A.-G. Can.* (Natural Products Marketing) [1937] A.C. 377.

[8]§ 15:5 note 8, above.

[9]Severance can be applied to instuments other than statutes, e.g., *Ross v. New Brunswick School District No. 15*, [1995] 1 S.C.R. 827 (severing and striking down one part of a human rights tribunal's order as an unjustified infringement of a Charter right).

[10]*Hunter v. Southam*, [1984] 2 S.C.R. 145.

[11]*R. v. Vaillancourt*, [1987] 2 S.C.R. 636.

[12]*R. v. Big M Drug Mart*, [1985] 1 S.C.R. 295.

[13]Other instances are: *Sask. Federation of Labour v. Sask.*, [2015] 1 S.C.R. 246, paras. 97, 103 (Public Service Essential Services Act, S.S. 2008, c. P-42.2 struck down in its entirety under the Charter; declaration of invalidity suspended for 1 year); *Alta. v. United Food and Commercial Workers*, [2013] 3 S.C.R. 733, paras. 40-41 (Personal Information Protection Act, S.A. 2003, c. P-6.5 struck down in its entirety under the Charter; declaration of invalidity suspended for 12 months). See also *Nova Scotia v. Martin*, [2003] 2 S.C.R. 504, para. 118 (Functional Restoration (Multi-Faceted Pain Services) Program Regulations, N.S. Reg. 57/96 struck down under the Charter; declaration of invalidity suspended for 6 months); *Mackin v. N.B.*, [2002] 1 S.C.R. 405, para. 88 (amending statute, the Act to Amend the Provincial Court Act, S.N.B. 1987, c. 45, struck down in its entirety; declaration of invalidity suspended for 6 months).

[14]In some cases, although there is no question of invalidating the entire statute, there is a question as to how much of the statute should be struck down: e.g., *R. v. Morgentaler*, [1988] 1 S.C.R. 30, 80; *Devine v. Que.*, [1988] 2 S.C.R. 790, 814. In some cases, the courts have awarded remedies other than severance: see ch. 40, Enforcement of Rights.

important tool of judicial restraint, because it circumscribes the impact of a successful Charter attack on a law. The law that falls is normally only a small portion of the legislative structure, and the rest of the structure remains standing.[15]

§ 15:15 Reading down

The "reading down" doctrine requires that, whenever possible, a statute is to be interpreted as being within the power of the enacting legislative body. What this means in practice is that general language in a statute which is literally apt to extend beyond the power of the enacting Parliament or Legislature will be construed more narrowly so as to keep it within the permissible scope of power. Reading down is simply a canon of construction (or interpretation). It is only available where the language of the statute will bear the (valid) limited meaning as well as the (invalid) extended meaning; it then stipulates that the limited meaning be selected. Reading down is like severance in that both techniques mitigate the impact of judicial review; but reading down achieves its remedial purpose solely by the interpretation of the challenged statute, whereas severance involves holding part of the statute to be invalid.[1] Reading down is sometimes said to depend upon a presumption of constitutionality: the enacting legislative body is presumed to have meant to enact provisions which do not transgress the limits of its constitutional powers; general language which appears to transgress the limits must therefore be "read down" so that it is confined within the limits.[2]

There are many examples of reading down. The Federal Court Act has been read down to exclude from the jurisdiction of the Federal Court cases that are governed by provincial law, because s. 101 of the Constitution Act, 1867, under which the Federal Court Act was enacted, authorizes the establishment of federal courts only for the purpose of deciding cases governed by federal law."[3] The Family Relations Act of British Columbia, which authorizes the division of family assets on divorce, has been read down to exclude property on an Indian reserve, because the right to property on an Indian reserve is exclusively within

---

[15]In Charter cases, in addition to the normal function described in this section of the book, severance serves a distinctive remedial purpose. It is sometimes used to delete words that create a constitutional problem and thereby change the meaning of the rest of the statute in order to bring it into conformity with the Charter. In this use, it is a close cousin of the more radical technique, reading in, where new words are added to a statute to bring it into conformity with the Charter. These two techniques are discussed in ch. 40, Enforcement of Rights, under headings § 40:5, "Severance", and § 40:6, "Reading in".

[Section 15:15]

[1]Severance is treated in the previous section of this chapter.

[2]Reading down is also available to bring a statute into conformity with the Charter of Rights or the Canadian Bill of Rights: ch. 40, Enforcement of Rights, under heading § 40:7, "Reading down".

[3]E.g., *Que. North Shore Paper Co. v. CP*, [1977] 2 S.C.R. 1054.

federal power."[4] A limitation period in the federal Railway Act has been read down to bar only causes of action created by the Act itself, because the barring of a common law cause of action in tort is exclusively within provincial power."[5] And, as the next section of this chapter[6] will show, provincial statutes have often been read down to exclude federally-regulated undertakings from otherwise valid and ostensibly applicable language.[7]

The general idea that a law should not be held to be wholly invalid just because it overreaches the limits of jurisdiction in certain respects is obviously in accord with a properly restrained role for the courts. Reading down allows the bulk of the legislative policy to be accomplished, while trimming off those applications that are constitutionally bad. The trouble is that it is not easy to tell when a law which is valid in most of its applications has trespassed outside its proper field. It must be recalled that the "pith and substance" doctrine, exemplified by *Bank of Toronto v. Lambe*,[8] is that a law which is in relation to a matter within jurisdiction (in that case taxation) is not objectionable just because it affects a matter outside jurisdiction (in that case banking). The limits of the pith and substance doctrine mark out an ill-defined zone of "interjurisdictional immunity", which is discussed in the next section of this chapter.

VI. INTERJURISDICTIONAL IMMUNITY

§ 15:16 Definition of interjurisdictional immunity

The term interjurisdictional immunity does not have a precise meaning.[1] A law that purports to apply to a matter outside the jurisdiction of the enacting legislative body may be attacked in three different

[4] *Derrickson v. Derrickson*, [1986] 1 S.C.R. 285.

[5] *Clark v. CNR*, [1988] 2 S.C.R. 680.

[6] §§ 15:16 to 15:21, "Interjurisdictional immunity".

[7] For other examples of reading down, see *Re Industrial Relations and Disputes Investigation Act* (Stevedores Reference) [1955] S.C.R. 529, esp. 535, 566, 582 (limiting scope of federal labour relations law); *CBC v. Cordeau*, [1979] 22 S.C.R. 618, 640 (provincial tribunal's powers read down to exclude s. 96 power to punish for contempt); *The Queen (Man.) v. Air Can.*, [1980] 2 S.C.R. 303 (provincial sales tax read down to exclude aircraft flying over province); *Friends of Oldman River Society v. Can.*, [1992] 1 S.C.R. 3 (federal environmental statute read down to limit environmental assessment to matters within federal legislative jurisdiction); *R. v. Grant*, [1993] 3 S.C.R. 223 (police power to search without warrant read down to apply only in exigent circumstances). On the other hand, a law that is excessively vague and broad so that it cannot be characterized as in relation to a matter within a head of power will not be rehabilitated by a massive exercise in reading down: see *Saumur v. Que.*, [1953] 2 S.C.R. 299, 333 per Rand J.

[8] *Bank of Toronto v. Lambe* (1887), 12 App. Cas. 575.

[Section 15:16]

[1] See D. Gibson, "Interjurisdictional Immunity in Canadian Federalism" (1969) 47 Can. Bar Rev. 40; R.M. Elliot, Comment (1988) 67 Can. Bar Rev. 523; E.R. Edinger, Comment (1989) 68 Can. Bar Rev. 631; P.W. Hogg and R. Godil, "Narrowing Interjurisdictional Immunity" (2008) 42 Supreme Court L.R. (2d) 623; R.M. Elliot, "Interjurisdictional Immunity after *Canadian Western Bank* and *Lafarge Canada Inc.*" (2008), 43

ways. The attack may go to (1) the validity of the law, or (2) the applicability of the law, or (3) the operability of the law.

First, it may be argued that the law is *invalid*, because the matter of the law (or its pith and substance) comes within a class of subjects that is outside the jurisdiction of the enacting legislative body. That is why the provincial law imposing a tax on banks was struck down in the *Alberta Bank Taxation Reference* (1938).[2] The provincial law was classified as in relation to banking (a federal matter), rather than direct taxation in the province (a provincial matter), and was accordingly held to be invalid. The question of validity depends upon the characterization of the law, which has been discussed in earlier sections of this chapter, and will not be revisited in this section of the chapter.

A second way of attacking a law that purports to apply to a matter outside the jurisdiction of the enacting body is to acknowledge that the law is valid in most of its applications, but to argue that the law should be interpreted so as not to apply to the matter that is outside the jurisdiction of the enacting body. If this argument succeeds, the law is not held to be invalid, but simply *inapplicable* to the extra-jurisdictional matter. The technique for limiting the application of the law to matters within jurisdiction is the reading down doctrine, which was discussed in the previous section of this chapter. The occasions when it is appropriate to use the technique will be discussed in this section of the chapter. It is this issue that I treat as interjurisdictional immunity.

A third way of attacking a law that applies to a matter outside the jurisdiction of the enacting body is to argue that the law is *inoperative* through the doctrine of paramountcy. The doctrine of paramountcy stipulates that, where there are inconsistent federal and provincial laws, it is the federal law that prevails; paramountcy renders the provincial law inoperative to the extent of the inconsistency. Thus, paramountcy is a form of attack that is available only against a provincial law, and then only when there is a conflicting federal law in existence. The doctrine of paramountcy is the topic of the next chapter.

It is the second issue—the issue of applicability—that I am treating under the present rubric of interjurisdictional immunity.[3]

Supreme Court L.R. (2d) 433.

[2] *A.-G. Alta. v. A.-G. Can.* (Bank Taxation) [1939] A.C. 117.

[3] The correct order of application of the three doctrines is as set out in the text. The second issue, interjurisdictional immunity, is logically prior to paramountcy, because paramountcy applies only if there are two valid laws applicable to the same facts and in conflict with each other (in which case the provincial law is rendered inoperative). There can be no conflict if one law is wholly unconstitutional (issue one), or cannot constitutionally apply to these facts (issue 2). And, of course, if immunity from federal law is sought for a head of provincial jurisdiction, paramountcy is not available anyway. Of course, dealing with issues in the wrong order will not normally change the result, which may be a reason not to cavil with the obiter dictum in the majority opinion in *Can. Western Bank v. Alta.*, [2007] 2 S.C.R. 3, para. 78, suggesting that while "in theory" interjurisdictional immunity should be considered prior to paramountcy, "in practice" a court should often deal with paramountcy before interjurisdictional immunity. For criticism, see

§ 15:17 Federally-incorporated companies

The idea of interjurisdictional immunity finds its genesis in cases concerning federally-incorporated companies.[1] It has been held that an otherwise valid provincial law may not impair the status or essential powers of a federally-incorporated company. Thus, a provincial law prohibiting all extra-provincial companies from operating in the province,[2] and a provincial law imposing a licensing scheme for the raising of corporate capital,[3] have been "read down" to exempt federally-incorporated companies. On the other hand, provincial laws whose impact on corporate status or powers was deemed less serious have been held applicable to federally-incorporated companies.[4]

§ 15:18 Federally-regulated undertakings

From the company cases a similar idea of immunity was carried over to cases concerning federally-regulated undertakings.[1] It is now well settled that undertakings engaged in interprovincial or international transportation or communication, which come within federal jurisdiction under the exceptions to s. 92(10) of the Constitution Act, 1867, are immune from otherwise valid provincial laws which would have the effect of "sterilizing" the undertakings. On this basis, an interprovincial telephone company has been held immune from provincial law requiring the consent of a municipality for the erection of telephone poles and

---

Bastarache J. concurring in the same case, paras. 113–114; R.M. Elliot, "Interjurisdictional Immunity after *Canadian Western Bank* and *Lafarge Canada Inc.*" (2008), 43 Supreme Court L.R. (2d) 433, 495–496.

[Section 15:17]

[1]The rationale of the old cases granting immunity from provincial laws to federally-incorporated companies is not entirely clear, and some scholars believe the cases were decided on the basis of federal paramountcy: J.S. Ziegel, in J.S. Ziegel (ed.), Studies in Canadian Company Law (Butterworths, Toronto, 1967), 165–167; R.M. Elliot, "Interjurisdictional Immunity after *Canadian Western Bank* and *Lafarge Canada Inc.*" (2008), 43 Supreme Court L.R. (2d) 433, 440. Even the old cases granting immunity to federally-regulated undertakings are less than clear in their rationale, and Elliot, 453, argues that the doctrine of interjurisdictional immunity did not emerge clearly until *Commission du Salaire Minimum v. Bell Telephone Co.*, [1966] S.C.R. 767.

[2]*John Deere Plow Co. v. Wharton*, [1915] A.C. 330; *Great West Saddlery v. The King*, [1921] 2 A.C. 91.

[3]*A.-G. Man. v. A.-G. Can.* (Manitoba Securities) [1929] A.C. 260.

[4]*Lymburn v. Mayland*, [1932] A.C. 318; *Can. Indemnity Co. v. A.-G. B.C.*, [1977] 2 S.C.R. 504; *Re Upper Churchill Water Rights*, [1984] 1 S.C.R. 297. This "status and essential powers" immunity is discussed in ch. 23, Companies.

[Section 15:18]

[1]The issue is not quite the same. The federal incorporation power does not authorize regulation of the activities of federally-incorporated companies, and therefore there can be no immunity from provincial laws regulating the activities of such companies. Undertakings (whether incorporated federally or provincially or outside Canada or even if unincorporated) operating in fields of federal legislative competence are, by definition, subject to federal regulation of their activities, and therefore some immunity from provincial laws purporting to regulate the activities of such undertakings is possible.

wires,[2] an international bus line has been held immune from provincial regulation as to routes, rates, etc.,[3] and an interprovincial pipeline has been held immune from provincial mechanics liens legislation.[4]

Until 1966, the provincial laws that were held inapplicable to federally-regulated undertakings were laws that asserted a power to sterilize (paralyze or impair) the federally-authorized activity. This possibility, however unlikely in practice, was the basis of each decision. In the *Bell 1966* case (1966),[5] the Supreme Court of Canada abandoned the language of sterilization, and held that the Bell Telephone Company (an interprovincial undertaking) was immune from a provincial minimum wage law on the lesser ground that such a law "affects a vital part of the management and operation of the undertaking".[6]

The new "vital part" test carved out a much broader field of immunity from provincial law than the old sterilization test, because the vital part test precluded the application of provincial laws that could not possibly paralyze or even impair the operation of the federally-regulated undertaking. The expansion of the immunity was criticized by commentators, who argued that such an extensive immunity was unnecessary, and undesirable in a federation where so many laws for the protection of workers, consumers and the environment (for example) are enacted and enforced at the provincial level.[7] In the *Bell 1966* case itself, the decision meant that workers in federal industries were not protected by minimum wage laws, because at that time there was no federal minimum wage. (There is now.) In a case where there is federal law in existence, the doctrine of paramountcy would of course force any directly conflicting provincial law out of the field, so that no immunity is needed for that situation.

In *Bell 1988*,[8] the Supreme Court of Canada reaffirmed its commitment to the vital part test. The case, along with two others decided at

[2] *Toronto v. Bell Telephone Co.*, [1905] A.C. 52.

[3] *A.-G. Ont. v. Winner*, [1954] A.C. 541; *Registrar of Motor Vehicles v. Can. American Transfer*, [1972] S.C.R. 811. On the other hand, less radical regulation, e.g., speed limits and other rules of the road, licence plates, weight limits, etc., are undoubtedly competent to the provinces. The application of provincial laws to aeronautics and to radio and television is discussed in ch. 22, Transportation and Communication. With respect to harbours, see *Hamilton Harbour Commrs. v. City of Hamilton* (1978), 21 O.R. (2d) 459 (Ont. C.A.) (provincial land-use laws apply).

[4] *Campbell-Bennett v. Comstock Midwestern*, [1954] S.C.R. 207.

[5] *Commission du Salaire Minimum v. Bell Telephone Co.*, [1966] S.C.R. 767.

[6] *Commission du Salaire Minimum v. Bell Telephone Co.*, [1966] S.C.R. 767, 774 per Martland J. For criticism, see D. Gibson, "Interjurisdictional Immunity in Canadian Federalism" (1969) 47 Can. Bar Rev. 40, 53–56; P.C. Weiler, "The Supreme Court and the Law of Canadian Federalism" (1973) 23 U. Toronto L.J. 307, 340–342; and see ch. 21, Property and Civil Rights, under heading § 21:11, "Federal power".

[7] See D. Gibson, "Interjurisdictional Immunity in Canadian Federalism" (1969) 47 Can. Bar Rev. 40, 53–56; P.C. Weiler, "The Supreme Court and the Law of Canadian Federalism" (1973) 23 U. Toronto L.J. 307, 340–342; the 2nd ed. (1985) of this book, 329–332, 465–466.

[8] *Bell Canada v. Quebec*, [1988] 1 S.C.R. 749.

the same time,[9] presented the question whether provincial occupational health and safety laws could apply to undertakings engaged in interprovincial transportation and communication. The precise question was whether Bell Canada, which is an interprovincial telephone company, was bound in Quebec by a Quebec law that required the protective reassignment of pregnant workers who work with video monitors. The Supreme Court of Canada, in an opinion written by Beetz J., held that the provincial law was constitutionally incapable of applying to the federal undertaking, and had to be read down so that it did not apply to the federal undertaking. Beetz J. acknowledged that a law requiring the reassignment of a small number of workers, like the minimum wage law in the *Bell 1966*, could not paralyze or impair the operation of the federal undertaking. But he held that "it is sufficient that the provincial statute which purports to apply to the federal undertaking affects a vital or essential part of that undertaking, without necessarily going as far as impairing or paralyzing it".[10] In his lordship's view, occupational health and safety laws, because they regulated labour relations within a firm, affected a vital part of the management and operation of the firm.[11] Therefore, occupational health and safety laws enacted by a province could not constitutionally apply to a federal undertaking.

In *Bell 1988*, Beetz J. rejected the view that there could be concurrent provincial jurisdiction over a vital part of a federal undertaking. In principle, "a basic, minimum and unassailable content" had to be assigned to each head of federal legislative power, and, since federal legislative power is exclusive, provincial laws could not affect that unassailable core.[12] In practice, "twofold jurisdiction" would encourage a "proliferation" of regulations, and the application of the paramountcy rule, far from solving the conflicts between "rival systems of regulation", would be a "source of uncertainty and endless disputes".[13] With this emphatic language, Beetz J. repudiated the overlapping of authority—the de facto concurrency—that had been urged by the critics of the vital part immunity.[14]

Shortly after reaffirming the vital part test in *Bell 1988*, the Supreme

[9] *CNR v. Courtois*, [1988] 1 S.C.R. 868 (CNR not bound by provincial law authorizing accident investigation); *Alltrans Express v. B.C.*, [1988] 1 S.C.R. 897 (Alltrans Express not bound by provincial law requiring safety committee and protective footwear).

[10] *Bell Canada v. Quebec*, [1988] 1 S.C.R. 749, 859–860.

[11] *Bell Canada v. Quebec*, [1988] 1 S.C.R. 749, 762.

[12] *Bell Canada v. Quebec*, [1988] 1 S.C.R. 749, 839.

[13] *Bell Canada v. Quebec*, [1988] 1 S.C.R. 749, 843.

[14] See D. Gibson, "Interjurisdictional Immunity in Canadian Federalism" (1969) 47 Can. Bar Rev. 40, 53–56; P.C. Weiler, "The Supreme Court and the Law of Canadian Federalism" (1973) 23 U. Toronto L.J. 307, 340–342; the 2nd ed. (1985) of this book, 329–332, 465–466. In the 2nd edition of this book (1985), I attacked the whole notion of interjurisdictional immunity. Beetz J. quoted extensively from my book, and criticized my views in a detailed fashion more like a law review article than a judgment. My views were also criticized by R.M. Elliot, Comment (1988) 67 Can. Bar Rev. 523. I have been persuaded by Beetz J. and Professor Elliot that some degree of interjurisdictional immunity is entailed by the Constitution of Canada's dual lists of exclusive powers.

Court of Canada had to decide whether a Quebec law that prohibited advertising directed at children could apply to advertising on television, which is of course a federally-regulated medium. In *Irwin Toy v. Quebec* (1989),[15] the Court held that the law was applicable to advertising on television. The Court acknowledged that advertising was "a vital part of the operation of a television broadcast undertaking".[16] But now the Court said that the vital part test applied only to provincial laws that purported to apply *directly* to federal undertakings. Where a provincial law had only an "indirect effect" on the undertaking, the law would be inapplicable only if the law impaired a vital part of the undertaking. An indirect effect falling short of impairment, even if it affected a vital part of the undertaking, would not render the provincial law constitutionally inapplicable.[17] In this case, the provincial prohibition on advertising applied to advertisers, not to the media: the advertiser was prohibited from placing the prohibited category of advertising, but the media were not directly prohibited from carrying the advertising.[18] Since the effect of the provincial law on a television undertaking was indirect, it did not matter that the law affected a vital part of the undertaking. Only *impairment* would render the law inapplicable, and the loss of children's advertising could not impair the operation of the television undertaking. Therefore, the provincial law was valid and effective to preclude advertisers in Quebec from placing advertisements directed at children on television.

Irwin Toy constituted an important qualification of the vital part test, and it made little sense. If it is the case, as *Bell 1988* had held, that any vital part of a federal undertaking is within the unassailable, exclusive core of federal power, then surely that core should be as protected from indirect invasion by provincial law as it is from direct invasion. Dale Gibson[19] speculated that the Court in *Irwin Toy* had become concerned that the vital part test was too tight a restriction on provincial power over federal undertakings operating within the province, and "saw this new refinement as a way of loosening the constraints".[20]

Another suggestion that the Supreme Court of Canada was wavering in its commitment to the vital part test came in *Ontario v. Canadian*

Otherwise, what would be incompetent to a legislative body in a narrowly framed law would be permitted if the law were framed more broadly. That cannot be right.

[15]*Irwin Toy v. Quebec*, [1989] 1 S.C.R. 927. The five-judge bench, consisting of Dickson C.J., Beetz, McIntyre, Lamer and Wilson JJ., divided three to two on the Charter issue (the majority upholding the law under s. 1), but were unanimous on the interjurisdictional immunity issue.

[16]*Irwin Toy v. Quebec*, [1989] 1 S.C.R. 927, 957.

[17]*Irwin Toy v. Quebec*, [1989] 1 S.C.R. 927, 955.

[18]This had been the basis of the earlier decision in *A.G. Que. v. Kellogg's Co. of Can.*, [1978] 2 S.C.R. 211, holding that restrictions on advertising directed at children could validly apply to television advertising.

[19]D. Gibson, Comment (1990) 69 Can. Bar Rev. 339.

[20]D. Gibson, Comment (1990) 69 Can. Bar Rev. 339, 353. The decision in *Irwin Toy* was rendered only eleven months after the decision in *Bell Canada*, and four of the five judges who sat on *Irwin Toy*, including Beetz J., had also sat on *Bell Canada*.

Pacific (1995).[21] In that case, Canadian Pacific, which operates an interprovincial railway and is an undertaking within federal jurisdiction, was held to be bound by Ontario's Environmental Protection Act. The company was under an obligation, provided by the federal Railway Act, to keep its right-of-way free of dead grass, weeds and other unnecessary combustible matter. In order to accomplish this task on the part of the right-of-way that ran through the town of Kenora, the company conducted a controlled burning of the dry grass on the right-of-way. Some smoke escaped into adjoining residential areas, causing a nuisance to the residents and provoking complaints. The company was charged with discharging a contaminant into the natural environment in breach of the Ontario Act. The Ontario Court of Appeal held that the Act validly applied to the company.[22] The Court pointed out that there were other ways of keeping the right-of-way clear of combustible matter, so that "controlled burning [was] not essential to the [company's] ability to fulfil its statutory mandate".[23] The Court also held that the Act was not aimed at the management and control of an undertaking.[24] These tests were much more favourable to the application of the provincial law than the vital part test, which the Court never recited or attempted to apply. And yet it could hardly be doubted that the right-of-way was a vital part of the railway, and that a provincial law that regulated the clearance of the right-of-way affected a vital part of the operation of the railway. The company appealed to the Supreme Court of Canada, which dismissed the appeal on this issue orally without written reasons.[25] The Court's brief oral explanation did not indicate how the outcome could be reconciled with the vital part test.[26]

In *Canadian Western Bank v. Alberta* (2007),[27] a majority of the Court confirmed that it had indeed changed its mind about the test for

---

[21]*Ontario v. Canadian Pacific*, [1995] 2 S.C.R. 1028.

[22]*Ontario v. Canadian Pacific* (1993) 13 O.R. (3d) 389 (C.A.).

[23]*Ontario v. Canadian Pacific* (1993) 13 O.R. (3d) 389, 393 (C.A.).

[24]*Ontario v. Canadian Pacific* (1993) 13 O.R. (3d) 389, 397–398 (C.A.).

[25]The Court did write at length on whether the Environmental Protection Act was unconstitutionally vague or overbroad: [1995] 2 S.C.R. 1028, 1031.

[26]The Court, while affirming the decision of the Court of Appeal, did not express any approval of the reasons of the Court of Appeal. What Lamer C.J. said at the conclusion of the oral argument was: "We are all of the view that the judgment *CPR v. Notre Dame de Bonsecours*, [1899] A.C. 367 governs the first issue in this appeal and, accordingly, the appeal with respect to that ground fails": [1995] 2 S.C.R. 1028, 1029. The *Bonsecours* case had not been referred to by the Court of Appeal. In that case, the Privy Council decided that the Canadian Pacific Railway had to comply with a municipal order, made under provincial law, to clear a drainage ditch on its right-of-way; the ditch was blocked and flooding adjacent land. The case is similar to the 1995 appeal, but one might wonder whether it is still good law since the vital part test was unknown in 1899, having been invented in 1966 by the Supreme Court of Canada with no prior judicial support (as explained in the text accompanying § 15:18 note 6, above).

[27]*Canadian Western Bank v. Alberta*, [2007] 2 S.C.R. 3. Binnie and LeBel JJ. wrote for the eight-judge majority. Bastarache J. wrote a concurring opinion, agreeing that the provincial law did not affect a vital part of banking (the ratio decidendi of the majority), but disagreeing with the reformulation of the interjurisdictional immunity doctrine (the

interjurisdictional immunity. Binnie and LeBel JJ., who wrote the majority opinion, announced that the Court was completing "the reassessment begun in *Irwin Toy*".[28] Interjurisdictional immunity would apply only if a "core competence" of Parliament or "a vital or essential part of an undertaking it duly constitutes" would be *impaired* by a provincial law. If the core competence or vital part would merely be *affected* (without any adverse consequence) by a provincial law, no immunity applied. The direct-indirect distinction that had complicated the law since *Irwin Toy* was erased. It no longer mattered whether the effect of a provincial law on the core or vital part was direct or indirect. In either case, the rule was the same: "in the absence of impairment, interjurisdictional immunity does not apply".[29] Impairment, Binnie and LeBel JJ. said, would involve an "adverse consequence" that placed the core or vital part "in jeopardy", although "without necessarily 'sterilizing' or 'paralyzing' ".[30] While disapproving the breadth of the vital part test as articulated by Beetz J. in *Bell 1988*, Binnie and LeBel JJ. did not disapprove of the outcome. The "management" of a federally-regulated undertaking was a vital part of the undertaking, and the provincial occupational health and safety laws at issue in *Bell 1988* would have intruded deeply into the management of the undertakings to which they purported to apply.[31] Evidently, that would have counted as an impairment had Beetz J. applied the test of impairing (instead of simply affecting) the vital part of the undertaking.

The issue in *Canadian Western Bank* was whether Alberta's Insurance Act could constitutionally apply to the banks. The Act required a "deposit-taking institution" (which included the federally-regulated banks as well as provincially-regulated trust companies and credit unions) to obtain a licence from the province and comply with provincial consumer-protection laws in order to promote insurance to its customers. (The Act did not purport to regulate banks in requiring customers to obtain insurance as collateral for loans; only if the banks promoted the

---

obiter dicta of the majority).

[28] *Canadian Western Bank v. Alberta*, [2007] 2 S.C.R. 3, para. 49.

[29] *Canadian Western Bank v. Alberta*, [2007] 2 S.C.R. 3 , para. 49.

[30] *Canadian Western Bank v. Alberta*, [2007] 2 S.C.R. 3, para. 48.

[31] *Canadian Western Bank v. Alberta*, [2007] 2 S.C.R. 3, paras. 52, 62–63. Perhaps the emphasis on management would also have saved the outcome in *Bell 1966* (application of provincial minimum wage to federal undertaking), although that seminal decision received only passing notice in the majority opinion. The notion of impairment is very difficult to apply because in this context it does not make much sense. If the purpose of interjurisdictional immunity is to preserve the exclusivity of the essential core of a nominally exclusive legislative power, then (as Eliott, below, argues) the former test of affecting (rather than impairing) is the more coherent one. Now that the Court has held otherwise, what precisely is it that has to be impaired? See the difference of opinion in *Que. v. Canadian Owners and Pilots Assn.*, [2010] 2 S.C.R. 536 between the majority opinion of McLachlin C.J. (para. 46) and the dissenting opinion of Deschamps J. (para. 142). The case is discussed at § 15:18 note 46, below, and see the commentary on this point by R. Elliot, "Ancillary Powers, Interjurisdictional Immunity and The Local Interest in Land Use Planning against the National Interest in a Unified System of Aviation Navigation" (2011) 55 Supreme Court L.R. 403, 428–437.

sale of the insurance were they subject to provincial law.) The federal Bank Act had been amended in 1991 to grant the banks the power to promote (not sell) to their customers certain types of creditors' insurance against events that would impair their borrowers' ability to repay a loan from the bank, for example, the death, disability or loss of employment of the borrower. Although the insurance promoted by the banks was normally optional, the great majority of their borrowers did in fact take out creditors' insurance; the beneficiary of each policy was the bank; and the effect of the widespread insurance was to enhance the security of the bank's portfolio of loans. There was no doubt that the lending of money and the taking of security by banks were vital functions of banking, and the banks argued that the close relationship of creditors' insurance to those functions made the promotion of insurance by banks a vital part of banking as well. The Court held that the vital part of an undertaking should be limited to functions that were "essential" or "indispensable" or "necessary" to the federal character of the undertaking; and that the promotion of insurance by banks was too far removed from the core of banking to qualify as a vital part of the banking undertaking.[32] Therefore, the Alberta Insurance Act could validly apply to the banks when they promoted insurance.

The general tenor of the majority opinion in *Canadian Western Bank* was unsympathetic to the doctrine of interjurisdictional immunity, on the basis that "a court should favour, where possible, the ordinary operation of statutes enacted by *both* levels of government".[33] The doctrine operated in practice as a restraint on provincial power, which undermined the principle of subsidiarity that decision-making should take place at the level of government closest to the individuals affected.[34] The doctrine was often superfluous, since the rule of federal paramountcy already limited the ability of provincial Legislatures to intrude into federal jurisdiction—at least where there was federal regulation in place.[35] Despite all this, the majority allowed that the doctrine still had "a proper

[32]*Canadian Western Bank v. Alberta*, [2007] 2 S.C.R. 3, paras. 51, 63. Bastarache J. (paras. 118–123), while not supporting the concept of a core "that is overly restrictive", agreed with the majority that the promotion of insurance by banks was outside the core of banking. This was in fact the only point necessary for the decision. Nothing turned on the distinction between impairing and merely affecting, and the majority's prolonged justification of the new rule of impairment was all obiter dicta.

[33]*Canadian Western Bank v. Alberta*, [2007] 2 S.C.R. 3, para. 37 (emphasis in original).

[34]*Canadian Western Bank v. Alberta*, [2007] 2 S.C.R. 3, para. 45. See also § 15:21, "Provincial entities". On subsidiarity, see ch. 5 Federalism, under heading § 5:7, "Subsidiarity".

[35]*Canadian Western Bank v. Alberta*, [2007] 2 S.C.R. 3, para. 46. The banks also argued that the Alberta insurance requirements were inconsistent with the federal Bank Act and therefore inoperative through federal paramountcy. This argument was unanimously rejected by the Court. It is discussed in ch. 16, Paramountcy, under heading § 16:5, "Covering the field".

part to play in appropriate circumstances",[36] but should be "applied with restraint".[37]

A second decision was handed down by the Supreme Court at the same time as *Canadian Western Bank*. The issue in *British Columbia v. Lafarge Canada* (2007)[38] was authority over land use regulation at the port of Vancouver. On the federal side, the Canada Marine Act, enacted under the federal power over navigation and shipping (s. 91(10)), authorizes land-use regulation in Canada's ports, and in Vancouver it is the Vancouver Port Authority that is the regulator. On the provincial side, no fewer than eight municipalities intersect with the port, each with the authority under provincial law to enact zoning by-laws and require land-use approvals. Lafarge proposed to build a concrete batch plant at a site in the port. The marine location was good for the mixing of concrete, because the aggregate (gravel), could be shipped by barge and directly unloaded at the plant, where the aggregate would then be mixed with cement and transported to construction sites in the Vancouver area. The Vancouver Port Authority approved the development. The development was challenged by a local ratepayers' association, which relied on the fact that the proposed site was also within the boundaries of the City of Vancouver, and which argued that the City by-law requiring a development permit should have also been complied with. If ever there was a case for interjurisdictional immunity, this was it. How could the Vancouver Port Authority (or any other port authority for that matter) develop and implement coherent land-use policies for the port if the port was also blanketed by a patchwork of municipal land-use regimes? As Bastarache J. said in his concurring opinion, the prospect was a "jurisdictional nightmare" of competing zoning rules, approvals and delays.[39]

Binnie and LeBel JJ., wrote the opinion for six of the seven judges who sat on the *Lafarge* case. Apparently undeterred by the nightmare, they remained true to their new policy of restraint on interjurisdictional immunity. Although the development of a marine facility on port lands for the mixing of concrete was within the federal power over navigation and shipping in s. 91(10), they held that the regulation of the development "lies beyond the core of s. 91(10)".[40] Therefore, interjurisdictional immunity did not apply. They did not seem to be entirely persuaded of

---

[36]*Canadian Western Bank v. Alberta*, [2007] 2 S.C.R. 3, para. 47.

[37]*Canadian Western Bank v. Alberta*, [2007] 2 S.C.R. 3, para. 67; and see also para. 77 ("interjurisdictional immunity is of limited application and should in general be reserved for situations already covered by precedent"). For criticism of these phrases and the uncertainty they inject into the question of which provincial laws must be complied with by federally-regulated undertakings, see P.W. Hogg and R. Godil, "Narrowing Interjurisdictional Immunity" (2008) 42 Supreme Court L.R. (2d) 623.

[38]*British Columbia v. Lafarge Canada*, [2007] 2 S.C.R. 86. As with the companion case, Binnie and LeBel JJ. wrote the majority opinion; Bastarache J. wrote a concurring opinion.

[39]*British Columbia v. Lafarge Canada*, [2007] 2 S.C.R. 86, paras. 140–141.

[40]*British Columbia v. Lafarge Canada*, [2007] 2 S.C.R. 86, para. 72. Title to the site was in the Vancouver Port Authority, which was not for that purpose an agent of the

their reasoning, however, because they went on to hold on flimsy grounds (that looked very like interjurisdictional-immunity reasoning) that the Vancouver by-law was inoperative by reason of federal paramountcy.[41] Moreover, and perhaps this was simply a mistake, they gave an unqualified "yes" to the constitutional question that had been stated for decision by the Chief Justice, which was whether the Vancouver by-law was "constitutionally inapplicable to the proposed development on the property in view of Parliament's legislative authority over 'navigation and shipping' under s. 91(10)."[42] This is the language of interjurisdictional immunity, not paramountcy.[43] Bastarache J., in his concurring opinion, placed his decision firmly on interjurisdictional immunity. He held that the regulation of land use in support of port operations on port lands was within "the core" of navigation and shipping,[44] and therefore immune from provincial or municipal laws that would impair the federal regime. In the end, then, the Court was unanimous that the Vancouver Port Authority's approval was all that was needed for the Lafarge development.

Only three years after *Canadian Western Bank*[45] had purported to restrict the application of the doctrine of interjurisdictional immunity, the majority of the Supreme Court gave it a robust application in *Quebec v. Canadian Owners and Pilots Association* (2010).[46] The issue in that case was whether a provincial law, which designated areas of the province as agricultural zones from which all non-agricultural uses were prohibited, applied to prohibit the operation of an airstrip on private land within an agricultural zone. The owners of the land had selected the site without any prior approval from the federal Department of Transport (or any other federal agency): no approval was required by the federal Aeronautics Act to establish or operate a private "aerodrome". (The Act did provide an optional procedure for registration with the Department of Transport, and the owners had registered their aerodrome; the effect of registration was to subject the aerodrome to federal standards and make

federal Crown. If, however, the VPA had been a Crown agent, or if the site had been federal Crown land, then its development would have been "exclusively within federal jurisdiction" (para. 51).

[41]For criticism of the paramountcy reasoning, see ch. 16, Paramountcy, under heading § 16:3, "Impossibility of dual compliance".

[42]*British Columbia v. Lafarge Canada*, [2007] 2 S.C.R. 86, para. 91.

[43]The Court apparently had enormous difficulty deciding the case, which was under reserve from the date of oral argument on November 8, 2005 to the date of judgment on May 31, 2007—a period of more than 18 months, during which the Lafarge project had to remain on hold.

[44]*British Columbia v. Lafarge Canada*, [2007] 2 S.C.R. 86, paras. 127–133.

[45]*Canadian Western Bank v. Alberta*, [2007] 2 S.C.R. 3.

[46]*Quebec v. Canadian Owners and Pilots Association*, [2010] 2 S.C.R. 536. McLachlin C.J. wrote the opinion of the seven-judge majority. LeBel and Deschamps JJ. wrote dissenting opinions. See also the companion case of *Quebec v. Lacombe*, [2010] 2 S.C.R. 453. For commentary on the two cases, see R. Elliot, "Ancillary Powers, Interjurisdictional Immunity and The Local Interest in Land Use Planning against the National Interest in a Unified System of Aviation Navigation" (2011) 55 Supreme Court L.R. 403, 428–437.

it available to anyone who needed to land.) The Supreme Court of Canada held unanimously that the provincial law was a valid law in relation to land use planning and/or agriculture, and two judges held that the law could have the valid incidental effect of restricting the location of aerodromes in the province. But the seven-judge majority applied the doctrine of interjurisdictional immunity to hold that the provincial law was "inapplicable to the extent that it prohibits aerodromes in agricultural zones".[47] McLachlin C.J., who wrote for the majority, held that the location of aerodromes was "essential" to the federal power over aeronautics, and was therefore within the "core" of the power. The effect of the provincial law on that core was sufficiently serious to count as an "impairment", which she described as a "midpoint between sterilization and mere effects".[48] Arguing for the application of its law, the province had pointed out that Parliament had not in fact regulated the location of aerodromes, and, if it did so, any contrary provincial law would then have to yield to the federal regulation by virtue of federal paramountcy.[49] In the absence of a conflicting federal law, why should a valid provincial law not apply? But the Chief Justice replied that "acceptance of this argument would narrow Parliament's legislative options and impede the exercise of its core jurisdiction".[50] In the end, therefore, the doctrine of interjurisdictional immunity exempted the aerodrome from the provincial law prohibiting non-agricultural uses.[51]

In *Vancouver International Airport v. Lafarge Canada* (2011),[52] the issue was whether creditors of the contractors who had constructed improvements to the Vancouver International Airport could register liens against the leasehold interest of the Vancouver International Airport Authority, which was the company that leased the Airport land and operated the Airport. British Columbia's Builders Lien Act authorized persons who worked on construction projects who had not been paid for their work to register a lien against the owner's interest (whether leasehold or freehold) in the underlying land; the lien imposed a charge on the owner's interest in the land, which, if not discharged by payment of the debt, entitled the holder of the lien to obtain a court order for the sale of the owner's interest. There was no doubt that the Act,

[47] *Quebec v. Canadian Owners and Pilots Association*, [2010] 2 S.C.R. 536, para. 4.

[48] *Quebec v. Canadian Owners and Pilots Association*, [2010] 2 S.C.R. 536, para. 44.

[49] In this case, there was no federal paramountcy because the Court was unanimous that the permissive language of the federal law with respect to the location of aerodromes gave rise to no conflict between the federal and provincial laws.

[50] *Quebec v. Canadian Owners and Pilots Association*, [2010] 2 S.C.R. 536, para. 53.

[51] Contrast this robust application of interjurisdictional immunity with *Marine Services International v. Ryan Estate*, [2013] 3 S.C.R. 53, 2013 SCC 44, para. 64, holding that a provincial law could bar a maritime negligence claim, and distinguishing *Ordon Estate v. Grail*, [1998] 3 S.C.R. 437; and with *Desgagnés Transport v. Wärtsilä Canada*, 2019 SCC 58, holding that the Civil Code of Quebec applied to a maritime contract claim, and casting further doubt on *Ordon*. These cases are described in ch. 22, Transportation and Communication, under heading § 22:12, "Transportation by water".

[52] *Vancouver International Airport v. Lafarge Canada* (2011), 331 D.L.R. (4th) 737 (B.C.C.A.). Smith J.A. wrote the opinion of the Court.

which has its counterparts in the other provinces, was a valid exercise of the province's legislative power over property and civil rights in the province (s. 92(13)).[53] The Registrar of the province's Land Title Office registered the liens of the Airport creditors against the leasehold interest of the Airport Authority. The Airport Authority applied for judicial review of the action of the Registrar, relying on the doctrine of interjurisdictional immunity. The Court of Appeal of the province relied on the *Canadian Owners and Pilots* case for the proposition that airports come within the core of the federal power over aeronautics. The Airport Authority was an aeronautics undertaking. The Court held that the mere registration of a lien on the leasehold interest in the Airport land would impair a vital part of the undertaking by diminishing the Airport Authority's ability to finance the construction, improvement or maintenance of airport facilities, and the execution of the lien by the sale of the leasehold interest would bring the operations of the airport to a halt. The Court concluded that the doctrine of interjurisdictional immunity applied to the Act, which accordingly had to be read down so as to render it inapplicable to the owner and operator of an airport.[54]

Seven years after *Canadian Western Bank*,[55] another banking case reached the Supreme Court. The issue in *Bank of Montreal v. Marcotte* (2014)[56] was whether the banks were bound by provisions in Quebec's Consumer Protection Act (CPA.) which required the issuers of credit cards to disclose their fees. A group of banks were sued by credit-card holders for failing to disclose a foreign-currency "conversion fee" which the banks charged to credit-card holders when their cards were used to purchase goods outside Canada. The civil action was for restitution of fees not disclosed and for punitive damages, both remedies authorized by the CPA. Regulations under the federal Bank Act also required disclosure of these fees, although the banking regulations provided only for criminal sanctions and did not authorize civil actions by consumers. The banks argued that lending money and extending credit by banks (including by means of credit cards) was part of the core of banking and, by virtue of interjurisdictional immunity, could only be regulated by Parliament. The Court agreed that lending at least was part of the core of banking: "lending, broadly defined, is central to banking and has been recognized as such by this Court in previous decisions";[57] but the Court also made clear that it had not forgotten or repented of its counsels of

---

[53]*Vancouver International Airport v. Lafarge Canada* (2011), 331 D.L.R. (4th) 737 (B.C.C.A.), para. 14.

[54]Accord, *Greater Toronto Airports Authority v. Mississauga* (2000), 50 O.R. (3d) 641 (C.A.) (provincial building code inapplicable to airport construction project because of its impact on a vital part of the aeronautics undertaking). For other cases involving aeronautics, see ch. 22, Transportation and Communication, under heading §§ 22:13 to 22:15, "Transportation by Air".

[55]*Canadian Western Bank v. Alberta*, [2007] 2 S.C.R. 3.

[56]*Bank of Montreal v. Marcotte*, [2014] 2 S.C.R. 725, 2014 SCC 55. Rothstein and Wagner JJ. wrote the opinion of the seven-judge panel of the Court.

[57]*Bank of Montreal v. Marcotte*, [2014] 2 S.C.R. 725, 2014 SCC 55, para. 66.

restraint in *Canadian Western Bank*.[58] The Court rejected the banks' argument, reasoning that a mere disclosure requirement could not be said to "*impair* . . . the manner in which Parliament's legislative jurisdiction over bank lending can be exercised".[59] "Banks cannot avoid the application of all provincial statutes that in any way touch on their operations, including lending and currency conversion."[60] Therefore, interjurisdictional immunity did not apply, and the CPA requirement was applicable to the banks as well as to the non-bank issuers of credit cards. (The banks' paramountcy arguments were also rejected.)[61] The plaintiffs succeeded in their civil action against the banks for restitution of the fees that had not been disclosed and for punitive damages.

Interjurisdictional immunity was applied by the Supreme Court in *Rogers Communications v. Châteauguay* (2016).[62] The issue in the case was whether the municipality of Châteauguay in Quebec could stop Rogers Communications (Rogers), a mobile telephone provider, from installing an antenna system on a particular property in the municipality. The antenna was needed to improve Rogers' mobile telephone service in that area. The location had been approved by the federal Minister of Industry acting under power conferred by the federal Radiocommunication Act. There was local opposition to the installation based on fears of risks to the health of persons living nearby. What the municipality did was to issue a "notice of a reserve" that under Quebec's municipal law prohibited all construction on the property. The prohibition lasted for two years, but it was renewable, and shortly before it expired the municipality renewed it for two additional years. Rogers successfully challenged the notice on constitutional grounds. The Supreme Court was unanimous that the doctrine of interjurisdictional immunity applied to render the notice inapplicable to Rogers.[63] *Bell 1966*[64] was a precedent for the application of interjurisdictional immunity to the siting of the telecommunication poles and cables which were essential to a land-line telephone network. The siting of a radiocommunication antenna system

---

[58]*Bank of Montreal v. Marcotte*, [2014] 2 S.C.R. 725, 2014 SCC 55, para. 63.

[59]*Bank of Montreal v. Marcotte*, [2014] 2 S.C.R. 725, 2014 SCC 55, para. 66 (emphasis added). Presumably, provincial laws that directly regulated lending by banks would impair a core of banking and be barred by interjurisdictional immunity.

[60]*Bank of Montreal v. Marcotte*, [2014] 2 S.C.R. 725, 2014 SCC 55, para. 68.

[61]The paramountcy arguments are discussed in ch. 16, Paramountcy, under heading § 16:7, "Constitutional significance".

[62]*Rogers Communications v. Châteauguay*, [2016] 1 S.C.R. 467, 2016 SCC 23. Wagner and Côté JJ. wrote the opinion of the majority. Gascon J. wrote a concurring opinion, but agreed with the majority on interjurisdictional immunity.

[63]The majority of the Court held that the pith and substance of the notice was the choice of radiocommunication infrastructure, a matter within federal jurisdiction, and held the notice invalid on that ground: for discussion, see ch. 22, Transportation and Communication, under heading § 22:22, "Communication by telephone", at note 12, below. Gascon J. did not agree with the pith and substance reasons. However, the majority also held that the notice was inapplicable by virtue of interjurisdictional immunity, and Gascon J. (para. 118) agreed with those reasons, making them unanimous.

[64]*Commission du Salaire Minimum v. Bell Telephone Co.*, [1966] S.C.R. 767.

was just as essential to a mobile telephone network. The municipal notice "compromised the orderly development and efficient operation of radiocommunication and impaired the core of the federal power over radiocommunication in Canada".[65] The notice was held to be inapplicable to Rogers by reason of interjurisdictional immunity.

Is the service of liquor a vital part of the undertaking of an airline? In *Air Canada v. Ontario* (1997),[66] an airline objected to paying a mark-up charged by the provincial liquor monopoly on liquor that was loaded onto aircraft from a bonded warehouse for consumption in the air. The airline took the position that the charge was an attempt by the province to regulate a vital part of its undertaking. Iacobucci J. for the Supreme Court of Canada acknowledged that in some circumstances the provision of food or beverages would form a vital part of the airline's undertaking. For example, food and water on aircraft were essential for long flights. But the provision of liquor, however attractive to the airline's customers, "is not essential to the operation of aircraft".[67] The airline was required to pay the mark-up.

§ 15:19 Other federal matters

The doctrine of interjurisdictional immunity also applies outside the fields of transportation and communication.[1] Provincial labour laws have been held inapplicable to postal workers[2] and to teachers on a military base.[3] A provincial driving licence requirement has been held inapplicable to members of the armed forces.[4] Provincial laws respecting inquiries and police discipline have been held inapplicable to the Royal Canadian Mounted Police.[5] A variety of provincial laws respecting hunting, adoption and family property have been held inapplicable to Indians or on Indian reserves.[6] A provincial bus licence requirement has been held inapplicable to a bus service provided by a federal agency in a

---

[65] *Rogers Communications v. Châteauguay*, [2016] 1 S.C.R. 467, 2016 SCC 23, para. 71.

[66] *Air Canada v. Ontario*, [1997] 2 S.C.R. 581.

[67] *Air Canada v. Ontario*, [1997] 2 S.C.R. 581, para. 74.

[Section 15:19]

[1] Not covered in the list that follows are the Crown: see. ch. 10, The Crown, under heading §§ 10:16 to 10:21, "Federal complications"; and taxation: see ch. 31, Taxation, under heading §§ 31:21 to 31:23, "Interjurisdictional taxation".

[2] *Re Minimum Wage Act (Sask.)*, [1948] S.C.R. 248; *Letter Carriers' Union of Can. v. Can. Union of Postal Workers*, [1975] 1 S.C.R. 178.

[3] *A.G. Can. v. St.-Hubert Base Teachers' Assn.*, [1983] 1 S.C.R. 498.

[4] *R. v. Anderson* (1930), 54 C.C.C. 321 (Man. C.A.).

[5] *A.G. Que. and Keable v. A.G. Can.*, [1979] 1 S.C.R. 218; *A.G. Alta. v. Putnam*, [1981] 2 S.C.R. 267.

[6] See ch. 28, Aboriginal Peoples, under heading §§ 28:7 to 28:12, "Provincial legislative power".

federal park.[7] A municipal by-law prohibiting the display of signs on residential property has been held inapplicable to federal election signs.[8]

§ 15:20 Rationale of interjurisdictional immunity

These interjurisdictional immunity cases do not concern provincial laws that single out federal undertakings, works, persons or services for special treatment.[1] On the contrary, in every case the provincial law that was held inapplicable was a law of general application that was indisputably valid in most of its applications. Nor were the decisions based on the paramountcy doctrine: in most of the cases, there was no competing federal law in existence.[2] The theory behind the results is that each head of federal power not only grants power to the federal Parliament but, being exclusive, denies power to the provincial Legislatures. There is no doubt, of course, that a provincial law (or municipal by-law) that specifically prohibited the posting of federal election signs would be invalid, because it would be characterized as in relation to a federal matter (federal elections). The doctrine of interjurisdictional immunity insists that the same result cannot be accomplished by the enactment of a broader law that, by reason of its non-federal applications, could be characterized as in relation to a provincial matter (land use).[3]

The difficulty is to distinguish the occasions when the interjurisdictional immunity doctrine applies from the occasions when the pith and substance doctrine applies. The pith and substance doctrine, it will be recalled, stipulates that a law "in relation to" a provincial matter may validly "affect" a federal matter.[4] Thus, the *McKay* case (1965),[5] which is the case that held that a municipal sign law could not extend to federal election signs, may be contrasted with the *Oil, Chemical Workers* case (1963),[6] which decided that a provincial prohibition on union donations to political parties could validly prohibit donations to federal as well as

---

[7]*National Battlefields Commn. v. CTCUQ*, [1990] 2 S.C.R. 838.

[8]*McKay v. The Queen*, [1965] S.C.R. 798.

[Section 15:20]

[1]Singling out would not by itself be a ground of invalidity, but would be a factor indicating that the law should be characterized as "in relation to" the federal undertaking: § 15:6, "Singling out".

[2]The rationale of the early cases was not entirely clear, issues of paramountcy and interjurisdictional immunity not being clearly distinguished: § 15:17 note 1. The recent interjurisdictional immunity decisions are not based on paramountcy: see *Re Minimum Wage Act (Sask.)*, [1948] S.C.R. 248, 253, 257, 269; *Campbell-Bennett v. Comstock Midwestern*, [1954] S.C.R. 207, 222; *Commission du Salaire Minimum v. Bell Telephone Co.*, [1966] S.C.R. 767, 771, 776–777; *Natural Parents v. Superintendent of Child Welfare*, [1976] 2 S.C.R. 751, 760–761; *Bell Can. v. Que.*, [1988] 1 S.C.R. 749, 867.

[3]*McKay v. The Queen*, [1965] S.C.R. 798. The restriction on freedom of expression would now attract a Charter attack as well.

[4]§ 15:5, "Matter".

[5]*McKay v. The Queen*, [1965] S.C.R. 798.

[6]*Oil, Chemical and Atomic Workers v. Imperial Oil*, [1963] S.C.R. 584.

provincial parties. A similar decision was given in the *OPSEU* case (1987),[7] where the Court held that a provincial law prohibiting provincial public servants from running as candidates in elections could validly prohibit participation in federal as well as provincial elections.

The pith and substance doctrine, which allows a provincial law to "affect" a federal matter, is applied much more frequently than the interjurisdictional immunity doctrine, which reads down the provincial law to exclude the federal matter. As well as the *Oil Chemical Workers* and *OPSEU* cases, there are many other well-known examples.[8] The leading case is, of course, *Bank of Toronto v. Lambe* (1887),[9] which decided that a provincial tax could validly apply to a bank, although a bank is a federal undertaking. Provincial taxes do of course routinely apply to federal undertakings operating in the province. Provincial workers compensation laws also apply to federal undertakings.[10] Provincial labour laws have been held to apply to a contractor building a runway for an airport (a federal undertaking) on federal Crown land (also within federal jurisdiction),[11] and to a business owned by Indians on an Indian reserve (within federal jurisdiction).[12] A provincial limitation statute has been held applicable to an action against a interprovincial railway (a federal undertaking).[13] Provincial consumer protection laws have been held to apply to banks (within federal jurisdiction).[14] Provincial laws dealing with tort and contract have been held to apply to maritime negligence and contract claims (also within federal jurisdiction).[15]

In *Bell 1988*,[16] Beetz J. made an effort to define the boundary between the pith and substance doctrine, on the one hand, and the interjurisdictional immunity doctrine, on the other. He suggested that the inapplicability to federal undertakings of provincial occupational safety laws was "one facet of a more general rule", which he expressed in these terms:[17]

> Works, such as federal railways, things, such as land reserved for Indians, and persons, such as Indians, who are within the special and exclusive jurisdiction of Parliament, are still subject to provincial statutes that are general in their application, . . . provided however that the application of

[7]*OPSEU v. Ont.*, [1987] 2 S.C.R. 2.

[8]§ 15:5 note 14, above.

[9]*Bank of Toronto v. Lambe* (1887), 12 App. Cas. 575.

[10]*Workmen's Comp. Bd. v. CPR*, [1920] A.C. 184; for discussion, see ch. 33, Social Security, under heading § 33:4, "Workers' compensation".

[11]*Construction Montcalm v. Minimum Wage Commn.*, [1979] 1 S.C.R. 754.

[12]*Four B Manufacturing v. United Garment Workers*, [1980] 1 S.C.R. 1031.

[13]*Clark v. CNR*, [1988] 2 S.C.R. 680.

[14]*Canadian Western Bank v. Alta.*, [2007] 2 S.C.R. 3; *Bank of Montreal v. Marcotte*, [2014] 2 S.C.R. 725.

[15]*Marine Services International v. Ryan Estate*, [2013] 3 S.C.R. 53 (negligence claim); *Desgagnés Transport v. Wärtsilä Canada*, 2019 SCC 58 (contract claim).

[16]*Bell Canada v. Quebec*, [1988] 1 S.C.R. 749.

[17]*Bell Canada v. Quebec*, [1988] 1 S.C.R. 749, 762.

these provincial laws does not bear upon those subjects in what makes them specifically of federal jurisdiction.

According to this formulation, provincial laws may validly extend to federal subjects unless the laws "bear upon those subjects in what makes them specifically of federal jurisdiction". The rule that emerged from this formulation was this: if the provincial law would affect the "basic, minimum and unassailable" core of the federal subject, then the interjurisdictional immunity doctrine stipulated that the provincial law must be restricted in its application (read down) to exclude the federal subject.[18] If, on the other hand, the provincial law did not affect the core of the federal subject, then the pith and substance doctrine stipulated that the provincial law validly applied to the federal subject.

In the *Canadian Western Bank* case,[19] the Supreme Court accepted Beetz J.'s rationale for the interjurisdictional immunity doctrine, and in particular the need to protect a "basic, minimum and unassailable" core of each head of legislative power, rooted in the exclusivity of each head of power in ss. 91 and 92 of the Constitution Act, 1867.[20] However, the majority narrowed the doctrine by insisting that, if a provincial law merely affected (without having an adverse effect on) the core of a federal subject, then the doctrine did not apply. In that case, the pith and substance doctrine would prevail, enabling the provincial law to apply to the core of the federal subject. Only if the provincial law would "impair" the core of the federal subject, would interjurisdictional immunity apply. The majority indicated a strong preference for the pith and substance doctrine as the default position when otherwise valid provincial laws intruded into federal matters. This was on the basis that "a court should favour, where possible, the ordinary application of statutes enacted by *both* levels of government".[21] While interjurisdictional immunity had a role to play, it should be applied "with restraint".[22]

§ 15:21 Provincial subjects

The cases discussed to this point have all concerned the impact of *provincial* laws on federally-incorporated companies, federally-regulated undertakings and other federal persons or subjects. The doctrine of interjurisdictional immunity ought to be reciprocal, protecting provincial subjects from incursion by *federal* laws. This is because the rationale for

---

[18]See also *Ordon Estate v. Grail*, [1998] 3 S.C.R. 437, where the Court held (para. 85) that provincial law could not apply to maritime negligence actions, because that would be "an intrusion upon the unassailable core of federal maritime law". The Court also made the point (para. 89) that maritime law should be uniform throughout Canada and stressed "the importance of exclusive federal jurisdiction to the preservation of that uniformity".

[19]*Canadian Western Bank v. Alta.*, [2007] 2 S.C.R. 3.

[20]*Canadian Western Bank* v. Alta., [2007] 2 S.C.R. 3, paras. 33–34 per Binnie and LeBel JJ.; Bastarache J. concurring did not disagree with this.

[21]*Canadian Western Bank* v. Alta., [2007] 2 S.C.R. 3, para. 37 (emphasis in original).

[22]*Canadian Western Bank* v. Alta., [2007] 2 S.C.R. 3, para. 67.

the doctrine is the exclusivity of the principal heads of legislative power, and the provincial heads of power in s. 92 of the Constitution Act, 1867 are just as exclusive as the federal heads in s. 91. It is true that the federal heads of power are paramount in the event of conflict between federal and provincial laws. But the paramountcy doctrine cuts both ways. On the one hand, it is true that federal paramountcy attributes some degree of superior force to the federal heads of power. On the other hand, federal paramountcy suggests the need to protect the provincial heads of power from federal law. The federal Parliament can protect its creatures from provincial law by enacting protective laws that will be paramount over conflicting provincial laws. The provincial Legislatures cannot do this. It really would be perverse if the federal heads of power had the (additional) protection of interjurisdictional immunity and the provincial heads of power did not.[1] There is nothing in the text of ss. 91 and 92 to suggest that exclusivity means anything different for s. 92 than it does for s. 91. The inescapable conclusion must be that each provincial head of power, no less than each federal head of power, has a "basic, minimum and unassailable content" that is immune from incursion by the other level of government.

There are judicial dicta that support the position that the doctrine of interjurisdictional immunity operates both ways.[2] Robin Elliot has argued for that position,[3] and he is right that there are some cases where federal laws have been read down so as to minimize their encroachment on provincial heads of power. Perhaps the clearest example is *Clark v. CNR* (1988),[4] where a limitation period in the federal Railway Act was read down to apply only to civil causes of action created by the Act, thereby excluding common law tort actions (a core provincial subject). The opinion in this case (like other cases reading down federal laws) was not framed in the language of interjurisdictional immunity (vital part, core, or suchlike), but the outcome is certainly consistent with that doctrine. The structure of Canada's federal-provincial

---

[Section 15:21]

[1]Note, however, the asymmetrical result of cases dealing with laws binding the Crown. Federal laws can bind the provincial Crowns, but some cases hold (wrongly I believe) that provincial laws cannot bind the federal Crown: ch. 10, The Crown, under heading §§ 10:16 to 10:21, "Federal complications".

[2]*Caron v. The King*, [1924] A.C. 999, 1006 (by "parity of reason" the immunity should be reciprocal); *City of Medicine Hat v. A.G. Can.* (1985), 18 D.L.R. (4th) 428 (Alta. C.A.) (holding that federal law did not affect vital part of municipality, but assuming that municipality would be immune if it did); *Canadian Western Bank v. Alta.*, [2007] 2 S.C.R. 3, para. 35 ("In theory the doctrine is reciprocal" but its application has produced "asymmetrical" results), and see also paras. 45, 67, 77 (all recognizing the reciprocal force of the doctrine, at least in theory).

[3]R.M. Elliot, Comment (1988) 67 Can. Bar Rev. 523, 542–543; R.M. Elliot, "Interjurisdictional Immunity after *Canadian Western Bank* and *Lafarge Canada Inc.*" (2008), 43 Supreme Court L.R. (2d) 433, 468–469.

[4]*Clark v. CNR*, [1988] 2 S.C.R. 680; and see ch. 15, Judicial Review on Federal Grounds, under heading § 15:15, "Reading down", for other cases where federal laws have been read down, arguably to protect a core provincial power.

distribution of legislative powers, consisting (mainly) of twin lists of exclusive powers, entails the conclusion that the doctrine of interjurisdictional immunity be reciprocal, protecting the core of exclusive provincial heads of power from federal legislation—as well as protecting the core of exclusive federal heads of power from provincial legislation.

Canada v. PHS Community Services Society (2011),[5] the *Insite* case, was the first case in which an exemption from federal law for a provincial entity was sought on the explicit basis of the reciprocal effect of interjurisdictional immunity. Insite was a safe injection clinic in Vancouver that provided a safe and supervised environment with trained staff and clean equipment (but no drugs) to assist injection drug addicts to inject their illicit drugs (which they had to bring with them). The clinic's operations reduced deaths by overdose, reduced injuries from incompetent injections, and reduced the spread of infectious disease from shared equipment. The clinic was established by a provincial regional health authority acting under provincial powers to provide health care services. The clinic had obtained an exemption from the criminal offences associated with illegal drugs from the federal Minister of Health, acting under a power granted by s. 56 of the federal Controlled Drugs and Substances Act. The exemption was needed because without it the patients and staff would be committing the criminal offence of possession of narcotics. After a change of policy by a new federal government, the Minister of Health refused to extend the exemption, which would have forced the closing of the clinic. Proceedings were brought by the operator of the clinic and two patients to obtain a declaration that the federal Act did not apply to the provincial clinic on the ground that a clinic established by provincial law to provide health services in the province was protected from federal criminal law by the doctrine of interjurisdictional immunity. If this claim had succeeded (as it did in the provincial Court of Appeal), the federal Act would have been inapplicable to Insite and no ministerial exemption would have been needed to allow the clinic to continue its operations. In the Supreme Court of Canada, however, the Court rejected the argument that the clinic was protected from federal law by interjurisdictional immunity. McLachlin C.J., who wrote for the unanimous Court, confirmed that the doctrine was not "in principle" confined to the protection of the core of only federal powers.[6] But she held that the provincial power over health care, which came from ss. 92(7) (hospitals), 92(13) (property and civil rights) and 92(16) (local and private matters), was not immune from federal interference.[7] The provincial power was so "broad and extensive" that it was not possible to identify a "core" of exclusively provincial power. This was particularly difficult in view of the well established capacity of the federal power over criminal law to touch on health. To now exclude health matters from the federal power over criminal law

[5] *Canada v. PHS Community Services Society*, [2011] 3 S.C.R. 134. McLachlin C.J. wrote the opinion of the Court.

[6] *Canada v. PHS Community Services Society*, [2011] 3 S.C.R. 134, para. 65.

[7] *Canada v. PHS Community Services Society*, [2011] 3 S.C.R. 134, paras. 66–70.

would "disturb settled competencies and introduce uncertainties for new ones". It might even result in "legal vacuums" from which both levels of government were excluded.[8] It followed that the doctrine of interjurisdictional immunity did not apply, and therefore the federal criminal law applied to the Insite clinic.[9]

VII. INTERPRETATION OF CONSTITUTION

§ 15:22 Relevance

Once the matter (or pith and substance) of a challenged law has been identified, the second stage in judicial review is to assign the matter to one of the "classes of subjects" (or heads of legislative power) specified in the Constitution. What is involved here, of course, is the interpretation of the power-distributing language of the Constitution. This is the principal topic of many of the succeeding chapters and so nothing need be said in this chapter about the meaning of particular heads of power. However, there are certain general principles which cut across particular heads of power, and which will be treated in this chapter.

§ 15:23 Exclusiveness

Each list of classes of subjects in s. 91 or s. 92 of the Constitution Act, 1867 is exclusive to the Parliament or Legislature to which it is assigned.[1] This means that a particular "matter" will come within a class of subjects in only one list. One corollary of exclusiveness is that if either the Parliament or a Legislature fails to legislate to the full limit of its power this does not have the effect of augmenting the powers of the other level of government.[2] However, the exclusiveness of the two lists does not mean that similar or even identical laws may not be enacted by both levels of government. Some laws are available to both levels, but that is

---

[8]The *Insite* case was followed in *Carter v. Can.*, [2015] 1 S.C.R. 331, 2015 SCC 5, para. 53 (physician-assisted dying was not part of any protected core of provincial power over health, but was within the jurisdiction of both Parliament and the provinces).

[9]The clinic stayed open nevertheless because the Court ordered the Minister to grant the exemption under s. 56 on the ground that his discretion had to be exercised in compliance with s. 7 of the Charter, and, in view of the impact that closure would have on life, liberty and security of the person, the only compliant course was to grant the exemption.

[Section 15:23]

[1]This is explicit in the opening words of ss. 91 and 92 and the other power-conferring sections, except for ss. 92A(3), 94A and 95, which confer concurrent powers. Concurrency in the Constitution is discussed in § 15:25, "Concurrency".

[2]*Union Colliery Co. v. Bryden*, [1899] A.C. 580, 588. It is obvious that the powers of one level of government cannot expand or contract depending upon the absence or presence of laws enacted by the other level of government. Nonetheless, courts do occasionally make reference to the absence or presence of such laws, and it seems likely that in practice they are sometimes influenced in favour of validity by the failure of the other jurisdiction to act. See *Fulton v. Energy Resources Conservation Bd.*, [1981] 1 S.C.R. 153, 162, 164 (explicit references to federal legislative inaction with implication that provincial power augmented).

because such laws have a double aspect (or two matters),[3] not because the classes of subjects duplicate or overlap each other; they do not.[4]

On the face of it, the terse descriptions of the classes of subjects (or heads of power) appear to give rise to a good deal of duplication and overlapping. For example, "property and civil rights in the province" (s. 92(13)) appears apt to include "the regulation of trade and commerce" (s. 91(2)). The courts have dealt with this kind of apparent overlapping by interpreting each head of power as excluding the other. Thus, "trade and commerce" has been narrowed down to interprovincial or international trade and commerce, while "property and civil rights" has been interpreted as including the regulation of only local trade and commerce. Similar accommodations have been made between "property and civil rights" and other heads of federal power, such as "interest" (s. 91(19)) and "bankruptcy and insolvency" (s. 91(21)). Another case of apparent overlapping is the federal class of subject "marriage and divorce" (s. 91(26)) and the provincial class "the solemnization of marriage in the province" (s. 92(12)). In all these cases the courts have narrowed the meaning of the broader class in order to exclude the narrower class. This process of "mutual modification"[5] is necessary in order to place each head of power in its context as part of two mutually exclusive lists.[6]

§ 15:24 Ancillary power

In the United States and Australia, the enumerated federal powers include an "ancillary" power. For the United States Congress, it is a power "to make all laws which shall be necessary and proper for carrying into execution the foregoing [enumerated] powers".[1] For the Australian Parliament, it is a power to make laws with respect to "matters incidental to the execution of any power vested by this Constitution in the Parliament".[2] In the United States and Australia, there is no list of enumerated state powers: the states simply retain a general residuary

---

[3] § 15:7, "Double aspect". The pith and substance doctrine occasionally has the same effect, in that a provision that would normally be within the jurisdiction of the provinces (e.g., custody of children) may be validly enacted federally as part of a law the pith and substance of which comes within the jurisdiction of the federal Parliament (e.g., divorce): see *Papp v. Papp*, [1970] 1 O.R. 331 (Ont. C.A.) and discussion of ancillary power in the next section of this chapter.

[4] There is one arguable violation of this proposition, namely, the taxation powers of ss. 91(3) and 92(2): see ch. 31, Taxation, under heading § 31:2, "For provincial purposes".

[5] Lederman, Continuing Canadian Constitutional Dilemmas (1981), 243.

[6] In the Constitutions of the United States, and Australia, where only the federal powers are enumerated (see heading § 15:4 "Reasoning of judicial review"), there is no similar basis for limiting the scope of the enumerated powers, with the result in both countries of a more expansive interpretation of federal powers than has occurred in Canada.

[Section 15:24]

[1] Constitution of the United States, art. 1, s. 8, cl. 18.

[2] Constitution of Australia, s. 51(39).

power of legislation,[3] and so there is no ancillary clause applicable to the states.

The Constitution of Canada does not include an ancillary power in the enumerated powers of either the federal Parliament or the provincial Legislatures. There have been suggestions from time to time that an ancillary power should be implied.[4] The better view, however, is that no such power is needed. The pith and substance doctrine enables a law that is classified as "in relation to" a matter within the competence of the enacting body to have incidental or ancillary effects on matters outside the competence of the enacting body. With respect to those incidental or ancillary effects, legislative power is, of course, concurrent rather than exclusive, but it does not seem to be necessary or helpful to introduce the concept of an ancillary power to explain results that can just as easily be regarded as flowing from well-established rules of classification.

The existence of an ancillary power was rejected as redundant in *A.-G. Can. v. Nykorak* (1962),[5] in which the Supreme Court of Canada upheld legislation which conferred on the federal Crown a civil right of action for loss of the services of an injured serviceman. Judson J. for a majority of the Court said that "legislation of this kind comes squarely under head 7 of s. 91 [the defence power], notwithstanding the fact that it may incidentally affect property and civil rights within the province". And he added that it was "meaningless" to rely on a "necessarily incidental" (or ancillary) doctrine to support the effect on property and civil rights.[6]

The same point was made by Laskin J.A., sitting alone as the Ontario Court of Appeal, in *Papp v. Papp* (1970).[7] In upholding the custody provisions of the federal Divorce Act, he said that he did not favour the language of "necessarily incidental" or "ancillary" to explain the valid impact of a federal law in relation to "divorce" on a provincial matter, such as custody of children:[8]

> Where there is admitted competence, as there is here, to legislate to a certain point, the question of limits (where that point is passed) is best answered by asking whether there is a rational, functional connection between what is admittedly good and what is challenged.

Laskin J.A.'s "rational, functional connection" (or rational connection

---

[3]Constitution of the United States, tenth amendment; Constitution of Australia, s. 107.

[4]*Grand Trunk Ry. v. A.G. Can.*, [1907] A.C. 65, 68; *R. v. Thomas Fuller Construction*, [1980] 1 S.C.R. 695, 713; *Fowler v. The Queen*, [1980] 2 S.C.R. 213, 224, 226; *Regional Municipality of Peel v. MacKenzie*, [1982] 2 S.C.R. 9, 18.

[5]*A.-G. Can. v. Nykorak*, [1962] S.C.R. 331.

[6]*A.-G. Can. v. Nykorak*, [1962] S.C.R. 331, 335. This dictum was cited with approval in *Papp v. Papp*, [1970] 1 O.R. 331 (Ont. C.A.) and *A.-G. Can. v. CN Transportation*, [1983] 2 S.C.R. 206, 228 per Laskin C.J.

[7]*Papp v. Papp*, [1970] 1 O.R. 331 (Ont. C.A.).

[8]*Papp v. Papp*, [1970] 1 O.R. 331, 335–336 (Ont. C.A.) (page 336 starts at "whether").

test, as it will hereafter be described) allows each enumerated head of power to embrace laws that have some impact on matters entrusted to the other level of government, and it provides a flexible standard which gives the enacting body considerable leeway to choose the legislative techniques it deems appropriate, while providing a judicial check on an unjustified usurpation of powers. In other words, the rational connection test directly confronts the appropriate questions in interpreting a federal constitution. Not being burdened with the complication of an express ancillary power, why should Canadian courts invent one?

The rational connection test was applied in two subsequent decisions of the Supreme Court of Canada. In *R. v. Zelensky* (1978),[9] in which the Supreme Court of Canada upheld a provision in the federal Criminal Code authorizing the payment of compensation to a victim of crime, Laskin C.J. for the majority of the Court cited *Papp v. Papp* and employed the rational connection test to reject the argument that the criminal law power would not authorize the quasi-civil sanction of compensation.[10] In *Multiple Access v. McCutcheon* (1982),[11] the Supreme Court of Canada, in a majority opinion written by Dickson J., upheld a provision of federal corporation law granting a civil remedy for insider trading, on the basis that the provision had a "rational, functional connection" with company law.[12]

It would be nice if the discussion of the ancillary power (or rather its absence) could stop at this harmonious point. But, alas, there are some discordant notes to be reported. In several cases, the same Supreme Court of Canada that decided *Zelensky* and *Multiple Access* referred to an ancillary power.[13] This would not matter—it would just be a question of semantics—if the ancillary power were defined by reference to the rational connection test in *Papp v. Papp*. But the references were accompanied by some heretical doctrine. The most puzzling reference occurs in the dissenting opinion of Laskin C.J. in *A.-G. Que. v. Kellogg's Company* (1978),[14] a case in which the majority of the Court held that a provincial law regulating advertising directed at children could validly apply to advertising on television (television being within federal jurisdiction). In dissenting from this result, Laskin C.J. said that "in so far as the British North America Act may be said to recognize an ancillary power or a power to pass legislation necessarily incidental to enumerated powers, such a power resides only in the Parliament of

[9] *R. v. Zelensky*, [1978] 2 S.C.R. 940.

[10] *R. v. Zelensky*, [1978] 2 S.C.R. 940, 955.

[11] *Multiple Access v. McCutcheon*, [1982] 2 S.C.R. 161.

[12] *Multiple Access v. McCutcheon*, [1982] 2 S.C.R. 161, 183.

[13] *Grand Trunk Ry. v. A.G. Can.*, [1907] A.C. 65, 68; *R. v. Thomas Fuller Construction*, [1980] 1 S.C.R. 695, 713; *Fowler v. The Queen*, [1980] 2 S.C.R. 213, 224, 226; *Regional Municipality of Peel v. MacKenzie*, [1982] 2 S.C.R. 9, 18.

[14] *A.-G. Que. v. Kellogg's Company*, [1978] 2 S.C.R. 211.

Canada".[15] The acknowledgement that there may be an ancillary power after all is surprising, coming from Laskin C.J., who had of course expressly rejected the concept in *Papp v. Papp*. The further suggestion that the ancillary power applies only to the federal Parliament is even more surprising. The rational connection test of *Papp v. Papp* applies with equal force to provincial as to federal powers, and there are many cases in which provincial laws, held to be in relation to a matter coming within a provincial class of subject, have been held to have a valid incidental effect on a matter within federal jurisdiction.[16] I think it is plain both on principle[17] and on authority that the provincial enumerated powers have exactly the same capacity as the federal enumerated powers to "affect" matters allocated to the other level of government.[18]

In *R. v. Thomas Fuller Construction* (1979),[19] the Supreme Court of Canada held that the Federal Court Act could not confer on the Federal Court jurisdiction to determine an issue of provincial law raised by a third party notice issued in proceedings that otherwise raised issues of federal law. Pigeon J. for the majority referred to "the ancillary power doctrine" and said that it was "limited to what is truly *necessary* for the effective exercise of Parliament's legislative authority".[20] This is obviously a much stricter test than the rational connection test of *Papp v. Papp*, and indeed the result of the case was to impose an inconveniently restrictive interpretation on the federal Parliament's power to establish federal courts under s. 101 of the Constitution Act, 1867.[21] It is tempting to dismiss *Fuller Construction* as an aberration to be explained by the Court's hostility to federal jurisdiction, but the dictum on the ancillary power was cited with approval in *Regional Municipality of Peel v. MacKenzie* (1982).[22] In that case, the Court held that the federal Parliament's criminal law power would not extend so far as to impose upon a municipality an obligation to contribute to the support of a juvenile

[15]*A.-G. Que. v. Kellogg's Company*, [1978] 2 S.C.R. 211, 216.

[16]The cases cited in *Papp v. Papp*, [1970] 1 O.R. 331, include more provincial laws than federal laws. If there was any room for doubt before the *Kellogg's* case, it has certainly been resolved by the *Kellogg's* case itself and by the later decisions in *Construction Montcalm* and *Four B Manufacturing* (both cited in § 15:5 note 14), in both of which Laskin C.J. also dissented.

[17]Laskin C.J.'s statement may have been an importation of doctrine from the United States or Australia, where only the federal Congress or Parliament is empowered by a list of enumerated powers. In Canada, where both the federal Parliament and the provincial Legislatures are empowered by lists of enumerated powers, there is no basis for a distinction.

[18]This statement in the 2nd edition (1985) was approved by Dickson C.J. for the Court in *General Motors v. City National Leasing*, [1989] 1 S.C.R. 641, 670. Accord, *Global Securities Corp. v. B.C.*, [2000] 1 S.C.R. 494, para. 45 (dictum that ancillary power applies to provincial laws).

[19]*R. v. Thomas Fuller Construction*, [1980] 1 S.C.R. 695.

[20]*R. v. Thomas Fuller Construction*, [1980] 1 S.C.R. 695, 713 (emphasis in original).

[21]The decision is criticized in ch. 7, Courts, under heading § 7:11, "Federal Court of Canada".

[22]*Regional Municipality of Peel v. MacKenzie*, [1982] 2 S.C.R. 9.

delinquent. Martland J. for a unanimous Court, after citing the *Fuller Construction* dictum,[23] held that it had not been "demonstrated that it is essential to the operation of the legislative scheme provided in the Juvenile Delinquents Act that the cost of supporting juvenile delinquents must be borne by the municipalities".[24] Clearly, the stipulation that the impugned provision be "essential" to the legislative scheme is stricter than the rational connection test of *Papp v. Papp*.

In *General Motors v. City National Leasing* (1989),[25] Dickson C.J. for a unanimous Court attempted to reconcile the various approaches that the Court had taken to defining the extent of the legislative power to affect matters outside the competence of the enacting body. Dickson C.J. said: "As the seriousness of the encroachment on provincial powers varies, so does the test required to ensure that an appropriate constitutional balance is maintained".[26] According to this theory, the Court must measure the degree of encroachment of a legislative scheme on the other government's sphere of power, and then the Court must determine how necessary the impugned provision is to the otherwise valid legislative scheme.[27] For minor encroachments, the rational connection test is appropriate. For major encroachments, a stricter test (such as "truly necessary" or "essential") is appropriate. In the *General Motors* case itself, the impugned law was the civil remedy in the federal competition statute. This law did intrude into provincial power over property and civil rights, but only "in a limited way". Therefore, it was sufficient to test the validity of the law by the rational connection test, and applying that test the Court upheld the validity of the civil remedy.[28] The rational connection to the legislative scheme was that the civil remedy, by providing a means and an incentive to private enforcement, would improve the efficacy of the competition law.[29]

The *General Motors* judgment was followed by the Supreme Court of Canada in *Kirkbi v. Ritvik Holdings* (2005),[30] which was a constitutional attack on s. 7(b) of the Trade-marks Act. Section 7(b) provided a civil remedy for the infringement of an unregistered trade mark. The remedy

[23]*Regional Municipality of Peel v. MacKenzie*, [1982] 2 S.C.R. 9, 18. He also referred to *Fowler v. The Queen*, [1980] 2 S.C.R. 213 (pollution of water frequented by fish outside federal power over fisheries), where the phrase "necessarily incidental" is used (at pp. 224, 226).

[24]*Regional Municipality of Peel v. MacKenzie*, [1982] 2 S.C.R. 9, 19.

[25]*General Motors v. City National Leasing*, [1989] 1 S.C.R. 641.

[26]*General Motors v. City National Leasing*, [1989] 1 S.C.R. 641, 671.

[27]*General Motors v. City National Leasing*, [1989] 1 S.C.R. 641, 668–669.

[28]*General Motors v. City National Leasing*, [1989] 1 S.C.R. 641, 683–684.

[29]In *Kitkatla Band v. B.C.*, [2002] 2 S.C.R. 146, the Supreme Court of Canada unanimously upheld a provincial heritage property law, despite its impact on federal power over Indians, on the ground that the law's effect on native heritage property was "a closely integrated part of this scheme" (para. 75); no reference to rational connection or necessity tests.

[30]*Kirkbi v. Ritvik Holdings*, [2005] 3 S.C.R. 302. LeBel J. wrote the opinion of the Court. I disclose that I was one of the counsel for the plaintiff seeking to uphold the validity of the civil remedy.

was an action for passing off against a competitor who branded his goods or services in a way that caused confusion with the trade mark holder's goods or services. The remedy was not materially different from the tort (or delict) of passing off that exists in the common law (or civil law) of the provinces. Standing on its own, therefore, the remedy would be a matter of property and civil rights, and would be incompetent to the federal Parliament. However, the remedy did not stand on its own. It was part of the Trade-marks Act, which was a valid federal law authorized by the trade and commerce power. Could the remedy survive in that context? Yes, said the Court. The intrusion into provincial jurisdiction was "minimal", so that a "functional relationship" with the scheme of the Act was all that was necessary to sustain the remedy.[31] The Court held that this relationship existed, because the Act sought to regulate unregistered as well as registered trade marks, and a uniform national remedy for the protection of unregistered marks was a useful part of the scheme of regulation. The Court concluded that the remedy was "sufficiently integrated into the federal scheme" to be a valid law in relation to trade marks.[32]

The *General Motors* judgment is a valiant attempt to give coherence to the inconsistent approaches of the Court. With respect, however, it is not satisfactory. If a provision is a rational, functional part of a federal legislative scheme, why should it be regarded as "encroaching" or "intruding" on provincial powers? Indeed, it may be doubted whether the provincial Legislatures would have been competent to enact the civil remedy provision that was under attack, since its purpose was to improve the enforcement of a federal law. The idea of encroachment or intrusion, however appealing in common sense, does not stand up to analysis. If I am wrong on this, there still remain serious difficulties. How is the encroachment or intrusion, once found, to be measured? And, once measured, how is the unique test for validity[33] to be formulated for that particular encroachment or intrusion? In my view, the *General Motors* approach makes the answer to a simple question too complicated, too discretionary, and therefore too unpredictable.[34]

The two different ways of viewing the ancillary aspects of legislative competence are nicely illustrated by the two concurring judgments in *Re GST* (1992).[35] In that case, the Supreme Court of Canada upheld the col-

[31] *Kirkbi v. Ritvik Holdings*, [2005] 3 S.C.R. 302, paras. 32–33.

[32] *Kirkbi v. Ritvik Holdings*, [2005] 3 S.C.R. 302, paras. 35–36.

[33] *General Motors v. City National Leasing*, [1989] 1 S.C.R. 641, 669 ("A careful case by case assessment of the proper test is the best approach.")

[34] E.g., the difference of opinion in *Re Assisted Human Reproduction Act*, [2010] 3 S.C.R. 457, paras. 138 per McLachlin C.J. (rational connection is the test; ancillary provisions valid), 275 per LeBel and Deschamps JJ. (necessity is the test; ancillary provisions invalid). Admittedly, even when the test is agreed upon, judges may differ as to the result, e.g., *Que. v. Lacombe*, [2010] 2 S.C.R. 453, paras. 58 per McLachlin C.J. (rational connection is the test; ancillary provision invalid), 147 per Deschamps J. (same test; ancillary provision valid).

[35] *Re GST*, [1992] 3 S.C.R. 445.

lection provisions of the federal Goods and Services Tax, which involved payment of tax on the value added to a good or service at each stage of production and distribution. Faithful to the approach in *General Motors*, Lamer C.J. for the majority said that the provisions (whose only purpose was to collect the federal tax) were an "intrusion upon provincial jurisdiction",[36] but he upheld the provisions under what he described as the "necessarily incidental" doctrine.[37] La Forest J.'s concurring opinion was, with respect, the more orthodox one. He avoided all language implying an intrusion upon provincial jurisdiction. Once it was determined that the GST was a valid federal tax, it was "of no moment" that the collection provisions affected property and civil rights.[38]

The proper course for the Court is to return to the true path marked out by *Nykorak, Papp, Zelensky* and *Multiple Access*. Each head of legislative power, whether federal or provincial, authorizes all provisions that have a rational connection to the exercise of that head of power. There is no theoretical or practical need for a separate ancillary power. The rational connection test is to be preferred to stricter alternatives, such as the "truly necessary" or "essential" tests, simply because it is less strict. The more liberal test respects the limits imposed by the Constitution's distribution of powers by requiring a rational connection, but it still allows considerable leeway to the legislative judgment of both the federal Parliament and the provincial Legislatures. It thus accords with the refrain of this text in favour of judicial restraint.

§ 15:25 Concurrency

As noted in the earlier section of this chapter on "Exclusiveness",[1] in the Canadian Constitution most of the classes of subjects (heads of legislative power) are exclusive to the Parliament or Legislature to which they are assigned. There are, however, three provisions that explicitly confer concurrent powers. First, s. 92A(2) of the Constitution Act, 1867 (added in 1982) confers on the provincial Legislatures the power to make laws in relation to the export of natural resources, and s. 92A(3) is explicit that the power is concurrent with the federal Parliament's trade and commerce power. Secondly, s. 94A (added in 1951 and revised in 1964) confers on the federal Parliament the power to make laws in relation to old age pensions and supplementary benefits, and the section acknowledges the existence of concurrent provincial power. Thirdly, s. 95 confers on both the federal Parliament and the provincial Legislatures concurrent powers over agriculture and immigration. These three provisions[2] obviously cover only a small portion of the field of legislative power. In the Canadian scheme of distribution, exclusivity is the rule and concurrency the exception.

---

[36] *Re GST*, [1992] 3 S.C.R. 445, 471.

[37] *Re GST*, [1992] 3 S.C.R. 445, 469.

[38] *Re GST*, [1992] 3 S.C.R. 445, 490.

[Section 15:25]

[1] § 15:23, "Exclusiveness".

[2] A fourth case of concurrency could be added, although the concurrency is not

It is otherwise in the United States and Australia, where concurrency is the rule and exclusivity the exception. In each of the American and Australian Constitutions there is a single list of subjects of legislation; that list is allotted to the federal Congress or Parliament, but for the most part the listed subjects are concurrent with the states. The states do not have a list of powers at all: they simply retain the plenary powers which they possessed prior to the union.[3] This is the contrast which is emphasized in the common description of the American or Australian federal government as being one "of enumerated powers". It follows that the American or Australian states, as well as possessing exclusive residual power, also possess concurrent power over most of the topics which have been allotted to the federal Congress or Parliament. The states are free to legislate upon these topics unless and until the federal Congress or Parliament decides to exercise its power. Once a federal law has been enacted, of course, the federal law will prevail over any inconsistent state law.[4] If the federal law is deemed to be comprehensive on a particular topic, state legislation on that topic is precluded altogether; in that case, the federal power, although still formally concurrent, becomes practically exclusive.

The contrast between the two exclusive lists of Canada and the single concurrent list of the United States or Australia is not as sharp as might be thought. There is, in practice, a substantial area of concurrency in Canada, even with respect to topics covered by the two exclusive lists. This result flows from two doctrines that have been explained earlier in this chapter. The first is the "double aspect" doctrine, which recognizes that a law may have a double aspect, that is, one aspect (or characteristic) coming within the federal list, and another aspect coming within the provincial list. For example, a law prohibiting careless driving has a criminal (federal) aspect and a highway regulation (provincial) aspect. Such a law is competent to both levels of government. Upon this and other legislative subjects with double aspects, there is in practice concurrent legislative power.[5]

The second judge-made doctrine that leads to concurrency is the "pith and substance" doctrine. Under that doctrine, if the "pith and substance" of a law comes within the list of the legislative body that enacted it, then the law is valid, and it is no objection to the law that it also incidentally regulates a matter falling within the other list. For example, the custody of children may be regulated incidentally under the federal

---

express: the provincial taxing powers of s. 92(2) and s. 92A(4) are effectively concurrent with the federal taxing power of s. 91(3): see ch. 31, Taxation.

[3]The federal enumerated powers are in art. 1, s. 8, of the United States Constitution and in ss. 51, 52 of the Australian Constitution. The states' plenary power is in the tenth amendment to the United States Constitution and in s. 107 of the Australian Constitution.

[4]Federal paramountcy has been held to be implicit in the supremacy clause (art. 6, clause 2) of the United States Constitution, and is explicit in s. 109 of the Australian Constitution.

[5]§ 15:7, "Double aspect".

divorce power, although the custody of children is otherwise a matter coming within provincial competence. This is one of many subjects upon which legislative power is in practice concurrent.[6]

Whenever legislative power is concurrent, there is the possibility of conflict between federal and provincial laws. In Canada, as in the United States and Australia, conflict between federal and provincial (or state) laws is resolved by a rule of federal paramountcy. Paramountcy is the topic of the next chapter of this book.

§ 15:26 Exhaustiveness

As has been explained in chapter 12, Parliamentary Sovereignty, the distribution of powers between the federal Parliament and the provincial Legislatures is exhaustive: the totality of legislative power is distributed between the federal Parliament and the provincial Legislatures. As the earlier chapter explained, there are important exceptions to the doctrine of exhaustive distribution, including the subjects protected by the Charter of Rights. But the exceptions have not eaten up the rule, and the rule is still helpful in understanding the structure of the Constitution.

It goes without saying that the framers of the Constitution could not foresee every kind of law which has subsequently been enacted; nor could they foresee social, economic and technological developments which have required novel forms of regulation. But they did make provision for new or unforeseen kinds of laws. The last of the enumerated provincial classes of subjects in s. 92 is "generally all matters of a merely local or private nature in the province" (s. 92(16)). And for matters which do not come within this or any other enumerated class of subjects, the opening words of s. 91 give to the federal Parliament the residuary power "to make laws for the peace, order, and good government of Canada in relation to all matters not coming within the classes of subjects assigned exclusively to the Legislatures of the Provinces". Thus, any matter which does not come within any of the specific classes of subjects will be provincial if it is merely local or private (s. 92(16)) and will be federal if it has a national dimension (s. 91, opening words).[1]

The consequence that is usually claimed to flow from the principle of exhaustive distribution is that every conceivable law is competent to one level of government or the other. That is generally true. But a law that is excessively broad or vague will be incompetent to both levels of government. A law must be sufficiently particular that it can be attributed to a "matter" coming within one of the classes of subjects in relation to which the enacting body is authorized to legislate. In *Saumur v.*

---

[6]The pith and substance doctrine is discussed from this point of view in § 15:5, "Matter", and § 15:24, "Ancillary power".

[Section 15:26]

[1]See ch. 17, Peace, Order, and Good Government.

Quebec (1953),[2] Rand J. articulated this doctrine as one reason for striking down a municipal by-law that forbade the distribution of literature on the streets of Quebec City without the permission of the chief of police. The by-law could have been administered as a mechanism for the regulation of the streets to prevent harassment of pedestrians and reduce littering, but the evidence showed that the by-law was in fact administered as a vehicle of censorship by the chief of police, whose decisions were based on his attitude towards the contents of the material to be distributed. For Rand J., the absence of any standards in the by-law to guide the chief of police's discretion was, by itself, fatal to the validity of the by-law. Without more precision in the drafting of the by-law, it was impossible to classify it as in relation to any particular matter.[3]

It might perhaps have been thought that a law that did not fit into any of the enumerated classes of subjects (including s. 92(16)) would come within the federal Parliament's residuary peace, order, and good government power. Again, that is generally true. But in the *Anti-Inflation Reference* (1976),[4] Beetz J., speaking for the majority of the Court on this issue (he dissented from the result), denied that a topic as broad as "the containment and reduction of inflation" could be authorized by the peace, order, and good government power. Except in times of emergency, even the p.o.g.g. power would embrace a new matter only where it "was not an aggregate but had a degree of unity that made it indivisible, an identity which made it distinct from provincial matters and a sufficient consistence to retain the bounds of form".[5] The point is that the federal Parliament should not be able to extend its authority into fields of provincial competence by enacting laws upon subjects so diffuse and pervasive that they do not fit within any enumerated power. In other words, a federal law that purports to regulate matters within provincial (as well as federal) competence cannot be saved by classifying the law as in relation to a matter as broad and diffuse as inflation.

§ 15:27 Progressive interpretation

Since confederation in 1867, Canada has changed a great deal. Its territory and population have expanded many times. Agriculture has ceased to be the dominant activity, supplanted by mining, manufacturing, financial and service industries. The population has become concentrated in large cities. Technological developments, including electricity, the internal combustion engine, the telephone, aviation, radio, television and now the computer, have transformed the modes of communication

---

[2] *Saumur v. Quebec*, [1953] 2 S.C.R. 299.

[3] *Saumur v. Quebec*, [1953] 2 S.C.R. 299, 333. The full text of this dictum is set out in ch. 14, Delegation, under heading § 14:7, "Classification of laws". None of the other judges used this mode of reasoning.

[4] *Re Anti-Inflation Act*, [1976] 2 S.C.R. 373.

[5] *Re Anti-Inflation Act*, [1976] 2 S.C.R. 373, 458. Accord, *R. v. Crown Zellerbach*, [1988] 1 S.C.R. 401, 432; Lederman, Continuing Canadian Constitutional Dilemmas (1981), 310–311.

and transportation, the appearance of the landscape, and the ways in which people live, work and play. Governments have grown immensely, as they have undertaken the building of railways, roads, dams, airports, pipelines and other public projects; and as the increasing acceptance of egalitarian, collectivist and humanitarian values has required the regulation of industry for the protection of workers, consumers and the environment, the regulation of labour relations to permit collective bargaining, and the expansion of public education, public health and social security systems. While all this change was occurring, the nation also had to endure the first world war, the great depression, the second world war and periodic bouts of inflation.

During this time the Constitution changed very little, and only four small changes were made in the distribution of powers.[1] The doctrine of progressive interpretation is one of the means by which the Constitution Act, 1867 has been able to adapt to the changes in Canadian society. What this doctrine stipulates is that the general language used to describe the classes of subjects (or heads of power) is not to be frozen in the sense in which it would have been understood in 1867. For example, the phrase "undertakings connecting the provinces with any other or others of the provinces" (s. 92(10)(a)) includes an interprovincial telephone system, although the telephone was unknown in 1867;[2] the phrase "criminal law" (s. 91(27)) "is not confined to what was criminal by the law of England or of any province in 1867";[3] the phrase "banking" (s. 91(15)) is not confined to "the extent and kind of business actually carried on by banks in Canada in 1867".[4] On the contrary, the words of the Act are to be given a "progressive interpretation", so that they are continuously adapted to new conditions and new ideas.

It is true that the Privy Council did not always follow this precept, and occasionally denied its validity.[5] Indeed, in the *Labour Conventions* case (1937),[6] Lord Atkin gave eloquent expression to a contrary point of view, saying, "while the ship of state now sails on larger ventures and into foreign waters she still retains the watertight compartments which are an essential part of her original structure". That Lord Atkin did not conceive of the "watertight compartments" expanding or contracting in

[Section 15:27]

[1]In 1940, unemployment insurance was added to the federal list (s. 91(2A)). In 1951, power over old age pensions was granted to the federal Parliament (s. 94A). In 1964, the new power over old age pensions was expanded to include supplementary benefits (s. 94A). In 1982, provincial powers over natural resources were added (s. 92A). The most important changes since 1867, not affecting the federal distribution of powers, have been the adoption of the amending procedures and the Charter of Rights in 1982.

[2]*Toronto v. Bell Telephone Co.*, [1905] A.C. 52.

[3]*P.A.T.A. v. A.-G. Can.*, [1931] A.C. 310, 324. Accord, *R. v. Zelensky*, [1978] 2 S.C.R. 940, 951 (upholding compensation provision in federal Criminal Code).

[4]*A.-G. Alta. v. A.-G. Can.* (Alberta Bill of Rights) [1947] A.C. 503, 553.

[5]Browne, The Judicial Committee and the British North America Act (1967), 20–29.

[6]*A.-G. Can. v. A.-G. Ont.* (Labour Conventions) [1937] A.C. 326, 354.

response to new developments is made clear from the actual holding in the *Labour Conventions* case, which was an emphatic refusal to give a progressive interpretation to the treaty power. But the authority of the *Labour Conventions* case, even on the point which it decided, is now suspect;[7] and the "watertight compartments" metaphor is not a reliable guide to judicial attitudes to the Constitution. Lord Sankey's metaphor would now be more generally accepted: "the B.N. A. Act planted in Canada a living tree capable of growth and expansion within its natural limits".[8]

The doctrine of progressive interpretation is rejected by some scholars, who argue that the courts are forever bound by the "original understanding" of the Constitution. This position, often called "originalism", is criticized later in this book.[9] It suffices to say here that originalism has never enjoyed significant support in Canada, either in the courts or the academy.[10] The issue was squarely raised in the *Same-Sex Marriage Reference* (2004),[11] where the question was whether Parliament's power over "marriage" would extend to legalizing same-sex marriage. No one doubted that the original understanding in 1867 would have been that marriage was by its nature the union of a man and a woman with a view to the procreation of children. At that time, marriage and religion were inseparable and sexual acts between consenting adults of the same sex were criminal (as they remained until 1969). The Supreme Court of Canada denied that it was bound by the original understanding, which it described as "frozen concepts" reasoning. Our Constitution, the Court said, "is a living tree which, by way of progressive interpretation, accom-

---

[7]See ch. 11, Treaties, under heading § 11:11, "Labour Conventions case".

[8]*Edwards v. A.-G. Can.*, [1930] A.C. 114, 136; Lord Sankey did emphasize that the case was not concerned with the distribution of legislative powers, but his idea was reformulated and approved in *British Coal Corp. v. The King*, [1935] A.C. 500, 518 and *A.-G. Ont. v. A.-G. Can.* (Privy Council Appeals) [1947] A.C. 127, 154, the latter of which did involve the distribution of powers. The Supreme Court of Canada has approved the living tree metaphor in *A.-G. Que. v. Blaikie*, [1979] 2 S.C.R. 1016, 1029 (interpretation of language rights); *A.-G. B.C. v. Can. Trust Co.*, [1980] 2 S.C.R. 466, 478 (interpretation of taxing power); *Re Residential Tenancies Act*, [1981] 1 S.C.R. 714, 723 (interpretation of s. 96). The living tree doctrine is also applied in Charter cases: ch. 36, Charter of Rights, under heading § 36:18, "Progressive interpretation".

[9]Chapter 60, Proof, under heading § 60:5, "Originalism".

[10]See I. Binnie, "Constitutional Interpretation and Original Intent" (2004) 23 Supreme Court L.R. (2d) 345. However, there is a small group of authors that advocates a form of originalism for Canada: see e.g. F.L. Morton and R. Knopff, "Permanence and Change in a Written Constitution: The 'Living Tree' Doctrine and the Charter of Rights" (1990) 1 Supreme Court L.R. 533; G. Huscroft, "The Trouble with Living Tree Interpretation" (2006) 25 U.Q.L.J. 1; B.W. Miller, "Beguiled by Metaphors: The Living Tree and Originalist Constitutional Interpretation in Canada" (2009) 22 Can. J.L. & Jur. 331; K.A. Froc, "Is Originalism Bad for Women? The Curious Case of Canada's 'Equal Rights Amendment' " (2015) 19 Rev. Const. Stud. 237; B. Oliphant & L. Sirota, "Has the Supreme Court of Canada Rejected 'Originalism'?" (2016) 42 Queen's L.J. 107; A. Honickman, "The Original Living Tree" (2019) 28 Const Forum Const 29.

[11]*Re Same-Sex Marriage*, [2004] 3 S.C.R. 698. The unanimous opinion was by "the Court".

modates and addresses the realities of modern life".[12] Canada in 2004 was a pluralistic society. Marriage, from the perspective of the state, was a civil institution. What was "natural" to marriage was now contested. Same-sex marriage had been legislatively recognized by two European countries (Belgium and the Netherlands), and judicially recognized by several Canadian provinces. A progressive interpretation of s. 91(26) led to the conclusion that it should be expanded to include same-sex marriage. Following this decision, Parliament enacted a law to legalize same-sex marriage.[13]

Another *Re Employment Insurance Act* (2005),[14] which was a challenge to the validity of the provisions of the federal Employment Insurance Act that granted maternity benefits to pregnant workers who left work to have a baby and parental benefits to mothers and fathers (natural or adoptive) who left work to care for a baby. The federal power over "unemployment insurance" was contained in s. 91(2A) of the Constitution Act, 1867, a head of power that was added by amendment in 1940. The first statute enacted under that power in 1940 did not provide for either maternity or parental benefits, and indeed virtually excluded married women from benefits. The assumption at the time was that married women would stop working after getting married, when they would be supported by their husbands. In 1940, it could hardly have been anticipated that married women would become a major part of the workforce, that they would want to take only temporary leave to have a child, and that they would want to maintain their employment afterwards. Nor would it have been anticipated that there was any need for fathers to take time off from work to help care for babies; that was the duty of their wives. Looking at Canada 65 years later, the Supreme Court of Canada emphasized the "living tree" quality of the Constitution: "the Court takes a progressive approach to ensure that Confederation can be adapted to new social realities".[15] Those social realities included "the evolution of the role of women in the labour market and of the role of fathers in child care".[16] A "generous interpretation" of s. 91(2A) would include income-replacement benefits to parents who must take time off work to give birth to or care for children. The maternity and parental benefits were therefore upheld.

Needless to say, the doctrine of progressive interpretation does not liberate the courts from the normal constraints of interpretation. Constitutional language, like the language of other texts, must be "placed in its proper linguistic, philosophical and historical contexts".[17] Nor is the original understanding (if it can be ascertained) irrelevant.

---

[12] *Re Same-Sex Marriage*, [2004] 3 S.C.R. 698, para. 22.

[13] Civil Marriage Act, S.C. 2005, c. 33.

[14] *Re Employment Insurance Act*, [2005] 2 S.C.R. 669. Deschamps J. wrote the opinion of the Court.

[15] *Re Employment Insurance Act*, [2005] 2 S.C.R. 669, para. 9.

[16] *Re Employment Insurance Act*, [2005] 2 S.C.R. 669, para. 77.

[17] *R. v. Big M Drug Mart*, [1985] 1 S.C.R. 295, 344 per Dickson J.

On the contrary, the interpretation of a constitutional provision "must be anchored in the historical context of the provision".[18] All that progressive interpretation insists is that the original understanding is not binding forever. If new inventions, new conditions or new ideas will fairly fit within the constitutional language, contemporary courts are not constrained to limit their interpretations to meanings that would have been contemplated in 1867 (or whenever the text was created).

The idea underlying the doctrine of progressive interpretation is that the Constitution Act, 1867, although undeniably a statute, is not a statute like any other: it is a "constituent" or "organic" statute, which has to provide the basis for the entire government of a nation over a long period of time. An inflexible interpretation, rooted in the past, would only serve to withhold necessary powers from the Parliament or Legislatures, and deny remedies to hitherto unrecognized victims of injustice. It must be remembered too that the Constitution Act, 1867, like other federal constitutions, differs from an ordinary statute in that it cannot easily be amended when it becomes out of date, so that its adaptation to changing conditions must fall to a large extent upon the courts.

§ 15:28 Unwritten constitutional principles

The interpretation of a constitution is of course the interpretation of an authoritative text, but over a long period of time, as precedents accumulate, the judicial exegesis may come to achieve more importance than the original text, and may bear only a tenuous relationship to the original text. The previous section of this chapter on progressive interpretation explains the phenomenon of the accommodation of the text to changes in the economy, technology, living patterns and ideas about the role of government. Obviously, the judges have played a creative role in that accommodation. But, even if the world remained the same, the courts would still have to apply the text to unpredictable human and institutional behaviour. Perhaps the best example of the interpretative process building an elaborate structure on a slender textual foundation is the case law under s. 96 of the Constitution Act, 1867. Section 96, the text of which provides simply for the federal appointment of the judges of the superior, district and county courts in each province, is now encrusted with an elaborate body of doctrine that protects the jurisdiction of superior courts and restricts the creation and empowering of inferior courts and administrative tribunals.[1] While s. 96 provides an extreme example, there is nothing unusual about this process. Cases come before the courts that were not foreseen when the text was drafted, and the courts see implications in the text that were not obvious when it

---

[18] *R. v. Blais*, [2003] 2 S.C.R. 236 (holding that the word "Indians" in the Natural Resources Agreements scheduled to the Constitution Act, 1930 originally excluded Métis and should not be expanded on the basis of the "living tree" approach).

[Section 15:28]

[1] The case law is explained in ch. 7, Courts, under heading §§ 7:15 to 7:20, "Implications of Constitution's judicature sections".

was drafted; each new case becomes a precedent, and before long there is a lot of detailed doctrine to supplement some brief phrase in the general language of the Constitution. In this sense, no one doubts that judges make new law.

An entirely different order of judicial law-making is the discovery (meaning invention) by the courts of "unwritten constitutional principles", the word "unwritten" being a frank acknowledgment that the "principles" are not to be found in the written constitutional text and cannot be derived by normal processes of interpretation from the text. It goes without saying that the Constitution of Canada is constructed on a set of unwritten or implicit principles that have profoundly influenced the drafting of the text and that continue to influence its interpretation.[2] Democracy, constitutionalism, the rule of law, the independence of the judiciary, the protection of civil liberties and federalism are among those principles. Any capsule description of the Constitution of Canada (to a foreigner, for example) would make use of those ideas. But the normal assumption of Canadian lawyers is that only the actual text of the Constitution— a text that is admittedly subject to interpretation— creates enforceable rights and obligations.[3] There are, however, a number of cases where the Supreme Court of Canada has found an "unwritten constitutional principle" in the Constitution, and has treated the principle as an implied term of the Constitution that is enforceable in precisely the same way as if it were an express term.[4] When an unwritten constitutional principle is directly enforced in that fashion, it is hard to avoid the conclusion that the Constitution has been amended by judicial fiat in defiance of the procedure laid down by the Constitution for its amendment.

In the *Manitoba Language Reference* (1985),[5] the Supreme Court of Canada held that "in the process of constitutional adjudication, the Court may have regard to unwritten postulates which form the very foundation of the Constitution of Canada". In that case, the applicable

[2]Even administrative powers are interpreted in the light of unwritten principles of the Constitution: *Lalonde v. Ont.* (2002), 56 O.R. (3d) 505 (C.A.) (setting aside government decision to reduce functions of French-language community hospital, insufficient attention having been paid to minority rights).

[3]P.W. Hogg and C.F. Zwibel, "The Rule of Law in the Supreme Court of Canada" (2005) 55 U. Toronto L.J. 715; see also ch. 1, Sources, under heading § 1:1, "Constitutional Law".

[4]See B. McLachlin, "Unwritten Constitutional Principles: What is Going On?" (2006) 4 N.Z.J. Public & Int. L. 147; J. Leclair, "Canada's Unfathomable Unwritten Constitutional Principles" (2002) 27 Queen's L.J. 389. Compare P. Hughes, "Recognizing Substantive Equality as a Foundational Constitutional Principle" (1999) 22 Dal. L.J. 5 (arguing for the recognition of an unwritten principle of substantive equality to make up for deficiencies in the written guarantee of s. 15 of the Charter of Rights). The phenomenon is not restricted to Canada: Tribe, The Invisible Constitution (2008) (demonstrating the significance of unwritten (invisible) constitutional principles in the constitutional law of the United States); L.B. Tremblay, "Les principes constitutionnels non écrits" (2012) 17 Review of Con. Studies 15.

[5]*Re Manitoba Language Rights*, [1985] 1 S.C.R. 721, 752 per the Court.

unwritten postulate was "the principle of rule of law".[6] This was no rhetorical flourish. The Court invoked the principle to solve the crisis that would have resulted from the Court's holding that all of the laws of Manitoba enacted since 1890 were invalid. They had been enacted in English only, in defiance of a constitutional requirement to enact the laws in English and French. The rule of law required that the Manitoba Legislature must follow the law of the constitution, which in turn required the Court to hold the laws to be invalid. But another aspect of the rule of law called for a community regulated by law, which would be violated if Manitoba were left with a vacuum of law. The solution to these conflicting aspects of the rule of law was to hold the laws enacted in English to be invalid, but also to hold that the laws were to remain in force for a temporary period stipulated by the Court while the existing laws were translated and re-enacted. By virtue of the unwritten "constitutional guarantee of rule of law",[7] the people of Manitoba continued to be governed temporarily by a body of law that had been invalidly enacted, and that owed its force solely to the fiat of the Court.

In *Re Remuneration of Judges* (1997),[8] the Supreme Court of Canada, by a majority, held that three provincial statutes reducing the salaries of provincial court judges were unconstitutional, because they violated judicial independence. Lamer C.J., speaking for the majority, held that the Constitution of Canada contained an "unwritten constitutional principle" of judicial independence. It did not matter that there were explicit guarantees of judicial independence for superior court judges in s. 99 of the Constitution Act, 1867, and for the judges of inferior courts with criminal jurisdiction in s. 11(d) of the Charter of Rights. These were merely exemplary of a broader unwritten principle. The unwritten principle applied to the courts deliberately left out of the explicit guarantees, and it required, on pain of invalidity, that elaborate procedures (designed by the Court) be followed to remove a judge and even to set judicial salaries. This assertion of an unwritten constitutional principle was technically an obiter dictum, because the Court decided the case on the basis of the explicit guarantee of judicial independence in s. 11(d). However, in later cases, the Court treated the unwritten principle as established law,[9] and in *Mackin v. New Brunswick* (2002)[10] the Court actually struck down a provincial statute abolishing

---

[6] *Re Manitoba Language Rights*, [1985] 1 S.C.R. 721, 752.

[7] *Re Manitoba Language Rights*, [1985] 1 S.C.R. 721, 758.

[8] *Re Remuneration of Judges*, [1997] 3 S.C.R. 3; discussed in ch. 7, Courts, under heading §§ 7:1 to 7:9, "Provincial courts".

[9] *Re Therrien*, [2001] 2 S.C.R. 3 (upholding removal of judge on ground that unwritten constitutional principle had been complied with); *Ocean Port Hotel v. B.C.*, [2001] 2 S.C.R. 781 (holding that unwritten constitutional principle did not apply to administrative tribunals—a contrary decision would have invalidated dozens of statutes in every province); *Babcock v. Can.*, [2002] 3 S.C.R. 3 (holding that unwritten constitutional principle did not invalidate statute allowing government to withhold cabinet documents from court proceedings).

[10] *Mackin v. New Brunswick*, [2002] 1 S.C.R. 405; discussed in ch. 7, Courts, under heading §§ 7:1 to 7:9, "Provincial courts".

supernumerary status for provincial court judges on the ground that the removal of an economic advantage of judicial employment offended the unwritten principle of judicial independence (as well ass. 11(d)).[11]

In the *Secession Reference* (1998),[12] the Supreme Court of Canada held that the secession of a province could not take place unilaterally but must proceed in accordance with the amending procedures of the Constitution. This was straight-forward constitutional law based on the text of the Constitution. But the Court went on to hold that any secession must respect four unwritten principles of the Constitution, those of democracy, federalism, constitutionalism and the protection of minorities. These four principles, which are without doubt leading characteristics of the Constitution of Canada, were not invoked merely for rhetorical effect. The Court said that two of the principles, namely, democracy and federalism, required that, if a province voted to secede, the rest of Canada would come under a legal obligation to negotiate the terms of secession with that province. This newly-discovered obligation to negotiate made the Court's decision much more palatable in the province of Quebec, and since there has been no affirmative vote to secede, the meaning and implications of the ruling remain unknown.

Unwritten constitutional principles are vague enough to arguably accommodate virtually any grievance about government policy. Fortunately, lower courts have maintained a wise reluctance to invalidate government initiatives on the basis of unwritten constitutional principles,[13] and the Supreme Court of Canada shows some sign of reining in its creative impulses.[14] In *Babcock v. Canada* (2002),[15] the Court rejected a challenge to s. 39 of the Canada Evidence Act, which allows the federal government to withhold cabinet documents from court proceedings to which the documents are relevant. The challengers invoked three unwritten constitutional principles, namely, the rule of law, the separation of powers and the independence of the judiciary. McLachlin C.J. for the unanimous Court said that "the unwritten principles must be balanced against the principle of Parliamentary sovereignty",[16] a salutary caution notably absent from the majority opinions in the *Remuneration* and *Mackin* cases, where statutes were struck down. Indeed, what is so extreme about those two decisions is not just the assumption that judicial independence is impaired by any reduction in judicial salaries

[11]R. Millen, "The Independence of the Bar: An Unwritten Constitutional Principle" (2005) 84 Can. Bar Rev. 107, argues for the recognition of the independence of the bar as an unwritten constitutional principle, because it is a precondition to the protection of individual rights and the maintenance of the rule of law.

[12]*Re Secession of Quebec*, [1998] 2 S.C.R. 217; discussed in ch. 5, Federalism, under heading §§ 5:24 to 5:26, "Secession".

[13]But note the successful blocking of a government initiative in the *Lalonde* case, *Lalonde v. Ont.* (2002), 56 O.R. (3d) 505 (C.A.).

[14]See *Ocean Port Hotel v. B.C.*, [2001] 2 S.C.R. 781, refusing to extend the unwritten principle of judicial independence to administrative tribunals.

[15]*Babcock v. Can.*, [2002] 3 S.C.R. 3.

[16]*Babcock v. Can.*, [2002] 3 S.C.R. 3, para. 55.

and perquisites, but the twin assumption that judicial independence is superior to and unqualified by any other principles of the Constitution, including parliamentary supremacy (or democratic control of public spending). *Babcock* may indicate some second thoughts on the second assumption.

Another unsuccessful attempt to invoke the unwritten principles of the constitution came in *British Columbia v. Imperial Tobacco* (2005).[17] British Columbia enacted a statute for the purpose of recouping from the tobacco companies the health-care costs incurred by the province for tobacco-related disease. This involved the creation of a new tort, which was solely applicable to the tobacco companies, which was retroactive, which involved the abolition of existing limitation periods, which was supported by rebuttable presumptions of fact that were designed to relieve the government of affirmatively proving important elements of the new tort, which denied the defendants access to individual health care records (to rebut the presumptions), and for which the maximum damages would be all present and future health care costs incurred by the province for tobacco-related disease, divided up among each company in accordance with its market share. The defendant tobacco companies challenged the validity of the statute, relying on the independence of the judiciary and the rule of law. Both these challenges failed. With respect to judicial independence, there was, of course, no doubt that a breach would lead to the invalidity of the statute. However, the Supreme Court of Canada held that there was no such breach; this ruling is described earlier in this book.[18] With respect to the rule of law, the Court held that a breach could not lead to the invalidity of a statute (except for the rare case where a statute was not enacted in the correct manner and form).[19] In particular, there was no constitutional objection to laws that singled out an industry for special treatment, laws that were retroactive,[20] or laws that conferred special advantages on government. Even if the statute had denied the tobacco companies a fair trial (as the companies claimed but which the Court denied), that would not be a basis for invalidity of the statute.[21] The Court's basic point was that an unwritten principle as potentially broad and vague as the rule of law would, if it

[17] *British Columbia v. Imperial Tobacco*, [2005] 2 S.C.R. 473. Major J. wrote the opinion of the Court.

[18] Chapter 7, Courts, under heading § 7:3, "Tenure of provincial judges: s. 99".

[19] *British Columbia v. Imperial Tobacco*, [2005] 2 S.C.R. 473, para. 60.

[20] The Charter of Rights, by s. 11(g), prohibits the retroactive creation of criminal liability, but not civil liability.

[21] The Charter of Rights, by s. 11(d), requires a fair criminal trial, and, by s. 7, requires a fair civil trial where life, liberty or security of the person is in issue. But there is no Charter guarantee of a fair civil trial where only money is in issue. Accord, *B.C. v. Christie*, [2007] 1 S.C.R. 873 (holding that rule of law does not provide general right to counsel above and beyond ss. 7 and 10(b)); discussed in ch. 50, Rights on Arrest or Detention, under heading § 50:15, "Legal aid".

led to invalidity, create broader versions of written rights and render redundant the specific language of much of the written constitution.[22]

The statement in *Imperial Tobacco* that a breach of the unwritten constitutional principle of the rule of law could not lead to the invalidity of a statute seems to have been forgotten by the majority of the Supreme Court in *Trial Lawyers' Association of British Columbia v. British Columbia* (2014).[23] In that case, the Court struck down a rule of the superior court of British Columbia that imposed a hearing fee on a litigant who set down a civil case for trial. The fee escalated with the length of the trial, and amounted to $3,500 for a ten-day trial. The majority of the Court found that a fee that large was unaffordable to a person of modest means, and that the fee had the effect of denying access to the superior court to potential litigants of modest means. The majority struck down the hearing fee as an unconstitutional restriction on access to the superior court of the province. The main reason offered for this conclusion was s. 96 of the Constitution Act, 1867, which provides for the appointment of superior court judges.[24] But the unwritten constitutional principle of the rule of law was offered as a second reason: "access to the courts is essential to the rule of law".[25] Rothstein J., who dissented on the constitutional issue, criticized both lines of the majority's reasoning. The majority's interpretation of s. 96 was "overly broad" and "novel". The rule of law reasons not only ignored the restraint insisted upon in *Imperial Tobacco*, but also ignored the presence in the Constitution of express, but limited, guarantees of access to the courts. Section 11(d) of the Charter guaranteed a fair and public hearing for a person charged with an offence. Section 24(1) of the Charter provided that a person whose Charter rights have been infringed or denied may apply to a court of competent jurisdiction for a remedy. "These provisions would be unnecessary if the Constitution already

[22]*British Columbia v. Imperial Tobacco*, [2005] 2 S.C.R. 473, para. 65. Note that this objection did not deter the Court from developing an unwritten principle of judicial independence despite the specific guarantees in s. 99 of the Constitution Act, 1867 and s. 11(d) of the Charter: text accompanying § 15:25 note 3, above. Nor did this objection deter the Court from developing a "residuary" theory of s. 7, under which the specific guarantees of s. 11 are merely exemplary of a broader guarantee in s. 7, which will cover cases excluded from s. 11: ch. 47, Fundamental justice, under heading § 47:14, "Procedure and substance".

[23]*Trial Lawyers' Association of British Columbia v. British Columbia*, [2014] 3 S.C.R. 31, 2014 SCC 59. McLachlin C.J. wrote the majority opinion for five members of the seven-judge bench. Cromwell J. wrote a concurring opinion which relied solely on non-constitutional reasons. Rothstein J. wrote a dissenting opinion.

[24]The s. 96 reasons of the Court are explained in ch. 7, Courts, under heading § 7:18 "Superior courts".

[25]*Trial Lawyers' Association of British Columbia v. British Columbia*, [2014] 3 S.C.R. 31, 2014 SCC 59, para. 38. It is not entirely clear from the majority opinion whether the rule of law was regarded as a stand-alone reason (as implied by paras. 40, 64) or simply a reinforcement of the majority's interpretation of s. 96 (as implied by paras. 38, 39). Rothstein J., dissenting, criticized both lines of reasoning, but clearly took the former view.

contained a more general right to access superior courts."[26] The majority view prevailed of course, and the Constitution now does contain a general right to access superior courts, although the provenance of the right (s. 96 or rule of law or both) is not clear.

It must be acknowledged that the phenomenon of unwritten constitutionalism is not a new one. In *De Savoye v. Morguard Investments* (1990),[27] La Forest J. for a unanimous Supreme Court of Canada invoked a principle of federalism to articulate a full faith and credit rule of the Constitution, which requires the courts of each province to recognize judgments issued by the courts of other Canadian provinces. In the constitutions of the United States and Australia, there is an explicit full faith and credit clause. Canada's unwritten one is however sufficient to invalidate inconsistent provincial legislation.[28] The "implied bill of rights" is another unwritten doctrine that developed in a line of cases starting with the *Alberta Press* case in 1938.[29] The theory was that the Constitution, although lacking an explicit bill of rights (a deliberate choice of the framers in 1867), nonetheless contained an implied bill of rights that restrained the provincial Legislatures and perhaps the federal Parliament from restricting freedom of expression and other fundamental freedoms. With the adoption of an explicit Charter of Rights in 1982, the implied bill of rights theory has lost its rationale, but it is an early example of an unwritten constitutional principle.

§ 15:29 Legislative history

To what extent is the legislative history of the Constitution Act, 1867 admissible as an aid to the interpretation of the language of the Act? This issue is considered in chapter 60, Proof.[1]

§ 15:30 Precedent

The need for judicial adaptation of a constitution, coupled with the difficulty of amendment, invites the question whether the doctrine of precedent (or stare decisis) should not be relaxed in constitutional cases. This question has been considered in chapter 8, Supreme Court of

---

[26] *Trial Lawyers' Association of British Columbia v. British Columbia*, [2014] 3 S.C.R. 31, 2014 SCC 59, para. 101, following *Imperial Tobacco*'s warning that a broad application of the rule of law would "render many of our written constitutional rights redundant and, in doing so, undermine the delimitation of those rights chosen by our constitutional framers".

[27] *De Savoye v. Morguard Investments*, [1990] 3 S.C.R. 1077; discussed in ch. 13, Extraterritorial Competence, under heading § 13:11, "Recognition of judgments".

[28] *Hunt v. T & N*, [1993] 4 S.C.R. 289 (enforcing B.C. court order for production of documents notwithstanding Quebec statute forbidding the removal of the documents from the province).

[29] *Re Alta. Statutes*, [1938] S.C.R. 100; discussed in ch. 34, Civil Liberties, under heading § 34:7, "Implied bill of rights".

[Section 15:29]

[1] Chapter 60, Proof, under heading §§ 60:1 to 60:7, "Legislative history".

Canada.[1]

[Section 15:30]

[1]Chapter 8, Supreme Court of Canada, under heading § 8:13, "Precedent".

Chapter 16

Paramountcy

I. PROBLEM OF INCONSISTENCY

§ 16:1 Problem of inconsistency

II. DEFINITION OF INCONSISTENCY

§ 16:2 Definition of inconsistency

III. EXPRESS CONTRADICTION

§ 16:3 Impossibility of dual compliance
§ 16:4 Frustration of federal purpose

IV. NEGATIVE IMPLICATION

§ 16:5 Covering the field
§ 16:6 Express extension of paramountcy

V. OVERLAP AND DUPLICATION

§ 16:7 Constitutional significance
§ 16:8 Double criminal liability
§ 16:9 Double civil liability

VI. EFFECT OF INCONSISTENCY

§ 16:10 Effect of inconsistency

I. PROBLEM OF INCONSISTENCY

§ 16:1 Problem of inconsistency

Every legal system has to have a rule to reconcile conflicts between inconsistent laws. The solution of the common law, which is applicable in unitary states such as the United Kingdom or New Zealand, is the doctrine of implied repeal: where there are two inconsistent (or conflicting) statutes[1] the later is deemed to have impliedly repealed the earlier to

[Section 16:1]

[1]The rule applies only to statute law, because the normal development of the common law eliminates inconsistencies. Where two inconsistent rules of common law are announced by the courts, a later court will choose one of them as "correct", either overruling the other decision as wrong or declaring it to be applicable only to some narrow set of facts or even "its own" facts.

the extent of the inconsistency.[2] The doctrine of implied repeal applies in Canada to resolve conflicts between laws enacted by the same legislative body, for example, conflicts between two statutes of the federal Parliament[3] or two statutes of the Ontario Legislature.[4] But in a federal system there is also the possibility of conflict between the statutes of different legislative bodies within the federation.[5]

In Canada, conflict between the statutes of different provincial Legislatures is unlikely to occur because the legislative authority of each province is confined within its own territory.[6] But conflict between a statute of the federal Parliament and a statute of a provincial Legislature is bound to occur from time to time because federal and provincial laws are applicable in the same territory, and by virtue of the double aspect and pith and substance (incidental effect) doctrines may be applicable to the same facts.[7] The doctrine of implied repeal is of no help in resolving a federal-provincial conflict, because neither the federal Parliament nor a provincial Legislature has the power to repeal either expressly or impliedly each other's laws. For the same reason, the order in which the two laws were enacted is irrelevant: there is no reason to prefer the later over the earlier, or vice versa.

The rule that has been adopted by the courts is the doctrine of "federal

---

[2]Sullivan, Sullivan and Driedger on the Construction of Statutes (4th ed., 2002), 275–280; Côté, The Interpretation of Legislation in Canada (3rd ed., 2000), 348–365; J. Burrows, "Implied Repeal" (1976) 3 Otago L. Rev. 601. An exception of uncertain scope is where the earlier statute is "special" and the later statute is "general"; in that case the general yields to the special, on the basis that the general statute should be construed as allowing an exception for the special statute; e.g., *Re B.C. Teachers' Federation* (1985), 23 D.L.R. (4th) 161 (B.C. C.A.); *Lévis v. Fraternité des policiers de Lévis*, [2007] 1 S.C.R. 591 (one statute was both later and special).

[3]E.g., *Can. v. Schmidt*, [1987] 1 S.C.R. 500.

[4]E.g., *Winnipeg School Division No. 1 v. Craton*, [1985] 2 S.C.R. 150. In all these cases, there is a threshold question as to whether there is a conflict between the two laws, and whether it can be reconciled by interpretation: *Lévis v. Fraternité des policiers de Lévis*, [2007] 1 S.C.R. 591 (where the Court divided on this issue). In *114957 v. Hudson*, [2001] 2 S.C.R. 241, paras. 36, 46, the Court used the rule of express contradiction that governs federal-provincial controversies to decide that a Quebec provincial statue and a Quebec municipal by-law were not in conflict.

[5]The doctrine of implied repeal also resolves conflicts between a federal statute or a provincial statute and a pre-confederation statute, where the pre-confederation statute is upon a subject within the competence of the body that enacted the post-confederation law: *Moore v. Johnson*, [1982] 1 S.C.R. 115.

[6]In *Interprovincial Cooperatives v. The Queen*, [1976] 1 S.C.R. 477, an apparent conflict between the laws of two provinces was resolved in three different ways, but each opinion assumed that the two laws could not both be applicable to a single set of facts, and that one of the laws had to be held either invalid or inapplicable by reason of the extraterritorial limitation on provincial legislative power. This case is discussed in ch. 13, Extraterritorial Competence, under heading § 13:6, "Regulation of extraprovincial activity".

[7]These doctrines are described, along with the three constitutional provisions that explicitly confer concurrent powers (ss. 92A(2), 94A, 95), in ch. 15, Judicial Review on Federal Grounds, under heading § 15:25, "Concurrency".

paramountcy":[8] where there are inconsistent (or conflicting) federal and provin-cial laws, it is the federal law[9] which prevails.[10] A similar rule has been adopted in the United States and Australia,[11] and apparently by most modern federal constitutions.[12] The doctrine of paramountcy applies where there is a federal law and a provincial law which are (1) each valid, and (2) inconsistent.

Most of this chapter will be devoted to the difficulty of determining when two laws are inconsistent for the purpose of paramountcy, but it should not be overlooked that the issue does not arise unless each law has first been held to be valid as an independent enactment. In determining the validity of each law, the existence and terms of the other law are irrelevant. Validity depends upon the principles discussed

---

[8]W.R. Lederman, "The Concurrent Operation of Federal and Provincial Laws in Canada" (1963) 9 McGill L.J. 185; B. Laskin, "Occupying the Field: Paramountcy in Penal Legislation" (1963) 41 Can. Bar Rev. 234; Laskin, Canadian Constitutional Law (5th ed., 1986 by Finkelstein), 262–291; E. Brouillet, "The Federal Principle and the 2005 Balance of Powers in Canada" (2006) 34 Supreme Court L.R. (2d) 307; B. Ryder, "The End of Umpire: Federalism and Judicial Restraint" (2006) 34 Supreme Court L.R. (2d) 345; R. Elliot, "Safeguarding Provincial Autonomy from the Supreme Court's New Federal Paramountcy Doctrine: A Constructive Role for the Intention to Cover the Field Test?" (2007) 38 Supreme Court L.R. (2d) 629.

[9]There is a strong argument that federal paramountcy should be attributed only to statutes enacted by the federal Parliament (and to regulations or orders made thereunder). There is, however, some authority that paramount status is possessed by pre-confederation laws in fields of federal jurisdiction: *Hellens v. Densmore*, [1957] S.C.R. 768, 784; *Re Broddy* (1982), 142 D.L.R. (3d) 151, 157 (Alta. C.A.). There was also some authority that paramount status is possessed by common law rules in fields of federal jurisdiction: *Bisaillon v. Keable*, [1983] 2 S.C.R. 60, 108. But the Supreme Court of Canada has since decided that common law rules and other non-statutory laws in fields of federal jurisdiction do not possess paramount status: *Marine Services International Ltd. v. Ryan Estate*, [2013] 3 S.C.R. 53, paras. 66-67; *Desgagnés Transport v. Wärtsilä Canada*, 2019 SCC 58, paras. 101-103; both cases are discussed in greater depth in ch. 22, Transportation and Communication, under heading § 22:12, "Transportation by Water".

[10]The Constitution Act, 1867 is curiously silent on the point, though there have been occasional suggestions that paramountcy flows from the notwithstanding clause in the opening words of s. 91 or the concluding clause of s. 91: *Re Exported Natural Gas Tax*, [1982] 1 S.C.R. 1004, 1031; Laskin, Canadian Constitutional Law (5th ed., 1986 by Finkelstein), 263. Two of the three provisions conferring concurrent powers, namely, ss. 92A and 95, expressly stipulate that the federal power is to be paramount. The third provision, s. 94A, conferring federal power over old age pensions and supplementary benefits, arguably goes beyond the recognition of concurrency and confers "reverse paramountcy" on conflicting provincial laws: so held in *Hislop v. Can.* (2009), 95 O.R. (3d) 81 (C.A.), para. 61; although the reverse paramountcy was held to be inapplicable in that case. Accord, *Que. v. Lacombe*, [2010] 2 S.C.R. 453, para. 95 per Deschamps J. (obiter dictum that "where old age pensions are concerned, provincial legislation is paramount"). Laskin, Canadian Constitutional Law (5th ed., 1986 by Finkelstein), 263–264 (not referred to in *Hislop* or *Lacombe)*, denies that s. 94A confers reverse paramountcy.

[11]The result has been held to be implicit in the "supremacy clause" in the United States' Constitution, art. 6, cl. 2; and is explicit in s. 109 of the Australian Constitution.

[12]Wheare, *Federal Government* (4th ed., 1963), 74. While most federal states seem to have some form of *federal* paramountcy, this is not true of all federal states: see e.g. Constitution of the Republic of Iraq, 2005, Articles 115, 121.

in the previous chapter: does the "matter" (or pith and substance) of the law come within the "classes of subjects" (or heads of power) allocated to the enacting Parliament or Legislature? If one law fails this test, then the problem is resolved without recourse to the doctrine of paramountcy. It is only if each law independently passes the test of validity that it is necessary to determine whether the laws are inconsistent. This may appear to be labouring the obvious, but there are a startling number of judicial opinions which confuse the issue of consistency with the antecedent, and entirely different, issue of validity.[13]

II. DEFINITION OF INCONSISTENCY

§ 16:2 Definition of inconsistency

When are two laws deemed to be inconsistent (or conflicting) so as to attract the doctrine of paramountcy? The question has profound implications for the scope of judicial review and for the balance of power in the federal system. Given the overriding force of federal law, a wide definition of inconsistency will result in the defeat of provincial laws in "fields" which are "covered" by federal law; a narrow definition, on the other hand, will allow provincial laws to survive so long as they do not "expressly contradict" federal law. The wide definition is the course of judicial activism in favour of central power; the narrow definition is the course of judicial restraint, leaving all but the irreconcilable conflicts to be resolved in the political arena. We shall see that Canadian courts have followed the course of restraint.[1]

III. EXPRESS CONTRADICTION

§ 16:3 Impossibility of dual compliance

The only clear case of inconsistency, which I call express contradiction,[1] occurs when one law expressly contradicts the other. For laws which directly regulate conduct, an express contradiction occurs when it is impossible for a person to obey both laws; or, as Martland J. put it in *Smith v. The Queen* (1960),[2] "compliance with one law involves breach of the other".

---

[13]See § 16:7 note 7, below.

[Section 16:2]

[1]The principle of subsidiarity (ch. 5, Federalism, under heading § 5:7, "Subsidiarity") also supports the preservation of laws made by the level of government closest to the people affected: *114957 Can. v. Hudson*, [2001] 2 S.C.R. 241, para. 3 per L'Heureux-Dubé J.

[Section 16:3]

[1]Laskin, Canadian Constitutional Law (5th ed., 1986 by Finkelstein), 264, uses the term "operating incompatibility", but he evidently has in mind a broader test than express contradiction because he includes in the test the negative implication which arises when a federal penal law is more restrictive than a provincial penal law. I prefer "express contradiction" because it clearly excludes negative implication and duplication, and makes it easier to analyze the three situations separately.

[2]*Smith v. The Queen*, [1960] S.C.R. 776, 800.

In *Multiple Access v. McCutcheon* (1982),[3] the question was whether the insider-trading provisions of provincial securities law were in conflict with the insider-trading provisions of federal corporate law. The Supreme Court of Canada answered "no". Dickson J. for the majority of the Court had this to say about the conflict that would trigger the rule of federal paramountcy:[4]

> In principle, there would seem to be no good reason to speak of paramountcy and preclusion except where there is actual conflict in operation, as where one enactment says "yes" and the other says "no"; "the same citizens are being told to do inconsistent things"; compliance with one is defiance of the other.

Since the federal and provincial laws provided essentially the same remedy for essentially the same conduct, namely, profiting from inside knowledge in the trading of stocks and bonds, there was no express contradiction. On the contrary, the two laws were in harmony, imposing the same standards of conduct on persons dealing in corporate securities. It followed that the rule of federal paramountcy did not apply. The provincial law was operative, despite its duplication of federal law.[5]

It is not always clear whether two laws are in conflict. This may involve interpretation. Where it is possible to interpret either the federal law or the provincial law so as to avoid the conflict that would trigger paramountcy, then that interpretation should be preferred to an alternative that brings about a conflict between the two laws. This is essentially the same presumption of constitutionality that applies in other kinds of federalism cases: where two possible interpretations of a law are possible, and one would make the law unconstitutional, the court should normally choose the one that supports the constitutional validity of the law.[6]

In *Marine Services International v. Ryan Estate* (2013),[7] the plaintiffs brought a tort action for maritime negligence arising from an accident at sea. They were covered by a provincial workers' compensation statute and had applied for and received workers' compensation for the accident. The question was whether there was a conflict between a *federal* marine liability law that entitled persons who were injured or killed at sea by the negligence of another to bring an action in tort for maritime negligence and the *provincial* workers' compensation law that barred actions in tort arising out of an accident for which workers' compensation benefits were payable. At first blush, the federal law said "yes" and the provincial law said "no" to a plaintiff who was covered by workers' compensation and who wanted to bring an action for maritime

---

[3]*Multiple Access v. McCutcheon*, [1982] 2 S.C.R. 161.

[4]*Multiple Access v. McCutcheon*, [1982] 2 S.C.R. 161, 191.

[5]For more discussion of duplication, see §§ 16:7 to 16:9, "Overlap and duplication".

[6]Chapter 15, Judicial Review on Federal Grounds, under heading § 15:13, "Presumption of constitutionality".

[7]*Marine Services International v. Ryan Estate*, [2013] 3 S.C.R. 53, 2013 SCC 44. LeBel and Karakatsanis JJ. wrote the opinion of the Court.

negligence. If paramountcy applied, the federal "yes" would prevail because the provincial "no" would inoperative. That was not the answer given by the Supreme Court. The Court emphasized that there was a threshold issue of interpretation: "when a federal statute can be properly interpreted so as not to interfere with a provincial statute, such an interpretation is to be applied in preference to another applicable construction that would bring about a conflict between the two statutes".[8] In this case, the federal law used language that restricted the right to bring a maritime negligence action to "circumstances" that would have "entitled" a person "to recover damages". The Court held that the provincial bar was a circumstance that *disentitled* the plaintiffs from recovering damages. Therefore the federal law did not apply to persons who were covered by provincial workers' compensation. This was not an implausible interpretation because the bar on tort actions was universal in Canadian workers' compensation schemes and a federal law should not be lightly interpreted as negating the rule in maritime cases. In the result, therefore, the Court held that there was no conflict between the two laws: the provincial workers' compensation law was a valid provincial law that was operative in its application to maritime workers,[9] and the plaintiffs were accordingly barred from bringing a tort action for maritime negligence.[10]

The decided cases offer only a few examples of impossibility of dual compliance. Where there are insufficient assets to pay a person's debts, it is impossible to comply with a federal law stipulating the order of priority of payment and a provincial law stipulating a different order of priority.[11] Where a federal law stipulates that Japanese citizens in Canada are to be afforded the same employment opportunities as Canadian citizens, and a provincial law stipulates that Japanese are not to be employed in mines, another express contradiction occurs.[12] Where two spouses are separated, and a court order made under federal law grants custody of their child to the wife, while a court order made under provincial law grants custody to the husband, another express contradiction occurs.[13] Where a federal law stipulates that defined standard weights and measures be used and a provincial law requires purchasers of natural gas to pay a tax by reference to a non-standard unit of

[8]*Marine Services International v. Ryan Estate*, [2013] 3 S.C.R. 53, 2013 SCC 44, para. 79.

[9]The Court also rejected the plaintiffs' arguments based on frustration of federal purpose (para. 84) and interjurisdictional immunity (para. 64).

[10]See also *Desgagnés Transport v. Wärtsilä Canada*, 2019 SCC 58, holding that part of a provincial law (the Civil Code of Quebec) was not rendered inoperative in the context of a maritime contract claim, because the federal law was non-statutory, and so the federal paramountcy doctrine did not apply.

[11]*Royal Bank of Can. v. LaRue*, [1928] A.C. 187; *Re Bozanich*, [1942] S.C.R. 130: *A.-G. Ont. v. Policy-holders of Wentworth Ins. Co.*, [1969] S.C.R. 779; *Sun Indalex Finance v. United Steelworkers*, [2013] 1 S.C.R. 271, 2013 SCC 6, paras. 53–60, 242, 265.

[12]*A.-G. B.C. v. A.-G. Can.* (Employment of Japanese) [1924] A.C. 203.

[13]*Gillespie v. Gillespie* (1973), 36 D.L.R. (3d) 421 (N.B. C.A.); discussed in ch. 27, The Family, under heading § 27:10, "General principles".

measurement, another express contradiction occurs.[14] Where a federal law provides that federal pension benefits cannot be assigned or charged and a provincial class-action law provides that legal fees are a first charge on a monetary award, if the monetary award in a class action is of federal pension benefits, another express contradiction occurs.[15] Where a federal law provides that Canada Post will determine the locations of "community mail boxes" and a municipal law provides that the municipality will determine the locations within the municipality, another express contradiction occurs.[16]

In *M & D Farm v. Manitoba Agricultural Credit Corporation* (1999),[17] the question arose whether the Manitoba Agricultural Credit Corporation, which held a mortgage on the farm owned by the plaintiffs, had validly foreclosed on the mortgage. Under the federal Farm Debt Review Act, the plaintiffs had obtained a 120-day stay of proceedings to halt any proceedings to recover the arrears owing by them to the corporation under the mortgage. (The purpose of the stay was to provide an opportunity for a consensual settlement with a farmer's creditors.) While the stay was in force, the corporation obtained a court order under the provincial Family Farm Protection Act granting permission to foreclose on the mortgage. The corporation did nothing more until the federal stay expired, and then continued the proceedings for foreclosure to a conclusion culminating in the corporation obtaining title to the farm. When the plaintiffs were faced with a demand by the corporation for possession of the farm, they argued that the court order granting permission to foreclose was a nullity, and that all the steps that followed were consequently also void. The Supreme Court of Canada agreed with the plaintiffs, and held that the foreclosure was invalid. The Court held that the effect of the stay, issued under federal law, was to prohibit any proceedings to enforce the mortgage, and an application for permission to foreclose was one of the prohibited proceedings. Therefore, the court order granting permission to foreclose was directly prohibited by the federal law. Since the court order permitting foreclosure proceedings was made under provincial law, and the court order staying proceedings was made under federal law, the doctrine of paramountcy required that the federal law prevail. There was an express contradiction between two court orders, one of which, made under federal law, prohibited enforcement proceedings for 120 days, and the other of which, made under provincial law within the 120-day period of the stay, was itself an enforcement proceeding.

---

[14] *Re Min. of Finance (B.C.) and Pacific Petroleums* (1979), 99 D.L.R. (3d) 491 (B.C. CA.).

[15] *Hislop v. Can.* (2009), 95 O.R. (3d) 81 (C.A.). Note the interesting argument that this case was governed by the "reverse paramountcy" rule of s. 94A of the Constitution Act, 1867; the Court held otherwise and applied the general rule of federal paramountcy (paras. 61–63).

[16] *Canada Post Corp. v. Hamilton* (2016), 134 O.R. (3d) 502, 2016 ONCA 767, para. 87.

[17] *M & D Farm v. Manitoba Agricultural Credit Corporation*, [1999] 2 S.C.R. 961. Binnie J. wrote the judgment of the Court.

The opposite result was reached in the *Saskatchewan Breathalyzer* case (1958).[18] In that case, a federal law provided that "no person is required to give a sample of. . .breath" as evidence of driving while intoxicated, and a provincial law suspended the driving licence of any person who refused to comply with a police request for a sample. In the Supreme Court of Canada, three judges held that the provincial law "required" the giving of a sample, which meant that the provincial law expressly contradicted the federal law ("no person is required"). But the majority decided otherwise. They held that the provincial sanction for a refusal to give a sample was not severe enough—merely the denial of "a questionable privilege"—to amount to a requirement of giving a sample. Therefore, the provincial law did not contradict the federal law, and was not rendered inoperative by paramountcy.

Is there an impossibility of dual compliance if a federal law requires the consent of a federal agency for a particular project and provincial law requires the consent of a provincial agency for the same project? In principle, the answer would seem to be no. Both levels of government may give their consent, which would obviate any conflict. Even if one level of government imposes stricter conditions on the project than the other, compliance with the stricter conditions obviates any conflict. Only if one level of government denies consent and the other grants consent, is there an impossibility of dual compliance, which would cause the federal decision to prevail over the provincial decision in that particular case. In *British Columbia v. Lafarge Canada* (2007),[19] it was clear that it was necessary to obtain approval from the Vancouver Port Authority (established under federal law) for the development of a marine facility on a site in the (federally-regulated) port of Vancouver. However, the site was also within the boundaries of the City of Vancouver (established under provincial law), and the question was whether the development also needed the approval of the City under its land-use by-law. Binnie and LeBel JJ, who wrote the majority opinion in the case, held that the mere requirement of municipal approval would give rise to "operational conflict", and therefore it was not even necessary to seek the permission of the City (which had already informally approved the project).[20] Bastarache J., who based his concurring reasons on interjurisdictional immunity, was surely correct in pointing out that "until the City refuses a permit, dual compliance is not 'impossible' here".[21]

In 2015, the Supreme Court decided three cases on the question

[18] *Re s. 92(4) of the Vehicles Act 1957 (Sask.)*, [1958] S.C.R. 608.

[19] *British Columbia v. Lafarge Canada*, [2007] 2 S.C.R. 86.

[20] *British Columbia v. Lafarge Canada*, [2007] 2 S.C.R. 86, paras. 81–82. As a separate point, Binnie and LeBel JJ. argued (paras. 83–85) that municipal permission would frustrate the purpose of the federal law governing land use at the port, but they never explained what that purpose was. In the absence of an identifiable, conflicting federal purpose, this is either a reversion to the discredited covering-the-field test (§ 16:5, "Covering the field") or it is just interjurisdictional immunity in disguise. The interjurisdictional-immunity point of the case is discussed in ch. 15, Judicial Review on Federal Grounds, under heading § 15:18, "Federally-regulated undertakings".

[21] *British Columbia v. Lafarge Canada*, [2007] 2 S.C.R. 86, para. 113.

whether the federal Bankruptcy and Insolvency Act (BIA) contradicted provincial laws. There was no doubt about the independent validity of the BIA, which was authorized by the federal power over "bankruptcy and insolvency" (s. 91(21)), or the three provincial laws, each of which was authorized by the provincial power over "property and civil rights in the province" (s. 92(13)).

In the first case, *Alberta v. Moloney* (2015),[22] the apparent conflict was between the fresh-start provision of the BIA, which provides that when a bankrupt debtor is discharged from bankruptcy, the debtor is released from all debts that are claims provable in bankruptcy, and Alberta's Traffic Safety Act, which provides that, if an uninsured driver fails to pay a damages award to the victim of an accident (in which case the province pays the award), the driver's vehicle permit and licence to drive are suspended until the driver has repaid the province the amount of the damages award. In this case, Moloney, a truck driver, caused an accident while driving without insurance. The victim of the accident sued Moloney and obtained judgment for $194,875. The province of Alberta paid the judgment debt and received an assignment of the debt, as provided by Alberta law. Moloney did not pay the debt to the province. Some time later Moloney went bankrupt. After three years, he was discharged from bankruptcy. The judgment debt was one of his debts provable in bankruptcy. In fact it was his largest debt and the reason for his financial difficulties. After his discharge from bankruptcy, because the judgment debt had not been paid, the province suspended his driving privileges, relying on the Traffic Safety Act. Moloney took the position that he was now released from the judgment debt, relying on the BIA's fresh-start provision. The Supreme Court held that there was a conflict between the two laws and the federal BIA therefore prevailed to discharge the judgment debt and render inoperative the provisions of the Traffic Safety Act denying driving privileges to Moloney. Gascon J., who wrote for the majority, held that the two laws could not operate concurrently: "This is a case where the provincial law says 'yes' ('Alberta can enforce this provable claim'), while the federal law says 'no' ('Alberta cannot enforce this provable claim')".[23] He also held that the second branch of paramountcy (frustration of federal purpose)[24] was satisfied. An important purpose of the fresh-start provision was to give the former bankrupt a fresh start in life, no longer encumbered by the debts that had overwhelmed him. The provincial law frustrated debts that the BIA discharged.[25] Côté J. disagreed that dual compliance was impossible. In her view, it was possible for Moloney to obey both laws, either by giving up driving or by paying the judgment

---

[22]*Alberta v. Moloney*, [2015] 3 S.C.R. 327, 2015 SCC 51. Gascon J. wrote the opinion of the majority. Côté J. (with McLachlin C.J.) wrote a concurring opinion.

[23]*Alberta v. Moloney*, [2015] 3 S.C.R. 327, 2015 SCC 51, para. 63.

[24]The frustration of federal purpose analysis in the decision is discussed in the next section of the book: see § 16:4, "Frustration of federal purpose", note 1, below.

[25]*Alberta v. Moloney*, [2015] 3 S.C.R. 327, 2015 SCC 51, para. 77.

debt.[26] However, she agreed that the provincial law frustrated the fresh-start objective of the BIA and she therefore concurred in the result.

The second 2015 case, *407 ETR Concession Co. v. Canada* (2015),[27] raised a similar issue to *Moloney*. The claimed conflict was between the fresh-start provision of the BIA (again) and the provision for enforcing payment of highway tolls in Ontario's Highway 407 Act. Highway 407 is a private toll highway that does not use toll booths to block entry to vehicles that have not paid the toll. It is an open-access highway: an electronic system reads each car's licence plate (or a transponder in the car) at the points of entry and exit and calculates the toll payable for that journey. An invoice is then mailed to the address of the owner of the licence plate (or transponder). If the invoice is not paid, the owner of the highway (ETR) is authorized by the Act to notify the province's Registrar of Motor Vehicles. Until the Registrar is advised that the debt has been paid, the Act requires the Registrar to refuse to issue or renew the debtor's vehicle permit. Mr Moore used Highway 407 1,973 times running up a toll debt of $34,977. He then went bankrupt. After he was discharged from bankruptcy, the Registrar continued to refuse to issue or renew his vehicle permit. He sought an order compelling the Registrar to issue his vehicle permit. The Supreme Court followed *Moloney* to hold that there was a conflict between the two laws rendering inoperative the Highway 407 Act's provisions for the enforcement of the toll debt. Gascon J. again wrote for the majority and again held that the two laws could not operate concurrently: "the 407 Act says 'yes' to the enforcement of a provable claim, while [the fresh-start provision] of the BIA says 'no', such that the operation of the provincial law makes it impossible to comply with the federal law."[28] Gascon J. also again held that the provincial law frustrated the purpose of the fresh-start provision of the BIA.[29] Côté J. again wrote a concurring opinion, denying that it was impossible to comply with both laws: "If a debtor chooses not to drive, the province simply cannot enforce its claim. The same is true if [ETR] opts not to notify the Registrar of Motor Vehicles of the debtor's failure to pay . . .".[30] However, she again agreed with Gascon J. that the Highway 407 Act frustrated the purpose of the fresh-start provision of the BIA.[31] Therefore, she ended up concurring with the majority in the result.

In the third case, *Saskatchewan v. Lemare Lake Logging* (2015),[32] the claimed conflict was between the power of a secured creditor to apply for

---

[26]*Alberta v. Moloney*, [2015] 3 S.C.R. 327, 2015 SCC 51, para. 123.

[27]*407 ETR Concession Co. v. Canada*, [2015] 3 S.C.R. 397, 2015 SCC 52. Gascon J. wrote the opinion of the majority. Côté J.(with McLachlin C.J.) wrote a concurring opinion.

[28]*407 ETR Concession Co. v. Canada*, [2015] 3 S.C.R. 397, 2015 SCC 52, para. 24.

[29]The frustration of federal purpose analysis in the decision is discussed in the next section of the book: see § 16:4, "Frustration of federal purpose", note 1, below.

[30]*407 ETR Concession Co. v. Canada*, [2015] 3 S.C.R. 397, 2015 SCC 52, para. 39.

[31]*407 ETR Concession Co. v. Canada*, [2015] 3 S.C.R. 397, 2015 SCC 52, para. 41.

[32]*Saskatchewan v. Lemare Lake Logging*, [2015] 3 S.C.R. 419, 2015 SCC 53. Abella

the appointment of a receiver over the debtor's assets under the BIA, which required a 10-day period of advance notice to the debtor, and, since the debtor was a farmer in Saskatchewan, the provincial Saskatchewan Farm Security Act, which required a 150-day period of advance notice to the debtor coupled with a mandatory review and mediation process. In this case, the Court was unanimous that there was no express contradiction: the creditor applying for a receiver could comply with both Acts by complying with the longer waiting period and other requirements of the provincial law. The Court also held, by a majority, that the provincial law did not frustrate the purpose of the federal law.[33]

In *Moloney* and *407 ETR* (but not in *Lemare Lake*, which turned more on frustration of federal purpose), Gascon and Côté JJ. adopted different approaches to the impossibility of dual compliance test. As Côté J. noted in her concurring opinions in both cases, it was not actually impossible to comply with the relevant federal and provincial laws. In *Moloney*, it was possible for Moloney to comply with both the federal BIA and Alberta's Traffic Safety Act, either by giving up driving or paying the judgment debt. Similarly, in *407 ETR*, it was possible for a debtor (like Moore) to comply with both the federal BIA and Ontario's Highway 407 Act, either by giving up driving or paying any toll debt. However, in both cases, Gascon J. held that there was an impossibility of dual compliance. He emphasized that an impossibility of dual compliance analysis "cannot be limited to asking whether [a party] can comply with both [federal and provincial] laws by renouncing the protection afforded to him or her under the federal law or the privilege he or she is otherwise entitled to under the provincial law".[34] The focus of the analysis must, he said, be "on the effect of the provincial law", which requires looking at its "substance . . . rather than its form", with an eye to determining whether it is allowing a province to "do indirectly what it is precluded from doing directly" by the federal law.[35] Côté J. criticized Gascon J.'s approach to impossibility of dual compliance, arguing that it blurred the lines between an impossibility of dual compliance and frustration of federal purpose analysis, and would lead to more provincial laws being rendered inoperative under the federal paramountcy doctrine. She defended a stricter approach to impossibility of dual compliance, one that looks at whether there is an "express conflict" between the "actual words" used in the relevant federal and provincial laws, read in their "literal" sense.[36]

Gascon and Côté JJ. did ultimately reach the same conclusion about federal paramountcy in *Moloney* and *407 ETR*; although Côté J. found there to be no impossibility of dual compliance in both cases, she agreed

---

and Gascon JJ. wrote the opinion of the majority. Côté J. wrote a dissenting opinion.

[33]The frustration of federal purpose analysis in the decision is discussed in the next section of the book: see § 16:4, "Frustration of federal purpose", note 1, below.

[34]*Alta. v. Moloney*, [2015] 3 S.C.R. 327, para. 60; see also para. 69.

[35]*Alta. v. Moloney*, [2015] 3 S.C.R. 327, para. 28.

[36]*Alta. v. Moloney*, [2015] 3 S.C.R. 327, paras. 97, 105, 108.

with Gascon J. that there was a conflict due to a frustration of federal purpose. This may suggest that Gascon and Côté JJ.'s different approaches to impossibility of dual compliance will not make a significant difference in practice. However, their decisions do reveal an element of (and may also generate additional) uncertainty about when an impossibility of dual compliance will be held to occur – uncertainty that Gascon J.'s majority opinion does little to resolve, since it is not entirely clear how to apply his substantive approach to impossibility of dual compliance. In addition, Gascon J.'s substantive approach to impossibility of dual compliance could make a difference in some cases, because it seems possible that it will lead to conflicts being found to occur due to an impossibility of dual compliance where there is no frustration of federal purpose. And if this is right, Côté J.'s claim that Gascon J.'s approach to impossibility of dual compliance will result in more provincial laws being rendered inoperative would be vindicated.

The Court should abandon Gascon J.'s approach to impossibility of dual compliance, and (re)affirm Côté J.'s stricter approach to impossibility of dual compliance. The concern that animated Gascon J. in *Moloney* – that a provincial law may allow a province to do indirectly what a federal law precludes it from doing directly – should be addressed as a potential frustration of federal purpose. Under this approach, a provincial law that appeared to allow a province to do indirectly what a federal law precludes it from doing directly would be rendered inoperative under the federal paramountcy doctrine *only if the result would be to frustrate the purpose of the federal law*. This approach may not produce absolute clarity – an approach that turns so much on identifying federal purposes hardly can, as the discussion in the next section clearly shows – but it would help alleviate the uncertainty introduced by *Moloney*, which, as Côté J. noted, blurred the line between an impossibility of dual compliance and frustration of federal purpose analysis.

The Supreme Court of Canada had the opportunity to consider another alleged conflict between the federal Bankruptcy and Insolvency Act (BIA) and provincial (in this case, environmental) law in *Orphan Well Association v. Grant Thornton* (2019).[37] Alberta law governing oil drilling imposed end-of-life duties on a licensed operator who had exhausted an oil well. The well had to be "abandoned" in compliance with Alberta law which required the sealing of the well and the remediation of the site—costly obligations. Redwater Energy was an insolvent oil company that owned some valuable producing wells as well as "orphan" wells that were at the end of their life and were subject to unfulfilled abandonment obligations. The company's trustee in bankruptcy wanted to disclaim the orphan wells and sell the valuable wells so as to maximize the value of the estate for the creditors. The Alberta Energy Regulator took the position that this was not permissible, claiming that a sufficient portion of the sale proceeds from the valuable wells

[37] *Orphan Well Association v. Grant Thornton*, [2019] 1 S.C.R. 150. Wagner C.J. wrote the opinion for the five-judge majority of the seven-judge bench. Côté J. wrote a dissenting opinion, which was joined by Moldaver J.

had to be set aside to meet the cost of remediating the orphan wells. The trial judge and the majority of the Alberta Court of Appeal agreed with the trustee that the end-of-life remediation obligations imposed by Alberta law conflicted with the BIA, and thus were rendered inoperative by the federal paramountcy doctrine. When the case reached the Supreme Court, the majority of the Court reached the opposite conclusion, agreeing with the Alberta Energy Regulator – and with their new colleague, Justice Martin, who had been in dissent in the Alberta Court of Appeal – that the end-of-life remediation obligations did not conflict with the BIA.[38]

Wagner C.J., who wrote for the majority of the Court, rejected two impossibility of dual compliance arguments offered by the trustee. First, he rejected the trustee's argument that Alberta's extension of its end-of-life remediation obligations to trustees that sought to disclaim assets of a bankrupt estate conflicted with s. 14.06 of the BIA, which provides that a trustee is "not personally liable for failure to comply" with an order "to remedy any environmental condition or environmental damage affecting property involved in a bankruptcy" if the trustee disclaims the property within a prescribed timeframe. He said that, properly interpreted, s. 14.06 is only "concerned with the personal liability of trustees, and does not empower a trustee to walk away from the environmental liabilities of the estate it is administering".[39] There was thus no impossibility of dual compliance, because the trustee could be – and was being – required to satisfy the environmental liabilities that resulted from Alberta's end-of-life remediation obligations out of Redwater Energy's assets, not its own assets. The trustee argued that, even if s. 14.06 only shielded it from personal liability for Redwater Energy's environmental liabilities, a conflict still arose because, under Alberta law, it was *possible* for the Alberta Energy Regulator to hold it personally liable for the costs of satisfying Redwater Energy's end-of-life remediation obligations in the future. Wagner C.J. dismissed this variation on the trustee's first impossibility of dual compliance argument as well, emphasizing that provincial laws should not be rendered inoperative under the federal paramountcy doctrine "by the mere theoretical possibility of a conflict".[40]

Wagner C.J. also rejected the trustee's second impossibility-of-dual compliance argument – that Alberta's end-of-life remediation obligations conflicted with the distribution scheme for the settlement of debts in the BIA. He said that the environmental liabilities that resulted from Alberta's end-of-life remediation obligations were not "claims provable in bankruptcy", and so were not subject to the distribution scheme set

[38]Martin J. was not part of the Supreme Court panel that heard the appeal due to her earlier involvement.

[39]*Orphan Well Association v. Grant Thornton*, [2019] 1 S.C.R. 150, para. 7.

[40]*Orphan Well Association v. Grant Thornton*, [2019] 1 S.C.R. 150, para. 105. Wagner C.J. did say (para. 107) that the federal paramountcy doctrine would be triggered due to an "operational conflict" if the Alberta Energy Regulator did attempt to hold the trustee personally liable in the future.

out in the BIA; rather, they resulted from statutory duties, which served the public interest. It was true that these environmental liabilities would diminish the value of the bankrupt estate for its creditors, but its value had to account for the costs of complying with the general law of Alberta.[41]

Côté J. dissented in *Orphan Well*. She agreed with the trustee that there was an impossibility of dual compliance. Unlike Wagner C.J., she read s. 14.06 of the BIA to allow a trustee to walk away from the environmental liabilities of an estate that it is administering by disclaiming assets, and she said that there was "an unavoidable operational conflict" because Alberta's end-of-life remediation obligations did "not recognize these disclaimers as lawful".[42]

In *Orphan Well*, neither Wagner C.J. nor Côté J. attempted to resolve the disagreement in *Moloney* about the impossibility of dual compliance test for conflict. Indeed, whereas Wagner C.J. distinguished *Moloney*,[43] Côté J. criticized the majority in *Orphan Well* for failing to respect *Moloney*, by allowing the province to "do indirectly what it is precluded from doing directly".[44]

§ 16:4 Frustration of federal purpose

Canadian courts also accept a second case of inconsistency, namely, where a provincial law would frustrate the purpose of a federal law. Where there are overlapping federal and provincial laws, and it is possible to comply with both laws, but the effect of the provincial law would be to frustrate the purpose of the federal law, that is also a case of inconsistency.[1] As we shall see, this form of inconsistency started its life as a subset of express contradiction, but it is best treated as a separate

[41]Wagner C.J. also rejected the trustee's argument that Alberta's end-of-life remediation obligations would frustrate the purpose of the BIA's disclaimer provisions and distribution scheme. This aspect of his opinion is discussed later in this chapter: see § 16:4, "Frustration of federal purpose".

[42]*Orphan Well Association v. Grant Thornton*, [2019] 1 S.C.R. 150, para. 169.

[43]*Orphan Well Association v. Grant Thornton*, [2019] 1 S.C.R. 150, para. 106.

[44]*Orphan Well Association v. Grant Thornton*, [2019] 1 S.C.R. 150, para. 280. This criticism came in the context of Côté J.'s discussion of frustration of federal purpose, and so her approach in *Orphan Well* was consistent with her suggestion in *Moloney* – and the approach recommended in this book – that this concern about allowing a province to do indirectly what it cannot do directly should be addressed as a potential frustration of federal purpose.

[Section 16:4]

[1]The frustration of federal purpose test was first articulated clearly in *Law Society of B.C. v. Mangat*, [2001] 3 S.C.R. 113, para. 72. However, it is the best explanation of two early paramountcy cases, namely, *Tennant v. Union Bank of Can.*, [1894] A.C. 31 (provincial law limiting legal effect of warehouse receipts frustrated purpose of federal law providing that title to goods could pass by warehouse receipt) and *Crown Grain Co. v. Day*, [1908] A.C. 504 (provincial law barring appeal from mechanics lien decision frustrated purpose of federal law providing for appeal to the Supreme Court of Canada from any final judgment in a province). The same test explains the cases striking down provincial attempts to provide for the punishment of young offenders in the face of

kind of inconsistency. It is certainly much less "express" than the impossibility of dual compliance, and accordingly much more vulnerable to judicial discretion. The courts have to interpret the federal law to determine what the federal purpose is, and then they have to decide whether the provincial law would have the effect of frustrating the federal purpose.

In *Bank of Montreal v. Hall* (1990),[2] the question arose whether there was a conflict between the federal Bank Act, which provided a procedure for the foreclosure of a mortgage held by a bank, and a provincial Act, which stipulated, as a prelude to foreclosure proceedings, that the creditor must serve on the debtor a notice giving the debtor a last opportunity to repay the loan. In this case, the bank had taken foreclosure proceedings in compliance with the federal law, but had not served the notice in compliance with the provincial law. Note that it was not impossible for the bank to obey both laws. If the bank had served the notice required by the provincial law, the bank would not have been in breach of the federal law. The sole effect of compliance with the provincial law would be to delay the bank in realizing its security. Nevertheless, the Supreme Court of Canada held that the bank was not obliged to obey the provincial law, because it was inconsistent with the federal law. La Forest J., who wrote the opinion of the Court, claimed that there was an "actual conflict in operation" and that "compliance with the federal statute necessarily entails defiance of its provincial counterpart".[3] What he seemed to mean by these statements was that the *purpose* of the federal law would be frustrated if the bank had to comply with the provincial law.[4]

The theory that it is a sufficient conflict to trigger federal paramountcy if a provincial law is incompatible with the purpose of a federal law[5] was reinforced (and better explained) in *Law Society of B.C. v. Mangat* (2001).[6] In that case, the federal Immigration Act provided that, in proceedings before the Immigration and Refugee Board, a party could be represented by a non-lawyer. British Columbia's Legal Profession Act provided that non-lawyers were prohibited from practising law (and appearing before a federal administrative tribunal would come within the definition of the practice of law). Gonthier J., who wrote the opinion of the Supreme Court of Canada, acknowledged that a party before the Board could comply with both laws by obeying the stricter provincial one

federal procedures: *A.G.B.C. v. Smith*, [1967] S.C.R. 702; *R. v. Wilson* (1980), 119 D.L.R. (3d) 558 (B.C.C.A.); *A.G. Que. v. Lechasseur*, [1981] 2 S.C.R. 253. For a more complex explanation, based on conflict between "secondary rules", see E. Colvin, "Legal Theory and the Paramountcy Rule" (1979) 25 McGill L.J. 82 (written before the *Mangat* case).

[2]*Bank of Montreal v. Hall*, [1990] 1 S.C.R. 121.

[3]*Bank of Montreal v. Hall*, [1990] 1 S.C.R. 121, 152, 153.

[4]*Bank of Montreal v. Hall*, [1990] 1 S.C.R. 121, 152, 154–155, referring to "legislative purpose".

[5]Compare *Tennant v. Union Bank of Can.*, [1894] A.C. 31, which could be explained by this theory.

[6]*Law Society of B.C. v. Mangat*, [2001] 3 S.C.R. 113.

and retaining a lawyer as his or her counsel. But he pointed out that the purpose of the federal law was to establish an informal, accessible and speedy process, and that purpose required that parties before the Board be able to retain counsel who spoke their language, understood their culture and were inexpensive. That purpose would often be defeated if only lawyers were permitted to appear before the Board. Therefore, compliance with the provincial law "would go contrary to Parliament's purpose in enacting [the representation provisions] of the Immigration Act".[7] In that sense, there was a conflict in operation between the provincial and the federal law, and the provincial law was therefore inoperative in its application to proceedings before the Immigration and Refugee Board.[8]

In *Rothmans, Benson & Hedges v. Saskatchewan* (2005),[9] the federal Tobacco Act prohibited the promotion of tobacco products, except as authorized elsewhere in the Act, and the Act went on to provide that "a person may display, at retail, a tobacco product". The Saskatchewan Tobacco Control Act banned the display of tobacco products in any premises in which persons under 18 years of age were permitted. The Supreme Court of Canada, speaking through Major J., interpreted the federal permission to display as intended to circumscribe the prohibition on promotion, and not to create a positive "entitlement" to display. That meant that a retailer could comply with both laws, either by refusing to admit persons under 18 or by not displaying tobacco products. But what about the frustration of the federal purpose? Did not the express permission to display indicate a federal purpose to allow retailers to display tobacco products? No, answered the Court. Both the general purpose of the Tobacco Act (which was "to address a national health problem") and the specific purpose of the permission to display (which was "to circumscribe the Tobacco Act's general prohibition on promotion") "remain fulfilled".[10]

With respect, there is much to be said on the other side of this issue. Parliament did, no doubt, recognize a national health problem, but it chose to "regulate" tobacco use only by restricting Charter-protected commercial expression. Parliament had to do so within the reasonable limits allowed by s. 1 of the Charter of Rights.[11] The express permission to retailers to display the product was an effort to impose a reasonable

---

[7] *Law Society of B.C. v. Mangat*, [2001] 3 S.C.R. 113, para. 72.

[8] Folld. in *Que. v. Can.*, [2011] 3 S.C.R. 635 (provincial law exempting workers compensation payments from seizure would frustrate the purpose of the federal employment insurance law authorizing recovery of employment insurance overpayments from third-party creditors; paramountcy applied).

[9] *Rothmans, Benson & Hedges v. Saskatchewan*, [2005] 1 S.C.R. 188. Major J. wrote the opinion of the Court.

[10] *Rothmans, Benson & Hedges v. Saskatchewan*, [2005] 1 S.C.R. 188, para. 25. The Supreme Court also found no frustration of federal purpose in *Que. v. Can. Owners and Pilots Assn.*, [2010] 2 S.C.R. 536, paras. 62–74, 92 (federal permissive legislation on location of aerodromes; provincial restriction on location; no conflict).

[11] The previous version of the Act had been struck down as an unreasonable limit on freedom of expression, as guaranteed by s. 2(b) of the Charter of Rights: *RJR-MacDonald*

limit on the prohibition of commercial speech about a product that retailers were lawfully entitled to sell. By narrowing the federal limit on the prohibition of commercial speech, the provincial law arguably frustrated an important *general* purpose of the federal Act, which was to comply with the Charter of Rights.[12] And, having regard to the impracticality of excluding persons under 18 from the supermarkets, convenience stores, news stands, gas stations and other retail outlets where cigarettes are sold, the provincial law surely frustrated the *specific* purpose of the explicit permission to display. The Court, however, decided otherwise, holding that the provincial law did not frustrate the purpose of the federal law, and, therefore, was not rendered inoperative by paramountcy. The Court acknowledged that it was influenced[13] by the curious decision of the Attorney General of Canada (normally so careful to protect federal turf) to intervene in the litigation on the side of the province, despite the fact that the provincial law undermined a federal law that expressly granted permission to display tobacco products at retail.

Two of the three paramountcy cases decided in 2015, which are discussed in the previous section of this chapter as cases of impossibility of dual compliance, were also decided on the ground of frustration of federal purpose. In both *Alberta v. Moloney*[14] and *407 ETR Concession Co. v. Canada*,[15] the issue was whether a provincial law which provided a process for enforcing payment of a debt incurred by a driver for causing an accident (*Moloney*) or for road tolls (*407*) was inconsistent with the federal Bankruptcy and Insolvency Act. The method of enforcement of the provincial laws was to deny driving privileges (registration of vehicle or driver's licence or both) to the debtor as long as the debt remained unpaid. In both cases, the driver had later become bankrupt and had later still been discharged from bankruptcy, but, because the road-related debt had never been paid, the province continued to deny driving privileges to the debtor. The Supreme Court held that the fresh-start provision of the Bankruptcy and Insolvency Act, under which, on discharge from bankruptcy, a debtor is released from all debts that are claims provable in bankruptcy, prevailed over the provincial enforcement provisions, rendering them inoperative by reason of paramountcy. As explained in the previous section of the chapter, a majority of the Court (Gascon J.) held that there was an impossibility of dual compliance, but a minority of the Court (Côté J.) held that a provincial law that simply withheld driving privileges could be complied with by not

---

v. Can., [1995] 3 S.C.R. 199. The new version of the Act was also under challenge in the Quebec courts as a breach of s. 2(b).

[12]The Court did not address the interesting question of whether the imposition by federal law of reasonable limits on a Charter right could be undermined by supplementary provincial laws that expand the violation of the Charter right beyond the federally-set limits.

[13]*Rothmans, Benson & Hedges v. Saskatchewan*, [2005] 1 S.C.R. 188, para. 26.

[14]*Alberta v. Moloney*, [2015] 3 S.C.R. 327, 2015 SCC 51.

[15]*407 ETR Concession Co. v. Canada*, [2015] 3 S.C.R. 397, 2015 SCC 52.

driving so that there was no impossibility of dual compliance. However, the Court was unanimous that the provincial laws frustrated the purpose of the fresh-start provision. The fresh-start provision reflected an important purpose of bankruptcy law, which was to free the debtor from the debts that had driven him into bankruptcy so that he could make a fresh start in his economic and personal life. Whether or not the provincial laws directly contradicted the fresh-start provision (the point on which the Court divided), the effect of the provincial laws was to keep a debt alive that had been discharged by the federal Act. All judges agreed that the provincial laws frustrated the purpose of the federal law.

The *Moloney* and *ETR* cases are rather clear examples of frustration of federal purpose (as is the earlier case of *Mangat*),[16] but the federal purpose is often unclear, and courts are faced with the question whether to frame what they think is the purpose narrowly or broadly. In the third 2015 paramountcy decision, *Saskatchewan v. Lemare Lake Logging*,[17] the issue was whether the provincial Saskatchewan Farm Security Act was rendered inoperative by a remedial provision of the federal Bankruptcy and Insolvency Act that allowed a secured creditor to apply for the appointment of a national receiver to take control of an insolvent or bankrupt debtor's business assets. The BIA required ten days of advance notice to the debtor before the application for the remedy could be made. In this case, the debtor was a farmer in Saskatchewan and the provincial Act required any action by a creditor with respect to farmland to be preceded by 150 days of advance notice to the debtor, during which time mandatory review by a provincial Farm Land Security Board and mandatory mediation assisted by the Board were to take place. It was clear that both laws could be complied with by following the long process mandated by the provincial law, but did that long process frustrate the purpose of the federal law? The decision of the majority of the Supreme Court was no. Abella and Gascon JJ., who wrote the opinion of the majority, emphasized "the guiding principle of cooperative federalism [that] paramountcy must be narrowly construed" and said that "harmonious interpretations of federal and provincial legislation should be favoured over interpretations that result in incompatibility".[18] Their conclusion from the legislative history of the amendment to the BIA that created the national receivership remedy was that the purpose was simply to provide for a national receiver so as to eliminate the former need for multiple provincial receivers. It followed that "Parliament's purpose of providing bankruptcy courts with the power to appoint a national receiver is not frustrated by the procedural and substantive conditions set out in the provincial legislation".[19] Côté J. dissented. She agreed that cooperative federalism was "an important principle", but "a yearning for

[16] *Law Society of B.C. v. Mangat*, [2001] 3 S.C.R. 113.

[17] *Saskatchewan v. Lemare Lake Logging*, [2015] 3 S.C.R. 419, 2015 SCC 53.

[18] *Saskatchewan v. Lemare Lake Logging*, [2015] 3 S.C.R. 419, 2015 SCC 53, para. 21.

[19] *Saskatchewan v. Lemare Lake Logging*, [2015] 3 S.C.R. 419, 2015 SCC 53, para.

a harmonious interpretation of both federal and provincial legislation cannot lead this Court to disregard obvious purposes that are pursued in federal legislation and that are, by this Court's jurisprudence, paramount."[20] She pointed out that the receivership remedy and the 10-day waiting period had been in the BIA for more than a decade before receivership was expanded to a national remedy, and the federal purpose could not be restricted to the creation of a national remedy. In her view, the federal purpose was to provide for a receivership remedy that would be timely, flexible and responsive to the context of insolvency. She emphasized the urgency that often attends creditors' remedies on the insolvency of a debtor, including the appointment of a receiver to protect secured assets. She did not claim that the BIA excluded all provincial regulation of creditors' remedies in insolvency, but the Saskatchewan law placed such "important obstacles" in the way of secured creditors that the provincial law frustrated "the federal purpose of providing a timely, flexible and context-sensitive remedy for secured creditors."[21]

In *Orphan Well Association v. Grant Thornton* (2019),[22] which has already been discussed in the previous section of this chapter, there was another disagreement in the Supreme Court of Canada about whether the purpose of an aspect of the BIA would be frustrated by the operation of a provincial law. Recall that, in this case, a trustee in bankruptcy wanted to disclaim the exhausted "orphan" wells of Redwater Energy, an insolvent oil company, so that it could maximize the value of the company's valuable producing wells for its creditors. The Alberta Energy Regulator disapproved of this plan. It took the position that an adequate share of the sale proceeds from the valuable wells had to be set aside to satisfy the cost of meeting the end-of-life remediation obligations that Alberta law imposed on the licensed operators of orphan wells. The trustee challenged Alberta's end-of-life remediation obligations, arguing that they conflicted with the BIA, and thus were rendered inoperative by the federal paramountcy doctrine. The Supreme Court of Canada held that Alberta's end-of-life remediation obligations did not conflict with the BIA.

The trustee, as explained in the previous section of this chapter, made two impossibility of dual compliance arguments, both of which were rejected by Wagner C.J., writing for the majority of the Court. The trustee also made two frustration of federal purpose arguments, which mirrored its impossibility of dual compliance arguments. Wagner C.J. rejected these two frustration of federal purpose arguments as well. First, he rejected the trustee's argument that Alberta's extension of its

73.

[20]*Saskatchewan v. Lemare Lake Logging*, [2015] 3 S.C.R. 419, 2015 SCC 53, para. 78.

[21]*Saskatchewan v. Lemare Lake Logging*, [2015] 3 S.C.R. 419, 2015 SCC 53, paras. 119.

[22]*Orphan Well Association v. Grant Thornton*, [2019] 1 S.C.R. 150. Wagner C.J. wrote the opinion for the five-judge majority of the seven-judge bench. Côté J. wrote a dissenting opinion, which was joined by Moldaver J.

end-of-life remediation obligations to trustees that sought to disclaim assets of a bankrupt estate conflicted with s. 14.06 of the BIA, which provides that a trustee is "not personally liable for failure to comply" with an order "to remedy any environmental condition or environmental damage affecting property involved in a bankruptcy" if the trustee disclaims the property within a prescribed timeframe. The purpose of this provision was to "protect trustees from personal liability",[23] not to allow trustees to walk away from the environmental liabilities of the estates that they are administering. This purpose was not being frustrated because the Alberta Energy Regulator was not seeking to hold the trustee liable *personally* for the environmental liabilities resulting from Redwater Energy's end-of-life remediation obligations. It was seeking to ensure that Redwater Energy's assets would be used for this purpose. Second, Wagner C.J. also rejected the trustee's argument that allowing Alberta's end-of-life remediation obligations to operate in this context would frustrate the purpose of the distribution scheme in the BIA for the settlement of debts. The purpose of the BIA's distribution scheme was not frustrated because the environmental liabilities that resulted from Alberta's end-of-life remediation obligations were not "claims provable in bankruptcy", and so were not subject to the distribution scheme; rather, they resulted from statutory duties, which served the public interest and were imposed by "valid provincial laws which define the contours of the bankrupt estate available for distribution".[24] Indeed, allowing Alberta's end-of-life remediation obligations to operate would actually "facilitate" one of the specific purposes of the BIA – "to permit regulators to place a first charge on real property of a bankrupt affected by an environmental condition or damage in order to fund remediation".[25]

IV. NEGATIVE IMPLICATION

§ 16:5 Covering the field

Cases where one law expressly contradicts another obviously call for the application of the paramountcy doctrine. We have seen that the courts have expanded the concept of express contradiction to include the case where a provincial law would frustrate the purpose of a federal law. The question to be examined in this section is whether they are the only cases that attract the doctrine or whether lesser kinds of incompatibility will also suffice. Where the federal Parliament has enacted a law on a particular topic, does this preclude a province from enacting a different

[23] *Orphan Well Association v. Grant Thornton*, [2019] 1 S.C.R. 150, para. 110.

[24] *Orphan Well Association v. Grant Thornton*, [2019] 1 S.C.R. 150, para. 160.

[25] *Orphan Well Association v. Grant Thornton*, [2019] 1 S.C.R. 150, para. 159. Côté J., in dissent, said that the environmental liabilities that resulted from Alberta's end-of-life remediation obligations were "claims provable in bankruptcy", and thus were subject to the BIA's distribution scheme. She said that an "essential purpose" of the BIA – to distribute the value of a bankrupt estate in accordance with this distribution scheme – would thus be frustrated by the operation of these obligations: *Orphan Well Association v. Grant Thornton*, [2019] 1 S.C.R. 150, para. 170.

law on the same topic? If the provincial law does not contradict the federal law, but adds to it or supplements it, is the provincial law rendered inoperative by the federal law? And what if the provincial law is exactly the same as the federal law? The short answer to these questions is that only express contradiction suffices to invoke the paramountcy doctrine. A provincial law that is supplementary or duplicative of a federal law is not deemed to be inconsistent with the federal law.

Canadian courts, by confining the doctrine of paramountcy to such a narrow compass, have rejected a "covering the field" (or negative implication) test of inconsistency, which is employed by the courts of the United States and Australia.[1] Under this test, a federal law may be interpreted as covering the field and precluding any provincial laws in that field, even if they are not contradictory of the federal law.[2] In other words, a federal law may be read as including not only its express provisions, but also a "negative implication" that those express provisions should not be supplemented or duplicated by any provincial law on the same subject. Under this test, the question is whether the provincial law is in the same "field", or is upon the same subject, as the federal law: if so, the provincial law is deemed to be inconsistent with the federal law.

The negative implication (or covering the field) test of inconsistency seems to have been applied on one occasion by the Privy Council. In the *Local Prohibition* case (1896),[3] the Privy Council held that federal local-option temperance legislation would render inoperative similar provincial legislation if both laws were ever adopted in the same district. Both laws prohibited the retail sale of liquor, the only differences residing in the definition of quantities which made a sale "wholesale" and therefore permitted. It was possible to comply with both laws by complying with the stricter of the two, that is, by selling liquor only in quantities which fitted the narrowest definition of wholesale sale. The direct contradiction test was therefore not satisfied,[4] and their lordships' find-

[Section 16:5]

[1]For an authoritative statement of the rule of "preemption" (as it is usually called) in the United States, see *Pennsylvania v. Nelson* (1956), 359 U.S. 497, 501–505; but compare *Wyeth v. Levine* (2009), 555 U.S. xxx (federal drug labelling requirements imposed by federal law do not pre-empt duty to warn imposed by the state's common law of negligence; both federal and state laws can be obeyed by giving the stronger warning called for by the stricter state law); and for the rule of "inconsistency" (as it is usually called) in Australia, *see Ex parte McLean* (1930), 43 C.L.R. 472, 483. These broad definitions of inconsistency are, of course, consistent with the more centralized interpretation of the federal distribution of powers in the United States and Australia. For a detailed comparison of the Australian and Canadian law, see Gilbert, Australian and Canadian Federalism 1867–1984 (1986), chs. 8, 9.

[2]This interpretation is not automatic, but turns on a judicial finding that the federal law was to be the sole and exclusive law in the field. This finding, and the definition of the "field" that has been covered, confer a degree of judicial discretion that makes the law quite unpredictable.

[3]*A.-G. Ont. v. A.G. Can.* (Local Prohibition) [1896] A.C. 348.

[4]Contra, W.R. Lederman, "The Concurrent Operation of Federal and Provincial

ing of inconsistency, although not explained in the opinion, must have been premised on a negative implication or coverage of the field.[5]

A statement of the negative implication (or covering the field) test of inconsistency is to be found in the dissenting opinion of Cartwright J. in *O'Grady v. Sparling* (1960).[6] In that case, a federal law (the Criminal Code) made it an offence to drive a motor vehicle recklessly; a provincial law (Manitoba's Highway Traffic Act) made it an offence to drive carelessly ("without due care and attention"). The two laws did not expressly contradict each other because it was possible to obey both of them by adhering to the stricter provincial standard. Nonetheless, Cartwright J. (who had dissented in the *Saskatchewan Breathalyzer* case) would have held that the two laws were inconsistent. With the concurrence of Locke J., he said:[7]

> In my opinion when Parliament has expressed in an Act its decision that a certain kind or degree of negligence in the operation of a motor vehicle shall be punishable as a crime against the state it follows that it has decided that no less culpable kind or degree of negligence in such operation shall be so punishable. By necessary implication the Act says not only what kinds or degrees of negligence shall be punishable but also what kinds or degrees shall not.

The premise of this reasoning is the inference that Parliament covered the field of bad driving when it enacted the Criminal Code offence of reckless driving, and thereby preempted any provincial law in the same field. What Cartwright J. was willing to do was to add to the express terms of the federal statute an implication that there should be no provincial regulation of the same subject matter.

In *O'Grady v. Sparling*, Cartwright J.'s opinion was a dissenting one. The majority of the Court, in an opinion written by Judson J., rejected the negative implication (or covering the field) test, holding that "both provisions can live together and operate concurrently".[8] The two laws were therefore not inconsistent and paramountcy did not apply. The negative implication test was also rejected in two other cases which the Court decided at the same time. In *Stephens v. The Queen* (1960),[9] the question was whether there was inconsistency between a federal (Criminal Code) offence of failing to remain at the scene of an accident "with intent to escape civil or criminal liability", and a provincial (Highway Traffic Act) offence of failing to remain at the scene of an accident. In this case, as in *O'Grady*, it was possible to obey both laws by complying

---

Laws in Canada" (1963) 9 McGill L.J. 185, 190–191; B. Laskin, "Occupying the Field: Paramountcy in Penal Legislation" (1963) 41 Can. Bar Rev. 234, 243.

[5]This part of the decision was not obiter, because it formed part of their lordships' answer to one of the questions referred for decision; on the other hand, the existence of inconsistency was described as "obvious" and was not carefully considered.

[6]*O'Grady v. Sparling*, [1960] S.C.R. 804.

[7]*O'Grady v. Sparling*, [1960] S.C.R. 804, 820–821.

[8]*O'Grady v. Sparling*, [1960] S.C.R. 804, 811.

[9]*Stephens v. The Queen*, [1960] S.C.R. 823.

with the stricter of the two, which was the provincial one because it lacked the ingredient of intention to escape liability. Again the majority of the Court, in an opinion written this time by Kerwin C.J., held that there was no inconsistency; and again Cartwright J. (with Locke J.) dissented on the basis of a negative implication. In *Smith v. The Queen* (1960),[10] the two laws were virtually identical in their effect: the federal (Criminal Code) offence was making, circulating or publishing a false prospectus; the provincial (Securities Act) offence was furnishing false information in a prospectus. Again the Court held that the two laws were not inconsistent. Kerwin C.J., who wrote one of the two concurring opinions, said that the two laws could "co-exist";[11] Martland J., who wrote the other, made his already-quoted statement that there was "no conflict in the sense that compliance with one law involves breach of the other";[12] Cartwright J. again dissented, this time attracting the support of Ritchie J. as well as Locke J.

In *O'Grady, Stephens* and *Smith*, none of the majority or concurring opinions attempted to deal with Cartwright J.'s argument that inconsistency could arise by negative implication. In fact, with the exception of Martland J.'s "compliance" dictum in *Smith*, none of the opinions even offered a rival definition of inconsistency. These failures left in doubt the exact status of negative implication (or covering the field) as a test of inconsistency. It was not clear whether the majority judges had rejected negative implication in principle for all cases, or whether they had decided merely that no negative implication should be drawn from the particular federal laws in issue in *O'Grady, Stephens* and *Smith*. Since those cases were decided, the Supreme Court of Canada has made clear that the former view is correct. A series of cases has decided that the negative implication test no longer has any place in Canadian constitutional law.

The first case is *Mann v. The Queen* (1966).[13] This case concerned a new federal Criminal Code offence of driving a motor vehicle "in a manner that is dangerous to the public". This "dangerous driving" offence stipulated a stricter standard of care than the "reckless driving" offence which was the federal offence in issue in *O'Grady v. Sparling*. Did this new offence render inoperative the provincial "careless driving" offences? In *Mann*, the Court held unanimously that paramountcy did not apply. This case was a clearer one for Cartwright J.'s negative implication than *O'Grady v. Sparling*, because the federal standard was now so close to the provincial one. But Cartwright J. wrote a concurring opinion in *Mann*, following *O'Grady v. Sparling* and not mentioning the negative implication test. Obviously, Cartwright J. was bowing to the doctrine of precedent, but it is significant that he did not consider that the clearer facts of *Mann* justified his persisting with the negative implication test.

---

[10] *Smith v. The Queen*, [1960] S.C.R. 776.

[11] *Smith v. The Queen*, [1960] S.C.R. 776, 781.

[12] *Smith v. The Queen*, [1960] S.C.R. 776, 800, quoted at § 16:3 note 4, above.

[13] *Mann v. The Queen*, [1966] S.C.R. 238.

In *Ross v. Registrar of Motor Vehicles* (1973)[14] and *Bell v. A.-G. P.E.I.* (1973),[15] the question arose whether there was inconsistency between a federal law conferring a judicial discretion to prohibit a convicted "drunk driver" from driving and a provincial law imposing an automatic suspension of a convicted drunk driver's driving licence. The question had first arisen in *Provincial Secretary of P.E.I. v. Egan* (1941),[16] when the Criminal Code included as a penalty for certain impaired driving offences the power to prohibit the convicted defendant from driving anywhere in Canada for up to three years. Egan was convicted of impaired driving, but the magistrate in imposing sentence exercised his discretion to make no order prohibiting Egan from driving. However, Egan's driving licence had been issued by Prince Edward Island, and that province's Highway Traffic Act automatically suspended for 12 months the licence of anyone who, like Egan, had been convicted of an impaired driving offence. Egan therefore lost his licence for a year and was effectively prohibited from driving his car for that period of time. The Supreme Court of Canada unanimously decided that Egan had indeed lost his licence: the provincial suspension was not inconsistent with the federal discretion. Cartwright J. was not on the Court in 1941, and no judge made the argument that a federal discretion to prohibit driving carried the negative implication that there should be no automatic suspension of the convicted driver's licence to drive. Although the reasoning of the judges confuses validity with inconsistency and does not clarify the ground for decision on the latter question, the reason for the result must have been that both enactments could be obeyed by Egan by not driving for a year!

The new point which had to be decided in *Ross* and *Bell* arose out of an amendment to the Criminal Code in 1972 which enlarged the discretion of the court in sentencing impaired drivers. Whereas before 1972 any court-imposed prohibition on driving had to be for a continuous period of time, the 1972 amendment authorized the sentencing court to prohibit driving on an intermittent basis "at such times and places as may be specified in the order". In *Ross*, the sentencing Court had prohibited the defendant "from driving for a period of six months, except Monday to Friday, 8 a.m. to 5:45 p.m., in the course of employment and going to and from work". The purpose of the 1972 amendment, as exemplified by the order in *Ross*, was to enable the sentencing court to tailor its prohibition order to the facts of the case; and, in particular, to impose a more lenient restraint on a defendant who was dependent upon driving for his livelihood. It was obviously contemplated by the amendment, and by the Court which sentenced Ross, that the defendant would be free to drive in those periods which were exempt from the federal prohibition.[17] An automatic, blanket suspension of the defendant's licence would nullify the effect of the amendment and make a mockery

[14] *Ross v. Registrar of Motor Vehicles*, [1975] 1 S.C.R. 5.

[15] *Bell v. A.-G. P.E.I.*, [1975] 1 S.C.R. 25.

[16] *Provincial Secretary of P.E.I. v. Egan*, [1941] S.C.R. 396.

[17] The sentencing Court in Ross actually held that the provincial licence was not to

of the criminal court's carefully tailored order. Surely, if ever a negative implication was warranted, it was here. But the Supreme Court of Canada refused to draw the implication. In *Bell*, where no intermittent order had in fact been made, the Court unanimously followed *Egan* and held operative an automatic provincial suspension of the convicted driver's licence. In *Ross*, where the intermittent order had been made, the Court reached the same conclusion by a majority of five to two. Pigeon J. for the majority admitted that "this means that as long as the provincial licence suspension is in effect, the person concerned gets no benefit from the indulgence granted under the federal legislation", but dismissed the point by asking rhetorically, "is the situation any different in law from that which was considered in the *Egan* case . . .?"[18] The two dissenting judges, Judson and Spence JJ., held that the making of the intermittent order in Ross did create a "direct conflict"[19] to which the provincial suspension had to yield.

The Supreme Court of Canada's rejection of negative implication (or covering the field) has continued in more recent cases. In *Robinson v. Countrywide Factors* (1977),[20] the Court held that a provincial law avoiding fraudulent preferences by insolvent debtors could stand in the face of a federal bankruptcy law. In *Construction Montcalm v. Minimum Wage Commission* (1978),[21] the Court held that a provincial minimum wage law was applicable to a Crown contractor constructing an airport runway, despite the fact that there was an applicable (less onerous) federal minimum wage law. In *Schneider v. The Queen* (1982),[22] the Court held that a provincial Heroin Treatment Act was not inconsistent with the federal Narcotic Control Act. In *Multiple Access v. McCutcheon* (1982),[23] the Court applied a provincial "insider trading" law to shares in a federally incorporated company, despite the existence of an applicable federal law prohibiting insider trading. In *Rio Hotel v. New Brunswick* (1987),[24] the Court held that a provincial prohibition of "nude entertainment" in taverns was not inconsistent with the federal Criminal Code offences involving public nudity. In *Irwin Toy v. Quebec* (1989),[25] the Court held that a provincial prohibition of advertising directed at children applied to television, despite the existence of federal guidelines for

be suspended. Pigeon J. was surely correct in holding that the Court lacked the power to suspend the operation of a provincial law; Judson J. in dissent did not rely on this aspect of the sentencing Court's order; Spence J. in dissent held that the sentencing Court did have the power it asserted.

[18] *Ross v. Registrar of Motor Vehicles*, [1975] 1 S.C.R. 5, 13. Pigeon J. went on to suggest (at p.15) that his decision was compatible with the negative implication (or covering the field) test, but it is difficult to see how that test could have produced the same result.

[19] *Ross v. Registrar of Motor Vehicles*, [1975] 1 S.C.R. 5, 20.

[20] *Robinson v. Countrywide Factors*, [1977] 2 S.C.R. 753.

[21] *Construction Montcalm v. Minimum Wage Commission*, [1979] 1 S.C.R. 754.

[22] *Schneider v. The Queen*, [1982] 2 S.C.R. 112.

[23] *Multiple Access v. McCutcheon*, [1982] 2 S.C.R. 161.

[24] *Rio Hotel v. New Brunswick*, [1987] 2 S.C.R. 59.

[25] *Irwin Toy v. Quebec*, [1989] 1 S.C.R. 927.

television advertising directed at children. In *Clarke v. Clarke* (1990),[26] the Court held that provincial matrimonial property legislation required the sharing of a military pension, despite a federal prohibition on the alienation of the pension. In *114957 Canada v. Hudson* (2001),[27] a municipal by-law restricting the use of pesticides was not rendered inoperative by federal legislation setting standards for pesticides or provincial legislation setting standards for vendors and commercial users of pesticides. In *Canadian Western Bank v. Alberta* (2007),[28] a provincial law requiring a licence for the promotion of insurance in the province was not rendered inoperative to banks by the federal Bank Act, which authorized banks to promote eight specified kinds of credit-related insurance.

It is clear from these cases that the Supreme Court of Canada does not infer an inconsistency between federal and provincial laws based on an imputation that federal law "covers the field" or carries a "negative implication" forbidding supplementary provincial law in the same field. However, as we noted earlier, the Court will infer an inconsistency where it concludes that a federal law has a purpose that would be frustrated by a provincial law. Cases where the provincial law frustrates the purpose of a federal law[29] are not easily distinguishable from the cases that deny the imputation that the federal law intended to cover the field or foreclose supplementary provincial law.[30] The Court has to make a judgment as to whether the two laws can indeed live together, bearing in mind not just the compatibility of the provincial law with the literal requirements of the federal law, but also the compatibility of the provincial law with the purpose of the federal law.

§ 16:6 Express extension of paramountcy

If the federal Parliament occupied a field of legislation by express words, would that be effective? For example, s. 88 of the federal Indian Act[1] provides that provincial laws are inapplicable to Indians "to the extent that such laws make provision for any matter for which provision

[26] *Clarke v. Clarke*, [1990] 2 S.C.R. 795.

[27] *114957 Canada v. Hudson*, [2001] 2 S.C.R. 241.

[28] *Canadian Western Bank v. Alberta*, [2007] 2 S.C.R. 3.

[29] E.g., *Bank of Montreal v. Hall*, [1990] 1 S.C.R. 121; *Law Society of B.C. v. Mangat*, [2001] 3 S.C.R. 113.

[30] R. Elliot, "Safeguarding Provincial Autonomy from the Supreme Court's New Federal Paramountcy Doctrine: A Constructive Role for the Intention to Cover the Field Test?" (2007) 38 Supreme Court L.R. (2d) 629, proposes that the covering the field test should be resurrected as a preliminary step so that the tests of inconsistency (impossibility of dual compliance, frustration of federal purpose) would only be applied if there were a parliamentary intention to cover the field. His intention is to narrow the doctrine of paramountcy, but the proposal would make the law more complicated and (in my view) more uncertain than it is now.

[Section 16:6]

[1] R.S.C. 1985, c. I-5.

is made by or under this Act". On the face of it,[2] this provision purports to extend the doctrine of paramountcy by rendering inoperative provincial laws upon the same matters as the Indian Act, even if the provincial laws do not contradict the Indian Act. Is it open to the federal Parliament to extend the doctrine of paramountcy beyond the case of an actual conflict in operation?

In principle, the answer to this question should be yes. Assuming that the express federal paramountcy provision was valid under federalism rules, that is, it was part of a law in relation to a federal head of power, there seems no reason why it should not be valid. If that is so, then a provincial law in the same field would be inconsistent with the federal law, and would therefore be rendered inoperative by the doctrine of paramountcy. For the most part, it has been assumed that this is indeed the law.[3] However, in *Dick v. The Queen* (1985),[4] Beetz J., who wrote the opinion of the five-judge bench, said that "it would not be open to Parliament in my view to make the Indian Act paramount over provincial laws simply because the Indian Act occupied the field. Operational conflict would be required to this end". This dictum was not strictly necessary to the decision, but it was part of the reasoning process, and it must be taken as a considered view of the issue.[5] For the reasons given above,[6] I think the better view is that an express covering-the-field clause would be effective.[7]

---

[2]The various interpretations of s. 88 are discussed in ch. 28, Aboriginal Peoples, under heading §§ 28:13 to 28:16, "Section 88 of the Indian Act". In *Dick v. The Queen*, [1985] 2 S.C.R. 309, it was held that s. 88 applied only to those provincial laws that could not apply to Indians of their own force. For those laws, Parliament, having made them applicable by referential incorporation, can adopt any paramountcy rule it chooses.

[3]*A.-G. B.C. v. Smith*, [1967] S.C.R. 702, 714 (holding that federal law, which defined juvenile delinquency as including breaches of provincial laws, precluded prosecutions under provincial laws); *R. v. Francis*, [1988] 1 S.C.R. 1025, 1031 (dictum that "sufficient intent" to cover field would be effective); compare *Ross v. Registrar of Motor Vehicles*, [1975] 1 S.C.R. 5, 16 (dictum leaving point open). The cases holding that s. 88 makes Indian treaties override provincial laws also support my view, because they proceed on the assumption that Parliament has the power to expand paramountcy in that way. See ch. 28, Aboriginal Peoples, under heading § 28:16, "Treaty exception".

[4]*Dick v. The Queen*, [1985] 2 S.C.R. 309, 327–328.

[5]The point was made in support of interpreting s. 88 as applying only to provincial laws that could not apply of their own force to Indians: § 16:6 note 2. The case is more fully discussed in ch. 29, Aboriginal Peoples, under heading § 28:14, "Laws of general application".

[6]Accord, P.J. Monahan and A.J. Petter, "Developments in Constitutional Law: The 1985–86 Term" (1987) 9 Supreme Court L.R. 69, 163.

[7]It appears that paramountcy may be expressly waived by the federal Parliament, as it has purported to do in the (now repealed) Juvenile Delinquents Act, R.S.C. 1970, c. J-3, s. 39, and possibly also in the Lord's Day Act: *Lord's Day Alliance of Can. v. A.-G. B.C.*, [1959] S.C.R. 497; and see also ch. 14, Delegation, under heading § 14:17, "Conditions as legislative interdelegation".

V. OVERLAP AND DUPLICATION

§ 16:7 Constitutional significance

The four paramountcy cases decided in the 1960s, namely, *O'Grady, Smith, Stephens* and *Mann* all concerned penal enactments which overlapped. In the case of each pair of laws, many fact situations would constitute an offence under both the federal and the provincial law. However, all of the majority and concurring opinions in the four cases (including that of Martland J. in *Smith*, which contained the "dual compliance" dictum) placed emphasis on the fact that the competing federal and provincial laws were different in some respect; by "different" they usually seemed to mean that there was some imaginable set of facts to which one law would apply and not the other. The implication of this kind of reasoning is that a provincial law which duplicated the provisions of a federal law would be held to be inoperative. Curiously, none of the majority or concurring judges said this, but their opinions are only explicable on this basis.[1]

There is no reason why duplication should be a case of inconsistency once the negative implication or covering the field test is rejected. On the contrary, duplication is "the ultimate in harmony".[2] The argument that it is untidy, wasteful and confusing to have two laws when only one is needed[3] reflects a value which in a federal system often has to be subordinated to that of provincial autonomy. Nor does the latter value disappear when provincial law merely duplicates federal law, because the suspension of a provincial law may create a gap in a provincial scheme of regulation which would have to be filled by federal law—a situation as productive of untidiness, waste and confusion as duplication.

In any event, arguments against duplication of federal and provincial laws can have little weight once overlapping is admitted. After all, overlapping legislation is duplicative to the extent of the overlap, and yet it is clear that provincial law is not inoperative to the extent of its overlap with federal law. It must be remembered too that the differences between the federal and provincial laws in *O'Grady* and *Stephens* were small, and in *Smith* and *Mann* they were virtually non-existent. If paramountcy does not apply when 999 cases out of 1,000 are covered by both laws, why should paramountcy apply when all 1,000 are covered by both laws? It is submitted that duplication is not a test of inconsistency.

[Section 16:7]

[1]Only the dissenting judges in *Smith*, namely Locke, Cartwright, and Ritchie JJ., held that the substantial identity between the two laws in that case amounted to an inconsistency.

[2]W.R. Lederman, "The Concurrent Operation of Federal and Provincial Laws in Canada" (1963) 9 McGill I.J. 185, 195.

[3]W.R. Lederman, "The Concurrent Operation of Federal and Provincial Laws in Canada" (1963) 9 McGill I.J. 185, 196.

The argument contained in the previous two paragraphs, which appeared in the first edition (1977) of this book,[4] was accepted by Dickson J. for a majority of the Supreme Court of Canada in *Multiple Access v. McCutcheon* (1982).[5] He held that the provisions of Ontario securities law relating to insider trading were not rendered inoperative by the substantially identical provisions of federal corporate law. This case is a considered and unequivocal ruling that duplication is not a test of paramountcy, and it probably settles the question, although there are two earlier cases to the contrary,[6] neither of which was referred to by Dickson J. Probably, the two earlier cases should be treated as overruled by *Multiple Access*.

Once it is determined that duplication is not a test of paramountcy, there is obviously no point in searching for minor differences between essentially similar laws, which was the approach taken by the Supreme Court of Canada in *O'Grady, Smith, Stephens* and *Mann*. This approach, which has not been used in cases decided after *Mann*, seems muddled. Occasionally, the search for differences—any differences— has led judges to point out that the competing laws had different "purposes" or "aspects", and that they were consistent for that reason, even though they were substantially the same in operation. This kind of reasoning confuses validity with consistency.[7] The existence of different purposes or aspects is relevant only to the question whether each law is valid in the first place. The double aspect doctrine[8] "opens two gates to the same field", but it does not help to resolve the subsequent question of whether the two laws are inconsistent.[9] Whether the laws are inconsistent or not

---

[4]Pages 110–111.

[5]*Multiple Access v. McCutcheon*, [1982] 2 S.C.R. 161, 185–191.

[6]*Home Insurance Co. v. Lindal and Beattie*, [1934] S.C.R. 33, 40; *N.S. Bd. of Censors v. McNeil*, [1978] 2 S.C.R. 662, 699. In both cases, it was assumed without question that duplication would give rise to federal paramountcy. There was no deliberate consideration of the issue, as there was in *Multiple Access*.

[7]On the distinction between validity and consistency, text accompanying § 16:1 note 13, above. For dicta indicating confusion of validity with consistency, either by treating the aspect doctrine as relevant to consistency, or by treating the existence or terms of one law as relevant to the validity of the other, or by treating inconsistency as a withdrawal of provincial power to enact the inconsistent legislation, see *Prov. Secretary of P.E.I. v. Egan*, [1941] S.C.R. 396, 400–403 per Duff C.J.; *Johnson v. A.-G. Alta.*, [1954] S.C.R. 127, 136–138 per Rand J.; *Smith v. The Queen*, [1960] S.C.R. 776, 781 per Kerwin C.J., 786–787 per Locke J.; *O'Grady v. Sparling*, [1960] S.C.R. 804, 811 per Judson J., 821 per Cartwright J.; *Stephens v. The Queen*, [1960] S.C.R. 823, 829 per Cartwright J.; *A.-G. Ont. v. Barfried Enterprises*, [1963] S.C.R. 570, 583 per Martland J.; *Mann v. The Queen*, [1966] S.C.R. 238, 251 per Ritchie J.; *N.S. Bd. of Censors v. McNeil*, [1978] 2 S.C.R. 662, 695, 698–699 per Ritchie J.; *Husky Oil Operations v. M.N.R.*, [1995] 3 S.C.R. 453, para. 87 per Gonthier J., criticized para. 213 per Iacobucci J.

[8]See ch. 15, Judicial Review on Federal Grounds, under heading § 15:7, "Double aspect".

[9]W.R. Lederman, "The Concurrent Operation of Federal and Provincial Laws in Canada" (1963) 9 McGill L.J. 185, 197; accord, B. Laskin, "Occupying the Field: Paramountcy in Penal Legislation" (1963) 41 Can. Bar Rev. 234, 242, 247; P.C. Weiler, "The Supreme Court and the Law of Canadian Federalism" (1973) 23 U. Toronto L.J.

depends not on their dominant purpose or aspect but upon whether they are compatible in operation.

The Supreme Court strongly reaffirmed its toleration of duplicative federal and provincial laws in *Bank of Montreal v. Marcotte* (2014).[10] The issue in the case was whether Quebec's Consumer Protection Act (CPA), which required the disclosure of foreign-exchange conversion fees by the issuers of credit cards, applied to the banks as well as to non-bank issuers. The regulations made under the federal Bank Act, which were applicable only to the banks, imposed the same disclosure requirement on the banks. The issue arose because the CPA, but not the banking regulations, authorized a civil action for restitution of any fees that had not been disclosed and punitive damages, and at trial restitution and punitive damages had been ordered against non-compliant banks. The Court held (rejecting an argument based in interjurisdictional immunity)[11] that the CPA requirement was valid and applicable to the banks. The Court also held that the CPA required the same straightforward disclosure as the banking regulations. (The trial judge had held that the CPA required the fees to be folded into the interest rate, creating a confusing form of disclosure that was different from that required by the banking regulations.) Having held that the federal and provincial laws were duplicative, the Court held that there was no inconsistency to trigger federal paramountcy and relieve the banks from civil liability under the CPA: "Duplication is not, on its own, enough to trigger paramountcy."[12] However, in this case the duplication was not quite "on its own"; it appeared to frustrate a federal purpose. The Bank Act provided in a preamble that "it is desirable and in the national interest to provide for clear, *comprehensive, exclusive* national standards applicable to banking products and banking services offered by banks" (emphasis added). The Court held that this made no difference: the disclosure provisions of the CPA "do not provide for 'standards applicable to banking products and banking services offered by banks', but rather articulate a contractual norm in Quebec"—just like "the basic rules of contract".[13] This was an implausible characterization of the complex disclosure provisions of the CPA,[14] but it was enough for the Court to hold that the duplicative requirements of the CPA "cannot be said to

---

307, 359.

[10]*Bank of Montreal v. Marcotte*, [2014] 2 S.C.R. 725, 2014 SCC 55. Rothstein and Wagner JJ. wrote the opinion of the seven-judge panel of the Court.

[11]For discussion, see ch. 15, Judicial Review on Federal Grounds, under heading § 15:18, "Federally-regulated undertakings", at § 15:18 note 27, above.

[12]*Bank of Montreal v. Marcotte*, [2014] 2 S.C.R. 725, 2014 SCC 55, para. 80. The Court acknowledged that a paramountcy argument would have been available if, as the trial judge had held (but without applying paramountcy), that the CPA required a mode of disclosure different from that of the Bank Act (para. 80); and see § 16:7 note 14, below.

[13]*Bank of Montreal v. Marcotte*, [2014] 2 S.C.R. 725, 2014 SCC 55, para. 79.

[14]The CPA provided different disclosure rules for fees characterized as "credit charges", which had to be folded into the interest rate, and "net capital", which had to be disclosed separately. The Court devotes 13 paragraphs to this difficult interpretative issue, concluding that the conversion fees were net capital and overruling the trial judge's

frustrate or undermine a goal of exclusive national standards".[15] Nor did the CPA's provincial regulatory oversight or its civil remedies of restitution and punitive damages frustrate the comprehensive, exclusive national standards,[16] although the Bank Act provided for separate federal regulatory oversight reinforced by criminal sanctions, not civil remedies, for breach of the disclosure obligations. Nor did the CPA's nullification of non-compliant contracts frustrate the comprehensive, exclusive national standards, although the Bank Act did not nullify non-compliant contracts; the Court was content to point out that the plaintiffs had not sought nullification.[17]

§ 16:8 Double criminal liability

The existence of overlapping or duplicative penal provisions raises the possibility that a person may be liable to conviction under both a federal law and a provincial law for the same conduct. There is nothing in paramountcy doctrine which precludes multiple prosecutions or convictions under federal and provincial laws.[1]

However, there is no reason why s. 11(h) of the Charter of Rights, which precludes double jeopardy,[2] and the various rules of criminal procedure that have a similar purpose,[3] should not be applicable where an accused is charged with an offence under a federal statute and an offence under a provincial statute.[4] For the purpose of double-jeopardy law, the differing jurisdictional sources of the multiple offences should

---

conclusion that they were credit charges: *Bank of Montreal v. Marcotte*, [2014] 2 S.C.R. 725, 2014 SCC 55, paras. 48–61. The complicated rules applicable to credit cards bear no resemblance to "basic rules of contract".

[15]*Bank of Montreal v. Marcotte*, [2014] 2 S.C.R. 725, 2014 SCC 55, para. 81; note the omission here of the word "comprehensive" from the preamble.

[16]*Bank of Montreal v. Marcotte*, [2014] 2 S.C.R. 725, 2014 SCC 55, para. 84.

[17]The Court acknowledged that a paramountcy argument would be available if the remedy of nullity had been sought by the plaintiffs: *Bank of Montreal v. Marcotte*, [2014] 2 S.C.R. 725, 2014 SCC 55, para. 83.

[Section 16:8]

[1]*R. v. Gautreau* (1978), 88 D.L.R. (3d) 718, 723 (N.B. A.D.).

[2]See ch. 51, Rights on Being Charged, under heading §§ 51:27 to 51:30, "Double jeopardy". There is no comparable guarantee in Australia. In the United States, the fifth amendment includes a guarantee against double jeopardy under federal law, and the same guarantee applies to state law through the due process clause of the fourteenth amendment: *Benton v. Maryland* (1969), 395 U.S. 784; but it has been held that the guarantee does not apply where one offence is federal and the other is state: *Bartkus v. Illinois* (1959), 359 U.S. 121; *Abbate v. United States* (1959), 359 U.S. 187; compare *Can. v. Schmidt*, [1987] 1 S.C.R. 500 (rejecting argument that extradition to U.S. should be refused, because of this limitation to the double-jeopardy rule).

[3]The doctrines of autrefois acquit, autrefois convict, issue estoppel, res judicata (as expanded in *Kienapple v. The Queen*, [1975] 1 S.C.R. 729) and abuse of process all bear on issues of double jeopardy. See similarly, *Chatterjee v. Ont.*, [2009] 1 S.C.R. 624, para. 51 (citing *Toronto v. C.U.P.E.*, [2003] 3 S.C.R. 77, para. 37.) See generally Friedland, Double Jeopardy (1969).

[4]Accord, *R. v. Wigglesworth*, [1987] 2 S.C.R. 541, 554, 556, 560 (obiter dicta); M.L. Friedland, "Double Jeopardy and the Division of Legislative Authority in Canada" (1967)

be irrelevant. In other words, double jeopardy issues should be dealt with as if Canada was a unitary state. Indeed, the administration of criminal justice in each province is to a large extent unitary. It is the provincial police and prosecutors who enforce most of the federal criminal law as well as all provincial penal law, and it is the provincial court system in which both federal and provincial offences are tried.[5] This means that nearly all relevant decisions are taken by the same provincial officials or judges, regardless of whether the offences are federal or provincial. The paucity of case law suggests that the issues of double jeopardy across jurisdictional boundaries are in fact usually resolved by prosecutorial or judicial discretion.

§ 16:9 Double civil liability

Double civil liability is also a possibility under overlapping or duplicative federal and provincial laws. The Privy Council has upheld double income taxation, saying that federal and provincial taxes "may co-exist and be enforced without clashing", because the Dominion "reaps part of the field", while the province "reaps another part".[1] The Supreme Court of Canada has upheld duplicative civil remedies for insider trading, one in a federal corporations statute, the other in an Ontario securities statute.[2] To the objection that a plaintiff should not be permitted to recover double damages from the insider, Dickson J. for the majority of the Court pointed out that no court would award damages to a plaintiff who had already been fully compensated.[3] Like the possibility of double criminal liability, the issue of double civil liability did not need to be resolved by the doctrine of paramountcy.[4]

VI. EFFECT OF INCONSISTENCY

§ 16:10 Effect of inconsistency

Once it has been determined that a federal law is inconsistent with a provincial law, the doctrine of federal paramountcy stipulates that the provincial law must yield to the federal law. The most usual and most accurate way of describing the effect on the provincial law is to say that it is rendered inoperative to the extent of the inconsistency. Notice that the paramountcy doctrine applies only to the extent of the inconsistency.

---

17 U. Toronto L.J. 66. Contra, *R. v. Kissick*, [1942] 2 W.W.R. 418 (Man. C.A.). The Criminal Code, R.S.C. 1985, c. C-46, s. 12, prohibiting double punishment for the same offence, is expressly confined to federal offences, but much of the ground covered by s. 12 is now also covered by the *Kienapple* rule.

[5]Courts of criminal jurisdiction, policing and prosecution are discussed in ch. 19, Criminal Justice.

[Section 16:9]

[1]*Forbes v. A.-G. Man.*, [1937] A.C. 260, 274.

[2]*Multiple Access v. McCutcheon*, [1982] 2 S.C.R. 161.

[3]*Multiple Access v. McCutcheon*, [1982] 2 S.C.R. 161, 191.

[4]See also *Lamb v. Lamb*, [1985] 1 S.C.R. 851 (provincial order for exclusive possession of matrimonial home not inconsistent with federal order for maintenance).

The doctrine will not affect the operation of those parts of the provincial law which are not inconsistent with the federal law, unless of course the inconsistent parts are inseparably linked up with the consistent parts.[1] There is also a temporal limitation on the paramountcy doctrine. It will affect the operation of the provincial law only so long as the inconsistent federal law is in force. If the federal law is repealed, the provincial law will automatically "revive" (come back into operation) without any reenactment by the provincial Legislature.[2]

It is not accurate to describe the effect of the paramountcy doctrine as the "repeal" of the provincial law. The federal Parliament cannot repeal a provincial law. Moreover, a repealed law does not revive on the repeal of the repealing law. Nor is it accurate to describe the effect of the paramountcy doctrine as rendering the provincial law ultra vires, invalid or unconstitutional. Such a description confuses validity with consistency. The federal Parliament cannot unilaterally take away from a provincial Legislature any power that the Constitution confers upon the Legislature.[3] The provincial power to enact the law is not lost; it continues to exist (so does the provincial law), although it remains in abeyance until such time as the federal Parliament repeals the inconsistent federal law. This is why the only satisfactory description of the effect of the paramountcy doctrine is that it renders inoperative the inconsistent provincial law.

It is even misleading to describe the effect of the paramountcy doctrine as rendering a provincial law "inapplicable". This description is not literally wrong, but it invites confusion with the doctrine of interjurisdictional immunity. The doctrine of interjurisdictional immunity is a limitation on the power of the provincial Legislatures to enact laws that extend into core areas of exclusive federal jurisdiction. In the *Quebec Minimum Wage* case (1966),[4] for example, it was held that Quebec's minimum wage law could not constitutionally apply to the Bell Telephone Company. This was not based on the existence of an inconsistent federal law; there was no federal minimum wage law in existence at that time.[5] The decision was based on the rule that a provincial law cannot affect a "vital part" of an undertaking within federal jurisdiction (such as a

[Section 16:10]

[1]This would depend upon the ordinary rules as to severance: ch. 15, Judicial Review on Federal Grounds, under heading, § 15:14, "Severance".

[2]It is otherwise of course if the provincial Legislature has formally repealed the law in the meantime.

[3]Compare *A.-G. N.S. v. A.-G. Can.* (Nova Scotia Inter-delegation) [1951] S.C.R. 31, holding that neither Parliament nor Legislature can confer additional powers on each other; a fortiori, neither can take existing powers away.

[4]*Commission du Salaire Minimum v. Bell Telephone Co.*, [1966] S.C.R. 767; discussed in ch. 15, Judicial Review on Federal Grounds, under heading §§ 15:16 to 15:21, "Interjurisdictional immunity".

[5]Even if there had been a federal minimum wage law, the existence of a different federal standard has been held not to qualify as an inconsistency: *Construction Montcalm v. Minimum Wage Commn.*, [1979] 1 S.C.R. 754.

telephone company). In a case of this kind, the law is said to be inapplicable, not inoperative, which makes clear that the provincial law is yielding not merely to an inconsistent federal law, but to an implied prohibition in the Constitution which makes the application of the law ultra vires.[6]

---

[6]It is sometimes unclear whether a provincial law has been held to be *inapplicable* on account of interjurisdictional immunity or *inoperative* on account of inconsistency with federal law. A line of cases that holds that provincial law cannot alter the ranking of debts in bankruptcy could be explained *either* on the (ultra vires) basis that the law affects a vital part of bankruptcy (a federal head of power) *or* on the (paramountcy) basis that the law is inconsistent with the Bankruptcy Act (a federal law). The cases are discussed in *Husky Oil Operations v. MNR*, [1995] 3 S.C.R. 453, where Gonthier J. for the majority (at para. 87) uses the word "inapplicable" for some (but not all) paramountcy conflicts. Iacobucci J. for the dissenting minority (at para. 213) criticizes Gonthier J.'s usage as "[confusing] the doctrines of vires and paramountcy, as these have been traditionally understood".

Chapter 17

Peace, Order, and Good Government

I. RESIDUARY NATURE OF POWER

§ 17:1 Residuary nature of power

II. THE "GAP" BRANCH

§ 17:2 The "gap" branch

III. THE "NATIONAL CONCERN" BRANCH

§ 17:3 History of national concern
§ 17:4 Definition of national concern
§ 17:5 Distinctness
§ 17:6 Newness

IV. THE "EMERGENCY" BRANCH

§ 17:7 The non-emergency cases
§ 17:8 War
§ 17:9 Apprehended insurrection
§ 17:10 Inflation
§ 17:11 Temporary character of law

V. RELATIONSHIP BETWEEN NATIONAL CONCERN AND EMERGENCY

§ 17:12 Relationship between national concern and emergency

I. RESIDUARY NATURE OF POWER

§ 17:1 Residuary nature of power

The opening words of s. 91 of the Constitution Act, 1867 confer on the federal Parliament the power:

> to make laws for the peace, order, and good government of Canada, in relation to all matters not coming within the classes of subjects by this Act assigned exclusively to the Legislatures of the provinces; . . .

This power to make laws for the "peace, order, and good government of Canada" (hereinafter called the p.o.g.g. power)[1] is residuary in its rela-

---

[Section 17:1]

[1]See B. Laskin, "Peace, Order and Good Government Re-examined" (1947) 25 Can.

tionship to the provincial heads of power, because it is expressly confined to "matters not coming within the classes of subjects by this Act assigned exclusively to the Legislatures of the provinces". It is clear from this language that any matter which does not come within a provincial head of power must be within the power of the federal Parliament. By this means the distribution of legislative powers was to be exhaustive. With only a few exceptions, of which the most important is the Charter of Rights, the residuary nature of the federal power ensures that every possible subject of legislation belongs to one or other of the federal Parliament or the provincial Legislatures.[2]

The residuary nature of the federal power in Canada is in contrast to the distribution of legislative powers in the earlier Constitution of the United States (1787) and the later Constitution of Australia (1900). In those two countries, the federal Congress or Parliament has only enumerated powers and the Legislatures of the States have the residue.[3] There are reasons for supposing that this difference between the Constitution Act, 1867 and its only real precedent, the Constitution of the United States, was part of a design to create a stronger central government in Canada than existed in the United States.[4] Of course, there is no logical reason why this result should follow from the mere fact that the federal Parliament has the residue of power: the actual extent and importance of the residue depends by definition on the extent and importance of the provincial powers which are subtracted from the residue.

In Canada the provincial heads of power include one of great extent and importance. This is s. 92(13), "property and civil rights in the province", a phrase which is apt to include most of the private law of property, contracts and torts and their many derivatives. Indeed, at the hands of the Privy Council, s. 92(13) became a kind of residuary power itself, and one which was much more important than the federal peace, order, and good government power.[5] A second potentially sweeping head of provincial power is s. 92(16), "generally all matters of a merely local or private nature in the province". Albert S. Abel used the existence of s.

Bar Rev. 1054; A.S. Abel "What Peace, Order and Good Government?" (1968) 7 West. Ont. L. Rev. 1: A.S. Abel, "The Neglected Logic of 91 and 92" (1969) 19 U. Toronto L.J. 487; W.R. Lederman, "Unity and Diversity in Canadian Federalism" (1975) 53 Can. Bar Rev. 597; K. Lysyk, "Constitutional Reform and the Introductory Clause of s. 91" (1979) 57 Can. Bar. Rev. 531; Beaudoin, La Constitution du Canada (3rd ed., 2004), ch. 8; Tremblay, Droit Constitutionnel-Principes (2nd ed., 2000), Part II, ch. 1; Monahan, Constitutional Law (2nd ed., 2002), ch. 8. For a whimsical comparison of the Privy Council's early constitutional decisions with Stephen Leacock, Sunshine Sketches of a Little Town (1912), see E. Morgan, "Sunshine Cases of a Little Constitution" (2009) 43 J. Can. Studies 146.

[2]See ch. 15, Judicial Review on Federal Grounds, under heading § 15:26, "Exhaustiveness".

[3]Constitution of the United States, art. 1, s. 8 (enumerated powers), 10th amendment (residue); Constitution of Australia, ss. 51, 52 (enumerated powers), 107 (residue).

[4]See ch. 5, Federalism, under heading §§ 5:9 to 5:18, "Federalism in Canada".

[5]See ch. 21, Property and Civil Rights.

92(16) as the basis for an argument that there is no residuary power in the Constitution Act, 1867 at all. He said that p.o.g.g. and s. 92(16) were two complementary grants of power which distributed the residue between the two levels of government.[6] But, as Abel himself conceded, one might just as easily speak of two residuary clauses as none, and of the two s. 92(16) has in practice turned out to be quite unimportant, because its work has been done for it by s. 92(13).[7]

The exact nature of the relationship between the p.o.g.g. language at the beginning of s. 91, and the enumerated heads of federal legislative power which follow it, has been more controversial. The O'Connor Report (1939) claimed, and other commentators have agreed, that it is incorrect to describe the p.o.g.g. power as residuary in its relationship with the enumerated heads of power.[8] The p.o.g.g. power, in O'Connor's view, does not comprise what is left after subtraction of the federal (as well as the provincial) enumerated heads; on the contrary, the p.o.g.g. power is the entire federal power, that is to say, all power not allocated to the provincial Legislatures. The enumerated heads of federal power are merely examples of the peace, order, and good government of Canada; they are not heads of power which exist independently of the opening words. This thesis finds support in the opening language[9] of s. 91, which asserts that the enumerated heads of federal power are listed "for

[6]A.S. Abel, "What Peace, Order and Good Government?" (1968) 7 West. Ont. L. Rev. 1. This theory is articulated by Lord Watson in *A.-G. Ont. v. A.-G. Can.* (Local Prohibition) [1896] A.C. 348, 365.

[7]In the same article Abel insisted that the phrase "peace, order and good government of Canada" should not be treated as "a jingle" (p. 4) or a "package deal" (p. 5), but should be unpacked so that a court asks of a statute: "does this involve the peace of Canada? the order of Canada? the good government of Canada?" (p. 6). This suggestion not only finds no support in Canadian case law (as he conceded), it seems to me to be historically inaccurate. The phrase, "peace, order, and good government", or some close variant thereof, is to be found in nearly all the British-derived constitutions, including the constitutions of unitary states such as New Zealand, and the phrase has everywhere been interpreted as "a compendious means of delegating full powers of legislation", subject to any limitations which may be derived from other language of the constitution: Jennings, Constitutional Law of the Commonwealth (1957), vol. 1, 49; *Ibralebbe v. The Queen*, [1964] A.C. 900, 923 (Ceylon). It is consistent with this understanding that s. 4 of the Constitution Act, 1871, intending to confer upon the federal Parliament plenary legislative power over the territories, empowered the Parliament to "make provision for the administration, peace, order, and good government of any territory not for the time being included in any Province". There is no doubt that plenary legislative power was in fact conferred in the sense explained by Jennings: *Riel v. The Queen* (1885), 10 App. Cas. 675; see also *A.-G. Sask. v. CPR*, [1953] A.C. 594; *CLRB v. Yellowknife*, [1977] 2 S.C.R. 729.

[8]*Report of the Parliamentary Counsel relating to the British North America Act, 1867* (Senate of Canada, 1939, Annex I), 61–63. This view was shared by Laskin, among others. See Laskin, Canadian Constitutional Law (5th ed., 1986 by Finkelstein), 401; B. Laskin, "Peace, Order, and Good Government Re-examined" (1947) 25 Can. Bar Rev. 1054, 1057; this important article includes references to the voluminous earlier commentary on the p.o.g.g. power.

[9]The deeming clause in the closing language of s. 91 expressly refers only to the s. 91 enumeration and gives it priority over s. 92(16) or, possibly, all of the s. 92 enumeration. The controversy as to its meaning, and the conflicting dicta, are reported in Browne,

greater certainty, but not so as to restrict the generality of the foregoing terms of this section [i.e., the p.o.g.g. language]". This thesis has led to the common description of the p.o.g.g. power as the "general" power.

Nevertheless, my view is that this "general" theory of the p.o.g.g. power, as including the whole of federal legislative power, is not a particularly helpful way of reading the Constitution Act, 1867. In the first place, despite the apparent import of the reference in s. 91 to "for greater certainty, etc.", it is reasonably clear that many of the enumerated heads of federal power are not merely examples of the opening words. Topics such as "trade and commerce" (s. 91(2)), "banking" (s. 91(15)), "bills of exchange and promissory notes"(s. 91(18)), "interest" (s. 91(19)), "bankruptcy and insolvency" (s. 91(21)), "patents of invention and discovery" (s. 91(22)), "copyrights" (s. 91(23)), and "marriage and divorce" (s. 91(26)) would probably have been held to come within the provincial head of "property and civil rights in the province"(s. 92(13)) if they had not been specifically enumerated in the federal list.[10] If not specifically enumerated they would therefore have been excluded from the p.o.g.g. language, since it does not include provincial heads of power. It seems to me, therefore, that W.R. Lederman is correct in his conclusion that "the federal list was not just superfluous grammatical prudence, it was compelled by historical necessity [the broad scope of "property and civil rights"] and has independent standing".[11]

A second reason for rejecting the general theory of the p.o.g.g. power is that it does not accord with the practice of the courts in applying the power-distributing provisions of the Constitution. For whatever a judge or commentator may say about the process of constitutional classification, the normal practice is to start by looking for a particular enumerated head of power which will sustain the impugned statute. Nor is there anything perverse about such a practice. When lawyers are called upon to decide which of two provisions in a text—be it a constitution, statute, deed, contract, will, or whatever—is applicable to a situation, they will usually choose the more specific of the two. This is often assumed to be the author's intention, because it means that there is a sphere of operation for both provisions, not merely the more general provision. It is also a more economical practice since the meaning of the more specific provision is usually clearer. "The more difficult exploration

---

The Judicial Committee and the British North America Act (1967), 37, 45–46, 59, 165–167. See also K. Lysyk, "Constitutional Reform and the Introductory Clause of s. 91" (1979) 57 Can. Bar Rev. 531, 540–541.

[10]This point is incontrovertible with respect to one federal head of power, namely, "unemployment insurance" (s. 91(2A)), because that topic was held to be within property and civil rights in the province in *A.-G. Can. v. A.-G. Ont.* (Unemployment Insurance) [1937] A.C. 355, and was added to s. 91 by an amendment in 1940.

[11]W.R. Lederman, "Unity and Diversity in Canadian Federalism" (1975) 53 Can. Bar Rev. 597, 603; K. Lysyk, "Constitutional Reform and the Introductory Clause of s. 91" (1979) 57 Can. Bar Rev. 531, 539.

of the big classes of subjects need not be undertaken if the little ones prove fruitful."[12]

In my view, therefore, the residuary theory of the p.o.g.g. power is more helpful than the competing general theory. The discussion which follows will proceed on the assumption that matters which come within enumerated federal or provincial heads of power should be located in those enumerated heads, and the office of the p.o.g.g. power is to accommodate the matters which do not come within any of the enumerated federal or provincial heads.[13]

The p.o.g.g. power has been the trunk from which three branches of legislative power have grown: (1) the "gap" branch; (2) the "national concern" branch; and (3) the "emergency" branch.[14] Each will be discussed in turn in the text that follows.

II. THE "GAP" BRANCH

§ 17:2 The "gap" branch

One of the offices of the p.o.g.g. power is to fill lacunae or gaps in the scheme of distribution of powers. There are very few undoubted gaps in the scheme of distribution which have to be filled in this way. One gap

---

[12] A.S. Abel, "The Neglected Logic of 91 and 92" (1969) 19 U. Toronto L.J. 487, 516, and see also 510.

[13] The theory that p.o.g.g. is essentially a residuary power, which appears to me to be correct, does not imply that the opening words of s. 91 are subordinate to the enumeration in the sense of conferring a weaker kind of legislative power. Under the "trenching doctrine" the enumerated heads of s. 91 were said to have the capacity to authorize encroachments on provincial subject matters (trenching), while the opening words had a lesser capacity to do so. The trenching theory is not useful and it has faded into well-deserved obscurity: Laskin, Canadian Constitutional Law (5th ed., 1986 by Finkelstein), 255. The true position is that both enumeration and opening words are subject to the same rules, and the exercise of both powers may have an important impact on property and civil rights in the province or other provincial subject matters. This can occur either by virtue of the "double-aspect" doctrine, e.g. *Munro v. National Capital Comm.*, [1966] S.C.R. 663, where the p.o.g.g. power gave land use planning power to create a national capital region concurrent with provincial power, or by virtue of the incidental effect doctrine, *e.g.*, *Johannesson v. West St. Paul*, [1952] 1 S.C.R. 292, where the p.o.g.g. power gave authority over aeronautics which pre-empted municipal zoning by-laws. The double-aspect doctrine and the incidental effect doctrine are discussed in ch. 15, Judicial Review on Federal Grounds.

[14] Monahan, Constitutional Law (2nd ed., 2002), 273–278, argues that there is an emerging fourth branch, namely, "matters of interprovincial concern or significance". This fourth branch would differ from the national concern branch in not requiring a "distinct" subject matter: see § 17:5, "Distinctness". The authority for this development consists entirely of brief obiter dicta by La Forest J. in three cases: *R. v. Crown Zellerbach*, [1988] 1 S.C.R. 401, 447–448; *Morguard Investments v. De Savoye*, [1990] 3 S.C.R. 1077, 1100; *Hunt v. T. & N.*, [1993] 4 S.C.R. 289, 326. Whether these vague dicta do support a fourth branch, and whether there is any need for a fourth branch, must, I think, await more definite rulings.

exists in the provision for the incorporation of companies.[1] The Constitution Act, 1867, by s. 92(11), empowers the provincial Legislatures to make laws in relation to "the incorporation of companies with provincial objects", but there is no equivalent enumerated federal power of incorporation. The courts have held that the power to incorporate companies with objects other than provincial must fall within the federal p.o.g.g. power because of its residuary nature.[2]

A similar argument can be made with respect to the treaty power.[3] Section 132 of the Constitution Act, 1867 confers upon the federal Parliament the power to enact laws for performing the obligations of Canada "as part of the British Empire, towards foreign countries, arising under treaties between the Empire and such foreign countries". The framers of the Constitution Act, 1867 evidently did not contemplate that Canada would eventually acquire the power to enter into treaties on its own behalf. Accordingly, s. 132 is silent about performing the obligations of Canada arising under treaties entered into by Canada in its own right as an international person. In the *Radio Reference* (1932),[4] the Privy Council held that the p.o.g.g. power filled this gap. Viscount Dunedin said that the power to perform Canadian (as opposed to imperial) treaties came within p.o.g.g. because it was "not mentioned explicitly in either s. 91 or s. 92".[5] This reasoning appears to be a faithful reading of the Constitution Act, 1867. However, it was later emphatically rejected by a differently-constituted Privy Council, speaking through Lord Atkin, in the *Labour Conventions* case (1937).[6] Recent dicta by the Supreme Court of Canada suggest that the reasoning in the *Radio Reference* could be returning to judicial favour.[7]

A less obvious example of the gap test is *Jones v. A.-G. N.B.* (1974),[8] in which the Supreme Court of Canada upheld the validity of the federal Official Languages Act, an Act which, broadly speaking, attempted to guarantee the equal status of French and English in the institutions of the Parliament and government of Canada. Laskin C.J. for the unanimous Court pointed out that, since federal institutions and agencies are "clearly beyond provincial reach", they must be within federal reach under the opening p.o.g.g. words of s. 91, "on the basis of the purely residuary character of the legislative power thereby conferred."[9] As in the federal company cases and the *Radio Reference*, no definition of p.o.g.g.

[Section 17:2]

[1] This topic is discussed in detail in ch. 23, Companies.

[2] *Citizens' Insurance Co. v. Parsons* (1881), 7 App. Cas. 96.

[3] This topic is discussed in detail in ch. 11, Treaties.

[4] *Re Regulation and Control of Radio Communication in Can.*, [1932] A.C. 304.

[5] *Re Regulation and Control of Radio Communication in Can.*, [1932] A.C. 304, 312.

[6] *A.-G. Can. v. A.-G. Ont.* (Labour Conventions) [1937] A.C. 326.

[7] See ch. 11, Treaties, under heading § 11:12, "Evaluation of Labour Conventions case".

[8] *Jones v. A.-G. N.B.*, [1975] 2 S.C.R. 182.

[9] *Jones v. A.-G. N.B.*, [1975] 2 S.C.R. 182, 189.

was offered. It was sufficient to note that the matter of the legislation was not included in any of the enumerated heads of power of ss. 91 and 92.[10]

The cases dealing with legislative jurisdiction over offshore mineral resources have employed a similar analysis. Because the seabed off the shore of British Columbia and the seabed off the shore of Newfoundland lay outside the boundaries of each province, the offshore minerals were outside each province's legislative jurisdiction.[11] The offshore minerals therefore had to come within the federal Parliament's p.o.g.g. power "in its residual capacity".[12]

It is of course always possible to classify a law by labelling its "matter" or "pith and substance" with a name which does not appear to come within any of the enumerated heads of power.[13] This could be said, and has been said, of aeronautics, atomic energy and the national capital region.[14] But the decisions concerning these topics are not based on the same reasoning as the cases on federal incorporation, treaties, official languages and offshore resources. These latter cases depend upon a lacuna or gap in the text of the Constitution: a reference to companies with provincial objects but no mention of companies with broader objects; a reference to imperial treaties but no mention of Canadian treaties; references to executive and legislative power but no mention of regulating the agencies that exercise that power; and a withdrawal of provincial extraterritorial competence but no grant of federal extraterritorial competence. In these cases, the Constitution recognizes certain topics as being classes of subjects for distribution-of-powers purposes, but fails to deal completely with each topic. The p.o.g.g. language completes the incomplete assignment of power. The gap branch of p.o.g.g. covers these limited and unusual cases, where the application of the p.o.g.g. power is almost logically required. In most cases a "new" or hitherto unrecognized kind of law does not have any necessary or logical claim to come within p.o.g.g. It might come within property and civil rights in the province (s.

---

[10]*Jones* was followed in *R. v. Appleby (No. 2)* (1976), 76 D.L.R. (3d) 110 (N.B. A.D.) (p.o.g.g. authorizes National Library Act provision for the compulsory taking of two copies of all new books published in Canada) and *Friends of Oldman River Society v. Can.*, [1992] 1 S.C.R. 3 (p.o.g.g. authorizes procedures for assessment of environmental impact of projects affecting federal heads of power).

[11]The provincial Legislatures' lack of extraterritorial competence is explained in ch. 13, Extraterritorial Competence.

[12]In *Re Offshore Mineral Rights of B.C.*, [1967] S.C.R. 792, the Court also buttressed this reasoning with the national concern branch of p.o.g.g., asserting (at p. 817) that the offshore minerals were "of concern to Canada as a whole and go beyond local or provincial concern or interest". In *Re Nfld. Continental Shelf*, [1984] S.C.R. 86, 127, which is where the quotation in the text comes from, this "residual capacity" was the only reason given for federal legislative jurisdiction.

[13]G. Le Dain, "Sir Lyman Duff and the Constitution" (1974) 12 Osgoode Hall L.J. 261, 293; quoted with approval by Beetz J. in *Re Anti-Inflation Act*, [1976] 2 S.C.R. 373, 451.

[14]See *Johannesson v. West St. Paul*, [1952] 1 S.C.R. 292, *Re Regulation and Control of Aeronautics in Can.*, [1932] A.C. 54, *Munro v. National Capital Commission*, [1966] S.C.R. 663, *R. v. Crown Zellerbach*, [1988] 1 S.C.R. 401.

92(13)) or matters of a merely local or private nature in the province (s. 92(16)). Which head of power is appropriate depends on the nature of the "new" matter, and the scope which is attributed to the various competing heads of power of which p.o.g.g. is only one.[15]

III. THE "NATIONAL CONCERN" BRANCH

§ 17:3 History of national concern

The "national concern" branch of p.o.g.g. takes its name from a dictum in the *Canada Temperance Federation* case (1946), a case that will shortly be described. But its roots may be traced back to the previous century.

The history starts with *Russell v. The Queen* (1882),[1] although no definition of p.o.g.g. was actually articulated in that case. The statute in issue was the Canada Temperance Act, a federal statute which established a local-option temperance scheme. Sir Montague Smith for the Privy Council upheld the statute on the basis that it did not fall within any of the provincial heads of legislative power. Therefore, he held, it must be within federal power, but he did not commit himself as to which head of federal power was applicable.

The decision in *Russell* was later explained by Lord Watson for the Privy Council in the *Local Prohibition* case (1896)[2] as resting on the p.o.g.g. power, and in the course of this explanation Lord Watson enunciated for the first time a "national dimensions" definition of p.o.g.g.:[3]

> Their Lordships do not doubt that some matters, in their origin local and provincial, might attain such dimensions as to affect the body politic of the Dominion, and to justify the Canadian Parliament in passing laws for their regulation or abolition in the interest of the Dominion. But great caution must be observed in distinguishing between that which is local or provincial and that which has ceased to be merely local or provincial, and has become a matter of national concern, in such sense as to bring it within the jurisdiction of the Parliament of Canada.

The idea that some matters of legislation, in their origin local and provincial, could acquire "national dimensions" or (as it is usually now expressed) "national concern" and thereby come within the federal Parliament's p.o.g.g. power, is the core of the national concern branch of p.o.g.g.

Ironically, although it was the *Local Prohibition* case which explained *Russell* as resting on the p.o.g.g. power, the two decisions are not easy to reconcile. The *Local Prohibition* case concerned a provincial local-option temperance scheme which was very similar to the federal scheme up-

---

[15]The relevance of "newness" is examined later in this chapter, under heading § 17:6, "Newness".

[Section 17:3]

[1]*Russell v. The Queen* (1882), 7 App. Cas. 829.

[2]*A.-G. Ont. v. A.-G. Can.* (Local Prohibition) [1896] A.C. 348.

[3]*A.-G. Ont. v. A.-G. Can.* (Local Prohibition) [1896] A.C. 348, 361.

held in *Russell*. In the *Local Prohibition* case, their lordships upheld the provincial statute as being in relation to either "property and civil rights in the province" (s. 92(13)) or "matters of a merely local or private nature in the province" (s. 92(16)). This reasoning is directly contradictory of *Russell*, which was based on the holding that a local-option temperance scheme did not come within s. 92(13) or s. 92(16). By this time, of course, it had been established that the "double aspect" doctrine would sometimes permit both levels of government to enact laws in the same general field.[4] But this would explain the co-existence of *Russell* and *Local Prohibition* only if a federal aspect could be attributed to the Canada Temperance Act. The Privy Council in *Russell* appeared to assume that whenever Parliament regarded a problem as being "one of general concern to the Dominion, upon which uniformity of legislation is desirable", then it acquired the power to deal with it.[5] If this were the law, there would be no limit to the reach of federal power. And yet Lord Watson's national dimensions test, while accompanied by the exhortation to "great caution" in its application, did not indicate what were the limits of the p.o.g.g. power.[6]

In 1911, Viscount Haldane joined the ranks of the law lords and thereby became a member of the Judicial Committee of the Privy Council. He wrote many of the opinions in Canadian constitutional appeals until his death in 1928. During this period, the Privy Council severely contracted each of the major federal powers. The impact of the decisions of this period on the criminal law power and the trade and commerce power is related in the later two chapters on those topics. With respect to the p.o.g.g. power, Viscount Haldane's Privy Council ignored Lord Watson's national dimensions dictum, and instead insisted that only an emergency would justify the exercise of the p.o.g.g. power. The decisions that expounded this view are discussed later in this chapter.[7]

---

[4]*Hodge v. The Queen* (1883), 9 App. Cas. 117; and see ch. 15, Judicial Review on Federal Grounds, under heading § 15:7, "Double aspect".

[5]*Russell v. The Queen* (1882) 7 App. Cas. 829, 841.

[6]The authority of *Russell v. The Queen* was also impaired by the fact that the case was a private prosecution and neither the federal Attorney-General nor any provincial Attorney-General was represented in the proceedings. Moreover, counsel for Russell conceded that Parliament had the power to enact the Canada Temperance Act without the local-option features. This led Duff J. in *Re Board of Commerce Act* (1920), 60 S.C.R. 456, 507 to describe Russell as "in great part an unargued case". See also *A.-G. Ont. v. A.G. Can.* (Local Prohibition) [1896] A.C. 348, 362 per Lord Watson; *Natural Products Marketing Act Reference*, [1936] S.C.R. 398, 420, per Duff C.J. Not long after *Russell*, legislation was enacted in Quebec and Ontario requiring, whenever the validity of a statute was challenged, that notice be given to the appropriate Attorney-General, and that he or she be entitled to intervene in the proceedings. These requirements exist now in all Canadian jurisdictions: see ch. 59, Procedure, under heading §§ 59:12 to 59:13, "Intervention".

[7]§§ 17:7 to 17:11, "The "emergency" branch".

Viscount Haldane's view that p.o.g.g. was only an emergency power persisted until after the second world war.[8] Its inconsistency with the national dimensions view of p.o.g.g. was not directly confronted until *A.-G. Ont. v. Canada Temperance Federation* (1946).[9] In that case, a frontal attack was mounted against *Russell v. The Queen* (1882).[10] The Canada Temperance Act, which had been upheld in *Russell*, was challenged a second time. In opposition to the statute, two alternative arguments were presented: either *Russell* was wrongly decided because it was not based on an emergency, or, if *Russell* was based on an emergency (as Viscount Haldane had claimed in *Toronto Electric Commissioners v. Snider)*,[11] the alleged emergency of drunkenness had now passed away. In light of the Privy Council's insistence on an emergency in every p.o.g.g. case since 1896, these arguments looked unanswerable. But in the *Canada Temperance* case, the Privy Council, now speaking through Viscount Simon, refused to overrule *Russell*. While stopping short of actually approving the decision, their lordships pointed out that it had stood for over sixty years, and for that reason "must be regarded as firmly embedded in the constitutional law of Canada".[12] Moreover, they held that *Russell* had not been decided on the basis of an emergency, and the p.o.g.g. power was not confined to emergencies.

The *Canada Temperance* case thus repudiated the line of cases that asserted that only an emergency could serve as the basis for an exercise of the p.o.g.g. power. In place of that doctrine, Viscount Simon formulated a new test, in the following words:[13]

> In their Lordships' opinion, the true test must be found in the real subject matter of the legislation: if it is such that it goes beyond local or provincial concern or interests and must from its inherent nature be the concern of the Dominion as a whole (as, for example, in the *Aeronautics* case and the *Radio* case), then it will fall within the competence of the Dominion Parliament as a matter affecting the peace, order and good government of Canada, although it may in another aspect touch on matters specially reserved to the provincial legislatures. War and pestilence, no doubt, are instances; so, too, may be the drink or drug traffic, or the carrying of arms. In *Russell v. The Queen*, Sir Montague Smith gave as an instance of valid Dominion legislation a law which prohibited or restricted the sale or exposure of cattle having a contagious disease. Nor is the validity of the legislation, when due to its inherent nature, affected because there may still be room for enactments by a provincial legislature dealing with an aspect of the same subject in so far as it specially affects that province.

---

[8]After Viscount Haldane's death in 1928, some fragmentation of opinion in the Privy Council emerged, and the national dimensions test was referred to obiter, without disapproval, in the *Re Regulation and Control of Aeronautics in Can.*, [1932] A.C. 54, the *Re Regulation and Control of Radio Communication in Can.*, [1932] A.C. 304 (at least by implication) and in *CPR v. A.-G. B.C.* (Empress Hotel) [1950] A.C. 122.

[9]*A.-G. Ont. v. Canada Temperance Federation*, [1946] A.C. 193.

[10]*Russell v. The Queen* (1882), 7 App. Cas. 829.

[11]*Toronto Electric Commissioners v. Snider*, [1925] A.C. 396.

[12]*A.-G. Ont. v. Canada Temperance Federation*, [1946] A.C. 193, 206.

[13]*A.-G. Ont. v. Canada Temperance Federation*, [1946] A.C. 193, 205–206.

This dictum, which bears a close resemblance to Lord Watson's "national dimensions" dictum in the *Local Prohibition* case, is now established as the definition of the "national concern" branch of p.o.g.g. The test is whether the matter of the legislation "goes beyond local or provincial concern or interests and must from its inherent nature be the concern of the Dominion as a whole". If this test is satisfied, then the matter comes within the p.o.g.g. power in its national concern branch. Of course, as will be elaborated later in this chapter, the emergency cases are still good law in the sense that an emergency will also provide a basis for legislation under the p.o.g.g. power. But the *Canada Temperance* case established that there was a national concern branch of p.o.g.g. as well as an emergency branch.[14]

The national concern branch of p.o.g.g. has been recognized in many cases since 1946,[15] and it has provided the sole basis for the decision in three cases in the Supreme Court of Canada. The first case was *Johannesson v. West St. Paul* (1952),[16] in which the Court held that aeronautics satisfied the national concern test. Of the five opinions written, four cited and relied upon the *Canada Temperance* dictum,[17] but only Locke J. attempted to define the characteristics of aeronautics that he thought were relevant. He pointed to the rapid growth of passenger and freight traffic by air, the use of aircraft for the carriage of mails especially to the more remote northern parts of the country, and the necessity for the development of air services to be controlled by a national government responsive to the needs of the nation as a whole.[18]

The second case was *Munro v. National Capital Commission* (1966),[19] in which the Court held that the national capital region—an area around Ottawa straddling Ontario and Quebec that had been designated by federal legislation—satisfied the national concern test. Cartwright J. for

[14]The relationship between the two branches, that is, the question when an emergency is required and when national concern will suffice, is taken up in the last section of this chapter.

[15]At first, it seemed to be destined for oblivion. The emergency test was applied (as the sole test) in *Co-op. Committee on Japanese Canadians v. A.-G. Can.*, [1947] A.C. 87; *Re Wartime Leasehold Regulations*, [1950] S.C.R. 124; *Can. Federation of Agriculture v. A.-G. Que.*, [1951] A.C. 179.

[16]*Johannesson v. West St. Paul*, [1952] 1 S.C.R. 292.

[17]*Re Regulation and Control of Aeronautics in Can.*, [1932] A.C. 54 had already decided that the federal Parliament had authority over aeronautics, but the decision had been based primarily on the existence of a British Empire treaty binding Canada. In 1947 the British Empire treaty was denounced and replaced by a new treaty to which Canada was a party in its own right. This rendered the treaty power arguably unavailable (§ 17:2 note 6), Treaties, under heading § 11:12, "Evaluation of Labour Conventions case".), and necessitated the finding of a new basis for legislative jurisdiction. In *Johannesson*, Rinfret C.J. still thought that the issue was concluded by the *Aeronautics Reference:*, [1952] 1 S.C.R. 292, 303; but the other four opinions each cited and relied upon the *Canada Temperance*, [1952] 1 S.C.R. 292, 308–309, 311, 318, 328. On aeronautics, see ch. 22, Transportation and Communication.

[18][1952] 1 S.C.R. 292, 326–327.

[19]*Munro v. National Capital Commission*, [1966] S.C.R. 663.

a unanimous Court referred to the unsuccessful efforts to zone the national capital region through the cooperative action of the two provinces of Ontario and Quebec.[20] Then, later on, he said:[21]

> I find it difficult to suggest a subject-matter of legislation which more clearly goes beyond local or provincial interests and is the concern of Canada as a whole than the development, conservation and improvement of the National Capital Region in accordance with a coherent plan in order that the nature and character of the seat of the Government of Canada may be in accordance with its national significance. Adopting the words of the learned trial judge, it is my view that the Act "deals with a single matter of national concern".

The third case was *R. v. Crown Zellerbach* (1988),[22] in which the Court held that marine pollution satisfied the national concern test. The federal Ocean Dumping Control Act, which prohibited dumping "at sea", was upheld in its application to marine waters within the boundaries of British Columbia. Le Dain J. for the majority of the Court[23] held that[24] "marine pollution, because of its predominantly extra-provincial as well as international character and implications, is clearly a matter of concern to Canada as a whole".

A fourth case could be added to the list, although the national concern branch of p.o.g.g. was not the sole ground of decision. In *Ontario Hydro v. Ontario* (1993),[25] the Supreme Court of Canada upheld the federal Atomic Energy Control Act. Federal jurisdiction over atomic energy (or nuclear power) was derived from both the declaratory power of s. 92(10)(c)[26] and the national concern branch of p.o.g.g. With respect to the national concern branch of p.o.g.g., La Forest J. for the majority of the Court said[27] that "the production, use and application of atomic energy constitute a matter of national concern", because "it is predominantly extra-provincial and international in character and implications"; he also pointed to the "strategic and security aspects of nuclear power in

---

[20] *Munro v. National Capital Commission*, [1966] S.C.R. 663, 667.

[21] *Munro v. National Capital Commission*, [1966] S.C.R. 663, 671.

[22] *R. v. Crown Zellerbach*, [1988] 1 S.C.R. 401.

[23] Le Dain J. was joined by Dickson C.J., McIntyre and Wilson JJ. La Forest J., joined by Beetz and Lamer JJ., dissented on the ground that the requirement of distinctness (see following text) was not satisfied.

[24] *R. v. Crown Zellerbach*, [1988] 1 S.C.R. 401, 436.

[25] *Ontario Hydro v. Ontario*, [1993] 3 S.C.R. 327. La Forest J., with L'Heureux-Dubé and Gonthier J., held that labour relations in a nuclear-powered electrical generating station were within federal jurisdiction. Lamer C.J., in a separate concurring opinion, reached the same result. Iacobucci J., with Sopinka and Cory JJ., dissented. However, all three opinions agreed that the federal Parliament had regulatory jurisdiction over nuclear power by reason of both the declaratory power and the national concern branch of p.o.g.g.

[26] See ch. 22, Transportation and Communication, under heading § 22:10, "Works for the general advantage of Canada".

[27] *Ontario Hydro v. Ontario*, [1993] 3 S.C.R. 327, 379.

relation to national defence" and to its potential for environmental catastrophes.[28]

The cumulative effect of the cases is to establish firmly the national concern branch of p.o.g.g.[29] In the following sections of the chapter, an attempt will be made to analyze the elements of the national concern branch.

§ 17:4 Definition of national concern

When does a subject matter of legislation become "the concern of the Dominion as a whole" so as to satisfy the national concern test?

About all that can be gleaned from the dicta in *Johannesson* and *Munro* is a sense that it is the nation-wide importance of a subject of legislation that determines whether or not it has the requisite national concern. But such a subjective criterion as importance could hardly serve as a justiciable test. Moreover, it would be difficult to argue that matters coming within federal legislative competence are generally more important than matters coming within provincial legislative competence. What could be more important than the law of contract or property, or municipal institutions, or education—all matters within provincial legislative competence? The notion of importance can be refined a little if one adds a geographic dimension to it. A matter of national concern must be "of import or significance to all parts of Canada".[1]

If a geographic sense of national concern is accepted, this could be thought to imply that it is the desirability of uniform legislation across Canada on a particular topic which gives that topic a national dimension. But this cannot be correct either. Uniformity is desirable with respect to many topics, and for many reasons, but of course the distribution of legislative powers in a federal system necessarily involves a substantial subordination of the value of uniformity to that of provincial autonomy even where there is no objective necessity for regional variations. In legislative fields which are entrusted to the provinces, it is for the provinces to decide whether or not they desire uniformity: they can achieve it whenever they wish through the enactment of uniform laws. If, as is common, some provinces do not enact the uniform statute, or enact it with variations, no great harm is done: a substantial degree of uniformity will still have been achieved and will still be valuable. Even in fields entrusted to the federal Parliament, while uniform laws are

---

[28] See also *Re Offshore Mineral Rights of B.C.*, [1967] S.C.R. 792 (offshore mineral resources satisfied national concern test and gap test). *Re Can. Metal Co.* (1982), 144 D.L.R. (3d) 124 (Man. Q.B.) (air pollution satisfied national concern test).

[29] For criticism of the cases, see J. Leclair, "The Elusive Quest for the Quintessential 'National Interest' " (2005) 38 U.B.C.L. Rev. 355.

[Section 17:4]

[1] D. Gibson, "Measuring National Dimensions" (1976) 7 Man. L.J. 15, 31.

usual, federal laws occasionally impose different rules on different parts of the country.[2] There is no constitutional requirement of uniformity.[3]

There are, however, cases where uniformity of law throughout the country is not merely desirable, but essential, in the sense that the problem "is beyond the power of the provinces to deal with it".[4] This is the case when the failure of one province to act would injure the residents of the other (cooperating) provinces. This "provincial inability" test goes a long way towards explaining the cases. The often cited case of an epidemic of pestilence is a good example. The failure by one province to take preventative measures would probably lead to the spreading of the disease into those provinces which had taken preventative measures. The national concern cases can be explained in these terms. In the case of aeronautics *(Johannesson)*,[5] the failure of one province to accept uniform procedures for the use of air space and ground facilities would endanger the residents of other provinces engaged in interprovincial and international air travel. In the case of the national capital region *(Munro)*,[6] the failure of either Quebec or Ontario to cooperate in the development of the national capital region would have denied to all Canadians the symbolic value of a suitable national capital. Indeed, in the *Munro* case the Supreme Court of Canada took judicial notice of the fact that the "zoning" of the national capital region was only undertaken federally after unsuccessful efforts by the federal government to secure cooperative action by Ontario and Quebec.[7] In the case of marine pollution *(Crown Zellerbach)*,[8] the failure of one province to protect its waters would probably lead to the pollution of the waters of other provinces as well as the (federal) territorial sea and high sea. In the case of nuclear power *(Ontario Hydro)*,[9] the failure of one province to enact adequate regulatory measures would expose the people of other provinces to the

[2]E.g., introduction of English divorce and annulment law in Ontario: Divorce Act, S.C. 1930, c. 14, (since repealed); differential rates of income tax caused by transfer of tax points to Quebec: ch. 6, Financial Arrangements, under heading § 6:7, "Conditional federal grants"; local-option liquor prohibition: *Russell v. the Queen* (1882), 7 App. Cas. 829; *A.-G. Ont. v. Can. Temperance Federation*, [1946] A.C. 193; and compare *Gold Seal v. Dom. Express Co.* (1921), 62 S.C.R. 424; opting-out clauses in the Lord's Day Act: *Lord's Day Alliance of Can. v. A.-G. B.C.*, [1959] S.C.R. 497; adoption of provincial highway transport regulation: *Coughlin v. Ont. Highway Transport Bd.*, [1968] S.C.R. 569; provincial variations in criminal procedure or punishment: *A.-G. B.C. v. Smith*, [1967] S.C.R. 702, 710–711; *R. v. Burnshine*, [1975] 1 S.C.R. 693; *R. v. Cornell*, [1988] 1 S.C.R. 461; *R. v. Turpin*, [1989] 1 S.C.R. 1296; *R. v. S.(S.)*, [1990] 2 S.C.R. 254.

[3]Not only is no requirement of uniformity imposed by federalism principles, challenges to non-uniform federal laws based on the equality guarantees of the Canadian Bill of Rights and the Charter of Rights have also failed: see ch. 55, Equality, under heading § 55:49, "Place of residence".

[4]D. Gibson, "Measuring National Dimensions" (1976) 7 Man. L.J. 15, 33.

[5]*Johannesson v. West St. Paul*, [1952] 1 S.C.R. 292.

[6]*Munro v. National Capital Commission*, [1966] S.C.R. 663.

[7]*Munro v. National Capital Commission*, [1966] S.C.R. 663, 667.

[8]*R. v. Crown Zellerbach*, [1988] 1 S.C.R. 401.

[9]*Ontario Hydro v. Ontario*, [1993] 3 S.C.R. 327.

risk of an environmental catastrophe as well as the risks created by the proliferation of nuclear weapons.

In the *Crown Zellerbach* case,[10] Le Dain J. for the majority of the Court relied on the provincial inability test as a reason for finding that marine pollution was a matter of national concern. "It is because of the interrelatedness of the intraprovincial and extra-provincial aspects of the matter that it requires a single or uniform legislative treatment."[11] It seems, therefore, that the most important element of national concern is a need for one national law which cannot realistically be satisfied by cooperative provincial action because the failure of one province to cooperate would carry with it adverse consequences for the residents of other provinces. A subject-matter of legislation which has this characteristic has the necessary national concern to justify invocation of the p.o.g.g. power.[12]

§ 17:5 Distinctness

In the *Anti-Inflation Reference* (1976),[1] a case that is discussed later in this chapter,[2] the Supreme Court of Canada upheld federal wage and price controls under the emergency branch of the p.o.g.g. power. Laskin C.J. (with whom Judson, Spence and Dickson JJ. agreed) left open the possibility that the federal wage and price controls could also have been supported under the national concern branch,[3] but Beetz J. (with whom, on this point, Martland, Ritchie, Pigeon and de Grandpré JJ. agreed) denied that the wage and price controls could have been supported under the national concern branch. Beetz J.'s opinion was that inflation was too broad and diffuse a topic to qualify as a "matter" coming within the national concern branch of the p.o.g.g. power. In order to qualify as a matter, a topic must be "distinct": it must have "a degree of unity that makes it indivisible, an identity which makes it distinct from provincial

---

[10] *R. v. Crown Zellerbach*, [1988] 1 S.C.R. 401.

[11] *R. v. Crown Zellerbach*, [1988] 1 S.C.R. 401, 434. He went on (also at p. 434) to caution against the fallacy "that there must be plenary jurisdiction in one order of government or the other to deal with any legislative problem". This is a reference to the requirement of distinctness, which Le Dain J. described as "singleness or indivisibility", which is discussed next in the text. He regarded (still at p. 434) the provincial inability test as useful in determining whether a matter has the requisite singleness or indivisibility. I find this passage difficult to understand. To me, the provincial inability test identifies the requirement of national concern, but is not relevant to the requirement of distinctness.

[12] As well as the *Crown Zellerbach* case, the provincial inability test is referred to with approval in *Labatt Breweries v. A.-G. Can.*, [1980] 1 S.C.R. 914, 945; *Schneider v. The Queen*, [1982] 2 S.C.R. 112, 131; *The Queen v. Wetmore*, [1983] 2 S.C.R. 284, 296.

[Section 17:5]

[1] *Re Anti-Inflation Act*, [1976] 2 S.C.R. 373.

[2] *Re Anti-Inflation Act*, [1976] 2 S.C.R. 373.

[3] *Re Anti-Inflation Act*, [1976] 2 S.C.R. 373, 419.

matters and a sufficient consistence to retain the bounds of form".[4] This opinion was supported by a majority of five of the nine judges.

The requirement of distinctness was the issue that divided the Supreme Court of Canada in *R. v. Crown Zellerbach* (1988).[5] In that case, a majority of the Court[6] upheld the federal Ocean Dumping Control Act, which prohibited dumping "at sea", on the basis that marine pollution[7] was a matter of national concern. La Forest J. dissented, because in his view marine pollution lacked the distinctness required of a matter of national concern. Marine waters intermingled with fresh waters, and were affected by coastal activity and by deposits from the air. The power to regulate marine pollution thus intruded too deeply into industrial and municipal activity, resource development, construction, recreation and other matters within provincial jurisdiction. Le Dain J. for the majority, while not asserting federal authority over pollution in general, held that marine pollution, although obviously affected by the air and by fresh water flowing into the sea, did have "ascertainable and reasonable limits, in so far as its impact on provincial jurisdiction is concerned".[8]

The requirement of distinctness was articulated in the *Crown Zellerbach* case,[9] in Le Dain J.'s usual felicitous style, as follows:

> For a matter to qualify as a matter of national concern . . . it must have a singleness, distinctiveness and indivisibility that clearly distinguishes it from matters of provincial concern and a scale of impact on provincial jurisdiction that is reconcilable with the fundamental distribution of legislative power under the Constitution.

As this passage emphasizes, the requirement of distinctness is an essential safeguard, allaying the justifiable concern that the national concern branch of p.o.g.g. would tend to absorb the entire catalogue of provincial powers if subject matters as broad as inflation and pollution were within federal authority.[10]

The requirement of "distinctness" is a necessary but not a sufficient

---

[4] *Re Anti-Inflation Act*, [1976] 2 S.C.R. 373, 457–458.

[5] *R. v. Crown Zellerbach*, [1988] 1 S.C.R. 401.

[6] Le Dain J. was joined by Dickson C.J., McIntyre and Wilson JJ. La Forest J., joined by Beetz and Lamer JJ., dissented on the ground that the requirement of distinctness was not satisfied.

[7] Federal jurisdiction over the waters outside the boundaries of any province could not be, and was not, doubted: see ch. 13, Extraterritorial Competence, under heading § 13:4, "Territory of province". The problem was that the Act applied to all dumping "at sea", and "sea" included inland waters within the boundaries of the provinces. The offence alleged against Crown Zellerbach had taken place within the boundaries of British Columbia.

[8] *R. v. Crown Zellerbach*, [1988] 1 S.C.R. 401, 438.

[9] *R. v. Crown Zellerbach*, [1988] 1 S.C.R. 401, 432.

[10] See also *Schneider v. The Queen*, [1982] 2 S.C.R. 112, 142 ("health" is another "amorphous topic" in the same category); *General Motors v. City National Leasing*, [1989] 1 S.C.R. 641, 682 ("competition is not a single matter any more than inflation or pollution"); *Friends of Oldman River Society v. Can.*, [1992] 1 S.C.R. 3, 63–64, (the environment is in the same category); *R. v. Hydro-Québec*, [1997] 3 S.C.R. 213, paras. 78, 115 (control of toxic substances for environmental protection not sufficiently distinct);

condition for a matter to be admitted to the national concern branch of p.o.g.g. A distinct matter would also have to satisfy the provincial inability test (or other definition of national concern) in order to be admitted to the national concern branch of p.o.g.g. A distinct matter would come within provincial power if it came within "property and civil rights in the province" (s. 92(13)) or if it were "of a merely local or private nature in the province"(s. 92(16)).

§ 17:6 Newness

In *The Queen v. Hauser* (1979),[1] the Supreme Court of Canada, by a majority of four to three, held that the federal Narcotic Control Act was a valid exercise of the p.o.g.g. power. This was a surprising result, because the Act had previously been upheld by the Supreme Court of Canada as a criminal law.[2] The criminal classification seems more plausible, because nearly all of the Act is concerned to prohibit the production, trafficking and possession of illicit drugs, and to provide for the prosecution and punishment of offenders; indeed, the penalties in the Act go as high as life imprisonment (for trafficking), an extraordinary sanction to find in a regulatory statute. To be sure, in favour of the p.o.g.g. classification, there is an affinity between alcohol and drugs, which suggests an analogy with *Russell v. The Queen* (1882),[3] in which a temperance law was upheld under the p.o.g.g. power. But *Russell* has always been an anomaly which was difficult to justify under orthodox constitutional doctrine, and it seemed to have been finally discredited in the *Anti-Inflation Reference* (1976),[4] where Beetz J. described *Russell* as a "special" case, an "extraordinary" case, a case with a "chequered" history, and a case that was "not easy to reconcile with the *Local Prohibition* case". It accordingly came as something of a surprise in *Hauser* to find Pigeon J., with the concurrence of Martland, Ritchie and Beetz JJ., referring to *Russell* with approval.[5]

The reasons given in Pigeon J.'s majority opinion for his reliance on the p.o.g.g. power are perfunctory and unsatisfactory.[6] No indication is given of why narcotics have attained the requisite degree of national

Kitkatla Band v. B.C., [2002] 2 S.C.R. 146, para. 51 ("culture" is divided between the two levels of government). Monahan, Constitutional Law (2nd ed., 2002), 273–278, argues for the existence of a fourth branch of p.o.g.g., matters of interprovincial concern or significance, to which the requirement of distinctness would not apply.

[Section 17:6]

[1] *The Queen v. Hauser*, [1979] 1 S.C.R. 984.

[2] *Industrial Acceptance Corp. v. The Queen*, [1953] 2 S.C.R. 273.

[3] *Russell v. The Queen* (1882), 7 App. Cas. 829.

[4] *Re Anti-Inflation Act*, [1976] 2 S.C.R. 373, 453–457.

[5] *The Queen v. Hauser*, [1979] 1 S.C.R. 984, 997. All of these judges had joined with Beetz J. in his dismissal of *Russell* in the *Anti-Inflation Reference*.

[6] Dickson J., with the agreement of Pratte J., dissented. With respect, his opinion is an impeccable account of the constitutional basis (as criminal law) of the Narcotic Control Act. Spence J. wrote a separate concurring opinion, and did not discuss this issue.

concern. Indeed, the phrase "national concern" is never used, and no reference is made to the *Canada Temperance* case, or to *Johannesson, Munro* or the *Anti-Inflation Reference.* (The *Crown Zellerbach* case had not then been decided.) The sum and substance of the reasoning is contained in the following paragraph of the opinion:[7]

> In my view, the most important consideration for classifying the Narcotic Control Act as legislation enacted under the general residual federal power, is that this is essentially legislation adopted to deal with a genuinely new problem which did not exist at the time of Confederation and clearly cannot be put in the class of "Matters of a merely local or private nature". The subject-matter of this legislation is thus properly to be dealt with on the same footing as such other new developments as aviation *(Re Aeronautics)* and radio communications *(Re Radio Communication).*

In this passage, the emphasis on "distinctness" which is found in the *Anti-Inflation Reference* (and in the later *Crown Zellerbach* case) is replaced by an emphasis on "newness". To be sure, Beetz J. in the *Anti-Inflation Reference* had referred several times to a "new matter" or "new subject-matter", and had described inflation as "a very ancient phenomenon".[8] But, in context, I think he was referring to a *conceptually* new subject-matter, that is to say, one which was not clearly covered by an enumerated head and had not previously been considered by the courts. He was using the word "new" in the sense of "arising for consideration for the first time": a new matter would therefore be one "that the courts have yet to allocate to either a provincial or a federal head of power".[9] It is hard to accept that a matter comes within the national concern branch of p.o.g.g. only if it is *historically* new. Newness in the historical sense seems to have no relevance in this context. Pigeon J.'s examples of aeronautics and radio do not help his argument. While it is true that aeronautics was placed under p.o.g.g. in *Johannesson*, the Court has held that television (and therefore radio) is not covered by p.o.g.g., but by an enumerated federal power (s. 92(10)(a)).[10] Other new inventions, such as, buses, trucks, telephones and movies have all been located outside p.o.g.g. Aeronautics is an anomaly, not the illustration of a general rule.[11] And, on the other side of the coin, if we accept the rapid (and unexplained) rehabilitation of *Russell*, what is "new" about liquor abuse? What about the actual problem at issue in *Hauser*, namely, drug abuse? Pigeon J. said that "drug abuse did not become a problem in this country during the last century".[12] Yet, surely neither Pigeon J. nor anyone else would disagree with Dickson J.'s dissenting opinion that

---

[7] *The Queen v. Hauser*, [1979] 1 S.C.R. 984, 1000–1001.

[8] *Re Anti-Inflation Act*, [1976] 2 S.C.R. 373, 458.

[9] R. Elliot, Note (1979) 14 U.B.C.L. Rev. 163, 197.

[10] *Capital Cities Communications v. CRTC*, [1978] 2 S.C.R. 141.

[11] Ch. 22, Transportation and Communications, deals with (inter alia) aeronautics, radio, television, trucks, buses, telephones and movies.

[12] *The Queen v. Hauser*, [1979] 1 S.C.R. 984, 997.

"drug abuse is a very ancient phenomenon", and the most that can be said is that it was "not a pressing problem at the time of Confederation".[13]

I conclude that "newness" is irrelevant and unhelpful in this context. As Lysyk has said, "the newness, or lack of newness, of the matter ought to be an entirely neutral factor in the process of determining the content of the federal residuary power."[14]

The reader will be wondering why Pigeon J. engaged in such tortured reasoning in order to locate the Narcotic Control Act within p.o.g.g., when the criminal classification was available to sustain the law. The answer is that Pigeon J. was straining to avoid facing the question whether the federal Parliament had the power to provide for the prosecution of criminal laws. At that time, the Court was deeply split on this question. As long as the federal power to prosecute criminal law was thought not to exist or was in doubt, the manifest inconvenience of that disability would inevitably create a tendency in the Court to move laws out of the "criminal" category and into another category, such as p.o.g.g., where federal enforcement power was clear. Since *Hauser*, the Court has decided that the federal government has the same power of enforcement over its criminal laws as it has over its other laws.[15] There is no longer any reason for the Court to shun the criminal classification.

The Narcotic Control Act's criminalization of the possession of marihuana was challenged on a variety of grounds in *R. v. Malmo-Levine* (2003).[16] The Supreme Court of Canada held that the Act was a valid exercise of the criminal law power, and overruled the decision in *Hauser* that the Act came within the national concern branch of p.o.g.g. However, the majority of the Court pointed out that, if Parliament chose to decriminalize the possession of marihuana, the federal authority "to deal with marihuana use on a purely regulatory basis might well be questioned".[17] The majority expressly left open the question whether there was some "residual authority to deal with drugs in general (or marihuana in particular) under the p.o.g.g. power".[18]

The foregoing discussion of *Hauser* was compelled by Pigeon J.'s introduction of the concept of "newness" as a pre-condition for a matter to be admitted to the national concern branch of p.o.g.g. My conclusion, of course, is that there is no requirement of "newness".

---

[13] *The Queen v. Hauser*, [1979] 1 S.C.R. 984, 1059.

[14] K. Lysyk, "Constitutional Reform and the Introductory Clause of Section 91" (1979) 57 Can. Bar Rev. 531, 571–572. Accord, *R. v. Crown Zellerbach*, [1988] 1 S.C.R. 401, 432 per Le Dain J. for majority, but note the cautious reference to newness by La Forest J. dissenting at 458.

[15] The history of this controversy is related in ch. 19, Criminal Justice, under heading §§ 19:14 to 19:15, "Prosecution".

[16] *R. v. Malmo-Levine*, [2003] 3 S.C.R. 571. Gonthier and Binnie JJ. wrote the opinion of the majority, which on this issue was agreed to by Arbour J. (para. 205) and Deschamps J. (para. 282) and was not disagreed with by LeBel J.

[17] *R. v. Malmo-Levine*, [2003] 3 S.C.R. 571, para. 72.

[18] *R. v. Malmo-Levine*, [2003] 3 S.C.R. 571, para. 72.

IV. THE "EMERGENCY" BRANCH

§ 17:7 The non-emergency cases

It is now necessary to go back in time to the period from 1911 to 1928, when Lord Haldane sat on the Privy Council. This was the period, it will be recalled, when the Privy Council ignored Lord Watson's "national dimensions" dictum in the *Local Prohibition* case,[1] and instead consistently expounded and applied the view that only an emergency would serve to enable the federal Parliament to exercise its p.o.g.g. power.[2]

Viscount Haldane's first consideration of the p.o.g.g. power came in the *Insurance Reference* (1916).[3] In that case, the Privy Council, through Viscount Haldane, held that the federal Insurance Act of 1910, which purported to license insurance companies, was unconstitutional. The Privy Council rejected arguments based on the trade and commerce power and the p.o.g.g. power. With respect to the latter, all that Viscount Haldane said was that the p.o.g.g. power "does not . . . enable the Dominion Parliament to trench on the subject-matters entrusted to the provincial Legislatures by the enumeration in s. 92."[4] He did not go on to specify any exceptions to this proposition, not even the case of an emergency; and he did not refer to the national dimensions test or consider the question whether the insurance industry satisfied that test.

The emergency test first emerged in the *Board of Commerce* case (1922),[5] although the word emergency was not used in the opinion. In that case, the Privy Council through Viscount Haldane struck down legislation which, as well as containing anti-combines provisions, prohibited the hoarding of "necessaries of life" (defined as food, clothing and fuel) and required stocks of such necessaries to be sold at fair prices. Their lordships rejected the p.o.g.g. power as authority for the statute on the ground that "highly exceptional" or "abnormal" circumstances would be required to justify the invocation of p.o.g.g.; as examples, they suggested "war or famine".[6]

In *Toronto Electric Commissioners v. Snider* (1925),[7] the question arose whether federal legislation for the settlement of industrial disputes—the labour legislation of the period—was valid. The Privy Council through Viscount Haldane held that it was not. The relations between employers and employees was a matter of civil rights in the

---

[Section 17:7]

[1]*A.-G. Ont. v. A.-G. Can.* (Local Prohibition) [1896] A.C. 348.

[2]The only exemption from this requirement was the incorporation of federal companies, where federal power could be justified as filling a gap in the distribution-of-powers provisions of the Constitution: see the discussion of the "gap branch" earlier in this chapter.

[3]*A.G. Can. v. A.-G. Alta.* (Insurance) [1916] 1 A.C. 588.

[4]*A.G. Can. v. A.-G. Alta.* (Insurance) [1916] 1 A.C. 588, 595.

[5]*Re Board of Commerce Act*, [1922] 1 A.C. 191.

[6]*Re Board of Commerce Act*, [1922] 1 A.C. 191, 197, 200.

[7]*Toronto Electric Commissioners v. Snider*, [1925] A.C. 396.

province, and therefore within provincial jurisdiction. The p.o.g.g. power was available only in "cases arising out of some extraordinary peril to the national life of Canada, such as the cases arising out of a war".[8]

In neither of these two important cases did the Privy Council make any reference to the "national dimensions" test. The difficulty of reconciling *Russell*[9] with the new emergency doctrine was hinted at in *Board of Commerce*,[10] and resolved in *Snider* by characterizing intemperance in Canada as an emergency: an evil "so great and so general that at least for the period it was a menace to the national life of Canada so serious and so pressing that the National Parliament was called on to intervene to protect the nation from disaster".[11]

Lord Haldane died in 1928. In 1932 the national dimensions test briefly surfaced again in the *Aeronautics Reference*.[12] But in the "new deal" cases[13] the Privy Council reverted to the emergency doctrine. In the depression of the 1930s, Prime Minister R.B. Bennett had proposed and secured the enactment of a Canadian new deal—a series of statutes designed to effect far-reaching social and economic reforms. However, in 1935, before the statutes could be implemented, his Conservative government was defeated, and the Liberal government of Prime Minister Mackenzie King referred the statutes to the courts for an opinion as to their validity. Most of the statutes were held to be invalid. The Privy Council, now speaking through Lord Atkin, held that laws providing for a weekly rest, minimum wages and maximum hours of labour were simply labour laws which, by virtue of *Snider*, were incompetent to the federal Parliament.[14] Unemployment insurance was also a matter within property and civil rights in the province and incompetent to the federal Parliament.[15] And the same was true of regulating the marketing of natural products.[16] Their lordships neither asked nor answered the question whether the various subject matters of the new deal statutes might not

---

[8] *Toronto Electric Commissioners v. Snider*, [1925] A.C. 396, 412.

[9] *Russell v. The Queen* (1882), 7 App. Cas. 829.

[10] *Re Board of Commerce Act*, [1922] 1 A.C. 191, 200.

[11] [1925] A.C. 396, 412. This "national binge" explanation of *Russell* was roundly condemned in *The King v. Eastern Terminal Elev. Co.*, [1925] S.C.R. 434, 438, by Anglin C.J. whose views were often in conflict with the Privy Council of this period.

[12] *Re Regulation and Control of Aeronautics in Can.*, [1932] A.C. 54, 77.

[13] The "new deal cases" in the Privy Council consisted of: *A.-G. Can. v. A.-G. Ont.* (Labour Conventions) [1937] A.C. 326; *A.-G. Can. v. A.-G. Ont.* (Unemployment Insurance) [1937] A.C. 355; *A.-G. B.C. v. A.-G. Can.* (Price Spreads) [1937] A.C. 368; *A.-G. B.C. v. A.-G. Can.* (Natural Products Marketing) [1937] A.C. 377; *A.-G. B.C. v. A.-G. Can.* (Farmers' Creditors Arrangement) [1937] A.C. 391; *A.-G. Ont. v. A.-G. Can.* (Canada Standard Trade Mark) [1937] A.C. 405. The decisions are the subject of a symposium in (1937) 15 Can. Bar Rev. 393–507; see also W.H. McConnell, "The Judicial Review of Prime Minister Bennett's New Deal" (1968) 6 Osgoode Hall L.J. 39; W.H. McConnell, "Some Comparisons of the Roosevelt and Bennett New Deals" (1971) 9 Osgoode Hall L.J. 221.

[14] *A.-G. Can. v. A.-G. Ont.* (Labour Conventions) [1937] A.C. 326.

[15] *A.-G. Can. v. A.-G. Ont.* (Unemployment Insurance) [1937] A.C. 355.

[16] *A.-G. B.C. v. A.-G. Can.* (Natural Products Marketing) [1937] A.C. 377.

have acquired a "national dimension" through the existence of an economic depression requiring national action for its alleviation. On the contrary, they held that only an emergency would justify the invocation of the p.o.g.g. power. One might have thought that the depression would qualify as an emergency,[17] but their lordships denied that the depression was an emergency.[18]

Finally, in the *Margarine Reference* (1951),[19] the Privy Council through Lord Morton of Henryton held that a federal prohibition on the manufacture and sale of margarine was invalid. Among other arguments, that based on p.o.g.g. was rejected on the basis of the emergency test.[20]

The denials of federal power in the "p.o.g.g. cases" of the Haldane period and the new deal period had profound effects on the nature of the Canadian federation. The *Insurance Reference*[21] confirmed that p.o.g.g. (like trade and commerce) could not be used to regulate a particular industry merely because the industry is nation-wide and important to the national economy. This has ensured that much regulation of industry has to be provincial.[22] The *Board of Commerce* case,[23] as well as reinforcing the lack of federal power over much economic regulation, discouraged the federal Parliament from enacting wage or price controls in peacetime until the Anti-Inflation Act of 1975.[24] The same case forced the substitution of narrower and less effective competition laws which could be upheld as criminal law.[25]

Toronto Electric Commissioners v. Snider[26] altered the character of the nation's labour law by remitting most of it to the provinces for enactment, although federal laws continue to govern the federal public sector and industries within federal jurisdiction.[27] The *Labour Conventions* case,[28] as well as extending the holding in *Snider* to labour standards,

---

[17]In *A.-G. v. A.-G. Ont.* (Unemployment Insurance) [1937] A.C. 355, counsel for the federal government included in his factum data showing the unemployment, lost production, lowering of living standards, etc., caused by the depression, but their lordships were unmoved.

[18]I think it was also a relevant factor that the new deal legislation was permanent, rather than temporary: see § 17:11, "Temporary character of law".

[19]*Can. Federation of Agriculture v. A.G. Que.*, [1951] A.C. 179.

[20]*Can. Federation of Agriculture v. A.G. Que.*, [1951] A.C. 179, 197–198.

[21]*A.G. Can. v. A.-G. Alta.* (Insurance) [1916] 1 A.C. 588.

[22]See ch. 21, Property and Civil Rights, under heading §§ 21:5 to 21:7, "Insurance".

[23]*Re Board of Commerce Act*, [1922] 1 A.C. 191.

[24]*Re Anti-Inflation Act*, [1976] 2 S.C.R. 373.

[25]See ch. 18, Criminal Law, under heading § 18:11, "Competition law".

[26]*Toronto Electric Commissioners v. Snider*, [1925] A.C. 396.

[27]See ch. 21, Property and Civil Rights, under heading §§ 21:10 to 21:11, "Labour relations".

[28]*A.-G. Can. v. A.-G. Ont.* (Labour Conventions) [1937] A.C. 326.

divided up the power to implement treaties in a way which still controls Canadian treaty-making practices.[29]

The *Unemployment Insurance Reference*[30] carried forward the logic of the insurance and labour cases to preclude the development of federal social security programmes of a contributory insurance character. It was reversed so far as unemployment insurance was concerned by an amendment to the Constitution Act in 1940, which added "unemployment insurance" as head 2A to the list of federal enumerated powers; but it cast its shadow over old age and other pensions, leading to an amendment in 1951 which added s. 94A to the Constitution Act and a further amendment in 1964 altering the new s. 94A. Other national social insurance plans covering health care and welfare services have been established under provincial legislation with the federal government setting the standards and sharing the cost.[31]

The *Natural Products Marketing Reference*[32] confirmed that p.o.g.g. did not offer a solution to the problem of enacting effective marketing schemes, a problem to which some partial solutions have been devised—but only partial solutions.[33]

The emergency period of the Privy Council thus wrote an exceedingly important chapter of Canadian constitutional law. While, as we shall see, the pendulum has subsequently tended to swing back to a position which allows larger use of the principal federal powers, it is likely that the broad lines of constitutional authority which were established by the Privy Council will continue to be controlling, and the expectations and patterns of legislative activity which they generated will certainly not be quickly revised. Recognizing this, constitutional lawyers have tended to lose interest in the once-heated debate over whether or not the Privy Council "misread" the Constitution in so limiting federal power. One can debate a fait accompli for only so long.

§ 17:8 War

The p.o.g.g. power did not entirely wither away in the Haldane and post-Haldane period. There were cases in which the emergency test was satisfied.[1]

During the first world war, the federal Parliament enacted the War

---

[29]See ch. 11, Treaties.

[30]*A.-G. Can. v. A.-G. Ont.* (Unemployment Insurance) [1937] A.C. 355.

[31]See ch. 6, Financial Arrangements, under heading § 6:7, "Conditional federal grants"; ch. 33, Social Security.

[32]*A.-G. B.C. v. A.-G. Can. (Natural Products Marketing)* [1937] A.C. 377.

[33]See ch. 21, Property and Civil Rights, under heading §§ 21:12 to 21:14, "Marketing".

[Section 17:8]

[1]See generally, H. Marx, "The Emergency Power and Civil Liberties" (1970) 16 McGill L.J. 39; W.S. Tarnopolsky, "Emergency Powers and Civil Liberties" (1972) 15 Can. Pub. Admin. 194; L.E. Weinrib, "Situations of Emergency in Canadian Constitutional Law" in Contemporary Law: Canadian Reports to the 1990 International Congress of

Measures Act,[2] a statute which came into force on the issue by the federal government of a proclamation "that war, invasion, or insurrection, real or apprehended, exists". The Act then empowered the federal government to make regulations on almost any conceivable subject. The War Measures Act was proclaimed into force for both world wars, and during both wars the federal government embarked on extensive economic and other controls in regulations made under the Act. In the *Fort Frances* case,[3] the Privy Council held that the regime of price control which had been established during the first world war, and which was continued temporarily after the war, was constitutional. In "a sufficiently great emergency such as that arising out of war", the p.o.g.g. power would authorize laws which in normal times would be competent only to the provinces.[4] Rent control during and after the second world war was upheld on the same basis by the Supreme Court of Canada in the *Wartime Leasehold Regulations Reference* (1950).[5] The deportation of Japanese Canadians after the second world war was upheld on the same basis by the Privy Council in the *Japanese Canadians Reference* (1947).[6]

Each of these three wartime cases arose after the actual hostilities had ceased, and one issue was whether wartime measures could be continued in time of peace. In the *Fort Frances* case, Viscount Haldane deferred to the federal government on this point, saying that "very clear evidence" would be required to justify the Court "in overruling the decision of the Government that exceptional measures were still requisite".[7] The other cases gave essentially the same answer.[8]

The cases that upheld the War Measures Act under the emergency branch of p.o.g.g. did not consider any possible role for the federal power over "defence" in s. 91(7). In Australia (where there is no p.o.g.g. power), it is the defence power that has authorized national economic and social regulation in time of war.[9] In Canada, the defence power of s. 91(7) should be regarded as the authority for legislation relating to the armed

Comparative Law (1990), 466.

[2]The War Measures Act was enacted in 1914 and remained in force until 1988, when it was repealed by the Emergencies Act, S.C. 1988, c. 29. The Emergencies Act provides for, in ascending order of threat, four kinds of emergencies: (1) public welfare emergencies (e.g., natural disaster, disease, accident, pollution); (2) public order emergencies (e.g., the October crisis of 1970); (3) international emergencies (e.g., oil shortages caused by wars or embargoes elsewhere); and (4) war emergencies. See E. Tenofsky, "The War Measures and Emergencies Acts" (1989) 19 Amer. Rev. of Can. Studies 293.

[3]*Fort Frances Pulp and Power Co. v. Man. Free Press Co.*, [1923] A.C. 695.

[4]*Fort Frances Pulp and Power Co. v. Man. Free Press Co.*, [1923] A.C. 695, 705.

[5]*Wartime Leasehold Regulations Reference*, [1950] S.C.R. 124.

[6]*Co-op. Committee on Japanese Canadians v. A.-G. Can.*, [1947] A.C. 87.

[7]*Fort Frances Pulp and Power Co. v. Man. Free Press Co.*, [1923] A.C. 695, 706.

[8]*Co-op. Committee on Japanese Canadians v. A.-G. Can.*, [1947] A.C. 87, 101–102; [1950] S.C.R. 124, 130–131, 135, 141, 151, 157, 166.

[9]The Australian and Canadian wartime powers are compared in C. Gilbert, "There Will be Wars and Rumours of Wars" (1980) 18 Osgoode Hall L.J. 307. The war power has filled the same function in the United States. See generally Laskin, Canadian Constitutional Law (5th ed., 1986 by Finkelstein), 345–347.

forces and other traditional military matters.[10] The emergency branch of p.o.g.g. should be confined to the temporary and extraordinary role required for national regulation in time of actual war (or other emergency).[11]

§ 17:9 Apprehended insurrection

Apart from the two world wars, the War Measures Act was proclaimed in force on only one other occasion, and that was the "October crisis" of October 1970 when the Front de Libération du Québec, a violent Quebec separatist group, had kidnapped a British diplomat and a Quebec cabinet minister (who was later killed by his captors) and had made various demands as the condition of their release.[1] The federal government of Prime Minister Trudeau responded by issuing a proclamation declaring that "apprehended insurrection exists", and thereby bringing the War Measures Act into force. The government then used the powers conferred by the Act to make the Public Order Regulations; these regulations outlawed the F.L.Q., and gave the police new powers of arrest, search, seizure and detention.[2] Under these powers, no fewer than 497 people were arrested and detained. Only 62 of those arrested were charged, and less than one-third of those charged were convicted. It was a remarkable suspension of civil liberties; and the facts which emerged later, especially during the trials of the kidnappers, suggested that there was

---

[10] *A.-G. Can. v. Nykorak*, [1962] S.C.R. 331, 335, 337 (law conferring cause of action for loss of services of members of armed forces); *McKay v. The Queen*, [1980] 2 S.C.R. 370, 390 (law providing for trial by court martial of military offenders). For discussion of s. 91(7) and s. 15 (command of armed forces vested in Crown), see P. Lagassé, "The Crown's Powers of Command-in-Chief: Interpreting s. 15 of Canada's Constitution Act, 1867" (2013) 18 Review of Constitutional Studies 189.

[11] In *Re Anti-Inflation Act*, [1976] 2 S.C.R. 373, 461, Beetz J. emphasized that "in practice, the emergency doctrine operates as a partial and temporary alteration of the distribution of powers between Parliament and the provincial Legislatures".

[Section 17:9]

[1] For an account of the October crisis and the legal measures employed to deal with it, see Tarnopolsky, The Canadian Bill of Rights (2nd ed., 1975), 331–348, who also refers to the other literature on the topic.

[2] The proclamation of the War Measures Act and the Public Order Regulations were revoked on December 3, 1970 by the Public Order (Temporary Measures) Act, S.C. 1970-71-72, c. 2, which continued in force a more limited version of the laws previously contained in the regulations. This Act, which enjoys the distinction of being the only example of a statute containing a "notwithstanding clause" exempting its provisions from the Canadian Bill of Rights (s. 12), was to expire automatically on April 30, 1971 unless extended by resolution of both Houses of Parliament (s. 15). It never was extended. There are other examples of temporary measures which have been enacted by the federal Parliament under its emergency power, but which have never been litigated: The Emergency Powers Act, S.C. 1950–51, c. 5, enacted during the Korean War; The Energy Supplies Emergency Act, S.C. 1973–74, c. 52, enacted after the 1973 Yom Kippur War when there was a threat of an oil shortage; see H. Marx, "The Energy Crisis and the Emergency Power" (1975) 2 Dalhousie L.J. 446. The Emergencies Act, replaced the War Measures Act in 1988. The Emergencies Act is intended to reserve the most draconic powers for the most serious emergencies and to authorize more limited measures for less serious emergencies.

never any possibility of an insurrection from the small and ill-organized F.L.Q. or from any other group. However, the constitutionality of the invocation of the War Measures Act was never reviewed by the courts,[3] and many of those who had been arrested or mistreated by the police were compensated by the Quebec government.

§ 17:10 Inflation

The most recent application of the emergency doctrine is to be found in the *Anti-Inflation Reference* (1976),[1] in which the federal Anti-Inflation Act was upheld as an emergency measure. The Anti-Inflation Act, 1975, and regulations made thereunder, controlled increases in wages, fees, prices, profits, and dividends ("wage and price controls" for short). The control scheme was administered by federal tribunals and officials. The scheme was temporary, the Act automatically expiring at the end of 1978 unless terminated earlier or extended by the government with parliamentary approval. After the Act had been in force for six months (and many collective agreements and prices had been adjusted under its provisions), the federal government referred the Act to the Supreme Court of Canada for a decision as to its constitutionality. The Court, by a majority of seven to two, held that the Act was valid as an exercise of the federal Parliament's emergency power. At the time when the control programme was announced, there had been a period of about twenty months of double-digit inflation in Canada, and the inflation had been accompanied by relatively high rates of unemployment. The majority of the Court held that this situation could be characterized by the government and Parliament as an emergency.[2]

The most serious difficulty with this conclusion[3] was that the Act itself, although it contained a preamble which purported to recite the reasons for the legislation, did not assert the existence of an emergency. This omission pointed to the conclusion, which was accepted only by the two dissenting judges,[4] that the government and Parliament had proceeded on the basis that federal power existed under the national

---

[3]There was some litigation in which lower courts refused to review the government's proclamation of apprehended insurrection: see H. Marx, "The Apprehended Insurrection of October 1970 and the Judicial Function" (1972) 7 U.B.C. L. Rev. 55; J.N. Lyon, "Constitutional Validity of Public Order Regulations" (1972) 18 McGill L.J. 136.

[Section 17:10]

[1]*Re Anti-Inflation Act*, [1976] 2 S.C.R. 373.

[2]Laskin C.J. used the word "crisis", but did not suggest that it meant anything different from emergency. Ritchie J. used the term "emergency".

[3]My criticism of this decision should be taken with a grain of salt, since I was one of the counsel (representing the Canadian Labour Congress) on the losing side!

[4]Beetz J., with whom de Grandpré J. agreed, held that Parliament cannot rely on its emergency power "unless it gives an unmistakable signal that it is acting pursuant to its extraordinary power": [1976] 2 S.C.R. 373, 463. Compare *MacDonald v. Vapor Can.*, [1977] 2 S.C.R 134, where Laskin C.J. insisted (at p. 171) that an exercise of federal power to implement a treaty "must be manifested in the implementing legislation and not left to inference". Yet Laskin C.J. in the *Anti-Inflation Reference* was content for an exercise of the emergency power to be left to inference.

concern branch of p.o.g.g. and that no showing of emergency was required.

The factual material that was filed in the *Anti-Inflation Reference*[5] included an economic study, which was agreed to by a substantial section of Canadian professional economic opinion, and which was not seriously challenged, asserting that Canadian inflation was not only on the wane when the controls were introduced in October 1975 but that it had never been particularly serious in its effects on living standards (which had continued to rise), or by comparison with the United States and other trading nations (whose rates of inflation were similar), or by comparison with other periods of recent Canadian history (this was Canada's third period of double-digit inflation since the second world war).[6]

Nevertheless, Laskin C.J., with whom Judson, Spence and Dickson JJ. agreed, held that the Court "would be unjustified in concluding, on the submissions in this case and on all the material put before it, that the Parliament of Canada did not have a rational basis for regarding the Anti-Inflation Act as a measure which, in its judgment, was temporarily necessary to meet a situation of economic crisis imperilling the well-being of Canada as a whole and requiring Parliament's stern intervention in the interests of the country as a whole".[7] It will be noted that this passage carefully disclaims any judicial duty to make a definitive finding that an emergency exists. All that the Court need do is to find that a "rational basis" exists for a finding of emergency. Moreover, it is not necessary for the proponents of the legislation to establish a rational basis, it is for the opponents of the legislation to establish the absence of a rational basis. Ritchie J., who wrote a concurring opinion with which Martland and Pigeon JJ. agreed, did not use the language of rational basis, but he also cast the burden of proof onto the opponents of the legislation. He adopted the test used in the war measures cases,[8] and held that "a judgment declaring the Act to be ultra vires could only be justified by reliance on very clear evidence that an emergency had not arisen when the statute was enacted".[9] And, without discussing the evi-

[5]The Canadian Labour Congress annexed to its factum a study of inflation in Canada by Richard G. Lipsey, a professor of economics at Queen's University, and it later filed telegrams from thirty-eight other economists associating themselves with Lipsey's conclusions. See ch. 60, Proof, under heading §§ 60:8 to 60:13, "Evidence".

[6]The recurring nature of double-digit inflation was demonstrated by its occurrence again in Canada (and other western nations) in 1980–82. However, this time the federal Parliament chose not to exercise the vast emergency powers which it had presumably acquired, contenting itself with wage controls in the federal public sector (five per cent of the workforce) and exhortations to voluntary restraint elsewhere. I cannot resist commenting that, if double-digit inflation really were an emergency, one would expect sterner remedies than these.

[7]*Re Anti-Inflation Act*, [1976] 2 S.C.R. 373, 425.

[8]*Fort Frances Pulp and Power Co. v. Man. Free Press Co.*, [1923] A.C. 695, 706.

[9]*Re Anti-Inflation Act*, [1976] 2 S.C.R. 373, 439.

dence to that effect which had been presented, he held that it did not satisfy his test.[10]

In a constitutional case, where the validity of legislation depends upon findings of fact concerning the social or economic condition of the country, it is obviously impossible for the Court to make definitive findings. Moreover, judicial restraint requires that a degree of deference be paid to the governmental judgment upon which the legislative policy was based. However, the formulations in the *Anti-Inflation Reference*, especially when read in the light of the persuasive factual material before the Court which denied the existence of an emergency, make it almost impossible to challenge federal legislation on the ground that there is no emergency.[11] This means that the federal Parliament can use its emergency power almost at will.

§ 17:11 Temporary character of law

There is one important limitation on the federal emergency power: it will support only temporary measures.[1] This is usually regarded as a self-evident proposition, based on the fact that an emergency is a temporary phenomenon. One is entitled to question, however, the usefulness of this limitation. It is in any case primarily formal, because an ostensibly temporary measure can always be continued in force by Parliament, while an ostensibly permanent measure can be repealed at any time. More importantly, an emergency, although itself temporary, may be caused by structural defects in the social or economic order which need to be corrected not only to cure the emergency, but also to prevent the occurrence of future emergencies. Yet preventive legislation would surely have to be permanent.[2]

The new deal statutes, which were enacted to deal with the depression of the 1930s, had this dual character: they were designed not only to help alleviate the immediate suffering of the depression, but also to provide permanent economic security which it was hoped would prevent a similar disaster in the future. Perhaps unemployment insurance is the best example of a permanent preventive measure, but minimum wage laws, anti-combine laws and natural products marketing regulation—other Canadian new deal measures—were also perceived by government in the same way. Nevertheless, in the *Unemployment Insurance Refer-*

---

[10]Beetz J., with whom de Grandpré J. agreed, dissented on the ground that the Act gave no indication that it was enacted to meet an emergency. Accordingly, he did not go on to consider the burden or standard of proof which was appropriate.

[11]For full discussion, see P.W. Hogg, "Proof of Facts in Constitutional Cases" (1976) 26 U. Toronto L.J. 386.

[Section 17:11]

[1]*Re Anti-Inflation Act*, [1976] 2 S.C.R. 373, 427, 437, 461, 467; *R. v. Crown Zellerbach*, [1988] 1 S.C.R. 401, 432.

[2]In other contexts "prevention" has been held to be on the same basis as "cure": *A.-G. Ont. v. Can. Temperance Federation*, [1946] A.C. 193, 207.

ence (1937)[3] and companion cases,[4] the Privy Council struck down most of the new deal legislation, and while it appears that their lordships' primary reason was that the depression did not qualify as a genuine emergency, it is a fair inference that they were influenced by the permanent nature of the new deal measures. Similarly, in the *Board of Commerce* case (1922),[5] federal legislation to control hoarding and profiteering caused by the economic dislocation which was the aftermath of the first world war was held to be unconstitutional. Once again, the Privy Council, while also doubting that a peacetime economic problem could be characterized as an emergency, was influenced by the ostensibly permanent character of the proposed controls.[6]

The contrast between the new deal cases and the *Board of Commerce* case, on the one hand, and the *Anti-Inflation Reference*,[7] on the other, is too obvious to require elaboration. It cannot be explained solely in conventional legal terms, but it is the fact that in the former cases the impugned legislation was permanent while in *the Anti-Inflation Reference* the legislation was temporary. No permanent measure has ever been upheld under the emergency power.[8]

V. RELATIONSHIP BETWEEN NATIONAL CONCERN AND EMERGENCY

§ 17:12 Relationship between national concern and emergency

The "gap" branch of p.o.g.g. stands on its own and requires no reconciliation with the "national concern" and "emergency" branches. But the relationship between the national concern and emergency branches does require examination.

One point has been settled by the course of decision since the abolition of appeals to the Privy Council. It is clear that the Privy Council was wrong in asserting that only an emergency would justify the invocation

---

[3]*A.-G. Can. v. A.-G. Ont. (Unemployment Insurance)*, [1937] A.C. 355.

[4]The "new deal cases" in the Privy Council consisted of: *A.-G. Can. v. A.-G. Ont.* (Labour Conventions) [1937] A.C. 326; *A.-G. Can. v. A.-G. Ont.* (Unemployment Insurance) [1937] A.C. 355; *A.-G. B.C. v. A.-G. Can.* (Price Spreads) [1937] A.C. 368; *A.-G. B.C. v. A.-G. Can.* (Natural Products Marketing) [1937] A.C. 377; *A.-G. B.C. v. A.-G. Can.* (Farmers' Creditors Arrangement) [1937] A.C. 391; *A.-G. Ont. v. A.-G. Can.* (Canada Standard Trade Mark) [1937] A.C. 405. The decisions are the subject of a symposium in (1937) 15 Can. Bar Rev. 393–507; see also W.H. McConnell, "The Judicial Review of Prime Minister Bennett's New Deal" (1968) 6 Osgoode Hall L.J. 39.

[5]*Re Board of Commerce Act*, [1922] 1 A.C. 191.

[6]*Re Board of Commerce Act*, [1922] 1 A.C. 191, 197 where the point is explicit.

[7]*Re Anti-Inflation Act*, [1976] 2 S.C.R. 373.

[8]A possible exception is *Lovibond v. Grand Trunk Ry. Co.*, [1939] O.R. 305 (Ont. C.A.), where the federal expropriation of shares in the Grand Trunk Ry. Co. was upheld. Masten J.A. (at p. 344), delivering one of two concurring opinions, offered the emergency branch of p.o.g.g. as one of two bases for the legislation.

of the p.o.g.g. power. *Johannesson*,[1] *Munro*,[2] *Crown Zellerbach*[3] and *Ontario Hydro*[4] establish that the emergency test cannot be the exclusive touchstone. Clearly, for some class of cases the national concern doctrine will suffice to justify the invocation of p.o.g.g. But, unless we are to repudiate the Haldane and post-Haldane decisions altogether, we must accept that there is a class of case for which only an emergency will suffice to found federal power. The problem then is to draw the line between these two different classes.

One possible dividing line must be rejected at the outset. It is not possible to argue that laws affecting property and civil rights must satisfy the emergency test, while laws not affecting property and civil rights need only satisfy the national concern test. In *Johannesson*,[5] what was in issue was the validity of a municipal zoning by-law which purported to limit the establishment of aerodromes in a municipality. In *Munro*,[6] what was in issue was the validity of a federal expropriation of a farmer's land to create a green belt in the national capital region. In *Crown Zellerbach*,[7] what was in issue was a federal law prohibiting the dumping of logging waste in provincial waters. Zoning, expropriation and logging are normally within property and civil rights in the province, and so all three cases had a profound impact upon property and civil rights in the province. Yet it was the national concern doctrine, not the emergency doctrine, which was applied in the cases.

W.R. Lederman, in an article which appeared in the Canadian Bar Review in 1975,[8] suggested a more sophisticated reconciliation of the cases. He pointed out that such subject matters as aviation, the national capital region and atomic energy each had "a natural unity that is quite limited and specific in its extent".[9] He contrasted these "limited and specific" subject matters with such sweeping categories as environmental pollution, culture or language. If the sweeping or pervasive categories were enfranchised as federal subject matters simply on the basis of national concern, then there would be no limit to the reach of federal legislative powers and the existing distribution of legislative powers would become unstable. Accordingly, in normal times, such categories had to be broken down into more specific and meaningful categories for the purpose of allocating legislative jurisdiction; on this basis some

[Section 17:12]

[1] *Johannesson v. West St. Paul*, [1952] 1 S.C.R. 292.

[2] *Munro v. National Capital Commission*, [1966] S.C.R. 663.

[3] *R. v. Crown Zellerbach*, [1988] 1 S.C.R. 401.

[4] *Ontario Hydro v. Ontario*, [1993] 3 S.C.R. 327.

[5] *Johannesson v. West St. Paul*, [1952] 1 S.C.R. 292.

[6] *Munro v. National Capital Commission*, [1966] S.C.R. 663.

[7] *R. v. Crown Zellerbach*, [1988] 1 S.C.R. 401.

[8] "Unity and Diversity in Canadian Federalism" (1975) 53 Can. Bar Rev. 597; see also G. Le Dain, "Sir Lyman Duff and the Constitution" (1974) 12 Osgoode Hall L.J. 261, 293.

[9] "Unity and Diversity in Canadian Federalism" (1975) 53 Can. Bar Rev. 597, 610.

parts of the sweeping categories would be within federal jurisdiction and other parts would be within provincial jurisdiction. Only in an emergency could the federal Parliament assume the plenary power over the whole of a sweeping category.

In the *Anti-Inflation Reference*,[10] Lederman appeared as counsel for one of the unions opposed to the legislation, and he and the other counsel urged his distinction upon the Court with a view to establishing that wage and price controls—a sweeping category—had to satisfy the stricter emergency test. The distinction was accepted by Beetz J., whose opinion constitutes the first, and so far the only,[11] attempt by a Canadian judge to reconcile the emergency cases with the national concern cases. Beetz J.'s opinion was a dissent, but it will be recalled that on this point Ritchie J. agreed with him. (The disagreement was over the question whether the legislation was in fact a recognizable response to an emergency.) This meant that Beetz J.'s opinion on this point enjoyed the support of five members—a majority of the Court, because de Grandpré J. agreed with Beetz J.; and Martland and Pigeon JJ. agreed with Ritchie J. Beetz J.'s opinion also seems to have been accepted by the Court in the later *Crown Zellerbach* case.[12]

In his opinion, Beetz J. expressly acknowledged his indebtedness to Lederman's article.[13] In accordance with the thesis of that article, he refused to accept that a subject matter as broad as "inflation" could be accepted as a new head of federal power: it was "totally lacking in specificity"; it was "so pervasive that it knows no bounds"; the recognition of such a "diffuse" subject matter "would render most provincial powers nugatory" and "destroy the equilibrium of the Constitution".[14] Rather, the Anti-Inflation Act should be classified for constitutional purposes not in terms of the Act's "ultimate purpose" (to contain infla-

[10] *Re Anti-Inflation Act*, [1976] 2 S.C.R. 373.

[11] In *Johannesson v. West St. Paul*, [1952] 1 S.C.R. 292, *Munro v. National Capital Comm.*, [1966] S.C.R. 663, and *R. v. Crown Zellerbach*, [1988] 1 S.C.R. 401, the Court applied the national concern doctrine without reference to the Privy Council cases that had held that only an emergency would suffice. However, in *Crown Zellerbach*, Le Dain J. for the majority said (at p. 431) that the national concern doctrine was "separate and distinct" from the emergency doctrine, and he applied the requirement of distinctness that had been insisted upon by Beetz J. This indicated agreement with Beetz J. La Forest, J., who dissented, also seemed to assume the correctness of Beetz J.'s analysis. In *Re Anti-Inflation Act*, [1976] 2 S.C.R. 373, Laskin C.J., with whom Judson, Spence and Dickson JJ. agreed, applied the emergency doctrine without reference to *Johannesson* and *Munro*. Laskin C.J. did suggest (at p. 419) that the national concern test could also have sustained the legislation, but he did not pursue this idea, and in particular he did not explain his disagreement with Beetz J.'s carefully reasoned opinion to the contrary, which was joined in on this point by all the other judges, and which is discussed in the following text.

[12] Previous note.

[13] *Re Anti-Inflation Act*, [1976] 2 S.C.R. 373, 451; he also acknowledged his indebtedness to G. Le Dain, "Sir Lyman Duff and the Constitution" (1974) 12 Osgoode Hall L.J. 261.

[14] *Re Anti-Inflation Act*, [1976] 2 S.C.R. 373, 458. Accord, *R. v. Crown Zellerbach*, [1988] 1 S.C.R. 401, 431–432.

tion) but in terms of its "operation" and "effects",[15] and in these more specific terms the Act was in relation to wages, prices and profits, which were matters within property and civil rights in the province. In normal times, therefore, wage and price controls were outside the competence of the federal Parliament. In an emergency, however, the power of the federal Parliament "knows no limit other than those which are dictated by the nature of the crisis. But one of those limits is the temporary nature of the crisis".[16]

The thesis advanced by Lederman and adopted by Beetz J. is that the p.o.g.g. power performs two separate functions in the Constitution. First, it gives to the federal Parliament *permanent* jurisdiction over "distinct subject matters which do not fall within any of the enumerated heads of s. 92 and which, by nature, are of national concern", for example, aeronautics and the national capital region.[17] Secondly, the p.o.g.g. power gives to the federal Parliament *temporary* jurisdiction over all subject matters needed to deal with an emergency. On this dual function theory, it is not helpful to regard an emergency as being simply an example of a matter of national concern. As Beetz J. said, "in practice the emergency doctrine operates as a partial and temporary alteration of the distribution of power between Parliament and the provincial Legislatures".[18]

This theory certainly explains most of the cases. The leading "emergency" cases did involve legislation which asserted a sweeping new category of federal power over property, prices, wages or persons, for example, combinations, hoarding, prices and profits in *Board of Commerce*,[19] prices in *Fort Frances*,[20] labour relations and standards in *Snider*[21] and *Labour Conventions*,[22] marketing of natural products in *Natural Products Marketing*,[23] rents in *Wartime Leasehold Regulations*,[24] and deportation in *Japanese Canadians.*[25] Accordingly, in these cases the legislation was upheld only if there was an emergency. The leading "national concern" cases each involved legislation over a more distinct and specific subject matter, for example, aeronautics in *Johannesson*,[26] the national capital in *Munro*,[27] atomic energy in *Ontario Hydro*,[28] and

[15]*Re Anti-Inflation Act*, [1976] 2 S.C.R. 373, 452.

[16]*Re Anti-Inflation Act*, [1976] 2 S.C.R. 373, 461.

[17]*Re Anti-Inflation Act*, [1976] 2 S.C.R. 373, 457.

[18]*Re Anti-Inflation Act*, [1976] 2 S.C.R. 373, 461.

[19]*Re Board of Commerce Act*, [1922] 1 A.C. 191.

[20]*Fort Frances Pulp and Power Co. v. Man. Free Press Co.*, [1923] A.C. 695.

[21]*Toronto Electric Commissioners v. Snider*, [1925] A.C. 396.

[22]*A.-G. Can. v. A.-G. Ont.* (Labour Conventions) [1937] A.C. 326.

[23]*A.-G. B.C. v. A.-G. Can.* (Natural Products Marketing) [1937] A.C. 377.

[24]*Wartime Leasehold Regulations Reference*, [1950] S.C.R. 124.

[25]*Co-op. Committee on Japanese Canadians v. A.-G. Can.*, [1947] A.C. 87.

[26]*Johannesson v. West St. Paul*, [1952] 1 S.C.R. 292.

[27]*Munro v. National Capital Commission*, [1966] S.C.R. 663.

[28]*Ontario Hydro v. Ontario*, [1993] 3 S.C.R. 327.

marine pollution in *Crown Zellerbach*[29] (where the issue of distinctness divided the Court). Accordingly, in these cases no emergency was called for, and the legislation was upheld if the subject matter was judged to be of national concern.[30]

Not all of the cases fit the theory. *Russell*[31] and *Margarine*[32] do not sit easily together. If the federal prohibition of one product—liquor or margarine—requires an emergency, as *Margarine* implies, then *Russell* is wrong. If, however, the subject matter of liquor or margarine is sufficiently specific that it requires only a showing of national concern, as *Russell* implies, then the courts were wrong to call for an emergency in *Margarine*. On the other hand, even if the national concern test is the appropriate one, one can justify the result of *Margarine* on the ground that the prohibition of a particular product lacking any special strategic importance was not sufficiently national in its dimensions; but it is not easy to see the national concern in *Russell*, especially as the legislation was brought into force by local votes. The *Unemployment Insurance Reference*[33] also gives difficulty. One would have thought that unemployment insurance was sufficiently specific to qualify as a new judge-made head of federal power, and that it had the requisite national concern. And, even if an emergency was necessary for this and the other "new deal" statutes, one would have thought that the depression of the 1930s qualified. But *Russell* and the *Unemployment Insurance Reference* are difficult to explain on any theory. Probably, both cases were wrongly decided.

---

[29]*R. v. Crown Zellerbach*, [1988] 1 S.C.R. 401.

[30]Monahan, "The Structure of Canadian Federalism" (1984) 34 U. Toronto L.J. 47, 73 has pointed out that the absence of criteria to determine whether a particular topic is distinct and indivisible, on the one hand, or sweeping and divisible, on the other, inevitably requires the judge to balance the national dimensions of the problem against the local or provincial dimensions.

[31]*Russell v. The Queen* (1882), 7 App. Cas. 829.

[32]*Can. Federation of Agriculture v. A.G. Que.*, [1951] A.C. 179.

[33]*A.-G. Can. v. A.-G. Ont.* (Unemployment Insurance) [1937] A.C. 355.

Chapter 18

Criminal Law

I. DISTRIBUTION OF POWERS

§ 18:1 Distribution of powers

II. DEFINITION OF CRIMINAL LAW

§ 18:2 Definition of criminal law

III. FOOD AND DRUGS

§ 18:3 Food and drug standards
§ 18:4 Illicit drugs
§ 18:5 Tobacco

IV. HEALTH

§ 18:6 Health

V. ENVIRONMENTAL PROTECTION

§ 18:7 Environmental protection

VI. ABORTION

§ 18:8 Abortion

VII. ASSISTED HUMAN REPRODUCTION

§ 18:9 Assisted human reproduction

VIII. GENETIC DISCRIMINATION

§ 18:10 Genetic Discrimination

IX. COMPETITION LAW

§ 18:11 Competition law

X. SUNDAY OBSERVANCE LAW

§ 18:12 Federal power
§ 18:13 Provincial power

XI. GUN CONTROL

§ 18:14 Gun control

XII. PREVENTION OF CRIME

§ 18:15 Prevention in general
§ 18:16 Young offenders

XIII. CRIMINAL LAW AND CIVIL REMEDY

§ 18:17 Federal power generally to create civil remedies
§ 18:18 Criminal law power to create civil remedies

XIV. CRIMINAL LAW AND REGULATORY AUTHORITY

§ 18:19 Criminal law and regulatory authority

XV. PROVINCIAL POWER TO ENACT PENAL LAWS

§ 18:20 Provincial power to enact penal laws

I. DISTRIBUTION OF POWERS

§ 18:1 Distribution of powers

The Constitution Act, 1867, by s. 91(27), confers on the federal Parliament the power to make laws in relation to:

> [t]he criminal law, except the constitution of courts of criminal jurisdiction, but including the procedure in criminal matters.

Under this provision, the criminal law is a federal responsibility. This stands in contrast with the United States and Australia, where the criminal law is a state responsibility. In Canada, since 1892, the criminal law has been codified in one federally-enacted Criminal Code.[1] The argument accepted by the United States and Australia that criminal law should reflect local conditions and sentiments was rejected by the fathers of confederation in favour of a national body of law.[2] However, as will be explained, for the most part, the Criminal Code is enforced by the provinces; and the decisions to investigate, charge and prosecute of-

---

[Section 18:1]

[1]R.S.C. 1985, c. C-46. There are as well other federal statutes enacted under the criminal law power, e.g., the Food and Drugs Act, the Hazardous Products Act. There are as well federal statutes enacted under other heads of federal power that also create offences for their enforcement, e.g., the Fisheries Act, the Income Tax Act. The enforcement provisions of the Income Tax Act do not depend upon the criminal law power for their validity: *Knox Contracting v. Can.*, [1990] 2 S.C.R. 338, 358 per Sopinka J. for majority on this issue; Cory J. for minority held that the enforcement provisions of the Act were criminal law, not tax law. The majority view is the better one: the enforcement provisions of a statutory scheme come under the same constitutional power as the scheme itself. In *Kourtessis v. M.N.R.*, [1993] 2 S.C.R. 53, 72, 102, the Court was unanimous that the offence provisions of the Income Tax Act were supportable under both the taxation power and the criminal law power. Query whether the reference to the criminal law power is necessary or correct.

[2]The legislative history of s. 91(27) is related in M.L. Friedland, A Century of Criminal Justice (Carswell, Toronto, 1984), ch. 2; J. Edwards, "The Advent of English (Not French) Criminal Law and Procedure into Canada" (1984) 26 Crim. Law Q. 464.

fences are therefore matters of provincial policy which will no doubt be framed in response to local conditions and sentiments. In this way, the criminal law is not as centralized as other fields of federal legislative competence, where federal administration normally follows federal enactment.

The provincial role in criminal justice derives from s. 92(14) of the Constitution Act, 1867, which confers on the provincial Legislatures the power to make laws in relation to:

> The administration of justice in the province, including the constitution, maintenance, and organization of provincial courts, both of civil and of criminal jurisdiction, and including procedure in civil matters in those courts.

This is the provision that authorizes provincial policing[3] and prosecution[4] of offences under the Criminal Code, although there is (unexercised) concurrent federal power as well on the basis that federal legislative power over the criminal law (or any other subject matter) carries with it the matching power of enforcement.

The establishment of courts of criminal jurisdiction[5] is expressly included in provincial power by s. 92(14), and is expressly excluded from federal power by s. 91(27). Criminal trials accordingly take place in provincial courts. But the rules of procedure and evidence[6] in a criminal trial are federal: the "procedure in criminal matters" is expressly included in federal power by s. 91(27).

Jurisdiction over correctional institutions[7] is divided between the two levels of government. Under s. 91(28), the federal Parliament has jurisdiction over "penitentiaries", which hold offenders sentenced to imprisonment for two years or more. Under s. 92(6), the provinces have jurisdiction over "prisons", which hold offenders sentenced to imprisonment for less than two years.

Another provincial head of power is relevant in this context, namely, s. 92(15), which authorizes the provincial Legislatures to make laws in relation to:

> The imposition of punishment by fine, penalty, or imprisonment for enforcing any law of the province made in relation to any matter coming within any of the classes of subjects enumerated in this section.

---

[3]Policing is discussed in the next chapter, Criminal Justice, under heading §§ 19:8 to 19:13, "Policing".

[4]Chapter 19, Criminal Justice, under heading §§ 19:14 to 19:15, "Prosecution".

[5]Chapter 19, Criminal Justice, under heading §§ 19:2 to 19:5, "Courts of criminal jurisdiction".

[6]Chapter 19, Criminal Justice, under headings § 19:6, "Procedure", and § 19:7 "Evidence".

[7]Chapter 19, Criminal Justice, under heading §§ 19:17 to 19:20, "Punishment".

This provision authorizes the provincial Legislatures to enact penal sanctions for the enforcement of provincial laws.[8] However, the closing language of the provision makes clear that it is an ancillary power, authorizing the creation of provincial offences only for the purpose of enforcing laws which are authorized under some other head of provincial power. Nevertheless, we shall see that s. 92(15) has imported a substantial degree of concurrent provincial jurisdiction to enact penal laws which are indistinguishable from federal criminal laws. This in turn has given rise to difficult issues of paramountcy where similar federal and provincial laws co-exist.

I have divided these topics into two chapters. This chapter, Criminal Law, covers the substantive criminal law, including the provincial power to enact penal laws. The next chapter, Criminal Justice, covers the adjectival aspects of criminal justice from policing through to punishment.

II. DEFINITION OF CRIMINAL LAW

§ 18:2 Definition of criminal law

The federal Parliament's power to enact "criminal law" has proved very difficult to define.[1] In the *Board of Commerce* case (1922),[2] Viscount Haldane held that the power was applicable only "where the subject matter is one which by its very nature belongs to the domain of criminal jurisprudence". Like Viscount Haldane's definitions of the peace, order, and good government power[3] and the trade and commerce power,[4] this definition of criminal law appeared to be too narrow.[5] Although Viscount Haldane did not spell out what he meant by a "domain of criminal jurisprudence", the phrase could be read as freezing the criminal law into a mould established at some earlier time, presumably 1867.[6]

After Viscount Haldane's death in 1928, Lord Atkin in the *P.A.T.A.*

[8]§ 18:14, "Provincial power to enact penal laws".

[Section 18:2]

[1]See L.M. Leigh, "The Criminal Law Power" (1967) 5 Alta. L. Rev. 237; B.C. McDonald, "Constitutional Aspects of Canadian Anti-Combines Law Enforcement" (1969) 47 Can. Bar Rev. 161; F. Chevrette, "La notion de droit criminel" (1969) 3 Revue Juridique Thémis 294; Laskin, Canadian Constitutional Law (5th ed., 1986 by Finkelstein), ch. 14; Beaudoin, La Constitution du Canada (3rd ed., 2004), ch. 16; Monahan, Constitutional Law (2nd ed., 2002), ch. 11.

[2]*Re Board of Commerce Act*, [1922] 1 A.C. 191, 198–199; folld. in *Toronto Electric Commrs. v. Snider*, [1925] A.C. 396.

[3]See ch. 17, Peace, Order, and Good Government.

[4]See ch. 20, Trade and Commerce.

[5]In fairness to Viscount Haldane, it must be said that the regulatory scheme in issue in the *Board of Commerce* case, administered as it was by an administrative tribunal, could not plausibly be characterized as a criminal law; and Viscount Haldane's only real fault lay in his failure to spell out what he meant by "the domain of criminal jurisprudence".

[6]This would be inconsistent with the doctrine of progressive interpretation, discussed in ch. 15, Judicial Review on Federal Grounds.

case (1931)[7] repudiated the domain of criminal jurisprudence theory and made clear that the federal power was "not confined to what was criminal by the law of England or of any Province in 1867", and that "the power may extend to legislation to make new crimes". Lord Atkin in the *P.A.T.A.* case offered a rival definition of criminal law:[8]

> The criminal quality of an act cannot be discerned by intuition; nor can it be discovered by reference to any standard but one: Is the act prohibited with penal consequences?

This definition appeared to be too wide in that it would enable the federal Parliament to expand its jurisdiction indefinitely, simply by framing its legislation in the form of a prohibition coupled with a penalty. Nor was this definition sufficiently qualified when Lord Atkin later said that "the only limitation on the plenary power of the Dominion to determine what shall or shall not be criminal is the condition that Parliament shall not in the guise of enacting criminal legislation in truth and in substance encroach on any of the classes of subjects enumerated in s. 92".[9] This says no more than the trite proposition that a law must be properly classifiable as in relation to the criminal law, and it no doubt contemplates the possibility of a statute in which the prohibition and penalty are unimportant appendages to provisions which really seek to accomplish the legislative goal by other means. Even setting aside this kind of "colourable" statute, which no one would seriously seek to defend as criminal, the *P.A.T.A.* definition is still too wide, because it would uphold any federal law which employs a prohibition and penalty as its primary mode of operation. If the only characteristics of the criminal law are the formal ones of a prohibition and a penalty, then there is no principled basis for denying to a law with those characteristics the criminal classification.

It is clear that a proper balance in the distribution of legislative powers requires some third ingredient in the definition of criminal law. This was demonstrated in the *Margarine Reference* (1951),[10] where the law in issue simply prohibited the manufacture, importation or sale of margarine. It was common ground that the purpose of this law was to protect the dairy industry. The Privy Council held that, although the law perfectly fitted the criminal form of a prohibition coupled with a penalty, the economic object of protecting an industry from its competitors made the law in pith and substance in relation to property and civil rights in the province.

It follows from the *Margarine Reference* that the elusive third ingredient of a criminal law is a typically criminal public purpose. In the Supreme Court of Canada, Rand J., whose reasoning was adopted by the Privy Council, said that a prohibition was not criminal unless it served

---

[7] *P.A.T.A. v. A.-G. Can.*, [1931] A.C. 310, 324.

[8] *P.A.T.A. v. A.-G. Can.*, [1931] A.C. 310, 324.

[9] *A.-G. B.C. v. A.-G. Can.* (Price Spreads) [1937] A.C. 368, 375.

[10] *Can. Federation of Agriculture v. A.-G. Que.*, [1951] A.C. 179.

"a public purpose which can support it as being in relation to the criminal law".[11] And what were the public purposes which would qualify? "Public peace, order, security, health, morality: these are the ordinary though not exclusive ends served by that law . . .".[12] It will be noticed that Rand J. was careful not to give an exhaustive definition of the purposes of the criminal law. It was enough for him to be confident that the protection of the dairy industry was not a qualifying purpose. But while he characterized that purpose as "to benefit one group of persons as against competitors in business",[13] no doubt the proponents of such protective legislation would deny that such a narrow definition was appropriate and would define the purpose in terms of national economic policy of benefit to all Canadians. Rand J.'s tendentious description of the margarine law, and his failure to provide a test for the identification of a typically criminal public purpose, detract from the value of his much-quoted opinion.[14] Indeed, it is fair to say that the requirement of a typically criminal public purpose is really only a slightly more sophisticated formulation of Viscount Haldane's "domain of criminal jurisprudence".[15]

The *Margarine Reference* should not be read as denying that the criminal law can serve economic ends. A large part of the criminal law is devoted to the protection of private property—a purpose, one might add, which confers a larger benefit on those who own property than on those who do not. But, apart from the traditional crimes of theft and its many variants, various forms of economic regulation have been upheld as criminal law. The *P.A.T.A.* case[16] itself upheld anti-combines (competition) laws under the criminal law power, and under this general rubric a variety of federal laws have been upheld, including prohibitions on price discrimination[17] and resale price maintenance[18] and a judicial power to enjoin some of the prohibited practices.[19] The false prospectus provisions of the Criminal Code have been upheld as criminal law, establishing that securities regulation—at least in crude form—is within the crimi-

[11]*Can. Federation of Agriculture v. A.-G. Que.*, [1949] S.C.R. 1, 50.

[12]*Can. Federation of Agriculture v. A.-G. Que.*, [1949] S.C.R. 1, 50.

[13]*Can. Federation of Agriculture v. A.-G. Que.*, [1949] S.C.R. 1, 50.

[14]Accord, P.C. Weiler, "The Supreme Court and the Law of Canadian Federalism" (1973) 23 U. Toronto L.J. 307, 326.

[15]A definition was suggested by Dickson C.J. (dissenting, but not on this issue) in *R. v. Hauser*, [1979] 1 S.C.R. 984, 1026, which was approved by Cory J. for the majority in *Knox Contracting v. Can.*, [1990] 2 S.C.R. 338, 348, as follows:

> Head 27 of s. 91 of the B.N.A. Act empowers Parliament to make substantive laws prohibiting, with penal consequences, acts or omissions considered to be harmful to the State, or to persons or property within the State. In this formulation, the typically criminal public purpose is said to be the prevention of harm to the State or to persons or property within the State.

[16]*P.A.T.A. v. A.-G. Can.*, [1931] A.C. 310, 324.

[17]*A.-G. B.C. v. A.-G. Can.* (Price Spreads) [1937] A.C. 368.

[18]*R. v. Campbell* (1965), 58 D.L.R. (2d) 673 (S.C.C.).

[19]*Goodyear Tire and Rubber Co. v. The Queen*, [1956] S.C.R. 303. See generally § 18:11, "Competition law".

nal law.[20] In short, there is abundant support for Laskin's assertion that "resort to the criminal law power to proscribe undesirable commercial practices is today as characteristic of its exercise as has been resort thereto to curb violence or immoral conduct."[21]

In *Boggs v. The Queen* (1981),[22] the Supreme Court of Canada, in a unanimous opinion written by Estey J., struck down the federal Criminal Code offence of driving a motor vehicle while one's provincial driver's licence was suspended. This offence would have been constitutionally unimpeachable if a provincial driver's licence could be suspended only for breach of Criminal Code provisions concerned with fitness to drive. If that were the case, the offence of driving while disqualified could be related to the public purpose of safety on the roads. In fact, Boggs' licence had been suspended for just such a cause: he had been convicted of the Criminal Code offences of impaired driving and refusing to take a breath test; and under Ontario's highway legislation these convictions had resulted in the automatic suspension of his driver's licence. But Estey J. discovered, on reviewing the highway legislation of all the provinces, that drivers' licences could also be suspended for breach of a variety of provincial regulations, and in particular for failure to pay insurance premiums, civil judgments, taxes and licence fees. These latter grounds for licence suspensions bore "no relationship in practice or in theory to the owner's ability to drive and hence to public safety on the highways of the nation".[23] A criminal prohibition premised on such grounds was simply an enforcement measure for a variety of provincial regulatory and taxation regimes, and did not pursue the kind of public purpose required by Rand J. in the *Margarine Reference*. The Criminal Code offence of driving while suspended was accordingly unconstitutional. It is clear that a re-framed version, in which the offence was confined to cases where the provincial disqualification resulted from a violation of a Criminal Code offence, would be sustained.[24]

The protection of the environment is a public purpose that will sustain laws enacted under the criminal law power.[25] So is the protection of animals from cruelty.[26] However, in *Ward v. Canada* (2002),[27] the Supreme Court of Canada held that a federal regulation that prohibited the *sale* of baby seals could not be upheld under the criminal law power,

---

[20]*Smith v. The Queen*, [1960] S.C.R. 776. See generally ch. 21, Property and Civil Rights, under heading §§ 21:15 to 21:16, "Securities regulation".

[21]Laskin, Canadian Constitutional Law (5th ed., 1986 by Finkelstein), 849; the whole of chapter 14 is a valuable collection of cases and textual notes on the scope of the criminal law power.

[22]*Boggs v. The Queen*, [1981] 1 S.C.R. 49.

[23]*Boggs v. The Queen*, [1981] 1 S.C.R. 49, 59.

[24]Estey J. held (at p. 65) that the Court itself could not correct the drafting through severance or reading down.

[25]*R. v. Hydro-Québec*, [1997] 3 S.C.R. 213; discussed under heading § 18:7, "Environmental protection".

[26]*Ward v. Can.*, [2002] 1 S.C.R. 569, para. 53 per McLachlin C.J. obiter.

[27]*Ward v. Can.*, [2002] 1 S.C.R. 569.

despite the fact that the purpose of the prohibition was to limit the *killing* of baby seals. The Court found that the law had been driven, not by the widely publicised concern about inhumane methods of killing, but by the concern about the depletion of the resource through large-scale commercial harvesting. The ultimate purpose of the law was to manage the fishery, and that was not a purpose that could sustain a criminal law. However, although the law could not be upheld under the criminal law power, it did come within the federal power over fisheries (s. 91(12)) and was upheld on that ground. Since the law was upheld, the discussion of the criminal law power was obiter—and it was brief. The Court offered no reason for the distinction between a law for the protection of the environment, which has been upheld as a criminal law,[28] and a law for the protection of a natural resource, which according to this case cannot be upheld as a criminal law.

In *R. v. Malmo-Levine* (2003),[29] the Supreme Court of Canada rejected the argument that a "harm principle" was a requirement of a valid criminal law. At issue was the validity of the criminalization of the possession of marihuana, something that did not, it was argued, cause any harm. Although the majority of the Court did succeed in identifying some harms to others that flowed from marihuana use, they made clear that the presence of harm to others was not a requirement of a valid criminal law. Harm to the accused and moral concerns, both of which underlay the marihuana prohibition, were adequate bases for the enactment of criminal law.[30] In other words, a purpose that will qualify to sustain a law as a criminal law does not necessarily involve the prevention of harm to other human beings. Indeed, the protection of the environment and the prevention of cruelty to animals (discussed in the previous paragraph) illustrate the point (although they were not relied upon in *Malmo-Levine).*

A variant of the harm principle was suggested by four of nine judges of the Supreme Court of Canada in *Re Assisted Human Reproduction Act* (2010).[31] In this case, the Court was unanimous that *absolute* prohibitions in the federal Assisted Human Reproduction Act on various practices associated with assisted human reproduction– for example, on the

---

[28]*R. v. Hydro-Québec*, [1997] 3 S.C.R. 213.

[29]*R. v. Malmo-Levine*, [2003] 3 S.C.R. 571. Gonthier and Binnie JJ. wrote the opinion for the majority. Arbour, LeBel and Deschamps JJ. wrote dissenting opinions. However, there was no disagreement with the proposition that harm to others was not a requirement of a valid criminal law.

[30]The Court (Arbour J. dissenting on this point) also rejected the argument that a harm principle was one of the principles of fundamental justice under s. 7 of the Charter. Indeed, the opinions are primarily focused on the fundamental justice issue, and the holding with respect to s. 91(27) has to be inferred (note especially paras. 76–78, 115–118). Only Arbour J. was clear about the distinction, holding (para. 215) that the harm principle was "*not* a constraint inherent in Parliament's criminal law power" (her emphasis), although it was her dissenting view that the harm principle was a principle of fundamental justice, and the marihuana law infringed the principle.

[31]*Re Assisted Human Reproduction Act*, [2010] 3 S.C.R. 457. For fuller discussion, see § 18:19, "Criminal law and regulatory authority", § 18:19 note 27, below.

sale and purchase of human embryos – were a valid exercise of the federal criminal law power. However, the Court divided on whether various *qualified* prohibitions and "controlled activities" in the Act relating to assisted human reproduction were valid under the criminal law power. McLachlin C.J., with the approval of three others, would have upheld the Act in its entirety under the criminal law power, relying on the presence of prohibitions, penalties and the criminal law purposes of morality, public health and the personal security of donors, donees and the unborn. LeBel and Deschamps JJ., with the agreement of two others, would have invalidated the qualified prohibitions and the controlled activities provisions, on the basis that they failed to satisfy the criminal law purpose requirement of the criminal law power. The requirement was not satisfied, they said, because the evidence showed that Parliament viewed assisted human reproduction as "beneficial", "not inherently harmful" or "an evil needing to be suppressed".[32] Cromwell J. cast the decisive vote. He agreed with McLachlin C.J. that the qualified prohibitions, and one of the controlled activities provisions, were valid exercises of the criminal law power. However, he also agreed with LeBel and Deschamps JJ. that most of the controlled activities provisions, and most of the licensing and regulatory scheme that supported them, were not valid exercises of the criminal law power.

There was a disagreement between McLachlin C.J. and LeBel and Deschamps JJ. as to the role that harm should play under the criminal law purpose requirement of the federal criminal law power. McLachlin C.J.'s opinion contains references to harm, but it would appear that she did not intend harm to operate as a significant restriction on the scope of the criminal law power. For example, she affirmed that health is a valid criminal law purpose, and although she seemed to accept that "the need to establish a reasonable apprehension of harm means that conduct with little or no threat of harm is unlikely to qualify as a 'public health evil' ", she also said that "[n]o threshold level of harm, as such, constrains Parliament's ability to target conduct causing these evils".[33] Moreover, other aspects of McLachlin C.J.'s discussion of the criminal law purpose requirement seemed to sidestep harm altogether as a relevant consideration. For example, she affirmed that morality is also a valid criminal law purpose, and said that "Parliament need only have a reasonable basis to expect that its legislation will address a moral concern of fundamental importance, even if hard evidence is unavailable on some points because 'the jury is still out' ".[34] The implication was that actual proof of harm was not necessary – that the criminal law purpose requirement would be satisfied if Parliament merely perceives a risk of

[32] *Re Assisted Human Reproduction Act*, [2010] 3 S.C.R. 457, paras. 250-251.

[33] *Re Assisted Human Reproduction Act*, [2010] 3 S.C.R. 457, paras. 54-56 (emphasis in original).

[34] *Re Assisted Human Reproduction Act*, [2010] 3 S.C.R. 457, para. 50.

harm to, or an injurious or desirable effect on, one of the criminal law purposes in Rand J.'s list or "some similar purpose".[35]

LeBel and Deschamps JJ., in contrast, took the position that a threshold level of harm must be established to satisfy the criminal law purpose requirement of the criminal law power. They suggested that Rand J.'s list of criminal law purposes "does little to clarify the content of this substantive component [of the criminal law power]".[36] And they said that the only public purposes that would support a valid federal criminal law would be ones that "involve suppressing an evil or safeguarding a threatened interest" – a requirement that would be met, they said, only if there is adequate evidence to show that there is a "*real* evil and a *reasonable* apprehension of harm".[37]

The LeBel-Deschamps approach to the criminal law purpose requirement of the federal criminal law power would "substitute[] a judicial view of what is good and what is bad for the wisdom of Parliament".[38] It is also hard to square with the case law on the criminal law power,[39] especially the use of the criminal law power to regulate food and drugs for health and safety,[40] since food and medicine are neither inherently harmful nor an evil in need in suppression. It seems telling that LeBel and Deschamps JJ. referred to the harm requirement as merely "implied" in Rand J.'s definition of the criminal law purpose requirement (which, recall, they also said did little to clarify the scope of the requirement), and that they drew the reasonable apprehension of harm standard largely from cases under the Charter rather than the criminal law power.[41] The LeBel-Deschamps approach failed to attract the support of a majority of the Court: it was flatly rejected by McLachlin C.J. (for four judges);[42] and the ninth judge, Cromwell J., who expressly agreed with part of the LeBel-Deschamps opinion, withheld his agreement from

[35] *Re Assisted Human Reproduction Act*, [2010] 3 S.C.R. 457, para. 43.

[36] *Re Assisted Human Reproduction Act*, [2010] 3 S.C.R. 457, para. 232.

[37] *Re Assisted Human Reproduction Act*, [2010] 3 S.C.R. 457, paras. 232-233, 236, 240 (emphasis added).

[38] *Re Assisted Human Reproduction Act*, [2010] 3 S.C.R. 457, para. 76 per McLachlin C.J.

[39] *Re Assisted Human Reproduction Act*, [2010] 3 S.C.R. 457, para. 76 per McLachlin C.J. (suggesting that the LeBel-Deschamps approach was breaking "new ground in enlarging the judiciary's role in assessing valid criminal law objectives"). Contrast *Re Genetic Non-Discrimination Act*, 2020 SCC 17, paras. 265-266 per Kasirer J. ("[r]equiring a reasoned apprehension of harm . . . accords with the bulk of the jurisprudence"; "the concept of 'harm' is evident throughout much of this Court's jurisprudence").

[40] *R. v. Wetmore*, [1983] 2 S.C.R. 284 (federal Food and Drugs Act offences of insanitary storage and deceptive labelling of drugs upheld as criminal law).

[41] *Re Assisted Human Reproduction Act*, [2010] 3 S.C.R. 457,, para. 236. It is noteworthy that the Court rejected the harm principle as a principle of fundamental justice under s. 7, partly on the basis that it does not provide a "manageable standard" for the courts to apply: *R. v. Malmo-Levine; R. v. Caine*, [2003] 3 S.C.R. 571, para. 129.

[42] *Re Assisted Human Reproduction Act*, [2010] 3 S.C.R. 457,, paras. 74-76 (rejecting the LeBel-Deschamps approach).

their discussion of the scope of the criminal law power.[43] Even so, given that both McLachlin C.J. and LeBel and Deschamps JJ. wrote for only four judges each, and that Cromwell J., the ninth judge, failed to address the role of harm under the criminal law power, *Re Assisted Human Reproduction Act* did generate uncertainty about the role of harm in determining the scope of the criminal law power.

The Supreme Court of Canada had the opportunity to resolve the disagreement and uncertainty about the role of harm under the criminal law power in *Re Genetic Non-Discrimination Act* (2020),[44] another reference that dealt with another health-related issue. The Genetic Non-Discrimination Act set out various prohibitions backed by penalties relating to genetic testing. Quebec, which opposed the Act, directed a reference to the Quebec Court of Appeal, asking it to consider whether ss. 1 to 7 of the Act – the provisions that prohibited forced genetic testing and disclosure, and the unauthorized use of genetic tests, as a condition of providing goods and services or contracting – were authorized by the criminal law power.[45] The Court of Appeal agreed unanimously with Quebec (and the federal government)[46] that the challenged provisions were not authorized by the criminal law power. On appeal, the Supreme Court of Canada, by a bare 5-4 majority, reached the opposite conclusion, concluding that the challenged provisions were authorized by the criminal law power. The Court was unanimous that the Act contained prohibitions backed by penalties, satisfying the first two requirements of the criminal law power. However, as in *Re Assisted Human Reproduction Act*, the Court disagreed about whether the challenged provisions also satisfied the third requirement of the criminal law power – a criminal law purpose. Karakatsanis J., writing for a plurality of three judges, said that the challenged provisions addressed several criminal law purposes: equality, autonomy, privacy and public health. Moldaver J., in a concurring opinion that was joined by Côté J., agreed with Karakatsanis J. that the challenged provisions satisfied the criminal law purpose

[43]*Re Assisted Human Reproduction Act*, [2010] 3 S.C.R. 457,, para. 287 seems careful to withhold agreement from the LeBel-Deschamps analysis of the scope of the criminal law power.

[44]*Re Genetic Non-Discrimination Act*, 2020 SCC 17. Karakatsanis J. wrote a plurality opinion, which was joined by Abella and Martin JJ. Moldaver J. wrote a concurring opinion, which was joined by Côté J. Kasirer J. wrote a dissenting opinion, which was joined by Wagner C.J. and Brown and Rowe JJ.

[45]Quebec did not challenge ss. 8 and 9 of the Act; s. 8 amended the Canada Labour Code, by protecting federally-regulated employees from forced genetic testing and forced disclosure of genetic test results, as well as the collection, disclosure and use of genetic test results without consent, and s. 9 amended the Canadian Human Rights Act, by adding "genetic characteristics" as a prohibited ground of discrimination for the purposes of the Act.

[46]The Act began as a non-government bill in the Senate and was not supported by the federal government – or by the federal Minister of Justice, who expressed concerns about its constitutionality. The government did not require its backbenchers to oppose the bill, and it passed with their support. However, in keeping with the Minister's constitutional concerns, the federal government took the unusual step of supporting Quebec in the reference.

requirement, but he focused on only one criminal law purpose: public health. There were therefore five judges who concluded that the challenged provisions were authorized by the criminal law power. Kasirer J. wrote a dissenting opinion, which was joined by three other judges. He agreed with Karakatsanis and Moldaver JJ. that the challenged provisions implicated public health, but he concluded that the criminal law purpose requirement was not satisfied because the challenged provisions promoted "*beneficial* health practices" by encouraging genetic testing, not a *threat* to public health.[47]

The Court split once again on the role that harm should play in determining the scope of the criminal law power. Justice Karakatsanis (for three judges) endorsed an approach to the criminal law purpose requirement similar to that favoured by McLachlin C.J. in *Re Assisted Human Reproduction Act*. She read McLachlin C.J.'s opinion to require a "reasoned apprehension of harm" to a public interest.[48] As noted earlier, it is possible to read McLachlin C.J.'s opinion to resist such a requirement,[49] but Karakatsanis J., in keeping with what she called "McLachlin C.J.'s deferential posture", did seem to accept that this requirement would do little work in restricting the scope of the criminal law power. She said that "no degree of seriousness of harm need be proved before [Parliament] can make criminal law".[50] Parliament's apprehension of harm must merely be "reasoned", and its "legislative action . . . a response to that apprehended harm".[51]

In contrast, Kasirer J. (for four judges) endorsed an approach reminiscent of the LeBel-Deschamps approach to the criminal law purpose requirement – an approach that, recall, understands harm to play an important role in limiting the reach of the criminal law power. He set out a three-stage test to be used in determining whether a federal law satisfies the criminal law purpose requirement. Under this three-stage test, a court must determine whether: (1) the federal law relates "to a 'public purpose', such as public peace, order, security, health or morality"; (2) the federal law seeks to suppress or prevent a "well-defined threat" to the specific public purpose; and (3) the threat to the specific public purpose is " 'real', in the sense that Parliament had a concrete basis and a reasoned apprehension of harm when enacting the" federal law.[52]

Moldaver J. (for two judges) explicitly refused to resolve the disagreement between his colleagues about the role of harm in determining the scope of the criminal law power.[53] In his view, the challenged provisions had a valid criminal law purpose under both the Karakatsanis (and

[47]*Re Genetic Non-Discrimination Act*, 2020 SCC 17, para. 239 (emphasis added).

[48]*Re Genetic Non-Discrimination Act*, 2020 SCC 17, para. 75.

[49]See the text accompanying notes § 18:2 notes 33-35, above.

[50]*Re Genetic Non-Discrimination Act*, 2020 SCC 17, para. 79.

[51]*Re Genetic Non-Discrimination Act*, 2020 SCC 17, para. 78.

[52]*Re Genetic Non-Discrimination Act*, 2020 SCC 17, para. 234.

[53]*Re Genetic Non-Discrimination Act*, 2020 SCC 17, para. 138.

McLachlin) approach and the Kasirer (and LeBel-Deschamps) approach to the criminal law purpose requirement. Since Moldaver J. (for two judges) refused to endorse either of these two approaches to harm, neither approach managed to attract the support of a majority of the Court.

Re Genetic Non-Discrimination Act was a missed opportunity. It was a missed opportunity for the Supreme Court to provide clarity as to the role that harm plays in determining the scope of the criminal law power. In addition, it was a missed opportunity for (at least a majority) of the Court to affirm the McLachlin-Karakatsanis approach to harm under the criminal law power.

III. FOOD AND DRUGS

§ 18:3 Food and drug standards

In the *Margarine Reference* (1951),[1] as we have just noticed, a prohibition on the manufacture or sale of margarine was struck down on the basis that the purpose of the legislation was the economic one of protecting the dairy industry. When the margarine legislation was originally enacted by the federal Parliament in 1886, the statute included a preamble asserting that margarine was "injurious to health". If that had been the continuing basis of the legislation, there is no doubt that it would have satisfied the requirement of a typically criminal public purpose. It is well-established that food and drug legislation making illegal the manufacture or sale of dangerous products, adulterated products or misbranded products is within the criminal law power.[2] But in the *Margarine Reference* it was conceded by the federal government that margarine was not injurious to health. This concession, which had to be made in light of the medical facts, destroyed what was originally a secure criminal law foundation for the legislation.[3]

In *Labatt Breweries v. A.-G. Can.* (1979),[4] the Supreme Court of Canada held that the part of the federal Food and Drugs Act that authorized regulations prescribing compositional standards for food was unconstitutional. Regulations made under the Act prescribed the ingredients of "beer" and "light beer" (along with hundreds of other foods and beverages), and in particular stipulated that any product described as "light beer" must contain no more than 2.5 per cent alcohol. Labatt Breweries violated the regulations by retailing a product they described as "lite" beer (which the Court held to be equivalent to "light" beer), which had an alcoholic content of 4 per cent, that is, more than the prescribed standard of 2.5 per cent. The brewery argued that the

---

[Section 18:3]

[1] *Can. Federation of Agriculture v. A.-G. Que.*, [1951] A.C. 179.

[2] *R. v. Wetmore*, [1983] 2 S.C.R. 284 (federal Food and Drugs Act offences of insanitary storage and deceptive labelling of drugs upheld as criminal law).

[3] Now see *UL Can. v. Que.*, [2005] 1 S.C.R. 143 (upholding provincial prohibition of sale of yellow-coloured margarine).

[4] *Labatt Breweries v. A.-G. Can.*, [1980] 1 S.C.R. 914.

compositional standard was unconstitutional, and Estey J., writing for a majority of the Supreme Court of Canada, so held.[5] Estey J. acknowledged that the criminal law power could be used to enact laws for the protection of health (and much of the Food and Drugs Act is plainly directed to that end),[6] but he found that the alcoholic requirement for light beer was not related to health. He also acknowledged that the criminal law power could be used to enact laws for the prevention of deception (and some of the Food and Drugs Act is also plainly directed to that end),[7] but he found that the specification of the compositional standards for light beer could not be supported on this ground either. It followed that the compositional standards authorized by the Food and Drugs Act could not be supported under the criminal law power. Since they could not be supported under the peace, order, and good government power,[8] or the trade and commerce power,[9] either, it followed that they were invalid. Although Estey J. confined his ruling to federal compositional standards "in so far as they relate to malt liquors",[10] the decision must mean that all the federal standards are invalid, except those few that can be related to health.

The *Labatt* decision is unfortunate in precluding a national regime of compositional standards for food. Most sectors of the food industry (beer is a good example) have become highly concentrated, with a few large manufacturers or suppliers marketing the products nation-wide. It would be costly and inconvenient for such manufacturers to comply with a variety of provincially-established standards. Of course, manufacturers might be content with no standards at all, and this invites the question: what is the public policy justification for a national regime of compositional standards for food?

In my view, Estey J. rejected too quickly the deception rationale for federal compositional standards. He was impressed by the fact that Labatt Breweries specified on the label of their "lite" beer that it contained 4 per cent alcohol. Obviously, this meant that the careful and knowledgeable reader of the label would not be deceived as to the product's alcohol content. But surely Parliament could rationally conclude that consumers often do not read or understand labels, and that consumers should be able to count on the fact that certain product names imply particular characteristics of the product: for example, that "light beer" was a low-alcohol beer; that "mayonnaise" contained egg; that "jam" and

---

[5]Estey J. was joined by Martland, Ritchie, Dickson, Beetz and Pratte JJ. Laskin C.J., Pigeon and McIntyre JJ. dissented. The dissenting opinions relied on the trade and commerce power, not the criminal law power, and are accordingly ignored in the account that follows.

[6]E.g., *R. v. Wetmore*, [1983] 2 S.C.R. 284.

[7]*R. v. Wetmore*, [1983] 2 S.C.R. 284.

[8]This aspect of the decision is discussed in ch. 17, Peace, Order, and Good Government, under heading § 17:4, "Definition of national concern".

[9]This aspect of the decision is discussed in ch. 20, Trade and Commerce, under heading § 20:4, "General trade and commerce".

[10]*Labatt Breweries v. A.-G. Can.*, [1980] 1 S.C.R. 914, 947.

"juice" were made from fruit, "ice-cream" from milk (or cream), and "chocolate" from cacao beans; that "ground beef" consisted only of beef; and so on.[11] Departures from these standards were not prohibited, but they had to be signalled by calling the unqualified product by a different name. With respect, the denial that this kind of regulation is directed to the prevention of consumer deception[12] is essentially the substitution of the Court's opinion as to the nature and likelihood of consumer deception for that of the Parliament.[13] In my view, a proper deference to a rationally defensible legislative policy required the regulation in *Labatt* to be upheld as a criminal law.

§ 18:4 Illicit drugs

The non-medical use of drugs such as cocaine and heroin is proscribed by the federal Controlled Drugs and Substances Act (replacing the Narcotic Control Act), which (among other things), prohibits the production, importation, sale and possession of a variety of illicit drugs. The Act has been upheld as a criminal law.[1] The non-medical use of marijuana also used to be proscribed by the Controlled Drugs and Substances Act, but marijuana was legalized in 2018, and is now regulated by a combination of federal and provincial legislation. The key federal statute is the Cannabis Act.[2] Before marijuana was legalized, the Supreme Court of Canada indicated (in 2003) that, if marijuana (for example) were to be legalized, the criminal law basis for a federal purely regulatory statute "might well be questioned".[3] The Court left open the question whether there was some "residual authority to deal with drugs

[11]These examples are all taken from the actual regulations of which the "light beer" rule was one.

[12]Having rejected the legislative purpose of preventing deception, Estey J. did not say what he thought the real purpose was. He described the impugned regulation (at p. 934) as "this detailed regulation of the brewing industry in the production and sale of its product". But the production and sale of 4 per cent beer (for example) was only affected in that it had to be described by some term other than "light" (or "lite"). Similarly, a manufacturer of candy could use any ingredients it chose, but could not describe the product as "chocolate" unless it contained cacao beans. To describe this as "detailed regulation" of an industry does not seem plausible, and in any event the description does not tell us what the purpose of the regulation is and it is the purpose which is critical to the characterization of a law as criminal or not.

[13]J.C. MacPherson, "Economic Regulation and the British North America Act" (1980) 5 Can. Bus. L. J. 172, 183, criticizes the *Labatt* decision on a number of grounds, including this one. The aftermath of the decision is described in Monahan, Politics and the Constitution (1987), 228–234.1.

[Section 18:4]

[1]*Industrial Acceptance Corp. v. The Queen*, [1953] 2 S.C.R. 273; *R. v. Malmo-Levine*, [2003] 3 S.C.R. 571 (overruling *The Queen v. Hauser*, [1979] 1 S.C.R. 984, which had upheld the Act under peace, order, and good government); *Can. v. PHS Community Services Society*, [2011] 3 S.C.R. 134, para. 52.

[2]S.C. 2018, c. 16.

[3]*R. v. Malmo-Levine*, [2003] 3 S.C.R. 571, para. 72.

in general (or marihuana in particular) under the peace, order, and good government power".[4]

The federal Controlled Drugs and Substances Act, by s. 56, empowers the federal Minister of Health to grant exemptions from the prohibitions in the Act "if, in the opinion of the Minister, the exemption is necessary for a medical or scientific purpose or is otherwise in the public interest". Acting under this power, the Minister granted an exemption to Insite, a safe-injection clinic located in Vancouver which was established by a regional health authority operating under provincial law. Insite provided trained staff and clean equipment (but no illicit drugs) to enable injection drug addicts (who brought their own drugs, mainly heroin and cocaine) to inject their drugs in a safe and supervised environment. The exemption under s. 56 was needed because without it the staff and patients of the clinic would be committing the offence of possession under the Act. A change of policy by a new federal government caused the Minister to refuse to extend the exemption, which would have forced the closing of the clinic. The province, the city and the police, not to mention the users of the clinic, were all in support of the continuance of the clinic, which, evidence showed, had dramatically reduced deaths by overdose, injuries from incompetent injections, and the spread of infectious diseases from shared needles. In *Canada v. PHS Community Services Society* (2011),[5] the Supreme Court of Canada ordered the Minister to grant the exemption on the ground that the closing of the clinic would endanger life, liberty and security of the person in breach of s. 7 of the Charter. The Minister had to exercise his discretion in compliance with the Charter, and he had to pay attention to the evidence in exercising the discretion. The Court held that, based on the evidence, the only Charter-compliant choice was to renew the exemption, and accordingly ordered the Minister to renew the exemption, thereby allowing the clinic to continue its operations—and no doubt opening a path for other safe injection sites that would require exemptions.

In *Schneider v. The Queen* (1982),[6] the Supreme Court of Canada upheld British Columbia's Heroin Treatment Act, which provided for the compulsory apprehension, assessment and treatment of "narcotic addicts"; the treatment could include compulsory detention in a treatment centre for up to six months. The argument that this was really a criminal law was based on the deprivations of liberty that were authorized by the Act. Of course, the Act was designed to treat and cure drug users, not to deter or punish them; but in some ways this made the legislation more rather than less oppressive, since the coercive features of the legislation were not accompanied by the procedural safeguards which

[4]*R. v. Malmo-Levine*, [2003] 3 S.C.R. 571, para. 72. Compare the cases dealing with the regulation of alcohol: ch. 17, Peace, Order, and Good Government, under heading § 17:3 "History of national concern".

[5]*Canada v. PHS Community Services Society*, [2011] S.C.R. 134; discussed in § 47:25, "Disproportionate laws".

[6]*Schneider v. The Queen*, [1982] 2 S.C.R. 112.

surround the criminal justice process.[7] Nevertheless, the Court was unanimous in classifying the legislation as within provincial competence. Dickson J., who wrote for seven of the nine judges, held that the medical treatment of drug addiction came within provincial authority over public health as a "local or private" matter within s. 92(16) of the Constitution Act, 1867. The coercive elements of the Act were incidental to its public health purpose.[8] Laskin C.J. and Estey J., in separate concurring opinions, reached similar conclusions.[9]

§ 18:5 Tobacco

In *RJR-MacDonald v. Canada* (1995),[1] the Supreme Court of Canada had to review the validity of the federal Tobacco Products Control Act, which prohibited the advertising of cigarettes and other tobacco products and required the placement of health warnings on packages. Was this a valid criminal law? The Act contained a prohibition and a penalty, but was there a typically criminal public purpose? In the case of the requirement of warnings, the Court was unanimous that the protection of public health supplied the required purpose to support the exercise of the criminal law power.[2] But what of the ban on advertising? It was clear that the criminal law power permitted Parliament to prohibit the manufacture, sale or possession of dangerous products.[3] But Parliament had not done that: the manufacture, sale and possession of tobacco remained lawful, and all that was prohibited was the advertising of tobacco products. Advertising itself was not a dangerous act, and the advertising of consumer goods was normally within the legislative jurisdiction of the provinces under their power over property and civil rights.[4] In the Supreme Court of Canada, Major J.'s dissenting view was that

[7]Section 7 of the Charter of Rights was not considered, because the case pre-dated the Charter.

[8]Compulsory detention of the mentally incompetent under provincial law was upheld in the pre-Charter case of *Fawcett v. A.-G. Ont.*, [1964] S.C.R. 625; but there the compulsion can be more easily justified on the basis that mental incompetence destroys the capacity to consent. This may be the point of Dickson J.'s description in *Schneider* (at p. 138) of narcotic addiction as a "compulsive condition over which the individual loses control".

[9]Laskin C.J. agreed generally with Dickson J. Estey J. placed the provincial power in s. 92(7) (hospitals) as well as in s. 92(13) (property and civil rights) and s. 92(16) (local or private matters).

[Section 18:5]

[1]*RJR-MacDonald v. Canada*, [1995] 3 S.C.R. 199. On the criminal law power, La Forest J.'s opinion is the majority one, attracting the support of six other judges. Major J. dissented on this issue, attracting the support of Sopinka J.

[2]*RJR-MacDonald v. Canada*, [1995] 3 S.C.R. 199, para. 41 per La Forest J., para. 196 per Major J.

[3]*R. v. Wetmore*, [1983] 2 S.C.R. 284, and previous section of this chapter under heading § 18:4, "Illicit drugs".

[4]*Irwin Toy v. Que.*, [1989] 1 S.C.R. 927. Compare *R. v. Sobey's Inc.* (1998), 172 D.L.R. (4th) 111 (N.S.C.A.) (upholding provincial prohibition on sale of cigarettes to minors; law was in relation to health).

the prohibition of the advertising of a legal product lacked a "typically criminal purpose" and was outside the federal criminal law power. But La Forest J., for the majority, disagreed. In his view, the power to prohibit the use of tobacco on account of its harmful effects on health also encompassed the power to take the lesser step of prohibiting the advertising of tobacco products. Although it was impracticable to ban the product itself in view of the large number of Canadians who were smokers,[5] it was clear from the legislative history that the ban on advertising still pursued the same underlying public purpose, namely, the protection of the public from a dangerous product. The fact that Parliament chose a "circuitous path" to its destination did not alter the pith and substance of the law, which was criminal. The majority of the Court held accordingly that the Act was within the criminal law power of Parliament. (The Act was struck down by a majority of the Court under the Charter of Rights, because of the impact of the advertising ban on freedom of expression.)[6]

In a sequel case,[7] the Supreme Court upheld a new federal Tobacco Act, which was a less sweeping ban on the advertising of tobacco products. The Court unanimously reaffirmed the *RJR* ruling that "restrictions on tobacco advertising are a valid exercise of Parliament's criminal law power".[8] (This version of the Act survived Charter attack; the more limited ban was upheld under s. 1 as a reasonable limit on freedom of expression.)[9]

IV. HEALTH

§ 18:6 Health

Health is not a single matter assigned by the Constitution exclusively to one level of government. Like inflation[1] and the environment,[2] health is an "amorphous topic" which is distributed to the federal Parliament or the provincial Legislatures depending on the purpose and effect of the particular health measure in issue. As the previous section of this chapter (food and drugs) illustrates, there is a criminal-law aspect of health, authorizing federal legislation under s. 91(27) to punish conduct

---

[5]A similar explanation was given for the exemption from the ban of advertising in foreign media imported into Canada (which meant that Canadians continued to be exposed to a great deal of lawful advertising of tobacco products). La Forest J. said (para. 56) that it would not be practical to censor foreign publications.

[6]Chapter 43, Expression, under heading § 43:23, "Advertising restrictions".

[7]*Can. v. JTI-Macdonald Corp.*, [2007] 2 S.C.R. 610. McLachlin C.J. wrote the opinion of the Court.

[8]*Can. v. JTI-Macdonald Corp.*, [2007] 2 S.C.R. 610, para. 20. Major J., who had dissented on this issue in *RJR*, was no longer on the Court.

[9]Chapter 43, Expression, under heading § 43:23, "Advertising restrictions".

[Section 18:6]

[1]*Re Anti-Inflation Act*, [1976] 2 S.C.R. 373, 458 per Beetz J.

[2]*Friends of Oldman River Society v. Can.*, [1992] 1 S.C.R. 3, 63, 64, 70 per La Forest J.

that is dangerous to health. Legislative authority over health is discussed in chapter 32, Health.

V. ENVIRONMENTAL PROTECTION

§ 18:7 Environmental protection

Closely related to health, and equally amorphous, is the subject matter of environmental protection. Legislative authority over environmental protection is discussed in the later chapter on Natural Resources.[1] However, it should be noted here that, in *R. v. Hydro-Québec* (1997),[2] all of the judges of the Supreme Court of Canada agreed that the protection of the environment (which extends beyond the protection of human health) was a public purpose that would support a federal law under the criminal law power, and the majority of the Court upheld the Canadian Environmental Protection Act under the criminal law power. The dissenting minority took the view that the Act was regulatory rather than criminal; that issue is taken up later in this chapter.[3]

VI. ABORTION

§ 18:8 Abortion

Canada's Criminal Code used to prohibit abortions, with the exception of an abortion approved by the therapeutic abortion committee of a hospital, which had to certify that the continuation of the pregnancy would be likely to endanger the mother's life or health. In *Morgentaler v. The Queen* (1975),[1] the validity of the prohibition was challenged on the basis that the safety of modern techniques of abortion made the prohibition inappropriate as a protection for the health of the pregnant woman. Therefore, the prohibition was not authorized by the criminal law power. Laskin C.J. held that it was open to Parliament under the criminal law power to prohibit the termination of pregnancy, even if the termination would not endanger the health of the woman.[2] The principal objective of the prohibition was "to protect the state interest in the foetus", and that was sufficient to make the prohibition a valid exercise of the criminal law power.[3]

The *Morgentaler* case of 1975 also rejected a challenge to the abortion

---

[Section 18:7]

[1]Chapter 30, Natural Resources, under §§ 30:31 to 30:33, "Environmental protection".

[2]*R. v. Hydro-Québec*, [1997] 3 S.C.R. 213.

[3]§ 18:19, "Criminal law and regulatory authority".

[Section 18:8]

[1]*Morgentaler v. The Queen*, [1976] 1 S.C.R. 616.

[2]*Morgentaler v. The Queen*, [1976] 1 S.C.R. 616, 624–628. Laskin C.J. dissented on another issue, but on this issue the Court was unanimous, although the majority did not express any reasons on the point.

[3]*R. v. Morgentaler*, [1988] 1 S.C.R. 30, 129 per Beetz J. following (and elaborating on) the 1975 *Morgentaler* case. In the 1988 case, all judges except Wilson J. held that

law based on the Canadian Bill of Rights. But another challenge was brought after the enactment of the Charter of Rights, and in the *Morgentaler* case of 1988[4] the Supreme Court of Canada struck down the law as contrary to s. 7 of the Charter. Parliament has not enacted a replacement law,[5] and the Criminal Code no longer prohibits abortion. A provincial prohibition would be held to be an invalid attempt to enact a criminal law,[6] even if the Charter obstacle could be surmounted.

VII. ASSISTED HUMAN REPRODUCTION

§ 18:9 Assisted human reproduction

The federal Assisted Human Reproduction Act was an attempted exercise of the criminal law power to regulate the use of assisted human reproduction techniques with a view to protecting morality, public health and the personal security of donors and donees of sperm and ova and persons not yet born. In *Re Assisted Human Reproduction Act* (2010),[1] the Supreme Court of Canada agreed that the outright prohibition of reprehensible practices, for example, the sale or purchase of human embryos, was a valid exercise of the criminal law power. However, a five-four majority of the Court held that most of the prohibitions in the Act that were subject to exceptions, or to a regulatory and licensing regime, were outside the criminal law power and unconstitutional. The regulation of assisted human reproduction, according to the majority, could not be governed by nation-wide rules because it came within provincial powers over hospitals, the medical profession, property and civil rights and local matters. This case deals with the intersection between criminal law and regulatory authority, and is discussed more fully in that context later in this chapter.[2]

VIII. GENETIC DISCRIMINATION

§ 18:10 Genetic Discrimination

Genetic testing involves looking at genetic material (like DNA) in order to determine whether an individual has a suspected genetic condition, or to help determine the individual's chance of developing or pass-

---

the prohibition was within the criminal law power, although the other judgments expressed no reasons on the point; Wilson J. did not mention the point.

[4] *R. v. Morgentaler*, [1988] 1 S.C.R. 30. The case is discussed in ch. 47, Fundamental Justice, under heading § 47:12, "Security of the person".

[5] Bill C-43, to re-criminalize abortion, but with a less restrictive law, was passed by the House of Commons, but defeated by the Senate on a 43-43 tie vote at third reading on January 31, 1991.

[6] *Re Freedom of Informed Choice (Abortions) Act* (1985), 25 D.L.R. (4th) 751 (Sask. C.A.) (provincial law requiring consent of husband or parents held invalid as criminal law); *R. v. Morgentaler (No. 3)*, [1993] 3 S.C.R. 463 (provincial law requiring abortions to be performed in hospitals held invalid as criminal law).

[Section 18:9]

[1] *Re Assisted Human Reproduction Act*, [2010] 3 S.C.R. 457.

[2] § 18:19, "Criminal law and regulatory authority", at § 18:19 note 22, below.

ing on a genetic condition. Genetic testing (or the results of it) can be sought by third parties (like insurance and financial companies) because the results can be used to determine whether to offer certain goods and services (like health or life insurance or annuities) or the price to charge for them – with individuals that have or might develop certain genetic conditions denied goods or services or charged more for them. In 2017, Parliament responded to concerns about this practice by enacting the Genetic Non-Discrimination Act. The Act set out various prohibitions – backed by penalties – related to genetic testing, carving out exceptions for healthcare practitioners and researchers. The Act was opposed by Quebec, which directed a reference to its Court of Appeal, asking whether the provisions of the Act (ss. 1 to 7) that prohibited forced genetic testing and disclosure, and the unauthorized use of genetic tests, as a condition of providing goods and services or contracting were beyond the scope of the criminal law power. The federal government took the unusual step of supporting Quebec in the reference in the courts.[1]

In *Re Genetic Non-Discrimination Act* (2020),[2] the Supreme Court of Canada, unlike the Court of Appeal, concluded that the challenged provisions of the Act were validly enacted under the criminal law power. The Court was unanimous that the challenged provisions contained prohibitions backed by penalties, satisfying the first two requirements of the criminal law power. However, the court divided about whether the challenged provisions also satisfied the third requirement of the criminal law power – a criminal law purpose. Karakatsanis J., writing for a plurality of three judges, said that the criminal law purpose requirement was satisfied: the challenged provisions represented Parliament's attempt to combat genetic discrimination, and safeguarded four criminal law purposes – equality, autonomy, privacy and public health. Moldaver J., with the agreement of Côté J., agreed with Karakatsanis J.'s conclusion that the criminal law purpose requirement was satisfied, but for different reasons. He said that the challenged provisions represented Parliament's attempt, not to combat genetic discrimination, but to prevent the negative health effects that can result when people forego genetic testing due to its potential misuse, and that the relevant criminal law purpose was public health, only one of the four criminal law purposes listed by Karakatsanis J. Kasirer J. wrote a dissenting opinion, with the agreement of three other judges. He said that, in pith and substance, the challenged provisions did not deal with either genetic discrimination or public health, but rather the regulation of contracts for the provision of goods and services, and that they did not satisfy the criminal purpose requirement because they promoted "*beneficial* health

[Section 18:10]

[1]For a discussion of this unusual move, see the text in § 18:2, note 49, above.

[2]*Re Genetic Non-Discrimination Act*, 2020 SCC 17. Karakatsanis J. wrote a plurality opinion, which was joined by Abella and Martin JJ. Moldaver J. wrote a concurring opinion, which was joined by Côté J. Kasirer J. wrote a dissenting opinion, which was joined by Wagner C.J. and Brown and Rowe JJ.

practices" by encouraging genetic testing, not a *threat* to public health.[3] In his view, the challenged provisions therefore fell, not within the criminal law power, but rather the provincial power over property and civil rights (s. 92(13)). However, because five judges concluded that the challenged provisions of the Act were valid under the criminal law power, it is now clear that Parliament has the jurisdiction to enact nation-wide prohibitions relating to genetic testing. There was another disagreement among the Court about the role of harm in determining the scope of the criminal law power; this aspect of the case is discussed earlier.[4]

IX. COMPETITION LAW

§ 18:11 Competition law

The encouragement of competition throughout much of the private sector of the Canadian economy has been a longstanding policy of Canada's federal governments. The argument is that a competitive market is the best means of promoting the efficient use of labour, capital and natural resources; and that in those sectors of the economy where the market is competitive, governmental regulation of industry is less necessary. However, because economic activity ignores provincial boundaries, and labour, capital and technology are highly mobile, it is difficult to regulate anti-competitive practices at a provincial level.[1] It is generally agreed that such regulation has to be federal if it is to be effective.[2]

In the second half of the nineteenth century, many industries became highly concentrated through mergers and other forms of combination which had the effect of limiting or eliminating competition. In the United States, the Congress acted against the combines or "trusts" which dominated many industries by enacting the Sherman Anti-Trust Act in 1890. In Canada, the federal Parliament passed a similar law a year earlier, in 1889. The Canadian law, which simply prohibited combinations designed to limit competition, was intended to be a criminal law, and in 1892 it was transferred to the Criminal Code. Machinery for investigation and for cease and desist orders was added in 1910. This first anti-combines (or competition) law was never challenged in the courts.[3]

In 1919, a more ambitious regime of regulation was enacted by the

---

[3]*Re Genetic Non-Discrimination Act*, 2020 SCC 17, para. 239 (emphasis added).

[4]§ 18:2, "Definition of criminal law".

[Section 18:11]

[1]Where an industry is regulated provincially, this usually involves the sanctioning of anticompetitive practices in that industry; the courts have resolved the potential paramountcy problem by holding that the federal Combines Investigation Act is inapplicable to provincially-regulated industries, e.g. *A.-G. Can. v. Law Society of B.C.*, [1982] 2 S.C.R. 307, 347–361; B.C. McDonald, "Constitutional Aspects of Canadian Anti-Combines Law Enforcement" (1969) 47 Can. Bar Rev. 161, 200–210.

[2]See Safarian, Canadian Federalism and Economic Integration (1974), esp. Parts 1 and III.

[3]B.C. McDonald, "Constitutional Aspects of Canadian Anti-Combines Law Enforce-

Combines and Fair Prices Act and the Board of Commerce Act. These two statutes prohibited combinations which in the opinion of an administrative agency, the Board of Commerce, were detrimental to the public interest. The Board had powers, not merely of investigation, but also to make cease and desist orders in respect of combinations or practices which it determined to be unlawful. In addition to those competition provisions, the statutes included provisions directed at hoarding and unduly profiting from necessaries of life (defined as staple foods, clothing and fuel), and conferred extensive powers on the board to determine when undue profits were being made and to make cease and desist orders which in effect fixed maximum prices. These two statutes were held to be unconstitutional in the famous *Board of Commerce* case (1921).[4] The Privy Council rejected the arguments in support which were based on the peace, order, and good government power,[5] the trade and commerce power[6] and the criminal law power. In reference to the criminal law power, it will be recalled that this was the case where Viscount Haldane uttered his "domain of criminal jurisprudence" dictum.[7]

After the *Board of Commerce* case, the federal Parliament enacted the Combines Investigation Act, 1923. This Act repealed the two statutes of 1919, and replaced them with a simpler prohibition of combines in restraint of trade. The new Act granted investigatory powers to a registrar and commissioners, but these officials were not given the power to order the cessation of anti-competitive activities. In the *P.A.T.A.* case (1931),[8] the Privy Council, now speaking through Lord Atkin, upheld the Act as a valid criminal law. It will be recalled that Lord Atkin repudiated the "domain of criminal jurisprudence" theory in this case,[9] and he held that "if Parliament genuinely determines that commercial activities which can be so described [as contrary to the public interest] are to be suppressed in the public interest, their Lordships see no reason why Parliament should not make them crimes".[10] This decision established that the criminal law power was capable of expansion into the world of commerce.[11]

The federal Parliament in 1935 enacted the Dominion Trade and Industry Commission Act. This Act established a Commission to

ment" (1969) 47 Can. Bar Rev. 161, is a study of the constitutional issues raised by Canadian combines law.

[4]*Re Board of Commerce Act, Board of Commerce*, [1922] 1 A.C. 191.

[5]See ch. 17, Peace, Order, and Good Government, under heading § 17:7 "The non-emergency cases".

[6]See ch. 20, Trade and Commerce, under heading § 20:2 "In the Privy Council".

[7]*Re Board of Commerce Act, Board of Commerce*, [1922] 1 A.C. 191, 198–199.

[8]*P.A.T.A. v. A.-G. Can.*, [1931] A.C. 310.

[9]*P.A.T.A. v. A.-G. Can.*, [1931] A.C. 310, 324.

[10]*P.A.T.A. v. A.-G. Can.*, [1931] A.C. 310, 323–324.

[11]Lord Atkin left open the possibility that the trade and commerce power could also have sustained the legislation, but he did not pursue this line of reasoning: [1931] A.C. 310, 326.

administer the Combines Investigation Act and conferred upon the Commission some new powers. One of the new powers was that of "advance clearance", under which the Commission could approve of certain agreements or practices and relieve them from prosecution. This power was held to be unconstitutional by the Supreme Court of Canada,[12] and the appeal to the Privy Council did not include that part of the decision. The Privy Council upheld the validity of the investigatory and prosecutorial powers of the Commission.[13]

Another statute enacted in 1935 was a prohibition of anti-competitive price discrimination which was added to the Criminal Code. This was upheld by the Privy Council as a criminal law.[14] In 1951, the federal Parliament prohibited resale price maintenance. This was upheld by the Supreme Court of Canada as a criminal law.[15] In 1952, the federal Parliament authorized the courts to make orders prohibiting the continuation of illegal practices or dissolving illegal mergers, in addition to their power to impose conventional criminal sanctions. The constitutionality of a prohibition order was challenged in *Goodyear Tire and Rubber Co. v. The Queen* (1956)[16] and upheld by the Supreme Court of Canada as within the criminal law power.

Canada's competition law[17] was radically altered by two phases of amendment, the first enacted in 1975 and the second in 1986. In 1975, the Combines Investigation Act was expanded to apply to the service industries.[18] The Restrictive Trade Practice Commission, which had formerly had only powers of inquiry, report and recommendation, was given the power to make orders compelling the cessation of certain anti-competitive practices. A new civil remedy was added to the Act. In 1986, the name of the Act was changed from the Combines Investigation Act to the Competition Act. The Restrictive Trade Practices Commission was replaced by the Competition Tribunal, which has only adjudicative functions. The Tribunal has power to make a variety of orders, including the cessation of certain anti-competitive trade practices, the prohibition of mergers or their approval subject to conditions, the divestiture of assets or shares, the dissolution of amalgamations, and consent orders.

---

[12]*Dominion Trade and Industry Comm. Act*, [1936] S.C.R. 379.

[13]*A.-G. Ont. v. A.-G. Can.* (Canada Standard Trade Mark) [1937] A.C. 405, varying judgment in previous note; this case also upheld, under the trade and commerce power, the creation of a national trade mark: see ch. 20, Trade and Commerce, under heading § 20:4, "General trade and commerce".

[14]*A.-G. B.C. v. A.-G. Can.* (Price Spreads) [1937] A.C. 368.

[15]*R. v. Campbell* (1965), 58 D.L.R. (2d) 673 (S.C.C.), affg. (1964) 46 D.L.R. (2d) 83 (Ont. C.A.).

[16]*Goodyear Tire and Rubber Co. v. The Queen*, [1956] S.C.R. 303.

[17]The current law is the Competition Act, R.S.C. 1985, c. C-34, as renamed and amended by S.C. 1986, c. 26, Part II. The Competition Tribunal is established by the Competition Act, S.C. 1986, c. 26, Part I. See W. Grover and R. Kwinter, "The New Competition Act" (1987) 66 Can. Bar Rev. 267.

[18]In *A.-G. Can. v. Law Society of B.C.*, [1982] 2 S.C.R. 307, 358 the Court upheld the extension of s. 32 of the Act to service industries as valid "criminal legislation", although the Court went on to hold that s. 32 did not apply to the Law Society of B.C.

These powers cannot be upheld as criminal law, because the Tribunal is not a court of criminal jurisdiction, and the orders can be made without any prior conviction for a criminal offence. Indeed, the provisions of the Act that are enforced by the Tribunal are civil: they do not carry a criminal sanction.

Although many anti-competitive practices are now de-criminalized, criminal sanctions have been retained for some practices. Obviously, however, the criminal aspect of the Act is greatly diminished in importance, and the criminal law power no longer provides a constitutional foundation for much of the Act. In the United States, the Sherman Act has been upheld under the commerce clause.[19] Canada's counterpart is the trade and commerce power, and the Supreme Court of Canada has now held that the trade and commerce power does provide the constitutional basis for the Act.

The Supreme Court of Canada's ruling came in *General Motors v. City National Leasing* (1989).[20] The case involved the civil remedy in the Act, which had been added in 1975. The civil remedy allowed any person who had suffered loss as a result of a breach of the Act to sue the person who committed the breach in a court of competent jurisdiction to recover damages for the loss. The civil remedy was not premised on the conviction of the defendant for a criminal offence, and it was not awarded by a court of criminal jurisdiction. The remedy was available to a private plaintiff in a court of civil jurisdiction in an ordinary action, and was governed by the civil rules of evidence and procedure. The criminal law power could not sustain such a proceeding.[21] Nevertheless, the Supreme Court of Canada upheld the constitutionality of the civil remedy. The Court held that the Act was a valid law under the trade and commerce power.[22] There was no reason, therefore, why its enforcement should be limited to criminal sanctions. The civil remedy was a valid part of the law, because it was designed to provide an incentive to private enforcement of the law, as a supplement to public enforcement.

The *City National Leasing* case did not address the validity of the extensive powers of the Competition Tribunal. The case actually arose before 1986, when those powers were added to the Act. However, the Court emphasized that the Act was an integrated regulatory scheme, and it is safe to assume that all parts, including the 1986 amendments, can be supported under the trade and commerce power. The resolution of this issue has not immunized the Act from constitutional attack, however. Charter attacks on the Tribunal, the investigatory powers in the Act and some of the criminal offences have met with success.[23] The constitutional battles to achieve an effective competition law never seem to end.

---

[19]J.E. Nowak and R.O. Rotunda, Constitutional Law (West, 7th ed., 2004), ch. 4.

[20]*General Motors v. City National Leasing*, [1989] 1 S.C.R. 641.

[21]See § 18:17, "Criminal law and civil remedy".

[22]For more discussion, see ch. 20, Trade and Commerce, under heading § 20:4, "General trade and commerce".

[23]E.g., *Hunter v. Southam*, [1984] 2 S.C.R. 145 (striking down search and seizure

X. SUNDAY OBSERVANCE LAW

§ 18:12 Federal power

The observance of days of religious significance[1] is obviously a matter upon which attitudes will vary from one locality to another. Moreover, limitations on work or play, albeit with religious motivation, could easily be regarded as in relation to civil rights or local matters in the province, and penalties could be justified under s. 92(15).[2] For these reasons, before 1903 it was generally assumed that laws regarding Sunday observance were competent to the provinces. That assumption was shattered by the Privy Council in *A.-G. Ont. v. Hamilton Street Railway* (1903),[3] in which Ontario's Lord's Day Act was struck down as a criminal law. This holding was re-affirmed, and indeed somewhat extended, by the Supreme Court of Canada in the *Henry Birks* case (1955),[4] in which a provincial law, which authorized a municipal by-law requiring the closing of shops on six days recognized as holy days by the Roman Catholic church, was held to be in the same category as a Sunday observance law and therefore unconstitutional. These cases establish that limitations on work or play which are imposed for religious reasons are criminal laws solely within the competence of the federal Parliament.

After the decision in the *Hamilton Street Railway* case, the federal Parliament moved to fill the void created by the invalidation of provincial Sunday observance laws. In 1906, the Parliament enacted the Lord's Day Act, which prohibited work and other commercial activities on Sunday (which the Act described as "the Lord's Day"). The Act included ingenious provisions enabling the provinces to "opt out" of the prohibitions if they chose. These opting out provisions were upheld under constitutional challenge in *Lord's Day Alliance of Canada v. A.-G. B.C.* (1959).[5] The basic prohibitions of the Lord's Day Act were not vulnerable to challenge—at least, not until after the enactment of the Charter of Rights, when they were challenged. In *R. v. Big M Drug Mart* (1985),[6] the Supreme Court of Canada confirmed that the Lord's Day Act was a

---

provisions of the pre-1986 Act); *Thomson Newspapers v. Can.*, [1990] 1 S.C.R. 425 (narrowly upholding examination for discovery provisions); *Stelco v. Can.*, [1990] 1 S.C.R. 617 (ditto); *Can. v. NutraSweet Co.* (1990), 32 C.P.R. (3d) 1 (Comp. Trib.) (upholding Tribunal); *Alex Couture v. A.G. Can.* (1991), 83 D.L.R. (4th) 577 (Que. C.A.) (upholding Tribunal); *R. v. Wholesale Travel Group*, [1991] 3 S.C.R. 154 (striking down part of false advertising offence); *R. v. N.S. Pharmaceutical Society*, [1992] 2 S.C.R. 606 (upholding conspiracy offence). For a survey, see M. Jamal, "Constitutional Issues in Canadian Competition Litigation" (2004) 41 Can. Bus. L.J. 66.

[Section 18:12]

[1]See K.M. Lysyk, Comment (1966) 2 U.B.C. L. Rev. 59, 60; R. Curtis, "Sunday Observance Legislation in Alberta" (1974) 12 Alta. L. Rev. 236.

[2]§ 18:20, "Provincial power to enact penal laws".

[3]*A.-G. Ont. v. Hamilton Street Railway*, [1903] A.C. 524.

[4]*Henry Birks & Sons v. Montreal*, [1955] S.C.R. 799.

[5]*Lord's Day Alliance of Canada v. A.-G. B.C.*, [1959] S.C.R. 497; see ch. 14, Delegation, under heading § 14:17, "Conditions as legislative inter-delegations".

[6]*R. v. Big M Drug Mart*, [1985] 1 S.C.R. 295; see ch. 42, Religion, under heading

valid exercise of the criminal law power, because it pursued the religious purpose of preserving the sanctity of the Christian sabbath.[7] The law came within the typically criminal purposes stipulated by Rand J. in the *Margarine Reference*,[8] because it was intended to safeguard morality.

The religious purpose that gave the Lord's Day Act its criminal character was of course essential to its validity as an enactment of the federal Parliament. Absent a religious purpose, the requirement of a uniform day of rest would be outside federal competence, for reasons that are elaborated in the next paragraph. But the same religious purpose that breathed life into the Act under the criminal law power was the kiss of death under the Charter of Rights. The Supreme Court of Canada in the *Big M* case held that the Act offended the Charter guarantee of freedom of religion, because its purpose was to compel the observance of the Christian sabbath. Moreover, a law that pursued a purpose so contradictory of Charter values could not be justified under s. 1. The Court accordingly held that the Lord's Day Act was unconstitutional.

§ 18:13 Provincial power

The provinces have the authority to regulate the conduct of most business or recreation in the province, along with labour relations, as matters of property and civil rights or local matters in the province. This authority certainly extends to the imposition of limits on hours of work for labour,[1] and in *Lieberman v. The Queen* (1963)[2] it was held that provincial authority also extends to the imposition of limits on the business hours of commercial establishments. In *Lieberman*, the Supreme Court of Canada upheld a provincial law which required the closing of pool rooms and bowling alleys between midnight and six a.m. on any weekday, and all day on Sunday. The Court sustained a conviction for operating a bowling alley on a Sunday. The Court distinguished *Hamilton Street Railway, Henry Birks* and other Sunday observance cases on the ground that the prohibition in those cases had a religious motivation, whereas the prohibition in *Lieberman*, including the special rule for Sunday, was "primarily concerned . . . with secular matters".[3] Ritchie J., who wrote the opinion of the Court, did not explain what could be the "secular" purpose of a prohibition of business on Sunday which did not apply to any other day of the week. Nor did he explain how the dominant purpose of such a prohibition was to be ascertained.

Provincial power to enact Sunday closing laws was attacked anew af-

§ 42:4, "Freedom of religion".

[7] *R. v. Big M Drug Mart*, [1985] 1 S.C.R. 295, 354.

[8] *Can. Federation of Agriculture v. A.-G. Que.*, [1949] S.C.R. 1, 50.

[Section 18:13]

[1] *Reference re Legislative Jurisdiction over Hours of Labour*, [1925] S.C.R. 505; *A.-G. Can. v. A.-G. Ont.* (Labour Conventions) [1937] A.C. 326.

[2] *Lieberman v. The Queen*, [1963] S.C.R. 643.

[3] *Lieberman v. The Queen*, [1963] S.C.R. 643, 649.

ter the enactment of the Charter of Rights. In *R. v. Edwards Books and Art* (1986),[4] the Supreme Court of Canada followed *Lieberman* to hold that a law providing a "pause day" for secular purposes "is properly characterized as relating to property and civil rights in the province".[5] The Court held that an Ontario law that prohibited retail stores from opening on Sundays had the requisite secular purpose: while Sunday had historically become accepted as the common pause day for religious reasons, the purpose of Ontario's law was now the secular one of providing a uniform pause day for retail workers. The Court made reference to statements in the legislative history of the Act to infer its secular purpose. *Edwards Books* thus confirmed that, provided the provinces proposed and enacted Sunday-closing laws in language that was secular, the provinces had recovered the power that they were denied in the *Hamilton Street Railway* case.[6]

In *Edwards Books*, the principal ground of attack on Ontario's Sunday-closing law was based on the Charter guarantee of freedom of religion. The Court held that, although the purpose of the law was secular, the *effect* of the law was to limit freedom of religion. However, the secular purpose of the law was an objective that could form the basis of justification under s. 1; and the Court held that the Act was justified under s. 1. The secular purpose thus distinguished the case from *Big M*, where the Court had refused to uphold the law under s. 1. In *Edwards Books*, the law was upheld.[7]

XI. GUN CONTROL

§ 18:14 Gun control

Canada's Criminal Code for many years before 1995 restricted access to guns, prohibiting some kinds of guns (mainly automatic weapons) and restricting others (mainly handguns) with registration and licensing requirements. In 1995, the federal Parliament amended the Criminal Code provisions by enacting the Firearms Act, which expanded the existing rules by requiring *all* guns to be registered and *all* gun owners to be licensed. The province of Alberta referred this Act to its Court of Appeal for a ruling on constitutionality, and, when the Act was upheld, appealed the decision to the Supreme Court of Canada. The Supreme Court of Canada in *Re Firearms Act* (2000)[1] held that the Act was a valid exercise of the criminal law power. The purpose of the Act was to restrict access to inherently dangerous things. The legislative history revealed a concern with violent crime, domestic violence, suicides and ac-

[4] *R. v. Edwards Books and Art*, [1986] 2 S.C.R. 713.

[5] *R. v. Edwards Books and Art*, [1986] 2 S.C.R. 713, 740–741.

[6] *A.-G. Ont. v. Hamilton Street Railway*, [1903] A.C. 524.

[7] Sunday-closing is discussed in more detail in ch. 42, Religion, under heading § 42:5, "Sunday observance".

[Section 18:14]

[1] *Re Firearms Act*, [2000] 1 S.C.R. 783. The unanimous opinion was the opinion of "the Court".

cidents, all of which could be facilitated or worsened by ready access to guns. The Act's requirements were all directed to public safety. The licensing criteria, for example, included checks of criminal records, past violent behaviour and mandatory safety courses. The registration provisions required each gun to be identified by serial number and connected with a licensed holder. The registration provisions were not concerned with priority between competing property interests in guns like a provincial property registry. It was true that guns were property, but the Act's focus on public safety distinguished the Act from provincial property registration schemes. The effect on property was incidental to the main purpose of public safety. The Court held as well that the Act was not merely regulatory.[2] Its provisions were enforced by the criminal-law means of a prohibition and penalty, because the Act prohibited possession of a gun without a licence and a registration certificate, and imposed penalties for breach of the prohibition.[3]

XII. PREVENTION OF CRIME

§ 18:15 Prevention in general

A law may be validly enacted "in relation to" the criminal law, although the law itself does not have the characteristics of a criminal law.[1] This would be true, for example, of a law which simply repealed a criminal law. Its most important application, however, is in support of laws aimed at the prevention of crime,[2] for example, binding over a person to keep the peace or controlling the possession of guns.[3] There is no doubt that laws of this kind are valid, although they depart from the traditional format of criminal law. The same rationale of prevention has been held to justify a provision in the Combines Investigation Act

---

[2]See § 18:19, "Criminal law and regulatory authority".

[3]There was a sequel to the *Firearms Reference*, which considered a constitutional issue that arose from the partial repeal of the gun-control regime: see *Que. v. Can. (Firearms Sequel)*, [2015] 1 S.C.R. 693, discussed in sec. § 18:19, "Criminal law and regulatory authority".

[Section 18:15]

[1]So held in *Que. v. Can. (Firearms Sequel)*, [2015] 1 S.C.R. 693, 2015 SCC 14, para. 43; the case is discussed in § 18:19, "Criminal law and regulatory authority", note 22 below.

[2]Laskin, Canadian Constitutional Law (5th ed., 1986 by Finkelstein), 850. The provinces may enact laws with a similar purpose so long as they can be classified as in relation to a provincial matter such as property use: *Bedard v. Dawson*, [1923] S.C.R. 681 (closing "disorderly" houses); or administration of justice: *Di Iorio v. Montreal Jail Warden*, [1978] 1 S.C.R. 152 (inquiry into organized crime); or the regulation of business: *N.S. Bd. of Censors v. McNeil*, [1978] 2 S.C.R. 662 (movie censorship); or the regulation of the municipal public domain (parks and streets): *A.-G. Can. and Dupond v. Montreal*, [1978] 2 S.C.R. 770 (temporary prohibition of assemblies and parades).

[3]*A.G. Can. v. Pattison* (1981), 123 D.L.R. (3d) 111 (Alta. C.A.). Note however that in *Re Firearms Act*, [2000] 1 S.C.R. 783, the Supreme Court of Canada did not rely on prevention of crime as the basis of upholding the 1995 federal gun control law as criminal law.

authorizing the courts to make orders prohibiting future conduct which would constitute an offence under the Act.[4]

The Criminal Code includes an elaborate regime of assessment, treatment and disposition to deal with accused persons who suffer from mental disorders. The first group covered by the regime is made up of accused who have been tried but found "not criminally responsible on account of mental disorder". (This group used to be described as acquitted on account of insanity.) The preventive aspect of the criminal law power permits the continued detention of these NCR offenders, despite the fact that they have not been convicted of any crime.[5] However, the role of the criminal law extends only to those NCR offenders who present a significant threat to society. "Once an NCR accused is no longer a significant threat to public safety, the criminal justice system has no further application."[6] The second group covered by the Criminal Code regime is made up of accused who have been charged, but who have not been tried on the ground that they are "unfit to stand trial" by reason of mental disorder. They remain in the criminal justice system, not because they pose a significant threat to public safety, but because they are subject to an unresolved criminal charge. It is the criminal procedure aspect of the criminal law power, not the preventive aspect, that permits the continued detention of accused who are unfit to stand trial.[7]

§ 18:16 Young offenders

For similar reasons, the federal Juvenile Delinquents Act was upheld under the criminal law power, despite its express stipulation that juvenile delinquents were not to be treated as "criminals", but were to be "subjected to such wise care, treatment and control as will tend to check their evil tendencies and strengthen their better instincts."[1] In 1984, the Juvenile Delinquents Act was replaced by the Young Offenders Act, which was "more closely tailored to our traditional conception of the criminal law", although it still pursued a similar curative and preven-

[4] *Goodyear Tire and Rubber Co. v. The Queen*, [1956] S.C.R. 303, 308–309.

[5] The automatic, indefinite detention of NCR offenders was struck down on Charter grounds in *R. v. Swain*, [1991] 1 S.C.R. 933. The assessment, treatment and disposition regime that was enacted following *Swain* was upheld against Charter attack in *Winko v. B.C.*, [1999] 2 S.C.R. 625.

[6] *Winko v. B.C.*, [1999] 2 S.C.R. 625, para. 33.

[7] *R. v. Demers*, [2004] 2 S.C.R. 489, paras. 22–24. While upholding the unfit-to-stand-trial provisions under the criminal law power (LeBel J. dissenting on that point), the Court went on to hold that the absence of any power to discharge the accused person who was permanently unfit to stand trial, and who was not a significant threat to public safety, was a breach of the accused's liberty interest under s. 7 of the Charter. This power has since been added to the Criminal Code.

[Section 18:16]

[1] *A.-G. B.C. v. Smith*, [1967] S.C.R. 702. But a provision in the Act purporting to authorize a court to order a municipality to contribute to the support of a delinquent child is invalid as going beyond the scope of criminal law: *Regional Municipality of Peel v. MacKenzie*, [1982] 2 S.C.R. 9.

tive philosophy.[2] In pursuit of that philosophy, the Young Offenders Act made provision for diversion programmes under which young offenders could be diverted away from the criminal courts and not subjected to traditional criminal sanctions. These programmes were upheld as an exercise of the preventive aspect of the criminal law power.[3] In 2003, the Young Offenders Act was replaced by the Youth Criminal Justice Act,[4] which makes more detailed provision for diversion of less serious offences, including specific provisions for non-judicial measures such as police warnings and cautions and referral to community programmes in place of charges. With respect to more serious offences, the Act makes provision for young offenders to be given adult sentences, although young offenders cannot be tried in adult court.[5] All young offenders are tried in Youth Justice Courts and the determination of whether an adult sentence should be imposed is made by the judge at the end of the trial.[6]

XIII. CRIMINAL LAW AND CIVIL REMEDY

§ 18:17 Federal power generally to create civil remedies

This section of the chapter will examine the extent to which the federal Parliament's criminal law power will authorize the creation of a civil right of action for breach of a criminal statute. But first it is appropriate to comment on the broader question of the federal Parliament's power to create a civil right of action under other heads of federal power.

The federal Parliament has no independent power to create civil remedies akin to its power over criminal law. This means that if the pith and substance of a federal law is the creation of a new civil cause of action, the law will be invalid as coming within the provincial head of power "property and civil rights in the province" (s. 92(13)). In *MacDonald v. Vapor Canada* (1976),[1] the Supreme Court of Canada held that s. 7(e) of the federal Trade Marks Act was invalid on this basis. Section 7(e) prohibited business practices "contrary to honest industrial or commercial usage in Canada." A later section of the Act authorized a court to grant civil relief—injunction, damages or accounting of profits—for

---

[2]*R. v. S.(S.)*, [1990] 2 S.C.R. 254, 279 (upholding validity of Act, following *Smith).*

[3]*R. v. S.(S.)*, [1990] 2 S.C.R. 254, 282. The validity of provincial legislation making non-criminal and non-curial provision for young offenders was left open in *A.-G. Que v. Lechasseur*, [1981] 2 S.C.R. 253, 259 (diversion procedure under Quebec's Youth Protection Act rendered inoperative through paramountcy on laying of charge under federal Criminal Code).

[4]S.C. 2002, c. 1.

[5]Where the Youth Criminal Justice Act is silent, the Criminal Code applies, including the right of the Attorney General to prefer a direct indictment against an accused, which denies the young person a preliminary inquiry: *R. v. S.J.L.-G.*, [2009] 1 S.C.R. 426.

[6]But note that it is a breach of fundamental justice for the Act to impose on a convicted youth the onus of avoiding an adult sentence by establishing that a youth sentence would be sufficient to make him accountable: *R. v. D.B.*, [2008] 2 S.C.R. 3.

[Section 18:17]

[1]*MacDonald v. Vapor Canada*, [1977] 2 S.C.R. 134.

breach of s. 7(e). The Act did not provide a criminal sanction for breach of s. 7(e).[2] Laskin C.J. for the majority of the Court described s. 7(e) as essentially an extension of tortious liability, which therefore came within property and civil rights in the province.[3]

Where the pith and substance of a federal law is not the creation of a civil remedy, but is some other matter within federal power, there is no reason to doubt the validity of a civil remedy provided for enforcement of the law. The remedy is valid as incidental to the main purpose of the law. This point emerges clearly from Laskin C.J.'s opinion in *Vapor*. He was at pains to emphasize that s. 7(e) was a "detached provision", and was not part of a broader regulatory scheme.[4] He contrasted another provision in the same Act which provided "for enforcement of its trade mark provisions at the suit of an injured person",[5] and he clearly assumed that the trade-mark civil remedy was valid.[6] There is also a dictum in the *Vapor* case to the effect that a civil remedy could be associated with patent or copyright laws,[7] and federal patent[8] and copyright[9] laws do of course confer civil rights of action on persons injured by their breach. Although the reasoning behind the *Vapor* dicta is not spelled out, the assumption is that a law validly enacted in relation to trade marks (trade and commerce power),[10] or patents (s. 91(22)) or copyrights (s. 91(23)) may validly include appropriate means of enforcement.[11]

The cases upholding the corollary relief provisions of the federal Divorce Act of 1968 are suggestive. In *Papp v. Papp* (1969),[12] the issue was whether the Divorce Act could validly provide for the custody of the children of a dissolved marriage. It was clearly established that custody of children was a matter coming within property and civil rights in the province, and until 1968 custody had been exclusively regulated by the

[2]The Criminal Code, R.S.C. 1985, c. C-46, s. 126, does impose a penalty for breach of any federal law that does not include its own penalty provision. The argument that s. 126 converted s. 7(e) into a criminal law was peremptorily rejected by the Court: [1977] 2 S.C.R. 134, 145.

[3]*MacDonald v. Vapor Canada*, [1977] 2 S.C.R. 134, 149 ("simply a formulation of the tort of conversion, perhaps writ large and in a business context"), 165 ("supplementing existing tort liability"). Laskin C.J.'s opinion was written for six judges, de Grandpré J. wrote a separate concurring opinion for three judges which agreed with Laskin C.J.'s conclusion and did not indicate any disagreement with Laskin C.J.'s reasoning.

[4]*MacDonald v. Vapor Canada*, [1977] 2 S.C.R. 134, 165.

[5]*MacDonald v. Vapor Canada*, [1977] 2 S.C.R. 134, 142.

[6]*MacDonald v. Vapor Canada*, [1977] 2 S.C.R. 134, 172.

[7]*MacDonald v. Vapor Canada*, [1977] 2 S.C.R. 134, 172.

[8]Patent Act, R.S.C. 1985, c. P-4, ss. 54–60.

[9]Copyright Act, R.S.C. 1985, c. C-42, ss. 34–41.

[10]See ch. 20, Trade and Commerce, under heading § 20:4, "General trade and commerce".

[11]So held in *Kirkbi v. Ritvik Holdings*, [2005] 3 S.C.R. 302 (upholding civil remedy for passing off in the federal Trade-marks Act).

[12]*Papp v. Papp*, [1970] 1 O.R. 331 (C.A.).

provinces. Nevertheless, Laskin J.A., sitting alone as the Ontario Court of Appeal, upheld the custody provisions of the federal Divorce Act. They were valid, he held, because there was a "rational, functional connection" between them and the admittedly valid provisions of the Act concerning divorce.[13] In a series of subsequent cases, *Papp v. Papp* has been followed and its reasoning also used to uphold the provisions of the Divorce Act providing for the maintenance of children and spouses and for alimony, despite the fact that maintenance and alimony would in other contexts come within property and civil rights in the province.[14]

Since *Papp v. Papp*, the Supreme Court of Canada has used the functional connection test to uphold a civil remedy in federal corporation law, against persons who engage in insider trading,[15] a civil remedy in federal competition law, against persons who engage in anti-competitive practices,[16] and a civil remedy in federal trade mark law, against persons who pass off their products as those of a trade mark holder.[17] There are also other cases in which civil rights of action in federal statutes have been upheld: a right of action for loss of services to the federal Crown against a person who injures a member of the armed forces;[18] the extension of the civil liability of the federal Crown;[19] a right of action in a "common informer" to recover penalties for bribery in a federal election;[20] a right of action for breach of the federal Railway Act;[21] a provision prohibiting railway companies from contracting out of their liability for negligence;[22] a provision imposing a limitation period on actions against railway companies;[23] a provision limiting the tortious liability of shipowners;[24] and a provision providing a cause of action to the dependants of a deceased victim in fatal accidents occurring in navigable waters.[25]

---

[13] *Papp v. Papp*, [1970] 1 O.R. 331, 336 (C.A.).

[14] The cases are discussed in ch. 27, The Family.

[15] *Multiple Access v. McCutcheon*, [1982] 2 S.C.R. 161.

[16] *General Motors v. City National Leasing*, [1989] 1 S.C.R. 641; and see discussion at § 18:11 note 20, above.

[17] *Kirkbi v. Ritvik Holdings*, [2005] 3 S.C.R. 302; and see discussion in ch. 15, Judicial Review on Federal Grounds, under heading § 15:24, "Ancillary power".

[18] *Nykorak v. A.-G. Can.*, [1962] S.C.R. 331.

[19] Ch. 10, The Crown.

[20] *Doyle v. Bell* (1884), 11 O.A.R. 326 (C.A.).

[21] *Curran v. Grand Trunk Ry. Co.* (1898), 25 O.A.R. 407 (Ont. C.A.).

[22] *Grand Trunk Ry. Co. v. A.-G. Can.*, [1907] A.C. 65.

[23] *Greer v. C.P.R.* (1915), 51 S.C.R. 338; *Can. Northern Ry. Co. v. Pszenicnzy* (1916), 54 S.C.R. 36; *Williams v. CNR* (1976), 75 D.L.R. (3d) 87 (N.S. A.D.). However, a federal limitation period on common law actions against railway companies has been held to be ultra vires as an invasion of property and civil rights in the province: *Clark v. CNR*, [1988] 2 S.C.R. 680, (reading down limitation period to cover only civil causes of action created by the Railway Act; obiter dictum at p. 710 that such causes of action are valid).

[24] *Whitbread v. Walley*, [1990] 3 S.C.R. 1273.

[25] *Ordon Estate v. Grail*, [1998] 3 S.C.R. 437.

§ 18:18 Criminal law power to create civil remedies

Does the criminal law power, like the other heads of federal power, authorize the federal Parliament to confer a civil right of action for breach of a statutory prohibition? This issue is more difficult, because the criminal law power differs from the other heads of federal power in that the criminal law power, by its very nature, contemplates public rather than private enforcement.

In *R. v. Zelensky* (1978),[1] the Supreme Court of Canada, by a majority of six to three, upheld a provision of the Criminal Code that authorized a criminal court, upon convicting an accused of an indictable offence, to order the accused to pay to the victim compensation for any loss or damage caused by the commission of the offence. This power to award compensation had three civil characteristics: (1) the order was to be made, not at the request of the prosecutor or at the initiative of the court, but only on the application of the victim; (2) the amount of compensation was to be related, not to the degree of blameworthiness of the accused, but to the value of the victim's loss; and (3) the order was to be enforced, not by the state as a fine would be, but by the victim as if it were a civil judgment. The civil characteristics of the compensation provision persuaded Pigeon J., writing for three dissenting judges, that the provision could not be upheld as criminal law. But Laskin C.J., writing for the majority, emphasized the "criminal" characteristics of the provision. The order for compensation was to be made as part of the sentencing process in the criminal proceedings, not in a separate civil action. As well, the order was discretionary, unlike an award of damages in a successful civil action. Indeed, Laskin C.J. held that this was a case where the trial judge should not have exercised his discretion to make the order.[2] There was dispute as to the appropriate amount of compensation, and Laskin C.J. held that this dispute could only be satisfactorily resolved in a separate civil action, in which the parties would have the benefit of discovery and production of documents and a proper trial of issues bearing on the quantum of the defendant's liability. The absence of such procedures from a criminal trial did not make the power to award compensation unconstitutional, but it did call for restraint in its exercise.[3]

What *Zelensky* does not decide is whether the federal Parliament

[Section 18:18]

[1]*R. v. Zelensky*, [1978] 2 S.C.R. 940.

[2]This made a ruling on the constitutional question unnecessary. However, the Court decides constitutional issues that go beyond the necessity of the case even more frequently than it articulates the alleged rule that the Court ought not to do so.

[3]Although the constitutional ruling in *Zelensky* applied only to s. 653 (now s. 738) of the Criminal Code, Laskin C.J. (at p. 946) assumed the validity of the restitution provision in s. 655 (now s. 738) of the Code, and it is clear that other sections of the Code providing for compensation or restitution are valid as well: J.C. MacPherson, "The Constitutionality of the Compensation and Restitution Provisions of the Criminal Code" (1979) 11 Ottawa L. Rev. 713. Forfeiture of property used in the commission of a criminal offence was upheld in *Industrial Acceptance Corp. v. The Queen*, [1953] 2 S.C.R. 273;

could authorize a person, who had suffered loss as the result of the breach of a criminal law, to bring a separate civil action to recover damages (or other relief) outside the criminal process.[4] The civil remedy[5] could not, of course, be the only sanction for breach of a criminal statute: the presence of traditional criminal sanctions as the primary mode of enforcement would be essential to the classification of the statute as a criminal law.[6] But it does not follow that the criminal law power will never authorize the creation of a civil remedy. Such a simple proposition ignores the fundamental principle that laws are classified in accordance with their pith and substance, and the corollary that a law which is valid under the pith and substance test may incidentally affect matters which ordinarily lie outside the power of the enacting body.[7] Where a federal statute with all the traditional characteristics of a criminal law purports to confer a civil right of action as a supplementary mode of enforcement, the question of the validity of the civil remedy should depend upon the answer to the question that was posed in *Papp v. Papp*, namely, whether there is a "rational, functional connection between what is admittedly good [the prohibition coupled with a penalty] and what is challenged [the civil remedy]". However, it must be acknowledged that the fact that the Court divided in *Zelensky*, and the emphasis in the majority opinion of the fact that the compensation order was a discretionary part of the sentencing process, suggest that the Court will

see also *R. v. Manning*, [2013] 1 S.C.R. 3, 2013 SCC 1 (upholding forfeiture of truck driven while committing offence of impaired driving; no constitutional question considered). Forfeiture of property representing the proceeds of crime in the hands of a third party was upheld in *R. v. Rosenblum* (1998), 167 D.L.R. (4th) 639 (B.C.C.A.). An order prohibiting the repetition of criminal conduct was upheld in *Goodyear Tire and Rubber Co. v. The Queen*, [1956] S.C.R. 303.

[4]The federal Competition Act contains just such a provision, but in *General Motors v. City National Leasing*, [1989] 1 S.C.R. 641, where the provision was upheld, the Court avoided this issue by holding that the Act was valid under the trade and commerce power, not the criminal law power.

[5]A related issue is whether there is any constitutional bar to the courts inferring a civil right of action for breach of a federal statute that provides only for criminal penalties. There are conflicting dicta on this issue: *Transport Oil Co. v. Imperial Oil Co.*, [1935] O.R. 215, 219 (C.A.); *Direct Lumber Co. v. Western Plywood Co.*, [1962] S.C.R. 646, 649. However, since these dicta were uttered, the Supreme Court has held that a judicially-inferred civil right of action for breach of a statute arises from the common law tort of negligence, not from the statute: *The Queen (Can.) v. Sask. Wheat Pool*, [1983] 1 S.C.R. 205. Although no constitutional conclusions were drawn in this case, the reasoning would free the federal Parliament from responsibility for the new cause of action and would seem to finesse any constitutional problem. If this is so, however, it means in practice that the federal Parliament may do indirectly (create a civil cause of action by silence through judicial interpretation) what it perhaps may not do directly (create a civil cause of action by express words). This is an argument in favour of a liberal view of the Parliament's ancillary criminal law power (discussed in following text).

[6]*MacDonald v. Vapor Canada*, [1977] 2 S.C.R. 134.

[7]Ch. 15, Judicial Review on Federal Grounds.

be unwilling to uphold a separate civil right of action as ancillary to a criminal law.[8]

XIV. CRIMINAL LAW AND REGULATORY AUTHORITY

§ 18:19 Criminal law and regulatory authority

The question to be considered here is whether the criminal law power will sustain the establishment of a regulatory scheme in which an administrative agency or official exercises discretionary authority. A criminal law ordinarily consists of a prohibition which is to be self-applied by the persons to whom it is addressed. There is not normally any intervention by an administrative agency or official prior to the application of the law. The law is "administered" by law enforcement officials and courts of criminal jurisdiction only in the sense that they can bring to bear the machinery of punishment after the prohibited conduct has occurred. Lord Atkin's definition of a criminal law as a prohibition coupled with a penalty[1] suggested that these formal characteristics were essential to any law which could be classified as criminal.[2]

The competition and insurance cases encourage the view that the criminal law power will not sustain a regulatory scheme which relies upon more sophisticated tools than a simple prohibition and penalty. It will be recalled from the earlier consideration of federal competition law that in the two cases where the law vested prohibitory or regulatory powers in an administrative agency, the courts held that these powers could not be sustained as criminal law.[3] The insurance cases present a similar picture. After the Privy Council had struck down a federal statute purporting to regulate by licensing the insurance industry, the Parliament added a section to the Criminal Code making it an offence to carry on the business of insurance without a licence from the Minister of Finance. The Privy Council held that the pith and substance of the new law was the establishment of licensing authority in the Minister of

---

[8]Compare *Regional Municipality of Peel v. McKenzie*, [1982] 2 S.C.R. 9 (Parliament cannot require municipalities to contribute to support of delinquent child, as ancillary to criminal law power).

[Section 18:19]

[1]*P.A.T.A. v. A.-G. Can.*, [1931] A.C. 310, 324.

[2]The contrast here is with a regulatory law. Some kinds of laws, e.g., those aimed at the prevention of crime, may be valid laws "in relation to" the criminal law without conforming to the traditional format: see § 18:15, "Prevention of crime".

[3]*Re Board of Commerce Act*, [1922] 1 A.C. 191; *Reference re Dominion Trade and Industry Comm. Act*, [1936] S.C.R. 379; and see § 18:10, "Competition Law". It should be noted that s. 96 and associated provisions of the Constitution Act, 1867 would not be an impediment, because those provisions do not restrain the federal Parliament in the establishment of federal courts or tribunals; but if the authority vested in the tribunal were characterized as "criminal jurisdiction", the questions would arise whether the federal Parliament had constituted a court of criminal jurisdiction, and if so whether it had the power to do so: see ch. 19, Criminal Justice, under heading §§ 19:2 to 19:5, "Courts of criminal jurisdiction".

Finance and accordingly struck down the law as a colourable attempt to do indirectly what the Parliament could not do directly.[4]

In *Nova Scotia Board of Censors v. McNeil* (1978),[5] the Supreme Court of Canada, by the narrow majority of five to four, held that the censorship of films was not criminal. The Court upheld Nova Scotia's censorship law as being the regulation of an industry within the province (property and civil rights under s. 92(13)) or a local or private matter under s. 92(16). Laskin C.J. for the minority held that the law was invalid as being a criminal law. Ritchie J. for the majority pointed out that the censorship law did not take the criminal form of a prohibition coupled with a penalty. On the case law to this point, Ritchie J. had the better argument. The salient characteristic of censorship is an administrative process that imposes a prior restraint on material deemed by the censorship tribunal to be offensive. There is, of course, always a prohibition, coupled with a penalty, on the sale or exhibition of uncensored material, but this is designed to enforce recourse to the administrative process. It is true that the suppression of ideas that are contrary to current morality[6] is a typically criminal objective, but the prior case-law indicated a requirement of form as well as a typically criminal objective.

The Criminal Code used to contain an abortion provision which took the form of a prohibition coupled with a dispensation. Abortion was prohibited with a dispensation for abortions approved by the therapeutic abortion committee of a hospital. In 1988, that law was held to be unconstitutional on Charter grounds.[7] There had been a pre-Charter challenge on federalism grounds, which was rejected in *Morgentaler v. The Queen* (1975).[8] In the latter case, only Laskin C.J. addressed himself to the point now in issue, asserting that "Parliament may determine what is not criminal as well as what is, and may hence introduce dispensations or exemptions in its criminal legislation".[9] This view appears to be too sweeping, since an elaborate regulatory scheme may easily be cast in the form of a "dispensation" or "exemption" from a "criminal" law. Indeed, this was the mechanism unsuccessfully employed to regulate

[4] *A.-G. Ont. v. Reciprocal Insurers*, [1924] A.C. 328.

[5] *Nova Scotia Board of Censors v. McNeil*, [1978] 2 S.C.R. 662.

[6] Since the adoption of the Charter of Rights in 1982, Ontario's censorship law has been successfully challenged as abridging freedom of expression under s. 2(b) of the Charter: *Re Ont. Film and Video Appeciation Society and Ont. Bd. of Censors* (1984), 45 O.R. (2d) 80 (C.A.).

[7] Bill C-43, to re-criminalize abortion, but with a less restrictive law, was passed by the House of Commons, but defeated by the Senate on a 43-43 tie vote at third reading on January 31, 1991.

[8] *Morgentaler v. The Queen*, [1976] 1 S.C.R. 616.

[9] *Morgentaler v. The Queen*, [1976] 1 S.C.R. 616, 626–627. Laskin C.J.'s opinion was dissenting, but on the constitutionality of the abortion law the Court was unanimous, although the majority did not express any reasons on the point. Compare *Lord's Day Alliance v. A.-G. B.C.*, [1959] S.C.R.497, discussed in ch. 14, Delegation, under heading § 14:17, "Conditions as legislative inter-delegation".

the insurance industry.[10] Perhaps the required qualification is simply that of colourability: the more elaborate the regulatory scheme, the more likely it is that the Court will classify the dispensation or exemption as being regulatory rather than criminal.[11]

In *R. v. Furtney* (1991),[12] a challenge was mounted against the Criminal Code provisions respecting lotteries. The Code prohibited lotteries, but made an exception for organizations licensed by the Lieutenant Governor in Council of a province. The five accused were licensed to conduct lotteries, but they were alleged to have violated the conditions stipulated in their provincial licences, which limited the profits that could be made by management. The Supreme Court of Canada held that the Criminal Code provision was a valid criminal law, despite the fact that it delegated regulatory power to the provincial Lieutenant Governor in Council. Stevenson J. for the Court accepted the suggestion in an earlier edition of this book that colourability was the issue, and held that "the decriminalization of lotteries licensed under prescribed conditions is not colourable".[13] He viewed the licensing provisions as constituting "a definition of the crime, defining the reach of the offence"; and he held that it was "a constitutionally permissive exercise of the criminal law power, reducing the area subject to criminal law prohibition where certain conditions exist".[14]

The Canadian Environmental Protection Act is a federal law that establishes a scheme for (among other things) the regulation of toxic substances. The Ministers of Environment and Health have authority to examine the effects of any substance and to recommend to the Governor in Council that the substance be classified as "toxic", which involves a finding that the substance is harmful to the environment or a danger to human health. Once classified as toxic, the substance comes under the regulatory authority of the Governor in Council, which may make regulations governing its release into the environment, and the manner and conditions under which it can be manufactured, imported, processed, transported, stored, sold, used and discarded. Where a substance has not yet been classified as toxic, but either Minister believes that immediate action is called for with respect to the substance, the Minister may make an "interim order" without following the full procedure of classification. The interim order is temporary, but may contain any regulation that could be imposed on a toxic substance. A breach of a regulation or an interim order is an offence punishable by fine or imprisonment.

---

[10] *A.-G. Ont. v. Reciprocal Insurers*, [1924] A.C. 328.

[11] Compare *R. v. Cosman's Furniture* (1976), 73 D.L.R. (3d) 312 (Man. C.A.) (upholding federal Hazardous Products Act as criminal law); *R. v. Malmo-Levine*, [2003] 3 S.C.R. 571 (upholding Narcotic Control Act as criminal law).

[12] *R. v. Furtney*, [1991] 3 S.C.R. 89.

[13] *R. v. Furtney*, [1991] 3 S.C.R. 89, 106.

[14] *R. v. Furtney*, [1991] 3 S.C.R. 89, 106.

In *R. v. Hydro-Québec* (1997),[15] Hydro-Québec was prosecuted for violating an interim order that restricted the emission of a substance (chlorobiphenyls or PCBs) to one gram per day. The corporation argued that the Act, and therefore the interim order, was outside the criminal law power of the federal Parliament. The argument was accepted by Lamer C.J. and Iacobucci J., who wrote for the four dissenting judges. In their view, although the protection of the environment was a legitimate purpose for a criminal law, this Act lacked the prohibitory character of a criminal law. There was no prohibition until the administrative process to classify the substance (or to make an interim order) had been completed, and "it would be an odd crime whose definition was made entirely dependent on the discretion of the Executive".[16] The dissenters were also troubled by a provision of the Act that exempted a province from a regulation if that province already had an equivalent law in place; they pointed out that such an exemption "would be a very unusual provision for a criminal law".[17] But La Forest J., writing for the majority, upheld the Act as a criminal law. In his view, because the administrative procedure for assessing the toxicity of substances culminated in a prohibition enforced by a penal sanction, the scheme was sufficiently prohibitory. And he characterized the exemption for provinces with equivalent provincial laws as recognizing the reality that much of the field of environmental protection is effectively concurrent. In the end, the Act was upheld as a criminal law, and the trend of the modern cases to permit an extensive degree of regulation under the criminal law power was emphatically reinforced.

In *Re Firearms Act* (2000),[18] a challenge was mounted to Canada's gun control legislation, which is part of the Criminal Code. The main techniques of control consisted of requirements to register all firearms and to license all firearms owners. The Supreme Court of Canada held that the purpose of gun control was public safety, which was a typically criminal purpose. The purpose was ultimately effected by a prohibition of unregistered guns and unlicensed holders, and the prohibition was backed by penalties. However, it was argued that the Act was regulatory rather than criminal legislation, because of the complexity of the regime and the discretionary powers vested in the licensing and registration authorities. Only an outright prohibition of guns, it was argued, would be a valid criminal law. The Court relied on its prior decision in *R. v. Hydro-Québec*[19] for the proposition that the criminal law power authorizes complex legislation, including discretionary administrative

---

[15]*R. v. Hydro-Québec*, [1997] 3 S.C.R. 213. The majority opinion was written by La Forest J. with the agreement of L'Heureux-Dubé, Gonthier, Cory and McLachlin JJ. The dissenting opinion was written by Lamer C.J. and Iacobucci J. with the agreement of Sopinka and Major JJ.

[16]*R. v. Hydro-Québec*, [1997] 3 S.C.R. 213, para. 55.

[17]*R. v. Hydro-Québec*, [1997] 3 S.C.R. 213, para. 57.

[18]*Re Firearms Act*, [2000] 1 S.C.R. 783. The unanimous opinion was the opinion of "the Court".

[19]*R. v. Hydro-Québec*, [1997] 3 S.C.R. 213.

authority. And the Court relied on its prior decision in *RJR-MacDonald v. Canada*[20] for the proposition that a criminal purpose may be pursued by indirect means. Just as the health risks of tobacco did not require the outright banning of cigarettes, nor did the safety risks of guns require the outright banning of guns. Measures that would indirectly advance the legislative purpose, such as the advertising ban in *RJR-MacDonald* or the licensing and registration requirements of the gun control legislation, were authorized by the criminal law power.[21]

There was an interesting sequel to the *Firearms Reference.* After a change of government in 2006, the Conservative government of Prime Minister Harper introduced into Parliament a bill to repeal the portion of the gun-control regime that covered "long guns". Quebec, whose police forces had been making use of the long-gun registry, announced that it would establish a provincial registry for the long guns, which the province would undoubtedly have the power to do under its power over property and civil rights in the province. The province asked the federal government to hand over the Quebec data now collected in the long-gun registry. The federal government not only refused the request, it amended the bill to add a provision requiring the destruction of all the long-gun data "as soon as feasible"! The bill was enacted with the destruction provision, and Quebec brought proceedings to challenge the constitutionality of the destruction provision. In *Quebec v. Canada (Firearms Sequel)* (2015),[22] the Supreme Court, by a majority, upheld the provision. The Court accepted that the purpose of the destruction provision "may well have been to prevent Quebec from creating its own long-gun registry",[23] but they upheld the provision nonetheless. The Court reasoned that the long-gun registry had been established under the federal criminal law power, and it could be repealed under the same power.[24] The repeal could validly include the destruction provision: "The power to repeal a criminal law provision must logically be wide enough to give Parliament the power to destroy the data collected for the purpose of a criminal law provision."[25] The Court rejected Quebec's argument that, in the circumstances of this case, the criminal law power was

---

[20] *RJR-MacDonald v. Canada*, [1995] 3 S.C.R. 199.

[21] By the same token, measures that appear criminal, but are enacted to achieve indirectly a noncriminal purpose, are outside the criminal law power: *Ward v. Can.*, [2002] 1 S.C.R. 569 (prohibition on sale of baby seals really intended to protect the fishery).

[22] *Quebec v. Canada (Firearms Sequel)*, [2015] 1 S.C.R. 693, 2015 SCC 14. Cromwell and Karakatsanis JJ. wrote the opinion of the five-judge majority. LeBel, Wagner and Gascon (with Abella J.) wrote a dissenting opinion.

[23] *Quebec v. Canada (Firearms Sequel)*, [2015] 1 S.C.R. 693, 2015 SCC 14, para. 38.

[24] *Quebec v. Canada (Firearms Sequel)*, [2015] 1 S.C.R. 693, 2015 SCC 14, para. 43.

[25] *Quebec v. Canada (Firearms Sequel)*, [2015] 1 S.C.R. 693, 2015 SCC 14, para. 43. The majority went on to point out (para. 44) that the provinces would lack the power to destroy the data contained in a federally enacted long gun registry; and therefore, if Parliament lacked the power to do so (as Quebec argued), no legislative body could do so. This would be contrary to the principle that the Constitution Act, 1867 "provides for a complete division of powers between both orders of governments".

constrained by an unwritten constitutional principle of "cooperative federalism".[26]

In *Re Assisted Human Reproduction Act* (2010),[27] Parliament, acting under its criminal law power, enacted an Act to regulate the practices and technologies associated with assisted human reproduction. Some of the provisions of the Act were absolute prohibitions, for example, of human cloning, the creation of human embryos for a purpose other than creating a human being, the determination of an embryo's sex for non-medical reasons, the payment of consideration to surrogate mothers, the purchase of human sperm or ova, and the sale or purchase of human embryos. Other prohibitions (which can be called the qualified prohibitions) were qualified by exceptions. Still other prohibitions (referred to in the Act as "controlled activities") applied to activities unless they were carried out in accordance with regulations made under the Act, under licence and in licensed premises. These included altering, manipulating, storing, transferring, destroying, importing and exporting human embryos or other human reproductive material, combining the human genome with that of another species, and reimbursing expenses incurred by the donor of sperm or ova or a surrogate mother. All the prohibitions were backed by penalties. The Act included the power to make regulations and established the Assisted Human Reproduction Agency of Canada to administer the licensing and regulatory functions. Quebec directed a reference to its Court of Appeal to challenge the constitutionality of most of the Act, including the qualified prohibitions and the controlled activities. (Together, these can be called the challenged provisions.) The absolute prohibitions were conceded to be valid criminal law and were not challenged. The Quebec Court of Appeal accepted Quebec's arguments and held that all of the challenged provisions were unconstitutional. The Government of Canada appealed to the Supreme Court of Canada.

McLachlin C.J., with the support of three other judges, would have upheld the Act in its entirety under the criminal law power. In her view, the Act consisted of prohibitions that were either absolute in the case of conduct that was always reprehensible or qualified in the case of conduct

---

[26] *Quebec v. Canada (Firearms Sequel)*, [2015] 1 S.C.R. 693, 2015 SCC 14, paras. 15–21. The dissenting minority accepted this argument. They took the view that the establishment of the long gun registry, although based on federal legislation, involved a "partnership" with the provinces (who were responsible for much of the administration), and the termination of the registry had to respect the principle of cooperative federalism by not destroying the collected data until it had been offered to any province that wanted to continue the registry under provincial law. Because the destruction provision in the Act was not qualified in this way, the dissenters would have struck it down.

[27] *Re Assisted Human Reproduction Act*, [2010] 3 S.C.R. 457. The Court split in three ways, McLachlin C.J., with the support of Binnie, Fish and Charron JJ., would have upheld the Act in its entirety. LeBel and Deschamps JJ., with the support of Abella and Rothstein JJ., would have struck down all but the absolute prohibitions of the Act. Cromwell J. occupied a middle ground, partly agreeing with the LeBel/Deschamps opinion and partly with the McLachlin opinion. Only Cromwell J.'s opinion attracts a majority of the Court. One of the co-authors of this book (Peter Hogg) was co-counsel for the Attorney General of Canada on the appeal to the Supreme Court.

that was generally reprehensible but was beneficial in the exceptional or licensed situations contemplated by the Act. She cited *Hydro-Quebec*[28] for the proposition that: "The complexity of modern problems often requires a nuanced scheme consisting of a mixture of absolute prohibitions, selective prohibitions based on regulations, and supporting administrative provisions."[29] The purpose of these various prohibitions was to safeguard morality, public health and the personal security of donors, donees and persons not yet born. For her, therefore, the requirements of a valid criminal law—(1) prohibition, (2) penalty, and (3) typical criminal purpose—were satisfied. In light of the decided cases, especially *Hydro-Quebec*, her opinion seemed to be the correct answer to the constitutional question, but it only attracted the support of four judges.

LeBel and Deschamps JJ., with the approval of two others, held (in essential agreement with the Quebec Court of Appeal) that what Parliament had enacted as a single Act was, for constitutional purposes, two Acts: the absolute prohibitions were prohibitions of reprehensible practices and were properly classified as criminal law, but the qualified prohibitions and controlled activities—those subject to exceptions or to regulatory or licensing requirements—were in relartion to the promotion of beneficial practices and outside the realm of criminal law.[30] The pith and substance of the qualified prohibitions and controlled activites was "the regulation of assisted human reproduction as a health service".[31] This matter fell within exclusive provincial jurisdiction over hospitals, the medical profession, property and civil rights and local matters. LeBel and Deschamps JJ. regarded most of the Act as "colourable", although they did not use that word. They said that "Parliament has therefore made a specious attempt to exercise its criminal law power by merely juxtaposing provisions falling within provincial jurisdiction with others that in fact relate to the criminal law".[32] And they added that "Parliament's intention was to enact legislation in relation to a matter outside its jurisdiction".[33] This opinion also had the support of only four judges.

Cromwell J., writing alone, said that he disagreed with "the results proposed by both the Chief Justice and by Justices LeBel and

---

[28] *R. v. Hydro-Québec*, [1997] 3 S.C.R. 213.

[29] *Re Assisted Human Reproduction Act*, [2010] 3 S.C.R. 457, para. 36.

[30] This involved a considerable contraction of the received scope of the criminal law power, discussed in § 18:2, "Definition of criminal law" at footnote 31.

[31] [2010] 3 S.C.R. 457, para. 227. In fact, assisted human reproduction is not a "health service" in any obvious sense. While the Act applied to some procedures that are performed by doctors in hospitals, the Act also applied to scientists, researchers, technicians, laboratories, clinics, sperm banks, donors of sperm or ova, surrogate mothers, persons who seek to exploit women and children or who seek to profit from selling the means to the artificial creation of life—as well as healthy persons seeking assistance to have children.

[32] *Re Assisted Human Reproduction Act*, [2010] 3 S.C.R. 457, para. 278; it would appear that the word spécieux in the French version, which is "specious" in the English version, is often translated as colourable.

[33] *Re Assisted Human Reproduction Act*, [2010] 3 S.C.R. 457, para. 280.

Deschamps".[34] He could not accept the McLachlin criminal classification for the entire Act, but he also thought that the LeBel-Deschamps health-service classification for the challenged provisions was too narrow. In his view, the pith and substance of the challenged provisions was the "regulation of virtually every aspect of research and clinical practice in relation to assisted human reproduction".[35] However, he agreed with LeBel and Deschamps JJ. that this was a matter that came within exclusive provincial jurisdiction over hospitals, the medical profession, property and civil rights and matters of a local nature. He parted company with LeBel and Deschamps JJ. only with respect to three provisions which they would have struck down, but which he thought should be upheld as criminal law because they were prohibitions of negative practices associated with assisted human reproduction.[36] For those three provisions, Cromwell J. added his (fifth) vote to the McLachlin four to uphold the provisions. For the other challenged provisions, Cromwell J. added his (fifth) vote to the LeBel-Deschamps four to strike down the provisions.

In the result, the absolute and qualified prohibitions in the Act were upheld as criminal law, but the controlled activities and the licensing and regulatory scheme that supported some of the controlled activities were mostly struck down. As a matter of policy, the result is unfortunate. At the time of the Supreme Court hearing only one province, Quebec, had enacted a statute to regulate assisted human reproduction—and that statute was passed only after Quebec brought the reference to challenge the federal Act. None of the other provinces had sought to regulate the field and six provinces did not even intervene in the reference. It seems likely that in some provinces there will be no legislation, and therefore no regulatory oversight of practices that may be unsafe for the biological mother, the surrogate or the eventual offspring.[37] Persons desperate to have children may be undeterred by these risks and attracted to those provinces. The solution of a comprehensive national regime for assisted human reproduction has been ruled out by the Court.

---

[34] *Re Assisted Human Reproduction Act*, [2010] 3 S.C.R. 457, para. 282.

[35] *Re Assisted Human Reproduction Act*, [2010] 3 S.C.R. 457, para. 285.

[36] *Re Assisted Human Reproduction Act*, [2010] 3 S.C.R. 457, paras. 288–291, upholding s. 8 (use of reproductive material without donor's consent), s. 9 (use of sperm or ova from a person under 18, except for the purpose of creating a human being who will be raised by the donor), and s. 12 (reimbursement of expenses incurred by donor or surrogate, except in accordance with the regulations and a licence). The first two provisions (ss. 8 and 9) are the qualified prohibitions. The last provision (s. 12) was one of the controlled activities.

[37] Of course, the medical profession will continue to be governed by the provincial Colleges of Physicians and Surgeons, but there is a lack of agreed-upon standards specific to assisted human reproduction and medical oversight is traditionally focused on the welfare of the patient (rather than eventual offspring). In any event, the Colleges have no jurisdiction over many of the actors (and institutions) who are involved in assisted human reproduction (§ 18:19 note 26), for example, the technicians who create in vitro embryos, test them, freeze them and store them.

XV. PROVINCIAL POWER TO ENACT PENAL LAWS

§ 18:20 Provincial power to enact penal laws

At the beginning of this chapter, it was explained that the provincial Legislatures have the power under s. 92(15) of the Constitution Act, 1867 to impose "punishment by fine, penalty or imprisonment" for the purpose of enforcing otherwise valid provincial laws.[1] This ancillary power would no doubt have been read into the Constitution by the courts if it had not been expressly included, because it is obvious that the provinces require the power to use penalties for enforcement of their legislation. However, the power requires the courts to draw a distinction between a valid provincial law with an ancillary penalty and a provincial law which is invalid as being in pith and substance a criminal law. The elusiveness of that distinction creates uncertainty about the scope of provincial power under s. 92(15) as well as the scope of federal power under s. 91(27).

The dominant tendency of the case law has been to uphold provincial penal legislation. In *Bedard v. Dawson* (1923),[2] the Supreme Court of Canada upheld a provincial law authorizing the closing of "disorderly houses", which were primarily defined as houses in respect of which there had been Criminal Code convictions for gambling or prostitution. On the face of it, the provincial law appeared to be simply supplementing undoubted criminal laws by adding new penalties, but the Court upheld the law as in relation to the use of property, and at most as aimed at suppressing the conditions likely to cause crime rather than at the punishment of crime.[3] In *Provincial Secretary of Prince Edward Island v. Egan* (1941),[4] the Supreme Court of Canada upheld a provincial law automatically suspending the driver's licence of anyone convicted of the Criminal Code's impaired driving offences. The Court held that the provincial law was in relation to the regulation of highway traffic and

[Section 18:20]

[1]Section 92(15) seems to place no limit on the severity of the sanction provided it is limited to "fine, penalty or imprisonment": *R. v. Wason* (1890), 17 O.A.R. 221, 250 (C.A.) (obiter dictum that s. 92(15) confers "power to inflict penalty without limit in amount, and imprisonment without limit in duration"); *R. v. Chief* (1963), 42 D.L.R. (2d) 712, affd. (1964) 44 D.L.R. (2d) 108 (Man. C.A.) (maximum five years' imprisonment upheld); *Re Skelley and the Queen* (1982), 140 D.L.R. (3d) 186 (B.C. C.A.) (mandatory imprisonment for seven or fourteen days upheld). This phrase is broad enough to include forfeiture of property: *R. v. Nat Bell Liquors Ltd.*, [1922] 2 A.C. 128, 138; but its language excludes some kinds of sanctions, for example, capital punishment: Laskin, Canadian Constitutional Law (5th ed., 1986 by Finkelstein), 851.

[2]*Bedard v. Dawson*, [1923] S.C.R. 681.

[3]Legislation for the prevention of crime is within the power of the federal Parliament, but there is an extensive area of concurrency flowing from provincial authority over the administration of justice, property, local businesses, roads, and other local institutions: see heading § 18:15 "Prevention in general".

[4]*Provincial Secretary of Prince Edward Island v. Egan*, [1941] S.C.R. 396.

therefore within provincial competence.[5] A paramountcy argument was also resolved in favour of the provincial law.

A series of cases in the 1960s were even more generous to provincial power. Provincial offences of careless driving,[6] failing to remain at the scene of an accident[7] and furnishing false information in a prospectus[8] were each upheld. In each case there existed in the Criminal Code a very similar federal offence, and in each case the Criminal Code offence was upheld as a valid criminal law. Moreover, as we have noticed in an earlier chapter, in each case the existence of similar federal and provincial laws was not regarded by the Court as an inconsistency which would render the provincial law inoperative under the doctrine of paramountcy.[9] The result is that over much of the field which may loosely be thought of as criminal law legislative power is concurrent.

The tendency to uphold provincial penal laws has continued. We have already noticed that in *N.S. Board of Censors v. McNeil* (1978),[10] provincial film censorship was upheld over a dissent by Laskin C.J., who regarded censorship as a matter coming within criminal law. In *A.-G. Can. and Dupond v. Montreal* (1978),[11] a municipal by-law prohibiting all assemblies, parades or gatherings in the public domain (parks and streets) of Montreal was upheld. Beetz J., for a majority of six judges, held that the by-law was a valid regulation of the municipal public domain, and that its purpose was not punitive, but preventive of public disturbances.[12] Laskin C.J., for a minority of three judges, again dissented on the ground that the by-law was a criminal law: in his view, the by-law did not have a regulatory purpose, but was simply addressed to apprehended breaches of the peace and the maintenance of public order—exclusively criminal concerns.[13]

Laskin C.J.'s view of the criminal law power as a substantial limitation on provincial power to enact penal laws finds little support in the

[5]The opinions are unspecific as to the appropriate provincial head of power; the opinions of Duff C.J., Hudson and Taschereau JJ. assert the existence of provincial power without reference to any head of s. 92, while that of Rinfret C.J. suggests three heads, namely, ss. 92(9), 92(13) and 92(16) (but not, curiously, s. 92(10)). See also *Buhlers v. B.C.* (1999), 170 D.L.R. (4th) 344 (B.C.C.A.) (upholding provincial law empowering police officer to cancel driver's licence of person failing breathalyser test; no particular head of provincial power identified).

[6]*O'Grady v. Sparling*, [1960] S.C.R. 804; *Mann v. The Queen*, [1966] S.C.R. 238.

[7]*Stephens v. The Queen*, [1960] S.C.R. 823.

[8]*Smith v. The Queen*, [1960] S.C.R. 776.

[9]Chapter 16, Paramountcy, under heading § 16:5, "Covering the field".

[10]*N.S. Bd. of Censors v. McNeil*, [1978] 2 S.C.R. 662.

[11]*A.-G. Can. and Dupond v. Montreal*, [1978] 2 S.C.R. 770.

[12]Now that the Charter of Rights is in force, such a by-law would be vulnerable as an abridgement of freedom of assembly under s. 2.

[13]Provincial power to enact penal laws was also upheld in *Montreal v. Arcade Amusements*, [1985] 1 S.C.R. 368 (regulation of location of video games); *Rio Hotel v. N.B.*, [1987] 2 S.C.R. 59 (prohibition of "nude entertainment" in taverns); *Devine v. Que.*, [1988] 2 S.C.R. 790 (requirement of French only in public signs); *Irwin Toy v. Que.*, [1989] 1 S.C.R. 927 (prohibition of advertising directed at children).

test at the police station, which can be demanded by a police officer under s. 254 of the Criminal Code. Under the Criminal Code, a breathalyser test that was failed at the roadside had to be confirmed at the police station. The provincial suspensions of driving privileges, which were premised on a fail score at the police station, have been held to be within provincial legislative power.[23] In 2010, British Columbia streamlined the process by imposing a 90-day driving suspension based on a fail score of the breathalyser test taken at the roadside, so that for the purpose of the provincial suspension it was unnecessary to take the driver to the police station to confirm the test result. As well as the driving suspension, the driver who registered a fail score was charged a variety of penalties and costs totaling over $4,000. This Automatic Roadside Prohibition (ARP) scheme was challenged in *Goodwin v. British Columbia* (2015)[24] on the ground that the law was outside the powers of the province because it was in pith and substance a criminal law.[25] The claimant's argument was that the purpose and effect of the provincial regime was to replace the Criminal Code's impaired driving provisions with a regime of automatic and severe penalties: crime control without the costs and delays of criminal-justice procedural protections; and this argument was supported by the fact that in British Columbia the police generally preferred to apply the provincial scheme rather than lay charges under the Criminal Code. The Supreme Court, in an opinion written by Karakatsanis J., rejected the argument. She acknowledged that the provincial law "targets, in part, specific criminal activity and imposes serious consequences, without the protections attendant on criminal investigations and prosecutions", but she pointed out that "the consequences relate to the regulation of driving privileges", and she characterized the pith and substance of the law as "the licensing of drivers, the enhancement of traffic safety, and the deterrence of persons from driving on highways when their ability is impaired by alcohol."[26] The regulation of highway traffic, including laws respecting drunk driving, and laws that rely incidentally on Criminal Code provisions (as this law did with respect to the breathalyser tests) was a matter within provincial competence, and it was no objection to the provincial law that "its purpose is to target conduct that is also captured by the Criminal Code."[27] The ARP scheme was held to be valid.

[23] *Buhlers v. Superintendent of Motor Vehicles (B.C.)* 1999 BCCA 0114; 119 B.C.A.C. 207 (B.C.C.A.).

[24] *Goodwin v. British Columbia*, [2015] 3 S.C.R. 250, 2015 SCC 46. Karakatsanis J. wrote the opinion of the majority. McLachlin C.J. wrote an opinion dissenting from the search and seizure holding of the majority.

[25] There were two other grounds of challenge, one based on s. 8 of the Charter, discussed in ch. 48, Unreasonable search and seizure, under heading § 48:30, "Regulatory inspections", and the other based on s. 11(d) of the Charter, discussed in ch. 51, Rights on being charged, under heading § 51:3, "Offence".

[26] *Goodwin v. British Columbia*, [2015] 3 S.C.R. 250, 2015 SCC 46, para. 29.

[27] *Goodwin v. British Columbia*, [2015] 3 S.C.R. 250, 2015 SCC 46, para. 32.

Chapter 20

Trade and Commerce

I. RELATIONSHIP TO PROPERTY AND CIVIL RIGHTS

§ 20:1 Relationship to property and civil rights

II. INTERPROVINCIAL OR INTERNATIONAL TRADE AND COMMERCE

§ 20:2 In the Privy Council
§ 20:3 In the Supreme Court of Canada

III. GENERAL TRADE AND COMMERCE

§ 20:4 General trade and commerce

IV. SPECIFIC TOPICS

§ 20:5 Specific topics

I. RELATIONSHIP TO PROPERTY AND CIVIL RIGHTS

§ 20:1 Relationship to property and civil rights

Section 91(2) of the Constitution Act, 1867 confers upon the federal Parliament the power to make laws in relation to "the regulation of trade and commerce".[1]

The generality of the language of s. 91(2) contrasts with the restrictive language of the commerce power of the Congress of the United States: "to regulate commerce with foreign nations, and among the several States, and with the Indian tribes".[2] Despite its broader language, the Canadian trade and commerce clause has turned out to be a much more limited power than its American cousin.[3] The divergence in result

---

[Section 20:1]

[1]See Laskin, Canadian Constitutional Law (5th ed., 1986 by Finkelstein), ch. 8; Monahan, Constitutional Law (2nd ed., 2002), ch. 9.

[2]Constitution of the United States, art. 1, s. 8(3).

[3]For example, the United States Congress has more extensive powers than the Canadian Parliament over anti-trust, insurance, labour, marketing, securities regulation and transportation and communication. These comparisons are made in the appropriate places in this text. At a technical level, the key to the difference lies in the absence from the Constitution of the United States of any state power equivalent to Canada's s. 92(13). The states possess no enumerated powers, simply an undefined plenary power recognized by the tenth amendment. There is, therefore, no principled way to limit the

is the product of judicial interpretation, which in Canada has narrowed the scope of the clause, and in the United States has expanded it.[4]

The interpretative problem for Canada lay in the accommodation of the federal power over "the regulation of trade and commerce" (s. 91(2)) with the provincial power over "property and civil rights in the province" (s. 92(13)). On the face of it, these powers appear to overlap. Trade and commerce is carried on by means of contracts which give rise to "civil rights" over "property". However, the courts, by a process of "mutual modification",[5] have narrowed the two classes of subjects so as to eliminate the overlapping and make each power exclusive. The leading case is *Citizens' Insurance Co. v. Parsons* (1881),[6] in which the issue was the validity of a provincial statute which stipulated that certain conditions were to be included in all fire insurance policies entered into in the province. The Privy Council, speaking through Sir Montague Smith, held that the statute was a valid law in relation to property and civil rights in the province. It did not come within the federal trade and commerce power, because that power should be read as not including "the power to regulate by legislation the contracts of a particular business or trade, such as the business of fire insurance in a single province".[7] What the phrase "the regulation of trade and commerce" did include was "political arrangements in regard to trade requiring the sanction of Parliament, regulation of trade in matters of inter-provincial concern, and it may be that they would include general regulation of trade affecting the whole dominion".[8]

Since the *Parsons* case, it has been accepted that, in general,

---

reach of the commerce clause or of the Congress's other enumerated powers. However, the Supreme Court of the United States has held that federal laws that have little connection to commercial activity cannot be sustained under the commerce clause: *United States v. Lopez* (1995), 514 U.S. 549 (striking down federal prohibition of firearms in "school zones"); *United States v. Morrison* (2000), 529 U.S. 598 (striking down federal law providing civil remedy for victims of gender-motivated violence); *National Federation of Independent Businesses v. Sebelius* (2012), 567 U.S. xxx (upholding federal law mandating the purchase of health insurance, but as a tax, not as an exercise of the commerce clause). Despite these decisions, the American commerce clause remains a much broader power than the Canadian trade and commerce power, reflecting, no doubt, the prevalence in the United States of a much more centralized conception of federalism: *Gonzales v. Raich* (2005), 545 U.S. 1 (upholding federal prohibition on growing and possession of marihuana for personal medicinal purposes).

[4]For comparisons, see Smith, The Commerce Power in Canada and the United States (1963); Mackinnon, Comparative Federalism (1964); S.F. Ross, "Insights from Canada for American Constitutional Federalism" (2014) 16 U. Penn. J. Constitutional Law 891. In Australia, the commerce clause (Constitution s. 51(1)) is very similar to the American clause, but it has not received a similarly expansive interpretation, partly because of s. 92, guaranteeing freedom of interstate trade. For comparison, see Gilbert, Australian and Canadian Federalism 1867–1984 (1986), chs. 4, 5.

[5]Mutual modification is discussed in ch. 15, Judicial Review on Federal Grounds, under heading § 15:23, "Exclusiveness".

[6]*Citizens' Insurance Co. v. Parsons* (1881), 7 App. Cas. 96.

[7]*Citizens' Insurance Co. v. Parsons* (1881), 7 App. Cas. 96, 113.

[8]*Citizens' Insurance Co. v. Parsons* (1881), 7 App. Cas. 96, 113.

intraprovincial trade and commerce is a matter within provincial power, under "property and civil rights in the province" (s. 92(13)),[9] and the federal trade and commerce power is confined to (1) interprovincial or international trade and commerce, and (2) "general" trade and commerce. Each of these categories will be considered in turn.

II. INTERPROVINCIAL OR INTERNATIONAL TRADE AND COMMERCE

§ 20:2 In the Privy Council

The history of the trade and commerce power closely parallels the history of the peace, order, and good government power.[1] In many of the most important constitutional cases, both the peace, order, and good government power and the trade and commerce power were relied upon, and many of the cases examined in the earlier chapter on peace, order, and good government will accordingly be encountered again in this chapter. Like the peace, order, and good government power, the trade and commerce power was severely contracted by the Privy Council, but has been permitted to expand somewhat by the Supreme Court of Canada since the abolition of appeals to the Privy Council.

The *Parsons* case did not define when trade and commerce became sufficiently interprovincial so as to come within the federal power. This definition was left to the Haldane period. The *Insurance Reference* (1916)[2] set the pattern. The federal Insurance Act of 1910 purported to establish a licensing regime for insurance companies, other than provincial companies carrying on business wholly within the province of incorporation. The exemption emphasized that the aim of the Act was to impose federal regulation on an industry which spread across the country without regard for provincial boundaries. But the Privy Council held that the scope of the industry or of particular companies was irrelevant. Viscount Haldane said:[3]

> It must now be taken that the authority to legislate for the regulation of trade and commerce does not extend to the regulation by a licensing system of a particular trade in which Canadians would otherwise be free to engage in the provinces.

---

[9]It has been suggested that the appropriate head of power is "matters of a merely local or private nature in the province" (s. 92(16)), because "legislation on 'trade' is not on civil rights as such, and especially so where in the Act the two subjects are expressly differentiated": I.C. Rand, Foreword to Smith, The Commerce Power in Canada and the United States (1963), xii; *Re Farm Products Marketing Act*, [1957] S.C.R. 198, 211–212. The more usual attribution has been to s. 92(13).

[Section 20:2]

[1]Ch. 17, Peace, Order, and Good Government.

[2]*A.-G. Can. v. A.-G. Alta.* (Insurance) [1916] 1 A.C. 588.

[3]*A.-G. Can. v. A.-G. Alta.* (Insurance) [1916] 1 A.C. 588, 596. Other attempts by the federal Parliament to regulate the insurance industry were also struck down as colourable versions of what had previously been held invalid: see ch. 21, Property and Civil Rights, under heading §§ 21:5 to 21:7, "Insurance".

The trade and commerce power was also rejected as a support for the legislation in the *Board of Commerce* case (1922).[4] The legislation there included anticombines provisions, and also provisions regulating hoarding and excessive prices of certain "necessaries of life" (food, clothing and fuel). In argument, Viscount Haldane suggested that the trade and commerce power had no independent content and could be invoked only as ancillary to other federal powers.[5] In his actual opinion, Viscount Haldane dismissed the trade and commerce power in one uninformative sentence: s. 91(2) "did not, by itself, enable interference with particular trades in which Canadians would, apart from any right of interference conferred by these words above [p.o.g.g.], be free to engage in the Provinces".[6] The ancillary theory of the trade and commerce power was repeated in *Toronto Electric Commissioners v. Snider* (1925),[7] where the power was again rejected, this time as a support for federal labour laws.[8] In these two cases, the interprovincial character of the laws resided in the fact that they attempted to control, not particular trades, but more general aspects of the economy—combinations, prices, labour—which were governed by economic forces that ignored provincial boundaries. But the pervasiveness and interdependence of the legislations' subject matters was not sufficient to carry them out of property and civil rights and into the federal fold.

In the *P.A.T.A.* case (1931),[9] the Privy Council through Lord Atkin upheld as a "criminal law" (s. 91(27)) a narrower form of anti-combines law (which had been redrafted following the *Board of Commerce* case). In an obiter dictum, Lord Atkin repudiated Viscount Haldane's ancillary theory of the trade and commerce power, saying that the words of s. 91(2) "must receive their proper construction where they stand as giving an independent authority to Parliament over the particular subject-matter".[10] However, he did not cast doubt on the results in *Board of Commerce* and *Snider*, and he expressly forbore from giving any rival definition to s. 91(2).[11]

Federal attempts to use the trade and commerce power to regulate marketing[12] were also struck down by the Privy Council, and by the

---

[4] *Re Board of Commerce Act*, [1922] 1 A.C. 191.

[5] Laskin, Canadian Constitutional Law (5th ed., 1986 by Finkelstein), 425.

[6] *Re Board of Commerce Act*, [1922] 1 A.C. 191, 198. See now *General Motors v. City National Leasing*, [1989] 1 S.C.R. 641; ch. 18, Criminal Law, under heading § 18:11, "Competition law".

[7] *Toronto Electric Commissioners v. Snider*, [1925] A.C. 396, 410.

[8] See ch. 21, Property and Civil Rights, under heading §§ 21:10 to 21:11, "Labour relations".

[9] *P.A.T.A. v. A.-G. Can.*, [1931] A.C. 310.

[10] *P.A.T.A. v. A.-G. Can.*, [1931] A.C. 310, 326.

[11] Lord Atkin did leave open the intriguing possibility that the *P.A.T.A.* legislation could have been upheld under s. 91(2), but he did not pursue the point: *P.A.T.A. v. A.-G. Can.*, [1931] A.C. 310, 326.

[12] See ch. 21, Property and Civil Rights, under heading §§ 21:12 to 21:14,

Supreme Court of Canada while still subject to appeals to the Privy Council. In *The King v. Eastern Terminal Elevator Co.* (1925),[13] the Supreme Court of Canada by a majority struck down a statute which regulated the grain trade. As is common knowledge (and was recognized by the judges in the case), very little of Canada's grain is consumed in the province of production, and the great bulk of it is exported. Nevertheless, the federal statute had to fasten onto some local operations, and in particular to license and regulate grain elevators, in order to make the scheme effective. The Court held that the regulation of local works, such as elevators, made the entire scheme invalid.[14] Similarly, in the *Natural Products Marketing Reference* (1937),[15] one of the "new deal" cases,[16] a statute was held invalid which provided for the establishment of marketing schemes for those natural products whose principal market was outside the province of production, or some part of which was for export. The Privy Council through Lord Atkin held that the entire statute was invalid because it included within its purview some transactions which could be completed within the province. That was a matter within property and civil rights in the province.

The Privy Council's last consideration of the trade and commerce power came in the *Margarine Reference* (1951),[17] in which their lordships held that a federal prohibition of the manufacture, sale or possession of margarine (for the purpose of protecting the dairy industry) was wholly invalid, because it proscribed not only interprovincial transactions but also transactions that could be completed within a province. A provision in the statute which prohibited the *importation* of margarine had been upheld by the Supreme Court of Canada as a valid exercise of the trade and commerce power.[18] The appeal to the Privy Council did not include the question of importation, and the Privy Council did not express any opinion on it; but there is no doubt that the federal trade and commerce power will authorize the regulation or prohibition[19] of the importation of goods into Canada.[20]

"Marketing".

[13]*The King v. Eastern Terminal Elevator Co.*, [1925] S.C.R. 434.

[14]This decision was overcome by the use of the declaratory power (s. 92(10)(c)). The federal Parliament enacted a statute declaring all grain elevators and warehouses to be for the general advantage of Canada: Canada Grain Act, S.C. 1926, c. 33, s. 234. A later form of this declaration was upheld in *Jorgenson v. A.-G. Can.*, [1971] S.C.R. 725 and *Chamney v. The Queen*, [1975] 2 S.C.R. 151. See ch. 22, Transportation and Communication, under heading § 22:10, "Works for the general advantage of Canada".

[15]*A.-G. B.C. v. A.-G. Can.* (Natural Products Marketing) [1937] A.C. 377.

[16]See ch. 17, Peace, Order, and Good Government, under heading § 17:7, "The non-emergency cases".

[17]*Can. Federation of Agriculture v. A.-G. Que.*, [1951] A.C. 179.

[18][1949] S.C.R. 1.

[19]There are dicta in early cases to the effect that the "regulation" of trade and commerce does not include its prohibition. Whatever validity this proposition may have in interpreting the powers of a municipality or administrative agency, it cannot be correct for s. 91(2), because it would leave a gap in legislative power: neither the Parliament nor

§ 20:3 In the Supreme Court of Canada

Since the abolition of appeals to the Privy Council there has been a resurgence of the trade and commerce power. A new attitude was discernible in the *Ontario Farm Products Marketing Reference* (1957),[1] a case concerning a provincial marketing statute, in which four judges indicated by implication that federal power would extend to some transactions which were completed within a province.[2] In *Murphy v. C.P.R.* (1958),[3] the Supreme Court of Canada upheld the validity of the federal Canadian Wheat Board Act, which provided for the compulsory purchase by the Canadian Wheat Board of all grain destined for markets outside the province of production, and for the marketing, pooling of proceeds and equalizing of the return to producers. The transaction which gave rise to the *Murphy* litigation was an interprovincial one—a shipment of grain from one province to another in violation of the Act. But in *R. v. Klassen* (1959),[4] the Manitoba Court of Appeal had to decide whether the Act could validly apply to a purely local work—a feed mill which processed locally-produced wheat and sold it as feed to local farmers. The Act imposed on producers, and enforced through elevators and mills, a quota system which was designed to ensure equal access to the interprovincial and export market; it also applied to local processing and sale so that a producer could not obtain an unfair advantage by selling grain in excess of his quota to a local mill for locally-sold flour, seed or feed. The Manitoba Court of Appeal held that the application of the Act to such intraprovincial transactions was valid. It was incidental to the principal purpose of the Act, which was to regulate the interprovincial and export trade in grain.

The *Klassen* decision was a striking departure from the course of

---

the Legislatures could prohibit interprovincial or international trade in a product. See Laskin, Canadian Constitutional Law (5th ed., 1986 by Finkelstein), 236.

[20] *Gold Seal Ltd. v. Dominion Express Co.* (1921), 62 S.C.R. 424; *Caloil v. A.-G. Can.*, [1971] S.C.R. 543. Custom duties may be justified under s. 91(2) or (3): *A.-G. B.C. v. A.-G. Can.* (Johnny Walker) [1924] A.C. 222. In *A.-G. Ont. v. A.-G. Can.* (Local Prohibition) [1896] A.C. 348, the Privy Council held that a provincial Legislature has no power to prohibit the importation of intoxicating liquor into the province. However, it has been held that a provincial law prohibiting (with certain exceptions) the possession of liquor not purchased from the provincial government's liquor store is valid, notwithstanding that it has the effect of prohibiting the importation of liquor into the province: *R. v. Gautreau* (1978), 88 D.L.R. (3d) 718 (N.B. A.D.); see also *R. v. Comeau*, [2018] 1 S.C.R. 342, para. 124 (noting that "[i]t is common ground that provinces are able to enact schemes to manage the supply of and demand for liquor within their borders") (citing *Air Canada v. Ont.*, [1997] 2 S.C.R. 581, para. 55; and *Gautreau*, this note).

[Section 20:3]

[1] *Ontario Farm Products Marketing Reference*, [1957] S.C.R. 198.

[2] *Ontario Farm Products Marketing Reference*, [1957] S.C.R. 198, 204, 209, 231; the passages are set out in full in *Carnation Co. v. Que. Agricultural Marketing Bd.*, [1968] S.C.R. 238, 245–246.

[3] *Murphy v. C.P.R.*, [1958] S.C.R. 626.

[4] *R. v. Klassen* (1959), 20 D.L.R. (2d) 406 (Man. C.A.); see Laskin, Comment (1959) 37 Can. Bar Rev. 630.

Privy Council decisions, which had consistently decided that federal regulation under the trade and commerce power could not embrace wholly intraprovincial transactions, even when the main object was to regulate the interprovincial or export trade. Yet the Supreme Court of Canada refused leave to appeal the decision. The new development suggested by *Klassen* was confirmed in *Caloil v. A.-G. Can.* (1971),[5] when the Supreme Court of Canada unanimously upheld a federal prohibition on the transportation or sale of imported oil west of the Ottawa Valley. The purpose was to protect the domestic industry in the West from the then cheaper imported product. This prohibition clearly caught many transactions which would otherwise have been completed within a province. Nevertheless, the law was upheld as "an incident in the administration of an extra-provincial marketing scheme" and as "an integral part of the control of imports in the furtherance of an extraprovincial trade policy".[6]

It is not easy to be confident about the implications of these cases. The commodities concerned—grain and oil—flow across provincial lines from the province of production or importation to the province of consumption or export.[7] The existence of this interprovincial flow enabled the courts to uphold the regulation of intraprovincial transactions on the ground that such regulation was incidental to the main object of regulating the interprovincial flow.[8] It is not yet clear to what extent interprovincial elements of a less obvious kind would provide support for federal regulation. Whenever a market for a product is national (or international) in size, as opposed to local, there is a strong argument that effective regulation of the market can only be national; and this is the position which has been effectively established in the United States.[9] The Canadian decisions do not yet go that far.

In *Re Agricultural Products Marketing Act* (1978),[10] a federal marketing statute was upheld. The statute was the federal element of interlock-

[5]*Caloil v. A.-G. Can.*, [1971] S.C.R. 543.

[6]*Caloil v. A.-G. Can.*, [1971] S.C.R. 543, 551 per Pigeon J. with whom Fauteux C.J., Abbott, Ritchie, Hall and Spence JJ. agreed; Laskin C.J., with whom Martland and Judson JJ. agreed, wrote a very brief separate concurring opinion emphasizing that the impugned law governed the importation of goods.

[7]So does natural gas, and the federal Parliament has power under s. 91(2) to regulate the price when the gas is sold outside the province of production: *Sask. Power Corp. v. TransCan. Pipelines* (1988), 56 D.L.R. (4th) 416 (Sask. C.A.).

[8]Under the double aspect doctrine, an expanded federal power need not entail a diminished provincial power. Yet the Supreme Court of Canada has severely curtailed the powers of the provinces to regulate the marketing of goods imported from outside the province: *A.-G. Man. v. Man. Egg and Poultry Assn.*, [1971] S.C.R. 689; *Burns Foods v. A.-G. Man.*, [1975] 1 S.C.R. 494; or to regulate the production or pricing of goods produced in the province but destined for out-of-province markets: *Can. Industrial Gas and Oil v. Govt. of Sask.*, [1978] 2 S.C.R. 545; *Central Can. Potash v. Govt. of Sask.*, [1979] 1 S.C.R. 42. Provincial power over marketing is discussed in ch. 21, Property and Civil Rights, under heading §§ 21:12 to 21:14, "Marketing".

[9]W.H. Riker, Federalism, Origin, Operation, Significance (Little, Brown, Boston, 1964), 7175.

[10]*Re Agricultural Products Marketing Act*, [1978] 2 S.C.R. 1198. I disclose that I

ing federal and provincial statutes (and regulations and orders) that together (1) established and empowered a national egg marketing agency and provincial egg marketing agencies; (2) controlled the supply of eggs by the imposition of quotas on each province and, within each provincial quota, on each producer; (3) provided for the disposal of the surplus product; and (4) imposed levies on producers to finance the cost of the scheme and especially the cost of surplus disposal. The federal agency was elected by all egg producers regardless of whether their business was interprovincial or local; federal quotas were based on volumes of production, not volumes entering interprovincial trade; the purchase and disposal of the surplus product by the federal agency was not confined to interprovincial trade; and federal levies were imposed on all producers, regardless of whether their production was destined for a local or out-of-province market. This intervention in local markets was especially heavy in that evidence showed that 90 per cent of all eggs produced in Canada were consumed within the province of production: it was cheaper to ship the feed for the birds than the fragile, perishable eggs.

On the face of it, the Supreme Court of Canada's decision to uphold the federal Act in *Re Agricultural Products Marketing Act* is a major expansion of federal power into local markets. However, the case is an unusual one, and may not be an important precedent. The Court[11] was impressed by the fact that the federal Act was the centrepiece of a cooperative scheme designed to rationalize the national market in eggs. The scheme had been agreed to by all eleven governments, and had been executed by complementary legislation in all eleven jurisdictions. Indeed, one of the provincial statutes—that of Ontario—was also in issue, and was also upheld. As Pigeon J. remarked with disarming frankness, it was "a sincere cooperative effort", and "it would really be unfortunate if this was all brought to nought".[12] A related factor was the extreme difficulty of disentangling the federal and provincial elements of the actual marketing plan for eggs that had been established, under the aegis of the statutes, by a complex undergrowth of regulations and orders emanating from the two levels of government. In these circumstances, it was understandable that the Court would place reliance on the frequent references in the federal Act to interprovincial and export trade, even though it was clear that these references did not in practice exclude farmers producing for local markets from the crucial federal rules

was one of the counsel representing those who were interested in the invalidity of the marketing plan.

[11]Two essentially concurring opinions were written. Laskin C.J. wrote a very long opinion which attracted the agreement of Judson, Spence and Dickson JJ. Pigeon J. wrote a short opinion—he explained at p. 1289 that he was "pressed for time"—which essentially reacted to Laskin C.J.'s opinion with which he was in substantial agreement. Pigeon J's opinion, despite its perfunctory nature, attracted the agreement of Martland, Ritchie, Beetz and de Grandpré JJ. and accordingly qualifies as the majority opinion.

[12]*Re Agricultural Products Marketing Act*, [1978] 2 S.C.R. 1198, 1296.

regarding production quotas,[13] surplus disposal[14] and levies.[15] The result is that the two concurring opinions are very general and abstract and hard to relate to the actual operation of the marketing plan under consideration.[16]

After the egg marketing plan was upheld in *Re Agricultural Products Marketing Act*, the same model of interlocking federal and provincial legislation was used to create a national chicken marketing plan. Like the egg marketing plan, the chicken marketing plan divided the national market for chickens by allocating a quota to each province, and within each province the province's quota was divided up among the individual producers. Neither the province's quota nor the individual producers' quotas drew any distinction between chickens produced for export and chickens produced for local consumption. Producers were free to sell their chickens wherever they chose. In *Fédération des producteurs v. Pelland* (2005),[17] a chicken producer in Quebec who exported all of his chickens to Ontario challenged the validity of his quota (which he had grossly exceeded). Because the quotas of individual producers were set under the authority of the provincial legislation, he argued that the quotas were inapplicable to production that was destined for markets outside the province. On his argument, the quotas could only apply to production for intraprovincial trade, and federal quotas were needed for those producing for export from the province. The Supreme Court of Canada rejected this argument, following the earlier case to hold that, at least in the context of a cooperative federal-provincial scheme, the provinces could impose production quotas without regard for the destination of the product. Mr Pelland was therefore bound by his quota despite his decision to export his production. Although there was no direct chal-

[13]With respect to production quotas, both federal and provincial rules were upheld. Pigeon J. for the majority said (at p. 1293) that "the control of production, whether agricultural or industrial, is prima facie a local matter, a matter of provincial jurisdiction". Nevertheless, Laskin C.J. (with whom Pigeon J. agreed on this issue) said (at p. 1265) that: "I do not think Parliament is precluded from allocating quotas on an industry-wide basis if it relates them to its regulatory control in relation to interprovincial and export trade". He did not explain what the qualification meant.

[14]With respect to surplus disposal, Pigeon J. for the majority held (at p. 1292) that the federal agency could not be empowered to buy and sell surplus eggs in local trade. In this he disagreed with Laskin C.J. for the minority (at p. 1266). However, Pigeon J. did not explain the implications of his view for the rest of the marketing plan, of which surplus disposal was an important part.

[15]With respect to levies, Laskin C.J. (with whom Pigeon J. agreed on this issue) introduced (at p. 1263) the qualification that they be limited to interprovincial and export trade, and suggested that they could be levied at grading stations established to handle eggs in interprovincial and export trade. Laskin C.J. did not explain whether this meant that the actual levies in the case, which were based on production, were bad.

[16]The previous three notes illustrate the doubts left by the opinions, which led to further litigation, e.g., *Boulanger v. Fédération des producteurs d'oeufs* (1982), 141 D.L.R. (3d) 72 (Que. C.A.). For comment on *Re Agricultural Products Marketing Act*, see T.B. Smith in Law Society of Upper Canada, The Constitution and the Future of Canada, Special Lectures, 1978, 135.

[17]*Fédération des producteurs v. Pelland*, [2005] 1 S.C.R. 292. Abella J. wrote the opinion of the Court.

lenge to the federal part of the plan, the Court clearly reaffirmed the decision in the earlier case, including the upholding of a federally-imposed quota on each of the provinces without regard for the destination of the product.

In *Dominion Stores v. The Queen* (1979),[18] the Supreme Court of Canada, by a narrow five to four majority, struck down Part I of the federal Canada Agricultural Products Standards Act. The Act provided for the establishment of grades with appropriate grade names for agricultural products. Part II of the Act made it compulsory to use the grade names for products moving in interprovincial or international trade. Part I of the Act did not make it compulsory to use the grade names for products marketed within the province of production,[19] but it provided that, if the grade names were used in local trade, then the appropriate federal standards had to be complied with. Dominion Stores was charged under Part I with selling apples (which were assumed to be locally produced) under the federally-established grade name "Canada Extra Fancy", which did not comply with the standards stipulated for that grade of apples. The company was acquitted on the ground that Part I of the Act was an unconstitutional attempt to regulate local trade.

In my opinion, *Dominion Stores* was wrongly decided. It is incontrovertible that Part II of the Canada Agricultural Products Standards Act, which requires the use of the federal grade names and standards for products moving in interprovincial or international trade, is a valid exercise of power over trade and commerce. But if the same grade names could be used for locally-produced products, without compliance with the federal standards, then the grade names would lose their credibility. It seems to me, therefore, that Part I of the Act was necessary to protect the interprovincial and international scheme: if the grade names were used for locally-produced products, then the federal standards had to be complied with. Surely, such a modest intrusion into local trade has a "rational, functional connection"[20] with the regulation of interprovincial and international trade. In rejecting this intrusion into local trade, the Court seems to have inexplicably reverted to the bad old days of the

[18] *Dominion Stores v. The Queen*, [1980] 1 S.C.R. 844.

[19] These facts were blurred by the existence in Ontario of provincial legislation which made the use of the same grade names compulsory in local trade. This led Estey J. for the majority to emphasize, correctly, that the use of the federal grade names was in practice mandatory in Ontario. But, in assessing the validity of the federal law, the existence of the provincial law should have been treated as irrelevant. The federal law imposed no compulsion. To the extent that Estey J. relied on the provincial law in assessing the validity of the federal law, he was permitting the scope of the federal trade and commerce power to be contracted by the enactment of provincial legislation. Moreover, this approach assumes that the federal law would be valid in those provinces that did not have matching legislation. It also stands in sharp contrast with the Court's approach in *Re Agricultural Products Marketing Act*, [1978] 2 S.C.R. 1198, where the Court was obviously anxious to overlook elements of overreaching by each level of government in order to sustain a marketing plan that had been established by the cooperative action of both levels of government.

[20] Chapter 15, Judicial Review on Federal Grounds, under heading § 15:24, "Ancillary power".

Privy Council's "watertight compartments". Indeed, Estey J.'s majority opinion discussed the trade and commerce power by reference only to the old Privy Council decisions that had so narrowed the power. He did not mention any of the developments since the abolition of appeals. However, at the end of the opinion Estey J. said that "it may well be" that his account of law "is not now a correct description of the federal power under s. 91(2)".[21] This unusual acknowledgment is a welcome caveat against giving too much precedential weight to the reasoning, but it does not meet my criticism, which is that a more "correct description" of the law would have led to a different outcome.[22]

Labatt Breweries v. A.-G. Can. (1979)[23] is another case in which the federal trade and commerce power was rejected as a support for federal legislation. In that case, the Court struck down compositional standards for beer enacted under the federal Food and Drugs Act. In the earlier chapter on Criminal Law, where the case is discussed at some length, I argued that the standards should have been upheld under the criminal law power.[24] But, with respect, the Court was right to reject the power to regulate interprovincial trade as a ground of validity. As Estey J. for the majority pointed out, the standards were imposed without regard for the product's movements across provincial boundaries.[25] He also reaffirmed the rule established in the insurance cases that the trade and commerce power will not authorize the regulation of a single trade or industry, even if the industry is dominated by a few large firms which advertise and market their products on a nation-wide basis.[26]

Before confederation, the British North American colonies used tariffs (customs duties) as a source of revenue. After confederation, only Parliament could levy tariffs, which were indirect taxes and therefore incompetent to the provinces. However, no doubt out of an abundance of caution, the Constitution Act, 1867, by s. 121,[27] provides:

> 121 All articles of the growth, produce, or manufacture of any one of the provinces shall, from and after the union, be admitted free into each of the other provinces.

[21] *Dominion Stores v. The Queen*, [1980] 1 S.C.R. 844, 866.

[22] In my view, the law could also have been upheld under the "general" category of trade and commerce: see the discussion in the next section of this chapter.

[23] *Labatt Breweries v. A.-G. Can.*, [1980] 1 S.C.R. 914.

[24] See ch. 18, Criminal Law, under heading § 18:3, "Food and drug standards".

[25] *Labatt Breweries v. A.-G. Can.*, [1980] 1 S.C.R. 914, 939, 943. The "general" category of trade and commerce was also rejected: see the discussion in the next section of this chapter.

[26] *Labatt Breweries v. A.-G. Can.*, [1980] 1 S.C.R. 914, 941. The brewing industry is in fact highly concentrated. At that time, the market was dominated by only three large firms. Estey J. pointed out, however (at p. 839), that the industry's production facilities tend to be local: Labatts had a brewery in every province except Quebec and Prince Edward Island. It is hard to see the relevance of this. Would the federal standards be valid in their application to an industry with centralized production facilities?

[27] This provision is also discussed elsewhere in this book: see ch. 31, Taxation, under heading § 31:4, "Limitations on the powers", below; and ch. 46, Mobility, under heading § 46:8, "Section 121 of the Constitution Act, 1867".

In *R. v. Comeau* (2018),[28] there was a challenge under s. 121 of the Constitution Act, 1867 to s. 134(b) of New Brunswick's Liquor Control Act, which prohibited residents of the province from keeping a quantity of liquor in excess of a prescribed threshold unless it had been purchased from the New Brunswick Liquor Corporation. Mr. Comeau had driven to Quebec and purchased a quantity of liquor in excess of the prescribed threshold. On his return to New Brunswick with his purchases, he was stopped by police and charged with an offence under s. 134(b). His defence – which was accepted at trial, leading to his acquittal – was that s. 134(b) infringed s. 121, and was therefore of no force and effect. The case advanced on appeal to the Supreme Court of Canada, which reversed the decision at trial and held, in an opinion of "the Court", that s. 134(b) did not infringe s. 121. The Court said that s. 121 precludes customs duties (tariffs)[29] as well as "tariff-like measures".[30] The latter would capture measures that "in *essence and purpose* burden the passage of goods across a provincial border", but not measures "*directed to other goals* that have *incidental effects* on the passage of goods across provincial borders", or that "form rational parts of broader legislative schemes with purposes unrelated to impeding provincial trade".[31] Section 134(b), by making it an offence to stock amounts of liquor in excess of a prescribed threshold unless it was purchased from the New Brunswick Liquor Corporation, had the effect of imposing restrictions on liquor purchased from outside of the province. It therefore restricted trade across a provincial border. However, the primary purpose of s. 134(b) was "not to impede trade"; its "primary purpose [was] to restrict access to *any* non-Corporation liquor, not just liquor brought in from another province like Quebec".[32] The effect that s. 134(b) had on interprovincial trade was "only incidental in light of the objective of the provincial scheme in general".[33]

The decision in *Comeau* would appear to leave s. 121 with little work to do, at least as far as provincial laws are concerned.[34] This is because any provincial law that is "in essence and purpose" related to interprovincial trade would likely be a law in relation to trade and commerce under s. 91(2), and therefore invalid under the federal-provincial division of powers. If this is right, s. 121 is likely only to have a role to play in precluding *federally*-imposed tariffs, or tariff-like measures that "in

[28] *R. v. Comeau*, [2018] 1 S.C.R. 342. The opinion is attributed to "the Court".

[29] *R. v. Comeau*, [2018] 1 S.C.R. 342, paras. 53, 98. Prior to *Comeau*, it appeared that any customs duties (tariffs) between the provinces would be precluded by s. 121: see *Gold Seal v. A.-G. Alta.* (1921), 62 S.C.R. 424. However, *Comeau* seems to contemplate that tariffs will not be precluded by s. 121 if they "form rational parts of broader legislative schemes with purposes unrelated to impeding interprovincial trade" (para. 114).

[30] *R. v. Comeau*, [2018] 1 S.C.R. 342, para. 53.

[31] *R. v. Comeau*, [2018] 1 S.C.R. 342, paras. 53, 114 (emphasis added).

[32] *R. v. Comeau*, [2018] 1 S.C.R. 342, para. 122.

[33] *R. v. Comeau*, [2018] 1 S.C.R. 342, para. 125.

[34] M. Lavoie, "Supreme Court's 'free-the-beer' decision privileges one part of the Constitution over another" CBC News (19 April 2018).

essence and purpose burden the passage of goods across a provincial border". And yet, *Comeau* left unresolved whether s. 121 "applies equally to federal and provincial laws".[35] If s. 121 does not apply equally to federal laws, it may have very little work to do indeed.

III. GENERAL TRADE AND COMMERCE

§ 20:4 General trade and commerce

It will be recalled that in the leading case of *Citizens' Insurance Co. v. Parsons* the Privy Council had suggested two categories of trade and commerce. The first, namely, interprovincial or international trade and commerce, we have just considered. The second was "general regulation of trade affecting the whole dominion"—the so-called "general" category of trade and commerce.[1]

Until the decision of the Supreme Court of Canada in *General Motors v. City National Leasing* (1989), which is discussed later in this chapter,[2] the general category of trade and commerce had been rather consistently rejected as a support for federal policies of economic regulation. For example, it was rejected as a support for the regulation of the insurance industry in the *Insurance Reference*, the regulation of combines, prices and profits in the *Board of Commerce* case, the regulation of labour relations in *Toronto Electric Commissioners v. Snider*, the regulation of marketing in *The King v. Eastern Terminal Elevator Co.* and the *Natural Products Marketing Reference*, and the prohibition of margarine in the *Margarine Reference*.[3]

Until 1989, the only unequivocal example of a valid exercise of the general trade and commerce power[4] was the *Canada Standard Trade*

---

[35]*R. v. Comeau*, [2018] 1 S.C.R. 342, para. 116. In *Comeau*, the Court noted that there is debate about this question, and that, in two previous cases, it had simply assumed "that federal laws may engage s. 121": *R. v. Comeau*, [2018] 1 S.C.R. 342, para. 116, citing *Gold Seal v. A.-G. Alta.* (1921), 62 S.C.R. 424; *Murphy v. CPR*, [1958] S.C.R. 626. The Court agreed with the suggestion made by Laskin C.J. in *Re Agricultural Products Marketing Act*, [1978] 2 S.C.R. 1198 (at 1267) that the application of s. 121 "may be different" if a federal law is involved: *R. v. Comeau*, [2018] 1 S.C.R. 342, para. 116. There is scholarship that argues that s. 121 should only apply to provincial legislation: see M. Lavoie, "*R. v. Comeau* and Section 121 of the Constitution Act, 1867: Freeing the Beer and Fortifying the Economic Union" (2017) 40 Dal. L.J. 189, 216-217.

[Section 20:4]

[1]*Citizens' Insurance Co. v. Parsons* (1881), 7 App. Cas. 96.

[2]*General Motors v. City National Leasing*, [1989] 1 S.C.R. 641.

[3]All of these cases are discussed in the previous section of this chapter, "Interprovincial or international trade and commerce", above.

[4]In *John Deere Plow Co. v. Wharton*, [1915] A.C. 330, 340, the Privy Council suggested that the federal Parliament's power over some aspects of the incorporation of companies was derived from the general trade and commerce power; this suggestion is replete with difficulties: see Smith, The Commerce Power in Canada and the United States (1963), 96–99; J.S. Ziegel in J.S. Ziegel (ed.), Studies in Canadian Company Law (Butterworths, Toronto, 1967), 159–160; and it is probably better to regard the whole topic of the incorporation of companies with other than provincial objects as derived

Mark case (1937),[5] in which the Privy Council upheld a federal statute which established a national mark called "Canada Standard". The use of the mark was voluntary, but if the mark was used, federal standards as to the quality of the product so marked had to be complied with. The use of the mark was not confined to interprovincial and international trade. The case seemed to decide that the general trade and commerce power would authorize federal standards of production or manufacture for products traded locally, provided that the federal standards were tied to the voluntary use of a distinctive mark.[6]

A shadow was cast on the *Canada Standard* case by the decision of the Supreme Court of Canada in *Dominion Stores v. The Queen* (1979).[7] That case presented very similar facts. The Canada Agricultural Products Standards Act established a system of grades for agricultural products, and provided that, if the grades were voluntarily used for products traded locally, then the products had to comply with the associated federal standards. The four dissenting judges regarded the *Canada Standard* case as indistinguishable: the grade name "Canada Extra Fancy" when used by Dominion Stores for apples should attract the associated federal regulation in the same way and for the same reasons as the use of the trade mark "Canada Standard". But Estey J. for the majority fastened on what seems to me to be a mere difference of machinery, namely, that in the *Canada Standard* case the mark was formally vested in the Crown, and on this ground he distinguished the *Canada Standard* case. This kind of distinction is close to confining a case to its own facts.[8]

In *Labatt Breweries v. A.-G. Can.* (1979),[9] the Supreme Court of Canada struck down compositional standards for light beer which had been enacted under the federal Food and Drugs Act. These standards became applicable only through the voluntary use of the description "light beer". Two of the dissenting judges (Pigeon J. with whom McIntyre J. agreed) would have upheld the legislation as on all fours with that upheld in the

from the "peace, order, and good government" power: see ch. 23, Companies, under heading §§ 23:1 to 23:5, "Incorporation of companies". Another possible authority is *Re Alberta Statutes*, [1938] S.C.R. 100, 116–121, where Duff C.J. and Davis J. gave as one of their reasons for striking down some of Alberta's social credit legislation that the creation of a new system of credit to be used as a means of exchange was a matter within the federal trade and commerce power; the other three opinions in the case did not rely on the trade and commerce power.

[5] *A.-G. Ont. v. A.-G. Can.* (Canada Standard Trade Mark) [1937] A.C. 405.

[6] The Privy Council stated, obiter (at p. 417), that the power to create and regulate trade marks was within the trade and commerce power. The existence of this power was affirmed in *Kirkbi v. Ritvik Holdings*, [2005] 3 S.C.R. 302; discussed in the text that follows.

[7] *Dominion Stores v. The Queen*, [1980] 1 S.C.R. 844; and see text accompanying § 20:3 note 18, above.

[8] A second point of distinction, namely, that the use of the grade names was effectively mandatory by reason of matching provincial legislation seems wrong.

[9] *Labatt Breweries v. A.-G. Can.*, [1980] 1 S.C.R. 914; see also text accompanying § 20:3 note 23, above.

Canada Standard case. However, the third dissenting judge (Laskin C.J.) and the six majority judges did not regard the precedent as controlling. Estey J. for the majority referred to the "arrogation" by Parliament of "common names",[10] and it is certainly arguable that therein lies an essential difference between *Canada Standard* (and *Dominion Stores)* on the one hand and *Labatt Breweries* on the other. In *Canada Standard* (and *Dominion Stores)* the application of the federal standards depended upon the use of a distinctive description, namely, Canada Standard (or Canada Extra Fancy). In *Labatt Breweries* the application of the federal standard depended upon the use of a common description, namely, "light beer". As MacPherson has commented, the use of a distinctive description is genuinely voluntary, because it is easy for manufacturers who do not wish to comply with the federal standards to avoid the use of the distinctive description. But the use of a common description is virtually mandatory since it is often not practicable for a manufacturer to produce a marketable product without calling the product by its common name.[11] "Light beer" is perhaps not the clearest example, but there are compositional standards prescribed by regulations made under the Food and Drugs Act for "beer", "whisky", "gin", "rum", "brandy", "coffee", "tea", "chocolate", "cocoa", "ice cream", "margarine", and for dozens of other foods and drinks described by their ordinary names. Such a regulatory regime bears little resemblance to that in issue in the *Canada Standard* case.

The standards laid down under the federal Food and Drugs Act can be supported under the general trade and commerce power only if that power is held to extend to the mandatory prescription of nation-wide standards for the manufacture of foods and drugs. In *Labatt Breweries*, Laskin C.J. in his separate dissent was prepared to go that far. He said that under the general branch of the trade and commerce power Parliament "should be able to fix standards that are common to all manufacturers of foods, including beer, drugs, cosmetics and therapeutic devices, at least to equalize competitive advantages in the carrying on of businesses concerned with such products".[12] No other judge agreed with Laskin C.J., although Estey J. did say that the general branch of the trade and commerce power would authorize legislation that "affected industry and commerce at large or in a sweeping general sense".[13] The force of this assertion was severely attenuated by Estey J.'s concurrent holding that the Food and Drugs Act is not sufficiently "sweeping" or "general" in its scope, apparently because the regulations (not the Act, be it noted) were drafted on a commodity-by-commodity basis. Considering that the Act and regulations covered most of the common foods and

---

[10] *Labatt Breweries v. A.-G. Can.*, [1980] 1 S.C.R. 914, 926.

[11] J.C. MacPherson, "Economic Regulation and the British North America Act" (1980) 5 Can. Bus. L.J. 172, 187. This article includes an extensive critique of the *Dominion Stores and Labatt Breweries* decisions.

[12] *Labatt Breweries v. A.-G. Can.*, [1980] 1 S.C.R. 914, 921.

[13] *Labatt Breweries v. A.-G. Can.*, [1980] 1 S.C.R. 914, 943.

drugs which are consumed in Canada, it is not easy to imagine a more sweeping or general code of regulation.

In *MacDonald v. Vapor Canada* (1976),[14] the issue arose as to the validity of a federal law which prohibited, and provided a civil remedy for, any "act" or "business practice" which was "contrary to honest industrial or commercial usage in Canada". The Federal Court of Appeal had upheld the law on the basis that "a law laying down a set of general rules as to the conduct of businessmen in their competitive activities in Canada" was within the general category of trade and commerce.[15] The Supreme Court of Canada unanimously reversed this decision. Laskin C.J., who wrote the principal opinion,[16] pointed out that the creation or extension of civil causes of action of an essentially contractual or tortious character was a matter within property and civil rights in the province. While a new civil remedy could be upheld as an incident to an otherwise valid federal law, in this case the remedy stood alone.[17] The only federal aspect which could really be claimed for the law was the fact that it applied throughout Canada, but generality of application has never been sufficient of itself to shift a law dealing with property and civil rights in the province into a federal head of power.[18]

Although the general trade and commerce power proved unavailing once again in *Vapor*, Laskin C.J. did suggest some circumstances where it would be available. He implied several times that the result might well have been different if the law had been part of a "regulatory scheme" administered by a "federally-appointed agency".[19] This law was not part of a "regulatory scheme" and its enforcement was "left to the chance of private redress without public monitoring by the continued oversight of a regulatory agency".[20] His lordship did not define a "regulatory scheme"; nor did he explain why the existence of such a scheme, administered by a regulatory agency, would satisfy the general trade and commerce power. The suggestion finds no basis in the previous case law. On the contrary, many of the federal statutes which were held unconstitutional by the Privy Council established some form of regulatory scheme administered by a federally-appointed official or agency.[21]

---

[14]*MacDonald v. Vapor Canada,* [1977] 2 S.C.R. 134; for more extended discussion, see P.W. Hogg, Comment (1976) 54 Can. Bar Rev. 361.

[15]*Vapor Canada Ltd. v. MacDonald* (1972) 33 D.L.R. (3d) 434, 449.

[16]Laskin C.J.'s opinion was agreed to by Spence, Pigeon, Dickson and Beetz JJ.; a separate concurring opinion was written by de Grandpré J. and agreed to by Martland and Judson JJ.

[17]This aspect of the *Vapor* case is discussed in ch. 18, Criminal Law, under heading § 18:17, "Criminal law and civil remedy".

[18][1977] 2 S.C.R. 134, 156.

[19][1977] 2 S.C.R. 134, 156, 158, 163, 165, 167.

[20][1977] 2 S.C.R. 134, 165.

[21]E.g., *A.-G. Can. v. A.-G. Alta.* (Insurance) [1916] 1 A.C. 588; *Re Board of Commerce Act*, [1922] 1 A.C. 191; *Toronto Electric Commrs. v. Snider*, [1925] A.C. 396; *The King v. Eastern Terminal Elevator Co.*, [1926] S.C.R. 434; *A.-G. Can. v. A.-G. Ont.* (Unemploy-

In the *Anti-Inflation Reference* (1976),[22] the federal regime of wage and price control appeared to present the regulatory scheme and the administrative agency called for in Laskin C.J.'s *Vapor* dicta. However, counsel for the federal government chose not to argue that the Act could be upheld under the trade and commerce power, confining their argument to the peace, order, and good government power. The legislation was upheld under the emergency branch of the peace, order, and good government power.[23] In his opinion in the *Anti-Inflation Reference*, Laskin C.J. included one paragraph which indicated that he might have been favourably disposed to an argument that the general trade and commerce power could have sustained the Act.[24] The other opinions in the case made no reference to the trade and commerce power.[25] In the *Labatt Breweries* case, which has just been discussed, where the "general" trade and commerce power was relied upon in argument, Estey J.'s majority opinion and Pigeon J.'s dissenting opinion made only passing reference to the *Vapor* case, and the other opinions did not refer to it at all.[26]

Despite the absence of supporting authority, Laskin C.J.'s dicta in *Vapor* have proved to be very important, having become the basis for upholding the federal Competition Act. As noted in the earlier chapter on Criminal Law,[27] Canada's competition law had been upheld as a "criminal" law, but this characterization had become impossible to sustain after amendments in 1975 and 1986, which had the effect of decriminalizing much of the law. The constitutionality of the new legislation had to be resolved in *General Motors v. City National Leasing* (1989),[28] which was a challenge to the validity of the civil remedy that had been introduced into the legislation in 1975. The Supreme Court of Canada, in a unanimous judgment written by Dickson C.J., held that the Combines Investigation Act (now the Competition Act) was a valid exercise of the "general" trade and commerce power.

Dickson C.J. applied the *Vapor* test, which consisted of three elements:

---

ment Insurance) [1937] A.C. 355; *A.-G. B.C. v. A.-G. Can.* (Natural Products Marketing) [1937] A.C. 377. Laskin C.J. in *MacDonald v. Vapor Can.*, [1977] 2 S.C.R. 134, 163 appeared to place the marketing cases in a special category, asserting that in those cases "regulation by a public authority" would not alone be sufficient; the regulation must also apply "to the flow of inter provincial or foreign trade". Why these cases should be special is not explained, although, of course, marketing cases are numerous and the doctrine is therefore deeply entrenched.

[22] *Re Anti-Inflation Act*, [1976] 2 S.C.R. 373.

[23] See ch. 17, Peace, Order, and Good Government, under heading § 17:10, "Inflation".

[24] *Anti-Inflation Reference*, [1976] S.C.R. 373, 426–427.

[25] Laskin C.J.'s opinion was agreed with by Judson, Spence and Dickson JJ.; Ritchie J.'s separate concurring opinion was agreed with by Martland and Pigeon JJ.; Beetz J.'s dissenting opinion was agreed with by de Grandpré J.

[26] N. Finkelstein, Comment (1989) 68 Can. Bar Rev. 802 argues that both the *Anti-Inflation Reference* and *Labatt Breweries* should be reconsidered in the light of *General Motors v. City National Leasing*, [1989] 1 S.C.R. 641.

[27] Chapter 18, Criminal Law, under heading § 18:11, "Competition law".

[28] *General Motors v. City National Leasing*, [1989] 1 S.C.R. 641.

(1) the presence of a "general regulatory scheme", (2) the "oversight of a regulatory agency", and (3) a concern "with trade as a whole rather than with a particular industry".[29] To these three elements, Dickson C.J. added a fourth and fifth: (4) "the legislation should be of a nature that the provinces jointly or severally would be constitutionally incapable of enacting", and (5) "the failure to include one or more provinces or localities in a legislative scheme would jeopardize the successful operation of the scheme in other parts of the country".[30] In the case of the Competition Act, all five elements were present: (1) There was a regulatory scheme. (2) It operated under the oversight of a regulatory agency. (3) It was concerned with trade in general, not with a particular place or a particular industry. Moreover ((4) and (5)), only national regulation of competition could possibly be effective, because of the ability of factors of production to move freely from one province to another.[31]

It is important to notice that the general branch of the trade and commerce power authorizes the regulation of *intraprovincial* trade. Indeed, there would be no need for a general branch of trade and commerce if it did not extend beyond interprovincial and international trade. In *City National Leasing*, the allegations that gave rise to the litigation concerned price discrimination in the financing of the purchase of vehicles by companies that lease fleets of automobiles and trucks. These purchases, and the associated financing arrangements, were transactions that, individually, took place within a single province. Those facts gave rise to an argument that the federal legislation should be read down to exclude such intraprovincial activity, which could be left to provincial law. Dickson C.J.'s answer to this argument was a reference back to the provincial inability test, captured in elements (4) and (5) of his definition of general trade and commerce: "Competition cannot be successfully regulated by federal legislation which is restricted to interprovincial trade."[32] The conclusion was that Parliament (as well as the provinces) has the constitutional power to regulate intraprovincial aspects of competition.[33]

The Constitution Act, 1867 confers on Parliament authority to legislate in relation to patents (s. 91(22)) (which protect the right to exploit an invention) and copyrights (s. 91(23)) (which protect the right to

---

[29] *General Motors v. City National Leasing*, [1989] 1 S.C.R. 641, 661.

[30] *General Motors v. City National Leasing*, [1989] 1 S.C.R. 641, 662. The additional elements, and indeed the general line of reasoning, had been put forward by Dickson J. in *A.G. Can. v. CN Transportation*, [1983] 2 S.C.R. 206, in which he decided that the federal competition law could be upheld under the general branch of trade and commerce. In that case, however, only two other judges agreed with him. The four-judge majority did not need to, and did not, decide the appropriate constitutional characterization of the legislation.

[31] *General Motors v. City National Leasing*, [1989] 1 S.C.R. 641, 679.

[32] *General Motors v. City National Leasing*, [1989] 1 S.C.R. 641, 681.

[33] *General Motors v. City National Leasing*, [1989] 1 S.C.R. 641, 682, asserting that "competition is not a single matter, any more than inflation or pollution", and the provinces also had the power "to deal with competition in the exercise of their legislative powers in such fields as consumer protection, labour relations, marketing and the like".

reproduce original writings or works of art), but the Act is silent with respect to trade marks, that other important branch of intellectual property. However, Canada has had a federal Trade-marks Act[34] since shortly after confederation. The current Act provides a system of registration of trade marks, a right of exclusive use of registered marks, and remedies for their infringement. The Act also recognizes unregistered trade marks, and provides them with the protection of a civil remedy. The *Canada Standard Trade Mark* case (1937),[35] which has earlier been described, upheld a federal statute that authorized the use of a "Canada Standard" designation to denote compliance with federal standards. The case was not about a trade mark in the normal sense of a mark that is used by a private manufacturer (or seller) to distinguish its products from those of others. The Trade-marks Act itself was not challenged. However, in an obiter dictum, Lord Atkin said that "one obvious source of authority" for the Trade-marks Act was the trade and commerce power.[36] This dictum has generally been accepted as good law, and with good reason. Trade marks attach to goods and services. Goods and services move across provincial borders, as do consumers, who take their opinions about products and manufacturers with them. The uniform, national protection of trade marks is closely connected with the mobility of goods and services and individuals, and is part of the regulation of competition.

In *Kirkbi v. Ritvik Holdings* (2005),[37] the manufacturer of LEGO toy building blocks sued the manufacturer of a competing product, Mega Bloks, which used the same interlocking system as LEGO. The plaintiff, claiming that the defendant had improperly passed off its Mega Bloks as LEGO blocks, brought proceedings against the defendant in the Federal Court of Canada under s. 7(b) of the federal Trade-marks Act. Section 7(b) authorizes the holder of an unregistered trade mark to bring an action for passing off against a competitor who has branded its product in a way that causes confusion between the defendant's product and the trade mark holder's product. The defendant won the case on the ground that LEGO's interlocking system was a functional characteristic of the product that could not, as a matter of law, be a trade mark. In the Supreme Court of Canada, the defendant raised a constitutional issue, namely, that s. 7(b) of the Trade-marks Act was outside the power of the federal Parliament. This was not a challenge to the validity of the Act as a whole, but only to the civil remedy provided by s. 7(b). However, the Court had to determine the validity of the Act as a whole in order to determine the validity of s. 7(b). LeBel J., who wrote the opinion of the Court, said that he was governed by the five indicia of validity set out in

---

[34]Trade Mark and Design Act, 1868, 31 Vic., c. 55 (Can.). The current Act is the Trademarks Act, R.S.C. 1985, c. T-13.

[35]*A.-G. Ont. v. A.-G. Can.* (Canada Standard Trade Mark) [1937] A.C. 405.

[36]*A.-G. Ont. v. A.-G. Can.* (Canada Standard Trade Mark) [1937] A.C. 405, 417.

[37]*Kirkbi v. Ritvik Holdings*, [2005] 3 S.C.R. 302. LeBel J. wrote the opinion of the Court. I disclose that I was one of the counsel for the appellant, arguing in favour of the validity of the civil remedy in the Trademarks Act.

City National Leasing, and he accepted an earlier decision of the Federal Court of Appeal that found that all five criteria were present in the Trade-marks Act:[38]

> All of the criteria of Chief Justice Dickson are verified in the Act: a national regulatory scheme, the oversight of the Registrar of Trade Marks, a concern with trade in general rather than with an aspect of a particular business, the incapability of the provinces to establish such a scheme and the necessity for national coverage.

LeBel J. held that the national regulatory scheme embraced unregistered trade marks as well as registered trade marks. Section 7(b), which was the mechanism for the enforcement of unregistered trade marks, was sufficiently integrated into the regulatory scheme to be a valid part of the Act.[39] The result was that the Trademarks Act, including the civil remedy of s. 7(b), was held to be a valid exercise of the general branch of the trade and commerce power.

Securities regulation became the object of judicial review under the general branch of the trade and commerce power in *Re Securities Act* (2011).[40] That was a reference to the Supreme Court of Canada of a proposed federal Securities Act which had been tabled in Parliament by the Minister of Finance, and immediately referred to the Court for its answer to the question whether the proposed Act was within the legislative authority of the Parliament of Canada. The Act would have provided a comprehensive regime of securities regulation under the oversight of a national regulatory authority to be established by the Act.[41] No distinction was made between interprovincial (or international) aspects of securities regulation and purely intraprovincial aspects; coverage was comprehensive, the goal being to wholly displace provincial regulation of the field, which had been in place in one form or another since the 19th century. The impact on provincial jurisdiction was recognized by an opt-in formula for bringing the Act into force. The Act would apply only within the boundaries of those provinces (and territories) that opted into the federal regime. For any province that chose not to opt in, its provincial statute would continue to govern the field in that province. Unmollified by the opt-in feature, Quebec and Alberta objected to the

---

[38]*Kirkbi v. Ritvik Holdings*, [2005] 3 S.C.R. 302, para. 28, quoting from *Asbjorn Horgard v. Gibbs/Nortac Industries*, [1987] 3 F.C. 544, 559 per MacGuigan J.A.

[39]The connection of the civil remedy to the regulatory scheme distinguished *MacDonald v. Vapor Canada*, [1977] 2 S.C.R. 134, where the civil remedy that was struck down was unconnected to trade marks (or patents or copyrights or any other valid federal regulatory scheme). This part of the decision is discussed in ch. 15, Judicial Review on Federal Grounds, under heading § 15:24, "Ancillary power", and ch. 18, Criminal Law, under heading § 18:17, "Federal power generally to create civil remedies".

[40]*Re Securities Act*, [2011] 3 S.C.R. 837. The opinion of "the Court" was unanimous. I disclose that I was one of the counsel for the Attorney General of Canada, arguing for the validity of the proposed federal Securities Act.

[41]Not surprisingly, a national securities regulator was upheld under the commerce clause by the Supreme Court of the United States in *North American Co. v. SEC* (1946), 327 U.S. 686.

federal initiative on constitutional grounds,[42] and, along with other provinces, they intervened in the reference in opposition to the federal initiative. Ontario intervened in support. The Supreme Court of Canada held that the proposed Act was not authorized by the general branch of the trade and commerce power, which was the only ground advanced in its support.

Of the five indicators of federal authority, (1) a "general regulatory scheme", and (2) "the oversight of a regulatory agency", were satisfied. Indicator (3) "trade as a whole", however, was not satisfied. The Court acknowledged that "much of Canada's capital market is interprovincial and indeed international", and that "trade in securities is not confined to 13 provincial and territorial enclaves."[43] But the Court went on to say that "equally", however, "capital markets also exist within provinces that meet the needs of local businesses and investors".[44] The Court said that "we cannot ignore that the provinces have been deeply engaged in the regulation of the market over many years", and "the structure and terms of the proposed Act largely replicate the existing provincial schemes".[45] "We are unable to accept Canada's assertion that the securities market has been so transformed as to make the day-to-day regulation of all aspects of trading in securities a matter of national concern".[46] The Court concluded that the main thrust of the proposed Act "remains essentially a matter of property and civil rights within the provinces and therefore subject to provincial power".[47]

The fourth indicator (provincial inability) was satisfied in part in that the provinces would be constitutionally incapable of creating a stable national scheme "aimed at genuine national goals", because each province would retain the power at any time to withdraw from the scheme. However, this would not overcome "Canada's problem" that the proposed

[42]Each province directed a reference to its Court of Appeal for a ruling that the federal initiative was unconstitutional. Both Courts ruled that the proposed federal Act was unconstitutional before the hearing of the federal reference in the Supreme Court: 2011 ABCA 77; 2011 QCCA 591 (CanLII).

[43]*Re Securities Act*, [2011] 3 S.C.R. 837, para. 115.

[44]*Re Securities Act*, [2011] 3 S.C.R. 837, para. 115, ignoring the evidence that this was now a minor aspect of securities markets.

[45]*Re Securities Act*, [2011] 3 S.C.R. 837, paras. 115, 116, perhaps establishing a new doctrine of squatters' rights, and ignoring the rule that in classifying a federal Act for division of powers purposes the existence of provincial legislation in the same field is irrelevant.

[46]*Re Securities Act*, [2011] 3 S.C.R. 837, para. 118. The test is actually trade as a whole, not national concern. The reference to national concern is a confusing conflation of two entirely different ideas in Canadian constitutional law. National concern is the defining feature of the national concern branch of peace, order, and good government, for which purpose it is has a requirement of distinctness which is inconsistent with the notion of trade as a whole. See ch. 17, Peace, order, and good government, under heading §§ 17:3 to 17:6, "The 'national concern' branch".

[47]*Re Securities Act*, [2011] 3 S.C.R. 837, para. 115. The Court's opinion is replete with vague suggestions that "aspects" of the proposed Act would be within federal power, presumably because they deal with trade as a whole: see paras. 6, 97, 102, 103, 104, 105, 114, 123, 125, 126, 128, 130.

Act "goes well beyond these matters of undoubted national interest and concern and reaches down into the detailed regulation of all aspects of securities".[48] This was a difference with competition law, which regulates only anti-competitive contracts and conduct, "a particular aspect of economic activity that falls squarely within the federal domain".[49]

The fifth indicator ("whether the legislative scheme is such that the failure to include one or more provinces or localities in the scheme would jeopardize its successful operation in other parts of the country") was not satisfied, because "the day-to-day regulation of securities", which was the main thrust of the proposed Act, "would not founder if a particular province declined to participate in the federal scheme".[50] The Court reinforced this point by reference to the opt-in feature of the scheme, which "contemplates the possibility that not all provinces will participate". But it was obvious (and acknowledged by counsel for Canada) that the failure of some provinces to opt in would jeopardize the successful operation of the scheme. The goal of the proposed Act was to achieve a single national regulator, not to perpetuate the multiple regulators, divergent rules for market participants, uncoordinated enforcement and variable protections for investors that characterized the status quo. The goal was universal coverage, and the means of getting there through the voluntary participation of provinces was surely a matter on which Parliament deserved some deference. To use the opt-in as an argument for the unconstitutionality of the Act renders somewhat hollow the Court's frequent exhortations to cooperative federalism, which were actually repeated at the end of the opinion in this very case.[51]

The Court's conclusion in *Re Securities Act* was that comprehensive securities regulation did not come within the general branch of the trade and commerce power. According to the Court, securities regulation is primarily focused on "local concerns", and local concerns were "the main thrust" of the proposed Act.[52] The key to this surprising decision seems to be the longstanding provincial presence in the field, which somehow made the federal initiative an invalid intrusion on provincial power instead of, as in the case of trade mark and competition law, a subject matter with a double aspect. No one would deny the existence of provincial power to regulate contracts and property within the province, but if securities regulation is not also a matter of trade as a whole it is

[48]*Re Securities Act*, [2011] 3 S.C.R. 837, para. 122.

[49]*Re Securities Act*, [2011] 3 S.C.R. 837, para. 122. This is circular reasoning, since the provisions dealing with competition fall within the federal domain only because the Court had decided in the *General Motors v. City National Leasing*, [1989] 1 S.C.R. 641, that competition was within the general branch of trade and commerce. The impugned provisions deal only with securities regulation, a much narrower category of contract and conduct than is governed by competition law.

[50]*Re Securities Act*, [2011] 3 S.C.R. 837, para. 123.

[51]*Re Securities Act*, [2011] 3 S.C.R. 837, paras. 130–133.

[52]*Re Securities Act*, [2011] 3 S.C.R. 837, paras. 6, 28.

hard to know what is.[53] The Court's expressed concerns about "eviscerating"[54] the extensive provincial power over property and civil rights would surely have been better directed at the narrow federal power over trade and commerce. It has never been easy to construct a system of national regulation under the interprovincial and international branch of trade and commerce because of the difficulty of distinguishing between what is local and what is not. The general branch of trade and commerce, so far only applied to trade marks and competition, now seemed to have its categories closed.

New life was breathed into the general branch of trade and commerce when a more cautious proposal to regulate the securities industry on a national basis was finally upheld as constitutional by the Supreme Court of Canada in *Re Pan-Canadian Securities Regulation* (2018).[55] This proposal was for a "cooperative securities regulator", which would have two components: (1) a uniform model provincial act, broadly similar to the existing provincial securities acts, to be enacted by all participating provinces and territories; and (2) a federal act aimed at preventing and managing "systemic risk", establishing criminal offences relating to financial markets and creating a national securities regulator. What was new in the cooperative system was the federal proposal for a national securities regulator, which would have power over systemic risk, but would derive the bulk of its regulatory powers by delegation from the participating provinces in their uniform acts; the national securities regulator would become the sole regulator, responsible for administering both the federal and the provincial cooperative legislation. There was no doubt that Parliament had the power, as part of its criminal law power, to create criminal offences relating to financial markets. But did Parliament have the power to establish the national securities regulator and empower it to regulate systemic risk and to receive by delegation from the provinces the power to regulate the securities market in all the cooperating provinces? The Court now answered yes to all parts of this question. The general branch of trade and commerce would sustain the federal role in the proposed cooperative regime. Neither of the first two indicators was in doubt: the proposed federal act created a general regulatory scheme that would operate under the oversight of a federal agency. The third indicator (concern with trade as a whole) had

---

[53]See also ch. 21, Property and Civil Rights, under heading §§ 21:15 to 21:16, "Securities regulation".

[54]References to the risk of "eviscerating" provincial power (but not federal power) are to be found in paras. 7, 70, 71, 85. None of the references to evisceration made mention of the fact that the provinces would give up their regimes of securities regulation in favour of the federal regime only if they voluntarily chose for themselves to join the federal regime. Nor was the point ever made that the objecting provinces did not need to opt in; the only point of their opposition was to deny that choice to provinces who did wish to opt in. The opt-in feature of the federal proposal was never praised by the Court and was relied on only to deny constitutionality (previous paragraph). One is reminded of the adage that no good deed goes unpunished.

[55]*Re Pan-Canadian Securities Regulation*, 2018 SCC 48. The opinion of the nine-judge court was issued by "the Court".

been failed in the 2011 case, but the Court held that this proposed federal act was concerned with trade as a whole rather than the securities industry in particular. Unlike the 2011 proposal, the proposed federal act "does not descend into the detailed regulation of all aspects of trading in securities" and "is instead limited to addressing issues and risks of a systemic nature that may represent a material threat to the stability of Canada's financial system."[56] The fourth indicator (provincial incapacity) was satisfied: although each province could subsequently resile from the cooperative scheme, this would not impair the scheme's capacity to protect the Canadian economy from systemic risk, because the proposed federal act would enable Parliament to step in "to fill this constitutional gap."[57] The fifth indicator (effect of failure to include all provinces) largely flowed from the answer to the fourth: "the effective management of systemic risk requires market-wide regulation . . . the management of systemic risk across Canadian capital markets must be regulated federally, if at all."[58] The Court's conclusion was that the general branch of the trade and commerce power authorized the federal role in the proposed cooperative regime.

IV. SPECIFIC TOPICS

§ 20:5 Specific topics

This chapter has discussed the federal trade and commerce power in relatively general terms. When attention is directed to more specific topics, for example, the regulation of businesses, the regulation of professions and trades, labour relations, marketing and securities regulation, it is found that trade and commerce is not the dominant source of power: legislative power is for the most part provincial, under property and civil rights in the province. Accordingly, these and other topics are examined in the next chapter, entitled Property and Civil Rights. However, despite its title, the next chapter is not just an examination of provincial power. Under each specific topic, the elements of federal power are examined as well. The peace, order, and good government power, the criminal law power, and, especially, the trade and commerce power, are therefore important subsidiary themes of the next chapter.

---

[56] *Re Pan-Canadian Securities Regulation*, 2018 SCC 48, para. 111 (emphasis in original).

[57] *Re Pan-Canadian Securities Regulation*, 2018 SCC 48, para. 113.

[58] *Re Pan-Canadian Securities Regulation*, 2018 SCC 48, para. 115.

Chapter 21

Property and Civil Rights

I. IN GENERAL

§ 21:1 Importance of property and civil rights
§ 21:2 History of property and civil rights
§ 21:3 Civil liberties
§ 21:4 Local or private matters

II. INSURANCE

§ 21:5 Reasons for regulation
§ 21:6 Provincial power
§ 21:7 Federal power

III. BUSINESS IN GENERAL

§ 21:8 Business in general

IV. PROFESSIONS AND TRADES

§ 21:9 Professions and trades

V. LABOUR RELATIONS

§ 21:10 Provincial power
§ 21:11 Federal power

VI. MARKETING

§ 21:12 Reasons for regulation
§ 21:13 Federal power
§ 21:14 Provincial power

VII. SECURITIES REGULATION

§ 21:15 Provincial power
§ 21:16 Federal power

VIII. PROPERTY

§ 21:17 General
§ 21:18 Foreign ownership
§ 21:19 Heritage property

IX. DEBT ADJUSTMENT

§ 21:20 Debt adjustment

X. CONSUMER PROTECTION

§ 21:21 Consumer protection

XI. EXTRATERRITORIAL COMPETENCE

§ 21:22 Extraterritorial competence

I. IN GENERAL

§ 21:1 Importance of property and civil rights

Section 92(13) of the Constitution Act, 1867 confers upon the provincial Legislatures the power to make laws in relation to "property and civil rights in the province".[1] This is by far the most important of the provincial heads of power. Indeed, the previous chapters on the three major federal heads of power, namely, peace, order, and good government, trade and commerce and criminal law, have been as much concerned with property and civil rights in the province as they have been with their ostensible topics. Most of the major constitutional cases have turned on the competition between one or more of the federal heads of power, on the one hand, and property and civil rights, on the other.

§ 21:2 History of property and civil rights

In chapter 2, Reception, we noticed that the phrase "property and civil rights" has a history in British North America which starts before confederation.[1] It will be recalled that the phrase appeared in s. 8 of the Quebec Act, 1774, which restored the French civil law as the private law of the conquered colony of Quebec. In s. 8, the phrase meant the whole body of law governing relationships between individuals—the body of law that did not need to be supplanted by the conquest of a foreign power. It will also be recalled that the phrase occurred again in the first Act of the Legislature of the province of Upper Canada, which in 1792 adopted English law as the private law of the colony. In this context, the phrase plainly had the same meaning as in the Quebec Act, 1774.

[Section 21:1]

[1]Tremblay, Les compétences législatives au Canada et les pouvoirs provinciaux en matière de propriété et de droits civils (1967) is a study of s. 92(13). This important book has no counterpart in the English-language literature, which has tended to concentrate on the federal powers. See also Beaudoin, La Constitution du Canada (3rd ed., 2005), ch. 9. Section 92(13) has no counterpart in the Constitutions of the United States or Australia because they enumerate only the federal powers. However, Americans often speak of the "police power" of the states, meaning the power to promote the health, safety, morals and general welfare of the people: L.H. Tribe, American Constitutional Law (Foundation Press, New York, 3rd ed., 2000), 1046–1049.

[Section 21:2]

[1]See ch. 2, Reception, under heading § 2:6, "Ontario and Quebec". See also Tremblay, Les compétences législatives au Canada et les pouvoirs provinciaux en matière de propriété et de droits civils (1967), 19–45; O'Connor Report (Senate of Canada 1939), Annex I, 109–145; Stanley, A Short History of the Canadian Constitution (1969), chs. 2 and 3.

The phrase "property and civil rights in the province", as a head of provincial power in s. 91(13) of the Constitution Act, 1867, did not have precisely the same meaning as in the pre-confederation instruments, because the phrase now appeared in the context of a federal system in which extensive powers had been accorded to a new central Parliament.[2] But, subject to the qualifications required by the new federal scheme, it is clear that the framers of the Constitution Act understood the familiar phrase in the same sense it obtained in 1792 and 1774, that is to say, as a compendious description of the entire body of private law which governs the relationships between subject and subject, as opposed to the law which governs the relationships between the subject and the institutions of government.[3]

The Constitution Act, 1867 did make some changes in the historical definition of property and civil rights. If it had not done so, it would have left very little for the new central Parliament to do. The enumerated list of federal heads of legislative power in s. 91 included a number of matters which would otherwise have come within property and civil rights in the province, for example, trade and commerce (s. 91(2)), banking (s. 91(15)), bills of exchange and promissory notes (s. 91(18)), interest (s. 91(19)), bankruptcy and insolvency (s. 91(21)), patents of invention and discovery (s. 91(22)), copyrights (s. 91(23)), and marriage and divorce (s. 91(28)). These federal classes of subjects were withdrawn from property and civil rights by their exclusive vesting in the federal Parliament. In addition, the peace, order, and good government phrase in the opening language of s. 91 presumably contemplated that certain matters which would otherwise have come within property and civil rights could attain such a national dimension as to come within federal competence. The zoning of the national capital region has since been held to be an example of this kind of federal subject matter.[4]

It remains true, however, that even after proper accommodation has been made for the catalogue of exclusive federal powers, property and civil rights in the province still covers most of the legal relationships between persons in Canada. The law relating to property, succession, the family, contracts and torts is mainly within provincial jurisdiction under s. 92(13). Moreover, the original distinction between private and public law has tended to break down for constitutional purposes, as governments have increasingly intervened to regulate the economic life of the nation. Labour relations, once a private matter between employer and employee, is now so extensively regulated that it may be thought of as a

---

[2]In addition, the words "in the province" had been added to the phrase: see ch. 13, Extraterritorial Competence.

[3]*Citizens Insurance Co. v. Parsons* (1881), 7 App. Cas. 96, 110–111; Tremblay, Les compétences législatives au Canada et les pouvoirs provinciaux en matière de propriété et de droits civils (1967), passim; O'Connor Report (Senate of Canada 1939), Annex I, 135; W.R. Lederman, "Unity and Diversity in Canadian Federalism" (1975) 53 Can. Bar Rev. 597, 601.

[4]*Munro v. National Capital Comm.*, [1966] S.C.R. 663, and see generally ch. 17, Peace, Order and Good Government.

branch of public law. Much business activity is no longer governed simply by contract, but by statutory rules and the decisions of government officials. These governmental interventions in the marketplace, if they could not be fitted rather clearly into a particular head of legislative power, have for the most part been allocated by the courts to property and civil rights in the province. In other words, the evolution of our laws has now swept much public law into the rubric which was originally designed to exclude public law. This will be described in later sections of this chapter.

§ 21:3 Civil liberties

It will be clear from the history of the phrase "property and civil rights" that the term "civil rights" in this context does not bear the meaning which it has acquired in the United States, that is, as meaning the civil liberties which in that country are guaranteed by the Bill of Rights. Civil rights in the sense required by the Constitution Act, 1867 are juristically distinct from civil liberties. The civil rights referred to in the Constitution Act, 1867 comprise primarily proprietary, contractual or tortious rights; these rights exist when a legal rule stipulates that in certain circumstances one person is entitled to something from another. But civil liberties exist when there is an absence of legal rules: whatever is not forbidden is a civil liberty. While it is common to use the term "right" in reference to a freedom or liberty, it is important not to overlook the analytical distinction. To say that one has a "right" to criticize the government (for example) implies only that no law prohibits criticism of the government.[1] This is quite different from the right to have a loan repaid (for example), because the law of contract creates this right by stipulating that certain kinds of promises must be performed and by imposing sanctions for non-performance.[2]

The term "civil rights" in s. 92(13) is used in the older, stricter sense. It does not include the fundamental civil liberties of belief and expression. Of course, many provincial laws impinge on those civil liberties, but a law whose pith and substance is the restraint of belief or

---

[Section 21:3]

[1]Under a bill of rights, such as Canada's Charter of Rights, it may carry the further implication that no law could prohibit criticism of the government, that is, any such law would be unconstitutional.

[2]The distinction between rights and liberties, which is of course commonplace in legal writing, has been emphasized by Rand J. in *Saumur v. Que.*, [1953] 2 S.C.R. 299, 329 and *Switzman v. Elbling*, [1957] S.C.R. 285, 305. Even civil liberties which are guaranteed by an effective bill of rights are juristically distinct from civil rights arising from the law of property, contract or torts. A bill of rights is addressed to legislative bodies, not individuals, and it will prevent the making of, or render invalid, any law which purports to deny the guaranteed civil liberty. The bill of rights will not necessarily give any redress to an individual whose civil liberties are wrongly violated, although s. 24 of the Charter of Rights may well permit the granting of such redress. Section 24 of the Charter is discussed in ch. 40, Enforcement of Rights.

expression does not come within property and civil rights in the province.[3]

§ 21:4 Local or private matters

The provincial "residuary power"[1] in s. 92(16) over "all matters of a merely local or private nature in the province" has turned out to be relatively unimportant, because the wide scope of "property and civil rights in the province" has left little in the way of a residue of local or private matters.

Section 92(16) has not been completely ignored, but often it is suggested as a possible alternative to s. 92(13), rather than as an independent source of power. Jurisdiction over highway traffic, for example, is undoubtedly provincial, but the Supreme Court of Canada has not committed itself to a specific head of power: s. 92(16) has been suggested, along with s. 92(13).[2] A municipal by-law temporarily banning assemblies in the streets and parks of Montreal has been upheld primarily under s. 92(16), with s. 92(13) also relied upon.[3] Jurisdiction over local trade is also undoubtedly provincial, and the power has usually been attributed to s. 92(13), but it has been suggested that s. 92(16) is the more appropriate attribution.[4] Provincial film censorship has been upheld (before the adoption of the Charter of Rights), with s. 92(13) and s. 92(16) offered as alternative sources of power.[5] The regulation of gaming by video lottery terminal has been held to be competent to the province, with s. 92(13) and s. 92(16) offered as alternative sources of power.[6] Section 92(16) has been held to be the sole source of power to sustain the Heroin Treatment Act, a public health measure enacted by British Columbia.[7]

---

[3]See ch. 43, Expression, under heading §§ 43:1 to 43:4, "Distribution of powers". See also ch. 40, Civil Liberties, under heading § 34:6, "Distribution of powers", and ch. 55, Equality, under heading § 55:1, "Distribution of powers".

[Section 21:4]

[1]The double-residue theory is explained in ch. 17, Peace, Order, and Good Government, under heading § 17:1, "Residuary nature of power".

[2]*Provincial Secretary P.E.I. v. Egan*, [1941] S.C.R. 396 is the leading case, but the opinions of Duff C.J., Hudson and Taschereau JJ. do not refer to any particular head of s. 92, while Rinfret J. refers inconclusively (at p. 413) to three heads, namely, s. 92(9), (13) and (16).

[3]*A.-G. Can. and Dupond v. Montreal*, [1978] 2 S.C.R. 770, 792 (s. 92(8), (14) and (15) are also invoked).

[4]See ch. 20, Trade and Commerce, under heading § 20:1, "Relationship to property and civil rights". Compare *Rio Hotel v. N.B.*, [1987] 2 S.C.R. 59, 63, 67 (provincial authority to regulate the sale and consumption of alcohol comes from 92(16) and/or 92(13)).

[5]*N.S. Bd. of Censors v. McNeil*, [1978] 2 S.C.R. 662, 699.

[6]*Siemens v. Man.*, [2003] 1 S.C.R. 6, para. 22.

[7]*Schneider v. The Queen*, [1982] 2 S.C.R. 112. This was the view of all judges except Estey J., who in a separate concurrence suggested (at p. 141) s. 92(7) and (13), as well as (16).

II. INSURANCE

§ 21:5 Reasons for regulation

The insurance industry became the arena in which the two levels of government contended for the power to regulate business, or at least that part of business activity over which legislative power was not specifically allocated by the Constitution Act, 1867. Unlike banking (s. 91(15)), insurance is not specifically mentioned in the Constitution Act, 1867; but, like banking, insurance was one of the first industries to attract fundamental regulation.

Because the terms and conditions of insurance policies are in practice stipulated by the insurer, and are not well understood by the insured, governments sought to protect the insured by requiring the inclusion of certain conditions in every policy. Because the financial strength, probity and permanence of an insurer cannot in practice be judged by the insured, and are essential to the fulfilment of the policy, governments sought to control entry to, and supervise the performance of, the industry by licensing insurers, by requiring a security deposit, by limiting the insurers' powers of investment, and by official inspection of their books. Similar considerations apply to banks and loan and trust companies.

§ 21:6 Provincial power

In the latter part of the nineteenth century, both levels of government began to regulate the insurance industry. A provincial statute was the first to come before the courts. In the leading case of *Citizens' Insurance Co. v. Parsons* (1881),[1] the Privy Council upheld an Ontario statute which required that certain conditions be included in every policy of fire insurance entered into in Ontario. Their lordships held that regulation of the terms of contracts came within property and civil rights in the province (s. 92(13)), and did not come within trade and commerce (s. 91(2)).

The next statute to come before the courts was a federal one, the Insurance Act, 1910, which prohibited any company from carrying on the business of insurance unless it had a licence issued by the federal Minister of Finance; there was also a requirement of a security deposit and provision for official inspection and report upon solvency. Provincially-incorporated companies carrying on business wholly within the province of incorporation were exempt from the Act. The Privy Council in the *Insurance Reference* (1916)[2] held the statute to be unconstitutional. Rejecting the argument based on trade and commerce,[3] their lordships held that the regulation of a particular industry came

---

[Section 21:6]

[1] *Citizens' Insurance Co. v. Parsons* (1881), 7 App. Cas. 96.

[2] *A.-G. Can. v. A.-G. Alta.* (Insurance) [1916] 1 A.C. 588.

[3] In the United States, after an initial ruling that insurance was not "commerce" (*Paul v. Virginia* (1868), 75 U.S. 168), the Supreme Court changed its mind and decided that regulation of the insurance industry was competent to the federal Congress under

within property and civil rights in the province, even when the industry and particular firms extended beyond the boundaries of any one province.[4]

The *Insurance Reference* was followed by a series of cases in which the courts had to pass on a variety of federal attempts to regain the jurisdiction which had been denied to the Dominion. The federal government's persistence in this enterprise, the ingenuity of the expedients employed, and the intransigence of provincial opposition, apparently stemmed from rivalries between permanent officials in Ottawa and Toronto.[5] The first response to the Privy Council's decision was an attempt by the federal Parliament to compel the licensing of insurance companies by a provision in the Criminal Code making it an offence to carry on the business of insurance without a licence from the federal Minister of Finance. This device was condemned by the Privy Council as a colourable attempt to use the cloak of the criminal law "to interfere with the exercise of civil rights in the Provinces".[6] Then the Privy Council struck down provisions which required nonresident British subjects and aliens to obtain a licence to carry on the business of insurance, and which imposed a special tax on persons taking out insurance with unlicensed British and foreign insurers. Here was a reliance on the powers over immigration (non-residents), aliens and taxation; but the Privy Council held that all three powers were being employed colourably "to intermeddle with the conduct of insurance business".[7] The final case in the series concerned another federal statute directed only at British and foreign insurers and coupled with a special tax on the customers of unregistered insurers. The Supreme Court of Canada adopted the reasoning of the Privy Council's last insurance decision to hold this statute also invalid.[8]

In the middle of this series of decisions, the Privy Council also struck down the scheme of unemployment insurance which was part of the Canadian "new deal" to combat the depression of the 1930s. The brief

---

the commerce clause: *U.S. v. South-Eastern Underwriters Assn.* (1944), 322 U.S. 533. The Congress in fact delegated the power back to the states: Smith, The Commerce Power in Canada and the United States (1963), 266–273; P.R. Benson, The Supreme Court and the Commerce Clause, 1937–1970 (Dunellen, New York, 1970), 147–169.

[4]In *Can. Indemnity Co. v. A.-G. B.C.*, [1977] 2 S.C.R. 504, the insurance industry emphasized the interprovincial and international character of its operations in an attempt to defeat a provincial law establishing a provincial monopoly of automobile insurance; the Supreme Court of Canada upheld the law notwithstanding its incidental impact on interprovincial trade and commerce.

[5]The fascinating tale is told in C. Armstrong, "Federalism and Government Regulation: the Canadian Insurance Industry 1927–34" (1976) 19 Can. Pub. Admin. 88.

[6]*A.-G. Ont. v. Reciprocal Insurers*, [1924] A.C. 328, 336.

[7]*Reinsurance Act of Can.*, [1932] A.C. 41, 51.

[8]*Re s.16 of Special War Revenue Act*, [1942] S.C.R. 429; leave to appeal to the P.C. refused [1943] 4 D.L.R. 657. The issue reappeared when British Columbia took over the automobile insurance industry in the province. Once again provincial authority was reaffirmed, this time to uphold the challenged law: *Can. Indemnity Co. v. A.-G. B.C.*, [1977] 2 S.C.R. 504. See also *Can. Western Bank v. Alta.*, [2007] 2 S.C.R. 3, paras. 80, 116 (provincial Insurance Act validly applicable to banks when they promote insurance).

reasons delivered in the *Unemployment Insurance Reference* (1937)[9] do not make the ground of decision crystal clear, but it seems to have been decided partly on the basis that the scheme related to employment, and partly on the basis that the scheme related to insurance. Both these matters came within property and civil rights in the province. This decision was overcome by an amendment to the Constitution in 1940.[10]

§ 21:7 Federal power

Despite all these setbacks in the courts, the federal government continues to regulate a substantial part of the insurance industry.[1] For a time, it did so under separate statutes covering British and foreign companies, federally-incorporated companies and, on a voluntary basis,[2] provincially-incorporated companies.[3] It now regulates foreign companies, federally-incorporated companies and provincially-incorporated companies under the same statute.[4] Presumably, the provinces and the industry are now content with, or at least reconciled to, the continued federal presence, because there has been no constitutional attack on it since 1942. The previous federal statutes included preambles which indicated that the powers over trade and commerce, aliens and insolvency were being relied upon as supporting their constitutionality. The first two of these heads have, of course, been relied upon in the past. But in all the litigation between 1916 and 1942 the federal power over "insolvency" (s. 91(21)) was never considered as a possible basis of federal jurisdiction. The current federal statute does not contain a similar preamble.

In the *Wentworth Insurance* case (1969),[5] a federal law applicable to insolvent insurance companies was upheld. The federal Winding-Up Act provided a certain order of priority for the distribution by the liquidator to creditors of securities which insurance companies were required by provincial law to keep on deposit. The Ontario Insurance Act provided a different administration and a different order of priority for the distribution of the same fund. On the winding-up of the Wentworth Insurance Company, the question arose whether the company's deposit should be

---

[9] *A.-G. Can. v. A.-G. Ont.* (Unemployment Insurance) [1937] A.C. 355.

[10] Constitution Act, 1940, adding "unemployment insurance" as head 2A of s. 91: see ch. 33, Social Security, under heading § 33:2, "Unemployment insurance".

[Section 21:7]

[1] Marine insurance is a special case; it is within federal jurisdiction under s. 91(10) (navigation and shipping); *Triglav v. Terrasses Jewellers*, [1983] 1 S.C.R. 283.

[2] In *Can. Pioneer Management v. Labour Relations Bd. Sask.*, [1980] 1 S.C.R. 433, it was held that a provincially-incorporated life insurance company, which was voluntarily registered under the Canadian and British Insurance Companies Act, was still subject to provincial labour relations law.

[3] Canadian and British Insurance Companies Act, R.S.C. 1985, c. I-12; Foreign Insurance Companies Act, R.S.C. 1985, c. I-13; Department of Insurance Act, R.S.C. 1985, c. I-14.

[4] Insurance Companies Act, S.C. 1991, c. 47.

[5] *A.-G. Ont. v. Policy-holders of Wentworth Insurance Co.*, [1969] S.C.R. 779.

administered in accordance with the federal or the provincial law. The Supreme Court of Canada divided sharply on the question, but decided by a majority of five to four to adopt the reasoning of Laskin J.A. in the Ontario Court of Appeal to the effect that the federal law was a valid law in relation to insolvency, and that the federal law was the applicable provision. Hall J. for the minority said that the federal law was "a foray into the field of insurance, an area forbidden to Parliament", and that it was "colourable legislation and, because of this, ultra vires".[6] Certainly the majority's decision was a startling departure from the course of decision between 1916 and 1942 when so many and various federal attempts to enter the field of insurance were rebuffed. Now entry had been gained through the "insolvency" door. Whether the same point of entry would lead to the regulation of solvent companies, for the purpose of preventing insolvency, is of course much more doubtful.

III. BUSINESS IN GENERAL

§ 21:8 Business in general

The insurance cases discussed in the previous section of this chapter established the proposition that the regulation of business was ordinarily a matter within property and civil rights in the province. To this proposition there are a number of exceptions. Some industries fall within federal jurisdiction because they are enumerated in s. 91, such as navigation and shipping (s. 91(10)) and banking (s. 91(15)), or because they are excepted from s. 92(10), namely, interprovincial or international transportation and communications undertakings (s.92(10)(a) and (b)) and works declared to be for the general advantage of Canada (s. 92(10)(c)). Some industries have been held to fall within federal jurisdiction under the peace, order, and good government power, namely, aeronautics and the production of atomic energy. Other federal powers confer a limited power to regulate business, for example, trade and commerce (s. 91(2)), taxation (s. 91(3)), interest (s. 91(19)), the criminal law (s. 91(27)) and peace, order, and good government (s. 91 opening words).

But the gaps in federal power are very important and extensive. The trade and commerce power will authorize a federal prohibition of the importation of margarine, but not a prohibition of its manufacture or sale.[1] The trade and commerce power will also authorize the regulation of interprovincial marketing, but not local marketing.[2] The trade and commerce power will also authorize the regulation of competition, but not the regulation of wages and prices, product standards or particular

[6] *A.-G. Ont. v. Policy-holders of Wentworth Insurance Co.*, [1969] S.C.R. 779, 806.

[Section 21:8]

[1] *Can. Federation of Agriculture v. A.-G. Que.* (Margarine) [1951] 1 A.C. 179. See also *UL Can. v. Que.*, [2005] 1 S.C.R. 143 (upholding provincial law prohibiting sale of yellow-coloured margarine).

[2] See §§ 21:12 to 21:14, "Marketing".

industries such as insurance.[3] The taxation power may be used to provide various kinds of incentives or disincentives with a view to the control of business activity,[4] but may not be used as a device to assume regulatory control over the insurance industry.[5] The interest power may be used to control interest rates, but not to control other terms of loans.[6] The criminal law power may be used to prohibit undesirable commercial practices, but if the law departs from the conventional criminal format the criminal law power will not sustain it.[7] The criminal law power may also be used to enforce closing hours on businesses for religious reasons, but not for secular reasons.[8] The peace, order, and good government power will authorize the control of rents, prices and profits in times of emergency, but not in normal times.[9]

The previous paragraph is not intended to be an exhaustive list of the gaps in the federal power to regulate business. It is simply a recitation of the better-known arenas of controversy. The gaps in federal power are covered by the provincial power over property and civil rights. The double-aspect doctrine also ensures substantial areas of concurrency even when federal power exists. The point is that the regulation of an industry, or the more general regulation of prices or profits or combinations, has traditionally been regarded by the courts, not in terms of its ultimate, often nation-wide objectives, but in terms of its immediate impact upon freedom of contract and property rights.[10] In these terms, of course, restraints on business fall into the category of property and civil rights in the province.[11]

IV. PROFESSIONS AND TRADES

§ 21:9 Professions and trades

Regulation of professions and trades typically takes the form of restrictions on entry, coupled with rules of conduct, which often include fee-setting, and administration by a governing body. Such regulation is no

[3]See ch. 20, Trade and Commerce, under heading § 20:4, "General trade and commerce".

[4]*Reader's Digest Assn. v. A.-G. Can.* (1965), 59 D.L.R. (2d) 54 (Que. C.A.).

[5]*Re Insurance Act of Can.*, [1932] A.C. 41.

[6]*A.-G. Ont. v. Barfried Enterprises*, [1963] S.C.R. 570.

[7]See ch. 18, Criminal Law, under heading § 18:2, "Definition of criminal law".

[8]See ch. 18, Criminal Law, under heading § 18:12, "Sunday observance law".

[9]See ch. 17, Peace, Order and Good Government, under heading §§ 17:7 to 17:11, "The emergency branch". For provincial power to control prices, see *Home Oil Distributors v. A.-G. B.C.*, [1940] S.C.R. 444; *Carnation Co. v. Que. Agricultural Marketing Bd.*, [1968] S.C.R. 238.

[10]The same approach has been taken in the labour relations cases: see §§ 21:10 to 21:11, "Labour relations".

[11]*N.S. Bd. of Censors v. McNeil*, [1978] 2 S.C.R. 662 (film censorship characterized as regulation of film business and upheld under s. 92(13)).

different for constitutional purposes than that of other industries, and comes within property and civil rights in the province.[1]

In *Krieger v. Law Society of Alberta* (2002),[2] the question arose whether the Law Society of Alberta had the power to discipline a provincial Crown prosecutor who had failed to make timely disclosure to the defence of exculpatory evidence in his possession. The Supreme Court of Canada held that the Law Society, which was empowered by provincial law to regulate the legal profession in the province, did have the jurisdiction. Although the duty of prosecutors to make timely disclosure was a rule of criminal procedure (a federal responsibility),[3] a default could also be a breach of professional responsibility. Crown prosecutors, whether federal or provincial, who practised in the province were all members of the Law Society. Like other lawyers in the province, they came within the jurisdiction of the Law Society to enforce professional standards of behaviour.

V. LABOUR RELATIONS

§ 21:10 Provincial power

The regulation of labour relations[1] over most of the economy is within provincial competence under property and civil rights in the province. The leading case is *Toronto Electric Commissioners v. Snider* (1925),[2] which concerned the validity of a federal attempt to regulate labour relations—the Industrial Disputes Investigation Act of 1907. This Act afforded compulsory conciliation procedures for the settlement of industrial disputes in mining, transportation, communication and public service utilities, and optional procedures for the settlement of disputes not compulsorily covered. The Privy Council held that the Act was unconstitutional. We have noticed in earlier chapters that their lordships rejected arguments that the Act could be sustained under the

---

[Section 21:9]

[1]*Beaule v. Corp. of Master Electricians* (1969), 10 D.L.R. (3d) 93 (Que. C.A.) (electricians); *Re Imrie*, [1972] 3 O.R. 275 (H.C.) (realtors); *R. v. Buzunis* (1972), 26 D.L.R. (3d) 502 (Man. C.A.) (accountants); *Re Levkoe* (1977), 18 O.R. (2d) 265 (Div. Ct.) (pharmacists); *Re Underwood McLellan* (1979), 103 D.L.R. (3d) 268 (Sask. C.A.) (engineers); *A.-G. Can. v. Law Society of B.C.*, [1982] 2 S.C.R. 307 (lawyers); *Global Securities Corp. v. B.C.*, [2000] 1 S.C.R. 494 (securities dealers); *Law Society of B.C. v. Mangat*, [2001] 3 S.C.R. 113, paras. 38–47 (lawyers, relying on s. 92(14) as well as s. 92(13)).

[2]*Krieger v. Law Society of Alberta*, [2002] 3 S.C.R. 372. Iacobucci and Major JJ. wrote the opinion of the Court.

[3]It is also a constitutional requirement: *R. v. Stinchcombe*, [1991] 3 S.C.R. 326; discussed in ch. 47, Fundamental Justice, under heading § 47:34, "Pre-trial disclosure by the Crown".

[Section 21:10]

[1]For discussion, see Tremblay, Les compétences législatives au Canada et les pouvoirs provinciaux en matière de propriété et de droits civils (1967), 227–253; Laskin, Canadian Constitutional Law (5th ed., 1986 by Finkelstein), 523–548; Tremblay, Droit Constitutionnel-Principes (2nd éd., 2000), Part II, ch. 3.

[2]*Toronto Electric Commissioners v. Snider*, [1925] A.C. 396.

peace, order, and good government power, or the trade and commerce power, or the criminal law power, and held instead that the Act came within property and civil rights in the province.

The decision of the Privy Council in *Snider* seems to have been both unexpected and unwelcome in Canada at the time. The federal Act had been upheld in the Ontario courts, and in previous litigation in the Quebec courts. Immediately after the decision, the federal Act was amended to confine its operation to industries which were otherwise within federal legislative authority, and in this more limited form the Act was upheld.[3] The amendment also made the Act applicable to any dispute within provincial jurisdiction "which by the legislation of the province is made subject to the provisions of this Act". This invitation to cooperate was accepted by all provinces except Prince Edward Island, each province enacting legislation adopting the federal law and thereby restoring the fact of uniform federal labour law. However, after the Wagner Act of 1935[4] in the United States had introduced the modern model of North American labour law with its concepts of certification, compulsory collective bargaining and unfair labour practices, new legislation came to be enacted in Canada by the provinces. Apart from the second world war, when a uniform federal law on the Wagner model was proclaimed under the War Measures Act,[5] labour law became provincial again. This is the present situation and it shows no sign of changing.[6]

The legislation in *Snider* was concerned with industrial peace—the prevention of strikes and lockouts through compulsory conciliation. In the *Labour Conventions* case (1937),[7] the decision was extended to labour standards legislation. Federal statutes providing for a weekly rest in employment, limitations on working hours and minimum wages were all held to be unconstitutional. Their lordships rejected arguments based on the peace, order, and good government power and the treaty power, and held that laws imposing labour standards came within property and civil rights in the province. A similar decision was rendered in the

---

[3] *Re Industrial Relations and Disputes Investigation Act (Can.)*, [1955] S.C.R. 529.

[4] The Wagner Act (National Labour Relations Act, 1935), a federal statute, was upheld in *Nat. Labour Relations Bd. v. Jones & Laughlin Steel Corp.* (1937), 301 U.S. 1. The federal Fair Labour Standards Act, 1938 was upheld in *U.S. v. Darby* (1941), 312 U.S. 100. Both decisions were based on the commerce clause. In Australia, the Constitution, by s. 51(35), expressly empowers the federal Parliament to make laws with respect to "conciliation and arbitration for the prevention and settlement of industrial disputes extending beyond the limits of any one state".

[5] Order-in-Council P.C. 1003, sometimes called the "Canadian Wagner Act", was replaced after the war with the Industrial Relations and Disputes Investigation Act, S.C. 1948, c. 54, which was confined to "federal" industries.

[6] The history is related in F.R. Scott, "Federal Jurisdiction over Labour Relations" (1960) 6 McGill L.J. 153.

[7] *A.-G. Can. v. A.-G. Ont.* (Labour Conventions) [1937] A.C. 326.

Empress Hotel case (1950),[8] where the Privy Council held that minimum hours of work in a hotel could only be stipulated by the province.[9]

Even a scheme of unemployment insurance, involving as it did compulsory contributions by employers and employees, was held to be incompetent to the federal Parliament in the *Unemployment Insurance Reference* (1937).[10] This decision was overcome by an amendment to the Constitution adding "unemployment insurance" as a new head of federal power (s. 91(2A)).[11] In the *Oil, Chemical Workers* case (1963),[12] the Supreme Court of Canada held that a province could validly prohibit the use for political contributions of trade union funds obtained by compulsory deduction from wages. This decision and the *Unemployment Insurance Reference* are companions in their insistence that the modification of the employment relationship is exclusively within property and civil rights, notwithstanding the important federal aspects presented by the relief of nation-wide unemployment and by the funding of federal election campaigns.

§ 21:11 Federal power

Despite the consistent affirmations of provincial power over labour relations, there is still a substantial federal presence in the field. In 1925, immediately after the decision in *Toronto Electric Commissioners v. Snider*,[1] the federal Parliament amended its labour legislation to apply only to "employment upon or in connection with any work, undertaking or business that is within the legislative authority of the Parliament of Canada".[2] The Act went on to list a number of industries which were within federal authority, such as navigation and shipping and interprovincial transportation and communication, "but not so as to restrict the generality of the foregoing". Aside from the period of the second world war,[3] this has been the pattern of coverage for federal labour law ever since, although the drafting has been slightly changed and the list of federal industries expanded.[4]

The theory that the federal Parliament could regulate labour relations

---

[8]*CPR v. A.-G. B.C.* (Empress Hotel) [1950] A.C. 122. Accord, *Re Hours of Labour*, [1925] S.C.R. 505.

[9]Compare *OPSEU v. Ont.*, [1987] 2 S.C.R. 2 (province may legislate conditions of employment in provincial public sector, including restrictions on political activities).

[10]*A.-G. Can. v. A.-G. Ont.* (Unemployment Insurance) [1937] A.C. 355.

[11]Constitution Act, 1940; see ch. 33, Social Security under heading § 33:2, "Unemployment Insurance".

[12]*Oil, Chemical and Atomic Wkrs. v. Imperial Oil*, [1963] S.C.R. 584.

[Section 21:11]

[1]*Toronto Electric Commissioners v. Snider*, [1925] A.C. 396.

[2]Industrial Disputes Investigation Amendment Act, S.C. 1925, c. 14.

[3]Order-in-Council P.C. 1003, sometimes called the "Canadian Wagner Act", was replaced after the war with the Industrial Relations and Disputes Investigation Act, S.C. 1948, c. 54, which was confined to "federal" industries.

[4]See now Canada Labour Code, R.S.C. 1985, c. L-2.

in those industries which were otherwise within federal legislative competence seemed plausible and was not directly challenged until the *Stevedores Reference* (1955).[5] In that case, two unions were claiming to represent a group of stevedores in the port of Toronto; one union was certified under provincial law, the other was certified under federal law. The federal law specifically applied to "businesses carried on for or in connection with navigation or shipping". The subject of "navigation and shipping" is, of course, a federal head of power unders. 91(10) of the Constitution Act, 1867. The Supreme Court of Canada held that the federal law was valid, and that it was applicable to the stevedores because their work of loading and unloading ships was an essential part of navigation and shipping.[6] Since this decision, it has been clear that the federal Parliament has the power to regulate employment in works, undertakings or businesses within the legislative authority of the federal Parliament.[7]

The legislation upheld in the *Stevedores Reference* covered only what may be termed the federal private sector. Needless to say, there is no doubt that the federal Parliament also has jurisdiction to regulate labour relations in the federal public sector, that is to say, employment in the departments and agencies of the federal government.[8]

The *Stevedores Reference* has been followed in many subsequent cases, litigation being caused by doubt as to whether or not a particular bargaining unit of employees is an integral part of an undertaking that is within federal jurisdiction. The required connection with the federal undertaking is a functional or operational one.[9] The fact that the employer is an interprovincial railway will not sweep a group of employees into federal jurisdiction, if they operate a hotel which is functionally separate from the railway.[10] The fact that employees are engaged in constructing a runway at an airport will not sweep them into federal jurisdiction, if their work is simply construction, unrelated to the tasks of design or operation that would be an integral part of aeronautics.[11] The fact that the employer is a company operated by Indians, and the

---

[5]*Re Industrial Relations and Disputes Investigation Act (Can.)*, [1955] S.C.R. 529.

[6]Later cases have narrowed the holding of the *Stevedores Reference* to stevedoring activity that is an essential part of *extraprovincial* transportation by ship (which was the factual situation in the case). Stevedoring activity that serves only intraprovincial shipping would remain within provincial jurisdiction: *Tessier v. Que.*, [2012] 2 S.C.R. 3, para. 34: and see ch. 22, Transportation and Communication, under heading § 22:12, "Transportation by water".

[7]E.g., *Ont. Hydro v. Ont.*, [1993] 3 S.C.R. 327 (employees on works, declared under s. 92(10)(c) to be for the general advantage of Canada, are within federal jurisdiction).

[8]*Re Hours of Labour*, [1925] S.C.R. 505, 510; *Re Minimum Wage Act (Sask.)*, [1948] S.C.R. 248; *Letter Carriers' Union v. Can. Union of Postal Wkrs.*, [1975] 1 S.C.R. 178; *Can. Labour Relations Bd. v. Yellowknife*, [1977] 2 S.C.R. 729; *A.-G. Can. v. St. Hubert Base Teachers' Assn.*, [1983] 1 S.C.R. 498.

[9]See also ch. 22, Transportation and Communication, under heading §§ 22:7 to 22:9, "Related undertakings".

[10]*CPR v. A.-G. B.C.* (Empress Hotel) [1950] A.C. 122.

[11]*Construction Montcalm v. Minimum Wage Comm.*, [1979] 1 S.C.R. 754.

business is on an Indian reserve, will not sweep employees into federal jurisdiction, if their work is simply the manufacturing of shoes.[12] The fact that employees' wages are subsidized by the federal government, as part of a federal job creation programme, will not sweep construction workers into federal jurisdiction.[13] The Court has approached these cases on the basis that provincial competence over labour relations is the rule, and federal competence is the exception.[14] Federal competence exists only where it is found that the work performed by the employees is an integral part of an undertaking within federal jurisdiction, and that finding depends upon "legislative authority over the operation, not over the person of the employer".[15]

Issues of constitutional jurisdiction over labour relations usually arise initially before a labour board, which is asked to certify a union as the bargaining agent of a group of employees. If certification is opposed on constitutional grounds, the labour board must decide the issue of "constitutional jurisdictional fact" that is thereby raised: do these employees form an integral part of a federal undertaking? So long as the labour board asks itself the right question, it is surely prudent for the courts to defer to the judgment of the board, informed as it will be by a closer and more expert examination of the facts.[16] The Supreme Court of Canada has, however, made clear that, when an administrative tribunal decides a constitutional issue involving the federal-provincial division of powers, it is subject to review by a superior court on the standard of correctness, not reasonableness.[17] The tribunal is to receive no deference.[18]

In the "federal sectors" of the economy, where there is federal jurisdiction over labour relations, is the federal jurisdiction exclusive, or is it concurrent with that of the provincial Legislatures? This question did not receive a definitive answer until *Commission du Salaire Minimum v. Bell Telephone Co.* (1966).[19] The issue in that case was whether Quebec's minimum wage law applied to the Bell Telephone Company, which was within federal jurisdiction as an interprovincial communications undertaking.[20] At the time when the case arose, there was no federal minimum wage law (there is now). The Supreme Court of Canada held nevertheless that the provincial law was inapplicable to Bell.

---

[12]*Four B Manufacturing v. United Garment Workers*, [1980] 1 S.C.R. 1031. Folld. in *NIL/TU,O Child and Family Services Society v. B.C.G.S.E.U.*, [2010] 2 S.C.R. 696 (provincial labour law applies to child welfare agency established by First Nations, operated by Indians and serving only Indian families on reserves).

[13]*YMHA Jewish Community Centre v. Brown*, [1989] 1 S.C.R. 1532.

[14]*Four B Manufacturing v. United Garment Workers*, [1980] 1 S.C.R. 1031, 1045.

[15]*Can. labour Relations Bd. v. Yellowknife*, [1977] 2 S.C.R. 729, 736.

[16]For the same reason, a ruling by a court as to constitutional jurisdiction over a unit of employees would normally be premature until the labour board had considered the issue: *Re 50478 Ont.* (1986), 56 O.R. (2d) 781 (H.C.).

[17]*Can. v. Vavilov*, 2019 SCC 65, para. 55.

[18]*Can. v. Vavilov*, 2019 SCC 65, para. 55.

[19]*Commission du Salaire Minimum v. Bell Telephone Co.*, [1966] S.C.R. 767.

[20]*Toronto v. Bell Telephone Co.*, [1905] A.C. 52.

The Court held that rates of pay and hours of work were "vital parts" of the interprovincial undertaking, and that all such vital parts were subject to the exclusive legislative control of the federal Parliament. Therefore, although the provincial law was valid in its application to most employment in the province, it could not constitutionally apply to employment in a federally-regulated industry.[21]

The *Quebec Minimum Wage* case was criticized in earlier editions of this book, on the basis that there was no good reason to immunize federal undertakings from provincial labour standards where the federal standards were lower or (as in the *Quebec Minimum Wage* case) non-existent.[22] However, in *Bell Canada v. Quebec* (1988),[23] the Supreme Court of Canada rejected the criticism and followed its earlier decision. The issue in the *Bell Canada* case was whether a provincial occupational health and safety law was applicable to an interprovincial telephone company. The provincial law gave to workers who used video monitors the right to be assigned to other duties while they were pregnant. The Court held that the provincial law was inapplicable to the telephone company. By interfering in the labour relations of the company, the law would affect a vital part of the management and operation of the federal undertaking. The Court thus reaffirmed its position that labour relations in federally-regulated industries is the exclusive preserve of federal law.

Federal jurisdiction over labour relations will extend outside the federal sectors of the economy in times of national emergency.[24] Both of the world wars counted as emergencies, although the depression of the 1930s did not. However, in the *Anti-Inflation Reference* (1976),[25] the Supreme Court of Canada held that a period of double-digit inflation (Canada's third since the second world war) counted as an emergency, and on this basis upheld temporary federal wage (and price) controls which substantially transformed labour relations outside as well as inside the federal sectors of the economy. This decision was rendered in the face of economic evidence that the inflationary situation was not particularly critical, and in spite of the fact that the preamble to the statute did not allege the existence of an emergency. This attenuation of the concept of an emergency makes federal intervention in labour relations an ever present possibility, since the Canadian economy (like that of all other countries) is nearly always beset by some difficulty, whether it be high unemployment, poor growth or an adverse balance of payments, which could be characterized as an emergency with as much (or as little) plausibility as inflation. Needless to say, throughout these

---

[21]The case was followed in *Letter Carriers' Union of Can. v. Can. Union of Postal Wkrs.*, [1975] 1 S.C.R. 178.

[22]The criticism is summarized in ch. 15, Judicial Review on Federal Grounds, under heading § 15:18, "Federally regulated undertakings".

[23]*Bell Canada v. Quebec*, [1988] 1 S.C.R. 749.

[24]See ch. 17, Peace, Order, and Good Government, under heading §§ 17:7 to 17:11, "The emergency branch".

[25]*Re Anti-Inflation Act*, [1976] 2 S.C.R. 373.

"emergencies" provincial power is concurrent, and provincial laws will operate unless and to the extent that inconsistent federal laws have been enacted.

VI. MARKETING

§ 21:12 Reasons for regulation

The reasons for regulating markets[1] may be found in the interests of both producers and consumers. Producers wanted to combine together to improve their bargaining power. They also wanted uniform standards of quality, enforced by grading, inspection and labelling, so that variations in kind or quality would be fairly reflected in prices. Sometimes, they sought a pooling of proceeds and an equalization of returns so that the short-term rises and falls in the market would be shared by all. In some cases, producers, through a producer-controlled board, would seek to control the market itself by determining the time, quantity and place at which the product should be sold, or even by controlling production and directly fixing prices. The interests of consumers, while by no means identical to those of producers, especially in the matter of prices, also called for regulation of some market practices. Uniform standards of quality, enforced by inspection and labelling, were needed to eliminate dangerous or unhealthy goods and deceptive marketing practices.

§ 21:13 Federal power

We have already seen that early attempts by the federal Parliament to enact marketing schemes under the trade and commerce power (s. 91(2)) were struck down by the Privy Council.[1] Their lordships started with a strong presumption that any interference with contracts was a matter within property and civil rights in the province. Even where the market to be regulated was primarily interprovincial or international, the Privy Council struck down statutes in their entirety if they had any application to purely local transactions.[2] This attitude made the federal enactment of an effective marketing scheme impossible.

[Section 21:12]

[1]The regulation of marketing raises several constitutional issues in addition to those discussed in the following text. On the federal declaratory power, see ch. 22, Transportation and Communication, under heading § 22:10, "Works for the general advantage of Canada"; on marketing levies as indirect taxation, see ch. 31, Taxation, under heading § 31:16, "Regulatory charges"; on the guarantee of free admission of goods (s. 121), see ch. 46, Mobility, under heading §§ 46:7 to 46:10, "Goods"; on the limited scope of the concurrent power over agriculture (s. 95), see *A.-G. Sask. v. A.-G. Can.* (Farm Security) [1949] A.C. 110; *Can. Federation of Agriculture v. A.-G. Que.* (Margarine) [1951] A.C. 179, 198–200; Laskin, Canadian Constitutional Law (5th ed., 1986 by Finkelstein), 500–501; McConnell, Commentary on the British North America Act (1977), 300–303; on federal-provincial inter-delegation, see ch. 14, Delegation.

[Section 21:13]

[1]See ch. 20, Trade and Commerce.

[2]The Supreme Court of the United States, in contrast, held that where intrastate

Since the abolition of appeals to the Privy Council, the Canadian courts have interpreted the trade and commerce power more liberally. Federal regulation of the trade in grain[3] and in oil[4] has been upheld, even though the regulation extended to purely local transactions. The reasoning was that the marketing of products which flow across interprovincial boundaries from the province of production or importation to the province of consumption or export could be regulated by the federal Parliament, and that some local transactions could also be regulated where that was an incident of the regulation of the interprovincial trade. These decisions represent a departure from the Privy Council precedents, and a significant expansion of federal power. Whether the power will be permitted to expand to the point of enabling the federal Parliament to regulate any market which extends beyond any one province remains to be seen, but it would be a rational development of the trade and commerce power.

§ 21:14 Provincial power

Contracts of sale and purchase are prima facie matters within "property and civil rights in the province" (s. 92(13)), and therefore amenable to provincial legislation. There is no doubt that under s. 92(13) the provinces have the power to regulate intraprovincial trade, although they lack the power to regulate interprovincial trade.[1] In the context of marketing, this distinction is not easy to apply. A provincial marketing scheme will nearly always have an impact on producers or consumers in other provinces. The question is to what extent should a province be permitted to burden interprovincial trade in the course of regulating intraprovincial trade?[2]

In *Shannon v. Lower Mainland Dairy Products Board* (1938),[3] the Privy Council upheld a provincial scheme for the compulsory marketing of milk through provincial boards. This scheme applied to all milk sold in the province, including milk produced in other provinces. The application to milk produced out of the province was upheld as an incident of an essentially intraprovincial scheme. In *Home Oil Distributors v. A.-G.*

---

and interstate transactions were commingled, the Congress was empowered under the commerce clause to regulate the whole: Smith, The Commerce Power in Canada and the United States (1963), 142.

[3]*Murphy v. CPR*, [1958] S.C.R. 626; *R. v. Klassen* (1959), 20 D.L.R. (2d) 406 (Man. C.A.).

[4]*Caloil v. A.-G. Can.*, [1971] S.C.R. 543.

[Section 21:14]

[1]See ch. 20, Trade and Commerce.

[2]The language of "burdens" on interstate commerce is conventional in the United States, where the essential problem is exactly the same, but is confronted more openly by the courts than in Canada: see P.R. Benson, The Supreme Court and the Commerce Clause, 1937–1970 (Dunellen, New York, 1970), ch. 7.

[3]*Shannon v. Lower Mainland Dairy Products Board*, [1938] A.C. 708.

B.C. (1940),[4] the Supreme Court of Canada upheld provincial regulation of the prices of all gasoline and fuel oil sold in the province. Once again the application of the scheme to products produced out of the province was upheld. In *Carnation Co. v. Quebec Agricultural Marketing Board (1968)*,[5] the Supreme Court of Canada upheld a provincial marketing plan for the sale of raw milk by farmers to the Carnation Company which processed the milk. Under this plan, Carnation had to pay higher prices for its milk than would have been payable in a free market, and indeed higher prices than other processors purchasing from farmers in the same area. In fact, Carnation shipped the bulk of its product out of the province. The Supreme Court of Canada held nevertheless that the marketing law was "in relation to" intraprovincial trade, and that it merely "affected" interprovincial trade.[6]

These three cases, spanning as they do both the Privy Council period and the post-appeals period, suggest a very extensive power to regulate marketing within the province, notwithstanding the burdens incidentally placed on the residents of other provinces. It is true that in the *Ontario Farm Products Marketing Reference* (1957)[7] there were dicta in the Supreme Court of Canada warning that provincial power over intraprovincial transactions would not extend to transactions which were really part and parcel of interprovincial trade. But these dicta had been cited in the *Carnation* case[8] the following year, and the Court had not regarded them as applicable, despite the fact that in *Carnation* the bulk of the regulated product was destined for export. However, in the *Manitoba Egg Reference* (1971),[9] the Supreme Court of Canada unexpectedly struck down a provincial scheme to regulate the marketing of eggs. The scheme applied to all eggs sold in Manitoba, including eggs produced elsewhere. The reason for the application of the scheme to eggs produced out-of-province was that the scheme could otherwise be undermined by imports of an unregulated and cheaper product. Moreover, the application of provincial regulation to a product produced outside the province had been upheld in the *Shannon* and *Home Oil* cases.[10] But, without explaining why these precedents and *Carnation* were not controlling, Martland J. for a majority of the Court held that "the Plan now in issue not only affects interprovincial trade in eggs, but that it aims at the

[4] *Home Oil Distributors v. A.-G. B.C.*, [1940] S.C.R. 444.

[5] *Carnation Co. v. Quebec Agricultural Marketing Board*, [1968] S.C.R. 238; folld. in *Can. Indemnity Co. v. A.-G. B.C.*, [1977] 2 S.C.R. 504.

[6] Accord, *UL Can. v. Que.*, [2005] 1 S.C.R. 143 (upholding provincial prohibition on sale of yellow-coloured margarine, notwithstanding its application to imported as well as locally manufactured margarine).

[7] *Re Farm Products Marketing Act*, [1957] S.C.R. 198.

[8] *Carnation Co. v. Quebec Agricultural Marketing Board*, [1968] S.C.R. 238, 245–246.

[9] *A.-G. Man. v. Man. Egg & Poultry Assn.*, [1971] S.C.R. 689.

[10] *Shannon v. Lower Mainland Dairy Products Board*, [1938] A.C. 708, *Home Oil Distributors v. A.-G. B.C.*, [1940] S.C.R. 444.

regulation of such trade".[11] The plan was accordingly held to be unconstitutional in its entirety.[12]

The *Manitoba Egg Reference* arose out of a much-publicized "chicken and egg war" between Ontario (which produced a surplus of eggs) and Quebec (which produced a surplus of chickens). Those provinces had established marketing plans for eggs in Quebec and for chickens in Ontario which, according to the press, gave undue preference to the locally-produced product. Manitoba, which as a producer of agricultural surpluses claimed to be injured by both plans, created an egg marketing plan of its own on the Quebec model and referred it to the courts for a judicial decision which would also effectively determine the validity of the Quebec and Ontario plans.[13] This background of the case may be relevant, because, although it is not mentioned in the opinions, it must have been present in the minds of the judges, and it may well have suggested to them that the various marketing plans could be used as vehicles by which a province could discriminate against the out-of-province product. Discrimination would of course make the plan unconstitutional, at least in operation,[14] and would be a clear distinction between this case and *Shannon* and *Home Oil*. Unfortunately, none of the opinions clearly stated that the decision was based on the discriminatory character of the plan, and Laskin J. denied that his opinion was based on discrimination against out-of-province producers.[15] A literal reading of the opinions would seem "to bar subjection of extraprovincial

[11]*A.-G. Man. v. Man. Egg & Poultry Assn.*, [1971] S.C.R. 689, 703 per Martland J. with whom Fauteux C.J., Abbott, Judson, Ritchie and Spence JJ. agreed. Separate concurring opinions by Laskin J., with whom Hall J. agreed, and Pigeon J. are to the same effect.

[12]In *Burns Foods v. A.-G. Man.*, [1975] 1 S.C.R. 494, the Supreme Court of Canada, by a majority of six to one, reached a similar decision, but held that only that part of the Manitoba Hog Producers' Marketing Plan which purported to bind the product purchased out-of-province was invalid. Even this more restrained result seems open to criticism, however, on the basis that the application to the imported product was necessary to the integrity of the plan and was merely an incidental effect of a plan whose primary purpose was to control the marketing of hogs in the province. This was the basis of Ritchie J.'s dissent.

[13]Weiler, In the Last Resort (1974), ch. 6, describes the background to the *Manitoba Egg Reference*, criticizes the use by the Manitoba government of the reference in these circumstances, and criticizes the decision of the Supreme Court.

[14]However, if discrimination was not inherent in the plan, and it could be administered fairly, then it would follow that only its unfair administration would be unconstitutional, and there would be no basis for the Court to hold invalid the plan itself.

[15]*A.-G. Man. v. Man. Egg & Poultry Assn.*, [1971] S.C.R. 689, 716, but note Laskin J.'s next paragraph, which refers to a province's "figurative sealing of its borders to entry of goods from others" (717), and which does appear to assume discrimination. The other opinions could be read as regarding the plan as inherently discriminatory: see especially 701 per Martland J., 723 per Pigeon J. In *Burns Foods v. A.-G. Man.*, [1975] 1 S.C.R. 494, 506, Pigeon J. (with the agreement of Fauteux C.J., Abbott, Martland, Judson and Spence JJ.) referred to "the features of discrimination present in the *[Manitoba] Egg* case". However, he went on to say that discrimination was absent in the *Burns Foods* case, and yet the hog marketing plan in that case could not be extended to hogs purchased out-of-province.

products even to a fairly administered, provincial regulatory scheme".[16] Such a principle is inconsistent with prior authority and with any effective provincial capacity to regulate marketing.

The decision in the *Manitoba Egg Reference* was followed by a federal-provincial agreement involving all 11 governments which settled a national marketing plan for eggs. The plan allocated production quotas to each province, and stipulated a higher price for eggs sold outside the province of production. Within each province, production quotas were to be imposed on producers so as to control supply and support prices; the surplus product (surplus to the table market) was to be sold in the industrial market by a marketing board; and the plan was to be financed by levies on all producers. The plan was to be administered by a national marketing board and ten provincial marketing boards. This ambitious national project was set up under the aegis of a federal marketing statute and ten provincial marketing statutes, and each marketing board was granted powers by inter-delegations from both levels of government. Through the cooperative action of both levels of government, it was hoped to fill the gaps in federal and provincial legislative power.

In *Re Agricultural Products Marketing Act* (1978),[17] the Supreme Court of Canada upheld the principal elements of the plan. Both the federal marketing statute and the Ontario statute were upheld, on the basis that the federal statute regulated the interprovincial elements of the plan, and the provincial statute regulated the intraprovincial elements of the plan. As noted in the discussion of the case in the previous chapter,[18] it was doubtful whether each level of government had succeeded in remaining within its proper sphere, but the Court was willing to give the benefit of the doubt to both the federal and the provincial sides of the cooperative enterprise. With respect to the provincial statute, perhaps the most important aspect of the decision is the holding that the provincial statute could impose production quotas on all producers "irrespective of the destination of their output".[19]

The Court has not adhered to this ruling about provincial power to

---

[16]Weiler, In the Last Resort (1974), 162. One of the many puzzles of the decision is how the Court was able to reach its conclusion without the aid of any factual information as to the actual impact of the plan on out-of-province eggs. It is possible that the impact would have been trivial in that Manitoba appears to have been a net exporter of eggs (Weiler, 156). Laskin J. deplored the absence of any "factual underpinning", but still went on to hold the scheme invalid.

[17]*Re Agricultural Products Marketing Act*, [1978] 2 S.C.R. 1198.

[18]Chapter 20, Trade and Commerce, under heading § 20:3, "In the Supreme Court of Canada".

[19]*Re Agricultural Products Marketing Act*, [1978] 2 S.C.R. 1198, 1296 per Pigeon J. for majority. Laskin C.J. for concurring minority was a little more cautious, upholding production controls (at p. 1286) on the basis that the "primary object" of the Act was "to regulate marketing in intraprovincial trade". The holding was reaffirmed in *Fédération des producteurs v. Pelland*, [2005] 1 S.C.R. 292 (chicken producer who exported all his production challenged the applicability to him of provincial production quota in chicken marketing plan structured on the model of the egg marketing plan; held, quota valid and applicable to him).

control the production of natural resources. In *Central Canada Potash v. Government of Saskatchewan* (1978),[20] the Court struck down Saskatchewan's prorationing scheme for potash produced in the province. The scheme, which was established by regulations made under statutory authority, imposed production quotas on producers of potash in the province.[21] The Saskatchewan Court of Appeal upheld the controls as measures "to protect and maintain the potash industry as a viable economic industry within the province".[22] But the Supreme Court of Canada reversed. Laskin C.J. for a unanimous Court acknowledged that *Re Agricultural Products Marketing Act* had held that production controls were "ordinarily" matters within provincial authority; but he said that "the situation may be different, however, where a province establishes a marketing scheme with price fixing as its central feature".[23] He did not explain why price fixing would make the situation different, and it is very hard to see why, since price fixing was also a central feature of the egg marketing plan in *Re Agricultural Products Marketing Act*. The controls in each case pursued exactly the same economic purpose: by reducing the supply of the product, the price could be maintained at a level above its free-market level.[24] The political object in both cases was to increase returns to producers and make the producing industry more prosperous.

In order to account for the different outcomes in the two cases, it seems necessary to look to the destination of the product. In *Re Agricultural Products Marketing Act*, it was established that 90 per cent of the eggs produced in Canada were consumed within the province of production. In *Central Canada Potash*, it was established that virtually all of the potash produced in Saskatchewan was exported. This led Laskin C.J. to characterize the prorationing scheme as "directly aimed at the production of potash destined for export".[25] With respect, this is not a plausible characterization. The prorationing controls were imposed at the mine without regard for the ultimate destination of the potash. The controls would have applied in exactly the same way if the fertilizer industry (the consumer of potash) had been located within the province. The purpose of the controls was not to reduce the export trade (though that was certainly their effect), but to protect the local mining industry. The Court's reasoning produces the unfortunate consequence that those

---

[20]*Central Canada Potash v. Government of Saskatchewan*, [1979] 1 S.C.R. 42.

[21]The case did not concern potash owned by the province itself. As proprietor, a province is free to control production and (if possible) price even if the product is destined for export. In this case, the resource was privately owned, and the controls involved an exercise of legislative, not proprietary power. The distinction is referred to by Laskin C.J. (at p. 72).

[22]*Central Canada Potash v. Government of Saskatchewan*, [1979] 1 S.C.R. 42, 68, quoting the relevant passage from the opinion of the Court of Appeal.

[23]*Central Canada Potash v. Government of Saskatchewan*, [1979] 1 S.C.R. 42, 74.

[24]Moreover, where supply can be controlled in the relevant market, the power to fix prices is not very significant, since the control of supply is by itself sufficient to manage the price.

[25]*Re Agricultural Products Marketing Act*, [1979] 1 S.C.R. 42, 74.

provinces that, like Saskatchewan, are mainly primary producers have less control over their natural resources than those provinces that, like Ontario, have more integrated economies.[26]

Neither in *Re Agricultural Products Marketing Act* nor in *Central Canada Potash*, could it be argued that the production controls had a physical (as opposed to economic) conservation purpose. Eggs are a renewable resource that can be produced in any quantity for the indefinite future. Potash is not a renewable resource, of course, but the trial judge found that Saskatchewan possessed reserves sufficient to supply world demand for 1,500 years; so it was plain, as Laskin C.J. held, that the prorationing scheme "could not be said to be a response to threatened shortages of the mineral or to conservation needs".[27] Where production controls are imposed for a physical conservation purpose, there is no doubt about the existence of provincial power. In *Spooner Oils v. Turner Valley Gas Conservation Bd.* (1933),[28] the Supreme Court of Canada upheld legislation enacted by Alberta to limit the production of natural gas in the Turner Valley gas field. The purpose of the controls was to prevent producers from extracting large quantities of gas, then separating naphtha from the gas, and then burning the gas. This wasteful practice had developed because there was a strong market for the naphtha, and no market for most of the gas. The Supreme Court of Canada did not discuss the location of the market for the naphtha, but it is safe to assume that it was outside Alberta. The Court rejected the argument that the province was purporting to regulate trade and commerce, saying that the production controls were imposed "from a point of view which is provincial and for a purpose which is provincial— the prevention of what the legislature conceives to be a waste of natural gas in the working of [the gas wells]."[29]

The Constitution Act, 1982, by s. 50, added a new s. 92A to the Constitution Act, 1867, enlarging provincial powers over natural resources.[30] Two provisions are arguably relevant to production controls in market-

---

[26]The Court followed its prior decision in *Can. Industrial Gas and Oil v. Govt. of Sask.*, [1978] 2 S.C.R. 545, where the Court struck down a Saskatchewan law purporting to fix the price of oil at the wellhead. The price was not an "export price", being imposed without regard for the destination of the oil. However, because the evidence showed that 98 per cent of Saskatchewan's oil was exported to eastern Canada, the Court, by majority, held that the province was attempting to fix the price in the export market, which was an unconstitutional attempt to regulate interprovincial trade and commerce. This reasoning is, in my view, open to the same line of criticism as that offered in the text in respect of the *Central Can. Potash* case. The two cases have attracted an extensive and generally critical commentary, of which perhaps the best article is W.D. Moull, "Natural Resources: The Other Crisis in Canadian Federalism" (1980) 18 Osgoode Hall L.J. 1.

[27]*Re Agricultural Products Marketing Act*, [1979] 1 S.C.R. 42, 50.

[28]*Spooner Oils v. Turner Valley Gas Conservation Bd.*, [1933] S.C.R. 629.

[29]*Spooner Oils v. Turner Valley Gas Conservation Bd.*, [1933] S.C.R. 629, 649.

[30]For analysis of s. 92A, see W.D. Moull, "Section 92A of the Constitution Act, 1867" (1983) 61 Can. Bar Rev. 715; R.D. Cairns, M.A. Chandler, W.D. Moull, "The Resource Amendment (Section 92A) and the Political Economy of Canadian Federalism" (1985) 23 Osgoode Hall L.J. 253; R.D. Cairns, M.A. Chandler, W.D. Moull, "Constitutional Change and the Private Sector: The Case of the Resource Amendment" (1987) 24 Osgoode Hall

ing plans. First, s. 92A(1)(b) confers on the provincial Legislatures the power to make laws in relation to:

> development, conservation and management of nonrenewable natural resources and forestry resources in the province, including laws in relation to the rate of primary production therefrom;

It will be noticed that this power applies only to "non-renewable natural resources and forestry resources". It therefore has no application to eggs and other agricultural products. It does apply to potash and other minerals, and it does contemplate "laws in relation to the rate of primary production". But the references at the beginning of the paragraph to "development, conservation and management", and the absence of any reference to the case where the resources are destined for export (which, it will be recalled, was the fatal element of the potash prorationing scheme), suggest that the paragraph may be no more than declaratory of pre-1982 provincial power as determined in *Central Canada Potash.*

The second new provision that may be relevant to production controls in marketing plans is s. 92A(2), which provides:

> In each province, the legislature may make laws in relation to the export from the province to another part of Canada of the primary production from non-renewable natural resources and forestry resources in the province and the production from facilities in the province for the generation of electrical energy, but such laws may not authorize or provide for discrimination in prices or in supplies exported to another part of Canada.

This provision is certainly an enlargement of pre-1982 provincial power, since laws in relation to the export of resources were previously incompetent to the provinces, as is illustrated by *Central Canada Potash.*[31] However, the new power does not extend to agricultural products; and, even with respect to "non-renewable natural resources" (and lumber and electricity), the new power only authorizes laws in relation to the export of the resources "to another part of Canada". The export of resources from Canada remains outside provincial legislative power. The facts of *Central Canada Potash*, where the bulk of the potash was destined for markets in the United States, would be outside the new power.[32]

L.J. 299.

[31]Section 92A(3) provides that the new power is not exclusive: federal power exists as well, and federal laws are paramount over inconsistent provincial laws.

[32]The facts of *Can. Industrial Gas and Oil v. Govt. of Sask.*, [1978] 2 S.C.R. 545, would be mainly within the new power, since Saskatchewan's oil was mainly exported to eastern Canada, not to the United States.

VII. SECURITIES REGULATION

§ 21:15 Provincial power

In line with the insurance cases and the marketing cases, the provinces have the power to regulate the trade in corporate securities.[1] This is a matter within property and civil rights in the province. In fact, the provinces have regulatory regimes which establish securities commissions, and which provide for the licensing of brokers and the regulation of the market for corporate securities.

There is one important exception to the generality of provincial power over securities regulation.[2] It has been held that the province has no power to confer upon a provincial agency discretionary power over the issue of securities by a federally-incorporated company, because the capacity to raise capital is an essential attribute of corporate status.[3] This does not preclude all provincial regulation of the issue of securities by federally-incorporated companies; for example, such companies can be required to issue their securities only through provincially-licensed brokers,[4] and a remedy can be provided for "insider trading" in their securities.[5] The question in each case is whether the degree of provincial control amounts to a denial of an essential attribute of corporate status. The scope of this immunity from provincial law is more fully discussed in the later chapter on Companies.[6]

Except for the limited immunity of federally-incorporated companies, the provincial power has been given a broad scope by the courts. The Ontario Securities Act's offence of furnishing false information in a prospectus has been held to be valid and operative, notwithstanding the existence of a similar offence in the federal Criminal Code.[7] The British Columbia Securities Commission's power to seize documents in the province for the purpose of handing them over to the securities commission of another jurisdiction has been upheld on the basis of its contribution to the regulation of the securities market in British Columbia.[8] The Quebec Securities Act's provision freezing deposits of funds or securities

---

[Section 21:15]

[1]The existence of provincial power was resoundingly affirmed in *Re Securities Act*, [2011] 3 S.C.R. 837, paras. 43–45, 126 (striking down federal proposed Securities Act).

[2]In *Re Securities Act*, [2011] 3 S.C.R. 837, there are a number of vague suggestions of federal power, some of which may be intended as denials of provincial power: see paras. 6, 97, 102, 103, 104, 105, 114, 123, 125, 126, 128, 130; but if so this is never spelled out.

[3]*A.-G. Man. v. A.-G. Can.* (Manitoba Securities) [1929] A.C. 260.

[4]*Lymburn v. Mayland*, [1932] A.C. 318.

[5]*Multiple Access v. McCutcheon*, [1982] 2 S.C.R. 161.

[6]Chapter 23, Companies, under heading §§ 23:7 to 23:9, "The status and essential powers immunity".

[7]*Smith v. The Queen*, [1960] S.C.R. 776; see also *Multiple Access v. McCutcheon*, [1982] 2 S.C.R. 161 (provincial insider trading remedy upheld despite existence of similar federal remedy).

[8]*Global Securities Corp. v. B.C.*, [2000] 1 S.C.R. 494; discussed in ch. 13, Extrater-

pending an investigation by the Commission has been held to be valid and applicable to a bank, notwithstanding the singling out of banks and other institutions holding deposits.[9] The Quebec Act has also been held applicable to a broker operating in the province whose business was confined to customers outside the province;[10] and the Manitoba Act has been held applicable to a broker operating outside the province but selling stock to customers inside the province.[11] In these cases where the provincial legislation has been applied to operations which, overall, are interprovincial, the court may have been influenced by the absence of federal securities legislation.[12]

§ 21:16 Federal power

Provincial legislation on securities regulation dates from the 19th century, when stock markets were primarily local.[1] Investors put their money into local businesses, trusting their local knowledge about enterprises and their owners to weed out corrupt and fraudulent promoters. But as communications became faster, local markets gave way to regional, national and international ones which offered a wider range of investments and economies of scale for investors. The largest investors are now pension funds and mutual funds, which normally want to diversify their holdings geographically as well as in terms of industrial sectors. In Canada, stock exchanges were consolidated until most trading is now done on the Toronto Stock Exchange with smaller specialized exchanges surviving in Montreal and Vancouver. On modern stock exchanges, the transactions are fully automated, and buyers and sellers never even discover the names or residences of their counterparties, who are unlikely to be in the same province, and may not even be in the same country. When companies issue new stocks or bonds to the public, only a tiny minority sell only to purchasers in a single province, and in any event resales in the secondary market would normally spread the securities across the country and outside the country. The securities markets are truly interprovincial and international, all large Canadian companies are ultimately dependent on those markets for their capital requirements, and nearly all Canadians are dependent on those markets for their financial security, especially through mutual funds and pension funds (including the Canada Pension Plan, which is invested in stocks and bonds).

---

ritorial Competence, under heading § 13:6, "Regulation of extraprovincial activity".

[9] *Gregory & Co. v. Imperial Bank*, [1960] C.S. 204 (Que. S.C.).

[10] *Gregory & Co. v. Que. Securities Comm.*, [1961] S.C.R. 584. The Court did not determine the constitutionality of this application of the Act.

[11] *R. v. W. McKenzie Securities Ltd.* (1966), 56 D.L.R. (2d) 56 (Man. C.A.). In this case the constitutional issue was determined in favour of the legislation.

[12] The marketing cases suggest that incidents of an interprovincial operation may only be regulated federally: see §§ 21:12 to 21:14, "Marketing".

[Section 21:16]

[1] Not entirely, for example, money was often raised by the issue of stock or bonds in London.

Similar developments have occurred in other countries with a predictable regulatory response. The international reach of securities markets and the corresponding need for international cooperation in matters of policy and enforcement is recognized by the International Organization of Securities Commissions (IOSCO), which has 109 members representing nearly all of the world's securities markets. Many of the members are federal countries like Canada. Only Canada lacks a national securities regulator, and only Canada is represented by two subnational regulators, namely, Ontario and Quebec. Members of IOSCO are supposed to be able to make commitments on behalf of their countries, but of course Ontario and Quebec have no mandate or power to bind the rest of Canada to decisions emanating from IOSCO.

The scope of securities activity and its importance to the prosperity and financial health of the nation invite the question whether Canada should have a national securities regulator. That has been the recommendation of a series of expert panels starting in 1964 and culminating in the Hockin panel in 2009.[2] However, only the Hockin panel led to an actual federal initiative to establish a national regulator, and, as will be related, that initiative was struck down by the Supreme Court of Canada. In earlier cases, while the Court had consistently affirmed provincial jurisdiction over securities regulation, the Court had also held that Parliament had some jurisdiction in the field under the criminal law power (offence of issuing a false statement in a prospectus)[3] and under the power over federally-incorporated companies (remedy for insider trading in their shares).[4] In each of those cases, the federal law basically duplicated provincial law. The Court held that both the federal law and the provincial law were valid on the basis that securities regulation had a double aspect, and it was no objection to either law that it essentially duplicated a law enacted by the other level of government. Obviously, however, neither the criminal law power nor the power over federally-incorporated companies would authorize a comprehensive national regime of securities regulation.

There was never any doubt that Parliament could enact a regime of securities regulation that was restricted to the interprovincial and international trade in securities. Parliament's trade and commerce power (s. 91(2)) clearly extended to interprovincial and international trade.[5] But, although a federal law restricted in that way would capture most of the field, it was not a very attractive prospect, since it would add a 14th regulator to the 13 that now exist, and would give rise to endless

---

[2]Expert Panel on Securities Regulation, *Final Report and Recommendations* (Department of Finance, Canada, January 2009) (Hockin report). The history is related in *Re Securities Act*, [2011] 3 S.C.R. 837, paras. 11–27.

[3]*Smith v. The Queen*, [1960] S.C.R. 776.

[4]*Multiple Access v. McCutcheon*, [1982] 2 S.C.R. 161; see also *A.-G. Man. v. A.-G. Can.* (Manitoba Securities) [1929] A.C. 260; *Esso Standard v. J.W. Enterprises*, [1963] S.C.R. 144 (takeover regulation).

[5]Chapter 20, Trade and Commerce, under heading § 20:2, "Interprovincial or international trade and commerce".

argument about what was local (intraprovincial) and what was interprovincial or international. The practical question was whether Parliament could enact a comprehensive regime of federal securities regulation, which covered local transactions as well as interprovincial and international transactions and which could replace the multiple provincial and territorial regulators with a single regulator.[6]

There was in fact a strong legal case for the power of Parliament to enact a comprehensive regime of securities regulation. The precedent was *General Motors v. City National Leasing* (1989),[7] where the Supreme Court confirmed that the trade and commerce power had two branches, the interprovincial and international trade branch and the "general" branch, which covers "trade as a whole", and which had already been held to cover trade mark law.[8] The Court upheld the federal Competition Act (then the Combines Investigation Act) under the general branch. The general branch of the trade and commerce power authorized Parliament to enact a *comprehensive* regulatory scheme to control anti-competitive practices: the scheme could validly extend to intraprovincial aspects of competition no less than interprovincial and international aspects. Dickson C.J. for the Court said: "Competition cannot be successfully regulated by federal legislation which is restricted to interprovincial trade."[9] Why would the same reasoning not apply to securities regulation?

This question had to be answered when the federal Minister of Finance tabled a proposed Canadian Securities Act in the House of Commons, and referred the Act to the Supreme Court to answer the question whether the proposed Act was within the legislative authority of the Parliament of Canada. The proposed Act was broadly similar[10] to the existing provincial statutes: prospectus filing requirements for the issue of new securities to the public, continuous disclosure requirements for companies that had existing securities in the public marketplace, regulation of takeover bids, regulation of insider trading and other unfair practices, registration of securities dealers and advisers, regulation of the stock exchanges, and a range of enforcement mechanisms (administrative, civil and criminal). The Act was comprehensive in its scope, mak-

[6]The provinces and territories have made some efforts to harmonize their laws, and have created a "passport system" under which many recurring regulatory decisions (prospectus clearance, registration of dealers, for example) require a decision by only one jurisdiction. But Ontario is not part of the passport system (and there is no guarantee that any other province will stay in it), enforcement measures are not covered, and national policies can be formed (or changed) only by the unanimous decision of 13 regulators.

[7]*General Motors v. City National Leasing*, [1989] 1 S.C.R. 641. The case is discussed in more detail in ch. 20, Trade and Commerce, under heading § 20:4, "General trade and commerce".

[8]Chapter 20, Trade and Commerce under heading § 20:4, "General trade and commerce".

[9]*General Motors v. City National Leasing*, [1989] 1 S.C.R. 641, 681.

[10]The Act differed from the provincial statutes in many details, as well as in its inclusion of criminal offences and provisions dealing with systemic risk.

ing no distinctions between interprovincial aspects and intraprovincial aspects.[11] The Act was supported by Canada, Ontario and private interveners as an exercise of the general branch of the trade and commerce power.

In *Re Securities Act* (2011),[12] the Supreme Court held unanimously that the proposed Act was unconstitutional. They reached this conclusion by an unorthodox route. In considering whether the proposed Act concerned "trade as a whole", they said that "we cannot ignore that the provinces have been deeply engaged in the regulation of the market over many years", and they noted that "the structure and terms of the proposed Act largely replicate the existing provincial schemes".[13] These observations should have been irrelevant to the classification of a proposed *federal* Act, but they formed the primary basis for the Court's conclusion that "the day-to-day regulation of securities within the provinces, which represents the main thrust of the Act, remains essentially a matter of property and civil rights within the provinces and therefore subject to provincial power."[14] "Aspects of the Act, for example those aimed at management of systemic risk and at national data collection" were concerned with trade as a whole,[15] but "they do not, on the record before us, justify a complete takeover of provincial regulation."[16]

The Court's division of what was drafted as a single comprehensive regulatory scheme into "day-to-day regulation of securities within the province" (not concerned with trade as a whole) and ill-defined federal "aspects" (concerned with trade as a whole) became the Court's distinction with competition law: "Competition law, by contrast, regulates *only* anti-competitive contracts and conduct—a particular aspect of economic

[11]The Act only applied in those provinces (and territories) that voluntarily opted into it; the ultimate goal was universal coverage—but only with the consent of the provinces.

[12]*Re Securities Act*, [2011] 3 S.C.R. 837. The unanimous opinion is by "the Court". The decision is discussed in more detail in ch. 20, Trade and Commerce, under heading § 20:4, "General trade and commerce".

[13]*Re Securities Act*, [2011] 3 S.C.R. 837, paras. 115, 116.

[14]*Re Securities Act*, [2011] 3 S.C.R. 837, para. 116.

[15]*Re Securities Act*, [2011] 3 S.C.R. 837, para. 117. Other suggestions of federal power can be found in paras. 6 ("aspects of the securities market are national in scope"), 97 ("fostering fair, efficient and competitive markets"), 102 (systemic risk and data collection), 103–104 (systemic risk, including examples), 105 (nationwide data collection), 114 (preservation of capital markets, minimum standards), 123 ("genuine national goals"), 125 ("measures directed at the control of the Canadian securities market as a whole"), 126 ("federal aspects"), 128 ("the preservation of capital markets and the maintenance of Canada's financial stability"), 130 ("genuinely national concerns"). Of course, the effect of the actual decision in the case is that the creation of a single national regulator by comprehensive federal legislation cannot be supported by any of these phrases, no matter how seemingly broad.

[16]*Re Securities Act*, [2011] 3 S.C.R. 837, para 117. A "complete takeover of provincial regulation" (and also in para. 117: "wholesale displacement of provincial regulation") was a considerable exaggeration, since (as explained in § 21:16 note 11, above) the Act would come into force in a province only if that province voluntarily opted into the Act. For those provinces which did not opt in, provincial regulation would continue as before.

activity that falls squarely within the federal domain."[17] The conclusion was that comprehensive securities regulation did not come within the general branch of the trade and commerce power. The effect of the decision is to maintain in place the status quo of 13 provincial and territorial regulators to regulate a market that is predominantly interprovincial and international, and certainly is not confined within 13 provincial and territorial enclaves.[18] No other federal country allows its securities markets to be regulated only by subnational regulators.[19]

In *Re Pan-Canadian Securities Regulation* (2018),[20] the Supreme Court, on an appeal from the Quebec Court of Appeal, was asked to review a new proposal by the governments of Canada, Ontario, British Columbia. Saskatchewan, New Brunswick, Prince Edward Island and Yukon for a "cooperative securities regulator". The two legal components of this proposal were (1) a uniform model provincial (and territorial) act, broadly similar to the existing provincial securities acts, to be enacted by all participating provinces; and (2) a federal act aimed at preventing and managing "systemic risk",[21] establishing criminal offences relating to financial markets and establishing a national securities regulator. What was new in the cooperative system was the federal proposal for a national securities regulator, which would have power over systemic risk, but which would derive the bulk of its regulatory powers by delegation from the participating provinces in the uniform provincial acts; the national securities regulator would become the sole regulator responsible for administering both the federal and provincial cooperative legislation. The national securities regulator would operate under the supervision of a Council of Ministers, which would comprise the federal minister of finance and the provincial ministers responsible for securities regulation in all of the participating provinces. The Supreme Court, after commenting that "Canada is one of the only industrialized countries in the world

[17]*Re Securities Act*, [2011] 3 S.C.R. 837, para. 122 (emphasis in original). The distinction is weak. Competition law falls squarely within the federal domain only because it was held to be within the general branch of trade and commerce in the *General Motors* case, and in that case the Court was very clear that similar provincial laws providing remedies for anti-competitive practices within a province were also valid under property and civil rights in the province.

[18]The Court acknowledged as much: *Re Securities Act*, [2011] 3 S.C.R. 837, para. 115; but went on to claim (also in para. 115) that "equally" "capital markets also exist within provinces that meet the needs of local businesses and investors", despite the evidence that this was now a minor aspect of securities markets.

[19]The United States has had a national regulator since 1933, established by Congress under the commerce clause of the United States constitution: Smith, *The Commerce Power in Canada and the United States* (1963), 461–465. The states retain jurisdiction as well, but the American doctrine of pre-emption (which is more robust than the Canadian doctrine of paramountcy) has greatly reduced the role of the states.

[20]*Re Pan-Canadian Securities Regulation*, 2018 SCC 48. The opinion of the nine-judge court was issued by "The Court".

[21]*Re Pan-Canadian Securities Regulation*, 2018 SCC 48, para. 107 provided a definition of systemic risk.

that does not have a national securities regulator",[22] held that, if this co-operative system were implemented as proposed, it would be constitutional. Parliament had the power, under the general branch of the trade and commerce power,[23] to regulate systemic risk and create a national securities regulator, as well as the criminal law power to establish criminal offences. The provincial Legislatures had the power, under their powers over property and civil rights in the province, to enact the proposed uniform model provincial act, including the delegation of regulatory power to the single national regulator to be created by Parliament.

VIII. PROPERTY

§ 21:17 General

The creation of property rights, their transfer and their general characteristics are within property and civil rights in the province. Thus, the law of real and personal property and all its various derivatives, such as landlord and tenant, trusts and wills, succession on intestacy, conveyancing, and land use planning, are within provincial power.

Difficulty has arisen, however, in cases where a province has sought to control the ownership or use of property in order to accomplish a non-proprietary objective which it could not accomplish by more direct means. For example, in *Switzman v. Elbling* (1957)[1] a provincial law which prohibited the use of a house "to propagate communism or bolshevism" was characterized as either a criminal law or a law in relation to speech, and not as a property law. By contrast, in *Bedard v. Dawson* (1923)[2] a provincial law which prohibited the use of a house as a "disorderly house" was characterized as a property law, and not as a mere supplement to Criminal Code offences in respect of disorderly houses.[3] And in *Johnson v. A.-G. Alta.* (1954)[4] the Court divided evenly on the question whether a provincial law which denied property rights

[22] *Re Pan-Canadian Securities Regulation*, 2018 SCC 48, para. 8 (emphasis in original).

[23] *Re Pan-Canadian Securities Regulation*, 2018 SCC 48, paras 108–116; and see also ch. 20, Trade and Commerce, under heading § 20:4, "General trade and commerce".

[Section 21:17]

[1] *Switzman v. Elbling*, [1957] S.C.R. 285.

[2] *Bedard v. Dawson*, [1923] S.C.R. 681.

[3] In *N.S. Bd. of Censors v. McNeil*, [1978] 2 S.C.R. 662, Ritchie J. for the majority upheld (at p. 688) a provincial film censorship law on the implausible basis that it was "concerned with dealings in and the use of property (i.e., films) which take place wholly within the province". He also upheld the law (at p. 688) as the regulation of the "film business" and (at p. 699) as the regulation of a local or private matter.

[4] *Johnson v. A.-G. Alta.*, [1954] S.C.R. 127.

in slot machines and provided for the confiscation of slot machines was a property law or a criminal law.[5]

§ 21:18 Foreign ownership

The question whether a province can control foreign ownership of land was litigated in *Morgan v. A.-G. P.E.I.* (1975),[1] in which the Supreme Court of Canada upheld a statute of Prince Edward Island which provided that "no person who is not a resident of the province" could acquire holdings of real property of more than a specified size except with the permission of the provincial cabinet. The qualification for unrestricted landholding was residence, not citizenship, and so the prohibition applied to non-resident citizens as well as non-resident aliens.[2] The decision would have been more difficult if the discrimination had been against aliens instead of non-residents, because "naturalization and aliens" (s. 91(25)) is a federal head of legislative power.[3] The authorities are divided on the extent of provincial power to discriminate against aliens,[4] but a dictum in the *Morgan* case suggests that a provincial law which imposed property-owning restraints on aliens could still be sustained as a valid property law.[5]

The federal Parliament has also asserted jurisdiction over foreign ownership of property in the Investment Canada Act,[6] which was enacted in 1985, and which provides screening procedures for certain takeovers of Canadian businesses by "non-Canadians". In the insurance cases, the "aliens" power was never held to be sufficient to authorize the regulation of foreign insurance companies, but there are dicta in those cases to the effect that the federal Parliament could "by properly framed legislation" impose restrictions on aliens seeking to do business in Canada.[7] The same dicta suggested that the trade and commerce power would also be available in support of this kind of legislation, and the undoubted federal

---

[5]See also *Walter v. A.-G. Alta.*, [1969] S.C.R. 383, upholding provincial restrictions on the communal holding of land which were intended to limit the expansion of Hutterite "colonies"; *Re Firearms Act*, [2000] 1 S.C.R. 783, upholding federal gun control as criminal law in light of its public safety purpose.

[Section 21:18]

[1]*Morgan v. A.-G. P.E.I.*, [1976] 2 S.C.R. 349.

[2]*Morgan* was followed in *Re Min. of Revenue (Ont.) and Hala* (1977), 18 O.R. (2d) 88 (Ont. H.C.), upholding a provincial tax on the acquisition of land, which was levied at the rate of less than one per cent on residents and twenty per cent on non-residents. The object of the tax was to discourage absentee ownership.

[3]See ch. 26, Citizenship.

[4]See ch. 55, Equality, under heading § 55:1, "Distribution of powers".

[5]*Morgan v. A.-G. P.E.I.*, [1976] 2 S.C.R. 349, 364–365. Contra, Spencer, "The Alien Landowner in Canada" (1973) 51 Can. Bar Rev. 389.

[6]R.S.C. 1985, c. 28 (1st Supp.), repealing and replacing the Foreign Investment Review Act, 1973.

[7]*A.-G. Can. v. A.-G. Alta.* (Insurance) [1916] 1 A.C. 588, 597; *A.-G. Ont. v. Reciprocal Insurers*, [1924] A.C. 328, 346; *Re Insurance Act of Can.*, [1932] A.C. 41, 51.

authority over the import and export of goods[8] provides an analogy. At the time of writing there has been no constitutional challenge[9] to this Act, or to its predecessor, the Foreign Investment Review Act, enacted in 1973.[10]

§ 21:19 Heritage property

In *Kitkatla Band v. British Columbia* (2002),[1] the Supreme Court of Canada held that the protection of heritage or cultural property was within provincial jurisdiction under property and civil rights in the province (s. 92(13)). In that case, the Court upheld British Columbia's Heritage Conservation Act, the purpose of which was to protect objects, artifacts and sites within the province which had heritage value. The Act included a discretion in the minister to license the destruction of heritage property, and the challenge to the Act was prompted by a ministerial decision to license the destruction of some "culturally modified trees" which had heritage value to Aboriginal people. The Court upheld the Act, including the ministerial power and its exercise in this case.

IX. DEBT ADJUSTMENT

§ 21:20 Debt adjustment

The law of contract is mainly within provincial power under property and civil rights in the province.[1] Provincial power extends to the annulment or reformation of harsh or unconscionable contracts.[2] But the provincial power to modify creditors' rights is circumscribed by a number of provisions of the Constitution Act, 1867. One is the extraterritorial limitation imposed by the words "in the province" in s. 92(13) itself. Another is the allocation of "interest" (s. 91(19)) and "bankruptcy and insolvency" (s. 91(21)) to the federal Parliament, which withdraws those subjects from provincial power. These various infirmities in provincial power have not deterred the provinces from extensive regulation of the debtor-creditor relationship, often with the purpose of protecting local debtors from the enforcement efforts of out-of-province creditors. The

---

[8]See ch. 20, Trade and Commerce, under heading § 20:2, "In the Privy Council".

[9]The Act was challenged unsuccessfully under the Canadian Charter of Rights and Freedoms and the Canadian Bill of Rights, not the division of powers, in *United States Steel v. Can.* (2011), 333 D.L.R. (4th) 1 (F.C.A.).

[10]For general discussion, see C.T.A. MacNab, "Constitutionality of Federal Control of Foreign Investment" (1965) 23 U. Toronto Fac. L. Rev. 95; E.J. Arnett, "Canadian Regulation of Foreign Investment" (1972) 50 Can. Bar Rev. 213.

[Section 21:19]

[1]*Kitkatla Band v. British Columbia*, [2002] 2 S.C.R. 146.

[Section 21:20]

[1]§ 21:2 "History of property and civil rights".

[2]*A.-G. Ont. v. Barfried Enterprises*, [1963] S.C.R. 570.

resulting constitutional challenges have created a substantial body of case-law, which is described in ch. 25, Bankruptcy and Insolvency.[3]

X. CONSUMER PROTECTION

§ 21:21 Consumer protection

Many of the laws that have been upheld within the various rubrics described in this chapter had the purpose of consumer protection. This illustrates that much consumer protection law is open to the province under the power over property and civil rights in the province. For example, provincial restrictions on advertising directed at children have been described as "in relation to consumer protection" and upheld under s. 92(13).[1] But much *federal* law could just as accurately be described as in relation to consumer protection. The phrase consumer protection is too broad and vague to serve as a "matter" for the purpose of the federal distribution of powers. Like inflation, pollution or health, consumer protection must be broken out into smaller, more distinct, concepts, before a consumer protection law can be placed in its correct constitutional slot.

XI. EXTRATERRITORIAL COMPETENCE

§ 21:22 Extraterritorial competence

The legislative power conferred by s. 92(13) is over property and civil rights in the province. The words "in the province" make clear that there is a territorial limitation on the power. The nature of that limitation has been discussed in ch. 13, Extraterritorial Competence.

---

[3]Chapter 25, Bankruptcy and Insolvency, under heading §§ 25:5 to 25:9, "Adjustment of debts".

[Section 21:21]

[1]*Irwin Toy v. Que.*, [1989] 1 S.C.R. 927, 953.

Chapter 22

Transportation and Communication

I. DISTRIBUTION OF POWER

§ 22:1 Distribution of power

II. WORKS AND UNDERTAKINGS

§ 22:2 Works and undertakings

III. TRANSPORTATION AND COMMUNICATION

§ 22:3 Transportation and communication

IV. CONNECTION WITH ANOTHER PROVINCE

§ 22:4 Connection with another province

V. UNDIVIDED JURISDICTION

§ 22:5 Undivided jurisdiction

VI. CONTINUOUS AND REGULAR SERVICE

§ 22:6 Continuous and regular service

VII. RELATED UNDERTAKINGS

§ 22:7 Common ownership
§ 22:8 Common management
§ 22:9 Dependency

VIII. WORKS FOR THE GENERAL ADVANTAGE OF CANADA

§ 22:10 Works for the general advantage of Canada

IX. TRANSPORTATION BY LAND

§ 22:11 Transportation by land

X. TRANSPORTATION BY WATER

§ 22:12 Transportation by water

XI. TRANSPORTATION BY AIR

§ 22:13 Basis of legislative jurisdiction

§ 22:14 Intraprovincial aeronautics
§ 22:15 Provincial jurisdiction

XII. COMMUNICATION BY RADIO

§ 22:16 Basis of legislative jurisdiction
§ 22:17 Intraprovincial broadcasting
§ 22:18 Content regulation

XIII. COMMUNICATION BY TELEVISION

§ 22:19 Broadcast television
§ 22:20 Cable television
§ 22:21 Pay television

XIV. COMMUNICATION BY TELEPHONE

§ 22:22 Communication by telephone

XV. COMMUNICATION BY OTHER MEANS

§ 22:23 Film
§ 22:24 Theatre
§ 22:25 Literature

I. DISTRIBUTION OF POWER

§ 22:1 Distribution of power

Legislative power over transportation and communication[1] is divided between the federal Parliament and the provincial Legislatures. There is no mention of either transportation or communication in the Constitution Act, 1867, although several modes of transportation and communication are mentioned. The most important of these references occurs in s. 92(10). Section 92(10) is, of course, part of the list of provincial powers. It confers upon the provincial Legislatures the power to make laws in relation to:

> Local works and undertakings other than such as are of the following classes:

[Section 22:1]

[1]C.H. McNairn, "Transportation, Communication and the Constitution" (1969) 47 Can. Bar Rev. 355; C.H. McNairn, "Aeronautics and the Constitution" (1971) 49 Can. Bar Rev. 411; D. Mullan and R. Beaman, "The Constitutional Implications of the Regulation of Telecommunications" (1973) 2 Queen's L.J. 67; I.H. Fraser, "Some Comments on Subsection 92(10) of the Constitution Act, 1867" (1984) 29 McGill L.J. 557; P.J. Monahan, "Constitutional Jurisdiction over Transportation: Recent Developments and Proposals for Change" in Directions: Final Report of the Royal Commission on National Passenger Transportation (1992), vol. 3, c. 9; Laskin, Canadian Constitutional Law (5th ed., 1986 by Finkelstein), ch. 9; Beaudoin, La Constitution du Canada (3rd ed., 2004), ch. 11; Rémillard, Le Fédéralisme Canadien (2nd ed., 1983), vol. 1, ch. 4; Monahan, Constitutional Law (2nd ed., 2002), ch. 12.

(a) Lines of steam or other ships, railways, canals, telegraphs, and other works and undertakings connecting the province with any other or others of the provinces, or extending beyond the limits of the province;
(b) Lines of steam ships between the province and any British or foreign country;
(c) Such works as, although wholly situate within the province, are before or after their execution declared by the Parliament of Canada to be for the general advantage of Canada or for the advantage of two or more of the provinces.

The three listed exceptions from provincial power are heads of federal legislative power by virtue of s. 91(29), which includes in the federal enumeration those classes of subjects which are expressly excepted from the provincial enumeration. Indeed, the exceptions have turned out to be more important than the primary grant of power over "local works and undertakings", because the courts have often preferred to rest provincial power on s. 92(13) (property and civil rights in the province) or s. 92(16) (matters of a merely local or private nature in the province), each of which is apt to cover much the same ground as s. 92(10).[2]

The essential scheme of s. 92(10) is to divide legislative authority over transportation and communication on a territorial basis. The specific references in s. 92(10)(a) to "lines of steam or other ships, railways, canals, telegraphs" do not allocate those modes of transportation or communication unqualifiedly to the federal Parliament. The references must be read in the context of the later reference to "other works and undertakings connecting the province with any other or others of the provinces, or extending beyond the limits of the province", and the whole of paragraph (a) must be read as an exception to the grant of provincial authority over local works and undertakings. The effect is to allocate to the federal Parliament the authority over *interprovincial* or *international* shipping lines, railways, canals, telegraphs and other modes of transportation or communication; and to allocate to the provincial Legislatures the authority over *intraprovincial* shipping lines, railways, canals, telegraphs and other modes of transportation or communication.[3]

Section 92(10)(c) forms an exception to the territorial distinction which generally differentiates federal and provincial jurisdiction under s. 92(10). Paragraph (c) enables the federal Parliament to assume jurisdiction over a purely local work by the simple (and unilateral) device of declaring the work to be "for the general advantage of Canada or for the advantage of two or more of the provinces". This declaratory power is available over any local "works", and is not confined to works related to

[2]C.H. McNairn, "Transportation, Communication and the Constitution" (1969) 47 Can. Bar Rev. 355, 356.

[3]For example, local railways are within provincial jurisdiction: *Montreal v. Montreal St. Ry.*, [1912] A.C. 333; *B.C. Elec. Ry. v. CNR*, [1932] S.C.R. 161; *UTU v. Central Western Ry.*, [1990] 3 S.C.R. 1112. Even local shiplines are within provincial jurisdiction, notwithstanding s. 91(10) ("navigation and shipping"); *Agence Maritime v. Can. Labour Relations Bd.*, [1969] S.C.R. 851.

transportation or communication.[4] However, the power will be discussed in this chapter. Paragraphs (a) and (b) of s. 92(10), by contrast, are confined to works and undertakings related to transportation or communication.[5]

There are other heads of legislative power which bear on transportation and communication. The peace, order, and good government power, which formed the subject of chapter 17, has been held to give the federal Parliament jurisdiction over aeronautics.[6] Several of the federal Parliament's enumerated powers also cover aspects of transportation and communication: "beacons, buoys, lighthouses, and Sable Island" (s. 91(9)); "navigation and shipping" (s. 91(10)),[7] and "ferries between a province and any British or foreign country or between two provinces" (s. 91(13)).[8] The federal "trade and commerce" power, on the other hand, has never been held to confer any federal power over transportation or communication.[9] This is in striking contrast with the commerce clause in the Constitution of the United States, which has been held to authorize federal regulation of interstate transportation and communication.[10]

The scheme of this chapter will be, first, to examine the powers over interprovincial or international undertakings and over works for the general advantage of Canada, and, secondly, to examine the powers over each of the principal modes of transportation and communication.

---

[4] *UTU v. Central Western Ry.*, [1990] 3 S.C.R. 1112.

[5] § 22:3, "Transportation and communication".

[6] §§ 22:13 to 22:15, "Transportation by air".

[7] § 22:12, "Transportation by water".

[8] Transportation and communication arrangements were crucial to the confederation of the provinces. Section 145 of the British North America Act (repealed in 1893) provided for the construction by the Government of Canada of the Intercolonial Railway, linking the St. Lawrence valley with the ice-free port of Halifax. Section 11 of the B.C. Terms of Union provided for the construction of the Canadian Pacific Railway, "to connect the seaboard of British Columbia with the railway system of Canada": see *B.C. v. Can.*, [1994] 2 S.C.R. 41. The P.E.I. Terms of Union included an undertaking that the Government of Canada would provide ferry service between the Island and the mainland: see *The Queen Can. v. The Queen P.E.I.*, [1978] 1 F.C. 533 (C.A.); *P.E.I. v. CNR*, [1991] 1 F.C. 129 (C.A.). Section 31 of the Newfoundland Terms of Union included the takeover by the Government of Canada of (among other things) the Newfoundland Railway and the telecommunications system, which thereby came within federal legislative jurisdiction: *CNR v. Commrs. of Public Utilities*, [1976] 2 S.C.R. 112. Section 32 was an undertaking by the Government of Canada to provide a ferry service between the mainland and the Island. See P.J. Monahan, "Constitutional Jurisdiction Over Transportation: Recent Developments and Proposals for Change" in Directions: Final Report of the Royal Commission on National Passenger Transportation (1992), vol. 3, ch. 9.

[9] C.H. McNairn, "Transportation, Communication and the Constitution" (1969) 47 Can. Bar Rev. 355.

[10] The abundant authorities start in the Supreme Court of the United States with *Gibbons v. Ogden* (1824), 9 Wheat. (22 U.S.) 1.

II. WORKS AND UNDERTAKINGS

§ 22:2 Works and undertakings

We have already noticed that s. 92(10)(a), read with s. 91(29), of the Constitution Act, 1867 confers on the federal Parliament the power to make laws in relation to:

> Lines of steam or other ships, railways, canals, telegraphs, and other works and undertakings connecting the province with any other or others of the provinces, or extending beyond the limits of the province.

We have also noticed that this power is confined to interprovincial (or international) works and undertakings, and that intraprovincial works and undertakings are within provincial jurisdiction.

Section 92(10)(a) refers to "works and undertakings", while s. 92(10)(c) refers only to "works". This suggests a distinction between the two terms which has usually been ignored, but has occasionally been adverted to in the cases. It has been said that a work is a "physical thing",[1] while an undertaking is "not a physical thing, but an arrangement under which . . . physical things are used".[2] The term "undertaking" is the one which has been most often invoked in the cases under s. 92(10)(a), and it seems to be equivalent to "organization"[3] or "enterprise",[4] although in the case of radio and television broadcasting the word has been held apt to encompass the entire broadcasting activity and not just particular broadcasting firms.[5]

III. TRANSPORTATION AND COMMUNICATION

§ 22:3 Transportation and communication

Section 92(10)(a) is confined to works and undertakings involved in transportation or communication. The general phrase "other works or undertakings connecting the province with any other", etc., is to be read ejusdem generis with the specific examples which precede it, and the specific examples are all modes of transportation or communication. The word "connecting" in this context is to be confined to connections by transportation or communication. Section 92(10)(a) has never been held applicable to any work or undertaking which is not of a transportation

---

[Section 22:2]

[1] *Montreal v. Montreal St. Ry.*, [1912] A.C. 333, 342; see also text accompanying § 22:10 note 6.

[2] *Re Regulation and Control of Radio Communication in Can.*, [1932] A.C. 304, 315.

[3] *CPR v. A.-G. B.C.* (Empress Hotel) [1950] A.C. 122, 142.

[4] *A.-G. Ont. v. Winner*, [1954] A.C. 541, 580; and see McNairn (1969) 47 Can. Bar Rev. 355, 358.

[5] Text accompanying § 22:16 note 13, below.

or communication character.[1] It is well established that the regulation of business enterprises which operate in more than one province, such as insurance companies, is for the most part within provincial authority under property and civil rights in the province.[2] The argument that s. 92(10)(a) would authorize federal regulation of labour relations in a construction firm that was participating in a nation-wide federal job creation programme has been rejected on the ground that s. 92(10)(a) covers only works and undertakings involved in transportation or communication.[3]

IV. CONNECTION WITH ANOTHER PROVINCE

§ 22:4 Connection with another province

According to s. 92(10)(a), an undertaking in a province is within federal jurisdiction if it is an undertaking "connecting the province with any other or others of the provinces, or extending beyond the limits of the province". The courts have held that the connection (or extension) that is contemplated by s. 92(10)(a) is an operational connection, and not a merely physical connection. For example, a local railway[1] or pipeline[2] does not come within federal jurisdiction just because it is physically connected to an interprovincial railway or pipeline. The local undertaking will remain within provincial jurisdiction despite the physical connection and despite regular cooperation between the two undertakings to facilitate through traffic. An undertaking will come within s. 92(10)(a) only if (1) the undertaking's own business operations extend beyond the provincial border, or (2) the undertaking has a close operational relationship[3] with an interprovincial undertaking.

[Section 22:3]

[1]Note however that particular facilities or activities that are not themselves engaged in transportation or communication may be so integrally connected with a transportation or communication enterprise as to be part of a single undertaking to which s. 92(10)(a) applies: *Westcoast Energy v. Can.*, [1998] 1 S.C.R. 322 (holding that gas processing plants were part of a single interprovincial gas transportation undertaking).

[2]*Can. Indemnity Co. v. A.G.B.C.*, [1977] 2 S.C.R. 504; *Consolidated Fastfrate v. Western Canada Council of Teamsters*, [2009] 3 S.C.R. 407, para. 76.

[3]*YMHA Jewish Community Centre v. Brown*, [1989] 1 S.C.R. 1532, 1552. Accord, *CPR v. A.G.B.C.* (Empress Hotel) [1950] A.C. 122, 142 (obiter dictum); *Re National Energy Bd. Act*, [1988] 2 F.C. 196, 220 (C.A.) (contractual arrangements to purchase gas from another province not within s. 92(10)(a)); *Conklin & Garrett v. Ont.* (1989), 70 O.R. (2d) 713 (Div. Ct.) (midway rides that are moved around North America to fairs and exhibitions not within s. 92(10)(a)); C.H. McNairn, "Transportation, Communication and the Constitution" (1969) 47 Can. Bar Rev. 355.

[Section 22:4]

[1]*Montreal v. Montreal St. Ry.*, [1912] A.C. 333; *B.C. Elec. Ry. v. CNR*, [1932] S.C.R. 161; *UTU v. Central Western Ry.*, [1990] 3 S.C.R. 1112.

[2]*Re National Energy Bd. Act*, [1988] 2 F.C. 196 (C.A.).

[3]The nature of the relationship is described later in this chapter under heading

In *Alberta Government Telephones v. CRTC* (1989),[4] the question arose whether Alberta Government Telephones (AGT) was within the regulatory jurisdiction of the federal or provincial government. AGT was an Alberta Crown corporation that operated a telephone system in Alberta. The AGT system connected at the four borders of the province with the telephone companies of British Columbia, Saskatchewan, the Northwest Territories and Montana. The AGT system was confined to the province of Alberta, and could carry telephone messages only within the province. AGT's subscribers could of course make calls to points outside Alberta and receive calls from outside Alberta, but this service was available only through the cooperation of extraprovincial telephone companies, who carried the messages through their own territories. Despite the intraprovincial scope of the AGT system, the Supreme Court of Canada held that AGT was an interprovincial undertaking. The Court said that "the facts demonstrate much more than mere physical interconnection of AGT's system at provincial borders."[5] The facts referred to were the bilateral agreements that AGT had entered into with the four neighbouring carriers, and AGT's membership of Telecom Canada, which was an unincorporated association of the major Canadian telephone companies to form a national telecommunications network. It seems to have been the scope and complexity of these bilateral and multilateral arrangements, enabling AGT to provide interprovincial and international service to its Alberta subscribers, that led the Court to characterize AGT as an interprovincial undertaking.[6]

The result in *AGT* probably owes a good deal to the unique character of telecommunication, which permits instantaneous two-way communication between people in different provinces and different countries. In other contexts, cooperative arrangements between an independently-managed local undertaking and extraprovincial undertakings would not suffice to transform the local undertaking into an interprovincial undertaking. We have already noticed the railway and pipeline cases, which have held that cooperative arrangements with a connecting interprovincial undertaking were insufficient to transform an independently-managed local undertaking into an interprovincial undertaking.

The freight-forwarding cases are similar to the railway and pipeline

---

§§ 22:7 to 22:9, "Related undertakings".

[4] *Alberta Government Telephones v. CRTC*, [1989] 2 S.C.R. 225. The majority opinion was written by Dickson C.J., with whom four others agreed. Wilson J. dissented on an issue of Crown immunity, but she agreed with Dickson C.J. on the constitutional issue. I disclose that I was one of the counsel on the losing side.

[5] *Alberta Government Telephones v. CRTC*, [1989] 2 S.C.R. 225, 262.

[6] It is not easy to capture exactly what moved the Court to classify AGT as interprovincial: see P.W. Hogg, Comment (1990) 35 McGill L.J. 480. In *UTU v. Central Western Ry.*, [1990] 3 S.C.R. 1112, 1135, Dickson C.J. for the Court said:

> The linchpin in the *A.G.T. v. CRTC* decision was this court's finding that A.G.T., by virtue of its role in Telecom Canada and its bilateral contracts with other telephone companies, was able to provide its clients with an interprovincial and, indeed, international telecommunications service.

cases. A freight forwarder is a company that takes delivery of goods from a customer and arranges to ship them to their destination. The company pools the shipments of many customers into full truck loads or rail-car loads, and realizes economies of scale that reduce the cost of shipping to the customer. In *Re Cannet Freight Cartage* (1976),[7] a freight forwarder took delivery of goods in Ontario, consolidated them into larger shipments, and made arrangements with Canadian National Railway to ship the goods by rail to Western Canada. The freight forwarder, whose operations were limited to the province of Ontario, was held to be a local undertaking. It did not become an interprovincial undertaking simply by virtue of being a shipper on an interprovincial railway. The only interprovincial undertaking was the Canadian National Railway which carried the goods outside the province of Ontario.

A more difficult case was *Consolidated Fastfrate v. Western Canada Council of Teamsters* (2009).[8] In that case, the freight forwarder, Fastfrate, had branches across the country, and it not only collected freight from customers in the province of origin, but, after the arrival of the shipment in the province of destination, Fastfrate de-consolidated the shipment and delivered it to the various consignees. In the Supreme Court of Canada, Binnie J., dissenting, would have classified Fastfrate as an interprovincial undertaking because (as was not the case in *Cannet)* Fastfrate handled the shipment in both the province of origin and the province of destination. But Rothstein J., who wrote for the majority, held that Fastfrate was a local undertaking that was subject to provincial jurisdiction over its labour relations in each of the provinces in which it had employees. He emphasized that Fastfrate itself did not carry the goods over provincial boundaries; it provided only local services in each of the provinces in which it operated; and (following *Cannet)* its contractual arrangements to ship goods over provincial boundaries did not make it an interprovincial undertaking. The only interprovincial undertaking was the railway or trucking company that actually transported the goods from the province of origin to the province of destination.

V. UNDIVIDED JURISDICTION

§ 22:5 Undivided jurisdiction

What is the appropriate classification of a business or group of associated businesses which is engaged in intraprovincial transportation or communication as well as interprovincial (or international) transportation or communication? Does one sever the intraprovincial part from the interprovincial part, and divide legislative jurisdiction accordingly? Or does one look to the dominant characteristic of the business and allocate

[7]*Re Cannet Freight Cartage*, [1976] 1 F.C. 174 (C.A.).

[8]*Consolidated Fastfrate v. Western Canada Council of Teamsters*, [2009] 3 S.C.R. 407. Rothstein J. wrote the opinion of the six-judge majority. Binnie J. wrote the dissenting opinion of the three-judge minority.

legislative jurisdiction over the entire business according to whether the dominant characteristic is intraprovincial or interprovincial? We shall see that neither of these approaches has been adopted by the courts; instead, they have held that a business which is engaged in a significant amount of continuous and regular interprovincial transportation or communication is wholly within federal jurisdiction.

The courts early rejected the idea of dividing legislative jurisdiction over a single undertaking. In *Toronto v. Bell Telephone Co.* (1905),[1] it was held that the Bell Telephone Company was an interprovincial undertaking within s. 92(10)(a). The Privy Council rejected the argument that the company's long-distance business and its local business should be separated for the purpose of allocating legislative jurisdiction. Their lordships held that the company carried on "one single undertaking", and that it fell within s. 92(10)(a). Nor did their lordships embark on an inquiry as to which aspect of the company's undertaking was dominant: the local or the long-distance. In fact, at the time of the litigation, the company had not actually established any connections outside Ontario, and so the interprovincial connection, far from being the dominant feature of the business, was no more than a "paper connection".[2] But their lordships held that the mere fact that the company's objects "contemplate extension beyond the limits of one province"[3] sufficed to stamp the entire undertaking with an interprovincial character.

The same resistance to dual jurisdiction over transportation and communication undertakings is evident in *A.-G. Ont. v. Winner* (1954).[4] The question in that case was whether the province of New Brunswick had regulatory authority over a bus line which operated from the United States, through New Brunswick, and into Nova Scotia. The bus line picked up and put down passengers at various points within New Brunswick; and the provincial highway board, purporting to act under statutory authority, sought to regulate (in fact, to prohibit) this part of the bus line's business. The Supreme Court of Canada held that the province could not regulate an interprovincial or international journey, even if it began or ended in New Brunswick, but that the province could regulate the journeys which began and ended in New Brunswick without crossing a provincial border. The Privy Council reversed this holding, denying the province even the regulatory authority over the local journeys. The dual legislative authority contemplated by the Supreme Court would be acceptable only "if there were evidence that Mr. Winner was engaged in two enterprises; one within the Province and the other

[Section 22:5]

[1] *Toronto v. Bell Telephone Co.*, [1905] A.C. 52.

[2] *Toronto v. Bell Telephone Co.*, [1905] A.C. 52, 58.

[3] *Toronto v. Bell Telephone Co.*, [1905] A.C. 52, 57.

[4] *A.-G. Ont. v. Winner*, [1954] A.C. 541.

of a connecting character".[5] As it was, however, the same buses carried both the local and the long-distance passengers: the undertaking was "in fact one and indivisible".[6] Their lordships therefore relied on the *Bell Telephone* case to hold that the entire undertaking was within federal jurisdiction.[7]

The *Bell Telephone* and *Winner* cases established an important rule, which has been consistently reaffirmed in later cases, that a transportation or communication undertaking is subject to the regulation of only one level of government. Once an undertaking is classified as interprovincial, all of its services, intraprovincial as well as interprovincial, are subject to federal jurisdiction.[8] And, by the same token, once an undertaking is classified as local, all of its services, including any casual or irregular interprovincial services,[9] are subject to provincial regulation. In this way, the courts have avoided the complications of divided regulation of a single undertaking. However, the one-undertaking-one-regulator rule loads all the freight on the initial question of classification (or characterization): everything turns on whether the undertaking is interprovincial or local. As Dickson C.J. commented in the *AGT* case, the question of jurisdiction is "an all or nothing affair".[10]

VI. CONTINUOUS AND REGULAR SERVICE

§ 22:6 Continuous and regular service

In *Winner*, as in *Bell Telephone*, their lordships did not inquire into the volume in dollars or passenger miles of Winner's local New Brunswick business, or make any attempt to compare it with the interprovincial and international business. In later cases, where this kind of information has been available, the courts have not shrunk from the implication of *Winner*, and especially *Bell Telephone*, that an interprovincial connection need not be the major part of the undertaking's activity in order to bring the undertaking within s. 92(10)(a). So long as the interprovincial services are a "continuous and regular" part of the undertaking's operations, the undertaking will be classified as interprovincial.

A good example of the "continuous and regular" rule is *Re Ottawa-*

[5]*A.-G. Ont. v. Winner*, [1954] A.C. 541, 580.

[6]*A.-G. Ont. v. Winner*, [1954] A.C. 541, 581.

[7]The sequel to the *Winner* case was a scheme of inter-delegation under which the federal Parliament delegated its authority over interprovincial road transport back to the provinces: see ch. 14, Delegation, under heading § 14:13, "Anticipatory incorporation by reference".

[8]*The Queen (Ont.) v. Bd. of Transport Commrs.*, [1968] S.C.R. 118 (commuter service on interprovincial railway line); *Sask. Power Corp. v. Trans Can. Pipelines*, [1979] 1 S.C.R. 297 (local gas delivery in interprovincial pipeline); *Re Ottawa-Carleton Regional Transit Commn.* (1983), 44 O.R. (2d) 560 (C.A.) (labour relations in municipal transit system).

[9]If the interprovincial services were continuous and regular, the undertaking would be classified as interprovincial: see the next section of this chapter.

[10]*Alberta Government Telephones v. CRTC*, [1989] 2 S.C.R. 225, 257.

Carleton Regional Transit Commission (1983).[1] In that case, a municipal transit system serving the Ottawa area in Ontario operated some bus routes between Ottawa and Hull in Quebec. The bus routes to and from Quebec accounted for less than one per cent of the total distance travelled by the system's vehicles, and they carried only about three per cent of the system's passengers. This interprovincial service, although small in relation to the local service, was regularly scheduled, and the Ontario Court of Appeal held that it was "continuous and regular". Therefore, the Court concluded that the transit system was an interprovincial undertaking, which meant that its labour relations (among other things) came within federal jurisdiction.

In the *Ottawa-Carleton* case, the interprovincial service was part of the transit system's regularly scheduled bus service. This supported the finding that the interprovincial service was "continuous and regular". In the trucking business, there is typically no published schedule or other predetermined timetable: hauls are made as and when customers call for them. Even in this situation, Ontario courts have been willing to find that a small proportion of interprovincial business satisfied the "continuous and regular" rule. In *Re Tank Truck Transport (1960)*,[2] it was held that a trucking company came within s. 92(10)(a), although 94 per cent of its trips were confined to the province and only six per cent were to points outside the province. McLennan J. of the Ontario High Court, whose decision was affirmed by the Court of Appeal, held that the interprovincial connections were "continuous and regular". In that case, there were interprovincial hauls to be made nearly every day. *Tank Truck* was followed in the *Liquid Cargo* case (1965),[3] where another trucking business was held to be within s. 92(10)(a), although its interprovincial business comprised only 1.6 per cent of its trips and ten per cent of its mileage. Haines J. of the Ontario High Court held that the "continuous and regular" test was satisfied, despite the fact that as much as two to three weeks could go by between interprovincial hauls.[4]

If the continuous and regular standard is not met, and the interprovincial service is held to be merely casual, then the undertaking will be classified as local (intraprovincial), which will place its activity within provincial regulatory jurisdiction. For example, in *Agence Maritime v. Canada Labour Relations Board* (1969),[5] vessels plying coastal ports within Quebec made three trips outside the province over a period of

[Section 22:6]

[1] *Re Ottawa-Carleton Regional Transit Commission* (1983), 44 O.R. (2d) 560 (C.A.).

[2] *Re Tank Truck Transport*, [1960] O.R. 497 (H.C.); affd. without written reasons [1963] 1 O.R. 272 (C.A.).

[3] *R. v. Cooksville Magistrate's Court; ex parte Liquid Cargo Lines*, [1965] 1 O.R. 84 (H.C.).

[4] See also *Re Pacific Produce Delivery and Warehouses* (1974), 44 D.L.R. (3d) 130 (C.A.); *Re A.-G. Que. and Baillargeon* (1978), 97 D.L.R. (3d) 447 (C.A.).

[5] *Agence Maritime v. Canada Labour Relations Board*, [1969] S.C.R. 851.

two years. The shipping company was held to be within provincial labour relations jurisdiction.[6]

There is one qualification which must be made to the rule that "continuous and regular" interprovincial service constitutes an interprovincial connection within the meaning of s. 92(10)(a). The rule will not apply to a carrier who artificially organizes its business so as to acquire an interprovincial connection, for example, by unnecessarily detouring across a provincial border or by unnecessarily locating a terminal just across a border. Such a "subterfuge" or "camouflage" will be disregarded by the courts in determining whether or not the undertaking is really interprovincial. As the Privy Council said in *Winner,* "The question is whether in truth and in fact there is an internal activity prolonged over the border in order to enable the owner to evade provincial jurisdiction or whether in pith and substance it is interprovincial".[7] In effect this is the colourability doctrine[8] applied to interprovincial undertakings.

VII. RELATED UNDERTAKINGS

§ 22:7 Common ownership

The decisions in *Bell Telephone, Winner, Ottawa-Carleton, Tank Truck* and *Liquid Cargo* were each premised on the finding that the company (or individual) was engaged in one indivisible undertaking. But a company may engage in more than one undertaking, in which case that company's operations may become subject to dual legislative authority. The fact that various business operations are carried on by a single proprietor does not foreclose inquiry as to whether or not those operations consist of more than one undertaking for constitutional purposes. It is the degree to which the operations are integrated in a functional or business sense that will determine whether they constitute one undertaking or not.

For example, in the *Empress Hotel* case (1950),[1] the Privy Council held that the Empress Hotel in Victoria, although owned by the Canadian Pacific Railway Company, was a separate undertaking from the company's interprovincial railway. It followed that employment in the hotel was regulated by provincial law, while employment on the railway was regulated by federal law. In reaching this conclusion, their lordships examined the business relationship between the hotel and the railway. If the hotel had catered principally to railway travellers, like a station restaurant, then it would have been classified as part of the

---

[6]Cf. *Construction Montcalm v. Minimum Wage Comm.*, [1979] 1 S.C.R. 754 (construction company with occasional work on airport; held, within provincial jurisdiction).

[7]*A.-G. Ont. v. Winner*, [1954] A.C. 541, 582.

[8]See ch. 15, Judicial Review on Federal Grounds, under heading § 15:11, "Colourability".

[Section 22:7]

[1]*CPR v. A.-G. B.C.* (Empress Hotel) [1950] A.C. 122.

railway undertaking. But in fact the Empress Hotel carried on a general hotel business, drawing its customers from all sections of the travelling public in the same way as an independently-owned hotel. Their lordships did not doubt that the hotel and the railway complemented each other in the sense that each helped the business of the other, but they concluded that "that does not prevent them from being separate businesses or undertakings".[2]

In *Total Oilfield Rentals v. Can.* (2014),[3] the issue was whether Total Oilfield's trucking operations came within federal or provincial jurisdiction. The company had been levied an administrative monetary penalty for violations of the transportation regulations enacted under the federal Motor Vehicle Transportation Act. The company applied to review the administrative monetary penalty on the ground that the company was a provincial undertaking to which the federal regulations did not apply. The company's primary business was the renting of industrial equipment needed in the oilfield services industry. The company maintained a fleet of trucks that were used mainly to deliver and retrieve its own rental equipment to and from its customers' job sites. The company's head office was in Alberta, but it had branches in other provinces, and its operations extended to all the oil-producing provinces and territories. Customers' job-site needs often required cross-border transportation, and its trucks were licensed to operate in multiple jurisdictions. The Alberta Court of Appeal, by a majority, held that the company's trucking operations were a transportation undertaking, and that the volume of cross-border journeys (21 per cent) satisfied the "continuous and regular" test. Therefore, the transportation undertaking extended beyond the limits of the province and was subject to federal regulation, including the challenged administrative penalties.

The complication in *Total Oilfield* was that the company's primary business, the renting of oilfield equipment, was unquestionably within provincial jurisdiction. The trucking operations supported the rental business by delivering and retrieving the rental equipment. The majority of the Court agreed that the company was not a transportation company, but they held, relying on *Empress Hotel*, that for constitutional purposes one company may own several undertakings. The company's trucking operations were a separate *undertaking* that was engaged in interprovincial transportation which was subject to federal jurisdiction.[4] Slatter J., who dissented, held that there was no separate transportation undertaking. In his view, the company was "an integrated equip-

---

[2]*CPR v. A.-G. B.C.* (Empress Hotel) [1950] A.C. 122, 144.

[3]*Total Oilfield Rentals v. Can.* (2014), 375 D.L.R. (4th) 433 (Alta.C.A.); leave to appeal to the SCC denied. O'Ferrall and Veldhuis JJ.A. wrote the opinion of the majority. Slatter J.A. dissented.

[4]*Total Oilfield Rentals v. Can.* (2014), 375 D.L.R. (4th) 433 (Alta.C.A.), paras. 85–86. The case did not concern jurisdiction over labour relations, but the majority commented, obiter, that labour relations would be governed by the nature of the company's primary business and would therefore be entirely provincial: *Total Oilfield Rentals v. Can.* (2014), 375 D.L.R. (4th) 433 (Alta.C.A.), paras. 65–69. For this proposition they relied on *Tessier v. Que.*, [2012] 2 S.C.R. 3.

ment rental company that happens to deliver its equipment."[5] Constitutional jurisdiction over the company depended on the "core", or the "essential operational nature" of its business.[6] That was equipment rental, which came within provincial jurisdiction. Because the core business was not transportation, the "continuous and regular" inquiry was irrelevant. Slatter J. would have decided that the company's entire operation, including trucking, was within provincial jurisdiction.

The inconclusiveness of ownership works in both directions. Just as one proprietor may own and operate two separate undertakings, so two (or more) proprietors may own and operate different parts of a single undertaking. A business which, regarded by itself, is entirely local may be so closely tied into another business which is interprovincial that the two businesses will be classified as forming a single interprovincial undertaking. There are two situations in which a local undertaking will be treated for constitutional purposes as part of a separately-owned interprovincial undertaking. One (common management) is where the two undertakings are managed in common as a single enterprise. The other (dependency) is where the interprovincial undertaking is dependent on the local undertaking for the performance of an essential part of the interprovincial transportation or communication services. These two situations are the topics of the next two sections of the chapter.

§ 22:8 Common management

The first situation where a local undertaking will be held to be part of a separately-owned interprovincial undertaking is where the two undertakings are actually operated in common as a single enterprise. That was the case in *Luscar Collieries v. McDonald* (1927),[1] where a short railway line located within the province of Alberta was held to be part of the interprovincial undertaking of the Canadian Northern Railway. The short line was owned by a colliery, which had built the line in order to be able to move coal onto the interprovincial railway to which the short line was connected (via another branch). Under a formal management agreement, the short line was operated by CNR. Although the Privy Council's reasons for judgment are ambiguous, the case was later explained by the Supreme Court of Canada as turning on the common management by CNR of both the local and the interprovincial line.[2] Later cases have made clear that a mere physical connection, even

[5] *Total Oilfield Rentals v. Can.* (2014), 375 D.L.R. (4th) 433 (Alta.C.A.), para. 132.

[6] *Total Oilfield Rentals v. Can.* (2014), 375 D.L.R. (4th) 433 (Alta.C.A.), paras. 142–144, relying on *Tessier v. Quebec*, [2012] 2 S.C.R. 3.

[Section 22:8]

[1] *Luscar Collieries v. McDonald*, [1927] A.C. 925.

[2] *B.C. Elec. Ry. Co. v. CNR*, [1932] S.C.R. 161, 169; *UTU v. Central Western Ry.*, [1990] 3 S.C.R. 1112, 1133.

combined with regular cooperatively-organized through traffic, will not make a local railway part of an interprovincial railway.[3]

In the *GO-Train* case (1968),[4] the Government of Ontario established the GO-Train commuter rail service, located entirely within the province, to serve the city of Toronto. No new railway track was built. The GO-Train trains made use of a short stretch of the Canadian National Railway's interprovincial network of rail. The Supreme Court of Canada held that the use of the interprovincial railway line made the commuter service part of the interprovincial undertaking. All of the services provided on the interprovincial line came within the same federal jurisdiction. This decision is not exactly a case of common management, because, unlike the *Luscar Collieries* case, the commuter service was not managed by CNR.[5] However, it is close to common management, because of the constraints imposed on the commuter service by CNR's control of the CNR tracks. The Court cited *Luscar Collieries*, and treated it as on all fours.

In *Westcoast Energy v. Canada* (1998),[6] Westcoast Energy owned and operated gathering pipelines that collected natural gas from the wells and carried the gas to processing plants, also owned and operated by Westcoast Energy, that removed impurities from the gas. These facilities were wholly located in the province of British Columbia. The question in the case was whether the facilities came within federal or provincial jurisdiction. The Supreme Court of Canada held that the facilities came within federal jurisdiction, because the processed gas was transported into an interprovincial pipeline that was also owned and operated by Westcoast Energy. The gathering pipelines, the processing plants and the interprovincial pipeline were managed in common as a single enterprise. It made no difference that the processing plants were not themselves engaged in transportation; their dedication to the common enterprise made them part of the transportation undertaking. The case was like *Luscar Collieries* with the added feature that in *Westcoast Energy* there was common ownership of the local and interprovincial facilities as well as common management. The Court held that the facilities constituted a single interprovincial undertaking for the purpose of s. 92(10)(a).

---

[3]*B.C. Elec. Ry. Co. v. CNR*, [1932] S.C.R. 161, 169; *UTU v. Central Western Ry.*, [1990] 3 S.C.R. 1112, 1133. Also, *Montreal v. Montreal St. Ry.*, [1912] A.C. 333. Compare *Kootenay and Elk Ry. v. CPR*, [1974] S.C.R. 955, 980, 982 (obiter dicta implying that something less than common management would suffice), but note discussion of *Kootenay and Elk* and affirmation of common management requirement in *UTU v. Central Western Ry.*, [1990] 3 S.C.R. 1112, 1133–1135.

[4]*The Queen Ont. v. Bd. of Transport Commrs.*, [1968] S.C.R. 118.

[5]I.H. Fraser, "Some Comments on Subsection 92(10) of the Constitution Act, 1867" (1984) 29 McGill L.J. 557, 605 regards the case as wrongly decided.

[6]*Westcoast Energy v. Canada*, [1998] 1 S.C.R. 322. The opinion of the majority was written by Iacobucci and Major JJ. and agreed with by L'Heureux-Dubé, Gonthier, Cory and Bastarache JJ. A dissenting opinion was written by McLachlin J.

§ 22:9 Dependency

The second situation where a local undertaking will be held to be part of a separately-owned interprovincial undertaking is where the interprovincial undertaking is dependent on the local undertaking for the performance of an essential part of the interprovincial transportation or communication services.[1] The leading example of this situation is the *Stevedores Reference* (1955).[2] The issue in the case was whether employment in a stevedoring company came within federal or provincial jurisdiction. The company furnished stevedoring services (the loading and unloading of ships) to several shipping companies in Canadian ports. It was common ground that the shipping companies were within federal jurisdiction under s. 92(10)(a), or possibly s. 91(10) ("navigation and shipping"). But the stevedoring company was independent of the shipping companies, and its operations in each port were entirely local. Nevertheless, the Supreme Court of Canada, by a majority of eight to one, held that the stevedores came within federal jurisdiction. The Court held that the stevedoring operations were "part and parcel" of a shipping undertaking,[3] and the shipping undertaking was "entirely dependent" on the stevedoring activity.[4]

Another example of the dependency rule is provided by the *Letter Carriers* case (1973).[5] In that case, a private company delivered and collected mail under contract with the Post Office. The postal work comprised most of the company's business. The Supreme Court of Canada held that the company's employees came within federal jurisdiction. Ritchie J. for the Court held that the work of the employees was "essential to the function of the postal service", and "an integral part of the effective operation of the Post Office".[6]

The relationship of dependency that will bring a local undertaking into federal jurisdiction must be a permanent, or at least ongoing, relationship. A casual, exceptional or temporary relationship will not suffice. Otherwise, "the Constitution could not be applied with any

---

[Section 22:9]

[1] *UTU v. Central Western Ry.*, [1990] 3 S.C.R. 1112, 1137.

[2] *Re Industrial Relations and Disputes Investigation Act*, [1955] S.C.R. 529.

[3] *Re Industrial Relations and Disputes Investigation Act*, [1955] S.C.R. 529, 537.

[4] *Re Industrial Relations and Disputes Investigation Act*, [1955] S.C.R. 529, 534. See also *Tessier v. Que.*, [2012] 2 S.C.R. 3, para. 34, confirming that the activity of stevedoring would not, by itself, bring a local undertaking into federal jurisdiction; dependency of interprovincial or international shipping on the stevedoring activity is necessary.

[5] *Letter Carriers' Union of Can. v. Can. Union of Postal Workers*, [1975] 1 S.C.R. 178.

[6] *Letter Carriers' Union of Can. v. Can. Union of Postal Workers*, [1975] 1 S.C.R. 178, 183, 186. See also *Northern Telecom Can. v. Communications Workers of Can.*, [1983] 1 S.C.R. 733 (telephone installation "an integral element" of the telephone undertaking); *Bernshine Mobile Maintenance v. CLRB*, [1986] 1 F.C. 422 (C.A.) (truck washing essential to interprovincial trucking undertaking).

degree of continuity and regularity".[7] For example, employees of a construction company that had been engaged by Canadian National Railway to replace bridges on the interprovincial railway line were certainly performing a function that was essential to the operation of the interprovincial railway. But the company's relationship with CNR was temporary in that it was limited to the particular construction projects contracted for. The relationship lacked the ongoing character that would have constitutional significance, and the employees were accordingly within provincial labour relations jurisdiction.[8] A more permanent relationship for the purpose of maintenance or repair would have brought the employees into the federal fold as an essential part of the interprovincial undertaking.[9]

A similar case is *Tessier v. Quebec* (2012),[10] where a company that rented out cranes and provided operating services to the renters was held to be within provincial jurisdiction for labour relations purposes. The company's operations were limited to the province of Quebec, but some of the company's cranes were used for stevedoring, which is the loading and unloading of ships, and some of those ships took their cargoes outside the province. It was argued that this function brought the company's employees into federal jurisdiction. The difficulty for this argument was that the stevedoring operations accounted for only 14 per cent of the company's earnings and 20 per cent of the company's payroll. Moreover, the stevedoring services were not performed by a separate unit of the company: an employee who operated a crane at the port one day might be working on a construction site the next day. The Supreme Court held that, even if the stevedoring operations were vital to the operation of extraprovincial shipping, they would not convert a local undertaking into a federal one if they were only "a minor part" of the local undertaking. Only if the "dominant character" of the local undertaking was the service of interprovincial transportation would the local undertaking come within federal jurisdiction.[11] That was not the case here.

The relationship of dependency that will bring a local undertaking into federal jurisdiction is the dependency of the interprovincial undertaking on the local undertaking, not the other way around.[12] A local railway that serves grain elevators is dependent upon its connection

---

[7]*Northern Telecom Can. v. Communications Workers (No. 1)*, [1980] 1 S.C.R. 115, 132 (obiter dictum); compare *Construction Montcalm v. Minimum Wage Commn.*, [1979] 1 S.C.R. 754 (employees of construction firm building runway at airport not within federal authority over aeronautics).

[8]*Re Can. Labour Code*, [1987] 2 F.C. 30 (C.A.).

[9]E.g., *Bernshine Mobile Maintenance v. CLRB*, [1986] 1 F.C. 422 (C.A.) (company that washed trucks held to be essential part of interprovincial undertaking).

[10]*Tessier v. Quebec*, [2012] 2 S.C.R. 3. Abella J. wrote the opinion of the Court.

[11]*Tessier v. Quebec*, [2012] 2 S.C.R. 3, paras. 50, 52, 59.

[12]I.H. Fraser, "Some Comments on Subsection 92(10) of the Constitution Act, 1867" (1984) 29 McGill L.J. 557, 605.

with an interprovincial railway that will carry the grain to port.[13] A local pipeline that supplies a factory with natural gas is dependent upon its connection with an interprovincial pipeline for all of its gas.[14] And a freight forwarder that collects goods in Toronto for shipment to the West is dependent upon its connection with an interprovincial railway to carry the goods to their destinations.[15] In each of these cases, the interprovincial undertaking could function effectively without the local undertaking. It was the local undertaking that depended upon the interprovincial undertaking. That relationship of dependency is constitutionally irrelevant. It does not transform the railway, the pipeline and the freight forwarder into parts of interprovincial undertakings. They remain as local undertakings within provincial jurisdiction, as the footnoted cases have decided.

The same cases establish that a connection between a local undertaking and an interprovincial undertaking, combined with a mutually beneficial commercial relationship, is not enough to make the local undertaking a part of the interprovincial undertaking.[16] The only[17] kinds of commercial relationships that will produce this result are (1) where the local undertaking is managed in common with the interprovincial undertaking (the topic of the previous section of this chapter), or (2) where the local undertaking performs a function that is essential to the delivery by the interprovincial undertaking of the interprovincial services (the topic of this section of the chapter).[18]

VIII. WORKS FOR THE GENERAL ADVANTAGE OF CANADA

§ 22:10 Works for the general advantage of Canada

Section 92(10)(c), read with s. 91(29), gives the federal Parliament the power to make laws in relation to:

---

[13]*UTU v. Central Western Ry.*, [1990] 3 S.C.R. 1112.

[14]*Re National Energy Bd. Act*, [1988] 2 F.C. 196 (C.A.).

[15]*Re Cannet Freight Cartage*, [1976] 1 F.C. 174 (C.A.). Folld. in *Consolidated Fastfrate v. Western Canada Council of Teamsters*, [2009] 3 S.C.R. 407; and see discussion in § 22:4, "Connection with another province".

[16]*UTU v. Central Western Ry.*, [1990] 3 S.C.R. 1112, 1147.

[17]The cable television cases, namely, *Capital Cities Communications v. CRTC*, [1978] 2 S.C.R. 141, and *Public Service Board v. Dionne*, [1978] 2 S.C.R. 191, do not quite fit the analysis. The cable systems, although located within a province, were held to be within federal jurisdiction. The cable systems were managed independently of the broadcasters (although with respect to broadcast signals the companies could exercise very little management discretion—they were "no more than a conduit for signals from the telecast"). The broadcasters were not dependent upon the cable systems for distribution of the signals, because the signals could be received off the air (although the cable systems provided a better quality of distribution). Critical to the decisions was the avoidance of the awkward dual regulatory jurisdiction that would result if cable reception was provincial and off-air reception was federal.

[18]This issue of the correct constitutional classification of an undertaking arises most frequently in a labour relations context, where it is necessary to determine which labour board, federal or provincial, has jurisdiction: see ch. 21, Property and Civil Rights, under heading §§ 21:10 to 21:11, "Labour relations".

(c) Such works as, although wholly situate within the province, are before or after their execution declared by the Parliament of Canada to be for the general advantage of Canada or for the advantage of two or more of the provinces.

This "declaratory power" enables the federal Parliament to assume jurisdiction over a local work by declaring the work to be "for the general advantage of Canada".[1] For example, an intraprovincial railway would be within provincial jurisdiction as a local work or undertaking (s. 92(10)),[2] but if the federal Parliament declared the railway to be a work for the general advantage of Canada, then the railway would be withdrawn from provincial jurisdiction by virtue of s. 92(10)(c) and brought into federal jurisdiction by virtue of s. 91(29).[3] If the declaration were repealed by the federal Parliament, then the railway would revert to provincial jurisdiction.[4]

The declaratory power has been exercised no less than 472 times, the majority of which have been in respect of local railways. Other instances include tramways, canals, bridges, dams, tunnels, harbours, wharves, telegraphs, telephones, mines, mills, grain elevators, hotels, restaurants, theatres, oil refineries and factories of various kinds.[5] Not all of these declarations relate to works involved in transportation or communication, and it is clear that the power is not so limited.[6]

The power under s. 92(10)(c) is confined to "works", which contrasts with s. 92(10)(a)'s reference to "works and undertakings". We have already noticed that there are dicta which distinguish between a "work" and an "undertaking", on the basis that a work is a tangible thing while

---

[Section 22:10]

[1]Lajoie, Le pouvoir déclaratoire du Parlement (1969) is a monograph on the declaratory power. See also V.C. MacDonald, "Parliamentary Jurisdiction by Declaration", Annotation [1934] 1 D.L.R. 1 (also, somewhat altered, in Dominion Law Annotations, vol. 3, 206); P. Schwartz, "Fiat by Declaration" (1960) 2 Osgoode Hall L.J. 1; K. Hanssen, "The Federal Declaratory Power" (1968) 3 Man. L.J. 87; Laskin, Canadian Constitutional Law (5th ed., 1986 by Finkelstein), 627–631; and for further literature see Lajoie, Le pouvoir déclaratoire du Parlement (1969), 153 (bibliography).

[2]*Montreal v. Montreal St. Ry.*, [1912] A.C. 333; *B.C. Elec. Ry. v. CNR*, [1932] S.C.R. 161; *UTU v. Central Western Ry.*, [1990] 3 S.C.R. 1112.

[3]*B.C. v. Can.*, [1994] 2 S.C.R. 41, 116. The declaration will not affect the ownership of the declared work, just legislative jurisdiction over it; although that jurisdiction might authorize a subsequent expropriation by federal statute: see ch. 29, Public Property, under the heading § 29:5, "Expropriation".

[4]*UTU v. Central Western Ry.*, [1990] 3 S.C.R. 1112.

[5]Lajoie, Le pouvoir déclaratoire du Parlement (1969), 54 and appendix which lists 470 declarations; K. Hanssen, "The Federal Declaratory Power" (1968) 3 Man. L.J. 87, has a similar appendix although it is less complete. Since Lajoie compiled her list, a few more declarations have been made: § 22:10 note 24, below.

[6]*Jorgenson v. A.-G. Can.*, [1971] S.C.R. 725 (grain elevators); *Chamney v. The Queen*, [1975] 2 S.C.R. 151 (grain elevators); *Ont. Hydro v. Ont.*, [1993] 3 S.C.R. 327 (electrical generating stations); Laskin, Canadian Constitutional Law (5th ed., 1986 by Finkelstein), 627.

an undertaking is an intangible "arrangement" or "organization" or "enterprise".[7] However, the drafters of federal declarations have not always observed such niceties and there are many federal statutes which contain declarations in respect of "works and undertakings" or even "undertakings" alone.[8] No declaration has ever been held to be invalid on the ground that it purported to apply to an "undertaking", and one such declaration has been expressly upheld.[9] Lajoie explains the validity of such declarations by suggesting that a declaration may be applied to undertakings linked with works, but not to undertakings which exist without the aid of works, for example, a society of accountants or lawyers or a social service agency.[10]

The distinction between works and undertakings is further blurred by the fact that the effect of a declaration over a work "must surely be to bring within federal authority not only the physical shell of the activity but also the integrated activity carried on therein; in other words, the declaration operates on the work in its functional character".[11] That this is correct is demonstrated by cases in which the declaration has been followed by an assertion of regulatory jurisdiction over the activity related to the work. Perhaps the clearest examples are the declarations that grain elevators and various kinds of mills and warehouses are works for the general advantage of Canada. The purpose of these declarations was to assume the regulatory jurisdiction over the grain trade which had been denied to the federal Parliament by *The King v. Eastern Terminal Elevator Co.* (1925).[12] It has been held that these declarations are effective to authorize federal regulation of the delivery, receipt, storage and processing of the grain, that is to say, the activities created on, in or about the "works".[13]

In *Ontario Hydro v. Ontario* (1993),[14] the Supreme Court of Canada held that a declaration over a work conferred on the federal Parliament

---

[7] *Montreal v. Montreal St. Ry.*, [1912] A.C. 333, 342.

[8] K. Hanssen, "The Federal Declaratory Power" (1968) 3 Man. L.J. 87 (appendix) lists many examples; see also C.H. McNairn, "Transportation, Communication and the Constitution" (1969) 47 Can. Bar Rev. 355, 359.

[9] *Que. Ry. Light and Power Co. v. Beauport*, [1945] S.C.R. 16.

[10] Lajoie, Le pouvoir déclaratoire du Parlement (1969), 61. She also suggests, though less confidently, that the declaratory power would not be available with respect to undertakings in which the physical works are of secondary importance to the provision of services, for example, universities or hospitals. See also Laskin, Canadian Constitutional Law (5th ed., 1986 by Finkelstein), 628, who says that the declaratory power is not available with respect to "undertakings existing without works".

[11] Laskin, Canadian Constitutional Law (5th ed., 1986 by Finkelstein), 629; K. Hanssen, "The Federal Declaratory Power" (1968) 3 Man. L.J. 87, 93–95.

[12] *The King v. Eastern Terminal Elevator Co.*, [1925] S.C.R. 434; see ch. 20, Trade and Commerce, under heading § 20:2, "In the Privy Council".

[13] *Jorgenson v. A.-G. Can.*, [1971] S.C.R. 725; *Chamney v. The Queen*, [1975] 2 S.C.R. 151.

[14] *Ontario Hydro v. Ontario*, [1993] 3 S.C.R. 327. La Forest J., with L'Heureux-Dubé and Gonthier JJ., wrote the majority opinion. Lamer C.J. wrote a separate concurring opinion. Iacobucci J., with Sopinka and Cory JJ., wrote a dissenting opinion, taking the

jurisdiction over labour relations in the declared work. Ontario Hydro was a provincially-owned and provincially-regulated corporation that produced and distributed electricity. The corporation produced the electricity at 81 generating stations, of which five were operated by nuclear power. The five nuclear plants had been declared to be works for the general advantage of Canada by a provision in the federal Atomic Energy Act.[15] The Supreme Court of Canada, by a majority, held that the declaration conferred on Parliament power over "the work as a going concern", which involved "control over its operation and management".[16] That included "power to regulate the labour relations between management and labour engaged in operating the work".[17] It followed that, although the rest of Hydro's workforce was governed by provincial labour law, the workers in the nuclear plants were governed by federal labour law.

The language of s. 92(10)(c) makes clear that a declaration may be made not only in respect of existing works, but also in respect of works to be constructed in the future. Until recently there was some doubt as to how specific a declaration had to be, especially if it was to apply to works not in existence at the time of the declaration. Obviously, any declaration had to sufficiently identify the works to which it applied, but did identification require that each work be individually specified by name or other description? In *Jorgensen v. A.-G. Can.* (1971),[18] the Supreme Court of Canada answered no, holding that a declaration which referred to a class of works was valid. At issue were the declarations in the Canada Grain Act and the Canada Wheat Board Act. The first of these applied to "all [grain] elevators in Canada heretofore or hereafter constructed"; the second applied to "all flour mills, feed mills, feed warehouses and seed cleaning mills, whether heretofore constructed or hereafter to be constructed". Both these sweeping "class" declarations were upheld.

While the definition of a work is subject to judicial interpretation, the courts have made no attempt to give content to the words "for the general advantage of Canada". The courts have treated this phrase as imposing a requirement of form rather than substance. No work is caught by s. 92(10)(c) by implication. There must be an explicit declaration by Parliament that the work is for the general advantage of Canada.[19] Once an explicit declaration has been made, it is conclusive: the question whether a particular work really is for the general

---

view that legislative jurisdiction over the declared work did not extend to labour relations.

[15]The declaration is now found in Nuclear Safety and Control Act, S.C. 1997, c. 9, s. 71.

[16]*Ontario Hydro v. Ontario*, [1993] 3 S.C.R. 327, 367.

[17]*Ontario Hydro v. Ontario*, [1993] 3 S.C.R. 327, 368.

[18]*Jorgensen v. A.-G. Can.*, [1971] S.C.R. 725; also *Chamney v. The Queen*, [1975] 2 S.C.R. 151. See also *Ont. Hydro v. Ont.*, [1993] 3 S.C.R. 327 (upholding a class declaration in the Atomic Energy Control Act).

[19]*YMHA Jewish Community Centre v. Brown*, [1989] 1 S.C.R. 1532, 1552.

advantage of Canada has been seen as an issue of policy for the Parliament, not subject to judicial review.[20]

In the earlier chapter on Federalism, I commented that the federal Parliament's power under s. 92(10)(c) is in conflict with classical principles of federalism because it enables the federal Parliament, by its own unilateral act, to increase its own powers and diminish those of the provinces.[21] The Constitutions of the United States and Australia confer no comparable power on their federal (or state) legislative bodies. The Canadian power has been the subject of provincial objection,[22] and it has been suggested that it should be amended to require the consent of the province in which the work is situated, or the consent of a majority of the provinces.[23] It appears, however, that the federal government and Parliament are sensitive to the anomalous character of the power and are now inclined to use the power only sparingly. It has been used very rarely in recent times.[24]

IX. TRANSPORTATION BY LAND

§ 22:11 Transportation by land

Legislative jurisdiction over transportation by land depends upon the principles explained in the previous sections of this chapter. Jurisdiction over trains,[1] buses,[2] trucks,[3] taxis, limousines,[4] pipelines,[5] and electricity

---

[20]Lajoie, Le pouvoir déclaratoire du Parlement (1969), 69–70; Laskin, Canadian Constitutional Law (5th ed., 1986 by Finkelstein), 628; K. Hanssen, "The Federal Declaratory Power" (1968) 3 Man. L.J. 87, 102–105.

[21]Chapter 5, Federalism, under heading § 5:17, "Declaratory power".

[22]Lajoie, Le pouvoir déclaratoire du Parlement (1969), 70–72.

[23]Lajoie, Le pouvoir déclaratoire du Parlement (1969), 118. The unsuccessful Charlottetown Accord of 1992 (see ch. 4, Amendment, under heading § 4:3, "The failure to accommodate Quebec") proposed the amendment of s. 92(10)(c) to require the consent of the province in which the work was situated.

[24]The most recent declarations would appear to be: Cape Breton Development Corporation Act, R.S.C. 1985, c. C-25, s. 35 (since repealed and replaced by Cape Breton Development Corporation Divestiture Authorization and Dissolution Act, S.C. 2000, c. 23, s. 5); Teleglobe Canada Reorganization and Divestiture Act, S.C. 1987, c. 12, s. 9; International Bridges and Tunnels Act, S.C. 2007, c. 1, s. 5; and New Bridge for the St. Lawrence Act, S.C. 2014, c. 20 s. 375, s. 5. Of course, old declarations are re-enacted when a statute that includes a declaration is replaced by a new statute: see e.g. Nuclear Safety and Control Act, S.C. 1997, c. 9, s. 71; Marketing Freedom for Grain Farmers Act, S.C. 2011, c. 25, s. 45.

[Section 22:11]

[1]*Montreal v. Montreal St. Ry.*, [1912] A.C. 333; *Luscar Collieries v. McDonald*, [1972] A.C. 925; *B.C. Elec. Ry. v. C.N.R.*, [1932] S.C.R. 161; *The Queen (Ont.) v. Bd. of Transport Commrs.*, [1968] S.C.R. 118; *Re Can. Labour Code*, [1987] 2 F.C. 30 (C.A.); *UTU v. Central Western Ry.*, [1990] 3 S.C.R. 1112. For discussion of the development of railways in Canada, and the variety of constitutional provisions which have been called in aid, see C.H. McNairn, "Transportation, Communication and the Constitution" (1969) 47 Can. Bar Rev. 355, 365–373; and see also heading § 22:1 "Distribution of power".

[2]*A.-G. Ont. v. Winner*, [1954] A.C. 541; *Re Ottawa-Carleton Regional Transit Comm.*

transmission lines[6] depends primarily on whether they are operated as part of an interprovincial (or international) undertaking, in which case jurisdiction is federal under s. 92(10)(a), or whether they are operated as part of an intraprovincial undertaking, in which case jurisdiction is provincial under s. 92(10).[7] Some intraprovincial undertakings, including many local railways, have been brought under federal jurisdiction by exercise of the declaratory power under s. 92(10)(c).

The postal service has a special constitutional status in that it is a separate federal head of power in s. 91(5) ("postal service"), specifically listed because of the national importance of the postal service for the economic development of the new federation and in creating a single nation from the uniting provinces. (At the time of confederation each of the uniting provinces had its own postal service.) Of course, the national postal service would in any case come within federal jurisdiction as an interprovincial undertaking under s. 92(10)(a), as would a local private transportation company that delivered mail under contract with Canada Post as an integral part of the operations of the national postal service.[8]

In *TurnAround Couriers v. Canadian Union of Postal Workers* (2012),[9] the question to be decided was which level of government had jurisdiction over the labour relations of a courier company that operated solely in Ontario. The company picked up and delivered, usually on the same day, letters and packages within the Greater Toronto Area. If the company was providing "postal service" within s. 91(5), then its labour relations came within federal jurisdiction. If not, then it was a local undertaking within s. 92(10), and its labour relations came within provincial jurisdiction. The company had no contractual or other rela-

(1983), 44 O.R. (2d) 560 (C.A.); *Ferguson Bus Lines v. ATU*, [1990] 2 F.C. 586 (C.A.).

[3]*Re Tank Truck Transport*, [1960] O.R. 497 (H.C.); affd. [1963] 1 O.R. 272 (C.A.); *R. v. Cooksville Magistrate's Court; ex parte Liquid Cargo Lines*, [1965] 1 O.R. 84 (H.C.); *R. v. Man. Lab Bd.; ex parte Invictus* (1968), 65 D.L.R. (2d) 517 (Man. Q.B.); *Re A.-G. Que. and Baillargeon* (1987), 97 D.L.R. (3d) 447 (Que. C.A.); *Bernshine Mobile Maintenance v. CLRB*, [1986] 1 F.C. 422 (C.A.).

[4]*Re Colonial Coach Lines*, [1967] 2 O.R. 25 (H.C.); *Re Windsor Airline Limousine Service* (1980), 30 O.R. (2d) 732 (Div. Ct.).

[5]*Campbell-Bennett v. Comstock Midwestern*, [1954] S.C.R. 207; *Sask. Power Corp. v. Trans Can. Pipelines*, [1979] 1 S.C.R. 297; *Re National Energy Bd. Act*, [1988] 2 F.C. 196 (C.A.); *Re Bypass Pipelines* (1988), 64 O.R. (2d) 293 (C.A.), *Westcoast Energy v. Can.*, [1998] 1 S.C.R. 322; *Re Environmental Management Act* (2019), 434 D.L.R. (4th) 213 (B.C.C.A.), affd. 2020 SCC 1.

[6]*Fulton v. Energy Resources Conservation Bd.*, [1981] 1 S.C.R. 153; *Re Town of Summerside and Maritime Electric Co. (No. 2)* (1983), 3 D.L.R. (4th) 577 (P.E.I. S.C. in banco).

[7]An undertaking may still be bound by the valid laws of the level of government which lacks primary jurisdiction over the undertaking under the incidental effect doctrine, or the double aspect doctrine, but subject to the interjurisdictional immunity doctrine: see ch. 15, Judicial Review on Federal Grounds.

[8]*Letter Carriers' Union of Can. v. Can. Union of Postal Workers*, [1975] 1 S.C.R. 178; text accompanying § 22:9 note 5.

[9]*TurnAround Couriers v. Canadian Union of Postal Workers* (2012), 347 D.L.R. (4th) 149 (F.C.A.). Evans J.A. wrote the opinion of the Court.

tionship with Canada Post (or any interprovincial courier company), and it was able to operate notwithstanding the statutory monopoly of Canada Post because there was an exemption in the Canada Post Corporation Act for courier services that delivered "letters of an urgent nature". It was argued that the company was providing a service that could in principle be provided by Canada Post, and could indeed only be provided by Canada Post if the urgency exemption in the Act were repealed, something Parliament obviously had the power to do. Therefore, it was argued, the company's operations must be "postal service" within s. 91(5). This argument prevailed at the Canada Industrial Relations Board (a federal board), which certified a union as the bargaining agent for the company's employees. On an application for judicial review, the Federal Court of Appeal set aside this decision. The better view, according to the Court, was that "postal service" in s. 91(5) meant only the national delivery system now provided by Canada Post Corporation and previously by the Post Office. That accorded with the nation-building role of the postal service, which was an objective of the framers in 1867.[10] It was also the easiest interpretation to apply, since it did not require a case-by-case analysis of how much of a courier's business was devoted to the collection and delivery of mailable items and how much to other items.[11] It followed that the courier company was a local undertaking within provincial jurisdiction.

The Canada Post Corporation, which now has the statutory responsibility to operate the postal service, decided to eliminate home delivery as an economy measure. (No-one in government apparently questioned whether you can have a postal service that does not deliver the mail.) To this end, Canada Post embarked on a process of building and installing "community mail boxes" (CMBs) to which the mail would be delivered and from which the addressees in that community could come and pick up their mail. Unsurprisingly, this project attracted opposition, not only for its inconvenience to the addressees who were used to home delivery, but also for ancillary problems of traffic congestion, littering and snow removal in the vicinity of each CMB. When the rollout of CMBs reached the dense, settled neighbourhood of downtown Hamilton, the City adopted a by-law giving the City control over the placement of equipment, including CMBs, on municipal roads. Canada Post challenged the by-law on constitutional grounds and was successful in the Ontario Court of Appeal.[12] Miller J.A., who wrote the opinion of the Court, held that Canada Post was acting in accordance with the Mail Receptacles Regulations, which Canada Post had validly promulgated, and which authorized Canada Post to install "in any public place, including a public roadway, any receptacle to be used for the collection, delivery or stor-

---

[10] *TurnAround Couriers v. Canadian Union of Postal Workers* (2012), 347 D.L.R. (4th) 149 (F.C.A.), para. 53.

[11] *TurnAround Couriers v. Canadian Union of Postal Workers* (2012), 347 D.L.R. (4th) 149 (F.C.A.), para. 55.

[12] *Canada Post Corp. v. Hamilton (City)* (2016) 134 O.R. (3d) 502, 2016 ONCA 767. Miller J.A. wrote the opinion of the Court.

age of mail." He also held that the by-law was a valid exercise of the City's municipal powers. But, because the by-law would give the City a veto over the placement of CMBs in Hamilton, it was in conflict with the federal CMB regulation, which empowered Canada Post to decide the location of the CMBs. The doctrine of paramountcy resolved the conflict by rendering the by-law inoperative in its purported application to CMBs.[13]

The building, maintenance and repair of public roads or highways is an exercise of the spending power, and can be undertaken by either the federal or the provincial governments (or by municipalities acting under provincially-delegated power).[14] Once a road is built and connected to other roads, it provides entry to a seamless highway network that permits interprovincial and international journeys as well as local ones.[15] Nonetheless, the cases have consistently held that the regulation of the roads, including the imposition of tolls (the first constitutional case),[16] the rules of the road,[17] and the licensing of drivers[18] are within provincial jurisdiction. It is not clear whether provincial jurisdiction comes from s. 92(10) (local works), s. 92(16) (local or private matters) or s. 92(13) (property and civil rights); the cases have not been specific. The federal Parliament's authority over criminal law (s. 91(27)) provides power to prohibit dangerous conduct, and the federal Criminal Code enacts a federal level of traffic regulation by creating offences of (among other things) reckless, dangerous and drunken driving.[19]

X. TRANSPORTATION BY WATER

§ 22:12 Transportation by water

Jurisdiction over transportation by water depends upon some of the same principles as those applicable to transportation by land. Section 92(10)(a) expressly refers to "lines of steam or other ships" and to

[13]Before the Court's decision was rendered, the general election of 2015 had caused the defeat of the Conservative government of Stephen Harper, under whose watch the CMB project was undertaken, and its replacement by the Liberal government of Prime Minister Justin Trudeau, who ordered the discontinuance of the CMB roll-out: (2016) 134 O.R. (3d) 502, 2016 ONCA 767, para. 97. This did not distract the Court from resolving the dispute, as recounted in the text, but it may spell the end of the CMB project, at least for those communities not yet supplied with CMBs.

[14]Chapter 6, Financial Arrangements, under heading § 6:8, "Spending power".

[15]Compare § 22:22, "Communication by telephone" (even local companies are within federal jurisdiction by virtue of the access they provide to interprovincial and international networks).

[16]*O'Brien v. Allen* (1900), 30 S.C.R. 340.

[17]*O'Grady v. Sparling*, [1960] S.C.R. 804; *Stephens v. The Queen*, [1960] S.C.R. 823; *Mann v. The Queen*, [1966] S.C.R. 238.

[18]*Re s. 92(4) of the Vehicles Act 1957 (Sask.)*, [1958] S.C.R. 608; *Provincial Secretary of P.E.I. v. Egan*, [1941] S.C.R. 396; *Ross v. Registrar of Motor Vehicles*, [1975] 1 S.C.R. 5; *Bell v. A.G.P.E.I.*, [1975] 1 S.C.R. 25.

[19]The cases cited in the previous two notes each concerned a Criminal Code offence and its interaction with related provincial traffic and licensing regulation. The cases are discussed in ch. 16, Paramountcy.

"canals". In addition, however, s. 91(10) confers on the federal Parliament jurisdiction over "navigation and shipping". The Supreme Court of Canada has developed a test—the "integral connection test"—that is to be applied in determining whether a matter falls within Parliament's jurisdiction over navigation and shipping in s. 91(10). This test was first articulated in *International Terminal Operators v. Miida Electronics* (1986),[1] and has been refined in subsequent cases, including *Desgagnés Transport v. Wärtsilä Canada* (2019).[2] Under this test, the courts must determine "whether the maritime elements of a matter are sufficient to render it integrally connected to navigation and shipping".[3] In making this determination, the courts are to consider a number of factors, including the spatial, functional and temporal relationship between the maritime and non-maritime elements of the matter; "the context surrounding the relationship of the parties to the dispute"; "the practical importance or necessity of legal uniformity" in relation to the particular matter; whether "the matter implicates standards, principles and practices that are specific to the marine context"; "the historical connection with English maritime law"; and any "relevant precedents".[4] In *Desgagnés*, the Court emphasized that this test must be applied rigorously so as to avoid unduly broadening the scope of federal power to matters only remotely related to navigation and shipping.[5]

Section 91(10)[6] confers federal legislative competence over navigable waters,[7] works of navigation,[8] harbours,[9] and a far-reaching body of maritime or admiralty law. This body of maritime or admiralty law includes laws regarding rules of navigation,[10] liability for maritime accidents,[11] liability for loss or delay of a ship's cargo,[12] marine insurance,[13] the sale,

---

[Section 22:12]

[1]*ITO-International Terminal Operators v. Miida Electronics*, [1986] 1 S.C.R. 752. However, there are signs of the test in earlier cases: for references, see *Desgagnés Transport v. Wärtsilä Canada*, 2019 SCC 58, para. 50.

[2]*Desgagnés Transport v. Wärtsilä Canada*, 2019 SCC 58. In this case, Gascon, Côté and Rowe JJ., writing jointly for a six-judge majority of the Court, affirmed the integral connection test (para. 58). However, Wagner C.J. and Brown J. wrote a concurring opinion, which was joined by Abella J., in which they said that, read properly, *ITO* had not endorsed the "integral connection test", and that the Court should not do so here (paras. 142-147). This case is discussed more fully later in this section.

[3]*Desgagnés Transport v. Wärtsilä Canada*, 2019 SCC 58, para. 52.

[4]*Desgagnés Transport v. Wärtsilä Canada*, 2019 SCC 58, para. 56.

[5]*Desgagnés Transport v. Wärtsilä Canada*, 2019 SCC 58, para. 52.

[6]On the scope of the power, see Laskin, Canadian Constitutional Law (5th ed., 1986 by Finkelstein), 631–639; McConnell, Commentary on the British North America Act (1977), 196–201.

[7]*Re Waters and Water Powers*, [1929] S.C.R. 200.

[8]*Re Waters and Water Powers*, [1929] S.C.R. 200. See also s. 91(9) ("beacons, buoys, lighthouses and Sable Island").

[9]*Hamilton Harbour Commrs. v. City of Hamilton* (1978), 21 O.R. (2d) 459 (C.A.); *B.C. v. Lafarge Canada*, [2007] 2 S.C.R. 86, paras. 62–68.

[10]*Whitbread v. Walley*, [1990] 3 S.C.R. 1273.

purchase and ownership of ships,[14] the construction, repair and maintenance of ships[15] and parts (like marine engine parts) essential to their operation,[16] and pilotage and towage.[17]

Federal power over navigation and shipping is not territorially restricted: it applies to vessels engaged in local shipping, and to pleasure boats as well as commercial vessels.[18] Nor is it confined to the high seas, or even to tidal waters: it extends up navigable rivers as well. All waterways are "part of the same navigational network" and must be subject to the "uniform legal regime" of Canadian maritime law.[19] All boats share that system of waterways, and they must obey the same federal "rules of the road" and be subject to the same federal regime of tortious liability.[20] The legislative authority over navigation and shipping that is conferred on the federal Parliament by s. 91(10) is, therefore, much more extensive than the authority over other forms of transportation and communication, where s. 92(10)(a) is the sole source of authority. For example, the tortious liability of a company operating an interprovincial railway is governed by provincial law, while the tortious liability of those engaged in navigation and shipping is (as explained above) governed by Canadian maritime law.[21]

The unqualified language of s. 91(10) does not authorize Parliament to regulate labour relations in undertakings engaged in intraprovincial

[11]The federal Parliament has jurisdiction over maritime negligence law, which includes limitations on tortious liability arising from accidents occurring on navigable waters: *Whitbread v. Walley*, [1990] 3 S.C.R. 1273; the range of possible claimants, the scope of available damages and the effect of contributory negligence: *Ordon Estate v. Grail*, [1998] 3 S.C.R. 437. Federal power also extends to tortious liability for "land based activities that are sufficiently connected with navigation and shipping": *Whitbread v. Walley*, [1990] 3 S.C.R. 1273, 1292, citing *ITO-International Terminal Operators v. Miida Electronics*, [1986] 1 S.C.R. 752. But this does not extend to transporting a pleasure boat by road to or from a dock: *Isen v. Simms*, [2006] 2 S.C.R. 349.

[12]*Tropwood A.G. v. Sivaco Wire and Nail Co.*, [1979] S.C.R. 157; *Aris Steamship Co. v. Associated Metals*, [1980] 2 S.C.R. 322.

[13]*Triglav v. Terrasses Jewellers*, [1983] 1 S.C.R. 283.

[14]*Antares Shipping Corp. v. The Ship "Capricorn"*, [1980] 1 S.C.R. 553.

[15]*Wire Rope Industries v. B.C. Marine Shipbuilders*, [1981] 1 S.C.R. 363.

[16]*Desgagnés Transport v. Wärtsilä Canada*, 2019 SCC 58.

[17]*Wire Rope Industries v. B.C. Marine Shipbuilders*, [1981] 1 S.C.R. 363.

[18]*Whitbread v. Walley*, [1990] 3 S.C.R. 1273 (Canadian maritime law applied to accident caused by pleasure boat making short journey on intraprovincial waterways); *Ordon Estate v. Grail*, [1998] 3 S.C.R. 437 (same decision); *MacKay v. Russell* (2007), 284 D.L.R. (4th) 528 (N.B. C.A.) (Canadian maritime law applied to accident aboard a whale-watching boat). But maritime law does not extend to a pleasure boat once it has been removed from the water for transportation by road: *Isen v. Simms*, [2006] 2 S.C.R. 349 (Canada Shipping Act limitation of liability inapplicable to accident occurring while pleasure boat being strapped onto trailer on land for towing by car).

[19]*Whitbread v. Walley*, [1990] 3 S.C.R. 1273, 1295.

[20]*Whitbread v. Walley*, [1990] 3 S.C.R. 1273, 1297. Compare aeronautics, where the shared use of airspace and ground facilities makes it impractical to divide up legislative jurisdiction according to whether the carrier is local or not.

[21]*Whitbread v. Walley*, [1990] 3 S.C.R. 1273, 1300.

shipping. In *Agence Maritime v. Canada Labour Relations Board* (1969),[22] it was held that labour relations on ships plying the waters of the St. Lawrence River within the province of Quebec were within provincial, not federal, jurisdiction. Of course ships with a continuous and regular trade to the ports of more than one province (or more than one country) would be within federal jurisdiction.[23] Labour relations on the ships supplying and servicing the oil drilling rigs off the coast of Newfoundland have been held to be within federal jurisdiction: although each voyage began and ended in a single province (Newfoundland), the major part of the voyage was in international waters.[24] However, ferries passing briefly through American waters on journeys between ports in British Columbia have been held to be within provincial jurisdiction.[25] Labour relations over stevedoring, which is the loading and unloading of ships, are subject to federal jurisdiction if the service is essential to shipping to or from other provinces or countries, but are subject to provincial jurisdiction if the stevedoring serves only local shipping (that is, shipping without a continuous and regular trade outside the province).[26]

To what extent can provincial laws validly affect navigation and shipping? In *Ordon Estate v. Grail* (1998),[27] two boating accidents that resulted in death and injury gave rise to four negligence actions. Although the accidents concerned pleasure boats on lakes in Ontario, because the accidents occurred in navigable waters, there was no doubt that the governing law was federal maritime law. However, the plaintiffs in the actions attempted to rely on several Ontario statues, which permitted negligence claims to be brought by the siblings of a deceased or injured victim, which permitted the recovery of damages for the loss of guidance, care and companionship of a deceased or injured victim, and which permitted apportionment of damages in cases of contributory negligence (rather than barring the plaintiff's action). These causes of action were unavailable under federal maritime law. The Supreme Court of Canada held that none of the Ontario statutes could apply to a maritime negligence case, and the statutes should be read down to exclude maritime negligence cases. The Court said that the application of any provincial statute that "would have the effect of regulating indirectly an issue of maritime negligence law" would be "an intrusion upon the unassailable core of federal maritime law" and would therefore be "constitu-

[22]*Agence Maritime v. Canada Labour Relations Board*, [1969] S.C.R. 851.

[23]Federal jurisdiction would flow from s. 92(10)(a). See also s. 91(13) ("ferries between a province and any British or foreign country or between two provinces"). With respect to ferries, see also § 22:1 note 8, above.

[24]*Seafarers' International Union v. Crosbie Offshore Services*, [1982] 2 F.C. 855 (C. A.). The Court relied on s. 91(10), but s. 92(10)(a) seems to be the applicable head of power.

[25]*Singbeil v. Hansen* (1985), 19 D.L.R. (4th) 48 (B.C.C.A.).

[26]*Tessier v. Que.*, [2012] 2 S.C.R. 3, para. 34, interpreting *Re Industrial Relations and Disputes Investigation Act*, [1955] S.C.R. 529 (the *Stevedores Reference*), discussed in text accompanying § 22:9 note 2.

[27]*Ordon Estate v. Grail*, [1998] 3 S.C.R 437. Iacobucci and Major JJ. wrote the opinion of the Court.

tionally impermissible".[28] The reason for this broad doctrine of interjurisdictional immunity was the need for uniformity across Canada of maritime law, which would be impaired by the application in provincial waters of provincial statutes. Did this mean that the unfortunate plaintiffs were denied causes of action in tort that had been generally adopted into provincial law, but had never been adopted in the Canada Shipping Act or other federal legislation? No, said the Court, and, in an unprecedented display of judicial activism, the Court simply "reformed" the maritime law to bring it into line with the provincial law. So, although the provincial laws were held to be constitutionally inapplicable, they were used as the models for the judicial reform of federal maritime law to bring it into accord with modern notions of justice.[29]

After *Ordon*, it seemed obvious that a provincial law purporting to bar tort actions would be inapplicable to maritime negligence claims. But the Supreme Court decided otherwise in *Marine Services International v. Ryan Estate* (2013).[30] In that case, two commercial fishermen died when their boat sank off the coast of Labrador and Newfoundland. Because the accident occurred in the course of the fishermens' employment, their dependants applied for and received compensation under the province's workers' compensation statute. That statute contained the standard bar on bringing a tort action in respect of any accident for which workers' compensation benefits were payable. The dependants nonetheless brought actions for negligence against the persons who designed and built the boat and against the federal government which was responsible for inspecting the boat. The plaintiffs argued that, under the doctrine of interjurisdictional immunity, a province could not prohibit the bringing of a maritime negligence claim. The Court agreed that the provincial bar on maritime negligence claims "affected" the core of the federal power over navigation and shipping, but held that the law did not have a sufficiently serious impact to "impair" the core of the federal power.[31] According to the Court, the impact of the provincial bar was "not significant or serious when one considers the breadth of the federal power over navigation and shipping, the absence of an impact on the uniformity of Canadian maritime law, and the historical application

[28]*Ordon Estate v. Grail*, [1998] 3 S.C.R 437, para. 85.

[29]The one "reform" that the Court refused to adopt into maritime law was the expansion of eligible dependants in fatal accident claims to include siblings. Parliament had spoken on this issue, because the Canada Shipping Act contained a list of eligible dependants that did not include siblings. "For this Court to reform the law to expand the class would be to effect a legislative and not a judicial change in the law": para. 106. This reasoning did not deter the Court from the other reforms, all of which had required legislation for their accomplishment in Ontario (and the other provinces).

[30]*Marine Services International v. Ryan Estate*, [2013] 3 S.C.R. 53, 2013 SCC 44. LeBel and Karakatsanis JJ. wrote the opinion of the Court.

[31]The requirement of impairment was introduced in *Canadian Western Bank v. Alta.*, [2007] 2 S.C.R. 3, that is, after *Ordon* was decided. The Court in *Marine Services* distinguished *Ordon* on that ground: *Marine Services International v. Ryan Estate*, [2013] 3 S.C.R. 53, 2013 SCC 44, para. 64.

of workers' compensation schemes in the maritime context".[32] The Court concluded that interjurisdictional immunity did not apply; therefore the provincial law did apply and barred the plaintiffs' actions for maritime negligence.

The Supreme Court's decision in *Marine Services* leaves more room than its decision in *Ordon* for provincial laws to affect maritime negligence claims. In *Marine Services*, the Court did not explicitly overrule *Ordon*, but it did distinguish *Ordon*, on the basis that *Ordon* was decided before *Canadian Western Bank v. Alberta* (2007)[33] and *Quebec v. Canadian Owners and Pilots Association* (2010)[34]—two cases in which the Court had "clarified" its approach to interjurisdictional immunity, including by raising the threshold that must be met to engage it.[35] The clear implication was that *Ordon*'s suggestion that provincial laws cannot "have the effect of regulating an issue of maritime negligence law" had been, if not outright abandoned, then significantly qualified. However, it was unclear whether the more permissive approach in *Marine Services* to provincial laws affecting maritime negligence law applied to provincial laws affecting navigation and shipping more broadly or was restricted to maritime negligence law.

The Supreme Court of Canada's decision in *Desgagnés Transport v. Wärtsilä Canada* (2019)[36] suggests a broader reach for the *Marine Services* approach—and accordingly more room for provincial laws to affect navigation and shipping. In *Desgagnés*, a shipping company, Desgagnés Transport, and a supplier, Wärtsilä Canada, entered into a contract for the purchase and sale of engine parts that were used to fix the engine of an oceangoing ship. The contract included a six-month warranty and a clause limiting Wärtsilä's liability as supplier to €50,000. After the warranty had expired, a latent defect in the parts resulted in a major failure of the ship's engine. Desgagnés sued Wärtsilä for damages for the latent defect. At issue in the case was whether Canadian maritime law or the Civil Code of Quebec governed the contractual claim. Wärtsilä argued that Canadian maritime law governed the dispute; if it was right, the clause limiting its liability to €50,000 was likely enforceable.

---

[32] *Marine Services International v. Ryan Estate*, [2013] 3 S.C.R. 53, 2013 SCC 44, para. 64. The Court also rejected an argument that the provincial bar was rendered inoperative by federal paramountcy: *Marine Services International v. Ryan Estate*, [2013] 3 S.C.R. 53, 2013 SCC 44, paras. 65–84.

[33] *Canadian Western Bank v. Alberta*, [2007] 2 S.C.R. 3.

[34] *Quebec v. Canadian Owners and Pilots Association*, [2010] 2 S.C.R. 536

[35] *Marine Services International v. Ryan Estate*, [2013] 3 S.C.R. 53, para. 64. It is somewhat ironic that the Court cited the *COPA* case, as in *COPA*, the Court gave the interjurisdictional immunity doctrine a more robust application than it did in its decision in *Canadian Western Bank*. The Court's interjurisdictional immunity analysis in the two cases is discussed in an earlier section of this book: see ch. 15, Judicial Review on Federal Grounds, under heading § 15:18, "Federally-regulated undertakings".

[36] *Desgagnés Transport v. Wärtsilä Canada*, 2019 SCC 58. Gascon, Côté and Rowe JJ. wrote a joint opinion for the majority, which was joined by Moldaver, Karakatsanis and Martin JJ. Wagner C.J. and Brown J. wrote a concurring opinion, which was joined by Abella J.

Desgagnés, however, argued that the Civil Code of Quebec governed the dispute; if it was right, the Civil Code of Quebec rendered the limitation of liability clause unenforceable, and Wärtsilä's liability was over $5.6 million.[37]

The Supreme Court of Canada agreed unanimously with Desgagnés that the Civil Code of Quebec governed the dispute. However, the judges arrived at this result in different ways. Wagner C.J. and Brown J. wrote a joint concurring opinion (for three judges). They characterized the matter involved broadly, as the sale of goods in the maritime context, and held that this matter *did not* fall within the federal power over navigation and shipping, but rather the provincial power over property and civil rights (s. 92(13)). For these three judges, therefore, the Civil Code of Quebec applied directly because the matter fell within provincial jurisdiction. In contrast, Gascon, Côté and Rowe JJ., writing jointly for a six-judge majority of the Court, characterized the matter more narrowly, as the sale of marine engine parts for use on a commercial ship, and held that this matter *did* fall within the federal navigation and shipping power. For the joint majority, this did not resolve the issue, though, because the relevant Civil Code of Quebec provisions were also valid provincial law, and could also be engaged, unless rendered inapplicable under the interjurisdictional immunity doctrine or inoperative under the federal paramountcy doctrine. Under *Ordon*, the Civil Code of Quebec provisions would likely have been rendered inapplicable by the interjurisdictional immunity doctrine. However, the joint majority concluded that the interjurisdictional immunity doctrine did not apply because the contractual issue did not engage the core of Parliament's power over navigation and shipping. They also held that the federal paramountcy doctrine did not apply. The federal law Wärtsilä sought to have govern the dispute, as with much of Canadian maritime law, was "non-statutory",[38] and non-statutory federal law could not, they said, render statutory provincial law inoperative under the federal paramountcy doctrine. Left with a choice between non-statutory federal law and statutory provincial law, the majority decided that, as a legislative enactment, the Civil Code of Quebec took precedence, and therefore governed the dispute.

The *Desgagnés* decision suggests that the more permissive approach in *Marine Services* to the application of provincial laws is not restricted to the maritime negligence context, but rather applies to navigation and shipping more broadly. The joint majority said that "a finding that Canadian maritime law can validly regulate a dispute does not end the analysis in the presence of an overlapping provincial rule".[39] The matter could also be governed by the province, pursuant to provincial power

[37]The most salient portion of the Civil Code of Quebec was art. 1733, which provides as follows: "A seller may not exclude or limit his liability unless he has disclosed the defects of which he was aware or could not have been unaware and which affect the right of ownership or the quality of the property."

[38]*Desgagnés Transport v. Wärtsilä Canada*, 2019 SCC 58, para. 103.

[39]*Desgagnés Transport v. Wärtsilä Canada*, 2019 SCC 58, para. 81.

over property and civil rights (s. 92(13)). If the restrictive approach to provincial laws in *Ordon* still applied, this suggestion might not be all that significant, as any analysis might then simply go on to find that any provincial law is inapplicable under the interjurisdictional immunity doctrine. However, the joint majority went on to say that *Marine Services* had also made it clear "that *Canadian Western Bank* had displaced prior jurisprudence on the interaction between the rules of Canadian maritime law and provincial statutes", and driving the point home further, they said that "the doctrines of interjurisdictional immunity and federal paramountcy must be applied to navigation and shipping in the same way as in all division of powers cases".[40]

British Columbia v. Lafarge Canada (2007),[41] concerned jurisdiction over a proposal by Lafarge to build a concrete batch plant in the port of Vancouver. The plant was to be a marine facility to which aggregate (or gravel) would be shipped by barge and unloaded directly into the plant, where it would be mixed with cement, and then trucked to construction sites in the Vancouver area. The Supreme Court held that the project was sufficiently integrated with navigation and shipping that the land-use regulatory powers conferred by the federal Canada Marine Act on the Vancouver Port Authority (a federal agency) were applicable to the project. The Vancouver Port Authority did review the project and approve it. The proposed site of the plant in the port was also within the boundaries of the city of Vancouver, and the question was whether the permission of the city under its land-use by-law (passed under the authority of provincial law) was also necessary. The Supreme Court divided on the answer, but the majority held that the proposed marine facility, although within the rubric of navigation and shipping in s. 91(10), was "beyond the *core* of s. 91(10)".[42] Since interjurisdictional immunity only applied to the "core" of federal powers, the municipal by-law was constitutionally applicable to the project. However, the majority went on to decide that the by-law was inoperative in its application to the project because the by-law was inconsistent with the Canada Marine Act. Bastarache J., in a concurring opinion, took the view that the regulation of land use on port lands was within the core of s. 91(10), and the municipal by-law was ousted by interjurisdictional immunity. In the end, therefore, the Court was unanimous that no municipal permission was required for the Lafarge project.

---

[40]*Desgagnés Transport v. Wärtsilä Canada*, 2019 SCC 58, paras. 88-89. The joint concurring opinion of Wagner C.J. and Brown J. includes similar suggestions (at paras. 129 and 154).

[41]*British Columbia v. Lafarge Canada*, [2007] 2 S.C.R. 86. Binnie and LeBel JJ. wrote the opinion of the majority; Bastarache J. wrote a concurring opinion. The case is more fully discussed in ch. 15, Judicial Review on Federal Grounds, under heading § 15:18, "Federally-regulated undertakings".

[42]*British Columbia v. Lafarge Canada*, [2007] 2 S.C.R. 86, para. 72.

XI. TRANSPORTATION BY AIR

§ 22:13 Basis of legislative jurisdiction

The subject of aeronautics[1] is not governed by the same principles as apply to other modes of transportation. It started off on a different constitutional track, because the first legislation was enacted by the federal Parliament to perform Canada's obligations under an international treaty. In the *Aeronautics Reference* (1931),[2] the Privy Council held that the legislation was valid by virtue of the treaty power in s. 132 of the Constitution Act, 1867.[3] The possibility that the peace, order, and good government power might also sustain the legislation was suggested as an alternative basis of jurisdiction.[4] This suggestion became important when the original treaty, which was a "British Empire" treaty to which s. 132 applied, was replaced by a new treaty, which was a "Canadian" treaty to which s. 132 did not apply; and it became necessary to attribute jurisdiction to some head of power other than the treaty power. In *Johannesson v. West St. Paul* (1952),[5] the Supreme Court of Canada held that the peace, order, and good government power gave the federal Parliament the claimed jurisdiction. This was on the basis that aeronautics was a distinct "matter" which satisfied the *Canada Temperance* test, that is to say, "it goes beyond local or provincial concern or interests and must from its inherent nature be the concern of the Dominion as a whole".[6]

Johannesson contains surprisingly little discussion of the reasons for attributing aeronautics to the peace, order, and good government power. Kerwin, Kellock and Estey JJ. contented themselves with a recitation of the *Canada Temperance* test,[7] apparently regarding it as self-evident that aeronautics satisfied the test. Only Locke J. attempted to spell out some reasons, referring to the growth of the air industry, its role in the carriage of mail and in opening up the more remote parts of the country.[8] But the same points could be made about other modes of transportation, especially the railways in their hey-day, and yet it has never been sug-

---

[Section 22:13]

[1]See generally C.H. McNairn, "Aeronautics and the Constitution" (1971) 49 Can. Bar Rev. 411; R. Paquette, "Les compétences constitutionnelles en matière d'aéronautique" (1979) 57 Can. Bar Rev. 281.

[2]*Re Regulation and Control of Aeronautics in Can.*, [1932] A.C. 54.

[3]Chapter 11, Treaties.

[4]*Re Regulation and Control of Aeronautics in Can.*, [1932] A.C. 54, 77.

[5]*Johannesson v. West St. Paul*, [1952] 1 S.C.R. 292.

[6]*A.-G. Ont. v. Can. Temperance Federation*, [1946] A.C. 193, 205, citing the *Aeronautics Reference* as an example. In *Johannesson*, four of the five opinions cited and relied upon the *Canada Temperance*: [1952] 1 S.C.R. 292, 308–309 per Kerwin J., 311 per Kellock J., 318 per Estey J., 328 per Locke J.; while Rinfret C.J. (at 303) thought the issue was concluded by the *Aeronautics Reference*. Peace, Order, and Good Government is the subject of ch. 17.

[7]See previous note.

[8]*Johannesson v. West St. Paul*, [1952] 1 S.C.R. 292, 326-327.

gested that the federal Parliament could assume jurisdiction over the railways under the peace, order, and good government power. On the contrary, federal jurisdiction over railways has always been placed under s. 92(10)(a), with the important result that local railways are outside federal jurisdiction.[9] It is true that railways are expressly mentioned in s. 92(10)(a), but road transportation (bus and truck) is not expressly mentioned and yet has been held to be within the same head of power by virtue of the phrase "other works and undertakings" in s. 92(10)(a). Why is aeronautics not caught by the same phrase? No court has ever asked or answered this question, and yet it now appears to be accepted without doubt that jurisdiction resides in the peace, order, and good government power.[10]

§ 22:14 Intraprovincial aeronautics

Because jurisdiction over aeronautics has been held to depend upon its national dimension or national concern, the question whether a particular undertaking is interprovincial or merely local is probably irrelevant. There are obiter dicta in both the *Aeronautics Reference*[1] and *Johannesson*[2] cases to the effect that federal jurisdiction extends to purely intraprovincial airlines, and this has been distinctly decided by the British Columbia Court of Appeal in *Jorgenson v. North Vancouver Magistrates* (1959).[3] The most plausible reason for subjecting local airlines to the same regime as the interprovincial and international airlines is the fact that both kinds of carriers share the same airspace and ground facilities, so that their operations are necessarily closely integrated.[4] Divided control over navigation and ground facilities would be impossible. In *Quebec v. Canadian Owners and Pilots Association* (2010),[5] the point was reargued before the Supreme Court of Canada. The issue was whether the location of a small local aerodrome came within the federal power over aeronautics. The Court agreed with earlier

---

[9] *Montreal v. Montreal St. Ry.*, [1912] A.C. 333; *B.C. Elec. Ry. v. CNR*, [1932] S.C.R. 161; *UTU v. Central Western Ry.*, [1990] 3 S.C.R. 1112.

[10] *Que. v. Lacombe*, [2010] 2 S.C.R. 453, para. 26; *Que. v. Can. Owners and Pilots Assn.*, [2010] 2 S.C.R. 536, para. 2. It has, however, been held that an international airport is part of a federal work or undertaking under s. 92(10)(a): *Greater Toronto Airports Authority v. Mississauga* (2000), 50 O.R. (3d) 641 (C.A.), paras. 59–61 per Laskin J.A. for the Court.

[Section 22:14]

[1] *Re Regulation and Control of Radio Communication in Can.*, [1932] A.C. 54, 77.

[2] *Johannesson v. West St. Paul*, [1952] 1 S.C.R. 292, 314.

[3] *Jorgenson v. North Vancouver Magistrates* (1959), 28 W.W.R. 265 (B.C.C.A.); see C.H. McNairn, "Aeronautics and the Constitution" (1971) 49 Can. Bar Rev. 411, 418–419; contra, R. Paquette, "Les compétences constitutionnelles en matière d'aéronautique" (1979) 57 Can. Bar Rev. 281, 291.

[4] This explanation was approved, obiter, in *Whitbread v. Walley*, [1990] 3 S.C.R. 1273, 1299; see also § 22:12 note 26.

[5] *Quebec v. Canadian Owners and Pilots Association*, [2010] 2 S.C.R. 536. Neither of the two dissenting opinions took issue with the holding that intraprovincial aviation was within federal jurisdiction.

dicta that "it is impossible to separate intraprovincial flying from interprovincial flying", and that the regulation and location of airports could not be "separated from aerial navigation as a whole". The "reality", said the Court, is "that Canada's airports and aerodromes constitute a network of landing places that together facilitate air transportation and ensure safety".[6] It followed that federal power over aeronautics extended to local aviation and to local aerodromes.

While it is easy to agree that divided control over navigation and ground facilities would be impossible, it is arguable that divided control over economic regulation—fares and perhaps routes—would be possible, but it is most unlikely that the courts would at this late stage be willing to fragment the subject of aeronautics into navigational and economic aspects.[7] The better view is that both aspects of aeronautics come within federal jurisdiction.[8]

§ 22:15 Provincial jurisdiction

Given that federal legislative jurisdiction exists over aeronautics, there remains the question of the degree to which provincial laws are precluded. Where there are inconsistent federal laws, then provincial laws are of course rendered inoperative by the paramountcy doctrine, but the tendency of the decisions is to deny the application of provincial laws to airports and related activity even where the federal Parliament has not acted.

The most extreme example is the *Johannesson* case[1] itself. At issue in the case was a municipal by-law, made under the authority of a provincial statute, which prohibited aerodromes in part of the municipal-

---

[6]*Quebec v. Canadian Owners and Pilots Association*, [2010] 2 S.C.R. 536, para. 33.

[7]C.H. McNairn, "Aeronautics and the Constitution" (1971) 49 Can. Bar Rev. 411, 427–429. Radio and television are close analogies, the argument for unified control of local and long-distance broadcasting depending on the shared use of the frequency spectrum. It has never been suggested that economic regulation should be treated any differently than technical regulation, although there is some room for argument that content regulation should be treated differently: see § 22:18, "Content regulation". Another analogy is *The Queen (Ont.) v. Bd. of Transport Commrs.*, [1968] S.C.R. 118, in which the shared use of interprovincial trackage brought a local rail service within federal jurisdiction, including jurisdiction over fares.

[8]There is, of course, room for argument as to where aeronautics ends and related local undertakings begin; for example, a company which services aircraft has been held to be within the federal power over aeronautics: *Field Aviation Co. v. Indust. Relations Bd. (Alta.)*, [1974] 6 W.W.R. 596 (Alta. A.D.); while a company engaged in constructing airport runways has been held to be a separate local undertaking: *Construction Montcalm v. Minimum Wage Commn.*, [1979] 1 S.C.R. 754. The provision of porter service in the airport, and limousine service to and from the airport, have also been held to be local undertakings outside federal power: *Re Colonial Coach Lines*, [1967] 2 O.R. 25 (H.C.); *Murray Hill Limousine Service v. Batson*, [1965] B.R. 788 (Que. C.A.); C.H. McNairn, "Aeronautics and the Constitution" (1971) 49 Can. Bar Rev. 411, 431–438. Compare *Stevedores Reference*, [1955] S.C.R. 529; discussed in text accompanying § 22:15 note 7.

[Section 22:15]

[1]*Johannesson v. West St. Paul*, [1952] 1 S.C.R. 292.

ity and required a licence for their establishment elsewhere. Johannesson, who owned a small airline, found a site in the municipality which was suitable for an air strip where he planned to establish a service depot for his planes. He purchased the land and brought proceedings to have the by-law declared invalid. The Supreme Court of Canada held that the by-law was invalid because of its interference with aeronautics. There were federal regulations providing for the licensing of a site for use as an aerodrome, and if Johannesson's site had been licensed the by-law would have had to yield to the federal licence under the paramountcy doctrine. But Johannesson's site had not been licensed; Johannesson had selected the site because it appeared to him to satisfy general federal regulations with respect to aerodromes, and because it was suitable for his business. When one considers that the control of land use is ordinarily within property and civil rights in the province, and is always a question of vital local concern, it would surely have been wiser for the Court to treat the by-law as valid under the double-aspect doctrine.[2] On this basis, the by-law would override a private business decision to construct an aerodrome, at least until the appropriate federal regulatory authority had directed its construction.[3]

Johannesson was followed by the Ontario Court of Appeal in *Re Orangeville Airport* (1976),[4] in which it was held that municipal zoning by-laws could not apply to an airport. In this case, however, the airport was federally licensed and in operation, and the by-law would have had the effect of preventing the building of new hangars, the plans of which had been approved by the federal Minister of Transport. In *Re Walker and Minister of Housing* (1983),[5] the same Court invalidated height restrictions imposed by the province on land adjacent to an airport. Once again, the airport was federally licensed and in operation. The purpose of the height restrictions was to facilitate the use of the airport by larger aircraft. Both these cases were very much clearer than *Johannesson*, since it was plain that the provincial law in each case affected a vital part of the design or operation of a functioning airport.

In *Greater Toronto Airports Authority v. Mississauga* (2000),[6] the local authority that operated Toronto's Pearson International Airport was engaged in a massive development project, which included the construction of a new passenger terminal, a new air traffic control tower and three new runways. Ontario's Building Code Act prescribed standards

---

[2]Compare *R. v. Pearsall* (1977), 80 D.L.R. (3d) 285 (Sask. C.A.), upholding provincial law prohibiting use of aircraft for hunting game; *Re The Queen and Van Goal* (1987), 36 D.L.R. (4th) 481 (B.C.C.A.), upholding municipal by-law permitting use of land as private airport.

[3]P.C. Weiler, "The Supreme Court and the Law of Canadian Federalism" (1973) 23 U. Toronto L.J. 207, 324.

[4]*Re Orangeville Airport* (1976), 11 O.R. (2d) 546 (C.A.).

[5]*Re Walker and Minister of Housing* (1983), 41 O.R. (2d) 9 (C.A.).

[6]*Greater Toronto Airports Authority v. Mississauga* (2000), 50 O.R. (3d) 641 (C.A.). The opinion of the unanimous Court was written by Laskin J.A. Leave to appeal to the SCC was denied on June 14, 2001.

for the construction of buildings and required building permits. This law, unlike a planning or zoning law, did not address the location or design or use of buildings, but merely their safe and sound construction. On the other hand, decisions taken under the laws would be permanently reflected in the structure of the finished buildings and would affect their operational qualities. The Court of Appeal for Ontario held that the law[7] could not apply. The development of the airport came within the federal power over aeronautics, and the province's building code regime was sufficiently intrusive as to affect a vital part of the aeronautics undertaking.[8]

In *Quebec v. Lacombe* (2010),[9] a Quebec municipality passed a by-law prohibiting the use of lakes in part of the municipality as aerodromes. The validity of the by-law was challenged by the operators of a commercial air taxi service that made use of one of the lakes as a water aerodrome for its float planes. In order to operate a commercial air service, the federal Aeronautics Act required that a licence by obtained from the federal Department of Transport, and the operators had obtained that licence.[10] However, the location of the aerodrome did not require prior approval under the Act. The operators had selected the lake themselves (they had a cottage on it), and had then registered their choice with the Department, which was all that was required by the Act. The Supreme Court of Canada, by a majority, rejected the argument that the by-law was in relation to the zoning of land use with an incidental effect on aeronautics.[11] McLachlin C.J., who wrote for the majority, held that the pith and substance of the by-law, like the by-law in *Johannesson*, was in relation to aeronautics; and the by-law was unconstitutional for that reason. The air taxi service was entitled to continue notwithstanding the contrary by-law.

In *Lacombe*, McLachlin C.J. had added that, even if the by-law had

[7]As well as the Building Code Act, the Development Charges Act authorized municipalities to impose development charges on building projects to defray the anticipated capital costs of increased demand for municipal services. The vital-part reasoning would not immunize the airport from development charges, but these development charges only applied if the building code applied, and so they fell along with the building code. The Court pointed out (paras. 8691) that the Crown, although exempt from taxes on its property, was under a common law obligation to pay for any municipal services received. As well, under the federal Municipal Grants Act, the municipality could apply to the federal government for a grant in lieu of real property tax.

[8]Folld. in *Vancouver International Airport v. Lafarge Canada* (2011), 331 D.L.R. (4th) 737 (B.C.C.A.) (provincial builders liens legislation, if applied to airport land, would impair a vital part of the aeronautics undertaking and accordingly inapplicable).

[9]*Quebec v. Lacombe*, [2010] 2 S.C.R. 453. McLachlin C.J. wrote the opinion of the seven-judge majority. LeBel J. wrote a concurring opinion. Deschamps J. wrote a dissenting opinion.

[10]LeBel J., para. 70, relied on the licence for his concurring opinion that the doctrine of paramountcy precluded the municipal by-law from applying to the licence-holders.

[11]That was the dissenting view of Deschamps J. (para. 131). LeBel J., who based his concurrence on paramountcy (previous note), is not entirely clear on this issue of classification, but (para. 72) seems to agree with Deschamps J.

been a valid law in relation to land use, the law would have been inapplicable to the water aerodrome by virtue of interjurisdictional immunity.[12] That was the holding in the companion case of *Quebec v. Canadian Owners and Pilots Association* (2010),[13] which was another case in which the owners of a small local aerodrome in Quebec were apparently in breach of zoning regulation. In this case the regulation was not a municipal by-law, but a provincial law that designated various areas of the province as agricultural zones from which all non-agricultural uses were prohibited.[14] The law did not single out aeronautics in any way, but it did preclude the use of the land in issue, which was within an agricultural zone, as an aerodrome. McLachlin C.J. for the majority held that the provincial law was in pith and substance in relation to land use and was therefore valid. But, she held, it was inapplicable to the extent that it prohibited aerodromes in agricultural zones, because that would impair the protected core of the federal jurisdiction over aeronautics. Although the location of the aerodrome had been selected by the owners (who had registered their choice with the federal Department of Transport), the provincial law was inapplicable to the aerodrome by virtue of interjurisdictional immunity.[15]

In *Construction Montcalm v. Minimum Wage Commission* (1978),[16] the question arose whether a provincial minimum wage law could apply to a construc-tion firm that was engaged in building the runways of an airport. The Supreme Court of Canada held that the provincial law was validly applicable. Beetz J. for the majority[17] confined the immunity from provincial law to "an integral part of aeronautics".[18] The location of an airport (which was the issue in *Johannesson)*, its design (which was the issue in *Orangeville)*, and its operation (which was the issue in *Walker)* would each be an integral part of aeronautics from which provincial power was excluded, but the physical construction (in accordance with federal specifications) of the runways was not. Therefore,

[12] *Quebec v. Lacombe*, [2010] 2 S.C.R. 453, para. 66. LeBel and Deschamps JJ. both disagreed with the majority on that point.

[13] *Quebec v. Canadian Owners and Pilots Association*, [2010] 2 S.C.R. 536. McLachlin C.J. wrote the opinion of the seven-judge majority. LeBel and Deschamps JJ. wrote dissenting opinions.

[14] A provincial agency could approve a non-conforming use, but the owners of the aerodrome had not received approval.

[15] For fuller discussion of interjurisdictional immunity, see ch. 15, Judicial Review on Federal Grounds, under heading §§ 15:16 to 15:21, "Interjurisdictional immunity".

[16] *Construction Montcalm v. Minimum Wage Commission*, [1979] 1 S.C.R. 754.

[17] Beetz J.'s opinion was agreed to by Martland, Ritchie, Pigeon, Dickson, Estey and Pratte JJ. Laskin C.J. with Spence J. dissented, holding that provincial law could not apply on an airport or on federal public property. The general issue of interjurisdictional immunity, upon which Laskin C.J. was usually in dissent, is discussed in ch. 15, Judicial Review on Federal Grounds.

[18] *Construction Montcalm v. Minimum Wage Commission*, [1979] 1 S.C.R. 754, 770.

provincial law regarding minimum wages could validly apply to the construction firm.[19]

Provincial or municipal environmental laws that do not regulate the location, design or operation of an airport or aerodrome will apply to the construction of an airport or aerodrome. In *Burlington Airpark v. City of Burlington* (2013),[20] Burlington Airpark (the company), which was the owner and operator of an aerodrome in the City of Burlington, undertook an expansion of the aerodrome, adding to and improving the runways, taxiways, aprons, hangars and terminal facilities. Some of the affected land was below the grade of the existing runway, and had to be elevated. The company embarked on fill operations to raise the elevation of the land. The city received complaints about the cleanliness of the material being used for the fill and the possible contamination of the groundwater. The city by-law required that a permit be obtained for fill operations in the city, and also required, among other things, that the fill contain no contaminants within the meaning of the provincial Environmental Protection Act. The company refused to comply with the by-law on the ground that the aerodrome was subject only to federal regulation (which did not, however, cover fill operations). The city applied for an order directing the company to comply with the by-law. The Superior Court of Ontario granted the city's application. Murray J. held that the by-law, which was authorized by the province's Municipal Act, was a valid exercise of the province's power over property and civil rights. He acknowledged that matters such as the slopes, surfaces and strengths of runways and runway shoulders were matters within the core of the aeronautics power that could not be regulated by the province. But regulating the quality of the fill used to bring runways and associated facilities up to grade, while it might affect the method and cost of constructing aerodrome improvements, would have no effect upon the operational qualities or suitability for aeronautics of the finished product.[21] The fill by-law, like the minimum wage law in *Construction Montcalm*, had no impact on the core of the federal aeronautics power and was therefore applicable to the project.

Construction Montcalm was followed in *Air Canada v. Ontario* (1997).[22] In that case, it was held that a province could validly require an airline to pay a mark-up on liquor that was loaded onto aircraft from an airport in the province for consumption by passengers in the air. The supply of

[19]Beetz J. (at pp. 775–776) also rejected the argument that the construction firm was itself an "aeronautics undertaking": its business was that of a general building contractor and its connection with aeronautics was only "casual or temporary". Compare *Re Forest Industries Flying Tankers* (1980), 108 D.L.R. (3d) 686 (B.C. C.A.) (company operating aircraft solely to prevent and fight forest fires held to be an aeronautics undertaking immune from provincial human rights legislation).

[20]*Burlington Airpark v. City of Burlington*, 2013 ONSC 6990 (Murray J.).

[21]*Burlington Airpark v. City of Burlington*, 2013 ONSC 6990, paras. 19–20, following *2241906 v. Scugog Township*, 2011 ONSC 2337 (Div. Ct.) ("fill" by-law applicable to construction of aerodrome).

[22]*Air Canada v. Ontario*, [1997] 2 S.C.R. 581. Iacobucci J. wrote the opinion of the Court.

food and water might affect the operation of aircraft by restricting the distances that could be travelled, but the supply of liquor did not affect the operation of aircraft, and could therefore be regulated by the province. (Once the aircraft was in the air, the province could no longer regulate the sale of liquor to the passengers, not because of the "vital part" immunity, but because the airspace above the province is outside the territory of the province.)[23]

XII. COMMUNICATION BY RADIO

§ 22:16 Basis of legislative jurisdiction

Radio broadcasting[1] (like television broadcasting)[2] takes place by means of electromagnetic waves of various frequencies which are transmitted in space. Only a limited number of frequencies are available, and regulation is therefore necessary to control the use of a scarce public resource. Because radio waves do not observe national boundaries, international agreement on the allocation of frequencies has been necessary to avoid transnational interference with radio reception. The International Radiotelegraph Convention, 1927, was a treaty which assigned frequencies among the various signatory states, one of which was Canada. In order to comply with this treaty, it was necessary for the assignment of radio frequencies in Canada to be regulated by statute. In the *Radio Reference* (1932),[3] decided just four months after the *Aeronautics Reference*,[4] the Privy Council held that the federal Parliament had the "jurisdiction to regulate and control radio communication". This jurisdiction existed by virtue of both the power over the peace, order, and good government of Canada (s. 91 opening words) and the power over interprovincial undertakings (s. 92(10)(a)).

The peace, order, and good government power was treated in the *Radio Reference* as authorizing laws implementing treaties. The treaty of 1927 had been entered into by Canada in its own right. Therefore, it was not a "British Empire" treaty, and s. 132 of the Constitution Act, 1867 did not authorize implementing legislation. Their lordships held that the peace, order, and good government power filled the gap and authorized legislation to implement "Canadian" treaties. This mode of reasoning was repudiated by a differently constituted Privy Council in the *Labour Conventions* case (1937).[5] But even if we disregard the existence of the treaty (as dictated by *Labour Conventions)*, it is possible that the

---

[23]Chapter 13, Extraterritorial Competence, under heading § 13:4, "Territory of province".

[Section 22:16]

[1]See D. Mullan and R. Beaman, "The Constitutional Implications of the Regulation of Telecommunications" (1973) 2 Queen's L.J. 67, 69–74.

[2]Exactly the same constitutional considerations apply to broadcast television as apply to radio: see §§ 22:19 to 22:21, "Communication by television".

[3]*Re Regulation and Control of Radio Communication in Can.*, [1932] A.C. 304.

[4]*Re Regulation and Control of Aeronautics in Can.*, [1932] A.C. 54.

[5]*A.-G. Can. v. A.-G. Ont.* (Labour Conventions) [1937] A.C. 326. The subject of

peace, order, and good government power still gives to the federal Parliament the jurisdiction over radio broadcasting.

Aeronautics[6] provides an analogy. It will be recalled that federal jurisdiction over aeronautics was first attributed to the existence of a treaty; then, after the treaty could no longer be relied upon, federal jurisdiction was attributed to the peace, order, and good government power. The attribution to peace, order, and good government was based on the view that aeronautics satisfied the *Canada Temperance* test, that is to say, it "goes beyond local or provincial concern or interests and must from its inherent nature be the concern of the Dominion as a whole".[7] It is clear that radio broadcasting has a similar, and perhaps stronger, claim to a national dimension or concern. The fact that radio frequencies do not respect provincial boundaries means that the limited range of frequencies cannot be assigned on a provincial basis, and the role of radio as an interprovincial and international communications link and as a force for national identity and unity also gives it an important national dimension. In *Re CFRB* (1973),[8] the Ontario Court of Appeal decided that the analogy between radio and aeronautics was compelling, and the Court held that radio broadcasting was a matter within federal jurisdiction under the *Canada Temperance* definition of peace, order, and good government. The Supreme Court of Canada refused leave to appeal.[9]

While the analogy with aeronautics has force, it will be recalled that the attribution of aeronautics to the peace, order, and good government power is something of an anomaly: federal jurisdiction over all other modes of transportation has been derived from s. 92(10)(a), the power over "undertakings connecting the province with any other or others of the provinces, or extending beyond the limits of the province". In the case of radio, s. 92(10)(a) was suggested as an additional basis of jurisdiction in both the *Radio Reference*[10] and *Re CFRB.*[11] In *Capital Cities Communications v. CRTC* (1977),[12] the Supreme Court of Canada held that s. 92(10)(a) was the basis of jurisdiction over broadcast television—and broadcast radio would obviously be in the same constitutional situation as broadcast television. The Court made no reference at all to peace, order, and good government, an omission that is so striking that it should probably be interpreted as a disapproval of that basis of jurisdiction.

In view of the *Capital Cities* holding, it is probably safe to conclude that federal jurisdiction over radio comes from the federal power over interprovincial or international "undertakings" in s. 92(10)(a). It will be

---

implementing treaties is dealt with in ch. 11, Treaties.

[6]§§ 22:13 to 22:15, "Transportation by air".

[7]*A.-G. Ont. v. Can. Temperance Federation*, [1946] A.C. 193, 205.

[8]*Re CFRB*, [1973] 3 O.R. 819 (C.A.).

[9]November 13, 1973.

[10]*Re Regulation and Control of Radio Communication in Can.*, [1932] A.C. 304, 315.

[11]*Re CFRB*, [1973] 3 O.R. 819, 822.

[12]*Capital Cities Communications v. CRTC*, [1978] 2 S.C.R. 141.

recalled that it was in the *Radio Reference* that Viscount Dunedin gave his often-quoted definition of an undertaking as "not a physical thing, but an arrangement under which . . . physical things are used".[13] But it is clear that the word "arrangement" in this context is not confined to a particular organization or enterprise, which is how the term "undertaking" in s. 92(10)(a) has usually been interpreted. Viscount Dunedin seems to have been thinking of the entire field of radio broadcasting as one vast undertaking. This extraordinarily broad definition of undertaking was accepted without demur in *Re CFRB*, Kelly J.A. for the Ontario Court of Appeal asserting that the *Radio Reference* decided that "the whole of the undertaking of broadcasting" was within federal jurisdiction.[14] Laskin C.J. for the majority in the *Capital Cities* case was less specific, but he seemed to be using the word undertaking in the same broad sense.[15]

§ 22:17 Intraprovincial broadcasting

Does federal jurisdiction extend to purely intraprovincial radiobroadcasting? In the *Radio Reference*,[1] the Privy Council considered this question and answered it yes. If federal jurisdiction is placed under the peace, order, and good government power, then the analogy of aeronautics[2] suggests that this must be the correct answer. If federal jurisdiction is placed under s. 92(10)(a), the correctness of the answer is less clear. It must be remembered that authority over most forms of transportation and communication— railways, bus lines, trucking lines, pipelines, and telephone systems—is divided on a territorial basis: the intraprovincial systems are within provincial jurisdiction as "local works and undertakings" (s. 92(10)), and only interprovincial or international systems are within federal jurisdiction under s. 92(10)(a). And yet radio is different from all of these other modes of transportation or communication in that all radio broadcasters must use the same kind of radio waves in the same frequency spectrum. The shared use of the frequency spectrum does give plausibility to the broader meaning attributed to the term "undertaking" in the *Radio Reference, CFRB* and *Capital Cities* cases.[3] The need to allocate space in the frequency spectrum in order to avoid interference suggests that the power to regulate the interprovincial broadcaster must carry with it the power to regulate the

---

[13]*Re Regulation and Control of Radio Communication in Can.*, [1932] A.C. 304, 315.

[14]*Re CFRB*, [1973] 3 O.R. 819, 822; see also *Re Public Utilities Comm. and Victoria Cablevision* (1965), 51 D.L.R. (2d) 716 (B.C. C.A.).

[15]*Capital Cities Communications v. CRTC*, [1978] 2 S.C.R. 141, 161.

[Section 22:17]

[1]*Re Regulation and Control of Radio Communication in Can.*, [1932] A.C. 304, 313. In one of those distressing lapses for which the Privy Council became notorious in Canada, their lordships referred consistently to "inter-provincial" broadcasting, although in the context it is clear that they meant *intra* provincial broadcasting.

[2]See § 22:14, "Intraprovincial aeronautics".

[3]*Re Regulation and Control of Radio Communication in Can.*, [1932] A.C. 304; *Re CFRB*, [1973] 3 O.R. 819; *Capital Cities Communications v. CRTC*, [1978] 2 S.C.R. 141.

intraprovincial broadcaster as well.[4] Certainly, the federal Radiocommunication and Broadcasting Acts[5] assert federal regulatory jurisdiction over intraprovincial as well as interprovincial and international broadcasters.

§ 22:18 Content regulation

The *Radio Reference* was concerned with the technical aspects of transmitting and receiving radio signals, that is, the problem of allocating frequencies and regulating transmission so as to avoid technical interference. In deciding that regulation of this kind could be accomplished at the national level, the Privy Council was not addressing itself to the question whether the federal Parliament could regulate the content of radio broadcasting. It is arguable therefore that the *Radio Reference* leaves open the possibility that the federal Parliament can regulate the medium but not the message.[1]

In *Re CFRB* (1973),[2] the Ontario Court of Appeal had to determine the validity of a provision in the federal Broadcasting Act which prohibited the broadcasting of partisan political programmes on the day before a federal, provincial or municipal election. The radio station that was prosecuted for breach of the provision argued that the federal Parliament's power over broadcasting did not extend to programme content. The Ontario Court of Appeal rejected the argument. The Court said that "it would be flying in the face of all practical considerations and logic to charge Parliament with the responsibility for the regulation and control of the carrier system and to deny it the right to exercise legislative control over what is the only reason for the existence of the carrier system, i.e., the transmission and reception of intellectual material".[3] The Court accordingly held that Parliament's jurisdiction over radio did extend to "the control and regulation of the intellectual content of radio communication".[4] It followed that the impugned section of the Broadcasting Act was valid. An application was made to the Supreme Court of Canada for leave to appeal this decision, and leave was refused.[5]

---

[4]There is an analogy in the shared use of airspace and ground facilities by aircraft, although aeronautics has not been treated as an undertaking under s. 92(10)(a), jurisdiction having been placed solely under the peace, order, and good government power.

[5]Radiocommunication Act, R.S.C. 1985, c. R-2; Broadcasting Act, S.C. 1991, c. 11.

[Section 22:18]

[1]R.I. Cohen, "Advertising to Children" (1974) 12 Can. Pat. Rep. (2d) 173, 188.

[2]*Re CFRB*, [1973] 3 O.R. 819 (C.A.).

[3]*Re CFRB*, [1973] 3 O.R. 819, 824 (C.A.).

[4]*Re CFRB*, [1973] 3 O.R. 819, 824 (C.A.).

[5]November 13, 1973. This was before the Charter of Rights. Compare *Thomson Newspapers Co. v. Can.*, [1998] 1 S.C.R. 877 (striking down under s. 2(b) Elections Act prohibition on publication of opinion surveys during last three days of election campaign); *Harper v. Can.*, [2004] 1 S.C.R. 827 (upholding under s. 1 Elections Act prohibition of election advertising on polling day).

In *Capital Cities Communications v. CRTC* (1977),[6] the Supreme Court of Canada had to determine the question whether a federal regulatory agency could authorize cable television companies to delete the commercials from American television programmes captured by the cable companies from the air, and to replace the deleted commercials with Canadian commercials; the American programmes with the Canadian commercials would then be distributed by the cable television companies to their subscribers. The question whether this practice could be authorized by the federal agency raised the constitutional question whether the federal Parliament had authority over the content of cable television. The Court held that the cable system was "no more than a conduit for signals from the telecast",[7] and that federal power over broadcast television extended to the cable system. Thus, the decision determined the scope of authority over broadcast television—and therefore broadcast radio—as well as cable television. The Court held that Parliament could regulate the content of the programmes. The regulation of programme content was inseparable from the regulation of the technical and economic aspects of television.

The *CFRB* and *Capital Cities* cases settle the question of federal power to regulate programme content. They are consistent with the judge-made policy, evident in earlier cases,[8] of refusing to divide legislative authority over transportation or communications undertakings.

The existence of exclusive federal authority over the programme content of radio and television does not exclude provincial law altogether. Under the pith and substance doctrine, a law that is in pith and substance in relation to a matter within provincial legislative competence may validly have an incidental effect on the programme content of radio or television. This is illustrated by *A.-G. Que. v. Kellogg's Co.* (1978),[9] where the question arose whether a Quebec law that prohibited the use of cartoons in advertising intended for children could validly apply to advertising on television. The Attorney General of Quebec had sought an injunction against the Kellogg's Company to restrain it from advertising its cereals on television by animated cartoons. The Supreme Court of Canada granted the injunction. Martland J. for the majority of the Court held that the pith and substance of the law was the control of commercial activity in the province, which was valid under s. 92(13) or s. 92(16). Such a law could incidentally also restrict what was shown on television. Martland J. suggested the analogy of defamation: just as provincial restrictions on defamatory statements could not be evaded by the use of a federal medium such as television, nor could the provincial restrictions on advertising be so evaded.[10]

In the *Kellogg's* case, the law applied to all advertising media, not just

[6] *Capital Cities Communications v. CRTC*, [1978] 2 S.C.R. 141.

[7] *Capital Cities Communications v. CRTC*, [1978] 2 S.C.R. 141, 159.

[8] See § 22:5, "Undivided jurisdiction".

[9] *A.-G. Que. v. Kellogg's Co.*, [1978] 2 S.C.R. 211.

[10] See also *Irwin Toy v. Que.*, [1989] 1 S.C.R. 927, following *Kellogg's* and upholding

television, although it seems obvious that cartoon advertising for children would be a much less significant problem in any medium other than television. But the more general scope of the law helped the Court to classify the law as in relation to advertising generally, rather than to advertising on television. The Quebec government, the plaintiff in the case, had also employed a wise procedural tactic in not seeking to enjoin the television station that had been showing the offending advertisements. The injunction had been sought only against the Kellogg's Company, the advertiser.[11] Martland J. stressed that he was not forced to decide whether an injunction would lie against the television station, and that he was not deciding that question.[12]

In ch. 43, Expression, the limits on the powers of both levels of government to control the expression of ideas on television or other media, including the limits imposed by the Charter of Rights, are considered more fully.

XIII. COMMUNICATION BY TELEVISION

§ 22:19 Broadcast television

Television[1] was almost unknown as a means of communication in 1932 when the *Radio Reference*[2] was decided. But it had been invented, and the reference to the Court asked for its opinion as to the constitutional jurisdiction not only over sound radio, but also over the transmission and reception of "pictures". A report by the Minister of Justice which was placed before the Court described television and included it in the term "radio".[3] Thus, although their lordships of the Privy Council made no specific reference to television in their opinion, their answer to the question referred did literally apply to television as well as radio. And, of course, the reasoning in the case applies with the same force to television—at least broadcast television—as to radio. Broadcast television also utilizes electromagnetic waves in space, and its hardware or

---

a provincial ban on advertising directed at children, including advertising on television.

[11]In *Irwin Toy v. Que.*, [1989] 1 S.C.R. 927, the law applied to advertisers, not to the media that carried the advertisements. But the law had the indirect effect of excluding advertising directed at children from all media, including radio and television.

[12]*A.-G. Que. v. Kellogg's Co.*, [1978] 2 S.C.R. 211, 225. Martland J. was probably concerned about the rule that a provincial law may not "sterilize"—now impair—a federal undertaking. The issue of an injunction against the television station might have been precluded by that rule. On the sterilization of federal undertakings, see ch. 15, Judicial Review on Federal Grounds, under heading §§ 15:16 to 15:21, "Interjurisdictional immunity".

[Section 22:19]

[1]See D. Mullan and R. Beaman, "The Constitutional Implications of the Regulation of Telecommunications" (1973) 2 Queen's L.J. 67, 80–88; M.K. Miazga, "Cable Television" (1978) 43 Sask. L. Rev. 1; S. Wilkie, "The Radio Reference and Onward" (1980) 18 Osgoode Hall L.J. 49.

[2]*Re Regulation and Control of Radio Communication in Can.*, [1932] A.C. 304.

[3]*Re Regulation and Control of Radio Communication in Can.*, [1931] S.C.R. 541, 542.

carrier system requires national regulation just as much as radio and for the same reasons. Moreover, the argument for national regulation of programme content has exactly the same force in relation to broadcast television as it has in relation to radio.

In *Capital Cities Communications v. CRTC* (1977),[4] the Supreme Court of Canada held that the *Radio Reference* supplied the same rule for broadcast television (and for cable television) as it did for radio. It is clear that for constitutional purposes there is no distinction between radio and broadcast television, and the preceding discussion of radio is all relevant to broadcast television as well. Indeed, as will be seen in the next section of this text, cable television is also in the same constitutional position as radio and broadcast television, except, perhaps, for cable systems carrying only the local programming that is possible on cable television.

§ 22:20 Cable television

Cable television differs from broadcast television in that viewers receive their signals through a cable rather than through the air. A cable television system consists essentially of two parts. The first part is the "head end", which is an antenna placed to pick up the signals from the television-broadcasting stations in the area or from satellites. The second part is the "distribution system", which is the network of cable that carries the signal from the head end into the homes of subscribers who pay rent to the cable company for the service. The notable feature of a cable television system is that it does not require radio frequency space, because it only uses a receiving antenna. The transmitting occurs on the cable, which places a strict geographical limit on the range of the signals, and which ensures that the cable system's signals cannot interfere with the signals of radio or television broadcasting stations or with the signals of other cable systems. It is also possible for programmes to be originated by the cable operator. Programmes can be made in a local studio, or purchased in tape form, or relayed from some local place such as a sports stadium or meeting hall. These "local programmes" can be supplied on one or more "community channels" of the cable system.

In the *Radio Reference*,[1] it was argued by the provinces that, even if radio transmitters had to be regulated federally because of the limitations of the radio frequency spectrum, the receivers did not require regulation because they did not interfere with other users of the radio frequency spectrum. The Privy Council refused to draw a distinction between transmitters and receivers. Their lordships held that once it was determined that the transmitter came within federal control, the receiver "must share its fate".[2]

Broadcasting as a system cannot exist without both a transmitter and a

---

[4] *Capital Cities Communications v. CRTC*, [1978] 2 S.C.R. 141.

[Section 22:20]

[1] *Re Regulation and Control of Radio Communication in Can.*, [1932] A.C. 304, 315.

[2] *Re Regulation and Control of Radio Communication in Can.*, [1932] A.C. 304, 315.

> receiver. The receiver is indeed useless without a transmitter and can be reduced to a nonentity if the transmitter closes. The system cannot be divided into two parts, each independent of the other.[3]

And their lordships added, finally, that "a divided control between transmitter and receiver could only lead to confusion and inefficiency".[4] This holding that transmitter and receiver must be treated as parts of one system for constitutional purposes resolves any question about legislative jurisdiction over the head end or receiving apparatus of a cable television system: the jurisdiction must be federal.

In *Capital Cities Communications v. CRTC* (1977),[5] the question arose whether the federal Parliament had constitutional authority to regulate the programme content of cable television. It was conceded that the federal Parliament had constitutional authority over the reception of broadcast signals by the cable operator's head end or receiving apparatus. But it was argued that the distribution system—the network of cable that carries the signals from the head end to the television sets in the homes of the cable subscribers—was a separate local undertaking within provincial jurisdiction. This argument was rejected by Laskin C.J. for the majority of the Supreme Court of Canada.[6] He held that the head end and the distribution system were parts of an indivisible communications undertaking within the legislative competence of the federal Parliament. The cable system could not be separated from the telecast, because it was "no more than a conduit for signals from the telecast".[7] It would be "incongruous", he held, "to deny the continuation of regulatory authority because the signals are intercepted and sent on to ultimate viewers through a different technology".[8]

The *Capital Cities* case sustained federal regulation of cable television. On the same day, the Supreme Court of Canada handed down its decision in *Public Service Board v. Dionne* (1977),[9] which scotched any argument that there was concurrent provincial authority over cable television. Laskin C.J. for the majority[10] struck down a Quebec law purporting to authorize a provincial agency to license cable television systems within the province. Laskin C.J. affirmed the exclusivity of federal regulatory power over cable television, and reaffirmed the Court's

[3] *Re Regulation and Control of Radio Communication in Can.*, [1932] A.C. 304.

[4] *Re Regulation and Control of Radio Communication in Can.*, [1932] A.C. 304, 317.

[5] *Capital Cities Communications v. CRTC*, [1978] 2 S.C.R. 141. The case is briefly discussed in *Re CFRB*, [1973] 3 O.R. 819, 822.

[6] Laskin C.J.'s opinion was agreed with by Martland, Judson, Ritchie, Spence and Dickson JJ. Pigeon J., with the agreement of Beetz and de Grandpré JJ., dissented.

[7] *Capital Cities Communications v. CRTC*, [1978] 2 S.C.R. 141, 159.

[8] *Capital Cities Communications v. CRTC*, [1978] 2 S.C.R. 141, 162.

[9] *Public Service Board v. Dionne*, [1978] 2 S.C.R. 191.

[10] The Court split in the same way as in the *Capital Cities* case, *Capital Cities Communications v. CRTC*, [1978] 2 S.C.R. 141.

refusal to countenance "divided constitutional control of what is functionally an inter-related system".[11]

Both *Capital Cities* and *Dionne* were concerned with the distribution by cable of "off-air" signals, that is, programmes that had originated as broadcast signals that had been captured from the air by the cable operator. In both cases, Laskin C.J. emphasized that the Court was not deciding which level of government had jurisdiction over "local" programmes, that is, the programmes produced in a local studio, or purchased in tape form, or relayed by cable from some local place. That question was left open. The important distinction between local programmes and off-air programmes is that the local programmes have never been received by the head end as broadcast signals. So far as local programmes are concerned, the cable system cannot be characterized as "a conduit for signals from the telecast,"[12] and the reasoning of *Capital Cities* and *Dionne* has no obvious application. If we postulate a cable television system which carries only programmes originated by the cable operator, the local origin of all programmes suggests the analogy of a closed-circuit television system of the kind commonly organized in schools or universities, or even a concert hall, theatre or cinema which uses television to serve a spillover audience in an adjoining hall.[13] Here, there does not seem to be any plausible claim to federal jurisdiction. The system is within provincial jurisdiction as a local work or undertaking under s. 92(10).

What most cable operators actually supply, of course, is at most only a few "community channels" carrying local programmes and a larger number of channels carrying programmes received from broadcast television stations. So long as the cable operator provides off-air programmes as well as local programmes, it is arguable that the local programmes are part of one undertaking whose characteristics are predominantly interprovincial. The courts have not been willing, for example, to sever into two undertakings a telephone company or a bus line or a trucking

[11]*Capital Cities Communications v. CRTC*, [1978] 2 S.C.R. 191, 197. A provincial law in relation to a matter within provincial competence could validly apply incidentally to a cable television system: *A.-G. Que. v. Kellogg's Co.*, [1978] 2 S.C.R. 211; discussed in text accompanying § 22:18 note 9.

[12]*Capital Cities Communications v. CRTC*, [1978] 2 S.C.R. 141, 159.

[13]Even if intraprovincial broadcasting is within federal jurisdiction, as argued in § 22:17, "Intraprovincial broadcasting", cable transmission presents distinctive features. A cable television system which carries only local programmes differs from a local airline or broadcasting station in that the cable system is self-contained. An intraprovincial airline must compete with interprovincial airlines for airport facilities and air routes. Similarly an intraprovincial radio or television broadcaster must compete with interprovincial broadcasters for frequency space. Clearly, in both cases the need to share facilities and the possibility of interference makes unified control highly desirable if not essential. But a cable television system carrying only local programmes is entirely self-contained. Its signals originate within the cable system and are confined to the system by the cable. The system need not use any facilities in common with broadcasters or other cable systems, and its signals cannot interfere with any broadcast or cabled signals.

company which does both local and long-distance business.[14] In each case the courts have held that a significant amount of "continuous and regular" interprovincial business turns the entire enterprise into an interprovincial undertaking. It is likely that the courts would view a cable television undertaking in the same light.[15]

§ 22:21 Pay television

The term "pay television" encompasses a variety of different systems, although they all utilize a cable to bring their product to their customers. Constitutional jurisdiction over pay television depends upon the same considerations as apply to cable television generally. In essence, this means that a self-contained, purely local, system will be within provincial jurisdiction, while a system which is added to the standard cable television mixed offering will be within federal jurisdiction.

XIV. COMMUNICATION BY TELEPHONE

§ 22:22 Communication by telephone

Legislative authority over communication by telephone (telecommunication)[1] depends upon s. 92(10) of the Constitution Act, 1867. We have already examined *Toronto v. Bell Telephone Co.* (1905)[2] and seen that the federal Parliament has legislative authority over the Bell Telephone Company, because it is an interprovincial undertaking under s. 92(10)(a). At the time of the decision, Bell was operating only in Ontario but it was planning to extend its system into Quebec, and the Privy Council took the wish for the deed. Bell did in fact extend its service into Quebec. By virtue of the *Bell Telephone* decision, Bell has always been federally regulated.[3]

Until the decision of the Supreme Court of Canada in the AGT case

---

[14] § 22:5, "Undivided jurisdiction".

[15] This line of reasoning is suggested in an obiter dictum in *Public Service Bd. v. Dionne*, [1978] 2 S.C.R. 191, where Laskin C.J. said (at p. 197) that the case did not involve cable operators that *"limit* their operations to programmes locally produced by them" (my emphasis), and (at p. 198) that "an argument based on relative percentages of original programming and of programmes received from broadcasting stations" would be of no avail.

[Section 22:22]

[1] D. Mullan and R. Beaman, "The Constitutional Implications of the Regulation of Telecommunications" (1973) 2 Queen's L.J. 67, 74–80. Buchan and others, *Telecommunications Regulation and the Constitution* (Institute for Research on Public Policy, 1982); R.A. Brait, "Constitutional Jurisdiction to Regulate Telephone Services" (1981) 13 Ottawa L. Rev. 53; R.J. Schultz, "Federalism and Telecommunications" (1982) 20 Osgoode Hall L.J. 745; W. Grieve, "Constitutional Structure and Regulation of Telecommunications in Canada" [2000] Mich. State U.—Detroit C.L. Law Rev. 23; M. H. Ryan, "Telecommunications and the Constitution: Re-setting the Bounds of Federal Authority" (2010) 89 Can. Bar Rev. 695.

[2] *Toronto v. Bell Telephone Co.*, [1905] A.C. 52.

[3] See also *Commission du Salaire Minimum v. Bell Telephone Co.*, [1966] S.C.R. 767; *Bell Canada v. Quebec*, [1988] 1 S.C.R. 749. Each case held that provincial law was

(1989),[4] it was assumed that a telephone company that was confined to a single province would be a local undertaking within provincial jurisdiction under s. 92(10), and such companies were in fact regulated provincially. However, in the *AGT* case, which was examined earlier in this chapter,[5] the Supreme Court of Canada held that Alberta Government Telephones (AGT) was within federal jurisdiction. Although AGT's operations did not extend beyond the province of Alberta, the Court held that the company was properly classified as an interprovincial undertaking under s. 92(10)(a). The Court pointed out that the company had the capacity to provide interprovincial and international service to its subscribers. This capacity stemmed from the company's connections at the Alberta border with the telephone systems of neighbouring jurisdictions and the company's membership of Telecom Canada, which was an unincorporated association of the major Canadian telephone companies to form a national telecommunications network.

After the *AGT* case, all that remained for decision was the constitutional status of a number of local telephone companies. In Ontario, Quebec and British Columbia, there were a number of small local telephone companies that served small communities and rural areas. These companies lacked cross-border connections, and they were not members of a national telecommunications network. Each company was able to provide full interprovincial and international service to its customers by cooperative arrangements with the major telephone company in the same province. The constitutional status of these local telephone companies depended on the correct interpretation of the AGT case. If the *AGT case* turned on AGT's cross-border connections and its membership in a national telecommunications network then local companies lacking these characteristics would remain within provincial jurisdiction. If, on the other hand, the *AGT* case turned on AGT's capacity to provide interprovincial and international service to its customers, then the local companies would be in the same federal boat.

The issue arose for decision in *Téléphone Guèvremont v. Quebec* (1994).[6] Téléphone Guèvremont was a local telephone company located in Quebec with 5,400 subscribers. It was not a member of a national telecommunications network and it had no connections at any of Quebec's borders (its territory being "in the heart" of the province). The company was interconnected with Bell, and through Bell's facilities the company could send and receive messages to and from anywhere in Canada and the rest of the world. The company, which was being regulated by a provincial agency (the Régie des télécommunications) brought proceedings to obtain a ruling that the province (and therefore the Régie) lacked

---

inapplicable to Bell based on the doctrine of interjurisdictional immunity; for discussion, see ch. 15, Judicial Review on Federal Grounds, under heading §§ 15:16 to 15:21, "Interjurisdictional immunity".

[4] *Alberta Government Telephones v. CRTC*, [1989] 2 S.C.R. 225.

[5] Text accompanying § 22:4 note 4.

[6] *Téléphone Guèvremont v. Quebec*, [1994] 1 S.C.R. 878. The opinion of the unanimous Court was written by Lamer C.J.

any regulatory authority over the company. The company was successful in the Superior Court, the Quebec Court of Appeal and the Supreme Court of Canada. The Quebec Court of Appeal,[7] in an opinion written by Rousseau-Houle J.A., held that the company's lack of cross-border connections and lack of membership in a national telecommunications network was not decisive. What was decisive was that the company was "the medium by which its local subscribers receive interprovincial and international communications".[8] It was therefore an interprovincial telephone system under s. 92(10)(a). This decision was affirmed by the Supreme Court of Canada. Lamer C.J.'s reasons for the unanimous Court read in full as follows:[9]

> We are all of the view that Téléphone Guèvremont Inc. is an interprovincial work and undertaking within the legislative authority of the Parliament of Canada by virtue of ss. 92(10)(a) and 91(29) of the *Constitution Act, 1867* by reason of the nature of the services provided and the mode of operation of the undertaking, which provides a telecommunication signal carrier service whereby its subscribers send and receive interprovincial and international communications as set out in the reasons of Rousseau-Houle J.A.

With those few words, the issue was settled. All telephone companies are within federal jurisdiction.

At the time of the decisions in *AGT* (1989) and *Téléphone Guèvremont* (1994), telecommunications were transmitted over a network of wires strung along poles or buried underground. Mobile phones did not exist (at least in the marketplace); they now provide telecommunications over wireless networks that do not rely on "land lines" but instead use the same spectrum as radio. It is no longer necessary for a telecommunications provider to have a land-based network and some have no land-based facilities at all. This change in the technology has probably made no change in the constitutional jurisdiction over telecommunications.[10] Since all telecommunications providers have the capacity to provide interprovincial and international service to their customers, the rationale of the *AGT* and *Téléphone Guèvremont* decisions would apply to the wireless providers no less than the wired providers.[11] They are all within federal jurisdiction under s. 92(10)(a).

---

[7] *Téléphone Guèvremont c. Québec* (1992) 99 D.L.R. (4th) 241 (Que. C.A.).

[8] *Téléphone Guèvremont c. Québec* (1992) 99 D.L.R. (4th) 241, 256 (Que. C.A.).

[9] *Téléphone Guèvremont c. Québec* [1994] 1 S.C.R. 878, 879.

[10] M. H. Ryan, "Telecommunications and the Constitution: Re-setting the Bounds of Federal Authority" (2010) 89 Can. Bar Rev. 695, 708, cautiously raises the possibility, based on the freight-forwarding cases (§ 22:4), that "some physical involvement in the conveyance of traffic is demanded by section 92(10(a)". But he acknowledges that it would be "rash" to rely too heavily on the analogy with freight-forwarding, because the telephone can provide interprovincial and international services without any physical connection, and the reasoning in *AGT* and *Téléphone Guèvremont* relied on the services provided by the companies (which extended beyond the province), not the physical facilities (which did not extend beyond the province).

[11] In the case of the wireless undertakings, there has to be a regulatory allocation of spectrum, which provides a close analogy with radio (§§ 22:16 to 22:18), reinforcing the

Federal jurisdiction over mobile telephones (wireless telephony) was confirmed by the Supreme Court in *Rogers Communications v. Châteauguay* (2016).[12] In that case, the federal Minister of Industry, exercising power conferred by the federal Radiocommunication Act, authorized Rogers Communications, a mobile telephone provider, to install an antenna system on a particular named property in the municipality of Châteaugay in Quebec. The antenna was needed to improve Rogers' mobile telephone service in that area. Responding to local opposition to the installation, the municipality adopted a resolution claiming that the health and well-being of people living near the installation would be at risk and issued a "notice of a reserve" that under municipal law prohibited all construction on the property. Rogers challenged the notice of a reserve on constitutional grounds, which were upheld by the Court. Wagner and Côté JJ., who wrote for the majority, held that "Parliament has exclusive jurisdiction over radiocommunication" and "this jurisdiction includes the power to choose the location of radiocommunication infrastructure."[13] In their view, the purpose and effect of the municipal notice was to prevent Rogers from installing its antenna system on the property approved by the minister. The pith and substance of the municipal notice was the choice of radiocommunication infrastructure, a matter that was within the exclusive federal power over radiocommunication. The municipal notice was invalid on that ground. This decided the case, although the judges went on to hold that the municipal notice impaired the core of the federal power over radiocommunication and was also invalid under the doctrine of interjurisdictional immunity.[14] Gascon J.'s concurring opinion disagreed with the majority's characterization of the pith and substance of the municipal notice—he held that the municipal notice was issued for valid municipal purposes[15]—but he agreed with the majority on the federal power over radiocommunications and with the majority's interjurisdictional immunity reasons.

XV. COMMUNICATION BY OTHER MEANS

§ 22:23 Film

The exhibition of films, like most businesses, comes within the legislative competence of the provinces. The location and design of cinemas,

---

federal characterization of the undertakings.

[12]*Rogers Communications v. Châteauguay*, [2016] 1 S.C.R. 467, 2016 SCC 23. Wagner and Côté JJ. wrote the opinion of the eight-judge majority. Gascon J. wrote a concurring opinion.

[13]*Rogers Communications v. Châteauguay*, [2016] 1 S.C.R. 467, 2016 SCC 23, para. 42.

[14]The interjurisdictional immunity reasons are described in more detail in ch. 15, Judicial Review on Federal Grounds, under heading § 15:18, "Federally-regulated undertakings", at footnote 62.

[15]Gascon J. (para. 79) took the view that the notice "relates first and foremost to ensuring the harmonious development of the territory of the [municipality] and protecting the well-being and health of the people living there."

safety and health requirements, the qualifications of projectionists and other personnel, the storage and rental of films, advertisements for film showings, times of showings and ticket prices, would all be matters within "property and civil rights in the province" (s. 92(13)) or "matters of a merely local or private nature in the province" (s. 92(16)).[1] This conclusion is not affected by the interprovincial or international elements of the film industry, such as the fact that the films shown may be imported from other countries,[2] or that a particular cinema may be part of a chain of cinemas stretching across the country.[3] Each province is free to impose its own regime of regulation upon the cinemas within its borders.

In *Nova Scotia Board of Censors v. McNeil* (1978),[4] the Supreme Court of Canada held that provincial authority over the exhibition of films extended to regulating the content of films by a system of censorship administered by a provincial agency with authority to ban films altogether, to permit their exhibition with cuts, and to permit their exhibition with age-based admission restrictions. Ritchie J. for the majority assumed that the provincial agency would limit its powers to issues of primarily local significance, namely, the depiction of violence or sex.[5] Censorship on political or religious grounds would be outside provincial power. In ch. 43, Expression,[6] the limits on the powers of both levels of government to control the expression of ideas in film or other media, including the limits imposed by the Charter of Rights, are considered more fully.

§ 22:24 Theatre

Live theatre, by which term I mean all forms of stage production, including plays, vaudeville, and concerts,[1] is within provincial regulatory authority upon the same constitutional grounds as film. The degree to which a province can regulate the content of a live production, for example, to restrict depictions of sex or violence, depends upon the same considerations as apply to film and literature, and is examined in ch. 43, Expression.

[Section 22:23]

[1] *N.S. Bd. of Censors v. McNeil*, [1978] 2 S.C.R. 662, discussed in following text.

[2] In *N.S. Bd. of Censors v. McNeil*, [1978] 2 S.C.R. 662, the film in issue was imported.

[3] Compare *Can. Indemnity Co. v. A.-G. B.C.*, [1977] 2 S.C.R. 504 (provincial authority over insurance industry unaffected by national and multi-national scope and operation of insurance companies).

[4] *N.S. Bd. of Censors v. McNeil*, [1978] 2 S.C.R. 662.

[5] *N.S. Bd. of Censors v. McNeil*, [1978] 2 S.C.R. 662, 700–701. The control of commercial advertising is also within provincial power: *A.-G. Que. v. Kellogg's Co.*, [1978] 2 S.C.R. 211; *Irwin Toy v. Que.*, [1989] 1 S.C.R. 927.

[6] Esp. under heading § 43:29, "Pornography".

[Section 22:24]

[1] Sporting events and other local entertainments are in the same constitutional category as theatre.

§ 22:25 Literature

By literature I mean all forms of written communication, including books, pamphlets, magazines and newspapers.[1] The publication, distribution and sale of all these forms of literature may be regulated by the province within which the publication, distribution or sale occurs. These are matters within property and civil rights in the province. This conclusion is not affected by the fact that the literature was imported from other provinces or countries,[2] or that the publisher or distributor is a nation-wide organization.[3] However, as in the case of film and theatre, the degree to which a province can regulate the content of literature is a difficult question that is considered more fully in ch. 43, Expression.

[Section 22:25]

[1]Records, tapes, videodiscs, and videotapes are in the same constitutional category as literature.

[2]*N.S. Bd. of Censors v. McNeil*, [1978] 2 S.C.R. 662.

[3]*Can. Indemnity Co. v. A.-G. B.C.*, [1977] 2 S.C.R. 504.

Chapter 28

Aboriginal Peoples

I. FEDERAL LEGISLATIVE POWER

§ 28:1 Section 91(24)
§ 28:2 Indians
§ 28:3 Lands reserved for the Indians
§ 28:4 Canadian Bill of Rights
§ 28:5 Charter of Rights
§ 28:6 Treaties

II. PROVINCIAL LEGISLATIVE POWER

§ 28:7 Application of provincial laws
§ 28:8 First exception: singling out
§ 28:9 Second exception: Indianness
§ 28:10 Third exception: paramountcy
§ 28:11 Fourth exception: Natural Resources Agreements
§ 28:12 Fifth exception: section 35

III. SECTION 88 OF THE INDIAN ACT

§ 28:13 Text of s. 88
§ 28:14 Laws of general application
§ 28:15 Paramountcy exception
§ 28:16 Treaty exception

IV. NATURAL RESOURCES AGREEMENTS

§ 28:17 Natural resources agreements

V. ABORIGINAL RIGHTS

§ 28:18 Recognition of aboriginal rights
§ 28:19 Definition of aboriginal rights
§ 28:20 Aboriginal self-government
§ 28:21 Aboriginal title
§ 28:22 Extinguishment of Aboriginal rights

VI. TREATY RIGHTS

§ 28:23 Introduction
§ 28:24 History
§ 28:25 Definition of treaty
§ 28:26 Interpretation of treaty rights

§ 28:27 Extinguishment of treaty rights

VII. THE NEED FOR CONSTITUTIONAL PROTECTION

§ 28:28 The need for constitutional protection

VIII. SECTION 35

§ 28:29 Text of s. 35
§ 28:30 Outside Charter of Rights
§ 28:31 "Aboriginal peoples of Canada"
§ 28:32 "Aboriginal and treaty rights"
§ 28:33 "Existing"
§ 28:34 "Recognized and affirmed"
§ 28:35 Application to treaty rights
§ 28:36 Application to extinguishment
§ 28:37 Application to provincial laws
§ 28:38 Duty to consult Aboriginal people
§ 28:39 Jurisdiction of the provincial courts
§ 28:40 Remedies for breach of s. 35

IX. SECTION 25

§ 28:41 Section 25

X. SECTION 35.1

§ 28:42 Section 35.1

XI. CHARLOTTETOWN ACCORD

§ 28:43 Charlottetown Accord

I. FEDERAL LEGISLATIVE POWER

§ 28:1 Section 91(24)

Section 91(24) of the Constitution Act, 1867 confers upon the federal Parliament the power to make laws in relation to "Indians, and lands reserved for the Indians".[1]

The main reason for s. 91(24) seems to have been a concern for the

[Section 28:1]

[1]See K.M. Lysyk, "The Unique Constitutional Position of the Canadian Indian" (1967) 45 Can. Bar Rev. 513; K.M. Lysyk "Constitutional Developments relating to Indians and Indian Lands" in Law Society of Upper Canada, The Constitution and the Future of Canada (Special Lectures, 1978), 201; D. Sanders, "Prior Claims: Aboriginal People in the Constitution of Canada" in Beck and Bernier (eds.), Canada and the New Constitution (1983), vol. 1, 225; J. Woodward, Native Law (Carswell, Toronto, 1989); Beaudoin, La Constitution du Canada (3rd ed., 2004), ch. 15; R. A. Reiter, The Fundamental Principles of Indian Law (First Nations Resource Council, 1993, looseleaf); K. McNeil, "Aboriginal Title and the Division of Powers" (1998) 61 Sask. L. Rev. 431.

protection of the aboriginal peoples against local settlers, whose interests lay in an absence of restrictions on the expansion of European settlement. The idea was that the more distant level of government—the federal government—would be more likely to respect the Indian reserves that existed in 1867, to respect the treaties with the Indians that had been entered into by 1867, and generally to protect the Indians against the interests of local majorities.[2] A second reason was probably the desire to maintain uniform national policies respecting the Indians.[3] The Royal Proclamation of 1763 had established that treaty-making with the Indians was the sole responsibility of the (imperial) Crown in right of the United Kingdom.[4] After confederation, the federal government was the natural successor to that responsibility.[5]

It will be noticed that s. 91(24) contains two heads of power: a power over "Indians" and a power over "lands reserved for the Indians". The first power may be exercised in respect of Indians (and only Indians) whether or not they reside on, or have any connection with, lands reserved for the Indians. The second power may be exercised in respect of Indians and non-Indians so long as the law is related to lands reserved for the Indians.

§ 28:2 Indians

The federal power over "Indians"—the first branch of s. 91(24)—invites two questions: (1) Who is an Indian? and (2) What kinds of laws may be made in relation to Indians?

Who is an Indian? In Canada, the word "Indian" has been used to mean the aboriginal peoples who had been living there long before European contact. The word has a dubious provenance, having originated in a mistake by Christopher Columbus, who thought he had discovered India in his voyages across the Atlantic Ocean. There are those who shun the word for that reason. There are others who shun the word because it conceals the diversity of the aboriginal peoples who are lumped together by the word. However, as we shall see, the use of the word in the Indian Act and in constitutional instruments makes it unavoidable in a legal text.

---

[2]D. Sanders, "Prior Claims: Aboriginal People in the Constitution of Canada" in Beck and Bernier (eds.), Canada and the New Constitution (1983), vol. 1, 238.

[3]See C. Bell, "Have You Ever Wondered Where s. 91(24) Comes From?" (2004) 17 Can. J. Con. Law 285.

[4]R.S.C. 1985, Appendix II, No. 1. The Royal Proclamation of 1763 is briefly described in ch. 2, Reception, under heading § 2:6, "Ontario and Quebec". With respect to Indians, the Proclamation recognized their rights to unceded lands in their possession, and established that the rights could be ceded only to the Crown.

[5]Aboriginal peoples did not participate in the confederation process, so that they had no influence over constitutional developments of profound significance to them.

The federal Indian Act[1] defines the term "Indian" for the purpose of that Act, and establishes a register to record the names of qualified persons. The statutory definition traces Indian status from particular bands whose charter members were normally determined at the time of the establishment of a reserve or the making of a treaty. The status then devolves from these charter members to their descendants.[2] Persons within the statutory definition of the Indian Act are known as "status Indians". They alone enjoy the right to live on Indian reserves[3] and various other Indian Act privileges.[4] There are about 700,000 status Indians in Canada.

It is probable that all status Indians are "Indians" within the meaning of s. 91(24) of the Constitution Act, 1867.[5] But there are also many persons of Indian blood and culture who are outside the statutory definition.[6] These "non-status Indians", which number about 400,000,

---

[Section 28:2]

[1]R.S.C. 1985, c. 1-5.

[2]The status provisions of the Act were substantially amended in 1985 by S.C. 1985, c. 27. The historical roots of status are now buried in s. 6(1)(a), which brings the charter group forward to those entitled to be registered in 1985. The amendments eliminate certain provisions that had been attacked as discriminatory, in particular, the provision that caused an Indian woman to lose status if she married a non-Indian man: see *A.G. Can. v. Lavell*, [1974] S.C.R. 1349 (provision upheld under Canadian Bill of Rights); *Lovelace v. Can.* (1983), 1 Can. Human Rights Yearbook 305 (U.N. Human Rights Committee) (provision held contrary to International Covenant on Civil and Political Rights). The amendments permit persons who before 1985 lost status under this and other provisions of the Act, including voluntary enfranchisement (which is no longer possible), and their children, to regain status. The amendments also separate Indian status from band membership; control over the latter, but not the former, has been conferred on the bands. See Scarsgard, "Indian Status and Band Membership" (University of Saskatchewan Native Law Centre, Update 1986). In *McIvor v. Can.* (2009), 306 D.L.R. (4th) 193 (B.C.C.A.), it was held that the 1985 amendments had not wholly cleansed the status provisions of the Indian Act of discrimination on the ground of sex, and that they were partially unconstitutional. The Government of Canada did not appeal to the Supreme Court, but Parliament followed up with corrective amendments to the Indian Act: S.C. 2010, c.18. See S.E. Hamill, "McIvor v. Canada and the 2010 Amendments to the Indian Act: A Half-Hearted Remedy to Historical Injustice" (2011) 19 Constitutional Forum 75.

[3]Any liberalization of the definition of a status Indian, such as occurred in 1985 (previous note), has the effect of enlarging the population that is entitled to live on the reserves.

[4]E.g., exemption from payment of tax on personal property situated on a reserve (s. 87), which has been held to include income tax: *Nowegijick v. The Queen*, [1983] 1 S.C.R. 29. Before 1950, status Indians resident on a reserve had no right to vote, so that the voluntary termination of status became known as "enfranchisement". In 1950, the franchise was extended to those Indians who waived their exemption from tax. Only in 1960 was an unconditional right to vote finally extended to status Indians.

[5]The Court would accept a statutory definition that could be supported as a reasonable, bona fide definition: see *A.-G. Can. v. Canard*, [1976] 1 S.C.R. 170, 206 per Beetz J., implying the validity of the provision (repealed in 1985) under which a white woman became an "instant Indian" on marrying an Indian man.

[6]Even a full-blooded Indian does not necessarily have Indian status under the Indian Act. His or her ancestors may not have belonged to the charter group for whom a

are also "Indians" within the meaning of s. 91(24), although they are not governed by the Indian Act.[7]

The Inuit people are also outside the reserve system, and are therefore not covered by the Indian Act definition, but they have been held to be "Indians" within the meaning of s. 91(24).[8] There are about 50,000 Inuit people in Canada.

The Métis people, who originated in the west from intermarriage between French Canadian men and Indian women during the fur trade period, received "half-breed" land grants in lieu of any right to live on reserves, and were accordingly excluded from the charter group from whom Indian status devolved. There are about 200,000 Métis in Canada. Although the prevailing view of commentators was that the Métis must also be "Indians" within the meaning of s. 91(24),[9] the federal government had usually responded to claims by Métis for legislation by saying that it had no authority over them. And, when Métis turned to provincial governments, they were often refused on the basis that the issue was a federal one. The effect of this buck-passing was that the Métis were deprived of funding, programs and services that were recognized by all governments as needed.[10] In 1999, in *Daniels v. Canada* (2016),[11] Métis plaintiffs brought an action for a declaration "that Métis and non-status Indians are 'Indians' under s. 91(24) of the Constitution Act, 1867". The Supreme Court of Canada granted the declaration. Abella J., who wrote the opinion of the Court, refused to provide a definition of Métis or of non-status Indians, saying that there was no consensus on who is considered Métis or non-status Indian "nor need there be": some mixed-ancestry communities identify as Métis, others as Indian; some non-status Indians regard themselves as Indian, others as Métis; but the "definitional ambiguities" do not preclude a determination as to whether the two groups, however they are defined, are within the scope of s. 91(24).[12] She held "that 'Indians' in s. 91(24) includes *all* Aboriginal peoples, including non-status Indians and Métis."[13] Since there was not much room for doubt about the "Indian" status of non-status Indians, she elaborated only on the Métis question. She pointed out that "Indians" "has long been used as a general term referring to all Indigenous peoples,

---

reserve was established or with whom a treaty was made. Even a "treaty Indian", whose ancestors signed a treaty, could lack status under the Indian Act, because status could be lost in a variety of ways. See generally J. Woodward, Native Law (Carswell, Toronto, 1989), 5–12. As well, some full-blooded Indians were classified as "half-breeds".

[7]So held in *Daniels v. Can.*, [2016] 1 S.C.R. 99, 2016 SCC 12, para. 50.

[8]*Re Eskimos*, [1939] S.C.R. 104.

[9]This was the view expressed in an earlier edition of this book, and quoted by Abella J. at the beginning of her discussion of the status of the Métis: *Daniels v. Can.*, [2016] 1 S.C.R. 99, 2016 SCC 12, para. 22.

[10]See *Daniels v. Can.*, [2016] 1 S.C.R. 99, 2016 SCC 12, paras. 13–14.

[11]*Daniels v. Can.*, [2016] 1 S.C.R. 99, 2016 SCC 12. Abella J. wrote the opinion of the Court.

[12]*Daniels v. Can.*, [2016] 1 S.C.R. 99, 2016 SCC 12, paras. 17–19.

[13]*Daniels v. Can.*, [2016] 1 S.C.R. 99, 2016 SCC 12, para. 19 (emphasis in original).

including mixed-ancestry communities like the Métis." She also pointed out that a major goal of confederation was to expand British North America westward across Rupert's Land and the North-West Territories and to build a national railway over that land. That goal could not easily have been achieved without authority over the Métis people who were a big presence on the prairies.[14] Finally, she held that the case-law on the meaning of "Indians", while not providing a single definitive answer, was generally consistent with recognition of the Métis as Indians.[15]

The Parliament of Canada is, of course, under no obligation to legislate to the full limit of its authority,[16] and, with respect to Indians, it has certainly not done so: non-status Indians, Métis and Inuit are not governed by the Indian Act.[17]

A risk of the *Daniels* decision, holding that the Métis people are within federal jurisdiction under the s. 92(24) power over "Indians", is that provincial laws dealing with Métis might be struck down as unconstitutional. For example, Alberta has enacted the Métis Settlements Act and related laws setting aside land in the province for Métis communities. Are these laws now unconstitutional? This issue did not have to be considered in *Daniels*, but Abella J. went out of her way to reassert the Court's belief that "courts should favour, where possible, the ordinary operation of statutes enacted by *both* levels of government", and added that "federal authority under s. 91(24) does not bar valid provincial schemes that do not impair the core of the 'Indian' power".[18] It is safe to assume that challenges on federalism grounds to provincial laws dealing with Métis are unlikely to be successful.

What kinds of laws may be made in relation to Indians? The federal Parliament has taken the broad view that it may legislate for Indians on matters which otherwise lie outside its legislative competence, and on which it could not legislate for non-Indians. The most conspicuous examples are the provisions of the Indian Act that govern succession to the property of deceased Indians. There are also provisions for the administration of the property of mentally incompetent Indians and infant Indians, and provisions for the education of Indian children. Whether these provisions are valid or not is of course a question of

---

[14] *Daniels v. Can.*, [2016] 1 S.C.R. 99, 2016 SCC 12, paras. 25–26.

[15] *Daniels v. Can.*, [2016] 1 S.C.R. 99, 2016 SCC 12, paras. 38–49. The one discordant note was provided by *R. v. Blais*, [2003] 2 S.C.R. 236, which held that a reference to "Indians" in Manitoba's Natural Resources Transfer Agreement did not include Métis, although at para. 36, the Court expressly left open the question of whether the same interpretation should be given to s. 91(24). Abella J. distinguished this case (para. 45) on the basis that the interpretation of a constitutional agreement would not necessarily be the same as the interpretation of the Constitution.

[16] *Daniels v. Can.*, [2016] 1 S.C.R. 99, 2016 SCC 12, para. 15.

[17] The guarantees of native rights in ss. 25 and 35 of the Constitution Act, 1982 (discussed later in this chapter) use the phrase "aboriginal peoples of Canada", which is defined in s. 35(2) as including "the Indian, Inuit and Métis peoples of Canada". The *Daniels* case confirms that "Indians" in s. 91(24) encompasses the same people.

[18] *Daniels v. Can.*, [2016] 1 S.C.R. 99, 2016 SCC 12, para. 51 (emphasis in original).

characterization: are they in pith and substance in relation to Indians, or in relation to succession or property or education? Lysyk rightly points out that this inquiry "will not be concluded by the fact that the enactment is limited in its application to a class of persons mentioned in the B.N.A. Act",[19] and he expresses doubt as to the validity of the Indian Act's forays into the law of property.

If s. 91(24) merely authorized Parliament to make laws for Indians which it could make for non-Indians, then the provision would be unnecessary. It seems likely, therefore, that the courts would uphold laws which could be rationally related to intelligible Indian policies, even if the laws would ordinarily be outside federal competence. This is not to deny Lysyk's caveat about the danger of assuming that a law which applies only to Indians is a law "in relation to" Indians. For example, a law which stipulated a special speed limit for Indians driving automobiles on public highways would be hard to sustain as an "Indian" law, because it does not seem to bear any relationship to any intelligible legislative policy in regard to Indians. But laws in regard to Indian property and Indian education have traditionally been part of federal Indian policy, and could probably be justified as aiming at peculiarly Indian concerns.[20] Whether such laws are wise or unwise is of course a much-controverted question, but it is not relevant to their constitutional validity.

§ 28:3 Lands reserved for the Indians

Section 91(24), by its second branch, confers on the federal Parliament legislative power over "lands reserved for the Indians". This phrase[1] obviously includes the lands set aside as Indian reserves in various ways[2] before and after confederation. However, it also includes the huge

---

[19]K.M. Lysyk, "The Unique Constitutional Position of the Canadian Indian" (1967) 45 Can. Bar Rev. 513, 533–534. On singling out, see ch. 15, Judicial Review on Federal Grounds.

[20]The succession provisions were upheld in *A.-G. Can. v. Canard*, [1976] 1 S.C.R. 170, where there was a distribution-of-powers challenge as well as a bill-of-rights challenge. This is an important holding, because the succession provisions are among the few provisions that deal with off-reserve property. It has been argued, however, that the off-reserve public drunkenness provisions (repealed in 1985) were unconstitutional (as well as in conflict with the Canadian Bill of Rights) because the racial classification was not reasonable in that context: P.N. McDonald, "Equality before the Law and the Indian Act" (1977) 3 Dalhousie L.J. 726. In *Brown v. The Queen* (1980), 107 D.L.R. (3d) 705 (B.C.C.A.), the Indian Act exemption from tax for personal property situated on a reserve was upheld in its application to provincial tax, following *Canard*.

[Section 28:3]

[1]For discussion, see La Forest, Natural Resources and Public Property under the Canadian Constitution (1969), ch. 7; J. Woodward, Native Law (Carswell, Toronto, 1989), ch. 8.

[2]The creation of reserves is a prerogative power that is "usually" exercised by the Governor in Council, although reserves can also be created by a duly authorized agent of the Crown: *Ross River Dena Council Band v. Can.*, [2002] 2 S.C.R. 816, paras. 63–66 (no

area of land recognized by the Royal Proclamation of 1763[3] as "reserved" for the Indians, that is, all land within the territory covered by the Proclamation that was in the possession of the Indians and that had not been ceded to the Crown. In *Delgamuukw v. British Columbia* (1997),[4] the Supreme Court of Canada went even further, holding that the phrase extends to all "lands held pursuant to aboriginal title". For that reason, only the federal Parliament had the power to extinguish aboriginal title.[5]

A grant of legislative power does not carry with it proprietary rights over the subject matter of the power.[6] In the *St. Catherine's Milling* case (1889),[7] the Privy Council held that lands reserved for the Indians were not among the properties transferred to the Dominion by the property provisions of the Constitution Act, 1867.[8] Accordingly, the underlying title to the land remained in the Crown in right of the province.[9] The title of the provincial Crown is subject to the aboriginal rights of the Indians,[10] and those rights, along with other matters pertaining to the control and administration of the reserves, are subject to the legislative authority of the federal Parliament.[11] But if the Indians surrender their rights over particular lands, which they can only do to the Crown, then full title to the lands is assumed by the province, not the Dominion.[12]

---

reserve created).

[3]R.S.C. 1985, Appendix II, No. 1. The Royal Proclamation of 1763 is briefly described in ch. 2, Reception, under heading § 2:6, "Ontario and Quebec". With respect to Indians, the Proclamation recognized their rights to unceded lands in their possession, and established that the rights could be ceded only to the Crown.

[4]*Delgamuukw v. British Columbia*, [1997] 3 S.C.R. 1010, para. 74 per Lamer C.J. for majority.

[5]See § 28:21, "Aboriginal title", and § 28:22, "Extinguishment of aboriginal rights".

[6]See ch. 29, Public Property, under heading § 29:4, "Legislative power and proprietary interests".

[7]*St. Catherine's Milling and Lumber Co. v. The Queen* (1888), 14 App. Cas. 46.

[8]The property provisions are discussed in ch. 29, Public Property, under heading § 29:1, "Distribution of public property".

[9]La Forest, Natural Resources and Public Property under the Canadian Constitution (1969), 113–114.

[10]As to the nature of aboriginal rights, see §§ 28:18 to 28:22, "Aboriginal rights".

[11]Federal and provincial legislative authority is now limited by s. 35 of the Constitution Act, 1982, discussed later in this chapter.

[12]*St. Catherine's Milling and Lumber Co. v. The Queen* (1889), 14 App. Cas. 46; *A.-G. Can. v. A.-G. Ont.* (Indian Annuities) [1897] A.C. 199; *Smith v. The Queen*, [1983] 1 S.C.R. 554. The rule is otherwise in the prairie provinces, where the Dominion retained title to public lands until the Natural Resources Agreements of 1930; those Agreements, while generally transferring public lands to the provinces, provided for reserve lands to continue as federal lands after 1930, even including reserves established after 1930. In the other provinces, except for Quebec, Prince Edward Island and Newfoundland (although there are no reserves in Newfoundland), the provinces have entered into agreements with the Dominion, granting the Dominion the right to manage, sell and lease surrendered lands on reserves. The agreements and other instruments relative to the ownership and management of reserve lands are listed in D.E. Sanders, Legal Aspects of

§ 28:4 Canadian Bill of Rights

The Canadian Bill of Rights, which is the subject of ch. 35, applies only to federal laws.[1] It contains, in s. 1(b), a guarantee of "equality before the law", and it specifically forbids "discrimination by reason of race".

The federal Indian Act[2] appears on its face to offend the guarantee of equality in the Canadian Bill of Rights. Yet special laws for Indians and Indian reserves are clearly contemplated by s. 91(24) of the Constitution Act, 1867. Indeed, legislation enacted in relation to "Indians"—the first branch of s. 91(24)—must normally be confined to Indians, that is to say, it must employ a racial classification,[3] in order to be constitutional. Legislation in relation to "lands reserved for the Indians"—the second branch of s. 91(24)—need not necessarily employ a racial classification; it could apply to anyone on a reserve.[4]

In *R. v. Drybones* (1969),[5] the Supreme Court of Canada held that the use of the racial classification "Indian" in s. 94 of the Indian Act, which made it an offence for an Indian to be intoxicated off a reserve, violated the equality guarantee in the Canadian Bill of Rights. The majority of the Court did not even notice the problem that the racial classification "Indian" seemed to be requisite to the constitutional validity of s. 94, although Pigeon J. emphasized this point in dissent. This decision cast doubt on all of the provisions of the Indian Act,[6] and on the whole principle of a special regime of law for Indians. Later cases, however,

---

Economic Development on Indian Reserve Lands (Dept. of Indian and Northern Affairs, Ottawa, 1976), Appendix A.

[Section 28:4]

[1]It may apply to provincial laws that are incorporated by reference by s. 88 of the Indian Act (discussed later in this chapter): *Jack and Charlie v. The Queen*, [1985] 2 S.C.R. 332, 338 (obiter dictum).

[2]R.S.C. 1985, c. 1-5.

[3]Note, however, the leeway accorded to the federal Parliament in defining the term "Indian": § 28:2 note 5.

[4]It is of course arguable that any law that is applicable only on a reserve, even if literally applicable to anyone, is so predominantly applicable to Indians that, in substance if not in form, the law does employ a racial classification. This argument was accepted in *R. v. Hayden* (1983), 3 D.L.R. (4th) 361 (Man. C.A.).

[5]*R. v. Drybones*, [1970] S.C.R. 282.

[6]A distinction could be drawn between those provisions that (like s. 94—the off-reserve drunkenness offence) applied only to Indians, and those provisions that (like s. 96—the on-reserve drunkenness offence) applied on a reserve to non-Indians as well as Indians. At first, s. 96 was upheld on this basis: *R. v. Whiteman (No. 1)*, [1971] 2 W.W.R. 316 (Sask. Dist. Ct.). In *R. v. Hayden* (1983), 3 D.L.R. (4th) 361 (Man. C.A.), s. 96 was struck down on the ground that, although s. 96 was not confined to Indians, since Indians were the "predominant residents of reservations", s. 96 was just as discriminatory as s. 94, and *Drybones* should be followed. In *R. v. Lefthand* (1985), 19 D.L.R. (4th) 720 (Alta. C.A.), s. 96 was upheld, following *Whiteman* and disapproving *Hayden*. Sections 94 and 96 were repealed in 1985.

have tended to confine *Drybones* "to its own facts",[7] and it now appears that the special regime of law for Indians is not threatened by the decision.[8]

§ 28:5 Charter of Rights

The Charter of Rights, by s. 15, also contains an equality guarantee. The Indian Act has not yet been challenged under s. 15 by reason of its use of the "Indian" classification. It seems likely, however, that the Constitution's various recognitions of Indian special status, reinforced by the long history of the reserve system, and by the desire of aboriginal peoples to preserve their identity and culture through some form of special legal status, would lead the courts to reject an equality challenge, perhaps by recognizing an exception to s. 15, or under the Charter's affirmative action clause (s. 15(2)), or under the Charter's general limitation clause (s. 1), or under the Charter's saving clause for "aboriginal, treaty or other rights or freedoms that pertain to the aboriginal peoples of Canada" (s. 25).[1] In *Ermineskin Indian Band and Nation v. Canada* (2009),[2] the special constitutional status of Indians was ignored by the Supreme Court in a s. 15 challenge by Indian bands to the investment provisions of the Indian Act, which precluded external investment of Indian funds held by the Crown. However, the Court rejected the challenge on the ground that the restrictions entailed prudent investment practices that were not "discriminatory".

Needless to say, the Indian Act, like any other statute, is vulnerable to attack if it offends s. 15 for any reason other than its use of the "Indian" classification. For example, in *Corbiere v. Canada* (1999),[3] the Supreme Court of Canada struck down the provision of the Indian Act that made residence on the reserve a requirement for voting in band elections. The Court held that the distinction between Indians who lived on the reserve (and could vote) and Indians who lived off the reserve (and could not vote) was a breach of s. 15. On the other hand, in *Lovelace*

---

[7] *A.-G. Can. v. Lavell*, [1974] S.C.R. 1349 (Indian Act status provision upheld); *A.-G. Can. v. Canard*, [1976] 1 S.C.R. 170 (Indian Act succession provision upheld). For more discussion of the relationship between s. 91(24) and equality, see P.W. Hogg, Comment (1974) 52 Can. Bar Rev. 263; D.E. Sanders, "The Renewal of Indian Special Status" in Bayefsky and Eberts (eds.), Equality Rights and the Canadian Charter of Rights and Freedoms (1985), ch. 12. See also ch. 55, Equality under heading §§ 55:23 to 55:27, "Race".

[8] Special status for the aboriginal peoples has been given constitutional recognition by ss. 25, 35 and 35.1 of the Constitution Act, 1982, discussed later in this chapter, under heading §§ 28:13 to 28:16, "Aboriginal rights".

[Section 28:5]

[1] See ch. 55, Equality, under headings § 55:34, "Race in s. 91(24)", and § 55:39, "Race". Section 25 is discussed later in § 28:41, "Section 25".

[2] *Ermineskin Indian Band and Nation v. Canada*, [2009] 1 S.C.R. 222.

[3] *Corbiere v. Canada*, [1999] 2 S.C.R. 203.

v. Ontario (2000),[4] the Supreme Court of Canada rejected a challenge to the distribution of the Casino Rama gambling profits that was limited to communities registered as bands under the Indian Act. The Court held that the exclusion of non-status bands from the distribution of the profits was not a breach of s. 15.

§ 28:6 Treaties

Before 1982, when s. 35 of the Constitution Act, 1982 was adopted, it was clear that federal legislative power over Indians and lands reserved for the Indians was not limited by the terms of treaties entered into with other countries or with Indian tribes or bands. So far as treaties with other countries are concerned, the general rule is that they have no effect on the internal law of Canada unless they are implemented by legislation.[1] Thus, although a treaty entered into with the United States exempted the Indians from payment of customs duties at the Canadian border, the Supreme Court of Canada held that customs duties were still payable by the Indians, because the Customs Act did not include the agreed-upon exemption.[2]

So far as treaties with Indian tribes or bands are concerned,[3] before 1982 they too could not stand against inconsistent federal[4] legislation. Thus, although a treaty entered into with certain Indian tribes guaranteed their right to hunt for food at any time of the year, the Supreme Court of Canada held that the Indians were still prohibited by federal law from shooting migratory birds out of season, because the Migratory Birds Convention Act did not include the agreed-upon exemption.[5]

Section 35 of the Constitution Act, 1982 now gives constitutional protection to rights created by treaties entered into with Indian tribes or bands and perhaps to rights created by provisions in international treaties. Section 35 operates as a limitation on the powers of the federal

---

[4]*Lovelace v. Ontario*, [2000] 1 S.C.R. 950.

[Section 28:6]

[1]See ch. 11, Treaties.

[2]*Francis v. The Queen*, [1956] S.C.R. 618; the decision is criticized by K.M. Lysyk, "The Unique Constitutional Position of the Canadian Indian" (1967) 45 Can. Bar Rev. 513, 527–528, on the basis that the Customs Act could have been construed as not violating the treaty.

[3]The legal status of these treaties is discussed in §§ 28:23 to 28:27, "Treaty rights".

[4]The treaties are effective against provincial legislation, by virtue of s. 88 of the Indian Act, which makes provincial laws "subject to the terms of any treaty". However, s. 88 is inapplicable to federal laws: *R. v. George*, [1966] S.C.R. 267. Section 88 of the Indian Act is discussed later in this chapter in §§ 28:13 to 28:16, "Section 88 of the Indian Act".

[5]*Sikyea v. The Queen*, [1964] S.C.R. 642; *R. v. George*, [1966] S.C.R. 267. For other cases affirming the effectiveness of the Migratory Birds Convention Act, see *Daniels v. White*, [1968] S.C.R. 517; *R. v. Catagas* (1977), 81 D.L.R. (3d) 396 (Man. C.A.).

Parliament, as well as the provincial Legislatures. Section 35 is the subject of a later section of this chapter.[6]

II. PROVINCIAL LEGISLATIVE POWER

§ 28:7 Application of provincial laws

The general rule is that provincial laws apply to Indians and lands reserved for the Indians.[1] In *R. v. Hill* (1907),[2] the Ontario Court of Appeal held that a provincial law confining the practice of medicine to qualified physicians applied to Indians; an Indian was convicted of the offence of the unauthorized practice of medicine. The offence in *Hill* did not take place on a reserve, but the result would have been the same if it had. In *Four B Manufacturing v. United Garment Workers* (1979),[3] the Supreme Court of Canada held that provincial labour law applied to a shoe-manufacturing business, which was located on a reserve, which was owned (through a corporation) by Indians, which employed mainly Indians, and which had been funded by the Department of Indian Affairs. In *R. v. Francis* (1988),[4] the Court held that provincial traffic laws applied to an Indian driving a vehicle on an Indian reserve.[5] In *Paul v. British Columbia* (2003),[6] the Court held that British Columbia's Forest Practices Act applied to an Indian who had been cutting timber in breach of a prohibition in the Act; the Act applied of its own force, and s. 88 of the Indian Act (discussed in the next section of this chapter) was not needed to make the Act applicable.

These decisions establish that the provincial Legislatures have the

---

[6]§§ 28:29 to 28:39, "Section 35".

[Section 28:7]

[1]See generally K.M. Lysyk, "The Unique Constitutional Position of the Canadian Indian" (1967) 45 Can. Bar Rev. 513; K.M. Lysyk "Constitutional Developments relating to Indians and Indian Lands" in Law Society of Upper Canada, The Constitution and the Future of Canada (Special Lectures, 1978), 201; D. Sanders, "Prior Claims: Aboriginal People in the Constitution of Canada" in Beck and Bernier (eds.), Canada and the New Constitution (1983), vol. 1, 225; J. Woodward, Native Law (Carswell, Toronto, 1989); Beaudoin, La Constitution du Canada (3rd ed., 2004), ch. 15; R. A. Reiter, The Fundamental Principles of Indian Law (First Nations Resource Council, 1993, looseleaf); K. McNeil, "Aboriginal Title and the Division of Powers" (1998) 61 Sask. L. Rev. 431; P. Hughes, "Indians and Lands Reserved for the Indians" (1983) 21 Osgoode Hall L.J. 82.

[2]*R. v. Hill* (1907), 15 O.L.R. 406 (C.A.).

[3]*Four B Manufacturing v. United Garment Workers*, [1980] 1 S.C.R. 1031. Folld. in *NIL/TU,O Child and Family Services Society v. B.C.G.S.E.U.*, [2010] 2 S.C.R. 696, described below under heading § 28:9 "Second exception: Indianness".

[4]*R. v. Francis*, [1988] 1 S.C.R. 1025.

[5]None of the three decisions relied on s. 88 of the Indian Act, discussed in the next section of this chapter. Section 88 did not exist when the *Hill* case was decided; s. 88 was referred to but not relied upon in the *Four B* case; s. 88 was expressly held to be inapplicable in the *Francis* case. According to *Dick v. The Queen*, [1985] 2 S.C.R. 309, s. 88 has no application to provincial laws that can apply to Indians of their own force.

[6]*Paul v. British Columbia*, [2003] 2 S.C.R. 585, para. 12 per Bastarache J. for the Court, explicitly making the point that the Act was applicable "to the extent it does not touch on the 'core of Indianness' ".

power to make their laws applicable to Indians and on Indian reserves, so long as the law is in relation to a matter coming within a provincial head of power. The situation of Indians and Indian reserves is thus no different from that of aliens, banks, federally-incorporated companies and interprovincial undertakings. These, too, are subjects of federal legislative power, but they still have to pay provincial taxes, and obey provincial traffic laws, health and safety requirements, social and economic regulations and the myriad of other provincial laws which apply to them in common with other similarly-situated residents of the province.[7]

The *Four B* and *Francis* cases definitely rejected the theory that Indian reserves are federal "enclaves" from which provincial laws are excluded. This theory was advanced by Laskin as a professor in his casebook,[8] and in a number of his judicial opinions as Chief Justice—all of them in dissent.[9] The theory was always implausible, because it involved a distinction between the first and second branches of s. 91(24) for which there is no textual warrant, and it placed the second branch ("lands reserved for the Indians") in a privileged position enjoyed by no other federal subject matter.[10] It is plain that there is no constitutional distinction between "Indians" and "lands reserved for the Indians", and that provincial laws may apply to both subject matters.

There are five exceptions to the general rule that provincial laws apply to Indians and lands reserved for the Indians.

§ 28:8 First exception: singling out

The first exception is singling out. A provincial law that singled out Indians or Indian reserves for special treatment would run the risk of being classified as a law in relation to Indians or Indian reserves; and, if so classified, the law would be invalid.[1]

---

[7]See ch. 15, Judicial Review on Federal Grounds, under §§ 15:16 to 15:21, "Interjurisdictional immunity".

[8]Laskin, Canadian Constitutional Law (4th ed. rev., 1975), 523 ("provincial laws are inapplicable on a reservation"). This position has been abandoned in the 5th edition by N. Finkelstein, the editor.

[9]*Cardinal v. A.-G. Alta.*, [1974] S.C.R. 695; *Natural Parents v. Superintendent of Child Welfare*, [1976] 2 S.C.R. 751 (concurring opinion, but dissenting on this issue); *Four B Manufacturing v. United Garment Workers*, [1980] 1 S.C.R. 1031.

[10]Laskin, Canadian Constitutional Law (4th ed. rev., 1975), 529, appeared to accord a similar status to the federal power over "the public debt and property" (s. 91(1A)). The enclave theory has also been rejected in that context: *Construction Montcalm v. Minimum Wage Comm.*, [1979] 1 S.C.R. 754 (Laskin C.J. dissenting).

[Section 28:8]

[1]*R. v. Sutherland*, [1980] 2 S.C.R. 451, 455 (provincial law struck down); *Dick v. The Queen*, [1985] 2 S.C.R. 309, 322 (obiter dictum); *Leighton v. B.C.* (1989), 57 D.L.R. (4th) 657 (B.C.C.A.) (provincial law struck down); *Kitkatla Band v. B.C.*, [2002] 2 S.C.R. 146, paras. 6768 (obiter dictum); see ch. 15, Judicial Review on Federal Grounds, under heading § 15:6, "Singling out".

§ 28:9 Second exception: Indianness

The second exception to the general rule that provincial laws apply to Indians and lands reserved for the Indians is "Indianness". A provincial law that affects "an integral part of primary federal jurisdiction over Indians and lands reserved for the Indians"[1] will be inapplicable to Indians and lands reserved for the Indians, even though the law is one of general application that is otherwise within provincial competence. This vague exception, which has been framed as precluding laws that impair the "status or capacity" of Indians,[2] or that affect "Indianness",[3] has its analogy in the immunity from provincial laws that impair a vital part of undertakings within federal jurisdiction; it is a branch of interjurisdictional immunity.[4]

There were cases that held that the Indianness exception precluded provincial laws that impaired aboriginal rights[5] or treaty rights:[6] such laws were assumed to be within the "core" of the federal power over "Indians, and lands reserved for the Indians", and therefore off limits to the provinces. In *Tsilhqot'in Nation v. British Columbia* (2014),[7] the Supreme Court of Canada overruled these cases. McLachlin C.J., who wrote for the Court, held that the doctrine of interjurisdictional immunity had to yield to s. 35 of the Constitution Act, 1982, under which "the existing aboriginal and treaty rights of the aboriginal peoples of Canada are recognized and affirmed". In *R. v Sparrow* (1990),[8] s. 35 had been interpreted as a constitutional guarantee of aboriginal and treaty

---

[Section 28:9]

[1] *Four B Manufacturing v. United Garment Workers*, [1980] 1 S.C.R. 1031, 1047 per Beetz J.

[2] This is the phraseology used by Dickson J. in *Kruger and Manuel v. The Queen*, [1978] 1 S.C.R. 104, 110.

[3] This is the phraseology used by Laskin C.J. in *Natural Parents v. Superintendent of Child Welfare*, [1967] 2 S.C.R. 751, 760–761, and by Beetz J. in *Dick v. The Queen*, [1985] 2 S.C.R. 309, 326.

[4] See ch. 15, Judicial Review on Federal Grounds, under §§ 15:16 to 15:21, "Interjurisdictional immunity".

[5] *Delgamuukw v. B.C.*, [1997] 3 S.C.R. 1010, para. 178 per Lamer C.J. for the Court on this issue. With respect to aboriginal rights (but not treaty rights), the disability is partially removed by s. 88 of the Indian Act (§§ 28:13 to 28:16), which however would not permit an extinguishment of aboriginal rights, because s. 88 "does not evince the requisite clear and plain intent to extinguish aboriginal rights": *Delgamuukw v. B.C.*, [1997] 3 S.C.R. 1010, para. 183. Since 1982, any effect on aboriginal rights (which would have to be through s. 88) would be blocked by s. 35 of the Constitution Act, 1982, unless the affecting law satisfied the *Sparrow* test of justification. See also *Paul v. B.C.*, [2003] 2 S.C.R. 585, paras. 10, 24, 49 (to the same effect).

[6] *Simon v. The Queen*, [1985] 2 S.C.R. 387, 411; *R. v. Sundown*, [1999] 1 S.C.R. 393, para. 47; *R. v. Morris*, [2006] 2 S.C.R. 915, para. 43. With respect to treaty rights (but not aboriginal rights), the disability is reinforced by s. 88 of the Indian Act (§§ 28:13 to 28:16), which is expressly made "subject to the terms of any treaty".

[7] *Tsilhqot'in Nation v. British Columbia*, [2014] 2 S.C.R. 257, 2014 SCC 44, para. 150. McLachlin C.J. wrote the opinion of the Court.

[8] *R. v Sparrow*, [1990] 1 S.C.R. 1075.

rights, that is, a restriction on legislative power; in *Tsilhqot'in*, McLachlin C.J. held that it was not appropriate to think of a restriction on legislative power as part of the core of the power. *Sparrow* had also decided that s. 35 authorized a framework of justification for limits on aboriginal and treaty rights, which called for a "compelling and substantial" legislative objective and was generally similar to the *Oakes* framework for the justification under s. 1 of limits on Charter rights.[9] McLachlin C.J. held that the *Sparrow* framework should be applied to provincial as well as federal laws. She pointed out that the effect of applying interjurisdictional immunity to aboriginal and treaty rights would be to preclude the provinces from enacting any law that impinged on aboriginal or treaty rights, even if the law was a reasonable and justifiable regulation of a matter otherwise within exclusive provincial jurisdiction (the case concerned a provincial forest). This would lead to gaps in regulation (of provincial forests, for example) that would be very difficult to fill. McLachlin C.J. concluded that the *Sparrow* framework "is fairer and more practical from a policy perspective than the blanket inapplicability imposed by the doctrine of interjurisdictional immunity".[10] The result is that provincial laws do apply to aboriginal and treaty rights, although any infringement of those rights would have to serve a compelling and substantial objective and otherwise satisfy the *Sparrow* framework of justification.

The holding in *Tsilhqot'in*, that interjurisdictional immunity did not apply to provincial laws affecting aboriginal and treaty rights, did not cast doubt on the decisions that had applied interjurisdictional immunity to provincial laws affecting other aspects of the federal power over Indians and lands reserved for the Indians. There have been a number of these decisions. For example, provincial laws cannot take away Indian status. In *Natural Parents v. Superintendent of Child Welfare* (1975),[11] the Supreme Court of Canada held that, while provincial adoption law would permit white parents to adopt an Indian child, the provincial law had to be read down so as not to deprive the child of his Indian status.[12] Provincial laws cannot affect the right to possession of land on an Indian reserve,[13] and probably cannot affect at least some uses of land on a reserve. Hunting on a reserve is such a significant element of traditional Indian ways that it should probably be free of provincial regulation.[14] However, it is less obvious that the construction of housing and other buildings on a reserve should be free

---

[9]For full discussion, see § 28:34, "Recognized and affirmed".

[10]*Tsilhqot'in Nation v. British Columbia*, [2014] 2 S.C.R. 257, 2014 SCC 44, para. 150.

[11]*Natural Parents v. Superintendent of Child Welfare*, [1976] 2 S.C.R. 751.

[12]This was the end result, although a variety of opinions reached the result by a variety of routes. The protection for Indian status was affirmed, obiter, by Beetz J. in *Four B Manufacturing v. United Garment Workers*, [1980] 1 S.C.R. 1031, 1047.

[13]*Derrickson v. Derrickson*, [1986] 1 S.C.R. 285 (division of assets on divorce or separation); *Paul v. Paul*, [1986] 1 S.C.R. 306 (occupancy of family residence).

[14]So held in *R. v. Jim* (1915), 26 C.C.C. 236 (B.C.S.C.); *R. v. Isaac* (1976), 13 N.S.R.

of provincial regulation, although there are decisions of provincial courts of appeal that so decide.[15]

The Indianness exception was relied on in *Lovelace v. Ontario* (2000)[16] to challenge a provincial programme that sent the profits from a casino located on an Indian reserve to other First Nation communities. The challenge was brought by non-status communities, who were excluded from the programme, and who argued that the province had strayed into the field of exclusive federal jurisdiction by defining which communities counted as "First Nations" for the casino programme. The argument was that the exclusion of non-status aboriginal communities undermined their Indianness. The Supreme Court of Canada held that a provincial spending programme that used the definitions of the Indian Act to prescribe its scope did not impair the status or capacity of non-status Indians, did not impair any aboriginal or treaty right, and consequently did not affect Indianness. A challenge based on the equality guarantee of s. 15 was also rejected. The programme was upheld.

The Indianness exception was relied on again in *Kitkatla Band v. British Columbia* (2002)[17] to challenge a provision of British Columbia's Heritage Conservation Act that conferred a discretion on the responsible minister to license the destruction of heritage property. The challenge was prompted by a ministerial decision to license the destruction by a logging company of some "culturally modified trees", which were trees that had been altered in some fashion by Aboriginal people, who had removed some of the bark or a limb (for example) for some traditional use, and who thenceforth attributed cultural significance to the trees. The argument was that the licensing of the destruction of aboriginal heritage property impaired the status or capacity of Aboriginal people, because these artifacts were at "the core of Indianness". The Supreme Court of Canada rejected the argument, holding that the Act was a valid exercise of provincial power over property and civil rights in the prov-

---

(2d) 460 (N.S.A.D.). Query whether hunting by Indians off a reserve is a characteristic of Indianness that is immune from provincial law. Compare *Kruger and Manuel v. The Queen*, [1978] 1 S.C.R. 104 (held, no) with *Dick v. The Queen*, [1985] 2 S.C.R. 309, 320–321 (assuming, without deciding, yes). Of course, in a case where hunting was an aboriginal right or a treaty right, *Tsilhqot'in Nation v. British Columbia*, [2014] 2 S.C.R. 257, 2014 SCC 44, would apply: provincial law could regulate the exercise of the right if the law satisfied the Sparrow framework of justification.

[15] *Surrey Corp. v. Peace Arch Enterprises* (1970), 74 W.W.R. 380 (B.C.C.A.) (zoning and health laws); *Re Whitebear Band Council* (1982), 135 D.L.R. (3d) 128 (Sask. C.A.) (labour law). Compare *Western Industrial Contractors v. Sarcee Developments* (1979), 98 D.L.R. (3d) 424 (Alta. C.A.) (provincial builder's lien applies to leasehold interest on reserve lands); *Re Stony Plain Indian Reserve* (1981), 130 D.L.R. (3d) 636, 652 (Alta. C.A.) (reaffirming *Sarcee*). In *Construction Montcalm v. Minimum Wage Comm.*, [1979] 1 S.C.R. 754, the Supreme Court of Canada held that provincial minimum wage law applied to a construction firm building a runway at an airport. The reasoning of Beetz J. for the majority is difficult to reconcile with the *Peace Arch* and *Whitebear* decisions, because the construction of buildings on a reserve seems only tenuously related to "Indianness".

[16] *Lovelace v. Ontario*, [2000] 1 S.C.R. 950.

[17] *Kitkatla Band v. British Columbia*, [2002] 2 S.C.R. 146.

ince (s. 92(13)). The main purpose of the Act was to protect heritage property, including Aboriginal heritage property, and it was a valid part of the scheme to permit destruction in exceptional cases in pursuit of other social goals. The Court held that the Aboriginal people had not established any aboriginal right or title to the culturally modified trees, which were on Crown land, and, despite the cultural significance of the trees, the application of the Act to the trees did not affect Indianness.[18]

In *Paul v. British Columbia* (2003),[19] the Forest Appeals Commission of British Columbia, an administrative tribunal established under provincial law, was trying a contravention of the province's Forest Practices Code. The defendant, an Indian, claimed that he was exercising an aboriginal right when he cut down trees in a provincial forest in apparent violation of the Code. He argued that the tribunal had no jurisdiction over his case once an aboriginal right was put in issue. The Supreme Court of Canada had decided in a companion case[20] that a provincial administrative tribunal with power to determine questions of law had authority to determine the constitutionality under the Charter of Rights of a potentially applicable law. Did the same rule apply to a determination of aboriginal rights? Aboriginal rights came within the essential core of Indianness. Therefore, it was argued, the province could not empower an administrative tribunal to make a ruling about the existence or applicability of aboriginal rights. The Court rejected this argument on the basis that adjudication was distinct from legislation. To be sure, the province could not legislate to extinguish or alter aboriginal rights, and could not confer on an administrative tribunal the power to extinguish or alter aboriginal rights. But the function conferred on the Forest Appeals Commission (which included the power to decide questions of law) was solely an adjudicative one. The Commission had no authority to extinguish or alter aboriginal rights. It could only determine as a matter of law whether a claimed right existed. The determination would be binding on the parties, of course, but it would not be a precedent that would be binding on other tribunals or courts, and it would be subject to judicial review by a superior court on a standard of correctness. Therefore, the jurisdiction of the Commission could extend to the determination of a claim of aboriginal right without any unconstitutional effect on Indianness. The Court held that the Commission should proceed to determine whether the cutting down of the trees was a valid exercise of an aboriginal right.

In *NIL/TU,O Child and Family Services Society v. B.C.G.S.E.U.* (2010),[21] a child welfare agency had been established by seven First Nations to provide "culturally appropriate" services to the members of the

---

[18]*Kitkatla Band v. British Columbia*, [2002] 2 S.C.R. 146, paras. 70–71.

[19]*Paul v. British Columbia*, [2003] 2 S.C.R. 585.

[20]*Nova Scotia v. Martin*, [2003] 2 S.C.R. 504.

[21]*NIL/TU,O Child and Family Services Society v. B.C.G.S.E.U.*, [2010] 2 S.C.R. 696. Abella J., with the agreement of five others, wrote the majority opinion. McLachlin C.J. and Fish J., with the agreement of one other, wrote a concurring opinion. Folld. in a companion case, *Communications, Energy and Paperworkers Union of Canada v. Native*

First Nations. It was located on one of the reserves, its employees were aboriginal, as were its clients, who were aboriginal people living on the reserves. Its mandate was to serve the distinct cultural, physical and emotional needs of the children and families of the seven First Nations. It received federal funding from the Department of Indian Affairs. The question before the Supreme Court of Canada was whether its labour relations came within federal or provincial jurisdiction, and the Court answered unanimously that the jurisdiction was provincial. The delivery of child welfare services was a matter of provincial jurisdiction. This remained the case even though its work was delivered by and focused on aboriginal people and partially funded by the federal government.[22] For the majority, the fact that the agency was a provincial undertaking was the answer to the question: no inquiry into the "core of Indianness" was called for.[23] For the concurring minority, that inquiry was essential to the disposition of the appeal, but they concluded that the activities of the agency (which did not include adoption) did not "touch on issues of Indian status or rights" and were therefore outside the core of Indianness.[24]

Provincial laws that do affect Indianness cannot apply to Indians of their own force. However, as will be explained in the next section of this chapter, some such laws could become applicable to Indians through s. 88 of the Indian Act, which incorporates by reference provincial laws of general application.

§ 28:10 Third exception: paramountcy

The third exception to the general rule that provincial laws apply to Indians and lands reserved for the Indians is the doctrine of federal paramountcy. If a provincial law is inconsistent with a provision of the Indian Act (or any other federal law), the provincial law is rendered inoperative by the doctrine of federal paramountcy.[1]

§ 28:11 Fourth exception: Natural Resources Agreements

The fourth exception to the general rule that provincial laws apply to Indians and lands reserved for the Indians is a right of Indians to take game and fish for food, which is defined and protected in the three prairie provinces by the "Natural Resources Agreements". Provincial laws cannot deprive Indians of this right. The Natural Resources Agree-

---

Child and Family Services of Toronto, [2010] 2 S.C.R. 737 (same decision, same split of Court).

[22]The Court followed *Four B Manufacturing v. United Garment Workers*, [1980] 1 S.C.R. 1031, for this conclusion.

[23]*NIL/TU,O Child and Family Services Society v. B.C.G.S.E.U.*, [2010] 2 S.C.R. 696, para. 46.

[24]*NIL/TU,O Child and Family Services Society v. B.C.G.S.E.U.*, [2010] 2 S.C.R. 696, para. 76.

[Section 28:10]

[1]Chapter 16, Paramountcy.

ments, which are part of the Constitution of Canada, are discussed in a later section of this chapter.[1]

§ 28:12 Fifth exception: section 35

Section 35 of the Constitution Act, 1982 provides that: "The existing aboriginal and treaty rights of the aboriginal peoples of Canada are hereby recognized and affirmed." Section 35 is not properly regarded as an exception to the general rule that provincial laws apply to Indians and lands reserved for the Indians. As has been explained in the earlier discussion of "Indianness",[1] in *Tsilhqot'in Nation v. British Columbia* (2014),[2] the Supreme Court of Canada held that provincial laws did apply of their own force to aboriginal and treaty rights, but subject to a major constitutional restriction. If a provincial law infringed (limited) an aboriginal or treaty right, the law must serve a "compelling and substantial objective" and satisfy the other elements of the *Sparrow* framework for the justification of limits on the s. 35 rights.[3] What had been unclear before *Tsilhqot'in* was whether the *Sparrow* framework applied to both federal and provincial laws (as some cases had decided), or whether provincial laws (however reasonable and justifiable) were categorically barred from any impact on s. 35 rights (as other cases had decided). *Tsilhqot'in* overruled the latter line of cases, upheld the former line of cases, and made clear that provincial laws applied to aboriginal and treaty rights subject to the constitutional limits laid down in *Sparrow*.

III. SECTION 88 OF THE INDIAN ACT

§ 28:13 Text of s. 88

Section 88 of the Indian Act, which was first enacted in 1951 (it was then s. 87), provides as follows:

> Subject to the terms of any treaty and any other Act of the Parliament of Canada, all laws of general application from time to time in force in any province are applicable to and in respect of Indians in the province, except to the extent that such laws are inconsistent with this Act or any order, rule, regulation or by-law made thereunder, and except to the extent that such laws make provision for any matter for which provision is made by or under this Act.

[Section 28:11]

[1] § 28:17, "Natural Resources Agreements".

[Section 28:12]

[1] § 28:9, "Second exception: Indianness".

[2] *Tsilhqot'in Nation v. British Columbia*, [2014] 2 S.C.R. 257, 2014 SCC 44.

[3] The *Sparrow* framework is explained in § 28:34, "Recognized and affirmed".

Section 88 makes clear that provincial[1] "laws of general application" apply to "Indians".[2] The section makes no reference to lands reserved for the Indians, but there is no doubt that the section extends to Indians on a reserve.[3] Section 88 operates as a federal adoption, or incorporation by reference, of provincial laws, making the provincial laws applicable as part of federal law. This technique is valid, despite the fact that it comes close to a delegation of federal legislative power to the provinces.[4]

§ 28:14 Laws of general application

What is meant by the phrase "laws of general application" in s. 88 of the Indian Act? The phrase certainly excludes provincial laws that single out Indians for special treatment. As noted earlier, such laws are likely to be classified as being in relation to Indians and therefore as invalid.[1] Section 88 does not invigorate such laws.

Does the phrase "laws of general application" also exclude laws that, while not singling out Indians for special treatment, have a specially severe effect on Indians by affecting Indianness? As noted earlier, such laws cannot apply to Indians of their own force.[2] The Supreme Court of Canada in 1978 held that s. 88 did not make provincial laws affecting Indianness applicable to Indians.[3] Since other provincial laws of general application would apply to Indians of their own force anyway,[4] this interpretation made s. 88 merely declaratory of the general constitutional

[Section 28:13]

[1]Section 88 does not apply to federal laws, with the important consequence (before the adoption of s. 35 of the Constitution Act, 1982) that Indian treaties do not take precedence over federal laws. As noted later in the text, the opening words of s. 88 accord precedence to Indian treaties over provincial laws.

[2]Because s. 88 is part of the Indian Act, the word "Indians" excludes non-status Indians, and the Inuit and Métis peoples: see § 28:2, "Indians".

[3]La Forest, Natural Resources and Public Property under the Canadian Constitution (1969), 179. Query, however, whether s. 88 would incorporate a provincial law that applied to lands reserved for the Indians: *Derrickson v. Derrickson*, [1986] 1 S.C.R. 285, 299 (leaving the question open); K. McNeil, "Aboriginal Title and Section 88 of the Indian Act" (2000) 34 U.B.C.L.R. 159 (arguing that s. 88 cannot incorporate provincial laws that relate to Indian lands).

[4]See ch. 14, Delegation, under heading §§ 14:12 to 14:14, "Referential legislation". See also *Wewaykum Indian Band v. Can.*, [2002] 4 S.C.R. 245, paras. 115–116 (upholding Federal Court Act's adoption of provincial limitation statutes, which "as federal law" could extinguish aboriginal cause of action).

[Section 28:14]

[1]This is the first exception to the general rule that provincial laws apply to Indians: see heading § 28:8 "First exception: singling out". A valid provincial law of special application to Indians would not be covered by s. 88, but would be applicable of its own force: K.M. Lysyk, "The Unique Constitutional Position of the Canadian Indian" (1967) 45 Can. Bar Rev. 513, 536–539.

[2]This is the second exception to the general rule that provincial laws apply to Indians: text accompanying § 28:8 note 1, above.

[3]*Kruger and Manuel v. The Queen*, [1978] 1 S.C.R. 104, 110.

[4]This is the general rule: text accompanying § 28:7 note 1, above.

position. Section 88 did not expand the body of provincial law that applied to Indians.

In *Dick v. The Queen* (1985),[5] the Court changed its mind about the scope of s. 88. Beetz J. for the Court held that s. 88 did apply to provincial laws that affected Indianness by impairing the status or capacity of Indians. These were the only laws to which s. 88 needed to apply, because these were the laws that could not apply to Indians of their own force. Indeed, Beetz J. held, these were the only laws to which s. 88 applied. Those "provincial laws that can be applied to Indians without touching their Indianness, like traffic legislation", applied to Indians of their own force. Section 88 was not needed to make those laws applicable to Indians, and s. 88 should be interpreted as not extending to those laws.[6]

The *Dick* interpretation of "laws of general application" in s. 88 has been reaffirmed in later cases,[7] and seems to be firmly established. It means that s. 88 is not merely declaratory of the existing constitutional position. On the contrary, s. 88 expands the body of provincial law that is applicable to Indians. Provincial laws affecting Indianness, which do not apply to Indians of their own force, are made applicable by s. 88.

Provincial laws not affecting Indianness, which apply to Indians of their own force, are not caught by s. 88. Since the *Tsilhqot'in* decision (2014),[8] this includes provincial laws that apply to aboriginal and treaty rights. Aboriginal and treaty rights are of course protected by s. 35 of the Constitution Act, 1982. An infringement of those rights, whether by federal or provincial law, will lead to the invalidity of the infringing law. However, a law, whether federal or provincial, that serves a "compelling and substantial objective", and otherwise satisfies the *Sparrow* framework of review,[9] will be upheld as a justified limit on the right. In other words, the validity of a provincial law that applies to aboriginal and treaty rights does not depend on its incorporation into federal law by s. 88 (which is inapplicable), but on the *Sparrow* framework of justification (which directly applies to provincial law—as well as to federal law).

§ 28:15 Paramountcy exception

Section 88 of the Indian Act, by its opening words, is expressly subject to "any other Act of the Parliament of Canada", so that any conflict between a federal statute and a provincial law of general application has to be resolved in favour of the federal statute. A provincial law of general application is also inapplicable where it is "inconsistent with this Act or any order, rule, regulation or by-law made thereunder". These

[5] *Dick v. The Queen*, [1985] 2 S.C.R. 309.

[6] *Dick v. The Queen*, [1985] 2 S.C.R. 309, 326–327.

[7] *Derrickson v. Derrickson*, [1986] 1 S.C.R. 285, 297; *R. v. Francis*, [1988] 1 S.C.R. 1025, 1030.

[8] *Tsilhqot'in Nation v. British Columbia*, [2014] 2 S.C.R. 257, 2014 SCC 44.

[9] The *Sparrow* framework is explained in § 28:34, "Recognized and affirmed".

two parts of the section seem to be intended to make clear that the paramountcy doctrine continues to apply to provincial laws of general application, notwithstanding their adoption by a federal statute.

The closing language of s. 88 goes on to provide that provincial laws of general application are applicable "except to the extent that such laws make provision for any matter for which provision is made by or under this Act". This language in its context seems to contemplate that a provincial law of general application which makes provision for any matter for which provision is made by (or under) the Indian Act must yield to the provisions of the Indian Act. The doctrine of paramountcy, on the other hand, at least as it has been interpreted recently, applies only where there is an express contradiction between a federal and a provincial law. It does not apply where the federal and provincial laws, while not in direct conflict, are merely occupying the same field, or in other words making provision for the same matters.[1] It seems probable therefore that the closing words of s. 88 go further than the paramountcy doctrine and will render inapplicable to Indians some provincial laws of general application which are not in direct conflict with the Indian Act.

It is important to notice that this expansion of the paramountcy doctrine operates as an exception to s. 88. Since the laws of general application to which s. 88 applies are only those provincial laws that affect Indianness, it is only those laws that are subject to the wider paramountcy rule.[2] Provincial laws that do not affect Indianness are not caught by s. 88, and are not affected by the exception to s. 88. Provincial laws that do not affect Indianness apply to Indians of their own force, not through s. 88, and they are subject to the ordinary rule of paramountcy, not the expanded rule of s. 88.

§ 28:16 Treaty exception

Section 88 of the Indian Act, by its opening words, is "subject to the terms of any treaty". This means that any conflict between a treaty made with the Indians[1] and a provincial law of general application has to be resolved in favour of the treaty provision. Section 88 has been the ground upon which courts have held that provincial laws cannot impair Indian treaty rights.[2] The cases have assumed that s. 88 has this protective effect against all provincial laws, and they have not considered the

---

[Section 28:15]

[1] Chapter 16, Paramountcy.

[2] In *Dick v. The Queen*, [1985] 2 S.C.R. 309, 328, Beetz J. drew this conclusion. He even asserted that Parliament could not validly enact a broader paramountcy rule for provincial laws that applied to Indians of their own force. This assertion is questioned in ch. 16, Paramountcy, under heading § 16:7, "Constitutional significance".

[Section 28:16]

[1] According to one dictum, the reference to a treaty in s. 88 does not include international treaties: *Francis v. The Queen*, [1956] S.C.R. 618, 631 per Kellock J.

[2] *R. v. White and Bob* (1965), 52 D.L.R. (2d) 481n (S.C.C.); *Simon v. The Queen*, [1985] 2 S.C.R. 387; *Saanichton Marina v. Tsawout Indian Band* (1989), 57 D.L.R. (4th)

implications of the *Dick* holding that s. 88 applies only to provincial laws that affect Indianness. According to *Dick*, s. 88 does not apply to provincial laws that do not affect Indianness, and therefore s. 88 would not confer on Indian treaties paramountcy over provincial laws that do not affect Indianness.

In *Tsilhqot'in Nation v. British Columbia* (2014),[3] the Supreme Court held that provincial laws applying to aboriginal or treaty rights did not affect Indianness and their application to aboriginal and treaty rights was to be determined under s. 35 of the Constitution Act, 1982 by the Sparrow framework of justification—the same framework as applies to federal laws limiting s. 35 rights.[4] *Tsilhqot'in* was not a treaty case, and the Court made no reference to s. 88, or to its effect as a shield protecting Indian treaties from provincial law. However, it is clear that the ruling would take provincial laws applying to treaties out of the s. 88 shield, and leave the treaty language of s. 88 with no work to do. In the later case of *Grassy Narrows First Nation v. Ontario* (2014),[5] where it was argued that the province had infringed a treaty, the Court held that the issue was to be resolved under s. 35 by the *Sparrow* framework: "The doctrine of interjurisdictional immunity [Indianness in the aboriginal cases] does not preclude the province from justifiably infringing treaty rights".[6] Once again no reference was made to the treaty cases decided under s. 88, but the ineluctable conclusion is that they have been implicitly overruled.

IV. NATURAL RESOURCES AGREEMENTS

§ 28:17 Natural resources agreements

A further limitation on provincial competence to make laws applicable to Indians is to be found in the "Natural Resources Agreements", which were entered into between Canada and the three prairie provinces, and which were given constitutional status by an amendment to the Constitution Act in 1930.[1] The following clause is to be found in the Agreement

---

161 (B.C.C.A.); *R. v. Sioui*, [1990] 1 S.C.R. 1025; *R. v. Sundown*, [1999] 1 S.C.R. 393, para. 47.

[3]*Tsilhqot'in Nation v. British Columbia*, [2014] 2 S.C.R 257, 2014 SCC 44; described in text accompanying *Tsilhqot'in Nation v. British Columbia*, [2014] 2 S.C.R. 257, 2014 SCC 44.

[4]The *Sparrow* framework is explained in § 28:34, "Recognized and affirmed".

[5]*Grassy Narrows First Nation v. Ontario*, [2014] 2 S.C.R. 447, 2014 SCC 48.

[6]*Grassy Narrows First Nation v. Ontario*, [2014] 2 S.C.R. 447, 2014 SCC 48, para. 53.

[Section 28:17]

[1]Constitution Act, 1930, R.S.C. 1985, Appendix II, No. 26. The history of these agreements is related in ch. 29, Public Property, under heading § 29:1, "Distribution of public property". The impact of the agreements on Indian hunting and fishing rights is the main theme of the symposium "The Natural Resources Transfer Agreements at 75" (2007) 12 Rev. of Con. Studies 127–300.

with Alberta (clause 12), Saskatchewan (clause 12) and Manitoba (clause 13):[2]

> In order to secure to the Indians of the Province the continuance of the supply of game and fish for their support and subsistence, Canada agrees that the laws respecting game in force in the Province from time to time shall apply to the Indians within the boundaries thereof, provided, however, that the said Indians shall have the right, which the Province hereby assures to them of hunting, trapping and fishing game for food at all seasons of the year on all unoccupied Crown lands and on any other lands to which the said Indians may have a right of access.

In Alberta, Saskatchewan and Manitoba, therefore, the Indians[3] are guaranteed the right to take game and fish "for food" at all seasons of the year on the lands specified.[4] Provincial laws[5] to the contrary are inapplicable to the Indians.[6]

The words "for food" are an important restriction on the hunting and fishing rights conferred by the Natural Resources Agreements. Those Indians in the prairie provinces who, under the numbered treaties, had a right to hunt and fish for commercial purposes as well as for food had their rights cut down by the Agreements. The Supreme Court of Canada in *R. v. Horseman* (1990)[7] held that an Alberta Indian's treaty right to hunt commercially, which had been conferred by Treaty 8 in 1899, had been "merged and consolidated" in clause 12 of the Alberta Agreement, and his rights were now only those specified in the Agreement.[8] This meant that Indian treaty rights had been partially extinguished by a constitutional amendment enacted without the consent of the Indians, who were not even consulted on the terms of the Natural Resources Agreements.

V. ABORIGINAL RIGHTS

§ 28:18 Recognition of aboriginal rights

Section 35 of the Constitution Act, 1982 gives constitutional protec-

---

[2]There is also an agreement with British Columbia, but it does not include this clause, although there is a clause respecting Indians in the Terms of Union with British Columbia: see *Jack v. ne Queen*, [1980] 1 S.C.R. 294; K.M. Lysyk, "The Unique Constitutional Position of the Canadian Indian" (1967) 45 Can. Bar Rev. 513, 522.

[3]The word "Indians" in this context excludes the Métis: *R. v. Blais*, [2003] 2 S.C.R. 236.

[4]The clause has been frequently applied or interpreted by the courts: e.g., *Daniels v. White*, [1968] S.C.R. 517; *Frank v. The Queen*, [1978] 1 S.C.R. 95; *The Queen v. Mousseau*, [1980] 2 S.C.R. 89; *Elk v. The Queen*, [1980] 2 S.C.R. 166; *The Queen v. Sutherland*, [1980] 2 S.C.R. 451; *Moosehunter v. The Queen*, [1981] 1 S.C.R. 282; *R. v. Horse*, [1988] 1 S.C.R. 187.

[5]The clause gives no protection against federal laws: *Daniels v. White*, [1968] S.C.R. 517; *Elk v. The Queen*, [1980] 2 S.C.R. 166.

[6]*R. v. Badger*, [1996] 1 S.C.R. 771.

[7]*R. v. Horseman*, [1990] 1 S.C.R. 901.

[8]See also *R. v. Badger*, [1996] 1 S.C.R. 771 (treaty right to hunt for food amended but not extinguished by Natural Resources Agreement).

tion to "the existing aboriginal and treaty rights of the aboriginal peoples of Canada". The nature of that protection is explained later in §§ 28:29 to 28:40 of this chapter. The nature of "aboriginal rights" is examined in this section of the chapter. The nature of "treaty rights" is examined in the next section of the chapter.

The survival of aboriginal rights with respect to land was placed beyond doubt by the *Calder* case (1973).[1] In that case, six of the seven judges held that the Nishga people of British Columbia possessed aboriginal rights to their lands that had survived European settlement. The actual outcome of the case was inconclusive, because the six judges split evenly on the question of whether the rights had been validly extinguished or not. However, the recognition of the rights was highly significant, and in fact, as will be noted later, caused the Government of Canada to start the negotiation of modern treaties—usually styled land claims agreements—in the regions of Canada where there were no treaties.

Aboriginal rights that have not been extinguished are recognized by the common law and are enforceable by the courts. The leading case is *Guerin v. The Queen* (1984),[2] in which the majority of the Supreme Court of Canada recognized the aboriginal title of the Musqueam Indian Band to land in British Columbia. Dickson C.J. described aboriginal title as "a legal right derived from the Indians' historic occupation and possession of their tribal lands".[3] The Band had surrendered the land to the Crown in order to enable the Crown to lease it to a golf club. The Crown did lease it to the golf club, but on terms less favourable than those agreed to by the Band. The Court held that the aboriginal title to the land gave rise to a fiduciary duty on the part of the Crown to deal with the land for the benefit of the surrendering Indians. The Court held that this fiduciary duty had been broken, and awarded damages to the Band.[4] It should be noted that this outcome did not depend upon s. 35 of the Constitution Act, 1982, which was not in force at the time of the surrender and which was not relied upon by the Court.

In *R. v. Sparrow* (1990),[5] the Supreme Court of Canada unanimously recognized the aboriginal right of a member of the Musqueam Indian Band to fish for salmon in the Fraser River "where his ancestors had

[Section 28:18]

[1] *Calder v. A.G.B.C.*, [1973] S.C.R. 313.

[2] *Guerin v. The Queen*, [1984] 2 S.C.R. 335.

[3] *Guerin v. The Queen*, [1984] 2 S.C.R. 335, 376 per Dickson C.J.; see also 349 per Wilson J. Only Estey J., who concurred in the result, decided the case on the basis of the law of agency.

[4] The *Guerin* ruling was followed and expanded in *Blueberry River Indian Band v. Can.*, [1995] 4 S.C.R. 344, where damages were awarded against the Crown for breach of fiduciary duty following a surrender of land by the Band to the Crown. In *Blueberry*, unlike *Guerin*, the Crown had done with the land what the Band wanted it to do; nevertheless, the Court held that the transaction (a sale that included mineral rights) was not in the best interests of the Band.

[5] *R. v. Sparrow*, [1990] 1 S.C.R. 1075.

fished from time immemorial". The defendant had been charged with a violation of the federal Fisheries Act, and, because the charge related to facts occurring after 1982, he was able to invoke s. 35 of the Constitution Act, 1982. The Court held that s. 35 did provide constitutional protection for the aboriginal right, and the Court laid down the principles that govern s. 35; this aspect of the case is addressed later in this chapter.[6] The Court enlarged upon the fiduciary duty that had been recognized in *Guerin*. The purpose of the discussion was to derive principles for the application of s. 35, but the Court made clear that in all dealings with aboriginal peoples (including legislation since the enactment of s. 35) "the Government has the responsibility to act in a fiduciary capacity".[7]

The effect of *Guerin* and *Sparrow* is to confirm that aboriginal rights do exist at common law, and that they are enforceable at the suit of aboriginal peoples.[8] The cases also recognize a fiduciary, or trust-like, obligation on the part of the Crown of ill-defined scope and ramifications.[9] *Sparrow* decides as well that aboriginal rights, including the fiduciary duty, are now constitutionally guaranteed through s. 35 of the Constitution Act, 1982.

§ 28:19 Definition of aboriginal rights

Aboriginal rights[1] are rights held by aboriginal peoples, not by virtue of Crown grant, legislation or treaty, but "by reason of the fact that

[6] Text accompanying § 28:33 note 1, below.

[7] *R. v. Sparrow*, [1990] 1 S.C.R. 1075, 1108 per Dickson C.J. and La Forest J. for the Court.

[8] See also *Roberts v. Can.*, [1989] 1 S.C.R. 322, 340 (aboriginal title is a matter of federal common law and within the jurisdiction of the Federal Court); *Ont. v. Bear Island Foundation*, [1991] 2 S.C.R. 570 (aboriginal right was established, but it had been extinguished by treaty); *Paul v. B.C.*, [2003] 2 S.C.R. 585 (aboriginal right constitutional law is within the jurisdiction of a provincial administrative tribunal).

[9] In *Guerin v. The Queen*, [1984] 2 S.C.R. 335, 387, Dickson C.J. said that "the fiduciary obligation which is owed to the Indians by the Crown is *sui generis*". This raises the possibility that it involves duties that are foreign to the traditional meaning of a fiduciary. In particular, there is a fiduciary duty to consult with aboriginal people before their interests are affected by governmental action: § 28:38, "Duty to consult aboriginal people"; although a traditional trustee is rarely under any obligation to consult the beneficiaries in the course of administering the trust.

[Section 28:19]

[1] There is a vast literature on aboriginal rights, much of it emphasizing constitutional aspects. A few particularly useful sources are B. Slattery, "The Constitutional Guarantee of Aboriginal and Treaty Rights" (1983) 8 Queen's L.J. 232; D. Sanders, "The Rights of the Aboriginal Peoples in Canada" (1983) 61 Can. Bar Rev. 314; B. Slattery, "Understanding Aboriginal Rights" (1987) 66 Can. Bar Rev. 727; W. Pentney, "The Rights of the Aboriginal Peoples of Canada" (1988) 22 U.B.C. L. Rev. 21 (Part I), 207 (Part II); J. Woodward, Native Law (Carswell, Toronto, 1989), ch. 2; R. A. Reiter, The Fundamental Principles of Indian Law (First Nations Resource Council, 1993, looseleaf), ch. 1; W.I.C. Binnie, "The Sparrow Doctrine" (1990) 15 Queen's L.J. 217; J. Borrows, "Frozen Rights in Canada" (1997) 22 Am. Indian Law Review 37; Macklem, Indigenous Difference and the Constitution of Canada (2001); B. Slattery, "Making Sense of

aboriginal peoples were once independent, self-governing entities in possession of most of the lands now making up Canada".[2] Lamer C.J. in *R. v. Van der Peet* (1996)[3] pointed out that "when Europeans arrived in North America, aboriginal peoples were already here, living in communities on the land, and participating in distinctive cultures, as they had done for centuries." This fact distinguishes aboriginal peoples from all other minority groups in Canada, and explains why aboriginal rights have a special legal, and now constitutional, status. Although aboriginal rights had been recognized and enforced in *Guerin* and *Sparrow*, before *Van der Peet* the Supreme Court of Canada had made no attempt to define their characteristics. The Court had simply noted that aboriginal rights were "unique" or "sui generis".[4]

In *R. v. Van der Peet*,[5] Lamer C.J. for the majority of the Supreme Court of Canada articulated the legal test that was to be used to identify an "existing aboriginal right" within the meaning of s. 35 of the Constitution Act, 1982: "in order to be an aboriginal right an activity must be an element of a practice, custom or tradition integral to the distinctive culture of the aboriginal group asserting the right".[6] In order for a practice to be "integral", the practice must be "of central significance" to the aboriginal society: it must be a "defining" characteristic of the society, "one of the things that made the culture of the society distinctive".[7] The practice must have developed before "contact", that is, "before the arrival of Europeans in North America".[8] The practice could evolve over the years as the result of contact, for example, the bone hook would be replaced by the steel hook, the bow and arrow by the gun, and so on,[9] but a practice that has evolved into modern forms must trace its origins back to the pre-contact period. Contemporary practices that developed "solely as a response to European influences" do not qualify.[10]

In *Van der Peet*, the aboriginal defendant had been convicted of selling fish that she had caught under the authority of a Indian food-fish

---

Aboriginal and Treaty Rights" (2000) 79 Can. Bar Rev. 196; McNeil, Emerging Justice (2001); Lajoie, Conceptions autochtones des droits ancestraux au Québec (2008); Morellato (ed.), Aboriginal Law Since Delgamuukw (2009).

[2]B. Slattery, "The Constitutional Guarantee of Aboriginal and Treaty Rights" (1983) 8 Queen's L.J. 232, 242.

[3]*R. v. Van der Peet*, [1996] 2 S.C.R. 507, para. 30.

[4]*Guerin v. The Queen*, [1984] 2 S.C.R. 335, 342; *R. v. Sparrow*, [1990] 1 S.C.R. 1075, 1112.

[5]*R. v. Van der Peet*, [1996] 2 S.C.R. 507. Lamer C.J. wrote the opinion of the seven-judge majority. L'Heureux-Dubé and McLachlin JJ. wrote dissenting opinions.

[6]*R. v. Van der Peet*, [1996] 2 S.C.R. 507, para. 45.

[7]*R. v. Van der Peet*, [1996] 2 S.C.R. 507, para. 55.

[8]*R. v. Van der Peet*, [1996] 2 S.C.R. 507, paras. 60–62. The two dissenting judges disagreed with this requirement as being arbitrary and unduly difficult to prove, and each offered less demanding time-period tests.

[9]Treaty rights also evolve to accommodate modern ways of doing whatever was authorized by the treaty: § 28:26, "Interpretation of treaty rights".

[10]*R. v. Van der Peet*, [1996] 2 S.C.R. 507, para. 73.

licence. The licence, which had been issued under the federal Fisheries Act, restricted the holder to fishing for food; the sale of fish caught under the licence was prohibited by regulations made under the Act. The question for decision was whether the defendant had an aboriginal right to sell fish (for money or other goods). The majority of the Supreme Court of Canada held that the exchange of fish did occur in the society of the Sto:lo people before contact with Europeans, but it was incidental to their practice of fishing for food. Unlike the practice of fishing for food, the practice of selling fish was not an "integral" part of the Sto:lo culture. It was only after contact that the Sto:lo people had begun fishing to supply a market, one created by European demand for the fish. Therefore, the aboriginal defendant was unsuccessful in establishing an aboriginal right to sell fish, and was properly convicted.

Van der Peet was followed in a companion case, *R. v. N.T.C. Smokehouse* (1996),[11] where the majority of the Court relied on a finding at trial that exchanges of fish by the Sheshaht and Obetchesaht people were "few and far between" and occurred mainly at potlatches and other ceremonial occasions. Therefore, the practice of exchanging fish was not sufficiently central to the aboriginal culture to qualify as an aboriginal right.[12] In another companion case, *R. v. Gladstone* (1996),[13] the Court held, by a majority, that the claimed aboriginal right, which was to sell herring spawn on kelp, was established. The evidence showed that, before contact, the Heiltsuk people habitually sold large quantities of herring spawn on kelp to other Indian tribes. The purpose of this activity was not to dispose of surplus food (as in *Van der Peet);* nor was it incidental to social and ceremonial traditions (as in *Smokehouse).* The trade in herring spawn on kelp was "a central and defining feature of Heiltsuk society".[14]

In *Mitchell v. Minister of National Revenue* (2001),[15] the Supreme Court of Canada rejected the claim by the Mohawk people of Akwesasne to an aboriginal right to bring goods purchased in the United States across the St. Lawrence River (the international border) into Canada without paying customs duty on the goods. McLachlin C.J., writing for the majority, reversed the findings of the trial judge (and the majority of the Federal Court of Appeal) to hold that the evidence adduced by the claimants did not establish pre-contact trade by the Mohawks (whose

---

[11]*R. v. N.T.C. Smokehouse*, [1996] 2 S.C.R. 672.

[12]Accord, *Lax Kw'alaams Indian Band v. Can.*, [2011] 3 S.C.R. 535 (pre-contact practice of rendering and trading eulachon grease could not evolve into the "different right" of a modern commercial fishery catching and trading all species of fish; continuity not established).

[13]*R. v. Gladstone*, [1996] 2 S.C.R. 723.

[14]*R. v. Gladstone*, [1996] 2 S.C.R. 723, para. 29 per Lamer C.J. for the majority. See also *R. v. Adams*, [1996] 3 S.C.R. 101 (upholding aboriginal right to fish for food); *R. v. Côté*, [1996] 3 S.C.R. 139 (upholding aboriginal right to fish for food).

[15]*Mitchell v. Minister of National Revenue*, [2001] 1 S.C.R. 911. The seven-judge bench was unanimous in rejecting the claim of aboriginal right. McLachlin C.J. wrote the majority opinion with the agreement of Gonthier, Iacobucci, Arbour and LeBel JJ.; Binnie J. wrote a concurring opinion with the agreement of Major J.

ancestors lived south of the river in what is now New York State)[16] in a northerly direction across the river. Forays across the river were mostly for military purposes. At most, the occasions of trade were few and far between, and participation in northerly trade was "not a practice integral to the distinctive culture of the Mohawk people".[17] Binnie J., with the agreement of Major J., wrote a concurring opinion agreeing that Mohawk pre-contact trade across the river was only occasional and not integral to Mohawk culture. This produced a unanimous decision that rejected the claimed right and required the Mohawk people to pay customs duty on goods brought into Canada. But Binnie J. went on to devote most of his long opinion to elaborating a further reason rejecting the claim to an aboriginal right. In his view, even if the evidence of pre-contact trade had supported an aboriginal right, such a right would be incompatible with Crown sovereignty. Control over the movement of people and goods into a country was a "fundamental attribute of sovereignty", and the asserted aboriginal right to bring in goods free of duty was incompatible with that sovereignty.[18] On this basis, the asserted right could never have survived the transition to Crown sovereignty and could never have come into existence as a right protected by s. 35(1). The majority opinion of McLachlin C.J. refused to address this argument, and so it is not yet clear whether there is a sovereign incompatibility principle that must be satisfied in order to establish an aboriginal right.[19]

A First Nation's freedom of religion was a central issue in *Ktunaxa Nation v. British Columbia* (2017).[20] In that case, the Ktunaxa Nation[21] applied for judicial review of the decision of the B.C. Minister of Forests to grant a permit for the construction of a ski resort in a valley in southeastern B.C. The First Nation lived in the valley and objected to the proposal on the ground that the proposed resort was within an area of spiritual significance to the First Nation because it was home to an important population of grizzly bears and to Grizzly Bear Spirit, a principal spirit within the Ktunaxa religion. The court application had been preceded by 20 years of consultations by the Crown (the B.C. Minister) and the promoter of the resort with the Ktunaxa and the Shuswap First Nation, which also inhabited the valley. As the result of

---

[16]Akwesasne, the current home of the claimant Mohawk people, is a string of islands in the St. Lawrence River which is bisected by the international boundary, causing daily inconvenience in their routine patterns of life: *Mitchell v. Minister of National Revenue*, [2001] 1 S.C.R. 911, para. 77.

[17]*Mitchell v. Minister of National Revenue*, [2001] 1 S.C.R. 911, para. 60.

[18]*Mitchell v. Minister of National Revenue*, [2001] 1 S.C.R. 911, paras. 160, 163.

[19]*Mitchell v. Minister of National Revenue*, [2001] 1 S.C.R. 911, para. 64, but there are references to the argument at paras. 10, 62 and 63, the last implying that Crown claims based on sovereignty should be dealt with under the doctrines of extinguishment, infringement and justification.

[20]*Ktunaxa Nation v. British Columbia*, [2017] 2 S.C.R. 386, 2017 SCC 54. McLachlin C.J. and Rowe J. wrote the seven-judge majority opinion. Moldaver J. (with Côté J.) wrote a concurring opinion.

[21]Ktunaxa is pronounced "too-nah-ha".

the consultations, significant accommodations had been made to the ski-resort proposal, including the removal of areas critical to First Nation use and to grizzly bear habitat. The Shuswap eventually supported the proposal because of the benefits that the ski resort would bring to their people and the region. However, late in the process, the Ktunaxa took the position that no accommodation was possible because they believed that the development would drive the Grizzly Bear Spirit out of the valley which would irrevocably impair their religious beliefs and practices. After fruitless attempts to revive the consultation process, the Minister declared that reasonable consultation had occurred and approved the project. The Supreme Court decided that the Minister's decision to end consultation and approve the project was reasonable, and since reasonableness was the standard of review for issues of mixed fact and law like this one, the Court unanimously upheld the Minister's decision. The key to understanding this decision is that the Court did not treat the facts as raising a claim of an aboriginal right. Indeed, the criterion of emergence before European contact was not mentioned by the Court and could not have been met because the Court accepted evidence that the First Nation's "knowledge keeper" had decided only in 2004 that the construction of the ski resort would drive the Grizzly Bear Spirit out of the valley, and McLachlin C.J. and Rowe J. for the majority said that "whether this belief is ancient or recent plays no part in our *s. 2(a) analysis.*"[22] In other words, although the case was about a First Nation's religious belief, rooted in a particular territory, "the Ktunaxa stand in the same position as non-Aboriginal litigants."[23] The majority went on to hold that the Minister's decision did not impair the Ktunaxa's freedom of religion: the Ktunaxa continued to be free to believe in the Grizzly Bear Spirit (although of course they would believe that the Spirit had departed the valley), and to engage in any religious practices that followed the belief (likely none, since the Spirit would have departed). The Court held that the Ktunaxa claim was to protect the presence of the Grizzly Bear Spirit itself, but s. 2(a) did not "protect the object of beliefs such as Grizzly Bear Spirit", but protected "everyone's freedom to hold such beliefs and to manifest them in worship and practice or by teaching and dissemination".[24] From this premise the majority reached the implausible conclusion that the Minister's decision did not impair the Ktunaxa's freedom of religion. Moldaver J. (with Côté J.) wrote a concurring opinion. He accepted that the proposed resort would be an infringement of s. 2(a) because the Ktunaxa belief that the proposed resort would cause the Grizzly Bear Spirit to depart would render their religious beliefs devoid of religious significance. However, he held that the infringement was saved by s. 1 of the Charter. The Minister had taken account of the Ktunaxa's beliefs and had appropriately balanced their s. 2(a) right with his statutory objectives of administering Crown land and disposing of it in the public interest.

---

[22] *Ktunaxa Nation v. British Columbia*, [2017] 2 S.C.R. 386, 2017 SCC 54, para. 69.

[23] *Ktunaxa Nation v. British Columbia*, [2017] 2 S.C.R. 386, 2017 SCC 54, para. 58.

[24] *Ktunaxa Nation v. British Columbia*, [2017] 2 S.C.R. 386, 2017 SCC 54, para. 71.

Can a practice that was adopted by an aboriginal people purely for survival count as one that was integral to a distinctive culture? Although the pre-contact practice of fishing for food had been upheld as the foundation of an aboriginal right in several cases,[25] this question was not asked or answered until the case of *R. v. Sappier* (2006).[26] Before contact with Europeans, the Maliset and Mi'kmaq Indians were migratory people, living from hunting and fishing over a large territory and using the rivers and lakes of Eastern Canada for transportation. They harvested wood for the building of temporary shelters and other domestic uses (such as canoes, tools and firewood), which any human society would have had to do in order to survive. Could such a practice evolve into a modern right to cut a truckload of timber on Crown lands for the purpose of building a permanent home? That was the issue in the case, where the Indian defendants relied on that aboriginal right as their defence to a charge of unauthorized possession of Crown timber, which was an offence under New Brunswick's forestry law. The Supreme Court of Canada held that the harvesting of wood for domestic uses was integral to the distinctive culture of the Maliset and Mi'kmaq people. It was immaterial that the practice had developed as a necessity of survival. Moreover, the Court held that the pre-contact practice of harvesting of wood for the construction of temporary shelters had evolved into the modern right to harvest wood by modern means for the construction of a permanent dwelling. "Any other conclusion would freeze the right in its pre-contact form."[27] The Indian defendants were therefore successful in establishing their aboriginal right, and were entitled to be acquitted.

The *Van der Peet* definition of aboriginal rights is based on the existence of an aboriginal practice before "contact", meaning before the arrival of Europeans. This time frame does not work for Métis rights, because the Métis people (who originated from the intermarriage of French Canadian men and Indian women during the fur trade period) did not exist before contact. Lamer C.J. for the majority in *Van der Peet* acknowledged this difficulty, and left open the question whether the time frame would need to be modified for the purpose of identifying Métis rights.[28] The alternative would be to hold that the Métis had no aboriginal rights. A possible later time frame would be the time of assertion of European sovereignty, which is the time at which aboriginal occupation of land must be established in order to establish aboriginal title.[29] However, that is not what the Supreme Court of Canada has

---

[25] *R. v. Sparrow*, [1990] 1 S.C.R. 1075; *R. v. Adams*, [1996] 3 S.C.R. 101; *R. v. Côté*, [1996] 3 S.C.R. 139.

[26] *R. v. Sappier*, [2006] 2 S.C.R. 686. Bastarache J. wrote the opinion of the eight-judge majority. Binnie J. wrote a short concurring opinion.

[27] *R. v. Sappier*, [2006] 2 S.C.R. 686, para. 48 per Bastarache J. for a Court that was unanimous on this point.

[28] *R. v. Van der Peet*, [1996] 2 S.C.R. 507, para. 67.

[29] *Delgamuukw v. B.C.*, [1997] 3 S.C.R. 1010, para. 145; see § 28:21, "Aboriginal title".

decided. In *R. v. Powley* (2003),[30] the Court held that, for Métis claimants of aboriginal rights, the focus on European contact had to be moved forward, not to the time of European sovereignty, but to "the time of effective European control".[31] Apart from this shift in the time frame, the same *Van der Peet* definition was to be used to identify Métis rights.

In *Powley*, two Métis[32] claimed an aboriginal right to hunt for food in the Sault Ste. Marie area of Ontario. The Court held that effective control of the Upper Great Lakes area had passed from the Indian and Métis people to the European settlers in approximately 1850. At the time, a distinctive Métis community had emerged in Sault Ste. Marie. (The assertion of Crown sovereignty over the area would have been in 1763, when the Treaty of Paris ceded jurisdiction to the British Crown. The Métis community was not established that early.) The practice of hunting for food was integral to the culture of the historic community, and the practice had continued to the present time. Since the Métis claimants in the case were members of the modern community, and traced their ancestry back to the pre-control community, they were entitled to the aboriginal right of hunting for food in the area.

§ 28:20 Aboriginal self-government

The aboriginal right of self-government must exist by virtue of the fact that aboriginal people were living in self-governing communities before the arrival of Europeans.[1] The existence of "the inherent right of self-government within Canada" was agreed to by all the First Ministers in the Charlottetown Accord of 1992, which, if it had been ratified, would have explicitly protected (and regulated) this right in a new s. 35.1 of the Constitution Act, 1982.[2] In *R. v. Pamajewon* (1996),[3] the Supreme Court of Canada rejected a claim by the Shawanaga and Eagle Lake First Nations to conduct high-stakes gambling on their reserves. In each case, the gambling operations were conducted pursuant to a law enacted by the band council. The gambling law was not a by-law made in accordance with the Indian Act; the law was claimed to be an exercise of the First Nation's power of self-government. The validity of the gambling law had to be determined when members of the First Nations were charged with gaming offences under the federal Criminal Code. Lamer C.J., for the majority of the Court, "assuming without deciding that s.

---

[30]*R. v. Powley*, [2003] 2 S.C.R. 207. The opinion was given by "the Court".

[31]*R. v. Powley*, [2003] 2 S.C.R. 207, para. 18.

[32]The Court also discussed the definition of Métis: see § 28:31, "Aboriginal peoples of Canada".

[Section 28:20]

[1]See B. Slattery, "First Nations and the Constitution: A Question of Trust" (1992) 71 Can. Bar Rev. 727.

[2]§ 28:43, "Charlottetown Accord".

[3]*R. v. Pamajewon*, [1996] 2 S.C.R. 821. The Court was unanimous. Lamer C.J. wrote the opinion for eight judges; L'Heureux-Dubé J. wrote a concurring opinion.

35(1) includes self-government claims",[4] held that such claims were to be resolved by the same *Van der Peet* test as claims to other kinds of aboriginal rights. He refused to characterize the claimed right as "a broad right to manage the use of their reserve lands" (which would surely have passed the *Van der Peet* test), and instead characterized the claimed right as a right "to participate in, and to regulate, gambling activities on their respective reserve lands". While the evidence showed that the Ojibwa people gambled before the arrival of Europeans, the gambling was informal and on a small scale, and it was never part of the means by which the communities were sustained. Lamer C.J. concluded that before the arrival of Europeans gambling was not an integral part of the distinctive cultures of the First Nations, and, therefore, that the First Nations had no aboriginal right to regulate gambling. The defendants were properly convicted of breaching the gaming provisions of the Criminal Code.

According to *Pamajewon*, the aboriginal right of self-government extends only to activities that took place before European contact, and then only to those activities that were an integral part of the aboriginal society.[5] These restrictions are very severe even for rights to hunt and fish and harvest, but they are singularly inappropriate to the right of self-government. In order to give meaning to self-government in a modern context, it should be couched in much wider terms. Here is what the Charlottetown Accord[6] would have put into the Constitution Act, 1982, as s. 35.1(3):

> The exercise of the right referred to in subsection (1) ["the inherent right of self-government within Canada"] includes the authority of duly constituted legislative bodies of the Aboriginal peoples, each within its own jurisdiction,
>
> (a) to safeguard and develop their languages, cultures, economies, identities, institutions and traditions, and
>
> (b) to develop, maintain and strengthen their relationship with their lands, waters and environment,
>
> so as to determine and control their development as peoples according to their own values and priorities and to ensure the integrity of their societies.

The Accord went on to make provision for the negotiation of self-government agreements to implement the right of self-government, and, in order to encourage that process, denied direct judicial enforcement of the new inherent-right provision for a period of five years. But, if an

---

[4]*R. v. Pamajewon*, [1996] 2 S.C.R. 821, para. 24.

[5]In *Mitchell v. M.N.R.*, [2001] 1 S.C.R. 911, discussed at § 28:19, note 15, the concurring opinion of Binnie J., which was agreed to by Major J., suggested a "sovereign incompatibility principle" as a restriction on aboriginal rights, and at paras. 134, 165–169 he implied that the principle would restrict the scope of an aboriginal right of self-government, although perhaps not of "*internal* self-government": para. 165 (his italics, the term internal not defined). The majority opinion of McLachlin C.J. did not express a view on whether the sovereign incompatibility principle existed as an independent restriction on the scope of aboriginal rights, but note references at paras. 10, 61–64.

[6]Charlottetown Accord, Draft Legal Text, October 9, 1992, pp. 37–38.

aboriginal nation had not negotiated an agreement within the five-year period, the right was, in principle, enforceable without an agreement.

In *Pamajewon*, the Court was obviously concerned about the ability of aboriginal people to immunize themselves from the rules of the Criminal Code, but the question whether federal (or provincial) laws apply in the face of an inconsistent aboriginal law is a separate question from the extent of the power of self-government. If the Court had decided that an aboriginal right of self-government did authorize an aboriginal law regulating gambling, this would not necessarily mean that the inconsistent Criminal Code provisions would have to yield to the aboriginal law. A question of paramountcy would be presented, and should probably be resolved by application of the *Sparrow* test: if the Criminal Code provision satisfied the *Sparrow* test of justification,[7] then the Criminal Code provision should prevail; if not, then the aboriginal law should prevail. The details of the extent of a First Nation's powers of self-government, and the paramountcy rules that would govern the application of federal and provincial (or territorial) law to aboriginal lands and people, are of course much better embodied in self-government agreements (with the status of treaties) between aboriginal nations and governments.[8] These agreements can deal comprehensively with all the issues of governance, and supply enough clarity to keep the issues out of the courts. However, the agreements have not proved easy to negotiate, and there is a danger that, if the aboriginal right of self-government is defined too narrowly by the Court, the bargaining power of aboriginal nations will be impaired, and the incentive of governments to reach agreements will be reduced.

In *Delgamuukw v. British Columbia* (1997),[9] aboriginal people brought proceedings for a declaration that they had aboriginal title and self-government rights over a territory in northern British Columbia. The Supreme Court of Canada did not grant the declaration sought, but ordered a new trial. The Court also declined to comment directly on the claim for self-government rights.[10] However, Lamer C.J. for the majority of the Court did provide extensive reasons as to the nature of aboriginal title, and these are discussed in the next section of this chapter. Two of the things that the Chief Justice said about aboriginal title have relevance to self-government rights. First, land held under aboriginal title is "held communally", and decisions with respect to the land are "made by that community".[11] Secondly, aboriginal title "encompasses the right to choose to what uses land can be put".[12] These characteristics of aboriginal title imply a necessary role for aboriginal laws and customs

---

[7]See § 28:34, "Recognized and affirmed".

[8]See P.W. Hogg and M.E. Turpel, "Implementing Aboriginal Self-Government: Constitutional and Jurisdictional Issues" (1995) 74 Can. Bar Rev. 187.

[9]*Delgamuukw v. British Columbia*, [1997] 3 S.C.R. 1010. The case is discussed more fully in the next section of this chapter.

[10]*Delgamuukw v. British Columbia*, [1997] 3 S.C.R. 1010, para. 171.

[11]*Delgamuukw v. British Columbia*, [1997] 3 S.C.R. 1010, para. 115.

[12]*Delgamuukw v. British Columbia*, [1997] 3 S.C.R. 1010, para. 166.

as to how the land is to be shared by the members of the community, how the land is to be managed, and how the land is to be developed. As well, Professor Slattery points out that "since decisions with respect to [aboriginal] lands must be made communally, there must be some internal structure for communal decision-making", and "the need for a decision-making structure provides an important cornerstone for the right of aboriginal self-government."[13]

§ 28:21 Aboriginal title

Aboriginal *title* is the right to the exclusive occupation of land,[1] which (as will be explained) permits the aboriginal owners to use the land for a variety of purposes. Aboriginal title would obviously permit the owners to hunt, fish and harvest on their land. However, rights to particular activities, such as hunting, fishing and harvesting may also exist on land to which the aboriginal people do not have title. That has been held to be the case with the right to fish, for example.[2] Even though the right to fish was defined in site-specific terms, in that it could only be exercised at a particular location, it was not necessary for the aboriginal claimants to establish title to the site of the fishing right. (Of course, they did have to satisfy the *Van der Peet* test by showing that the practice of fishing in that location had arisen before European contact and was integral to their distinctive culture.) In one case where a fishing right was established, title to the land had actually been surrendered by the aboriginal people.[3]

As noted earlier, the Supreme Court of Canada in the *Calder*[4] and *Guerin*[5] cases recognized that aboriginal title survived European settlement and the assumption of sovereignty by the British Crown. The use and occupation of land by aboriginal people before the assumption of sovereignty created an aboriginal title to the land. The theory of the common law was that the Crown mysteriously acquired the underlying title to all land in Canada, including land that was occupied by aboriginal people.[6] But the common law recognized that aboriginal title, if not surrendered or lawfully extinguished, survived as a burden on the

---

[13]B. Slattery, "Making Sense of Aboriginal and Treaty Rights" (2000) 79 Can. Bar Rev. 196, 215.

[Section 28:21]

[1]See B. Slattery, "The Metamorphosis of Aboriginal Title" (2006) 85 Can. Bar Rev. 255; Morellato (ed.), Aboriginal Law Since Delgamuukw (2009), ch. 7 (B. Slattery).

[2]*R. v. Adams*, [1996] 3 S.C.R. 101, paras. 26–28, 49; *R. v. Côté*, [1996] 3 S.C.R. 139, paras. 38-39.

[3]*R. v. Adams*, [1996] 3 S.C.R. 101.

[4]*Calder v. B.C.*, [1973] S.C.R. 313.

[5]*Guerin v. R.*, [1984] 2 S.C.R. 335.

[6]In Crown land that is burdened by aboriginal title, the Crown's title, after aboriginal title has been subtracted from it, is a legal but not a beneficial interest. It contains two elements: (1) a fiduciary duty owed by the Crown to the aboriginal (beneficial) owners, and (2) a right to encroach on aboriginal title if the Crown can justify this "in the broader public interest" under s. 35 of the Constitution Act, 1982: *Tsilhiqot'n*

Crown's title.[7] Since 1982, aboriginal title, like other aboriginal rights, has been protected by s. 35 of the Constitution Act, 1982.

Aboriginal title was recognized by the Royal Proclamation of 1763, which governed British imperial policy for the settlement of British North America. As settlement advanced across the country, in most of the settled areas, treaties were entered into with the aboriginal people, who surrendered portions of their land to the Crown, thereby freeing up the surrendered land for settlement and development by non-aboriginal people.[8] British Columbia, where most of the land was occupied by Indians when the Europeans arrived, was a notable exception to the practice of treaty-making. In that province, European settlement took place without treaties with the aboriginal people, and, while a treaty process has now been established, it is a very slow process. This has led to litigation, as aboriginal people have turned to the courts to define their rights.

Delgamuukw v. British Columbia (1997),[9] was an action by aboriginal people for a declaration that they had aboriginal title to a tract of land in British Columbia. After a prolonged trial, followed by appeals, the result of the case was inconclusive. The Supreme Court of Canada found that the trial judge had wrongly rejected (or given insufficient weight to) much of the aboriginal evidence that was proffered in support of the claim, and the Court ordered a new trial to make new factual findings. However, the Court did lay down the rules of evidence and substance that were to govern the new trial, and the majority opinion of Lamer C.J. is an important account of the law. It is summarized in the text that follows.

Aboriginal title has its source in the occupation of land by aboriginal people before the Crown assumed sovereignty over the land. It does not derive from a Crown grant, something that could only take place after the assumption of sovereignty by the Crown. Aboriginal title is proved, not by showing a chain of title originating in a Crown grant, but by showing that an aboriginal people occupied the land prior to sovereignty. The mere fact of pre-sovereignty occupation is sufficient to show that

---

Nation v. B.C., [2014] 2 S.C.R. 257, 2014 SCC 44, para. 71.

[7]Section 109 of the Constitution Act, 1867 makes clear that the Crown's title is "subject to . . . any interest other than that of the province" in the land. *Delgamuukw* confirms that aboriginal title is such an interest. If Indian title is surrendered, the title passes to the Crown in right of the province, not Canada: § 28:3, "Lands reserved for the Indians".

[8]§ 28:24, "History".

[9]*Delgamuukw v. British Columbia*, [1997] 3 S.C.R. 1010. The Court was unanimous in its conclusion. The majority opinion was written by Lamer C.J. with the agreement of Cory, Major and McLachlin JJ. A concurring opinion was written by La Forest J. with the agreement of L'Heureux-Dubé J. and the "substantial agreement" of McLachlin J. La Forest J. said that he disagreed "with various aspects of [Lamer C.J.'s] reasons", but I was not able to detect any inconsistency between the accounts of the law in the two opinions. McLachlin J. evidently had the same difficulty, since she agreed with both opinions. It is perhaps fair to say that the Court was virtually unanimous in its reasons. Only six judges participated in the decision.

title to the land is "of central significance to the culture of the claimants", and so the centrality requirement of *Van der Peet* does not have to be separately established in order to make out a claim to aboriginal title.[10] The pre-sovereignty occupation by the first nation has to be exclusive. If the land was used by others, then it is necessary to show that the claimants' first nation had the intention to retain exclusive control and had the power to exclude others if they chose.[11]

The point of time at which aboriginal occupation of the land must be proved in order to make out aboriginal title is "prior to sovereignty", not "prior to contact". This is a relaxation of the *Van der Peet* time requirement for the proof of activity-based rights, which is "prior to contact", because the time of contact is earlier and less certain than the time of the assumption of Crown sovereignty. The less stringent time frame for proof of aboriginal title follows from the fact that aboriginal title is a burden on the Crown's underlying title, and the Crown's underlying title only came into existence when sovereignty was assumed by the Crown. Therefore, so far as the common law was concerned, "aboriginal title crystallized at the time sovereignty was asserted".[12] If present occupation is relied upon, then it is necessary to show "a continuity between present and pre-sovereignty occupation". That continuity might have been disrupted for a time, but so long as there was a "substantial maintenance of the connection" the requirement of continuity is satisfied.[13]

Proof of pre-sovereignty occupation does not involve adherence to strict rules of evidence. Because aboriginal societies did not keep written records at the time of sovereignty, their account of the past would typically be contained in "oral histories"—stories that had been handed down from generation to generation in oral form. The admission of oral histories to prove occupation would violate the hearsay rule, but the rules of evidence have to be adapted to the realities of pre-sovereignty aboriginal societies. Otherwise, proof of occupation would become impossible and theoretical entitlements to aboriginal title would be rendered nugatory.[14] This danger was illustrated by this case, in which the trial judge had found that the claimants had not established their title to the claimed lands. The trial judge had reached this finding after rejecting (or giving little weight to) much of the oral-history evidence that had been proffered to him. This caused the Supreme Court to hold that the factual findings at trial could not stand, and that a new trial was required in which oral histories would be admitted and given appropriate weight.

---

[10] *Delgamuukw v. British Columbia*, [1997] 3 S.C.R. 1010, para. 151.

[11] *Delgamuukw v. British Columbia*, [1997] 3 S.C.R. 1010, paras. 155–156.

[12] *Delgamuukw v. British Columbia*, [1997] 3 S.C.R. 1010, para. 145. In the case of British Columbia, that date was 1846, when the Oregon Boundary Treaty was entered into. Notice the anomaly that aboriginal title (which carries with it the right to hunt, fish and harvest on the land) is established by reference to the date of sovereignty, while the activity-based rights to hunt, fish and harvest, if claimed independently of aboriginal title, call for proof that goes back to the date of "contact".

[13] *Delgamuukw v. British Columbia*, [1997] 3 S.C.R. 1010, para. 153.

[14] *Delgamuukw v. British Columbia*, [1997] 3 S.C.R. 1010, para. 87.

Delgamuukw never did go back to trial, and so the claim of aboriginal title was never resolved in the courts. However, in *Tsilhqot'in Nation v. British Columbia* (2014),[15] the Supreme Court applied the principles laid down in *Delgamuukw* and made a finding of aboriginal title. The Tsilhqot'in Nation was a group of six bands who occupied the Cariboo Chilcotin region of central British Columbia. The issue of their title arose when the province granted to a private lumber company a licence to cut trees on provincial Crown land that was part of the First Nation's traditional territory. The First Nation brought legal proceedings against the province for a declaration of aboriginal title over the land.[16] *Delgamuukw* had decided that aboriginal title had to be established by proving that the First Nation occupied the land at the date of the British assumption of sovereignty over the territory of British Columbia in 1846. This case called for clarification of what was "sufficient" occupation. The evidence showed that the Tsilhqot'in people occupied the sites of villages "intensively", but were otherwise "semi-nomadic", ranging over the rest of the claimed land to forage, harvest, hunt, trap and fish according to the season. The trial judge concluded that the First Nation had established sufficient occupation over the entire territory which their ancestors had used regularly and exclusively. The Court of Appeal took a narrower view, holding that sufficient occupation would be established only over those sites that had been intensively occupied and that had reasonably definite boundaries in 1846. This would have resulted in "small islands of title" surrounded by larger territories over which the aboriginal people would have no title (although they would of course have rights to engage in their traditional activities). The Supreme Court sided with the trial judge. The sufficiency of occupation was a "context-specific inquiry".[17] The Tsilhqot'in land was extensive but it was harsh and could only support a small number of people; the semi-nomadic way of life was driven by the limited carrying capacity of the land. What amounted to sufficient occupation should reflect this reality and should acknowledge that semi-nomadic aboriginal people "might conceive of possession of land in a somewhat different manner than did the common law".[18] The pre-sovereignty occupation was "sufficient", not just over specific sites of settlement, but over the entire territory that their ances-

---

[15]*Tsilhqot'in Nation v. British Columbia*, [2014] 2 S.C.R. 257, 2014 SCC 44. McLachlin C.J. wrote the opinion of the Court. The implications of the decision for the development of land encumbered by aboriginal title or claims of title are well analyzed in H. Swain and J. Baillie, "*Tsilhqot'in Nation v. British Columbia*: Aboriginal Title and Section 35" (2015) 56 Can. Bus. L. J. 265.

[16]The First Nation also challenged the validity of the logging licence on the ground that, although their title had not been established at the time of issue, they had not been consulted; the Court upheld that claim as well as the claim of title: *Tsilhqot'in Nation v. British Columbia*, [2014] 2 S.C.R. 257, 2014 SCC 44, para. 153. See also § 28:38, "Duty to consult aboriginal people".

[17]*Tsilhqot'in Nation v. British Columbia*, [2014] 2 S.C.R. 257, 2014 SCC 44, para. 37.

[18]*Tsilhqot'in Nation v. British Columbia*, [2014] 2 S.C.R. 257, 2014 SCC 44, para. 41. This seems to be inconsistent with the Court's earlier decision in *R. v. Marshall*, [2005] 2 S.C.R. 220 (*Marshall No. 3*), where the Court relied on the common law of pos-

tors had used regularly and exclusively. The Court also accepted the findings of the trial judge that the occupation had been "continuous" to the present day and that it had been "exclusive" to the Tsilhqot'in people. The three criteria of sufficiency, continuity and exclusivity were all satisfied, and the Court granted a declaration of title.

In *Delgamuukw*, Lamer C.J. frequently repeated the proposition, which is found in all the earlier cases,[19] that aboriginal title is sui generis (one of a kind). By this he meant that there are a number of important differences between aboriginal title and non-aboriginal title. There are five such differences. The first, which has already been discussed, relates to the source of aboriginal title, which derives from pre-sovereignty occupation rather than a post-sovereignty grant from the Crown.

The second difference relates to the range of uses to which aboriginal-title land may be put. Aboriginal title confers the right to exclusive use and occupation of the land, which includes the right to engage in a variety of activities on the land, and those activities are not limited to those that have been traditionally been carried on, and are certainly not limited to those that were integral to the distinctive culture. For example, the exploitation of oil or gas existing in aboriginal lands would be a possible use. However, the range of uses to which the land could be put is subject to the limitation that the uses "must not be irreconcilable with the nature of the attachment to the land which forms the basis of the particular group's aboriginal title".[20] This means that land occupied for hunting purposes could not be converted to strip mining, for example. Perhaps a better way of explaining this restriction on the use of aboriginal land is that the land is held "not only for the present generation but for all succeeding generations", and cannot be abused or encumbered "in ways that would prevent future generations of the group from using and enjoying it."[21] This inherent limit on the uses to which the land could be put may be contrasted with the lack of any comparable restrictions on a fee simple title (although there will usually be *statutory* restrictions on a fee simple title, such as zoning by-laws).

The third difference between aboriginal title and non-aboriginal title is that aboriginal title is inalienable, except to the Crown. This was well established in the prior case-law. The doctrine of inalienability means that the Crown has to act as an intermediary between the aboriginal

session to deny aboriginal title to a semi-nomadic aboriginal nation. In *Tsilhqot'in*, para. 44, McLachlin C.J. distinguished the earlier decision on the ground that "regular and exclusive use" of the land had not been established in that case.

[19] E.g., *Guerin v. The Queen*, [1984] 2 S.C.R. 335, 382 per Dickson J. See also *Tsilhqot'in Nation v. British Columbia*, [2014] 2 S.C.R. 257, 2014 SCC 44, para. 72 per McLachlin C.J.

[20] *Delgamuukw v. British Columbia*, [1997] 3 S.C.R. 1010, para. 111.

[21] *Tsilhqot'in Nation v. British Columbia*, [2014] 2 S.C.R. 257, 2014 SCC 44, para. 74 per McLachlin C.J.

owners and third parties.[22] In order to pass title to a third party, the aboriginal owners must first surrender the land to the Crown. The Crown then comes under a fiduciary duty to deal with the land in accordance with the best interests of the surrendering aboriginal people, for example, by ensuring that adequate compensation is received by the aboriginal owners.[23] During the period of European settlement, the doctrine of inalienability was a safeguard against unfair dealings by settlers trying to acquire aboriginal land and an encouragement to the process of treaty making. The doctrine also supplied certainty to land titles in Canada, because it made clear that a Crown grant was the only valid root of title for non-aboriginal people and for non-aboriginal land. In *Delgamuukw*, Lamer C.J. made the interesting suggestion that the doctrine of inalienability was a subset of the inherent limit on the uses permitted by aboriginal title. Alienation would be irreconcilable with the nature of the aboriginal attachment to the land—indeed, it would end the attachment—and was barred for that reason.[24] Of course, an aboriginal nation that wants to alienate its lands, or to use its lands in a way that aboriginal title does not permit, can do so indirectly by surrendering the lands to the Crown, which can convert them by grant to a fee simple.

The fourth difference between aboriginal title and non-aboriginal title is that aboriginal title can only be held communally. "Aboriginal title cannot be held by individual aboriginal persons; it is a collective right to land held by all members of an aboriginal nation."[25] Decisions with respect to the land are made by the community, not by an individual owner as would be the case with a fee simple title. In the previous section of this chapter, we noticed that the communal holding of land implies some mechanisms of governance to decide how the land is to be shared and used. This is an element of aboriginal self-government.

The fifth (and last) difference between aboriginal title and non-aboriginal title is that aboriginal title is constitutionally protected. As is explained in the next section of this chapter, even before 1982, aboriginal title could not be extinguished by provincial legislation, because provincial extinguishment would conflict with the exclusive federal power over "Indians, and lands reserved for the Indians" in s. 91(24) of the Constitution Act, 1867. Before 1982, aboriginal title could be extinguished by federal legislation, but the legislation would have that effect only if it showed a "clear and plain" intention to extinguish aboriginal title. In 1982, s. 35 of the Constitution Act, 1982 was adopted. The effect of s. 35 is to confer constitutional protection on any aboriginal

---

[22]La Forest, Natural Resources and Public Property under the Canadian Constitution (1969), 110–111, 120.

[23]*Guerin v. The Queen*, [1984] 2 S.C.R. 335; *Blueberry River Indian Band v. Can.*, [1995] 4 S.C.R. 344.

[24]*Delgamuukw v. British Columbia*, [1997] 3 S.C.R. 1010, para. 129.

[25]*Delgamuukw v. British Columbia*, [1997] 3 S.C.R. 1010, para. 115.

title that was "existing" (unextinguished) in 1982.[26] The constitutional protection accorded by s. 35 is not absolute, but it does require that any infringement of the right must be enacted by the competent legislative body (which could be either the federal Parliament or a provincial Legislature depending on the subject matter),[27] and must satisfy the *Sparrow* test of justification.[28] At a minimum, the test of justification would normally require prior consultation with the aboriginal owners before any of the incidents of their title was impaired as well as fair compensation for any impairment.[29] A fee simple, or any other non-aboriginal interest in land, has no constitutional protection.[30] It can be extinguished or impaired by the competent legislative body (which would usually be the provincial Legislature) without any constitutional obligation of prior consultation or compensation (or any other justification).

Despite the five important differences between non-aboriginal (fee simple) title and aboriginal title, the similarities must not be lost sight of. In particular, it goes without saying that any activity or development on aboriginal-title land requires the consent of the aboriginal title holders—just as consent would be required from fee simple title holders.[31] Of course, as explained in the previous paragraph, a refusal of consent can be overcome by legislation. In the case of fee simple title, legislation would be enacted by the normal legislative process, and (no constitutional rights being engaged) no special justification would be called for, and judicial review would not be available. In the case of aboriginal title (which is protected by s. 35 of the Constitution Act, 1982), any encumbering legislation would have to satisfy the *Sparrow* test of justification, a matter that if contested would be subject to judicial review.

Much land in Canada is subject to claims of aboriginal title that have not yet been proved. As long as a claim remains unproved, the aboriginal claimants have no right to insist on their consent to activity such as logging or hunting on the claimed land or to physical developments such as the building of a road or pipeline through the claimed land. However, because the claim is to a constitutionally protected right, the aboriginal claimants do have the right to be consulted by government and if necessary have their interests accommodated, and judicial review is available to determine the sufficiency of the consultation and accommodation.[32] But, if a court determines that consultation and accommodation have

[26] *Delgamuukw v. British Columbia*, [1997] 3 S.C.R. 1010, para. 133.

[27] *Tsilhqot'in Nation v. B.C.*, [2014] 2 S.C.R. 257, 2014 SCC 44, paras. 131–152, held (reversing prior decisions) that the doctrine of interjurisdictional immunity did not apply to block provincial laws that applied to aboriginal or treaty rights, and that the application of provincial laws to aboriginal or treaty rights was governed by the same s. 35 framework established in *Sparrow* for federal laws.

[28] The doctrine of justification is explained in § 28:34, "Recognized and affirmed".

[29] *Delgamuukw v. British Columbia*, [1997] 3 S.C.R. 1010, paras. 168–169.

[30] See ch. 29, Public Property, under heading § 29:8, "Compensation".

[31] *Tsilhqot'in Nation v. British Columbia*, [2014] 2 S.C.R. 257, 2014 SCC 44, para. 76.

[32] § 28:38, "Duty to consult with aboriginal people".

been sufficient on a standard of reasonableness, the proposed use of the land will be confirmed even if the aboriginal people are not satisfied with the outcome.[33] There is, however, some hazard in proceeding with a project in the absence of aboriginal consent. In *Tsilhqot'in Nation*, McLachlin C.J. commented that, after the aboriginal people have succeeded in establishing their title, it may be necessary to "reassess" any project that was undertaken without consent: the Crown, she said, "may be required to cancel the project upon establishment of the title if continuation of the project would be unjustifiably infringing."[34] This comment was an obiter dictum, and it was made in a case where the issue was logging, but it would literally extend to a project involving the construction of a permanent facility such as a road or pipeline.

§ 28:22 Extinguishment of Aboriginal rights

Aboriginal rights (including aboriginal title) can be extinguished in two ways: (1) by surrender and (2) by constitutional amendment. As to the first way, the surrender of aboriginal rights must be voluntary, and must be to the Crown. Surrenders have occurred in treaties entered into between an aboriginal nation and the Crown.[1] A treaty will confer treaty rights on the aboriginal people in substitution for the surrendered aboriginal rights. The second way of extinguishing aboriginal rights is by constitutional amendment.[2] In the past, constitutional amendments affecting aboriginal or treaty rights have been enacted without the consent of the affected aboriginal people.[3] It is now clear that it would be a breach of the Crown's fiduciary duty to the aboriginal people to proceed with a constitutional amendment affecting aboriginal rights without at least the active participation of the affected aboriginal people.[4]

Before 1982, there was a third way of extinguishing aboriginal rights, and that was by legislation,[5] although after confederation only the

---

[33]E.g., *Taku River Tlingit First Nation v. B.C.*, [2004] 3 S.C.R. 550 (approval of reopening of old mine confirmed despite aboriginal objection); *Beckman v. Little Salmon/Carmacks First Nation*, [2010] 3 S.C.R. 103 (land grant to non-aboriginal farmer confirmed despite aboriginal objection).

[34]*Tsilhqot'in Nation v. British Columbia*, [2014] 2 S.C.R. 257, 2014 SCC 44, para. 92.

[Section 28:22]

[1]E.g., *Ont. v. Bear Island Foundation*, [1991] 2 S.C.R. 570; *R. v. Howard*, [1994] 2 S.C.R. 299 (fishing right extinguished by treaty); *Grassy Narrows First Nation v. Ont.*, [2014] 2 S.C.R. 447, 2014 SCC 48, para. 2 (aboriginal title extinguished by treaty).

[2]*R. v. Horseman*, [1990] 1 S.C.R. 901 (treaty right).

[3]*R. v. Horseman*, [1990] 1 S.C.R. 901 (treaty right).

[4]Section 35.1 probably does not apply to constitutional amendments that make no direct change to any of the identified constitutional provisions but which do impair aboriginal or treaty rights. However, the fiduciary duty of the Crown recognized in *Sparrow* would, in my view, preclude such action without aboriginal participation.

[5]*Sikyea v. The Queen*, [1964] S.C.R. 642 (treaty right); *R. v. George*, [1966] S.C.R. 267 (treaty right); *R. v. Derriksan* (1976), 71 D.L.R. (3d) 159 (S.C.C.) (aboriginal right);

federal Parliament was competent to enact an extinguishing law.[6] In 1982, the power to extinguish by legislation was removed by s. 35 of the Constitution Act, 1982. Section 35 (as interpreted in the *Sparrow* case) permits the *regulation* of aboriginal and treaty rights by a federal law that satisfies strict standards of justification,[7] but does not permit the *extinguishment* of aboriginal and treaty rights.[8]

Extinguishment, whether by voluntary surrender or constitutional amendment, or (before 1982) by statute, will not be inferred from unclear language. Only a "clear and plain" intention to extinguish is accepted by the courts as having that effect. This was decided by the Supreme Court of Canada in the *Sparrow* case,[9] resolving the question that had caused the even division of the Court in *Calder*.[10]

VI. TREATY RIGHTS

§ 28:23 Introduction

Before 1982, Indian treaty rights[1] were explicitly protected from derogation by provincial law, but not federal law, by s. 88 of the Indian Act.[2] Since 1982, Indian treaty rights have been protected by s. 35 of the Constitution Act, 1982 from derogation by either federal or provincial law. Section 35 is discussed later in this chapter.[3]

§ 28:24 History

In eastern North America, from the earliest stages of French and English settlement, treaties of peace and friendship were entered into with the Indian nations. These treaties of the seventeenth and eighteenth centuries conferred (among other things) hunting and fishing rights in

---

R. v. Sparrow, [1990] 1 S.C.R. 1075, 1111 (aboriginal right—obiter dictum).

[6]*Delgamuukw v. B.C.*, [1997] 3 S.C.R. 1010, para. 178.

[7]*Tsilhqot'in Nation v. B.C.*, [2014] 2 S.C.R. 257, 2014 SCC 44, para. 152, and *Grassy Narrows First Nation v. Ont.*, [2014] 2 S.C.R 447, 2014 SCC 48, para. 53, expanded the s. 35 capacity to regulate aboriginal and treaty rights to the provinces, acting on matters otherwise within provincial jurisdiction such as provincial forests, and subject to the same strict standards of justification.

[8]§ 28:36, "Application to extinguishment".

[9]*R. v. Sparrow*, [1990] 1 S.C.R. 1075. Folld. in *R. v. Gladstone*, [1996] 2 S.C.R. 723 (aboriginal right to sell herring spawn on kelp not extinguished by extensive regulation, including at times prohibition, of the trade); *R. v. Adams*, [1996] 3 S.C.R. 101 (surrender of aboriginal title did not demonstrate clear and plain intention to extinguish the "freestanding" aboriginal right to fish in water adjacent to the surrendered lands); *R. v. Sappier*, [2006] 2 S.C.R. 686 (aboriginal right to harvest timber on Crown land not extinguished by regulation through a licensing scheme).

[10]*Calder v. A.G.B.C.*, [1973] S.C.R. 313.

[Section 28:23]

[1]See Henderson, Treaty Rights in the Constitution of Canada (2007).

[2]§ 28:16, "Treaty exception". Treaty rights were also protected from provincial law by the "Indianness" exception: see § 28:9 note 5, above.

[3]§§ 28:29 to 28:40, "Section 35".

return for peace, and typically did not involve the cession by the Indians of their lands.[1] As European settlement moved westward, so did treaty-making. In 1850, the Robinson treaties were signed on the shores of Lakes Huron and Superior;[2] and, between 1871 and 1921, a series of 11 numbered treaties were entered into, covering a large part of Canada in Ontario and the prairie provinces.[3] These treaties do on their face cede Indian lands to the Crown[4] in return for (among other things) hunting and fishing rights, as well as the reservation of portions of the treaty lands for the Indians. By the 1920s, when the last of the numbered treaties had been entered into, there remained vast areas of Canada where no treaty-making had taken place. These included Inuit lands in Labrador, northern Quebec and the Northwest Territories, and Indian lands in northern Quebec, British Columbia, the Yukon and the Northwest Territories.

After the *Calder* case (1973)[5] recognized the validity of aboriginal rights, the Government of Canada reversed its policy of 50 years,[6] and resumed the process of treaty-making. Modern treaties—styled land claims agreements—have been entered into with the Inuit and Cree of the James Bay area of northern Quebec, with the Inuit of the eastern Arctic (now Nunavut), and with a number of the First Nations in the Yukon and Northwest Territories and British Columbia.[7] These land claims agreements reserve large areas of land (settlement land) to the aboriginal signatories as well as considerable sums of money in return for the surrender of aboriginal rights over non-settlement land. As well, however, the agreements constitute sophisticated codes with respect to such matters as development, land use planning, water management, fish and wildlife harvesting, forestry and mining. These codes assure a continuing role for the aboriginal people in the management of the re-

---

[Section 28:24]

[1] *Simon v. The Queen*, [1985] 2 S.C.R. 387 recognized a treaty of peace and friendship made in 1752.

[2] *Ont. v. Bear Island Foundation*, [1991] 2 S.C.R. 570 recognized the Robinson-Huron Treaty of 1850.

[3] *R. v. Swimmer* (1971), 17 D.L.R. (3d) 476 (Sask. C.A.) recognized Treaty No. 6 of 1876.

[4] There is room for doubt as to whether the written terms of the numbered treaties accurately express the Indian understanding of their terms, and whether there was fully informed consent to the apparent extinguishment of rights: see, e.g., *Re Paulette* (1973), 42 D.L.R. (3d) 8 (N.W.T. S.C.).

[5] *Calder v. A.G.B.C.*, [1973] S.C.R. 313.

[6] Department of Indian Affairs and Northern Development, "Statement on Claims of Indian and Inuit People" (Queen's Printer, Ottawa, 1973).

[7] J. Merritt and T. Fenge, "The Nunavut Land Claims Settlement" (1990) 15 Queen's L.J. 255; A.R. Thompson, "Land Claim Settlements in Northern Canada" (1991) 55 Sask. L. Rev. 127.

sources of the entire region covered by the agreement, not just their own settlement land.[8]

Section 35 of the Constitution Act, 1982 explicitly includes rights acquired under modern land claims agreements in its protected treaty rights. Therefore, as land claims agreements are ratified, they acquire constitutional status.[9]

§ 28:25 Definition of treaty

An Indian treaty has been described as "unique" or "sui generis".[1] It is not a treaty at international law, and is not subject to the rules of international law. It is not a contract, and is not subject to the rules of contract law. It is an agreement between the Crown and an aboriginal nation with the following characteristics:

1. Parties: The parties to the treaty must be the Crown, on the one side, and an aboriginal nation, on the other side.[2]
2. Agency: The signatories to the treaty must have the authority to bind their principals, namely, the Crown and the aboriginal nation.[3]
3. Intention to create legal relations: The parties must intend to create legally binding obligations.
4. Consideration: The obligations must be assumed by both sides, so that the agreement is a bargain.
5. Formality: there must be "a certain measure of solemnity".

The foregoing characteristics are my extrapolation from the two leading cases on the meaning of a treaty. The cases are *Simon v. The Queen* (1985) and *R. v. Sioui* (1990). Both cases were applying s. 88 of the Indian Act, not s. 35 of the Constitution Act, 1982, but it is safe to assume that the word "treaty" would bear the same meaning in both instruments.

---

[8]Self-government agreements have also been negotiated with some aboriginal nations. These have not formed part of constitutionally-protected land claims agreements, but have been separate agreements, implemented by federal legislation.

[9]Section 35(3) makes clear that modern land claims agreements are protected regardless of whether they were entered into before or after 1982, when s. 35 came into force: so held in *Que. v. Moses*, [2010] 1 S.C.R. 557, para. 15 (James Bay Treaty, signed by aboriginal and government signatories in 1975, has constitutional status under s. 35(3)).

[Section 28:25]

[1]*Simon v. The Queen*, [1985] 2 S.C.R. 387, 404; *R. v. Sioui*, [1990] 1 S.C.R. 1025, 1043. These two cases are fully examined in text accompanying § 28:25 notes 4 and 5, below.

[2]The argument that an Indian tribe was not an entity possessing the legal personality or the capacity to enter into treaties was summarily rejected in *Simon* (at 398–401) and not raised again in *Sioui*.

[3]This was in issue in both *Simon* and *Sioui*, and it was determined in both cases that the signatories possessed the requisite authority.

In *Simon v. The Queen* (1985),[4] the question arose whether legal recognition should be given to a "peace and friendship" treaty signed in 1752 by the governor of Nova Scotia and the Chief of the Micmac Indians. The document purported to guarantee to the Indians "free liberty of hunting and fishing as usual" in the treaty area. The Supreme Court of Canada held that this was a valid treaty, which, by virtue of s. 88 of the Indian Act, exempted the Micmac defendant from the game laws of Nova Scotia. Dickson C.J. for the Court indicated his definition of an Indian treaty in two passages. At page 401:

> In my opinion, both the Governor and the Micmac entered into the Treaty with the intention of creating mutually binding obligations which would be solemnly respected.

And at p. 410:

> The treaty was an exchange [of] solemn promises between the Micmacs and the King's representative entered into to achieve and guarantee peace. It is an enforceable obligation between the Indians and the white man and, as such, falls within the meaning of the word "treaty" in s. 88 of the Indian Act.

In *R. v. Sioui* (1990),[5] what was in issue was a short document signed only by the Governor of Quebec in 1760, which "certified" that the Chief of the Huron Indians had come "in the name of his nation" to make peace, and henceforth the Huron Indians were under his protection and were to be allowed "the free exercise of their religion, their customs and liberty of trading with the English". The Supreme Court of Canada held that this was a valid treaty, which, by virtue of s. 88 of the Indian Act, exempted the Huron defendants, who were practising customary religious rites in a provincial park, from provincial park regulations. Lamer C.J. for the Court quoted the extracts from the *Simon* case, and said at p. 1044:

> From the extracts it is clear that what characterizes a treaty is the intention to create obligations, the presence of mutually binding obligations and a certain measure of solemnity.

These elements, he held, were all satisfied by the document of 1760.

In both *Simon* and *Sioui*, the treaties did not involve a cession of land by the Indians; and in *Sioui*, the right to religious exercise that was successfully asserted by the Huron Indians was not even over their traditional territory. These cases make clear that the surrender of aboriginal rights is not a requirement of a valid treaty. Nor does a treaty have to be concerned with territory; it could be "an agreement about political or social rights".[6] In each case, however, there was consideration moving from the Indian side, namely, a promise to cease hostilities. The Indians had made a bargain, and the Crown should be held to its side of the bargain.

---

[4] *Simon v. The Queen*, [1985] 2 S.C.R. 387.

[5] *R. v. Sioui*, [1990] 1 S.C.R. 1025.

[6] *R. v. Sioui*, [1990] 1 S.C.R. 1025, 1043.

It is a well established principle of interpretation that "treaties and statutes relating to Indians should be liberally construed and doubtful expressions resolved in favour of the Indians".[7] The idea is to construe treaties "in the sense in which they would naturally be understood by the Indians". In *Sioui*, Lamer C.J. for the Court said that the same approach should be applied to the question whether a particular document constituted a treaty: "we should adopt a broad and generous interpretation of what constitutes a treaty",[8] and also "in examining the preliminary question of the capacity to sign a treaty".[9] The Court has to attempt to transport itself back to the time of signing the treaty to determine whether the Indians had reasonable grounds for believing that they were dealing with an authorized agent of the Crown, and that the resulting document created binding obligations. In *Sioui*, this approach helped the Court to resolve in favour of the Indians any doubt about the Governor's authority and the status of his rather informal certificate.

§ 28:26 Interpretation of treaty rights

The rule for the interpretation of treaties between the Crown and aboriginal nations is that they "should be liberally construed and doubtful expressions resolved in favour of the Indians".[1] The reasons for this rule include the unequal bargaining power of the Crown and the aboriginal people. As well, the representatives of the Crown typically created the written text and the written records of the negotiations, and those writings often differed from or did not fully express the Indians' oral understanding of the arrangement.[2] The honour of the Crown and the fiduciary duty of the Crown demand a rule that removes even the appearance or suspicion of sharp practice in treating with aboriginal people.

A clear example of the generous interpretation of a treaty is *R. v. Marshall (Marshall 1)* (1999).[3] The issue here was whether a Mi'kmaq man, who had been charged with fishing for eels and selling eels without

---

[7]*Nowegijick v. The Queen*, [1983] 1 S.C.R. 29, 36 (statute); *Simon v. The Queen*, [1985] 2 S.C.R. 387, 402 (treaty); *R. v. Sioui*, [1990] 1 S.C.R. 1025, 1036 (treaty).

[8]*R. v. Sioui*, [1990] 1 S.C.R. 1025, 1035.

[9]*R. v. Sioui*, [1990] 1 S.C.R. 1025, 1035, 1036.

[Section 28:26]

[1]*Nowegijick v. The Queen*, [1983] 1 S.C.R. 29, 36 (statute); *Simon v. The Queen*, [1985] 2 S.C.R. 387, 402 (treaty); *R. v. Sioui*, [1990] 1 S.C.R. 1025, 1036 (treaty). See also *R. v. Sundown*, [1999] 1 S.C.R. 393 (treaty right to hunt in provincial park interpreted as including by implication right to construct log cabin in park, which overrode provincial regulation prohibiting construction of dwellings in park).

[2]"It has been held that it is unconscionable for the Crown to ignore oral terms and rely simply on the written words of a treaty": *Ermineskin Indian Band and Nation v. Can.*, [2009] 1 S.C.R. 222, para. 54 per Rothstein J. for the Court. In that case, it was held that the oral understanding of the Indian signatories, based on an oral statement by the Crown agent who negotiated the treaty, was to be treated as part of the treaty.

[3]*R. v. Marshall*, [1999] 3 S.C.R. 456. Binnie J. wrote the majority judgment, which

a licence, had a treaty right to catch and sell eels. The applicable treaty was a brief "peace and friendship" treaty entered into in 1760 between the British Governor of Nova Scotia and the Mi'kmaq chief. The treaty said nothing directly about fishing, and with respect to trade said only that the Indians would no longer trade "any commodities in any manner" except with the managers of "truck houses" established by the Governor. A truck house was a government trading post which existed in Nova Scotia in 1760, but which was discontinued in 1780. The point of the truck house clause was that the Indians, who had formerly been allies of the French, were now agreeing to trade only with the British. It was a considerable stretch to interpret this clause, in form nothing more than a negative restraint on the ability of the Mi'kmaq to trade with non-governmental purchasers, as a protection for the defendant's commercial fishing activity. But that is what the Supreme Court of Canada decided. The Court held, by a majority, that the clause should be interpreted as conferring a right to hunt, fish and gather, because only by hunting, fishing and gathering would the Indians be in a position to bring "commodities" to the truck house. The clause should also be interpreted as conferring a right to trade the products of hunting, fishing and gathering sufficiently to make "a moderate livelihood". The right to trade persisted after the abolition of truck houses, which the Court characterized as "a mere disappearance of the mechanism created to facilitate the right".[4] The defendant's rights to "moderate" fishing and trading were treaty rights within the meaning of s. 35 of the Constitution Act, 1982, and the rights prevailed over the statutory licensing regime that the defendant had not complied with. The defendant's activity was accordingly protected by the treaty, and he was entitled to be acquitted of the charges of fishing and trading without a licence.

The logic of *Marshall 1* seemed to confer an aboriginal treaty right over the commercial exploitation of most of the natural resources of Nova Scotia and New Brunswick, where truck house clauses were contained in Indian treaties of peace and friendship. In response to an application for a rehearing, the Court in *Marshall 2* (1999)[5] issued a second set of reasons, clarifying and somewhat narrowing its earlier reasons, but not changing the decision or the ratio decidendi, which was that the truck house clause conferred a modern right to hunt, fish and gather the things that in 1760 were to be traded at the truck house. Relying on this principle, the Mi'kmaq Indians in Nova Scotia and New Brunswick commenced commercial logging operations on Crown lands without the authorization required by statute in each province. They were charged with offending the forest management laws of the two provinces, and they invoked the truck house clause in defence. Their ancestors used wood in 1760 as firewood, and to make a variety of things, such as buildings, sleds, canoes, snowshoes and baskets. The things that

---

was agreed to by Lamer C.J., L'Heureux-Dubé, Cory and Iacobucci JJ.; McLachlin J. wrote a dissenting judgment, which was agreed to by Gonthier J.

[4]*R. v. Marshall*, [1999] 3 S.C.R. 456, para. 54.

[5]*R. v. Marshall*, [1999] 3 S.C.R. 533. Binnie J. wrote the opinion of the Court.

they made of wood were occasionally traded. Logging, they argued, was simply a modern use of the same products and was therefore protected. In *Marshall 3* (2005),[6] the Supreme Court of Canada, now speaking through McLachlin C.J. (who had dissented in *Marshall 1*), rejected this argument. While modern eel fishing was the logical evolution of a traditional trading activity, as decided in *Marshall 1*, the same case could not be made for logging. Logging (unlike eel fishing) was not a traditional Mi'kmaq activity in 1760. And, while treaty rights are not frozen in time, modern logging activity could not be characterized as the natural evolution of the minor trade in wood products that took place at the time of the treaty. The Mi'kmaq defendants therefore had no treaty right[7] to cut down trees for commercial purposes without a licence.[8]

Another example of the progressive (or dynamic) interpretation of an Indian treaty is *R. v. Morris* (2006).[9] The treaty in that case had been made in 1852 by the Governor of the Colony of Vancouver Island with the Saanich Nation. In exchange for the surrender by the Saanich of their lands, the Crown promised (among other things) that the Indians would be "at liberty to hunt over the unoccupied lands" of the Island "as formerly". Two members of the Tsartlip Band of the Saanich Nation, who had been hunting in their traditional territory at night, driving a truck along a road, using a spotlight to identify game and a rifle to shoot the game, were charged with offences under British Columbia's Wildlife Act that prohibited hunting at night and hunting with a spotlight. Their defence was the treaty right in the 1852 treaty. They led evidence that the Saanich had traditionally hunted at night, using sticks with flaming pitch on the end of them. The Supreme Court of Canada had no difficulty in holding that "the use of guns, spotlights and motor vehicles is the current state of the evolution of the Tsartlip's historic hunting practices"; these modern ways of hunting "do not change the essential character of the practice, namely, night hunting with illumination".[10] The majority of the Court held that the practice was protected by the treaty, and the two accused were entitled to be acquitted.[11] The dissenting minority agreed that the treaty right should be adapted to modern methods of transportation, illumination and weaponry, but they held that the power of the modern rifle made hunting at night more danger-

[6]*R. v. Marshall*, [2005] 2 S.C.R. 220. McLachlin C.J. wrote the opinion of the majority. LeBel J., with the agreement of Fish J., wrote a concurring opinion.

[7]They also claimed aboriginal title to the forest lands on which their logging took place, but this claim was also rejected: § 28:21, "Aboriginal title".

[8]Another example of the generous interpretation of Indian treaties is *Mikisew Cree First Nation v. Can.*, [2005] 3 S.C.R. 388; described in § 28:38, "Duty to consult aboriginal people".

[9]*R. v. Morris*, [2006] 2 S.C.R. 915. Deschamps and Abella JJ. wrote the majority judgment which was agreed to by Binnie and Charron JJ. McLachlin C.J. and Fish J. wrote a dissenting judgment which was agreed to by Bastarache J.

[10]*R. v. Morris*, [2006] 2 S.C.R. 915, para. 33 per Deschamps and Abella JJ.

[11]The Court relied on s. 88 of the Indian Act for this decision (§ 28:16, "Treaty exception"), not on s. 35 of the Constitution Act, 1982 (which would presumably have yielded the same result).

ous than it had been in 1852. In the dissenting view, the treaty should not be interpreted as protecting an inherently dangerous activity, and the prohibition on night hunting was consistent with the treaty.[12] The dissenting view, although it did not prevail, makes clear that the progressive (or dynamic) interpretation of treaty rights does not necessarily have the effect of expanding the rights.

In the case of "modern treaties", the rules of interpretation are much more straightforward. In *First Nation of Nacho Nyak Dun v. Yukon* (2017),[13] the treaty to be interpreted was the First Nation of Nacho Nyak Dun Final Agreement, which was concluded with Canada and Yukon in 1993. The Final Agreement was based on the Umbrella Final Agreement, also entered into in 1993 by Nacho Nyak Dun and all the other Yukon First Nations.[14] Karakatsanis J., for a unanimous Supreme Court, said that "[b]ecause modern treaties are 'meticulously negotiated by well-resourced parties', courts must 'pay close attention to their terms' ".[15] She also said that "[c]ompared to their historic counterparts, modern treaties are detailed documents and deference to their text is warranted".[16] However, she did acknowledge in an *obiter dictum* that even a modern treaty is "subject to such constitutional limitations as the honour of the Crown."[17] The question in the case was whether Yukon had the power unilaterally to adopt a regional land use plan for the Peel Watershed, a remote region of the territory, which would increase access to and development of the region. The answer to the question was no, because the Final Agreement stipulated in detail a robust process of consultation with the First Nation for a land use plan of this kind and Yukon had not followed that process. Karakatsanis J. quashed the Yukon plan, explaining that it could be revived only by following the Final-Agreement process of consultation with the First Nation.

---

[12] *R. v. Morris*, [2006] 2 S.C.R. 915, paras. 116–119. The majority agreed that the treaty should not be interpreted as authorizing dangerous activity, but their answer to the dissenters (para. 59) was that not all night hunting, even with modern weaponry, was dangerous, and "something less than an absolute prohibition of night hunting can address the concern for safety".

[13] *First Nation of Nacho Nyak Dun v. Yukon*, [2017] 2 S.C.R. 576, 2017 SCC 58. Karakatsanis J. wrote the opinion of the nine-judge court.

[14] *Beckman v. Little Salmon/Carmacks First Nation*, [2010] 3 S.C.R. 103, 2010 SCC 53 is another Yukon First Nation case in which the Final Agreement is also based on the Umbrella Final Agreement. I acknowledge that I played a minor role as one of the counsel advising the Yukon First Nations in the negotiation and drafting of the Umbrella Final Agreement.

[15] *First Nation of Nacho Nyak Dun v. Yukon*, [2017] 2 S.C.R. 576, para. 36, citing *Quebec v. Moses*, [2010] 1 S.C.R. 557, para. 7.

[16] *First Nation of Nacho Nyak Dun v. Yukon*, [2017] 2 S.C.R. 576, para. 36, citing J. Jai, "The Interpretation of Modern Treaties and the Honour of the Crown: Why Modern Treaties Deserve Judicial Deference" (2012) 26 Nat. J. Con. Law 25, 41.

[17] *First Nation of Nacho Nyak Dun v. Yukon*, [2017] 2 S.C.R. 576, 2017 SCC 58, para. 37, citing *Beckman v. Little Salmon/Carmacks First Nation*, [2010] 3 S.C.R. 103, 2010 SCC 53, para. 54.

§ 28:27 Extinguishment of treaty rights

Treaty rights may be extinguished in the same two ways as aboriginal rights, that is: (1) by voluntary surrender to the Crown, and (2) by constitutional amendment. Before 1982, there was a third way: treaty rights could also be extinguished by federal (but not provincial) legislation; but that possibility ended with the enactment of s. 35 of the Constitution Act, 1982. Extinguishment by any of these means will not be lightly inferred; a "clear and plain" intention to extinguish must be established.[1]

In addition, if a treaty makes provision for its own amendment or repeal, then obviously the treaty can be amended or repealed as contemplated. Such a provision, which would of course have been agreed to by the aboriginal parties to the treaty, would establish a procedure for future amendment or repeal, and that procedure would normally include a requirement of aboriginal consent.

In addition, it is probable that treaty rights would be at least voidable in the event of a fundamental breach by one of the parties.[2] However, evidence of longstanding non-exercise of treaty rights does not cause an extinguishment.[3] Nor could international treaties or treaties with other Indian nations cause an extinguishment. Without competent legislation (before 1982) or a constitutional amendment, "a treaty cannot be extinguished without the consent of the Indians concerned".[4]

VII. THE NEED FOR CONSTITUTIONAL PROTECTION

§ 28:28 The need for constitutional protection

Aboriginal and treaty rights suffered from four serious infirmities. One was the uncertainty as to the precise legal status of the rights. Both the relationship of the aboriginal peoples to the land and the treaties between the Crown and the aboriginal peoples lacked close analogies in the common law. This uncertainty has been partially lifted by recent decisions recognizing aboriginal and treaty rights, but uncertainties persist, especially as to the definition of aboriginal rights. The second infirmity was the doctrine of parliamentary sovereignty, which meant that aboriginal rights were vulnerable to change or abolition by the action of the competent legislative body. The third infirmity was the liberal idea of equality, which gained increasing acceptance in Canada after the second world war. As well as creating a political climate unsympathetic

---

[Section 28:27]

[1]See § 28:22, "Extinguishment of aboriginal rights", where the authorities for treaty rights as well as aboriginal rights are cited.

[2]Cf. *Simon v. The Queen*, [1985] 2 S.C.R. 387, 404 (obiter dictum).

[3]*R. v. Sioui*, [1990] 1 S.C.R. 1025, 1066.

[4]*R. v. Sioui*, [1990] 1 S.C.R. 1025, 1063. Lamer C.J. does not qualify his assertion by reference to legislative extinguishments before 1982 or constitutional extinguishments, but he is not addressing those modes of extinguishment, and it is clear that they do not require the consent of the Indians.

to the recognition of special rights peculiar to a group defined by race, the idea of equality, when guaranteed by the Canadian Bill of Rights and, later, by the Charter of Rights, suggested that special status might actually be unconstitutional. The fourth infirmity was that aboriginal and treaty rights could be modified or extinguished by constitutional amendment, and the aboriginal peoples' representatives were not entitled to participate in the decisive phases of the amending process.

The Constitution Act, 1982, supplemented by an amendment adopted in 1984, has taken steps to eliminate these four infirmities. Section 35 of the Constitution Act, 1982 provides that "the existing aboriginal and treaty rights of the aboriginal peoples of Canada are hereby recognized and affirmed". This gives constitutional recognition (but not definition) to "aboriginal and treaty rights", and protects them from legislative attack. Section 25 of the Constitution Act, 1982, which is part of the Charter of Rights, provides that the Charter of Rights is not to be construed as derogating from "aboriginal, treaty or other rights or freedoms that pertain to the aboriginal peoples of Canada". This makes clear that the equality guarantee in s. 15 of the Charter does not invalidate aboriginal or treaty rights. Finally, s. 35.1 declares that constitutional amendments to the native rights provisions of the Constitution Acts, 1867 and 1982 that directly apply to aboriginal peoples will not be made without a prior constitutional conference involving participation by representatives of the aboriginal peoples of Canada. These three provisions—ss. 35, 25 and 35.1—reinforce s. 91(24) in their recognition of special status for the aboriginal peoples.[1] They are discussed in more detail in the next three sections of this chapter.

VIII. SECTION 35

§ 28:29 Text of s. 35

Section 35 of the Constitution Act, 1982[1] provides as follows:[2]

35. (1) The existing aboriginal and treaty rights of the aboriginal peoples of Canada are hereby recognized and affirmed.

[Section 28:28]

[1]D.E. Sanders, "The Renewal of Indian Special Status" in Bayefsky and Eberts (eds.), Equality Rights and the Canadian Charter of Rights and Freedoms (1985), ch. 12, traces the history of special status in the face of these forces. As to the place of s. 35 in Canada's "constitutional culture", see B.L. Berger, "Children of two logics: A way into Canadian constitutional culture" (2013) 11 Int. J. of Con. Law 319, 333–336.

[Section 28:29]

[1]For commentary, see heading §§ 28:18 to 28:22 "Aboriginal rights".

[2]Section 35 was not in the October 1980 version of the Constitution Act, 1982. It was in the April 1981 version, but without the word "existing" in subsection (1). The entire section was dropped, apparently at the request of the Premiers of the resource-based provinces, in the November 5, 1981 federal-provincial agreement. This development attracted severe criticism and, later in November, the first ministers agreed to restore the section, but with the addition of the word "existing". Subsections (3) and (4) were not in the original version; they were added by the Constitution Amendment Proclamation, 1983.

(2) In this Act, "aboriginal peoples of Canada" includes the Indian, Inuit and Métis peoples of Canada.

(3) For greater certainty, in subsection (1) "treaty rights" includes rights that now exist by way of land claims agreements or may be so acquired.

(4) Notwithstanding any other provision of this Act, the aboriginal and treaty rights referred to in subsection (1) are guaranteed equally to male and female persons.

§ 28:30 Outside Charter of Rights

Section 35 is outside the Charter of Rights, which occupies ss. 1 to 34 of the Constitution Act, 1982. The location of s. 35 outside the Charter of Rights provides certain advantages. The rights referred to in s. 35 are not qualified by s. 1 of the Charter, that is, the rights are not subject to "such reasonable limits prescribed by law as can be demonstrably justified in a free and democratic society", although, as we shall see, they are subject to reasonable regulation according to principles similar to those applicable to s. 1. Nor are the rights subject to legislative override under s. 33 of the Charter. Nor are the rights effective only against governmental action, as stipulated by s. 32 of the Charter. On the other hand, the location of s. 35 outside the Charter carries the disadvantage that the rights are not enforceable under s. 24, a provision that permits enforcement only of Charter rights.

§ 28:31 "Aboriginal peoples of Canada"

The rights referred to in s. 35 are possessed by the "aboriginal peoples of Canada". That phrase, which is also used in ss. 25, 37 and 37.1, is defined in s. 35(2) as including "the Indian, Inuit and Métis peoples of Canada", but none of these three terms is given further definition. It is obvious that the phrase includes not only status Indians, but also non-status Indians, as well as the Inuit and Métis peoples. As noted earlier in this chapter,[1] the federal Parliament has the power under s. 91(24) to supply some degree of definition to the word "Indians" in s. 91(24), although it has never attempted a comprehensive definition. The courts would probably accept federally legislated definitions of the words "Indian", "Inuit" and "Métis" in s. 35(2), provided that the definitions employed reasonable criteria.[2]

Perhaps the most difficult of definition is the Métis people (or peoples),

---

[Section 28:31]

[1]Any liberalization of the definition of a status Indian, such as occurred in 1985 (previous note), has the effect of enlarging the population that is entitled to live on the reserves.

[2]The definition of "Indians" in s. 91(24) is discussed in § 28:2, "Indians", and the opinion offered that the term would extend to non-status Indians, Inuit and Métis peoples. In other words, the term "Indians" in s. 91(24) is just as wide as the term "aboriginal peoples of Canada" in s. 35(2). The word "Indian" in s. 35(2) has a narrower meaning than the word "Indians" in s. 91(24), because the Inuit and Métis peoples are separately identified in s. 35(2). The word "Indian" in the Natural Resources Agreements (§ 28:17) has been held to exclude the Métis people: *R. v. Blais*, [2003] 2 S.C.R. 236.

who originated from the intermarriage of French Canadian men and Indian women during the fur trade period. In *R. v. Powley* (2003),[3] a father and son, who lived in Sault Ste. Marie, Ontario, shot a moose for food. They had not obtained the hunting licence that was required by provincial law. They were charged with a breach of the provincial law. They defended the charge on the basis that they were Métis who had an aboriginal right to hunt for food in the Sault Ste. Marie area. In the absence of any definition of "Métis" in s. 35 or anywhere else, the Supreme Court of Canada had to decide whether the defendants were in truth Métis. The Court held that:[4]

> The term "Métis" does not encompass all individuals with mixed Indian and European heritage; rather it refers to distinctive peoples who, in addition to their mixed ancestry, developed their own customs, way of life, and recognizable group identity separate from their Indian or Inuit or European forebears.

The Court made clear that it was not setting down a "comprehensive definition of who is Métis for the purpose of asserting a claim under s. 35", but the Court articulated "three broad factors as indicia of Métis identity".[5] The first factor was "self-identification", meaning that the claimant must self-identify as a member of a Métis community. The second factor was "ancestral connection", meaning that the claimant must trace his ancestry to an historic Métis community. The third factor was "community acceptance", meaning that the claimant must be a member of and participant in the modern Métis community.

The key to these vague factors was the existence, before the assumption of effective control by European settlers and continuing to the present, of a community of distinctive people of mixed ancestry with "their own customs, way of life, and recognizable group identity".[6] The Court in *Powley* concluded that there was a distinctive Métis community in Sault Ste. Marie which dated back to before the early nineteenth century, when effective control in the Upper Great Lakes area passed from the Indian and Métis people to the European settlers. The two defendants self-identified as members of that community, traced their ancestry back to the historic community and were accepted as members of the modern community. They therefore satisfied the three criteria, and were entitled to Métis rights, which, the Court went on to hold, included the claimed right to hunt for food. The provincial regulation of hunting did not therefore apply to their hunting (which was for food), and they were entitled to be acquitted.

§ 28:32 "Aboriginal and treaty rights"

The rights referred to in s. 35 are "aboriginal and treaty rights". The

[3] *R. v. Powley*, [2003] 2 S.C.R. 207. The opinion was given by "the Court".

[4] *R. v. Powley*, [2003] 2 S.C.R. 207, para. 10.

[5] *R. v. Powley*, [2003] 2 S.C.R. 207, para. 30.

[6] *R. v. Powley*, [2003] 2 S.C.R. 207, para. 10.

nature of these rights has been explained in earlier sections of this chapter.[1]

§ 28:33 "Existing"

Section 35 protects "existing aboriginal and treaty rights". What is the force of the word "existing"? The word obviously has reference to April 17, 1982, which is when the Constitution Act, 1982 was proclaimed into force.

It is clear from the text of s. 35 itself that the word "existing" does not exclude rights that come into existence after 1982. Such rights could only be treaty rights, of course, since aboriginal rights pre-date European settlement. Subsection (3) of s. 35 provides:

> For greater certainty, in subsection (1) "treaty rights" includes rights that now exist by way of land claims agreement or may be so acquired.

The last phrase, "or may be so acquired", makes clear that treaty rights acquired after 1982 are protected by s. 35. The first phrase, "For greater certainty", makes clear that, although "land claims agreements" are the only kind of modern treaties expressly mentioned, future treaty rights derived from treaties that did not settle land claims would also be protected.

What is the status of aboriginal or treaty rights that had been extinguished or regulated before 1982? This was the issue that had to be resolved in *R. v. Sparrow* (1990).[1] In that case, a member of the Musqueam Indian Band was charged under the federal Fisheries Act with the offence of fishing with a drift net that was longer than permitted by the Band's Indian food fishing licence, which had been issued under regulations made under the Fisheries Act. The Supreme Court of Canada, as noted earlier,[2] held that the Indian defendant was exercising an aboriginal right to fish within the meaning of s. 35. However, the question remained: was it an "existing" right? The right to fish had for many years before 1982 been subject to a system of discretionary licensing under the Fisheries Act that, the Crown argued, was inconsistent with the continued existence in 1982 of any right to fish.

The Supreme Court of Canada in *Sparrow* held that the word "existing" in s. 35 meant "unextinguished".[3] A right that had been validly extinguished before 1982 was not protected by s. 35.[4] In other words, s. 35 did not retroactively annul prior extinguishments of aboriginal rights so as to restore the rights to their original unimpaired condition.

[Section 28:32]

[1] § 28:21, "Definition of aboriginal rights"; § 28:25, "Definition of treaty".

[Section 28:33]

[1] *R. v. Sparrow*, [1990] 1 S.C.R. 1075. Dickson C.J. and La Forest J. wrote the opinion of the Court.

[2] *R. v. Sparrow*, [1990] 1 S.C.R. 1075.

[3] *R. v. Sparrow*, [1990] 1 S.C.R. 1075, 1091.

[4] See also *R. v. Howard*, [1994] 2 S.C.R. 299 (s. 35 does not protect fishing right

The Court in *Sparrow* refused to imply an extinguishment from the admittedly extensive regulatory control of the Fisheries Act. While an aboriginal right could be extinguished by federal statute before 1982,[5] a federal statute would have that effect only if the intention to extinguish was "clear and plain". The Fisheries Act and its regulations (although they prohibited fishing, except under a statutory licence) did not demonstrate "a clear and plain intention to extinguish the Indian aboriginal right to fish".[6] Therefore, the right was an "existing" right within the meaning of s. 35.

The Court in *Sparrow* also refused to treat regulation as a partial extinguishment of the regulated right. Before *Sparrow*, it was arguable that an existing right was only that part of the right that was not regulated in 1982. On that approach, the scope of an existing right would be defined by the regulatory laws that limited the right in 1982. Those laws would, in effect, be frozen and constitutionalized by s. 35. Only the unregulated residue would be an "existing" right. The Court in *Sparrow* rejected this approach, pointing out that it would give constitutional status to a host of statutes and regulations, which might differ from place to place, and which would draw no distinction between the important and the trivial, the permanent and the temporary, or the reasonable and the unreasonable.[7] Instead, the Court held that an aboriginal right, provided it had not been extinguished before 1982 by clear and plain language, should be treated as existing in its unregulated form.

According to *Sparrow*, the effect of the word "existing" in s. 35 was to exclude from constitutional protection those rights that had been validly extinguished before 1982. This was a much less severe restriction of the scope of s. 35 than the incorporation-of-regulations interpretation that the Court rejected, but it was a restriction nonetheless. However, the Court also attributed an expansive or liberalizing effect to the word "existing". The Court held that the word "existing" meant that the guaranteed rights are "affirmed in a contemporary form rather than in their primeval simplicity and vigour".[8] This would mean that aboriginal rights to hunt and fish (for example) were not simply rights to hunt and fish by bow and arrow, bone hook, and other techniques available before European settlement, but were rights that would evolve to take advantage of the progress of technology. Similarly, a right to trade in

---

extinguished by treaty in 1923).

[5]*R. v. Sparrow*, [1990] 1 S.C.R. 1075, 1091, 1111. Folld. in *R. v. Gladstone*, [1996] 2 S.C.R. 723 (aboriginal right to sell herring spawn on kelp not extinguished by extensive regulation, including at times prohibition, of the trade); *R. v. Adams*, [1996] 3 S.C.R. 101 (surrender of aboriginal title did not demonstrate clear and plain intention to extinguish the "free-standing" aboriginal right to fish in water adjacent to the surrendered lands).

[6]*R. v. Sparrow*, [1990] 1 S.C.R. 1075, 1099.

[7]*R. v. Sparrow*, [1990] 1 S.C.R. 1075, 1092, following B. Slattery, "Understanding Aboriginal Rights" (1987) 66 Can. Bar Rev. 727, 781–782.

[8]*R. v. Sparrow*, [1990] 1 S.C.R. 1075, 1093, again following B. Slattery, "Understanding Aboriginal Rights" (1987) 66 Can. Bar Rev. 727, 782.

the form of barter would in modern times extend to the use of currency, credit and the normal commercial facilities of distribution and exchange.

§ 28:34 "Recognized and affirmed"

Section 35 provides that existing aboriginal and treaty rights are "recognized and affirmed". What is the effect of this language?

The Court in *Sparrow* held that the phrase "recognized and affirmed" should be interpreted according to the principle that "treaties and statutes relating to Indians should be liberally construed and doubtful expressions resolved in favour of the Indians".[1] The phrase should also be read as incorporating the fiduciary obligation that government owes to the aboriginal peoples. From these two premises, the Court concluded that s. 35 should be interpreted as a constitutional guarantee of aboriginal and treaty rights. As a constitutional guarantee, s. 35 had the effect of nullifying legislation that purported to abridge the guaranteed rights.

Because s. 35 is not part of the Charter of Rights, it is not subject to s. 1 of the Charter of Rights, which makes clear that Charter rights are not absolute, but are subject to "such reasonable limits prescribed by law as can be demonstrably justified in a free and democratic society". However, the Court held that the rights protected by s. 35 were not absolute either. They were subject to regulation by federal laws, provided the laws met a standard of justification not unlike that erected by the Court for s. 1 of the Charter.[2] Any law that had the effect of impairing an existing aboriginal right would be subject to judicial review to determine whether it was a justified impairment. A justified impairment would have to pursue an objective that was "compelling and substantial".[3] The conservation and management of a limited resource would be a justified objective, but "the public interest" would be too vague to serve as a justification.[4] If a sufficient objective was found, then the law had to employ means that were consistent with "the special trust relationship" between government and the aboriginal peoples.[5] In the context of the fishery, this would require that the Indian claims be given priority over the claims of other interest groups who could not assert an aboriginal right.[6] In other contexts, other questions would have to be addressed:[7]

These include the questions of whether there has been as little infringe-

[Section 28:34]

[1]*Nowegijick v. The Queen*, [1983] 1 S.C.R. 29, 36 (statute); *Simon v. The Queen*, [1985] 2 S.C.R. 387, 402 (treaty); *R. v. Sioui*, [1990] 1 S.C.R. 1025, 1036 (treaty).

[2]Chapter 38, Limitation of Rights.

[3]*R. v. Sparrow*, [1990] 1 S.C.R. 1075, 1113.

[4]*R. v. Sparrow*, [1990] 1 S.C.R. 1075, 1113.

[5]*R. v. Sparrow*, [1990] 1 S.C.R. 1075, 1113.

[6]*R. v. Sparrow*, [1990] 1 S.C.R. 1075, 1113, 1116.

[7]*R. v. Sparrow*, [1990] 1 S.C.R. 1075, 1113, 1119.

ment as possible in order to effect the desired result; whether, in a situation of expropriation, fair compensation is available; and, whether the aboriginal group in question has been consulted with respect to the conservation measures being implemented.

In the *Sparrow* case itself, the Court did not feel able to decide whether the net-length restriction would satisfy the standard of justification. The Court ordered a new trial to permit findings of fact that would enable the issue of justification to be resolved. If the net-length restriction were found to satisfy the standard of justification, then the restriction would be valid and Mr. Sparrow would be guilty as charged. If the net-length restriction were found not to satisfy the standard of justification, then the net-length restriction would be invalid as a violation of s. 35 and Mr. Sparrow would be entitled to an acquittal.

The *Sparrow* test of justification was applied in *R. v. Adams* (1996),[8] where the issue was whether an aboriginal right to fish for food had been validly limited by the federal Quebec Fishery Regulations, which provided for the issue of licences for sport and commercial fishing, but not for food fishing, although there was provision for a special permit to be issued by the minister to an Indian for food fishing. The Supreme Court of Canada held that the Regulations failed the *Sparrow* test of justification. The evidence showed that, after conservation, it was the promotion of sport fishing that was the major goal, and that did not qualify as a compelling and substantial objective. Even if the objective were sufficient, the scheme "fails to provide the requisite priority to the aboriginal right to fish for food, a requirement laid down by this Court in *Sparrow*".[9] The ministerial discretion to issue Indian fishing permits was unstructured, and did not include standards directing the minister to accord priority to the aboriginal right to fish for food.[10]

In *R. v. Gladstone* (1996),[11] the question was whether restrictions on the sale of herring spawn on kelp could be justified in their application to aboriginal people who had an aboriginal right to sell the spawn. In this case, the majority of the Supreme Court of Canada, speaking through Lamer C.J., qualified the Court's earlier ruling in *Sparrow* that

[8] *R. v. Adams*, [1996] 3 S.C.R. 101. The Court was unanimous. The opinion of eight judges was written by Lamer C.J.; L'Heureux-Dubé J. wrote a brief concurring opinion. A companion case, *R. v. Côté*, [1996] 3 S.C.R. 139, decided the same issue the same way.

[9] *R. v. Adams*, [1996] 3 S.C.R. 101, para. 59, per Lamer C.J.

[10] Folld. *R. v. Marshall*, [1999] 3 S.C.R. 456, para. 64; *R. v. Marshall (No. 2)*, [1999] 3 S.C.R. 533, para. 33 (licensing regime failed to include standards to protect treaty right to fish). Compare *R. v. Nikal*, [1996] 1 S.C.R. 1013 (requirement of licence for conservation purpose not a breach of the aboriginal right to fish, but conditions of the licence were a breach that Crown had adduced no evidence to justify; held, entire licence invalid).

[11] *R. v. Gladstone*, [1996] 2 S.C.R. 723. The opinion of six judges was written by Lamer C.J. L'Heureux-Dubé J., who wrote a separate concurring opinion, agreed with Lamer C.J. on the issue of justification. Neither McLachlin J., who also wrote a separate concurring opinion, nor La Forest J., who dissented, discussed the issue of justification. However, in *R. v. Van der Peet*, [1996] 2 S.C.R. 507, McLachlin J., in a dissenting opinion (at S.C.R. 507, paras. 301–315), strongly disagreed with Lamer C.J.'s *Gladstone* opinion on the issue of justification.

the holders of aboriginal rights would have to be given priority in access to a resource such as the fishery. Now the Court said that priority was required only when the aboriginal right was limited by its own terms, as was the case of a right to fish *for food*, which is internally limited by the fact that the right-holders need only so many fish for food. Giving priority to an internally limited aboriginal right would still leave room for non-aboriginals to gain access to the resource (assuming conservation goals were not transgressed). The right to engage in *commercial* fishing, such as the right to harvest herring spawn for sale in the open market, has no internal limitation; it is limited only by external factors, namely, the availability of the resource and the demands of the market. To give priority to a right with no internal limitations would confer on the aboriginal right-holders the power to absorb the entire fishery, effectively eliminating all non-aboriginal access to the resource. The Court held that this was not an acceptable outcome, and held that, for a right without internal limitations, the *Sparrow* requirement of justification did not require aboriginal priority, but could be satisfied by "objectives such as the pursuit of economic and regional fairness, and the recognition of the historical reliance upon, and participation in, the fishery by non-aboriginal groups".[12] The Court concluded that there was insufficient evidence to determine whether the regulatory scheme for the sale of herring spawn was justified, and remitted the issue to a new trial.

The *Gladstone* ruling on justification seems to be a departure from *Sparrow*'s insistence on "compelling and substantial" objectives. The reference to "the pursuit of economic and regional fairness" is almost as vague as the "public interest", which was rejected in *Sparrow* as an objective that would qualify as justification.[13] And the reference to "the historical reliance upon, and participation in, the fishery by non-aboriginal groups" comes close to saying that "the Crown may convey a portion of an aboriginal fishing right to others, not by treaty or with the consent of the aboriginal people, but by its own unilateral act."[14] These phrases carry the risk that later courts will not impose strict standards of justification on regulatory schemes that derogate from those aboriginal or treaty rights that are not limited by their own terms.

In *Delgamuukw v. British Columbia* (1997),[15] Lamer C.J. for the majority of the Supreme Court of Canada discussed, obiter, the kind of justification that would be required for an infringement of aboriginal title. He pointed out that the Crown's fiduciary duty would normally involve a "duty of consultation" with aboriginal people before decisions

---

[12] *R. v. Gladstone*, [1996] 2 S.C.R. 723, para. 75. Folld. *R. v. Marshall (No. 2)*, [1999] 3 S.C.R. 533, para. 41 (treaty right to fish commercially can be limited to protect non-aboriginal fishers).

[13] Lamer C.J. (at para. 63) acknowledged the vagueness of his ruling, and tried to give some guidance, suggesting, for example, that justification might involve "something less than exclusivity but which nevertheless gives priority to the aboriginal right".

[14] *R. v. Van der Peet*, [1996] 2 S.C.R. 507, para. 315 per McLachlin J. dissenting, criticizing Lamer C.J.'s opinion on justification in *Gladstone*.

[15] *Delgamuukw v. British Columbia*, [1997] 3 S.C.R. 1010.

were taken with respect to their lands.[16] He also pointed out that "fair compensation" would normally be required when aboriginal title was infringed.[17] "In the wake of *Gladstone*", he acknowledged that "the range of legislative objectives that can justify the infringement of aboriginal title is fairly broad", and he elaborated:[18]

> In my opinion, the development of agriculture, forestry, mining, and hydroelectric power, the general economic development of the interior of British Columbia, protection of the environment or endangered species, the building of infrastructure and the settlement of foreign populations to support those aims, are the kinds of objectives that are consistent with this purpose [of reconciliation] and, in principle, can justify the infringement of aboriginal title.

This language offers some reassurance that the economic development of British Columbia will carry considerable weight in the process of reconciliation with the many aboriginal peoples who have claims of title over land in the province.

In *Tsilhqot'in Nation v. British Columbia* (2014),[19] McLachlin C.J. for the Court quoted the passage from *Delgamuukw* with evident approval, and she went on to comment on provincial laws and aboriginal title.[20] She explained that "general regulatory legislation such as legislation aimed at managing the forests in a way that deals with pest invasions or prevents forest fires [on aboriginal-title land] will often pass the *Sparrow* test as it will be reasonable, not impose undue hardships, and not deny the holders of the right their preferred means of exercising it."[21] In such cases, "no infringement will result", and no justification would need to be established. The issue in this case, however, was the validity of logging licences issued under the authority of the province's Forest Act to a private company. The assignment of aboriginal property rights to a third party was an infringement that, if done without aboriginal consent (as in this case), would have to be justified. The justification asserted by the province for the licences was "the economic

---

[16]Consultation with the affected aboriginal people is a prerequisite to justification in most contexts: *R. v. Marshall (No. 2)*, [1999] 3 S.C.R. 533, para. 43.

[17]*Delgamuukw v. British Columbia*, [1997] 3 S.C.R. 1010, paras. 168–169.

[18]*Delgamuukw v. British Columbia*, [1997] 3 S.C.R. 1010, para. 165.

[19]*Tsilhqot'in Nation v. British Columbia*, [2014] 2 S.C.R. 257, 2014 SCC 44, para. 83.

[20]*Tsilhqot'in Nation v. British Columbia*, [2014] 2 S.C.R. 257, 2014 SCC 44, paras. 123–127. The discussion was not necessary for the decision of the case which was resolved in favour of the aboriginal people by the failure of the province to consult with them and if necessary accommodate their interests before issuing logging licences over the land. At the time of the issue of the licences, no aboriginal title had been established. The Court decided that the aboriginal people had now established their title to the land, and went on to comment "for the benefit of all parties going forward" on the issue of licences over aboriginal-title land.

[21]*Tsilhqot'in Nation v. British Columbia*, [2014] 2 S.C.R. 257, 2014 SCC 44, para. 123.

benefits" that would be realized from the licensed logging.[22] McLachlin C.J. had no difficulty in deciding that, on these facts, this was not a sufficiently "compelling and substantial" objective for *Sparrow* justification. The economic benefits were dubious in light of the trial judge's finding that the cutting sites were not economically viable; any benefits would in any case not be shared with the aboriginal title-holders; and any benefits were outweighed by the detrimental effects on the value of the aboriginal resource. The grant of the licences could not be justified.[23]

§ 28:35 Application to treaty rights

Sparrow was concerned with an aboriginal right, not a treaty right. In *R. v. Badger* (1996),[1] the Supreme Court of Canada held that, because s. 35 applied to treaty rights as well as aboriginal rights, the doctrine laid down in *Sparrow* applied to treaty rights as well as aboriginal rights. Before this decision, it was arguable that treaty rights ought to receive absolute protection from s. 35, on the basis that the Crown's fiduciary duty is to do exactly what it bargained to do in the treaty. Cory J., writing for the majority in *Badger*, acknowledged that the ruling meant that treaty rights that had been created by mutual agreement could be abridged unilaterally.[2] In *R. v. Côté* (1996),[3] the Supreme Court of Canada repeated that the *Sparrow* doctrine applied to treaty as well as aboriginal rights. We are left with the unsatisfactory position that treaty rights have to yield to any law[4] that can satisfy the *Sparrow* standard of justification.[5] In *Côté*, the impugned law (which imposed a fee on vehicles entering a fishing area) was held not to infringe a treaty right to fish, so

---

[22]A second objective that had been claimed at trial was to prevent the spread of a mountain beetle infestation. This would probably have been a compelling and substantial objective, and might indeed not have been an infringement of the right at all (reference to "pest invasions" in quotation supported by previous note). However, the trial judge found as a matter of fact that this was not one of the province's objectives, and on appeal the province abandoned the claim: *Tsilhqot'in Nation v. British Columbia*, [2014] 2 S.C.R. 257, 2014 SCC 44, paras. 126–127.

[23]For an effort to synthesize the case law, see P.W. Hogg and D. Styler, "Statutory Limitation of Aboriginal or Treaty Rights: What Counts as Justification?" (2015) 1 Lakehead L.J. 3.

[Section 28:35]

[1]*R. v. Badger*, [1996] 1 S.C.R. 771. The Court was unanimous, but only the majority opinion of Cory J. addressed the application of *Sparrow* to treaty rights. Sopinka J.'s concurring opinion did not need to address this point.

[2]*R. v. Badger*, [1996] 1 S.C.R. 771, para. 77.

[3]*R. v. Côté*, [1996] 3 S.C.R. 139. The Court was unanimous on this issue.

[4]In both *Badger* and *Côté*, the law was a provincial law: for discussion, see § 28:37, "Application to provincial laws".

[5]Cory J. in *Badger* left a little gap in his ruling by saying (para. 75) that the *Sparrow* criteria would apply to infringements of treaty rights "in most cases". But Lamer C.J. in *Côté*, went further by saying (para. 33) "the *Sparrow* test for infringement and justification applies with the same force and the same considerations to both species of constitutional rights". With respect, this cannot be right. In the case of a modern land claims agreement, in which the rights and obligations of the Crown and the Indian nation are set out in great detail, and in which there is provision for amendments to be

that the issue of justification was never reached. In *Badger*, the impugned law (which established a hunting season) was held to infringe a treaty right to hunt for food, and so the issue of justification was reached, but the Court held that there was not enough evidence to decide the issue. The Court ordered a new trial to determine whether the restrictions on hunting could be justified according to the *Sparrow* standard. In my view, the standard of justification for a law impairing a treaty right should be very high indeed.

In *R. v. Marshall* (1999),[6] the Supreme Court of Canada affirmed its earlier rulings that a treaty right could be regulated, provided the *Sparrow* test of justification was satisfied, and the Court did not say or imply that any higher standard of justification would be required for the regulation of a treaty right than for the regulation of an aboriginal right.[7] Moreover, the Court went a step further, holding that some kinds of laws limiting treaty rights would not need to satisfy any standard of justification. In that case, the treaty right was to fish "for a moderate livelihood", and the Court held that there was a difference between *defining* the treaty right and *regulating* the treaty right. Laws imposing catch limits or other restrictions on aboriginal fishing that had as their purpose limiting the aboriginal catch to a "moderate livelihood" were simply "defining" the treaty right, and such laws would not need to satisfy the *Sparrow* test of justification. Only those laws that would take the aboriginal catch below the quantities reasonably expected to produce a moderate livelihood should be regarded as "regulating" the treaty right, and only those laws would need to satisfy the *Sparrow* test of justification.

§ 28:36 Application to extinguishment

Before 1982, aboriginal and treaty rights could be extinguished by federal legislation, provided clear and plain words were used for the purpose.[1] It is implicit in *Sparrow* that s. 35 now protects aboriginal and treaty rights from extinguishment by federal legislation. The justificatory tests propounded in *Sparrow* would, if satisfied, save a federal law that purported to *regulate* an aboriginal or treaty right, but not a federal law that purported to *extinguish* the right.[2]

The effect of s. 35 is that aboriginal and treaty rights can only be

---

made (invariably by mutual agreement), it seems wrong to me to permit Parliament unilaterally to amend the treaty rights, however strong the justification. At the very least, a higher standard of justification should be demanded for the infringement of treaty rights than for the infringement of Aboriginal rights.

[6] *R. v. Marshall*, [1999] 3 S.C.R. 456, para. 60; for fuller discussion of this issue, see the decision on the application for a rehearing: *R. v. Marshall (No. 2)*, [1999] 3 S.C.R. 533, paras. 36–39.

[7] Accord, *Grassy Narrows First Nation v. Ont.*, [2014] 2 S.C.R. 447, 2014 SCC 48, para. 53 per McLachlin C.J. for the Court.

[Section 28:36]

[1] § 28:22, "Extinguishment of Aboriginal rights".

[2] Note, however, that Dickson C.J. and La Forest J, in the passage quoted at [1990]

extinguished in two ways: (1) by surrender and (2) by constitutional amendment.[3] The first involves the consent of the aboriginal right-holders. The second does not, but it would surely be contrary to the federal government's fiduciary duty to the aboriginal peoples to proceed with a constitutional amendment affecting aboriginal or treaty rights without at least the active participation of the aboriginal peoples.[4]

§ 28:37 Application to provincial laws

What effect does s. 35 have on provincial laws? The Court in *Sparrow* did not have to consider that question, because the only law at issue, the Fisheries Act, was a federal law. However, the Court said: "It [that is, s. 35] also affords aboriginal people constitutional protection against provincial legislative power".[1] It was not clear whether this meant that s. 35 imposed an absolute bar on any infringement of aboriginal or treaty rights by provincial law, or whether s. 35 would permit an infringement by provincial law if the law satisfied the justificatory standards of *Sparrow*.[2] The latter view was approved in *Tsilhqot'in Nation v. British Columbia* (2014).[3]

In *Tsilhqot'in*, the Supreme Court of Canada finally resolved the inconsistency between two lines of its own decisions. One line of decisions held that the justificatory standards of Sparrow were available to provincial laws impairing aboriginal or treaty rights on the same basis as federal laws.[4] That was the line that was accepted in *Tsilhqot'in*. The other line of decisions held that no province had any power to enact a law that impaired aboriginal or treaty rights, no matter how reasonable or justifiable the provincial law.[5] This line of decisions was based in the doctrine of interjurisdictional immunity, which precludes provincial

---

1 S.C.R. 1075, 1119, referred to "a situation of expropriation". I assume that what is contemplated here is the expropriation of a parcel of Indian land which, if fully justified and fully paid for, would not be a violation of s. 35, although the aboriginal rights in that parcel of land would be extinguished. This example does, however, show the difficulty of distinguishing justified regulation (valid) from expropriation (invalid).

[3]In the case of treaty rights, a fundamental breach of the treaty may be a third mode of extinguishment: § 28:27, "Extinguishment of treaty rights".

[4]Section 35:1 probably does not apply to constitutional amendments that make no direct change to any of the identified constitutional provisions but which do impair aboriginal or treaty rights. However, the fiduciary duty of the Crown recognized in *Sparrow* would, in my view, preclude such action without aboriginal participation.

[Section 28:37]

[1]*R. v. Sparrow*, [1990] 1 S.C.R. 1075, 1105.

[2]In *Mitchell v. Peguis Indian Band*, [1990] 2 S.C.R. 85, 108–109, Dickson C.J. in a separate concurring judgment made clear, obiter, that the Crown's fiduciary obligation to the Indians was owed by provincial governments as well as the federal government. The other judges said nothing on this point.

[3]*Tsilhqot'in Nation v. British Columbia*, [2014] 2 S.C.R. 257, 2014 SCC 44. McLachlin C.J. wrote the opinion of the Court.

[4]*R. v. Badger*, [1996] 1 S.C.R. 771; *R. v. Côté*, [1996] 3 S.C.R. 139.

[5]*Simon v. The Queen*, [1985] 2 S.C.R. 387, 411; *R. v. Sundown*, [1999] 1 S.C.R. 393, para. 47; *R. v. Morris*, [2006] 2 S.C.R. 915, para. 43.

laws that impair the "core" of a federal power, in this case the federal power over "Indians, and lands reserved for the Indians" in s. 91(24).[6] McLachlin C.J., who wrote for the Court in *Tsilhqot'in*, recognized that the two lines of decisions could not stand together and she gave two reasons why it was the doctrine of interjurisdictional immunity that should yield to the *Sparrow* doctrine of s. 35 justification. First, she held that, at least since the enactment of s. 35 in 1982, it was no longer appropriate to think of aboriginal and treaty rights as part of the "core" of federal power. Section 35, like the guarantees in the Charter of Rights, is not a grant of power, but a "limit" on governmental powers, both federal and provincial; s. 35 has the effect of prohibiting some laws respecting aboriginal and treaty rights that governments would otherwise be competent to enact. As in the case of the guarantees in the Charter, no different limit should be applied to provincial power than to federal power. Secondly, she pointed to the Court's decision in *Canadian Western Bank* (2007), which had insisted on restraint in the application of interjurisdictional immunity on the ground that "a court should favour, where possible, the ordinary operation of statutes enacted by both levels of government".[7] She concluded that the cases categorically barring provincial regulation of aboriginal and treaty rights "should no longer be followed".[8] The application of provincial laws to aboriginal and treaty rights should be determined by the same *Sparrow* framework as applies to federal laws.[9]

§ 28:38 Duty to consult Aboriginal people

Section 35 protects aboriginal and treaty rights, but, as we have seen, the proof of an aboriginal right (or title) can be a difficult and lengthy process, and the negotiation of a treaty (land claims agreement) can also be a difficult and lengthy process. Indeed, the two processes are closely related and are often going on at the same time. This is because the ability of a First Nation to negotiate a treaty will depend on persuading government that there is a credible claim to aboriginal title. During the

[6]The doctrine of interjurisdictional immunity creates an exception to the general rule that provincial laws apply to Indians and lands reserved for the Indians: § 28:9, "Second exception: Indianness".

[7]*Tsilhqot'in Nation v. British Columbia*, [2014] 2 S.C.R. 257, 2014 SCC 44, para. 149, quoting from *Canadian Western Bank v. Alta.*, [2007] 2 S.C.R. 3, para. 37.

[8]*Tsilhqot'in Nation v. British Columbia*, [2014] 2 S.C.R. 257, 2014 SCC 44, para. 150, mentioning only *R. v. Morris*, [2006] 2 S.C.R. 915, the most recent of that line of cases.

[9]The Chief Justice made no reference to s. 88 of the Indian Act, which provides that provincial laws of general application are applicable to and in respect of Indians in the province. By virtue of s. 88, provincial laws of general application that impair *aboriginal* rights are adopted as federal law in which case the s. 35 framework would apply even if interjurisdictional immunity continued to apply. However, provincial laws of general application that impair *treaty* rights are not adopted by s. 88, so that the s. 35 framework would not apply to those laws if the doctrine of interjurisdictional immunity continued to apply. Section 88 adds some complexity to the issues, but it probably makes no difference to the law as now declared by the Chief Justice, which may be why she did not discuss it. Section 88 is analyzed in §§ 28:13 to 28:16, "Section 88 of the Indian Act".

period of proof and/or negotiation, which will certainly take years and may take decades, the First Nation is in an awkward situation. It is not yet able to invoke a proved aboriginal right or title, and it does not have a treaty. And yet logging or mining activities, or other forms of development, on land claimed by the First Nation, may diminish the value of the resource. Does s. 35 provide any interim protection for aboriginal interests that are still unproved or under negotiation? The Supreme Court of Canada has answered this question yes. Section 35 not only guarantees existing aboriginal and treaty rights, it also imposes on government the duty to engage in various processes even before an aboriginal or treaty right is established. Section 35 gives constitutional protection to a special relationship between the Crown and aboriginal peoples under which the honour of the Crown must govern all dealings. The honour of the Crown entails a duty to negotiate aboriginal claims with First Nations.[1] And, while aboriginal claims are unresolved, the honour of the Crown entails a duty to consult, and if necessary accommodate the interests of, the aboriginal people, before authorizing action that could diminish the value of the land or resources that they claim.[2]

The duty to consult and accommodate was established in *Haida Nation v. British Columbia* (2004).[3] In that case, the government of British Columbia had issued a licence to the Weyerhaeuser Company authorizing the company to cut trees on provincial Crown land in the Queen Charlotte Islands. The Queen Charlotte Islands were the traditional homeland of the Haida people. The Islands were the subject of a land claim by the Haida Nation which had been accepted for negotiation, but had not been resolved at the time of the issue of the licence. The cutting of trees on the claimed land would have the effect of depriving the Haida people of some of the benefit of their land if and when their title was established. The Supreme Court of Canada held that, in these circumstances, s. 35 obliged the Crown to consult with the Haida people, and, if necessary, accommodate their concerns. The extent of consultation and accommodation "is proportionate to a preliminary assessment of the strength of the case supporting the existence of the right or title, and to the seriousness of the potentially adverse effect upon the right or title claimed".[4] In this case, a preliminary assessment indicated that there was a prima facie case for aboriginal title and a strong prima facie case for an aboriginal right to harvest the red cedar growing on the Islands. The logging contemplated by the company's licence, which included old-growth red cedar, would have an adverse effect on the claimed right. Since the province was aware of the Haida claim at the time of issuing

---

[Section 28:38]

[1]*Haida Nation v. B.C.*, [2004] 3 S.C.R. 511, para. 20. McLachlin C.J. wrote the opinion of the Court.

[2]See B. Slattery, "Aboriginal Rights and the Honour of the Crown" (2005) 29 Supreme Court L.R. (2d) 433; Newman, The Duty to Consult: New Relationships with Aboriginal Peoples (2009).

[3]*Haida Nation v. B.C.*, [2004] 3 S.C.R. 511.

[4]*Haida Nation v. B.C.*, [2004] 3 S.C.R. 511, para. 39.

the licence, it was under a duty to consult with the Haida before issuing the licence. Not having done so, the Crown was in breach of s. 35, and the licence was invalid.[5]

The duty to consult will lead to a duty to accommodate where the consultations indicate that the Crown should modify its proposed action in order to accommodate aboriginal concerns. In *Haida Nation*, since the required consultation never took place, the Court did not have to decide whether consultation would have given rise to a duty to accommodate. But the Court suggested that the circumstances of the case "may well require significant accommodation to preserve the Haida interest pending resolution of their claims".[6]

Does the duty to consult extend to a private party like the Weyerhaeuser Company? The Court answered no to this question. The honour of the Crown imposed obligations only on the Crown. The Court accordingly rejected the argument that the Weyerhaeuser Company was under a constitutional duty to consult (although the terms of its licence imposed a contractual obligation to engage in some consultations with the Haida). Although a private party cannot satisfy the constitutional duty to consult, it is foolish for a private party contemplating development of land that might be subject to aboriginal claims not to engage in discussions with the First Nation and learn about any objections or concerns. In one case, where a provincial logging licence had been granted to a private company over provincial Crown land within a First Nation traditional territory, aboriginal people blockaded the logging site, stopping all access by loggers, and causing the abandonment of the project. When the company sued the provincial Crown for breach of contract and negligent misrepresentation, it was held that the logging licence did not impliedly guarantee access to the site licensed by the Crown for the logging, that the Crown was under no duty to convey to the company an early warning received from members of the First Nation of their intention to stop any future logging, and that in any case an exclusion clause in the (non-negotiable) terms of the licence protected the Crown from any liability for disruptive actions by third parties.[7]

Can the Crown's duty to consult be exercised by a federal statutory regulatory body? This question arose in *Clyde River v. Petroleum Geo-Services* (2017)[8] and the answer that was provided was yes. The Inuit of the hamlet of Clyde River (on the northeast coast of Baffin Island) sought

---

[5]See also *Musqueam Indian Band v. B.C.* (2005), 251 D.L.R. (4th) 717 (B.C.C.A.) (Crown under duty to consult before selling land to which aboriginal title was claimed); *Tsilhqot'in Nation v. B.C.*, [2014] 2 S.C.R. 257, 2014 SCC 44, paras. 95–96 (Crown under duty to consult before issuing logging licences on land to which aboriginal title was claimed).

[6]*Haida Nation v. B.C.*, [2004] 3 S.C.R. 511, para. 77.

[7]*Moulton Contracting v. B.C.* (2015), 381 D.L.R. (4th) 263, 2015 BCCA 89, leave to appeal denied October 22, 2015. Levine J.A. wrote the opinion of the three-judge Court. This case is a sequel to *Behn v. Moulton Contracting*, [2013] 2 S.C.R. 227, discussed below.

[8]*Clyde River v. Petroleum Geo-Services*, [2017] 1 S.C.R. 1069, 2017 SCC 40. Karakatsanis and Brown JJ. wrote the opinion of the Court.

judicial review of a decision of the National Energy Board (NEB) authorizing offshore seismic testing for oil and gas resources in water over which the Inuit had a treaty right to hunt for the marine mammals (whale, narwhal, seal, polar bear) that they relied upon for food and for their economic, cultural and spiritual well-being. It was undisputed that the testing could impair their hunting rights. The Crown was not a party to the NEB process and did not participate in it. The Inuit complained that they had not been consulted by the Crown at any time before the NEB decision was made, although they had attended a meeting in Clyde River organized by the NEB (where the proponents of the project had been unable to answer the Inuit's questions about the effect of the testing on the marine mammals of the region).[9] The Supreme Court held that: "While the Crown always owes the duty to consult, regulatory processes can partially <u>or completely</u> fulfill this duty."[10] The Court acknowledged that "the NEB is not, strictly speaking, 'the Crown' ". "Nor is it, strictly speaking, an agent of the Crown, since—as the NEB operates independently of the Crown's ministers—no relationship of control exists between them."[11] The conclusion that may seem to follow from these premises may seem to be that the NEB could not exercise the Crown's duty to consult, but the Court's conclusion was otherwise: "In this context, the NEB is the vehicle through which the Crown acts."[12] The NEB had "a significant array of powers", which included "the procedural powers necessary to implement consultation" and "the remedial powers to, where necessary, accommodate affected Aboriginal claims, or Aboriginal and treaty rights".[13] It followed that the NEB could exercise the Crown's duty to consult the Inuit before reaching a final decision. In this case, however, the NEB's consultation was insufficient for the "deep consultation" that was required, and, tellingly, the NEB report permitting the testing made no mention of the Inuit hunting rights or that consultation was required. The Court quashed the NEB's authorization in this case, but the Court's opinion made clear that, when the NEB is seized of an issue affecting aboriginal rights, the task of consultation may be carried out by the NEB: no independent

---

[9]The proponents later provided a 3,926-page document to the NEB which the NEB forwarded to the Inuit applicants. The Court was not impressed (para. 49): "furnishing answers to questions that went to the heart of the treaty rights at stake in the form of a practically inaccessible document dump months after the questions were initially asked in person is not true consultation."

[10]*Clyde River v. Petroleum Geo-Services*, [2017] 1 S.C.R. 1069, 2017 SCC 40, para. 1 (emphasis added). See also para. 22 ("while the Crown may rely on steps undertaken by a regulatory agency to fulfill its duty to consult in whole or in part and, where appropriate, accommodate, the Crown always holds ultimate responsibility for ensuring consultation is adequate").

[11]*Clyde River v. Petroleum Geo-Services*, [2017] 1 S.C.R. 1069, 2017 SCC 40, para. 29, citing Hogg, Monahan and Wright, Liability of the Crown (4th ed., 2011), 465.

[12]*Clyde River v. Petroleum Geo-Services*, [2017] 1 S.C.R. 1069, 2017 SCC 40, para. 29.

[13]*Clyde River v. Petroleum Geo-Services*, [2017] 1 S.C.R. 1069, 2017 SCC 40, para. 34.

Crown process of consultation is needed if the NEB does the work properly.

That was the Court's conclusion in the companion case of *Chippewas of the Thames First Nation v. Enbridge Pipelines* (2017).[14] The Chippewas of the Thames First Nation, who live near the Thames River in southwestern Ontario, have an Enbridge oil pipeline crossing their traditional territory. Enbridge applied to the NEB for approval of a modification of the pipeline that would reverse the flow of part of the pipeline and increase its capacity. These changes would increase the risk of oil spills. The Chippewas requested federal ministers to engage in Crown consultation before NEB approval, but no response was received until after an NEB public hearing on the proposal when the federal Minister of Natural Resources finally replied that the government would be relying on the NEB's public-hearing process to satisfy the Crown's duty to consult. The Chippewas had been granted funding by the NEB to participate in the hearing and they had filed evidence and delivered oral argument explaining their concerns that the project would increase the risk of oil spills on their territory which would impair their use of their land for traditional purposes. The NEB approved the project, finding that any impacts on Aboriginal groups "are likely to be minimal and will be appropriately mitigated", the scope of the project was limited, no new land was needed by Enbridge, and most of the work would take place in Enbridge's facilities or on Enbridge's existing right of way. The NEB decision also required Enbridge to file an environmental protection plan, to prepare a report providing details of its present and future discussions with aboriginal groups, and to include aboriginal groups in the company's continuing education program which included emergency preparedness and response. The Chippewas argued that there had been inadequate Crown consultation, and brought review proceedings that went on up to the Supreme Court of Canada. The Court followed *Clyde River*, decided at the same time, to hold that the Crown was entitled to rely on a regulatory agency to fulfill its duty to consult. And, in this case, unlike *Clyde River*, the NEB process, which included the hearing at which the Chippewas were a fully funded, active participant, was sufficient to satisfy the Crown's duties of consultation and accommodation. The NEB decision was upheld.

Does the duty to consult extend to the Crown in right of a province (the provincial government)? It is the Crown in right of Canada (the federal government) that has the primary responsibility for aboriginal affairs, matching the federal legislative grant over "Indians, and lands reserved for the Indians" in s. 91(24). Obviously, in the appropriate case, the federal government would be under a duty to consult. But in this case it was provincial Crown land that was the subject of the aboriginal claim, and it was the action of the provincial government in licensing the cutting of trees that potentially impaired the value of the claim. The Court held that the public lands of the province were subject to

[14]*Chippewas of the Thames First Nation v. Enbridge Pipelines*, [2017] 1 S.C.R. 1099, 2017 SCC 41. Katakatsanis and Brown JJ. wrote the opinion of the Court.

aboriginal interests, and the duty to consult extended to the Crown in right of the province.[15]

Does the duty to consult extend to a municipality? A municipality is created by provincial law under the province's legislative power over "municipal institutions in the province" (s. 91(8) of the Constitution Act, 1867). Every province has a municipal statute, and in the case of larger cities, sometimes a special statute relating to that city alone. The municipal legislation invariably establishes an elected council and delegates to the council the power to levy taxes and enact by-laws under a long list of heads of power over matters of local concern. The municipality is not an agent of the provincial Crown, because it is not controlled by the provincial government: the council, having been elected by residents of the municipality, acts independently of the provincial government. Does it follow that the municipality is under no duty to consult with aboriginal peoples when municipal actions could have an adverse impact on existing or claimed aboriginal or treaty rights? "Yes" was the answer of the British Columbia Court of Appeal in *Neskonlith Indian Band v. Salmon Arm* (2012).[16] In that case, the province's Local Government Act had delegated much of the province's responsibility for flood management to municipalities; the Act required a permit from the municipality for any development of land in the municipality that was vulnerable to flooding. The City of Salmon Arm issued a permit for the construction of a shopping centre on private land that was vulnerable to flooding. Adjacent to (and downstream from) the shopping-centre site was a block of land which the Neskonlith First Nation claimed as part of its traditional territory. The First Nation took the view that the shopping centre should be built at an elevation 1.5 metres higher than the elevation allowed by the terms of the permit, and that their land would be adversely affected by flooding if the development were not elevated. They challenged the validity of the permit on the ground that they had not been adequately consulted by the City before the permit was issued. The Court rejected the challenge on the ground that a municipality is under no duty to consult with First Nations when municipal action could have an adverse effect on aboriginal or treaty rights.[17] Newbury J.A., writing for the Court, held that, in principle, "the honour of the Crown cannot be delegated", and that, in practice, no "remedial powers" had been

[15]*Chippewas of the Thames First Nation v. Enbridge Pipelines*, [2017] 1 S.C.R. 1099, 2017 SCC 41, para. 59. Folld. *Musqueam Indian Band v. B.C.* (2005), 251 D.L.R. (4th) 717 (B.C.C.A.); *Grassy Narrows First Nation v. Ont.*, [2014] 2 S.C.R. 447, 2014 SCC 48, paras. 50–53.

[16]*Neskonlith Indian Band v. Salmon Arm*, 2012 BCCA 379. Newbury J.A. wrote the opinion of the three-judge Court.

[17]This was the main ground of decision, but the Court also held that, if there had been a duty to consult, the Court would have found that the City had in fact adequately consulted the First Nation, and that in any event the adverse effect of the development on the First Nation land was too "hypothetical" and "speculative" to trigger a duty to consult.

delegated to municipalities to enable them to accommodate First Nation's concerns.[18]

The reasons given in *Neskonlith* for refusing to impose a duty to consult on municipalities are not persuasive. It is one thing to deny that the honour of the Crown can be delegated to a private person, as *Haida Nation* decided, but quite another to deny that the honour of the Crown can be delegated to a local *government*.[19] Just as Charter obligations flow down to any statutory bodies to which statutory powers are granted, so the honour-of-the-Crown obligations should also flow down to municipalities exercising statutory powers. A Legislature cannot grant broader powers to statutory bodies than the Legislature itself possesses. Otherwise, the Crown, simply by delegating its responsibilities to a municipality (over flood management for example), could evade the honour-of-the-Crown duties that are supposed to protect aboriginal and treaty rights. As for remedial powers, surely it is the municipality and not the province that has the remedial power by virtue of its power to make the decision to issue the permit. If, after consultation, the municipality were to decide that the First Nation's solution was the best answer, the municipality would have the legal power to do exactly what the First Nation had urged, namely, issue the permit for a development with a 1.5 metre higher elevation. As the legislation now stands, the province lacks the power to do this, having delegated the power to the municipality. The province would need to enact new legislation to recover the power.[20] But there seems no point to such an elaborate effort to restructure decision-making over flood management, since the municipality is likely to be a better judge of the impact of its decisions on aboriginal land in the municipality.[21]

Does the Crown's duty to consult extend to the legislative process? That was the issue before the Supreme Court in *Mikisew Cree (No. 2)* (2018),[22] where the Mikisew Cree First Nation argued that the Crown in right of Canada was under a duty to consult the First Nation before Par-

---

[18]*Neskonlith Indian Band v. Salmon Arm*, 2012 BCCA 379, paras. 66, 68.

[19]*Rio Tinto*, discussed at § 28:38 note 52, below, made clear that the duty to consult could be delegated to a statutory tribunal, provided the tribunal were also given "remedial powers". This conclusion was affirmed, and expanded upon, several years later in the *Clyde River* and *Chippewas of the Thames* decisions, which are discussed above at note § 28:38 note 8 and § 28:38 note 14 respectively.

[20]Oddly, Newbury J.A. did not suggest that as a solution. Citing *Rio Tinto*, para. 63, she suggested (para. 69) that the only remedy for the First Nation would be in the courts, although she acknowledged (para. 70) that "First Nations may experience difficulty in seeking appropriate remedies in the courts in cases like this one". Why ignore the simple solution of imposing the duty to consult on the municipality?

[21]Newbury J.A. said (para. 72) that it would be "completely impractical" for municipalities to consult with First Nations, but she then went on to find (para. 90) that, if the City of Salmon Arm were under a duty to consult in this case (contrary to her decision), the City had in fact consulted adequately, causing "material modifications of the planned development". In other words, consultation (and accommodation) was not impractical at all.

[22]*Mikisew Cree First Nation v. Can.*, [2018] 2 S.C.R. 765. There were four opinions on the duty to consult issue: one by Karakatsanis J. (with Wagner C.J. and Gascon J.);

liament enacted environmental legislation that had the potential to adversely affect the First Nation's treaty rights to hunt, trap and fish. Abella J. agreed with the First Nation: she reasoned that the honour of the Crown required that the duty to consult apply to "all contemplated government conduct with the potential to adversely impact asserted or established Aboriginal and treaty rights, including . . . legislative action"; the duty to consult arose from "the effect, not the source, of the government action".[23] However, this was the dissenting view. The majority of the Court—in three separate opinions by Karakatsanis, Brown and Rowe JJ.—held that the duty to consult is not engaged by any stage of the legislative process, including the ministerial and cabinet activities related to the development of legislation. In their separate opinions, the reasons that Karakatsanis, Brown and Rowe JJ. offered for this conclusion varied to some extent, but they each said that extending the duty to consult to the legislative process would result in improper interferences by the judicial branch with the workings of the legislative branch, contrary to the principles of parliamentary sovereignty, parliamentary privilege and the separation of powers.[24] However, Karakatsanis, Brown and Rowe JJ. divided as to whether other obligations arising from the honour of the Crown might be engaged in this context. Karakatsanis J., writing for three judges, said that, even though the duty to consult is not engaged in the legislative process,[25] the honour of the Crown *is* engaged in this context. And she expressly left the door open for the courts to develop "other forms of recourse" to ensure that the honour of the Crown is respected where "legislation may adversely affect—but does not necessarily infringe—Aboriginal or treaty rights".[26] Brown J. rejected and strongly criticized this suggestion by Karakatsanis J. The honour of the

---

one by Brown J.; one by Rowe J. (with Moldaver and Côté JJ.), who expressly agreed with the opinion of Brown J. (para. 148); and a dissenting opinion by Abella J. (with Martin J.). This case is called *Mikisew Cree No. 2* in order to distinguish it from *Mikisew Cree First Nation v. Canada*, [2005] 3 S.C.R. 388, discussed at § 28:38 note 39, below, which is called *Mikisew Cree*.

[23]*Mikisew Cree First Nation v. Can.*, [2018] 2 S.C.R. 765, [2017] 2 S.C.R. 576, para. 55.

[24]*Mikisew Cree First Nation v. Can.*, [2018] 2 S.C.R. 765, [2017] 2 S.C.R. 576, paras. 35-37 per Karakatsanis J. (invoking all three); paras. 115-126 per Brown J. (invoking only parliamentary privilege and the separation of powers); and paras. 148, 153, 160-171 per Rowe J. (invoking all three).

[25]Brown J. reads Karakatsanis J.'s refusal to extend the duty to consult to the legislative process to be "less than categorical": *Mikisew Cree First Nation v. Can.*, [2018] 2 S.C.R. 765, para. 103. However, her refusal to extend the duty seems clear enough: see e.g. *Mikisew Cree First Nation v. Can.*, [2018] 2 S.C.R. 765, paras. 1-2, 32. Karakatsanis J. did say that her conclusion that the duty to consult does not extend to the legislative process does not include "the process by which subordinate legislation (such as regulations or rules) is adopted", or "treaty provisions, implemented through legislation, that explicitly require pre-legislative consultation": *Mikisew Cree First Nation v. Can.*, [2018] 2 S.C.R. 765, para. 51.

[26]*Mikisew Cree First Nation v. Can.*, [2018] 2 S.C.R. 765, [2017] 2 S.C.R. 576, paras. 3, 25, 43-49, 52.

Crown, he said, "does not bind Parliament".[27] Rowe J., writing for three judges, agreed expressly with the opinion of Brown J., and wrote separately to offer three additional reasons that the duty to consult should not be extended to the legislative process.[28]

Taking the various opinions together, seven judges therefore refused to extend the duty to consult to the legislative process, but three (and possibly as many as five) judges seemed prepared to accept that judicial recourse may still be available where legislation adversely affects, but does not infringe, s. 35 rights in order to ensure that the honour of the Crown is respected in the legislative process.[29] (And of course, if legislation did infringe s. 35 rights, it could be challenged on that basis.) Even though the duty to consult is not engaged by the legislative process, it would be a prudent precaution, but also in keeping with the spirit of mutual respect and reconciliation, for governments to engage in consultation with Indigenous communities as part of any legislative process that seems to be heading in the direction of s. 35 Aboriginal and treaty rights.

On the Aboriginal side, the duty to consult is owed to "the Aboriginal group that holds the s. 35 rights, which are collective in nature".[30] Individual members of the entitled group do not have a right to be consulted, although "an Aboriginal group can authorize an individual or an organization to represent it for the purpose of asserting its s. 35 rights".[31] This issue was raised by *Behn v. Moulton Contracting* (2013),[32] where the government of British Columbia had issued licences to a logging company to harvest timber on sites on provincial Crown land within the territory of the Fort Nelson First Nation. Consultations had taken place with the First Nation. The Behn family, who were members of the First Nation, erected a camp that blocked the company's access to the logging sites. The company sued the Behns for interference with contractual relations; the Behns defended the action on the basis that they had not been consulted before the licences were issued, which, they argued, rendered the licences invalid. The Supreme Court of Canada rejected the defence, holding that the right to be consulted was not possessed by

---

[27] *Mikisew Cree First Nation v. Can.*, [2018] 2 S.C.R. 765, [2017] 2 S.C.R. 576, 135.

[28] *Mikisew Cree First Nation v. Can.*, [2018] 2 S.C.R. 765, [2017] 2 S.C.R. 576, para. 148.

[29] Karakatsanis J., and the two judges that joined her opinion (Wagner C.J. and Gascon J.), were clearly prepared to contemplate this result. The qualification "possibly as many as five" is added because Abella J. (with Martin J. concurring) did not explicitly reject her colleague's alternative approach—although she did express doubts about whether such an alternative approach made sense (para. 78), which may reflect her view that the duty to consult should extend to the legislative process, and not so much a complete rejection of the alternative proposed by Karakatsanis J.

[30] *Benn v. Moulton Contracting*, [2013] 2 S.C.R. 227, 2013 SCC 26, para. 30 per LeBel J., who wrote for the Court.

[31] *Benn v. Moulton Contracting*, [2013] 2 S.C.R. 227, 2013 SCC 26, para. 30.

[32] *Behn v. Moulton Contracting*, [2013] 2 S.C.R. 227. For more discussion of the case, see § 28:40, "Remedies for breach of s. 35".

the Behns, but by the First Nation, who had not authorized the Behns to represent it.

Who is to be the judge of whether the Crown's consultation and accommodation were sufficient in the unique circumstances of any given case? The Court in *Haida Nation* said that the Crown's actions were reviewable by the courts under general principles of judicial review. While pure questions of law were reviewable on a standard of correctness, the existence and extent of a duty to consult or accommodate would typically be inextricably entwined with assessments of fact. In such a case, reasonableness would be the standard of review. "Reasonable efforts" on the part of government to inform itself, to consult, and to accommodate, were all that were called for.[33]

In *Haida Nation*, the Supreme Court of Canada, while indicating that the precise nature of the consultation and accommodation that was required would depend on the circumstances of the case, emphasized that the duties of consultation and accommodation did not involve a duty to *agree* with the aboriginal people.[34] In the absence of a proved aboriginal right, or a treaty right, the aboriginal people did not have a veto over the development of land in which they claimed an interest. In the companion case of *Taku River Tlingit First Nation v. British Columbia* (2004),[35] a mining company applied to the British Columbia government for permission to reopen an old mine in an area that was the subject of an unresolved land claim by the Taku River Tlingit First Nation. This application triggered a statutory environmental assessment process, which ended with approval of the application to reopen the mine. The First Nation objected to the outcome. The Supreme Court of Canada held that this was a case where there were duties to consult and accommodate: there was a prima facie case for the aboriginal claim, and the reopening of the mine was potentially harmful to the claim. However, the Crown's duty had been discharged in this case. The environmental assessment took three and a half years. The First Nation was included in the process. Its concerns were fully explained and were listened to in good faith, and the ultimate approval contained measures to address the concerns. Although those measures did not satisfy the First Nation, the process fulfilled the province's duties of consultation and accommodation. Meaningful consultation did not require agreement, and accommodation required only a reasonable balance between the aboriginal concerns and competing considerations.[36]

The *Haida Nation* duty to consult was an interim protection measure, designed to safeguard aboriginal interests while rights were in dispute or a treaty was under negotiation. One might assume that the duty would fall away once a treaty had been entered into, and the rights of

---

[33]*Haida Nation v. B.C.*, [2004] 3 S.C.R. 511, para. 62.

[34]*Haida Nation v. B.C.*, [2004] 3 S.C.R. 511, paras. 10, 42, 48, 49.

[35]*Taku River Tlingit First Nation v. British Columbia*, [2004] 3 S.C.R. 550. McLachlin C.J. wrote the opinion of the Court.

[36]*Taku River Tlingit First Nation v. British Columbia*, [2004] 3 S.C.R. 550, para. 2.

the parties were spelled out in writing. But the Supreme Court of Canada has held otherwise. In *Mikisew Cree First Nation v. Canada* (2005),[37] the federal government proposed to build a road in a national park on federal Crown land in northern Alberta. The route of the road was through the traditional hunting grounds of the Mikisew Cree First Nation, which objected to the project for that reason. The road proposal was all within the Treaty 8 area of northern Alberta. Under Treaty 8, entered into 1899, the aboriginal people who lived in the territory had surrendered the entire area to the federal Crown. In return, the aboriginal people were promised reserves and some other benefits.

Treaty 8 gave to the aboriginal signatories (which included the ancestors of the Mikisew Cree) the right to hunt, trap and fish throughout the surrendered territory "saving and excepting such tracts as may be required or taken up from time to time for settlement, mining, lumbering, trading or other purposes". The proposed road involved an exercise of the Crown's right to take up land under this clause. Was taking up land under the Treaty subject to a constitutional duty of consultation? It was true, of course, that land taken up for development would have the effect of diminishing the area available to aboriginal people for hunting, trapping and fishing, but that was what was agreed to in 1899. The Supreme Court of Canada held, however, that "treaty making is an important stage in the long process of reconciliation [of aboriginal and non-aboriginal peoples], but it is only a stage"; and Treaty 8 was "not the complete discharge of the duty arising from the honour of the Crown".[38] Where the exercise of treaty rights by the Crown could have an "adverse impact" on aboriginal people, the honour of the Crown required consultation with the affected people.[39] In "appropriate" cases (not defined), the duty of consultation would lead to a duty to accommodate the aboriginal interests, although it did not require that aboriginal consent be obtained. In this case, the diminution of the Mikisew Cree's hunting and trapping rights in their traditional territory was a clear consequence of the proposed road. That adverse impact triggered the duties of consultation and accommodation. The discussions that had taken place between park officials and the Mikisew Cree were not sufficient to satisfy those duties. The Court quashed the minister's decision to approve the road project and sent the project back for reconsideration in accordance with the Court's reasons.[40]

Mikisew Cree is a striking example of interpreting treaties in favour of

[37] *Mikisew Cree First Nation v. Canada*, [2005] 3 S.C.R. 388. Binnie J. wrote the opinion of the Court.

[38] *Mikisew Cree First Nation v. Canada*, [2005] 3 S.C.R. 388, para. 54. Binnie J. added (para. 56) that "the 1899 negotiations were the first step in a long journey that is unlikely to end any time soon".

[39] An adverse impact did not include one that was "remote or unsubstantial": *Mikisew Cree First Nation v. Canada*, [2005] 3 S.C.R. 388, para. 55.

[40] *Mikisew Cree* was followed in *Grassy Narrows First Nation v. Ont.*, [2014] 2 S.C.R. 447, 2014 SCC 48, where the Court held that Ontario had a duty to consult before taking up land covered by Treaty 3 (1873), which included a taking-up power very similar in its terms to that of Treaty 8.

aboriginal peoples.[41] The purpose of the numbered treaties was to provide certainty in the rights of the Crown and the aboriginal peoples so as to open up land for settlement and development. Obviously, the new duties to consult and accommodate are important unwritten qualifications to the treaty language, and they are sufficiently vague and open-ended to make compliance difficult. Since non-compliance will invalidate a decision by the Crown, the certainty that is the goal of treaty-making is diminished by the *Mikisew Cree* decision. The Court did not discuss the value of certainty, but it obviously preferred to view treaties as a stage in a long process of reconciliation rather than the final step in that process. And the Court did make clear that "any administrative inconvenience incidental to managing the process" is irrelevant.[42] Modern comprehensive treaties (land claims agreements) tend to emphasize the goal of certainty. Unlike the historical treaties, the modern comprehensive treaties are the product of lengthy negotiations in which the aboriginal side (as well as the government side) is represented by sophisticated negotiators who have access to the resources needed to retain lawyers and other experts. The modern treaties are vastly more detailed than the historical treaties, running into the hundreds of pages, and they make express provision for consultation and dispute resolution processes to manage the continuing relationships between First Nations and government. Do the modern treaties leave room for some residue of the honour of the Crown to impose additional unwritten obligations of consultation on the Crown?

Mikisew Cree suggested that the answer to that question would be "yes", and this was confirmed in *Beckman v. Little Salmon / Carmacks First Nation* (2010).[43] At issue was the effect of the Little Salmon/Carmacks First Nation Final Agreement, which was ratified by members of the First Nation in 1997. The treaty was one of eleven that implemented an umbrella agreement signed in 1993 after 20 years of negotiations between representatives of all of the Yukon First Nations and the federal and territorial governments, well described by Binnie J. as a "monumental achievement".[44] The treaty conferred on the First Nation a right of access to Crown land forming part of its traditional territory (although outside its "settlement land") for hunting and fishing for subsistence. The treaty also contemplated (as in *Mikisew Cree)* that Crown land could be taken up for other purposes, including agriculture, with a consequent diminution of the hunting and fishing rights. The treaty included a definition of consultation and required or made reference to consultation in 60 places, but the taking up of land for grants to

---

[41]See § 28:26, "Interpretation of treaty rights".

[42]*Mikisew Cree First Nation v. Canada*, [2005] 3 S.C.R. 388, para. 50.

[43]*Beckman v. Little Salmon / Carmacks First Nation*, [2010] 3 S.C.R. 103. Binnie J. wrote the opinion of the seven-judge majority. Deschamps J., with the agreement of Lebel J., wrote a concurring opinion.

[44]*Beckman v. Little Salmon / Carmacks First Nation*, [2010] 3 S.C.R. 103, para. 2. I disclose that I played a minor, part-time role in the representation of the Yukon First Nations for ten of those years.

private persons was not one of them. An official of the Yukon government was authorized by statute, subject to the treaty provisions, to issue land grants of non-settlement land for agricultural purposes and he approved a grant of 65 hectares to a Yukon farmer. The granted land was within the First Nation's traditional territory. The First Nation applied for judicial review of the land-grant decision on the ground that the First Nation had not been adequately consulted by the territorial government. The territorial government responded that the treaty was a "complete code" of its responsibilities to the First Nation, and, since the treaty imposed no obligation of consultation on the take-up power, no consultation was required. The Supreme Court of Canada unanimously rejected this argument. For Binnie J., who wrote for the majority, *Mikisew Cree* continued to govern the action of government whenever its decisions would adversely affect the rights of aboriginal people, including rights recognized by a modern treaty. The duty to consult flowed from the honour of the Crown which was independent of any treaty, and, while it could be "shaped" by agreement of the parties, "the Crown cannot contract out of its duty of honourable dealing with Aboriginal people".[45] Nevertheless, in deference to the existence of the treaty,[46] the consultation requirement for the take-up power was at "the lower end of the spectrum",[47] and was satisfied on the facts of this case, where the First Nation had received "ample notice" of the application for the land grant and had successfully made its views known to the territorial decision-maker. Binnie J. therefore concluded that there was a common law duty of consultation and that it had been adequately discharged. Deschamps J., who concurred in the result, did not agree that the common law duty to consult was superimposed on all government decision-making on matters covered by the treaty. That was inconsistent with the "legal certainty" that was "the primary objective of all parties to a comprehensive land claim agreement."[48] She accepted that the treaty was not a complete code, but she held that the duty to consult would only apply to gaps in the provisions of the treaty, and she did not agree that the power to take up land for agricultural purposes was a gap of the kind that would leave room for the duty to consult.[49]

What kind of "adverse impact" on aboriginal claims or rights will trig-

---

[45]*Beckman v. Little Salmon/Carmacks First Nation*, [2010] 3 S.C.R. 103, para. 61.

[46]It is not entirely clear what weight Binnie J. placed on the treaty. As well as describing the treaty as a "monumental achievement": *Beckman v. Little Salmon/Carmacks First Nation*, [2010] 3 S.C.R. 103, para. 2, he quoted from the preamble of the treaty, which recited that the parties intended "to achieve certainty with respect to their relationships with each other": *Beckman v. Little Salmon/Carmacks First Nation*, [2010] 3 S.C.R. 103, para. 68; but, in an obscure passage of faint praise, he also said that "their efforts [the work of the successful treaty negotiators] should be encouraged", and "the Court should strive to respect their handiwork": *Beckman v. Little Salmon/Carmacks First Nation*, [2010] 3 S.C.R. 103, para. 54.

[47]*Beckman v. Little Salmon/Carmacks First Nation*, [2010] 3 S.C.R. 103, para. 57.

[48]*Beckman v. Little Salmon/Carmacks First Nation*, [2010] 3 S.C.R. 103, para. 109.

[49]While the tone of Deschamps J.'s opinion, with its emphasis on certainty, was certainly different from that of Binnie J.'s opinion, the two positions are not very far

ger the duty to consult? This was the question in *Rio Tinto Alcan v. Carrier Sekani Tribal Council* (2010).[50] In the 1950s, the government of British Columbia had authorized Alcan to build a dam for the production of hydro electricity for the smelting of aluminum. The dam changed the water flows into the Nechako River, which the Carrier Sekani First Nations had traditionally used for fishing, and which flowed through lands that were now the subject of a land claim by the First Nations. This was done without consulting (let alone compensating) the First Nations. Alcan needed the power for the production of aluminum, but its plant generated a surplus which for many years Alcan sold to BC Hydro for use as part of the province's general power supply. Contracts for the sale of power required the approval of the British Columbia Utilities Commission, which was charged with determining whether a contract was in the public interest. The Commission approved a 2007 contract under which Alcan's surplus power would continue to be sold to BC Hydro until 2034. The Commission decided that the contract would not introduce any new adverse effects to the interests of the First Nations, and there was no duty to consult with them. The First Nations applied for judicial review on the basis that they had a constitutional right to be consulted before the Commission declared the contract to be in the public interest. The First Nations' argument was based on the premises that their rights had been infringed when the dam was built in the 1950s, that the infringement was a continuing one, and that the contract was part of the project that continued to infringe their rights. The Supreme Court of Canada did not doubt that these premises were correct, but the Court held that "prior and continuing breaches, including prior failures to consult, will only trigger a duty to consult if the present decision has the potential of causing a novel adverse impact on a present claim or existing right".[51] The issue for decision, therefore, was the narrow one of whether the approval of the 2007 power-sale contract would have any fresh adverse impact on aboriginal claims or rights. Alcan owned the power and the evidence showed that it would continue to produce power at the same rate regardless of whether the sales to BC Hydro were approved; Alcan would sell its surplus elsewhere if necessary. On this evidence, it was not unreasonable for the Commission to conclude that the 2007 contract would have no new effect on water levels in the Nechako River, and would therefore have no adverse ef-

---

apart, as Deschamps J. acknowledges at para. 124. She said (para. 94) that the duty to consult applies only if the parties to the treaty "have said nothing about consultation in respect of the right the Crown seeks to exercise under the treaty". It is not clear whether Binnie J. disagreed with this formulation since he did not comment on it and he interpreted the treaty as saying nothing about consultation in respect of the Crown's right to take up land for agricultural purposes. But Deschamps J. interpreted chapter 12 of the treaty (not mentioned by Binnie J.) as applying duties of consultation (which had been discharged) to the Crown's take-up power, thereby filling the gap and negating the common law duty to consult: *Beckman v. Little Salmon/Carmacks First Nation*, [2010] 3 S.C.R. 103, para. 124.

[50] *Rio Tinto Alcan v. Carrier Sekani Tribal Council*, [2010] 2 S.C.R. 650. McLachlin C.J. wrote the opinion of the Court.

[51] *Rio Tinto Alcan v. Carrier Sekani Tribal Council*, [2010] 2 S.C.R. 650, para. 49.

fect on the claims or rights of the First Nations. The Commission's approval of the contract, including its determination that there was no constitutional duty to consult with the First Nations,[52] was therefore confirmed.

§ 28:39 Jurisdiction of the provincial courts

An earlier chapter of this book addresses the issues that arise when the provincial courts are asked to consider cases that raise extraterritorial elements, including the jurisdiction of the provincial courts to decide cases in which the facts or the parties are outside of the province.[1] Indigenous peoples occupied what is now called Canada long before the arrival of European settlers, and the imposition of colonial provincial borders. As a result, when Indigenous peoples assert claims for Aboriginal and treaty rights under s. 35 of the Constitution Act, 1982, it is inevitable that situations will arise in which the territorial scope of claims will straddle provincial borders. This raises an important question: how should the jurisdiction of provincial courts be determined when a s. 35 claim straddles provincial borders? Should the ordinary approach that is used to determine the jurisdiction of a provincial court to decide a case with extraterritorial elements be applied, or should some sort of different approach be applied—and if so, what is it?

The Supreme Court of Canada considered this question in *Newfoundland and Labrador v. Uashaunnuat (Innu of Uashat and of Mani-Utenam)* (2020).[2] This case involved two Innu First Nations, whose traditional territory (which they call Nitassinan) straddles the border of Quebec and Newfoundland and Labrador. The First Nations, and several Innu Chiefs and councillors, filed suit against two Quebec-based mining companies who were responsible for a large mining project on their traditional territory. The project, which consisted of pit mines, a railway and other industrial facilities, also straddled the border of Quebec and Newfoundland and Labrador. The Innu sought, among other things, a permanent injunction ordering the mining companies to stop all work related to the project, damages and a declaration that the project violates their Aboriginal title to their traditional territory and vari-

---

[52] *Rio Tinto Alcan v. Carrier Sekani Tribal Council*, [2010] 2 S.C.R. 650, paras. 55–94, holding that the Commission, which had the statutory power to decide questions of law, had the authority to make this determination, and would, if the determination had been otherwise, have had the authority to decide whether adequate consultation had taken place, but would not have had the authority to engage in the actual consultation (which presumably would have to be done by the province itself). This aspect of the case is discussed in ch. 40, Enforcement of Rights, under heading § 40:26, "With power to decide questions of law".

[Section 28:39]

[1] Chapter 13, Extraterritorial Competence, under heading §§ 13:9 to 13:14, "Courts".

[2] *Newfoundland and Labrador v. Uashaunnuat (Innu of Uashat and of Mani-Utenam)*, 2020 SCC 4. Wagner C.J. and Abella and Karakatsanis JJ wrote a joint opinion for the majority of the Court, which was joined by Gascon and Martin JJ. Brown and Rowe JJ. wrote a joint dissenting opinion, which was joined by Moldaver and Côté JJ.

ous Aboriginal rights associated with it. The Innu filed their claim in the Superior Court of Quebec, asking the Superior Court to consider the aspects of the claim relating to territory, not just in Quebec, but also in Newfoundland and Labrador. The two mining companies and Newfoundland and Labrador each filed motions arguing that the Superior Court did not have jurisdiction over the aspects of the claim that related to Newfoundland and Labrador, and therefore should be struck out. This provided an opportunity for the Court to consider how to approach the aspects of Book Ten of the Civil Code of Quebec that govern the jurisdiction of Quebec courts over extraterritorial claims where a cross-border s. 35 claim is involved.

The Court held, by a five-four majority, that the Superior Court of Quebec had jurisdiction over all aspects of the claim. Under a conventional approach to Book Ten, there was a strong argument that the Superior Court lacked jurisdiction over the aspects of the claim relating to Newfoundland and Labrador. However, Wagner C.J. and Abella and Karakatsanis JJ., writing jointly for the majority of the Court, emphasized that, where a s. 35 claim straddles provincial borders, Book Ten must be interpreted "flexibly so as not to prevent Aboriginal peoples from asserting their constitutional rights, including their traditional rights to land".[3] The joint majority offered several arguments for this flexible approach. First, it would recognize the nature of Aboriginal rights, including Aboriginal title, under s. 35—which are not only unique ("sui generis") rights, but also "operate uniformly across the country".[4] Second, it would facilitate access to justice for Indigenous peoples, ensuring that Indigenous claimants are not required "to litigate the same issues in separate courts multiple times"—a result that would "be particularly unjust given that the rights claimed pre-date the imposition of provincial borders on Indigenous peoples".[5] Finally, it would respect the honour of the Crown, which—like access to justice—"requires increased attention to minimizing costs and complexity when litigating s. 35 claims".[6] Applying their flexible approach, the joint majority said that the Innu's claim involved a new category of action—a "*non-classical* mixed action"—and that the Superior Court had jurisdiction over all aspects of the claim, including those relating to Newfoundland and Labrador.[7]

Brown and Rowe JJ. wrote a joint dissenting opinion (for four judges)

---

[3]*Newfoundland and Labrador v. Uashaunnuat (Innu of Uashat and of Mani-Utenam)*, 2020 SCC 4, para. 50.

[4]*Newfoundland and Labrador v. Uashaunnuat (Innu of Uashat and of Mani-Utenam)*, 2020 SCC 4, para. 64.

[5]*Newfoundland and Labrador v. Uashaunnuat (Innu of Uashat and of Mani-Utenam)*, 2020 SCC 4, para. 49.

[6]*Newfoundland and Labrador v. Uashaunnuat (Innu of Uashat and of Mani-Utenam)*, 2020 SCC 4, para. 51.

[7]*Newfoundland and Labrador v. Uashaunnuat (Innu of Uashat and of Mani-Utenam)*, 2020 SCC 4, paras. 57-59 (emphasis added). The joint majority also rejected another argument—a Crown immunity argument that Newfoundland and Labrador cannot be sued in the courts of another province—on the basis that the Innu

in *Innu*. They agreed with the joint majority that the courts should strive to "do justice to" Aboriginal and treaty rights claims under s. 35 that straddle provincial borders, but they disagreed with its solution.[8] They offered an alternative solution—allowing the provincial superior courts to draw on their statutory jurisdiction (or, where necessary, their inherent jurisdiction) to sit together and hold a joint hearing.[9] This alternative solution, they said, would give cross-border s. 35 claims "a better chance of being resolved in an efficient, timely and cost-effective manner".[10]

The *Innu* case was focused on the jurisdiction of Quebec courts under Book Ten where a s. 35 claim straddles provincial borders. However, there is nothing in the joint majority's opinion to suggest that it intended its calls for flexibility to be limited to the jurisdiction of the provincial courts in Quebec under Book Ten. Certainly, the access to justice and honour of the Crown arguments that the joint majority offered for this flexible approach would apply equally to cross-border s. 35 claims involving provincial courts in other provinces. It therefore seems highly likely that the joint majority's calls for a flexible approach to jurisdiction will apply equally where provincial courts outside of Quebec encounter s. 35 claims that straddle provincial borders.

§ 28:40 Remedies for breach of s. 35

It has already been explained that s. 35 of the Constitution Act, 1982 is outside Part I of the Act, which comprises the Charter of Rights.[1] Among other things, that means that the remedial discretion provided to a court of competent jurisdiction by s. 24 of the Charter for breaches of the Charter is not available for breaches of s. 35. That is not normally a serious disability, since it leaves aboriginal claimants with all the same remedies that are available for breaches of other (non-Charter) constitutional laws, such as the federalism rules. Generally speaking, a law that has been held to infringe s. 35 (like any other constitutional requirement) will be a nullity and will not authorize any regulatory action.[2] This opens up a wide range of remedies, most commonly a declaration that a law or other governmental act is invalid, sometimes an injunction to prevent action that is not authorized by a valid law, and

---

were not seeking relief from the Crown in right of the province, but rather from the mining companies.

[8] *Newfoundland and Labrador v. Uashaunnuat (Innu of Uashat and of Mani-Utenam)*, 2020 SCC 4, para. 256.

[9] *Newfoundland and Labrador v. Uashaunnuat (Innu of Uashat and of Mani-Utenam)*, 2020 SCC 4, paras. 218-219, citing *Endean v. B.C*, [2016] 2 S.C.R. 163. The *Endean* decision is discussed in an earlier section of this book: see ch. 13, Extraterritorial Competence, under heading § 13:10, "Jurisdiction".

[10] *Newfoundland and Labrador v. Uashaunnuat (Innu of Uashat and of Mani-Utenam)*, 2020 SCC 4, para. 223.

[Section 28:40]

[1] § 28:30, "Outside Charter of Rights".

[2] This is explained in much more detail in Part IV (chs. 58 to 60).

occasionally damages in tort, contract or breach of fiduciary duty for acts causing damage unauthorized by a valid law.[3]

In *Manitoba Métis Federation v. Can.* (2013),[4] the Supreme Court of Canada created a new cause of action that is unique to Aboriginal cases, namely, a breach of the honour of the Crown. The facts arose out of the establishment of the province of Manitoba in 1870. The Manitoba Act, 1870, which is part of the Constitution of Canada,[5] provided in s. 31 for the distribution of Crown land to the children of Métis families, a complex process that took a long time but was finally completed in 1885. The Manitoba Métis Federation and individual Métis plaintiffs sued the federal Crown for declarations that that the long process of implementation of s. 31 was a breach of the Crown's fiduciary obligation and of the honour of the Crown. The Court held that the facts did not rise to the level of a breach of fiduciary obligation (a recognized cause of action), but the Court did issue a declaration "that the Crown failed to implement the land-grant provision set out in s. 31 of the Manitoba Act, 1870 in accordance with the honour of the Crown". Although the honour of the Crown is a well-established principle governing the interpretation of s. 35 of the Constitution Act, 1982, and of treaties and statutes creating obligations to aboriginal people, it had not before this case been treated as giving rise to a cause of action for its breach. The majority of the Court held that s. 31 of the Manitoba Act, 1870 engaged the honour of the Crown and imposed an obligation of due diligence in its implementation. Although s. 31 had, after much delay, eventually been implemented, the majority held that the Crown had not exercised due diligence in the implementation, and that this was a breach of the honour of the Crown.[6] The question then arose what remedy could be granted for the breach. A "personal" (coercive) remedy such as damages was well and truly time-barred by Manitoba's limitation statutes—the proceedings had been commenced in 1981 relying on facts that occurred between 1870 and 1885.[7] But the plaintiffs claimed only a *declaration*

[3]Monetary compensation would be available under s. 24 for breaches of the Charter of Rights that did not necessarily fit into the causes of action that would give rise to damages at common law or civil law, but breaches of the Charter that cause damage are usually torts or delicts that would give rise to damages without s. 24.

[4]*Manitoba Métis Federation v. Can.*, [2013] 1 S.C.R. 623, 2013 SCC 14. McLachlin C.J. and Karakatsanis J. wrote the opinion of the six-judge majority of the eight-judge bench. Rothstein J. (with Moldaver J.) wrote a dissenting opinion.

[5]The power of Parliament to create provinces out of federal territories was retroactively granted by the Constitution Act, 1871, and the Manitoba Act was expressly confirmed.

[6]The Court was very clear that the decision was based on the honour of the Crown, but I am not sure that the Court needed to create a novel cause of action. Could not s. 31 of the Manitoba Act, 1870 (interpreted in accordance with the honour of the Crown) have been held to implicitly impose an obligation of diligent implementation on the Crown?

[7]Limitation periods apply to aboriginal claims: *Wewaykum Indian Band v. Can.*, [2002] 4 S.C.R. 245, para. 121; *Can. v. Lameman*, [2008] 1 S.C.R. 372, para. 13. In some limitation statutes, but not that of Manitoba, there is an exemption for aboriginal claims.

that the honour of the Crown had been breached.[8] The majority of the Court, explaining that the plaintiffs sought the declaratory relief "in order to assist them in extra-judicial negotiations with the Crown",[9] issued the declaration. Rothstein J. dissented, arguing that the honour of the Crown was too vague a concept to be the basis of a new cause of action, and that in any case the claim, based as it was on disputed facts occurring over 100 years ago, was statute-barred.

In s. 35 cases, as in other constitutional cases, for the most part, the normal rules of procedure and evidence must be followed, and issues of standing may arise, depending on who brings (or defends) the proceedings.[10] In *Behn v. Moulton Contracting* (2013),[11] the Behn family, who were members of the Fort Nelson First Nation, erected a camp that blocked access by a logging company to sites on Crown land within the territory of the First Nation. The logging company had obtained licences from the British Columbia Ministry of Forests to harvest timber on those sites. The Ministry had consulted the First Nation before issuing the licences. The company sued the Behns for damages for the tort of interference with contractual relations. The Behns defended the action on the ground that their s. 35 rights had been infringed, first, because they had not been consulted before the licences were issued, and second, because the logging operations were a breach of their treaty rights to hunt and trap under Treaty No. 8. The Supreme Court of Canada rejected the s. 35 defences. As to consultation, the Court held that the right to be consulted was held by the First Nation, and could not be asserted by individual members of the First Nation. As to the treaty, the Court pointed out that it was the First Nation that was the party to the treaty, but the Court left open the possibility that some treaty rights could be asserted by individuals.[12] However, the Court did not decide whether the Behns had standing to assert the treaty rights because their defences were in any case defeated by the doctrine of abuse of process. Having taken no legal steps to seek judicial review of the logging licences when they were issued,[13] it was an abuse of process to block the company's operations and force the company to either cease

---

[8]On the application of limitation periods to declaratory relief and "personal" relief, see ch. 59, Remedies, under heading §§ 59:18 to 59:19, "Limitation periods".

[9]*Manitoba Métis Federation v. Can.*, [2013] 1 S.C.R. 623, 2013 SCC 14, para. 137.

[10]In *Manitoba Métis Federation v. Can.*, [2013] 1 S.C.R. 623, 2013 SCC 14, there was a challenge to the standing of the Manitoba Métis Federation; the Court (paras. 43–44, 160) granted public interest standing to the Federation.

[11]*Behn v. Moulton Contracting*, [2013] 2 S.C.R. 227, 2013 SCC 26. LeBel J. wrote the opinion of the Court.

[12]There was some evidence that the First Nation had assigned particular tracts of land (called "traplines") to particular families for the exercise of treaty rights to hunt and trap, and the logging sites were within the Behns' trapline. The Court acknowledged that "it might be argued" that these facts provided the Behns with standing to raise the treaty rights in their defence to the company's action: *Behn v. Moulton Contracting*, [2013] 2 S.C.R. 227, 2013 SCC 26, para. 36.

[13]The Court recognized that the Behns might lack standing to take such steps, but they should have "raised the issue [by legal means] at the appropriate time": *Behn v.*

operations or take them to court. To allow the Behns to assert s. 35 rights in that way "would be tantamount to condoning self-help remedies and would bring the administration of justice into disrepute".[14]

IX. SECTION 25

§ 28:41 Section 25

Section 25 of the Constitution Act, 1982[1] is part of the Charter of Rights. It provides:[2]

> 25. The guarantee in this Charter of certain rights and freedoms shall not be construed so as to abrogate or derogate from any aboriginal, treaty or other rights or freedoms that pertain to the aboriginal peoples of Canada including
>
> (a) any rights or freedoms that have been recognized by the Royal Proclamation of October 7, 1763; and
>
> (b) any rights or freedoms that now exist by way of land claims agreements or may be so acquired.

Section 25 is part of the Charter of Rights, but it does not create any new rights. It is an interpretative provision, included to make clear that the Charter is not to be construed as derogating from "any aboriginal, treaty or other rights or freedoms that pertain to the aboriginal peoples of Canada". In the absence of s. 25, it would perhaps have been arguable that rights attaching to groups defined by race were invalidated by s. 15 (the equality clause) of the Charter.

In *Corbiere v. Canada* (1999),[3] an equality challenge was mounted against a provision of the Indian Act that restricted voting rights in band elections to those who lived on the band's reserve. In response, it was argued that the provision was one of the "other rights or freedoms" referred to in s. 25 of the Charter of Rights and was therefore shielded from constitutional attack. The Court acknowledged that "other rights

---

Moulton Contracting, [2013] 2 S.C.R. 227, 2013 SCC 26, para. 37. It would probably have been better for the Court to resolve the issue of standing to assert treaty rights (previous note), because, if the Behns did indeed have no legal recourse at any time for the impact of the logging licences on their traditional hunting and trapping activities, they might well have concluded that their only remedy was of the self-help variety.

[14]*Behn v. Moulton Contracting*, [2013] 2 S.C.R. 227, 2013 SCC 26, para. 42.

[Section 28:41]

[1]For commentary, see § 28:19 note 1, above; also, Wildsmith, Aboriginal Peoples and s. 25 of the Charter (1988).

[2]Section 25 was not in the October 1980 version of the Charter, although there was a reference to "rights or freedoms that pertain to the native peoples of Canada" in the October 1980 version of s. 26. Section 25 was included for the first time in the April 1981 version, and the reference to native peoples was removed from s. 26. Paragraph (b) was substituted by the Constitution Amendment Proclamation, 1983. The former paragraph provided:

> (b) any rights or freedoms that may be acquired by the aboriginal peoples of Canada by way of land claims settlement.

[3]*Corbiere v. Canada*, [1999] 2 S.C.R. 203.

or freedoms" might include statutory rights, but did not suggest which statutory rights would qualify. For the purpose of disposing of this case, it was sufficient to hold that "the fact that legislation relates to Aboriginal people cannot alone bring it within the scope of the 'other rights or freedoms' included in s. 25".[4] The Court struck down the residence provision under s. 15 on the basis that it discriminated against those Indian band members who lived off the band's reserve.

The previous section of this chapter has described s. 35 of the Constitution Act, 1982, under which "the existing aboriginal and treaty rights of the aboriginal peoples of Canada are hereby recognized and affirmed". Section 35 is not merely a saving provision, but affords constitutional protection from legislative impairment for the rights that it covers. Section 35 obviously leaves s. 25 with very little work to do. However, as was suggested in *Corbiere*, the class of rights saved by s. 25 is probably wider than the class of rights guaranteed by s. 35, by reason of the reference in s. 25 to "other" rights or freedoms.[5] It may also be significant that the rights referred to in s. 25 are not qualified by the word "existing" and they expressly include rights recognized by the Royal Proclamation of 1763.

Section 25 is the same as s. 35 in its description of the rights-holders as the "aboriginal peoples of Canada". As noted in the discussion of s. 35, that phrase is defined by s. 35(2) as including "the Indian, Inuit and Métis peoples of Canada".

X. SECTION 35.1

§ 28:42 Section 35.1

Section 91(24) of the Constitution Act, 1867 and ss. 25 and 35 of the Constitution Act, 1982 can, of course, be repealed or amended by the process of constitutional amendment. The appropriate procedure would be the general (seven-fifty) amending procedure of s. 38 of the Constitution Act, 1982.[1] That procedure, it will be recalled, requires the assent of the federal Parliament and the Legislatures of two-thirds of the provinces representing 50 per cent of the population of the provinces. Aboriginal peoples have been concerned that their constitutional protections are still vulnerable, in the sense that they could be impaired by a

[4] *Corbiere v. Canada*, [1999] 2 S.C.R. 203, para. 52 per L'Heureux-Dubé J.; agreed to by majority, para. 20.

[5] In *R. v. Kapp*, [2008] 2 S.C.R. 483, Bastarache J., concurring, held that an Indian fishing licence (not reflecting an aboriginal right to fish) was an "other" right or freedom, protected from challenge under s. 15(1). McLachlin C.J. and Abella J., writing for the eight-judge majority, decided the case under s. 15(2) (affirmative action), and they expressed "concern" about Bastarache J.'s reasoning, suggesting without deciding (para. 63) that s. 25 protected "only rights of a constitutional character".

[Section 28:42]

[1] If an amendment affected aboriginal rights only within a single province, s. 38 would still be the appropriate procedure. Section 43 applies to the amendment of "any provision that applies to one or more, but not all, provinces". Sections 91(24), 25 and 35 are not so limited.

process in which their organizations play no formal role. In fact, ss. 25 and 35 of the Constitution Act, 1982 have already been amended once,[2] but in ways that were agreed to by representatives of the aboriginal peoples at a constitutional conference of first ministers held in March 1983 to which representatives of the aboriginal peoples were invited.[3]

The changes agreed to in March 1983 did not include a veto for aboriginal peoples on constitutional amendments affecting their rights, but a new section 35.1 was added, which went some distance in that direction. Section 35.1 declares that the federal and provincial governments "are committed to the principle" that, before any amendment is made to s. 91(24) or to s. 35 or to s. 25,[4] a constitutional conference will be convened to which representatives of the aboriginal peoples of Canada will be invited to participate in discussions of the proposed amendment.[5] Through s. 35.1, the aboriginal peoples have gained entry to the constitutional amendment process. This privilege is accorded to no other group outside government, which emphasizes that the special status of the aboriginal peoples is now firmly accepted in Canada.

XI. CHARLOTTETOWN ACCORD

§ 28:43 Charlottetown Accord

The Charlottetown Accord of 1992[1] proposed an elaborate set of new constitutional provisions respecting aboriginal peoples. A new section

---

[2]Constitution Amendment Proclamation, 1983, R.S.C. 1985, Appendix II, No. 46, substituting new s. 25(b), adding new s. 35(3) and (4), and adding new ss. 35.1, 37.1, 54.1 and 61 of the Constitution Act, 1982.

[3]This conference, including the participation of representatives of the native peoples, had been mandated by s. 37 of the Constitution Act, 1982. Section 37.1, agreed to at that same conference, mandated two further such conferences. These conferences were held in 1985 and 1987, and they attempted to agree on language that would expressly recognize a right of aboriginal self-government. Unfortunately, agreement could not be reached.

[4]§ 35:1 probably does not apply to constitutional amendments that make no direct change to any of the identified constitutional provisions but which do impair aboriginal or treaty rights. However, the fiduciary duty of the Crown recognized in *Sparrow* would, in my view, preclude such action without aboriginal participation.

[5]Schwartz, First Principles, Second Thoughts (Institute for Research on Public Policy, Montreal, 1986), 127–131, argues that s. 35.1 is invalid. The argument is that s. 35.1 is, in effect, an amendment to Part V of the Constitution Act, 1982 (which contains the amending procedures); such an amendment requires unanimous provincial consent (s. 41(e)); and the Constitution Amendment Proclamation, 1983 (which added s. 35.1) was ratified by only nine provincial legislative assemblies because at that time (1983) Quebec was boycotting the constitutional amending process. The premise of this argument is dubious. Section 35.1 is not literally an amendment to Part V, and s. 35.1 is not addressed to the Governor General, Senate, House of Commons or legislative assemblies which are governed by Part V.

[Section 28:43]

[1]Chapter 4, Amendment, under heading § 4:3, "The failure to accommodate Quebec". I disclose that I was one of the legal advisers to the Assembly of First Nations in the discussions leading to the Charlottetown Accord, and I have also given advice to the Council for Yukon First Nations and other aboriginal organizations in their land

35.1 would recognize that the aboriginal peoples of Canada "have the inherent right of self-government within Canada". This right would not be enforceable in the courts for a period of five years, during which time (as well as afterwards) the federal and provincial governments would be committed to the negotiation of self-government agreements. The self-government agreements would be enforceable, and they would create treaty rights that were protected by s. 35. The Charter of Rights would apply to the institutions of self-government. These provisions were supplemented by ancillary provisions that attempted to give some definition to aboriginal self-government and to set up the framework for a "political accord" that would guide the process of self-government negotiations.

The defeat of the Charlottetown Accord in the referendum of 1992 spelled the end of the aboriginal provisions of the Accord. However, the Accord will have some lasting effects on the status of aboriginal peoples. In the first place, the leaders of the four national aboriginal organizations,[2] along with the eleven first ministers and the two territorial leaders, were full parties to all the discussions that led up to the Accord. Aboriginal participation was not confined to the aboriginal provisions of the Accord, but extended to all its far-reaching provisions. In this way, the aboriginal organizations were treated as if they were already a third order of government, as was contemplated by the Accord. In the second place, the agreement by all first ministers and territorial leaders that the aboriginal peoples have an "inherent" right of self-government should probably be regarded as an informal recognition that the right exists now, albeit in inchoate form, despite the failure to ratify the express declaration to that effect in the Accord. This recognition by all governments should facilitate the negotiation of self-government agreements between governments and first nations, which can of course take place under the existing constitutional provisions, and which is already in progress in some parts of the country. Nor is there any reason why the provisions of self-government agreements, which are modern treaties, should not have constitutional status as treaty rights protected under s. 35.[3] The movement to self-government can and will proceed despite the failure of the Charlottetown Accord.

---

claim and self-government processes.

[2]The four organizations that were represented were the Assembly of First Nations, representing most status Indians (Indians, as defined in the Indian Act), the Native Council of Canada, representing mainly non-status Indians, the Métis National Council, representing Métis, and the Inuit Tapirisat of Canada, representing Inuit.

[3]Constitutional status as aboriginal rights is also arguable, based on the inherent (aboriginal) right of self-government. Aboriginal rights in the event of secession by Quebec are discussed in Grand Council of the Crees, *Sovereign Injustice* (study by P. Joffe, 1995) and are referred to in *Re Secession of Quebec*, [1998] 2 S.C.R. 217, paras. 82, 96, 139.

Chapter 32

Health

I. PROVINCIAL POWER OVER HEALTH

§ 32:1 Provincial power over health

II. FEDERAL POWER OVER HEALTH

§ 32:2 Federal power over health

III. CANADA HEALTH ACT

§ 32:3 Canada Health Act

IV. UNIVERSALITY OF PUBLIC HEALTH CARE

§ 32:4 Universality of public health care

V. COMPREHENSIVENESS OF PUBLIC HEALTH CARE

§ 32:5 Comprehensiveness of public health care

VI. ACCESSIBILITY OF PUBLIC HEALTH CARE

§ 32:6 Accessibility of public health care

I. PROVINCIAL POWER OVER HEALTH

§ 32:1 Provincial power over health

Health[1] is not a single matter assigned exclusively to one level of government by the Constitution Act, 1867. Like inflation[2] and the environment,[3] it is an amorphous topic, which in its entirety encompasses matters within federal as well as provincial jurisdiction. A law dealing with some aspect of health will come within federal or provincial jurisdiction depending upon the purpose and effect of the law.[4]

The Constitution Act, 1867, by s. 92(16) confers on the provincial

---

[Section 32:1]

[1]A. Lajoie and P.A. Molinari, "Partage constitutionnel des compétences en matière de santé au Canada" (1978) 56 Can. Bar Rev. 579; J. Downie, T. Caulfield and C.M. Flood (eds.), Canadian Health Law and Policy (Butterworths, Toronto, 2nd ed., 2002), esp. ch. 1 by C.M. Flood.

[2]*Re Anti-Inflation Act*, [1976] 2 S.C.R. 373, 458.

[3]*Friends of Oldman River Society v. Can.*, [1992] 1 S.C.R. 3, 63, 64, 70.

[4]*Schneider v. The Queen*, [1982] 2 S.C.R. 112, 142; *RJR-MacDonald v. Can.*, [1995]

Legislatures the power to make laws in relation to "all matters of a merely local or private nature in the province". This head of power has had little work to do, because of the broad scope attributed by the courts to "property and civil rights in the province" in s. 92(13). But s. 92(16) is the source of provincial authority over some matters of public health. In *Schneider v. The Queen* (1982),[5] for example, British Columbia's Heroin Treatment Act, which provided for the compulsory apprehension, assessment and treatment of drug users, was challenged on the ground that it was really a criminal law and therefore outside the powers of the province. The Supreme Court of Canada held that the law came within provincial authority over public health as a local or private matter under s. 92(16).[6] Provincial mental health legislation, providing for the compulsory apprehension, assessment and treatment of persons suffering from a "mental disorder", is valid on the same basis, even when a compulsory power of psychiatric assessment is used in aid of the sentencing of a convicted criminal.[7]

Section 92(13), the power over "property and civil rights in the province", which covers contract, tort and property, is the main provincial power over health (as of so much else). It authorizes the provincial Legislatures to regulate business in the province (except for those industries coming within federal jurisdiction). This covers the insurance industry, including the public provision of health insurance and the regulation of the private provision of health insurance. It covers the professions, including the health care professions, all of which are regulated provincially. It covers food and drug standards, as well as the regulation of the preparation and service of food and drink in restaurants and bars. It covers the field of labour relations and labour standards (except in those industries coming within federal jurisdiction), including employment-related health benefits and occupational health and safety requirements.[8]

Section 92(7) authorizes the provinces to make laws in relation to "the establishment, maintenance, and management of hospitals, asylums, charities, and eleemosynary institutions in and for the province, other than marine hospitals". This authorizes the provinces to establish and regulate hospitals, and to regulate hospital-based health care services.[9] Marine hospitals are expressly excluded from s. 92(7), because they are

---

3 S.C.R. 199, para. 32; *Eldridge v. B.C.*, [1997] 3 S.C.R. 624, para. 24; *Carter v. Can.*, [2015] 1 S.C.R. 331, 2015 SCC 5, para. 53.

[5] *Schneider v. The Queen*, [1982] 2 S.C.R. 112.

[6] This was the reasoning of Dickson J. for seven of the nine judges. In separate concurring opinions, Laskin C.J. agreed generally with Dickson J. and Estey J. agreed in the result but relied on s. 92(7) and (13) as well as (16).

[7] *R. v. Lenart* (1998), 39 O.R. (3d) 55 (C.A.). The Court was vague about which head of power authorized the legislation, but s. 92(16) is the obvious one.

[8] Chapter 21, Property and Civil Rights, expands on these well-settled points.

[9] Assisted human reproduction is a matter that has been upheld under the provincial power over health, combined with powers over the medical profession, property and civil rights and local matters, although this matter is shared with the federal

included in the list of federal powers (s. 91(11)). Marine hospitals used to exist for the inspection and treatment of immigrants arriving by sea. The close connection to immigration (as well as navigation and shipping) is undoubtedly the reason for the allocation of marine hospitals to federal power.

In *Canada v. PHS Community Services Society* (2011),[10] the Supreme Court of Canada confirmed that the provinces have a "broad and extensive" power over health, and that the power comes from ss. 92(7), 92(13) and 92(16). The case concerned a safe-injection clinic, established under provincial law, which provided a safe, supervised environment, trained staff and clean equipment to enable injection drug users to inject drugs (which they brought with them). There was no doubt that the province had the power to establish such a facility, which provided health care services in the province. The issue was whether the clinic was also subject to the federal criminal law, which prohibited the possession of narcotics, and which would force the closure of the clinic, since both staff and patients would be guilty of that crime. The Court held that the clinic was not entitled to a constitutional exemption under the doctrine of interjurisdictional immunity,[11] but that it was entitled to be granted a *statutory* exemption by the federal Minister of Health because the Minister's attempt to deny the exemption was a breach of s. 7 of the Charter in light of evidence showing the impact that the closure of the clinic would have on life, liberty and security of the person.

II. FEDERAL POWER OVER HEALTH

§ 32:2 Federal power over health

The federal Parliament's power over the peace, order, and good government of Canada, which is in the opening words of s. 91 of the Constitution Act, 1867, is the national analogue of the provincial power over local or private matters in s. 92(16). The peace, order, and good government power extends to public health matters that have attained national dimensions, either under the national concern branch of the power, or under the emergency branch of the power.[1] The Privy Council contemplated the emergency branch as the source of authority to deal with an "epidemic of pestilence".[2]

While the provinces have the power to regulate most industries and their labour relations, there is a set of industries that is within federal

---

Parliament under its power over criminal law: *Re Assisted Human Reproduction Act*, [2010] 3 S.C.R. 457.

[10] *Canada v. PHS Community Services Society*, [2011] 3 S.C.R. 134.

[11] This part of the case is discussed in ch. 15, Judicial Review on Federal Grounds, under heading § 15:21, "Provincial subjects".

[Section 32:2]

[1] Chapter 17, Peace, Order, and Good Government, expands on this description.

[2] *Toronto Electric Commrs. v. Snider*, [1925] A.C. 396, 412.

jurisdiction. Banking is one of these,[3] as is much of the transportation and communications sector, including ships, railways, airlines, telephone systems and radio and television stations.[4] In this federal sector, employment-related health benefits and occupational health and safety come within federal jurisdiction. The federal Parliament also has authority over some classes of people: veterans (s. 91(7)), aboriginal people (s. 91(24)) and immigrants (s. 91(25)); and (concurrently with the provinces) has authority over their health care.

The federal power over criminal law in s. 91(27) authorizes laws to punish or regulate conduct that is dangerous to health, such as the use of narcotics and tobacco, and the regulation of hazardous products.[5] The federal Criminal Code used to prohibit abortion (unless approved by a therapeutic abortion committee) until the law was struck down by the Supreme Court of Canada for breach of s. 7 of the Charter of Rights.[6] The Criminal Code no longer prohibits a person from attempting suicide (or committing suicide). The Criminal Code used to prohibit all third parties from assisting a person to commit suicide. However, in response to the decision of the Supreme Court of Canada in *Carter v. Canada* (2015),[7] which struck down the offence under s. 7 of the Charter, but only with respect to physician-assisted death, the Criminal Code was amended. The Criminal Code now makes an exception for physician-assisted death, which is subject to various restrictions.[8] Non-physician-assisted death is still an offence.[9]

The federal power over patents in s. 91(22) obviously includes the regulation of pharmaceutical patents, which has been held to extend to the compulsory licensing of the manufacture of patented drugs so as to improve access by bringing prices down to competitive levels.[10]

The federal spending power allows Parliament to impose conditions on federal grants to the provinces, including conditions that come within provincial jurisdiction and which for that reason could not be directly legislated by Parliament.[11] Parliament has used this power to impose national standards on the provinces' health care insurance plans as a

---

[3]Chapter 21, Property and Civil Rights, and ch. 24, Financial Institutions.

[4]Chapter 22, Transportation and Communication.

[5]Chapter 18, Criminal Law. This was affirmed in *Can. v. PHS Community Services Society*, [2011] 3 S.C.R. 134, described in the previous section of this chapter. On assisted human reproduction, see *Re Assisted Human Reproduction Act*, [2010] 3 S.C.R. 457.

[6]*R. v. Morgentaler (No. 2)*, [1988] 1 S.C.R. 30; discussed in § 32:6, "Accessibility of public health care".

[7]*Carter v. Canada*, [2015] 1 S.C.R. 331, not following the s. 7 analysis of *Rodriguez v. B.C.*, [1993] 3 S.C.R. 519 (upholding validity of offence against attack under ss. 7, 12 and 15 of the Charter).

[8]The Criminal Code amendments are discussed in more detail in ch. 40, Enforcement of Rights, under heading § 40:4, "Temporary validity".

[9]*R. v. Latimer*, [2001] 1 S.C.R. 3 (mercy killing is murder).

[10]*Smith, Kline & French Laboratories v. Can.*, [1986] 1 F.C. 274 (T.D.).

[11]Chapter 6, Financial Arrangements, under heading § 6:8, "Spending power".

condition of federal cash contributions to the provinces. The Canada Health Act[12] is the law that sets the standards; it is discussed in the next section of this chapter.

III. CANADA HEALTH ACT

§ 32:3 Canada Health Act

The provision of health care services to individuals in each province is a matter that comes within the jurisdiction of the provinces. The relevant provisions of the Constitution Act, 1867 were described earlier in this chapter.[1] They are s. 92(7), which confers jurisdiction over hospitals, and s. 92(13) (property and civil rights), which confers jurisdiction over the health care professions and health insurance.

In exercise of its powers over the provision of health care, each provincial Legislature has enacted a health care insurance plan, which governs the delivery of hospital and physician services and some other medical services. Each provincial plan establishes a publicly-funded insurance system for the health care services that it specifies (they are described as "insured services"). All residents of the province (who have, of course, paid for the services through taxes or premiums) are entitled to receive those services free of charge at the time of use. Hospitals, physicians and other providers of the publicly insured services are paid directly by the provincial government. They are not permitted to bill patients directly for the insured services; nor are they permitted to impose fees or charges over and above those provided by the government.

There is more uniformity to these provincial health care insurance plans than might be expected of provincial laws in a federal system. Indeed, despite the terms of the Constitution, Canadians usually speak of Medicare as a national program. This is because the Government of Canada contributes to the cost of each province's health care insurance plan, and imposes national standards on the provinces as a condition of accepting the federal contribution. The federal conditions are enacted in the Canada Health Act,[2] which stipulates that, in order for a province's health care insurance plan to qualify for "a full cash contribution" by the Government of Canada to the province, the province's plan must satisfy five criteria. The criteria are: (1) public administration; (2) comprehensiveness; (3) universality; (4) portability; and (5) accessibility. The Canada Health Act does not directly impose these rules on the delivery of health care in the provinces; that would be an unconstitutional intrusion into provincial legislative power over the delivery of health care. The Act simply stipulates the terms on which federal funding can be granted to each province. Because the Act only applies to federal spend-

---

[12] R.S.C. 1985, c. C-6.

[Section 32:3]

[1] § 32:1, "Provincial power over health".

[2] R.S.C. 1985, c. C-6, ss. 7-12.

ing, and does not regulate the delivery of health care in each province, it is a valid exercise of the Parliament of Canada's spending power.[3]

Medicare as a national program began in 1968. It was originally a "shared-cost program", with the federal and provincial governments each bearing 50 per cent of the cost of each provincial health care insurance plan. However, in order to limit the growth of federal expenditures and provide more incentive to provinces to control costs generally, in 1977 Parliament modified the formula for the federal contributions so that they are now based on the growth in the gross national product and the population rather than on the actual growth in provincial expenditures for health care.[4] This has caused a steep decline in the percentage of the federal contribution, because the cost of each provincial health care plan has increased more rapidly than the growth in the gross national product and the population.[5] Nevertheless, the federal contribution is still sufficiently important to the provinces that they all choose to accept the federal funding—and the Canada Health Act conditions that come with the funding. If a province chose to forego the federal funding, it would no longer be bound by the Canada Health Act, and would be legally free of the five conditions. As a political matter, however, the Canada Health Act enjoys strong popular support, so that, even for a province that could afford to finance a universal system of public health care on its own, radical departures from the Act are not politically attractive.

IV. UNIVERSALITY OF PUBLIC HEALTH CARE

§ 32:4 Universality of public health care

For a provincial health care insurance plan to be "universal", the Canada Health Act stipulates in s. 10 that the plan must cover all of the "residents" of the province on the same terms and conditions. This extends to non-citizens (permanent residents) as well as to citizens. The Act, by s. 2, permits a province to impose a waiting period of up to three months for new arrivals. This short period is probably in accord with the mobility rights in s. 6 of the Charter of Rights. Section 6 guarantees to "citizens" the right "to move and take up residence in any province", but the section explicitly permits provinces to enact "reasonable residency requirements as a qualification for the receipt of publicly provided social services".

---

[3]*Eldridge v. B.C.*, [1997] 3 S.C.R. 624, para. 25 (obiter dictum). See also S. Choudhry, "Bill 11, the Canada Health Act and the Social Union" (2000) 38 Osgoode Hall L.J. 39.

[4]The story is related in ch. 6, Financial Arrangements, § 6:7, "Conditional federal grants".

[5]An initial part of the federal contribution was "tax points" (a reduction of federal income tax to allow room for increased provincial income tax), but this contribution is effectively beyond recall by the Government of Canada. The Canada Health Act, by s. 7, provides that its conditions apply only to the "cash contribution" of the Government of Canada. Non-compliance by a province would not lead to a withdrawal of tax points from that province.

In *Eldridge v. British Columbia* (1997),[1] a group of deaf residents of British Columbia challenged the province's failure to fund sign-language interpretation as part of the province's health care insurance plan. The Supreme Court of Canada held that this was a violation of s. 15 (the equality guarantee) of the Charter of Rights. Since effective communication with health care practitioners was essential to the provision of medical services, and since effective communication was automatically available to the hearing population, the failure to include sign-language interpretation in the health care insurance plan was the denial of a benefit to deaf people that was available to hearing people. This constituted discrimination on the ground of physical disability in breach of s. 15 of the Charter. The province was ordered to include in its health care insurance plan the funding for sign-language interpretation "where necessary for effective communication in the delivery of medical services".[2] This ruling covers doctors' offices as well as hospitals, wherever publicly-funded medical services are delivered, throughout the province.

The Court in *Eldridge* did not consider whether the constitutional requirement of public provision of interpretation services applied to minority-language speakers, who (like the deaf) would also need interpretation for effective communication with medical practitioners. Their case is not quite as clear, because s. 15 expressly lists physical disability as a prohibited ground of discrimination, and is silent about language.[3] Nor has language been judicially accepted as an analogous ground of discrimination.[4] However, an inability to speak English or French is a product of foreign national origin, and national origin is one of the grounds listed in s. 15. It is therefore arguable that a failure to provide interpretation to minority-language speakers seeking health care services constitutes unconstitutional discrimination on the basis of national origin.[5]

[Section 32:4]

[1] *Eldridge v. British Columbia*, [1997] 3 S.C.R. 624. La Forest J. wrote the opinion of the Court.

[2] *Eldridge v. British Columbia*, [1997] 3 S.C.R. 624, para. 96.

[3] The language rights of ss. 16–23 of the Charter cover only English or French, and in any case would not cover this situation. The right to an interpreter in s. 14 of the Charter (which is not limited to English or French) is limited to court proceedings.

[4] The various elements of a s. 15 constitutional challenge are described in ch. 55, Equality.

[5] Obviously, this would be a very expensive undertaking in provinces that have received immigrants from many different language groups. No doubt, the Court would be receptive to reasonable limitations on the right based on cost. The discussion of cost in *Eldridge* is unsatisfactory, because the Court, in what I can only describe as a lapse of its critical faculty, accepted uncontradicted evidence that the total cost of providing sign-language interpretation in every hospital and doctor's office in the province would be only $150,000 per annum! See ch. 38, Limitation of Rights, under heading § 38:17, "Cost".

V. COMPREHENSIVENESS OF PUBLIC HEALTH CARE

§ 32:5 Comprehensiveness of public health care

For a provincial health care insurance plan to be "comprehensive", the Canada Health Act stipulates in s. 9 that the plan must cover all "insured health services", which means all "medically necessary" hospital services, all "medically required" physician services and all "medically or dentally required" surgical-dental procedures performed in a hospital. Curiously, the Act does not define the crucial phrases "medically necessary" or "medically required", and nor do the various provincial statutes. In practice, each province determines which services are medically required, and only those services become the "insured services" that are covered by the province's plan. The Canada Health Act does not require that prescription drugs or non-surgical dental services be covered, and the provincial plans mostly do not cover these costs. Nor does the Canada Health Act require that the services of non-physicians be covered, and the provincial plans mostly do not cover the services of such health-care providers as ambulance paramedics, optometrists, audiologists, pharmacists, physiotherapists, chiropractors, psychologists, therapists, home-care nurses and other non-physicians.

Every provincial health care insurance plan is "comprehensive" according to the criterion stipulated by the Canada Health Act, but (as explained above) that only means that the plans all cover "medically necessary" or "medically required" hospital and physician services. The provincial plans are far from comprehensive in any ordinary sense. The lack of public funding for prescription drugs, dental services and other non-physician services causes most Canadians to take out private health insurance (often through their workplace) to fill the gaps in public coverage.

The lack of comprehensiveness of the provincial health care insurance plan of British Columbia has led to a constitutional challenge. In *Auton v. British Columbia* (2004),[1] autistic children and their parents brought proceedings to challenge the province's failure to fund "applied behavioural therapy", which was a therapy that, according to the evidence at trial, was the most effective treatment for autism. The claimants argued that the failure to fund the autism therapy discriminated against sufferers of autism, and was unconstitutional by virtue of the equality guarantee of s. 15 of the Charter. The province's statutory health care insurance plan provided full funding for all medically required services provided by physicians—as is required by the Canada Health Act. The plan also covered some (but by no means all) medically required services that were provided by persons other than physicians, but it did not cover the autism therapy. Both the trial judge and the Court of Appeal held that the province was in breach of s. 15, because it

---

[Section 32:5]

[1] *Auton v. British Columbia*, [2004] 3 S.C.R. 657. McLachlin C.J. wrote the opinion of the Court.

funded some medically required therapies, but did not fund the autism therapy. The Supreme Court of Canada reversed. McLachlin C.J., writing for the Court, held that the error in the lower courts was in the selection of the comparator group. It was wrong to compare the autism claimants with the recipients of fully funded therapies, because this ignored the fact that the autism therapy had only recently become recognized as medically required. Funding of new therapies "may be legitimately denied or delayed because of uncertainty about a program and administrative difficulties related to its recognition and implementation".[2] Because the claimants had adduced no evidence that the province was funding "other comparable, novel therapies", they could not show disadvantage or unequal treatment.[3]

No doubt, cash-strapped provinces breathed a sigh of relief when British Columbia won the *Auton* case. But the opinion is not entirely reassuring to those provinces that wish to preserve discretion as to whether or how much they fund non-physician services (which, it will be recalled, are not required by the Canada Health Act to be covered, even if they are medically required). The straightforward reading of the opinion[4] is that, if the autism therapy had been an established treatment, instead of being "novel", then s. 15 of the Charter would have been applicable, and the claimants would have been constitutionally entitled to full public funding from the province.[5] Since no province provides full public funding for dentistry and many other non-physician services that are medically required,[6] we may expect further litigation to clarify the extent of the constitutional obligation to provide funding.[7]

---

[2]*Auton v. British Columbia*, [2004] 3 S.C.R. 657, para. 55.

[3]*Auton v. British Columbia*, [2004] 3 S.C.R. 657, para. 62.

[4]The Court also held (*Auton v. British Columbia*, [2004] 3 S.C.R. 657, para. 47) that the benefit claimed "is not a benefit provided by law", which McLachlin C.J. also regarded as fatal to the claim. This ground of decision is hard to understand, since the claimants were arguing that the therapies that were provided by law were underinclusive in that they should have included the autism therapy. Perhaps the point was that the province's health care insurance plan did not purport to be comprehensive with respect to even medically required services that were not provided by physicians.

[5]Compare *Eldridge v. B.C.*, [1997] 3 S.C.R. 624 (province obliged by s. 15 of Charter to provide sign-language interpretation for deaf people seeking medical services); *Nova Scotia v. Martin*, [2003] 2 S.C.R. 504 (province obliged by s. 15 of Charter to provide full workers' compensation benefits to sufferers from work-related "chronic pain").

[6]Of course, it is the most costly treatments (for which public insurance is most needed) that the provinces are most reluctant to add to the list of services covered by their health care insurance plans. The Supreme Court of Canada accepts that high cost is a valid ground for a "reasonable limit" on a Charter right: *Nfld. v. N.A.P.E.*, [2004] 3 S.C.R. 381 (upholding a delay in the implementation of pay equity for female public employees on the ground of a financial crisis in Newfoundland). This will enable provinces to plead cost as a reason for limiting the funding of health care services as well. Curiously, the Court in *Auton* made no reference to the high cost of the autism therapy, although that was presumably the reason the province did not want to pay for it.

[7]One such case is *Wynberg v. Ont.* (2006), 82 O.R. (3d) 561 (C.A.) (Ontario funds autism therapy for pre-school children, but cuts off the funding at age 6; held, no breach of s. 15: no discrimination on the basis of age or disability).

VI. ACCESSIBILITY OF PUBLIC HEALTH CARE

§ 32:6 Accessibility of public health care

For medical services under a provincial health care insurance plan to be "accessible", the Canada Health Act, by s. 12, stipulates that the plan must provide for the services to be supplied free of charge, and there must be no extra-billing or user fees imposed directly on the patients. This is specific and clear, but s. 12 also includes the more general requirement that the plan must provide for "reasonable access" to the services. "Reasonable access" is not defined in the Act, or in any of the provincial plans. Inevitably, there is huge demand by Canadians for health care services that are absolutely free. Inevitably, government financing falls short of what is needed to meet the demand. And, equally inevitably, in such a huge and complex system, central management leads to shortages of the personnel and equipment that a free market would allocate to meet changes in medical knowledge and practice, changes in technology and drugs, and changes in the demand for particular treatments. This leads to long waits to see specialists in some fields, to gain access to some kinds of diagnostic equipment and for some kinds of surgery. Are long waiting times for medically necessary procedures a denial of accessibility? And, if so, is there a constitutional guarantee of accessibility?

Canada is unusual among the countries of the world in making its publicly-funded system of health care effectively exclusive.[1] With few exceptions, there is no parallel privately-funded alternative to the publicly-funded system. The reasons for this are complicated. The Canada Health Act, while requiring that each province's public health care insurance plan be "universal" (available to everyone in the province regardless of means), does not prohibit a parallel system of privately-funded health care. Nor does any provincial health care insurance plan directly prohibit a physician (or a private hospital) from opting out of the public plan and charging patients directly. However, the provincial health care insurance plans include a variety of regulations that are very effective in deterring physicians from opting out of the public plan.[2] For example, six of the ten provinces require that, in respect of "insured services", opting-out must be complete: physicians cannot mix their practices between private (direct-billed) patients and public (government-billed) patients. Three provinces prohibit opted-out physicians from charging more than they would get under the public plan. Six provinces prohibit their residents from purchasing private insurance for medical

---

[Section 32:6]

[1]Note that the funding of the system is all that is public. The "insured services" that are publicly funded are actually delivered privately. Physicians are not employed by the state but are private contractors. Hospitals are usually misleadingly described as "public", but they are mostly private (although not for profit) institutions that (unlike public hospitals in the United Kingdom and New Zealand) are not owned or managed by the state.

[2]For details, see *Chaoulli v. Quebec*, [2005] 1 S.C.R. 791, paras. 70–73.

services that are covered by the public plan—even though most Canadians carry private health insurance (for prescription drugs, dentistry and some other medical services that are not covered by the public plan). The cumulative effect of all these regulations is that a parallel privately-funded health care system has not been able to develop in any of the provinces. Those services covered by the public plan typically cannot be purchased privately (unless, of course, the patient is willing and able to travel outside the country to purchase the needed care).[3] This means that a person faced with a denial of timely access to publicly-funded health care does not have the option of purchasing the needed care privately.

Is it a breach of the Charter of Rights for a province to deny a patient timely access to publicly-funded medically-required health care *and* the right to purchase that care privately? That was the issue in *Chaoulli v. Quebec* (2005).[4] In that case, a physician who wanted to practise outside the public system and a patient who had suffered delays in receiving treatment in the public system brought a proceeding in Quebec. The law that they singled out for challenge was Quebec's prohibition on the purchase of private insurance for health care that was covered by the public system. The plaintiffs rightly identified that law as a critical component in the cluster of deterrents to the development of a private health care sector in the province. The plaintiffs succeeded in the Supreme Court of Canada, which struck down Quebec's prohibition on private insurance for breach of s. 7 of the Charter and s. 1 of the Quebec Charter of Human Rights and Freedoms.[5]

Section 7 of the Charter is the topic of a later chapter, where the *Chaoulli* case is more fully described.[6] It suffices to say here that the plaintiffs in *Chaoulli* had to persuade the Court of three points: (1) that the plaintiffs' interest in "life" or "security of the person" was affected; (2) a law (or other government act) deprived the plaintiffs of that interest; and (3) the law was a breach of "the principles of fundamental justice".

On the first point, the Court had no difficulty in deciding unanimously that life or security of the person was affected. The evidence in the case showed shocking delays in the delivery of services under Quebec's health

[3]A private system has developed to service persons who are not covered by the provincial health care plans (for example, workers' compensation patients, R.C.M.P. officers, penitentiary inmates and visitors from other countries) and services that are not covered by the provincial health care plans (for example, cosmetic surgery, laser eye correction).

[4]*Chaoulli v. Quebec*, [2005] 1 S.C.R. 791. Three opinions were written. McLachlin C.J. and Major J., with the agreement of Bastarache J., wrote what became the majority opinion. Deschamps J. wrote a separate concurring opinion. Binnie and LeBel JJ., with the agreement of Fish J., wrote a dissenting opinion. I disclose that I appeared as counsel in the case for an intervener who argued that a prohibition of private health care was a breach of s. 7 if the public system could not provide necessary treatment in a timely fashion.

[5]R.S.Q., c. C-12.

[6]Chapter 47, Fundamental Justice, under heading § 47:26, "Arbitrary laws".

care insurance plan. These delays impaired the right to life, because they sometimes increased the risk of death. They also impaired the right to security of the person, because they always prolonged pain and stress and sometimes prevented fully successful treatment.

Second, did Quebec's prohibition on private health care insurance cause the deprivations of life and security of the person? Yes, answered the Court, again unanimously. The purpose and effect of the prohibition was to make the public health care insurance plan exclusive. Faced with excessive delays in the public system, persons needing treatment were effectively precluded from obtaining timely care privately. *So long as the public system failed to provide medically-required services in a timely fashion*, it was a deprivation of life and security of the person for Quebec to prohibit people from obtaining health care insurance privately.

Third, was Quebec's prohibition on private health care insurance a breach of the principles of fundamental justice? On this issue, the seven-judge bench split evenly (three-three, one judge declining to answer). For McLachlin C.J. and Major J. (writing with the agreement of Bastarache J.), the Quebec law prohibiting private health care insurance offended the principles of fundamental justice, because it was "arbitrary". That was the case here, they said, because the evidence showed that other developed countries with universal public health care plans permitted parallel access to private care without injury to the public system. For Binnie and LeBel JJ. (writing with the agreement of Fish J.), the law was not arbitrary. They relied on expert evidence given at the trial that the development of a private system would divert resources away from the public system, ultimately reducing the quality of the public system. For them, the discouragement of private health care was a rational means of supporting the public health care system, and was therefore not arbitrary.

Deschamps J., the seventh judge, who could have broken the tie, confined herself to s. 1 of Quebec's Charter of Human Rights and Freedoms, which guaranteed personal inviolability (equivalent to security of the person) without the need to show a breach of the principles of fundamental justice. She held that the delays in the public system were a breach of the guarantee of personal inviolability. She did not need to decide whether the law was a breach of the principles of fundamental justice, and she did not do so. However, she did consider whether the ban on private insurance could be justified under the Quebec equivalent of s. 1 of the Charter (which authorizes reasonable limits on Charter rights).[7] She held that the law was not a justified limit on the right of inviolability. She pointed to the experience of other developed countries as contradicting the theory that private health care is a threat to a healthy public system, and the tenor of her opinion was similar to that of the McLachlin-Major opinion. She agreed with the McLachlin-Major

[7]The Quebec Charter's standard of justification is in s. 9.1. While it uses different language than s. 1 of the Canadian Charter, it has been interpreted as having the same meaning as s. 1. The provision is set out in para. 46 of Deschamps J.'s opinion, and the interpretation is set out in paras. 47–48.

opinion that the law was unconstitutional—but only in Quebec. Her opinion created a majority in favour of striking down the Quebec law, but, by confining her opinion to the Quebec Charter, she denied national effect to the ruling. It will take another case to determine the validity of the legal restrictions on access to private health care that exist in the other provinces and territories.[8]

After the decision in *Chaoulli*, the Government of Quebec sought and obtained from the Supreme Court a one-year stay of the judgment. This maintained in force the prohibition on the purchase of private health care insurance for publicly-insured services for one year from the date of the judgment, a period that expired on June 9, 2006.[9] On December 13, 2006, the Quebec Legislature enacted Bill 33[10] as an amendment to the health care legislation of the province. Bill 33 permitted the purchase of private health care insurance for procedures that can be performed by private clinics, namely, hip and knee replacements and cataract surgery, with ministerial power to add other procedures.[11] Subject to this exception, Bill 33 restored the general prohibition on the purchase of private health insurance for publicly-funded medical procedures that was struck down in *Chaoulli*. These provisions were made retroactive to June 9, 2006, the date when the suspension of the *Chaoulli* ruling expired.[12]

Chaoulli was not the first case to decide that the accessibility of a medical procedure was constitutionally guaranteed. In *R. v. Morgentaler (No.2)* (1988),[13] the Supreme Court of Canada struck down the restrictions on abortion that were contained in the Criminal Code. Abortion was an offence unless the procedure was approved by a therapeutic abortion committee of an approved hospital. The evidence in the case showed that the requirement of committee approval caused delays that increased the risk to the health of the woman seeking the procedure. The majority of the Court held that the state-induced delay was a violation of the woman's security of the person under s. 7 of the Charter, and

---

[8]In *Allen v. Alta.*, 2015 ABCA 277 (Alta. C.A.), the Alberta Court of Appeal rejected a s. 7 challenge to Alberta's ban on private health insurance due to insufficient evidence. In *Cambie Surgeries Corp. v. B.C.*, 2020 BCSC 1310, the British Columbia Supreme Court rejected—in a decision numbering 2,943 paragraphs!—a decade-long ss. 7 and 15 challenge to British Columbia's ban on private health insurance.

[9]Supreme Court of Canada order of August 4, 2005.

[10]S.Q. 2006, c. 43.

[11]Regulations have added other procedures, including cosmetic surgery, vascular and lymphatic surgery, orthopaedic surgery and ear surgery.

[12]Bill 33 introduced a care guarantee by permitting those procedures that can be performed in private clinics to be paid for publicly if the Minister of Health determines that the waiting time for the procedure in the public system is unreasonable. The holder of private insurance would not have to wait for such a determination. The Bill also required hospitals to establish and administer a centralized mechanism for recording and managing waiting lists for all of the services provided by the hospital. For comment, see P.J. Monahan, "*Chaoulli v. Quebec* and the Future of Canadian Healthcare: Patient Accountability as the 'Sixth Principle' of the Canada Health Act" (2006) C.D Howe Institute, Toronto, Benefactors Lecture 2006.

[13]*R. v. Morgentaler (No.2)*, [1988] 1 S.C.R. 30; discussed in ch. 47, Fundamental Justice, under heading § 47:12, "Security of the person".

that the unnecessarily burdensome procedural requirements were a breach of the principles of fundamental justice. The criminal law respecting abortion was accordingly struck down, and the procedure is no longer subject to the delay-inducing requirement of approval by a therapeutic abortion committee.

In *Chaoulli*, the majority regarded *Morgentaler* as a controlling precedent[14] and surely they were right. The dissenters in *Chaoulli* distinguished *Morgentaler* on the basis that the prohibition on abortion and the requirement of the approval of a therapeutic abortion committee were matters of criminal law rather than public health policy.[15] With respect, this difference seems unimportant in comparison with the substantive similarities. The similarities are that, in both cases, medical treatment inside the legislatively provided system was not provided in time to avoid risks to life or security of the person, while medical treatment outside the system was effectively prohibited. Both cases decide that, when the state assumes a monopoly power over the provision of a medical service that affects life or security of the person, it is under a constitutional duty to ensure that the service is provided in a timely fashion. What that means for Canada's public health system is that it is no longer constitutional for the provinces to ration health-care resources by allowing dangerous waiting times to develop for procedures that affect life or security of the person.[16] The "reasonable access" to health care services that is required in theory by the Canada Health Act has become a constitutional obligation that is required in practice.

---

[14]*Chaoulli v. Quebec*, [2005] 1 S.C.R. 791, paras. 43 per Deschamps J., 118–121 per McLachlin C.J. and Major J.

[15]*Chaoulli v. Quebec*, [2005] 1 S.C.R. 791, paras. 167, 180, 259–262 per Binnie and Fish JJ.

[16]*Chaoulli* does not require that the province pay for medical treatment that is obtained privately outside the country, even if the treatment could not be obtained in the province and is needed to save the patient's life: *Flora v. Ont.* (2008), 91 O.R. (3d) 412 (C.A.) (upholding province's refusal to reimburse cost of life-saving liver transplant refused in Ontario and obtained in England).

Part III

CIVIL LIBERTIES

Chapter 34

Civil Liberties

I. DEFINITIONS OF CIVIL LIBERTIES

§ 34:1 Definition of civil liberties

II. COMMON LAW

§ 34:2 Common law

III. STATUTE

§ 34:3 Human rights codes
§ 34:4 Statutory bills of rights

IV. CONSTITUTION ACT, 1867

§ 34:5 Express guarantees
§ 34:6 Distribution of powers
§ 34:7 Implied bill of rights

V. CONSTITUTION ACT, 1982

§ 34:8 Constitution Act, 1982

I. DEFINITIONS OF CIVIL LIBERTIES

§ 34:1 Definition of civil liberties

Civil liberties[1] encompass a broad range of values that support the freedom and dignity of the individual, and that are given recognition in various ways by Canadian law. The political civil liberties include the freedoms of speech, religion, assembly and association; the right to vote

---

[Section 34:1]

[1]See Scott, Civil Liberties and Canadian Federalism (1959); Schmeiser, Civil Liberties in Canada (1964); Tarnopolsky, The Canadian Bill of Rights (2nd ed., 1975); Beaudoin and Mendes (eds.), The Canadian Charter of Rights and Freedoms (4th ed., 2005); Tremblay, Droit Constitutionel-Principes (2nd ed., 2000), Part II, ch. 4; Sharpe and Roach, The Charter of Rights and Freedoms (3rd ed., 2005).

and be a candidate for elected office; and the freedom to enter and leave Canada and to move from one province to another. Legal civil liberties include the freedom from search, seizure, arrest, imprisonment, cruel and unusual punishment and unfair trial procedures. Egalitarian civil liberties include equality of access to accommodation, employment, education and other benefits, implying, at least, an absence of racial, sexual or other illegitimate criteria of discrimination. Particular to Canada are language rights, covering the right to use the English or the French language; and educational rights, covering the rights of denominational (or separate) schools.

All of these civil liberties are discussed in the chapters that follow. The basic point to be made here, however, is that all of these civil liberties come into competition with other values recognized by the legal system, and indeed they come into competition with each other. When we speak of the protection of civil liberties in a society, we are really speaking about the nature of the compromises which that society has made between civil libertarian values of the kind described and the competing values recognized by social and economic regulation, which limits individual freedom in pursuit of collective goals, such as public order and morality, health and safety, fair dealing, environmental protection and a more equitable distribution of wealth.

II. COMMON LAW

§ 34:2 Common law

The English common law, which was inherited by the colonies of British North America,[1] includes many rules that are protective of civil liberties, but it does not provide any positive guarantees of their continued recognition. The common law's position is that a person is free to do anything that is not positively prohibited, and various doctrines help to narrow the scope of what is positively prohibited. For the common law, civil liberties do not derive from positive law or governmental action, but from an absence of positive law or governmental action. Take freedom of speech as an example. At common law, one is free to speak one's mind so long as there is no positive law prohibiting such action. The laws of defamation, contempt of court, sedition, hate propaganda, obscenity, fraud, false advertising, television and radio licensing are among the laws which prohibit (or regulate) various forms of speech; what is left unprohibited is the civil liberty of speech. The doctrine of parliamentary sovereignty meant that in the United Kingdom those unregulated residues of individual liberty had no constitutional protection. Parliament could make any law whatever, even if it curtailed

---

[Section 34:2]

[1]The French civil law was inherited in Quebec, but the criminal law and public law generally were supplanted by the English law: see ch. 2, Reception, under heading § 2:6, "Ontario and Quebec".

a cherished civil liberty.[2] Only a bill of rights that was immune from ordinary legislative change could guarantee civil liberties from legislative encroachment, and the United Kingdom has never had a bill of rights of that kind.[3]

After the newly-independent American colonies federated in 1787, they added various guarantees of civil liberties to their new Constitution;[4] these "amendments" became a Bill of Rights which could not be altered except by further constitutional amendment. This was a radical departure from British tradition. When the loyal British North American colonies federated in 1867, they did not include a bill of rights in their Constitution. On the contrary, as recited in the preamble to the Constitution Act, 1867, the Canadian federation was to have "a Constitution similar in principle to that of the United Kingdom". Thus the Canadian Parliament and Legislatures, provided they stayed within the limits of the federal distribution of powers and a few other restraints,[5] received powers as "plenary and ample" as those of the United Kingdom Parliament.[6]

Civil liberties in Canada have now received some direct constitutional protection. In 1960, the Canadian Bill of Rights was adopted, but it was only a statute, not a constitutional amendment, and it was applicable only to the federal level of government, not to the provinces. For these and other reasons, the Canadian Bill of Rights made little change in Canada's law.[7] In 1982, the Charter of Rights was adopted. The Charter is a constitutional instrument; it is applicable to both levels of government, and it now fulfils an important role in protecting the civil liberties

---

[2] See ch. 12, Parliamentary Sovereignty, under heading § 12:1 "Sovereignty in the United Kingdom".

[3] The Magna Carta of 1215 (adopted by Parliament in 1297), the Bill of Rights of 1689, and the Human Rights Act 1998 are simply statutes amenable to ordinary legislative change. Human rights or civil liberties are a relatively modern concern. The Ten Commandments, recognized as authority in the Hebrew Bible, the Old Testament of the Christian Bible and the Islamic Koran, are all concerned with responsibilities rather than rights. The same is true of other ancient texts, for example, the Dead Sea Scrolls, which also have 10 commandments, and the Egyptian Book of the Dead, which has 42 commandments. The preoccupation is the responsibility of the individual, to God and fellow citizens and (in the case of the Egyptian commandments) to the environment, and to live a good life. The idea that the individual might have rights that could be demanded from God or government or fellow citizens is not there. See W. Thorsell, "How to Be Good—What the Ancient Texts Say" (2009) Royal Ontario Museum Magazine, vol. 42, no. 1, p. 3.

[4] The first ten amendments, the original "bill of rights", were passed by Congress in 1789 (the first year of the Union) and ratified by three-fourths of the states in 1791. Other bill of rights amendments, of which the fourteenth (1868) is the most important, were adopted later.

[5] The impact on civil liberties of the Constitution Act, 1867 is discussed in a later section of this chapter.

[6] See ch. 12, Parliamentary Sovereignty, under heading §§ 12:2 to 12:8, "Sovereignty in Canada".

[7] See ch. 35, Canadian Bill of Rights.

that it guarantees.[8] But the fact remains that, for most of its history, Canada, like the United Kingdom, Australia and New Zealand, has had few direct constitutional protections of civil liberties.

Despite the lack of a bill of rights, Canada, like the United Kingdom, Australia and New Zealand, has a good record of respect for civil liberties. Tolerance of political and religious dissent, and of racial and linguistic minorities, freedom of movement, control of police powers and fair and open trials are among the criteria by which a nation's record is judged. Canada's record, while far from perfect, seems to be much better than that of most of the countries of the world, although nearly all countries have bills of rights in their constitutions. The basic reason for this has very little to do with the contents of Canada's (or any other country's) constitutional law. It is to be found in the democratic character of Canada's political institutions, supported by long traditions[9] of free elections, opposition parties and a free press. Democracy is without doubt the most important safeguard of civil liberties.[10]

A second safeguard of civil liberties is the independence of the judiciary, which in Canada is partly secured by constitutional provisions, and partly by "unwritten constitutional principles", but is most effectively secured by a long political tradition stretching back to the beginning of the eighteenth century in Britain.[11] A supporting tradition is that of the independence of the legal profession. This ensures that an individual with a legal case can obtain legal representation even if his or her cause is opposed by government or by the wealthy or by a majority of the people.

A third safeguard of civil liberties is the common law, which, for the most part, tends to favour individual rights and freedoms (as traditionally understood) when they come into conflict with state interests. This is perhaps seen most clearly in the criminal law. For example, mens rea (or a guilty mind) was an ingredient of common law offences and is presumed by the courts to be an ingredient of statutory offences; in other respects, the definitions of crime are construed strictly (in favour of the defendant), the defendant is presumed to be innocent and the Crown is required to prove guilt beyond a reasonable doubt, confessions are inadmissible unless they have been freely obtained, the defendant cannot be compelled to testify and no-one can be compelled to incriminate himself.[12]

Outside the realm of criminal law, the state and the individual usually come into conflict as the result of the exercise by officials of

---

[8] See ch. 36, Charter of Rights.

[9] There are a few relevant provisions in the Constitution Act, 1867: see especially s. 133; and, since 1982, in the Charter of Rights, ss. 3-5: see ch. 45, Voting.

[10] P.H. Russell, "A Democratic Approach to Civil Liberties" (1969) 19 U. Toronto L.J. 109.

[11] See ch. 7, Courts, under heading § 7:3, "Tenure of provincial judges".

[12] These rights have now been guaranteed by the Charter of Rights, and are discussed in later chapters, especially ch. 51, Rights on Being charged.

governmental powers over persons or private property. In Britain, common law doctrine early developed that the King and his officials had no powers other than those granted by the law. It is true that "the law" included certain royal prerogatives as well as statute law, but the courts successfully asserted the power to determine the existence and extent of the prerogatives.[13] With few exceptions, actions which infringe the liberty of the subject require the authority of a statute.[14] This was settled in the great case of *Entick v. Carrington* (1765),[15] in which it was held that neither a search warrant signed by a minister of the Crown, nor a claim of "state necessity", could justify Crown servants in entering the premises of the plaintiff and seizing his papers. The plaintiff's action in trespass against the Crown servants was successful, because they could not show that their actions were authorized by law.

The principle of validity—that every official act must be justified by law—has to be reaffirmed periodically. One of the best-known Canadian cases is *Roncarelli v. Duplessis* (1959),[16] in which Premier Duplessis of Quebec ordered the cancellation of restaurateur Roncarelli's liquor licence because Roncarelli was a Jehovah's Witness who had made a practice of acting as bondsman for the numerous Jehovah's Witnesses who were arrested for distributing their literature in breach of municipal by-laws. The Supreme Court of Canada awarded damages to Roncarelli. Duplessis could not rely on his high office, nor his judgment as to the demands of the public interest, as justification for his act. Only a statute would suffice to authorize the cancellation of the licence, and the statute which did authorize licence cancellations gave the power to another official, not the Premier.[17] The Duplessis regime in Quebec offered the courts many other opportunities to protect civil liberties. In the present context, we may notice *Chaput v. Romain* (1955),[18] in which police broke up an assembly of Jehovah's Witnesses who were meeting peacefully in a private house, and *Lamb v. Benoit* (1959),[19] in which police arrested a Jehovah's Witness who was distributing pamphlets on a street corner. In both those cases, the Supreme Court of Canada awarded damages against the responsible policemen on the ground that they had acted without legal authority.[20]

A corollary of cases such as *Entick v. Carrington* and *Roncarelli v. Duplessis* is that the Prime Minister (or Premier) or a Minister of the Crown or any other representative of the government has no power to

[13] *Case of Proclamations* (1610), 12 Co. Rep. 74, 77 E.R. 1352.

[14] See ch. 1, Sources, under heading § 1:9, "Prerogative".

[15] *Entick v. Carrington* (1765), 19 St. Tr. 1030, 95 E.R. 807 (K.B.).

[16] *Roncarelli v. Duplessis*, [1959] S.C.R. 121.

[17] In any event, the Court made clear that the exercise of the power by the correct official, but for a purpose extraneous to the service and consumption of liquor, would have been unauthorized.

[18] *Chaput v. Romain*, [1955] S.C.R. 834.

[19] *Lamb v. Benoit*, [1959] S.C.R. 321.

[20] Another important decision was *Boucher v. The King*, [1951] S.C.R. 265 (Jehovah's Witness not guilty of sedition).

suspend the operation of a law for a time, or to dispense with a law in favour of a particular person or group. These "suspending" and "dispensing" powers were asserted by the Stuart Kings, but were abolished by the Bill of Rights of 1688. From time to time, modern governments assert such powers, and the assertions are repudiated by the courts, who always add a stern admonition that the Crown is not above the law.[21]

A second feature of the common law protection of civil liberties is the availability of remedies to citizens injured by illegal official action. If an official acts outside his or her statutory authority, the official enjoys no more powers than a private individual; if the act is tortious, then the official may be sued in an ordinary action in tort by the injured citizen. This is true even if the tort were committed in the course of employment, although in that case the Crown itself will ordinarily be liable as well.[22] In addition to the ordinary action in tort, the courts developed the "prerogative writs" for the express purpose of allowing speedy challenge to contested official action or inaction. The most famous of these writs is habeas corpus, to determine the legality of imprisonment; but the writs of mandamus, certiorari, prohibition and quo warranto also provide mechanisms which are available to secure judicial review of administrative action. Of more recent vintage is the action for a declaration (declaratory judgment), which is also often available to review administrative action. In most jurisdictions, a single statutory remedy, often styled an application for judicial review, has been introduced to do the work of several of these common law remedies.

Because of the doctrine of parliamentary sovereignty, if a statute plainly takes away a civil liberty or plainly authorizes an official to take away a civil liberty, then the courts can provide no protection. The statute prevails over the common law. Therefore, the principle of validity is satisfied; no legal wrong has occurred; and no remedy is available. However, it is still the function of the courts to interpret any statute which is relied upon as the justification for a denial of a civil liberty and many civil libertarian values have been introduced into the law as canons of interpretation.

The governing canon of interpretation is that "statutes which encroach on the rights of the subject, whether as regards person or property, are subject to a 'strict' construction".[23] This is a principle which is no longer universally applauded because of cases where courts have given rein to laissez-faire prejudices and interpreted social legislation so strictly as to

[21]*Fitzgerald v. Muldoon*, [1976] 2 N.Z.L.R. 615 (N.Z. S.C.) (N.Z. Prime Minister may not suspend statutory obligation to contribute to state pension plan); *Re Anti-Inflation Act*, [1976] 2 S.C.R. 373 (Lieutenant Governor in Council may not change law by agreement with Governor in Council); *Man. Govt. Employees Assn v. Govt. of Man.*, [1978] 1 S.C.R. 1123 (same decision); *R. v. Catagas* (1977), 81 D.L.R. (3d) 396 (Man. C.A.) (Minister may not dispense with Migratory Birds Convention Act in favour of native people.)

[22]See ch. 10, The Crown, under heading § 10:12, "Liability of Crown in tort".

[23]*A.G. Can. v. Hallet & Carey*, [1952] A.C. 427, 450.

stultify its objects.[24] But now that state intervention in the social and economic life of the nation is generally accepted, even by judges, these hostile interpretations have ceased to be a problem. In my opinion, the principle of strict construction is sound: it is reasonable for the courts to insist that invasions of personal or proprietary rights be clearly authorized by the statutory language. For example, there is a presumption against interference with vested rights and a presumption against the retroactive operation of a statute. As well, the courts have confined the scope of official discretion by holding that power conferred in broad terms may not be "abused" by exercise in bad faith or for an improper purpose or upon irrelevant considerations or "unreasonably". The courts have also structured the mode of exercise of some statutory powers by insisting upon official compliance with the procedural guarantees of "natural justice", now usually seen as part of a more general duty of "procedural fairness". All of these results have been achieved without any denial of parliamentary sovereignty, and without the aid of a bill of rights, simply by "interpreting" statutory language, wherever possible, into conformity with civil libertarian values.[25]

It is worth noting at this point that democracy, the independence of the judiciary and the protection of individual rights are also preconditions to sustained economic development, because they are essential to the reliability of property and contractual rights upon which a stable currency, investment, banking, insurance and commercial transactions depend. Civil liberties are not luxuries that only prosperous countries can afford; they are the basic requirements for prosperity.[26]

III. STATUTE

§ 34:3 Human rights codes

Since the latter part of the second world war, Canadian provincial Legislatures have been active in promoting egalitarian civil liberties by statute. The purpose of the statutes is to prohibit discrimination by landlords and employers on grounds such as race, national origin, colour, religion, sex or age. Early statutes simply prohibited various forms of discrimination and imposed a penalty for breach. But, following the model of a New York statute of 1945, the provinces passed statutes which employed labour relations techniques of investigation, conciliation and arbitration to combat discrimination in accommodation and employment. In 1962, Ontario took the step of consolidating its law into a Human Rights Code, to be administered by a Human Rights Commission. All of the other provinces followed suit, and, finally, in 1977, the federal Parliament enacted its own Code with a Commission

---

[24]See Jennings, The Law and the Constitution (5th ed., 1959), 253.

[25]See R. Sullivan, Sullivan and Driedger on the Construction of Statutes (Butterworths, Markham, Ont., 4th ed., 2002), chs. 13, 14.

[26]Mancur Olson, Power and Prosperity: Outgrowing Communist and Capitalist Dictatorships (Basic Books, 2000), esp. preface and chs. 1, 2 and 10; see also Hernando De Soto, The Mystery of Capital (Basic Books, 2000), esp. ch. 1.

to administer it. These codes prohibit discriminatory practices in hiring and employment, and in the renting of accommodation; they tend to provide for investigation and conciliation of complaints by a commission, and for adjudication by a board of inquiry or tribunal if conciliation fails. As well as their administrative functions, the commissions have educational and promotional functions.[1]

The importance of the various human rights codes has not been diminished by the adoption in 1982 of the Charter of Rights. The human rights codes apply to discrimination by private individuals or firms, especially in the hiring and paying of employees, and in the renting of commercial and residential accommodation.[2] This fills a gap in the Charter of Rights, which applies only to governmental activity, not private activity.[3] Moreover, the codes' informal and inexpensive procedures, which are initiated by a complaint to the human rights commission, have no counterpart under the Charter, which contemplates judicial enforcement of its provisions.[4]

§ 34:4 Statutory bills of rights

Statutory bills of rights are another source of civil liberties. Saskatchewan led the way in 1947 with the Saskatchewan Bill of Rights Act,[1] which went beyond fair employment and accommodation to guarantee the fundamental freedoms of speech, press, assembly, religion and association. In 1960, the federal Parliament enacted the Canadian Bill of Rights,[2] which guaranteed a wide range of civil liberties and had the effect of overriding inconsistent federal (but not provincial) statutes. In 1972, Alberta enacted the Alberta Bill of Rights;[3] and, in 1975, Quebec

---

[Section 34:3]

[1]See Tarnopolsky, Discrimination and the Law in Canada (1982), of which ch. 2 relates the history of the legislation. See also Macdonald and Humphrey (eds.), The Practice of Freedom (1979), chs. 3 (Cheffins and Tucker), 4 (Leavy), 5 (Hunter), 15 (Tarnopolsky), 16 (Fairweather).

[2]The Codes also apply to activity by governments and to that extent overlap with s. 15 of the Charter of Rights. Presumably, the courts would insist that Code remedies be exhausted before exercising their discretion to give a remedy under s. 24 of the Charter.

[3]See ch. 37, Application of Charter.

[4]D.S. Days, "Civil Rights in Canada: An American Perspective" (1984) 32 Am. J. Comp. Law, 307, 316, is struck by the leadership role played by the Canadian provinces (rather than the federal government, as in the United States) and by the dominance of legislative and administrative bodies (rather than the courts, as in the United States).

[Section 34:4]

[1]S.S. 1947, c. 35, but note that the Act did not purport to have overriding effect on inconsistent legislation. It was repealed and replaced by the Saskatchewan Human Rights Code, S.S. 1979, c. S-24.1, s. 44 of which provides that an inconsistent law is inoperative unless the law contains a notwithstanding clause.

[2]S.C. 1960, c. 44. See next chapter on Canadian Bill of Rights.

[3]S.A. 1972, c. 1.

enacted the Quebec Charter of Human Rights and Freedoms.[4] Each of these statutes was similar to the Canadian Bill of Rights in guaranteeing a range of civil liberties and overriding inconsistent statutes. These four statutory bills of rights have lost much of their importance since the adoption in 1982 of the Charter of Rights, which is a constitutional instrument applicable to both the federal and provincial levels of government. But the statutory bills of rights remain in force, and remain effective to the extent that they are broader in scope than the Charter, as they are in a few respects.[5] In one case, the Supreme Court, while expressly acknowledging that there was no relevant difference in the meaning of the freedom-of-religion guarantees of the Canadian Charter and the Quebec Charter, chose to decide the case on the basis of the Quebec Charter.[6]

The Canadian Bill of Rights is the topic of the next chapter.

IV. CONSTITUTION ACT, 1867

§ 34:5 Express guarantees

We have already noticed that the framers of the Constitution Act, 1867 rejected the American precedent of the Bill of Rights, and sought instead to make an exhaustive distribution of legislative powers.[1] We have also noticed some exceptions to the principle of exhaustion. In the context of civil liberties, the important exceptions are s. 93, guaranteeing rights and privileges of denominational schools;[2] s. 99, guaranteeing the tenure of superior court judges;[3] and s. 133, guaranteeing the English and French languages in legislative and judicial proceedings in Quebec and the federal jurisdiction.[4] These provisions[5] do constitute a small bill of rights.[6]

---

[4]S.Q. 1975, c. 6. For commentary, see Macdonald and Humphrey (eds.), The Practice of Freedom (1979), ch. 21 (by Brun).

[5]E.g., *Singh v. Minr. of Emplt. and Imm.*, [1985] 1 S.C.R. 177 (s. 2(e) of Canadian Bill of Rights extends beyond s. 7); *MacBain v. Lederman*, [1985] 1 F.C. 856 (C.A.) (same point); *Ford v. Que.*, [1988] 2 S.C.R. 712 (Charter had been overridden under s. 33, but Quebec Charter had not been); *Godbout v. Longueuil*, [1997] 3 S.C.R. 844 (Quebec Charter guaranteed right of privacy); *Syndicat Northcrest v. Amselem*, [2004] 2 S.C.R. 551 (Quebec Charter applied to private contract); *Chaoulli v. Que.*, [2005] 1 S.C.R. 791, paras. 15, 30 per Deschamps J. (Quebec Charter's equivalent to s. 7 contained no requirement of breach of fundamental justice); *Bruker v. Marcovitz*, [2007] 3 S.C.R. 607 (Quebec Charter applied to private contract).

[6]*Mouvement laïque québécois v. Saguenay*, [2015] 2 S.C.R. 3, 2015 SCC 16, para. 68.

[Section 34:5]

[1]See ch. 12, Parliamentary Sovereignty, under heading §§ 12:2 to 12:8, "Sovereignty in Canada".

[2]See ch. 57, Education.

[3]See ch. 7, Courts, under heading § 7:3, "Tenure of provincial judges".

[4]See ch. 56, Language.

[5]See also s. 20 (annual session of Parliament), ss. 50, 91(1) (five year limit to Par-

§ 34:6 Distribution of powers

The distribution of powers in Canada (or any other federal state) denies plenary power to any one legislative body. This raises impediments to legislative action in many fields, and thus often has the indirect effect of safeguarding civil liberties. For example, the provincial Legislatures have no power to enact criminal law; if a province attempts to suppress gambling[1] or communism[2] or prostitution,[3] and the law is classified as a criminal law, the law will be invalid, and gamblers, communists and prostitutes will remain free to continue their activities. As another example, the federal Parliament has no power to regulate property and civil rights in the province; if the federal Parliament attempts to prohibit the sale of margarine[4] or regulate the labelling of beer,[5] and the law is classified as a law in relation to property and civil rights in the province, the law will be invalid, and sellers of margarine and beer will be free from the purported federal constraints.

The foregoing examples illustrate the obvious proposition that a law affecting civil liberties, like any other law, is valid only if it is authorized by a grant of power in the Constitution Act, 1867. But a more subtle question then calls for an answer: to what extent is the law's impact on civil liberties a relevant factor in determining the appropriate classification of the law? The same question may be reframed by asking, to what extent are civil liberties "matters" (or constitutional values) which must be recognized as coming within the classes of subjects (or heads of power) in ss. 91 and 92 of the Constitution Act, 1867?[6]

The broad range of claims which can be encompassed by the term

---

liament), ss. 51, 51A, 52 (representation by population), s. 86 (annual sessions of Legislatures of Ontario and Quebec), s. 121 (free admission of goods to provinces), s. 125 (no taxation of land or property belonging to Canada or province).

[6]My use in an earlier edition of the phrase "a small bill of rights" in reference to denominational school rights was disapproved in *Greater Montreal Protestant School Bd. v. Que.*, [1989] 1 S.C.R. 377, 401 per Beetz J. for majority; his point was that the school rights should not be given the liberal interpretation that is appropriate to rights guaranteed by the Charter of Rights; otherwise, I think the description is accurate. The suggestion of an "implied bill of rights" is discussed later in this chapter, in § 34:7, "Implied bill of rights". The suggestion that the federal power of disallowance is available to invalidate provincial violations of civil liberties is referred to in ch. 5, Federalism, under heading § 5:13, "Disallowance".

[Section 34:6]

[1]*Johnson v. A.-G. Alta.*, [1954] S.C.R. 127 (provincial law confiscating slot-machines struck down).

[2]*Switzman v. Elbling*, [1957] S.C.R. 285 (provincial law authorizing padlocking of any house used to propagate communism struck down).

[3]*Westendorp v. The Queen*, [1983] 1 S.C.R. 43 (municipal by-law prohibiting street prostitution struck down).

[4]*Can. Federation of Agriculture v. A.-G. Que.*, [1951] A.C. 179 (federal law prohibiting manufacture or sale of margarine struck down).

[5]*Labatt Breweries v. A.-G. Can.*, [1980] 1 S.C.R. 914 (federal law prescribing compositional standards for product labelled "light beer" struck down).

[6]See ch. 15, Judicial Review on Federal Grounds. Note also that civil liberties are

"civil liberties" renders any single or simple answer impossible.[7] Accordingly, this question is taken up with respect to particular civil liberties in the chapters that follow. However, to anticipate the more detailed discussion, as a broad generalization, it may be said that a law's impact on civil liberties has not been treated by the courts as the leading characteristic in determining the law's classification. The courts have instead relegated the impact of a law on civil liberties to an incidental or subordinate position. The effect of this approach to classification is that the power to affect civil liberties is distributed between the two levels of government, depending upon which level of government has jurisdiction over the activities regulated by the law. For example, the provincial Legislatures may prohibit racial discrimination in occupations subject to provincial jurisdiction, and the federal Parliament may prohibit discrimination in occupations subject to federal jurisdiction. In other words, it is the nature of the regulated occupation that determines the law's classification, not the law's impact on racial discrimination. It should be added that the federal Parliament could probably enact a universal prohibition of racial discrimination (though not a more sophisticated scheme) under the criminal law power, but this would depend upon the law's classification as a criminal law, and in making that classification, the courts will look for the ingredients of a criminal law—a prohibition, a penalty and a typically criminal public purpose—and not primarily to the law's impact on racial discrimination.[8]

§ 34:7 Implied bill of rights

Restraints on legislative power that are derived only from the federal distribution of powers are incomplete, in that a law which is denied to one level of government will be open to the other level of government. For example, when Ontario's Lord's Day Act was held to be unconstitutional, on the ground that the observance of days of religious significance was a matter of criminal law,[1] the federal Parliament enacted a Lord's Day Act that was held to be constitutional for precisely the reason that had defeated it as a provincial measure.[2] Only under a bill of rights can the courts consider the question whether any legislative body should be able to impose Christian days of religious observance upon a pluralistic society.[3]

In the absence of a bill of rights, when a law abridging a civil liberty

---

not equivalent to civil rights in the phrase "property and civil rights in the province" (s. 92(13)): see ch. 21, Property and Civil Rights, under heading § 21:3, "Civil liberties".

[7]On the distribution of powers over civil liberties, see Tarnopolsky, The Canadian Bill of Rights (2nd ed., 1975), ch. 2; Swinton, The Supreme Court and Canadian Federalism (1990), ch. 6.

[8]This is offered as an example only. The egalitarian civil liberties are discussed more fully in ch. 55, Equality, under heading § 55:1, "Distribution of powers".

[Section 34:7]

[1]*A.G. Ont. v. Hamilton Street Ry.*, [1903] A.C. 524.

[2]*Lord's Day Alliance of Can. v. A.-G. B.C.*, [1959] S.C.R. 497.

[3]After the adoption of the Canadian Bill of Rights in 1960, the Lord's Day Act was

is challenged, the issue is "which jurisdiction should have power to work the injustice, not whether the injustice should be prohibited completely".[4] The theory that there are some "injustices" that should be "prohibited completely" is, of course, the impulse to adoption of a bill of rights. Indeed, some judges have professed to find in the Constitution Act, 1867 an "implied bill of rights". In the *Alberta Press* case (1938),[5] where the Supreme Court of Canada held that a province could not require newspapers to give the government a right of reply to criticism of provincial policies, Duff C.J.'s opinion could be read as suggesting that the Constitution Act, 1867 impliedly forbade both the Legislatures and the Parliament from curtailing political speech.[6] In *Switzman v. Elbling* (1957),[7] where the Court held that a province could not prohibit the use of a house to propagate communism, Rand J. left open the possibility that Parliament as well as the Legislatures might be incompetent to curtail political speech;[8] but Abbott J. went further, saying explicitly that "Parliament itself could not abrogate this right of discussion and debate".[9] Abbott J.'s obiter dictum was an unequivocal expression of the implied bill of rights theory.

The implied bill of rights theory was forgotten, or at least was never mentioned, by the Supreme Court of Canada from 1963 until 1978, when the Court decided the *Dupond* case (1978).[10] In that case, Beetz J., for the majority, said that none of the fundamental freedoms that were inherited from the United Kingdom "is so enshrined in the Constitution as to be beyond the reach of competent legislation". This seemed to have given the theory its quietus. However, like freeway proposals and snakes, the theory does not die easily. Since the adoption of the Charter

---

unsuccessfully challenged under the Bill: *Robertson and Rosetanni v. The Queen*, [1963] S.C.R. 651; and, after the adoption of the Charter of Rights in 1982, the Act was successfully challenged under the Charter: *R. v. Big M Drug Mart*, [1985] 1 S.C.R. 295. See ch. 42, Religion.

[4]P.C. Weiler, "The Supreme Court and the Law of Canadian Federalism" (1973) 23 U. Toronto L.J. 307, 344, although Weiler points out that the Supreme Court of Canada occasionally used federalism as a surreptitious bill of rights, allocating jurisdiction to that level of government which had not exercised it in order to invalidate a law which it really believed should not be enacted at all.

[5]*Re Alta. Statutes*, [1938] S.C.R. 100; this case is discussed in ch. 43, Expression, under heading §§ 43:1 to 43:4, "Distribution of powers".

[6]*Re Alta. Statutes*, [1938] S.C.R. 100, 133-134. This passage was quoted with approval in *Saumur v. City of Quebec*, [1953] 2 S.C.R. 299 by Rand J. at 331, Kellock J. at 353-354 and Locke J. at 373-374; and Kellock J. at 354 and Locke J. at 363 each suggested the possibility of an implied bill of rights.

[7]*Switzman v. Elbling*, [1957] S.C.R. 285; this case is discussed in ch. 43, Expression, under heading §§ 43:1 to 43:4, "Distribution of powers".

[8]*Switzman v. Elbling*, [1957] S.C.R. 285, 307.

[9]*Switzman v. Elbling*, [1957] S.C.R. 285, 328. He cautiously repeated the proposition in *Oil, Chemical and Atomic Wkrs. v. Imperial*, Oil [1963] S.C.R. 584, 600.

[10]*A.G. Can. and Dupond v. Montreal*, [1978] 2 S.C.R. 770, 796; this case is discussed in ch. 43, Expression, under heading §§ 43:1 to 43:4, "Distribution of powers". The quoted dictum was quoted with approval by Estey J. for the Court in *A.G. Can. v. Law Society of B.C.*, [1982] 2 S.C.R. 307, 364.

of Rights in 1982, it has been revived in a number of obiter dicta, the clearest of which was uttered by Beetz J., who had been so dismissive of the theory in *Dupond*. In the *OPSEU* case (1987),[11] speaking for the majority, Beetz J. quoted with evident approval the dicta in the *Alberta Press* case and *Switzman v. Elbling*, and said that "quite apart from Charter considerations, the legislative bodies in this country must conform to these basic structural imperatives and can in no way override them". In context, it is clear that by "basic structural imperatives" he meant the political freedoms, including freedom of expression, that were necessary to preserve "the essential structure of free parliamentary institutions".

Two reasons have been suggested in the dicta as supporting the existence of an implied bill of rights. The first is the language of the preamble to the Constitution Act, 1867, which refers to "a Constitution similar in principle to that of the United Kingdom".[12] The reasoning here is that civil liberties that were enjoyed in the United Kingdom in 1867 were intended to be enjoyed in Canada as well. The difficulty with this reasoning is that the central feature of the Constitution of the United Kingdom, and of its Parliament, was in 1867, and still is, parliamentary sovereignty: any of the civil liberties, including freedom of political speech, can be abolished by the Parliament at Westminster at any time. In the United Kingdom, the tradition of respect for civil liberties is not reflected in the law of the Constitution. It therefore seems likely that "a Constitution similar in principle to that of the United Kingdom" would not contain implied guarantees of civil liberties.

A second reason which has been offered in favour of an implied bill of rights is the Constitution Act, 1867's establishment of representative parliamentary institutions. The reasoning here is that free political speech is "the breath of life of parliamentary institutions", and therefore the establishment of such institutions must be implicitly accompanied by a guarantee of the conditions that are necessary to the effective functioning of the institutions. This is a stronger argument,[13] but it is subject to a similar difficulty to the argument based on the preamble.

---

[11]*OPSEU v. Ont.*, [1987] 2 S.C.R. 2, 57 per Beetz J.; 25 per Dickson C.J. is to the same effect. Other implied bill of rights dicta are to be found in *Fraser v. Public Service Staff Relations Bd.*, [1985] 2 S.C.R. 455, 462-463 per Dickson C.J.; *RWDSU v. Dolphin Delivery*, [1986] 2 S.C.R. 573, 584 per McIntyre J.; *Re Remuneration of Judges*, [1997] 3 S.C.R. 3, paras. 94-105 per Lamer C.J.

[12]Compare *New Brunswick Broadcasting Co. v. N.S.*, [1993] 1 S.C.R. 319, 375 per McLachlin J. for majority, holding that preamble incorporates into Constitution of Canada the rules of parliamentary privilege; *Re Remuneration of Judges*, [1997] 3 S.C.R. 3, para. 105 per Lamer C.J. for majority, holding that preamble protects judicial independence.

[13]It can be buttressed by the suggestion in *Re Initiative and Referendum Act*, [1919] A.C. 935, 945, that the establishment in the Constitution Act of representative parliamentary institutions guarantees the existence of those institutions. It is conceivable that this argument could be pushed so far as to guarantee freedom of political discussion: see P.H. Russell, "The Political Role of the Supreme Court of Canada in its First Century" (1975) 53 Can. Bar Rev. 576, 592; although the ironic result would be that the establishment of institutions in a written constitution radically distinguishes

When the Canadian Constitution established parliamentary institutions on the Westminster model, the plausible assumption would be that they were intended to exercise powers of the same order as those of the Parliament at Westminster, and, of course, those powers included the power to curtail civil liberties, including freedom of political speech. Any limitations on legislative power, such as those entailed by the federal system, could be expected to be expressed, or at least very clearly implied. This seems especially clear with respect to a bill of rights. The framers of the Constitution had the United States Constitution before them; it was their only useful precedent. They followed its federal character, but they deliberately did not copy its bill of rights.[14]

The conventional wisdom is that legislative powers are exhaustively distributed in Canada. As has been explained in chapter 12, Parliamentary Sovereignty, while there are undoubted exceptions to exhaustive distribution, the principle is certainly inconsistent with the theory of an implied bill of rights. It seems to me that it is the principle of exhaustive distribution that is more faithful to the history and text of the Constitution Act, 1867. We have noticed that the adoption of the Charter of Rights in 1982 seems to have provoked the Supreme Court of Canada into a renewal of its lagging faith in the implied bill of rights.[15] This is surely a perverse reaction. Since s. 2 of the Charter explicitly guarantees freedom of expression, it is now even harder to argue that an implicit guarantee is to be derived from the Constitution Act, 1867.[16]

V. CONSTITUTION ACT, 1982

§ 34:8 Constitution Act, 1982

The Charter of Rights, which is Part I of the Constitution Act, 1982, is a bill of rights that is part of the Constitution of Canada. It is the topic of Chapters 36 to 55.

---

the institutions from those upon which they were modelled!

[14]The implied bill of rights is supported by Scott, Civil Liberties and Canadian Federalism (1959), 18-21; Schmeiser, Civil Liberties in Canada (1964), 203 (but compare 15) and D. Gibson, "Constitutional Amendment and the Implied Bill of Rights" (1967) 12 McGill L.J. 497; and is opposed by B. Laskin, "An Inquiry into the Diefenbaker Bill of Rights" (1959) 37 Can. Bar Rev. 77, 103 and P.C. Weiler, "The Supreme Court and the Law of Canadian Federalism" (1973) 23 U. Toronto L.J. 307, 344.

[15]*OPSEU v. Ont.*, [1987] 2 S.C.R. 2, 57 per Beetz J.; 25 per Dickson C.J. is to the same effect. Other implied bill of rights dicta are to be found in *Fraser v. Public Service Staff Relations Bd.*, [1985] 2 S.C.R. 455, 462-463 per Dickson C.J.; *RWDSU v. Dolphin Delivery*, [1986] 2 S.C.R. 573, 584 per McIntyre J.; *Re Remuneration of Judges*, [1997] 3 S.C.R. 3, paras. 94-105 per Lamer C.J.

[16]Such an argument would normally be pointless since the explicit guarantee could be relied upon. Note, however, that s. 2 of the Charter is subject to the power of override in s. 33, while the implied bill of rights (if it exists) would not be subject to override.

Chapter 35

Canadian Bill of Rights

I. HISTORY OF BILL OF RIGHTS

§ 35:1 History of Bill of Rights

II. APPLICATION TO FEDERAL LAWS

§ 35:2 Application to federal laws

III. EFFECT OF INCONSISTENT STATUTES

§ 35:3 Meaning of s. 2
§ 35:4 Effect on earlier statutes
§ 35:5 Effect on later statutes
§ 35:6 Conclusions

IV. CONTENTS OF BILL OF RIGHTS

§ 35:7 Contents of Bill of Rights

V. JUDICIAL INTERPRETATION

§ 35:8 Judicial interpretation

VI. SCRUTINY BY MINISTER OF JUSTICE

§ 35:9 Scrutiny by Minister of Justice

I. HISTORY OF BILL OF RIGHTS

§ 35:1 History of Bill of Rights

We have already noticed that the Constitution Act, 1867 did not include a bill of rights.[1] This was an omission which never seems to have been regretted until after the second world war, when concern for civil liberties surfaced publicly and led to suggestions that a bill of rights should be adopted. Similar suggestions were being taken seriously elsewhere in the world. In 1948, the Universal Declaration of Human Rights was adopted by the United Nations; and a bill of rights became an indispensable part of the constitution of each of the many developing countries which attained independence in the post-war era.

[Section 35:1]

[1]See previous chapter, Civil Liberties, under heading §§ 34:5 to 34:7, "Constitution Act, 1867".

In 1960, the Progressive Conservative government of Prime Minister Diefenbaker secured the enactment of the Canadian Bill of Rights.[2] It was enacted as an ordinary statute of the federal Parliament, and it was made applicable only to federal laws.[3] Apparently the government was reluctant to resort to the anachronistic procedure for amending the Constitution, and was convinced that the provinces would not agree to the adoption of a bill of rights which was applicable to them.[4] However, the failure to entrench the Bill of Rights by constitutional amendment meant that it could be amended[5] or repealed at any time by the federal Parliament, and raised the question whether it could be effective at all. The failure to extend the Bill of Rights to the provinces (which would have required an amendment) meant that provincial violations of civil liberties were not covered at all.[6]

The Canadian Bill of Rights lost most of its importance in 1982, with the adoption of the Charter of Rights.[7] Most of the rights and freedoms guaranteed by the Bill are now guaranteed by the Charter. The Charter is part of the Constitution of Canada, and can be amended only by the constitutional amending procedures. The Charter is applicable to the provincial as well as to the federal level of government. In these circumstances, it would not have been surprising if the Charter had repealed the Bill. But it did not do so, and it is plain that the Bill remains in force, despite the fact that most of its provisions are duplicated by the Charter.[8] Those provisions of the Bill that are not duplicated by the Charter are two in number: (1) the Bill's "due process" clause (s. 1(a)), which extends to the protection of property, and (2) the Bill's guarantee

[2]The Canadian Bill of Rights, S.C. 1960, c. 44; R.S.C. 1985, Appendix III, is set out in an appendix to this book. For discussion, see Tarnopolsky, The Canadian Bill of Rights (2nd ed., 1975); Tremblay, Droit Constitutionel-Principes (2nd ed., 2000), 366-370.

[3]§ 35:2, "Application to federal laws".

[4]Tarnopolsky, The Canadian Bill of Rights (2nd ed., 1975), 88-92.

[5]The Canadian Bill of Rights has been amended once by the ordinary action of the federal Parliament: Statute Law (Canadian Charter of Rights and Freedoms) Amendment Act, S.C. 1985, c. 26, s. 105 (amending s. 3 regarding pre-enactment scrutiny of bills and regulations).

[6]It is of course open to the provinces to enact their own bills of rights, and Saskatchewan, Alberta and Quebec have done so: see previous chapter, Civil Liberties, under heading § 34:4, "Statutory bills of rights".

[7]See P.W. Hogg, "A Comparison of the Charter of Rights with the Canadian Bill of Rights" in Beaudoin and Ratushny (eds.), The Canadian Charter of Rights and Freedoms (2nd ed., 1989), ch. 1. (This chapter does not appear in subsequent editions.)

[8]In P.W. Hogg, "A Comparison of the Charter of Rights with the Canadian Bill of Rights" in Beaudoin and Ratushny (eds.), The Canadian Charter of Rights and Freedoms (2nd ed., 1989), ch. 1, at p. 4, I argue that duplicative provisions of the Canadian Bill of Rights are of no force and effect. Curiously, this has never been the subject of a ruling by the Supreme Court, and it is possible that the Canadian Bill of Rights, the Quebec Charter of Rights and Freedoms and other provincial statutory bills of rights simply operate concurrently with the Charter. However, the cases rely on the statutory guarantees only when the comparable Charter guarantee is narrower or inapplicable for some reason. The cases are footnoted in the previous ch. 34, Civil Liberties, under heading § 34:4, "Statutory bills of rights".

(s. 2(e)) of a fair hearing for the determination of rights and obligations.[9] Both these provisions go beyond the guarantees in the Charter, and will therefore continue to be operative restraints on federal (but not provincial) activity.

II. APPLICATION TO FEDERAL LAWS

§ 35:2 Application to federal laws

The Canadian Bill of Rights applies to every "law of Canada". This phrase is defined in s. 5(2) as follows:

> The expression "law of Canada" in Part I means an Act of the Parliament of Canada enacted before or after the coming into force of this Act, any order, rule or regulation thereunder, and any law in force in Canada or in any part of Canada at the commencement of this Act that is subject to be repealed, abolished or altered by the Parliament of Canada.

This definition covers existing and future federal legislation, including "any order, rule or regulation thereunder", which would include subordinate legislation[1] and all administrative action taken under the authority of primary or subordinate federal legislation.[2] The definition also covers existing (but not future) laws that are "subject to be repealed, abolished or altered by the Parliament of Canada". This phrase is copied from s. 129 of the Constitution Act, 1867, and is intended to catch pre-confederation laws within the legislative authority of the federal Parliament which were continued in force in 1867 by s. 129. Very few of these would still be in force.

The definition does not cover provincial laws, not even provincial laws in fields of concurrent jurisdiction.[3] However, provincial laws that are incorporated by reference into a federal statute would be transformed by the incorporation (or adoption) into federal laws, and would become subject to the Canadian Bill of Rights.[4]

---

[9]Both these provisions are discussed in ch. 47, Fundamental Justice, under heading § 47:13, "Property".

[Section 35:2]

[1]In legal theory, this is the status of the laws of the three territories. However, in *Re Branigan* (1986), 26 D.L.R. (4th) 268 (Y.T.S.C.), it was held that the constitutional development of Yukon made it inappropriate to apply the Bill to territorial laws.

[2]Query whether the common law in fields of federal legislative jurisdiction is covered. L. Taman, "The Adversary Process on Trial" (1975) 13 Osgoode Hall L.J. 251, 276 and J.N. Lyon, "A Progress Report on the Canadian Bill of Rights" (1976) 3 Dalhousie L.J. 39, 41 say yes.

[3]Provincial laws are not covered by the closing language of the definition, because, although provincial laws in fields of concurrent jurisdiction may be rendered inoperative through paramountcy by inconsistent federal laws, it is not accurate to describe a provincial law that has been rendered inoperative by paramountcy as "repealed, abolished or altered": see ch. 16, Paramountcy, under heading § 16:10, "Effect of inconsistency".

[4]*Jack and Charlie v. The Queen*, [1985] 2 S.C.R. 332, 338 (obiter dictum suggesting that Canadian Bill of Rights might apply to provincial laws adopted by s. 88 of the

III. EFFECT OF INCONSISTENT STATUTES

§ 35:3 Meaning of s. 2

The Canadian Bill of Rights does not expressly state what is to be its effect on a federal statute that violates its precepts. Is the Bill merely a canon of interpretation for doubtful or equivocal language in federal statutes? Or is it a "constitutional" instrument which will override inconsistent federal statutes? The latter alternative would, of course, raise the constitutional question whether Parliament could bind itself in this way by enactment of a simple statute.

The effect of the Bill on inconsistent statutes turns on the meaning of the opening words of s. 2, which state:

> Every law of Canada shall, unless it is expressly declared by an Act of the Parliament of Canada that it shall operate notwithstanding the Canadian Bill of Rights, be so construed and applied as not to abrogate, abridge or infringe or to authorize the abrogation, abridgment or infringement of any of the rights or freedoms herein recognized and declared, and in particular, no law of Canada shall be construed or applied so as to. . . .

These opening words are followed by a detailed list of legal civil liberties. A due process clause and the main political and egalitarian civil liberties are "recognized and declared" separately in s. 1 of the Act; but it is clear that the s. 1 liberties are included in the phrase in s. 2 "any of the rights or freedoms herein recognized and declared" and that they, as well as the s. 2 liberties, accordingly obtain their force from the opening words of s. 2.[1] It is also clear from s. 2 that the federal Parliament may exempt a statute from compliance with the Canadian Bill of Rights by enacting an express declaration that the statute "shall operate notwithstanding the Canadian Bill of Rights".[2]

What is not so clear in s. 2 is the meaning of the phrase "construed and applied". Does this require the courts simply to "construe" each statute so as to avoid as far as possible any conflict with the Bill of Rights, and then "apply" the statute as so construed? On this view, s. 2 is merely a rule of construction or interpretation. If a statute plainly infringed the Bill of Rights, so that the conflict could not be avoided by interpretation,

---

Indian Act).

[Section 35:3]

[1]*Curr v. The Queen*, [1972] S.C.R. 889, 896 per Laskin J.; *Miller and Cockriell v. The Queen*, [1977] 2 S.C.R. 680, 686 per Laskin C.J.

[2]The exemption clause has been used only once: Public Order (Temporary Measures) Act, S.C. 1970-71-72, c. 2, s. 12. This is the statute which superseded the Public Order Regulations which were made under the War Measures Act of 1914 to deal with the F.L.Q. "October crisis" in Quebec in 1970. The War Measures Act itself was exempted from the Bill of Rights not by a notwithstanding clause (curiously) but by a different form of words in s. 6(5), which was added to the Act by the same statute which enacted the Bill of Rights: S.C. 1960, c. 44, s. 6. The War Measures Act is discussed in ch. 17, Peace, Order, and Good Government, under headings § 17:8, "War" and § 17:9, "Apprehended insurrection". As noted there, the Act was repealed and replaced by the Emergencies Act, S.C. 1988, c. 29, which contains no notwithstanding clause or other exemption from the Canadian Bill of Rights.

then the effect of s. 2 would be exhausted and the statute would have to be applied despite its conflict with the Bill of Rights. This would follow even if the conflicting statute did not include the express declaration that it was to operate notwithstanding the Canadian Bill of Rights. A rule of construction cannot avail against a clear statutory intention to the contrary.

The alternative reading of s. 2 (which has now been judicially accepted) is to give the word "apply" in s. 2 some independent force, which can be done by reading it as a direction not to apply a statute which is inconsistent with the Bill of Rights. On this view, the courts should first "construe" a statute to avoid as far as possible any conflict with the Bill of Rights, but if the conflict cannot be avoided by interpretation, then the courts should hold the statute to be inoperative. This reading is strongly supported by the language of the exemption clause in s. 2. A statute is exempt from the Bill of Rights if it is expressly declared that it "shall operate notwithstanding the Canadian Bill of Rights". The use of the word "operate" implies that in the absence of such a declaration the statute would be inoperative. Even more persuasive is the point that the Bill of Rights would hardly have introduced the exemption clause as a formula merely to escape from a rule of construction. A rule of construction will yield to any clear language; no special formula is needed for the purpose.

Anyway, after nearly ten years of doubt reinforced by conflicting judicial opinions, the Supreme Court of Canada by a majority of six to three rejected the view that s. 2 was merely a rule of interpretation and held that s. 2 had the effect of overriding inconsistent federal statutes by rendering them inoperative. This was decided in *R. v. Drybones* (1969).[3] In that case, s. 94(b) of the Indian Act, which made it an offence for "an Indian" to be intoxicated anywhere off a reserve, was held to be inconsistent with s. 1(b) of the Bill of Rights, which guarantees to the individual "equality before the law".[4] Ritchie J. for the majority of the Court[5] held that s. 94(b) was rendered inoperative by the Bill of Rights.[6] He held that the term "inoperative" was the appropriate one to describe the effect of the Bill of Rights on an inconsistent statute, and that the effect on the inconsistent statute was "somewhat analogous to a case

[3] *R. v. Drybones*, [1970] S.C.R. 282.

[4] The meaning of "equality before the law" is addressed in ch. 55, Equality, under heading § 55:2, "Canadian Bill of Rights".

[5] Fauteux, Martland, Judson, and Spence JJ. agreed with Ritchie J.; Hall J. wrote a brief concurring opinion, but also expressed his agreement with Ritchie J.; Cartwright C.J., Abbott and Pigeon JJ. each wrote dissenting opinions.

[6] *R. v. Drybones* was followed in *R. v. Hayden* (1983), 3 D.L.R. (4th) 361 (Man. C.A.), in which the Indian Act offence of being drunk on a reserve was held to be inoperative (*Drybones* had concerned the off-reserve offence). However, *Hayden* was not followed in *R. v. Lefthand* (1985), 19 D.L.R. (4th) 720 (Alta. C.A.) (upholding the on-reserve offence). Both of these Indian Act drunkenness offences were repealed in 1985.

where valid provincial legislation in an otherwise unoccupied field ceases to be operative by reason of conflicting federal legislation".[7]

The decision in *Drybones* made clear that the Canadian Bill of Rights was not a statute like any other. In *Hogan v. The Queen* (1975),[8] Laskin J. described its status in these terms: "The Canadian Bill of Rights is a half-way house between a purely common law regime and a constitutional one; it may aptly be described as a quasi-constitutional instrument". Despite this and other affirmations of the overriding effect of the Canadian Bill of Rights,[9] Canadian courts continued to be very reluctant to apply the Bill. There have, however, been a few cases where it has been applied.[10]

In *Singh v. Minister of Employment and Immigration* (1985),[11] a challenge was brought by persons who claimed to be refugees to the refugee-determination process of the federal Immigration Act. That process could, and did in this case, result in a denial of refugee status without an oral hearing before an official with power to make the determination. The Supreme Court of Canada unanimously granted a remedy to the applicants, holding that they were entitled to an oral hearing notwithstanding the contrary provisions of the Immigration Act. However, the Court divided evenly on the legal basis for its decision. Wilson J., with the concurrence of Dickson C.J. and Lamer J., decided on the basis of s. 7 of the Charter of Rights, and said nothing about the Canadian Bill of Rights. Beetz J., with the concurrence of Estey and McIntyre JJ., decided on the basis of s. 2(e) of the Canadian Bill of Rights. Beetz J. did not rely on s. 7 of the Charter, because of doubt as to whether "life, liberty and security of the person" were affected by the refugee-determination process. (Wilson J. had decided that security of the person was affected.) Beetz J. preferred to rely on s. 2(e) of the Canadian Bill of Rights, because s. 2(e) afforded a right to a fair hearing whenever there was federal power to determine a person's "rights and obligations".

In *Singh*, while Wilson J. held that the offending provisions of the Immigration Act were "of no force or effect" by virtue of their conflict with

[7] *R. v. Drybones*, [1970] S.C.R. 282, 294-295.

[8] *Hogan v. The Queen*, [1975] 2 S.C.R. 574, 579.

[9] For obiter dicta reaffirming the overriding effect of the Bill of Rights, see *Lavell v. A.-G. Can.*, [1974] S.C.R. 1349, 1364-1365 per Ritchie J., 1374 per Abbott J., 1382 per Laskin J.; *R. v. Burnshine*, [1975] 1 S.C.R. 693, 714 per Laskin J.; *Hogan v. The Queen*, [1975] 2 S.C.R. 574, 584 per Ritchie J., 589-590 per Laskin C.J.; *A.-G. Can. v. Canard*, [1976] 1 S.C.R. 170, 205 per Beetz J.; *R. v. Miller and Cockriell*, [1977] 2 S.C.R. 680, 686 per Laskin C.J.

[10] As well as *R. v. Hayden* (1983), 3 D.L.R. (4th) 361 (Man. C.A.), *Singh v. Minr. of Emplmt. and Imm.*, [1985] 1 S.C.R. 177, and *MacBain v. Lederman*, [1985] 1 F.C. 856 (C. A.), there are the following cases: *Brownridge v. The Queen*, [1972] S.C.R. 926, *Lowry and Lepper v. The Queen*, [1974] S.C.R. 195, *A.-G. Ont. v. Reale*, [1975] 2 S.C.R. 624, and *R. v. Shelley*, [1981] 2 S.C.R. 196. See also *Bell Canada v. Can. Telephone Employees Assn.*, [2003] 1 S.C.R. 884, para. 28; *Authorson v. Can.*, [2003] 2 S.C.R. 40; *Kazemi Estate v. Islamic Republic of Iran*, [2014] 3 S.C.R. 176, 2014 SCC 62.

[11] *Singh v. Minr. of Emplmt. and Imm.*, [1985] 1 S.C.R. 177.

the Charter of Rights,[12] Beetz J. held that the provisions were "inoperative" by virtue of their conflict with the Canadian Bill of Rights.[13] Beetz J. pointed out that s. 26 of the Charter of Rights expressly preserved "any other rights or freedoms that exist in Canada", which made clear that the Canadian Bill of Rights and the various provincial bills of rights remained in force. "Because these constitutional or quasi-constitutional instruments are drafted differently", he noted, "they are susceptible of producing cumulative effects for the better protection of rights and freedoms".[14] For this reason, these instruments should not be allowed to "fall into neglect".[15]

In *MacBain v. Lederman* (1985),[16] a challenge was brought to the provisions of the federal Human Rights Code that provided for the appointment of a tribunal to determine complaints under the Code. The objection to the provisions was that they allowed the Commission, which was in effect the prosecutor, to select the members of the tribunal; this gave rise, so it was argued, to a reasonable apprehension of bias. This objection could not be raised under s. 7 of the Charter of Rights, because the tribunal had no power that could affect "life, liberty and security of the person". However, the tribunal did have the power to determine "rights and obligations". The Federal Court of Appeal, taking its cue from Beetz J. in *Singh*, held that s. 2(e) of the Canadian Bill of Rights applied, and that it rendered inoperative the appointment provisions of the Human Rights Code.

§ 35:4 Effect on earlier statutes

The Canadian Bill of Rights is a statute of the federal Parliament. What is the constitutional basis for preferring it over another statute of the federal Parliament? The general rule of the common law for resolving conflicts between two laws of the same legislative body is the doctrine of implied repeal: the later is deemed to have impliedly repealed the earlier to the extent of the inconsistency.[1] In *Drybones*, it was the Indian Act which was the earlier of the two statutes. This fact seems to eliminate any constitutional difficulty. To be sure, Ritchie J. denied that the inconsistent provision of the Indian Act was repealed, saying that it

[12]Singh v. *Minr. of Emplmt. and Imm.*, [1985] 1 S.C.R. 177, 221.

[13]*Singh v. Minr. of Emplmt. and Imm.*, [1985] 1 S.C.R. 177, 239, following *Drybones*. The word inoperative was also used in *MacBain v. Lederman*, [1985] 1 F.C. 856, 883 (C. A.), following *Drybones* and *Singh*.

[14]*Singh v. Minr. of Emplmt. and Imm.*, [1985] 1 S.C.R. 177, 224.

[15]*Singh v. Minr. of Emplmt. and Imm.*, [1985] 1 S.C.R. 177, 224. Beetz J. for a unanimous Court in *Ford v. Que.*, [1988] 2 S.C.R. 712, applied the Quebec Charter of Rights and Freedoms to strike down a Quebec law that was protected from Charter attack by a notwithstanding clause under s. 33 of the Charter.

[16]*MacBain v. Lederman*, [1985] 1 F.C. 856 (C.A.).

[Section 35:4]

[1]See ch. 16, Paramountcy, under the heading § 16:1, "Problem of inconsistency".

was merely "inoperative",[2] but in respect of constitutional power the difference is immaterial: if a later statute can repeal an earlier one, it can surely do something less drastic, such as suspend it or render it inoperative.[3]

§ 35:5 Effect on later statutes

What is the effect of the Canadian Bill of Rights on statutes enacted after the Bill of Rights? The Bill of Rights certainly purports to apply to later statutes. Section 5(2) defines "law of Canada" as including a federal statute "enacted before or after the coming into force of this Act", and the exemption clause in s. 2 contemplates that the Bill of Rights will be applicable to later statutes (since earlier statutes obviously could not include the express declaration). The courts have assumed without discussion that the Bill of Rights applies to post-1960 statutes. Both *Singh*[1] and *MacBain*[2] applied the Bill of Rights to post-1960 statutes, and no court has suggested that there is any distinction to be drawn between statutes enacted before the Bill of Rights and those enacted after.[3]

What is the constitutional basis for the application of the Bill of Rights to later statutes? The difficulty is that, according to the orthodox doctrine of parliamentary sovereignty, the later (and more specific) statute should be regarded as impliedly repealing the earlier statute (the Bill of Rights) to the extent of the inconsistency.[4] On this basis, the Bill of Rights, although effective in rendering inoperative earlier inconsistent statutes, could not be anything more than a canon of construction with respect to later inconsistent statutes. For this reason, early commentators on the Canadian Bill of Rights emphatically denied that the Bill could override future legislation.[5] There is one possible escape from the remorseless logic of parliamentary sovereignty. If it is accepted, as I think it must be, that the federal Parliament can bind itself as to the

---

[2] *R. v. Drybones*, [1970] S.C.R. 282, 294.

[3] He did not explain the difference between repealing and rendering inoperative, but presumably the latter is suspensory only: the inconsistent statute (the Indian Act) would revive if the Canadian Bill of Rights were repealed. That is the effect of the paramountcy doctrine, which also renders statutes "inoperative" and which Ritchie J. suggested was analogous.

[Section 35:5]

[1] *Singh v. Minr. of Emplmt. and Imm.*, [1985] 1 S.C.R. 177.

[2] *MacBain v. Lederman*, [1985] 1 F.C. 856 (C.A.).

[3] The only exception is *R. v. Drybones*, [1970] S.C.R. 282, 301, where Pigeon J. (who dissented) said, obiter, that "different considerations may conceivably apply in the case of subsequent statutes".

[4] Chapter 16, Paramountcy, under the heading § 16:1, "Problem of inconsistency".

[5] D.M. Gordon, "The Canadian Bill of Rights" (1961) 4 Can. Bar J. 431, 440 ("the attempt must be futile"); B. Laskin, "An Inquiry into the Diefenbaker Bill of Rights" (1959) 37 Can. Bar Rev. 77, 132 ("an unentrenched non-constitutional enactment [cannot] be given force to limit Parliamentary action"); Schmeiser, Civil Liberties in Canada (1964), 42 (the Bill "cannot possibly apply to future legislation").

"manner and form" of its future legislation,[6] then it is arguable that the notwithstanding clause in s. 2 of the Bill of Rights is a manner-and-form limitation.[7] The argument would be that Parliament has bound itself to enact laws inconsistent with the Bill of Rights only in a specified manner and form: that manner and form is the inclusion of an express declaration that the statute "shall operate notwithstanding the Canadian Bill of Rights". The conclusion of this argument would be that the Bill of Rights is entrenched, and that a later statute inconsistent with it is invalid unless it contains the express declaration described in s. 2 (the exemption clause).[8]

In my view, the manner-and-form analysis has considerable force, although it is not helped at all by the insistence of Ritchie J. in *Drybones*[9] that the Bill of Rights renders inconsistent statutes "inoperative". The manner-and-form analysis would force us to say that later statutes inconsistent with the Bill of Rights were not merely inoperative, but invalid; the absence of the exemption clause would have the same effect as the absence of assent by the Governor General (for example), namely, complete invalidity. Of course, the word "inoperative" could still be accepted with respect to earlier statutes, for which the manner-and-form argument is irrelevant, since the special manner and form was not part of the law when they were enacted.

If the foregoing analysis is correct, the ironic result is that the exemption clause in the Canadian Bill of Rights, far from detracting from the efficacy of the Bill, is essential to its efficacy, at least in its application to later statutes. If it were not for the exemption clause, the Bill would be unable to prevail over later statutes.[10]

§ 35:6 Conclusions

The effect of the Canadian Bill of Rights on prior inconsistent federal statutes is to render them inoperative. The constitutional basis for this effect is the doctrine of implied repeal: since Parliament can repeal an earlier statute, it can do something less than repeal, that is, render a statute inoperative.

The effect of the Bill of Rights on subsequent inconsistent federal statutes which do not include an express declaration of exemption is

---

[6]See ch. 12, Parliamentary Sovereignty, under heading §§ 12:9 to 12:10, "Self-imposed restraints on legislative power".

[7]Tarnopolsky, The Canadian Bill of Rights (2nd ed., 1975), 143.

[8]Cf. *Bell Canada v. Can. Telephone Employees Assn.*, [2003] 1 S.C.R. 884, para. 28 (describing the Canadian Bill of Rights as "quasi-constitutional legislation").

[9]*R. v. Drybones*, [1970] S.C.R. 282, 294. The word "inoperative" was also used in the two cases where the Bill of Rights has actually been applied to a post-1960 statute, namely, *Singh v. Minr. of Emplmt. and Imm.*, [1985] 1 S.C.R. 177, 239 and *MacBain v. Lederman*, [1985] 1 F.C. 856, 883 (C.A.).

[10]Note, however, that the Supreme Court of Canada has upheld "primacy clauses" in human rights codes which were not accompanied by notwithstanding procedures: ch. 12, Parliamentary Sovereignty, under heading § 12:10, "Manner and form of future laws".

also said to be to render them inoperative. Probably, however, the Bill of Rights renders such statutes invalid, not inoperative. The constitutional basis for this effect is the manner-and-form doctrine. Parliament has bound itself to enact laws inconsistent with the Bill of Rights only in the manner and form prescribed by the Bill of Rights.

IV. CONTENTS OF BILL OF RIGHTS

§ 35:7 Contents of Bill of Rights

The Canadian Bill of Rights guarantees the fundamental freedoms of religion, speech, assembly and association (s. 1(c), (d), (e), (f)). It guarantees a number of legal rights, including protection against arbitrary detention or imprisonment, protection against cruel and unusual treatment or punishment, the right to counsel, protection against self-incrimination, the presumption of innocence, the right to a fair and public trial and the right to an interpreter (s. 2). It guarantees equality before the law (s. 1(b)). As noted at the beginning of this chapter, these guarantees all have their counterparts in the Charter of Rights, which was adopted in 1982, and the replicated provisions of the Bill have lost their importance.[1]

There are two guarantees in the Canadian Bill of Rights that are not substantially replicated in the Charter of Rights. These are s. 1(a), which protects property rights through a "due process" clause, and s. 2(e), which guarantees a fair hearing whenever a person's rights and obligations are to be determined. Section 7 of the Charter covers some of the same ground as ss. 1(a) and 2(e) of the Bill, but s. 7 does not protect property rights and does not guarantee a fair hearing where only economic interests are at stake.[2] These provisions are discussed in ch. 47, Fundamental Justice.[3] For present purposes, the point is that ss. 1(a) and 2(e) of the Canadian Bill of Rights are the only provisions[4] that still have work to do following the adoption of the Charter of Rights in 1982.

[Section 35:7]

[1]See § 35:1 note 8, above, and accompanying text.

[2]It was the broader scope of s. 2(e) that caused it, rather than s. 7 of the Charter, to be relied on in *Singh v. Minr. of Emplmt. and Imm.*, [1985] 1 S.C.R. 177, *MacBain v. Lederman*, [1985] 1 F.C. 856 (C.A.), *Bell Canada v. Can. Telephone Employees Assn.*, [2003] 1 S.C.R. 884, para. 28 (although s. 2(e) did not avail in that case) and in *Authorson v. Can.*, [2003] 2 S.C.R. 40 (although neither s. 2(e) nor s. 1(a) availed in that case). See also *Kazemi Estate v. Islamic Republic of Iran*, [2014] 3 S.C.R. 176, 2014 SCC 62 (s. 2(e) provides no right to a hearing of a claim of torture by a foreign state that is outside the jurisdiction of Canadian courts by virtue of the federal State Immunity Act; nor does s. 7 of the Charter).

[3]§ 47:13, "Property".

[4]The Bill's prohibition (s. 2(a)) of "arbitrary. . .exile" is not reproduced in the Charter, but would be covered by the Charter's mobility clause (s. 6). The Bill's guarantee of "equality before the law" (s. 1(b)) stood on its own for the first three years of the Charter's life (see s. 32(2) of Charter), but on April 17, 1985 s. 1(b) was replicated by the coming into force of the Charter's equality clause (s. 15).

V. JUDICIAL INTERPRETATION

§ 35:8 Judicial interpretation

The Canadian Bill of Rights has, of course, left a legacy of case-law interpreting its provisions.[1] With respect to those provisions of the Bill of Rights that are not replicated by the Charter of Rights (ss. 1(a) and 2(e) are the only ones), the case-law is obviously of continuing relevance. With respect to those provisions of the Bill of Rights that are replicated by the Charter of Rights, the case-law is of little continuing relevance, even where the Bill right is expressed in the same language as the Charter right.

The Supreme Court of Canada was much criticized for its "timid" approach to the Bill of Rights. In the 22 years that elapsed between the Bill's enactment in 1960 and the Charter's adoption in 1982, the *Drybones* case[2] was the only one[3] in which the Supreme Court of Canada held a statute to be inoperative for breach of the Bill.[4] This cautious attitude stemmed in large part from the fact that the Bill was simply a statute,[5] which "did not reflect a clear constitutional mandate to make judicial decisions having the effect of limiting or qualifying the traditional sovereignty of Parliament".[6] A reinforcing factor was that the Bill contained no limiting provision comparable to s. 1 of the Charter, so that the courts were inclined to avoid broad interpretations of the rights for fear that reasonable statutory limits on the rights would have to be struck down.[7]

The restraint that led the courts to defer to the legislative choices that were presented for judicial review under the Bill of Rights has not continued under the Charter. The courts have assumed that the constitutional status of the Charter resolves their former uncertainty as to the legitimacy of judicial review. Moreover, broad interpretations of

---

[Section 35:8]

[1]See Tarnopolsky, The Canadian Bill of Rights (2nd ed., 1975), chs. 5-8.

[2]*R. v. Drybones*, [1970] S.C.R. 282.

[3]The *Drybones* case was followed in *R. v. Hayden* (1983), 3 D.L.R. (4th) 361 (Man. C.A.). Since 1982, there have been two more applications of the Canadian Bill of Rights, namely, *Singh v. Minr. of Emplmt. and Imm.*, [1985] 1 S.C.R. 177, and *MacBain v. Lederman*, [1985] 1 F.C. 856 (C.A.). See also *Bell Canada v. Can. Telephone Employees Assn.*, [2003] 1 S.C.R. 884, para. 28; *Authorson v. Can.*, [2003] 2 S.C.R. 40; *Kazemi Estate v. Islamic Republic of Iran*, [2014] 3 S.C.R. 176, 2014 SCC 62.

[4]In some cases, however, a remedy was afforded which did not involve holding a statute to be inoperative: *Brownridge v. The Queen*, [1972] S.C.R. 926 (right to counsel before taking breath test); *Lowry and Lepper v. The Queen*, [1974] S.C.R. 195 (right to hearing before sentencing); *A.-G. Ont. v. Reale*, [1975] 2 S.C.R. 624 (right to interpreter during judge's charge to jury); *R. v. Shelley*, [1981] 2 S.C.R. 196 (Crown required to prove additional element of offence notwithstanding "reverse onus" clause).

[5]The restrained attitude is well expressed by Laskin J. in *Curr v. The Queen*, [1972] S.C.R. 889, 899, emphasizing the statutory root of the Bill; quoted with approval by Martland J. in *R. v. Burnshine*, [1975] 1 S.C.R. 693, 707.

[6]*R. v. Therens*, [1985] 1 S.C.R. 613, 639 per Le Dain J.

[7]*R. v. Therens*, [1985] 1 S.C.R. 613, 639.

the Charter rights are automatically subject to the qualification that reasonable legislation in derogation of a right may be justified under s. 1. These seem to be the principal reasons[8] why the Supreme Court of Canada has consistently refused to follow its Bill of Rights decisions when the same point has arisen for decision under the Charter.

The Supreme Court of Canada had decided that mandatory Sunday closing did not offend the guarantee of "freedom of religion" in the Bill of Rights;[9] but in *R. v. Big M Drug Mart* (1985)[10] the Court held that mandatory Sunday closing did offend the guarantee of "freedom of conscience and religion" in the Charter of Rights. The Court had decided that a police demand for a breath sample was not a detention, so that there was no right to counsel under the Bill of Rights;[11] but in *R. v. Therens* (1985)[12] the Court reached the opposite conclusion under the similar language of the Charter of Rights. The Court had decided that a rational "reverse onus" clause did not offend the presumption of innocence in the Bill of Rights;[13] but in *R. v. Oakes* (1986)[14] the Court held that all reverse onus clauses offended the presumption of innocence in the Charter of Rights. These cases[15] have made it abundantly clear that there is no presumption that language carried over from the Bill of Rights to the Charter bears the same meaning in its new context. On the contrary, the cautious, restrictive interpretations of the Bill of Rights are more likely to be repudiated in favour of a generous interpretation of Charter rights. In other words, decisions rendered under the Bill of Rights are of little precedential value in determining the meaning of the Charter.

VI. SCRUTINY BY MINISTER OF JUSTICE

§ 35:9 Scrutiny by Minister of Justice

The Canadian Bill of Rights contains an interesting noncurial enforcement clause. Section 3 of the Canadian Bill of Rights requires the federal Minister of Justice to scrutinize all proposed federal statutes and regulations "in order to ascertain whether any of the provisions thereof are in-

---

[8]For extended discussion, see P.W. Hogg, "A Comparison of the Charter of Rights with the Canadian Bill of Rights" in Beaudoin and Ratushny (eds.), The Canadian Charter of Rights and Freedoms (2nd ed., 1989), ch. 1.

[9]*Robertson and Rosetanni v. The Queen*, [1963] S.C.R. 651 (upholding federal Lord's Day Act).

[10]*R. v. Big M Drug Mart*, [1985] 1 S.C.R. 295 (striking down federal Lord's Day Act).

[11]*Chromiak v. The Queen*, [1980] 1 S.C.R. 471.

[12]*R. v. Therens*, [1985] 1 S.C.R. 613.

[13]*R. v. Appleby*, [1972] S.C.R. 303; *R. v. Shelley*, [1981] 2 S.C.R. 196. These cases established that a reverse onus clause was valid if there was a "rational connection" between the proved fact and the presumed fact.

[14]*R. v. Oakes*, [1986] 1 S.C.R. 103 (rational connection relevant only under s. 1). Accord, *R. v. Whyte*, [1988] 2 S.C.R. 3.

[15]See also *Singh v. Minr. of Emplmt. and Imm.*, [1985] 1 S.C.R. 177, 209 per Wilson J.; *Re B.C. Motor Vehicle Act*, [1985] 2 S.C.R. 486, 509-512 per Lamer J.

consistent with [the Canadian Bill of Rights]", and it goes on to require that "he shall report any such inconsistency to the House of Commons at the first convenient opportunity".[1] As Peter Russell has noted, it is a weakness of this provision that it "entrusts the government itself with the responsibility of testing its own proposals against the Bill of Rights"; and he points out that "to put real teeth into such a provision, a standing committee of the House of Commons would have to be established".[2] Nevertheless, although only one report of inconsistency has ever been made,[3] the contemplated scrutiny does take place within the Department of Justice, and legislative proposals are sometimes modified before they achieve their final form.[4]

The Charter of Rights contains no obligations of pre-enactment scrutiny and report like those imposed by s. 3 of the Bill of Rights. However, in 1985 the federal Parliament amended the Department of Justice Act to require a similar scrutiny and report for compliance with the Charter.[5] As a result of this amendment (which confirmed a pre-existing practice), the scrutiny by the Minister of Justice of proposed statutes and regulations must encompass compliance with the Charter as well as the Bill.[6]

[Section 35:9]

[1]Section 3 was repealed and replaced by S.C. 1985, c. 26, s. 105, but the changes were not significant. The quoted language is in both versions.

[2]P.H. Russell, "A Democratic Approach to Civil Liberties" (1969) 19 U. Toronto L.J. 109, 125-126.

[3]Report to the House of Commons by the Minister of Justice pursuant to s. 3 of the Canadian Bill of Rights", March 27, 1975 (a report concerning an amendment to the Feeds Act).

[4]Tarnopolsky, The Canadian Bill of Rights (2nd ed., 1975), 125-128, gives examples.

[5]S.C. 1985, c. 26, which by s. 105 repealed and replaced s. 3 of the Canadian Bill of Rights, and by s. 106 added a new s. 4.1 to the Department of Justice Act, R.S.C. 1985, c. J-2. With respect to regulations, the obligation of scrutiny under the foregoing provisions (which cover regulations as well as bills) is duplicated by s. 3 of the Statutory Instruments Act, R.S.C. 1985, c. S-22. The existence of s. 3 is expressly recognized in the 1985 version of s. 3 of the Canadian Bill of Rights that was the reason for its amendment in 1985—and in s. 4.1 of the Department of Justice Act.

[6]See J.L. Hiebert, "Rights-Vetting in New Zealand and Canada" (2005) 3 N.Z. J. of Public and Int. Law 63. See further ch. 40, Enforcement of Rights, under heading § 40:30, "Scrutiny by Minister of Justice".

Chapter 36

Charter of Rights

I. IN GENERAL

§ 36:1 History of Charter
§ 36:2 Protection of civil liberties
§ 36:3 Enhancement of national unity

II. EXPANSION OF JUDICIAL REVIEW

§ 36:4 New grounds of review
§ 36:5 Vagueness of concepts
§ 36:6 Role of s. 1
§ 36:7 Role of s. 33

III. DIALOGUE WITH LEGISLATIVE BRANCH

§ 36:8 The idea of dialogue
§ 36:9 Second look cases
§ 36:10 Remedial discretion
§ 36:11 Dialogue within government

IV. POLITICAL QUESTIONS

§ 36:12 Political questions

V. CHARACTERIZATION OF LAWS

§ 36:13 Comparison with federalism review
§ 36:14 Purpose or effect
§ 36:15 Trivial effects
§ 36:16 Severance
§ 36:17 Reading down

VI. INTERPRETATION OF CHARTER

§ 36:18 Progressive interpretation
§ 36:19 Generous interpretation
§ 36:20 Purposive interpretation
§ 36:21 Process as purpose
§ 36:22 Hierarchy of rights
§ 36:23 Conflict between rights
§ 36:24 English-French discrepancies
§ 36:25 Interpretation of exceptions

VII. SOURCES OF INTERPRETATION

§ 36:26 Pre-Charter cases
§ 36:27 American cases
§ 36:28 International sources
§ 36:29 Legislative history

VIII. PRIORITY BETWEEN FEDERAL AND CHARTER GROUNDS

§ 36:30 Priority between federal and Charter grounds

IX. COMMENCEMENT OF CHARTER

§ 36:31 Commencement of Charter

X. UNDECLARED RIGHTS

§ 36:32 Undeclared rights

I. IN GENERAL

§ 36:1 History of Charter

We have already noticed the absence of a bill of rights in the Constitution Act, 1867, the increased interest in bills of rights following the second world war, and the enactment in 1960 of the Canadian Bill of Rights.[1] The enactment of the Canadian Bill of Rights did not satisfy those who advocated a bill of rights for Canada. It was a merely statutory instrument. It did not apply to the provinces. And it had been given little effect even in its application to the federal government. Indeed, the inadequacies of the Canadian Bill of Rights were often offered as reasons for the adoption of a more effective bill.

The most prominent of the advocates of a bill of rights was Pierre Elliott Trudeau, who was elected to Parliament in 1965, became Minister of Justice in the Liberal government of Prime Minister Pearson in 1967, and became Prime Minister in 1968. His government, which remained in office with only one brief interruption from 1968 until his retirement in 1984, steadily sought to achieve provincial consent to an amendment of the Constitution which would include a new amending formula and a new bill of rights. That long quest culminated in November 1981 with an agreement which included nine of the ten provinces (Quebec dissenting), and which was followed by the enactment of the Constitution Act, 1982[2] of which Part I is the Canadian Charter of Rights and Freedoms.[3]

[Section 36:1]

[1]See previous chapter, Canadian Bill of Rights, under heading § 35:1, "History of Bill of Rights".

[2]The Constitution Act, 1982 is Schedule B of the Canada Act 1982, c. 11 (U.K.).

[3]The history of the Constitution Act, 1982 is more fully related in ch. 4, Amend-

The Charter of Rights[4] has quickly proved itself to be a more effective instrument than the old Canadian Bill of Rights (which has, however, not been repealed).[5] Whereas the Bill is merely a statute, the Charter is part of the Constitution of Canada and can be altered only by constitutional amendment.[6] Whereas the Bill's effect on inconsistent statutes is (or was) not clear, the Charter expressly overrides inconsistent statutes.[7] And whereas the Bill applies only to the federal level of government, the Charter applies to both levels.[8]

§ 36:2 Protection of civil liberties

The Charter of Rights, like any other bill of rights,[1] guarantees a set of civil liberties that are regarded as so important that they should

---

ment, under heading § 4:2, "The search for a domestic amending procedure". For further discussion, see Bayefsky, Canada's Constitution Act 1982 and Amendments: A Documentary History (1989); L.E. Weinrib, "Of Diligence and Dice: Reconstituting Canada's Constitution" (1992) 42 U.Toronto L.J. 207; B.L. Strayer, Canada's Constitutional Revolution (2013), chs. 10-14.

[4]For commentary on the Charter of Rights, see Gilliland (ed.), The Charter at Thirty (2012); Gibson, Law of the Charter: General Principles (1986); Weiler and Elliot (eds.), Litigating the Values of a Nation: The Canadian Charter of Rights and Freedoms (1986); Sharpe (ed.), Charter Litigation (1987); Finkelstein and Rogers (eds.), Charter Issues in Civil Cases (1988); Beaudoin and Mendes (eds.), The Canadian Charter of Rights and Freedoms (4th ed., 2005); Tremblay, Droit Constitutionnel-Principes (2nd ed., 2000), 370-406; Mandel M., The Charter of Rights and the Legalization of Politics in Canada (2nd ed., 1994); Hutchinson, Waiting for Coraf: A Critique of Law and Rights (1995); Bakan, Just Words: Constitutional Rights and Social Wrongs (1977); Greene, The Charter of Rights (1989); Beatty, Talking Heads and the Supremes (1990); Sharpe and Roach, The Charter of Rights and Freedoms (4th ed., 2009); McLeod, Takach, Morton, Segal, The Canadian Charter of Rights (Carswell, loose-leaf service); Canadian Charter of Rights Annotated (Canada Law Book, loose-leaf service). The last work contains an excellent bibliography of the periodical literature, which is kept up to date, and I make no attempt to list it here, except for the outstanding article by S.R. Peck, "An Analytical Framework for the Application of the Charter" (1987) 25 Osgoode Hall L.J. 1.

[5]Most of the guarantees of the Canadian Bill of Rights duplicate guarantees now contained in the Charter. However, several provisions do go beyond the Charter, and these provisions will continue to be effective as against the federal government. See previous chapter on the Canadian Bill of Rights, under headings § 35:1, "History of Bill of Rights", and § 35:7, "Contents of Bill of Rights".

[6]The "Constitution of Canada" is defined in s. 52(2) of the Constitution Act, 1982, and the definition includes "this Act" of which the Charter is Part I. By virtue of s. 52(3), the constitutional amending procedure must be employed to alter the Charter. By virtue of s. 38, the general (seven-fifty) procedure is the appropriate one. This procedure involves the concurrence of the federal Parliament and the Legislatures of two-thirds of the provinces having at least fifty per cent of the population of all the provinces.

[7]Constitution Act, 1982, s. 52(1) (supremacy clause). The effect of the Bill on inconsistent statutes is discussed in the previous chapter on the Canadian Bill of Rights, under heading § 35:3, "Effect on inconsistent statutes".

[8]Constitution Act, 1982, s. 32(1), discussed in ch. 37, Application of Charter.

[Section 36:2]

[1]The purposes and effects of a bill of rights are the subject of a vast literature. Outstanding Canadian contributions are P.H. Russell, "A Democratic Approach to Civil Liberties" (1969) 19 U. Toronto L.J. 109; D.V. Smiley, "The Case against the Canadian

receive immunity, or at least special protection, from state action. This purpose is partially accomplished through the legislative and executive branches of government, which will normally do their best to avoid actions that would violate Charter rights.[2] Indeed, after the adoption of the Charter, all Canadian jurisdictions except for Quebec (which was protesting the adoption of the Charter) engaged in a review of the statute book and enacted amendments to a large number of statutes to correct perceived violations of Charter rights.[3] In the federal jurisdiction, there is a continuing statutory obligation on the Minister of Justice to review all proposed statutes and regulations for compliance with the Charter, and to report instances of non-compliance to the House of Commons.[4] In each province, some degree of scrutiny (admittedly not followed by any public report) would be undertaken by the Attorney General or Minister of Justice as part of his or her duty to keep governmental action within constitutional limits. It would be a mistake to underestimate the extent of executive and legislative compliance with the Charter, although for the most part it goes unnoticed and unrecorded.[5]

If the Charter's effect depended exclusively on the voluntary acts of government, there would obviously be no guarantee of compliance. Ultimately, the Charter is enforced by the sanction of nullification administered by the courts. If a law (or a governmental act) is challenged, and if it is found by a court to violate one of the civil liberties guaranteed by the Charter, the court will declare the law (or act) to be nugatory. In that way, the guaranteed civil liberties are protected from the actions of Parliament, Legislatures, government agencies and officials.

The Charter will never become the main safeguard of civil liberties in Canada. The main safeguards will continue to be the democratic character of Canadian political institutions, the independence of the judiciary and a legal tradition of respect for civil liberties. The Charter is no substitute for any of these things, and would be ineffective if any of these things disappeared. This is demonstrated by the fact that in many countries with bills of rights in their constitutions the civil liberties which are purportedly guaranteed do not exist in practice.

Charter of Human Rights" (1969) 2 Can. J. Pol. Sci. 277; R.A. Macdonald, "Postscript and Prelude the Jurisprudence of the Charter" (1982) 4 Supreme Court L.R. 321; P.H. Russell, "The Political Purposes of the Canadian Charter of Rights and Freedoms" (1983) 61 Can. Bar Rev. 30.

[2]The second edition of this book (1985) was criticized for placing insufficient emphasis on Charter compliance by the legislative and executive branches of government: B. Slattery, "A Theory of the Charter" (1987) 25 Osgoode Hall L.J. 701.

[3]E.g., Statute Law (Canadian Charter of Rights and Freedoms) Amendment Act, S.C. 1985, c. 26. Each province except for Quebec and each territory enacted a comparable statute between 1985 and 1987.

[4]Department of Justice Act, R.S.C. 1985, c. J-2, s. 4.1 (added in 1985). This provision is modelled on s. 3 of the Canadian Bill of Rights, discussed in the previous chapter, Canadian Bill of Rights, under heading § 35:9, "Scrutiny by Minister of Justice".

[5]See also §§ 36:8 to 36:11, "Dialogue with legislative branch".

§ 36:3 Enhancement of national unity

It is sometimes said that a bill of rights is a centralizing force in a federal state.[1] This is not true in any obvious sense. The Charter of Rights did not confer any additional powers on the federal Parliament. On the contrary, it limited the powers of the federal Parliament as well as the provincial Legislatures. But the Charter is a centralizing force in a subtle sense. It supplies a set of uniform national standards for the protection of civil liberties. These apply throughout the country, and in fields of formerly exclusive provincial jurisdiction. Some of these standards, namely, the mobility rights of s. 6 and the language rights of ss. 16 to 23, are avowedly directed to national unity, facilitating personal mobility and attempting to make the whole of Canada a homeland for French-speaking as well as English-speaking Canadians. But all of the provisions of the Charter give to persons whose civil liberties have been abridged by provincial (or federal) action the right to appeal to national norms which will be enforced by the court system, and ultimately by a national court, the Supreme Court of Canada.

It is true that the decisions of the Supreme Court of Canada on Charter issues will not be unifying in the sense of attracting national concurrence. Judicial decisions on matters such as pornography, school prayers, the funding of denominational schools, Sunday closing, minority language education, the right to strike, police powers, same-sex marriage and abortion are highly controversial and divisive. But the debates engendered by such decisions are national debates, on issues that transcend the federal-provincial or regional differences that occupy so much of Canada's public debates. Charter issues do not call in question the legitimacy of Canada as a national political community. They assume that legitimacy, and they strengthen it by the further assumption that on issues of human rights it is appropriate to have a single Canadian policy.[2]

In short, the Charter's conferral of a right to invoke national standards and a national court for the protection of civil liberties adds a dimension of allegiance to Canada as a whole that did not exist before 1982. The Charter is to that extent a unifying instrument.

[Section 36:3]

[1]P.H. Russell, "The Political Purposes of the Canadian Charter of Rights and Freedoms" (1983) 61 Can. Bar Rev. 30, 31-43, to which the following text is indebted. See also A.C. Cairns, "Recent Federalist Constitutional Proposals" (1979) 5 Can. Public Policy 348; P.W. Hogg, "Federalism Fights the Charter of Rights" in Shugarman and Whitaker (eds.), Federalism and Political Community (1989), 249; L. Weinrib, "Canada's Charter: Rights Protection in the Cultural Mosaic" (1996) 4 Cardozo J. of Int'l and Comp. L. 395.

[2]Section 1 of the Charter makes room for some diversity on civil liberties issues, but it also exerts a homogenizing influence on provincial policy-making, because the requirement of "least drastic means" discourages variations in provincial laws that derogate from Charter rights: see ch. 38, Limitation of Rights, under heading §§ 38:20 to 38:21, "Least drastic means".

II. EXPANSION OF JUDICIAL REVIEW

§ 36:4 New grounds of review

The major effect of the Charter has been an expansion of judicial review. Judicial review is not new in Canada. Since confederation, Canadian courts have assumed and exercised the power to hold laws and acts to be invalid for inconsistency with the Constitution.[1] Until the adoption of the Charter in 1982, however, the provisions of the Constitution that yielded most of the invalidating inconsistencies were the provisions that distribute legislative powers between the federal Parliament and the provincial Legislatures. The Charter adds a new set of constitutional provisions that will invalidate inconsistent laws. Thus, whereas before 1982 judicial review in Canada was for the most part confined to federalism grounds, since 1982 judicial review can also be based on Charter grounds.

The addition of the Charter's grounds of judicial review has proved to be a substantial expansion of judicial review. Not only are Charter cases much more numerous than federalism cases, they are also more policy-laden. This is because many of the Charter rights are expressed in exceedingly vague terms, and all of the rights come into conflict with other values respected in Canadian society. The result is that judicial review under the Charter involves a much higher component of policy than any other line of judicial work.[2]

The theory that rights are best protected by judicial review of legislation, based on a constitutional bill of rights, has been a basic assumption of American constitutional law for about 200 years.[3] Judicial review could no doubt be abolished by a constitutional amendment, but it is safe to say that it is a permanent feature of the American constitutional arrangements. The theory has been an extremely popular export, since adopted by many other countries (including Canada, of course). However, even in the United States, it has given rise to periodic controversy. The controversy centres around two institutional questions: (1) the question whether it is legitimate in a free and democratic society to empower non-elected judges to strike down the decisions of elected legislators (the

[Section 36:4]

[1]See ch. 5, Federalism, under heading §§ 5:20 to 5:22, "Role of the courts".

[2]A vast literature addresses the interpretation of the Charter, building on a (much larger) literature on the American Bill of Rights. The most radical commentators are those who regard the constitutional text as so indeterminate that it does not constrain the judges at all, with the consequence that the judge's role of "interpretation" is actually purely a political one. The more conventional view, certainly held by textbook writers, is that the judges have a distinctive legal role, constrained by the language of the constitutional text. However, the severity and nature of the text's constraints are open to much room for argument. For a useful survey, see S.M. Sugunasiri, "Contextualism: The Supreme Court's New Standard of Judicial Analysis and Accountability" (1999) 22 Dal. L.J. 126.

[3]*Marbury v. Madison* (1803), 5 U.S. (1 Cranch) 137 (not a rights case) was the decision that established that legislation was invalid if it conflicted with a provision of the U.S. Constitution.

"counter-majoritarian" question);[4] and (2) the question whether judges are better qualified than legislators to decide policy-laden rights issues.

Jeremy Waldron[5] argues against the institution of judicial review. His view is that, in a society with democratic institutions that are in reasonably good working order, there is no reason to depart from the usual rules of democratic governance to resolve the inevitable disagreements about rights. Issues such as abortion, affirmative action, freedom of expression or same-sex marriage should be decided definitively by the people using the normal legislative procedures. He also takes the view that democratic legislative assemblies are likely to be respectful of individual and minority rights and to debate the issues more fully and fairly than courts and for that reason are more likely to achieve wise outcomes than courts. For Waldron, there is no point in allowing a court of non-elected judges to overrule what has been determined by elected legislative assemblies. Richard Fallon[6] responds that, even if Waldron is right that courts are no better than legislatures in defining individual and minority rights, that does not make the case against judicial review. The presence of judicial review imposes no impediment to legislatures refraining from infringing rights or affirmatively protecting rights.[7] But, if the goal is to protect fundamental rights as carefully as possible, then there is advantage in giving to courts as well as legislatures the power to veto legislation that might reasonably be thought to violate rights. For example, a legislature might decide not to prohibit the picketing of employers by labour unions on the ground that it would infringe the employees' freedom of expression. In that case, the legislature has decided not to infringe the right and no judicial review would be demanded. But if the legislative decision went the other way, judicial review would be demanded and a court would hold that the picketing ban did infringe the right. Judicial review prevents errors in only one direction (under-protection or infringement), and is certain to produce more protection of rights; it may indeed give rise to the over-protection of rights, but, Fallon argues, that is preferable to the risk of under-protection (infringement) of rights.[8]

While there is no conclusive way to decide whether legislatures or

---

[4]The much-used phrase comes from Alexander M. Bickel, The Least Dangerous Branch (2nd ed, 1986), 17-18 ("judicial review is a counter-majoritarian force in our system. . .[thwarting] the will of representatives of the actual people of the here and now. . .".

[5]J. Waldron, "The Core of the Case Against Judicial Review" (2006) 115 Yale L.J. 1346; see also M. Tushnet, Taking the Constitution Away from the Courts (1999); L. Kramer, The People Themselves: Popular Constitutionalism and Judicial Review (2004); A.C. Hutchinson, "A 'Hard Core' Case Against Judicial Review" (2008) 121 Harv. L. Rev. Forum 57.

[6]R. H. Fallon, "The Core of an Uneasy Case For Judicial Review" (2008) 121 Harv. L. Rev. 1693.

[7]It is sometimes argued that the availability of judicial review diminishes the motivation of legislators to respect rights, but there does not seem to be any evidence to support that supposition: Fallon, 1704-1705.

[8]Fallon, 1699 ("If errors of underprotection—that is, infringements of rights—are

courts are the best institutions to resolve disagreements about rights, courts do have some significant advantages. Both Waldron and Fallon argue on the basis that it is *moral* rights that are in issue, but the effect of an entrenched bill or charter of rights is to define *legal* rights, and to give them priority over other (unentrenched) laws. Disagreements about the scope of the rights or their application to particular cases have to be resolved by reference to the constitutional text and any relevant decided cases.[9] That is something that the courts are better at than legislatures. Indeed, there is no real way for an individual who claims that his or her rights will be infringed by a proposed law or have been infringed by an existing law to bring the claim before the legislature. Political action to stop the legislature from enacting a law or to obtain an amendment of a law is no doubt a desirable reaction to a concern about infringement of rights, and occasionally it will be successful. But, most of the time, if an individual wants to enforce an entrenched right, the only realistic venue is a court, which will examine the evidence adduced by both sides, listen to legal argument on both sides, and decide whether the right has been infringed and if so what is the appropriate remedy. The facts of the case are usually important, and they may not have been foreseen by the legislators.

As for legitimacy, in Canada, before 1982 there was no judicial review on most rights issues. The adoption of the Charter of Rights in 1982 followed a full political debate about the desirability of an entrenched bill of rights and of judicial review by courts. The notwithstanding clause of the Charter, which is discussed later in this chapter,[10] was introduced to win over opponents of judicial review. That clause empowers legislatures to overrule the decisions of the Supreme Court on rights issues. In fact, the clause has been rarely used, because legislators recognize that the exercise of the power would be very unpopular. Nevertheless, that course is open to legislatures, and the combination of the notwithstanding clause (s. 33) and the limitation clause (s. 1)[11] have made judicial review weaker in Canada than it is in the United States.[12] There is undoubtedly little popular awareness of such niceties as the notwithstanding clause and the limitation clause. But opinion polls consistently report strong popular support for the Charter in all regions of Canada (including Quebec), and even polls taken after an unpopular decision are not much affected. The counter-majoritarian difficulty is obviously taken in stride by the people and by their elected representatives, who approve

---

more morally serious than errors of overprotection, then there could be outcome-related reasons to prefer a system with judicial review to one without it").

[9]Waldron, 1379-1385, criticizes the courts' reliance on text and precedent as a distraction from the "real issues of human interests and human liberties that are at stake".

[10]§ 36:7, "Role of s. 33"; and for fuller discussion see ch. 39, Override of Rights.

[11]§ 36:6, "Role of s. 1"; and for fuller discussion, see ch. 38, Limitation of Rights.

[12]This point is elaborated in §§ 36:8 to 36:11, "Dialogue with the legislative branch". See also J.B. Kelly and M.A. Hennigar, "The Canadian Charter of Rights and the minister of justice; Weak-form review within a constitutional bill of rights" (2010) 10 Int. J. Con. Law 35.

the decision made in 1982 to adopt the Charter, and who evidently believe that rights are better protected in a system with judicial review than they would be without judicial review.

Stephen Gardbaum[13] praises the weaker form of judicial review exemplified by Canada's Charter of Rights, under which rights are protected by judicial review, but there is a legislative power to override (under s. 33) or amend (under s. 1) a judicial decision invalidating a law for infringement of a Charter right. He describes this as "the new Commonwealth model of constitutionalism". Also exemplifying the new Commonwealth model are the statutory bills of rights that have been adopted by New Zealand (New Zealand Bill of Rights Act 1990) and the United Kingdom (Human Rights Act 2000), under which courts have no power to invalidate a law for infringement of a right, but they do have the power to interpret the law into compliance with the bill of rights, and, where that is not possible, to declare that the statute is incompatible with the bill of rights—the expectation being that Parliament will then correct the infringement found by the court. Obviously, the U.K. and N.Z. have opted for a much weaker form of judicial review than Canada, where the court does have the power to invalidate a law that is incompatible with the Charter. However, Canada shares with these countries (and not the United States) the preservation of the final word in the legislature. All three countries occupy an intermediate stage between parliamentary supremacy and judicial supremacy which were once seen as the only options. Gardbaum argues that these intermediate systems provide a "better balance"[14] between the roles of court and legislature in resolving rights disagreements than untrammelled parliamentary supremacy with its risk of under-protection (infringement) of rights and untrammelled judicial supremacy with its risk of over-protection of rights and concerns about the counter-majoritarian difficulty.

§ 36:5 Vagueness of concepts

It is certainly true that the rights guaranteed by a bill of rights tend to be expressed in broad and vague terms, and the Charter of Rights is no exception. While some of the Charter rights are fairly specific, most are not. They depend upon vague words or phrases, including, "thought, belief, opinion and expression", "assembly", "association", "life, liberty and security of the person", "fundamental justice", "fair and public hearing", "cruel and unusual treatment or punishment" and "equal protection and equal benefit of the law". The meaning of these phrases has to be determined by the courts. In performing that task, the judges will inevitably be influenced by their own social, economic and political values. They will also be influenced by their attitudes towards the appropriate relationship between the courts and the other branches of government. An attitude of judicial restraint would be deferential to the decisions of

---

[13] S. Gardbaum, "Reassessing the new Commonwealth model of constitutionalism" (2012) 8 Int. J. Con. Law 167

[14] Gardbaum, 171.

the political branches, resulting in judicial invalidation of political decisions only in clear cases of Charter violations. An attitude of judicial activism would be sympathetic to the expansion of the guaranteed civil liberties, resulting in frequent invalidation of the decisions of the political branches.

The history of the interpretation of the American Bill of Rights[1] teaches us how malleable is the vague language of a bill of rights, and how dramatically its interpretation varies with changes in the attitudes of the judges who have to apply it. Until the school desegregation case of 1954,[2] which brought the "equal protection" clause of the fourteenth amendment into prominence, the main area of controversy was the "due process" clauses of the fifth and fourteenth amendments. (The fifth amendment applies to the federal Congress; the fourteenth amendment applies to the states.) Those clauses provide that no person is to be deprived of "life, liberty, or property" without "due process of law". The due process clause of the fifth amendment was one of the grounds of decision in the *Dred Scott* case (1857).[3] In that case, the Supreme Court of the United States held that a federal law purporting to ban slavery from certain parts of the United States could not have the effect of freeing slaves brought into those states, because that would be a deprivation of the owner's property rights in his slaves. The American Bill of Rights thus became an obstacle to the emancipation of the slaves, an obstacle that was removed after the civil war by constitutional amendments.[4]

Another notorious case is *Lochner v. New York* (1905),[5] in which the Supreme Court of the United States struck down a New York law that limited hours of work in a bakery to 60 per week and 10 per day. This law violated the due process clause of the fourteenth amendment, because it was a denial of "liberty"—the employer's liberty to contract with his workers—without due process of law. Holmes J.'s dissent has become famous: he pointed out that this legal argument masked a laissez-faire economic theory which had been deliberately rejected by

---

[Section 36:5]

[1]The American Bill of Rights is made up of the first ten amendments to the Constitution of the United States. These amendments were passed by the Congress in 1789 (the first year of the union) and were ratified by three-fourths of the states in 1791. Other civil rights amendments, of which the fourteenth (1868) is the most important, were added later. The term "American Bill of Rights" is often used to include all the civil rights amendments, and that is the usage in this book. There are also some civil rights provisions in the original Constitution, namely, prohibitions on ex post facto laws or bills of attainder (art. I, s. 9, cl. 3; art. I, s. 10, cl. 1), a provision prohibiting the states from impairing the obligation of contracts (art. I, s. 10, cl. 1), and a guarantee of jury trials in federal criminal prosecutions (art. III, s. 2, cl. 3).

[2]*Brown v. Bd. of Education* (1954), 347 U.S. 483.

[3]*Dred Scott v. Sandford* (1857), 60 U.S. (19 How.) 393.

[4]The thirteenth amendment (1865) proscribed slavery. The fourteenth amendment (1868) conferred citizenship and equality rights on Black and White people alike. The fifteenth amendment (1870) provided that the right to vote was not to be denied or abridged on account of race, colour, or previous condition of servitude.

[5]*Lochner v. New York* (1905), 198 U.S. 45.

the New York legislature.[6] The *Lochner* case was not an isolated one. In more than a hundred later cases, the Supreme Court of the United States applied broad conceptions of "property", "liberty" and "due process" to strike down state laws attempting to prescribe maximum hours of work, minimum wages, maximum prices and to restrain anti-union activity by employers. Only after President F.D. Roosevelt, in an attempt to save his "New Deal" legislation, had proposed his "court-packing" plan, did the Court change its mind and reverse these decisions.[7]

The American Court's rejection of *Lochner* and the other "substantive due process" cases is sometimes described as the "constitutional revolution" of 1937. That revolution brought to an end a remarkable period of judicial activism. However, in 1953, when Chief Justice Warren was appointed, the Court entered upon another controversial activist phase, which lasted until several years after the Chief Justice's retirement in 1969. The Warren Court gave broad readings to several of the clauses of the American Bill of Rights. The equal protection clause of the fourteenth amendment was held to require the desegregation of segregated schools[8] and the reapportionment of malapportioned state Legislatures.[9] The first amendment prohibition of an establishment of religion was held to require a ban on voluntary school prayers.[10] The fifth and sixth amendments were held to confer a number of rights on criminal defendants, and upon breach to require the exclusion of reliable evidence or the setting aside of convictions.[11] The eighth amendment's ban on cruel and unusual punishments was held to cover capital punishment.[12] Even substantive due process was revived, not to invalidate social legislation, but to protect from state law a woman's "liberty" to have an abortion.[13]

---

[6]Holmes' own political views, unlike those of his friends Brandeis and Frankfurter, were conservative: he had no particular sympathy for the laws that he would have upheld: S.M. Novick, Honorable Justice: The Life of Oliver Wendell Holmes (Little Brown, Boston 1989). His decisions were based on his interpretation of the Constitution, and his belief in the appropriate limits of judicial authority.

[7]*West Coast Hotel v. Parrish* (1937), 300 U.S. 379. See also L.H. Tribe, American Constitutional Law (Foundation Press, New York, 3rd ed., 2000), ch. 8; J.E. Nowak and R.D. Rotunda, Constitutional Law (West, St. Paul, Minn., 7th ed., 2004), ch. 11.

[8]*Brown v. Bd. of Education* (1954), 347 U.S. 483.

[9]*Baker v. Carr* (1962), 369 U.S. 186; *Reynolds v. Sims* (1964), 377 U.S. 533.

[10]*Engel v. Vitale* (1962), 370 U.S. 421; *Abington School District v. Schempp* (1963), 347 U.S. 203.

[11]*Mapp v. Ohio* (1961), 367 U.S. 643 (excluding illegally obtained evidence); *Gideon v. Wainwright* (1963), 372 U.S. 335 (right to counsel); *Escobedo v. Illinois* (1964), 378 U.S. 478 (right to be informed of right to remain silent); *Miranda v. Arizona* (1966), 384 U.S. 436 (right to be informed of right to counsel).

[12]*Furman v. Georgia* (19972), 408 U.S. 238. For the revival of capital punishment in the U.S.A., see ch. 53, Cruel and Unusual Punishment.

[13]*Roe v. Wade* (1973), 410 U.S. 113.

The constitutional decisions of the Warren Court were, and still are, highly controversial.[14] They differed from the decisions of the *Lochner* era in that the Warren Court decisions vindicated values then current among American liberals, whereas those of the *Lochner* era vindicated values then current among American conservatives. Judicial activism can take any political direction depending in large measure on the political predilections of the judges.

The Canadian Charter of Rights contains no protection of "property" and no reference to "due process of law"—omissions that are explained by concern about the substantive due process decisions of the *Lochner* era. However, s. 7 does confer protection on "liberty", and s. 7 substitutes for the phrase "due process" the equally vague phrase "fundamental justice". The Charter's other guarantees include language that is similar to, or even wider than, the American Bill, for example, the freedom of religion and freedom of speech clauses of s. 2, the rights of criminal defendants in s. 11, the cruel and unusual punishment clause of s. 12, and the equality clause of s. 15. As the later chapters of this book will show, the Supreme Court of Canada has willingly embraced the new powers conferred on it by this vague language. The Court has interpreted "fundamental justice" as a substantive concept, and used it to strike down a range of criminal and other laws,[15] including restrictions on abortion.[16] The rights of criminal defendants and the concept of cruel and unusual punishment have been carried well beyond the decisions of the Warren Court (and its successors) in the United States.[17] Freedom of religion and expression have also been interpreted more broadly than in the United States.[18] In short, the Charter has ushered in a period of extraordinarily active judicial review.

This period of judicial activism since 1982 has been described as "the

[14]After Chief Justice Warren's retirement in 1969, the Court's active phase continued for a few years (see *Furman v. Georgia* (19972), 408 U.S. 238 and *Roe v. Wade* (1973), 410 U.S. 113), but then the Court became more restrained. There were no more civil libertarian initiatives comparable to those cited in the previous notes, and a tendency emerged to qualify some of the criminal defendant rulings. But none of the major decisions has been reversed. Nor have the frequent attempts to overturn the decisions by constitutional amendment been successful.

[15]*Re B.C. Motor Vehicle Act*, [1985] 2 S.C.R. 486; *R. v. Vaillancourt*, [1987] 2 S.C.R. 636; *R. v. Martineau*, [1990] 2 S.C.R. 633; *R. v. Logan*, [1990] 2 S.C.R. 731; *R. v. Hess*, [1990] 2 S.C.R. 906.

[16]*R. v. Morgentaler*, [1988] 1 S.C.R. 30.

[17]The comparison is carefully documented in R. Harvie and H. Foster, "Ties that Bind? The Supreme Court of Canada, American Jurisprudence and the Revision of Canadian Criminal Law under the Charter" (1990) 28 Osgoode Hall L.J. 729; R. Harvie and H. Foster, "Different Drummers, Different Drums: the Supreme Court of Canada, American Jurisprudence and the Continuing Revision of Criminal Law under the Charter" (1992) 24 Ottawa L. Rev. 39.

[18]E.g. *R. v. Big M Drug Mart*, [1985] 1 S.C.R. 295 (holding Sunday closing to be in violation of freedom of religion, notwithstanding American decisions to the contrary). A balanced appraisal of this area would need to factor in s. 1, which has had the effect of qualifying the Court's extremely broad definitions of religion and expression: see ch. 42, Religion, and ch. 43, Expression.

Charter revolution".[19] There is no doubt that the role of law, lawyers and judges in the public life of the country has been greatly increased. Understandably, commentators have become interested in who are the political winners and losers from active judicial review. Some have seen the Supreme Court's decisions as favouring a right-wing pro-business agenda,[20] while others have seen an opposite trend in favour of a left-wing anti-business agenda.[21] The more balanced view is that there is no consistent trend in the decisions that can be identified with a political ideology.[22] Moreover, the commentators often exaggerate the political impact of judicial review. Judicial review in Canada is weaker than judicial review in the United States. As will be explained, judicial review on Charter grounds rarely defeats a desired legislative objective. After a law is struck down by the Court, the mechanisms of ss. 1 and 33 (next two sections of this chapter) typically leave room for the law to be replaced with another version that still carries out the legislative objective, and most of the time a replacement law is in fact enacted.[23] The controversy about the political role of the Court has mainly taken place in academic journals, books and conferences. The *public* controversy about the role of the highest court that has become the standard fare of politics in the United States is muted and sporadic in Canada. It is not clear whether this is because Canadians are more respectful of their Court, or because they are less disturbed by the anti-majoritarian outcomes. It may be a bit of both.[24]

§ 36:6 Role of s. 1

The previous section has addressed the problem of vagueness in the language of the Charter, and the discretion which vagueness inevitably confers on the courts whose duty it is to apply the Charter. But even if there were perfect agreement on the precise scope of every guaranteed right, the application of the Charter would still be a difficult, policy-laden undertaking. This is because the civil liberties guaranteed by the Charter occasionally come into conflict with each other and frequently come into conflict with other values that are respected in Canadian society. A moment's reflection is enough to show that the Charter's values should not always take precedence over non-Charter values.

---

[19] Morton and Knopff, The Charter Revolution and the Court Party (2000).

[20] E.g., Mandel, The Charter of Rights and the Legalization of Politics in Canada (1994); Hutchinson, Waiting for Coraf: A Critique of Law and Rights (1995); Bakan, Just Words: Constitutional Rights and Social Wrongs (1997).

[21] E.g., Morton and Knopff, The Charter Revolution and the Court Party (2000).

[22] P.W. Hogg, "The Charter Revolution: Is it Undemocratic?" (2001) 12 Constitutional Forum 1; R. Elliot, "The Charter Revolution and the Court Party: Sound Critical Analysis or Blinkered Political Polemic" (2002) 35 U.B.C.L.Rev. 271.

[23] §§ 36:8 to 36:11, "Dialogue with legislative branch".

[24] The former ground accords with the conventional wisdom, which holds that Canadians are more respectful of authority than Americans; the latter ground is inconsistent with the conventional wisdom, which holds that Americans are more devoted to individual liberty.

Take freedom of expression, for example. This freedom is undeniably limited by many laws that restrict what a person is free to say or write, for example, laws respecting fraud, defamation, misleading advertising or labelling, sedition, official secrecy, blasphemy, obscenity and contempt of court. No one would seriously suggest that s. 2 of the Charter should be applied to eliminate all laws limiting expression, because the purposes of some at least of these laws are just as valuable in their place as is freedom of expression. What is called for, obviously, is a compromise between the conflicting values.

Section 1 of the Charter, which is the subject of a later chapter,[1] implicitly authorizes the courts to balance the guaranteed rights against competing societal values. Section 1 provides:

> The Canadian Charter of Rights and Freedoms guarantees the rights and freedoms set out in it subject only to such reasonable limits prescribed by law as can be demonstrably justified in a free and democratic society.

Section 1 makes clear that a law limiting a Charter right is valid if the law is a "reasonable" one that "can be demonstrably justified in a free and democratic society". Who is to decide whether a law satisfies the requirements of s. 1? Initially, decisions will be made by the government that introduces a bill in derogation of a Charter right, and by the legislative body that enacts the bill into law. But these decisions are not conclusive. When a law is challenged in the courts, the reviewing court will reach its own determination on the question whether s. 1 is satisfied. When appeals have been exhausted, it is the final decision of the courts that prevails over the judgment of the government and legislature that enacted the law.

Because of s. 1, judicial review of legislation under the Charter of Rights is a two-stage process. The first stage of judicial review is to determine whether the challenged law derogates from a Charter right. If it does not, then the review is at an end: the law must be upheld. But if the law is held to derogate from a Charter right, then the review moves to the second stage. The second stage is to determine whether the law is justified under s. 1 as a reasonable limit prescribed by law that can be demonstrably justified in a free and democratic society. In the second stage of judicial review, the reviewing court must decide whether the law should be upheld despite the fact that it limits a Charter right. In other words, the Court must decide whether the enacting legislative body has made an appropriate compromise between the civil libertarian value guaranteed by the Charter and the competing social or economic objectives pursued by the law. Before the adoption of the Charter in 1982, that compromise was worked out in the political arena. That will still occur, of course, but, under the Charter, the political judgment will be subject to judicial review. The courts will have to decide whether the Parliament or Legislature, in enacting an abridgement of a civil liberty,

---

[Section 36:6]

[1] Chapter 38, Limitation of Rights.

has drawn the line in the "right" place. In making that judgment, the courts will receive little guidance from the vague references in s. 1 to reasonable limits and demonstrable justification.[2]

§ 36:7 Role of s. 33

Judicial power under a bill of rights is naturally greatest when the court has a conclusive veto over legislation. This is the situation in the United States, of course, where the decisions of the Supreme Court of the United States can be overcome only by the difficult and time-consuming process of constitutional amendment. In Canada, however, the Charter includes, as s. 33, an override power, which enables the Parliament or a Legislature to enact a law that will override the guarantees in s. 2 and ss. 7 to 15 of the Charter.[1] All that is necessary is the enactment of a law containing an express declaration that the law is to operate notwithstanding the relevant provision of the Charter. Once this declaration has been enacted, the law that it protects will not be touched by the overridden provision of the Charter. This override power extends to s. 2 (expression), ss. 7 to 14 (legal rights) and s. 15 (equality). It does not extend to ss. 3-5 (democratic rights), s. 6 (mobility), ss. 16 to 23 (language rights) or s. 28 (sexual equality). With respect to these provisions, no override is possible. With respect to the provisions that can be overridden, any judicial decision could be overcome by the re-enactment of the invalid statute coupled with a declaration of override; in other words, the judicial veto is suspensory only. The fact that the elected legislative bodies have been left with the last word answers a good deal of the concern about the legitimacy of judicial review by unelected judges.[2]

III. DIALOGUE WITH LEGISLATIVE BRANCH

§ 36:8 The idea of dialogue

The presence in the Charter of Rights of the power of override in s. 33 means that most decisions striking down statutes on Charter grounds can be reversed by the competent legislative body. For example, a prohibition of the use of English in commercial signs that was struck down as

---

[2]The attempt to develop standards that would limit judicial discretion and render decisions more predictable is described in ch. 38, Limitation of Rights.

[Section 36:7]

[1]The override power is discussed in ch. 39, Override of Rights. The Canadian Bill of Rights, s. 2, includes a similar power, discussed in ch. 35, Canadian Bill of Rights, under heading § 35:3, "Effect of inconsistent statutes". So does the Alberta Bill of Rights, R.S.A. 2000, c. A-14, s. 2, the Quebec Charter of Human Rights and Freedoms, R.S.Q. 1977, c. C-12, s. 52, and the Saskatchewan Human Rights Code, S.S. 1979, s. S-24.1, s. 44.

[2]If there was an override power in the American Bill of Rights, it would have offered a solution to the substantive due process decisions of the *Lochner* era. President Roosevelt's court-packing plan would not have been necessary. It must be conceded as well that some of the Warren Court decisions would probably have been overridden in some states.

a breach of freedom of expression was revived by the Quebec Legislature, invoking s. 33.[1] Section 1 has the same effect, although it is less obvious. When a law is struck down on Charter grounds, it has failed the requirement of justification under s. 1. This nearly always means that a different law, one that still pursues the same objective, but which makes a less drastic encroachment on the Charter right, would be a reasonable limit that can be demonstrably justified in a free and democratic society. For example, when the Supreme Court of Canada struck down the prohibition on the advertising of tobacco products, it made clear that a more limited law, confined to "lifestyle advertising" or advertising directed at children, would be upheld.[2] As well, decisions that a search is "unreasonable" (under s. 8), or that a detention is "arbitrary" (under s. 9) can usually be corrected by crafting a law that includes more procedural protections but that still accomplishes the legislative goal. For example, the search and seizure provisions of the federal Competition Act have been struck down as unreasonable, but have been revived with ancillary safeguards for a requirement of a warrant to be issued by a judicial officer.[3]

A study published in 1997[4] showed that, from the inception of the Charter, there had been 66 cases in which the Supreme Court of Canada had struck down a law on Charter grounds. Of those 66 cases, all but 13 elicited some response from the competent legislative body. In seven cases, the response was simply to repeal the offending law, but in the other cases a new law was substituted for the old, invalid one. This data[5] illustrates that the decisions of the Court usually leave room for a legislative response, and they usually get a legislative response. In the end, if the democratic will is there, the legislative objective can usually be accomplished, albeit with some new safeguards to protect individual rights. It is helpful to think of the Court's Charter decisions, not as imposing a veto on desired legislative policies, but rather as starting a "dialogue" with the legislative branch as to how best to reconcile the individualistic values of the Charter with the accomplishment of social and economic policies for the benefit of the community as a whole.

The concept of a "dialogue" between the judicial and legislative branches has attracted the attention of commentators[6] and been referred

[Section 36:8]

[1]*Ford v. Que.*, [1988] 2 S.C.R. 712; followed by S.Q. 1988, c. 54.

[2]*RJR-MacDonald v. Can.*, [1995] 3 S.C.R. 199, paras. 164, 191; followed by S.C. 1997, c. 13; upheld in *Can. v. JTI-Macdonald Corp.*, [2007] 2 S.C.R. 610.

[3]*Hunter v. Southam*, [1984] 2 S.C.R. 145; followed by S.C. 1986, c. 26.

[4]P.W. Hogg and A.A. Bushell, "The Charter Dialogue between Courts and Legislatures" (1997) 35 Osgoode Hall L.J. 75.

[5]The data is updated to 2005 in P.W. Hogg, A.A.B. Thornton and W.K. Wright, "Charter Dialogue Revisited Or 'Much Ado About Metaphors' " (2007) 45 Osgoode Hall L.J. 1, reporting 23 more holdings of invalidity on Charter grounds, of which 14 (or 61 per cent) elicited a legislative response.

[6]F.L. Morton, "Dialogue or Monologue?" (1999) 20(3) Policy Options 23; J.L. Hiebert,

to in several cases by the Supreme Court of Canada.[7] However, the most striking recognition of the concept has come in the "second look" cases, which are considered next.

§ 36:9 Second look cases

In *R. v. Mills* (1999)[1] the issue was the validity of a 1997 statutory regime for the disclosure to the accused of confidential records in sexual assault cases. The Supreme Court of Canada had spoken on the issue two years earlier in *R. v. O'Connor* (1995),[2] and had laid down procedures for disclosure that tried to draw a balance between the accused's right under s. 7 to make full answer and defence (which called for disclosure) and the complainant's rights under s. 8 to privacy and under s. 15 to equality (which called for confidentiality). After the decision in *O'Connor*, Parliament enacted the 1997 statutory regime for the disclosure of confidential records in sexual assault cases.[3] The statutory regime was significantly more restrictive of disclosure than the procedures laid down by the Court, so that there was the likelihood that in some cases records that the Court in *O'Connor* had assumed would be needed by the accused in order to make full answer and defence would be withheld

---

"Why must a Bill of Rights be a Contest of Political and Judicial Wills?" (1999) 10 Public Law Review 22; C.P. Manfredi and J.B. Kelly, "Six Degrees of Dialogue: A Response to Hogg and Bushell" (1999) 37 Osgoode Hall L.J. 513; P.W. Hogg and A.A. Thornton, "Reply to 'Six Degrees of Dialogue' " (1999) 37 Osgoode Hall L.J. 529; Morton and Knopff, The Charter Revolution and the Court Party (2000), 160-166; P.W. Hogg, "The Charter Revolution: Is it Undemocratic?" (2001) 12 Constitutional Forum 1; Roach, The Supreme Court on Trial (2001), chs. 10-15; J. Waldron, "Some Models of Dialogue Between Judges and Legislators" (2004) 23 Supreme Court L.R. (2d) 5; K. Roach, "Dialogic Judicial Review and its Critics" (2004) 23 Supreme Court L.R. (2d) 49; C.P. Manfredi, "The Life of a Metaphor: Dialogue in the Supreme Court, 1998-2003" (2004) 23 Supreme Court L.R. (2d) 105; L.B. Tremblay, "The legitimacy of judicial review: the limits of dialogue between courts and legislatures" (2005) 3 Int. J. Con. Law 617; P.W. Hogg, A.A.B. Thornton and W.K. Wright, "Charter Dialogue Revisited Or 'Much Ado About Metaphors' " (2007) 45 Osgoode Hall L.J. 1, together with commentaries by scholars 67-91 and reply 193-202; R. Dixon, "The Supreme Court of Canada, Charter Dialogue and Deference" (2009) 47 Osgoode Hall L.J. 235; S. Gardbaum, "Reassessing the new Commonwealth model of constitutionalism" (2010) 8 Int. J. Con. Law 167, 178-183; E. Macfarlane, "Conceptual Precision and Parliamentary Systems of Rights: Disambiguating 'Dialogue' " (2012) 17 Rev. of Con. Studies 73; J. Cameron, "Collateral Thoughts on Dialogue's Legacy as Metaphor and Theory: A Favourite from Canada" (2016) 35 U. of Queensland L.J. 157; Stephenson, From Dialogue to Disagreement in Comparative Rights Constitutionalism (2016).

[7]*Vriend v. Alta.*, [1998] 1 S.C.R. 493, paras. 137-139, 178; *M. v. H.*, [1999] 2 S.C.R. 3, para. 328; *Corbiere v. Can.*, [1999] 2 S.C.R. 203, para. 116; *Little Sisters Book & Art Emporium v. Can.*, [2000] 2 S.C.R. 1120, para. 268; *Bell ExpressVu v. Rex*, [2002] 2 S.C.R. 559, paras. 65-66; *Harper v. Can.*, [2004] 1 S.C.R. 827, para. 37; and see also cases described in following text.

[Section 36:9]

[1]*R. v. Mills*, [1999] 3 S.C.R. 668.

[2]*R. v. O'Connor*, [1995] 4 S.C.R. 411.

[3]S.C. 1997, c. 46.

in the interests of the privacy and equality rights of the complainants.[4] This was of course a normal reaction of Parliament to a decision of which it did not fully approve, and s. 1 was available to uphold the 1997 statute, assuming that it could be justified as a reasonable limit on s. 7. Indeed, the statute contained a lengthy preamble, reciting Parliament's concern with the prevalence of sexual violence against women and children and the risk that the reporting of incidents of sexual violence would be deterred by the compelled production of records revealing personal information about complainants. The preamble had clearly been inserted with a view to bolstering the s. 1 justification.

The 1997 statute was upheld in *R. v. Mills* (1999),[5] but the decision was a surprising one, because the Court did not rely on s. 1 to uphold the statute. Instead, the Court repeatedly invoked the concept of dialogue as a reason for deferring to Parliament's judgment—not its judgment about legislative objective and other elements of s. 1 justification, but its judgment *as to where to draw the appropriate line between the competing rights.* The Court, speaking through McLachlin and Iacobucci JJ., said that *O'Connor* was "not necessarily the last word on the subject", and that "the law develops through a dialogue between courts and legislatures".[6] The Court pointed to a long process of consultation that had preceded the enactment of the statute, which had allowed time for Parliament to consider the constitutional standards laid down in *O'Connor* and also to consider how well they were working in practice. The Court described this process of consultation as "a notable example of the dialogue between the judicial and legislative branches discussed above".[7] What the Court in *O'Connor* had regarded as "preferable" was not a "rigid constitutional template" and "did not preclude Parliament from coming to a different conclusion".[8] The Court concluded that, although the statute did not place as much weight on the accused's s. 7 right to make full answer and defence as had the majority in *O'Connor*, in light of Parliament's careful deliberative process, the statute should be upheld as providing sufficient protection for the s. 7 right.

While *Mills* may be an extreme example, the idea of dialogue indicates that when Parliament (or a Legislature) has revised and re-enacted a law that the courts have found unconstitutional, the Court is likely to uphold the second attempt. After all, the new law was only enacted because of the Court's earlier decision and after taking into account the Court's reasons in the earlier decision.[9] In two cases in 2002, however,

---

[4]The story is related in more detail in ch. 47, Fundamental Justice, under heading §§ 47:32 to 47:37, "Fair trial".

[5]*R. v. Mills*, [1999] 3 S.C.R. 668.

[6]*R. v. Mills*, [1999] 3 S.C.R. 668, para. 20.

[7]*R. v. Mills*, [1999] 3 S.C.R. 668, para. 125.

[8]*R. v. Mills*, [1999] 3 S.C.R. 668, para. 133; for further comments on dialogue, see paras. 57, 143.

[9]The second look cases are analyzed in more detail in P.W. Hogg, A.A.B. Thornton and W.K. Wright, "Charter Dialogue Revisited Or 'Much Ado About Metaphors' " (2007)

the Court divided sharply on the degree of deference that a second try by Parliament should receive.

The first of these cases was *R. v. Hall* (2002),[10] which reviewed a second attempt by Parliament to define the grounds for denying bail to an accused person in custody. In an earlier case called *Morales*, the Supreme Court of Canada had struck down a provision of the Criminal Code that authorized the denial of bail when the continued detention of an accused person was "necessary in the public interest".[11] The Court held that the quoted phrase was too vague to satisfy s. 11(e) of the Charter, which prohibited the denial of bail without just cause. After this decision, Parliament replaced the invalid public-interest ground with a new provision that authorized the denial of bail "on any other just cause being shown and, without limiting the generality of the foregoing, where the detention is necessary in order to maintain confidence in the administration of justice . . .". In *Hall*, the Supreme Court of Canada held unanimously that the general phrase "on any other just cause being shown" was (like its public interest predecessor) unconstitutionally vague. But the Court divided five to four on the validity of the more specific ground, which authorized the denial of bail in order to maintain confidence in the administration of justice. McLachlin C.J., for the majority of the Court, upheld the provision as being sufficiently precise to pass constitutional muster under s. 11(e). She pointed out that Parliament, before enacting the challenged language, had taken into account the Court's reasons in *Morales*. She described this as "an excellent example" of the "constitutional dialogue" between the courts and Parliament.[12] But Iacobucci J., for the dissenting minority, held that the administration-of-justice language was still unconstitutionally vague. In his view, the case demonstrated how "constitutional dialogue can break down". Although Parliament had responded to the Court's decision in *Morales*, "it has not done so with due regard for the constitutional standards set out in that case". By upholding the new provision, the majority of the Court "has transformed dialogue into abdication".[13]

Just three weeks after its decision in *Hall*, the Supreme Court of Canada decided *Sauvé v. Canada* (2002),[14] which reviewed a second attempt by Parliament to impose voting disqualifications on prisoners. In earlier litigation by the same litigant, the Court had struck down a provision of the Canada Elections Act that disqualified all persons serving prison sentences from voting in federal elections. The Court had held that the disqualification infringed the right to vote in s. 3 of the Charter and was

---

45 Osgoode Hall L.J. 1.

[10] *R. v. Hall*, [2002] 3 S.C.R. 309.

[11] *R. v. Morales*, [1992] 3 S.C.R. 711; see ch. 51, Rights on Being Charged, under heading § 51:18, "Reasonable bail (s. 11 (e))".

[12] *R. v. Hall*, [2002] 3 S.C.R. 309, para. 43.

[13] *R. v. Hall*, [2002] 3 S.C.R. 309, para. 127.

[14] *Sauvé v. Canada*, [2002] 3 S.C.R. 519.

not justified under s. 1.[15] After this provision was struck down, Parliament amended the legislation to narrow the disqualification to prisoners serving a sentence of two years or more.[16] When the constitutional challenge to the new provision reached the Supreme Court of Canada, the Government of Canada conceded the infringement of s. 3, and the issue before the Court was whether the infringement was justified under s. 1. On that issue, the Court divided five to four, the majority holding that the law was not justified under s. 1. Gonthier J., writing for the four dissenters, invoked the concept of dialogue to argue that the Court should defer to Parliament's judgment as to what was a reasonable limit on the right to vote. Once Parliament had debated that issue, the dialogue metaphor suggested that the Court should not substitute its view for Parliament's reasonable choices among social and political philosophies. According to Gonthier J., this was a case where the Court should "let Parliament have the last word".[17] After *Hall*, one might have expected McLachlin C.J. to agree with this reasoning, but she now took a very different line. Writing for the majority (which included Iacobucci J.), she described the right to vote as "fundamental to our democracy" and of "special importance" and said that any limits on the right "require not deference, but careful examination".[18] Echoing the strong language of Iacobucci J. in *Hall*, she said: "The healthy and important promotion of a dialogue between the legislature and the courts should not be debased to a rule of 'if at first you don't succeed, try, try again'."[19] She dismissed the parliamentary debates as offering "more fulmination than illumination".[20] She described the reasons given by Government for limiting the right (enhancing civic responsibility, promoting respect for the rule of law, and strengthening the criminal sanction) as merely "symbolic", "abstract" and "rhetorical"; and she concluded that there was no pressing and substantial objective that would justify limiting the right.[21] The conclusion was that all persons serving prison sentences must be given the right to vote, notwithstanding that Parliament had made a clear choice, informed by the Court's previous decision, to limit the right.[22]

---

[15] *Sauvé v. Can.*, [1993] 2 S.C.R. 438.

[16] The amendment had been enacted by the time the appeal reached the Supreme Court of Canada, but it was not applicable to that appeal, and the Court did not comment on it.

[17] *Sauve v. Can.*, [2002] 3 S.C.R. 519, para. 104.

[18] *Sauve v. Can.*, [2002] 3 S.C.R. 519, paras. 9, 11.

[19] *Sauve v. Can.*, [2002] 3 S.C.R. 519, para. 17.

[20] *Sauve v. Can.*, [2002] 3 S.C.R. 519, para. 21.

[21] *Sauve v. Can.*, [2002] 3 S.C.R. 519, paras. 21-26.

[22] See also *Harper v. Can.*, [2004] 1 S.C.R. 827 (law restricting third-party election expenditures upheld under s. 1; law had been enacted after a prohibition had been struck down and after a second law imposing restrictions had also been struck down; dialogue not invoked by Bastarache J. for the majority, but referred to in para. 37 of the dissenting opinion of McLachlin C.J. and Major J.).

In *Canada v. JTI-Macdonald Corp.* (2007),[23] the Court reviewed a second attempt by Parliament to ban the advertising of tobacco products. The first Act had been struck down by the Court in the *RJR* case[24] as a breach of freedom of expression that was too sweeping to satisfy the minimum-impairment branch of s. 1 justification. In the *JTI* case, McLachlin C.J., who wrote for a unanimous Court, said that "the mere fact that the legislation represents Parliament's response to a decision of this Court does not militate for or against deference".[25] However, she described the second Act as "a genuine attempt by Parliament to craft controls on advertising and promotion that would meet its objectives as well as *the concerns expressed by the majority of this Court* in *RJR*".[26] The second Act took up suggestions from the *RJR* reasons that information advertising and brand-preference advertising should be excepted from the general ban, and that "lifestyle" advertising and advertising designed to be appealing to young persons should be specifically targeted. These changes to the original Act led the Court to hold that the minimum-impairment branch of s. 1 justification was now satisfied. The case illustrates that, without any increased deference by the second-look Court, the chances of a second statute being upheld are high.[27] The second statute will have been drafted with close attention to the reasons given by the Court in the earlier case for holding that the requirements for s. 1 justification were not satisfied. The drafters will also have taken note of any suggestions made by the Court in the earlier case as to how the constitutional infirmities could have been corrected. The second statute will typically include a preamble that recites the s. 1 justification for the statute, and this too will have been informed by the reasons in the earlier case. And evidence will have been prepared for the second-look litigation to create a record that is more persuasive on justification than was the record in the earlier case. With all these advantages, the second statute is likely to be upheld. Indeed, in most cases, the validity of the second statute is so clear that it is never even challenged.[28]

The easiest second-look cases are those in which the competent legislative body follows the suggestion of the Supreme Court as to how a constitutional infirmity could be corrected. That was what happened in *Canada v. Harkat* (2014),[29] where the Court reviewed an amendment to the security-certificate scheme of the Immigration and Refugee Protec-

---

[23] *Canada v. JTI-Macdonald Corp.*, [2007] 2 S.C.R. 610.

[24] *RJR-Macdonald v. Can.*, [1995] 3 S.C.R. 199.

[25] *Canada v. JTI-Macdonald Corp.*, [2007] 2 S.C.R. 610, para. 11, citing P.W. Hogg, A.A.B. Thornton and W.K. Wright, "Charter Dialogue Revisited Or 'Much Ado About Metaphors' " (2007) 45 Osgoode Hall L.J. 1.

[26] *Canada v. JTI-Macdonald Corp.*, [2007] 2 S.C.R. 610, para. 7 (emphasis added).

[27] R. Dixon, "The Supreme Court of Canada, Charter Dialogue and Deference" (2009) 47 Osgoode Hall L.J. 235, argues that the Court should take a more deferential approach to second-look cases.

[28] See the statistics reported at P.W. Hogg and A.A. Bushell, "The Charter Dialogue between Courts and Legislatures" (1997) 35 Osgoode Hall L.J. 75.

[29] *Canada v. Harkat*, [2014] 2 S.C.R. 33, 2014 SCC 37.

tion Act. The security-certificate scheme was designed to identify non-citizens who were threats to national security and who should be removed from Canada. A security certificate would be issued to a "named person" by two ministers; the named person would be arrested and detained; and then there would be a process before a designated Federal Court judge, whose duty was to review the grounds for the certificate and, if the judge found them "reasonable", the security certificate would be translated into a removal order against the named person. In the review proceedings before the judge, the relevant evidence that was secret on national security grounds could not be shown to the named person, and for the same reason the certificate hearing took place, at least in part, in a closed court from which the named person was excluded. In *Charkaoui v. Canada* (2007),[30] the Supreme Court had found that, although the named person was entitled to be heard at the open part of the certificate hearing, the named person might not have enough information about the case against him to answer that case. The Court held that the process did not satisfy the principles of fundamental justice under s. 7. McLachlin C.J., who wrote the opinion of the Court, also held that the process could not be justified under s. 1 because Parliament could have adopted measures to preserve secrecy that were less intrusive of the free-trial rights of the named person. She pointed with approval to a system of "special counsel", that had previously been used in Canada and had been adopted in other countries for national security cases, and she offered this as one measure that Parliament might consider. Parliament adopted this suggestion, amending the Act[31] to provide for "special advocates", who would be security-cleared lawyers to whom the entire record of the case against a named person could be disclosed, and whose duty would be to protect the interests of the named person in a closed hearing. The special advocate was not permitted to disclose secret information to the named person, and was permitted to communicate with the named person only as approved by the judge. In *Harkat*, the Court acknowledged that the system was still "an imperfect substitute for full disclosure in an open court".[32] However, while imperfect, the Court held that, bearing in mind the national security context, the security certificate scheme as amended did not violate s. 7. It was the provision for the special counsel, which was the change suggested in *Charkaoui*, that made the difference.

§ 36:10 Remedial discretion

Another way in which the concept of dialogue has affected the reasoning and results of constitutional cases is the Supreme Court of Canada's willingness to suspend a declaration of invalidity after a finding that a

[30] *Charkaoui v. Canada*, [2007] 1 S.C.R. 350.

[31] S.C. 2008, c. 3.

[32] *Canada v. Harkat*, [2014] 2 S.C.R. 33, 2014 SCC 37, para. 77.

law is unconstitutional.[1] Starting in 1985, the Court occasionally suspended the operation of a declaration of invalidity for a period of six months or a year or 18 months in order to allow the competent legislative body time to enact corrective legislation. This is a radical remedy, since the Court's declaration leaves in force (although only for a temporary period) a law that is unconstitutional. In *Schachter v. Canada* (1992),[2] the Court said that it would only be prepared to grant a temporary period of validity to an unconstitutional law in three circumstances. Those circumstances were where the immediate striking down of the law (1) would pose a danger to the public, (2) would threaten the rule of law, or (3) would result in the deprivation of benefits from deserving persons.

The exigent circumstances of danger, disorder or deprivation that were stipulated in *Schachter* as required to justify the suspension of a declaration of invalidity were indeed present in most of the cases in which suspensions had been ordered before *Schachter*. After *Schachter*, however, the Court has frequently ordered the suspension of declarations of invalidity in circumstances that do not fit the *Schachter* criteria.[3] This is because a dialogue rationale has supplanted the emergency rationale as a sufficient basis for the suspension of a declaration of invalidity. The new rationale is simply that, in many cases where the Court has found a law to be unconstitutional, the Court would prefer the legislature to design the appropriate remedy. According to Professors Choudhry and Roach, "the delayed declaration of invalidity has evolved beyond its origins as an emergency measure and emerged. . .as a powerful dialogic device that allows courts to remand complex issues to legislative institutions".[4] The dialogue rationale has typically gone unacknowledged by the Court, but it was articulated in *Corbiere v. Canada* (1999).[5] In that case, the Court suspended for 18 months a declaration that the on-reserve residence requirement for voting in Indian Act band elections was unconstitutional. In a concurring opinion, L'Heureux-Dubé J. pointed out that there were a number of ways in which the constitutional defect could be repaired, and the best solution would be one designed by Parliament after consultation with the aboriginal people affected. In her view, the principle of democracy should guide the exercise of the Court's

[Section 36:10]

[1]See ch. 40, Enforcement of Rights, under heading § 40:4, "Temporary validity".

[2]*Schachter v. Canada*, [1992] 2 S.C.R. 679, 719.

[3]S. Choudhry and K. Roach, "Putting the Past Behind Us?" (2003) 21 S.C.L.R. (2d) 205, 226-238 list all the suspended declarations that have been issued up to the date of the article, and describe the changed attitude of the Court. See also B. Ryder, "Suspending the Charter" (2003) 21 S.C.L.R. (2d) 267.

[4]S. Choudhry and K. Roach, "Putting the Past Behind Us?" (2003) 21 S.C.L.R. (2d) 205, 232.

[5]*Corbiere v. Canada*, [1999] 2 S.C.R. 203.

remedial discretion, and that principle "encourages remedies that allow the democratic process of consultation and dialogue to occur".[6]

Judicial respect for the autonomy of the other branches of government, which underlies the suspended declarations of invalidity, would also argue for restraint in crafting orders to compel the executive branch to rectify Charter breaches.[7] In *Doucet-Boudreau v. Nova Scotia* (2003),[8] a superior-court judge in Nova Scotia had found the provincial government in breach of the minority language educational rights of s. 23 of the Charter. Acting under s. 24(1) of the Charter (the remedial provision), he ordered the province to build new French-language schools in five districts of the province where the numbers of children of French-speaking parents warranted. The order not only stipulated the dates by which each of the schools should be built, but provided for the judge to retain jurisdiction to receive progress reports from the government "respecting [its] compliance with the order". The judge in fact held a series of "reporting hearings" throughout the period of construction. For each of these hearings, he required the government to file an affidavit as to its progress in building the schools, he allowed affidavits of rebuttal to be filed, and he provided for the cross-examination of the deponents. The Attorney General of Nova Scotia appealed only the retention of jurisdiction to hold the reporting hearings. By the time the case reached the Supreme Court of Canada, the reporting hearings were completed and the schools had been built, but the Court dealt with the appeal all the same. The majority of the Court upheld the judge's order, citing concerns about the assimilation of the French-speaking minority in the province and past delays in developing French-language facilities and programs. The majority took the view that, without the supervisory order, the order to build the schools might be "ineffective",[9] by which the Court could only mean that the government might not comply with the order.

The trial judge's supervisory order in *Doucet-Boudreau* reflected a high degree of distrust of the executive branch. The majority of the Supreme Court of Canada seemed to share the mistrust. They were willing to assume that there was a risk of government disobedience of the order to build the schools, even though the order to build the schools (as opposed to the order to participate in "reporting hearings") was not even appealed by the province. (And, in any case, as the majority acknowledged, disobedience could be remedied by a contempt order.) The dissenting minority pointed out that: "Canada has maintained a tradition of compliance by governments and public servants with judicial

[6]*Corbiere v. Canada*, [1999] 2 S.C.R. 203, para. 116.

[7]E.g., *Can. v. Khadr*, [2010] 1 S.C.R. 44, para. 2 (granting declaration that the applicant's rights had been infringed without any specific remedial order so as to leave the government "a measure of discretion in deciding how best to respond").

[8]*Doucet-Boudreau v. Nova Scotia*, [2003] 3 S.C.R. 3.

[9]*Doucet-Boudreau v. Nova Scotia*, [2003] 3 S.C.R. 3, para. 66.

interpretations of the law and court orders".[10] So far as I am aware, they might have truthfully added that there has not been a single instance of a failure by any Canadian government to comply with a s. 24(1) order. Canada has not faced the intransigent refusals to comply with constitutional rights that the federal courts of the United States had to cope with after the American Supreme Court ordered that the fourteenth amendment required the desegregation of schools and other public facilities. Obviously, when governments refuse to obey the constitution, there comes a point when dialogue must be replaced with coercion. But Canadian governments do not refuse to obey the constitution. The minority in *Doucet-Boudreau* did not use the word "dialogue" in support of their view that the supervisory order inappropriately invaded the sphere of the executive. However, the majority were obviously troubled by the dissonance between their espousal of dialogue in other contexts and their affirmation of the draconian supervisory order in this case. They said that "judicial restraint and metaphors such as 'dialogue' must not be elevated to the level of strict constitutional rules to which the words of s. 24 can be subordinated".[11]

§ 36:11 Dialogue within government

This section of the book, entitled "Dialogue with the legislative branch" has been devoted to the sequels to cases where a law has been struck down by the Supreme Court. The process of legislative reaction to a Supreme Court decision has been described as "dialogue". That is a highly artificial meaning of the word "dialogue"—it is simply a metaphor—because of course the Court and the legislative bodies never actually talk to each other. The Court simply issues its judgments and governments take whatever action they believe to be possible and appropriate in order to salvage their legislative policies without infringing the Charter.

Constitutional lawyers like to write about (and talk about) cases where a law has been struck down by the Supreme Court. That is always interesting! But the truth is that such cases are rare, especially when you consider that hundreds of new laws are enacted every year by Canada's fourteen legislative bodies—on top of the thousands of laws already on the books. Because of the vagueness of much of the Charter, and the tendency for the Charter rights to expand over time under judicial interpretation, many laws have at least an arguable impact on a Charter right. And yet laws are rarely struck down. One reason for this is that governments at all levels, regardless of political party, want to comply with the Charter. And to achieve that end, every Canadian government employs a staff of constitutional lawyers in the department headed by the Attorney General, which is usually called the Department of Justice or the Ministry of the Attorney General. One of the roles of these lawyers is to examine all legislative proposals that are being

[10] *Doucet-Boudreau v. Nova Scotia*, [2003] 3 S.C.R. 3, para. 106.

[11] *Doucet-Boudreau v. Nova Scotia*, [2003] 3 S.C.R. 3, para. 53.

considered by government, and to provide an assessment of the risk of a successful constitutional challenge to each proposal.[1] If a risk is identified, the lawyers will work with policy staff in the relevant government department to examine various options with a view to finding a way to accomplish the government's objectives in a fashion that is likely to be upheld by the courts. This debate within government about the impact of the Charter on government policy takes place *before* the enactment of legislation. It is an actual rather than a metaphorical dialogue, and one in which constitutional lawyers inevitably play an active role.[2]

There is no doubt that the Charter has given to lawyers a more important role in government than they possessed before 1982. Their considered opinions cannot be brushed aside on policy grounds because they ultimately report to the Attorney General. The Attorney General is the chief law officer of the Crown. Briefed by the lawyers in his or her department, the Attorney General advises the Prime Minister or Premier on the legality of whatever is proposed by the government. In fulfilling this role,[3] the Attorney General acts with a degree of independence from the other ministers in the cabinet.[4] By long tradition, the Attorney General upholds the rule of law, which means that he or she is under a duty

[Section 36:11]

[1]In the case of the federal Minister of Justice, there is a statutory obligation to review all statutes and regulations for compliance with the Charter (as well as the Canadian Bill of Rights): Department of Justice Act, R.S.C. 1985, c. J-2, s. 4.1 (added in 1985); and see ch. 35, Canadian Bill of Rights, under heading § 35:9, "Scrutiny by Minister of Justice". But all governments engage in a pre-enactment review of their proposed laws for Charter compliance.

[2]L.R. Sterling, "The Charter's Impact on the Legislative Process: Where the Real "Dialogue" Takes Place" (2007) 23 Nat. J. Con. Law 139. See also M. Dawson, "The Impact of the Charter on the Public Policy Process and the Department of Justice" (1992) 30 Osgoode Hall L.J. 595; Monahan and Finkelstein (eds.), The Impact of the Charter on the Public Policy Process (1993); Hiebert, Charter Conflicts: What is Parliament's Role? (2002); J.B. Kelly and M.A. Hennigar, "The Canadian Charter of Rights and the minister of justice: Weak-form review within a constitutional bill of rights" (2012) 10 Int. J. Con. Law 35, 51-68.

[3]An even more independent role is the Attorney General's oversight of the prosecution of persons accused of crime, which must be undertaken free of the influence of political goals (other than the suppression and punishment of crime). This is easier to keep free of politics in that the Attorney has exclusive authority to make decisions respecting prosecutions. J.B. Kelly and M.A. Hennigar, "The Canadian Charter of Rights and the minister of justice: Weak-form review within a constitutional bill of rights" (2012) 10 Int. J. Con. Law 35, argue that the roles of Minister of Justice and Attorney General, which are fused in Canadian practice, the names often being used interchangeably, should be separated. A separate Attorney General would have responsibility for the conduct of the government's litigation (civil as well as criminal), including providing legal opinions to government. A separate Minister of Justice would have responsibility for other matters within the Justice portfolio, for example, legislative policy (amendments to the Criminal Code and other justice-related laws), judicial appointments, administration of federal courts, etc. The responsibilities assigned to the Minister of Justice would not be different in principle from those of other cabinet ministers and would not call for a distinctively independent role.

[4]Compare *Sutcliffe v. Ont.* (2004), 69 O.R. (3d) 257 (C.A.) (Attorney General, by virtue of his independence from government, had standing to intervene in an appeal

to provide objective legal advice in order to make sure that government action complies with the Charter (and other laws). Canadian politicians understand that government is bound by the rule of law, and the Attorney General's advice on legal issues, even if it is unwelcome from a policy standpoint, normally has to be accepted by cabinet. If it were not accepted, and the Attorney General became convinced that the government was set on a policy course that was unconstitutional, it would be difficult for the Attorney General to remain in cabinet, where of course he would be under an obligation to support the policy.[5] Although there does not seem to have been a case in Canada where an Attorney General has actually resigned on an issue of legality, the Attorney General's voice on issues of law has much greater force in the formation of policy than that of other ministers.[6]

IV. POLITICAL QUESTIONS

§ 36:12 Political questions

"All constitutional interpretations have political consequences".[1] By denying government the power to do something it wants to do, or even by affirming the existence of the power, the courts are inescapably important parties to political controversies. Indeed, in Canada many political controversies find their way into courts. It is usually possible to construct an argument that any controversial government policy offends some part of the Constitution; and many organizations and individuals, and even some provincial governments, hold the puzzling view that losing an expensive constitutional case is a good way to advance their political objectives.

A constitutional challenge to a government policy will only succeed if the challenger can persuade a court that the policy is contrary to the

notwithstanding that the Minister of the Environment, one of two appellants, the other being a private company, had abandoned the appeal).

[5] I.G. Scott, "The Role of the Attorney General and the Charter of Rights" (1986) 29 Crim. L.Q. 187, 193-196, stops short of asserting that resignation is necessary, although he implies as much in that he does not indicate how else a conflict should be resolved. He does point out that, in practice, a constitutional issue is entwined with policy and, even if the legal issue can be isolated, it is rarely black or white. On all but the clearest legal issues, the Attorney General would obviously be entitled to provide tentative support for a position with which he disagreed. After all, only a judicial decision can provide a conclusive answer, and if the matter is decided by the courts, the government would comply, and the Attorney General's conflict would disappear. For discussion of the Attorney General's role in litigation, see G. Huscroft, "The Attorney General and Charter Challenges to Legislation: Advocate or Adjudicator?" (1995) 5 Nat. J. Con. Law 125.

[6] L.R. Sterling and H. Mackay, "The Independence of the Attorney General in the Civil Law Sphere" (2004), unpublished paper delivered to conference at Queen's University on "The Role of the Attorney General", offers a scholarly and realistic survey of the position, informed by their experience as law officers of the Crown.

[Section 36:12]

[1] This statement by Jackson J. of the Supreme Court of the United States is in his book: R. H. Jackson, The Supreme Court in the American System of Government (Harvard U. P., Cambridge, Mass., 1955), 56.

Constitution. Inside the courtroom, the issue is determined on the basis of the language of the Constitution. Of course, the language of the Constitution may not speak clearly to the point, and the Court will have to exercise choice in determining what is the best interpretation of vague or ambiguous language. Issues of standing, mootness, ripeness or remedy may also have to be resolved, again involving the exercise of choice. But judges are not free to decide cases in accordance with their personal preferences or their ideological predilections or their sense of political astuteness, although no doubt these factors may unconsciously influence judicial choices. Judges decide cases by the application of standards of legality that are derived from the Constitution, the statutes and the decided cases.[2] Decisions of single judges are of course subject to appeal, as are many decisions of appellate courts until the Supreme Court of Canada is reached, and even the Supreme Court of Canada is subject to professional and academic commentary. Departures from standards of legality are thus open to correction and criticism.

In the United States, there have been occasional refusals to decide cases on the basis of a "political questions" doctrine.[3] The general idea is that there are some questions that are inherently nonjusticiable because they are too "political" for judicial resolution. American commentators are divided on the question whether there is indeed a political questions doctrine. One school of thought holds that each of the decisions can be explained without recourse to any such doctrine. For example, even where a court has invoked the doctrine, the refusal to grant a remedy may well turn on (1) the court's obligation to respect those decisions of the executive or legislative branches that are made within their constitutional authority, or (2) the court's refusal to impose limitations or prohibitions on government activity where the Constitution does not prescribe any.

Whatever the position in the United States, it is clear that there is no political questions doctrine in Canada.[4] In *Operation Dismantle v. The Queen* (1985),[5] an action was brought by a peace organization for a declaration that the Canadian government's decision to permit the United States to test its air-launched "cruise missile" in Canada was a violation of the Charter of Rights. The Supreme Court of Canada struck out the statement of claim as disclosing no cause of action. The Court held that

---

[2]See B. Slattery, "Are Constitutional Cases Political?" (1989) 11 Supreme Court L.R. 507. For reference to the vast literature on the legitimacy of judicial review, see ch. 5, Federalism, under heading § 5:21, "Limitations of judicial review".

[3]See J.E. Nowak and R.D. Rotunda, Constitutional Law (West, St. Paul, Minn., 7th ed., 2004), 125-137; L.H. Tribe, American Constitutional Law (Foundation, N.Y., 3rd ed., 2000), 365-385.

[4]Sossin, Boundaries of Judicial Review (1999), 133, 199-200, argues that this assessment merits reconsideration on the basis that there is a variety of situations in which judicial refusals to decide cases can be best explained in terms of a political questions doctrine, albeit one that is still evolving and lacks clear governing principles. Chapter 4 of Sossin's book contains a comprehensive account of the cases that could be grouped under a political questions doctrine.

[5]*Operation Dismantle v. The Queen*, [1985] 1 S.C.R. 441.

the federal government was acting within its constitutional powers in permitting the tests, and that no prohibition in the Charter (or elsewhere in the Constitution) applied to the tests.[6] However, the Court declined to place its decision on a political questions doctrine. Wilson J., speaking for a unanimous Court on this issue, said that there was no doctrine of political questions in Canadian constitutional law. If a case raised the question whether executive or legislative action violated the Constitution, then the question had to be answered by the Court, regardless of the political character of the controversy.[7]

The question whether the Parliament of Canada could place a five per cent cap on the growth of its payments to the provinces under open-ended cost-sharing agreements was (at least to provincial politicians) a controversial political question in 1990, when the policy was announced in the federal budget. When the policy was challenged in court by four provinces, the federal government argued that the issue was a purely political one that was not suitable for judicial determination. But the reference to the courts had transformed the issue into a legal one: did the Constitution contain any prohibition on the unilateral introduction and enactment of legislation to curb spending by the federal government under shared-cost agreements with the provinces? The Supreme Court of Canada in *Re Canada Assistance Plan* (1991)[8] held that this was a legal question that could be answered by the Court; and the Court went on to hold that there were no prohibitions in Canada's constitutional law that would preclude the proposed legislation. Of course, if the Court had been asked whether the federal Parliament should as a matter of policy reduce its contributions to provincial social programmes, the Court would have refused to answer. The refusal might have been expressed in terms of the question being "political",[9] but the real point would be that the question was not one of law.

No question could be more "political" than the question whether the province of Quebec could secede unilaterally from Canada. And yet the question is also one of constitutional law, requiring a consideration of how the Constitution of Canada would govern the secession of a province. In the *Secession Reference* (1998),[10] the Supreme Court of Canada held that this was a question that should be answered on a reference. The Court held that, under the Constitution of Canada, a secession could be accomplished only in compliance with the amending procedures of the Constitution, and those procedures precluded a unilateral secession by a province. The Court also answered a second question that asked for a ruling as to the position under international law. That was also a "legal

---

[6]Section 7 was the basis argued for by the plaintiff.

[7]*Operation Dismantle v. The Queen*, [1985] 1 S.C.R. 441, 472. Wilson J.'s opinion was a separate concurrence, but on this issue Dickson J., who wrote for the rest of the Court, agreed with her: *Operation Dismantle v. The Queen*, [1985] 1 S.C.R. 441, 459.

[8]*Re Canada Assistance Plan*, [1991] 2 S.C.R. 525.

[9]*Re Canada Assistance Plan*, [1991] 2 S.C.R. 525, 545, asserting power not to answer a "purely political" question.

[10]*Re Secession of Quebec*, [1998] 2 S.C.R. 217.

aspect" of the question of secession. The Court held that international law would give the same answer as domestic constitutional law, namely, that secession by unilateral act was unauthorized.[11]

V. CHARACTERIZATION OF LAWS

§ 36:13 Comparison with federalism review

Under the two-stage process of judicial review of legislation under the Charter of Rights, the first stage is to determine whether the challenged law abridges a Charter right. (If it does, then the second stage is to determine whether the law can be justified under s. 1.) In the first stage of judicial review under the Charter, there are two related issues that have to be resolved in every case: one is the characterization of the challenged law, and the other is the meaning of the asserted right. The first issue requires an examination of the purpose or effect of the challenged law in order to determine whether it limits a Charter right. The second issue requires an interpretation of the language of the Charter of Rights in order to determine whether it has been abridged by the challenged law. Obviously, these two issues are inextricably linked in practice. However, for the purpose of analysis, this section will consider the techniques by which a law is characterized for the purpose of Charter review. Succeeding sections will consider the techniques by which the Charter of Rights is interpreted. (The question of justification under s. 1 is left to a later chapter.)[1]

The characterization of laws for the purpose of *federalism* review has earlier been explained.[2] The courts attempt to ascertain the "matter" (or "pith and substance") of a challenged law; then they decide whether that matter comes within one of the classes of subjects (heads of power) that are conferred upon the enacting legislative body. In determining the pith and substance of a law, the most important consideration is the *purpose* of the law. Once the pith and substance of the law has been held to be within the powers of the enacting legislative body, it is no objection that the law may have some *effect* on matters outside the powers of the enacting legislative body. For example, a provincial law enacted for the purpose of levying a direct tax has been held to be valid and applicable to a bank, notwithstanding that the taxation of a bank has a significant effect on banking, which is a matter that is outside provincial jurisdiction.[3]

The characterization of laws for the purpose of *Charter* review reflects

---

[11]See also *Chaoulli v. Que.*, [2005] 1 S.C.R. 791, paras. 183-185 per Binnie and LeBel JJ. dissenting but not on this point (legality of health care policy justiciable despite also being a political question).

[Section 36:13]

[1]Chapter 38, Limitation of Rights.

[2]Chapter 15, Judicial Review on Federal Grounds, under heading §§ 15:5 to 15:13, "Characterization of laws".

[3]This is the famous case of *Bank of Toronto v. Lambe* (1887), 12 App. Cas. 575; discussed in ch. 15, Judicial Review on Federal Grounds, under heading § 15:5, "Matter".

a similarity and a difference between Charter review and federalism review. If the *purpose* of a law is to abridge a Charter right, then the law will be unconstitutional. That rule is similar to the federalism rule that condemns a law with the purpose of regulating matters outside the jurisdiction of the enacting body. It is in the legal result to be attributed to the *effect* of a law that a crucial distinction emerges between Charter review and federalism review. If the effect of a law is to abridge a Charter right, then the law will be unconstitutional (unless saved by s. 1), even if the purpose of the law was entirely benign and constitutional. This rule is the reverse of the federalism rule that tolerates effects on matters outside the jurisdiction of the enacting legislative body so long as the purpose (more precisely, the matter or pith and substance) of the law is within the jurisdiction of the enacting body.

§ 36:14 Purpose or effect

A law will offend the Charter of Rights if either its purpose or its effect is to abridge a Charter right.[1] This point was established by the Sunday-closing cases. In *R. v. Big M Drug Mart* (1985),[2] the Supreme Court of Canada held that the federal Lord's Day Act, which prohibited commercial activity on a Sunday, abridged the guarantee of freedom of religion in s. 2(a) of the Charter of Rights. The Court held that the history of the Lord's Day Act established that its purpose was the religious one of compelling the observance of the Christian Sabbath. That purpose was an abridgement of freedom of religion, which invalidated the legislation. It was not necessary to consider whether the effect of the legislation was to abridge freedom of religion, because "effects can never be relied upon to save legislation with an invalid purpose".[3] Moreover, legislation with an invalid purpose could not be justified under s. 1.[4]

In *R. v. Edwards Books and Art* (1986),[5] the Court was presented with another Sunday-closing law, this one enacted by a province in a statute that prescribed holidays for retail businesses. The Court held that the history of this law established that its purpose was the secular one of prescribing a uniform pause day for retail workers. Therefore, the law passed the purpose test. However, the Court went on to consider the ef-

[Section 36:14]

[1] *R. v. Big M Drug Mart*, [1985] 1 S.C.R. 295, 331.

[2] *R. v. Big M Drug Mart*, [1985] 1 S.C.R. 295, para. 331. Dickson J. wrote the majority judgment. Wilson J. wrote a separate concurrence, arguing that only effect (not purpose) was relevant to the characterization of laws for the purpose of Charter review.

[3] *R. v. Big M Drug Mart*, [1985] 1 S.C.R. 295, 334.

[4] *R. v. Big M Drug Mart*, [1985] 1 S.C.R. 295, 353.

[5] *R. v. Edwards Books and Art*, [1986] 2 S.C.R. 713. The plurality opinion was written by Dickson C.J. with the concurrence of Chouinard and Le Dain JJ.; they held that the Act abridged freedom of religion, but was saved by s. 1. La Forest J. wrote a separate concurrence, reaching the same conclusions. Beetz J. with the concurrence of McIntyre J. wrote a separate concurrence, but on the ground that the Act did not abridge freedom of religion. Wilson J. dissented in part, because in her view the Sabbatarian exemption in the Act was too narrow to be saved by s. 1.

fect of the law, and the majority held that the effect of the law was to impose a burden on those retailers whose religious beliefs required them to abstain from work on a day other than Sunday. That effect was an abridgement of freedom of religion. Therefore, like the Lord's Day Act, this Sunday-closing law also abridged the Charter right. However, a majority of the Court relied on the benign purpose of the law to uphold it under s. 1.[6]

While either purpose or effect can invalidate legislation, Canadian legislative bodies rarely enact laws that have the purpose of abridging a Charter right. The Lord's Day Act has the special distinction of being one of the few laws to fail the purpose test in the Supreme Court of Canada. The purpose of a law is normally benign (as it was in *Edwards Books*), and the breach of the Charter is an incidental effect of the pursuit of the purpose. Where this is the case, the law may satisfy the justificatory standard of s. 1, in which case the law will be upheld as a reasonable limit that is demonstrably justified in a free and democratic society. (This was the outcome in *Edwards Books.*) If the law does not satisfy the justificatory standard of s. 1, then it will be invalid by virtue of its limiting effect on the Charter right.

§ 36:15 Trivial effects

In *R. v. Jones* (1986),[1] another claim to freedom of religion came before the Court. The accused was charged with a breach of Alberta's School Act, because instead of sending his children to school he was educating them himself in the basement of the fundamentalist church of which he was pastor. Alberta's School Act actually made liberal provision for alternative schooling, but it did require that the accused obtain from the province's Department of Education either approval of his basement operation as a private school or approval in the form of a certificate of efficient instruction for parental education. The accused refused to apply for either of these approvals, because he claimed that it was contrary to his religion to request the State for permission to do what was God's will. La Forest J. for a minority of three held that the School Act did violate freedom of religion in requiring the accused to apply to the State for permission to educate his children. However, he upheld the Act under s. 1. Wilson J. for the majority held that the Act did not violate freedom of religion. In her view, where the effect of a law on a Charter right was "trivial or insubstantial",[2] there was no breach of the Charter, and that was the case here.

---

[6]The two cases also present an interesting contrast of characterization for federalism purposes: see ch. 18, Criminal Law, under heading § 18:12, "Sunday observance law".

[Section 36:15]

[1]*R. v. Jones,* [1986] 2 S.C.R. 284.

[2]*R. v. Jones,* [1986] 2 S.C.R. 284, 314.

Jones was decided before *Edwards Books.*[3] In the latter case, the question arose whether the Sunday-closing law had any effect, or any substantial effect, on freedom of religion. The difficulty in the case was that any retailer who observed a sabbath placed himself or herself at a competitive disadvantage which would exist even if there was no Sunday-closing law. The Sunday-closing law removed that disadvantage from those retailers who observed Sunday as their sabbath, but that preference for Sunday-observers did not affect the practices of non-Sunday observers. This was the position taken by Beetz and McIntyre JJ. in *Edwards Books:* they held that the Sunday-closing law did not abridge freedom of religion. Dickson C.J.'s answer to this, for the majority, was that the Act, by relieving the Sunday observers of any financial penalty, exacerbated the competitive disadvantage of non-Sunday observers.[4] He went on to hold, after referring to *Jones*, that this increase in competitive advantage caused by the Act was not "insubstantial or trivial".[5]

§ 36:16 Severance

In *R. v. Big M Drug Mart* (1985),[1] the entire Lord's Day Act was held to be unconstitutional because of its inadmissible religious purpose. In only a few other Charter cases has the entire statute been struck down.[2] In the other cases where there has been a holding of unconstitutionality, the vice infected only one or a few provisions of the challenged statute; those provisions were usually "severed" from the rest of the statute, enabling the rest of the statute to survive. The principles upon which severance is applied in Charter cases are examined in a later chapter.[3]

§ 36:17 Reading down

Where the language of a statute will bear two interpretations, one of which would abridge a Charter right, and one of which would not, the Charter can be applied simply by selecting the interpretation that does

---

[3]*R. v. Edwards Books and Art*, [1986] 2 S.C.R. 713.

[4]*R. v. Edwards Books and Art*, [1986] 2 S.C.R. 713, 765.

[5]*R. v. Edwards Books and Art*, [1986] 2 S.C.R. 713, 765.

[Section 36:16]

[1]*R. v. Big M Drug Mart*, [1985] 1 S.C.R. 295.

[2]Other instances are: *Sask. Federation of Labour v. Sask.*, [2015] 1 S.C.R. 246, paras. 97, 103 (Public Service Essential Services Act, S.S. 2008, c. P-42.2 struck down in its entirety under the Charter; declaration of invalidity suspended for 1 year); *Alta. v. United Food and Commercial Workers*, [2013] 3 S.C.R. 733, paras. 40-41 (Personal Information Protection Act, S.A. 2003, c. P-6.5 struck down in its entirety under the Charter; declaration of invalidity suspended for 12 months). See also *Nova Scotia v. Martin*, [2003] 2 S.C.R. 504, para. 118 (Functional Restoration (Multi-Faceted Pain Services) Program Regulations, N.S. Reg. 57/96 struck down under the Charter; declaration of invalidity suspended for 6 months); *Mackin v. N.B.*, [2002] 1 S.C.R. 405, para. 88 (amending statute, the Act to Amend the Provincial Court Act, S.N.B. 1987, c. 45, struck down in its entirety; declaration of invalidity suspended for 6 months).

[3]Chapter 40, Enforcement of Rights, under heading § 40:5, "Severance".

not abridge the Charter right. This technique is known as "reading down". Its application in Charter cases is examined in a later chapter.[1]

VI. INTERPRETATION OF CHARTER

§ 36:18 Progressive interpretation

A constitution differs from an ordinary statute in that a constitution is expressed in language sufficiently broad to accommodate a wide and unpredictable range of facts; a constitution is difficult to amend; and a constitution is likely to remain in force for a long time. These considerations call for a flexible interpretation, so that the constitution can be adapted over time to changing conditions. That is the source of the doctrine of progressive interpretation, which was elegantly captured in *Edwards v. A.-G. Can.* (1930)[1] by Lord Sankey's metaphor of "a living tree capable of growth and expansion within its natural limits". The requirement of flexibility or progressive interpretation obviously applies to the Charter of Rights no less than other constitutional provisions,[2] although the Charter is still so recent that the requirement is not yet apparent.

It is never seriously doubted that progressive interpretation is necessary and desirable in order to adapt the Constitution to facts that did not exist and could not have been foreseen at the time when it was written. For example, in 1967, the Supreme Court of the United States applied the right against unreasonable search and seizure in the fourth amendment to electronic eavesdropping—a practice that could not have been anticipated in the eighteenth century, when the fourth amendment was adopted.[3] However, when progressive interpretation leads to more radical changes in the meaning of rights, it is more controversial. In the United States, a school of thought, sometimes called "originalism" or "interpretivism", holds that the courts ought to adhere faithfully to the

---

[Section 36:17]

[1]Chapter 40, Enforcement of Rights, under heading § 40:7, "Reading down".

[Section 36:18]

[1]*Edwards v. A.-G. Can.*, [1930] A.C. 124, 136. The doctrine of progressive interpretation is discussed in ch. 15, Judicial Review on Federal Grounds, under heading § 15:27, "Progressive interpretation".

[2]*A.-G. Que. v. Blaikie*, [1979] 2 S.C.R. 1016, 1029-1030 (interpreting s. 133 of the Constitution Act, 1867, one of the few bill-of-rights provisions); *Law Society of Upper Can. v. Skapinker*, [1984] 1 S.C.R. 375, 365-366 (interpreting s. 6 of the Charter); *Hunter v. Southam*, [1984] 2 S.C.R. 145, 155-157 (interpreting s. 8); *Re B.C. Motor Vehicle Act*, [1985] 2 S.C.R. 486, 509 (interpreting s. 7); *Re Prov. Electoral Boundaries (Sask.)*, [1991] 2 S.C.R. 158, 180 (interpreting s. 3); *Can. v. Hislop*, [2007] 1 S.C.R. 429, paras. 94, 144 (interpretation of Charter generally).

[3]*Katz v. United States* (1967), 389 U.S. 347. The Supreme Court of Canada, in *R. v. Duarte*, [1990] 1 S.C.R. 30, has given a similar interpretation to s. 8 of the Charter, but of course s. 8 dates from 1982, when electronic surveillance could reasonably have been assumed to be within the contemplation of the framers.

"original understanding" of the meaning of the Constitution.[4] Only in this way, it is argued, can the judges' own policy preferences be excluded from constitutional adjudication. Progressive interpretation is illegitimate, it is said, because it grants to unelected judges the power to amend the Constitution without recourse to the amending procedures provided by the Constitution. The amending procedures were included for the very purpose of keeping the Constitution up-to-date, and they constitute the only democratic way of accomplishing that purpose.

There are many theoretical difficulties with originalism, which are discussed elsewhere in this book.[5] From a practical standpoint, however, it is simply inevitable that judicial interpretations will change with changing societal values. Judges are not historians, and, even if they were, they would be rightly reluctant to decide modern controversies by reference to research as to the attitudes of people long dead and gone. When the deficiencies of a purely formal theory of equality had been demonstrated to the Supreme Court of the United States, should it nevertheless have adhered to the separate-but-equal doctrine and perpetuated the segregation of the races in public schools?[6] When exaggerated notions of an employer's "property" and "liberty" proved to be incompatible with new kinds of state regulation of labour standards, even including minimum wage and maximum hours, and much other social and economic regulation, should the Supreme Court of the United States have stood its ground and destroyed President Franklin Roosevelt's New Deal?[7] As the latter example shows, changes in interpretation need not always take the form of an expansion of the guaranteed rights; in some instances, old interpretations will come to be seen as too broad, and hence too restrictive of legislative policy. In my view, a continuing review by the courts of their former interpretations of the Constitution is essential if a bill of rights is not to become a force of reactionary conservatism.[8] Moreover, in the case of Canada's Charter of Rights, I think it is clear as a matter of fact that the original understanding of many of the framers of 1982 was not that the Charter rights should be

---

[4]See ch. 60, Proof, under heading § 60:5, "Originalism". For fuller discussions, see P.W. Hogg, "Legislative History in Constitutional Cases" in Sharpe (ed.), Charter Litigation (1987), ch. 6; P.W. Hogg, "The Charter of Rights and American Theories of Interpretation" (1987) 25 Osgoode Hall L.J. 87.

[5]Chapter 60, Proof, under heading § 60:5, "Originalism".

[6]*Brown v. Board of Education* (1954), 347 U.S. 483 overruled *Plessy v. Ferguson* (1896), 163 U.S. 537.

[7]*West Coast Hotel Co. v. Parrish* (1937), 300 U.S. 379 overruled *Lochner v. New York* (1905), 198 U.S. 45.

[8]Originalism can be reinforced by its close cousin, the theory of "natural rights", which are rights that are rooted in nature and therefore not subject to change. The famous debate between Blackstone, the conservative, and Bentham, the reformer, as to whether natural rights exist was revived by two lesser mortals in reference to Canada's Charter of Rights: F. Vaughan, "On being a Positivist: Does it really matter?" (1991) 29 Osgoode Hall L.J. 399; P.W. Hogg, "On being a Positivist: A Reply" (1991) 29 Osgoode Hall L.J. 411.

frozen in the shape that seemed good in 1982, but rather that the rights should be subject to changing judicial interpretations over time.[9]

§ 36:19 Generous interpretation

For Lord Sankey in *Edwards v. A.-G. Can.* (1930),[1] the primary implication of his living tree metaphor was that a constitution should receive a generous interpretation. He went on to say that the provisions of the Constitution Act, 1867 should not be "cut down" by "a narrow and technical construction", but should be given "a large and liberal interpretation".[2] This case decided that women were "persons" and accordingly eligible to be appointed to the Senate. It did not concern the federal distribution of powers. However, the dictum was taken up in later cases that did concern the federal distribution of powers.[3] The later cases emphasized that a large and liberal interpretation of the provisions of the Constitution that allocate powers to the federal Parliament and provincial Legislatures has the effect of conferring the "widest amplitude" of power on those bodies. In the context of federalism, the large and liberal interpretation is the course of judicial restraint; it tends to uphold challenged legislation, reinforcing a presumption of constitutionality.

The Charter of Rights does not confer power on the Parliament or Legislatures. On the contrary, it denies power to the Parliament and Legislatures. A generous interpretation of the Charter cannot be justified as increasing the powers of the legislative bodies; it will have the effect of reducing their powers. It is the course of judicial activism, since it will lead to more invalidations of laws than a narrow interpretation of the Charter. The justification for a generous interpretation of the Charter is that it will give full effect to the civil liberties that are guaranteed by the Charter.[4] That was the approach of the Supreme

---

[9]Chapter 60, Proof, under heading § 60:6, "Progressive interpretation".

[Section 36:19]

[1]*Edwards v. A.-G. Can.*, [1930] A.C. 124.

[2]*Edwards v. A.-G. Can.*, [1930] A.C. 124.

[3]*British Coal Corp. v. The King*, [1935] A.C. 500, 518; *A.-G. Ont. v. A.-G. Can.* (Privy Council Appeals), [1947] A.C. 127, 154. Both cases gave a liberal interpretation to s. 101, which empowers Parliament to establish a general court of appeal for Canada.

[4]The assumption, of course, is that the Charter of Rights is a benign influence on society; a generous interpretation is good because it will extend its influence. This assumption is vehemently denied by a group of scholars who regard the Charter as drawing a veil of legalism over decisions that are really political, thereby masking and legitimizing neo-conservative policies and inhibiting progressive policies: e.g., Mandel, The Charter of Rights and the Legalization of Politics in Canada (1994); Bakan, Just Words: Constitutional Rights and Social Wrongs (1997); Petter, The Politics of the Charter: The Illusive Promise of Constitutional Rights (2008). Morton and Knopff, The Charter Revolution and the Court Party (2000) agree that the Charter draws a veil of legalism over decisions that are really political, but they criticize the use of the Charter by the courts to implement social policies that equality-seeking groups, civil liberties associations and other proponents (the "Court party") were unable to obtain through

Court of Canada in *A.-G. Que. v. Blaikie* (1979),[5] in giving a broad interpretation to s. 133 of the Constitution Act, 1867, the language guarantee that is one of the few bill of rights provisions in the 1867 instrument. With respect to the Charter, the Court has agreed that it calls for "a generous interpretation, avoiding what has been called 'the austerity of tabulated legalism', suitable to give to individuals the full measure of the fundamental rights and freedoms referred to".[6]

When the judges speak of a generous or broad interpretation of the Charter, they are referring to the scope of the guaranteed rights. It should not be overlooked, however, that there is a second stage to judicial review under the Charter, and that is the application of the standard of justification under s. 1. There is a relationship between the scope of the rights guaranteed by the Charter and the standard of justification under s. 1. In *R. v. Oakes* (1986),[7] which is examined at length in a later chapter[8] the Court decided to prescribe a single standard of s.1 justification for all rights, to make that standard a high one, and to cast the burden of satisfying it on the government. This insistence that the test of justification be a stringent one is, in practice, inconsistent with the insistence that the guaranteed rights be given a generous (broad) scope. If the scope of the guaranteed rights is wide, they are bound to reach conduct that is not really worthy of constitutional protection. If Parliament or a Legislature attempts to regulate conduct that is guaranteed only by virtue of an artificially wide definition of the Charter rights, the courts are going to strive to uphold the legislation. Since the courts can uphold the legislation only under s. 1, they will strive to find that s. 1 is satisfied, and the inevitable result will be the erosion of the *Oakes* standard of justification.[9]

Freedom of expression may be the most obvious example of the connection between the scope of a right and the stringency of s. 1 justification. It is obvious that any attempt to regulate political debate should have to face a stringent standard of justification under s. 1. But if the Court decides, as it has done, that almost every communicative

---

democratic channels, for example, the expansion of rights of criminal defendants, abortion rights and LGBTQ rights.

[5] *A.-G. Que. v. Blaikie*, [1979] 2 S.C.R. 1016, 1029-1030, justifying the decision that the reference to courts in s. 133 included administrative tribunals.

[6] *Min. of Home Affairs v. Fisher*, [1980] A.C. 319, 328 (P.C., Bermuda) per Lord Wilberforce in reference to Bermuda's bill of rights; quoted in *Hunter v. Southam*, [1984] 2 S.C.R. 145, 156. The Court has reiterated this point in numerous decisions: see e.g. *R. v. Big M Drug Mart*, [1985] 1 S.C.R. 295, 344; *Re B.C. Motor Vehicle Act*, [1985] 2 S.C.R. 486, 509; *United States v. Cotroni*, [1989] 1 S.C.R. 1469, 1480; *Re Prov. Electoral Boundaries (Sask.)*, [1991] 2 S.C.R. 158, 179; *Eldridge v. B.C.*, [1997] 3 S.C.R. 624, para. 53; *Doucet-Boudreau v. N.S.*, [2003] 3 S.C.R. 3, paras. 23-24; *R. v. Grant*, [2009] 2 S.C.R. 353, paras. 15-16; *Ont. v. Fraser*, [2011] 2 S.C.R. 3, paras. 90, 97, 117; *Mounted Police Association of Ontario v. Can.*, [2015] 1 S.C.R. 3, para. 47.

[7] *R. v. Oakes*, [1986] 1 S.C.R. 103.

[8] Chapter 38, Limitation of Rights, under heading § 38:11, "Oakes test".

[9] This thesis is advanced in more detail in P.W. Hogg, "Interpreting the Charter of Rights: Generosity and Justification" (1990) 28 Osgoode Hall L.J. 817.

act, no matter how trivial, false or harmful, enjoys constitutional protection, then it is inevitable that the Court will relax the standard of s. 1 justification in order to accommodate laws that are generally approved. For example, the Court has held that advertising is constitutionally protected, but has sustained provincial regulation of advertising directed at children—despite a weak case of justification under s. 1.[10] Soliciting for the purpose of prostitution is also protected by the Constitution, which would no doubt surprise many Canadians, but few would be surprised to find that the Criminal Code offence has been upheld under s. 1—although the case for justification was weak.[11] Similar comments could be made about hate propaganda,[12] obscenity,[13] defamation[14] and nude dancing,[15] which are some of the other activities caught by the broad scope of s. 2(b) of the Charter of Rights.[16]

Does it make much difference whether the Court gives a wide interpretation to rights and relaxes the standard of justification under s. 1, or gives a narrow interpretation[17] to rights and maintains the stringent standard of justification called for by *Oakes?* If we assume that the outcomes of cases will be much the same under either approach, the second approach is surely preferable, because it will reduce the volume of litigation and limit the policy-making role of the courts. If the scope of the guaranteed rights is wide, and the standard of justification is relaxed, then a large number of Charter challenges will come before the courts, and will fall to be determined under s. 1. Since s. 1 requires that the policy of the legislation be balanced against the policy of the Charter, and since it is difficult to maintain meaningful standards to constrain the balancing process, judicial review will become even more unpredictable than it is now. While there are signs that some judges welcome such extensive powers, most judges will be concerned to stem the wasteful floods of litigation, to limit the occasions when they have to review the policy choices of legislative bodies, and to introduce meaningful

---

[10] *Irwin Toy v. Que.*, [1989] 1 S.C.R. 927; but note the failure of s. 1 justification in *Ford v. Que.*, [1988] 2 S.C.R. 712, *Rocket v. Royal College of Dental Surgeons*, [1990] 2 S.C.R. 232 and *RJR-MacDonald v. Can.*, [1995] 3 S.C.R. 199.

[11] *Re ss. 193 and 195.1 of Crim. Code*, [1990] 1 S.C.R. 1123.

[12] *R. v. Keegstra*, [1990] 3 S.C.R. 697 (prohibition on hate propaganda upheld under s. 1).

[13] *R. v. Butler*, [1992] 1 S.C.R. 452 (prohibition on obscenity upheld under s. 1); *R. v. Sharpe*, [2001] 1 S.C.R. 45 (prohibition on child pornography upheld under s. 1).

[14] *Hill v. Church of Scientology*, [1995] 2 S.C.R. 1130 (tort of defamation upheld under s. 1); *R. v. Lucas*, [1998] 1 S.C.R. 439 (criminal libel upheld under s. 1).

[15] E.g., *Re Koumoudouros* (1984), 45 O.R. (2d) 426 (Div. Ct.) (prohibition on nude dancing upheld under s. 1).

[16] See ch. 43, Expression.

[17] I use narrow in contradistinction to wide, but, as I argue in the next section, the correct approach is a purposive one, which will usually (but not always) have the effect of narrowing the right.

rules to the process of Charter review. These purposes can be accomplished only by restricting the scope of the Charter rights.[18]

§ 36:20 Purposive interpretation

How can the scope of the Charter rights be restricted without abandoning or undermining the civil libertarian values that the Charter protects? The Supreme Court of Canada has answered this question in its insistence on a "purposive" interpretation of the Charter rights.[1] What this involves is an attempt to ascertain the purpose of each Charter right, and then to interpret the right so as to include activity that comes within the purpose and exclude activity that does not. Of course, this cannot be anything more than a general approach to interpretation. The actual purpose of a right is usually unknown, and so a court has a good deal of discretion in deciding what the purpose is, and at what level of generality it should be expressed. But some guidance can be obtained from the language in which the right is expressed, from the implications to be drawn from the context in which the right is to be found, including other parts of the Charter, from the pre-Charter history of the right and from the legislative history of the Charter. Moreover, as a body of case-law develops on the meaning of a particular right, the core of the definition tends to become settled.[2]

The Court has generally assumed that a "purposive" approach and a "generous" approach are one and the same thing—or at least are not inconsistent. Indeed, statements of the purposive approach have frequently been accompanied—often in the same sentence—by statements of the generous approach.[3] In the case of some rights, that is

---

[18]In American parlance, I am advocating more "definitional balancing" (by applying the purposive approach to yield a definition of the right: see next section) and less "ad hoc balancing" (under s. 1): see S.R. Peck, "An Analytical Framework for the Application of the Charter" (1987) 25 Osgoode Hall L.J. 1, 21-31. I here part company with Beatty, Talking Heads and the Supremes (1990), who holds the view that the presence of s. 1 in the Charter precludes definitional balancing; on his view, all balancing should take place under s. 1.

[Section 36:20]

[1]E.g., *Hunter v. Southam*, [1984] 2 S.C.R. 145, 156; *R. v. Big M Drug Mart*, [1985] 1 S.C.R. 295, 344; *Re B.C. Motor Vehicle Act*, [1985] 2 S.C.R. 486, 499; *Eldridge v. B.C.*, [1997] 3 S.C.R. 624, para. 53; *Ont. v. Fraser*, [2011] 2 S.C.R. 3, paras. 90, 97, 117; *Mounted Police Association of Ontario v. Can.*, [2015] 1 S.C.R. 3, para. 47.

[2]For analysis of purposive interpretation of the Charter, see S.R. Peck, "An Analytical Framework for the Application of the Charter" (1987) 25 Osgoode Hall L.J. 1, 6-31. See generally A. Barak, Purposive Interpretation in Law (Princeton U.P., 2005); A. Barak, The Judge in a Democracy (Princeton U.P., 2006), ch 5.

[3]Note, however, that in *R. v. Big M Drug Mart*, [1985] 1 S.C.R. 295, which contains the fullest explanation of the purposive approach, Dickson J. warned (at 344) that judges should not "overshoot" the purpose of the right. See similarly, *R. v. Grant*, [2009] 2 S.C.R. 353, para. 17 (citing this paragraph with approval); *R. v. Stillman*, 2019 SCC 40, para. 21 (ditto); *R. v. Poulin*, 2019 SCC 47, paras. 53-55 (ditto).

correct: a purposive interpretation will yield a broad scope for the right.[4] In the case of most rights, however, the widest possible reading of the right, which is the most generous interpretation, will "overshoot" the purpose of the right, by including behaviour that is outside the purpose and unworthy of constitutional protection. The effect of a purposive approach is normally going to be to narrow the scope of the right.[5] Generosity is a helpful idea as long as it is subordinate to purpose. Obviously, the courts in interpreting the Charter should avoid narrow, legalistic interpretations that might be appropriate to a detailed statute.[6] But if the goal of generosity is set free from the limiting framework of purpose, the results of a generous interpretation will normally be inconsistent with the purposive approach.

The purposive approach, it seems to me, works in perfect harmony with the stringent standard of justification under s. 1. Once a right has been confined to its purpose, it seems obvious that a government ought to have to satisfy a stringent standard of justification to uphold legislation limiting the right.

§ 36:21 Process as purpose

The undoubted usefulness of a purposive interpretation invites the question whether the Charter has a single over-arching purpose which would illuminate each provision. In the United States, Ely has argued that the purpose of the Bill of Rights is to protect the *process* of decision-making.[1] In the case of some rights, it is process writ small, namely, procedural fairness in the resolution of individual disputes. In the case of other rights, it is process writ large, namely, reinforcing the democratic political process. All rights are ultimately directed to one of these two kinds of process. In principle, Ely's argument could easily be adapted to fit Canada's Charter, and Fairley and Monahan have both

[4]This is the case for s. 8: *Hunter v. Southam*, [1984] 2 S.C.R. 145 (stipulating standards of reasonableness); *R. v. Duarte*, [1990] 1 S.C.R. 30 (extending s. 8 to electronic surveillance).

[5]E.g., *Law Society of Upper Can. v. Skapinker*, [1984] 1 S.C.R. 357 (s. 6 does not guarantee a general right to work); *Andrews v. Law Society of B.C.*, [1989] 1 S.C.R. 143 (s. 15 prohibits discrimination only on the stated grounds or analogous grounds); *R. v. Sinclair*, [2010] 2 S.C.R. 310 (s. 10(b) does not demand the continued presence of counsel throughout an interrogation); *R. v. Poulin*, 2019 SCC 47 (s. 11(i) does not protect a "global" right to a lesser punishment upon conviction; it protects only a less generous "binary" right").

[6]Neither the federal nor the provincial Interpretations Acts apply to the Charter: *Law Society of Upper Can. v. Spakinker*, [1984] 1 S.C.R. 357, 370. Technically, of course, the Charter is Part I of the Constitution Act, 1982, which is a schedule to a U.K. statute, the Canada Act 1982 (U.K.), 1982, c. 11; but the two Acts were entirely drafted in Canada and passed in the form of a resolution by the federal Parliament; it would be absurd to apply the U.K. Interpretation Act to them.

[Section 36:21]

[1]J.H. Ely, Democracy and Distrust: A Theory of Judicial Review (Harvard U.P., Cambridge, Mass., 1980).

taken that step.[2] In Monahan's words, the Charter does not require the courts "to test the substantive outcomes of the political process against some theory of the right or the good"; rather, the Charter guarantees the integrity of the political process itself by enhancing "the opportunities for public debate and collective deliberation".[3]

This process-based theory of judicial review offers two important advantages. The first advantage is that it supplies a helpful context for interpreting particular guarantees. The guarantees of free speech or expression, for example, should be seen not as constitutive of personal autonomy (a substantive value), but as an instrument of democratic government (a process-based value). The guarantees of due process or fundamental justice should be seen not as requiring substantively just (or good) outcomes, but as requiring a fair procedure.

The second advantage of the process-based theory of judicial review is that it offers a solution to the problem of the legitimacy of judicial review. Under this theory, the judges need never take positions on controversial substantive issues, because the constitution does not address such issues. All that the judges are concerned with is the fairness of the process by which legislative bodies or other agencies or officials reach their decisions. It is not the wisdom, justice or Tightness of the outcomes of the political process, but the integrity of the process itself, that is the proper subject of judicial review. When a bench of non-elected judges strikes down a statute enacted by an elected legislative body, it is doing so either because the process of enacting the statute was flawed or because the statute itself places impediments in the way of a fair political process. Such decisions may be controversial, butthey involve judgments only on matters of process or procedure; they do not trespass on the exclusive power of elected officials to determine the substantive values by which society is to be governed. Viewed in this light, the power of judicial review is not incompatible with democracy; indeed, process-based judicial review casts the judges in the role of "servants of democracy even as they strike down the actions of supposedly democratic governments".[4]

At first glance, the process-based theory is attractive. Even if the crucial distinction between process and substance is hard to draw, the theory provides a means of limiting the scope of some of the broader Charter guarantees and thereby reduces the political element of judicial decision-making. I have no doubt that judicial review is best addressed to process rather than substance, but I do not think that process provides

[2] H.S. Fairley, "Enforcing the Charter: Some Thoughts on an Appropriate and Just Standard for Judicial Review" (1982) 4 Supreme Court L.R. 217; P.J. Monahan, "Judicial Review and Democracy: A Theory of Judicial Review" (1986) 21 U.B.C. L. Rev. 87.

[3] P.J. Monahan, "Judicial Review and Democracy: A Theory of Judicial Review" (1986) 21 U.B.C. L. Rev. 87, 89. Compare H.S. Fairley, "Enforcing the Charter: Some Thoughts on an Appropriate and Just Standard for Judicial Review" (1982) 4 Supreme Court L.R. 217, 234.

[4] L. Tribe, "The Puzzling Persistence of Process-Based Constitutional Theories" (1980) 89 Yale L.J. 1063.

a satisfactory general or comprehensive theory of judicial review, either under the American Bill of Rights or under the Charter of Rights. With respect to the American Bill of rights, Tribe[5] and Dworkin[6] have effectively criticized Ely's thesis. With respect to the Charter of Rights, I have attempted to do the same thing,[7] and I will just summarize the points here. First, many of the broader Charter guarantees are inescapably substantive, or have been interpreted to be so; and only a few are truly supportive of the democratic political process.[8] Secondly, the legal rights guarantees, although procedural in form, are ultimately directed to the substantive goal of respect for individual liberty, dignity and privacy. Indeed, all the Charter guarantees respect some aspect of individual liberty, dignity or privacy. They cannot be subsumed under a single process rubric. There is no escaping the fact that judicial review enables the judges to strike down those products of the democratic political process that fail to respect those aspects of individual autonomy that are guaranteed by the Charter.

§ 36:22 Hierarchy of rights

The Charter of Rights, by s. 33, provides for the override of some rights by the inclusion of a notwithstanding clause in the overriding statute.[1] The rights that can be overridden in this way are those guaranteed by s. 2 (freedom of religion, expression, assembly and association), ss. 7-14 (legal rights) and s. 15 (equality). The rights that cannot be overridden in this way are those guaranteed by ss. 3-5 (democratic rights), s. 6 (mobility), ss. 16-23 (language) and s. 28 (sexual equality). Section 33 thus creates two tiers of rights: the "common rights" that are subject to override, and the "privileged rights" that are not. One right, namely, the right to sexual equality (s. 28), may even be exempt from the limitation power of s. 1 as well as the override power of s. 33.[2] That places s. 28 at the top of the hierarchy.[3] Aboriginal and treaty rights, which are guaranteed by s. 35, are similarly privileged in that

---

[5]L. Tribe, "The Puzzling Persistence of Process-Based Constitutional Theories" (1980) 89 Yale L.J. 1063.

[6]R.M. Dworkin, "The Forum of Principle" (1981) 56 N.Y.U.L. Rev. 469.

[7]P.W. Hogg, "The Charter of Rights and American Theories of Interpretation" (1987) 25 Osgoode Hall L.J. 87.

[8]Language rights certainly do not fit the model, as both Monahan and Fairley acknowledge. But freedom of conscience and religion, freedom of expression and mobility, while certainly contributing to an open political process, extend well beyond that purpose. Equality, as limited in *Andrews v. Law Society of B.C.*, [1989] 1 S.C.R. 143, fits the process model better than I acknowledged in my article, which was written before *Andrews*.

[Section 36:22]

[1]Chapter 39, Override of Rights.

[2]Chapter 55, Equality, under heading § 55:43, "Section 28".

[3]Also in a privileged position is the guarantee of judicial independence in s. 11(d), because it is reinforced by an "unwritten constitutional principle" of judicial independence, and this means, among other things, that "the standard application of s. 1 of the

they are subject to neither s. 1 nor s. 33; this is because s. 35 is outside the Charter of Rights.[4] However, being outside the Charter of Rights, is not entirely beneficial, because it means that s. 24, which provides a remedy for breach of Charter rights, does not provide a remedy for breach of aboriginal and treaty rights.

There seems to be no rational basis for the Charter's distinctions between rights. It could, I think, be argued that the right to vote is more valuable than other rights, but why are mobility rights and language rights also exempt from s. 33? Why is Parliament free to restrict political debate by overriding s. 2, or impose a cruel and unusual punishment by overriding s. 12, but is not free to invoke s. 33 to restrict personal mobility or the guaranteed uses of the English or French language? With respect to equality, the distinctions are even harder to defend. Why is racial discrimination possible by the invocation of s. 33, while sexual discrimination is absolutely precluded? Those who regard the Charter as reflecting a transcendent set of norms rooted in nature or stipulated by God ought to have difficulty with these distinctions. Those who regard the Charter as the handiwork of politicians, responding in their usual way to the pressures of interest groups and other practical exigencies, will be less surprised by its irrational structure.

§ 36:23 Conflict between rights

The hierarchy of rights that I have described reflects differences in the vulnerability of the right to legislative abridgement. It does not imply that the "privileged rights" must take priority over the "common rights" when they come into conflict. There are two provisions of the Charter that contemplate conflict between rights. One is s. 25, which recognizes that aboriginal and treaty rights, which are available to people who are defined by their race, may be regarded as in conflict with the equality guarantee, which prohibits discrimination on the ground of race. Section 25 recognizes this possibility of conflict, and provides that the aboriginal and treaty rights are to prevail.[1] Another recognized potential for conflict is between the denominational school rights of s. 93, which are available to people who are defined by their religion, and the equality rights of s. 15, which prohibits discrimination on the ground of religion; s. 29 recognizes this possibility of conflict, and provides that the denominational school rights are to prevail.[2]

Charter could not alone justify an infringement of that independence": *Mackin v. N.B.*, [2002] 1 S.C.R. 405, para. 72 per Gonthier J. for the majority.

[4]Chapter 28, Aboriginal Peoples, under heading §§ 28:29 to 28:39, "Section 35".

[Section 36:23]

[1]Chapter 28, Aboriginal Peoples.

[2]So held in *Re Bill 30* (Ont. Separate School Funding), [1987] 1 S.C.R. 1148 and *Adler v. Ont.*, [1996] 3 S.C.R. 609; and see ch. 57, Education.

The Charter makes no provision for other kinds of conflicts between rights.[3] In *B.C. Government Employees' Union v. British Columbia* (1988),[4] the Chief Justice of British Columbia had issued an injunction against a union to prohibit its members from picketing the courthouses. The union applied to have the injunction set aside, invoking their members' right to freedom of expression. The government supported the injunction, invoking a right of access to the courts, which is not mentioned in the Charter, but which (it was argued) is implied by the fact that the Charter is enforced through access to the courts. The Supreme Court of Canada unanimously upheld the injunction. Dickson C.J. for the majority seemed to agree that the Charter did guarantee a right of access to the courts, but he did not explicitly recognize that he was faced with a conflict between two rights; he held that the injunction was a limit on freedom of expression, but that it was justified under s. 1 as a reasonable and demonstrably justified limit. McIntyre J., in a separate concurrence, held that a right of access to the court was "Charter-protected", and, therefore, he reasoned, the injunction could not be a breach of freedom of expression. McIntyre J. thus assumed, without saying so, that freedom of expression should give way to the more specific (but less explicit) right of access to the courts.

In *R. v. Keegstra* (1990),[5] a person accused of wilfully promoting hatred against an identifiable group (Jews in this case), which is the hate propaganda offence of the Criminal Code, attacked the offence as an abridgement of freedom of expression. The prosecution defended the Criminal Code provision on the ground that, by protecting racial, religious and ethnic groups from hateful messages, it furthered the values of equality (in s. 15) and multiculturalism (in s. 27) that were also recognized by the Charter. The Supreme Court of Canada, by a majority, upheld the Criminal Code provision. Dickson C.J. for the majority followed the same approach as in the *BCGEU* case, holding that the provision did abridge freedom of expression, and the rights invoked in support of the legislation were relevant only through s. 1; he held that the law was justified under s. 1. McLachlin J., for the dissenting minority, agreed that the values of equality and multiculturalism were of relevance only through s. 1; she held that the law was not justified under s. 1, not because equality and multiculturalism should be subordinated to freedom of expression, but because in her view the hate propaganda law was neither a rational nor a least drastic means of suppressing hatred against identifiable groups.

In both the *BCGEU* and *Keegstra* cases, the conflict between rights

---

[3]See A. Petter and A.C. Hutchinson, "Rights in Conflict: The Dilemma of Charter Legitimacy" (1989) 23 U.B.C.L. Rev. 531.

[4]*B.C. Government Employees' Union v. British Columbia*, [1988] 2 S.C.R. 214. Dickson C.J. wrote the majority opinion, which was agreed to by Lamer, Wilson, La Forest and L'Heureux-Dubé JJ. McIntyre J. wrote a concurring opinion.

[5]*R. v. Keegstra*, [1990] 3 S.C.R. 697. Dickson C.J. wrote the majority opinion, which was agreed to by Wilson, L'Heureux-Dubé and Gonthier JJ. McLachlin J. wrote a dissenting opinion, which was agreed to by La Forest and Sopinka JJ.

was resolved through s. 1. Only McIntyre J., concurring separately in *BCGEU*, took the position that the scope of a right (in that case, freedom of expression) should be narrowed to accommodate the exercise of another right (in that case, access to the courts). That technique of "mutual modification" is the way in which the conflicting heads of legislative power have been accommodated in federalism cases. For example, the federal Parliament's exclusive power to legislate in relation to "trade and commerce" (s. 91(2)) has been held to exclude intraprovincial trade so as not to conflict with the provincial Legislatures' exclusive power to legislate in relation to "property and civil rights in the province" (s. 92(13)).[6] But the Court has generally avoided engaging in mutual modification in its Charter jurisprudence. In *Keegstra*, both the majority and minority explicitly rejected this approach to the interpretation of Charter rights.[7] According to that case, the scope of each right should be defined without regard for the existence of other rights. When other rights are invoked in support of a challenged law, the conflict is to be resolved by application of the justificatory principles of s. 1.[8] In that way, the Court does not assign priorities to rights, except in the context of a specific law in a particular case. In other words, the Court prefers "ad hoc balancing" to "definitional balancing" when resolving conflicts between rights.

However the Supreme Court of Canada has not always avoided the definitional balancing of Charter rights. In *R. v. O'Connor* (1995),[9] the Court was called upon to decide whether and how an accused in a sexual assault case should be able to gain access to the counselling and medical records of the complainants (or other witnesses). The records sought were not held by the Crown and were not part of the Crown's case; the records were in the possession of the persons and institutions that had provided the therapeutic counselling. Unlike most other Charter cases, here there was no law to be challenged or supported. The Court itself had to establish for the first time the common law principles which would strike the proper balance between the accused's right (under s.7)

---

[6]See ch. 15, Judicial Review on Federalism Grounds, under heading § 15:23, "Exclusiveness".

[7]*R. v. Keegstra*, [1990] 3 S.C.R. 697, 734, 755-758 per Dickson C.J., 833-837 per McLachlin J.

[8]Accord *Dagenais v. CBC*, [1994] 3 S.C.R. 835 (court-ordered publication ban made to protect fair trials of accuseds struck down; Charter right to fair trial taken into account under s. 1); *R. v. Mentuck*, [2001] 3 S.C.R. 442 (court-ordered publication ban a justified limit on freedom of expression with respect to identities of police officers but not police methods); *R. v. N.S.*, [2012] 3 S.C.R. 726 (trial judge ordered to find balance between claim of complainant to testify behind veil—freedom of religion—and trial fairness to accused, based on facts of individual case); *Sask. v. Whatcott*, [2013] 1 S.C.R. 467, 2013 SCC 11, paras. 6, 66, 154 (provincial prohibition of hate speech a justified limit on freedom of expression and religion).

[9]*R. v. O'Connor*, [1995] 4 S.C.R. 411. On this issue, the majority judgment was that of Lamer C.J. and Sopinka J. Major J. and Cory J. wrote separate concurring judgements. Iacobucci J. concurred with Cory J. The main dissenting opinion was that of L'Heureux-Dubé J., with the concurrence of La Forest and Gonthier JJ. McLachlin J. concurred with L'Heureux-Dubé J. but wrote a separate opinion.

to full answer and defence, and the witness's right (under s. 7 or s. 8) to a reasonable expectation of privacy. In this context, it would have been nonsensical for the Court to consider full answer and defence without regard for privacy, or privacy without regard to full answer and defence. Instead, the majority of the Court considered how privacy rights could be accommodated to "reasonably limit" full answer and defence;[10] the dissenting minority considered how the right to a fair trial could "demonstrably justify" limits on privacy.[11] Both the majority and the minority set up procedures for an application to the trial judge for disclosure of third-party records, and stipulated the factors to be weighed by the judge in determining whether to make an order for disclosure. Although the Supreme Court of Canada employs the language of s. 1, the effect of the decision is to narrow the scope of one Charter right to accommodate the exercise of another. *O'Connor* therefore establishes that definitional balancing (or mutual modification) does indeed have a place in Charter jurisprudence, albeit one that only arises in special circumstances.[12]

§ 36:24 English-French discrepancies

The rules to deal with discrepancies between the English and French versions of the Charter of Rights are discussed in ch. 56, Language.

§ 36:25 Interpretation of exceptions

The Charter contains several exceptions that qualify particular rights and freedoms. For example, s. 11(f) guarantees the right to a trial by jury where the maximum punishment for the offence is imprisonment of five years or more, "except in the case of an offence under military law tried before a military tribunal", and s. 13 guarantees witnesses a right not to have incriminating testimony used in other proceedings, "except in a prosecution for perjury or for the giving of contradictory evidence". The Supreme Court of Canada has articulated several interpretive principles that should be taken into account in interpreting exceptions in the Charter. First, it has indicated that, as a general rule, "the same core interpretive principles that apply to *rights* stated in the Charter also apply to *exceptions* stated in the Charter".[1] Second, the Court has indicated that, just as the courts must be careful not to overshoot the

---

[10] *R. v. O'Connor*, [1995] 4 S.C.R. 411, para. 30 per Lamer C.J. and Sopinka J.

[11] *R. v. O'Connor*, [1995] 4 S.C.R. 411, para 131 per L'Heureux-Dubé J.

[12] *In R. v. Mills*, [1999] 3 S.C.R. 668, which was a sequel to *O'Connor*, reviewing (and upholding) the statutory regime for disclosure of records that was enacted after *O'Connor*, McLachlin and Iacobucci JJ. for the majority were explicit that they were engaged in definitional balancing. They said that "the first question to ask is how to *define* full answer and defence, privacy and equality in this context, and not how they may justifiably be limited" (para. 68, their emphasis). For discussion of their answer to the question, see §§ 36:8 to 36:11, "Dialogue with legislative branch"; also ch. 47, Fundamental Justice, under heading § 47:37, "Statutory limits on pre-trial disclosure".

[Section 36:25]

[1] *R. v. Stillman*, 2019 SCC 40, para. 22 (emphasis in original).

purposes of Charter rights through overly generous interpretations, they must also be careful not to undershoot the purposes of Charter exceptions through overly narrow interpretations.[2] Finally, the Court has emphasized that an exception in the *Charter* can only be properly understood in the context of the right that it qualifies.[3] For example, in the case of the military exception to the right to a jury trial in s. 11(f), the exception can only be understood in the context of the right to a jury trial conferred by s. 11(f).

VII. SOURCES OF INTERPRETATION

§ 36:26 Pre-Charter cases

In interpreting the Charter, the doctrine of precedent will apply in the same way as it applies to the interpretation of other constitutional provisions.[1] However, there will be few Canadian cases decided before the adoption of the Charter in 1982 that will be relevant.

The closest cases would appear to be those interpreting the Canadian Bill of Rights. But, as noted in the previous chapter on the Canadian Bill of Rights, the Supreme Court of Canada exercised extraordinary restraint in interpreting the Bill, relying in part on its statutory, as opposed to constitutional, status. The Charter does have constitutional status, and it also contains internal indications that it affords stronger protections for the guaranteed rights than did the Bill.[2] In this new context, the Court has consistently departed from previous decisions interpreting language in the Bill which is similar to language in the Charter.[3]

The cases interpreting the distribution-of-powers provisions of the Constitution Act, 1867 will usually be irrelevant to the interpretation of the Charter.[4] The issue in each of those cases is whether a law is in relation to a matter coming within a class of subject allocated to the enacting legislative body. The answer to that question will rarely have any bearing on the question whether that law (or a similar law) abridges a Charter right. It is true that both questions involve the characterization (or classification) of the impugned statute, but the classes into which laws must be sorted are totally different for the distribution-of-powers decision from what they are for the Charter decision; none of the phrases that distribute power between the federal Parliament and provincial

---

[2]*R. v. Stillman*, 2019 SCC 40, para. 22.

[3]*R. v. Stillman*, 2019 SCC 40, para. 22.

[Section 36:26]

[1]See ch. 8, Supreme Court of Canada, under heading § 8:13, "Precedent".

[2]For example, the limitation clause (s. 1), the supremacy clause (s. 52(1)), the remedy clause (s. 24), the absence of "frozen concepts" language, and the stronger equality clause (s. 15).

[3]See ch. 35, Canadian Bill of Rights, under heading § 35:8, "Judicial interpretation".

[4]The contrary position is argued by N. Finkelstein, "The Relevance of Pre-Charter Case Law for Post-Charter Adjudication" (1982) 4 Supreme Court L.R. 267.

Legislatures are to be found in the Charter.[5] More than that, classification of laws for distribution-of-powers purposes turns on the "matter" or "pith and substance" of the law; and incidental effects on matters outside jurisdiction are valid.[6] Classification for Charter purposes does not disregard the incidental effects of a law. If the law has the effect of abridging a Charter right, then the Charter is implicated and, if s. 1 does not supply justification, the law will be to that extent invalid.[7]

§ 36:27 American cases

The American Bill of Rights[1] was an important source of inspiration for the Charter (as it was for most other countries' bills of rights), and much of the language of the Charter can be traced back to phrases in the American Bill of Rights. Obviously, the decisions of the Supreme Court of the United States interpreting language that is similar to the language of the Charter are useful precedents for Canadian courts. Even where the language is dissimilar, the American cases are a useful source of ideas and parallels. Nor must secondary materials be overlooked. The long American experience with the Bill of Rights has generated a highly sophisticated commentary on civil libertarian values, such as speech or equal protection, and on the role of judicial review in a democratic society, which it would be folly to ignore. The American sources, which are of course set against a familiar common law background, and a social and economic milieu that is also familiar to Canadians, are in fact frequently, but not systematically, referred to in Charter cases.[2]

Despite the obvious usefulness of American cases, their results have

---

[5]E.g., *Re Ont. Film and Video Appreciation Soc.* (1984), 45 O.R. (2d) 80 (C.A.), holding that a censorship law violated s. 2 of the Charter. The Court made no reference to *N.S. Bd. of Censors v. McNeil*, [1978] 2 S.C.R. 662, holding that a similar censorship law was valid as a regulation of business or local matter. Plainly, although *McNeil* was determinative of the distribution-of-powers issue (at least in any court below the Supreme Court of Canada), it was irrelevant to the Charter issue.

[6]See §§ 36:13 to 36:17, "Characterization of laws".

[7]§§ 36:13 to 36:17, "Characterization of laws". As is there explained, classification for Charter purposes does look to the "purpose" of a law as well as to its "effect". Classification by purpose can yield similar results to classification by pith and substance: e.g., *R. v. Big M Drug Mart*, [1985] 1 S.C.R. 295.

[Section 36:27]

[1]For definition, see § 35:5 note 1 above.

[2]See P. Bender, "The Canadian Charter and the U.S. Bill of Rights" (1983) 28 McGill L.J. 811; McKercher (ed.), The U.S. Bill of Rights and the Canadian Charter of Rights and Freedoms (1983); S.I. Bushnell, "The Use of American Cases" (1986) 35 U.N.B.L.J. 157; J. Cameron, "The Motor Vehicle Reference and the Relevance of American Doctrine" in Sharpe (ed.), Charter Litigation (1987), ch. 4; Charles, Cromwell and Jobson, Evidence and the Charter of Rights and Freedoms (1989), 27-35; R. Harvie and H. Foster, "Ties that Bind? The Supreme Court of Canada, American Jurisprudence and the Revision of Canadian Criminal Law under the Charter" (1990) 28 Osgoode Hall L.J. 729; R. Harvie and H. Foster, "Different Drummers, Different Drums: the Supreme Court of Canada, American Jurisprudence and the Continuing Revision of Criminal Law under the Charter" (1992) 24 Ottawa L. Rev. 39.

not always been followed in Canada. The Supreme Court of Canada has exhorted the courts to "be wary of drawing too ready a parallel between constitutions born to different countries in different ages and in different circumstances".[3] Where the Canadian Court has departed from American precedents, it has usually been to give a broader interpretation to the rights in the Charter. Thus, freedom of religion, freedom of expression, fundamental justice (due process) and the rights of persons accused of crime have all been extended beyond the American precedents.[4]

One reason for the broader interpretation of the rights in Canada is the presence of s. 1 in the Canadian Charter of Rights. The Canadian Court regards s. 1 as an important difference between the two constitutions, and one that suggests a broader scope for the guaranteed rights in Canada.[5] The Canadian Court has felt free to give Charter rights a broad interpretation, knowing that s. 1 will allow laws imposing reasonable limits on the rights to be upheld. Without any limitation clause like s. 1 of the Charter, the American Court is driven to do more "definitional balancing" in which the scope of the rights themselves are narrowed so as to accommodate laws that the Court regards as reasonable limits that ought not to be struck down. The presence in the Canadian Charter of s. 33—the power of override—probably also tends in the same direction.[6] An overly broad application of the Charter can, after all, be overcome by an ordinary statute containing a notwithstanding clause. An overly broad application of the American Bill of Rights can be overcome only by a constitutional amendment. Once again, the Canadian Court has less reason than the American Court to be cautious in drawing the boundaries of the guaranteed rights.

§ 36:28 International sources

Canada is bound by a number of treaties dealing with human rights,[1] of which the most important for present purposes is the International

[3]*R. v. Rahey*, [1987] 1 S.C.R. 598, 639 per La Forest J.; *R. v. Keegstra*, [1990] 3 S.C.R. 697, 740 per Dickson C.J.

[4]See § 36:5 notes 7 to 18 and accompanying text, above.

[5]*Re B.C. Motor Vehicle Act*, [1985] 2 S.C.R. 486, 498 per Lamer J.; *R. v. Keegstra*, [1990] 3 S.C.R. 697, 743 per Dickson C.J. For my criticism of this approach, see heading § 36:19, "Generous interpretation".

[6]Section 33 is expressly linked with s. 1 in the defence of a more generous interpretation of rights in *Re B.C. Motor Vehicle Act*, [1985] 2 S.C.R. 486.

[Section 36:28]

[1]M. Cohen and A.F. Bayefsky, "The Canadian Charter of Rights and Freedoms and Public International Law" (1983) 61 Can. Bar Rev. 265, 285 list 23 treaties on human rights that have been ratified by Canada. On the relevance of international human rights law to Canada, see the same article; also, A.F. Bayefsky, "The Impact of the European Convention on Human Rights in the United Kingdom" (1981) 13 Ottawa L. Rev. 507; J. Claydon, "The Application of International Human Rights Law by Canadian Courts" (1981) 30 Buffalo L. Rev. 727; J. Claydon, "International Human Rights Law and the Interpretation of the Charter" (1982) 4 Supreme Court L.R. 287; E.P. Mendes, "Interpreting the Charter: Applying International and European Jurisprudence" (1982)

Covenant on Civil and Political Rights,[2] to which Canada became a party in 1976. As treaties, these instruments are only binding at international law. They are not incorporated into Canada's domestic law, and are not enforceable in Canadian courts.[3] However, the International Covenant on Civil and Political Rights covers much of the same ground and, although its provisions are more detailed, uses similar language to the Charter of Rights.[4] The terms of the Covenant are relevant to the interpretation of the Charter, by virtue of the rule that a statute (and presumably a constitution) should be interpreted as far as possible into conformity with international law.[5] Where (as is common) the Covenant makes detailed provision for a right that is also guaranteed by the Charter, but in language that is less clear or complete, the terms of the Covenant may well indicate the appropriate interpretation of the Charter language.

For example, s. 10(b) of the Charter, which confers upon an arrested person the right "to retain and instruct counsel without delay", does not make clear whether counsel is to be paid for by the accused or by the government. The Covenant, however, by article 14(3)(d), confers upon an accused person the right to "legal assistance", and goes on to stipulate that the legal assistance is to be provided "without payment by him. . .if he does not have sufficient means to pay for it". The terms of the Covenant thus impose upon Canada an obligation under international law to supply legal aid to an indigent accused. Canadian courts could interpret the equivocal language of s. 10(b) of the Charter as having constitutionalized that international obligation.[6] Note, however, that this interpretation of s. 10(b) is not compelled by the terms of the Covenant, because Canada could fulfil the terms of the Covenant by providing legal aid on

---

20 Alta. L. Rev. 383; A.A. Hayward, "International Law and the Interpretation of the Charter" (1985) 23 U. Western Ont. L. Rev. 9; Schabas, International Human Rights Law and the Canadian Charter (2nd ed., 1996); Bayefsky, International Human Rights Law (1992); J. Brunnée and S.J. Toope, "A Hesitant Embrace: The Application of International Law by Canadian Courts" (2002) 41 Can. Y.B. Int'l Law 3.

[2]The text of the Covenant is set out in Appendix VI to this book.

[3]See ch. 11, Treaties, under heading §§ 11:6 to 11:9, "Implementing treaties".

[4]W.S. Tarnopolsky, "A Comparison between the Charter and the International Covenant on Civil and Political Rights" (1983) 8 Queen's L.J. 211. Note that, while Canada's ratification of the International Covenant was one of the reasons urged in Canada for the adoption in 1982 of the Charter, the Charter does not purport to implement the Covenant, although many Charter provisions no doubt do implement particular provisions of the Covenant.

[5]*Re Powers to Levy Rates on Foreign Legations*, [1943] S.C.R. 208; *Health Services and Support—Facilities Subsector Bargaining Assn. v. B.C.*, [2007] 2 S.C.R. 391, para. 69; *Divito v. Can.*, [2013] 3 S.C.R. 157, 2013 SCC 47, paras. 22-27; *Sask. Federation of Labour v. Sask.*, [2015] 1 S.C.R. 245, 2015 SCC 4, paras. 62-71; *Loyola High School v. Quebec*, [2015] 1 S.C.R. 613, 2015 SCC 12, paras. 65, 96-97; *Henry v. B.C.*, [2015] 2 S.C.R. 214, 2015 SCC 24, paras. 135-137; *R. v. Appulonappa*, [2015] 3 S.C.R. 754, 2015 SCC 59, paras. 40-45; Jacomy-Millette, Treaty Law in Canada (1975), 280-290; Sullivan, Sullivan and Driedger on the Construction of Statutes (4th ed., 2002), 330-333.

[6]*R. v. Brydges*, [1990] 1 S.C.R. 190, 214 (obiter dictum). Other references to the International Covenant by Canadian courts are listed in Schabas, International Human Rights Law and the Canadian Charter (2nd ed., 1996), Appendix 2.

a statutory, as opposed to a constitutional, basis. The Covenant does not require that all of its stipulations be embodied in the constitutions of the states that are parties to the Covenant. Compliance can take the form of statutory or administrative measures.[7]

The International Covenant on Civil and Political Rights includes an optional protocol,[8] to which Canada is a party, which provides that individuals in the states that are parties to the protocol, who claim that any of their rights under the Covenant have been violated, and who have exhausted all available domestic remedies, may petition the Human Rights Committee of the United Nations. The Committee receives submissions from the petitioner and from the state against which the violation is alleged, and decides whether or not the state has violated the Covenant. The decision cannot be directly enforced,[9] of course, but it is reported to the petitioner, the state and the General Assembly of the United Nations.[10] This procedure yields decisions which constitute a body of jurisprudence interpreting the Covenant.[11] Since this jurisprudence elaborates the terms of obligations at international law which

[7]W.S. Tarnopolsky, "A Comparison between the Charter and the International Covenant on Civil and Political Rights" (1983) 8 Queen's L.J. 211, 212.

[8]The text of the optional protocol, to which Canada became a party in 1976, is set out in Appendix VII to this book.

[9]In *Ahani v. Can.* (2002), 58 O.R. (3d) 107 (C.A.), a petitioner to the Human Rights Committee applied for a stay of his deportation order to await the decision of the Committee on his petition. The petition claimed that he would be tortured if deported, and the Committee requested Canada to delay the deportation until the Committee had considered the petition. Canada refused the request, and proposed to deport the petitioner without waiting for the decision of the Committee. The Ontario Court of Appeal refused to grant the stay, despite the fact that immediate deportation would make the right to petition illusory. After the Supreme Court of Canada denied leave to appeal (May 17, 2002), Ahani was deported. The decision is criticized by J. Harrington, "Punting Terrorists, Assassins and Other Undesirables" (2003) 48 McGill L.J. 55.

[10]The procedure is described by T.J.M. Zuijdwijk, "The Right to Petition the United Nations because of Alleged Violations of Human Rights" (1981) 59 Can. Bar Rev. 103. The Human Rights Committee and the equivalent committee under the International Covenant on Economic, Social and Cultural Rights have repeatedly criticized Canada for breaches of the two treaties, including failures by Canadian courts to interpret the Charter into conformity with Canada's obligations: C. Scott, "Canada's International Human Rights Obligations and Disadvantaged Members of Society" (1999) 10 Constitutional Forum 97.

[11]The Convention and the optional protocol only became effective in 1976, not only for Canada but for other party states as well. The Human Rights Committee reports annually to the United Nations General Assembly and each annual report of the Human Rights Committee contains the full text of the decisions of the Committee, and is to be found in vol. 2 of the 40th Supplement to the Official Records of the General Assembly (GAOR). Decisions are also reported in the Human Rights Law Journal, the International Law Reports and the International Human Rights Reports. Decisions on petitions against Canada are reported in the Canadian Human Rights Yearbook. Also relevant to Canada's Charter jurisprudence are the decisions of the Committee against Torture, which interprets the Convention against Torture to which Canada is a party. Decisions of this Committee are reported in the 44th Supplement to GAOR and are also available through the Treaty Body Database.

have been accepted by Canada, it is as relevant to the interpretation of the Charter as the terms of the Covenant itself.

The decisions of the Human Rights Committee of the United Nations are relevant to the interpretation of the Charter, not only because Canada is a party to the Covenant which they interpret, but also because they are considered interpretations by distinguished jurists of language and ideas that are similar to the language and ideas of the Charter. Even if Canada were not a party to the Covenant, the Committee's decisions would enjoy the same kind of persuasive value for Canadian courts as the decisions of the courts of a foreign country: the search for wisdom is not to be circumscribed by national boundaries.[12]

Canada is a member of the Organization of American States (OAS). The American Declaration of the Rights and Duties of Man of 1948 is applicable to the members of OAS. Canadians may petition the Inter-American Commission on Human Rights if they claim a breach by Canada of their rights under the Declaration. Few cases have been brought against Canada, but the Commission's jurisprudence is another possible source of interpretation of the Canadian Charter.[13]

The European Convention on Human Rights[14] is another source of international jurisprudence that has persuasive value for Canadian courts interpreting the Charter.[15] The European Convention came into force in 1953 and has been ratified by the United Kingdom and 43 other European countries.[16] Canada is not a party and cannot become one, because the treaty is a regional one. The Convention guarantees many of the same civil liberties as the Charter, although, like the International Covenant, the Convention tends to be more detailed in its provisions. Before 1999, individuals in party states who claimed a violation of the Convention could petition the European Commission of Human Rights and the Commission had the power to make a decision itself or refer the petition to the European Court of Human Rights. In 1999, a treaty known as Protocol 11 to the European Convention on Human Rights came into force. Protocol 11 abolished the Commission, and individuals now petition the Court directly.[17]

Even customary (non-treaty) international law can occasionally serve

---

[12]J. Claydon, "International Human Rights and the Interpretation of the Charter" (1982) 4 Supreme Court L.R. 287, 295.

[13]The decisions of the Inter-American Commission on Human Rights are contained in its annual reports to OAS, which are available on the OAS website: http://www.oas.org.

[14]The text of the Convention is set out in Schabas, International Human Rights Law and the Canadian Charter (2nd ed., 1996), 255.

[15]References to the Convention by Canadian courts are listed in Schabas, International Human Rights Law and the Canadian Charter (2nd ed., 1996), Appendix III. See also G. Zellick, "The European Convention on Human Rights: Its Significance for Charter Litigation" in Sharpe (ed.), Charter Litigation (1987), ch. 5.

[16]Current information on ratifications is available at http://conventions.coe.int.

[17]Until 2015, the decisions of the European Court of Human Rights were reported in a series called Reports of Judgments and Decisions. The decisions are also available online from the Human Rights Documentation (HUDOC) database maintained by the

as an aid to interpretation of the Charter. In *R. v. Hape* (2007),[18] the issue was whether the Charter applied to the investigations of Canadian police in a foreign country (the Turks and Caicos Islands). Section 32 of the Charter governs the application of the Charter, making clear that the Charter applies to Canadian government officials, including police officers, but s. 32 is silent on the issue of territoriality. LeBel J. for the majority of the Supreme Court of Canada held that s. 32 should be interpreted into conformity with applicable principles of customary international law, of which the most relevant principle was that of "respect for the sovereignty of foreign states".[19] While respect for the sovereignty of foreign states did not preclude Parliament from *making* laws with extraterritorial effect, it did preclude Canada from *enforcing* its laws in the territory of a foreign state. LeBel J. took the view that it would be tantamount to enforcing a Canadian law in a foreign state if the Court were to hold that the Charter applied to searches and seizures in the Turks and Caicos Islands by Canadian police who were looking for evidence of Canadian crime (money laundering of drug proceeds).[20] He concluded that s. 32 should be interpreted as confining the application of the Charter to actions taken by Canadian actors inside the boundaries of Canada.[21]

§ 36:29 Legislative history

The legislative history of the Charter is admissible as an aid to its interpretation. Thus, earlier versions of the Charter, testimony given before the parliamentary committee which examined an earlier version, and debates in the Senate and House of Commons are all relevant and admissible. This topic will be addressed in a later chapter.[1]

Council of Europe at http://hudoc.echr.coe.int/. The decisions are also reported in the European Human Rights Reports. A selection is reported in the Human Rights Law Journal.

[18]*R. v. Hape*, [2007] 2 S.C.R. 292. LeBel J. wrote the majority opinion for himself and four others. Bastarache J. (agreed to by two others) and Binnie J. wrote concurring opinions, but, while agreeing that the Charter did not apply to the facts of this case, they disagreed with LeBel J.'s view that the Charter did not apply outside the boundaries of Canada. For fuller discussion, see ch. 37, Application of Charter, under heading § 37:14, "Extraterritorial application". See also H.S. Fairley, "International Law Comes of Age: *Hape v. The Queen*" (2008), 87 Can. Bar Rev. 229.

[19]*R. v. Hape*, [2007] 2 S.C.R. 292, para. 40. LeBel J. also referred to equality of states (para. 44), comity of nations (para. 47), and obviously regarded them as relevant to the interpretative issue as well.

[20]The Canadian police were working with the consent and cooperation of the Turks and Caicos police, and in compliance with Turks and Caicos law, which was not, however, fully consistent with Charter norms.

[21]*R. v. Hape*, [2007] 2 S.C.R. 292, para. 85 ("Since extraterritorial enforcement is not possible, and enforcement is necessary for the Charter to apply, extraterritorial application of the Charter is impossible.")

[Section 36:29]

[1]Chapter 60, Proof, under heading §§ 60:1 to 60:7, "Legislative history".

VIII. PRIORITY BETWEEN FEDERAL AND CHARTER GROUNDS

§ 36:30 Priority between federal and Charter grounds

When a law is challenged on both federal and Charter grounds, it is the federal ground that is the more fundamental of the two, and that ought to take priority over the Charter ground. This point has been argued, and its implications explained, in an earlier chapter.[1]

IX. COMMENCEMENT OF CHARTER

§ 36:31 Commencement of Charter

Section 58 of the Constitution Act, 1982 provides that the Act is to come into force on a day to be fixed by proclamation. That proclamation was issued by the Queen, who came to Canada for the purpose, at a ceremony in Ottawa on April 17, 1982; and the proclamation fixed April 17, 1982 as the day upon which the Constitution Act, 1982 was to come into force.[1] The Charter of Rights accordingly came into force on that day, and operates only prospectively from that day.[2]

A statute (or regulation or by-law or other legislative instrument) which was enacted before April 17, 1982, and which is inconsistent with the Charter, will be rendered "of no force or effect" by the supremacy clause of the Constitution,[3] but only as from April 17, 1982.[4] In *Mack v. Canada* (2002),[5] an attempt was made to seek redress under the Charter for the federal Chinese Immigration Acts that were in force from 1885 to 1923. These laws imposed a "head tax" on persons of Chinese origin upon entering Canada, and made it very difficult to immigrate to Canada from China. The claimants included a few people who had actually

---

[Section 36:30]

[1]Chapter 15, Judicial Review on Federal Grounds, under heading § 15:2 "Priority between federal and Charter grounds".

[Section 36:31]

[1]The proclamation is published in a special issue of The Canada Gazette, Part III, September 21, 1982, p. 33.

[2]The coming into force of s. 15 (the equality guarantee) was postponed for three years, until April 17, 1985: Constitution Act, 1982, s. 32(2). The purpose of the postponement was to allow the various governments time to review their statutes for compliance with s. 15. All governments, except for Quebec, conducted a review and secured the enactment of legislation to correct any perceived breaches of the Charter (not just s. 15).

[3]Constitution Act, 1982, s. 52(1) (supremacy clause).

[4]*R. v. Stevens*, [1988] 1 S.C.R. 1153 (accused, charged with an offence that took place before 1982, cannot challenge law on Charter grounds). Query correctness of *Ravndahl v. Sask.*, [2009] 1 S.C.R. 181, holding that the termination of a workers compensation pension on the ground of remarriage was a breach of s. 15, although the termination took place in 1984, before the coming into force of s. 15. The Court said that the pensioner's cause of action arose on April 17, 1985 (para. 23). However, the Court held that the cause of action was statute-barred.

[5]*Mack v. Canada* (2002), 60 O.R. (3d) 737 (C.A.). The opinion of the Court was written by Moldaver and MacPherson JJ.A.

paid the head tax; the others were descendants of persons who had paid the head tax or suffered in other ways from the laws. They sought the return with interest of the head taxes paid and damages. The Ontario Court of Appeal, affirming the trial judge, acknowledged that the laws discriminated on the ground of race, and would today offend the Charter. But the laws were repealed in 1923. Since the laws were not in force at the commencement of the Charter, those whose rights were denied by the laws had no remedy under the Charter.

Action of an executive or administrative kind, such as search, seizure, arrest or detention, which was taken before April 17, 1982, cannot be a violation of the Charter, because the Charter was not in force at the time of the action.[6] No remedy under s. 24(1) would be available in respect of action taken before April 17, 1982, because the remedy is available only to anyone whose rights or freedoms, "as guaranteed by this Charter", have been infringed or denied.[7] Even s. 24(2) (exclusion of evidence) would not apply to evidence which, although tendered after April 17, 1982, was obtained before April 17, 1982; s. 24(2) applies only to evidence "obtained in a manner that infringed or denied any rights or freedoms guaranteed by this Charter", and no rights or freedoms were guaranteed by the Charter until April 17, 1982.[8]

Some of the provisions of the Charter have been interpreted in such a way that events occurring before April 17, 1982 are relevant to their application, despite the exclusively prospective operation of the Charter. One example is provided by s. 13, which stipulates that a witness who testifies in any proceedings has the right not to have any incriminating evidence that the witness may have given in earlier proceedings used against him or her in the later proceedings. It has been held that this right takes effect at the time of the later proceedings, when the Crown seeks to use the incriminating testimony from the earlier proceedings. Therefore, the right can be invoked even if the earlier proceedings took place before April 17, 1982, provided that the later proceedings took place after April 17, 1982.[9] Another example is provided by s. 11(b), which guarantees the right "to be tried within a reasonable time". It has been held that a period of delay occurring before April 17, 1982 should be taken into account in determining whether a person, whose trial had still not occurred by a date after April 17, 1982, had been denied the right to be tried within a reasonable time.[10] Another example is provided by s. 12, which guarantees the right "not to be subjected to any cruel and unusual treatment or punishment". Where a person was sentenced to a cruel and unusual punishment before April 17, 1982, but the

---

[6] *R. v. James*, [1988] 1 S.C.R. 669 (seizure took place before 1982).

[7] *R. v. James*, [1988] 1 S.C.R. 669.

[8] *R. v. James*, [1988] 1 S.C.R. 669.

[9] *Dubois v. The Queen*, [1985] 2 S.C.R. 350. The rule is the same for s. 11(h) (double jeopardy): the right becomes effective at the time of the later proceedings, and it is irrelevant that the earlier proceedings took place before April 17, 1982: *Corp. Professionnelle des Médecins v. Thibault*, [1988] 1 S.C.R. 1033.

[10] *R. v. Antoine* (1983), 41 O.R. (2d) 607, 613 (C.A.).

sentence continued after April 17, 1982, the continuation of the sentence would constitute a breach of s. 12.[11] But even in these two examples, where events occurring prior to April 17, 1982 are relevant, the application of the Charter is prospective only.

Another way in which events occurring before April 17, 1982 may be relevant to the application of the Charter is where they create a status or condition that continues after April 17, 1982 and that leads to a breach of the Charter. This is illustrated by *Benner v. Canada* (1997).[12] The statutory provision under challenge in that case was a section of the federal Citizenship Act that provided for the citizenship of children born outside Canada of Canadian parents. For children born before 1977, the Act distinguished between those born of a Canadian father, who were automatically entitled to register as citizens, and those born of a Canadian mother, who had to apply for citizenship, which involved passing a security check. Mr. Benner had been born in 1962 to a Canadian mother and an American father. In 1987, when he applied for Canadian citizenship, the required security check revealed that he had been charged with a murder (he subsequently pleaded guilty to manslaughter), and he was refused citizenship. Had his father (instead of his mother) been the Canadian citizen, he would have had an automatic right to register as a citizen regardless of his criminal record. He brought proceedings to quash the refusal of citizenship on the ground that it was a breach of his equality rights to treat the children of Canadian mothers differently than the children of Canadian fathers. The trial judge and the Federal Court of Appeal held that the Charter did not apply, because his complaint related to the circumstances of his birth, which had occurred 20 years before the Charter came into force in 1982. The Supreme Court of Canada allowed his appeal. Iacobucci J., writing for a unanimous Court, held that the better way to characterize his complaint was in terms of a status or condition that imposed a disadvantage on him that persisted after 1982. The discrimination occurred when the applicant was refused citizenship on the basis of that status, and the refusal took place in 1987. Therefore, the applicant was entitled to challenge the refusal of citizenship under the Charter of Rights. (The Court went on to hold that there was a breach of his equality rights, and he was successful in challenging the decision and the statutory provision that underlay it.)[13]

---

[11] *Re Mitchell and the Queen* (1983), 42 O.R. (2d) 481 (H.C.); *R. v. Konechny* (1983), 6 D.L.R. (4th) 350 (B.C. C.A.). See also *R. v. Gamble*, [1988] 2 S.C.R. 595 (continuing deprivation of liberty remediable, despite fact that breach of fundamental justice occurred before 1982).

[12] *Benner v. Canada*, [1997] 1 S.C.R. 358. Iacobucci J. delivered the judgment of the unanimous Court.

[13] Note however that the discriminatory provision was contained in the current Citizenship Act. *Contrast Taylor v. Can.* (2007), 286 D.L.R. (4th) 385 (F.C.A.), paras. 57-72 (application for citizenship in 2003 defeated by discriminatory provision of Canadian Citizenship Act, 1947 that was repealed in 1977; no Charter challenge available).

X. UNDECLARED RIGHTS

§ 36:32 Undeclared rights

Section 26 of the Charter[1] provides as follows:

> 26. The guarantee in this Charter of certain rights and freedoms shall not be construed as denying the existence of any other rights or freedoms that exist in Canada.

Section 26 is a cautionary provision, included to make clear that the Charter is not to be construed as taking away any existing undeclared rights or freedoms.[2] Rights or freedoms protected by the common law or by statute[3] will continue to exist notwithstanding the Charter.[4] Section 26 does not incorporate these undeclared rights and freedoms into the Charter, or "constitutionalize" them in any other way. They continue to exist independently of the Charter, and receive no extra protection from the Charter. They differ from the rights or freedoms guaranteed in the Charter in that, as creatures of common law or statute, the undeclared rights can be altered or abolished by the action of the competent legislative body.[5] As well, the remedy under s. 24 is not available for their enforcement.

[Section 36:32]

[1]In the October 1980 version of the Charter, s. 26 (then numbered s. 24) was included in its present form, but with the addition (at the end, after the word "Canada", which was followed by a comma) of the words "including any rights or freedoms that pertain to the native peoples of Canada". These words were dropped in the April 1981 version of s. 26 (then numbered s. 26), because of the inclusion of s. 25, which appeared for the first time in the April 1981 version.

[2]Section 26 has its equivalent in the ninth amendment of the Constitution of the United States, a provision that has rarely been invoked: M.N. Goodman, The Ninth Amendment (Exposition Press, Smithtown, New York, 1981).

[3]Among the statutory rights preserved by s. 26 are those contained in the Canadian Bill of Rights and the statutory bills of rights of Saskatchewan, Alberta and Quebec. *Singh v. Minr. of Emplmt. and Immigration*, [1985] 1 S.C.R. 177, 224.

[4]The Constitution Act, 1867, by s. 133, contains a guarantee of language rights, and, by s. 93, a guarantee of denominational schools. There are also some equivalent provisions in the Manitoba Act, the Alberta Act, the Saskatchewan Act and the Terms of Union of Newfoundland. These rights would also be preserved by s. 26. However, they are the subject of more specific preservation by s. 21 (language) and s. 29 (denominational schools) of the Charter. Aboriginal rights are specifically preserved by ss. 25 and 35.

[5]Note, however, the existence of "unwritten constitutional principles", which are immune from legislative change: ch. 15, Judicial Review on Federal Grounds, under heading § 15:28, "Unwritten constitutional principles".

Chapter 37

Application of Charter

I. BENEFIT OF RIGHTS

§ 37:1 The issue
§ 37:2 Everyone, anyone, any person
§ 37:3 Individual
§ 37:4 Citizen
§ 37:5 Permanent resident

II. BURDEN OF RIGHTS

§ 37:6 Both levels of government
§ 37:7 Parliament or Legislature
§ 37:8 Statutory authority
§ 37:9 Amending procedures
§ 37:10 Government
§ 37:11 Courts
§ 37:12 Common law
§ 37:13 Private action
§ 37:14 Extraterritorial application

III. WAIVER OF RIGHTS

§ 37:15 Definition of waiver
§ 37:16 Rationale of waiver
§ 37:17 Waiver of presumption of innocence
§ 37:18 Waiver of right to silence
§ 37:19 Waiver of unreasonable search and seizure
§ 37:20 Waiver of right to counsel
§ 37:21 Waiver of speedy trial
§ 37:22 Waiver of right to jury
§ 37:23 Waiver of right to interpreter
§ 37:24 Waiver by contract

I. BENEFIT OF RIGHTS

§ 37:1 The issue

Who is entitled to the benefit of the rights guaranteed by the Charter of Rights? In particular, is a corporation entitled to the benefit of all rights? This question turns on the language by which the rights are defined; this language is surprisingly various and surprisingly silent on its applicability to corporations.

§ 37:2 Everyone, anyone, any person

Sections 2, 7, 8, 9, 10, 12 and 17 of the Charter open with the phrase, "Everyone has the right". In ss. 11 and 19 "any person" replaces "everyone"; s. 20 uses "any member of the public"; and s. 24 uses "anyone". It seems likely that these various terms are synonymous[1] and that each is apt to include a corporation as well as an individual.[2] Indeed, some of the rights would be seriously attenuated if they did not apply to corporations. For example, newspapers, television stations and other media of communication require significant capital for their operation and are usually operated by corporations; "freedom of the press and other media of communication" (s. 2(b)) would be a hollow right if it could not be invoked by a corporation. Nor is there any reason to assume that the Charter denies to a corporation charged with an offence the basic safeguards of a fair trial (s. 11).

Some of the rights, although guaranteed to "everyone" or "any person", are by their very nature not available to a corporation. For example, the right to "freedom of conscience and religion" in s. 2(a) does not apply to a corporation, because a corporation cannot hold a religious belief or any other belief.[3] The right to fundamental justice under s. 7 does not apply to a corporation, because it is limited to deprivations of "life, liberty and

---

[Section 37:2]

[1]In the French version of the Charter, the word "chacun" is used in place of "everyone" in ss. 2, 8, 9, 10, 12 and 17; and the same word "chacun" is used in place of "person" in s. 19. This reinforces the commonsense conclusion that nothing turns on at least the variation between "everyone" and "any person".

[2]*Hunter v. Southam*, [1984] 2 S.C.R. 145 (applying s. 8 at suit of corporation); *Edmonton Journal v. Alta.*, [1989] 2 S.C.R. 1326 (applying s. 2 at suit of corporation). *R. v. CIP*, [1992] 1 S.C.R. 843 (holding that s. 11(b) applies to corporation). The word "person" in the American Bill of Rights (where it appears in the fifth and fourteenth amendments) has been held to include a corporation: *Covington and Lexington Turnpike Road Co. v. Sandford* (1896), 164 U.S. 578; *Smyth v. Ames* (1897), 169 U.S. 466; *First Nat. Bank of Boston v. Bellotti* (1978), 435 U.S. 765.

[3]*R. v. Big M Drug Mart*, [1985] 1 S.C.R. 295, 314. There may be some corporations that are formed for the exercise of religious beliefs, for example, a church organized as a corporation. No doubt, such a corporation could invoke s. 2(a). In Loyola High School v. Quebec, [2015] 1 S.C.R. 613, Loyola High School was a denominational school organized as a corporation which claimed successfully that its freedom of religion was infringed by Quebec's curriculum regulations. Abella J. for the majority (para. 34) did not need to decide whether the corporation enjoyed the benefit of s. 2(a) because the teachers, parents and students were enough to support the Charter claim. McLachlin C.J. and Moldaver J., for the concurring minority (paras. 89-102) held that Loyola, as a religious, non-profit corporation, did enjoy the benefit of s. 2(a). In *Law Society of British Columbia v. Trinity Western University*, [2018] 2 S.C.R. 293, the joint majority declined to address whether Trinity Western University, a private evangelical Christian university, could possess rights under s. 2(a) as an institution (para. 61; see similarly para. 219 per Rowe J. concurring); Côté and Brown JJ., dissenting, implied a willingness to accept that institutions can possess rights under s. 2(a) (para. 315). These cases are discussed in ch. 42, Religion, under heading § 42:9, "Denominational schools". It is unlikely that a Canadian court would follow the surprising American case of *Burwell v. Hobby Lobby Stores* (2014), 134 S.Ct. 2751, holding, by majority, that business corporations that were closely held were entitled to a religious exemption from the obligation to provide health

security of the person", which are attributes of individuals, not corporations.[4] The right not to be "arbitrarily detained or imprisoned" in s. 9, and other rights that arise only on "arrest or detention" in s. 10, as well as the right to reasonable bail in s. 11(e), cannot be enjoyed by a corporation, because a corporation cannot be detained, imprisoned or arrested.[5] A corporation cannot testify, so that the right of an accused person not to be compelled to be a witness against himself in s. 11(c),[6] the right against self-incrimination in s. 13,[7] and the right of a witness to an interpreter in s. 14, are not available to a corporation.

Those rights that do not apply to corporations cannot be invoked by a corporation to obtain a remedy under s. 24.[8] Section 24 itself is available to "anyone", which includes a corporation,[9] and can therefore be used by a corporation to enforce a right that does apply to a corporation. However, it is wrong to assume that a corporation can never invoke a right that does not apply to a corporation. In *R. v. Big M Drug Mart* (1985),[10] the Supreme Court of Canada held that a corporation could invoke the right to freedom of religion in s. 2(a) as a defence to a criminal charge of selling goods on a Sunday. The charge was laid under the federal Lord's Day Act, which the corporation successfully argued was unconstitutional on the ground that the Act abridged the freedom of religion of individuals. The corporation had standing to make this argument, despite the fact that s. 2(a) did not apply to a corporation, because "no-one can be convicted of an offence under an unconstitutional law".[11] The corporation was not seeking a remedy under s. 24. As a defendant to a criminal charge, the corporation was entitled to rely on any constitutional defect in the law. This ruling means that rights that do not apply to corporations by their own terms may nevertheless operate to the benefit of corporations. The rationale and limits of this ruling are discussed in a later chapter.[12]

A foetus is not a legal person, either at common law or civil law, until the child is born by being separated alive from the mother. A foetus is

---

insurance for contraceptive drugs by reason of the sincere religious beliefs about contraception of the controlling shareholders.

[4]*Irwin Toy v. Que.*, [1989] 1 S.C.R. 927, 1004; *Dywidag Systems v. Zutphen Bros.*, [1990] 1 S.C.R. 705, 709.

[5]Query correctness of Re *PPG Industries Can.* (1983), 146 D.L.R. (3d) 261 (B.C.C.A.) (corporation not entitled to trial by jury because of reference to imprisonment in s. 11(f)).

[6]*R. v. Amway Corp.*, [1989] 1 S.C.R. 21, 37-40.

[7]Compare *United States v. White* (1944), 322 U.S. 694, 698 (privilege against self-incrimination essentially personal, applying only to natural individuals).

[8]See ch. 40, Enforcement of Rights, under heading § 40:14, "Standing".

[9]*R. v. Big M Drug Mart*, [1985] 1 S.C.R. 295, 313.

[10]*R. v. Big M Drug Mart*, [1985] 1 S.C.R. 295.

[11]*R. v. Big M Drug Mart*, [1985] 1 S.C.R. 295, 313.

[12]Chapter 59, Procedure, under heading §§ 59:2 to 59:6, "Standing".

not entitled to a right to life under s. 7, or any other right under the Charter.[13]

Is there a requirement of some connection to Canada for a person to be the holder of Charter rights? Of course, s. 32 requires that there must be action by a Canadian legislative body or government for the Charter to apply. That requirement, which is considered later in this chapter under the heading "Burden of rights", imposes a connection with Canada of a kind. But it seems likely that there is no independent requirement of a connection with Canada in order to receive the benefit of Charter rights. In *Singh v. Minister of Employment and Immigration* (1985),[14] Wilson J., speaking for three members of a six-member bench of the Supreme Court of Canada, held that anyone who entered Canada, however illegally, was instantly entitled to assert s. 7 rights, which apply to "everyone". Beetz J., speaking for the other three judges, decided the case under the Canadian Bill of Rights, which he assumed could also be invoked by anyone who succeeded in crossing a Canadian border. In the context of that case, this meant that everyone who entered Canada and made a refugee claim was entitled to a hearing before a person with authority to decide the issue.[15]

In *R. v. Cook* (1998),[16] a majority of the Supreme Court of Canada held that an American citizen, who was arrested and detained in the United States, was entitled to the right to counsel under s. 10(b) of the Charter, which applies to "everyone". The issue reached the Canadian court system, because the detainee was later removed to Canada and tried for a murder allegedly committed in Canada. He successfully challenged the admissibility of a statement made in the United States to Canadian police officers in violation of his right to counsel. The majority did not notice the implications of this decision for the scope of the class that could hold Charter rights, and L'Heureux-Dubé J., for the dissenting minority, pointed out that the majority had not directed their minds to the crucial first step of determining whether the person claiming a Charter right "is indeed the holder of a right under the Canadian

[13]*Tremblay v. Daigle*, [1989] 2 S.C.R. 530 (foetus not a "human being" for purpose of right to life in Quebec Charter of Rights and Freedoms or for purpose of civil rights under Quebec Civil Code); *R. v. Sullivan*, [1991] 1 S.C.R. 489 (foetus not a "person" within Criminal Code offence of death by criminal negligence); *Borowski v. A.G. Can.* (1987), 39 D.L.R. (4th) 731 (Sask. C.A.) (foetus not included in s. 7's "everyone" or s. 15's "individual"). The *Borowski* case went up to the Supreme Court of Canada, but in that Court these rulings were not addressed, because the issue, which was the validity of the abortion provisions of the Criminal Code, had become moot: *Borowski v. Can.*, [1989] 1 S.C.R. 342. The abortion provisions of the Criminal Code were held to be unconstitutional in *R. v. Morgentaler (No. 2)*, [1988] 1 S.C.R. 30 on the ground that they infringed the mother's right under s. 7; there was no ruling on whether the foetus had any rights.

[14]*Singh v. Minister of Employment and Immigration*, [1985] 1 S.C.R. 177.

[15]Accord, *Suresh v. Can.*, [2002] 1 S.C.R. 3, para. 44 ("everyone" in s. 7 includes a refugee in Canada facing deportation).

[16]*R. v. Cook*, [1998] 2 S.C.R. 597.

constitution".[17] She said that she was "not convinced that the passage of the Charter necessarily gave rights to everyone in the world, of every nationality, wherever they might be, even if certain rights contain the word 'everyone' ".[18] However, since this issue had not been argued, and since she considered that the Charter did not apply for other reasons, she contented herself with flagging the issue and did not base her dissent on this ground.

§ 37:3 Individual

Section 15 confers its equality rights on "every individual". This is a more specific term than "everyone", "any person" or "anyone", and it probably excludes a corporation, at least in the context of an instrument which also contains the more general terms. The word "individual" was substituted for "everyone" during the parliamentary committee's deliberations on the Charter, and the explanation given to the committee was that the change was intended "to make it clear that this right would apply to natural persons only".[1] Within s. 15, the reference to "discrimination based on race, national or ethnic origin, colour, religion, sex, age or mental or physical disability" also reinforces the exclusion of corporations: the listed attributes are all personal characteristics of human beings, and only "national origin" could apply to corporations as well. But in that company, national origin should probably be read down to exclude foreign corporations.[2] While I think that this is the better view, the position is not clear. It can be argued that the French version of s. 15, which uses the word "personne" in subsection (1) in place of individual (although it uses "individus" in subsection (2)), suggests that artificial persons are covered. It can also be argued that it is anomalous to make the act of incorporation deny to a business proprietor a right that he or she enjoyed before incorporation.[3]

At the time of writing, the Supreme Court of Canada has decided two cases where corporations have invoked s. 15; finding against the equality claim on other grounds, the Court studiously refused to decide this issue,[4] which may indicate that the Court has some doubt as to the

---

[17] *R. v. Cook*, [1998] 2 S.C.R. 597, para. 85.

[18] *R. v. Cook*, [1998] 2 S.C.R. 597, para. 86.

[Section 37:3]

[1] For reference to the legislative history, see Gibson, The Law of the Charter: Equality Rights (1990), 53-55.

[2] The stipulated grounds are not exclusive, but only "analogous grounds" can be added, and the common feature of the stipulated grounds may well be the personal characteristic of a human being: see ch. 55, Equality, under heading § 55:16, "Discrimination".

[3] See Gibson, The Law of the Charter: Equality Rights (1990), 53-55; G.D. Chipeur, Section 15 of the Charter protects People and Corporations Equally" (1986) 11 Can. Bus. L.J. 304; E. Gertner, "Are Corporations entitled to Equality?" (1986) 19 Can. Rts. Reporter 288.

[4] *Rudolf Wolff & Co. v. Can.*, [1990] 1 S.C.R. 695, 703; *Dywidag Systems v. Zutphen*

answer.[5] Lower courts have held that s. 15 does not extend to corporations.[6]

Even if s. 15 does not extend to corporations, corporations will still be able to rely on s. 15 as a defence to a criminal charge laid under a law that is invalid by virtue of unconstitutional discrimination against individuals. This is the principle established by *Big M Drug Mart*, discussed above.[7]

The word "individual" does not include a foetus.[8] Nor does "individual" include the estate of a deceased individual: "s. 15 rights die with the individual".[9]

§ 37:4 Citizen

Generally speaking, a person need not be a Canadian citizen in order to invoke Charter rights. "Everyone" in s. 7 has been held to include "every human being who is physically present in Canada and by virtue of such presence amenable to Canadian law".[1] The same would apply to "anyone", "any person" and "individual". Even persons who have entered

---

Bros., [1990] 1 S.C.R. 705, 709. The decisions hold that the Crown is not an individual.

[5]Compare *R. v. Big M Drug Mart*, [1985] 1 S.C.R. 293, 313 where Dickson J. uses the word "individuals" to include "real persons or artificial ones"; but he is not referring to s. 15.

[6]The cases are referred to in the sources in § 37:3 note 3, above.

[7]*R. v. Big M Drug Mart*, [1985] 1 S.C.R. 295.

[8]*Tremblay v. Daigle*, [1989] 2 S.C.R. 530 (foetus not a "human being" for purpose of right to life in Quebec Charter of Rights and Freedoms or for purpose of civil rights under Quebec Civil Code); *R. v. Sullivan*, [1991] 1 S.C.R. 489 (foetus not a "person" within Criminal Code offence of death by criminal negligence); *Borowski v. A.G. Can.* (1987), 39 D.L.R. (4th) 731 (Sask. C.A.) (foetus not included in s. 7's "everyone" or s. 15's "individual"). The Borowski case went up to the Supreme Court of Canada, but in that Court these rulings were not addressed, because the issue, which was the validity of the abortion provisions of the Criminal Code, had become moot: *Borowski v. Can.*, [1989] 1 S.C.R. 342. The abortion provisions of the Criminal Code were held to be unconstitutional in *R. v. Morgentaler (No. 2)*, [1988] 1 S.C.R. 30 on the ground that they infringed the mother's right under s. 7; there was no ruling on whether the foetus had any rights.

[9]*Can. v. Hislop*, [2007] 1 S.C.R. 429, para. 73 (denying s. 15 claim to CPP survivor benefits on behalf of individuals who had died before the conclusion of the hearing of the s. 15 claim).

[Section 37:4]

[1]*Singh v. Minr. of Emplmt. and Immig.*, [1985] 1 S.C.R. 177, 202 per Wilson J. for half of the six-judge bench. Beetz J. for the other half decided the case on the basis of the Canadian Bill of Rights rather than the Charter. While Beetz J. said nothing on this point, he probably agreed with it, because he assumed that illegal immigrants were entitled to the rights under the Canadian Bill of Rights. The issue was definitively decided by a unanimous Supreme Court in *R. v. Appulonappa*, [2015] 3 S.C.R. 754, 2015 SCC 59, para. 23 ("Charter applies to foreign nationals entering Canada without the required documentation"), in which Tamils fleeing from Sri Lanka without documentation arrived by boat in British Columbia and brought a partially successful s. 7 challenge to the human-smuggling offence in the Immigration and Refugee Protection Act.

Canada illegally are entitled to most of the Charter rights simply by virtue of their presence on Canadian soil.[2]

Citizenship is a required qualification for some rights. Voting rights (s. 3), mobility rights (s. 6) and minority language educational rights (s. 23) are conferred upon a "citizen".

Canadian citizenship is a relatively recent concept,[3] established for the first time by federal statute in 1947.[4] It is clear that citizenship is a matter coming within the legislative authority of the federal Parliament.[5] Now that the concept has constitutional implications, how will the courts define it? It seems unlikely that the courts would develop their own definition of "citizen", since the concept has no meaning apart from statute.[6] Yet it would be unfortunate if the courts were to hold that the statutory rules defining citizenship in 1982 (when the Charter came into force) constituted the rigid, unchangeable definition for constitutional purposes. The best course is for the courts to accept that citizenship is a creature of federal statute law and that it can be changed from time to time by the federal Parliament, even though the consequence of any such change is also to change the scope of ss. 3, 6 and 23 of the Charter.[7] Of course, the courts should review any amendment to the citizenship law to satisfy themselves that it is reasonably related to a legitimate national objective, and is not simply a device to limit Charter rights.

If I am right that the term "citizen" essentially means citizenship as legislated from time to time by the federal Parliament, it follows that the term excludes corporations, at least until such time as the Parliament establishes a concept of citizenship for corporations.[8] The contexts in which the term "citizen" appears in the Charter reinforce the view that corporate citizenship is not contemplated. The term appears only in ss. 3, 6 and 23. It is obvious that a corporation could not possess the

[2]*Singh v. Minr. of Emplmt. and Immig.*, [1985] 1 S.C.R. 177, 202. In *R. v. A.*, [1990] 1 S.C.R. 995, a majority of the Court seems to have held that even persons outside Canada are entitled to Charter rights. This entitlement must surely be restricted to citizens. But see *R. v. Cook*, [1998] 2 S.C.R. 597.

[3]See ch. 26, Citizenship, under heading § 26:3, "Citizenship".

[4]Canadian Citizenship Act, S.C. 1946, c. 15; see now Citizenship Act, R.S.C. 1985, c. C-29.

[5]It is not clear whether the power is derived from s. 91(25) (naturalization and aliens) or from the opening words of s. 91 (peace, order, and good government): McConnell, Commentary on the British North America Act (1911) 227-232.

[6]Contrast the word "Indian" in s. 91(24), which is obviously not a purely statutory concept, and which has been held to include persons outside the definition in the federal Indian Act: *Re Eskimos*, [1939] S.C.R. 104.

[7]Compare *Cunningham v. Tomey Homma*, [1903] A.C. 151, 156 (Parliament has power to define "aliens" in s. 91(25)); *A.-G. Can. v. Canard*, [1976] 1 S.C.R. 170, 206 (Parliament has power to define "Indians" in s. 91(24) although Parliament has not attempted to do so exhaustively: see previous note).

[8]If, on the other hand, the courts were prepared to give the term "citizen" some significance independent of federal statute law, it is possible that a corporation could be held to be a Canadian citizen, based on either incorporation within Canada or control by Canadian citizens.

right to vote under s. 3, or the right to educate its "children" in the minority language under s. 23. That leaves only the mobility rights of s. 6. Certainly, it is not impossible for mobility rights to be extended to corporations, but this would represent a radical change in Canada's constitutional law, which has hitherto always denied full legal status to a corporation outside its jurisdiction of incorporation.[9] A change in this fundamental rule would call for a clearer provision than one applying to "every citizen".

§ 37:5 Permanent resident

The mobility rights of s. 6(2) (but not s. 6(1)) apply, not only to "every citizen", but also to "every person who has the status of a permanent resident of Canada".

The term "permanent resident" is to be found in the federal Immigration and Refugee Protection Act,[1] where it is defined (unhelpfully) as "a person who has acquired permanent resident status". It is a technical term in immigration law, meaning a person who has been officially admitted to Canada as a permanent resident, but who has not taken out Canadian citizenship. Section 6(2) of the Charter rather plainly uses the term in this technical sense, because it refers to a person who has "the status" of a permanent resident, which seems to imply some official recognition of the status, and not just the fact of permanent residence. If this is correct, then the courts should interpret "permanent resident" as meaning its statutory definition from time to time in the Immigration and Refugee Protection Act.[2] On that basis, of course, a corporation would not be included.

If, contrary to the opinion just advanced, the courts did not confine the term "permanent resident" to its technical immigration-law meaning, then it could easily encompass a corporation. A corporation can be a "person",[3] and it is well established in income-tax law that a corporation can be a "resident" of Canada,[4] and there seems to be no reason why a corporation could not be a "permanent" resident of Canada. Of course, as noted in the previous discussion of citizenship, the extension of mobility rights to corporations would constitute a radical change in the constitutional law respecting corporate recognition outside the province

---

[9]See ch. 23, Companies, under heading § 23:2, "Territorial limitation".

[Section 37:5]

[1]S.C. 2001, c. 27, s. 2(1). The term was defined in the previous Immigration Act, S.C. 1976-77, c. 52, s. 2(1), as a person who "has been granted landing". The term was not used or defined in the Immigration Act before 1977.

[2]The problem of a statutory definition controlling the scope of a constitutional right is discussed in the previous section of this chapter with reference to citizenship, § 37:4.

[3]§ 37:1 note 2 and accompanying text, above.

[4]The leading case, which makes corporate residence depend upon the location of "central management and control", is *De Boers Consolidated Mines v. Howe*, [1906] A.C. 455 (H.L.).

of incorporation, and the courts would be reluctant to take this step in the absence of clearer language in the Charter.[5]

II. BURDEN OF RIGHTS

§ 37:6 Both levels of government

The previous section of this chapter examined who is entitled to the *benefit* of Charter rights. This section examines who is subject to the *burden* of Charter rights, or, in other words, who is bound by the Charter. This latter question is governed by s. 32(1) of the Charter,[1] which provides as follows:

> **32.** (1) This Charter applies
>
> (a) to the Parliament and government of Canada in respect of all matters within the authority of Parliament including all matters relating to the Yukon Territory and Northwest Territories; and
>
> (b) to the legislature and government of each province in respect of all matters within the authority of the legislature of each province.

Section 32(1) expressly provides that the Charter applies to "the Parliament and government of Canada" and to "the legislature and government of each province". This makes clear that both levels of government are bound by the Charter.

It will be recalled that the Canadian Bill of Rights applied (and still applies) only to the federal level of government.[2]

The original American Bill of Rights, namely, the first ten amendments to the Constitution of the United States, was proposed by the first Congress in response to concerns about civil liberties that had been expressed during the debates on the ratification of the Constitution. These concerns seem to have been directed only to the new federal government, and the first ten amendments, which were ratified by the states in 1791,[3] applied only to the federal government. After the civil war, however, the fourteenth amendment was adopted (it was ratified in 1868), and it did apply to the states (and only to the states). The due

---

[5] § 37:4 note 9 and accompanying text, above.

[Section 37:6]

[1] For commentary on s. 32, see Gibson, The Law of the Charter: General Principles (1986), 88120; Beaudoin and Mendes (eds.), The Canadian Charter of Rights and Freedoms (4th ed., 2005), ch. 3 (by Tassé); Lokan and Dassios, Constitutional Litigation in Canada (Carswell, loose-leaf), ch. 2; McLeod, Takach, Morton, Segal, The Canadian Charter of Rights (Carswell, loose-leaf), ch. 3; Canadian Charter of Rights Annotated, (Canada Law Book, loose-leaf), annotation to s. 32. The last work provides a bibliography of the relevant literature.

[2] See ch. 35, Canadian Bill of Rights under heading § 35:2, "Application to federal laws".

[3] The Constitution of the United States, by article V, provides that an amendment must be proposed by the federal Congress by a two-thirds majority of both Houses, and must be ratified by the Legislatures (or constitutional conventions) of three-fourths of the states.

process clause of the fourteenth amendment has been interpreted as "incorporating" most (but not all) of the guarantees of the first ten amendments. Through this doctrine of "selective incorporation", the incorporated guarantees have become applicable to the states.[4] In the opposite direction, the equal protection clause of the fourteenth amendment, which has no counterpart in the first ten amendments, has been incorporated into the due process clause of the fifth amendment, and has thereby become applicable to the federal level of government.[5] By these circuitous routes, most of the guarantees of the American Bill of Rights have become applicable to both levels of government.

§ 37:7 Parliament or Legislature

The references in s. 32 to the "Parliament" and a "legislature" make clear that the Charter operates as a limitation on the powers of those legislative bodies.[1] Any statute enacted by either Parliament or a Legislature which is inconsistent with the Charter will be outside the power of (ultra vires) the enacting body and will be invalid.[2]

The word "Parliament" means the federal legislative body, which consists (in the language of s. 17 of the Constitution Act, 1867) "of the Queen, an upper house styled the Senate, and the House of Commons". Of these three elements, the first, namely the Queen, is represented in Canada by the Governor General, who gives the royal assent. The second element, the Senate, is the upper house, which is an appointed legislative chamber. The third element, the House of Commons, is the lower house, which is an elected legislative chamber.[3]

The word "legislature" means the provincial legislative body, which consists, in the case of Ontario (in the language of s. 69 of the Constitution Act, 1867), "of the Lieutenant Governor and of one house, styled the Legislative Assembly of Ontario". Ontario's two elements of a Lieutenant Governor, who gives the royal assent, and a Legislative Assembly, which is an elected chamber, have their counterparts in the other nine

---

[4]The Supreme Court of the United States never accepted "total incorporation" of the first ten amendments. Selective incorporation covered only the more fundamental guarantees; however, this has steadily been extended to all but a few of the guarantees, thus coming close to total incorporation. The position is well explained in J.E. Nowak and R.D. Rotunda, Constitutional Law (West, St. Paul, Minn., 7th ed., 2004), sec. 11.6. A shorter account is in L.H. Tribe, American Constitutional Law (Foundation Press, N.Y., 2nd ed., 1988), 772-774.

[5]J.E. Nowak and R.D. Rotunda, Constitutional Law (West, St. Paul, Minn., 7th ed., 2004), sec. 14.1; L.H. Tribe, American Constitutional Law (Foundation Press, N.Y., 2nd ed., 1988), 1437.

[Section 37:7]

[1]On the effect of the phrases "in respect of all matters", etc. in both paragraphs, see ch. 15, Judicial Review on Federal Grounds, under heading § 15:2, "Priority between federal and Charter grounds".

[2]This result would follow even without the supremacy clause of s. 52(1), but that clause reinforces the ultra vires conclusion.

[3]The Parliament is more fully described in ch. 9, Responsible Government, under heading §§ 9:8 to 9:12, "The legislative branch".

provinces as well. Five provinces used to have an upper house, styled a Legislative Council, but all five abolished it.[4]

In *New Brunswick Broadcasting Co. v. Nova Scotia* (1993),[5] the question arose whether the Nova Scotia legislative assembly, which had prohibited the televising of its proceedings, was bound by the Charter of Rights. The Supreme Court of Canada, by a majority,[6] held that the word "legislature" in s. 32 should be interpreted as making the Charter applicable to a legislative assembly, even when the assembly acted independently of the Lieutenant Governor and was for that reason less than the full Legislature. Presumably, the same conclusion would apply to the word "Parliament" in s. 32, making the Charter applicable to actions of the Senate or the House of Commons as well as to those of Parliament as a whole.

What the Supreme Court of Canada in *New Brunswick Broadcasting* gave with the one hand it took away with the other. Having held that the Charter applied to the legislative assembly of Nova Scotia, the Court went on to hold by a majority[7] that the power of the assembly "to exclude strangers" (including the television media) from its deliberations was immune from Charter review. This odd result was premised on the theory that the parliamentary privileges that are needed to secure the orderly functioning of a legislative assembly, and which include the power to exclude strangers, are part of the "Constitution of Canada". If that was so, then it followed (according to the majority) that the Charter did not apply, because "one part of the Constitution cannot be abrogated or diminished by another".[8]

The reasoning in *New Brunswick Broadcasting* is open to criticism.

---

[4]Forsey, Freedom and Order (1974), 222.

[5]*New Brunswick Broadcasting Co. v. Nova Scotia*, [1993] 1 S.C.R. 319.

[6]On this issue, only Lamer C.J., who concurred in the result, dissented, holding that "legislature" included only the body capable of enacting laws, and not its component parts.

[7]McLachlin J. wrote the majority opinion, with the concurrence of La Forest, L'Heureux-Dubé, Gonthier and Iacobucci JJ. Lamer C.J. based his concurring opinion on the interpretation of s. 32. Sopinka J., concurring, and Cory J., dissenting, both disagreed with McLachlin J. on this issue, holding that the Charter applied to the actions of the legislative assembly in the exercise of parliamentary privilege.

[8]*New Brunswick Broadcasting Co. v. Nova Scotia*, [1993] 1 S.C.R. 319, 373; folld. in *Ont. v. Ont.* (2001), 54 O.R. (3d) 595 (C.A.) (recital of Lord's prayer as part of daily opening exercises of Ontario's Legislative Assembly immune from Charter challenge). In *Harvey v. N.B.*, [1996] 2 S.C.R. 876, McLachlin J. (with L'Heureux-Dubé J.) in a separate concurring opinion, held that the power of the New Brunswick Legislature to expel and disqualify a member guilty of a corrupt or illegal practice was a parliamentary privilege that was immune from Charter review. La Forest J., for the majority of the Court, did not decide that issue on the ground that it had not been raised by the parties (para. 20); he held that the power was a limit on s. 3 that was justified under s. 1. Lamer C.J. held that the Charter applied where the power was contained in a statute, as this one was. In *Can. v. Vaid*, [2005] 1 S.C.R. 667, para. 33, Binnie J. for the Court, while holding that no parliamentary privilege was involved in the dismissal of the Speaker of the House of Commons' chauffeur, said that it "must now be taken as settled" that "legislated" privilege was exempt from the Charter no less than "inherent" privilege.

The point has earlier been made that there was insufficient basis to add parliamentary privilege to the definition of the Constitution of Canada, considering that that definition is expressed solely in terms of written instruments and appears (despite the use of the word "includes") to be exhaustive.[9] But the next step in the Court's reasoning is even harder to justify. The fact that a power is conferred by the Constitution of Canada does not immunize the power from the Charter of Rights.[10] On the contrary, the purpose of the Charter of Rights is to diminish the powers of the legislative and executive branches of government, including those powers that are conferred by the Constitution. This is illustrated by the application of the Charter of Rights to the legislative powers of the federal Parliament and the provincial Legislatures. All of the legislative powers of the federal Parliament and the provincial Legislatures are conferred by the Constitution of Canada, chiefly by ss. 91 and 92 of the Constitution Act, 1867. The Charter of Rights applies to these powers. Indeed, there would be no point in applying the Charter to the Parliament and the Legislatures if powers conferred by other parts of the Constitution were exempt from its constraints.

In my opinion, the decision that the legislative assembly of Nova Scotia came within the word "legislature" in s. 32 of the Charter of Rights entailed the legal conclusion that all of the assembly's powers, including those conferred by the Constitution, were subject to the Charter of Rights. As a matter of policy too, it is surely unacceptable that every exercise of parliamentary-privilege powers by a legislative assembly should be exempt from Charter review. Could a legislative assembly choose to exclude all members of the public from its deliberations? Could it refuse to allow members of the opposition to speak, or allow them to speak but refuse to record their speeches? These questions answer themselves. This is not to say that a legislative assembly may never act in derogation of a guaranteed right; it is only to say that a rule adopted by a legislative assembly in derogation of a Charter right would have to be justified as a reasonable limit under s. 1. As Sopinka and Cory JJ. pointed out in their opinions in the *New Brunswick Broadcasting* case,[11] restrictions on the use of television cameras in or-

---

[9]Chapter 1, Sources under heading § 1:4, "Constitution of Canada".

[10]In *New Brunswick Broadcasting Co. v. Nova Scotia*, [1993] 1 S.C.R. 319, at 373, McLachlin J. said, that "one part of the Constitution cannot be abrogated or diminished by another part of the Constitution". The words "or diminished" are what is wrong in this statement. They reflect a misunderstanding of *Re Bill 30* (Ontario Separate School Funding), [1987] 1 S.C.R. 1148, the case she cites as authority. That case decided that a power to distinguish between school supporters on the basis of religion was implicit in s. 93 of the Constitution Act, 1867, which expressly authorized the establishment of denominational schools, and was not an infringement of s. 15 of the Charter of Rights. The case did not decide that the provincial power over education was in any other respect undiminished by the Charter of Rights. On the contrary, discrimination on any basis other than religion (such as race or sex) would be unconstitutional, and infringements of Charter rights other than those in s. 15 would also be unconstitutional.

[11]*New Brunswick Broadcasting Co. v. Nova Scotia*, [1993] 1 S.C.R. 319, 397 per Sopinka J. concurring separately, 413-414 per Cory J. dissenting.

der to maintain order and decorum in the legislative assembly would be readily upheld by the courts under s. 1.[12]

To what extent is legislative *silence* subject to Charter review? In *Vriend v. Alberta* (1998),[13] the plaintiff, who alleged that he had been dismissed from his employment because he was a gay man, challenged the Alberta human rights statute under s. 15 of the Charter. The constitutional defect, he argued, was that the statute failed to prohibit discrimination in employment on the ground of sexual orientation. The government of Alberta argued in response that the Legislature had chosen not to deal with the issue, and the Charter did not apply to a failure by the Legislature to act. This argument was accepted by one judge in the Alberta Court of Appeal, who said: "When they choose silence provincial legislatures need not march to the Charter drum. In a constitutional sense they need not march at all."[14] In the Supreme Court of Canada, Cory J., speaking for the entire Court on this issue, pointed out that the Alberta Legislature had acted in the sense that it had enacted a prohibition on discrimination in employment that covered discrimination based on race, sex, religion, disability, national origin, marital status and other grounds. Having gone so far, the question was whether it was open to the Legislature to deny to LGBTQ people the same protections that had been granted to other groups who suffered discrimination. Cory J. held that this was a denial of equal benefit of the law, and upheld the Charter challenge. If Alberta had had no human rights statute at all, or perhaps one that dealt only with discrimination on the basis of age (for example), then the Charter challenge would have failed at the threshold, because there would be no statute or other governmental act to which the Charter could apply. As a general proposition, the Charter does not impose positive duties to act on legislative bodies or governments.[15] But, having enacted a relatively comprehensive statute providing redress for acts of discrimination, the Legislature subjected itself to the Charter, including the obligation to cover everyone who, under s. 15, had a constitutional right to be included.[16]

To what extent is a legislative *exclusion* subject to Charter review? In

---

[12]The Court has since partly mitigated the impact of its conclusion that the powers protected by parliamentary privilege are exempt from Charter review. In *Chagnon v. Syndicat de la fonction publique et parapublique du Québec*, [2018] 2 S.C.R. 687, Karakatsanis J., writing for the majority of the Court, said that the necessity test that is applied in determining the scope of parliamentary privilege is "stringent" because "parliamentary privilege has the potential to shield parliamentary decision-making from judicial oversight, including for Charter compliance" (para. 42); see also paras. 25, 28, 56. Côté and Brown JJ., dissenting jointly, criticized this aspect of Karakatsanis J.'s opinion, arguing that it improperly "subordinates parliamentary privileges to the Charter" (para. 147).

[13]*Vriend v. Alberta*, [1998] 1 S.C.R. 493.

[14]*Vriend v. Alta.* (1996), 132 D.L.R. (4th) 595, 605 (Alta. C.A.) per McClung J.A.

[15]In some contexts, including s. 23 (minority educational language rights), there are positive duties imposed on legislatures: [1998] 1 S.C.R. 493, paras. 60-64, where Cory J. reviews this issue.

[16]Judicial review of under-inclusive statutes is discussed in ch. 40, Enforcement of

Dunmore v. Ontario (2001),[17] a challenge was brought to the exclusion of agricultural workers from Ontario's labour relations statute. The majority of the Supreme Court of Canada rejected the equality guarantee of s. 15 as the basis for the challenge without reasons, but no doubt because employment status is not an analogous ground that is protected by s. 15. As for freedom of association under s. 2(d), while the statutory regime would obviously be much preferable for the workers, the difficulty was that previous decisions made clear that the constitutional freedom to associate did not require legislation, and the mere exclusion from the statutory regime did not in any way impair the agricultural workers' freedom to organize at common law. The workers were in no different situation than if the labour relations statute had never been enacted. This logic prevailed with Major J., who dissented, but did not prevail with a majority of the Court. Speaking for the majority, Bastarache J. held that this was not a case where "no legislation had been enacted in the first place".[18] The enactment of the labour relations statute provided the "minimum of state action" that was required for the invocation of the Charter.[19] Having gone this far, the Legislature was under a positive duty to extend the protections of labour relations law to those employee groups who could not otherwise successfully organize. The exclusion of the agricultural workers was a breach of s. 2(d) and the provision excluding them was severed from the statute.

§ 37:8 Statutory authority

Because s. 32 makes the Charter of Rights applicable to the federal Parliament and the provincial Legislatures, the Parliament and Legislatures have lost the power to enact laws that are inconsistent with the Charter of Rights. It follows that any body exercising statutory authority, for example, the Governor in Council or Lieutenant Governor in Council, ministers, officials, municipalities, administrative tribunals and police officers, is also bound by the Charter.

Action taken under statutory authority is valid only if it is within the scope of that authority. Since neither Parliament nor a Legislature can itself pass a law in breach of the Charter, neither body can authorize action which would be in breach of the Charter. Thus, the limitations on statutory authority which are imposed by the Charter will flow down the chain of statutory authority and apply to regulations, by-laws, orders, decisions and all other action (whether legislative, administrative or judicial) which depends for its validity on statutory authority. That is the way in which limitations on statutory authority imposed by ss. 91 and 92 of the Constitution Act, 1867 (and other distribution-of-powers rules) work. There is no reason to treat limitations on statutory authority imposed by the Charter any differently.

Rights, under headings § 40:5, "Severance", and § 40:6, "Reading in", and ch. 55, Equality, under heading § 55:16, "Discrimination".

[17] *Dunmore v. Ontario*, [2001] 3 S.C.R. 1016.

[18] *Dunmore v. Ontario*, [2001] 3 S.C.R. 1016, para. 29.

[19] *Dunmore v. Ontario*, [2001] 3 S.C.R. 1016, para. 28.

The distinctive characteristic of action taken under statutory authority is that it involves a power of compulsion that is not possessed by a private individual or organization. It is that power of compulsion that must conform to the Charter. A private corporation is a creature of statute in the sense that its existence and powers depend upon the statute that authorized its incorporation. But a private corporation is empowered to exercise only the same proprietary and contractual powers that are available to a natural person. It does not possess the coercive power of governance to which the Charter applies. This is the reason why the Supreme Court of Canada has held that the mandatory retirement policies of a university and a hospital are not reviewable under the Charter. Although the university and the hospital were both established and empowered by statute, the bodies were not possessed of powers any larger than those of a natural person.[1]

Where the Parliament or a Legislature has delegated a power of compulsion to a body or person, then the Charter will apply to the delegate. For example, the Charter has been held to apply to a municipal by-law, made under statutory authority, that purported to prohibit postering on municipal public property.[2] The Charter has been held to apply to an arbitrator awarding a remedy for an unjust dismissal; the arbitrator ordered the employer to provide the dismissed employee with a letter of reference—a requirement that was possible because the arbitrator was exercising powers conferred by statute.[3] Had the arbitrator's authority simply come from the consent of the parties, no exercise of statutory power would have been involved, and the Charter would not have applied. The Charter has been held applicable to the rules of the Law Society of Alberta, which purported to restrict the entry

---

[Section 37:8]

[1]*McKinney v. U. of Guelph*, [1990] 3 S.C.R. 229; *Stoffman v. Vancouver General Hospital*, [1990] 3 S.C.R. 483. If the bodies had been controlled by government, they would have been covered by the Charter by virtue of s. 32's reference to "government". That was the case in *Douglas/Kwantlen Faculty Assn. v. Douglas College*, [1990] 3 S.C.R. 570 and *Lavigne v. OPSEU*, [1991] 2 S.C.R. 211, where community colleges were held to be subject to the Charter.

[2]*Ramsden v. Peterborough*, [1993] 2 S.C.R. 1084. All of the powers of a municipality are subject to the Charter: *Godbout v. Longueuil*, [1997] 3 S.C.R. 844, paras. 50-51, 118 (Charter applicable to resolution of council requiring contracts with employees to include condition of residence within municipality). In *Greater Vancouver Transportation Authority v. Can. Federation of Students*, [2009] 2 S.C.R. 295, paras. 17-24, the Court held correctly that the Charter applied to the "policy" (which the Court held was a binding rule of general application made under statutory authority) of a local transit authority banning political messages on the sides of its buses. However, the Court put the holding on the ground that the transit authority was controlled by a local government and therefore came within "government" in s. 32. With respect, the application of the Charter in that case followed from the transit authority's statutory power to regulate advertising on buses. The word "government" in s. 32 is limited to the senior (federal and provincial) levels of government: § 37:10, "Government".

[3]*Slaight Communications v. Davidson*, [1989] 1 S.C.R. 1038. Folld. in *Blencoe v. B.C.*, [2000] 2 S.C.R. 307 (Charter applies to Human Rights Commission with adjudicatory functions because it exercises statutory authority).

of out-of-province law firms to the legal profession in Alberta—something that required the exercise of statutory authority.[4] The rules of an organization that are binding on the members simply by virtue of their consent are not subject to the Charter.[5] The Charter has also been held applicable to an automobile insurance policy that excluded common-law spouses from spousal accident benefits; although both the insurer and the insured were private parties, the terms of the policy were stipulated by statute.[6] A private person making a citizen's arrest under statutory authority is subject to the Charter.[7]

The foregoing examples illustrate that bodies or persons possessing statutory authority are often independent of the federal government or the provincial government. The Charter applies to the exercise of statutory authority regardless of whether the actor is part of the government or is controlled by the government. It is the exertion of a power of compulsion granted by statute that causes the Charter to apply. As we shall see in the next section of this chapter, the Charter also applies to the action of the federal and provincial governments, including all bodies or persons controlled by a government, even if the governmental action was not based on statutory authority. But, outside the sphere of government, the Charter will apply only to persons or bodies exercising statutory authority.

In my view, it is the exercise of a power of compulsion that makes the Charter applicable to bodies exercising statutory authority. It must however be acknowledged that the courts have occasionally deviated from this position. In one case (*Eldridge*), it was held that the Charter was applicable despite the absence of any power of compulsion, and in two other cases (*Bhindi* and *Lavigne*) it was held that the Charter was inapplicable despite the presence of a power of compulsion. These cases are described in the text that follows, where it is argued that they are wrongly decided. Certainly, these cases offer no predictable or principled basis for the application of the Charter.

In *Eldridge v. British Columbia* (1997),[8] one issue was whether a hospital was bound by the Charter. The hospital did not provide sign-language interpretation for deaf persons seeking medical services, an

---

[4]*Black v. Law Society of Alta.*, [1989] 1 S.C.R. 591.

[5]*Tomen v. FWTAO* (1989), 70 O.R. (2d) 48 (C.A.).

[6]*Miron v. Trudel*, [1995] 2 S.C.R. 418.

[7]*R. v. Lerke* (1986), 25 D.L.R. (4th) 403 (Alta. C.A.). Contra, *R. v. Skeir* (2005), 253 D.L.R. (4th) 221 (N.S. C.A.). While *Lerke* seems right in principle, in favour of *Skeir* there is the practical point (not relied on in the decision) that a private person who makes a citizen's arrest is unlikely to be aware of the Charter obligations under s. 10 of the Charter to inform the arrested person of the reasons for the arrest and of his right to counsel. It is unrealistic to impose those obligations. On the other hand, security guards with powers of arrest no greater than those of a private citizen could be trained to comply with the Charter. Compare *R. v. Buhay*, [2003] 1 S.C.R. 631 (security guards treated as private actors); *R. v. Dell* (2005), 256 D.L.R. (4th) 271 (Alta. C.A.) (bouncer in bar a private actor).

[8]*Eldridge v. British Columbia*, [1997] 3 S.C.R. 624. La Forest J. wrote the opinion of the Court.

omission that would be a breach of s. 15 (the equality guarantee) if it were made by an entity that was bound by the Charter. In an earlier case, *Stoffman v. Vancouver General Hospital* (1990),[9] the Supreme Court of Canada had held that the Charter did not apply to the mandatory retirement policy of a hospital that required its doctors to give up their admitting privileges when they reached the age of 65. This case seemed to settle the question. Although established and empowered by statute, and undeniably performing a public service, the hospital did not exercise any powers of compulsion in providing medical services (and it was not controlled by government). Therefore, the hospital was not bound by the Charter. But in *Eldridge*, La Forest J. for a unanimous Supreme Court of Canada pointed to British Columbia's Hospital Services Act, which funded the provision of hospital services, and held that the hospital was "implementing a specific government policy or program."[10] This case was different from *Stoffman*, he said, because *Stoffman* only decided that the Charter did not apply to the "day-to-day operations" of the hospitals; *Stoffman* did not decide what the position was when a hospital was implementing a specific government policy or program.[11] With respect, this distinction seems weak, since the only reason for the day-to-day operations of the hospital, and in particular for the employment of doctors, was to perform the medical services that the Court in *Eldridge* characterizes as the implementation of a specific government policy or program. In any case, it seems implausible to characterize the provision of medical services by hospitals as an exercise of statutory authority, considering that the hospitals did not need any power conferred by statute to provide a full range of medical services—they were doing so long before funding under the hospital insurance program started in 1958. It is submitted that *Eldridge* is inconsistent with *Stoffman*, and the absence of statutory compulsion should have led to the conclusion that the Charter did not apply in *Eldridge*.[12]

In *Re Bhindi* (1986),[13] the British Columbia Court of Appeal had to consider whether a "closed-shop" provision in a collective agreement violated the guarantee of freedom of association in the Charter of Rights. A closed shop is a workplace in which the employer has agreed to hire only members of the union. The majority of the Court, pointing out that the collective agreement was between a private employer and the union

---

[9] *Stoffman v. Vancouver General Hospital*, [1990] 3 S.C.R. 483.

[10] *Eldridge v. British Columbia*, [1997] 3 S.C.R. 624, para. 43.

[11] *Eldridge v. British Columbia*, [1997] 3 S.C.R. 624, para. 51.

[12] The understandable sympathy for the plight of the deaf hospital patients may have driven the decision. The Court did not discuss the possible application of the Human Rights Act, S.B.C. 1984, c. 22, s. 2, which prohibits discrimination on the basis of physical or mental disability (among other grounds) in the provision of any service customarily available to the public. This provision, which has its counterpart in the human rights codes of the other provinces and the federal jurisdiction, applies to private as well as public entities.

[13] *Re Bhindi* (1986), 29 D.L.R. (4th) 47 (B.C.C.A.). The majority opinion was written by Nemetz C.J. with the agreement of Hinkson and Craig JJ.A. Dissenting opinions were written by Anderson and Hutcheon JJ.A.

of its employees, held that the collective agreement was a private contract to which the Charter did not apply. The fallacy in this ruling, as the two dissenting judges pointed out, is that the closed-shop provision was not only expressly authorized by the applicable labour legislation, it would have been ineffective without the statutory authority. At common law, a contract is binding by virtue of the consent of the parties. A collective agreement that forces unwilling employees to join the union could not be effective through the common law of contract. In all jurisdictions, collective agreements are authorized by statute so that their terms and conditions will be binding on all employees in the bargaining unit, including those who do not agree with the terms and conditions. The terms and conditions of a collective agreement thus have a coercive force that goes beyond what could be achieved in a common law (or civil law) contract. Therefore, the terms and conditions of a collective agreement should be subject to the Charter.

In *Lavigne v. OPSEU* (1991),[14] the Supreme Court of Canada had to consider whether an "agency-shop" provision in a collective agreement violated the guarantees of freedom of expression and association in the Charter of Rights. An agency shop is a workplace in which all employees are not required to join the union (as is the case in a closed shop or a union shop), but all employees are required to pay dues to the union. The Supreme Court of Canada held that the Charter applied, because the employer was an agent of the provincial government, which made the collective agreement a governmental act.[15] But the Court seemed to be unanimous that, if the employer had not been a part of government, then the collective agreement would be a private contract to which the Charter would not have applied. La Forest J. for the majority, after referring to *Bhindi* with approval, said that the fact that the provision for the compulsory payment of dues was authorized (but not required) by statute did not make the Charter applicable. He said that the "parties to collective agreement negotiations would be free to agree to [the agency shop provision] independently of any legislative 'permission' ".[16] With respect, La Forest J. is correct that the Charter should not become applicable by virtue of permissive statutory authority which grants power no greater than would be possessed by a natural person anyway. But that is not this case. Without statutory authority, an obligation to pay union dues could be created only by the agreement of the employee. In my opinion, it is clear that the dissident employee was being subjected

[14] *Lavigne v. OPSEU*, [1991] 2 S.C.R. 211. On the status of the collective agreement, the majority opinion of La Forest J. attracted the agreement of Sopinka, Gonthier, Cory and McLachlin JJ. Wilson J.'s concurring opinion was agreed with by L'Heureux-Dubé J.

[15] See text accompanying § 37:10 note 4, below.

[16] *Lavigne v. OPSEU*, [1991] 2 S.C.R. 211, 310. Wilson J. was less categorical, saying (at p. 247) that "in a great many instances, 'permissive legislation' does not connote governmental approval of what is permitted but connotes at most governmental acquiescence in it". With respect, the issue is not whether governmental approval or governmental acquiescence (whatever the difference may be) has been given, but whether a statutory power of compulsion has been delegated by the Legislature and exercised by the Legislature's delegates, and the answer to that question is surely yes.

to a statutory power of compulsion as surely as if the statute had directly ordered him to pay the dues.

It was not necessary for the Court in *Lavigne* to rule on the status of collective agreements in the private sector. Because the government was a party to the collective agreement, the Charter applied.[17] The discussion of statutory authority was therefore obiter. I hope that when the issue has to be decided, the Court will reconsider its approval of *Bhindi* and its comments on statutory authority. As the cases stand at present, a Legislature that is itself powerless to abridge freedom of association (or any other Charter right) has the mysterious capacity to grant to employers and unions (or anyone else outside of government) the power to abridge the right. That cannot be good law.

§ 37:9 Amending procedures

The extent to which s. 32 of the Charter makes the Charter binding on the process of constitutional amendment has been discussed in the earlier chapter on Amendment.[1] Briefly, the position is that those amending procedures that require the concurrence of several legislative houses (under ss. 38, 41, 43) are not constrained by the Charter. However, the limited powers of amendment that are possessed by the federal Parliament alone (under s. 44) and by each provincial Legislature alone (under s. 45) are constrained by the Charter.

§ 37:10 Government

The application of the Charter to all action taken under statutory authority follows simply from the references in s. 32 to "Parliament" and "legislature". What is added by the references to the "government" of Canada and of each province?[1] To the extent that government acts under statutory authority, the reference to government adds nothing. But government sometimes acts under prerogative powers, which are common law powers possessed only by government, for example, when government awards honours, issues passports or conducts foreign affairs. Government also acts under common law powers that are possessed by everyone, for example, when government enters into contracts, or buys

---

[17]This was also the case in *Douglas/Kwantlen Faculty Assn. v. Douglas College*, [1990] 3 S.C.R. 570, where the Charter was held applicable to a collective agreement. See also *Health Services and Support—Facilities Subsector Bargaining Assn. v. B.C.*, [2007] 2S.C.R. 391, para. 88 per McLachlin C.J. and LeBel J. for majority, obiter (private employer, as party to collective agreement, not bound by Charter).

[Section 37:9]

[1]Chapter 4, Amendment, under heading § 4:7, "Charter of Rights".

[Section 37:10]

[1]The references to government in s. 32 are expressly confined to the governments of Canada and the provinces. Therefore, actions by foreign governments cannot be breaches of the Charter: § 37:14, "Extraterritorial application". The municipal level of government is not "government" within s. 32, but the Charter applies to municipal by-laws (and other kinds of binding municipal rules) by virtue of the fact that the municipality acts under statutory authority: § 37:8 note 2, above.

or sells property. The references in s. 32 to "government" will make the Charter applicable to governmental action taken under both kinds of common law powers. The Supreme Court of Canada has held that the Charter applies to expression that takes place on government-owned property, such as airports and streets.[2] The Court has also held that the Charter applies to a cabinet decision taken under the prerogative to allow the United States to test its cruise missile in Canada.[3] The Court has also applied the Charter to the making by a Crown agent of a contract of employment with its employees.[4] In the last case, La Forest J. said: "To permit government to pursue policies violating Charter rights by means of contracts or agreements with other persons or bodies cannot be tolerated".[5]

What is included in the term "government"? Obviously, it includes action taken by the Governor General in Council or the Lieutenant Governor in Council, by the cabinet, by individual ministers and by public servants within the departments of government. Also included are those Crown corporations and public agencies that are outside the formal departmental structure, but which, by virtue of a substantial degree of ministerial control, are deemed to be "agents" of the Crown.[6] Thus, the Supreme Court of Canada has held[7] that a community college in British Columbia was subject to the Charter, because it was subject to a substantial degree of government control.[8] All the members of the governing board were appointed by the Lieutenant Governor in Council, and held office at pleasure. As well, the Minister of Education had power to issue directives to the college. In other cases involving a university and a hospital, the Court has held that both institutions were sufficiently independent of government that they were not subject to the Charter.[9]

The control test looks to an *institutional* or *structural* link with govern-

---

[2]Chapter 43, Expression, under heading § 43:30, "Access to public property".

[3]*Operation Dismantle v. The Queen*, [1985] 1 S.C.R. 441. The claim that "life, liberty and security of the person" had been placed at risk was rejected.

[4]*Douglas/Kwantlen Faculty Assn. v. Douglas College*, [1990] 3 S.C.R. 570, 585 (collective agreement contained provision for mandatory retirement); *Lavigne v. OPSEU*, [1991] 2 S.C.R. 211, 313 (collective agreement required employees to pay union dues, even if they were not union members).

[5]*Douglas/Kwantlen Faculty Assn. v. Douglas College*, [1990] 3 S.C.R. 570. The same passage is in both cases. There was in fact statutory authority for the collective agreement in both cases, but the Court placed its decision on the presence of a government party to the agreement, and clearly intended to lay down a rule governing common law contracts.

[6]See ch. 10, The Crown, under heading §§ 10:2 to 10:4, "Crown agency".

[7]*Douglas/Kwantlen Faculty Assn. v. Douglas College*, [1990] 3 S.C.R. 570; folld. in *Lavigne v. OPSEU*, [1991] 2 S.C.R. 211 (Council of Regents, governing Ontario's community colleges, controlled by Minister of Education).

[8]The college was also expressly stipulated by statute to be an agent of the Crown, but the Court did not rely on this fact. The rule for Crown-agent status is that an express stipulation will create the status even if the body so stipulated is not controlled by government: ch. 10, The Crown, under heading § 10:4, "Agent by statute". It is submitted that the same rule should apply to the application of the Charter as well.

[9]*McKinney v. U. of Guelph*, [1990] 3 S.C.R. 229; *Stoffman v. Vancouver General*

ment to determine whether a public body is covered by the Charter. This is a principled approach to the issue, and one that makes use of the jurisprudence defining the Crown and Crown agents. The majority of the Court has wisely rejected *a functional* link with government as the test for the coverage of the Charter.[10] Thus, it was irrelevant that the university and the hospital were each performing a "public service", as long as they were performing it independently of government.[11] And it would be irrelevant that a public body was performing a "private" function if it was performing it under the control of government.[12] There is no principled way to classify the functions of public bodies into "governmental" (or "public") and "commercial" (or "private") categories. The only useful question is whether government has assumed control of the function. The existence of control is the only sure guide to whether the function is one of government to which the Charter should apply.

It must be emphasized that the scope of the term "government" is important only if the body alleged to have breached the Charter was not relying on a statutory power. If the body alleged to have breached the Charter was relying on a statutory power, the Charter will apply by virtue of that fact,[13] and regardless of whether or not the body is within the term "government".

§ 37:11 Courts

Does the Charter apply to the courts? The Supreme Court of Canada has answered this question yes and no.

The no answer came in *Retail, Wholesale and Department Store Union v. Dolphin Delivery* (1986).[1] The question in that case was whether Dolphin Delivery, a courier company, could obtain an injunction to restrain a union from picketing Dolphin Delivery's premises. The union represented the employees of another courier company against whom it

---

Hospital, [1990] 3 S.C.R. 483.

[10]In *McKinney v. U. of Guelph*, [1990] 3 S.C.R. 229, and *Stoffman v. Vancouver General Hospital*, [1990] 3 S.C.R. 483, Wilson J. dissented on the issue of the application of the Charter. In her view, the Court ought to apply three tests (1) a "control" test, (2) a "governmental functions" test, and (3) a "government entity" test; and none of the three tests were to be determinative. Fortunately, the majority rejected this approach, which would have been a recipe for unbridled judicial discretion.

[11]*McKinney v. U. of Guelph*, [1990] 3 S.C.R. 229, 269; *Stoffman v. Vancouver General Hospital*, [1990] 3 S.C.R. 483, 511. But see *Eldridge v. B.C.*, [1997] 3 S.C.R. 624, holding that a hospital was subject to the Charter, because it was "implementing a specific government policy or program".

[12]*Lavigne v. OPSEU*, [1991] 2 S.C.R. 211, 314 (". . . government activities which are in form 'commercial' or 'private' transactions are in reality expressions of government policy . . .").

[13]§ 37:7, "Parliament or Legislature".

[Section 37:11]

[1]*RWDSU* v. Dolphin Delivery, [1986] 2 S.C.R. 573. The majority opinion was written by McIntyre J., with the agreement of Dickson C.J., Estey, Chouinard and Le Dain JJ. Concurring opinions were written by Beetz and Wilson JJ., but they both agreed with McIntyre J. on the applicability of the Charter.

was on strike. Since Dolphin Delivery was not part of that dispute, the picketing of Dolphin Delivery's premises would be "secondary picketing". The courts in British Columbia held that the picketing would constitute the common law tort of inducing a breach of contract, and they granted an injunction to prevent the picketing. In the Supreme Court of Canada, the union argued that the injunction should be set aside, because it abridged the Charter guarantee of freedom of expression. The Court rejected the argument on the ground that the Charter had no application to the order of a court. McIntyre J., speaking for a unanimous Court on this issue, held that the word "government" in s. 32 meant only the executive branch of government, and did not include the judicial branch.[2] A court order was not governmental action, and therefore the injunction issued by the Supreme Court of British Columbia was not subject to the Charter.

The yes answer came in *R. v. Rahey* (1987).[3] In that case, the Supreme Court of Canada had to determine whether a criminal court had denied to a defendant the s. 11(b) right to be tried within a reasonable time. The trial judge had delayed unreasonably in reaching a decision on the application by the defendant, made at the close of the Crown's case, for a directed verdict of acquittal. The trial judge had adjourned the application 19 times and taken 11 months to reach his decision; his decision was to deny the application. The Supreme Court of Canada held that the delay was a breach of s. 11(b) of the Charter and the Court ordered a stay of the proceedings. In this case, the action that was held to be a breach of the Charter was the action of a court, and the remedy was directed to a court. In the Supreme Court of Canada, of the four judges who wrote opinions, only La Forest J. adverted to this point, saying: "it seems obvious to me that the courts, as custodians of the principles enshrined in the Charter, must themselves be subject to Charter scrutiny in the administration of their duties".[4] This statement is, of course, contradictory of the ruling in *Dolphin Delivery*, given only five months earlier, that the Charter does not apply to the courts. Yet *Dolphin Delivery* was not referred to by La Forest J. or by any of the other judges who wrote opinions.

The yes answer was confirmed in *British Columbia Government Employees' Union v. British Columbia* (1988).[5] In that case, a union, on lawful strike, had formed picket lines outside the courts in British Columbia, where some of the union members worked. The Chief Justice of

[2]*RWDSU* v. Dolphin Delivery, [1986] 2 S.C.R. 573, 598-600.

[3]*R. v. Rahey*, [1987] 1 S.C.R. 588. Four concurring opinions were written: by Lamer J. (with Dickson C.J.), Wilson J. (with Estey J.), Le Dain J. (with Beetz J.) and La Forest J. (with McIntyre J.).

[4]*R. v. Rahey*, [1987] 1 S.C.R. 588, 633.

[5]*BCGEU v. B.C.*, [1988] 2 S.C.R. 214. Dickson C.J. wrote the majority opinion, with the agreement of Lamer, Wilson, La Forest and L'Heureux-Dubé JJ. McIntyre J. wrote a concurring opinion agreeing with Dickson C.J. that the Charter applied, but disagreeing with Dickson C.J.'s opinion that there had been a violation of freedom of expression.

British Columbia, discovering the picketers outside the courthouse on his way to work, immediately, on his own motion and without notice to the union, issued an injunction prohibiting the picketing of the courts. The union, on learning of the injunction, applied to have it set aside on the ground that it abridged the s. 2(b) right to freedom of expression. The Supreme Court of Canada refused to set aside the injunction. The majority of the Court held that, although the injunction did limit freedom of expression, it was justified under s. 1. Although the Charter issue was thus resolved in favour of the injunction, Dickson C.J. for a unanimous Court (on this issue), did hold that a court order was subject to Charter review. He referred to *Dolphin Delivery*, distinguishing it on the basis that the injunction in that case was issued to resolve "a purely private dispute".[6] In this case, "the court is acting on its own motion and not at the instance of any private party", and the court's motivation "is entirely 'public' in nature, rather than 'private' ".[7]

The *Rahey* and *BCGEU* decisions have, in effect, repudiated McIntyre J.'s ruling in *Dolphin Delivery* that the word "government" in s. 32 excludes the courts. Obviously, in the circumstances of those two cases, "government" did include the courts. Also, many of the Charter rights contemplate that the courts are bound by the Charter. Nearly all of the rights guaranteed to criminal defendants by s. 11 entail action by courts: holding a trial within a reasonable time (s. 11(b)), not compelling the defendant to testify (s. 11(c)), respecting the presumption of innocence and providing a fair and public trial (s. 11(d)), granting reasonable bail (s. 11(e)) and so on. The same is true of the s. 12 right not to be subjected to cruel and unusual treatment or punishment, the s. 13 right against self-incrimination, and the s. 14 right to an interpreter. These provisions supply a context in which it is reasonable to interpret the word "government" in s. 32 as including the judicial branch. The references in s. 32 to "Parliament" and "Legislature" could also be regarded as catching court action, because courts are established (or continued) by statute, and their powers to grant injunctions and make other orders are granted (or continued) by statute. Since other statutory tribunals have to comply with the Charter,[8] the courts should have to do so too.

If it is impossible to reconcile the definition of "government" in *Dolphin Delivery* with the decisions in *Rahey* and *BCGEU*, is it still possible to accommodate the actual decision in *Dolphin Delivery* with the two later cases? There are two elements of the court order in *Dolphin Delivery* that make it distinctive: (1) the court order resolved a dispute between two private parties, and (2) the court order was based upon the common law. No government was involved in the dispute, and no statute applied to the dispute. Therefore, there was no governmental action that could

[6]*BCGEU v. B.C.*, [1988] 2 S.C.R. 214, 243.

[7]*BCGEU v. B.C.*, [1988] 2 S.C.R. 214, 244. Accord, *UNA v. Alta.*, [1992] 1 S.C.R. 901, 930.

[8]*Slaight Communications v. Davidson*, [1989] 1 S.C.R. 1038 (Charter applies to statutory arbitrator exercising judicial functions); *Blencoe v. B.C.*, [2000] 2 S.C.R. 307 (Charter applies to Human Rights Commission exercising judicial functions).

make the Charter applicable, at least up to the point of the making of the court order (the issue of the injunction). The question then becomes: does the making of the court order, supported as it is by "the full panoply of state power", supply the requisite element of governmental action?[9] The ratio decidendi of *Dolphin Delivery* must be that a court order, when issued as a resolution of a dispute between private parties, and when based on the common law, is not governmental action to which the Charter applies.[10] And the reason for the decision is that a contrary decision would have the effect of applying the Charter to the relationships of private parties that s. 32 intends to exclude from Charter coverage,[11] and that ought in principle to be excluded from Charter coverage.[12] Where, however, a court order is issued on the court's own motion for a public purpose (as in *BCGEU*), or in a proceeding to which government is a party (as in any criminal case, such as *Rahey*), or in a purely private proceeding that is governed by statute law, then the Charter will apply to the court order.

§ 37:12 Common law

Does the Charter apply to the common law? This question is closely related to the question whether the Charter applies to the courts, since the courts "make" the common law. It is not surprising, therefore, that in the *Dolphin Delivery* case (1986)[1] the Supreme Court of Canada answered the question no: the Charter does not apply to the common

[9] *Shelley v. Kraemer* (1948), 334 U.S. 1, 19 (where the quotation comes from) answers the question yes, holding that an injunction to enforce a racially-discriminatory restrictive covenant was "state action" to which the Bill of Rights applied. The decision has been much criticized: e.g., in the famous article by H. Wechsler, "Toward Neutral Principles of Constitutional Law" (1959) 73 Harv. L. Rev. 1, 29-31. L.H. Tribe, American Constitutional Law (Foundation Press, New York, 2nd ed., 1988), 1697, joins the criticism, commenting that "such reasoning, consistently applied, would require individuals to conform their private agreements to constitutional standards whenever, as almost always, the individuals might later seek the security of potential judicial enforcement".

[10] In *Young v. Young*, [1993] 4 S.C.R. 3, L'Heureux-Dubé J. (with La Forest and Gonthier JJ.) held that the Charter did not apply to a court order, resolving a dispute between two private parties, granting custody of children to their mother and access to their father (there were restrictions on access relating to religion that were argued to be in breach of s. 2(a)). However, the majority of the Court left open the question whether the Charter applied or not. They did not say why they did not agree with L'Heureux-Dubé J., but it may have been because the court order could be traced to a power in the Divorce Act.

[11] This is explicit in McIntyre J.'s opinion: *RWDSU v. Dolphin Delivery*, [1986] 2 S.C.R. 573, 600 ("To regard a court order as an element of governmental intervention necessary to invoke the Charter would, it seems to me, widen the scope of Charter application to virtually all private litigation"). This is Tribe's point as well, L.H. Tribe, *American Constitutional Law* (Foundation Press, New York, 2nd ed., 1988), 1697.

[12] The rationale for the exclusion of private action is examined in § 37:13, "Private action".

[Section 37:12]

[1] *RWDSU v. Dolphin Delivery*, [1986] 2 S.C.R. 573.

law, or at least those rules of the common law that regulate relationships between private parties.

In *Dolphin Delivery*, an injunction against picketing had been issued against a union. The basis for the injunction was a rule of the common law that secondary picketing (in the circumstances there presented) would amount to the tort of inducing a breach of contract. The union, seeking to set aside the injunction, argued that this rule of the common law was an unconstitutional abridgement of freedom of expression. McIntyre J., for a Court that was unanimous on this issue, said that the Charter had no application to such a rule: "where . . . private party 'A' sues private party 'B' relying on the common law, and where no act of government is relied upon to support the action, the Charter will not apply".[2] With this language, the Court excluded from Charter review the rules of the common law that regulate relationships between private parties.

The Supreme Court of the United States has decided this issue the other way. The leading case is *New York Times v. Sullivan* (1963).[3] In that case, it was held that the Bill of Rights' guarantees of freedom of speech and of the press applied to the common law of defamation, shielding a newspaper from tortious liability for defamatory criticism of a public official, unless the criticism was actuated by malice. In this way, the Bill of Rights modified the common law of Alabama by adding a new ingredient to the tort of defamation, namely, malice, where the defamatory statement took the form of political speech. There is an earlier American case that is on all fours with *Dolphin Delivery*. In *American Federation of Labour v. Swing* (1941),[4] the Supreme Court of the United States held that an injunction issued by a state court to restrain a union from secondary picketing was an unconstitutional violation of the guarantee of freedom of speech. The injunction was based on the common law, and the effect of the decision was to modify the common law of the state of Illinois. As the result of these decisions, in the United States, it is well settled "that common law is state action—that is, that the state 'acts' when its courts create and enforce common law rules".[5]

In Canada, the exclusion of the common law from Charter review makes it necessary to determine the source of any law that is claimed to abridge a Charter right. If the applicable law is a rule of the common law, the Charter does not apply. If, however, the law is a rule of statute law, the Charter does apply: the statute supplies the needed element of governmental action.[6] This anomaly is starkly presented by the facts of *Dolphin Delivery* itself. Because the prohibition on secondary picketing

---

[2]*RWDSU v. Dolphin Delivery*, [1986] 2 S.C.R. 573, 603.

[3]*New York Times v. Sullivan* (1963), 376 U.S. 254.

[4]*American Federation of Labour v. Swing* (1941), 312 U.S. 321.

[5]L.H. Tribe, American Constitutional Law (Foundation Press, New York, 2nd ed., 1988), 1711.

[6]§ 37:7, "Parliament or Legislature".

had not been enacted in the Canada Labour Code,[7] it remained a matter of common law, and the Charter did not apply. But in most jurisdictions, including British Columbia, the prohibition on secondary picketing has been enacted in the Labour Code; in those jurisdictions, the Charter will apply.[8] It seems odd that the applicability of the Charter should turn on the question whether the applicable law is a rule of the common law or a rule of statute law.[9]

In support of the Court's decision in *Dolphin Delivery*, it could be said that the exclusion of private action from the operation of the Charter does entail the exclusion of at least some of the common law. In an expansive sense, the common law could be said to authorize any private action that is not prohibited by a positive rule of law. On this view, if I were to refuse to permit Anglicans to enter my house, my refusal would be an act authorized by the common law, and therefore subject to Charter review. This line of reasoning would make the Charter applicable to all private action. The American courts have not allowed themselves to be beguiled down that slippery slope, but the Supreme Court of Canada is right to be concerned that the application of the Charter to any rule of the common law would later require difficult distinctions to be drawn if a zone of private action is to be shielded from Charter review.[10]

The Charter applies when a police officer exercises a common law power to search an accused person as an incident of an arrest.[11] The Charter applies when a Crown prosecutor exercises a common law power to adduce evidence of the accused's insanity, causing the accused to be acquitted but held in custody.[12] The Charter applies when the Crown acts under a prerogative power, for example, by authorizing the testing

[7] The applicable law was federal, because the union represented employees of an undertaking engaged in interprovincial transportation.

[8] Just as a common law rule becomes subject to the Charter if the rule is transformed into statute law, a convention (defined § 1:10, "Conventions") that is enacted into statutory form also becomes subject to the Charter: *Osborne v. Can.*, [1991] 2 S.C.R. 69 (restrictions on political activity by public servants held unconstitutional).

[9] B. Slattery, "The Charter's Relevance to Private Litigation: Does Dolphin Deliver?" (1987) 32 McGill L.J. 905 criticizes the exclusion of the common law from the Charter on the basis that in most Canadian jurisdictions the original reception of the common law from England, and its continuing force, depends upon a statute. He points out as well that the Civil Code of Quebec, which substitutes for the common law in that civilian jurisdiction, is a statute. With respect to the latter point, the Court has now held that the rules of the civil law governing relations between private parties are also exempt from the Charter: *Tremblay v. Daigle*, [1989] 2 S.C.R. 530, 571. This removes the intolerable anomaly of the Charter having a far more extensive application in Quebec than it has in the nine common law provinces.

[10] The rationale for the exclusion of private action is examined in § 37:13, "Private action".

[11] *R. v. Golden*, [2001] 3 S.C.R. 679.

[12] *R. v. Swain*, [1991] 1 S.C.R. 933 (the breach of the Charter was cured by the Court directly modifying the common law rule).

of American cruise missiles on Canadian soil.[13] The Charter also applies when the Crown acts under a general common law power, for example, by entering into a contract with its employees requiring mandatory retirement[14] or mandatory payment of union dues.[15] It is questionable whether one ought to describe the Charter as applicable to the common law[16] in these situations,[17] because it is the presence of the governmental actor, not the source of the actor's power, that makes the Charter applicable.

While the Charter does not apply directly to the common law (where no governmental actor is involved), the Charter does have an indirect effect on the common law. This was suggested by McIntyre J. in *Dolphin Delivery*, when he asserted that "the judiciary ought to apply and develop the principles of the common law in a manner consistent with the fundamental values enshrined in the Constitution"; and he went on to say that "in this sense, then, the Charter is far from irrelevant to private litigants whose disputes fall to be decided at common law".[18] In that case, McIntyre J. did examine the Charter argument, holding that secondary picketing "would have involved the exercise of the right of freedom of expression",[19] but that the common law's prohibition of the practice would have been justified under s. 1.[20] Although this part of the opinion appeared to be obiter, and was never connected to the dictum about developing the common law, it was clear that the majority of the Court[21] did not believe that the common law respecting secondary picketing was inconsistent with the values of the Constitution. Therefore, that case did not present the occasion for developing the common law so as to make it consistent with the values of the Constitution.

[13]*Operation Dismantle v. The Queen*, [1985] 1 S.C.R. 441.

[14]*Douglas / Kwantlen Faculty Assn. v. Douglas College*, [1990] 3 S.C.R. 570.

[15]*Lavigne v. OPSEU*, [1991] 1 S.C.R. 211; see § 37:10 notes 1 to 5 and accompanying text, above.

[16]The common law offence of contempt of court is subject to the Charter: *R. v. Kopyto* (1987), 62 O.R. (2d) 449 (C.A.); *BCGEU v. B.C.*, [1988] 2 S.C.R. 214. These were cases of criminal contempt, where the court is, in effect, a party, and the dispute is not a private one. The position is less clear with respect to civil contempt for breach of a court order, where the dispute retains a private character (although the defendant is liable to imprisonment): see *Vidéotron v. Industries Microlec*, [1992] 2 S.C.R. 1065, 1071, 1079, 1100, where the majority opinions seem to assume that the Charter would apply.

[17]McIntyre J.'s opinion in *RWDSU v. Dolphin Delivery*, [1986] 2 S.C.R. 573 was confusing, because early in the opinion (at 592) he insisted that the Charter did apply to the common law, but he later (at 599) made it clear that he meant only when "the common law is the basis of some governmental act".

[18]*RWDSU v. Dolphin Delivery*, [1986] 2 S.C.R. 573, 603.

[19]*RWDSU v. Dolphin Delivery*, [1986] 2 S.C.R. 573, 588.

[20]Beetz J. wrote a separate concurring opinion, holding that picketing was not a form of expression that was protected under s. 2(b). Wilson J. also wrote a separate concurring opinion disagreeing with McIntyre J.'s opinion on the application of the Charter.

[21]Only Wilson J. seemed to decide (the brief opinion is not perfectly clear on the point) that the prohibition on secondary picketing would have violated the Charter had the Charter been applicable.

In *Dolphin Delivery*, the injunction against the secondary picketing was premised on the finding that the picketing amounted to the tort of inducing breach of contract, and that may be why McIntyre J. rather quickly agreed that the injunction did not offend Charter values. In *Pepsi-Cola Canada Beverages v. R.W.D.S.U.* (2002),[22] a more sweeping injunction was in issue. In that case, a union that was on strike against its employer, Pepsi-Cola, set up picket lines not only around the bottling plant where the employees worked but also around a variety of secondary locations. Pepsi-Cola obtained an injunction against all the secondary picketing, and the validity of this injunction came before the Supreme Court of Canada. As in *Dolphin Delivery*, the dispute was between private parties and was regulated by the common law, so that the Charter did not apply directly. However, as in *Dolphin Delivery*, the Court held that it had the power to "develop" the common law in order to make it consistent with "Charter values".[23] The union had been picketing the retail stores that sold Pepsi-Cola products. The pickets were effective in preventing the delivery of Pepsi-Cola products to the stores, but they were peaceful and did not commit any tort, not even the tort of inducing breach of contract. Did the common law authorize an injunction against secondary picketing where no "wrongful act" (whether tort or crime) was committed? There was a line of pre-Charter cases that answered yes to that question, but the Supreme Court of Canada held that these cases were not sufficiently respectful of the Charter value of freedom of expression. The Court therefore overruled these cases and held that picketing could be enjoined only if it involved the commission of a wrongful act. Since no wrongful act was involved in the picketing of the stores, the Court discharged that part of the injunction. The union had also been picketing the homes of Pepsi-Cola management personnel, but those picket lines had not been peaceful and had been committing the tort of intimidation. Under the new wrongful act doctrine, that part of the injunction was not inconsistent with Charter values and was accordingly affirmed by the Court.

In *Dagenais v. CBC* (1994),[24] a Charter challenge was brought to an injunction (publication ban) that had been issued by a trial judge to prohibit the CBC[130] from broadcasting a television programme that could have had the effect of influencing the juries in a series of criminal trials

---

[22] *Pepsi-Cola Canada Beverages v. R.W.D.S.U.*, [2002] 1 S.C.R. 156. McLachlin C.J. and LeBel J. wrote the opinion of the unanimous Court.

[23] *Pepsi-Cola Canada Beverages v. R.W.D.S.U.*, [2002] 1 S.C.R. 156, paras. 18-20.

[24] *Dagenais v. CBC*, [1994] 3 S.C.R. 835. The majority opinion was written by Lamer C.J., with whom Sopinka, Cory, Iacobucci and Major JJ. agreed; McLachlin J. wrote a separate concurring opinion; La Forest, L'Heureux-Dubé and Gonthier JJ. each wrote dissenting opinions. All nine judges agreed that the Charter applied to the publication ban, but there was some diversity in the reasons. Lamer C.J.'s majority opinion is described in the accompanying text. McLachlin J., with whom (on this issue) La Forest J. agreed, held (at p. 944) that the Charter applied to "Court orders in the criminal sphere". Gonthier J. held (at p. 918) that the Charter applied to the common law in "criminal matters". L'Heureux-Dubé J. held (at p. 912) that the Charter applied to the common law without limitation.

of Christian brothers who were charged with abusing young boys in their care. The applicants for the injunction were the Christian brothers who had been charged with abuse, and the respondent was the CBC, which, although publicly owned, is not an agent of the Crown to which the Charter would apply. Since the legal basis for the injunction was the common law, the case was on all fours with *Dolphin Delivery* in that it was a dispute between private parties governed by the common law.[25] Lamer C.J. for the majority of the Supreme Court of Canada relied upon McIntyre J.'s dictum in *Dolphin Delivery* to hold that the common law should be developed in a manner consistent with the values of the Constitution. After reviewing the common law respecting publication bans, the Chief Justice decided that the law gave insufficient weight to the Charter value of freedom of expression. He held that it was "necessary to reformulate the common law rule . . . in a manner that reflects the principles of the Charter".[26] He proceeded to do this by formulating a more restrictive common law rule for the issue of publication bans, and by striking down the ban that was under appeal.[27]

In *Hill v. Church of Scientology* (1995),[28] a Crown attorney employed by the government of Ontario brought an action for defamation against the Church of Scientology and its lawyer, who had falsely accused the plaintiff of violating a court order. The defendants argued that their statements were protected by the Charter of Rights. They pointed to the facts that the plaintiff was employed as an agent of the Crown, that the defamatory statements related to his official duties, and that his defamation action was being funded by the Crown. The Supreme Court of Canada held that these facts did not supply the element of governmental action that was required by s. 32 of the Charter. In the context of a defamation action, the plaintiff was a private party, because the action was brought, not as part of his governmental duties, but to vindicate his personal reputation. Since it was the common law that governed the cause of action, it followed that the Charter did not apply. However, although the Charter did not apply directly to the common law of defamation, it was still necessary to consider whether the common law was con-

[25]But see *Hill v. Church of Scientology*, [1995] 2 S.C.R. 1130, para. 94 (discussed in following text), in which Cory J. said that *Dagenais* should not be regarded as a case of "purely private civil litigation", because "the court was called upon to consider the operations of the court and to determine the extent of its own jurisdiction to consider matters which were essentially public in nature". However, in *Dagenais* itself, this was not the rationale for the application of the Charter in the majority judgment of Lamer C.J. to which Cory J. agreed, or in the opinion of L'Heureux-Dubé J., although it seems closer to the opinion of McLachlin J. with which (on this issue) La Forest J. agreed and perhaps to the opinion of Gonthier J. On the division of opinion, see previous note.

[26]*Dagenais v. CBC*, [1994] 3 S.C.R. 835, 878.

[27]For discussion of this aspect of the decision, see ch. 43, Expression, under heading § 43:32, "Restrictions on reporting".

[28]*Hill v. Church of Scientology*, [1995] 2 S.C.R. 1130. Cory J. wrote the opinion of the majority. L'Heureux-Dubé J., who wrote a short concurring opinion, agreed with Cory J. on all but one issue having nothing to do with the application of the Charter. The Court was therefore unanimous on the application of the Charter.

sistent with "Charter values",[29] and to modify the common law if necessary. Cory J., who wrote for the Court on this issue, said that this exercise was not exactly the same as applying the Charter directly to the common law. The balancing of the competing values "must be more flexible than the traditional s. 1 analysis undertaken in cases involving governmental action", and the Charter claimant "should bear the onus of proving both that the common law fails to comply with Charter values and that, when these values are balanced, the common law should be modified".[30] The concern here was that a private party relying on the common law should not be put in the position of carrying the burden of defending the law against a Charter attack. (Of course, a private party relying on a statute is placed in precisely this position.) Having established these preliminaries, Cory J. went on to balance the competing interests that are accommodated by the common law of defamation, namely, the personal reputation of plaintiffs and the freedom of expression of defendants.[31] The Court concluded that "in its application to the parties in this action, the common law of defamation complies with the underlying values of the Charter and there is no need to amend or alter it".[32]

Grant v. Torstar Corp. (2009)[33] was another defamation action, this one by a private individual against the Toronto Star newspaper, which had published a story about the plaintiff that the trial court had found to be defamatory. The Supreme Court followed the *Hill* decision on the application of Charter values to the common law of defamation: "The common law, though not directly subject to Charter scrutiny where disputes between private parties are concerned, may be modified to bring it into harmony with the Charter."[34] Then, in a stunning reversal of the ruling in *Hill*, the Court held that the common law of defamation did not give adequate weight to the Charter value of freedom of expression, and should be modified to introduce a new defence of responsible communication on matters of public interest.[35]

---

[29] *Hill v. Church of Scientology*, [1995] 2 S.C.R. 1130, para. 95.

[30] *Hill v. Church of Scientology*, [1995] 2 S.C.R. 1130, paras. 97, 98; there is of course no onus of proof on issues of law (as opposed to fact) in Charter cases (or any other kinds of cases), and the statement about onus of proof is presumably intended to relate only to issues of fact.

[31] This part of the opinion is discussed in ch. 43, Expression, under heading § 43:28, "Defamation".

[32] *Hill v. Church of Scientology*, [1995] 2 S.C.R. 1130, para. 141. This is not the end of the story: *WIC Radio v. Simpson*, [2008] 2 S.C.R. 420, paras. 2, 16, 18-25 per Binnie J. for majority (obiter dicta presaging change in the common law of defamation by reason of Charter values).

[33] *Grant v. Torstar Corp.*, [2009] 3 S.C.R. 640. McLachlin C.J. wrote the opinion of the majority. Abella J. wrote a short concurring opinion. The Court was unanimous on the application of the Charter and the impact of Charter values on the law of defamation.

[34] *Grant v. Torstar Corp.*, [2009] 3 S.C.R. 640, para. 44.

[35] This part of the opinion is discussed in ch. 43, Expression, under heading § 43:28, "Defamation".

The result of these cases[36] is that the exclusion of the common law from Charter review is not particularly significant. The rule that the common law should be developed into conformity with "Charter values" means that, although the Charter does not apply directly to the common law, it does apply indirectly. Despite some differences in the way s. 1 justification is assessed, the indirect application is much the same in its effect as the direct application. The Charter applies directly to statute law, of course, and no recourse to Charter values is necessary. However, the Supreme Court of Canada has also rejected the idea that statutes should automatically be interpreted into conformity with Charter values. Charter values are relevant to statutory interpretation only where the statute is ambiguous and reference to a Charter value would help resolve the ambiguity.[37]

§ 37:13 Private action

Section 32 provides, as we have seen, that the Charter applies to "the Parliament and government of Canada" and to "the legislature and government of each province". This is an exhaustive statement of the binding application of the Charter. It follows that the Charter applies only where there has been governmental action of some kind, that is, action by the Parliament or government of Canada or by the Legislature or government of a province. The rights guaranteed by the Charter take effect only as restrictions on the power of government over the persons entitled to the rights. The Charter regulates the relations between government and private persons, but it does not regulate the relations between private persons and private persons.[1] Private action is therefore excluded from the application of the Charter. Such actions as an employer restricting an employee's freedom of speech or assembly, a parent restricting the mobility of a child or a landlord discriminating on

---

[36]See also *M.(A.) v. Ryan*, [1997] 1 S.C.R. 157 (Charter values applied in determining claim of privilege by plaintiff in civil action for psychiatric records sought by defendant; partial disclosure ordered); *R. v. National Post*, [2010] 1 S.C.R. 477, para. 50 (Charter values applied in restating the common law to recognize a journalistic secret-source privilege).

[37]*Bell ExpressVu v. Rex*, [2002] 2 S.C.R. 559, paras. 61-66 per Iacobucci J. for the Court; *Medovarski v. Can.*, [2005] 2 S.C.R. 539, para. 48 per McLachlin C.J. for the Court. The Court has not always followed this admonition: *Can. Foundation for Children, Youth and the Law v. Can.*, [2004] 1 S.C.R. 76; *Montreal v. 2952-1366 Que.*, [2005] 3 S.C.R. 141; for discussion, see ch. 40, Enforcement of Rights, under heading § 40:9, "Reconstruction".

[Section 37:13]

[1]*RWDSU v. Dolphin Delivery*, [1986] 2 S.C.R. 573 (Charter inapplicable to union picketing of private company); *Tremblay v. Daigle*, [1989] 2 S.C.R. 530 (Charter inapplicable to father's attempt to stop an abortion); *McKinney v. U. of Guelph*, [1990] 3 S.C.R. 229 (Charter inapplicable to mandatory retirement rules within university); *Stoffman v. Vancouver General Hospital*, [1990] 3 S.C.R. 483 (same result within hospital); *Syndicat Northcrest v. Amselem*, [2004] 2 S.C.R. 551 (Charter inapplicable to condominium by-laws, but Quebec Charter applicable); *Sagen v. Vancouver Organizing Committee* (2009), 313 D.L.R. (4th) 393 (B.C. C.A.) (Charter inapplicable to body organizing 2010 Olympic winter games).

the basis of race in his selection of tenants cannot be breaches of the Charter, because in no case is there any action by the Parliament or government of Canada or by the Legislature or government of a province. In cases where private action results in a restriction of a civil liberty, there may be a remedy for the aggrieved person under a human rights code, under labour law, family law, tort law, contract law or property law, or under some other branch of the law governing relations between private persons; but there will be no breach of the Charter.[2]

In *R. v. Buhay* (2003),[3] two security guards at the Winnipeg bus depot detected the smell of marijuana coming from a locker that had been rented to someone and locked up. They asked a manager of the bus depot to open the locker with his master key, which he did. The security guards found drugs inside the locker. They replaced the drugs in the locker, and called the police. When the police arrived, the security guards again got the manager to reopen the locker with the master key, and the police seized the drugs. The police later arrested the person who had rented the locker and charged him. The Supreme Court of Canada held that the initial opening of the locker was not a search within the meaning of s. 8 of the Charter (the guarantee against unreasonable search and seizure), because the security guards were private actors. Private security guards in Manitoba were subject to "a loose framework of statutory regulation", but they were "not subject to government control".[4] Nor were they acting as agents of the police in opening the locker; they had acted "totally independently of the police in their initial search".[5] However, the second opening of the locker was in a different category. When the police took over, private action was replaced by state action. Since the police acted without a warrant, the search and seizure were unreasonable, which was a breach of s. 8 of the Charter.

After the Charter was adopted in 1982 there was some speculation as to whether it was restricted to governmental action. Some commentators took the view that it was not so restricted. Section 32, it was suggested, was a cautionary provision, inserted to make clear that

---

[2]This idea is commonly expressed by saying that the Charter lacks the "horizontal effect" of directly imposing on private persons a duty to refrain from infringing the guaranteed rights of others. The absence of horizontal application does not foreclose the possibility that the Charter might be interpreted as imposing on the *state* a constitutional duty to enact laws to impose on private persons a statutory duty not to infringe the guaranteed rights of others. This "protective function" of the state has been explicitly recognized in other countries and some Canadian Charter decisions can be interpreted as imposing a protective function on the state: V.A. MacDonnell, "The Protective Function and Section 7 of the Canadian Charter of Rights and Freedoms" (2012) 17 Review of Con. Studies 53, 60.

[3]*R. v. Buhay*, [2003] 1 S.C.R. 631. Arbour J. wrote the opinion of the Court.

[4]*R. v. Buhay*, [2003] 1 S.C.R. 631, para. 28.

[5]*R. v. Buhay*, [2003] 1 S.C.R. 631, para. 29. Accord, *R. v. Dell* (2005), 256 D.L.R. (4th) 271 (Alta. C.A.) (detention and search by bouncer in bar not covered by Charter). In *R. v. Skeir* (2005), 253 D.L.R. (4th) 221 (N.S. C.A.), it was held that, even when making a citizen's arrest under statutory authority, a private security guard is not bound by the Charter. Contra, *R. v. Lerke* (1986), 25 D.L.R. (4th) 403 (Alta. C.A.) (Charter applies to citizen's arrest under statutory authority).

governmental action was covered, but not intended to confine the guaranteed rights to governmental action. This view was never particularly plausible, running into contradictory indications within the text of the Charter,[6] in the legislative history of the Charter[7] and in the American jurisprudence, which confines the Bill of Rights to governmental action ("state action").[8] In deciding that the Charter does not extend to private action, the Supreme Court of Canada has affirmed the normal role of a constitution. A constitution establishes and regulates the institutions of government, and it leaves to those institutions the task of ordering the private affairs of the people.

The restriction of the Charter to "governmental action" (which may take the form of a legislative or executive or in some situations a judicial act) is sometimes regarded as creating a public-private distinction in our law. The terms "public" and "private" are no doubt convenient labels, but they reflect a rather complex body of law, and they can be seriously misleading. Much "public" activity is not covered by the Charter, because there is no statutory or governmental presence that would make the Charter applicable.[9] Much "private" activity has been regulated by statute, or been joined by government, and if so the statutory or governmental presence will make the Charter applicable as well. If the Parliament chooses to give a power of arrest to private citizens, a citizen's arrest will be subject to the Charter.[10] If the Parliament chooses to criminalize abortion, its statute will be subject to the Charter, and the Court will investigate the constitutionality of regulating a woman's decision to have an abortion.[11] If the Legislature chooses to prohibit employers from discriminating on the basis of race, sex, religion, national origin and other grounds, the statute will have to conform to the Charter by including sexual orientation as a ground of discrimination.[12] If the Legislature chooses to prohibit discrimination by sex, its statute will be subject to

---

[6]Section 1, for example, affords justification only to Charter limits that are "prescribed by law", which would never be true of private action in derogation of a Charter right.

[7]Testimony of F.J.E. Jordan, Senior Counsel, Public Law, federal Department of Justice, in Minutes of Proceedings and Evidence of the Special Joint Committee of the Senate and of the House of Commons on the Constitution of Canada, First Session of Thirty-second Parliament, 1980-81, pp. 48:27 (January 29, 1981), 49:47 (January 30, 1981).

[8]L.H. Tribe, American Constitutional Law (Foundation Press, N.Y., 2nd ed., 1988), 772-774, ch. 18; J.E. Nowak and R.D. Rotunda, Constitutional Law (West, St. Paul, Minn., 7th ed., 2004), ch. 14.

[9]E.g., *McKinney v. U. of Guelph*, [1990] 3 S.C.R. 229 (public university not covered by Charter); *Stoffman v. Vancouver General Hospital*, [1990] 3 S.C.R. 483 (public hospital not covered by Charter).

[10]*R. v. Lerke* (1986), 25 D.L.R. (4th) 403 (Alta. C.A.). Contra, *R. v. Skeir* (2005), 253 D.L.R. (4th) 221 (N.S. C.A.).

[11]*R. v. Morgentaler (No. 2)*, [1988] 1 S.C.R. 30.

[12]In *Vriend v. Alta.*, [1998] 1 S.C.R. 493, Cory J. (paras. 105-106) denied that the decision meant that human rights legislation had to "mirror" the Charter by including all the listed and analogous grounds of discrimination that are covered by s. 15. That "would have the undesirable result of unduly constraining legislative choice and allow-

the Charter, and the Court will investigate the constitutionality of a statutory exemption for boys-only sports teams.[13] If the Government chooses to contract with its employees for mandatory retirement, the contractual provision to which government is a party will be subject to the Charter, and the Court will investigate the constitutionality of mandatory retirement.[14] If the police enlist the aid of a private individual, for example, to obtain information from a prisoner or to obtain medical records, the private informers are regarded as agents of the police, and the Court will investigate the constitutionality of their actions.[15] Therefore, when it is said that the Charter does not apply to "private" action, the word "private" is really a term of art, denoting a residual category from which it is necessary to subtract those cases where the existence of a statute or the presence of government does make the Charter applicable. Without this understanding, the claim that the Charter does not apply to private action would be grossly misleading.

An interesting phenomenon has been the Supreme Court of Canada's use of a remedy of "extension", under which the Court extends the reach of a statute that the Court finds to be "under-inclusive". An under-inclusive statute is one that excludes some group that has a constitutional right to be included. Sometimes this is accomplished by "severance", deleting from the statute the language that excludes the group.[16] Other times, this is accomplished by "reading in", inserting new language into the statute to add the excluded class.[17] Whatever the judicial technique, the result is to extend the statute to previously unregulated activity. The equality guarantee of s. 15 is usually the Charter right that is invoked to support the remedy of extension. For example, in *Vriend v. Alberta* (1998),[18] the Supreme Court of Canada held that the failure of Alberta's human rights statute to extend protection against discrimination on the ground of sexual orientation was a breach of s. 15, and the Court, by reading in, directly added the ground of sexual orientation to the statute. In *Dunmore v. Ontario* (2001),[19] the Court held that the exclusion of agricultural workers from Ontario's labour relations statute was a breach, not of s. 15, but of s. 2(d) (freedom of association), and the Court severed the exclusion clause from the stat-

---

ing the Charter to indirectly regulate private conduct". Yet that is exactly the effect of the decision, because it makes clear that the omission of a Charter ground in human rights legislation could survive only if the omission could be justified under s. 1, which is hard to imagine.

[13] *Re Blainey* (1986), 54 O.R. (2d) 513 (C.A.).

[14] *Douglas/Kwantlen Faculty Assn. v. Douglas College*, [1990] 3 S.C.R. 570.

[15] *R. v. Broyles*, [1991] 3 S.C.R. 595 (statement obtained from prisoner in breach of s. 7); *R. v. Dersch*, [1993] 3 S.C.R. 768 (medical records given in breach of s. 8).

[16] Chapter 40, Enforcement of Rights, under heading § 40:5, "Severance".

[17] Chapter 40, Enforcement of Rights, under heading § 40:6, "Reading in".

[18] *Vriend v. Alberta*, [1998] 1 S.C.R. 493.

[19] *Dunmore v. Ontario*, [2001] 3 S.C.R. 1016.

ute, thereby sweeping the agricultural workers in.[20] In these cases, by virtue of the judicial decree, the common law is supplanted by statute, and private action is private no longer.[21]

Even noting that the potential scope of "public" action is not fixed, there remain critics who take issue with the legitimacy of the public/private distinction as it has been applied to the Charter. They assert that government is really everywhere, even if only by facilitation or abstention. Moreover, some of these critics see a nasty bias in the public/private distinction. It is the sphere of the "private", from which the Charter is excluded, that includes the relationships of hierarchy and dominance that serve to oppress workers (in the socialist critique) or women (in the feminist critique).[22] The Charter and Charter jurisprudence are attacked on the grounds that nothing in the Charter addresses the really bad stuff that is left unregulated. But the real risks of unmitigated oppression in the private sphere are rather overstated. Legislatures have never accepted that they are limited in their actions by some mythical divide between public matters and private ones, and have actually extensively regulated the employment relationship (to provide for collective bargaining, employment standards, health and safety standards, pay equity, etc.), family relationships (to regulate marriage, divorce, support, family property, child welfare, physical abuse, etc.) and much else that is "private". If the laws are inadequate, it has little to do with the public/private distinction, and much to do with the power of competing political forces. Indeed the constitutional power (and the evident political willingness) of Canadian governmental institutions to regulate the private spheres of life makes it unnecessary (and undesirable) to extend the Charter's reach to matters outside the fluid boundaries set by governmental action. If private abuse exists, the democratic political process can drive the legislative bodies to produce the laws that are needed to provide the remedy. A legislative body can design a remedial instrument that is appropriate to the problem—in contrast to the limited range of relatively crude remedies that could be fashioned as Charter remedies by the courts.[23]

It is arguable that if a private abuse exists, there ought to be a Charter

---

[20]The Court postponed the order of severance for 18 months in case the Legislature wished to enact a different regime of labour law for the agricultural workers (as it later did)—but the Legislature did not have the option of leaving the organization of agricultural workers unregulated.

[21]V.A. MacDonnell, "The Protective Function and Section 7 of the Canadian Charter of Rights and Freedoms" (2012) 17 Review of Con. Studies 53, 55, would take these cases a step beyond the extension of a statute, arguing for the recognition of a "protective function", imposed on the state by the Charter, to legislate obligations on private persons not to infringe the rights of others.

[22]E.g., H. Lessard, "The Idea of the Private: A Discussion of State Action Doctrine and Separate Sphere Ideology" (1986) 10 Dal. L.J. 107; A.C. Hutchinson and A. Petter, "Private Rights/Public Wrongs: The Liberal Lie of the Charter" (1988) 38 U. Toronto L.J. 278; J. Fudge, "The Public/Private Distinction: The . . . Use of Charter Litigation to Further Feminist Struggles" (1987) 25 Osgoode Hall L.J. 485.

[23]See P.C. Weiler, "The Charter at Work" (1990) 40 U. Toronto L.J. 117, 148-155.

remedy, in case no remedy is provided by the competent governmental institutions, or in case the legislated remedy is inadequate. If the Charter were extended to private activity, s. 24 would authorize a court-imposed remedy. This would create an extensive new body of "constitutional tort law", co-existing uneasily with the labour codes, family law, human rights codes and other bodies of law, not forgetting the criminal law and the law of torts. The existence of these new remedies would vastly expand the role of the courts. The Charter of Rights, and the judicial review that inescapably accompanies its prescriptions, would be intolerably pervasive, applying to even the most intimate relationship.[24] The effect of the governmental action restriction is that there is a private realm in which people are not obliged to subscribe to "state" values, and into which constitutional norms do not intrude.[25] The boundaries of that realm are marked, not by an a priori definition of what is "private", but by the absence of statutory or other governmental intervention. The boundaries will expand or contract as the scope of governmental intervention, driven by democratic political forces, contracts or expands. But, at any given time, the boundaries can be ascertained by the courts, and the scope of the Charter can therefore be determined.

§ 37:14 Extraterritorial application

The references in s. 32 to "the Parliament and government of Canada" and to "the legislature and government of each province" confine the application of the Charter to the legislative bodies and governments of Canada and the provinces. Foreign governments are not bound by the Charter, and their actions cannot be breaches of the Charter. This means, for example, that an accused person in Canada cannot object to a statement given to American police officers who failed to comply with the standards of the Canadian Charter.[1] Generally speaking, it is also not a breach of the Charter when Canadian law exposes a person to foreign sanctions, for example, by compelling testimony that forces the witness to violate a foreign secrecy law.[2]

Canada has entered into extradition treaties with other states under which Canada agrees to surrender to the other state a person who has been charged with or convicted of an offence in the other state but who has fled to Canada. Within Canada, an application by a foreign state to extradite a fugitive is dealt with in a two-stage process. First, a judge holds a hearing to determine whether the foreign state has sufficient evidence of the commission by the fugitive of an extraditable offence in the

---

[24] See *McKinney v. U. of Guelph*, [1990] 3 S.C.R. 229, 262-263 per La Forest J.

[25] See J.D. Whyte, "Is the Private Sector affected by the Charter?" in Smith (ed.), Righting the Balance: Canada's New Equality Rights (1986), 145, 149.

[Section 37:14]

[1] *R. v. Harrer*, [1995] 3 S.C.R. 562; *R. v. Terry*, [1996] 2 S.C.R. 207.

[2] *Spencer v. The Queen*, [1985] 2 S.C.R. 278.

foreign state.[3] Second, and only if the extradition judge finds the evidence to be sufficient, the Minister of Justice decides whether to surrender the fugitive to the requesting state. At the second (surrender) stage, extradition of a fugitive who is a Canadian citizen is a denial of the right to remain in Canada that is guaranteed by s. 6 of the Charter. However, extradition is justified as a reasonable limit under s. 1.[4] At both stages of the extradition process, extradition is a deprivation of liberty in Canada, and s. 7 of the Charter is therefore applicable. It would be a breach of the principles of fundamental justice under s. 7 if a fugitive (whether or not a Canadian citizen) were to be extradited to a country where he or she may be treated in a fashion that "shocks the conscience".[5] However, the Supreme Court of Canada, not relishing the idea of Canada becoming a safe haven for foreign criminals, has generally been reluctant to interfere with extradition orders. The Court has allowed extraditions to the United States when the fugitive faced penalties that were more severe than penalties for similar crimes in Canada or that were even contrary to the Charter.[6]

What about the extradition of a fugitive who may face the death penalty in the requesting state? Canada's extradition treaty with the United States expressly provides that extradition may be refused if the United States does not provide assurances "that the death penalty shall not be imposed, or, if imposed, shall not be exercised". (The Minister of Justice would in any case have the discretionary power to require such assurances before surrendering a fugitive even if this provision were not in the treaty.) In *Kindler v. Canada* (1991),[7] Kindler was an American citizen who was convicted of murder in Pennsylvania. After the sentencing hearing required by Pennsylvania law, the jury recommended that he be sentenced to death. Before the sentence was formally imposed, he

---

[3]Section 7 of the Charter requires that this hearing be conducted in accordance with the principles of fundamental justice. It can be contaminated by actions occurring outside Canada, as in *United States v. Cobb*, [2001] 1 S.C.R. 587, *United States v. Tsioubrios*, [2001] 1 S.C.R. 613 and *United States v. Shulman*, [2001] 1 S.C.R. 616, where threats were made against the Canadian fugitives by a prosecutor and judge in the United States. The Supreme Court of Canada held that to continue the extradition process in the face of these threats would be a breach of fundamental justice, and the Court stayed the hearing. See also ch. 47, Fundamental Justice, under heading § 47:32, "The right to a fair trial".

[4]Chapter 46, Mobility, under heading § 46:2, "International movement".

[5]*Can. v. Schmidt*, [1987] 1 S.C.R. 500, 522.

[6]*United States v. Jamiesun*, [1996] 1 S.C.R. 465 (mandatory 20-year sentence); *United States v. Whitley*, [1996] 1 S.C.R. 467 (mandatory 20-year sentence); *United States v. Ross*, [1996] 1 S.C.R. 469 (mandatory 15-year sentence); *Lake v. Can.*, [2008] 1 S.C.R. 761 (mandatory 10-year sentence). These sentences, if imposed in Canada, would probably all be contrary to s. 12 of the Charter: ch. 53, Cruel and Unusual Punishment, under heading § 53:4, "Minimum sentence". See also *Can. v. Barnaby*, [2015] 2 S.C.R. 563, 2015 SCC 31 (extradition to U.S. to face fourth trial for murder upheld).

[7]*Kindler v. Canada*, [1991] 2 S.C.R. 779. Majority opinions to the same effect were written by La Forest and McLachlin JJ. and both opinions were agreed to by L'Heureux-Dubé and Gonthier JJ. Dissenting opinions were written by Sopinka and Cory JJ. and both opinions were agreed to by Lamer C.J. A companion case was decided at the same time with the same result: *Re Ng Extradition*, [1991] 2 S.C.R. 858.

escaped from custody and fled to Canada where he was caught and arrested. At the conclusion of the extradition process in Canada, the Minister decided to surrender the fugitive without seeking assurances that the death penalty would not be imposed. On review of the Minister's decision, the majority of the Supreme Court of Canada held that the decision did not shock the conscience and that therefore there was no breach of the principles of fundamental justice.[8] The majority noted that if extradition were denied there would be no legal basis for keeping Kindler in custody, and Canada would become a safe haven for the most violent American criminals.[9]

Ten years after *Kindler* was decided, the Supreme Court of Canada had a change of heart. The conversion occurred in *United States v. Burns* (2001),[10] in which the United States sought extradition of two fugitives who had been charged with brutal murders in the State of Washington and who had fled across the border to British Columbia where they were arrested. At the conclusion of the extradition process in Canada, the Minister of Justice decided to surrender the two fugitives to the United States. Under the criminal code of the State of Washington, they were liable if convicted to either the death penalty or life imprisonment without parole. The Minister did not seek assurances that the death penalty would not be imposed. On review of the Minister's decision, the Supreme Court of Canada now held that it would be a breach of fundamental justice to extradite the fugitives without obtaining assurances that the death penalty would not be imposed. The Court could have distinguished *Kindler* on the basis that the two accused in *Burns* were Canadian citizens and were only 18 years old when they allegedly committed the murders. But the Court chose not to follow its earlier decision in *Kindler*, holding that an extradition to face the death penalty would shock the conscience and would breach s. 7. "In the absence of exceptional circumstances, which we refrain from trying to anticipate, assurances in death penalty cases are always constitutionally required".[11] The main reason for departing from *Kindler* was the Court's belief that over the last decade the arguments against the death penalty, and in particular the concern about wrongful convictions, had become stronger. The "safe haven" argument was dismissed on the basis that there was "little indication" that United States' governments would ever fail to

[8]*Kindler v. Can.*, [1991] 2 S.C.R. 779, 832 per La Forest J., 852 per McLachlin J.

[9]*Kindler v. Can.*, [1991] 2 S.C.R. 779, 836 per La Forest J., 853 per McLachlin J. If the Court had held that Kindler could not be extradited to face the death penalty, then he would have to be released from custody, because he had not offended against any Canadian law. Not being a Canadian citizen, he would be illegally in Canada, but his deportation would be blocked by Canadian courts for the same reason as his extradition, since deportation to the United States would inevitably lead to his arrest and return to custody to await execution.

[10]*United States v. Burns*, [2001] 1 S.C.R. 283. The unanimous opinion was written by "the Court". The nine-judge bench included three of the four members of the majority (La Forest J. had retired) in *Kindler* and *Ng*.

[11]*United States v. Burns*, [2001] 1 S.C.R. 283, para. 65.

give assurances.[12] Therefore, violent criminals could be extradited, and would not be left to roam free in Canada. If this is true, even in cases like *Kindler*, where the American fugitive had already been convicted and had undergone a sentencing hearing before fleeing to Canada, then it is indeed a strong (but not conclusive)[13] reason to reject the safe haven argument.

In *Suresh v. Canada* (2002),[14] the question arose whether it would be a breach of s. 7 to deport a person (in this case, a citizen of Sri Lanka) from Canada if that person was likely to face torture in the country to which he was returned. The Supreme Court of Canada held that deportation was not materially different from extradition, and followed *Burns* to hold that a deportation to face torture would "usually" be a breach of the principles of fundamental justice.[15] The reason for the qualification "usually" was that the Court recognized that Canada was entitled to protect itself by expelling someone who was truly dangerous, and s. 7 allowed a balancing of the danger to public safety within Canada against the risk of harm to the deported person outside Canada. The Court upheld the provision in the Immigration Act that permitted the Minister of Immigration to deport noncitizens who were found to be a "danger to the security of Canada", but the Court held that there must be cogent evidence that the person is indeed dangerous before the Minister could constitutionally deport a person who would face torture in the country to which he was returned. Moreover, s. 7 required that a person making a credible claim that he would be tortured on return to his country of citizenship must be given full information of the case for deportation, be given an opportunity to respond and be provided with reasons for the ultimate decision. Because Suresh had not been given a sufficient opportunity to substantiate his claims that he would face torture if deported to Sri Lanka and that in any event he was not a danger to public safety in Canada, the Court set aside the deportation order and ordered the Minister to reconsider. In the companion case of *Ahani v.*

---

[12] *United States v. Burns*, [2001] 1 S.C.R. 283, para. 138. After the decision of the Court in this case, the Minister requested assurances that the death penalty would not be sought for the two accused, and the assurances were given: *Globe and Mail* newspaper, March 10, 2001, p. A2.

[13] A weaker form of the safe haven argument is that American criminals will still have an incentive to flee to Canada, because, although they are liable to be arrested and extradited (once assurances are provided), the flight to Canada will relieve them of the risk of the death penalty. Any encouragement to American criminals to sojourn even temporarily in Canada could properly be regarded with concern by the Minister of Justice. La Forest J. pointed out in *Kindler* (*Kindler v. Canada*, [1991] 2 S.C.R. 779, 836) that, although the accused in that case and in the companion case of *Ng* were eventually arrested and extradited, they still managed to commit some crimes in Canada while they were on the loose. Indeed, it was only by committing crimes in Canada that they came to the attention of the police who then initiated the extradition process.

[14] *Suresh v. Canada*, [2002] 1 S.C.R. 3. The unanimous opinion was written by "the Court".

[15] *Suresh v. Canada*, [2002] 1 S.C.R. 3, para. 58. Para. 76 is to the same effect, using the word "generally".

Canada (2002),[16] the Court upheld the deportation of an Iranian citizen. In that case, the Minister had followed the appropriate procedures and had concluded that there was only a minimal risk that the deportee would be tortured if he were returned to Iran and that the deportee was a danger to the security of Canada. The Court accordingly affirmed the Minister's decision.[17]

In *Schreiber v. Canada* (1998),[18] the question arose whether the Charter applied to a letter of request from the Canadian Department of Justice to government authorities in Switzerland requesting the seizure of records of Swiss bank accounts that were wanted by the Royal Canadian Mounted Police for a criminal investigation. The letter of request had not been authorized by a search warrant or other judicial authorization that would, under s. 8 of the Charter, be constitutionally necessary for the seizure of bank records in Canada. The Swiss government, acting without judicial authorization but in compliance with Swiss law, carried out the request and seized the documents. The Canadian owner of the bank accounts did not challenge the action of the Swiss government, to which the Charter clearly did not apply. What he did challenge was the letter of request that had been issued by the Canadian government. The majority of the Supreme Court of Canada rejected the challenge on the basis that the letter of request had no legal effect and was not subject to Charter review for that reason. All the actions that were legally effective had been carried out by a foreign government in accordance with foreign law, and were not subject to Charter review. The dissenting minority took the view that this was a "formalistic" disposition of the case. The Canadian officials who issued the letter of request initiated a process that they expected to result in a seizure of documents that invaded the privacy of the Canadian owner. According to the dissenters, Charter standards should have been complied with before making the request.[19]

In *R. v. Cook* (1998),[20] an American citizen was arrested in the United States by a United States marshall for a murder that had been commit-

---

[16]*Ahani v. Canada*, [2002] 1 S.C.R. 72. The unanimous opinion was written by "the Court".

[17]A subsequent proceeding, seeking a stay of deportation pending a decision by the United Nations Human Rights Committee, was also unsuccessful: *Ahani v. Can.* (2002), 58 O.R. (3d) 107 (C.A.) (leave to appeal to S.C.C. denied on May 16, 2002).

[18]*Schreiber v. Canada*, [1998] 1 S.C.R. 841. The majority opinion was written by L'Heureux-Dubé J. with whom McLachlin, Bastarache and Binnie JJ. agreed; a concurring opinion was written by Lamer C.J.; and a dissenting opinion was written by Iacobucci J. with whom Gonthier J. agreed.

[19]Lamer C.J., in a separate concurring opinion, took a middle ground. He agreed with the dissenters that the Charter applied to the letter of request, but he held that there was no breach of a reasonable expectation of privacy, because the person who chooses to place funds in a foreign bank account must expect to be governed by the law of the place where the account is located.

[20]*R. v. Cook*, [1998] 2 S.C.R. 597. The majority opinion was written by Cory and Iacobucci JJ. with whom Lamer C.J., Binnie and Major JJ. agreed; a concurring opinion was written by Bastarache J. with whom Gonthier J. agreed; and a dissenting opinion

ted in Canada. After the arrest, two police officers from Canada travelled to the prison in New Orleans where the accused was being held and interrogated him. The interrogation did not comply with Charter standards, because there was an inadequate warning of the right to counsel. The accused was extradited to Canada for trial, and the statement was used by the Crown at the trial. The Supreme Court of Canada held, by a majority, that the Charter applied to the interrogation because, although the interrogation took place in the United States, it had been carried out by Canadian police officers. According to the majority, there was no interference with American sovereignty in holding that the Canadian police officers continued to be bound by the Charter even after entering the United States. The majority concluded that the statement had been obtained in breach of the Charter. The dissenting view of L'Heureux-Dubé J. was premised on the proposition that the Canadian police officers had no legal authority to act in the United States. Since the interrogation could take place only with the cooperation of the American authorities and in compliance with American law, she would have decided that it would be an unconstitutional extraterritorial effect to impose the Charter of Rights on the proceedings.[21]

Cook was the first case where the Supreme Court had given direct extraterritorial effect to the Charter by applying it to actions taken outside Canada by Canadian government actors. However, nine years later, *Cook* was overruled by a five-four majority of the Court in *R. v. Hape* (2007).[22] That case was a prosecution in Canada for money laundering. The evidence consisted mainly of documents that had been searched for and seized by Canadian police officers in the Turks and Caicos Islands. The police officers acted under the supervision of a senior officer of the Turks and Caicos Police Force. The case proceeded on the assumption that all the various searches and seizures that yielded the evidence were made in compliance with Turks and Caicos law,[23] but at least one of the searches took place without a warrant in circumstances that would have been a breach of the Canadian Charter if it were applicable. It should be noted that *Hape* is a very different case from *Cook*, in that requiring the Turks and Caicos legal system to develop a procedure for the issue of a warrant simply in order to comply with the

---

was written by L'Heureux-Dubé J. with whom McLachlin J. agreed.

[21]See also *Purdy v. Can.* (2003), 230 D.L.R. (4th) 361 (B.C.C.A.) (Canadian citizen charged with offence in U.S.A. entitled under Charter to disclosure of material obtained by R.C.M.P. in the course of investigating the offence jointly with the F.B.I.).

[22]*R. v. Hape*, [2007] 2 S.C.R. 292. The majority opinion was written by LeBel J. with whom McLachlin C.J., Deschamps, Fish and Charron JJ. agreed; concurring opinions were written by Bastarache J. (with whom Abella and Rothstein JJ. agreed) and Binnie J.

[23]An oddity of the case is that the Turks and Caicos law respecting searches and seizures was never proved by either the Crown or the defence, and no Turks and Caicos warrants for any of the various searches and seizures that took place were produced by the Crown. However, it was common ground that one of the searches that would have required a warrant under the Canadian Charter did not have a Turks and Caicos warrant.

Canadian Charter would be an objectionable interference with Turks and Caicos sovereignty. As Bastarache and Binnie JJ. pointed out in their concurring opinions, the ruling in *Cook* would not require the application of the Canadian Charter to the facts in *Hape*. LeBel J. for the majority in *Hape* agreed that the Charter should not apply, but he took the occasion to engage in a reappraisal of the law respecting the extraterritorial reach of the Charter. In effect,[24] he took the same view as the dissenting opinion in *Cook:* the Charter applied only to actions taken by Canadian actors inside Canada. His reasoning was that s. 32 of the Charter of Rights should be read down to conform to principles of international law that respect the sovereignty of foreign states. This led him to the syllogism: "Since extraterritorial enforcement [of Canadian law] is not possible, and enforcement is necessary for the Charter to apply, extraterritorial application of the Charter is impossible".[25]

LeBel J. for the majority in *Hape* acknowledged that there would be no breach of a foreign state's sovereignty if the only consequence of a Charter breach in the foreign state was that evidence was excluded from a Canadian criminal trial; but he held that this was not a sufficient basis for the application of the Charter to the acts of Canadian police in a foreign country, because the Charter was intended as a guide to action by Canadian police, not merely as a vehicle for *ex post facto* review of evidence obtained in the foreign state. However, if the police action in the foreign state yielded evidence that would make the Canadian trial unfair, then the evidence could and should be excluded under ss. 7 and 11(d) of the Charter. That would not be an extraterritorial application of the Charter, but a measure to control the process of the Canadian court.[26] A failure to meet Charter standards in the search for or seizure of evidence in a foreign country would not by itself make a Canadian trial unfair. In this case, the evidence had been obtained in compliance with Turks and Caicos law (to which the defendant had willingly entrusted his affairs), and its admission did not make the trial in Canada unfair.

---

[24]LeBel J. never said that *Cook* was no longer good law, but, as Binnie J. pointed out (para. 182), that seems to be the inevitable conclusion from his reasoning. His position differed from the dissent in *Cook* in that LeBel J. made two exceptions to the territorial restriction on the Charter. The first exception (para. 101) was for "activities [outside Canada] that violate Canada's international obligations", which, he said, "might justify a remedy under s. 24(1) of the Charter because of the impact of those activities on Charter rights in Canada". He did not explain how activities outside Canada could have an impact on Charter rights "in Canada". The second exception (para. 106) was for the case "where the host state consents", and he found (without explanation) that consent was "neither demonstrated nor argued" in this case. He did not explain what he meant by consent. As Bastarache J. pointed out (paras. 145, 178), an investigation by Canadian police in a foreign country must always take place with the consent of the foreign country; otherwise there would be a breach of the international law of state sovereignty. And in this case the Canadian police officers worked under the supervision of a Turks and Caicos officer apparently a common arrangement in foreign investigations. LeBel J. is using consent in a special sense that is never elucidated, but, whatever he means by consent, he says (para. 106) that it would be "rare".

[25]*R. v. Hape*, [2007] 2 S.C.R. 292, para. 85 per LeBel J.

[26]*R. v. Hape*, [2007] 2 S.C.R. 292, paras. 91, 100, 108.

Less than a year after the decision in *Hape*, the Supreme Court decided another extraterritorial case, *Canada v. Khadr* (2008).[27] Khadr was a Canadian citizen who was captured by American forces in Afghanistan as part of the military action against Taliban and Al Qaeda forces following the terrorist attacks in the United States on September 11, 2001. Along with other prisoners, he was held in a detention camp at the American military base in Guantanamo Bay, Cuba. He was charged with murder and terrorist activities against U.S. forces. The charges were to be tried before a U.S. Military Commission at Guantanamo Bay. After the charges were laid against him in 2005, he applied to the Federal Court of Canada for an order under s. 24(1) of the Charter compelling the Government of Canada to disclose to him the records of interviews that were conducted with him in 2003 by officials of the Canadian Security Intelligence Service (CSIS). The Canadian officials had interviewed him in Cuba and had made records of the interviews and given a copy of those records to American officials. The Supreme Court held that he was entitled to disclosure of the records of the interviews that were in the possession of the government of Canada. The Court reasoned that if everything had taken place in Canada, including the criminal process, Khadr would have been entitled, by s. 7 of the Charter, to the *Stinchcombe* right of full disclosure of all relevant material in the possession of the Crown.[28] While *Hape* had held that the Charter did not have extraterritorial effect, the opinion in *Hape* had suggested an exception for the case where Canada was in breach of its international obligations. The Court held that the Guantanamo Bay process was contrary to the 1949 Geneva Conventions to which Canada (as well as the United States) was a party; and, by handing over the records of the Khadr interviews to the United States, Canada was "involved" in the process. Therefore, *Hape* did not apply and the Charter acquired extraterritorial effect.[29] Neither the interviews nor the handing over of the records was a breach of the Charter,[30] but, by analogy with *Stinchcombe*, it was a breach of the Charter not to provide disclosure to Khadr of the records of the interviews and any other relevant material in the possession of the Canadian government. The end result of this tortuous

[27]*Canada v. Khadr*, [2008] 2 S.C.R. 125. The unanimous opinion was an opinion of "the Court".

[28]*R. v. Stinchcombe*, [1991] 3 S.C.R. 326 decided that, where an accused's liberty is at stake in a criminal prosecution, s. 7 requires full disclosure by the prosecution to the accused: see ch. 47, Fundamental Justice, under heading § 47:34, "Pre-trial disclosure by the Crown".

[29]The Court in *Khadr* neither quoted nor mentioned the language used by LeBel J. in outlining the exception in *R. v. Hape*, [2007] 2 S.C.R. 292, para. 101, which seemed to call for some "impact . . . on Charter rights in Canada".

[30]*Canada v. Khadr*, [2008] 2 S.C.R. 125, para. 27. However, in sequel litigation, the Court held that the interviews and the handing over of the records was a breach of Khadr's s. 7 rights: *Can. v. Khadr*, [2010] 1 S.C.R. 44, para. 48 per the Court ("Canada actively participated in a process contrary to Canada's international human rights obligations and contributed to Mr. Khadr's ongoing detention so as to deprive him of his right to liberty and security of the person . . . contrary to the principles of fundamental justice").

reasoning was that Khadr was entitled to the s. 24(1) remedy of disclosure of the records held by the Canadian government.[31]

Canada's State Immunity Act, codifying a longstanding principle of customary international law, provides that "a foreign state is immune from the jurisdiction of any court in Canada." In *Kazemi Estate v. Islamic Republic of Iran* (2014),[32] Kazemi, a Canadian citizen, visited Iran as a freelance photographer and journalist, where her interest in protest movements caused her to be arrested, detained in prison and tortured to death. Her son in Canada brought proceedings in Quebec against Iran and the responsible officials claiming damages for the torture and killing of his mother in Iran. The proceedings were defeated by the State Immunity Act. The plaintiff argued that the Act was unconstitutional, at least in so far as it immunized foreign states and officials from liability in Canada for torture. LeBel J., writing for the majority, was prepared to assume for the purpose of the argument that the psychological distress suffered by the plaintiff in Canada was a breach of "security of the person" within the meaning of s. 7 of the Charter, but he denied that there was any breach of "the principles of fundamental justice". It was argued that "where there was a right [to be free from torture] there must be a remedy. LeBel J. agreed that this was a legal maxim, but he denied that it was a principle of fundamental justice. There were often procedural limitations that restricted the remedy for breach of a right and "state immunity is a procedural bar which prevents an individual from bringing a civil claim against a foreign state."[33] The State Immunity Act was valid and applicable despite the tragic circumstances and the universal abhorrence of torture. The plaintiff, who obviously had good reason to assume that proceedings in Iran would not be successful, was left without a remedy.[34]

The mobility rights of s. 6 of the Charter contemplate some degree of extraterritorial application in that s. 6(1) grants to every citizen of Canada the right to "enter" Canada. By its terms, the benefit of that right is possessed by a person outside Canada (who wishes to enter). The burden of the right (to permit entry) falls on the Government of Canada and

[31]Disclosure was to be made, not directly to Khadr, but to a Federal Court judge, who would review each item and rule on any claims of public interest immunity or other privilege that were made by the Crown for a particular item. Disclosure was duly made to Mosley J. of the Federal Court, who, after hearing from counsel for the Attorney General and an amicus curiae to represent the interests of the applicant, and after reviewing all the items, ordered extensive disclosure to Khadr: *Khadr v. Canada* (2008), 331 F.T.R. 1 (F.C.). Khadr then released the material to the news media: Globe and Mail newspaper, Thursday July 10, 2008, A1.

[32]*Kazemi Estate v. Islamic Republic of Iran*, [2014] 3 S.C.R. 176, 2014 SCC 62. LeBel J. wrote the opinion of the majority. Abella J. wrote a dissenting opinion.

[33]*Kazemi Estate v. Islamic Republic of Iran*, [2014] 3 S.C.R. 176, 2014 SCC 62, para. 161.

[34]An argument based on s. 2(e) of the Canadian Bill of Rights was also rejected. Abella J., who dissented, did not rely on either s. 7 or s. 2(e). In her view, the State Immunity Act should be interpreted as not precluding legal action against individual torturers because torture could not be an "official" act that attracted immunity.

would normally be carried out within Canada, either by immigration officials at the point of entry or by the passport office in the Department of Foreign Affairs in Ottawa. In *Abdelrazik v. Canada* (2009),[35] the Federal Court held that the Government of Canada was in breach of s. 6(1) in refusing to issue a passport to permit the return to Canada of a Canadian citizen in Sudan whose passport had expired while he was languishing in a Sudanese prison (without having been charged with or convicted of anything). The Court not only ordered the Minister of Foreign Affairs to issue a passport to enable the applicant to return to his family in Montreal, but also ordered the Minister to provide an escort to accompany the applicant on his journey. The Court was not troubled by any extraterritorial scruples in making that order.[36]

III. WAIVER OF RIGHTS

§ 37:15 Definition of waiver

A constitutional right can sometimes be "waived" by the right-holder.[1] Waiver requires an informed, clear and voluntary choice by the right-holder to surrender the right.[2] The issue usually arises in the context of the criminal-justice process of investigation, charge, prosecution, and trial. For example, the right to counsel, which is guaranteed by s. 10(b) of the Charter,[3] may be waived by an accused person who does not wish to be represented by counsel. If the right to counsel is waived, then the police are free to question the accused without infringing s. 10(b).

---

[35]*Abdelrazik v. Canada*, [2010] 1 F.C.R. 267 (Zinn J.). The case is more fully described in § 46:2, "International movement".

[36]Zinn J. was plainly troubled by the concern (based on his finding that the Canadian government had been complicit in the imprisonment in Sudan) that the Government would not use its best efforts to facilitate the return of the applicant, who was the subject of a United Nations travel ban. The judge even went so far as to order the Minister to produce the applicant for inspection by the Court for the purpose of satisfying the Court that the applicant had in fact returned to Canada.

[Section 37:15]

[1]For discussion, see E.L. Rubin, "Toward a General Theory of Waiver" (1981) 28 U.C.L.A. L. Rev. 478; A. Young, " 'Not Waving but Drowning': A look at Waiver and Collective Constitutional Rights in the Criminal Process" (1989) 53 Sask. L. Rev. 47; J.D.R. Craig, "Guilty Plea Revocation, Constitutional Waiver, and the Charter. 'A Guilty Plea is not a Trap' " (1997) 20 Dal. L. J. 161.

[2]*Korponay v. Can.*, [1982] 1 S.C.R. 41, 49 (waiver of trial by jury must be "clear and unequivocal", with "full knowledge" of the right and the effect that waiver of the right will have on the proceedings); *Clarkson v. The Queen*, [1986] 1 S.C.R. 383, 394-395 (waiver of right to counsel must be "clear and unequivocal" and must be made "with full knowledge of the rights the procedure was enacted to protect and of the effect the waiver will have on those rights in the process"); *R. v. Lee*, [1989] 2 S.C.R. 1384, 1411 (waiver of trial by jury must be "clear and unequivocal" and made with knowledge of the consequences of the waiver). See also *Johnson v. Zerbst* (1938), 404 U.S. 458, 464 ("an intentional relinquishment. . .of a known right or privilege"); E.L. Rubin, "Toward a General Theory of Waiver" (1981) 28 U.C.L.A. L. Rev. 478, criticizes the last definition on the ground that U. S. courts have not adhered to the "intentional" and the "known"—but Canadian courts have usually been strict in requiring knowledge and voluntariness.

[3]§ 37:20, "Waiver of right to counsel".

Waiver must be distinguished from *failure to exercise a right*, which is a broader category than waiver; waiver is a sub-set of the failure to exercise a right. One may fail to exercise a right without knowing of the existence of the right, or without making any conscious decision on the matter or without knowledge of the consequences of a waiver. In any of those cases, the failure to exercise the right would not be a waiver of the right. In the case of the right to counsel (for example), the police would not be free to treat the right as waived merely because the accused had not in fact retained counsel. The police would first be obliged to satisfy themselves (and ultimately a reviewing court) that the accused had the requisite knowledge of the right and understanding of the consequences to make a truly informed, clear and voluntary choice that could serve as a waiver.

Waiver must also be distinguished from *forfeiture* of a right. A right may be forfeited by bad behaviour which is stipulated by statute as having the effect of forfeiting the right. For example, the right to trial by jury, which is guaranteed by s. 11(f) of the Charter for serious offences, was lost by an accused person who failed to appear for his trial without a legitimate excuse; after burdening the system with the cost of futilely empanelling a jury, he could not object to being tried by judge alone.[4] The right to be present at one's trial on a criminal charge, which is implicitly guaranteed by s. 11(d), was lost by a defendant who absconded in the course of the trial; the trial could validly continue in his absence.[5] And the right to be a candidate for election to a provincial legislature, which is guaranteed by s. 3 of the Charter, was lost by a person who had committed an illegal practice under the electoral legislation.[6] These kinds of cases are often described as examples of waiver, but the disqualified person, although he has behaved badly, has not waived the right: he has made no informed, clear and voluntary choice to relinquish the right. They are cases of forfeiture, and "the forfeiture occurs by operation of law without regard to the defendant's state of mind."[7] Forfeiture is effective only if it is authorized by statute. Moreover, since the forfeiting provision of the statute restricts a constitutional right, the statutory provision must be justified as a reasonable limit on the right under s. 1 of the Charter.

---

[4]*R. v. Lee*, [1989] 2 S.C.R. 1384. The consequence was stipulated by the Criminal Code, which was held to be justified under s. 1 as a reasonable limit on the right to a jury trial.

[5]*R. v. Czuczman* (1986), 54 O.R. (2d) 574 (C.A.) (defendant, by absconding, had "waived" his right to be present at his trial). By classifying the absconding as a waiver (instead of a forfeiture), the Court was distracted from the need to justify the Criminal Code provision allowing the continuance of the trial as a reasonable limit under s. 1 of the Charter; no s. 1 analysis was undertaken.

[6]*Harvey v. New Brunswick*, [1996] 2 S.C.R. 876. The consequence was stipulated by the provincial Elections Act, which was held to be justified under s. 1 as a reasonable limit on the right to candidacy.

[7]A. Young, " 'Not Waving but Drowning': A look at Waiver and Collective Constitutional Rights in the Criminal Process" (1989) 53 Sask. L. Rev. 47, 67.

§ 37:16 Rationale of waiver

The waiver of a constitutional right presupposes that the right is for the benefit of the individual who chooses to waive it. If anyone else would be affected by the waiver, the concurrence of that other person would also be required. And a right that has a "collective" or "public" quality cannot be waived by any individual (or group of individuals), even when waiver would be advantageous to the individual. For example, the right to a "public" trial, which is guaranteed by s. 11(d), is not a right of the accused's alone; the right has the public purpose of ensuring that the criminal-justice process is open to public scrutiny. Therefore, an accused who would prefer his trial to take place privately or anonymously is not permitted to give effect to his individual preference and waive the right to a public trial.[1] By contrast, the right to trial within a reasonable time, which is guaranteed by s. 11(b), can be waived by an accused person who seeks (or gives an informed consent to) a delay that would otherwise be unreasonably long.[2] Needless to say, the absence of a collective or public quality to a Charter right is not always explicitly revealed, and Alan Young has argued that all the legal rights that protect the integrity of the criminal-justice system should be regarded as having a collective quality, constraining governmental power for the benefit of everyone. He concludes that none of the "core" rights should be waivable by an individual accused, although less important "derivative" rights should continue to be waivable.[3] The courts of Canada and the other countries with common law criminal-justice traditions have never accepted this position. Rather the judicial assumption is that most rights are intended to protect the dignity and autonomy of the individual, and the practice of waiver is consistent with that purpose. "The essence of autonomy is choice, and the individual is permitted either to insist upon or waive a right in accordance with that individual's perception of her self-interest."[4]

Take, for example, the mother of all waivers, namely, the guilty plea. When an accused pleads guilty to a charge, he waives the most fundamental criminal-justice right of all, which is the presumption of in-

[Section 37:16]

[1] *R. v. D. (G.)* (1991), 2 O.R. (3d) 498 (C.A.) (denying the defendant's application for a publication ban on his name).

[2] *R. v. D. (G.)* (1991), 2 O.R. (3d) 498, 507 (C.A.), with the important qualification that the resulting trial is not unfair, because (except in the case of a plea of guilty, which obviates any trial at all) there is no right to waive the constitutional right to a fair trial. On waiver of speedy trial, see § 37:21.

[3] A. Young, " 'Not Waving but Drowning': A look at Waiver and Collective Constitutional Rights in the Criminal Process" (1989) 53 Sask. L. Rev. 47. The most dramatic of his "core" of unwaivable rights would include unreasonable search and seizure (cannot be waived by consent) and the presumption of innocence (cannot be waived by a guilty plea).

[4] A. Young, " 'Not Waving but Drowning': A look at Waiver and Collective Constitutional Rights in the Criminal Process" (1989) 53 Sask. L. Rev. 47, 51 (articulating the current position, which he goes on to criticize).

nocence guaranteed by s. 11(d) of the Charter. That guarantee requires the prosecution to prove the commission of the offence beyond a reasonable doubt (not simply the civil standard of the balance of probabilities) in a fair and public hearing before an independent and impartial tribunal. When this right is coupled with the right to silence guaranteed by s. 7 (before trial) and by s. 11(c) (at trial), the person accused of crime is "entitled to sit back, secure in his or her silence, and put the Crown to its proof".[5] These are valuable safeguards against false accusations of crime against innocent persons. But suppose the accusation of crime is true? It is easy to see the attraction to the guilty party of a plea of guilty, especially if the defence and prosecution are able to agree on a recommendation of sentence which is likely to be accepted by the sentencing court. Why should the accused be forced to wait for and endure a trial to establish the guilt that he acknowledges? And why should the resources of the state be applied to the prosecutorial and judicial effort of running a futile trial? These are no doubt some of the reasons why 90 per cent of convictions in Canada's criminal justice system arise from guilty pleas—and it seems undeniable that major additions to police, prosecutorial and judicial resources would be needed if guilty pleas were abolished.[6] The person who pleads guilty is exercising an informed, voluntary and clear choice to forego a trial. No one else seems to be affected: the guilty plea of one accused does not stop another accused from pleading not guilty and putting the Crown's case to the test of trial. And the right to a fair trial remains a reassuring and realistic safeguard for those members of society who are in fact law abiding.

As the guilty plea example shows, waiver may offer significant advantages to the right-holder, speeding up the resolution of a criminal charge, and reducing the risk of an uncertain result. And it offers society the parallel advantages of cost and time saving in the criminal process. On the other hand, the right-holder's choice to plead guilty may be unduly influenced by the police, the prosecution or even the accused's own counsel—making it imperative for the court accepting the plea to satisfy itself that the plea was in fact informed, voluntary and clearly articulated.[7]

---

[5]J.D.R. Craig, "Guilty Plea Revocation, Constitutional Waiver, and the Charter. 'A Guilty Plea is not a Trap' " (1997) 20 Dal. L. J. 161, 162.

[6]A. Young, " 'Not Waving but Drowning': A look at Waiver and Collective Constitutional Rights in the Criminal Process" (1989) 53 Sask. L. Rev. 47, favours the abolition of the guilty plea, but he acknowledges (p. 111) that this "may be a difficult task", and suggests that before this recommendation is implemented "it will be necessary to collect empirical data which might indicate how this proposal would affect the allocation of resources in the justice system".

[7]Like any other waiver, the guilty plea must be informed, voluntary and clear. A judge will inquire into those elements in the case of an unrepresented accused, but will not usually do so when an accused is represented by counsel. It may be that this inquiry should be the norm, because there does seem to be reason for concern that some guilty pleas result from pressure on the accused by overburdened defence counsel to accept a plea bargain with the prosecution even when a trial would be likely to yield a verdict of not guilty: A. Young, " 'Not Waving but Drowning': A look at Waiver and Collective

§ 37:17 Waiver of presumption of innocence

Section 11(d) of the Charter prescribes that a person charged with an offence has the right "to be presumed innocent until proven guilty according to law in a fair and public hearing by an independent and impartial tribunal".[1] As explained in the previous section, the proof of guilt has to be proof beyond a reasonable doubt, but, if that standard of proof is met, then the presumption of innocence is rebutted, the accused is legally guilty, and will be sentenced by the criminal court that conducted the trial.

As also explained in the previous section, the accused may waive the presumption of innocence (and the trial that it entails) by pleading guilty. A plea of guilty is usually thought of as the only way in which the presumption of innocence can be waived. However, in *R. v. Richard* (1996),[2] the Supreme Court held that an accused person, who failed to pay the fine stipulated on a traffic ticket and failed to appear in court to defend the charge at the time and place stipulated on the ticket, had waived the presumption of innocence (and the right to a fair trial), and could validly be convicted in absentia and fined the amount stipulated on the ticket. According to La Forest J., who wrote for the Court, the traffic ticket accurately explained the consequences of a failure to appear, and there was a statutory right to set aside the conviction within 45 days if the defendant satisfied a judge that the failure to appear was the result of events outside his or her control. On these facts, a sufficient level of knowledge and voluntariness could be attributed to the accused to treat his absence from court as an implicit waiver of the right to a trial. This lowers the bar for a waiver, since the accused's behavior falls well short of a "clear and unequivocal" waiver, and it is informed and voluntary only if one assumes that the traffic ticket has been read and understood. On the other hand, the result seems reasonable given the high volume of traffic tickets and the relatively low penalties normally at stake. Perhaps the Court's decision is best analyzed as a finding of forfeiture rather than waiver, although the Court did not engage in the s. 1 analysis that would be required to justify the statutory provision that authorized a finding of guilt without a trial.[3]

If an entire trial is validly waived by a guilty plea or validly forfeited by failure to attend at court, then of course no trial takes place and all the safeguards of a criminal trial become irrelevant. If an accused pleads not guilty and a trial ensues, the accused cannot necessarily waive any of the elements of the Charter's requirements for a fair trial, even if the

---

Constitutional Rights in the Criminal Process" (1989) 53 Sask. L. Rev. 47, 71-74, 109-111; J.D.R. Craig, "Guilty Plea Revocation, Constitutional Waiver, and the Charter. 'A Guilty Plea is not a Trap' " (1997) 20 Dal. L. J. 161, 166-167.

[Section 37:17]

[1]See ch. 51, Rights on Being Charged, under heading §§ 51:13 to 51:17, "Presumption of innocence (s. 11(d))", especially § 51:17, "Waiver of presumption of innocence".

[2]*R. v. Richard,* [1996] 3 S.C.R. 525.

[3]Text accompanying § 37:15 notes 4 to 7.

accused would prefer not to take advantage of them. We have already noticed that an accused who would prefer his trial to take place privately and anonymously cannot waive his s. 11(d) right to a "public" trial.[4] That is because the right to a public trial is not a right that only benefits the accused; it also serves the public interest of keeping the criminal-justice process open to public scrutiny. It is not easy to imagine why an accused might want to waive the s. 11(d) requirements of proof beyond a reasonable doubt, a "fair" trial, and "an independent and impartial tribunal", but these requirements too not only protect the accused, but serve the public interest that justice must be seen to be done—by observers in the courtroom and by the wider public through media reports from the courtroom.

§ 37:18 Waiver of right to silence

The right to silence finds its source in ss. 7 and 11(c) of the Charter.[1] Section 7 of the Charter has been interpreted as constitutionalizing the common law right of an individual to remain silent following arrest or detention. This was decided in *R. v. Hebert* (1990),[2] where the accused was warned of his right to retain and instruct counsel. He did so, and after consulting counsel he advised the police that he did not want to make a statement. He was then placed in a cell with an undercover police officer, disguised as another prisoner, who engaged the accused in conversation and to whom the accused made an incriminatory statement. The Supreme Court held that this statement had been obtained in violation of the accused's right to silence, and should be excluded from evidence under s. 24(2). There is no doubt that an accused who has refused to talk to the police is free to change his mind.[3] But in this case the statement to the undercover police officer had been obtained by a police trick. Not knowing that he was talking to a police officer, the accused was unaware of the consequences of his act. The statement, although voluntary, was not sufficiently informed to serve as a waiver of the right to silence.

The s. 7 right to silence applies to an accused person who has been arrested or detained and is questioned by police before trial. At trial, s. 11(c) provides that an accused person has the right "not to be compelled to be a witness" at his own trial. The accused person's right to silence is thus extended to the trial. The accused is however a competent witness, and can testify on his own behalf if he chooses to do so. This is not

[4] *R. v. D. (G.)* (1991), 2 O.R. (3d) 498 (C.A.).

[Section 37:18]

[1] For fuller discussion, see ch. 47, Fundamental Justice, under heading § 47:31, "Right to silence".

[2] *R. v. Hebert*, [1990] 2 S.C.R. 151. McLachlin J. wrote the opinion of the majority of seven. Sopinka and Wilson JJ. wrote separate concurring opinions.

[3] So held in *R. v. Singh*, [2007] 3 S.C.R. 405 (initial refusal to talk to the police; eventually, voluntary statement made to the police; not obtained by threats, promises, oppression or trickery; held no breach of right to silence).

technically a waiver: the only right is not to be *compelled*; voluntary testimony is not caught by the s. 11(c) right, which need not therefore be waived by the accused who wishes to testify.

§ 37:19 Waiver of unreasonable search and seizure

Section 8 of the Charter guarantees against "unreasonable search and seizure".[1] The general rule is that a search or seizure must be carried out with a court-authorized warrant, which will only be issued on a sworn statement establishing reasonable and probable cause to believe that an offence has been committed and that evidence of the offence will be found in the place to be searched. With some exceptions, a search or seizure without a warrant is unreasonable and an infringement of s. 8. The s. 8 right can be waived if the person whose privacy is protected gives a police officer an informed, clear and voluntary consent to the search or seizure.[2] In that case, a police search without a warrant will not infringe s. 8. Waiver enables a person to cooperate with a police investigation. This is one of the situations where a person has the option to waive a constitutional right, and it would surely be pointless to require the police to obtain a warrant to make a consensual search. If the police investigation is at an early stage, the police may in any case lack the evidence needed to obtain a warrant and have no choice but to depend upon cooperation to obtain information.

A reality of any police interaction with the public is that people are not well informed about the extent of police powers. A person may therefore consent to a police search in the mistaken belief that the police had the legal power to make the search. If a consensual search turns up incriminating evidence, it will be necessary to determine whether the consent was truly a waiver of the right to be free from unreasonable search and seizure. What the courts have wisely insisted upon is that consent is not sufficiently informed to count as a waiver if the suspect was unaware that he or she had the power to refuse the police request for a search. For example, in *R. v. Mellenthin* (1992),[3] the police, having lawfully stopped a car for a roadside check, saw an open gym bag on the passenger seat of the car and asked the driver what was in it. The driver produced some empty glass vials of a kind commonly used for storing cannabis. The police officer then searched the bag and found that it contained illegal drugs. The Supreme Court held that the accused's voluntary production of the vials should not be construed as a waiver of the right to be free from an unreasonable search. The accused was not aware of his right to refuse to respond to the police question,

---

[Section 37:19]

[1]For fuller discussion, see ch. 48, Unreasonable Search and Seizure.

[2]A. Young, " 'Not Waving but Drowning': A look at Waiver and Collective Constitutional Rights in the Criminal Process" (1989) 53 Sask. L. Rev. 47, 56-62; G. Luther, "Consent Search and Reasonable Expectation of Privacy: Twin Barriers to the Reasonable Protection of Privacy in Canada" (2008) 41 U.B.C. L. Rev. 1.

[3]*R. v. Mellenthin*, [1992] 3 S.C.R. 615.

and without that awareness a waiver could not be inferred. The search of the gym bag, which was unauthorized by a warrant, was a breach of s. 8.

In *R. v. Wills* (1992),[4] the accused, who had been involved in an automobile accident, voluntarily submitted to a breathalyzer test at the police station, even though he had not failed the roadside screening test. The police suggested to the accused that he take the breathalyzer test on the ground that it would help him in the event of a civil suit arising out of the accident. Unbeknown to the accused (and to the police), the roadside screening device had been malfunctioning, and the level of alcohol in the accused's blood was in fact above the legal limit. When the breathalyzer registered above the legal limit, the police charged the accused with impaired driving causing death. There was no doubt that the accused had consented to take the breathalyzer test with the knowledge that he had the right to refuse. But the Ontario Court of Appeal held that the accused's consent was not a waiver of his right to refuse because the consent was not sufficiently informed by knowledge of the consequences of taking the test. He was unaware that the roadside device was unreliable (as were the police), and he was also unaware that the victim of his accident had died (something the police had not told him). Without full information as to the possible consequences of his voluntary act, there was no waiver, and the breathalyzer test was taken in breach of s. 8.

If property is voluntarily given to the police, then it has not been seized—so long as the handing over of the property is informed as to the use that would be made of the property.[5] In *R. v. Dersch* (1993),[6] the accused, who was a victim of a traffic accident, agreed to provide a blood sample to the hospital for medical purposes. A doctor at the hospital prepared a report on the level of alcohol in the accused's blood, and concluded that he had been intoxicated at the time of the accident. The hospital gave this report to the police who charged the accused with impaired driving. The Supreme Court held that the accused's voluntary provision of the blood sample for medical diagnosis should not be interpreted as consent to its use by the police for the purpose of investigating or proving the commission of a crime. The accused retained a reasonable expectation of privacy in his hospital records. The obtaining of the report from the hospital was an unreasonable search by the police. If the hospital had voluntarily given the actual blood sample to the police, that would have been an unreasonable seizure by the police

[4] *R. v. Wills* (1992), 7 O.R. (3d) 337 (C.A.).

[5] *R. v. Arp*, [1998] 3 S.C.R. 339 (accused consented to the police taking hair samples for the investigation of a crime; held, the consent extended to the use of the samples for the investigation of another crime); compare *R. v. Borden*, [1994] 3 S.C.R. 145 (opposite result; query correctness).

[6] *R. v. Dersch*, [1993] 3 S.C.R. 768.

because only the person with the privacy interest can waive his right to be free from unreasonable seizure.[7]

In *R. v. Cole* (2012),[8] a school principal handed over to the police a school-board-owned laptop computer that had been issued to the accused, who was a teacher in the school. A school board technician performing routine maintenance on the computer had discovered a file in the computer containing nude photographs of one of the school's female students. He had notified the principal of the school who confiscated the computer and handed it over to the police. The police, without a warrant, reviewed the contents of the computer and charged the accused with possession of child pornography. At his trial, the accused objected to the evidence of the photographs on the ground that it had been obtained in breach of s. 8. The Supreme Court held that, although the computer was owned by the school board and was intended primarily for work-related use, the teacher did have a reasonable expectation of privacy in the personal matters stored on the computer.[9] The police search of the computer without a warrant was therefore in breach of s. 8. The Court acknowledged that the employer—the school board—had consented to the search by the police, but a third party could not waive the accused's privacy interest. There was no doctrine of "third party consent" in Canada (unlike the United States)[10] because that would be inconsistent with the requirement that a waiver be an informed, clear and voluntary choice by the right-holder.[11] It followed that "the school board's 'third party consent' to the search was of no legal consequence."[12]

The Supreme Court of Canada revisited third party consent in *R. v. Reeves* (2018).[13] In this case, the accused and his common-law spouse shared a computer that was located in a common area of a house that was co-owned and (most of the time) co-occupied by them. During a pe-

[7]Compare *R. v. Colarusso*, [1994] 1 S.C.R. 20 (blood and urine samples taken by hospital by consent for medical purposes; samples validly seized by coroner for investigation of a death; samples given by coroner to police; held, unreasonable seizure by police).

[8]*R. v. Cole*, [2012] 3 S.C.R. 34.

[9]I have elsewhere criticized this holding on the ground that the school board maintained full access to the computer, and had a policy denying privacy to any of its contents: ch. 48, Search and Seizure, under heading §§ 48:5 to 48:12, "From property to privacy".

[10]A doctrine of third party consent has been accepted in the U.S.A. when the person with the privacy interest has voluntarily assumed the risk that the third party might provide his information to the police: *United States v. Matlock* (1974), 415 U.S. 164; *Illinois v. Rodriguez* (1990), 497 U.S. 177; *United States v. Ziegler* (2007), 474 F.3d 1184 (9th Circ.), 1191.

[11]*R. v. Cole*, [2012] 3 S.C.R. 34, para. 78.

[12]*R. v. Cole*, [2012] 3 S.C.R. 34, para. 10. Accord, *R. v. McNeice*, 2013 BCCA 98 (work computer given to police by employer; employee retained reasonable expectation of privacy in the personal files).

[13]*R. v. Reeves*, [2018] 3 S.C.R. 531. Karakatsanis J. wrote the opinion for the majority of the Court, with the agreement of six other judges. Moldaver and Côté JJ. each wrote concurring opinions.

riod when the accused was not permitted in the home (after a domestic assault charge, the accused was prohibited from being in the home without the spouse's consent, which she withdrew), the spouse discovered child pornography on the computer. She reported this to the police. In response, a police officer came to the house without a warrant, was admitted to the house by the spouse and, with her consent, took the computer. The police did not search the computer until they had obtained a search warrant to do so, and their search revealed child pornography. The accused was charged with possessing and accessing child pornography. He applied to exclude the computer-based evidence under s. 24(2) on the basis that it was obtained in breach of s. 8. The Supreme Court of Canada held that the accused had a diminished but still reasonable expectation of privacy in the computer, and that the police seizure of the computer without a warrant was therefore in breach of s. 8. The Crown argued that there was no breach of s. 8 because the spouse's consent to the taking of the computer waived his s. 8 rights in the computer. The Court's decision in *Cole* obviously posed a challenge for this argument, but the Crown attempted to distinguish *Cole*, arguing that the spouse was "not a 'true' third party because she had an equal and overlapping privacy interest in the computer".[14] Karakatsanis J., who wrote for the majority of the Court, rejected this argument. She affirmed *Cole's* rejection of the third party consent doctrine, and she said that a person cannot waive the s. 8 rights of another even if they share "an equal and overlapping privacy interest".[15]

§ 37:20 Waiver of right to counsel

Section 10(b) of the Charter guarantees to everyone "on arrest or detention" the right "to retain and instruct counsel without delay and to be informed of that right". This is a very important right since counsel will advise his or her client of the various criminal-justice rights, and especially the right to remain silent. Nevertheless, it is not mandatory for an accused person to be represented by counsel either before or during a criminal trial, and the right to counsel can be waived. Like other waivers, it must be informed, clear and voluntary. The discussion of the right to counsel later in the book[1] explains the waiver rules in detail, including the nature of the warning that must be given to the accused by the police in order to be sure that any waiver is fully informed, the opportunity that must be provided by the police to enable the accused to retain counsel, the requirements that any waiver be "clear and unequivocal" and be informed by an understanding of the extent of the accused's

---

[14] *R. v. Reeves*, [2018] 3 S.C.R. 531, para. 51.

[15] *R. v. Reeves*, [2018] 3 S.C.R. 531, para. 48. Côté J. wrote a concurring opinion; she agreed that the spouse's consent did not waive the accused's privacy interests, but did take it into account in finding that the accused lacked a reasonable expectation of privacy.

[Section 37:20]

[1] Chapter 50, Rights on Arrest or Detention, under heading §§ 50:5 to 50:16, "Right to counsel", especially § 50:13, "Waiver of right".

jeopardy. The police are under a duty to refrain from questioning the accused until he has either retained counsel or validly waived the right.[2] The accused's answers to police questions in violation of any of these various rules will have been obtained in breach of s. 10(b) and will be liable to be excluded from evidence under s. 24(2).

§ 37:21 Waiver of speedy trial

Section 11(b) of the Charter confers on an accused person the right "to be tried within a reasonable time".[1] The right can be waived, but, like other waivers, the waiver must be informed, clear and voluntary. The issue typically arises over an adjournment or the setting of a late trial date, which would cause the trial to move outside the limit of "reasonable time". If defence counsel requests the adjournment or the late trial date, with full knowledge of the 11(b) right, that will be regarded as a partial waiver of the right, and the agreed-upon delay will not be counted in assessing the reasonableness of the time of trial.[2] If it is the Crown or the court itself that requests or causes a delay, and if the defence objects, then of course there is no waiver of the right. Even passive acquiescence by defence counsel would not typically be "clear and unequivocal" enough to be treated as an implicit waiver of the right,[3] but it is obviously more prudent for defence counsel, in acquiescing to a delay, to state expressly that the 11(b) right is not being waived.

§ 37:22 Waiver of right to jury

Section 11(f) of the Charter confers on an accused person the right to "the benefit of trial by jury where the maximum punishment for the offence is imprisonment for five years or a more severe punishment".[1] The Criminal Code used to make trial by jury mandatory for the most serious offences. When persons accused of one of these offences applied to be tried by judge alone, the Supreme Court agreed that they had waived their s. 11(f) right, but the Court held that s. 11(f) did not confer any right to any alternative mode of trial, and at that time nor did the Criminal Code, which stipulated that the trial must be by jury. Their application to be tried by judge alone could not be granted.[2]

The Criminal Code now makes general provision for an accused to

---

[2]Chapter 50, Rights on Arrest or Detention, under heading § 50:12, "Duty to refrain from questioning".

[Section 37:21]

[1]See ch. 52, Trial Within a Reasonable Time, especially, § 52:9, "Waiver of delay".

[2]If the defendant is unrepresented, the trial judge will have to talk to the defendant, and satisfy himself that an informed, clear and voluntary waiver is being given in return for the requested delay.

[3]*R. v. Morin*, [1992] 1 S.C.R. 771, 790.

[Section 37:22]

[1]See ch. 51, Rights on Being Charged, under heading §§ 51:19 to 51:25, "Trial by jury (s. 11(f))", especially § 51:22, "Waiver of right".

[2]*R. v. Turpin*, [1989] 1 S.C.R. 1296.

elect against trial by jury, in which case a trial by judge alone is provided for. The election should presumably be informed, clear and voluntary, since it is equivalent to a waiver of the right to trial by jury. However, it does not seem to be necessary to invoke the idea of waiver to explain the justification for this statutory power of election. So long as the mode of trial (jury or judge alone) is the choice of the accused, the accused has "the benefit" of trial by jury.

In *R. v. Lee* (1989),[3] the accused elected to be tried by jury, but then failed to appear for his trial without a legitimate excuse. In that circumstance, the Criminal Code provided that the accused was to be tried by judge alone. The accused still wanted to be tried by jury, and argued that he had a constitutional right to that mode of trial. The Supreme Court held that he had not waived his right to trial by jury. His failure to attend for trial was not sufficiently "clear and equivocal", or sufficiently informed as to the consequences, to be regarded as a waiver of the right to be tried by a jury.[4] However, the right was forfeited by the Criminal Code provision that imposed trial by judge alone. Lamer J., for the majority, held that the forfeiture was a limit on the right that was justified under s. 1. It was appropriate to deny the right to trial by jury to those who had burdened the system with the cost of futilely empanelling a jury.[5] Wilson J. dissented, arguing that "reducing administrative inconvenience and reducing expense are not, in my view, sufficient objectives to override such a vital constitutional right".[6]

§ 37:23 Waiver of right to interpreter

Section 14 of the Charter confers on a party or witness in court proceedings who does not understand or speak the language in which the proceedings are conducted "the right to the assistance of an interpreter".[1] In *R. v. Tran* (1994),[2] Lamer C.J. for the Supreme Court said that the right to an interpreter "is not only a fundamental constitutional guarantee in its own right, but also an important means of ensuring a full, fair and public hearing". That would seem to give the right a "public" quality that would make it unwaivable by the individual who was entitled to claim the right. However, Lamer C.J. went on to say only that "there will be situations where the right *cannot*, in the greater public interest, be waived".[3] Despite the emphatic "cannot", this statement implied that there will be situations where the right can be waived, but he did not elucidate—and he went on to consider whether the right had been waived in the case before him. The issue in the case was

---

[3] *R. v. Lee*, [1989] 2 S.C.R. 1384.

[4] *R. v. Lee*, [1989] 2 S.C.R. 1384, 1411-1412.

[5] *R. v. Lee*, [1989] 2 S.C.R. 1384, 1390-1391.

[6] *R. v. Lee*, [1989] 2 S.C.R. 1384, 1420.

[Section 37:23]

[1] See ch. 56, Language, under heading § 56:13, "Right to interpreter".

[2] *R. v. Tran*, [1994] 2 S.C.R. 951, 996.

[3] *R. v. Tran*, [1994] 2 S.C.R. 951 (emphasis in original).

whether there had been a breach of s. 14 in the trial in English of an accused who only spoke Vietnamese. One of the witnesses, who spoke English and Vietnamese, and who was called by the defence, testified in English only, just adding a short summary in Vietnamese at the end of his testimony. The accused's counsel did not object to the absence of the verbatim, contemporaneous, and continuous interpretation that had been provided for the rest of the evidence. After his conviction, however, the accused appealed on the ground that he had been denied his right to an interpreter. The Court held that counsel's failure to object to the inadequate interpretation was not a sufficiently informed, clear and voluntary choice by the accused to serve as a waiver. The Court held that s. 14 had been infringed and ordered a new trial.

§ 37:24 Waiver by contract

As the foregoing discussion has demonstrated, issues of waiver have typically arisen in criminal proceedings where it is arguable that an accused person has waived one of the Charter's criminal-justice rights. Another situation is where a governmental entity (bound by the Charter) enters into a contract in which the contracting party agrees to waive a constitutional right, for example, a right to be free of age-related discrimination or a right to engage in a religious practice or a right of free expression. Assuming that the private contracting party freely entered into the contract, the contract must provide benefits that offset the loss of the constitutional right. Unless the contract would offend public policy for some good reason, a contract would seem to be an informed, clear and voluntary act which should count as a waiver. Indeed, it is arguable that "any prohibition of contracting out is itself a denial of a very fundamental right: the liberty of personal choice".[1] The issue is less clear with a collective agreement, since not all the employees in the bargaining unit do in fact necessarily agree with all the terms negotiated by the union they selected as their bargaining agent, but the union must have concluded that the package was for their advantage, and of course it must have been ratified by at least a majority of the employees. However, the Supreme Court of Canada has never said unequivocally that constitutional rights can be waived by contract, and it is impossible to discern any clear doctrine from the few decided cases, which are discussed in the following text.

The issue of waiver has arisen with collective agreements that provide for mandatory retirement at age 65. This may well be discrimination on the ground of age contrary to s. 15 of the Charter. But it usually comes as part of a package which is advantageous to employees, including, for example, higher pay at an earlier age, more security of tenure, less continuous performance evaluation, and pension benefits that are payable at the stipulated retirement age. However, in the pre-Charter case

[Section 37:24]

[1] Gibson, The Law of the Charter: General Principles (1986), 167. There is an inconclusive discussion of waiver at pp. 163-168.

of *Craton v. Winnipeg School Division No. 1* (1986),[2] the Supreme Court held that a collective agreement providing for mandatory retirement at age 65 for school teachers was not a valid waiver of equality rights under Manitoba's Human Rights Act. McIntyre J. for the Court announced without elaboration that the Act "is legislation declaring public policy and may not be avoided by private contract".[3] The mandatory retirement provision was held to be invalid.

The Charter challenge came in *McKinney v. University of Guelph* (1990),[4] where professors at Ontario universities challenged their universities' mandatory retirement policies as infringements of the equality right in s. 15. (The Ontario Human Rights Code at that time permitted mandatory retirement at age 65.) The Supreme Court held, by a majority, that the Charter did not apply to the universities, but the Court went on to discuss what the position would be if the Charter did apply. The majority of the Court held that, if the Charter did apply, mandatory retirement would infringe s. 15, but that it would be justified as a reasonable limit under s. 1. In several of the universities, mandatory retirement had been agreed to by unionized faculty in a collective agreement, which raised the question whether the equality right could be waived by them as part of a package that provided offsetting benefits (which included tenure to retirement and a pension thereafter). La Forest J., writing for himself and two others, suggested, obiter, that "the acceptance of a contractual obligation could, in some circumstances, constitute a waiver of a Charter right especially in a case like mandatory retirement, which not only imposes burdens, but benefits on employees". However, in an unacknowledged departure from previous (criminal-justice) waiver cases, he went on to say that "such an arrangement would usually require justification as a reasonable limit under s. 1".[5] Cory J. agreed that the equality right could be waived, and added that it would be "unfortunate" if a union could not agree to mandatory retirement as part of a package that would be for the benefit of the employees.[6] He did not comment on La Forest J.'s suggestion that s. 1 justification would be necessary. Wilson J. wrote a dissenting opinion, holding that the Charter did apply to the universities and that mandatory retirement could not be justified under s. 1. On waiver, she took a similar line to that of McIntyre J. in Craton, saying that "equality rights lie at the heart of the Charter", and that she had "serious reservations" about whether they could be waived by contract.[7]

In *Godbout v. Longueuil* (1997),[8] the City of Longueuil passed a resolution requiring permanent employees of the city to live within the city

---

[2]*Craton v. Winnipeg School Division No. 1*, [1985] 2 S.C.R. 150.

[3]*Craton v. Winnipeg School Division No. 1*, [1985] 2 S.C.R. 150, 154.

[4]*McKinney v. University of Guelph*, [1990] 3 S.C.R. 229.

[5]*McKinney v. University of Guelph*, [1990] 3 S.C.R. 229, 277.

[6]*McKinney v. University of Guelph*, [1990] 3 S.C.R. 229, 447-448.

[7]*McKinney v. University of Guelph*, [1990] 3 S.C.R. 229, 406.

[8]*Godbout v. Longueuil*, [1997] 3 S.C.R. 844.

limits. The claimant was hired by the city to a temporary position, and she signed a contract in which she agreed to live within the city limits if she were granted a permanent position. She was granted a permanent position, but later moved outside the city limits, and was dismissed for that reason. She successfully sued the city for reinstatement and damages for wrongful dismissal, and the Supreme Court of Canada upheld these remedies. The Court was unanimous in holding that the city's resolution violated the claimant's rights. Six of the judges rested their decision solely on s. 5 of the Quebec Charter of Human Rights and Freedoms, which guarantees respect for one's private life; they held that s. 5 included a right to choose one's place of residence. They did not discuss the question whether the claimant had waived this right. La Forest J., with the agreement of L'Heureux-Dubé and McLachlin JJ., agreed with the other six judges that s. 5 of the Quebec Charter had been infringed. But La Forest J. also rested his decision on the Canadian Charter, which is of course applicable to municipalities. He held that the guarantee of "liberty" in s. 7 conferred on the claimant a right to choose her place of residence. In that context, he discussed the question of waiver, and he decided that the contract signed by the claimant was not a valid waiver of the right. He pointed out that the claimant had no choice but to sign the contract if she wanted to be employed by the municipality; it was really a contract of adhesion because, in view of council's resolution, there was no possibility to negotiate that particular term. Signing a contract of adhesion to get a job was not sufficiently voluntary to count as a waiver of a constitutional right. Obviously, there is some force in this reasoning, but the result does not seem entirely satisfactory. She had, after all, signed the contract, and must have thought at the time that the package of employment conditions was sufficiently advantageous to her that she could accept the residence condition. In the end, she kept the job that she had obtained by agreeing to the residence condition and she got rid of the residence condition.

The Supreme Court followed *Godbout* in *Syndicat Northwest v. Amselem* (2004),[9] where the claimants were purchasers of condominium apartments in a building that prohibited the building of structures on the (communally-owned) balconies of the apartments. The balconies were part of the fire-escape routes, so that there were safety (as well as aesthetic) reasons for the prohibition. On purchase, each purchaser had signed an agreement promising to abide by the by-laws that included the prohibition. After abiding by the by-laws for several years, the claimants (who were orthodox Jews) invoked a sincere religious belief that required them to build "succahs" (temporary dwellings) on their balconies and live in the succahs for a nine-day period during the festival of "Succot". The Supreme Court held that the claimants had the right to build the succahs notwithstanding their agreement to the prohibiting by-law. Iacobucci J. for the majority of the Court rejected the argument that the claimants had waived their right to engage in the religious

[9] *Syndicat Northwest v. Amselem*, [2004] 2 S.C.R. 551; for further discussion, see ch. 42, Religion, under heading § 42:7, "Waiver of religious practice".

practice[10] on the grounds[11] that the claimants "did not read" the by-laws that they signed, and in any case "had no choice" but to agree to the by-laws in order to live in that building. Binnie J., who dissented, answered that the claimants had a choice of places to live, and they "undertook by contract to the owners of this building to abide by the rules of this building even if (as is apparently the case) they accepted the rules without reading them".[12] It seems to me that Binnie J. (though dissenting) has the better of the argument. The claimants should have been treated as having voluntarily waived a right to engage in a religious practice on the communally-owned balconies that was incompatible with their condominium contract and that defeated the reasonable expectations of the other condominium owners who relied on the contract.[13]

In most kinds of employment, employees have access to confidential information, which it would be contrary to the interests of their employer (or its clients or customers) to disclose, and disclosure would be a breach of at least an implied term of the contract of employment. In the case of public employees, who are employed by some unit of government to which the Charter applies, any contractual requirement of confidentiality would be a limit on their s. 2(b) right to freedom of expression. Some degree of confidentiality is a bona fide occupational requirement for some employees, and the s. 2(b) right should be waivable by contract at least to that extent. Material classified as secret ought to be able to be kept secret, and the s. 2(b) right should be waivable to that extent too.

In *Snepp v. United States* (1980),[14] a CIA agent had entered into a contract of employment in which he agreed not to publish anything relating to the activities of the Agency, either during or after his term of employment, "without specific prior approval by the Agency". Mr Snepp, after his retirement from the Agency, published a book about the activities of the Agency in Vietnam during the Vietnam War. He did not seek or obtain prior approval by the Agency. The Agency sued him for a declaration that he was in breach of his contract, for an accounting of profits from the sales of the book, and for an injunction to enjoin the publica-

---

[10]Because this was a contract between private parties, the Canadian Charter was not applicable, but the Quebec Charter did apply: *Syndicat Northwest v. Amselem*, [2004] 2 S.C.R. 551, para. 38.

[11]*Syndicat Northwest v. Amselem*, [2004] 2 S.C.R. 551, paras. 98-99; he gave a variety of other reasons as well: *Syndicat Northwest v. Amselem*, [2004] 2 S.C.R. 551, paras. 91-102.

[12]*Syndicat Northwest v. Amselem*, [2004] 2 S.C.R. 551, paras. 184-185 (emphasis in original).

[13]Note that in this case (*McKinney v. University of Guelph*, [1990] 3 S.C.R. 229) the burden of compliance with the Quebec Charter fell on private persons (the other condominium owners) rather than government. Another private contract case, covered by the Quebec Charter, but not the Canadian Charter is *Bruker v. Marcovitz*, [2007] 3 S.C.R. 607 (husband's religious right to refuse a "get" to his wife overridden by his contractual promise to grant the get, but the Court did not find the husband's "binding promise" conclusive by itself); for discussion, see ch. 42, Religion, under heading § 42:7, "Waiver of religious practice".

[14]*Snepp v. United States* (1980), 444 U.S. 507.

tion of future manuscripts without prior approval. The Supreme Court of the United States, by a majority, granted all these remedies. Although the Court's opinion is not framed in the language of waiver, the Court held that a government agency had the power to impose reasonable restrictions on its employees' First Amendment right to freedom of speech, and that Mr Snepp was bound by the terms of his contract. Stevens J., who (with two others) dissented, pointed out that the effect of the majority decision was "to enforce a species of prior restraint on a citizen's right to criticize his government".[15] He would have denied the Agency any remedy on the basis that the book disclosed no classified information (as the Agency acknowledged), and the employment contract should be read down to prohibit only the disclosure of classified information so as to limit the First Amendment right as little as possible. The "national security context" of Snepp may have led to a broader decision by the majority than would be appropriate in other "whistleblowing" contexts.[16] In general, a contractual waiver of freedom of expression would be contrary to the public interest and should be ineffective to the extent that it had the effect of keeping expression critical of government out of the public domain. In that situation, the constitutional right serves a public purpose that cannot be surrendered by an individual.

---

[15] *Snepp v. United States* (1980), 444 U.S. 507, 526.

[16] So argued by B.K. Weinstein, "In Defense of Jeffrey Wigand: A First Amendment Challenge to the Enforceability of Employee Confidentiality Agreements against Whistleblowers" (1997) 49 South Carolina L. Rev. 129 (arguing that First Amendment should generally trump employee confidentiality agreements, and distinguishing *Snepp* on the ground that "the national security context was determinative" in that case).

Chapter 38

Limitation of Rights

I. OVERVIEW OF S. 1

§ 38:1 Introduction to s. 1
§ 38:2 Rationale of s. 1
§ 38:3 Relationship between s. 1 and rights

II. BURDEN OF PROOF

§ 38:4 Burden of proof

III. PRESUMPTION OF CONSTITUTIONALITY

§ 38:5 Presumption of constitutionality

IV. LIMITS

§ 38:6 Limits

V. PRESCRIBED BY LAW

§ 38:7 Definition of prescribed by law
§ 38:8 Discretion
§ 38:9 Vagueness

VI. REASONABLE AND DEMONSTRABLY JUSTIFIED

§ 38:10 Introduction
§ 38:11 Oakes test

VII. SUFFICIENTLY IMPORTANT OBJECTIVE

§ 38:12 Identification of objective
§ 38:13 Importance of objective
§ 38:14 Quebec's distinct society
§ 38:15 Inadmissible objectives
§ 38:16 Shifting objectives
§ 38:17 Cost

VIII. RATIONAL CONNECTION

§ 38:18 Definition
§ 38:19 Causation

IX. LEAST DRASTIC MEANS

§ 38:20 Minimum impairment

§ 38:21 Margin of appreciation

X. PROPORTIONATE EFFECT; APPLICATION TO EQUALITY RIGHTS

§ 38:22 Proportionate effect
§ 38:23 Application to equality rights

XI. APPLICATION TO QUALIFIED RIGHTS

§ 38:24 Scope of s. 1
§ 38:25 Section 7
§ 38:26 Section 8
§ 38:27 Section 9
§ 38:28 Section 11
§ 38:29 Section 12
§ 38:30 Section 23

XII. APPLICATION TO COMMON LAW

§ 38:31 Application to common law

XIII. APPLICATION TO DISCRETIONARY DECISIONS

§ 38:32 Application to discretionary decisions
§ 38:33 Emergency measures

I. OVERVIEW OF S. 1

§ 38:1 Introduction to s. 1

Section 1 of the Charter of Rights[1] provides as follows:

> The Canadian Charter of Rights and Freedoms guarantees the rights and freedoms set out in it subject only to such reasonable limits prescribed by law as can be demonstrably justified in a free and democratic society.

Section 1 guarantees the rights and freedoms set out in the Charter, but makes clear that they are not absolutes; they are subject "to such rea-

---

[Section 38:1]

[1]There is a huge literature on s. 1: see the up-to-date bibliography in Canadian Charter of Rights Annotated, Canada Law Book, looseleaf service, vol. 4. Especially valuable is Gibson, The Law of the Charter: General Principles (1986), ch. 4; S.R. Peck, "An Analytical Framework for the Application of the Canadian Charter of Rights and Freedoms" (1987) 25 Osgoode Hall L.J. 1; R.M. Elliot, "The Supreme Court of Canada and Section 1" (1987) 12 Queen's L.J. 277; L.E. Weinrib, "The Supreme Court of Canada and Section 1 of the Charter" (1988) 10 Supreme Court L.R. 469; E. Mendes, "In Search of a Theory of Social Justice: The Supreme Court Reconceives the Oakes Test" (1990) 24 Thémis 1; M. Jackman, "Protecting Rights and Promoting Democracy: Judicial Review under Section 1 of the Charter" (1996) 34 Osgoode Hall L.J. 661; Tremblay and Webber (eds.), The Limitation of Charter Rights: Critical Essays (2009).

sonable limits prescribed by law as can be demonstrably justified in a free and democratic society".[2]

Section 1 of the Charter contemplates that judicial review of legislation under the Charter should proceed in two stages. In the first stage, the court must decide whether the challenged law has the effect of limiting one of the guaranteed rights. If the challenged law does have this effect, the second stage is reached: the court must then decide whether the limit is a reasonable one that can be demonstrably justified in a free and democratic society.[3] The first stage involves the interpretation and application of the provisions of the Charter that define the guaranteed rights. The second stage involves the interpretation and application of s. 1 of the Charter.[4]

The existence of the general limitation clause of s. 1, and the two-stage review process which s. 1 mandates, reflect the influence of international human rights instruments, and especially the European Convention on Human Rights and the International Covenant on Civil and Political Rights. In these instruments, the guaranteed rights are qualified by limitation clauses expressed in terms quite similar to Canada's s. 1. The cases before the European Court of Human Rights (under the European Convention) and the Human Rights Committee of the

---

[2]In the October 1980 version of the Charter, s. 1 was as follows:

> The Canadian Charter of Rights and Freedoms guarantees the rights and freedoms set out in it subject only to such reasonable limits as are generally accepted in a free and democratic society with a parliamentary system of government.

This version of s. 1 attracted a great deal of criticism, and it was amended to its present form in the April 1981 version of the Charter. Three potentially significant changes were made: (1) the phrase "prescribed by law" was added; (2) the phrase "as can be demonstrably justified" replaced the phrase "as are generally accepted"; and (3) the phrase "with a parliamentary system of government" (which might have implied the irrelevance of American experience) was dropped from the final version. Each of these changes tended to raise the standard of justification under s. 1. See generally J. Hiebert, "The Evolution of the Limitation Clause" (1990) 28 Osgoode Hall L.J. 103.

[3]In *Frank v. Can.*, [2019] 1 S.C.R. 3, Côté and Brown JJ., in a joint dissenting opinion, argued (paras. 120-122) that a clear distinction should be drawn between Charter *limitations* and Charter *infringements* during this two-stage analysis; under their approach, an *infringement* of the Charter would arise only where a *limit* on a Charter right (at stage one) is found to be unjustifiable (at stage two). This approach would treat the reasonable and demonstrably justified limits recognized at stage two "as inherent in the right itself, shaping the right's outer boundaries": *Frank v. Can.*, [2019] 1 S.C.R. 3, para. 120. Wagner C.J., writing for the majority, rejected this distinction, suggesting that it is "largely semantic in nature", and also "novel, since a cursory review of the jurisprudence reveals that the terms 'infringement' and 'limit' are often used interchangeably": *Frank v. Can.*, [2019] 1 S.C.R. 3, para. 40. This distinction certainly does seem to be "novel". However, it is not obvious that it is merely "largely semantic", because there does seem to be an important difference between defining the scope ("outer boundaries") of a right and justifying an infringement of a right.

[4]Since s. 1 has to be considered (stage 2) in every case where a law is held to infringe a Charter right (stage 1), it is not surprising that s. 1 "has become the hungriest, the greediest, of Charter provisions, absorbing most issues of genuine constitutional dispute into its analytic grasp": B.L. Berger, "Section 1, Constitutional Reasoning and Cultural Difference: Assessing the Impacts of *Alberta v. Hutterian Brethren of Wilson Colony*" (2010) 51 Supreme Court L.R. (2d) 25, 26.

United Nations (under the International Covenant) constitute a body of jurisprudence[5] as to the meaning of the limitation clauses[6] which has been relied upon by academic commentators on s. 1 of the Charter and which is starting to be used by Canadian courts.

In contrast to the international instruments which have just been described, the American Bill of Rights contains no limitation clause, and many of the guaranteed rights are expressed in unqualified terms. Since rights to "freedom of speech" and "equal protection" (to name the two most obvious examples) cannot be absolute, the American courts have had to imply qualifications on the rights in order to accommodate legitimate restraints on free speech and legitimate distinctions between different groups.[7] This has been accomplished as a matter of "judicial legislation" and without any express direction in the Bill of Rights. In Canada, the courts can point to s. 1 as authorizing the development of limits on the guaranteed rights. This formal difference between the American Bill and the Canadian Charter does not make the American jurisprudence irrelevant, of course, but it does require the Canadian courts to develop their own patterns of reasoning, which must take into account not only the guaranteed rights but also the limitation clause of s. 1.

During the public debate that preceded the adoption of the Charter, there was controversy about the desirability of a limitation clause, the conventional view being that the clause "weakened" the Charter. But s. 1 has probably had the effect of strengthening the guaranteed rights. As will be explained, s. 1 has been interpreted as imposing stringent requirements of justification. Those requirements may be more difficult for the government to discharge than the requirements that would have been imposed by the courts in the absence of a limitation clause. In any event, there is merit in the frank avowal that the guaranteed rights are not absolutes, and in the establishment of procedural and substantive rules defining the requirements of justification. These rules, which the Court has derived from s. 1, are the topic of this chapter.

It should be remembered that s. 1 is not the only route to the enactment of laws in derogation of Charter rights. Under s. 33 (the override clause), it is possible to enact a law that overrides a Charter right by including in the law a notwithstanding clause. Thus, a law that cannot satisfy the standard of justification required by s. 1 may still be

[5]For discussion of this jurisprudence, and its relevance to the Charter, see ch. 36, Charter of Rights, under heading § 36:28, "International sources".

[6]See B. Hovius, "The Limitation Clauses of the European Convention on Human Rights" (1985) 17 Ottawa L. Rev. 213; B. Hovius, "The Limitation Clauses of the European Convention on Human Rights and Freedoms" (1986) 6 Yearbook of European Law 1; de Mestral (ed.), The Limitation of Human Rights in Comparative Constitutional Law (1986) H.C. Yourow, The Margin of Appreciation Doctrine in the Dynamics of European Human Rights Jurisprudence (S.J.D. thesis, U. of Michigan, 1993).

[7]E.g., *Central Hudson Gas & Electric Corp. v. Public Service Commn. of N.Y.* (1980), 447 U.S. 557, 566, setting out a four-part test as the standard for the validity of restrictions on commercial speech. This test bears striking similarities to the *Oakes* test, developed by the Supreme Court of Canada six years later: § 38:11, "Oakes test".

competent to the Parliament or Legislature under s. 33. Section 33 is the topic of §§ 39, Override of Rights, which follows this chapter.

§ 38:2 Rationale of s. 1

The idea that rights can be limited in pursuit of other legislative objectives is a difficult one. If a right can be limited, what is its value? Indeed, this question should really be reformulated as, what is a right? In the absence of rights, it is normally a sufficient moral or political justification for a law (or any political decision) that the law is calculated to increase the general welfare. The law may make some people worse off, but so long as these costs are outweighed by the benefits to others, there is a net increase in the general welfare.[1]

In a famous essay, "Taking Rights Seriously" (1970),[2] Ronald Dworkin pointed out that rights are not "taken seriously" if they can be overridden simply by an appeal to the general welfare. It should not be possible to take away a right just because, on balance, the benefits to others will outweigh the cost to the right-holder. If a right could be taken away for only the reasons that would be sufficient if no right existed, then the claim to a right is pointless. Dworkin's argument was directed to "moral rights", but his argument has more obvious force to constitutionally protected rights, and its practical significance in that context is clear. Section 1 of the Charter would undermine everything that follows it if it were interpreted as permitting the Court to uphold a limit on a guaranteed right whenever the benefits of the law imposing the limit outweighed the costs. Moreover, there is no reason in a democracy why a non-elected Court should be given the task of re-doing the political calculus of costs and benefits that has already been performed by an elected legislative body. Not only does the Court lack the democratic mandate that is provided by electoral accountability, the Court also lacks the expertise and resources to review the legislative judgment that a particular law will increase the general welfare.[3]

[Section 38:2]

[1] Utilitarianism holds that the principle of "utility" is the only sure guide to public policy. Jeremy Bentham held that the principle of utility was satisfied if a policy would advance "the greatest happiness of the greatest number". This required that, if a law inflicted some pains, those pains were outweighed by the pleasures that the law produced. Bentham went so far as to catalogue the various pleasures and pains and to provide standards for measuring them, so that the pleasures could be added and the pains subtracted in order to determine whether the principle of utility was satisfied: J. Bentham, An Introduction to the Principles of Morals and Legislation (Burns and Hart eds., Clarendon Press, Oxford, 1996), chs. 1-5. Of course, no one now believes that pleasures and pains can be identified and measured in the scientific way suggested by Bentham. But it is probably the case that legislators do attempt some kind of utilitarian calculus, weighing advantages against disadvantages, or benefits against costs, in formulating policy.

[2] This essay was originally published in the New York Review of Books. It now forms ch. 7 of Dworkin, Taking Rights Seriously (rev. ed., 1978).

[3] See L.E. Weinrib, "The Supreme Court of Canada and Section 1 of the Charter"

In *R. v. Oakes* (1986),[4] the Supreme Court of Canada attempted to grapple with these profound questions. Dickson C.J. wrote a brilliant opinion for a Court that was unanimous on this issue. He pointed out[5] that the words "free and democratic society" in s. 1 set the standard of justification under s. 1. Only the values of a free and democratic society would suffice to limit the guaranteed rights. Since the guaranteed rights were themselves derived from the values of a free and democratic society, there was an "identity of values" underlying both the rights and their limits.[6] "The underlying values of a free and democratic society both guarantee the rights in the Charter and, in appropriate circumstances, justify limitations upon those rights".[7] What are these values? Dickson C.J. suggested,[8] as examples:

> respect for the inherent dignity of the human person, commitment to social justice and equality, accommodation of a wide variety of beliefs, respect for cultural and group identity, and faith in social and political institutions which enhance the participation of individuals and groups in society.

It is implicit in the Court's emphasis on the values of a free and democratic society that some kinds of considerations[9] can never justify limits on rights.[10] However, the reference to a free and democratic society is too vague to provide much assistance in assessing the manifold worthy objectives that legislative bodies attempt to pursue in derogation of rights. As we shall see later in the chapter,[11] the Court has accepted a wide variety of legislative objectives as justifications under s. 1.

As well as its reference to a free and democratic society, s. 1 provides other indications as to the relationship between the guaranteed rights and legislated limits on those rights. In *Oakes*, Dickson C.J. pointed out[12] that s. 1 performed two functions. It not only provided for limits on the guaranteed rights; it also, by its opening words, expressly guaranteed the rights and freedoms set out in the Charter. The primacy of the rights and freedoms was also implied by the requirement that limits be "demonstrably" justified. These indications led Dickson C.J. to stipulate strict rules as to the burden and standard of proof of justification, and

(1988) 10 Supreme Court L.R. 469, esp. 486-492.

[4] *R. v. Oakes*, [1986] 1 S.C.R. 103.

[5] *R. v. Oakes*, [1986] 1 S.C.R. 103, 136.

[6] L.E. Weinrib, "The Supreme Court of Canada and Section 1 of the Charter" (1988) 10 Supreme Court L.R. 469, 494.

[7] *Slaight Communications v. Davidson*, [1989] 1 S.C.R. 1038, 1056; *R. v. Keegstra*, [1990] 3 S.C.R. 697, 736.

[8] *R. v. Oakes*, [1986] 1 S.C.R. 103, 136.

[9] Compare J. Rawls, A Theory of Justice (Harvard U.P. Camb., Mass., 1972), 61, 250, arguing that (except for the maintenance of public order—a vague exception) a right can be defeated only by another right.

[10] L.E. Weinrib, "The Supreme Court of Canada and Section 1 of the Charter" (1988) 10 Supreme Court L.R. 469, 494-495.

[11] §§ 38:12 to 38:17, "Sufficiently important objective".

[12] *R. v. Oakes*, [1986] 1 S.C.R. 103, 135.

as to the substantive criteria that would qualify a law as a "reasonable limit" that "can be demonstrably justified in a free and democratic society". Thus, the Court insisted upon a "stringent standard of justification"[13] before it would accept a limit under s. 1. In this way, the Court has attempted to lay down rules that will preserve the guaranteed rights against much legislative encroachment,[14] but will permit the enactment of limits where there is a strong demonstration that the exercise of the rights "would be inimical to the realization of collective goals of fundamental importance".[15] The various elements of this approach are discussed in the balance of this chapter.

§ 38:3 Relationship between s. 1 and rights

There is a close relationship between the standard of justification required under s. 1 and the scope of the guaranteed rights.[1] If the courts give to the guaranteed rights a broad interpretation that extends beyond their purpose, it is inevitable that the court will relax the standard of justification under s. 1 in order to uphold legislation limiting the extended right. For example, if the guarantee of freedom of expression in s. 2(b) were held to protect perjury, fraud, deception and conspiracy—all forms of expression in an extended sense—it would be foolish to require a legislative body to satisfy a high standard of justification in order to regulate or prohibit such obviously harmful behaviour.

In fact, as has been briefly mentioned, and will be more fully described later in this chapter, in *R. v. Oakes* (1986),[2] the Supreme Court of Canada decided to prescribe a single standard of justification for all rights, and to make that standard a high one, and to cast the burden of satisfying it on the government. In my opinion, this decision entails a corresponding caution in defining the guaranteed rights. Each right should be so interpreted as not to reach behaviour that is outside the purpose of the right—behaviour that is not worthy of constitutional protection. If this is ignored, the inevitable result will be the erosion of the *Oakes* standard of justification, because it can be taken for granted that the

---

[13] *R. v. Oakes*, [1986] 1 S.C.R. 103, 136.

[14] Dworkin has popularized the metaphor that rights are "trumps", because they will defeat a general utilitarian justification for a law: see, e.g., Dworkin, Taking Rights Seriously (rev. ed., 1978), 365. But in Dworkin's theory of rights, the metaphor is not entirely apt, because in bridge the trump card always takes the trick: a trump can be defeated only by another (higher) trump, whereas Dworkin makes clear at 191 that a right can be defeated not only by another (conflicting) right but by a powerful utilitarian justification. Rawls' theory of rights, on the other hand, takes the stronger position that a right can be defeated only by another right: J. Rawls, A Theory of Justice (Harvard U.P. Camb., Mass., 1972), 61, 250.

[15] *R. v. Oakes*, [1986] 1 S.C.R. 103, 136.

[Section 38:3]

[1] The argument in this section of the chapter is made more fully in P.W. Hogg, "Interpreting the Charter of Rights: Generosity and Justification" (1990) 28 Osgoode Hall L.J. 817.

[2] *R. v. Oakes*, [1986] 1 S.C.R. 103.

courts will find a way of upholding legislation in the face of Charter claims that are regarded by the judges as weak.

It may well be that it makes little difference in result whether the courts opt for a stringent standard of justification coupled with a purposive interpretation of rights, or for a relaxed standard of justification coupled with a broad interpretation of rights. However, it certainly makes a great deal of difference to the scope of judicial review. If the rights are broad, and the standard of justification is low, then many more Charter challenges will come before the courts, and will fall to be determined under s. 1. Since the standard of justification under s. 1 would be low, it would be difficult to devise meaningful constraints on the process of judicial review. The result would be that judicial review would become even more pervasive, even more policy-laden, and even more unpredictable than it is now. In my view, therefore, the courts should adhere to the strict standard of justification prescribed by *Oakes*, and should give a purposive (rather than a generous) interpretation to the guaranteed rights.[3] That approach will help to stem the wasteful floods of litigation,[4] to limit the occasions when courts have to review the policy choices of legislative bodies and to introduce meaningful rules to the process of Charter review.

II. BURDEN OF PROOF

§ 38:4 Burden of proof

Who bears the burden of proof of factual issues in Charter litigation? At the first stage of Charter review, the court must decide whether a Charter right has been infringed. This issue is subject to the normal rules as to burden of proof, which means that the burden of proving all elements of the breach of a Charter right rests on the person asserting the breach. In the case of those rights that are qualified by their own terms, for example, by requirements of unreasonableness or arbitrariness, the burden of proving the facts that establish unreasonableness or arbitrariness, or whatever else is part of the definition of the right, rests on the person asserting the breach.

The second stage of Charter review, which is reached only if a Charter right has been infringed, is the inquiry into justification under s. 1. At this stage, the burden of persuasion shifts to the government (or other party) seeking to support the challenged law. It is for the government to persuade the court that the challenged law is a "reasonable limit", and

[3]On the difference between a "purposive" interpretation and a "generous" interpretation, see ch. 36, Charter of Rights, under heading §§ 36:18 to 36:24, "Interpretation of Charter".

[4]An indication of the danger is provided by the flood of equality challenges that entered the judicial system before *Andrews v. Law Society of B.C.*, [1989] 1 S.C.R. 143 severely narrowed the scope of s. 15. In the first three years that s. 15 was in force, there were 599 cases in which a law was challenged, usually unsuccessfully, under s. 15: Brodsky and Day, Canadian Charter Equality Rights for Women (Canadian Advisory Council on the Status of Women, 1989), 277. The great majority of these cases could not even be brought after the ruling in *Andrews*.

that it "can be demonstrably justified in a free and democratic society".[1] This was established by the judgment of Dickson C.J. for the unanimous Court in *R. v. Oakes* (1986).[2] The standard of proof, the Court held, was "the civil standard, namely, proof by a preponderance of probability".[3] The criminal standard of proof beyond a reasonable doubt would be too onerous, given the vagueness of the controlling concepts of reasonableness, justifiability and free and democratic society, but "the preponderance of probability test must be applied rigorously".[4]

In order to satisfy the burden of proving justification under s. 1, Dickson C.J. said that evidence would "generally" be required, although he added that "there may be cases where certain elements of the s. 1 analysis are obvious or self-evident".[5] It is risky for a government not to adduce evidence of justification[6] in defence of a Charter challenge, but in several cases the Supreme Court has been prepared to make justificatory findings of a factual nature without evidence,[7] or with very little evidence,[8] relying on the "obvious" or "self-evident" character of the findings. These cases have been criticized,[9] but the Supreme Court of Canada has to make do with the factual record developed at trial, and it would be unfortunate if a law was struck down because of a deficiency in the evidence which could be supplied by a common-sense finding. Indeed, the Court occasionally relies on evidence that seems to violate common sense, presumably because of the absence of any contradictory evidence. For example, in ordering the province of British Columbia to provide sign-language interpretation around the clock seven days a week in every hospital in the province, the Court took comfort in its finding that this service would cost the province a total of $150,000 per year. The rights of the deaf were being denied by the province merely to save this paltry sum![10]

Evidence in Charter cases gives rise to many problems. One is the

---

[Section 38:4]

[1]The question whether a Charter limit is "prescribed by law" is a pure question of law to which no burden of proof could attach.

[2]*R. v. Oakes*, [1986] 1 S.C.R. 103, 136-137.

[3]*R. v. Oakes*, [1986] 1 S.C.R. 103, 137.

[4]*R. v. Oakes*, [1986] 1 S.C.R. 103, 137.

[5]*R. v. Oakes*, [1986] 1 S.C.R. 103, 138.

[6]Note that evidence has often been adduced informally in constitutional cases, in the form of social-science briefs, and extracts from studies and reports of various kinds. The admissibility of this material is examined in ch. 60, Proof, under heading §§ 60:8 to 60:13, "Evidence".

[7]*R. v. Jones*, [1986] 2 S.C.R. 284, 299-300, 315; *R.W.D.S.U. v. Dolphin Delivery*, [1986] 2 S.C.R. 573, 590.

[8]*R. v. Edwards Books and Art*, [1986] 2 S.C.R. 713, 769-770; *R v. Bryan*, [2007] 1 S.C.R. 527, para. 20.

[9]A.J. Petter and P.J. Monahan, "Developments in Constitutional Law (The 1986-87 Term)" (1988) 10 Supreme Court L.R. 61, 71-96.

[10]*Eldridge v. B.C.*, [1997] 3 S.C.R. 624, para. 87. In *Nfld. v. N.A.P.E.*, [2004] 3 S.C.R. 381, where the high cost of Charter compliance was held to justify a limit on a Charter

point already made, that the validity or invalidity of a law will often turn on the state of the evidentiary record at trial.[11] Another problem is cost. A parade of expert witnesses is extremely costly, and this cost is borne not just by the defending government, but also by the challenger, who, although not bearing the burden of proof, must in all prudence adduce evidence to rebut the government's evidence of justification.[12] Another problem is that, in the realm of public policy, cogent social-science evidence often does not exist for a perceived harm, and yet the legislators do have a "reasoned apprehension of harm".[13] For these reasons, in my opinion, it would be desirable for Charter review to become less dependent on evidence,[14] even if the courts have to strain somewhat to make "obvious" or "self-evident" findings.[15]

III. PRESUMPTION OF CONSTITUTIONALITY

§ 38:5 Presumption of constitutionality

When a statute is attacked on federal grounds, there is, or ought to be, a presumption of constitutionality.[1] This presumption carries three legal consequences. First, the court should exercise restraint in judicial review, striking down the law only if it clearly offends constitutional restrictions on the power of the enacting Parliament or Legislature.

---

right, the Court (at para. 84) distinguished *Eldridge* on the basis of the "tiny" $150,000 number.

[11]E.g., *Corp. Professionnelle des Médecins v. Thibault*, [1988] 1 S.C.R. 1033 (Quebec statute allowing prosecutor to appeal from acquittal by way of trial de novo struck down for breach of s. 11(h); s. 1 justification not considered for lack of evidence).

[12]In the normal course, each party to litigation tenders all of that party's evidence at the same time. Therefore, a plaintiff challenging a law on Charter grounds will tender all of the plaintiff's evidence before the defendant government tenders any evidence. The plaintiff's evidence will include not only the stage 1 evidence of the Charter breach, but also the stage 2 evidence in rebuttal of the anticipated evidence of justification. Since the latter evidence is given before the government has tendered any evidence of justification, some of the advantage of the government's burden of proof is lost. A trial court would have the power to split the trial, and allow the plaintiff's reply evidence to follow the defendant's evidence but no such practice seems to have developed.

[13]E.g., *R. v. Bryan*, [2007] 1 S.C.R. 527, para. 20 (upholding requirement of delay in publication of election results from East so that voters in the West will not know the likely result of a national election before they vote); S. Choudhry, "So What is the Real Legacy of *Oakes*? Two Decades of Proportionality Analysis under the Canadian *Charter's* Section 1" (2006) 34 Supreme Court L.R. 501 (emphasizing (p. 503) the need for the Court to recognize "the reality of policy making under conditions of factual uncertainty").

[14]It is sworn evidence that is costly. Judicial notice dispenses with the need for evidence of facts that are notorious or publicly accessible: ch. 60, Proof, under heading § 60:8, "Modes of proof.

[15]Accord, *Sauvé v. Can.*, [2002] 3 S.C.R. 519, paras. 18 per McLachlin C.J. for majority, 90 per Gonthier J. for minority; *B.C. Freedom of Information and Privacy Assn. v. B.C.*, [2017] 1 S.C.R. 93, 2017 SCC 6, para. 58 per McLachlin C.J. for the Court (no evidence, but "logic and reason" were sufficient).

[Section 38:5]

[1]See ch. 15, Judicial Review on Federal Grounds, under heading § 15:13, "Presumption of constitutionality".

Secondly, where the validity of a law turns on a finding of fact (for example, the existence of an emergency), that finding of fact need not be proved strictly by the government; it is sufficient that there be a "rational basis" for the finding.[2] Thirdly, where a law is open to two interpretations, under one of which it would be unconstitutional, and under the other of which it would be constitutional, the latter interpretation is the one that should be selected; this mode of interpretation is known as "reading down".[3] These are three doctrines of judicial restraint, designed to minimize intrusion by the judicial branch in the affairs of the legislative branch.

In federalism cases, whatever the form of the litigation, the constitutional contest is essentially between two levels of government: what is denied to one level of government belongs to the other. In that context, a presumption of constitutionality tilts the scale in favour of upholding the law that has been enacted by one of the levels of government. In Charter cases, the constitutional contest is between a government and an individual, who asserts that a right has been violated. In that context, it is not appropriate to tilt the scale in favour of the government. There should be no special obstacles placed in the way of an individual who seeks to vindicate a Charter right. In Charter cases, therefore, there is no presumption of constitutionality,[4] except in the third sense indicated above, namely, reading down.[5] There is no derogation of individual rights if the individual wins through a reading down of the statute as opposed to a holding of invalidity. The application of reading down in Charter cases is discussed in a later chapter.[6]

With respect to evidence in Charter cases, in the stage-one inquiry into whether the law infringes a Charter right, the burden of proof does rest on the individual asserting the infringement. That, however, is simply a consequence of the rule of civil procedure that "the one who asserts must prove".[7] The burden of proof is the normal civil one, uncomplicated by any doctrine that the government need have only a "rational basis" for its legislation. Once the stage-one inquiry has been answered yes, there is no presumption that the law is a reasonable limit that can be demonstrably justified in a free and democratic society. On

---

[2]See ch. 60, Proof, under heading § 60:13, "Standard of proof.

[3]See ch. 15, Judicial Review on Federal Grounds, under heading § 15:15, "Reading down".

[4]*Man. v. Metropolitan Stores*, [1987] 1 S.C.R. 110, 121-125 per Beetz J., giving as his reason (at 122) "the innovative and evolutive character of the Charter". Contra, D. Pinard, "Le principe d'interprétation issue de la présomption de constitutionnalité" (1990) 35 McGill L.J. 305; A.S. Butler, "A Presumption of Statutory Conformity with the Charter" (1993) 19 Queen's L.J. 209.

[5]*Man. v. Metropolitan Stores*, [1987] 1 S.C.R. 110, 125, where Beetz J. leaves the point open.

[6]Chapter 40, Enforcement of Rights, under heading § 40:7, "Reading down".

[7]*Man. v. Metropolitan Stores*, [1987] 1 S.C.R. 110, 124-125.

the contrary, the burden is on the government to prove that the elements of s. 1 justification are present.[8]

IV. LIMITS

§ 38:6 Limits

Section 1 provides that the Charter rights are subject "to such reasonable limits prescribed by law as can be demonstrably justified in a free and democratic society". There is one decision of the Supreme Court of Canada that holds that not every Charter infringement is a "limit", and any infringement that is more severe than a limit cannot be justified under s. 1.

This distinction was announced in the *Quebec School Board* case (1984).[1] In that case, the Court had to determine the validity of the "Quebec clause" of Quebec's Charter of the French Language (Bill 101), which limited admission to English-language schools in Quebec to the children of persons who had been educated in English in Quebec. The Quebec clause was inconsistent with s. 23(1)(b) (the "Canada clause") of the Charter of Rights, which guaranteed admission to minority-language schools to the children of persons who had been educated in the minority language anywhere in Canada.[2] The Supreme Court of Canada held that the Quebec clause infringed s. 23(1)(b), but the Court refused to be drawn into any inquiry into justification under s. 1. The opinion of "the Court", pointed out that the detailed definition of the classes of parents entitled to protection was the heart of s. 23 of the Charter. A redefinition of those classes was not a "limit" contemplated by s. 1 of the Charter as open to legislative enactment. The Court concluded that "the provisions of [the Quebec clause] collide directly with those of s. 23 of the Charter, and are not limits which can be legitimized by s. 1 of the Charter".[3]

The distinction invoked by the Court in the *Quebec School Board* case is a distinction between "limits", which can be justified under s. 1, and "denials", which cannot be. The obvious criticism of the distinction is that there is no legal standard by which the various Charter infringements can be sorted into the two categories.[4] The Court seems to have taken this criticism to heart, and, without actually overruling the *Quebec School Board* case, has signalled that it will no longer use the distinction to obviate the requirement of s. 1 justification, "apart from the rare

[8] See ch. 60, Proof, under heading §§ 60:8 to 60:13, "Evidence".

[Section 38:6]

[1] *A.G. Que. v. Que. Protestant School Bds.*, [1984] 2 S.C.R. 66.

[2] See ch. 56, Language, under heading §§ 56:17 to 56:25, "Language of education".

[3] *A.G. Que. v. Que. Protestant School Bds.*, [1984] 2 S.C.R. 66, 88.

[4] This criticism was elaborated at undue length in the second edition of this book (1985), 682-684. For approval of the distinction, see L.E. Weinrib, "The Supreme Court of Canada and Section 1 of the Charter" (1988) 10 Supreme Court L.R. 469, 479-483.

case of a truly complete denial" of a guaranteed right.[5] The result seems to be that even severe restrictions on Charter rights will count as limits, and will therefore be susceptible to s. 1 justification. The severity of the contravention would not be irrelevant, of course, because it would be harder to establish that a severe contravention was reasonable and demonstrably justified.

V. PRESCRIBED BY LAW

§ 38:7 Definition of prescribed by law

Section 1 provides that the Charter rights are subject to "such reasonable limits *prescribed by law* as can be demonstrably justified in a free and democratic society". The words "prescribed by law" make clear that an act that is not legally authorized can never be justified under s. 1, no matter how reasonable or demonstrably justified it may appear to be.[1] Charter violations that take place on the initiative of a police officer (or other official), acting without clear legal authority,[2] are outside the protection of s. 1. For example, in *Little Sisters Book and Art Emporium v. Canada* (2000),[3] it was held that customs officials had discriminated against LGBTQ literature in administering the statutory prohibition on the importation of obscene materials. This was a breach of the equality right in s. 15 of the Charter, and it could not be justified under s. 1. The customs legislation did not authorize any distinction between LGBTQ and heterosexual literature, and therefore the actions of the customs officials were not prescribed by law.

The requirement that any limit on rights be prescribed by law reflects two values that are basic to constitutionalism or the rule of law. First, in order to preclude arbitrary and discriminatory action by government officials, all official action in derogation of rights must be authorized by law. Secondly, citizens must have a reasonable opportunity to know what is prohibited so that they can act accordingly. Both these values

---

[5]*Ford v. Que.*, [1988] 2 S.C.R. 712, 771-774, where the distinction is cogently criticized, the only implausible element being the description (at 773) of the *Quebec School Board* case as exemplifying a "complete denial" of the right. Compares, *R. v. Big M Drug Mart*, [1985] 1 S.C.R. 295, holding that Sunday-closing legislation could not be justified under s. 1, because its purpose was to compel religious observance, which was itself a violation of freedom of religion. This line of reasoning is a possible explanation of the *Quebec School Board* case. See § 38:15, "Inadmissible objectives".

[Section 38:7]

[1]E.g., *R. v. Therens*, [1985] 1 S.C.R. 613 (no law authorized denial by police of right to counsel); *R. v. Mannion*, [1986] 2 S.C.R. 272 (no law authorized use by Crown prosecutor of accused's previous incriminating testimony); *R. v. Simmons*, [1988] 2 S.C.R. 495 (no law authorized denial by customs officials of right to counsel); *R. v. Hebert*, [1990] 2 S.C.R. 151 (no law authorized denial by police of right to silence); *R. v. Broyles*, [1991] 3 S.C.R. 595 (no law authorized denial by police of right to silence); *R. v. Dersch*, [1993] 3 S.C.R. 768 (no law authorized access by police to medical records).

[2]*R. v. Hebert*, [1990] 2 S.C.R. 151 205 per Sopinka J. ("The word 'prescribe' connotes a mandate for specific action, not merely permission for that which is not prohibited.")

[3]*Little Sisters Book and Art Emporium v. Canada*, [2000] 2 S.C.R. 1120.

are satisfied by a law that fulfils two requirements: (1) the law must be adequately accessible to the public, and (2) the law must be formulated with sufficient precision to enable people to regulate their conduct by it, and to provide guidance to those who apply the law.

These two requirements have been held to be inherent in the phrase "prescribed by law" by the European Court of Human Rights, interpreting that same phrase in the European Convention on Human Rights.[4] In the *Sunday Times* case (1979),[5] the Court had to decide whether the contempt power of the British courts, which had been exercised to restrain the Sunday Times from publishing an article on pending litigation by thalidomide victims against a drug company, was a breach of the right to freedom of expression, which was guaranteed by the Convention. The Convention provided that the right to freedom of expression was "subject to such. . . restrictions. . . as are prescribed by law and are necessary in a democratic society". It was argued that the law of contempt could not satisfy this limitation clause, because it was a creature of common law and not of legislation. The Court rejected this argument, holding (1) that a common law rule was adequately accessible to the public, and (2) that the common law of contempt was formulated with sufficient precision to enable a newspaper to regulate its reporting of pending judicial proceedings.[6]

The Supreme Court of Canada has held that the phrase "prescribed by law" in s. 1 entails the same two requirements of accessibility and precision.[7] As to accessibility, the clearest example is a statute. Indeed, it has been argued that only statute law qualifies, on the ground that a limit on a Charter right is a matter that ought to be subject to the democratic safeguards of the full legislative process, including debate in the legislature. This narrow definition has been rejected by the Supreme Court of Canada, which has held that "law" in s. 1 is not limited to primary legislation: it is also satisfied by delegated legislation (made under statutory authority), such as a regulation,[8] municipal by-law[9] or rule of a regulatory body.[10] The courts have also accepted a rule of the common

---

[4] See ch. 36, Charter of Rights, under heading § 36:28, "International sources".

[5] *Sunday Times v. United Kingdom* (1979), 2 European Human Rights Reports 245 (Eur. Ct. of Hum. Rts.). The discussion of "prescribed by law" is at pp. 270-273.

[6] The Court held nevertheless that the contempt law was not justified under the limitation clause, because it was not "necessary in a democratic society".

[7] *Greater Vancouver Transportation Authority v. Can. Federation of Students*, [2009] 2 S.C.R. 295, para. 50, citing this text.

[8] *R. v. Therens*, [1985] 1 S.C.R. 613, 645 (dictum); *Irwin Toy v. Que.*, [1989] 1 S.C.R. 927, 981; *Alta. v. Hutterian Brethren of Wilson Colony*, [2009] 2 S.C.R. 567, paras. 40, 46 (argument that Charter limits may be prescribed only by primary legislation expressly rejected).

[9] *Ramsden v. Peterborough*, [1993] 2 S.C.R. 1084; *Montreal v. 2952-136 Que.*, [2005] 3 S.C.R. 141; *Greater Vancouver Transportation Authority v. Can. Federation of Students*, [2009] 2 S.C.R. 295, para. 53.

[10] *Black v. Law Society of Alberta*, [1989] 1 S.C.R. 591; *Greater Vancouver Transportation Authority v. Can. Federation of Students*, [2009] 2 S.C.R. 295, para. 53.

law[11] and a prerogative order governing the issue of passports.[12] Even government policies will count as law if the government entity has the statutory power to enact binding rules of general application and if that is what the policies really are (legislative policies). But, in order for policies to count as law, the requirements of accessibility and precision must be satisfied. The status of government policies was decided in *Greater Vancouver Transportation Authority v. Canadian Federation of Students* (2009),[13] where the Supreme Court held that the policies of transit authorities restricting advertising on the sides of buses were limits on freedom of expression that were prescribed by law. The transit authorities had the statutory power to enact binding rules of general application. The advertising policies were rules of general application that were binding on the transit authorities and the general public. Although the policies were not officially published as delegated legislation, they were set out clearly in writing and made available to those who wished to advertise on the buses. They were sufficiently accessible and precise to be "law" for the purpose of s. 1.[14] The Court distinguished the "legislative" policies in this case from "administrative" policies that were intended for internal use within government as aids in the interpretation of regulatory powers.[15] Administrative policies, which were often informal and inaccessible outside government, would not count as law for the purpose of s. 1.[16]

As to precision, the Supreme Court of Canada has held that a limit on a right need not be express, but can result "by necessity from the terms of a statute or regulation or from its operating requirements".[17] For example, a statutory requirement that a roadside breath test be administered "forthwith", which in practice precluded contact by the

[11] *R. v. Therens*, [1985] 1 S.C.R. 613, 645 (dictum); *R.W.D.S.U. v. Dolphin Delivery*, [1986] 2 S.C.R. 573; *B.C.E.G.U. v. B.C.*, [1988] 2 S.C.R. 214; *R. v. Swain*, [1991] 1 S.C.R. 933, 968.

[12] *Can. v. Kamel*, [2009] 4 F.C.R. 449 (F.C.A.). On the prerogative, see ch. 1, Sources, under heading § 1:9, "Prerogative".

[13] *Greater Vancouver Transportation Authority v. Canadian Federation of Students*, [2009] 2 S.C.R. 295. Deschamps J. wrote the opinion of the majority. Fish J. wrote a concurring opinion which did not disagree with the prescribed-by-law ruling.

[14] See also *Canadian Broadcasting Corp. v. Can.*, [2011] 1 S.C.R. 19, paras. 58-62 (Quebec Ministry of Justice "directive" restricting journalistic activity in courthouses, made under statutory authority, intended to be binding on journalists, and posted in courthouses, held to be law within s. 1).

[15] *Canadian Federation of Students v. Greater Vancouver Transportation Authority,*, [2009] 2 S.C.R. 295, paras. 48-73.

[16] See also *Re Ont. Film and Video Appreciation Society* (1984), 45 O.R.(2d) 80 (C.A.) (standards published by Ont. Board of Censors not law, because not binding on the Board); *Committee for Cth. of Can. v. Can.*, [1991] 1 S.C.R. 139 (Court divided on whether Airport's internal directives were law); *Little Sisters Book and Art Emporium v. Can.*, [2000] 2 S.C.R. 1120, para. 85 (interpretative memorandum was an "internal administrative aid to Customs inspectors" and not law). Compare *Martineau v. Matsqui Institution Inmate Disciplinary Bd.*, [1978] 1 S.C.R. 118 (Court divided on whether departmental directives were law within s. 28 of the Federal Court Act).

[17] *R. v. Therens*, [1985] 1 S.C.R. 613, 645.

suspected motorist with counsel, was held to be a limit "prescribed by law" on the right to counsel, although the statute was silent on the right to counsel.[18]

§ 38:8 Discretion

A law that confers a discretion on a board or official to act in derogation of a Charter right will satisfy the prescribed-by-law requirement if the discretion is constrained by legal standards. In *Re Ontario Film and Video Appreciation Society* (1984),[1] a statute authorizing film censorship failed the requirement, because the censor board was given an unfettered discretion to ban or cut films proposed for public exhibition; the statute did not stipulate the criteria to be applied by the board. The board had in fact developed its own criteria, which were publicly available, but those criteria, the Court held, were insufficient, because they were not binding on the board. Had they been contained in the statute itself, or in a regulation, the limit on freedom of expression would have been prescribed by law.[2]

The *Ontario Film and Video* case was a decision of the Ontario Court of Appeal. The Supreme Court of Canada has also held that a statutory discretion in derogation of a Charter right must be subject to an "intelligible standard".[3] However, the Court has upheld discretions that were not constrained by meaningful legal standards. In *R. v. Hufsky* (1988),[4] the Court upheld a provincial statute authorizing the police at their unfettered discretion to stop vehicles. The police used the power to stop vehicles at random, in a programme of spot checks for drunkenness and other traffic violations. The Court held that the general discretion conferred by the statute should be interpreted to extend to random stops; and that the statute, so interpreted, was, by implication, a limit prescribed by law on the right not to be arbitrarily detained.

The random stop that led to the arrest in *Hufsky* was part of an organized programme, which took place at a pre-determined location at

---

[18] *R. v. Thomsen*, [1988] 1 S.C.R. 640. Folld. *R. v. Orbanski*, [2005] 2 S.C.R. 3 (statute implicitly authorized police to ask roadside questions without first warning of right to counsel). Also, *R. v. Hufsky*, [1988] 1 S.C.R. 621; *R. v. Ladouceur*, [1990] 1 S.C.R. 1257; *Slaight Communications v. Davidson*, [1989] 1 S.C.R. 1038.

[Section 38:8]

[1] *Re Ontario Film and Video Appreciation Society* (1984), 45 O.R. (2d) 80 (C.A.).

[2] After the decision, the Legislature amended the Theatres Act to require the censor board to follow criteria prescribed by regulations, and a regulation was made under the authority of the Act stipulating the cinematic images that would justify a refusal to permit exhibition or distribution of a film. *In R. v. Glad Day Bookshops* (2004), 70 O.R. (3d) 691 (S.C.J.), Juriansz J. held that the new regulatory criteria satisfied the prescribed-by-law requirement (although some "adult sex guidelines" developed by the board without statutory authority did not do so) (paras. 89-91); however, he held that the new regulatory criteria were too broad to constitute a reasonable limit on freedom of expression (para. 150).

[3] *Irwin Toy v. Que.*, [1989] 1 S.C.R. 927, 983.

[4] *R. v. Hufsky*, [1988] 1 S.C.R. 621.

which several police officers were present. In *R. v. Ladouceur* (1990),[5] the Court was presented with a roving random stop, taken at the initiative of an individual police officer, and not part of any organized programme. The Court, by a narrow majority of five to four, followed *Hufsky* and held that the same statute authorized the stop, and that it was a limit prescribed by law on the right not to be arbitrarily detained. The dissenting minority held that the decision in *Hufsky* should be confined to stops at organized check-points, and that s. 1 could not extend to a statute that authorized a police officer to stop any vehicle at any time, at any place and for any reason.

A similar decision was reached in *Slaight Communications v. Davidson* (1989).[6] In that case, an adjudicator found that an employer had unjustly dismissed an employee. The adjudicator ordered the employer to provide a letter of reference to the employee, reciting certain stipulated facts about the employee's achievements, and also ordered the employer not to make any comments other than the stipulated facts in response to any enquiry about the employee's performance. The purpose of the negative order was to prevent the employer from undermining the effect of the positive order. The majority of the Supreme Court of Canada held that both the positive and negative orders, although limits on the employer's freedom of expression, were justified under s. 1. The Court held that the prescribed-by-law requirement was satisfied, because the adjudicator's order was made under the authority of a statute. But the statute simply gave to the adjudicator a general power to order compensation, reinstatement or other equitable remedy. There was no explicit authority to require a letter of reference or otherwise limit freedom of expression. Nevertheless, the statutory discretion was held to be, by implication, a limit prescribed by law on freedom of expression.[7]

In *Slaight Communications*,[8] Lamer C.J., whose opinion on this issue was accepted by all members of the Court, drew a distinction between two types of statutory conferrals of discretion. One type was the statute that expressly or by necessary implication authorized a decision that would infringe a Charter right. In that case, which is exemplified by *Ontario Film and Video, Husky* and *Ladouceur*, the statute itself, not the decision, had to be justifiable under s. 1. The second type was the statute that conferred a discretion in language that was apparently broad enough to encompass decisions infringing a Charter right, although the language did not expressly or by necessary implication authorize infringements of the Charter. In that case, which is exemplified by *Slaight Communications*, the broad empowering language should be read down so as not to authorize decisions that would infringe the

[5]*R. v. Ladouceur*, [1990] 1 S.C.R. 1257.

[6]*Slaight Communications v. Davidson*, [1989] 1 S.C.R. 1038.

[7]See also *United States v. Cotroni*, [1989] 1 S.C.R. 1469, 1497-1498 (upholding prosecutorial discretion in the context of extradition); *Irwin Toy v. Que.*, [1989] 1 S.C.R. 927; *R. v. Ladouceur*, [1990] 1 S.C.R. 1257.

[8]*Slaight Communications v. Davidson*, [1989] 1 S.C.R. 1038, 1077-1080; see also *Eaton v. Brant County Bd. of Education*, [1997] 1 S.C.R. 241, paras. 1-4.

Charter. Any decision that did infringe the Charter would therefore be ultra vires the empowering statute. However, Lamer C.J. pointed out that the Charter included s. 1, and therefore a decision that limited a Charter right in a way that was justifiable under s. 1 would not infringe the Charter right. It followed that, when a decision limiting a Charter right was made under a broad statutory discretion, it was the decision, not the statute, that had to satisfy the s. 1 standard of justification.[9]

§ 38:9 Vagueness

It is a principle of fundamental justice in Canada, and of due process in the United States, that a statute is "void for vagueness" if its prohibitions are not clearly defined.[1] A vague law offends the values of constitutionalism. It does not provide sufficiently clear standards to avoid arbitrary and discriminatory applications by those charged with enforcement. It does not provide reasonable notice of what is prohibited so that citizens can govern themselves safely. Indeed, as American judges have noted, a vague law may lead citizens to steer far wider of the unlawful zone than they would if the boundaries were clearly marked.[2]

In Canada, the idea that a law may be void for vagueness is also implicit in the requirement that a limit on a Charter right be prescribed by law. That follows from the rule described above[3] that precision is one of the ingredients of the prescribed-by-law requirement.[4]

Irwin Toy v. Quebec (1989)[5] was a challenge to a provincial statute that prohibited "commercial advertising directed at persons under thirteen years of age". The statute stipulated three factors that were to be taken into account in determining whether an advertisement was directed at persons under 13 years of age, but even with these factors, the scope of the prohibited class of advertisements was highly uncertain. It was argued that such a vague prohibition could not be a limit on freedom of expression that was prescribed by law. The majority of the Court held that it was not practicable to seek "absolute precision" in a statute. A law would fail the prescribed-by-law test only "where there is no intelligible standard and where the legislature has given a plenary

---

[9]For discussion of the approach that is to be applied where a discretionary administrative decision is challenged on Charter grounds, see § 38:32, "Application to discretionary decisions".

[Section 38:9]

[1]Chapter 47, Fundamental Justice, under heading §§ 47:27 to 47:29, "Vague laws".

[2]See *Groyned v. City of Rockford* (1972), 408 U.S. 104, 108-109 (holding that an anti-noise bylaw was not unconstitutionally vague).

[3]§ 38:7, "Definition of prescribed by law".

[4]A law that was excessively vague would also not be a "reasonable" limit within s. 1: *Osborne v. Can.*, [1991] 2 S.C.R. 69, 94.

[5]*Irwin Toy v. Quebec*, [1989] 1 S.C.R. 927.

discretion to do whatever seems best in a wide set of circumstances".[6] That was not the case here, the Court held, because the three statutory factors provided an "intelligible standard" for the application of the prohibition.[7]

The requirement of an "intelligible standard" is itself vague. However, it is intended to capture the two values protected by the phrase "prescribed by law". Those are the provision of fair notice to citizens of what is prohibited, and the provision of checks on enforcement discretion. The requirement is not a demanding one.[8] The Court has upheld a prohibition on communicating for the purpose of prostitution,[9] a prohibition on communicating hatred or contempt towards minorities,[10] a prohibition on political campaigning by civil servants,[11] a prohibition on the sale of obscene materials,[12] and a prohibition on tobacco advertising that was "likely to create an erroneous impression" of the health hazards of tobacco.[13] In each case, there was a limit on freedom of expression that was couched in relatively vague terms; and, in each case, the Court held that the law supplied a sufficiently intelligible standard to meet the requirement of s. 1 that a limit be prescribed by law.[14]

VI. REASONABLE AND DEMONSTRABLY JUSTIFIED

§ 38:10 Introduction

Section 1 provides that the Charter rights are subject to "such *reasonable* limits prescribed by law as can be *demonstrably justified* in a free and democratic society". The requirements of reasonableness and demonstrable justification are cumulative, not alternative. Although both must be satisfied, there does not seem to be much point in treating each separately. Indeed, the requirement of reasonableness may be redundant, because a limit that is demonstrably justified must surely be

---

[6] *Irwin Toy v. Quebec*, [1989] 1 S.C.R. 927, 983.

[7] See also *Luscher v. Deputy Minr., Revenue Can.*, [1985] 1 F.C. 85 (C.A.) (striking down a prohibition of the importation of "immoral or indecent" books; such a vague law could not be a "reasonable limit"); *Re Blainey and Ont. Hockey Assn.* (1986), 54 O.R. (2d) 513 (C.A.) (striking down exemption from Human Rights Code for sex-segregated sport: "It prescribes no limits and provides no guidelines."); *Can. v. Kamel*, [2009] 4 F.C.R. 449 (F.C.A.) (upholding power to refuse passport on grounds of "national security").

[8] Another formulation that has been suggested is whether the impugned law "is so obscure as to be incapable of interpretation using the ordinary tools": *Osborne v. Can.*, [1991] 2 S.C.R. 69, 94.

[9] *Re ss. 193 and 195.1 of Crim. Code*, [1990] 1 S.C.R. 1123.

[10] *Can. v. Taylor*, [1990] 3 S.C.R. 892.

[11] *Osborne v. Can.*, [1991] 2 S.C.R. 69.

[12] *R. v. Butler*, [1992] 1 S.C.R. 452.

[13] *Can. v. JTI-Macdonald Corp.*, [2007] 2 S.C.R. 610, paras. 62-66.

[14] It has been suggested that vagueness could also be relevant under the third branch of the *Oakes* test (§ 38:20, "Minimum impairment"). A law that passed the "prescribed by law" threshold might still, by reason of its imprecision, fail the minimum impairment branch of the *Oakes* test: *CBC v. N.B.*, [1996] 3 S.C.R. 480, para. 56; *Can. v. JTI-Macdonald Corp*, [2007] 2 S.C.R. 610, para. 77.

reasonable. The courts have not attempted to distinguish between the two requirements, but have assumed that the language of reasonableness and demonstrable justification articulates a single standard to be applied to all laws limiting Charter rights.

§ 38:11 Oakes test

In *R. v. Oakes* (1986),[1] Dickson C.J., for a Court that was unanimous on this issue, laid down the criteria that must be satisfied to establish that a limit is reasonable and demonstrably justified in a free and democratic society. Because this judgment has taken on some of the character of holy writ, I set out below the main passages:[2]

> To establish that a limit is reasonable and demonstrably justified in a free and democratic society, two central criteria must be satisfied. First, the objective, which the measures responsible for a limit on a Charter right or freedom are designed to serve, must be "of sufficient importance to warrant overriding a constitutionally protected right or freedom" . . . The standard must be high in order to ensure that objectives which are trivial or discord ant with the principles integral to a free and democratic society do not gain s. 1 protection. It is necessary, at a minimum, that an objective relate to concerns which are pressing and substantial in a free and democratic society before it can be characterized as sufficiently important.
>
> Second, once a sufficiently significant objective is recognized, then the party invoking s. 1 must show that the means chosen are reasonable and demonstrably justified. This involves "a form of proportionality test" . . . Although the nature of the proportionality test will vary depending on the circumstances, in each case court's will be required to balance the interests of society with those of individuals and groups. There are, in my view, three import ant components of a proportionality test. First, the measures adopted must be carefully designed to achieve the objective in question. They must not be arbitrary, unfair or based on irrational considerations. In short, they must be rationally connected to the objective. Second, the means, even if rationally connected to the objective in this first sense, should impair "as little as possible" the right or freedom in question . . . Third, there must be a proportionality between the *effects* of the measures which are responsible for limiting the Charter right or freedom, and the objective which has been identified as of "sufficient importance".

In summary, there are four criteria to be satisfied by a law that qualifies as a reasonable limit that can be demonstrably justified in a free and democratic society:

1. Sufficiently important objective: The law must pursue an objective that is sufficiently important to justify limiting a Charter right.
2. Rational connection: The law must be rationally connected to the objective.
3. Least drastic means: The law must impair the right no more than is necessary to accomplish the objective.

[Section 38:11]

[1] *R. v. Oakes*, [1986] 1 S.C.R. 103.

[2] *R. v. Oakes*, [1986] 1 S.C.R. 103, 138-139 (emphasis in original).

4. Proportionate effect: The law must not have a disproportionately severe effect on the persons to whom it applies.

Each of these criteria will be examined in turn in the text that follows.

To anticipate the later discussion, it is step 3—least drastic means—that is the centre of the inquiry into s. 1 justification. Only in a rare case will a court reject the legislative judgment that the objective of the law is sufficiently important to justify limiting a Charter right (step 1). It is an even rarer case where the law is not rationally connected to the objective (step 2). And the inquiry into disproportionate effect (step 4) is normally, if not always, precluded by the judgment that the law's objective is sufficiently important to justify the impact on the Charter right (step 1). What is left for serious inquiry is the question whether the law has impaired the Charter right no more than is necessary to accomplish the objective (step 3). As we shall see, nearly all the s. 1 cases have turned on the answer to this inquiry.

VII. SUFFICIENTLY IMPORTANT OBJECTIVE

§ 38:12 Identification of objective

The identification of the objective of a challenged law is a task of considerable practical and theoretical difficulty. At the practical level, the objective of the legislators in enacting the challenged law may be unknown. To be sure, the courts will now willingly receive the legislative history of the law,[1] but this is often silent or unclear with respect to the provision under attack. Courts have not been troubled by this difficulty as much as one might expect. They usually assume that the statute itself reveals its objective, and they may pronounce confidently on the point even if there is no supporting evidence.

Even if one could be absolutely certain of what the legislators were hoping to achieve when they enacted the challenged law, the statement of the objective can be expressed at various levels of generality. Take *Andrews v. Law Society of British Columbia* (1989)[2] as an example. The challenged law imposed a requirement of Canadian citizenship for admission to the legal profession of British Columbia. The Supreme Court of Canada was unanimous that the law infringed the guarantee of equality, but the Court divided on the question whether the law could be justified under s. 1. The objective of the law could be expressed at a high level of generality: to restrict entry to the legal profession to persons who are qualified to practise law. Stated in this way, who could doubt that the objective was sufficiently important for the purpose of s. 1? Or the objective of the law could be stated at a low level of generality: to restrict entry to the legal profession to persons who are Canadian citizens. Stated in this way, the value of the objective is by no means obvious. There is no logical or factual basis for preferring one version of the law's

---

[Section 38:12]

[1] See ch. 60, Proof, under heading §§ 60:1 to 60:7, "Legislative history".

[2] *Andrews v. Law Society of British Columbia*, [1989] 1 S.C.R. 143.

objective to the other; they are simply expressed at different levels of generality.

The higher the level of generality at which a legislative objective is expressed, the more obviously desirable the objective will appear to be. This will move the s. 1 inquiry into the proportionality of the means that the law employs to accomplish the objective, that is, steps 2, 3 and 4 of the *Oakes* analysis. However, when step 3 is reached—least drastic means—the high level of generality will become a serious problem for the justification of the law. If the objective has been stated at a high level of generality, it will be easy to think of other ways in which the wide objective could be accomplished with less interference with the Charter right. If the objective has been stated at a low level of generality, perhaps simply restating the terms of the challenged law, then it will be hard to think of other ways in which the narrow objective could be accomplished with less interference with the Charter right. In the *Andrews* case, the difference of opinion between the majority, who held that the citizenship requirement could not be justified under s. 1, and the minority, who held that it could be, can be traced in large part to the different levels of generality employed by the judges in characterizing the purpose of the law.[3]

In arriving at the appropriate level of generality at which to cast a legislative objective, it must be remembered that the only reason for embarking on the search for the legislative objective is to determine whether there is a sufficient justification for an infringement of the Charter. The statement of the objective should therefore be related to the infringement of the Charter, rather than to other goals. In other words, the statement of the objective should supply a reason for infringing the Charter right.[4] In *RJR-MacDonald v. Canada* (1995),[5] the challenged law was one that banned the advertising of tobacco products. The infringement of the Charter was the breach of freedom of expression. If Parliament had chosen to ban the harmful product itself, there would have been no basis for a Charter challenge. Instead, Parliament chose the lesser path of banning the advertising of the product, and exposed its law to a Charter challenge. It was not therefore relevant to s. 1 justification to characterize the objective as the protection of public health from the use of tobacco, and to establish the importance of the

[3]Wilson J., with whom Dickson C.J. and L'Heureux-Dubé J. agreed, articulated the purpose at a high level of generality, but held that the proportionality tests were failed (p. 156). McIntyre J., with whom Lamer J. agreed, articulated the purpose at a low level of generality; he acknowledged that it could not meet the "pressing and substantial" standard, but he held that that standard was inappropriately high, and that the law was justified under an appropriately lower standard (pp. 184-186). La Forest J. agreed with McIntyre J.'s account of s. 1, but still agreed with Wilson J. that the law could not be justified.

[4]C. Sherrin, "Objectionable Objectives?: An Analysis of the First Branch of the Oakes Test" (D.Jur. thesis, Osgoode Hall Law School, York University, 1994), 137 ("[The court's] primary focus must remain upon the characterization which most directly relates to the reason for violating the constitutional right.")

[5]*RJR-MacDonald v. Canada*, [1995] 3 S.C.R. 199.

objective by reviewing the evidence that showed the harmful effects of tobacco on health. This way of looking at the objective was too broad because it did not focus on the reason for infringing the Charter. McLachlin J., writing for the majority of the Supreme Court of Canada, said that "the objective that is relevant to the s. 1 analysis is *the objective of the infringing measure*". On that basis, the objective of the advertising ban "must be to prevent people in Canada from being persuaded by advertising and promotion to use tobacco products".[6] This was a narrower and "less significant" objective than the broad objective of protecting the health of Canadians from use of tobacco, but she held that it was still an objective of sufficient importance to justify overriding the right of free expression.[7] She went on to hold, however, that the law failed the least drastic means branch of the s. 1 inquiry, because the total ban encompassed purely informational and brand-recognition advertising that played no role in persuading people to use tobacco products. The law was therefore struck down.[8]

In *Vriend v. Alberta* (1998),[9] the law under challenge was Alberta's human rights legislation, which prohibited discrimination in employment on a variety of grounds, including age, sex, race and disability. The basis of the challenge was that the legislation did not protect against discrimination on the basis of sexual orientation. The Supreme Court of Canada held that the failure to include sexual orientation in the prohibited grounds of discrimination was a breach of s. 15 (the equality guarantee) of the Charter. When the Court moved on to the s. 1 analysis, Iacobucci J., who wrote that part of the reasons, pointed out that the benign objective of the legislation—to eliminate discriminatory practices by employers—could not be invoked to justify the breach, because the breach of the Charter lay in what was omitted from the Act. The relevant objective for the purpose of the s. 1 analysis was the Legislature's objective in failing to cover sexual orientation. Since the province of Alberta had failed to adduce any evidence of this objective, and the objective could not be discerned from the legislation itself, the province had failed to establish the existence of an important objective that would satisfy the first step of the *Oakes* analysis.[10] Therefore, the limit could not be justified under s. 1 and the omission was unconstitutional.[11] A

---

[6]*RJR-MacDonald v. Canada*, [1995] 3 S.C.R. 199, para. 144 (emphasis in original).

[7]*RJR-MacDonald v. Canada*, [1995] 3 S.C.R. 199, para. 146.

[8]The idea that it is the objective of the *infringing* measure that must be considered under s. 1 has been reiterated in a variety of later cases: see e.g. *R. v. K.R.J.*, [2016] 1 S.C.R. 906, para. 62; *Que. v. Alliance du personnel professionnel et technique de la santé et des services sociaux*, [2018] 1 S.C.R. 464, para. 45; *Frank v. Can.*, [2019] 1 S.C.R. 3, para. 46; *Fraser v. Can.*, 2020 SCC 28, para. 125.

[9]*Vriend v. Alberta*, [1998] 1 S.C.R. 493. The section 1 reasons were written by Iacobucci J. with whom all members of the Court agreed.

[10]*Vriend v. Alberta*, [1998] 1 S.C.R. 493, paras. 113-116.

[11]The Court's remedy was to "read in" the omitted ground.

similar result was reached in *Rosenberg v. Canada* (1998),[12] where the Court of Appeal of Ontario held that the federal Income Tax Act offended s. 15 of the Charter in requiring all private pension plans that qualified for tax benefits to restrict survivor benefits to spouses of the opposite sex. A pension plan that conferred survivor benefits on same-sex partners did not qualify for tax benefits under the Act. In holding that the failure to include same-sex spouses could not be justified under s. 1, the Court decided that the objective of favouring heterosexual unions was itself discriminatory and could not form the basis of s. 1 justification. The restriction to opposite-sex spouses was held to be unconstitutional.[13]

In *Irwin Toy v. Quebec* (1989),[14] the majority of the Supreme Court of Canada upheld a Quebec law that prohibited advertising directed at children under 13. The law infringed freedom of expression, but was held to be justified under s. 1. The majority of the Court defined the objective of the law at a very low level of generality, as the protection of children (a vulnerable group) from advertising.[15] No attempt was made to define the objective in terms of the injury to the children that the law was presumably designed to prevent.[16] Nonetheless, the majority held that the objective was "pressing and substantial". Having defined the objective in narrow terms, it was then easy to find that the proportionality tests were satisfied. Indeed, the proportionality reasoning became no more than a pair of tautologies. If the objective of the law was to protect children from advertising, then a ban on advertising directed at children must be rationally connected to the objective,[17] and nothing less than a ban on advertising could possibly satisfy the objective.[18]

The trouble with the reasoning of the majority in *Irwin Toy* is that the narrow statement of the objective of the law, essentially repeating the text of the law, left the proportionality tests with no work to do. The *Oakes* test necessarily implies that it is possible to make independent assessments of the objective of a challenged law and of the means employed by the law to accomplish its objective. This requires that the objective of the law be formulated at a higher level of generality than a mere paraphrase of the law. Of course, the question remains: how high a level of generality is appropriate? The answer cannot be captured in any verbal formula. It is inevitably a discretionary choice by the review-

[12] *Rosenberg v. Canada* (1998), 38 O.R. (3d) 577 (C.A.).

[13] The Court's remedy was to "read in" language that would make the definition of spouse include persons of the same sex. See also *Can. v. Hislop*, [2007] 1 S.C.R. 429, paras. 45-55 (rejecting s. 1 justification for denying Canada Pension Plan survivors' benefits to same-sex couples).

[14] *Irwin Toy v. Quebec*, [1989] 1 S.C.R. 927.

[15] *Irwin Toy v. Quebec*, [1989] 1 S.C.R. 927, 987.

[16] McIntyre J., who, with the agreement of Beetz J., dissented, held that the law could not be justified under s. 1, because there was no evidence that children were harmed by advertising directed at them.

[17] *Irwin Toy v. Quebec*, [1989] 1 S.C.R. 927, 991.

[18] *Irwin Toy v. Quebec*, [1989] 1 S.C.R. 927, 999.

ing court. Yet that choice will often dictate the answers to the four *Oakes* questions. Obviously, the attitude of the reviewing court to its function of review—activism or restraint—will play a crucial but inarticulate role in the choice.[19]

§ 38:13 Importance of objective

According to *R. v. Oakes* (1986),[1] the only kind of law that can serve as a justified limit on a Charter right is one that pursues an objective that is sufficiently important to justify overriding a Charter right. When does an objective achieve this degree of importance? Dickson C.J. in his *Oakes* judgment attempted to provide some guidance on this question. First of all, as emphasized earlier in this chapter,[2] the legislative objective must meet the standard implied in the words "free and democratic society" in s. 1. Only objectives that are consistent with the values of a free and democratic society will qualify. Secondly, he suggested that the objective must "relate to concerns which are "pressing and substantial", rather than merely trivial.[3] Thirdly, the objective must be directed to "the realization of collective goals of fundamental importance".[4]

These phrases all indicate that a reviewing court should engage in a rigorous scrutiny of the legislative objective. In practice, however, the requirement of a sufficiently important objective has been satisfied in all but one or two of the Charter cases that have reached the Supreme Court of Canada. It has been easy to persuade the Court that, when the Parliament or Legislature acts in derogation of individual rights, it is doing so to further values that are acceptable in a free and democratic society, to satisfy concerns that are pressing and substantial and to realize collective goals of fundamental importance. Some of the cases are examined in the sections of this text that follow.

§ 38:14 Quebec's distinct society

Quebec's "distinct society" provides the motivation for laws respecting language, education and culture that have no counterparts in the other provinces. When Dickson C.J. in *Oakes* gave examples of the values of a free and democratic society, he included "respect for cultural and group

---

[19]The thesis of S.R. Peck, "An Analytical Framework for the Application of the Canadian Charter of Rights and Freedoms" (1987) 25 Osgoode Hall L.J. 1, is that the *Oakes* test, although clearly intended to mandate active review, is sufficiently malleable to protect restraint as well.

[Section 38:13]

[1]*R. v. Oakes*, [1986] 1 S.C.R. 103, 138.

[2]See heading § 38:2, "Rationale of s. 1".

[3]*R. v. Oakes*, [1986] 1 S.C.R. 103, 138-139.

[4]*R. v. Oakes*, [1986] 1 S.C.R. 103, 136.

identity".[1] This suggested that the Court would be willing to use s. 1 to enable the national norms of the Charter to accommodate at least some of the diversity that it is the role of the federal system to permit.[2]

It was perhaps unfortunate that the very first Charter case to reach the Supreme Court of Canada raised a conflict between a Charter right and cultural identity. In the *Quebec School Board* case (1984),[3] the question was whether Quebec could restrict admission to its English-language public schools to the children of persons who had been educated in English in Quebec. This was an infringement of the minority language educational right in s. 23(1)(b) of the Charter.[4] The question was whether it could be justified under s. 1. A lengthy trial was held at which the Attorney General of Quebec adduced evidence of the need to protect the French language and culture and reduce the assimilation of Quebec children into the nationally-dominant English-speaking culture. The trial judge reviewed this evidence, and held that the infringement of s. 23(1)(b) would make such a trivial contribution to Quebec's cultural and linguistic objectives that it could not be regarded as a reasonable limit under s. 1.[5] However, the Supreme Court of Canada finessed the question of justification altogether. As explained earlier in this chapter,[6] the Court held that the Quebec law was such a severe infringement of the Charter right that it should be characterized as a "denial" rather than a "limit" of the right, and a denial of the right could not be justified under s. 1. The Court therefore discarded the evidence of justification, and refused to even entertain a line of argument based on Quebec's distinct society.

In *Attorney General of Quebec v. Ford* (1988),[7] the Court was faced with another of Quebec's unique laws, this one requiring that public signs be solely in the French language. The Court held that the law infringed freedom of expression, and that it could not be justified under s. 1. However, now the Court recognized the vulnerable position of the French language in Quebec, and recognized that the protection and enhancement of the language was a sufficiently important objective to justify a limit on freedom of expression. The law was struck down, not because of any doubt as to the legitimacy of the purpose, but because

[Section 38:14]

[1] *R. v. Oakes*, [1986] 1 S.C.R. 103, 136.

[2] The accommodation of federal values by the Charter of Rights is the topic of my essay, "Federalism Fights the Charter of Rights" in Shugarman and Whitaker (eds.), Federalism and Political Community (1989), 249-266.

[3] *A.G. Que. v. Que. Protestant School Bds.*, [1984] 2 S.C.R. 66.

[4] Section 23(1)(b) is discussed in ch. 56, Language, under heading §§ 56:17 to 56:25, "Language of education".

[5] (1982) 140 D.L.R. (3d) 33, 71-90 (Que. S.C.). The trial judge also held, in the alternative, that the Quebec law was the "denial" of a right that could not be justified under s. 1. The Quebec Court of Appeal affirmed on the latter ground: (1983) 1 D.L.R. (4th) 573 (Que. C.A.).

[6] § 38:6, "Limits".

[7] *Attorney General of Quebec v. Ford*, [1988] 2 S.C.R. 712.

the banning of English was a disproportionate impairment of the rights of English speakers. However, the mandatory use of French was valid,[8] and, the Court held, it would have been valid to require that French be predominant over English. It was the banning of English that went too far. (The sequel to the decision was that Quebec re-enacted a ban on English-language signs, protecting the new law by including in the law the notwithstanding clause that is permitted by s. 33 of the Charter.)[9]

The Meech Lake Accord of 1987[10] would have amended the Constitution by adding a clause recognizing "that Quebec constitutes within Canada a distinct society". This clause turned out to be the most controversial element of the Accord, attracting opposition on account of its vagueness, its possible effect on Charter rights and its suggestion of special status for the province of Quebec. These concerns seemed to me to be exaggerated in light of the Court's willingness in *Ford* to take into account Quebec's distinctness despite the absence of a distinct society clause in the Constitution. Yet it was the distinct society clause, above all, that precluded the Accord from winning the support of all the provincial Legislatures.

§ 38:15 Inadmissible objectives

Dickson C.J. in *R. v. Oakes* (1986)[1] made it clear that a legislative objective would not count as justification if it was not sufficiently important to override a Charter right. Subsumed in the vague notion of importance were the requirements that the objective would have to be consistent with the values of a "free and democratic society", and relate to concerns that were "pressing and substantial".

Despite the vigour of these strictures, there has so far been only one case in which the Supreme Court of Canada has unequivocally rejected the legislative objective.[2] In *R. v. Big M Drug Mart* (1985),[3] the Court held that the Lord's Day Act, which was a federal Sunday-closing law,

[8] So held in the companion case of *Devine v. Que.*, [1988] 2 S.C.R. 790.

[9] S.Q. 1988, c. 54, An Act to Amend the Charter of the French Language.

[10] See ch. 4, Amendment, under heading § 4:3, "The failure to accommodate Quebec". A distinct society clause was also proposed in the Charlottetown Accord of 1992, which was defeated in a popular referendum.

[Section 38:15]

[1] *R. v. Oakes*, [1986] 1 S.C.R. 103, 138-139.

[2] Where a law providing government benefits is under-inclusive, that is, it fails to provide the benefits to a class of persons who is (by virtue of s. 15) entitled to be included, the program itself normally has laudable objectives, but there is normally no sufficiently important objective for the discriminatory omission. These cases could perhaps be added to the unequivocally inadmissible objective class, e.g., *Vriend v. Alta.*, [1998] 1 S.C.R. 493, para. 116 (failure to include sexual orientation as prohibited ground of discrimination in human rights legislation); *Rosenberg v. Can.* (1998), 38 O.R. (3d) 577, para. 31 (C.A.) (failure of Income Tax Act to recognize pension plans that provided survivor benefits to same-sex spouses); *Can. v. Hislop*, [2007] 1 S.C.R. 429, paras. 45-55 (failure to include same-sex couples in CPP survivor benefits). See also *Sauvé v. Can.*, [2002] 3 S.C.R. 519 (objectives of restricting right of prisoners to vote dismissed by majority as merely "symbolic", "abstract" (para. 23) and "rhetorical" (para. 24), but majority went on

infringed the guarantee of freedom of religion. Its purpose, the majority of the Court held, was "to compel the observance of the Christian sabbath".[4] That was a purpose that was directly contradictory of the Charter right, and could not be a purpose that justified limiting the right.

The Court in *Big M* acknowledged that the secular objective of providing a common day of rest would be sufficiently important to justify overriding a Charter right, but the Court refused to attribute that purpose to the Lord's Day Act for two reasons. First, the legislative history of the Act indicated that the purpose was religious, not secular. Secondly, under federalism principles, the Act was constitutionally valid as a criminal law only if the purpose was religious.[5] It followed that the legislative objective could not justify the limiting of freedom of religion, and the Act was unconstitutional.[6] Not long after *Big M*, the Court was invited to review a *provincial* Sunday-closing law in the case of *R. v. Edwards Books and Art* (1986).[7] The Court held that the provincial law pursued the secular objective of providing a common day of rest for workers in the province. This distinguished the case from *Big M*, and, since the other elements of s. 1 justification were also satisfied, the provincial law was upheld under s. 1.

Three rules emerge from the decision in *Big M*. The first is that an objective cannot provide the basis for s. 1 justification if the objective is incompatible with the values entrenched by the Charter of Rights. The religious objective of compelling the observance of a Christian sabbath was incompatible with the guarantee of freedom of religion. However, as *Edwards Books* held, the objective of providing a common day of rest, although entailing some limitation of freedom of religion, could be accommodated by a society that respected freedom of religion.

The second rule is that an objective cannot provide the basis for s. 1 justification if the objective is ultra vires the enacting legislative body on federal distribution of powers grounds.[8] Therefore, the provision of a common day of rest could not be accepted as the objective of the federal law in *Big M*, although it could be accepted as the objective of the provincial law in *Edwards Books*.

The third rule to be derived from *Big M* is the rule against shifting objectives, which is the topic of the next section.

---

to do proportionality analysis).

[3] *R. v. Big M Drug Mart*, [1985] 1 S.C.R. 295. Query whether the *Quebec School Board* case is another example: see [1984] 2 S.C.R. 66.

[4] *R. v. Big M Drug Mart*, [1985] 1 S.C.R. 295, 351.

[5] *R. v. Big M Drug Mart*, [1985] 1 S.C.R. 295, 352-353.

[6] Followed in *Zylberberg v. Sudbury Bd. of Ed.* (1988), 65 O.R. (2d) 641 (C.A.) (s. 1 cannot save provincial law requiring religious exercises in the schools); *Can. Civil Libs. Assn. v. Ont.* (1990), 71 O.R. (2d) 341 (C.A.) (s. 1 cannot save provincial law requiring religious instruction in the schools if the instruction amounts to Christian indoctrination).

[7] *R. v. Edwards Books and Art*, [1986] 2 S.C.R. 713.

[8] *R. v. Big M Drug Mart*, [1985] 1 S.C.R. 295, 353.

§ 38:16 Shifting objectives

In *R. v. Big M Drug Mart* (1985),[1] the Supreme Court of Canada held that an objective cannot provide the basis for s. 1 justification if that objective did not in fact cause the enactment of the law. Dickson C.J. rejected the notion that the purpose of a law might change over time with changing social conditions. This would create uncertainty and invite the relitigation of Charter issues previously settled. Therefore, he held: "Purpose is a function of the intent of those who drafted and enacted the legislation at the time, and not of any shifting variable".[2] This rule was fatal to the legislation in *Big M*, because the religious motivation of the legislators in 1906, when the law was enacted, was clear, although it was certainly arguable that the law had been maintained on the books in recent times only because it fulfilled the secular function of requiring a common day of rest.

The rule against shifting objectives was again considered by the Supreme Court of Canada in *R. v. Butler* (1992),[3] in which the Court upheld under s. 1 the anti-obscenity provision of the Criminal Code. Sopinka J., writing for a unanimous Court, acknowledged that the original objective of the provision was the promotion of morality, and he held that this objective was insufficiently important to justify a limit on freedom of expression. However, he went on to uphold the provision on the basis that, as interpreted in recent cases, the provision promoted sexual equality. Was this an impermissible shift in the objective of the law? No, answered Sopinka J. The objective had always been the protection of society from the harms caused by obscene materials. The change in the way in which the courts defined those harms was merely "a permissible shift in emphasis".[4] The modern "emphasis" made the law's objective sufficiently important to serve as a justification under s. 1.

What Sopinka J. did in *Butler* was to formulate the objective of the law at a level of generality that could be regarded as remaining constant over time, even though the "emphasis" (which is really just a more par-

---

[Section 38:16]

[1] *R. v. Big M Drug Mart*, [1985] 1 S.C.R. 295.

[2] *R. v. Big M Drug Mart*, [1985] 1 S.C.R. 295, 335. This part of the *Big M* opinion is to be found in the first stage of the Charter analysis, when the Court considered whether the law infringed a Charter right. By implication, but not expressly, the Court applied the same rule to the identification of the objective of the law in the section 1 analysis. Query whether the same rule applies to the assessment of purpose for the federal distribution of powers. In the *Margarine Reference, Can. Federation of Agriculture v. A.G. Que.*, [1951] A.C. 179, the Privy Council struck down a federal prohibition on the manufacture and sale of margarine, although the law had originally been enacted in 1886 on the secure criminal-law basis that margarine was injurious to health. In subsequent reenactments of the statute, a preamble reciting the health rationale was dropped, and the federal Attorney General acknowledged that the original health rationale was false. The Act was judged (and found wanting) on the basis that its purpose was the protection of the dairy industry.

[3] *R. v. Butler*, [1992] 1 S.C.R. 452.

[4] *R. v. Butler*, [1992] 1 S.C.R. 452, 496.

ticular formulation of the objective) had changed with changing community values. This technique offers a path around the rule against shifting objectives. In *R. v. Zundel* (1992),[5] the majority of the Supreme Court of Canada refused to take that path. At issue was the Criminal Code offence of spreading false news, which was held to be a limit on freedom of expression. The original objective of the law was to protect "the great men of the realm" from malicious lies. In *Zundel*, however, the law had been used to prosecute the purveyor of Holocaust-denial literature that was deeply offensive to Jews. For Cory and Iacobucci JJ., who wrote the dissenting opinion, the false-news law had always had as its purpose the prevention of harm from deliberate falsehoods. Citing *Butler*, they characterized the modern objective of racial harmony as a "permissible shift in emphasis" in response to current values.[6] They would have upheld the law under s. 1. McLachlin J., who wrote for the majority, held that the prevention of harm from deliberate falsehoods was too general a statement of the law's objective. In her view, "to convert [the false-news law] into a provision directed at encouraging racial harmony is to go beyond any permissible shift in emphasis".[7] She applied the rule against shifting objectives to hold that the modern objective could not be attributed to the law. Since the law had not been enacted for an objective that was sufficiently important today to justify a limit on freedom of expression, the law was struck down.

§ 38:17 Cost

Is it a possible justification of a limit on a Charter right that the limit will save money?

This was one of the issues in *Singh v. Minister of Employment and Immigration* (1984),[1] where the question was whether an oral hearing by a body with decision-making power had to be afforded to every person who arrived at Canada's borders and claimed to be a refugee. It was argued by the Attorney General of Canada that such a procedure, if applied to the many thousands of refugee-claimants who arrive each year, would impose an "unreasonable burden" on the resources of government. Wilson J., who wrote for three of six judges of the Supreme Court of Canada, said:[2]

I have considerable doubt that the type of utilitarian consideration brought

---

[5] *R. v. Zundel*, [1992] 2 S.C.R. 731.

[6] *R. v. Zundel*, [1992] 2 S.C.R. 731, 823.

[7] *R. v. Zundel*, [1992] 2 S.C.R. 731, 761.

[Section 38:17]

[1] *Singh v. Minr. of Emplmt. and Imm.*, [1985] 1 S.C.R. 177.

[2] *Singh v. Minr. of Emplmt. and Imm.*, [1985] 1 S.C.R. 177, 218-219. See also *Re B.C. Motor Vehicle Act*, [1985] 2 S.C.R. 486, 518 per Lamer J. ("administrative expediency" would be relevant under s. 1 "only in cases arising out of exceptional conditions, such as natural disasters, the outbreak of war, epidemics and the like"); *R. v. Schwartz*, [1988] 2 S.C.R. 443, 472 per Dickson C.J. ("administrative convenience . . . is rarely if ever an objective of sufficient importance").

> forward by Mr. Bowie [counsel for the Attorney General of Canada] can constitute a justification for a limitation on the rights set out in the *Charter*. Certainly the guarantees of the *Charter* would be illusory if they could be ignored because it was administratively convenient to do so. No doubt considerable time and money can be saved by adopting administrative procedures which ignore the principles of fundamental justice but such an argument, in my view, misses the point of the exercise under s. 1. The principles of natural justice and procedural fairness which have long been espoused by our courts, and the constitutional entrenchment of the principles of fundamental justice in s. 7, implicitly recognize that a balance of administrative convenience does not override the need to adhere to these principles. Whatever standard of review eventually emerges under s. 1, it seems to me that the basis of the justification for the limitation of rights under s. 7 must be more compelling than any advanced in these appeals.

The other three judges in *Singh* did not address this issue—indeed, they did not decide the case on the basis of the Charter—but the Court was unanimous that the full hearing right had to be provided. (Compliance with the Court's ruling has in fact proved to be very difficult, leading to a huge backlog of refugee claimants, who typically endure delays of two years or more awaiting adjudication.)[3]

In *R. v. Lee* (1989),[4] a challenge was brought against the section of the Criminal Code that provided that an accused who had elected trial by jury, but who had failed to appear for trial without a legitimate excuse, was to be tried by judge alone. Was this the denial of the Charter right to "the benefit of trial by jury" (s. 11(f))? The majority of the Supreme Court of Canada held that the right had been denied, but that the section was saved by s. 1. Lamer J. for the majority held that it was appropriate to deny the right to those who had burdened the system with the cost of futilely empanelling a jury.[5] Wilson J. dissented, holding that "reducing administrative inconvenience and reducing expense are not, in my view, sufficient objectives to override such a vital constitutional right".[6]

In *R. v. Chaulk* (1990),[7] the question was whether the Criminal Code's presumption of sanity offended the Charter of Rights. The majority of the Supreme Court of Canada held that the presumption of sanity offended the presumption of innocence guaranteed by s. 11(d), because it relieved the Crown of the burden of proving that an accused person was sane. However, Lamer C.J. (with four others) was willing to uphold the rule under s. 1; in his view, to relieve the Crown of the great difficulty of proving sanity was a sufficient objective.[8] Wilson J. disagreed, holding that a "purely procedural" objective could not be sufficiently important

---

[3]See ch. 47, Fundamental Justice, under heading § 47:5, "Immigrants".

[4]*R. v. Lee*, [1989] 2 S.C.R. 1384.

[5]*R. v. Lee*, [1989] 2 S.C.R. 1384, 1390-1391.

[6]*R. v. Lee*, [1989] 2 S.C.R. 1384, 1420.

[7]*R. v. Chaulk*, [1990] 3 S.C.R. 1303.

[8]*R. v. Chaulk*, [1990] 3 S.C.R. 1303, 1337.

to satisfy s. 1.[9] She acknowledged that the prospect of guilty persons escaping conviction through false pleas of insanity could be a "pressing social problem" that would afford justification under s. 1, but she held that there was no evidence to establish such a concern.[10]

In *New Brunswick v. G.(J.)* (1999),[11] the Supreme Court of Canada held that it was a breach of s. 7 not to provide legal aid to a parent whose children were the subject of removal proceedings to bring them under the wardship of the state. The failure to provide legal aid was said to be justified by the need to control government expenditures. Lamer C.J., writing for the majority, did not categorically deny that cost could be a sufficiently important objective to justify the denial of a fair hearing to the parent. He did not need to reach the issue of principle, because he rejected the justification on the ground that the proposed budgetary savings would be "minimal".[12]

In the case of a workers' compensation scheme, the speedy payment of benefits and the reduction in transaction costs are usually seen as calling for systems of classification of injuries and standardization of benefits. But the Supreme Court of Canada has rejected claims of cost and administrative expediency as grounds of justification for a standard program to deal with "chronic pain" (pain without any physical manifestations). In *Nova Scotia v. Martin* (2003),[13] the Court held that the standard program violated the equality rights of workers who suffered from chronic pain and could not be justified under s. 1 on the basis of cost or administrative expediency (or anything else). Never mind the cost, individualized assessment of chronic pain cases was required by the Charter.

Professor Weinrib must be correct when she says that:[14] "It is inherent in the nature of constitutional rights that they must receive a higher priority in the distribution of available government funds than policies or programmes that do not enjoy that status". She concludes that: "A different preference for allocation of resources cannot justify encroachment on a right". As well, cost-benefit analysis is not particularly useful in considering the rectification of Charter breaches, because of the incomparability of cost and benefit: the cost of rectifying the breach can usually be calculated in dollars, but the benefit to be derived is rarely

---

[9]*R. v. Chaulk*, [1990] 3 S.C.R. 1303, 1373.

[10]Three judges held that the presumption of sanity did not offend s. 11(d); they did not need to consider s. 1.

[11]*New Brunswick v. G.(J.)*, [1999] 3 S.C.R. 46.

[12]*New Brunswick v. G.(J.)*, [1999] 3 S.C.R. 46, para. 100. This was a weak answer, because Lamer C.J. considered only state custody proceedings, failing to recognize the full cost implications of a ruling that legal aid must be made available to indigent persons whenever s. 7 would call for a fair hearing. L'Heureux-Dubé J., who wrote a concurring opinion, did not address the s. 1 issue.

[13]*Nova Scotia v. Martin*, [2003] 2 S.C.R. 504, paras. 109, 110.

[14]L.E. Weinrib, "The Supreme Court of Canada and Section 1 of the Charter" (1988) 10 Supreme Court L.R. 469, 486. See also § 38:2, "Rationale of s. 1".

measurable.[15] Nevertheless, there is a point at which the cost of rectification is so high that it would justify the limiting of a Charter right.[16] Even Wilson J. seemed to accept that "prohibitive" cost could have this effect.[17] Where the cost of complying with the Charter is high, but not prohibitive, it would surely be a reasonable limit on the right for government to be permitted to achieve compliance over a period of time, on the basis of a plan that would spread the cost over the compliance period.[18]

In only one case has the Supreme Court of Canada accepted that the saving of government money is a sufficiently important objective to justify a limit on a Charter right.[19] In *Newfoundland v. N.A.P.E.* (2004),[20] the government of Newfoundland had signed a pay-equity agreement with female workers in the hospital sector, which provided for a series of pay increases over five years to bring their pay up to that of comparable male workers. Before the payments had started, the Legislature enacted the Public Sector Restraint Act. The Act modified the agreement by deferring the commencement of the payments to a date three years later than the agreed-upon date. The Act also closed 360 hospital beds, reduced the scope of Medicare coverage, laid off 2000 public employees, and froze or cut the budgets of school boards and other government programs. While the implementation of pay equity was only delayed, no provision was made for retroactive pay for the period of delay, so that the government's contractual obligation to make the first three years of payments was erased. This caused a savings to government (and a denial of pay to the workers) of $24 million. The reason given by government for the Act was an unexpected shortfall of $200 million in the province's revenues. The workers sued for the pay-equity adjustments, arguing that the Act was unconstitutional. When the case reached the Supreme Court of Canada, the Court agreed with the workers that the Act discriminated on the basis of sex in breach of s. 15 of the Charter. But the Court held that the Act was saved by s. 1. The financial crisis of the province supplied a sufficiently important objective to justify the limit on the female workers' equality rights.

Binnie J., who wrote for the Court, said that financial considerations would not "normally" suffice as the objective of a limit on a Charter right, but in this case the government was managing a "financial crisis"

---

[15]*Rosenberg v. Can.* (1998), 38 O.R. (3d) 577 (C.A.), para. 42 per Abella J.A.

[16]*Figueroa v. Can.*, [2003] 1 S.C.R. 912, para. 66 per Iacobucci J. for majority (cost of "sufficient magnitude" might justify limiting right to vote).

[17]See *Singh v. Minr. of Emplmt. and Imm.*, [1985] 1 S.C.R. 177, 220, where this is strongly implied.

[18]For discussion of cost as a justification for limiting Charter rights, see M.D. Lepofsky, "A Report Card on the Charter's Guarantee of Equality to Persons with Disabilities After 10 Years" (1997) 7 N.J.C.L. 263, 394-398.

[19]But note obiter dictum in *Divito v. Can.*, [2013] 3 S.C.R. 157, 2013 SCC 47, para. 66 per LeBel and Fish JJ. for concurring minority ("greater administrative and financial costs. . .may be relevant at the s. 1 justification stage").

[20]*Newfoundland v. N.A.P.E.*, [2004] 3 S.C.R. 381. Binnie J. wrote the opinion of the Court.

that had attained a dimension that called for remedial measures.[21] But did those remedial measures need to include the limiting of the claimants' equality rights? After all, the government of Newfoundland could have financed the payment of the pay-equity adjustments by making cuts in programs that were not protected by the Charter. Binnie J. emphasized that the Act in fact made cuts to many other programs in addition to pay-equity. There were "numerous legitimate claims on the public purse by disadvantaged people which the government was bound to mediate".[22] It was wrong to analyze the case as one of "rights versus dollars"; it was also a case of "rights versus hospital beds, rights versus layoffs, rights versus education and rights versus social welfare".[23] It was "not convincing simply to declare that an expenditure to achieve a s. 15 objective must necessarily rank ahead of hospital beds or school rooms".[24] In this case, the Court accepted the legislative judgment as to the necessity of limiting Charter rights in the service of other values of a free and democratic society.[25]

The Supreme Court of Court considered another cost-related objective under s. 1 in *Conseil scolaire francophone de la Colombie-Britannique v. British Columbia* (2020).[26] In this case, the Court held that British Columbia's French-language education system infringed the right to minority language education in s. 23 in various ways. Wagner C.J., writing for the majority of the Court, held that the courts below erred in concluding that some of the s. 23 infringements were justified under s. 1. In doing so, he disagreed with their conclusion that "the fair and rational allocation of limited public funds" is a pressing and substantial objective under s. 1.[27] He noted that the courts below relied heavily on *N.A.P.E.* in concluding to the contrary, and he treated *N.A.P.E.* as an exceptional case, albeit more by implication. He said—citing the Court's more recent decision in *Health Services and Support - Facilities Subsector Bargain-*

[21] *Newfoundland v. N.A.P.E.*, [2004] 3 S.C.R. 381, para. 64.

[22] *Newfoundland v. N.A.P.E.*, [2004] 3 S.C.R. 381, para. 94.

[23] *Newfoundland v. N.A.P.E.*, [2004] 3 S.C.R. 381, para. 75.

[24] *Newfoundland v. N.A.P.E.*, [2004] 3 S.C.R. 381, para. 95.

[25] But see *Health Services and Support—Facilities Subsector Bargaining Assn. v. B.C.*, [2007] 2 S.C.R. 391, para. 147 (rejecting cost as justification for restricting job-security provisions of collective agreements in health care sector despite acknowledging that health care costs in province had for ten years been growing at rate three times that of provincial economy (para. 4), creating a "health care crisis" (para. 144).

[26] *Conseil scolaire francophone de la Colombie-Britannique v. British Columbia*, 2020 SCC 13. Wagner C.J. wrote the opinion for the majority of the Court, which was joined by Abella, Moldaver, Karakatsanis, Côté, Martin and Kasirer JJ. Brown and Rowe JJ. wrote a joint opinion dissenting in part. This decision is discussed elsewhere in this book; the most detailed discussion is in ch. 56, Language, under heading § 56:23, "Where numbers warrant".

[27] Brown and Rowe JJ., who dissented in part, agreed that this was not a pressing and substantial objective, but for different reasons: *Conseil scolaire francophone de la Colombie-Britannique v. British Columbia*, 2020 SCC 13, paras. 257-260.

ing Assn. v. British Columbia (2007),[28] which cited *N.A.P.E.*—that an objective to "cut costs . . . is suspect as a pressing and substantial objective", and that "strong scepticism" was therefore warranted in determining whether this objective qualifies as pressing and substantial.[29] Applying this skeptical approach, he said that adding the words "fair and rational" to the words "allocation of limited public funds" did not transform this it into a pressing and substantial objective. "Public funds", he said, "are limited by definition", and "[t]he fair and rational allocation of limited public funds represents the daily business of government".[30] As a result, treating this as a pressing and substantial objective "would risk watering down the scope of the Charter".[31]

It should also be noted that cost may have an impact on the content of some of the Charter rights, and thus be relevant to the first stage of Charter review. What is entailed by the principles of fundamental justice may well vary from situation to situation, depending at least in part on the resources involved in providing hearing and appeal rights of differing extent. Similarly, the right to equal benefit of the law can hardly be defined without regard for the claims on resources of policies and programmes that compete with a challenged programme: all roads cannot be paved at once. The right to a trial within a reasonable time and the right not to be subjected to cruel and unusual punishment do not require that the facilities of criminal justice and corrections should be allocated the resources now allocated to health care or education.

VIII. RATIONAL CONNECTION

§ 38:18 Definition

The second step in the *Oakes* tests of justification (the first element of proportionality)[1] of a law that limits a Charter right is to determine whether the law is "rationally connected" to the objective of the law. This second step is reached of course only after the first step has been taken and the objective of the law has been found to be sufficiently important to justify in principle the limiting of the Charter right. "The requirement of rational connection calls for an assessment of how well the legislative garment has been tailored to suit its purpose".[2] The law

---

[28] *Health Services and Support—Facilities Subsector Bargaining Assn. v. B.C.*, [2007] 2 S.C.R. 391, para. 147.

[29] *Conseil scolaire francophone de la Colombie-Britannique v. British Columbia*, 2020 SCC 13, para. 152.

[30] *Conseil scolaire francophone de la Colombie-Britannique v. British Columbia*, 2020 SCC 13, para. 153.

[31] *Conseil scolaire francophone de la Colombie-Britannique v. British Columbia*, 2020 SCC 13, para. 153.

[Section 38:18]

[1] Text accompanying § 38:11 note 1, above.

[2] *R. v. Edwards Books and Art*, [1986] 2 S.C.R. 713, 770.

must be "carefully designed to achieve the objective in question"; it should not be "arbitrary, unfair, or based on irrational considerations".[3]

The *Oakes* case itself[4] was determined by the Supreme Court of Canada's finding that the law failed the rational connection requirement. At issue was the validity of a provision of the federal Narcotic Control Act, which provided that proof that the accused was in possession of an illegal drug raised a presumption that the accused was in possession for the purpose of trafficking. The effect of the provision was to cast on the accused the burden of proving that he was not in possession for the purpose of trafficking. The Supreme Court of Canada held that this "reverse onus" clause was an infringement of s. 11(d) of the Charter, which guarantees the presumption of innocence. This moved the Charter inquiry into its second stage: could the reverse onus clause be justified under s. 1?

The Court in *Oakes* readily agreed that the objective of the reverse onus clause—to protect society from drug trafficking—was sufficiently important to justify limiting a Charter right. But the Court held that the law failed the rational connection test. "There must be", Dickson C.J. said, "a rational connection between the basic fact of possession and the presumed fact of possession for the purpose of trafficking".[5] This reverse onus clause could not satisfy this requirement because it did not make any stipulation as to the quantity of narcotics in the possession of the accused: "possession of a small or negligible quantity of narcotics does not support the inference of trafficking".[6] The Court stopped the s. 1 inquiry at this point, holding that the reverse onus clause could not be justified under s. 1 and was therefore unconstitutional.

Had the Court moved its inquiry on to step 3—least drastic means—there is no doubt that the law would have failed that requirement. By raising the presumption of trafficking on the basis of possession of any quantity of narcotics, however small, the law did not impair the presumption of innocence as little as possible. Indeed, the requirement of least drastic means seems to me to provide a much stronger ground for the decision than does the requirement of rational connection.[7] Surely, the defect in the reverse onus clause was that it was too harsh, not that it was irrational. It seems to me that the reverse onus clause would tend to discourage both the possession of drugs (because the possessor would be in jeopardy of the serious charge of trafficking) and the trafficking in drugs (because the Crown's ability to prove a trafficking

---

[3]*R. v. Oakes*, [1986] 1 S.C.R. 103, 139.

[4]*R. v. Oakes*, [1986] 1 S.C.R. 103.

[5]*R. v. Oakes*, [1986] 1 S.C.R. 103, 141.

[6]*R. v. Oakes*, [1986] 1 S.C.R. 103, 142.

[7]Accord, S.R. Peck, "An Analytical Framework for the Application of the Canadian Charter of Rights and Freedoms" (1987) 25 Osgoode Hall L.J. 1, 70; E. Mendes, "In Search of a Theory of Social Justice: The Supreme Court Reconceives the Oakes Test" (1990) 24 Thémis 1, 8-10; Beatty, Talking Heads and the Supremes (1990), 31.

purpose would be facilitated).[8] Both these tendencies have a rational connection to the objective of protecting society from drug trafficking.

Another case that failed the rational-connection step of the *Oakes* test is *Benner v. Canada* (1997).[9] In that case, the Supreme Court of Canada held that it was a breach of equality rights to impose more stringent requirements for Canadian citizenship on a person born outside Canada before 1977 to a Canadian *mother* than on a person born outside Canada before 1977 to a Canadian *father*. Under the federal Citizenship Act, the person born to a Canadian mother had to apply for citizenship and pass a security check, while the person born to a Canadian father was entitled to citizenship automatically upon registering the birth in Canada. The federal government attempted to justify the impugned provison by submitting that the requirement of a security check was a rational means of screening potential citizens in order to keep out dangerous persons. (The applicant in this case illustrated the point, because he had been charged with a murder and subsequently pleaded guilty to manslaughter; he therefore failed the security check.) The Supreme Court of Canada assumed that the screening out of dangerous persons was an important objective,[10] but the Court held that there was no rational connection between the objective and the discrimination. The children of Canadian mothers could not rationally be regarded as more dangerous than the children of Canadian fathers. Therefore, the legislation failed the requirement of rational connection, and it was not necessary to go on and consider whether it also failed the requirement of least drastic means.

Greater Vancouver Transportation Authority v. Canadian Federation of Students (2009)[11] is another case where the Supreme Court held that the challenged law failed the rational-connection test. The challenged law prohibited the placing of political messages on the sides of buses (where commercial advertisements were permitted). This was held to be a limit on freedom of expression. Under s. 1, the Court held that the objective of a "safe, welcoming transit system" was sufficiently important to justify some limits on freedom of expression, for example, advertisements that were discriminatory or advocated violence or terrorism. But the Court held that the political character of a message had no bearing on whether the message created an unwelcoming environment for tran-

---

[8]It is difficult to catch a trafficker in the act of selling drugs. That is the reason for the offence of possession for the purpose of trafficking. But it is also difficult to prove the purpose. That is the reason for the reverse onus.

[9]*Benner v. Canada*, [1997] 1 S.C.R. 358.

[10]In my opinion, the legislation should have failed this first step, because the issue was not whether there was a sufficiently important reason for screening applicants for citizenship but whether there was a sufficiently important reason for the breach of the Charter, which was the discrimination between the two categories of children: see § 38:12, "Identification of objective". The reason for the discrimination was the historical evolution of the Citizenship Act, which was clearly not good enough for the same reasons that the Court offered in rejecting the rational-connection step.

[11]*Greater Vancouver Transportation Authority v. Cdn. Federation of Students*, [2009] 2 S.C.R. 295.

sit users, and therefore there was no rational connection between the objective and the law banning political messages. The Court went on to hold that the law also failed the minimum impairment test, because a ban on all political messages was broader than was needed to accomplish the legislative purpose. With respect, the latter ground is stronger than the former. It was surely not irrational for the transit authorities to conclude that harsh political messages on strongly-felt issues like abortion or the Middle East would offend the sensibilities of some of their riders. Indeed, Deschamps J., who wrote the opinion of the majority, almost conceded as much by asserting that "citizens, including bus riders, are expected to put up with some controversy in a free and democratic society".[12] The long-suffering commuter just had to get a little bit tougher.

In *Saskatchewan v. Whatcott* (2013),[13] the Supreme Court severed some words from the Saskatchewan Human Rights Code on the ground that they failed the rational-connection step of the Oakes test. The Code prohibited the publication of any representation "that exposes or tends to expose to hatred, ridicules, belittles or otherwise affronts the dignity of any person or class of persons on the basis of a prohibited ground [sexual orientation in this case]". The Court held that this was a limitation on freedom of expression, but that prohibiting the exposure of minorities to "hatred" was justified under s. 1. However, the Court held that the language following the word "hatred" ("ridicules, belittles or otherwise affronts the dignity of") should be severed from the Code prohibition because it could not be justified under s. 1. Rothstein J. for the Court claimed that these words "are not rationally connected to the legislative objective of addressing systemic discrimination of protected groups".[14] But, with respect, the protection of minorities from ridicule, belittlement and other forms of verbal abuse (falling short of hatred) has a rational (indeed a strong) connection to the legislative purpose of addressing discrimination against minorities. The only plausible constitutional objection to the language was that it was too severe a limitation on freedom of expression—a point that is captured by the least-drastic-means (minimum impairment) branch of the *Oakes* test. In fact, Rothstein J. went on to give that as a second reason for the language failing the Oakes test: "I also find them [the severed words] constitutionally invalid because they do not minimally impair freedom of expression".[15] In my view, it is that second reason that provides the only sound ground for denying s. 1 justification.

Mounted Police Association v. Canada (2015),[16] was a challenge to the legislative provision that excluded the RCMP from the general federal

[12]*Greater Vancouver Transportation Authority v. Cdn. Federation of Students*, [2009] 2 S.C.R. 295, para. 77.

[13]*Saskatchewan v. Whatcott*, [2013] 1 S.C.R. 467, 2013 SCC 11.

[14]*Saskatchewan v. Whatcott*, [2013] 1 S.C.R. 467, 2013 SCC 11, para. 92.

[15]*Saskatchewan v. Whatcott*, [2013] 1 S.C.R. 467, 2013 SCC 11, para. 108.

[16]*Mounted Police Association v. Canada*, [2015] 1 S.C.R. 3, 2015 SCC 1.

public employees labour relations statute, which granted collective bargaining rights to federal public employees. The RCMP had a non-unionized statutory process which afforded them opportunities to make employment-related demands and grievances to RCMP management, but in the end their employment terms and conditions were fixed not by any form of collective bargaining but by decision of the federal Treasury Board. The Supreme Court held that the exclusion of the RCMP from the general labour-relations regime infringed s. 2(d) of the Charter of Rights, because "freedom of association" included the right of collective bargaining. The Court held that the challenged law could not be justified under s. 1 because "the government had failed to establish a rational connection between denying RCMP members their s. 2(d) right to meaningful collective bargaining, and maintaining a neutral, stable and reliable police force".[17] This was the only ground on which s. 1 justification was rejected, and, with respect, it seems insufficient. A principal reason for keeping the RCMP out of the general labour-relations regime was undoubtedly to deny the force the right to strike, although the Court said nothing about the right to strike. How can one say that there is no rational connection between the exclusion and the maintenance of a reliable police force without even mentioning the right to strike?[18] The Court did postpone the declaration of invalidity for 12 months, and made clear that Parliament could if it wished explore "other collective bargaining processes that could better address the specific context in which members of the RCMP discharge their duties".[19] But the default position, if Parliament did not act within 12 months, was to put the RCMP into the general labour-relations regime with a right to strike.

The few cases described seem to be the only ones where a law has been struck down for failure to satisfy the requirement of rational connection.[20] All of the other s. 1 cases where the objective has been approved have turned on the requirement of least drastic means. Obviously, the requirement of rational connection has very little work to do.[21] Indeed, for a time I held the theory that the requirement of rational connection was redundant, because the few laws that would fail it would also fail the requirement of least drastic means. But I am now per-

[17] *Mounted Police Association v. Canada*, [2015] 1 S.C.R. 3, 2015 SCC 1, para. 148.

[18] The omission is even more surprising since only two weeks later the same Court held that "freedom of association" included a constitutional right to strike: *Sask. Federation of Labour v. Sask.*, [2015] 1 S.C.R. 245, 2015 SCC 4.

[19] *Mounted Police Association v. Canada*, [2015] 1 S.C.R. 3, 2015 SCC 1, para. 137.

[20] In *RJR-MacDonald v. Can.*, [1995] 3 S.C.R. 199, discussed in § 38:19, while the challenged legislation generally satisfied the rational connection test, one provision failed the test: *Mounted Police Association v. Canada*, [2015] 1 S.C.R. 3, 2015 SCC 1, para. 137.

[21] This point is strengthened if one agrees that *Oakes* could more easily have been decided under the requirement of least drastic means (text accompanying § 38:18 note 7, above) and *Benner* could more easily have been decided under the requirement of sufficiently important objective.

suaded[22] that it is possible to imagine a case where the rational connection test has an independent role to play. A law could be so poorly designed to meet its (important) objective that the law would fail the s. 1 justification, even though it had only a minimal effect on a guaranteed right, and even though a better designed law would have a more severe impact on the guaranteed right. In such a case, the law would fail the requirement of rational connection even though it would pass the requirement of least drastic means.

A silly variant of *Oakes* might serve as an example. Suppose that the Narcotic Control Act cast on persons accused of drug trafficking the burden of proving their names. This burden would be very easy to discharge (and could be discharged without the accused himself actually testifying), and therefore would be only a minimal infringement of the presumption of innocence. But it would not contribute in any significant way to the goal of impeding the trade in drugs. This law would fail the requirement of rational connection, although it is a less drastic measure than a reverse onus clause affecting an important element of the offence.

§ 38:19 Causation

The essence of rational connection is a causal relationship between the objective of the law and the measures enacted by the law. This is often a difficult matter to establish by evidence, and the Supreme Court of Canada has not always insisted on direct proof of the causal relationship.

A striking example of the Court substituting it own intuition for admissible evidence is *RJR-MacDonald v. Canada* (1995).[1] In that case, the objective of the law, which banned the advertising of tobacco products, was to reduce the consumption of tobacco. The law was certainly a limit on freedom of expression. Could it be justified under s. 1? At the trial (which took 71 sitting days), a parade of expert witnesses called by both sides from all over the world debated the issue of whether the ban on advertising would indeed reduce consumption. The trial judge found that the steady decline in tobacco use in all developed countries (some of which had enacted advertising bans and some of which had not) was unaffected by the presence or absence of advertising, and he specifically rejected the evidence to the contrary as being unreliable and without probative value. He concluded that there was no rational connection between the advertising ban and the objective of reduced consumption, and that the law (which also failed the minimum impairment test) was unjustified under s. 1. In the Supreme Court of Canada, however, there was unanimity on the position that the rational

---

[22] A benefit of teaching, which is much underrated by professors, is that students often challenge cherished professorial "insights". I am indebted to first-year student Stephen L. Szikora, class of '92, for the destruction in the classroom of the redundancy theory.

[Section 38:19]

[1] *RJR-MacDonald v. Canada*, [1995] 3 S.C.R. 199.

connection test was satisfied. La Forest J., for the four dissenting judges (who would have upheld the law under s. 1), held that "the common-sense connection between advertising and consumption" was "sufficient to satisfy the rational connection requirement".[2] McLachlin J., for the five-judge majority (who struck the law down on the basis that it failed the minimum impairment test), agreed with La Forest J. that the rational connection test was satisfied. She said that a causal connection based on "reason" or "logic" would suffice, even though the evidence was "admittedly inconclusive".[3] For all the judges, therefore, the finding at trial based on the evidence had to give way to the appellate judges' "common sense", "reason" or "logic".[4]

IX. LEAST DRASTIC MEANS

§ 38:20 Minimum impairment

The requirement of least drastic means is the third step in the *Oakes* tests of justification[1] of a law that limits a Charter right. *In R. v. Oakes*,[2] it was described as the second element of proportionality, and it was said to require that the law "should impair 'as little as possible' the right or freedom in question". The idea is that the law should impair the right no more than is necessary to accomplish the desired objective, or, in other words, that the law should pursue the objective by the least drastic means. This branch of the *Oakes* test can also be described as the minimum impairment test, because it insists that the limit on the Charter right be the minimum that is necessary to accomplish the desired objective. It is not, however, accurate (although it has become popular) to describe the test as the *minimal* impairment test, because the word "minimal" carries the connotation of trivial or slight, and a justified limit on a Charter right might be quite a severe limit on the right.

---

[2]*RJR-MacDonald v. Canada*, [1995] 3 S.C.R. 199, para. 86; he also reviewed the evidence and, in direct contradiction to the careful judgment of the trial judge, held (para. 87) that "there was, in any event, sufficient evidence adduced at trial to bear out the rational connection between advertising and consumption".

[3]*RJR-MacDonald v. Canada*, [1995] 3 S.C.R. 199, paras. 156-158. She did, however, hold (para. 159) that one provision of the Act, s. 8, which prohibited the use of the tobacco trademark on articles other than tobacco products (such as a tobacco brand logo on a cigarette lighter), did not satisfy even a "causal connection based on logic or reason", and failed the rational connection test.

[4]See also *R. v. Butler*, [1992] 1 S.C.R. 452, 503 ("reasonable to presume" that there is a causal relationship between obscenity and harm to society); *Ross v. New Brunswick School District No. 15*, [1996] 1 S.C.R. 825, para. 101 ("reasonable to anticipate" that there is a causal relationship between anti-semitic activity by schoolteacher outside school and discriminatory attitudes within school); *R. v. Sharpe*, [2001] 1 S.C.R. 45, paras. 84-94 (social science evidence, "buttressed by experience and common sense", establishes a rational connection); *Harper v. Can.*, [2004] 1 S.C.R. 827, paras. 77-79, 104 (lower courts erred in requiring the government "to establish an empirical connection"; a rational connection can be established "on the basis of reason or logic").

[Section 38:20]

[1]Text accompanying § 38:11 note 1, above.

[2]*R. v. Oakes*, [1986] 1 S.C.R. 103, 139.

The law of defamation, for example, is hardly a "minimal" restraint on freedom of expression, affecting as it does all expression that is critical of others, but it has been held to be the minimum impairment required to safeguard the value of personal reputation.[3]

The requirement of least drastic means has turned out to be the heart and soul of s. 1 justification. We have noticed that courts have usually readily accepted that a legislative purpose is sufficiently important to justify overriding a Charter right (first step).[4] We have also noticed that courts have usually readily accepted that a law is rationally connected to its objective (second step).[5] We shall shortly notice that courts have usually readily accepted that a law does not have a disproportionately severe impact on the persons to whom it applies (fourth step).[6] In short, for the great majority of cases, the arena of debate is the third step, the requirement of least drastic means.

A number of laws have failed the requirement of least drastic means. The Criminal Code's felony-murder rule has been held to be too drastic a means of discouraging the use of weapons by criminals.[7] Quebec's prohibition of the use of English in commercial signs has been held to be too drastic a means of protecting the French language,[8] although requiring the use of French is acceptable.[9] Alberta's rule prohibiting Alberta lawyers from entering into partnership with lawyers not resident in Alberta has been held to be too drastic a means of regulating the standards of the legal profession.[10] Alberta's prohibition of the publication of accounts of matrimonial litigation has been held to be too drastic a means of safeguarding the privacy of individuals.[11] Ontario's prohibition on advertising by dentists has been held to be too drastic a means of maintaining high professional standards.[12] A federal ban on all advertising of tobacco products has been held to be too drastic a means of curtailing the consumption of tobacco.[13] A board of inquiry order that a person employed in a non-teaching position by a school board must be fired if he continued his dissemination of anti-semitic ideas has been held to be

---

[3] *Hill v. Church of Scientology*, [1995] 2 S.C.R. 1130.

[4] See §§ 38:12 to 38:17, "Sufficiently important objective".

[5] See §§ 38:18 to 38:19, "Rational connection".

[6] See § 38:22, "Proportionate effect".

[7] *R. v. Vaillancourt*, [1987] 2 S.C.R. 636. See also *R. v. Martineau*, [1990] 2 S.C.R. 633; *R. v. Logan*, [1990] 2 S.C.R. 731; *R. v. Hess*, [1990] 2 S.C.R. 906, all cases in which Criminal Code provisions failed the least-drastic-means test.

[8] *Ford v. Que.*, [1988] 2 S.C.R. 712.

[9] *Devine v. Que.*, [1988] 2 S.C.R. 790.

[10] *Black v. Law Society of Alta.*, [1989] 1 S.C.R. 591.

[11] *Edmonton Journal v. Alta.*, [1989] 2 S.C.R. 1326.

[12] *Rocket v. Royal College of Dental Surgeons*, [1990] 2 S.C.R. 232.

[13] *RJR-MacDonald v. Can.*, [1995] 3 S.C.R. 199. A reformulated (less sweeping) ban was upheld in *Can. v. JTI-Macdonald Corp.*, [2007] 2 S.C.R. 610.

too drastic a means of rectifying a discriminatory climate in the school.[14] Restricting spending in referendum campaigns to those affiliated with an official Yes committee or No committee has been held to be too drastic a means of equalizing the financial resources available to both sides of the campaign.[15] Prohibiting the publication of opinion polls in the final three days of an election campaign has been held to be too drastic a means of protecting voters from inaccurate information.[16] Prohibiting the peaceful distribution of leaflets by a striking union at sites not involved in the labour dispute has been held to be too drastic a means of minimizing disruption to businesses not involved in the dispute.[17] In each of these cases, the Supreme Court of Canada held that other laws were available to the enacting legislative body which would still accomplish the desired objective but which would impair the Charter right less than the law that was enacted.

In *Dunmore v. Ontario* (2001),[18] the Supreme Court of Canada, by a majority, held that the exclusion from Ontario's labour relations statute of agricultural workers was a breach of the workers' freedom of association guaranteed by s. 2(d). The objective of the exclusion was to relieve the farm economy of Ontario of the formalism of collective bargaining, which was seen as inappropriate in a sector with many family-owned farms, and of the risk of strikes, to which agriculture was peculiarly vulnerable because of its seasonal character. The Court accepted these objectives, which would seem to answer the question of why agricultural workers had been excluded. But the Court went on to hold that the exclusion failed the least drastic means (or minimum impairment) test, because it was a "total exclusion".[19] By this the Court meant that some other regime of labour law, one that did not include rights to collective bargain and to strike, could have been devised and enacted for the agricultural workers. The Court went on to hold that the Legislature was under a positive duty to devise and enact some new regime of labour relations law for the agricultural workers. In order to hold the attention of the Legislature, the Court struck down the provision excluding them from the statute, so that they were automatically included in a statute that the Court acknowledged was inappropriate, and the Court postponed this order for 18 months to allow the Legislature to substitute a new statute that would be appropriate. This was an innovative application of s. 1 of the Charter and an extraordinary intervention in the

---

[14] *Ross v. New Brunswick School District No. 15*, [1996] 1 S.C.R. 825 (the order removing the person from a teaching position to a non-teaching position did satisfy the least drastic means test).

[15] *Libman v. Que.*, [1997] 3 S.C.R. 569.

[16] *Thomson Newspapers Co. v. Can.*, [1998] 1 S.C.R. 877.

[17] *U.C.F.W. v. KMart Canada*, [1999] 2 S.C.R. 1083.

[18] *Dunmore v. Ontario*, [2001] 3 S.C.R. 1016.

[19] *Dunmore v. Ontario*, [2001] 3 S.C.R. 1016, para. 63 per Bastarache J. for the majority.

legislative process, since it imposed on the Legislature a duty to regulate an activity that the Legislature wished to leave unregulated.[20]

§ 38:21 Margin of appreciation

It is rarely self-evident that a law limiting a Charter right does so by the least drastic means.[1] Indeed, "a judge would be unimaginative indeed if he could not come up with something a little less 'drastic' or a little less 'restrictive' in almost any situation, and thereby enable himself to vote to strike legislation down".[2] This is especially so if judges are unaware of the practicalities of designing and administering a regulatory regime, and are indifferent to considerations of cost. If s. 1 is to offer any real prospect of justification, the judges have to pay some degree of deference to legislative choices.

A related point concerns the accommodation by the Charter of federal values. A strict application of the least-drastic-means requirement would allow only one legislative response to an objective that involved the limiting of a Charter right. The law that least impaired the Charter right would be acceptable; all alternatives would fail. In a federal country like Canada, there ought to be some room for distinctive provincial responses to similar social objectives. The uniformity of provincial laws that would be entailed by a stringent requirement of least drastic means is in conflict with the federal values of distinctiveness, diversity and experimentation. If s. 1 is to permit some accommodation of these federal values, the judges have to allow to provincial Legislatures a "margin of appreciation",[3] a zone of discretion within

[20]The Legislature followed up with the Agricultural Employees Protection Act, 2002, S.O. 2002, c. 16, which maintained the bar on collective bargaining and striking. A challenge to the Act invoking ss. 2(d) and 15 of the Charter was rejected in *Ont. v. Fraser*, [2011] 2 S.C.R. 3.

[Section 38:21]

[1]We have noticed that it can be made to appear self-evident by articulating the objective of the law in terms so close to the actual text of the law that no other law could possibly fulfil the objective: § 38:12, "Identification of objective".

[2]*Illinois Elections Bd. v. Socialist Workers Party* (1979), 440 U.S. 173, 188-189 per Blackmun J.

[3]The European Court of Human Rights, interpreting the limitation clauses in the European Convention on Human Rights, has allowed member states "une marge d'appréciation", which is usually mechanically rendered into English as "margin of appreciation", although measure of discretion would be much better. This concept allows the Court to tolerate different levels of derogation of Convention rights out of respect for the different conditions and values of the European states that adhere to the Convention. See B. Hovius, "The Limitation Clauses of the European Convention on Human Rights" (1985) 17 Ottawa L. Rev. 213; B. Hovius, "The Limitation Clauses of the European Convention on Human Rights and Freedoms" (1986) 6 Yearbook of European Law 1; de Mestral (ed.), The Limitation of Human Rights in Comparative Constitutional Law (1986) H.C. Yourow, The Margin of Appreciation Doctrine in the Dynamics of European Human Rights Jurisprudence (S.J.D. thesis, U. of Michigan, 1993).

which different legislative choices in derogation of a Charter right could be tolerated.[4]

The categorical language that Dickson C.J. employed in *Oakes* to delineate the function of the Supreme Court of Canada under s. 1 appeared to leave little room for even a narrow margin of appreciation. The only law that was qualified to enter into the kingdom of validity was the law that impaired the Charter right "as little as possible".[5] In view of the ease with which a less drastic alternative to virtually any law could be imagined, the process of s. 1 justification looked like the camel passing through the eye of the needle.

Not surprisingly, the Supreme Court of Canada quickly recognized that some margin of appreciation had to mitigate the least-drastic-means requirement. The problem became evident in *R. v. Edwards Books and Art* (1986).[6] In that case, the Court upheld the Ontario Sunday-closing law that applied to retail businesses in the province. The Court held that the law infringed freedom of religion, but that it was justified under s. 1. The Court held that the objective of the law, which was to provide a common day of rest, was sufficiently important to justify overriding a Charter right. The question was whether the law satisfied the requirement of least drastic means. The law contained a "sabbatarian exemption" for retailers who observed Saturday as the sabbath. However, only small retailers—those employing no more than seven people and using no more than 5,000 square feet of retail space—were entitled to the exemption. The issue in the case resolved itself into whether the law had made an adequate accommodation of those who observed Saturday as their sabbath. On this point the Court fractured into three camps.

Dickson C.J., who had written the *Oakes* opinion, now softened his language considerably. With the concurrence of Chouinard and Le Dain JJ., he said that the test was whether the law abridged the freedom of religion of Saturday observers "as little as is reasonably possible".[7] The word "reasonably" had not appeared in that phrase in the *Oakes* case. As to the precise form of the legislative limit, it was "one that was rea-

---

[4]This argument is advanced at more length in "Federalism Fights the Charter of Rights", which is my contribution to Shugarman and Whitaker (eds.), Federalism and Political Community (1989), 249. As noted there, s. 1 is not the only vehicle by which the Charter of Rights can accommodate federal values. Section 33 (the power of override) is also available. See also *R. v. Advance Cutting & Coring*, [2001] 3 S.C.R. 209, para. 277 per LeBel J. ("the principle of federalism means that the application of the Charter in fields of provincial jurisdiction does not amount to a call for legislative uniformity"). For example, as a derogation from freedom of expression, compare the law of defamation of the common-law provinces (*Hill v. Church of Scientology*, [1995] 2 S.C.R. 1130) with the very different law of defamation in the Quebec Civil Code (*Néron v. Chambre des notaires du Québec*, [2004] 3 S.C.R. 95).

[5]*R. v. Oakes*, [1986] 1 S.C.R. 103, 139.

[6]*R. v. Edwards Books and Art*, [1986] 2 S.C.R. 713.

[7]*R. v. Edwards Books and Art*, [1986] 2 S.C.R. 713, 772.

sonable for the legislature to impose".[8] The courts were "not called upon to substitute judicial opinions for legislative ones as to the place at which to draw a precise line".[9] The exemption in the Act "represents a satisfactory effort on the part of the Legislature of Ontario to that end [the accommodation of Saturday observers] and is, accordingly, permissible".[10] La Forest J. was even more deferential in his attitude to the provincez's policy choice. He would have upheld the law, even if it had contained no Sabbatarian exemption. He said that "a legislature must be given reasonable room to manoeuvre".[11] In particular, it seemed to him that "the choice of having or not having an exemption for those who observe a day other than Sunday must remain, in essence, a legislative choice".[12] Only Wilson J. applied the remorseless logic of "least drastic means" to insist that the law must contain a Sabbatarian exception, and that the exception must extend to all Saturday-observing retailers, not just those with no more than seven employees and 5,000 square feet of space.[13]

The majority opinions in *Edwards Books* in effect recognized a margin of appreciation, which would tolerate a variety of different Sunday-closing laws. Indeed, the Court has since used the phrase "margin of appreciation" to describe its approach to the requirement of least drastic means.[14] Certainly, the cases after *Edwards Books* have applied the requirement in a flexible fashion, looking for a reasonable legislative effort to minimize the infringement of the Charter right, rather than insisting that only the least possible infringement could survive.

In *R. v. Whyte* (1988),[15] the Court upheld the Criminal Code provision that presumes that a person occupying the driver's seat of a vehicle has the care and control of the vehicle for the purpose of the drunk driving offence. This reverse onus clause infringed the presumption of innocence in order to make it easier to secure convictions. Dickson C.J. for the Court described[16] the clause as a "restrained parliamentary response to a pressing social problem" and "a minimal interference with the presumption of innocence".

---

[8] *R. v. Edwards Books and Art*, [1986] 2 S.C.R. 713, 781-782.

[9] *R. v. Edwards Books and Art*, [1986] 2 S.C.R. 713, 782.

[10] *R. v. Edwards Books and Art*, [1986] 2 S.C.R. 713, 782.

[11] *R. v. Edwards Books and Art*, [1986] 2 S.C.R. 713, 795.

[12] *R. v. Edwards Books and Art*, [1986] 2 S.C.R. 713, 796.

[13] *R. v. Edwards Books and Art*, [1986] 2 S.C.R. 713, 810. Beetz J. (with McIntyre J.) did not discuss s. 1 at all, because in his view the Sunday closing law did not breach freedom of religion.

[14] *Irwin Toy v. Que.*, [1989] 1 S.C.R. 927, 999. See also *Alta. v. Hutterian Brethren of Wilson Colony*, [2009] 2 S.C.R. 567, paras. 35 ("measure of leeway"), 53 ("measure of deference"); the question is whether the legislative choice "falls within a range of reasonable alternatives" (para. 37).

[15] *R. v. Whyte*, [1988] 2 S.C.R. 3.

[16] *R. v. Whyte*, [1988] 2 S.C.R. 3, 26-27.

In *Canadian Newspapers Co. v. Attorney General of Canada* (1988),[17] the Court upheld a Criminal Code provision authorizing a court order banning the disclosure of the identity of the complainant in a case of sexual assault. The making of the order by the Court was mandatory if it was requested by the complainant or the prosecutor. It was argued that a discretionary ban would be a less severe limit on freedom of the press. Lamer J. for the Court held[18] that only a mandatory ban would provide assurance to a complainant that her identity would not be disclosed, and therefore only a mandatory ban would serve the purpose of fostering complaints by victims of sexual assault.

In *British Columbia Government Employees' Union v. Attorney General of British Columbia* (1988),[19] the Court upheld an injunction prohibiting the union, which was on strike, from picketing the courts of British Columbia, where some of its members worked. Holding that "a picket line *ipso facto* impedes public access to justice",[20] Dickson C.J. for the Court held that the injunction limited freedom of expression by the least drastic means because the union was free to picket workplaces other than the courts.

In *United States v. Cotroni* (1989),[21] the Court upheld the extradition to the United States of a Canadian citizen. Extradition infringed the citizen's mobility right under s. 6 of the Charter, but the objective of suppressing crime was sufficiently important to support a limit on the right. Wilson and Sopinka JJ., who dissented, held that in this case extradition did not limit the right as little as possible, because the accused was charged with a crime that had allegedly been committed in Canada; he could therefore have been prosecuted in Canada as an alternative to his extradition. La Forest J. for the majority answered this by insisting that the requirement of least drastic means must be applied "flexibly".[22] Because there could be procedural or evidentiary reasons why the other country was a preferable forum, he held that the right "is infringed as little as possible, or at the very least as little as reasonably possible".[23]

---

[17] *Canadian Newspapers Co. v. Attorney General of Canada*, [1988] 2 S.C.R. 122.

[18] *Canadian Newspapers Co. v. Attorney General of Canada*, [1988] 2 S.C.R. 122, 130-133.

[19] *B.C.G.E.U. v. B.C.*, [1988] 2 S.C.R. 214.

[20] *B.C.G.E.U. v. B.C.*, [1988] 2 S.C.R. 214, 231. The *ipso facto* suggested that a picket line in front of a courthouse would always impede access to justice. However, in this case, the evidence established that, in addition to everyone's normal ability to cross the picket line, those with business in the courts could obtain a pass from the picketers. In my view, these facts showed that the injunction was an unnecessarily severe response to the picketing, and s. 1 should have been held to be unavailable to save the injunction.

[21] *United States v. Cotroni*, [1989] 1 S.C.R. 1469.

[22] *United States v. Cotroni*, [1989] 1 S.C.R. 1469, 1489.

[23] *United States v. Cotroni*, [1989] 1 S.C.R. 1469, 1490. This approach was unanimously affirmed by the Court in two subsequent cases involving the extradition of Canadian citizens to be tried for crimes in the United States: *United States v. Whitley*, [1996] 1 S.C.R. 467; *United States v. Ross*, [1996] 1 S.C.R. 469.

In the *Prostitution Reference* (1990),[24] the Court upheld the offence of communicating for the purpose of prostitution. This was a limit on freedom of expression that was justified by the objective of eliminating the nuisance of street solicitation. Wilson J. in dissent pointed out[25] that the law prohibited communications between prostitutes and customers regardless of whether or not traffic congestion, noise, or any other form of nuisance was caused by the activity; she thought that the law failed the least-drastic-means test. Dickson C.J. and Lamer J. for the majority emphasized the difficulty of devising legislative solutions, and the Court's inability "to second-guess the wisdom of policy choices made by our legislators".[26] They held that the law passed the least-drastic-means test.

In *Harvey v. New Brunswick* (1996),[27] the Court upheld a provision of a provincial elections law that imposed a five-year disqualification on a member of the legislative assembly who had been found guilty of a corrupt or illegal practice. This was a breach of the right of a citizen to be a candidate for election to a legislative assembly under s. 3, and of course it would have been a lesser infringement of the right if the disqualification were for less than five years. La Forest J. for the majority of the Court quoted from *Edwards Books* for the proposition that the Court ought not to substitute its opinion as to where to draw a line that is inevitably somewhat arbitrary.[28]

In each of the foregoing cases,[29] it does not take a vivid imagination to devise a law that would be less intrusive of the applicable Charter right than the law that was enacted. But the Court was willing to defer to the legislative choice on the basis that the choice was within a margin of appreciation, a zone of discretion in which reasonable legislators could disagree while still respecting the Charter right. Among the considerations that are invoked by the Court in support of a degree of deference to the legislative choice are: where the law is designed to protect a vulnerable group (children, for example),[30] where the law is premised on complex social-science evidence (about the effect of advertising, for example), where the law deals with a "complex social issue" (smoking, for example),[31] where the law reconciles the interests of competing groups (mandatory retirement, for example) and where the law allocates scarce resources. The result makes for an unpredictable jurisprudence, but

---

[24] *Re ss. 193 and 195.1 of Criminal Code*, [1990] 1 S.C.R. 1123.

[25] *Re ss. 193 and 195.1 of Criminal Code*, [1990] 1 S.C.R. 1123, 1214-1215.

[26] *Re ss. 193 and 195.1 of Criminal Code*, [1990] 1 S.C.R. 1123, 1199 per Lamer J; 1138 per Dickson C. J. is to the same effect.

[27] *Harvey v. New Brunswick*, [1996] 2 S.C.R. 876.

[28] *Harvey v. New Brunswick*, [1996] 2 S.C.R. 876, para. 47.

[29] Many other cases could be added to this account, e.g., cases respecting hate propaganda laws (§ 43:27), pornography laws (§ 43:29) and mandatory retirement laws (§ 55:44), all of which have survived the least-drastic-means test and been upheld under s. 1.

[30] *Irwin Toy v. Que.*, [1989] 1 S.C.R. 927, 993-994.

[31] *Can. v. JTI-Macdonald Corp.*, [2007] 2 S.C.R. 610, para. 43.

there is no practical way to avoid uncertainty in the application of the requirement of least drastic means.

X. PROPORTIONATE EFFECT; APPLICATION TO EQUALITY RIGHTS

§ 38:22 Proportionate effect

The requirement of proportionate effect is the fourth and last step in the *Oakes* tests of justification.[1] In *R. v. Oakes*,[2] it was described by Dickson C.J. as the third element of proportionality, and it was said to require "a proportionality between the *effects* of the measures which are responsible for limiting the Charter right or freedom, and the objective which has been identified as of 'sufficient importance' ". In *R. v. Edwards Books and Art* (1986),[3] Dickson C.J. rephrased the requirement by saying that "their effects [that is, the effects of the limiting measures] must not so severely trench on individual or group rights that the legislative objective, albeit important, is nevertheless outweighed by the abridgement of rights". In *Dagenais v. CBC* (1994),[4] Lamer C.J. added to the requirement by saying that the third element of proportionality should also take into account the "proportionality between the deleterious and the salutory effects of the measures".

Although this fourth step is offered as a test of the means rather than the objective of the law, it has nothing to do with means. The fourth step is reached, it must be remembered, only after the means have already been judged to be rationally connected to the objective (second step), and to be the least drastic of all the means of accomplishing the objective (third step). What the requirement of proportionate effect requires is a balancing of the objective sought by the law against the infringement of the Charter. It asks whether the Charter infringement is too high a price to pay for the benefit of the law.

Obedient to *Oakes*, when the Court engages in s. 1 analysis, it nearly always goes through the motion of this fourth step. So far as I can tell, however, this step has never had any influence on the outcome of any case.[5] And I think that the reason for this is that it is redundant. It is really a restatement of the first step, the requirement that a limiting law pursue an objective that is sufficiently important to justify overrid-

---

[Section 38:22]

[1]Text accompanying § 38:11 note 1, above.

[2]*R. v. Oakes*, [1986] 1 S.C.R. 103, 139 (emphasis in original).

[3]*R. v. Edwards Books and Art*, [1986] 2 S.C.R. 713, 768.

[4]*Dagenais v. CBC*, [1994] 3 S.C.R. 835, 889.

[5]A possible exception is *R. v. K.R.J.*, [2016] 1 S.C.R. 906, 2016 SCC 31, where the Court struck down a law that had apparently passed the first three steps, relying on step 4. However, when one goes back to step 1, what Karakatsanis J. for the majority says (para. 66) is only that "this objective is sufficiently important to warrant further scrutiny". This is not an answer to step 1 (which is inconsistent with the rule that each step of Oakes must be answered in sequence), but it avoids my problem with step 4, namely, that it is inconsistent with step 1.

ing a Charter right. If the objective of a law is sufficiently important to justify overriding a Charter right (first step), and if the law is rationally connected to the objective (second step), and if the law impairs the Charter right no more than is necessary to accomplish the objective (third step), how could its effects then be judged to be too severe? A judgment that the effects of the law were too severe would surely mean that the objective was *not* sufficiently important to justify limiting a Charter right.[6] If the objective is sufficiently important, and the objective is pursued by the least drastic means, then it must follow that the effects of the law are an acceptable price to pay for the benefit of the law.[7] I conclude, therefore, that an affirmative answer to the first step—sufficiently important objective—will always yield an affirmative answer to the fourth step—proportionate effect.[8] If this is so, then the fourth step has no work to do, and can safely be ignored.

The thesis advanced in the previous paragraph—that the fourth step has no work to do—seems to me to have an irresistible logic, but this is a lonely view. Obviously Dickson C.J., who proposed the fourth step, did not regard it as redundant. Nor does Aharon Barak, former President of the Supreme Court of Israel, who is perhaps the foremost scholar of

[6]Contra, *Can. v. JTI-Macdonald Corp.*, [2007] 2 S.C.R. 610, para. 46, where McLachlin C.J. for the Court described the fourth step as "essential", and said that if the analysis were to end after the third step 'the result might be to uphold a severe impairment on a right in the face of a less important objective". My respectful answer would be that the feared result should have been avoided by the first step, namely, a finding that the objective of the law was not sufficiently important to justify the limitation of the right.

[7]Contra, *Rocket v. Royal College of Dental Surgeons*, [1990] 2 S.C.R. 232, where McLachlin J. for Court held that the impugned law (restricting advertising by dentists) pursued a sufficiently important objective (first step) but failed the fourth step. Even here, however, the fourth step seemed redundant, because the supporting reasons basically repeated the reasons given under least-drastic-means (third step). *In New Brunswick v. G. (J.)*, [1999] 3 S.C.R. 46, Lamer C.J. for the majority purported to decide (para. 98) the s. 1 issue under the fourth step, but in that case the only objective offered to justify the denial of legal aid (which was held to be a breach of s. 7) was cost, and Lamer C.J. went on to describe (para. 100) the cost savings as "minimal". If the steps had been taken in order, the fourth one would never have been reached. In *R. v. Sharpe*, [2001] 1 S.C.R. 45, McLachlin C.J. for the majority used the fourth step to conclude that the Criminal Code offence of possession of child pornography covered some situations that should be excluded because they posed no risk of harm to children. But this seems a classic outcome of the third step which she did not bring to a conclusion. In *R. v. Bryan*, [2007] 1 S.C.R. 527, Abella J. in dissent would have relied on the fourth step to hold that the impugned law (restricting the publication of election results) was an unjustified limit on freedom of expression, but she skipped the third step and her finding on the fourth step (para. 125) seems to me to contradict her finding that the objective was sufficiently important (para. 104). In *Alta. v. United Food and Commercial Workers*, [2013] 3 S.C.R. 733, 2013 SCC 62, Abella and Cromwell JJ. for the Court relied on the 4th step to hold that Alberta's privacy legislation was an unjustified limit on freedom of expression in the context of a labour dispute, but they skipped the third step which would have been failed because the vice of the legislation was that it was overbroad in making no exception for labour relations disputes.

[8]This conclusion follows only insofar as the full proportionality analysis has indeed been completed under the first three steps.

proportionality.[9] Nor does the Supreme Court of Canada. McLachlin C.J., writing for the majority of the Supreme Court (and the minority did not disagree) in *Alberta v. Hutterian Brethren of Wilson Colony* (2009),[10] explicitly considered my argument and rejected it. She explained:

> It may be questioned how a law which has passed the rigours of the first three stages of the proportionality analysis—pressing goal, rational connection, and minimum impairment—could fail at the final inquiry of proportionality of effects. The answer lies in the fact that the first three stages of *Oakes* are anchored in an assessment of the law's purpose. Only the fourth branch takes full account of the 'severity of the deleterious effects of a measure on individuals or groups'. As President Barak explains:
>
> > Whereas the rational connection test and the least harmful measure test are essentially determined against the background of the proper objective, and are derived from the need to realize it, the test of proportionality *(stricto sensu)* examines whether the realization of this proper objective is commensurate with the deleterious effects upon the human right. . . . It requires placing colliding values and interests side by side and balancing them according to their weight.
>
> In my view, the distinction drawn by Barak is a salutary one, though it has not always been followed by Canadian courts. Because the minimal impairment and proportionality of effects analyses involve different kinds of balancing, analytical clarity and transparency are well served by distinguishing between them. Where no alternative means are reasonably capable of satisfying the government's objective, the real issue is whether the impact of the rights infringement is disproportionate to the likely benefits of the impugned law. Rather than reading down the government's objective within the minimum impairment analysis, the court should acknowledge that no less drastic means are available and proceed to the final stage of *Oakes*.

The point is a subtle one, but perhaps it can be captured in this way: a legislative objective may, *in principle*, be sufficiently important to justify limiting the claimants' right (step 1), but the least drastic means of accomplishing the objective may still have too drastic an effect on the claimants' rights for the law to be a reasonable limit under s. 1 (step 4). In that case, step 4 would in fact be decisive in denying s. 1 justification to the impugned law.[11] I have emphasized "in principle", because an alternative way of analyzing this case is to say that the objective is not

---

[9]A. Barak, "Proportional Effect: The Israeli Experience" (2007) 57 U. Toronto L.J. 369, 374, quoted with approval in *Alberta v. Hutterian Brethren of Wilson Colony*, [2009] 2 S.C.R. 567, para. 76.

[10]*Alberta v. Hutterian Brethren of Wilson Colony*, [2009] 2 S.C.R. 567, paras. 75-76; see also the previous notes to this section which report more judicial disagreement with my argument.

[11]B.L. Berger, "Section 1, Constitutional Reasoning and Cultural Difference: Assessing the Impacts of *Alberta v. Hutterian Brethren of Wilson Colony*" (2010) 51 Supreme Court L.R. (2d) 25, 33, points out that McLachlin C.J.'s opinion (para. 74) reinforces the new emphasis on step 4 by suggesting a more forgiving analysis of step 3, so that minimal impairment is more easily satisfied and the Court can proceed to step 4 and resolve the justification issue (and therefore the outcome) by the balancing of good and bad effects—as occurred in *Hutterian Brethren*.

in fact important enough to justify limiting the claimants' rights—in which case step 4 would not be reached (and nor would steps 2 and 3).

In the *Hutterian Brethren* case, Alberta's highway traffic law required a photograph of each holder of a driver's licence. The Court held that the law limited the religious freedom of the Hutterian Brethren because they believed that the Bible forbade them from having their photographs taken. The Court held by a majority that the law was justified under s. 1. The law passed the first three steps of the *Oakes* test, but McLachlin C.J. for the majority made clear that (contrary to my argument) the fourth step also had to be satisfied. She determined that the fourth step was satisfied because the salutary effects of the universal photo requirement outweighed the deleterious effects on the claimants' religious rights. If she had reached the opposite conclusion, I confess that I still have difficulty in seeing how one could conclude that the objective of the law was sufficiently important to justify limiting the claimants' religious rights (step 1).[12] The distinction between the first and fourth steps remains, for me at least, a difficult one.[13]

Accepting that the Supreme Court follows the full *Oakes* structure and considers step 4 after the first three steps have been passed, it is very important to remember that the four steps must be taken in order: each must be passed before moving to the next. There have been cases where the Court has skipped the crucial step 3 of minimum impairment and resolved the issue of justification by the balancing exercise of step 4.[14] With respect, that is a mistake. A right is not a right if it can be limited by a mere balancing of deleterious and salutary effects—the same appeal to the general welfare that moves legislative bodies to enact laws that do not implicate rights.[15] The point of the *Oakes* structure is to impose a more rigorous analysis on s. 1 justification than the cost-benefit analysis that is the normal moral and political justification for a law that does not implicate a right. In the case of a law that does implicate a right, the s. 1 inquiry into justification potentially involves *all* steps of the *Oakes* structure, taken in sequence, not just step 4 (or even steps 1, 2 and 4). At the heart of the *Oakes* structure is the step 3 finding that the limiting law should impair the right no more than is reasonably necessary to accomplish the (sufficiently important) objective of the law. To move to the balancing exercise of step 4 without having made that crucial finding entails the risk that the balancing exercise might result in the upholding of a law that was a more drastic infringe-

[12]The three dissenting judges did reach the opposite conclusion on the balance between salutary and deleterious effects, and were not troubled by any inconsistency with their concurrent finding that the law had a sufficiently important objective to justify limiting the claimants' rights.

[13]See *R. v. K.R.J.*, [2016] 1 S.C.R. 906, 2016 SCC 31, where the difficulty was avoided by not answering step 1.

[14]See in particular, *R. v. Sharpe*, [2001] 1 S.C.R. 45; *R. v. Bryan*, [2007] 1 S.C.R. 527 (dissent only); *Alta. v. United Food and Commercial Workers*, [2013] 3 S.C.R. 733, 2013 SCC 62.

[15]This point is elaborated in § 38:2, "Rationale of s. 1".

ment of the right than was necessary to accomplish the legislative objective. Since steps 1 (important objective) and 2 (rational connection) are relatively easy to pass, the skipping of step 3 takes much of the rigour out of the *Oakes* structure, and undermines Dickson C.J.'s admirable vision of a structured approach to justification—an approach that he assumed would yield a "stringent standard of justification".[16] A Charter right should not be subject to limitation on the basis of little more than a balancing of deleterious and salutary effects.

§ 38:23 Application to equality rights

The *Oakes* test is offered by Dickson C.J. as a universal rule, applicable to all Charter infringements. Whether this is indeed the position was left in some doubt by *Andrews v. Law Society of British Columbia* (1989).[1] In that case, McIntyre J. took the view that the *Oakes* test was "too stringent for application in all cases".[2] That was an equality case, in which the question was whether British Columbia's requirement of Canadian citizenship as a qualification for admission to the legal profession infringed s. 15 of the Charter. The Court held unanimously that it did, but the Court then divided on the question whether the law was saved by s. 1. McIntyre J., who dissented, in effect rejected the *Oakes* test, at least for equality cases. He said:[3]

> There is no single test under s. 1; rather, the Court must carefully engage in the balancing of many factors in determining whether an infringement is reasonable and demonstrably justified.

What McIntyre J. was concerned about was the fact that legislative bodies had to make "innumerable distinctions" between groups and individuals in the pursuit of "desirable social goals", and in making these distinctions it was not reasonable to demand "the standard of perfection" that was contemplated by *Oakes.*[4] Applying a more flexible standard, McIntyre J. held that the citizenship requirement was justified under s. 1. Lamer J., the other dissenter, agreed with McIntyre J. La Forest J. said that he was "in general agreement" with McIntyre J.'s views on s. 1, although he held that, even on the basis of a lower standard than *Oakes*, the citizenship requirement could not be justified under s. 1.[5] La Forest J. therefore voted with the majority to strike down the citizenship requirement.

There would be a great deal of force to McIntyre J.'s argument if it were the case that s. 15 condemned innumerable legislative distinctions, and required that each be justified under s. 1. But, as will be explained

---

[16] *R. v. Oakes*, [1986] 1 S.C.R. 103, 136.

[Section 38:23]

[1] *Andrews v. Law Society of British Columbia*, [1989] 1 S.C.R. 143.

[2] *Andrews v. Law Society of British Columbia*, [1989] 1 S.C.R. 143, 184.

[3] *Andrews v. Law Society of British Columbia*, [1989] 1 S.C.R. 143, 185.

[4] *Andrews v. Law Society of British Columbia*, [1989] 1 S.C.R. 143, 185.

[5] *Andrews v. Law Society of British Columbia*, [1989] 1 S.C.R. 143, 197.

in a later chapter,[6] the decision in *Andrews* severely limited the scope of s. 15, confining it to discrimination on the basis of the listed grounds of "race, national or ethnic origin, colour, religion, sex, age or mental or physical disability", and "analogous grounds". This restriction led Wilson J. to hold that the *Oakes* test "remains an appropriate standard" for s. 15 cases: "Given that s. 15 is designed to protect those groups that suffer social, political and legal disadvantage in our society, the burden resting on government is appropriately an onerous one".[7] She therefore applied the *Oakes* test, and held that the citizenship requirement could not pass it. Her opinion was concurred in by Dickson C.J. and L'Heureux-Dubé J.

In the result, the six judges in *Andrews* voted by a majority of four to two to strike down the British Columbia law. But, because La Forest J., although voting with the majority, expressed himself as in general agreement with McIntyre J.'s statement of s. 1 principles (although not his application of those principles), the Court actually divided evenly on whether the *Oakes* test should apply in equality cases. Given the restrictions on the scope of s. 15,[8] an infringement of s. 15 calls for the same stringent standard of justification as does the infringement of any other Charter right. The *Oakes* test ought to apply to s. 15 cases. This has been the implicit assumption of the Court in the many equality cases that have been decided since *Andrews*. Although McIntyre J.'s view has never been discussed, it seems safe to say that it has been implicitly overruled.[9]

XI. APPLICATION TO QUALIFIED RIGHTS

§ 38:24 Scope of s. 1

Does s. 1 have a role to play in justifying infringements of Charter rights that are by their own terms qualified by notions of reasonableness or regularity? The general answer is yes.[1] The principal qualified rights are examined in the text that follows.

§ 38:25 Section 7

Section 7 of the Charter guarantees the right not to be deprived of life, liberty and security of the person "except in accordance with the principles of fundamental justice". It is clear from the text of s. 7 that

[6]Chapter 55, Equality.

[7]*Andrews v. Law Society of British Columbia*, [1989] 1 S.C.R. 143, 154.

[8]The relationship between s. 15 and s. 1 is discussed in ch. 55, Equality, under heading § 55:31, "Justification under s. 1".

[9]Another question about the application of the *Oakes* test is whether it applies to those Charter rights, such as ss. 7, 8, 9 and 12, which are by their own terms limited by notions of reasonableness or regularity. This is really a broader question about the application of s. 1, and is accordingly treated separately in the next section of this chapter: §§ 38:24 to 38:29, "Application to qualified rights".

[Section 38:24]

[1]Gibson, The Law of the Charter: General Principles (1986), 135-142.

the right to life, liberty and security of the person can be limited by a law that conforms to the principles of fundamental justice. Does s. 1 permit other limits? Could a law that violated the principles of fundamental justice still be upheld under s. 1 as a reasonable limit prescribed by law that could be demonstrably justified in a free and democratic society?

In the *B.C. Motor Vehicle Reference* (1985),[1] Lamer J. said, obiter, that the answer was yes, "but only in cases arising out of exceptional conditions, such as natural disasters, the outbreak of war, epidemics, and the like".[2] Wilson J. took the contrary view, also obiter, that a law that violated the principles of fundamental justice could never be either "reasonable" or "demonstrably justified in a free and democratic society".[3]

In *R. v. Morgentaler (No. 2)* (1988),[4] the Supreme Court of Canada, by a majority, held that the abortion offence in the Criminal Code infringed s. 7 of the Charter. Each of the three majority opinions, including that of Wilson J., went on to consider whether the law could nonetheless be justified under s. 1 (and held that it could not be). I think it is fair to say, however, that the discussions of s. 1 justification essentially rehearsed points already discussed under fundamental justice.[5] The finding that the abortion law offended fundamental justice virtually entailed a finding that the law was not a "reasonable limit" and was not "demonstrably justified in a free and democratic society".

In other cases, the Supreme Court of Canada has usually applied s. 1 before holding that a breach of s. 7 invalidated a law.[6] The s. 1 justifica-

---

[Section 38:25]

[1] *Re B.C. Motor Vehicle Act*, [1985] 2 S.C.R. 486.

[2] *Re B.C. Motor Vehicle Act*, [1985] 2 S.C.R. 486, 518. In context, it is possible that Lamer J. was dealing only with infringements of s. 7 for "administrative expediency", in which case he was not restricting the use of s. 1 in justification of laws pursuing more lofty objectives. In *New Brunswick v. G.(J.)*, [1999] 3 S.C.R. 46, para. 99, Lamer C.J. for the majority repeated the dictum, but then went on to consider (and admittedly reject) cost as a justification for a s. 7 violation!

[3] *Re B.C. Motor Vehicle Act*, [1985] 2 S.C.R. 486, 523. Wilson J. repeated this view in *R. v. Jones*, [1986] 2 S.C.R. 284, 322; *Re ss. 193 and 195.1 of Criminal Code* (Prostitution Reference), [1990] 1 S.C.R. 1123, 1223; *R. v. Swain*, [1991] 1 S.C.R. 933, 1034.

[4] *R. v. Morgentaler (No. 2)*, [1988] 1 S.C.R. 30.

[5] This is clear in the case of the opinions of Dickson, C.J. (with whom Lamer J. agreed) and Beetz J. (with whom Estey J. agreed). Wilson J.'s opinion arguably applies a somewhat different analysis to the s. 1 reasoning (at 180-184) than to the fundamental justice reasoning (at 174-180).

[6] *R. v. Vaillancourt*, [1987] 2 S.C.R. 636; *R. v. Logan*, [1990] 2 S.C.R. 731; *R. v. Hess*, [1990] 2 S.C.R. 906; *United States v. Burns*, [2001] 1 S.C.R. 283, para. 133 ("rare" for violation of s. 7 to be justified under s. 1); *Suresh v. Can.*, [2002] 1 S.C.R. 3, para. 128 ("exceptional conditions" required); *R. v. Demers*, [2004] 2 S.C.R. 489, para. 46 (overbreadth can never be saved under s. 1); *Chaoulli v. Que.*, [2005] 1 S.C.R. 791, para 155 ("we question whether an arbitrary provision. . .will ever meet the rational connection test"); *Charkaoui v. Can.*, [2007] 1 S.C.R. 350, para. 66 ("the task may not be impossible"); *R. v. D.B.*, [2008] 2 S.C.R. 3, para. 89 ("seldom salvageable by s. 1"); *Can v. Bedford*, [2013] 3 S.C.R. 1101, 2013 SCC 72, para. 129 ("possibility. . .cannot be

tion has been upheld in minority opinions,[7] but never by a majority of the Court.

The Ontario Court of Appeal has upheld a limitation of s. 7 under s. 1. In *R. v. Michaud* (2015),[8] the issue was the validity of a regulation made under Ontario's Highway Traffic Act that required trucks to be equipped with speed limiters set to 105 km per hour. The appellant was a commercial truck driver whose truck was equipped with a speed limiter but one that was set to 109.4 km per hour. He was charged with a breach of the speed-limiter regulation, and he defended on the ground that the regulation was unconstitutional under s. 7 of the Charter. Lauwers J.A., who wrote the opinion of the Court of Appeal, held that the requirement did breach s. 7 of the Charter. He accepted the expert evidence that in about 2 per cent of "traffic conflicts" it was necessary for a truck driver to accelerate beyond 105 km per hour in order to avoid a collision. In that situation, the speed-limiter regulation forced the driver (and others in the immediate vicinity) into an unsafe situation, infringing "security of the person" in breach of a principle of fundamental justice (overbreadth).[9] The regulation was, however, justified under s. 1. The purpose of improving highway safety by reducing the number and severity of collisions in the great majority of truck-related traffic conflicts was sufficiently important to justify a limit on the Charter right. There was a rational connection between the regulation and its purpose because the evidence showed that the speed limiters did enhance traffic safety by reducing the speed of the truck. As to minimum impairment, the regulatory choices of the required speed limiter and the 105 km limit (5 km. over the speed limit) were well within the regulator's margin of appreciation and were minimally impairing. As to proportionality, the benefits of enhanced road safety and reduced greenhouse gas emissions exceeded the detrimental effects on the s. 7 right of truck drivers.[10] Lauwers J.A concluded that the regulation was justified under s. 1. The Supreme Court of Canada denied leave to appeal.[11]

§ 38:26 Section 8

Section 8 of the Charter guarantees the right to be secure against "unreasonable" search and seizure. One may well question whether a search that is "unreasonable" within the meaning of s. 8 could be justified as "reasonable" within the meaning of s. 1. On the other hand, the Supreme

---

discounted"); *Carter v. Can.*, [2015] 1 S.C.R. 331, 2015 SCC 5, para. 95 ("in some situations" a restriction on s. 7 rights may be upheld under s. 1); *R. v. Safarzadeh-Markhali*, [2016] 1 S.C.R. 180, 2016 SCC 14, para. 57 ("difficult, but not impossible").

[7] *R. v. Penno*, [1990] 2 S.C.R. 865 per Lamer J. concurring; *R. v. Hess*, [1990] 2 S.C.R. 906, per McLachlin J. dissenting.

[8] *R. v. Michaud* (2015), 127 O.R. (3d) 81; 2015 ONCA 585. Lauwers J.A. wrote the opinion of the Court.

[9] *R. v. Michaud* (2015), 127 O.R. (3d) 81; 2015 ONCA 585, paras. 59-80.

[10] *R. v. Michaud* (2015), 127 O.R. (3d) 81; 2015 ONCA 585, paras. 114-145.

[11] May 5, 2016.

Court of Canada in *Hunter v. Southam* (1984)[1] has elaborated a set of requirements for legislation that authorizes a search or seizure, and by this ruling has given a particular meaning to the word "unreasonable" in s. 8. The word "reasonable" in the entirely different context of s. 1 is not restricted in the same fashion. Although the words are the same, the tests they require are different. In principle, therefore, it is possible to imagine a law that fails the narrow test of reasonableness in s. 8, but passes the broader test of reasonableness in s. 1.[2] Finkelstein is correct, it seems to me, when he argues that, after a law has been found in violation of s. 8, "s. 1 must then become operative to allow the Crown to lead evidence of reasonableness and demonstrable justification to support the search or seizure".[3] However, the fact is that s. 1 has never saved a law found in breach of s. 8, and s. 1 is rarely even mentioned in s. 8 decisions.

§ 38:27 Section 9

Section 9 of the Charter guarantees the right not to be "arbitrarily" detained or imprisoned. Can an arbitrary detention be reasonable and demonstrably justified under s. 1?

That question arose in *R. v. Hufsky* (1988).[1] The case involved a Charter challenge to a spot-check programme by police, under which motor vehicles were stopped at random at a check-point to check for drunkenness and other traffic violations. The Supreme Court of Canada held that a driver stopped by police under the spot-check programme had been arbitrarily detained in breach of s. 9, but the Court held that the procedure was justified under s. 1. The objective of preventing highway accidents was sufficiently important to justify arbitrary detentions, and nothing less than a random stopping procedure would be as effective in detecting and deterring the commission of traffic offences. The Court assumed without discussion that s. 1 was applicable to salvage an infringement of s. 9.[2]

§ 38:28 Section 11

Several of the rights of accused persons in s. 11 are qualified by

---

[Section 38:26]

[1]*Hunter v. Southam*, [1984] 2 S.C.R. 145; see ch. 48, Unreasonable Search or Seizure, under heading §§ 48:21 to 48:35, "Reasonableness".

[2]Contra, *R. v. Noble* (1984), 48 O.R. (2d) 643, 667-668 (C.A.). Compare *Hunter v. Southam*, [1984] 2 S.C.R. 145, 169 ("I leave to another day the difficult question of the relationship between these two sections [ss. 1 and 8]. . ."); *Canada v. Federation of Law Societies*, [2015] 1 S.C.R. 401; 2015 SCC 7, para. 58 ("The government has a difficult task in seeking to uphold as reasonable provisions. . .which have been found to authorize unreasonable searches.").

[3]N. Finkelstein, Comment on Hunter v. Southam (1985) 63 Can. Bar Rev. 178, 197.

[Section 38:27]

[1]*R. v. Hufsky*, [1988] 1 S.C.R. 621.

[2]Followed in *R. v. Ladouceur*, [1990] 1 S.C.R. 1257 (roving random stop upheld under s. 1).

requirements of reasonableness. A person charged with an offence has the right: to be informed without "unreasonable" delay of the specific offence (s. 11(a)); to be tried within a "reasonable" time (s. 11(b)); and not to be denied "reasonable" bail without just cause (s. 11(e)). It seems probable that infringements of these rights could, perhaps only in the rarest of cases, be "reasonable" limits under s. 1. As was argued with respect to s. 8,[1] the requirement of reasonableness takes on a unique meaning in the context of the definition of a particular Charter right. Therefore, it is in principle possible for a law to fail a requirement of reasonableness in s. 11 and still pass the more generous requirement of reasonableness in the different context of s. 1.

Section 11(d), which guarantees the right to a trial by an "independent and impartial tribunal", is in a special situation, because the Supreme Court of Canada has held that s. 11(d) is reinforced by an "unwritten constitutional principle" of judicial independence. This means, among other things, that "the standard application of s. 1 [presumably meaning the *Oakes* tests] could not alone justify an infringement of that independence". This proposition was announced in *Mackin v. New Brunswick* (2002),[2] in which a majority of the Supreme Court of Canada struck down a New Brunswick statute abolishing supernumerary status for judges of the provincial court, on the ground that it impaired the financial security required for judicial independence. The alleged breach of judicial independence strains credulity, but the refusal to consider s. 1 justification goes even further. Gonthier J. for the majority acknowledged that the statute was passed for the "legitimate purpose" of enhancing the flexibility and efficiency of the provincial court,[3] but he refused to examine the statute through the normal *Oakes* tests. Instead, he held that the financial security of the judges could be reduced only "in cases of dire and exceptional financial emergencies caused by extraordinary circumstances such as the outbreak of war or imminent bankruptcy."[4] Since these conditions did not obtain in New Brunswick when the statute was enacted, s. 1 justification was not available.

§ 38:29 Section 12

It may simply be a failure of imagination, but it is difficult to accept

---

[Section 38:28]

[1] § 38:26, "Section 8".

[2] *Mackin v. New Brunswick*, [2002] 1 S.C.R. 405, para. 72.

[3] *Mackin v. New Brunswick*, [2002] 1 S.C.R. 405, para. 70.

[4] *Mackin v. New Brunswick*, [2002] 1 S.C.R. 405, para. 72, quoting from *Re Remuneration of Judges*, [1997] 3 S.C.R. 3, para. 137. In para. 73, this impossible burden is made even more onerous by the suggestion that the Government of New Brunswick had to justify, not just the decision to repeal supernumerary status (which according to the quotation called for some showing akin to war or bankruptcy), but also the decision to "circumvent" the procedure of prior report by a judicial compensation commission. That procedure had been stipulated by *Re Remuneration of Judges*, which had been decided two years after the supernumerary repeal, so that the Government of New Brunswick had no knowledge of the requirement at the time of the repeal.

that the right not to be subjected to any "cruel and unusual treatment or punishment" contrary to s. 12 could ever be justifiably limited. This may be an absolute right. Perhaps it is the only one.

The Supreme Court of Canada has left open the possibility that "cruel and unusual treatment or punishment" could be justified under s. 1.[1] Even so, and unsurprisingly, it has indicated that "only in exceedingly rare cases can a s. 12 infringement be justified under s. 1".[2] It has also indicated—referring to one of the grounds upon which a measure can be challenged as cruel and unusual treatment or punishment—that "[i]t will be difficult to show that a mandatory minimum sentence that has been found to be grossly disproportionate under s. 12 is proportionate as between the deleterious and salutary effects of the law under s. 1".[3]

§ 38:30 Section 23

The right to minority language education in s. 23 is also a qualified right.[1] Section 23 confers upon "citizens of Canada" who are members of the English-speaking minority in Quebec or the French-speaking minority in the other provinces "the right to have their children receive primary and secondary school instruction in [the minority] language in that province". However, this right to instruction – which is conferred on three categories of parents described in s. 23—is only engaged where the "number[s] of [qualifying] children . . . warrant", and includes the right to "minority language educational facilities" only where "the number of those children so warrants". These where-numbers-warrant thresholds qualify the right to minority language education in s. 23.

Can an infringement of s. 23 be justified under s. 1? The Supreme Court of Canada has said that, in principle, the answer is yes.[2] However, it has also said that an infringement of s. 23 is "especially difficult to justify" and that "a very stringent standard" of justification is required.[3]

[Section 38:29]

[1]See e.g., *R. v. Smith*, [1987] 1 S.C.R. 1045, where majority of Court, having decided that a minimum prison sentence for importing narcotics was cruel and unusual, proceeded to consider (and reject) a s. 1 justification. Only Le Dain J., concurring (at 1111) and McIntyre J., dissenting (at 1085), regarded s. 1 as unavailable to justify a limit on s. 12.

[2]*R. v. Boudreault*, [2018] 3 S.C.R. 599, para. 97, citing *R. v. Nur*, [2015] 1 S.C.R. 773, para. 111.

[3]*R. v. Nur*, [2015] 1 S.C.R. 773, para. 111.

[Section 38:30]

[1]Section 23 is discussed in more detail later in this book: ch. 56, Language, under heading §§ 56:17 to 56:25, "Language of education".

[2]*Que. v. Nguyen*, [2009] 3 S.C.R. 208, para. 37; *Conseil scolaire francophone de la Colombie-Britannique v. B.C.*, 2020 SCC 13, para. 143.

[3]*Conseil scolaire francophone de la Colombie-Britannique v. B.C.*, 2020 SCC 13, para. 151.

And tellingly perhaps, the Court has yet to find an infringement of s. 23 to be justified.[4]

In *Conseil scolaire francophone de la Colombie-Britannique v. British Columbia* (2020),[5] the Supreme Court of Canada said that this strict standard of justification was justified by, among other things,[6] s. 23's internal limits (the where-numbers-warrant thresholds).[7] The Court explained that many aspects of a where-numbers warrant analysis under s. 23—which is described in more detail later in this book[8]—closely resemble parts of a s. 1 *Oakes* analysis, and it said that "[i]t would make no sense if considerations that justify the exercise of the right at one stage could also justify its infringement at a second stage".[9] The Court held that the infringements of s. 23 in this case were not justified under s. 1, but it accepted that it was possible for an infringement of s. 23 to be justified under s. 1. The Court emphasized, however, that this justification must not rest on factors already considered during a where-numbers-warrant analysis.

In *Conseil scolaire*, the Supreme Court emphasized an additional point about how to do an *Oakes* analysis under s. 1 in the s. 23 context. In this case, at the final stage of their *Oakes* analysis, the proportionate effects stage,[10] the lower courts had discounted the high rate of assimilation of French-speaking students in British Columbia. They took the view that the evidence did not show that the existence of minority language instruction and facilities would significantly reduce the rate of assimilation, and thus that this high rate of assimilation was not a particularly deleterious effect. Wagner C.J., who wrote for the majority of the Court, said that this reasoning "defies logic", because it is inconsistent with one of the purposes of s. 23 – "to counter the assimilation of

---

[4] *Conseil scolaire francophone de la Colombie-Britannique v. B.C.*, 2020 SCC 13, para. 143 (making this point). In *Conseil scolaire*, the lower courts did find various infringements of s. 23 to be justified, but the Court held that the lower courts erred in doing so. This aspect of the decision is discussed in more detail earlier in this chapter: see § 38:17, "Cost".

[5] Wagner C.J. wrote the opinion for the majority of the Court, which was joined by Abella, Moldaver, Karakatsanis, Côté, Martin and Kasirer JJ. Brown and Rowe JJ. wrote a joint opinion dissenting in part. This decision is discussed elsewhere in this book; the most detailed discussion is in ch. 56, Language, under heading § 56:23, "Where numbers warrant".

[6] The Court also said that a strict standard of justification was justified in the s. 23 context by the remedial purpose of the provision, and the fact that the provision is not subject to the s. 33 notwithstanding clause: *Conseil scolaire francophone de la Colombie-Britannique v. B.C.*, 2020 SCC 13, paras. 147-149.

[7] *Conseil scolaire francophone de la Colombie-Britannique v. B.C.*, 2020 SCC 13, para 150.

[8] Chapter 56, Language, under heading § 56:23, "Where numbers warrant".

[9] *Conseil scolaire francophone de la Colombie-Britannique v. B.C.*, 2020 SCC 13, para. 150.

[10] See § 38:22, "Proportionate effect".

official language minority communities".[11] He emphasized that the courts should not discount the risks or realities of assimilation in determining whether a s. 23 infringement is justified under s. 1; they should "take assimilation fully into account as a deleterious effect".[12] Brown and Rowe JJ., who dissented in part, but not on this point, put the matter even more pointedly: they said that the high rate of assimilation of French-speaking students in British Columbia ought to have led the lower courts to the "opposite inference"—that the rate of assimilation is "*gravely* deleterious".[13]

XII. APPLICATION TO COMMON LAW

§ 38:31 Application to common law

The *Oakes* test applies to common law limits on rights. It is well established that a rule of the common law may be a limit "prescribed by law" under s. 1,[1] and in two cases common law rules in derogation of Charter rights have been held to be justified under s. 1.[2] In both cases, it was assumed that the *Oakes* tests applied, but the tests were not applied with much care. It is hard to apply the various tests to a rule of the common law, where there is no specific enactment that can be examined in terms of objective, rational connection, least drastic means and proportionate effect.

In *R. v. Swain* (1991),[3] however, the Supreme Court of Canada applied the *Oakes* tests to the common law rule that a Crown prosecutor may adduce evidence of the insanity of the accused against the wish of the accused. This rule was a violation of s. 7 of the Charter, because the evidence of insanity, if led by the Crown, limited the accused's right to control his or her own defence. The majority of the Court held that the rule failed the least-drastic-means branch of the *Oakes* tests, and could not, therefore, be upheld under s. 1. At this point, an interesting difference emerged between a rule of statute law and a rule of the common law. While a rule of statute law that violated the Charter would have to be struck down, a rule of the common law could be amended by the Court itself. A less drastic rule, which would satisfy s. 1, would allow the Crown to adduce evidence of insanity only after the accused had been found otherwise guilty of the offence charged. The issue of insanity

---

[11]*Conseil scolaire francophone de la Colombie-Britannique v. B.C.*, 2020 SCC 13, para. 156.

[12]*Conseil scolaire francophone de la Colombie-Britannique v. B.C.*, 2020 SCC 13, para. 156.

[13]*Conseil scolaire francophone de la Colombie-Britannique v. B.C.*, 2020 SCC 13, para. 264 (emphasis in original).

[Section 38:31]

[1]§ 38:7 note 1, above.

[2]*RWDSU v. Dolphin Delivery*, [1986] 2 S.C.R. 573 (common law tort of inducing breach of contract by secondary picketing upheld); *BCEGU v. B.C.*, [1988] 2 S.C.R. 214 (common law prohibition of picketing of courthouses based on contempt of court upheld).

[3]*R. v. Swain*, [1991] 1 S.C.R. 933.

would then be tried (in front of the same trier of fact) before any final verdict was entered. Lamer C.J., speaking for the majority of the Court, said that he could see "no conceptual problem with the Court simply enunciating such a rule to take the place of the old rule".[4] With those words, the offending rule of the common law was immediately transformed into a new rule that was compatible with the Charter of Rights![5]

In R. v. Daviault (1994),[6] the Supreme Court of Canada held, by a majority, that the common law rule that self-induced intoxication was no defence to a criminal charge offended ss. 7 and 11(d) of the Charter. The Court immediately constructed a new rule, that extreme intoxication was a defence, and that the defence had to be established by the accused on the balance of probabilities. The imposition of the onus of proof on the accused was a breach of the presumption of innocence of s. 11(d), but the Court held that it was justified under s. 1. The s. 1 analysis was very brief, and did not follow the *Oakes* tests at all.[7]

In *R. v. Stone* (1999),[8] the Court held that the common law defence of automatism had to be established by the accused on the balance of probabilities. The Court acknowledged that this was a change in the law, and that it was a breach of s. 11(d), but held that the shift to the accused of the onus of proof was justified under s. 1. As in the case of *Daviault*, the s. 1 analysis was brief and did not follow the *Oakes* tests.

Swain, Daviault and *Stone* were criminal cases in which the Charter of Rights applied by virtue of the presence of the Crown as a party to the proceedings. The Charter of Rights does not apply to the common law in its application to private parties, that is, where no governmental actor is involved.[9] However, the Supreme Court of Canada has held that the Charter of Rights applies indirectly to the common law, because the Court will examine whether the common law is consistent with "Charter values", and, if it is not, the Court will modify the common law to make it consistent with Charter values. In *Hill v. Church of Scientology*

---

[4] *R. v. Swain*, [1991] 1 S.C.R. 933, 978; Wilson J. agreed at 1036.

[5] After this decision, Parliament enacted legislation which details the conditions under which a court may order the accused to undergo a mental assessment. According to this legislation, a court may make such an order either of its own motion, on application of the accused, or on application of the Crown prosecutor. Unless the accused has put his or her mental capacity in issue, the court may only make an order for assessment on application of the prosecutor if the prosecutor satisfies the court that there are "reasonable grounds to doubt that the accused is criminally responsible for the alleged offence, on account of mental disorder": S.C. 1991, c. 43, s. 672.12(3)(b). This provision does not limit the prosecutor to applying for an assessment only after the trier of fact has found the accused to be otherwise guilty.

[6] *R. v. Daviault*, [1994] 3 S.C.R. 63.

[7] *R. v. Daviault*, [1994] 3 S.C.R. 63, 101-102. Compare *R. v. Robinson*, [1996] 1 S.C.R. 683, para. 42, in which Lamer C.J. for the majority claimed that "a strict application of the Oakes test" was called for in justifying a common law rule; the common law rule respecting intoxication for offences of specific intent was struck down and a new rule substituted.

[8] *R. v. Stone*, [1999] 2 S.C.R. 290, para. 180.

[9] Chapter 37, Application of Charter, under heading § 37:12, "Common law".

(1995),[10] which was a defamation action between private parties, the Supreme Court of Canada considered whether the common law of defamation was consistent with Charter values. Cory J., who wrote for the Court on this issue, said that it was not appropriate to apply "the traditional s.1 analysis" in cases where the Charter was not directly applicable. Instead, he said, there should be a "more flexible" balancing of the competing values, and the onus rested with the Charter claimant to persuade the Court that the common law should be modified.[11] He concluded that the law of defamation struck an appropriate balance between the Charter value of freedom of expression and the non-Charter (but important) value of personal reputation; therefore, there was no need to modify the common law.[12] Cory J.'s approach to the balancing of Charter values was upheld, but his actual decision was reversed in *Grant v. Torstar Corp.* (2009),[13] where the Court held that the common law of defamation did not give adequate weight to the constitutional value of free expression. McLachlin C.J., who wrote for the Court on this issue, held that the common law should be modified to introduce a new defence (in addition to truth) of responsible communication on matters of public interest.[14]

XIII. APPLICATION TO DISCRETIONARY DECISIONS

§ 38:32 Application to discretionary decisions

Administrative tribunals and other decision-makers exercising discretionary power under the authority of a statute have to comply with the Charter of Rights.[1] But if a discretionary decision has the effect of limiting a Charter right, can the decision be justified under s. 1? And, if so, is it the *Oakes* framework that supplies the applicable standards of justification?

In *Doré v. Barreau du Québec* (2012),[2] the issue was the constitutionality of a decision by the Disciplinary Council of the Barreau du Québec to discipline a lawyer, Mr Doré, by suspending him from practice for 21 days and reprimanding him. The cause of the discipline was a "rude and insulting" letter that the lawyer wrote to a judge at the conclusion of a hearing before the judge. The Council found that this breached the prov-

[10] *Hill v. Church of Scientology*, [1995] 2 S.C.R. 1130.

[11] *Hill v. Church of Scientology*, [1995] 2 S.C.R. 1130, paras. 97, 98.

[12] See also *Dagenais v. CBC*, [1994] 3 S.C.R. 835 (modifying common law power to issue publication ban injunction).

[13] *Grant v. Torstar Corp.*, [2009] 3 S.C.R. 640.

[14] For a fuller account of the two cases, see ch. 43, Expression, under heading § 43:28, "Defamation".

[Section 38:32]

[1] *Slaight Communications v. Davidson*, [1989] 1 S.C.R. 1038 (arbitrator exercising statutory powers); *Blencoe v. B.C.*, [2000] 2 S.C.R. 307 (Human Rights Commission exercising statutory powers).

[2] *Doré v. Barreau du Québec*, [2012] 1 S.C.R. 395. Abella J. wrote the opinion of the Court.

ince's Code of Ethics of Advocates, which required an advocate to behave with "moderation and dignity". The Council acknowledged that its decision limited the lawyer's freedom of expression but held that the decision was a reasonable limit in a system in which "lawyers and judges must work together in the interest of justice". The lawyer applied unsuccessfully for judicial review of this decision and eventually appealed the matter to the Supreme Court of Canada. Abella J., who wrote for the Court, held that the *Oakes* framework was poorly suited to the review of a discretionary decision. A discretionary decision was not like a statute that could be assessed in terms of its objective, rational connection, least drastic means and proportionate effect.[3] The better framework was that provided by administrative-law principles, which in the case of a discretionary decision by an expert tribunal would simply call for judicial review of the decision for reasonableness. The fact that a Charter right was implicated would not alter the standard of review to one of correctness, but did require the reviewing court to satisfy itself that the tribunal had given appropriate weight to the Charter right in reaching its decision. "If, in exercising its statutory discretion, the decision-maker has properly balanced the relevant Charter value with the statutory objectives, the decision will be found to be reasonable."[4] On the facts of this case, the Council had to balance "the fundamental importance of open, and even forceful, criticism of our public institutions with the need to ensure civility in the profession".[5] Proper respect for expressive rights "may involve disciplinary bodies tolerating a degree of discordant criticism".[6] However, in light of the "excessive degree of vituperation" in the lawyer's letter to the judge, the Council's decision "cannot be said to represent an unreasonable balance of Mr Doré's expressive rights with the statutory objectives."[7] The disciplinary decision was affirmed.[8]

In pre-*Doré* cases, the Court had divided about the approach to apply

[3]*Doré v. Barreau du Québec*, [2012] 1 S.C.R. 395, para. 4; see also para. 39, analogizing the difficulties in applying the *Oakes* framework to the common law and citing § 38:31.

[4]*Doré v. Barreau du Québec*, [2012] 1 S.C.R. 395, para. 58.

[5]*Doré v. Barreau du Québec*, [2012] 1 S.C.R. 395, para. 66.

[6]*Doré v. Barreau du Québec*, [2012] 1 S.C.R. 395, para. 65.

[7]*Doré v. Barreau du Québec*, [2012] 1 S.C.R. 395, para. 71.

[8]For commentary on the decision, much of it critical, see E. Fox-Decent and A. Pless, "The Charter and Administrative Law: Cross-Fertilization or Inconstancy?" in C.M. Flood and L. Sossin (eds.), *Administrative Law in Context* (2nd ed. 2013); H.L. Kong, "Doré, Proportionality and the Virtues of Judicial Craft" (2013) 63 S.C.L.R. (2d) 501; P. Daly, "Prescribing Greater Protection for Rights: Administrative Law and Section 1 of the Canadian Charter of Rights and Freedoms" (2014) 65 S.C.L.R. (2d) 249; C. D. Bredt and E. Krajewska, "*Doré*: All That Glitters Is Not Gold" (2014) 67 S.C.L.R. (2d) 339; A. Macklin, "Charter Right or Charter-Lite? Administrative Discretion and the Charter" (2014) 67 S.C.L.R. (2d) 561; T. Hickman, "Adjudicating Constitutional Rights in Administrative Law" (2016) 66 U.T.L.J. 121; M. Liston, "Administering the Charter, Proportioning Justice: Thirty-five Years of Development in a Nutshell" (2017) 30 Can. J. Admin. L. & Prac. 211. See also *Gehl v. Can.* (2017), 138 O.R. (3d) 52, paras. 78-83 per Lauwers and Miller J.A. concurring (C.A.); *E.T. v. Hamilton-Wentworth District School Board* (2017), 140 O.R. (3d) 11, paras. 108-25 per Lauwers J.A. concurring (C.A.).

in determining whether a discretionary administrative decision respects the Charter.[9] However, in *Doré*, the Court was unanimous. As a result, it appeared that at least seven members of the Court[10] were supportive of the framework that *Doré* prescribed for determining whether a discretionary administrative decision respects the Charter. And yet, disagreement quickly emerged over the *Doré* framework among the Court. The decision of the Court in *Law Society of British Columbia v. Trinity Western University* (2018)[11] is particularly revealing in this respect.[12] In this case, the Court was asked to consider whether a decision by the Law Society of British Columbia to deny accreditation to a law school proposed by Trinity Western University (TWU), a private evangelical Christian university, respected the right of the TWU community to freedom of religion under s. 2(a) of the Charter.[13] At the heart of the controversy around the proposed law school was a prohibition on "sexual intimacy that violates the sacredness of marriage between a man and a woman" that was included in an existing religiously-based "Community Covenant Agreement" that TWU was planning to require all students to sign and obey as a condition of acceptance. The majority of the Court rejected the freedom of religion claim of the TWU community, in a divided decision involving four separate opinions.[14] Abella, Moldaver, Karakatsanis, Wagner and Gascon JJ., who wrote jointly for a bare majority of the Court, affirmed and applied the *Doré* framework (as clarified in *Loyola High School v. Quebec* (2015)),[15] emphasizing in doing so

---

[9]See e.g. *Multani v. Commission scolaire Marguerite-Bourgeoys*, [2006] 1 S.C.R 256 (striking down decision not to grant exemption to Sikh student from rule prohibiting weapons in schools; disagreement between majority, which applied a s. 1 analysis to the decision, and the concurring minority, which called for an administrative-law review of the decision).

[10]Not all nine because a panel of only seven judges heard and decided *Doré*.

[11]*Law Society of British Columbia v. Trinity Western University*, [2018] 2 S.C.R. 293 [*LSBC*]. Abella, Moldaver, Karakatsanis, Wagner and Gascon JJ. wrote a joint opinion for the majority of the Court. McLachlin C.J. and Rowe J. each wrote separate concurring opinions. Côté and Brown JJ. wrote a joint dissenting opinion.

[12]An earlier example is *Loyola High School v. Quebec*, [2015] 1 S.C.R. 613. In this case, the majority of the Court applied the *Doré* framework in setting aside the discretionary administrative decision of a minister that was challenged on s. 2(a) freedom of religion grounds. However, in a joint opinion concurring partially in the result, McLachlin C.J. and Moldaver J. (who were joined by Rothstein J.) did not apply the *Doré* framework, at least explicitly (para. 114 contains an oblique reference)—even though they acknowledged that it had been applied by the Quebec Court of Appeal (para. 87), and even though McLachlin C.J. and Rothstein J. both joined Abella J.'s opinion in *Doré*. For further discussion of the case, see ch. 42, Religion, under heading § 42:9, "Denominational schools".

[13]*LSBC* was heard together with a companion case involving the same issue, also involving TWU: *Trinity Western University v. Law Society of Upper Canada*, [2018] 2 S.C.R. 453 [*LSUC*]. In *LSUC*, the Court divided exactly as it did in *LSBC*.

[14]The freedom of religion claim is discussed more fully later in this book: see ch. 42, Religion, under heading § 42:9, "Denominational schools".

[15]*Loyola High School v. Quebec*, [2015] 1 S.C.R. 613. See further, note xx, above.

that "*Doré* and *Loyola* are binding precedents of this Court".[16] They reiterated that "[u]nder the *Doré* framework, [an] administrative decision will be reasonable if it reflects a proportionate balancing of the Charter protection with the statutory mandate"—and that it will reflect such a proportionate balance if it "gives effect as fully as possible to the Charter protections at stake given the particular statutory mandate".[17] However, in separate concurring opinions, McLachlin C.J. and Rowe J. each took the opportunity to address the *Doré* framework; in doing so, both expressed concerns about aspects of the framework and suggested various refinements or "clarifications" to it. The refinements or clarifications that they suggested would assimilate a *Doré* analysis more to a classic *Oakes* analysis.[18] In a joint dissenting opinion, Côté and Brown JJ. went even further, identifying a variety of "fundamental concerns" about the *Doré* framework, and implying a willingness to abandon it altogether.[19]

§ 38:33 Emergency measures

The Charter of Rights makes no explicit provision for the enactment of emergency measures.[1] On the three occasions when the War Measures Act was proclaimed in force—during the first world war, the second world war and the "October crisis" of 1970—civil liberties were severely restricted by regulations made under the Act.[2] The War Measures Act was repealed in 1988, and replaced by the Emergencies Act,[3] which also authorizes restrictions on civil liberties. It will be for the courts to decide, in a situation of emergency, whether such restrictions are reasonable

---

[16]*Law Society of British Columbia v. Trinity Western University*, [2018] 2 S.C.R. 293, para. 59.

[17]*Law Society of British Columbia v. Trinity Western University*, [2018] 2 S.C.R. 293, paras. 79-80.

[18]Among the suggested "clarifications" were: (1) that the analysis should focus on the impact that a discretionary administrative decision has on a Charter *right*, *not* a Charter *value* (*Law Society of British Columbia v. Trinity Western University*, [2018] 2 S.C.R. 293, para. 115 per McLachlin C.J., para. 166 per Rowe J.; see similarly para. 307 per Côté and Brown JJ. dissenting); and (2) that the onus should be on the relevant government actor to demonstrate that any limitation on a Charter right is justifiable under s. 1 (*Law Society of British Columbia v. Trinity Western University*, [2018] 2 S.C.R. 293,, para. 117 per McLachlin C.J., paras. 195-196, 206 per Rowe J.; see similarly para. 312 per Côté and Brown JJ. dissenting).

[19]*Law Society of British Columbia v. Trinity Western University*, [2018] 2 S.C.R. 293, paras. 266, 302-314. In *Can. v. Vavilov*, 2019 SCC 65, a case that reconsidered substantive review in administrative law, the joint majority of the Court (which included Côté and Brown JJ.) declined to revisit "the approach to the standard of review" prescribed in *Doré* (para. 57), but did not close the door on the idea of doing so in a future case.

[Section 38:33]

[1]The Canadian Bill of Rights, by s. 6, amended the War Measures Act to exempt it from the provisions of the Canadian Bill of Rights. The War Measures Act has since been repealed by the Emergencies Act, R.S.C. 1985, c. 22 (4th Supp.), which does not, however, contain a similar exemption.

[2]See ch. 17, Peace, Order and Good Government, under heading §§ 17:7 to 17:11, "The 'emergency' branch".

[3]R.S.C. 1985, c. 22 (4th Supp.).

and demonstrably justified in a free and democratic society.[4]

---

[4]In *Re B.C. Motor Vehicle Act*, [1985] 2 S.C.R. 486, 518, Lamer J. suggests an expanded role for s. 1 in a situation of emergency; for commentary, see L.E. Weinrib, "The Supreme Court of Canada and Section 1 of the Charter" (1988) 10 Supreme Court L.R. 469, 489-491.

Chapter 39

Override of Rights

I. SECTION 33

§ 39:1 Section 33

II. HISTORY OF S. 33

§ 39:2 History of s. 33

III. RIGHTS THAT MAY BE OVERRIDDEN

§ 39:3 Rights that may be overridden

IV. FIVE-YEAR LIMIT

§ 39:4 Five-year limit

V. SPECIFICITY OF DECLARATION

§ 39:5 Specificity of declaration

VI. RETROACTIVE EFFECT

§ 39:6 Retroactive effect

VII. JUDICIAL REVIEW

§ 39:7 Judicial review

VIII. EVALUATION OF S. 33

§ 39:8 Evaluation of s. 33

I. SECTION 33

§ 39:1 Section 33

Section 33 of the Charter of Rights[1] provides as follows:

[Section 39:1]

[1]See S.A. Scott, "Entrenchment by Executive Action" (1982) 4 Supreme Court L.R. 303 (arguing that the Lieutenant Governor should be instructed to refuse royal assent to any bill containing a s. 33 declaration); B. Slattery, "Override Clauses under Section 33" (1983) 61 Can. Bar Rev. 391 (arguing that s. 33 is subordinate to s. 1); D.J. Arbess, "Limitations on Legislative Override" (1983) 21 Osgoode Hall L.J. 113 (also arguing that s. 33 is subordinate to s. 1); S.V. LaSelva, "Only in Canada: Reflections on the Charter's

33.(1) Parliament or the legislature of a province may expressly declare in an Act of Parliament or of the legislature, as the case may be, that the Act or a provision thereof shall operate notwithstanding a provision included in section 2 or sections 7 to 15 of this Charter.

(2) An Act or a provision of an Act in respect of which a declaration made under this section is in effect shall have such operation as it would have but for the provision of this Charter referred to in the declaration.

(3) A declaration made under subsection (1) shall cease to have effect five years after it comes into force or on such earlier date as may be specified in the declaration.

(4) Parliament or a legislature of a province may re-enact a declaration made under subsection (1).

(5) Subsection (3) applies in respect of a re-enactment made under subsection (4).

Section 33 enables the Parliament or a Legislature to "override" s. 2 or ss. 7 to 15 of the Charter. If a statute contains an express declaration that it is to operate notwithstanding a provision included in s. 2 or ss. 7 to 15 of the Charter, then by virtue of s. 33(2) the statute will operate free from the invalidating effect of the Charter provision referred to in the declaration. Through the use of this override power, the Parliament or a Legislature is enabled to enact a statute limiting (or abolishing) one or more of the rights or freedoms guaranteed by s. 2 or ss. 7 to 15. If the override power did not exist (or if it were not exercised), such a statute

---

Notwithstanding Clause" (1983) 63 Dalhousie Review 383 (arguing that s. 33 leaves a law exposed to review under pre-Charter federalism principles); P.C. Weiler, "Rights and Judges in a Democracy: A New Canadian Version" (1984) 18 U. of Michigan J. of Law Reform, 51 (general discussion); D. Greschner and K. Norman, "The Courts and Section 33" (1987) 12 Queen's L.J. 155 (arguing that s. 33 can only be used to protect a law after a judicial decision invalidating the law); L.E. Weinrib, "Learning to Live with the Override" (1990) 35 McGill L.J. 541 (comment on *Ford* case); Gibson, The Law of the Charter: General Principles (1986), 124-131 (general discussion); Beaudoin and Mendes (eds.), The Canadian Charter of Rights and Freedoms (4th ed., 2005), 106-110 (by Tassé) (general discussion); J.D. Whyte, "On Not Standing for Notwithstanding" (1990) 28 Alta. L. Rev. 347 (criticism of s. 33); P.H. Russell, "Standing Up for Notwithstanding" (1991) 29 Alta. L. Rev. 293 (defence of s. 33); T. Macklem, "Engaging the Override" (1991) 1 Nat. J. Con. Law 274 (criticism of s. 33); L.G. MacDonald, "Promoting Social Equality through the Legislative Override" (1993) 4 Nat. J. Con. Law 1 (defence of s. 33); P. Lougheed, "Why a Notwithstanding Clause?" (Constitutional Forum, U. of Alta., 1998) (defence of s. 33); H. Leeson, "Section 33, The Notwithstanding Clause: "Paper Tiger?" (2000) 6 Choices, no. 4, p. 3 (general discussion); T. Kahana, The Partnership Model of the Canadian Notwithstanding Mechanism: Failure and Hope (S.J.D. thesis, University of Toronto, 2000) (general discussion); T. Kahana, "The Notwithstanding Mechanism and Public Discussion: Lessons from the Ignored Practice of Section 33" (2001) 43 J. Can. Public Admin. 225; T. Kahana, "Understanding the Notwithstanding Mechanism" (2002) 52 U. Toronto L.J. 221; J. Cameron, "The Charter's Legislative Override" (2004) 23 Supreme Court L.R. (2d) 135; J.L. Hiebert, "Is it Too Late to Rehabilitate Canada's Notwithstanding Clause?" (2004) 23 Supreme Court L.R. (2d) 169; T. Kahana, "What Makes for a Good Use of the Notwithstanding Mechanism?" (2004) 23 Supreme Court L.R. (2d) 191; L.E. Weinrib, "The Canadian Charter's Override Clause: Lessons for Israel" (2016) 49 Israel L. Rev. 67.

would be valid only if it came within s. 1 of the Charter: a court would have to be persuaded, in accordance with the rules described in the previous chapter, that the statute came within "such reasonable limits prescribed by law as can be demonstrably justified in a free and democratic society". The override power, if exercised, would remove the statute containing the express declaration from the reach of the Charter provisions referred to in the declaration without the necessity of any showing of reasonableness or demonstrable justification.[2]

II. HISTORY OF S. 33

§ 39:2 History of s. 33

Section 33 was not in any of the earlier versions of the Charter. It was the crucial element of the federal-provincial agreement of November 5, 1981 that secured the consent of those provinces (other than Quebec) that had until then been opposed to the Charter on the ground that it limited the sovereignty of their Legislatures.[1] Section 33 preserved that sovereignty, provided the Legislature satisfied the requirements of the section.

Quebec was the one province that did not join the agreement of November 5, 1981, and the province has never given its assent to the Constitution Act, 1982, including the Charter of Rights. After the Charter came into force on April 17, 1982, Quebec's Parti Québécois Government secured the passage by the Legislature of Bill 62, entitled An Act respecting the Constitution Act, 1982.[2] This Act, which was intended to be a protest against the Charter,[3] added a standard-form notwithstanding clause to each of the statutes in force in Quebec on April 16, 1982.[4] In addition, each new Act enacted by the Quebec Legislature routinely included a standard-form notwithstanding clause. The latter practice was discontinued after December 2, 1985, when a provincial election installed a Liberal Government in Quebec City with a policy of reaching a constitutional accommodation with the rest of Canada.[5] The Liberal Government also allowed the blanket override to lapse in 1987, when it came to the end of its five-year life; no attempt was made to re-enact it for another five-year term.

---

[2]This point has been the subject of some controversy: see § 39:7, "Judicial review".

[Section 39:2]

[1]The other major concession achieved by the seven provinces was the substitution of their preferred amending formula for the one preferred by the federal government and its two provincial allies (Ontario and New Brunswick). The history of the Constitution Act, 1982 is related in ch. 4, Amendment, under heading § 4:2, "The search for a domestic amending procedure".

[2]S.Q. 1982, c. 21.

[3]The Act did not override the Quebec Charter of Human Rights and Freedoms, thus making clear that the purpose was not to abridge civil liberties, but only to protest the imposed national Charter.

[4]The validity of this use of the override was upheld in *Ford v. Que.*, [1988] 2 S.C.R. 712; the case is discussed in the text that follows.

[5]That policy caused the Government to agree to the Meech Lake Accord, which,

The Liberal Government of Quebec that was elected on December 2, 1985, while not continuing the previous government's routine uses of s. 33, did nevertheless insert a notwithstanding clause in twelve statutes in order to preclude Charter attacks on the statutes.[6] These uses of the clause seem to have attracted no controversy, with one notable exception. The controversial use of s. 33 was in Bill C-178, entitled An Act to Amend the Charter of the French language,[7] in which the Legislature of Quebec prohibited the use of English in outside commercial signs. This was a response to the decision of the Supreme Court of Canada in *Ford v. Quebec* (1988),[8] which had held that a law banning the use of languages other than French in commercial signs was an infringement of the Charter right to freedom of expression. After this decision, the Legislature re-enacted the prohibition with respect to exterior signs (while allowing bilingual interior signs), and protected the new prohibition with a notwithstanding clause. Section 33 was thus used to support a language policy that enjoyed widespread support among French-speakers within Quebec, although the law (and the use of s. 33) was very unpopular outside Quebec and contributed to opposition to the then-unratified Meech Lake Accord. In 1993, when the notwithstanding clause reached the end of its five-year life, the Quebec Legislature lifted the ban on English language signs and replaced it with legislation that required only that French be predominant. This new legislation was not protected by a notwithstanding clause.[9]

Quebec invoked s. 33 again in 2019 in the Laicity Act.[10] The Act prohibits various categories of public employees, such as court staff, government lawyers, police officers and teachers, from wearing religious symbols (like turbans and kippahs) while performing their functions.

---

however, failed to achieve two of the required eleven legislative ratifications in the three-year period allowed for ratifications, and therefore lapsed. See ch. 4, Amendment, under heading § 4:3, "The failure to accommodate Quebec".

[6]The twelve uses occurred in statutes dealing with the language of commercial signs (one statute, discussed in following text), pension plans (four statutes, different treatment of men and women), education (six statutes, religious distinctions) and agriculture (one statute, age distinction). Three of these twelve uses of s. 33 were renewed, either on the expiry of the notwithstanding clause or on the revision of the statute. The Liberal Government was defeated in 1994 and the Parti Québécois Government that replaced it enacted two of the renewals but did not use s. 33 on any of its own statutes. A comprehensive account of the uses of s. 33 is to be found in T. Kahana, The Partnership Model of the Canadian Notwithstanding Mechanism: Failure and Hope (S.J.D. thesis, University of Toronto, 2000); T. Kahana, "The Notwithstanding Mechanism and Public Discussion: Lessons from the Ignored Practice of Section 33" (2001) 43 J. Can. Public Admin. 225; T. Kahana, "Understanding the Notwithstanding Mechanism" (2002) 52 U. Toronto L.J. 221; T. Kahana, "What Makes for a Good Use of the Notwithstanding Mechanism?" (2004) 23 Supreme Court L.R. (2d) 191.

[7]S.Q. 1988, c. 54.

[8]*Ford v. Quebec*, [1988] 2 S.C.R. 712, 737-742.

[9]S.Q. 1993, c. 40. For an accounting of uses of the notwithstanding clause in Quebec up to and including 2014, see G. Rousseau & F. Côté, "A Distinctive Quebec Theory and Practice of the Notwithstanding Clause: When Collective Interests Outweigh Individual Rights" (2017) 47 Revue générale de droit 343.

[10]An Act respecting the laicity of the State, C.Q.L.R., c. L-0.3, s. 34.

The Act includes a similar prohibition on face coverings (like hijabs). The prohibition on wearing religious symbols does not apply to those employed as of March or June 2019, but it does apply to those being hired into or promoted within these categories of public employment. Unsurprisingly, as with the Quebec language law referred to in the previous paragraph, a fierce debate erupted, both inside and outside of Quebec, about the Act's wisdom and constitutionality. Those that defend the Act claim that it protects an important aspect of Quebec's identity—its secularism—whereas those that oppose it worry, quite rightly, about its impact on religious freedom, and religious, racial and gender equality. Unsurprisingly, shortly after the Act was enacted, its constitutionality was challenged in several cases, including under the rights to religious freedom and equality in ss. 2(a) and 15 of the Charter.[11] These cases have provided the courts a (thus far) rare chance to consider a constitutional challenge involving a notwithstanding clause.[12]

Before 2018, the power of override was used just three times outside of Quebec.[13] The first was enacted by the Yukon Territory in a statute that was never brought into force and so scarcely counts as an example.[14] The second use of s. 33 was by Saskatchewan to protect a back-to-work law[15] of a kind that the Saskatchewan Court of Appeal in an earlier case[16] had held was contrary to the guarantee of freedom of association (s. 2(d)). When Saskatchewan enacted the override clause, the Government was in the process of appealing the earlier case to the Supreme Court of Canada. The Supreme Court of Canada later allowed the appeal, vindicating the Saskatchewan Government's view that the back-to-

[11]One argument that was invoked to circumvent the notwithstanding clause included in the Act is s. 28 of the Charter, which provides that "[n]otwithstanding anything in this Charter, the rights and freedoms referred to in it are guaranteed equally to male and female persons". The argument is that the "notwithstanding anything in this Charter" language in s. 28 operates to ensure that discrimination on the basis of sex in laws—like the Act, which adversely impacts Muslim women who wear face coverings—cannot be protected by a notwithstanding clause.

[12]In one of the constitutional challenges, the Quebec Superior Court rejected an application for a provisional stay of certain provisions of the Act pending a decision on the merits: *Hak v. Que.*, 2019 QCCS 2989. The majority of the Quebec Court of Appeal dismissed an appeal of this decision: 2019 QCCA 2145, leave to appeal to the S.C.C. denied April 9, 2020. Four of the constitutional challenges were heard together by the Quebec Superior Court, in a hearing that concluded in December 2020; as of the time of writing, the Court's decision is under reserve.

[13]A comprehensive account of the uses of s. 33 is to be found in T. Kahana, The Partnership Model of the Canadian Notwithstanding Mechanism: Failure and Hope (S.J.D. thesis, University of Toronto, 2000); T. Kahana, "The Notwithstanding Mechanism and Public Discussion: Lessons from the Ignored Practice of Section 33" (2001) 43 J. Can. Public Admin. 225; T. Kahana, "Understanding the Notwithstanding Mechanism" (2002) 52 U. Toronto L.J. 221; T. Kahana, "What Makes for a Good Use of the Notwithstanding Mechanism?" (2004) 23 Supreme Court L.R. (2d) 191 above (thesis and articles).

[14]Land Planning and Development Act, S.Y. 1982, c. 22, s. 39(1) (providing for nominations to boards by the Council for Yukon Indians).

[15]The SGEU Dispute Settlement Act, S.S. 1984-85-86, c. 111, s. 9.

[16]*RWDSU v. Govt. of Sask.*, [1985] 5 W.W.R. 97 (Sask. C.A.).

work law did not offend the Charter.[17] Thus, the use of the power of override was shown to be unnecessary. The third use of s. 33 was by Alberta to protect a law that stipulated that marriage could not be between same-sex spouses.[18]

Beginning in 2018, the notwithstanding clause seemed to enjoy something of a renaissance. We have already seen that Quebec invoked the notwithstanding clause in 2019 in the Laicity Act. In May 2018, Saskatchewan, which is one of the three provinces that had already invoked the notwithstanding clause, also invoked it again in the School Choice Protection Act.[19] The Act was passed in response to the decision of the Court of Queen's Bench in *Good Spirit School Division No. 204 v. Christ The Teacher Roman Catholic Separate School Division No. 212* (2017),[20] which held that a provincial scheme that funded non-Catholic students to attend Catholic schools violated s. 2(a) (religious freedom) and s. 15 (equality) of the Charter. The Saskatchewan Court of Appeal overturned the trial-level decision,[21] rendering the notwithstanding clause in the Act unnecessary.

In September 2018, Ontario was added to the list of provinces that have (almost) invoked the notwithstanding clause. In August 2018, the government of Progressive Conservative Premier Doug Ford introduced the Better Local Government Act,[22] which reduced the size of Toronto City Council from 47 to 25 wards in the middle of a Toronto municipal election. The notwithstanding clause was not included in the Act, but rather in Bill 31, the Efficient Local Government Act, 2018.[23] Bill 31 was a response to a decision of the Superior Court of Justice, which held that the Act infringed the right of candidates and voters to freedom of expression under s. 2(b) of the Charter by reducing the size of Toronto City Council in this way.[24] However, Bill 31 was not taken to a final vote in the Legislature, because the Ontario Court of Appeal stayed the Superior Court's decision pending the resolution of an appeal,[25] allowing the mu-

[17] *RWDSU v. Sask.*, [1987] 1 S.C.R. 460.

[18] Marriage Amendment Act, S.A. 2000, c. 3, s. 5. A notwithstanding declaration was also included in Bill 26 of 1988, which would have limited the amount of compensation payable to victims of a (long discontinued) provincial sterilization program; but the bill was withdrawn by the government after a public outcry.

[19] S.S. 2018, c. 39, s. 3.

[20] *Good Spirit School Division No. 204 v. Christ The Teacher Roman Catholic Separate School Division No. 212*, [2017] 9 W.W.R. 673, 2017 SKQB 109 (Sask. Q.B.).

[21] (2020) 445 D.L.R. 4th 179, 2020 SKCA 34 (Sask. C.A.).

[22] S.O. 2018, c. 11.

[23] The Bill involved amendments to four provincial Acts, and four notwithstanding clauses: see Bill 31, 1st Reading, September 12, 2018, Schedule 1, s. 456.1, Schedule 2, s. 218.3, Schedule 3, s. 10.3, Schedule 4, s. 58.02.

[24] *City of Toronto v. Ont.*, 2018 ONSC 5151 (S.C.J.).

[25] *Toronto (City) v. Ont.* (2018) 142 O.R. (3d) 481, 2018 ONCA 761 (C.A.).

nicipal election for a smaller Toronto City Council to proceed without a notwithstanding clause.[26]

Finally, in November 2019, the Progressive Conservative government of New Brunswick added New Brunswick to the list of provinces that have (almost) invoked the notwithstanding clause, when it introduced Bill 11, An Act Respecting Proof of Immunization.[27] Bill 11 would have required students to provide proof of vaccination before attending school, and eliminated the ability of parents to exempt their children from vaccinations on religious, personal or other non-medical grounds. A notwithstanding clause was inserted into the Bill in an attempt to circumvent Charter challenges by anti-vaccination groups and parents. The provincial government had only a minority in the Legislature, and Bill 11 was defeated on third reading. Before this defeat, a legislative committee had already voted to remove the notwithstanding clause from Bill 11.

These invocations of the notwithstanding clause may suggest the beginning of a less cautious approach to s. 33, including outside of Quebec. It is true that two of the uses of s. 33 (in Ontario and New Brunswick) were contained in bills that were never actually enacted, and that one of these two bills (in New Brunswick) was defeated on a vote in the Legislature. It is also true that five of the ten provinces (seven if Ontario and New Brunswick are not counted because the bills there were not enacted), two of the three territories and the federal Parliament have never used the notwithstanding clause. However, the number of (almost) uses of s. 33 in such short order, coupled with the fact that two of the provinces were provinces that had yet to invoke the notwithstanding clause, may suggest a greater willingness on the part of political actors to invoke s. 33.

III. RIGHTS THAT MAY BE OVERRIDDEN

§ 39:3 Rights that may be overridden

Not all Charter rights may be overridden by the use of s. 33. The section applies only to the rights in s. 2 and ss. 7 to 15 of the Charter. This includes the fundamental freedoms (s. 2), the legal rights (ss. 7 to 14) and the equality rights (s. 15). It does not include the democratic rights (ss. 3 to 5), the mobility rights (s. 6), the language rights (ss. 16 to 23), the enforcement provision (s. 24) or the sexual equality clause (s. 28). As well, in order to be effective under s. 33(2), the declaration must refer specifically to the Charter provision that is to be overridden. It is clear that more than one provision can be referred to, or even all of the provi-

---

[26]The Court of Appeal subsequently rejected the appeal on the merits as well: *Toronto (City) v. Ont.* (2019), 146 O.R. (3d) 705, 2019 ONCA 732 (C.A.), leave to appeal to the S.C.C. granted on March 26, 2020. As of the time of writing, the Court has not released a decision in the appeal.

[27]Bill 11, 3rd Reading, June 18, 2020, s. 4.

sions contained in s. 2 and ss. 7 to 15,[1] but a declaration that did not specify any particular Charter provision would not be effective.[2]

IV. FIVE-YEAR LIMIT

§ 39:4 Five-year limit

The override power is subject to a temporal restriction. Section 33(3) is a sunset clause, under which an express declaration will automatically expire at the end of five years. Section 33(4) permits the express declaration to be re-enacted, but the re-enacted declaration will also expire at the end of five years (s. 33(5)). It is not perfectly clear whether a re-enacted declaration can be re-enacted a second time (to add a third period of five years), because s. 33(4) authorizes the re-enactment of only "a declaration *made* under subsection (1)". However, a declaration re-enacted under subsection (3) should probably be regarded as a declaration made under subsection (1), in which case the declaration is perpetually renewable.[1] The purpose of the sunset clause is to force reconsideration by the Parliament or Legislature of each exercise of the power at five-year intervals (intervals in which elections will have been held).

V. SPECIFICITY OF DECLARATION

§ 39:5 Specificity of declaration

Section 33 stipulates that the Parliament or Legislature must "expressly" declare that a statute is to operate notwithstanding a Charter right. The exercise of the override power must therefore be express. It is not to be inferred by implication from the fact that a particular statute has been enacted in violation of the Charter. The express declaration contemplated by s. 33(1) thus becomes a "manner and form" requirement[1] that is essential to the validity of any statute enacted in violation of a provision contained in s. 2 or ss. 7 to 15 of the Charter.

Secondly, the express declaration contemplated by s. 33(1) must be

---

[Section 39:3]

[1]*Ford v. Que.*, [1988] 2 S.C.R. 712, 737-742; discussed in § 39:5, "Specificity of declaration".

[2]Some uses of s. 33 have been broadly framed, whereas others have referred only to the particular Charter right that might have been infringed by the particular statute: T. Kahana, "The Notwithstanding Mechanism and Public Discussion: Lessons from the Ignored Practice of Section 33" (2001) 43 J. Can. Public Admin. 225.

[Section 39:4]

[1]There are examples in Quebec of more than one renewal of the declaration (in pension legislation and education legislation): the details are provided by T. Kahana, "The Notwithstanding Mechanism and Public Discussion: Lessons from the Ignored Practice of Section 33" (2001) 43 J. Can. Public Admin. 225.

[Section 39:5]

[1]Manner and form requirements are discussed in ch. 12, Parliamentary Sovereignty, under heading § 12:10, "Manner and form of future laws".

specific as to the statute[2] that is thereby exempted from the provisions of the Charter. Indeed, the express declaration must be in the statute itself, although it can be added to a pre-existing statute by amendment (on the basis that an amending statute is construed as part of the statute that it amends). Whether s. 33(1) would authorize a blanket declaration which purported to apply to all statutes, or to a class of statutes described in general terms, is a question that was raised by Quebec's Bill 62, entitled An Act respecting the Constitution Act, 1982. This was the Act, mentioned earlier,[3] that was passed by Quebec as a kind of protest against the Charter of Rights (to which Quebec had not agreed). The Act added a standard-form notwithstanding clause to "each of the Acts adopted [by the National Assembly of Quebec] before 17 April 1982". The Acts referred to were not listed; they were identified only by the quoted phrase. In *Ford v. Quebec* (1988),[4] the Supreme Court of Canada held that this exercise of the override power was legally sufficient; the express declaration had been effectively inserted in each of the Acts coming within the omnibus description.

Thirdly, the express declaration contemplated by s. 33(1) must be specific as to the Charter right which is to be overridden. In the *Ford* case,[5] it was argued that the declaration should refer to the very right that was infringed by the particular Act in which the declaration appeared. That argument would have been fatal to the standard form of declaration that was in issue in that case. That declaration referred to "the provisions of sections 2 and 7 to 15 of the Constitution Act, 1982",[6] which is, of course, a reference to all of the Charter rights that s. 33 makes vulnerable to the override. The Supreme Court of Canada held[7] that this omnibus reference to the rights was sufficient. It was not reasonable to require a reference that was particular to the statute containing the declaration, because a legislative body "might not be in a position to judge with any degree of certainty what provisions of the [Charter] might be successfully invoked against various aspects of the Act in question". For this reason, a legislative body "must be permitted in a particular case to override more than one provision of the Charter and indeed all of the provisions which it is permitted to override by the

[2]The express declaration must be contained in a statute. In the context of s. 33, "an Act of Parliament or of the legislature" would not extend to regulations, by-laws or other forms of delegated legislation, because that would enable the Charter to be overridden without full parliamentary debate: Gibson, The Law of the Charter: General Principles (1986), 127-128; Beaudoin and Mendes (eds.), The Canadian Charter of Rights and Freedoms (4th ed., 2005), 124-125 (by Tassé).

[3]S.Q. 1982, c. 21.

[4]*Ford v. Quebec*, [1988] 2 S.C.R. 712, 742-743.

[5]*Ford v. Quebec*, [1988] 2 S.C.R. 712, 740-742.

[6]There were actually two declarations in issue in the case; both were in the language quoted in the text.

[7]*Ford v. Quebec*, [1988] 2 S.C.R. 712, 741.

terms of s. 33".[8] Nor did the word "expressly" in s. 33 require that the Charter rights be identified in words (such as "freedom of expression"). A reference to the numbers of the sections of the Charter was "sufficiently express".

VI. RETROACTIVE EFFECT

§ 39:6 Retroactive effect

In the *Ford* case,[1] the Supreme Court of Canada had to rule on the validity of Bill 62, entitled An Act respecting the Constitution Act, 1982, which was the Quebec statute that purported to insert a standard override clause in every one of Quebec's statutes. In the previous section of this chapter, we noticed that the Court upheld this exercise of the override power, despite the omnibus character of its specification of the statutes that it would protect and the rights that it would override. In one respect, however, Bill 62 was held to be unconstitutional, and that was its attempt to make the declaration retroactive. Bill 62 was enacted on June 23, 1982, but was expressed to take effect from April 17, 1982, which was the date when the Charter of Rights came into force. The Court held that the normal presumption against retroactivity should be applied to the language of s. 33, and the section should be construed as permitting "prospective derogation only".[2] The derogation of rights therefore came into force on June 23, 1982, the date of enactment, not on April 17, 1982, the date stipulated in Bill 62.

There is considerable appeal to the idea that rights should not be able to be taken away retroactively. As Weinrib has commented, the rule of law requires that a person be aware of his or her constitutional rights at the time of taking action, and not be vulnerable to retroactive change.[3] However, the ruling against retroactivity will probably encourage the use of s. 33. Before the *Ford* case was decided, it had always been assumed that a decision striking down a statute for breach of the Charter could be retroactively reversed by the competent legislative body by the exercise of its override power. Indeed, one learned article had argued that this was the *only* permissible use of s. 33.[4] Now that this option is no longer open, it might be expected that legislative bodies, when limiting rights, will sometimes include cautionary override clauses to insure against the risk of an adverse judicial decision on s. 1 justification.[5]

---

[8]For criticism, see L.E. Weinrib, "Learning to Live with the Override" (1990) 35 McGill L.J. 541.

[Section 39:6]

[1]*Ford v. Quebec*, [1988] 2 S.C.R. 712.

[2]*Ford v. Quebec*, [1988] 2 S.C.R. 712, 744.

[3]L.E. Weinrib, "Learning to Live with the Override" (1990) 35 McGill L.J. 541, 559.

[4]D. Greschner and K. Norman, "The Courts and Section 33" (1987) 12 Queen's L.J. 155.

[5]Where the statute deals with a temporary problem, such as an emergency, or a labour dispute, the damage may be irremediable by the time a court has ruled on the

VII. JUDICIAL REVIEW

§ 39:7 Judicial review

To what extent is the exercise of the override power subject to judicial review?

A declaration under s. 33 will be held to be invalid by the courts if it fails to satisfy the various requirements of s. 33 that have been described earlier in this chapter. The declaration must be confined to the rights specified in s. 33; it must be specific as to the statute that is exempted from the Charter, and as to the rights that are overridden; and it may not be given retroactive effect. These requirements are mainly formal, and, as we have noticed, are not very demanding.

Are there any other grounds upon which a declaration under s. 33 could be successfully attacked? It has been suggested that any declaration under s. 33 would have to satisfy the s. 1 standards of reasonableness and demonstrable justification.[1] Of course, those standards would have to be lower than they are for statutes unprotected by s. 33, because otherwise there would be no point in a legislative body exercising the power of override. But the application of s. 1 would introduce a degree of judicial review to the exercise of the override power, enabling courts to strike down those statutes that were in fundamental conflict with the values of a free and democratic society.

The thesis that s. 33 is subject to s. 1 is a difficult one to sustain. It is true that s. 33 does not expressly state that s. 1 of the Charter can be overridden. However, it is implicit in s. 33 that, once a Charter provision has been overridden by an express declaration in a statute, the Charter provision has no application whatsoever to the statute, and therefore there is no need for any showing of reasonableness or justification under s. 1. This view seems to have been accepted in the *Ford* case. Although the Court made no explicit reference to the s. 1 argument, the Court upheld the validity of the s. 33 override without considering its reasonableness or demonstrable justification. And the Court said[2] that s. 33 "lays

---

Charter issue. In other cases, it may be reasonable to await the Charter decision, even though it can only be overturned prospectively. T. Kahana argues that the cautionary use attracts less public attention and less political opposition: T. Kahana, The Partnership Model of the Canadian Notwithstanding Mechanism: Failure and Hope (S.J.D. Thesis, University of Toronto, 2000); T. Kahana, "The Notwithstanding Mechanism and Public Discussion: Lessons from the Ignored Practice of Section 33" (2001) 43 J. Can. Public Admin. 225; T. Kahana, "Understanding the Notwithstanding Mechanism" (2002) 52 U. Toronto L.J. 221; T. Kahana, "What Makes for a Good Use of the Notwithstanding Mechanism?" (2004) 23 Supreme Court L.R. (2d) 191. But in most jurisdictions it seems likely that any use of s. 33 would be treated by the opposition and the media as a red flag to a bull.

[Section 39:7]

[1] B. Slattery, "Override Clauses under Section 33" (1983) 61 Can. Bar Rev. 391; D.J. Arbess, "Limitations on Legislative Override" (1983) 21 Osgoode Hall L.J. 113.

[2] *Ford v. Quebec*, [1988] 2 S.C.R. 712, 740.

down requirements of form only", and that there was "no warrant for importing into it grounds for substantive review".[3]

VIII. EVALUATION OF S. 33

§ 39:8 Evaluation of s. 33

Section 33 is viewed by many as an anomaly that is simply incompatible with constitutionally guaranteed rights. Certainly, s. 33 invites the question whether it is meaningful to speak about rights when the principal provisions of the Charter can be overcome by the enactment of an ordinary statute containing a notwithstanding declaration. A similar question was earlier addressed under s. 1,[1] but under s. 1 the decision whether a law can survive conflict with a guaranteed right is made by a court upon a showing that the law is a reasonable limit that can be demonstrably justified in a free and democratic society. Under s. 33, the Parliament or Legislature makes the decision for whatever reasons seem good to it.

The fact is, however, that if we put aside the special case of Quebec, which has never given its approval to the Charter of Rights, we are left with very few uses of the power of override.[2] It is clear that governments are exceedingly reluctant to use s. 33. The reluctance stems partly from a principled commitment to the Charter and partly from the political resistance that could be expected from opposition parties, the press, the organized bar and civil liberties groups. The inclusion of a notwithstanding clause in a bill performs a "signalling function", alerting critics to the fact that the government believes that its proposed legislation is inconsistent with the Charter, and causing a public debate on the issue—a debate that is normally unwelcome to the government. In practice, therefore, it seems clear that s. 33 will be used infrequently and only when the legislating government is persuaded that there are powerful reasons of public policy to justify its use. Despite s. 33, the fact that a right is in the Charter constitutes a significant obstacle to its abridgement, and places it in a much stronger position than a right that is not in the Charter.

We have earlier noticed the longstanding debate about the legitimacy of judicial review.[3] Of course, there is widespread agreement that certain rights ought to take priority over the wish of the majority, and that result can only be accomplished by giving to courts the power to strike

---

[3]The thesis of D. Greschner and K. Norman, "The Courts and Section 33" (1987) 12 Queen's L.J. 155, which would restrict the use of s. 33 to situations where there had been a prior judicial invalidation of a statute, is also contradicted by *Ford*, where there had been no such prior decision.

[Section 39:8]

[1]Chapter 38, Limitation of Rights, under heading § 38:3, "Relationship between s. 1 and rights".

[2]§ 39:2, "History of s. 33".

[3]See ch. 36, Charter of Rights, under heading §§ 36:4 to 36:7, "Expansion of judicial review".

down the majority's legislation when it unjustifiably abridges those rights. The difficulty is that in a civilized society like Canada the courts are rarely confronted with unequivocal examples of majority oppression. What tends to come before the courts are delicate questions of public policy in which community objectives are in opposition to individual rights. Aid to Catholic schools, Sunday closing, hate propaganda, obscenity, prostitution, mandatory retirement and the protection of the French language are examples, taken almost at random from the cases. There is no general agreement as to the appropriate legislative response to such issues, because there is no general agreement on the weight to be accorded the various competing values. When legislation is enacted, it inevitably finds its way into the courts as a Charter case. There is no clear answer to such a case, either in morality or in law. The question of legitimacy is this: why should the views of non-elected judges prevail over the views of the elected legislators?

Once it is acknowledged that the definition of rights is often unclear, and that even clearly acknowledged rights must occasionally yield to other values, it is obvious that there is room for argument over the question of which institutions should have the power to determine questions of rights. The British solution is the doctrine of parliamentary sovereignty, under which there is no judicial review of statutes, and judgments of the Parliament are final. The American solution is judicial review, under which the courts have the power to review the legislative choices, and the judgments of the courts are final. The power of override places Canada in an intermediate position. Judicial review of statutes is, of course, a longstanding part of the Canadian Constitution, because it has been needed since 1867 to impose the rules of federalism on the two levels of government. But judicial review on Charter grounds dates only from 1982, and, by virtue of s. 33, a judicial decision to strike down a law for breach of s. 2 or ss. 7 to 15 of the Charter is not final. The judicial decision is subject to legislative review. If the competent legislative body still wants the law, it can re-enact it by including the notwithstanding clause contemplated by s. 33.

It is wrong to assume that a judicial decision on a rights issue closes the debate on that issue. On the contrary, citizens and their elected representatives will inevitably want to continue the debate, and in some cases there will be a strong sentiment in favour of reversing the decision of the Court. This can, of course, be accomplished by constitutional amendment, but this is such a difficult process that it can rarely be invoked with any prospect of success. In the United States, where the Bill of Rights is unqualified by an override power, the political response to a decision considered unjust or harmful is to attack the Court, and to attempt to change its composition. We have noticed that the threat of packing the Supreme Court of the United States was used by President Franklin Roosevelt in 1937 to influence the Court in favour of his new deal legislation. And in recent times a series of appointments by Republican Presidents has been made with the avowed purpose of reversing some of the controversial civil libertarian decisions of the Warren Court. These kinds of reactions, which draw the Court itself deeply into the realm of partisan politics, are much less likely in Canada, where the power of legislative override is always on standby. The override power is exercised after a reasoned debate in a public forum addressed to a particular issue of justice and public policy, and this is preferable (I think) to the court-bashing and the court-packing that is a staple of federal politics in the United States.[4]

It is also wrong to assume that a judicial decision at the highest level is always "right". There are no right and wrong decisions on the issues that reach the Supreme Court of Canada. More than this, however, judges have their biases and blind spots, like the rest of humanity. And they are often poorly informed about the costs and other consequences of their decisions. If the judges have the last word on the issues of social and political justice that arise in the form of Charter litigation, there is no guarantee that the issues will always be decided more wisely than if the last word rests with the peoples' elected representatives. The power of override allows for the rare case where the elected representatives are convinced that a judicial decision is an inappropriate answer to the rights issue. By that device, citizens are able to participate in the policy choices for their political community.[5]

While s. 33 looks odd to non-Canadian observers, it has precedents in the Canadian Bill of Rights[6] Saskatchewan,[7] Alberta[8] and Quebec.[9] Each of those instruments confers a power of override on the Parliament or

---

[4]A judicial decision striking down a statutory provision for breach of the Charter is rarely the last word on the issue. In most cases, the competent legislative body relies on s. 1 (or other justificatory doctrine) to enact a new statute to achieve the objective of the statute struck down. This phenomenon of "dialogue" is described in ch. 36, Charter of Rights, under heading §§ 36:8 to 36:11, "Dialogue with legislative branch".

[5]For a defence of s. 33 to which the foregoing account is indebted, see P.H. Russell, "Standing Up for Notwithstanding" (1991) 29 Alta. L. Rev. 293.

[6]Canadian Bill of Rights, R.S.C. 1985, Appendix III. By s. 2, the Bill applies "unless it is expressly declared by an Act of the Parliament of Canada that it shall operate notwithstanding the Canadian Bill of Rights". This provision undoubtedly provided the model for s. 33 of the Charter. But the override power in the Bill is a less refined instrument in that it applies to all of the provisions of the Bill (instead of just some of them), it does not require that particular provisions be referred to in the declaration, and it does not impose any time-limit on the duration of the declaration. The override power in the Bill has been used just once: Public Order (Temporary Measures) Act, S.C. 1970-71-72, c. 2, s. 12.

[7]The Saskatchewan Human Rights Code, 2018, S.S. 2018, c. S-24.2 includes an override power (s. 52). Its predecessor, the Saskatchewan Human Rights Code, S.S. 1979, c. S-24.1, also included an override power (s. 44). Section 44, the earlier iteration of the override power, was used in the same provincial statutes that overrode the Charter of Rights: see (1) SGEU Dispute Settlement Act, S.S. 1984-85-86, c. 111, s. 9, discussed at § 39:2 note 15, above, and accompanying text; and (2) School Choice Protection Act, S.S. 2018, c. 39, s. 3, discussed at § 39:2 note 19, above, and accompanying text.

[8]The Alberta Bill of Rights, R.S.A. 2000, c. A-14, includes an override power (s. 2) which is similar to the one in the Canadian Bill of Rights. It was used in the same Act that overrode the Charter of Rights, namely, the Marriage Amendment Act, S.A. 2000, c. 3, s. 5.

[9]Quebec's Charter of Human Rights and Freedoms, C.Q.L.R. c. C-12 includes an override power (s. 52). This override power has been used various times, including in

Legislature. The power of override seems to be a uniquely Canadian invention,[10] which makes judicial review suspensory only. So long as the last word remains with the competent legislative body, there can be no acute or longstanding conflict between the judicial and legislative branches, and much of the American debate over the legitimacy of judicial review is rendered irrelevant. That is why Paul Weiler has described s. 33 as "an intrinsically sound solution to the dilemma of rights and courts".[11]

2019, in a provincial Act that also overrode the Charter of Rights, namely, An Act respecting the laicity of the State, C.Q.L.R., c. L-0.3, s. 33, discussed at § 39:2 note 10, above, and accompanying text. For an accounting of uses of this override power up to and including 2014, see G. Rousseau & F. Côté, "A Distinctive Quebec Theory and Practice of the Notwithstanding Clause: When Collective Interests Outweigh Individual Rights" (2017) 47 Revue générale de droit 343.

[10]The power of override was adopted by Israel in 1992, although only for one right, freedom of occupation: Basic Law: Freedom of Occupation, s. 8; discussed by T. Kahana, The Partnership Model of the Canadian Notwithstanding Mechanism: Failure and Hope (S.J.D. thesis, University of Toronto, 2000), ch. 2.

[11]P.C. Weiler, "Rights and Judges in a Democracy: A New Canadian Version" (1984) 18 U. of Michigan J. of Law Reform 51, 80. Accord, L.E. Weinrib, "The Canadian Charter's Override Clause: Lessons for Israel" (2016) 49 Israel L. Rev. 67, 82-97, a very strong and persuasive defence of the override clause.

Chapter 40

Enforcement of Rights

I. SUPREMACY CLAUSE

§ 40:1 Section 52(1)
§ 40:2 Section 24(1) compared
§ 40:3 Nullification
§ 40:4 Temporary validity
§ 40:5 Severance
§ 40:6 Reading in
§ 40:7 Reading down
§ 40:8 Constitutional exemption
§ 40:9 Reconstruction
§ 40:10 Limitation of actions

II. REMEDY CLAUSE

§ 40:11 Section 24(1)
§ 40:12 Applicable to Charter only
§ 40:13 Non-exclusive remedy
§ 40:14 Standing
§ 40:15 Apprehended infringements
§ 40:16 Court of competent jurisdiction
§ 40:17 Range of remedies
§ 40:18 Declaration
§ 40:19 Damages
§ 40:20 Costs
§ 40:21 Exclusion of evidence
§ 40:22 Remedies outside s. 24(1)
§ 40:23 Supervision of court orders
§ 40:24 Appeals
§ 40:25 Limitation of actions

III. ADMINISTRATIVE TRIBUNALS

§ 40:26 With power to decide questions of law
§ 40:27 Without power to decide questions of law
§ 40:28 Preliminary inquiry judge
§ 40:29 Provincial court judge

IV. SCRUTINY BY MINISTER OF JUSTICE

§ 40:30 Scrutiny by Minister of Justice

V. LEGISLATIVE ENFORCEMENT

§ 40:31 Legislative enforcement

I. SUPREMACY CLAUSE

§ 40:1 Section 52(1)

Section 52(1) of the Constitution Act, 1982[1] provides as follows:

> The Constitution of Canada is the supreme law of Canada, and any law that is inconsistent with the provisions of the Constitution is, to the extent of the inconsistency, of no force or effect.

This supremacy clause gives to the Charter overriding effect. Since the Charter is part of the "Constitution of Canada",[2] any law[3] that is inconsistent with the Charter is "of no force or effect". Since it inevitably falls to the courts to determine whether or not a law is inconsistent with the Charter, s. 52(1) provides an explicit basis for judicial review of legislation in Canada. Of course, as related in chapter 5 on Federalism,[4] Canadian courts long ago assumed and exercised the power of judicial review to enforce the distribution-of-powers rules of federalism and other restrictions contained in the British North America Act, and they would have enforced the Charter in the same way. Section 52(1) merely articulates the previous practice.

Before the adoption of the Charter of Rights in 1982, judicial review of legislation could take place in a wide variety of legal proceedings; for example, review could occur on a reference for an advisory opinion, an action for a declaratory judgment or an injunction, an application to review the decision of an administrative agency or official, or as a collateral issue in a criminal or civil proceeding. Whenever the constitutionality of a statute was properly placed in issue, and was relevant to the outcome of the case, the presiding court was obliged to determine the

---

[Section 40:1]

[1] For commentary on ss. 24(1) and 52(1), see Gibson, The Law of the Charter: General Principles (1986), chs. 6, 8; Beaudoin and Mendes (eds.), The Canadian Charter of Rights and Freedoms (4th ed., 2005), 131-162 (by L. Tassé), ch. 19 (by D. Gibson); Lokan and Dassios, Constitutional Litigation in Canada (Carswell loose-leaf), ch. 6; McLeod, Takach, Morton, Segal, The Canadian Charter of Rights (Carswell, loose-leaf), chs. 28, 30; Fitzgerald, Understanding Charter Remedies (Carswell, loose-leaf); Roach, Constitutional Remedies in Canada (Canada Law Book, loose-leaf); Canadian Charter of Rights Annotated (Canada Law Book, loose-leaf), annotations to ss. 24 and 52. The last work provides a bibliography of the relevant literature.

[2] The term "Constitution of Canada" is defined in s. 52(2)(a) as including the Constitution Act, 1982, of which the Charter is Part I.

[3] *Greater Vancouver Transportation Authority v. Can. Federation of Students*, [2009] 2 S.C.R. 295, paras. 87-89 ("policy" of transit authority banning political messages on the sides of its buses was a binding rule of general application made under statutory authority; such a policy was a "law" within s. 52(1); and since the policy infringed the Charter a declaration of invalidity was issued under s. 52(1)).

[4] Chapter 5, Federalism, under heading §§ 5:20 to 5:22, "Role of the Courts".

constitutional question.[5] This continues to be true under the Charter: all the remedies that have been available in the past continue to be available.

§ 40:2 Section 24(1) compared

As noted in the previous section, the effect of the supremacy clause (s. 52(1)) is to preserve all pre-existing remedies for unconstitutional action and to extend those remedies to the Charter of Rights. In addition, however, the Charter contains its own remedy clause, namely, s. 24. Section 24(1) authorizes a court of competent jurisdiction to award a remedy for breach of the Charter. Section 24(2) authorizes a court of competent jurisdiction to exclude evidence obtained in breach of the Charter; the power to exclude evidence is the topic of the next chapter.[1]

The remedy clause of s. 24(1) is examined in the latter part of this chapter.[2] However, it is worth setting it out here, and briefly noting the differences between s. 24(1) and s. 52(1). Section 24(1) provides:

> Anyone whose rights or freedoms, as guaranteed by this Charter, have been infringed or denied may apply to a court of competent jurisdiction to obtain such remedy as the court considers appropriate and just in the circumstances.

The differences between s. 24(1) and s. 52(1), which will be elaborated as the chapter progresses, may be briefly noted at this point. First, s. 24(1) is applicable only to breaches of the Charter of Rights; s. 52(1) is applicable to the entire Constitution of Canada, including the Charter of Rights. Secondly, s. 24(1) is available only to a person whose rights have been infringed; s. 52(1) is available in some circumstances to persons whose rights have not been infringed.[3] Thirdly, s. 24(1) may be applied only by a "court of competent jurisdiction"; s. 52(1) may be applied by any court or tribunal with power to decide questions of law.[4] Fourthly, s. 24(1) authorizes the award of a wide range of remedies; s. 52(1) appears to authorize only a holding of invalidity, leaving it to the general law to authorize the particular remedy. Fifthly, s. 24(1) confers a discretion on the court as to whether any remedy should be awarded; s. 52(1) appears to confer no discretion on the court, requiring the court to make a holding of invalidity if it concludes that a law or act is inconsistent with the Constitution.

In the fourth and fifth propositions of the previous paragraph, I have pointed out that s. 52(1) expressly contemplates only a holding of invalidity as a remedy for inconsistency between a statute and the Constitution of Canada and that s. 52(1) does not in terms confer any discretion

---

[5] See ch. 59, Procedure.

[Section 40:2]

[1] Chapter 41, Exclusion of Evidence.

[2] §§ 40:11 to 40:25, "Remedy clause".

[3] § 40:14, "Standing".

[4] §§ 40:26 to 40:29, "Administrative tribunals".

on the courts. However, in Charter cases, the courts have in fact developed a number of variations on a simple declaration of invalidity, and have assumed the power to choose from a range of possible remedies.[5] There are in fact six choices available to a court under s. 52(1):

1. Nullification, that is, striking down (declaring invalid) the statute that is inconsistent with the Constitution;
2. Temporary validity, that is, striking down the statute that is inconsistent with the Constitution, but temporarily suspending the coming into force of the declaration of invalidity;
3. Severance, that is, holding that only part of the statute is inconsistent with the Constitution, striking down only that part and severing it from the valid remainder;
4. Reading in, that is, adding words to a statute that is inconsistent with the Constitution so as to make the statute consistent with the Constitution and valid;
5. Reading down, that is, interpreting a statute that could be interpreted as inconsistent with the Constitution so that it is consistent with the Constitution; and
6. Constitutional exemption, that is, creating an exemption from a statute that is partly inconsistent with the Constitution so as to exclude from the statute the application that would be inconsistent with the Constitution.

Each of these six remedies is discussed in the text that follows. It must be emphasized that each of the six remedies is authorized by the supremacy clause of s. 52(1), and does not require the authority of the remedy clause of s. 24(1). The distinctive role of s. 24(1) is the topic of the latter part of this chapter.[6]

§ 40:3 Nullification

Section 52(1) (the supremacy clause) stipulates that "any law that is inconsistent with the provisions of the Constitution is, to the extent of the inconsistency, of no force or effect". This language requires a court to hold that an unconstitutional law is invalid. If a law is found by a court to be inconsistent with the Charter of Rights, the court is obliged to strike the law down. The effect of such a holding is that the litigation will be determined as if the unconstitutional law did not exist.[1] If the litigation is a criminal prosecution, the person charged under the invalid law will be entitled to be acquitted. If the litigation is a civil action, the party relying on the invalid law will lose the legal basis for his or her case.

---

[5]The remedies available, and the criteria of choice, are fully discussed by Lamer C.J. in *Schachter v. Can.*, [1992] 2 S.C.R. 679, 695-719.

[6]§§ 40:11 to 40:25, "Remedy clause".

[Section 40:3]

[1]The effect of an unconstitutional law is examined in more detail in ch. 58, Effect of Unconstitutional Law.

§ 40:4 Temporary validity

While s. 52(1) requires a court to hold that an unconstitutional statute is invalid, the courts have assumed the power to postpone the operation of the declaration of invalidity. When a court exercises this power, the effect is to grant a period of temporary validity to an unconstitutional statute, because the statute will remain in force until the expiry of the period of postponement.

In *Re Manitoba Language Rights* (1985),[1] a case that is discussed more fully later in this book,[2] the Supreme Court of Canada assumed the power to hold that unconstitutional laws were to be given "temporary force and effect" to allow the Legislature time to enact the required corrective legislation. That was a highly unusual case in that the Manitoba Legislature's failure to enact laws in French as well as English had invalidated the entire Manitoba statute book. The Court invoked the "rule of law" ("necessity" would have been the more conventional rubric) to keep the unconstitutional laws temporarily in force in order to avoid a vacuum of law in the province. This was a radical exercise of judicial power, because a body of unconstitutional law was maintained in force solely by virtue of the Court's order.[3]

The *Manitoba Language* case appeared to be unique at the time. However, it turned out that the laws of Saskatchewan and Alberta were in a similar plight, because a pre-confederation statute required that they be enacted in French as well as English, and the laws had in fact been enacted in English only. The Supreme Court of Canada followed its earlier decision and filled the vacuum of law by declaring a period of temporary validity to allow the two Legislatures the time to take curative action.[4] In yet another case,[5] the Court employed the same technique to maintain in force the by-laws and other acts of a Quebec municipality that had been invalidly incorporated, but which had in fact been functioning for a period of six years. These cases are discussed more fully later in this book.[6]

The *Manitoba Language* case and its companions were not Charter cases. In each case, the invalidity flowed from a failure to comply with a

---

[Section 40:4]

[1] *Re Manitoba Language Rights*, [1985] 1 S.C.R. 721.

[2] Chapter 58, Effect of Unconstitutional Law, under heading § 58:9, "The Manitoba Language Rights Reference". That same chapter, under heading § 58:1, "Invalidity of unconstitutional law", discusses the technique of prospective overruling, which bears a close affinity to the remedy ordered in the *Manitoba Language* case.

[3] There has been remarkably little criticism of this practice, but a sterling exception is Peltomaa, Understanding Unconstitutionality: How a Country Lost its Way (2018).

[4] *R. v. Mercure*, [1988] 1 S.C.R. 234 (Sask.); *R. v. Paquette*, [1990] 2 S.C.R. 1103 (Alta.).

[5] *Sinclair v. Que.*, [1992] 1 S.C.R. 579.

[6] Chapter 58, Effect of Unconstitutional Law, under headings § 58:11, "The Mercure case," and § 58:12, "The Paquette case".

non-Charter rule of the Constitution. But the Supreme Court of Canada has several times given delayed effect to a Charter ruling in order to allow governmental authorities time to accommodate to the ruling. In *R. v. Brydges* (1990),[7] Lamer J. for the majority of the Supreme Court of Canada, after deciding that the police were under a constitutional duty to advise all persons under arrest of the availability of legal aid, allowed a "transition period" of 30 days to enable the police forces to prepare new cautions.[8] In *R. v. Askov* (1990),[9] Cory J. for the majority of the Supreme Court of Canada, after deciding that the District of Peel in Ontario had unreasonable systemic delay in its criminal court process, raised the possibility of "a transitional period of lenient treatment of systemic delay".[10] Unfortunately, he decided not to allow any such period of leniency, which caused thousands of criminal charges to be stayed over the next few months, because the District's huge backlog of cases could not be cleared overnight.

In *R. v. Feeney* (1997),[11] the Supreme Court of Canada held that, by virtue of s. 8 of the Charter, a warrant was required to enter a dwelling house in order to make a lawful arrest. This was a change from the common law, which permitted a police officer to enter a dwelling house without a warrant if the purpose was to make a lawful arrest. The Criminal Code made no provision for the issue of the entry warrant contemplated by the Court, but Sopinka J. for the majority held that the provision should be "read in".[12] After the decision, the Crown applied for a stay of the requirement of the entry warrant for a period of six months from the date of the Court's judgment. This was granted without any reasons.[13] The stay was expressed so as not to affect the disposition of the *Feeney* case itself, but for all other dwelling house arrests made prior to the decision or for six months thereafter the common law remained in place. Parliament then enacted an amendment to the Criminal Code,[14] which made provision for the issue of a warrant to enter a dwelling house for the purpose of making an arrest.[15]

Brydges, Askov and *Feeney* did not involve unconstitutional legisla-

---

[7] *R. v. Brydges*, [1990] 1 S.C.R. 190. Lamer J. wrote for the majority of four. La Forest J. wrote a concurring judgment for a minority of three; he found it unnecessary to deal with the question of whether the police needed to prepare new cautions.

[8] *R. v. Brydges*, [1990] 1 S.C.R. 190, 217.

[9] *R. v. Askov*, [1990] 2 S.C.R. 1199. Cory J. wrote for five judges. There were four short concurring opinions which made no reference to the possibility of a transitional period.

[10] *R. v. Askov*, [1990] 2 S.C.R. 1199, 1231.

[11] *R. v. Feeney*, [1997] 2 S.C.R. 13.

[12] *R. v. Feeney*, [1997] 2 S.C.R. 13, para. 48.

[13] *R. v. Feeney (No. 2)*, [1997] 2 S.C.R. 117, the stay was extended in *R. v. Feeney (No. 3)*, [1997] 3 S.C.R. 1008.

[14] S.C. 1997, c. 39, s. 2, amending s. 529 of the Criminal Code.

[15] See also *Eldridge v. B.C.*, [1997] 3 S.C.R. 624 (suspending for six months order that s. 15 required sign-language interpretation for deaf persons seeking medical services).

tion; but there is now a series of cases in which courts have maintained legislation in force after holding it to be invalid for breach of the Charter of Rights. In *Dixon v. British Columbia* (1989),[16] McLachlin C.J., who was then the Chief Justice of the Supreme Court of British Columbia (she was later elevated to the Supreme Court of Canada), held that the provincial legislation prescribing electoral districts for the province was unconstitutional; the disparity between the voting populations of different districts was so great as to violate s. 3 of the Charter (which guarantees the right to vote). Having reached this decision, she pointed out that the nullification of the legislation would leave the province without the means of holding an election, and in a system of responsible government it was possible for an election to be called at any time. This qualified as "an emergency" comparable to that recognized in *Re Manitoba Language Rights*, and a similar order was required.[17] She therefore held that the unconstitutional legislation "will stay provisionally in place to avoid the constitutional crisis which would occur should a precipitate election be required".[18] The legislation would remain in place for the time that "may reasonably be required to remedy the legislation", and she left that period to be fixed by a later order of the court.[19] An order was subsequently sought before another judge, who declined to impose any deadline on the Legislature, holding that the Legislature should be left "to do what is right in its own time".[20] New legislation was in fact enacted in time for the next provincial election,[21] which took place more than two years later—in October, 1991.

In *R. v. Swain* (1991),[22] the majority of the Supreme Court of Canada struck down the provisions of the Criminal Code that required the detention in a psychiatric facility of a person acquitted on the ground of insanity. The Criminal Code provisions were held to be contrary to ss. 7 and 9 of the Charter. The invalidity of the provisions meant that a person acquitted on the ground of insanity would simply be released like any other accused who had been found not guilty at his or her trial. Since a person acquitted on the ground of insanity has usually committed a serious offence, and may well be a continued danger to the public, his or her release into the community would often involve serious risks. (This, of course, was the reason for the provisions requiring the detention of a person acquitted on the ground of insanity.) The Court held that there was to be a six-month "period of temporary validity" so that judges would not be compelled to release into the community all insan-

[16]*Dixon v. British Columbia* (1989), 59 D.L.R. (4th) 247 (B.C.S.C.).

[17]*Dixon v. British Columbia* (1989), 59 D.L.R. (4th) 247, 283 (B.C.S.C.).

[18]*Dixon v. British Columbia* (1989), 59 D.L.R. (4th) 247, 284 (B.C.S.C.).

[19]*Dixon v. British Columbia* (1989), 59 D.L.R. (4th) 247, 284 (B.C.S.C.).

[20]*Dixon v. British Columbia* (1989) 60 D.L.R. (4th) 445, 448 (B.C.S.C.).

[21]S.B.C. 1990, c. 39.

[22]*R. v. Swain*, [1991] 1 S.C.R. 933.

ity acquittees.[23] The Court evidently assumed that the six-month period would enable the federal government to prepare, and Parliament to enact, replacement provisions which, perhaps by providing additional standards and a separate hearing on the necessity for detention, could overcome the constitutional disabilities of its predecessor.[24]

In *R. v. Bain* (1992),[25] the majority of the Supreme Court of Canada struck down the provisions of the Criminal Code that allowed the Crown prosecutor, but not the accused, to "stand by" prospective jurors. The provisions were held to be contrary to the guarantee of a fair trial in s. 11(d) of the Charter, because they gave the Crown more influence than the accused in the selection of the jury. In this case too, the declaration of invalidity was suspended for six months in order to "provide an opportunity for Parliament to remedy the situation if it considers it appropriate to do so".[26] There was no explanation of how the six-month period was arrived at, or, indeed, why the declaration of invalidity should be suspended. The invalidity of the stand-by provisions certainly did not pose a danger to the public or a threat to the rule of law.

In *Schachter v. Canada* (1992),[27] the Supreme Court of Canada held that a provision of the federal Unemployment Insurance Act offended the guarantee of equality in s. 15 of the Charter of Rights, because the provision allowed more generous child care benefits to adoptive parents than to biological parents.[28] (The case used the term "natural parents".) This meant that the statute was "under-inclusive",[29] meaning that it failed to include a class of people (biological parents, in this case) that had an equality-based constitutional right to be included. Lamer C.J. for the majority of the Court pointed out that striking down an under-inclusive statute would have the perverse result of denying the statutory benefits to the deserving class that was covered by the statute (adoptive parents in this case), while granting no benefit to the class that was unconstitutionally excluded (biological parents in this case). He concluded that: "The logical remedy is to strike down but suspend the declaration of invalidity to allow the government to determine whether

[23] *R. v. Swain*, [1991] 1 S.C.R. 933, 1021, 1037.

[24] Seven months after the Court handed down its decision, Parliament repealed the offending provisions and replaced them with provisions that established more comprehensive standards and mandatory hearings on the necessity for detention: S.C. 1991, c. 43, adding new Part XX.1 (Mental Disorder) to the Criminal Code.

[25] *R. v. Bain*, [1992] 1 S.C.R. 91.

[26] *R. v. Bain*, [1992] 1 S.C.R. 91, 104, 165. Parliament did remedy the situation by repealing the Crown's power of stand-by and giving the Crown the same powers as the accused with respect to jury selection: S.C. 1992, c. 41, s. 2, amending s. 634 of the Criminal Code.

[27] *Schachter v. Canada*, [1992] 2 S.C.R. 679. The opinion of Lamer C.J. was concurred in by Sopinka, Gonthier and McLachlin JJ. La Forest J. wrote a short concurring opinion that was concurred in by L'Heureux-Dubé J.

[28] This point was actually conceded by the Government of Canada, and the Court proceeded on the basis of the concession, despite doubt as to whether the concession was correct: *Schachter v. Canada*, [1992] 2 S.C.R. 679, 695, 727.

[29] *Schachter v. Canada*, [1992] 2 S.C.R. 679, 715.

to cancel or extend the benefits".[30] In fact, by the time the Court rendered its decision in *Schachter*, Parliament had amended the Act so as to equalize the position of adoptive and biological parents. The Court held, therefore, that there was "no need for a declaration of invalidity or a suspension thereof".[31]

In *Schachter*, although the Court was willing to grant a temporary period of validity in that case, Lamer C.J. recognized the radical character of the remedy. In the first place, it maintains in force a statute that has been found to be unconstitutional. In the second place, it is a "serious interference" with the legislative process, because the delayed nullification "forces the matter back onto the legislative agenda at a time not of the choosing of the legislature, and within time limits under which the legislature would not normally be forced to act".[32] For these reasons, Lamer C.J. held that it was preferable for the Court to rectify the statute by severance (discussed next) or reading in (discussed after severance) where those remedies were appropriate. Where those remedies were not appropriate (as in this case), and a declaration of invalidity had to be made, then the Court could provide for a temporary suspension of the declaration of invalidity in certain cases. Those cases were those in which the immediate striking down of the legislation (1) "would pose a danger to the public" (as in *Swain)*, (2) "would threaten the rule of law" (as in the *Manitoba Language* case), or (3) "would result in the deprivation of benefits from deserving persons" (as in *Schachter* itself).[33]

The three *Schachter* "guidelines" essentially limited the courts' use of suspended declarations of invalidity to exigent situations where danger, disorder or deprivation would be caused by an immediate declaration of invalidity. The guidelines explained most (but not all)[34] of the suspended declarations of invalidity that had been issued by the Supreme Court of Canada before *Schachter*. Some of the subsequent cases also fit the guidelines,[35] but the guidelines "have largely been ignored in subsequent

---

[30] *Schachter v. Canada*, [1992] 2 S.C.R. 679, 716.

[31] *Schachter v. Canada*, [1992] 2 S.C.R. 679, 725. The result was that the Court granted no remedy at all to the unfortunate plaintiff, despite his success on the substantive issue of equality rights. However, the Court did order the Crown to pay his costs. The benefits to biological and adopted parents were altered again and challenged again, this time unsuccessfully, in *Schafer v. Can.* (1997), 35 O.R. (3d) 1 (C.A.), leave to appeal to S.C.C. denied January 29, 1998.

[32] *Schachter v. Canada*, [1992] 2 S.C.R. 679, 716-717.

[33] *Schachter v. Canada*, [1992] 2 S.C.R. 679, 719. These guidelines were reaffirmed in *Can. v. Hislop*, [2007] 2 S.C.R. 391, paras. 121, 161.

[34] *R. v. Bain*, [1992] 1 S.C.R. 91, although decided only six months before *Schachter*, fits none of the guidelines.

[35] *Re Remuneration of Judges (No. 2)*, [1998] 1 S.C.R. 3, para. 18 (suspending for one year requirement of judicial compensation commission required for judicial independence so that "the orderly administration of justice is not disrupted in the interim"); *M. v. H.*, [1999] 2 S.C.R. 3, paras. 145-147 (suspending for six months declaration of invalidity of opposite-sex definition of "spouse", because its repair was complicated and support obligations between common-law spouses would be interrupted); *Nova Scotia v. Martin*,

cases".[36] That is because a new rationale, which can be captured by the notion of "dialogue",[37] has developed for the suspended declaration of invalidity. That new rationale is simply that, in many cases where the Court has found a law to be unconstitutional, the Court would prefer the legislature to design the appropriate remedy. "The suspended declaration of invalidity can be viewed as a form of legislative remand, whereby unconstitutional legislation is sent back for reconsideration in light of the court's judgment."[38] This is not an abdication of responsibility by the Court, because, if the legislature chooses to take no action during the period of suspension, the Court's declaration of invalidity will take effect. But the period of suspension gives to the legislature the first opportunity to remedy the constitutional wrong.

In *Re Eurig Estate* (1998),[39] where the Supreme Court of Canada invalidated Ontario's probate fees, the Court suspended the declaration of invalidity for six months, citing only the potential loss of revenue to the province. In *Corbiere v. Canada* (1999),[40] where the Court invalidated the on-reserve residence requirements in the Indian Act for Indian band elections, the Court suspended the declaration of invalidity for 18 months to enable new provisions to be drafted after consultation with Aboriginal people. In *UFCW v. Kmart Canada* (1999),[41] where the Court invalidated an overbroad prohibition of secondary picketing, the Court suspended the declaration of invalidity for six months to allow time for a

---

[2003] 2 S.C.R. 504, para. 119 (suspending for six months declaration of invalidity of chronic-pain provisions of workers' compensation scheme "to preserve the limited benefits of the current program until an appropriate legislative response to chronic pain can be implemented"); *R. v. Demers*, [2004] 2 S.C.R. 489 (suspending for one year Criminal Code regime for persons found unfit to stand trial so that persons who presented a danger to the public would not be released); *Charkaoui v. Can.*, [2007] 1 S.C.R. 350, para. 140 (suspending for one year the invalidity of the security certificate process under the immigration statute, so that persons who presented a danger to national security would not be released); *R. v. Tse*, [2012] 1 S.C.R. 531 (suspending for one year the invalidity of the police power to intercept private communications in emergencies where serious harm is anticipated).

[36] S. Choudhry and K. Roach, "Putting the Past Behind Us?" (2003) 21 Supreme Court L.R. (2d) 205, 232. This article (Table A, p. 253) lists all the suspended declarations of invalidity that had been issued by Canadian courts up to the date of the article. There are 42 of them, of which 14 were issued by the Supreme Court of Canada. See also B. Ryder, "Suspending the Charter" (2003) 21 Supreme Court L.R. (2d) 267, an article which also has an appendix, this one listing all the declarations of invalidity (immediate and suspended) in the Supreme Court of Canada.

[37] See ch. 36, Charter of Rights, under heading §§ 36:8 to 36:11, "Dialogue with legislative branch".

[38] S. Choudhry and K. Roach, "Putting the Past Behind Us?" (2003) 21 Supreme Court L.R. (2d) 205, 233.

[39] *Re Eurig Estate*, [1998] 2 S.C.R. 565, para. 44. The suspension of the declaration of invalidity did not apply to the claimant estate, which was expressly granted a refund of the probate fees that it had paid under protest: para. 45.

[40] *Corbiere v. Canada*, [1999] 2 S.C.R. 203, paras. 23, 118-119.

[41] *UFCW v. Kmart Canada*, [1999] 2 S.C.R. 1083, para. 79.

new provision to be drafted. In *Dunmore v. Ontario* (2001),[42] where the Court invalidated a provision excluding agricultural workers from Ontario's labour relations statute, the Court suspended the declaration of invalidity for 18 months to allow time for amending legislation to be drafted and enacted. In *R. v. Guignard* (2002),[43] where the Court invalidated a by-law restricting advertising signs in the municipality, the Court suspended the declaration of invalidity for six months to allow time to redraft the by-law. In *Trociuk v. British Columbia* (2003),[44] where the Court invalidated powers given to a mother but not a father in a provincial birth-registration law, the Court suspended the declaration of invalidity for 12 months to allow time to redraft the law. In *Figueroa v. Canada* (2003),[45] where the Court invalidated restrictions that disqualified small political parties from registration for the purpose of federal elections, the Court suspended the declaration of invalidity for 12 months "in order to enable the government to comply with these reasons". In the *Health Services Bargaining* case (2007),[46] where the Court invalidated a statute that increased health-care employers' rights to manage their unionized workforce, the Court suspended the declaration of invalidity for 12 months "to allow the government to address the repercussions of this decision". In *Confédération des syndicats nationaux v. Canada* (2008),[47] where the Court held that the employment insurance premiums levied during a three-year period were invalid, the Court suspended the declaration of invalidity for 12 months "to allow the consequences of that invalidity to be rectified". In *Nguyen v. Quebec* (2009),[48] where the Court invalidated amendments to Quebec's Charter of the French Language restricting access to English-language public schools, the Court suspended the declaration of invalidity for 12 months "to enable Quebec's National Assembly to review the legislation". In *Canada v. Bedford* (2013),[49] where the Court held that three prostitution-related offences in the Criminal Code were invalid, the Court decided that "considering all the interests at stake, the declaration of invalidity should be suspended for one year".[50]

In all of these *post-Schachter* cases, there were a variety of solutions

[42] *Dunmore v. Ontario*, [2001] 3 S.C.R. 1016, para. 66.

[43] *R. v. Guignard*, [2002] 1 S.C.R. 472, para. 32.

[44] *Trociuk v. British Columbia*, [2003] 1 S.C.R. 835, para. 43.

[45] *Figueroa v. Canada*, [2003] 1 S.C.R. 912, para. 93.

[46] *Health Services and Support—Facilities Subsector Bargaining Assn. v. B.C.*, [2007] 2 S.C.R. 391, para. 168.

[47] *Confédération des syndicats nationaux v. Canada*, [2008] 3 S.C.R. 511, para. 94.

[48] *Nguyen v. Quebec*, [2009] 3 S.C.R. 208, paras. 46, 51. In a rare acknowledgment of the impact of suspension on claimants, the suspension was not applied to the claimants in the case; they were given the immediate benefit of the amendments' invalidity: para. 51 (but see also *Re Eurig Estate*, [1998] 2 S.C.R. 565).

[49] *Canada v. Bedford*, [2013] 3 S.C.R. 1101, 2013 SCC 72, para. 169.

[50] See also *Alta. v. United Food and Commercial Workers*, [2013] 3 S.C.R. 733, 2013 SCC 62, para. 44 (holding that provincial privacy legislation was invalid for failure to make provision for labour relations disputes, but suspending the declaration of invalid-

available to the competent legislative body to correct the constitutional defect. Clearly, the legislative body would be the best judge of the best solution. Of course, the legislative body could, and probably would, still act even if the declaration of invalidity were given immediate effect, but an immediate declaration of invalidity would leave a gap in the law for the period required to draft and enact new legislation. Obviously, the Court was implicitly acknowledging that the preservation in force of an unconstitutional law was preferable to the legal discontinuity that would otherwise result.[51] However, in none of the cases described in the previous paragraph did the gap in the law give rise to the exigent circumstances that, according to *Schachter*, were required to justify the postponement of a declaration of invalidity.[52] With one exception, none of the cases offered an alternative rationale for postponing the declaration of invalidity. The exception was *Corbiere*,[53] where the concurring opinion of L'Heureux-Dubé J. articulated the dialogue rationale for the postponement of the declaration. She pointed out that there were a number of ways in which the unconstitutional on-reserve residence requirement for Indian Act elections could be corrected, and the best solution would be the one determined by Parliament after consulting with the Aboriginal people who were affected by the decision. In her view, the principle of democracy should guide the exercise of the Court's remedial discretion, and that principle "encourages remedies that allow the democratic process of consultation and dialogue to occur".[54] The 18-month suspension of the declaration of invalidity in that case gave to Parliament time to develop and enact a new voting regime, should it choose to do so. If Parliament decided not to act, the Court's declaration of invalidity of the residence requirement would take effect after 18 months, enfranchising for all purposes all those band members who lived off the reserve.

---

ity for 12 months "to give the legislature time to decide how best to make the legislation constitutional"); *Mounted Police Assn. v. Can.*, [2015] 1 S.C.R. 3, 2015 SCC 1, para. 158 (invalidating the exclusion of the RCMP from the federal public service labour relations statute, but suspending the declaration of invalidity for 12 months); *Sask. Federation of Labour v. Sask.*, 2014 SCC 4, para. 103 (invalidating provincial legislation denying the right to strike to essential services public employees, but suspending the declaration of invalidity for one year).

[51]B. Ryder, "Suspending the Charter" (2003) 21 Supreme Court L.R. (2d) 267, 283, criticizes the Court for its "casual" approach to the suspension of declarations of invalidity, and argues that the Court should require government to demonstrate that the costs of an immediate declaration outweigh the benefits of a suspended declaration.

[52]In *Can. v. Hislop*, [2007] 1 S.C.R. 429, paras. 121, 161, the Court mysteriously reaffirmed the *Schachter* guidelines without any explanation and without reference to the eight previous Supreme Court cases that contradicted the guidelines. Then, just three months later, in *Health Services and Support—Facilities Subsector Bargaining Assn. v. B.C.*, [2007] 2 S.C.R. 391, para. 168, the Court, without any explanation and without reference to either *Schachter* or *Hislop*, issued yet another suspended declaration of invalidity that contradicted the guidelines.

[53]*Corbiere v. Canada*, [1999] 2 S.C.R. 203.

[54]*Corbiere v. Canada*, [1999] 2 S.C.R. 203, para. 116.

In *Canada v. Bedford* (2013),[55] the Supreme Court held that the three prostitution-related provisions of the federal Criminal Code, namely, communicating in a public place for the purpose of prostitution, keeping or being found in a common bawdy house, and living off the avails of prostitution, were unconstitutional under s. 7 of the Charter. The Court postponed the declaration of invalidity for 12 months to give Parliament time to amend the provisions. The federal government, which had defended the three provisions in court, was left with the problem of developing a new policy on prostitution. The government launched a month of on-line consultations to obtain public input as to what that new policy might be.[56] Eventually, a bill emerged and was introduced into Parliament and enacted.[57] Under the old law, prostitution itself was not an offence. Under the new law, prostitution becomes an offence for the purchaser of sexual services, but not the seller (that is the Swedish model), although advertising for sale is prohibited. Communicating for sale continues to be prohibited, but only where persons under 18 are found. Keeping a common bawdy house continues to be prohibited, but with a narrower definition of bawdy house (now a place kept "for the practice of acts of indecency"). Living off the avails of prostitution continues to be prohibited, but is narrowed to limit it to pimping. Those who had hoped that the success of the constitutional challenge would lead to the decriminalization of prostitution were disappointed.

In *Carter v. Canada* (2015),[58] the Supreme Court held that the Criminal Code prohibition of physician-assisted death was unconstitutional under s. 7 of the Charter "for a competent adult person who (1) clearly consents to the termination of life and (2) has a grievous and irremediable medical condition (including an illness, disease or disability) that causes enduring suffering that is intolerable in the circumstances of his or her condition."[59] One of the issues in the case was whether safeguards could be erected to guard against error of abuse. The Court accepted the finding of the trial judge, based on experience in other jurisdictions, that safeguards could be designed and enacted, but left that important task to Parliament (or the legislatures), and postponed the declaration of invalidity for one year (later extended to 16 months) to allow time for legislation to be enacted. Parliament enacted an amendment to the Criminal Code[60] which did provide detailed procedural requirements to make sure that the request for assistance was fully informed, and had

---

[55]*Canada v. Bedford*, [2013] 3 S.C.R. 1101, 2013 SCC 72. For a fuller description of the decision, see ch. 47, Fundamental Justice, under headings § 47:24, "Overbroad laws" and § 47:25, "Disproportionate laws".

[56]Department of Justice, News Release, "Government of Canada Launches On-Line Consultations to Seek Views on Criminal Code Prostitution-Related Offences" (Ottawa, February 17, 2014).

[57]Protection of Communities and Exploited Persons Act, S.C. 2014, c. 25.

[58]*Carter v. Canada*, [2015] 1 S.C.R. 331, 2015 SCC 5. For a fuller description of the decision, see ch. 47, Fundamental Justice, under heading § 47:24, "Overbroad laws".

[59]*Carter v. Canada*, [2015] 1 S.C.R. 331, 2015 SCC 5, para. 147.

[60]S.C. 2016, c. 3.

not been withdrawn, and that two medical practitioners had confirmed in writing that the patient met all the criteria for entitlement to the assistance. The Court had expressly stipulated that the legislation be "consistent with the constitutional parameters set out in [the Court's] reasons",[61] but the legislation purported to narrow the class of entitled persons to those who were near the end of life, a limitation that had been argued before the Court in *Carter* and not accepted, as two subsequent cases had confirmed.[62] This produced the result that people who had the s. 7 right after the Supreme Court's decision in *Carter* were now denied the right by the legislation. This was not consistent with the constitutional parameters set out in *Carter*; it was a disagreement with those parameters.[63] This was unfortunate, especially for those people who apparently lost the right granted to them by *Carter*, but also because it required more litigation to determine the scope of the *Carter* right.[64]

A suspended declaration of invalidity is not to be confused with a *prospective* ruling. A suspended declaration of invalidity is delayed in coming into force, but if and when it comes into force it has the normal retroactive effect of a court order. It operates to invalidate the unconstitutional statute from the time of its enactment. Of course, a suspended declaration of invalidity will not come into force at all if during the period of suspension the competent legislative body enacts corrective legislation that replaces the unconstitutional statute with one

[61] *Carter v. Canada*, [2015] 1 S.C.R. 331, 2015 SCC 5, para. 126.

[62] *Canada v. E.F.*, 2016 ABCA 155, 34 Alta. L.R. (6th) 1, para. 41 (Alta. C.A.); *IJ v. Canada*, 2016 ONSC 3380 paras. 18-23 (Perell J.). In both cases the grievous and irremediable medical condition was not terminal, and both courts confirmed that the applicant's condition satisfied the *Carter* test.

[63] A Charter right can, of course, be limited under s. 1, but this law had to be consistent with the constitutional parameters set out in *Carter* and it is implausible to argue that the s. 1 power of limitation was contemplated by a Court that had rejected the argument that the right should be restricted to end-of-life conditions.

[64] In *Truchon c. Procureur général du Canada*, 2019 QCCS 3792, the Superior Court of Quebec held that the Criminal Code's requirement that death be reasonably foreseeable to obtain physician assistance in dying infringed both ss. 7 and 15 of the Charter. (The Court also held that a similar requirement in Quebec's physician assistance in dying law, the Act respecting end-of-life care, R.S.Q. c. S-32.0001, infringed s. 15.) The Court granted the federal (and provincial) government a six-month suspension of the declaration of invalidity. The federal government did not appeal the Superior Court's decision. Instead, in February 2020, and again in October 2020 (after a prorogation of Parliament), the federal government introduced legislative amendments to the Criminal Code. The amendments (which were passed and came into force in March 2021) repealed the requirement that a person's death be reasonably foreseeable in order to be eligible for physician assistance in dying: see An Act to amend the Criminal Code (medical assistance in dying), S.C. 2021, c. 2. The initial suspension of the declaration of invalidity in *Truchon* was set to expire in March 2020. However, the suspension was extended by the Superior Court until July 2020 (*Truchon c. Procureur général du Canada*, 2020 QCCS 772); then, due to the COVID-19 pandemic, until December 2020 (*Truchon c. Procureur général du Canada*, 2020 QCCS 2019); then until February 2021 (*Truchon c. Procureur général du Canada*, 2020 QCCS 4388); and then until March 2021 (*Truchon c. Procureur général du Canada*, 2021 QCCS 590). Of course, all of this could have been avoided if the reasonable foreseeability of death requirement had not been added in the first place.

that is constitutional. It would seem to follow from the retroactive effect of a declaration of invalidity (including one that is suspended), that the corrective legislation would also have to be retroactive in its effect. Otherwise, the litigants who successfully asserted their constitutional rights and obtained their declaration of invalidity would be left without a remedy (or at least without a complete remedy). In *Canada v. Hislop* (2007),[65] this important point was overlooked. The majority of the Supreme Court of Canada said that "the purpose of a suspended declaration of invalidity can be to facilitate the legislature's function in crafting a *prospective* remedy".[66] And the Court upheld a corrective statute that conferred survivor-pension rights on same-sex couples, but for the future only, thus denying the claimants the past benefits to which they would have been entitled had the pension legislation been enacted in compliance with s. 15 (the equality guarantee) of the Charter. In my view, this was a limit on Charter rights that should have been upheld only if the prospective legislation satisfied the *Oakes* standards of s. 1 justification, but the Court upheld the prospective legislation without engaging in a s. 1 analysis.[67]

§ 40:5 Severance

The topic of severance, in Charter cases as well as other constitutional cases, has been examined earlier.[1] Severance is the appropriate remedy when only part of the statute is held to be invalid, and the rest can independently survive. In that case, a court will hold that the bad part of the statute should be struck down and severed from the good part, thereby preserving the part that complies with the Constitution. Severance occurs in most Charter cases because it is unusual for a Charter breach to taint a statute in its entirety. For example, the invalidity of the search and seizure power of the Competition Act does not entail the striking

[65]*Canada v. Hislop*, [2007] 1 S.C.R. 429. LeBel and Rothstein JJ. wrote the majority opinion. Bastarache J. wrote a separate concurring opinion. For fuller discussion, see ch. 58, Effect of Unconstitutional Law, under heading § 58:1, "Invalidity of unconstitutional law".

[66]*Canada v. Hislop*, [2007] 1 S.C.R. 429, para. 92 (emphasis added). They interpreted the suspended declaration of invalidity in *M. v. H.*, [1999] 2 S.C.R. 3 as having that intention, although the suspended declaration was directed to the Ontario Legislature, not Parliament, which had enacted the legislation in issue in *Hislop*.

[67]The decision is internally inconsistent. The Court insisted that the corrective legislation had to make the *eligibility* requirements for the survivorship pension retroactive; the Court applied the *Oakes* standards and found them unmet by the legislation. But the Court permitted the legislation to make the *payment* provisions prospective without applying the *Oakes* standards. If the former was a limit on constitutional rights, surely the latter was as well. However, this curious compromise meant that the claimants were not excluded altogether from the pension scheme (which is what the statute purported to do): persons who had become eligible for survivor-pensions in the past were entitled to receive future (but not past) payments.

[Section 40:5]

[1]Chapter 15, Judicial Review on Federal Grounds, under heading § 15:14, "Severance".

down of the entire Act,[2] and the invalidity of the felony-murder rule of the Criminal Code does not entail the striking down of the entire Criminal Code.[3] Severance is a doctrine of judicial restraint, because its effect is to minimize the impact of a successful Charter attack on a law: the court's intrusion into the legislative process goes no further than is necessary to vindicate the Charter right.

Severance, as traditionally employed, is not designed to alter the meaning or effect of the remainder of the statute that survives. The remainder of the statute survives on its own merits, because in the form that it was enacted it was from the beginning consistent with the Constitution (and severable from the unconstitutional part). In a few Charter cases, however, the Supreme Court of Canada has used the doctrine of severance in order to repair a statutory provision that was invalid in the language in which it was enacted. In these cases, severance is used to amend the defective statutory provision by deleting the words that caused the constitutional problem.

In *R. v. Hess* (1990),[4] the Supreme Court of Canada reviewed the statutory rape provision of the Criminal Code. The provision made it an offence for a male person to have intercourse with a female person under 14 years of age, "whether or not he believes that she is fourteen years of age or more". The quoted language caused the offence to violate s. 7, because it eliminated the requirement of mens rea for an essential element of the offence, namely, the age of the young woman. The constitutional problem could be corrected by excising the quoted words. The rest of the section would make sense without the words, and the normal requirement of mens rea would apply if there was no longer any language eliminating the requirement. The Court accordingly invoked the power of severance to strike out the unconstitutional words. No new words had to be inserted in order to import the requirement of mens rea. The result, of course, was a significant change in the statutory provision. The alternative would have been to strike down the entire offence, which would mean that intercourse with a young woman under fourteen would no longer be an offence, even for a man who was aware of her age—at least until Parliament amended the Criminal Code to reintroduce the offence.

In *Tétreault-Gadoury v. Canada* (1991),[5] the Supreme Court of Canada held that it was a breach of s. 15 of the Charter to restrict unemployment insurance benefits to persons under the age of 65. There was an age-65 bar in the Unemployment Insurance Act, which took the form of an exception to the general rules of entitlement. If the age-65 bar were excised from the Act, the normal rules of entitlement would operate without any limitation as to age. The Court therefore simply invoked the power of severance to remove the age-65 bar from the Act. The effect

---

[2] *Hunter v. Southam*, [1984] 2 S.C.R. 145.

[3] *R. v. Vaillancourt*, [1987] 2 S.C.R. 636.

[4] *R. v. Hess*, [1990] 2 S.C.R. 906.

[5] *Tétreault-Gadoury v. Canada*, [1991] 2 S.C.R. 22.

of this was to require payment of unemployment insurance benefits to persons over 65. This meant that the plaintiff became entitled to benefits, because she was a person over 65 who was otherwise qualified. As in *Hess*, the Court's decision caused a significant change in the statutory provision.

In *Tétreault-Gadoury*, the statutory scheme of unemployment insurance was "under-inclusive", meaning that the scheme failed to include a class of people (those over 65) who had a constitutional right to be included. In such a case, the obvious remedy is to hold the statute unconstitutional, but this produces the harsh result of denying unemployment insurance benefits to persons under 65. The alternative[6] is to "extend"[7] the statutory benefits to persons over 65 by striking out the words that make the statutory scheme under-inclusive. However, the remedy of extension directly alters the statutory scheme and requires new expenditures by the federal government that have never been authorized by Parliament. Thus, a court faced with an under-inclusive statute has an unpalatable choice between the draconic remedy of nullification and the radical remedy of extension. In choosing the remedy of extension, the Court in *Tétreault-Gadoury* was influenced by the fact that by the time the case was decided Parliament had repealed the age-bar (although not with retroactive effect so as to entitle the applicant).[8] La Forest J. for the Court also said (rather cryptically) that "there was no evidence put forth that the government could not afford to extend benefits to those over sixty-five".[9]

In *Benner v. Canada* (1997),[10] the Supreme Court of Canada held that the federal Citizenship Act was in breach of the equality rights of s. 15, because it drew a distinction between the children of Canadian mothers born abroad before 1977 and the children of Canadian fathers born abroad before 1977. In order to become a Canadian citizen, the child of a Canadian mother had to apply for citizenship and pass a security test; the child of a Canadian father was automatically entitled to citizenship on registering his or her birth in Canada. Having concluded that this statutory distinction was unconstitutional, what was the remedy? One approach would have been to impose the more stringent mother-derived rules on all persons born abroad before 1977 to a Canadian parent of ei-

[6]Another option is the suspended declaration of invalidity, which was held to be the appropriate remedy for an under-inclusive statute in the *Schachter* case, discussed at § 40:4 note 27, above, and § 40:6 note 2, below.

[7]For American writing on the remedy of extension, see D. Beers, "Extension versus Invalidiation of Underinclusive Statutes" (1975) 12 Columbia J. Law and Soc. Problems 115; E.H. Caminker, "A Norm-Based Remedial Model for Underinclusive Statutes" (1986) 95 Yale L.J. 1185. The remedy of extension in Canada is discussed further in the next section, heading § 40:6.

[8]*Tétreault-Gadoury v. Canada*, [1991] 2 S.C.R. 22, 46.

[9]*Tétreault-Gadoury v. Canada*, [1991] 2 S.C.R. 22. La Forest J. did not indicate what kind of evidence he would find persuasive. It is not clear whether he was unwilling to take judicial notice of what was then a notorious federal deficit, or whether he did not regard the deficit as making new expenditures unaffordable.

[10]*Benner v. Canada*, [1997] 1 S.C.R. 358.

ther sex. This would have denied a remedy to the applicant, who was the child of a Canadian mother and had been refused citizenship on the ground that he failed the security test. The other approach was to extend the father-derived automatic right of citizenship to all persons born abroad before 1977. This was the remedy sought by the applicant in this case, because it would grant him citizenship despite a criminal record. Either of the two possible remedies was a marked change in the Citizenship Act that had been enacted by Parliament. The Court decided on the latter approach, giving as their reason that the automatic right of citizenship was already the rule for children born abroad to a Canadian parent of either sex after 1977. Therefore, the legislative scheme would be less disturbed by the extension of the automatic right of citizenship. It turned out that the result ordered by the Court could be achieved by excising several phrases from the Act, and the Court ordered that those phrases be severed.[11]

What is new about the use of severance in these Charter cases is that in each case words were deleted from a statutory provision that were integral to the operation of the provision. The remainder of the provision could survive only because it had been *altered* by the Court's deletion of the severed words.[12] The provision was invalid in the language in which it was enacted by Parliament, and could be upheld only after the Court had amended it.[13]

§ 40:6 Reading in

Although the remedy in *Tétreault-Gadoury*[1] was a radical one, it did not involve adding new words to the Unemployment Insurance Act. The age-65 bar was simply deleted by the exercise of the Court's power of severance, leaving the plaintiff in a position to rely upon the general rules of entitlement. A much more difficult problem was presented to the Supreme Court of Canada in *Schachter v. Canada* (1992).[2] In that case, a claim was made by biological parents (or "natural parents", the term used in this case) to child care benefits that were conferred only on

---

[11]*Benner v. Can. (No. 2)*, [1997] 3 S.C.R. 389.

[12]See also *R. v. Lucas*, [1998] 1 S.C.R. 439, paras. 84-86 (severing language in order to uphold the offence of defamatory libel); *Dunmore v. Ont.*, [2001] 3 S.C.R. 1016, para. 66 (severing exclusion clause in order to bring agricultural workers into the labour relations statute); *Charkaoui v. Can.*, [2007] 1 S.C.R. 350, para. 142 (severing language and reading in language to a statute that provided for early review of security detention to permanent residents, so as to give foreign nationals the same right); *Sask. v. Whatcott*, [2013] 1 S.C.R. 467, 2013 SCC 11 (severing language from Human Rights Code prohibition on anti-minority speech so as to confine it to hate speech, which was all that could be justified under s. 1).

[13]For further discussion, see P.W. Hogg, "Judicial Amendment of Statutes to Conform to the Charter of Rights" in G.-A. Beaudoin and others (eds.) Mélanges Jean Beetz (Les Èditions Thémis, 1995), 497.

[Section 40:6]

[1]*Tétreault-Gadoury v. Canada*, [1991] 2 S.C.R. 22.

[2]*Schachter v. Canada*, [1992] 2 S.C.R. 679; the case is also discussed at § 40:4.

adoptive parents by the federal Unemployment Insurance Act. The Act treated adoptive parents more generously than biological parents, which was agreed on appeal to be a denial of equal benefit of the law in violation of s. 15 of the Charter of Rights. But what was the remedy? There was no severable provision excluding biological parents from the child care benefits. The Act simply limited the benefits to adoptive parents. If that provision were excised, the perverse result would be to deny child care benefits to all adoptive parents.

In *Schachter*, the Supreme Court of Canada held that it possessed the power not only to sever language from a statute, but also to "read in" new language if that were necessary to remedy a constitutional defect. In principle, therefore, the defect in *Schachter* could be cured by "reading in" the class of "natural parents" to the statutory provision benefiting adoptive parents. Lamer C.J., speaking for a unanimous Court on this issue, explained that reading in would be a "legitimate remedy akin to severance",[3] despite the fact that it involved adding to a statute words that had never been enacted by Parliament. In other words, a judicial remedy was available to cure the under-inclusive statutory scheme even if new language had to be added to the statute in order to accommodate the unconstitutionally excluded class.

The Court in *Schachter* acknowledged that caution was called for in exercising the newly-assumed power of reading in. Reading in would be appropriate only in "the clearest of cases",[4] which seemed to mean cases where (1) the addition of the excluded class was consistent with the legislative objective, (2) there seemed to be little choice as to how to cure the constitutional defect, (3) the reading in would not involve a substantial change in the cost or nature of the legislative scheme, and (4) the alternative of striking down the under-inclusive provision would be an inferior remedy.[5] The Court concluded that the *Schachter* case was not an appropriate one for correction by reading in. The objective of the Act in making special provision for adoptive parents was not clear, and therefore it could not be assumed that the addition of "natural parents" to the provision would be consistent with the legislative objective. Furthermore, the reading in of "natural parents" (who are of course more numerous than adoptive parents) would cause a major increase in the scope and cost of the child care benefits legislated by Parliament. The Court concluded that "to read in natural parents would in these circumstances constitute a substantial intrusion into the legislative

[3]*Schachter v. Canada*, [1992] 2 S.C.R. 679, 702. Reading *in*, which involves adding new words to a statute to remove a constitutional defect, should not be confused with reading *down*, which involves giving a narrow interpretation to a statute in order to avoid a constitutional defect. Reading down is the topic of the next section of this chapter.

[4]*Schachter v. Canada*, [1992] 2 S.C.R. 679, 718 per Lamer C.J., 727 per La Forest J.

[5]*Schachter v. Canada*, [1992] 2 S.C.R. 679, 718.

domain".[6] Instead, as related earlier in this chapter,[7] the Court held that the appropriate remedy was a declaration of invalidity suspended for a sufficient time to enable Parliament to amend the Act into conformity with the Constitution.

In *Miron v. Trudel* (1995),[8] the Supreme Court of Canada applied the remedy of reading in.[9] The Court in that case held that Ontario's Insurance Act, which stipulated the terms of the compulsory automobile insurance policies in the province, contained an unconstitutional provision for an accident benefit that was payable to the "spouse" of an insured person. Because the definition of spouse in the Act was restricted to a person who was legally married to the insured person, the Court held by a majority that this provision discriminated against the claimant, who was the common-law spouse of an insured person. The exclusion of common-law spouses was discrimination on the basis of marital status, which was a denial of the claimant's s. 15 equality rights.[10] The Court held that the appropriate remedy for the constitutional defect was to read into the definition of spouse new language that would include the unconstitutionally-excluded class of common-law spouses.[11] The problem of formulating the appropriate language to read into the Act was solved by the fact that the Legislature had already amended the definition by adding common-law spouses, although it had done so after the claimant's cause of action arose by an amendment that was only prospective in its effect. This amendment also indicated how the Legislature would have remedied the constitutional defect had it been required to do so in time to qualify the claimant. The Court accordingly ordered that the language of the subsequent amendment be made retroactive to cover the claimant's claim of spousal status.[12]

In *Vriend v. Alberta* (1998),[13] the Supreme Court of Canada reviewed Alberta's Individual Rights Protection Act, which prohibited discrimina-

---

[6]*Schachter v. Canada*, [1992] 2 S.C.R. 679, 723 per Lamer C.J.; La Forest J. agreed.

[7]Text accompanying § 40:4 note 27, above.

[8]*Miron v. Trudel*, [1995] 2 S.C.R. 418. The majority opinion was written by McLachlin J., with the agreement of Sopinka, Cory and Iacobucci JJ. L'Heureux-Dubé J. wrote a separate concurring opinion, agreeing with McLachlin J. as to remedy. Gonthier J. dissented, with the agreement of Lamer C.J., La Forest and Major JJ.

[9]See also *R. v. Laba*, [1994] 3 S.C.R. 965 (unconstitutional reverse onus clause saved by striking out language imposing burden of persuasion on accused and reading in new language to substitute an evidentiary burden).

[10]The case is discussed in ch. 55, Equality, under heading § 55:18, "Addition of analogous grounds".

[11]This would also have been the remedy of the dissenting minority in *Egan v. Can.*, [1995] 2 S.C.R. 513, 620, para. 220, per Iacobucci J., who would have held that the exclusion of same-sex couples from the spouse's allowance under the federal Old Age Security programme was a breach of s. 15.

[12]*Miron v. Trudel*, [1995] 2 S.C.R. 418, 510, para. 180 per McLachlin J. The Court did not provide the time limit of retroactivity, but presumably the read-in language would take effect from April 17, 1985, when s. 15 of the Charter came into force (three years after the rest of the Charter).

[13]*Vriend v. Alberta*, [1998] 1 S.C.R. 493. The majority opinion was written by Cory

tion in employment, accommodation, public facilities and the supply of goods and services. The case had been brought by a plaintiff who had been discharged from his employment because he was a gay man. His attempt to seek a remedy under the Act from the Alberta Human Rights Commission had been unsuccessful because the Act, while prohibiting discrimination on a variety of grounds, did not cover discrimination based on sexual orientation. The Court agreed that the omission of sexual orientation from the Act was a denial of the plaintiff's equality rights under the Charter. The Court ordered that the constitutional defect be cured by reading into the statutory list of grounds of prohibited discrimination the words "sexual orientation". According to Iacobucci J., who wrote for the majority on this issue, the addition of this language to the Act would be consistent with the objective of the Act, could be accomplished with precision, would not greatly add to the cost of administering the Act, and would be a less intrusive remedy than striking down the entire Act.[14]

Miron and *Vriend* are both examples of the remedy of "extension". In these cases, as in *Tétreault-Gadoury*,[15] the Court had to review an "under-inclusive" statute, that is, a statute that conferred a benefit on a class that failed to include all persons who had an equality-based right to be included.[16] In *Tétreault-Gadoury*, the extension of the statute could be accomplished by severing words from the statute. Severance would not repair the defect in *Miron* and *Vriend*, where the Court was required to read new words into the statute in order to extend its benefits to those who had been unconstitutionally excluded.

The remedy of reading in was denied in *Trial Lawyers' Association of British Columbia v. British Columbia* (2014).[17] In that case, the Supreme Court of Canada decided that hearing fees imposed on litigants by the superior court of British Columbia were sufficiently burdensome to deny

J. (on ss. 32 and 15) and Iacobucci J. (on s. 1 and remedy), with the agreement of each other and Lamer C.J., Gonthier, McLachlin and Bastarache JJ. L'Heureux-Dubé J. wrote a separate concurring opinion. Major J. dissented on only the issue of reading in.

[14]The Court followed *Haig v. Can.* (1992), 9 O.R. (3d) 495 (C.A.), in which sexual orientation had been read into the Canadian Human Rights Act. *Vriend* was itself followed in *Rosenberg v. Can.* (1998), 38 O.R.(3d) 577 (C.A.), in which "or same sex" was read into the definition of spouse in the Income Tax Act after the language that required a spouse to be of the opposite sex. See also *Charkaoui v. Can.*, [2007] 1 S.C.R. 350, para. 142 (reading in "foreign nationals" to a statute that provided for early review of security detention only to permanent residents).

[15]*Tétreault-Gadoury v. Canada*, [1991] 2 S.C.R. 22.

[16]The opposite problem is when a statute is over-inclusive or overbroad, and this can also be corrected by reading in language to exclude the situations that are constitutionally entitled to be excluded: *R. v. Sharpe*, [2001] 1 S.C.R. 45 (reading in exceptions to the Criminal Code offence of possession of child pornography for situations that, in the opinion of the majority, posed no risk of harm to children).

[17]*Trial Lawyers' Association of British Columbia v. British Columbia*, [2014] 3 S.C.R. 31, 2014 SCC 59. McLachlin C.J. wrote the majority opinion for five members of the seven-judge bench. Cromwell J. wrote a concurring opinion. Rothstein J. wrote a dissenting opinion. Neither of the two individual opinions commented on the reading-in point.

access to the court to litigants of modest means. The Supreme Court, by a majority, held that the fees were unconstitutional on the basis of either s. 96 of the Constitution Act, 1867[18] or the unwritten constitutional principle of the rule of law.[19] The Court of Appeal, which had also found the fees unconstitutional, had repaired the constitutional defect by reading into the hearing-fee rule an exception for litigants "in need". McLachlin C.J., for the majority of the Supreme Court, held that this was not the appropriate remedy. She held that reading in should be "sparingly used", and "only where it is clear that the legislature, faced with a ruling of unconstitutionality, would have made the change proposed".[20] It was true that an exemption from the fee for litigants "in need" would be one corrective option for the rule-maker, but other options were to abandon or modify the fee. "The proper remedy", she held, "is to declare the hearing fee scheme as it stands unconstitutional and leave it to the legislature or the [rule-maker] to enact new provisions, should they choose to do so."[21]

Once it is accepted that severance is available to extend the reach of a statute to make it conform to the Charter of Rights, as the Court decided in *Tétreault-Gadoury*, it is only a short step to reading in. If severance allows the Court to delete something improperly included in a statute, it seems only appropriate to allow the Court to add something improperly excluded. As Lamer C.J. commented in *Schachter*,[22] it seems wrong that the "style of drafting" of a statute should be "the single critical factor in the determination of a remedy".[23] This line of reasoning leads inexorably to reading in as the twin of severance. Where the constitutional deficiency consists not in what the statute included but in what it excluded, reading in is a possible remedy.

There is no doubt that reading in is a serious intrusion by the courts on the functions of the legislative branch of government. So is severance, when it is employed (as in *Tétreault-Gadoury)* to extend the reach of an under-inclusive statute. However, the alternative of striking down the unconstitutional legislative scheme is also very intrusive. This is illustrated by *Nova Scotia v. Phillips* (1986).[24] In that case, the Nova Scotia Court of Appeal held that a welfare benefit that was available only to single mothers was in breach of s. 15, because the benefit was

[18]The s. 96 reasons of the Court are explained in ch. 7, Courts, under heading § 7:18, "Superior Courts".

[19]The rule-of-law reasons of the Court are explained in ch. 15, Judicial Review on Federal Grounds, under heading § 15:28, "Unwritten constitutional principles".

[20]*Trial Lawyers' Association of British Columbia v. British Columbia*, [2014] 3 S.C.R. 31, 2014 SCC 59, para. 66.

[21]*Trial Lawyers' Association of British Columbia v. British Columbia*, [2014] 3 S.C.R. 31, 2014 SCC 59, para. 68. Folld. in *Canada v. Federation of Law Societies*, [2015] 1 S.C.R. 401; 2015 SCC 7, paras. 64-66 (refusing reading in and declaring provision unconstitutional).

[22]*Schachter v. Canada*, [1992] 2 S.C.R. 679.

[23]*Schachter v. Canada*, [1992] 2 S.C.R. 679, 698.

[24]*Nova Scotia v. Phillips* (1986), 34 D.L.R. (4th) 633 (N.S.C.A.).

not available to single fathers as well. Being unwilling to extend the statutory provision by reading in the excluded group of single fathers, the Court was driven to nullify the provision, which denied the benefit to single mothers. This restored equality, but it was obviously an ironic and harsh result. Moreover, while the decision does not directly amend the unconstitutional statute, it does force the Legislature to act promptly to restore the nullified benefits, as well as to correct the constitutional defect.

A variation on the remedy of striking down an unconstitutional statute is to declare the statute unconstitutional, but suspend the declaration of invalidity for a stipulated period of time. As explained earlier,[25] this was held to be the appropriate remedy in the *Schachter* case. The attraction of the suspended declaration of invalidity is that it avoids the disruptive effects of the immediate retroactive nullification of a statutory programme, which is the normal consequence of a declaration of invalidity. However, the making of a suspended declaration of invalidity is close to a legislative function. To be sure, the court does not directly amend the unconstitutional statute, as the court does when it exercises its powers of severance and reading in. But the court takes upon itself the power to maintain in force for a temporary period a statute that is unconstitutional. And the time limit on the suspension has the effect of imposing on the competent legislative body a deadline to which it must conform on pain of the declaration of invalidity taking effect. Obviously, this is a major interference by the judicial branch of government with the agenda, priorities and procedures of the legislative branch.

One way or another, a group that has been unconstitutionally excluded from a legislated programme has to be added. None of the solutions is free from difficulty. In cases like *Tétreault-Gadoury, Miron* and *Vriend*, where severance or reading in effects the necessary repair in a straightforward fashion that seems consistent with the legislative objective, and that does not significantly alter the legislative scheme, there is much to be said for the direct judicial amendment of the statute by severance or reading in. Although severance takes away words that the legislative body enacted, and reading in adds words that the legislative body did not enact, these radical results need not be other than temporary. It is always open to the competent legislative body to enact a new legislative scheme—in compliance with constitutional requirements, needless to say—if the legislators are not content with the scheme as amended by the court.[26] In this sense, the democratic legislative process retains the last word.

---

[25]Text accompanying § 40:4 note 27 and § 40:6 note 7, above.

[26]In *Vriend v. Alberta*, [1998] 1 S.C.R. 493, Major J. dissented on the issue of remedy. In his view, the preferable remedy was a postponed declaration of invalidity, allowing the Legislature to determine its response, which could be to add the words sexual orientation to the grounds of discrimination and thus come into compliance with the Charter, but could also be to protect the existing Act by a notwithstanding clause under s. 33, or to allow the statute to fall so that the province would have no human rights statute at all. (Of course, these options remained open to the Legislature after the Court-ordered reading in, because the statute was still subject to amendment or repeal

§ 40:7 Reading down

The topic of reading down in federalism cases has been examined earlier.[1] Reading down is also a remedy in Charter cases; it is the appropriate remedy when a statute will bear two interpretations, one of which would offend the Charter of Rights and the other of which would not. In that case, a court will hold that the latter interpretation, which is normally the narrower one (hence reading *down*), is the correct one. When a statute is read down to avoid a breach of the Charter, there is no holding of invalidity. The vindication of the Charter right is accomplished solely by interpretation.[2] Reading down is another doctrine of judicial restraint, because it minimizes the impact of a successful Charter attack on a law.[3]

Reading down should not be confused with reading *in*, which was the topic of the previous section of this chapter. Reading in involves the insertion into a statute of words that Parliament never enacted. It is not a technique of interpretation, but rather a technique of judicial amendment, altering the statute to make it conform to the Constitution. Reading in usually has the effect of extending the scope of the statute. Reading down, on the other hand, involves giving a statute a narrow interpretation in order to avoid a constitutional problem that would arise if the statute were given a broad interpretation.

Most discussion, judicial and academic, of reading down assumes that the statutory provision that is too broad to be constitutional will plausibly bear the narrower interpretation that would make it constitutional. When that is the case, the constitutional remedy is achieved solely by statutory interpretation. To be sure, the saving statu-

---

by the Legislature.)

[Section 40:7]

[1]Chapter 15, Judicial Review on Federal Grounds, under heading § 15:15, "Reading down".

[2]But note disagreements about the extent to which reading down should be used as a remedy in Charter cases: *Can. Foundation for Children, Youth and the Law v. Can.*, [2004] 1 S.C.R. 76; *Montreal v. 2952-1366 Que.*, [2005] 3 S.C.R. 141; the cases are discussed in § 40:9, "Reconstruction". See also the debate between H. Stewart, "In Defence of Constitutionalized Interpretation" (2016) 36 Nat. J. Con. Law 195 and K. Roach, "Constitutionalized Interpretation, Reading Down/In and the Wisdom of *Schachter*" (2016) 36 Nat. J. Con. Law 211.

[3]E.g., *Ruby v. Can.*, [2002] 4 S.C.R. 3 (reading down provision of Privacy Act requiring in camera hearings); *Solski v. Que.*, [2005] 1 S.C.R. 201 (reading down provision of Quebec Charter of the French Language restricting access to English-language schools); *United States v. Ferras*, [2006] 2 S.C.R. 77, para. 42 (reading down provision of Extradition Act defining role of extradition judge); *Canada v. Federation of Law Societies*, [2015] 1 S.C.R. 401, 2015 SCC 7, para. 63 (reading down search and seizure provisions of federal Proceeds of Crime (Money Laundering) and Terrorist Financing Act to protect solicitor-client privilege); *R. v. Appulonappa*, [2015] 3 S.C.R. 485, 2015 SCC 59, para. 86 (reading down human-smuggling offence in Immigration and Refugee Protection Act to exclude persons who give humanitarian, mutual or family assistance to undocumented refugee claimants); *Can. v. Chambre des notaires du Québec*, [2016] 1 S.C.R. 336, 2016 SCC 20, para. 92 (reading down Income Tax Act's grant of power to demand documents or information to protect solicitor-client privilege).

tory interpretation is driven by constitutional considerations, but it can reasonably be presumed that the enacting legislative body would not have wanted to pass an unconstitutional law. More controversial is the case, which I will call "radical reading down", where the narrower interpretation that would be needed to save the statute is not a plausible reading of the statutory provision, and is really a judicial reconstruction of the statute. In that case, it cannot reasonably be presumed that the reviewing court's new version of the statute is the one that would have been chosen by the competent legislative body if it had been aware of the risk of judicial invalidation. On the other hand, the radical reading down does save the bulk of the statute from invalidation, and is not in principle very different from reading in or severance, two remedies where the court actually redrafts the statutory provision. In that case (as in the case of reading in or severance), it will be a judgment call by the reviewing court as to whether it would be better to strike down the statute and leave to the competent legislative body the decision as to what should replace it. Eric Fish, writing in the United States,[4] argues that these two kinds of reading down (or constitutional avoidance) should be distinguished, but he does not take the view that the second kind (radical reading down) is necessarily an illegitimate exercise of judicial power: it is a remedy not unlike reading in and severance, and should be governed by similar considerations to those remedies. This seems to be the better view of the Canadian position as well. The "spanking case", discussed later in this chapter,[5] may be the best example of radical reading down. In that case, a Criminal Code exemption from criminal assault for teachers and parents who applied "reasonable" force "by way of correction" against the children in their charge was saved from invalidity (void for vagueness) by a majority of the Supreme Court, which read the exemption down by incorporating into it a series of detailed limits on the use of force by teachers and parents. This was a narrower interpretation than could possibly be derived from the exemption's text or legislative history or prior judicial interpretation. The three dissenting judges objected that the majority had drafted an entirely new provision; they would have struck down the exemption, leaving it to Parliament to decide whether or not it wanted to replace the exemption with more specific standards for corrective discipline.

§ 40:8 Constitutional exemption

The Supreme Court of Canada has occasionally indicated, obiter, that it might be willing to grant a "constitutional exemption" from "otherwise

---

[4]E.S. Fish, "Constitutional Avoidance as Interpretation and as Remedy" (2016) 114 Michigan L. Rev. 1275; see also by the same author "Choosing Constitutional Remedies" (2016) 63 UCLA L. Rev. 322; "Judicial Amendment of Statutes" (2016) 84 Geo. Washington L. Rev. 563.

[5]*Canadian Foundation for Children,Youth and the Law v. Can.*, [2004] 1 S.C.R. 76; described in § 40:9, "Reconstruction". Another example of radical reading down is *R. v. Sharpe*, [2001] 1 S.C.R. 45, reading in exemptions from offence of child pornography; described in ch. 43, Expression, under heading § 43:29 "Pornography".

valid legislation" that would be unconstitutional in its application to particular individuals or groups.[1] In the context of Sunday closing, the dicta seemed to indicate that a prohibition of retailing on a Sunday could be salvaged by reading into the legislation an exemption for those who observed some day other than Sunday as the sabbath. With this exemption, the Sunday-closing law would no longer offend the guarantee against freedom of religion. The advantage of the constitutional exemption is that it enables the Court to uphold a law that is valid in most of its applications by creating an exemption for those applications that would offend the Charter. The disadvantage of the constitutional exemption is that its scope must be defined by the Court, and the task of definition is likely to involve choice among a range of equally constitutional solutions; that is the kind of choice that should be made by the legislative body itself.

In *R. v. Seaboyer* (1991),[2] the Supreme Court of Canada considered the constitutional validity of the Criminal Code provision restricting the evidence that may be adduced by the accused in sexual assault cases of the past sexual activity of the complainant. This provision, which has been enacted in most jurisdictions of the United States, is known as a rape-shield law, because its main purpose is to shield the complainant in a sexual assault (or rape) case from cross-examination at trial. The Ontario Court of Appeal[3] had taken the view that in some situations the rape-shield section would violate s. 7 (or s. 11(d)) of the Charter, because it would deprive the accused of the right to make full answer and defence. Nonetheless, the Court of Appeal, following American authority, had upheld the section on the basis that there would only be rare cases where the section would exclude relevant evidence, and those cases could be accommodated by the doctrine of the constitutional exemption. In that way, the section could remain in force for the generality of cases, while leaving it open to an accused to establish that in the circumstances of a particular case the section should not be applied.

The Supreme Court of Canada reversed the Ontario Court of Appeal. The Court, by a majority, agreed that in some situations the rape-shield section would deprive an accused of the right to make full answer and defence.[4] However, the Supreme Court of Canada held that this made the section unconstitutional. McLachlin J., who wrote for the majority, refused to salvage the section through the doctrine of constitutional

---

[Section 40:8]

[1] *R. v. Big M Drug Mart*, [1985] 1 S.C.R. 295, 315; *R. v. Edwards Books and Art*, [1986] 2 S.C.R. 713, 783. A constitutional exemption from a Sunday closing law was granted in *R. v. Westfair Foods* (1989), 65 D.L.R. (4th) 56 (Sask. C.A.). See also *Osborne v. Can.*, [1991] 2 S.C.R. 69, 77 per Wilson J. obiter (constitutional exemption not available), 105 per Sopinka J. obiter (constitutional exemption available).

[2] *R. v. Seaboyer*, [1991] 2 S.C.R. 577.

[3] *R. v. Seaboyer*, (1987) 61 O.R. (2d) 290 (C.A.).

[4] L'Heureux-Dubé J. who, with Gonthier J., dissented, would have upheld the rape-shield section on the ground that it excluded only evidence that was either irrelevant or, if relevant, unduly prejudicial to the fairness of the trial.

exemption. The constitutional exemption would operate by importing into the section a discretionary power of dispensation by the trial judge. In her view, since Parliament deliberately chose to exclude any discretion on the part of the trial judge, the importation into the section of judicial discretion, "while perhaps saving the law in one sense, dramatically alters it in another".[5] In her view, the constitutional exemption would have much the same effect as striking down the section, because the admissibility of evidence under the constitutional exemption would be governed by common law notions of relevance. Finally (and perhaps inconsistently with the previous point), she noted that it would be difficult to define the scope of the constitutional exemption so as to provide guidance to trial judges.[6]

Seaboyer thus rejects the constitutional exemption as the salvation of what the Court regarded as the overbroad rape-shield law, but McLachlin J. made clear that she was not rejecting the solution in principle, and she said that "it may be appropriate in some other case".[7]

For a time it looked as though that "other case" was the crime that carries a mandatory minimum sentence, a topic more fully explored later in the book.[8] The Supreme Court of Canada has held that a punishment that is grossly disproportionate to the offence is unconstitutional for breach of the Charter guarantee (s. 12) against cruel and unusual punishment. Where an offence carries a mandatory minimum sentence, for example, seven years imprisonment for importing illegal drugs, what is one to do if the punishment is grossly disproportionate in a rare, unusual or exceptional case (the university student carrying a small amount of marijuana pre-legalization), but is not grossly disproportionate in the general run of cases for which it was intended (the drug trafficker)? In *R. v. Smith* (1987),[9] the Supreme Court of Canada came up with the surprising conclusion that the minimum sentence was uncon-

---

[5]*R. v. Seaboyer*, [1991] 2 S.C.R. 577, 628.

[6]*R. v. Seaboyer*, [1991] 2 S.C.R. 577, 629.

[7]*R. v. Seaboyer*, [1991] 2 S.C.R. 577, 630. McLachlin J. found that "other case" in *Rodriguez v. B.C.*, [1993] 3 S.C.R. 519, where she and three others, Lamer C.J., L'Heureux-Dubé and Cory JJ., all dissenting, would have allowed a constitutional exemption from the prohibition of assisting suicide for persons physically unable to commit suicide unassisted. However, Lamer C.J. (by himself) asserted (at 577) that a constitutional exempton could only be granted in concert with a suspended declaration of invalidity. Sopinka J. for the majority upheld the prohibition without any constitutional exemption. The Supreme Court refused to follow *Rodriguez* in *Carter v. Can.*, [2015] 1 S.C.R. 331, 2015 SCC 5, holding that the prohibition of physician-assisted death offended s. 7, but the Court (para. 125) rejected the remedy of a constitutional exemption, granting instead a declaration of invalidity suspended for one year to enable Parliament to design the exemption from the general prohibition of third-party-assisted death. See also *Corbiere v. Can.*, [1999] 2 S.C.R. 203, para. 22 (denying constitutional exemption from residence requirement for voting in Indian band elections).

[8]Chapter 53, Cruel and Unusual Punishment, under heading § 53:4, "Minimum sentence".

[9]*R. v. Smith*, [1987] 1 S.C.R. 1045. A variety of concurring opinions were written. Only McIntyre J. dissented, advocating something like a constitutional exemption for the rare case, should it ever come to the courts.

stitutional for all cases, even if the rare case was hypothetical. While the idea of a constitutional exemption was inconsistent with the reasoning in *Smith*, it was not expressly rejected, and it certainly had much to be said for it. It would enable the courts to keep in force a minimum sentence that was not disproportionate in the great majority of its applications, while applying normal sentencing principles to the rare set of facts where the defendant's lack of moral culpability would make the minimum sentence cruel and unusual. However, the idea was definitively rejected by a unanimous Supreme Court in *R. v. Ferguson* (2008).[10]

The defendant in *Ferguson* was a police officer who was attacked by a violent prisoner whom he was trying to put into a cell. In the course of the struggle that ensued, the defendant's gun went off and killed the prisoner. The defendant was acquitted of murder, but convicted of manslaughter. The Criminal Code imposed a minimum sentence of four years for manslaughter with a firearm. However, the trial judge (having heard the evidence) took the view that four years' imprisonment was a grossly disproportionate punishment on these facts. Without striking down the minimum sentence, the judge held that the defendant was entitled to a constitutional exemption from the sentence, and he imposed a sentence of two years less a day. On appeal, the Supreme Court disagreed, holding that there was "no basis" for concluding that the four-year sentence was grossly disproportionate "on the facts of this case".[11] It followed from this finding that there was no need to consider the availability of a constitutional exemption. However, the Court went on to do so anyway, and it held that a constitutional exemption from a minimum sentence was not a remedy that was available to a defendant in a rare, exceptional or unusual case where the minimum sentence would be grossly disproportionate. The remedy in such a case was to strike down the law in its entirety. The Court thus reaffirmed the holding in *Smith* that, if a minimum-sentence law is grossly disproportionate in any of its applications, however rare, exceptional or unusual, the duty of the sentencing court is to strike down the law. The overbroad law cannot be salvaged by creating a constitutional exemption for the particular rare case.

The opinion of the unanimous Court in *Ferguson* was written by McLachlin C.J., and her main reason was similar to her main reason in *Seaboyer*. The intention of Parliament in creating a minimum sentence was to eliminate the discretion of the sentencing judge to impose a sentence less than the stipulated minimum. If the courts assumed the power to grant constitutional exemptions from the minimum sentence, the effect would be "to read in a discretion to a provision where Parliament clearly intended to exclude discretion", and this would be "an inap-

[10] *R. v. Ferguson*, [2008] 1 S.C.R. 96. McLachlin C.J. wrote the opinion of the Court.

[11] *R. v. Ferguson*, [2008] 1 S.C.R. 96, para. 29. As well, she could not find a reasonable hypothetical application of the sentence that would be a grossly disproportionate punishment.

propriate intrusion into the legislative sphere."[12] The Chief Justice was also concerned that rule-of-law values of "certainty, accessibility, intelligibility, clarity and predictability" would be offended if the minimum sentence remained in the statute book, but was in fact subject to discretionary case-by-case exceptions: as constitutional exemptions were granted, the law in the statute book would "increasingly diverge from the law as applied".[13] For these reasons, *Ferguson* rejects the constitutional exemption as the salvation of an overbroad minimum-sentence law. The decision is limited to minimum sentences, and does not necessarily foreclose the granting of a constitutional exemption in some other kind of case. However, the reasons do not leave much room for constitutional exemptions of any kind, and the Chief Justice did not repeat what she had said in *Seaboyer* that a constitutional exemption "may be appropriate in some other case".[14]

§ 40:9 Reconstruction

So far this chapter has been devoted to reporting the various techniques that are available to a court that finds a statute to be unconstitutional. Some of these techniques are highly intrusive of the legislative function, and two of them, namely, severance and reading in, have occasionally been used by courts to directly amend a statute in order to bring the statute into conformity with the Charter of Rights. After all this, it may seem disingenuous to claim that the general rule is that the courts may not reconstruct an unconstitutional statute in order to render it constitutional. That, however, is the general rule; and the creative use of the techniques of temporary validity, severance, reading in, reading down and the constitutional exemption should be seen as exceptions to the general rule.

There is a point at which a court will recognize that an unconstitutional statute cannot be salvaged except by changes that are too profound, too policy-laden and too controversial to be carried out by a court. It is all a matter of degree, which is difficult to articulate and to predict. As Lamer C.J. commented in *Schachter v. Canada* (1991):[1]

> In some cases, the question of how the statute ought to be extended in order to comply with the Constitution cannot be answered with a sufficient degree of precision on the basis of constitutional analysis. In such a case, it is the legislature's role to fill in the gaps, not the court's.

This dictum serves as a reminder of the caution that should be exercised by non-elected courts in fashioning new laws. In a democracy, the primary responsibility for the enactment of new laws must always be that of the elected legislative bodies.

---

[12] *R. v. Ferguson*, [2008] 1 S.C.R. 96, para. 56.

[13] *R. v. Ferguson*, [2008] 1 S.C.R. 96, paras. 69-70.

[14] *R. v. Seaboyer*, [1991] 2 S.C.R. 577, 630.

[Section 40:9]

[1] *Schachter v. Canada*, [1992] 2 S.C.R. 679, 705.

The general rule prohibiting a court from reconstructing an unconstitutional statute is illustrated by *Hunter v. Southam* (1984).[2] In that case, the Supreme Court of Canada held that the search and seizure power in the Competition Act was unconstitutional under s. 8 of the Charter, because the Act did not stipulate a standard of reasonable and probable cause for the issue of a search warrant, and did not invest an impartial judicial body with the power to issue the warrant. It was argued that the Court should "read in" the required standards, and uphold the power as judicially modified. Dickson J. for the Court refused to salvage the provision in this way; he asserted that "it is the legislature's responsibility to enact legislation that embodies appropriate safeguards to comply with the Constitution's requirements".[3] The Court therefore struck down the statutory provision, leaving Parliament to enact an amendment that would satisfy the constitutional requirements. Parliament did in fact amend the Act to that end.[4]

A similar argument in favour of the reconstruction of unconstitutional legislation was made and rejected in *Singh v. Minister of Employment and Immigration* (1985).[5] The Supreme Court of Canada held that the refugee-determination provisions of the Immigration Act were unconstitutional, because they did not provide for a hearing by an official with power to decide.[6] It was suggested that this result could be achieved by a cleverly designed order of the Court. But Beetz J. pointed out that there was "probably more than one way to remedy the constitutional shortcomings of the Immigration Act", and it was "not the function of this Court to re-write the Act".[7] There were occasions when "crude surgery" could be performed by the Court, "but not plastic or reconstructive surgery".[8] The Court accordingly struck down the refugee-determination procedure, leaving it to Parliament to fill the lacuna with a new, and constitutional, provision. Parliament did in fact enact the required amendment.[9]

The Supreme Court of Canada again refused to reconstruct defective legislation in *Rocket v. Royal College of Dental Surgeons* (1990).[10] The offending legislation was a prohibition on advertising by dentists, with some limited exceptions. The Court held that the prohibition was a

[2] *Hunter v. Southam*, [1984] 2 S.C.R. 145.

[3] *Hunter v. Southam*, [1984] 2 S.C.R. 145, 169.

[4] S.C. 1986, c. 26.

[5] *Singh v. Minister of Employment and Immigration*, [1985] 1 S.C.R. 177.

[6] Beetz J. with two others reached his conclusion—technically, that the Act was inoperative rather than unconstitutional—on the basis of s. 2(e) of the Canadian Bill of Rights. Only Beetz J. commented on the Court's refusal to reconstruct the offending provision. Wilson J. with two others reached her conclusion on the basis of s. 7 of the Charter, and her principal reason was the Minister's failure to disclose reasons for rejection to the refugee claimant.

[7] *Singh v. Minr. of Emplmt. and Imm.*, [1985] 1 S.C.R. 177, 235.

[8] *Singh v. Minr. of Emplmt. and Imm.*, [1985] 1 S.C.R. 177, 236.

[9] S.C. 1986, c. 13.

[10] *Rocket v. Royal College of Dental Surgeons*, [1990] 2 S.C.R. 232.

breach of freedom of expression and was not saved by s. 1. The Court made clear that some restrictions on professional advertising would be saved by s. 1, but it still struck the prohibition down in its entirety. McLachlin J. for the Court said that it was "for the legislators" to determine what kinds of advertising should be prohibited.[11]

A striking departure from the general rule against salvage by reconstruction occurred in *Canadian Foundation for Children, Youth and the Law v. Canada* (2004).[12] That was a decision of the Supreme Court of Canada rejecting a constitutional challenge to s. 43 of the Criminal Code. Section 43 provides a defence to a charge of assault for teachers and parents who apply "reasonable" force "by way of correction" against the children in their charge. The challenge to the provision was based on the void for vagueness doctrine of s. 7 of the Charter.[13] Arbour J.'s dissenting opinion reviewed many decisions of the lower courts in which defendants had been acquitted under s. 43 despite their use of violent, abusive or ineffective force against children. Arbour J. concluded that the provision failed to provide meaningful standards for the use of force by teachers and parents, and that it should be struck down. This would send the problem back to Parliament to consider whether some version of s. 43 was necessary and, if so, to draft more specific standards for corrective discipline. However, Arbour J.'s powerful reasoning did not prevail. McLachlin C.J., for the majority of the Court, issued a new "interpretation" of the provision. Ignoring the lower-court decisions which decided the contrary, she held[14] that the provision "exempts from criminal sanction only minor corrective force of a transitory and trifling nature". This excluded all "harmful conduct", which meant that the provision did not apply to corporal punishment of children under two or corporal punishment of teenagers. Nor did it apply to discipline by the use of objects such as belts or rulers, or by blows or slaps to the head. So interpreted, she held that the provision established a sufficiently clear standard to avoid the charge of unconstitutional vagueness. Arbour J. objected that the Chief Justice was not engaged in "mere interpretation", but had drafted "an entirely new provision".[15] Similar criticisms were expressed by Binnie and Deschamps JJ., the other dissenting judges.[16] Of course, the majority view prevailed, so that s. 43 was upheld—but subject to the restrictions read into it by the Chief Justice.

---

[11] *Rocket v. Royal College of Dental Surgeons*, [1990] 2 S.C.R. 232, 252.

[12] *Canadian Foundation for Children, Youth and the Law v. Canada*, [2004] 1 S.C.R. 76. McLachlin C.J. wrote the opinion of the majority. Binnie, Arbour and Deschamps JJ. wrote dissenting opinions.

[13] See ch. 47, Fundamental Justice, under heading § 47:28, "Standard of precision", where the case is more fully described.

[14] *Canadian Foundation for Children, Youth and the Law v. Canada*, [2004] 1 S.C.R. 76, para. 40.

[15] *Canadian Foundation for Children, Youth and the Law v. Canada*, [2004] 1 S.C.R. 76, para. 190.

[16] *Canadian Foundation for Children, Youth and the Law v. Canada*, [2004] 1 S.C.R. 76, para. 81 per Binnie J, paras. 216, 243 per Deschamps J.

Disagreement within the Supreme Court about salvage by reconstruction surfaced again in *Montreal v. 2952-1366 Quebec* (2005).[17] In that case, a city by-law prohibited noise produced by sound equipment that could be heard outside a building. The by-law included no stipulations as to the level of noise or the impact on neighbours or passers-by. The by-law was a limit on freedom of expression, and, without any such standards, it would be too broad to count as a reasonable limit under s. 1. McLachlin C.J. and Deschamps J., who wrote for the majority, solved this problem by interpreting the by-law as applying only to "noise that adversely affects the enjoyment of the environment".[18] So interpreted, they held that the by-law should be upheld under s. 1. Binnie J. (who had been one of the dissenters in *Canadian Foundation)* dissented. He pointed out that the by-law by its terms purported to prohibit "any audible signal from 'sound equipment' without regard to the potential, if any, for disturbance or annoyance";[19] and he would have held that this was too broad to be a reasonable limit under s. 1. He described the majority's "interpretation" of the by-law as "radical surgery" which had left the realm of interpretation and entered the realm of amendment.[20] It would be "more respectful of our place in the constitutional scheme", he said, to declare the by-law invalid, and "send it back to the legislators for consideration and possible re-enactment".[21]

There is one exception to the general rule that a court will not redraft a law in order to bring the law into compliance with the Charter. This is the rare case where the offending law is a rule of the common law. In *R. v. Swain* (1991),[22] the Supreme Court of Canada reviewed the common law rule that allows the Crown prosecutor in a criminal trial to adduce evidence of the accused's insanity against the wish of the accused. The Court held that this rule violated s. 7 of the Charter, because the evidence of insanity, if believed, would limit the right of the accused to conduct his or her own defence. The Court held that the rule would be saved by s. 1 if the issue of insanity were raised by the Crown in a separate hearing, in front of the same trier of fact, which would take place after the conclusion of the criminal trial, and which would only take place if the accused had been found otherwise guilty of the offence charged. The Court held that it was not necessary to strike down the

---

[17]*Montreal v. 2952-1366 Quebec*, [2005] 3 S.C.R. 141. McLachlin C.J. and Deschamps J. wrote for the six-judge majority. Binnie J. dissented. Only seven judges sat on the case.

[18]*Montreal v. 2952-1366 Quebec*, [2005] 3 S.C.R. 141, para. 34.

[19]*Montreal v. 2952-1366 Quebec*, [2005] 3 S.C.R. 141, para. 109.

[20]*Montreal v. 2952-1366 Quebec*, [2005] 3 S.C.R. 141, paras. 110, 147.

[21]*Montreal v. 2952-1366 Quebec*, [2005] 3 S.C.R. 141, para. 160. Binnie J.'s comment could as well apply to *Ontario v. Fraser*, [2011] 2 S.C.R. 3; discussed more fully in ch. 44, Freedom of Association, under heading § 44:5, "Purpose of association", where the majority of the Court (which included Binnie J.) upheld the constitutionality of Ontario's Agricultural Employees' Protection Act by interpreting the Act as imposing on employers a duty to engage in collective bargaining—something the Act rather clearly withheld, only requiring the employers to "listen to" or "read" representations by their employees.

[22]*R. v. Swain*, [1991] 1 S.C.R. 933.

existing law. Because the existing law was a rule of the judge-made common law, not statute, the Court had the power to replace the existing rule with a new rule that complied with the Charter. The Court therefore simply declared that a new rule, fashioned by it to comply with the Charter, was now the law![23]

§ 40:10 Limitation of actions

An action or other form of proceeding for a declaration that a statute is unconstitutional, including all the many variants of the declaration that have been described, is not subject to any limitation period. A declaration of unconstitutionality that is not accompanied by any other form of relief simply declares the existing state of the law; there is no cause of action to which a statute of limitation can apply. It does not matter how long ago the challenged statute was enacted.[1] If the reviewing court holds that the statute is unconstitutional, then the statute will be declared to have been unconstitutional from its inception,[2] and the newly discovered rights and obligations that flow from the retroactive disappearance of the statute will take effect automatically. If the plaintiff in the declaratory proceeding needs additional relief, such as damages or an injunction, those "personal remedies", although based on a constitutional ground, will be subject to any applicable statute of limitations of general application.[3]

II. REMEDY CLAUSE

§ 40:11 Section 24(1)

Section 24(1) of the Charter[1] provides as follows:

Anyone whose rights or freedoms, as guaranteed by this Charter, have

[23]*R. v. Swain*, [1991] 1 S.C.R. 933, 978, 1036. New common law rules were substituted for their Charter-defective predecessors in *R. v. Daviault*, [1994] 3 S.C.R. 63; *R. v. Robinson*, [1996] 1 S.C.R. 683.

[Section 40:10]

[1]The Charter of Rights came into force on April 17, 1982 for all provisions other than s. 15, which has a commencement date of April 17, 1985: ch. 36, Charter of Rights, under heading § 36:31, "Commencement of Charter". No declaration of invalidity on Charter grounds will be issued in respect of a statute enacted and repealed before the coming into force of the Charter, but that is because the Charter does not apply to such a statute: *Mack v. Can.* (2002), 60 O.R. (3d) 737 (C.A.). However, a statute enacted before the coming into force of the Charter that is unrepealed at the time of the coming into force of the Charter can be declared invalid on Charter grounds at the suit of a person with standing to seek a declaration. In that case, the declaration of invalidity will date back only to the coming into force of the Charter (because that is when the statute became unconstitutional), not the enactment of the statute.

[2]Chapter 58, Effect of Unconstitutional Law.

[3]§ 40:25, "Limitation of actions".

[Section 40:11]

[1]See J. Krane, "Proprietary Rights and Remedies under the Charter" (2008) 54 Crim. L. Q. 215. For larger works covering the supremacy clause as well as s. 24(1), see Gibson, The Law of the Charter: General Principles (1986), chs. 6, 8; Beaudoin and

been infringed or denied may apply to a court of competent jurisdiction to obtain such remedy as the court considers appropriate and just in the circumstances.

Section 24(1) provides for the granting of a remedy to enforce the rights or freedoms guaranteed by the Charter.[2]

§ 40:12 Applicable to Charter only

Section 24(1) is available only for a breach of the Charter. It is not a remedy for unconstitutional action in general. Breaches of other parts of the Constitution of Canada may only be challenged by the traditional methods referred to in the earlier discussion of the supremacy clause. In respect of enforcement, the Charter is thus in a preferred position. While many of the rights or freedoms guaranteed by the Charter existed before the Charter, in the sense that before April 17, 1982 Canadian law afforded some protection to them, the inclusion of a pre-existing right or freedom in the Charter has the effect of significantly strengthening the right: it becomes part of "the supreme law of Canada" to which inconsistent laws must yield (s. 52(1)), it becomes entrenched (alterable only by the process of constitutional amendment) (s. 52(3)), and it becomes enforceable under s. 24.

§ 40:13 Non-exclusive remedy

Section 24(1) is not the exclusive remedy for a breach of the Charter of Rights.[1] It will be recalled that the supremacy clause of s. 52(1), which is the topic of the earlier part of this chapter, renders "of no force or effect" any law that is inconsistent with the Constitution of Canada. As has been explained, s. 52(1) authorizes a court to hold that a law that abridges a Charter right is invalid. Whenever the validity of a statute (or other official act) is relevant to the outcome of a dispute, the court that is seized of the dispute has the power and the duty to determine whether or not the statute (or other act) is valid. For example, a court trying a criminal case is obliged to rule on the validity of the statute creating the offence if the defendant argues that the statute violates the Charter of Rights; if the court accepts the defendant's argument, then the court will acquit the defendant on the ground that the offence

---

Mendes (eds.), The Canadian Charter of Rights and Freedoms (4th ed., 2005), 131-162 (by L. Tassé), ch. 19 (by D. Gibson); Lokan and Dassios, Constitutional Litigation in Canada (Carswell loose-leaf), ch. 6; McLeod, Takach, Morton, Segal, The Canadian Charter of Rights (Carswell, loose-leaf), chs. 28, 30; Fitzgerald, Understanding Charter Remedies (Carswell, loose-leaf); Roach, Constitutional Remedies in Canada (Canada Law Book, loose-leaf); Canadian Charter of Rights Annotated (Canada Law Book, loose-leaf), annotations to ss. 24 and 52.

[2]The legislative history of s. 24(1) is related by Gibson, The Law of the Charter: General Principles (1986), 192-195.

[Section 40:13]

[1]*R. v. Big M Drug Mart*, [1985] 1 S.C.R. 295, 313.

charged is not known to the law.[2] In this example, the ruling of invalidity is authorized by s. 52(1) and the remedy of acquittal is authorized by the Criminal Code. Section 24(1) is not needed in such a case, and it is not applicable.

As will be explained later in this chapter, an administrative tribunal will be a "court of competent jurisdiction" for the purpose of s. 24(1) if it has the power to decide questions of law.[3] But, without the need to rely on s. 24(1), an administrative tribunal with the power to decide questions of law has the power to rule on the validity of a statute that is potentially applicable and that is argued to be in violation of the Charter.[4] For example, if a union applies to a labour board for certification as the collective bargaining agent of agricultural workers, and a statute excludes agricultural workers from collective bargaining, the labour board would have the power to rule on the question whether the statutory exclusion of agricultural workers violated the Charter.[5] If the board held that the statutory exclusion was a violation of the Charter, then the board would also have the power to certify the union. In this example, the ruling of invalidity is authorized by s. 52(1), and the remedy of certification is authorized by the board's empowering statute. Section 24(1) is not applicable.

As these examples show, s. 24(1) is not needed to provide a remedy for a Charter infringement where a holding of invalidity is all that the applicant needs in order to obtain an appropriate remedy that is available under the general law. Section 24(1) is needed only where a remedy provided by the general law is not available for some reason, or will not provide satisfactory redress. Generally speaking, it will be the declaration of invalidity under s. 52(1) that provides the remedy for *laws* that violate a Charter right (or indeed any constitutional right), while s. 24(1) provides the remedy for *government acts* that violate an individual's Charter right. Section 24(1) provides a "personal remedy against unconstitutional government action".[6] That is why the only person who has standing to seek a remedy under s. 24(1) is the very person whose Charter right has been infringed. Standing is the topic of the next section of this chapter.

Charter claimants have occasionally sought individual relief under s. 24(1) in the same proceeding as they have sought a declaration of invalidity under s. 52(1). In principle, there is no reason why both remedies should not be available in the same proceeding in the rare case where

---

[2] *R. v. Big M Drug Mart*, [1985] 1 S.C.R. 295, 313.

[3] § 40:16, "Court of competent jurisdiction".

[4] §§ 40:26 to 40:29, "Administrative tribunals".

[5] *Cuddy Chicks v. Ont.*, [1991] 2 S.C.R. 5.

[6] *R. v. Ferguson*, [2008] 1 S.C.R. 96, para. 61 per McLachlin C.J. for the Court. Followed in *Greater Vancouver Transportation Authority v. Can. Federation of Students*, [2009] 2 S.C.R. 295, paras. 85-90 (declaration of invalidity under s. 52(1) granted as remedy for rules of general application that infringe the Charter; remedy under s. 24(1) not appropriate).

both remedies are needed to provide full relief to the claimant.[7] That was the situation in *R. v. Demers* (2004),[8] where the Supreme Court of Canada held that the provisions of the Criminal Code respecting accused persons who were found permanently unfit to stand trial were unconstitutional for overbreadth.[9] The Court suspended the declaration of invalidity for a period of one year to permit Parliament to enact a new law. That, of course, was a remedy under s. 52(1).[10] But the Court was concerned that, if Parliament failed to act, persons unfit to stand trial would still be subject to criminal charges and to the restrictions on their liberty that follow from criminal charges. The Court therefore added a second remedy. Acting under s. 24(1), the Court ordered that, in the event of Parliament not acting within a year, those persons permanently unfit to stand trial who were found to be no danger to the public should have their proceedings stayed.[11]

§ 40:14 Standing

Standing to apply for a remedy under s. 24(1) is granted to "anyone"[1] whose Charter rights "have been infringed or denied". This imposes stricter requirements of standing than are applicable to many remedies under the general law.[2]

Section 24(1) contemplates that it is the applicant's own rights that have been infringed or denied. For example, it has been held that an accused could not complain about an unreasonable search of his girlfriend's apartment, even though the search yielded evidence (a cache of drugs) that was relied upon by the Crown as part of its case against the accused. Since the accused had no reasonable expectation of privacy in someone else's apartment, the search was not a breach of the accused's s. 8 right

[7] *Schachter v. Can.*, [1992] 2 S.C.R. 679, 720 per Lamer C.J. for majority ("An individual remedy under s. 24(1) will rarely be available in conjunction with an action under s. 52 . . ."); *R. v. Ferguson*, [2008] 1 S.C.R. 96, para. 63 per McLachlin C.J. for the Court (s. 24(1) remedy is available "in connection with a s. 52(1) declaration of invalidity in unusual cases where additional s. 24(1) relief if necessary to provide the claimant with an effective remedy").

[8] *R. v. Demers*, [2004] 2 S.C.R. 489. Iacobucci and Bastarache JJ. wrote the opinion of the eight-judge majority. LeBel J. wrote a concurring opinion. On the remedial issue, he disagreed with the majority that the s. 24(1) remedy should be postponed for a year; he would have granted to the claimant an immediate stay of proceedings: § 40:15, "Apprehended infringements".

[9] Chapter 47, Fundamental Justice, under heading § 47:24, "Overbroad laws".

[10] § 40:4, "Temporary validity".

[11] A new law was enacted within one year. S.C. 2005, c. 22, s. 33, adds a new section to the Criminal Code (s. 672.851), which authorizes a court to order a stay of proceedings if the court is satisfied that the accused is not likely ever to become fit to stand trial and does not pose a significant threat to the public.

[Section 40:14]

[1] The meaning of "anyone" is examined in ch. 37, Application of Charter, under heading §§ 37:1 to 37:5, "Benefit of rights".

[2] Standing under the general law is examined in ch. 59, Procedure, under heading §§ 59:2 to 59:6, "Standing".

to be secure against unreasonable search or seizure. Only the tenant of the apartment could pursue a remedy under s. 24.[3]

A corporation cannot obtain a remedy under s. 24(1) for a denial of freedom of religion, because a corporation cannot hold a religious belief.[4] But, in *R. v. Big M Drug Mart* (1985),[5] the Supreme Court of Canada held that a corporation could defend a criminal charge under a Sunday closing law on the ground that the law was a denial of the freedom of religion of individuals. The Court held that a defendant to a criminal charge was at liberty to raise any constitutional defect in the law under which the charge is laid, because "no one can be convicted of an offence under an unconstitutional law".[6] The fact that the corporation had no standing under s. 24(1) to challenge the law was irrelevant. The challenge was based on the supremacy clause of s. 52(1): "Where, as here, the challenge is based on the unconstitutionality of legislation, recourse to s. 24 is unnecessary and the particular effect on the challenged party is irrelevant".[7]

In *R. v. Big M Drug Mart*, the corporation was allowed to invoke a right that did not extend to corporations in order to escape criminal liability under a statute that purported to apply to it. Sometimes a person, motivated by public interest, wishes to make a Charter challenge to a statute that does not even apply to the challenger. This cannot be done under s. 24(1). However, in *Minister of Justice v. Borowski* (1981),[8] the Supreme Court of Canada granted standing to an anti-abortion activist to bring an action for a declaration that the Criminal Code's abortion provisions were unconstitutional. Those provisions could never actually be applied to the applicant, who was neither a doctor nor a woman, but he was granted standing nevertheless. This illustrates that the availability of a declaration of invalidity under s. 52(1) is governed by more generous standing requirements than are the remedies authorized by s. 24(1).[9]

---

[3] *R. v. Edwards*, [1996] 1 S.C.R. 128; folld. in *R. v. Belnavis*, [1997] 3 S.C.R. 341 (passenger in someone else's car).

[4] However, the cases leave open whether s. 2(a) applies to religious, non-profit corporations: see ch. 37, Application of Charter, under heading § 37:2, "Everyone, anyone, any person".

[5] *R. v. Big M Drug Mart*, [1985] 1 S.C.R. 295.

[6] *R. v. Big M Drug Mart*, [1985] 1 S.C.R. 295, 313.

[7] *R. v. Big M Drug Mart*, [1985] 1 S.C.R. 295, 313. Accord, *R. v. Morgentaler*, [1988] 1 S.C.R. 30 (male doctor acquitted of performing an illegal abortion on ground that women's Charter right to liberty or security of the person infringed by law); *R. v. Wholesale Travel Group*, [1991] 3 S.C.R. 154 (corporation successfully attacked part of law under which it was charged on ground that it infringed liberty of individual); *Can. Egg Marketing Agency v. Richardson*, [1998] 3 S.C.R. 157 (corporate defendant in civil suit by government allowed standing to invoke mobility rights of individual).

[8] *Minister of Justice v. Borowski*, [1981] 2 S.C.R. 575.

[9] See also *R. v. Ferguson*, [2008] 1 S.C.R. 96, para. 61 per McLachlin C.J. for the Court (distinguishing between the remedy under s. 52(1) and that under s. 24(1)).

§ 40:15 Apprehended infringements

Section 24(1) stipulates that the applicant's rights "have been" infringed or denied, which contemplates that the infringement has occurred at the time of the application. It does not authorize an application in respect of a merely apprehended future infringement. For example, no one could bring a s. 24(1) application after nothing more than an announcement of a new police interrogation procedure, even if the announced procedure was going to infringe the Charter. However, it seems to be generally accepted that the imminent threat of a Charter violation will satisfy s. 24(1).[1] For example, s. 24(1) will authorize a remedy for English-speaking parents who are denied by statute their Charter right under s. 23 to send their children to an English-speaking school, even if the application is made before the school year has started, and therefore before any parent's child has actually been refused admission.[2] It is not clear whether s. 24(1) will extend as far as the general remedies of declaration and injunction, which are both available in respect of threatened violations of rights.[3]

In *R. v. Demers* (2004),[4] the Supreme Court of Canada awarded a s. 24(1) remedy for an infringement that it feared might occur in the future. The Court had issued a suspended declaration of invalidity that gave Parliament one year to replace the provisions in the Criminal Code dealing with accused persons who had been charged with an offence, but who had been found unfit to stand trial. The existing provisions, the Court held, were unconstitutional for overbreadth under s. 7 of the Charter. However, the majority of the Court added a second remedy to the suspended declaration of invalidity.[5] Acting under s. 24(1), the majority ordered that, in the event that Parliament did not act within the one-year period, those persons who were permanently unfit to stand trial and who had been found not to be a danger to the public should receive a stay of proceedings. LeBel J., who wrote a concurring opinion, disagreed with this remedy. He was concerned that the majority's prospective remedy provided no immediate relief to the claimant (an accused person permanently unfit to stand trial) whose liberty had been restricted by an unconstitutional law. The majority's order left him in this condition for another year (or until a corrective law was enacted).

[Section 40:15]

[1] E.g., Gibson, The Law of the Charter: General Principles (1986), 195-198; Cromwell, Locus Standi (1986), 99-100.

[2] *Que. Assn. of Protestant School Bds. v. A.-G. Que.* (1982), 140 D.L.R. (3d) 33 (Que. S.C.). This decision was affirmed by the Quebec Court of Appeal ((1983) 1 D.L.R. (4th) 573) and by the Supreme Court of Canada ([1984] 2 S.C.R. 66), although neither appellate court commented on the remedial issue. Accord, *New Brunswick v. G.(J.)*, [1999] 3 S.C.R. 46, paras. 50-51 (ordering provision of state-funded counsel for custody hearing in order to remedy prospective breach of s. 7).

[3] S.A. de Smith, Lord Woolf and J. Jowell, Judicial Review of Administrative Action (Sweet & Maxwell, London, 5th ed., 1995), 637-648.

[4] *R. v. Demers*, [2004] 2 S.C.R. 489.

[5] The second remedy is discussed in § 40:13, "Non-exclusive remedy".

LeBel J. would have ordered an immediate stay of proceedings for those accused persons who were permanently unfit to stand trial and whose release into the community would not create a risk of danger.

§ 40:16 Court of competent jurisdiction

Section 24(1)'s remedies may be granted only by a "court of competent jurisdiction". We have already noticed the important point that the power to make a finding of invalidity on Charter grounds under the supremacy clause of s. 52(1) is not restricted to a court of competent jurisdiction, but is possessed by any court or tribunal (with power to decide questions of law) before which the validity of the law is brought into contention.[1] The meaning of the phrase "court of competent jurisdiction" is thus relevant only to the availability of a remedy under s. 24(1).

A superior court, which is a court of general jurisdiction, is always a court of competent jurisdiction.[2] Moreover, the power of a superior court to grant a remedy under s. 24(1) cannot be limited by statute.[3] (As will be explained, inferior courts and administrative tribunals have been held to be bound by statutory restrictions on their remedial powers.) Therefore, an application for a remedy under s. 24(1) can always be made to a superior court. This does not mean that the application will always be successful if a Charter violation is established, because the award of a remedy under s. 24(1) is discretionary. If, for example, the applicant interrupted a trial in an inferior court in order to bring a s. 24(1) application before a superior court, the superior court should normally refuse the application on the ground that the trial court is the most convenient forum to hear the s. 24(1) application.[4]

A trial court, even if it is not a superior court, is a court of competent jurisdiction to hear an application for a remedy that relates to the conduct of the trial, for example, the exclusion of evidence that has been obtained in violation of the Charter or a stay of proceedings that have gone on for an unreasonable time or an award of costs against the Crown for failure to make timely disclosure to the defence.[5] It is not necessary to make a separate application to a superior court, although a superior court would also be a court of competent jurisdiction. If a separate application were made to a superior court, the superior court should generally decline to grant any remedy, because it is the trial judge who is in the best position to assess what is the remedy that is just and

---

[Section 40:16]

[1]§§ 40:1 to 40:10, "Supremacy clause".

[2]*R. v. Rahey*, [1987] 1 S.C.R. 588; *R. v. Smith*, [1989] 2 S.C.R. 1120.

[3]*Doucet-Boudreau v. Nova Scotia*, [2003] 3 S.C.R. 3, paras. 51, 105, and note explicit contrast (para. 49) with the situation of inferior courts and administrative tribunals.

[4]*R. v. Smith*, [1989] 2 S.C.R. 1120, 1129.

[5]*R. v. 974649*, [2001] 3 S.C.R. 575 (provincial offences court, during trial, awarded costs against the Crown for late disclosure in breach of Charter).

appropriate.[6] However, a defendant to a criminal charge who has not been given a trial date, and is not likely to get one for a long time, has no trial court within reach, and therefore may apply to a superior court to stay the proceedings on the ground of unreasonable delay.[7] Even after the trial has commenced, an application to a superior court may be appropriate if it is the action of the trial judge that is the subject of the complaint; for example, when the trial judge has failed to render a decision on a motion for a directed verdict.[8]

The Supreme Court of Canada has held that a judge conducting a preliminary inquiry into a criminal charge is not a court of competent jurisdiction.[9] This means that a preliminary inquiry judge has no power to stay proceedings on the ground of unreasonable delay under s. 11(b), and no power to exclude evidence on the ground that the evidence was obtained in breach of the Charter. This is a rather surprising result when one considers that the preliminary inquiry judge would have to rule on non-Charter grounds on the validity of the charge and the admissibility of the evidence adduced.[10] In the case where the defendant claims that the trial of a criminal charge has been unreasonably delayed because too much time has elapsed even before the preliminary inquiry has been held, the defendant can make a separate application to a superior court to stay the proceedings.[11] But, in the normal course of events, Charter applications have to await the trial.

Can an *administrative tribunal* be a court of competent jurisdiction? The Supreme Court of Canada answered yes to that question in 1995, holding that an administrative tribunal was a court of competent jurisdiction if its constituent statute gave it power over (1) the parties to the dispute, (2) the subject matter of the dispute, and (3) the Charter remedy that was sought.[12] In that case, an administrative tribunal had power to grant a remedy under s. 24 for breach of the Charter. The Court continued to apply this definition until 2010 when it noticed that it had been applying a somewhat different definition to identify those administrative tribunals that had the power to hold invalid those laws that were apparently applicable to the proceedings but which the tribunal found to be in breach of the Charter. On this latter issue, which was a remedy under s. 52 not s. 24, the Court had held that an

---

[6]*R. v. 974649*, [2001] 3 S.C.R. 575.

[7]*R. v. 974649*, [2001] 3 S.C.R. 575.

[8]*R. v. Rahey*, [1987] 1 S.C.R. 588.

[9]*R. v. Hynes*, [2001] 3 S.C.R. 623.

[10]Even more surprising is the holding in *R. v. Seaboyer*, [1991] 2 S.C.R. 577 that the preliminary inquiry judge has no power to determine Charter issues under s. 52(1): see text accompanying § 40:24 note 5, below.

[11]*R. v. Smith*, [1989] 2 S.C.R. 1120.

[12]*Weber v. Ont. Hydro*, [1995] 2 S.C.R. 929 (labour arbitrator had power to award declaration and damages for breach of Charter). See also *Mooring v. Can.*, [1996] 1 S.C.R. 75 (National Parole Board had no power to exclude evidence for breach of Charter); *R. v. 974649*, [2001] 3 S.C.R. 575 (provincial offences court had power to award costs for breach of Charter).

administrative tribunal with jurisdiction over the parties and subject matter could apply the Charter only if it had the power (express or implied) to decide questions of law (provided its constituent legislation did not exclude Charter issues from the tribunal's authority over questions of law).[13] There seemed to be no good reason why an administrative tribunal's authority over questions of law was necessary to empower the tribunal to grant a Charter remedy under s. 52, but was not necessary to empower the tribunal to grant a Charter remedy under s. 24.

In *R. v. Conway* (2010),[14] the Supreme Court decided to merge the two lines of remedial cases by holding that an administrative tribunal *with authority to decide questions of law* was a court of competent jurisdiction for the purpose of s. 24 (unless Charter issues had been clearly withdrawn from the tribunal's jurisdiction). It was the authority to decide questions of law that qualified an administrative tribunal to decide constitutional questions, whether those questions arose under s. 24 or s. 52.[15] The applicant in *Conway* had in 1984 been charged with a crime and found not guilty by reason of insanity (in modern parlance not criminally responsible by reason of mental disorder—an NCR patient). The Criminal Code required that he be incarcerated in mental health facilities subject to regular reviews of his case by the Ontario Review Board, which was an administrative tribunal established by the Criminal Code for the province of Ontario with supervisory jurisdiction over NCR patients. The Board held an annual hearing for each patient. In 2006, in advance of his annual review by the Board, the applicant applied to the Board under s. 24 of the Charter for an absolute discharge from custody on the ground that his Charter rights had been infringed. The application was initially denied by the Board (and on appeal by the Ontario Court of Appeal), using the three-part test that prevailed before 2010: the Board was held not to be a court of competent jurisdiction because it lacked the power to grant the remedy sought. The Supreme Court, applying its new test, held that the Board was a court of competent jurisdiction because it was authorized by the Criminal Code to decide questions of law. However, as will be explained in the next paragraph, the Court agreed that the Board lacked the power to grant the remedy sought, and therefore dismissed the applicant's appeal.

Once it is determined that an administrative tribunal is a court of competent jurisdiction, the remaining question is whether the tribunal can grant the remedy sought. A literal reading of s. 24 would suggest that the tribunal should not be restricted to the remedies authorized by its constituent statute because a court of competent jurisdiction is empowered by s. 24 itself to grant "such remedy as the court considers appropriate and just in the circumstances". However, there is much to be said for the proposition that an administrative tribunal (or even an inferior court) should be confined to its normal range of remedies, so

---

[13]§§ 40:26 to 40:29, "Administrative tribunals".

[14]*R. v. Conway*, [2010] 1 S.C.R. 765. Abella J. wrote the opinion of the Court.

[15]*R. v. Conway*, [2010] 1 S.C.R. 765, paras. 80-81.

that a Charter claim does not move it beyond its statutory mandate, which alone is the sphere of its undoubted competence.[16] This was the position taken in *Conway*, where the Court, following previous authority,[17] held that the tribunal was restricted by its constituent statute as to the remedies that could be granted under s. 24. The tribunal did not need to have explicit statutory authority over the precise remedy sought, but the tribunal was restricted to "the kind of remedy that the legislature intended would fit within the statutory framework of the particular tribunal".[18] In this case, the Criminal Code imposed some restrictions on the remedial powers of a Review Board. In particular, the Board was explicitly prohibited from granting an absolute discharge to an NCR patient who had been found by the Board to be "a significant threat to the safety of the public". The Board had found that the applicant was a significant threat to the safety of the public, and therefore the Board had no *statutory* power to grant an absolute discharge. The applicant argued that s. 24 freed the Board from statutory limits to its jurisdiction, but the Court disagreed. The withdrawal of the power to grant an absolute discharge to an NCR patient who was dangerous was consistent with the Board's mandates to protect public safety and to adequately prepare NCR patients for their reintegration into society. For the Board to grant such a remedy under s. 24 "would be a clear contradiction of Parliament's intent". The application for an absolute discharge had to be denied.

§ 40:17 Range of remedies

The argument made in the previous section was that the phrase "court of competent jurisdiction" did not limit the range of remedies available under s. 24(1). Section 24(1) does limit the range of remedies by the phrase "such remedy as the court considers appropriate and just in the circumstances". While this phrase confers a discretion on the court, the cases are slowly developing principles that will structure and limit the discretion. For example, the courts have usually insisted that existing procedures be employed for s. 24(1) applications, so that well-understood procedural values are not ignored simply because a constitutional point

---

[16]So held in the case of an inferior court in *R. v. 974649*, [2001] 3 S.C.R. 575, paras. 26, 43 (enabling legislation granted provincial offences court only narrow power to award costs; held, legislation should be interpreted as conferring by implication the power to award costs for Charter breaches). The power of a *superior* court to grant a s. 24 remedy cannot be limited by statute: *Doucet-Boudreau v. Nova Scotia*, [2003] 3 S.C.R. 3, paras. 51, 105.

[17]*Weber v. Ont. Hydro*, [1995] 2 S.C.R. 929 (labour arbitrator had power to award declaration and damages for breach of Charter). See also *Mooring v. Can.*, [1996] 1 S.C.R. 75 (National Parole Board had no power to exclude evidence for breach of Charter); *R. v. 974649*, [2001] 3 S.C.R. 575 (provincial offences court had power to award costs for breach of Charter).

[18]*R. v. Conway*, [2010] 1 S.C.R. 765, para. 82.

is in issue.[1] This is why applications respecting the conduct of a trial should normally be made to the trial judge, who is in the best position to determine whether a trial should be delayed or interrupted.[2] For the same reason, the courts have generally refused to countenance the creation of new procedural mechanisms, such as the pre-trial motion to suppress evidence, despite its common use in the United States.[3] This kind of procedural caution would obviously bar the award of damages or other civil remedies in a criminal trial, where the person against whom the remedy is sought was not represented by counsel and has not received the normal civil safeguards of pleadings, discovery and the like, which ensure a proper trial of the issue of civil liability.[4]

Subject to the important qualification that a remedy must be appropriate and just in all the circumstances of the case, there is no limit to the remedies that may be ordered under s. 24(1).[5] They include "defensive" remedies,[6] where the court nullifies or stops some law or act, for example, by dismissing a charge, staying a proceeding,[7] quashing a search warrant or a committal or a conviction, enjoining an act, or declaring a law to be invalid.[8] The exclusion of evidence obtained in breach of the Charter also falls into the defensive category, but the exclusion of evidence is subject to a special set of rules under s. 24(2), and it is discussed in the next chapter.[9] The remedies available under s. 24(1) also include "affirmative" remedies, such as ordering a province to provide state-funded counsel to an indigent litigant,[10] ordering the return of goods improperly seized[11] or a mandatory injunction requiring positive action.[12]

[Section 40:17]

[1]See Gibson, The Law of the Charter: General Principles (1986), 284-286.

[2]*R. v. Smith*, [1989] 2 S.C.R. 1120, 1129.

[3]*Re Blackwoods Beverages* (1984), 15 D.L.R. (4th) 231 (Man. C.A.).

[4]*Mills v. The Queen*, [1986] 1 S.C.R. 863, 971 per La Forest J., obiter. Compare *R. v. Zelensky*, [1978] 2 S.C.R. 940 (upholding validity of Criminal Code provision providing for compensation to victim, but suggesting circumstances in which compensation award should not be made).

[5]The numerous cases in which remedies have been awarded by courts are collected in the two loose-leaf services cited in § 40:1 note 1.

[6]The distinction between defensive and affirmative constitutional remedies is made by A. Hill, "Constitutional Remedies" (1969) 69 Columb. L. Rev. 1109 and W.E. Dellinger, "Of Rights and Remedies: the Constitution as a Sword" (1972) 85 Harv. L. Rev. 1532.

[7]E.g., *R. v. Bellusci*, [2012] 2 S.C.R. 509 (upholding stay of proceedings against accused who had been assaulted by prison guard while in custody of guard); *R. v. Singh* (2013), 118 O.R. (3d) 253 (C.A.) (ordering stay of proceedings against accused who had been beaten by police officers during interrogation).

[8]Note that defensive remedies will often be available under s. 52(1) (the supremacy clause), and no recourse to s. 24(1) will be necessary: §§ 40:1 to 40:10, "Supremacy clause".

[9]Chapter 41, Exclusion of Evidence.

[10]*New Brunswick v. G.(J.)*, [1999] 3 S.C.R. 46.

[11]E.g., *Re Chapman* (1984), 46 O.R. (2d) 65 (C.A.); *Lagiorgia v. Can.*, [1987] 3 F.C. 28 (C.A.).

In one case,[13] the court contemplated ordering a provincial Legislature to enact legislation to make provision for absentee voting, but the court contented itself with issuing a declaration that the absence of any provision for absentee voting was a breach of s. 3 of the Charter.

Selecting from the broad range of remedies which are possible under s. 24(1) of the Charter presents the courts with a difficult and value-laden task. As L'Heureux-Dubé J. has eloquently stated:[14]

> It is important to recognize that the *Charter* has now put into judges' hands a scalpel instead of an axe: a tool that may fashion, more carefully than ever, solutions taking into account the sometimes complementary and sometimes opposing concerns of fairness to the individual, societal interests, and the integrity of the judicial system.

It has been suggested that the court's discretion should be governed by three factors: (1) the redress of the wrong suffered by the applicant; (2) the encouragement of future compliance with the Constitution; and (3) the avoidance of unnecessary interference with the exercise of governmental power.[15] To these might be added: (4) the ability of the court to administer the remedy awarded. But, as L'Heureux-Dubé J. has emphasized, each case will also present its own unique set of considerations. The trial judge is normally in the best position to weigh the relevant considerations and select the appropriate and just remedy, and the decision of the trial judge is accordingly entitled to deference from an appellate court, even if the appellate court would have selected a different remedy. The decision at first instance should be disturbed on appeal "only if the trial judge misdirects himself or if his decision is so clearly wrong as to amount to an injustice".[16]

§ 40:18 Declaration

The declaration is a remedy that declares the legal position, but does not actually order the defendant to do anything. However, a simple declaration that the government is in default of its Charter duties would almost invariably be obeyed, and would therefore usually be an effective

---

[12]See R.J. Sharpe, "Injunctions and the Charter" (1984) 22 Osgoode Hall L.J. 473. As the author explains, in the United States, despite the absence of any equivalent of s. 24, it has been held that the "civil rights injunction" is available to enforce the Bill of Rights.

[13]*Re Hoogbruin* (1985), 24 D.L.R. (4th) 718 (B.C.C.A.).

[14]*R. v. O'Connor*, [1995] 4 S.C.R. 411, para. 69.

[15]M.L. Pilkington, "Damages as a Remedy for Infringement of the Canadian Charter of Rights and Freedoms" (1984) 62 Can. Bar Rev. 517.

[16]*R. v. Regan*, [2002] 1 S.C.R. 297, para. 117 (but still reversing the trial judge's remedy of a stay of proceedings on the ground that he made palpable and overriding errors of fact and misdirected himself on the law); *R. v. Bellusci*, [2012] 2 S.C.R. 509, 2012 SCC 44, para.17 (upholding trial judge's remedy of a stay of proceedings); *R. v. Singh* (2013), 118 O.R. (3d) 253 (C.A.) (reversing trial judge's denial of a stay of proceedings on the ground that it was "so clearly wrong as to amount to an injustice").

remedy.[1] The declaration is especially appropriate if the court is not sure what would be the appropriate remedial action by government, and is content to leave that choice to the government—informed, obviously, by the court's reasons for holding that the government is in breach of the Charter. In *Canada v. Khadr* (2010),[2] a Canadian citizen, who was being held for trial by the United States at a military base in Cuba, applied to the Federal Court for an order that Canada request the United States to return him to Canada. The accused was alleged to have killed an American soldier in Afghanistan, and the evidence against him included the record of interviews by Canadian officials. The Supreme Court of Canada held that the Canadian officials had acted in breach of the Charter, and that the breach contributed to the accused's ongoing detention by the United States. But the Court refused to order Canada to request the return of the accused to Canada. The Court recognized that the making of representations to foreign governments was a complex matter upon which the courts should generally defer to the executive branch. The Court granted only a declaration that the accused's Charter rights had been infringed, thereby leaving to the government "a measure of discretion in deciding how best to respond."[3]

§ 40:19 Damages

The award of damages is sometimes an appropriate and just remedy for a breach of the Charter.[1] This was the case in *Vancouver v. Ward*

[Section 40:18]

[1]E.g., *Re Hoogbruin* (1985), 24 D.L.R. (4th) 718 (B.C.C.A.); *Re Gamble*, [1988] 2 S.C.R. 595 (declaration that prisoner held in violation of s. 7 was eligible for parole); *Vancouver v. Ward*, [2010] 2 S.C.R. 28, paras. 74-78 (declaration that car seized in violation of s. 8; no actual harm done to owner).

[2]*Canada v. Khadr*, [2010] 1 S.C.R. 44. The opinion is by "the Court". The case is a sequel to *Can. v. Khadr*, [2008] 2 S.C.R. 125; discussed in ch. 37, Application of Charter, under heading § 37:14, "Extraterritorial application".

[3]*Canada v. Khadr*, [2010] 1 S.C.R. 44, para. 2, and see also paras. 33-39 (reasons), 48 (text of declaration). After the decision, Canada sent a diplomatic note to the United States requesting that the U.S. not use any of the information provided by Canadian officials in the prosecution of the accused. The U.S. responded with a diplomatic note that did not give a direct answer to the request, but which assured Canada that evidence obtained through torture or other improper means would not be admissible in military commission proceedings: *Can. v. Khadr* (2010), 321 D.L.R. (4th) 448 (F.C.A.), paras. 7, 8 (sequel proceedings). In 2010, Khadr agreed to a plea agreement with the U.S., in which he pled guilty to all five charges against him in the U.S. in exchange for an eight-year sentence and the possibility of a transfer to Canada after one year and parole after three years. In 2012, Khadr was transferred to Canada to serve the rest of his sentence. He was released on bail in 2015, pending an appeal of his conviction in the U.S. In 2017, the Canadian government reached a $10.5 million settlement with Khadr as compensation for its handling of his case. Khadr's sentence was declared complete in 2019.

[Section 40:19]

[1]M.L. Pilkington, "Damages as a Remedy for Infringement of the Canadian Charter of Rights and Freedoms" (1984) 62 Can. Bar Rev. 517; K. Cooper-Stephenson, "Tort Theory for the Charter Damages Remedy" (1988) 52 Sask. L. Rev. 1; Cooper-Stephenson,

(2010),[2] where the plaintiff, a Vancouver lawyer, was mistakenly identified by the police as a person who was planning to throw a pie at the Prime Minister, who was attending a public ceremony in Vancouver. The city police confronted the plaintiff and handcuffed him, and when he protested and created a scene they arrested him for a breach of the peace and took him to a police lock-up, where provincial corrections officers took charge of him. They strip-searched him and held him in a cell for more than four hours before releasing him without laying any charges. During this time the police also seized his car, but realized that they did not have enough evidence to obtain a warrant to search it, and returned it to him when he was released. The plaintiff sued, and at trial was awarded damages under s. 24(1) of $5,000 from the province for the strip search in breach of s. 8 (unreasonable search or seizure) and of $100 from the city for the seizure of the car (another breach of s. 8). (He was also awarded damages of $5,000 from the city for the tort of wrongful imprisonment.) The awards of Charter damages (but not the tort damages) were appealed on up to the Supreme Court of Canada, which agreed that the plaintiff's rights under s. 8 had been infringed, and upheld the award of damages for the strip search, but held that a declaration was a sufficient remedy for the seizure of the car.

McLachlin C.J., who wrote for the Court in *Ward*, held that damages was an appropriate and just remedy for a breach of the Charter when they served a useful function. That function was threefold: not only (1) to compensate the plaintiff for his loss, but also (2) to vindicate Charter rights and (3) to deter future Charter breaches.[3] Because vindication and deterrence pursued societal goals, Charter damages under s. 24(1) would not necessarily be the same as common-law damages (which are purely compensatory).[4] Even where no personal loss was suffered, a damages award might be appropriate and just under s. 24(1). For example, in an earlier case, an arrest of a soldier by military police in violation of s. 9 (arbitrary detention or imprisonment) attracted a damages award of $5,000, although the claimant had not suffered any harm that would be compensable by common law damages.[5] In another case, the action of police officers in removing a sick man from his car to at-

---

Charter Damages Claims (1990); Hogg and Monahan, Liability of the Crown (3rd ed., 2000), sec. 6.5(d); G.S. Gildin, "Allocating Damages Caused by Violation of the Charter: The Relevance of American Constitutional Remedies Jurisprudence" (2009) 24 Nat. J. Con. Law 121; K. Roach, "A Promising Late Spring for Charter Damages: Ward v. Vancouver" (2011) 29 Nat. J. Con. Law 135.

[2] *Vancouver v. Ward*, [2010] 2 S.C.R. 28. McLachlin C.J. wrote the opinion of the Court.

[3] *Vancouver v. Ward*, [2010] 2 S.C.R. 28, para. 25.

[4] McLachlin C.J. did not allude to the possibility of punitive damages, which are available at common law to punish a defendant where a tort (or breach of contract or other cause of action) consists of "misconduct that represents a marked departure from ordinary standards of decent behaviour", and where purely compensatory damages would not be a sufficient punishment for the misconduct: *Whiten v. Pilot Insurance Co.*, [2002] 1 S.C.R. 595, para. 36.

[5] *Du-Lude v. Can.* (2000), 192 D.L.R. (4th) 714 (F.C.A.).

tend court in breach of s. 7 (security of the person) attracted a damages award of $5,000, despite the absence of any harm to the claimant.[6] In the *Ward* case itself, the Court upheld the trial judge's award of $5,000 damages for the strip search on the ground that his humiliating experience should receive some compensation, and that the functions of vindication and deterrence also justified some damages. However, the Court showed no sympathy for merely symbolic awards of damages, and reversed the trial judge's award of $100 for the seizure of the plaintiff's car: this caused the plaintiff no harm, the car was not searched, and, although the seizure was a breach of s. 8, it was not a serious one. For that breach, the remedy of a declaration, which was sufficient to fulfil the functions of vindication and deterrence, was all that should be granted.[7]

McLachlin C.J., in her review of s. 24(1) damages, explained that, even when damages are "functionally required" to fulfil one or more of the objects of compensation, vindication or deterrence, there could be countervailing considerations that would render an award of damages inappropriate and unjust. She offered two examples, while warning that this was not a complete catalogue. One countervailing consideration was the availability of alternative remedies. "The Charter entered an existent remedial arena which already housed tools to correct violative state conduct."[8] This was illustrated by the denial of damages for the seizure of the plaintiff's car: the alternative remedy of the declaration was available and was sufficient. Moreover, if private actions in tort would adequately address the Charter breach, then Charter damages would be duplicative and should not be awarded. The Chief Justice said that a tort claim could be joined with a Charter claim, and it would be "useful" for the court to consider the tort claim first in case it rendered recourse to s. 24(1) unnecessary; but it was not "essential" to exhaust the tort remedies first.[9] In this case, the plaintiff's tort action for wrongful imprisonment was successful and yielded damages of $5,000 for his detention in the police lock-up; on appeal, he did not pursue any additional Charter damages for the detention. No tort damages were awarded for the strip search or the seizure of the car, and so no issue of duplicative remedies arose for those causes of action.

A second consideration that could negate the appropriateness of Charter damages is "concern for effective governance".[10] Of course, Charter damages would usually promote good governance, since they should deter Charter breaches by government. However, what the Chief Justice had in mind was the line of cases (in particular, *Mackin v. New Brunswick* (2002)) holding that, "absent conduct that is clearly wrong, in bad faith, or an abuse of power", no damages are available "for the harm

[6]*Hawley v. Bapoo* (2005), 76 O.R. (3d) 649 (Ont. S.C.J.).

[7]*Canada v. Khadr*, [2010] 1 S.C.R. 44, paras. 74-78.

[8]*Canada v. Khadr*, [2010] 1 S.C.R. 44, para. 34.

[9]*Canada v. Khadr*, [2010] 1 S.C.R. 44, para. 59.

[10]*Canada v. Khadr*, [2010] 1 S.C.R. 44, paras. 38-43.

suffered as the result of the mere enactment or application of a law that is subsequently held to be unconstitutional."[11] According to McLachlin C.J. in *Ward*, this doctrine is exemplary of the principle of good governance, because damages awards would "chill the exercise of policy-making discretion" and deter public officials from carrying out their duties under apparently valid statutes.[12] She did not mention the indeterminate extent of Crown liability that would be opened up if damages claims could be brought by all who had suffered harm as the result of the enactment and implementation of a statute that was subsequently held to be unconstitutional. Perhaps that is an issue of good governance as well. In *Ward* itself, however, the good governance immunity was not relevant: the public officials had not been acting on the faith of statutes subsequently held to be unconstitutional.

Ward establishes that there is a four-stage approach that is to be followed in determining whether damages is an appropriate and just remedy for a breach of the Charter. At the first stage, the question is whether a Charter right or freedom has been breached. At the second stage, the question is whether "damages are a just and appropriate remedy" for the Charter breach, which involves considering whether an award of damages would serve "one or more of the related functions of compensation, vindication of the right, and/or deterrence of future breaches".[13] At the third stage, the government has the opportunity to raise countervailing considerations—like the availability of an alternative remedy or good governance concerns – that show why an award of damages would nonetheless not be a just or appropriate remedy for the Charter breach. At the fourth and final stage, it is necessary to determine the amount of damages that should be awarded.

The Supreme Court of Canada clarified the scope of the immunity from damages affirmed in *Ward* (which drew, as noted, on *Mackin* and other cases) in *Conseil scolaire francophone de la Colombie-Britannique v. British Columbia* (2020).[14] In this case, various decisions made in accordance with policies of the British Columbia government about the province's French-language education system were found to have breached the right to minority language education under s. 23 of the *Charter*. The trial judge had awarded damages of $6 million to the Conseil scolaire francophone de la Colombie-Britannique, the province's

[11]*Mackin v. N.B.*, [2002] 1 S.C.R. 405, para. 78 (refusing damages for enactment of legislation in breach of Charter right to judicial independence), following the pre-Charter cases of *Wellbridge Holdings v. Greater Winnipeg*, [1971] S.C.R. 957 and *Central Canada Potash v. Govt. of Sask.*, [1979] 1 S.C.R. 42 as well as the Charter case of *Guimond v. Que.* [1996] 3 S.C.R. 347.

[12]*Vancouver v. Ward*, [2010] 2 S.C.R. 28, 2010 SCC 27, paras. 40-41.

[13]*Vancouver v. Ward*, [2010] 2 S.C.R. 28, para. 4.

[14]*Conseil scolaire francophone de la Colombie-Britannique v. British Columbia*, 2020 SCC 13. Wagner C.J. wrote the opinion for the majority of the Court, which was joined by Abella, Moldaver, Karakatsanis, Côté, Martin and Kasirer JJ. Brown and Rowe JJ. wrote a joint opinion dissenting in part. The decision is discussed elsewhere in this book; the most detailed discussion is in ch. 56, Language, under heading § 56:23, "Where numbers warrant".

French-language school board, as a remedy for a deficit it incurred due to one of these s. 23 infringements. The British Columbia Court of Appeal had reversed this aspect of the trial judge's decision, citing *Ward* and *Mackin* for the proposition that the immunity from damages for decisions made in accordance with a law that is later declared unconstitutional includes decisions made in accordance with "government policies" later found to be unconstitutional. The Supreme Court restored the trial judge's damages award, and also awarded the Conseil scolaire an additional $1.1 million in damages for another infringement of s. 23 that the trial judge had improperly held to be justified under s. 1. Wagner C.J., writing for the majority of the Court, held that the immunity from damages recognized in *Ward* and *Mackin* does not extend beyond decisions made in accordance with subsequently-invalidated legislation to decisions made in accordance with subsequently-invalidated government policies.[15] He said that, unlike a law, the concept of a "government policy" lacks a precise definition and could be said to include "any form of directives or guidelines issued by the government".[16] In addition, if the immunity from damages was extended to decisions stemming from government policies, a government would be able to "avoid liability for damages simply by showing that its unlawful actions are authorized by policies".[17] The Court's decision in *Conseil scolaire* makes it clear that the immunity from damages affirmed in *Ward* and *Mackin* does not extend to decisions that stem from "government policies that infringe fundamental rights".[18]

Henry v. British Columbia (2015)[19] was an action for damages against the Attorney General of British Columbia by a man who had been wrongfully imprisoned for 27 years. He had been convicted of a number of sexual offences in 1983, and had been sentenced to prison where he had remained until 2010, when the British Columbia Court of Appeal quashed all his convictions and substituted acquittals on the grounds that there had been serious errors in the conduct of his trial and that the guilty verdicts were unreasonable in light of the evidence as a whole. The plaintiff's action for damages was based on the allegation that the

[15]Wagner C.J. left open whether the immunity from damages is engaged where regulations or orders in council are involved: *Conseil scolaire francophone de la Colombie-Britannique v. British Columbia*, 2020 SCC 13, para. 178.

[16]*Conseil scolaire francophone de la Colombie-Britannique v. British Columbia*, 2020 SCC 13, para. 173.

[17]*Conseil scolaire francophone de la Colombie-Britannique v. British Columbia*, 2020 SCC 13, para. 172.

[18]*Conseil scolaire francophone de la Colombie-Britannique v. British Columbia*, 2020 SCC 13, para. 179. Brown and Rowe JJ., dissenting in part, disagreed with Wagner C.J. that the immunity from damages does not extend to decisions that stem from subsequently-invalidated government policies. However, they agreed with him that damages were appropriate in this case, because the immunity should, they said, not apply to s. 23 breaches.

[19]*Henry v. British Columbia*, [2015] 2 S.C.R. 214, 2015 SCC 24. Moldaver J. wrote the opinion of the four-judge majority of the six-judge court. McLachlin C.J. and Karakatsanis J. wrote a separate opinion, concurring in the result but dissenting on the constitutional issue.

Crown prosecutors at his trial had committed a breach of the Charter by failing to disclose relevant information to him. The issue before the Supreme Court was whether *Ward*'s countervailing consideration of "concern for effective governance" required the action for damages to be limited by requiring the plaintiff to establish malice or some other element of fault when (as in this case) the claimed Charter breach was misconduct by Crown prosecutors. The province argued that, if it was too easy to claim damages for prosecutorial misconduct, Crown prosecutors would be fearful of personal liability when they should be giving priority to their duty to prosecute crime, and they would be distracted from their public duty by the need to defend a host of damages claims in court. The analogy was the tort of malicious prosecution, which is a damages claim against Crown prosecutors, but which (as the name implies) requires the plaintiff to establish malice (in this context an improper purpose) on the part of the defendant prosecutor. The Supreme Court was unanimous in holding that the malicious-prosecution analogy was not very strong. The tort of malicious prosecution is based on an exercise of *discretion* by an individual Crown prosecutor to initiate an improperly motivated prosecution. The Charter action under s. 24(1) is based on the breach of a Charter *duty* owed by the Crown to disclose relevant information to the defence. When the Charter duty is breached, it is the state and not the individual prosecutor that faces liability. The Court unanimously decided that it was not appropriate to burden the Charter claimant with a requirement of proving malice. However, Moldaver J., writing for the majority, held that effective-governance concerns did support a higher threshold of proof in a Charter action based on prosecutorial misconduct. He held that, in a Charter action for breach of the disclosure duty, the plaintiff should have to prove not merely the failure to disclose relevant information (the Charter breach), but also that the failure was "intentional" with knowledge on the part of the prosecutor that the information withheld from the defendant is "material to the defence and that the failure to disclose will likely impinge on the accused's ability to make full answer and defence".[20] McLachlin C.J. and Karakatsanis J., who dissented on this point, took the view that it was not appropriate to impose any additional requirement of fault where what the Charter claimant alleges is the breach of an absolute obligation: "Good governance is strengthened, not undermined, by holding the state to account where it fails to meet its Charter obligations."[21] In their view, the Charter claimant should only have to establish the breach of the duty of disclosure and that damages would be an "appropriate and just" remedy for the breach (as they clearly would be on the facts alleged in this case); there should be no need for the plaintiff to prove that the breach was intentional in order to succeed.[22] That however was the dissenting view.

[20] *Henry v. British Columbia*, [2015] 2 S.C.R. 214, 2015 SCC 24, para. 82.

[21] *Henry v. British Columbia*, [2015] 2 S.C.R. 214, 2015 SCC 24, para. 129.

[22] *Henry v. British Columbia*, [2015] 2 S.C.R. 214, 2015 SCC 24, para. 138.

Ernst v. Alberta Energy Regulator (2017)[23] was an action for Charter damages brought against the Alberta Energy Regulator (the Board), which was a statutory, independent, quasi-judicial body responsible for regulating the province's energy, resource and utility sectors. The plaintiff alleged that the Board, of which she was a public critic, had punished her for her criticisms by preventing her for a period of 16 months from speaking to officers of the Board. She sought Charter damages of $50,000 for this infringement of her freedom of expression. The new element to this case was that the Board was protected by an immunity clause in its constating statute that provided that "no action or proceeding may be brought against the Board. . .in respect of any act or thing done purportedly in pursuance of this Act. . .or a decision, order or direction of the Board". The Board applied to strike the plaintiff's claim based on the immunity clause, and this application proceeded on up to the Supreme Court of Canada, where it divided the Court. Cromwell J., who wrote the opinion of four judges, held that it was plain and obvious that the immunity clause barred the plaintiff's claim, even though the claim was for Charter damages. He reinforced this conclusion by deciding that Charter damages would not in any case be an appropriate and just remedy for two reasons. The first reason was that judicial review was an alternative remedy which would not be barred by an immunity clause[24] (although it would not yield damages). The second reason was that the good governance of the Board would be impaired by the distraction of defending or worrying about damages claims against the Board.[25] Abella J., who wrote a concurring opinion, agreed that the immunity clause barred the plaintiff's claim and agreed that it was "likely" that Charter damages were not an appropriate and just remedy[26] because judicial review was the appropriate remedy. Her substantial agreement with Cromwell J. yielded a five-judge majority in favour of striking the plaintiff's claim solely on the basis of the pleadings. McLachlin C.J., Moldaver and Brown JJ. (with whom Côté J. agreed) wrote a dissenting opinion. They denied that it was plain and obvious that the immunity clause barred proceedings to redress "punitive conduct" by the Board.[27] And they also denied that it was plain and obvious that Charter damages could in no circumstances be an appropriate and just remedy in a claim against the Board for punitive conduct. They noted that damages were not recoverable on judicial review, and an award of Charter damages could vindicate the plaintiff's right and deter future breaches. They held that "it would be premature to conclude, based on the pleadings alone, that judicial review would provide an ef-

[23]*Ernst v. Alberta Energy Regulator*, [2017] 1 S.C.R. 3, 2017 SCC 1. Cromwell J. wrote for four judges. Abella J. wrote a concurring opinion. McLachlin C.J., Moldaver and Brown JJ, with whom Côté J. agreed, wrote a dissenting opinion.

[24]*Ernst v. Alberta Energy Regulator*, [2017] 1 S.C.R. 3, 2017 SCC 1, para. 33, citing *Crevier v. Que.*, [1981] 2 S.C.R. 220.

[25]*Ernst v. Alberta Energy Regulator*, [2017] 1 S.C.R. 3, 2017 SCC 1, para. 47.

[26]*Ernst v. Alberta Energy Regulator*, [2017] 1 S.C.R. 3, 2017 SCC 1, para. 123.

[27]*Ernst v. Alberta Energy Regulator*, [2017] 1 S.C.R. 3, 2017 SCC 1, para. 180.

fective alternative remedy to Charter damages in this case, let alone *all* cases, against the Board."[28]

The action for Charter damages under s. 24(1) is commonly described (following American terminology) as a "constitutional tort". However, it is not literally a species of tort. In *Ward*, McLachlin C.J. described damages under s. 24(1) as "a unique public law remedy"; it was not "a private law action in the nature of a tort claim".[29] For one thing, the Charter action "lies against the state and not against individual actors". Since individual actors are not bound by the Charter, they are not liable for damages under s. 24(1), and the Crown is not liable vicariously for their Charter breaches. The Crown is liable directly (not vicariously) for breaches of the Charter. Any personal liability of individual actors such as police or corrections officers would have to be found in the private law of tort, and if so found the Crown would be vicariously liable for the tort, provided it was committed by an official in the course of employment. Another distinction between the public-law remedy under the Charter and the private-law remedy of tort is that the quantum of damages may differ. As explained above, in assessing Charter damages, vindication and deterrence must be taken into account, and these could justify a damages award where no loss cognizable by the common law had been suffered. Still these two differences are not so marked as to require the abandonment of the common phrase "constitutional tort"—since the adjective "constitutional" signals the existence of some distinctions from the private law of tort.

§ 40:20 Costs

The award of costs[1] is sometimes an appropriate and just remedy for those Charter breaches that cause inconvenience or delay to a litigant. Default in the Crown's Charter obligation to make pre-trial disclosure to a criminal defendant[2] has often been sanctioned by an award of costs against the Crown. A stay of proceedings would normally be too severe a sanction and a mere adjournment not severe enough. The Supreme Court of Canada has upheld an award of costs against the Crown for delay in making disclosure, although the Court warned that this remedy

---

[28]*Ernst v. Alberta Energy Regulator*, [2017] 1 S.C.R. 3, 2017 SCC 1, para. 167 (emphasis in original).

[29]*Ernst v. Alberta Energy Regulator*, [2017] 1 S.C.R. 3, 2017 SCC 1, paras. 22, 30, 31. Compare the restitutionary remedy against the Crown for unconstitutional taxes, which is not based on s. 24(1), because it is not based on a breach of the Charter. The Court has insisted that this is a special public-law remedy, although it is very similar to the private-law remedy for restitution based on unjust enrichment: *Kingstreet Investments v. N.B.*, [2007] 1 S.C.R. 3, para. 40; discussed in ch. 58, Effect of Unconstitutional Law, under heading § 58:8, "Unconstitutional taxes".

[Section 40:20]

[1]On costs in constitutional cases generally, see ch. 59, Procedure, under heading §§ 59:14 to 59:17, "Costs".

[2]Chapter 47, Fundamental Justice, under heading § 47:34, "Pre-trial disclosure by the Crown".

was appropriate and just only in exceptional cases: "costs awards will not flow from every failure to disclose in a timely fashion", but are restricted to "circumstances of a marked and unacceptable departure from the reasonable standards expected of the prosecution".[3]

§ 40:21 Exclusion of evidence

Evidence that has been obtained in breach of the Charter may be excluded as a remedy for the Charter breach, but this remedy is regulated by s. 24(2), which provides that the evidence shall only be excluded if its admission "would bring the administration of justice into disrepute". That has turned out to be the topic of much litigation, and so s. 24(2) is the topic of the next chapter, namely, 41, Exclusion of Evidence.

Evidence that has been obtained in compliance with the Charter is not covered by s. 24(2) (or by the next chapter of this book), and yet in some situations the exclusion of the evidence will be an appropriate and just remedy *under s. 24(1)*. In *R. v. White* (1999),[1] an accident report, which had been given to the police by the accused under the (valid) compulsion of a provincial law that required the reporting of all serious traffic accidents, was excluded from the accused's trial for leaving the scene of the accident. The exclusion was ordered under s. 24(1) on the ground that the admission of the accused's report would offend one of the principles of fundamental justice under s. 7, namely, the principle against self-incrimination.

In *R. v. Bjelland* (2009),[2] the question arose whether the exclusion of evidence was an appropriate and just remedy under s. 24(1) when the Charter breach was the late disclosure of the evidence by the Crown to the accused. It is a principle of fundamental justice under s. 7 that the Crown must, in advance of a criminal trial, make timely disclosure to the accused of all evidence in the possession of the Crown.[3] In *Bjelland*, a criminal trial for drug offences, the Crown, after making timely disclosure to the defence of what was thought to be most of the evidence, discovered and disclosed further evidence shortly before the date set for trial. The trial judge excluded the late-breaking evidence for breach of the Charter obligation of timely disclosure. The trial proceeded and the accused was acquitted. An appeal by the Crown went up to the Supreme Court of Canada, which ordered that the evidence be admitted and a

---

[3]*R. v. 974649*, [2001] 3 S.C.R. 575, para. 87 per McLachlin C.J. for the Court. For discussion, see K. Jull, "Costs, the Charter and Regulatory Offences: the Price of Fairness" (2002) 81 Can. Bar Rev. 646.

[Section 40:21]

[1]*R. v. White*, [1999] 2 S.C.R. 417; the case is more fully discussed in ch. 47, Fundamental Justice, under heading § 47:31, "Right to silence".

[2]*R. v. Bjelland*, [2009] 2 S.C.R. 651. Rothstein J. (with three others) wrote the opinion of the majority. Fish J. (with two others) wrote a dissenting opinion.

[3]*R. v. Stinchcombe*, [1991] 3 S.C.R. 326; discussed in ch. 47, Fundamental Justice, under heading § 47:34, "Pre-trial disclosure by the Crown".

new trial held. Rothstein J., who wrote for the majority, held that the trial judge had erred in excluding the evidence when the less drastic remedy of an adjournment was available as a remedy under s. 24(1).[4] Because the exclusion of relevant evidence impairs the truth-seeking function of a trial, the normal remedy for a Crown default in timely disclosure should be an adjournment of the trial to give the defence time to consider the new evidence. The exclusion of the new evidence should be ordered only in exceptional cases affecting the fairness of the trial or the integrity of the justice system.[5] Examples of exceptional cases would be where the postponement of the trial would lead to a breach of the accused's Charter right to be tried within a reasonable time, or where the accused was in pre-trial custody and the postponement of the trial would significantly prolong the custody. Another possible (but less clear) example would be where the Crown had abused the process by deliberately withholding the evidence from the accused. None of these exceptional circumstances was present in this case, and the prejudice to the accused would have been cured by the less drastic remedy of postponing the trial.

§ 40:22 Remedies outside s. 24(1)

It is not always necessary for a court to rely on s. 24(1) to remedy a Charter breach. In exercising a statutory discretion, for example, a court may properly be influenced by a relevant Charter breach. *In R. v. Nasogaluak* (2010),[1] the accused had pleaded guilty and been convicted of impaired driving and fleeing from the police, offences that would normally attract a sentence of imprisonment. Instead, the trial judge granted him a 12-month conditional discharge coupled with a 12-month driving prohibition. The police had used excessive force in making the arrest and in preventing flight, and they had inflicted injuries on the accused. The trial judge held that the police actions were a breach of the accused's s. 7 right to security of the person, and a reduced sentence was an appropriate and just remedy for the breach under s. 24(1). The Supreme Court of Canada agreed that there had been a breach of s. 7, and that it justified a reduction of the accused's sentence. However, the Court held that the trial judge had been wrong to rely on s. 24(1) as the justification for the reduced sentence. Sentence reduction was not an ap-

[4]As Fish J. pointed out in dissent, the most drastic remedy is a stay of proceedings, which would terminate the prosecution entirely. The accused actually applied for a stay of proceedings, and the trial judge made the "intermediate" order to exclude the evidence, which allowed the prosecution to continue, but without the late evidence. The least drastic remedy is an adjournment of the trial, which the majority holds is to be the normal remedy, although it causes a delay of the trial and provides only a weak incentive for Crown compliance with the duty of timely disclosure.

[5]Fish J., dissenting, disagreed with these "novel" restrictions on the discretion of the trial judge to exclude evidence under s. 24(1). In his view, the Supreme Court should have deferred to the trial judge's exercise of remedial discretion, which was to exclude the evidence.

[Section 40:22]

[1]*R. v. Nasogaluak*, [2010] 1 S.C.R. 206. LeBel J. wrote the opinion of the Court.

propriate remedy under s. 24(1), except in the exceptional case where it was the "sole effective remedy" for a Charter breach.[2] However, under normal sentencing principles, a Charter breach that related to the circumstances of the offence or the offender could properly be taken into account in sentencing. Even state misconduct that did not amount to a Charter breach could be taken into account in sentencing. In this case, the police breach of the accused's Charter rights was properly taken into account in fixing the accused's sentence without the need to invoke s. 24(1). The Court upheld the reduced sentence. The implication of this case, never clearly spelled out, is that s. 24(1) is a remedy of last resort, to be invoked only where a Charter breach cannot be remedied by the application of the general law. We noticed the same implication in the discussion of Charter damages, above: if a tort action would provide adequate redress for the harm suffered from the Charter breach, then no damages should be awarded under s. 24(1).[3]

§ 40:23 Supervision of court orders

In *Doucet-Boudreau v. Nova Scotia* (2003),[1] a superior-court judge in Nova Scotia, acting on the application of French-speaking parents, ordered the government of Nova Scotia to use its "best efforts" to build French-language schools in five districts of the province and to develop programs of instruction for the schools. The order was made under s. 24(1) of the Charter, and its purpose was to enforce the guarantee of minority language educational rights in s. 23 of the Charter. The judge's order was unusual in that it not only specified the dates by which each school should be built, but it provided that "the Court shall retain jurisdiction to hear reports from [the government] respecting the [government's] compliance with the order". Under this last provision, the judge presided over a series of "reporting hearings" throughout the period of construction of the schools. For each hearing, the judge required the government to file an affidavit as to its progress in building the schools and developing their curricula, he permitted affidavits in rebuttal to be filed, and he made provision for the cross-examination of all deponents. The Attorney General of Nova Scotia appealed only the part of the order that retained jurisdiction to hear reports of compliance. By the time the appeal reached the Supreme Court of Canada, the hearings were completed, the schools were all built, and the appeal was moot. However,

---

[2] *R. v. Nasogaluak*, [2010] 1 S.C.R. 206, paras. 6, 64. Both these paragraphs contemplate that a sentence reduction under s. 24(1) could even go "outside statutory limits", that is, reduce a mandatory minimum sentence. That was an obiter dictum in the circumstances of this case where no mandatory minimum was applicable. But see *R. v. Donnelly* (2016), 135 O.R. (3d) 336 (C.A.) (refusing to reduce sentence below statutory limit under s. 24(1)); *R. v. Gowdy* (2016), 135 O.R. (3d) 371 (C.A.) (same decision).

[3] § 40:19, "Damages".

[Section 40:23]

[1] *Doucet-Boudreau v. Nova Scotia*, [2003] 3 S.C.R. 3. Iacobucci and Arbour JJ. wrote the opinion for the five-judge majority. LeBel and Deschamps JJ. wrote the opinion for the four-judge dissenting minority.

the Court proceeded to decide the question anyway. The question was whether a judge could retain jurisdiction to supervise compliance with a remedial order under s. 24(1). The Court split five-four on the question, but the answer of the five-judge majority was yes.

Iacobucci and Arbour JJ., who wrote for the majority in *Doucet-Boudreau*, pointed out that the Charter was supposed to receive a large and liberal construction, and this applied to the remedial power of s. 24(1) no less than to the substantive rights. Section 24(1) authorized a court of competent jurisdiction to grant the remedy that is "appropriate and just in the circumstances". It was "difficult to imagine language which could give the court a wider and less fettered discretion".[2] Remedies under s. 24(1) could include "novel and creative features when compared with traditional and historical remedial practice".[3] In this case, the trial judge had been concerned about the progressive assimilation of the French-speaking minority in the province, and the delays in building French-language schools that had occurred in the past (before any court order had been issued). The judge was concerned that, without the reporting requirement, the order to build the schools would be "ineffective"[4] (meaning, of course, that the government might refuse to comply with the court order). Iacobucci and Arbour JJ. concluded that the trial judge's supervisory order was appropriate and just in the circumstances. LeBel and Deschamps JJ. wrote the dissenting opinion. In their view, once the order to build the schools was made, the judge had fully discharged his duty (functus officio), and it became the function of the executive to carry out the order. They pointed out that "Canada has maintained a tradition of compliance by governments and public servants with judicial interpretations of the law and court orders".[5] The court was entitled to assume compliance and should "resist the temptation to directly oversee and supervise the administration of their orders".[6] In the unlikely event that a government failed to comply with a s. 24(1) order, contempt proceedings would be available to the parents to enforce compliance.

In my opinion, the dissenting view in *Doucet-Boudreau* is the better one. A supervisory order should be a remedy of last resort, to be employed only against governments who have refused to carry out their constitutional responsibilities. The courts exhaust their expertise when they find the facts, apply the law to those facts, and order the defendant to rectify any wrong. After that, no legal issue remains, just the practical details of implementation, and that is a function of the executive. Moreover, the courts cannot easily be apprised of all the information and other considerations that are required to evaluate progress in the funding, planning and development of school curricula and school

---

[2] *Doucet-Boudreau v. Nova Scotia*, [2003] 3 S.C.R. 3, para. 52.

[3] *Doucet-Boudreau v. Nova Scotia*, [2003] 3 S.C.R. 3, para. 59.

[4] *Doucet-Boudreau v. Nova Scotia*, [2003] 3 S.C.R. 3, para. 66.

[5] *Doucet-Boudreau v. Nova Scotia*, [2003] 3 S.C.R. 3, para. 106.

[6] *Doucet-Boudreau v. Nova Scotia*, [2003] 3 S.C.R. 3, para. 111.

building. To the extent that judicial supervision is intended to put pressure on the executive, the task is akin to that of the political opposition, and could easily draw the courts into political conflict. Curiously, neither the majority nor the minority in the Supreme Court of Canada referred to the extensive American experience with judicial orders of supervision to achieve the desegregation of school systems, police forces and public facilities, and to impose constitutional standards on prisons and mental hospitals. But the federal courts of the United States were driven to these highly controversial expedients by the intransigent refusal of some governments to comply with their constitutional duties. Supervision orders are remedies of last resort.[7] Canada has had no history of governmental defiance of the constitution, and, until it does, there is no need for judicial supervision orders.[8]

A judicial supervision order was made by the Federal Court in *Abdelrazik v. Canada* (2009).[9] In that case, a Canadian citizen, who had made a visit to Sudan (the land of his birth), was arrested without charge, imprisoned for several years and tortured by the Sudanese authorities. When he was released, his Canadian passport had expired, and efforts to obtain a new one, even just a temporary one to get him back home to Montreal where his family awaited him, all proved unavailing. The applicant brought an application for a declaration that his right to enter Canada under s. 6(1) of the Charter of Rights had been violated, and for an appropriate and just remedy for the violation under s. 24(1). The Federal Court found that the Canadian government had been complicit in the applicant's arrest and imprisonment (but not in the torture) by Sudan. The Court also found that, after the applicant's release from prison in Sudan, when he was staying in the Canadian embassy, the Canadian government in Ottawa, while giving him assurances of aid and comfort, had actually been doing its best to block his return to Canada. The Court held that the applicant had a constitutional right to return to Canada under s. 6(1), and that the right had been violated.[10] The Court ordered that an emergency passport be issued to enable the applicant to return to Canada. But, based on the past history of governmental bad faith in dealing with the applicant, the Court also ordered that the applicant be brought before the Court after his return for the purpose of satisfying the Court that he had in fact returned to

---

[7] D.L. Horowitz, "Decreeing Organizational Change: Judicial Supervision of Public Institutions" [1983] Duke L.J. 1265, 1281; M.L. Pilkington, "Enforcing the Charter: The Supervisory Role of Superior Courts" (2004) 25 Supreme Court L.R. (2d) 77.

[8] Compare *Assn. des parents de l'école Rose-des-vents v. B.C.*, [2015] 2 S.C.R. 139, 2015 SCC 21, paras. 65-67 (granting only declaration and no positive remedy in hope that simple declaration would cause government to remedy constitutional defect by bringing French-language school facilities up to par).

[9] *Abdelrazik v. Canada*, [2010] 1 F.C.R. 267 (F.C.) (Zinn J.).

[10] For discussion, see ch. 46, Mobility, under heading § 46:2 "International movement".

Canada.[11] And, in case that did not happen in a timely fashion, the Court reserved the right "to issue further orders as may be required to safely return Mr. Abdelrazik to Canada".[12] The government did not appeal the Court's orders and fully complied with them. The applicant was able to return to Canada and he was duly produced to the Court, which pronounced itself "satisfied that the judgment has been respected."[13]

§ 40:24 Appeals

Section 24(1) does not authorize an appeal from the decision of a court of competent jurisdiction.[1] The existence of a right of appeal will depend upon the rules of the court to which the s. 24(1) application was made. Where there is no existing right of appeal, as will often be the case in applications in criminal proceedings before the trial is over, there will be no appeal from the Charter ruling by the court of competent jurisdiction.[2]

In *Knox Contracting v. Canada* (1990),[3] the Supreme Court of Canada, by a majority, held that there was no appeal from a refusal by a judge to quash a search warrant issued under the Income Tax Act. The Court held that, because neither the Income Tax Act nor the Criminal Code provided for any right of appeal, there was no right of appeal, despite the fact that the applicant claimed that the warrant had been issued in breach of the Charter of Rights.[4] In *Kourtessis v. Minister of National Revenue* (1993),[5] another attempt was made to quash a search warrant issued under the Income Tax Act. This time the applicant applied for a declaration that the statutory provision authorizing the warrant and the warrant itself were unconstitutional for breach of the Charter. The Supreme Court of Canada was unanimous that an appeal was available

---

[11]*Abdelrazik v. Canada*, [2010] 1 F.C.R. 267, para. 167. There was a second reason for the order (paras. 162-165): the applicant was the subject of a United Nations travel ban to which an exception was the fulfillment of a "judicial process".

[12]*Abdelrazik v. Canada*, [2010] 1 F.C.R. 267, para. 168.

[13]Federal Court Index and Docket (online), entry for July 7, 2009.

[Section 40:24]

[1]*Mills v. The Queen*, [1986] 1 S.C.R. 863; *James Doyle v. Anderson* (1990), 71 D.L.R. (4th) 731 (Nfld. C.A.).

[2]A wrong decision on a Charter issue by a court of competent jurisdiction, unless "manifestly and palpably wrong", will not be a jurisdictional error giving rise to judicial review by prerogative writ or other extraordinary remedy: *Re Corbeil* (1986), 27 C.C.C. (3d) 245 (Ont. C.A.). Of course, if the court of competent jurisdiction is a superior court, the prerogative writs and other extraordinary remedies would not normally be available to review the decision, although it is possible that the invocation of the Charter would remove the superior court's immunity: *Kourtessis v. M.N.R.*, [1993] 2 S.C.R. 53, 90 per La Forest J., obiter; compare cases denying Crown immunity to shield an unconstitutional act: Hogg and Monahan, Liability of the Crown (3rd ed., 2000), secs. 2.4(d), 2.6(d), 4.5(d).

[3]*Knox Contracting v. Canada*, [1990] 2 S.C.R. 338.

[4]Sopinka J., dissenting, would have avoided this unfortunate result by classifying the Income Tax Act as a taxation law rather than a criminal law, and by allowing the appellant to invoke the appeal procedures allowed by provincial law.

[5]*Kourtessis v. Minister of National Revenue*, [1993] 2 S.C.R. 53.

in these proceedings. An application (or action) for a declaration of invalidity was a civil proceeding. The declaration "is not transformed from a civil remedy to a criminal remedy merely because the declaration relates to a criminal statutory provision".[6] It followed that the application for a declaration in this case was governed by the provincial rules of civil procedure, which made provision for an appeal. In this way, the rules of criminal procedure were bypassed, although the Court emphasized that there would be a discretion to refuse to issue the declaration if another procedure were available to resolve the constitutional issue.[7]

§ 40:25 Limitation of actions

Where proceedings are brought, whether under s. 24(1) or under the general law, for a "personal remedy",[1] such as the recovery of unconstitutional taxes or damages for breach of the Charter, statutes of limitation of general application will apply to the proceedings.[2] In general, constitutional claimants are not liberated from the rules of practice and procedure of the court in which a claim is made, despite the fact that failure to comply with the rules will sometimes defeat proceedings. In the case of limitation periods, the policy reasons for bringing finality to disputes and relieving defendants of the risk of stale claims, when evidence is likely to be lost or unreliable, do not disappear whenever the constitution is invoked by a claimant. Indeed, the Supreme Court of Canada has required persons convicted of unconstitutional crimes to serve out their time in prison if they were outside the time limits for appeals from conviction.[3]

The leading case on limitation of actions is *Kingstreet Investments v. New Brunswick* (2007),[4] which was an action by taxpayers against the Crown in right of New Brunswick to recover taxes that had been imposed

[6]*Kourtessis v. Minister of National Revenue*, [1993] 2 S.C.R. 53, 114 per Sopinka J.

[7]*Kourtessis v. Minister of National Revenue*, [1993] 2 S.C.R. 53, 86, 115.

[Section 40:25]

[1]A personal remedy such as damages is to be contrasted with a declaration of invalidity under s. 52(1) (the supremacy clause). There is no limitation period on the making of a declaration of invalidity of a statute no matter how long ago the statute was passed, and the new state of the law will take effect from the time when the invalid statute was passed (or when a valid statute became invalid, for example, by the passage of the Constitution Act, 1982), and the benefits and obligations flowing from the new state of the law will take effect automatically. However, if legal proceedings are needed to obtain a personal remedy under the new state of the law, statutes of limitation of general application will apply to the proceedings. These distinctions are explained and applied in *Ravndahl v. Sask.*, [2009] 1 S.C.R. 181, para. 27.

[2]Statutes of limitation also apply to aboriginal claims against the Crown: *Can. v. Lameman*, [2008] 1 S.C.R. 372 (claim statute-barred).

[3]*R. v. Thomas*, [1990] 1 S.C.R. 713 (person convicted of felony-murder three years before the offence was held to be unconstitutional could not obtain relief because accused no longer "in the judicial system").

[4]*Kingstreet Investments v. New Brunswick*, [2007] 1 S.C.R. 3. Bastarache J. wrote the opinion of the Court.

by the provincial Legislature without constitutional authority. (The taxes, which were on the sale of liquor, were held to be indirect and outside the provincial power of taxation, which is limited to "direct" taxes.) The plaintiffs' cause of action was of course based on the unconstitutionality of the taxes, but s. 24(1) was not applicable because there had been no breach of the Charter. The plaintiffs simply relied on the law of restitution to recover the taxes that had unjustly enriched the Crown. The Supreme Court of Canada held that the plaintiffs were entitled to recover the taxes under the law of restitution, but the Court held that the recovery was subject to the province's limitation statute, which included a residuary limitation period (for all actions not otherwise provided for) of six years after the cause of action arose. That period applied to the plaintiffs' action, and their recovery was accordingly limited to those taxes that had been paid during the six-year period preceding the commencement of the action.

In *Kingstreet*, Bastarache J., who wrote the opinion of the Court, distinguished the Court's earlier decision in *Amax Potash v. Government of Saskatchewan* (1977),[5] where the Court had struck down a provincial law that purported to bar the recovery of unconstitutional taxes. The bar had been enacted for the sole purpose of denying relief for things done under an unconstitutional law. The invalidity of the bar was said to be demanded by a principle of federalism: a constitutional restriction on the power of the province to tax could not be evaded by the indirect means of barring the recovery of a tax that had been levied in violation of the restriction.[6] In *Kingstreet*, Bastarache J. drew a distinction between a law that was enacted for the purpose of barring the recovery of an unconstitutional tax from the Crown (*Amax Potash*) and a law of general application that imposed a limitation period on a class of generally-described causes of action. There was no reason, he said, why a general limitation statute should not be effective to bar stale claims for the recovery of unconstitutional taxes.[7]

In *Ravndahl v. Saskatchewan* (2009),[8] the widow of a person who had been killed in the course of his employment received a workers compensation pension from 1975, the date of her husband's death, until 1984, when she remarried. On her remarriage the workers compensation legislation of that time terminated her pension. The Supreme Court of Canada held that the termination of her pension was a violation of s. 15 of the Charter, and that she had a cause of action against the Crown in right of Saskatchewan under s. 24(1) for damages for breach of the

[5] *Amax Potash v. Government of Saskatchewan*, [1977] 2 S.C.R. 576.

[6] *Amax Potash* was followed in *Air Canada v. B.C.*, [1986] 2 S.C.R. 539 (petition of right to recover unconstitutional taxes, levied at a time when the petition of right was the only means of suing the Crown, cannot be blocked by discretionary refusal of fiat).

[7] *Kingstreet Investments v. New Brunswick*, [2007] 1 S.C.R. 3, paras. 59-61.

[8] *Ravndahl v. Saskatchewan*, [2009] 1 S.C.R. 181. McLachlin C.J. wrote the opinion of the Court.

Charter.[9] However, that cause of action arose on April 17, 1985, when s. 15 came into force. Following *Kingstreet*, the Court held that her proceedings, which had been commenced in 2000, were defeated by the province's limitation statute, which imposed a residuary limitation period (for all actions not otherwise provided for) of six years after the cause of action arose.[10]

The distinction between the limitation period of general application that was applied in *Kingstreet* and *Ravndahl* and the specific bar on the recovery of an unconstitutional tax that was struck down in *Amax Potash* is clear and sound in principle. There is, however, a middle case exemplified by *Prete v. Ontario* (1993).[11] In that case, the plaintiff brought an action for damages under s. 24(1) of the Charter alleging various Charter breaches by the law officers of the Crown, who had prosecuted him unsuccessfully. The plaintiff brought his action outside the six-month limitation period that was then prescribed for proceedings against the Crown and public officials by Ontario's Public Authorities Protection Act. The Ontario Court of Appeal held that the limitation period did not bar the action. Carthy J.A., who wrote for the Court on this issue, explained that governments should not, even by statute, be permitted "to decide when they would like to be free of [constitutional] controls".[12] The result was that the plaintiff was allowed to proceed with his action, although an action framed in tort for malicious prosecution (which the plaintiff's constitutional claim closely resembled) would have been statute-barred.

Prete was decided before *Kingstreet* and *Ravndahl*, and was (surprisingly) not referred to by the Supreme Court in either of the later cases. It is possible that *Prete* has been implicitly overruled by the later cases. The limitation period in the Public Authorities Protection Act had not been passed for the specific purpose of barring constitutional claims, and it was not limited to constitutional claims. On the other hand, the Public Authorities Protection Act was hardly a law of general application, since it applied only to proceedings against public authorities (including the Crown) and imposed a very short limitation period on those proceedings. In my view, *Prete* was rightly decided, and for the reason given by Carthy J.A. The Crown should not be allowed to immunize itself from constitu-

---

[9] The Court did not address the problem that this involved giving retroactive effect to the Charter of Rights, since the remarriage and consequent termination of the pension had taken place before the coming into force of s. 15: see ch. 36, Charter of Rights, under heading § 36:31, "Commencement of Charter".

[10] The limitation period did not bar her actions for declarations that the applicable legislation was unconstitutional: § 40:25 note 1, above; however, the Court did not deal with the claims for declaratory relief.

[11] *Prete v. Ontario* (1993), 16 O.R. (3d) 161 (C.A.). Carthy J.A. wrote for the majority; Weiler J.A. dissented on another point, but agreed with the majority that the limitation period was inapplicable.

[12] *Prete v. Ontario* (1993), 16 O.R. (3d) 161, 168 (C.A.). The only limitation Carthy J.A. suggested was the doctrine of laches. In this case, the action had been commenced within 18 months, which he evidently did not consider to be the kind of unreasonable delay that would amount to laches.

tional controls by enacting special, short limitation periods for proceedings against itself. While most special limitation periods in favour of the Crown have been repealed (including Ontario's Public Authorities Protection Act), there are still some on the statute books.[13] Such special limitation periods are, of course, effective to bar claims in tort or contract or other non-constitutional causes of action,[14] but in my view they will not apply to constitutional claims.

III. ADMINISTRATIVE TRIBUNALS

§ 40:26 With power to decide questions of law

Can administrative tribunals decide Charter issues? The Supreme Court of Canada has answered yes to this question. In *Douglas/Kwantlen Faculty Association v. Douglas College* (1990),[1] the Court held that an arbitration board, which had been appointed by the parties under a collective agreement, but which was empowered by statute to decide questions of law, had the power to determine the constitutionality of a mandatory retirement provision in the collective agreement. In *Cuddy Chicks v. Ontario* (1991),[2] the Court held that a labour relations board, which had been created and empowered by statute to decide questions of law, had the power to determine the constitutionality of a provision in the empowering statute that denied collective bargaining rights to agricultural workers. In both cases, it was necessary for the tribunal to resolve the constitutional issue in order to exercise its statutory jurisdiction. In the *Douglas College* case, La Forest J., for the Court, said: "A tribunal must respect the Constitution so that if it finds invalid a law that it is called upon to apply, it is bound to treat it as having no force or effect".[3] This conclusion was entailed by the supremacy clause in s. 52(1) of the Constitution Act, 1982. In effect, the tribunal was obliged to apply all of the relevant law, which included the Constitution as well as the relevant portions of contracts and statutes.

---

[13]Hogg, Monahan and Wright, Liability of the Crown (4th ed., 2010), sec. 4.5, "Limitation of actions".

[14]Constitutional challenges to Crown privileges in litigation, which have been based on the equality guarantee of s. 15 of the Charter, have been unsuccessful for lack of a listed or analogous ground: ch. 55, Equality, under heading § 55:17, "Requirement of a listed or analogous ground".

[Section 40:26]

[1]*Douglas/Kwantlen Faculty Association v. Douglas College*, [1990] 3 S.C.R. 570. On the ability of the arbitrator to decide Charter issues, all judges agreed with La Forest J.'s opinion, except that Wilson J. (with L'Heureux-Dubé J.) preferred "to leave open the question whether a tribunal may have such jurisdiction even in the absence of specific provisions in the governing legislation" (606-607). (This reservation related to the fact that the arbitrator had express power to decide questions of law.)

[2]*Cuddy Chicks v. Ontario*, [1991] 2 S.C.R. 5. The principal opinion was written by La Forest J., with whom all judges agreed, although Wilson J. (with L'Heureux-Dubé J.) added brief concurring reasons, making the same reservation as she had made in *Douglas/Kwantlen Faculty Association v. Douglas College*, [1990] 3 S.C.R. 570.

[3]*Douglas/Kwantlen Faculty Association v. Douglas College*, [1990] 3 S.C.R. 570, 594.

The power to decide the Charter issues in *Douglas College* and *Cuddy Chicks* did not come from the remedial provision in s. 24 of the Charter. Section 24's remedies are available only to a court of competent jurisdiction. (The Supreme Court has since decided that an administrative tribunal with power to decide questions of law is a court of competent jurisdiction.)[4] In both cases, the Supreme Court of Canada expressly refused to decide whether an administrative tribunal could be a court of competent jurisdiction. Section 24 was irrelevant, because the applicants were not seeking any remedy for breach of the Charter, not even a declaration of invalidity.[5] The applicant was seeking a remedy that the tribunal was empowered to grant in the normal course of its jurisdiction: the reinstatement of wrongfully dismissed employees in *Douglas College* and the certification of a union in *Cuddy Chicks*. The Charter issue arose in the course of determining whether the remedy should be granted, because the Charter if applicable directed the tribunal to disregard a law that would otherwise bar the tribunal from granting the remedy sought. Thus, in *Douglas College*, the professors who had been mandatorily retired were entitled to be reinstated only if the mandatory retirement provision was invalid; and, in *Cuddy Chicks*, the union that had organized the agricultural workers was entitled to certification only if the agricultural workers exclusion was invalid. But the applicants did not look to s. 24 for any remedy. Once s. 52(1) had invalidated the apparently applicable law, the exercise of the tribunal's ordinary statutory jurisdiction over the parties, the subject matter and the remedy would give to the applicants all that they asked for.

Where an administrative tribunal decides a constitutional question, its decision will be subject to judicial review by a superior court.[6] Indeed, an attempt by Parliament or a Legislature to enact a privative clause to bar judicial review would be unconstitutional.[7] Nevertheless, the tribunal's initial determination of the constitutional question is likely to make a useful contribution to the ultimate resolution of the issue. The tribunal's expert knowledge of the regulated field is likely to produce a well informed assessment of the strength of the constitutional arguments.[8] This fact was acknowledged by La Forest J. in both *Douglas*

---

[4] § 40:16, "Court of competent jurisdiction".

[5] The power to make a general declaration of invalidity is part of the jurisdiction of a superior court, but unless specifically granted by statute is not possessed by an inferior court or an administrative tribunal: [1990] 3 S.C.R. 570, 592. The determination by a tribunal that a law, which it is called upon to apply, is unconstitutional is not equivalent to a formal declaration of invalidity: [1990] 3 S.C.R. 570, 599.

[6] There is no right to appeal from a decision of an administrative tribunal unless the right has been conferred by statute. However, all administrative tribunals are subject to judicial review by superior courts, not to reconsider the merits, but to determine whether jurisdiction has been exceeded, and, depending on the review remedy sought, to correct some other kinds of errors, often including errors of law.

[7] Chapter 7, Courts, under heading § 7:20, "Privative clauses".

[8] See generally J.M. Evans, "Administrative Tribunals and Charter Challenges" (1988) 2 Can. J. of Admin. Law and Practice 13; D.M. McAllister, "The Role of

College[9] and *Cuddy Chicks*[10] but he also added in both cases that constitutional determinations by administrative tribunals should receive "no curial deference".[11] In other words, according to La Forest J. in both *Douglas College and Cuddy Chicks*, the standard of judicial review[12] was correctness.[13] Under this approach, when a superior court reviews the decision of an administrative tribunal on a constitutional issue, the court does not defer to the decision of the tribunal, even if the tribunal has made a reasonable interpretation of the constitutional text. The superior court must decide the constitutional question in the way that the superior court believes to be correct.

A more fine-grained approach has since emerged to the standard of review that is to be applied to constitutional questions. When a superior court reviews the decision of an administrative tribunal as to its *jurisdiction* to consider a challenge to the constitutionality of legislation, the standard of review remains correctness.[14] The standard of review also remains correctness when a superior court reviews the decision of an administrative tribunal actually addressing the constitutionality of *legislation*, on Charter or any other constitutional grounds.[15] However, the standard of review when a superior court reviews the substance of an administrative *decision* that is itself alleged to unjustifiably limit a Charter right is *reasonableness*, which is a more deferential standard of review than correctness.[16] Importantly, the reasonableness standard of review *does not* apply any time a superior court reviews an administra-

---

Administrative Tribunals in Constitutional Adjudication" (1991) 1 Nat. J. Con. Law 25; P. Anisman, "Jurisdiction of Administrative Tribunals to Apply the Canadian Charter of Rights and Freedoms" (LSUC Special Lectures, 1992); M. Priest, "Charter Procedure in Administrative Cases: The Tribunal's Perspective" (1994) 7 Can. J. Admin. Practice 151.

[9] *Douglas/Kwantlen Faculty Association v. Douglas College*, [1990] 3 S.C.R. 570, 605.

[10] *Cuddy Chicks v. Ontario*, [1991] 2 S.C.R. 5, 18.

[11] *Cuddy Chicks v. Ontario*, [1991] 2 S.C.R. 5, 17; *Douglas/Kwantlen Faculty Association v. Douglas College*, [1990] 3 S.C.R. 570, 605.

[12] There are two standards of judicial review of administrative action—reasonableness and correctness: *Dunsmuir v. N.B.*, [2008] 1 S.C.R. 190. The reasonableness standard of review applies presumptively: *Can. v. Vavilov*, 2019 SCC 65, para. 23. This presumption will be rebutted where: (1) the legislative branch has indicated that it intends a different standard of review to apply, either by prescribing a different standard of review or by including a statutory right of appeal; or (2) the rule of law requires that correctness be the standard of review: *Vavilov*, this note, paras. 33, 53.

[13] Accord, *Nova Scotia v. Martin*, [2003] 2 S.C.R. 504, para. 31 per Gonthier J. for the Court; *Paul v. British Columbia*, [2003] 2 S.C.R. 585, paras. 31, 32 per Bastarache J. for the Court; *Okwuobi v. Lester B. Pearson School Bd.*, [2005] 1 S.C.R. 257, paras. 44-45 per "the Court"]; *Multani v. Commission scolaire Marguerite-Bourgeoys*, [2006] 1 S.C.R. 256, para. 20 per Charron J. for the majority; *Dunsmuir v. N.B.*, [2008] 1 S.C.R. 190, para. 58.

[14] *Nova Scotia v. Martin*, [2003] 2 S.C.R. 504, para. 31; *Dunsmuir v. N.B.*, [2008] 1 S.C.R. 190, para. 58 (citing *Martin*, among others).

[15] *Dunsmuir v. N.B.*, [2008] 1 S.C.R. 190, para. 58; *Can. v. Vavilov*, 2019 SCC 65 note 256, above, para. 57.

[16] *Doré v. Barreau du Québec*, [2012] 1 S.C.R. 395, paras. 43-45. For a discussion of

tive *decision* that engages some aspect of the Constitution. When the basis of the constitutional challenge is "the division of powers between Parliament and the provinces, the relationship between the legislature and the other branches of the state, the scope of Aboriginal and treaty rights under s. 35 of the Constitution Act, 1982, and other constitutional matters",[17] the standard of review remains correctness.[18]

There is another limitation on the power of an administrative tribunal to decide constitutional issues. The Supreme Court of Canada has insisted that the administrative tribunal has no power to make a *declaration* of invalidity.[19] What the Court seems to mean by this is that a decision by a tribunal that a law is unconstitutional is no more than a decision that the law is inapplicable in the particular case. It is not a binding precedent. According to the Court, only "superior courts" have the power to issue binding declarations of invalidity that will invalidate a law with general effect.[20]

In both *Douglas College* and *Cuddy Chicks*, the tribunals' empowering statutes expressly granted to the tribunals the power to decide questions of law. In two subsequent decisions, a majority of the Supreme Court of Canada held that the absence of an *express* power to decide questions of law precluded an administrative tribunal from deciding Charter issues.[21] These decisions were rather odd, because any statutory tribunal, whether or not it has an express power to decide questions of law, must decide all questions of law or fact that are necessary to carry out its mandate. Except for the rare case where questions of law are actually withdrawn from the jurisdiction of the tribunal by its empowering statute, a tribunal cannot fold its hands and refuse to reach a decision just because the matter before it raises a question of law. Nearly all tribunals have an *implied* power to decide all questions of law that are relevant to reaching decisions that are called for by their mandate.[22] Once this is accepted, it is hard to see why the terms of the Constitution should be excluded from the body of law that the tribunal may consider,

---

what this reasonableness analysis involves, see ch. 38, Limitation of Rights, under heading § 38:31, "Application to discretionary decisions". In *Can. v. Vavilov*, 2019 SCC 65 note 256, above, the Court declined to revisit this aspect of *Doré* (para. 57); however, it did not close the door to the possibility that it might be willing to do so in a future case.

[17]*Can. v. Vavilov*, 2019 SCC 65, note 256, above, para. 55; see also *Dunsmuir v. N.B.*, [2008] 1 S.C.R. 190, para. 58.

[18]The standard of review of correctness does not apply whenever a superior court reviews an administrative decision that somehow relates to, or impacts, Aboriginal and treaty rights under s. 35 of the Constitution Act, 1982. For example, a more fine-grained approach has also been applied when the duty to consult is involved: see § 40:26 note 24, below.

[19]This point is made in the passages referred to in the previous note. See also *Tranchemontagne v. Ont.*, [2006] 1 S.C.R. 513, para. 79 per Abella J. dissenting.

[20]*Cuddy Chicks v. Ont.*, [1991] 2 S.C.R. 5, 17 per La Forest J. for the majority.

[21]*Tétreault-Gadoury v. Can.*, [1991] 2 S.C.R. 22 (Employment Insurance Board of Referees); *Cooper v. Can.*, [1996] 3 S.C.R. 854 (Canadian Human Rights Commission).

[22]*McLeod v. Egan*, [1975] 1 S.C.R. 517 (arbitrator under collective agreement bound to interpret any statute potentially applicable to the dispute).

especially since the terms of the Constitution are declared (by s. 52 of the Constitution Act, 1982) to be "the supreme law of Canada". It is true that some administrative tribunals are not well placed to decide constitutional issues, whether because of the lack of expertise of their members or because of the volume of cases they have to decide. But these prudential considerations cannot overcome the theoretical objection to requiring administrative tribunals to apply laws that are contrary to the Charter of Rights. Indeed, one might wonder whether Parliament or a Legislature, which is itself powerless to enact a law in violation of the Charter, has the power to create an administrative tribunal that must apply a law that is in violation of the Charter.[23]

The Supreme Court of Canada has now repudiated the two rulings that stipulated that only an express grant of power over questions of law would authorize an administrative tribunal to decide whether a potentially applicable law offends the Charter. In *Nova Scotia v. Martin* (2003),[24] the Workers' Compensation Appeals Tribunal of Nova Scotia was faced with a claim that the benefits provided by the province's workers' compensation plan for chronic pain were unconstitutional for violation of s. 15 of the Charter of Rights. (Sufferers from work-related chronic pain were provided with a standard, temporary program for their rehabilitation and were otherwise excluded from the benefits of the workers' compensation plan.) The Supreme Court of Canada, in an opinion written by Gonthier J., held that the Tribunal had the power to rule on the Charter issue. The Tribunal had express power to determine questions of law, and so the case fell squarely within *Douglas College* and *Cuddy Chicks*, and it was not really necessary to rule on the case where the power to determine questions of law was merely implied. However, the Court took the opportunity to "reappraise and restate" the law.[25] The Court held that a tribunal with power to determine questions of law, *whether the power was express or implied*,[26] was presumed to have the power to determine the constitutional validity of any potentially applicable law. That presumption could be rebutted only by showing that the legislation empowering the tribunal "clearly intended to exclude

[23]In *Tétreault-Gadoury v. Can.*, [1991] 2 S.C.R. 22, the Supreme Court of Canada held that the Board of Referees was obliged to exclude persons over 65 from unemployment insurance benefits, and the Board's decision could not be upset on appeal or judicial review, despite the fact that the exclusion of persons over 65 was, according to the Court, contrary to the Charter of Rights. In *Cooper v. Can.*, [1996] 3 S.C.R. 854, the Court held that the Canadian Human Rights Commission could not even consider the question whether its empowering statute violated the Charter in providing that it was not a discriminatory practice for an employer to dismiss an employee who had reached "the normal age of retirement". Contrast these decisions with the caution articulated in *Nova Scotia v. Martin*, [2003] 2 S.C.R. 504, para. 44.

[24]*Nova Scotia v. Martin*, [2003] 2 S.C.R. 504. The opinion of the Court was written by Gonthier J.

[25]*Nova Scotia v. Martin*, [2003] 2 S.C.R. 504, para. 3.

[26]*Nova Scotia v. Martin*, [2003] 2 S.C.R. 504, para. 41.

Charter issues from the tribunal's authority over questions of law".[27] That clear intention would normally be evidenced by legislative provision for an alternative route for the resolution of Charter issues coming before the tribunal.[28] In this case, there was nothing in the Appeal Tribunal's empowering legislation that indicated an intention to exclude Charter issues from the Tribunal's authority. It followed that the Tribunal could decide the Charter issue. (The Court, applying its review standard of correctness, went on to hold that the chronic pain provisions were contrary to the Charter of Rights; the Court postponed the declaration of invalidity to give the Legislature time to make better provision for workers incapacitated by chronic pain.)

The constitutional question in *Martin* was whether a law was unconstitutional for breach of the Charter of Rights. In *Paul v. British Columbia* (2003),[29] which was decided by the Supreme Court of Canada at the same time as *Martin*, the question was whether a law was unconstitutional for breach of the aboriginal rights guaranteed by s. 35 of the Constitution Act, 1982. This question came before the Forest Appeals Commission of British Columbia, which had to determine whether Mr Paul, a registered Indian, had violated the statutory Forest Practices Code of the province. Mr Paul had cut down three trees on Crown land, intending to use the timber to build a deck on his home. The Code prohibited the cutting of Crown timber, but Mr Paul asserted that he had an aboriginal right to harvest the trees. The Commission decided that it had the power to deal with this defence, but Mr Paul immediately sought judicial review to stop the Commission from determining his aboriginal rights. The Supreme Court of Canada, in an opinion written by Bastarache J., held that the power of an administrative tribunal to determine whether a law was overridden by an aboriginal right was governed by the same rules as *Martin* stipulated were to be applied to Charter issues. In this case, the Commission had the power, under its empowering statute, to decide questions of law. That power was presumed to include the power to determine whether a potentially applicable law was unconstitutional in its application to an Indian by reason of s. 35 of the Constitution Act, 1982. There was nothing in the empowering statute to indicate an intention to withdraw aboriginal rights issues from the jurisdiction of the Commission. Therefore, the Commission had the power to hear and determine Mr Paul's defence of aboriginal right, and the Commission should resume its proceeding in order to receive his evidence and determine the issue.

In *Paul*, it was argued that the provincial Legislature could not enact

[27] *Nova Scotia v. Martin*, [2003] 2 S.C.R. 504, para. 3.

[28] Gonthier J. (para. 44) expressly reserved the question of the constitutionality of "a provision that would place procedural barriers in the way of claimants seeking to assert their rights in a timely and effective manner, for instance by removing Charter jurisdiction from a tribunal without providing an effective administrative route for Charter claims".

[29] *Paul v. British Columbia*, [2003] 2 S.C.R. 585. The opinion of the Court was written by Bastarache J.

a law that had the effect of empowering a tribunal to determine questions relating to aboriginal rights. That would encroach on the federal power over "Indians, and lands reserved for the Indians" in s. 91(24) of the Constitution Act, 1867. Aboriginal rights came within the essential core of "Indianness", which lay outside the power of the province. The Supreme Court of Canada rejected this argument on the basis that adjudication was distinct from legislation. The power conferred by the British Columbia Legislature on its Forest Appeals Commission was solely an adjudicative one. The Commission was not granted the power to alter or extinguish aboriginal rights; it could only determine whether or not they existed. The Commission's determinations would be binding on the parties, of course, but they would not constitute precedents that were binding on other tribunals or courts, and they would be subject to judicial review on a standard of correctness.[30] Bastarache J. drew the analogy of a provincial court, which has jurisdiction to apply the entire body of law, including federal law and constitutional law, to resolve disputes properly before it; a provincial administrative tribunal with power to adjudicate questions of law must also take account of all applicable legal rules, whether provincial, federal or constitutional.[31]

Section 35 of the Constitution Act, 1982 imposes on governments (both federal and provincial) a duty to consult with aboriginal people where proposed action by the government would adversely affect an aboriginal right or claim.[32] In *Rio Tinto Alcan v. Carrier Sekani Tribal Council* (2010),[33] the question was whether an administrative tribunal had any role to play respecting the process of consultation. The British Columbia Utilities Commission possessed a statutory power to review contracts for the sale of electricity and confirm those that were in the "public interest". The Commission had approved a contract for the sale of electricity from Alcan (which generated hydro electricity in excess of its requirements for aluminum smelting) to BC Hydro (which used the electricity as part of its general power supply). The Carrier Sekani First Nations applied for judicial review of the Commission's decision on the ground that they should have been consulted before the Commission found the contract to be in the public interest. The Commission had put its mind to this issue and determined that there was no duty to consult with the First Nations because the contract of sale would have no adverse impact on the First Nations' rights or claims. The Supreme Court of Canada held that the question whether there was a constitutional duty to consult aboriginal people was a question of constitutional law that came within the jurisdiction of an administrative tribunal with power to decide questions of law. In this case, the Commission had the power to decide questions of law, and there were no indications in its

---

[30] *Paul v. British Columbia*, [2003] 2 S.C.R. 585, para. 31.

[31] *Paul v. British Columbia*, [2003] 2 S.C.R. 585, para. 21.

[32] Chapter 28, Aboriginal People, under heading § 28:38, "Duty to consult aboriginal people".

[33] *Rio Tinto Alcan v. Carrier Sekani Tribal Council*, [2010] 2 S.C.R. 650. McLachlin C.J. wrote the opinion of the Court.

empowering statute that would exclude from that power questions respecting consultation. The decision of the Commission was reviewable on the standard of correctness, and the Court held that the Commission was correct in determining that there was no duty to consult the First Nations before entering into the disputed contract.[34]

If the decision in *Rio Tinto* had been otherwise—that there was a duty to consult—it would have been within the jurisdiction of the Commission to determine whether the duty to consult had been adequately exercised by government. The adequacy of government consultation was also a question of constitutional law.[35] But a tribunal's power to decide questions of law would not by itself include a power to engage in the actual process of consultation: "Consultation itself is not a question of law, but a distinct constitutional process requiring powers to effect compromise and do whatever is necessary to achieve reconciliation of divergent Crown and Aboriginal interests."[36] The Legislature could, if it chose, delegate to a tribunal (or other regulatory body or official) the power to consult,[37] but that had not been done in this case: the Commission's empowering statute did not expressly or impliedly include the power to consult with aboriginal people.[38]

Ontario's Human Rights Code, like those of other jurisdictions, is

[34]As with Charter issues a more fine-grained approach has emerged to the standard of review that is applied to administrative decisions involving the duty to consult. In *Haida Nation v. B.C.*, [2004] 3 S.C.R. 511, the Court distinguished the "existence or extent of the duty to consult" (which it said was a legal issue that would attract a correctness standard of review) from the process of consultation (which it said would attract a reasonableness standard of review) (paras. 61-62). However, the Court also noted that the existence or extent of the duty to consult "is typically premised on an assessment of the facts", and it left open the possibility that a reasonableness standard may also be appropriate in this context if the decision-maker has expertise and the issue involved is factual or involves legal and factual issues that are "inextricably intertwined" (para. 61). In *Beckman v. Little Salmon/Carmacks First Nation*, [2010] 3 S.C.R. 103, the Court appeared to suggest that the process of consultation (which it seemed to lump in with the "adequacy of consultation") may attract a correctness standard of review (para. 48), even though *Haida*, as noted, indicated that it would attract a reasonableness standard of review. Understandably, the result has been uncertainty and inconsistency in the cases: compare e.g. *Ahousaht First Nation v. Can.* (2008), 297 D.L.R. (4th) 722, para. 34 (F.C.A.) and *Mi'kmaq of PEI v. PEI*, 2019 PECA 26, paras. 42-43 (P.E.I.C.A.), which adopt different standards of review.

[35]*Rio Tinto Alcan v. Carrier Sekani Tribal Council*, [2010] 2 S.C.R. 650, paras. 72-73.

[36]*Rio Tinto Alcan v. Carrier Sekani Tribal Council*, [2010] 2 S.C.R. 650, para. 74.

[37]It is clear that it is "open to legislatures to empower regulatory bodies to play a role in fulfilling the Crown's duty to consult", but "the Crown always holds ultimate responsibility for ensuring consultation is adequate": *Clyde River (Hamlet) v. Petroleum Geo-Services*, [2017] 1 S.C.R. 1069, paras. 21-22, 30. This is because "the honour of the Crown cannot be delegated": *Haida Nation v. B.C.*, [2004] 3 S.C.R. 511, para. 53. This is not a distinction without a difference. It means, for example, that the Crown has continuing oversight responsibilities, even if it does empower an administrative tribunal to play a role in fulfilling its duty to consult: *Clyde River (Hamlet) v. Petroleum Geo-Services*, [2017] 1 S.C.R. 1069, paras. 22-23.

[38]Compare *Clyde River (Hamlet) v. Petroleum Geo-Services*, [2017] 1 S.C.R. 1069 (power to fulfil the Crown's duty to consult delegated to the National Energy Board;

expressly given primacy over other Ontario statutes. These primacy clauses have been held to be effective, which gives a "quasi-constitutional" status to human rights codes.[39] In *Tranchemontagne v. Ontario* (2006),[40] the question arose whether Ontario's Social Benefits Tribunal had the power to decide that a provision in its empowering statute was inoperative for conflict with the Ontario Code. The provision in question denied a disability benefit (but not general social assistance) to a person whose incapacity resulted from addiction to alcohol or drugs. The claimant argued that this provision was discriminatory and for that reason contrary to the Code. The Tribunal, which had power to determine income-support decisions on appeal from a statutory official, held that it had no power to entertain this argument, and denied the disability benefit on the ground of the claimant's addiction. The Tribunal's empowering statute authorized it to decide questions of law, but expressly denied the power to determine the "constitutional validity" of a statute or regulation. Did this restriction on its powers deny to the Tribunal the power to determine whether the addiction provision was contrary to the Code? Bastarache J., writing for the majority of the Supreme Court, answered "no". While the Tribunal was precluded from "invalidating" a statutory provision on constitutional grounds, it was not precluded from refusing to apply a statutory provision on the ground of conflict with the Code. Aside from the constitutional issues that were expressly withdrawn from its powers, the Tribunal was empowered to apply "the whole law", and that included the Code and its primacy clause.[41] Abella J. dissented. She pointed out that administrative tribunals have no jurisdiction to make declarations of invalidity,[42] so that the distinction between invalidity and inoperability (or non-application) should not be treated as determinative. In her view, the denial of power over constitutional compliance should be interpreted as extending by implication to Code compliance as well. She pointed out that the Tribunal had to deal with many thousands of cases every year, and its process was meant to be "efficient, effective and quick" in order to avoid delay in getting payments to eligible applicants. Inquiries into discrimination under the Code, like Charter inquiries, were contrary to this mandate: they were likely to be "complex, lengthy and inevitably delaying" in their effect.[43] Needless to say, the majority view prevailed,

---

duty to consult *not* satisfied in the context); *Chippewas of the Thames First Nation v. Enbridge Pipelines*, [2017] 1 S.C.R. 1099 (power to fulfil the Crown's duty to consult delegated to the National Energy Board; duty to consult satisfied in the context).

[39] *Tranchemontagne v. Ont.*, [2006] 1 S.C.R. 513, para. 33, per Bastarache J. for majority. For discussion, see ch. 12, Parliamentary Sovereignty, under heading § 12:10, "Manner and form of future laws".

[40] *Tranchemontagne v. Ontario*, [2006] 1 S.C.R. 513. Bastarache J., with McLachlin C.J., Binnie and Fish JJ., wrote the opinion of the four-judge majority. Abella J., with LeBel and Deschamps J., wrote a dissenting opinion.

[41] *Tranchemontagne v. Ontario*, [2006] 1 S.C.R. 513, para. 40.

[42] *Tranchemontagne v. Ontario*, [2006] 1 S.C.R. 513, para. 79.

[43] *Tranchemontagne v. Ontario*, [2006] 1 S.C.R. 513, paras. 90-91.

and the case was sent back to the Tribunal to rule on the applicability of the Code.

§ 40:27 Without power to decide questions of law

Administrative tribunals that lack the power to decide questions of law also lack the power to refuse to apply laws on the ground of unconstitutionality. The previous section of this chapter has reported that the Supreme Court of Canada has held that the power to decide questions of law may be implied as well as express. This means that most administrative tribunals with adjudicative functions will possess the power to decide questions of law. The power to decide normally carries with it the implicit power to determine all issues of fact or law that are needed to reach a decision. Where that is the case, s. 52(1) of the Constitution Act, 1982 requires the tribunal to resolve any constitutional issues that affect the validity or applicability of any relevant law.

§ 40:28 Preliminary inquiry judge

In *R. v. Seaboyer* (1991),[1] the Supreme Court of Canada held that the judge presiding at the preliminary inquiry of an indictable offence had no jurisdiction under s. 52(1) of the Constitution Act, 1982 to determine the constitutionality of a rape-shield law which purported to limit the accused's right to cross-examine the victim of a sexual assault. The Court acknowledged that the preliminary inquiry judge would in the course of conducting the inquiry have the power (and the duty) to rule on the admissibility of the evidence presented at the inquiry. But this power did not extend to determining the constitutionality of a statute that purported to prohibit the admission of evidence. In order to determine whether there was sufficient evidence to make the accused stand trial, the preliminary inquiry judge was obliged "to accept the rules of evidence as they stand".[2] Any Charter challenge to the rules of evidence had to await the trial, where the trial judge would be permitted to look at the Constitution of Canada as part of the body of law to be applied.[3]

The decision in *Seaboyer* predates the decisions in *Martin*[4] and *Paul*,[5] and is inconsistent with those decisions. Clearly, the preliminary inquiry judge has an implied power to decide questions of law, since he or she has to rule on the validity of the charge and the admissibility of evidence presented at the inquiry. Under the doctrine laid down in *Martin*

[Section 40:28]

[1]*R. v. Seaboyer*, [1991] 2 S.C.R. 577. The decision is also examined in § 40:8, "Constitutional exemption".

[2]*R. v. Seaboyer*, [1991] 2 S.C.R. 577, 638.

[3]It has been held that a preliminary inquiry judge is not a court of competent jurisdiction within s. 24(1): *R. v. Hynes*, [2001] 3 S.C.R. 623; but this was irrelevant in *Seaboyer*, where it was s. 52(1), not s. 24(1), that was being relied upon by the accused.

[4]*Nova Scotia v. Martin*, [2003] 2 S.C.R. 504.

[5]*Paul v. British Columbia*, [2003] 2 S.C.R. 585.

and *Paul*, the power to decide questions of law raises the presumption that the decision-maker also has the power to determine the constitutionality of any potentially applicable law. There seems to be no ground to rebut that presumption. Indeed, it is hard to see how the preliminary inquiry judge can properly decide whether the accused should stand trial if the judge must blindly follow unconstitutional legislation. Unfortunately, despite the announced intention of the Supreme Court of Canada in *Martin* and *Paul* to "reappraise and restate" the law, in neither case did the Court make any mention of *Seaboyer*. However, I think it is safe to regard *Seaboyer* as impliedly overruled. The preliminary inquiry judge has the power to decide constitutional questions that affect the validity of the charge or the admissibility of the evidence tendered in support of the charge.

§ 40:29 Provincial court judge

The previous section of this chapter, "Preliminary inquiry judge", concluded that a judge presiding over a preliminary inquiry would have the power to decide constitutional questions that affected the validity of the charge or the admissibility of evidence tendered in support of the charge. The preliminary inquiry judge would normally be a provincial court judge. But provincial court judges are not restricted to preliminary inquiries: they actually try the overwhelming majority of criminal cases, including the most serious indictable offences.[1]

In *R. v. Lloyd* (2016),[2] the defendant was charged with a drug offence for which the federal Controlled Drugs and Substances Act prescribed a mandatory minimum sentence of one year. He argued that the one-year sentence was cruel and unusual punishment which was banned by s. 12 of the Charter. The case was tried by a provincial court judge, who considered and accepted the argument and "declared" that the mandatory minimum sentence was unconstitutional. One of the issues before the Supreme Court of Canada was whether the provincial court judge had the power to make that decision. The Court held that a provincial court judge did not have the power to make a binding declaration that a law is of no force and effect; only superior court judges of inherent jurisdiction could make such a declaration. However, "provincial court judges do have the power to determine the constitutionality of a law where it is properly before them."[3] This was on the basis that no one should be convicted or sentenced under an invalid statute. The effect of a finding of unconstitutionality by a provincial court judge is to enable that judge to refuse to apply the unconstitutional law in that case. However, "the law remains in full force or effect, absent a formal declaration of invalid-

[Section 40:29]

[1]Chapter 19, Criminal Justice.

[2]*R. v. Lloyd*, 2016 SCC 13. McLachlin C.J. wrote the opinion of the majority which on this issue was agreed to by the dissenting judges (para. 61).

[3]*R. v. Lloyd*, 2016 SCC 13, para. 15.

ity by a court of inherent jurisdiction."[4] In this case, although the judge used the word "declare", his ruling should not be interpreted as a formal declaration of invalidity, but just as a refusal to apply the unconstitutional law to the defendant before him. The judge had the power to do that. (The Supreme Court, by a majority, went on to issue a formal declaration that the mandatory minimum sentence was indeed unconstitutional.)

IV. SCRUTINY BY MINISTER OF JUSTICE

§ 40:30 Scrutiny by Minister of Justice

The Charter of Rights makes no provision for the pre-enactment scrutiny of proposed statutes and regulations to ensure that they comply with the Charter. The Canadian Bill of Rights, it will be recalled, imposes an obligation of scrutiny on the Minister of Justice, including an obligation to report to the House of Commons any inconsistency between the Bill and a proposed statute or regulation.[1] In 1985, the Department of Justice Act[2] was amended to require that the Minister of Justice's scrutiny and report encompass compliance with the Charter as well as with the Bill.[3] In 2019, the Department of Justice Act was amended again to require the Minister of Justice "for every Bill introduced in or presented to either House of Parliament by a minister or other representative of the Crown, . . . to . . . table[] . . . a statement that sets out potential effects of the Bill on the rights and freedoms that are guaranteed by the *Canadian Charter of Rights and Freedoms*".[4] The purpose of these so-called Charter statements "is to inform members of the Senate and the House of Commons as well as the public of those potential effects."[5]

V. LEGISLATIVE ENFORCEMENT

§ 40:31 Legislative enforcement

The federal Parliament and the provincial Legislatures, acting within their own legislative jurisdictions, are of course free to make whatever

---

[4] *R. v. Lloyd*, 2016 SCC 13, para. 19. Needless to say, other provincial court judges may choose to follow their colleague and refuse to apply the law in the cases before them, but they will not be bound to do so.

[Section 40:30]

[1] This provision is discussed in ch. 35, Canadian Bill of Rights, under heading § 35:9 "Scrutiny by Minister of Justice".

[2] R.S.C. 1985, c. J-2, s. 4.1.

[3] See ch. 35, Canadian Bill of Rights, under heading § 35:9, "Scrutiny by Minister of Justice".

[4] R.S.C. 1985, c. J-2, s. 4.2(1).

[5] R.S.C. 1985, c. J-2, s. 4.2(2). For discussion of a proposed reform to these provisions, which would expand them to the Constitution of Canada as a whole, see W.K. Wright, "Against Privileging the Charter: The Case of Federal Pre-enactment Constitutional Review" (2021) 25 Rev. Const. Stud. 49.

provision they choose for the better enforcement of Charter rights. But the Charter of Rights does not confer any new legislative power. Section 31 declares that "nothing in this Charter extends the legislative powers of any body or authority".

Section 93(4) of the Constitution Act, 1867 expressly authorizes the federal Parliament to enact "remedial laws" to redress a breach by a province of the denominational school rights guaranteed by s. 93.[1] The American Bill of Rights expressly authorizes the federal Congress to enact laws to "enforce" against the states the guarantee against slavery,[2] the rights to due process and equal protection[3] and the right to vote without discriminatory restrictions.[4] It is clear from s. 31 of the Charter that no similar remedial or enforcement power in the federal Parliament is to be inferred from the provisions of the Charter. Enforcement of the Charter is the function of the courts, by virtue of s. 52(1) or s. 24.

[Section 40:31]

[1]See ch. 57, Education, under heading § 57:5, "Federal power to enact remedial laws".

[2]Thirteenth amendment, s. 2.

[3]Fourteenth amendment, s. 5.

[4]Fifteenth amendment, s. 2.

Chapter 41

Exclusion of Evidence

I. SCOPE OF CHAPTER

§ 41:1 Scope of chapter

II. ORIGIN OF S. 24(2)

§ 41:2 Origin of s. 24(2)

III. TEXT OF S. 24(2)

§ 41:3 Text of s. 24(2)

IV. CAUSATION

§ 41:4 Causation

V. BURDEN OF PROOF

§ 41:5 Burden of proof

VI. REASONABLE PERSON TEST

§ 41:6 Reasonable person test

VII. DEFINITION OF DISREPUTE

§ 41:7 Definition of disrepute

VIII. NATURE OF EVIDENCE

§ 41:8 Nature of evidence

IX. NATURE OF OFFICIAL CONDUCT

§ 41:9 Deliberate violations
§ 41:10 Extenuating circumstances
§ 41:11 Good faith

X. NATURE OF CHARTER BREACH

§ 41:12 Nature of Charter breach

XI. EFFECT OF EXCLUDING EVIDENCE

§ 41:13 Effect of excluding evidence

XII. CONCLUSION

§ 41:14 Conclusion

I. SCOPE OF CHAPTER

§ 41:1 Scope of chapter

The previous chapter, Enforcement of Rights, has considered the remedies that are available for breach of the Charter of Rights. That chapter omitted one remedy, namely, the exclusion of evidence that has been obtained in breach of the Charter. The reason for the omission is that the exclusion of evidence is separately provided for in s. 24(2) of the Charter, and has accumulated its own distinctive body of case-law.[1] This chapter is devoted to s. 24(2) and its exegesis.

II. ORIGIN OF S. 24(2)

§ 41:2 Origin of s. 24(2)

Before the adoption of the Charter of Rights in 1982, Canadian courts followed the rule of the English common law that evidence obtained by illegal means was admissible if relevant.[1] The Canadian Bill of Rights of 1960 was silent on the question of the admissibility of evidence, and the Supreme Court of Canada held that even a breach of the Canadian Bill of Rights did not render inadmissible any evidence obtained by the breach.[2]

The Canadian rule of admissibility stood in contrast with the American exclusionary rule. The American courts held that evidence obtained in violation of the Bill of Rights was inadmissible.[3] When Canada's Charter of Rights was being drafted, a debate ensued as to whether the American exclusionary rule should be adopted. In favour of the American rule, it could be argued that lawless behaviour by law enforcement officers should not be rewarded by allowing them to use the fruits of such behaviour. On the other side of the argument was the point that when reliable evidence is excluded, a guilty person usually goes free; it is arguable that it would be more sensible to discipline the police officer

---

[Section 41:1]

[1]Section 24(2) applies only if evidence has been obtained in breach of the Charter. Where evidence has been *obtained* in conformity with the Charter, but its *use* would be a breach of the Charter, then the exclusion of the evidence is authorized by s. 24(1), not s. 24(2): ch. 40, Enforcement of Rights, under heading § 40:21, "Exclusion of evidence".

[Section 41:2]

[1]*The Queen v. Wray*, [1971] S.C.R. 272, following *Kuruma v. The Queen*, [1955] A.C. 197 (P.C.). In *Wray*, the majority denied the existence of a discretion to exclude evidence where its admission would bring the administration of justice into disrepute. The Police and Criminal Evidence Act 1984 (U.K.), 1984, c. 60, s. 78, now authorizes the exclusion of evidence that would have "such an adverse effect on the fairness of the proceedings that the court ought not to admit it".

[2]*Hogan v. The Queen*, [1975] 2 S.C.R. 574.

[3]*Mapp v. Ohio* (1961), 367 U.S. 643.

directly than to confer such a windfall on the undeserving accused.[4] However, despite widespread popular and academic hostility to the exclusionary rule, American courts have persisted with it on the theory, which is controversial, that it is required in order to deter police misconduct. In the United States, deterrence is the rationale of the exclusionary rule.[5]

In Canada, the outcome of the debate between admission and exclusion was a compromise between the two alternatives.[6] The compromise is embodied in s. 24(2) of the Charter of Rights.

III. TEXT OF S. 24(2)

§ 41:3 Text of s. 24(2)

Section 24(2) of the Charter of Rights[1] provides as follows:

> Where, in proceedings under subsection (1), a court concludes that evidence was obtained in a manner that infringed or denied any rights or freedoms guaranteed by the Charter, the evidence shall be excluded if it is established that, having regard to all the circumstances, the admission of it in the proceedings would bring the administration of justice into disrepute.

Section 24(2) bases its exclusionary rule on the good reputation of the administration of justice, rather than the deterrence of official misconduct.[2] If the admission of evidence obtained in breach of the Charter "would bring the administration of justice into disrepute", then the evidence must ("shall") be excluded. If the admission of the evidence would not bring the administration of justice into disrepute, then the

---

[4]"Our way of upholding the Constitution is not to strike at the man who breaks it, but to let off somebody else who broke something else": Wigmore on Evidence (1961), vol. 8, 31.

[5]*Segura v. United States* (1984), 468 U.S. 796; *Illinois v. Krull* (1987), 480 U.S. 340.

[6]In the October 1980 version of the Charter, there was no provision for the exclusion of evidence obtained in breach of the Charter. Indeed, there was a section affirming the pre-existing law:

> 26. No provision of this Charter, other than section 13 [privilege against self-incrimination], affects the laws respecting the admissibility of evidence in any proceedings or the authority of the Parliament or a legislature to make laws in relation thereto.

This section was deleted and the present s. 24(2) was inserted in the April 1981 version.

[Section 41:3]

[1]For commentary on s. 24(2), see Gibson, The Law of the Charter: General Principles (1986), ch. 7; Charles, Cromwell and Jobson, Evidence and the Charter of Rights and Freedoms (1989), ch. 3; Beaudoin and Mendes (eds.), The Canadian Charter of Rights and Freedoms (4th ed., 2005), 1384-1396 (by Gibson); Stuart, Charter Justice in Canadian Criminal Law (3rd ed., 2000); Sopinka, Lederman, Bryant, The Law of Evidence in Canada (2nd ed., 1999), ch. 9; Schiff, Evidence in the Litigation Process (1993); Roach, Constitutional Remedies in Canada (Canada Law Book, loose-leaf) McLeod, Takach, Morton, Segal, The Canadian Charter of Rights (Carswell, loose-leaf), ch. 29; Canadian Charter of Rights Annotated (Canada Law Book, loose-leaf), annotation to s. 24(2). The last work provides a bibliography of the relevant literature.

[2]*R. v. Collins*, [1987] 1 S.C.R. 265, 281 ("s. 24(2) is not a remedy for police misconduct").

general rule of admissibility will apply.[3] Of course, if the evidence was obtained without any breach of the Charter of Rights, even if the police action involved a trick[4] or an illegality, then the general rule of admissibility will apply.

In *R. v. Calder* (1996),[5] a statement had been obtained from the accused in breach of his right to counsel, and had been excluded by the trial judge under s. 24(2). This meant, of course, that the Crown could not use the statement as part of its case in chief. However, when the accused testified in his own defence, he told a story that differed from the earlier excluded statement. The Crown applied to have the statement admitted for the sole purpose of cross-examining the accused as to his credibility. This raised the question whether evidence that had been excluded for one purpose (establishing the guilt of the accused) could be admitted for another purpose (impeaching the accused's credibility). Section 24(2) calls for the court to have regard to "all the circumstances" in determining whether the admission of evidence would bring the administration of justice into disrepute. Was the accused's inconsistent testimony one of the relevant circumstances? And could evidence have different effects on the administration of justice depending on the purposes for which it was used? Sopinka J., writing for the majority of the Supreme Court of Canada, gave a cautious yes answer to both questions. He left open the possibility that evidence that, if admitted without restriction, would tend to bring the administration of justice into disrepute might be admissible if its use in the proceedings were restricted. However, he said that the admission of evidence for the restricted purpose of impeaching credibility would be appropriate only in "very limited circumstances", and he did not say what those circumstances would be.[6] In this case, he held that the Crown's application to use the evidence for the purpose of impeaching credibility had been cor-

---

[3]In *R. v. Therens*, [1985] 1 S.C.R. 613, 648, Le Dain J., with the agreement of five of the seven other judges on this issue, held that, after a finding that the admission of the evidence would not bring the administration of justice into disrepute, the court had no discretion to exclude the evidence, even if the court concluded that the exclusion of the evidence would be an "appropriate and just" remedy under s. 24(1). This point did not have to be decided in *Therens*, and Dickson C.J. (at p. 619) and Lamer J. (at p. 626) left the point open.

[4]A police tactic that was in use before the Charter of Rights was the placing of a police officer disguised as a prisoner in the same cell as the accused. In apparently casual conversation, the police officer would attempt to elicit an incriminating statement from an unsuspecting accused. Before the Charter of Rights, such a statement was admissible: *Rothman v. The Queen*, [1981] 1 S.C.R. 640 (statement admitted). The position now is that this tactic is a breach of s. 7 of the Charter of Rights, and the statement is therefore vulnerable to exclusion under s. 24(2): *R. v. Hebert*, [1990] 2 S.C.R. 151 (statement excluded).

[5]*R. v. Calder*, [1996] 1 S.C.R. 660. The majority opinion was that of Sopinka J., with the concurrence of Gonthier, Cory, Iacobucci and Major JJ. La Forest J. wrote a brief concurring opinion. McLachlin J. dissented.

[6]*R. v. Calder*, [1996] 1 S.C.R. 660, para. 35. La Forest J., concurring, said (para. 1) that he could not envisage any circumstances where the distinction would be appropriate. In *R. v. Cook*, [1998] 2 S.C.R. 597, Cory and Iacobucci JJ. for the majority, following

rectly denied by the trial judge, although the trial (on sexual misconduct charges) essentially turned on whether the accused (a police officer) or the complainant (a prostitute) was telling the truth. The jury had acquitted the accused, and this verdict was upheld by the majority of the Supreme Court of Canada. The dissenting opinion of McLachlin J. was that the inability of the Crown to cross-examine the accused on his earlier statement would tend to bring the administration of justice into disrepute.

Section 24(2) provides for the exclusion of evidence, not the inclusion of evidence. For example, the Criminal Code prohibits the use of wiretap evidence not obtained in conformity with the Code; such evidence is inadmissible by virtue of its express statutory exclusion, whether or not its admission would bring the administration of justice into disrepute.[7] Section 24(2) has no application to evidence that is excluded by a common law or statutory exclusionary rule. A statutory exclusionary rule may be vulnerable to Charter attack, but not under s. 24(2). For example, in *R. v. Seaboyer* (1991),[8] the Supreme Court of Canada held that the "rape-shield" law, which excluded from a criminal trial for sexual assault evidence of the complainant's past sexual activity, was unconstitutional. Because the law excluded evidence that might be necessary to make full answer and defence, the law violated ss. 7 and 11 (d) of the Charter.[9]

IV. CAUSATION

§ 41:4 Causation

Section 24(2) applies when evidence has been "obtained in a manner" that infringed or denied a Charter right. This requirement would be satisfied if the evidence was obtained as a result of the Charter infringement. For example, a weapon may be found during an unreasonable search. In that case, there would be a causal connection between the Charter violation and the discovery of the evidence.[1] But the Supreme Court of Canada in *R. v. Strachan* (1988)[2] has held that a causal connection is not necessary. It is not necessary to show that the evidence was discovered by reason of the Charter violation. And it is

---

Calder, refused to admit evidence for the limited purpose of impeaching credibility and said that the circumstances when that would be allowed would be "very rare indeed" (para. 76); however, L'Heureux-Dubé J. in dissent would have admitted the evidence for the limited purpose (paras. 107-109).

[7]*R. v. Thompson*, [1990] 2 S.C.R. 1111.

[8]*R. v. Seaboyer*, [1991] 2 S.C.R. 577.

[9]See also Paciocco, "The Constitutional Right to Present Defence Evidence in Criminal Cases" (1985) 63 Can. Bar Rev. 519.

[Section 41:4]

[1]E.g., *R. v. I. (L.R.)*, [1993] 4 S.C.R. 504 (first confession obtained in breach of Charter; second confession excluded on basis of causal connection to first confession).

[2]*R. v. Strachan*, [1988] 2 S.C.R. 980; followed in *R. v. Debot*, [1989] 2 S.C.R. 1140 (reasonable "frisk" search not preceded by advice of right to counsel).

certainly not necessary to show that the evidence would not have been discovered but for the Charter violation. It is sufficient that there be a temporal connection between the Charter violation and the discovery of the evidence.

The facts of the *Strachan* case were these. The police held a valid search warrant to search the accused's apartment for illegal drugs. When they arrived at the apartment they arrested the accused for possession of marijuana, and they searched the apartment, where they found drugs. The Supreme Court of Canada held that the police had denied the accused's right to counsel, because, although they had advised the accused of his right to retain and instruct counsel, they had not allowed him to contact a lawyer until after the search was over and they had taken him back to the police station. The question then arose whether the evidence found in the search should be excluded. It was clear that there was no causal relationship between the breach of the Charter and the discovery of the evidence. The police held a valid search warrant, and they would have searched the apartment and found the evidence even if the accused's counsel had been present. Nevertheless, the Court held that s. 24(2) applied. The Charter violation and the discovery of the evidence were part of a single "chain of events";[3] the Charter violation occurred "in the course of" obtaining the evidence.[4] This temporal connection between the Charter violation and the discovery of the evidence was enough to establish that the evidence was "obtained in a manner" that infringed or denied a Charter right. (The Court went on to admit the evidence on the ground that there were extenuating circumstances that mitigated the police conduct, so that the admission of the evidence would not bring the administration of justice into disrepute.)

In *Strachan*, the Court was intentionally vague about the precise nature of the connection between the Charter violation and the discovery of the evidence. The temporal connection that existed in that case sufficed, but such a connection was not "determinative":[5] "there can be no hard and fast rule for determining when evidence obtained following the infringement of a Charter right becomes too remote",[6] For example, there might be a causal connection, but not a temporal connection. This would be so with respect to "secondary" (or "derivative") evidence, which is evidence obtained as an indirect result of a Charter violation. An example of secondary evidence would be a weapon found elsewhere as the result of lawful police work based on information discovered during an unreasonable search. The secondary evidence may be found some time after the Charter violation, but it would be causally connected to

[3] *R. v. Strachan*, [1988] 2 S.C.R. 980, 1005.

[4] *R. v. Strachan*, [1988] 2 S.C.R. 980, 1005. Compare *R. v. Graham* (1991), 1 O.R. (3d) 499 (C.A.) (lapse of seven days between Charter violation and inculpatory statement negated any temporal connection).

[5] *R. v. Strachan*, [1988] 2 S.C.R. 980, 1005.

[6] *R. v. Strachan*, [1988] 2 S.C.R. 980, 1006.

the Charter violation.[7] In the United States, the exclusionary rule applies to secondary evidence ("the fruit of the poisoned tree") as well as to the primary product of a constitutional violation.[8] This seems to be a reasonable interpretation of s. 24(2) as well.[9] Of course, as the causal connection between the Charter violation and the discovery of the evidence becomes more tenuous, the likelihood increases that a court would hold that the evidence was not obtained in a manner that infringed a Charter right.

The facts of *R. v. Grant* (1993)[10] presented another situation where there was no causal connection between the breach of the Charter and the obtaining of the evidence. In that case, the police had conducted two warrantless searches of the perimeter of the accused's house, which the police suspected was being used to cultivate marijuana. Having observed indications that the basement of the house was being used to cultivate something, the police applied for and obtained a warrant to search the house itself. They searched the house and found and seized marijuana plants, marijuana and drug paraphernalia. The Supreme Court of Canada, in an opinion written by Sopinka J., held that the warrantless perimeter searches had been made in breach of s. 8 of the Charter, but he also held that the search warrant for the house itself was valid, because the police had presented to the issuing judge sufficient evidence of reasonable and probable cause for a search of the house quite apart from the perimeter-search observations, which should not have been relied upon. Sopinka J. held, nonetheless, that the valid warrant did not wash away the sins of the past. There was "a sufficient temporal connection between the warrantless perimeter searches and the evidence ultimately offered at trial to require a determination as to whether the evidence should be excluded".[11] (He went on to admit the evidence on the grounds that it was real evidence and it had been obtained in good faith, so that the admission of the evidence would not bring the administration of justice into disrepute.)

In *R. v. Burlingham* (1995),[12] police persuaded a murder suspect to provide a statement and to lead them to the murder weapon in violation of his right to counsel under s. 10(b) of the Charter. Obviously, the direct fruits of the unconstitutional police actions (the accused's state-

---

[7] *R. v. Strachan*, [1988] 2 S.C.R. 980, 1004, using derivative evidence as an example of a causal connection.

[8] *Silverthorne Lumber Co. v. United States* (1920), 251 U.S. 385; *Wong Sun v. United States* (1963), 371 U.S. 471.

[9] *R. v. Strachan*, [1988] 2 S.C.R. 980, 1004 (obiter dictum recognizing application of s. 24(2) to derivative evidence); *R. v. Feeney*, [1997] 2 S.C.R. 13, paras. 69-70 (explaining when "derivative" evidence is "conscriptive" evidence).

[10] *R. v. Grant*, [1993] 3 S.C.R. 223. The opinion of the Court was written by Sopinka J. Two other cases raising the same issues were decided at the same time, namely, *R. v. Wiley*, [1993] 3 S.C.R. 263 and *R. v. Plant*, [1993] 3 S.C.R. 281.

[11] *R. v. Grant*, [1993] 3 S.C.R. 223, 255.

[12] *R. v. Burlingham*, [1995] 2 S.C.R. 206; see also ch. 50, Rights on Arrest or Detention, under heading §§ 50:5 to 50:16, "Right to counsel".

ment and the weapon) required a determination as to their admissibility under s. 24(2) (all of this evidence was ultimately excluded). However, the accused had also recounted to his girlfriend how he had led police to the weapon, and, at his trial, she testified about that conversation. The accused's statement to his girlfriend was voluntary, and, since the girlfriend was not a police agent, the statement to her had not been elicited by the police and was not in violation of the right to counsel. Nevertheless, the Supreme Court of Canada held that the statement to the girlfriend was caught by s. 24(2). The Court reasoned from *Strachan* that there was a sufficient temporal connection with the breach of the accused's Charter rights to taint the statement to the girlfriend.[13] The Court went on to hold that the admission of the girlfriend's testimony would bring the administration of justice into disrepute, and a new trial was ordered from which her testimony was to be excluded.

A *causal* connection between a Charter violation and the discovery of evidence was found to be too remote in *R. v. Goldhart* (1996).[14] In that case, an unreasonable search had uncovered evidence of an illegal narcotics operation and had led police to arrest the accused, Goldhart, and another suspect for drug-related offences. Both men were advised by their counsel, accurately as it turned out, that the evidence discovered in the search would probably be excluded by the trial judge under s. 24(2) of the Charter. However, only Goldhart chose to exercise his Charter rights. The co-accused pleaded guilty, explaining that he had become a "born-again Christian" and wanted to clear his conscience. The co-accused also volunteered to testify against Goldhart, and Goldhart was convicted. On appeal, counsel for the defence objected to the testimony of Goldhart's co-accused on the grounds that the Crown had only "discovered" its witness by virtue of the unreasonable search which led to the two arrests. That causal connection, the defence argued, made the testimony of Goldhart's co-accused the product of an unreasonable search and seizure. The Supreme Court of Canada, by a majority, held that the testimony of the co-accused had not been obtained in a manner that breached the Charter. Rather, the co-accused's decision to testify had been the product of the co-accused's own conscience and free will. The causal connection between the Charter breach and the evidence was too remote to be caught by s. 24(2), and the evidence had been properly admitted at the trial.

A causal connection was found to be sufficient in *R. v. Wittwer* (2008).[15] In that case, a police officer had obtained an incriminating statement from the accused (who was charged with sexual assault) without warning him of his right to counsel. When the police realized that the state-

---

[13]The Court was unanimous that a sufficient proximate connection to the Charter breach existed, but L'Heureux-Dubé J., the lone dissenter, felt that the testimony should still have been admitted. A majority of six judges concurred with Iacobucci J.'s opinion that the evidence was both tainted by the Charter breach and should have been excluded.

[14]*R. v. Goldhart*, [1996] 2 S.C.R. 463. Sopinka J. wrote for an eight-judge majority. La Forest dissented.

[15]*R. v. Wittwer*, [2008] 2 S.C.R. 235. Fish J. wrote the opinion of the Court.

ment had been obtained in breach of the Charter, a different police officer interviewed the accused again, this time giving him the proper warning and opportunity to retain counsel. The interviewing officer initially denied any knowledge of the accused's earlier statement, but over the course of four hours was unsuccessful in eliciting a repetition of the statement. The officer left the interview room and after a short absence returned to announce that he had just been told what the accused had said in his earlier statement. The accused immediately then acknowledged the truth of what he had earlier said and repeated a similar account of the facts. The Supreme Court of Canada held that the later statement was tainted by the earlier Charter breach, because the earlier statement was "a substantial factor contributing to the making of the second statement".[16] The Court went on to exclude the later statement on the ground that its admission would enable the police "to reap the benefit of their own infringements of a suspect's constitutional rights", which would bring the administration of justice into disrepute.[17]

V. BURDEN OF PROOF

§ 41:5 Burden of proof

The exclusionary rule of s. 24(2) applies "if it is established" that the admission of the evidence would bring the administration of justice into disrepute. The phrase "if it is established" casts the burden of proving that the admission of the evidence would bring the administration of justice into disrepute onto the person seeking to exclude the evidence.[1] The standard of proof is the civil standard of the balance of probability.[2] Thus, the person seeking to exclude the evidence must persuade the trial court that it is more probable than not that the admission of the evidence would bring the administration of justice into disrepute. Of course, without a clear definition of the matter to be proved, namely, disrepute, the location of the burden of proof and the standard of proof are not of much significance. Certainly, the cases in the Supreme Court of Canada, to be described shortly, do not suggest that the Court uses the burden of proof to resolve uncertainty. Rather, they suggest a leaning in favour of exclusion, even when one would expect at least a division of opinion among reasonable people as to whether disrepute had been established.[3] In fact, the Court has frankly acknowledged that, while "theoretically" the burden is placed on the accused to establish that the administration of justice would be brought into disrepute, "in

---

[16] *R. v. Wittwer*, [2008] 2 S.C.R. 235, paras. 23-25. There was also a close temporal connection between the two statements.

[17] *R. v. Wittwer*, [2008] 2 S.C.R. 235, para. 26.

[Section 41:5]

[1] *R. v. Collins*, [1987] 1 S.C.R. 265, 280.

[2] *R. v. Collins*, [1987] 1 S.C.R. 265, 280.

[3] E.g., the cases where the police acted in good faith, in ignorance that they were in violation of the Charter, and obtained reliable evidence. The Court had often excluded the evidence in these circumstances: see cases cited in § 41:11, "Good faith".

practice" the burden will fall on the Crown when the Crown "possesses superior knowledge".

VI. REASONABLE PERSON TEST

§ 41:6 Reasonable person test

When s. 24(2) speaks of bringing the administration of justice "into disrepute", it does not say in whose eyes the disrepute must appear. Disrepute to a police officer (for example) might be quite different from disrepute to a law professor. In *R. v. Collins* (1987),[1] where Lamer J. for the majority of the Supreme Court of Canada laid down the basic guidelines for s. 24(2), he said that it is disrepute in the "community at large" that is the touchstone. But he hastened to add that no attempt should be made to ascertain the actual state of opinion in the community at large, whether by opinion polls or other direct evidence. Instead, he stipulated a "reasonable person" test: the trial court would have to decide whether the admission of the evidence would bring the administration of justice into disrepute in the eyes of a reasonable person.[2] "The reasonable person is usually the average person in the community, but only when the community's current mood is reasonable".[3]

It is difficult to know how a judge is to ascertain the views of the "average person". Indeed, the whole exercise is so hypothetical that it is doubtful whether it is even meaningful to ask what the average person would think about the admission of evidence in a particular case. It seems inevitable that judges will regard themselves as barometers of public opinion for the purpose of s. 24(2), so that disrepute is likely to reflect "the views of the judiciary more closely then that of the citizenry at large".[4] And yet, this is one topic upon which the attitudes of the judiciary, nurtured in a professional climate of concern for scrupulous adherence to constitutional norms, are unlikely to be shared by the citizenry at large, who would probably give much greater weight to securing the conviction of criminals.[5]

VII. DEFINITION OF DISREPUTE

§ 41:7 Definition of disrepute

There were suggestions in the pre-Charter case-law that evidence

---

[Section 41:6]

[1] *R. v. Collins*, [1987] 1 S.C.R. 265.

[2] *R. v. Collins*, [1987] 1 S.C.R. 265, 282.

[3] *R. v. Collins*, [1987] 1 S.C.R. 265, 282.

[4] D. Gibson, "Shocking the Public" (1983) 13 Man. L.J. 495, 498.

[5] A.W. Bryant and others, "Public Attitudes towards the Exclusion of Evidence" (1990) 69 Can. Bar Rev. 1; M. Gold and others, "Public Support for the Exclusion of Unconstitutionally Obtained Evidence" (1990) 1 Supreme Court L.R. (2d) 555. In *R. v. Burlingham*, [1995] 2 S.C.R. 206, para. 74, L'Heureux-Dubé J., dissenting, suggested that public opinion surveys did constitute a periodic "reality check" that was both "healthy and necessary" for the judges. No other judge agreed with her opinion!

obtained by a dirty trick (such as by a police officer impersonating a priest) should be excluded on the ground that its admission would "shock" the community.[1] In *R. v. Collins* (1987),[2] Lamer J. said that community shock was not the standard of disrepute under s. 24(2). A lower standard was sufficient, for two reasons. One reason is that s. 24(2) contemplates that a breach of the Charter has taken place, which is much more serious than a trick,[3] and does not call for such a powerful additional ground of exclusion. The other reason is to be found in the softer language of the French version of s. 24(2). The English version uses the phrase "would bring the administration of justice into disrepute". In the French version, the word "would" is replaced by "est susceptible de". The French version is closer to "could" than "would", which implies a less onerous standard than that of community shock.

While *Collins* establishes the negative proposition that community shock is not the test of disrepute, the case does not provide a positive definition of disrepute. However, Lamer J. did set out three factors to be weighed in determining disrepute. The factors were as follows: (1) the nature of the evidence; (2) the nature of the conduct by which the evidence was obtained; and (3) the effect on the system of justice of excluding the evidence.[4] These three *Collins* factors governed the exclusion of evidence from 1987 until 2009 when the Court decided *R. v. Grant* (2009).[5] In that case, the Court substituted three new factors to be weighed in determining disrepute. The *Grant* factors are (1) "the seriousness of the Charter-infringing state conduct"; (2) "the impact of the breach on the Charter-protected interests of the accused"; and (3) "society's interest in the adjudication of the case on its merits".[6] The new framework is not markedly different from the *Collins* framework, and the three *Collins* factors will continue to be relevant, albeit in new rubrics. However, the omission of *Collins* factor (1), the nature of the evidence, is of great significance, because of the way in which the Court had applied that factor before 2009. That is the topic of the next section of this chapter. Then the following three sections of the chapter will deal in turn with the three *Grant* factors.

[Section 41:7]

[1] *Rothman v. The Queen*, [1981] 1 S.C.R. 640, 697 per Lamer J.

[2] *R. v. Collins*, [1987] 1 S.C.R. 265, 286-288.

[3] Note, however, that some "tricks" are breaches of the Charter § 41:3 note 4, above.

[4] *R. v. Collins*, [1987] 1 S.C.R. 265, 284-286.

[5] *R. v. Grant*, [2009] 2 S.C.R. 353. McLachlin C.J. and Charron J. wrote the opinion of the majority. Binnie J. wrote a concurring opinion, disagreeing with some aspects of the majority reasons but agreeing (para. 150) on the new three-factor framework. Deschamps J. also wrote a concurring opinion, disagreeing with the new three-factor framework and proposing instead (para. 223) "a simple test that takes into account both the public interest in protecting Charter rights and the public interest in an adjudication on the merits".

[6] *R. v. Grant*, [2009] 2 S.C.R. 353, para. 71.

VIII. NATURE OF EVIDENCE

§ 41:8 Nature of evidence

The first branch of the *Collins* test called for an examination of the nature of the evidence that had been obtained in breach of the Charter. Under *Grant*, that is no longer one of the factors to be weighed in assessing the admissibility of the evidence. Of course, it cannot be doubted that the nature of the evidence will continue to be relevant even under the new *Grant* framework. Evidence obtained in breach of the Charter that was unreliable, for example, would obviously not be admitted, perhaps under *Grant* factors (2) or (3). But the nature of the evidence is no longer a separate factor to be weighed in the balance, and that is because the Court in *Grant* rejected the large body of jurisprudence that the Court had developed in interpreting *Collins* factor (1).

What the Supreme Court had done with *Collins* factor (1), the nature of the evidence, was to develop a set of rules under which evidence was routinely excluded in disregard not only of *Collins* factors (2) and (3) but also of s. 24(2)'s stipulation that "all the circumstances" be taken into account. On the assumption that the Court has turned over a new leaf, this text will abandon its former long (and critical) account[1] and content itself with a brief description of the jurisprudence that has now been superseded. The Court started with the proposition that evidence should be excluded if its admission would make the trial of the accused "unfair". No one could disagree with the general proposition that an unfair trial would bring the administration of justice into disrepute. The Court then went on to hold that the admission of "conscriptive" evidence obtained in breach of the Charter would make a trial unfair. If conscriptive really meant conscripted (compelled), that step might be an easy one to accept as well, but the Court's view of what was conscriptive had nothing to do with compulsion and included any evidence that was self-incriminatory (such as an incautious admission made by the accused before he was warned of his right to counsel), even if it was perfectly voluntary, totally reliable, the product of good-faith behaviour by the police, and essential to the case for the prosecution. The Court then turned its attention to "derivative" evidence, which was real evidence that existed independently of the Charter breach (such as a gun or drugs), but which was discovered with the aid of a "conscriptive" statement by the accused. Derivative evidence, despite its reliability, was also excluded on the basis that its admission would make the trial unfair, unless the prosecution proved that the evidence would have been "discoverable" if no breach of the Charter had occurred.[2] This had the effect of sidetracking a criminal trial into a hypothetical inquiry into whether the police would have

---

[Section 41:8]

[1]The bound version of the 5th edition of this book, § 41:8, "Nature of evidence", contains my account of the *pre-Grant* law. It is to be hoped that there will be no longer be any occasion to consult it (despite the time lavished on its preparation).

[2]The leading case was *R. v. Stillman*, [1997] 1 S.C.R. 607; criticized by D.M. Paciocco, "*Stillman*, Disproportion and the Fair Trial Dichotomy under Section 24(2)"

discovered the evidence if no Charter breach had taken place—a considerable distraction from the factors initially laid down in *Collins*.

In *Grant*, the Court was frank in acknowledging the wrong path that it had travelled since *Collins* stipulated "the nature of the evidence" as the first factor to be considered under s. 24(2).[3] The Court in *Grant* banished consideration of trial fairness and conscription from s. 24(2), recognizing that those concepts had created "new problems of their own". Neither concept should any longer be determinative of admissibility. Trial fairness was in other contexts a "multifaceted and contextual concept" which was not consistent with "a near-automatic presumption that admission of a broad class of evidence will render a trial unfair, regardless of the circumstances in which it was obtained." The assumption that conscripted evidence always makes a trial unfair was in any case "open to challenge", and the inquiry into whether evidence had been conscripted "should be replaced by a flexible test based on all the circumstances, as the wording of s. 24(2) requires". As for derivative evidence, the inquiry into discoverability was "overly speculative", and discoverability should no longer be determinative of admissibility.[4] The admissibility of every type of evidence obtained in breach of the Charter should be assessed by weighing the same three *Grant* factors in order to determine under s. 24(2) whether in "all the circumstances" its admission "would bring the administration of justice into disrepute".

The *Grant* ruling simplifies the law and makes it more faithful to the text of s. 24(2), which is after all the governing constitutional provision. However, *Grant* does substitute a judicial balancing exercise for rules that sometimes contributed predictability to judicial decisions under s. 24(2). The decisions derived from balancing the three *Grant* factors are likely to be unpredictable, especially since appellate courts are instructed to pay "considerable deference" to the decisions of trial judges—provided they have considered "the proper factors".[5] More predictability would better advance the important goal[6] of deterring unconstitutional behav-

---

(1997) 2 Can. Crim. L.R. 163.

[3]*R. v. Grant*, [2009] 2 S.C.R. 353, paras. 59-128. The phrases quoted in the rest of this paragraph of text are to be found at paras. 62, 65, 107, 120.

[4]*R. v. Grant*, [2009] 2 S.C.R. 353, para. 121, but note that in para 122 McLachlin C.J. and Charron J. say that discoverability still "retains a useful role" in assessing the impact of the breach on the Charter-protected interests of the accused (*Grant* factor (2)). See also *R. v. Côté*, [2011] 3 S.C.R. 215, paras. 65-88 per Cromwell J. for majority, 106-113 per Deschamps J. dissenting. Query as to how much weight should be given to such a speculative and hypothetical concept.

[5]*R. v. Grant*, [2009] 2 S.C.R. 353, para. 86. E.g., *R. v. Beaulieu*, [2010] 1 S.C.R. 248, para. 5.

[6]In *R. v. Grant*, [2009] 2 S.C.R. 353, paras. 67-70, the majority said that the goal of s. 24(2) was not to punish the police or compensate the accused, but was to maintain the good reputation of the administration of justice. They did not talk about deterring unconstitutional behaviour by the police, but that surely is an important subsidiary goal.

iour by the police.[7] It may well be that *Grant* factor (1) (the seriousness of the Charter-infringing state conduct) will develop into the dispositive consideration, considering that factor (2) (the impact of the breach on the Charter-protected interests of the accused) will normally weigh in on the side of exclusion, while factor (3) (society's interest in the adjudication of the case on its merits) will normally weigh in on the side of admission.[8] If factor (1) was normally dispositive, the police could become reasonably confident that intended (or reckless) breaches of the Charter would lead to exclusion, while unintended breaches of the Charter, made in good faith in situations of legal or factual uncertainty, would not lead to exclusion. Even that degree of predictability would serve as an incentive for the police (reinforcing their training and good instincts) to obey the Charter to the best of their ability.

What happened in *Grant* itself was that the accused had been stopped on the sidewalk by police officers who had no reasonable grounds to suspect him of anything, although they did have vague suspicions (a police hunch) that turned out to be well founded. The police asked him whether he had anything on him that he should not have, and he said that he was carrying a gun. He was then arrested, searched, and, when a gun was found, he was charged with several firearms offences. At his trial, the gun was entered in evidence against him, and he was convicted of the charges. He argued that the evidence of the gun should have been excluded under s. 24(2). The Supreme Court of Canada held that the accused's statement that he was carrying a gun had been elicited in breach of his Charter right not to be arbitrarily detained (s. 9) and his Charter right to counsel (s. 10(b)).[9] Under the *Collins* framework, the gun would have had to be excluded. It was "derivative" evidence—real evidence discovered by reason of a "conscripted" statement—that was not otherwise discoverable by the police. Its admission would therefore make the trial "unfair". But the *Grant* Court, applying the new framework, held that the gun was properly admitted.[10] The concepts of trial unfairness and conscripted evidence were no longer part of the analysis. The police conduct *(Grant* factor (1)) occurred in a context of legal uncertainty about when the warning of the right to counsel had to be given; it was "neither deliberate nor egregious", and "cannot be characterized as hav-

---

[7] S. Penney, "Taking Deterrence Seriously: Excluding Unconstitutionally Obtained Evidence" (2003) 49 McGill L.J. 105, 134. Penney, who argues that the deterrence of unconstitutional behaviour is the sole defensible purpose of s. 24(2), would prefer a bright-line rule that excludes all evidence obtained in breach of the Charter, except where the police have acted in good faith. See § 41:11, "Good faith".

[8] Research supports the accuracy of this prediction that *Grant* factor (1) would be the dispositive consideration in the cases: see P. McGuinty, "Section 24(2) of the Charter: Exploring the Role of Police Conduct in the Grant Analysis" (2018) 41:4 Man. L.J. 273, para. 3 (conducting an empirical study of 100 cases from 2016).

[9] This was based on a holding that the accused was detained before he was arrested; this aspect of the decision is discussed in ch. 50, Rights on Arrest or Detention, under heading § 50:3, "Requirement of restraint".

[10] *R. v. Grant*, [2009] 2 S.C.R. 353, paras. 129-140.

ing been in bad faith".[11] The impact of the Charter breach on the accused's rights *(Grant* factor (2)) was admittedly "significant" and was to be weighed in the balance on the side of exclusion, but it was outweighed by factor (1). (The Court found that factor (3) was of little assistance, although it surely should have weighed strongly in favour of admission since the gun was reliable evidence that was essential to the prosecution's case.). The Court's conclusion was that the admission of the gun into evidence would not, on balance, bring the administration of justice into disrepute, and the gun was properly admitted at the trial.

IX. NATURE OF OFFICIAL CONDUCT

§ 41:9 Deliberate violations

The first factor that was identified in *Grant*[1] as relevant in determining disrepute was "the seriousness of the Charter-infringing state conduct". This is essentially the same as the second *Collins* factor which was the conduct by which the evidence was obtained. The jurisprudence that developed before *Grant* was decided in 2009 under *Collins* factor (2) has therefore continued to be relevant under *Grant* factor (1).[2] As reported in the discussion of *Grant* in the previous section of the book, this factor was the dispositive one: it was the good faith of the police conduct that tipped the balance of factors in favour of admitting the gun that had been discovered in breach of the Charter. In my view, *Grant* factor (1) will normally be the dispositive factor since *Grant* factors (2) and (3) will normally pull in opposite directions.[3] Moreover, I argue, *Grant* factor (1) *should* be the dispositive factor because it provides the police with enough pre-dictability to provide them with an incentive to obey the Charter to the best of their ability.

Where the police have deliberately violated the Charter in order to obtain incriminating evidence, then the use of the evidence would tend to bring the administration of justice into disrepute. Where the police arrested several accuseds without reasonable and probable cause, in circumstances where the police must have been aware of the absence of a legal basis for the arrests, the Court excluded the confessions, fingerprints and stolen property that the police obtained after the arrest.[4] Where the police made a search under an invalid warrant, and also used excessive force in executing the search, the Court excluded the evidence

[11] Compare the companion case of *R. v. Harrison*, [2009] 2 S.C.R. 494 (police conduct, although not a deliberate breach of the Charter, was reckless in its insufficient regard for Charter rights; evidence excluded under the *Grant* factors).

[Section 41:9]

[1] *R. v. Grant*, [2009] 2 S.C.R. 353.

[2] See e.g. *R. v. Côté*, [2011] 3 S.C.R. 215, para. 71; *R. v. Paterson*, [2017] 1 S.C.R. 202, paras. 44, 46; *R v. Le*, 2019 SCC 34, para. 143.

[3] This prediction has been confirmed: see P. McGuinty, "Section 24(2) of the Charter: Exploring the Role of Police Conduct in the Grant Analysis" (2018) 41:4 Man. L.J. 273, para. 3 (conducting an empirical study of 100 cases from 2016).

[4] *R. v. Duguay*, [1989] 1 S.C.R. 93.

of the illegal weapons that were found in the search.[5] Where the police entered private property without a warrant and made a "perimeter search" of a house, the Court excluded the evidence of the marijuana plants that were later found in the house.[6] In each of these cases, the police knew or ought to have known that they were acting in breach of the Charter.

In *R. v. Taylor* (2014),[7] the police, on arriving at the scene of a one-vehicle accident, arrested the driver and charged him with impaired driving. The police informed the accused of his rights and asked him if he wished to speak to a lawyer; he replied that he did. However, he was not taken back to the police station; instead, he was taken by ambulance to a hospital for assessment. Two police officers also went to the hospital and were present during his medical examination. Blood samples were taken by the hospital shortly after the arrival of the accused. Although the accused was in the hospital for several hours, neither police officer made any effort to provide him with access to a phone, an omission that they described as "a mistake" when they testified at his trial. Next day, under the authority of a warrant, the police seized the blood samples that had been taken by the hospital. The analysis of those blood samples was the evidence that was relied upon by the prosecution at the trial where the accused was convicted of impaired driving. The Supreme Court took the view that there was a breach of the accused's right to counsel before the taking of the blood samples.[8] Were the blood samples admissible under s. 24(2)? The police failure to facilitate the accused's access to counsel "was not the result of a wilful disregard for [the accused's] rights", but it did constitute "a significant departure from the standard of conduct expected of police officers".[9] The first *Grant* factor ("seriousness" of breach) accordingly weighed in favour of exclusion, as did the second factor (effect of breach on the accused). Although the evidence was reliable and essential to the prosecution case (third factor), the Court concluded that on balance the evidence should be excluded; the accused was entitled to be acquitted.

---

[5] *R. v. Genest*, [1989] 1 S.C.R. 59.

[6] *R. v. Kokesch*, [1990] 3 S.C.R. 3. See also *R. v. Paterson*, [2017] 1 S.C.R. 202, 2017 SCC 15 (police entered private dwelling uninvited and without a warrant and saw incriminating evidence in plain view; evidence excluded).

[7] *R. v. Taylor*, [2014] 2 S.C.R. 495, 2014 SCC 50. Abella J. wrote the opinion of the Court.

[8] *R. v. Taylor*, [2014] 2 S.C.R. 495, 2014 SCC 50, para. 37. The trial judge took the view that no phone need be provided at the accident scene, and that there was no reasonable opportunity to provide a phone at the hospital, at least in the short time (20 to 30 minutes) before the hospital took the blood samples. (Some later samples had been taken on the demand of the police, but it was the earlier ones that were put in evidence.) On that reasoning, although the police behaved badly in never subsequently providing a phone, no breach of the right to counsel occurred before the blood samples were taken. The trial judge therefore admitted the evidence and the accused was convicted. Abella J. never explained what was wrong with that reasoning; she focused on the long period at the hospital when no phone was provided, but only the very beginning of that period was relevant.

[9] *R. v. Taylor*, [2014] 2 S.C.R. 495, 2014 SCC 50, para. 39.

§ 41:10 Extenuating circumstances

On the other hand, where the action in breach of the Charter was taken in circumstances that were particularly difficult or complicated, the Court has been willing to excuse the breach to the extent of admitting the evidence. In *R. v. Tremblay* (1987),[1] the accused was being obstructive, and the police thought that he was using the opportunity to contact a lawyer as a delaying tactic; the Court admitted the evidence of a breath test, despite the fact that it had been administered before there had been enough time for the lawyer to be contacted by the accused's wife. In *R. v. Strachan* (1988),[2] the police, after arresting the accused in his apartment, exercised a tight control over him and two other people in the apartment, because the police feared that attempts would be made to use weapons or destroy drugs that they thought (correctly as it turned out) were concealed in the apartment; the Court admitted the evidence of the drugs found by the police, despite the fact that the police delayed too long in allowing the accused to call his lawyer. In *R. v. Silveira* (1995),[3] police officers entered the accused's home without a search warrant and exercised control over its occupants (who did not include the accused) while a search warrant was being obtained. The officers had already arrested the accused in a public place, and they feared that, unless they secured the house immediately, someone connected to the accused might destroy or remove evidence of drugs before they could get a warrant to search the house. Although the Crown did not contest that the securing of the house was a breach of the accused's Charter right to be secure from unreasonable search or seizure, a majority of the Supreme Court of Canada admitted the evidence on the basis that the police action was a reaction to a real risk that evidence might be destroyed.

§ 41:11 Good faith

In the absence of the extenuating circumstances that are illustrated by the cases in the previous section, the Supreme Court of Canada initially showed itself to be surprisingly impervious to a plea of good faith on the part of police officers who gathered evidence in inadvertent breach of the Charter. This situation arose in several of the early cases, where the precise requirements of the Charter were unsettled at the time when the police acted, and were only settled when the accused's appeal reached the Supreme Court of Canada several years later.

In *R. v. Therens* (1985),[1] the police took a breath sample from the accused, who was suspected of impaired driving, without first informing

---

[Section 41:10]

[1] *R. v. Tremblay*, [1987] 2 S.C.R. 435.

[2] *R. v. Strachan*, [1988] 2 S.C.R. 980.

[3] *R. v. Silveira*, [1995] 2 S.C.R. 297.

[Section 41:11]

[1] *R. v. Therens*, [1985] 1 S.C.R. 613.

him of his right to retain and instruct counsel. Most lower courts had held that the accused was not "detained" in this situation, so that s. 10(b) of the Charter did not apply and there was no right to retain and instruct counsel. Indeed, the Supreme Court of Canada itself, in *Chromiak v. The Queen* (1980),[2] had recently held that in this situation there was no right to counsel under the similar language of the Canadian Bill of Rights. In these circumstances, the police could surely be forgiven for assuming that they need not offer the accused the opportunity to retain and instruct counsel, which would of course delay the taking of the breath test. The Supreme Court of Canada disagreed. The Court overruled its earlier decision in *Chromiak*, and held that, when a breath test was demanded at the police station, there was a detention and a right to counsel. Then, in an astonishing passage, the majority of the Court said that the police had "flagrantly violated a Charter right", and that such an "overt violation" would bring the administration of justice into disrepute.[3] The breath sample was therefore excluded. This condemnation of the police action seems to have been based solely on the police's inability to predict that the Supreme Court of Canada would overrule its earlier decision in *Chromiak*.[4]

The Supreme Court of Canada excluded evidence in a number of other early Charter cases that were similar to *Therens*. The Court excluded two other breath samples that had been taken without prior warning of the right to counsel.[5] The Court excluded a vial of blood taken by a doctor from an unconscious accused.[6] The Court excluded a statement made by an accused who was intoxicated,[7] and a statement made by an accused who had said that he wished to exercise his right to counsel but who had made no attempt to do so.[8] In each of these cases, the police action, although held to be a breach of the Charter, had never been so characterized at the time when the police acted. In each case, the action fell into a grey area where reasonable lawyers and judges could and did

[2] *Chromiak v. The Queen*, [1980] 1 S.C.R. 471.

[3] *R. v. Therens*, [1985] 1 S.C.R. 613, 621 per Estey J. Le Dain J., with the agreement of McIntyre J., dissented on the basis of the police's good-faith reliance on *Chromiak*.

[4] The Court continues to like this rhetoric: *R. v. Stillman*, [1997] 1 S.C.R. 607, para. 123 per Cory J. for majority, describing as a "blatant disregard for the fundamental rights of the appellant" the taking of DNA samples from an arrested person; the police had taken the samples only after getting a Crown Attorney's opinion (for which there was appellate level authority) that the power of search incident to arrest authorized the taking; *R. v. Feeney*, [1997] 2 S.C.R. 13, para. 80 *per* Sopinka J. for majority, describing as a "flagrant" disregard of the accused's rights a search and seizure that had been upheld as lawful and constitutional by the trial judge, the unanimous Court of Appeal, as well as the four dissenting judges, one of whom (L'Heureux-Dubé J., para. 197) commented that "if the conduct of the police was truly of such a horrific nature, I find it peculiar that neither the trial judge nor three judges of the Court of Appeal had a similar appreciation of the facts".

[5] *Trask v. The Queen*, [1985] 1 S.C.R. 655; *Rahn v. The Queen*, [1985] 1 S.C.R. 659.

[6] *R. v. Dyment*, [1988] 1 S.C.R. 417.

[7] *Clarkson v. The Queen*, [1986] 1 S.C.R. 383.

[8] *R. v. Manninen*, [1987] 1 S.C.R. 1233.

disagree. In each case, the police did not know, and could not have known, that they were violating the rights of the accused. In these circumstances, the conclusion that the use of the evidence would bring the administration of justice into disrepute was quite implausible.

The *Therens* line of cases appears to hold that the question of whether the police acted in good faith or not is irrelevant to bringing the administration of justice into disrepute. This is certainly a rather startling conclusion, especially as the American courts have carved a good-faith exception out of their exclusionary rule.[9] It now seems clear that good faith is in fact a relevant consideration in Canadian law.

In *R. v. Simmons* (1988),[10] the accused, who was charged with importing illegal drugs into Canada, had been searched at the airport without having first been informed of her right to retain and instruct counsel. The drugs were found taped to her body. The majority of the Supreme Court of Canada held that the search violated the accused's right to counsel, and was therefore in breach of the Charter. Should the evidence be excluded? In a 180-degree turn from the *Therens* line of cases, the Court said no. Dickson C.J. pointed out that at the time when the search was conducted, the customs officers had no way of knowing that they were in breach of the Charter. He said:[11]

> The breaches occurred not long after the Charter came into force and several years before the decision of this Court in *Therens* on the meaning of detention in s. 10(b). At the time of this search the decision of this Court in *Chromiak, supra*, stood for the proposition that investigative detentions of this sort were not detentions of the type requiring persons to be advised of their right to counsel.

With respect, this seems eminently sensible. But, of course, every word of the quotation would apply with even greater force to *Therens* itself, where the police failure to advise of the right to counsel was described as a "flagrant" breach of the Charter.

In *Simmons*, the Chief Justice did not attempt to explain the Court's characterization of the police action in *Therens*, but he did offer an explanation for the different outcome in *Therens*. *Therens*, he said, was a case where the accused was "conscripted against [himself]", and the use of the breath sample would "tend to affect adversely the fairness of the trial process".[12] By this he meant that Therens had been forced to create incriminating evidence in the form of the breath sample. In *Simmons*, he pointed out, "the evidence obtained as a result of the search

---

[9] *United States v. Leon* (1984), 468 U.S. 897 (police relied in good faith on apparently valid warrant); *Massachusetts v. Sheppard* (1984), 468 U.S. 981 (same result); *Illinois v. Krull* (1987), 480 U.S. 340 (police relied in good faith on a statute subsequently held to be unconstitutional).

[10] *R. v. Simmons*, [1988] 2 S.C.R. 495.

[11] *R. v. Simmons*, [1988] 2 S.C.R. 495, 535.

[12] *R. v. Simmons*, [1988] 2 S.C.R. 495, 534.

was real evidence that existed irrespective of the Charter violations".[13] In other words, it was not the police conduct that caused the exclusion of the evidence in the *Therens* line of cases, but rather the nature of the evidence—self-incriminatory evidence that would not have existed apart from the Charter violation.[14] This explanation of the cases paves the way to the development of a good-faith doctrine under s. 24(2).

As well as *Simmons*, there are other cases in which the Supreme Court of Canada has held that good-faith action by the police justified the admission of the evidence. Two cases[15] involved evidence discovered in searches conducted under writs of assistance (writs that authorized warrantless searches) that had been issued under the federal Narcotic Control Act. The Supreme Court of Canada held that the writs of assistance had been rendered unconstitutional by the adoption of s. 8 of the Charter of Rights in 1982, so that the evidence had been obtained in breach of the Charter. However, the Court held that the admission of the evidence would not bring the administration of justice into disrepute, because the police "believed in good faith" that the writs of assistance, which at the time of the searches had not been challenged under the Charter, were valid.[16] Three cases[17] involved warrantless searches made under the authority of another provision of the Narcotic Control Act. The Supreme Court of Canada held that the statutory provision violated s. 8 of the Charter, but held that the police could not be expected to predict the outcome of a Charter challenge to their statutory power of search. The police had acted in good faith in relying on the statute, and the evidence resulting from the search should not be excluded.

Four other cases involved evidence obtained by various types of surreptitious electronic surveillance.[18] The Supreme Court of Canada held that surreptitious electronic surveillance was a breach of s. 8 of the Charter, but noted that this was not clear at the time when the police obtained their evidence. The Court held that the admission of the evidence would not bring the administration of justice into disrepute. The police officers who conducted the surveillance were acting "in good faith. . .in accordance with what they had good reason to believe was the law".[19] In another case,[20] police had a warrant to seize drugs, but, because the warrant was grounded on information which had been

[13]*R. v. Simmons*, [1988] 2 S.C.R. 495, 534.

[14]See also *R. v. Hebert*, [1990] 2 S.C.R. 151 (good faith action by police, but Charter violation caused self-incrimination); *R. v. Broyles*, [1991] 3 S.C.R. 595 (same result).

[15]*R. v. Sieben*, [1987] 1 S.C.R. 295; *R. v. Hamill*, [1987] 1 S.C.R. 301.

[16]*R. v. Sieben*, [1987] 1 S.C.R. 295, 299.

[17]*R. v. Grant*, [1993] 3 S.C.R. 223; *R. v. Wiley*, [1993] 3 S.C.R. 263; *R. v. Plant*, [1993] 3 S.C.R. 281.

[18]*R. v. Duarte*, [1990] 1 S.C.R. 30; *R. v. Wiggins*, [1990] 1 S.C.R. 62; *R. v. Thompson*, [1990] 2 S.C.R. 1111; *R. v. Wong*, [1990] 3 S.C.R. 36.

[19]*R. v. Duarte*, [1990] 1 S.C.R. 30, 59. Similar findings were made in the three other electronic surveillance cases. Similar findings were also made in *R. v. Généreux*, [1992] 1 S.C.R. 259 (drugs admitted); *R. v. Wise*, [1992] 1 S.C.R. 527 (evidence of location of car admitted); *R. v. Colarusso*, [1994] 1 S.C.R. 20 (blood sample admitted).

discovered through a previous and unreasonable "olfactory search", s. 8 of the Charter had been breached. A majority of the Court found that the police had acted in good faith on an honest but mistaken understanding of the scope of their investigatory powers. The majority concluded that the administration of justice would not be brought into disrepute by admitting the evidence.[21]

In the end, therefore, one can say with some confidence that good-faith action by the police, in reliance on the ostensible state of the law at the time of obtaining the evidence, is a factor that weighs in the scale on the side of admitting the evidence.[22]

The Supreme Court of Canada has held that "good faith cannot be claimed if a Charter violation is committed on the basis of a police officer's unreasonable error or ignorance as to the scope of his or her authority".[23] In theory, that makes perfect sense. In practice, the Court has a tendency to hark back to its reasoning in *Therens*, and to condemn as unreasonable any police judgment on a doubtful point if it differs from the after-the-fact judgment of the Court. In *R. v. Buhay* (2003),[24] for example, the police obtained evidence from a locker in a bus station that had already been opened and searched by private security guards. The police did not obtain a warrant for the seizure of the evidence. The Manitoba Court of Appeal held unanimously that there was no search or seizure by the police, but simply a handing over of evidence from the security guards to the police. The Supreme Court disagreed, holding that the police had made a seizure and should have first obtained a warrant. The Court unanimously condemned the police for taking "a casual approach to infringing the [accused's] rights", held that the Charter breach was "serious", and excluded the evidence.[25] *In R. v. Mann* (2004),[26] the police stopped a suspect on an "investigative detention" and searched him, finding drugs in his pocket. The Manitoba Court of Appeal held unanimously that, although the search was supposed to be limited to weapons, when drugs were in fact found, the police were acting within their powers in seizing them. The Supreme Court disagreed, holding that the police should not have looked at the soft package that their search for weapons revealed. A majority of the Court denied that there was any "reasonable foundation" for the discovery of the drugs, held

---

[20]*R. v. Evans*, [1996] 1 S.C.R. 8. This case is discussed in more detail in ch. 48, Unreasonable Search or Seizure, in § 48:14 "Plain view".

[21]See also *R. v. Grant*, [2009] 2 S.C.R. 353, para. 133 (good faith on part of police; evidence admitted); *R. v Harrison*, [2009] 2 S.C.R. 494, para. 27 ("blatant disregard for Charter rights" on part of police; evidence excluded).

[22]Accord, *R. v. Aucoin*, [2012] 3 S.C.R. 408, para. 50 per Moldaver J. for majority (law "still evolving"; police acted "in good faith"; drugs seized by police in violation of Charter should be admitted).

[23]*R. v. Buhay*, [2003] 1 S.C.R. 631, para. 59; *R. v. Mann*, [2004] 3 S.C.R. 59, para. 55.

[24]*R. v. Buhay*, [2003] 1 S.C.R. 631.

[25]*R. v. Buhay*, [2003] 1 S.C.R. 631, para. 66.

[26]*R. v. Mann*, [2004] 3 S.C.R. 59.

that the Charter breach was "serious", and excluded the evidence.[27] In both these cases, the police officers acted in good faith on a view of the law that was sufficiently reasonable to be upheld by a unanimous Court of Appeal. But it was not reasonable enough for the Supreme Court, who excluded reliable evidence, obtained in good faith, on the basis of the "seriousness" of the Charter breach by the police.

The use of a "sniffer dog" in a police investigation led to the exclusion of evidence in *R. v. Kang-Brown* (2008).[28] In that case, police stationed at the Calgary bus terminal became suspicious about the accused, a passenger alighting from the overnight bus from Vancouver. A police dog, trained to detect the odour of drugs, was directed to the accused's bag, and, after sniffing the air around the bag, the dog sat down, which was its signal that it had smelled drugs. A police officer then searched the bag manually and found drugs. The accused was charged with possession of drugs for the purpose of trafficking. At trial and on appeal in Alberta, the courts held that a sniff by a sniffer dog was not a search at all, and that the dog's signal provided a reasonable ground for the subsequent manual search. The Supreme Court of Canada unanimously held that the sniff was a search, and a majority held that the sniffer dog could not be used unless the police officer either had reasonable and probable cause to believe that drugs would be found in the luggage of the accused (the view of four judges), or had a reasonable suspicion based on objectively verifiable evidence that drugs would be found (the view of two judges). The majority held that the sniff and the subsequent manual search were illegal and violated s. 8 of the Charter. Should the evidence of the drugs be excluded under s. 24(1)? There was no doubt that the police had acted in good faith in the belief that they were in compliance with the Charter. Moreover, while the state of the law was uncertain, not having been addressed by the Supreme Court at the time of the search, the police assessment of the law could not be said to be unreasonable, since their action was upheld by the trial judge, two of the three appeal judges, and three dissenting Supreme Court judges. And yet, the six-judge majority in the Supreme Court, who acknowledged that they were making new common-law rules for sniffer dogs, held that the "seriousness" of the breach of the Charter required them to exclude the evidence under s. 24(2).[29] In a companion case, *R. v. M. (A.)* (2008),[30] where a sniffer dog had signalled the presence of illegal drugs in an unattended knapsack in a school gymnasium, the same majority of six held that the sniff was a breach of the Charter and was so "serious" that the

[27] *R. v. Mann*, [2004] 3 S.C.R. 59, paras. 56, 57. Deschamps and Bastarache JJ. dissented; they would have admitted the evidence.

[28] *R. v. Kang-Brown*, [2008] 1 S.C.R. 456. The case is more fully described in under heading §§ 48:5 to 48:12 "From property to privacy" under subheading "Sniffer dog".

[29] *R. v. Kang-Brown*, [2008] 1 S.C.R. 456, para. 17 per LeBel J. for four judges ("given the seriousness of the breach"), para. 104 per Binnie J. for two judges ("a warrantless search on inadequate grounds"). Binnie J. does not use any variant of the word serious in this case, but he does in the companion case of *R. v. M. (A.)*, [2008] 1 S.C.R. 569.

[30] *R. v. M. (A.)*, [2008] 1 S.C.R. 569.

evidence should be excluded under s. 24(2).[31] Once again, a peculiar and plastic notion of seriousness trumped the good faith of the police, leading to an implausible finding that the admission of reliable evidence would bring the administration of justice into disrepute.

It will be recalled that in *Grant* itself (2009)[32] good faith police action (the Court actually only said that it was not in bad faith), in a context of legal uncertainty, led the Supreme Court to admit reliable evidence (a gun in that case). That decision reflected a more realistic attitude by the Court to good faith action by the police.

In *R. v. Vu* (2013),[33] the police found three computers in a house for which they had a search warrant. The search warrant did not expressly mention the search of computers found on the premises. The police searched the contents of the computers and found relevant evidence. The Supreme Court held that this was a breach of s. 8 of the Charter: the search of the computers required a separate search warrant or a specific express authority in the search warrant for the house. The decision created a new exception for computers from the general rule that a search warrant for premises authorizes the search of all receptacles on the premises; the cupboards, drawers, filing cabinets, and the like, do not need to be specified in the warrant. The Supreme Court found that the police had acted in the belief that their search of the computers was authorized by the warrant. The law at the time was uncertain, having only been clarified after the fact by the present decision. The good faith of the police persuaded the Court that the breach of the Charter was not serious within *Grant* factor (1),[34] and the Court concluded that the reliable evidence extracted from the computers should not be excluded.

The same conclusion was reached in *R. v. Spencer* (2014),[35] where the Court again broke new ground, this time in holding (contrary to the trial judge and the Court of Appeal) that a police request that an Internet Service Provider disclose the identity of one of its subscribers (a disclosure that would reveal nothing about the lifestyle of the subscriber, except that there was a computer in the household) was a search requiring a warrant. On the basis of the answer to this request (and other evidence obtained separately), the police had obtained a warrant to search the house and any computer found in the house, and had found evidence of possession of child pornography by the accused (who was not the subscriber but a relative living in the same household). The police had not obtained a warrant to authorize the preliminary request for subscriber information because they believed that no warrant was necessary. The

---

[31] *R. v. M. (A.)*, [2008] 1 S.C.R. 569, para. 2 per LeBel J. for four judges (repeating his reasons in *Kang-Brown*), para. 32 per Binnie J. for two judges ("The breach was serious.").

[32] *R. v. Grant*, [2009] 2 S.C.R. 353.

[33] *R. v. Vu*, [2013] 3 S.C.R. 657, 2013 SCC 60. The case is more fully described under heading §§ 48:5 to 48:12 "From property to privacy" under subheading "Computer".

[34] *R. v. Vu*, [2013] 3 S.C.R. 657, 2013 SCC 60, para. 69.

[35] *R. v. Spencer*, [2014] 2 S.C.R. 212, 2014 SCC 43. The case is more fully described under heading §§ 48:5 to 48:12 "From property to privacy" under subheading "Computer".

Court held that the failure to obtain a warrant for this preliminary step meant that virtually all of the evidence against the accused had been obtained in breach of the Charter. In a highly unusual recognition that a different opinion on a previously-unsettled constitutional issue might be reasonable, the Court held that "in light of the fact that the trial judge and three judges of the Court of Appeal concluded that [the police officer who made the request] had acted lawfully, his belief was clearly reasonable".[36] The reasonableness of the police action—the Court did not use the words "good faith", although those words seem equally applicable—meant that the breach of the Charter was not serious within *Grant* factor (1) and the Court concluded that the reliable evidence extracted from the computer should not be excluded.[37]

A different conclusion was reached by the Supreme Court in *R. v. Marakah* (2017).[38] In that case, the sender had sent text messages on his cell phone to the recipient regarding illegal transactions in firearms. The police, without a warrant, unlawfully seized and searched the recipient's cell phone and charged the sender with firearms offences, proffering the text messages as evidence against the sender. The Court held that the sender retained a reasonable expectation of privacy in the messages, and the police had therefore obtained the messages in breach of the sender's s. 8 right to be free of unreasonable search and seizure.[39] In order to determine whether the messages could still be admitted as evidence, an assessment had to be made of "the seriousness of the infringing state conduct" (*Grant*, first factor). McLachlin C.J., for the majority of the Court, held that: "The police's Charter-infringing conduct was sufficiently serious to favour the exclusion of the evidence."[40] The police had committed a "serious breach of the Charter" in searching the recipient's cell phone without a warrant which led them to the sender's messages, and the police error, even if made "in good faith", could not be regarded as "reasonable". The police action also had a "significant" impact on the sender's Charter-protected privacy interest (*Grant*, second factor). And, although society's interest in the adjudication of the case on the merits (*Grant*, third factor) would have favoured admission, she concluded that "on balance" the admission of the evidence would bring the administration of justice into disrepute, and it had to be excluded under s. 24(2).

One relevant consideration in determining whether the police acted in

---

[36] *R. v. Spencer*, [2014] 2 S.C.R. 212, 2014 SCC 43, para. 77.

[37] Accord, *R. v. Fearon*, [2014] 3 S.C.R. 621, 2014 SCC 77 (evidence obtained from search of cellular phone in breach of s. 8 admitted: police acted in good faith in a situation where the law was unsettled).

[38] *R. v. Marakah*, [2017] 2 S.C.R. 608, 2017 SCC 59. McLachlin C.J. wrote the opinion of the majority of the seven-judge court. Rowe J. wrote a concurring opinion, essentially agreeing with the Chief Justice's reasons. Moldaver J. (with Côté J.) wrote a dissenting opinion.

[39] This part of the decision is related in ch. 48, Unreasonable search or seizure, under heading §§ 48:5 to 48:12, "From property to privacy" under subheading "Computer".

[40] *R. v. Marakah*, [2017] 2 S.C.R. 608, 2017 SCC 59, para. 61. The rest of her reasoning on this point is in paras. 62-66.

good faith will be whether they engaged in racial profiling. This was implied by the Supreme Court of Canada in *Grant*,[41] and confirmed explicitly by the Court in *R. v. Le* (2019).[42] In *Le*, Brown and Martin JJ., who wrote for the majority of a five-judge bench, acknowledged that "racial profiling is a reality in policing in Canada that is 'supported by significant social science research' ".[43] They defined racial profiling to include any action that is "based on actual or presumed membership in a group defined by race, colour, ethnic or national origin or religion, without factual grounds or reasonable suspicion, that results in the person or group being exposed to differential treatment or scrutiny".[44] They emphasized that racial profiling will be relevant in determining whether the police have arbitrarily detained an individual in breach of s. 9 of the Charter, and that it will also be "relevant under s. 24(2) when assessing whether the police conduct was so serious and lacking in good faith that admitting the evidence at hand under s. 24(2) would bring the administration of justice into disrepute".[45] They did not say that a finding of racial profiling will necessarily lead to the exclusion of the evidence involved under s. 24(2), but it will certainly support a finding of lack of good faith (or bad faith), and as a result, it will—or at least should—weigh heavily in the direction of exclusion. In *Le*, the police had detained five racialized young men—Le, who was Asian, and four other young men, who were Black—in the backyard of a townhouse in a low-income housing co-operative in Toronto. Brown and Martin JJ. held that Le had been detained arbitrarily in breach of s. 9.[46] The trial judge had held that there was no racial profiling on the facts, and this determination was not challenged on appeal in the Supreme Court. Brown and Martin JJ. said that an absence of bad faith in the form of racial profiling did "not equate to a positive finding of good faith", and went on to exclude the evidence gathered under s. 24(2) for other reasons, including on the basis that the misconduct of the police had been serious.[47]

---

[41]*R. v. Grant*, [2009] 2 S.C.R. 353, para. 133 per McLachlin C.J. and Charron J. (referring to an absence of "racial profiling or other discriminatory police practices" in discounting the seriousness of improper police conduct).

[42]*R. v. Le*, 2019 SCC 34. Brown and Martin JJ. wrote a joint opinion for a three-judge majority of the five-judge bench; Karakatsanis J. joined their joint opinion. Moldaver J. wrote a dissenting opinion, which was joined by Wagner C.J.

[43]*R. v. Le*, 2019 SCC 34, para. 145; see similarly para. 80.

[44]*R. v. Le*, 2019 SCC 34, para. 77, citing *Que. v. Bombardier Inc. (Bombardier Aerospace Training Center)*, [2015] 2 S.C.R. 789, para. 33.

[45]*R. v. Le*, 2019 SCC 34, para. 78.

[46]For a more detailed discussion of the Court's s. 9 analysis, see ch. 49, Arbitrary Detention or Imprisonment, under heading § 49:11, "Requirement of standards"; and ch. 50, Rights on Arrest or Detention, under heading § 50:2 to 50:3, "Requirement of restraint".

[47]*R. v. Le*, 2019 SCC 34, para. 145-147, 150. Moldaver J., in dissent (with Wagner C.J. concurring), agreed with the joint majority that s. 9 had been breached, although for different reasons, but would not have excluded the evidence under s. 24(2).

X. NATURE OF CHARTER BREACH

§ 41:12 Nature of Charter breach

The second factor that was identified in *Grant*[1] as relevant in determining disrepute is "the impact of the breach on the Charter-protected interests of the accused". This was not one of the *Collins* factors, and so there is no *pre-Grant* jurisprudence to flesh out its content.[2] The Court in *Grant* explained that the impact of a Charter breach on the accused "may range from fleeting and technical to profoundly intrusive", and "the more serious the impact on the accused's protected interests, the greater the risk [of] bringing the administration of justice into disrepute".[3] In that case, where the accused in response to a police question had confessed that he was carrying a gun, there was a breach of two Charter rights, namely, s. 9 (not to be arbitrarily detained) and s. 10(b) (to counsel). The Court classified the impact on the accused's rights as "significant".[4] However, the Court held that the gun had been properly admitted in evidence on the basis that *Grant* factor (2) was outweighed by factor (1) (the police had acted in good faith)—a conclusion that was reinforced by factor (3) (the evidence was reliable and essential to the prosecution's case).

XI. EFFECT OF EXCLUDING EVIDENCE

§ 41:13 Effect of excluding evidence

The third factor that was identified in *Grant*[1] as relevant in determining disrepute was "society's interest in the adjudication of the case on its merits". This factor invites the inquiry into "whether the truth-seeking function of the criminal trial process would be better served by admission of the evidence, or by its exclusion".[2] Where the evidence that was obtained in breach of the Charter is reliable and is important to the case for the prosecution, its admission would be unlikely to bring the administration of justice into disrepute—and indeed in many cases its *exclusion* would be more likely to bring the administration of justice into disrepute.[3] This factor normally weighs heavily on the side of admitting

---

[Section 41:12]

[1] *R. v. Grant*, [2009] 2 S.C.R. 353.

[2] A possible exception is the pre-*Grant* discoverability rule, which survives in weakened form: § 41:8 note 4. The theory is that a Charter breach that yields evidence that would have been discovered anyway has a lesser impact on the Charter-protected interests of the accused than a Charter breach that yields evidence that would not otherwise have been discovered.

[3] *R. v. Grant*, [2009] 2 S.C.R. 353, para. 76.

[4] *R. v. Grant*, [2009] 2 S.C.R. 353, para. 138.

[Section 41:13]

[1] *R. v. Grant*, [2009] 2 S.C.R. 353.

[2] *R. v. Grant*, [2009] 2 S.C.R. 353, para. 79.

[3] *R. v. Grant*, [2009] 2 S.C.R. 353, paras. 81-83. The seriousness of the alleged of-

the evidence. This factor (*Grant* factor (3)) is essentially the same as *Collins* factor (3), which was "the effect of excluding the evidence". In the *pre-Grant* cases, however, *Collins* factor (3) was rarely explicitly considered by the Court, and was obviously regarded as less important than *Collins* factors (1) (the nature of the evidence) and (2) (the nature of the official conduct).[4] This pattern seems to be perpetuated in *Grant* itself, where the gun that had been discovered in breach of the Charter was admitted in evidence, but the Court did so primarily on the basis of *Grant* factor (1) (the good faith of the police), holding that "we do not find [*Grant* factor (3)] to be of much assistance".[5] This was a puzzling treatment of *Grant* factor (3), since the gun was reliable evidence of the firearms offences with which the accused was charged, and the gun was essential to the prosecution's case.

In *R. v. Feeney* (1997),[6] a five-judge majority of the Supreme Court of Canada came close to stating that the effect of excluding evidence is no longer a consideration under s. 24(2). In that case, the accused had been convicted of the violent and unprovoked murder of an old man. The majority of the Court (differing from the trial judge and the unanimous Court of Appeal) found that much of the evidence used to convict the accused had been obtained in breach of the Charter. The Court held that the evidence was to be excluded. In the case of a confession and fingerprints, the exclusion was based on trial unfairness. In the case of the accused's blood-stained shirt and shoes, and cigarettes and money apparently stolen from the victim, the exclusion was based on what the majority found to be police misconduct. Sopinka J., who wrote for the majority, acknowledged that the effect of excluding all this evidence would probably be that there was insufficient evidence to convict the accused. But, he said:[7]

> If the exclusion of this evidence is likely to result in an acquittal of the accused. . ., then the Crown is deprived of a conviction based on illegally obtained evidence. Any price to society occasioned by the loss of such a conviction is fully justified in a free and democratic society which is governed by the rule of law.

If the acquittal of a person who has been convicted of murder on the basis of reliable evidence is not enough to merit consideration by the

---

fence may also be "a valid consideration" under *Grant* factor (3), but "it has the potential to cut both ways": failure to prosecute a serious charge upon which there is reliable evidence of guilt arguably tends to bring the administration of justice into disrepute; but so does a conviction obtained with evidence obtained in breach of the Charter: *R. v. Grant*, [2009] 2 S.C.R. 353, para. 84. But see *R. v. Cularussu*, [1994] 1 S.C.R. 20, 78 ("appalling" and "shocking" offence; evidence admitted); *R. v. Evans*, [1996] 1 S.C.R. 8 (serious drug offence for which accused would be acquitted if evidence excluded; evidence admitted).

[4] *R. v. Feeney*, [1997] 2 S.C.R. 13, para. 83 (conviction for murder based on reliable evidence overturned; "any price to society occasioned by the loss of such a conviction is fully justified").

[5] *R. v. Grant*, [2009] 2 S.C.R. 353, para. 139.

[6] *R. v. Feeney*, [1997] 2 S.C.R. 13.

[7] *R. v. Feeney*, [1997] 2 S.C.R. 13, para. 83.

Court under the third branch of the *Collins* test (now the *Grant* test), it is hard to imagine any situation in which the effect of excluding the evidence would be relevant to the admissibility of evidence obtained in breach of the Charter of Rights.

XII. CONCLUSION

§ 41:14 Conclusion

Given the vague language of s. 24(2), it is not surprising that the Supreme Court of Canada has had difficulty in developing a consistent body of jurisprudence. The early decisions, especially *Therens*, treated s. 24(2) as if it were an absolute exclusionary rule. This was ironic, because s. 24(2) was intended to be a compromise between the American exclusionary rule and the Canadian inclusionary rule. And yet, the American Court, true to its rationale of deterrence, had created a good-faith exception to the American rule, and would almost certainly have admitted the breath sample in *Therens*. After *Therens*, Canada had a stricter exclusionary rule than the United States.

In *Collins*, Lamer J. suggested a set of guidelines for the application of s. 24(2), under which the nature of the evidence, the nature of the police conduct and the cost of excluding the evidence would all be taken in to consideration. While the strict *Therens* approach lingered on in a few cases, *Collins* provided a framework for a recognition that some kinds of evidence were more unfair to the accused than others, that police conduct in breach of the Charter varied in its culpability, and that the social costs of allowing persons accused of serious crimes to go unprosecuted could also be taken into account. The early decisions had recognized none of these propositions. The *Collins* guidelines provided a more nuanced approach to the exclusion of evidence, which was truer to the idea of a compromise between the extremes of invariable inclusion and invariable exclusion.

Unfortunately, the *Collins* guidelines were transformed by later decisions into strict exclusionary rules, based on elaborate (and implausible) theories of "trial unfairness", "conscriptive evidence" and "discoverability", and once again entire classes of evidence were being excluded in what seemed to be a departure from the text of s. 24(2), which calls for evidence to be excluded only if "having regard to all the circumstances" its admission of it in the proceedings would bring the administration of justice into disrepute". In *Grant* (2009), the Court recognized the wrong path that it had taken and substituted new guidelines for the *Collins* guidelines. The justification was to rid the jurisprudence of the theories that had developed into exclusionary rules. The goal was to return to a balancing test which would take account of all the circumstances before excluding evidence obtained in breach of the Charter. Since this had also been the goal of the *Collins* guidelines and it had not been achieved, it remains to be seen whether the *Grant* guidelines will be more successful in maintaining the compromise between a rule that excludes all evidence obtained in breach of the Charter (the American model) and a rule that admits all such evidence (the pre-Charter common law). That is what s. 24(2) was enacted to achieve, but its governing principle of the good reputation of the administration of justice is highly indeterminate, and judges are likely to continue to have difficulty in applying it.

Chapter 42

Religion

I. DISTRIBUTION OF POWERS

§ 42:1 Distribution of powers

II. SECTION 2(A) OF THE CHARTER

§ 42:2 Section 2(a) of the Charter

III. FREEDOM OF CONSCIENCE

§ 42:3 Freedom of conscience

IV. FREEDOM OF RELIGION

§ 42:4 Freedom of religion

V. SUNDAY OBSERVANCE

§ 42:5 Sunday observance

VI. OTHER RELIGIOUS PRACTICES

§ 42:6 Other religious practices

VII. WAIVER OF RELIGIOUS PRACTICE

§ 42:7 Waiver of religious practice

VIII. RELIGION IN PUBLIC SCHOOLS

§ 42:8 Religion in public schools

IX. DENOMINATIONAL SCHOOLS

§ 42:9 Denominational schools

X. RELIGION IN PUBLIC BODIES OTHER THAN SCHOOLS

§ 42:10 Religion in public bodies other than schools

XI. RELIGIOUS MARRIAGE

§ 42:11 Religious marriage

I. DISTRIBUTION OF POWERS

§ 42:1 Distribution of powers

Which legislative body—the federal Parliament or the provincial Legislatures—has the power to enact laws in relation to religion?

This question first arose in the litigation over the validity of Sunday observance laws. As has been explained in ch. 18, Criminal Law, a long line of cases has held that laws compelling the observance of Sundays or holy days are within the exclusive competence of the federal Parliament under its power over criminal law.[1] Of course, these laws took the classical criminal law form of a prohibition coupled with a penalty, and there was a long history of the criminalization of profaning the Sabbath. These cases need not be interpreted as holding that all laws with a religious purpose are within federal jurisdiction. There are, however, other cases where it has been held or assumed that any law restricting freedom of religion is within exclusive federal competence.[2] On the other hand, s. 92(12) expressly allocates to the provincial Legislatures the power over the solemnization of marriages, a subject with important religious dimensions; and s. 93(3) makes clear that the provincial Legislature's power over education extends to the establishment of denominational schools.

In *R. v. Edwards Books and Art* (1986),[3] the Supreme Court of Canada upheld provincial legislation that prohibited retail stores from opening on Sundays. The law came within provincial power over property and civil rights, the Court said, because it pursued the secular purpose of providing a pause day for retail workers, rather than the religious purpose of compelling observance of the Christian sabbath. However, the law contained an exemption for stores of less than a specified size that observed Saturday as a holiday. This "sabbatarian" exemption admittedly had the religious purpose of accommodating those who observed Saturday as their sabbath. Did the religious purpose render the exemption unconstitutional? Dickson J., speaking for the whole Court on this issue, held that it did not. It was open to a provincial Legislature "to attempt to neutralize or minimize the adverse effects of otherwise valid provincial legislation on human rights such as freedom of religion".[4]

Dickson J. in *Edwards Books* concluded that "the Constitution does not contemplate religion as a discrete constitutional 'matter' falling

---

[Section 42:1]

[1]Chapter 18, Criminal Law, under heading § 18:12, "Sunday observance law".

[2]In *Saumur v. City of Quebec*, [1953] 2 S.C.R. 299, Rand, Kellock, Locke, Estey, Cartwright and Fauteux JJ. all took this position, although Rinfret, C.J., Taschereau and Kerwin JJ. rejected it. Federal jurisdiction over religion is also assumed in *Walter v. A.G. Alta.*, [1969] S.C.R. 383 (communal property law not in relation to religion, despite its special impact on Hutterite colonies).

[3]*R. v. Edwards Books and Art*, [1986] 2 S.C.R. 713.

[4]*R. v. Edwards Books and Art*, [1986] 2 S.C.R. 713, 751.

exclusively within either a federal or provincial class of subjects".[5] Legislation concerning religion could therefore be competent to either the federal Parliament or the provincial Legislatures, depending upon the other characteristics of the law. In other words, in classifying a law for the purpose of the federal distribution of powers, the law's impact on religion would not necessarily be the critical factor. In *Edwards Books*, the requirement of a common pause day for retail workers could be relieved for some groups for religious reasons without destroying the law's classification as coming within property and civil rights in the province. The power to make laws respecting religion is thus like the power to make laws respecting other civil liberties, which is also for the most part divided between the two levels of government, and is not the exclusive preserve of either one.[6]

Since the adoption of the Charter of Rights in 1982, any law that affects freedom of religion will be vulnerable to challenge under s. 2(a) of the Charter. The rest of this chapter is addressed to s. 2(a) of the Charter.

II. SECTION 2(A) OF THE CHARTER

§ 42:2 Section 2(a) of the Charter

Section 2(a) of the Charter of Rights[1] guarantees to "everyone"[2] the "fundamental freedom" of "freedom of conscience and religion".[3]

Section 2(a), like other Charter rights, is subject to s. 1 (the limitation clause) of the Charter. A law that limits freedom of conscience and religion will be valid under s. 1 if it comes within the phrase "such reasonable limits prescribed by law as can be demonstrably justified in a free and democratic society". Section 1 was examined in ch. 38, Limitation of Rights.

The comparable provision of the American Bill of Rights is the first amendment, which on the topic of religion provides that "Congress shall make no law respecting an establishment of religion, or prohibiting the free exercise thereof. This provision contains no reference to freedom of conscience. With respect to religion, the provision contains two clauses,

---

[5] *R. v. Edwards Books and Art*, [1986] 2 S.C.R. 713, 750.

[6] Chapter 34, Civil Liberties, under heading § 34:6, "Distribution of powers".

[Section 42:2]

[1] For commentary on s. 2(a), see Beaudoin and Mendes (eds.), The Canadian Charter of Rights and Freedoms (4th ed., 2005), ch. 5 (by B.A. Elberg and M.C. Power); McLeod, Takach, Morton, Segal, The Canadian Charter of Rights (Carswell, loose-leaf service), ch. 23; Canadian Charter of Rights Annotated (Canada Law Book, loose-leaf service), annotation to s. 2(a). The last work contains a bibliography of the relevant literature.

[2] On the meaning of "everyone", see ch. 37, Application of Charter, under heading §§ 37:1 to 37:5, "Benefit of rights".

[3] The comparable provision of the Canadian Bill of Rights is s. 1(c), which guarantees "freedom of religion".

an "establishment" clause and a "free exercise" clause.[4] The first amendment by its terms binds the federal Congress only, but it is also applicable to the states through the fourteenth amendment.[5] The establishment clause, which was intended to prohibit the establishment of an official church or religion in the United States, has no counterpart in s. 2(a). The free exercise clause is closer to s. 2(a).

III. FREEDOM OF CONSCIENCE

§ 42:3 Freedom of conscience

Section 2(a)'s reference to "conscience",[1] which is not found in the first amendment, would protect systems of belief which are not theocentric (centred on a deity), and which might not be characterized as religions for that reason (or for some other reason).[2]

In *Mouvement laïque québécois v. Saguenay* (2015),[3] the claimant was an atheist who invoked freedom of conscience and religion to object to a municipal council's practice, later formalized by by-law, of the Mayor saying a prayer to God at the beginning of council's proceedings. Although the prayer (in its later formulation) was not intended to favour any one religion, it still excluded those who, like the claimant, did not believe in God. The Supreme Court struck down the by-law and ordered the municipal council to cease the practice. The guarantee of freedom of conscience and religion included the "freedom to have no religious beliefs whatosoever"; non-belief, atheism and agnosticism were all protected.[4] A public body, like a municipal council, was under a duty to observe religious neutrality in its public proceedings, and this duty was breached by the recitation of a prayer that professed a belief in God.

---

[4]For commentary on the religion clauses of the first amendment, see L.H. Tribe, American Constitutional Law (Foundation Press, New York, 2nd ed., 1986), ch. 14; J.E. Nowak and R.D. Rotunda, Constitutional Law (West, St. Paul, Minn., 7th ed., 2004), ch. 17.

[5]The doctrine of "selective incorporation", which accomplishes this result, is explained in ch. 37, Application of Charter, under heading § 37:6, "Both levels of government".

[Section 42:3]

[1]See Moon, Freedom of Conscience and Religion (2014), ch. 7.

[2]In *R. v. Morgentaler*, [1988] 1 S.C.R. 30, where the Court struck down the abortion provisions of the Criminal Code, Wilson J. in a separate concurring judgment held that the regulation of abortion was a denial of freedom of conscience, which she defined (at p. 178) as "personal morality which is not founded in religion" and as "conscientious beliefs which are not religiously motivated". The decision to terminate a pregnancy was (at pp. 175-176) a "matter of conscience", which was accordingly protected. None of the other judges made any reference to freedom of conscience.

[3]*Mouvement laïque québécois v. Saguenay*, [2015] 2 S.C.R. 3, 2015 SCC 16. Gascon J. wrote the opinion of the majority. Abella J. wrote a concurring opinion, disagreeing only with the standards of administrative review of the majority.

[4]*Mouvement laïque québécois v. Saguenay*, [2015] 2 S.C.R. 3, 2015 SCC 16, para. 71.

IV. FREEDOM OF RELIGION

§ 42:4 Freedom of religion

The leading case on freedom of religion[1] is *R. v. Big M Drug Mart* (1985),[2] in which the Supreme Court of Canada struck down the Lord's Day Act, a federal statute that prohibited (with exceptions) commercial activity on Sunday. Dickson J. for the majority of the Court held that the purpose of the Act, which he derived from the history and terms of the Act, was "to compel the observance of the Christian Sabbath".[3] That purpose was an infringement of the freedom of religion of non-Christians, because, by virtue of the guarantee of freedom of religion, "government may not coerce individuals to affirm a specific religious practice for a sectarian purpose".[4]

In *Big M*, Dickson J. offered the following definition of freedom of religion:[5]

> The essence of the concept of freedom of religion is the right to entertain such religious beliefs as a person chooses, the right to declare religious beliefs openly and without fear of hindrance or reprisal, and the right to manifest religious belief by worship and practice or by teaching and dissemination.

The last part of this quotation makes clear that s. 2(a) protects religious practices as well as religious beliefs. Dickson J.'s language borrows from the International Covenant on Civil and Political Rights, which, by article 18, provides that freedom of religion includes the right "to manifest [one's] religion or belief in worship, observance, practice or teaching".

The "free exercise" clause of the Constitution of the United States also protects religious practices as well as religious beliefs. In *Employment Division, Department of Human Resources of Oregon v. Smith* (1990),[6] the Supreme Court of the United States had to decide whether an Oregon law banning the use of narcotics could validly apply to members of the Native American Church who ingested peyote for sacramental purposes as part of the established ceremony of the Church. Peyote is a hallucinogenic drug prepared from the peyote cactus. The Oregon law expressly included peyote in the list of banned drugs, and made no

---

[Section 42:4]

[1] See Moon, Freedom of Conscience and Religion (2014); Berger, Law's Religion: Religious Difference and the Claims of Constitutionalism (2015).

[2] *R. v. Big M Drug Mart*, [1985] 1 S.C.R. 295. Dickson J. wrote the opinion for the majority. Wilson J. wrote a separate concurrence, disagreeing only with Dickson J.'s reliance on the purpose of the Act, as opposed to its effect, to show the breach of the Charter.

[3] *R. v. Big M Drug Mart*, [1985] 1 S.C.R. 295, 351.

[4] *R. v. Big M Drug Mart*, [1985] 1 S.C.R. 295, 347; see also 350 for a different formulation of the same idea.

[5] *R. v. Big M Drug Mart*, [1985] 1 S.C.R. 295, 336.

[6] *Employment Division, Department of Human Resources of Oregon v. Smith* (1990), 494 U.S. 872.

exception for sacramental use. Scalia J. for a five-judge majority of the Court acknowledged that the law had the effect of prohibiting a religious practice. A law that had as its object the prohibition (or burdening) of a religious practice would be invalid. But in this case the prohibition of peyote in the Church ceremony was merely an "incidental effect" of a generally applicable and otherwise valid provision. Therefore, he held, the law was validly applicable to the Church ceremony. O'Connor J., for a minority of four judges, held that the state should have to show that the application of the law to a religious practice was required by a compelling state interest. She concurred in the result, because she held that there was a compelling state interest in the universal application of the ban. But the other three minority judges, speaking through Blackmun J., held that there was no compelling state interest in banning the use of drugs in a limited ceremonial context, and that the law should be constitutionally inapplicable to the religious use of peyote.

In response to the decision in *Smith*, the United States Congress enacted the Religious Freedom Restoration Act of 1993, which essentially adopted as a statutory rule the position of the dissenting minority in the case. The Act prohibited the Federal Government from substantially burdening a person's sincere exercise of religion, even by a law of general application, unless the Government could establish that the burden was in furtherance of a compelling government interest and was the least restrictive means of furthering that interest. After the enactment of this Act, a religious exemption was applied to peyote.[7] In *Gonzales v. O Centro Espirita Beneficente Uniao do Vegetal* (2006),[8] a Christian Spiritist sect based in Brazil used a tea called hoasca for sacramental purposes. The tea included a hallucinogenic drug derived from a plant found in the Amazon rainforest. The use of this drug was banned in the United States by the federal Controlled Substances Act. After the seizure by American customs of a shipment of hoasca intended for the American branch of the sect, the sect sued for an injunction to prevent enforcement of the ban against it. The lower courts granted the injunction, and their decisions were upheld by the Supreme Court of the United States. The case was very like *Smith*, but now the controlling law was the Religious Freedom Restoration Act. The Court held unanimously that the application of the ban to the sect would substantially burden their sincere exercise of religion, and that the Government had failed to establish any compelling government interest in the application of the ban to the religious ceremonies of the 130 members of the sect who lived in the United States. The fact that a religious exception for peyote had been in place for 35 years reinforced the absence of any compelling pub-

---

[7]The Religious Freedom Restoration Act would have permitted the use of peyote for sacramental purposes, but that result was in fact accomplished by the enactment of a specific religious exception for the use of peyote by American Indians.

[8]*Gonzales v. O Centro Espirita Beneficente Uniao do Vegetal* (2006), 546 U.S. 418.

lic interest in the denial of a religious exemption for the much less widely used hoasca.[9]

The division of the U.S. Court in the peyote case, the response to the decision by the Congress (an American example of dialogue), and the continued efforts by government to ban religious practices involving the use of banned drugs illustrate the struggle by all three branches of American government over the degree to which laws of general application should be made to accommodate religious practices. In the succeeding sections of this chapter, we look at similar struggles in the short history of the Charter. However, it will become apparent that the majority decision in the peyote case could not have been reached by the Canadian Supreme Court, which has been willing to go to great lengths to require the accommodation of minority religious practices.

V. SUNDAY OBSERVANCE

§ 42:5 Sunday observance

We have already noticed the decision in *R. v. Big M Drug Mart* (1985),[1] in which the Supreme Court of Canada struck down the federal Lord's Day Act, which prohibited (with exceptions) commercial activity on Sunday. The decision was made easier than it would otherwise have been by the Court's finding from the legislative history and text of the Act that the *purpose* of the Act was "to compel the observance of the Christian Sabbath".[2] Such a purpose was not compatible with s. 2(a). The Court did not have to wait long for the hard case, which was *R. v. Edwards Books and Art* (1986),[3] in which Ontario's Retail Business Holidays Act was under challenge. The Act prohibited retail stores from opening on Sunday. The legislative history of this Act showed that its purpose was the secular one of providing a common pause day for retail workers. The Court held nonetheless that the law infringed s. 2(a), because its *effect* was to impose an economic burden on those retailers who observed a sabbath on a day other than Sunday. That effect created a "competitive pressure"[4] to abandon a non-Sunday sabbath, which was an abridgement of freedom of religion.[5]

In *Edwards Books*, the law was not actually struck down, because the Court upheld the law under s. 1 of the Charter. The secular purpose of

[9]See also *Burwell v. Hobby Lobby Stores* (2014), 134 S.Ct. 2751 (applying RFRA to uphold exemption of Christian owners of closely held corporations with sincere religious beliefs about contraception from mandatory health insurance provision for contraceptive drugs).

[Section 42:5]

[1]*R. v. Big M Drug Mart*, [1985] 1 S.C.R. 295; discussed at § 42:4.

[2]*R. v. Big M Drug Mart*, [1985] 1 S.C.R. 295, 351.

[3]*R. v. Edwards Books and Art*, [1986] 2 S.C.R. 713; discussed with reference to the distribution of powers at § 42:1.

[4]*R. v. Edwards Books and Art*, [1986] 2 S.C.R. 713, 766.

[5]See the discussion of these cases in ch. 36, Charter of Rights, under the headings § 36:14, "Purpose or effect", and § 36:15, "Trivial effects".

providing a common pause day was sufficiently important to justify a limit on freedom of religion. However, some division of the Court occurred on the question whether the Legislature had used the least drastic means of accomplishing the objective. The answer to that question turned on the extent to which the law should have made accommodation for non-Sunday observers. As has already been explained,[6] the Act did in fact contain a "sabbatarian exemption" for retailers who closed their stores on Saturdays, but the exemption was hedged with a size restriction that made it applicable only to small stores.[7] Having regard to the restriction on the availability of the exemption, could it be said that the law pursued its objective by the least drastic means, that is, with the minimum intrusion on freedom of religion? The majority of the Court answered yes to that question, allowing the Legislature some leeway in designing the exemption.[8] Wilson J., however, dissenting on this point, would have required the exemption to be extended to all Saturday-observing retailers, large as well as small, and she would have struck down the size limits in the exemption.

Although the Ontario Act with its restricted Sabbatarian exemption was upheld by the majority in *Edwards Books*, the Ontario Legislature later amended the Act in the fashion called for in Wilson J.'s dissent by removing the size limits on the exemption. After the amendment, the Act exempted any retail store that closed on a day other than Sunday by reason of the religion of the owner of the store; such a store was free to open on Sunday. The amended Act was challenged and upheld by the Ontario Court of Appeal in *Peel v. Great Atlantic and Pacific Co.* (1991).[9] The Court held that the opening up of the exemption eliminated the "competitive pressure" on non-Christians that the Supreme Court in *Edwards Books* had held to be an infringement of freedom of religion. Therefore, the amended Act did not fall foul of s. 2(a) of the Charter, and was valid without recourse to s. 1.[10]

VI. OTHER RELIGIOUS PRACTICES

§ 42:6 Other religious practices

The previous section of this chapter discussed the Sunday-closing cases, which establish that there is a constitutional obligation under s. 2(a) to accommodate those persons whose religion calls for observance of

---

[6]See the discussion of these cases in ch. 36, Charter of Rights, under the headings § 36:14, "Purpose or effect", and § 36:15, "Trivial effects", above.

[7]The exemption also did not cover those who observed a weekday as the sabbath, but apparently no evidence was adduced and no attack mounted on this ground, which was not discussed by the Court.

[8]The s. 1 reasoning is discussed more fully in ch. 38, Limitation of Rights, under heading §§ 38:20 to 38:21, "Least drastic means".

[9]*Peel v. Great Atlantic and Pacific Co.* (1991), 2 O.R. (3d) 65 (C.A.).

[10]Accord, *London Drugs v. Red Deer* (1988), 52 D.L.R. (4th) 203 (Alta C.A.) (Sunday closing law with wide exemption not in breach of s. 2(a)); compare *R. v. Westfair Foods* (1989), 65 D.L.R. (4th) 56 (Sask. C.A.) (Sunday closing law without Sabbatarian exemption upheld by creating a "constitutional exemption" for non-Sunday observers).

a sabbath on a day other than Sunday. This section of the chapter considers the extent to which freedom of religion entails the tolerance of other minority religious practices.[1] In *R. v. Big M. Drug Mart* (1985),[2] Dickson J. said that freedom of religion included the right "to manifest religious belief by worship and practice". However, he added the proviso that "such manifestations do not injure his or her neighbours or their parallel rights to hold and manifest beliefs and opinions of their own".[3] The proviso implies that freedom of religion would not protect minority religious groups in such practices as human sacrifice, or refusals of schooling or medical treatment of children. However, there are many other practices that have a religious compulsion for a minority religion, such as (to take examples from pre-Charter cases), refusing to salute the flag or sing the national anthem,[4] distributing proselytizing tracts,[5] chanting a mantra,[6] or holding land communally.[7] Such practices could, and therefore should, be tolerated by the majority. Where there is no compelling governmental interest to the contrary, s. 2(a) of the Charter would require the law to accommodate minority religions by according exemptions for their practices.[8]

In *Young v. Young* (1993),[9] a judge had granted custody to the mother of three young children, and had granted access to the father, but with the restriction that the father not discuss the Jehovah's Witness religion with the children, or take them to religious services. The reason for the restriction was that the father's strong religious views were not shared by the mother, and were a source of conflict between them. The father attacked the restriction on the ground, among others, that it denied his right to freedom of religion. The British Columbia Court of Appeal struck down the restriction, holding that it was a breach of freedom of religion to preclude a parent from sharing his religious beliefs with his children.

[Section 42:6]

[1]For analysis, see the series of articles by B.L. Berger, "Law's Religion: Rendering Culture" (2007) 45 Osgoode Hall L.J. 277; "The Cultural Limits of Legal Tolerance" (2008) 21 Can. J. Law & Jurisprudence 245; "Section 1, Constitutional Reasoning and Cultural Difference: Assessing the Impacts of *Alberta v. Hutterian Brethren of Wilson Colony*" (2010) 51 Supreme Court L.R. (2d) 25.

[2]*R. v. Big M. Drug Mart*, [1985] 1 S.C.R. 295, 336.

[3]*R. v. Big M. Drug Mart*, [1985] 1 S.C.R. 295, 346.

[4]*Donald v. Hamilton Bd. of Education*, [1945] O.R. 518 (C.A.) (Jehovah's Witnesses held exempt from flag salute and national anthem).

[5]*Saumur v. City of Quebec*, [1953] 2 S.C.R. 299 (Jehovah's Witnesses held exempt from municipal street by-law).

[6]*R. v. Harrold* (1971), 19 D.L.R. (3d) 471 (B.C. C.A.) (Hare Krishnas held bound by municipal anti-noise by-law).

[7]*Walter v. A.-G. Alta.*, [1969] S.C.R. 383 (Hutterites held bound by landholding statute).

[8]Compare *Employment Division, Dept. of Human Resources of Oregon v. Smith* (1990), 494 U.S. 872.

[9]*Young v. Young*, [1993] 4 S.C.R. 3. Concurring opinions were written by McLachlin J., Cory and Iacobucci JJ. and Sopinka J.; dissenting opinions were written by La Forest and L'Heureux-Dubé JJ.

On appeal to the Supreme Court of Canada, the British Columbia Court of Appeal's decision was upheld by a narrow majority of four to three, but only Sopinka J. followed the same line of reasoning as the British Columbia Court of Appeal. According to Sopinka J., the restriction on religious communication, although imposed in the best interests of the children, would offend freedom of religion, unless it could be shown that the restriction was needed to avoid a "risk of substantial harm" to the children; since, in his view, the evidence established no such risk, the restriction should be struck down. The other six members of the Court held that no order respecting custody or access that was made in the best interests of the children could violate freedom of religion.[10] The right to freedom of religion did not guarantee any religious activity that would not be in the best interests of the children. Because s. 2(a) was inherently limited in this way, no consideration of s. 1 was needed, and the propriety of the judge's order was to be determined without reference to the Charter. McLachlin J. (with Cory and Iacobucci JJ.) still agreed with the British Columbia Court of Appeal that the restriction should be struck down, because in her view the restriction was not in the best interests of the children. L'Heureux-Dubé J. (with La Forest and Gonthier JJ.) dissented on the ground that the trial judge's finding that the restriction was in the best interests of the children should be upheld.[11]

The idea that freedom of religion authorizes religious practices only so far as they do not injure others has been abandoned by the Supreme Court of Canada in favour of an unqualified right to do anything that is dictated by a religious belief. In *B.(R.) v. Children's Aid Society* (1995),[12] a majority of the Supreme Court of Canada held that the decision of parents to prohibit doctors from giving a blood transfusion to their baby daughter was protected by freedom of religion, because it was dictated by their beliefs as Jehovah's Witnesses. The doctors attending the child, who was in hospital, considered that her life would be in danger if she did not receive a blood transfusion. In the face of this advice, an application was made under Ontario's child welfare statute to make the child a temporary ward of the Children's Aid Society. The application was granted by a provincial court judge, and the Children's Aid Society consented to the blood transfusion, which was duly given to the child.

---

[10]There was a question whether the Charter applied to a court order resolving a dispute between two private parties. L'Heureux-Dubé J., dissenting, held that the Charter did not apply; but the majority assumed without deciding that the Charter did apply.

[11]In the companion case of *P.(D.) v. S.(C.)*, [1993] 4 S.C.R. 141, the Court, by a majority, upheld a prohibition on the access parent "continually" indoctrinating the child with the Jehovah's Witness religion; in this case, a majority (Sopinka and McLachlin JJ. dissenting) accepted the trial judge's view that the prohibition on indoctrination was in the best interests of the child.

[12]*B.(R.) v. Children's Aid Society*, [1995] 1 S.C.R. 315. On the freedom of religion issue, the opinion of La Forest J. attracted the support of L'Heureux-Dubé, Sopinka, Gonthier and McLachlin JJ. The contrary opinion of Iacobucci and Major JJ. attracted the support of Lamer C.J. and Cory J.

The order was then terminated and the child was returned to her parents. The parents challenged this procedure as a violation of their freedom of religion, and five judges (a majority) of the Supreme Court of Canada agreed. Speaking for the majority, La Forest J. said that the right of a parent to choose the medical treatment of the child in accordance with the parent's religious beliefs was a "fundamental aspect of freedom of religion",[13] and that the statutory procedure that had been employed in this case was a "serious" infringement of the parents' rights.[14] However, he held that the statutory procedure was justified under s. 1. Iacobucci and Major JJ., with the agreement of two others, took the view that there were intrinsic limits on freedom of religion, and "a parent's freedom of religion does not include the imposition on the child of religious practices which threaten the safety, health or life of the child".[15]

Another blood transfusion case reached the Supreme Court in *A.C. v. Manitoba* (2009).[16] In that case, A.C., a 14-year-old girl who was a Jehovah's Witness, was admitted to hospital with an illness involving internal bleeding. A blood transfusion was prescribed by doctors as a matter of urgency, which she refused on account of her religious belief. The Director of Child and Family Services, acting under powers conferred by Manitoba's Child and Family Services Act, apprehended her as a child in need of protection, and sought a treatment order under the Act, which authorized a court to order treatment that "the court considers to be in the best interests of the child". No order could be made with respect to a child that was 16 or older unless the court was satisfied that she lacked the capacity to decide on her medical treatment, but this presumption of capacity did not apply to children under 16. The judge who heard the application accepted that A.C., although under 16, was mature enough to make decisions about her medical treatment. He concluded nevertheless that, because she was in imminent danger if not of death then of serious damage, a treatment order would be in her best interests. He ordered that the blood transfusion be given immediately; this was done; the treatment was successful; and A.C. recovered. Although the validity of the treatment order was moot, A.C. (and her parents) appealed the treatment order in order to bring a constitutional challenge to the power conferred by the Manitoba Act to override the wishes of a child under 16 on a matter of religious belief.[17] The Supreme Court, by a majority, upheld the power in the Act. Abella

[13] *B.(R.) v. Children's Aid Society*, [1995] 1 S.C.R. 315, para. 105.

[14] *B.(R.) v. Children's Aid Society*, [1995] 1 S.C.R. 315, para. 111.

[15] *B.(R.) v. Children's Aid Society*, [1995] 1 S.C.R. 315, para. 225.

[16] *A.C. v. Manitoba*, [2009] 2 S.C.R. 181. Abella J., with the agreement of LeBel, Deschamps and Charron JJ. wrote the opinion of the majority of the seven-judge bench. McLachlin C.J., with the agreement of Rothstein J., wrote a concurring opinion. Binnie J. wrote a dissenting opinion.

[17] The constitutional challenge was based not only on s. 2(a), but also s. 7 (discussed in ch. 47, Fundamental Justice, under heading § 47:26, "Arbitrary laws") and s. 15 (discussed in ch. 55, Equality, under heading § 55:44, "Age").

J. for the majority held that there was no breach of s. 2(a) because the best-interests standard of the Act required the judge to take account of the child's religious convictions and to give increasing weight to the child's wishes as her age, maturity and independence increased. McLachlin C.J., concurring in the result, held the power to override the child's religious convictions was a breach of s. 2(a), but was justified under s. 1 as a measure to protect the life and health of vulnerable young people. Binnie J., who dissented, held that the power to override the religious convictions of a child under 16 who had been found mature enough to make decisions about her own treatment was a breach of s. 2(a) that could not be justified under s. 1.

In *Ross v. New Brunswick School District No. 15* (1996),[18] the Supreme Court of Canada again held that a damaging practice was protected by freedom of religion. Ross was a schoolteacher who publicly disseminated (not in his teaching, but in the form of books, letters to the newspaper and television appearances) the opinion that Christian civilization was being destroyed by an international Jewish conspiracy. The Supreme Court of Canada held unanimously that this activity was protected by freedom of religion. La Forest J., who wrote the opinion of the Court, did not articulate which of the tenets of Christianity called for this anti-semitic activity. He recited no evidence on the issue, other than that of Ross himself, who had described his writings as "honest religious statements". And La Forest J. relied on his opinion in *B. (R.) v. Children's Aid Society* for the proposition that freedom of religion was to be given a broad interpretation, unlimited by consideration of the impact of an allegedly religious practice on the rights of other people.[19] In this case, Ross had been removed from his teaching position by the order of a board of inquiry constituted under New Brunswick's human rights statute. The board of inquiry, after hearing the evidence of Jewish students and their parents, had found that the school board's failure to dismiss or discipline Ross amounted to discrimination in the provision of educational services. The Court held that the board of inquiry's order infringed Ross's freedom of religion (as well as his freedom of expression). However, the Court held that most of the board's order could be justified under s. 1 as a measure to remedy an anti-semitic environment in the school. This justified the removal of Ross from his teaching position to a non-teaching position with the school board, but it did not justify a part of the order that required that Ross be dismissed from a non-teaching position if he resumed his anti-semitic activity. That part of the order was therefore held to be unconstitutional and was severed from the rest of the order.

An analogous case arose under Saskatchewan's Human Rights Code, s. 14 of which prohibited the publication of representations that exposed

[18] *Ross v. New Brunswick School District No. 15*, [1996] 1 S.C.R. 825. La Forest J. wrote the opinion of the nine-judge Court.

[19] *Ross v. New Brunswick School District No. 15*, [1996] 1 S.C.R. 825, para. 73. Note that the judges who rejected this proposition in *B. (R.) v. Children's Aid Society*, [1995] 1 S.C.R. 315 agreed with La Forest J.'s opinion in this case.

the victim to "hatred" on the basis of a prohibited ground—one of which was sexual orientation. The claimant, a self-proclaimed "Christian Truth Activist", had distributed flyers that condemned "homosexuality" in very strong language, some of which was held to be hate speech by the Supreme Court of Canada in *Saskatchewan v. Whatcott* (2013).[20] He said that he had a sincere religious belief in the practice of propagating his extreme views about "homosexuality". The simple assertion of a sincere religious belief, despite the lack of any objective evidence of relevant Christian doctrine, and despite the Court's finding that there was a reasoned apprehension of harm to his targets, was of course sufficient to establish his constitutional right to disseminate the flyers.[21] The protection under s. 2(a) was as broad as the protection under s. 2(b) (freedom of expression); there were no internal limits on either right other than violence and threats of violence. The conflict with the competing Charter value of equality was to be resolved under s. 1.[22] The Court held that the prohibition of hate speech was a justified limit on s. 2(a) under s. 1, although speech that was merely derogatory, offensive or hurtful—not rising to the level of hatred—could not be prohibited. Those flyers adjudged by the Court to be hateful could be banned under the Human Rights Code, despite the limitation on the claimant's religious practice.

The definition of the religious practices that are protected under s. 2(a) was expanded even further in *Syndicat Northcrest v. Amselem* (2004).[23] At issue was the right, claimed by condominium owners who were orthodox Jews, to build "succahs" (temporary dwellings) on the balconies of their condominium apartments where they would live for a nine-day period each year during the festival of "Succot". The condominium by-laws prohibited "constructions of any kind whatever" on the balconies.[24] This rule had the aesthetic purpose of preserving the harmonious external appearance of the building and the practical

[20]*Saskatchewan v. Whatcott*, [2013] 1 S.C.R. 467, 2013 SCC 11. Rothstein J. wrote the opinion of the Court. Most of the opinion is directed to the claim to freedom of expression, and the case is more fully discussed in ch. 43, Expression, under heading § 43:27, "Hate propaganda".

[21]*Saskatchewan v. Whatcott*, [2013] 1 S.C.R. 467, 2013 SCC 11, paras. 155-156.

[22]*Saskatchewan v. Whatcott*, [2013] 1 S.C.R. 467, 2013 SCC 11, para. 154.

[23]*Syndicat Northcrest v. Amselem*, [2004] 2 S.C.R. 551. Iacobucci J. wrote the opinion for the majority of five. Bastarache J. wrote a dissenting opinion for three. Binnie J. also wrote a dissenting opinion. For commentary, see D.M. Brown, "Where Can I Pray? Sacred Space in a Secular Land" (2004) 17 Nat. J. Con. Law 121; R. Moon, "Religious Commitment and Identity" (2005) 29 S.C.L.R. (2nd) 201.

[24]The by-laws were agreed to by each owner, who, on the purchase of each apartment, signed a "declaration of co-ownership" containing the by-laws. The contractual basis of the by-laws would protect them from Charter attack for lack of governmental action: ch. 37, Application of Charter, under heading § 37:13, "Private action", above. The claimants avoided this problem by making their claim under the guarantee of freedom of religion in Quebec's statutory Charter of Human Rights and Freedoms, which applies to private as well as governmental action. Other than this point, however, eight of the nine judges explicitly assumed that freedom of religion had the same meaning under the Quebec Charter as it did under s. 2(a) of the Charter of Rights: [2004] 2 S.C.R. 551, paras. 37 per Iacobucci J., 132 per Bastarache J; Binnie J. did not opine on the

purpose of keeping the balconies free of obstruction as fire escape routes. The other condominium owners sought an injunction to prevent the building of the succahs. The Supreme Court of Canada (reversing both the trial judge and the unanimous Quebec Court of Appeal) held that the claimants were entitled to erect their succahs in defiance of the by-laws. In doing so, Iacobucci J. for the majority of the Court defined protected religious practice in an extraordinarily broad fashion. The practice need not be part of an established belief system, or even a belief system shared by some others; it could be unique to the claimant. The practice need not be perceived as obligatory by the claimant; "voluntary expressions of faith" were equally protected.[25] All that was necessary to qualify a practice for Charter protection was that the claimant sincerely believed that the practice was "of religious significance".[26] Religious belief was "intensely personal and can easily vary from one person to another".[27] The test was wholly subjective. Expert evidence was not necessary, because the claimant only had to show the sincerity of his belief. And even the inquiry into sincerity of belief was to be "as limited as possible".[28] For example, it did not matter that the claimants had not attempted to build their own succahs in the past, because "individuals change and so can their beliefs".[29]

It is not surprising that freedom of religion confers a constitutional right to hold and profess religious views that are purely personal and private. The remarkable feature of the majority opinion in *Syndicat Northcrest* is that a person also has a constitutional right to *act* on those views.[30] Bastarache J., dissenting, rejected this second step. For him, a purely personal and private religious commitment was not enough to provide constitutional protection for a practice prohibited by law. In his view, religion was a collective enterprise, and its precepts were susceptible of objective proof.[31] Since the expert evidence in this case denied that orthodox Jews were under obligation to build their own personal succahs, Bastarache J.'s position would have defeated the claimants. Binnie J.'s dissent relied on the fact that the claimants had chosen to purchase a condominium in a building with by-laws that prohibited constructions on the balconies. The majority's decision to al-

---

point.

[25] *Syndicat Northcrest v. Amselem*, [2004] 2 S.C.R. 551, para. 47.

[26] *Syndicat Northcrest v. Amselem*, [2004] 2 S.C.R. 551, para. 47.

[27] *Syndicat Northcrest v. Amselem*, [2004] 2 S.C.R. 551, 54.

[28] *Syndicat Northcrest v. Amselem*, [2004] 2 S.C.R. 551, para. 52.

[29] *Syndicat Northcrest v. Amselem*, [2004] 2 S.C.R. 551, para. 53.

[30] In *S.L. v. Commission scolaire des Chênes*, [2012] 1 S.C.R. 235, discussed in § 42:8, the Supreme Court drew a distinction between the *existence* of a protected religious practice, which was to be ascertained simply by reference to the claimants' sincere subjective belief, and an *infringement* of that practice, which was to be ascertained by proof of objective facts. *Syndicat Northcrest v. Amselem* was distinguished on the ground that in *S.L.* infringement was in issue and the claimants' subjective belief was not enough.

[31] *Syndicat Northcrest v. Amselem*, [2004] 2 S.C.R. 551, paras. 137-139.

low the claimants to defy the by-laws on religious grounds went "too far in relieving private citizens of the responsibility of ordering their own affairs under contracts which they chose to enter into and upon which other people rely".[32]

In *Congrégation des Témoins de Jéhovah v. Lafontaine* (2004),[33] the Jehovah's Witnesses applied to the municipality of Lafontaine for permission to build a place of worship (a Kingdom Hall) on a parcel of land that was located in a residential zone in which a place of worship was a prohibited use. In order to comply with the request, the zoning by-law would have to be amended, which involved a cumbersome process that included a public hearing and a referendum. Despite the fact that land was available in another zone where the place of worship would be permitted, McLachlin C.J. for the majority of the Supreme Court of Canada sent the issue back to the municipality to reconsider its decision not to set in train the process for amending the zoning by-law. McLachlin C.J. rested her decision on administrative-law grounds, and made only one passing reference to freedom of religion.[34] However, the decision is only explicable on the basis that a religious practice was in issue, since a proposal to build a factory or an office building in a residential zone would surely not require such intensive consideration by a municipality. The four dissenting judges explicitly addressed the issue of freedom of religion.[35] They held that the building of a place of worship was protected by freedom of religion, and a municipality would come under a constitutional duty to amend its zoning by-laws if there was no land available for the building of a place of worship.[36] In this municipality, however, there was a zone in which a church could be built, and land was available in that zone. Religious adherents were not entitled to build a place of worship anywhere they chose, and could not insist on the municipality changing its zoning to accommodate a preference as to location. On the dissenting view, therefore, compliance with the zoning by-laws did not cause a breach of freedom of religion.

In *Multani v. Commission scolaire Marguerite-Bourgeoys* (2006),[37] the issue was whether a thirteen-year-old Sikh boy was constitutionally entitled to wear a "kirpan" (a dagger with a metal blade) to his public school in the face of a school board regulation (in a statutorily authorized code of conduct) that prohibited students from bringing weapons and other dangerous objects to school. The Supreme Court of Canada

---

[32]*Syndicat Northcrest v. Amselem*, [2004] 2 S.C.R. 551, para. 207.

[33]*Congrégation des Témoins de Jéhovah v. Lafontaine*, [2004] 2 S.C.R. 650. McLachlin C.J. wrote the opinion for the majority of five. LeBel J. wrote a dissenting opinion for three. Major J. wrote a dissenting opinion.

[34]*Congrégation des Témoins de Jéhovah v. Lafontaine*, [2004] 2 S.C.R. 650, para. 30.

[35]On this issue, Major J. agreed with the reasons of LeBel J.

[36]*Congrégation des Témoins de Jéhovah v. Lafontaine*, [2004] 2 S.C.R. 650, para. 79 per LeBel J.

[37]*Multani v. Commission scolaire Marguerite-Bourgeoys*, [2006] 1 S.C.R. 256. The eight-judge Court was unanimous. Charron J. wrote the opinion of the five-judge majority. Deschamps and Abella JJ. wrote a concurring opinion, as did LeBel J.

held unanimously that the regulation infringed the student's freedom of religion. The Court found that the student sincerely believed that his religion required him to wear a kirpan made of metal at all times. Following *Syndicat Northcrest*, this was all that the student had to show: "that his personal and subjective belief in the religious significance of the kirpan is sincere".[38] The student had refused to wear a harmless symbolic kirpan, as suggested by the review committee that considered the student's request for exemption. It was irrelevant that "other Sikhs accept such a compromise", because this student sincerely believed that a dagger without a metal blade would not comply with his religion. Since the school regulation prevented the student from acting on a sincere religious belief, the regulation contravened s. 2(a) of the Charter.

Turning to s. 1, Charron J. for the majority agreed that safety in the schools was a sufficiently important objective to justify limiting a Charter right, and there was no doubt that a bladed weapon could cause injury, whether by the owner or by another student, and whether by deliberate use or by accident. But she held that the prohibition on weapons was too broad to satisfy the minimum impairment branch of the *Oakes* test. In order to limit the student's freedom of religion as little as possible, she ordered the school to permit the wearing of the kirpan, but on condition that it be kept in a wooden sheath and sewn into the student's clothing so that it could not be easily removed—a solution the governing board and the review committee had rejected. This was well short of a guarantee that the kirpan would never emerge in the course of rough play, bullying or fighting, but she held that it was a reasonable accommodation that the school was required to make. Charron J. readily accepted and agreed with lower court decisions upholding an absolute prohibition of the kirpan in aircraft and even in courtrooms, commenting that each environment would justify "a different level of safety".[39] But the unanimous Court concluded that the school's governing board and the review committee were wrong to insist on the same high level of safety in the schools as judges insist on in their courtrooms![40]

In *Alberta v. Hutterian Brethren of Wilson Colony* (2009),[41] a colony of Hutterian Brethren brought proceedings against the government of

---

[38]*Multani v. Commission scolaire Marguerite-Bourgeoys*, [2006] 1 S.C.R. 256, para. 37 per Charron J.

[39]*Multani v. Commission scolaire Marguerite-Bourgeoys*, [2006] 1 S.C.R. 256, para. 66.

[40]Deschamps and Abella JJ. disagreed with Charron J.'s s. 1 analysis. In their view, the s. 1 analysis should simply be part of judicial review on administrative-law grounds of the decision of the governing board and review committee not to relax the no-weapons rule for the kirpan-wearer (para. 103). The decision, they held, should be reviewed on the standard of reasonableness (not correctness) (para. 96), but they went on to concur in the result on the ground that the governing board's insistence on the highest level of safety in the schools was not reasonable (para. 99)! LeBel J., also concurring, took a middle ground, saying that there was room for an administrative-law analysis as well as a s. 1 analysis (para. 155).

[41]*Alberta v. Hutterian Brethren of Wilson Colony*, [2009] 2 S.C.R. 567. McLachlin C.J. wrote the opinion of the four-judge majority. Abella, LeBel and Fish JJ. each wrote

Alberta to obtain an exemption, on religious grounds, from the requirement of provincial law that a driver's licence must display a photograph of the holder. The Hutterian Brethren are a Christian denomination who live in communal colonies and who believe that having their photos taken (even under compulsion of law) is forbidden by the Bible. Alberta (in common with the other provinces) requires a driver's licence to display a photograph of the holder. The purposes are to enable police officers to identify any driver involved in an accident or suspected of a driving offence, and to confirm that the driver is indeed the holder of a licence. However, Alberta did not rely on these obvious purposes as the justification for imposing the requirement on the Hutterian Brethren, and the reason seems to have been that the province had from 1974 to 2003 permitted a religious exemption from the photo requirement without any apparent negative effects on roadside enforcement. What changed in 2003 was the establishment by the province of a data bank of digital photographs of all licensed drivers, which was to be used to prevent identity theft. For this purpose to be fully realized, all drivers had to be photographed and have their images placed in the data bank. That was the reason for the province amending its licensing regulations in 2003 to make the photo requirement universal. The Supreme Court held that the Hutterian claimants had a sincere religious belief that prohibited their being photographed, and that belief was protected by s. 2(a) of the Charter. However, the majority held that the universal photo requirement was justified under s. 1: it served an important purpose and did not impose a severe burden on the claimants, who could avoid the requirement by using alternative means of transport. According to the majority, the requirement was a reasonable limit on freedom of religion and the Hutterian claimants were not entitled to an exemption.

Polygamy is a practice sanctioned by the religious beliefs of the community of Bountiful in British Columbia.[42] In the *Polygamy Reference* (2011),[43] the government of the province directed a reference to the province's Supreme Court (that is the trial court) to determine whether the prohibition of polygamy in the federal Criminal Code was applicable to the sect—and therefore whether those engaging in the practice could be prosecuted by the province. Bauman C.J. held that the Criminal Code prohibition was a limitation on a constitutionally protected religious practice, but one that was justified under s. 1. The evidence of harm to women in polygamous communities and to the men who were left without spouses persuaded the judge that harmful effects were

---

dissenting opinions.

[42]The practice of the Bountiful community was polygyny (one husband, several wives) not polyandry (one wife, several husbands). Both are encompassed by the word polygamy, and both are prohibited by ss. 290 (bigamy) and 293 (polygamy) of the Criminal Code.

[43]*Re s. 293 of the Criminal Code* (2011), 28 B.C.L.R. (5th) 96 (B.C. S.C.). B.C. is unusual in allowing references to be made to the trial court (as opposed to the Court of Appeal), but the extensive evidence required to determine the case made the trial court an appropriate venue. However, because the decision was not appealed, it remains a trial-level decision.

"endemic" to the practice of polygamy[44] and the Criminal Code's prohibition was a reasonable limit on the right to engage in the practice.

In *R. v. N.S.* (2012),[45] the complainant in a sexual assault case sought to testify at the preliminary hearing and the subsequent trial wearing a niqab, which is a veil that covers the face except for the eyes. As a Muslim woman, she held the sincere religious belief that she must wear a niqab while testifying in front of any man who is not a direct family member. The cases discussed earlier in this section of the book made clear that this was a religious practice protected by s. 2(a). The two accused asserted their right to make full answer and defence to the criminal charges against them, a right protected by ss. 11(d) and 7 of the Charter. Their argument was that, if the complainant did not bare her face in court, she could not be effectively cross-examined by their counsel and her credibility could not be properly assessed by the trial judge. McLachlin C.J., who wrote the opinion of the four-judge majority of the seven-judge bench of the Supreme Court of Canada, held that, in the absence of "compelling evidence" to the contrary, seeing a witness's face was an important factor in cross-examination and credibility assessment, and therefore important to the right to make full answer and defence. She proceeded on the basis that freedom of religion and trial fairness were in conflict, and, following the *Dagenais/Mentuck* approach,[46] she said that "the answer lies in a just and proportionate balance between freedom of religion on the one hand and trial fairness on the other, based on the particular case before the Court".[47] She left that balance to be found by the trial judge in the case, although she devoted several pages[48] to outlining the considerations that should be taken into account by the unfortunate trial judge, who would likely face a major trial within a trial. The Chief Justice contemplated that the complainant would testify because, although the claimant's sincerity was not questioned on appeal in this case, one consideration was "how important is the practice to the complainant?", a consideration that would no doubt expose the complainant to intrusive personal questioning to find out when she did take off the niqab.[49] The Chief Justice also contemplated that the complainant would lead expert evidence because other relevant considerations included the "scientific exploration of the importance of seeing a witness's face" and "broader social harms" like the reluctance of Muslim women to report sexual assaults. These were "but some of the factors" to be weighed by the trial judge.

---

[44]*Re s. 293 of the Criminal Code* (2011), 28 B.C.L.R. (5th) 96 (B.C. S.C.), para. 1045.

[45]*R. v. N.S.*, [2012] 3 S.C.R. 726. McLachlin C.J. wrote the majority opinion for four of the seven-judge bench. LeBel J. (with Rothstein J.) wrote a concurring opinion. Abella J. wrote a dissenting opinion.

[46]Chapter 43, Expression, under heading § 43:32, "Restrictions on reporting".

[47]*R. v. N.S.*, [2012] 3 S.C.R. 726, para. 31.

[48]*R. v. N.S.*, [2012] 3 S.C.R. 726, paras.15-45.

[49]Sincerity is subject to a very low bar of proof: *Syndicat Northcrest v. Amselem*, [2004] 2 S.C.R. 551, para. 49. But "importance" clearly invites cross-examination. Abella J., *R. v. N.S.*, [2012] 3 S.C.R. 726, para. 88, criticizes this factor as leading to "inappropriate inquiries into a claimant's past practices".

The weighing of the factors required by the majority in *N.S.* does supply an analytical framework for the solution of the difficult issue of conflicting rights. But it imposes heavy evidentiary burdens on the claimant (and the accused in reply), and (with respect) it does not seem likely to present an easy solution to the trial judge's problem of finding a "just and proportionate balance" of the conflicting rights.[50] The other three judges in *N.S.* proposed a clear rule to resolve the conflicting rights. For LeBel J. (with whom Rothstein J. agreed), the credibility of a key witness in a criminal prosecution was so critical to the accused whose guilt or innocence was at stake that the balancing process should always be resolved in favour of the accused. He concluded that, in a criminal trial, the clear rule should be that the wearing of the niqab by a witness is not allowed. Abella J. reached the opposite conclusion: the clear rule should be that the wearing of the niqab is allowed.[51] She agreed that "seeing more of a witness's facial expressions is better than seeing less", but she did not agree that "seeing less is so impairing of a judge's or an accused's ability to assess the credibility of a witness that the complainant will have to choose between her religious rights and her ability to bear witness against an alleged aggressor."[52] She pointed out that the niqab presented only a partial obstacle to the assessment of demeanour, and witnesses often present partial obstacles to the assessment of demeanour. For example, child witnesses are sometimes allowed to testify behind a screen, witnesses who are unable to speak English or French are allowed to use an interpreter, and witnesses sometimes have physical or mental disabilities that impair facial expression or speech. In any case, demeanour is only one factor in assessing credibility, and an imprecise one at that, leading Abella J. to ask the rhetorical question of "why we demand full 'demeanour access' when religious belief prevents it."[53] Despite the merits of a clear rule, the majority view prevailed of course, so that the issue of whether the niqab can be worn is to be determined on a case-by-case basis by the trial judge, who must try to balance the competing rights after hearing evidence on that issue.

---

[50]Abella J., *R. v. N.S.*, [2012] 3 S.C.R. 726, para. 85, said: "In the context of a witness wearing the niqab, I see very little realistic possibility of accommodation." That was also the view of LeBel J., who said (para. 69) that the application of the Chief Justice's criteria "looks highly problematic", "could trigger new motions", and "add a new layer of complexity to a trial process that is not always a model of simplicity".

[51]She made an exception for the case where witness's face is a central issue in the trial, for example, where it is the identity of the witness that is in issue, rather than merely part of the assessment of demeanour: *R. v. N.S.*, [2012] 3 S.C.R. 726, para. 83.

[52]*R. v. N.S.*, [2012] 3 S.C.R. 726, para. 89.

[53]*R. v. N.S.*, [2012] 3 S.C.R. 726, para. 108.

VII. WAIVER OF RELIGIOUS PRACTICE

§ 42:7 Waiver of religious practice

In *Syndicat Northwest v. Amselem* (2004),[1] the condominium case discussed in the previous section, the Supreme Court of Canada held that a party to a contract could invoke freedom of religion to resile from a contractual obligation, in that case, a promise not to build structures on the balconies of condominiums owned by the claimants. The majority of the Court brushed aside the argument of their co-owners that the claimants had waived their religious right. Iacobucci J., writing for the majority, held that the claimants' sincere religious belief that they should build and occupy "succahs" on their balconies for the nine-day festival of "Succot" (something that most of them had not done in previous years) trumped the by-laws of the condominium to which the claimants had agreed on purchasing their units.[2] Iacobucci J. for the majority of the Court provided a veritable pot-pourri of reasons for denying the primacy of the by-laws.[3] He wondered whether a religious practice could be waived at all, he wondered if the by-law was sufficiently clear to amount to a waiver, he thought the by-law should have made explicit reference to the Charter right to freedom of religion, he held that the claimants "had no choice" but to sign their agreement to the by-laws in order to live in that building (that is the building that prohibited building on the balconies!), and that in any case the claimants "did not read" the by-laws (which they signed and were given a copy of on purchase). Binnie J., who dissented, replied that the claimants had a choice of places to live, and that they "undertook by contract to the owners of *this* building to abide by the rules of *this* building even if (as is apparently the case) they accepted the rules without reading them". Therefore, he reasoned, the claimants should be defeated by their "contract with their co-owners, that they would not insist on construction of a personal succah on the communally owned balconies of the building".[4]

It is an extraordinary doctrine that permits a contracting party to invoke a sincere religious belief as the basis for ignoring a contractual promise that the promisor freely made but no longer wishes to keep. After all, as Binnie J. emphasised, the counterparties will have ordered their affairs in reliance on the external manifestation of agreement, and will be rightly disturbed by the promisor's assertion of a hitherto secret religious scruple to justify not keeping the promise. In *Bruker v. Marco-*

[Section 42:7]

[1] *Syndicat Northwest v. Amselem*, [2004] 2 S.C.R. 551.

[2] The Charter of Rights did not actually apply to the by-laws as private contracts, but Quebec's statutory Charter did: § 42:6 note 24, above.

[3] *Syndicat Northwest v. Amselem*, [2004] 2 S.C.R. 551, paras. 91-102.

[4] *Syndicat Northwest v. Amselem*, [2004] 2 S.C.R. 551, paras. 184-185 (emphasis in original).

vitz (2007),[5] a husband and wife, as part of a divorce settlement, negotiated and signed a corollary relief agreement, which provided for spousal support, child support, custody and access. Because the two spouses were Orthodox Jews, the agreement included a promise to attend before a rabbinical court to obtain a "get". A get is a Jewish divorce, and it must be granted by the husband and agreed to by the wife. If the husband refuses the get, the wife is an "agunah" or "chained wife". Even if the couple are divorced under Canadian civil law (as this couple was), any new marriage by the wife would be unrecognized by Jewish law, the relationship would be treated as adulterous and any children would be treated as illegitimate. In this case, despite his promise, the husband refused for 15 years to grant the get, and did so only after the wife brought an action against him for breach of contract. Not surprisingly in light of *Amselem*, he invoked freedom of religion[6] as the basis for his absolute right to withhold the get in spite of his signed contract to grant it.[7] The Supreme Court of Canada, by a majority, rejected this argument and upheld an award of damages for breach of contract against the husband. Abella J., writing for the majority, held that the husband, by entering into the corollary relief agreement, had converted his religious right to withhold the get into a contractual obligation to grant the get. He was bound by contract to fulfil that obligation despite its religious aspect. If it were not for *Amselem*, the reasons would no doubt have stopped there. But Abella J. evidently felt compelled to add that the husband's "binding promise" was "only one of the factors that weighs against his claim"; the most important factors were "the public policies of equality, religious freedom and autonomous choice in marriage and divorce".[8] The claim that these factors were more important than the contract is puzzling, since the husband would certainly not have been held liable for withholding the get in the absence of a legally binding contract to grant it.[9] Perhaps what she meant was that a contract that waived a right to a religious practice would not be enforced if it were contrary to public policy to do so. It should be noted, however, that there was nothing contrary to public policy in the *Amselem* contract to keep condominium balconies free of construction: that promise was demanded by the co-owners and given by the claimants for intelligible aesthetic and fire-safety reasons.

---

[5] *Bruker v. Marcovitz*, [2007] 3 S.C.R. 607. Abella J. wrote the opinion of the seven-judge majority. Deschamps J. (with Charron J.) dissented.

[6] The Charter of Rights is not applicable to a private contract, but, as in *Anselem*, the case arose in Quebec and Quebec's statutory charter was applicable.

[7] There was no doubt that the corollary relief agreement was voluntary. Both sides were legally represented, and the attendance to grant the get was just one of a number of reciprocal promises.

[8] *Bruker v. Marcovitz*, [2007] 3 S.C.R. 607, para. 80.

[9] Deschamps J. in dissent took the view that even the inclusion in a contract of the promise to provide the get did not change its character as "a purely moral obligation that may not be enforced civilly": *Bruker v. Marcovitz*, [2007] 3 S.C.R. 607, para. 175.

VIII. RELIGION IN PUBLIC SCHOOLS

§ 42:8 Religion in public schools

In *Zylberberg v. Sudbury Board of Education* (1988),[1] a challenge was brought to an Ontario regulation, made under statutory authority, that required a public school to open or close each school day with "religious exercises consisting of the reading of the Scriptures or other suitable readings and the repeating of the Lord's Prayer or other suitable prayers". The regulation conferred a right on each pupil not to participate in the religious exercises. The Ontario Court of Appeal, by a majority, held that the regulation was unconstitutional, because it "imposed Christian observances upon non-Christian pupils and religious observances on non-believers".[2] The regulation was not saved by the fact that it was wide enough to authorize non-Christian prayers and readings. In Sudbury, where the case originated, the school board had in fact prescribed only Christian exercises (which was what had caused the litigation); but the Court held that, even if the school board had in fact prescribed non-Christian exercises as well as Christian exercises, the regulation would still be bad because it authorized a school board to prescribe only Christian exercises. Nor was the regulation saved by a pupil's right to be exempted from the religious exercises. The regulation still exerted an indirect coercion[3] on pupils to participate, because of the pressure to conform to the majority's norms, which would make it difficult in practice for a minority pupil to claim the exemption.

Ontario did not appeal the decision in *Zylberberg* and the province removed the requirement of "religious exercises" from its public school regulations. However, the province kept in place a regulation dating from 1944 that required a public school to devote two periods per week to "religious education". A parent had the right to apply to the principal of the school to exempt a pupil from the religious education. In *Canadian Civil Liberties Association v. Ontario* (1990),[4] the Ontario Court of Appeal struck down this regulation too. The Court concluded from the legislative history of the regulation and the curricula that were placed before it that the purpose of the regulation was the indoctrination of Christian belief, as opposed to education about many religions. The Court followed *Zylberberg* to hold that the regulation was an unconstitutional attempt to impose the majority's Christian beliefs on all school children, and that it was not saved by the provision for exemption, which parents would be reluctant to utilize for fear of embarrassing their children.

In the United States, the Supreme Court has struck down many at-

---

[Section 42:8]

[1] *Zylberberg v. Sudbury Board of Education* (1988), 65 O.R. (2d) 641 (C.A.).

[2] *Zylberberg v. Sudbury Board of Education* (1988), 65 O.R. (2d) 641, 654 (C.A.).

[3] Compare the indirect coercion imposed by the "competitive pressure" in *R. v. Edwards Books and Art*, [1986] 2 S.C.R. 713.

[4] *Canadian Civil Liberties Association v. Ontario* (1990), 71 O.R. (2d) 341 (C.A.).

tempts to introduce religious exercises or instruction in the public schools, including a government-written "nondenominational" prayer,[5] voluntary Christian prayer and bible reading,[6] the posting of the ten commandments on classroom walls,[7] a period of silence for "meditation or voluntary prayer",[8] and equal time for the teaching of "creation science" and evolution.[9] All of these cases were decided under the establishment clause of the first amendment, not the free exercise clause.[10] What was unconstitutional was the active support of government for religious views or practices, which tended to "an establishment of religion". This line of reasoning cannot be directly transferred to s. 2(a) of the Charter, which lacks an establishment clause.

In the United States, judges and commentators have speculated as to whether the decisions barring religious exercises or instruction in the public schools could have been reached under the free exercise clause, which is much closer to s. 2(a). This turns on the question whether a mandatory programme with a power of exemption (or a voluntary programme) is sufficiently coercive in practice to constrain a minority child's freedom not to participate. As we have noticed, the Ontario Court of Appeal in the *Zylberberg* and *Canadian Civil Liberties* cases, after hearing evidence on the point, took the view that the embarrassment of nonconformity did operate as a significant practical barrier to the exercise by minority children (or their parents) of a power of exemption from religious exercises or instruction. That finding, which seems sound, means that programmes of religious exercises or instruction in public schools will normally violate the guarantee of freedom of religion.

What does not infringe the guarantee of freedom of religion is a course on religion that examines various religions in a neutral way, not promoting any one religion or assuming the superiority of any one religion. That was decided by the Supreme Court of Canada in *S.L. v. Commission scolaire des Chênes* (2012),[11] where Roman Catholic parents objected to their children being enrolled in a course in "Ethics and Religious Culture", which was compulsory in both the elementary and secondary levels of Quebec's public school system. Their complaint was that they believed (1) that they had a religious obligation to impart the precepts of Catholicism to their children, and (2) that the presentation in school of the beliefs of other religions on an equal footing with Catholicism would impair their ability to pass their faith on to their children. There was no doubt about the sincerity of these beliefs. On the basis of *Syndicat*

---

[5] *Engel v. Vitale* (1962), 370 U.S. 421.

[6] *Abingdon School District v. Schempp* (1963), 374 U.S. 203.

[7] *Stone v. Graham* (1980), 449 U.S. 39.

[8] *Wallace v. Jaffree* (1985), 472 U.S. 38.

[9] *Edwards v. Aguillard* (1987), 482 U.S. 578.

[10] The text of the two clauses is set out in § 42:2, "Section 2(a) of the Charter".

[11] *S.L. v. Commission scolaire des Chênes*, [2012] 1 S.C.R. 235. Deschamps J., with the agreement of six others, wrote the opinion of the majority. LeBel J., with the agreement of Fish J., wrote a concurring opinion.

Northcrest v. Amselem,[12] it was argued that the parents' sincerity of belief was decisive, and they had a constitutional entitlement to an exemption for their children. What the Court held was that the parents' belief (1) was indeed decisive on the existence of a protected religious practice, namely, to impart their faith to their children. But belief (2) was not decisive. The question whether the parents' religious practice would be infringed by the school's curriculum was not resolved by their subjective belief that it would be. "At the stage of establishing an *infringement*, it is not enough for a person to say that his or her rights have been infringed. The person must prove the infringement on a balance of probabilities. This may of course involve any legal form of proof, but it must nonetheless be based on facts that can be established *objectively*".[13] The Court held that "exposing children to a variety of religious facts" simply reflected the "multicultural reality of Canadian society", and, while it might be "a source of friction", it did not constitute an infringement of the parents' freedom of religion.[14]

IX. DENOMINATIONAL SCHOOLS

§ 42:9 Denominational schools

It goes without saying that private schools may offer religious exercises and instruction, and of course that is a major appeal of private schools to many parents. The Supreme Court of Canada has implied that s. 2(a) requires a province to permit children to be educated outside the secular public system,[1] although the province must have the right to regulate alternative schools, including denominational schools, in order to ensure that a core curriculum and adequate facilities and standards of teaching are offered.

The previous section of this chapter described *S.L. v. Commission*

[12]*Syndicat Northcrest v. Amselem*, [2004] 2 S.C.R. 551.

[13]*S.L. v. Commission scolaire des Chênes*, [2012] 1 S.C.R. 235, para. 23 (emphasis added).

[14]*S.L. v. Commission scolaire des Chênes*, [2012] 1 S.C.R. 235, para. 40. No evidence was proffered as to how the course was actually taught. The Court only had the written curriculum before it. This led LeBel J. to write a concurring opinion agreeing that the parents had not proved their case, but cautioning (para. 58) that the course might, "in the future, possibly infringe the rights of [parents]". This was only a minority view, and was probably not intended as an invitation to future litigation, in which schoolteachers would be forced under subpoena to testify as to the religious neutrality of their presentations, but it could be read as contemplating a sequel of that kind.

[Section 42:9]

[1]*R. v. Jones*, [1986] 2 S.C.R. 284 held by a majority of four to three that it was not a violation of s. 2(a) to require that an application be made to the provincial Department of Education for approval of a private school or a certificate of efficient instruction for teaching at home. The minority held that this requirement was contrary to s. 2(a) (although it was saved by s. 1) for a person who believed on religious grounds that he ought to be able to teach his children without reference to the state. It is a reasonable inference that for both majority and minority a prohibition on alternative, religious schooling would violate s. 2(a).

scolaire des Chênes (2012),[2] in which the Supreme Court held that "Ethics and Religious Culture" (ERC), which was a compulsory course in the public schools of Quebec, did not infringe the freedom of religion of Roman Catholic parents of children in the public school system. The course, which required neutral instruction about the beliefs and practices of the main religions of the world, was also compulsory in the denominational schools of the province, all of which were private. In the case of the private schools, however, the responsible Minister had the regulatory power to exempt a school from the course if, in the Minister's opinion, the school was offering an "equivalent" course. In *Loyola High School v. Quebec* (2015),[3] Loyola High School, a Catholic school, had applied to the Minister for an exemption from the ERC course on the ground that the Loyola curriculum covered the same ground, albeit from a Catholic viewpoint. The Minister denied the exemption; in her view, a course could not be equivalent if any part of the course, including instruction on the beliefs and practices of Catholicism itself, was not taught from a neutral standpoint. The school applied for judicial review of the Minister's decision on the ground that she had not properly respected the Charter guarantee of the religious freedom of the Loyola teachers, students and parents who sought to offer or wished to receive a Catholic education.[4] The Supreme Court accepted this argument and granted judicial review. Applying the *Doré* framework, which applies where a discretionary administrative decision (rather than a law) is challenged on Charter grounds,[5] Abella J., who wrote for the majority, held that a discretionary administrative decision that affected freedom of religion had to take account of the Charter right and ensure that the right was limited no more than necessary to achieve the statutory purposes that the decision-maker was obliged to pursue. In her view, the Minister's prescription that Loyola teach Catholicism from a neutral standpoint was a serious interference with freedom of religion which did little or nothing to advance the ERC objectives of understanding and respect for other religions. So far as those other religions were concerned, Abella J. agreed that the Minister could insist that Loyola explain their beliefs and practices "in as objective and neutral way as possible, rather than from a Catholic perspective."[6] The Court's remedy was to set aside the Minister's decision, and require the Minister to reconsider in light of the

---

[2]*S.L. v. Commission scolaire des Chênes*, [2012] 1 S.C.R. 235.

[3]*Loyola High School v. Quebec*, 2015 SCC 12. Abella J. wrote the opinion of the majority of four. McLachlin C.J. and Moldaver J (with Rothstein J.) wrote a partially concurring opinion.

[4]Abella J., for the majority, did not need to decide whether Loyola itself, as a corporation, could possess s. 2(a) rights: *Loyola High School v. Quebec*, 2015 SCC 12, para. 34. McLachlin C.J. and Moldaver J., concurring, held that Loyola, as a religious, non-profit corporation, did possess s. 2(a) rights: *Loyola High School v. Quebec*, 2015 SCC 12, paras 89-102.

[5]For further discussion of the *Doré* framework (which was laid out in *Doré v. Barreau du Québec*, [2012] 1 S.C.R. 395), see ch. 38, Limitation of Rights, under heading § 38:31, "Application to discretionary decisions".

[6]*Loyola High School v. Quebec*, 2015 SCC 12, para. 6.

ruling that Loyola could not be made to teach Catholicism from a neutral perspective.[7]

The Supreme Court of Canada considered a freedom of religion claim involving another denominational school three years later in two companion cases—*Law Society of British Columbia v. Trinity Western University* (2018)[8] and *Trinity Western University v. Law Society of Upper Canada* (2018).[9] Both cases arose from a proposal by Trinity Western University (TWU), a private evangelical Christian university, to start a law school where all students would be required to sign and obey the University's existing Community Covenant Agreement, a religiously-based code of conduct. The mandatory Covenant includes a prohibition on "sexual intimacy that violates the sacredness of marriage between a man and a woman". This prohibition forbids all sexual intimacy outside of marriage, regardless of the sexual orientation of those involved, but it singles out LGBTQ people for harsher treatment, as it prohibits all same-sex sexual intimacy, regardless of whether those involved are married. This prohibition—and the mandatory Covenant more broadly—was to extend to all aspects of the students' lives, including when they were off campus. TWU applied for accreditation of its proposed law school from the provincial law societies, which regulate, among other things, who is entitled to practice law. The Law Society of British Columbia and the Law Society of Upper Canada (now the Law Society of Ontario) both denied accreditation.[10] Although neither law society provided formal written reasons, it was clear from the record of their deliberations that the mandatory Covenant's prohibition on same-sex sexual intimacy was a key reason for both decisions.[11] TWU and a prospective student sought judicial review of these decisions in separate proceedings in British Columbia and Ontario, arguing, among other

---

[7]McLachlin C.J. and Moldaver J., concurring, agreed that the Minister's decision should be set aside, agreed that Loyola must be permitted to teach Catholicism from a Catholic point of view, and agreed that Loyola could be required to teach other religions from a neutral point of view, but they also would have held that ethics could be taught from a Catholic point of view; and instead of remitting the matter to the Minister for reconsideration they would have issued a mandamus requiring the Minister to grant the exemption in accordance with their guidelines.

[8]*Law Society of British Columbia v. Trinity Western University*, [2018] 2 S.C.R. 293 [*LSBC*]. Abella, Moldaver, Karakatsanis, Wagner and Gascon JJ. wrote a joint opinion for the majority of the Court. McLachlin C.J. and Rowe J. each wrote separate concurring opinions. Côté and Brown JJ. wrote a joint dissenting opinion.

[9]*Trinity Western University v. Law Society of Upper Canada*, [2018] 2 S.C.R. 453 [*LSUC*]. The bench in this case broke down exactly as it did in *LSBC* (see previous note). *LSBC* is the lead companion case; the opinions in *LSUC* refer regularly to, and adopt significant portions of, the corresponding opinions in *LSBC*.

[10]The Nova Scotia Barristers' Society also denied accreditation, but after the Nova Scotia Court of Appeal overturned its decision, it decided not to appeal: *The Nova Scotia Barristers' Society v. Trinity Western University*, 2016 NSCA 59.

[11]In the case of the Law Society of Upper Canada, the decision was made by a majority of the Benchers. In the case of the Law Society of British Columbia, the decision was made by the Benchers following a referendum in which a large majority of the Law Society's members voted against accrediting TWU's proposed law school.

things, that each law society did not properly respect their freedom of religion under s. 2(a). The cases ended up on appeal in the Supreme Court, which heard the appeals together.

The majority of the Court rejected the freedom of religion claims, in divided decisions each involving four separate opinions.[12] Applying the *Doré* framework, Abella, Moldaver, Karakatsanis, Wagner and Gascon JJ., who wrote jointly for the majority of the Court, agreed that the freedom of religion of the TWU community was "engaged".[13] By denying accreditation to the proposed law school due to the mandatory Covenant, the two law societies had made decisions that interfered with "the ability of religious adherents to come together and create cohesive communities of belief and practice".[14] However, the joint majority concluded that the limitation on freedom of religion that resulted from the denial of accreditation was proportionate, and therefore reasonable. Citing *Doré* and *Loyola*, they reiterated that a discretionary administrative decision that engages freedom of religion "will be reasonable if it reflects a proportionate balancing of the Charter protection with the statutory mandate".[15] TWU argued that, in determining whether to accredit a proposed law school, the statutory mandate of the two law societies did not permit them to examine TWU's admissions policies—that it extended only to the academic qualifications and competence of potential graduates, which were not disputed. The joint majority rejected this argument. Both law societies had an overarching statutory mandate to protect "the public interest in the administration of justice", and it was open to them to consider a discriminatory admissions policy in determining whether to accredit a law school, because "promoting equality by ensuring equal access to the legal profession, supporting diversity within the bar, and preventing harm to LGBTQ law students" were reasonable means to further the public interest in the administration of justice.[16] With this public interest statutory mandate in mind, the joint majority said that the two law societies were presented with only two options—accrediting

[12]Portions of the various opinions (particularly of the concurring opinions of McLachlin C.J. and Rowe J. and joint dissenting opinion of Brown and Côté JJ.) were given over to discussion of and disagreement about the *Doré* framework. The description here focuses on the discussion of the freedom of religion claim. For further discussion of the *Doré* framework, see ch. 38, Limitation of Rights, under heading § 38:31, "Application to discretionary decisions".

[13]The joint majority declined to address whether TWU could possess rights under s. 2(a) as an institution: *Law Society of British Columbia v. Trinity Western University*, [2018] 2 S.C.R. 293, para. 61; see similarly para. 219 per Rowe J. Compare *Law Society of British Columbia v. Trinity Western University*, [2018] 2 S.C.R. 293, para. 315 per Côté and Brown JJ. dissenting, implying a willingness to accept that institutions can possess rights under s. 2(a).

[14]*Law Society of British Columbia v. Trinity Western University*, [2018] 2 S.C.R. 293, para. 64.

[15]*Law Society of British Columbia v. Trinity Western University*, [2018] 2 S.C.R. 293, para. 79.

[16]*Law Society of British Columbia v. Trinity Western University*, [2018] 2 S.C.R. 293, para. 40; see also *Trinity Western University v. Law Society of Upper Canada*, [2018] 2 S.C.R. 453, paras. 20, 27.

or not accrediting the proposed law school—and that accreditation was not an alternative, less-impairing option because approving the proposed law school would not have furthered this statutory mandate. In addition, the two law societies had struck a proportionate balance between freedom of religion and their statutory mandate: the impact of their decisions on the freedom of religion of the TWU community was minimal and their decisions "significantly advanced" their statutory mandate.[17]

McLachlin C.J. wrote a concurring opinion in both cases.[18] She agreed with the joint majority that the freedom of religion of the TWU community was "limited" or "infringed" by the law societies' decisions.[19] However, unlike the joint majority, she focused more on the expressive and associational harms of their decisions. She said that the two law societies had infringed religious freedom not merely by limiting religious beliefs and practices, but also by limiting the ability of the TWU community to *express* those beliefs and practices, and to *associate* with those "who accept these beliefs and practices or are prepared to respect and conform to them".[20] She also agreed with the joint majority that the limitation on the freedom of religion of the TWU community resulting from the law societies' decisions was proportionate. However, unlike the joint majority, she focused her analysis on a different aspect of the law societies' statutory mandate to protect the public interest—their "imperative" to protect the public interest by "refusing to condone discrimination against LGBTQ people".[21] She also disagreed with the joint majority that the impact of the law societies' decisions on the freedom of religion of the TWU community was minimal. Even so, she said that their decisions struck a proportionate balance because the imperative of refusing to condone discrimination against LGBTQ people outweighed the impact of the decisions on the freedom of religion of the TWU community.[22]

Côté and Brown JJ. wrote a joint dissenting opinion in both cases. Unlike the joint majority and McLachlin C.J., they agreed with TWU that, in determining whether to accredit a proposed law school, the statutory mandate of the two law societies did not permit them to examine TWU's admissions policies—that it extended only to the academic qualifications and competence of potential graduates, which were not disputed. They

---

[17] *Law Society of British Columbia v. Trinity Western University*, [2018] 2 S.C.R. 293, paras. 92; see also *Trinity Western University v. Law Society of Upper Canada*, [2018] 2 S.C.R. 453, para. 39.

[18] In *LSUC*, McLachlin C.J. largely adopted her opinion in *LSBC*: see *Trinity Western University v. Law Society of Upper Canada*, [2018] 2 S.C.R. 453, paras. 44-46.

[19] Unlike the joint majority, McLachlin C.J. used the terms limited or infringed more than the word "engages" in referring to the impact on the Charter: see e.g. *Law Society of British Columbia v. Trinity Western University*, [2018] 2 S.C.R. 293, paras. 120, 122.

[20] *Law Society of British Columbia v. Trinity Western University*, [2018] 2 S.C.R. 293, paras. 124-126.

[21] *Law Society of British Columbia v. Trinity Western University*, [2018] 2 S.C.R. 293, para. 137.

[22] *Law Society of British Columbia v. Trinity Western University*, [2018] 2 S.C.R. 293, paras. 146-148.

also said that, even if the statutory mandate of the two law societies did extend this far, their decisions did not strike a proportionate balance.

Taking the various opinions together, eight judges (the joint majority, McLachlin C.J. and the joint dissent) agreed that freedom of religion was "engaged", "limited" or "infringed" by the law societies' decisions; only one judge (Rowe J.) took the view that freedom of religion was not infringed by the decisions.[23] However, of these eight judges, six (the joint majority and McLachlin C.J.) took the view that the claims could not succeed because the limitation on freedom of religion that resulted from the decisions was proportionate, and therefore reasonable. A total of seven judges (the joint majority, McLachlin C.J. and Rowe J.) thus rejected the religious freedom claims.

In the United States, the establishment clause prohibits most state aid to denominational schools.[24] In Canada, systems of state aid to minority Protestant and Catholic schools have existed since confederation and are actually guaranteed by s. 93 of the Constitution Act, 1867.[25] Moreover, the Protestant and Catholic schools that are recognized by s. 93 may receive public funding that is denied to the schools of religious denominations not recognized by s. 93.[26] In *Adler v. Ontario* (1996),[27] the Supreme Court of Canada held that a province's failure to fund the schools of religious denominations not recognized by s. 93 was not a breach of freedom of religion under s. 2(a) or of equality under s. 15. In *R. v. Big M Drug Mart* (1985),[28] Dickson J. left open the question whether s. 2(a), despite its lack of an establishment clause, prohibits state aid to denominational schools other than those entitled under s. 93. It is hard to see why s. 2(a) should be regarded as infringed by a programme of state aid,[29] provided all religions are treated equally.[30]

---

[23]Rowe J. took the view—not accepted by his colleagues—that freedom of religion was not infringed in the cases because freedom of religion does not protect the right to impose religious beliefs and practices on others.

[24]L.H. Tribe, American Constitutional Law (Foundation Press, New York, 2nd ed., 1986), 1215; J.E. Nowak and R.D. Rotunda, Constitutional Law (West, St. Paul, Minn., 7th ed., 2004), 1429-1430.

[25]Section 93 and its counterparts are discussed in ch. 57, Education.

[26]*Re Bill 30*, (Ontario Separate School Funding) [1987] 1 S.C.R. 1148.

[27]*Adler v. Ontario*, [1996] 3 S.C.R. 609. With respect to s. 2(a), the decision was unanimous. With respect to s. 15, L'Heureux-Dubé J. dissented and McLachlin J. dissented in part. The s. 15 reasoning is discussed in ch. 55, Equality, under heading § 55:35, "Religion in s. 93".

[28]*R. v. Big M Drug Mart*, [1985] 1 S.C.R. 295, 340-341.

[29]The issue did not have to be decided in *Adler v. Ontario*, [1996] 3 S.C.R. 609, where the issue was the province's failure to fund private religious schools, but the opinions strongly suggest that there would be no constitutional impediment to funding: see, especially, para. 48 per Iacobucci J. for majority.

[30]The requirement of equal treatment would probably flow from s. 2(a), having regard to *R. v. Big M Drug Mart*, [1985] 1 S.C.R. 295 (preference for Christian sabbath violated s. 2(a)). As well, "religion" is expressly named as a prohibited ground of discrimination in s. 15.

X. RELIGION IN PUBLIC BODIES OTHER THAN SCHOOLS

§ 42:10 Religion in public bodies other than schools

In the earlier discussion of "Religion in public schools" we noticed the case of *S.L. v. Commission scolaire des Chênes* (2012),[1] which held that curricular requirements in public schools must be neutral with respect to religion, even if neutrality offends the religious beliefs of a parent or child. The same duty of religious neutrality applies to public bodies other than schools. *Mouvement laïque québécois v. Saguenay* (2015),[2] imposed this duty on a municipal body, namely, the municipal council of the City of Saguenay in Quebec. At meetings of the council, the mayor would open the proceedings by reciting a prayer. The mayor would stand during the prayer and make the sign of the cross while saying "in the name of the Father, the Son and the Holy Spirit" at the beginning and end of the prayer. The other councilors and municipal officials would also stand and cross themselves at the beginning and end of the prayer. The claimant was an atheist who, although not a member of council, attended the meetings. He complained to the mayor, asking him to stop the religious practice. When the mayor refused, he complained to Quebec's human rights tribunal. The Mouvement laïque québécois, a non-profit organization promoting the secularization of the province, joined in the complaint. The City then formalized its practice by by-law, adopting a new non-denominational prayer addressed to "Almighty God" and closing with "Amen". The by-law also stipulated that, to accommodate council members and the public who wished to attend a council meeting but to avoid the recitation of the prayer, the mayor would not open the session until two minutes after the recitation of the prayer. The new prayer and two-minute wait did not satisfy the claimants, who amended their complaint to attack the new arrangements. The proceedings advanced to the Supreme Court of Canada. Gascon J., who wrote for the majority, decided the case on the basis of Quebec's Charter of human rights and freedoms, which also guarantees freedom of conscience and religion, but made clear that the interpretation was no different from that of the Canadian Charter's guarantee of freedom of conscience and religion.[3] The guarantee was not limited to religious beliefs. "The freedom not to believe, to manifest one's non-belief and to refuse to participate in religious observance is also protected."[4] An atheist like the individual claimant was therefore entitled to invoke the guarantee. The state's duty of religious neutrality was not explicit in either the Quebec

---

[Section 42:10]

[1] *S.L. v. Commission scolaire des Chênes*, [2012] 1 S.C.R. 235; discussed at § 42:8.

[2] *Mouvement laïque québécois v. Saguenay*, [2015] 2 S.C.R. 3, 2015 SCC 16. Gascon J. wrote the opinion of the majority. Abella J. wrote a concurring opinion, disagreeing only with the standards of administrative review applied by the majority.

[3] *Mouvement laïque québécois v. Saguenay*, [2015] 2 S.C.R. 3, 2015 SCC 16, para. 68.

[4] *Mouvement laïque québécois v. Saguenay*, [2015] 2 S.C.R. 3, 2015 SCC 16, para. 70, citing Dickson C.J. in *R. v. Big M Drug Mart*, [1985] 1 S.C.R. 295, 346-347.

or the Canadian Charter, but it "results from an evolving interpretation of freedom of conscience and religion",[5] and it "helps preserve and promote the multicultural nature of Canadian society enshrined in s. 27 of the Canadian Charter".[6] The second prayer (the one adopted by by-law), although intended not to favour any one religion, was not in fact fully inclusive because it had the effect of excluding those who (like the claimant) did not believe in an "Almighty God". The reference to "the supremacy of God" in the preamble to the Canadian Charter[7] "cannot lead to an interpretation of freedom of conscience and religion that authorizes the state to consciously profess a theistic faith."[8] The attempt at accommodation provided by the two-minute waiting period did not temper the discrimination, but exacerbated it by emphasizing the exclusion of the non-believers who would be expected to come into the council meeting after the prayer. The Court's conclusion was that the City's by-law and practice were in breach of the state's duty of religious neutrality; the Court held that the by-law was invalid and ordered the City to cease the recitation of the prayer in the municipal council's chambers.

XI. RELIGIOUS MARRIAGE

§ 42:11 Religious marriage

In all Canadian provinces, under provincial law, marriages may be solemnized in civil or religious ceremonies. Provided the statutory formalities are observed, which usually involve obtaining a licence before the ceremony and registration afterwards, both civil and religious ceremonies lead to valid marriages. A civil ceremony must be provided for all persons who want to get married and have the capacity to marry, and certainly cannot be denied on the basis of religion. But it has always been accepted without question that a religious ceremony can be denied by a church, synagogue or mosque to persons who want to get married, but who are not adherents of that particular faith. Equally accepted is the right to refuse to perform a religious ceremony that would be contrary to the particular faith. For example, a church that does not recognize divorce may refuse to marry divorced persons. Needless to say, couples wishing to get married who are denied a religious ceremony can get married in a civil ceremony.

---

[5]*Mouvement laïque québécois v. Saguenay*, [2015] 2 S.C.R. 3, 2015 SCC 16, para. 71.

[6]*Mouvement laïque québécois v. Saguenay*, [2015] 2 S.C.R. 3, 2015 SCC 16, para. 74.

[7]The preamble (in full) is: "Whereas Canada is founded upon principles that recognize the supremacy of God and the rule of law".

[8]*Mouvement laïque québécois v. Saguenay*, [2015] 2 S.C.R. 3, 2015 SCC 16, para. 147, citing with approval L. Sossin, "The Supremacy of God, Human Dignity and the Charter of Rights and Freedoms" (2003) 52 U.N.B.L.J. 227, 229.

In the *Same-Sex Marriage Reference* (2004),[1] the Supreme Court of Canada was asked if Parliament could enact a bill legalizing same-sex marriage for civil purposes. The Court held that Parliament could do so under its power over "marriage" in s. 91(26) of the Constitution Act, 1867. The bill also included a section that provided: "Nothing in this Act affects the freedom of officials of religious groups to refuse to perform marriages that are not in accordance with their religious beliefs." The Court held that this provision was ultra vires Parliament, because it related to "the solemnization of marriage", which was a provincial head of power under s. 92(12). But the Court went on to hold that the protection intended by the invalid section was provided by s. 2(a) of the Charter. The Court said: "The performance of religious rites is a fundamental aspect of religious practice."[2] Therefore, "absent unique circumstances with respect to which we will not speculate, the guarantee of religious freedom in s. 2(a) of the Charter is broad enough to protect religious officials from being compelled by the state to perform civil or religious same-sex marriages that are contrary to their religious beliefs".[3] Setting aside the obscure qualification about "unique circumstances", that means that the provinces could not use their power over solemnization of marriage to compel (in a human rights code, for example) a religious official to perform a same-sex marriage ceremony that would be contrary to his or her religious beliefs. The Court indicated, obiter, that "the compulsory use of sacred places [a church hall, for example] for the celebration of such marriages" would also be forbidden by s. 2(a) of the Charter.[4] The bill to legalize same-sex marriage "for civil purposes" was subsequently enacted.[5]

The Supreme Court's holding that the right to freedom of religion would protect "religious officials" from state compulsion to solemnize same-sex marriages if that were contrary to their religious beliefs applied to *religious* marriages. The Court said nothing about state compulsion to solemnize *civil* marriages that would be contrary to the civil official's personal religious beliefs. In *Re Marriage Commissioners* (2011),[6] the Government of Saskatchewan proposed a law allowing "marriage commissioners" to refuse to solemnize any marriages that would be contrary to their personal religious beliefs. Marriage commissioners were civil officials appointed by the province to perform civil marriages in the

[Section 42:11]

[1] *Re Same-Sex Marriage*, [2004] 3 S.C.R. 698. The unanimous opinion was given by "the Court".

[2] *Re Same-Sex Marriage*, [2004] 3 S.C.R. 698, para. 57.

[3] *Re Same-Sex Marriage*, [2004] 3 S.C.R. 698, para. 60.

[4] *Re Same-Sex Marriage*, [2004] 3 S.C.R. 698, para. 59.

[5] Civil Marriage Act, S.C. 2005, c. 33. The provision to protect the freedom of officials of religious groups was retained (s. 3), but revised into purely declaratory form.

[6] *Re Marriage Commissioners* (2011), 327 D.L.R. (4th) 669 (Sask. C.A.). Richards J.A. (with Klebuc C.J. and Ottenbreit J.) wrote the majority opinion. Smith J.A. (with Vancise J.A.) wrote a concurring opinion, agreeing with the result and most of the reasoning.

province. They were the only persons with power to administer a non-religious ceremony of marriage. The province referred its proposed law to the Saskatchewan Court of Appeal for an opinion as to its validity. The Court unanimously struck down the proposed law on the ground that it would infringe s. 15 of the Charter by discriminating on the ground of sexual orientation. Richards J.A., who wrote the majority opinion, acknowledged that the proposed law was not expressly limited to same-sex marriages; it permitted a marriage commissioner to refuse to solemnize any marriage based on any personal religious scruple. Nor was the *purpose* of the law discriminatory: the purpose was to accommodate the religious beliefs of marriage commissioners rather than to deny the rights of same-sex couples. But, while the law was neutral in its expression and purpose, its *effect* would be to restrict the ability of couples to obtain same-sex marriages. Religious marriage was often foreclosed to same-sex couples because so many religious denominations did not recognize same-sex marriages. The affidavits filed by marriage commissioners in this case made clear that, if the proposed law were enacted, some marriage commissioners would also refuse to conduct civil same-sex marriages. The result would be that same-sex couples would face more obstacles to getting married than opposite-sex couples would face. This was a "negative distinction based on sexual orientation", and one that perpetuated the historical disadvantage of LGBTQ people and stereotypes about the lesser worthiness of their unions.[7] Richards J.A. accepted the argument that requiring marriage commissioners to solemnize same-sex marriages would impair the right to freedom of religion of those commissioners who had to act contrary to their religious beliefs. But he held that, when the competing rights were balanced under s. 1, the religious freedom of civil officials had to "yield to the larger public interest" in the "impartial and non-discriminatory" delivery of public services.[8] The Court's conclusion was that the proposed law could not be justified under s. 1 and would be unconstitutional if enacted.

[7] *Re Marriage Commissioners* (2011), 327 D.L.R. (4th) 669 (Sask. C.A.), paras. 44-45. Smith J.A. is to the same effect: *Re Marriage Commissioners* (2011), 327 D.L.R. (4th) 669 (Sask. C.A.), paras. 106-108.

[8] *Re Marriage Commissioners* (2011), 327 D.L.R. (4th) 669 (Sask. C.A.), paras. 98, 100. Smith J.A. is to the same effect: *Re Marriage Commissioners* (2011), 327 D.L.R. (4th) 669 (Sask. C.A.), para. 161.

Chapter 43

Expression

I. DISTRIBUTION OF POWERS

§ 43:1 Classification of laws
§ 43:2 Political speech
§ 43:3 Provincial power
§ 43:4 Federal power

II. SECTION 2(B) OF THE CHARTER

§ 43:5 Section 2(b) of the Charter

III. COMPARISON WITH FIRST AMENDMENT

§ 43:6 Comparison with first amendment

IV. REASONS FOR PROTECTING EXPRESSION

§ 43:7 Reasons for protecting expression

V. MEANING OF EXPRESSION

§ 43:8 Definition of expression
§ 43:9 Criminal expression
§ 43:10 Violence
§ 43:11 Content neutrality

VI. WAYS OF LIMITING EXPRESSION

§ 43:12 Prior restraint
§ 43:13 Border control
§ 43:14 Penal prohibition
§ 43:15 Civil prohibition
§ 43:16 Forced expression
§ 43:17 Language requirement
§ 43:18 Search of press premises
§ 43:19 Disclosure of journalists' sources
§ 43:20 Time, manner and place

VII. COMMERCIAL EXPRESSION

§ 43:21 Protection of commercial expression
§ 43:22 Language requirements
§ 43:23 Advertising restrictions

§ 43:24 Signs
§ 43:25 Prostitution

VIII. PICKETING; HATE PROPAGANDA; DEFAMATION

§ 43:26 Picketing
§ 43:27 Hate propaganda
§ 43:28 Defamation

IX. PORNOGRAPHY

§ 43:29 Pornography

X. ACCESS TO PUBLIC PROPERTY

§ 43:30 Access to public property

XI. ACCESS TO COURTS

§ 43:31 Fair trial concerns
§ 43:32 Restrictions on reporting
§ 43:33 Restrictions on access

XII. ACCESS TO LEGISLATIVE ASSEMBLY

§ 43:34 Generally

XIII. CONTEMPT OF COURT; PUBLIC SERVICE; MANDATORY LETTERS OF REFERENCE

§ 43:35 Contempt of court
§ 43:36 Public service
§ 43:37 Mandatory letters of reference

XIV. ELECTION EXPENDITURES; VOTING

§ 43:38 Election expenditures
§ 43:39 Voting

XV. ACCESS TO GOVERNMENT; ACCESS TO GOVERNMENT DOCUMENTS

§ 43:40 Access to government
§ 43:41 Access to government documents

I. DISTRIBUTION OF POWERS

§ 43:1 Classification of laws

Laws abridging civil liberties, like all other laws, are subject to the federal distribution of powers. A law is valid only if it is classified as in relation to a matter coming within a class of subjects allocated by the Constitution to the enacting Parliament or Legislature. As noted in ch.

34, Civil Liberties, generally speaking, a law's impact on civil liberties has not been treated by the courts as the leading characteristic in determining the law's classification; the impact on civil liberties has been treated as an incidental or subordinate feature of the law.[1] Freedom of expression does not fit the general rule perfectly. As we shall see, *political* speech may well be a distinct matter that is assigned exclusively to the federal Parliament. Other kinds of speech are distributed between the two levels of government by reference to the facility or activity wherein the speech is regulated. This makes the position quite complicated. For example, commercial advertising is generally within provincial jurisdiction as an incident of the sale of goods or services in the province; but advertising in a federally-regulated medium, such as radio or television, is within federal jurisdiction. As a further complication, a general prohibition of false or misleading advertising could be enacted by the federal Parliament as a criminal law.

§ 43:2 Political speech

With respect to political speech,[1] the story begins with the *Alberta Press* case (1938),[2] in which the Supreme Court of Canada struck down an Alberta statute that compelled newspapers in Alberta to publish a government reply to any criticism of provincial government policies.[3] In that case, Duff C.J. and Cannon J. asserted that free political discussion ("the breath of life of parliamentary institutions")[4] was so important to the nation as a whole that it could not be regarded as a value that was subordinate to other legislative objectives; nor could it be regarded as a local or private matter (s. 92(16)) or as a civil right "in the province" (s. 92(13)). It followed that it was outside the power of the provinces, and within the exclusive power of the federal Parliament. In Cannon J.'s view, the federal power stemmed from the criminal law power; Duff C.J. did not commit himself as to which head of federal legislative power would be applicable, but he appeared to assume that it would be the peace, order, and good government power.

[Section 43:1]

[1]Chapter 34, Civil Liberties, under heading § 34:6, "Distribution of powers".

[Section 43:2]

[1]For discussion of the cases, see Schmeiser, Civil Liberties in Canada (1964), chs. 4, 5; Tarnopolsky, The Canadian Bill of Rights (2nd ed., 1975), 37-46.

[2]*Re Alberta Statutes*, [1938] S.C.R. 100.

[3]Five of the six judges gave as their primary reason that the law was ancillary to and dependent upon other social credit legislation which was invalid. Duff C.J. (with Davis J.) added, obiter, the remarks that are described in the text. Cannon J., who alone did not rely on the ancillary point, found the law invalid on the grounds described in the text. An appeal was taken to the Privy Council, but their lordships decided that the validity of the Press bill (and other bill) was moot, and the appeal proceeded only on a third bill, the Bank Taxation bill: *A.-G. Alta. v. A.-G. Can.* (Bank Taxation) [1939] A.C. 117.

[4]*Re Alberta Statutes*, [1938] S.C.R. 100, 133 per Duff C.J.

In *Saumur v. City of Quebec* (1953),[5] in which the Court struck down a by-law that required the permission of the Chief of Police for the distribution of pamphlets in the city streets, three of the five majority judges, namely, Rand, Kellock and Locke JJ., used the dicta of Duff C.J. and Cannon J. in the *Alberta Press* case as the basis for their decision.[6]

In *Switzman v. Elbling* (1957),[7] the Supreme Court of Canada had to determine the validity of Quebec's "Padlock Act", which made it illegal to use a house "to propagate communism or bolshevism by any means whatever". The Act had been upheld in the Quebec courts, but the Supreme Court of Canada, by a majority of eight to one, held it to be invalid. The dissenting judge, Taschereau J., classified the statute as a law in relation to the use of property, and upheld it on that basis. But the other eight judges held that the control of the use of property was colourable, and that the pith and substance of the law was the prohibition of certain political ideas. However, only three of the eight majority judges, namely, Rand, Kellock and Abbott JJ., classified the law as in relation to speech and assigned it to the federal jurisdiction on that basis. The other five judges, namely, Kerwin C.J., Locke, Cartwright, Fauteux and Nolan JJ., did not express an opinion as to legislative jurisdiction over speech, because they held that the prohibition of the propagation of communism with sanctions for breach was tantamount to the creation of a new crime and was within federal jurisdiction as a criminal law.

It seems plausible to conclude from this line of cases, which ended in the 1950s, that at least some forms of regulation of political speech should be characterized as the denial of a fundamental freedom of national dimensions, which is competent only to the federal Parliament, either under its criminal law power or under its peace, order, and good government power. Paul Weiler has criticized the decisions, arguing that the Court was using doctrines of federalism as a kind of surreptitious bill of rights, allocating jurisdiction to that level of government that had not exercised it, in order to invalidate a law that the Court really believed should not be enacted at all.[8] However, the cases did not suggest that the entire topic of speech was competent only to the federal Parliament.[9] Since the 1950s, the tendency of the cases has been to expand provincial power over speech, even in cases where the power was exercised in derogation of civil libertarian values.

---

[5]*Saumur v. City of Quebec*, [1953] 2 S.C.R. 299.

[6]Estey J. held that the by-law was in relation to religion and invalid on that ground. Kerwin J. held that the by-law was inconsistent with a pre-confederation statute and was invalid on that ground. The four minority judges held that the by-law was in relation to the use of the streets and was valid on that ground.

[7]*Switzman v. Elbling*, [1957] S.C.R. 285.

[8]P.C. Weiler, "The Supreme Court and the Law of Canadian Federalism" (1973) 23 U. Toronto L.J. 307, 342-352. Compare the discussion of the "implied bill of rights" in ch. 34, Civil Liberties, under heading § 34:7, "Implied bill of rights".

[9]For example, in the *Alberta Press* case, Duff C.J. was not sure whether the impugned law passed beyond the legitimate provincial realm of regulating newspapers and into the forbidden free speech category: [1938] S.C.R. 100, 135.

§ 43:3 Provincial power

The provincial power over speech, while it may not extend to the regulation or prohibition of political ideas, does authorize the regulation of speech on commercial or local grounds. The tort of defamation, for example, is provincial, despite its impact on speech, because the redress of injury to reputation supplies a dominant tortious aspect to the law, and the law of torts is within provincial power (s. 92(13)).[1] As another example, advertising is within provincial jurisdiction, because it is part of the regulation of business and of consumer protection that is within provincial power (s. 92(13)).[2]

The first case taking an expansive view of provincial power over speech was *Nova Scotia Board of Censors v. McNeil* (1978).[3] In that case, the Supreme Court of Canada upheld provincial censorship of films, on the basis that the exhibition of films was a business within provincial jurisdiction and censorship was part of the regulation of the business (s. 92(13)), or, alternatively, was a regulation of a local matter (s. 92(16)). A difficulty with these characterizations of the censorship law was that the law did not supply any criteria for the censor board, which could therefore have exercised its power to suppress political or religious ideas. But Ritchie J. for the majority of the Court finessed this difficulty by holding that the powers of the censor board should be "read down" to exclude the censorship of political or religious ideas.[4] The censor board's power was thus limited to applying moral standards to the depiction of sex and violence, issues of primarily local significance.[5]

In *A.-G. Can. and Dupond v. Montreal* (1978),[6] the Supreme Court of Canada upheld a Montreal by-law that imposed a temporary prohibition on assemblies, parades and gatherings on municipal parks and streets. Beetz J. for the majority of the Court held that this was a regulation of the municipal public domain that was within the provincial power over local matters (s. 92(16)). He also said that "none of [the freedoms of speech, of assembly and association, of the press and of religion] is a

[Section 43:3]

[1]E.g., *Hill v. Church of Scientology*, [1995] 2 S.C.R. 1130 (upholding common law of defamation); *Néron v. Chambre des notaires du Québec*, [2004] 3 S.C.R. 95 (upholding civil law of defamation).

[2]E.g., *A.-G. Que. v. Kellogg's Co.*, [1978] 2 S.C.R. 211 (upholding provincial regulation of advertising directed to children); *A.G. Can. v. Law Society of B.C.*, [1982] 2 S.C.R. 307 (upholding provincial regulation of advertising by lawyers); *Irwin Toy v. Que.*, [1989] 1 S.C.R. 927 (upholding provincial regulation of advertising directed to children). Compare *Devine v. Que.*, [1988] 2 S.C.R. 790 (upholding provincial regulation of the language of commercial signs).

[3]*Nova Scotia Board of Censors v. McNeil*, [1978] 2 S.C.R. 662.

[4]Contrast Rand J.'s comments on the breadth of discretion of the chief of police in *Saumur v. City of Que.*, [1953] 2 S.C.R. 299, 333.

[5]Accord, *Rio Hotel v. N.B.*, [1987] 2 S.C.R. 59 (upholding provincial prohibition of "nude entertainment" in taverns); *R. v. Glad Day Bookshops* (2004), 70 O.R. (3d) 691 (S.C.J.) (upholding provincial censorship of films).

[6]*A.-G. Can. and Dupond v. Montreal*, [1978] 2 S.C.R. 770.

single matter coming within exclusive federal or provincial competence".[7] However, this was probably not intended as a rejection of the 1950s cases, because he went on to hold that the by-law's prohibition did not involve a denial of free speech, saying that "demonstrations are not a form of speech but of collective action".[8] Of course, the by-law did not just ban "demonstrations", but would have had the effect of prohibiting an assembly that had gathered quietly to listen to speakers.

Civil libertarian concerns about the extensive powers ceded to the provinces by the *McNeil* and *Dupond* decisions are now of primarily historical interest. Such laws would now have to survive Charter review based on freedom of expression and assembly. What the cases establish, however, is an extensive provincial power to regulate speech or assembly in local parks and streets, and to regulate speech in the media that come within provincial jurisdiction, including films, live theatre, books, magazines, newspapers, tapes and records. That power may not extend to the denial of political speech, but this is a narrow category after *McNeil* and *Dupond.*

§ 43:4 Federal power

The federal Parliament has the power to regulate political speech for the reasons given earlier.[1] The federal Parliament also has the power, by a prohibition coupled with a sanction, to make particular kinds of speech criminal, as it has done, for example, in the crimes of sedition, fraud, obscenity,[2] hate propaganda[3] and communicating for the purpose of prostitution.[4] And the federal Parliament has the power to regulate speech in the media that come within federal jurisdiction, namely, radio and television.[5]

II. SECTION 2(B) OF THE CHARTER

§ 43:5 Section 2(b) of the Charter

Section 2(b) of the Charter of Rights[1] guarantees to "everyone"[2] the "fundamental freedom" of:

---

[7] *A.-G. Can. and Dupond v. Montreal*, [1978] 2 S.C.R. 770, 796-797.

[8] *A.-G. Can. and Dupond v. Montreal*, [1978] 2 S.C.R. 770, 797.

[Section 43:4]

[1] The dicta in the *Alberta Press* case were referred to with approval by Martland J. for a majority of the Court in *Gay Alliance Toward Equality v. Vancouver Sun*, [1979] 2 S.C.R. 435, 455 (upholding a newspaper's power to refuse to publish an advertisement for a magazine directed to gay and lesbian people).

[2] *R. v. Butler*, [1992] 1 S.C.R. 452; *R. v. Sharpe*, [2001] 1 S.C.R. 45.

[3] *R. v. Keegstra*, [1990] 3 S.C.R. 697.

[4] *Re ss. 193 and 195.1 of Criminal Code*, [1990] 1 S.C.R. 1123.

[5] *Capital Cities Communications v. CRTC*, [1978] 2 S.C.R. 141 (upholding federal content regulation of television).

[Section 43:5]

[1] For commentary on s. 2(b), see Anisman and Linden (eds.), The Media, the Courts

freedom of thought, belief, opinion and expression, including freedom of the press and other media of communication;

Section 2(b),[3] like other Charter rights, is subject to s. 1 (the limitation clause) of the Charter. A law that limits freedom of expression will be valid under s. 1 if it comes within the phrase "such reasonable limits prescribed by law as can be demonstrably justified in a free and democratic society". Because of s. 1, judicial review under the Charter is a two-stage process: first is the question whether the law (or action) has the purpose or effect of limiting a guaranteed right; and, secondly, if the law does have that purpose or effect, the question is whether the law satisfies the standards of justification under s. 1. A law will be held to be unconstitutional only if both questions are answered adversely to the law. While this two-stage process is appropriate for judicial review under all the Charter rights, we shall see that the unqualified language of s. 2(b), reinforced by the broad interpretation that has been given to that language, means that, in most of the freedom of expression cases, it is easy to decide that, yes, the impugned law does limit s. 2(b). In that case, the constitutionality of the law will turn on the outcome of the second stage of review, that is, the s. 1 inquiry. However, this chapter is not concerned directly with the s. 1 inquiry. Section 1 was examined in ch. 38, Limitation of Rights, above. This chapter is about the scope of s. 2(b).

III. COMPARISON WITH FIRST AMENDMENT

§ 43:6 Comparison with first amendment

The comparable provision of the American Bill of Rights is the first amendment, which on the topic of expression provides that "Congress shall make no law . . . abridging the freedom of speech, or of the press".[1] This provision by its terms binds only the federal Congress, but it is applicable to the states as well through the fourteenth amendment.[2]

The first amendment uses the word "speech". Section 2(b) uses the

---

and the Charter (1986); Beaudoin and Mendes (eds.), The Canadian Charter of Rights and Freedoms (4th ed., 2005), ch. 6 (by K. Roach and D. Schneiderman); Schneiderman (ed.), Freedom of Expression and the Charter (1991); Moon, The Constitutional Protection of Freedom of Expression (2000); McLeod, Takach, Morton, Segal, The Canadian Charter of Rights (Carswell, loose-leaf service), ch. 23; Canadian Charter of Rights Annotated (Canada Law Book, loose-leaf service), annotation to s. 2(b). The last work contains a bibliography of the relevant literature.

[2]On the meaning of "everyone", see ch. 37, Application of Charter, under heading §§ 37:1 to 37:5, "Benefit of rights".

[3]The comparable provisions of the Canadian Bill of Rights are s. 1 (d), which guarantees "freedom of speech", and s. 1(f), which guarantees "freedom of the press".

[Section 43:6]

[1]For commentary on the guarantee of free speech in the first amendment, see L.H. Tribe, American Constitutional Law (Foundation Press, N.Y., 2nd ed., 1986), ch. 12; J.E. Nowak and R.D. Rotunda, Constitutional Law (West, St. Paul, Minn., 7th ed., 2005); ch. 16.

[2]The doctrine of "selective incorporation", which accomplishes this result, is

phrase "thought, belief, opinion and expression". The references to "thought, belief, opinion" will have little impact, since even a totalitarian state cannot suppress unexpressed ideas. It is the reference to "expression" in s. 2(b) that is the critical one, and the word expression is very broad—broader than "speech".

Because the first amendment is framed in absolute language, and the American Bill of Rights contains no limitation clause like s. 1, American courts have had difficulty in supplying a principled justification for upholding laws that restrict speech.[3] No attempt will be made here to describe the complex American jurisprudence, except to note that laws restraining speech have generally been struck down.

IV. REASONS FOR PROTECTING EXPRESSION

§ 43:7 Reasons for protecting expression

What is the rationale for a guarantee of freedom of expression?

Perhaps the most powerful rationale for the constitutional protection of freedom of expression is its role as an instrument of democratic government. This rationale was well expressed by Rand J. in *Switzman v. Elbling* (1957),[1] when he said that parliamentary government was "ultimately government by the free public opinion of an open society", and that it demanded "the condition of a virtually unobstructed access to and diffusion of ideas".[2] In the same case, Abbott J. said that "the right of free expression of opinion and of criticism" were "essential to the working of a parliamentary democracy such as ours".[3] Canadian judges have always placed a high value on freedom of expression as an element of parliamentary democracy and have sought to protect it with the limited tools that were at their disposal before the adoption of the

---

explained in ch. 37, Application of Charter, under heading § 37:6, "Both levels of government".

[3]For example, the Supreme Court of the United States upheld restrictions on falsehoods, on insulting, profane or fighting words, on advertising and on obscenity by the bizarre expedient of denying that these things were speech at all! The Court has backed away from that position, and now accords a degree of first amendment protection to all these things, except for obscenity: *New York Times v. Sullivan* (1964), 376 U.S. 254 (false and defamatory statement in newspaper protected); *Cohen v. California* (1971), 403 U.S. 15 (profane slogan on jacket protected); *Virginia State Bd. of Pharmacy v. Virginia Citizens Consumer Council* (1976), 425 U.S. 748 (advertising of prescription drugs protected); *Greater New Orleans Broadcasting Assn. v. U.S.* (1999), 527 U.S. 173 (advertising of casino gambling protected); *Lorillard Tobacco Co. v. Mass.* (2001), 533 U.S. 525 (advertising of tobacco products protected). But compare *Morse v. Frederick* (2007), 551 U.S. 393 (banner advocating illegal drug use displayed by student at school event not protected).

[Section 43:7]

[1]*Switzman v. Elbling*, [1957] S.C.R. 285.

[2]*Switzman v. Elbling*, [1957] S.C.R. 285, 358.

[3]*Switzman v. Elbling*, [1957] S.C.R. 285, 369.

Charter of Rights.[4] It is obvious that political speech is at the core of s. 2(b) of the Charter, and could be curtailed under s. 1 only in service of the most compelling governmental interest.[5]

A second, broader rationale for the constitutional protection of freedom of expression is its role as an instrument of truth. It was John Stuart Mill in his essay *On Liberty* (1859) who argued that suppression of opinion was wrong, because it is only by "the collision of adverse opinions" that truth is discovered or confirmed. This idea became Oliver Wendell Holmes's rationale for the guarantee of freedom of speech in the first amendment: the truth was to be found in a "free trade in ideas", in "the power of thought to get itself accepted in the competition of the market".[6] This "marketplace of ideas" rationale for freedom of expression would include political speech, of course, but would also extend to the ideas of philosophy, history, the social sciences, the natural sciences, medicine and all the other branches of human knowledge. It is obvious that the expression of all these ideas is also protected by s. 2(b) of the Charter.

A third, even broader, rationale for the constitutional protection of freedom of expression is its role as an instrument of personal fulfilment. On this theory, which is to be found in some American judicial decisions, expression is protected not just to create a more perfect polity, and not just to discover the truth, but to "enlarge the prospects for individual self-fulfilment",[7] or to allow "personal growth and self-realization".[8] If expression is conceived in these broad terms, it covers much that is not speech at all: art, music and dance, for example.

The idea of expression as an instrument of personal fulfilment goes too far if it does not include a communicative purpose. After all, any act could be characterized as an instrument of personal fulfilment. Both "speech" and "expression" should be limited to attempts to communicate ideas. The courts of both the United States and Canada have insisted upon a communicative purpose to qualify an act as protected speech or expression. It might be thought that the word "speech", which is narrower than "expression", would exclude even some acts that were done with a communicative purpose. But the Supreme Court of the United States has readily accepted a variety of forms of "expressive conduct" as

---

[4]See the discussion of the *Alberta Press* case, *Saumur* case and *Switzman v. Elbling* under heading § 43:2 "Political speech".

[5]E.g., *Libman v. Que.*, [1997] 3 S.C.R. 569 (striking down law prohibiting third-party expenditures in referendum campaigns); *Thomson Newspapers Co. v. Can.*, [1998] 1 S.C.R. 877 (striking down law prohibiting publication of opinion poll results during last three days of election campaign); but contrast *Harper v. Can.*, [2004] 1 S.C.R. 827 (upholding restrictions on third-party election expenditures under s. 1); *R. v. Bryan*, [2007] 1 S.C.R. 527 (upholding a prohibition, since repealed, on the broadcasting of election results on election day until polling stations are closed in all parts of the country).

[6]*Abrams v. United States* (1919), 250 U.S. 616, 630 (dissenting).

[7]J.E. Nowak and R.D. Rotunda, *Constitutional Law* (West, St. Paul, Minn., 7th ed., 2005).

[8]L.H. Tribe, American Constitutional Law (Foundation Press, N.Y., 2nd ed., 1986), 787.

being "symbolic speech", which is entitled to first amendment protection, for example, a refusal to salute the flag,[9] the burning of a flag,[10] the burning of a draft card,[11] the covering of a motto on a car licence plate,[12] and the wearing of a black armband.[13] If "speech" will go this far, it is clear that "expression" in s. 2(b) of the Charter will do so as well.

In *Irwin Toy v. Quebec* (1989),[14] Dickson C.J., Lamer and Wilson JJ., in their joint majority judgment, embraced all of the three reasons for protecting freedom of expression, which they summarized in the following terms:[15]

> (1) seeking and attaining the truth is an inherently good activity; (2) participation in social and political decision-making is to be fostered and encouraged; and (3) the diversity in forms of individual self-fulfilment and human flourishing ought to be cultivated . . . .

The acceptance of all three reasons as the basis for the right to freedom of expression entails a very broad definition of the right.[16]

The breadth of the right that is entailed by acceptance of the third rationale for protection of expression—as an instrument of personal fulfilment—is illustrated by *R. v. Sharpe* (2001),[17] in which a constitutional challenge was mounted to the Criminal Code offence of possession of child pornography. Child pornography was defined in very specific terms as pictures of children engaged in sexual activity, pictures of children's sexual organs or anal areas, and material promoting sexual activity with children that would be a Criminal Code offence. The Supreme Court of Canada acknowledged that such material made no contribution to democratic government and made no contribution to the search for truth. But the Court held that it should be constitutionally protected under s. 2(b) because of its role as an instrument of personal fulfilment. The majority was even prepared to say that purely private child pornography of certain kinds (material created by the accused and recordings of lawful sexual activity by the accused) "deeply implicates s. 2(b) freedoms, engaging the values of self-fulfilment and self-

---

[9] *West Virginia State Bd. of Education v. Barnette* (1943), 319 U.S. 624.

[10] *Texas v. Johnson* (1989), 491 U.S. 397.

[11] *United States v. O'Brien* (1968), 391 U.S. 367.

[12] *Wooley v. Maynard* (1977), 430 U.S. 705 (the New Hampshire plate's motto was "Live free or die"!).

[13] *Tinker v. Des Moines School District* (1969), 393 U.S. 503.

[14] *Irwin Toy v. Que.*, [1989] 1 S.C.R. 927, 968-971; see *also RWDSU v. Dolphin Delivery*, [1986] 2 S.C.R. 573, 583-586; *R. v. Keegstra*, [1990] 3 S.C.R. 697, 727-728, 827-828.

[15] *Irwin Toy v. Que.*, [1989] 1 S.C.R. 927, 976.

[16] Accord, *Montreal v. 2952-1366 Que.*, [2005] 3 S.C.R. 141, para. 74 per McLachlin C.J. and Deschamps J. for majority (describing "purposes which s. 2(b) are intended to serve" as "(1) democratic discourse, (2) truth-finding and (3) self-fulfilment"). The case decided that the broadcast into the street of the proceedings of a strip club was protected under s. 2(b), although a by-law prohibiting the broadcast was upheld under s. 1.

[17] *R. v. Sharpe*, [2001] 1 S.C.R. 45. For discussion, see § 43:29, "Pornography".

actualization and engaging the inherent dignity of the individual".[18] The concurring minority also accepted the rationale of personal fulfilment but did so reluctantly, describing it as self-fulfilment "at a base and prurient level".[19] The Court was unanimous that the Criminal Code offence was justified under s. 1 of the Charter, although the majority carved out exceptions for the purely private forms of child pornography referred to above (which were not in issue in the case except as hypothetical examples).

The next section of the chapter addresses the definition of freedom of expression that has emerged from the rationales discussed in this section of the chapter.

V. MEANING OF EXPRESSION

§ 43:8 Definition of expression

The Supreme Court of Canada has defined "expression" in these terms: "Activity is expressive if it attempts to convey meaning".[1] This broad definition has been supported by a willing acceptance of the broadest rationale for the protection of expression—the realization of individual self-fulfilment[2]—as well as the Court's view that the Charter should be given a generous interpretation.[3]

Is there any activity that is *not* expression under the Court's definition? The answer is not much, because "most human activity combines expressive and physical elements"; what is excluded is that which is "purely physical and does not convey or attempt to convey meaning".[4] Obviously, all forms of art are sufficiently communicative to be protected: novels, plays, films, paintings, dances and music.[5] A speaker's choice of language is protected, so that a requirement that commercial signs be in French only is a violation of s. 2(b).[6] Indeed, the Court has acknowledged that parking a car would be an expressive activity, and therefore protected under s. 2(b), if it were done with an expressive purpose—and

---

[18] *R. v. Sharpe*, [2001] 1 S.C.R. 45, para. 107 per McLachlin C.J.

[19] *R. v. Sharpe*, [2001] 1 S.C.R. 45, para. 242 per L'Heureux-Dubé, Gonthier and Bastarache JJ.

[Section 43:8]

[1] *Irwin Toy Ltd. v. Que.*, [1989] 1 S.C.R. 927, 968. Accord, *Re ss. 193 and 195.1 of Criminal Code* (Prostitution Reference) [1990] 1 S.C.R. 1123, 1180; *Rocket v. Royal College of Dental Surgeons*, [1990] 2 S.C.R. 232, 244; *R. v. Keegstra*, [1990] 3 S.C.R. 697, 729, 826.

[2] *Irwin Toy v. Quebec*, [1989] 1 S.C.R. 927, 968-971; see *also RWDSU v. Dolphin Delivery*, [1986] 2 S.C.R. 573, 583-586; *R. v. Keegstra*, [1990] 3 S.C.R. 697, 727-728, 827-828.

[3] Chapter 36, Charter of Rights, under heading § 36:19, "Generous interpretation".

[4] *Irwin Toy v. Que.*, [1989] 1 S.C.R. 927, 969.

[5] *Re ss. 193 and 195.1 of Criminal Code* (Prostitution Reference) [1990] 1 S.C.R. 1123, 1182.

[6] *Ford v. Que.*, [1988] 2 S.C.R. 712.

a protest against the parking regulations would be a sufficiently expressive purpose![7]

§ 43:9 Criminal expression

In the *Prostitution Reference* (1990),[1] the Court held that communicating for the purpose of prostitution, which was an offence under the Criminal Code, was protected expression under s. 2(b). (A majority of the Court upheld the law under s. 1.) Lamer J. in a concurring judgment pointed out that activities should not be denied s. 2(b) protection "solely because they have been made the subject of criminal offences",[2] and he listed 25 Criminal Code offences that prohibited some form of expression. In other words, s. 2(b) protects falsehoods (perjury or fraud, for example) and other harmful (but communicative) activity (counselling a suicide, for example). Lamer J.'s dictum was confirmed in the later cases of *R. v. Keegstra* (1990)[3] and *R. v. Zundel* (1992),[4] in which the Criminal Code offences of publishing hate propaganda and publishing false news were held to be in violation of s. 2(b). (The hate-propaganda offence, but not the false news offence, was upheld under s. 1 by a narrow majority of the Court.) In *R. v. Lucas* (1998),[5] the Criminal Code offence of publishing a defamatory libel with knowledge of its falsity was held to be in violation of s. 2(b) (although the provision was upheld under s. 1). So long as the activity is communicative, and falls short of the direct infliction of violence, it is protected by s. 2(b).

§ 43:10 Violence

Expressive activity that takes the *form* of violence is not protected by s. 2(b): "a murderer or a rapist cannot invoke freedom of expression in justification of the form of expression he has chosen".[1] Nor can a person

[7] *Irwin Toy v. Que.*, [1989] 1 S.C.R. 927, 969. Fortunately, most drivers are unaware of their constitutional right to disregard parking restrictions of which they disapprove.

[Section 43:9]

[1] *Re ss. 193 and 195.1 of Criminal Code* (Prostitution Reference) [1990] 1 S.C.R. 1123. Dickson C.J., with whom La Forest and Sopinka JJ. agreed, wrote the plurality opinion. Lamer J. wrote a concurring opinion. Wilson J., with the agreement of L'Heureux-Dubé J., dissented. In *Can. v. Bedford*, [2013] 3 S.C.R. 1101, 2013 SCC 72, the communicating offence was struck down, not on the basis of s. 2(b) but on the basis of s. 7: ch. 47, Fundamental Justice, under heading § 47:25, "Disproportionate laws".

[2] *Re ss. 193 and 195.1 of Criminal Code* (Prostitution Reference) [1990] 1 S.C.R. 1123, 1183.

[3] *R. v. Keegstra*, [1990] 3 S.C.R. 697.

[4] *R. v. Zundel*, [1992] 2 S.C.R. 731.

[5] *R. v. Lucas*, [1998] 1 S.C.R. 439.

[Section 43:10]

[1] *Irwin Toy v. Que.*, [1989] 1 S.C.R. 927, 970; *R. v. Keegstra*, [1990] 3 S.C.R. 697, 731.

invoke s. 2(b) to challenge his deportation from Canada for "conduct associated with violent activity".[2]

What about *threats* of violence? Initially, the Court held that threats of violence were also unprotected by s. 2(b).[3] Then the Court changed its mind and held that threats of violence were protected by s. 2(b)[4] on the theory that a threat of violence could be identified only by its content, and there should be no content-related restrictions on the s. 2(b) right.[5] The Court has since changed its mind again, holding that "it makes little sense to exclude acts of violence from the ambit of s. 2(b), but to confer protection on threats of violence. Neither are worthy of protection."[6]

What about the *depiction* of violence? There is no doubt that the depiction of violence would be protected expression under the Court's content-neutral definition,[7] although obviously s. 1 would be available to justify limits on the most extreme depictions of violence.[8]

§ 43:11 Content neutrality

It will be evident from the preceding text that content neutrality is the governing principle of the Supreme Court of Canada's definition of expression. "The content of a statement cannot deprive it of the protection accorded by s. 2(b), no matter how offensive it may be".[1] Therefore, in *R. v. Keegstra* (1990),[2] the Supreme Court of Canada held unanimously that the promotion of hatred against the Jews or another racial group, which is a Criminal Code offence, is protected by s. 2(b). The offence was upheld under s. 1, but by the bare majority of four to three. In *Keegstra*, the Court even rejected the argument that s. 2(b) should be narrowed by reference to other provisions of the Charter, such as the guarantee of

---

[2]*Suresh v. Can.*, [2002] 1 S.C.R. 3, para. 105.

[3]*RWDSU v. Dolphin Delivery*, [1986] 2 S.C.R. 573, 588.

[4]*R. v. Keegstra*, [1990] 3 S.C.R. 697, 733 per Dickson C.J. for majority; McLachlin J. at 829 disagreed.

[5]*R. v. Keegstra*, [1990] 3 S.C.R. 697, 732.

[6]*R. v. Khawaja*, [2012] 3 S.C.R. 555, para. 70 per McLachlin C.J. for the Court. The case upheld the terrorism offences of the Criminal Code, rejecting a challenge under s. 2(b) on the ground that the offence that arguably limited expression "is confined to the realm of acts of violence and threats of violence" (para. 73).

[7]So held in the United States: *Brown v. Entertainment Merchants Assn.* (2011), 564 U.S. xxx (striking down California law prohibiting the sale or rental of violent video games to minors). This case might have been decided differently in Canada, not on the definition of expression (speech), but by upholding the law as a reasonable limit under s. 1, which was essentially Breyer J.'s dissenting opinion (despite the absence of any equivalent of s. 1). Thomas J. also dissented, but on the basis that "freedom of speech" would not have been understood by the founders as including a right to speak to (sell video games to) minors without going through their parents.

[8]E.g., sexual violence: § 43:29, "Pornography".

[Section 43:11]

[1]*R. v. Keegstra*, [1990] 3 S.C.R. 697, 828.

[2]*R. v. Keegstra*, [1990] 3 S.C.R. 697.

equality in s. 15 and the recognition of multiculturalism in s. 27. The fact that the Criminal Code provision was attempting to vindicate the values reflected in ss. 15 and 27 was relevant only to the s. 1 inquiry.[3]

In *R. v. Zundel* (1992),[4] the Supreme Court of Canada struck down the false-news provision of the Criminal Code, which made it an offence for a person to "wilfully publish a statement, tale or news that he knows is false and causes or is likely to cause injury or mischief to a public interest". This prohibition covered only statements that were false, and that were known by the accused to be false. Zundel, who had published a pamphlet denying that the Holocaust occurred, was convicted under the false-news law. The Supreme Court of Canada reversed the conviction on the ground that the law was unconstitutional. The Court was unanimous that s. 2(b)'s protection extended to deliberate falsehoods, because the truth or falsity of a statement can be determined only by reference to its content. The principle of content-neutrality therefore dictated the answer. The Court, by a bare majority of four to three, also held that the law could not be justified under s. 1. The law was therefore struck down, and Zundel was acquitted and left free to continue his dissemination of deliberate falsehoods under the protection of the Constitution.[5]

In *R. v. Lucas* (1998),[6] the Supreme Court of Canada confirmed that deliberate falsehoods were protected by s. 2(b). At issue was the constitutionality of the Criminal Code's offence of defamatory libel, which made it an offence to publish material that was known to be false and that would expose the victim to hatred, contempt or ridicule. The Court held that the publication of defamatory libels was an activity that was protected by s. 2(b), but the Court upheld the prohibition under s. 1 as a justifiable means of protecting reputation from false attack. In the course of the s. 1 analysis, Cory J. for the majority commented that defamatory libel, consisting as it did of deliberate and harmful lies, was "so far removed from the core values of freedom of expression that it merits but scant protection".[7] In a separate concurring opinion, McLachlin J. expressed concern about allowing "the perceived low value of the expression to lower the bar of justification from the outset of the

---

[3]*R. v. Keegstra*, [1990] 3 S.C.R. 697, 734, 755-758, 833.

[4]*R. v. Zundel*, [1992] 2 S.C.R. 731.

[5]Zundel had not been charged under the hate-propaganda offence that was upheld in *Keegstra*, because a prosecution for that offence requires the consent of the Attorney General, and the Attorney General of Ontario, perhaps fearing that Holocaust denial was not caught by the hate-propaganda offence, refused to give his consent. That refusal was followed by the laying of a charge by a private citizen under the false-news provision, which does not require that the consent of the Attorney General be obtained.

[6]*R. v. Lucas*, [1998] 1 S.C.R. 439. The court was unanimous in upholding the offence of defamatory libel. The opinion of the majority was written by Cory J. and agreed with by Lamer C.J., Gonthier, Iacobucci and Bastarache JJ.; separate opinions were written by L'Heureux-Dubé, McLachlin and Major JJ.

[7]*R. v. Lucas*, [1998] 1 S.C.R. 439, para. 94.

s. 1 analysis".[8] However, she also agreed that the offence should be upheld under s. 1.

The same result occurred in *Canada v. JTI-Macdonald Corp.* (2007),[9] where the Court upheld the prohibition by the federal Tobacco Act of "false, misleading or deceptive" advertising of tobacco products. This activity was expression that was protected by s. 2(b), and, like the regulation of other falsehoods, had to be justified under s. 1 of the Charter. However, false advertising of products that were harmful to health was of "low value",[10] and its prohibition was justified under s. 1.

The principle of content neutrality means that s. 2(b) extends to much activity that is not worthy of constitutional protection. Indeed, the Court has acknowledged that "not all expression is equally worthy of protection".[11] The evaluation of the worthiness of the expression is however relevant only to the s. 1 inquiry. If the Court regards a particular kind of expression as of little value, then this makes the objective of a limiting law easier to justify, and invites more relaxed standards of proportionality. Because communicating for the purpose of prostitution, or promoting racial hatred, or defamation, or false advertising, are of "limited importance",[12] it is relatively easy to justify laws that prohibit those activities.[13] This illustrates my earlier point that the expansion of the guaranteed right, in this case, s. 2(b), inevitably leads to an erosion of the severe standards of justification that the Court originally erected for s. 1. That in turn leads to decisions that depend heavily on the judges' balancing of costs and benefits, a process that is unprincipled and unpredictable.[14]

VI. WAYS OF LIMITING EXPRESSION

§ 43:12 Prior restraint

Expression may be restricted in a variety of different ways. The restriction that is usually regarded as the most severe is a "prior restraint" on publication. A prior restraint is a law that prohibits the publication of particular material either absolutely or under a requirement of prior approval by a censor. Expression that is never published cannot contribute in any way to the democratic process, to the marketplace of ideas or to personal fulfilment. The courts have taken under review a variety of

---

[8] *R. v. Lucas*, [1998] 1 S.C.R. 439, para. 115.

[9] *Canada v. JTI-Macdonald Corp.*, [2007] 2 S.C.R. 610.

[10] *Canada v. JTI-Macdonald Corp.*, [2007] 2 S.C.R. 610, paras. 68, 94, per McLachlin C.J. for Court.

[11] *R. v. Zundel*, [1992] 2 S.C.R. 731, 760.

[12] *R. v. Zundel*, [1992] 2 S.C.R. 731, 762.

[13] Note, however, that the Court divided on the issue of s. 1 justification in the prostitution and hate propaganda cases.

[14] Chapter 38, Limitation of Rights, under heading § 38:3, "Relationship between s. 1 and rights".

prior restraints, including the censorship of films,[1] restrictions on the importation of books and magazines,[2] restrictions on access to the courts[3] and the reporting of judicial proceedings,[4] a publication ban on a fictional television programme,[5] a prohibition on the publication of public opinion polls in the final three days of an election campaign,[6] a prohibition of election advertising on polling day,[7] a prohibition on charitable solicitation without government permission,[8] restrictions on access to public property[9] and injunctions against picketing.[10] Needless to say, in all these cases, it was held that the prior restraint was a limit on freedom of expression. The courts have also held that a restriction on election campaign expenditures, which would be used to purchase time or space in the media for campaign messages, is a form of prior restraint that is prohibited by s. 2(b).[11] In contrast to the United States, where prior restraints are nearly (but not quite) always struck down,[12] in Canada the general standards of s. 1 justification are applicable to prior restraints as well as to other limits on expression, and a number of prior restraints have been upheld under s. 1.[13]

§ 43:13 Border control

An important kind of prior restraint is the prohibition on the importation of pornographic books and magazines. The prohibited material can be stopped and confiscated at the border, with customs officials serving as the censors. The federal Customs Tariff Act used to prohibit the importation of "immoral or indecent" books and magazines, and this was struck down as being too vague to serve as a reasonable limitation under

---

[Section 43:12]

[1] *Re Ont. Film and Video Appreciation Society* (1984), 41 O.R. (2d) 583 (C.A.) (struck down); *R. v. Glad Day Bookshops* (2004), 70 O.R. (3d) 691 (S.C.J.) (struck down).

[2] See § 43:13, "Border control".

[3] *Re Southam and The Queen (No. 1)* (1983), 41 O.R. (2d) 113 (C.A.) (struck down); *Re Southam and The Queen (No. 2)* (1986), 53 O.R. (2d) 663 (C.A.) (saved under s. 1).

[4] *Canadian Newspapers Co. v. Can.*, [1988] 1 S.C.R. 122 (saved under s. 1); *Edmonton Journal v. Alta.*, [1989] 2 S.C.R. 1326 (struck down).

[5] *Dagenais v. CBC*, [1994] 3 S.C.R. 835 (struck down).

[6] *Thomson Newspapers Co. v. Can.*, [1998] 1 S.C.R. 877 (struck down).

[7] *Harper v. Can.*, [2004] 1 S.C.R. 827 (saved under s. 1).

[8] *Epilepsy Can. v. Alta.* (1994), 115 D.L.R. (4th) 501 (Alta. C.A.) (struck down).

[9] *Committee for Cth. of Can. v. Can.*, [1991] 1 S.C.R. 139 (struck down).

[10] *BCGEU v. B.C.* (Vancouver Courthouse) [1988] 2 S.C.R. 214 (saved under s. 1).

[11] § 43:38, "Election expenditures".

[12] L.H. Tribe, American Constitutional Law (Foundation Press, N.Y., 2nd ed., 1986), 1039-1061; J.E. Nowak and R.D. Rotunda, Constitutional Law (West, St. Paul, Minn., 7th ed., 2005); secs. 16.16-16.17.

[13] The outcomes of the prior restraint cases are indicated in § 43:11 notes 12-14 and § 43:12 notes 1-4.

s. 1.[1] The "immoral or indecent" standard was replaced by the definition of "obscene" in the Criminal Code. In *R. v. Butler* (1992),[2] the Supreme Court of Canada held that the definition of "obscene" in the Criminal Code was a sufficiently clear standard and served sufficiently justified social purposes to serve as the basis of the criminal offence of possession or sale of obscene materials. The criminal offence was a valid limitation of freedom of expression under s. 1.

In *Little Sisters Book and Art Emporium v. Canada* (2000),[3] the Little Sisters bookstore challenged the prohibition in the Customs Tariff Act that used the same obscenity standard. The bookstore, which catered to the LGBTQ communities in Vancouver, had experienced great difficulty in importing LGBTQ erotica because of the frequency of seizures by customs officers. The bookstore attacked not only the definition of obscenity but also the customs border review procedures which disproportionately withheld LGBTQ literature. The Supreme Court of Canada held that the prohibition on obscenity, having been upheld under s. 1 as a Criminal Code offence within the country, could also be used at the border. Binnie J. for the majority of the Court acknowledged that the implementation of the prohibition by customs officials had been unconstitutionally discriminatory against LGBTQ literature, but he held that this outcome was not inherent in the definition of obscenity. He enumerated the inadequacies of resources, training, direction and procedure in the customs department which led to the excessive delays, seizures and confiscations that Little Sisters had endured, and he directed the government to repair the problems. The solution did not have to involve amendment of the legislation, because failures at the implementation level could be addressed at the implementation level. The legislation was accordingly upheld.[4] Iacobucci J. for the dissenting minority held that the maladministration flowed "from the very nature of prior restraint itself", and the legislation should contain procedural safeguards to "minimize the dangers posed by prior restraint".[5] He would have struck down the legislation with a postponement of 18 months in order to enable Parliament to put procedural safeguards into the legislation.

[Section 43:13]

[1] *Luscher v. Revenue Can.*, [1985] 1 F.C. 85 (C.A.).

[2] *R. v. Butler*, [1992] 1 S.C.R. 452; discussed in § 43:29, "Pornography".

[3] *Little Sisters Book and Art Emporium v. Canada*, [2000] 2 S.C.R. 1120; also discussed in § 43:29, "Pornography".

[4] The majority did strike down a reverse onus provision in the customs legislation that placed the burden of challenging customs classifications on the importer (paras. 97-105). The majority held that, in its application to expressive material, the Crown should bear the burden of proving that the material was obscene. This was a minor point in that the reverse onus applied only when an issue got to court and did not apply to the determinations made at the departmental level, which was the source of the problems.

[5] *Little Sisters Book and Art Emporium v. Canada*, [2000] 2 S.C.R. 1120, para. 237.

§ 43:14 Penal prohibition

The most common restriction on speech is a prohibition coupled with a penal sanction, for example, the Criminal Code offences of perjury or counselling suicide. To the extent that the prospect of punishment deters the uttering of the prohibited expression, a legal prohibition operates in the same way as a prior restraint. However, some speakers may not be deterred, and their ideas will enter the public domain. The courts have struck down a prohibition on advertising by dentists,[1] and a prohibition on the advertising of tobacco products.[2] The courts have upheld under s. 1 a prohibition on advertising directed at children,[3] a prohibition on communicating for the purpose of prostitution,[4] a prohibition on publication of defamatory libel[5] and a prohibition on hate propaganda.[6]

Falling just short of a criminal prohibition is the prohibition of "discriminatory practices" in the Canadian Human Rights Act. One of those practices was the use of the telephone to spread messages of hatred against minority groups.[7] A discriminatory practice does not give rise to an immediate penalty, but a Human Rights Tribunal has the power to order that the practice cease. Once the order has been made, it can be entered as an order of the Federal Court, and disobedience is then punishable as a contempt of court. In *Canada v. Taylor* (1990),[8] this entire process was followed, and, when Mr. Taylor continued his telephonic messages of anti-semitism in defiance of the court order, he was committed to prison for contempt. He appealed the committal on constitutional grounds up to the Supreme Court of Canada, which held that the ban on telephone messages violated s. 2(b). However, the Court held that the ban was justified under s. 1, and so Mr. Taylor stayed in prison.[9]

In *Ross v. New Brunswick School District No. 15* (1996),[10] the public dissemination (outside the classroom) by a schoolteacher of anti-semitic messages was found to be a prohibited discriminatory practice by a board of inquiry constituted under New Brunswick's human rights statute. The board of inquiry ordered the school board that employed the teacher to remove him from his teaching position to a non-teaching

---

[Section 43:14]

[1] *Rocket v. Royal College of Dental Surgeons*, [1990] 2 S.C.R. 232.

[2] *R.J.R.-MacDonald v. Can.*, [1995] 3 S.C.R. 199.

[3] *Irwin Toy v. Que.*, [1989] 1 S.C.R. 927.

[4] *Re ss. 193 and 195.1 of Criminal Code* (Prostitution Reference) [1990] 1 S.C.R. 1123.

[5] *R. v. Lucas*, [1998] 1 S.C.R. 439.

[6] *R. v. Keegstra*, [1990] 3 S.C.R. 697.

[7] The relevant provision (s. 13 of the Act) was amended to apply also to messages communicated over the Internet, but then was ultimately repealed in 2013: S.C. 2013, c. 37, s. 2.

[8] *Canada v. Taylor*, [1990] 3 S.C.R. 892.

[9] Compare *BCGEU v. B.C.* (Vancouver Courthouse) [1988] 2 S.C.R. 214 (injunction issued against courthouse picketing on basis that picketing was a contempt of court).

[10] *Ross v. New Brunswick School District No. 15*, [1996] 1 S.C.R. 825.

position. The Supreme Court of Canada held that the order of the board of inquiry was a breach of s. 2(b), but that it was justified under s. 1 as a measure to reduce the climate of anti-semitism that had developed at the school. However, the Court held that the board of inquiry had overstepped the reasonable limit of s. 1 in also ordering the school board to dismiss the teacher from his non-teaching post if at any time in the future he were to resume his antisemitic activities. That part of the order was struck down as an unjustified breach of s. 2(b).

§ 43:15 Civil prohibition

A prohibition on expression that is sanctioned by only a civil remedy is exemplified by the tort of defamation or a contract to keep some matter confidential. Breach of a civil obligation does not attract a penal sanction, such as a fine or imprisonment; the breach entitles the aggrieved party to recover damages or to obtain some other civil remedy such as an injunction. Where a civil obligation is created by the common law (which includes the law of contract), there will normally be no Charter remedy, because the Charter does not apply to the rules of the common law that govern relations between private parties.[1] Where the civil prohibition is created by statute, the Charter will apply, and the prohibition will offend s. 2(b).[2]

§ 43:16 Forced expression

Occasionally a person is forced by law to make a statement.[1] For example, in *R.J.R.-MacDonald v. Canada* (1995),[2] a federal statute, the Tobacco Products Control Act, required cigarettes and other tobacco products to be sold in packages that displayed prescribed warnings of the health dangers of smoking. The warnings were unattributed, so that they could be interpreted as coming from the manufacturers (instead of the true author, the federal government), and the manufacturers were prohibited from displaying any information of their own on the packages (except for the name of the product). The Supreme Court of Canada, by a majority, held that the requirement of unattributed warnings was a breach of s. 2(b), on the basis that "freedom of expression necessarily entails the right to say nothing or the right not to say certain things".[3] The majority of the Court held that a simple requirement of health

---

[Section 43:15]

[1] *RWDSU v. Dolphin Delivery*, [1986] 2 S.C.R. 573 (Charter inapplicable to tort of inducing breach of contract).

[2] See ch. 37, Application of Charter.

[Section 43:16]

[1] A famous pre-Charter case is *Re Alberta Statutes*, [1938] S.C.R. 100 (striking down provincial law requiring newspapers to publish a government reply to any criticism of government policy).

[2] *R.J.R.-MacDonald v. Canada*, [1995] 3 S.C.R. 199.

[3] *R.J.R.-MacDonald v. Canada*, [1995] 3 S.C.R. 199, para. 124 per McLachlin J. for the majority. La Forest J. for the dissenting minority would have held that warnings of

warnings on cigarette packages could be justified under s. 1, but that the government had failed to establish the justification for the non-attribution of the warnings or for the prohibition of additional information on the packages. The requirement of unattributed warnings was therefore struck down.

After *RJR*, the Government of Canada secured the enactment of a new Tobacco Act, which continued the requirement of warnings on cigarette packages. However, now the warnings were to be attributed to Health Canada. They were also required to occupy 50 per cent of the surface of the package. In a sequel case, *Canada v. JTI-Macdonald Corp.* (2007),[4] the Court unanimously upheld the new requirement. Indeed, McLachlin C.J., who wrote the opinion of the Court, mused that "minor restrictions or requirements with respect to packaging" might not infringe s. 2(b) at all. But she acknowledged that a warning, albeit attributed to government, that occupied half of the space on the package, "arguably rises to the level of interfering with how they [the manufacturers] choose to express themselves".[5] Despite her "arguably", she held that s. 2(b) was infringed by the warning requirement. She went on to hold that the requirement was justified under s. 1. Although the infringement would have been less if the size of the warnings were less, "the evidence established that bigger warnings *may* have a greater effect. Parliament is not required to implement less effective alternatives".[6]

In *Slaight Communications v. Davidson* (1989),[7] an adjudicator, exercising statutory powers conferred by the Canada Labour Code, ordered an employer to provide a letter of reference to an unjustly dismissed employee, and also stipulated the facts that were to be recited in the mandatory letter of reference. The Supreme Court of Canada, by a majority, held that it was a breach of s. 2(b) to order a person to make a statement, but, because the statement included "only objective facts that are not in dispute", the order was justified under s. 1.

In *Lavigne v. OPSEU* (1991),[8] the question arose whether an "agency shop" clause in a collective agreement, which required non-members of the union to pay union dues, was a breach of s. 2(b). The evidence

---

danger on packaging that were not expressly attributed to the manufacturers did not infringe their freedom of expression, and required no justification under s. 1: *R.J.R.-MacDonald v. Canada*, [1995] 3 S.C.R. 199, para. 115.

[4]*Canada v. JTI-Macdonald Corp.*, [2007] 2 S.C.R. 610. McLachlin C.J. wrote the opinion of the Court.

[5]*Canada v. JTI-Macdonald Corp.*, [2007] 2 S.C.R. 610, para. 132.

[6]*Canada v. JTI-Macdonald Corp.*, [2007] 2 S.C.R. 610, para. 137 (emphasis added). The word "may" indicates how soft the evidentiary requirements are for the regulation of commercial speech. It seems likely to me that the prominent warnings, if they have any effect at all, make the product more attractive to the 15- to 19-year-olds, who, according to the Court (para. 16), are the only demographic group whose incidence of smoking has recently been on the increase.

[7]*Slaight Communications v. Davidson*, [1989] 1 S.C.R. 1038.

[8]*Lavigne v. OPSEU*, [1991] 2 S.C.R. 211.

established that the union used some of its funds, which included the forced dues, to promote left-wing causes of which the complaining non-member (Lavigne) disapproved. La Forest J. for the majority of the Supreme Court of Canada held that the payments to the union were not expressive activity, and therefore did not come within s. 2(b). Wilson J. for the concurring minority held that a voluntary payment of dues could be expressive activity, but that the forced payment of dues under an agency shop requirement did not imply support for the union's views or preclude the payer from holding and expressing contrary views; she therefore agreed that there was no breach of s. 2(b).[9]

Applicants for Canadian citizenship are required, by the federal Citizenship Act, to take an oath (or make an affirmation) of allegiance in the following terms:

> I swear (or affirm) that I will be faithful and bear true allegiance to Her Majesty Queen Elizabeth the Second, Queen of Canada, Her Heirs and Successors, and that I will faithfully observe the laws of Canada and fulfil my duties as a Canadian citizen.

In *McAteer v. Canada* (2014),[10] several permanent residents of Canada applied for a declaration that the oath was unconstitutional in its present form. They did not object to making an oath of allegiance to Canada in terms that made no reference to the Queen, but they claimed that swearing allegiance to the Queen violated their right to freedom of expression. They objected to swearing allegiance to a person who was a foreign monarch, unelected by Canadians and head of the Church of England. They did not believe that such a person should be Canada's head of state, and they claimed it was contrary to their freedom of expression to be forced to make an express commitment to that person. The Ontario Court of Appeal, in an opinion written by Weiler J.A., held that the requirement of the oath of allegiance did not infringe their freedom of expression. Weiler J.A. reasoned that the oath did not mean what the applicants thought it meant. To interpret the oath as a commitment to an individual person, as it appears on its face, was a mistaken literal interpretation of an anachronistic reference. Canada was a *constitutional* monarchy. The development of the conventions of responsible government now meant that the Queen no longer "reigned" personally, but only through elected Canadian ministers. In today's context, the reference in the oath to the Queen of Canada and her heirs and successors was not a reference to a foreign monarch, but to the Canadian institutions she represented. "[A] patently incorrect understanding of a provision cannot ground a finding of unconstitutionality."[11] Based on the correct understanding of the oath, Weiler J.A.'s conclusion

---

[9]Accord, *McKay v. Man.*, [1989] 2 S.C.R. 357 (public funding of candidates for election does not abridge the freedom of expression of taxpayers).

[10]*McAteer v. Canada* (2014), 121 O.R. (3d) 1, 2014 ONCA 578 (Ont. C.A.), leave to appeal denied February 26, 2015. Weiler J.A. wrote the opinion of the three-judge bench. This case was a second try. *Roach v. Can.*, [1994] 2 F.C. 406 (C.A.) had upheld the oath of allegiance on the same grounds against the same constitutional objections.

[11]*McAteer v. Canada* (2014), 121 O.R. (3d) 1, 2014 ONCA 578 (Ont. C.A.), para. 63,

was that the purpose of the oath was not to compel expression, but to obtain from prospective citizens a commitment to Canada's form of government. The oath did have an effect on freedom of expression in that the prospective citizen was obliged to say the words of the oath in order to become a citizen. But the effect was trivial (or benign) since, after taking the oath, the new citizen had the Charter right of freedom of expression and was free to express any political opinions, including support for a republican form of government. Therefore, there was no breach of s. 2(b) of the Charter.[12]

§ 43:17 Language requirement

A Quebec law requiring that public signs and advertisements be in French only has been struck down as a violation of s. 2(b). The law did not restrict the content of signs or advertisements; they could contain any message at all, provided the message was in the French language. In *Ford v. Quebec* (1988),[1] the Supreme Court of Canada rejected the argument that language was "merely a means or medium of expression"; rather, the Court held, "it colours the content and meaning of expression".[2] The Court concluded that freedom of expression included "the freedom to express oneself in the language of one's choice".[3] On that basis, the requirement of the exclusive use of French, involving as it did a prohibition of the use of any language other than French, was unconstitutional. In *Devine v. Quebec* (1988),[4] the Court considered a Quebec law requiring the non-exclusive use of French for brochures, orders, invoices and other business documents; the documents had to be in French, but English (or any other language) could be used as well. The Court held that this law was also a breach of s. 2(b): "freedom consists in the absence of compulsion as well as an absence of restraint".[5] However, the Court did uphold the non-exclusive requirement under s. 1.

---

citing *R. v. Khawaja*, [2012] 3 S.C.R. 555, para. 82.

[12]The Court also rejected arguments based in freedom of religion (s. 2(a)) and equality (s. 15). On freedom of religion, although the Queen is head of the Church of England, the oath was not to the Queen as a person, and it was a secular requirement that did not compel the new citizen to conform to any religious belief (para. 120). On equality, the oath had no discriminatory purpose or effect (paras. 121-129).

[Section 43:17]

[1]*Ford v. Quebec*, [1988] 2 S.C.R. 712.

[2]*Ford v. Quebec*, [1988] 2 S.C.R. 712, 748.

[3]*Ford v. Quebec*, [1988] 2 S.C.R. 712, 748. The same argument is advanced in L. Green, "Freedom of Expression and Choice of Language" (1991) 13 Law and Policy 215.

[4]*Devine v. Quebec*, [1988] 2 S.C.R. 790.

[5]*Devine v. Quebec*, [1988] 2 S.C.R. 790, 813.

§ 43:18 Search of press premises

In two cases,[1] the Supreme Court of Canada has reviewed the issue of a search warrant to the police to obtain film taken by television crews of a crime in progress. It was argued, and accepted by McLachlin J. in dissent, that the search warrant was invalid as a breach of freedom of the press, because of the chilling effect on newsgathering that would be caused if the information gathered was available to the police. However, the majority of the Court, while suggesting caution in the issue of search warrants for press premises, upheld the warrants, placing emphasis on the fact that the film had already been shown. For the majority, there was no breach of s. 2(b).

§ 43:19 Disclosure of journalists' sources

Journalists often obtain information, for example from "whistle-blowers" within government or other organizations, only after promising the person who offers the information that his or her identity would be kept confidential. In *R. v. National Post* (2010),[1] a journalist employed by the National Post newspaper was offered some information on a story he was pursuing on condition that the identity of the informant be kept confidential. The journalist was authorized by the newspaper to make promises of confidentiality, and he made the promise demanded in this case. In due course a plain brown envelope arrived in the mail which contained a document that appeared to indicate improper behaviour by the Prime Minister. The journalist made some inquiries to check the authenticity of the document, and was told that it was a forgery. One of the persons to whom these inquiries were directed informed the RCMP of the journalist's possession of the document, and the RCMP obtained a search warrant to require the newspaper to give up the document (and its envelope) on the ground that it was evidence of the offence of forgery. The newspaper applied to quash the warrant on the ground that police testing of the document (and its envelope) might lead to the identification of the person who had mailed it to the journalist, causing the journalist's promise of confidentiality to be broken. The Supreme Court of Canada, by a majority of eight to one, rejected the newspaper's application, holding that the search warrant was valid and had to be obeyed even if there was a risk of disclosing the identity of the

---

[Section 43:18]

[1] *CBC v. Lessard*, [1991] 3 S.C.R. 421; *CBC v. N.B.*, [1991] 3 S.C.R. 459.

[Section 43:19]

[1] *R. v. National Post*, [2010] 1 S.C.R. 477. Binnie J. wrote the opinion of the seven-judge majority. LeBel J. wrote a concurring opinion (disagreeing with only the procedural point that in his view the media should have been given prior notice of the issue of the search warrant, but holding that the default did not invalidate the warrant). Abella J. wrote a dissenting opinion, agreeing with Binnie J.'s four-part test for disclosure of confidential sources, but disagreeing with his conclusion in favour of disclosure. She also thought that the media should have been given prior notice and a timely opportunity to oppose the issue of the warrant before it was issued.

confidential source. In the course of getting to this conclusion, Binnie J., who wrote for the majority, restated the law respecting disclosure of journalists' confidential sources.

Binnie J. acknowledged that the freedom to publish the news, which was guaranteed by s. 2(b) of the Charter, necessarily involved a freedom to gather the news, and an important element of the news-gathering function was the ability of the media to make use of confidential sources. If the media were unable to provide anonymity to sources of information, some important sources would dry up and freedom of expression on matters of public interest "would be badly compromised".[2] However, he rejected the argument that there was a *constitutional* immunity against compelled disclosure of confidential sources. He pointed out that not all techniques of news gathering should be constitutionally protected. And an absolute immunity for confidential sources would be too sweeping, since it would be hard to limit it to the traditional media, and it would impair law enforcement too severely. Nevertheless, the common law could "properly be developed to reflect Charter values",[3] and he held that the common law of Canada should recognize a journalist-source privilege[4] which is closely aligned with the Charter guarantee of freedom of the press, but which would not have constitutional force and which would be applied on a case-by-case basis. There were four elements to the privilege:[5] (1) the journalist must have received a communication that originated in a confidence that the identity of the informant would not be disclosed; (2) the confidence must be essential to the relationship in which the communication arises; (3) the relationship must be one that should be "sedulously fostered" in the public good; and finally (4) the public interest served by protecting the identity of the informant must outweigh the public interest in getting at the truth. The fourth and last element requires the judge to weigh the protection of the valuable confidential relationship against the countervailing public interest in the investigation of crime (as in this case) or national security, public safety or other public good. Because of this balancing exercise, "no journalist can give a source a total assurance of confidentiality". In this case, while the first three elements were satisfied, the balance of public interest was in favour of disclosing the document, because it was physical evidence that would be essential to the investigation and proof of a serious crime. Therefore, the search warrant was properly issued and had to be complied with despite the risk of breaching the confidence that had been promised to the source.

---

[2] *R. v. National Post*, [2010] 1 S.C.R. 477, para. 33.

[3] *R. v. National Post*, [2010] 1 S.C.R. 477, para. 50.

[4] As a creature of the common law, which is not provided for in Quebec's Civil Code or Code of Civil Procedure, it was unclear whether the privilege would be available in civil litigation in Quebec until *Globe and Mail v. Can.*, [2010] 2 S.C.R. 592 held that the privilege was part of the law of Quebec as well.

[5] *R. v. National Post*, [2010] 1 S.C.R. 477, paras. 56-59.

§ 43:20 Time, manner and place

The least severe form of restriction on expression is the regulation of the time, manner or place of expression.[1] For example, a law might prohibit the use of cartoons in advertising directed at children, or a law might authorize a public official to stipulate the time and route of a parade.[2] These laws restrict expression, and are therefore in violation of s. 2(b); but, because they do not regulate the content of expression, a court would be likely to uphold the laws under s. 1.

The regulation of time, manner and place can be so broad as to amount to a significant restriction on expression. This was the case in *Ramsden v. Peterborough* (1993),[3] where a municipal by-law prohibited the placing of posters anywhere on municipal public property. The by-law was content-neutral, and it prohibited only one kind of expression (postering) on only one kind of property (municipal public property). Nonetheless, the by-law did close off the most obvious public places to affix posters, such as utility poles. Moreover, because public postering is inexpensive, it was traditionally used by poorly-funded groups to publicize their ideas, causes or events. These considerations persuaded the Supreme Court of Canada that the ban on postering was too broad to be upheld under s. 1, although the Court implied that a narrower by-law, more carefully targeted at such legitimate concerns as littering, aesthetic blight, traffic hazards and impediments to persons repairing utility poles, would be upheld.

In *Thomson Newspapers Co. v. Canada* (1998),[4] the Supreme Court of Canada struck down a prohibition on the publication of new opinion polls during the last three days of an election campaign. The purpose was to prevent the voters from being misled by inaccurate polls that came out too late to be analyzed and corrected. Although the prohibition lasted for only three days, the Court still held that the measure was too severe a restriction on expression to be upheld under s. 1.

In *U.F.C.W. v. KMart Canada* (1999),[5] the Supreme Court of Canada struck down a provision in the Labour Relations Code of British Columbia that prohibited a striking union from handing out leaflets at

---

[Section 43:20]

[1]In the United States, it is accepted that restrictions may be imposed on the time, manner and place of speech, so long as they are content-neutral, narrowly tailored to serve a significant governmental interest, and leave open alternative channels of communication: *Ward v. Rock against Racism* (1989), 491 U.S. 781, 798-799.

[2]E.g., *R. v. Spratt* (2008), 298 D.L.R. (4th) 317 (B.C. C.A.) (upholding under s. 1 a provincial law creating an "access zone" to an abortion clinic in which anti-abortion protests and related activities were prohibited); *Canadian Broadcasting Corp. v. Can.*, [2011] 1 S.C.R. 19 (upholding under s. 1 rules of court restricting to designated areas of courthouses the news gathering activities of journalists).

[3]*Ramsden v. Peterborough*, [1993] 2 S.C.R. 1084. The opinion of the Court was written by Iacobucci J.

[4]*Thomson Newspapers Co. v. Canada*, [1998] 1 S.C.R. 877.

[5]*U.F.C.W. v. KMart Canada*, [1999] 2 S.C.R. 1083.

workplaces other than the struck premises. This prohibition, which was part of a prohibition of secondary picketing, applied only during a strike or lockout, and did not apply to the site of the strike or lockout. The Court held that the goal of minimizing disruption to businesses that are not involved in the labour dispute would justify a prohibition of conventional picketing, but not a prohibition of leafleting, which, like postering, was a traditional means of communicating information by poorly-funded groups.

In the *KMart* case, the prohibition on secondary picketing had been enacted by statute. In *Pepsi-Cola Canada Beverages v. R.W.D.S.U.* (2002),[6] the Supreme Court of Canada considered the question whether a prohibition on secondary picketing existed at common law. In Saskatchewan, where secondary picketing was not governed by statute, a court had issued an injunction prohibiting all secondary picketing by employees of Pepsi-Cola, who were on strike against their employer. The employees had picketed, not only the bottling plant where they worked (the primary location), but also the shops that sold Pepsi-Cola products and a variety of other secondary locations. The injunction was limited by location, but was very sweeping in that only the primary location was open to picketing. The Court held that the common law[7] did not authorize an injunction that applied to all secondary locations regardless of the nature of the picketing activity. In order to protect freedom of expression, only a more limited injunction could be issued, one that was premised on the commission of a wrongful act (a tort or a crime). Since the picketing of the shops was peaceful and did not involve the commission of a wrongful act, that part of the injunction was discharged. However, the union had also been picketing the homes of Pepsi-Cola management personnel. Those pickets had been guilty of the tort of intimidation. That part of the injunction was accordingly affirmed.

VII. COMMERCIAL EXPRESSION

§ 43:21 Protection of commercial expression

"Commercial expression",[1] of which the most important example is advertising, is expression that is designed to promote the sale of goods and services. Because of the obvious public need to forbid false or misleading claims, to require warnings of danger and disclosure of other

---

[6]*Pepsi-Cola Canada Beverages v. R.W.D.S.U.*, [2002] 1 S.C.R. 156. The opinion of the Court was written by McLachlin C.J. and LeBel J.

[7]The Charter does not apply to private disputes governed by the common law, but the Court held (paras. 18-20) that it had the power to "develop" the common law to make it consistent with "Charter values". The Court also made clear (para. 86) that restrictions on secondary picketing that were enacted as part of statutory scheme of labour relations regulation would probably be upheld (presumably under s. 1).

[Section 43:21]

[1]See R.J. Sharpe, "Commercial Expression and the Charter" (1987) 37 U. Toronto L.J. 229; L.E. Weinrib, "Does Money Talk?: Commercial Expression in the Canadian Constitutional Context" in Schneiderman (ed.) Freedom of Expression and the Charter (1991).

matters (such as food ingredients), commercial expression is in all jurisdictions subject to a good deal of regulation. Indeed, the Supreme Court of the United States, not wanting to inhibit regulation, initially held that commercial expression was not speech at all, so that it was unprotected by the guarantee of "freedom of speech" in the first amendment.[2] In 1976, the Court reversed this implausible position, and held that commercial speech was protected by the first amendment.[3] The Court made clear that it would still uphold laws against false or deceptive claims, and reasonable restrictions as to the time, place and manner of speech.[4] But restrictions on the content of commercial speech have since 1976 generally been struck down.[5]

There are two reasons why commercial expression ought to be protected under a guarantee of freedom of expression (in Canada) or speech (in the United States). First, it does literally fall within the meaning of the word "expression" (or "speech"), and it does make a contribution to the "marketplace of ideas" that is fostered by the constitutional guarantee. Secondly, it is very difficult to distinguish commercial speech from other kinds of speech, in that a variety of political, economic and social ideas are inevitably inherent in commercial speech. However, to the extent that commercial expression deals with ascertainable facts regarding price, quality, effectiveness and safety, regulation designed to ensure that consumers have sufficient, accurate information to make informed choices must be upheld. In Canada, the balancing of the value of free expression against the value of consumer protection has to take place within s. 1 of the Charter.

§ 43:22 Language requirements

The Supreme Court of Canada has held from the beginning that commercial expression is protected by the guarantee of freedom of expression in s. 2(b). The first case to reach the Court was *Ford v. Quebec* (1988),[1] in which the Court held that a Quebec law requiring commercial signs to be in French only was unconstitutional. The Court discussed the American commercial speech cases, and reviewed some of the American literature. While not expressly approving the detail of the American jurisprudence, the Court concluded that:[2]

---

[2]*Valentine v. Chrestenson* (1942), 316 U.S. 52.

[3]*Virginia State Bd. of Pharmacy v. Virginia Citizens Consumer Council* (1976), 425 U.S. 748.

[4]*Virginia State Bd. of Pharmacy v. Virginia Citizens Consumer Council* (1976), 425 U.S. 748, 771, 777-778.

[5]L.H. Tribe, American Constitutional Law (Foundation Press, N.Y., 2nd ed., 1986), ch. 12 secs. 16.26-16.31, 890-904; J.E. Nowak and R.D. Rotunda, Constitutional Law (West, St. Paul, Minn., 7th ed., 2005); ch. 16, secs. 16.26-16.31, and see cases listed in § 43:6 note 3.

[Section 43:22]

[1]*Ford v. Quebec*, [1988] 2 S.C.R. 712. A single opinion of "the Court" was rendered.

[2]*Ford v. Quebec*, [1988] 2 S.C.R. 712, 767.

> Over and above its intrinsic value as expression, commercial expression which, as has been pointed out, protects listeners as well as speakers plays a significant role in enabling individuals to make informed economic choices, an important aspect of individual self-fulfilment and personal autonomy.

The Court held that the language-of-signs law violated s. 2(b) by prohibiting signs in the English language. The Court held that the law could not be justified under s. 1, because, although it pursued an important purpose, namely, the protection of the French language, it impaired the rights of English-speakers more than was necessary to accomplish the purpose. A requirement of French, even a requirement that French be predominant, would have been a "reasonable limit" under s. 1, but a complete prohibition of English went too far.[3]

§ 43:23 Advertising restrictions

In *Irwin Toy v. Quebec* (1989),[1] the Court upheld a Quebec law that prohibited all commercial advertising directed at children under 13 years of age. The Court followed its earlier decision in Ford to decide that advertising was constitutionally protected by s. 2(b) of the Charter. However, the Court divided on the issue whether this law could be justified as a "reasonable limit" under s. 1. By a majority of three to two, the Court held that the protection of a particularly vulnerable group, namely, young children, was a sufficiently important purpose, and the Quebec Legislature should be allowed some leeway in deciding to accomplish that purpose by a ban on advertising directed at children. The ban was not an absolute one, in the sense that products such as toys and breakfast cereals could still be advertised, provided the advertising did not use cartoons and other techniques directed at children. The majority of the Court accordingly upheld the law.

Professionals such as lawyers, doctors and dentists are typically subject to restrictions on advertising of varying degrees of stringency. The object of the restrictions is to maintain the dignity of a learned profession, although the implausible claim that advertising of professional services is inevitably misleading is sometimes made as well. In *Rocket v. Royal College of Dental Surgeons* (1990),[2] a particularly severe regulation came under judicial review. Under Ontario's Health Disciplines Act, dentists were prohibited from advertising their services, with only trivial exceptions for an exterior sign, business cards and the like. The Supreme Court of Canada held unanimously that the dental regulation was a violation of s. 2(b). With respect to s. 1, the Court held

---

[3]In the companion case of *Devine v. Que.*, [1988] 2 S.C.R. 790, the Court held that a requirement of French for various business forms was also a breach of s. 2(b), but, because other languages were not prohibited, the requirement was upheld under s. 1.

[Section 43:23]

[1]*Irwin Toy v. Quebec*, [1989] 1 S.C.R. 927. A joint opinion of Dickson C.J., Lamer and Wilson JJ. was the majority opinion. McIntyre J., with Beetz J., dissented.

[2]*Rocket v. Royal College of Dental Surgeons*, [1990] 1 S.C.R. 232. McLachlin J. wrote the opinion of the Court.

that the objective of maintaining high standards of professional conduct would justify the regulation of advertising by professionals, but this particular regulation was far broader than was necessary to accomplish that purpose. For example, the regulation prohibited a dentist from advertising office hours or languages spoken—"information which would be useful to the public and present no serious danger of misleading the public or undercutting professionalism".[3] The Court struck down the regulation.

In *RJR-MacDonald v. Canada* (1995),[4] the federal Tobacco Products Control Act was held to be unconstitutional. The Act prohibited the advertising of cigarettes and other tobacco products.[5] Obviously, the Act infringed s. 2(b). With respect to s. 1, the main difficulty for the federal government was that the product itself was lawful.[6] The government argued that a ban on the product was impracticable, because so many Canadians were smokers.[7] Instead, Parliament chose the weaker alternative of banning advertising, intending thereby to reduce consumption, which would reduce the harmful effects of smoking.[8] The Quebec Superior Court, at the conclusion of a long trial, held that the evidence failed to establish a causal connection between a ban on advertising and a reduction in smoking. In the face of this finding, the Supreme Court of Canada was still unanimously prepared to find that there was enough evidence to establish a rational connection between the advertising ban and the objective of reducing consumption. However, a majority of the Court could not accept that a total ban on all forms of advertising, including purely informational advertising, was the least drastic means of accomplishing the objective. The majority concluded that the Act could not be justified under s. 1, and held that it was unconstitutional. The Court would have upheld a ban more carefully targeted at the

---

[3] *Rocket v. Royal College of Dental Surgeons*, [1990] 1 S.C.R. 232, 250.

[4] *RJR-MacDonald v. Canada*, [1995] 3 S.C.R. 199. The principal majority opinion was written by McLachlin J.; Lamer C.J., Sopinka, Iacobucci and Major JJ. each wrote concurring opinions. The principal dissenting opinion was written by La Forest J., with the agreement of L'Heureux-Dubé and Gonthier JJ.; Cory J. wrote a brief dissenting opinion, agreeing with La Forest J. except on one point.

[5] The Act also required that unattributed health warnings be displayed on the packaging: see text accompanying § 43:16 note 2.

[6] Compare the subsequent decisions of the Supreme Court of the United States, striking down restrictions on the advertising of lawful businesses: *Greater New Orleans Broadcasting Assn. v. U.S.* (1999), 527 U.S. 173 (casino gambling); *Lorillard Tobacco Co. v. Mass.* (2001), 533 U.S. 525 (tobacco products).

[7] Ironically, the ban on the product itself would not attract Charter of Rights review, since freedom of expression is not engaged (and nor is any other right): *Rosen v. Ont.* (1996), 131 D.L.R. (4th) 708 (Ont. C.A.) (prohibition of the sale of tobacco products in pharmacies not an infringement of freedom of expression).

[8] This invited the question of whether Parliament could use the criminal law power to ban advertising of a harmful but legal product. The Court, by a majority of seven to two, held that the criminal law power did authorize a law of this kind: see ch. 18, Criminal Law, under heading § 18:5, "Tobacco".

recruitment of new smokers, for example, advertising directed to young people or advertising associating smoking with an attractive lifestyle.[9]

After the decision in *RJR*, the Government of Canada went back to the drawing board and a new Tobacco Act was enacted. The new Act continued to ban the advertising of tobacco products, but there were now limited exceptions for "information advertising" and "brand-preference advertising", provided they were not "lifestyle advertising" or "advertising that could be construed on reasonable grounds to be appealing to young persons" (all the quoted terms being defined). Sponsorship of events by tobacco companies was also banned. In *Canada v. JTI-Macdonald Corp.* (2007),[10] the Supreme Court upheld the Act. McLachlin C.J., who wrote for the unanimous Court, described the Act as "more restrained and nuanced than its predecessor", and as "a genuine attempt by Parliament to craft controls on advertising and promotion that would meet its objectives as well as the concerns expressed by the majority of this Court in *RJR*".[11] She held that the Act was justified under s. 1. The public-health objective of the Act was important, the commercial expression that it restricted was of "low value",[12] and a sufficient effort had been made to meet the minimum-impairment concerns that had defeated the predecessor Act in *RJR*.

§ 43:24 Signs

Commercial signs are protected by s. 2(b). It was the regulation of the language of commercial signs that was struck down in *Ford v. Quebec* (1988),[1] which was the Supreme Court of Canada's first commercial speech case.

In *R. v. Guignard* (2002),[2] a municipal by-law in Quebec prohibited advertising signs and billboards except in industrial zones of the municipality. The defendant was prosecuted under the by-law for erecting a sign on his property complaining about the delays of his insurance company in settling a claim. Because the sign named the insurance company, it fell within the by-law's definition of an advertising sign (despite its negative message). The Supreme Court of Canada acquitted the defendant, holding that the by-law infringed his freedom of expression. The municipality attempted to justify the by-law as a reasonable limit that was "designed to prevent visual pollution and driver distraction", and the Court acknowledged that a municipality might well want to maintain "a pleasant environment for the residents". But the Court rejected the claimed justification, describing the by-law as "arbitrary",

---

[9] *R.J.R.-MacDonald v. Canada*, [1995] 3 S.C.R. 199, paras. 164, 191.

[10] *Canada v. JTI-Macdonald Corp.*, [2007] 2 S.C.R. 610.

[11] *Canada v. JTI-Macdonald Corp.*, [2007] 2 S.C.R. 610, para. 7.

[12] *Canada v. JTI-Macdonald Corp.*, [2007] 2 S.C.R. 610, paras. 68, 94, 115.

[Section 43:24]

[1] *Ford v. Quebec*, [1988] 2 S.C.R. 712.

[2] *R. v. Guignard*, [2002] 1 S.C.R. 472. LeBel J. wrote the opinion of the Court.

as not being a "reasonable solution", and as "disproportionate to any benefit that it secures for the municipality".[3] The Court struck down the by-law, but gave the municipality six months to revise it. The six-month delay suggests that the Court would be willing to entertain some restrictions on billboards, but very little guidance is to be found in the opinion as to what would be acceptable. One would have thought that the fact that the bylaw did not catch signs that lacked any trade name would be a strong point in its favour, since non-commercial messages were not banned, but the Court went out of its way to condemn this limitation as "arbitrary". This suggests that the ban was too narrow, but other passages in the opinion suggest that the ban was too wide. It would be unfortunate if a formula could not be found for provinces and municipalities to impose restrictions on roadside advertising that would not infringe the Charter.

In *Vann Niagara v. Oakville* (2003),[4] the Supreme Court of Canada accepted a municipal by-law that banned "billboard signs" throughout the municipality. Billboard signs were defined as ground signs measuring more than 80 square feet. Because of this definition, signs measuring less than 80 square feet were not prohibited. Arbour J., in a very brief opinion of the Court, simply agreed with the dissenting opinion of MacPherson J.A. in the Ontario Court of Appeal.[5] MacPherson J.A. (in disagreement with the other two judges on the panel) had held that the prohibition of only large signs could be justified under s. 1 on the basis that it left room for commercial expression on smaller signs, and the larger signs were the most likely to cause distraction to motorists and visual blight. The Court of Appeal had unanimously struck down a second by-law that banned "third party signs" (signs that advertised products or services that were not produced on the premises where the sign was located). In the Supreme Court of Canada, Arbour J. (para. 1) simply commented that no appeal had been taken from that decision.[6] Once again, municipal efforts to restrict roadside advertising in the interests of environmental aesthetics and safety, while partly successful in this case, ran into a Charter barrier.[7]

---

[3] *R. v. Guignard*, [2002] 1 S.C.R. 472, paras. 29-31 contain the discussion of s. 1 justification.

[4] *Vann Niagara v. Oakville*, [2003] 3 S.C.R. 158. Arbour J. wrote the opinion of the Court.

[5] *Vann Niagara v. Oakville* (2002), 60 O.R. (3d) 1 (C.A.)

[6] The municipality adopted a new by-law that allowed third-party signs but imposed restrictions on their location. In *Vann Media v. Oakville* (2008), 311 D.L.R. (4th) 556 (Ont. C.A.), the new by-law was quashed on the basis that the restrictions were too severe to withstand s. 1 analysis.

[7] See also *Ont. v. Miracle* (2005), 74 O.R. (3d) 161 (C.A.) (upholding provincial statutory prohibition on large signs within 400 metres of controlled-access highways, except with permission of minister).

§ 43:25 Prostitution

Prior to 2014, prostitution, like tobacco, was lawful in Canada.[1] However, the Criminal Code made it an offence to communicate in a public place for the purpose of engaging in prostitution. In this, the Court was unanimous. The Supreme Court of Canada, in the *Prostitution Reference* (1990),[2] held that this type of "commercial speech" is protected by s. 2(b). However, a majority of the Court upheld the Criminal Code provision under s. 1. For the majority, the purpose of eradicating the nuisance of street-solicitation justified the limit on expression. For the dissenting minority, the law was overbroad, because it prohibited communications between prostitutes and customers regardless of whether they were causing any harm to others.

VIII. PICKETING; HATE PROPAGANDA; DEFAMATION

§ 43:26 Picketing

Picketing is the activity of members of a trade union on strike, who will assemble outside a workplace, often carrying signs.[1] The purposes of picketing are to advise the public that the picketers are on strike, to dissuade strikebreakers from entering the workplace, and to encourage consumers to boycott the goods or services produced by the struck firm. Picketing is a form of industrial action that is intended to bring economic pressure to bear on the struck employer in order to encourage the employer to settle its differences with its workers.[2] There is also a communicative element to a picket line, and therefore it constitutes "expres-

---

[Section 43:25]

[1]In 2014, the Criminal Code was amended, in response to the Supreme Court of Canada's decision in *Can. v. Bedford*, [2013] 3 S.C.R. 1101, to make it an offence to purchase (but not to sell) "sexual services".

[2]*Re ss. 193 and 195.1 of Criminal Code* (Prostitution Reference) [1990] 1 S.C.R. 1123. Dickson C.J., with La Forest and Sopinka JJ., wrote the plurality opinion; Lamer J. concurred separately; Wilson J., with L'Heureux-Dubé J., dissented. In *Can. v. Bedford*, [2013] 3 S.C.R. 1101, 2013 SCC 72, the Court struck down the prohibition on communicating in a public place, not on the basis of s. 2(b), but on the basis of s. 7: the prohibition deprived street prostitutes of their security of the person because the inability to screen customers in a public place made their work more dangerous; the imposition of increased risk was also a breach of the principles of fundamental justice which could not be justified under s. 1. The Court did not revisit the reasoning in the *Prostitution Reference* because "it is possible to resolve the case entirely on s. 7 grounds" (paras. 47, 160). For discussion of *Bedford*, see ch. 47, Fundamental Justice, under heading § 47:25, "Disproportionate laws". The Criminal Code was amended in response to *Bedford*; the amendments introduced a narrower prohibition on communicating "for the purpose of offering or providing sexual services for consideration" that applies in any "public place . . . that is or is next to a school ground, playground or daycare centre" (s. 213(1.1)).

[Section 43:26]

[1]The term is sometimes extended to demonstrations outside the labour relations setting, where persons carrying signs assemble at a particular location to protest against the policies of a government or a corporation that has offices at that location.

[2]The Supreme Court of the United States has described picketing as "speech plus", and has accorded it a lower level of constitutional protection on the basis that the "plus"

sion" within s. 2(b) of the Charter. Picketing is probably best regarded as a kind of commercial expression, since its main purpose is to encourage employees not to work and consumers not to buy. However, like other kinds of commercial expression, the picket line may also convey an implicit, or even explicit, political message. Of course, under the broad definition of "expression" established by the Supreme Court of Canada,[3] it does not matter whether the expression is categorized as commercial or political: both kinds are protected.

In the *Dolphin Delivery* case (1986),[4] a union challenged the constitutionality of an injunction that had been issued by the courts of British Columbia to prohibit the members of the union, which was on strike, from picketing the workplace of a firm that was not their employer. This "secondary picketing" was not provided for by the applicable federal labour law legislation, but the British Columbia courts had held that secondary picketing in the circumstances of this case was prohibited by the common law; it constituted the tort of inducing a breach of contract. The courts had issued the injunction in order to stop the commission of the tort. The Supreme Court of Canada held that the Charter of Rights had no application to a dispute between two private parties that was governed by the common law. Therefore, the Court refused to discharge the injunction. However, McIntyre J. for the majority of the Court, in an extended obiter dictum, recognized the "element of expression in picketing",[5] and held that it was protected expression under the Charter. He also went on to indicate that a prohibition on secondary picketing would be justified under s. 1 as a measure to prevent industrial conflict from spreading beyond the parties in dispute.

In the *Vancouver Courthouse* case (1988),[6] the Chief Justice of British Columbia, who had encountered a picket line at the courthouse on his way to work, as soon as he reached his chambers, on his own motion, and without notice to the union, issued an injunction to prohibit the picketing of the courts. The union was on lawful strike, and was picketing the courts because that was where some of their members worked. The union made application to have the injunction set aside on constitutional grounds, and this application was denied by the Supreme Court of Canada. The Court held that there was a legal basis for the injunction in that the picketing was a criminal contempt of court. The Court also held that the Charter applied to an injunction to prevent a

---

could be regulated: J.E. Nowak and R.D. Rotunda, Constitutional Law (West, St. Paul, Minn., 7th ed., 2005); sec. 16.55. In Canada, the interplay of s. 2(b) and s. 1 is likely to produce similar outcomes.

[3] §§ 43:8 to 43:11, "Meaning of expression".

[4] *RWDSU v. Dolphin Delivery*, [1986] 2 S.C.R. 573. McIntyre J., with Dickson C.J., Estey, Chouinard and Le Dain JJ., wrote the majority judgment. Beetz and Wilson JJ. wrote short concurring opinions.

[5] *RWDSU v. Dolphin Delivery*, [1986] 2 S.C.R. 573, 588.

[6] *BCGEU v. B.C.*, [1988] 2 S.C.R. 214. Dickson C.J., with Lamer, Wilson, La Forest and L'Heureux-Dubé JJ., wrote the majority opinion. McIntyre J. wrote a concurring opinion.

criminal contempt of court; and that this injunction, by prohibiting picketing, was a limit on freedom of expression. However, the Court held that the injunction was justified under s. 1. "Assuring unimpeded access to the courts" was a sufficiently important objective, and the injunction was not overly broad because it "left the union and its members free to express themselves in other places and other ways so long as they did not interfere with the right of access to the courts".[7] These two cases make clear that picketing is protected by s. 2(b) of the Charter. But the readiness with which the courts were prepared to accept the rather slender s. 1 justification in the two cases[8] indicates that laws or court orders limiting picketing in order to avoid the spread of an industrial dispute, or to facilitate access to a public facility, or to reduce the risk of violent confrontations, or for some other purpose, are likely to be upheld under s. 1.

In *U.C.F.W. v. KMart Canada* (1999),[9] a retail workers' union challenged the secondary picketing provisions in British Columbia's statutory labour code. The union, which was on strike against certain KMart stores, asserted the right to hand out leaflets to people entering and leaving KMart stores that were not involved in the dispute. The leaflets urged consumers to boycott KMart to help the union eliminate "the exploitation of employees" by the company. The union did not put up a picket line and made no attempt to impede public access to the stores. The labour code included a prohibition on secondary picketing, and the definition of picketing was wide enough to catch the union's activity of "leafleting" at secondary sites. The Labour Relations Board accordingly enjoined the union activity. On judicial review of the Board's decision, the Supreme Court of Canada followed the dictum in *Dolphin Delivery* to hold that a prohibition of picketing was a limitation of freedom of expression, and also followed the same dictum to hold that a prohibition on secondary picketing was justified by the labour-relations goal of minimizing disruption to businesses not involved in the labour dispute. However, the Court held that this prohibition was too broad in prohibiting the peaceful distribution of leaflets by union members who were not carrying placards or formed into a picket line. The prohibition of this form of expression was not justified by the legislative goal and was therefore unconstitutional. The Court struck down the prohibition on secondary picketing, but suspended the declaration of invalidity for six months to allow time for the Legislature to enact a narrower version that no longer prohibited the peaceful distribution of leaflets at secondary sites.

---

[7] *BCGEU v. B.C.*, [1988] 2 S.C.R. 214, 248. McIntyre J. in a concurring opinion held the right of access to the courts was protected by the Charter, and therefore an injunction to secure access could not be a breach of s. 2(b).

[8] In *Dolphin Delivery*, McIntyre J. said (at 590) that this was a case "where certain elements of the s. 1 analysis are obvious or self-evident", meaning that they did not require evidence. In *Vancouver Courthouse*, Dickson C.J. recited uncontradicted evidence (at 221) that indicated that the picketers were not impeding access to the courts.

[9] *U.C.F.W. v. KMart Canada*, [1999] 2 S.C.R. 1083. Cory J. wrote the opinion of the Court.

In *Pepsi-Cola Canada Beverages v. R.W.D.S.U.* (2002),[10] the union representing workers at a Pepsi-Cola bottling plant in Saskatchewan went on a legal strike against the employer, Pepsi-Cola. The union not only picketed the primary location (the bottling plant) but also secondary locations, including shops that sold Pepsi-Cola products and the homes of Pepsi-Cola management personnel. Pepsi-Cola obtained an injunction against the picketing at the secondary locations, and the question that reached the Supreme Court of Canada was whether that injunction should be confirmed or discharged. Unlike *KMart*, where the union was merely handing out leaflets at the secondary locations, in this case the union had put up picket lines at the secondary locations, and, in the case of the shops, the pickets had successfully prevented Pepsi-Cola from delivering its products to the shops. Also unlike *KMart*, where the British Columbia labour code regulated secondary picketing, in Saskatchewan secondary picketing had not been regulated by statute, so that this was a case like *Dolphin Delivery* of a dispute between private parties governed by the common law. The Court held that, while the Charter was not directly applicable, the common law should be "developed" by the courts to make it consistent with "Charter values". This was especially important in the present case, because the common law was unclear. One line of cases held that all secondary picketing was unlawful and could be enjoined. The Court rejected these (pre-Charter) cases as being insufficiently respectful of the Charter value of freedom of expression. Another line of cases held that secondary picketing was lawful provided it was peaceful and did not involve the commission of a wrongful act, meaning a crime or a tort. The "wrongful act" doctrine made no distinction between primary and secondary picketing and therefore allowed labour disputes to spread beyond the contending parties and injure neutral third parties. Nevertheless, the Court accepted the wrongful act doctrine, because it gave better protection to "labour speech".

In *Pepsi-Cola*, the Court addressed the problem of labour disputes spreading beyond the disputing parties by relying on the law of torts to avoid many (but not all) of the harms caused by picketing to neutral third parties. The Court mentioned the torts of trespass, nuisance, intimidation and inducing breach of contract. (The injunction against secondary picketing in *Dolphin Delivery* was premised on the tort of inducing breach of contract.) And if unforeseen harms occurred, the various torts, "themselves the creatures of common law, may grow and be adapted to current needs".[11] As well, the Court emphasized that the case concerned the common law, and the Court implied that if a Legislature enacted a labour relations regime that was more restrictive of secondary picketing, the Court would likely uphold the legislation

[10] *Pepsi-Cola Canada Beverages v. R.W.D.S.U.*, [2002] 1 S.C.R. 156. McLachlin C.J. and LeBel J. wrote the opinion of the unanimous Court.

[11] *Pepsi-Cola Canada Beverages v. R.W.D.S.U.*, [2002] 1 S.C.R. 156, paras. 73, 106.

(presumably under s. 1).[12] In the present case, the Court concluded that the secondary picketing of the shops that sold pepsi-cola was peaceful and did not involve the commission of a crime or a tort, and therefore could not be enjoined despite its harm to the picketed businesses. However, the picketing of the homes of the management personnel amounted to the tort of intimidation and could be enjoined.

The expression involved in picketing usually takes the form of signs publicly carried by the picketers which inform the world that the union is on strike and sometimes say something about the union point of view in the dispute with the employer. These are instances of protected expression which do not infringe personal privacy. In *Alberta v. United Food and Commercial Workers* (2013),[13] however, the union, which was on strike against a casino, videotaped the picket line at the main entrance of the casino, and posted a sign nearby stating that images of people crossing the picket line might be placed on a website called "casinoscabs". Some of the images of management personnel who crossed the line were used on a poster displayed at the picket line and in union newsletters and strike leaflets accompanied by humorous captions. The main purpose of these practices was to deter anyone from crossing the picket line. This use of private pictures without consent was forbidden by the general provisions of Alberta's privacy legislation (which did not specifically address the context of labour relations), and following complaints an adjudicator appointed under the privacy legislation ordered the union to stop collecting the private information. The union applied for judicial review of the prohibitory order, and the application made its way up to the Supreme Court of Canada. The Court held that the union tactics of collecting and disclosing personal information in the context of picketing during a lawful strike were protected by s. 2(b). The issue then became whether the privacy legislation was a justified limit under s. 1. Although the Court acknowledged that privacy was a fundamental value in a free and democratic society, and even described privacy legislation as "quasi-constitutional",[14] the Court concluded that the privacy legislation was not a justified limit on the use of personal information "for legitimate labour relations purposes".[15] Since the only vice of the legislation was its failure to take account of union tactics in a labour dispute, this would seem to be a perfect case for a constitutional

[12] *Pepsi-Cola Canada Beverages v. R.W.D.S.U.*, [2002] 1 S.C.R. 156, para. 86 ("Within the broad parameters of the Charter, legislatures remain free to craft their own statutory provisions for the governance of labour disputes, and the appropriate limits of secondary picketing.")

[13] *Alberta v. United Food and Commercial Workers*, [2013] 3 S.C.R. 733, 2013 SCC 62. Abella and Cromwell JJ. wrote the opinion of the Court.

[14] *Alberta v. United Food and Commercial Workers*, [2013] 3 S.C.R. 733, 2013 SCC 62, paras. 19, 22.

[15] *Alberta v. United Food and Commercial Workers*, [2013] 3 S.C.R. 733, 2013 SCC 62, para. 38.

exemption, which is what the Alberta Court of Appeal had granted.[16] But the Supreme Court took the extraordinary step of striking down the legislation in its entirety,[17] while suspending the declaration of invalidity for 12 months to give the legislature "time to decide how best to make the legislation constitutional".[18]

§ 43:27 Hate propaganda

Hate propaganda is material that promotes hatred against minority groups. Racial, religious and sexual minorities seem to be the most common targets. Hate propaganda is usually called "group libel" in the United States, where it probably may not be banned without offence to the first amendment.[1]

Hate propaganda is prohibited by the Criminal Code, which makes it an offence to wilfully promote hatred against "any section of the public distinguished by colour, race, religion or ethnic origin." This is of course a limit on expression, albeit expression of a worthless and harmful kind. The purpose of the ban is to promote the value of equality, because the effect of hate propaganda is to reinforce the malign attitudes towards minorities that are important barriers to the achievement of equality. It is arguable that the scope of s. 2(b) should be narrowed to make way for a ban on expression that has as its purpose the advancement of equality, which is of course guaranteed by s. 15. That approach would support a ban on hate propaganda without recourse to s. 1.[2]

In *R. v. Keegstra* (1990),[3] the Supreme Court of Canada was faced with a challenge to the hate propaganda section of the Criminal Code.

---

[16] *Alberta v. United Food and Commercial Workers*, [2013] 3 S.C.R. 733, 2013 SCC 62, para. 8.

[17] The Court based this decision on the submissions in oral argument of counsel for the province, who said that if they were unsuccessful they would prefer this remedy: *Alberta v. United Food and Commercial Workers*, [2013] 3 S.C.R. 733, 2013 SCC 62, para. 40.

[18] *Alberta v. United Food and Commercial Workers*, [2013] 3 S.C.R. 733, 2013 SCC 62, para. 41. The suspension of the declaration of invalidity would leave in force the adjudicator's order, which would mean that the union's application for judicial review would have been unsuccessful. The Court made no mention of this problem, which could have been solved by exempting the instant case from the suspension. However, although the decision mentions no dates, the strike took place in 2006 and was no doubt well and truly over by 2013 when the Court rendered its decision. This would make the union's application for relief moot, although the Court did not mention the issue of mootness.

[Section 43:27]

[1] Compare *Beauharnais v. Illinois* (1952), 343 U.S. 250 (group libel law upheld) with *R.A.V. v. St. Paul* (1992), 505 U.S. 377 (group libel law struck down but four of nine judges would have upheld a narrower law).

[2] This was the mode of reasoning employed by McIntyre J. in the *Vancouver Courthouse* case, but it was not adopted by the majority: *BCGEU v. B.C.*, [1988] 2 S.C.R. 214.

[3] *R. v. Keegstra*, [1990] 3 S.C.R. 697. Dickson C.J., with Wilson, L'Heureux-Dubé and Gonthier JJ., wrote the majority opinion; McLachlin J., with La Forest and Sopinka JJ. dissented. The companion case of *Can. v. Taylor*, [1990] 3 S.C.R. 892 upheld a ban

The Court rejected the notion that there were any content-based restrictions on the s. 2(b) right. Section 2(b) covered all messages, "however unpopular, distasteful or contrary to the mainstream".[4] The Court also rejected the notion that s. 2(b) could be narrowed by reference to the equality rights of s. 15 (or any other rights).[5] It followed that Mr. Keegstra, a schoolteacher who had been found guilty of making anti-semitic statements to his students, had been engaged in constitutionally protected activity. For the purpose of the s. 1 inquiry, however, it was relevant to take account of the competing equality values, which tended to strengthen the importance of the law's objective, and thus make it easier to uphold under s. 1.[6] The Court did go on to uphold the law under s. 1, but only by the slim margin of four to three.[7]

The Criminal Code used to contain the offence of spreading false news, which was committed by anyone who published a statement that he knew was false and that caused or was likely to cause injury to a public interest. In *R. v. Zundel* (1992),[8] the accused was charged with this offence.[9] He had published a pamphlet that claimed that the Holocaust was a fraud invented by an international conspiracy of Jews. The accused was convicted at trial, but the Supreme Court of Canada, by a majority, held that he was entitled to be acquitted on the ground that the false-news prohibition was unconstitutional. The Court was unanimous

---

imposed by the Canadian Human Rights Act on hate propaganda over the telephone. The same judges split the same way on the s. 1 issue. For commentary on the *Keegstra* case, see Weinrib, "Hate Promotion in a Free and Democratic Society: *R. v. Keegstra*" (1991), 36 McGill L.J. 1416.

[4] *R. v. Keegstra*, [1990] 3 S.C.R. 697, 729.

[5] *R. v. Keegstra*, [1990] 3 S.C.R. 697, 734, 755-758.

[6] Accord, *Ross v. New Brunswick School District No. 15*, [1996] 1 S.C.R. 825, in which the Supreme Court of Canada upheld under s. 1 the order of a human rights tribunal that required the removal from his teaching post of a schoolteacher who disseminated anti-semitic statements outside the classroom. The unanimous Court included the judges who had dissented in *R. v. Keegstra*, [1990] 3 S.C.R. 697 and *Can. v. Taylor*, [1990] 3 S.C.R. 892.

[7] After being convicted, Keegstra appealed the conviction and the case went on to the Supreme Court of Canada. Keegstra unsuccessfully applied for leave to re-argue s. 2(b) (and ss. 7 and 15): *R. v. Keegstra (No. 2)*, [1995] 2 S.C.R. 381. He was able to re-argue s. 11(d) in *R. v. Keegstra (No. 3)*, [1996] 1 S.C.R. 458, albeit without success in the outcome: ch. 51, Rights On Being Charged, under heading § 51:14, "Reverse onus clauses".

[8] *R. v. Zundel*, [1992] 2 S.C.R. 731. McLachlin J., with La Forest, L'Heureux-Dubé and Sopinka JJ., wrote the majority opinion; Cory and Iacobucci JJ., with Gonthier J., wrote the dissenting opinion.

[9] The accused was not prosecuted under the hate-propaganda provision of the Criminal Code, because that provision requires the consent of the Attorney General to the laying of a charge. The Attorney General of Ontario had refused his consent, presumably because he was unsure whether denying the Holocaust constituted an offence under that provision. A private citizen then laid a charge under the false-news provision, which had no requirement of consent by the Attorney General. The Attorney General, who in Ontario always intervenes in private prosecutions of indictable offences, decided not to stay the proceedings and instead continued the prosecution, despite his earlier decision not to consent to the laying of a charge under the hate-propaganda provision.

in deciding that the accused's activity of publishing deliberate falsehoods was protected by s. 2(b). The doctrine of content-neutrality protected falsehoods as well as truths, because the question whether a statement is true or false can be determined only by reference to the content of the statement. The Court divided four to three on the s. 1 issue, the majority holding that the false-news offence could not be justified under s. 1. The offence was therefore struck down.

The different results in *Keegstra* and *Zundel* depended on the different outcomes of the s. 1 reasoning. The hate-propaganda law that was upheld in *Keegstra* was specifically directed at the wilful promotion of hatred against identifiable groups and it was easy to accept that the prevention of harm caused by that activity was an important objective. The false-news law that was struck down in *Zundel* did not specify any particular type of statement and did not specify what type of injury to the public interest was contemplated. The false-news law was so broad that it was difficult to identify an objective that was sufficiently important to justify the limit on freedom of expression. Indeed, the objective of the false-news law in its original 13th-century form in England was to prevent the spreading of falsehoods concerning the "great men of the realm". The majority of the Court held that this could not serve as an adequate purpose today, and they refused to reinterpret the purpose as the pursuit of racial harmony (as the minority would have done) on the ground that this would be a departure from the actual historical purpose.

In *Saskatchewan v. Whatcott* (2013),[10] the claimant had distributed four flyers containing messages which condemned "homosexuality" in very strong language. In response to complaints, a tribunal appointed by the Saskatchewan Human Rights Commission issued an order prohibiting the claimant from distributing the flyers and requiring the payment of compensation to those who had filed complaints with the Commission. The statutory authority for the order was s. 14 of the province's Human Rights Code, which prohibited the publication of any representation "that exposes or tends to expose to hatred, ridicules, belittles or otherwise affronts the dignity of any person or class of persons on the basis of a prohibited ground". One of the Code's prohibited grounds was "sexual orientation". The case moved on up to the Supreme Court of Canada, where the issue was the constitutionality of s. 14 of the Code. Rothstein J., who wrote the opinion of the Court, held that s. 14 was a limit on freedom of expression. Was it a reasonable limit justified under s. 1? The objective of the law was to advance the Charter value of equality by protecting minorities from discrimination. The conflict between the claimant's right to freedom of expression and the complainants' right to equality had to be resolved by the s. 1 analysis as structured by *Oakes*.[11] As to the objective of the law, the objective of prohibiting discrimination was sufficiently important to justify a limit on freedom of

[10]*Saskatchewan v. Whatcott*, [2013] 1 S.C.R. 467, 2013 SCC 11. Rothstein J. wrote the opinion of the Court.

[11]*Saskatchewan v. Whatcott*, [2013] 1 S.C.R. 467, 2013 SCC 11, paras. 6, 66, 154.

expression. As to rational connection, there was a rational connection between the objective and the prohibition of hateful messages. However, s. 14 not only prohibited a message that exposed persons to "hatred", but also one that "ridicules, belittles or otherwise affronts the dignity" of a person. Such a message might be offensive and hurtful, but, unless it rose to the level of promoting hatred, it was not rationally connected to the prohibition of discrimination.[12] Rothstein J. held, however, that the softer language could all be severed from s. 14, leaving only the reference to "hatred", and on that basis the rational connection test was passed. As to minimum impairment, the severance of the non-hatred language also saved the provision from overbreadth—as modified, s. 14 did not limit expression any further than was necessary to combat discrimination. It was not necessary for the government to show that the prohibited speech caused actual harm; Rothstein J. took judicial notice, based on "common sense and experience", that there was a "reasonable apprehension of harm" from hate speech.[13] Rothstein J. concluded that, once the prohibition in the Code was restricted to hate speech, it was a limit on freedom of expression[14] that was justified under s. 1, and was therefore constitutional. He went on to hold that two of the flyers distributed by the claimant were properly characterized by the tribunal as hate speech, and two were not; and he modified the order of the tribunal (which had banned all four) accordingly.

§ 43:28 Defamation

The tort of defamation provides a civil remedy for a person whose reputation has been damaged by false statements made by the defendant. Under the content-neutral definition of expression, the defendant's freedom of expression is abridged by this prohibition against statements that are both false and harmful. In the United States, while there does not seem to have been a challenge to the law of defamation in general, the case where the defamed person is a public official has been held to attract the protection of the first amendment right to freedom of speech.

In *New York Times v. Sullivan* (1964),[1] the plaintiff, a public official of the city of Montgomery, Alabama, sued the New York Times newspaper for publishing an advertisement which criticized his handling of civil

[12] *Saskatchewan v. Whatcott*, [2013] 1 S.C.R. 467, 2013 SCC 11, paras. 92-95. I criticize this part of the reasoning in ch. 38, Limitation of Rights, under heading § 38:18, "Definition [of rational connection]".

[13] *Saskatchewan v. Whatcott*, [2013] 1 S.C.R. 467, 2013 SCC 11, para. 132.

[14] The claimant also claimed a sincere religious belief to justify his condemnation of "homosexuality", but the prohibition on hate speech was held to be a justified limit on freedom of religion as well: paras. 156-164; and see ch. 42, Religion, under heading § 42:6, "Other religious practices".

[Section 43:28]

[1] *New York Times v. Sullivan* (1964), 376 U.S. 254. The opinion of the majority was written by Brennan J. Black, Douglas and Goldberg JJ. concurred in the dismissal of the plaintiff's action, but they favoured an absolute bar on defamation actions by public officials.

rights demonstrations in Montgomery. The criticism included falsehoods which were defamatory of the plaintiff. Under the common law, which constituted the law of defamation in Alabama, proof of a false and defamatory statement, without more, entitled the plaintiff to damages; and the Alabama courts accordingly awarded damages. The Supreme Court of the United States reversed. Because the defamatory speech was critical of a public official, it was entitled to a degree of first amendment protection. That protection took the form of a requirement of "malice": a public official could successfully sue for defamation only if he established that the defendant made the defamatory statement with malice, that is, with the knowledge that the statement was false or at least with a reckless disregard of whether or not the statement was false. The presence of malice was required to strip the speech of its constitutional protection. In this case, the plaintiff was able to show that, if the defendant newspaper had taken the trouble to check the facts stated in the advertisement against its own news stories, it would have become aware that the facts stated in the advertisement were false. But the Court held that this carelessness on the part of the newspaper did not rise to the level of recklessness. Therefore, no malice was present; the statement was protected by the first amendment; and the plaintiff recovered nothing.

The demonstrated falsity of the speech in *New York Times v. Sullivan* did not disqualify the speech from constitutional protection. However, the point of the decision was not to protect false statements. The tort of defamation is anomalous in that it is a tort of absolute liability. Outside privileged occasions, there is no requirement of either intention or negligence. Truth (or "justification") is the only defence for factual statements, and truth must be proved by the defendant by admissible evidence. The Court in *New York Times v. Sullivan* recognized that, under the common law of defamation, "would-be critics of official conduct may be deterred from voicing their criticism, even though it is believed to be true and even though it is in fact true, because of doubt whether it can be proved in court or fear of the expense of having to do so."[2] The tendency of the law of defamation to deter the publishing of statements critical of public officials is the "libel chill" that has caused a constitutional restriction to be engrafted onto the common law where the plaintiff is a public official. Later cases have extended the constitutional requirement of proof of malice to public figures other than public officials, for example, a prominent university football coach[3] and a retired army general.[4]

After *New York Times v. Sullivan*, the highest courts of the United

[2]*New York Times v. Sullivan* (1964), 376 U.S. 254, 279 per Brennan J.

[3]*Curtis Publishing Co. v. Butts* (1967), 388 U.S. 130.

[4]*Associated Press v. Walker* (1967), 388 U.S. 130 (same report as *Curtis Publishing Co. v. Butts).* For an account of the United States' law, see L.H. Tribe, American Constitutional Law (Foundation Press, N.Y., 2nd ed., 1986), 861-886; J.E. Nowak and R.D. Rotunda, Constitutional Law (West, St. Paul, Minn., 7th ed., 2005); secs. 16.33-16.35; R.E. Brown, The Law of Defamation in Canada (Carswell, Scarborough, Ont., 2nd

Kingdom, Australia, New Zealand and South Africa eventually came to accept the concern about libel chill and modified the common law of defamation by broadening the defences available to media defendants.[5] The same development occurred in Canada, but it took longer. Before the adoption of the Charter, the Supreme Court refused to extend any special privilege to the media in reporting on the actions of public officials.[6] The protection of individual reputation took priority over freedom of the press. Even for a media defendant, the only defence to a defamatory statement of fact was proof of its truth. After the Charter of Rights elevated freedom of expression to constitutional status, the Supreme Court revisited the issue in *Hill v. Church of Scientology* (1995).[7] In this case, a Crown attorney brought an action for defamation against the Church of Scientology and its lawyer, who in a press conference had falsely claimed that the plaintiff had breached a court order. Cory J., who wrote for the Court, acknowledged that freedom of expression was now constitutionally protected, but (ignoring the risk of libel chill) he said that false and injurious statements were outside the core values protected by s. 2(b) and were not deserving of much protection. Reputation, on the other hand, although not explicitly protected by the Charter, "reflected the innate dignity of the individual" and was "related to the right of privacy which has been accorded constitutional protection".[8] Having weighed the competing values in this fashion, Cory J. concluded that the common law of defamation was not "unduly restrictive or inhibiting",[9] and required no significant modification[10] to conform to Charter values.[11] The Court upheld the trial court's award of

---

ed., 1994), vol. 2, ch. 27.

[5]The position in all four countries was reviewed and was clearly influential in *Grant v. Torstar Corp.*, [2009] 3 S.C.R. 640, paras. 66-87.

[6]*Douglas v. Tucker*, [1952] 1 S.C.R. 275; *Globe & Mail v. Boland*, [1960] S.C.R. 203; *Banks v. Globe & Mail*, [1961] S.C.R. 474; *Jones v. Bennett*, [1969] S.C.R. 277.

[7]*Hill v. Church of Scientology*, [1995] 2 S.C.R. 1130. Cory J. wrote for a Court that was unanimous on the main issues. L'Heureux-Dubé J. wrote a concurring judgment disagreeing with Cory J. on one point that did not affect the outcome. I disclose that I appeared as counsel for a coalition of media organizations to argue that the common law should be modified to give more weight to freedom of political expression.

[8]*Hill v. Church of Scientology*, 1995] 2 S.C.R. 1130, paras. 120-121. The value of protecting reputation was again invoked by Cory J. for the majority in *R. v. Lucas*, [1998] 1 S.C.R. 439, para. 94 (upholding the Criminal Code offence of defamatory libel as a reasonable limitation on freedom of expression). See also *Aubry v. Editions Vice-Versa*, [1998] 1 S.C.R. 591 (where a photograph is published without the subject's consent, the right to privacy trumps freedom of expression under the Quebec Charter of Human Rights and Freedoms, and the publisher is liable in damages).

[9]*Hill v. Church of Scientology*, 1995] 2 S.C.R. 1130, para. 137.

[10]On one point, the Court, by a majority, did hold that that the common law was unduly restrictive, and the Court extended the common law privilege that attaches to reports of judicial proceedings held in open court to pleadings and other documents publicly filed: *Hill v. Church of Scientology*, 1995] 2 S.C.R. 1130, paras. 143-156. This was the issue upon which L'Heureux-Dubé J. disagreed with the majority.

[11]The Charter of Rights did not directly apply to the proceedings (despite Hill's pub-

$1.6 million in damages—then an unprecedented award in a defamation case.[12]

There was no media defendant in *Hill*,[13] which left open the possibility that it was not the last word on the impact of the Charter on defamation, especially as the cases from other Commonwealth countries left Canada increasingly isolated[14] in its retention of the pristine common law.[15] The sea change came in *Grant v. Torstar Corp.* (2009),[16] which was an action against the Toronto Star newspaper by a wealthy landowner in northern Ontario. The newspaper had published a story reporting on the plaintiff's proposal to expand the golf course on his lakefront estate; environmental issues were raised and the concerns of residents that the plaintiff's political influence would result in the necessary approvals from the provincial government. The newspaper had repeatedly asked the plaintiff to comment on the residents' concerns, which he had refused to do. The article was published, and the plaintiff sued for defamation. The case was tried by a judge and jury. The judge directed the jury on the basis of the traditional common law. The jury rejected the defence of truth and held the newspaper liable, awarding general, aggravated and punitive damages totalling $1.475 million. This stunning verdict punished the newspaper for publishing the article, despite its high public interest in northern Ontario, and despite the newspaper's efforts to obtain the plaintiff's side of the story. On appeal, the Supreme Court of Canada, explicitly acknowledging the influence of developments in other common law countries and especially the United Kingdom, held that the common law of defamation should be modified to recognize a defence of "responsible communication on matters of public interest".[17]

---

lic position), but the common law should be modified to conform to Charter values: § 43:28 note 20, below.

[12]In catastrophic personal injury cases, the Supreme Court has established a cap of $100,000 in 1978 currency for non-pecuniary damages, which with inflation had a value of about $250,000 in 1991 (para. 173 per Cory J.). In *Hill*, ignoring the aggravated ($500,000) and punitive ($800,0000) damages, the general damages of $300,000 exceeded the personal injury cap, which of course would apply to only the most catastrophic injuries, but Cory J. held that the cap did not apply to damages for defamation, despite the Charter value at stake.

[13]The plaintiff had sued the media which carried the story of the press conference, but the media defendants settled in advance of the trial.

[14]§ 43:28 note 5, above.

[15]As for the civil law of Quebec, see *Néron v. Chambres des notaries du Québec*, [2004] 3 S.C.R. 95.

[16]*Grant v. Torstar Corp.*, [2009] 3 S.C.R. 640. McLachlin C.J. wrote the opinion for the eight-judge majority; Abella J. wrote a concurring opinion, which disagreed with the Chief Justice on the respective roles of judge and jury (discussed in the following text) and otherwise agreed with the Chief Justice.

[17]*Grant v. Torstar Corp.*, [2009] 3 S.C.R. 640, para. 7. An important progenitor of the new defence was *Cusson v. Quan* (2007), 87 O.R. (3d) 241 (C.A.), in which Sharpe J.A. for a unanimous Court proposed a public interest defence of responsible journalism. This case advanced to the Supreme Court, where it was decided as a companion to *Grant*, essentially agreeing with Sharpe J.A.'s reasons, but with some modification to

The Court reversed the damages award and ordered a new trial at which the new defence would be available to the newspaper.

McLachlin C.J., who wrote for a Court that was unanimous on all but one point,[18] rejected the central thesis of *Hill* that defamatory statements were outside the core values protected by s. 2(b). The chilling effect on the media of the nofault common law "may have the effect of inhibiting political discourse and debate on matters of public importance, and impeding the cut and thrust of discussion necessary to discovery of the truth."[19] She concluded that "the current law with respect to statements that are reliable and important to public debate does not give adequate weight to the constitutional value of free expression."[20] While the law of defamation must continue to protect reputation, it must be modified to include the new defence of responsible communication on matters of public interest. The new defence does not supplant the existing defence of truth, which continues to protect the publisher, but is an additional defence for the case where the publisher cannot prove the truth of a defamatory statement but can prove that it acted responsibly in publishing the statement. The defence is available to the traditional media, but also applies to commentary on matters of public interest by persons other than journalists. That is why the defence is called "responsible communication" rather than "responsible journalism", as it is in the United Kingdom.[21]

There are two elements to the new defence. One is that the publication must be on a matter of "public interest".[22] Public interest is not confined to government and political matters, as it has been restricted in Australia and New Zealand. Nor is it necessary that the plaintiff be a "public figure", which is the requirement in the United States. These qualifications cast the public interest too narrowly, since "the public has a genuine stake in knowing about many matters, ranging from science to the environment, religion and morality". On the other hand, "mere curiosity or prurient interest", for example, in the lives of well-known people, does not amount to a "genuine interest" that converts what is essentially a private matter into a public one for the purpose of defamation law. It will be for the trial judge to determine whether a publication is on a matter of "genuine" public interest.

---

form the new defence of responsible communication on matters of public interest: *Quan v. Cusson*, [2009] 3 S.C.R. 712.

[18]Disagreement on the respective roles of judge and jury led to a concurring opinion by Abella J.

[19]*Grant v. Torstar Corp.*, [2009] 3 S.C.R. 640, para. 57.

[20]*Grant v. Torstar Corp.*, [2009] 3 S.C.R. 640, para. 65. The Charter did not directly apply to the common law, but the Court followed *Hill* to hold that it had the power to modify the common law to bring it into conformity with "Charter values": *Grant v. Torstar Corp.*, [2009] 3 S.C.R. 640, para. 44. See ch. 37, Application of the Charter, under heading § 37:12, "Common law".

[21]The leading cases are *Reynolds v. Times Newspapers*, [2001] 2 A.C. 127 (H.L.); *Jameel v. Wall Street Journal*, [2007] 1 A.C. 359 (H.L.).

[22]*Grant v. Torstar Corp.*, [2009] 3 S.C.R. 640, paras. 99-109.

The second element of the new defence is that the publication must be "responsible".[23] This will apply where the publisher exercised due diligence in trying to verify the defamatory allegation. What amounts to due diligence depends on all the circumstances, including the seriousness of the allegation, the public importance of the matter, its urgency, the status and reliability of the source of the information, and whether the plaintiff's side of the story was sought and accurately reported. While no particular factor is dispositive, the last-mentioned factor will normally be of great significance because to publish defamatory allegations of fact without giving the target an opportunity to respond is not only unfair but increases the risk of inaccuracy. The inquiry into the due diligence of the publisher "obviates the need for a separate inquiry into malice".[24]

The point on which the Court divided in *Grant* was the respective roles of judge and jury. According to McLachlin C.J. for the eight-judge majority,[25] the question whether the publication is on a matter of public interest is for the judge to decide, on the basis that this is primarily a question of law;[26] but the question whether the publisher has acted responsibly is for the jury to decide, on the basis that this is primarily a question of fact. According to Abella J.,[27] the judge should decide the second issue as well as the first. She viewed both issues as conceptually similar, predominantly legal, and having "constitutional dimensions". In my view, Abella J.'s lonely view is the better one. The new defence of responsible communication would better serve its purpose of protecting freedom of expression if the judge were to decide both issues, since there is a risk of jury bias in cases like *Grant* (and *New York Times v. Sullivan* was the same) where a local plaintiff is suing a remote city newspaper, or where the defamatory story presents an unpopular point of view.

The common law of defamation has always been more forgiving to statements of *opinion* about individuals in the public eye than it has historically been to statements of fact. The defence of "fair comment" is available to the publisher of an opinion so long as the opinion (1) is based on fact, (2) is related to a matter of public interest, and (3) is one that an honest (but not necessarily reasonable) person could hold. In

---

[23] *Grant v. Torstar Corp.*, [2009] 3 S.C.R. 640, paras. 110-125.

[24] *Grant v. Torstar Corp.*, [2009] 3 S.C.R. 640, para. 125. That is because malice is irrelevant; due diligence is the test. Unfortunately, McLachlin C.J. muddied the water by going on to say (para. 125) that: "A defendant who has acted with malice in publishing defamatory allegations has by definition not acted responsibly". But a publisher motivated by malice might still have exercised the utmost care in investigating and publishing a news story, in which case the publisher is surely entitled to the defence of responsible communication. Any other conclusion would be an invitation for "a separate inquiry into malice", the very inquiry she said was precluded, and which she obviously intended to preclude.

[25] *Grant v. Torstar Corp.*, [2009] 3 S.C.R. 640, paras. 127-135.

[26] Public interest is also a requirement for the defence of fair comment (discussed in the next paragraph of text), where it is also an issue for the judge.

[27] *Grant v. Torstar Corp.*, [2009] 3 S.C.R. 640, paras. 142-145.

WIC Radio v. Simpson (2008),[28] a case that was decided a year before *Grant* introduced the defence of responsible communication on matters of public interest to defamatory statements of fact, the Supreme Court held that the law of fair comment did not require any modification to bring it into line with Charter values: "Commentators are allowed broad latitude under the existing law of fair comment."[29] The case certainly illustrated the latitude. The defendants were Rafe Mair, a radio talk show host in Vancouver, and the radio station that carried his show. Mair had criticized the plaintiff on air and implied that she would condone violence against the "homosexual community". This was false and, because it injured the reputation of the plaintiff, it was defamatory. However, because the statement was one of opinion, not fact, no demonstration of truth was required. The plaintiff had been conducting a public campaign to promote "family values" in the schools and had often made public pronouncements against "homosexuality" in extreme terms. The Court held that all three elements of the defence of fair comment were present. The statement was based on fact (element (1)) and related to a matter of public interest (element (2)). The difficult point was honest belief (element (3)), because Mair had testified that he himself did not believe that the plaintiff would condone violence, and that he did not intend the imputation that his words carried. But the Court held that the plaintiff's public pronouncements "could support an honest belief on the part of at least some of her listeners that she 'would condone violence against gay people' ".[30] That was enough to sustain the defence of fair comment, and the action for defamation was dismissed.

The Quebec Civil Code, unlike the common law jurisdictions of the world, does not provide for a separate tort (delict) of defamation with its own distinctive rules. Actions for defamation fall under the general rubric of actions for injury caused by "fault" under article 1457 of the Code. In *Néron v. Chambre des notaires du Québec* (2004),[31] an action for defamation was brought in Quebec against the CBC. The CBC had broadcast a program that criticized the Chambre des notaires du Québec (the body that governs notaries in the province) for delays in dealing with complaints by members of the public. Néron, who was a communications consultant to the Chambre, wrote a letter to the CBC, alleging errors in the program. The CBC aired a follow-up program, in which they quoted part of the letter and pointed out (correctly) that on two points the letter was wrong (and the program had been right). Néron sued the CBC for defamation, alleging that the CBC's second program had injured his reputation. The trial judge awarded heavy damages of $673,153, and this award was upheld by a majority of the Supreme Court of Canada. The "fault" of the CBC in its broadcast consisted in using only those

[28]*WIC Radio v. Simpson*, [2008] 2 S.C.R. 420. Binnie J. wrote the opinion of the seven-judge majority; LeBel and Rothstein JJ. wrote concurring opinions.

[29]*WIC Radio v. Simpson*, [2008] 2 S.C.R. 420, para. 25.

[30]*WIC Radio v. Simpson*, [2008] 2 S.C.R. 420, para. 60.

[31]*Néron v. Chambre des notaires du Québec*, [2004] 3 S.C.R. 95. LeBel J. wrote for the six-judge majority of the seven-judge panel. Binnie J. wrote a dissenting opinion.

parts of the letter that made false statements, in not allowing the plaintiff time to check up on his errors and retract them, and in adopting a defensive tone. These were breaches of professional journalistic standards. LeBel J. for the majority of the Court said that, in an action for defamation under the Quebec Civil Code, "fault is measured against professional journalistic standards".[32] The CBC was therefore liable for the injury to the plaintiff's reputation.

What is astonishing about the decision in *Néron* is that the CBC's statements were true, and the broadcast (on the deficiencies of self-regulation of notaries) was in the public interest. This was acknowledged by LeBel J., who explained that "truth and public interest are merely factors to consider in the overall contextual analysis of fault"; and in this case they were not "the determinative factors".[33] The determinative factor was the breach of professional journalistic standards. Surely, this ruling loses sight of the principle that the law of defamation must be justified as a reasonable limit on freedom of the press. Binnie J., alone in dissent, was troubled by the impact on the freedom of the press. He said:[34]

> My deeper concern is that in balancing press freedom against the respondents' interest in the protection of their reputation, my colleague [LeBel J.] puts insufficient weight on the constitutional right of members of the Quebec public to have access to true and accurate information about matters of legitimate interest and concern. An award of this size built on such a thin foundation can only discourage the fulfilment by the media of their mandate in a free and democratic society to afflict the comfortable and to comfort the afflicted. . . .

But that was the dissenting view. The effect of *Néron* is that, in Quebec, any statement in the media that lowers someone's reputation, however true and however important the statement may be, will expose the publisher to liability for defamation if the publisher was guilty of some lapse of professional journalistic standards.[35] The new common law defence of responsible communication in the public interest now shares with the civil law a focus on due diligence on the part of the publisher, but of course the common law defence is needed only to protect statements that are false whereas the civil law defence is needed to protect statements that are true (as well as those that are false).

---

[32] *Néron v. Chambre des notaires du Québec*, [2004] 3 S.C.R. 95, para. 132.

[33] *Néron v. Chambre des notaires du Québec*, [2004] 3 S.C.R. 95, para. 60. See also *Bou Malhab v. Diffusion Métromédia*, [2011] 1 S.C.R. 214, para. 25 (In an action for defamation in Quebec: "The truth of the message will be only one of the factors used to determine whether conduct is wrongful.").

[34] *Néron v. Chambre des notaires du Québec*, [2004] 3 S.C.R. 95, para. 83.

[35] For criticism of *Néron*, see M.J. Freiman, "The Public Law Consequences of Private Disputes: *Néron v. CBC* and the Law of Defamation" (2005) 29 Supreme Court L.R. (2d) 321.

IX. PORNOGRAPHY

§ 43:29 Pornography

Attempts to ban the description or depiction of sexual activity have traditionally been justified as protecting public morality by preventing the dissemination of material that is morally objectionable. They have been a serious threat to freedom of expression, resulting in many jurisdictions in the banning of the works of some of the greatest novelists, including D. H. Lawrence, James Joyce and Vladimir Nabokov. Another way of looking at pornography that has been suggested by feminist writers and is now widely accepted is as a first cousin to hate propaganda. On this basis, what is offensive about pornography is not the explicit portrayal of sex, nor the flouting of conventional morality, but rather the reinforcement of discrimination against women.[1] On this basis, the emphasis of pornography law would shift to focus on the depiction of violence, cruelty, degradation and humiliation which is apparently a feature of much pornography, and which promotes the attitudes that help to bar the achievement of equality by women. Even on this basis, laws banning pornography raise major problems of definition and create risks of the suppression of serious ideas. However, the advancement of the value of equality does constitute a far more important objective than the protection of conventional morality, and greatly strengthens the argument that can be made for s. 1 justification.

The Supreme Court of the United States has distinguished between pornography and obscenity, and has held that the latter is not protected by the first amendment's guarantee of freedom of speech. In *Miller v. California* (1973),[2] the Court settled on a three-part test to identify obscenity: (1) the material must appeal to the prurient interest; (2) it must be patently offensive in light of community standards; and (3) it must lack any serious literary, artistic, political, or scientific value.[3] The Court has not revised this test since 1973 and has not shifted the emphasis to the equality value now espoused by the Supreme Court of Canada.[4] (The Supreme Court of the United States, unlike the highest courts of all the other common law countries, pays no attention to developments in other countries.) However, the American test is a narrow one and the reference to community standards arguably builds in a shift in emphasis as community standards increasingly tolerate explicit descriptions of consensual sexual activity, but not depictions of violence, cruelty and humiliation of the kind that the Canadian Court has singled out as obscenity.

[Section 43:29]

[1]See, e.g., K.A. Lahey, "The Charter and Pornography" in Weiler and Elliot (eds.) Litigating the Values of a Nation (1986), 265; other points of view are developed in the essays by L. Arbour (at 294) and R. Elliot (at 308).

[2]*Miller v. California* (1973), 413 U.S. 15, 24.

[3]Compare *Roth v. United States* (1957), 354 U.S. 476, 484 (obscenity is "utterly without redeeming social importance").

[4]*Ashcroft v. Free Speech Coalition* (2002), 535 U.S. 234 (applying *Miller* test and striking down the Child Pornography Prevention Act).

The expression cases in the Supreme Court of Canada make clear that pornography, including obscenity, is protected expression in Canada. Pornography, however defined, can only be identified by reference to the content of the challenged material. Since there are no content-based restrictions on s. 2(b),[5] it follows that pornography is covered by the guarantee.

In *R. v. Butler* (1992),[6] the accused, who operated a sex shop, was found guilty of various charges of selling obscene material and possessing obscene material for sale. He challenged the constitutionality of these prohibitions of obscenity, which were enacted by the Criminal Code. The Code's definition of obscenity was as follows:

> For the purposes of this Act, any publication a dominant characteristic of which is the undue exploitation of sex, or of sex and any one or more of the following subjects, namely, crime, horror, cruelty and violence, shall be deemed to be obscene.

The Supreme Court of Canada held unanimously that the prohibition of obscenity offended s. 2(b) of the Charter. The purpose and the effect of the prohibition was "to restrict the communication of certain types of materials based on their content".[7] Since there are no content-based restrictions on s. 2(b), it followed that obscene material was covered by the guarantee. The Court held, however, that the prohibition could be upheld under s. 1.

Sopinka J. for the majority of the Supreme Court of Canada held that the "undue" exploitation of sex contemplated material that (1) portrayed explicit sex with violence, or (2) portrayed explicit sex without violence, but in a degrading or dehumanizing manner by "[placing] women (and sometimes men) in positions of subordination, servile submission or humiliation".[8] These forms of pornography, when not required by the internal necessities of a serious work of art, were intolerable to the Canadian community, "not because [they offended] against morals but because [they were] perceived by public opinion to be harmful to society, particularly to women".[9] Sopinka J. acknowledged that the perception of harm was "not susceptible of exact proof, but he referred to" a substantial body of opinion that holds that the portrayal of persons being subjected to degrading or dehumanizing sexual treatment results in harm, particularly to women and therefore to society as a whole", and

---

[5]§§ 43:8 to 43:11, "Meaning of expression".

[6]*R. v. Butler*, [1992] 1 S.C.R. 452. The majority opinion was written by Sopinka J. with the concurrence of six others. A concurring opinion was written by Gonthier J. with the concurrence of L'Heureux-Dubé J. Gonthier J. generally agreed with Sopinka J., but would have interpreted the definition of obscenity and the prospect of harm to society somewhat more broadly than Sopinka J.

[7]*R. v. Butler*, [1992] 1 S.C.R. 452, 489.

[8]*R. v. Butler*, [1992] 1 S.C.R. 452, 479.

[9]*R. v. Butler*, [1992] 1 S.C.R. 452, para. 479.

he said that "it would be reasonable to conclude that there is an appreciable risk of harm to society in the portrayal of such material".[10]

These findings could not of course overcome the rule that all expressive activity, no matter how repulsive its content, was protected by s. 2(b). However, they did provide the basis to allow the Court to uphold the obscenity law under s. 1. Section 1 requires that a limit on a right be "prescribed by law", which means that a law must not be excessively vague; and this has been a fatal flaw in some attempts to control pornography.[11] Sopinka J. pointed out that the test of vagueness had to be applied to the language of a statute as it had been interpreted, and the gloss of harmfulness placed by judicial decisions on the language of the Code gave it enough precision to count as an "intelligible standard".[12]

The same judicial gloss enabled Sopinka J. to hold that the objective of the Code was not merely moral disapprobation but "the avoidance of harm to society".[13] This was a sufficiently important objective to justify a limit on freedom of expression. It was similar to the prevention of the influence of hate propaganda, which had been accepted as a legitimate reason for the limitation of freedom of expression in the *Keegstra* case.[14] The prohibition also satisfied the proportionality tests stipulated by *Oakes* in that it did not extend beyond material that created a risk of harm to society, and in particular did not prohibit sexually explicit material that was neither accompanied by violence nor degrading or dehumanizing. Nor did it prohibit material that was required by the internal necessities of serious artistic work. Nor did the Code's prohibition touch the private possession or viewing of the obscene materials. Therefore, the prohibition was no wider than was necessary to accomplish the legislative purpose of preventing harm to society. For these reasons, Sopinka J. concluded that the prohibition of obscenity was justified under s. 1.

The Criminal Code's definition of obscenity is also used as the standard for border control of pornography. The federal Customs Tariff Act prohibits the importation into Canada of books, magazines and pictures that are obscene under the Criminal Code definition. In *Little Sisters Book and Art Emporium v. Canada* (2000),[15] the Little Sisters bookstore challenged the validity of the prohibition on a number of grounds includ-

---

[10] *R. v. Butler*, [1992] 1 S.C.R. 452, 479-480.

[11] *Re Ont. Film and Video Appreciation Society* (1984), 41 O.R. (2d) 583 (C.A.) (film censorship law invalid for failure to supply standards of censorship); *Luscher v. Revenue Can.*, [1985] 1 F.C. 85 (C.A.) (prohibition of importation of "immoral" or "indecent" books too vague to satisfy s. 1).

[12] *R. v. Butler*, [1992] 1 S.C.R. 452, 491.

[13] *R. v. Butler*, [1992] 1 S.C.R. 452, 493. For criticism of this definition of the objective of obscenity law, see B.W. Miller, "Morals Laws in an Age of Rights: Hart and Devlin at the Supreme Court of Canada" (2010) 55 Am. J. of Jurisprudence 79.

[14] *R. v. Keegstra*, [1990] 3 S.C.R. 697.

[15] *Little Sisters Book and Art Emporium v. Canada*, [2000] 2 S.C.R. 1120. Binnie J. wrote the opinion for the majority (who upheld the legislation), consisting of himself, McLachlin C.J., L'Heureux-Dubé, Gonthier, Major and Bastarache JJ. Iacobucci J. wrote

ing a frontal assault on the *Butler* test itself. Little Sisters was a company that operated a LGBTQ bookstore in Vancouver. The company had had great difficulty in importing LGBTQ erotica into Canada because of frequent seizures by customs officials. The company argued that the *Butler* test was inherently discriminatory, because the harm-based approach used a single community standard that was inevitably insensitive to the nature and significance of erotica directed to the minority LGBTQ communities. The Supreme Court of Canada held that it was not inappropriate to use a single community standard of obscenity, pointing out that the Little Sisters bookstore was open to the public. Moreover, although it was true that the customs legislation had been administered in a way that was discriminatory, the *Butler*-interpreted definition of obscenity in the legislation targeted harm in the form of violence, degradation and dehumanization that could occur in the context of same-sex as well as heterosexual relationships. The Supreme Court of Canada unanimously denied the claim that the *Butler* test was unconstitutional in its application to LGBTQ erotica. Iacobucci J., writing for a dissenting minority, would still have struck down the prohibition of obscenity in the Customs Tariff Act, with a postponement of 18 months to require Parliament to supplement the prohibition by the enactment of procedural safeguards to ensure fairer, speedier, more expert and more objective adjudication of potentially obscene material. Binnie J., writing for the majority, was content to identify the administrative failures that had permitted the discriminatory behaviour to occur, and to lay down guidelines for the future use of the officials who would be administering the prohibition. The majority accordingly upheld the legislation.[16]

Most provinces attempt to regulate the exhibition and distribution (sale or rental) of films by empowering a statutory review board to classify movies according to a system that will help viewers choose age-appropriate films, and alert them to sexual or violent content. This power of classification is not controversial, and may not even be a limit on freedom of expression. However, many provinces also confer on the board a power of censorship, namely, the power to deny approval to exhibit or distribute a film that is regarded as pornographic (or to insist on cuts before approval is granted). This power of censorship (or prior restraint) is the most severe kind of limit on freedom of expression.[17] Can such a limit be justified under s. 1?

Ontario established a system of film censorship that allowed a film review board to ban or cut films proposed for public exhibition. This law was struck down at the threshold of the s. 1 analysis, because the Court

---

the opinion for the dissenting minority (who would have struck down the legislation), consisting of himself, Arbour and LeBel JJ.

[16]The majority did strike down a reverse onus clause that placed the burden of challenging a customs classification on the importer. The majority held (paras. 97-105) that, in its application to expressive materials, the burden of proving that the material was obscene had to be on the Crown.

[17]§ 43:12, "Prior restraint".

of Appeal held that the discretion of the censor board was not sufficiently constrained by legal standards to meet the s. 1 requirement of "prescribed by law".[18] The Legislature enacted a new law that bound the board to follow criteria prescribed by regulation, and authorized the making of a regulation to prescribe the criteria. The government exercised this authority by making a regulation that stipulated a number of cinematic images that would justify refusal to permit a film to be exhibited or distributed. The Superior Court of Justice held that the new regulation satisfied the requirement of "prescribed by law", but that it was not a "reasonable limit" under s. 1, because the power of censorship that it granted extended to material that would not be obscene under the *Butler* test. (The regulation had been drafted before the decision in *Butler.)* The regulation was therefore struck down.[19] The government did not appeal this decision, which was clearly correct, but went back to the drawing board a second time. New regulations were enacted to narrow the scope of the power to refuse approval, the object being to keep the power within the *Butler* test.[20]

In *R. v. Sharpe* (2001),[21] the accused challenged the constitutionality of the Criminal Code offence of possession of "child pornography". Child pornography was defined as a picture of a child engaged in explicit sexual activity, a picture of a child's sexual organ or anal region, and written material that advocated sexual activity with a child that would be a Criminal Code offence. The Supreme Court of Canada held that the offence was a limit on freedom of expression under s. 2(b), and the only question was whether it could be justified under s. 1. This turned entirely on whether the mere possession of child pornography was harmful to children. The Court held that possession contributed to the market for child pornography and the market caused the production of child pornography which often involved the exploitation of children. As well, possession "may facilitate the seduction and grooming of victims and may break down inhibitions or incite potential offences".[22] While these effects were not susceptible of scientific proof, the Court followed *Butler* to hold that there was a "reasoned apprehension of harm", and that was

[18] *Re Ont. Film and Video Appreciation Society* (1984), 45 O.R. (2d) 80 (C.A.); *Re Ont. Film and Video Appreciation Society* (1984), 41 O.R. (2d) 583 (C.A.).

[19] *R. v. Glad Day Bookshops* (2004), 70 O.R. (3d) 691 (S.C.J.).

[20] Ont. Reg. 2004/04, effective July 5, 2004. This regulation was made under the Theatres Act, R.S.O. 1990, c. T.6. The Theatres Act was then replaced by the Film Classification Act, 2005, S.O. 2005, c. 17, which was then replaced by the Film Content Information Act, 2020, S.O. 2020, c. 36. The Film Content Information Act eliminates the Ontario Film Review Board, along with the film classification and licensing requirements for film exhibitors, retailers and distributors, and instead requires exhibitors to provide publicly-available information about the content of films; the Act maintains the existing requirements for adult movies and video games.

[21] *R. v. Sharpe*, [2001] 1 S.C.R. 45. McLachlin C.J. wrote the opinion for the majority, consisting of herself, Iacobucci, Major, Binnie, Arbour and LeBel JJ. A concurring opinion was written by L'Heureux-Dubé, Gonthier and Bastarache JJ.

[22] *R. v. Sharpe*, [2001] 1 S.C.R. 45, para. 28 per McLachlin C.J.

enough.[23] Once harm to children was inferred,[24] the various elements of the *Oakes* test fell into place, and the prohibition of possession of child pornography was upheld under s. 1.[25]

In the United States, a very similar case yielded the opposite result. The issue in *Ashcroft v. Free Speech Coalition* (2002)[26] was the validity of the federal Child Pornography Prevention Act, which banned child pornography in terms not markedly different from Canada's Criminal Code prohibition. The Supreme Court of the United States found the Act to be unconstitutional on its face. There was no constitutional problem in banning material that was obscene under the *Miller* test (described above), because that speech was unprotected.[27] Nor was there any constitutional problem in banning material that, although not obscene, depicted sexual activity by real children, because of the state's interest in protecting children from exploitation in the production process. But the Act (like its Canadian counterpart) also banned child pornography that used artificial images of children or used adults who looked like children, and those depictions did not involve real children. The Act also reached material that was not obscene under the *Miller* test, for example, because it had some redeeming literary or artistic value. The Court held—and this was the difference between the outcome of this case and that of the Canadian decision in *Sharpe*—that the tendency of child pornography to encourage or support unlawful acts by pedophiles was not a sufficient constitutional justification for the ban. Because the Act banned a substantial amount of protected speech, the majority of the Court held that the Act was wholly unconstitutional.

X. ACCESS TO PUBLIC PROPERTY

§ 43:30 Access to public property

Does s. 2(b) confer a right to use public property as a forum of expression?

[23]*R. v. Sharpe*, [2001] 1 S.C.R. 45, para. 85 per McLachlin C.J.

[24]McLachlin C.J. for the majority of the Court discussed at length the question whether hypothetical examples of child pornography could be imagined that would be caught by the definition but where possession would create no risk of harm to children. She took the view that there were two such examples, namely, private material created by the accused and private recordings of lawful sexual activity by the accused, and she read into the legislation exceptions for those two categories. The minority disagreed that these two situations were free of harm to children, and would not have read in the exceptions.

[25]The case went back to trial, and Sharpe was convicted of two charges involving photographs; he was acquitted of the charges involving his own writings, on the ground that they did not advocate sexual activity with children, and therefore did not come within the Criminal Code definition of child pornography: *R. v. Sharpe*, [2002] B.C.J. No. 610 (QL).

[26]*Ashcroft v. Free Speech Coalition* (2002), 535 U.S. 234. The opinion of the majority was written by Kennedy J. Thomas J. wrote a brief concurring opinion. Rehnquist C.J. (with Scalia J.) and O'Connor J. wrote partially dissenting opinions; they would have upheld the Act in part.

[27]*Miller v. California* (1973), 413 U.S. 15.

With respect to *private* property, the general rule (of both the common law and the civil law) is that the owner has the power to determine who uses the property and for what purpose. This means that the owner has the power to determine the extent if at all that the property can be used as the location of signs, placards, pickets, speeches or other forms of expression. This rule of proprietary power obviously affects the kind and amount of expression in our society. But the rule is not affected by s. 2(b) of the Charter, because the Charter does not apply to private action. It is therefore clear that s. 2(b) confers no right to use private property as a forum of expression.[1]

With respect to *public* property, since the Charter applies to governmental action, s. 2(b) is potentially applicable.[2] In *Committee for the Commonwealth of Canada v. Canada* (1991),[3] the question arose whether the manager of Crown-owned Dorval Airport in Montreal could prohibit the distribution of political leaflets in the Airport. The Supreme Court of Canada held unanimously that the prohibition was unconstitutional. The Court was unanimous that s. 2(b) conferred a right to use public property for expression purposes; the government did not possess the absolute power of a private owner to control access to and use of public property. However, the Court splintered into three camps in its attempt to define the scope of the right of expression.

The most expansive view of the right of expression on public property was taken by L'Heureux-Dubé J., who held that s. 2(b) conferred a right to use all governmental property for purposes of expression. In her view, any limitation of access or use, even in respect of places not generally accessible by the public, would have to be justified under s. 1. McLachlin J. disagreed with her colleague, but proposed an alternative that in my view is virtually indistinguishable. She said that a prohibition on expression on governmental property would violate s. 2(b) only if the person seeking access was pursuing one of the three purposes of the guarantee of freedom of expression. Those purposes, it will be recalled, are (1) seeking truth, (2) participation in decision-making, and (3) individual self-fulfilment.[4] McLachlin J. assumed that a person or group demanding an audience in "the Prime Minister's office, an airport control tower, a prison cell or a judge's private chambers" would be unable to fit within

---

[Section 43:30]

[1] *Committee for Cth. of Can. v. Can.*, [1991] 1 S.C.R. 139, 228 per McLachlin J.

[2] Note, however, that not all "public" institutions are covered by the Charter. Universities and hospitals, for example, are sufficiently independent of government to be largely outside the application of the Charter: see ch. 37, Application of Charter, under heading §§ 37:6 to 37:14, "Burden of rights". Their property therefore counts largely as private property for this purpose.

[3] *Committee for Cth. of Can. v. Can.*, [1991] 1 S.C.R. 139. While the seven-judge bench was unanimous, there were three concurring opinions: Lamer C.J.'s opinion was agreed to by Sopinka and Cory JJ.; McLachlin J.'s opinion was concurred in by La Forest and Gonthier JJ.; L'Heureux-Dubé J. wrote a third opinion.

[4] *Committee for Cth. of Can. v. Can.*, [1991] 1 S.C.R. 139, 238-239, following the dictum in *Irwin Toy v. Quebec*, [1989] 1 S.C.R. 927, 976.

one of the three purposes. But why not? The purposes are easily wide enough to embrace any statement or demonstration in any imaginable forum. In the end, therefore, McLachlin J. is in the same camp as L'Heureux-Dubé: any restriction on access for the purpose of expression anywhere on government property would need to be justified under s. 1. Nor should it be assumed that justification under s. 1 would necessarily be easy to establish. Where access to a particular building or office is not governed by carefully formulated rules, but is controlled on an ad hoc basis, the exclusion of religious proselytizers or political protesters (for example) would probably not satisfy s. 1's requirement of "prescribed by law".[5]

It seems obvious to me that proprietary control over government property ought not to disappear entirely even in the face of an assertion of expression rights. That was the view of Lamer C.J. in the *Commonwealth of Canada* case. Lamer C.J. would allow proprietary controls over access or use to the extent necessary to carry out the principal function of the governmental place. Thus a rule of silence in the parliamentary library would not violate s. 2(b), and would not need to be justified under s. 1, because silence is essential to the function of the library. Only if expression would be compatible with the function of the place, would a limitation on expression offend s. 2(b) and require justification under s. 1. Lamer C.J.'s functional test is not free of difficulty. As McLachlin J. pointed out, it does involve identifying and defining the function of any governmental place in which expression rights have been asserted; it involves determining what degree of expressive activity would be compatible with the function; and, because these inquiries take place within s. 2(b) rather than s. 1, the onus of proof rests on the person asserting freedom of expression. However, the functional test provides more certainty than the s. 1 inquiry that would be required by the opinions of L'Heureux-Dubé and McLachlin JJ. Nor is the functional test unduly restrictive of the guarantee of freedom of expression. It is far wider than the American doctrine of "public forum", under which restrictions on speech on public property require substantial justification (strict scrutiny) only if they apply to places that have traditionally been used for free speech, such as streets, sidewalks and parks.[6] Lamer C.J.'s functional test would extend the constitutional guarantee to expression on any governmental property so long as the expression was compatible with the principal function of the property. In the *Commonwealth* case itself, because the distribution of political leaflets was compatible with the airport's function of serving the travelling public, Lamer C.J. concluded that the plaintiffs had a constitutional

[5]Even a carefully framed rule, if it took the form only of an "internal directive or policy", would not satisfy "prescribed by law", according to Lamer J. (with two others) in this case. McLachlin J. (also with two others) on the other hand, held that internal directives as to the management of Crown property would qualify as "prescribed by law". The seventh judge, L'Heureux-Dubé, did not express an opinion on this issue.

[6]L.H. Tribe, American Constitutional Law (Foundation Press, N.Y., 2nd ed., 1986), at 986; J.E. Nowak and R.D. Rotunda, Constitutional Law (West, St. Paul, Minn., 7th ed., 2005); secs. 16.45-16.47.

right to carry out the practice. L'Heureux-Dubé and McLachlin JJ., relying on their wider views of the constitutional right of access, reached the same conclusion, so that the Court was unanimous in its result.

In *Ramsden v. Peterborough* (1993),[7] the Supreme Court of Canada struck down a municipal by-law that prohibited the placing of posters "on any public property" within the municipality. The defendant was a musician who advertised performances of his band by placing posters on hydro poles (utility poles carrying electrical transmission lines) on public property in the municipality. He was charged with a breach of the by-law. He defended the charge on the basis that the by-law was unconstitutional. The opinion of the Supreme Court of Canada was written by Iacobucci J., who had not been a member of the Court at the time of the *Commonwealth* case. There was no doubt, of course, that "postering" was a form of expression. Was postering on public property protected by s. 2(b)? In answering this question, Iacobucci J. noted the three different approaches that were taken in the *Commonwealth* case, but made no attempt to resolve the conflict. Instead, he held that, under each of the three approaches, postering on at least some kinds of public property, including utility poles, would be protected by s. 2(b). That moved the issue to s. 1. Iacobucci J. recognized that the municipality's objectives in enacting the by-law, which were to reduce littering, aesthetic blight, traffic hazards and hazards to persons engaged in the repair of utility poles, were sufficiently important to justify some limitation of freedom of expression. He held, however, that a complete ban on postering on all public property was broader than necessary to accomplish the objectives. The by-law therefore failed the leastdrastic-means requirement of s. 1 justification, and was unconstitutional.[8]

In *Montreal v. 2952-1366 Quebec* (2005),[9] a strip club in Montreal set up a loudspeaker at its street entrance which it used to broadcast the music and commentary that accompanied the show within. The club was charged under a city by-law that prohibited noise produced by sound equipment that could be heard outside a building. The by-law did not contain language stipulating any particular level of noise or any disturbance of neighbours or passers-by, but McLachlin C.J. and Deschamps J., writing for the majority of the Supreme Court of Canada, interpreted the by-law as applying only to "noise that adversely affects the enjoy-

[7] *Ramsden v. Peterborough*, [1993] 2 S.C.R. 1084. The opinion of the Court was written by Iacobucci J.

[8] A by-law prohibiting postering on utility poles and buildings and a by-law prohibiting postering on roads were both struck down as too broad in *Toronto v. Quickfall* (1994), 16 O.R. (3d) 665 (C.A.). A by-law placing a cap on the annual increase in number of billboards in the municipality, and on the ultimate total, was upheld under s. 1 on aesthetic grounds in *Urban Outdoor Trans Adv. Scarborough* (2001), 196 D.L.R. (4th) 304 (Ont. C.A.).

[9] *Montreal v. 2952-1366 Quebec*, [2005] 3 S.C.R. 141. McLachlin C.J. and Deschamps J. wrote the opinion of the six-judge majority. Binnie J. wrote a dissenting opinion. Only seven judges heard the case.

ment of the environment".[10] On that basis, they held that the by-law was authorized by the city's statutory power to define and prohibit nuisances. That answered the administrative-law question, and led to the constitutional question: was the by-law contrary to s. 2(b)? The broadcast conveyed a message about the show that was going on in the club. That was expression. Although the message originated in private premises where s. 2(b) would not apply, it was the transmission into the public street (public property) that was prohibited by the by-law. Did s. 2(b) protect expression that was transmitted into a public street? McLachlin C.J. and Deschamps J. now created a single test from the three approaches in the *Commonwealth* case by combining elements of the Lamer opinion and the McLachlin opinion. (The L'Heureux-Dubé opinion was not mentioned.) The reformulated test for the application of s. 2(b) on public property was:[11]

> whether the place is a public place where one would expect constitutional protection for free expression on the basis that expression in that place does not conflict with the purposes which s. 2(b) is intended to serve, namely (1) democratic discourse, (2) truth-finding and (3) self-fulfillment.

To answer the question it was necessary to consider the "historical function" of the place, the "actual function of the place", and "whether other aspects of the place suggest that expression within it would undermine the values underlying free expression".[12] In this case, the streets "are clearly areas of public, as opposed to private, concourse, where expression of many varieties has long been accepted".[13] Therefore, the club's broadcast into the street was protected by s. 2(b). The majority went on to hold that the by-law was justified as a reasonable limit under s. 1, despite its lack of standards with respect to the level or effects of the prohibited noise.

The public property in *Greater Vancouver Transportation Authority v. Canadian Federation of Students* (2009)[14] was the sides of buses, where two public transit bodies permitted the posting of advertising messages. The two bodies had adopted the same advertising policies, which included a prohibition of political messages. The Supreme Court of Canada applied the *Montreal* test to determine whether expression on the sides of buses was protected by s. 2(b). While the sides of buses had not historically been used for expressive purposes, they were so used now (although not for political advocacy), and the expressive activity was not

---

[10] *Montreal v. 2952-1366 Quebec*, [2005] 3 S.C.R. 141, para. 34. Binnie J. dissented on this administrative-law issue, which he described as "radical surgery" by the majority (para. 110), and this also led him to dissent on the constitutional issue, since the prohibition of "any audible signal from 'sound equipment' " (para. 109) was too broad to be justified under s. 1.

[11] *Montreal v. 2952-1366 Quebec*, [2005] 3 S.C.R. 141, para. 74.

[12] *Montreal v. 2952-1366 Quebec*, [2005] 3 S.C.R. 141, para. 74.

[13] *Montreal v. 2952-1366 Quebec*, [2005] 3 S.C.R. 141, para. 81.

[14] *Greater Vancouver Transportation Authority v. Canadian Federation of Students*, [2009] 2 S.C.R. 295. Deschamps J. wrote the opinion of the majority. Fish J. wrote a concurring opinion.

incompatible with the primary function of the bus as a vehicle for public transportation. The side of a bus was a public place like a city street "where individuals can openly interact with each other and their surroundings", and expression there could enhance the purposes of s. 2(b) "by furthering democratic discourse, and perhaps even truth finding and self-fulfillment".[15] The Court had no trouble in concluding that the prohibition of political messages was a breach of s. 2(b), and the Court went on to hold that it was not justified under s. 1. Clearly the Court envisaged a bus as a kind of democracy wall on which a robust exchange of ideas, including political ideas, could take place. But buses are hardly a promising ground for political debate: advertisements on buses have to be purchased, probably have to be professionally prepared, and certainly have to be very short. Moreover, they are inevitably in the faces of those who have to ride the buses. In my view, the Court should have found some room in the *Montreal* test for deference to the judgment of the transit bodies, whose goal was a "safe, welcoming public transit system", and who had concluded that some of their riders would be disturbed by the harsher kind of political messages.[16]

XI. ACCESS TO COURTS

§ 43:31 Fair trial concerns

Section 2(b) expressly provides that freedom of expression includes "freedom of the press and other media of communication". The freedom of the press occasionally comes into conflict with the right of persons accused of crime to receive a fair trial.[1] For example, pre-trial publicity may bias potential jurors or judges, and may damage the reputation of someone subsequently exonerated of the charge. As well, extensive publicity of pending cases, and intemperate criticism of decisions, may tend to draw the courts into political controversy and impair their capacity, or public perception of their capacity, for neutral adjudication.

§ 43:32 Restrictions on reporting

Freedom of the press includes the freedom to publish reports of proceedings in court. For example, in *Edmonton Journal v. Alberta*

---

[15] *Greater Vancouver Transportation Authority v. Canadian Federation of Students*, [2009] 2 S.C.R. 295, para. 43.

[16] The messages whose rejection led to the litigation were in fact quite mild (urging students to vote and condemning cuts to education funding), but no doubt messages on strongly-felt issues like abortion or the Middle East will now find their place on the buses. The Court's answer to that risk was: "Citizens, including bus riders, are expected to put up with some controversy in a free and democratic society." (para. 77 per Deschamps J. for the majority).

[Section 43:31]

[1] See generally Lepofsky, Open Justice (1985).

(1989),[1] the Supreme Court of Canada struck down an Alberta statute that prohibited, with some limited exceptions, press reports of matrimonial litigation. The Court was unanimous that the statute violated s. 2(b): "the courts must be open to public scrutiny and to public criticism of their operation by the public".[2] With respect to s. 1, the Court agreed that the protection of the privacy of individuals engaged in matrimonial litigation would justify some limits on the right to report judicial proceedings. However, a majority of the Court held that the Alberta ban was wider than was necessary to safeguard privacy, and could not be upheld under s. 1.[3]

In *Canadian Newspapers Co. v. Canada* (1988),[4] the Criminal Code made provision for a court order prohibiting the media from disclosing the identity of the complainant in a case of sexual assault. The making of the order was mandatory if it was requested by the complainant or the prosecutor; in other cases, the making of the order was discretionary. The Supreme Court of Canada held that the Criminal Code section was valid. Although it limited the freedom of the press as guaranteed by s. 2(b), the limit was justified under s. 1. The purpose of fostering complaints by victims of sexual assault justified some limit on s. 2(b). The mandatory nature of the ban did not limit the right excessively, because only a mandatory ban would provide assurance to the complainant that her identity would not be disclosed. A merely discretionary ban would not eliminate the fear of publication that it was the purpose of the section to eliminate.

In *Dagenais v. CBC* (1994),[5] a superior court had issued an injunction prohibiting the CBC from broadcasting a television programme called "The Boys of St. Vincent". This publication ban did not apply to reports of judicial proceedings, because the programme was a fictional one. The programme portrayed the abuse of children in a Catholic institution and

---

[Section 43:32]

[1]*Edmonton Journal v. Alberta*, [1989] 2 S.C.R. 1326. The principal judgment was written by Cory J., with whom Dickson C.J. and Lamer J. agreed; Wilson J. wrote a separate concurring opinion; La Forest J., with L'Heureux-Dubé and Sopinka JJ., dissented on the s. 1 issue.

[2]*Edmonton Journal v. Alberta*, [1989] 2 S.C.R. 1326, 1337.

[3]Parliament subsequently repealed s. 166 of the Criminal Code, which was similar to the Alberta legislation: S.C. 1994, c. 44, s. 9. Although the Court seemed to indicate that a more carefully drafted provision was what was needed, there has been no replacement legislation.

[4]*Canadian Newspapers Co. v. Canada*, [1988] 1 S.C.R. 122. Lamer J. wrote the opinion of the Court.

[5]*Dagenais v. CBC*, [1994] 3 S.C.R. 835. The majority opinion was written by Lamer C.J., with whom Sopinka, Cory, Iacobucci and Major JJ. agreed. A concurring opinion was written by McLachlin J., and dissenting opinions by La Forest J., L'Heureux-Dubé J., and Gonthier J. On the issue of the validity of the publication ban, both McLachlin J. and La Forest J. were essentially in agreement with Lamer C.J. to strike down the ban, while Gonthier J. (who wrote the main dissenting opinion on this issue) and L'Heureux-Dubé J. (who essentially agreed with the dissenting opinion of Gonthier J. on this issue) would have upheld the ban.

the subsequent trials of the priests who were responsible for the abuse. The injunction was sought by four Catholic priests who had been charged with the abuse of children under their care in circumstances resembling those depicted in the programme. The injunction had been granted under a common-law power to prevent "a real and substantial risk of interference with the fairness of the trial," and was limited to the period of the four trials. At the conclusion of the fourth trial, the injunction would be at an end, and the CBC would be free to air the programme.

The Supreme Court of Canada, by a majority, struck down the injunction. Lamer C.J., who wrote the opinion of the majority, held that the common law rule gave too much weight to the right to a fair trial and not enough weight to freedom of expression. Since the injunction was a limit on freedom of expression, the injunction had to be justified under s. 1 of the Charter by reference to *Oakes*-derived standards of justification. This required, among other things, a judicial finding that "reasonably available alternative measures" would not prevent the risk to the fairness of the trial.[6] In this case, he held, alternative measures were available, namely, "adjourning trials, changing venues, sequestering jurors, allowing challenges for cause and voir dires during jury selection, and providing strong judicial direction to the jury".[7] Therefore, the injunction could not be justified under s. 1.

Gonthier J. wrote the main dissenting opinion on the validity of the publication ban.[8] He accepted the trial judge's finding, based on the evidence, that there was a risk of influencing potential jurors, and he was reluctant to require a prolonged, American-style jury-selection process as an alternative remedy. He pointed out that the only effect of the ban was to delay the presentation of the programme for the duration of the trials, which was expected to be about eight months, when it would be just as timely and interesting to its audience. Not being a news programme, its value was not premised on immediate publication. Nor did the ban affect access to the courts or the publication of their proceedings. Therefore, in his dissenting view, the impact of the ban on freedom of the press was minor, and was justified by the objective of securing a fair trial for the four accused.

In *R. v. Mentuck* (2001),[9] the evidence against the accused, who was charged with murder, had been gathered by an elaborate operation of deception carried out by undercover police officers (who claimed to be members of a fictitious criminal organization that would help the accused to establish his innocence). Because there were other similar undercover operations under way, the Crown applied to the trial judge for an order prohibiting the publication of evidence that would disclose the identity of the undercover officers and the operational methods they had employed. In this case, unlike *Dagenais*, the accused opposed the or-

---

[6] *Dagenais v. CBC*, [1994] 3 S.C.R. 835, 878.

[7] *Dagenais v. CBC*, [1994] 3 S.C.R. 835, 881.

[8] § 43:32 note 5, above.

[9] *R. v. Mentuck*, [2001] 3 S.C.R. 442. Iacobucci J. wrote the opinion of the Court.

der, invoking his Charter right to a "public" hearing under s. 11(d) of the Charter, as well as s. 2(b) of the Charter. The trial judge granted the order with respect to the identities of the officers and denied the order with respect to the operational methods. The Supreme Court of Canada held that the judge was correct. The Crown had to establish "a serious risk to the proper administration of justice" and that "reasonable alternative measures will not prevent the risk".[10] The Court held that this test was satisfied as to the identities of the undercover police officers, because disclosure of their identities would create a serious risk to police operations in which those same officers were engaged. But the disclosure of the police methods would not, according to the Court, pose a serious threat to the efficacy of police operations. The publication ban was accordingly upheld as a justified limit on freedom of the press only with respect to the identities of the police officers.[11]

In *Toronto Star Newspapers v. Ontario* (2005),[12] the Supreme Court again affirmed the rule that court proceedings were to be "open" unless "disclosure would subvert the ends of justice or unduly impair its proper administration".[13] The question in the case was whether the rule applied to the reporting of pre-trial phases of court proceedings. The police had obtained warrants to search meat packing plants that they suspected of violating health laws. After the searches had taken place, and the media had become aware of the investigation, the Crown applied to the provincial court for an order sealing the search warrants and the supporting information on which they had been based. The reason for sealing was to protect the identity of the "whistle-blower" who was the police's confidential source. The provincial court sealed the warrants, and the Toronto Star newspaper brought proceedings to quash the sealing order, invoking s. 2(b) of the Charter. The proceedings ended up in the Supreme Court, which said that: "Once a search warrant is executed, the warrant and the information on which it was issued must be made available to the public unless an applicant seeking a sealing order can demonstrate that public access would subvert the ends of justice".[14] The Court held that this test was not met, and quashed the sealing order, subject only to the editing of the material to conceal the identity of the confidential informant.

An important pre-trial phase of criminal proceedings is the bail hearing, when it is determined by a judge whether there is "just cause" to

[10] *R. v. Mentuck*, [2001] 3 S.C.R. 442, para. 32.

[11] See also *Globe and Mail v. Can.*, [2010] 2 S.C.R. 592 *(Dagenais/Mentuck* test applied; publication ban quashed); *Canadian Broadcasting Corp. v. Can.*, [2011] 1 S.C.R. 19 (s. 1 test applied; prohibition on broadcasting recordings of court hearings upheld); *Canadian Broadcasting Corp. v. Can.*, [2011] 1 S.C.R. 65 *(Dagenais/Mentuck* test should have been applied by trial judge before prohibiting the broadcasting of an audio recording that had been produced as an exhibit at trial; issue now moot).

[12] *Toronto Star Newspapers v. Ontario*, [2005] 2 S.C.R. 188. Fish J. wrote the opinion of the Court.

[13] *Toronto Star Newspapers v. Ontario*, [2005] 2 S.C.R. 188, para. 5.

[14] *Toronto Star Newspapers v. Ontario*, [2005] 2 S.C.R. 188, para. 18.

deny bail to the accused, and if not what conditions should be imposed on his release on bail. Two questions are usually critical: (1) is the continued detention of the accused necessary to be sure that he will show up for his trial?, and (2) is the accused likely to commit crimes if released on bail? The evidence at the bail hearing is focused on the character of the accused, and may include evidence that would be prejudicial and inadmissible at his trial, such as previous convictions and post-offence conduct. That is why the Criminal Code provides for a publication ban of the evidence, the arguments and the judge's reasons in a bail hearing. If the prosecutor seeks such a publication ban, the judge has a discretion to grant it. If the accused seeks a publication ban, the ban must be granted automatically. In *Toronto Star Newspapers v. Canada* (2010),[15] the Toronto Star newspaper challenged the constitutionality of the accused's entitlement to an automatic publication ban. The Supreme Court of Canada rejected the challenge, upholding the Criminal Code provision by a majority of eight to one. Deschamps J., who wrote for the majority, acknowledged that a publication ban is a limit on freedom of expression. Discretionary bans are constitutional, she said, because the test developed in *Dagenais/Mentuck* incorporates the essence of the *Oakes* test.[16] But where as here the legislation *requires* the judge to order a publication ban (if requested by the accused), its constitutionality was to be determined by subjecting the legislation to the *Oakes* test itself. In this case, the objectives of the bail-hearing publication ban were twofold: (1) to safeguard the right to fair trial by preventing any prejudicial evidence about the accused from going beyond the bail courtroom; and (2) to ensure expeditious bail hearings by precluding arguments for and against a ban, which would in high-profile cases likely entail media interventions and delays. These were pressing and important objectives. The resulting ban was not an absolute one in that the press was free to report on the identity of the accused, the charge against him, and the outcome of the bail hearing. And the ban was not permanent, ending automatically with the end of the subsequent trial. For these reasons, the ban did not limit freedom of expression any more than was necessary to achieve its objectives, and the ban was therefore held to be justified under s. 1.

In *A.B. v. Bragg Communications* (2012),[17] a teenage girl, who had been the victim of "cyberbullying", sought an order from a judge in Nova Scotia requiring an internet provider to supply the name of the person or persons who had created a false and malicious Facebook profile; she needed the names for the purpose of pursuing an action for defamation. The applicant also sought an order that her identity as the applicant be kept secret, and that the Facebook profile (which had in fact been

---

[15] *Toronto Star Newspapers v. Canada*, [2010] 1 S.C.R. 722. Deschamps J. wrote the opinion of the eight-judge majority. Abella J. wrote a dissenting opinion, holding that the automatic publication ban was not justified under s. 1.

[16] *Toronto Star Newspapers v. Canada*, [2010] 1 S.C.R. 722, para. 18.

[17] *A.B. v. Bragg Communications*, [2012] 2 S.C.R. 567. Abella J. wrote the opinion of the Court.

removed by Facebook) be the subject of a publication ban. The Supreme Court of Canada applied the *Dagenais/Mentuck* test to determine whether these exceptions to the open court principle could be ordered: (1) were the proposed measures necessary to protect an important legal interest? and (2) did they impair free expression as little as possible? The Court concluded that preserving the privacy of a child and protecting her from cyberbullying were important legal interests which would justify an exception to the open court principle. The applicant's request for anonymity was granted for that reason.[18] However, the publication ban was not granted. The Facebook profile had to be cleansed of any identifying content, and, once that was done, it could be published: the privacy interest of the applicant would no longer outweigh the open court principle. On that basis, the applicant could proceed anonymously with her application to seek the name of the person who had defamed her.

§ 43:33 Restrictions on access

Freedom of the press also includes the right of the press and the public to be present in court.[1] That right was not affected in the *Edmonton Journal* and *Canadian Newspaper* cases, where the press were not denied access to the courtroom; they were simply prohibited from reporting part of the proceedings.

In *Re Southam and the Queen (No. 1)* (1983),[2] the Ontario Court of Appeal had to consider the validity of s. 12(1) of the Juvenile Delinquents Act, which provided that "the trials of children shall take place without publicity". (The phrase "without publicity" had been held to require a trial closed to the press and the general public.) A newspaper challenged the validity of this provision, claiming that freedom of expression entailed a right of access to the courts.[3] The Court upheld the newspaper's claim, and struck down the closed-court provision. The Court acknowledged that in some cases the interests of the child would justify restrictions on press access to the trial, but the Court held that an absolute ban could not be justified under s. 1, because it did not

---

[18]The media interest in publishing the identity of the applicant was described (para. 28) as "minimal". This should no doubt be interpreted in the context of these facts because in other contexts there is surely a powerful public interest against anonymous court proceedings.

[Section 43:33]

[1]*Edmonton Journal v. Alta.*, [1989] 2 S.C.R. 1326, 1337 (obiter dictum). Compare *BCGEU v. B.C.* (Vancouver Courthouse) [1988] 2 S.C.R. 214 (injunction to stop picketing outside courthouses upheld in order to provide access to courts); *R. v. Squires* (1992), 11 O.R. (3d) 385 (C.A.) (statutory prohibition on filming persons entering and leaving courtrooms upheld in order to maintain order and decorum and facilitate access to courts); *B.C. v. Christie*, [2007] 1 S.C.R. 873 (right of access does not include right to retain counsel outside ss. 7 and 10(b)).

[2]*Re Southam and the Queen (No. 1)* (1983), 41 O.R. (2d) 113 (C.A.).

[3]The newspaper could not invoke s. 11(d) of the Charter, which requires a "public" criminal trial, because s. 11(d) is available only to the "person charged with an offence".

pursue the "least restrictive means" of attaining its objective. The Court refused to reconstruct the Act by reading a judicial discretion into it. The Juvenile Delinquents Act was repealed by the Young Offenders Act, which replaced the absolute requirement of a closed hearing for trials of young offenders with a requirement that hearings be open to the press and public subject to a discretion in the judge to order that a hearing be closed.[4] In *Re Southam and the Queen (No. 2)* (1986),[5] the discretionary provision was upheld under s. 1.

There is a provision of the Criminal Code that provides that proceedings against an accused are to be held "in open court", but the provision goes on to confer on the trial judge the power "to exclude all or any members of the public from the court room for all or part of the proceedings". This power is exercisable if the judge forms the opinion that access should be restricted in the interest of "the proper administration of justice". In *CBC v. New Brunswick* (1996),[6] the trial judge excluded the public and the media from part of the sentencing hearing of a prominent citizen who had pleaded guilty to various sexual offences involving young girls. The exclusion order covered the part of the hearing detailing the acts committed by the accused, and it remained in force for about 20 minutes. The order was consented to by both the Crown and the accused, but the CBC, whose reporter had been denied access by the order, brought a proceeding for a declaration that the statutory provision authorizing the exclusion order was unconstitutional. The Supreme Court of Canada unanimously upheld the provision. La Forest J., who wrote the opinion of the Court, held that freedom of the press included the right of the media to have access to court proceedings. It followed that any power to exclude the media from the court room was a breach of s. 2(b) of the Charter. However, La Forest J. held that the provision was justified under s. 1. Parliament was pursuing an important objective in providing a power to make an exclusion order when openness would be inimical to the proper administration of justice, and, because the power was discretionary, the provision was no broader than necessary. This reasoning disposed of the constitutional challenge, but La Forest J. added some comments on the exclusion order that had been made in the case that prompted the challenge. He said that the kind of evidence that establishes sexual assault charges, even when the victims are very young, should not normally be regarded as a sufficient reason to deny access to the court room, and any hardship that prejudicial publicity would impose on the accused should be given little weight at the sentencing stage, when the accused has been found guilty. In considering an exclusion order, the judge had to give appropriate weight to the value of subjecting sentencing proceedings to public scrutiny, and only exceptional circumstances of hardship to the accused or the complainants would override this value.

---

[4] A similar provision is in the current law: Youth Criminal Justice Act, S.C. 2002, c. 1, s. 132.

[5] *Re Southam and the Queen (No. 2)* (1986), 53 O.R. (2d) 663 (C.A.).

[6] *CBC v. New Brunswick*, [1996] 3 S.C.R. 480. La Forest J. wrote the judgment of the Court.

The Criminal Code provides for a "pre-inquiry" by a justice of the peace into whether to commence criminal proceedings against a person against whom an information has been laid. The person accused is not entitled to be present at a pre-inquiry, and any hearing is also closed to the public. In *Southam v. Coulter* (1990),[7] a private citizen had sworn an information against several cabinet ministers and senior police officers alleging bribery and corruption. Because of the prominence of the accused persons, the press were anxious to attend the pre-inquiry into the charges. The Ontario Court of Appeal held that the constitutional right of public access to the court included pre-trial proceedings as well as trials. However, the Court held that the protection of a falsely accused person and risk to a properly accused person that the subsequent trial would be prejudiced by pre-trial publicity were values that justified the closure of the pre-inquiry. The Court upheld the closure under s. 1.[8]

In *Re Vancouver Sun* (2004),[9] the Supreme Court of Canada reviewed a "judicial investigative hearing" that had been held in camera (closed to the public) by a superior court judge. This kind of hearing was an innovation authorized by the Anti-Terrorism Act, a federal statute that had been enacted in 2001 in the aftermath of the terrorist attacks in the United States on September 11 of that year.[10] The Act authorized a peace officer, with the approval of the Attorney General, to apply to a judge for an order for "the gathering of information" in relation to a "terrorism offence" (a defined term). If the order was granted, the court would then order a judicial investigative hearing, which would consist of the attendance before a judge of a named person for examination under oath by counsel for the Attorney General. The Act was silent on the question whether a judicial investigative hearing was to be held, in whole or in part, in camera. In this case, a judicial investigative hearing was held by a judge in relation to acts of terrorism that had caused explosions in an airport in Japan and on an Air India flight (which crashed with total loss of life). The presiding judge closed the hearing to the public and press. The Vancouver Sun, learning by accident of the proceedings, applied to be given access, and when that application was refused, appealed to the Supreme Court of Canada.

The Supreme Court emphasized that the "open court principle" was guaranteed by s. 2(b) of the Charter. It could be limited under s. 1 only

---

[7]*Southam v. Coulter* (1990), 75 O.R. (2d) 1 (C.A.).

[8]See also *Ruby v. Can.*, [2002] 4 S.C.R. 3 (upholding under s. 1 in camera procedure for part of judicial review proceedings in respect of requests under the Privacy Act for personal information affecting national security).

[9]*Re Vancouver Sun*, [2004] 2 S.C.R. 332. Iacobucci and Arbour JJ. wrote the opinion of the six-judge majority. LeBel J. wrote a short concurring opinion, essentially agreeing with the majority. Bastarche J. wrote a dissenting opinion that was agreed to by Deschamps J.

[10]This measure was subject to a sunset clause, and it expired on February 27, 2007, along with two other anti-terrorism measures, when the proposal of the minority Conservative government of Prime Minister Harper to extend the three measures for three more years was defeated by the votes of the three opposition parties.

if the standards of justification established in *Dagenais*[11] and *Mentuck*[12] were satisfied. Although those cases concerned publication bans, the same principles applied to orders limiting access to court proceedings. Those principles were: (a) that the order is "necessary in order to prevent a serious risk to the proper administration of justice because reasonable alternative measures will not prevent the risk"; and (b) that "the salutary effects of [the order] outweigh the deleterious effects on the rights and interests of the parties and the public".[13] The Court acknowledged that an application for a judicial investigative hearing would have to be held in camera, for the same reason as an application for a search warrant or a wiretap authorization. But Iacobucci and Arbour JJ., for the majority of the Court, held that the hearing itself should have been held in open court, although the hearing judge would maintain a discretion (to be exercised in accordance with the *Dagenais/Mentuck* principles) to exclude the public from parts of the hearing and/or ban publication of parts of the evidence. Bastarache J., who dissented, took the view that the open court principle should not apply to a judicial investigative hearing. Closed proceedings were needed to maintain the secrecy of the investigation from those who may be engaged in the terrorist activity under investigation, and to protect innocent witnesses from injury to their reputations or even to their lives.

Canadian Broadcasting Corp. v. Canada (2011)[14] was a challenge by media organizations to restrictions by the Superior Court of Quebec on media access, not to the court hearing itself, but to the public areas of courthouses, where journalists had traditionally interviewed and filmed parties, witnesses, lawyers and others who were on their way to or from a courtroom where a newsworthy case was being heard. This would sometimes cause crowding and jostling in front of courtroom doors, and was often distressing to participants. In order to regulate the activity, the Superior Court adopted rules of practice that restricted interviews and the use of cameras to designated areas of each courthouse. After the rules were adopted (and a more detailed directive was issued by the Ministry of Justice), the designated areas were posted and marked in each courthouse. The Supreme Court of Canada held that the guarantee of freedom of the press extended beyond the courtroom itself to the newsgathering activities of the media in the public areas of the courthouses. The restrictions on media access were therefore limits on the s. 2(b) right. However, the Court held that the restrictions were justified under s. 1. The important objective of the rules was to preserve the order, decorum and serenity of judicial proceedings, and, by avoiding a total ban through the creation of designated media areas, the rules limited the freedom of the press no more than was reasonably necessary to accomplish the objective.

---

[11] *Dagenais v. CBC*, [1994] 3 S.C.R. 835.

[12] *R. v. Mentuck*, [2001] 3 S.C.R. 442.

[13] *Re Vancouver Sun*, [2004] 2 S.C.R. 332, para. 29 per Iacobucci and Arbour JJ. for majority.

[14] *Canadian Broadcasting Corp. v. Canada*, [2011] 1 S.C.R. 19. Deschamps J. wrote the opinion of the Court.

XII. ACCESS TO LEGISLATIVE ASSEMBLY

§ 43:34 Generally

In *New Brunswick Broadcasting Co. v. Nova Scotia* (1993),[1] the Supreme Court of Canada, by a majority, upheld a ban on television cameras in the legislative chamber that had been imposed by the Nova Scotia House of Assembly. The reasoning was that parliamentary privilege included the power of a legislative assembly to exclude "strangers" from the legislative chamber, and that power was not subject to the Charter of Rights. Sopinka J., who wrote a separate concurring opinion, and Cory J., who dissented, would have held that the Charter applied, and that s. 2(b) conferred a right of access to a legislative assembly on the press and other media. But the majority, by denying that the Charter was applicable at all, effectively rejected any such right.[2]

XIII. CONTEMPT OF COURT; PUBLIC SERVICE; MANDATORY LETTERS OF REFERENCE

§ 43:35 Contempt of court

A contempt of court is an act that offends against the administration of justice. A failure to obey a court order is the most common form of contempt. A failure to obey a court order may have no significance beyond the parties to the order, in which case the contempt is a "civil contempt". If the court order resolved a dispute between two private parties, and if it was based on the common law, the Charter of Rights will have no application to the court order,[1] or to any proceedings between the private parties to enforce the order by civil contempt proceedings. Therefore, even if the effect of the contempt proceedings were to enforce a restraint on freedom of expression (such as an injunction against picketing), the Charter cannot be called in aid to resist the contempt proceedings.

A "criminal contempt" is one where the offence to the administration of justice has a public significance that goes beyond the immediate parties. Criminal contempt is a criminal offence at common law that has

---

[Section 43:34]

[1] *New Brunswick Broadcasting Co. v. Nova Scotia*, [1993] 1 S.C.R. 319. The majority opinion was written by McLachlin J. with the agreement of La Forest, L'Heureux-Dubé, Gonthier and Iacobucci JJ.; Lamer C.J. and Sopinka J. wrote separate concurring opinions; Cory J. dissented. Folld. *Zundel v. Boudria* (1999), 46 O.R. (3d) 410 (C.A.) (refusing to review House of Commons resolution denying plaintiff admission to House of Commons). Compare *Weisfeld v. Can.* (1994), 116 D.L.R. (4th) 232 (Fed. C.A.) (regulation authorizing removal of protesters' "peace camp" from Parliament Hill held to be a limit on s. 2(b) that was justified under s. 1 for protection of safety, health, security and aesthetics).

[2] The majority's reasoning is more fully explained, and criticized, in ch. 37, Application of Charter, under heading § 37:7, "Parliament or Legislature".

[Section 43:35]

[1] *RWDSU v. Dolphin Delivery*, [1986] 2 S.C.R. 573.

been preserved in Canada by s. 8 of the Criminal Code.[2] There are two kinds of criminal contempt. A "direct contempt" is a contempt in the face of the court. This is committed by words or acts inside the courtroom that are intended to disrupt the proceedings, for example, where a person insults the judge, interrupts the proceedings, refuses to be sworn as a witness or refuses to testify. An "indirect contempt" is a contempt not in the face of the court. This is committed by words or acts outside the courtroom that are intended to obstruct the administration of justice, for example, an article in a newspaper that would prejudice the fairness of an ongoing or pending trial. Although criminal contempt is a matter of common law, and the Charter does not generally apply to the common law, the public character of criminal contempt makes the Charter applicable.

In the *Vancouver Courthouse* case (1988),[3] the Chief Justice of British Columbia issued an injunction prohibiting a union from picketing the courthouses where some of the striking employees worked. The basis for the injunction was the offence of criminal contempt, which was allegedly being committed by the picketers by restricting access to the courts. The Supreme Court of Canada held that the Charter applied to an injunction for criminal contempt, and that the injunction was a limit on freedom of expression. However, the Court went on to decide that the assurance of unimpeded access to the courts was a sufficiently important objective to justify a limit on freedom of expression, and the injunction in this case was justified as a reasonable limit under s. 1.

In *R. v. Kopyto* (1987),[4] a lawyer, after his client had lost a civil suit against police officers, made a statement to the press in which he claimed that: "The courts and the RCMP are sticking so close together you'd think they were put together with Krazy Glue". Mr. Kopyto was charged with, and convicted of, "scandalizing the court", which was a branch of criminal contempt that had been recognized by the common law since 1900, although it had been rarely invoked. The Ontario Court of Appeal allowed Kopyto's appeal, holding by a majority that the offence of scandalizing the court had not survived Canada's adoption of the Charter of Rights. The critical feature of Kopyto's statement was that it was made *after* the end of a judicial proceeding, so that it could not prejudice an ongoing or pending trial. The only effect of the statement was therefore its general tendency to lower the reputation and the authority of the court. The Ontario Court of Appeal held that criticism of the courts, however unrestrained, made after a decision had been rendered, was constitutionally protected expression, and a law attempting to restrict such criticism could not be justified under s. 1.

[2]The lack of a statutory definition of the criminal offence is not a breach of fundamental justice under s. 7: *UNA v. Alta.*, [1992] 1 S.C.R. 901.

[3]*BCGEU v. B.C.* (Vancouver Courthouse) [1988] 2 S.C.R. 214.

[4]*R. v. Kopyto* (1987), 62 O.R. (2d) 449 (C.A.). The majority judgments were written by Cory, Goodman and Houlden JJ.A.; Dubin and Brooke JJ.A. dissented on the constitutional issue, although they gave a narrow definition of the (constitutional) offence, and held that Kopyto had not committed it.

§ 43:36 Public service

Public servants in all jurisdictions in Canada are subject to restrictions on their partisan political activities. This is because the entire public service is a professional career service that is supposed to serve governments of all political stripes with equal diligence, and to be impervious to partisan political considerations in the administration of government programmes. The maintenance of the political neutrality of the service is necessary for its effective functioning, both in its relationships with its political masters and in its relationships with the public. While the general rule of neutrality is widely if not universally accepted, it does not provide a sure answer to the question of how much political activity by an individual public servant could be tolerated without serious risk to the integrity of the service.

In *OPSEU v. Ontario* (1986),[1] public servants in Ontario challenged provisions in Ontario's Public Service Act that prohibited public servants from engaging in a variety of political activities, including running for the federal Parliament without taking a leave of absence, fundraising on behalf of federal political parties, and expressing opinions in public on federal political issues. This was a pre-Charter case, and so the plaintiffs took aim at the restrictions on political activity only insofar as they precluded *federal* political activity. The plaintiffs argued that such restrictions were outside the powers of a provincial Legislature. The argument was unsuccessful. The Supreme Court of Canada held unanimously that the province had the power to regulate its own public service,[2] and in pursuit of political neutrality the regulation could extend to restrictions on federal as well as provincial political activity.

The inevitable Charter challenge[3] came in *Osborne v. Canada* (1991),[4] in which federal public servants attacked provisions in the federal Public Service Employment Act that prohibited them from "engaging in work" for or against a candidate for election to Parliament or for or against a federal political party. The Supreme Court of Canada held that the Act did limit freedom of expression under s. 2(b), and that it was not justified under s. 1. The objective of maintaining a neutral public service would justify limits on expression, but these limits did not pursue that objective by the least drastic means; the Act was overinclusive as to both the range of activity that was prohibited, and the

---

[Section 43:36]

[1]*OPSEU v. Ontario*, [1987] 2 S.C.R. 2.

[2]There was some disagreement as to the source of the power. Beetz J., writing with the agreement of McIntyre, Le Dain and La Forest JJ., held that the political restrictions were not simply labour relations laws but were part of the constitution of the province under s. 92(1) (now s. 45 of the Constitution Act, 1982) or the tenure of provincial offices under s. 92(4). Dickson C.J., concurring, relied on s. 92(4) and s. 92(13). Lamer J., concurring, relied only on s. 92(4).

[3]The Ontario legislation was challenged unsuccessfully under the Charter in *OPSEU v. Ont.* (1988), 65 O.R. (2d) 689 (H.C.).

[4]*Osborne v. Canada*, [1991] 2 S.C.R 69.

range of public servants who were covered. A narrower prohibition would have been sufficient to protect the value of neutrality with less impact on freedom of expression.

§ 43:37 Mandatory letters of reference

Occasionally, labour boards or adjudicators order an employer to give a letter of reference to an employee who has been unjustly dismissed. Such an order is a breach of the employer's Charter right to freedom of expression. Where the order requires the employer to provide an opinion about the employee that the employer does not truly hold, then the breach of the Charter right cannot be justified under s. 1.[1] However, where the stipulated letter of reference contains "only objective facts that are not in dispute", then the order can be justified under s. 1.[2]

XIV. ELECTION EXPENDITURES; VOTING

§ 43:38 Election expenditures

Restrictions on election expenditures[1] are indirect restrictions on political speech, because expenditures are required to purchase time or space in the media for campaign messages. Restrictions on expenditures are therefore bound to diminish the capacity of candidates to communicate their ideas, and thereby diminish the quantity of political speech. This has caused the Supreme Court of the United States to strike down a variety of restrictions on campaign expenditures and contributions on the basis that they offend the first amendment guarantee of freedom of speech.[2] The reason for such restrictions is to reduce the risk that wealthy or well-financed candidates will have an

---

[Section 43:37]

[1]*National Bank of Can. v. RCIU*, [1984] 1 S.C.R. 269 (Canada Labour Code should not be interpreted as conferring power to order employer to state opinion not held; Charter not relied upon directly).

[2]*Slaight Communications v. Davidson*, [1989] 1 S.C.R. 1038.

[Section 43:38]

[1]See J. A. Fraser, "Canada's Election Law: A Constitutional Analysis" (LL.M. thesis, Osgoode Hall Law School, York University, 1995). Compare *Lavigne v. OPSEU*, [1991] 2 S.C.R. 211 (compelled payment of union dues not a denial of payer's freedom of expression, although dues were used for advocacy purposes); *MacKay v. Man.*, [1989] 2 S.C.R. 357 (statutory funding of candidates for election not a denial of taxpayer's freedom of expression). For closely related cases, see ch. 45, Voting, under heading § 45:4, "Regulation of elections".

[2]*Citizens United v. Federal Election Commn.* (2010), 558 U.S. 310 (federal prohibition on election campaign expenditures by corporations and unions struck down); *McCutcheon v. Federal Election Commn.* (2014), 572 U.S. xxx (federal limits on aggregate election campaign contributions by individuals struck down). See also L.H. Tribe, American Constitutional Law (Foundation Press, N.Y., 2nd ed., 1986), 1132-1153; J.E. Nowak and R.D. Rotunda, Constitutional Law (West, St. Paul, Minn., 7th ed., 2005); sec. 16.51.

unfair advantage by reason of their greater access to the media: the well-financed point of view may drown out opposing views.[3]

The federal Canada Elections Act imposes spending limits on parties and candidates during an election. As well, by an amendment enacted in 1983, the Act absolutely prohibited anyone who was not a candidate for election, and who was not acting on behalf of a registered party or a candidate for election, from incurring "election expenses" during the period from the date of the issue of the writ for the election to polling day. Election expenses were defined as money paid "for the purpose of promoting or opposing. . .a particular registered party or the election of a particular candidate". In *National Citizens' Coalition v. A.-G. Can.* (1984),[4] a court challenge was mounted against the prohibition on third-party election expenditures that had been enacted by the 1983 amendment. The Alberta Court of Queen's Bench held that the prohibition was a breach of the guarantee of freedom of expression, and that it could not be justified under s. 1. The prohibition was therefore struck down. This decision was rendered not long before the federal election that was held on September 4, 1984. Because of the imminence of the election, the federal government did not appeal the decision, and so the issue did not advance to a higher court. The 1984 federal election was held without any prohibition on third-party expenditures, and so was the 1988 federal election, in which the main issue was free trade with the United States, an issue that provoked heavy spending by lobby groups.

In 1993, Parliament amended the Canada Elections Act, replacing the prohibition on third-party expenditures with a monetary ceiling. Under the 1993 amendment, third-party expenditures to promote a candidate or party during an election campaign were permitted, but only up to a limit of $1,000. This provision was struck down by the Alberta Court of Appeal in *Somerville v. Canada* (1996)[5] as a breach of the guarantee of freedom of expression. On the issue of s. 1 justification, Conrad J.A. for the majority of the Court held that there was no evidence of the danger of the well-financed point of view monopolizing the media, and that the true objective of the law was to exclude ordinary citizens from the electoral process in favour of the "privileged voice" of political parties and official candidates. That objective, she held, was so contrary to freedom of expression that it could not form the basis for s. 1 justification.

---

[3]*McCloy v. New South Wales*, [2015] HCA 34 (High Court of Australia) (upholding caps and other restrictions on private funding of candidates in state and local elections). Compare *Reform Party of Can. v. Can.* (1995), 123 D.L.R. (4th) 366 (Alta. C.A.) (upholding most of the Elections Act rules for the allocation of free broadcast time between political parties); *Thomson Newspapers Co. v. Can.*, [1998] 1 S.C.R. 877 (striking down Elections Act prohibition on the publication of opinion surveys during the last three days of an election campaign).

[4]*National Citizens' Coalition v. A.-G. Can.* (1984), 11 D.L.R. (4th) 481 (Alta. Q.B.).

[5]*Somerville v. Canada* (1996), 136 D.L.R. (4th) 205 (Alta. C.A.). Conrad J.A. wrote the majority opinion for herself and Harradence J.A. Kerans J.A. wrote a concurring opinion, which included some reservations about the majority's categorical rejection of the risk of electoral distortion.

In 2000, Parliament again amended the Canada Elections Act, this time raising the ceiling on third-party election expenditures from the $1,000 that had been struck down in *Somerville* to a total of $150,000, of which no more than $3,000 could be incurred in a single electoral district. These restrictions applied during an election campaign. The national limit of $150,000 was less than half the cost of a one-time full-page advertisement in major Canadian newspapers. The district limit of $3,000 was less than half the cost of a single bulk mailing in one electoral district. These restrictions, like their more draconian predecessors, essentially made election campaigns the exclusive reserve of registered political parties and their candidates, who were also subject to spending limits, but limits that were more than 60 times greater. There was no doubt that the third-party expenditure restrictions were limits on freedom of expression. Were they saved by s. 1? In *Harper v. Canada* (2004),[6] the Supreme Court of Canada, by a majority of six to three, said yes. Although there was no evidence that in election campaigns the voices of the wealthy drowned out those of others, the Court accepted that the prevention of that evil was the objective of the restrictions, and that the objective was sufficiently important to justify limiting freedom of expression. They did not mention, and obviously did not agree with, Conrad J.A.'s view in *Somerville*, which was that the purpose of the third-party restrictions was to exclude ordinary citizens from the electoral process.[7] Where the Court divided was on the least drastic means branch of the *Oakes* test. Did the statutory restrictions impair the right of free expression as little as reasonably possible? For McLachlin C.J. and Major J., who dissented, the third-party restrictions were too stringent to pass constitutional muster, because they effectively deprived those who did not speak through political parties of any political voice during an election campaign. But for Bastarache J. who wrote for the majority, the restrictions did not go too far. They allowed third parties to use modest means of advertising "to inform the electorate of their message in a manner that will not overwhelm candidates, political parties or other third parties".[8] The restrictions on third-party expenditures were accordingly upheld.

Harper also upheld under s. 1 a registration requirement for third parties who spend at least $500 on election advertising.[9] This ruling was followed in *B.C. Freedom of Information and Privacy Association v. Brit-*

---

[6]*Harper v. Canada*, [2004] 1 S.C.R. 827. Bastarache J. wrote the opinion of the six-judge majority. McLachlin C.J. and Major J. wrote a dissenting opinion which was agreed to by Binnie J. The Court was unanimous in holding that the spending restrictions did not breach s. 3 of the Charter (right to vote). The Act also prohibited election advertising on polling day. The Court was unanimous in upholding that prohibition: it was a breach of s. 2(b) that was justified under s. 1.

[7]The Court had already indicated its disagreement with that characterization of the objective in *Libman v. Quebec*, [1997] 3 S.C.R. 569, para. 79.

[8]*Harper v. Canada*, [2004] 1 S.C.R. 827, para. 118.

[9]*Harper v. Canada*, [2004] 1 S.C.R. 827, paras. 142-146 (Bastarache J.), para. 48 (McLachlin C.J. and Major J.).

ish Columbia (2017).[10] In that case, the province imposed a registration requirement on third-party "sponsors" of "election advertising" during an election campaign regardless of how much they spent during the campaign period. Obviously, this was a limit on freedom of expression, and the question was whether it was justified under s. 1. The main objection to the registration requirement was the claim that it would apply to persons who conveyed political messages through individual election activities like displaying homemade signs in their windows, putting bumper stickers on their cars, or wearing T-shirts with political messages on them. Could that be justified under s. 1? McLachlin C.J., who wrote the opinion of the Supreme Court, dismissed this objection by pointing out that the registration requirement applied only to "sponsors" of election advertising, persons who either pay for advertising services or receive the services without charge as a contribution. Sponsorship involved at least two people. There was no registration requirement for "those engaged in individual self-expression."[11] Once individual self-expression was removed from the equation, the case looked very like *Harper*. The federal legislation upheld in *Harper* imposed a quantitative threshold ($500), while the B.C. legislation here imposed a qualitative threshold (sponsorship); both thresholds were low, but each was high enough to permit small-scale individual election advertising without registration. In both cases, the purpose of the registration requirement was to increase transparency, openness and public accountability in the electoral process which was a pressing and substantial objective.[12] The registration requirement was rationally connected to this objective. In the case of the B.C. legislation, by confining the registration requirement to "sponsors", the requirement was tailored to the objective of the legislation. And the benefits of public transparency outweighed the deleterious effects on those who wished to sponsor election advertising without registering. The claimants argued that the province was obliged to lead social-science evidence to establish the benefits of the registration requirement. McLachlin C.J. agreed that evidence would have been helpful in establishing justification, but held that in this case "logic and reason" were sufficient.[13]

The Supreme Court of Canada has also had to review the validity of restrictions on third-party expenditures in the context of a referendum. Quebec's Referendum Act provided that, when a referendum was held in the province, each side of the campaign had to organize into Yes or No committees. The expenses that each committee could incur were strictly controlled with a view to ensuring that equal resources were deployed

[10]*B.C. Freedom of Information and Privacy Association v. British Columbia*, [2017] 1 S.C.R. 93, 2017 SCC 6. McLachlin C.J. wrote the opinion of the Court.

[11]*B.C. Freedom of Information and Privacy Association v. British Columbia*, [2017] 1 S.C.R. 93, 2017 SCC 6, para. 21.

[12]*B.C. Freedom of Information and Privacy Association v. British Columbia*, [2017] 1 S.C.R. 93, 2017 SCC 6, para. 51.

[13]*B.C. Freedom of Information and Privacy Association v. British Columbia*, [2017] 1 S.C.R. 93, 2017 SCC 6, para. 58.

on both sides. However, no expenses could be incurred by persons who were outside the umbrella of one of the two committees. In *Libman v. Quebec* (1997),[14] the Court held that the prohibition on third-party expenditures, which was obviously a breach of freedom of expression, could not be justified under s. 1. The Court accepted the importance of the purpose of restricting the expenditures of the committees, which was to equalize access to the media by both sides of a referendum campaign. That purpose entailed restrictions on third-party expenditures as well, because if they were left unregulated the controls on the committees would be able to be by-passed. But the Court reasoned that respect for freedom of expression should allow some room for participation by those who could not fit themselves under one of the committee umbrellas, for example, those who argued for abstention. This law failed the least drastic means branch of the *Oakes* test, because the total prohibition on third-party expenditures was a more drastic infringement of freedom of expression than was necessary to accomplish the legislative objective. The Court said that a financial ceiling on third-party expenditures of something like $1,000 (the third-party ceiling in the Canada Elections Act at that time) would be a "far less intrusive" limit than a total prohibition.[15] After this decision, the Legislature of Quebec amended the legislation to allow third-party expenditures up to the limit of $1,000 suggested by the Court.

In *Hogan v. Newfoundland* (2000),[16] a referendum was held by the Government of Newfoundland to seek popular approval for an amendment of the constitution that would take away from denominational schools their constitutional right to public funding. The "Yes" side received 72 per cent of the vote, and the proposed amendment was duly enacted by the joint action of the Legislative Assembly of Newfoundland and the two Houses of the Parliament of Canada, using the amending procedure of s. 43 of the Constitution Act, 1982. A group of Roman Catholic school supporters who had opposed the amendment sought compensation from the Government for the disparity in expenditures incurred during the referendum campaign. The Government had actively campaigned for the Yes side and had spent more on the campaign than the No side could muster. It was argued that the Government was under a constitutional responsibility to equalize expenditures on both sides, either by imposing limits on both sides or by providing public funding for the No side. The trial judge accepted the argument and ordered the Government to pay damages to the plaintiffs, but the Newfoundland Court of Appeal reversed. While the imposition of spending limits on po-

[14]*Libman v. Quebec*, [1997] 3 S.C.R. 569. The unanimous opinion was attributed to "the Court".

[15]*Libman v. Quebec*, [1997] 3 S.C.R. 569, para. 80. This figure seems absurdly low, but the Court was influenced by the fact that it had been recommended by the Lortie Commission for the Canada Elections Act. The Court was also making clear that it disagreed with the decision of the Alberta Court of Appeal in *Somerville v. Canada* (1996), 136 D.L.R. (4th) 205 (Alta. C.A.), which had just struck down the $1,000 restriction in the Canada Elections Act.

[16]*Hogan v. Newfoundland* (2000), 183 D.L.R. (4th) 225 (Nfld. C.A.).

litical campaigns was a limit on freedom of expression that could be justified by fairness, the right to freedom of expression did not demand spending limits, and the fact that the Government-sponsored Yes side spent more than the No side was not a breach of the freedom of expression of the No side.[17] Since there was no breach of freedom of expression (or freedom of religion), there was no basis for an award of damages.

§ 43:39 Voting

The right to vote is guaranteed by s. 3 of the Charter, but the right is limited to elections of the members of the federal House of Commons and of the provincial legislative assemblies.[1] In *Haig v. Canada* (1993),[2] the plaintiff, a Canadian citizen who had slipped through the cracks of the residency requirements,[3] found himself unable to vote in the federal referendum that was held to approve the set of constitutional amendments known as the Charlottetown Accord. Being unable to rely on s. 3 of the Charter, he argued that the failure of the federal Parliament to make provision for him to vote was a breach of freedom of expression, guaranteed by s. 2(b) of the Charter. The Supreme Court of Canada agreed that the casting of a ballot in a referendum was a means of expression. However, the majority of the Court held that s. 2(b) did not impose on the federal (or a provincial) government any positive duty to consult its citizens by referendum, and, if a government did choose to hold a referendum, there was no duty to consult everyone.[4] The plaintiff could complain of his exclusion only if it amounted to a breach of his s. 15 equality right, but the majority of the Court held that the exclusion of citizens who did not satisfy the residency requirement was not discrimination that was prohibited by s. 15.[5] The conclusion was that the plaintiff had no constitutional right to vote in the referendum.

Elections to the federal House of Commons and the provincial legislative assemblies, to which s. 3 applies, are extensively regulated by federal law (in the case of the House of Commons) and by provincial

[17] *Hogan v. Newfoundland* (2000), 183 D.L.R. (4th) 225 (Nfld. C.A.), para. 149.

[Section 43:39]

[1] Chapter 45, Voting, under heading § 45:2, "Section 3 of Charter".

[2] *Haig v. Canada*, [1993] 2 S.C.R. 995. On the point in the text, seven members of the Court agreed with the majority opinion of L'Heureux-Dubé J.; Iacobucci J. wrote a dissenting opinion that was concurred in by Lamer C.J.

[3] The problem was created by the fact that two referenda were held, a federal one in nine provinces and a provincial one in Quebec. The plaintiff had moved from Ontario to Quebec in August of 1992. When the referendum was held in October, he was not qualified to vote in the federal referendum, because in October he was not resident in Ontario or any of the other eight provinces where the federal referendum was held (the federal law's requirement). He was not qualified to vote in the Quebec referendum, because he had not been resident in Quebec for six months (the Quebec law's requirement).

[4] This was the point upon which Iacobucci J., with Lamer C.J., dissented. In his view (at 1066-1067), s. 2(b) conferred a right to participate in the referendum.

[5] See ch. 55, Equality, under heading § 55:49, "Place of residence".

laws (in the case of the legislative assemblies). In the previous section of this chapter, we noticed the litigation on the regulation of election expenditures. Other fields of regulation include such matters as the qualifications to vote, the boundaries of electoral districts, limits on advertising, polling and publication of electoral results, and the registration and funding of parties. Challenges to the regulation of elections have often been brought under s. 3 and sometimes under s. 2(b). They are discussed in the later ch. 45, Voting.

XV. ACCESS TO GOVERNMENT; ACCESS TO GOVERNMENT DOCUMENTS

§ 43:40 Access to government

In *Native Women's Assn. of Canada v. Canada* (1994),[1] the Native Women's Association of Canada (NWAC) argued that the Government of Canada had denied its right to freedom of expression[2] by providing funding to other aboriginal organizations but not to NWAC, and by inviting other aboriginal organizations, but not NWAC, to participate in the constitutional discussions that eventually led to the constitutional proposals known as the Charlottetown Accord. NWAC, which promoted the rights of aboriginal women, argued that the other aboriginal organizations were dominated by men, and the exclusion of NWAC would deny a voice to aboriginal women. As in the earlier *Haig* case,[3] this raised the question whether s. 2(b) imposed positive duties on governments, in this case, a duty to fund and consult with particular groups. Sopinka J. for the majority of the Supreme Court of Canada held that *Haig* "establishes the principle that generally the government is under no obligation to fund or provide a specific platform of expression to an individual or a group".[4] The government could not provide access or funding in a fashion that amounted to discrimination under s. 15,[5] but s. 15 should not be interpreted as constraining the government in its choice of advisers, or requiring the government to listen to every

---

[Section 43:40]

[1] *Native Women's Assn. of Canada v. Canada*, [1994] 3 S.C.R. 627. The Court was unanimous. The opinion of the majority was written by Sopinka J., with the agreement of Lamer C.J., La Forest, Gonthier, Cory, Iacobucci and Major JJ. Brief concurring opinions were written by L'Heureux-Dubé and McLachlin JJ.

[2] Sections 15 and 28 were invoked as well as s. 2(b). The Court gave some indication of the respective roles of ss. 2(b) and 15 (see [1994] 3 S.C.R. 627, 664), but said nothing of substance about s. 28.

[3] *Haig v. Canada*, [1993] 2 S.C.R. 995.

[4] *Native Women's Assn. of Canada v. Canada*, [1994] 3 S.C.R. 627, 655. L'Heureux-Dubé J.'s separate concurring opinion (at p. 666) disagreed with this reading of *Haig*, but the difference of opinion was very slight, since Sopinka J. acknowledged (at p. 655) that the government must not act "in a discriminatory fashion", which was L'Heureux-Dubé J.'s concern. McLachlin J.'s separate concurring opinion was that governments were not constrained by the Charter (including, presumably, s. 15) in choosing and funding their advisers on matters of policy.

[5] *Native Women's Assn. of Canada v. Canada*, [1994] 3 S.C.R. 627, 664 (discrimina-

point of view. In any event, in this case, the Court held, the evidence did not support NWAC's contentions that the funded groups were not representative of aboriginal women and were adopting positions inimical to the interests of aboriginal women.

In *Baier v. Alberta* (2007),[6] the question arose whether Alberta could enact a law that disqualified teachers and other employees of school boards from serving as trustees of school boards. The applicants were teachers who had been elected as trustees and who would be disqualified by the new law. They argued that the law was an infringement of their freedom of expression. The Supreme Court of Canada rejected the argument and upheld the law. The law did not prevent the teachers from expressing opinions on any issues relating to education (or anything else); its purpose and effect was to disqualify them[7] from participation in the management of the schools[8] because of their conflict of interest in labour relations matters.[9] There is much to be said for LeBel J.'s concurring view that freedom of expression was not engaged at all. Rothstein J., for the majority, was prepared to accept that "expressive activity" was in issue, but all that was restricted was access to a "statutory platform" for expression,[10] and he held that s. 2(b) did not provide a right of access to any particular statutory platform.[11] Fish J., the sole dissenter, characterized the case as involving "political expression" and its "deliberate suppression by Alberta";[12] he would have struck down the law.

§ 43:41 Access to government documents

Ontario, in common with all other Canadian governments, has enacted freedom of information legislation to provide access to the public to documents held by government. The Ontario Act, like the other statutes,

---

tory treatment should be examined under s. 15, not s. 2(b)).

[6]*Baier v. Alberta*, [2007] 2 S.C.R. 673. Rothstein J. wrote the five-judge majority opinion; LeBel J. wrote a three-judge concurring opinion; Fish J. wrote a dissenting opinion. For comment, see R.E. Charney, "The Shaky Foundation of 'Statutory Platforms': a comment on *Baier v. Alberta*" (2008), 42 S.C.L.R. (2d) 115.

[7]Section 15 (equality) was also argued, but the Court held that a statutory distinction based on occupational status is not a listed or analogous ground of discrimination: ch. 55, Equality, under heading § 55:50, "Occupation".

[8]The right to be a candidate for elected office is protected by s. 3 of the Charter, but only for the House of Commons and provincial legislative assemblies: ch. 45, Voting, under heading § 45:6, "Candidacy".

[9]The teachers were already disqualified from serving as trustees of their own board and did not challenge that disqualification; the new law would disqualify them from serving as trustees of any Alberta school board. The wider geographic scope of the disqualification recognized an indirect conflict of interest.

[10]*Baier v. Alberta*, [2007] 2 S.C.R. 673, paras. 33, 36.

[11]Compare *Greater Vancouver Transportation Authority v. Can. Federation of Students*, [2009] 2 S.C.R. 295, paras. 26-36 (transit authorities, having created a statutory platform by permitting commercial messages on the sides of their buses, were not entitled to exclude political messages).

[12]*Baier v. Alberta*, [2007] 2 S.C.R. 673, para. 79.

provides a right of public access to certain classes of documents, and exempts other classes of documents from the right of access. The exemption may be absolute (for example, cabinet records, personal information) or subject to the discretion of the responsible minister. In *Ontario v. Criminal Lawyers' Association* (2010),[1] an association of criminal defence lawyers made a request under the Ontario Act for access to three documents in the hands of the Crown, one being the report of a police inquiry into police misconduct in a murder investigation, the other two being memoranda of legal advice related to the inquiry. The request was refused by the minister responsible for the police and on review (under the Act) by the information and privacy commissioner. The basis for the refusal was that the Act contained two discretionary exemptions from disclosure, one for law enforcement records (covering the report) and the other for solicitor-client privileged memoranda (covering the memoranda). The Act contained a provision (the "public-interest override") that certain exemptions from disclosure did not apply "where a compelling public interest in the disclosure of the record clearly outweighs the purpose of the exemption", but the exemptions for law enforcement and solicitor-client privilege were not included in this "public-interest override". The case advanced into the Ontario courts and up to the Supreme Court of Canada. The association argued that the public-interest override provision infringed the guarantee of freedom of expression because it did not extend to law-enforcement records or solicitor-client privileged records. The Supreme Court rejected the constitutional argument, although it did remit the request back to the commissioner to re-consider whether any or all of the law-enforcement report (but not the solicitor-client privileged memoranda) could be disclosed notwithstanding the inapplicability of the express public-interest override.

The Court first considered whether s. 2(b) protected access to information, and the Court gave a qualified "yes" to that question.[2] Although s. 2(b) guaranteed freedom of expression, not access to information, the Court held that "access is a derivative right which may arise where it is a necessary precondition to meaningful expression on the functioning of government". Where it can be shown that, without the desired access, "meaningful public discussion and criticism on matters of public interest would be substantially impeded", then there will be a prima facie case for access to records under s. 2(b). If the records are covered by a common-law privilege, like solicitor-client privilege, or a statutory privilege, like cabinet confidences, the privileges, although "in principle open to constitutional challenge", are "in practice" likely to be upheld to maintain predictability and certainty as to what remains protected from

[Section 43:41]

[1]*Ontario v. Criminal Lawyers' Association*, [2010] 1 S.C.R. 815. McLachlin C.J. and Abella J. wrote the opinion of the Court.

[2]*Ontario v. Criminal Lawyers' Association*, [2010] 1 S.C.R. 815, paras. 30-40.

production.[3] In some cases, "a particular government function is incompatible with access to government documents", for example, occasions like the preparation of a judicial decision (after the hearing) or a cabinet discussion, where full and frank deliberation must not be compromised. In summary: "Access to documents in government hands is constitutionally protected only where it is shown to be a necessary precondition of meaningful expression, does not encroach on protected privileges, and is compatible with the function of the institution concerned".[4] In this case, the plaintiff association had not established that meaningful discussion of the investigation and prosecution in the murder trial required access to the documents since there was a great deal of information already in the public domain. Therefore, the s. 2(b) right of access did not apply. Even if it did apply, the addition of the public-interest override to the two exemptions would not add much to them. Both were already discretionary, and it was open to the minister or commissioner to exercise the discretion to release documents where there was a compelling public interest in disclosure. That would be unlikely in the case of the solicitor-client privileged documents, since solicitor-client privilege is "close to absolute", but in the case of the law enforcement document (the report of the inquiry into police conduct), the matter should be remitted back to the commissioner to consider whether the public interest would warrant its discretionary disclosure.

Although the Supreme Court in *Criminal Lawyers' Association* is cautious in its recognition of the "derivative" right of access to government information, the decision is very important.[5] Before the decision, for example, a legislature would have been free to repeal its freedom of information legislation. That is no longer the case.[6]

---

[3]*Ontario v. Criminal Lawyers' Association*, [2010] 1 S.C.R. 815, para. 39.

[4]*Ontario v. Criminal Lawyers' Association*, [2010] 1 S.C.R. 815, para. 5.

[5]See D. Guttman, "*Criminal Lawyers' Assn. v. Ontario*: A Limited Right to Government Information under Section 2(b) of the Charter" (2010) 51 Supreme Court L.R. (2d) 199; R.L. Gilliland, "Supreme Court Recognizes (a Derivative) Right to Access Information" (2010) 51 Supreme Court L.R. (2d) 223.

[6]See *Can. v. Can.*, [2011] 2 S.C.R. 306, para. 40 per Charron J. for majority (denying access to information in ministerial offices, but describing the [federal] Access to Information Act as "quasi-constitutional"); para.79 per LeBel J. concurring ("quasi-constitutional").

Chapter 44

Assembly and Association

I. DISTRIBUTION OF POWERS

§ 44:1 Distribution of powers

II. FREEDOM OF ASSEMBLY

§ 44:2 Freedom of assembly

III. FREEDOM OF ASSOCIATION

§ 44:3 Section 2(d) of Charter
§ 44:4 Formation of association
§ 44:5 Purpose of association
§ 44:6 Exercise of constitutional rights
§ 44:7 Exercise of non-constitutional rights
§ 44:8 Freedom not to associate

I. DISTRIBUTION OF POWERS

§ 44:1 Distribution of powers

Legislative authority over *assembly* is divided between the two levels of government, depending upon the type of assembly. For example, the provincial Legislatures have the power to regulate meetings, parades and gatherings on parks and streets by virtue of the provincial legislative authority over "matters of a merely local or private nature in the province" (s. 92(16)).[1] The federal Parliament has the power to prohibit riots and other breaches of the peace by virtue of the federal legislative authority over criminal law (s. 91(27)). The regulation of picketing is a matter of labour law, which comes within the power of whichever level of government has authority over the industry in which the picketers are employed.[2]

Legislative authority over *association* is also divided between the two levels of government, depending upon the type of association. For example, the provincial Legislatures have the power to regulate clubs, societies, partnerships and other unincorporated associations, by virtue

---

[Section 44:1]

[1]*A.G. Can and Dupond v. Montreal*, [1978] 2 S.C.R. 770 (municipal by-law restricting public meetings and parades upheld).

[2]See ch. 21, Property and Civil Rights, under heading §§ 21:10 to 21:11, "Labour relations".

of the provincial legislative authority over property and civil rights in the province (s. 91(13)).[3] The federal Parliament has the power to prohibit conspiracies to commit offences by virtue of the federal legislative authority over criminal law (s. 91(27)), and the power to regulate mergers and monopolies in restraint of trade by virtue of federal legislative authority over criminal law (s. 91(27)) and trade and commerce (s. 91(2)).[4] In the labour field, the power to regulate trade unions is possessed by the level of government that has authority over the particular industry in which the trade union members are employed. This means that most trade union regulation is provincial; but in the federal public service and in federally-regulated industries, such as banking and interprovincial transportation and communication, where federal labour law applies, the regulation of trade unions is federal.[5]

II. FREEDOM OF ASSEMBLY

§ 44:2 Freedom of assembly

Section 2(c) of the Charter of Rights[1] guarantees to "everyone"[2] the "fundamental freedom" of "freedom of peaceful assembly". The word "peaceful", which is not used in the Canadian Bill of Rights,[3] is closer to the first amendment of the United States Constitution ("the right of the people peaceably to assemble"), and is presumably included to make clear that no doubt is cast on laws regarding breaches of the peace or riots. However, municipal by-laws restricting public meetings or parades will be limitations on s. 2(c) that will have to be justified under s. 1.[4] Section 1 was examined in ch. 38, Limitation of Rights.

Picketing by striking workers has been held to be an exercise of freedom of expression.[5] For that reason, it is a constitutionally protected activity, and any restrictions have to be justified under s. 1. The Supreme Court of Canada has not treated picketing as an exercise of the right of assembly, although that would also be a plausible analysis.

---

[3]Legislative power over the incorporation of companies depends upon s. 92(11) (provincial) and the opening words of s. 91 (federal): see ch. 23, Companies.

[4]See ch. 18, Criminal Law, under heading § 18:11, Competition law.

[5]Chapter 21, Property and Civil Rights, under heading §§ 21:10 to 21:11, "Labour relations".

[Section 44:2]

[1]For commentary on s. 2(c) and (d), see Beaudoin and Mendes (eds.), The Canadian Charter of Rights and Freedoms (4th ed., 2005), ch. 7 (by Norman); McLeod, Takach, Morton, Segal, The Canadian Charter of Rights (Carswell, loose-leaf service), ch. 23; Canadian Charter of Rights Annotated (Canada Law Book, loose-leaf service), annotations to s. 2(c) and (d). The last work contains a bibliography of the relevant literature.

[2]On the meaning of "everyone", see ch. 37, Application of Charter, under heading §§ 37:1 to 37:5, "Benefit of rights".

[3]The comparable provision of the Canadian Bill of Rights is s. 1(e), which guarantees "freedom of assembly".

[4]*A.G. Can and Dupond v. Montreal*, [1978] 2 S.C.R. 770, was a pre-Charter case.

[5]See ch. 43, Expression, under heading § 43:26, Picketing.

III. FREEDOM OF ASSOCIATION

§ 44:3 Section 2(d) of Charter

Section 2(d) of the Charter of Rights[1] guarantees to "everyone"[2] the "fundamental freedom" of "freedom of association".[3]

Section 2(d), like other Charter rights, is subject to s. 1 (the limitation clause) of the Charter, which means that limits on freedom of association will be valid if they come within the phrase "such reasonable limits prescribed by law as can be demonstrably justified in a free and democratic society". Section 1 was examined in ch. 38, Limitation of Rights.

Freedom of association is not explicitly guaranteed by the first amendment of the United States Constitution, but it has been held to be guaranteed by implication as a derivative of the guarantees of free speech and assembly.[4]

§ 44:4 Formation of association

Freedom of association in s. 2(d) includes "the freedom to establish, belong to and maintain an association".[1] In the labour context, for example, s. 2(d) accords to employees the right to form an employee association to represent their interests against the employer. However, the Supreme Court of Canada initially held that the right of association did not require that the competent legislative body enact a statutory regime of compulsory collective bargaining on the model that is now general in

---

[Section 44:3]

[1]For commentary on s. 2(d), see Beaudoin and Mendes (eds.), The Canadian Charter of Rights and Freedoms (4th ed., 2005), ch. 7 (by Norman); McLeod, Takach, Morton, Segal, The Canadian Charter of Rights (Carswell, loose-leaf service), ch. 23; Canadian Charter of Rights Annotated (Canada Law Book, loose-leaf service), annotations to s. 2(c) and (d). For references to freedom of association in contexts not discussed in the text that follows, see *Catholic Children's Aid Society v. S.(T)* (1989), 69 O.R. (2d) 189 (C.A.) (s. 2(d) is not applicable to family relationships, and does not protect adopted child's access to biological parents); *Black v. Law Society of Alta.*, [1989] 1 S.C.R. 591, 636 (minority per McIntyre J. held that restrictions on legal partnerships with out-of-province lawyers violated s. 2(d); majority rested decision only on mobility right of s. 6); *R. v. Skinner*, [1990] 1 S.C.R. 1235, 1250-1251 (minority per Wilson J. held that prohibition on communication for the purpose of prostitution violated s. 2(d) as well as s. 2(b); majority at 1234 rejected s. 2(d)); *Alex Couture v. Can.* (1991), 83 D.L.R. (4th) 477 (Que. C.A.) (s. 2(d) not violated by merger restrictions in Competition Act).

[2]On the meaning of "everyone", see ch. 37, Application of Charter, under heading §§ 37:1 to 37:5, "Benefit of rights".

[3]The comparable provision of the Canadian Bill of Rights is s. 1(e), which also guarantees "freedom of association".

[4]*NAACP v. Alabama* (1958), 357 U.S. 449; see generally L.H. Tribe, American Constitutional Law (Foundation Press, N.Y., 2nd ed., 1988), 1010-1022; J.E. Nowak and R.D. Rotunda, Constitutional Law (West St. Paul, Minn., 7th ed., 2004), sec. 16.41.

[Section 44:4]

[1]*Professional Institute v. N.W.T.*, [1990] 2 S.C.R. 367, 402 per Sopinka J., whose opinion (at 401-403) contains an excellent review of the law.

North America. This was established in *Delisle v. Canada* (1999)[2]—a case that has since been overruled,[3] but is important to the history now being related. In *Delisle*, it was held that the exclusion of the members of the Royal Canadian Mounted Police from the federal Public Service Staff Relations Act, which regulates labour relations in the federal civil service, was not a breach of s. 2(d).[4] While the exclusion meant that the members of the RCMP could not form a trade union that would be certified under the Act, it did not impair their right to form an independent employee association (which they had in fact done), and indeed their right to do so was guaranteed by s. 2(d) of the Charter.[5]

In *Delisle*, Bastarache J. for the majority emphasized that "the fundamental freedoms protected by s. 2 of the Charter do not impose a positive obligation of protection or inclusion on Parliament or the government, except perhaps in exceptional circumstances which are not at issue in the instant case."[6] This point seems to have been rather quickly forgotten, because two years later in *Dunmore v. Ontario* (2001),[7] the Supreme Court of Canada, with Bastarache J. again writing for the majority, held that the Legislature of Ontario was under a constitutional obligation under s. 2(d) of the Charter to enact legislation to facilitate the organization of employees' associations by agricultural workers. Ontario's Labour Relations Act, which provided the legislative framework for union certification, collective bargaining and strikes, excluded a number of categories of employees from its provisions. One of these was agricultural workers, who challenged the constitutionality of their exclusion from the Act. On the face of it, this was exactly the same issue

---

[2] *Delisle v. Canada*, [1999] 2 S.C.R. 989. The opinion of the majority was written by Bastarache J. with the concurrence of Gonthier, McLachlin and Major JJ. L'Heureux-Dubé J. wrote a separate concurring opinion. Cory and Iacobucci JJ. wrote a dissenting opinion, holding that the exclusion of the RCMP from the collective bargaining regime was a breach of freedom of association.

[3] *Mounted Police Assn. v. Can.*, [2015] 1 S.C.R. 3, 2015 SCC 1.

[4] If the exclusion had been based on a ground listed in s. 15 of the Charter, or an analogous ground, then there would have been a breach of equality rights, but the Court held (para. 44) that a distinction based on a group's employment status as members of the RCMP was not a listed or analogous ground that qualified for protection under s. 15.

[5] The RCMP as a branch of government was directly bound by the Charter. A private employer would not have been directly bound by the Charter (but note that the common law must respect "Charter values", so that in practice this distinction is not a sharp one).

[6] *Delisle v. Canada*, [1999] 2 S.C.R. 989, para. 33 (and see also paras. 36, 37); this was in answer to the obiter suggestion by L'Heureux-Dubé J. in her concurring opinion (para. 7) that there might be some positive obligation to legislate against unfair labour practices in the private sector (where the Charter did not directly apply) in order to check interference by employers with the formation of employee associations.

[7] *Dunmore v. Ontario*, [2001] 3 S.C.R. 1016. The opinion of the majority was written by Bastarache J. with the concurrence of McLachlin C.J. and Gonthier, Iacobucci, Binnie, Arbour and LeBel JJ. A concurring opinion was written by L'Heureux-Dubé J. and a dissenting opinion by Major J.

as had been resolved in *Delisle*, but now the Court held that the exclusion was a breach of s. 2(d) that could not be saved under s. 1.[8]

How did *Dunmore* differ from *Delisle?* The Court offered two reasons. One was that, unlike the police officers in *Delisle*, who had formed their own association without the benefit of labour relations legislation, it was not feasible for the agricultural workers to form an employees' association without some assistance from the Legislature. The second was that, unlike the police officers in *Delisle*, who were employed by government, the agricultural workers were employed by private firms or individuals and could not rely on the direct application of the Charter to support their efforts to form an association. But surely the ratio decidendi of *Delisle* is equally applicable in *Dunmore*. The freedom to organize existed independently of any statute, and the exclusion of agricultural workers from the superior regime of the Labour Relations Act did not impair their freedom to organize. The agricultural workers were in the same position as if there were no Labour Relations Act.[9] Their difficulties in forming an association stemmed from the inherent character of farm work and from resistance by their private employers, not from any action by the Legislature or government to which the Charter applied. This was the dissenting view of Major J., as well as the unanimous view of the Ontario judges at trial and in the Court of Appeal.

In *Dunmore*, the Supreme Court of Canada did not resile from its earlier rulings that s. 2(d) conferred on employees' associations no rights to collective bargaining or to strike.[10] And yet the Court's remedy was to sever from the Labour Relations Act the provision excluding agricultural workers. This had the effect of conferring on the formerly excluded workers the rights to collective bargaining and strike. This would be a particularly bizarre result in that the Court, in its discussion of s. 1 justification, acknowledged that many farms in Ontario were family owned and operated and were not suitable to formal processes of decision-making; the Court also acknowledged that the seasonal character of agriculture made it peculiarly vulnerable to work stoppages. These characteristics of Ontario's farm economy would justify the Legislature in withholding the rights to collective bargaining and strike. The Court solved this problem by postponing its declaration of invalidity for 18 months to allow the Legislature time to enact a special regime of labour law for agricultural workers. This regime would not have to

[8]The majority did not rely on s. 15 for the result (para. 2). Although no reason was given, no doubt the reason (which had been explicit in *Delisle v. Canada*, [1999] 2 S.C.R. 989, para. 44) was that a distinction based on a person's employment status was not a listed or analogous ground that qualified for protection under s. 15. L'Heureux-Dubé J. argued that occupational status was an analogous ground (para. 170) and gave s. 15 along with s. 2(d) as her reasons for concurrence in the result. Major J., dissenting, explicitly argued that s. 15 did not apply because of the absence of a listed or analogous ground (para. 215).

[9]Bastarache J. argues (paras. 43-48) that the exclusion of agricultural workers from the statute somehow makes their situation worse. Like Major J. in dissent (para. 214), I did not find the argument persuasive.

[10]*Dunmore v. Ontario*, [2001] 3 S.C.R. 1016, para. 17.

include rights to collective bargaining and strike, but it should include a "statutory freedom to organize" along with "protections judged essential to its meaningful exercise, such as freedom to assemble, to participate in the lawful activities of the association and to make representations, and the right to be free from interference, coercion and discrimination in the exercise of these freedoms."[11] Since these rights exist at common law (which must itself reflect Charter values),[12] the Court apparently believed that enacting them into a statute would make them more likely to be exercised (even if no collective bargaining or strike rights could be acquired by the effort).[13] In any event, the end result was the imposition by the Court on the Legislature of a positive duty to enact a statute to facilitate the organization of agricultural workers.

Dunmore fitted uneasily into the prior jurisprudence, but it turned out to be the precursor of a 180-degree shift in the jurisprudence. The shift came in the *Health Services Bargaining* case (2007),[14] which decided that, in the labour context, the formation of a union carried with it the right of the union to engage in collective bargaining. This case and its important sequels are discussed in the next section of this chapter.

§ 44:5 Purpose of association

The Supreme Court of Canada initially held that freedom of association was an individual right, not a collective right. It was possessed by individuals who wished to associate, but not by the associations that they formed. From that premise, the Court reasoned that an association, once formed, was not guaranteed the right to engage in a collective activity, even if the activity was "a foundational or essential purpose of the association".[1] In the labour context, the concept of s. 2(d) as a right of individuals meant that trade unions had no constitutional rights that were not possessed by individuals. Trade unions could be deprived of the statutory right to engage in collective bargaining,[2] or could be restricted in their power to bargain by wage controls,[3] or could be denied the right

---

[11]*Dunmore v. Ontario*, [2001] 3 S.C.R. 1016, para. 67.

[12]E.g., *Pepsi-Cola Canada Beverages v. R.W.D.S.U*, [2002] 1 S.C.R. 156 (affirming common law right to engage in secondary picketing).

[13]The Legislature followed up with the Agricultural Employees Protection Act, 2002, S.O. 2002, c. 16, which continued the exclusion of agricultural workers from the Labour Relations Act and continued the denial of collective bargaining and striking. The new law was immediately but unsuccessfully challenged by the agricultural workers as a breach of ss. 2(d) and 15: *Ont. v. Fraser*, [2011] 2 S.C.R. 3.

[14]*Health Services and Support—Facilities Subsector Bargaining Assn. v. B.C.*, [2007] 2 S.C.R. 391.

[Section 44:5]

[1]*Professional Institute v. N.W.T.*, [1990] 2 S.C.R. 367, 402. Folld. *Can. Egg Marketing Agency v. Richardson*, [1998] 3 S.C.R. 157 (activity of egg marketing not protected under s. 2(d) despite fact that it is impossible to market eggs by oneself).

[2]*Professional Institute v. N.W.T.*, [1990] 2 S.C.R. 367.

[3]*PSAC v. Can.*, [1987] 1 S.C.R. 424. I disclose that I was one of the counsel for the

to strike,[4] or having struck could be ordered back to work,[5] all without infringing s. 2(d). The one discordant (or perhaps prescient) note was sounded by Bastarache J. in *Dunmore.* In an obiter dictum (but speaking for the majority), he said that some collective activities should be protected by s. 2(d), because they were "central to freedom of association, even though they are inconceivable on the individual level."[6] That dictum was taken up in the *Health Services Bargaining* case (2007),[7] where the Court held that the *Dunmore* dictum was now the law. Reversing its earlier decisions, the Court unanimously held that collective bargaining by unions (although not the right to strike) was protected by s. 2(d).

The issue in the *Health Services Bargaining* case (2007)[8] was the validity of the Health and Social Services Delivery Act, a law enacted by British Columbia in 2002 that attempted to enable hospitals to deliver their services more efficiently and to rein in the costs of the province's public health care system, which had for the last ten years been increasing at a rate three times that of the provincial economy. The Act gave to publicly-funded health care employers, who were bound by collective agreements, more freedom in managing their unionized employees. Some of the provisions of the Act conflicted with the terms of the applicable collective agreements. Of course, according to the pre-2007 rules of constitutional law, a statute would in any case prevail over a collective agreement, and to make matters doubly certain the Act expressly provided that its terms were to prevail over the applicable collective agreements. The unions challenged the Act as contrary to the Charter guarantee of freedom of association. The Supreme Court held for the first time that "members of labour unions" have the constitutional right to engage in "collective bargaining on fundamental workplace issues" ("a process of collective action to achieve workplace goals"). If the government "substantially interferes" with that right, it violates s. 2(d) of the Charter.[9] According to the Court, the importance of collective bargaining as a goal of trade unions, its role in enhancing "workplace democracy",

---

union in this case.

[4]*Re Public Service Employees Relations Act*, [1987] 1 S.C.R. 313.

[5]*RWDSU v. Sask.*, [1987] 1 S.C.R. 460. See also *ILWU v. Can.*, [1994] 1 S.C.R. 150 (holding that back-to-work legislation does not violate the liberty of the employees under s. 7).

[6]*Dunmore v. Ontario*, [2001] 3 S.C.R. 1016, para. 17.

[7]*Health Services and Support—Facilities Subsector Bargaining Assn. v. B.C.*, [2007] 2 S.C.R. 391, paras. 27-28.

[8]*Health Services and Support—Facilities Subsector Bargaining Assn. v. B.C.*, [2007] 2 S.C.R. 391. McLachlin C.J. and LeBel J. wrote the opinion of the six-judge majority. Deschamps J. dissented in part. She agreed (para. 174) that s. 2(d) protected collective bargaining, and she agreed that five of the Act's provisions infringed s. 2(d), but she would have saved all but one of them under s. 1.

[9]*Health Services and Support—Facilities Subsector Bargaining Assn. v. B.C.*, [2007] 2 S.C.R. 391, para. 19 per majority. Deschamps J. disagreed with the "substantial interference" test, which she pointed out (para. 181) led the majority to "indirectly protect the substance of clauses in collective agreements". Her own test (para. 180)

its history as a union right in Canada, and the recognition of unions in multilateral treaties ratified by Canada, all led to the conclusion that freedom of association should now be interpreted as including the right of collective bargaining. The Act substantially interfered with *past* collective bargaining by substituting, for the seniority-based employee-security provisions of the collective agreements, rules that permitted employers greater freedom to contract-out services and to lay off employees, and that restricted the bumping options of laid-off employees. Those provisions infringed s. 2(d) and were not saved by s. 1.

The majority in the *Health Services Bargaining* case repeatedly emphasized that what it was constitutionalizing was the "procedure" or "process" of collective bargaining, and they pointed out correctly that "it is entirely possible to protect the 'procedure' known as collective bargaining without mandating constitutional protection for the fruits of the bargaining process".[10] But they immediately ignored this distinction, granting constitutional protection to the collective agreements precisely because they were the fruits of the bargaining process. The Act breached s. 2(d), not merely by limiting *future* collective bargaining, but also "by invalidating existing collective agreements and consequently undermining the *past* bargaining processes that formed the basis for these agreements".[11] The Act's provisions respecting seniority, layoffs, bumping and contracting out were held to be unconstitutional because they were a substantial interference[12] with the terms of collective agreements. This ruling elevated collective agreements above statutes in the hierarchy of laws, and granted them virtually the same status as the provisions of the Charter itself.[13] Any substantial interference by statute with the terms of a collective agreement dealing with workplace issues is unconstitutional unless it can be justified as a reasonable limit under s. 1. Indeed, the majority of the Court actually posited a stricter test for s. 1 justification for substantial interference with collective bargaining rights than for breach of other Charter rights. Section 1 justification, they said,

---

focussed more on the process of collective bargaining, but produced similar conclusions.

[10] *Health Services and Support—Facilities Subsector Bargaining Assn. v. B.C.*, [2007] 2 S.C.R. 391, para. 29, and see to the same effect paras. 66, 68, 89, 111.

[11] *Health Services and Support—Facilities Subsector Bargaining Assn. v. B.C.*, [2007] 2 S.C.R. 391, para. 113 (emphasis added). The Act, by limiting what could go into future collective agreements, also breached s. 2(d) by "undermining future collective bargaining over these matters". The "undermining" of either past or future collective bargaining constituted a breach of s. 2(d).

[12] The Act's provisions respecting transfer and reassignment of workers were held to be insufficiently important to the trade unions to amount to substantial interference with collective bargaining.

[13] See ch. 1, Sources, under heading § 1:4, "Constitution of Canada". As explained earlier in this section, the protection differed from that accorded to other Charter rights in that only a "substantial interference" would qualify as a breach, and only "workplace" provisions (although presumably that would normally be all provisions) were protected. On the other hand, as explained in the following text, stricter standards of s. 1 justification were demanded by the majority of the Court for interferences with collective bargaining. None of these new rules have any basis in the text of the Charter or in the earlier case law.

"may" be available "on an exceptional and typically temporary basis, in situations, for example, involving essential services, vital state administration, clear deadlocks and national crisis."[14] Deschamps J., dissenting, disagreed with the majority on this ruling. She pointed out that it was the first time that a standard of exceptional and temporary circumstances had been applied to s. 1 justification.[15] Not surprisingly, the majority found that none of the five infringing provisions of the Act was justified under s. 1, while Deschamps J. would have found all but one of the infringing provisions to be justified.

Trade union goals for the ordering of the workplace that have not found their way into collective agreements are also apparently protected by s. 2(d). "Seniority", the majority of the Court said, "is one of the most important and far-reaching benefits which the trade union movement has been able to secure for its members by virtue of the collective bargaining process."[16] Therefore, seniority was now protected by s. 2(d), despite the rigidity it introduces into a workplace. Even if the existing collective agreements had been silent on the seniority issues covered by the Act (layoffs and bumping) and on contracting out, the provisions of the Act would still have been invalid as a substantial interference with *future* collective bargaining![17] This all goes way beyond the "procedure" or "process" of collective bargaining.

It will be recalled that, in *Dunmore v. Ontario* (2001),[18] a case that is discussed in the previous section of this chapter, the Supreme Court of Canada decided that it was unconstitutional for Ontario to exclude agricultural workers from its labour relations statute. After this decision, the province enacted the Agricultural Employees Protection Act, 2002, which continued the exclusion of agricultural workers from the general labour relations statute, but which did enact some protections for the associational rights of agricultural workers. The Act conferred on agricultural workers the "right to form or join an employees' association" and the "right to make representations to their employers". However, under the Act the duties of the employer were only to "listen to the representations if made orally, or read them if made in writing", and if the representations were made in writing to "give the association a written acknowledgment that the employer has read them". There was no duty on the employer to bargain in good faith with the representatives of the association. The Act was quickly challenged by a union represent-

[14]*Health Services and Support—Facilities Subsector Bargaining Assn. v. B.C.*, [2007] 2 S.C.R. 391, para. 108.

[15]*Health Services and Support—Facilities Subsector Bargaining Assn. v. B.C.*, [2007] 2 S.C.R. 391, para. 196.

[16]*Health Services and Support—Facilities Subsector Bargaining Assn. v. B.C.*, [2007] 2 S.C.R. 391, para. 130.

[17]*Health Services and Support—Facilities Subsector Bargaining Assn. v. B.C.*, [2007] 2 S.C.R. 391, para. 113 ("prohibiting provisions dealing with specified matters in future collective agreements" would have the unconstitutional effect of "undermining future collective bargaining over those matters").

[18]*Dunmore v. Ontario*, [2001] 3 S.C.R. 1016.

ing agricultural workers. At first instance, the Act was upheld on the basis that *Dunmore* did not insist that organized workers be granted collective bargaining rights.[19] Then the Supreme Court rendered the decision in *Health Services*[20] with its new holding that the freedom of association of employees to pursue workplace goals had to be accompanied by a statute-imposed duty on employers to bargain in good faith with the representatives of the employees' association. This development caused the Ontario Court of Appeal to strike down the Act on the ground that it failed to impose on employers the duty to bargain in good faith with the representatives of the employees.[21] The Court of Appeal's decision seemed to be a straightforward application of *Health Services.* But, when it was appealed to the Supreme Court in *Ontario v. Fraser* (2011),[22] the Supreme Court splintered into four different camps. A majority of eight reversed the Court of Appeal, and only one judge (Abella J. in dissent) affirmed the reasoning and result of the Court of Appeal.

In describing the Supreme Court decision in *Fraser*, it is perhaps easiest to start with the dissenting opinion of Abella J. As explained, she followed the same straightforward route as the Ontario Court of Appeal. She agreed that, after *Health Services* created a "completely different jurisprudential universe", the Agricultural Employees Protection Act could no longer be upheld. The new constitutional requirement of a statutory duty on the part of the employer to bargain in good faith with the representatives of the employees' association was "missing in action", and without that piece the Act was unconstitutional. How did the other judges avoid this seemingly ineluctable conclusion? The answer is: by three different routes. First, Rothstein J. (with Charron J.) held that *Health Services* was wrongly decided and that *Fraser* should be decided on the basis of the pre-*Health-Services* law, which did not include a constitutional requirement of a statutory duty on the part of the employer to bargain in good faith; on that basis, the Act was constitutional. Second, Deschamps J. held that *Health Services* did not need to reach a conclusion about the duty to bargain in good faith, and, since the dicta in the decision on that point were merely obiter, the decision should be interpreted as not having decided the point. That took her back to the pre-*Health-Services* law, under which the Act was constitutional. Third—and this is the majority reasoning—McLachlin C.J. and LeBel J. (with Binnie, Fish and Cromwell JJ.) held that *Health Services* was controlling; it imposed a constitutional requirement that the Act impose a duty on the part of the employer to bargain in good faith; and, although the Act did not do that expressly (just requiring the

---

[19] *Fraser v. Ont.* (2006), 79 O.R. (3d) 219 (S.C.J.).

[20] *Health Services and Support—Facilities Subsector Bargaining Assn. v. B.C.*, [2007] 2 S.C.R. 391.

[21] *Fraser v. Ont.* (2008) 92 O.R. (3d) 481 (C.A.).

[22] *Ontario v. Fraser,* [2011] 2 S.C.R. 3. McLachlin C.J. and LeBel J., with the agreement of Binnie, Fish and Cromwell JJ., wrote the majority opinion. Rothstein J., with the agreement of Charron J., and Deschamps J. wrote opinions concurring in the result. Abella J. wrote a dissenting opinion.

employer to "listen" to oral representations and to "read" written representations), it should be interpreted as implicitly requiring the employer to bargain in good faith.[23] That implausible interpretation of the Act meant that it complied with the new *Health Services* jurisprudence and was therefore constitutional. It meant as well, of course, that the agricultural workers had acquired by judicial fiat a right to insist on their employers bargaining with them in good faith. However, the simple announcement that the statute implicitly required collective bargaining is no guarantee that collective bargaining will be effective: labour relations statutes find it necessary to include a host of other safeguards to support the right to collective bargaining.[24] If the Court had struck down the law, as Abella J. proposed, the government would have had to return to the drafting table and prepare legislation that made express provision for collective bargaining, along with the associated provisions to make it effective, or perhaps simply put the agricultural workers back into the general labour relations statute. Express legislative provision for collective bargaining would surely have been a much better result for the agricultural workers than a ruling by a court that has no ongoing responsibility or accountability for the management of the regime that it has put in place.

In *Mounted Police Association v. Canada* (2015),[25] the Supreme Court revisited the question of whether the exclusion of the Royal Canadian Mounted Police (RCMP) from the collective bargaining regime of the federal Public Service Labour Relations Act (the general federal public service labour relations statute) was constitutional. The Court had upheld the exclusion of the RCMP in *Delisle v. Canada* (1999).[26] The scheme that was substituted by regulation for the RCMP denied the members the collective bargaining rights possessed by other members of the federal public service, but it did grant the members of the RCMP a right to elect "staff relations representatives" to represent their interests directly to management. As well, the members had formed voluntary

---

[23]*Ontario v. Fraser*, [2011] 2 S.C.R. 3, para. 101 per McLachlin C.J. and LeBel J. ("By implication" the Act's duties to "listen" and "read" include "a requirement that the employer consider employee representations in good faith."). To consider something in good faith is a unilateral act falling well short of collective bargaining, but without further explanation the judges move on to conclude (para. 117) that the Act confers on the agricultural workers "a right to collective bargaining. . .requiring engagement by both parties".

[24]Abella J., in dissent, following the decision of the Ontario Court of Appeal, held that, in order for the collective bargaining process to be effective, the Act also needed a provision requiring the employer to bargain only with the union selected by a majority of the employees in the bargaining unit (majoritarian exclusivity). It may be too that some process of certification of bargaining units and their majority representatives would be necessary, as well as prohibitions of unfair labour practices by employers and rules of dispute-resolution to resolve impasses in collective bargaining and settle differences in the interpretation of the resulting collective agreements.

[25]*Mounted Police Association v. Canada*, [2015] 1 S.C.R. 3, 2015 SCC 1. McLachlin C.J. and LeBel J. wrote the opinion of the six-judge majority of the seven-judge bench. Rothstein J. wrote a dissenting opinion.

[26]*Delisle v. Canada*, [1999] 2 S.C.R. 989.

regional associations which were not unions, but which (among other things)[27] communicated workplace concerns to the elected staff relations representatives for consideration by management. The trial judge had found that members' workplace concerns were considered in good faith by management. The process, which was a consultative (or collaborative) one, did not allow for collective bargaining, and at the end of the process RCMP salaries were fixed by the federal Treasury Board. Did this regime pass muster under s. 2(d) of the Charter? The Court, by a majority,[28] said no. The Court held that "the s. 2(d) guarantee of freedom of association protects a *meaningful process of collective bargaining* that provides employees with a degree of *choice* and *independence* sufficient to enable them to determine and pursue their collective interests."[29] The RCMP process did not provide for collective bargaining, and the criteria of choice and independence were not satisfied: RCMP members had to present their workplace claims within the management organization of the force—"an organization they did not choose and do not control".[30] The Court concluded that the RCMP process was a "substantial interference with the right to associate for the purpose of addressing workplace goals through a meaningful process of collective bargaining free from employer control."[31] The Court refused to follow *Delisle* and held that the exclusion of the RCMP from the collective bargaining regime of the Public Service Staff Relations Act was a breach of s. 2(d).[32] This did not mean that Parliament must include the RCMP in the Public Service Staff Relations Act; "it remains open to the federal government to explore other collective bargaining processes that could better address the

---

[27]Two of the associations were the applicants in the proceedings.

[28]Rothstein J. in dissent would have held that the RCMP's "collaborative" process provided effective representation of the employees and was adequate to satisfy s. 2(b). In his view, no one model of labour relations should be given constitutional status, and he disagreed with the majority's insistence on a collective bargaining model that closely approximated the Wagner model and would normally yield an adversarial rather than a collaborative process.

[29]*Mounted Police Association v. Canada*, [2015] 1 S.C.R. 3, 2015 SCC 1, para. 5 (emphasis added). Rothstein J., in dissent, took the view that collective bargaining should not be a constitutional requirement if the employees were effectively represented in the labour-relations process, which he held was true of the RCMP.

[30]*Mounted Police Association v. Canada*, [2015] 1 S.C.R. 3, 2015 SCC 1, para. 106.

[31]*Mounted Police Association v. Canada*, [2015] 1 S.C.R. 3, 2015 SCC 1, para. 105.

[32]The Court held that the invalidity could not be saved under s. 1: "We conclude that the government has failed to establish a rational connection between denying RCMP members their s. 2(d) right to meaningful collective bargaining, and maintaining a neutral, stable and reliable police force" (para. 148). This statement is made with no discussion of the right to strike, despite the fact that removing the right to strike would have to be an important consideration in constructing a labour relations regime for a police force. If "meaningful collective bargaining" includes the right to strike, how could one possibly deny the rational connection? And yet, just two weeks later, in *Sask. Federation of Labour v. Sask.*, [2015] 1 S.C.R. 245, 2015 SCC 4, the same Court held that "meaningful collective bargaining" includes the right to strike!

specific context in which members of the RCMP discharge their duties."[33] The Court suspended the declaration of invalidity for 12 months to provide an opportunity for the government to take up the suggestion of constructing a different (but "meaningful") collective bargaining process for the RCMP.[34]

The consultative process that was condemned as unconstitutional in *Mounted Police* may not have been "meaningful collective bargaining", but it was by no means ineffective. As the result of the process, in 2008, the federal Treasury Board awarded pay increases for the RCMP of 3.32% for 2008, 3.5% for 2009 and 2% for 2010, three years of little or no inflation. However, later in 2008, the global financial crisis set in, and the federal government decided to impose wage restraints on the entire federal public sector, including the RCMP. In 2009 Parliament passed the Expenditure Restraint Act (ERA), which limited pay increases in the federal public sector to 1.5% for each of 2008, 2009 and 2010. Obedient to the new policy, the Treasury Board rolled back the previously announced RCMP increases to 1.5% per annum. In *Meredith v. Canada* (2015),[35] the RCMP's elected staff relations representatives applied for judicial review of the Treasury Board's rollback decision, arguing that the ERA was unconstitutional. The argument seemed strong. If the regular consultative RCMP process was a "substantial interference" with collective bargaining, as decided in *Mounted Police*, the unilateral ERA rollback seemed to be an even more substantial interference. In the Supreme Court, Abella J. took this view: she would have held that the ERA was unconstitutional at least in its application to RCMP pay; but she was a sole dissenter. The majority reached the contrary conclusion primarily by finding that "the level at which the ERA capped wage increases for members of the RCMP was consistent with the going rate reached in agreements concluded with other bargaining agents inside and outside of the core public administration and so reflected an outcome consistent with actual bargaining processes".[36] With respect, this reasoning seems weak if not circular. For bargaining agents covered by the ERA, "agreements" were concluded at the ERA level under the compulsion of the ERA, but of course it was the validity of the ERA that the applicants had put in issue. However, for the majority of the Court, the ERA did not substantially impair the collective pursuit of workplace goals by the RCMP: s. 2(d) was not breached,[37] and it was not even necessary to consider a s. 1 justification of the rollbacks. Of course, the

---

[33] *Mounted Police Association v. Canada*, [2015] 1 S.C.R. 3, 2015 SCC 1, para. 137.

[34] *Mounted Police Association v. Canada*, [2015] 1 S.C.R. 3, 2015 SCC 1, para. 158.

[35] *Meredith v. Canada*, [2015] 1 S.C.R. 125, 2015 SCC 2. McLachlin C.J. and LeBel J. wrote the opinion of the five-judge majority. Rothstein J. wrote a concurring opinion. Abella J. wrote a dissenting opinion.

[36] *Meredith v. Canada*, [2015] 1 S.C.R. 125, 2015 SCC 2, para. 28.

[37] The majority also seemed to be influenced by the temporary character of the rollback (affecting three years only) (para. 29). Another factor was that the RCMP were in fact able to obtain some "additional allowances" despite the rollback (para. 29), perhaps suggesting that wage-restraint legislation is only valid if it is ineffective.

damaging effects of the unexpected 2008 financial crisis on Canada's economy and tax revenues would have provided a case for s. 1 justification.[38] The fact that the Court upheld the ERA, albeit with such inadequate reasons, will be an important precedent for the validity of temporary, across-the-board public sector wage-restraint legislation in future circumstances of financial difficulty. And, of course, legislative bodies have not lost the power of unilateral changes to minor public employment conditions which (more clearly than the ERA) would not amount to "substantial interference" with collective bargaining.[39]

In *Mounted Police*, the Court had repeatedly referred to "meaningful collective bargaining" as the labour-relations requirement of s. 2(d), but never talked about whether that included the right to strike, which was a curious omission in a case reviewing the labour-relations process for a police force. In an earlier case, *Re Public Service Employees Relations Act* (1987),[40] the Court had held that s. 2(d) did not constitutionalize the right to strike. The issue came back to the Court in *Saskatchewan Federation of Labour v. Saskatchewan* (2015),[41] a case that was decided two weeks after *Mounted Police* and *Meredith* (which were decided on the same day). At issue was the validity of a Saskatchewan law, the Public Service Essential Services Act (PSESA),[42] which prohibited "essential services employees" from participating in a work stoppage against their public employer. Essential services were defined as services that were necessary for a public employer to prevent "danger to life, health or public safety", "the destruction or serious deterioration of machinery, equipment or premises", "serious environmental damage", or "disruption of any of the courts of Saskatchewan". The PSESA had been enacted in 2007 by a newly elected government after strikes by nurses, highway workers, snow plow operators and corrections workers had created concerns about public health and safety. The law only prohibited work stoppages; those workers who were unionized retained all the other attributes of union membership under the province's public-service labour relations legislation, which provided for collective bargaining. The Supreme Court, by a majority, held that the PSESA was unconstitutional. Abella J., who wrote for the majority, assumed that she was free to depart from the 1987 decision ("the arc bends increas-

---

Rothstein J. concurred in the result, although he reasoned from the dissenting view he had expressed in *Mounted Police*.

[38]Abella J., whose dissenting view required her to consider s. 1 justification, was not persuaded that the unilateral action by government was justified under s. 1: *Meredith v. Canada*, [2015] 1 S.C.R. 125, 2015 SCC 2, paras. 64-71.

[39]This was acknowledged in the *Health Services and Support—Facilities Subsector Bargaining Assn. v. B.C.*, [2007] 2 S.C.R. 391, para. 95.

[40]*Re Public Service Employees Relations Act*, [1987] 1 S.C.R. 313.

[41]*Saskatchewan Federation of Labour v. Saskatchewan*, [2015] 1 S.C.R. 245, 2015 SCC 4. Abella J. wrote the opinion of the five-judge majority. Rothstein and Wagner JJ. wrote a dissenting opinion.

[42]Also challenged was a statute that introduced stricter requirements for unions to be certified. The Court unanimously upheld this statute, holding that it did not substantially interfere with collective bargaining.

ingly towards workplace justice").[43] She held that the right to strike was an "indispensable component" of "meaningful collective bargaining", and that it was time to give this proposition "constitutional benediction" by holding that the right to strike was protected by s. 2(d).[44] Indeed, she asserted (in agreement with the trial judge) that without a right to strike "a constitutionalized right to bargain collectively is meaningless."[45] She did acknowledge that public sector employees who perform essential services "undoubtedly have unique functions which may argue for a less disruptive mechanism [than the strike] when collective bargaining reaches an impasse",[46] but the PSESA did not provide any alternative dispute resolution mechanism for the essential workers who were denied the right to strike. She said that, if essential services legislation provided for "one of the meaningful dispute resolution mechanisms commonly used in labour relations" (probably meaning compulsory arbitration), the legislation would "more likely be justified under s. 1 of the Charter".[47] In her s. 1 analysis of the PSESA, Abella J. held that the objective of maintaining essential public services was sufficiently important to justify a limitation of the s. 2(d) right, but the absence of a "meaningful dispute resolution mechanism" meant that the law was not minimally impairing of the right and could not be justified under s. 1. She postponed the declaration of invalidity for one year without giving a reason, but presumably to give the province time to enact substitute legislation with an alternative dispute resolution mechanism. As Rothstein and Wagner JJ. emphasized in dissent,[48] the decision to constitutionalize the right to strike is a radical one that injects the Court even more deeply into the regulation of labour relations with its difficult issues of balance between the rights of employees, employers and the public. The Court's earlier view that it should defer to the decisions of the competent legislative bodies on labour-relations issues has been decisively repudiated.

§ 44:6 Exercise of constitutional rights

The expansion of freedom of association to include collective rights, such as the right of unions to collective bargaining, does not mean that individual rights are not also protected by s. 2(d). When an individual

---

[43] *Saskatchewan Federation of Labour v. Saskatchewan*, [2015] 1 S.C.R. 245, 2015 SCC 4, para. 1.

[44] *Saskatchewan Federation of Labour v. Saskatchewan*, [2015] 1 S.C.R. 245, 2015 SCC 4, para. 3.

[45] *Saskatchewan Federation of Labour v. Saskatchewan*, [2015] 1 S.C.R. 245, 2015 SCC 4, para. 24.

[46] *Saskatchewan Federation of Labour v. Saskatchewan*, [2015] 1 S.C.R. 245, 2015 SCC 4, para. 4.

[47] *Saskatchewan Federation of Labour v. Saskatchewan*, [2015] 1 S.C.R. 245, 2015 SCC 4, para. 25.

[48] They took the view that the right to strike was an implausible extension of "freedom of association" in s. 2(d) and an unwarranted rejection of the Court's previous jurisprudence.

has a *constitutional* right to freedom of expression or freedom of religion (for example), the right continues to be protected if the individual chooses to exercise the right in association with others. The right is not lost just because it is exercised in common with others. No decision yet illustrates this point, but it has been widely recognized in dicta.[1]

§ 44:7 Exercise of non-constitutional rights

Does freedom of association also protect the exercise in association of the *lawful but non-constitutional* rights of individuals? In the *Labour Trilogy*,[1] three of the six judges asserted that freedom of association protected any activity by an association that was permitted for an individual. However, the other three judges pointedly made no reference to this element of the right. In *Professional Institute v. Northwest Territories*,[2] two of the six judges made the same claim for freedom of association but over the silence of the other four. In none of the cases did the point have to be decided, because the judges all took the view that the point was not raised by the claims to a right to strike and collective bargaining in the *Labour Trilogy* and the *Professional Institute* cases. But this view is disputable. It is at least arguable that the right to strike is simply the associational analogue of an individual's right to withdraw his or her services at the termination of an individual contract of employment (a common phenomenon in the world of professional sport, for example), and the right to bargain collectively is simply the associational analogue of the right to bargain individually.[3]

The fact is that the costs (and benefits) of collective action are so different from those of individual action that different regimes of regulation are often appropriate. The fixing of prices is a good example: what is lawful for an individual seller is properly prohibited by our competition law when performed in concert with other sellers. It is surely an undue extension of freedom of association to expand its protection to

---

[Section 44:6]

[1] *Professional Institute v. N.W.T.*, [1990] 2 S.C.R. 367, 402-403 per Sopinka J. referring to supporting dicta.

[Section 44:7]

[1] *Re Public Service Employees Relations Act*, [1987] 1 S.C.R. 313, 366-367 per Dickson J. (with Wilson J.), 408-409 per McIntyre J. These opinions were repeated in *PSAC v. Can.*, [1987] 1 S.C.R. 424; *RWDSU v. Sask.*, [1987] 1 S.C.R. 460.

[2] *Professional Institute v. Northwest Territories*,, [1990] 2 S.C.R. 367, 403 per Sopinka J. (with L'Heureux-Dubé J.). La Forest J., who otherwise agreed with Sopinka J., at 390-391 reserved his opinion on this point.

[3] This issue can be argued either way, depending upon how many characteristics of the statutory rights to strike and bargain collectively are taken into account. In support of the analogy (and of the extended right) is D. Beatty and S. Kennett, "Striking Back" (1988) 67 Can. Bar Rev. 573, 589-593. Also in support of the analogy (but not of the extended right) is P.C. Weiler, "The Charter at Work" (1990) 40 U. Toronto L.J. 117, 146-147.

every activity by an association that is permitted to an individual.[4] If the right is so extended, we must expect to find judges denying analogies between collective activity and apparently similar individual activity in order to avoid conferring constitutional protection on collective activity that legislators have reasonably decided to regulate.[5]

In the *Health Services Bargaining* case (2007),[6] the Supreme Court decided that freedom of association was not restricted to the rights of individuals, but included some collective rights of associations as well. This means that it is no longer necessary to find an individual analogue for every right of an association. A right that is essential to the purpose of an association, such as the right of collective bargaining for a union, is guaranteed by s. 2(d) regardless of whether it has an individual analogue. The artificial inquiry into which rights of individuals can be translated into associational rights is no longer necessary.

§ 44:8 Freedom not to associate

Does freedom of association include the freedom not to associate—freedom *from* association? This issue is raised by the union security arrangements that Canadian labour laws typically permit and sometimes require. The strictest arrangement is the "closed shop", under which a person must be a member of the union before he or she can be hired by the employer. The "union shop" does not require an employee to be a member of the union before being hired, but does require that all employees join the union after being hired. The "agency shop", which is the most common arrangement, does not require that all employees be members of the union, but does require that all employees, including non-members, pay dues to the union. In all three cases, an employee who would prefer not to belong to (or pay dues to) a union is compelled to do so on pain of losing his or her job.

The Supreme Court of Canada first had to consider the third type of union security arrangement, that is, the agency shop.[1] In *Lavigne v. OPSEU* (1991),[2] the plaintiff, Lavigne, was a teacher at a community college. The collective agreement between the college and the teachers' union included an agency shop provision, under which all employees

[4]Accord, P.C. Weiler, "The Charter at Work" (1990) 40 U. Toronto L.J. 117, 146-147.

[5]Alternatively, a relaxation of the standards of justification under s. 1 could be used to uphold regulation of collective activity. The better approach, in my opinion, is to confine the right to those activities worthy of protection (because they are within the purpose of the right), and maintain strict standards of justification under s. 1 This approach is argued for in ch. 38, Limitation of Rights, under heading § 38:3, "Relationship between s. 1 and rights".

[6]*Health Services and Support—Facilities Subsector Bargaining Assn. v. B.C.*, [2007] 2 S.C.R. 391.

[Section 44:8]

[1]Compare *R. v. Allen* (2005), 257 D.L.R. (4th) 458 (N.S.C.A.) (upholding provincial law requiring all licensed fishers to pay dues to a fisheries organization; fishers did not have to join the organization).

[2]*Lavigne v. OPSEU*, [1991] 2 S.C.R. 211.

had to pay dues to the union. Lavigne, who was not a member of the union, did not directly challenge the agency shop provision. He brought an action for a declaration that his obligation to pay dues was a breach of his Charter right to freedom of association to the extent that the dues were used by the union to fund political parties or causes unrelated to the representation of employees. This was not a frontal attack on the agency shop provision: the plaintiff made no objection to his obligation to pay for the union's services as his bargaining agent. What he objected to was the use of the compelled funds to contribute to the New Democratic Party and to various left-wing causes of which Lavigne disapproved. This kind of objection has been sustained under the first amendment in the United States.[3] The Supreme Court of Canada was unanimous in upholding the agency shop provision without any conditions as to the uses to which the compelled dues could be put. However, the Court divided on the reasons for this result.

In *Lavigne*, a narrow majority of the Supreme Court of Canada held that the right to freedom of association included the right not to associate. This was the view of four judges. La Forest J. (with Sopinka and Gonthier JJ.) followed the American approach in holding that the forced payment of dues was not a forced association to the extent that it only required the employee to pay for the union's services as the employees' bargaining representative, but was a forced association to the extent that the dues were used to support purposes other than employee representation. Therefore, the agency shop provision did limit Lavigne's freedom of association. However, La Forest J. held that the provision was justified under s. 1 as a measure to encourage healthy democratic debate. McLachlin J. was the fourth judge who agreed that the right to freedom of association included the right not to associate. However, in her view, the forced payment of dues was not a forced association, because the payments to the union did not indicate support by the payor for the causes financed by the union. Therefore, in McLachlin J.'s view, the agency shop provision did not limit Lavigne's freedom of association. Wilson J., with L'Heureux-Dubé J. and, on this issue, Cory J., formed a minority of three to hold that freedom of association did not include a right not to associate. In *Lavigne*, the three-way split of the Supreme Court of Canada came together in the result, producing a unanimous decision that the agency shop provision was valid.[4]

Bernard v. Canada (2014)[5] concerned another agency shop (or Rand formula) workplace, this one in the federal public service. The applicant

[3]In the United States, it has been held that the first amendment is infringed by agency shop collective agreements to the extent that the compelled dues are available to the union for political purposes unrelated to the union's duty of representation of the employees: *Abood v. Détruit Bd. of Education* (1977), 431 U.S. 209; *Chicago Teachers' Union v. Hudson* (1986), 475 U.S. 292; *Lehnert v. Ferris Faculty Assn.* (1991), 111 S. Ct. 1950.

[4]The Court was also unanimous that there was no breach of freedom of expression: see ch. 43, Expression, under heading § 43:38, "Election expenditures".

[5]*Bernard v. Canada*, [2014] 1 S.C.R. 227, 2014 SCC 13. Abella and Cromwell JJ. wrote the opinion of the seven-judge majority. Rothstein J. (with Moldaver J.) wrote an

was a member of the bargaining unit, but (like Mr. Lavigne) was a Rand formula employee who paid the union dues without belonging to the union. She challenged an order of the Public Service Labour Relations Board that required all members of the bargaining unit (including non-union members) to provide their home contact information to the union. She argued that this order was a compelled association in breach of s. 2(d). The Supreme Court unanimously rejected the argument. The Court accepted the Board's finding that the union needed the home contact numbers in order to effectively carry out its obligations to represent all members of the bargaining unit. The applicant had the right not to join the union, but she could not waive her right to be fairly represented by the union, which owed its duty of representation to all members of the bargaining unit. The compelled disclosure of her home contact information for the purpose of facilitating the union's obligation of representation was integral to her inevitable association with her fellow employees in the same workplace, and should not be characterized as compelled association with the union.[6]

In *R. v. Advance Cutting & Coring* (2001),[7] the Supreme Court of Canada had to consider the validity of a unique form of union shop, which had been established by Quebec's Construction Act for the construction industry in the province. The Act required all workers in the construction industry to join one of five unions, which were actually specified in the legislation. The Court, by a majority of five to four, upheld the requirement. LeBel J., with the agreement of Gonthier and Arbour JJ., held that s. 2(d) included a negative right not to associate only if the forced association imposed "ideological conformity" on the individual; and he held that "the bare obligation to belong to a union" did not impose any such conformity.[8] He accordingly upheld the legislation. Bastarache J., with the agreement of McLachlin C.J., Major and Binnie JJ., essentially agreed with LeBel J.'s formulation of the constitutional test, but Bastarache J. held that "ideological conformity" was imposed simply by requiring a worker to join a union against his or her will. He also held that the union shop requirement could not be justified under s. 1, and so he would have struck down the legislation. Iacobucci J., writing for himself alone, rejected the ideological conformity test on the ground that it was too "elusive and abstract".[9] As an alternative, he proposed (what seems to be equally elusive and abstract) that the forced association would be acceptable if it furthered the "common good" or the "collective social welfare", which (he held) the union shop in this case did not

---

opinion concurring on the merits, but dissenting on the issue of costs.

[6]*Bernard v. Canada*, [2014] 1 S.C.R. 227, 2014 SCC 13, paras. 37-38 per Abella and Cromwell JJ., 107 per Rothstein J.

[7]*R. v. Advance Cutting & Coring*, [2001] 3 S.C.R. 209. The breakdown of the judges' voting is explained in the text.

[8]*R. v. Advance Cutting & Coring*, [2001] 3 S.C.R. 209, para. 218.

[9]*R. v. Advance Cutting & Coring*, [2001] 3 S.C.R. 209, para. 284.

do.[10] He therefore held that the legislation was in breach of s. 2(d), but he upheld the legislation under s. 1 as a measure to bring peace to Quebec's turbulent construction industry. It is noteworthy that all eight judges agreed on the proposition that s. 2 included the right not to associate. L'Heureux-Dubé J., the ninth member of the Court, was the lone adherent to the view that s. 2(d) did not include the right not to associate, and she, writing for herself alone, upheld the legislation on that basis. The divergent reasons of LeBel J. (with two others), Iacobucci J. and L'Heureux-Dubé J. all supported the validity of the legislation, forming a majority of five, with Bastarache J. (and three others) dissenting. The union shop requirement was therefore upheld.

The close result, divergent reasons and construction-industry context in *Advance Cutting* make it difficult to predict the validity of other union shop (or closed shop) arrangements. However, it must be remembered that many union security arrangements will not be caught by the Charter at all; an arrangement that is contained in a collective agreement with a private employer is deemed to be "private action" to which the Charter does not apply.[11] Where the Charter does apply, either because the arrangement is directly stipulated by statute (as in *Advance Cutting)*, or because the employer is an agency of government (as in *Lavigne)*, there will always be a powerful s. 1 argument for a union security arrangement, which is designed to strengthen the bargaining position of employees and to avoid free-riding by non-union employees who could otherwise share all the benefits of collectively improved terms of employment without sharing any of the burdens of union membership. Whether these considerations could outweigh the deprivation of liberty involved in compelled membership of a union is, at bottom, the issue upon which the Supreme Court has not yet been able to agree.

---

[10] *R. v. Advance Cutting & Coring*, [2001] 3 S.C.R. 209, paras. 285-287.

[11] *Re Bhindi* (1986), 29 D.L.R. (4th) 47 (B.C.C.A.) (closed shop provision in collective agreement upheld on basis that Charter did not apply); see also ch. 37, Application of Charter, under heading § 37:8, "Statutory authority".

Chapter 45

Voting

I. VOTING

§ 45:1 Pre-Charter law
§ 45:2 Section 3 of Charter
§ 45:3 One person, one vote
§ 45:4 Regulation of elections
§ 45:5 Contested elections

II. CANDIDACY

§ 45:6 Candidacy

III. DURATION OF LEGISLATIVE BODIES

§ 45:7 Duration of legislative bodies

IV. ANNUAL SITTINGS OF LEGISLATIVE BODIES

§ 45:8 Annual sittings of legislative bodies

I. VOTING

§ 45:1 Pre-Charter law

Despite the fundamental importance of the right to vote, and the central position of democratic institutions in the Canadian system of government, there was no constitutional right[1] to vote before the adoption of the Charter. Each legislative body was free to enact its own voting qualifications,[2] and these could exclude certain classes of citizens, such as citizens of Japanese or Chinese origin (who once could not vote

---

[Section 45:1]

[1] The right to vote was protected by the courts to the extent possible through statutory interpretation: clear statutory language was required to take away the right: Boyer, Political Rights (1981), 124. The right was (and still is) also protected by the Quebec Charter of Rights and Freedoms, s. 22, and by the Saskatchewan Human Rights Code, s. 8. The right was not (and still is not) protected by the Canadian Bill of Rights or by the Alberta Bill of Rights.

[2] The federal Parliament's power was derived from the peace, order, and good government power until 1949, when s. 91(1) was adopted, and after 1949 from s. 91(1), which has now been replaced by s. 44 of the Constitution Act, 1982. The provincial Legislatures' powers were derived from s. 92(1), which has now been replaced by s. 45 of the Constitution Act, 1982. See ch. 4, Amendment, above, for discussion of ss. 44 and 45.

in British Columbia),[3] or women (who could not vote in federal elections until 1918),[4] or Indigenous peoples (who could not vote in federal elections until 1960),[5] or persons under the age of 18 (who still cannot vote in federal elections).[6]

§ 45:2 Section 3 of Charter

Section 3 of the Charter of Rights[1] provides as follows:

> 3. Every citizen of Canada has the right to vote in an election of members of the House of Commons or of a legislative assembly and to be qualified for membership therein.

Section 3 confers on "every citizen"[2] the right to vote in federal and provincial elections. The right does not extend to municipal or school board elections or to referenda or plebiscites.[3]

Section 3 of the Charter is among those provisions that are not subject to override under s. 33.[4]

However, s. 3 is subject to s. 1.[5] The right to vote can be limited by any law that comes within the phrase "such reasonable limits prescribed by law as can be demonstrably justified in a free and democratic society".[6] In every jurisdiction, the qualifications for voting are prescribed by stat-

---

[3]*Cunningham v. Tomey Homma*, [1903] A.C. 151 (disqualification of Japanese and Chinese upheld).

[4]Women were granted the right to vote in federal elections in 1918 by S.C. 1918, c. 20.

[5]Indigenous peoples were granted the right to vote in federal elections in 1960 by S.C. 1960, c. 39.

[6]Canada Elections Act, R.S.C. 1985, c. E-2, s. 50. The qualifying age was reduced from twenty-one to eighteen by S.C. 1969-70, c. 49.

[Section 45:2]

[1]For commentary on ss. 3 to 5 of the Charter, see Beaudoin and Ratushny (eds.), The Canadian Charter of Rights and Freedoms (4th ed., 2005), ch. 8 (by Beaudoin); McLeod, Takach, Morton, Segal, The Canadian Charter of Rights (Carswell, loose-leaf), ch. 27; Canadian Charter of Rights Annotated (Canada Law Book, loose-leaf service), annotations to ss. 3-5; The last work contains a bibliography of the relevant literature. See also C.D. Bredt and M.F. Kremer, "Section 3 of the Charter: Democratic Rights at the Supreme Court of Canada" (2004) 17 Nat. J. Con. Law 19; Y. Dawood, "Democracy and the Right to Vote: Rethinking Democratic Rights under the Charter" (2013) 51 Osgoode Hall L. J. 251.

[2]On the meaning of "citizen" see ch. 37, Application of Charter, under heading §§ 37:1 to 37:5, "Benefit of rights".

[3]*Haig v. Can.*, [1993] 2 S.C.R. 995 (s. 3 confers no right to vote in federal referendum; arguments based on ss. 2(b) and 15 also rejected).

[4]See ch. 39, Override of Rights.

[5]See ch. 38, Limitation of Rights.

[6]Section 3 of the Charter was in the October 1980 version in the following terms:

> 3. Every citizen of Canada has, without unreasonable distinction or limitation, the right to vote in an election of members of the House of Commons or of a legislative assembly and to be qualified for membership therein.

ute, and various people are disqualified. The federal statute[7] used to exclude from the franchise not only persons who are not Canadian citizens and persons who are under the age of 18, but also (1) persons who are mentally incompetent, (2) federally-appointed judges, (3) inmates of penal institutions, and (4) most citizens who are absent from Canada. Each of these four categories of exclusion has been held to be unconstitutional.[8] In 1993, the federal statute was amended[9] to remove the disqualifications of mentally incompetent persons and judges. The disqualification of prisoners was retained but restricted to inmates "serving a sentence of two years or more"; however, this narrower disqualification was held to be unconstitutional by a majority of the Supreme Court of Canada,[10] so that all prisoners are now eligible to vote. The disqualification of absent citizens was removed for those citizens who had been absent from Canada for less than five years and who intended to return to Canada as residents. However, this limited disqualification was struck down by the Supreme Court in 2019 in *Frank v. Canada*, which is discussed in the next paragraph. Provincial and territorial requirements of six months' or 12 months' residency as a qualification for voting in provincial or territorial elections have been upheld under s. 1 by the courts.[11] The disqualification of non-citizens is of course in conformity with s. 3 of the Charter.

Frank v. Canada (2019)[12] was the case in which the Canada Elections Act's disqualification from voting of citizens who have been absent from Canada for five years was struck down by the Supreme Court of Canada. The two plaintiffs in the case were Canadian citizens who lived outside Canada and had attempted to vote in the Canadian federal election of 2011. They were both notified that they were not entitled to receive a ballot because they had been residing outside Canada for more than five

---

The April 1981 version contained the final version of s. 3. In the final version the words "without unreasonable distinction or limitation" are deleted. The reason for the deletion was, no doubt, that the words were redundant having regard to s. 1.

[7]Canada Elections Act, R.S.C. 1985, c. E-2, ss. 50-51.

[8]*Can. Disability Rights Council v. The Queen*, [1988] 3 F.C. 622 (T.D.) (mentally incompetent persons); *Muldoon v. Can.*, [1988] 3 F.C. 628 (T.D.) (judges); *Sauvé v. Can.*, [1993] 2 S.C.R. 438 (prison inmates); *Frank v. Can.*, [2019] 1 S.C.R. 3 (absent citizens). See also *Re Hoogbruin* (1985), 24 D.L.R. (4th) 718 (B.C.C.A.) (dealing with temporary absentees under a *provincial* statute).

[9]S.C. 1993, c. 19, amending s. 51 and adding a new s. 51.1.

[10]*Sauvé v. Can.*, [2002] 3 S.C.R. 519 (breach of s. 3 conceded by Crown; Court held breach unjustified under s. 1 by majority of five to four).

[11]*Re Yukon Election Residency Requirement* (1986), 27 D.L.R. (4th) 146 (Y.T. C.A.) (12 months upheld); *Arnold v. Ont.* (1987), 61 O.R. (2d) 481 (H.C.) (six months upheld); *Haig v. Can.*, [1993] 2 S.C.R. 995, 1029 (obiter dictum approving six months). Compare *Re Weremchuk* (1986), 35 D.L.R. (4th) 278 (B.C.C.A.) (requirement of cross on ballot upheld). Note that, as in the last case, some degree of administrative regulation is required to make the right to vote effective, and would not require justification under s. 1.

[12]*Frank v. Canada*, 2019 SCC 1. Wagner C.J. wrote the opinion of the majority of the seven-judge court. Rowe J. wrote a concurring opinion. Côté and Brown JJ. wrote a dissenting opinion.

years. They brought the case to challenge the constitutionality of their disqualification. They were successful in the Supreme Court. Wagner C.J., who wrote for the majority, pointed out that a citizen's right to vote was guaranteed by s. 3 of the Charter, and s. 3 "tethers voting rights to citizenship, and citizenship alone. The Charter does not mention residence".[13] If non-residence is to be a limit on the right, that has to be justified under s. 1. The Chief Justice had this to say about justification: "In the absence of evidence pointing to a concrete problem, the justification boils down to an argument based on worthiness: the non-resident citizens in question are deemed to be less deserving of the right to vote than the resident majority on the basis that they have voluntarily left Canada and severed their connection to the country. However, this Court has quite properly foreclosed the use of such worthiness rationales to justify restrictions on the right to vote in past cases." Wagner C.J concluded that: "Worthiness cannot be used to justify the disenfranchisement of non-resident Canadian citizens in the case at bar."[14] The Court struck from the eligibility provisions of the Act the words "a person who has been absent from Canada for less than five consecutive years and who intends to return to Canada as a resident", and replaced them with "an elector who resides outside Canada"—no stipulations as to time of absence or intention to return. It was a complete win for the non-resident plaintiffs and a broad and purposive interpretation of s. 3.

The American Bill of Rights contains no right to vote couched in such sweeping terms as s. 3 of the Charter. However, it is provided in the American Bill of Rights that the right to vote may not be denied "on account of race, colour, or previous condition of servitude" (fifteenth amendment), or "on account of sex" (nineteenth amendment), or "by reason of failure to pay any poll tax or other tax" (twenty-fourth amendment), or "on account of age" greater than 18 years (twenty-sixth amendment). In addition, the Supreme Court of the United States has held that the fourteenth amendment's guarantee of "equal protection of the laws" is violated when malapportioned electoral districts make some votes weightier than others.[15] These decisions, constitutionalizing the principle that each vote should be of equal weight, have led to judicial orders reapportioning state legislatures so that each electoral district contains an approximately equal number of voters.[16]

§ 45:3 One person, one vote

To what extent does the Charter require that each vote be of equal weight? As noted in the previous paragraph, the American courts have derived a principle of equality of voting power from the equal protection

---

[13] *Frank v. Canada*, 2019 SCC 1, para. 29.

[14] *Frank v. Canada*, 2019 SCC 1, para. 82.

[15] *Baker v. Carr* (1962), 369 U.S. 186; *Reynolds v. Sims* (1964), 377 U.S. 533.

[16] See generally L.H. Tribe, American Constitutional Law (Foundation Press, N.Y., 2nd ed., 1988), ch. 13; J.E. Nowak and R.D. Rotunda, Constitutional Law (West, St. Paul, Minn., 7th ed., 2004), secs. 14.31-14.33.

clause of the fourteenth amendment. The Supreme Court of Canada has held that a similar principle is to be derived, not from s. 15 (the equality guarantee),[1] but from s. 3 (the voting guarantee).

In the *Saskatchewan Electoral Boundaries Reference* (1991),[2] the Supreme Court of Canada was presented with a challenge to the electoral boundaries for Saskatchewan's legislative assembly. The province's Electoral Boundaries Commission Act called for 66 electoral districts (ridings, constituencies), of which two had to be "northern", 35 "rural" and 29 "urban". The two northern districts were allowed to vary from the electoral quotient (the number of voters divided by the number of districts) by 50 per cent. The other districts were allowed to vary by 25 per cent. An electoral commission, working under this mandate, drew the electoral boundaries, which were translated into law by a second Act. The resulting districts ranged from a northern district with a voting population of 6,309—38 per cent below the quotient of 10,147—to an urban district with a voting population of 12,567—24 per cent above the quotient. Although these were the extremes, the permissible variation of 25 per cent above or below the quotient produced considerable voter population disparities between districts. Also, the statutory requirement that 35 of the 66 districts be rural, while it did not cause any breach of the 25-per-cent-variance rule, did result in rural voters being somewhat over-represented: the rural districts on average were under the quotient, while the urban districts on average were over the quotient. This last point, which was the primary basis of the dissenting opinion, was particularly emphasized in support of the Charter challenge, because the Progressive Conservative government of Saskatchewan, which had caused the enactment of the 35-rural-districts requirement, drew more electoral support from rural voters than did the New Democratic opposition.

The Court held that the purpose of the right to vote in s. 3 was to confer on each citizen "effective representation" in the Legislature.[3] Effective representation in the Legislature did not require absolute parity of voting power, although parity of voting power was "of prime importance".[4] Deviations from parity that could be justified on the

[Section 45:3]

[1]Despite the success of the equal protection argument in the U.S.A., s. 15 does not extend to disparities in voting power because of the need to show discrimination on the basis of a listed or analogous ground: see ch. 55 Equality, under heading § 55:49, "Place of residence".

[2]*Re Prov. Electoral Boundaries (Sask.)*, [1991] 2 S.C.R. 158. The majority judgment was written by McLachlin J. and concurred in by La Forest, Gonthier, Stevenson, Iacobucci JJ and "substantially" by Sopinka J., who wrote brief concurring reasons. Cory J. dissented with the agreement of Lamer C.J. and L'Heureux-Dubé J.

[3]*Re Prov. Electoral Boundaries (Sask.)*, [1991] 2 S.C.R. 158, 183. Cory J.'s dissent did not seem to quarrel with this basic proposition, although he placed greater weight than the majority on the ideal of parity.

[4]*Re Prov. Electoral Boundaries (Sask.)*, [1991] 2 S.C.R. 158, 184.

grounds of effective representation were not breaches of s. 3.[5] Sparsely populated regions could have districts with lower voting populations than densely populated regions, because of the greater difficulty of representing the larger area. For this reason, the special treatment of the northern districts was constitutionally acceptable, as was the rural-urban disparity. Special geographic features, such as rivers and hills, and even municipal boundaries that formed natural community boundaries, did not have to be disregarded in order to achieve better voter parity. Population growth projections could also justify deviations that were projected to diminish through the life of a set of electoral boundaries.

For these reasons, the majority of the Court held that s. 3 was not violated by the liberal allowances for voter population disparities in the Saskatchewan legislation, nor by the actual boundaries drawn by the electoral commission. There was no need to rely on s. 1 to uphold either the legislation or the boundaries. This was so, despite the fact that (as we have noticed) the most populous Saskatchewan district was nearly double the size of the least populous district.[6] Obviously, the principle of effective representation is highly deferential to any electoral apportionment stipulated by a legislative body.[7]

§ 45:4 Regulation of elections

The electoral process is heavily regulated in all jurisdictions in Canada. Whenever restrictions are imposed on the process, such as ceilings on election expenditures or information blackouts, there is room for the argument that the right to vote has been limited by the reduction in information that these measures produce. These kinds of cases have often been decided under freedom of expression rather than the right to vote.[1] For example, in *Thomson Newspapers Co. v. Canada* (1998),[2] the Supreme Court of Canada was asked to review a provision of the Canada Elections Act that prohibited the publication of opinion polls during the last three days of an election campaign. The purpose of the measure was to reduce the risk of voters being misled by inaccurate polls that

---

[5]*Re Prov. Electoral Boundaries (Sask.)*, [1991] 2 S.C.R. 158, 185.

[6]See also *Re Electoral Boundaries Commission Act (Alta.)* (1991), 86 D.L.R. (4th) 447 (Alta. C.A.) (upholding electoral apportionment involving similar deviations to Saskatchewan, but an even more pronounced preference for rural voters); *Charlottetown v. Prince Edward Island* (1998), 168 D.L.R. (4th) 79 (P.E.I.C.A.) (upholding 25 per cent deviations from voter parity).

[7]The principle of effective representation is criticized as too deferential by R.E. Charney, "Sask. Election Boundary Reference: One Person—Half a Vote" (1991) 1 Nat. J. Con. Law 225. An examination of conflicting electoral values in Canada is undertaken by Smith, MacKinnon and Courtney (eds.) in Drawing Boundaries: Legislatures, Courts and Electoral Values (1992).

[Section 45:4]

[1]See ch. 43, Expression, under heading § 43:38, "Election expenditures".

[2]*Thomson Newspapers Co. v. Canada*, [1998] 1 S.C.R. 877. The unanimous judgment was rendered by "the Court".

came out too late for proper analysis and correction. One argument against the measure was that, by depriving voters of information relevant to the exercise of their right to vote, it violated s. 3 of the Charter. The Court did not rule on this argument, deciding the case on the basis that the measure offended the guarantee of freedom of expression in s. 2(b) and was too drastic to be upheld under s. 1.

Section 3 was a subsidiary part of the reasoning in *Harper v. Canada* (2004),[3] which upheld two kinds of electoral regulations in the Canada Elections Act. One was a prohibition on electoral advertising on polling day. The other was financial ceilings on expenditures during the election campaign by third parties (persons other than registered parties or candidates). The Supreme Court of Canada held that both kinds of regulation were breaches of freedom of expression under s. 2(b), but that both were saved by s. 1. The attack on the two provisions was also based on s. 3, but the Court was unanimous that there was no breach of s. 3. In the case of the advertising blackout, the Court held that the short duration of the ban (just polling day) would not deprive voters of the information needed to cast a well informed ballot. In the case of the third-party expenditure restrictions, the Court held that they were not sufficiently severe to deny to third parties a "meaningful role" in the electoral process.[4] The latter ruling was somewhat surprising in that the expenditure limits allowed very little access to the media by third parties, and nearly all electoral campaign activity would inevitably be reserved for registered political parties and their candidates.[5]

Section 3 was not relied upon at all in *R. v. Bryan* (2007),[6] which was a challenge based on s. 2(b) to a provision of the federal Canada Elections Act that prohibited any publication of the results of national elections as long as the polls were still open in more westerly parts of the country. The mischief to which this measure was directed was the "information imbalance" on election day caused by Canada's six time zones: voters in the West would know the results in the East (along with the inevitable computer-driven expert forecasts of the likely outcome of the election) before they had even cast their votes. (A complementary measure, which was not challenged, required that voting hours be staggered across the various regions of the country, thus reducing the duration of the publication ban.) The publication ban was a limit on freedom of expression, albeit a minor one, since it delayed the publication of the most easterly electoral results for only three hours. The Supreme Court

[3] *Harper v. Canada*, [2004] 1 S.C.R. 827; the case is more fully described in ch. 43, Expression, under heading § 43:38, "Election expenditures".

[4] *Harper v. Canada*, [2004] 1 S.C.R. 827, para. 74.

[5] Compare *Figueroa v. Canada*, [2003] 1 S.C.R. 912, which implies (although it does not decide) that persons outside the registered parties should be able to play a more significant role in the electoral process.

[6] *R. v. Bryan*, [2007] 1 S.C.R. 527. Bastarache and Fish JJ. each wrote a similar concurring opinion, and both opinions were agreed to by Deschamps, Charron and Rothstein JJ. Abella J. wrote a dissenting opinion which was agreed to by McLachlin C.J., Binnie and LeBel JJ.

of Canada, by a majority of five to four, held that the publication ban was justified under s. 1. All nine judges agreed that the objective of "information equality among voters", because it promoted "public confidence in the electoral system", was a sufficiently important objective to justify limiting freedom of expression.[7] For the majority, the publication ban (coupled with the staggering of the voting hours) satisfied the other branches of the *Oakes* tests of s. 1 justification. In particular, it was within "a range of reasonable alternatives" that satisfied the minimum-impairment branch[8] of the *Oakes* test. For the dissenting minority (and in contradiction to their support of the importance of the objective), the harm caused by informational imbalance "is highly theoretical and far from sufficiently persuasive to justify infringing the core right at issue in this case".[9]

The Supreme Court of Canada has held that the regulation of political parties engages s. 3 of the Charter. In *Figueroa v. Canada* (2003),[10] the Court struck down the requirement, imposed by federal legislation, that a party had to nominate candidates in at least 50 electoral districts in order to be "registered" for the purpose of contesting federal elections. The consequences for a party of achieving registered status included the right to issue tax receipts for donations, the right to keep unspent election funds (instead of remitting them to the government), and the right to list the party affiliation of its candidates on the ballot papers. As in the *Saskatchewan Electoral Boundaries Reference*,[11] no one was literally denied the right to vote by this law, but, following the *Reference*, the Court held that the Charter right to vote comprised more than "the bare right to place a ballot in a box"; it was intended to guarantee to every citizen "effective representation" in the House of Commons.[12] This in turn implied the broader right "to play a meaningful role in the electoral process".[13] The 50-candidate threshold diminished the ability of the supporters of small parties to play a meaningful role in the electoral process. By denying to small parties the privileges that were granted to large parties, the law gave a competitive advantage to large parties that made it more difficult for the supporters of small parties to be heard in the electoral debate.[14] This was a breach of s. 3 of the Charter that could not be justified under s. 1.

---

[7] *R. v. Bryan*, [2007] 1 S.C.R. 527, paras. 12 per Bastarache J., 62 per Fish J., 104 per Abella J.

[8] *R. v. Bryan*, [2007] 1 S.C.R. 527, paras. 42 per Bastarache J., 65 per Fish J.

[9] *R. v. Bryan*, [2007] 1 S.C.R. 527, para. 125 per Abella J. and compare her para. 104.

[10] *Figueroa v. Canada*, [2003] 1 S.C.R. 912. Iacobucci J. wrote the opinion of the six-judge majority. LeBel J. wrote the opinion of the three-judge concurring minority.

[11] *Re Prov. Electoral Boundaries (Sask.)*, [1991] 2 S.C.R. 158.

[12] *Figueroa v. Canada*, [2003] 1 S.C.R. 912, para. 19 per Iacobucci J.

[13] *Figueroa v. Canada*, [2003] 1 S.C.R. 912, para. 25 per Iacobucci J.

[14] By the time of the appeal, the 50-candidate threshold had been reduced to 12, and while the new threshold was not in issue, Iacobucci J. acknowledged that "the thrust of the reasons is that no threshold requirement is acceptable" (para. 92). LeBel J. said that

In *Figueroa*, the point of the 50-candidate requirement was to channel voter support to large parties with broad appeal that would be serious contenders in an election. No doubt, this requirement had the effect of discouraging the formation of small parties. But the chief discouragement to the formation of small parties in Canada is not the rules for the registration of parties, but the first-past-the-post (single member constituency) electoral system. The first-past-the-post electoral system denies a seat in the House of Commons to any party that fails to secure a plurality in an electoral district, and this has the effect of exaggerating the large parties' share of seats. Around 40 per cent of the popular vote is usually more than enough to secure a majority in the House of Commons. This electoral system encourages the formation of broadly based parties that seek to accommodate a variety of interests within the party. Proportional representation, on the other hand, provides seats in the representative assembly to all parties who achieve a stipulated proportion of the vote, even if they do not achieve a plurality in any electoral districts. Proportional representation encourages the formation of small parties, makes it rare for any one party to achieve a majority, and therefore usually leads to coalition governments. Canada (including the provinces and territories) has a long political tradition of first-past-the-post electoral systems, with their corollaries of broadly based parties and frequent majority governments. Yet in *Figueroa*, the general thrust of the two opinions, especially the majority opinion of Iacobucci J., and some of the dicta in both opinions,[15] could be interpreted as inviting a constitutional challenge to the first-past-the-post system!

§ 45:5 Contested elections

The Canada Elections Act[1] provides, by s. 3, that "every person who is a Canadian citizen and who on polling day is 18 years of age or older is qualified as an elector", and, by s. 6, that a person qualified as an elector "is entitled to have his or her name included in the list of electors for the polling division in which he or she is ordinarily resident and to vote at the polling station for that polling division". The Act follows with elaborate administrative provisions for the registration of electors and for their identification on polling day. The Act, by s. 524, makes provision for an unsuccessful candidate for election to apply to a competent court to "contest the election" on the ground that "there were irregularities. . .that affected the result of the election". In the general federal election of May 2, 2011, 52,794 votes were cast in the Etobicoke Centre riding ("electoral district"), and the Conservative candidate defeated the Liberal candidate by only 26 votes. In *Opitz v. Wrzesnewskyj*

"at least one candidate and perhaps more" would be acceptable (para. 149).

[15]Explicit discussion of the first-past-the-post system is to be found at paras. 37, 79-87, 106, 154-161.

[Section 45:5]

[1]S.C. 2000, c. 9.

(2012),[2] the unsuccessful candidate contested the election. He established that there were "irregularities" (not involving fraud or corruption) in the case of 79 votes. Since the number of irregular votes exceeded the "magic number"[3] of 26, the judge who heard the application annulled the election, which would have led to a by-election in that riding. On appeal, the Supreme Court of Canada, by a four-three majority, reversed the application judge and reinstated the May 2 outcome. Rothstein and Moldaver JJ., writing for the majority, took the view that administrative irregularities were not by themselves sufficient to overturn an election; under s. 524, the irregularities had to affect the result of the election. That required proof not only of irregular votes, but also that the persons who voted irregularly were "not entitled to vote". (Equally dispositive, but not relevant on these facts, would be proof that a person entitled to vote was denied the vote.) They went on to review the 79 votes that had been identified as involving mistakes by the electoral officials, and determined that in the case of 59 of them the voter was entitled to vote in the sense that he or she was a Canadian citizen of age and ordinarily resident in the riding; those votes should be reinstated. Because the remaining 20 irregular votes were fewer than the magic number of 26, the election should be upheld. McLachlin C.J., who wrote for the dissenting minority, held that all of the statutory requirements, including the administrative processes of registration and identification, were essential to entitlement to vote. On that basis, she found that 65 ballots had been cast by persons who were not entitled to vote, and she would have upheld the annulment of the election.

Opitz was not a constitutional case, but the right to vote in s. 3 of the Charter explicitly influenced the reasoning of Rothstein and Moldaver JJ., who wrote for the majority. In their view, the right to vote should govern the interpretation of the Act: "the central value is the Charter-protected right to vote".[4] The Act's requirements should not be interpreted as disenfranchising Canadian citizens by reason of administrative errors respecting registration or identification. A Canadian citizen, of age and resident in the riding, should be regarded as entitled to vote even if administrative mistakes vitiated his or her registration or identification. The judges pointed out that the complexity of administering a federal election, involving as it does tens of thousands of election workers, many of them without prior experience and with only a short period of training, made it "inevitable that administrative

---

[2]*Opitz v. Wrzesnewskyj*, [2012] 3 S.C.R. 76. Rothstein and Moldaver JJ. (with the agreement of Deschamps and Abella JJ.) wrote the opinion of the majority. McLachlin CJ (with the agreement of LeBel and Fish JJ.) wrote a dissenting opinion.

[3]The magic number test was the one applied in the Supreme Court as well, although, as the majority pointed out (para. 72), the test favours the challenger in its assumption that all the rejected votes were cast for the successful candidate, which is "highly improbable". They left open (para. 73) the possibility that "another, more realistic method for assessing contested election applications might be adopted by the court in a future case".

[4]*Opitz v. Wrzesnewskyj*, [2012] 3 S.C.R. 76, para. 44.

mistakes will be made".[5] The objective of s. 3 of the Charter to enfranchise Canadian citizens would be undermined if Canadian citizens could be disenfranchised by reason of administrative mistakes, and if elections could be easily annulled. If elections could be easily annulled, losers in close ridings would be encouraged to bring court applications to contest the results which would impair the finality and legitimacy of elections. Rothstein and Moldaver JJ. concluded that the integrity of the electoral system, which they took to be a constitutional objective, was best protected if the only irregularities that counted for the purpose of annulling an election were those that resulted in the denial of a vote by a person who was a Canadian citizen of age and resident in the riding or the allowance of a vote by a person who was not a Canadian citizen of age and resident in the riding.[6]

II. CANDIDACY

§ 45:6 Candidacy

Section 3 of the Charter covers candidacy as well as voting. It confers upon every citizen the right to be "qualified for membership" in the federal House of Commons or a provincial legislative assembly. The qualifications of a member of the House of Commons or a legislative assembly are prescribed by statute in each jurisdiction,[1] and various citizens are disqualified. A disqualification of provincial civil servants was unsuccessfully challenged before the Charter was adopted in a case that went to the Supreme Court of Canada.[2] All disqualifications of citizens are, of course, now contrary to the Charter, unless they can be justified under s. 1.[3] For example, in *Harvey v. New Brunswick* (1996),[4] the Supreme Court of Canada reviewed a provision of New Brunswick's Elections Act, which required that a member of the legislative assembly who was convicted of a corrupt or illegal practice be expelled from the assembly and be disqualified from being re-elected or sitting in the assembly for a period of five years. The majority of the Court[5] held that the provision limited s. 3 of the Charter, but that it was justified under

---

[5]*Opitz v. Wrzesnewskyj*, [2012] 3 S.C.R. 76, para. 2.

[6]McLachlin C.J.'s dissent did not explicitly emphasize the constitutional right to vote, but she did argue (para. 140) that the statutory requirements, including the administrative ones, "are fundamental safeguards for the integrity of the electoral system".

[Section 45:6]

[1]The source of power is the same as that to prescribe voting qualifications: see § 45:1 note 2, above.

[2]*OPSEU v. Ont.*, [1987] 2 S.C.R. 2 (disqualification upheld as incident of restrictions on political activity by public servants).

[3]*MacLean v. A.G.N.S.* (1987), 35 D.L.R. (4th) 306 (N.S.S.C., T.D.) (disqualification of convicted criminals struck down).

[4]*Harvey v. New Brunswick*, [1996] 2 S.C.R. 876.

[5]The Court was unanimous in the outcome, but McLachlin J., in a concurring judgment agreed with by L'Heureux-Dubé J., argued that the expulsion and disqualification were immune from Charter review, because they were within the parliamentary privi-

s. 1 as a reasonable measure to maintain the integrity of the electoral process.

Section 3 does not refer to the Senate. (None of the provinces has an upper house.) The qualifications of a Senator are prescribed by ss. 23 and 24 of the Constitution Act, 1867, as interpreted by *Edwards v. A.-G. Can.* (1930),[6] which held that "persons" who were qualified for appointment include women.

III. DURATION OF LEGISLATIVE BODIES

§ 45:7 Duration of legislative bodies

Section 4 of the Charter of Rights[1] provides as follows:

> **4.**(1) No House of Commons and no legislative assembly shall continue for longer than five years from the date fixed for the return of the writs at a general election of its members.
>
> (2) In time of real or apprehended war, invasion or insurrection, a House of Commons may be continued by Parliament and a legislative assembly may be continued by the legislature beyond five years if such continuation is not opposed by the votes of more than one-third of the members of the House of Commons or the legislative assembly, as the case may be.

Section 4(1) prescribes a maximum duration of five years for the House of Commons[2] and each provincial legislative assembly.[3] The purpose, of course, is to ensure that there are elections to those bodies at least every five years. The five-year period is a maximum term, not a fixed term. Under the conventions of responsible government, the Prime Minister or Premier has the power to advise an earlier dissolution, either because his or her government has lost the confidence of the house, or (usually) because he or she thinks the time is ripe for an election.[4] This important power of the Prime Minister or Premier is not disturbed by s. 4, except

---

lege of the Legislature.

[6] *Edwards v. A.-G. Can.*, [1930] A.C. 124.

[Section 45:7]

[1] For commentary on s. 4, see § 45:2 note 1, above.

[2] Section 4 does not change the law applicable in the federal jurisdiction. Sections 50 and 91(1) of the Constitution Act, 1867 (s. 91(1) was added by amendment in 1949) contained similar provisions to s. 4 of the Charter. Section 91(1) (but not s. 50) is one of the few provisions which were expressly repealed by s. 53 of the Constitution Act, 1982 (see Schedule, Item 1).

[3] Section 85 of the Constitution Act, 1867 prescribed a four-year maximum term for the legislative assemblies of Ontario and Quebec, but in both provinces that term was extended to five years by statutes enacted under the provincial amending power of s. 92(1). Section 19 of the Manitoba Act, 1870 prescribes a four-year maximum term for the legislative assembly of Manitoba. None of these provisions was expressly repealed or amended by s. 53 of the Constitution Act, 1982.

[4] See ch. 9, Responsible Government, under heading § 9:6, "The Prime Minister".

that the power must be exercised within five years of the previous election.[5]

Section 4(2) enables the five-year period to be extended by the Parliament or a Legislature, but only "in time of real or apprehended war, invasion or insurrection", and only if the extension "is not opposed by the votes of more than one-third of the members of the House of Commons or the legislative assembly".

IV. ANNUAL SITTINGS OF LEGISLATIVE BODIES

§ 45:8 Annual sittings of legislative bodies

Section 5 of the Charter of Rights[1] provides as follows:

> 5. There shall be a sitting of Parliament and of each Legislature at least once every twelve months.

Section 5 stipulates that there shall be a sitting of Parliament and of each Legislature "at least once every twelve months".[2] Section 5 does not say how long the sitting must continue; a very short sitting (one day, for example) would satisfy the requirement.

---

[5]Note that some Canadian jurisdictions have enacted fixed election dates at four-year intervals, while not disturbing the power of earlier dissolution: ch. 9, Responsible Government, under heading § 9:14, "Dissolution of Parliament".

[Section 45:8]

[1]For commentary on s. 5, see § 45:2 note 1, above.

[2]Section 5 has its counterparts in ss. 20 (Parliament) and 86 (Ontario and Quebec) of the Constitution Act, 1867 and in s. 20 of the Manitoba Act. Section 20 (but not s. 86) of the Constitution Act, 1867 and s. 20 of the Manitoba Act are repealed by s. 53 of the Constitution Act, 1982 (see Schedule, Items 1, 2).

Chapter 47

Fundamental Justice

I. DISTRIBUTION OF POWERS OVER LEGAL RIGHTS

§ 47:1 Distribution of powers over legal rights

II. SECTION 7 OF CHARTER

§ 47:2 Section 7 of Charter

III. APPLICATION OF S. 1

§ 47:3 Application of s. 1

IV. BENEFIT OF S. 7

§ 47:4 Corporations
§ 47:5 Immigrants
§ 47:6 Foetus

V. BURDEN OF S. 7

§ 47:7 Burden of s. 7

VI. LIFE

§ 47:8 Life

VII. LIBERTY

§ 47:9 Physical liberty
§ 47:10 Economic liberty
§ 47:11 Political liberty

VIII. SECURITY OF THE PERSON

§ 47:12 Security of the person

IX. PROPERTY

§ 47:13 Property

X. FUNDAMENTAL JUSTICE

§ 47:14 Procedure and substance
§ 47:15 Definition of fundamental justice

XI. ABSOLUTE AND STRICT LIABILITY

§ 47:16 Categories of offences

§ 47:17 Absolute liability offences
§ 47:18 Strict liability offences

XII. MURDER

§ 47:19 Murder

XIII. UNFORESEEN CONSEQUENCES

§ 47:20 Unforeseen Consequences

XIV. INVOLUNTARY ACTS

§ 47:21 Automatism
§ 47:22 Duress
§ 47:23 Intoxication

XV. OVERBROAD LAWS

§ 47:24 Overbroad laws

XVI. DISPROPORTIONATE LAWS

§ 47:25 Disproportionate laws

XVII. ARBITRARY LAWS

§ 47:26 Arbitrary laws

XVIII. VAGUE LAWS

§ 47:27 Void for vagueness
§ 47:28 Standard of precision
§ 47:29 Application to other Charter rights

XIX. WRONG LAWS

§ 47:30 Wrong laws

XX. RIGHT TO SILENCE

§ 47:31 Right to silence

XXI. FAIR TRIAL

§ 47:32 The right to a fair trial
§ 47:33 Full answer and defence
§ 47:34 Pre-trial disclosure by the Crown
§ 47:35 Pre-trial disclosure by third parties
§ 47:36 Preservation of evidence
§ 47:37 Statutory limits on pre-trial disclosure

XXII. FAIR ADMINISTRATIVE PROCEDURES

§ 47:38 Fair administrative procedures

I. DISTRIBUTION OF POWERS OVER LEGAL RIGHTS

§ 47:1 Distribution of powers over legal rights

This chapter deals with s. 7 of the Charter of Rights, which is the first of eight sections (ss. 7 to 14) of the Charter that are grouped under the heading "Legal Rights". The term legal rights does not have a precise legal or popular meaning. It certainly includes the rights of persons within the system of criminal justice, limiting the powers of the state with respect to investigation, search, seizure, arrest, detention, trial and punishment. However, as we shall see, s. 7 in particular spills over into civil justice as well.

The distribution of powers between the federal Parliament and the provincial Legislatures over the matters loosely encompassed by the vague term "legal rights" depends upon the characterization of each law. In characterizing a law, the law's impact on civil liberties is generally irrelevant, or at least of only subordinate importance. If the law is in relation to criminal law or criminal procedure, it will be within federal power under s. 91 (27) of the Constitution Act, 1867. The various stages of a criminal trial from arrest and charge through to acquittal or conviction and sentence are accordingly within federal legislative authority. On the other hand, provincial authority over the administration of justice in the province (s. 92(14)) includes the constitution of criminal and civil courts and civil procedure, and extends to some aspects of the investigation and prosecution of crime.[1] If a law establishes a legislative scheme, for example, for the raising of taxes, securities regulation or traffic regulation, the law may provide for investigation and enforcement of the scheme. The validity of these adjectival provisions depends upon the validity of the scheme to which they are incidental. There is no suggestion in the cases that the severity of the law's impact on civil liberties is of importance in assigning legislative jurisdiction.[2]

II. SECTION 7 OF CHARTER

§ 47:2 Section 7 of Charter

Section 7 of the Charter of Rights[1] provides as follows:

> 7. Everyone has the right to life, liberty and security of the person and

---

[Section 47:1]

[1]See ch. 7, Courts, and ch. 19, Criminal Justice, above.

[2]On the distribution of legislative power over legal civil liberties, see Tarnopolsky, The Canadian Bill of Rights (2nd ed., 1975), 55-56.

[Section 47:2]

[1]For commentary on s. 7, see Stewart, Fundamental Justice (2012); Paciocco, Charter Principles and Proof in Criminal Cases (1987); Beaudoin and Mendes (eds.), The Canadian Charter of Rights and Freedoms (4th ed., 2005), ch. 10 (by P. Garant); Finkelstein and Finkelstein, Constitutional Rights in the Investigative Process (1991), chs. 2, 3; Stuart, Charter Justice in Canadian Criminal Law (3rd ed., 2001), ch. 2; McLeod, Takach, Morton, Segal, The Canadian Charter of Rights (Carswell, loose-leaf) ch. 5; Canadian Charter of Rights Annotated (Canada Law Book, loose-leaf), annotation to s.

> the right not to be deprived thereof except in accordance with the principles of fundamental justice.

Section 7 protects the right of "everyone" to "life, liberty and security of the person", and imposes the requirement that any deprivation be "in accordance with the principles of fundamental justice".

It is arguable that s. 7 confers two rights: (1) a right to "life, liberty and security of the person" that is unqualified, except by s. 1 (the limitation clause) of the Charter; and (2) a right not to be deprived of life, liberty and security of the person except in accordance with the principles of fundamental justice. If this were correct, then every deprivation of life, liberty or security of the person would be a breach of s. 7, even if the principles of fundamental justice had been complied with. This two-rights interpretation of s. 7, although supported by the grammatical structure of the English (but not the French) version of the section,[2] is otherwise an unnatural reading of the section, and one that would give s. 7 an extraordinarily broad sweep. The better view is that s. 7 confers only one right, namely, the right not to be deprived of life, liberty or security of the person except in accordance with the principles of fundamental justice. The cases generally assume that the single-right interpretation is the correct one, so that there is no breach of s. 7 unless there has been a failure to comply with the principles of fundamental justice.[3]

The Canadian Bill of Rights, by s. 1(a) guarantees:

> the right of the individual to life, liberty and security of the person and enjoyment of property, and the right not to be deprived thereof except by due process of law. . . .

In addition, s. 2(e) provides that no law of Canada is to be construed or applied so as to:

> deprive a person of the right to a fair hearing in accordance with the principles of fundamental justice for the determination of his rights and obligations. . . .

Section 7 of the Charter can be seen as an amalgam of these two provisions, but s. 7 is significantly narrower in scope than either s. 1(a),

---

7; the last work provides a bibliography of the relevant literature.

[2]Contrast the grammatical structure of the fifth and fourteenth amendments of the Constitution of the United States, which clearly confer only one right, namely, the right not to be deprived of life, liberty or property without due process of law.

[3]E.g., *Can. v. Chiarelli*, [1992] 1 S.C.R. 711 (denial of liberty in compliance with fundamental justice is not a breach of s. 7). However, in *Re B.C. Motor Vehicle Act*, [1985] 2 S.C.R. 486, Lamer J. (at 500) expressly left the issue open, and Wilson J. (at 523) seemed to accept the two-right interpretation, because she said that even if fundamental justice were satisfied s. 1 would *also* have to be satisfied. Both positions are puzzling: Lamer J.'s elaborate discussion of fundamental justice would have little point if *any* denial of life, liberty or security of the person was a breach of s. 7; and Wilson J. had previously doubted the two-right interpretation in *Operation Dismantle v. The Queen*, [1985] 1 S.C.R. 441, 487. The two-right interpretation was espoused by Arbour J. in dissent in *Gosselin v. Que.*, [2002] 4 S.C.R. 429, paras. 338-343; L'Heureux-Dubé J., also dissenting, agreed with her, but the other seven judges did not.

which extends to "enjoyment of property", or s. 2(e), which extends to any determination of "rights and obligations". Section 7's protection is limited to "life, liberty and security of the person", a phrase which does not include property and which does not include a determination of rights and obligations respecting economic interests. As has earlier been explained, the Canadian Bill of Rights (which applies only to federal laws) remains in force, and ss. 1(a) and 2(e) are of continuing importance because their coverage is broader than s. 7.[4]

The Constitution of the United States, by the fifth amendment, which applies to the federal government, provides that no person "shall be deprived of life, liberty, or property, without due process of law". The fourteenth amendment, which applies to the states, also guarantees against the deprivation of "life, liberty, or property, without due process of law." These guarantees are also broader than s. 7, because they extend to "property", although they make no reference to "security of the person". Another difference is that the American guarantees refer to "due process of law" whereas s. 7 refers to "the principles of fundamental justice". The significance of this change is examined in the later discussion of fundamental justice.[5]

III. APPLICATION OF S. 1

§ 47:3 Application of s. 1

Section 7 makes clear that a law can deprive a person of life, liberty or security of the person if the law conforms to the principles of fundamental justice.[1] Could a law that did not conform to the principles of fundamental justice be upheld under s. 1? Could a violation of fundamental justice ever be a reasonable limit that can be demonstrably justified in a free and democratic society? In the Supreme Court of Canada, Wilson J. several times expressed the view that the answer to this question is no: a violation of fundamental justice could never be justified under s. 1. However, for the most part, the Court has routinely moved on to the issue of s. 1 justification before finding a breach of s. 7, and some judges (although never a majority) have held that a particular breach of s. 7 was justified under s. 1. The issue is examined in ch. 38, Limitation of Rights, above.[2]

---

[4] Chapter 35, Canadian Bill of Rights, under heading, § 35:7, "Contents".

[5] §§ 47:14 to 47:15, "Fundamental justice".

[Section 47:3]

[1] Note, however, that the two-right interpretation of s. 7 calls for s. 1 justification even if the principles of fundamental justice are satisfied: text accompanying § 47:2 note 2, below, above.

[2] Chapter 38, Limitation of Rights, under heading §§ 38:24 to 38:29, "Application to qualified rights".

IV. BENEFIT OF S. 7

§ 47:4 Corporations

Section 7 is applicable to "everyone", a word that is normally apt to include a corporation as well as an individual.[1] However, the Supreme Court of Canada has held that in the context of s. 7 "everyone" does not include a corporation. An artificial person such as a corporation is incapable of possessing "life, liberty or security of the person", because these are attributes of natural persons.[2] Therefore, s. 7 does not apply to a corporation.

This does not mean that a corporation can never invoke s. 7.[3] When a corporation is a defendant to a prosecution, the corporation is entitled to defend the charge on the basis that the law is a nullity. In *R. v. Wholesale Travel Group* (1991),[4] the Supreme Court of Canada held that this principle allows a corporation to defend a criminal charge on the ground that the law under which the charge was laid would be a violation of s. 7 in its application to an individual. The Court rejected the argument that a law could be unconstitutional for individuals, but constitutional for corporations. The Court also rejected the argument that a corporation could be convicted under an unconstitutional law, even though the defect in the law (a denial of "liberty" in breach of fundamental justice) was not one that was relevant to a corporation (because a corporation has no right to "liberty").[5]

§ 47:5 Immigrants

"Everyone" in s. 7 includes illegal immigrants to Canada. In *Singh v. Minister of Employment and Immigration* (1985),[1] Wilson J. said that s. 7 rights could be asserted by "every human being who is physically present in Canada and by virtue of such presence amenable to Canadian law".[2] What that meant, she held, was that any illegal immigrant who claimed to be a refugee was entitled to a hearing before an official or tribunal with authority to determine the issue. The argument that such

---

[Section 47:4]

[1]Chapter 37, Application of Charter, under heading §§ 37:1 to 37:5, "Benefit of rights".

[2]*Irwin Toy v. Que.*, [1989] 1 S.C.R. 927, 1004; *Dywidag Systems v. Zutphen Bros.*, [1990] 1 S.C.R. 705, 709.

[3]An individual may invoke s. 7, even when appearing as a witness as a representative of a corporation: *Thomson Newspapers v. Can.*, [1990] 1 S.C.R. 425.

[4]*R. v. Wholesale Travel Group*, [1991] 3 S.C.R. 154.

[5]See also ch. 59, Procedure, under heading §§ 59:2 to 59:6, "Standing".

[Section 47:5]

[1]*Singh v. Minr. of Emplmt. and Imm.*, [1985] 1 S.C.R. 177.

[2]*Singh v. Minr. of Emplmt. and Imm.*, [1985] 1 S.C.R. 177, 202 per Wilson J. for half of the six-judge bench. Beetz J. for the other half decided the case on the basis of the Canadian Bill of Rights rather than the Charter, but he assumed that illegal immigrants were entitled to the rights under the Canadian Bill of Rights.

a procedure would make it impossible to deal expeditiously with the many thousands of refugee claimants who arrive in Canada each year was rejected as an inadmissible "utilitarian" or "administrative" concern, which could not be permitted to vitiate individual rights.[3] In fact, after *Singh*, refugee claimants arrived in Canada at the rate of about 36,000 a year, and the federal government was not able to comply with the *Singh* rule in a timely fashion. As a result, a huge backlog of refugee claimants developed, and they endured delays of two or more years awaiting adjudication.[4]

§ 47:6 Foetus

"Everyone" in s. 7 does not include a foetus, and so a foetus is not entitled to a right to life.[1] The Supreme Court of Canada has in fact used s. 7 to strike down *restrictions* on abortion, the reasoning being that the restrictions deprived the mother of her right to liberty or security of the person.[2]

V. BURDEN OF S. 7

§ 47:7 Burden of s. 7

Section 7, like all the other Charter rights, applies only to "governmental action", as defined in s. 32 of the Charter. This is the subject of ch. 37, Application of Charter, above.[1]

VI. LIFE

§ 47:8 Life

Section 7 protects "life, liberty and security of the person". So far as "life" is concerned, the section has little work to do, because governmental action rarely causes death. The most obvious case is the death penalty, but this was removed from Canada's Criminal Code in 1976—before the

---

[3]*Singh v. Minr. of Emplmt. and Imm.*, [1985] 1 S.C.R. 177, 218-219.

[4]See, for example, the reports of refugee backlogs in The Globe and Mail newspaper, February 23, 26 and 27, 1991. At that time, the refugee-determination procedures occupied a 276-member Immigration and Refugee Board and 773 civil servants. Despite these resources, in 2003, the Immigration and Refugee Board had a backlog of more than 50,000 cases: Globe and Mail newspaper, November 22, 2003, p. A23. Mr Singh himself, the litigant in *Singh*, has fully availed himself of his constitutional rights. In 2005, 20 years after the Supreme Court ruling, he was still in Canada fighting his deportation to India: Globe and Mail newspaper, January 18, 2005, p. A17.

[Section 47:6]

[1]Chapter 37, Application of Charter, under heading § 37:2, "Everyone, anyone, any person".

[2]*R. v. Morgentaler (No. 2)*, [1988] 1 S.C.R. 30.

[Section 47:7]

[1]On the extent to which s. 7 could be infringed by the action of a foreign government, an issue that arises in extradition cases, among others, see ch. 37, Application of Charter, under heading § 37:14, "Extraterritorial application".

adoption of the Charter of Rights.[1] The Supreme Court of Canada has held, however, that excessive waiting times for treatment in the public health care system of Quebec increased the risk of death, and were a violation of the right to life (as well as security of the person).[2] The Court has also held that a prohibition of physician-assisted death was a deprivation of the right to life, because of evidence that some persons who were grievously ill took their own lives prematurely out of fear that they would be incapable of doing so when they reached the point where suffering was intolerable.[3]

Abortion is sometimes characterized as implicating a "right to life", meaning a right possessed by a foetus. That characterization does not work in this context. The s. 7 right is possessed by "everyone", and everyone does not include a foetus.[4] The Supreme Court of Canada has used s. 7 to strike down *restrictions* on abortion, reasoning that they infringed the liberty and security of the person of the mother, and did not comply with the principles of fundamental justice.[5]

VII. LIBERTY

§ 47:9 Physical liberty

Section 7 protects "life, liberty and security of the person". What is included in "liberty"?

"Liberty" certainly includes freedom from physical restraint. Any law that imposes the penalty of imprisonment, whether the sentence is mandatory[1] or discretionary,[2] is by virtue of that penalty a deprivation of liberty, and must conform to the principles of fundamental justice. A

[Section 47:8]

[1]A few death penalty provisions remained outside the Criminal Code (for espionage, mutiny with violence and war crimes). These were never challenged, no doubt because they were never exercised, and they were repealed in 1998. See ch. 53, Cruel and Unusual Punishment, under heading § 53:7, "Death penalty".

[2]*Chaoulli v. Que.*, [2005] 1 S.C.R. 791. The Court was unanimous on this ruling. The Court held by a majority of four to three that a ban on private health insurance was invalid for breach of Quebec's Charter of Human Rights and Freedoms. The Court split three-three (one judge not deciding) on whether the law was a breach of fundamental justice contrary to s. 7 of the Charter of Rights.

[3]*Carter v. Can.*, [2015] 1 S.C.R. 331, 2015 SCC 5, paras. 57-58.

[4]§ 47:6, "Foetus".

[5]§ 47:6, "Foetus".

[Section 47:9]

[1]*Re B.C. Motor Vehicle Act*, [1985] 2 S.C.R. 486, 515, 529 (mandatory term of imprisonment a denial of liberty); *R. v. Swain*, [1991] 1 S.C.R. 933 (automatic detention of person acquitted on ground of insanity a denial of liberty.)

[2]*Re ss. 193 and 195.1 of Criminal Code* (Prostitution Reference) [1990] 1 S.C.R. 1123, 1140, 1215 ("possibility of imprisonment" a denial of liberty); *R. v. Malmo-Levine*, [2003] 3 S.C.R. 571, para. 84 ("availability of imprisonment. . .is sufficient to trigger s. 7 scrutiny"); *R. v. Smith*, [2015] 2 S.C.R. 602, 2015 SCC 34, para. 17 (threat of imprisonment a deprivation of liberty); *R. v. Moriarity*, [2015] 3 S.C.R. 485, 2015 SCC 55, para. 18 ("risk of imprisonment").

law that imposes only the penalty of a fine is not a deprivation of liberty, and need not conform to the principles of fundamental justice.[3] Nor is the suspension of a driver's licence a deprivation of liberty.[4] Nor is the imposition on Department of Justice employees of mandatory standby shifts on evenings and weekends to deal with urgent immigration matters.[5] As well as imprisonment, statutory duties to submit to fingerprinting,[6] to produce documents,[7] to give oral testimony[8] and not to loiter in or near schoolgrounds, playgrounds, public parks and bathing areas,[9] are also deprivations of liberty attracting the rules of fundamental justice. On the other hand, the deportation of a non-citizen is not a deprivation of liberty, attracting the rules of fundamental justice, because a non-citizen has no right to enter or remain in Canada.[10]

Once a criminal defendant has been convicted and sentenced to a term of imprisonment, will a change in the terms of the sentence amount

---

[3]*Re B.C. Motor Vehicle Act*, [1985] 2 S.C.R. 486, 529; see also *R. v. Pontes*, [1995] 3 S.C.R. 44, paras. 9, 26, 47 (no deprivation of liberty from a fine alone); *R. v. Transport Robert (1973) Lteé* (2003), 68 O.R. (3d) 51, paras. 17-18 (C.A.) (ditto). In *Re B.C. Motor Vehicle Act*, [1985] 2 S.C.R. 486, Lamer J. left open whether "imprisonment as an alternative to the non-payment of a fine" could trigger s. 7 (at 515), as well as whether s. 7 could be triggered if imprisonment was not available as a sentence (at 516); see also *R. v. Pontes*, [1995] 3 S.C.R. 44, para. 26. These reservations raised the possibility of a huge scope for "liberty" in s. 7, since even civil orders are ultimately enforceable by imprisonment (for contempt). There are subsequent decisions of provincial appellate courts that have held that the risk of imprisonment as an alternative for non-payment of a fine is a deprivation of liberty sufficient to trigger s. 7: see *R. v. Burt*, [1988] 1 W.W.R. 385 (Sask. C.A.); *R. v. Gray*, [1989] 1 W.W.R. 66 (Man. C.A.); *R. v. Sutherland* (1990), 96 N.S.R. (2d) 271 (C.A.); *Entreprises M.G. de Guy Ltée v. Que.*, [1996] R.J.Q. 258 (Que. C.A.); *R. v. Zwicker*, 2003 NSCA 140, paras. 16-19 (C.A.). However, some decisions have held that, where the risk of imprisonment is too remote, there is no deprivation of liberty sufficient to trigger s. 7: see *London (City) v. Polewsky* (2005), 202 C.C.C. (3d) 257, para. 4 (Ont. C.A.); *R. v. Schmidt* (2014), 119 O.R. (3d) 145, para. 44 (C.A.); *Ont. v. Bogaerts*, 2019 ONCA 876, para. 49 (C.A.).

[4]*Buhlers v. B.C.* (1999), 170 D.L.R. (4th) 344 (B.C.C.A.).

[5]*Association of Justice Counsel v. Can.*, [2017] 2 S.C.R. 456, 2017 SCC 55, paras. 3, 48-53, per Karakatsanis J. for the seven-judge majority, para. 54 per Côté J. (with Moldaver J.), making the court unanimous on the "liberty" issue.

[6]*R. v. Beare*, [1988] 2 S.C.R. 387.

[7]*Thomson Newspapers v. Can.*, [1990] 1 S.C.R. 425.

[8]*Thomson Newspapers v. Can.*, [1990] 1 S.C.R. 425; *Stelco v. Can.*, [1990] 1 S.C.R. 617.

[9]*R. v. Heywood*, [1994] 3 S.C.R. 761.

[10]*Medovarski v. Can.*, [2005] 2 S.C.R. 539, para. 46 (deportation upheld); distinguished in *Charkaoui v. Can.*, [2007] 1 S.C.R. 350, para. 16 (when combined with detention as part of the "security certificate" process, deportation is a deprivation of liberty: para. 17). Deportation to torture is a deprivation of liberty: *Charkaoui v. Can.*, [2007] 1 S.C.R. 350, para. 17; *Suresh v. Can.*, [2002] 1 S.C.R. 3, para. 44 (and "barring extraordinary circumstance" will also be a breach of fundamental justice: para. 76). Deportation is also a deprivation of liberty if the non-citizen has made a refugee claim that has not been rejected in a fair hearing: *Singh v. Minr. of Emplmt. and Imm.*, [1985] 1 S.C.R. 177.

to a deprivation of liberty? In *Cunningham v. Canada* (1993),[11] the defendant had been sentenced in 1981 to 12 years' imprisonment for manslaughter. Under the Parole Act in force at the time of his sentencing, he was entitled to be released on mandatory supervision after serving two-thirds of the sentence, provided he had been of good behaviour. Before he reached the two-thirds point of his sentence (which was 1989), the Parole Act was amended (in 1986) to empower the National Parole Board to cancel the conditional release and require the continued detention of the prisoner for the rest of his sentence. This power was exercisable where there was reason to believe that the inmate, if released, was likely to commit an offence causing death or serious harm during the unexpired portion of his sentence. The Board exercised its new power in this case, and the defendant was accordingly not released on mandatory supervision in 1989. He applied for habeas corpus. The Supreme Court of Canada held that, although the amendment of the Parole Act had not had the effect of lengthening the defendant's 12-year sentence, it had altered the manner in which the sentence was to be served. Serving time on mandatory supervision was a lesser deprivation of liberty than serving time in prison. This change in the law should be treated as the deprivation of a liberty interest, making s. 7 of the Charter potentially applicable. The Court went on to hold that the change in the law was not a breach of the principles of fundamental justice,[12] so that the defendant remained in prison.

In *May v. Ferndale Institution* (2005),[13] the Court was asked to review a decision by the Correctional Service of Canada to transfer a prisoner in the federal penitentiary system from a minimum-security institution to a medium-security institution. The medium-security institution would be more restrictive of the prisoner's liberty than the minimum-security institution. Therefore, the Court held, following *Cunningham*, the decision to transfer the prisoner was a deprivation of his "residual liberty". Section 7 applied and the decision had to observe the principles of fundamental justice. In this case, the Court held that the failure of the Correctional Service to fulfil a statutory obligation to provide information as to the reasons for the transfer was not sufficiently important to amount to a breach of fundamental justice.[14] (It did make the transfer unlawful, however, and the Court ordered that the prisoner be returned to a minimum-security institution.)

For a time, the Supreme Court of Canada proved reluctant to extend

[11] *Cunningham v. Canada*, [1993] 2 S.C.R. 143. The opinion of the Court was written by McLachlin J.

[12] This part of the decision is discussed at § 47:13.

[13] *May v. Ferndale Institution*, [2005] 3 S.C.R. 809. LeBel and Fish JJ. wrote the opinion of the majority. Charron J. wrote a dissenting opinion, disagreeing only with the majority's ruling that the decision was unlawful.

[14] *May v. Ferndale Institution*, [2005] 3 S.C.R. 809, paras. 89-92, ruling that the *Stinchcombe* rules of disclosure (described in § 47:34, "Pre-trial disclosure by the Crown") did not apply outside criminal proceedings where the innocence of the accused was at stake.

liberty beyond freedom from physical restraint.[15] However, in *Blencoe v. British Columbia* (2000),[16] Bastarache J., speaking for a majority of five judges of the Supreme Court of Canada, asserted that liberty in s. 7 is "no longer restricted to mere freedom from physical restraint"; it applies whenever the law prevents a person from making "fundamental personal choices".[17] The case involved a claim by Mr Blencoe that his liberty interest had been impaired because of the unreasonable delay of the British Columbia Human Rights Commission in disposing of complaints of sexual harassment made against him by two women. It is very difficult to see how a plausible deprivation of liberty can be constructed out of these facts, and Bastarache J. with little discussion held that "in the circumstances of this case, the state has not prevented [Mr Blencoe] from making any fundamental personal choices' ".[18] Mr Blencoe was therefore denied a remedy. LeBel J. for the dissenting minority of four (who would have ordered an expedited hearing on administrative-law principles) pointedly refused to comment on the scope of s. 7 of the Charter.[19] With respect, LeBel J.'s caution seems the more appropriate position to take in a case that did not call for a ruling about the protection of such vague notions as fundamental personal choices.[20]

Bastarache J.'s dictum in *Blencoe* was quoted with approval by a unanimous Supreme Court in *Carter v. Canada* (2015).[21] At issue was the constitutionality of the Criminal Code offence of aiding or abetting a

---

[15]A notable exception was Wilson J., who consistently advocated a broad definition of liberty: *Singh v. Minr. of Emplmt. and Imm.*, [1985] 1 S.C.R. 177, 205; *Operation Dismantle v. The Queen*, [1985] 1 S.C.R. 441, 488; *R. v. Jones*, [1986] 2 S.C.R. 284, 318-319; *R. v. Morgentaler*, [1988] 1 S.C.R. 30, 164-166. Wilson J.'s definition gradually received increasing support, but until 2000, not from a majority of the Supreme Court of Canada: see *B.(R.) v. Children's Aid Society*, [1995] 1 S.C.R. 315, para. 80 per La Forest J. with the concurrence of L'Heureux-Dubé, Gonthier and McLachlin JJ. (liberty includes right to choose medical treatment of one's children); *R. v. O'Connor*, [1995] 4 S.C.R. 411, para. 111 per L'Heureux-Dubé J. with the concurrence of La Forest, Gonthier and McLachlin JJ. (liberty includes privacy; the other five judges acknowledged that privacy was a constitutional right but were silent as to its source); *Godbout v. Longueuil*, [1997] 3 S.C.R. 844, para. 66 per La Forest J. with the concurrence of L'Heureux-Dubé and McLachlin JJ. (liberty includes right to choose place of residence); *New Brunswick v. G.(J.)*, [1999] 3 S.C.R. 46, paras. 117-118 per L'Heureux-Dubé J. with the concurrence of McLachlin J. (liberty includes right to bring up children).

[16]*Blencoe v. British Columbia*, [2000] 2 S.C.R. 307.

[17]*Blencoe v. British Columbia*, [2000] 2 S.C.R. 307, paras. 49, 54.

[18]*Blencoe v. British Columbia*, [2000] 2 S.C.R. 307, para. 54. The Court also rejected the claim that Blencoe's security of the person was impaired: see § 47:12, "Security of the person".

[19]*Blencoe v. British Columbia*, [2000] 2 S.C.R. 307, para. 187; LeBel J. went on to say (para. 189) that it was unwise for the evolution of the common law and civil law to assume that the Charter "must solve every legal problem".

[20]In *R. v. Malmo-Levine*, [2003] 3 S.C.R. 571, paras. 85-87, the majority of the Supreme Court of Canada accepted, in obiter, that s. 7 protects fundamental personal choices, but they did not accept that the recreational use of marihuana qualified as a fundamental personal choice.

[21]*Carter v. Canada*, [2015] 1 S.C.R. 331, 2015 SCC 5, para. 64. The opinion was attributed to "the Court".

person to commit suicide. The plaintiff was a person who suffered from a fatal degenerative disease that was progressively robbing her of her physical abilities. She wanted to die peacefully at a time and in a manner of her own choice, but she knew that she would probably need the help of a doctor when that time came. She challenged the validity of the offence under s. 7, and was successful. On liberty, it was the disease not the law that restricted her physical liberty. However, the law certainly denied her the right to make a fundamental personal choice free from state interference (as contemplated by the dictum in *Blencoe*), but the Court did not leave it at that:[22]

> An individual's response to a grievous and irremediable medical condition is a matter critical to their dignity and autonomy. The law allows people in this situation to request palliative sedation, refuse artificial nutrition and hydration, or request the removal of life-sustaining medical equipment, but denies them the right to request a physician's assistance in dying. This interferes with their ability to make decisions concerning their bodily integrity and medical care and thus trenches on liberty.

The challenged law therefore involved a deprivation of liberty.[23] The Court went on to hold that the law was not in accordance with the principles of fundamental justice because it was overbroad.[24] The Court accordingly held that the law was invalid to the extent that it prohibited physician-assisted death by a competent adult person in a situation similar to that of the plaintiff.[25]

§ 47:10 Economic liberty

There are good reasons for caution in expanding the concept of liberty in s. 7. One reason is the unhappy experience of the United States during the *Lochner* era. Between 1905, when *Lochner v. New York*[1] was decided, and 1937, when the case was overruled, the Supreme Court of the United States protected the liberties of the owners of factories and mines against the efforts of Congress and the state Legislatures to limit hours of work, to require the payment of minimum wages, to impose health and safety standards and to protect union activity. As Oliver Wendell Holmes pointed out in his brilliant dissenting opinions, the Court used the Constitution to enforce a laissez-faire economic theory that had been rejected by the elected legislators. The Court had taken sides in a political conflict that was suitable for resolution only by elected legislators. In 1937, after an exasperated President Roosevelt had

---

[22]*Carter v. Canada*, [2015] 1 S.C.R. 331, 2015 SCC 5, para. 66.

[23]The Court also held (para. 64) that it was a deprivation of security of the person: see § 47:12, "Security of the person".

[24]This part of the reasoning is described in § 47:24, "Overbroad laws".

[25]See also *Association of Justice Counsel v. Can.*, [2017] 2 S.C.R. 456, paras. 48-51 (liberty protects fundamental personal choices).

[Section 47:10]

[1]*Lochner v. New York* (1905), 198 U.S. 45 (maximum hours of work law struck down over eloquent dissent of Holmes J.).

proposed his court-packing plan, the Court changed its mind and reversed these decisions. Since then, the Court has been extremely reluctant to review social and economic regulation, despite its inevitable interferences with the property and contract rights that the Constitution of the United States expressly guarantees.[2]

All this happened in the United States, but the *Lochner* era cast its shadow over Canada as well. The framers of Canada's Charter of Rights deliberately omitted any reference to property in s. 7, and they also omitted any guarantee of the obligation of contracts. These departures from the American model, as well as the replacement of "due process" with "fundamental justice" (of which more will be said later), were intended to banish *Lochner* from Canada.[3] The product is a s. 7 in which liberty must be interpreted as not including property, as not including freedom of contract, and, in short, as not including *economic* liberty.[4]

Another reason for caution in the definition of liberty is the placement of s. 7 within the Charter of Rights. Section 7 leads off a group of sections (ss. 7 to 14) entitled "Legal Rights". These provisions are mainly addressed to the rights of individuals in the criminal justice system: search, seizure, detention, arrest, trial, testimony and imprisonment are the concerns of ss. 8 to 14. It seems reasonable to conclude, as Lamer J. has done, that "the restrictions on liberty and security of the person that s. 7 is concerned with are those that occur as a result of an individual's interaction with the justice system, and its administration".[5] This line of reasoning also excludes economic liberty from s. 7.

The Supreme Court of Canada has held that s. 7 does not apply to

---

[2]The story is told in L.H. Tribe, American Constitutional Law (Foundation Press, New York, 3rd ed., 2000), ch. 8; J.E. Nowak and R.D. Rotunda, Constitutional Law (West, St. Paul, Minn., 7th ed., 2004), ch. 11.

[3]The legislative history is reviewed by Lamer J. in *Re B.C. Motor Vehicle Act*, [1985] 2 S.C.R. 486, 504-505.

[4]*Re ss. 193 and 195.1 of Criminal Code* (Prostitution Reference) [1990] 1 S.C.R. 1123, 1163-1166 per Lamer J. But see the decision in *Health Services and Support—Facilities Subsector Bargaining Assn. v. B.C.*, [2007] 2 S.C.R. 391, holding that s. 2(d) of the Charter (freedom of association) protects collective bargaining by unions, and the protection extends to the terms of collective agreements. The Court decided that a provincial statute that attempted to legislate working conditions in the health care sector was invalid to the extent that it conflicted with the terms of a collective agreement. Freedom of contract prevailed over the statute. For criticism, see R.E. Charney, "The Contract Clause Comes to Canada: The British Columbia *Health Services* Case and the Sanctity of Collective Agreements" (2007) 23 Nat. J. Con. Law 65.

[5]*Re ss. 193 and 195.1 of Criminal Code* (Prostitution Reference) [1990] 1 S.C.R. 1123. Accord, *Gosselin v. Que.*, [2002] 4 S.C.R. 429, paras. 77 per McLachlin C.J. for majority (but with suggestion that definition is capable of expansion), para. 216 per Bastarache J. dissenting but not on this point. In *Chaoulli v. Que.*, [2005] 1 S.C.R. 791 (prohibition on private health insurance struck down), McLachlin C.J. and Major J., who (with Bastarache J.) applied s. 7 to strike down the law as "arbitrary", seem to have surreptitiously abandoned the link with the administration of justice, and Binnie and LeBel JJ., who (with Fish J.) wrote the dissenting opinion, explicitly said (paras. 195-199) that the link was not essential. Deschamps J., whose concurring opinion made up a majority to strike down the law, did not do so under s. 7 and did not discuss this point.

corporations, because "liberty" does not include corporate activity.[6] Nor does "liberty" include the right to do business, for example, by selling goods on a Sunday.[7] Does "liberty" include the right of an individual to work? Despite some lower court decisions[8] to the contrary, which emphasize the role of work as an instrument of self-fulfilment, the regulation of trades and professions should be regarded as restrictions on economic liberty that are outside the scope of s. 7.[9]

§ 47:11 Political liberty

"Liberty" does not include freedom of conscience and religion, freedom of expression, freedom of assembly, freedom of association, the right to vote and be a candidate for election, or the right to travel. These rights are all guaranteed elsewhere in the Charter of Rights, and should be excluded from s. 7.[1]

VIII. SECURITY OF THE PERSON

§ 47:12 Security of the person

Section 7 protects "life, liberty and security of the person". What is included in "security of the person"?

---

[6] *Irwin Toy v. Que.*, [1989] 1 S.C.R. 927, 1004; *Dywidag Systems v. Zutphen Bros.*, [1990] 1 S.C.R. 705, 709.

[7] *R. v. Edwards Books and Art*, [1986] 2 S.C.R. 713, 786 (s. 7 does not confer "an unconstrained right to transact business whenever one wishes"); *Siemens v. Man.*, [2003] 1 S.C.R. 6, para. 46 (no right to operate video lottery terminals).

[8] E.g. *Wilson v. Medical Services Commn.* (1988), 53 D.L.R. (4th) 171 (B.C.C.A.) (s. 7 violated by restrictions on the practice of medicine); criticized by M.D. Lepofsky, "Comment" (1989) 68 Can. Bar Rev. 615.

[9] *Re ss. 193 and 195.1 of Criminal Code* (Prostitution Reference) [1990] 1 S.C.R. 1123, 1170-1171 per Lamer J. (disapproving *Wilson v. Medical Services Commn.* (1988), 53 D.L.R. (4th) 171 (B.C.C.A.)); *ILWU v. Can.*, [1994] 1 S.C.R. 150 (holding that back-to-work legislation does not violate the liberty of the employees). But see *Ruffo v. Conseil de la Magistrature*, [1995] 4 S.C.R. 267, para. 38, where Gonthier J., for the majority of the Court, asserted without discussion that s. 7 demanded that a provincial court judge's conduct be examined by "an independent and impartial tribunal". The disciplinary committee charged with investigating the matter had the power to recommend the judge's dismissal. The case could have been decided under s. 23 of Quebec's Charter of Human Rights and Freedoms, which guaranteed an independent and impartial tribunal for a "determination of . . . rights and obligations" and without reference to life, liberty or security of the person. In any case, no remedy was granted, because the Court rejected the allegation that the committee was biased.

[Section 47:11]

[1] But see *B.(R.) v. Children's Aid Society*, [1995] 1 S.C.R. 315, para. 83 per La Forest J. (with the concurrence of three others) (liberty includes the right of parents who were Jehovah's Witnesses to refuse a blood transfusion for their child, although this right was also included in freedom of religion); the overlap between ss. 7 and 2 was rejected by Lamer C.J. at para. 30.

The easy case is *Canadian Foundation for Children, Youth and the Law v. Canada* (2004),[1] where a challenge was brought to the provision of the Criminal Code that provides a defence to a charge of assault for teachers and parents who use "reasonable" force "by way of correction" against the children in their care. This provision exposed children to force that would amount to a criminal assault if committed against an adult. The Supreme Court of Canada, relying on a concession by the Crown, had no difficulty in finding that the provision adversely affected the security of the person of the children to whom it applied.[2] (The Court upheld the provision on the ground that there was no breach of the principles of fundamental justice.)[3]

In *R. v. Morgentaler (No. 2)* (1988),[4] the Supreme Court of Canada, by a majority of five to two, held that the Criminal Code's restrictions on abortion, which required that the abortion be approved by the therapeutic abortion committee of an approved hospital, were unconstitutional. The evidence showed that the requirement of approval by a therapeutic abortion committee restricted access to the procedure of an abortion (because some hospitals would not set up the required committees) and caused delays in treatment, which increased the risk to the health of the woman. All five majority judges agreed that the risk to health that was caused by the law was a deprivation of security of the person.[5] The breach of fundamental justice consisted (for four of the majority judges) in the unnecessarily restrictive procedural requirements for a therapeutic abortion and (for Wilson J.) in the deprivation of the woman's freedom of conscience. As the result of this decision, Canada no longer has any restrictions on abortion.[6]

[Section 47:12]

[1] *Canadian Foundation for Children, Youth and the Law v. Canada*, [2004] 1 S.C.R. 76.

[2] *Canadian Foundation for Children, Youth and the Law v. Canada*, [2004] 1 S.C.R. 76, para. 3.

[3] See also *R. v. Nasogaluak*, [2010] 1 S.C.R. 206, para. 38 (use of excessive force by police in making an arrest is a deprivation of security of the person not in accordance with principles of fundamental justice).

[4] *R. v. Morgentaler (No. 2)*, [1988] 1 S.C.R. 30. Four opinions were written: by Wilson J.; Dickson C.J. (with Lamer J.); by Beetz J. (with Estey J.); and, dissenting, by McIntyre J. (with La Forest J.). For a case commentary see L.E. Weinrib, "The *Morgentaler* Judgment: Constitutional Rights, Legislative Intention and Institutional Design" (1992) 42 U.Toronto L.J. 207.

[5] This was the lowest common denominator of the majority reasoning, espoused by Beetz J. and concurred in by Wilson J. and Dickson C.J. For Wilson J., the loss of control over the termination of pregnancy was a deprivation of liberty; and both she and Dickson C.J. regarded the loss of control as another aspect of the deprivation of security of the person.

[6] The Government of Canada introduced a less restrictive bill to re-criminalize abortion, which as Bill C-43 passed the House of Commons but was defeated by the Senate on a 43-43 tie vote on January 31, 1991.

In *Chaoulli v. Quebec* (2005),[7] the Supreme Court of Canada held that excessive waiting times in the public health care system of Quebec caused unnecessary pain and stress to those awaiting surgery and other medical procedures. This was a breach of the right to security of the person (as well as the right to life, since the risk of death was sometimes increased by the prolonged delays). Quebec law forbade the purchase of private health insurance. The law was designed to make the public system exclusive, and it had that effect. Although the seven-judge bench was unanimous that the law caused a breach of security of the person, there was an even (three-three) split on whether the law was a breach of the principles of fundamental justice under s. 7.[8] One judge (Deschamps J.) confined her decision to the Quebec Charter of Human Rights and Freedoms, which contains guarantees similar to those of the Canadian Charter, but does not use the phrase "fundamental justice". She held that there was a breach of the Quebec Charter. This became the majority position. The Quebec law was accordingly struck down, but the ruling does not extend beyond the province of Quebec. Bans on the purchase of private insurance or other impediments to access to private health care exist in the other provinces and territories, but it will take another case to determine whether they are in breach of the Charter.[9]

Canada v. Bedford (2013)[10] was a constitutional challenge to three prostitution-related offences in the federal Criminal Code: keeping or being found in a common bawdy house, living on the avails of prostitution, and communicating in a public place for the purposes of prostitution. Prostitution itself was not an offence for either the seller or the buyer of sexual services. Did the three offences limit security of the person so as to make s. 7 applicable? The Supreme Court of Canada answered yes.[11] Each provision imposed increased risks on the legal activity of prostitution. The bawdy-house provision prevented prostitutes from working on "in-calls" from a fixed indoor location, forcing them to work on the street or on "out-calls" with clients at different locations—both more dangerous practices. The living-off-the-avails provision prevented prostitutes from hiring drivers, bodyguards or receptionists who could make the work safer. The communicating-in-public provision

---

[7] *Chaoulli v. Quebec*, [2005] 1 S.C.R. 791. Three opinions were written. McLachlin and Major J., with the agreement of Bastarache J., wrote what became the majority opinion. Deschamps J. wrote a separate concurring opinion. Binnie and LeBel JJ., with the agreement of Fish J., wrote a dissenting opinion.

[8] McLachlin C.J and Major J., with the agreement of Bastarache J., held that the ban on private health insurance offended the principles of fundamental justice, because it was arbitrary: for discussion, see § 47:26, "Arbitrary laws".

[9] In *Allen v. Alta.*, 2015 ABCA 277 (Alta. C.A.), the Alberta Court of Appeal rejected a s. 7 challenge to Alberta's ban on private health insurance due to insufficient evidence. In *Cambie Surgeries Corp. v. B.C.* 2020 BCSC 1310, the British Columbia Supreme Court rejected a decade-long ss. 7 and 15 challenge to British Columbia's ban on private health insurance.

[10] *Canada v. Bedford*, [2013] 3 S.C.R. 1101, 2013 SCC 72. McLachlin C.J. wrote the opinion of the Court.

[11] *Canada v. Bedford*, [2013] 3 S.C.R. 1101, 2013 SCC 72, paras. 58-92.

prevented street prostitutes (who were the most vulnerable to personal risk) from doing any preliminary screening of clients for drunkenness or propensity to violence which could reduce the risks they faced. It was true that prostitutes knew that their chosen occupation was risky; and it was also true that the risks came from violent clients and pimps, not the state; but there was a "sufficient causal connection" between the legal prohibitions and the enhancement of the risks of prostitution to conclude that the legal prohibitions had a negative impact on the security of the person of prostitutes. Section 7 therefore applied. The Court went on to strike the laws down for breach of the principles of fundamental justice.[12]

Does security of the person go beyond health and safety? In *Morgentaler*, three of the five majority judges were willing to find a deprivation of security of the person, not only in the risk to the woman's health created by the law-related delays, but also in the loss of her control over the termination of the pregnancy. On this basis, security of the person would include some requirement of personal autonomy, at least with respect to medical treatment.

The extension of security of the person to include control over one's body was confirmed in *Rodriguez v. British Columbia* (1993).[13] In that case, a plaintiff who was terminally ill (with Lou Gehrig's disease) challenged the constitutionality of the Criminal Code offence of assisting a person to commit suicide. She pointed out that the law deprived a disabled person of the ability to commit suicide (which was not an offence); she wanted to die at a time of her own choosing, but could not do so without medical assistance, because she was (or soon would be) too disabled by her illness. Eight of the nine judges of the Supreme Court of Canada held that the removal from the plaintiff of an aspect of the control over her body was a deprivation of security of the person under s. 7.[14] However, the plaintiff was not successful in her challenge to the law, because five of the nine judges held that the law did not offend the

---

[12]*Canada v. Bedford*, [2013] 3 S.C.R. 1101, 2013 SCC 72, paras. 134 (bawdy-house provision grossly disproportionate), 142 (living-off-the-avails provision overbroad), 159 (communicating-in-public provision grossly disproportionate); for discussion, see § 47:24, "Overbroad laws", § 47:25, "Disproportionate laws".

[13]*Rodriguez v. British Columbia*, [1993] 3 S.C.R. 519. The majority opinion was written by Sopinka J. (with La Forest, Gonthier, Iacobucci, and Major JJ.). Dissenting opinions were written by McLachlin J. (with L'Heureux-Dubé J.), Lamer C.J. and Cory J. For the majority, Sopinka J. rejected arguments based on ss. 7, 12 and 15 of the Charter. Of the dissenting opinions, McLachlin J. relied on s. 7, Lamer C.J. on s. 15, and Cory J. on both ss. 7 and 15. Lamer C.J. expressed no view on security of the person or fundamental justice.

[14]Compare *Pretty v. United Kingdom* (2002), 35 E.H.R.R. 1 (European Court of Human Rights) (holding law prohibiting assisted suicide interfered with the disabled plaintiff's right to make choices about her own body under Article 8 of the European Convention on Human Rights, but was a justifiable limit of that right); *Washington v. Glucksberg* (1997), 521 U.S. 702 (assistance in dying not a "liberty" interest protected by the due process clause of the fourteenth Amendment). For a comparative review, see M. Cormack, "Euthanasia and Assisted Suicide in the Post-Rodriguez Era: Lessons from Foreign Jurisdictions" (2000) 38 Osgoode Hall L.J. 591.

principles of fundamental justice. Exactly the same issue came back to the Court in *Carter v. Canada* (2015).[15] In *Carter*, the Court refused to follow *Rodriguez* on the issue of fundamental justice, holding that the prohibition of physician-assisted death was overbroad,[16] but the Court reaffirmed its ruling in *Rodriguez* that the deprivation of control over the plaintiff's body was a breach of security of the person.[17]

Does a threat to "psychological integrity" constitute a deprivation of security of the person? In *New Brunswick v. G.(J.)* (1999),[18] the Supreme Court of Canada held that an application by the state to remove children from a parent and place them under the wardship of the state affected the security of the person of the parent. Security of the person was affected, because the government action would constitute "a serious interference with the psychological integrity of the parent."[19] The result was that s. 7 applied, and the removal proceedings had to be conducted in accordance with the principles of fundamental justice, which in this case led the Court to order that the parent be represented by state-funded counsel. This decision was followed in *Winnipeg Child and Family Services v. K.L.W.* (2000),[20] where the Supreme Court of Canada held that the warrantless apprehension of a child deemed to be "in need of protection" was a breach of the parents' security of the person, although a majority of the Court held that the principles of fundamental justice had not been breached. There was no requirement of a warrant or other pre-apprehension hearing, because any such procedure would cause delay and consequent risk of harm to the child. In this context, the principles of fundamental justice were satisfied by a post-apprehension hearing.

The protection of psychological integrity was relied upon in *Blencoe v. British Columbia* (2000)[21] to seek a remedy under s. 7 for unreasonable

---

[15]*Carter v. Canada*, [2015] 1 S.C.R. 331, 2015 SCC 5. The opinion was attributed to "the Court".

[16]The case is discussed in § 47:24, "Overbroad laws".

[17]*Carter v. Canada*, [2015] 1 S.C.R. 331, 2015 SCC 5, para. 64. See also *R. v. Smith*, [2015] 2 S.C.R. 602, 2015 SCC 34, para. 18 (holding Medical Marihuana Access Regulations infringed security of the person by allowing authorized medical marihuana users to possess and use only "dried marihuana", which denied them other forms of marihuana that would be safer and more effective for some medical conditions).

[18]*New Brunswick v. G.(J.)*, [1999] 3 S.C.R. 46. The majority opinion was written by Lamer C.J.; a concurring opinion was written by L'Heureux-Dubé J.

[19]*New Brunswick v. G.(J.)*, [1999] 3 S.C.R. 46, para. 61 per Lamer C.J.; see also para. 116 per L'Heureux-Dubé J. ("serious stigma and psychological stress").

[20]*Winnipeg Child and Family Services v. K.L.W.*, [2000] 2 S.C.R. 519. The majority opinion of L'Heureux-Dubé J. was agreed with by four judges; the dissenting opinion of Arbour J., with whom McLachlin C.J. agreed, would have required that a warrant be obtained from a judge before an apprehension in a non-emergency situation.

[21]*Blencoe v. British Columbia*, [2000] 2 S.C.R. 307. The majority opinion of Bastarache J. was agreed with by four judges; the dissenting opinion of LeBel J., who would have ordered an expedited hearing on administrative law grounds, and who refused to be drawn into discussion of the scope of s. 7, was agreed with by three judges. The case is also discussed in § 47:9, "Physical liberty".

delay by the British Columbia Human Rights Commission in disposing of complaints of sexual harassment made against the applicant. Bastarache J. for a majority of five of the Supreme Court of Canada held that state-induced psychological stress would be a breach of security of the person, but decided that the Commission's delays did not have a sufficiently severe impact on the applicant's psychological state to qualify as a breach. The stress was contributed to by a number of other causes, including the loss of his position in the British Columbia cabinet and the relentless attentions of the media. However, Bastarache J. said that the decision should not be construed as a ruling that delays in human-rights proceedings can never trigger an individual's s. 7 rights.[22] It would appear therefore that there may be a constitutional remedy for administrative delay if the person involved finds it sufficiently distressing.[23]

It has been suggested that "security of the person" includes the economic capacity to satisfy basic human needs.[24] John Whyte says that "state action which deprives a person of all (or a substantial portion) of his or her capacity to produce an income could be seen as invading security of the person". He gives the examples of "the removal of a person from the welfare scheme, the confiscation of property (tools, equipment, etc.) essential to a person's work, or the cancellation of a licence which is essential to the pursuit of one's occupation (taxi driver, lawyer or engineer)".[25] The trouble with this argument is that it accords to s. 7 an economic role that is incompatible with its setting in the legal rights portion of the Charter—a setting that the Supreme Court of Canada has relied upon as controlling the scope of s. 7.[26] The suggested role also involves a massive expansion of judicial review, since it would bring under judicial scrutiny all of the elements of the modern welfare state, including the regulation of trades and professions, the adequacy of labour standards and bankruptcy laws and, of course, the level of public expenditures on social programmes. As Oliver Wendell Holmes would have pointed out, these are the issues upon which elections are won and

---

[22] *Blencoe v. British Columbia*, [2000] 2 S.C.R. 307, para. 98.

[23] Several provincial appellate courts have rejected claims that (even significant) fines gave rise to the level of state-caused psychological stress sufficient to constitute a deprivation of security of the person: *R. v. Transport Robert (1973) Lteé* (2003), 68 O.R. (3d) 51, para. 28 (C.A.); *Lavallee v. Alta.* (2010), 317 D.L.R. (4th) 373, paras. 26-29 (Alta. C.A.); see also *R. v. Tinker*, 2017 ONCA 552, paras. 71-82 (C.A.) (rejecting a similar claim involving the mandatory victim surcharge).

[24] *Singh v. Minr. of Emplmt. and Imm.*, [1985] 1 S.C.R. 177, 207 per Wilson J. (obiter dictum, with supporting citations); *Irwin Toy v. Que.*, [1989] 1 S.C.R. 927, 1003 per Dickson C.J. (obiter dictum, leaving issue open).

[25] J.D. Whyte, "Fundamental Justice" (1983) 13 Man. L.J. 455, 474. See also M. Jackman, "Poor Rights: Using the Charter to Support Social Welfare Claims" (1993) 19 Queen's L.J. 65. Even if s. 7 cannot be used to guarantee particular levels of social services, there is a school of thought that holds that unsuccessful Charter litigation may serve a "signalling function" by alerting government to desirable law reform: R. Howse, "Another Rights Revolution?" in P.M. Grady and others (eds.), Redefining Social Security (1995), 99.

[26] See heading § 47:10, "Economic liberty".

lost; the judges need a clear mandate to enter that arena, and s. 7 does not provide that clear mandate.

In *Gosselin v. Quebec* (2002),[27] it was argued that s. 7 imposed on government a positive obligation to provide adequate welfare benefits to those who were without other sources of income. Quebec had enacted a welfare scheme under which persons under the age of 30 received only about one-third of the standard welfare benefit, which they could top up to the standard amount only if they participated in stipulated educational or work experience programmes. The plaintiff for various reasons had not been able to participate in the "workfare" programmes, and had been forced to subsist on the lower benefit. She sued to challenge the validity of the law (which had by then been repealed) and to recover the difference between the amount of the welfare benefit that she received and the standard amount. Her challenge was based on s. 15 (age discrimination)[28] as well as s. 7 and she failed on both grounds. With respect to s. 7, McLachlin C.J. for the majority pointed out that s. 7 had not been extended to economic rights or indeed to any rights wholly unconnected with the administration of justice.[29] She also pointed out that, while s. 7 prohibited state deprivations of life, liberty or security of the person, it had not been interpreted as imposing positive obligations on the state to ensure that each person enjoyed life, liberty or security of the person.[30] These two hurdles defeated the plaintiff's claim. McLachlin C.J.'s opinion was very cautiously expressed and she was careful not to close the door forever on a more expansive interpretation of s. 7. Arbour J., who dissented, was ready, willing and able to give s. 7 the more expansive interpretation that would condemn the Quebec law. In her view, s. 7 was not limited to rights connected with the administration of justice, and in particular guaranteed a level of welfare sufficient to meet basic needs.[31] Nor was s. 7 limited to deprivations of life, liberty or security of the person; on the contrary, the state was under a positive obligation to make provision for everyone's basic needs.[32] A workfare programme under which some people could not qualify for full welfare benefits was unconstitutional.[33] Arbour J.'s expansive view of s. 7 was

---

[27]*Gosselin v. Que.*, [2002] 4 S.C.R. 429. The opinion of the majority was written by McLachlin C.J. with the agreement of Gonthier, Iacobucci, Major and Binnie JJ. Dissenting opinions were written by L'Heureux-Dubé, Bastarache, Arbour and LeBel JJ.

[28]The equality point is explained in ch. 55, Equality, under heading § 55:44, "Age".

[29]*Gosselin v. Que.*, [2002] 4 S.C.R. 429, paras. 77-80.

[30]*Gosselin v. Que.*, [2002] 4 S.C.R. 429, paras. 81-82.

[31]*Gosselin v. Que.*, [2002] 4 S.C.R. 429, para. 316.

[32]*Gosselin v. Que.*, [2002] 4 S.C.R. 429, para. 358.

[33]It was the "workfare" or conditional nature of the scheme that defeated it in Arbour J.'s view, because she accepted (para. 333) that the precise amount of income that would be needed to meet basic needs could not be determined by the Court. This was not an impediment to a finding of unconstitutionality in this case, she held, because the failure to fulfil the workfare conditions left the plaintiff with benefits below the standard amount set by the Legislature (para. 334). Under Arbour J.'s view of s. 7, the precise amount of welfare is not reviewable, provided the Legislature has determined

agreed to by only one other judge.[34] Thus, the division of the Court was seven-two in favour of the narrower interpretation of s. 7.[35]

IX. PROPERTY

§ 47:13 Property

Section 7 protects "life, liberty and security of the person". The omission of property[1] from s. 7 was a striking and deliberate departure from the constitutional texts that provided the models for s. 7.[2] The due process clauses in the fifth and fourteenth amendments of the Constitution of the United States protect "life, liberty or property". And the due process clause in s. 1(a) of the Canadian Bill of Rights protects "life, liberty, security of the person and enjoyment of property".

The omission of property rights from s. 7 greatly reduces its scope. It means that s. 7 affords no guarantee of compensation or even of a fair procedure for the taking of property by government.[3] It means that s. 7 affords no guarantee of fair treatment by courts,[4] tribunals or officials with power over the purely economic interests of individuals or corporations.[5] It also requires, as we have noticed in the earlier discussions of "liberty" and "security of the person", that those terms be

---

that the amount meets basic needs, but any conditions or exclusions ("any differential treatment or underinclusion": para. 385) that would leave anyone not fully provided for would be unconstitutional as a denial of the right to security of the person (except in the unlikely event of their being justified under s. 1).

[34]L'Heureux-Dubé J. agreed with Arbour J. on s. 7 (para. 141). Bastarache and LeBel JJ., who also dissented (based on s. 15), essentially agreed with McLachlin C.J.'s majority opinion on s. 7.

[35]See also *Masse v. Ont.* (1996), 134 D.L.R. (4th) 20 (Ont. Div. Ct.) (rejecting constitutional challenge to law reducing provincial social assistance rates); *Flora v. Ont.* (2008), 91 O.R. (3d) 412 (C.A.) (rejecting constitutional duty on provincial government to pay for out-of-country life-saving medical treatments); *Tanudjaja v. Can.* (2013), 116 O.R. (3d) 574 (S.C.J.) (rejecting constitutional duty on governments to provide affordable housing).

[Section 47:13]

[1]The gap is not filled by s. 8's prohibition of unreasonable "seizure". Section 8 applies only to a seizure of property for investigatory or evidentiary purposes: *Re Becker* (1983), 148 D.L.R. (3d) 539 (Alta. C.A.) (s. 8 does not apply to an expropriation of property).

[2]However, the International Covenant on Civil and Political Rights, which in articles 6-11 includes elaborate provisions regarding life, liberty and security of the person, also omits any guarantee of property rights.

[3]The courts will imply these rights in the absence of an express legislative provision to the contrary: see ch. 29, Public Property, under heading § 29:5, "Expropriation"; but there is no constitutional impediment to an express legislative provision to the contrary, except for s. 1(a) of the Canadian Bill of Rights, which is applicable only to the federal Parliament.

[4]Section 7 does not protect the right of action for damages: *Wittman v. Emmott* (1991), 77 D.L.R. (4th) 77 (B.C.C.A.); *Budge v. Alta.* (1991), 77 D.L.R. (4th) 361 (Alta. C.A.).

[5]The courts will imply a duty to observe the rules of "natural justice" in the absence of an express legislative provision to the contrary, but there is no constitutional impedi-

interpreted as excluding economic liberty and economic security; otherwise, property, having been shut out of the front door, would enter by the back.[6]

The omission of property rights from s. 7 also ensures a continuing role for the Canadian Bill of Rights, which continues to apply to federal (but not provincial) laws.[7] In the Canadian Bill of Rights, "enjoyment of property" is guaranteed by the due process clause of s. 1(a); there is also, in s. 2(e), a guarantee of "a fair hearing in accordance with the principles of fundamental justice for the determination of his rights and obligations". Although s. 2(e) has been held to be only a guarantee of a fair procedure,[8] the reference to the determination of "rights and obligations" extends beyond s. 7's "life, liberty and security of the person". For example, in *Singh v. Minister of Employment and Immigration* (1985),[9] where the question was whether refugee claimants had been accorded a sufficient hearing under federal law, Beetz J., for half of the six-judge bench, being undecided whether life, liberty or security of the person was implicated, decided the case under s. 2(e) of the Canadian Bill of Rights. Wilson J., for the other half of the bench, held that s. 7 did apply, and she decided the case on that basis. Both judges were agreed in the result, which was that the Immigration Act's procedures did not measure up to the standard of fundamental justice, and were therefore inoperative or invalid.

MacBain v. Lederman (1985)[10] is another example of the broad reach of s. 2(e). The issue in that case was whether the federal Human Rights Code violated fundamental justice in the provisions establishing an adjudicatory tribunal. The Code provided that the members of the tribunal were to be appointed by the Human Rights Commission. It was argued that this mode of appointment gave rise to a reasonable apprehension of bias because the Commission was also in effect the prosecutor of the complaint. The Federal Court of Appeal upheld the claim of bias, and struck down the appointment provisions of the Code. The Court relied upon s. 2(e), which was clearly applicable, because the tribunal had the power to make a determination of the respondent's rights and obligations. The Court did not rely upon s. 7, presumably because the tribunal had no power over life, liberty or security of the

---

ment to an express legislative provision to the contrary. Once again, an exception must be made for the federal jurisdiction, because s. 2(e) of the Canadian Bill of Rights requires compliance with "the principles of fundamental justice" for the determination of "rights and obligations". Note also *Morguard Investments v. De Savoye*, [1990] 3 S.C.R. 1077, 1110 (obiter suggestions by La Forest J. that s. 7, "though not made expressly applicable to property", might play a role in conflict of laws cases in the courts).

[6]See *Irwin Toy v. Que.*, [1989] 1 S.C.R. 927, 1003.

[7]Chapter 35, Canadian Bill of Rights.

[8]This is clear from the context; and see § 47:2 note 2 and accompanying text, below.

[9]*Singh v. Minr. of Emplmt. and Imm.*, [1985] 1 S.C.R. 177.

[10]*MacBain v. Lederman*, [1985] 1 F.C. 856 (C.A.).

person.[11] Civil litigation, whether before the courts or tribunals, is usually about money or property or other purely economic interests. Section 7 does not apply to this kind of litigation, but s. 2(e) does apply, so long as the dispute is governed by federal law.

In *Authorson v. Canada* (2003),[12] a disabled veteran challenged a provision in the federal Department of Veterans Affairs Act that barred any claim to interest on moneys held by the Department on behalf of disabled veterans. The plaintiff was a disabled veteran who had been incapable of managing his own funds and for whom the Department had (in accordance with its normal practice) been collecting his veteran's pension payments. After the plaintiff became competent, the Department paid him the pension money that had accumulated over a 40-year period, but the Department paid him no interest on the money. The plaintiff sued for the interest. It was common ground that the Crown was under a fiduciary duty to the veterans for whom it was holding funds to pay interest on the funds. The problem for the plaintiff was the statute that unambiguously barred any claim by veterans to interest on the funds. Section 7 of the Charter was no help, since only property rights were at stake. The plaintiff accordingly invoked ss. 1(a) and 2(e) of the Canadian Bill of Rights. The Supreme Court of Canada denied relief under both provisions. With respect to s. 1(a), the plaintiff argued that he had been deprived of the "enjoyment of property" without "due process of law": Parliament had taken away his rights without notice or hearing. But the Court refused to impose any additional procedural obligations on Parliament: "the only procedure due any citizen of Canada is that proposed legislation receive three readings in the Senate and House of Commons and that it receive Royal Assent".[13] Nor did s. 2(e) impose its right to a "fair hearing" on Parliament (as opposed to courts and administrative tribunals). The Court also refused to interpret s. 1(a) as imposing a substantive obligation to provide compensation for expropriated property.[14]

---

[11]Compare *Blencoe v. B.C.*, [2002] 2 S.C.R. 307.

[12]*Authorson v. Canada*, [2003] 2 S.C.R. 40. Major J. wrote the opinion of the unanimous Court.

[13]*Authorson v. Canada*, [2003] 2 S.C.R. 40, para. 37. Folld. in *Taylor v. Can.* (2007), 286 D.L.R. (4th) 385 (F.C.A.), paras. 91-96 (Parliament under no duty to provide prior notice to persons potentially affected by statute containing loss of citizenship provisions).

[14]The plaintiff pressed on, with the ingenious argument that the Supreme Court decision extinguishing his right to interest should not be interpreted as extinguishing his right to damages for breach of fiduciary duty, although an "interest" figure would have to be deducted from the damages. This argument was accepted by a superior court judge in Ontario, who awarded damages (minus an interest figure). However the damages award was reversed on appeal by the Court of Appeal, which held that the Supreme Court decision had extinguished all relief for the Crown's breach of fiduciary duty: *Authorson v. Can.* (2007), 86 O.R. (3d) 321 (C.A.), leave to appeal denied by the SCC on January 17, 2008.

X. FUNDAMENTAL JUSTICE

§ 47:14 Procedure and substance

A deprivation of life, liberty or security of the person is a breach of s. 7 of the Charter only if the deprivation is not in accordance with "the principles of fundamental justice".[1]

When the Charter was adopted in 1982, the phrase "the principles of fundamental justice" did not have a firmly established meaning in Anglo-Canadian law. The phrase did appear in s. 2(e) of the Canadian Bill of Rights, which guarantees to a person "the right to a fair hearing in accordance with the principles of fundamental justice for the determination of his rights and obligations". In that context, which included a reference to "a fair hearing", the term fundamental justice was equivalent to natural justice,[2] a term that does have an established meaning in Anglo-Canadian law. The rules of natural justice are rules of procedure only: they require a hearing, unbiased adjudication and (a recent development) a fair procedure.[3] Therefore, if fundamental justice in s. 7 meant natural justice, the courts would be entitled to review the appropriateness and fairness of the *procedures* enacted for a deprivation of life, liberty or security of the person—but that would be all. The courts would not be entitled to review the *substantive* justice of the deprivation.

The legislative history of s. 7 makes clear that the framers thought that "fundamental justice" meant natural justice, and were anxious to avoid judicial review that went beyond issues of procedure. The concern, expressed at the hearings of the Special Joint Committee that examined the text of the Charter,[4] was to avoid any risk of the importation to Canada of the substantive due process doctrine of the *Lochner* era in the United States.[5] At that time (1905 to 1937), the Supreme Court of the United States applied a notion of substantive due process to strike down state and federal laws providing for maximum hours of work, minimum wages, health and safety standards, and the protection of union activity. These decisions were overruled in 1937,[6] but they demonstrated the hazard of granting to the judges the power to review legislation on a ground

---

[Section 47:14]

[1]This assumes that s. 7 confers only a single right: see § 47:2 note 3 and accompanying text, above.

[2]*Duke v. The Queen*, [1972] S.C.R. 917, 923. This interpretation of "fundamental justice" in s. 2(e) has been carried forward into the post-Charter period: *Bell Canada v. Can. Telephone Employees Assn.*, [2003] 1 S.C.R. 884, para. 28.

[3]See S.A. de Smith, Lord Woolf and J.L. Jowell, Judicial Review of Administrative Action (Sweet & Maxwell, London, 5th ed., 1995), chs. 4, 5; D.J.M. Brown and J.M. Evans, Judicial Review of Administrative Action in Canada (Canvasback Publishing, 2004), chs. 7-12.

[4]The principal passages in the proceedings of the Special Joint Committee are referred to in *Re B.C. Motor Vehicle Act*, [1985] 2 S.C.R. 486, 504-505.

[5]See heading § 47:10, "Economic liberty".

[6]Substantive due process is no longer used to review social and economic legislation, but it is still alive and well in other contexts, for example, the incorporation into

as inherently indeterminate as substantive due process. It is plain from the testimony before the Special Joint Committee that the phrase "due process" was omitted from s. 7 in order to make sure that s. 7 did not give rise to a Canadian doctrine of substantive due process.

The trouble was that the phrase that was selected to replace due process was not "natural justice", which would certainly have been restricted to procedure, but "fundamental justice", a term that lacked any substantial body of defining case-law. It was arguable that the term fundamental justice in s. 7, when liberated from the procedural context of s. 2(e) of the Canadian Bill of Rights, was apt to reach substantive as well as procedural justice. In the *B.C. Motor Vehicle Reference* (1985),[7] the Supreme Court of Canada held that fundamental justice did indeed cover substantive as well as procedural justice. The case was a reference by the government of British Columbia to determine the validity of a provision in the province's Motor Vehicle Act which made it an offence to drive a car while prohibited from driving or while one's driving licence was suspended. The Act imposed a mandatory term of imprisonment on anyone found guilty of the offence. The controversial provision was a subsection that declared that the offence was one of "absolute liability" in which "guilt is established by proof of driving, whether or not the defendant knew of the prohibition or suspension". The Court held that it was a breach of fundamental justice to impose a term of imprisonment for an offence that lacked the element of mens rea (a guilty mind). The Court made no attempt to characterize this as a procedural defect in the law; the absence of mens rea created a substantive injustice. Section 7 prohibited substantive as well as procedural injustice.

Lamer J., who wrote the principal opinion in the *B.C. Motor Vehicle Reference*, referred to the testimony in the Special Joint Committee in which fundamental justice was equated with natural justice, and in which the concern of the framers to avoid substantive due process was explained.[8] But he brushed this aside as being of "minimal weight"[9] in comparison to the reasons for giving fundamental justice a more extended meaning.

Lamer J.'s opinion gives three reasons for extending fundamental justice beyond procedure. The first reason is that the words "fundamental justice" are literally broader in scope than other formulations that could have been used, such as, "natural justice". The second reason is that the

---

the fourteenth amendment of most of the guarantees of the first ten amendments, the incorporation into the fifth amendment of the equal protection clause of the fourteenth amendment, and the recognition of a right of privacy. See L.H. Tribe, American Constitutional Law (Foundation Press, New York, 3rd ed., 2000), chs. 11, 15; J.E. Nowak and R.D. Rotunda, Constitutional Law (West, St. Paul, Minn., 7th ed., 2004), ch. 11.

[7]*Re B.C. Motor Vehicle Act*, [1985] 2 S.C.R. 486. The seven-judge bench was unanimous on this issue, and on the result, but three opinions were written: by Lamer J. with the agreement of four others; by McIntyre J.; and by Wilson J.

[8]*Re B.C. Motor Vehicle Act*, [1985] 2 S.C.R. 486, 504-505.

[9]*Re B.C. Motor Vehicle Act*, [1985] 2 S.C.R. 486, 509. The admissibility and weight of legislative history is examined in ch. 60, Proof, under heading §§ 60:1 to 60:7, "Legislative history".

expansion of the concept of fundamental justice has the effect of expanding the protection of life, liberty and security of the person. These two reasons are without doubt strong considerations cutting in the opposite direction to the legislative history. However, the third reason given by Lamer J. for extending fundamental justice beyond procedure into substance is much more dubious, and Wilson J. in her concurring opinion specifically disagreed with it. Lamer J. held that s. 7 is a kind of general residuary clause for all of the "legal rights" of the Charter. Sections 8 to 14 are merely "illustrative" of deprivations of fundamental justice that could just as easily be caught by s. 7. Since ss. 8 to 14 go beyond merely procedural guarantees (as in "unreasonable" search or seizure in s. 8, "arbitrary" detention or imprisonment in s. 9 and "cruel and unusual" treatment or punishment in s. 12), it follows that s. 7 also must go beyond a merely procedural guarantee.[10]

There are two difficulties with the residuary theory of s. 7, under which ss. 8 to 14 of the Charter are merely examples or illustrations of s. 7. One difficulty, which was pointed out by Wilson J., is that ss. 8 to 14 of the Charter are not in fact drafted in that way, but as "self-standing provisions".[11] A second difficulty is the fact that ss. 8 to 14 are not confined to life, liberty and security of the person, as s. 7 is. Thus, s. 8, which protects property from unreasonable search or seizure, is not premised on a denial of life, liberty or security of the person; this is why s. 8 applies to corporations, while s. 7 does not.[12] Section 11, with its long list of protections for "any person charged with an offence", is not confined to offences for which imprisonment is a penalty, but would also apply to offences punishable by a fine; such offences do not implicate life, liberty or security of the person.[13] The guarantees of s. 13 (self-incrimination) and s. 14 (interpreter) are also not confined to proceedings where life, liberty or security of the person is at stake.[14]

The theory that ss. 8 to 14 of the Charter are simply illustrations of s. 7 may help to provide some limits to the new substantive fundamental justice; the values protected by the term "fundamental justice" could be derived by analogy from the values explicitly protected by ss. 8 to 14. In the *B.C. Motor Vehicle Reference* itself, for example, the proposition that "a law that has the potential to convict a person who has not really done anything wrong offends the principles of fundamental justice" (which

---

[10] *Re B.C. Motor Vehicle Act*, [1985] 2 S.C.R. 486, 502-503.

[11] *Re B.C. Motor Vehicle Act*, [1985] 2 S.C.R. 486, 530.

[12] Compare *Hunter v. Southam*, [1984] 2 S.C.R. 145 (s. 8 applies to corporations) with *Irwin Toy v. Que.*, [1989] 1 S.C.R. 927 (s. 7 does not).

[13] It cannot seriously be contended that, just because a minor traffic offence leads to a very slight consequence, perhaps only a small fine, that offence does not fall within s. 11": *R. v. Wigglesworth*, [1987] 2 S.C.R. 541, 559 per Wilson J.

[14] The force of this criticism seems to be recognized in *R. v. CIP*, [1992] S.C.R., 843, 854, (p. 6) where Stevenson J. for a unanimous Court that included Lamer C.J. "explained" the residuary theory as relating only to the scope of the principles of fundamental justice, not the scope of life, liberty or security of the person.

was Lamer J.'s opening comment)[15] is a proposition which has affinities to s. 11(d) (presumption of innocence) and s. 12 (cruel and unusual treatment or punishment). But a case such as *Lochner v. New York* (1905),[16] where the Supreme Court of the United States applied substantive due process to strike down a law that limited the hours of work in bakeries, could not show affinities to anything in ss. 8 to 14. Thus, the Court's link between s. 7 and ss. 8 to 14, however implausible for other interpretative purposes, may help to shield social and economic legislation from judicial review under s. 7.[17] We have already noticed the usefulness of the link in interpreting "liberty" and "security of the person" in s. 7.[18]

The question whether the Court was right to extend fundamental justice into the substance of laws is not an easy one. If the Court had followed the legislative history and confined fundamental justice to procedural requirements, the distinction between procedure and substance would undoubtedly have proved to be unstable and indeterminate. The distinction has never been clear, and the courts would be constantly urged to characterize this or that unjust result as procedural so as to make it remediable under s. 7.[19] The Court's decision in the *B.C. Motor Vehicle Reference* does spare us that order of argument.

§ 47:15 Definition of fundamental justice

In the *B.C. Motor Vehicle Reference*,[1] the only definition of fundamental justice that was provided by the Court was Lamer J.'s assertion that "the principles of fundamental justice are to be found in the basic tenets of the legal system".[2] The inadequacy of this formulation to provide any real guidance for the future was acknowledged by Lamer J. when he said that "those words [fundamental justice] cannot be given any exhaustive content or simple enumerative definition, but will take on concrete meaning as the courts address alleged violations of s. 7".[3] Indeed, the Court never explained why absolute liability, which has long been a fa-

---

[15]*Re B.C. Motor Vehicle Act*, [1985] 2 S.C.R. 486, 492.

[16]*Lochner v. New York* (1905), 198 U.S. 45.

[17]Accord, E. Colvin, "Section 7 of the Charter of Rights and Freedoms" (1989) 68 Can. Bar Rev. 560.

[18]§ 47:10 note 5, § 47:12 note 26 and accompanying texts, above.

[19]*R. v. Morgentaler (No. 2)*, [1988] 1 S.C.R. 30 illustrates the difficulty: were the invalid restrictions on obtaining an abortion procedural requirements (as Dickson C.J. and Beetz J. claimed) or substantive requirements (as Wilson J. claimed)?

[Section 47:15]

[1]*Re B.C. Motor Vehicle Act*, [1985] 2 S.C.R. 486.

[2]*Re B.C. Motor Vehicle Act*, [1985] 2 S.C.R. 486, 503; Lamer J. (at 512) gives another, similar formulation; Wilson J. seems to accept this definition, referring (at 530) to "a fundamental tenet of our justice system"; McIntyre J. said (at 521-522) only that fundamental justice "includes as well a substantive element".

[3]*Re B.C. Motor Vehicle Act*, [1985] 2 S.C.R. 486, 513.

miliar (if unloved) part of Canada's system of criminal justice,[4] was now contrary to the basic tenets of the legal system. All that can be discerned from the opinions is the view that absolute liability is morally repugnant.

As will be seen in succeeding sections of this chapter, subsequent decisions have not succeeded in giving better definition to the basic tenets of the legal system. On the contrary, later decisions have demonstrated that there is little agreement as to what are the basic tenets of the legal system or even as to the sources from which the basic tenets might be derived. In *Thomson Newspapers v. Canada* (1990),[5] for example, a case that is discussed later,[6] five judges gave five different opinions as to the applicable basic tenet of the legal system!

The Supreme Court of Canada has not even been consistent in describing the principles of fundamental justice as the basic tenets of the legal system. In *Cunningham v. Canada* (1993),[7] the Supreme Court of Canada had to decide whether an amendment to the federal Parole Act was a breach of the principles of fundamental justice. The amendment empowered the National Parole Board to deny to a prisoner his release on mandatory supervision for the last one-third of his sentence. The new power was exercisable when there was reason to believe that the prisoner was likely to commit an offence causing death or serious harm if he was released for the unexpired portion of the sentence. Having determined that this change in the law was the deprivation of a liberty interest,[8] the Court had to decide whether it was a breach of the principles of fundamental justice. The Court, in an opinion written by McLachlin J., made no reference to the basic tenets of the legal system. Here is how McLachlin J. posed the question of fundamental justice.[9]

> The . . . question is whether, from a substantive point of view, the change in the law strikes the right balance between the accused's interests and the interests of society.

In other words, whenever a law deprives an individual of life, liberty or security of the person, the courts must determine whether the Parliament or Legislature struck "the right balance" between the competing values that the legislators had sought to reconcile. In this case, the Court agreed that "the balance is fairly struck",[10] and upheld the impugned law. Of course, if the legislators had got the balance wrong,

---

[4]Note the inclusion of absolute liability in Dickson C.J.'s taxonomy of criminal offences in *R. v. City of Sault Ste. Marie*, [1978] S.C.R. 1299.

[5]*Thomson Newspapers v. Canada*, [1990] 1 S.C.R. 425.

[6]Text accompanying § 47:15 note 46, below

[7]*Cunningham v. Canada*, [1993] 2 S.C.R. 143. The opinion of the Court was written by McLachlin J.

[8]This part of the decision is discussed at § 47:9.

[9]*Cunningham v. Canada*, [1993] 2 S.C.R. 143, 152. A little earlier on the same page she had required "a fair balance".

[10]*Cunningham v. Canada*, [1993] 2 S.C.R. 143, 153. The Court also held that the procedure established for making the determinations of the National Parole Board satisfied procedural fundamental justice.

then the law would have been struck down. For example, a total abolition of release on mandatory supervision would presumably strike the wrong balance, and would be unconstitutional. It is difficult to resist the conclusion that the Court was here interpreting substantive fundamental justice as justifying the Court in striking down a law whenever the Court disagreed with the policy implemented by the law. What else could "the right balance" or even "a fair balance" mean? At least the basic tenets of the legal system suggested, however vaguely, that there should be some basis in legal history or legal doctrine for the principles of fundamental justice.

The Supreme Court of Canada's broad approach to fundamental justice was evident again in *Rodriguez v. British Columbia* (1993).[11] In that case, the Court, on an application by a person who was terminally ill, had to decide whether the Criminal Code's prohibition of assisting a person to commit suicide offended the principles of fundamental justice. The common law had always prohibited assisting suicide, as well as counselling suicide, attempting suicide and even committing suicide. (The successful suicide could not be directly punished, of course, but the deceased's property was forfeited and indignities were visited on the body.) The modern Criminal Code, which no longer makes attempted suicide or suicide an offence, was already a substantial liberalization of the common law. For this reason, the effort to further liberalize the law could be characterized as directed to *changing* the basic tenets of the legal system rather than vindicating them. At bottom, this may well be the reason why Sopinka J., who wrote for the majority, held that the law did not offend the principles of fundamental justice. Certainly, he emphasized that the law was simply declaratory of the common law position. But he also asserted that the principles of fundamental justice must be " 'fundamental' in the sense that they would have general acceptance among reasonable people",[12] and he found no such consensus on the issue of euthanasia. Surely, a more orthodox view would be that the search for a consensus among reasonable people is a task that is more appropriate to Parliament than the courts; and, in any case, it is hard to see how it would illuminate any basic tenets of the legal system. The principal dissenting opinion in *Rodriguez* was written by McLachlin J. with the agreement of L'Heureux-Dubé J. and the "substantial" agreement of Cory J. In their view, a law would violate fundamental justice if

---

[11] *Rodriguez v. British Columbia*, [1993] 3 S.C.R. 519. On s. 7, Sopinka J. (with four others) wrote the majority opinion; McLachlin J. (with one other) and Cory J. wrote dissenting opinions. Lamer C.J. did not discuss s. 7; he also dissented, but he relied on s. 15. For commentary on the *Rodriguez* case, see L.E. Weinrib, "The Body and the Body Politic: Assisted Suicide Under the *Canadian Charter of Rights and Freedoms*" (1994), 39 McGill L.J. 618.

[12] *Rodriguez v. British Columbia*, [1993] 3 S.C.R. 519, 607. There is also a passage (at 590) in which he acknowledges that "the principles of fundamental justice leave a great deal of scope for personal judgment".

the law was "arbitrary"[13] or "unfair".[14] They held that the Criminal Code provision was arbitrary or unfair, because it precluded a disabled person (who would need assistance) from dying at a time of their own choosing while permitting an able-bodied person to do so. They would have struck down the prohibition on assisting suicide, but postponed the declaration of invalidity for one year to enable Parliament to enact safeguards against error or abuse. Exactly the same issue came back to the Court twenty two years later after developments in the s. 7 jurisprudence had established that "overbroad laws" were in violation of the principles of fundamental justice. In *Carter v. Canada* (2015),[15] the unanimous Court refused to follow *Rodriguez*, essentially accepted McLachlin J's dissenting view in that case, but now couched in the language of overbreadth. The prohibition of physician-assisted death was struck down as overbroad, and the declaration of invalidity was postponed for one year (later extended to 16 months) to enable Parliament to enact the necessary safeguards.

The Supreme Court of Canada has allowed s. 7 to drift even further away from the "basic tenets of the legal system" in its Charter review of extradition cases.[16] Sections 11 and 12 of the Charter are not applicable to charges or punishments under foreign law,[17] and have no direct bearing on extradition cases. The Court has maintained, however, that courts do have the right to overturn extradition decisions (which are an executive function of the federal Minister of Justice) if extradition would violate a fugitive's right to fundamental justice. In *Canada v. Schmidt* (1987),[18] the Court held that s. 7 would be breached by an extradition order where a fugitive faced a punishment under foreign law which would "shock the conscience" of, or be "simply unacceptable" to, reasonable Canadians. How do judges determine whether or not foreign laws are "shocking" or "unacceptable"? One might think that such determinations would be governed by the Supreme Court of Canada's jurisprudence under s. 12 of the Charter, which prohibits "cruel and unusual" punishments. But the Court has upheld extradition orders where fugitives faced drug charges in the United States carrying mandatory penal-

---

[13] *Rodriguez v. British Columbia*, [1993] 3 S.C.R. 519, 619. She added (at 619-620) that a limit will be arbitrary "if it bears no relation to, or is inconsistent with, the objective that lies behind the legislation".

[14] *Rodriguez v. British Columbia*, [1993] 3 S.C.R. 519, 621: "The principles of fundamental justice require that each person, considered individually, be treated fairly by the law".

[15] *Carter v. Canada*, [2015] 1 S.C.R. 331, 2015 SCC 5. The opinion of the Court was attributed to "the Court". McLachlin C.J. was the only member of the *Rodriguez* court who was still on the court that decided *Carter.* The discussion of the overbreadth part of *Carter* is in § 47:24, "Overbroad laws".

[16] See J. Harrington, "The Role for International Human Rights Obligations in Canadian Extradition Law" (2005) 43 Can. Yearbook of Int. Law 45.

[17] *Can. v. Schmidt*, [1987] 1 S.C.R. 500 (s. 11 does not apply); *Kindler v. Can.*, [1991] 2 S.C.R. 779 (s. 12 does not apply).

[18] *Canada v. Schmidt*, [1987] 1 S.C.R. 500, 522.

ties of 15 to 20 years imprisonment,[19] despite the fact that the Court has held that a seven-year minimum sentence for similar offences in Canada's Criminal Code is cruel and unusual.[20] This means that long mandatory minimum sentences for drug offences are cruel and unusual, but are not shocking or unacceptable![21] In two cases in 1991,[22] the Court held that extradition of a fugitive to face the death penalty (which is almost certainly cruel and unusual in Canada)[23] did not shock the Canadian conscience, and then a decade later the Court overruled itself and decided that it did.[24] The variety of these outcomes can be accounted for only by the enormous discretion that the Supreme Court of Canada has assumed for itself under the rubric of fundamental justice. Any change in the composition of the Court or even in the judges' perceptions of public opinion can lead to different results.

In *R. v. Malmo-Levine* (2003),[25] a challenge was brought to the criminalization of the possession of marihuana, which included the penalty of imprisonment, thereby impairing liberty and engaging s. 7. It was argued that a "harm principle" was a principle of fundamental justice, which was offended by criminalizing conduct which did not cause harm to others. The Supreme Court of Canada attempted to bring some order to the chaos of its previous attempts to define fundamental justice. The Court now denied that "striking the right balance" between individual and societal interests was a requirement of fundamental justice.[26]

---

[19]*United States v. Jamieson*, [1996] 1 S.C.R. 465; *United States v. Whitley*, [1996] 1 S.C.R. 467; *United States v. Ross*, [1996] 1 S.C.R. 469. In each of the three cases, the Court delivered no opinion other than to uphold the extradition order "substantially for the reasons" of the Court of Appeal. With respect, this seems a perfunctory disposition of such important issues. If the Supreme Court of Canada does not fully agree with the reasons of the court below it should provide its own reasons.

[20]*R. v. Smith*, [1987] 1 S.C.R. 1045.

[21]In *United States v. Ross* (1994), 119 D.L.R. (4th) 333, 370-371 (B.C.C.A.), Finch J.A. politely indicated that he found it difficult to apply the *Schmidt* test, and he sensibly suggested that the notion of the "reasonable man", however useful in determining standards of care, was not useful in assessing sentencing guidelines. In affirming the decision of the Court of Appeal, the Supreme Court of Canada did not address this opinion, rather they disposed of the case "substantially for the reasons" of Taylor J.A., with whom Finch J.A. had concurred.

[22]*Kindler v. Can.*, [1991] 2 S.C.R. 779; *Re Ng Extradition*, [1991] 2 S.C.R. 858.

[23]Chapter 53, Cruel and Unusual Punishment, under heading § 53:7, "Death penalty".

[24]*United States v. Burns*, [2001] 1 S.C.R. 283; folld. in *Suresh v. Can.*, [2002] 1 S.C.R. 3, para. 76 ("barring extraordinary circumstances" deportation to torture would "generally" offend s. 7). See also *Kazemi Estate v. Islamic Republic of Iran*, [2014] 3 S.C.R. 176, 2014 SCC 62 (State Immunity Act was not in breach of the principles of fundamental justice although it barred proceedings in Canada for damages for the torture and death of a Canadian citizen in Iran).

[25]*R. v. Malmo-Levine*, [2003] 3 S.C.R. 571. Gonthier and Binnie JJ. wrote the opinion of the majority. Arbour, LeBel and Deschamps JJ. each wrote opinions dissenting in part, although only Arbour dissented on the harm principle.

[26]*R. v. Malmo-Levine*, [2003] 3 S.C.R. 571, para. 96 per Gonthier and Binnie JJ. for majority. Accord, *Charkaoui v. Can.*, [2007] 1 S.C.R. 350, para. 21 per McLachlin C.J. for

Instead, the Court postulated[27] three requirements for a rule to qualify as a basic tenet of the legal system and therefore as a principle of fundamental justice. First, the rule must be a "legal principle". Secondly, there must be a "significant societal consensus that it is fundamental to the way in which the legal system ought fairly to operate". Thirdly, the rule must be capable of being "identified with sufficient precision to yield a manageable standard".[28] The Supreme Court of Canada, by a majority of eight to one, held that the harm principle did not satisfy any of the three requirements.[29] Therefore, it was open to Parliament to impose a sentence of imprisonment for crimes that did not involve harm to others, as it had done, for example, in the cases of cannibalism, bestiality, duelling and consensual incest.

In upholding the offence of possession of marihuana, *Malmo-Levine* addressed only the recreational use of marihuana. Could possession be prohibited for those who had a medical use for the drug? In *R. v. Parker* (2000),[30] the Ontario Court of Appeal answered no.[31] The possession of marihuana could not be prohibited (with imprisonment as a possible penalty) if the prohibition did not include an exemption for those with a medical need for the drug. An absolute prohibition that threatened health was a breach of the principles of fundamental justice. The Court suspended the declaration of invalidity for a year to provide time for a medical exemption to be enacted. Within the year, the federal government responded with the Marihuana Medical Access Regulations, which were enacted under a statutory power, and which created a process that enabled certain categories of ill people to obtain a permit to cultivate and possess the drug for therapeutic purposes. In *Hitzig v. Canada* (2003),[32] a challenge was brought to the new regulations, and the Ontario Court of Appeal held that they were unconstitutional, because in practice

---

Court.

[27]*R. v. Malmo-Levine*, [2003] 3 S.C.R. 571, para. 113. The definition basically follows that of Sopinka J. for the majority in *Rodriguez v. British Columbia*, [1993] 3 S.C.R. 519, 590-591, which included the requirement of societal consensus, which I criticize in my discussion of that case: text accompanying § 47:15 note 12, above. There is also a passage (at 590) in which he acknowledges that "the principles of fundamental justice leave a great deal of scope for personal judgment".

[28]This three-part test has been reaffirmed by the Court in later cases: see e.g. *R. v. D.B.*, [2008] 2 S.C.R. 3, para. 46; *Ewert v. Canada*, [2018] 2 S.C.R. 165, para. 76.

[29]*R. v. Malmo-Levine*, [2003] 3 S.C.R. 571, paras. 102-129 per Gonthier and Binnie JJ. for majority; 277 per LeBel J.; 285 per Deschamps J. Only Arbour J. (para. 244) accepted the harm principle and held that it was infringed by the offence of simple possession of marihuana. Arbour J. (para. 215) agreed with the majority that harm to others was not a requirement of a criminal law under s. 91 (27) of the Constitution Act, 1867: see ch. 18, Criminal Law, under heading § 18:2, "Definition of criminal law".

[30]*R. v. Parker* (2000), 49 O.R. (3d) 481 (C.A.).

[31]Contrast *Gonzales v. Raich* (2005), 545 U.S. 1 (upholding federal prohibition on growing and possession of marihuana for personal medicinal purposes; federal prohibition overrides California law authorizing use of marihuana for personal medicinal purposes).

[32]*Hitzig v. Canada* (2003), 231 D.L.R. (4th) 104 (Ont. C.A.), leave to appeal refused (2004) 112 C.R.R. (2d) 376(n) (S.C.C.).

they did not create a legal source of supply for many of those persons who were permitted to have the drug for medical purposes. To require those persons to purchase the drug from criminals was "inconsistent with the fundamental principle that the state must obey and promote compliance with the law".[33] The Court struck down those parts of the new regulations that provided the barriers to the creation of a lawful source of supply to medical users of marihuana.[34]

In *R v Smith* (2015),[35] the Supreme Court of Canada weighed in on the regulatory regime for the first time and struck down another element of the Medical Marihuana Access Regulations. The Regulations confined the exemption for those authorized to use medical marihuana to "dried marihuana", which was a cannabis product inhaled by smoking. The exemption did not extend to cannabis products which were taken orally in the form of cookies or capsules or applied topically to the skin in the form of oil or patches. The accused in the case worked for the Cannabis Buyers Club, an organization located on Vancouver Island, which sold a wide range of cannabis products to persons whose medical conditions might be relieved by the products. The accused, whose home was searched by the police, was found in possession of dried marihuana, cannabis cookies and jars of liquids derived from cannabis, in quantities that were assembled for sale by the Club. He was charged under the federal Controlled Drugs and Substances Act (to which the Regulations provided their medical exemption) with unlawful possession of cannabis products. At trial, he was acquitted on the ground that the Regulations were in breach of s. 7 in restricting the medical exemption to dried marihuana. The trial judge heard extensive expert and lay evidence and found that the derivatives of the cannabis plant conferred medical benefits, although the precise basis for the benefits was not yet established. He went on to find that for some conditions the oral and topical cannabis derivatives were more effective than the inhaling of marihuana smoke and they also lacked the harmful side effects of smoking. In the Supreme Court of Canada, these findings were accepted and the constitutional ruling was affirmed.[36] The users of medical marihuana were deprived of both their "liberty" and their "security of

[33]*Hitzig v. Canada* (2003), 231 D.L.R. (4th) 104 (Ont. C.A.), leave to appeal refused (2004) 112 C.R.R. (2d) 376(n) (S.C.C.), para. 118 per "the Court".

[34]After the decision, the federal government amended the regulations to bring them in line with the Court's decision (including provision for marihuana to be supplied by the government itself): Regulations Amending the Marihuana Medical Access Regulations, SOR/DORS/2003387. The Marijuana Medical Access Regulations were replaced by the Marihuana for Medical Purposes Regulations (in 2013), which were in turn replaced by the Access to Cannabis for Medical Purposes Regulations, SOR/2016-230 (in 2016). Cannabis was legalized in 2018 and is now regulated by a combination of federal and provincial legislation. The key federal statute is the Cannabis Act, S.C. 2018, c. 16. The 2016 regulation was repealed in 2018 as part of this change.

[35]*R v Smith*, [2015] 2 S.C.R. 602, 2015 SCC 34. The unanimous opinion was attributed to "the Court".

[36]The standing of the accused to make the constitutional argument was attacked by the Crown on the ground that the accused was not himself a user of medical marihuana. The Court held that the accused was entitled to raise the constitutional argument to

the person" by the restriction on their access to the cannabis products that were indicated for their medical conditions. The Court held that the objective of the prohibition of non-dried mariihuana was the protection of the health and safety of medical marihuana users, but that objective was "undermined" by effectively reducing the quality of their medical care: "The effects of the prohibition contradict its objective, rendering it arbitrary".[37] An arbitrary law was in breach of the principles of fundamental justice contrary to s. 7, and the prohibition on non-dried marihuana was accordingly invalid.[38]

In *Canadian Foundation for Children, Youth and the Law v. Canada* (2004),[39] a challenge was brought to the Criminal Code provision that provides a defence to an assault charge for teachers or parents who have used reasonable force by way of correction against the children in their charge. This provision exposed children to force that would be criminal if committed against an adult, and therefore impaired the security of the person of the child, thereby engaging s. 7. It was argued that the "best interests of the child" was a principle of fundamental justice, and that the exposure of children to corrective force was not in their best interests. The Supreme Court of Canada accepted the three requirements of fundamental justice that it had stipulated only a month earlier in *Malmo-Levine*. The Court held that the best interests of the child was a legal principle (first requirement), but it was not one that was generally regarded as fundamental to the justice of the legal system (second requirement), and it was not one that yielded a sufficiently precise standard (third requirement). Therefore, the best interests of the child was not a principle of fundamental justice, and, even if the corrective-force defence was not in the best interests of the child, it did not infringe s. 7.

In *R. v. D.B.* (2008),[40] the Supreme Court held unanimously that the presumption of diminished moral responsibility of young offenders was a principle of fundamental justice. It satisfied the three *Malmo-Levine* criteria as (1) a longstanding legal principle animating the criminal justice system, (2) generally agreed to be fundamental to the operation of a fair criminal justice system, and (3) sufficiently precise to yield a manageable standard. However, the Court split five-four on the question

---

avoid being convicted under an unconstitutional law: *R v Smith*, [2015] 2 S.C.R. 602, 2015 SCC 34, paras. 11-13.

[37]*R v Smith*, [2015] 2 S.C.R. 602, 2015 SCC 34, para. 25.

[38]The actual order of the Court was "a declaration that ss. 4 and 5 of the Controlled Drugs and Substances Act [the provisions under which the accused was charged] are of no force and effect to the extent that they prohibit a person with a medical authorization from possessing cannabis derivatives for medical purposes.": *R v Smith*, [2015] 2 S.C.R. 602, 2015 SCC 34, para. 33.

[39]*Canadian Foundation for Children, Youth and the Law v. Canada*, [2004] 1 S.C.R. 76. McLachlin C.J. wrote the opinion of the majority. Binnie, Deschamps and Arbour wrote dissenting opinions, but they did not address the issue in the text, namely, the alleged "best interests of the child" principle. Arbour J. held that s. 7 was infringed by vagueness.

[40]*R. v. D.B.*, [2008] 2 S.C.R. 3. Abella J. wrote for the five-judge majority. Rothstein J. wrote for the four-judge dissenting minority.

whether the challenged provision of the federal Youth Criminal Justice Act, enacted in 2002, breached the principle. The Act provided for lower sentences for young offenders, but the provision in question classified certain violent offences, including manslaughter, as "presumptive offences" for which the youth justice court was obliged to impose an adult sentence unless the young accused applied to the court and demonstrated, according to criteria set out in the Act (which included age, maturity, character, background and previous record), that an adult sentence should not be imposed. This provision recognized the diminished moral responsibility of young offenders in the sense that the offender was treated differently from an adult: he was subject to youth-justice-court procedure and was tried in a youth justice court; he had the opportunity to persuade the court not to sentence him as a adult; and, even if sentenced as an adult, he was allowed more generous eligibility for parole. For the dissenting minority, there was no breach of fundamental justice. For the majority, however, it was a breach of fundamental justice to reverse the normal criminal onus and cast on the accused the burden of establishing that an adult sentence should not be imposed. It could not be justified under s. 1 since the objectives of the legislation could as well be served by placing the burden of persuasion on the Crown. The reverse onus was therefore unconstitutional.

In *Canada v. Federation of Law Societies* (2015),[41] it was argued that the independence of the bar was a principle of fundamental justice. The Supreme Court did not reject the argument, but, by a majority, decided that a narrower subset of the independence of the bar was relevant to the case, namely, the lawyers' duty of commitment to the client's cause. The Court held that the duty of commitment to the client's cause was a principle of fundamental justice. It satisfied the three *Malmo-Levine* criteria as (1) a legal principle, (2) supported by a widespread consensus as to its fundamental importance, and (3) sufficiently precise to provide a workable standard.[42] The constitutional challenge was to provisions of the federal Proceeds of Crime (Money Laundering) and Terrorist Financing Act, which imposed duties on financial intermediaries—those who handle funds on behalf of others, including lawyers—to collect and keep information about those on whose behalf they pay or receive money, and to keep specified records of the transactions. The duty of commitment to the client's cause was breached in this case because the Act required the lawyer to create records that were not necessary for the ethical and effective representation of the client and might even be contrary to the lawyer's correctly formed opinion of the client's legitimate interests. The

---

[41]*Canada v. Federation of Law Societies*, [2015] 1 S.C.R. 401, 2015 SCC 7. Cromwell J. wrote the opinion of the majority. McLachlin C.J. and Moldaver J. wrote a joint concurring opinion.

[42]*Canada v. Federation of Law Societies*, [2015] 1 S.C.R. 401, 2015 SCC 7, paras. 87-103. McLachlin C.J. and Moldaver J., who concurred in the result, disagreed on the third criterion. In their opinion, the lawyer's commitment to the client's cause did not provide a workable constitutional standard. However, solicitor-client privilege was the applicable principle of fundamental justice, and it had been infringed: *Canada v. Federation of Law Societies*, [2015] 1 S.C.R. 401, 2015 SCC 7, paras. 119-120.

records then had to be maintained by the lawyer so that they were available for search by an administrative agency, and the power to search did not adequately protect solicitor-client privilege.[43] When the information gathering and retaining requirements were combined with the search provisions, there was a breach of fundamental justice, which was a breach of s. 7 of the Charter.[44]

The point has already been made that the scope of fundamental justice could be restricted by the placement of s. 7 in the legal rights portion of the Charter. The Court's residuary theory of s. 7, under which ss. 8 to 14 are simply illustrations of s. 7, emphasizes that s. 7 is directed to the protection of only those values that are reflected in the legal rights.[45] That offers some assurance that social and economic regulation, even if disliked by a majority of the Court, is not vulnerable to attack under s. 7. It must be remembered as well that a breach of fundamental justice is of no constitutional import if it does not cause a deprivation of life, liberty or security of the person. Outside the general sphere of criminal justice, fewer laws touch life, liberty or security of the person.

The Supreme Court of Canada's residuary theory of s. 7, under which ss. 8 to 14 are merely illustrations of s. 7, has a limiting effect on the scope of fundamental justice, as explained in the previous paragraph. But, on balance, the residuary theory introduces additional uncertainty to the interpretation of s. 7 and especially of ss. 8 to 14. The effect of the residuary theory is that the precise language of ss. 8 to 14 becomes relatively unimportant. If it is found that none of those provisions apply to a set of facts, that is not the end of the inquiry; on the contrary, the inquiry moves to s. 7, where it must be determined whether the facts of the case, although outside ss. 8 to 14, are within "the principles of fundamental justice".

In *Thomson Newspapers v. Canada* (1990),[46] for example, a corporation and its officers objected to a demand made under the Combines Investigation Act for oral examination of the officers. Although the purpose of the demand was to inquire into the possible commission of an offence by the corporation, neither of the two Charter guarantees against self-incrimination was applicable. Section 11(c), which provides that a person charged with an offence is not a compellable witness against himself, was not applicable, because no one had been charged with an offence. Section 13, which provides that self-incriminatory evidence given in one proceeding cannot be used against the witness in another proceeding, was not applicable, because this inquiry was the first proceeding. If ss. 11(c) and 13 expressed the full measure of the Charter's right against self-incrimination, then there would be no grounds upon

---

[43]The search provisions were held to be unconstitutional for breach of s. 8 of the Charter: see discussion in ch. 48, under heading § 48:31, "Search of law office".

[44]Section 7 applied because the lawyer's "liberty" interest was engaged, imprisonment being a potential penalty for infringement of the Act's gathering and retaining requirements.

[45]Text accompanying § 47:14 notes 15-18, above.

[46]*Thomson Newspapers v. Canada*, [1990] 1 S.C.R. 425.

which the demand for testimony could be resisted. But the five-judge bench of the Supreme Court of Canada, obedient to the logic of the *B.C. Motor Vehicle Reference*, was unanimous that the "principles of fundamental justice" in s. 7 could still contain some "residual" elements of the right against self-incrimination. In other words, the scope of the right was to be discerned not from the relatively precise language of ss. 11(c) and 13, which explicitly deal with the right, but from the vague language of s. 7, which refers only to the principles of fundamental justice.

The Supreme Court of Canada has often applied the residuary theory of s. 7 to grant a right in circumstances that do not fit within a more specific Charter guarantee.[47] A good example is afforded by the guarantee of trial within a reasonable time in s. 11(b). That right does not apply to pre-charge delay—delay that occurs before the accused is charged; nor does it apply to appellate delay—delay that occurs after the accused has been tried.[48] But the Court has held that excessive delay at either the pre-charge stage or the appellate stage of criminal proceedings may afford the accused a remedy under s. 7.[49]

It is obvious that the residuary theory of s. 7 introduces great uncertainty into all the legal rights, especially those that are couched in very specific language. With respect to each right, there is a possibility of a residue in s. 7, defined by the phrase "the principles of fundamental justice", which has been defined no more precisely than "the basic tenets of the legal system".[50] In effect, the residuary theory of s. 7 authorizes the judges to redraft the provisions of ss. 8 to 14 of the Charter. In *Thomson Newspapers*, the five judges came up with no less than five different theories as to what additional content s. 7 added to ss. 11(c) and 13: a right to remain silent (Sopinka J.), a right not to give an incriminating answer (Lamer J.), a right to have all evidence derived from the compelled testimony excluded from subsequent proceedings (Wilson J.), a right to have only that derivative evidence that could not have been discovered apart from the compelled testimony excluded from subsequent

[47]Accord, *R. v. Lyons*, [1987] 2 S.C.R. 309, 354 (no right to trial by jury under s. 11(f), but necessary to consider whether s. 7 conferred the right "for s. 11 does not limit s. 7 but simply serves to illustrate and, perhaps, amplify its potential applications"); *Dehghani v. Can.*, [1993] 1 S.C.R. 1053, 1076 ("there may be residual protection of the right to counsel under s. 7 in situations which do not fall within the parameters of "arrest or detention" in s. 10(b)"); *B.C. Securities Commn. v. Branch*, [1995] 2 S.C.R. 3 (s. 7 guarantees right to silence that goes beyond ss.1 1(c) and 13); *R. v. Brown*, [2002] 2 S.C.R. 185 (s. 7 confers right against self-incrimination where s. 13 does not apply). Contra, *R. v. Généreux*, [1992] 1 S.C.R. 259, 310 (rejecting s. 7 argument on basis that "s. 7 does not offer greater protection than the highly specific guarantee under s. 11(d)", but noting that in some unspecified circumstances "s. 7 provides a more compendious protection than these sections [ss. 8 to 14] combined").

[48]Chapter 52, Trial Within Reasonable Time, under headings § 52:6, "Pre-charge delay", § 52:7, "Appellate delay".

[49]*R. v. L.(W.K.)*, [1991] 1 S.C.R. 1091, 1100 (pre-charge delay); *R. v. Potvin*, [1993] 2 S.C.R. 880, 899, 915 (appellate delay).

[50]*Re B.C. Motor Vehicle Act*, [1985] 2 S.C.R. 486, 503; and see text accompanying § 47:14 note 7, above.

proceedings (La Forest J.), no right additional to ss. 11(c) and 13(L'Heureux-Dubé J.). The range of opinion is remarkable. Yet, each of the judges was confident that he or she was articulating a principle or tenet of the justice system that was so basic that, through s. 7, it should prevail over the inconsistent enactment of the Parliament of Canada.[51]

XI. ABSOLUTE AND STRICT LIABILITY

§ 47:16 Categories of offences

In the pre-Charter case of *R. v. City of Sault Ste. Marie* (1978),[1] Dickson J. for the Supreme Court of Canada divided offences into three categories:

1. Offences of "absolute liability", in which the offence consists simply of doing the prohibited act. There is no requirement of fault, either mens rea or negligence. The defendant could be convicted even if he or she had no intention of breaking the law and also exercised reasonable care to avoid doing so.
2. Offences of "strict liability", in which the offence again consists simply of doing the prohibited act; however, it is a defence if the defendant proves to the civil standard of the balance of probabilities that he or she exercised reasonable care (due diligence) to avoid committing the offence. In effect, there is a fault requirement of negligence, because the accused is liable only if he or she cannot prove the exercise of reasonable care.
3. Offences of "mens rea", in which the offence consists not only of doing the prohibited act, but of doing so with the guilty intent (mens rea) of intending to break the law (or being reckless as to whether or not the law would be broken).

§ 47:17 Absolute liability offences

The first category, *absolute liability*, came under judicial review in the *B.C. Motor Vehicle Reference* (1985).[1] That case concerned a section of the B.C. Motor Vehicle Act that made it an offence to operate a motor vehicle while one was prohibited or suspended from driving. A subsection explicitly stated that the offence was to be interpreted as "an absolute liability offence, for which guilt is established by proof of driving, whether or not the defendant knew of the prohibition or

---

[51]The Court, in subsequent cases, has continued the lively debate as to the existence of a residual right to silence in s. 7: § 47:31, "Right to silence".

[Section 47:16]

[1]*R. v. City of Sault Ste. Marie*, [1978] S.C.R. 1299, 1325-1326. This classification was re-affirmed in *Levis v. Tétreault*, [2006] 1 S.C.R. 420, paras. 15-19.

[Section 47:17]

[1]*Re B.C. Motor Vehicle Act*, [1985] 2 S.C.R. 486. The seven-judge bench was unanimous on this issue, and on the result, but three opinions were written: by Lamer J. with the agreement of four others; by McIntyre J.; and by Wilson J.

suspension".[2] The Supreme Court of Canada held that absolute liability was a denial of "the principles of fundamental justice". Since the offence carried a short term of imprisonment, a conviction would mean a deprivation of "liberty". The offence was therefore declared to be in violation of s. 7 and of no force or effect.

Another absolute liability case was *R. v. Hess* (1990),[3] which was a challenge to the statutory rape provision of the Criminal Code. This provision made it an offence for a male person to have intercourse with a female person under the age of 14, "whether or not he [the accused] believes that she is fourteen years of age or more". This offence was one of absolute liability, since it was no defence for the accused to show that he reasonably believed his act to be innocent: the accused's conduct could be lacking in mens rea and non-negligent. The offence carried a penalty of imprisonment. The Supreme Court of Canada followed the *B.C. Motor Vehicle Reference* to hold unanimously that an absolute liability offence that carried the penalty of imprisonment was a breach of fundamental justice in violation of s. 7. The result was not to strike down the offence entirely, since the deletion of the words "whether or not he believes that she is fourteen years of age or more" was sufficient to remove the element of absolute liability.[4]

R. v. Pontes (1995)[5] was the sequel to the *B.C. Motor Vehicle Reference.* The Supreme Court of Canada had to classify an amended version of the offence in the B.C. Motor Vehicle Act of driving while prohibited from driving. The Act provided that any driver who was convicted of a driving-related Criminal Code offence was "automatically and without notice" prohibited from driving for 12 months. Cory J. for the majority of the Court held that the quoted phrase meant that a duly diligent driver could be unaware of the prohibition, and could innocently commit the offence of driving while prohibited. The principle that ignorance of the law is no excuse would preclude the accused from raising his ignorance of the statutory suspension as a defence. Cory J. concluded that the statute effectively barred the defence of due diligence, which meant that the offence was one of absolute liability. The Motor Vehicle Act purported to impose a term of imprisonment for the offence, which would be an unconstitutional deprivation of liberty under s. 7. However, the amended Act now contained a saving provision to the effect that, notwithstanding the imprisonment penalty in the Act, "no person is liable to imprison-

---

[2]Motor Vehicle Act, R.S.B.C. 1979, c. 288 s. 94(2). After the decision, this subsection was repealed: S.B.C. 1986, c. 19. However the Court later held that the amended offence was still an absolute liability offence: *R. v. Pontes*, [1995] 3 S.C.R. 44.

[3]*R. v. Hess*, [1990] 2 S.C.R. 906. The Court was unanimous that s. 7 was violated, and held by a majority that s. 1 did not save the provision.

[4]In *R. v. Penno*, [1990] 2 S.C.R. 865, it was held that the offence of driving while impaired did not offend fundamental justice, although the offence excluded the defence of intoxication. The mental element of voluntarily becoming intoxicated was a sufficiently guilty mind to satisfy the *B.C. Motor Vehicle Reference.*

[5]*R. v. Pontes*, [1995] 3 S.C.R. 44. Cory J. wrote for the majority. Gonthier J., who wrote for the dissenting minority, would have held that the offence was one of strict liability on the ground that in his view there was some room for a due diligence defence.

ment for an absolute liability offence". Cory J. applied this provision to "read out" the penalty of imprisonment. The result was that there was no penalty of imprisonment for the offence of driving while prohibited. Therefore, there was no breach of liberty under s. 7 and no need for the law to comply with the principles of fundamental justice. The offence, although one of absolute liability, was accordingly upheld.

Pontes makes clear that s. 7 has no application to an offence that carries only the penalty of a fine, even a very large fine, because in that case "liberty" is not affected. Therefore, so long as no sentence of imprisonment is provided for, it is still possible for Parliament or the Legislatures to create offences of absolute liability.[6] For regulatory offences that are punishable only by fine, it is an issue of statutory interpretation, not constitutional law, as to whether they are offences of absolute liability (without a defence of due diligence) or of strict liability (with a defence of due diligence). However, because of the injustice of punishing a person who has acted without fault, and has taken reasonable precautions to comply with the law, the presumption is in favour of strict liability. LeBel J. in *Lévis v. Tétreault* (2006)[7] said: "Absolute liability offences still exist, but they have become an exception requiring clear proof of legislative intent." In that case, faced with statutory language that appeared to impose absolute liability, the Court held that offences under Quebec's Highway Safety Code of driving an unregistered car and driving without a licence were offences of strict liability. That ruling allowed a defence of due diligence to the two accused, whose excuses were that they had not received notices of renewal of the car registration (in one case) and the driver's licence (in the other). However, the accused were still convicted, because the Court held that the mere failure to receive a renewal notice, without any positive steps on their part to attempt to accomplish the renewal, did not amount to due diligence.

As the preceding text has made clear, an offence of absolute liability that carries the penalty of imprisonment is an infringement of s. 7 of the Charter. However, it does not follow that the offence must always be struck down. As the cases described in this section show, there are other remedial options that are open to the Court.[8] One option is to interpret the statute creating the offence as implicitly allowing a defence of due diligence, in which case the offence becomes one of strict liability. That is what saved the offence in *Lévis v. Tétreault*.[9] (As will be explained in the next section of the chapter, if the offence is a "regulatory" one, strict liability complies with s. 7 of the Charter.) Another option is to use the power of severance (or reading in) to convert the offence into one of

---

[6]Accord, *R. v. Transport Robert* (2003), 68 O.R. (3d) 51 (C.A.) (upholding absolute liability offence for the owner and operator of a truck if a wheel came off on a highway).

[7]*Lévis v. Tétreault*, [2006] 1 S.C.R. 420, para. 17. LeBel J. wrote for the Court.

[8]Remedies for unconstitutional statutes are discussed in ch. 40, Enforcement of Rights.

[9]*Lévis v. Tétreault*, [2006] 1 S.C.R. 420.

mens rea. That is what saved the offence in *R. v. Hess.*[10] Another option is to use the power of severance to eliminate the penalty of imprisonment, in which case the offence (if it is a regulatory one) can survive as one of absolute liability. That is what saved the offence in *R. v. Pontes.*[11]

§ 47:18 Strict liability offences

The second category in Dickson C.J.'s *Sault Ste. Marie* taxonomy is *strict liability*. This came under judicial review in *R. v. Wholesale Travel Group* (1991).[1] In that case, the accused corporation[2] was charged with the offence of false or misleading advertising under the Competition Act. The Crown alleged that the company had advertised travel packages at "wholesale" prices, while in fact charging "retail" prices. The Act made clear that there was no requirement of mens rea: the only defence was one of due diligence (reasonable care), and the burden of proving due diligence rested with the accused. The offence therefore followed the conventional pattern of strict liability. The penalty for the offence was a fine or imprisonment for up to five years or both. The accused relied on the *B.C. Motor Vehicle Reference* to argue that it was a violation of fundamental justice to place an individual in jeopardy of imprisonment for any lesser fault than mens rea. The Crown agreed that the *B.C. Motor Vehicle Reference* required an element of fault for an offence carrying the penalty of imprisonment, but the Crown argued that an absence of due diligence (negligence) satisfied the requirement.

The Supreme Court of Canada in *Wholesale Travel* was unanimous in its view that the offence of false or misleading advertising in the Competition Act was not a "true crime", but was merely a "regulatory offence" or "public welfare offence". Cory J. explained that the characteristic of a "true crime" was that "inherently wrongful conduct" was punished.[3] A regulatory offence, on the other hand, was designed to establish standards of conduct for activity that could be harmful to others; it did not imply moral blameworthiness; and it attracted less social stigma. Therefore, the Court reasoned, it was not a constitutional objection to the offence that it was premised on negligence (lack of due diligence) rather than mens rea. The Court treated it as obvious that the offence of misleading advertising fell into the "regulatory" category, despite the fact that it carried a maximum penalty of five years' imprisonment—

---

[10] *R. v. Hess*, [1990] 2 S.C.R. 906.

[11] *R. v. Pontes*, [1995] 3 S.C.R. 44.

[Section 47:18]

[1] *R. v. Wholesale Travel Group*, [1991] 3 S.C.R. 154.

[2] The corporation was able to invoke s. 7, despite the fact that s. 7 does not apply to corporations, because the corporation was a defendant to a criminal prosecution, and the law was applicable to individuals as well as to corporations: § 47:4, "Corporations".

[3] *R. v. Pontes*, [1991] 3 S.C.R. 154, 219.

quite a stretch for doing something that did not imply moral blameworthiness and attracted little social stigma![4]

The Competition Act contained a "reverse onus" clause which required the defendant to a charge of false or misleading advertising to prove (to the civil standard of the balance of probabilities) that he or she had exercised due diligence to avoid making the false or misleading claims. Even if the Act had been silent as to the defence and the burden of proof, the effect of the *Sault Ste. Marie* decision[5] was that a regulatory offence was to be regarded as one of strict liability, and two characteristics of strict liability were (1) that there was a defence of due diligence, and (2) that the burden of proving due diligence rested on the defendant. Therefore, in order to uphold the offence in *Wholesale Travel* (or any other strict liability offence involving imprisonment), the Court also had to decide whether the reversal of the burden of proof was defeated by the Charter of Rights. This issue was governed, not by s. 7 but by s. 11(d), the presumption of innocence clause, and the Court's decision will be described in this book's later discussion of the presumption of innocence.[6] However, for present purposes, we may note that the Court by a five to four majority upheld the reversal of the burden of proof.

The effect of the *Wholesale Travel* case is to settle the validity of strict liability.[7] In the case of a "regulatory offence" or a "public welfare offence", including those that carry the penalty of imprisonment, fundamental justice does not require that mens rea be an element of the offence. Fundamental justice is satisfied if there is a defence of reasonable care (due diligence), and the burden of proving reasonable care (to the civil standard) may be cast on the defendant.[8] In the case of "true crimes", however, fundamental justice requires that mens rea be an element of the offence, and the burden of proving mens rea (to the criminal standard) would have to be on the Crown.

The offence of dangerous driving causing death is in the Criminal

[4]As the discussion of the cases in the next section of this chapter (§ 47:19, "Murder") will show, the Supreme Court of Canada likes to premise radical constitutional results on findings of stigma. There is never any evidence on the point. In my view, the stigma attaching to a particular offence is unknown and perhaps unknowable, since it would depend upon a host of circumstances related to both the offence and the offender, and would vary according to the eye of the beholder. The concept is too uncertain to attract any constitutional consequence of any kind. In my view, the Court ought to abandon this idea completely and rely on more objective considerations. In this context, it would be preferable to use the presence of the penalty of imprisonment as the dividing line between those offences that require mens rea and those that require only an absence of due diligence.

[5]*R. v. City of Sault Ste. Marie*, [1978] S.C.R. 1299. The holding was subsequently reaffirmed in *Lévis v. Tétreault*, [2006] 1 S.C.R. 420.

[6]Chapter 51, Rights on Being Charged, under heading § 51:14, "Reverse onus clauses", above.

[7]*R. v. Martin*, [1992] S.C.R. 838 (strict liability upheld, following *Wholesale Travel)*; *R. v. Ellis-Don*, [1992] 1 S.C.R. 840 (same decision).

[8]In *Lévis v. Tétreault*, [2006] 1 S.C.R. 420, para. 22, a defence of officially induced error, of which the burden was also on the accused (para. 34), was recognized (in addition to due diligence).

Code, and it carries a maximum penalty of 14 years imprisonment. Surely, this must be a "true crime" for which mens rea would be constitutionally required. The Supreme Court of Canada held otherwise in *R. v. Hundal* (1993).[9] In that case, the accused had driven his truck through a red light and collided with another car in the intersection, killing the driver. The accused testified that he believed that he did not have time to stop safely when the light turned amber, so that he believed that his driving through the intersection was the prudent course of action. This evidence raised the question whether the accused had to be subjectively aware that his driving was dangerous in order to be convicted of dangerous driving. The Court cited *Wholesale Travel* for the proposition that "in the appropriate context, negligence can be an acceptable basis of liability which meets the fault requirement of s. 7 of the Charter".[10] That proposition governed this case: all that the Crown needed to establish was an objective departure by the accused from the appropriate standard of care. The fact that the accused believed that he was driving safely was irrelevant.

The opinion of the majority in *Hundal* was written by Cory J., who relied on *Wholesale Travel* for the holding that objective negligence was a sufficient fault requirement for dangerous driving causing death. In a puzzling attack of reticence, Cory J. did not actually describe the offence of dangerous driving causing death as a "regulatory offence", although that classification had formed the ratio decidendi of his opinion in *Wholesale Travel.* However, he did claim that "driving can only be undertaken by those who have a licence", and he described driving as a "regulated activity".[11] On the face of it, these statements seem irrelevant since unlicensed drivers can be (and often are) found guilty of dangerous driving. Presumably, Cory J. was using the licensing requirement to force driving offences into the "regulatory" category. McLachlin and La Forest JJ. each agreed with Cory J. but added brief concurring reasons. McLachlin J. added nothing on the appropriate classification of the offence. La Forest J. described dangerous driving causing death as a "quasi-regulatory offence",[12] but he did not expand on the characteristics of this new class of offence.

Later cases have modified *Hundal* somewhat by insisting that an element of fault (mens rea) is constitutionally required for the offence of dangerous driving causing death on top of the objective facts of dangerous driving and death (actus reus). The requirement of fault would of course be satisfied by proof of subjective mens rea, namely, that the accused was deliberately or recklessly driving dangerously, but that degree of fault is not necessary. In deference to the regulatory character of the offence, a "modified objective mens rea" is enough. That will be satisfied

[9] *R. v. Hundal*, [1993] 1 S.C.R. 867. Cory J. wrote the majority opinion; McLachlin J. (with Lamer C.J.) and La Forest J. agreed with Cory J. but added short concurring opinions.

[10] *R. v. Hundal*, [1993] 1 S.C.R. 867, 882.

[11] *R. v. Hundal*, [1993] 1 S.C.R. 867, 884.

[12] *R. v. Hundal*, [1993] 1 S.C.R. 867, 876.

by proof of a "marked departure" (as opposed to a "mere departure"), from the standard of care of a prudent driver: mens rea can properly be inferred from the marked departure. However—and this seems inconsistent with *Hundal*—the accused's actual state of mind is not irrelevant. If there is an explanation by the driver (or anything else in the evidence) that raises a reasonable doubt as to whether a reasonable person in the position of the accused would have behaved in much the same way, then that may rebut the finding of a marked departure and the inference of mens rea. The new requirement of fault has led to some remarkable acquittals. In *R. v. Beatty* (2008),[13] the accused drove his pick-up truck across the centre line of a busy highway, killing the three occupants of the first oncoming vehicle. The accused said that he was not sure what happened and that he must have fallen asleep at the wheel. The Supreme Court of Canada held unanimously that he was entitled to be acquitted. Charron J. for the majority held that the accused's driving (the actus reus) was dangerous, but that there was no mens rea because his driving was not a marked departure from that of a prudent driver. A "momentary lapse of attention" was not enough to ground criminal liability. In *R. v. Roy* (2012),[14] the accused drove his motor home out from a stop sign and into the path of an incoming tractor-trailer, killing a passenger in the motor home. The Supreme Court again held unanimously that he was entitled to be acquitted. The Court again agreed that the driving was dangerous, but again held that there was no mens rea. Although the evidence was unclear as to whether the accused had stopped at the stop sign before pulling out onto the highway, and there was no evidence as to the accused's actual state of mind at the time, Cromwell J. for the Court held that there was no marked departure from the standard of care of a prudent driver, just "a single and momentary error in judgment", admittedly with tragic consequences.

In *R. v. Nova Scotia Pharmaceutical Society* (1992),[15] the Supreme Court of Canada rejected a challenge to the Competition Act offence of conspiring to lessen competition unduly. The Act expressly eliminated the element of mens rea by providing that it was not necessary for the prosecution to prove that the accused intended that his actions would have the effect of lessening competition unduly. Did this provision violate the principles of fundamental justice guaranteed by s. 7 of the Charter?[16] Gonthier J., writing for a unanimous Court, answered no. He held that the challenged provision contained both a subjective mental element, namely, the requirement that the accused intended to enter into an agreement, and an objective mental element, namely, the requirement

---

[13] *R. v. Beatty*, [2008] 1 S.C.R. 49. Charron J. wrote the majority opinion. McLachlin C.J. and Fish J. each wrote concurring opinions, each defining the requirement of mens rea somewhat differently from Charron J. and from each other.

[14] *R. v. Roy*, [2012] 2 S.C.R. 60. Cromwell J. wrote the opinion of the Court.

[15] *R. v. Nova Scotia Pharmaceutical Society*, [1992] 2 S.C.R. 606. Gonthier J. wrote the opinion of the Court.

[16] The offence was also unsuccessfully challenged on the basis of the vagueness inherent in the word "unduly". This part of the decision is discussed at § 47:27.

that the accused *ought to have known* that the agreement would lessen competition. This was enough, he held, to satisfy the "minimum fault requirement" of s. 7.[17]

Gonthier J.'s word "minimum" was certainly the word to describe the fault requirement that he held was constitutionally sufficient. He pointed out[18] that proof by the Crown that the accused had entered into an agreement that had the effect of lessening competition unduly would "in most cases" be all that was needed, because the "logical inference" from proof that the accused had entered into such an agreement would be that the accused ought to have known that the agreement would have the effect of lessening competition unduly. The "objective" mental element—consisting of what the accused ought to have known—is close to no mental element at all. A businessperson who entered into an agreement that he or she believed would *enhance* competition would have committed the offence if a criminal court concluded that the actual effect of the agreement was to lessen competition unduly.

The opinion in *Nova Scotia Pharmaceutical*, like the opinions in *Hundal*, did not describe the offence under challenge as a "regulatory offence". On the contrary, Gonthier J. said that the offence of conspiring to lessen competition unduly was "at the core of the *criminal* part of the [Competition] Act".[19] If by that he meant that the offence was a "true crime", then the decision in *Nova Scotia Pharmaceutical* cannot stand with *Wholesale Travel*, which was as clear as it could be that true crimes required subjective mens rea. Gonthier J. purported to rely on *Wholesale Travel*, which he described as establishing a minimum fault requirement for "every criminal or regulatory offence".[20] If by that he meant that the minimum fault requirement was the same for a "criminal" offence as it was for a "regulatory" offence, then it is not an accurate description of the holding in *Wholesale Travel*, which carefully distinguished the fault requirement for the two different categories of offences. Gonthier J. did not mention the stigma or the maximum penalty (it was five years imprisonment) that was attached to the offence of conspiring to lessen competition unduly and did not offer any other reasons why he regarded a departure by the defendant from an objective standard as a sufficient fault requirement to satisfy s. 7.

In *R. v. Finlay* (1993),[21] the Supreme Court of Canada reviewed the Criminal Code offence of storing a firearm "in a careless manner". The maximum penalty was two years' imprisonment for a first offence and five years' imprisonment for a second or subsequent offence. Once again, it was necessary to decide whether negligence was a sufficient fault

---

[17] *R. v. Nova Scotia Pharmaceutical Society*, [1992] 2 S.C.R. 606, 659.

[18] *R. v. Nova Scotia Pharmaceutical Society*, [1992] 2 S.C.R. 606, 660.

[19] *R. v. Nova Scotia Pharmaceutical Society*, [1992] 2 S.C.R. 606, 649 (emphasis added).

[20] *R. v. Nova Scotia Pharmaceutical Society*, [1992] 2 S.C.R. 606, 659.

[21] *R. v. Finlay*, [1993] 3 S.C.R. 103. The opinion of Lamer C.J. was concurred in by all members of the Court, except for one point of disagreement not germane to the present account.

requirement for a Criminal Code offence. Lamer C.J. for the Court repeated the dictum in *Hundal*[22] that "in the appropriate context, negligence can be an acceptable basis of liability which meets the fault requirement of s. 7 of the Charter".[23] In a section of the opinion headed "Stigma Analysis" (an oxymoron in my view), Lamer C.J. held that the offence "does not give rise to sufficient stigma to require a subjective mens rea under s. 7 of the Charter".[24] He did not describe the offence as a regulatory offence, although he did make reference to *Wholesale Travel* as supporting the result. The fault requirement of negligence was upheld.

In *R. v. Naglik* (1993),[25] the provision under challenge was the Criminal Code offence of failing to provide necessaries of life to a child under the age of 16 years. The accused's baby had in fact been brutally beaten either by the accused or her common law spouse over a period of several weeks, and they had given the baby no medical treatment. The Supreme Court of Canada, in an opinion written by Lamer C.J., held that the offence did not require subjective mens rea: whether a parent had failed to provide necessaries of life to a child was to be measured by an "objective, societal standard", and not by the subjective belief of the accused. In other words, a negligent failure to provide necessaries of life was as culpable as an intentional failure to do so. Did this objective standard satisfy s. 7 of the Charter? The Court held that it did, relying again on the *Hundal* proposition[26] that "in the appropriate context" negligence will satisfy s. 7.[27] Why was this the appropriate context? Lamer C.J. did not claim that the offence was a "regulatory" one; and it seems obvious that it was a "true crime"—and a very serious one at that.[28] As for stigma, one would have guessed (it can only be a guess, of course) that the stigma associated with failing to obtain medical treatment for a battered baby was far greater than theft and comparable to attempted murder and murder, which indeed on these facts it closely resembled. But this was not Lamer C.J.'s approach. He acknowledged that the conviction would "stigmatize" the accused, but he held that "this stigmatization is neither unfairly disproportionate nor unrelated to the culpable conduct of which the accused was found guilty".[29] He also pointed out that "the sentencing judge can tailor the sentence to the circumstances of the particular offence and offender, eliminating the danger of the accused being punished to a degree out of proportion to the level of fault

[22] *R. v. Hundal*, [1993] 1 S.C.R. 867, 882.

[23] *R. v. Finlay*, [1993] 3 S.C.R. 103, 116-117.

[24] *R. v. Finlay*, [1993] 3 S.C.R. 103, 119.

[25] *R. v. Naglik*, [1993] 3 S.C.R. 122. The opinion of Lamer C.J. on the constitutional issue was agreed with by all members of the Court, except for one point of disagreement not germane to the present account.

[26] *R. v. Hundal*, [1993] 1 S.C.R. 867, 882.

[27] *R. v. Naglik*, [1993] 3 S.C.R. 122, 144.

[28] Oddly, the maximum penalty was only two years' imprisonment; however, Lamer C.J. did not suggest that the offence was not very serious.

[29] *R. v. Naglik*, [1993] 3 S.C.R. 122, 144.

actually found to exist."[30] These comments apply with equal force to nearly every offence in the Criminal Code.[31]

It is not easy to summarize the present state of the law. *B.C. Motor Vehicle Reference* still stands for the proposition that s. 7 of the Charter requires that offences that carry the penalty of imprisonment must include an element of fault. According to *Wholesale Travel*, that element of fault must be subjective mens rea if the offence is a true crime, but need only be negligence (departure from an objective standard of due diligence) if the offence is a regulatory offence. The acceptance of negligence as a sufficient element of fault is an abandonment of the broader principle of *B.C. Motor Vehicle* that the morally innocent should not be punished, because the merely negligent offender may sincerely believe that his or her conduct is lawful. Yet in *Hundal*, the Court held that negligence was the only constitutional requirement for an offence that carried a punishment of 14 years imprisonment, and the Court did not clearly state that the offence was a regulatory one. In *Nova Scotia Pharmaceutical* and *Naglik*, the Court also accepted that a departure from an objective standard was the only constitutional requirement for an offence that the Court implied was a true crime. The Court thus seems to be quietly abandoning its silly distinction between true crimes and regulatory offences. However, the Court leaves us with no guidance as to when subjective mens rea is constitutionally required and when a merely objective standard of fault will suffice.

XII. MURDER

§ 47:19 Murder

The Criminal Code's definition of murder[1] used to include the so-called felony-murder rule (sometimes called the constructive murder rule). If an accused caused a death in the course of committing certain serious offences, including robbery, while armed with a weapon, then the accused was guilty of murder. There was no requirement that the accused intended to cause the death, or that he knew that his actions were likely to cause the death (subjective foreseeability), or even that he ought to have known that his actions were likely to cause the death (objective foreseeability). In place of these culpable states of mind, the felony-murder rule required only proof of the felony, the use or carrying of the weapon and the ensuing death.

In *R. v. Vaillancourt* (1987),[2] the accused was charged with murder as the result of a poolroom robbery in which the accused's accomplice shot

---

[30] *R. v. Naglik*, [1993] 3 S.C.R. 122, 145.

[31] As noted in the text accompanying § 47:19 note 7, below, murder may be the only serious offence for which the penalty is non-discretionary (and constitutionally valid).

[Section 47:19]

[1] In *R. v. Arkell*, [1990] 2 S.C.R. 695, the Supreme Court of Canada rejected a s. 7 challenge to the distinction between "first degree murder" and "second degree murder".

[2] *R. v. Vaillancourt*, [1987] 2 S.C.R. 636. The principal opinion was written by Lamer J. with the concurrence of Dickson C.J., Estey and Wilson JJ., and, in separate

and killed a customer of the poolroom. The accused knew that his accomplice was carrying a gun, and of course he intended to rob the poolroom. He was charged under the felony-murder branch of murder,[3] and the appeal proceeded on the assumption that he did not foresee that a death was likely to ensue from the robbery (subjective foresight), and that there was at least a reasonable doubt as to whether he *ought* to have foreseen that a death was likely to ensue (objective foresight). The Supreme Court of Canada held that the felony-murder rule was a violation of fundamental justice under s. 7 of the Charter. The fact that an accused must have mens rea (a guilty mind) with respect to the underlying offence, in this case, the robbery, was not sufficient to satisfy s. 7. Before an accused could be found guilty of murder, s. 7 required that there be mens rea with respect to the death. Therefore, the felony-murder rule was unconstitutional.

The majority opinion in *Vaillancourt* was written by Lamer J. The ratio decidendi of the opinion is contained in the following passage:[4]

> there are, though very few in number, certain crimes where, because of the stigma attached to the conviction therefor or the available penalties, the principles of fundamental justice require a mens rea reflecting the particular nature of that crime. Such is theft, where, in my view, a conviction requires proof of some dishonesty. Murder is another such offence. The punishment for murder is the most severe in our society and the stigma that attaches to a conviction for murder is similarly extreme.

Thus, it was the extreme stigma and severe punishment associated with murder that entailed the requirement that the accused have some level of mens rea with respect to the death.

McIntyre J., who dissented, pointed out[5] that it must surely be open to Parliament to decide that a robbery that causes a death is a more serious offence than a robbery that does not cause a death. If this is so, then the objection to the felony-murder rule is simply an objection to the use of the name "murder". That objection could be corrected by changing the name of the offence to (for example) "manslaughter" or "killing during the commission of an offence". McIntyre J. took the view that the use of the word "murder" to classify an unintentional killing ought not to be regarded as a breach of fundamental justice. McIntyre J.'s point is illustrated by Lamer J.'s example of theft, which by reason of its stigma,

---

opinions giving cautious agreement, Beetz, Le Dain and La Forest JJ. McIntyre J. dissented.

[3]Under s. 21(2) of the Criminal Code, Vaillancourt was a party to the accomplice's crime, because they were functioning in concert, and the commission of the robbery (not the death) was foreseeable. In effect, there were two constructive elements to the charge of murder against Vaillancourt, namely, the felony-murder rule and the party rule. The constitutionality of the latter rule was not reviewed in *Vaillancourt*, but it was in *R. v. Logan*, [1990] 2 S.C.R. 731.

[4]*R. v. Vaillancourt*, [1987] 2 S.C.R. 636, 653-654.

[5]*R. v. Vaillancourt*, [1987] 2 S.C.R. 636, 663.

was said to require proof of some dishonesty.[6] Obviously, an offence of a different name, such as conversion of a motor vehicle, would not require proof of dishonesty. On this view, fundamental justice controls the names by which offences can be called, prohibiting those names that suggest a higher degree of culpability than is warranted.

Lamer J.'s theft example indicates that stigma is more important than penalty in attracting the *Vaillancourt* doctrine. The great majority of offences, including theft, carry discretionary penalties; and a sentencing court would tailor the penalty to fit the actual culpability of the accused.[7] Murder is exceptional in carrying a mandatory penalty of life imprisonment. It is a possible objection to the felony-murder rule that the same penalty must be applied to offenders whose culpability varies widely. Lamer J. did not seem to rely on this argument, although he did make reference to the severity of the punishment for murder. The trouble with this argument is that there is another guarantee of the Charter that is specifically addressed to unduly harsh penalties, and that is s. 12, the prohibition on cruel and unusual punishment. The Supreme Court of Canada[8] has held that a mandatory sentence of imprisonment that is disproportionately severe is unconstitutional for breach of s. 12. This means that s. 12 is the correct rubric under which to bring a complaint that a mandatory sentence is disproportionately severe. Section 7 is not needed to control penalties. That leaves only the control of the names of offences (based on stigma) as a rule for s. 7 in this context. But the control of names is a relatively trivial function that could well be left to the judgment of Parliament and excluded from judicial review, as McIntyre J. argued.

In *Vaillancourt*, the Supreme Court of Canada decided that "some level of mens rea"[9] with respect to the victim's death was required for the crime of murder. The Court did not have to decide, and did not decide, whether the required level of mens rea was *subjective* foreseeability, meaning that the accused did in fact foresee the likelihood of causing death, or was the lower level of *objective* foreseeability, meaning that the accused did not in fact foresee but ought to have foreseen the likelihood of causing death. In *R. v. Martineau* (1990),[10] the Supreme Court of Canada, by a majority, held that it was the higher level of mens rea—subjective foreseeability—that was required by s. 7. However, L'Heureux-Dubé J., who dissented, pointed out that it ought to be open

[6]Quotation accompanying § 47:19 note 4, above.

[7]This was acknowledged by Lamer C.J. in *R. v. Logan*, [1990] 2 S.C.R. 731, 743 (". . . the social stigma associated with a conviction is the most important consideration, not the sentence").

[8]*R. v. Smith*, [1987] 1 S.C.R. 1045; discussed in ch. 53, Cruel and Unusual Punishment, under heading § 53:4, "Minimum sentence".

[9]*R. v. Vaillancourt*, [1987] 2 S.C.R. 636, 653-654.

[10]*R. v. Martineau*, [1990] 2 S.C.R. 633. Lamer C.J. wrote for himself and four others; Sopinka J. concurred, but on the basis that it was not necessary to resolve the subjective-objective question; L'Heureux-Dubé J. dissented. The decision was followed in *R. v. Sit*, [1991] 3 S.C.R. 124, where the Court was unanimous.

to Parliament to enact that "flagrant, callous, ruthless or selfish acts, perpetrated by one whose purpose is already criminal, will be treated more harshly than a mere accidental killing".[11] That is a proposition that surely cannot be denied, and it reinforces the point made earlier that it is only Parliament's use of the name "murder" that offends s. 7.

In *Martineau*, L'Heureux-Dubé J. also pointed out that subjective foresight of death has never before been the exclusive standard for murder in Canada or in the other countries that inherited English principles of criminal law.[12] How then did it suddenly become a basic tenet of the legal system? The question points up the indeterminacy of the doctrine of substantive fundamental justice, and its dependence on the moral attitudes of the judges.

The ruling in *Martineau*, that the mens rea requirement for murder was subjective foresight of the likely death, quickly led to a s. 7 challenge to s. 21(2) of the Criminal Code, which defines who is a "party" to an offence. This provision makes persons party to an offence if they are carrying out an unlawful purpose together, and, although only one of them actually commits the offence, the others "knew *or ought to have known* that the commission of the offence would be a probable consequence of carrying out the common purpose". In *R. v. Logan* (1990),[13] the two accuseds were participants in the armed robbery of a store, in the course of which a third participant shot and severely injured the sales clerk of the store. The two accuseds were convicted as parties under s. 21(2) to the crime of attempted murder, on the basis that they ought to have known that the shooting was a probable consequence of their common purpose. The Supreme Court of Canada set aside their convictions.

In *Logan*, the Supreme Court of Canada held that the crime of attempted murder was one of those "very few offences" for which s. 7 stipulated a requirement of subjective mens rea. There was no mandatory penalty for attempted murder, but that did not matter because it was not the penalty, but "the social stigma associated with a conviction" for attempted murder that was "the most important consideration".[14] Since subjective mens rea was required by s. 7 for a conviction for attempted murder, the same level of mens rea was required for the conviction of a party to the offence. Therefore, the phrase "or ought to have known" in s. 21(2), which purported to make objective mens rea sufficient for the conviction of a party, was inapplicable whenever the principal offence was attempted murder or any other offence for which subjective mens rea was constitutionally required.

What then are the offences for which subjective mens rea is constitutionally required? We know that they include murder, because *Martineau*

---

[11] *R. v. Martineau*, [1990] 2 S.C.R. 633, 657 and see also 662.

[12] *R. v. Martineau*, [1990] 2 S.C.R. 633, 674.

[13] *R. v. Logan*, [1990] 2 S.C.R. 731. Lamer C.J. wrote the majority judgment. L'Heureux-Dubé J. dissented. The decision was followed in *R. v. Sit*, [1991] 3 S.C.R. 124, where the Court was unanimous.

[14] *R. v. Logan*, [1990] 2 S.C.R. 731, 743.

so decides, and attempted murder, because *Logan* so decides. They also include war crimes and crimes against humanity committed outside Canada.[15] We are told that they are "very few" in number, and are identified primarily by the "social stigma" that is associated with them.[16] We are told that the sentence for the offence is not the decisive consideration, and this is made clear by Lamer C.J.'s example of theft, which he gave in *Vaillancourt* and repeated in *Logan*.[17] Theft is one of the least severely punished offences in the Criminal Code: in some circumstances, theft attracts a *maximum* penalty of six months' imprisonment.[18] In these circumstances, it is difficult to identify which other offences fall into this small category. What is the status of treason, sabotage, mutiny, sedition, forgery, piracy, hijacking, perjury, fabricating evidence, bribery, fraud, cheating, procuring for prostitution, abandoning a child, infanticide, aggravated assault, sexual assault, kidnapping, abduction, torture, bigamy, extortion, breach of trust, breaking and entering and false pretences? How is a prosecutor to decide whether persons can be charged under the objective language of s. 21(2) as parties to these offences? If a charge is laid, how is a judge to decide whether it was properly laid? If it all depends upon the social stigma, how is that to be measured and compared, bearing in mind that only a "very few" offences qualify?[19]

In my opinion, it is most unsatisfactory to make radical constitutional consequences flow from such a vague, unproved and unprovable notion as social stigma. In any case, the notion cannot plausibly be derived from the basic tenets of the legal system, which have always countenanced the conviction for crimes such as murder and attempted murder of those who engage in flagrant, callous, ruthless or selfish acts in pursuit of criminal purposes. Whether it is morally wrong to continue to

---

[15] *R. v. Finta*, [1994] 1 S.C.R. 701 (holding by majority that the stigma required subjective knowledge of the facts that made the offence a war crime or crime against humanity).

[16] *R. v. Finta*, [1994] 1 S.C.R. 701. See similarly, *R. v. Morrison*, [2019] 2 S.C.R. 3, para. 75.

[17] *R. v. Finta*, [1994] 1 S.C.R. 701, 744.

[18] *R. v. Finta*, [1994] 1 S.C.R. 701, 744.

[19] The answer, of course, is that nothing short of a ruling by a majority of the Supreme Court of Canada can measure the stigma attached to each offence and then determine whether there is a constitutional requirement of subjective mens rea. So far, this has been the issue in the following cases, each of which has determined (after extensive discussion) that subjective mens rea is not required: *R. v. Wholesale Travel Group*, [1991] 3 S.C.R. 154 (false advertising); *R. v. Nova Scotia Pharmaceutical Society*, [1992] 2 S.C.R. 606 (conspiring to lessen competition); *R. v. DeSousa*, [1992] 2 S.C.R. 944 (unlawfully causing bodily harm); *R. v. Hundal*, [1993] 1 S.C.R. 867 (dangerous driving causing death); *R. v. Creighton*, [1993] 3 S.C.R. 3 (manslaughter by unlawful act); *R. v. Finlay*, [1993] 3 S.C.R. 103 (storing a firearm in a careless manner); *R. v. Naglik*, [1993] 3 S.C.R. 122 (failing to provide necessaries of life to a child). In *R. v. Morrison*, [2019] 2 S.C.R. 3, the Court was "very doubtful" that "purely subjective mens rea" is a constitutional requirement in relation to child luring, even though "child luring carries a high degree of stigma and a potentially severe punishment" (para. 79); however, it did not resolve the issue, because it said that, properly understood, subjective mens rea was already contemplated.

do so seems to me to be an issue that could safely be left to Parliament to decide. If, however, it must be accepted that fundamental justice requires that certain offences carry a constitutional requirement of subjective mens rea, then those offences should be identified, not by reference to their names, nor by reference to their social stigma, but by reference to an objective standard, which would have to be framed on the basis of the severity of the sentence.

XIII. UNFORESEEN CONSEQUENCES

§ 47:20 Unforeseen Consequences

There are Criminal Code offences in which the consequences of an unlawful act dictate the severity of the punishment for which the accused is liable. For example, the maximum term of imprisonment for dangerous driving is five years; but for dangerous driving causing bodily harm the maximum term is ten years; and for dangerous driving causing death the maximum term is 14 years. Assuming that the accused's mental state is the same for all three offences, is it a breach of fundamental justice to make an unintended and unforeseen consequence (bodily harm or death) the basis of a more serious charge?

In the previous section of this chapter, entitled "Murder", we noticed that the Supreme Court of Canada has held that, where an accused is charged with the offences of murder or attempted murder, then it is a requirement of fundamental justice that the accused must have actually intended or foreseen the death of the victim. However, the Court indicated that this requirement of subjective foresight of the consequences of an unlawful act applied only to "very few" offences, which were to be identified by reference to the "social stigma" and the penalty attaching to the offence.[1] I have already commented on the difficulty of identifying this narrow class of offences. Outside this narrow class, what mens rea elements are required by s. 7 for an offence that makes a person liable for the consequences of an unlawful act?

In *R. v. DeSousa* (1992),[2] the accused, while in a fight, threw a glass bottle that shattered against a wall, causing fragments of glass to injure an innocent bystander. The accused neither intended nor foresaw this injury. However, the injury was used as the basis of a Criminal Code charge of unlawfully causing bodily harm. This offence carried a penalty of imprisonment (ten years in fact), so that s. 7 of the Charter was applicable. The Supreme Court of Canada, in an opinion written by Sopinka J., held that the only mental element that was constitutionally required for the offence of unlawfully causing bodily harm was embedded in the word "unlawfully". That required an unlawful act, which Sopinka J. held must be a statutory offence with a constitutionally sufficient mental element. This ingredient of the offence was not in dispute.

[Section 47:20]

[1] *R. v. Logan*, [1990] 2 S.C.R. 731.

[2] *R. v. DeSousa*, [1992] 2 S.C.R. 944. Sopinka J. wrote the opinion for the Court.

What was in dispute was the mental element required for causing bodily harm. Sopinka J. held that there was "no constitutional requirement that intention, either on an objective or subjective basis, extend to the consequences of unlawful acts in general".[3] Therefore, the accused was properly convicted of unlawfully causing bodily harm despite his lack of intention or foresight with respect to the bodily harm.

Sopinka J. in *DeSousa* distinguished the line of cases involving murder and attempted murder,[4] on the basis that murder and attempted murder were among "those few offences which due to [their] stigma and penalty require fault based on a subjective standard".[5] The offence of unlawfully causing bodily harm did not carry sufficient stigma or penalty to be one of "those few offences". For all of the less serious offences, the element of mens rea that was required by the principles of fundamental justice did not include any foresight (subjective or objective) of the consequences of an unlawful act. In other words, under s. 7 of the Charter, "it is acceptable to distinguish between criminal responsibility for equally reprehensible acts on the basis of the harm that is actually caused".[6]

The ruling in *DeSousa* was reinforced in *R. v. Hundal* (1993),[7] where the Supreme Court of Canada reviewed the Criminal Code offence of dangerous driving causing death. In that case, the three concurring opinions were devoted exclusively to the mental element involved in dangerous driving.[8] Having decided that the mental element was an objective one, so that the accused's subjective belief that he was driving safely was no defence, the Court affirmed his conviction. Without even referring to *DeSousa*, the Court took for granted that the accused could be convicted of dangerous driving *causing death*, even though it was plain that the accused had no intention or foresight with respect to the death that he had caused. (He had gone through a red light and killed another motorist in the intersection.) Yet, the death elevated the maximum penalty from five years (for simple dangerous driving) to 14 years (for dangerous driving causing death). Evidently, neither the stigma of having killed an innocent person by dangerous driving nor the penalty of 14 years were sufficient to impose any constitutional requirement of a mental element with respect to the fatal consequence of the accused's dangerous driving.

---

[3]Sopinka J. held (at p. 961) that, as a matter of statutory intepretation, the Criminal Code offence required *objective* foresight of bodily harm, meaning that the accused *ought* to have foreseen the risk of the injury that ensued. But he emphasized in the language quoted in the text (at p. 965) that not even objective foresight was required by s. 7.

[4]The cases are discussed in the previous section of this chapter, under heading § 47:19, "Murder".

[5]*R. v. DeSousa*, [1992] 2 S.C.R. 944, 962.

[6]*R. v. DeSousa*, [1992] 2 S.C.R. 944, 967.

[7]*R. v. Hundal*, [1993] 1 S.C.R. 867.

[8]This aspect of the case is discussed at § 47:18, "Strict liability offences".

In *R. v. Creighton* (1993),[9] the Supreme Court of Canada had to determine what was the mental element of the offence of manslaughter by unlawful act, which consisted of causing the death of a human being by an unlawful act. The logical possibilities were: (1) the accused actually foresaw the risk of death (subjective foresight of death), (2) the accused ought (as a reasonable person) to have foreseen the risk of death (objective foresight of death), (3) the accused actually foresaw the risk of bodily harm (subjective foresight of bodily harm), and (4) the accused ought (as a reasonable person) to have foreseen the risk of bodily harm (objective foresight of bodily harm). The Criminal Code, as interpreted by the courts, imposed only requirement (4). In the world of substantive fundamental justice, the Court was free to substitute (1), (2) or (3), invoking s. 7 to justify the overruling of Parliament's choice. The Court approached the task by engaging in a long and subtle debate, uninformed by any evidence or social-science information, as to the degree of social stigma[10] that attached to a conviction for manslaughter. According to Lamer C.J. (with three others), the stigma was not enough for (1), but was too much for (3) and (4); it was just right for (2), and so the offence was unconstitutional in requiring only (4). According to McLachlin J. (with three others), the stigma was just right for (4), and so the offence was constitutional. La Forest J. (who alone did not measure the stigma) broke the tie by also coming out in favour of (4). In the end, therefore, the Court, by a five-four majority, upheld the constitutionality of the Criminal Code's requirement of objective foresight of bodily harm as the mental element of unlawful act manslaughter.[11] Foresight of the death was not required, despite the fact that the maximum penalty for manslaughter was imprisonment for life.

XIV. INVOLUNTARY ACTS

§ 47:21 Automatism

It is a tenet of the criminal law that a person should not be convicted of a criminal offence for an act that is not voluntary. Thus a blow inadvertently struck during a spasm or a convulsion is not an offence. The criminal courts have, however, become persuaded that a person can engage in very complex behaviour while in a state of "automatism", and that automatic behaviour cannot be an offence because it is involuntary. In *R. v. Parks* (1992),[1] for example, the accused got up in the middle of the night, drove his car 23 kilometres from his home to the home of his wife's parents, parked, got out, entered the home of the parents-in-law,

---

[9] *R. v. Creighton*, [1993] 3 S.C.R. 3. Concurring opinions were written by Lamer C.J. with three others, McLachlin J. with three others, and La Forest J.

[10] For those who can stand the tedious repetition of my criticisms of this concept as a constitutional "standard", see heading § 47:18, "Strict liability offences" and *R. v. Wholesale Travel Group Inc.*, [1991] 3 S.C.R. 154.

[11] Accord, *R. v. Jackson*, [1993] 4 S.C.R. 573, 587.

[Section 47:21]

[1] *R. v. Parks*, [1992] 2 S.C.R. 871.

killed his mother-in-law and wounded his father-in-law. He was charged with murder and attempted murder. His defence was that he was sleep-walking throughout, which resulted in a state of automatism. He testified to that effect, and his testimony was supported by five psychiatric experts, none of whom had of course actually observed the behaviour. The experts were not only confident that the accused was sleep-walking at the time of the attacks, they were also confident that he was not suffering from any "disease of the mind" (another interesting criminal-law concept) that would cause him to be classified as insane (and incarcerated for that reason). He was acquitted, and the acquittal was upheld by the Supreme Court of Canada.[2]

One need not be asleep to achieve a state of automatism. In the world of criminal law, a person who is awake and sane may suffer a "psychological blow" that induces a state of automatism, causing him to commit acts of violence that are involuntary (or unconscious).[3] In *R. v. Stone* (1999),[4] the accused, after relentless taunting by his wife, stabbed her to death. The behaviour of the wife was accepted by the jury as provocation, which reduces murder to manslaughter, and the accused was acquitted of murder and found guilty of manslaughter. Manslaughter is still a serious offence, and the accused was in fact sentenced to four years in jail. He appealed on the ground that he should have been acquitted, because the taunting by his wife was a psychological blow that had induced a state of (non-insane) automatism that freed him from criminal responsibility for the stabbing of his wife. A five-four majority of the Supreme Court of Canada held that this defence (which the trial judge had refused to put to the jury) was not available, because a "normal" person would not have shifted into a state of automatism as the result of the wife's taunts (although the Court did not doubt that a more severe psychological blow could have that effect on a normal person).[5] The minority of the Court would have ordered a new trial to enable the jury to consider whether the accused should be acquitted on the basis of automatism.

For a defence of automatism to succeed, it is only necessary for the defence to raise a reasonable doubt that the accused acted while in a

---

[2]Sexual assault charges are defended sufficiently frequently (with the support of sleep experts) on the basis that the accused was asleep while committing the assault that the defence has a name, "sexsomnia", and it has been successful on at least three occasions: K. Makin, "Sexsomniac will not face new rape trial, court decides", Globe and Mail newspaper, February 28, 2008.

[3]It is indicative of how little the law of automatism owes to objective medical science (as opposed to expert witnesses for the defence) that the courts have usually described behaviour in a state of automatism as "unconscious". However, since an unconscious person does not move at all, and therefore does not commit acts of violence, Bastarache J. for the majority of the Supreme Court of Canada took the view that it might be better to speak of "impaired consciousness" (para. 156).

[4]*R. v. Stone*, [1999] 2 S.C.R. 290.

[5]So held in *R. v. Graveline*, [2006] 1 S.C.R. 609 (upholding acquittal of abused wife, who shot her husband in a state of automatism).

state of automatism. In an obiter dictum in *R. v. Stone*,[6] Bastarache J. for the majority of the Court said that the defence of automatism, because it was "easily feigned and all knowledge of its occurrence rests with the accused", should have to be proved by the defence on the balance of probabilities. He acknowledged that this would be a breach of the presumption of innocence under s. 11(d) of the Charter of Rights, but he held that the shift of the burden of persuasion on this issue would be justified under s. 1. This was a remarkable ruling since (as Binnie J. pointed out in his dissenting opinion)[7] it was not necessary for the decision of the case, had not been argued by the Crown or any of the intervening Attorney Generals, and Bastarache J. did not follow the steps prescribed by *R. v. Oakes* to establish justification under s. 1.

The requirement of voluntariness is a basic tenet of the legal system that is protected by s. 7 of the Charter of Rights, at least for all offences carrying the penalty of imprisonment.[8] This means that the law respecting automatism now has constitutional status, and any attempt by Parliament to abolish the defence or restrict its availability would be unconstitutional, unless the limiting law could be justified under s. 1. That may be why Bastarache J. wanted the Court itself to interpose some difficulties in making out the defence of automatism, which does appear to offer too easy a route to escape criminal liability.

§ 47:22 Duress

The Criminal Code, by s. 17, makes duress an excuse for the commission of an offence: an offence committed "under compulsion" is excused from criminal liability. However, s. 17 stipulates that the compulsion must take the form of "threats of immediate death or bodily harm from a person who is present when the offence is committed". In *R. v. Ruzic* (2001),[1] the accused arrived at Pearson Airport in Toronto carrying heroin strapped to her body and a fake passport, and she was detected, arrested, charged and tried for unlawful importation of narcotics and use of a false passport. At her trial, she admitted both offences, but claimed that she had been forced to commit the offences by a man in Belgrade (where she lived) who threatened to harm her mother (who also lived in Belgrade) if the accused did not follow his order to take the drugs to Toronto. Although this story was entirely uncorroborated (she had not divulged her fears to the police or her mother or anyone else), it was evidently believed by the jury, who acquitted her. The Crown appealed on the ground that the limiting conditions of s. 17 were not satisfied. Since the bad man was in Belgrade when the offences were committed in Toronto, his threats were not "immediate" and he was not "present

[6] *R. v. Stone*, [1999] 2 S.C.R. 290, para. 180.

[7] *R. v. Stone*, [1999] 2 S.C.R. 290, paras. 44-53.

[8] The clearest rulings on this point come in the cases on duress and intoxication, described in the next two sections of this chapter.

[Section 47:22]

[1] *R. v. Ruzic*, [2001] 1 S.C.R. 687. The opinion of the Court was written by LeBel J.

when the offence was committed". Therefore, she did not qualify for the statutory excuse. The Supreme Court of Canada affirmed the acquittal of the accused. Section 7 of the Charter was applicable because the offences carried the penalty of imprisonment. LeBel J. for the unanimous Court held that it would be a breach of the principles of fundamental justice to convict a person of a crime when that person had not acted voluntarily. The immediacy and presence requirements of s. 17 were struck down as unconstitutional, because they had the potential, on facts like those of the present case, of convicting a person who had not acted voluntarily.

§ 47:23 Intoxication

In *R. v. Daviault* (1994),[1] the Supreme Court of Canada held that s. 7 requires that extreme intoxication be a defence to a criminal charge. Before this decision, a person could not escape responsibility for offences of general intent by pleading drunkenness. An offence of general intent is one for which the mental element of the offence (mens rea) is simply an intention to do the prohibited act (actus reus). An offence of specific intent is one for which there is a required mental element in addition to the intention to do the act. For example, assault to resist arrest is an offence of specific intent (because the intention to resist arrest is an added mental element), while simple assault is an offence of general intent (because the only mental element is the intention to commit the act of assault). In the case of an offence of specific intent, extreme intoxication may negative the additional intent and lead to the acquittal of the accused, but the accused would not normally escape criminal responsibility, because the accused could still be convicted of a lesser offence (such as simple assault) for which no specific intent was required.

The theory by which the courts refused to permit intoxication as a defence to offences of general intent was that the mental element required for an offence of general intent was so minimal that even a drunken person was capable of forming the intent. The fact that drunkenness might have caused the accused to give way more readily to a violent impulse was not enough to negative the mental element of an offence of general intent. What about those cases where it is claimed that the accused's intoxication was so extreme that he or she acted as an automaton without any awareness of doing the forbidden act? The courts rejected even that defence on the pragmatic ground that self-induced drunkenness was sufficiently blameworthy to substitute for the intention to perform the forbidden act. The intention or recklessness involved in voluntarily drinking so much alcohol that the drinker loses control over his or her actions was regarded as a sufficiently guilty mind to sup-

[Section 47:23]

[1] *R. v. Daviault*, [1994] 3 S.C.R. 63. The opinion of the majority was written by Cory J., with whom L'Heureux-Dubé, McLachlin and Iacobucci JJ. agreed. Short concurring opinions were written by Lamer C.J. and La Forest J., essentially agreeing with Cory J. The opinion of the dissenting minority was written by Sopinka J., with whom Gonthier and Major JJ. agreed.

port a conviction for an offence of general intent. This rule undoubtedly reflected a policy of protecting the public from drunken offenders, who could not escape responsibility for violent acts by becoming extremely drunk. It probably also reflected some scepticism as to the factual basis of the claim that drunkenness could rob a person so completely of any willed responsibility for his criminal act, especially where that act was a relatively complicated one, such as a rape.

In *R. v. Daviault*, the accused was charged with a sexual assault. The complainant, who was confined to a wheelchair, testified that the accused (who had been drinking in her apartment) had wheeled her into her bedroom, had thrown her onto the bed and sexually assaulted her. The accused testified that he had been drinking heavily during the day and evening, and that he awoke without any clothes on in the complainant's bed, but had no recollection of what had happened before that. An expert called by the accused testified that the accused had drunk so much alcohol that he could have been in a state akin to automatism when he committed the assault (if he committed the assault). The trial judge found that the accused had committed the act of sexual assault, but he acquitted the accused on the basis of a reasonable doubt as to whether the accused had the intent necessary to commit the offence. The Quebec Court of Appeal substituted a verdict of guilty on the ground that self-induced intoxication was no defence to a crime of general intent, and sexual assault was a crime of general intent.

The Supreme Court of Canada, by a majority of six to three, held that ss. 7 and 11(d) of the Charter were offended by the rule that self-induced intoxication was no defence to a criminal charge. Cory J., who wrote for the majority, held that, under s. 7, the requirement of mens rea for a crime of general intent could only be the intention to commit the prohibited act. The intention to become drunk could not be substituted for the intention to commit the forbidden act. Having derived this premise from the Charter, he reasoned that to eliminate the only permissible mental element from the crime was a breach of fundamental justice resulting in a breach of s. 7. Section 11(d) was also infringed, because the denial of the defence of drunkenness would enable an accused to be convicted notwithstanding a reasonable doubt as to whether the accused possessed the only permissible mental element of the crime. In short, the Charter required that self-induced intoxication, if it was so extreme as to be akin to automatism, must free the accused from criminal liability. Sopinka J., who wrote the dissenting opinion, took the view that self-induced intoxication was sufficiently blameworthy to count as the mental element for a crime of general intent, and that there were sound policy reasons for not permitting drunken offenders to escape criminal liability for acts of violence.

There are two passages near the end of Cory J.'s majority judgment that evidently seek to allay concerns about the public dangers of a constitutional requirement that has the effect of freeing extremely drunken offenders from criminal liability. The first passage requires the accused to establish the defence of extreme intoxication on the balance of probabilities.[2] By reversing the usual onus of proof in a criminal case, Cory J. created a new rule that offends the presumption of innocence in s. 11(d), and that preserves what he had earlier offered as one of the constitutional vices of the old law, namely, that a person could be convicted of a criminal offence notwithstanding a reasonable doubt as to whether he had the mens rea to commit the offence. But Cory J. explained that the reversal of the onus of proof (but apparently not the old common law) could be justified under s. 1 of the Charter.[3]

The second passage is one where Cory J. asserts "that it is always open to Parliament to fashion a remedy which would make it a crime to commit a prohibited act while drunk".[4] This passage is a puzzle, because every word of the opinion to this point has argued that it is not open to Parliament to make it a crime to commit a prohibited act while drunk. That, surely, is the state of the law that the Court is now striking down. What would the mens rea of this new crime be? It could hardly be the intention or recklessness of getting drunk, since that has been ruled constitutionally insufficient as a replacement for the intention of committing the prohibited act. This problem could hardly be overcome by describing drunkenness as the crime, rather than the prohibited act, since that is a transparent evasion of the constitutional rule laid down in this case. If the only problem with the prosecution of Daviault is that he could not be charged with drunkenness rather than the sexual assault, which is the actual reason for wanting to punish him, then all the words in the majority judgment add up to nothing of substance. Why not simply uphold the present state of the law, instead of insisting on Parliament switching the names of the offences?

The decision in *Daviault* attracted very unfavourable public comment. Public concern that drunken offenders would escape liability for violent acts was intensified when the newspapers reported three successful uses of the drunkenness defence within days of the Court's decision. The federal government was forced to take the issue up as a matter of urgency. The government did not follow Cory J.'s suggestion that Parliament could make drunkenness an offence. Instead, Parliament enacted an amendment to the Criminal Code that described extreme self-induced intoxication as a marked departure from "the standard of reasonable care generally recognized in Canadian society", and provided that this departure constituted the fault required for conviction of offences of violence.[5] This essentially enacts the common law rule that the majority in *Daviault* had struck down as offending the Charter of Rights. On the face of it, the amendment is subject to the same constitutional objections as the common law rule. Yet the amendment does not invoke the override power of s. 33: there is no notwithstanding clause to override ss. 7

[2] *R. v. Daviault*, [1994] 3 S.C.R. 63, 101.

[3] *R. v. Daviault*, [1994] 3 S.C.R. 63, 101, citing *R. v. Chaulk*, [1990] 3 S.C.R. 1303, which upheld under s. 1 the statutory reversal of the onus of proving the defence of insanity.

[4] *R. v. Daviault*, [1994] 3 S.C.R. 63, 100.

[5] S.C. 1995, c. 32, adding new s. 33.1 to the Criminal Code.

and 11(d) of the Charter. It will be interesting to see whether the Court will uphold the amendment, which it could only do under s. 1.[6]

In *R. v. Robinson* (1996),[7] the Supreme Court of Canada turned its attention to offences of *specific* intent. As explained at the beginning of this section, the common law did admit intoxication as a defence to offences of specific intent. However, the Supreme Court of Canada, in a case called *R. v. MacAskill* (1931),[8] had held that the defence of intoxication required evidence that the accused was so intoxicated that he was *incapable* of forming the required specific intent. *Robinson* was a case of murder, which is an offence of specific intent, because the intention to kill (or the foresight of death) is a specific intent that must be established for conviction. In *Robinson*, the accused had been drinking heavily before first beating his victim over the head with a stone, and then going and getting a knife and stabbing the victim several times in the stomach. In conformity with *MacAskill*, the trial judge instructed the jury that the accused was entitled to be acquitted only if there was a reasonable doubt as to his *capacity* to form the intention to kill. The jury found him guilty. The Supreme Court of Canada ordered a new trial, holding that this limitation on the defence of intoxication offended ss. 7 and 11(d) of the Charter of Rights. The objection to the *MacAskill* rule was that a jury would be compelled to convict a person of an offence of specific intent if the evidence of intoxication fell short of establishing that the accused was incapable of forming the required specific intent. This could lead to a person being convicted when there was a reasonable doubt as

---

[6]The amending Act contains a two-page preamble which recites what is close to a factual and legal rebuttal of the Court's reasoning, and which emphasizes the close association of intoxication and violence, especially violence against women and children. Recall, however, the Court's reluctance to employ s. 1 to overcome a breach of s. 7: ch. 38, Limitation of Rights, under heading § 38:25, "Section 7". The Globe and Mail newspaper reported in 2011 that the amendment had been held to be unconstitutional "at least" 10 times by trial judges, who have permitted defendants to raise the defence of drunkenness despite the amendment: Kirk Makin, "Drunkenness can be a defence, judge rules", May 6, 2011, p. All. In *R. v. Bouchard-Lebrun*, [2011] 3 S.C.R. 575, an accused appealed a conviction under s. 33.1 to the Supreme Court of Canada, but his only argument was that he was entitled to a verdict of not criminally responsible on account of mental disorder under s. 16 of the Criminal Code (which has now replaced the defence of insanity). The Court rejected this argument on the basis that an automatistic mental condition that was brought on by self-induced intoxication and that went away when the intoxication wore off was covered by s. 33.1, not s. 16, and the Court affirmed his conviction under s. 33.1. However, LeBel J. for the Court (para. 28) said that "[the accused] raises no arguments regarding the constitutionality of s. 33.1 *Cr. C.*, which means that only the interpretation and application of that provision are in issue"; and, while acknowledging (para. 35) that Parliament had "implicitly endorsed Sopinka J.'s dissent in *Daviault*", he made no direct comment on the constitutionality of s. 33.1. In *R. v. Sullivan* (2020), 151 O.R. (3d) 353 (C.A.), the Ontario Court of Appeal held that s. 33.1 infringes ss. 7 and 11(d) of the Charter, and that the infringements could not be justified under s. 1. The Supreme Court of Canada granted leave to appeal on December 23, 2020. As of the time of writing, the Court had not released a decision in the appeal.

[7]*R. v. Robinson*, [1996] 1 S.C.R. 683. The Court was unanimous. The majority opinion was written by Lamer C.J. L'Heureux-Dubé J. wrote a separate concurring opinion.

[8]*R. v. MacAskill*, [1931] S.C.R. 330.

to whether he in fact possessed the requisite intent. This offended s. 7's requirement of mens rea and s. 11(d)'s presumption of innocence. Therefore, the Court overruled *MacAskill* and held that, if drunkenness raised a reasonable doubt as to whether the accused in fact possessed the requisite specific intent, the accused was entitled to be acquitted even if there was no doubt that the accused possessed the capacity to form the requisite intent.

XV. OVERBROAD LAWS

§ 47:24 Overbroad laws

In *R. v. Heywood* (1994),[1] the Supreme Court of Canada established a new doctrine of "overbreadth",[2] which applies to a law that is broader than necessary to accomplish its purpose. Overbreadth is a breach of the principles of fundamental justice, and therefore a basis for a finding of unconstitutionality in a law that affects life, liberty or security of the person.

The law under challenge in *Heywood* was a provision of the Criminal Code that made it an offence (of "vagrancy") for a person who had been previously found guilty of the offence of sexual assault to be "found loitering in or near a schoolground, playground, public park or bathing area". The law obviously restricted the liberty of those convicted sex offenders to whom the prohibition applied. Was it also a breach of the principles of fundamental justice? The majority of the Supreme Court of Canada, in an opinion written by Cory J., held that the purpose of the law was to protect the safety of children. Cory J. acknowledged that a restriction on liberty for the purpose of protecting the safety of children would not be a breach of fundamental justice. But, he held, a law that restricted liberty more than was necessary to accomplish its purpose would be a breach of fundamental justice by reason of "overbreadth". In this case, the law was overbroad for three reasons: (1) its geographic scope was too wide, because parks and bathing areas included places where children were not likely to be found; (2) its duration was too long, because it applied for life without any possibility of review; and (3) the class of persons to whom it applied was too wide, because some of the offenders to whom it applied would not be a continuing danger to children.[3] Because the law was overbroad, it offended the principles of fundamental

[Section 47:24]

[1] *R. v. Heywood*, [1994] 3 S.C.R. 761. The opinion of the majority was written by Cory J., with the agreement of Lamer C.J., Sopinka, Iacobucci and Major JJ. The opinion of the dissenting minority was written by Gonthier J., with the agreement of La Forest, L'Heureux-Dubé and McLachlin JJ.

[2] In *R. v. Nova Scotia Pharmaceutical Society*, [1992] 2 S.C.R. 606, 632 ("overbreadth has no independent existence"), Gonthier J. for the Court had denied that there was such a doctrine in Canada.

[3] A fourth reason for holding that the law offended the principles of fundamental justice was that it made no provision for notice of the loitering prohibition to be given to those convicted offenders who came under the terms of the prohibition. This has nothing to do with overbreadth. The theory that a requirement of notice is a principle of

justice. It could not be upheld under s. 1, because its overbreadth would cause it to fail the minimum impairment (least drastic means) branch of the s. 1 analysis. The law was therefore struck down in its entirety.

Overbreadth is not the same as vagueness (a topic that is treated in a later section of this chapter).[4] Of course, a law that was excessively vague might also be excessively broad, and thus fail both requirements. Overbreadth and vagueness have this in common: either deficiency results in the invalidity of the entire law, including the part that is consistent with the purpose of the law and clear in its application.

It is hard to disagree with the basic premise of Cory J.'s opinion in *Heywood*, which is that a law that restricts liberty "for no reason" (to use Cory J.'s phrase)[5] offends the principles of fundamental justice. But the doctrine of overbreadth, as applied by the Court, raises serious practical and theoretical difficulties, and confers an exceedingly discretionary power of review on the Court. The doctrine requires that the terms of a law be no broader than is necessary to accomplish the purpose of the law. But the purpose of a law is a judicial construct, which can be defined widely or narrowly as the reviewing court sees fit.[6] In this case, for example, Cory J., who wrote for the majority, defined the purpose of the law as being for the protection of children, while Gonthier J., who wrote for the dissenting minority, defined the purpose of the law as being for the protection of adults as well as children. Much of the difference of opinion between majority and minority depended on these competing purposes, because the law was apt to cover persons and situations that presented a danger to adults as well as children. Even if agreement could be reached on the purpose of a law, the question whether the terms of the law are no broader than is needed to carry out the purpose raises a host of interpretative, policy and empirical questions. In this case, for example, Cory J. interpreted loitering as not involving anything more than mere presence in the prohibited areas, while Gonthier J. interpreted the term as requiring some malevolent intent. The two judges also disagreed on such issues as whether sex offenders can be reliably diagnosed as cured, and whether there is a pattern of crossover from one kind of past offence (for example, against adults) to a different kind (for example, against children). These kinds of disagreements among judges are not unusual and are not surprising. It must be recognized, however, that a judge who disapproves of a law will always be able to find that it is overbroad.

---

fundamental justice, namely, a basic tenet of the legal system, is not only novel, but contradicts what is undeniably a basic tenet of the legal system that ignorance of the law is no excuse. This was the dissenting view of Gonthier J. (In fact, the accused in this case had been given notice of the law when he was warned by police and not charged on an earlier occasion of loitering near a playground.)

[4]Section 47:27 to 47:29, "Vague laws".

[5]*R. v. Heywood*, [1994] 3 S.C.R. 761, 793.

[6]For a broader discussion of this point, see H. Schwartz, "Circularity, Tautology and Gamesmanship: 'Purpose' based Proportionality-Correspondence Analysis in Sections 15 and 7 of the Charter" (2015) 35 Nat. J. Con. Law 105.

A feature of Cory J.'s opinion is his use of hypothetical cases to demonstrate the overbreadth of the law. He was concerned about the application of the law to "remote wilderness parks",[7] and to "a man convicted at age 18 of sexual assault of an adult woman who was known to him in a situation aggravated by alcohol".[8] The case before the Court, however, was a man, who had been previously convicted of sexual assault, who was found standing at the edge of a children's playground in a public park in Victoria, taking photographs of the children with a camera with a telephoto lens; the film in the camera, and photographs found in his home, showed that he was taking pictures of young girls with their clothing disarranged from play so that their crotches, although covered by underclothes, were visible. The trial judge regarded the behaviour as sufficiently sinister to impose a three-month prison sentence followed by three years of probation. The Supreme Court of Canada could hardly have been indifferent to these facts, but the majority's analysis is based entirely on hypothetical cases involving the most innocent possible offenders.[9] This mode of reasoning is a very powerful tool of judicial review, since there must be few laws indeed in which it would not be possible to design a hypothetical case (disregarding the realities of police and prosecutorial discretion)[10] that is caught by the law although it falls outside the apparent purpose of the law. What law can withstand an attack of this kind?[11]

Why should the Supreme Court of Canada be in such a hurry to strike down a law for overshooting its purpose in a case where the law is clearly accomplishing its purpose?[12] After all, if the hypothetical cases are realistic, there will be future opportunities to review the law when it is applied too broadly. The reliance on hypothetical cases turns the courts into "roving commissions assigned to pass judgment on the valid-

---

[7] *R. v. Heywood*, [1994] 3 S.C.R. 761, 795.

[8] *R. v. Heywood*, [1994] 3 S.C.R. 761, 799.

[9] The most innocent possible offender principle has also been used to strike down minimum sentence requirements under s. 12 of the Charter's prohibition on cruel and unusual treatment or punishment. The law is described (and similar criticism is offered) in ch. 53, Cruel and Unusual Punishment, under heading § 53:4, "Minimum sentence". For judicial criticism, see *R. v. Biller* (1999), 174 D.L.R. (4th) 721, 737 (Sask. C.A.).

[10] The majority opinion is completely silent on the issue of police and prosecutorial discretion, although that discretion is likely to keep the wilderness bird watcher out of court, just as it protects the speeding motorist who is rushing a sick child to the hospital.

[11] Early in the opinion (at p. 793), Cory J. says that in analyzing a statutory provision to determine whether it is overbroad, a "measure of deference" should be paid to the means selected by the legislature. While a measure of deference is not (apparently) very much deference, this dictum should shield those laws whose overbreadth depends upon particularly fanciful hypotheticals.

[12] It is possible that the majority was emboldened by the fact that Parliament (responding to the decision of the British Columbia Court of Appeal in this case, which also struck down the law) had already replaced the law with a narrower version that amended the various characteristics of the law that the majority regarded as overbroad: S.C. 1993, c. 45, s. 1 (referred to by Cory J. at p.801). Therefore, although Heywood was acquitted, a valid law was in place for the future.

ity of the Nation's laws".[13] The American courts have not allowed this to happen. In the United States, it is well established that "a person to whom a statute may constitutionally be applied will not be heard to challenge that statute on the ground that it may conceivably be applied unconstitutionally to others, in other situations not before the Court".[14] Surely, this reflects a more appropriately restrained role for the courts.[15]

In *Heywood*, the law that was struck down was a direct restraint on the liberty of those to whom it applied, because their access to schoolyards, playgrounds, public parks and bathing areas was restricted. Such laws are unusual. But it must be remembered that any law that carries the possible sanction of imprisonment is deemed by the Supreme Court of Canada to be a deprivation of liberty requiring compliance with s. 7.[16] And it must also be remembered that a corporation, although not itself liable to the sanction of imprisonment, is permitted to rely on s. 7 as a defence to a criminal charge if the defence would be available to an individual.[17] The effect of these rules is to expose not only the criminal law, but virtually all regulatory law to s. 7 review, including review for overbreadth. Any law that includes the sanction of imprisonment is unconstitutional if a court determines, relying on hypothetical cases, that the scope of the law is broader than is required to carry out its purpose.

In *Ontario v. Canadian Pacific* (1995),[18] Canadian Pacific was charged with an offence under Ontario's Environmental Protection Act of discharging a contaminant, namely, smoke, into the natural environment. The company had been clearing the part of its railway right-of-way that ran through the town of Kenora, by burning the grass and weeds growing on the right-of-way. The resulting smoke caused some nuisance and discomfort to residents of the town whose complaints led to the laying of the charge. When the case reached the Supreme Court of Canada, the new doctrine of overbreadth had to be considered, which involved assessing the impact of the law on the most innocent possible offender. The discharge of smoke in a wilderness area (instead of in Kenora), or the placing of sand on icy sidewalks by homeowners

---

[13]*Broadrick v. Oklahoma* (1973), 413 U.S. 601, 611 per White J.

[14]*Broadrick v. Oklahoma* (1973), 413 U.S. 601, 610-611; the United States' law is described, and rejected, by Lamer C.J. and Gonthier J. in *Ont. v. Canadian Pacific*, [1995] 2 S.C.R. 1031, paras. 6-7, 73-78, although they do agree not to accept hypothetical cases in order to hold a statute unconstitutionally vague (as opposed to overbroad).

[15]Overbreadth does play a role in first amendment cases in the United States. If a law restricts "substantially" more speech than is justified by a compelling state interest, then the law is unconstitutional on its face: *Broadrick v. Oklahoma* (1973), 413 U.S. 601, 615; appld. in *Ashcroft v. Free Speech Coalition* (2002), 535 U.S. 234 (striking down Child Pornography Prevention Act).

[16]§ 47:9, "Physical liberty".

[17]Chapter 59, Procedure, under heading § 59:6, "Enforcing other people's rights".

[18]*Ontario v. Canadian Pacific*, [1995] 2 S.C.R. 1031. The Court was unanimous as to the outcome, upholding the law and its applicability to Canadian Pacific. The majority opinion was written by Gonthier J., with the agreement of La Forest, L'Heureux-Dubé, McLachlin, Iacobucci and Major JJ. A concurring opinion was written by Lamer C.J., with the agreement of Sopinka and Cory JJ.

(since the hypothetical case need have nothing to do with the actual facts) gave Lamer C.J. enormous difficulty, since they appeared to be discharges of contaminants that were caught by the literal words of the Act. And he explicitly recognized that the fact that police and prosecutors would not lay charges based on the wilderness smoke or the sandy sidewalks was irrelevant under the most innocent possible offender principle. Of course, recognition of the overbreadth argument in this case would be a serious blow to effective environmental regulation, which must rely on broad general language to capture the multitude of polluting activities that ought to be prohibited. Lamer C.J. solved the problem by invoking the presumption of constitutionality and adopting an artificially narrow interpretation of the Act that, he said, exempted the wilderness smoke and the sandy sidewalks. Gonthier J., who wrote for the majority of the Court, also managed to find an interpretation of the Act (a different one) that, he said, excluded speculative or imaginary uses of the environment. For both judges, then, the Act was not overbroad, and Ontario was permitted to continue to try to regulate its environment.

In *R. v. Clay* (2003),[19] it was argued that the law criminalizing the possession of marihuana (which included the penalty of imprisonment and therefore impaired liberty under s. 7) offended the principles of fundamental justice, because it was overbroad. The majority of the Supreme Court of Canada (the dissenters did not address this issue) held that the challenge failed. The Court did not need to come up with fanciful imaginary cases, because it was obvious that the law caught people who were in possession of marihuana in the privacy of a home, who were not about to drive a car or operate machinery, and who were not members of the "vulnerable groups" of "chronic users" who would be harmed by marihuana use. Indeed, the people who smoked marihuana in this harmless way were probably the great majority of users. Why should they be subject to criminal penalties? The majority of the Supreme Court of Canada gave this argument short shrift, asserting that "a narrower prohibition would not be effective"; and that there was "a rational basis for extending the prohibition to all users".[20] The conclusion was that the prohibition was not overbroad.

An overbreadth argument was also quickly dismissed in *Canadian Foundation for Children, Youth and the Law v. Canada* (2004).[21] That case was a challenge to the provision of the Criminal Code that permitted teachers and parents to use reasonable force for the purpose of correction against the children in their charge. Since this exposed children to conduct that would be a criminal assault if committed against an

---

[19] *R. v. Clay*, [2003] 3 S.C.R. 735. The majority opinion was written by Gonthier and Binnie JJ. Dissenting opinions (but not on the issue of overbreadth) were written by Arbour, LeBel and Deschamps JJ.

[20] *R. v. Clay*, [2003] 3 S.C.R. 735, para. 40.

[21] *Canadian Foundation for Children, Youth and the Law v. Canada*, [2004] 1 S.C.R. 76. The majority opinion was written by McLachlin C.J. Dissenting opinions (but not on the issue of overbreadth) were written by Binnie, Arbour and Deschamps JJ.

adult, it impaired the security of the person of the children to whom it applied, and therefore engaged s. 7. It was argued that the provision was overbroad, because it applied to children under two, who were not capable of learning from physical correction, and to teenagers, who could suffer psychological harm from physical correction. The majority of the Supreme Court of Canada acknowledged that the evidence bore out these claims, but answered them with a syllogism. Because the law "does not permit force that cannot correct or is unreasonable", and because all examples of overbreadth would involve applications where force could not correct or would be unreasonable, therefore the law could not be overbroad![22]

The consistent rejection of overbreadth challenges in the decade following the invention of the doctrine in *Heywood*[23] might have led one to conclude that the doctrine was dead if not formally buried.[24] Not so, said the Supreme Court of Canada in *R. v. Demers* (2004).[25] It is alive and well after all. What was in issue in that case was the regime established by the Criminal Code for accused persons who were found to be unfit to stand trial. This involved an annual hearing by a review board to determine whether the accused was still unfit to stand trial. If he was found fit to stand trial, he would be sent to trial. If not, the board would determine whether he should be undergoing treatment and whether he should be in custody or at liberty under conditions; and the situation would be reviewed at the next annual hearing. According to the Supreme Court of Canada, this regime worked appropriately for an accused person who was not permanently unfit to stand trial; such a person would remain in the process until he had recovered the capacity to stand trial, and would then be tried. But the Court held that the law was overbroad because of its application to a person who suffered from a mental disorder that made him permanently unfit for trial. A person who would never be fit to stand trial was trapped in the system, subject to the annual reviews and whatever restrictions on his liberty the review board chose to impose. As long as the charge remained outstanding,[26] there was no power in a court to order a discharge even if the accused person was not a threat to public safety. Since the law made no provision for an absolute discharge for the permanently unfit accused, it was overbroad;

---

[22]*Canadian Foundation for Children, Youth and the Law v. Canada*, [2004] 1 S.C.R. 76, para. 46.

[23]*R. v. Heywood*, [1994] 3 S.C.R. 761.

[24]See also *Cochrane v. Ont.* (2008), 92 O.R. (3d) 321 (C.A.) (ban on "pit bulls" not overbroad, although it applied to the kind and gentle ones as well as the dangerous ones).

[25]*R. v. Demers*, [2004] 2 S.C.R. 489. The Court was unanimous in its result. Iacobucci and Bastarache JJ. wrote the opinion of the eight-judge majority. LeBel J. wrote a concurring opinion, disagreeing with some of the majority reasons, but agreeing with the overbreadth reasons.

[26]The charges would come to an end if the Crown became unable to make out a prima facie case against the accused, in which case a court could discharge the accused. The same result would occur automatically if the Crown withdrew the charge. The Court held (para. 54) that this was not sufficient to correct the overbreadth.

and, since the law impaired liberty under s. 7, its overbreadth made the law unconstitutional. The Court struck down the law, but postponed the declaration of invalidity for 12 months to allow for Parliament to amend the law.[27] If the law were not amended during the 12-month period, the Court ordered that a stay of proceedings be granted to those permanently unfit accused who did not present a threat to the safety of the public.

After a further rest of nine years, overbreadth was applied again to strike down a law in *Canada v. Bedford* (2013).[28] The law in issue was one of three prostitution-related offences in the federal Criminal Code, all of which were successfully attacked under s. 7 in the same proceeding. The overbroad provision was the prohibition on living off the avails of prostitution. (The prohibitions on keeping a common bawdy house and communicating in public for the purpose of prostitution were struck down as grossly disproportionate, and are discussed in the next section of the book.)[29] With respect to the living-off-the-avails provision, the Court recognized that the purpose of the prohibition was to criminalize the pimp, the person who lived parasitically off a prostitute's earnings, and was commonly involved in recruiting and controlling the prostitute. But the law made no distinction between those who exploit prostitutes and those who would increase the safety and security of prostitutes, for example, legitimate drivers, managers or bodyguards. Because the law captured conduct that bore no relation to its purpose, it was overbroad; and, since the law impaired security of the person under s. 7, the overbreadth made the law unconstitutional. The Court struck down the law in its entirety, but postponed the declaration of invalidity for 12 months to allow for Parliament to amend the law.[30]

Overbreadth was applied again in *Carter v. Canada* (2015).[31] The law in issue was s. 241(b) of the Criminal Code, which made it an offence to aid or abet a person to commit suicide.[32] This provision had been upheld by a majority of the Supreme Court against a s.7 challenge in *Rodriguez*

[27]A new law was enacted within one year. S.C. 2005, c. 22, s. 33, adds a new provision to the Criminal Code (s. 672.851), which authorizes a court to order a stay of proceedings if the court is satisfied that the accused is not likely ever to become fit to stand trial and does not pose a significant threat to the safety of the public.

[28]*Can. v. Bedford*, [2013] 3 S.C.R. 1101, 2013 SCC 72. McLachlin C.J. wrote the opinion of the Court.

[29]See § 47:25 "Disproportionate laws". With respect to the living-off-the-avails provision, the Court said (para. 145) that, having found that the provision was overbroad, it was unnecessary to consider whether it was also grossly disproportionate.

[30]An account of the sequel legislation is in ch. 40, Enforcement of Rights, under heading § 40:4, "Temporary validity".

[31]*Carter v. Canada*, [2015] 1 S.C.R. 331, 2015 SCC 5. The unanimous opinion was attributed to "the Court".

[32]Section 241(b) was reinforced by s. 14, which provided that "consent of the deceased does not affect the criminal responsibility of any person by whom death may be inflicted on the person by whom consent is given." This provision was also held to be overbroad under the same conditions as s. 241(b).

v. British Columbia (1993),[33] a case that was decided before the doctrine of overbreadth had become established. The second challenge was successful, and *Rodriguez* was overruled. The Court in *Carter* held that the purpose of s. 241(b) was "to protect vulnerable persons from being induced to commit suicide in a moment of weakness".[34] The plaintiff in this case, like the plaintiff in *Rodriguez*, suffered from a fatal degenerative disease that was progressively robbing her of all of her physical abilities. She wanted to die peacefully at a time and in a manner of her own choice, but she knew that she would probably need the help of a doctor when that time came. The trial judge had found that the plaintiff was not a "vulnerable" person: she was competent, fully-informed and free from coercion or duress. Her situation (which was similar to that of others whose affidavits were filed in the case) showed that the prohibition extended to some people who were not "vulnerable" persons in need of protection and was therefore overbroad. In its discussion of s. 1, the Supreme Court recognized that, if the absolute prohibition of physician-assisted death were to be replaced with a regime less restrictive of life, liberty and security of the person, it was necessary to determine whether safeguards could be designed to remove the risks of error or abuse in a more permissive regime. This was a question on which the trial judge had heard extensive evidence and she had concluded that safeguards could be constructed that would sufficiently reduce the risks of error or abuse.[35] Since the Court applied a rule of deference to a trial judge's findings even on legislative and social facts, except in cases of "palpable and overriding error,"[36] which was not present in this case, the Court accepted the findings at trial. It followed that a constitutional regime less restrictive of life, liberty and security of the person could be constructed. The Court did not attempt to design the new regime itself, leaving that for Parliament. The Court issued a declaration that the prohibition of physician-assisted death was unconstitutional "for a competent adult person who (1) clearly consents to the termination of life and (2) has a grievous and irremediable medical condition (including an illness, disease or disability) that causes enduring suffering that is intolerable to the individual in the circumstances of his or her condition."[37] The Court suspended the declaration for 12 months (later extended to 16 months)

---

[33] *Rodriguez v. British Columbia*, [1993] 3 S.C.R. 519.

[34] *Carter v. Canada*, [2015] 1 S.C.R. 331, at para. 86. Note the great importance to the outcome of the judicial finding of legislative purpose as limited to the protection of "vulnerable" persons; that finding determined the overbroad classification.

[35] Neither the trial judge nor the Supreme Court found that the risks could be eliminated, but with proper safeguards they could be reduced to a level no higher than in other (lawful) situations of end-of-life medical decision-making, "risks that are already part and parcel of our medical system": *Carter v. Canada*, [2015] 1 S.C.R. 331, para. 115.

[36] This had been established in the earlier case of *Can. v. Bedford*, [2013] 3 S.C.R. 1101, 2013 SCC 72, where trial findings of legislative and social facts were equally critical: for discussion, see ch. 60, Proof, under heading § 60:8, "Modes of proof".

[37] *Carter v. Canada*, [2015] 1 S.C.R. 331, para. 147. Since the challenged Criminal Code provisions were not restricted to physician-assisted death, the declaration had the

to allow time for Parliament to design and enact the appropriate safeguards. Parliament did enact legislation, which is discussed earlier in the book.[38]

Overbreadth was considered and rejected in *R. v. Moriarity* (2015),[39] where it was argued that the National Defence Act's definition of "service offences", which were triable by military courts, was too broad in including general criminal law offences in the Criminal Code and the Controlled Drugs and Substances Act when committed by a member of the armed forces. The argument was that some military connection in the circumstances of the offence was necessary to comply with the principles of fundamental justice. The Supreme Court rejected this argument. Cromwell J., who wrote for the Court, held that the purpose of service offences, triable by military courts, was "to maintain the discipline, efficiency and morale of the military". The extension of service offences into the general criminal law was not overbroad because the commission of criminal offences by members of the armed forces, "even when they are not on duty, in uniform, or on a military base", would undermine trust and respect which would have an impact on the discipline, efficiency and morale of the military. No more military connection than the defendant's membership in the armed forces was needed to satisfy the principles of fundamental justice.

Overbreadth was applied in *R. v. Appulonappa* (2015)[40] to the human-smuggling offence in the Immigration and Refugee Protection Act. In that case, a boatload of Tamils from Sri Lanka bound for Canada was apprehended off the coast of British Columbia. The people on the boat all claimed refugee status in Canada. None had the required documentation. The organizers of the venture, the captain and main crew of the boat, who had been paid for their services by the passengers, were charged under s. 117 of the Act, which makes it an offence "to organize, induce, aid or abet" the coming into Canada of people in contravention of the Act. Conviction would make them liable to imprisonment and disqualification from consideration as a refugee. The defendants challenged the constitutionality of s. 117, not in its application to them, but on the basis that it was overbroad, because it could apply to hypothetical cases where penalties would be unwarranted. The hypothetical-cases line of argument had of course been applied to

---

effect of carving out an exception to the provisions, leaving them otherwise in force as prohibitions on non-physicians aiding or abetting another person to commit suicide.

[38]S.C. 2016, c. 3, is discussed in ch. 40, Enforcement of Rights, under heading § 40:4, "Temporary validity". In *Truchon c. Procureur général du Canada*, 2019 QCCS 3792, the Superior Court of Quebec struck down part of the revised law under ss. 7 and 15 of the Charter. The federal government did not appeal, and revised the law again to take into account the Court's decision. This is also discussed in ch. 40, Enforcement of Rights, under heading § 40:4, "Temporary validity".

[39]*R. v. Moriarity*, [2015] 3 S.C.R. 485, 2015 SCC 55. Cromwell J. wrote the opinion of the Court. This case is more fully described in § 51:24, "Offence under military law".

[40]*R. v. Appulonappa*, [2015] 3 S.C.R. 754, 2015 SCC 59. McLachlin C.J. wrote the opinion of the Court.

invalidate a law in *Heywood.*[41] McLachlin C.J., who wrote the opinion of the Court, accepted the argument, offering the hypothetical cases of "a father offering a blanket to a shivering child, or friends sharing food aboard a migrant vessel".[42] The language of s. 117 was broad enough to capture these cases, although, if the boat passengers included some kind fathers or generous friends, they had not been charged—only the paid organizers had been charged. The legislative history of s. 117 disclosed concerns about liability for family or humanitarian assistance, and the minister's answer was that the Act stipulated that all prosecutions under s. 117 had to be approved by the Attorney General, who would never approve such a prosecution. McLachlin C.J. denied that the requirement of the Attorney General's approval cured the overbreadth problem. It could not be said to be "impossible" that the Attorney General would approve a prosecution for acts of family or humanitarian assistance, and, if the Attorney General were to do so, "nothing remains in the provision to prevent conviction and imprisonment".[43] She concluded that s. 117 infringed s. 7 because it was overbroad. However, she then made an important (but unacknowledged) departure from Heywood: she did not strike down s. 117 in its entirety (so as to acquit the defendants). She "read down" s. 117 "as not applicable to persons who give humanitarian, mutual or family assistance", which left the rest of the prohibition on human smuggling in place.[44] The charges against the defendants were remitted for trial on that basis.

An overbreadth attack was again successful in *R. v. Safarzadeh-Markhali* (2016).[45] When a person is convicted of a criminal offence that is deserving of a sentence of imprisonment, an issue for the sentencing judge is how much credit should be granted for any period of pre-sentence custody. In Canada, this has been a matter of judicial discretion, but the usual practice was to grant an enhanced credit of two days for each day spent in pre-sentence custody. In 2009, Parliament enacted the Truth in Sentencing Act which reduced credit for pre-sentence custody to a maximum of one and a half days credit for each day in pre-sentence custody unless the reason for the refusal of bail was stated by the bail judge to be a prior conviction, in which case the credit would not be enhanced; it would be one for one. In this case, a constitutional challenge was brought to the denial of any enhancement where the refusal of bail was stated to be a prior conviction. The restriction on pre-sentence credit had the intended effect of making convicted criminals with prior convictions serve more time in prison, and so it affected liberty. McLachlin C.J., who wrote for the Supreme Court, held that the purpose

[41] *R. v. Heywood*, [1994] 3 S.C.R. 761.

[42] *R. v. Appulonappa*, [2015] 3 S.C.R. 754, 2015 SCC 59, para. 57.

[43] *R. v. Appulonappa*, [2015] 3 S.C.R. 754, 2015 SCC 59, para. 74.

[44] *R. v. Appulonappa*, [2015] 3 S.C.R. 754, 2015 SCC 59, para. 85.

[45] *R. v. Safarzadeh-Markhali*, [2016] 1 S.C.R. 180, 2016 SCC 14. McLachlin C.J. wrote the opinion of the Court. For extended analysis, see M. Moore, "*R. v. Safarzadeh-Markhali*: Elements and implications of the Supreme Court's new rigorous approach to construction of statutory purpose" (2017) 77 S.C.L.R. (2d) 223.

of the law was to enhance public safety and security, and the law was overbroad because the existence of a prior conviction was an "inexact proxy for the danger that an offender poses to public safety and security",[46] and this was reinforced by the absence of judicial review of the bail judge's finding of a prior conviction.[47]

The Supreme Court dealt with another sentencing-related overbreadth challenge one year later in *R. v. Boutilier* (2017).[48] This case involved the "dangerous offender" provisions of the Criminal Code. These provisions were first enacted in 1977, and then amended in 1996, and again in 2008. Mr. Boutilier, who the Crown sought (ultimately successfully) to have designated a dangerous offender, challenged several aspects of the dangerous offender provisions under s. 7 of the Charter on the basis that they were overbroad.[49] Boutilier argued that one of the key dangerous offender provisions was overbroad because, on his reading, the 2008 amendments to the provision prevented a sentencing judge from considering future treatment options before designating an offender dangerous, with the result that the provision could capture offenders who may cease to pose a threat to public safety in the future, after successful treatment. Boutilier also argued that another of the key dangerous offender provisions was overbroad because it carries the risk of indeterminate detention for offenders who could have been dealt with under the long-term offender regime in the Criminal Code (which does not contemplate indeterminate detention). Côté J., who wrote for the majority of the Court, rejected both overbreadth arguments. The first overbreadth argument could not succeed because, properly interpreted, the relevant provision not only permitted, but required sentencing judges to consider future treatment options before designating an offender dangerous. As a result, it did not capture offenders who may cease to be a threat to public safety in the future, after successful treatment.[50] The second overbreadth argument could not succeed because the dangerous offender criteria are "more onerous" than the long-term offender criteria, and thus the two regimes do not "target the same offenders".[51] Côté J. went on to find that the trial judge had not erred in designating Boutilier a dangerous offender, or in sentencing him to the indeterminate detention the designation allows.

---

[46]*R. v. Safarzadeh-Markhali*, [2016] 1 S.C.R. 180, 2016 SCC 14, para. 53.

[47]Compare *Ewert v. Canada*, [2018] 2 S.C.R. 165 (psychological and actuarial risk assessment tests used by the Correctional Service of Canada to make decisions about inmates not overbroad, despite "uncertainty about the extent to which the tests are accurate when applied to Indigenous offenders").

[48]*R. v. Boutilier*, [2017] 2 S.C.R. 936. Côté J. wrote the opinion for the majority of the Court, which was joined by McLachlin C.J. and Abella, Moldaver, Wagner, Gascon, Brown and Rowe JJ. Karakatsanis J. wrote an opinion dissenting in part.

[49]Boutilier also invoked s. 12 of the Charter. This aspect of the case is discussed later in this book: see ch. 53, Cruel and Unusual Punishment, under heading § 53:5, "Indeterminate sentence".

[50]Côté J. did imply that constitutional concerns may have arisen if this prospective analysis had been removed: [2017] 2 S.C.R. 936, para. 46.

[51][2017] 2 S.C.R. 936, para. 75.

XVI. DISPROPORTIONATE LAWS

§ 47:25 Disproportionate laws

The doctrine of overbreadth (previous § 47:24) has, despite my criticisms, become established as one of the breaches of the principles of fundamental justice, and it has been joined by two other related doctrines: gross disproportionality (this § 47.16) and arbitrariness (next § 47.17) which are also breaches of the principles of fundamental justice. Any (or all) of these doctrines will lead to a breach of s. 7 by a law that deprives anyone of life, liberty or security of the person. Hamish Stewart has identified the common features of the three doctrines as a "failure of instrumental rationality",[1] by which he means that the Court accepts the objective of a challenged law, but reviews the policy instrument enacted as the means to achieve the objective. If the policy instrument is not a rational means to achieve the objective, then the law is dysfunctional in terms of its own objective. In *Canada v. Bedford* (2013),[2] which is discussed more fully later in this section, McLachlin C.J. attempted to articulate the kind and degree of dysfunctionality that would condemn a law as arbitrary, overbroad, or grossly disproportionate.[3] Her taxonomy was as follows. If the law has no connection to its objective, then the s. 7 deprivation will be "arbitrary". If a law includes some conduct that has no connection to its objective, then it is arbitrary in those applications, but if it also includes other applications that are connected to the objective, then the s. 7 deprivation is classified as "overbreadth". If a law has a connection to its objective, but the s. 7 deprivation is so severe as to be out of all proportion to the objective, then the s. 7 deprivation is classified as "grossly disproportionate". As these sections of the book demonstrate, the three doctrines are powerful tools of judicial review (substantive due process in spades), which confer great power (and great discretion) on the Court to strike down laws affecting life, liberty or security of the person that the Court is persuaded are mistaken.

The topic of this section of the book is disproportionate laws. The doctrine of disproportionality got its start in *R. v. Malmo-Levine* (2003).[4] The doctrine of disproportionality, according to the majority of the Court, requires the Court to determine: (1) whether a law pursues a "legitimate

---

[Section 47:25]

[1]Stewart, Fundamental Justice (2012), 151.

[2]*Canada v. Bedford*, [2013] 3 S.C.R. 1101, 2013 SCC 72, paras. 96-123; the disproportionality part of the case is discussed at § 47:25.

[3]Before this clarification no one knew what were the elements of each doctrine, or the distinctions between them. See, for example, the differences of opinion in *R. v. Malmo-Levine*, [2003] 3 S.C.R. 571, paras. 135-183 (arbitrariness and disproportionality are two doctrines), paras. 277-280, 289-302 (disproportionality is the test for arbitrariness) and *R. v. Khawaja*, [2012] 3 S.C.R. 555, paras. 38-40 (wondering whether disproportionality and overbreadth are distinct doctrines). The different possibilities are analyzed by Stewart, Fundamental Justice (2012), 150-155.

[4]*R. v. Malmo-Levine*, [2003] 3 S.C.R. 571. The opinion of the majority was written by Gonthier and Binnie JJ. Dissenting opinions were written by Arbour, LeBel and Deschamps JJ.

state interest"; and, if it does, (2) whether the law is grossly disproportionate to the state interest.[5] As a preliminary point, one may note that this doctrine, like its sister "overbreadth" (discussed in the previous section of this chapter), is really an authority for the Court to undertake a review of the wisdom of legislative policy.

The issue in *Malmo-Levine* was the criminalization (with the possibility of imprisonment) of the possession of marihuana. Obedient to its self-defined mandate to examine the proportionality of the challenged law, the Court asked whether there was a legitimate state interest in the prohibition of marihuana use (yes was the answer), and whether the prohibition of possession was too extreme a response to that state interest. On the latter point, the majority concluded that it was not, so that there was no disproportionality, and no breach of s. 7. LeBel and Deschamps JJ., however, dissented on this point, holding that "the harm caused by using the criminal law to punish the simple use of marihuana far outweighs the benefits that its prohibition can bring".[6] On that basis, namely, a simple disagreement with the legislative policy with respect to marihuana, they would have struck down the law for breach of s. 7.

Canada v. PHS Community Services Society (Insite) (2011),[7] was another drug case arising out of the criminalization of drug use. Insite was a safe-injection clinic established under provincial law and located in the city of Vancouver. It provided a safe and supervised environment with trained staff and clean equipment (but not drugs) to enable drug addicts to inject their illegal drugs, mainly heroin and cocaine (which they had to bring with them). The clinic was very successful in reducing deaths by overdose, reducing injuries from incompetent injections, and reducing the spread of infectious disease from shared equipment. The federal Controlled Drugs and Substances Act prohibited, with a penalty of imprisonment, the possession of proscribed drugs (which included cocaine and heroin), and the clinic could not operate if the criminal prohibition were applied to it. Initially this problem was solved by the federal Minister of Health, who, under s. 56 of the Act, had the discretion to grant exemptions from the Act "if, in the opinion of the Minister, the exemption is necessary for a medical or scientific purpose or is otherwise in the public interest". The Minister granted an exemption to Insite on a trial basis. After a change of policy by a new federal government, and despite the evidence of the benign effects of the clinic, the new Minister refused to extend the exemption, which would have forced the closing of the clinic. The operator of the clinic and two of its patients brought proceedings for a declaration that the criminal prohibition of possession was, in its application to Insite, an infringement of s. 7 of the

[5] *R. v. Malmo-Levine*, [2003] 3 S.C.R. 571, para. 143.

[6] *R. v. Malmo-Levine*, [2003] 3 S.C.R. 571, para. 301 per Deschamps J.; see also 280 per LeBel J. The other dissenting judge, Arbour J., would also have struck down the law under s. 7, but on the basis of a "harm principle" that she alone found to be a principle of fundamental justice.

[7] *Canada v. PHS Community Services Society*, [2011] 3 S.C.R. 134. McLachlin C.J. wrote the opinion of the unanimous Court.

Charter. The Supreme Court of Canada held that the Act did indeed impair the "liberty" of the staff and patients of the clinic (who would all be vulnerable to the penalty of imprisonment for possession), as well as the "life" and "security of the person" of the patients (who would lose their access to a safe venue for injections). However, the Act itself was not in breach of the principles of fundamental justice, because the prohibition of possession was qualified by the power to grant exemptions in s. 56, which could prevent the Act from applying where its application would be "grossly disproportionate" or "arbitrary".[8] In this case, however, the Minister had denied an exemption to Insite, thereby reimposing the criminal prohibition on the clinic. The Minister's decision to deny the exemption was a denial of the principles of fundamental justice because it disregarded the evidence that Insite had saved lives and prevented injury and disease without any countervailing adverse effects on public safety. The effect of the Minister's decision (the closure of Insite) was "grossly disproportionate" to any state interest in maintaining an absolute prohibition of possession of illegal drugs on Insite's premises.[9] The Minister's decision was also "arbitrary, undermining the very purposes of [the Act], which include public health and safety".[10] The Minister was obliged to exercise his discretion under s. 56 in compliance with s. 7, and had failed to do so. Since the evidence indicated that there was only one Charter-compliant choice, the Court ordered the Minister to grant an exemption to Insite "forthwith".

Canada v. Bedford (2013)[11] was a challenge to three prostitution-related provisions in the federal Criminal Code. Prostitution itself was not a criminal offence, either for the seller or the buyer of sexual services; prostitution was therefore a lawful occupation. But it was an offence (1) to "live wholly or in part on the avails of prostitution of another person"; (2) to communicate with any person in a public place "for the purpose of prostitution"; and (3) to keep or be found in a "common bawdy house", which was a place that is used for "the purpose of prostitution". The Supreme Court held that all three provisions impaired "security of the person" because each of them had the effect of preventing prostitutes from taking sensible precautions to reduce the risk of the physical violence to which they were subject.[12] The Court went on to hold that all three provisions were contrary to the principles of fundamental justice and therefore in breach of s. 7. The infirmity of the living-off-the-avails provision was that the prohibition extended beyond those who would exploit prostitutes, for example, controlling and abusive pimps, and also covered those who would increase the safety and security of prostitutes,

---

[8] *Canada v. PHS Community Services Society*, [2011] 3 S.C.R. 134, para. 113. The topic of "arbitrary laws" is discussed in the next section of this chapter: § 47:26, "Arbitrary laws".

[9] *Canada v. PHS Community Services Society*, [2011] 3 S.C.R. 134, para. 136.

[10] *Canada v. PHS Community Services Society*, [2011] 3 S.C.R. 134, para. 136.

[11] *Canada v. Bedford*, [2013] 3 S.C.R. 1101, 2013 SCC 72. McLachlin C.J. wrote the opinion of the Court.

[12] For discussion, see § 47:12, "Security of the person".

for example, legitimate drivers or bodyguards. By prohibiting some conduct that bore no relation to the legislative purpose of preventing the exploitation of prostitutes, the provision was overbroad and contrary to the principles of fundamental justice for that reason; this reasoning was described in the previous section of the book.[13] The other two provisions fell on the sword of disproportionality.[14] The communicating-in-public provision had as its object the prevention of street nuisance, but had the effect of criminalizing any attempt by street prostitutes to screen potential customers by talking to them in a public place before getting into a vehicle or going to a private place. The bawdy-house provision had as its object the prevention of neighbourhood disorder, but had the effect of criminalizing all prostitution in a fixed indoor location (including the prostitute's own home) which could include security measures and would in any case be safer than the streets. Both these provisions increased the risks faced by prostitutes to an extent that was grossly disproportionate to the objectives of the provisions.[15] The Court struck down all three provisions, but postponed the declaration of invalidity for 12 months to allow for Parliament to amend the provisions.[16]

Proportionality is a guiding principle of sentencing: the sentencing judge should impose a fit sentence having regard to all relevant factors. In *R. v. Lloyd* (2016),[17] the defendant was charged with a drug offence for which the federal Controlled Drugs and Substances Act imposed a mandatory minimum sentence of 12 months. He successfully attacked the mandatory minimum as grossly disproportionate under s. 12 (cruel and unusual punishment).[18] But he also argued that proportionality in sentencing was a principle of fundamental justice and the sentence was

---

[13]For discussion, see § 47:24, "Overbroad laws".

[14]A complication was that the communicating-in-public and bawdy-house provisions had been upheld by the Court in *Re ss. 193 and 195.1 of the Criminal Code* (Prostitution Reference) [1990] 1 S.C.R. 1123. In that case, arguments based on s. 7 were rejected. In *Canada v. Bedford*, [2013] 3 S.C.R. 1101, 2013 SCC 72, para. 45, the Court held that the s. 7 reasoning of the earlier Prostitution Reference was not binding on it (or even on the lower courts) because the doctrines of arbitrariness, overbreadth and disproportionality had developed "only in the last 20 years". The s. 2(b) reasoning in the earlier Prostitution Reference was however binding on the lower courts (para. 46), and it was not necessary to determine whether it was binding on the Supreme Court itself because "it is possible to resolve the case entirely on s. 7 grounds" (paras. 47, 160). For discussion, see ch. 8, Supreme Court of Canada, under heading § 8:13, "Precedent".

[15]It was in fact not entirely clear what the objectives of the provisions were. The Court relied on dicta in earlier cases rather than legislative history, but the Court summarily rejected the Attorney General's argument that the objective of the provisions was to deter prostitution. If that objective had been accepted, it would have been difficult to make the disproportionality arguments that the Court accepted. As in the case of overbreadth, the Court's construction of the legislative objective is critical to the result.

[16]An account of the sequel legislation is in ch. 40, Enforcement of Rights, under heading § 40:4, "Temporary validity".

[17]*R. v. Lloyd*, [2016] 1 S.C.R. 130, 2016 SCC 13. McLachlin C.J. wrote the majority opinion, which was agreed to by the dissenting judges (para. 61) on the issue discussed in this section of the text.

[18]This part of the decision is described in ch. 53, Cruel and Unusual Punishment, under heading § 53:4, "Minimum sentence".

invalid under s. 7 as well as s. 12. The Supreme Court rejected this argument. McLachlin C.J., who wrote for a Court that was unanimous on the point, denied that proportionality in sentencing was a principle of fundamental justice. She pointed out that s. 7 should be read consistently with s. 12. The defendant's interpretation of s. 7 "would set a new constitutional standard for sentencing laws—a standard that is lower than the cruel and unusual punishment standard prescribed by s. 12."[19] It would be incoherent if s. 7 set a lower standard of review of sentences than s. 12. She concluded that proportionality in sentencing, although a very important principle of criminal law, is not a principle of fundamental justice under s. 7, and that the challenged mandatory minimum did not violate s. 7.[20]

XVII. ARBITRARY LAWS

§ 47:26 Arbitrary laws

In *Chaoulli v. Quebec* (2005),[1] a constitutional challenge was brought to Quebec's prohibition on the purchase of private health care insurance. The purpose and effect of the prohibition was to make the universal public health care plan exclusive. The evidence established that there were excessive delays in seeking treatment through the public health care system, and yet for all but the very rich (who could travel outside Canada for treatment) persons needing treatment were effectively precluded from obtaining timely care privately. The Supreme Court of Canada held unanimously that the failure to provide timely care in the public system led to breaches of the right to life (since delays sometimes increased the risk of death) and the right to security of the person (since delays prolonged pain and stress). In these circumstances, was a prohibition on the purchase of private health care insurance a breach of the principles of fundamental justice under s. 7? The seven-judge bench split evenly (three-three) on this issue. One judge, Deschamps J., declined to decide the issue, because she held that the law was in breach of the Quebec Charter of Human Rights and Freedoms, and that it was not necessary to consider the Canadian Charter. Her opinion created a majority in favour of striking down the Quebec law, but by confining her opinion to the Quebec Charter she denied national effect to the ruling. It will take another case to determine the validity of the legal restrictions

---

[19] *R. v. Lloyd*, [2016] 1 S.C.R. 130 at para. 41.

[20] Accord, *R. v. Safarzadeh-Markhali*, [2016] 1 S.C.R. 180, 2016 SCC 14, para. 73.

[Section 47:26]

[1] *Chaoulli v. Quebec*, [2005] 1 S.C.R. 791. Three opinions were written. McLachlin and Major J., with the agreement of Bastarache J., wrote what became the majority opinion. Deschamps J. wrote a separate concurring opinion. Binnie and LeBel JJ., with the agreement of Fish J., wrote a dissenting opinion. I disclose that I appeared as counsel in the case for an intervener who argued that a prohibition of private health care was a breach of s. 7 if the public system could not provide necessary treatment in a timely fashion.

on access to private health care that exist in the other provinces and territories.[2]

On the issue of fundamental justice, the Court was evenly divided. For McLachlin C.J. and Major J. (writing with the agreement of Bastarache J.) the Quebec law prohibiting private health insurance offended the principles of fundamental justice, because it was "arbitrary". They posited a somewhat different test from the test of disproportionality that the Court had recently laid down in *Malmo-Levine* (described in the previous section of this chapter). According to the McLachlin-Major opinion, a law is arbitrary if it "lacks a real connection on the facts to the purpose the [law] is said to serve".[3] That was the case here, because the evidence showed that other developed countries with universal public health care plans permitted parallel access to private care without injury to the public health system. The dissenting Binnie-LeBel opinion agreed that arbitrary laws were offensive to fundamental justice, and also agreed with the McLachlin-Major definition of arbitrary laws.[4] But the Binnie-LeBel opinion relied on expert evidence that the development of a private system would divert resources away from the public system, ultimately reducing the quality of the public health system. For them, the discouragement of private health care was a rational means of supporting the public health care system, and was therefore not arbitrary. Deschamps J., who could have broken the tie, confined herself to the Quebec Charter, which guaranteed personal inviolability (equivalent to security of the person) without the need to show a breach of the principles of fundamental justice. However, she held that, in light of the breach of personal inviolability caused by the delays in the public system, the ban on private insurance could not be justified under the Quebec equivalent of s. 1 of the Charter. She rejected the theory that private health care is a threat to a healthy public system, and the tenor of her opinion was similar to that of the McLachlin-Major opinion.[5]

There is a puzzling passage in the Binnie-LeBel dissenting opinion that may indicate some common ground between the dissent and the majority. Paragraph 264 reads (in full):

> The safety valve (however imperfectly administered) of allowing Quebec residents to obtain essential health care outside the province when they are unable to receive the care in question at home in a timely way is of importance. If, as the appellants' claim, the safety valve is opened too sparingly, the courts are available to supervise enforcement of the rights of

---

[2]There have been several unsuccessful challenges to the bans on private health insurance in other provinces: see further, § 47:12, "Security of the person", above.

[3]*Chaoulli v. Quebec*, [2005] 1 S.C.R. 791, para. 134.

[4]*Chaoulli v. Quebec*, [2005] 1 S.C.R. 791, para. 233.

[5]*Can. v. PHS Community Services Society*, [2011] 3 S.C.R. 134, discussed at § 47:25, was decided on the basis that the Minister's decision was both "grossly disproportionate" and "arbitrary". On the latter ground, McLachlin C.J. followed *Chaoulli*, while acknowledging (para. 132) differences between the McLachlin-Major and Binnie-LeBel definitions of arbitrary; the Minister's action in *PHS*, she said, "qualifies as arbitrary under both definitions".

> those patients who are directly affected by the decision on a case-by-case basis. Judicial intervention at this level on a case-by-case basis is preferable to acceptance of the appellants' global challenge to the entire single-tier health plan. It is important to emphasize that rejection of the appellants' global challenge to Quebec's health plan would not foreclose individual patients from seeking individual relief tailored to their individual circumstances.

In this passage, the reference to "the rights" of patients and the general tenor of the last two sentences seem to imply a *constitutional* right to receive timely health care. It is certainly a clear invitation to litigation by patients on waiting lists (however impractical that may often be). When the invitation is taken up, perhaps the courts will tease out the meaning of this apparent contradiction in the dissenting opinion.

In *A.C. v. Manitoba* (2009),[6] a constitutional challenge was brought to Manitoba's Child and Family Services Act, which contained powers to apprehend a child in need of protection and to apply to a court for an order imposing medical treatment that "the court considers to be in the best interests of the child". For a child aged 16 or over, no treatment order could be made unless the court was satisfied that the child lacked the capacity to give consent to treatment. But no such presumption of capacity applied to children under 16. In this case, A.C., a 14-year-old girl who was a Jehovah's Witness, refused her consent to a blood transfusion that hospital doctors regarded as urgently necessary to protect her from death or serious damage. Under the statutory powers, she was apprehended, and a judge ordered the blood transfusion. The judge recognized that A.C., although only 14, was sufficiently mature to make decisions about her medical treatment, but he decided nevertheless that, in light of the danger to her life or long-term health, the blood transfusion would be in her best interests. The treatment was given, and A.C. recovered. Although the validity of the treatment order was moot, A.C. (and her parents) appealed the order as a means of challenging the constitutionality of the statutory power to override the child's wishes with respect to medical treatment. The challenge was based on s. 7 (as well as ss. 2(a) and 15).[7] There was no doubt that the "liberty" and "security of the person" of A.C. was infringed by the compelled medical treatment. A.C. argued that the power to override the wishes of a child under 16 who was sufficiently mature to determine her own medical treatment was a breach of the principles of fundamental justice because it was arbitrary. In the Supreme Court of Canada, this argument was accepted by Binnie J. in dissent. He took the view that there was no valid state purpose to be served by permitting a judge to override the wishes of a mature minor as to her medical treatment. But the other six

[6] *A.C. v. Manitoba*, [2009] 2 S.C.R. 181. Abella J., with the agreement of LeBel, Deschamps and Charron JJ., wrote the opinion of the majority of the seven-judge bench. McLachlin C.J., with the agreement of Rothstein J., wrote a concurring opinion. Binnie J. wrote a dissenting opinion.

[7] The case is discussed with respect to s. 2(a) in ch. 42, Religion, under heading § 42:6, "Other religious practices", above, and with respect to s. 15 in ch. 55, Equality, under heading § 55:44, "Age".

members of the bench rejected the argument and upheld the constitutionality of the statutory power. Abella J., for the majority, agreed that it would be arbitrary to assume that no one under the age of 16 had the capacity to make medical-treatment decisions, but the best-interests standard enabled the judge to take increasingly serious account of the child's own wishes as her age, maturity and independence advanced. That was not arbitrary (and nor was it discriminatory or violative of religious freedom). Abella J. and McLachlin C.J. (who on this point concurred for essentially the same reasons as Abella J.) reaffirmed the McLachlin-Major definition of arbitrariness from *Chaoulli*, namely, that a law was arbitrary if it bore no real connection to the purpose of the law. In this case, the protective purpose of the law was served by the best-interests standard, which enabled the judge to take account of the choice of the child while weighing other considerations bearing on voluntariness such as the effect of parental influence on the choice of a dependent child.

We have already noticed that, in *Canada v. Bedford* (2013),[8] the Supreme Court settled for the first time on definitions of "overbroad laws" (§ 47:24)—"disproportionate laws" (§ 47:25) and "arbitrary laws" (this section), three categories that are all breaches of the principles of fundamental justice, but which before the *Bedford* clarification in 2013 had blurred or even overlapping boundaries. The *Bedford* definition of an "arbitrary law" was one that had no connection to its objective.[9] This definition was confirmed and applied in *R. v. Smith* (2015),[10] in which a constitutional challenge was brought to the Medical Marihuana Access Regulations, which provided an exemption from the criminal prohibitions of the federal Controlled Drugs and Substances Act for persons who had established the usefulness of marihuana for the relief of their medical conditions. The Regulations limited the medical exemption to "dried marihuana", the derivative of the cannabis plant that is inhaled by smoking. The accused was found in possession of cookies and oils that had the same active cannabis-derived ingredient as marihuana, and which were intended for sale to users of medical marihuana, in defiance of the restricted scope of the regulatory exemption. He was charged with possession of illegal drugs under the Act, and he defended the charge on the ground that the regulatory exemption was unconstitutional in arbitrarily restricting users of medical marihuana to just the one derivative of the cannabis plant. He succeeded at trial and in the Supreme Court. Based on extensive lay and expert evidence, the trial judge found that the oral and topical derivatives of cannabis were more

---

[8] *Canada v. Bedford*, [2013] 3 S.C.R. 1101, 2013 SCC 72.

[9] On this definition, the "fact that a government practice is in some way unsound or that it fails to further the government objective as effectively as a different course of action would is not sufficient to establish that the government practice is arbitrary": *Ewert v. Canada*, [2018] 2 S.C.R. 165, para 73. The fact that there is uncertainty about the extent to which a law furthers the government objective is also not sufficient to establish that the law is arbitrary: *Ewert v. Canada*, [2018] 2 S.C.R. 165, para. 73.

[10] *R. v. Smith*, [2015] 2 S.C.R. 602, 2015 SCC 34. The opinion was given by "the Court".

effective for some medical conditions then the inhaling of marihuana smoke and they also lacked the harmful side effects of smoking. The Supreme Court accepted these findings. The Court held that the Regulations, by restricting medical marihuana users to dried marihuana, deprived them of the choice of the products which might be the most suitable for their condition; that was a breach of "liberty" and "security of the person" under s. 7. That left the question whether the Regulations were arbitrary. The Court held that the objective of the Regulations was the protection of the health and safety of the patients who qualified for legal access to medical marihuana. But the prohibition of potentially useful cannabis derivatives other than dried marihuana had no connection to that objective: the prohibition actually "undermined" the objective, indeed "contradicted" it, "rendering it arbitrary" within the *Bedford* definition.[11] The Regulations were therefore in breach of the principles of fundamental justice and were accordingly invalid.[12]

XVIII. VAGUE LAWS

§ 47:27 Void for vagueness

A vague law[1] violates the principles of fundamental justice, which causes a breach of s. 7 if the law is a deprivation of life, liberty or security of the person. A vague law offends two values that are fundamental to the legal system. First, the law does not provide fair notice to persons of what is prohibited, which makes it difficult for them to comply with the law. Secondly, the law does not provide clear standards for those entrusted with enforcement, which may lead to arbitrary enforcement.

In the *Prostitution Reference* (1990),[2] it was argued (among other things) that the offence of communicating for the purpose of engaging in prostitution was in breach of s. 7, because the offence was unconstitutionally vague. The Supreme Court of Canada, while acknowledging that the prohibition was "broad and far reaching", denied that it was so

---

[11]*R. v. Smith*, [2015] 2 S.C.R. 602, 2015 SCC 34, para. 25.

[12]See also *Ewert v. Canada*, [2018] 2 S.C.R. 165 (psychological and actuarial risk assessment tests used by the Correctional Service of Canada to make decisions about inmates not arbitrary, despite "uncertainty about the extent to which the tests are accurate when applied to Indigenous offenders").

[Section 47:27]

[1]Vagueness can also have an invalidating effect under the federal distribution of powers, because it can cause difficulty in classifying the law as in relation to a matter coming within one of the heads of power of the enacting legislative body: *Saumur v. Que.*, [1953] 2 S.C.R. 299, 333; discussed in ch. 15, Judicial Review on Federal Grounds, under heading § 15:26, "Exhaustiveness". Vagueness also does not satisfy the requirement "prescribed by law" in s. 1 of the Charter, which means that a vague law in derogation of a Charter right cannot be saved by s. 1: ch. 38, Limitation of Rights, under heading § 38:9, "Vagueness".

[2]*Re ss. 193 and 195.1 of Criminal Code* (Prostitution Reference) [1990] 1 S.C.R. 1123. The discussion of vagueness is in the concurring judgment of Lamer J., with whom Dickson C.J. for the majority agreed on this issue. Wilson J., dissenting in the result, also rejected the argument based on vagueness, but did not express agreement (or disagreement) with Lamer J.

vague that a court could not give "sensible meaning" to its terms.[3] This attack on the provision was therefore rejected, as were the attacks based on freedom of expression and freedom of association.

In *United Nurses of Alberta v. Alberta* (1992),[4] it was argued that the criminal offence of contempt of court was unconstitutionally vague under s. 7. The offence of contempt of court is unique in Canada in that it has not been reduced to statutory form. Section 9 of the Criminal Code, while abolishing common law offences, makes an exception for contempt of court, which accordingly survives as a common law offence. The Supreme Court of Canada held that it was not a requirement of fundamental justice that a criminal offence be codified in statutory form. Although the elements of the common law offence were not as clear as could be achieved in a statutory definition, the offence was "neither vague nor arbitrary".[5]

In *R. v. Nova Scotia Pharmaceutical Society* (1992),[6] the Competition Act offence of conspiring to lessen competition "unduly" was attacked under s. 7 on the ground that the crucial word "unduly" was unconstitutionally vague. Once again, the argument was rejected by the Supreme Court of Canada. Gonthier J., for a unanimous Court, reviewed the cases that had interpreted the word "unduly", and concluded that "Parliament has sufficiently delineated the area of risk and the terms of debate to meet the constitutional standard".[7]

In *Ontario v. Canadian Pacific* (1995),[8] a challenge was brought to a provision in Ontario's Environmental Protection Act, which made it an offence to discharge a "contaminant" into the "natural environment" that could impair the quality of the environment "for any use that can be made of it". It was argued that the controlling concepts of "contaminant", "natural environment" and "use" were so vague that the offence was void for vagueness under s. 7. Gonthier J., for a Court that was unanimous on this issue, held that, although the legislation was very broad and general, its scope was "reasonably delineated" so that "legal debate can occur as to the application of the provision in a specific fact

[3] *Re ss. 193 and 195.1 of Criminal Code* (Prostitution Reference) [1990] 1 S.C.R. 1123, 1160.

[4] *United Nurses of Alberta v. Alberta*, [1992] 1 S.C.R. 901. The majority opinion was written by McLachlin J. Dissenting opinions were written by Cory and Sopinka JJ., but they did not discuss the vagueness issue.

[5] *United Nurses of Alberta v. Alberta*, [1992] 1 S.C.R. 901, 933.

[6] *R. v. Nova Scotia Pharmaceutical Society*, [1992] 2 S.C.R. 606. Gonthier J. delivered the opinion of the Court.

[7] *R. v. Nova Scotia Pharmaceutical Society*, [1992] 2 S.C.R. 606, 657.

[8] *Ontario v. Canadian Pacific*, [1995] 2 S.C.R. 1031. The majority opinion was written by Gonthier J., with whom La Forest, L'Heureux-Dubé, McLachlin, Iacobucci and Major JJ. agreed. A concurring opinion was written by Lamer C.J., with whom Sopinka and Cory JJ. agreed.

situation".[9] That was all that s. 7 required, and the challenge therefore failed.[10]

As was related in the previous section of this chapter, in the *Canadian Pacific* case, the law was also challenged for overbreadth. An overbreadth challenge relies, not on the vagueness of the law, but on the argument that the terms of the law are broader than is necessary to accomplish the purpose of the law. It will be recalled that the analysis employed by the Court to determine the overbreadth argument, is to examine hypothetical cases. If a hypothetical case can be imagined that is outside the purpose of the law, but is nevertheless caught by the terms of the law, then the law is overbroad and is unconstitutional in its entirety. I have already made the comment that the use of imaginary hypothetical cases makes it difficult to defend a law against a claim of overbreadth (although the claim was, with difficulty, successfully defended in the *Canadian Pacific* case). The Court in *Canadian Pacific* made an important distinction between overbreadth and vagueness. In the case of vagueness, the use of hypothetical cases is not permitted. Once the law has been determined to apply to the defendant on the facts of the case before the court, the defendant is not permitted to point to the vagueness of the law in its application to other (hypothetical) cases not before the court. As explained in the previous section of this chapter, I believe the same rule of restraint should have been applied to the overbreadth argument, but at least the issue is settled correctly for the vagueness argument: the use of hypothetical cases is not permitted.

§ 47:28 Standard of precision

What is the "constitutional standard" of precision that a law must meet in order to avoid the vice of vagueness? In the *Nova Scotia Pharmaceutical* case, Gonthier J. said:[1]

> A vague provision does not provide an adequate basis for legal debate, that is for reaching a conclusion as to its meaning by reasoned analysis applying legal criteria. It does not sufficiently delineate any area of risk, and thus can provide neither fair notice to the citizen nor a limitation of enforcement discretion. Such a provision is not intelligible, to use the terminology of previous decisions of this Court, and, therefore it fails to give sufficient indications that could fuel a legal debate.

A number of tests are suggested in this passage: whether the law is "intelligible", whether the law sufficiently delineates "an area of risk", and whether the law provides "an adequate basis for legal debate". Of these, the last—the legal debate test—seems to me to be the least useful, because almost any provision, no matter how vague, could provide a

[9] *Ontario v. Canadian Pacific*, [1995] 2 S.C.R. 1031, para. 70.

[10] See also *Winko v. B.C.*, [1999] 2 S.C.R. 625, paras. 68-69 (vagueness argument rejected on basis that challenged provision provided "sufficient guidance for legal debate").

[Section 47:28]

[1] *R. v. Nova Scotia Pharmaceutical Society*, [1992] 2 S.C.R. 606.

basis for legal debate. However, it was the legal debate test that Gonthier J. evidently preferred, that he applied in his conclusion, and that the Supreme Court of Canada has employed in subsequent cases.[2]

What is perhaps most useful in giving some content to the rule against vagueness is to refer back to the two values that the rule protects, namely, fair notice to citizens and limitation of enforcement discretion. A law is unconstitutionally vague if it fails to give fair notice of what conduct is prohibited by the law, and if it fails to impose real limitations on the discretion of those charged with enforcement of the law. These are the standards that are intended to be captured by the various shorthand tests, including the legal debate test.[3]

However formulated, the constitutional standard of precision cannot be very exacting.[4] Gonthier J. in the *Nova Scotia Pharmaceutical* case said that it was important not to require a law "to achieve a standard of precision to which the subject matter does not lend itself."[5] Certainly, there is no requirement that a law be "absolutely certain", because "no

---

[2]*R. v. Morales*, [1992] 3 S.C.R. 711; *Ontario v. Canadian Pacific*, [1995] 2 S.C.R. 1031; *R. v. Finta*, [1994] 1 S.C.R. 701 (rejecting vagueness attack on Criminal Code's war-crimes provisions); *Ruffo v. Conseil de la Magistrature*, [1995] 4 S.C.R. 267 (rejecting vagueness attack on Quebec Courts of Justice Act requirement that judges act in a "reserved manner"); *Can. Foundation for Children, Youth and the Law v. Can.*, [2004] 1 S.C.R. 76 (rejecting vagueness attack on Criminal Code's exemption for teachers and parents who apply reasonable force by way of correction against children).

[3]Accord, *Suresh v. Can.*, [2002] 1 S.C.R. 3, paras. 80-99 (holding that the phrases "danger to the security of Canada" and "terrorism" in the deportation provisions of the Immigration Act are not unconstitutionally vague by reference to the two values).

[4]A vagueness argument has never so far led to invalidity. Vagueness arguments were rejected in the following cases: *Re ss. 193 and 195.1 of Criminal Code* (Prostitution Reference) [1990] 1 S.C.R. 1123 (communicating for the purpose of engaging in prostitution); *R. v. Butler*, [1992] 1 S.C.R. 452 ("undue exploitation of sex"); *United Nurses of Alberta v. Alberta*, [1992] 1 S.C.R. 901 (common law offence of contempt); *R. v. Nova Scotia Pharmaceutical Society*, [1992] 2 S.C.R. 606 (lessening competition "unduly"); *Young v. Young*, [1993] 4 S.C.R. 3 ("best interests of the child"); *Ontario v. Canadian Pacific*, [1995] 2 S.C.R. 1031 (discharging a "contaminant" that "is likely to cause impairment of the natural environment for any use that can be made of it"); *Suresh v. Can.*, [2002] 1 S.C.R. 3 ("danger to the security of Canada", member of organization engaged in "terrorism"); *Canadian Foundation for Children, Youth and the Law v. Canada*, [2004] 1 S.C.R. 76 ("reasonable" force "by way of correction"); *Harper v. Can.*, [2004] 1 S.C.R. 827 (restriction on promotion of candidates with which one is "associated"); *Can. v. JTI-Macdonald Corp.*, [2007] 2 S.C.R. 610 ("likely to create an erroneous impression about the characteristics, health effects or health hazards of the. . .product or its emissions"); *Cochrane v. Ont.* (2008), 92 O.R. (3d) 321 (C.A.) (ban on "pit bulls", not a recognized breed); *R. v. Tse*, [2012] 1 S.C.R. 531 ("the urgency of the situation", "reasonable diligence", "unlawful act", "serious harm"); *R. v. Levkovic*, [2013] 2 S.C.R. 204 ("child [that] died before. . .birth"); *Wakeling v. United States of America*, [2014] 3 S.C.R. 549 ("where disclosure . . . is intended to be in the interests of the administration of justice in Canada or elsewhere"); *R v. Conception*, [2014] 3 S.C.R. 82 (consent requirement).

[5]*R. v. Nova Scotia Pharmaceutical Society*, [1992] 2 S.C.R. 606, 642; accord *Ruffo v. Conseil de la Magistrature*, [1995] 4 S.C.R. 267, para. 111-112 (judicial duty to act in a "reserved manner" is an ethical principle which defies a more precise definition).

law can meet that standard."[6] Nor is the vagueness doctrine offended if a law is open to more than one interpretation. A law is unconstitutionally vague only if it cannot, even with judicial interpretation, provide meaningful standards of conduct.[7]

To what extent is it possible for a court to repair potentially unconstitutional vagueness by interpreting a challenged law to supply more precision? Obviously, the nature of language is such that interpretation is often required to provide standards of conduct that are meaningful. This is a normal and necessary judicial function. But where does interpretation end and redrafting begin? That was the question in *Canadian Foundation for Children, Youth and the Law v. Canada* (2004),[8] which was a challenge to s. 43 of the Criminal Code, a provision that provides a defence to a charge of assault for teachers and parents who apply "reasonable" force "by way of correction" against the children in their charge. There was little doubt, based on the numerous cases decided by lower courts, which were described in Arbour J.'s dissenting opinion, that s. 43 had not in the past provided meaningful standards of conduct for teachers and parents. In many cases, defendants had been acquitted despite their use of violent, abusive or ineffective force against children, including the use of corporal punishment against children under two and against teenagers, blows to the face or head and the use of belts and other instruments. McLachlin C.J. for the majority of the Supreme Court of Canada ignored the large body of case law in the lower courts which had given s. 43 this broad reach, and instead relied on expert evidence as to the efficacy of corporal punishment against children. Based on that evidence, she issued a new interpretation of the section:[9]

> Generally, s. 43 exempts from criminal sanction only minor corrective force of a transitory and trifling nature. *On the basis of current expert consensus*, it does not apply to corporal punishment of children under two or teenagers. Degrading, inhuman or harmful conduct is not protected. Discipline by the use of objects or blows or slaps to the head is unreasonable. Teachers may reasonably apply force to remove a child from a classroom or secure compliance with instructions, but not merely as corporal punishment. . . . The gravity of the precipitating event is not relevant.

So interpreted, she held that s. 43 "sets real boundaries and delineates a risk zone for criminal sanction" that is a sufficiently clear standard to avoid the charge of unconstitutional vagueness.

Arbour J., dissenting, pointed out that the restrictions on s. 43 that

---

[6] *Re ss. 193 and 195.1 of Criminal Code* (Prostitution Reference) [1990] 1 S.C.R. 1122, 1156.

[7] *Re ss. 193 and 195.1 of Criminal Code* (Prostitution Reference) [1990] 1 S.C.R. 1122, 1157-1161; to the same effect is *R. v. Nova Scotia Pharmaceutical Society*, [1992] 2 S.C.R. 606, 626-627.

[8] *Canadian Foundation for Children, Youth and the Law v. Canada*, [2004] 1 S.C.R. 76. McLachlin C.J. wrote the opinion of the majority. Binnie, Arbour and Deschamps JJ. wrote dissenting opinions.

[9] *Canadian Foundation for Children, Youth and the Law v. Canada*, [2004] 1 S.C.R. 76, para. 40. Emphasis added.

were stipulated by the Chief Justice had "not emerged from the existing case law", were "far from self-evident and would not have been anticipated by many parents, teachers or enforcement officials".[10] In her view, the Chief Justice was not engaged in "mere interpretation", but had drafted "an entirely new provision".[11] In her view, it was wrong to pre-empt the constitutional question in this way. Section 43, as enacted by Parliament was unconstitutionally vague, and the Court should so hold. The other dissenting judges made similar comments about the Chief Justice's reinterpretation of the section. Binnie J. described it as "pushing the boundary between judicial interpretation and judicial amendment".[12] Deschamps J. said that it turned "the exercise of statutory interpretation into one of legislative drafting".[13] Of course, the majority view prevailed, so that s. 43 was upheld—but subject to the restrictions read into it by the Chief Justice.

§ 47:29 Application to other Charter rights

Vagueness, in a law that deprives a person of life, liberty or security of the person, is a breach of s. 7, because it is a principle of fundamental justice that a law should not be too vague. In *R. v. Morales* (1992),[1] the Supreme Court of Canada held that the doctrine of vagueness also applies to s. 11(e) of the Charter. Section 11(e) guarantees the right "not to be denied reasonable bail without just cause." Lamer C.J. for the majority of the Court said that "there cannot be just cause for a denial of bail within the meaning of s. 11(e) if the statutory criteria for denying bail are vague and imprecise".[2] At issue in the *Morales* case was a Criminal Code provision that authorized a judge to deny bail to an accused person on the ground "that his detention is necessary in the public interest." Lamer C.J. acknowledged that the value of "fair notice to the citizen" was "not relevant to a provision . . . which does not prohibit conduct".[3] However, the value of limiting the discretion of those charged with enforcement was relevant. The "public interest" criterion would authorize a "standardless sweep", because under that criterion "a court can

[10]*Canadian Foundation for Children, Youth and the Law v. Canada*, [2004] 1 S.C.R. 76, para. 190.

[11]*Canadian Foundation for Children, Youth and the Law v. Canada*, [2004] 1 S.C.R. 76, para. 190.

[12]*Canadian Foundation for Children, Youth and the Law v. Canada*, [2004] 1 S.C.R. 76, para. 81.

[13]*Canadian Foundation for Children, Youth and the Law v. Canada*, [2004] 1 S.C.R. 76, para. 216 and see also para. 243.

[Section 47:29]

[1]*R. v. Morales*, [1992] 3 S.C.R. 711. Lamer C.J. wrote the majority opinion. Gonthier J. wrote the dissenting opinion, disagreeing on the issue of vagueness.

[2]*R. v. Morales*, [1992] 3 S.C.R. 711, 728.

[3]*R. v. Morales*, [1992] 3 S.C.R. 711, 728.

order imprisonment whenever it sees fit".[4] Lamer C.J. concluded that the bail provision provided "no guidance for legal debate", and was therefore void for vagueness.[5]

Morales makes clear that the doctrine of vagueness is not confined to s. 7, but applies to any Charter right that carries an implicit requirement that laws not be vague. In *Morales*, it was the "just cause" standard in s. 11(e) that called for legislative precision. Similar holdings can be expected under Charter provisions that call for laws that are not unreasonable (s. 8) and laws that are not arbitrary (s. 9); vague laws could not satisfy those standards. Moreover, a law that limits *any* of the guaranteed rights can be upheld under s. 1 only if the limit is "prescribed by law." As had been explained earlier in the book, the requirement that a limit be prescribed by law also calls for fair notice to the citizen and limitations on enforcement discretion. Section 1 cannot be satisfied by a vague law.[6]

XIX. WRONG LAWS

§ 47:30 Wrong laws

In *R. v. Gamble* (1988),[1] the accused was tried and convicted for murder, and sentenced to life imprisonment. She was tried, convicted and sentenced under the Criminal Code provisions in force at the time of the trial, which was a mistake, because those provisions had just come into force, and were not in force at the time of the commission of the offence. Not only had the elements of the offence been changed, so had the rules regarding eligibility for parole. Had she been convicted under the old (correct) law, she would have been eligible for parole after ten years. Under the new (incorrect) law, she was ineligible for parole for 25 years. The trial and conviction took place in 1976, long before the Charter of Rights was in force. In 1986, when the Charter of Rights was in force, and she had served ten years of her sentence, she applied for habeas corpus to remove from her sentence the condition that she be ineligible for parole for 25 years. The Supreme Court of Canada granted the application.

In *Gamble*, Wilson J. for the majority of the Supreme Court of Canada

---

[4] *R. v. Morales*, [1992] 3 S.C.R. 711, 732.

[5] *R. v. Morales*, [1992] 3 S.C.R. 711, 732. After *Morales*, Parliament replaced the invalid public-interest provision with a power to deny bail "on any other just cause being shown" and "where the detention is necessary in order to maintain confidence in the administration of justice". In *R. v. Hall*, [2002] 3 S.C.R. 309, the Supreme Court of Canada held unanimously that the former phrase was still unconstitutionally vague, but held by a majority that the latter phrase was sufficiently precise to be valid.

[6] See heading § 47:27 "Void for vagueness". The standard of precision seems to be the same under s. 1 as it is under ss. 7 and 11(e): *R. v. Nova Scotia Pharmaceutical Society*, [1992] 2 S.C.R. 606, 631.

[Section 47:30]

[1] *R. v. Gamble*, [1988] 2 S.C.R. 595. Wilson J. wrote the opinion of the three-judge majority. Dickson C.J. wrote the opinion of the two-judge dissenting minority.

held that the continued detention of the prisoner without eligibility for parole was a breach of s. 7.[2] The principles of fundamental justice were to be found in "the basic tenets of our legal system".[3] It was a basic tenet of any legal system "that an accused must be tried and punished under the law in force at the time the offence is committed".[4] Since that did not happen in this case, there was a breach of s. 7, and the accused was entitled to be declared eligible for parole immediately.

XX. RIGHT TO SILENCE

§ 47:31 Right to silence

In *R. v. Hebert* (1990),[1] the accused had been arrested and advised of his right to counsel. He did retain counsel, and he advised the police that he did not wish to make a statement. However, he was then placed in custody with an undercover police officer, disguised as another prisoner, who engaged the accused in conversation, and to whom the accused made an incriminating statement. The Supreme Court of Canada held that the statement had been obtained in breach of the Charter. The obvious route to that result was the right to counsel in s. 10(b), because it is clear that the right to counsel is violated if the police continue questioning an accused who has exercised his right to counsel.[2] But the route the Court in fact took was a "right to silence", which was a principle of fundamental justice in s. 7.

In *Hebert*, the right to silence was said to be a "basic tenet of the legal system", although it was no part of the legal system as recently as 1981, when the Court had, in a pre-Charter case,[3] admitted a statement made by an accused to an undercover police officer posing as a prisoner. This new right to silence arose, according to the majority, only upon detention,[4] and it precluded only statements elicited by police questioning. A

[2]Dickson C.J. dissented, on the basis (at 610) that the majority's decision would be "a retrospective application of the Charter".

[3]*R. v. Gamble*, [1988] 2 S.C.R. 595, 647, citing the *B.C. Motor Vehicle Reference*.

[4]*R. v. Gamble*, [1988] 2 S.C.R. 595, 647.

[Section 47:31]

[1]*R. v. Hebert*, [1990] 2 S.C.R. 151. The Court was unanimous; McLachlin J. wrote for seven judges; Sopinka and Wilson JJ. wrote separate concurring opinions.

[2]See ch. 50, Rights on Arrest or Detention, under heading § 50:12, "Duty to refrain from questioning".

[3]*Rothman v. The Queen*, [1981] 1 S.C.R. 640.

[4]*R. v. Hebert*, [1990] 2 S.C.R. 151, 184 per McLachlin J. for majority. Sopinka J.'s concurring opinion held (at 201) that the right arose "whenever the coercive power of the state is brought to bear against the individual—either formally (by arrest or charge) or informally (by detention or accusation)"; according to this view (with which Wilson J. also agreed), the right could arise prior to detention. In *R. v. Broyles*, [1991] 3 S.C.R. 595, 606, discussed in the next paragraph of the text, Iacobucci J. for the Court said that "the right is triggered when the accused is subjected to the coercive powers of the state *through his or her detention*" (my emphasis).

voluntary statement to another prisoner,[5] or even to an undercover police officer,[6] would not offend the right if the police officer did not actively elicit the statement. In this case, however, the accused's statement had been elicited by the questioning of the undercover police officer. In effect, the police had used a trick to subvert the accused's election not to make a statement to the police. This was a breach of s. 7. The statement was excluded.[7]

R. v. Broyles (1991)[8] was another jailhouse confession case. In that case, the accused made a statement while in custody to a friend who visited him in the jail. Unknown to the accused, the friend had been recruited as a police informer, and was wearing a body pack upon which the accused's statement was recorded. These facts differed from *Hebert* in that the informer in *Broyles* was not a police officer. However, the Supreme Court of Canada held that the informer was acting as an agent of the state, and should be covered by the same constitutional restraints as a police officer. Since the recording showed that the informer had actively elicited the statement by his questions to the accused, the statement was obtained in breach of the right to silence. The statement was excluded.

In *R. v. Osmar* (2007),[9] undercover police officers, posing as organized crime figures, offered the accused the opportunity to join their organization. In order to join, however, he had to admit to the commission of a serious crime; that way he would show that he trusted the organization and that he could be counted on to carry out the criminal orders of Mr. Big. He confessed to the murder of two men. At his trial for the murders, the trial judge admitted the confession made to the police officers, and the accused was convicted. The Ontario Court of Appeal dismissed an appeal from the convictions. The confession was correctly admitted as evidence. The right to silence was not triggered by these facts, because the accused was not being detained by the police when he made his confession. The accused was unaware that he was talking to police officers and was not under any form of state coercion. The mere fact that the confession was elicited by police trickery did not engage the right to silence.

---

[5]*R. v. Gray* (1991), 4 O.R. (3d) 33 (C.A.) (statement made to fellow prisoner, who afterwards volunteered it to police, admitted).

[6]*R. v. Logan*, [1990] 2 S.C.R. 731 (statements made to undercover police officers posing as prisoners admitted; Lamer C.J. said (at 737) that the police officers "did not encourage the [accuseds] to talk, but merely provided the opportunity for the making of the statements"); *R. v. Johnston* (1991), 2 O.R. (3d) 771 (C.A.) (statement made to police informer in prison admitted; police informer did not "elicit" statement); *R. v. Liew*, [1999] 3 S.C.R. 227 (same decision).

[7]*Hebert* was distinguished in *R. v. Jones*, [1994] 2 S.C.R. 229 (statements made at pre-trial psychiatric assessment admissible in dangerous offender hearing, because it was a sentencing hearing). See also *R. v. Crawford*, [1995] 1 S.C.R. 858 (accused's pre-trial silence could be used by a co-accused to impeach his testimony at trial, but not as evidence of guilt).

[8]*R. v. Broyles*, [1991] 3 S.C.R. 595. Iacobucci J. wrote the opinion of the Court.

[9]*R. v. Osmar* (2007), 84 O.R. (3d) 321 (C.A.).

In *R. v. Singh* (2007),[10] the accused, while in police custody, was advised by his counsel not to talk to the police. He relayed that advice to the interviewing police officer, who nevertheless continued to go over the evidence with him and engage him in limited conversation. Eventually, when shown pictures of the crime scene (a pub) that had been taken by video surveillance, the accused identified himself in the video. At trial, this evidence was admitted on the basis of a finding by the trial judge that the admission was voluntary,[11] and the accused was convicted of second-degree murder. On appeal, the accused did not contest the finding of voluntariness, but he argued nevertheless that his right to silence under s. 7 had been breached by the police officer continuing to talk to him after he had stated clearly that he did not want to talk to the police. In the Supreme Court of Canada, this argument was accepted by Fish J., writing for the dissenting minority, who would have excluded the statement under s. 24(2) of the Charter. But Charron J., writing for the majority, held that the right to remain silent did not include "the right *not to be spoken to* by state authorities".[12] For a person who (unlike *Osmar)* is in detention and therefore covered by s. 7, but who (unlike *Hebert* and *Broyles)* knows that he is talking to a person in authority, the right to silence is not offended by a voluntary statement. In this case, the accused's statement was not induced by threats, promises, oppression or trickery, and had been found to be voluntary. It was properly admitted in evidence at the trial.

Charron J. in *Singh* distinguished the right to silence under s. 7 from the right to counsel under s. 10(b).[13] The right to counsel is outside the control of an accused who is in police custody; the accused is dependent on the help of the police to exercise the right. This explains why the right to counsel under s. 10(b) has been interpreted as requiring the police to refrain from questioning the accused until he has had a reasonable opportunity to contact counsel.[14] But, where as here the accused has contacted counsel, the right to silence under s. 7 should not be interpreted as continuing to preclude police questioning. The accused has an operating mind, and of his own free will may change his mind about whether to talk to the police. That change of mind may take place as the result of police persuasion, provided the police conduct does not

[10]*R. v. Singh*, [2007] 3 S.C.R. 405. Charron J. wrote the opinion of the five-judge majority. Fish J. wrote the opinion of the four-judge dissenting minority.

[11]The trial judge correctly applied the common-law rule for the admission of confessions, under which voluntariness must be proved by the prosecution beyond a reasonable doubt. Charron J. held (para. 38) that the s. 7 right to silence, which (unlike the common-law confessions rule) applies only to persons in custody (deprived of "liberty"), extends no further than the common-law confessions rule.

[12]*R. v. Singh*, [2007] 3 S.C.R. 405, para. 28 (her emphasis).

[13]A similar case to *Singh* is *R. v. Sinclair*, [2010] 2 S.C.R. 310 (requests by accused for reconsultations with counsel over course of long interrogation denied by police; held, no breach of right to counsel); discussed in ch. 50, Rights on Arrest or Detention, under heading § 50:12, "Duty to refrain from questioning".

[14]Chapter 50, Rights on Arrest or Detention, under heading § 50:8, "Duty to refrain from questioning".

deprive him of choice. Since a voluntary statement by an accused person is likely to be reliable, to impose a holding-off obligation on the police would run counter to "the state interest in the effective investigation of crime".[15] "The ultimate question", however, "is whether the accused exercised free will in choosing to make a statement".[16] The uncontested finding at trial that the accused's statement was voluntary entailed the conclusion that the right to silence had not been breached.[17]

The cases discussed so far concerned the right to silence before trial. At the trial stage of criminal proceedings, the Charter of Rights contains two specific guarantees that are aspects of a right to silence. One is s. 11(c), which provides that an accused person is not a compellable witness at his or her own trial. The other is s. 13, which provides that a witness who gives self-incriminatory evidence has the right not to have that evidence used against him or her in other proceedings. In the face of these two specific guarantees, does s. 7 afford any additional right to silence at the trial stage? The answer is yes, according to the Supreme Court of Canada: s. 7 contains a residue of the right to silence, and it supplements ss. 11(c) and 13.

Section 11(c),[18] which applies only to the accused in a criminal trial (making the accused non-compellable as a witness), is supplemented by a s. 7 right, which applies to any witness in any proceeding, and which makes the witness non-compellable if the true purpose of calling the witness was to obtain incriminating evidence against the witness.[19] For example, if a commission of inquiry was established with the purpose of inquiring into some public issue, and if the commission summoned a witness for the purpose, not of advancing the inquiry, but of obtaining incriminating testimony from the witness, s. 11(c) would not make the witness non-compellable, but s. 7 would. The basis of the witness's residual s. 7 right not to have to testify is that it would be a breach of fundamental justice for the coercive power of the state to be used for the purpose of obtaining self-incriminating testimony from a witness.[20]

R. v. Fitzpatrick (1995),[21] concerned the requirement of the federal Fisheries Act that records be kept by fishers and supplied to government on a daily basis detailing their daily catch of fish. The question was

---

[15] *R. v. Singh*, [2007] 3 S.C.R. 405, para. 45.

[16] *R. v. Singh*, [2007] 3 S.C.R. 405, para. 53.

[17] The finding of voluntariness was accepted by Fish J. in dissent (para. 74), and he also agreed that "detainees who have asserted their right to silence are entitled to change their minds" (para. 95), but he still found that in this case there was a breach of the right to silence on the grounds that the accused was "compelled" to make his statement (para. 95) and that he was "conscripted to provide evidence against himself" (para. 99).

[18] Chapter 51, Rights on Being Charged, under heading §§ 51:6 to 51:12, "Non-compellability (s.11(c))".

[19] *B.C. Securities Commn. v. Branch*, [1995] 2 S.C.R. 3, 15.

[20] Note, however, that if the evidence were admitted, s. 13 would apply, and the evidence would be inadmissible in later criminal proceedings against the witness.

[21] *R. v. Fitzpatrick*, [1995] 4 S.C.R. 154. La Forest J. wrote the opinion of the Court.

whether these records, which were required by government to regulate the fishery, could be used as evidence at the trial of a fisher for the offence of overfishing (catching fish in excess of statutory quotas), which carried the penalty of imprisonment. There was no breach of s. 11(c), because the accused was not being compelled to be a witness at his own trial. However, the accused argued that it would be a breach of s. 7 for the Crown to make use of the accused's own compelled statements about his fishing activities as evidence against him. The Supreme Court of Canada rejected the argument, holding that the records could be used at the accused's trial. In the context of a regulatory scheme to which the accused had voluntarily submitted by engaging in the business of fishing, fundamental justice did not provide an immunity against the use of statutorily compelled information.

In *R. v. White* (1999),[22] the issue was whether three reports, which had been made to the police under the compulsion of a provincial law requiring the reporting of serious traffic accidents, were admissible at the criminal trial of the person who made the reports, who was charged with failing to stop at the scene of an accident. Once again, s. 11(c) was not implicated, because the accused was not being compelled to be a witness at her own trial. Section 7 was implicated, however, because the offence of failing to stop at the scene of an accident carried the penalty of imprisonment. The Supreme Court of Canada held that, because the accident reports were provided under compulsion, their admission into evidence against the accused would violate a principle of fundamental justice under s. 7, namely, a principle against self-incrimination. This, of course, was the opposite result to that reached on the similar facts of *Fitzpatrick*, where the fishing catch reports were admitted. The Court distinguished *Fitzpatrick* on the grounds that "driving is not freely undertaken in precisely the same way as one is free to participate in a regulated industry such as the commercial fishery", and that the reporting of traffic accidents, unlike the reporting of fishing catches, was to the police whose duty was to investigate possible crimes arising out of the accidents reported.[23] Because of these differences, fundamental justice provided immunity against the use in the criminal trial of the statutorily compelled information.

The Income Tax Act confers on tax officials the power to require a taxpayer to produce books and records and the power to inspect books and records; neither power requires a search warrant or similar process. According to the Act, these powers to require and inspect are available for the "administration or enforcement" of the Act. In *R. v. Jarvis* (2002),[24] the Supreme Court of Canada drew a distinction between the *audit* function of tax officials (when the powers were available) and the *investigation* function (when they were not). The Court held that a

[22] *R. v. White*, [1999] 2 S.C.R. 417. Iacobucci J. wrote the opinion of the majority; L'Heureux-Dubé J. wrote a dissenting opinion.

[23] *R. v. White*, [1999] 2 S.C.R. 417, paras. 55, 58.

[24] *R. v. Jarvis*, [2002] 3 S.C.R. 757. Iacobucci and Major JJ. wrote the opinion of the Court.

regulatory statute such as the Income Tax Act could validly confer these powers, provided the powers were limited to the audit functions of tax officials, that is, when they were monitoring compliance with the Act. This was so, even though non-compliance with the filing and reporting requirements of the Act could expose the taxpayer to summary offences and civil penalties. However, the Act also created a set of mens rea offences that could loosely be regarded as tax evasion, and for those offences the Act provided severe penalties, including imprisonment. When the taxpayer was vulnerable to the penalty of imprisonment, s. 7 of the Charter was applicable. Section 7's residual principle against self-incrimination became applicable when "the predominant purpose" of a tax official's inquiries moved from audit to investigation, that is, an inquiry into the commission of an offence carrying the penalty of imprisonment.[25] At that point, the requirement and inspection powers ceased to be available. The Court did permit material compulsorily obtained during the audit phase to be used in the investigation phase (and as evidence in the criminal trial if one occurred), because of the low expectation of privacy in documents already surrendered to and inspected by tax officials. But, during the investigation phase, tax officials could not continue to use the audit powers to collect evidence for a criminal prosecution. If more material was sought from the taxpayer, it had to be obtained by standard criminal investigatory techniques, which would involve a search warrant.

Section 13,[26] which applies only to self-incriminatory evidence given by a witness (making it inadmissible to incriminate the witness in other proceedings), is supplemented by a s. 7 right, which applies to "derivative" or "secondary" evidence. Derivative evidence is evidence that is discovered as the result of the witness' testimony. Derivative evidence is not *self*-incriminatory because it was not created by the witness but existed independently of the witness' testimony. The s. 7 right expands on s. 13 by excluding derivative evidence that would probably not have been discovered but for the witness's testimony.[27] For example, on a trial for murder, the gun that is tendered by the Crown as the murder weapon may have been found in a hiding place that was discovered only because it was disclosed in the accused's compelled testimony when he was a witness in earlier proceedings against a person charged with the same crime. In this example, the murder weapon would not be excluded by s. 13, but it will be excluded by s. 7. The basis for the accused's residual s. 7 right to exclude the evidence is that it would be a breach of fundamental justice for the Crown to make use of evidence with such a direct connection to the compelled self-incriminatory testimony.

The foregoing cases make clear that a statutory compulsion to give testimony is a deprivation of liberty under s. 7 of the Charter, which gives rise to a right against self-incrimination, which is a principle of

[25]*R. v. Jarvis*, [2002] 3 S.C.R. 757, paras. 2, 88-94.

[26]Chapter 54, Self-incrimination.

[27]*B.C. Securities Commn. v. Branch*, [1995] 2 S.C.R. 3, 13-14, interpreting *R. v. S. (R.J.)*, [1995] 1 S.C.R. 451.

fundamental justice. The s. 7 right against self-incrimination may give rise to three different kinds of immunity. One is "use immunity", which protects the witness from having the compelled testimony used to incriminate him or her in a subsequent proceeding. This is provided to "a witness who testifies in any proceedings" by s. 13, and to persons other than witnesses by s. 7, as illustrated by *R. v. White.*[28] The second is "derivative use immunity", which protects the witness from having the compelled testimony used to obtain other evidence (derivative or secondary evidence) to incriminate him or her in a subsequent proceeding, unless the derivative evidence is discoverable independently of the compelled testimony. This is illustrated by the gun example (and footnoted cases) of the previous paragraph. The third is a constitutional exemption from testifying in the first place, which applies if an attempt is made to use a statutory compulsion to obtain testimony for the predominant purpose of obtaining evidence for the prosecution of the witness. This is illustrated by *R. v. Jarvis.*[29]

All three immunities were engaged by the Anti-Terrorism Act of 2001, which made provision for a "judicial investigative hearing", in which a person could be examined under oath before a judge in order to obtain information in relation to a "terrorism offence". In *Re Application under s. 82.28 of the Criminal Code* (2004),[30] the Supreme Court of Canada held that a witness could be compelled to testify in this proceeding, but that s. 7 of the Charter would protect the witness from self-incrimination through use immunity, derivative use immunity, and the constitutional exemption.[31] The Act expressly accorded use immunity and derivative use immunity to the testimony, and the Court held that the constitutional exemption would apply in accordance with *Jarvis* if the predominant purpose of the hearing was to obtain evidence for the prosecution of the witness.

XXI. FAIR TRIAL

§ 47:32 The right to a fair trial

The principles of fundamental justice obviously require that a person

---

[28] *R. v. White*, [1999] 2 S.C.R. 417.

[29] *R. v. Jarvis*, [2002] 3 S.C.R. 757.

[30] *Re Application under s. 82.28 of the Criminal Code*, [2004] 2 S.C.R. 248. Iacobucci and Arbour JJ., with the agreement of McLachlin C.J. and Major J., wrote the plurality opinion. Bastarache J., with the agreement of Deschamps J., wrote a brief concurring opinion. Binnie J. dissented, but only on the ground that the hearing in this case was an abuse of process by the Crown; he agreed with Iacobucci and Arbour JJ. that the statutory provision for the hearing was constitutional. LeBel J., with the agreement of Fish J., dissented on the ground that the judicial investigative hearing was unconstitutional for breach of the unwritten principle of judicial independence. This aspect of the case is discussed in ch. 7, Courts, under heading § 7:5, "Inferior courts".

[31] The Court made no mention of s. 13, although it would seem to be applicable, since the witness in a judicial investigative hearing is surely "a witness who testifies in any proceedings".

accused of a crime receive a fair trial.[1] In this respect, s. 7 overlaps with s. 11(d), which also guarantees to a person charged with an offence "a fair and public hearing by an independent and impartial tribunal".[2] Section 7 is, however, wider than s. 11(d), because s. 7 also applies to civil and administrative proceedings where they affect life, liberty or security of the person. In *New Brunswick v. G.(J.)*,[3] for example, it was held that an application by the state to remove children from the custody of a parent affected the parent's security of the person, and made s. 7 applicable. The principles of fundamental justice required that a fair hearing be provided, which in turn required that the parent be provided with representation by state-funded counsel. In *Winnipeg Child and Family Services v. K.L.W.* (2000),[4] it was held that the warrantless apprehension by the state of a child "in need of protection" was not a breach of the principles of fundamental justice. A requirement of a warrant issued by a judge or a hearing before a judge prior to apprehension would lead to delay which would create a risk of harm to the child. In this context, the principles of fundamental justice were satisfied by a post-apprehension hearing.[5]

In *R. v. Cawthorne* (2016),[6] it was argued by members of the armed forces that the system of military justice offended s. 7 because the National Defence Act conferred on the Minister of National Defence the power to appeal from the decision of a court martial (which is to the Court Martial Appeal Court) and from the decision of the Court Martial Appeal Court (which is to the Supreme Court of Canada). The argument was that a fair trial required an independent prosecutor, and the Minister, who supervised military prosecutions, was not independent because he was a minister and member of cabinet and was responsible for the control of the Canadian forces. The Supreme Court held that it was a principle of fundamental justice that a prosecutor "must not act

---

[Section 47:32]

[1]An abuse of process by a Crown prosecutor could be a breach of fundamental justice under s. 7: *R. v. Nixon*, [2011] 2 S.C.R. 566 (Crown's subsequent repudiation of a plea bargain not an abuse of process).

[2]Section 7 will be inapplicable if the offence is punishable by fine only, since a fine is not a deprivation of life, liberty or security of the person. Section 11(d) will be applicable even if the offence is only punishable by a fine. A civil action for damages is not caught by either s. 7 or s. 11(d): *Wittman v. Emmott* (1991), 77 D.L.R. (4th) 77 (B.C.C.A.); *Budge v. Alta.* (1991), 77 D.L.R. (4th) 361 (Alta. C.A.); *B.C. v. Imperial Tobacco*, [2005] 2 S.C.R. 473, paras. 73-76. But note *Sierra Club of Can. v. Can.*, [2002] 2 S.C.R. 522, para. 50 ("Although in the context of a civil proceeding this does not engage a Charter right, the right to a fair trial generally can be viewed as a fundamental principle of justice.").

[3]*New Brunswick v. G.(J.)*, [1999] 3 S.C.R. 46. See also ch. 50, Rights on Arrest or Detention, under heading § 50:15, "Legal aid".

[4]*Winnipeg Child and Family Services v. K.L.W.*, [2000] 2 S.C.R. 519.

[5]See also *Ruby v. Can.*, [2002] 4 S.C.R. 3 (upholding ex parte, in camera procedure for judicial review of refusals of requests under the Privacy Act for personal information affecting national security).

[6]*R. v. Cawthorne*, [2016] 1 S.C.R. 983, 2016 SCC 32. McLachlin C.J. wrote the opinion of the Court.

for improper purposes, such as purely partisan motives".[7] But there was no evidence of improper purposes in these cases. The dual role of the Minister was not enough because it was no different from that of the Attorney General, who was also a minister and member of cabinet with non-prosecutorial responsibilities. The Attorney General was "entitled to a strong presumption" that he "can and does set aside partisan duties in exercising prosecutorial responsibilities". There was "no compelling reason to treat the Minister differently in this regard."[8] There was no violation of s. 7's principles of fundamental justice.

The Canadian process for the extradition of a fugitive to face trial in another country starts with the arrest of the fugitive and a hearing before a judge to determine whether the requesting state has sufficient evidence to place the fugitive on trial for an extraditable offence. The process is obviously a denial of liberty to the fugitive and the hearing must be conducted in conformity with the principles of fundamental justice. The fugitive is not entitled to a full-dress criminal trial, because the determination of guilt or innocence will occur in the requesting state. All that the extradition judge in Canada can do is to determine whether the requesting state has a prima facie case against the fugitive.[9] While the fugitive is entitled to know the case against him, he is not entitled to the full disclosure of all relevant prosecution evidence that is required in a criminal trial.[10] In three cases, threats of severe penalties and conditions of imprisonment were made by a prosecutor and judge in the United States to attempt to persuade fugitives to avoid the Canadian extradition process and go voluntarily to the place of trial in the United States. Despite the fact that the United States had made out a prima facie case against the fugitives, the Supreme Court of Canada stayed the proceedings on the ground that the extradition of the fugitives in light of these threats would be a breach of the principles of fundamental justice.[11]

The right to a fair trial does not mean that all existing rules of procedure and evidence that are directed to a fair trial are constitutionalized and consequently immutable.[12] The Supreme Court of Canada has upheld a provision of the Criminal Code that allows for the videotaping of

---

[7]*R. v. Cawthorne*, [2016] 1 S.C.R. 983, 2016 SCC 32, para. 26.

[8]*R. v. Cawthorne*, [2016] 1 S.C.R. 983, 2016 SCC 32, para. 32.

[9]On the role of the extradition judge, see *United States v. Yang* (2001), 56 O.R. (3d) 52 (C.A.); *United States v. Ferras*, [2006] 2 S.C.R. 77.

[10]*United States v. Kwok*, [2001] 1 S.C.R. 532.

[11]*United States v. Cobb*, [2001] 1 S.C.R. 587; *United States v. Tsioubrios*, [2001] 1 S.C.R. 613; *United States v. Shulman*, [2001] 1 S.C.R. 616.

[12]For example, there is no constitutional right to an appeal: *Charkaoui v. Can.*, [2007] 1 S.C.R. 350, para. 136. Nor is there a constitutional right to a preliminary hearing or to any other form of oral discovery of prosecution witnesses: *R. v. L. (S.J.)*, [2009] 1 S.C.R. 426, paras. 21-23, 89 (upholding Criminal Code provision allowing Attorney General to prefer a direct indictment, even in the case of a young accused); *R. v. Bjelland*, [2009] 2 S.C.R. 651, paras. 32-36 (evidence admitted although Crown had not produced the witness at the preliminary hearing; no constitutional right to cross-examine witness at preliminary hearing).

the evidence of a witness who is under the age of 18, so that at the trial the witness need only adopt the contents of the tape instead of going over the whole story again.[13] The Court has also upheld another provision that allows a witness under the age of 18 to testify from behind a one-way screen, so that the witness cannot see the accused (although the accused can see the witness).[14] The Court upheld these departures from the traditional trial format on the ground that they would reduce the stress on young witnesses and enhance the reliability of their evidence. In both cases, the accused's right to cross-examine the witness was preserved. Neither innovation prejudiced the fairness of the trial in any other respect. However, if an unforeseen case should arise in which the use of the videotape or the screen would prejudice the fairness of the trial, the Court took comfort from the fact that the trial judge had been given a discretion to deny the use of the videotape or screen in that case.

The Supreme Court of Canada had to review a much more radical departure from the traditional trial format in *Charkaoui v. Canada* (2007).[15] At issue was the process for the issue of "security certificates" under the federal Immigration and Refugee Protection Act. The Act empowered two ministers to issue a certificate declaring a non-citizen named in the certificate to be a threat to national security. The certificate authorized the arrest and detention of the named person.[16] The certificate was to be automatically referred to a judge of the Federal Court for review on the standard of reasonableness, and, if the judge found the certificate to be reasonable, the certificate became a removal order, authorizing the deportation of the named person. The problem with the process was that at no stage did the named person necessarily know the nature of the case against him. There was no hearing on the original issue of the certificate. On review by the Federal Court judge, the named person was entitled to be heard, but the Act required the judge to "ensure the confidentiality of the information on which the certificate is based. . .if, in the opinion of the judge, its disclosure would be injurious to national security or to the safety of any person". This obligation meant that the judge would often be unable to disclose to the named person the information upon which the certificate had been based. The Supreme Court of Canada held that the issue of a security certificate was a deprivation of liberty under s. 7, and that the review process did not satisfy the principles of fundamental justice, because it did not provide the named person with a fair hearing. McLachlin C.J., who wrote the opinion of the Court, acknowledged that "the procedures required to meet the

[13]*R. v. L. (D.O.)*, [1993] 4 S.C.R. 419.

[14]*R. v. Levogiannis*, [1993] 4 S.C.R. 475; *R. v. J.Z.S.*, [2010] 1 S.C.R. 3.

[15]*Charkaoui v. Canada*, [2007] 1 S.C.R. 350. McLachlin C.J. wrote the opinion of the Court.

[16]In the case of a "permanent resident", the arrest and detention was authorized by the Act, but was not mandatory. In the case of a "foreign national" (a non-citizen who was not a permanent resident), it was mandatory. As to the categories of non-citizens, see ch. 26, Citizenship.

demands of fundamental justice depend on the context",[17] and she also acknowledged that "national security considerations can limit the extent of disclosure of information to the affected person",[18] but she held that "the secrecy required by the scheme denies the named person the opportunity to know the case put against him or her, and hence to challenge the government's case".[19] This was a breach of the principles of fundamental justice.

McLachlin C.J. then turned her attention to s. 1 of the Charter, applying the *Oakes* test[20] to determine whether the law could be justified as a reasonable limit on s. 7. There was no doubt that the protection of secret information respecting national security and intelligence sources was a sufficiently important objective, and the withholding of such information was rationally connected to the objective. But the law failed to limit the right by the least drastic means, because Parliament could have adopted procedures to protect secrecy that were less intrusive of individual rights. McLachlin C.J. pointed to a system of "special counsel" that had previously been used in Canada and was used in other countries in national security cases. Special counsel were independent counsel with security clearances who could be retained by the Federal Court judge, and to whom full disclosure could be made, and who could then scrutinize the evidence and do their best to defend the interests of named persons. One is surely entitled to be somewhat sceptical of the effectiveness of a special-counsel system, since the special counsel's advocacy will be impaired by his or her inability to disclose the secret information to the named person. For example, only the named person is likely to know whether personal information is true or false, and what evidence is available to disprove false information. However, a special-counsel system would no doubt compensate to some extent for the lack of informed participation by the named person. McLachlin C.J., although clearly attracted by the idea, did not offer it as the only answer, making clear that "precisely what is to be done is a matter for Parliament to decide".[21] But, without some effort to compensate for the non-disclosure of secret information, the security-certificate process could not be justified under s. 1.

After *Charkaoui*, the government took up Mclachlin C.J.'s suggestion and Parliament amended the Immigration and Refugee Protection Act

---

[17]*Charkaoui v. Canada*, [2007] 1 S.C.R. 350, para. 20.

[18]*Charkaoui v. Canada*, [2007] 1 S.C.R. 350, para. 58, citing *Chiarelli v. Can.*, [1992] 1 S.C.R. 711. In a sequel case, *Charkaoui v. Can.*, [2008] 2 S.C.R. 326, the Supreme Court held that it was a breach of s. 7 for the Canadian Security Intelligence Service (CSIS) to destroy operational notes related to the subject of a security certificate; all relevant information in the possession of CSIS must be retained and disclosed to the Federal Court judge charged with determining whether the certificate is reasonable.

[19]*Charkaoui v. Canada*, [2007] 1 S.C.R. 350, para. 65.

[20]See ch. 38, Limitation of Rights.

[21]*Charkaoui v. Canada*, [2007] 1 S.C.R. 350, para. 87.

to introduce "special advocates" into the security-certificate process.[22] Special advocates were security-cleared lawyers to whom the entire record of the case against a named person could be disclosed. One (or more) of them would be given the duty to protect the interests of a named person in a closed hearing. The special advocate was permitted to communicate with the named person, although each communication had to be authorized by the designated Federal Court judge. In *Canada v. Harkat* (2014),[23] the Supreme Court held that the provision for special advocates corrected the constitutional infirmity that had been identified in *Charkaoui*. McLachlin C.J., writing for a unanimous Court on the main issue, acknowledged that the amended scheme was still "an imperfect substitute for full disclosure in an open court",[24] but she held that it was nevertheless compliant with s. 7: the "gatekeeper role" of the designated judge was the saving grace. The restrictions on the special advocate's ability to communicate with the named person did not render the amended scheme unconstitutional because the judge had "a sufficiently broad discretion to allow all communications that are necessary for the special advocates to perform their duties"; and those duties were to "function as closely as possible to ordinary counsel in a public hearing".[25] Moreover, the judge was under a statutory duty to ensure that the named person received enough disclosure to be "reasonably informed" of the ministers' grounds for issuing the security certificate, and, if the scope of confidentiality made that impossible, the judge would have to grant a remedy under s. 24(1) of the Charter, including, if necessary, a stay of proceedings. In the national-security context, there were now enough safeguards of trial fairness for the amended Act to constitute a reasonable limit under s. 1.

§ 47:33 Full answer and defence

In *R. v. Seaboyer* (1991),[1] the Supreme Court of Canada held that both ss. 7 and 11(d) guaranteed to an accused "the right to present full answer and defence". The Court by a majority held that this right was abridged by a "rape-shield" provision in the Criminal Code, which restricted the right of a person charged with sexual assault to cross-examine the complainant about her past sexual activity. According to McLachlin J. for the majority, this provision would occasionally have the effect of excluding relevant evidence that was required to enable the accused to

---

[22]S.C. 2008, c. 3.

[23]*Canada v. Harkat*, [2014] 2 S.C.R. 33; 2014 SCC 37. McLachlin C.J. wrote the opinion of the majority. Abella and Cromwell JJ. wrote an opinion dissenting on an issue of informer privilege, but otherwise agreeing with McLachlin C.J.

[24]*Canada v. Harkat*, [2014] 2 S.C.R. 33; 2014 SCC 37, para. 77.

[25]*Canada v. Harkat*, [2014] 2 S.C.R. 33; 2014 SCC 37, para. 69-70.

[Section 47:33]

[1]*R. v. Seaboyer*, [1991] 2 S.C.R. 577.

make full answer and defence.[2] According to L'Heureux-Dubé J. for the dissenting minority, the rape-shield provision would exclude only evidence that was either irrelevant or so prejudicial to the fairness of the trial that it could properly be excluded. The majority view prevailed, of course, and the rape-shield provision was struck from the Criminal Code.[3]

R. v. R.V. (2019),[4] was a sexual assault case. At the trial, the complainant (aged 13) was pregnant and she testified that the only possible cause of the pregnancy was a sexual assault by the accused (aged 20) which she said took place on the Canada Day weekend of 2013. Aside from that single act of forced intercourse, she testified that she was a virgin. The accused denied that he had ever engaged in intercourse with the complainant, and, since she was undoubtedly pregnant, he applied to cross-examine her about her sexual activity with other men. The Supreme Court of Canada held that the accused's right to full answer and defence did confer a right to cross-examine the complainant, but that right was subject to restrictions giving effect to protections to safeguard the rights of the complainant. Section 276 of the Criminal Code provided that, in a proceeding for (defined) sexual offences, evidence that the complainant has engaged in sexual activity, "whether with the accused or with any other person", is not admissible to support an inference that the complainant "is more likely to have consented to the sexual activity that forms the subject matter of the charge" or "is less worthy of belief". With this language, the "twin myths" that used to justify intrusive and wide-ranging defence questioning of complainants are put to rest. Section 276 goes on to require that any evidence of the complainant's sexual activity must be limited to "specific instances of sexual activity", must be "relevant to an issue at trial", and must have "significant probative value that is not substantially outweighed by the danger of prejudice to the proper administration of justice". In this case,

---

[2]Compare *R. v. Corbett*, [1988] 1 S.C.R. 670 (no breach of fundamental justice to allow Crown to question accused about previous convictions for the purpose of assessing credibility); *R. v. Putvin*, [1989] 1 S.C.R. 525 (no breach of fundamental justice to admit at trial Crown evidence given at preliminary inquiry, provided accused had an opportunity to cross-examine at preliminary inquiry).

[3]Parliament subsequently replaced the rape-shield provisions with a set of provisions that closely followed the principles laid down in the majority judgment in *Seaboyer*. S.C. 1992, c. 38, s. 2, amending s. 276 of the Criminal Code. The new provisions render inadmissible any of the complainant's past sexual history either with a third party or with the accused. The latter exclusion is a significant step beyond the legislation that was struck down in *Seaboyer*, which rendered inadmissible all of the past sexual history of the complainant *except* that between the complainant and the accused. In order to comply with the Charter, however, the new provisions essentially give the trial judge the discretion to determine whether evidence of the complainant's past sexual history should be admitted, in exception to the general rule, in circumstances where it is "relevant to an issue at trial" and "has significant probative value that is not substantially outweighed by the danger of prejudice to the proper administration of justice". In *R. v. Darrach*, [2000] 2 S.C.R. 443, the new legislation was upheld on the basis that it faithfully reflected the principles laid down in *Seaboyer*.

[4]*R. v. R.V.*, 2019 SCC 41. Karakatsanis J. wrote the opinion of the five-judge majority. Brown and Rowe JJ. wrote a joint dissenting opinion.

the Supreme Court of Canada held that R.V.'s right to full answer and defence gave him the right to engage in a limited cross-examination of the complainant with respect to any other sexual activity. "The complainant's privacy must yield to cross-examination in order to avoid convicting the innocent."[5]

In *R. v. Cook* (1997),[6] the accused was convicted of assault, despite the fact that the Crown did not call the victim of the assault as a witness for the Crown. The accused argued that the Crown was under an obligation at common law[7] to call the victim, since he was competent and available. The inability of the accused to cross-examine his accuser was, he argued, a denial of the accused's right to make full answer and defence. The Supreme Court of Canada rejected the argument, holding that the Crown had a discretion as to the witnesses it chose to call, and the accused's right to make full answer and defence was protected by his right to cross-examine those witnesses that the Crown did call (and upon whose evidence the jury had found the accused guilty). The argument that the accused would be unfairly surprised by a trial at which the victim did not testify was rejected on the basis that the accused's pre-trial right to full disclosure of all relevant material in the possession of the Crown (the topic of the next section of this chapter) was a sufficient safeguard against surprise. The Court acknowledged that there might be rare cases where the suppression of potentially exculpatory evidence by the Crown amounted to an abuse of process, but the onus of proving misconduct lay on the accused and had not been discharged in this case.[8]

§ 47:34 Pre-trial disclosure by the Crown

Criminal proceedings are unlike civil proceedings in that there is no statutory provision for pre-trial discovery in criminal proceedings.[1] In most jurisdictions, however, a practice of voluntary disclosure by the

---

[5] *R. v. R.V.*, 2019 SCC 41, para. 65.

[6] *R. v. Cook*, [1997] 1 S.C.R. 1113. The opinion of the Court was written by L'Heureux-Dubé J.

[7] The case was not argued under s. 7 of the Charter, but L'Heureux-Dubé J. said (para. 54) that her reasoning would "likely" be consistent with a Charter analysis.

[8] See also *R. v. Rose*, [1998] 3 S.C.R. 262 (right to full answer and defence not infringed by Criminal Code requirement that, when defence calls evidence, defence gives closing address to jury before Crown); *R. v. Pan*, [2001] 2 S.C.R. 344 (right to full answer and defence not infringed by rule of jury secrecy); *R. v. Ahmad*, [2011] 1 S.C.R. 110 (right to full answer and defence not infringed by exclusive jurisdiction of Federal Court to determine claim of Crown privilege for evidence relevant to a criminal trial in provincial criminal court); *R. v. St-Onge Lamoureux*, [2012] 3 S.C.R. 187, para. 76 (right to full answer and defence not infringed by excluding evidence of alcohol consumption if proffered to prove that breathalyzer test was inaccurate).

[Section 47:34]

[1] Compare *Charkaoui v. Can.*, [2008] 2 S.C.R. 326 (duty of disclosure by Crown to federal judge in security certificate cases); *Canada v. Khadr*, [2008] 2 S.C.R. 125 (duty of disclosure by Crown to defendant in American criminal proceedings).

Crown developed. In *R. v. Stinchcombe* (1991)[2] the Supreme Court of Canada held that pre-trial disclosure by the Crown[3] of all information relevant to the conduct of the defence[4] is a constitutional obligation, entailed by the accused's right to make full answer and defence.[5] The obligation applies not only to statements obtained from witnesses that the Crown intends to call at trial, but also to statements obtained from persons that the Crown does not intend to call as witnesses.[6] The breadth of the duty is demonstrated by this case, where the Crown had failed to disclose statements obtained from a person whom the Crown did not call as a witness. The person had in fact testified at the preliminary inquiry so that her existence, identity and the general nature of her knowledge were all known to the defence, who could obviously have called her as a witness. Nevertheless, the Court held that the defence's right to make full answer and defence might have been impaired by the failure of the Crown to produce to the defence statements derived from Crown interviews of the person.[7] The Court ordered a new trial.[8]

---

[2]*R. v. Stinchcombe*, [1991] 3 S.C.R. 326. The opinion of the Court was written by Sopinka J.

[3]"In contrast, the defence has no obligation to assist the prosecution and is entitled to assume a purely adversarial role towards the prosecution.": *R. v. Stinchcombe*, [1991] 3 S.C.R. 326, 333, but note passage earlier on same page reserving question whether "the duty should be reciprocal".

[4]There is no duty to disclose irrelevant information, or privileged information; and the Crown retains a discretion as to the timing of disclosure, since premature disclosure could impede an ongoing investigation: *R. v. Stinchcombe*, [1991] 3 S.C.R. 326, 339. Accord, *R. v. Leipert*, [1997] 1 S.C.R. 281 (duty to disclose does not override police-informer privilege). Another exception was enacted by amendments to the Criminal Code in 1997 for confidential records in sexual assault cases; this exception was upheld in *R. v. Mills*, [1999] 3 S.C.R. 668; for discussion, see § 47:37, "Statutory limits on pre-trial disclosure".

[5]*R. v. Stinchcombe*, [1991] 3 S.C.R. 326, 336, referring to s. 7, but not s. 11(d); and see also 342, referring again only to s. 7, and indicating some doubt as to the application of the duty to summary conviction offences (as opposed to the indictable offences in issue in the case).

[6]Note however that the Crown does not have an obligation to "produce" its witnesses for oral discovery by the accused; the Crown cannot control people as it can physical evidence: *R. v. Khela*, [1995] 4 S.C.R. 201, para. 18 per Sopinka and Iacobucci JJ. for a Court that was unanimous on this point.

[7]Accord, *Dersch v. Can.*, [1990] 2 S.C.R. 1505 (accused entitled to see contents of "sealed package" of wiretap surveillance materials, subject to Crown's right to apply to have the materials edited); *R. v. Egger*, [1993] 2 S.C.R. 451 (Crown must disclose to accused its possession of a second blood sample and its availability to the accused, even though the Criminal Code prescribed that Crown must take second sample to permit analysis by accused); *R. v. Durette*, [1994] 1 S.C.R. 469 (excessive editing of wiretap affidavits before disclosure to accused held to be a denial of right to make full answer and defence.); *R. v. Chaplin*, [1995] 1 S.C.R. 727 (Crown need not disclose whether accused had been target of wiretap when accused had failed to establish that the fact was potentially relevant to the defence); *R. v. Dixon*, [1998] 1 S.C.R. 244 (failure to disclose did not affect fairness of trial); *R. v. Robart*, [1998] 1 S.C.R. 279 (same decision); *R. v. McQuaid*, [1998] 1 S.C.R. 285 (same decision); *R. v. Smith*, [1998] 1 S.C.R. 291 (new trial ordered for failure to disclose); *R. v. Skinner*, [1998] 1 S.C.R. 298 (same decision); *R v. Taillefer; R v. Duguay*, [2003] 3 S.C.R. 307 (new trial ordered in one case and stay of proceedings ordered in another for failure to disclose); *R v. Bjelland*, [2009] 2 S.C.R. 651

Disclosure of information under *Stinchcombe* must be timely, that is, it must be provided with enough time before the trial to enable the defence to consider it properly. If information comes into the possession of the Crown close to the time of the trial, it must still be disclosed, and the trial should be adjourned for enough time to enable the defence to consider the new evidence.[9] The obligation of disclosure does not cease with the trial, at least not if the accused is convicted. If information comes into the possession of the Crown after the trial, the Crown's obligation is to disclose "any information in respect of which there is a reasonable possibility that it may assist the [accused] in prosecuting an appeal."[10]

Section 24(1) authorizes an "appropriate and just remedy" for a breach of the Charter of Rights. For default in pre-trial disclosure by the Crown, the appropriate and just remedy would normally be an order for disclosure, coupled with an award of costs to the accused. If the default is that the Crown has made its disclosure (or some of it) too late (too close to the trial date), the appropriate remedy would normally be an adjournment of the trial to give the defence time to consider the tardily-produced evidence.[11] The exclusion of the tardily-produced evidence from the accused's trial is not normally an appropriate remedy, because it impairs the truth-finding function of the trial, but in exceptional circumstances the exclusion of the evidence would be an appropriate remedy.[12]

If a failure of pre-trial disclosure by the Crown is not discovered until after the accused has been convicted, more radical remedies are called for. If the failure to disclose casts doubt on the reliability of the verdict or the fairness of the trial, a new trial would be the normal remedy.[13] In one difficult case, the accused had pleaded guilty, been sentenced to 12 years imprisonment, and had actually served eight years by the time the Supreme Court of Canada found a violation of the Crown's duty of pre-trial disclosure. The Court allowed the accused to withdraw his guilty plea, quashed his conviction and prohibited a new trial by directing a stay of proceedings.[14] If a failure to disclose evidence to the defence is a deliberate or negligent default by the prosecutor, this will also be a

(disclosure was sufficient; no constitutional right to cross-examine a witness at preliminary hearing).

[8]Compare *R. v. Swain*, [1991] 1 S.C.R. 933, 972 (Crown's presentation of evidence of accused's insanity against wish of accused violates s. 7, because it is a basic tenet of the legal system that "an accused person have the right to control his or her own defence").

[9]*R. v. Bjelland*, [2009] 2 S.C.R. 651.

[10]*R. v. McNeil*, [2009] 1 S.C.R. 66, para. 17.

[11]*R. v. Bjelland*, [2009] 2 S.C.R. 651.

[12]*R. v. Bjelland*, [2009] 2 S.C.R. 651, paras. 22-27; more fully discussed in ch. 40, Enforcement of Rights, under heading § 40:21, "Exclusion of evidence".

[13]*R. v. Taillefer*, [2003] 3 S.C.R. 307 (new trial ordered for one of two accused).

[14]*R. v. Taillefer*, [2003] 3 S.C.R. 307 (stay of proceedings ordered for the other of the two accused).

breach of professional responsibility, exposing the prosecutor to discipline from the provincial law society.[15]

§ 47:35 Pre-trial disclosure by third parties

In *R. v. O'Connor* (1995),[1] the Supreme Court of Canada had to consider whether an accused's constitutional right to make full answer and defence included a right to obtain documents which were not in the Crown's possession, but were held by third parties.[2] The case arose out of charges of rape and indecent assault brought against a Catholic Bishop who had been the principal of a native residential school at the time of the alleged offences. The complainants were four women, all former students who were employees of the school at the time. The accused sought an order requiring disclosure of the complainants' counsellors' records, medical records and school records, all of which were in the possession of third parties. Because these records were not in the possession of the Crown, *Stinchcombe* imposed no obligation on the Crown to disclose them, which the Crown would in any case be unable to do. As well, the fact that the records were not in the possession of the Crown meant that they were not being relied upon by the Crown, so that they did not form part of the accused's "case to meet", and therefore might not be necessary for full answer and defence. Furthermore, the disclosure of the records would implicate constitutional rights besides those of the accused. The complainants, in common with other witnesses, had a right to a reasonable expectation of privacy in the confidential records of persons and institutions who had provided counselling and medical advice.[3] The Court also appreciated that there was a risk of a breach of equality rights: disclosure in sexual assault cases would bear disproportionately on women and could be premised on discriminatory stereotypes about how past sexual activity or psychological counselling might affect issues of consent and credibility.[4]

The Court held unanimously that access to private records in the possession of third parties *could* be necessary to an accused's right to make full answer and defence. However, this did not give an accused person

[15]*Krieger v. Law Society of Alberta*, [2002] 3 S.C.R. 372.

[Section 47:35]

[1]*R. v. O'Connor*, [1995] 4 S.C.R. 411. *A. (L.L.) v. B. (A.)*, [1995] 4 S.C.R. 536 was a companion case, also involving sexual assault charges, which was decided at the same time with the same outcome.

[2]*R. v. McNeil*, [2009] 1 S.C.R. 66 contains a careful review by Charron J. for the Court of the third-party obligation to disclose.

[3]The source of this right was not entirely clear. L'Heureux-Dubé J. ([1995] 4 S.C.R. 411, paras. 110-119) placed it in s. 7; the others were not specific as to its source.

[4]L'Heureux-Dubé J., referring to the "rape shield" provision of the Criminal Code, which restricts the evidence which may be adduced in court about a complainant's sexual activities, stated that "we must not allow the defence to do indirectly what it cannot do directly": [1995] 4 S.C.R. 411, para. 122. The recognition that constitutional rights attach to confidential records has also led to limits on disclosure in the context of civil proceedings: *M. (A.) v. Ryan*, [1997] 1 S.C.R. 157.

an automatic right of access to the records. Rather, the Court ruled that production must be governed by a procedure which would strike the proper balance between full answer and defence on the one hand, and the witness's privacy and equality rights on the other. The Court in *O'Connor* divided five to four over how to achieve this balance.[5] The majority view was as follows. The defence must apply to the trial judge for a disclosure order, and must establish on a balance of probabilities that the records are "likely relevant" to making full answer and defence. If likely relevance is established, the records must be produced into court, but at this stage only for the private inspection of the judge. The judge must inspect the records and determine whether a disclosure order should be made. That determination should be made only after considering the following five factors: (1) the records' importance for full answer and defence; (2) their "probative value"; (3) the nature and extent of privacy vested in them; (4) whether production would be premised on a discriminatory belief or bias; and (5) the effect that production would have on a witness's dignity, privacy and security of the person.[6] In this way, the majority of the Court[7] sought to accommodate the competing values. *O'Connor* makes clear that the right to make full answer and defence is not an absolute right, but one that must at times yield to other constitutional values.[8]

Solicitor-client privilege was the competing constitutional value in *R. v. McClure* (2001).[9] In that case, an accused, who was charged with sexual assault, obtained from the trial judge an order for the production of the civil litigation file of his alleged victim (who had brought a civil action for damages against the accused). The purpose of the production was to permit the accused to review the allegations that the victim had made to his solicitor about the accused's conduct, and to assess the mo-

---

[5]The majority opinion on this issue was that of Lamer C.J. and Sopinka J., which attracted the support of Cory, Iacobucci, and Major JJ. The main dissenting opinion was that of L'Heureux-Dubé J., which was concurred in by La Forest and Gonthier JJ. McLachlin J. wrote a separate dissent in which she agreed wholly with L'Heureux-Dubé J.

[6]Security of the person would be threatened if disclosure would cause psychological harm to the witness: see § 47:12, "Security of the person".

[7]L'Heureux-Dubé J., dissenting on this issue, took the view that the records should not be produced in court for inspection on the sole basis of likely relevance. She would have had the trial judge balance the salutary and deleterious effects of production into court *before* deciding to examine the records. With respect to the balancing process, she would have added two additional factors to the five stipulated by the majority, namely, (1) society's interest in encouraging the reporting of sexual offences, and (2) the integrity of the trial process. If a trial judge decided that the documents should be produced into court for inspection, L'Heureux-Dubé J. would have had the judge then reconsider all seven factors before deciding whether to make the order for disclosure which would release the records to defence counsel.

[8]After the decision in *O'Connor*, Parliament enacted amendments to the Criminal Code to regulate the disclosure of confidential records in sexual assault proceedings. These amendments followed the dissenting opinion of L'Heureux-Dubé J. (previous note) more closely than the majority opinion, but the amendments were upheld in *R. v. Mills*, [1999] 3 S.C.R. 668; for discussion, see § 47:37, "Statutory limits on pre-trial disclosure".

[9]*R. v. McClure*, [2001] 1 S.C.R. 445. Major J. wrote the opinion of the Court.

tive of the victim to fabricate or exaggerate the allegations. The Supreme Court of Canada held that the litigation file, because it contained communications between a solicitor and his client for the purpose of providing legal advice or assistance, was covered by solicitor-client privilege. This meant that, as a general rule, the privilege-holder (the victim in this case) could refuse to produce it in court proceedings. The Court held that, because of the fundamental importance of solicitor-client privilege, the privilege would yield to the accused's Charter right to full answer and defence only if the accused's innocence was at stake, that is, when the observance of the privilege (exclusion of the evidence) would probably lead to a wrongful conviction.[10] The Court established a two-stage process for a trial judge to determine when the innocence-at-stake test was passed. First, the judge had to determine whether there was an evidentiary basis to conclude that the privileged records *could* raise a reasonable doubt as to guilt. If that stage was passed, then the judge would proceed to a second stage and inspect the records privately to determine if they were *likely* to raise a reasonable doubt as to guilt. Only if both stages were passed, would the judge order production of the records to the accused in the face of solicitor-client privilege. In this case, the Supreme Court held, the first stage was not passed, because there was no evidence to suggest that the disclosure of the file could raise a reasonable doubt as to the guilt of the accused. The trial judge had erred by following the process stipulated in *O'Connor*, instead of the more stringent innocence-at-stake process. The Supreme Court therefore reversed the decision of the trial judge ordering disclosure of the victim's civil litigation file.

The innocence-at-stake test was applied again by the Supreme Court of Canada in *R. v. Brown* (2002).[11] In that case, the accused, who was charged with murder, sought production of another individual's solicitor's file, because there was evidence that the other individual had confessed to his solicitor to the murder for which the accused was charged. Once again, the Court reversed the trial judge's order for disclosure. While the first stage of the *McClure* inquiry was satisfied, the second stage was not. Although the evidence of the file was likely to raise a reasonable doubt as to guilt, the breach of solicitor-client privilege was to be a remedy of last resort. The judge had erred in not first investigating the admissibility of other evidence of the confession (which had allegedly been made to another person in addition to the solicitor). It was premature for the judge to order production of privileged records as long as the accused had other means of raising a reasonable doubt. One might have thought that, even if other evidence was available, the solicitor's file should still be produced, since its contents were so directly

---

[10]Major J. (para. 40) borrowed the test from the law of police-informer privilege, which yields to the right to full answer and defence only where the innocence-at-stake test is satisfied.

[11]*R. v. Brown*, [2002] 2 S.C.R. 185. Major J. wrote the opinion of the majority. Arbour J., with L'Heureux-Dubé J., wrote a concurring opinion, agreeing with Major J. but adding some further comments.

relevant to the accused's guilt. After all, the other witness to the confession might be disbelieved without the corroboration of the solicitor's records. But the Court's extreme solicitude for solicitor-client privilege led them to the contrary conclusion.

The previous section of this chapter describes the *Stinchcombe* pre-trial disclosure regime applicable to the Crown.[12] This section describes the *O'Connor* pre-trial disclosure regime applicable to third parties. The existence of these two pre-trial disclosure regimes in criminal proceedings raises an obvious question: how to determine which of the two regimes applies? The answer is important, because the *Stinchcombe* "first party" disclosure regime contemplates a more generous, less cumbersome form of disclosure for the accused than the *O'Connor* third party disclosure regime. In many cases, the answer as to which pre-trial disclosure regime applies will be obvious; the identity of the party that possesses the information (the Crown or a third party) will suggest an easy answer. However, in other cases, the answer will be less obvious.

The Supreme Court of Canada addressed how to determine which disclosure regime applies in *R. v. Gubbins* (2018).[13] In this case, the two accused were charged with impaired driving and with driving with blood alcohol above the legal limit. They provided breath samples that yielded blood alcohol readings well in excess of the legal limit. They asked the Crown to disclose various maintenance records for the breathalyzers used to measure the blood alcohol in their blood samples, invoking the *Stinchcombe* first party disclosure regime. The Crown refused, taking the position that the *O'Connor* third party disclosure regime applied to the maintenance records, and that the maintenance records did not need to be disclosed because they were not "likely relevant". This dispute about which of the two pre-trial disclosure regimes applied made its way to the Court. The Court indicated that the *Stinchcombe* first party disclosure regime will apply: 1) if the information is "in the possession or control of the prosecuting Crown"; or 2) if the information is in the possession or control of the police or "another Crown entity", which "ought to have supplied it to the prosecuting Crown" because it forms "part of the fruits of the investigation or [is] obviously relevant".[14] Otherwise, the information will be subject to the *O'Connor* third party disclosure regime. Applying this approach, the Court held that the maintenance records were subject to the *O'Connor* third party disclosure regime. Since neither of the two accused were able to establish that the maintenance records were "likely relevant", they did not need to be disclosed.

---

[12]Section 47:34, "Pre-trial disclosure by the Crown".

[13]*R. v. Gubbins*, [2018] 3 S.C.R. 35. Rowe J. wrote the opinion for the majority of the Court, with the agreement of seven other judges. Côté J. wrote a dissenting opinion.

[14]*R. v. Gubbins*, [2018] 3 S.C.R. 35, para. 33. Rowe J. cautioned that his opinion "should not be seen as detracting" from the limits on pre-trial disclosure that apply to applications to obtain records "relating to a complainant or a witness", which qualify *O'Connor*, and apply "even if those records are in the possession or control of the Crown": *R. v. Gubbins*, [2018] 3 S.C.R. 35, para. 33, fn. 1. These limits are discussed more fully in § 47:37, "Statutory limits on pre-trial disclosure".

§ 47:36 Preservation of evidence

The Crown's duty to disclose relevant evidence to the accused applies only to evidence that is in the possession or control of the Crown. Evidence that has been destroyed or lost (or never existed in the first place)[1] cannot be disclosed. For this reason, the Supreme Court of Canada has held that the Crown is under a duty to the accused to *preserve* relevant evidence once it comes into the possession or control of the Crown.[2]

R. v. La (1997)[3] was a sexual assault case in which potentially relevant evidence was unavailable to the accused. The evidence was a tape recording which had been taken of a conversation between a police officer and the complainant, a 13-year old prostitute. The recorded conversation took place before the police had decided to investigate criminal charges against the accused, and the conversation did not directly relate to the charges which were subsequently laid against the accused. Nevertheless, counsel for the accused argued, and the Court accepted, that the tape might have been useful for attacking the credibility of the complainant. The tape had not been transcribed, and was inadvertently lost by the police officer who made the recording. The Supreme Court of Canada held that the loss of the tape, and the consequent failure to disclose it to the defence, was not a breach of s. 7 of the Charter. Sopinka J., for the majority of the Court,[4] held that a breach of s. 7 would occur if the Crown could not provide a satisfactory explanation for the loss, which would be the case if the evidence had been deliberately destroyed or had been lost by "an unacceptable degree of negligent conduct".[5] In this case, the explanation was satisfactory in that it showed that the evidence had not been deliberately destroyed and, although the tape had simply been mislaid by the police, the Court accepted that there had been no unacceptable degree of negligence. Where, as in this case, the Crown had provided a satisfactory explanation for the loss of relevant evidence, there would still be a breach of s. 7 if the accused affirmatively established that the loss of the evidence would prejudice his ability to make full answer and defence and thus cause an unfair trial. In this case, the Court held that the tape was not

[Section 47:36]

[1]Compare *R. v. Wicksted*, [1997] 1 S.C.R. 307 (rejecting argument that police failure to take verbatim notes of interviews with complainant deprived defence of right to full anwer and defence by reducing opportunity to test complainant's credibility).

[2]Compare *Charkaoui v. Can.*, [2008] 2 S.C.R. 326 (duty of Crown to preserve evidence relevant to security certificate).

[3]*R. v. La*, [1997] 2 S.C.R. 680.

[4]The majority consisted of Sopinka J., Lamer C.J., Cory, Iacobucci and Major JJ. A minority opinion, which concurred in the result but not with the reasoning of the majority, was delivered by L'Heureux-Dubé J. and was concurred in by La Forest, Gonthier and McLachlin JJ.

[5]*R. v. La*, [1997] 2 S.C.R. 680, para. 22. L'Heureux-Dubé J., for the concurring minority, would have insisted on a showing that the loss of the evidence caused prejudice to the accused's right to make full answer and defence.

sufficiently critical to the case to establish prejudice to the accused's right to make full answer and defence.

In *R. v. Carosella* (1997),[6] the defendant, who was charged with sexual assault, had attempted to obtain the record of an interview of the complainant by a counsellor at a sexual assault crisis centre. The trial judge ordered the centre to produce its file on the complainant, but the file did not contain the notes of the interview with the complainant (or anything else of importance). The reason for the absence of the notes was that the centre had adopted a policy of shredding its counsellors' notes in those cases which were likely to lead to a prosecution. The notes of the interview with the complainant had been destroyed pursuant to that policy before the trial judge ordered their production. Counsel for the defence argued that the accused had been denied his right to full answer and defence by this deliberate destruction of relevant evidence. A five-four majority of the Supreme Court of Canada agreed, and ordered a stay of proceedings. Sopinka J., who wrote for the majority, was obviously upset that the sexual assault crisis centre had deliberately destroyed its clients' records for the express purpose of preventing defence counsel from gaining access to them. Since the records had been deliberately destroyed, it was not necessary for the accused to show that his right to make full answer and defence had been prejudiced by the loss of the evidence. It was enough that the evidence "*may* affect the conduct of the defence".[7] The possibility that the notes would reveal some inconsistency between the account the complainant made to her counsellor and her testimony at trial was enough to meet this low threshold.

With respect, the reasoning of the majority in *Carosella* does not stand up to analysis. In that case, the Crown had committed no breach of the duty to preserve or disclose relevant evidence, because the counsellor's notes had never been in the possession or control of the Crown. The crisis centre had committed no breach of any Charter duty, because it was a private body to which the Charter does not apply.[8] The centre, like any other private body, was free to preserve or destroy its files as it chose. And the mere fact that one piece of potentially relevant evidence had gone missing (for whatever reason) could hardly amount to a breach

---

[6] *R. v. Carosella*, [1997] 1 S.C.R. 80. The majority judgment was that of Sopinka J., with Lamer C.J., Cory, Iacobucci and Major JJ. concurring. A dissenting opinion was delivered by L'Heureux-Dubé J. and was concurred in by La Forest, Gonthier, and McLachlin JJ.

[7] *R. v. Carosella*, [1997] 1 S.C.R. 80, para. 36 per Sopinka J.

[8] In addressing the remedy of a stay (but not the application of the Charter), Sopinka J. noted (para. 56) that the sexual assault crisis centre was government funded, that its activities were "scrutinized" by the provincial government, and that its conduct would tend to bring the administration of justice into disrepute. However he did not suggest that the centre was a government body within the scope of s. 32 of the Charter; and the cases under s. 32 dealing with hospitals and universities (which Sopinka J. did not discuss) make clear that there was insufficient government control for the shredding of the documents to be considered "government action": ch. 37, Application of Charter, under heading § 37:10, "Government".

of the accused's right to make full answer and defence. There would be few if any criminal prosecutions in which every piece of relevant evidence in the world, however speculative its value, had been made available to the accused. Indeed, the *La* case,[9] which was decided just a few weeks after *Carosella*, makes clear that the accused's right to disclosure is not so broad as to cause a Charter breach every time evidence is lost or destroyed. The rules laid down in *La* seem to be fully satisfied in *Carosella*. In *Carosella*, as in *La*, the Crown made a perfectly satisfactory explanation for its failure to produce the counsellor's notes—they had been destroyed by an agency outside Crown control. And in *Carosella*, as in *La*, there was no reason to suppose that the counsellor's notes were critical to the accused's ability to make full answer and defence—their only relevance was the possibility that the counsellor might have recorded some observation by the complainant that was inconsistent with her evidence at trial. After *La, Carosella* seems to be a case that is unlikely to be followed.[10] As will be explained in the next section, Parliament has now prohibited the disclosure to the accused in sexual-assault cases of confidential records of which the only relevance is that they may disclose an inconsistent statement by the complainant or that they may relate to the credibility of the complainant. The *Carosella* issue will, therefore, not come up again, except perhaps in the form of a challenge to the new legislation.

§ 47:37 Statutory limits on pre-trial disclosure

The Supreme Court of Canada recognized in *O'Connor*[1] that the accused's right to disclosure from third parties must be limited in sexual assault cases, where the constitutional rights to privacy and equality of complainants and other witnesses must be weighed in the balance with the accused's right to make full answer and defence. In *Carosella*, however, the majority of the Court made no mention of the interests that could be impaired by the compelled production of the records of sexual assault crisis centres. After the *O'Connor* and *Carosella* decisions, Parliament enacted legislation, in the form of amendments to the Criminal Code, that placed severe restrictions on the disclosure of confidential records in sexual assault cases.[2] The statutory requirements purport to replace the procedure for the disclosure of third-party records that was developed by the majority of the Court in *O'Connor*, a procedure which was perceived by Parliament to give undue preference to the

---

[9] *R. v. La*, [1997] 2 S.C.R. 680.

[10] In *La*, Sopinka J. distinguished *Carosella* as a case of "deliberate frustration of the court's jurisdiction" ([1997] 2 S.C.R. 680, para. 26), but this ignores the fact that the deliberate destruction in *Carosella* was not the work of the Crown to which the Charter applies.

[Section 47:37]

[1] *R. v. O'Connor*, [1995] 4 S.C.R. 411.

[2] S.C. 1997, c. 46, s. 1, adding new ss. 278.1-278.91 to the Criminal Code.

rights of the accused over the rights of complainants and witnesses.[3] The legislation applies to *all* confidential records, including those in the Crown's possession, with the exception of records that are created in the course of a police investigation. This eliminates the distinction drawn by the Court in *O'Connor* between records in the possession of the Crown, which were always to be disclosed unless privileged, and records in the possession of third parties, which were only to be disclosed if they met the *O'Connor* test.

According to the Criminal Code amendments, a confidential record will be produced for inspection by the court if the defence can establish both that it is "likely relevant", and that its production is "necessary in the interests of justice". As to what is "likely relevant", the legislation supplies a list of 11 reasons which will *not* be sufficient to establish likely relevance. One of these is that "the record may disclose a prior inconsistent statement of the complainant or witness"; another is that "the record may relate to the credibility of the complainant or witness". As to "the interests of justice", the legislation supplies a list of eight factors that are relevant to the interests of justice:

(a) the extent to which the record is necessary for the accused to make a full answer and defence;
(b) the probative value of the record;
(c) the nature and extent of the reasonable expectation of privacy with respect to the record;
(d) whether production of the record is based on a discriminatory belief or bias;
(e) the potential prejudice to the personal dignity and right to privacy of any person to whom the record relates;
(f) society's interest in encouraging the reporting of sexual offences;
(g) society's interest in encouraging the obtaining of treatment by complainants of sexual offences; and
(h) the effect of the determination on the integrity of the trial process.

Once the judge has determined that the records are likely relevant and that the interests of justice favour production, the judge will order them to be produced, and will then inspect the records in the absence of the parties to determine whether, with reference to the eight factors listed above, it is in the interests of justice to release some or all of them to the defence, and whether they should be subject to editing or other conditions.[4]

These Criminal Code amendments, which were enacted in 1997, set restrictions on the pre-trial disclosure of confidential records in sexual assault proceedings that are significantly more severe than those set by the Supreme Court of Canada. With respect to records in the possession

[3]S.C. 1997, c. 46, preamble.

[4]The procedure mandated by Parliament is very similar to the procedure suggested by L'Heureux-Dubé J. for the minority of the Supreme Court of Canada in *R. v. O'Connor*, [1995] 4 S.C.R. 411.

of the Crown, *Stinchcombe*[5] had decided that, if they were relevant to the defence and not privileged, they should automatically be disclosed to the accused. The 1997 amendments protect records in the possession of the Crown with the same elaborate two-stage procedure for determining whether disclosure should be made as is applied to records in the possession of third parties.[6] Under that procedure, some records that the Court in *Stinchcombe* assumed were necessary to enable the accused to make full answer and defence might now be withheld as the result of balancing the eight listed factors. With respect to records in the possession of third parties, the 1997 amendments essentially follow, not the majority opinion in *O'Connor*[7] but the dissenting opinion of L'Heureux-Dubé J. whose standards for disclosure were stricter than those of the majority. In particular, the 1997 amendments call for the balancing of factors to take place at the first stage of review (production to the judge) as well as the second stage (production to the accused). In addition, the factors to be considered include two that were stipulated by L'Heureux-Dubé J. and rejected by the majority, namely, society's interest in encouraging the reporting of sexual offences, and the effect of the determination on the integrity of the trial process. Under the 1997 amendments, therefore, some records that the majority in *O'Connor* thought were necessary to enable the accused to make full answer and defence might now be withheld as the result of the higher barriers to disclosure.

Parliament braced itself for the inevitable challenge to the 1997 amendments by including a long preamble which recites Parliament's concern about the prevalence of sexual violence against women and children, the privacy and equality rights of victims of sexual violence and the risk that the reporting of incidents of sexual violence may be deterred by the compelled production of records of personal information about victims. The assumption underlying the preamble was that the amendments would have to be justified under s. 1 as a limit on the s. 7 right to make full answer and defence. The challenge came in *R. v. Mills* (1999),[8] when the Supreme Court of Canada upheld the amendments. What was surprising about the decision was that the Court did not rely on s. 1 to uphold the law. Rather, in a remarkable display of deference to Parliament, the Court said that *O'Connor* (and presumably *Stinchcombe)* was "not necessarily the last word on the subject", and that "the law develops through a dialogue between courts and legislatures".[9] The Court noted that Parliament had enacted the amendments only after a long consulta-

[5]*R. v. Stinchcombe*, [1991] 3 S.C.R. 326.

[6]There were two variations in the general regime for records in the possession of the Crown. First, the regime did not apply if the witness had waived the protection of the regime. Secondly, the prosecutor was required to notify the accused of the existence of any records in the Crown's possession.

[7]*R. v. O'Connor*, [1995] 4 S.C.R. 411.

[8]*R. v. Mills*, [1999] 3 S.C.R. 669. McLachlin and Iacobucci JJ. wrote the opinion of the majority; Lamer C.J. wrote a separate opinion dissenting in part (with respect to disclosure of records in the possession of the Crown).

[9]*R. v. Mills*, [1999] 3 S.C.R. 669, para. 20; see also references to dialogue in paras.

tion process that included consideration of the constitutional standards set in *O'Connor*, and that also included information as to how well the *O'Connor* regime was working.[10] What the Court in *O'Connor* regarded as "preferable" was not a "rigid constitutional template" and "did not preclude Parliament from coming to a different conclusion".[11] The Court concluded that, although the 1997 amendments gave more weight to the complainants' rights of privacy and equality than had the Court's previous decisions, the amendments still gave sufficient weight to the accuseds' rights to make full answer and defence, and the amendments were therefore constitutional.[12]

XXII. FAIR ADMINISTRATIVE PROCEDURES

§ 47:38 Fair administrative procedures

Earlier in this chapter we noticed the debate on the question whether "fundamental justice" in s. 7 was synonymous with "natural justice" at common law. That debate was settled by the *B.C. Motor Vehicle Reference*,[1] which held that s. 7 extended to substantive as well as procedural justice. As the bulk of this chapter illustrates, s. 7 goes far beyond natural justice, which is a requirement that administrative tribunals observe rules of *procedural* fairness.[2] However, s. 7 also includes a requirement of procedural fairness.[3] This requirement attaches only where a decision-maker has a power of decision over life, liberty or security of the person.[4] Where this is so, s. 7 will impose rules of procedural fairness on the decision-maker. Those rules are probably the same—but are at least as

57, 125, 133 and 143; and see also ch. 36, Charter of Rights, under heading §§ 36:8 to 36:11, "Dialogue with legislative branch".

[10] *R. v. Mills*, [1999] 3 S.C.R. 669, paras. 59, 125.

[11] *R. v. Mills*, [1999] 3 S.C.R. 669, para. 133.

[12] For criticism, see D. Stuart, "*Mills:* Dialogue with Parliament and Equality by Assertion at What Cost?" (2000) 28 C.R. (5th) 275; J. Cameron, "Dialogue and Hierarchy in Charter Interpretation: A Comment on *R. v. Mills*" (2001), 38 Alta. L. Rev. 1051.

[Section 47:38]

[1] *Re B.C. Motor Vehicle Act*, [1985] 2 S.C.R. 486.

[2] S.A. de Smith, Lord Woolf and J.L. Jowell, Judicial Review of Administrative Action (Sweet & Maxwell, London, 5th ed., 1995), chs. 4, 5; D.J.M. Brown and J.M. Evans, Judicial Review of Administrative Action in Canada (Canvasback Publishing, 2004), chs. 7-12.

[3] *Singh v. Minr. of Emplmt. and Imm.*, [1985] 1 S.C.R. 177, 212 per Wilson J.; *Pearlman v. Man. Law Society*, [1991] 2 S.C.R. 869, 882 per Iacobucci J.; *Idziak v. Can.*, [1992] 3 S.C.R. 631, 656 per Cory J.; *New Brunswick v. G.(J.)*, [1999] 3 S.C.R. 46; *Winnipeg Child and Family Services v. K.L.W.*, [2000] 2 S.C.R. 519; *Suresh v. Can.*, [2002] 1 S.C.R. 3; *Charkaoui v. Can.*, [2007] 1 S.C.R. 350; *Charkaoui v. Can.*, [2008] 2 S.C.R. 326; *Can. v. Khadr*, [2008] 2 S.C.R. 125; *Can. v. Harkat*, [2014] 2 S.C.R. 33.

[4] This explains the continuing significance of s. 2(e) of the Canadian Bill of Rights, which imposes on federal decision-makers with power to determine "rights and obligations" a duty to observe the procedural side of fundamental justice: *Singh v. Minr. of Emplmt. and Imm.*, [1985] 1 S.C.R. 177; *MacBain v. Lederman*, [1985] 1 F.C. 856 (C.A.). Compare *Amaratunga v. Northwest Atlantic Fisheries Organization*, [2013] 3 S.C.R. 866; and *Kazemi Estate v. Islamic Republic of Iran*, [2014] 3 S.C.R. 176.

generous—as those that would be required by the common law.[5] The common law rules are in fact basic tenets of the legal system, and they have evolved in response to the same values and objectives as s. 7.[6] For example, it has been held that a person claiming to be a refugee has a right to an oral hearing before the body with authority to determine the issue.[7] It has been held that a decision to deport a refugee does not require an oral hearing, although s. 7 does require disclosure of the case for deportation and an opportunity to reply in writing.[8] Where a person who has been ordered deported has petitioned the United Nations Human Rights Committee for relief, and the Committee has made a request that Canada stay the deportation until the Committee has had time to consider the petition, s. 7 does not require that Canada stay the deportation.[9]

The common law rules of procedural fairness must, of course, yield to any inconsistent statutory provision. Where s. 7 applies, the rules of procedural fairness have constitutional status and will prevail over any inconsistent statutory provision.[10] A statutory provision that was found to be in breach of s. 7 could in theory be justified under s. 1 of the Charter, but it would be difficult to justify a breach of the procedural norms of fundamental justice and no such justification has so far been successful.[11]

---

[5]In *Suresh v. Can.*, [2002] 1 S.C.R. 3, the Supreme Court of Canada indicated that "the principles of fundamental justice demand, at a minimum, compliance with the common law requirements of procedural fairness" (para. 113, citing *Singh v. Minr. of Emplmt. and Imm.*, [1985] 1 S.C.R. 177, 212-213 per Wilson J.). This suggests that the common law will be understood to set the floor, but not necessarily the ceiling, for procedural fairness under s. 7.

[6]J.M. Evans, "The Principles of Fundamental Justice" (1991) 29 Osgoode Hall L.J. 51.

[7]*Singh v. Minr. of Emplmt. and Imm.*, [1985] 1 S.C.R. 177 (Wilson J. for half the Court relied on s. 7; Beetz J. for the other half relied on s. 2(e) of the Canadian Bill of Rights).

[8]*Suresh v. Can.*, [2002] 1 S.C.R. 3.

[9]*Ahani v. Can.* (2002), 58 O.R. (3d) 107 (C.A., Rosenberg J.A. dissenting; leave to appeal to SCC refused on May 16, 2002).

[10]*Singh v. Minr. of Emplmt. and Imm.*, [1985] 1 S.C.R. 177 (striking down refugee-determination provisions of Immigration Act); *R. v. Swain*, [1991] 1 S.C.R. 993 (striking down insanity-determination provisions of Criminal Code).

[11]Chapter 38, Limitation of Rights, under heading §§ 38:24 to 38:29, "Application to qualified rights".

Chapter 55

Equality

I. IN GENERAL

§ 55:1 Distribution of powers
§ 55:2 Canadian Bill of Rights
§ 55:3 American Bill of Rights
§ 55:4 Section 15 of Charter

II. APPLICATION OF S. 15

§ 55:5 Individual
§ 55:6 "Law" in s. 15
§ 55:7 Private action

III. EQUALITY

§ 55:8 Four equalities of s. 15
§ 55:9 Absolute equality
§ 55:10 Aristotle's definition
§ 55:11 Similarly situated
§ 55:12 Formal and substantive equality
§ 55:13 Reasonable classification
§ 55:14 Valid federal objective
§ 55:15 Early applications of s. 15

IV. DISCRIMINATION

§ 55:16 Discrimination

V. LISTED OR ANALOGOUS GROUNDS

§ 55:17 Requirement of a listed or analogous ground
§ 55:18 Addition of analogous grounds

VI. HUMAN DIGNITY

§ 55:19 Ambiguity in Andrews
§ 55:20 Impairment of human dignity
§ 55:21 The factor of correspondence
§ 55:22 Discrimination without human dignity

VII. DISADVANTAGE

§ 55:23 Selection of comparator group

§ 55:24 Requirement of disadvantage
§ 55:25 Objective and subjective disadvantage
§ 55:26 Human dignity and disadvantage
§ 55:27 Group disadvantage

VIII. DIRECT AND INDIRECT DISCRIMINATION

§ 55:28 Substantive equality
§ 55:29 Unintended discrimination
§ 55:30 Reasonable accommodation

IX. JUSTIFICATION UNDER S. 1; AFFIRMATIVE ACTION

§ 55:31 Justification under s. 1
§ 55:32 Affirmative action

X. DISCRIMINATION PERMITTED BY CONSTITUTION

§ 55:33 Age in ss. 23, 29, 99
§ 55:34 Race in s. 91(24)
§ 55:35 Religion in s. 93
§ 55:36 Province of residence in ss. 91, 92
§ 55:37 Citizenship in s. 6
§ 55:38 Language in ss. 16-23

XI. RACE; RELIGION

§ 55:39 Race
§ 55:40 Religion

XII. SEX

§ 55:41 Direct discrimination
§ 55:42 Systemic discrimination
§ 55:43 Section 28

XIII. OTHER GROUNDS OF DISCRIMINATION

§ 55:44 Age
§ 55:45 Mental or physical disability
§ 55:46 Citizenship
§ 55:47 Marital status
§ 55:48 Sexual orientation
§ 55:49 Place of residence
§ 55:50 Occupation

I. IN GENERAL

§ 55:1 Distribution of powers

The distribution of powers over egalitarian values[1] presents two issues. The first issue is the extent to which each level of government may deny or limit egalitarian values, for example, by the enactment of laws that discriminate on the basis of characteristics such as race, national origin or sex. The second issue is the extent to which each level of government may promote egalitarian values, for example, by the enactment of laws that forbid discrimination in employment, accommodation and facilities open to the public.

On the first issue—the power to enact discriminatory laws—the position before April 17, 1985, when s. 15 of the Charter of Rights came into force, was dictated by the doctrine of parliamentary sovereignty: generally speaking, the Parliament or a Legislature could discriminate as it pleased in enacting otherwise competent legislation. Discrimination on the basis of sex, for example, has been upheld.[2] There are, however, some heads of legislative power which have enabled the courts to introduce egalitarian values into decisions reviewing the validity of statutes on federal grounds. The existence of federal power over "naturalization and aliens" (s. 91(25)) led the Privy Council in *Union Colliery v. Bryden* (1899)[3] to strike down a British Columbia law which prohibited the employment of Chinese persons in mines; their lordships reasoned that the pith and substance of the law was the imposition of a disability on aliens and naturalized subjects.[4] The existence of federal legislative power over "Indians, and lands reserved for the Indians" (s. 91(24)) would tend to preclude provincial laws which singled out Indians for special treatment.[5] In all these cases, one must remember that what is denied to one level of government is allowed to the other. Before the

[Section 55:1]

[1]See Schmeiser, Civil Liberties in Canada (1964), ch. 6; Tarnopolsky, The Canadian Bill of Rights (2nd ed., 1975), 46-55.

[2]*A.-G. Can. v. Lavell*, [1974] S.C.R. 1349. Even a challenge based on the Canadian Bill of Rights failed. Ritchie J.'s opinion was agreed to by three other judges. The fifth member of the majority, Pigeon J., expressed no opinion on whether the impugned provision was in conflict with the equality guarantee; he agreed in the result, because he persisted in the view he had expressed in dissent in *Drybones* that the Canadian Bill of Rights could not in any event override inconsistent legislation. Laskin C.J. dissented, on the basis that *Drybones* was controlling; and his opinion was agreed to by three other judges.

[3]*Union Colliery v. Bryden*, [1899] A.C. 580.

[4]But compare *Cunningham v. Tomey Homma*, [1903] A.C. 151; *Quong-Wing v. The King* (1914), 49 S.C.R. 440; *Brooks-Bidlake and Whittall v. A.-G. B.C.*, [1923] A.C. 450, where similarly discriminatory laws were upheld on the basis that the discrimination was merely incidental. Compare *A.-G. B.C. v. A.-G. Can.* (Japanese Employment) [1924] A.C. 203; *Co-op. Committee on Japanese Canadians v. A.-G. Can.*, [1947] A.C. 87; *Morgan v. A.-G. P.E.I.*, [1976] 2 S.C.R. 349. For discussion, see Schmeiser, Civil Liberties in Canada (1964), 257-262.

[5]The singling out would not be decisive of the law's classification: see ch. 15, Judicial Review on Federal Grounds under heading § 15:6, "Singling out".

coming into force of s. 15, discrimination against aliens and naturalized subjects, and against Indians, was undoubtedly competent to the federal Parliament.[6]

The bigger threat to equality in Canada comes not from legislative and official action, but from discrimination by private persons, such as employers, trade unions, landlords, realtors, restaurateurs and other suppliers of goods or services. The economic liberties of freedom of property and contract, which imply a power to deal with whomever one pleases, come into direct conflict with egalitarian values, and in all Canadian jurisdictions the former have now been subordinated to the latter by the enactment of human rights legislation, which forbids various discriminatory practices on pain of a penalty, and establishes a commission to administer the legislation.[7] The authority to enact legislation of this kind is distributed between the federal Parliament and the provincial Legislatures according to which has jurisdiction over the employment, accommodation, restaurants and other businesses or activities in which discrimination is forbidden.[8] Most of the field is accordingly provincial under property and civil rights in the province (s. 92(13)). However, there is little doubt that the federal Parliament could if it chose exercise its criminal law power (s. 91(27)) to outlaw discriminatory practices generally.[9]

§ 55:2 Canadian Bill of Rights

The Canadian Bill of Rights,[1] by s. 1(b), guarantees "equality before the law".[2] This provision, which applies only to the federal Parliament, was on April 17, 1985 superseded by s. 15 of the Charter of Rights, which applies to the federal Parliament and to the provincial Legislatures.

The Supreme Court of Canada held only once that the equality clause in s. 1(b) of the Canadian Bill of Rights had the effect of nullifying a

---

[6]Some kinds of discrimination by the federal Parliament (not the provincial Legislatures) were (after 1960) rendered inoperative by the equality clause in the Canadian Bill of Rights, which is the subject of the next section of this chapter. Saskatchewan, Alberta and Quebec also have bills of rights: see ch. 34, Civil Liberties, under heading § 34:4, "Statutory bills of rights".

[7]For a comprehensive survey of the law, see Tarnopolsky and Pentney, Discrimination and the Law in Canada (rev. ed., 1985).

[8]Tarnopolsky and Pentney, Discrimination and the Law in Canada (rev. ed., 1985), ch. 3.

[9]The analogy here is the prohibition of undesirable commercial practices, as in competition law: see ch. 18, Criminal Law, under heading § 18:11, "Competition law".

[Section 55:2]

[1]The Canadian Bill of Rights is the topic of ch. 35.

[2]For discussion of s. 1(b), see Tarnopolsky, The Canadian Bill of Rights (2nd ed., 1975), ch. 8; M.E. Gold, "Equality before the Law in the Supreme Court of Canada" (1980) 18 Osgoode Hall L.J. 336; Gibson, The Law of the Charter: Equality Rights (1990), 23-36.

statutory provision. That was in the case of *R. v. Drybones* (1969),[3] in which the Court struck down a provision of the Indian Act that made it an offence for "an Indian" to be intoxicated off a reserve. (A companion provision made it an offence to be intoxicated on a reserve.) Ritchie J. for the majority of the Court[4] held that the racial classification "Indian", which was employed by the challenged provision, was a breach of s. 1(b). This ruling cast doubt on all of the provisions of the Indian Act, which is for the most part applicable only to "Indians". Indeed, on principles of federalism, that racial classification is a prerequisite to the validity of the Act, which was enacted under the federal power (s. 91(24)) over "Indians, and lands reserved for the Indians".[5]

Drybones predictably led to challenges to other parts of the Indian Act. These were unsuccessful. In *A. G. Can. v. Lavell* (1973),[6] the majority of the Court upheld the provisions of the Act that defined the term "Indian", although the Act employed a patrilineal concept that discriminated against women. In *A.G. Can. v. Canard* (1975),[7] the Court upheld the provisions of the Act that established a special regime of succession to the property of deceased Indians, although the Act required estates to be administered by an official of the Department of Indian Affairs rather than a relative of the deceased. In both these cases, *Drybones*, although not overruled, was distinguished on implausible grounds, and equality in s. 1(b) was defined in a variety of inconsistent ways.[8] The end result was that the validity of the Indian Act (apart from the drunkenness provision) was settled, but the definition of equality in s. 1(b) was in serious disarray.

After the Indian Act cases, the Supreme Court of Canada began to develop a consistent definition of equality under s. 1 (b). The definition relied on the cryptic notion of a "valid federal objective". If a law pursued a valid federal objective, then it was not in breach of s. 1(b). In *R. v. Burnshine* (1974),[9] this doctrine enabled the Court to uphold sentencing provisions that exposed young offenders to longer sentences than adult

[3] *R. v. Drybones*, [1970] S.C.R. 282.

[4] Ritchie J.'s opinion was agreed to by five other judges; Hall J., who was one of the five, also added a separate concurring opinion. Cartwright C.J., Abbott and Pigeon JJ. dissented.

[5] See ch. 28, Aboriginal Peoples; see also § 55:34, "Race in s. 91(24)".

[6] *A. G. Can. v. Lavell*, [1974] S.C.R. 1349. Ritchie J.'s opinion was agreed to by three other judges. The fifth member of the majority, Pigeon J., expressed no opinion on whether the impugned provision was in conflict with the equality guarantee; he agreed in the result, because he persisted in the view he had expressed in dissent in *Drybones* that the Canadian Bill of Rights could not in any event override inconsistent legislation. Laskin C.J. dissented, on the basis that *Drybones* was controlling; and his opinion was agreed to by three other judges.

[7] *A.G. Can. v. Canard*, [1976] 1 S.C.R. 170. Four concurring opinions were written: by Ritchie J., Martland J. with whom Judson J. agreed, Pigeon J. and Beetz J. Laskin C.J., with whom Spence J. agreed, dissented. The bench comprised only seven judges.

[8] For more expansive criticism of these cases, see the 2nd edition of this book (1985), 787-789.

[9] *R. v. Burnshine*, [1975] 1 S.C.R. 693. Martland J.'s majority opinion was agreed

offenders; the young offenders were to serve "indeterminate" sentences in special correctional facilities which would be dedicated to the rehabilitation of the unfortunate inmates. The Court held that the rehabilitation of young offenders was a valid federal objective that justified the age-based distinction in the statute. In *Bliss v. A.G. Can.* (1979),[10] the Court upheld a provision of the Unemployment Insurance Act that denied benefits to a woman whose employment had been interrupted by pregnancy. An unspecified valid federal objective was invoked to justify the denial of benefits in that situation. In *MacKay v. The Queen* (1980),[11] the Court upheld a provision of the National Defence Act that exposed members of the armed forces to trial by military tribunal for offences for which a civilian would be tried in the ordinary courts. Because the National Defence Act had been enacted for a valid federal objective, it followed that any differentiation between members of the armed forces and other citizens could not be attacked.[12]

The valid federal objective doctrine was unsatisfactory in two ways. First, the Court never clarified what the term meant, although the Court always accepted that a statute containing a challenged provision did pursue a valid federal objective. Secondly, the Court (at least in *Bliss* and *MacKay)* did not relate the valid federal objective to the particular provision that was under challenge; if the Act as a whole pursued a valid federal objective, then every detailed provision was invulnerable to attack on equality grounds.[13] In effect, the Court automatically deferred to Parliament's judgment as to the distinctions that were required in order to establish a legislative scheme of sentencing, unemployment insurance, military justice or anything else.[14]

With the coming into force of s. 15 of the Charter of Rights, s. 1(b) of

---

with by five other judges, two of whom, Ritchie and Pigeon JJ., added brief additional reasons. Laskin J., with Spence and Dickson JJ., dissented.

[10]*Bliss v. A.G. Can.*, [1979] 1 S.C.R. 183. Ritchie J. wrote the judgment of the Court.

[11]*MacKay v. The Queen*, [1980] 2 S.C.R. 370. Ritchie J.'s opinion was agreed with by four other judges. McIntyre J., with Dickson J., wrote a separate concurring opinion. Laskin C.J., with Estey J., dissented.

[12]Charter challenges based, not on s. 15, but on s. 7 (overbreadth) and s. 11(f) have also failed: *R. v. Moriarity*, [2015] 3 S.C.R. 485 (National Defence Act not overbroad in including Criminal Code and other offences of general application as "service offences" for which members of the armed forces are tried by military courts); *R. v. Stillman*, 2019 SCC 40 (lack of jury trials in military courts does not infringe the right to a trial by jury in s. 11(f)). For fuller discussion, see ch. 51, Rights on Being Charged, under heading § 51:24, "Offence under military law".

[13]This brief account inevitably omits some complexities, including the valiant efforts of Beetz J. (in *Canard)*, McIntyre J. (in *MacKay)* and Laskin J. (in *Lavell, Canard* and *Burnshine)* to introduce more sophistication into the reasoning. An expanded account of the cases is provided in the 2nd edition of this book (1985), 787-794.

[14]In *Beauregard v. Can.*, [1986] 2 S.C.R. 56, a case which had arisen before s. 15 came into force, the Court by majority rejected a challenge under s. 1(b) to an amendment to the Judges Act that required newly appointed judges to contribute to the cost of their pensions while exempting existing judges from the obligation. Dickson C.J. for the majority said (at 90) that "the day has passed when it might have been appropriate . . . to reassess the direction this Court has taken in interpreting that document [the Cana-

the Canadian Bill of Rights, although still in force, has been rendered irrelevant.[15] Moreover, in applying s. 15, the Supreme Court of Canada has turned over a new leaf. The language of valid federal objective has been banished, and replaced by new doctrine that is less deferential to the legislative will.[16] That new doctrine is the subject of later sections of this chapter. First, however, is a brief description of the American equal protection jurisprudence.

§ 55:3 American Bill of Rights

The fourteenth amendment to the Constitution of the United States provides that no state shall deny to any person within its jurisdiction "the equal protection of the laws". Although the fourteenth amendment applies only to the states, the guarantee of equal protection has been held to be incorporated in the due process clause of the fifth amendment, which applies to the federal Congress.[1] In the result, both levels of government are bound by a guarantee of "equal protection of the laws".

This guarantee of equal protection is unqualified in its terms; and the Constitution of the United States contains no equivalent of s. 1 of the Canadian Charter of Rights, under which reasonable limits on rights are authorized, provided that they "can be demonstrably justified in a free and democratic society". And yet, recognizing that nearly all laws impose burdens or confer benefits on special groups, and deny the benefits or burdens to other groups, the Supreme Court of the United States has developed the doctrine of "reasonable classification", which saves those legislative classifications that are a reasonable means of achieving a legitimate legislative purpose.[2]

In applying the doctrine of reasonable classification, the Court has developed a "two-tier" standard of review. The upper tier includes laws that classify by race or national origin, which the Court describes as "suspect" classifications. Also included in the upper tier are laws which, although employing other kinds of classifications, abridge a "fundamental" right, such as the right to vote or the right of interstate travel. For laws coming within the upper tier, the standard of review is usually described as "strict scrutiny". It is presumed that such laws are not a

---

dian Bill of Rights]". Beetz J., with McIntyre J., dissented.

[15]On the relationship between the Canadian Bill of Rights and the Charter of Rights, see ch. 35, Canadian Bill of Rights.

[16]The leading case *is Andrews v. Law Society of B.C.*, [1989] 1 S.C.R. 143; see esp. 170, rejecting Canadian Bill of Rights doctrine.

[Section 55:3]

[1]The applicability of the American Bill of Rights to both levels of government is explained in ch. 37, Application of Charter, under heading § 37:6, "Both levels of government".

[2]For accounts of the equal protection jurisprudence, see J. Tussman and J. tenBroek, "The Equal Protection of the Laws" (1949) 37 Calif. L. Rev. 341; L.H. Tribe, American Constitutional Law (Foundation Press, N.Y., 2nd ed., 1986), ch. 16; J.E. Nowak and R.D. Rotunda, Constitutional Law (West, St. Paul, Minn., 7th ed., 2004), ch. 14.

reasonable means of securing a legitimate legislative purpose. Such laws are held to be unconstitutional unless the government establishes that the classification was justified by a "compelling state interest", and that there was no alternative means of vindicating that state interest. Because it is hard for the government to discharge this burden, the practical effect of including a law in the upper tier is that it is very likely to be held to be unconstitutional. In particular, with the exception of the wartime case of the detention of Japanese Americans[3] the modern Supreme Court of the United States has invariably struck down laws which classified by race. *Brown v. Board of Education* (1954),[4] the school desegregation case, is the most famous example.

Even programmes of affirmative action, which are designed to advance the members of racial minorities, are presumptively unconstitutional and have to meet the standard of strict scrutiny. University admissions policies that make use of racial quotas in order to admit more minority students are unconstitutional.[5] However, a majority of the Supreme Court of the United States has accepted that the educational benefit of a diverse student body is a "compelling state interest" that would justify an admissions program that is "narrowly tailored" to serve that interest without the use of quotas. The admissions program of the Law School of the University of Michigan, which used minority race as a "plus factor" in the evaluation of applicants, has been upheld on this ground.[6]

The lower tier of judicial review under the equal protection clause includes all legislative classifications that are not "suspect" and that do not affect fundamental rights. For these laws, a more relaxed standard of judicial review, usually described as "minimal scrutiny", is employed. It is sufficient if there is a "rational basis" for the classification. A good example is *Massachusetts Board of Retirement v. Murgia* (1976),[7] in which the Court upheld a state law requiring police officers to retire at age 50. The plaintiff police officer, who had been compulsorily retired at age 50, established that he was still in excellent physical and mental health and fully capable of continuing to serve in the police force. Nonetheless, the Court held that the mandatory retirement law satisfied the rational basis test. To remove from police service those officers whose competence had presumptively diminished with age was a reasonable means of achieving a legitimate legislative purpose, namely, securing the physical preparedness of the state's police officers. The Court explicitly rejected the argument that age ("a stage that each of us will reach if we live out our normal span") was a suspect category, inviting

---

[3]*Korematsu v. United States* (1944), 323 U.S. 214.

[4]*Brown v. Board of Education* (1954), 347 U.S. 483.

[5]*Regents of University of California v. Bakke* (1978), 438 U.S. 265 (16 of 100 places in medical school reserved for minorities; held invalid).

[6]*Grutter v. Bollinger* (2003), 539 U.S. 306. But compare *Parents v. Seattle School Dist. No. 1* (2007), 551 U.S. 701 (striking down use of race as a "tiebreaker" in assigning students to high schools in order to increase racial diversity in the schools).

[7]*Massachusetts Board of Retirement v. Murgia* (1976), 427 U.S. 307.

strict scrutiny.[8] As this case illustrates, it is not difficult for a government to find a rational basis for a law, so that the minimal scrutiny entailed by including a classification in the lower tier only occasionally results in a holding of unconstitutionality.[9]

Not all equal protection cases fit the neat two-tier analysis. In particular, classifications by sex, which used to be placed on the lower tier, have recently been subjected to a stricter standard of review than the rational basis test. The leading case is *Craig v. Boren* (1976),[10] where the Court struck down a state law that prohibited the sale of beer to males under 21 and females under 18. This discrimination against males aged 18 to 21 was supported by evidence showing a much higher incidence of drunkenness arrests and alcohol-related car accidents for young males than for young females. Despite this evidence, the Court held that the law was unconstitutional. Brennan J. for the majority of the Court said that "the showing offered by the [government] does not satisfy us that sex represents a legitimate, accurate proxy for the regulation of drinking and driving".[11] In getting to this result, Brennan J. articulated a standard of judicial review that fell somewhere in between strict scrutiny and minimal scrutiny. He said that "classifications by gender must serve important governmental objectives and must be substantially related to achievement of those objectives".[12] This test, which has come to be described as "intermediate scrutiny", has been applied in other cases.[13] However, it may turn out to be just a way station on the journey from the lower tier to the upper tier. It is quite possible that sex will soon be treated as no different from race and national origin, in which case few sexual classifications would survive judicial review under the equal protection clause.

The American cases are not directly relevant to the Canadian Charter of Rights, because the language of s. 15 and its interaction with ss.1 and 28 call for the development of indigenous Canadian doctrine. The rest of this chapter is devoted to explaining that doctrine.

---

[8]*Massachusetts Board of Retirement v. Murgia* (1976), 427 U.S. 307, 313-314.

[9]E.g., *Heller v. Doe* (1993), 509 U.S. 312 (discrimination on basis of mental disability receives rational basis review; procedures for the commitment of "mentally retarded" persons upheld, although less rigorous than those for mentally ill persons and unlikely to withstand heightened scrutiny).

[10]*Craig v. Boren* (1976), 429 U.S. 190.

[11]*Craig v. Boren* (1976), 429 U.S. 190, 204.

[12]*Craig v. Boren* (1976), 429 U.S. 190, 197.

[13]For an account of the cases, see L.H. Tribe, American Constitutional Law (Foundation Press, N.Y., 2nd ed., 1986), 1558-1588; J.E. Nowak and R.D. Rotunda, Constitutional Law (West, St. Paul, Minn., 7th ed., 2004), secs. 14.22-14.24.

§ 55:4 Section 15 of Charter

Section 15 of the Charter of Rights[1] provides as follows:

> 15.(1) Every individual is equal before and under the law and has the right to the equal protection and equal benefit of the law without discrimination and, in particular, without discrimination based on race, national or ethnic origin, colour, religion, sex, age or mental or physical disability.
>
> (2) Subsection (1) does not preclude any law, program or activity that has as its object the amelioration of conditions of disadvantaged individuals or groups including those that are disadvantaged because of race, national or ethnic origin, colour, religion, sex, age or mental or physical disability.

Section 15[2] confers its right on an "individual". Equality is expressed in four different ways: equality before the law, equality under the law, equal protection of the law and equal benefit of the law. The section also guarantees against "discrimination based on race, national or ethnic origin, colour, religion, sex, age or mental or physical disability". These are the named or listed grounds of discrimination. (The common practice of referring to them as "enumerated" grounds is not quite accurate, because the grounds are not numbered.) The section makes clear, by the phrase "in particular", that the named grounds are not exhaustive. Subsection (2) of s. 15 authorizes the creation of affirmative action programmes that have the purpose of ameliorating the conditions of disadvantaged groups. The function of each of the elements of s. 15, and the ways in which the various elements relate to each other and to s. 1 of the Charter, occupy the rest of this chapter.

Section 32(2) of the Charter delayed the coming into force of s. 15 for

---

[Section 55:4]

[1]See Gibson, The Law of the Charter: Equality Rights (1990); Bayefsky and Eberts (eds.), Equality Rights and the Charter of Rights (1985); Smith (ed.), Righting the Balance: Canada's New Equality Rights (1986); Weiler and Elliot (eds.), Litigating the Values of a Nation (1986), Part II; Boyle and others (eds.), Charterwatch: Reflections on Equality (1986); Mahoney and Martin, Equality and Judicial Neutrality (1987); Brodsky and Day, Canadian Charter Equality Rights for Women (1989); Beaudoin and Mendes (eds.), The Canadian Charter of Rights and Freedoms (4th ed., 2005), ch. 14 (by W. Black and L. Smith); Stuart, Charter Justice in Canadian Criminal Law (3rd ed., 2001), ch. 10; McLeod, Takach, Morton, Segal, The Canadian Charter of Rights (Carswell, loose-leaf), ch. 25; Canadian Charter of Rights Annotated (Canada Law Book, loose-leaf), annotation to s. 15. The last work provides a bibliography of the periodical literature.

[2]Section 15 was in the October 1980 version of the Charter, but in the following terms:

> (1) Everyone has the right to equality before the law and to the equal protection of the law without discrimination because of race, national or ethnic origin, colour, religion, age or sex.
>
> (2) This section does not preclude any law, program or activity that has as its object the amelioration of conditions of disadvantaged persons or groups.

The final version appeared in the April 1981 version. In the final version "every individual" replaced "everyone"; new and more various formulations of the idea of equality were substituted; the words "in particular" made clear that the specified grounds of discrimination were not exhaustive; "mental or physical disability" were added to the specified grounds of discrimination; and the "including" clause was added to s. 15(2). On the history of s. 15, see Symposium Issue, "Equality: The Heart of a Just Society" (2006) 5 J.L. & Equality 13 (B.L. Strayer), 25 (M. Dawson), 39 (D. Anderson), 47 (M. Eberts).

three years after the coming into force of the rest of the Charter. That brought s. 15 into force on April 17, 1985. The purpose of the delay was to provide time for the federal government and each province to review its body of laws and make those amendments that were necessary to bring the laws into conformity with s. 15. This review did take place in all Canadian jurisdictions except for Quebec, and each jurisdiction enacted amendments to a large number of statutes to correct perceived violations of s. 15 and other Charter rights.[3]

II. APPLICATION OF S. 15

§ 55:5 Individual

The *benefit* of the equality rights in s. 15 is conferred upon "an individual". The word individual has been analyzed earlier in this book, and the conclusion reached that it probably excludes a corporation.[1]

§ 55:6 "Law" in s. 15

The *burden* of the equality rights, like all other Charter rights, is imposed by s. 32 on the Parliament and government of Canada and the Legislature and government of each province. Section 32 has been analyzed earlier in this book, and the conclusion reached that it includes, among other things, all action taken under statutory authority.[1] Does the reference to "law" in the various formulations of the equality rights in s. 15 have the effect of narrowing the application of s. 15 so as to exclude governmental action that is not law?[2]

This question arose in *R. v. S.(S.)* (1990).[3] The federal Young Offenders Act authorized the Attorney General of each province to establish a programme of "alternative measures" to divert young offenders away from proceedings in the courts. The contemplated diversion programmes were established in nine provinces, but not in Ontario. A young person accused of a crime in Ontario argued that the failure of the Attorney General to establish a programme in Ontario was a violation of the accused's equality rights under s. 15. The Supreme Court of Canada rejected this argument on the ground that s. 15 applied only to "the

---

[3]Chapter 36, Charter of Rights, under heading § 36:2, "Protection of civil liberties".

[Section 55:5]

[1]Chapter 37, Application of Charter, under heading § 37:3, "Individual". This does not mean that a corporation can never invoke s. 15: see ch. 59, Procedure, under heading §§ 59:2 to 59:6, "Standing".

[Section 55:6]

[1]Chapter 37, Application of Charter, under heading § 37:7, "Parliament or Legislature".

[2]The issue is briefly and inconclusively raised in *Andrews v. Law Society of B.C.*, [1989] 1 S.C.R. 143, 164, 193.

[3]*R. v. S.(S.)*, [1990] 2 S.C.R. 254. Dickson C.J. wrote the unanimous opinion of the Court.

law".[4] Section 15 did not apply to an exercise of discretion conferred by law, but only to the enabling law itself. Therefore, the Attorney General of Ontario's decision not to establish a diversion programme could not be impeached under s. 15. In a companion case, *R. v. S.(G.)* (1990),[5] the Court also rejected an equality attack on a diversion programme that had been established, on the ground that the programme was an exercise of discretion under the Act.

These holdings that s. 15 has no application to an exercise of discretion conferred by a statute must surely be wrong. It makes no sense to say that Parliament itself lacks the power to abridge equality rights, but Parliament can confer on a delegate the power to abridge equality rights. The better view is that Parliament is unable to delegate a power that Parliament does not possess. Restrictions on the power of Parliament (or a Legislature) must apply to all bodies that draw their powers from the Parliament (or the Legislature). This does seem to be the latest view of the Supreme Court of Canada, because six months after the *S.* cases a majority of the Court asserted that the requirement of "law" in s. 15 is satisfied by conduct taken under the authority of law,[6] and a majority of the Court held that a collective agreement is "law" within s. 15.[7] In these two cases, no reference was made to the contrary rulings in the two *S.* cases. However, the later expression of opinion is the better one.

It now seems clear that the reference to law in s. 15 does not have the effect of excluding anything from the application of s. 15.[8] In other words, s. 15 applies to the same range of governmental action as other Charter rights[9] The range of governmental action is that defined in s. 32.[10]

---

[4]The Court held as well, following *R. v. Turpin*, [1989] 1 S.C.R. 1296, that province of residence was not a ground of discrimination under s. 15: § 55:49, "Place of residence". On this basis, the reasoning about "law" in s. 15 was not strictly necessary to the decision.

[5]*R. v. S.(G.)*, [1990] 2 S.C.R. 294. Dickson C.J. wrote the unanimous opinion of the Court.

[6]*McKinney v. U. of Guelph*, [1990] 2 S.C.R. 229, 276-278 per La Forest J. (with whom Dickson C.J. and Gonthier J. agreed), 380-386 per Wilson J. (with whom on this issue Cory J. agreed); Sopinka J. left the issue open at 444. Both La Forest and Wilson JJ. in the passages referred to assumed that even governmental action taken under common law authority, e.g., by contract, would be covered by "law" in s. 15 and caught by s. 15. They referred in support to the reference to "program or activity" in s. 15(2).

[7]*Douglas/Kwantlen Faculty Assn. v. Douglas College*, [1990] 3 S.C.R. 570, 585 per La Forest J. (with whom Dickson C.J. and Gonthier J. and on this issue Cory J. agreed), 614 per Wilson J. (with whom L'Heureux-Dubé J. agreed); Sopinka J. took the view at 616 that a consensual act could not be law within s. 15.

[8]See e.g. *R. v. Swain*, [1991] 1 S.C.R. 933 (common law rule subjected to s. 15 scrutiny); *Eldridge v. British Columbia*, [1997] 3 S.C.R. 624 (exercise of delegated statutory authority held to infringe s. 15); *Lovelace v. Ontario*, [2000] 1 S.C.R. 950 (exercise of delegated statutory authority subjected to s. 15 scrutiny); *Little Sisters Book and Art Emporium v. Canada*, [2000] 2 S.C.R. 1120 (exercise of delegated statutory authority held to infringe s. 15; legislation itself held not to infringe s. 15).

[9]This would include not only governmental action taken under statutory authority, but also governmental action taken under common law authority: previous two notes.

§ 55:7 Private action

There is no doubt that s. 32 of the Charter excludes private action from the application of the Charter. This means that s. 15 does not apply to private acts of discrimination, as where an employer hires only male employees, or a landlord rents only to white people, or a shopkeeper refuses to serve children. However, in all Canadian jurisdictions, Human Rights Codes have been enacted that prohibit private acts of discrimination in employment, accommodation and the provision of services.[1] The Codes are typically enforced by human rights commissions through investigation, mediation and, if necessary, adjudication. The Human Rights Codes are simply statutes. They do not enjoy constitutional status. However, some of the Codes contain primacy clauses making them superior to other statutes, and even without a primacy clause the Supreme Court of Canada has held that a Human Rights Code takes precedence over other statutes.[2]

The Human Rights Codes, as statutes, are themselves subject to the Charter of Rights.[3] In *Blainey v. Ontario Hockey Association* (1986),[4] a girl, who had been excluded by the Ontario Hockey Association from a boy's hockey team, challenged a provision of the Ontario Human Rights Code that permitted single-sex sports teams. The Code generally prohibited discrimination by sex, but made an exception for single-sex sports teams. The Ontario Court of Appeal by a majority held that the exception was a breach of s. 15, because it denied to the plaintiff the benefit of the Human Rights Code by reason of her sex. The effect of nullifying the exception was to make the general prohibition of discrimination applicable to sports teams, which gave the plaintiff a remedy under the Human Rights Code. The Charter of Rights did not apply directly to the action of the Ontario Hockey Association because the Association was a private organization. But by extending the scope of the Human Rights Code to action that the Code left unregulated, the Charter did have an indirect impact on private action.[5]

The argument that succeeded in *Blainey* was tried again in *McKinney*

---

[10]See ch. 37, Application of Charter.

[Section 55:7]

[1]See Tarnopolsky and Pentney, Discrimination and the Law (rev. ed., 1985).

[2]*Winnipeg School Division No. 1 v. Craton*, [1985] 2 S.C.R. 150; *Council of Canadians with Disabilities v. VIA Rail Canada*, [2007] 1 S.C.R. 650, para. 115; see ch. 12, Parliamentary Sovereignty, under heading § 12:10, "Manner and form of future laws".

[3]See R.G. Juriansz, "Section 15 and the Human Rights Codes" in Beaudoin (ed.), Your Clients and the Charter (1988), ch. 12.

[4]*Blainey v. Ontario Hockey Association* (1986), 54 O.R. (2d) 513 (C.A.).

[5]The Charter also had an indirect impact on the common law, which, by virtue of the exception to the Human Rights Code, governed the selection of members to sports teams. The effect of the Charter was to replace the common law rule permitting discrimination with the statutory rule prohibiting discrimination. Accord, *Vriend v. Alberta*, [1998] 1 S.C.R. 493 (extending Alberta's human rights legislation to cover discrimination on the basis of sexual orientation).

v. University of Guelph (1990),[6] in which a university professor who had reached the age of 65 challenged the mandatory retirement rule of his university. The Charter did not apply to the university, because by virtue of its independence from government the university was held to be a private body. However, the Charter did apply to the Ontario Human Rights Code, which indirectly permitted mandatory retirement: the Code's prohibition of discrimination by age in employment applied only up to age 65. The Supreme Court of Canada held that the age-65 limit was a breach of s. 15. However, the Court went on to hold that the limit was justified by s. 1. Therefore, the limit was upheld, and the Charter did not have the effect of extending the Code to cover mandatory retirement at age 65.

III. EQUALITY

§ 55:8 Four equalities of s. 15

Section 15 provides that every individual is "equal before and under the law and has the right to the equal protection and equal benefit of the law". The reason for having four formulations of the idea of equality[1] was to reverse the restrictive interpretations placed by the Supreme Court of Canada on the phrase "equality before the law", which, as we have already noticed, is the phrase used in s. 1(b) of the Canadian Bill of Rights.[2] Section 15 of the Charter speaks of being equal "before and under the law". The words "and under" were intended to abrogate a suggestion by Ritchie J. in the *Lavell* case,[3] that judicial review on equality grounds did not extend to the substance of the law but only to the way in which it was administered. Section 15 also speaks of "equal benefit of the law"; this phrase was intended to abrogate a suggestion by Ritchie J. in the *Bliss* case[4] that the legislative provision of "benefits" was not subject to equality standards. Finally, s. 15 uses the phrase "equal protection . . . of the law". This is very similar to the phrase "equal protection of the laws", which, as we have already noticed, is the phrase used in the fourteenth amendment of the Constitution of the United States.[5]

§ 55:9 Absolute equality

What is meant by a guarantee of equality? It cannot mean that the law must treat everyone equally. The Criminal Code imposes punishments on persons convicted of criminal offences; no similar burdens are

[6] *McKinney v. University of Guelph*, [1990] 3 S.C.R. 229.

[Section 55:8]

[1] The "four equalities" are analyzed by A.F. Bayefsky in Bayefsky and Eberts (eds.), Equality Rights and the Charter of Rights (1985), 3-25.

[2] § 55:2, "Canadian Bill of Rights".

[3] *A. G. Can. v. Lavell*, [1974] S.C.R. 1349, 1366.

[4] *Bliss v. A.G. Can.*, [1979] 1 S.C.R. 183, 191.

[5] § 55:3, "American Bill of Rights".

imposed on the innocent. Education Acts require children to attend school; no similar obligation is imposed on adults. Manufacturers of food and drugs are subject to more stringent regulations than the manufacturers of automobile parts. The legal profession is regulated differently from the accounting profession. The Wills Act prescribes a different distribution of the property of a person who dies leaving a will from that of a person who dies leaving no will. The Income Tax Act imposes a higher rate of tax on those with high incomes than on those with low incomes. Indeed, every statute or regulation employs classifications of one kind or another for the imposition of burdens or the grant of benefits. Laws never provide the same treatment for everyone.

§ 55:10 Aristotle's definition

Aristotle said that "justice considers that persons who are equal should have assigned to them equal things",[1] and "there is no inequality when unequals are treated in proportion to the inequality existing between them".[2] According to Aristotle's conception of equality, persons who are alike (similarly situated) should be treated alike, and persons who are not alike should be treated differently in proportion to the difference. Laws that single out groups for special treatment do not offend the principle of equality if they employ classifications that appropriately distinguish between people who are not alike, and if they provide for appropriately different treatment for those who are not alike. For example, a person who has committed a crime deserves to be punished, whereas a person who is innocent does not; and a person who has committed a serious crime deserves to be punished more severely than a person who has committed a minor offence. These people are not alike in respect of their liability to punishment, and the law need not—indeed, must not—treat them equally.

The trouble with Aristotle's idea of equality is that the idea is stated at too high a level of generality to be useful. It provides no criteria to determine whether one person is "like" another, or even as to who should be compared to whom; and it provides no criteria to assess the appropriateness of different legislative treatment of those who are not alike. Even the simple example of the treatment of persons who have committed a criminal offence illustrates these problems. What kind of conduct should be treated as criminal? How does one compare the seriousness of different kinds of criminal conduct? What variations in punishment are appropriate to different degrees of seriousness? We normally think of these questions as questions of criminal justice, not equality. The concept of equality is not really useful in answering the questions. This has led commentators to describe equality as an "empty

[Section 55:10]

[1]Aristotle, The Politics of Aristotle (trans. E. Barker, Clarendon Press, Oxford, 1946), Book III, xii, 1282b.

[2]Aristotle, The Politics of Aristotle (trans. E. Barker, Clarendon Press, Oxford, 1946), Book V, i, 1301a.

idea".[3] The idea is empty in the sense that it cannot be applied without first working out the criteria of likeness and like treatment, and the idea of equality cannot by itself supply those criteria.

§ 55:11 Similarly situated

Before the Supreme Court of Canada decided the *Andrews* case,[1] Canadian courts were applying a version of the Aristotelian principle of equality known as the "similarly situated" test.[2] According to that test, a denial of equality was made out if it could be shown that the law accorded the complainant worse treatment than others who were similarly situated. In *Andrews*, McIntyre J. said that this test was "seriously deficient", and that it could be used to justify laws that discriminated against Jewish or Black people.[3] He concluded that the similarly situated test should no longer be used, at least "as a fixed rule or formula for the resolution of equality questions".[4] With respect, this criticism is somewhat exaggerated. Equality is an inescapably "comparative concept" (as McIntyre J. acknowledged).[5] A person is treated unequally only if that person is treated worse than others, and those others (the comparison group) must surely be those who are similarly situated to the complainant. As Gibson has noticed, "no court facing an equality issue can avoid somehow determining whether the person or group relying on section 15 is sufficiently similar to other persons or groups in relevant respects to merit equal treatment".[6] The similarly situated test is not wrong in principle. Its vice is the one identified in the previous paragraph: the test does not supply the crucial criteria that are required to determine who is similarly situated to whom, and what kinds of differences in treatment are appropriate to those who are not similarly situated. The test is deficient in the sense that it provides too little guidance to a reviewing court.

§ 55:12 Formal and substantive equality

The most common criticism of the similarly-situated definition of equality (and of the Aristotelian definition of equality) is not that it provides too little guidance to a reviewing court (or is "empty"), but that it can mask discrimination that occurs indirectly rather than directly.

---

[3]P. Westen, "The Empty Idea of Equality" (1982) 95 Harv. L. Rev. 537; A.F. Bayefsky in Bayefsky and Eberts (eds.), Equality Rights and the Charter of Rights (1985), 2-3; contra, Gibson, The Law of the Charter: Equality Rights (1990), 59-62.

[Section 55:11]

[1]*Andrews v. Law Society of B.C.*, [1989] 1 S.C.R. 143.

[2]E.g., *R. v. Ertel* (1987), 20 O.A.C. 257 (C.A.).

[3]*Andrews v. Law Society of B.C.*, [1989] 1 S.C.R. 143, 166.

[4]*Andrews v. Law Society of B.C.*, [1989] 1 S.C.R. 143, 168.

[5]*Andrews v. Law Society of B.C.*, [1989] 1 S.C.R. 143, 164.

[6]Gibson, The Law of the Charter: Equality Rights (1990), 74. See also *Catholic Children's Aid Society v. S.(T.)* (1989), 69 O.R. (2d) 189, 205-206 per Tarnopolsky J.A., vigorously defending the similarly situated test *after* its repudiation in *Andrews!*

An apparently neutral law may have a disproportionate effect on a particular group, which, as a consequence, is being treated unequally. A law that prohibited women from serving in the police force would have the *direct* effect of discriminating against women. A law framed in gender-neutral language that prohibited persons under six feet in height from serving in the police force would have the *indirect* effect of discriminating against women, because their generally lower height will cause them, disproportionately, to fail to meet the height qualification. A theory that only covers the direct case is often described as "formal equality", and is often attributed to the similarly-situated definition (and to Aristotle). The conventional wisdom is that formal equality is "trivial, even insulting".[1] Robert Wintemute, writing about discrimination on the ground of sexual orientation, points out that formal equality "has tremendous material and symbolic value, which only those who have been denied it for many years can fully appreciate".[2] But, as Wintemute acknowledges, formal equality is not enough. It is also necessary to guarantee "substantive equality", meaning by that term a theory of equality that will capture indirect as well as direct discrimination.

It has never been clear to me that the similarly-situated definition (or the Aristotelian definition) was incapable of recognizing indirect discrimination. After all, the claim of the equality-seeking group is that unlike cases (men and women, for example) are being treated alike by the apparently neutral law (the height requirement, for example). What substantive equality requires[3] is that the identification of persons who are similarly situated must take account of contextual factors related to race, sex and disability (for example), that may make a person's situation sufficiently different to require different treatment in order to be treated fairly (with equal respect).[4] Notice, however, that even when one moves from formal equality to substantive equality, one is still left with the problem that the idea of equality does not by itself supply the criteria for determining which distinctions (whether they be direct or indirect) are consistent with the idea of equality and which are not.

[Section 55:12]

[1]R. Wintemute, "Sexual Orientation and the Charter" (2004) 49 McGill L.J. 1143, 1180.

[2]R. Wintemute, "Sexual Orientation and the Charter" (2004) 49 McGill L.J. 1143, 1180.

[3]I should note that academics are not agreed on precisely what is the difference between formal and substantive equality: for discussion, see P. Hughes, "Recognizing Substantive Equality as a Foundational Principle" (1999) 22 Dal. L.J. 5; D. Greschner, "Does *Law* Advance the Cause of Equality?" (2001) 27 Queen's L.J. 299; B. Ryder, C.C. Faria, E. Lawrence, "What's Law Good For: An Empirical Overview of Charter Equality Rights Decisions" (2004) 24 S.C.L.R. (2d) 103, 105-108.

[4]The current state of the law under s. 15 is explained in §§ 55:28 to 55:30, "Direct and indirect discrimination".

§ 55:13 Reasonable classification

American courts, as we have seen,[1] have found the criteria of equality in a doctrine of reasonable classification. If a law pursues a legitimate state purpose, and it employs classifications that are reasonably related to the accomplishment of that purpose, there is no violation of equal protection. This approach concentrates on the purpose of the law, and tests likeness by reference to that purpose. If the purpose of a law is to safeguard health, then it is appropriate to impose more stringent regulation on the manufacturers of food and drugs than on the manufacturers of products that are not eaten. However, that purpose could not justify a distinction between individual and corporate manufacturers, because risks to health turn on the nature of the product, not on the organizational form of the manufacturer.

The American doctrine of reasonable classification is like the similarly situated test in that it operates at a very high level of generality. Views will differ as to how the purpose of a law is to be ascertained and stated, and as to how perfectly the law's classifications must fit the purpose. The impact of judicial review will therefore depend upon whether the courts are prepared to accept the legislators' judgments on these inherently disputable issues, or whether the courts are prepared to substitute their own views for those of the legislators. As we have noticed, the American courts have developed "levels of scrutiny" that impose strict standards of review (strict scrutiny) on laws that use "suspect" classifications, such as race, or which burden the exercise of fundamental rights, and lax standards of review (minimal scrutiny) on laws that employ classifications that are not suspect and that regulate activities that are less fundamental. In that way, some measure of certainty has been introduced into judicial review on equal protection grounds in the United States.

§ 55:14 Valid federal objective

Before the adoption of the Charter of Rights, Canadian courts applied the guarantee of equality in the Canadian Bill of Rights.[1] As we have seen, the approach that became dominant in the Supreme Court of Canada was to uphold any distinction in a statute if the statute pursued a "valid federal objective". This test brought a high degree of judicial deference to the Court's review of the choices made by Parliament. It was even more deferential than the American standard of minimal scrutiny. The Court was severely criticized for its "timidity" in applying the Canadian Bill of Rights, and the legislative history of s. 15 of the Charter of

[Section 55:13]

[1] § 55:3, "American Bill of Rights".

[Section 55:14]

[1] § 55:2, "Canadian Bill of Rights".

Rights made abundantly clear that it was not to be given the same minimal effect as the Canadian Bill of Rights.[2]

§ 55:15 Early applications of s. 15

With the adoption of the Charter of Rights, Canadian courts faced a dilemma. On the one hand, they could not apply s. 15 so deferentially as to rob it of any serious force; that was the criticism of their decisions under the Canadian Bill of Rights. On the other hand, they could hardly review every distinction in the statute book; that would not be a wise use of judicial resources, and would constantly involve the courts in issues of legislative policy. Until the *Andrews* case was decided by the Supreme Court of Canada in 1989, most courts followed both approaches, that is, they assumed that every legislative distinction was a proper subject for equality review, but they upheld every distinction. The volume of cases was truly disturbing. A study prepared in 1988,[1] only three years after the coming into force of s. 15 (which occurred on April 17, 1985),[2] found 591 cases (two-thirds of which were reported in full) in which a law had been challenged on the basis of s. 15. Most of the challenges seemed unmeritorious, and most were unsuccessful; but the absence of any clear standards for the application of s. 15 encouraged lawyers to keep trying to use s. 15 whenever a statutory distinction worked to the disadvantage of a client.

In the *Andrews* case, which will be described more fully in the next section of this chapter, the Supreme Court of Canada started to develop rules to control the floodgates opened by s. 15. In that case, the Court held that s. 15 was a prohibition of "discrimination", and that discrimination could only be based on a ground that was listed in s. 15 or that was analogous to those listed in s. 15. This ruling had the merit of avoiding any inquiry into the abstract concept of equality, and the further merit of excluding from equality review those statutes that do not employ the listed classifications, or analogous classifications.

IV. DISCRIMINATION

§ 55:16 Discrimination

Section 15(1) of the Charter of Rights provides as follows:

> 15(1) Every individual is equal before and under the law and has the right to the equal protection and equal benefit of the law without discrimination and, in particular, without discrimination based on race, national or ethnic origin, colour, religion, sex, age or mental or physical disability.

The section guarantees equality, but goes on to stipulate "without

---

[2]A.F. Bayefsky in Bayefsky and Eberts (eds.), Equality Rights and the Charter of Rights (1985), 3-25.

[Section 55:15]

[1]Brodsky and Day, Canadian Charter Equality Rights for Women (1989), 277.

[2]Charter of Rights, s. 32(2).

discrimination and, in particular, without discrimination based on race, national or ethnic origin, colour, religion, sex, age or mental or physical disability". It is now clear that s. 15 should be read as prohibiting only those violations of equality that amount to "discrimination". Discrimination is the operative concept. What does it mean? The Supreme Court of Canada has struggled with the answer to this question, but the winding course of judicial interpretation[1] seems now to have settled itself into the following definition of discrimination:

(1) The challenged law imposes (directly or indirectly)[2] on the claimant a disadvantage (in the form of a burden or withheld benefit) in comparison to other comparable persons;[3]
(2) The disadvantage is based on a ground listed in or analogous to a ground listed in s. 15;[4] and
(3) The disadvantage also constitutes an impairment of the human dignity of the claimant.[5]

The claimant who persuades the Court of these three elements is entitled to a finding of discrimination, which means that the challenged law is in breach of s. 15. The burden then shifts to government to justify the discriminatory law under s. 1.[6] For reasons that will be explained, s. 1 justification is difficult, because the finding of an impairment of human dignity will involve much of the same inquiry as that required by s. 1. However, in an unusual case, s. 1 justification will still uphold a discriminatory law.

V. LISTED OR ANALOGOUS GROUNDS

§ 55:17 Requirement of a listed or analogous ground

What kinds of legislative distinctions count as discrimination, and are therefore prohibited by s. 15? Before the *Andrews* case was decided in the Supreme Court of Canada, a variety of views had been articulated by courts and commentators. At one extreme, was the theory, espoused by me in the second edition of this book,[1] that every distinction drawn in a statute counted as discrimination in breach of s. 15. The question

---

[Section 55:16]

[1]See J. Hendry, "The Idea of Equality in Section 15 and its Development" (2002) 21 Windsor Y.B. Access to Justice 153; D. M. McAllister, "Section 15—The Unpredictability of the *Law* test" (2003) 15 Nat. J. Con. Law 35; B. Ryder and others, "What's *Law* Good For: An Empirical Overview of Charter Equality Rights Decisions" (2004) 24 Supreme Court L.R. (2d) 103; P.W. Hogg, "What is Equality? The Winding Course of Judicial Interpretation" (2005) 29 Supreme Court L.R. (2d) 39.

[2]§§ 55:28 to 55:30, "Direct and indirect discrimination".

[3]§§ 55:23 to 55:27, "Disadvantage".

[4]§§ 55:17 to 55:18, "Listed or analogous grounds".

[5]§§ 55:19 to 55:22, "Human dignity".

[6]§ 55:31, "Justification under s. 1".

[Section 55:17]

[1]Hogg, Constitutional Law of Canada (2nd ed., 1985), 799-801.

whether it was justified or not would then have to be determined under s. 1. On this theory, the structure of analysis developed in *R. v. Oakes* (1986)[2] for justification under s. 1 (sufficiently important objective, rational connection to that objective, minimum impairment and proportionality)[3] would be the analysis that would be applied to all s. 15 challenges. The analogy was freedom of expression, which is guaranteed by s. 2(b) of the Charter; the Supreme Court has defined "expression" so broadly that freedom of expression cases are in practice nearly all decided under s. 1.[4]

At the other end of the spectrum was the position taken by McLachlin J. (who became the Chief Justice of Canada) when she was a judge of the British Columbia Court of Appeal. In the *Andrews* case (1986)[5]—the same case that went on to the Supreme Court of Canada—she held that the only legislative distinctions that would amount to discrimination were those that were "unreasonable or unfair". On this theory, s. 15 contained its own implicit requirement of justification, and the question whether a legislative distinction was justified or not would be determined by an assessment of its reasonableness or unfairness according to standards that the courts would have to develop within s. 15 itself. Presumably, s. 1 would play little or no role in s. 15 cases since s. 1 justifies only "reasonable" limits on Charter rights. The analogy was "unreasonable search and seizure", which is prohibited by s. 8 of the Charter; the justificatory principle for laws authorizing searches and seizures is embedded in s. 8 itself.[6]

Both of these competing theories of s. 15 shared the assumption that all legislative distinctions were open to review under s. 15. It was this assumption that opened the floodgates to equality challenges early on. Whether justification was to be found in s. 1 (as I had suggested) or within s. 15 itself (as McLachlin J. had suggested) was not likely to make much difference to the volume of cases coming before the courts. What was needed was some threshold barrier that would reduce the flow of cases to those where legislative distinctions were presumptively suspect, and where judicial intervention was less likely to disturb legitimate legislative line-drawing. In fact, s. 15 did contain some clues to its scope that were missing from its counterparts in the Canadian Bill of Rights and the Fourteenth Amendment. The listed grounds, although admittedly not exhaustive, did point to personal characteristics of individuals that cannot easily be changed and which have often been the target of prejudice or stereotyping. The reference in subsection (2) (the affirmative action clause) to "disadvantaged individuals or groups" suggested that the role of s. 15 was to correct discrimination against

---

[2]*R. v. Oakes*, [1986] 1 S.C.R. 103.

[3]Chapter 38, Limitation of Rights.

[4]Chapter 43, Expression.

[5]*Andrews v. Law Society of B.C.* (1986), 27 D.L.R. (4th) 600, 610 (B.C.C.A.).

[6]Chapter 48, Unreasonable Search or Seizure.

disadvantaged individuals or groups.[7] These features of s. 15 suggested that the proper role of s. 15 was not to eliminate all unfairness from our laws, let alone all classifications that could not be rationally defended, but rather to eliminate discrimination based on immutable personal characteristics.

Andrews v. Law Society of British Columbia (1989)[8] was the first s. 15 case to reach the Supreme Court of Canada. It was a challenge to the statutory requirement of the province of British Columbia that members of the bar had to be citizens of Canada. The Court held unanimously that this requirement was contrary to s. 15, and by a majority that it was not saved by s. 1. McIntyre J. wrote for the unanimous Court on the interpretation of s. 15 (although he ended up dissenting, because he thought the law should be upheld under s. 1). McIntyre J. discussed and rejected the theories advanced by me (that s. 15 condemned all legislative classifications) and by McLachlin J. (that s. 15 condemned unreasonable or unfair classifications). He held that there was a "middle ground" between those two positions, which was to interpret "discrimination" in s. 15 as applying to only the grounds listed in s. 15 and "analogous" grounds. This "enumerated and analogous grounds approach", he said, "most closely accords with the purposes of s. 15", and "leaves questions of justification to s. I".[9] The Court went on to hold (with surprisingly little discussion) that citizenship qualified as an analogous ground of discrimination.

After *Andrews*, it was clear that s. 15 was a prohibition of discrimination, and that discrimination involved the imposition of a disadvantage (the imposition of a burden or the denial of a benefit)[10] on an individual by reason of the individual's possession of a characteristic that was either listed in s. 15 or was analogous to those listed in s. 15. This immediately ruled out judicial review of all statutes that did not employ a listed or analogous classification.[11] This was a severe reduction in the scope of s. 15, but one that could certainly be supported by the text of the section. After *Andrews*, only L'Heureux-Dubé J., for a time, refused

---

[7]Subsection (2) of s. 15 is discussed in § 55:32, "Affirmative action".

[8]*Andrews v. Law Society of British Columbia*, [1989] 1 S.C.R. 143. The Court comprised six judges. Wilson J.'s majority opinion was agreed with by Dickson C.J. and L'Heureux-Dubé J. La Forest J. wrote a separate concurring opinion. McIntyre J.'s dissenting opinion was agreed with by Lamer J.

[9]*Andrews v. Law Society of British Columbia*, [1989] 1 S.C.R. 143, 182. The adjective "enumerated" is not quite accurate, since the listed grounds are not numbered.

[10]In the world of equality, few matters are straightforward. The question of whether a claimant has truly suffered a disadvantage is often difficult to determine, and the question of to whom the claimant should be compared in order to determine disadvantage is also often difficult to determine: see §§ 55:23 to 55:27, "Disadvantage".

[11]Another way of expressing the point would be to say that the restriction to listed and analogous grounds ruled out all equality challenges that were not based on a listed or analogous ground. This might be a preferable formulation in that it more clearly includes indirect as well as direct discrimination: §§ 55:28 to 55:30, "Direct and indirect discrimination".

to accept the new doctrine.[12] She advocated a more discretionary, case-by-case, assessment of whether discrimination existed.[13] No other judge agreed with her, and she rejoined the other members of the Court in *Law v. Canada* (1999),[14] in which the Court unanimously reaffirmed the restriction of s. 15 to listed and analogous grounds. The Court in *Law* also added a new restriction (which turned out to be short-lived), namely, that discrimination involved an impairment of "human dignity". That element of s. 15 is discussed later in this chapter.[15] For present purposes, the point is that the restriction of s. 15 to listed and analogous grounds is a permanent feature of the s. 15 jurisprudence.

§ 55:18 Addition of analogous grounds

Although the restriction to listed and analogous grounds was a severe reduction in the scope of s. 15, it did leave room for analogous grounds to be enrolled as bases for findings of discrimination. What are "analogous" grounds? Obviously, they are grounds that are similar in some important way to the grounds listed in s. 15, which are "race, national or ethnic origin, colour, religion, sex, age or mental or physical disability". These are all personal characteristics of individuals that are unchangeable (or immutable), or at least unchangeable by the individual except with great difficulty or cost.[1] They are not voluntarily chosen by individuals, but are an involuntary inheritance. They describe what a person is rather than what a person does. What is objectionable about using such characteristics as legislative distinctions is that consequences should normally follow what people do rather than what they are. It is morally wrong to impose a disadvantage on a person by reason of a characteristic that is outside the person's control.

The limitation of s. 15 to listed and analogous grounds restricts judicial review to laws that distinguish between individuals on the basis of their inherent attributes as opposed to their behaviour. Section 15 has nothing to say about laws that make special provision for those who have committed a crime, made a will, entered into a contract, become insolvent, manufactured food or drugs, joined the legal profession, purchased a taxable good or service, etc. It is true that individuals may claim to be treated unfairly by the law for conditions that are their own

[12]She had been a member of the Court in *Andrews*, but obviously had not interpreted McIntyre J.'s opinion (with which she agreed, except for the s. 1 issue) as imposing an absolute requirement of listed or analogous grounds.

[13]*Mirun v. Trudel*, [1995] 2 S.C.R. 418, para. 90; *Egan v. Canada*, [1995] 2 S.C.R. 513, para. 89.

[14]*Law v. Canada*, [1999] 1 S.C.R. 497.

[15]§§ 55:19 to 55:22, "Human dignity".

[Section 55:18]

[1]Religion is unlike the other listed characteristics in that there is no natural or legal impediment to a change of religion, and some people do in fact change their religion. However, for most people, religious affiliation is acquired at an early age and becomes an important part of their personal identity. It cannot be easily changed. See Gibson, The Law of the Charter: Equality Rights (1990), 158.

responsibility, but this kind of claim even if fully justified does not warrant a constitutional remedy. This kind of claim is the daily fare of politics, and is best remedied not by judges but by elected and accountable legislative bodies. What does warrant a constitutional remedy is the claim that a law has treated an individual unfairly by reason of a condition over which the person has no control. In that case, forces of prejudice may well have distorted the democratic political process, and it is appropriate for judges to review the law.

No doubt with these kinds of considerations in mind, the Supreme Court has held that an analogous ground is one based on "a personal characteristic that is immutable or changeable only at unacceptable cost to personal identity".[2]

The first analogous ground to be recognized was *citizenship*.[3] That occurred in *Andrews* itself. Although the Court in that case was unanimous that citizenship was an analogous ground, only La Forest J. attempted to articulate a reason. He pointed out that citizenship was a personal characteristic that is "typically not within the control of the individual and, in this sense, is immutable".[4] This ruling was affirmed in *Lavoie v. Canada* (2002),[5] where the issue was the validity of a statutory hiring preference for citizens in the federal public service. A majority of the Court, which divided on issues of human dignity and s. 1, upheld the preference, but all members of the Court agreed that citizenship was an analogous ground.

The second analogous ground to be recognized was *marital status*.[6] The recognition started in *Miron v. Trudel* (1995),[7] which concerned the statutory provision of accident benefits to a "spouse", a term that was defined as a person legally married to the victim. Although the claimant common-law spouse succeeded in striking down the requirement of legal marriage, only four judges actually held that marital status was an analogous ground. Four judges held that it was not. The fifth member of the majority (L'Heureux Dubé J.) held that it did not matter. This was less than a ringing endorsement of marital status as an analogous ground, but, in *Nova Scotia v. Walsh* (2002),[8] the Court (which included two of the judges who had dissented in *Miron v. Trudel)* was unanimous that marital status was an analogous ground. However, the majority of the Court held that the matrimonial property regime of Nova Scotia, which was restricted to persons who were legally married, did not breach s. 15, because it did not impair the human dignity of the common-law spouses who were excluded by reason of their marital status.

---

[2] *Corbiere v. Can.*, [1999] 2 S.C.R. 203, para. 13 per McLachlin and Bastarache JJ. for the majority.

[3] § 55:46, "Citizenship".

[4] *Andrews v. Law Society of B.C.*, [1989] 1 S.C.R. 143, 195.

[5] *Lavoie v. Canada*, [2002] 1 S.C.R. 769.

[6] § 55:47, "Marital status".

[7] *Miron v. Trudel*, [1995] 2 S.C.R. 418.

[8] *Nova Scotia v. Walsh*, [2002] 4 S.C.R. 325.

It is worth interpolating here that neither citizenship nor marital status is immutable in a strong sense. Each is a status that can often be chosen by the individual, although (as the Court has rightly emphasized) that choice is sometimes blocked by legal requirements or disadvantage or (in the case of marital status) by the contrary wish of another person. Indeed, the element of choice in citizenship and marital status has been important in persuading the Court to find ways to uphold legislative distinctions based on citizenship[9] and marital status.[10]

The third analogous ground to be recognized was *sexual orientation.*[11] In *Egan v. Canada* (1995),[12] eight of nine judges decided that sexual orientation was an analogous ground. La Forest J., writing for himself and three others, described sexual orientation as "a deeply personal characteristic that is either unchangeable or changeable only at unacceptable personal costs".[13] For complicated reasons, the claimants, a same-sex couple who were seeking a spousal allowance under the federal Old Age Security program, did not actually succeed.[14] But the ruling on analogous grounds was clear enough, and it paved the way for a series of cases that confirmed the ruling and upheld the equality rights of LGBTQ claimants. In *Vriend v. Alberta* (1998),[15] the Court held that Alberta's human rights code violated s. 15 by failing to include sexual orientation as a prohibited ground of discrimination. In *M. v. H.* (1999),[16] the Court held that Ontario's family law legislation violated s. 15 by excluding same-sex couples from spousal support obligations. In *Little Sisters Book and Art Emporium v. Canada* (2000),[17] the Court held that the practices of customs officials in obstructing the importation of books by a bookstore catering to the LGBTQ communities was a breach of s. 15. The Courts of Appeal of British Columbia and Ontario and other provincial courts held that the opposite-sex requirement for marriage was contrary to s. 15, thereby legalizing same-sex marriage in several provinces.[18] These decisions also helped the Supreme Court to decide that the federal power over "marriage" extended to same-sex marriage,[19] a ruling which was followed by legislation enacting a new national defi-

---

[9]*Lavoie v. Can.*, [2002] 1 S.C.R. 769.

[10]*Nova Scotia v. Walsh*, [2002] 4 S.C.R. 325.

[11]§ 55:48, "Sexual orientation".

[12]*Egan v. Canada*, [1995] 2 S.C.R. 513.

[13]*Egan v. Canada*, [1995] 2 S.C.R. 513, para. 5.

[14]At that time, four members of the Court were insisting that a distinction had to be "irrelevant" to count as discrimination. These four held that the exclusion of same-sex couples from spousal allowances was not irrelevant, and a fifth judge held that the exclusion was justified under s. 1.

[15]*Vriend v. Alberta*, [1998] 1 S.C.R. 493.

[16]*M. v. H.*, [1999] 2 S.C.R. 203.

[17]*Little Sisters Book and Art Emporium v. Canada*, [2000] 2 S.C.R. 1120.

[18]*EGALE v. Can.* (2003), 225 D.L.R. (4th) 472 (B.C.C.A.); *Halpern v. Can.* (2003), 225 D.L.R. (4th) 529 (Ont. C.A.).

[19]*Re Same-Sex Marriage*, [2004] 3 S.C.R. 698.

nition of marriage that no longer requires the couple to be of opposite sex.[20]

So far, these three grounds are the only ones that have been recognized.[21] *Place of residence*[22] has not been accepted as an analogous ground, except in the special case of residence on an Indian reserve.[23] Nor is *occupation*[24] an analogous ground, so that a law denying collective bargaining rights to police officers cannot be challenged under s. 15.[25] Nor is *substance orientation* an analogous ground, so that a law prohibiting the use of marihuana cannot be challenged under s. 15.[26] Every change in the law creates a distinction between those who were governed by the law before the change and those who are governed by the new law, but this is not discrimination under s. 15, because a *temporal* distinction is not an analogous ground.[27] And privileges for the Crown and other public authorities in litigation cannot be challenged under s. 15, because the existence of a claim against government is not an analogous ground.[28]

Where there is no distinction based on a listed or analogous ground, there is no remedy under s. 15. The Court, which of course created this restriction, has chafed against it in some cases where the Court wanted to grant a remedy. Malapportioned voting districts, which give rural votes more weight than urban votes, have been held to be unconstitutional under the right to vote in s. 3 of the Charter.[29] This decision allows place of residence to be a ground of unconstitutional discrimination where voting rights are involved. The exclusion of agricultural workers from Ontario's labour relations legislation has been held to be unconstitutional under the right to freedom of association in s. 2(d) of the Charter.[30] This decision allows occupation to be a ground of unconstitutional discrimination where freedom of association is involved. When the

---

[20]Civil Marriage Act, S.C. 2005, c. 33. See also ch. 27, The Family, under heading §§ 27:3 to 27:4, "Marriage".

[21]Language (or at least native language) may be a fourth analogous ground: *Gosselin v. Que.*, [2005] 1 S.C.R. 238, para. 12 (obiter dictum raising possibility). In *Fraser v. Can.*, 2020 SCC 28, it was left open whether family/parental status is an analogous ground (paras. 114-123 per Abella J., for the majority; paras. 182-183 per Brown and Rowe JJ. dissenting, but not on this point); Côté J., dissenting, appeared to close the door more firmly (para. 238).

[22]§ 55:49, "Place of residence".

[23]*Corbiere v. Can.*, [1999] 2 S.C.R. 203.

[24]§ 55:50, "Occupation".

[25]*Delisle v. Can.*, [1999] 2 S.C.R. 989.

[26]*R. v. Malmo-Levine*, [2003] 3 S.C.R. 571, paras. 184-185, 267.

[27]*Can. v. Hislop*, [2007] 1 S.C.R. 429, para. 39.

[28]*Rudolf Wolff & Co. v. Can.*, [1990] 1 S.C.R. 695 (upholding exclusive jurisdiction of Federal Court over actions against the Crown in right of Canada); *Mirhadizadeh v. Ont.* (1989), 69 O.R. (2d) 422 (C.A.) (upholding limitation period on action against public authorities); *Filip v. Waterloo* (1992), 98 D.L.R. (4th) 534 (Ont. C.A.) (same decision).

[29]*Re Prov. Electoral Boundaries (Sask.)*, [1991] 2 S.C.R. 158.

[30]*Dunmore v. Ont.*, [2001] 3 S.C.R. 1016.

Court imports equality values into other Charter rights,[31] it leaves out the restriction to listed and analogous grounds. (And it also leaves out the requirement of an impairment of human dignity or discrimination.)[32]

VI. HUMAN DIGNITY

§ 55:19 Ambiguity in Andrews

The simple (and most common) reading of *Andrews*[1] was that a breach of s. 15 occurred whenever a disadvantage (a burden or withheld benefit) was imposed on the basis of a listed or analogous ground. That finding would exhaust the role of s. 15, and issues of the reasonableness or fairness of the challenged law would be addressed under s. 1. This simple approach accorded appropriately distinct roles for s. 15 and s. 1 in the equality inquiry. This interpretation meant that "discrimination" in s. 15 had a very simple meaning. It meant the imposition of a disadvantage on the basis of a listed or analogous ground. However, McIntyre J.'s opinion contains hints of a more complicated theory of discrimination. There is one passage in which he says that it is "not enough to focus only on the alleged ground of discrimination and decide whether or not it is an enumerated or analogous ground".[2] This passage leaves the impression that something more than the breach of a listed or analogous ground is required to constitute discrimination under s. 15. But it is accompanied by no hint as to what that something more might be. And, it is accompanied by the assertion that "any justification, any consideration of the reasonableness of the enactment" is to take place under s. 1.[3] The implication of this assertion is that the reasons justifying the enactment are not part of the definition of discrimination in s. 15, because, if they are, the clear demarcation between the roles of s. 15 and s. 1 is destroyed. However, it must be acknowledged that there is some uncertainty as to whether McIntyre J. intended his simple "enumerated and analogous grounds" approach to exhaust the elements of "discrimination" in s. 15.

In the *Miron* and *Egan* cases, decided by the Supreme Court of Canada in 1995, four of the nine judges wanted to import into the s. 15 analysis (through the definition of discrimination) the requirement that the legislative classification not only be based on a listed or analogous ground, but also be "irrelevant" to "the functional values of the legislation".[4] If the legislative classification was relevant, then there was no discrimination. If there was no discrimination, there was no breach

---

[31]See P.W. Hogg, "Equality as a Charter Value in Constitutional Interpretation" (2003) 20 Supreme Court L.R. (2d) 113.

[32]§§ 55:19 to 55:22, "Human dignity".

[Section 55:19]

[1]*Andrews v. Law Society of British Columbia*, [1989] 1 S.C.R. 143.

[2]*Andrews v. Law Society of B.C.*, [1989] 1 S.C.R. 143, 182.

[3]*Andrews v. Law Society of B.C.*, [1989] 1 S.C.R. 143, 182.

[4]*Miron v. Trudel*, [1995] 2 S.C.R. 418, para. 15 per Gonthier J. dissenting (with the

of s. 15, and no requirement for the government to justify under s. 1 its use of a listed or analogous ground as the basis for the imposition of a disadvantage. One can readily agree that the relevance of a legislative distinction to a legitimate legislative purpose is important in assessing whether the distinction is justified or not. But an inquiry into relevance would essentially duplicate the *Oakes* tests for s. 1 justification.[5] Of the five other judges in *Miron* and *Egan*, four held that a disadvantage imposed on the basis of an analogous ground (marital status in *Miron*, sexual orientation in *Egan)* was enough to constitute discrimination, and immediately moved on to s. 1 justification. One judge, L'Heureux-Dubé J., took a different path entirely, rejecting the restriction of s. 15 to listed and analogous grounds, and investigating discrimination on a broader, more discretionary, case-by-case basis.

After *Miron* and *Egan*, the Supreme Court was splintered into three camps as to the interpretation of s. 15. This did not stop the Court from deciding some s. 15 cases unanimously. In *Eaton*,[6] *Benner*,[7] *Eldridge*[8] and *Vriend*,[9] decided between 1995 and 1998, the Court reached unanimous decisions,[10] but made no attempt to resolve the differences among the judges. It was not necessary, they claimed, because in each case all three interpretations of s. 15 would have led to the same result. This fragmentation of the Court lasted only until 1999, when *Law v. Canada* was decided. That case is described in the next section of the chapter.

§ 55:20 Impairment of human dignity

In *Law v. Canada* (1999),[1] the Supreme Court of Canada surprised observers by issuing a unanimous opinion, written by Iacobucci J., that provided a new interpretation of s. 15. The new interpretation differed from each of the three competing interpretations that had been offered in *Miron* and *Egan*. The new consensus was as follows:

(1) Section 15 applied only to legislative distinctions based on a listed or analogous ground (contrary to L'Heureux Dubé J.'s earlier view).

---

agreement of Lamer C.J., La Forest and Major JJ); *Egan v. Canada*, [1995] 2 S.C.R. 513, para. 13 per La Forest J. concurring (with the agreement of Lamer C.J., Gonthier and Major JJ.).

[5]In *Miron v. Trudel*, [1995] 2 S.C.R. 418, paras. 31-38, Gonthier J. argued that the requirement of irrelevance in s. 15 would still leave s. 1 with some work to do. The argument depends on the point that the "functional values" of the legislation are not the same as the objective of the legislation. This is a highly refined distinction.

[6]*Eaton v. Brant County Bd. of Ed.*, [1997] 1 S.C.R. 241, paras. 62-65.

[7]*Benner v. Can.*, [1997] 1 S.C.R. 358, paras. 60-68.

[8]*Eldridge v. B.C.*, [1997] 3 S.C.R. 624, paras. 58-59.

[9]*Vriend v. Alta.*, [1998] 1 S.C.R. 493, paras. 70-74.

[10]In *Vriend v. Alta.*, [1998] 1 S.C.R. 493, Major J. dissented, but only on the issue of remedy, not s. 15.

[Section 55:20]

[1]*Law v. Canada*, [1999] 1 S.C.R. 497. Iacobucci J. wrote the opinion of the Court.

(2) Discrimination in s. 15 involved an element additional to a distinction based on a listed or analogous ground (contrary to four judges' earlier view).

(3) That additional element was an impairment of "human dignity"[2] (contrary to all nine judges' earlier view).

The new requirement of an impairment of human dignity defeated the claimant in *Law*. Under the federal Canada Pension Plan, survivors' benefits were payable to the spouses of deceased contributors, unless the spouse was under the age of 35, in which case the spouse was not entitled to survivors' benefits. The claimant in *Law* was the survivor of a deceased contributor, but, because she was under the age of 35, she was ineligible for a survivor's benefit. The law withheld a benefit from her on the ground of her age, age being a listed ground under s. 15. On the simple interpretation of *Andrews*, this would have been enough to constitute discrimination under s. 15, which would have sent the issue on to s. 1, where the government would be required to satisfy the Court that the age-based distinction was justified under the standards established in *Oakes*. But, by adding the new requirement of human dignity to s. 15, the Court imposed on the claimant the burden of establishing that the age-based distinction was an impairment of her human dignity. She was unable to discharge that burden, and so her equality claim was denied without recourse to s. 1.

Why was the age-based distinction in *Law* not an impairment of human dignity? The Court's answer was that, in the context of the Canada Pension Plan's purpose, it recognized the reality that young widows and widowers would have less difficulty than older persons in finding and maintaining employment after the death of a spouse, and would in the long term be able to replace the lost income of the deceased spouse. This is very close to saying that the age-based distinction was a reasonable restriction on access to CPP benefits. And yet, if one point was clearly enunciated by McIntyre J. in *Andrews*, it was that, once discrimination was found under s. 15, issues of reasonableness should be left to s. 1.

Iacobucci J. in *Law* did not define "human dignity". What he did do was to suggest[3] four "contextual factors" (which were not to be taken as exhaustive) that were helpful to the inquiry. The factors were (1) the existence of "pre-existing disadvantage, stereotyping, prejudice or vulnerability"; (2) the correspondence between the distinction and the claimant's characteristics or circumstances; (3) the existence of ameliorative purposes or effects on other groups; and (4) the nature of the interest affected. In *Law* itself, it was the second ("correspondence") factor that was important. The age qualification for CPP survivor benefits corresponded to the actual characteristics and circumstances of youthful surviving spouses, who could more readily find or maintain employment than older surviving spouses. Later cases have also relied on this factor, as will be explained in the next section of this chapter.

---

[2] *Law v. Canada*, [1999] 1 S.C.R. 497, para. 88.

[3] *Law v. Canada*, [1999] 1 S.C.R. 497, para. 88.

After 1999, every case followed the *Law* analysis until *R. v. Kapp* (2008),[4] when the Supreme Court unexpectedly changed its mind and retracted the requirement of an impairment of human dignity, replacing it with what seems to be the very similar requirement of "discrimination".[5] Until the Court is more explicit about the differences if any between the two concepts, it is worth rehearsing the problems with the element of human dignity. It is vague, confusing and burdensome to equality claimants.[6] That it is vague is established by the fact that, in the cases following *Law*, the Supreme Court has often disagreed with lower courts and disagreed among itself on the question whether the challenged law impairs the human dignity of the claimant.[7] It is confusing, because it introduces an evaluative step into s. 15 which leaves it unclear as to how much work s. 1 is left to do. And it is burdensome to claimants, because it introduces a new element to s. 15, and the burden rests on the claimant to establish all the elements of s. 15. A failure to establish an impairment of human dignity is fatal to the claimant's case, which never advances to s. 1. The government must establish all the elements of s. 1 justification, but this burden never has to be discharged if the claimant fails to persuade the Court of an impairment of human dignity. Moreover, the inquiry into human dignity is highly unstructured compared with the inquiry into s. 1 justification. In particular, in the inquiry into human dignity, the court does not need to make a finding of minimum impairment (or least drastic means), which under s. 1 calls for an inquiry as to whether there are alternative legislative measures that would accomplish the legislative purpose without impairing the right as much.

In *Law*, the Court frankly acknowledged that it was imposing a new burden on the claimant, and could only offer in reply[8] that in some cases it would not be necessary for the claimant "to adduce evidence", because it would be "evident on the basis of judicial notice and logical reasoning" that human dignity had been impaired. The fact remains that a failure to persuade the Court (in one fashion or another) that human dignity is impaired causes the claimant to lose the case. As well as *Law* itself, in

---

[4]*R. v. Kapp*, [2008] 2 S.C.R. 483.

[5]The *Kapp* ruling is discussed in § 55:22, "Discrimination without human dignity".

[6]Commentators have been nearly unanimous in their criticism of the new element: e.g., B. Baines, "*Law v. Canada*: Formatting Equality" (2000) 11 Const. Forum 65; S. Martin, "Balancing Individual Rights to Equality and Social Goals" (2001) 80 Can. Bar Rev. 299, 319-332; J. Ross, "A Flawed Synthesis of the Law" (2000) 11 Constitutional Forum 74; C. Bredt and A. Dodek, "Breaking the Law's Grip on Equality: A New Paradigm for Section 15" (2003) 20 Supreme Court L.R. (2d) 33; D.M. McAllister, "Section 15—the Unpredictability of the *Law* test" (2003) 15 Nat. J. Con. Law 35; P.W. Hogg, "What is Equality? The Winding Course of Judicial Interpretation" (2005) 29 Supreme Court L.R. (2d) 39. D. Greschner, "Does *Law* Advance the Cause of Equality?" (2001) 27 Queen's L.J. 299, 315, agrees that there should be a third element to s. 15, but that it should be "protecting the interest in belonging" rather than human dignity.

[7]E.g., *M. v. H.*, [1999] 2 S.C.R. 203; *Lavoie v. Can.*, [2002] 1 S.C.R. 769; *Nuva Scutia v. Walsh*, [2002] 4 S.C.R. 325; *Gosselin v. Que.*, [2002] 4 S.C.R. 429; *Can. Foundation for Children, Youth and the Law v. Can.*, [2004] 1 S.C.R. 76.

[8]*Law v. Canada*, [1999] 1 S.C.R. 497, para. 88.

many subsequent equality cases, the claimant has established a disadvantage based on a listed or analogous ground, but has lost the case for failure to also establish an impairment of human dignity.[9] The law has been upheld without the need for the government to establish s. 1 justification.

§ 55:21 The factor of correspondence

As related in the previous section of this chapter, in *Law* the Supreme Court suggested four "contextual factors" that were to be taken into account in determining whether or not human dignity is impaired by a law that imposes a disadvantage on the basis of a listed or analogous ground.[1] The factor that was dispositive in that case was the "correspondence" factor. The Court described the factor in these words: "The correspondence, or lack thereof, between the ground or grounds on which the claim is based and the actual need, capacity, or circumstances of the claimant or others".[2] The denial of CPP survivor benefits to spouses under the age of 35 accurately corresponded to the circumstances of younger spouses of deceased income-earners, who could be expected to be more successful in finding and retaining employment than older spouses. Therefore, the claimant, who was denied the spousal benefit on the basis of her age, was unable to establish an impairment of her human dignity and lost her case.[3]

Another age-based case was *Gosselin v. Quebec* (2002),[4] where the Court upheld a workfare program that provided low welfare benefits for persons under 30, unless they attended training programs, in which case standard benefits were payable. According to the majority, the age-based requirement corresponded to the increased capability of young persons to benefit from training programs. According to the minority, the imposition of hardship on young persons did not respect them as full persons. The majority prevailed, of course. The claimant, who had been unable to access the training programs and had been forced to subsist on the low benefits, was unable to establish an impairment of her human dignity. She therefore lost her case.

---

[9]E.g, *Winko v. B.C.*, [1999] 2 S.C.R. 625 (mental disability); *Granovsky v. Can.*, [2000] 1 S.C.R. 2003 (physical disability); *Nova Scotia v. Walsh*, [2002] 4 S.C.R. 325 (marital status); *Gosselin v. Que.*, [2002] 4 S.C.R. 429 (age); *Can. Foundation for Children, Youth and the Law v. Can.*, [2004] 1 S.C.R. 76 (age); *Wynberg v. Ont.* (2006), 82 O.R. (3d) 561 (C.A.) (age).

[Section 55:21]

[1]*Law v. Canada*, [1999] 1 S.C.R. 497.

[2]*Law v. Can.*, [1999] 1 S.C.R. 497, para. 88.

[3]See also *Wynberg v. Ont.* (2006), 82 O.R. (3d) 561 (C.A.) (leave to appeal to S.C.C. denied April 12, 2007) (autism therapy limited to pre-school children corresponded to their needs and circumstances and did not impair human dignity of school-age children).

[4]*Gosselin v. Quebec*, [2002] 4 S.C.R. 429.

In *Nova Scotia v. Walsh* (2002),[5] the exclusion of common-law spouses from Nova Scotia's community property regime was held by a divided Supreme Court to correspond to real differences between common-law relationships and legal marriages. In *Canadian Foundation for Children, Youth and the Law v. Canada* (2004),[6] the Criminal Code's permission for parents and teachers to use reasonable corrective force against children was held by a divided Court to correspond to the needs of children. In these cases, the correspondence factor meant that there was no impairment of human dignity.

The correspondence factor pointed the other way in *Nova Scotia v. Martin* (2003),[7] where the Court held unanimously that Nova Scotia's provision of short-term remedial programs, instead of full workers' compensation benefits, for "chronic pain" did not correspond to the needs of injured workers who suffered from that condition.

While judicial discussion of human dignity often ranges far and wide, the correspondence factor seems to have become the key to the impairment of human dignity. It is the Court's evaluation of that factor that normally yields the outcome, even if the other factors point in the other direction. What does the correspondence factor really mean? It seems to come down to an assessment by the Court of the legitimacy of the statutory purpose and the reasonableness of using a listed or analogous ground to accomplish that purpose. If that is right, the correspondence factor leaves very little work for s. 1 to do.

§ 55:22 Discrimination without human dignity

The Supreme Court of Canada, after introducing human dignity as an essential element of a claim under s. 15, and after using the concept as the reason for denying many of the equality claims that came before it,[1] has apparently abandoned the concept. The change came in a brief obiter dictum in *R. v. Kapp* (2008),[2] where McLachlin C.J. and Abella J., writing for a Court that was unanimous on this point, unexpectedly revisited the issue of human dignity in the s. 15 jurisprudence. They did not doubt that "human dignity is an essential value underlying the s. 15 equality guarantee", but they acknowledged that *"as a legal test"* human dignity was "confusing and difficult to apply" and was "an *additional* burden on equality claimants, rather than the philosophical enhance-

---

[5] *Nova Scotia v. Walsh*, [2002] 4 S.C.R. 325.

[6] *Canadian Foundation for Children, Youth and the Law v. Canada*, [2004] 1 S.C.R. 76.

[7] *Nova Scotia v. Martin*, [2003] 2 S.C.R. 504.

[Section 55:22]

[1] § 55:20 note 9, above.

[2] *R. v. Kapp*, [2008] 2 S.C.R. 484. McLachlin C.J. and Abella J. wrote the eight-judge majority opinion, deciding the case under s. 15(2). Bastarache J., wrote a concurring opinion, deciding the case under s. 25; but he made a point of saying (para. 77) that "I am in complete agreement with the restatement of the test for the application of s. 15 that is adopted by the Chief Justice and Abella J. in their reasons for judgment".

ment it was intended to be".[3] They held that an impairment of human dignity should no longer be a required element of a s. 15 claim.

For this conclusion, the Court in *Kapp* referred to academic criticism, including my own. However, my point has always been that the only way to bring clarity and coherence to the law, and to remove any unnecessary burden on equality claimants, is to accept that discrimination under s. 15 is nothing more than a disadvantage imposed on a listed or analogous ground. In my view, that should be enough for the claimant to establish a breach of s. 15, leaving issues of reasonableness and justification to be established by the government under the standards set by *Oakes* for s. 1.[4] Unfortunately, the Court was unwilling to reverse *Law* quite so completely. Instead, the *Kapp* opinion assumes that there is still an element of s. 15 in addition to a disadvantage imposed on a listed and analogous ground. That element is no longer called "human dignity"—it has no name other than "discrimination"—but it is identified by the same four contextual factors that were formerly used to identify an impairment of human dignity.[5] Factors one (pre-existing disadvantage) and four (nature of interest affected) and possibly three (ameliorative purpose) went to "perpetuation of disadvantage and prejudice".[6] Factor two (correspondence), which (as argued in the previous section of this book) has normally been the decisive one, went to "stereotyping". The four factors, the Court said, "should not be read literally as if they were legislative dispositions, but as a way of focussing on the central concern of s. 15 identified in *Andrews*—combating discrimination, defined in terms of perpetuating disadvantage and stereotyping".[7] In other words, after *Kapp*, it is still necessary for an equality claimant to establish something in addition to disadvantage based on a listed or analogous ground. That additional element ("discrimination") is no longer an impairment of human dignity; it is now the perpetuation of prejudice or stereotyping.

The Court's object in banishing human dignity from its lexicon is the admirable one of reducing the vagueness, confusion and additional burden that *Law* imported into the s. 15 jurisprudence. But the *Kapp* restatement does not by itself achieve these goals. The definition of

---

[3]*R. v. Kapp*, [2008] 2 S.C.R. 484, paras 21-22 (emphasis in original).

[4]Oddly, in applying the prohibitions on discrimination in the statutory human rights codes, the Court does not impose any requirements on the claimant other than a showing of adverse treatment on a prohibited ground; the burden then moves to the respondent to show justification: e.g., *Moore v. B.C.*, [2012] 3 S.C.R. 360, para. 33 per Abella J. for the Court; for discussion, see B. Ryder, "The Strange Double Life of Canadian Equality Rights" (2013) to be published in the Supreme Court Law Review.

[5]*R. v. Kapp*, [2008] 2 S.C.R. 484, para. 23.

[6]Factor three has mainly been overtaken by the *Kapp* decision itself. An ameliorative purpose is not simply a "factor" in rebutting discrimination under s. 15(1); it is determinative of the validity of a program under s. 15(2).

[7]*R. v. Kapp*, [2008] 2 S.C.R. 484, para. 24. Note the slightly different formulation in para. 17 ("Does the distinction create a disadvantage by perpetuating prejudice or stereotyping?"). The latter formulation was the one applied in *Ermineskin Indian Band and Nation v. Canada*, [2009] 1 S.C.R. 222.

discrimination as the perpetuation of prejudice or stereotyping is almost as vague as human dignity, and it continues to rely on the same contextual factors as were used to identify human dignity. The inquiry into the reasonableness of a distinction that is based on a listed or analogous ground is not wholly remitted to s. 1 (as *Andrews* so wisely insisted), but continues to be divided in a confusing way between the s. 15 inquiry into discrimination and the s. 1 inquiry into justification. And, because the inquiry into discrimination is part of s. 15, it is the equality claimant who bears the burden of establishing that the use of a listed or analogous ground is a perpetuation of prejudice or stereotyping. In sum, the *Kapp* restatement does not seem to be successful either in clarifying the law or in removing an unnececessary burden from equality claimants. However, the restatement was announced in a case to which it had no relevance. The *Kapp* case was an equality challenge to a fishing licence that gave exclusive rights to aboriginal fishers, and the licence was upheld under the affirmative-action clause of s. 15(2).[8] No analysis under s. 15(1) was called for and none was attempted. That is not an ideal context for the development of new s. 15(1) doctrine. What the Court seemed to be doing is signalling a change of direction in its equality doctrine, but for that new direction to take hold more guidance is needed from the Court.

Ermineskin Indian Band and Nation v. Canada (2009)[9] was the first equality case to be decided after *Kapp*. In that case, four Indian bands had surrendered their interests in the oil and gas under their reserves to the federal Crown so that the Crown could make arrangements with third parties to exploit the resources. This was done and the Crown received and held the oil and gas royalties on behalf of the bands. The royalties were paid into the consolidated revenue fund, where separate accounts were maintained for each band, and each account was regularly credited with interest at a floating rate that was calculated by reference to the average rate for long-term government bonds over the period for which interest was paid. The bands sued the government for breach of fiduciary duty, claiming that the return on their money would have been higher if the government had invested the money in a diversified portfolio of investments. The Supreme Court of Canada dismissed this claim on the basis that the government was precluded by statute from external investment of the bands' money. The Indian Act required Indian money to be paid into the consolidated revenue fund, and other statutory provisions prohibited external investment of money held in the consolidated revenue fund.

The equality issue came up in *Ermineskin* because the bands argued that, if the effect of the Indian Act was to preclude the external investment of the bands' money (which is what the Court decided), then the applicable provisions of the Indian Act were unconstitutional for breach of s. 15 of the Charter. According to the bands, the Indian Act deprived

---

[8]The decision is discussed in § 55:32, "Affirmative action".

[9]*Ermineskin Indian Band and Nation v. Canada*, [2009] 1 S.C.R. 222. Rothstein J. wrote the opinion of the Court.

Indians,[10] a group distinguished by race, of the rights that were available to non-Indians[11] whose property was held in trust by the Crown. Rothstein J., who wrote for the Court, was prepared to assume that the Indian Act imposed a disadvantage on the bands, and that the disadvantage was based on the listed ground of race. However, as expected, he confirmed the *Kapp* ruling that it was not enough for an equality claimant to show a disadvantage based on a listed or analogous ground. The equality claimant also had to establish that the challenged law was "discriminatory", which involved establishing that the law "perpetuates prejudice or stereotyping".[12] A change from *Kapp* was that Rothstein J. made no reference to the four contextual factors from *Law* that the Court in *Kapp* had been so careful to preserve (while rejecting the concept of human dignity that they were supposed to establish). (Of course, the Court's silence does not necessarily mean that the four factors are now irrelevant.) In order to decide the issue before him, Rothstein J. held that the Indian Act requirement to keep the bands' funds in the consolidated revenue fund, as opposed to investing them, involved less control over the funds by the Crown, greater liquidity for the bands, and no risk of loss to the bands. These features of the statutory regime "do not draw a distinction that perpetuates disadvantage through prejudice or stereotyping".[13] This defeated the bands' equality claim without the need to go through a s. 1 analysis.[14]

In *Withler v. Canada* (2011),[15] the Supreme Court upheld a statutory pension plan for federal civil servants, which used the age of a plan member at the time of his or her death as a factor in determining the value of the benefit payable to a dependant. The claimants were widows of deceased civil servants whose pensions were reduced by reference to the age of their husbands at the time of death. They challenged the age-

---

[10]The Court did not consider the point that the Indian Act, having been enacted under s. 91(24) ("Indians, and lands reserved for the Indians"), was inescapably restricted in its application to Indians, and therefore its use of the classification "Indian" was invulnerable to s. 15 attack: § 55:34, "Race in s. 91(24)".

[11]The Court did not question this premise. However, in the federal jurisdiction, the general rule is that public money (including money held in trust by the Crown) must be paid into the consolidated revenue fund and cannot be invested in external investments: *Authorson v. Can.* (2007), 86 O.R. (3d) 321 (C.A.) (so held with respect to veterans' pensions received by Crown). The comparisons argued for by the bands were the Canada Pension Plan and federal employee pension funds which are segregated from the consolidated revenue fund and invested externally.

[12]*Ermineskin Indian Band and Nation v. Canada*, [2009] 1 S.C.R. 222, paras. 188, 190, 192, 201, 202.

[13]*Ermineskin Indian Band and Nation v. Canada*, [2009] 1 S.C.R. 222, para. 202.

[14]See also *Alta. v. Hutterian Brethren of Wilson Colony*, [2009] 2 S.C.R. 567, paras. 105-108 (*Kapp* applied; requirement of photo on driving licence not discriminatory; no reference to contextual factors); *Withler v. Can.*, [2011] 1 S.C.R. 396 (*Kapp* applied; reduction in statutory death benefits based on age not discriminatory; trial judge's contextual analysis based on *Law* factors approved).

[15]*Withler v. Canada*, [2011] 1 S.C.R. 396. McLachlin C.J. and Abella J. wrote the opinion of the Court. A fuller account of the case is to be found in § 55:23, "Selection of comparator group".

based provisions under s. 15. McLachlin C.J. and Abella J. wrote the opinion of the Court, and they took the opportunity to elaborate on what they had said in *Kapp*. They said that the *Law* factors "may be helpful", although "they need not be expressly canvassed in every case in order to fully and properly determine whether a particular distinction is discriminatory".[16] Without expressly canvassing the factors, they went on to consider whether "the [legislative] distinction perpetuates prejudice or stereotypes a particular group".[17] In answering that question, it was relevant to "take into account the fact that pension programs are designed to benefit a number of different groups and necessarily draw lines on factors like age."[18] They concluded that "the package of benefits, viewed as a whole and over time, does not impose or perpetuate discrimination."[19] Although the claimants had suffered a disadvantage on account of age, there was no breach of s. 15, and therefore no need for the Court to consider justification under s. 1.

In *Quebec v. A* (2013),[20] the Supreme Court reviewed the spousal-support and division-of-family-property provisions of the Civil Code of Quebec. These provisions conferred rights and imposed reciprocal obligations on spouses who had married,[21] but they did not apply to persons in de facto (common-law) unions. The claimant was a woman who had been in a de facto union with a wealthier man for seven years. She argued that the denial of the rights to support and a share of family property was a breach of her equality right under s. 15. There was no doubt that she had suffered a disadvantage by reason of her marital status, which is an analogous ground under s. 15.[22] But, in order to establish a breach of s. 15, she still had to satisfy the requirement of discrimination, which had defeated the claimants in *Ermineskin* and *Withler*. That requirement proved fatal to A's claim too. In the Supreme Court of Canada, all judges accepted that marital status was indeed an analogous ground, but LeBel J., writing for a plurality of four judges, held that the Quebec Legislature intended to offer cohabiting couples a choice of the legal regime to which they wished to adhere. The evidence showed that in Quebec de facto unions were far more common than they were in the rest of Canada, and that they were accepted as normal relationships in Quebec. The Legislature was not motivated by prejudice or stereotyping in leaving the de facto option unregulated. Since the claimant had not established prejudice or stereotyping, LeBel J. concluded that there was

---

[16]*Withler v. Canada*, [2011] 1 S.C.R. 396, para. 66, citing *Ermineskin*.

[17]*Withler v. Canada*, [2011] 1 S.C.R. 396, para. 67.

[18]*Withler v. Canada*, [2011] 1 S.C.R. 396, para. 67.

[19]*Withler v. Canada*, [2011] 1 S.C.R. 396, para. 81.

[20]*Quebec v. A*, [2013] 1 S.C.R. 61, 2013 SCC 5. LeBel J., with Fish, Rothstein and Moldaver, wrote the plurality opinion. McLachlin C.J. wrote a concurring opinion. Deschamps J., with Cromwell and Karakatsanis JJ., wrote a partially dissenting opinion. Abella J. wrote a dissenting opinion.

[21]The provisions also applied to persons in "civil unions", an alternative to marriage authorized by Quebec law.

[22]§ 55:47, "Marital status", where a fuller account of this case is to be found.

no breach of s. 15, and therefore it was not necessary to consider justification under s. 1. The LeBel four did not form a majority of the nine-judge bench, but McLachlin C.J., who held that there was a breach of s. 15, and therefore had to consider s. 1, held that the objective of providing choice to cohabiting couples was sufficient to justify the de facto regime. She provided the fifth vote to uphold the exclusion of de facto spouses from the Civil Code's provisions.

Abella J., who dissented in *Quebec v. A*, held that the exclusion of de facto spouses from the spousal support and division-of-property rights was a breach of s. 15 that could not be justified under s. 1. De facto spouses who were dependent and vulnerable had the same need of protection as married spouses. She held that their exclusion from the spousal protections "perpetuates historic disadvantage against them based on their marital status".[23] She acknowledged that attitudes towards de facto unions had changed in Quebec, and that the Legislature had not been motivated by prejudice or stereotyping, but she held that it was not necessary for the claimant to show prejudice or stereotyping: "what is relevant is not the *attitudinal* progress towards them, but the continuation of the *discriminatory* treatment".[24] Apart from her earlier reference to "historic disadvantage", Abella J. did not elaborate on why the "treatment" was discriminatory in the absence of prejudice or stereotyping,[25] and her opinion comes close to saying that the imposition of a disadvantage by reason of marital status is enough to serve as a breach of s. 15. Her s. 15 reasons were expressly agreed to by five judges[26]—a majority—and they at least suggest some rethinking of this elusive and burdensome requirement of discrimination.

[23] *Quebec v. A.*, [2013] 1 S.C.R. 61 at para. 356; see also para. 332 per Abella J. referring to historic disadvantage and para. 385 per Deschamps J. referring to historic disadvantage.

[24] *Quebec v. A.*, [2013] 1 S.C.R. 61, para. 357 (emphasis in original).

[25] Another passage, in her discussion of the previous cases earlier in the opinion (para. 331), refers to "a flexible and contextual inquiry into whether a distinction has the effect of perpetuating *arbitrary* disadvantage on the claimant because of his or her membership in an enumerated or analogous group" (my emphasis). She never uses the word "arbitrary" in characterizing the legislation in this case, but perhaps that is what she means.

[26] *Quebec v. A.*, [2013] 1 S.C.R. 61, para. 382 per Deschamps J. (with Cromwell and Karakatsanis JJ.); para. 416 per McLachlin C.J., although she added some reasons of her own which were largely but perhaps not fully consistent with all of Abella J.'s reasoning (para. 423 suggested that "prejudice" and "stereotype" had been perpetuated in the Quebec legislation). The five judges who comprised the s. 15 majority, split in three directions on s. 1 justification. McLachlin C.J. held that the exclusion of de facto spouses from both the spousal support and the division-of-property provisions was justified under s. 1. As explained in the text, that provided the fifth vote to uphold all of the challenged legislation and defeat the claimant. Deschamps J., with Cromwell and Karakatsanis JJ., dissented in part: they held that the exclusion from the division-of-property provision was justified under s. 1, but not the exclusion from the support provision. Abella J. dissented: she held that neither of the two exclusions was justified under s. 1.

In *Kahkewistahaw First Nation v. Taypotat* (2015),[27] the First Nation, acting under the authority of the Indian Act, had adopted an election code for their chief and band councillors which required that candidates for office must have at least a grade 12 education. The applicant, who was aged 76, and who had served as chief for 27 years before the election code was adopted, had only a grade 10 education. He brought an equality challenge to the election code, arguing that the new educational requirement had a disproportionate effect on older community members who lived on the reserve. The Supreme Court rejected the challenge, upholding the educational requirement. Abella J., who wrote the opinion of the Court, cited her opinion in *Quebec v. A.* and attempted a short restatement of the law. "The focus of s. 15 is therefore on laws that draw *discriminatory* distinctions—that is, distinctions that have the effect of perpetuating arbitrary disadvantage based on an individual's membership in an enumerated or analogous group."[28] The first stage in the analysis was to determine whether the impugned law "creates a distinction on the basis of an enumerated or analogous ground."[29] The second stage in the analysis "focuses on arbitrary—or discriminatory—disadvantage, that is whether the impugned law fails to respond to the actual capacities and needs of the members of the group and instead imposes burdens or denies a benefit in a manner that has the effect of reinforcing, perpetuating or exacerbating their disadvantage."[30] At this second stage, "evidence that goes to establishing a claimant's historical position of disadvantage will be relevant."[31] The claim in this case foundered at the first stage. The listed ground of "age" was not applicable because no relevant evidence was adduced of any correlation between educational attainment and age among the community members. And on-reserve residence was not an analogous ground.[32] It followed that the educational requirement for First Nation office did not create a distinction based on an enumerated or analogous ground, and there was no breach of s. 15. Abella J. did not need to and did not move on to the second stage of s. 15 review. But one may safely speculate that the First Nation's elevation of educational requirements for their officers was unlikely to be character-

[27]*Kahkewistahaw First Nation v. Taypotat*, [2015] 2 S.C.R. 548, 2015 SCC 30. Abella J. wrote the opinion of the Court.

[28]*Kahkewistahaw First Nation v. Taypotat*, [2015] 2 S.C.R. 548, 2015 SCC 30, para. 18 (emphasis in original).

[29]*Kahkewistahaw First Nation v. Taypotat*, [2015] 2 S.C.R. 548, 2015 SCC 30, para. 19.

[30]*Kahkewistahaw First Nation v. Taypotat*, [2015] 2 S.C.R. 548, 2015 SCC 30, para. 20.

[31]*Kahkewistahaw First Nation v. Taypotat*, [2015] 2 S.C.R. 548, 2015 SCC 30, para. 21.

[32]*Kahkewistahaw First Nation v. Taypotat*, [2015] 2 S.C.R. 548, 2015 SCC 30, para. 26, distinguishing *Corbiere v. Can.*, [1999] 2 S.C.R. 203, which held that off-reserve residence was an analogous ground.

ized as imposing an "arbitrary" disadvantage or as a failure to respond to the actual capacities and needs of the members of the First Nation.[33]

The Supreme Court of Canada returned to s. 15 three years later in two companion cases – *Quebec v. Alliance du personnel professionel et technique de la santé et des services sociaux* (2018)[34] and *Centrale des syndicats du Québec v. Quebec* (2018).[35] In both cases, several Quebec unions challenged different aspects of Quebec's Pay Equity Act[36] under s. 15. The Act imposes various obligations on public and private employers with ten or more employees that have as their overarching goal ensuring that women are provided with equal pay for work of equal value. In both cases, the majority of the Court adopted and applied a refined approach to the s. 15 test that had been articulated in *Taypotat*. However, in both cases, there were also dissenting opinions, which articulated and applied competing approaches to s. 15.

In *Alliance*,[37] the s. 15 challenge related to various amendments made to the Act in 2009. These amendments replaced the *ongoing* obligations that the Act had imposed on employers to monitor and adjust for pay inequities in their workplaces with a system of *periodic* five-year pay equity audits. The amendments also restricted the Pay Equity Commission's ability to remedy *past* pay inequities by limiting its ability to order retroactive adjustments to situations where an employer acted arbitrarily or in bad faith, and also denied employees and unions any information revealed by a five-year audit about when any pay inequities emerged. The apparent aim in making the pay equity scheme more friendly to employers in these ways was to increase employer compliance with the Act. The unions argued that these amendments unjustifiably infringed s. 15.

Abella J., who wrote for the majority of the Court in *Alliance*, set out a two-stage test that is to be applied in determining whether s. 15 has been infringed, citing her opinion in *Taypotat* in support. The first stage

---

[33] Abella J., at the beginning of her opinion, cited passages from the 1996 Report of the Royal Commission on Aboriginal Peoples, in which "education was identified as a top priority for promoting collective and individual well-being in Aboriginal communities, and for helping those communities prepare to assume the complete range of responsibilities associated with self-government": *Kahkewistahaw First Nation v. Taypotat*, [2015] 2 S.C.R. 548, 2015 SCC 30, para. 1.

[34] *Quebec v. Alliance du personnel professionel et technique de la santé et des services sociaux*, [2018] 1 S.C.R. 464. Abella J. wrote the opinion for the majority of the Court, which was joined by McLachlin C.J. and Moldaver, Karakatsanis, Wagner, and Gascon JJ. Côté, Brown and Rowe JJ. wrote a joint dissenting opinion.

[35] *Centrale des syndicats du Québec v. Quebec*, [2018] 1 S.C.R. 522. Abella J. wrote an opinion for four judges, which was joined by Moldaver, Karakatsanis and Gascon JJ. McLachlin C.J. wrote a brief opinion dissenting in the result, which agreed with Abella J. that s. 15 had been infringed, but disagreed with her that the infringement could be justified under s. 1. Côté J. wrote an opinion for four judges, which was joined by Wagner, Brown and Rowe JJ, and which disagreed with Abella J. and McLachlin C.J. that s. 15 was infringed.

[36] C.Q.L.R., c. E-12.001.

[37] *Quebec v. Alliance du personnel professionel et technique de la santé et des services sociaux*, [2018] 1 S.C.R. 464.

of the test is the same as the first stage of the test in *Taypotat*: "[d]oes the impugned law, on its face or in its impact, create a distinction based on enumerated or analogous grounds?"[38] However, in her restatement of the second stage of the test, Abella J. introduced a subtle but significant change, asking: "does the law impose 'burdens or den[y] a benefit in a manner that has the effect of reinforcing, perpetuating, or exacerbating disadvantage' "?[39] This reformulation omitted the references in the second stage of the *Taypotat* test to "arbitrary – or discriminatory – disadvantage", as well as to "whether the impugned law fails to respond to the actual capacities and needs of the members of the group",[40] language that had implicitly incorporated one of the *Law* factors (the correspondence factor) into the second stage of the test. The reformulation also omits any reference to prejudice and stereotyping, which had figured so prominently in *Kapp* (and the decisions following it),[41] and bypasses a consideration of the *Law* factors, which, although criticized, had never been entirely abandoned by the Court.[42] Abella J. said that it is "not necessary or desirable" to apply the *Law* factors, and that no case since *Kapp* had done so[43] – implicitly criticizing the joint dissenting opinion of Côté, Brown and Rowe JJ., which revived and applied all four factors.[44] Taken together, these changes affirmed what had already been hinted at by Abella J. in *Quebec v. A.*[45] – that the focus of the second stage of the s. 15 test should now be on whether a law reinforces, perpetuates or exacerbates *disadvantage*.

Applying this approach on the facts of *Alliance*, Abella J. held that most (but not all) of the impugned amendments infringed s. 15.[46] The flawed amendments satisfied the first stage of the two-stage test, because

---

[38] *Quebec v. Alliance du personnel professionel et technique de la santé et des services sociaux*, [2018] 1 S.C.R. 464, para. 25.

[39] *Quebec v. Alliance du personnel professionel et technique de la santé et des services sociaux*, [2018] 1 S.C.R. 464.

[40] *Kahkewistahaw First Nation v. Taypotat*, [2015] 2 S.C.R. 548, 2015 SCC 30, para. 20.

[41] Abella J. did not address the omission of prejudice and stereotyping explicitly, but did so implicitly, saying that at stage two "[t]he focus is not on 'whether a discriminatory attitude exists', or on whether a distinction 'perpetuates negative attitudes' about a disadvantaged group, but rather on the discriminatory *impact* of the distinction": *Quebec v. Alliance du personnel professionel et technique de la santé et des services sociaux*, [2018] 1 S.C.R. 464, para. 28 (emphasis in original).

[42] See text accompanying § 55:22 notes 5 to 7, above, discussing how the *Law* factors were also incorporated into an analysis of prejudice and stereotyping.

[43] *Quebec v. Alliance du personnel professionel et technique de la santé et des services sociaux*, [2018] 1 S.C.R. 464, para. 28.

[44] *Quebec v. Alliance du personnel professionel et technique de la santé et des services sociaux*, [2018] 1 S.C.R. 464, paras. 99-106 per Côté, Brown and Rowe JJ. dissenting.

[45] See text accompanying § 55:22 notes 25 and 26, above.

[46] Abella J. held that the impugned amendments that repealed the ongoing obligations that the Act had imposed on employers to monitor and adjust for pay inequities did not infringe s. 15: *Quebec v. Alliance du personnel professionel et technique de la santé et des services sociaux*, [2018] 1 S.C.R. 464, para. 59. It was therefore not the shift to periodic five-year pay equity audits, but rather the new restrictions imposed in between

they created a distinction based on the enumerated ground of sex. The Act itself created such a distinction because it "targets women in redressing the pay discrimination they have suffered".[47] In addition, the flawed amendments also created a distinction based on sex because they determined when and how inequities in "*women's* pay, in comparison to men" would be addressed.[48] The flawed amendments satisfied the restated second stage of the two-stage test because they perpetuated the disadvantage of women. They disadvantaged women in a substantive sense by making the obligation imposed on employers to monitor and adjust for pay inequities "an episodic, partial obligation" and "effectively giv[ing] an amnesty to the employer for discrimination" between the five-year pay equity audits.[49] The flawed amendments also disadvantaged women in a procedural sense by making the process to engage the limited avenues provided to challenge pay inequity between five-year audits "opaque and difficult to access".[50] Abella J. went on to hold that these infringements of s. 15 could not be justified under s. 1.[51]

Côté, Brown and Rowe JJ. wrote a joint dissenting opinion in *Alliance*. In their opinion, they rejected the reformulated s. 15 test articulated by Abella J. Like Abella J., they said that a two-stage test should be applied in determining whether s. 15 has been infringed, and cited *Taypotat* in support. And, like Abella J., they indicated that the first stage of the test involves a consideration of "whether a law, on its face or in its impact, creates a distinction on the basis of an enumerated or analogous ground".[52] However, unlike Abella J., they added a hurdle to the first stage of the test – a requirement that the distinction be found to be "disadvantageous or prejudicial".[53] In addition, unlike Abella J., they did not reformulate the second stage to focus solely on disadvantage; they maintained the suggestion in *Taypotat* that the law must fail "to respond to the actual capacities and needs of the members of the group".[54] And, unlike Abella J., and perhaps most unexpectedly, they revived and

---

them, that infringed s. 15.

[47] *Quebec v. Alliance du personnel professionel et technique de la santé et des services sociaux*, [2018] 1 S.C.R. 464, para. 29.

[48] *Quebec v. Alliance du personnel professionel et technique de la santé et des services sociaux*, [2018] 1 S.C.R. 464 (emphasis in original).

[49] *Quebec v. Alliance du personnel professionel et technique de la santé et des services sociaux*, [2018] 1 S.C.R. 464, para. 33.

[50] *Quebec v. Alliance du personnel professionel et technique de la santé et des services sociaux*, [2018] 1 S.C.R. 464, para. 34.

[51] Abella J. also rejected an alternative argument – offered by Côté, Brown and Rowe JJ. in dissent – based on s. 15(2); this aspect of the decision is discussed later in this chapter, in § 55:32, "Affirmative action".

[52] *Quebec v. Alliance du personnel professionel et technique de la santé et des services sociaux*, [2018] 1 S.C.R. 464, para. 70.

[53] *Quebec v. Alliance du personnel professionel et technique de la santé et des services sociaux*, [2018] 1 S.C.R. 464, para. 71.

[54] *Quebec v. Alliance du personnel professionel et technique de la santé et des services sociaux*, [2018] 1 S.C.R. 464, para. 94.

applied all four *Law* factors at stage two of the test.[55] Applying their approach to s. 15, the joint dissenting judges agreed that the impugned amendments created a distinction based on the enumerated ground of sex, but they held that neither the first nor the second stage of the s. 15 test were satisfied, largely on the basis that the form of disadvantage involved (gender-based pay inequity) already existed in the labour market, and the impugned amendments did not perpetuate this form of disadvantage, but rather ameliorated it.[56]

In *Centrale*,[57] the s. 15 challenge related to a different aspect of Quebec's Pay Equity Act. When the Act was enacted in 1996, it gave women who worked in female-dominated workplaces without male comparators (like childcare centers) a right to pay equity. However, it delegated the development and implementation of a method to assess pay equity in these workplaces to Quebec's Pay Equity Commission. The result was that women in workplaces with male comparators could access pay equity in November 2001, whereas women in workplaces without male comparators could not access pay equity until May 2007. In this case, the unions' s. 15 challenge was to s. 38 of the Act, the provision that was largely responsible for this almost six-year delay. In this case, unlike in *Alliance*, the majority of the Supreme Court ultimately rejected the unions' challenge, although some judges did so at the s. 15 stage of the analysis, and others did so under the s. 1 stage.

Abella J. wrote again in *Centrale*, but this time for only four judges.[58] She reiterated the two-stage s. 15 test that she set out in her majority opinion in *Alliance*.[59] Applying this test on the facts of *Centrale*, Abella J. said that the almost six-year delay in access to pay equity that resulted from s. 38 satisfied the first stage of the test because it created a distinction on the basis of the enumerated ground of sex. Echoing her reasoning in *Alliance*, she said that the Act as a whole drew "a distinction based on sex in targeting systemic pay discrimination against women".[60] She also said that s. 38 itself created a distinction based on sex, both on its face (by sorting women into two categories that were "expressly defined by the presence or absence of men") and in its impact

---

[55]Each of these differences were rejected by Abella J., explicitly or implicitly: *Quebec v. Alliance du personnel professionel et technique de la santé et des services sociaux*, [2018] 1 S.C.R. 464, paras. 26-28.

[56]*Quebec v. Alliance du personnel professionel et technique de la santé et des services sociaux*, [2018] 1 S.C.R. 464, paras. 98-106 (emphasis in original).

[57]*Centrale des syndicats du Québec v. Quebec*, [2018] 1 S.C.R. 522.

[58]Abella J.'s opinion was joined by only three others. McLachlin C.J., who joined Abella J.'s majority opinion (for six judges) in *Alliance*, rejected her conclusion in *Centrale* that the s. 15 breach could be justified under s. 1, and Wagner J., who also joined her majority opinion in *Alliance*, joined Côté J.'s opinion (for four judges) in *Centrale*. However, McLachlin C.J. agreed with Abella J. that s. 15 had been infringed, and in doing so, seemed to agree with her s. 15 analysis, with the result that it can be read to have the support of a majority of five judges: *Centrale des syndicats du Québec v. Quebec*, [2018] 1 S.C.R. 522, paras. 154-156.

[59]*Centrale des syndicats du Québec v. Quebec*, [2018] 1 S.C.R. 522, para 22.

[60]*Centrale des syndicats du Québec v. Quebec*, [2018] 1 S.C.R. 522, para. 24.

(by creating an almost six-year delay in access to pay equity for women who already "disproportionately suffer an adverse impact *because they are women*").[61] Applying her restatement of the second stage of the test, Abella J. concluded that the almost six-year delay in access to pay equity that resulted from s. 38 perpetuated the disadvantage of a class of women because it forced them to live with the consequences of pay inequity for longer without a remedy, with "a considerable economic impact".[62] Abella J. concluded that s. 38 therefore infringed s. 15. However, unlike in *Alliance*, she ultimately held that this infringement could be justified under s. 1, in essence because the issue (how to determine pay equity in workplaces that had no male comparators) was complex and required careful study, and the province had responded to it with reasonable diligence. Abella J. wrote for only four judges in finding that the infringement of s. 15 to be justified, because McLachlin C.J, in a brief separate opinion, agreed with Abella J. that s. 38 infringed s. 15, but disagreed with her that the infringement could be justified under s. 1.[63]

Côté J. wrote a separate opinion in *Centrale*, which was joined by her two co-authors in *Alliance* (Brown and Rowe JJ.), as well as by Wagner J., who had joined Abella J.'s majority opinion in *Alliance*. In her opinion, Côté J. did not adopt the reformulated s. 15 test articulated by Abella J. in her opinion. However, she also departed from the approach to s. 15 that she had taken in her joint dissenting opinion in *Alliance*, without offering an explanation and justification for doing so. As in *Alliance*, she said that a two-stage test is to be applied in determining whether s. 15 has been infringed. Moreover, as in *Alliance*, she resurrected and applied all four *Law* factors at stage two of the test. However, unlike in *Alliance*, she did not require proof of disadvantage or prejudice at stage one of the test. In addition, unlike in *Alliance*, she harkened back to the *Kapp* test in suggesting that the second stage of the test looks at whether the law "create[s] a discriminatory disadvantage by, among other things, *perpetuating prejudice or stereotyping*".[64] Applying this approach, Côté J. would have rejected the claim at the first stage on the basis that s. 38 created a distinction based on the place of work, which is not an enumerated or analogous ground of discrimination, and not, as Abella J. had concluded, on the basis of sex. Côté J. went on to say that she would have rejected the claim at the second stage of the s. 15 test as well, largely on the basis that pay inequity already existed in the labour market, and the Act did not perpetuate, but rather ameliorated it. Because Abella J. had held that the s. 15 infringement could be justified under s.

---

[61] *Centrale des syndicats du Québec v. Quebec*, [2018] 1 S.C.R. 522, paras. 28-29 (emphasis in original).

[62] *Centrale des syndicats du Québec v. Quebec*, [2018] 1 S.C.R. 522, paras. 31, 34.

[63] Abella J. also rejected – as she did in *Alliance* – an alternative argument that invoked s. 15(2); this aspect of her decision is discussed later in this chapter, in § 55:32, "Affirmative action".

[64] *Centrale des syndicats du Québec v. Quebec*, [2018] 1 S.C.R. 522, para. 117 (emphasis added).

1, the challenge in *Centrale* was rejected by an eight-to-one majority of the Court.

The *Alliance* and *Centrale* decisions appeared to mark another turning point in the Supreme Court's approach to s. 15. Without expressly acknowledging that she was doing so, Abella J. subtly reframed the s. 15 test from *Taypotat*. By applying a flexible approach to comparison at the first stage of the test, and also solidifying the shift to disadvantage and abandoning the requirement of arbitrariness at the second stage of the test, Abella J. made it easier for claimants to establish a s. 15 infringement, shifting more of the analysis to s. 1, where the burden is on the government to justify the infringement. This development is in keeping with the approach to s. 15 long recommended in this book. And yet, in both cases, Côté, Brown and Rowe JJ. (who were joined by Wagner J. in *Centrale*) rejected Abella J.'s reframed s. 15 test. In doing so, they set out their own competing approaches to s. 15. Abella J. did write for a solid majority of six judges in *Alliance*, but given the narrower result in *Centrale*, and the extent of the gap between the competing approaches to s. 15 evident in both cases, it was not clear whether her reformulated two-stage s. 15 test, and her broader approach to s. 15, would be embraced in future cases.

The answer seemed to come two years later in *Fraser v. Canada* (2020).[65] In this case, the three claimants were female members of the Royal Canadian Mounted Police (R.C.M.P.). In 1997, the R.C.M.P. had introduced a job-sharing program, which allowed R.C.M.P. members to split the duties of one full-time position. The three claimants, each of whom had young children, enrolled in the job-sharing program. R.C.M.P. members who participated in the job-sharing program – most of whom, like the claimants, were women with young children when they elected to participate – were not permitted to "buy back" full-time pension plan credit, whereas full-time R.C.M.P. members who took unpaid leave had this option.[66] The claimants initiated a s. 15 challenge, arguing that the pension plan arrangement for job-sharers discriminated against them – not directly, on its face, but indirectly, in its impact – because it adversely impacted them on the basis of their sex or, alternatively, family/parental status. The case made its way to the Supreme Court, giving the Court the opportunity to revisit s. 15, and perhaps resolve the disagreements that had emerged in *Alliance* and *Centrale*.

As in *Alliance*, Abella J. wrote an opinion for a six-judge majority of the Court (which included Wagner C.J., who had joined her opinion in *Alliance*, but not in *Centrale*). In her opinion, Abella J. affirmed the revised two-stage s. 15 test that she had set out in her opinions in *Alli-*

[65]*Fraser v. Canada*, 2020 SCC 28. Abella J. wrote the opinion for the majority of the Court, which was joined by Wagner C.J and Moldaver, Karakatsanis, Martin and Kasirer JJ. Brown and Rowe JJ. wrote a joint dissenting opinion. Côté J. also wrote dissenting opinion.

[66]The relevant legislation was the Royal Canadian Mounted Police Superannuation Act, R.S.C. 1985, c. R-11; and the Royal Canadian Mounted Police Superannuation Regulations, C.R.C., c. 1393.

ance and *Centrale*. Under this test, recall, a claimant must demonstrate that a law: (1) creates a distinction, on its face or in its impact, on the basis of an enumerated or analogous ground; and (2) imposes a burden or denies a benefit "in a manner that has the effect of reinforcing, perpetuating, or exacerbating disadvantage".[67] Abella J. also expanded on both stages of this test. Expanding on the first stage of the test, she reiterated that a law can create a distinction either: (1) directly, by creating a distinction that is evident on the face of the law itself; or (2) indirectly, by having a disproportionately adverse *impact* on a particular group. This case involved a claim of adverse impact discrimination, and Abella J. wrote at some length about the legal principles applicable to such claims; this aspect of her opinion is discussed in more detail later in this chapter.[68] Expanding on the second stage of the test, Abella J. clarified that, in determining whether a law has the effect of reinforcing, perpetuating or exacerbating disadvantage, the focus should be on "the impact of the harm caused to the affected group", and that harm for this purpose may include economic exclusion or disadvantage, social exclusion, psychological harm, physical harm or political exclusion – all of which "must be viewed in light of any systemic or historical disadvantages faced by the group".[69] Abella J. also explicitly confirmed two points that were more implicit in her opinions in *Alliance* and *Centrale* – that it is not necessary to establish the existence of prejudice or stereotyping to satisfy the second stage of the s. 15 test (although "[t]hey may assist in showing that a law has negative effects on a particular group"); and that a consideration of whether a distinction is "*relevant* to a legitimate state objective", or "arbitrary", should be deferred to s. 1.[70]

Applying this two-stage test, Abella J. held that the R.C.M.P.'s pension plan infringed s. 15. The first stage of the two-stage test was satisfied because the failure of the R.C.M.P.'s pension plan to grant the claimants – and other job-sharers – the ability to buy-back full-time pension benefits created a distinction, not on the face of the pension plan, but in its impact, on the basis of sex. The evidence showed – in keeping with the broader gendered patterns of part-time work – that it was primarily women with young children who participated in the job-sharing program, and hence "the RCMP's use of a temporary reduction in working hours as a basis for imposing less favourable pension consequences has an adverse impact on women".[71] The second stage of the two-stage test was satisfied because this adverse impact perpetuated the longstanding economic disadvantage of women. The "negative pension consequences of job-sharing perpetuate[d] a long-standing source of disadvantage to women: gender biases within pension plans, which have historically been designed 'for middle and upper-income full-time em-

---

[67] *Fraser v. Canada*, 2020 SCC 28, paras. 27, 50, 81.

[68] Section 55:28, "Substantive equality".

[69] *Fraser v. Canada*, 2020 SCC 28, para. 76.

[70] *Fraser v. Canada*, 2020 SCC 28, paras. 78-80.

[71] *Fraser v. Canada*, 2020 SCC 28, paras. 97, 106.

ployees with long service, typically male' ".[72] Abella J. went on to hold that the infringement of s. 15 could not be saved under s. 1, on the basis that the federal government had not offered a pressing and substantial objective for failing to grant the claimants – and other job-sharers – the ability to buy back full-time pension benefits.

The three judges that dissented in both *Alliance* and *Centrale* – Côté, Brown and Rowe JJ. – dissented again in *Fraser*, in two separate opinions, the first written jointly by Brown and Rowe JJ. and the second by Côté J. The dissenting judges disagreed with various aspects of the majority's approach to s. 15.[73] Unsurprisingly, they also disagreed with the majority's application of s. 15 to the facts of the case. All three judges would have concluded that the R.C.M.P.'s pension plan did not infringe s. 15. However, whereas Brown and Rowe JJ. would have rejected the claim at the second stage of the analysis (largely on the basis that the distinction created by the less favourable treatment of job-sharers under the R.C.M.P.'s pension plan was not arbitrary), Côté J. would have rejected the claim at the first stage of the analysis (largely on the basis that the distinction created was due to caregiving status, which is not an enumerated or analogous ground of discrimination).

The *Fraser* case answered a key question left open by the *Alliance* and *Centrale* cases – whether Abella J.'s reformulated approach to s. 15 would be embraced in future cases. The Court divided into two camps, as it did in *Alliance* and *Centrale*. However, a strong majority of the Court joined Abella J.'s opinion in *Fraser*, and although (as the previous discussion shows us) the Court often rallies around an approach to s. 15, only to reject or modify it a few years later, for now at least, Abella J.'s opinions in those cases would seem to capture the governing approach to s. 15. This approach involves a more flexible approach to comparison at the first stage of the analysis, and a focus on disadvantage (without a search for arbitrariness) at the second stage of the analysis.

VII. DISADVANTAGE

§ 55:23 Selection of comparator group

As explained in the previous section of this chapter, in order to suc-

---

[72] *Fraser v. Canada*, 2020 SCC 28, para. 108. Because Abella J. accepted the s. 15 argument based on the enumerated ground of sex, she declined to decide whether the alternative s. 15 argument based on a new analogous ground of parental/family status should also be accepted: *Fraser v. Canada*, 2020 SCC 28, para. 114.

[73] Brown and Rowe JJ. criticized aspects of the majority's approach to adverse impact discrimination under the first stage of the s. 15 test; they also disagreed with the majority that the analysis at the second stage of the test should focus on disadvantage, deferring any discussion of arbitrariness (whether the law fails "to respond to the actual capacities and needs of the group") to s. 1. Côté J. declined to engage in a comprehensive discussion of the proper approach to s. 15, and read her colleagues to agree on a two-stage s. 15 test that precisely mirrored the majority's two-stage s. 15, neglecting their disagreement about the role of arbitrariness under the second stage: *Fraser v. Canada*, 2020 SCC 28, para. 232. However, like Brown and Rowe JJ., she rejected aspects of the majority's approach to adverse impact discrimination. For Abella J.'s rather pointed response to some of these criticisms, see *Fraser v. Canada*, 2020 SCC 28, paras. 132-136.

ceed in an equality challenge under s. 15, the first step is for the claimant to establish that he or she has suffered a disadvantage by reason of his or her possession of one of the characteristics listed in s. 15 or an analogous characteristic. (The second step is for the claimant to establish that the disadvantage amounts to "discrimination".) It is the requirement of disadvantage that involves a comparison with others—others that are similarly situated to the claimant except for the presence of a listed or analogous personal characteristic. In *Andrews*,[1] for example, the claimant suffered a disadvantage by reason of his non-Canadian citizenship: he was denied admission to the legal profession, while others were entitled to be admitted to the profession, although their qualifications to practise law were no different from his, except for their Canadian citizenship.

The presence of disadvantage (or unequal treatment) requires a comparison between the legal position of the claimant and that of other people to whom the claimant may legitimately invite comparison.[2] This involves two inquiries. The first is whether the group to which the claimant compares herself is the appropriate comparator group. That is the topic of this section of the chapter. Once the appropriate comparator group has been selected, a second inquiry is presented, which is whether the distinction that the law draws between the claimant and the comparator group is disadvantageous to the claimant. That is the topic of the next section of the chapter.

The selection of the appropriate comparator group involves finding the group that shares with the claimant all the characteristics that qualify for the benefit (or burden), except for a personal characteristic that is listed in or analogous to those listed in s. 15. If a woman challenges a law that confers a benefit only on men, the comparator group will be men who qualify for the benefit, and if the claimant possesses all the qualifications for the benefit other than her sex, then it will be clear that she has suffered a disadvantage by reason of her sex. Some cases, however, are not this obvious.

In *Hodge v. Canada* (2004),[3] the claimant applied for a survivor's benefit under the Canada Pension Plan. The benefit was payable to a person who was the "spouse" of a CPP contributor at the time of the contributor's death. "Spouse" included not only persons legally married, but also common law partners. In this case, the claimant had been the common law

---

[Section 55:23]

[1]*Andrews v. Law Society of B.C.*, [1989] 1 S.C.R. 143. (The case held that citizenship was a personal characteristic analogous to those listed in s. 15.)

[2]The conventional wisdom is that equality is a comparative concept, and an equality claim always involves a comparison of the situation of the claimant with that of other similarly situated people. However, S.R. Moreau, "The Wrongs of Unequal Treatment" (2004) 54 U. Toronto L.J. 291, 303, 312 argues that no comparison is needed where the claimant is denied a benefit on the basis of a stereotype or where the claimant is denied access to basic goods. See also S.R. Moreau, "Equality Rights and the Relevance of Comparator Groups" (2006) 5 J.L. & Equality 81.

[3]*Hodge v. Canada*, [2004] 3 S.C.R. 357. Binnie J. wrote the opinion of the Court.

wife of a deceased CPP contributor, but she had left him shortly before his death. She was denied the benefit because she was no longer his spouse at the time of his death. She argued that the law discriminated on the ground of marital status, which is an analogous ground under s. 15. She pointed out that, as a separated common law spouse, she shared all relevant characteristics with a group that was entitled to the benefit, namely, separated married spouses, except for the personal characteristic of marital status. The Supreme Court of Canada held that she had selected the wrong comparator group. The correct comparator was not married spouses living apart at the time of the contributor's death (as she argued), but former spouses. Only a person who was a spouse at the time of death was entitled to the benefit. By terminating cohabitation (an essential element of a common law marriage), she had brought the common law marriage to an end. It was true that the termination of cohabitation would not have brought a legal marriage to an end, but the appropriate comparison was with married persons whose marriage had been brought to an end by divorce. They too were denied survivor benefits. All former spouses, whether the prior marriage was legal or common law, were treated equally. The claimant had therefore suffered no disadvantage on account of her marital status.

In Auton v. British Columbia (2004),[4] a claim of discrimination was made by autistic children and their parents, who complained that the province did not fund the "applied behavioural therapy" that was the most effective treatment for autism. The province's statutory health care plan provided full funding for all medically necessary services provided by physicians. Some medically necessary services that were provided by persons other than physicians were also funded, but not the autism therapy. Both the trial judge and the Court of Appeal held that the province was in breach of s. 15, because it funded some medically necessary therapies, but did not fund the equally necessary autism therapy. The Supreme Court of Canada reversed. McLachlin C.J., writing for the Court, held that the error in the lower courts was in the selection of the comparator group.[5] It was wrong to compare the autism claimants with the recipients of fully funded therapies, because this ignored the fact that the autism therapy had only recently become recognized as medically necessary. Funding of new therapies "may be legitimately denied or delayed because of uncertainty about a program and administrative difficulties related to its recognition and implementation".[6] Because the claimants had adduced no evidence that the province was funding "other

[4]*Auton v. British Columbia*, [2004] 3 S.C.R. 657. McLachlin C.J. wrote the opinion of the Court.

[5]She also held (para. 47) that the benefit claimed "is not a benefit provided by law", which she also regarded as fatal to the claim. I find this ground of decision hard to understand, since the claimants were arguing that the benefits that were provided by law were under-inclusive, because they excluded the sufferers from autism. Perhaps the point was that the statutory scheme did not purport to provide comprehensive funding for even medically necessary services if they were not provided by physicians.

[6]*Auton v. British Columbia*, [2004] 3 S.C.R. 657, para. 55.

comparable, novel therapies", they could not show disadvantage or unequal treatment.[7]

In a case like *Auton*, the outcome turns on the way in which the comparator group is defined. If the comparator group were defined as persons receiving medically necessary therapy, the autism claimants would be able to show unequal treatment. That is what the lower courts decided. But when the therapy is described as "novel", no comparator group can be found, and the claimants are unable to show unequal treatment. The introduction into the definition of the comparator group of a characteristic that was unique to the claimant group (the medical need for novel therapy) defeated the s. 15 claim at the outset. *Nova Scotia v. Martin* (2003)[8] provides a striking contrast. In that case, the Supreme Court of Canada held that Nova Scotia's statutory workers' compensation scheme violated s. 15 for providing only short-term benefits to sufferers from work-related "chronic pain". The Court acknowledged that chronic pain was unlike other work-related injuries in that it had no physical manifestations and there was no accepted method of diagnosis or treatment. If the Court had defined the comparator group with the same specificity that it did in *Auton*, the chronic-pain claimant in *Martin* would have had to find another group of persons suffering from work-related injuries that like chronic pain had no physical manifestations and no accepted method of diagnosis or treatment. That would have defeated the claim. But instead the Court brushed aside the problems of fully funding chronic pain cases and held that the comparator group is "the group of workers subject to the Act who do not have chronic pain and are eligible for compensation for their employment-related injuries".[9] That definition of the comparator group ensured that the claim of unequal treatment on the basis of the personal characteristic of physical disability was established.

These cases demonstrate that the definition of the comparator group is critical to the outcome of s. 15 cases. The claimant will compare himself to a group that is better treated than him *(Martin)*. The responding government will suggest a different comparator group that either receives worse treatment or the same treatment *(Hodge)* or that does not exist *(Auton)*. In choosing between the competing comparisons, a court works with little guidance, although it may be assisted by its sense of the purpose of the statutory scheme.[10] Perhaps *Auton* and *Martin* could be distinguished by reference to the different purposes of the

[7]*In Auton v. British Columbia*, [2004] 3 S.C.R. 657, para. 62.

[8]*Nova Scotia v. Martin*, [2003] 2 S.C.R. 504; discussed under heading § 55:45, "Mental or physical disability".

[9]*Nova Scotia v. Martin*, [2003] 2 S.C.R. 504, para. 71 per Gonthier J. for the Court.

[10]In *Law v. Canada*, [1999] 1 S.C.R. 497, paras. 57-58, Iacobucci J. suggested that the identification of the comparator group involves "a number of factors", including the subject-matter, purpose and effect of the legislation and "other contextual factors". He also suggested that the comparator group chosen by the claimant should be "the natural starting point", and he implied that the Court would only rarely depart from the claimant's choice.

statutory schemes. In *Auton*, the health care plan did not purport to be comprehensive in its funding of even medically necessary services if they were not provided by physicians. In *Martin*, the workers' compensation scheme did purport to provide comprehensive coverage for all work-related injuries (for which the tort action was barred). In a scheme that is supposed to be comprehensive, it is natural to make the comparison between those who are denied benefits and those who are granted benefits. The comparison is less persuasive (and the consequences more costly) where the scheme is not comprehensive and the claimant group is only one of a number of groups from whom benefits are withheld.

When the Court decides to choose a comparison that causes the claim to fail, the elaborate infrastructure of doctrine defining the elements of s. 15 and the elements of s. 1[11] is completely bypassed. Only if the claimant's choice of comparison is agreed to by the Court will the claim be able to proceed through the various stages of s. 15 and s. 1.

In *Withler v. Canada* (2011),[12] the Court suddenly resiled from its insistence on finding a precise comparator group to which the claimant's position was to be compared. In that case, the claimants were widows of deceased federal civil servants who had died over the age of 65. Under the federal statutory pension plan, the spouse of a deceased plan member was entitled to a death benefit (akin to life insurance). Where the plan member had died under the age of 65, the death benefit was a lump sum equal to twice the annual salary of the plan member at the time of death. However—and this was the point of the s. 15 challenge—where the plan member had died over the age of 65, the death benefit was reduced by ten per cent for each year by which the plan member had survived his 65th birthday. The claimants argued that they had suffered a disadvantage by reference to age. Their comparator group, namely, the spouses of plan members who died under the age of 65 (and received the full death benefit), perfectly matched the claimant group except for the claimed ground of discrimination, which was the age of the plan member at the time of death. Of course, "discrimination" still had to be established, but the claimants seemed to have established a disadvantage based on the listed ground of age. Not so fast, said the Court: "a mirror comparator group analysis may fail to capture substantive inequality";[13] "reliance on a mirror comparator group can occlude aspects of the full contextual analysis that s. 15(1) requires."[14] These statements are not easy to understand. The Court acknowledged that "equality is a

[11]In *Auton*, the evidence showed that the autism therapy was extremely expensive, and that was one reason for the lack of public funding (para. 10). Compare *Nfld. v. N.A.P.E.*, [2004] 3 S.C.R. 381, where the Court held that the high cost of pay equity, although required by s. 15, justified delay in its implementation. But to reach this decision the Court had to go through the various steps required for the establishment of s. 1 justification.

[12]*Withler v. Canada*, [2011] 1 S.C.R. 396. McLachlin C.J. and Abella J. wrote the opinion of the Court.

[13]*Withler v. Canada*, [2011] 1 S.C.R. 396, para. 60.

[14]*Withler v. Canada*, [2011] 1 S.C.R. 396, para. 81 ("occlude" means "stop, close up or obstruct").

comparative concept" and quickly concluded that the law did indeed create a "distinction on the basis of an enumerated or analogous ground"[15]—although the Court pointedly failed to identify any particular comparator group. The Court then went on to apply a contextual analysis to hold that the distinction was not discriminatory because "the package of benefits, viewed as a whole and over time, does not impose or perpetuate discrimination".[16] The decision would presumably have been exactly the same if the "mirror comparator group" had been relied upon. However, the Court was obviously signalling a concern about their reasoning in *Hodge* and *Auton*, where "the definition of the comparator group determines the analysis and the outcome".[17]

§ 55:24 Requirement of disadvantage

Once the appropriate comparator group has been selected, it is necessary to compare the treatment provided by the law to the claimant with the treatment provided to the comparator group. Only if the law treats the claimant less favourably, whether by withholding a benefit that is granted to the comparator group, or by imposing a burden that is not applicable to the comparator group, is the claim of disadvantage or unequal treatment made out.

In *Thibaudeau v. Canada* (1995),[1] the claimant was unable to establish that she had suffered a disadvantage by reason of her marital status. The claimant was a divorced woman who had custody of the children of the marriage and who received child-support payments from her former husband. She objected to a provision of the Income Tax Act that required her to pay income tax on the support payments that she received from her ex-spouse. She argued that the tax provision discriminated against separated custodial parents, because in an intact family the income tax on money spent on child support would be paid by the spouse who earned the income. The Supreme Court of Canada, by a majority, rejected the argument. The Court pointed out that the inclusion requirement on the recipient spouse was matched by a deduction for the payor spouse. Since the payor spouse was usually in a higher tax bracket than the recipient spouse, the tax saved by the deduction would normally exceed the tax incurred by the inclusion. This resulted in a reduction of tax for the majority of separated couples—a reduction that cost the treasury over $300 million per year.

While it was the payor who received the benefit of the deduction, and

---

[15] *Withler v. Canada*, [2011] 1 S.C.R. 396, paras. 68-69.

[16] *Withler v. Canada*, [2011] 1 S.C.R. 396, para. 81.

[17] *Withler v. Canada*, [2011] 1 S.C.R. 396, para. 56, citing the previous passages of this section of this book.

[Section 55:24]

[1] *Thibaudeau v. Canada*, [1995] 2 S.C.R. 627. The principal majority opinion of the seven-judge bench was written by Gonthier J. Short concurring opinions were written by Sopinka J., with whom La Forest J. agreed, and by Cory and Iacobucci JJ. McLachlin J. and L'Heureux-Dubé J. each wrote dissenting opinions.

the recipient who bore the burden of the tax, the family law system required that the tax consequences be taken into account in fixing the amount of child support. Therefore, in fixing the amount of child support, the payor's enhanced ability to pay should be recognized, and the amount of child support should be grossed-up to fully compensate the recipient for her additional tax liability. In Thibaudeau's case, the family court that made the support order had taken her additional tax liability into account, but it appeared that the liability had been underestimated, and the gross-up for tax was insufficient.[2] But the majority of the Court held that this deficiency should be remedied by a review of the support order by the family court. Although some separated custodial parents did not benefit from the deduction-inclusion system, as a group separated custodial parents did benefit. Therefore, the Income Tax Act did not discriminate against them, and there was no breach of s. 15 of the Charter of Rights.

Another way of looking at *Thibaudeau* is that it calls for any disadvantage imposed on the claimant group to be netted out against any advantage granted to the claimant group. The disadvantage of having to pay income tax on support payments was, if the family-law system worked properly,[3] offset by higher support payments, more faithfully paid.[4]

Another case in which there was a finding of no disadvantage was *Eaton v. Brant County Board of Education* (1997).[5] The Ontario Special Education Tribunal was a body empowered by Ontario's Education Act to make decisions about the placement of "exceptional pupils", a term that included those pupils who by virtue of mental or physical disability required placement in a special education programme. In this case, the Tribunal had determined that a 12-year-old child with cerebral palsy, who had for three years been educated in a regular classroom, should be placed in a special classroom. The child's parents took the view, which was accepted by the Ontario Court of Appeal, that the statutory power to place exceptional pupils in a separate classroom without parental consent was a violation of equality rights. The Supreme Court of Canada held unanimously that there was no breach of s. 15. To be sure, the distinction drawn by the Education Act between "exceptional pupils"

---

[2]The Court did not consider the question, upon which no evidence seemed to have been led, as to how much lower the support order would have been if the payor's deduction did not exist. Without some estimate of this, it is not apparent merely from the inadequacy of the tax gross-up that Thibaudeau was worse off than she would have been in a world without the deduction-inclusion system.

[3]McLachlin and L'Heureux-Dubé JJ. dissented primarily on the ground that the family-law system could not be relied upon to shift the tax benefit forward to the custodial spouse. By conferring the benefit of the deduction on the non-custodial spouse, and imposing the burden of the tax on the custodial spouse, the Act was discriminatory.

[4]Compare *Miron v. Trudel*, [1995] 2 S.C.R. 418, where the count disagreed on whether, on balance, it was more or less advantageous to be a common-law spouse.

[5]*Eaton v. Brant County Board of Education*, [1997] 1 S.C.R. 241. The opinion of the unanimous Court was written by Sopinka J. Lamer C.J. added brief concurring reasons on a point not germane to the outcome.

and other pupils was based on mental or physical disability, which was a listed s. 15 ground. But the purpose of the distinction was to identify children with special educational needs, and then to design special education programmes to meet those special needs. Although the parents wanted their child's education to continue in the regular classroom setting, the Tribunal had found that the evidence showed that the segregated setting was in the best interests of the child. The equality right was that of the child, not her parents, and the issue had to be resolved "from the child's point of view as opposed to that of the adults in his or her life".[6] The Court concluded that, given the Tribunal's findings, the placement of the child in a segregated setting could not be. Therefore, there was no discrimination under s. 15.[7]

§ 55:25 Objective and subjective disadvantage

How does one measure disadvantage? Is it a purely economic calculus, or are non-economic disadvantages also relevant? This question was presented by *Egan v. Canada* (1995),[1] in which a same-sex couple challenged the spouse's allowance that was payable under the federal Old Age Security Act to the "spouse" of a pensioner. The term spouse included persons in common-law relationships, but only if they were "of the opposite sex". The awkward element of the facts, however, was that in British Columbia, where the claimants lived, the combined effect of the provincial social assistance entitlements and the Old Age Security pension left the claimants better off as unmarried individuals than they would be if they were recognized as spouses under the Old Age Security Act. The Supreme Court of Canada denied the claim to spousal status by a majority of five to four for reasons that have earlier been explained.[2] But all nine judges accepted the proposition that the denial of the federal spousal allowance was a disadvantage that could in principle be the basis of a s. 15 equality right.

In *Egan*, none of the judges considered that the economic advantage of the claimants' non-recognition as spouses should defeat their s. 15 claim. La Forest J., who wrote for four of the five judges who upheld the legislation, dismissed the point by saying that, while there might be an advantage "in this specific instance" (which was the only one before the Court), "there was nothing to show that this is generally the case with

---

[6]*Eaton v. Brant County Board of Education*, [1997] 1 S.C.R. 241, para. 77.

[7]See also *R. v. Kokopenace*, [2015] 2 S.C.R. 398, para. 128 (Indigenous person convicted by jury of manslaughter claimed breach of s. 15 because Indigenous peoples were underrepresented on jury roll; held, no breach of s. 15: accused had received a fair trial and suffered no disadvantage from the deficient jury roll); *Ewert v. Canada*, [2018] 2 S.C.R. 165, paras. 77-79 (evidence of a risk that psychological and actuarial risk assessment tools used by the Correctional Service of Canada to make decisions about inmates were less accurate when applied to Indigenous inmates not sufficient to establish a breach of s. 15).

[Section 55:25]

[1]*Egan v. Canada*, [1995] 2 S.C.R. 513.

[2]See § 55:18, "Addition of analogous grounds".

homosexual couples" (meaning, presumably, couples in other provinces who were not before the Court).[3] Cory J., who dissented, but who on this point attracted the agreement of Sopinka J., as well as Iacobucci and McLachlin JJ., said that "the concept of equal benefit of the law should not be restricted to a simple calculation of economic profit or loss".[4] And L'Heureux-Dubé J. agreed that "it would take too narrow a view of the phrase "benefit of the law" [in s. 15] to define it strictly in terms of economic interests".[5] These sentiments are admirable, but it must not be overlooked that many people, especially those who are poor, place a higher value on additional income than on less tangible considerations. In *Egan*, if the s. 15 argument had prevailed, as the four dissenters would have held, the law would have been invalidated not only for Egan and his partner, but for all other same-sex couples in like circumstances. Those who preferred the extra money that came from their non-spousal status would have to accept the lower benefits that their newly acquired spousal status had brought. Nor is this a unique or unusual situation as La Forest J. implied. It is common for social legislation to combine spousal incomes for the purpose of determining eligibility for income-tested social programs, and common-law spouses are included for the very reason that two single individuals would draw higher benefits than a married couple.

Another way of framing the issue in *Egan* is to ask whether the presence of disadvantage is to be judged from the *subjective* standard of the individual who makes the claim of discrimination, or from an *objective* standard determined by the reviewing court. The Supreme Court of Canada was implicitly applying a subjective standard in *Egan:* the claimants were disadvantaged because, according to their subjective calculus of costs and benefits, the disadvantage of not being officially recognized as spouses outweighed the advantage of higher single-status social

[3]*Egan v. Canada*, [1995] 2 S.C.R. 513, 531, para. 12. In *Eldridge v. B.C.*, [1997] 3 S.C.R. 624, para. 83, LaForest J. referred to his *Egan* statement as authority for the proposition that equality-seeking plaintiffs "need not establish a violation of their own particular rights" so long as they establish that "the equality rights of members of the group to which they belong have been infringed". This statement was an obiter dictum, and must surely be wrong in light of the insistence in all cases other than *Egan* that particular disadvantage be established. Compare *Vriend v. Alta.*, [1998] 1 S.C.R. 493, paras. 43-44, requiring plaintiff to obtain discretionary public interest standing to challenge statutory provisions that did not disadvantage him personally, although they did disadvantage other members of the (LGBTQ) group to which the plaintiff belonged.

[4]*Egan v. Canada*, [1995] 2 S.C.R. 513, 593, para. 158. Cory J. also asserted that the economic advantage was "highly speculative and may well be incorrect" (593, para.157), although the factual issue was not regarded as speculative by La Forest J. or L'Heureux-Dubé J. He also held that the provincial law should be ignored in assessing the validity of the federal law (592, paras. 155-156), a point that seems inconsistent with *Thibaudeau v. Canada*, [1995] 2 S.C.R. 627, where the provincial family law rescued the Income Tax Act from discrimination. In *Thibaudeau*, Cory and Iacobucci JJ. explained the difference on the basis that the Income Tax Act "explicitly" incorporated family law, whereas in *Egan* the spousal allowance was allotted "independently of any reference to provincial social insurance legislation" (*Thibaudeau v. Canada*, [1995] 2 S.C.R. 627, 703).

[5]*Egan v. Canada*, [1995] 2 S.C.R. 513, 565, para. 86.

assistance. The same subjective standard seems to have been the (unarticulated) premise of the finding of disadvantage in *McKinney v. University of Guelph* (1990),[6] in which the Supreme Court of Canada held that mandatory retirement at age 65 constituted discrimination on the basis of age. The Court assumed without discussion that mandatory retirement was a disadvantage to employees aged 65. From an *objective* standpoint, this is probably wrong. The evidence in *McKinney* suggested that in a regime of mandatory retirement, wages rise faster with seniority than they would if there were no definite end to an individual's employment, continuous performance assessment is not usually imposed upon older workers, and pension rights are usually agreed to and contributed to by the employer. Assuming this to be so, one might well conclude that a person of 65, who admittedly now confronts the downside of the regime, has nonetheless received overall a net benefit from mandatory retirement. But none of the judges doubted that the individual plaintiffs, who had reached 65 and wished to continue their work (at full salary), were disadvantaged by the obligation to retire. From their own subjective standpoint, the plaintiff professors were disadvantaged.

If the subjective standard of disadvantage is the correct approach, then disadvantage will be present in all but the most unusual cases, since plaintiffs do not bring Charter cases (or any other legal proceedings) unless they believe that they have suffered a disadvantage. The case for the subjective standard would be conclusive if Charter decisions affected only the parties to those decisions. Who, one might ask, is in the position to do the calculus of costs and benefits for someone else? But Charter decisions do not affect only the parties who believe they are disadvantaged. If mandatory retirement had been struck down in *McKinney*, then its benefits would have been denied to all employees,[7] including those whose unions had voluntarily sought and negotiated mandatory retirement (and pensions) in their collective agreements. This radical result was in fact avoided in *McKinney*, because the Court held, by a majority, that mandatory retirement was justified under s. 1. As part of the s. 1 inquiry, the Court did attempt an objective weighing of the costs and benefits of mandatory retirement. The Court concluded that mandatory retirement offered significant benefits to individual university professors, as well as to the universities as centres of teaching and research. In the end, therefore, the Court's (objective) calculus of costs and benefits, rather than the (subjective) calculus of the plaintiffs, is the one that prevailed. Mandatory retirement was upheld.

The subjective standard of disadvantage in s. 15 (as opposed to s. 1) was not applied in *Thibaudeau*,[8] the case (discussed earlier) that upheld the Income Tax Act's deduction-inclusion system for taxing child support. In that case, it will be recalled, the claimant Thibaudeau regarded

---

[6] *McKinney v. University of Guelph*, [1990] 3 S.C.R. 229, see also § 55:44, "Age".

[7] The ruling applied to all workplaces, not just those of government, because the challenge was to a provision in the Human Rights Code, which applied to private as well as public workplaces.

[8] *Thibaudeau v. Canada*, [1995] 2 S.C.R. 627.

herself as disadvantaged by the Income Tax Act provisions, and she probably was disadvantaged by them since the amount of her support had not been grossed-up sufficiently to enable her to pay the additional income tax to which the support payments rendered her liable. But the Supreme Court of Canada held that the deduction-inclusion system was, on the whole, beneficial to separated custodial parents. Therefore, the Court did not want to strike the system down. But this reasoning all took place within s. 15. In contrast to *McKinney*, the Court did not need to advance to the s. 1 inquiry. In effect, without saying so, the Court in *Thibaudeau* applied an objective measure of disadvantage to the s. 15 equality claim. The claim failed for lack of objective disadvantage, despite the claimant's subjective sense of disadvantage.

The objective approach to disadvantage was also applied in *R. v. Swain* (1991),[9] where one of the issues was whether a person accused of a criminal offence, who had chosen not to raise the defence of insanity, would be discriminated against by a rule that permitted the Crown against the wish of the accused to raise the issue of insanity. If the accused were convicted of the criminal offence, he would be subject to a finite sentence imposed under the Criminal Code. If the accused were acquitted on the ground of insanity, he would be detained indefinitely at the pleasure of the Lieutenant Governor. One can easily understand why an accused would regard the indefinite detention as a worse alternative than the finite sentence. And this alternative, obviously, is triggered by the mental disability of the accused, which is one of the grounds of discrimination named in s. 15. Nevertheless, Lamer C.J. for a majority of the Supreme Court of Canada held that there was no discrimination because the accused who was acquitted on the ground of insanity did not really suffer a disadvantage; rather, he was spared the disadvantage of being convicted of an offence for which by reason of insanity he did not have the requisite guilty mind.[10] This conclusion obviously involved a rejection of the subjective measurement of disadvantage: the accused, who with the advice of counsel deliberately refused to use the defence of insanity, obviously feared the indeterminate detention more than the stigma of conviction. I agree that the point of view of the accused ought not to be decisive, but the Court's view that the stigma of a criminal conviction (coupled with a finite sentence) would be a greater detriment to the accused than an indefinite detention seems to me to be wrong on any basis.[11]

The fluctuations between objective and subjective in the Supreme

---

[9] *R. v. Swain*, [1991] 1 S.C.R. 933.

[10] *R. v. Swain*, [1991] 1 S.C.R. 933, 995-996. Lamer C.J. wrote for himself, Sopinka and Cory JJ., and his opinion on this issue was agreed with by Gonthier and La Forest JJ. Wilson and L'Heureux-Dubé JJ. did not need to, and did not, consider this issue.

[11] This is another example of the Supreme Court of Canada's confidence that it is able to identify and measure the stigma of a criminal conviction, and the Court's view that radical constitutional results should flow from a finding of stigma: see ch. 47, Fundamental Justice, under headings §§ 47:16 to 47:18, "Absolute and strict liability" (definition of "true crimes") and § 47:19, "Murder" (definition of "murder").

Court of Canada's inquiries into disadvantage may have been resolved in *Law v. Canada* (1999).[12] That case did not explicitly address the question of disadvantage. However, the case did introduce into the equality jurisprudence anew requirement of human dignity, and it addressed the question whether an impairment of human dignity was to be assessed from a subjective or an objective perspective. The Court's answer was that both perspectives must be employed! The inquiry was to be undertaken "from the perspective of the claimant and from no other perspective", but the claimant's assertion must be "supported by an objective assessment of the situation".[13] This seems to make the objective assessment the decisive one. Later cases have clarified the test as meaning that an impairment of human dignity is to be assessed from the perspective of a reasonable person (objective), but one who shares the attributes and circumstances of the claimant (subjective).[14] Presumably, this test would now be the appropriate one for the assessment of disadvantage as well.

§ 55:26 Human dignity and disadvantage

The element of human dignity that was part of the s. 15 analysis from 1999 to 2008 often led the Court to omit any explicit analysis of whether the claimant is truly disadvantaged by the challenged law. After all, if there is no impairment of human dignity, then the claimant loses regardless of whether she has suffered any disadvantage. Moreover, the indeterminate concept of human dignity tends to absorb the question of disadvantage, making it hard for the Court to keep the two ideas distinct. Judicial discussion of human dignity inevitably ranges far and wide, and often sounds very much like a discussion of disadvantage.

In *Nova Scotia v. Walsh* (2002),[1] for example, the majority of the Supreme Court of Canada seemed to decide that persons in common-law relationships were on the whole better off by not being included in the shared-property regime that was imposed on those who were formally married. The true position would seem to be that, in each relationship, one person would be better off and the other would be worse off, depending on who owned the most property. Needless to say, the claimant in the case owned less property than her common-law spouse. However, the Court avoided any analysis of this issue by deciding that a reasonable person who shared the attributes and circumstances of the claimant would find that the claimant's human dignity had not been impaired by her exclusion from the shared-property regime.[2]

In *Canadian Foundation for Children, Youth and the Law v. Canada*

---

[12] *Law v. Canada*, [1999] 1 S.C.R. 497. Iacobucci J. wrote the opinion of the Court.

[13] *Law v. Canada*, [1999] 1 S.C.R. 497, para 60.

[14] E.g., *Can. Foundation for Children, Youth and the Law v. Can.*, [2004] 1 S.C.R. 76, para. 53 per McLachlin C.J. for majority.

[Section 55:26]

[1] *Nova Scotia v. Walsh*, [2002] 4 S.C.R. 325.

[2] *Nova Scotia v. Walsh*, [2002] 4 S.C.R. 325, paras. 38, 62.

(2004),[3] the majority of the Supreme Court of Canada explicitly decided that the Criminal Code provision that permitted the reasonable use of corrective force against children by parents and teachers was on the whole beneficial to children.[4] But the Court did not rest its opinion on the absence of disadvantage. It held that the human dignity of children was not impaired, taking the perspective of "a reasonable person acting on behalf of a child, who seriously considers and values the child's views and developmental needs."[5]

When *Kapp* removed human dignity from the s. 15 analysis, it replaced the concept with "discrimination", a similarly indeterminate judicially-created element to be established by the equality claimant. The *Kapp* requirement has the same tendency to absorb the requirement of disadvantage. In *Ermineskin Indian Band and Nation v. Canada* (2009),[6] the Supreme Court dismissed an equality challenge by Indian bands to the investment provisions of the Indian Act, which precluded the external investment of band moneys held by the Crown. Rothstein J., who wrote for the Court, avoided the issue of disadvantage altogether by pointing out that "if the preclusion of investment by the Crown is a disadvantage, the legislation will violate s. 15(1) only if that disadvantage is one that is discriminatory, that is, if it perpetuates prejudice or stereotyping".[7] He then pointed out that the retention of Indian moneys in the consolidated revenue fund, where they were regularly credited with a reasonable rate of interest, reduced the power of the Crown to control the fund, avoided any risk of loss to the fund and maintained the liquidity of the fund. The conclusion that Rothstein J. drew was that these features were not discriminatory in the sense of perpetuating prejudice or stereotyping.[8] No doubt that was correct, but the more obvious conclusion was the straightforward one that the investment provisions entailed prudent practices that did not impose a disadvantage on the Indian bands.

§ 55:27 Group disadvantage

In *Andrews*,[1] it will be recalled, the Supreme Court of Canada struck down a British Columbia law that excluded non-citizens from admission

---

[3]*Canadian Foundation for Children, Youth and the Law v. Canada*, [2004] 1 S.C.R. 76.

[4]*Canadian Foundation for Children, Youth and the Law v. Canada*, [2004] 1 S.C.R. 76, para. 59.

[5]*Canadian Foundation for Children, Youth and the Law v. Canada*, [2004] 1 S.C.R. 76, para. 53.

[6]*Ermineskin Indian Band and Nation v. Canada*, [2009] 1 S.C.R. 222. Rothstein J. wrote the opinion of the Court.

[7]*Ermineskin Indian Band and Nation v. Canada*, [2009] 1 S.C.R. 222, para. 192.

[8]*Ermineskin Indian Band and Nation v. Canada*, [2009] 1 S.C.R. 222, paras. 201-202.

[Section 55:27]

[1]*Andrews v. Law Society of British Columbia*, [1989] 1 S.C.R. 143.

to the bar. Three opinions were written, and all three suggested that disadvantage or powerlessness was characteristic of the groups protected by s. 15. Both Wilson and McIntyre JJ. referred to non-citizens as an example of a "discrete and insular minority",[2] an obscure phrase which in the United States has become a code word to describe groups that typically experience discrimination.[3] Wilson J. elaborated by explaining that non-citizens were "a group lacking in political power and as such vulnerable to having their interests overlooked and their rights to equal concern and respect violated".[4] La Forest J. described non-citizens as "an example without parallel" of a group "who are relatively powerless politically, and whose interests are likely to be compromised by legislative decisions".[5]

In *R. v. Turpin* (1989),[6] a s. 15 challenge was mounted to a provision of the Criminal Code that stipulated that certain of the most serious offences, including murder, were to be tried by a judge and jury, and that gave no right to elect a trial by judge alone. The s. 15 argument was based on another provision of the Criminal Code, which was applicable only in Alberta, and which gave to an accused person the right to elect a trial by judge alone for all indictable offences, including murder.[7] In *Turpin*, there were three accused who were charged with murder in Ontario. They wished to be tried by judge alone, and they argued that the failure of the Criminal Code to accord that right to an accused person in Ontario was discriminatory, because the right was available to an accused person in Alberta.

In *Turpin*, the Supreme Court of Canada rejected the s. 15 argument on the basis that the three accused were not members of a disadvantaged group. Wilson J. for a unanimous Court said that it was not sufficient for the equality claimant to show that he or she was disadvantaged by the impugned law. That, obviously, was necessary, but it was not sufficient. The claimant had to go further and show that the distinction employed by the statute was one that defined a group that was disadvantaged in other respects. Wilson J. put it this way:[8]

> A finding that there is discrimination will, I think, in most but perhaps not all cases necessarily entail a search for disadvantage that exists apart from and independent of the particular legal distinction being challenged.

Province of residence (or trial) did not, at least in the context of this case, identify a disadvantaged group. It was impossible to identify "indicia of discrimination such as stereotyping, historical disadvantage

---

[2] *Andrews v. Law Society of B.C.*, [1989] 1 S.C.R. 143, 152, 157, 183.

[3] The phrase was drawn from *United States v. Carolene Products Co.* (1938), 304 U.S. 144.

[4] *Andrews v. Law Society of B.C.*, [1989] 1 S.C.R. 143, 152.

[5] *Andrews v. Law Society of B.C.*, [1989] 1 S.C.R. 143, 195.

[6] *R. v. Turpin*, [1989] 1 S.C.R. 1296.

[7] This curious provision has since been amended to extend throughout Canada the right to elect for trial by judge alone.

[8] *R. v. Turpin*, [1989] 1 S.C.R. 1296, 1332.

or vulnerability to political and social prejudice".[9] The claim would not, Wilson J. said, "advance the purposes of s. 15 in remedying or preventing discrimination against groups suffering social, political and legal disadvantage in our society".[10] Since the claim was outside the purpose of s. 15, it was also outside the scope of s. 15, and the claim accordingly was rejected.[11]

The view that systemic disadvantage and political powerlessness are essential characteristics of the groups protected by s. 15 reflects a theory of equality that finds its origin in the famous footnote 4 of *United States v. Carolene Products Co.* (1938).[12] In that footnote, Stone J. of the Supreme Court of the United States pointed out that "prejudice against discrete and insular minorities" could have the effect of distorting "those political processes ordinarily to be relied upon to protect minorities".[13] The point is that discrimination against racialized people (or other minorities) may reflect a flawed political process from which racialized people are effectively excluded. From this perspective, judicial review of discriminatory laws can be viewed as the correction of a failure of the political process—the failure to represent adequately a "discrete and insular minority". This line of reasoning has been offered in the United States by John Hart Ely as a defence of the legitimacy of judicial review on equal protection grounds.[14] According to Ely, when the judges strike down a discriminatory law, what they are really doing is removing impediments to access to the democratic political process. This view of equality casts the judges "in the role of servants of democracy even as they strike down the actions of supposedly democratic governments".[15]

The view of equality review as a correction of political powerlessness undoubtedly contains a valuable insight as to why discrimination by legislative bodies may properly be corrected by courts. But it is doubtful whether it is appropriate to regard the political powerlessness of a group as an essential ingredient of discrimination under s. 15. For one thing, a court is not normally in a position to measure the relative power of

---

[9] *R. v. Turpin*, [1989] 1 S.C.R. 1296, 1333.

[10] *R. v. Turpin*, [1989] 1 S.C.R. 1296, 1333. This line of reasoning was followed by L'Heureux-Dubé J. for the majority in *Haig v. Can.*, [1993] 2 S.C.R. 995, 1043-1044, to hold again that place of residence was not an analogous ground.

[11] Compare *McKinney v. U. of Guelph*, [1990] 3 S.C.R. 229, 293, where Wilson J. said that even a disadvantage imposed by reference to a named ground of discrimination (age in that case) would be discrimination only if there was also a finding of "prejudice". La Forest J. seems to reject the point in an inconclusive reference at 279.

[12] *United States v. Carolene Products Co.* (1938), 304 U.S. 144.

[13] *United States v. Carolene Products Co.* (1938), 304 U.S. 144, 153, footnote 4.

[14] J.H. Ely, Democracy and Distrust (Harvard U.P., Cambridge, Mass., 1980), ch. 6. This same theory is espoused in Canada by H.S. Fairley, "Enforcing the Charter" (1982) 4 Supreme Court L.R. 217, 243, 249-250 and P.J. Monahan, "Judicial Review and Democracy" (1986) 21 U.B.C.L. Rev. 87, 89-97.

[15] L. Tribe, "The Puzzling Persistence of Process-based Constitutional Theories" (1980) 89 Yale L.J. 1063, 1063. Tribe goes on to criticize the process-based theories. For criticism from a Canadian standpoint, see P.W. Hogg, "The Charter of Rights and American Theories of Interpretation" (1987) 25 Osgoode Hall L.J. 87.

groups within society. Wilson J.'s insistence in *Turpin* on a "search for disadvantage that exists apart from and independent of the particular legal distinction being challenged" would carry courts far beyond the facts and the law relevant to a particular case and into some of the most hotly contested areas of sociology and political science.[16]

Wilson J. herself acknowledged in *Andrews* that "the range of discrete and insular minorities has changed and will continue to change with changing political and social circumstances".[17] But how could a court possibly measure such changes? Would the economic success of some recently-arrived visible minorities from Asia, who have already achieved incomes higher than the national average,[18] disentitle an immigrant from Asia to a s. 15 remedy? Would the growing proportion of old people in the Canadian population be judged sufficient to disentitle an old person to a s. 15 remedy? Would the growing influence of women's groups on legislative agendas be judged sufficient to disentitle a woman to a s. 15 remedy? Of course, the answers to these questions should be no if an immigrant, an old person or a woman could show that a particular statute imposed a burden or denied a benefit solely by reason of the race, national origin, age or sex of the complainant. In my view, nothing more should have to be established.

Assuming that general disadvantage could be identified with particular groups, the awkward question arises as to how to deal with an individual who has been discriminated against on a named or analogous ground, although the individual belongs to a group that is in other respects not subject to disadvantage. The implication of *Turpin* is that an individual member of the advantaged part of a named or analogous group would not invoke s. 15, even if the individual could establish unjust treatment based on a named or analogous ground. Whatever the theoretical justification for such a stern doctrine, it is hard to square with the unqualified language of s. 15,[19] and it has in fact been rejected by the Supreme Court of Canada.

In *R. v. Hess* (1990),[20] a s. 15 attack was mounted against the statutory rape offence in the Criminal Code. This provision, since repealed,

---

[16]For example, it is widely held that discrete and insular minorities are relatively effective in the American political process, in comparison with anonymous and diffuse minorities (or majorities): B. Ackerman, "Beyond Carolene Products" (1985) 98 Harv. L. Rev. 713 (criticizing the phrase "discrete and insular minorities" in U.S. equal protection law).

[17]*Andrews v. Law Society of B.C.*, [1989] 1 S.C.R. 143, 152.

[18]On the basis of average incomes, one would be forced to conclude that many visible minority groups are not disadvantaged, and some invisible (white) groups are: see the review of some of the data in R.G. Juriansz, "Employment Equity and Pay Equity" in Tarnopolsky, Discrimination in the Law and the Administration of Justice (1993).

[19]Accord, Gibson, The Law of the Charter: Equality Rights (1990), 152-157.

[20]*R. v. Hess*, [1990] 2 S.C.R. 906. Wilson J.'s opinion was agreed to by Lamer C.J., La Forest and L'Heureux-Dubé JJ.; McLachlin J.'s opinion was agreed to by Gonthier J.; Sopinka J. wrote a concurring opinion siding with McLachlin J. on the s. 1 issue. There was also a s. 7 issue, upon which the Court divided: Wilson J. struck down the law; McLachlin J. dissented, upholding the law under s. 1; Sopinka J. agreed with Wilson J.

made it an offence for a male person to have intercourse with a female person under the age of fourteen. The s. 15 attack was based on discrimination by sex: the provision applied only to male offenders and protected only female victims. McLachlin J., with the agreement of three others, frankly noted that Wilson J.'s dictum in *Turpin* suggested that "a distinction against men as compared with women" could not be discrimination under s. 15, because men could "rarely show discrimination apart from the provision they are challenging". She rejected this view, saying that "these arguments take the language in *Turpin* further than is justified".[21] She held that the statutory rape provision did offend s. 15, because of its discrimination against men, although she went on to uphold the provision under s. 1. Wilson J., with the agreement of four other judges, held that the provision did not offend s. 15, because the definition of intercourse used the concept of penetration, which could as a matter of biological fact be committed only by a man; therefore, she held, it was not discriminatory to apply the offence only to men. This dubious reasoning is discussed later in the chapter.[22] For present purposes, the point to notice is that Wilson J., although finding no discrimination, did not repeat her general disadvantage argument from *Turpin*, and clearly assumed that discrimination against men was contrary to s. 15.

In *Weatherall v. Canada* (1993),[23] an inmate in a federal penitentiary brought a constitutional challenge under s. 15 to the penitentiary's practice of allowing female guards to perform frisk searches and observe the cells (and toilets) of male prisoners. These "cross-gender" indignities were not visited on female prisoners, who were always searched and observed by female guards. The Court held that there "may be" no discrimination against the male prisoners in this situation. The Court did not reach a definite conclusion, falling back on s. 1 to justify the challenged practice.[24] However, in the course of his brief (and probably obiter) comments about the probable lack of discrimination, La Forest J. for the Court did use the language of general disadvantage. He said that "women generally occupy a disadvantaged position in society in relation to men".[25] In my opinion, this proposition, however true of society in general, should play no role in the denial of redress to a male prisoner who complains of his treatment at the hands of female guards. In the prison setting, the man is the disadvantaged party. It is cold comfort to him that other men (not in prison) have nothing to complain about.

The question whether a showing of general (or group) disadvantage is a prerequisite to a s. 15 equality claim has probably been settled by

---

on the s. 7 issue.

[21] *R. v. Hess*, [1990] 2 S.C.R. 906, 943.

[22] Text accompanying § 55:41 note 7.

[23] *Weatherall v. Canada*, [1993] 2 S.C.R. 872.

[24] The justification (unsupported by any reference to evidence) was that the presence of female guards would "humanize" the institutions, and would aid in the achievement of "employment equity" in the correctional system.

[25] *Weatherall v. Canada*, [1993] 2 S.C.R. 872, 877.

Miron v. Trudel (1995)[26] and *Egan v. Canada* (1985),[27] two cases that were described earlier in this chapter. The claim of discrimination in each case was made by a member of a group that, the Court held, was generally disadvantaged. (It was common-law couples in *Miron* and same-sex couples in *Egan.)* In neither case, therefore, was it necessary to pronounce on the issue whether general disadvantage was a prerequisite to a s. 15 claim. Nonetheless, *in Miron*, eight judges said that membership in a disadvantaged group was not a prerequisite, but merely an "indicator"[28] or "indicium"[29] of an analogous ground. The ninth judge, L'Heureux-Dubé J., who rejected analogous grounds as a necessary basis for a s. 15 claim, said that the nature of the group affected should be considered but that it was a "factor" that was not by itself determinative.[30] In *Egan*, three judges agreed with Cory J., who said that: "while historical disadvantage or a group's position as a discrete and insular minority may serve as indicators of an analogous ground, they are not prerequisites for finding an analogous ground."[31]

When the *Law* case introduced human dignity into the s. 15 analysis in 1999,[32] Iacobucci J. for the Court made reference to group disadvantage as a "contextual factor" in determining whether there had been an impairment of the claimant's human dignity. He said that "the important purpose of s. 15(1) in protecting individuals or groups who are vulnerable, disadvantaged, or members of 'discrete and insular minorities' should always be a central consideration." However, the claimant's association with a "disadvantaged group or groups" was "not *per se* determinative" of an impairment of human dignity.[33] This seems to be the current position of the Court. The analysis no longer focuses on human dignity. It focuses on disadvantage, including group disadvantage. However, disadvantage has been defined broadly. As a result, it does not appear to be necessary for a claimant to establish that he or she is a member of a group that is generally disadvantaged, independent of the particular legal distinction under challenge—although this will clearly assist in establishing a s. 15 infringement. It appears to be enough to be

[26]*Miron v. Trudel*, [1995] 2 S.C.R. 418.

[27]*Egan v. Canada*, [1995] 2 S.C.R. 513.

[28]*Egan v. Canada*, [1995] 2 S.C.R. 418, 496, per McLachlin J., with the agreement of Sopinka, Cory and Iacobucci JJ.

[29]*Egan v. Canada*, [1995] 2 S.C.R. 418, 436, 455, per Gonthier J. dissenting, with the agreement of Lamer C.J., La Forest and Major JJ.

[30]*Egan v. Canada*, [1995] 2 S.C.R. 418, 468, per L'Heureux-Dubé J. concurring.

[31]*Egan v. Canada*, [1995] 2 S.C.R. 513, 599, per Cory J. dissenting (but not on this issue), with the agreement of Sopinka, McLachlin and Iacobucci JJ. L'Heureux-Dubé J. took the same view as in *Miron*, namely, that the nature of the group affected was an important factor in finding discrimination. La Forest J., who wrote the majority opinion, with the agreement of Lamer C.J., Gonthier and Major JJ., did not discuss general disadvantage.

[32]§ 55:20, "Impairment of human dignity".

[33]*Law v. Canada*, [1999] 1 S.C.R. 497, para. 88 (both quotations).

part of a group that is disadvantaged by the particular legal distinction under challenge in some measurable way.[34]

VIII. DIRECT AND INDIRECT DISCRIMINATION

§ 55:28 Substantive equality

A law may also be discriminatory *on its face.* A law that expressly excluded women from admission to the police force would be discriminatory on its face. We have already noticed that this is an example of "direct" discrimination. And we have also noticed that the term "formal equality" is normally used to indicate a theory of equality that covers only direct discrimination. Section 15 includes direct discrimination (obviously), and this leads to the invalidity of a law that is discriminatory on its face.

A law may be discriminatory *in its effect.* A law that imposed height or weight qualifications for admission to the police force would be discriminatory in its effect if the effect of the law (whether intended or not) was to disqualify a disproportionate number of women. We have already noticed that this is an example of "indirect" discrimination. Indirect discrimination is caused by a law that does not expressly employ any of the categories listed in s. 15 (or analogous to those listed), if the law has a disproportionately adverse effect on persons defined by any of the prohibited categories. Sometimes the terms "systemic" discrimination or "adverse effect" or "impact" discrimination are used as synonyms for indirect discrimination. The term "substantive equality" is normally used to indicate a theory of equality that covers indirect as well as direct discrimination. Because s. 15 includes substantive equality, it leads to the invalidity of a law that is discriminatory in its effect.

Finally, a law may be discriminatory *in its application.* A law that prescribed no discriminatory qualifications for admission to the police force would be discriminatory in its application if police recruitment procedures led to the rejection of a disproportionate number of female applicants. This is another kind of indirect discrimination, and it is also a breach of substantive equality and of s. 15.[1] Where a law is discriminatory only in its application, s. 15 will not lead to the invalidity of the law itself. Section 15 will deny validity to past applications of the law, and will require (in the police example) that gender-neutral procedures be established for its future administration.[2]

---

[34]See § 55:22, "Discrimination without human dignity".

[Section 55:28]

[1]On the application of s. 15 to action taken under statutory discretion, see § 55:6, "Law in s. 15".

[2]E.g., *Little Sisters Book and Art Emporium v. Can.*, [2000] 2 S.C.R. 1120 (customs law prohibiting importation of obscene books administered in a way that discriminated against LGBTQ literature; held, law valid, but application in breach of s. 15).

In *Andrews*,[3] the Supreme Court of Canada made clear that s. 15 required substantive and not merely formal equality. McIntyre J. for the majority of the Court pointed out that "identical treatment may frequently produce serious inequality".[4] In cases under the statutory human rights codes, the Court had already held that indirect discrimination was covered along with direct discrimination. McIntyre J. held that the same expansive view should be taken under s. 15.[5] Since that ruling in 1989, substantive equality has remained a central assumption of the interpretation of s. 15. Section 15 therefore applies to all of the three kinds of laws identified above: (1) the law that is discriminatory on its face; (2) the law that is discriminatory in its effect; and (3) the law that is discriminatory in its application.

Substantive equality is of great importance to equality-seeking groups such as women and visible minorities who have generally achieved formal equality. Substantive equality allows a court to drill beneath the surface of the facially neutral law and identify adverse effects on a class of persons distinguished by a listed or analogous personal characteristic. It is not necessary to show that the law was passed with the intention of discriminating; the mere fact that the law does have the disproportionately adverse effect is enough.[6] Despite the commitment of the Supreme Court to substantive equality, and despite the industry of women's groups and other equality-seeking groups in developing equality cases for litigation, few claims of indirect discrimination have been successful.[7] One is *Eldridge v. British Columbia* (1997),[8] where the challenge was to the failure of British Columbia's statutory health care plan to provide publicly-funded sign-language interpretation to deaf persons seeking medical services. British Columbia's law was neutral in that all persons were denied sign-language interpretation, but of course the denial only disadvantaged deaf people. The Court held that the law discriminated

[3]*Andrews v. Law Society of B.C.*, [1989] 1 S.C.R. 143.

[4]*Andrews v. Law Society of B.C.*, [1989] 1 S.C.R. 143, 164.

[5]*Andrews v. Law Society of B.C.*, [1989] 1 S.C.R. 143, 173-174.

[6]This mode of analysis is not unique to s. 15. Any provision of the Charter of Rights will be infringed by a law of which the purpose *or effect* is to abridge the right: ch. 36, Charter of Rights, under heading § 36:14, "Purpose or effect".

[7]Unsuccessful claims of indirect discrimination are *Rodriguez v. B.C.*, [1993] 3 S.C.R. 519 (prohibition on assisted suicide not discrimination on the basis of physical disability); *Symes v. Can.*, [1993] 4 S.C.R. 695 (disallowance of child care costs as business expenses for income tax purposes not discrimination on the basis of sex); *Adler v. Ont.*, [1996] 3 S.C.R. 609 (failure of province to fund private schools not discrimination on the basis of religion); *Health Services and Support – Facilities Subsector Bargaining Assn. v. B.C.*, [2007] 2 S.C.R. 391 (law interfering with collective bargaining rights of healthcare workers, most of whom were women, not discriminatory on the basis of sex); *Alta. v. Hutterian Brethren of Wilson Colony*, [2009] 2 S.C.R. 567 (photo requirement for a driver's licence in Alberta not discrimination on the basis of religion); *Kahkewistahaw First Nation v. Taypotat*, [2015] 2 S.C.R. 548 (education requirement for candidates for Chief and Band Councillor not discrimination on the basis of age or residence on a reserve).

[8]*Eldridge v. British Columbia*, [1997] 3 S.C.R. 624. The adverse-effect point is addressed at paras. 60-83 by La Forest J. for the unanimous Court.

against deaf people in breach of s. 15. Another case is *Vriend v. Alberta* (1998),[9] where the challenge was to the failure of Alberta's human rights legislation to include sexual orientation in the list of forbidden grounds of discrimination in employment. Alberta's law was neutral in that the denial of a remedy applied to those of all sexual orientations. However, the disproportionate impact of the law led the Court to hold that it discriminated against LGBTQ people in breach of s. 15.

In *Re Marriage Commissioners* (2011),[10] Saskatchewan proposed to enact a law allowing "marriage commissioners" (civil officials authorized to perform civil marriages) to refuse to solemnize a marriage that would be contrary to their personal religious beliefs. The province directed a reference to the Saskatchewan Court of Appeal for a ruling as to whether the proposed law would be valid. The Court found that the law was neutral in terms of the religious beliefs that it protected: any relevant religious belief would suffice to justify a refusal to perform a marriage ceremony—although the only religious belief that was seriously advanced in the evidence was an opposition to same-sex marriage. The Court found as well that the purpose of the law was not discriminatory: its purpose was "to accommodate the religious beliefs of marriage commissioners rather than to deny the rights of same-sex couples."[11] But the evidence showed that many religious denominations did not recognize or perform same-sex marriages so that the erection of obstacles to civil marriage would be disproportionately born by same-sex couples. The Court held that the effect of the proposed law would be to draw a "negative distinction based on sexual orientation", which would be invalid as an infringement of s. 15.[12]

As noted earlier, few claims of indirect (or adverse impact) discrimination have been successful in the Supreme Court of Canada.[13] The first stage of a s. 15 analysis requires a claimant to establish that a law creates a distinction, on its face or in its impact, on the basis of an enumerated or analogous ground. In *Withler v. Canada* (2011),[14] the Court acknowledged that this stage of the analysis "will be relatively straightforward" in cases of direct discrimination, where the claimant only needs to show that the distinction is evident on the face of the law itself, and that "the claimant will have more work to do" in cases of indirect discrimination, where the claimant must show that a law that

[9] *Vriend v. Alberta*, [1998] 1 S.C.R. 493. The adverse-effect point is addressed at paras. 82-86 by Cory J. for a Court that was unanimous on this issue.

[10] *Re Marriage Commissioners* (2011), 327 D.L.R. (4th) 669 (Sask. C.A.). For further discussion, see § 55:48, "Sexual orientation", and ch. 42, Freedom of Religion, under heading § 42:11, "Religious marriage".

[11] *Re Marriage Commissioners* (2011), 327 D.L.R. (4th) 669 (Sask. C.A.), para. 36.

[12] *Re Marriage Commissioners* (2011), 327 D.L.R. (4th) 669 (Sask. C.A.), para. 37, 44. The Court went on to hold that the law could not be justified under s. 1.

[13] See the text accompanying § 55:28 note 7, above.

[14] *Withler v. Canada*, [2011] 1 S.C.R. 396.

is neutral on its face creates a distinction in its impact.[15] However, the Court provided little guidance about how much extra work would be required, and what it might entail. This lack of guidance, coupled with the low rate of success of indirect discrimination claims in the Court, made it difficult for claimants to know how to go about making such claims.

The Supreme Court finally provided this much-needed guidance in *Fraser v. Canada* (2020).[16] This case, which is also discussed earlier in this chapter,[17] involved a s. 15 claim brought by three members of the Royal Canadian Mounted Police (R.C.M.P.), each of whom were women with young children who had participated in a job-sharing program that allowed R.C.M.P. members to split the duties of one full-time position. R.C.M.P. members who participated in the job-sharing program – most of whom, like the claimants, were women with young children when they elected to participate – were not permitted to "buy back" full-time pension plan credit, whereas full-time R.C.M.P. members who took unpaid leave had this option.[18] The claimants challenged the R.C.M.P.'s pension plan under s. 15, arguing that it discriminated against job-sharers on the basis of sex or, alternatively, family/parental status. The case made its way to the Supreme Court on appeal. The case involved a claim of indirect discrimination. The claimants argued that the R.C.M.P.'s pension plan arrangement for job-sharers discriminated on the basis of sex or family/parental status, not on its face, but in its impact. Abella J., who wrote for the majority, seized the opportunity the case provided the Court to provide guidance about the legal principles relating to indirect discrimination under s. 15.

Abella J. emphasized that the same two-stage test that is applied in cases alleging direct discrimination under s. 15 should be applied in cases alleging indirect discrimination. Under this two-stage test, recall, a claimant must show that a law: (1) creates a distinction, on its face or in its impact, on the basis of a protected ground; and (2) thereby perpetuates, reinforces or exacerbates a form of disadvantage. However, Abella J. acknowledged that the analysis at the first stage of test will vary in cases of indirect discrimination, where the allegation will be that the law creates a distinction, not on its face, but *in its impact*. The first stage of the test will be satisfied in a case of indirect discrimination if the law has a "disproportionate impact" on the members of a group

[15] *Withler v. Canada*, [2011] 1 S.C.R. 396, para. 64.

[16] *Fraser v. Canada*, 2020 SCC 28. Abella J. wrote the opinion for the majority of the Court, which was joined by Wagner C.J and Moldaver, Karakatsanis, Martin and Kasirer JJ. Brown and Rowe JJ. wrote a joint dissenting opinion. Côté J. also wrote dissenting opinion.

[17] See § 55:22, "Discrimination without human dignity".

[18] The relevant legislation was the Royal Canadian Mounted Police Superannuation Act, R.S.C. 1985, c. R-11; and the Royal Canadian Mounted Police Superannuation Regulations, C.R.C., c. 1393.

identified by a protected ground.[19] A law might have this kind of disproportionate impact: by imposing "rules, restrictions or criteria that operate in practice as 'built-in headwinds' for members of protected groups"; or by failing to put in place measures that accommodate the members of protected groups.[20] Abella J. pointed to two types of evidence that would be "especially helpful" in establishing these two forms of disproportionate impact.[21] The first would be evidence about the "physical, social, cultural or other barriers" faced by a protected group, which might "come from the claimant, from expert witnesses, or through judicial notice".[22] The second would be evidence about the actual impact of the law, which "may include statistics", especially if the law impacts "*both* members of a protected group *and* members of more advantaged groups".[23] Abella J. suggested that claims of indirect discrimination would "ideally" be supported by both types of evidence.[24] However, she also emphasized that claimants will not always be required to provide both types of evidence, and that "their significance will vary depending on the case".[25] In addition, she emphasized that if claimants succeed in establishing that a law has a disproportionate impact on a protected group, they do not also need to establish *why* the law has this disproportionate impact, or that the law created the background barriers or conditions underlying the disproportionate impact, or that the legislature *intended* to create the disproportionate impact.

Applying this approach, Abella J. held that first stage of the s. 15 test was satisfied, because the failure of the R.C.M.P.'s pension plan to grant job-sharers the ability to buy-back full-time pension benefits created a distinction on the basis of a protected ground – namely, sex – by disproportionately impacting the women in its ranks. The lower courts had taken the view that the pension plan did not create a distinction on the basis of a protected ground, on the basis that the claimants *chose* to participate in the job-sharing program, and by extension, a less favourable pension arrangement. Abella J. rejected this argument, noting that the "differential treatment can be discriminatory even if it is based on choices made by the affected individual or group", and that what may appear to be choices "often lie[] beyond the individual's effective

[19]*Fraser v. Canada*, 2020 SCC 28, para. 52.

[20]*Fraser v. Canada*, 2020 SCC 28, paras. 53-54.

[21]*Fraser v. Canada*, 2020 SCC 28, para. 56.

[22]*Fraser v. Canada*, 2020 SCC 28, para. 57. Abella J. cautioned that the barriers faced by certain groups may not be well-documented, in which case "claimants may have to rely more heavily on their own evidence or evidence from other members of their group": *Fraser v. Canada*, 2020 SCC 28, para. 57.

[23]*Fraser v. Canada*, 2020 SCC 28, para. 58 (emphasis in original). Abella J. cautioned that the weight to be given to statistics "will depend on, among other things, their quality and methodology", and that "[t]here is no universal measure for what level of statistical disparity is necessary to demonstrate that there is a disproportionate impact": *Fraser v. Canada*, 2020 SCC 28, para. 59.

[24]*Fraser v. Canada*, 2020 SCC 28, paras. 59-60.

[25]*Fraser v. Canada*, 2020 SCC 28, paras. 61-67.

control".[26] The evidence showed the barriers that women faced "as a group in balancing professional and domestic work", including that women as a group "have historically borne the overwhelming share of childcare responsibilities" and "are far more likely than men to work part-time due to childcare responsibilities".[27] The evidence also showed the impact of the law – that it was primarily women with young children who participated in the job-sharing program, most of whom "cited childcare as their reason for doing so".[28] This evidence, she said, established that "the RCMP's use of a temporary reduction in working hours as a basis for imposing less favourable pension consequences has an adverse impact on women".[29] Abella J. went on to conclude that the second stage of the 15 test was also satisfied, on the basis that the law perpetuated the economic disadvantage of women, and thus that s. 15 was infringed – and that the infringement could not be justified under s. 1, because the federal government had not offered a pressing and substantial objective for failing to grant job-sharers the ability to buy back full-time pension benefits.[30]

The *Fraser* case provides the Supreme Court's most helpful account of the law relating to indirect discrimination under s. 15 to date. It would go too far to suggest, as the dissenting judges seem to do,[31] that the majority of the Court effectively jettisoned altogether the evidentiary burden on claimants to show that a law "creates" a distinction on the basis of a protected ground.[32] However, Abella J.'s opinion for the majority does appear to be aimed at not only clarifying the law, but also easing the burden on claimants, increasing the potential for claims of indirect discrimination to succeed. Abella J. seemed to embrace this

[26] *Fraser v. Canada*, 2020 SCC 28, paras. 86, 91.

[27] *Fraser v. Canada*, 2020 SCC 28, paras. 97-98.

[28] *Fraser v. Canada*, 2020 SCC 28, para. 97.

[29] *Fraser v. Canada*, 2020 SCC 28, paras. 97, 106.

[30] There were two dissenting opinions in *Fraser* – one written jointly by Brown and Rowe JJ., and the other written by Côté J. The dissenting judges took issue with various aspects of Abella J.'s account of the law relating to s. 15, but a key focus of their dissent as it relates to claims of indirect discrimination was on the requirement of causation – that the law *create* a distinction in its impact on the basis of a protected ground. The dissenting judges disagreed with Abella J. that the R.C.M.P.'s pension plan infringed s. 15; whereas Brown and Rowe JJ. would have rejected the claim under the second stage of the analysis, Côté J. would have rejected the claim under the first stage of the analysis.

[31] *Fraser v. Canada*, 2020 SCC 28, para. 178 per Brown and Rowe JJ., paras. 243, 248 per Côté J.

[32] Abella J. did not explicitly deny – indeed, she appeared to accept – that claimants must establish that the impugned law caused ("created") a distinction, in its impact, on the basis of a protected ground: see e.g. paras. 27, 50, 52, 76. She explicitly rejected only the requirement that a claimant go on to prove that it was the protected ground that caused the disproportionate impact: para. 70. However, Abella J. did appear to accept that strict proof of a causative link between the impugned law and the disproportionate impact will not be required in all cases – that proof of a correlation between the law and the disproportionate impact may be enough to give rise to an inference of causation in some cases: see e.g. paras. 61-63. (Many thanks to Andy Yu for an interesting conversation about this aspect of the opinion.)

result, noting that claims of indirect discrimination can be one of the " 'most powerful' " tools "available to disadvantaged groups in society to assert their claims to justice' ", because it is "much more prevalent" than direct discrimination, and "often poses a greater threat" to the "equality aspirations" of such groups.[33]

§ 55:29 Unintended discrimination

Indirect discrimination may be unintended. This would be the case in the police-force example if the framers of height or weight qualifications believed the qualifications to be bona fide occupational requirements for a police officer. Indirect discrimination may also be intended, as would be the case if the height or weight requirements were a covert device to exclude women from the police force. However, because intention is not an ingredient of discrimination under s. 15, it is not necessary to make any judgment about whether a case of indirect discrimination is intended or not. The mere fact that a law has a disproportionately adverse effect on persons defined by a prohibited category (along with an impairment of human dignity) is enough to establish the breach of s. 15.[1]

Even direct discrimination may be unintended. In the *Andrews* case,[2] for example, it was never seriously suggested that the object of the British Columbia Legislature, in requiring that lawyers must be citizens, was to disadvantage noncitizens. On the contrary, all the judges assumed that the legislators thought that citizenship was a bona fide occupational requirement for the practice of law, and the disadvantage to non-citizens was simply the inevitable by-product of the requirement. Nevertheless, because the effect of the law was to disadvantage a person on the basis of citizenship (an analogous ground), there was a breach of s. 15. (This was before the element of an impairment of human dignity or discrimination was added to s. 15 by the Court.) The benign purpose of the law was irrelevant under s. 15. It was, however, relevant to the s. 1 inquiry, and was considered by all judges in that context—and two of the judges dissented on the ground that the law was justified under s. 1.

In the *Andrews* case, McIntyre J., speaking for the majority of the Court on this issue, explicitly addressed the issue of intention. In defining discrimination, he used the phrase "whether intentional or not".[3] And he followed the cases in which the Court had decided that discrimination under statutory human rights codes need not be intentional, holding that the same rule applied to s. 15.[4] From the beginning, therefore, the Supreme Court has committed itself to the doctrine that it is not necessary to show that the *purpose* of a challenged law is

---

[33] *Fraser v. Canada*, 2020 SCC 28, para. 35.

[Section 55:29]

[1] *Eldridge v. British Columbia*, [1997] 3 S.C.R. 624, para. 62 (unintended discrimination against deaf people held to be a violation of s. 15).

[2] *Andrews v. Law Society of B.C.*, [1989] 1 S.C.R. 143.

[3] *Andrews v. Law Society of B.C.*, [1989] 1 S.C.R. 143, 174.

[4] *Andrews v. Law Society of B.C.*, [1989] 1 S.C.R. 143, 173, 176.

to impose a disadvantage on a person by reason of a listed or analogous characteristic. It is enough to show that the challenged law has this *effect*.

The rule that discrimination under s. 15 need not be intentional is consistent with the rule developed by the Court with respect to other Charter rights. A law is in breach of a Charter right if *either* the purpose *or* the effect of the law is to abridge a Charter right.[5] Applied to s. 15, this doctrine leads to the conclusion that either a discriminatory purpose or a discriminatory effect will constitute a breach of s. 15. The purpose of the law will, however, always be relevant to justification under s. 1, because a law limiting a Charter right cannot be justified under s. 1 unless it serves an important purpose that is compatible with the values of a free and democratic society.[6] In the common case where the purpose of the law is benign, the law may be able to be saved under s. 1. In the rare case where a law has a discriminatory purpose, the law cannot be saved under s. 1.[7]

§ 55:30 Reasonable accommodation

Another concept that has become established in decisions under the human rights codes, and which will apply under s. 15 as well, is "reasonable accommodation". As Gibson points out,[1] it is a necessary corollary of the rule that discrimination may be indirect and unintended that a law may have to make reasonable accommodation for those who, by reason of religious affiliation or disability (for example), are discriminated against by otherwise neutral laws.[2]

For example, the Supreme Court of Canada has held[3] that an employer (a retailer) was under a duty to make reasonable adjustments to employee work schedules so that an employee who was a Seventh Day Adventist would not have to work on Friday evenings and Saturdays. The rule requiring employees to be available for work at those times was a reasonable requirement for a retailer, because those times were particularly busy in the retail trade. However, the rule had a disproportionately adverse effect on those observing a Saturday sabbath, and therefore constituted discrimination on the basis of religion. The discrimination could be cured by making reasonable accommodation for

---

[5]Chapter 36, Charter of Rights, under heading § 36:14, "Purpose or effect".

[6]Chapter 38, Limitation of Rights, under heading §§ 38:12 to 38:17, "Sufficiently important objective".

[7]The addition of judge-made elements to s. 15, whether in the form of human dignity or discrimination, means that much of the s. 1 analysis now takes place within s. 15 itself, leaving s. 1 with little work to do: §§ 55:19 to 55:22, "Human dignity", and § 55:31, "Justification under s. 1".

[Section 55:30]

[1]Gibson, The Law of the Charter: Equality Rights (1990), 133.

[2]See S. Day and G. Brodsky, "The Duty to Accommodate" (1996) 75 Can. Bar Rev. 433.

[3]*Ont. Human Rights Cummn. v. Simpsons-Sears*, [1985] 2 S.C.R. 536.

the person whose religious beliefs called for some deviation from the general rule. Or, to turn the proposition around, the discrimination consisted in the failure to make reasonable accommodation for a person whose religious practices were specially burdened by an otherwise neutral rule. This was a human rights code case, but the same principle would apply under s. 15 as well.[4]

Sometimes there is room for argument as to the form of accommodation that is required by s. 15. In *Eaton v. Brant County Board of Education* (1997),[5] the Supreme Court of Canada held that a school system was under a s. 15 duty to make a reasonable accommodation to the educational needs of children with mental or physical disabilities. But what form should that accommodation take? In that case, the parents of a disabled child objected to her being moved out of the regular classroom (where she had been for three years) and assigned to a separate special-education classroom. They argued that the equality guarantee of s. 15 conferred on the child a right to remain in the regular classroom, and that the school board was under a duty to accommodate her needs in the regular classroom setting. The Supreme Court of Canada held that there was no rule or presumption in favour of the regular classroom setting. The school board's duty of reasonable accommodation was to be driven by the best interests of the child, not the wishes of the parents.[6] In this case, there had been a careful assessment of the needs of the child, which included evidence of her difficulties in the regular classroom setting, and the assessment tribunal had determined that the segregated placement was in the child's best interests. This decision fulfilled the school board's duty of accommodation, and there was no breach of s. 15.

IX. JUSTIFICATION UNDER S. 1; AFFIRMATIVE ACTION

§ 55:31 Justification under s. 1

Section 1 of the Charter of Rights provides that all the Charter rights are subject to "such reasonable limits prescribed by law as can be demonstrably justified in a free and democratic society". The courts have articulated standards to assist in determining whether a law that infringes a Charter right is a reasonable limit that is justified under s.

[4]So held in *Eldridge v. B.C.*, [1997] 3 S.C.R. 624 (provision of medical services to deaf persons requires provision of sign-language interpretation in order to comply with s. 15). In *Alta. v. Hutterian Brethren of Wilson Colony*, [2009] 2 S.C.R. 567, paras. 66-71, McLachlin C.J. for the majority (and the minority did not disagree) drew a distinction between government *action* or administrative *practice* (her emphasis) to which the duty of reasonable accommodation would apply and laws of general application to which the s. 1 analysis mandated by *Oakes* (rather than the duty of reasonable accommodation) would apply. The *Eaton* case, discussed in the next para., was in the former category.

[5]*Eaton v. Brant County Board of Education*, [1997] 1 S.C.R. 241. The opinion of the unanimous Court was written by Sopinka J. Lamer C.J. wrote a brief concurring opinion on a secondary issue.

[6]For criticism of the failure to impose a presumption of inclusion, see M.D. Lepofsky, "A Report Card on the Charter's Guarantee of Equality to Persons with Disabilities" (1997) 7 Nat. J. Con. L. 263, 414-423.

1. Those standards are the topic of an earlier chapter.[1] Section 1 applies to laws that infringe s. 15 no less than to laws that infringe other rights. However, once *Law* imported human dignity into s. 15 in 1999, there were few cases in which s. 1 saved a law found to be in breach of s. 15.[2] In *Newfoundland v. N.A.P.E.* (2004),[3] the Court decided that Newfoundland, faced with a serious financial crisis, could enact a law postponing the implementation of collective agreements under which the government had undertaken to increase the wages of female hospital workers in order to achieve pay equity with men. The Court held that the law withheld a benefit on the basis of a listed ground, namely, sex. The Court also held that it was a breach of human dignity to maintain in force wages that did not do justice to the female workers' contribution. Therefore, there was a breach of s. 15. But the Court accepted that in 1991, when the law was enacted, the province had experienced a huge reduction in federal transfer payments, causing the province to make comparable cuts in expenditures, which it did by temporarily freezing the wages of all public sector employees, laying off many employees and not filling vacant positions, closing hospital beds, reducing medicare coverage, and freezing or reducing expenditures for education and other government programs. Although the pay equity agreements were mandated by the Charter, their postponement was justified under s. 1 as part of the response to the fiscal crisis.[4]

The *N.A.P.E.* case is an unusual one. In the great majority of cases, human dignity in s. 15 left no role for s. 1. It is obviously hard to justify a law that imposes a disadvantage on the basis of a listed or analogous ground and also impairs human dignity.[5] When the Court used the "correspondence" factor to decide the issue of human dignity,[6] it considered whether the purpose of the law is legitimate and the use of a listed or analogous ground to accomplish the purpose is reasonable. This inquiry was really a loose form of the inquiry into justification under s. 1. It is not surprising that s. 1 became less important in equality cases when the human dignity element was introduced by the Court in 1999. The

[Section 55:31]

[1]Chapter 38, Limitation of Rights.

[2]In *Lavoie v. Can.*, [2002] 1 S.C.R. 769, a majority of the Court upheld citizenship preferences for hiring into the federal public service. Four judges based their decision on s. 1. Two judges based their decision on an absence of impairment of human dignity. Three judges dissented.

[3]*Newfoundland v. N.A.P.E.*, [2004] 3 S.C.R. 381. Binnie J. wrote the opinion of the Court.

[4]The Court made no mention of s. 28 of the Charter of Rights, which guarantees rights "equally to male and female persons", and which applies "notwithstanding anything in this Charter". There had been speculation that s. 1 would not apply to sex equality, because of the notwithstanding clause in s. 28.

[5]This was the view of Bastarache J. (with the agreement of three others) in *Lavoie v. Can.*, [2002] 1 S.C.R. 769.

[6]§ 55:21, "The factor of correspondence".

Court's retraction of human dignity in *R. v. Kapp* (2008)[7] did not really restore s. 1 to its intended justificatory role, because the substituted concept of "discrimination" was very similar to a human dignity analysis, at least to the extent that it included a correspondence analysis.

The shift to a focus on disadvantage in the s. 15 analysis in *Quebec v. Alliance du personnel professionel et technique de la santé et des services sociaux* (2018),[8] *Centrale des syndicats du Québec v. Quebec* (2018)[9] and *Fraser v. Canada (Attorney General)* (2020)[10]—which was discussed earlier in this chapter[11] – may restore s. 1 to its intended justificatory role, because the disadvantage analysis contemplated does not involve a discussion of correspondence (or other similar ideas).

§ 55:32 Affirmative action

Subsection (2) of s. 15[1] provides as follows:

> 15.(2) Subsection (1) does not preclude any law, program or activity that has as its object the amelioration of conditions of disadvantaged individuals or groups including those that are disadvantaged because of race, national or ethnic origin, colour, religion, sex, age or mental or physical disability.

Subsection (2) of s. 15 makes clear that s. 15 does not preclude "affirmative action" or "equity" programmes in favour of "disadvantaged individuals or groups". If such a programme were attacked on equality grounds by a person who was not a member of the favoured (disadvantaged) group, subsection (2) provides an answer. What is not clear is whether s. 15(2) is an *exception* to s. 15(1) or whether it is simply a *clarification* of s. 15(1). Regarded as an exception to s. 15(1), s. 15(2) insulates from constitutional challenge those programmes that practise "reverse discrimination" by requiring that a member of a disadvantaged group be preferred to a person who is equally or better qualified but who is not a member of the favoured (disadvantaged) group.[2] Section 1 of the Charter is of course available to sustain a law that uses a racial or sexual clas-

---

[7] *R. v. Kapp*, [2008] 2 S.C.R. 483; § 55:22, "Discrimination without human dignity".

[8] *Quebec v. Alliance du personnel professionel et technique de la santé et des services sociaux*, [2018] 1 S.C.R. 464.

[9] *Centrale des syndicats du Québec v. Quebec*, [2018] 1 S.C.R. 522.

[10] *Fraser v. Canada (Attorney General)*, 2020 SCC 28.

[11] See § 55:22, "Discrimination without human dignity".

[Section 55:32]

[1] For commentary on s. 15(2), see Gibson, The Law of the Charter: Equality Rights (1990), ch. 7; P. Blache, "Affirmative Action" in Weiler and Elliot (eds.), Litigating the Values of a Nation (1986), 165-186; R.G. Juriansz, "Equality Rights, Affirmative Action" in Finkelstein and Rogers (eds.), *Charter Issues in Civil Cases* (1988), 109-150, M.A. Drumbl and J.D.R. Craig, "Affirmative Action in Question: A Coherent Theory for Section 15(2)" (1997) 4 Rev. of Const. Studies 80.

[2] In the United States, where there is no equivalent to s. 15(2), there is continuous litigation over the constitutionality (under the equal protection clause of the fourteenth amendment) and the legality (under the Civil Rights Act, 1964) of affirmative action programmes, e.g., *Ricci v. DeStefano* (2009), 557 U.S. xxx: see § 55:3, "American Bill of Rights".

sification (for example) for a benign purpose, but s. 15(2) makes it unnecessary to go to s. 1. Provided the programme meets the conditions stipulated by s. 15(2), it cannot be attacked under s. 15(1).

The foregoing explanation of s. 15(2) as an exception to s. 15(1), assumes that laws designed to ameliorate the conditions of disadvantaged individuals or groups are prima facie violations of s. 15(1). That is why they need to be "saved" by s. 15(2). But the Supreme Court of Canada has consistently interpreted s. 15(1) as implementing a substantive rather than a formal definition of equality. Under a substantive definition of equality, different treatment in the service of equity for disadvantaged groups is an expression of equality, not an exception to it. In *R. v. Kapp* (2008),[3] Mclachlin C.J. and Abella J. for the majority of the Supreme Court of Canada quoted the previous sentence of this book with approval and rejected the idea that s. 15(2) was an exception to s. 15(1). They described the two subsections as "confirmatory" of each other. The focus of subsection (1) was on *preventing* governments from discriminating; the focus of subsection (2) was on *enabling* governments to pro-actively combat discrimination.[4] However, they held that subsection (2) was not merely a clarification or an aid to the interpretation of subsection (1);[5] subsection (2) had an "independent role" to play.[6] If an affirmative action program met the criteria of subsection (2), then the program was valid under s. 15(2) and no s. 15(1) analysis was necessary. If the program failed to meet the criteria of s. 15(2), then a s. 15(1) analysis would have to be undertaken to determine whether the program was discriminatory.

The program in issue in *Kapp* was a special "communal" commercial fishing licence, which was authorized by the federal Fisheries Act, and available only to Indian bands. In this case, the licence authorized fishing by the members of three bands for salmon in the mouth of the Fraser River for an exclusive 24-hour period before non-aboriginal commercial fishing licences took effect. The members of the bands had an aboriginal right to fish, but only for food, not for sale. The effect of the communal licence was to enlarge that right to fishing for sale for the exclusive 24-hour period stipulated in the license. Commercial fishers who were not members of the three Indian bands held a "protest fishery" during the 24-hour period that the fishery was closed to them; they were duly

[3] *R. v. Kapp*, [2008] 2 S.C.R. 483. McLachlin C.J. and Abella J. wrote the opinion of the eight-judge majority. Bastarache J. wrote a concurring opinion, confining his reasoning to s. 25 of the Charter, but expressing his agreement (para. 77) with the restatement of the test for the application of s. 15. (He did not make clear whether his agreement included the majority's discussion of s. 15(2), as opposed to their discussion of s. 15(1).)

[4] *R. v. Kapp*, [2008] 2 S.C.R. 483, para. 37.

[5] An "ameliorative purpose" was one of the four factors listed in *Law v. Can.*, [1999] 1 S.C.R. 497, para. 88, as part of the s. 15(1) analysis, and in no previous case had it been determinative: *Lovelace v. Ont.*, [2001] 1 S.C.R. 950, para. 93, assembles the citations. In that case, which was an unsuccessful challenge to a program to send casino profits to First Nation communities, the Court refused to decide that s. 15(2) was an independent ground of validity, although the Court (para. 100) left the point open.

[6] *R. v. Kapp*, [2008] 2 S.C.R. 483, para. 38.

charged with fishing while prohibited; and they defended the charges by arguing that the communal licence was unconstitutional. The position of the non-aboriginal fishers was that the privileged access granted by the communal licence only to aboriginal fishers constituted discrimination on the ground of race. The Crown replied that the purpose of the communal licence was to ameliorate the conditions of disadvantaged groups. And so the issue was joined. The Court was unanimous in upholding the constitutionality of the communal licence, and McLachlin C.J. and Abella J., writing for eight of the nine judges, based their decision squarely on s. 15 (2).[7] The communal-licence program was indeed restricted by race, which was a listed ground under s. 15(1). However, the program had as its "object" the "amelioration of conditions" of the three Indian bands, which, the judges held, were "disadvantaged" groups.[8] The program was therefore covered by s. 15(2) and it was not necessary to engage in a s. 15(1) analysis to conclude that the program was not a breach of the equality guarantee of s. 15(1).

The decision in *Kapp* provides some security for the creation by government of affirmative-action programs. It is not a cast-iron guarantee of validity in that s. 15(2) only shields a program from attack under s. 15(1), that is, on equality grounds. If the program violated some other Charter guarantee, or an aboriginal or treaty right, or a federalism restriction on legislative power, or some other constitutional rule, s. 15(2) would not save it. But what *Kapp* makes clear is that a program cannot be attacked under s. 15(1) if it targets a group identified by one of the listed or analogous grounds in s. 15(1), so long as (1) the group is disadvantaged, and (2) the purpose of the program is the improvement of the conditions of the group.

Kapp was followed in *Alberta v. Cunningham* (2011),[9] which was a constitutional challenge to a provision of Alberta's Metis Settlements Act, which granted settlement land to eight Métis communities in the province, but which forbade status Indians from becoming members of any Métis settlement. The claimants, who had been members of the Métis settlement of Peavine, Alberta, were also entitled to be registered as status Indians under the Indian Act, and they opted to register as status Indians in order to obtain medical benefits under the Indian Act. The Registrar of the Métis Settlements Land Registry, obedient to the Métis Settlements Act, revoked their membership of Peavine. The claim-

---

[7]Bastarache J., concurring, decided the case on the basis that s. 25 of the Charter protected the aboriginal fishing licence from challenge under s. 15(1). The majority did not agree with his reasoning. See ch. 28, Aboriginal Peoples, under heading § 28:40, "Section 25".

[8]The disadvantage (described paras. 58-60) seemed to be by comparison with Canadian society at large rather than with the non-aboriginal fishers who were denied the fruits of the exclusive 24-hour fishery. There was no discussion of the wealth, social status, education or other indicia of advantage possessed by the non-aboriginal fishers. It may be surmised that they were not a particularly well-off group, and yet they bore the cost of ameliorating the conditions of the bands.

[9]*Alberta v. Cunningham*, 2011 SCC 37. McLachlin C.J. wrote the opinion of the Court.

ants applied for a declaration that their exclusion from membership of Peavine was a violation of s. 15 of the Charter. The Supreme Court of Canada denied the declaration, holding that s. 15(2) was a complete answer to the claim. The object of the Act was to enhance Métis identity, culture, and self-governance by creating a land base for Métis. Unlike Indians, the Métis had no reserves on which they could strengthen their identity and culture and govern themselves; not did they enjoy the protection of an equivalent to the Indian Act. If status Indians were allowed to become members of Métis settlements, the distinctive Métis identity (distinct from Indian identity) would be compromised, as would the goal of self-governance.

One question that lingered after *Kapp* and *Cunningham* was whether s. 15(2) could be invoked to defeat a s. 15(1) challenge brought by a member of a disadvantaged group if the purpose of the law being challenged is the improvement of the conditions of the same disadvantaged group. The Supreme Court answered this question with a resounding no in *Quebec v. Alliance du personnel professionel et technique de la santé et des services sociaux* (2018).[10] In this case, several Quebec unions brought a s. 15(1) challenge to various amendments that Quebec made to its Pay Equity Act[11] in 2009. The impugned amendments to the Act weakened various obligations that had been imposed on employers by the Act in 1996, ostensibly in order to *increase* employer compliance with the Act. Abella J., writing for a six-judge majority of the Court, held that most of the impugned amendments infringed s. 15(1), and that the infringements had not been justified under s. 1. Côté, Brown and Rowe JJ., in a joint dissenting opinion, said that the union's challenge to the impugned amendments could be rejected under s. 15(1) without taking s. 15(2) into account, but they also advanced an alternative argument that "the Act as a whole should be protected under s. 15(2)" – including, seemingly, from a claim brought by or for the disadvantaged group that the Act seeks to protect – because the Act "genuinely has the promotion and achievement of substantive equality as its object".[12] Abella J.'s majority opinion rejected this view. She said that "[s]ection 15(2) cannot bar s. 15(1) claims by the very group the legislation seeks to protect" – that s. 15(2) only "protects ameliorative programs for disadvantaged groups from [s. 15(1)] claims by those the program was not intended to benefit".[13]

[10]*Quebec v. Alliance du personnel professionel et technique de la santé et des services sociaux*, [2018] 1 S.C.R. 464. Abella J. wrote the opinion for the majority of the Court, which was joined by McLachlin C.J. and Moldaver, Karakatsanis, Wagner, and Gascon JJ. Côté, Brown and Rowe JJ. wrote a joint dissenting opinion.

[11]C.Q.L.R., c. E-12.001.

[12]*Quebec v. Alliance du personnel professionel et technique de la santé et des services sociaux*, [2018] 1 S.C.R. 464, paras. 107-111.

[13]*Quebec v. Alliance du personnel professionel et technique de la santé et des services sociaux*, [2018] 1 S.C.R. 464, paras. 31-32.

This makes it clear that s. 15(2) cannot be used to defeat s. 15(1) claims to ameliorative laws brought by their intended beneficiaries.[14]

X. DISCRIMINATION PERMITTED BY CONSTITUTION

§ 55:33 Age in ss. 23, 29, 99

What is the position if the Constitution itself requires or permits discrimination? For example, the Constitution Act, 1867, provides that a person under the age of 30 cannot be appointed to the Senate (s. 23), and that a senator must retire at the age of 75 (s. 29); it also provides that a judge must retire at the age of 75 (s. 99). These provisions impose a burden by reference to a ground of discrimination that is listed in s. 15, namely, age. The provisions would therefore be contrary to s. 15, and hence invalid (unless they did not perpetuate disadvantage[1] or were saved by s. 1[2]), if they were contained in an official instrument other than the Constitution itself. Are the provisions sheltered from Charter attack by reason of their constitutional status? Those particular provisions have never been attacked, but the cases on other constitutional provisions, which are discussed in the following text, make clear that the answer to this question is yes.

§ 55:34 Race in s. 91(24)

This issue arose under the equality clause of the Canadian Bill of Rights. In *R. v. Drybones* (1969),[1] the Supreme Court of Canada struck down a provision of the Indian Act that made it an offence for "an Indian" to be drunk off a reserve. (The offence was matched by another offence of being drunk on a reserve; both provisions have since been repealed.) The majority of the Court held that the use of the racial classification "Indian" as an ingredient of an offence was contrary to the equality clause of the Canadian Bill of Rights. What was not addressed by Ritchie J.'s opinion for the majority, although it was the basis of Pigeon J.'s dissent, was that the use of the racial classification "Indian" was prerequisite to the validity of all of the provisions of the Indian Act. The Constitution Act, 1867, by s. 91 (24), confers on the federal Parliament the power to make laws in relation to "Indians, and lands reserved for the

---

[14] Abella J. reiterated this view in her opinion in a companion case to *Alliance*: see *Centrale des syndicats du Québec v. Que.*, [2018] 1 S.C.R. 522, paras. 37-41 (s. 15(2) only "save[s] ameliorative programs" from "reverse discrimination" claims, which are claims that involve "someone [from] outside the scope of intended beneficiaries"). See also *Fraser v. Can.*, 2020 SCC 28, para. 69 ("ameliorative purpose [not] sufficient to shield legislation from s. 15(1) scrutiny").

[Section 55:33]

[1] § 55:22 "Discrimination without human dignity".

[2] § 55:31, "Justification under s. 1".

[Section 55:34]

[1] *R. v. Drybones*, [1970] S.C.R. 282. Ritchie J., with the agreement of five others, wrote the majority opinion; Hall J., who was one of the five, added a separate concurring opinion. Cartwright C.J., Abbott and Pigeon JJ. each wrote a dissenting opinion.

Indians". Obviously, any law enacted under this power will have to be explicitly restricted to "Indians" or will have a disproportionate impact on Indians who live on "lands reserved for the Indians". Did *Drybones* mean that the entire Indian Act was inoperative, and that s. 91(24) could no longer be used by the federal Parliament?

Drybones was predictably followed by attacks on other provisions of the Indian Act, and two of the cases went on to the Supreme Court of Canada. The Court quickly repented of its boldness in *Drybones*, and upheld, first, the status provisions of the Indian Act (which defined the term "Indian"),[2] and, secondly, the succession provisions of the Act (which governed succession to the property of deceased Indians residing on reserves).[3] In the second case, Ritchie J. for the majority held that differences between Indians and non-Indians were contemplated by s. 91(24) of the Constitution, and such differences should not be eradicated under the equality guarantee of the Canadian Bill of Rights.[4] This was flatly contradictory of his opinion in *Drybones*,[5] where he had held that a difference between Indians and non-Indians did have to be eradicated under the equality guarantee of the Canadian Bill of Rights. However, obviously, the later view had won over most of the Court.[6]

The position under s. 15 of the Charter should be the same as under the Canadian Bill of Rights. Laws enacted under s. 91(24) that employ the classification "Indian" (or that have a disproportionate impact on Indians or lands reserved for the Indians) should not be vulnerable to attack under s. 15.[7] However, in *Ermineskin Indian Band and Nation v. Canada* (2009),[8] which was a challenge to the Indian Act restrictions on the investment of Indian band moneys, the special constitutional status of Indians was not considered. The Court assumed that a s. 15 challenge was available if the Indian Act imposed a disadvantage on Indians, although it rejected the challenge on the ground that the investment provisions entailed prudent investment practices that were not "discriminatory".

§ 55:35 Religion in s. 93

The religious education provisions of s. 93 of the Constitution Act, 1867 raise a similar issue to the constitutional provisions for Indians.

---

[2]*A.G. Can. v. Lavell*, [1974] S.C.R. 1349.

[3]*A.G. Can. v. Canard*, [1976] 1 S.C.R. 170.

[4]*A.G. Can. v. Canard*, [1976] 1 S.C.R. 170, 191-192.

[5]*A.G. Can. v. Canard*, [1976] 1 S.C.R. 170, 192, attempting to distinguish *Drybones*, on the basis that it arose in the Northwest Territories, where both Indians and non-Indians were covered by federal law.

[6]Ritchie J.'s opinion on this issue was agreed to by Martland, Judson and Pigeon JJ. Beetz J. wrote a separate concurring opinion. Laskin C.J., with whom Spence J. agreed, dissented.

[7]See § 55:39, "Race"; see also ch. 28, Aboriginal Peoples, under heading § 28:5, "Charter of Rights".

[8]*Ermineskin Indian Band and Nation v. Canada*, [2009] 1 S.C.R. 222.

The point arose in the *Ontario Separate School Funding* case (1987).[1] That case reviewed the validity of an Ontario statute that extended full public funding to Roman Catholic separate secondary schools, which at the time were being funded to grade 10 only. This was attacked on the ground that it was a violation of s. 15 to confer a benefit on Roman Catholic separate school supporters, a class defined by their religion. In Ontario, at that time, the non-denominational public school system also received full public funding, but religious schools other than the Roman Catholic schools received no public funding. The Supreme Court of Canada unanimously upheld the statute on the basis that the distinctive treatment of Roman Catholic school supporters was expressly permitted by the Constitution.

The province's power to enact laws in relation to education came from s. 93 of the Constitution Act, 1867. However, s. 93 went on to guarantee the rights of Roman Catholic and Protestant school supporters that existed at the time of confederation,[2] and subsection (3) of s. 93 made reference to any system of separate schools "thereafter established", meaning established after confederation. The Supreme Court of Canada held, in the words of Estey J., that this language "contemplates that after confederation the Legislature may establish a new system of separate schools or may enlarge an existing system of separate schools".[3] This power, if it was to be exercised, required the Legislature to distinguish between school supporters on the basis of religion. Estey J. drew an analogy with s. 91(24) (Indians, and lands reserved for the Indians), pointing out (without referring to *Drybones)* that s. 91(24) "authorizes the Parliament of Canada to legislate for the benefit of the Indian population in a preferential, discriminatory, or distinctive fashion vis à vis others".[4] The Charter of Rights, he held, "cannot be interpreted as rendering unconstitutional distinctions that are expressly permitted by the Constitution Act, 1867".[5]

Essentially the same issue was relitigated in *Adler v. Ontario* (1996),[6] in which supporters of private religious schools in Ontario sought a declaration that the province's failure to fund private religious schools was

---

[Section 55:35]

[1]*Re Bill 30* (Ontario Separate School Funding) [1987] 1 S.C.R. 1148. The principal opinion was written by Wilson J. with three others; Estey J. with one other wrote a concurring opinion; Lamer J. also wrote a concurring opinion.

[2]Wilson J., but not Estey or Lamer JJ., gave as a second reason for decision that full funding was a right guaranteed by s. 93(1), and protected from Charter attack by s. 29 of the Charter of Rights. This ground of decision is discussed in ch. 57, Education, under heading § 57:9, "Regulation".

[3]*Re Bill 30* (Ontario Separate School Funding) [1987] 1 S.C.R. 1148, 1202; Wilson J. at 1176 is to the same effect; and Lamer J. at 1209 agrees with Wilson J. on this issue.

[4]*Re Bill 30* (Ontario Separate School Funding) [1987] 1 S.C.R. 1148, 1206.

[5]*Re Bill 30* (Ontario Separate School Funding) [1987] 1 S.C.R. 1148, 1207.

[6]*Adler v. Ontario*, [1996] 3 S.C.R. 609. The argument based on s. 2(a) of the Charter was also rejected.

a breach of s. 15 of the Charter of Rights. The Supreme Court of Canada unanimously decided that the comparison with the fully-funded Roman Catholic schools could not be invoked as a breach of equality, because of the special constitutional status of the Roman Catholic schools. The *Ontario Separate School Funding* case was followed. Iacobucci J. for the five-judge majority of the Court also held that the plaintiffs could not invoke a comparison with the fully-funded *public* system, because s. 93 of the Constitution Act, 1867 constituted a "comprehensive code", and the public schools as well as the Roman Catholic separate schools were "part and parcel" of that code.[7] Four of the nine judges disagreed with this reasoning, holding that s. 93 should not be interpreted as immunizing the public system from equality review. Of the four, Sopinka and Major JJ. held that the failure to fund religious schools was not a breach of s. 15, because it was the *private* nature of the schools that disqualified them from funding, and that distinction was not a listed or analogous ground of discrimination. McLachlin and L'Heureux-Dubé JJ. held that the non-funding of the private schools was a breach of s. 15, because it had the effect of imposing a disproportionate burden on those whose religious beliefs required them to send their children to religious schools; this constituted adverse-effect discrimination on the basis of religion. McLachlin J. was prepared to hold that the discrimination was justified under s. 1 for the objective of promoting a more tolerant multicultural society,[8] but L'Heureux-Dubé J. held that the discrimination could not be justified, and so she alone would have held that there was a constitutional obligation to fund private religious schools.

It seems clear, therefore, that the Charter of Rights, although adopted later in time than the Constitution Act, 1867, is not to be read as impliedly repealing or amending those provisions of the earlier instrument that are inconsistent with the unqualified language of s. 15 (or any other guarantee). Rather, s. 15 is to be read as qualified by the language of the earlier instrument.

§ 55:36 Province of residence in ss. 91, 92

A closely related issue, which is discussed more fully in a later section of this chapter,[1] is whether distinctions based on a person's province of residence could amount to discrimination under s. 15. The Supreme Court has in fact held that place of residence is not an analogous ground. However, if a claim of discrimination involves comparing the treatment accorded by the law of the claimant's province with the (more beneficial) treatment accorded by the law of another province, such a claim is a

[7] *Adler v. Ontario*, [1996] 3 S.C.R. 609, para. 44 per Iacobucci J. for majority.

[8] However, McLachlin J. dissented in part, because she took the view that the failure to provide health support services to children with disabilities in the private religious schools was a breach of s. 15 that (unlike the failure to fund generally) could not be justified under s. 1.

[Section 55:36]

[1] § 55:49, "Place of residence".

contradiction of the federal principle, under which the laws of each province are permitted to differ from each other. Differences between provincial laws cannot amount to discrimination under s. 15, because that would require a uniformity of provincial laws which would be inconsistent with the distribution of legislative powers in ss. 91 and 92 (and some other sections) of the Constitution Act, 1867. The federal system thus operates as a general qualification of s. 15's guarantee of equality.

§ 55:37 Citizenship in s. 6

The Charter of Rights itself contains some implicit qualifications of s. 15's guarantee of equality. Because s. 6(1)'s guarantee of the right to remain in Canada applies only to a "citizen", it has been held that the Immigration Act may validly provide for the deportation of non-citizens who have committed criminal offences,[1] or who have been certified as a threat to national security.[2] The imposition of a burden on non-citizens that does not also apply to citizens would normally be a breach of s. 15,[3] but in the case of the right to remain in Canada a difference in treatment was specifically contemplated by s. 6(1).

Outside the right to remain in Canada under s. 6(1), laws imposing disabilities on non-citizens have been held to be in breach of s. 15. *Andrews v. Law Society of British Columbia* (1989)[4] held that citizenship was an analogous ground of discrimination under s. 15, and struck down the provincial law that restricted entry to the province's legal profession to Canadian citizens. This decision was followed in *Lavoie v. Canada* (2002),[5] where a hiring preference for Canadian citizens in the federal public service was held by a majority of the Supreme Court of Canada to be a breach of s. 15, although the law was saved under s. 1. In this case, the law was a federal one, and it was urged in favour of the law's validity that the federal Parliament's power over citizenship, which comes from s. 91(25) (naturalization and aliens),[6] could hardly be exercised if no distinctions between citizens and non-citizens were permitted. This argument was rejected by the Court. Bastarache J., writing the principal majority opinion, held that laws imposing disabilities on non-citizens were not exempt from constitutional equality

---

[Section 55:37]

[1] *Chiarelli v. Can.*, [1992] 1 S.C.R. 711; *Medovarski v. Can.*, [2005] 2 S.C.R. 539.

[2] *Charkaoui v. Can.*, [2007] 1 S.C.R. 350.

[3] § 55:46, "Citizenship".

[4] *Andrews v. Law Society of British Columbia*, [1989] 1 S.C.R. 143.

[5] *Lavoie v. Canada*, [2002] 1 S.C.R. 769.

[6] There have also been suggestions that the power over citizenship derives from Parliament's authority over peace, order, and good government: *Winner v. S.M.T. Eastern*, [1951] S.C.R. 889, 919 per Rand J.; McConnell, *Commentary on the British North America Act* (1977), 227-232. See generally ch. 26, Citizenship.

standards, and he asserted that this would not abolish the concept of citizenship.[7]

§ 55:38 Language in ss. 16-23

Another qualification of s. 15 is created by the language rights of ss. 16 to 23 of the Charter. These implement a notion of equality of the French and English languages. However, by implication, they accord a "special status" to French and English "in comparison to all other linguistic groups in Canada".[1] For example, the right to minority language education in s. 23, which is explicitly limited to French and English, does not extend to other minority language speakers by the operation of s. 15.[2] The conferral of a benefit on French-speaking citizens that was denied to German-speaking citizens (for example) would normally be a breach of s. 15,[3] but in the case of the right to minority language education a difference in treatment is specifically contemplated by s. 23.

XI. RACE; RELIGION

§ 55:39 Race

"Race", as well as "national or ethnic origin" and "colour", is one of the grounds of discrimination that is expressly prohibited by s. 15. A racial distinction in a statute would be upheld if the statute established an affirmative action programme within the terms of s. 15(2), and might be upheld under s. 1 if the statute fell outside the strict terms of s. 15(2) but pursued a benign purpose of an affirmative action kind. Otherwise, it is difficult to imagine a situation in which a racial distinction could possibly be upheld. Canadian statutes were cleansed of explicit racial distinctions long before the adoption of the Charter of Rights in 1982, and there have been no successful challenges to federal or provincial laws on the basis of race in the Supreme Court of Canada.[1] To the extent that racial discrimination occurs in the private sphere, the remedy would

---

[7]*Lavoie v. Canada*, [2002] 1 S.C.R. 769, para. 40; to the same effect, para. 39 per McLachlin C.J. and L'Heureux-Dubé J., but note para. 117 per Arbour J. who held there was no breach of s. 15 ("legislating over matters of citizenship itself entails differential treatment between citizens and non-citizens").

[Section 55:38]

[1]*Mahe v. Alta.*, [1990] 1 S.C.R. 342, 369 per Dickson C.J.

[2]*Mahe v. Alta.*, [1990] 1 S.C.R. 342, para. 369. Indeed, it is limited to a particular subset of English and French speakers: *Gosselin v. Que.*, [2005] 1 S.C.R. 238 (rejecting equality challenge to Quebec law denying access by French speakers to English-language schools).

[3]I am assuming that language would be an analogous ground of discrimination; in some circumstances, there might be room for argument about whether a person's language is an immutable personal characteristic.

[Section 55:39]

[1]There have been successful challenges on the basis of race in the lower courts: see e.g. *R. v. Sharma* (2020), 152 O.R. (3d) 209 (C.A.), leave to appeal to the S.C.C. granted

be found under the human rights codes, not the Charter, which does not apply to private action.

The situation of the aboriginal peoples[2] is a special one. The Constitution Act, 1867, by s. 91(24), empowers the federal Parliament to make laws in relation to "Indians, and lands reserved for the Indians". We have already noticed the point that any law enacted under that head will either explicitly employ the racial classification "Indian" or will have disparate impact on Indians who live on "lands reserved for the Indians".[3] The special status of aboriginal peoples has been reinforced by the adoption of s. 35 of the Constitution Act, 1982, which guarantees "aboriginal and treaty rights". Such rights are restricted to aboriginal peoples, who are of course defined by their race. This is recognized by s. 25 of the Charter of Rights, which provides that the Charter should not be construed so as to abrogate or derogate from "any aboriginal, treaty or other rights or freedoms that pertain to the aboriginal peoples of Canada". By reason of these provisions, s. 15 has only a limited role to play with respect to aboriginal peoples.[4] A law enacted by the federal Parliament under s. 91(24) for the benefit of Indian people, and laws enacted to give effect to aboriginal or treaty rights, are not affected by s. 15 of the Charter.

§ 55:40 Religion

"Religion" is another of the grounds of discrimination that is expressly prohibited by s. 15. The public funding of the schools of a religious denomination without comparable provision for the supporters of the schools of other religious denominations would be forbidden by s. 15.[1] However, we have already noticed[2] the special provisions of s. 93 of the Constitution Act, 1867, which guarantee the rights of the supporters of denominational schools that existed at the time of confederation, and which authorize the enlargement of those rights. To the extent that a denominational school system is protected, or even contemplated, by s. 93, no s. 15 challenge is open.

January 14, 2021 (as of the time of writing, the Court has not released a decision in the appeal). For academic discussion, see J. Jai and J. Cheng, "The Invisibility of Race in Section 15: Why Section 15 Has Not Done More to Promote Racial Equality" (2006) 5 J.L. & Equality 125; A. Go, "Whose Charter is it anyways? An examination of Charter litigation as it relates to the Chinese Canadian community" (2007) 22 Nat. J. Con. Law 93.

[2]See generally ch. 28, Aboriginal Peoples.

[3]§ 55:34, "Race in s. 91(24)".

[4]Section 15 is still available to attack provisions dealing with aboriginal people so long as there is a basis of discrimination that avoids the various exceptions to s. 15 that are outlined in the text: *Corbiere v. Can.*, [1999] 2 S.C.R. 203 (striking down Indian Act provision making residence on a reserve a requirement for voting in band elections); compare *Lovelace v. Ont.*, [2000] 1 S.C.R. 950 (rejecting challenge to exclusion of non-status Indian bands from distribution of casino profits).

[Section 55:40]

[1]See also ch. 42, Religion, under heading § 42:9, "Denominational schools".

[2]§ 55:35, "Religion in s. 93".

The Charter of Rights, by s. 2(a), guarantees "freedom of conscience and religion". In chapter 42, Religion, we noticed that s. 2(a) has been held to be abridged by Sunday observance laws and by religious exercises in public schools. In very general terms, the reasoning was that the endorsement of Christian beliefs indirectly burdened those who did not accept those beliefs. These cases were not decided under s. 15, but they could easily be viewed as equality cases in which benefits are conferred on Christians that are denied to the adherents of other religions.

In *Alta. v. Hutterian Brethren of Wilson Colony* (2009),[3] the Hu7tterian Brethren, a Christian denomination, objected on religious grounds to the province's law requiring that a driver's licence display a photo of the licence holder. This offended their belief that having their photos taken was prohibited by the Bible. The Supreme Court accepted that the requirement was a limit on their freedom of religion, but, by a majority, upheld the law under s. 1. The claimants also made an argument under s. 15. The Court rejected the s. 15 argument, holding that a universal requirement of photo licences did not create a distinction based on religion.[4]

XII. SEX

§ 55:41 Direct discrimination

"Sex" is another of the grounds of discrimination that is expressly prohibited by s. 15.

The equality guarantee of the Canadian Bill of Rights gave rise to two cases of sexual discrimination. The first case was *A.G. Can. v. Lavell* (1973),[1] in which a challenge was brought against the provisions of the Indian Act that used to provide for the transmission of Indian status. The Act provided that an Indian woman who married a non-Indian man lost her Indian status, whereas an Indian man who married a non-Indian woman did not. This challenge was rejected by the Court on the basis of a theory of equality[2] that need not detain us since it is obviously indefensible and was later abandoned by the Court. The discriminatory provisions of the Indian Act were subsequently held by an international tribunal to be in violation of the International Covenant on Civil and Political Rights; and they were repealed in 1985.[3]

---

[3] *Alta. v. Hutterian Brethren of Wilson Colony*, [2009] 2 S.C.R. 567. McLachlin C.J. wrote the opinion of the majority. Abella, LeBel and Fish JJ. wrote dissenting opinions, but based on s. 2(a) not s. 15 (which they did not mention).

[4] *Alta. v. Hutterian Brethren of Wilson Colony*, [2009] 2 S.C.R. 567, para. 107.

[Section 55:41]

[1] *A.G. Can. v. Lavell*, [1974] S.C.R. 1349.

[2] The theory was that "equality *before* the law", the phrase used in s. 1(b) of the Canadian Bill of Rights, only prohibited discrimination in the administration of a law, and did not permit the law itself to be struck down. Of course, in the earlier case of *R. v. Drybones*, [1970] S.C.R. 282, the law itself had been struck down.

[3] See ch. 28, Aboriginal Peoples, under heading § 28:2, "Indians".

The second case was *Bliss v. A.G. Can.* (1979),[4] in which a challenge was brought to a provision of the Unemployment Insurance Act, which denied ordinary unemployment benefits to women whose employment was interrupted by pregnancy. (The Act did provide maternity benefits, but there was a longer period of qualification for them, a period designed to limit the benefits to women who were already employed when they became pregnant.) This challenge was rejected by the Court on the basis that the disadvantaged class was defined by pregnancy rather than by sex. This reasoning has been strongly criticized. The argument has been that, since pregnancy is a condition experienced by women in particular,[5] any disadvantage premised on pregnancy should be characterized as discrimination by sex. This criticism has been accepted by the Supreme Court of Canada, which overruled *Bliss* in a decision dealing with a Human Rights Code.[6]

Although *Bliss* itself has been overruled, its line of reasoning has been employed under s. 15 of the Charter of Rights. In *R. v. Hess* (1990),[7] a majority of the Supreme Court of Canada held that the offence of statutory rape (intercourse with a "female person" under the age of 14) did not offend s. 15, although the offence could only be committed by "a male person". Wilson J., writing for the majority, held that, since the prohibited act ("intercourse") was defined by reference to penetration, it could as a matter of biological fact be committed only by males. Therefore, she concluded, it was not discriminatory to subject only male persons to the offence. Is this not the *Bliss* argument all over again? The imposition of a legal distinction by reference to a biological characteristic attributed to only one sex (such as pregnancy or penetration) is held not to be discrimination by sex. The offence could easily have been recast to include acts of intercourse by older women with young men (or, more inclusively, older people with young people, regardless of sex and gender). McLachlin J., in dissent, did not accept Wilson J.'s reasoning. In McLachlin J.'s view, the offence did constitute discrimination on the basis of sex, although it could be justified under s. 1 as a measure for the protection of young women who, unlike young men, could get pregnant through intercourse. McLachlin J.'s reasoning is to be preferred over Wilson J.'s reasoning.[8]

In *Weatherall v. Canada* (1993),[9] a prisoner in a federal penitentiary for men challenged the constitutionality of frisk searches and cell

---

[4]*Bliss v. A.G. Can.*, [1979] 1 S.C.R. 183.

[5]It is not the case that *only* cisgendered women can get pregnant, because trans men and gender non-binary people can also become pregnant. This explains the use of the term "in particular" rather than "only" in the text.

[6]*Brooks v. Can. Safeway*, [1989] 1 S.C.R. 1219 (exclusion of pregnant women from employee group health insurance plan held to be discrimination on the basis of sex).

[7]*R. v. Hess*, [1990] 2 S.C.R. 906.

[8]Although, in keeping with the dominant thinking at the time, it does not acknowledge that trans men and gender non-binary people can also become pregnant.

[9]*Weatherall v. Canada*, [1993] 2 S.C.R. 872.

surveillance of male prisoners by female guards.[10] This was said to be an affront to the dignity of the prisoners, and to be discriminatory, because female prisoners were searched and observed only by guards of the same sex. La Forest J. for the Supreme Court of Canada pointed out (without referring to s. 28) that equality did not demand that men and women always be treated in the same way, and the effect of cross-gender searching was "different and more threatening for women than for men".[11] He did not seem to be entirely convinced by this reasoning, because he concluded only that there "may not be" discrimination, and that it was "doubtful" that s. 15 had been violated.[12] But he held that, even if there was a breach of s. 15, it was saved by s. 1. The "humanizing effect" of having women in male prisons and the enhancement of "employment equity" constituted sufficient justification[13] for the practices.[14]

In *Benner v. Canada* (1997),[15] a provision of the federal Citizenship Act that distinguished between men and women was struck down under s. 15. In regulating the citizenship status of persons born outside Canada before 1977, the Act provided that a person born to a Canadian father was automatically entitled to citizenship on registration in Canada of the birth, but a person born to a Canadian mother had to apply for citizenship and undergo a security check. The Supreme Court of Canada held that this was discrimination by sex, which was a breach of s. 15. The breach could not be justified under s. 1, because there was no rational basis to suppose that the children of Canadian mothers required a more rigorous screening process than the children of Canadian fathers. An interesting complication was that the complainant was a man. He had been born abroad before 1977 to a Canadian mother, and he had applied for citizenship in 1987. His application was refused because he failed the security test (he had a criminal record). The discrimination by sex applied to the parents of applicants and not to the applicants themselves. However, the Court held that the complainant had standing to invoke s. 15, because the denial of his citizenship showed that he was disadvantaged by the discriminatory provision.

In *Trociuk v. British Columbia* (2003),[16] a father challenged the provincial law that permitted a mother, on the birth of a child, to leave

---

[10]A challenge under s. 8 was rejected on the ground that a prisoner had no reasonable expectation of privacy with respect to the searches and surveillance.

[11]*Weatherall v. Canada*, [1993] 2 S.C.R. 872, 877.

[12]*Weatherall v. Canada*, [1993] 2 S.C.R. 872, 877-878.

[13]*Weatherall v. Canada*, [1993] 2 S.C.R. 872, 878. No evidence was referred to in support of these findings; nor was it explained why these findings outweighed the assumed breach of equality rights; nor was it explained how the "prescribed by law" requirement of s. 1 was satisfied.

[14]See also *Native Women's Assn. of Can. v. Can.*, [1994] 3 S.C.R. 627 (claim of sex discrimination in funding rejected); the case is discussed in ch. 43, Expression, under heading § 43:40, "Access to government".

[15]*Benner v. Canada*, [1997] 1 S.C.R. 358.

[16]*Trociuk v. British Columbia*, [2003] 1 S.C.R. 835. Deschamps J. wrote the opinion of the Court.

the father's name off the birth certificate, and, if she did that, to alone choose the surname of the child. In this case, the (unmarried) mother and father were estranged by the time they had children (triplets). As authorized by the law, the mother registered the births without acknowledging the name of the father, and she gave the children her surname without consulting the wishes of the father. The father challenged the validity of the law, because he wanted his name to appear on the birth certificate, and he wanted the children to have a hyphenated surname that included his surname. The Supreme Court of Canada held that the law distinguished on the basis of sex, since fathers were disadvantaged in comparison with mothers. The Court also held that the exclusion of fathers from the registration and naming process impaired their human dignity. Therefore, the law infringed s. 15, and (since the Court decided that the law was not justified under s. 1) the law was invalid.

In *Newfoundland v. N.A.P.E.* (2004),[17] the province of Newfoundland enacted the Public Sector Restraint Act, which delayed for three years the introduction of pay equity for female workers in the hospital sector. The Act modified a collective agreement that called for a five-year series of pay-equity adjustments to the pay of hospital workers in female-dominated jobs which would bring their pay up to that of comparable male workers. The Act only delayed the implementation of the collective agreement, but it made no provision for retroactive pay for the period of delay, so that the Act did cancel the government's obligation to make the first three years of payments. The Supreme Court of Canada held that the Act was a breach of s. 15. The Court left open the question whether s. 15 required governments to provide their female employees with equal pay for work of equal value, saying that "we do not get to that issue in this case".[18] But in this case the claimants had a contractual right to pay adjustments that were calculated to achieve equal pay for work of equal value. By postponing the implementation of that right, the Act singled out a group of women who were being paid less than men who performed work of equal value, and perpetuated their disadvantage. This was discrimination on the ground of sex. The Court went on to hold that the Act was saved by s. 1, because the Act was a response to a "financial crisis" in the province that provided justification for the limit on the claimants' Charter rights.[19]

§ 55:42 Systemic discrimination

The raising of consciousness about the position of women in society has led to the removal from the Canadian statute books of most provisions that create formal inequalities between the sexes. Those few that

---

[17] *Newfoundland v. N.A.P.E.*, [2004] 3 S.C.R. 381. Binnie J. wrote the opinion of the Court.

[18] *Newfoundland v. N.A.P.E.*, [2004] 3 S.C.R. 381, para. 37.

[19] For discussion of the s. 1 reasoning, see ch. 38, Limitation of Rights, under heading § 38:17, "Cost". Note that s. 28 of the Charter was not referred to by the Court: § 55:43, "Section 28".

remain will undoubtedly be reviewed by the courts under s. 15. Where a statutory provision that is gender-neutral on its face gives rise to a disproportionately adverse impact on women, s. 15 review will also be available by reason of the rules, discussed earlier,[1] that discrimination may be unintended, that discrimination may be indirect and that discrimination may require reasonable accommodation to be made to accommodate a special condition (such as pregnancy). To the extent that discrimination against women takes place in the private sphere from which the Charter is excluded, any remedy would have to lie under the human rights codes. In fact, as we have already noticed,[2] it has been in proceedings initiated by women under the human rights codes that the Supreme Court of Canada has established the expansive rules respecting discrimination which now apply to s. 15 as well as to the codes.[3]

In *Symes v. Canada* (1993),[4] it was argued that the Income Tax Act offended s. 15 of the Charter by not allowing businesspersons to deduct the full cost of child care. The Act allowed a deduction for child care, but it was limited to $2,000 per child in 1985 (the taxation year in issue). The taxpayer, a self-employed female lawyer with two children, had in fact paid $13,000 to a nanny to care for her children. In the Supreme Court of Canada, L'Heureux-Dubé and McLachlin JJ. (the only two female judges) held that, because women were more likely than men to bear child care responsibilities, the Act's denial of full deductibility for child care expenses had an adverse impact on women. The two judges concluded that the statutory provision, although neutral on its face, was in its effect discriminatory on the basis of sex. However, this was a dissenting view. The majority of the Court, in an opinion written by Iacobucci J., acknowledged that women disproportionately bore the *social* costs of child care, but held that the taxpayer had not established that women disproportionately bore the *financial* costs of child care. Since the deduction would be available with respect only to the financial costs of child care, it would benefit men as much as women, and its restriction did not amount to discrimination on the basis of sex.[5]

One way that systemic discrimination against women has manifested is in the gender-based pay gap, which continues to "impoverish women

---

[Section 55:42]

[1]These rules have been discussed in §§ 55:28 to 55:30, "Direct and indirect discrimination".

[2]§§ 55:28 to 55:30, "Direct and indirect discrimination".

[3]Note as well that s. 15 can sometimes reach private action indirectly by extending the reach of a Human Rights Code. This happened in *Blainey v. Ont. Hockey Assn.* (1986), 54 O.R. (2d) 513 (C.A.) (striking down provision of Human Rights Code permitting sex-segregated hockey teams). See generally § 55:7, "Private action".

[4]*Symes v. Canada*, [1993] 4 S.C.R. 695. Iacobucci J. wrote the opinion of the majority. L'Heureux-Dubé and McLachlin JJ. wrote dissenting opinions.

[5]Compare *Thibaudeau v. Can.*, [1995] 2 S.C.R. 627 (taxation of child-support payments did not indirectly discriminate against custodial parents who were mostly women, because the family-law rules respecting the calculation of support should take account of and nullify the tax disadvantage).

relative to men across the country and across the labour market".[6] In an attempt to remedy this gender-based pay gap, some provinces have enacted pay equity laws, which impose obligations on employers to provide their female employees with equal pay for work of equal value. In two companion cases, *Quebec v. Alliance du personnel professionel et technique de la santé et des services sociaux* (2018)[7] and *Centrale des syndicats du Québec v. Quebec* (2018),[8] several Quebec unions challenged aspects of Quebec's Pay Equity Act[9] under s. 15. The majority of the Supreme Court of Canada found s. 15 to be infringed in both cases. In *Centrale*, the claim failed under s. 1, but in *Alliance*, the claim did not fail under s. 1, and thus ultimately succeeded.

In *Alliance*,[10] the unions brought a s. 15 challenge to various amendments that Quebec made to the Act in 2009. These amendments replaced the *ongoing* obligations that the Act had imposed on employers to monitor and adjust for pay inequities in their workplaces with a system of *periodic* five-year pay equity audits. The amendments also restricted the Pay Equity Commission's ability to remedy *past* pay inequities retroactively, and denied employees and unions any information revealed by a five-year audit about when any pay inequities emerged. The rate of employer compliance with the Act had been poor, and the apparent aim in making the pay equity scheme more friendly to employers in these ways was to increase employer compliance with the Act. In this case, the unions argued that these amendments to the Act infringed s. 15.

Abella J., who wrote for the majority of the Court, held that most (but not all)[11] of the impugned amendments infringed s. 15.[12] The flawed amendments created a distinction based on the enumerated ground of

[6] F. Faraday, "One Step Forward, Two Steps Back? Substantive Equality, Systemic Discrimination and Pay Equity at the Supreme Court of Canada" (2020) 94 S.C.L.R. (2d) 301, para. 9.

[7] *Quebec v. Alliance du personnel professionel et technique de la santé et des services sociaux*, [2018] 1 S.C.R. 464. Abella J. wrote the opinion for the majority of the Court, which was joined by McLachlin C.J. and Moldaver, Karakatsanis, Wagner, and Gascon JJ. Côté, Brown and Rowe JJ. wrote a joint dissenting opinion.

[8] *Centrale des syndicats du Québec v. Quebec*, [2018] 1 S.C.R. 522. Abella J. wrote an opinion for four judges, which was joined by Moldaver, Karakatsanis and Gascon JJ. McLachlin C.J. wrote a brief opinion dissenting in the result, which agreed with Abella J. that s. 15 had been infringed, but disagreed with her that the infringement could be justified under s. 1. Côté J. wrote an opinion for four judges, which was joined by Wagner, Brown and Rowe JJ, and which disagreed with Abella J. and McLachlin C.J. that s. 15 was infringed.

[9] C.Q.L.R., c. E-12.001.

[10] *Quebec v. Alliance du personnel professionel et technique de la santé et des services sociaux*, [2018] 1 S.C.R. 464.

[11] Abella J. held that the impugned amendments that repealed the ongoing obligations that the Act had imposed on employers to monitor and adjust for pay inequities did not infringe s. 15: *Quebec v. Alliance du personnel professionel et technique de la santé et des services sociaux*, [2018] 1 S.C.R. 464, para. 59. It was therefore not the shift to periodic five-year pay equity audits, but rather the new restrictions imposed in between them, that infringed s. 15.

sex, and therefore satisfied the first stage of the two-stage s. 15 test. The Act itself created a distinction based on sex because it "targets women in redressing the pay discrimination they have suffered".[13] The flawed amendments also created a distinction based on sex because they determined when and how inequities in "*women's* pay, in comparison to men" would be addressed.[14] Moreover, the flawed amendments also perpetuated the disadvantage of women, and therefore satisfied the second stage of the two-stage s. 15 test. The flawed amendments disadvantaged women by making the obligation imposed on employers to monitor and adjust for pay inequities "an episodic, partial obligation" and "effectively giv[ing] an amnesty to the employer for discrimination" between five-year pay equity audits.[15] They also disadvantaged women by making the process to engage the limited avenues provided to employees and unions to challenge pay inequity between five-year audits "opaque and difficult to access".[16] Abella J. went on to hold that the s. 15 infringements could not be justified under s. 1, largely on the basis that there was "virtually no evidence" that other less impairing alternatives (like stricter enforcement) "would be ineffective, if indeed Quebec's objective was to improve compliance".[17] Côté, Brown and Rowe JJ., in a joint dissenting opinion, agreed with Abella J. that the impugned amendments created a distinction based on the enumerated ground of sex, but would have held that none of the impugned amendments infringed s. 15, largely on the basis that gender-based pay inequity already existed in the labour market, and the impugned amendments did not perpetuate this form of disadvantage, but rather ameliorated it.[18] However, this was a dissenting view, and because Abella J. wrote for a majority, the s. 15 challenge largely succeeded. This made *Alliance* the first case in which women have won a sex-based s. 15 claim in the Supreme Court of Canada.

In *Centrale*,[19] the companion case to *Alliance*, the s. 15 challenge related to a different aspect of Quebec's Pay Equity Act. When the Act was

---

[12]Abella J. articulated and applied a revised s. 15 test in the course of doing so. This revised s. 15 test is described earlier in this chapter, in § 55:22, "Discrimination without human dignity".

[13]*Quebec v. Alliance du personnel professionel et technique de la santé et des services sociaux*, [2018] 1 S.C.R. 464, para. 29.

[14]*Quebec v. Alliance du personnel professionel et technique de la santé et des services sociaux*, [2018] 1 S.C.R. 464, para. 29 (emphasis in original).

[15]*Quebec v. Alliance du personnel professionel et technique de la santé et des services sociaux*, [2018] 1 S.C.R. 464, para. 33.

[16]*Quebec v. Alliance du personnel professionel et technique de la santé et des services sociaux*, [2018] 1 S.C.R. 464, para. 34.

[17]*Quebec v. Alliance du personnel professionel et technique de la santé et des services sociaux*, [2018] 1 S.C.R. 464, para. 51. Abella J. also rejected an alternative argument – offered by Côté, Brown and Rowe JJ. in dissent – based on s. 15(2); this aspect of the decision is discussed earlier in this chapter, in § 55:32, "Affirmative action".

[18]*Quebec v. Alliance du personnel professionel et technique de la santé et des services sociaux*, [2018] 1 S.C.R. 464, paras. 98-106 (emphasis in original).

[19]*Centrale des syndicats du Québec v. Quebec*, [2018] 1 S.C.R. 522.

enacted in 1996, it gave women who worked in female-dominated workplaces without male comparators (like childcare centers) a right to pay equity. However, it delegated the development and implementation of a method to assess pay equity in these workplaces to Quebec's Pay Equity Commission. The result was that women in workplaces with male comparators were able to access pay equity almost six years earlier than women in workplaces without male comparators. In this case, the unions' s. 15 challenge was to s. 38 of the Act, the provision that was largely responsible for this almost six-year delay.

Abella J. wrote again in *Centrale*, but this time for only four judges.[20] As in *Alliance*, she held that the seven-year delay in pay equity that resulted from s. 38 infringed s. 15. The first stage of the two-stage s. 15 test was satisfied because the Act generally, and s. 38 specifically, created a distinction based on the enumerated ground of sex. On the Act generally, Abella J. echoed her reasoning in *Centrale* – that the Act as a whole drew "a distinction based on sex in targeting systemic pay discrimination against women".[21] On s. 38 specifically, she said that the provision created a distinction based on sex both on its face (by sorting women into two categories that were "expressly defined by the presence or absence of men") and in its impact (by creating an almost six-year delay in access to pay equity for women who already "disproportionately suffer an adverse impact *because they are women*").[22] The second stage of the two-stage s. 15 test was also satisfied because s. 38 perpetuated the disadvantage of a class of women – those in workplaces without male comparators. It did so by forcing them to live with the consequences of pay inequity for longer without a remedy, with "a considerable economic impact".[23] Up to this point, Abella J. was on track to reach the same result that she reached in *Alliance*. However, unlike in *Alliance*, she went on to hold that the s. 15 infringement could be justified under s. 1, in essence because the issue (how to determine pay equity in workplaces that had no male comparators) was complex and required careful study, and the province had responded to it with reasonable diligence.[24] McLachlin C.J, in a brief separate opinion, agreed with Abella J. that s. 38 infringed s. 15, but disagreed with her that the infringement could be

[20]Abella J.'s opinion was joined by only three others. McLachlin C.J., who joined Abella J.'s majority opinion (for six judges) in *Alliance*, rejected her conclusion in *Centrale* that the s. 15 breach could be justified under s. 1, and Wagner J., who also joined her majority opinion in *Alliance*, joined Côté J.'s opinion (for four judges) in *Centrale*. However, McLachlin C.J. agreed with Abella J. that s. 15 had been infringed, and in doing so, seemed to agree with her s. 15 analysis, with the result that it can be read to have the support of a majority of five judges: *Centrale des syndicats du Québec v. Quebec*, [2018] 1 S.C.R. 522, paras. 154-156.

[21]*Centrale des syndicats du Québec v. Quebec*, [2018] 1 S.C.R. 522, para. 24.

[22]*Centrale des syndicats du Québec v. Quebec*, [2018] 1 S.C.R. 522, paras. 28-29 (emphasis in original).

[23]*Centrale des syndicats du Québec v. Quebec*, [2018] 1 S.C.R. 522, paras. 31, 34.

[24]Abella J. also rejected – as she did in *Alliance* – an alternative argument that invoked s. 15(2); this aspect of her decision is discussed earlier in this chapter, in § 55:32, "Affirmative action".

justified under s. 1. Côté J. wrote a separate opinion, which was joined by her co-authors in *Alliance* (Brown and Rowe JJ.), as well as Wagner J., who had joined Abella J.'s majority opinion in *Alliance*. As in *Alliance*, Côté J. held that s. 38 did not infringe s. 15. However, in this case, unlike in *Alliance*, she said that the claim should founder at the first stage of the s. 15 test, because s. 38 created a distinction on the basis of place of work (which is not an enumerated or analogous ground) and not, as Abella J. held, on the basis of sex (which is of course an enumerated ground). This was enough for Côté J. to reject the claim, but she went on to say that the claim should fail at the second stage of the s. 15 test as well – again, largely on the basis that the Act did not perpetuate the pay inequity resulting from sex discrimination, but rather ameliorated it. Taking the various opinions together, five judges (Abella J., for four judges, and McLachlin C.J.) concluded that s. 38 infringed s. 15, but 8 judges dismissed the challenge (Abella J., for four judges, under s. 1, and Côté J., for four judges, under s. 15).

Another way that systemic discrimination against women has manifested is in the gendered pattern of part-time work, which sees more women engaged in part-time work than men, often to accommodate childcare responsibilities, which have been unequally distributed to women. The Supreme Court of Canada considered a case involving this issue in *Fraser v. Canada* (2020).[25] This case involved three claimants, each of whom were women with young children, and each of whom were members of the Royal Canadian Mounted Police (R.C.M.P.). The three claimants participated in a job-sharing program that the R.C.M.P. introduced in 1997; the program allowed R.C.M.P. members to split the duties of one full-time position. R.C.M.P. members who participated in the job-sharing program – most of whom, like the claimants, were women with young children when they elected to participate – were not permitted to "buy back" full-time pension plan credit, whereas full-time R.C.M.P. members who took unpaid leave had this option.[26] The claimants challenged the R.C.M.P.'s pension plan under s. 15, arguing that it discriminated against job-sharers on the basis of sex or, alternatively, family/parental status. The claimants did not argue that the R.C.M.P.'s pension plan arrangement for job-sharers was directly discriminatory on its face. Rather, they argued that it was indirectly discriminatory because it had an adverse impact on women. The case made its way to the Supreme Court on appeal. Claims of adverse impact discrimination had not had much success in the Court; the last (and indeed only) suc-

[25]*Fraser v. Canada*, 2020 SCC 28. Abella J. wrote the opinion for the majority of the Court, which was joined by Wagner C.J and Moldaver, Karakatsanis, Martin and Kasirer JJ. Brown and Rowe JJ. wrote a joint dissenting opinion. Côté J. also wrote dissenting opinion.

[26]The relevant legislation was the Royal Canadian Mounted Police Superannuation Act, R.S.C. 1985, c. R-11; and the Royal Canadian Mounted Police Superannuation Regulations, C.R.C., c. 1393.

cessful cases were in 1997 and 1998.[27] However, the majority of the Court accepted the claimants' adverse impact discrimination argument.

Abella J., who wrote again for the majority of the Court, said that the first stage of the two-stage s. 15 analysis was satisfied because the failure of the R.C.M.P.'s pension plan to grant the job-sharers the ability to buy-back full-time pension benefits created a distinction, not on its face, but in its impact, on the basis of sex. The evidence showed – in keeping with the broader gendered patterns of part-time work – that it was primarily women with young children who participated in the job-sharing program, and hence "the RCMP's use of a temporary reduction in working hours as a basis for imposing less favourable pension consequences has an adverse impact on women".[28] In reaching this conclusion, Abella J. rejected the argument – which had been accepted by both lower courts – that there was no adverse impact because the claimants had chosen to participate in the job-sharing program; she said that "differential treatment can be discriminatory even if it is based on choices made by the affected individual or group", and that "[f]or many women, the decision to work on a part-time basis, far from being an unencumbered choice, 'often lies beyond the individual's effective control' ".[29] Abella J. said that the second stage of the two-stage test was satisfied because this adverse impact perpetuated the longstanding economic disadvantage of women. The "negative pension consequences of job-sharing perpetuate[d] a longstanding source of disadvantage to women: gender biases within pension plans, which have historically been designed 'for middle and upper-income full-time employees with long service, typically male' ".[30] Abella J. went on to hold that the infringement of s. 15 could not be saved under s. 1, on the basis that the federal government had failed to offer a pressing and substantial objective for failing to grant the claimants – and other job-sharers – the ability to buy back full-time pension benefits.

The three judges that dissented in both *Alliance* and *Centrale* – Côté, Brown and Rowe JJ. – also dissented in *Fraser*, in two separate opinions. All three judges concluded that the R.C.M.P. pension plan did not infringe s. 15. In a joint dissenting opinion, Brown and Rowe JJ. said that the claim should fail at the second stage of the analysis, largely on the basis that the distinction created by the less favourable treatment of job-sharers under the R.C.M.P. pension plan was not arbitrary.[31] In a

[27]The two successful cases were: *Eldridge v B.C.*, [1997] 3 S.C.R. 624; and *Vriend v Alta.*, [1998] 1 S.C.R. 493. These cases are discussed more fully earlier in this chapter: see § 55:28, "Substantive equality".

[28]*Fraser v. Canada*, 2020 SCC 28, paras. 97, 106.

[29]*Fraser v. Canada*, 2020 SCC 28, paras. 86, 91.

[30]*Fraser v. Canada*, 2020 SCC 28, para. 108. Because Abella J. accepted that the s. 15 argument based on the enumerated ground of sex, she declined to decide whether the alternative s. 15 argument based on a new analogous ground of parental/family status should also be accepted: *Fraser v. Canada*, 2020 SCC 28, para. 114.

[31]Not arbitrary because it reflected the hours worked, and the job-sharing program itself provided a flexible working arrangement that sought to ameliorate, rather than perpetuate, "the pre-existing disadvantage of women in the workplace which arises in

separate dissenting opinion, Côté J. said that the claim should fail at the first stage of the analysis, because the distinction created by the less favourable treatment of job-sharers was not on the ground of sex ("being a *woman*"), but rather caregiving status ("being a woman *with children*"), and this was not an enumerated or analogous ground under s. 15.[32] However, these were dissenting views; as noted, the majority of the Court accepted the claimants' s. 15 challenge.

The three cases described above – *Alliance*, *Centrale* and *Fraser* – are each important sex discrimination cases. The majority of the Court was careful to emphasize that it was not constitutionalizing particular programs aimed at combatting sex discrimination, like pay equity laws, and that it was acceptable for governments to act incrementally in an attempt to combat the historical disadvantage of women.[33] However, the decisions send a clear signal that legislative measures that are ostensibly aimed at combatting the historical disadvantage of women should not "codif[y] the denial to women of benefits routinely enjoyed by men", either directly or indirectly[34] – unless, of course, such a result can be justified under s. 1, as in *Centrale* (which did not find the differential treatment itself, but rather the extra time required to address it, to be justified).

§ 55:43 Section 28

Section 28 of the Charter of Rights[1] provides as follows:

> 28. Notwithstanding anything in this Charter, the rights and freedoms referred to in it are guaranteed equally to male and female persons.

Section 28 provides that the rights and freedoms referred to in the Charter "are guaranteed equally to male and female persons".[2] This falls short of a requirement of the equal treatment of "male and female

---

part from unequal distribution of parental responsibilities": *Fraser v. Canada*, 2020 SCC 28, paras. 142, 168, 191-193, 198.

[32]*Fraser v. Canada*, 2020 SCC 28, para. 234 (emphasis in original).

[33]*Quebec v. Alliance du personnel professionel et technique de la santé et des services sociaux*, [2018] 1 S.C.R. 464, para. 42; see also para. 33.

[34]*Quebec v. Alliance du personnel professionel et technique de la santé et des services sociaux*, [2018] 1 S.C.R. 464, para. 38.

[Section 55:43]

[1]For commentary on s. 28, see Gibson, The Law of the Charter: Equality Rights (1990), 206-212; Bayefsky and Eberts (eds.), Equality Rights and the Charter of Rights (1985), ch. 11 (by de Jong); Beaudoin and Mendes (eds.), The Canadian Charter of Rights and Freedoms (4th ed., 2005), ch. 14, 1012-1015 (by Black and Smith); McLeod, Takach, Morton, Segal, The Canadian Charter of Rights (Carswell, loose-leaf), ch. 27; Canadian Charter of Rights Annotated (Canada Law Book, loose-leaf), annotation to s. 28; K.A. Froc, *The Untapped Power of Section 28 of the Canadian Charter of Rights and Freedoms* (PhD Thesis, Queen's University Faculty of Law, 2015) [unpublished].

[2]Section 28 has no equivalent in the Canadian Bill of Rights or in the American Bill of Rights. However, it was inspired by the Equal Rights Amendment, which was proposed by the Congress of the United States on March 22, 1972, and which was still being considered for ratification by the states when the Charter was drafted. The pro-

persons", presumably because that objective is attained by the general equality clause of s. 15.[3] All that s. 28 seems to require is that the other provisions of the Charter[4] be implemented without discrimination between the sexes. To the extent that the other provisions of the Charter would apply equally to male and female persons anyway, s. 28 has very little work to do.

Within its narrow sphere of application, s. 28 is a stronger guarantee than s. 15 in at least two, and perhaps three, respects: (1) the three-year delay in the coming into force of s. 15 (by virtue of s. 32(2)) did not apply to s. 28; (2) the power of legislative override (under s. 33) applies to s. 15, but not to s. 28;[5] and (3) it is possible that even the limitation clause (s. 1) does not qualify s. 28, having regard to s. 28's opening words, "Notwithstanding anything in this Charter".

XIII. OTHER GROUNDS OF DISCRIMINATION

§ 55:44 Age

"Age" is another of the grounds of discrimination that is expressly prohibited by s. 15.[1]

Like the other grounds of discrimination, age is a personal character-

---

posal subsequently lapsed, because it failed to secure ratification by three-fourths of the state legislatures by the deadline of June 30, 1982. The terms of the proposed amendment were as follows:

> Article—
>
> Section 1. Equality of rights under the law shall not be denied or abridged by the United States or by any State on account of sex.
>
> Section 2. The Congress shall have the power to enforce, by appropriate legislation, the provisions of this article.
>
> Section 3. This amendment shall take effect two years after the date of ratification.

[3]In *Nfld. v. N.A.P.E.*, [2004] 3 S.C.R. 381, a provincial statute that postponed pay-equity adjustments to the pay of female hospital workers was held to be a breach of s. 15 that was saved by s. 1 (because it was a response to a financial crisis in the province). Section 28 was apparently not argued by the claimants to resist the application of s. 1. There is no mention of s. 28 in the Court's opinion.

[4]The Charter does not include s. 35 of the Constitution Act, 1982, which guarantees aboriginal and treaty rights. However, by an amendment in 1984, s. 35(4) was added, which provides that:

> Notwithstanding any other provision of this Act, the aboriginal and treaty rights referred to in subsection (1) are guaranteed equally to male and female persons.

[5]Section 28 was not in the October 1980 version of the Charter, but was in the April 1981 version. At the federal-provincial agreement of November 5, 1981, when the override clause of s. 33 was first agreed to, the first draft of the override clause authorized the override not only of ss. 2 and 7 to 15, but also of "section 28 of this Charter in its application to discrimination based on sex referred to in section 15". This provoked a vigorous round of lobbying by women's groups, and the reference to s. 28 was removed from s. 33.

[Section 55:44]

[1]*See Schafer v. Can.* (1997), 35 O.R. (3d) 1 (C.A.) (federal law granting benefits for sick children, but only if they were six months or older, struck down as age discrimina-

istic that is immutable in the sense that it cannot be changed by the choice of the individual. There are, however, two differences between age and the other named grounds of discrimination.[2] First, age is a characteristic shared by everyone. In the course of a normal life span, each individual passes through the various stages of childhood, youth, adulthood, middle age and old age. Each individual of any age has personally experienced all earlier ages and expects to experience the later ages. A minority defined by age is much less likely to suffer from the prejudice of the majority than is a minority defined by race or religion or any other characteristic that the majority has never possessed and will never possess.

A second difference between age and most of the other named characteristics is that there is some correlation between age and ability. That is not true of race, national or ethnic origin, colour, religion or sex, although it is true to some extent of mental or physical disability. In fact, our laws are replete with provisions in which age is employed as the qualification for pursuits that require skill or judgment. Consider the laws regulating voting, driving, drinking, marrying, contracting, will-making, leaving school, being employed, etc. In regulating these matters, all jurisdictions impose disabilities on young people, employing age as a proxy for ability. Such stereotyping is inevitably inaccurate, because individuals mature at different rates. In principle, the use of age could be eliminated, because each individual could be tested for performance of each function. Age is used as a qualification for no other reason than to avoid or reduce the administrative burden of individualized testing. It might be argued that the disabilities imposed on young people by reference to the attainment of a qualifying age should be regarded as discrimination under s. 15, since a disadvantage is imposed by reference to a named ground of discrimination, but it seems likely that the courts will uphold – and there is a strong argument that they should uphold – these disabilities, if not under s. 15, then under s. 1, even though administrative expediency generally does not count towards s. 1 justification.[3]

Consent to medical treatment is one of the areas where legal disabilities are imposed on children. Manitoba's Child and Family Services Act used the age of 16 as a yardstick for capacity to consent, but did so in a much more nuanced way than most laws imposing disabilities on children. The Act authorized a judge to make an order for medical treatment of a child (a person under 18) based on "the best interests of the child". For a child aged 16 or older, there was a presumption of capacity: no treatment order could be made unless the judge was satisfied that the child lacked the capacity to consent to treatment. No such presump-

---

tion under s. 15).

[2]See the discussion by La Forest J. in *McKinney v. U. of Guelph*, [1990] 3 S.C.R. 229, 296-297.

[3]See § 38:17, "Cost".

tion existed with respect to a child under 16. In *A.C. v. Manitoba* (2009),[4] A.C., a 14-year-old girl who was a Jehovah's Witness refused her consent to a blood transfusion that hospital doctors regarded as urgently necessary to save her life or at least protect her from long-term damage to her health. A judge, acting under the power conferred by the Act, ordered that a blood transfusion be given to A.C. The judge acknowledged that A.C. was sufficiently mature to make decisions about her medical treatment, but he decided nevertheless that it was in her best interests to receive the blood transfusion. The blood transfusion was given, and A.C. recovered. Although the validity of the treatment order was moot, A.C. (and her parents) appealed the order as a means of challenging the constitutionality of the statutory power to override the wishes of a mature child under the age of 16. The challenge was based on s. 15 (as well as ss. 2(a) and 7).[5] The Supreme Court of Canada, by a majority, upheld the Act. Abella J., for the majority, pointed out that the Act did not use age 16 as a conclusive determinant of capacity, but merely as the basis for a presumption of capacity. For children under 16, the best-interests standard required the judge to take account of the child's wishes, and to give increasing weight to those wishes as the child's age, maturity and independence increased. Although a presumption of capacity arose at age 16, this was not a breach of s. 15 because the treatment of children both under and over 16 was calibrated in accordance with an individualized judgment of their capacity to make decisions in their own best interests, not their age.[6] For McLachlin C.J., concurring in the result, the Act did make a distinction based on age, but the distinction was not discriminatory because children under 16 were a vulnerable group in need of protection and they were in any case given an input into the ultimate decision on their treatment. Binnie J., who dissented, did not address the s. 15 issue (relying solely on ss. 2(a) and 7).

In *Law v. Canada* (1999),[7] the Supreme Court of Canada upheld a law that denied a benefit to young persons. The federal Canada Pension Plan provided that, on the death of a contributor to the Plan, benefits were to be paid to a surviving spouse. The law that was challenged was a provision that imposed an age qualification on the surviving spouse, excluding persons who were under the age of 35. Although the law imposed a distinction on the listed ground of age, the Court held that it was not discriminatory, because it did not impair human dignity (a now-

[4]*A.C. v. Manitoba*, [2009] 2 S.C.R. 181. Abella J., with the agreement of LeBel, Deschamps and Charron JJ., wrote the opinion of the majority of the seven-judge bench. McLachlin C.J., with the agreement of Rothstein J., wrote a concurring opinion. Binnie J. wrote a dissenting opinion, but did not address the s. 15 issue.

[5]The case is discussed with respect to s. 2(a) in ch. 42, Religion, under heading § 42:6, "Other religious practices", and with respect to s. 7 in ch. 47, Fundamental Justice, under heading § 47:26, "Arbitrary laws".

[6]I think the correct reading of Abella J.'s opinion is that she denies that the Act relies on age as a distinction (implied in para. 111), but she may mean (in agreement with McLachlin C.J.) that the Act does use age as a distinction but one that is not discriminatory (implied in para. 110).

[7]*Law v. Canada*, [1999] 1 S.C.R. 497.

abandoned element of s. 15 that the Court in this case introduced into the jurisprudence for the first time).[8] The Court took judicial notice of the fact that widows and widowers under the age of 35 were more capable than older persons of maintaining or finding employment and replacing the income lost through the death of their spouse. The exclusion of persons under 35 from the benefit scheme did not imply that they were less capable or less worthy, but was simply designed to recognize the reality that older people would be in greater need of support, and to apply limited resources to those in greater need.

Another case in which a law singled out younger people for lower benefits was *Gosselin v. Quebec* (2002).[9] Quebec's social assistance law provided that welfare recipients under the age of 30 received benefits of only about one-third of the standard amount that was payable to persons 30 or over; the lower benefits could be brought up to the standard amount if the under-30 recipient participated in stipulated educational or work experience programmes. In effect, this was a "workfare" scheme, but only for those under 30. The plaintiff, who had been a welfare recipient under the age of 30, and who had for various reasons been unable to access the stipulated workfare programmes, brought proceedings to challenge the validity of the law and to recover the difference between the amount of the welfare benefit that she received and the standard amount that she would have received had she been aged 30. The law imposed a distinction on the ground of age, obviously, but the Supreme Court of Canada, by a majority of five to four, followed *Law* to hold that the distinction was not discriminatory, because it did not impair human dignity. McLachlin C.J. for the majority acknowledged that the welfare scheme (which had been repealed by the time it reached the Court) "was harsh, perhaps even misguided", but held that it did not treat young people as "less worthy or less deserving of respect"; on the contrary, it assumed that they were more able than older people "to benefit from training and education, more able to get and retain a job, and more able to adapt to their situations and become fully participating and contributing members of society".[10] The dissenting judges disagreed, holding that the welfare scheme did impair human dignity. It imposed hardship on the under-30 recipients, "failed to respect them as full persons" and diminished their "feeling of self-worth".[11] The view of the majority prevailed, of course, and the welfare scheme was upheld (as in *Law*) without the need to resort to s. 1.[12]

---

[8]See §§ 55:19 to 55:22, "Human dignity".

[9]*Gosselin v. Quebec*, [2002] 4 S.C.R. 429. The majority opinion was written by McLachlin C.J. with the agreement of Gonthier, Iacobucci, Major and Binnie JJ. Dissenting opinions were written by L'Heureux-Dubé, Bastarache, Arbour and LeBel JJ.

[10]*Gosselin v. Quebec*, [2002] 4 S.C.R. 429, para. 69.

[11]*Gosselin v. Quebec*, [2002] 4 S.C.R. 429, para. 258 per Bastarache J., whose views were shared by the other dissenters.

[12]A challenge under s. 7 was also unsuccessful: see ch. 47, Fundamental Justice, under heading § 47:12, "Security of the person".

Wynberg v. Ontario (2006)[13] was a challenge to a provincial government program that supplied therapy to pre-school children with autism. The program ceased once a child attained the age of six. The distinction between those children (aged two to five) who benefited from the program and those who did not (aged six and over) was based on age. However, the Court of Appeal of Ontario upheld the program on the basis that it did not impair the human dignity of children aged six and over. The program was directed to children aged two to five, because expert opinion held that very young children responded best to the therapy. It was true that the autism did not cease at age six, even in the most successful cases, but the particular program was so time consuming and intensive (20 to 40 hours of one-on-one therapy) that it was only possible to deliver it to children who were not yet attending school full-time. The Court concluded that the program corresponded to the needs and circumstances of children aged two to five; and for this reason did not impair the human dignity of school-age children who were denied the therapy (and who were not provided with any alternative program in school for their autism).

In *Canadian Foundation for Children, Youth and the Law v. Canada* (2004),[14] the issue was the constitutionality of s. 43 of the Criminal Code, which made it a defence to a charge of assault for a schoolteacher or parent to use force "by way of correction toward a pupil or child" provided that "the force does not exceed what is reasonable in the circumstances". The law was unsuccessfully challenged under s. 15.[15] The law drew a distinction on the basis of age, since "a pupil or child" was left unprotected by the Criminal Code from force that would amount to an assault if committed against an adult. However, the distinction was not discriminatory, because it did not impair the dignity of the children who were exposed to the corrective force. In the Supreme Court of Canada, McLachlin C.J., writing for the majority, held that the decriminalization of corrective force against children was not based on a devaluation of children, but was based on the view that the criminal law should not intrude into normal school and family discipline. The criminal law remained available to punish force that was violent or abusive.[16] The criminal law was only excluded by s. 43 "where the force is part of a

---

[13]*Wynberg v. Ontario* (2006), 82 O.R. (3d) 561 (C.A.) (leave to appeal to S.C.C. denied April 12, 2007).

[14]*Canadian Foundation for Children, Youth and the Law v. Canada*, [2004] 1 S.C.R. 76. The majority opinion upholding the law was written by McLachlin C.J. with the agreement of Gonthier, Iacobucci, Major, Bastarache and LeBel JJ. Binnie J. dissented in part, holding that the law was invalid with respect to schoolteachers, but not parents. Arbour and Deschamps JJ. wrote dissenting opinions, holding that the law was invalid. Arbour J. based her decision on s. 7, and did not discuss s. 15. Deschamps J. based her decision on s. 15.

[15]Challenges under ss. 7 (fundamental justice) and 12 (cruel and unusual punishment) were also rejected by the Court.

[16]Arbour J. in her dissenting opinion (paras. 153-170, dealing with the s. 7 argument) listed numerous recent reported cases where teachers and parents had been charged with assault and acquitted under s. 43 despite the use of force that was far from

genuine effort to educate the child, poses no reasonable risk of harm that is more than transitory or trifling, and is reasonable under the circumstances".[17] The introduction of the criminal law into families or schools in such circumstances "would harm children more than help them".[18] She concluded that the s. 43 defence "is firmly grounded in the actual needs and circumstances of children", and therefore does not impair their dignity.[19] Binnie and Deschamps JJ., dissenting, held that s. 43 offended s. 15. In their view, the use of corrective force against children did impair their dignity, and the goal of keeping the criminal law out of schools and families was a justification that was more properly addressed under s. 1. For Binnie J., the law was justified under s. 1 in its application to parents, but not in its application to teachers. For Deschamps J., the law was unjustified in its entirety. (Arbour J., the third dissenting judge, would also have struck down the law, but under s. 7, not s. 15, which she did not discuss.)

Advancing age also leads to a decline in ability, culminating in death. This is reflected in the widespread adoption in workplaces of mandatory retirement rules, typically requiring an employee to retire at the age of 65. These rules are reinforced by pay scales that increase with seniority, by relatively lax assessment procedures for workers drawing near to retirement, by private and public pension schemes that commence payment at the retirement age and by human rights codes that withdraw their prohibitions on age discrimination at the age of 65.

The Supreme Court of Canada decided a group of four mandatory requirement cases in 1990. The principal decision was *McKinney v. University of Guelph* (1990),[20] in which a number of university professors in Ontario challenged the mandatory retirement policies of their universities. The second case[21] involved the same issue in universities in British Columbia. The third case[22] involved the admitting privileges of doctors at a hospital in British Columbia. The fourth case[23] involved professors at a community college in British Columbia. The first three cases were all held to be outside the scope of the Charter, because the universities and the hospital operated outside the control of government.

---

trifling and transitory. McLachlin C.J. answered this point (para. 40) with a detailed "interpretation" of s. 43 that would exclude various categories of force that she assumed to be abusive or violent or ineffective. The dissenting judges took the view (Binnie J., para. 81; Arbour J., paras 132-141; Deschamps J., paras. 215-217) that such a wholesale rewriting of the section went beyond permissible interpretation.

[17]*Canadian Foundation for Children, Youth and the Law v. Canada*, [2004] 1 S.C.R. 76, para. 59.

[18]*Canadian Foundation for Children, Youth and the Law v. Canada*, [2004] 1 S.C.R. 76, para. 59.

[19]*Canadian Foundation for Children, Youth and the Law v. Canada*, [2004] 1 S.C.R. 76, para. 68.

[20]*McKinney v. University of Guelph*, [1990] 3 S.C.R. 229.

[21]*Harrison v. U.B.C.*, [1990] 3 S.C.R. 451.

[22]*Stoffman v. Vancouver General Hospital*, [1990] 3 S.C.R. 483.

[23]*Douglas/Kwantlen Faculty Assn. v. Douglas College*, [1990] 3 S.C.R. 570.

Only the fourth case was within the scope of the Charter, because the community college was more tightly controlled by government than the other institutions. (These are leading cases on the application of the Charter, and are discussed from that standpoint in ch. 37, Application of Charter.) Despite the fact that the Charter did not apply to the universities and the hospital, the Court went on to examine the constitutionality of mandatory retirement in those institutions[24] as if s. 15 did apply. The Court held unanimously that mandatory retirement was discrimination by age and was therefore in violation of s. 15, but the Court by a majority[25] went on to decide that mandatory retirement was saved by s. 1. The result, therefore, was that mandatory retirement was upheld.

The Supreme Court of Canada in *McKinney* and the other mandatory retirement cases had no difficulty in finding discrimination within s. 15 of the Charter. The mandatory retirement rules imposed a disadvantage (retirement)[26] on a defined group by its age (65), and age was one of the grounds of discrimination named in s. 15. Therefore, there was a breach of s. 15. The issue then moved to s. 1. Could the mandatory retirement rules be justified as a reasonable limit that was demonstrably justified in a free and democratic society? The majority of the Court answered yes. Within the universities, the rules permitted faculty renewal by opening up positions for younger faculty, and they supported tenure (or employment security) by minimizing the need for continuous performance assessments of older faculty.[27] Within the hospital, the arguments were essentially the same: the termination of admitting privileges for doctors who had reached 65 created openings for younger doctors, and (despite the absence of a formal system of tenure) reduced the need for regular assessments of the competence of older doctors.

---

[24]In *Douglas/Kwantlen Faculty Assn. v. Douglas College*, [1990] 3 S.C.R. 570, the issue was not reached, because the only question before the Court was whether an arbitration board had jurisdiction to determine the Charter issue; the Court held that the board did have jurisdiction.

[25]In *McKinney v. University of Guelph*, [1990] 3 S.C.R. 229, on the s. 1 issue, La Forest J., with the agreement of Dickson C.J. and Gonthier J., wrote the plurality judgment; Sopinka and Cory JJ. wrote separate concurring judgments; Wilson and L'Heureux-Dubé JJ. wrote dissenting opinions. (The Court divided differently on the s. 32 issue.) The same division occurred in *Harrison v. U.B.C.*, [1990] 3 S.C.R. 451, where the issues were exactly the same. The same division occurred in *Stoffman v. Vancouver General Hospital*, [1990] 3 S.C.R. 483, except that Cory J. moved into the dissenting camp, because of the absence of tenure for doctors in hospitals.

[26]As to whether mandatory retirement is a disadvantage, see § 55:25, "Objective and subjective disadvantage".

[27]A provision of Ontario's human rights code, which excluded persons aged over 65 from the protection against age discrimination in employment, was also upheld on the basis that it was designed to permit (not require) mandatory retirement. In *Dickason v. U. of Alta.*, [1992] 2 S.C.R. 1003, the Supreme Court of Canada upheld mandatory retirement at the University of Alberta in the face of Alberta's human rights code, which prohibited age discrimination in employment (without any upper limit to the age), but which authorized "reasonable and justifiable" arrangements; the majority of the Court followed *McKinney* to hold that mandatory retirement was reasonable and justifiable.

In *Tétreault-Gadoury v. Canada* (1991),[28] the question arose whether a provision of the Unemployment Insurance Act, which denied benefits to persons over 65, was in breach of s. 15. The Supreme Court of Canada followed *McKinney* to hold that the provision violated s. 15. However, the Court departed from *McKinney* to hold that the age-65 bar could not be justified under s. 1. The result was to strike from the Act the provision imposing the age-65 bar.

The rejection of s. 1 justification in *Tétreault-Gadoury* suggests that age distinctions are vulnerable to Charter attack, and even that mandatory retirement in workplaces other than universities (and hospitals) may be unjustified under s. 1. The Court distinguished *McKinney* on three grounds: (1) that a university was "a closed system with limited resources"; (2) that "faculty renewal" was "crucial to extending the frontiers of knowledge"; and (3) that "academic freedom" required a minimum of performance review up to retirement age.[29] These points, especially the second and third, would be inapplicable in non-university workplaces, both public and private. Of course, other justifications might be persuasive in other contexts. In *Tétreault-Gadoury*, however, the Court rejected what seemed to me to be a powerful justification for the age-bar, which was to prevent the doubling up of pension income and unemployment insurance benefits. The applicant in that case was in fact receiving income from three pensions, presumably as a consequence of having attained age 65.

In *Tétreault-Gadoury*, the Court seemed to forget the salutary point that judicial intervention in the complex field of employee retirement is bound to be clumsy, and is likely to produce counterproductive results. If mandatory retirement is unconstitutional in some workplaces, and if benefit programmes cannot be stopped (or started?) at age 65, various consequences are likely to follow. If an employee cannot be counted upon to leave at age 65 (or other arbitrary age), then employee incomes would have to rise more slowly with seniority than they now do, employee performance would have to be monitored more closely than it is now, and the incentive for employers and governments to provide adequate pensions for retired workers would be diminished. No court can adequately measure these effects and weigh them against age-based mandatory retirement.

In *Withler v. Canada* (2011),[30] a statutory benefit programme was attacked as discriminatory on the basis of age. Federal civil servants were entitled to a package of employment benefits that included a death benefit akin to life insurance. When a plan member died under the age of 65, the death benefit was a lump sum equal to twice the annual salary of the deceased plan member. When a plan member died over the age of

[28]*Tétreault-Gadoury v. Canada*, [1991] 2 S.C.R. 22. The opinion of La Forest J. was agreed to by all members of the Court. L'Heureux-Dubé J. added brief concurring reasons not germane to the s. 15 issue.

[29]*Tétreault-Gadoury v. Canada*, [1991] 2 S.C.R. 22, 44.

[30]*Withler v. Canada*, [2011] 1 S.C.R. 396. McLachlin C.J. and Abella J. wrote the opinion of the Court.

65, the death benefit was reduced by ten per cent for each year by which the plan member had survived his 65th birthday. The claimants were widows of plan members who had died over the age of 65, and they attacked the reduction of the death benefit as discrimination based on age. The Supreme Court acknowledged that the statute did create a distinction based on age that was obviously disadvantageous to the claimants. But the Court held that there was no breach of s. 15 because the claimants had not established "discrimination": a "contextual analysis" of the statutory benefit plan justified the conclusion that "the package of benefits, viewed as a whole and over time, does not impose or perpetuate discrimination".[31] The Court did not even advance to the s. 1 stage of the analysis. The situation of the claimants in this case bears an obvious resemblance to *Tétreault-Gadoury*, and it would have been helpful if the Court had explained why it was not following that case, but the Court made no reference to *Tétreault-Gadoury*.

§ 55:45 Mental or physical disability

Mental or physical disability is another of the grounds of discrimination that is expressly prohibited by s. 15.[1] Like the other grounds of discrimination, mental or physical disability is immutable in the sense that it cannot be changed by the choice of the individual. It is not necessarily immutable in an absolute sense, since the condition may be curable. Unlike the other grounds of discrimination, mental or physical disability is often an impairment in ability; and some legal restrictions may properly be predicated on mental or physical disability. For example, a blind person is properly disqualified from holding a driver's licence; and a mentally incompetent person is properly disqualified from making a will. On the other hand, many disabilities can be accommodated by changes to workplaces and public facilities that permit those who are blind, deaf or in wheelchairs (for example) to function effectively. Thus, the rules that discrimination may be unintended, may be indirect, and may require reasonable accommodation,[2] are of special importance for this ground of discrimination.[3]

For example, in *Eaton v. Brant County Board of Education* (1997),[4] the question arose as to what form of accommodation was required by s.

---

[31] *Withler v. Canada*, [2011] 1 S.C.R. 396, para. 81.

[Section 55:45]

[1] See M.D. Lepofsky, "A Report Card on the Charter's Guarantee of Equality for Persons with Disabilities" (1997) 7 Nat. J. Con. L. 263; E. Chadha and C.T. Sheldon, "Promoting Equality: Economic and Social Rights for Persons with Disabilities under Section 15" (2004) 16 Nat. J. Con. L. 27.

[2] See §§ 55:28 to 55:30, "Direct and indirect discrimination".

[3] Sometimes, however, a law directly discriminates on the ground of disability: *O.N.A. v. Mount Sinai Hospital* (2005), 255 D.L.R. (4th) 195 (Ont. C.A.) (striking down provision of Ont. Employment Standards Act denying severance pay to persons whose contract of employment is frustrated by illness or injury).

[4] *Eaton v. Brant County Board of Education*, [1997] 1 S.C.R. 241. The opinion of the unanimous Court was written by Sopinka J. Lamer C.J. wrote a brief concurring judg-

15 in order for a school system to make provision for children with mental or physical disabilities. In that case, the parents of a 12-year-old child with cerebral palsy objected to a decision by a statutory tribunal to move the child out of the regular classroom, where she had been placed for three years, and place her in a separate special-education classroom. The Supreme Court of Canada made clear that the school system had to accommodate to the special educational needs of disabled children, but the Court refused to stipulate what form that accommodation should take. In this case, the decision to place the child in the separate classroom had been reached after a careful process of assessment, which included hearing the views of the parents. The Court held that the s. 15 right belonged to the child, not her parents, and the school system's accommodation must be driven by the best interests of the child. The tribunal's decision had been based solely on an informed determination as to what would be in the best interests of the child. Therefore, the child's placement in a special classroom was an accommodation of her special needs that fully complied with s. 15.

Another case where the parental preference for a particular kind of accommodation for a disabled child was rejected by the courts is *Wynberg v. Ontario* (2006).[5] In that case, parents of school-age children with autism brought proceedings to compel Ontario to provide special education programs in the public schools that would cater to children with autism. The province did provide a particular therapy for children aged two to five (who were not yet in school), and the parents wanted a similar program to be provided to their children, who were aged six and over (and who were in school). The parents' claim was based on two listed grounds of s. 15, namely, age and disability. The age-based claim was rejected by the Ontario Court of Appeal for reasons discussed in the previous section of this chapter.[6] The disability-based claim was also rejected by the Court. The Court held that the therapy that was provided to pre-school children would not be the appropriate accommodation for school children, because it was so time-consuming and intensive that it could not be fitted into a full-time school program without abandoning most of the other instruction. Ontario schools did provide some programs and services for autistic children, but there was little evidence as to the efficacy of these interventions. This meant that the claimants had failed to prove that what was provided was inappropriate, and their claim was dismissed. This case, like *Eaton* before it, illustrates the difficulty faced by parents who are dissatisfied with a school program that purports to accommodate the mental or physical disability of a child. The burden of proof is on the claimants to prove discrimination, and it is hard for persons who are outside the school system to muster the kind of evidence that would persuade a court that the school system has not responded appropriately to the needs of the child.

---

ment on a secondary issue.

[5] *Wynberg v. Ontario* (2006), 82 O.R. (3d) 561 (C.A.) (leave to appeal to S.C.C. denied April 12, 2007).

[6] § 55:44, "Age".

Winko v. B.C. (1999),[7] was a challenge to the provisions of the Criminal Code that provided for the disposition of the accused following a verdict of "not criminally responsible on account of mental disorder". The Criminal Code remitted the issue to a review board, the duty of which was to assess the risk that the accused posed for public safety, and then to direct that the accused be discharged absolutely, or be discharged conditionally, or be detained in custody in a hospital. The accused in this case, who was aggrieved at receiving a conditional rather than an absolute discharge, argued that the provisions violated s. 15 by treating mentally ill offenders differently from other offenders. The Supreme Court of Canada rejected the challenge and upheld the provisions. Although the Criminal Code created a distinction based on the listed ground of mental disability, the provisions did not impair the human dignity of those who were found not criminally responsible. On the contrary, the provisions recognized that mentally ill offenders should not be punished, but should be provided with rehabilitative treatment. Each individual received an assessment of his or her actual personal situation, received the treatment that was judged appropriate to that situation, and was restrained only to the extent judged necessary to protect the public.

Another case where an accommodation had been made to the special circumstances of a class of disabled persons is *Granovsky v. Canada* (2000),[8] which was a challenge to the provisions of the Canada Pension Plan that provided for a disability pension for those who had become unable to work by reason of disability. The federal legislation establishing the CPP required the person claiming the disability pension to establish not only that he suffered from a permanent disability but also that he had contributed to the Plan in five of the previous ten years or two of the previous three years. Mr Granovsky was unable to satisfy the contribution requirement because his disability (a back condition) had prevented him from working long enough in the previous ten years or the previous three years to make the required contributions. The CPP legislation permitted an applicant to drop out of the calculations those parts of the ten-year qualifying period when the required contributions had not been made by reason of a permanent disability. But Mr Granovsky could not take advantage of the drop-out provision, because his periods of non-contribution had been caused by a temporary rather than a permanent disability. He thus fell through the cracks of the legislation and claimed that his failure to qualify for a disability pension was a breach of s. 15. There was no doubt that he had been denied a benefit on the basis of a listed ground (physical disability), but the Supreme Court of Canada held that the denial was not a breach of s. 15.

---

[7]*Winko v. B.C.*, [1999] 2 S.C.R. 625. The opinion of the majority was written by McLachlin J. and agreed with by Lamer C.J., Cory, Iacobucci, Major, Bastarache and Binnie JJ.; a separate concurring opinion was written by Gonthier J. and agreed with by L'Heureux-Dubé J.

[8]*Granovsky v. Canada*, [2000] 1 S.C.R. 703. The opinion of the unanimous court was written by Binnie J.

By giving preference to the claims of those who had been permanently disabled during the qualifying period, Parliament was recognizing a greater need and not impairing the human dignity of those who had been temporarily disabled during the qualifying period.

In each of the cases described so far, an accommodation had been made to the special needs of a class of persons with disabilities. The constitutional challenge was to the appropriateness of the accommodation, and in each case the challenge failed. It was reasonable to conclude that the Supreme Court of Canada was likely to defer to a legislated effort to accommodate persons with disabilities and was not inclined to substitute different remedies, draw qualifying lines in different places, or otherwise redesign the legislated scheme.

This pattern of deference was broken in *Nova Scotia v. Martin* (2003),[9] where the Supreme Court of Canada struck down the provisions of Nova Scotia's statutory workers' compensation scheme that dealt with "chronic pain". Chronic pain is pain that persists after the injury that originally caused the pain appears to have fully healed. The workers' compensation scheme provided only for a four-week program of rehabilitation for a worker who was still suffering from chronic pain after the apparent healing of a work-related injury; after taking the program, the worker was supposed to return to work. The Court held that this program was not appropriate as a general answer to chronic pain, which often persisted beyond the four-week period. The restriction on benefits for chronic pain distinguished between workers with chronic pain and workers with other kinds of work-related injuries. The distinction was based on physical disability, even though the members of the comparison group were also disabled. The distinction also impaired the human dignity of chronic pain sufferers, and therefore counted as discrimination that was prohibited by s. 15. It could not be justified under s. 1. The Court accordingly struck down the chronic pain provisions of the workers' compensation scheme, and postponed the declaration of invalidity for six months to allow the Legislature to come up with some new method of dealing with chronic pain.

The *Martin* case is one where I would have expected the Court to defer to the legislative judgment. The Legislature had addressed the vexed issue of chronic pain, and had designed a plan to accommodate it. The Court frankly acknowledged that chronic pain has no physical manifestations, that there is no received method of diagnosis or treatment, that false claims are hard to detect, and that "the medical evidence before us does point to early intervention and return to work as the most promising treatment for chronic pain".[10] The Court also acknowledged that the benefits of government programs cannot be "fully

[9]*Nova Scotia v. Martin*, [2003] 2 S.C.R. 504. Gonthier J. wrote the opinion of the Court.

[10]*Nova Scotia v. Martin*, [2003] 2 S.C.R. 504, para. 97.

customized".[11] This is true in spades for workers' compensation systems, which are supposed to deliver universal, speedy payment of benefits to injured workers, without the costs, delays and uncertainties of the tort action. But speed and efficiency surely require systems of classification of injuries and standardization of benefits. And yet it seemed to be the lack of individualized assessment that was the fatal flaw in Nova Scotia's chronic pain provisions, a flaw that would surely have to be corrected by a more customized scheme. The Court, by allowing a six-month delay in its declaration of invalidity, was literally allowing the Legislature to find its own solution to the constitutional defect, but the language of the opinion seems to leave little room for any solution other than a costly, contentious case-by-case assessment of every claim of chronic pain. It is hard to resist the conclusion that the Court was directing a rather detailed, and perhaps impractical, redesign of Nova Scotia's workers' compensation scheme. The Court was, as usual, dismissive of concerns based on cost and administrative expediency.[12] The judicial assumption is that, once a Charter breach has been identified, the province simply has to do whatever is necessary to come into compliance. In this case, that would involve moving its workers' compensation plan to more customized benefits (presumably across the board, and not just in the assessment of chronic pain).[13]

The *Martin* case raised questions about the validity of provincial efforts to hold down the cost of the private automobile insurance that is compulsory in most provinces. In Nova Scotia, for example, in 2003, after a steep rise in automobile insurance premiums, the province legislated a cap of $2,500 on "non-monetary damages" (damages for pain and suffering) for "minor injuries" (a defined term) suffered in automobile accidents. (The cap did not apply to "monetary damages" for expenses such as lost wages and health care costs, all of which continued to be recoverable in full.) The purpose of the cap was to reduce damages awards to automobile accident victims, which enabled the province to legislate at the same time a 20 per cent reduction in automobile insurance premiums. In *Hartling v. Nova Scotia* (2009),[14] the cap was challenged by two motorists who had sustained "minor injuries" and had each been restricted to $2,500 in damages for pain and suffering. They argued that the cap infringed s. 15 because it treated those who suffered "minor injuries" differently from those who suffered more serious injuries which were not subject to the cap. The Court of Appeal of Nova Scotia upheld the cap. It was true that (following *Martin*) the cap created a

[11] *Nova Scotia v. Martin*, [2003] 2 S.C.R. 504, para. 82.

[12] *Nova Scotia v. Martin*, [2003] 2 S.C.R. 504, paras. 109, 110.

[13] Compare the more deferential approach in *Auton v. B.C.*, [2004] 3 S.C.R. 657, where the Court denied a s. 15 claim for public funding of therapeutic treatment of autism. See also *Wynberg v. Ont.* (2006), 82 O.R. (3d) 561 (C.A.) (Ontario funds autism therapy for preschool children, but cuts off the funding at age 6; held, no discrimination on the basis of disability or age).

[14] *Hartling v. Nova Scotia* (2009), 314 D.L.R. (4th) 114 (N.S. C.A.). The opinion of the Court was written by MacDonald C.J.N.S.

distinction based on physical disability, and this was disadvantageous to the claimants. Nonetheless, the Court held that there was no breach of s. 15 because the cap was not "discriminatory". The Court relied on the *Laws* factors[15] for this conclusion, but those factors were not very indicative of the outcome, and what the Court was really doing was deferring to the legislative judgment to enact a moderate measure to deal with a difficult issue of public policy—the control of automobile insurance premiums.[16]

An earlier case in which the Supreme Court of Canada granted a s. 15 remedy for discrimination on the ground of disability is *Eldridge v. British Columbia* (1997),[17] where, however, there had been no accommodation of the disability. In that case, the Supreme Court of Canada held that the administrators of British Columbia's health services plan had not accommodated the special needs of deaf people seeking medical services. Deaf persons seeking medical services were not provided with publicly-funded sign-language interpretation. The Court held that this failure was a breach of s. 15. Because communication was a crucial part of the provision of most medical services, it was a denial of equal benefit to deaf people not to provide the assistance that would enable effective communication to occur between a deaf patient and a hospital or doctor.

In *Rodriguez v. British Columbia* (1993),[18] a plaintiff, who suffered from a debilitating, fatal disease (Lou Gehrig's disease), challenged the constitutionality of the Criminal Code offence of assisting a person to commit suicide. She pointed out that this provision had the effect of prohibiting the commission of suicide by a person who was so physically disabled that she was unable to kill herself without assistance. Able-bodied persons, by contrast, were free to commit suicide (neither suicide nor attempted suicide is a Criminal Code offence), because they could do so without assistance. She argued that the prohibition on assisting suicide discriminated on the ground of physical disability, and was unconstitutional by virtue of s. 15.[19] In the Supreme Court of Canada, this argument was accepted by Lamer C.J. and Cory J., who dissented.[20] Sopinka J., who wrote for the majority, did not deal with the argument,

---

[15] *Hartling v. Nova Scotia* (2009), 314 D.L.R. (4th) 114 (N.S. C.A.), paras. 66-95. The factors are listed and discussed earlier in this chapter: §§ 55:19 to 55:22, "Human dignity".

[16] See also *Hernandez v. Palmer*, [1992] O.J. No. 2648 (Ont. Gen. Div.) (upholding serious-injury threshold that barred tort action for automobile accidents below the threshold, and imposed a no-fault scheme on claims that met the threshold); *Morrow v. Zhang* (2009), 307 D.L.R. (4th) 678 (Alta. C.A.) (upholding cap on damages for pain and suffering for minor injuries).

[17] *Eldridge v. British Columbia*, [1997] 3 S.C.R. 624. The opinion of the unanimous Court was written by La Forest J.

[18] *Rodriguez v. British Columbia*, [1993] 3 S.C.R. 519.

[19] The law was also unsuccessfully challenged under s. 7 (see §§ 47:12, 47:15) and s. 12 (see § 53:2). In *Carter v. Can.*, [2015] 1 S.C.R. 331, 2015 SCC 5, a new challenge was successful under s. 7, refusing to follow *Rodriguez* on s. 7. The *Carter* court did not address the equality arguments which were also made in that case.

[20] McLachlin J., with L'Heureux-Dubé J., also dissented, but she relied exclusively

contenting himself with the holding that the prohibition would in any case be justified under s. 1. The prohibition was therefore upheld.[21]

§ 55:46 Citizenship

Citizenship is not a ground of discrimination that is expressly mentioned in s. 15, but we know that it is analogous to those that are expressly mentioned, because the Supreme Court of Canada so held in *Andrews v. Law Society of British Columbia* (1989).[1] In that case, the Court decided that the requirement of British Columbia law that a person be a Canadian citizen as a qualification for admission to the bar of the province was a breach of s. 15 (and was not justified by s. 1). *Andrews* was followed in *Lavoie v. Canada* (2002),[2] in which a majority of the Supreme Court of Canada held that a statutory hiring preference for Canadian citizens in the federal public service was a breach of s. 15 (although the preference was upheld under s. 1). That case also rejected the argument that, because Parliament's power over citizenship entailed the drawing of distinctions between citizens and non-citizens, citizenship laws should be exempt from equality review. What has been accepted by the Court is that the statutory power of deportation can be (and indeed must be) limited to non-citizens. This is because s. 6 of the Charter of Rights guarantees to "every citizen of Canada" the right to remain in Canada.[3]

§ 55:47 Marital status

Marital status is not a ground of discrimination that is expressly mentioned in s. 15, but in *Miron v. Trudel* (1995)[1] the Supreme Court of Canada held that it was analogous to those that are expressly mentioned.[2] The case decided that Ontario's Insurance Act, which dictated the terms of automobile insurance policies in the province, of-

---

on s. 7, asserting (rather cryptically) (at 616) that "this is not at base a case about discrimination under s. 15". However, her reasoning under s. 7 was strikingly similar to Lamer C.J.'s under s. 15.

[21]The prohibition on assisted suicide in the United Kingdom was challenged under the guarantee against discrimination in Article 8 of the European Convention on Human Rights in *Pretty v. United Kingdom* (2002), 35 E.H.R.R. 1. The European Court of Human Rights upheld the law on the basis that an exemption from the prohibition for those who were incapable of committing suicide unaided would "seriously undermine the protection of life which the [challenged law] was intended to safeguard and greatly increase the risk of abuse" (para. 89).

[Section 55:46]

[1]*Andrews v. Law Society of British Columbia*, [1989] 1 S.C.R. 143. See § 55:18, "Addition of analogous grounds".

[2]*Lavoie v. Canada*, [2002] 1 S.C.R. 769.

[3]See §§ 55:33 to 55:38, "Citizenship in s. 6".

[Section 55:47]

[1]*Miron v. Trudel*, [1995] 2 S.C.R. 418. See § 55:18, "Addition of analogous grounds".

[2]See also *Hodge v. Canada*, [2004] 3 S.C.R. 357 (held, no discrimination on the basis of marital status).

fended s. 15 by limiting accident benefits to the legally-married spouse of an insured, which had the effect of excluding common-law spouses. This was discrimination on the basis of marital status.

In *Miron v. Trudel*, Gonthier J., who wrote the dissenting opinion for himself and three others, was obviously concerned that the enrolment of marital status as an analogous ground would strip the ceremony of marriage of all legal significance. And that did, indeed, seem to be the effect of the majority decision. Any legal consequences that were attached to legal marriages would have to be extended to common-law relationships, including same-sex relationships (see next section), and perhaps to all persons living together in relationships of mutual support and dependence without a sexual aspect. Otherwise, the marital-status distinction would cause an infringement of s. 15. To be sure, any legal consequence that purported to be restricted to legal marriages could be justified under s. 1, but this seemed unlikely, since the goal of supporting the institution of marriage would seem to be a discriminatory objective that could not form the basis of s. 1 justification.[3] These conclusions were counterintuitive, considering that s. 91(26) of the Constitution Act, 1867 confers on the Parliament of Canada legislative authority over "marriage and divorce", and s. 92(12) confers on the provincial Legislatures legislative authority over "the solemnization of marriage". Did not those powers imply that some legal significance could be attached to something called "marriage" that was solemnized in a formal ceremony?

After *Miron v. Trudel*, the Supreme Court of Canada added its new requirement of "human dignity" to s. 15.[4] Did that additional barrier to a s. 15 claim protect some elements of marriage? In *Nova Scotia v. Walsh* (2002),[5] the Court said yes. The issue was the validity of Nova Scotia's matrimonial property law, which imposed a regime of shared property on married spouses, which came into effect on the breakdown of the marriage. However, the law was restricted to legally-married spouses. The inevitable challenge came from a woman in a common-law relationship. When the relationship came to an end, her male partner owned more property than she did. She argued that the law was unconstitutional in excluding common-law spouses, and she sought an equal division of the matrimonial property. The Court now accepted unanimously that marital status was an analogous ground under s. 15.[6] But the Court moved on to decide that the exclusion of unmarried cohabitants did not impair human dignity. Bastarache J., who wrote for the majority, denied that the law treated unmarried cohabitants as less deserving of respect than married spouses. The law, he held, was premised on the assumption that only those persons who had made the choice to get

---

[3]Chapter 38, Limitation of Rights, under heading §§ 38:12 to 38:17, "Sufficiently important objective".

[4]*Law v. Can.*, [1999] 1 S.C.R. 497. See §§ 55:19 to 55:22, "Human dignity".

[5]*Nova Scotia v. Walsh*, [2002] 4 S.C.R. 325. Bastarache J. wrote the majority opinion. Gonthier J. wrote a concurring opinion. L'Heureux-Dubé J. wrote a dissenting opinion.

[6]*Nova Scotia v. Walsh*, [2002] 4 S.C.R. 325, paras. 32, 89, 190.

married had committed themselves to a relationship of such permanence that it would justify imposing on them the obligations to contribute to and share in each other's assets. The mere choice to live together, without getting married, could properly be viewed by the Legislature as not sufficient to trigger the radical revision of property rights required by the shared property regime.[7] He concluded that the distinction drawn by the law between legally-married spouses and common-law spouses corresponded to real differences between the relationships, and did not impair the dignity of common-law spouses. The matrimonial property law was upheld.

In Quebec, the family-law provisions of the Civil Code enabled couples to either marry or enter a civil union, in which case, on the break-up of the relationship, the dependent spouse had the right to support from the other spouse and a division of the family property. But a spouse in a common-law or de facto union[8] had no right to spousal support or division of family property.[9] *Quebec v. A* (2013),[10] was a challenge to the constitutionality of the Civil Code's provisions for support and family property based on their failure to extend to de facto couples. The challenge was brought by a woman who had been in a de facto union for seven years with a wealthier man. She had wanted to get married, but the man had refused. The Supreme Court of Canada, by a majority of five to four, upheld her exclusion from the entitlements to support and family property. All nine judges agreed that marital status was an analogous ground of discrimination under s. 15, and that the plaintiff had suffered a disadvantage by reason of her marital status. But the Court then splintered into four camps. LeBel J., with Fish, Rothstein and Moldaver JJ., followed *Walsh* to hold that it was not discriminatory for the Quebec Legislature to offer a choice of different legal regimes to cohabiting couples. By living together without the formality of marriage or

[7]Gonthier J., concurring (para. 203), distinguished *M. v. H.*, [1999] 2 S.C.R. 3 (discussed in the next § 55:48, "Sexual orientation") on the basis that the claimant in this case, as in *M. v. H.*, would be entitled to support from her partner, which would be based on need. But, not having married, she could be denied a division of the matrimonial assets, regardless of need. L'Heureux-Dubé J., who dissented, disagreed. In her view, it was an impairment of dignity to withhold from common-law spouses the division of matrimonial assets that was imposed on married spouses.

[8]The adjective "common law" is usually used outside Quebec; the adjective "de facto" is usually used in Quebec. The evidence in the A case, described next, showed that de facto unions were far more common in Quebec that in the rest of Canada, and were generally accepted as normal in Quebec society.

[9]There was an obligation of child support, and in the A case, described next, the claimant was the beneficiary of an order for child support for the three children of the de facto union. Her constitutional claim was for access to spousal support and a share of the family property.

[10]*Quebec v. A*, [2013] 1 S.C.R. 61, 2013 SCC 5. LeBel J., with Fish, Rothstein and Moldaver J., wrote the plurality opinion. McLachlin C.J. wrote a concurring opinion. Deschamps J., with Cromwell and Karakatsanis JJ., wrote a partially dissenting opinion. Abella J. wrote a dissenting opinion.

civil union,[11] de facto spouses chose to maintain their separate property and not to assume mandatory support obligations. This option did not reflect legislative prejudice or stereotyping (concepts that had replaced human dignity in the equality jurisprudence since *Walsh* was decided), but respect for the freedom of choice of those who wished to organize their relationship outside the mandatory statutory framework constructed for marriages and civil unions. It followed that the claimant had not established the requirement of discrimination, which meant that the de facto regime did not offend s. 15, and it was not necessary to consider justification under s. 1. LeBel J.'s opinion, representing the view of only four judges, was not the majority view on s. 15 because, as will be related, the other five judges held that the challenged provisions did offend s. 15. LeBel J.'s opinion nevertheless became the majority decision because McLachlin C.J. in a separate concurring opinion decided that the de facto regime, although contrary to s. 15, was justified under s. 1.

Abella J., who dissented in the *A* case, took the view that the exclusion of support and property-sharing obligations from the de facto regime offended s. 15. She pointed out that many de facto spouses shared the characteristics of married or civil-union spouses: they formed longstanding relationships, divided household responsibilities and developed a high degree of interdependence. It followed that "the economically dependent—and therefore vulnerable—spouse is faced with the same disadvantages when the union is dissolved".[12] That meant, she argued, that dependent de facto spouses should be entitled to the same economic protections that were provided to those in marriages or civil unions. She also argued that the choice to marry was constrained by so many factors (including the consent of the other spouse) that the failure to marry did not represent a choice that should carry adverse legal consequences. Indeed, she argued that, having accepted that marital status was an analogous ground, that is, one that is "immutable or changeable only at unacceptable cost to personal identity",[13] "it is contradictory to find not only that de facto spouses *do* have a choice about their marital status, but that it is that very choice that excludes them from the protection of s. 15(1) to which *Miron* said they were entitled".[14] That contradiction also infected the decision in *Walsh*, which had in any case been overtaken by developments in equality jurisprudence and should not be

[11]In answer to Abella J.'s point that the vulnerable party is left at the mercy of the other should the other refuse to marry, LeBel J. said (para. 260): "If we accept that an individual's freedom to decide and personal autonomy are not purely illusory, his or her decision to continue living with a spouse who refuses to marry has the same value as that of a spouse who gives in to insistent demands to marry".

[12]*Quebec v. A*, [2013] 1 S.C.R. 61, 2013 SCC 5, para. 283.

[13]*Quebec v. A*, [2013] 1 S.C.R. 61, 2013 SCC 5, para. 335, citing *Corbiere v. Can.*, [1999] 2 S.C.R. 203, para. 13.

[14]*Quebec v. A*, [2013] 1 S.C.R. 61, 2013 SCC 5, para. 335 (emphasis in original).

followed.[15] Finally, she denied that there was any need for the claimant to establish that a distinction based on a listed or analogous ground was motivated by or will perpetuate prejudicial or stereotypical attitudes. The fact that attitudes towards de facto unions had changed in Quebec did not matter; what mattered was "the continuation of their discriminatory *treatment*".[16] Abella J.'s conclusion was that the exclusion of de facto spouses from the economic protections mandated for married and civil-union spouses was discrimination on the ground of marital status and contrary to s. 15.

Abella J.'s opinion was a dissent, but her s. 15 reasoning was expressly approved by four other judges,[17] forming a majority of five. Among these five, however, there was a three-way split on s. 1 justification. All five agreed that the objective of Quebec's matrimonial regime was to preserve freedom of choice for cohabiting couples. For Abella J. herself, the choice that was provided was not sufficiently protective of the dependent party to a de facto union; if a presumptive protective regime had provided support and property-division obligations with an opt-*out* choice, then the choice would have been justified under s. 1, but that was not what the Legislature had done. For Deschamps J., with Cromwell and Karakatsanis JJ., the exclusion of the support obligation was not justified, but the exclusion of the property-division obligations was justified. For McLachlin C.J., who in her s. 15 reasons had condemned the de facto regime as resting on a "false stereotype of choice",[18] that same choice provided s. 1 justification to uphold the exclusions of both support and property-division. This surprising shift in her reasoning caused McLachlin C.J. to cast the fifth vote to create a majority (with the LeBel four) upholding the entirety of Quebec's challenged de facto union regime.

§ 55:48 Sexual orientation

Sexual orientation[1] is not listed in s. 15, but it has been held to be a ground of discrimination that is analogous to those listed in s. 15. In *Egan v. Canada* (1995),[2] a majority of the Supreme Court of Canada held that the federal Old Age Security Act offended s. 15 by making a

---

[15] *Quebec v. A*, [2013] 1 S.C.R. 61, 2013 SCC 5, para. 347.

[16] *Quebec v. A*, [2013] 1 S.C.R. 61, 2013 SCC 5, para. 357 (emphasis in original).

[17] *Quebec v. A*, [2013] 1 S.C.R. 61, 2013 SCC 5, para. 382 per Deschamps J., with Cromwell and Karakatsanis JJ.; para. 416 per McLachlin C.J., although she added some comments of her own on s. 15 (paras. 417-431) which were largely but perhaps not fully consistent with all of Abella J.'s reasoning (para. 423 suggested that "prejudice" and "stereotype" had been perpetuated in the Quebec legislation).

[18] *Quebec v. A*, [2013] 1 S.C.R. 61, 2013 SCC 5, para. 423.

[Section 55:48]

[1] See R. Wintemute, "Sexual orientation and the Charter" (2004) 49 McGill L.J. 1143; W.K. Wright, "The Tide in Favour of Equality: Same-Sex Marriage in Canada and England and Wales" (2006) 20 Int. J. Law, Policy and the Family 249; D. Elliott, "Secrets of the Lavender Mafia" (2006) 5 J.L. & Equality 97.

[2] *Egan v. Canada*, [1995] 2 S.C.R. 513. See § 55:18, "Addition of analogous grounds".

spousal allowance available to a spouse "of the opposite sex" but not to a same-sex partner. The provision was upheld under s. 1 by a narrow five-four majority.

In *Vriend v. Alberta* (1998),[3] the Supreme Court of Canada unanimously held that Alberta's human rights statute offended s. 15 by failing to provide a remedy for a person who had been discriminated against by his employer on the basis of sexual orientation. Since the statute provided a remedy for discrimination in employment on the basis of a host of grounds, including age, sex, race, religion, disability and marital status, the omission of sexual orientation was a denial of equal benefit of the law based on a ground analogous to those listed in s. 15. The omission was not saved under s. 1, because Alberta failed to adduce evidence of a legitimate legislative goal that would be advanced by the failure to protect LGBTQ persons from discrimination on the basis of their sexual orientation.[4]

In *M. v. H.* (1999),[5] the Supreme Court of Canada held by a majority that the exclusion of persons in same-sex relationships from the spousal support obligations in Ontario's family law legislation was unconstitutional. The definition of spouse that had this effect discriminated on the ground of sexual orientation, which was an analogous ground under s. 15, and it also impaired human dignity by implying that persons in same-sex relationships were less worthy of protection than persons in opposite-sex relationships. The definition was not saved under s. 1, because the goals of the legislation, which were to make equitable provision for the economically weaker spouse on the breakdown of a relationship and to ease the burden on the public purse, were not advanced by the exclusion of same-sex couples.

In *M. v. H.*, the Court suspended the declaration of invalidity for six months to give the Ontario government time to revise its legislation. Of course, at that time, the failure to recognize same-sex relationships was endemic to legislation in all Canadian jurisdictions, and they all had to enact amendments to give effect to the holding that same-sex relationships were to be treated equally with opposite-sex relationships. The Parliament of Canada enacted a remedial statute (the Modernization of Benefits and Obligations Act) in 2000, making changes to 68 statutes, of which one was the Canada Pension Plan. The Canada Pension Plan provided that, on the death of a contributor, the contributor's surviving spouse was entitled to apply for a pension. Because the definition of

---

[3] *Vriend v. Alberta*, [1998] 1 S.C.R. 493.

[4] See also *Haig v. Can.* (1992), 9 O.R. (3d) 495 (C.A.) (Canadian Human Rights Act offends s. 15 by failing to include sexual orientation as a prohibited ground of discrimination); *Rosenberg v. Can.* (1998), 38 O.R. (3d) 577 (C.A.) (Income Tax Act offends s. 15 by defining spouse so as to exclude same-sex partners). Compare *Romer v. Evans* (1996), 517 U.S. 620 (striking down amendment to Colorado constitution which would have prevented municipalities from enacting by-laws prohibiting discrimination on the basis of sexual orientation); *United States v. Windsor* (2013), 570 U.S. xxx (striking down federal Defence of Marriage Act which defined "marriage" and "spouse" for all Acts of Congress as excluding same-sex partners).

[5] *M. v. H.*, [1999] 2 S.C.R. 3.

spouse was restricted to opposite-sex couples, the remedial statute amended the definition to include same-sex couples. In *Canada v. Hislop* (2007),[6] a class action was commenced by survivors of same-sex relationships challenging the remedial law on the basis of s. 15 of the Charter. The constitutional infirmity asserted by the claimants was that the remedial law was prospective from January 1, 1998, so that persons whose same-sex partners had died before 1998 were ineligible for the survivors' pension. The Court held that s. 15 required that eligibility for the survivors' pension had to be made retroactive to April 15, 1985, when s. 15 came into force.[7] The appropriate comparison was between survivors of opposite-sex relationships whose partners died between 1985 and before 1998 (and who were eligible for the pension) and survivors of same-sex relationships whose partners died in the same time period (and who were ineligible for the pension). The failure to grant eligibility to the latter class was discrimination on the basis of sexual orientation, and could not be justified under s. 1. The Court accordingly struck down the restriction on eligibility in the remedial statute. The Court went on to make a surprising distinction between the rule governing *eligibility* for benefits (which had to be retroactive to the coming into force of the Charter) and the rule governing *payment* of benefits. Although the same reasoning would seem to apply with equal force to both rules, the Court held that Parliament could properly make the payment of benefits prospective only, and the payment provisions were upheld.[8] This produced the unjust result that survivors, who had successfully persuaded the Court that they had by virtue of the Charter become eligible to pensions before the coming into force of the remedial law, were only entitled to actually receive payments after the coming into force of the law and this despite the fact that LGBTQ CPP contributors had paid exactly the same premiums as heterosexual contributors.[9]

---

[6] *Canada v. Hislop*, [2007] 1 S.C.R. 429. LeBel and Rothstein JJ. wrote the opinion of the six-judge majority. Bastarache J. wrote a concurring opinion, disagreeing with the majority reasoning on the retroactivity of payments (but concurring in the result).

[7] Section 15 came into force three years after the rest of the Charter: § 55:4, "Section 15 of Charter".

[8] The text omits some irrelevant complications. The remedial statute came into force in July 2000. The statute was slightly retroactive in that (as explained in the text) the statute made the eligibility rule prospective from January 1, 1998. It made the payment rule prospective from July 2000. The Court held that a 12-month period of retroactivity had to be added to the payment rule, because the general rule under the CPP was that benefit arrears were payable for up to 12 months prior to the application for survivor benefits. But (as explained in the text) the Court unaccountably (and without engaging in s. 1 analysis) rejected the claimants' argument that, because they had been unconstitutionally denied eligibility to apply for benefits from 1985 to 2000, the payment of arrears should not be limited to 12 months from the date of application, but should go back to 1985.

[9] The failure to grant a retroactive remedy with respect to the payments is criticized in ch. 58, Effect of Unconstitutional Law, under heading § 58:1, "Invalidity of unconstitutional law".

In *Little Sisters Book and Art Emporium v. Canada* (2000),[10] it was argued that the federal customs legislation discriminated against the LGBTQ communities by prohibiting the importation of obscene books and magazines. The argument was made by the Little Sisters bookstore, which served the LGBTQ communities in Vancouver. The bookstore had suffered great difficulties in importing LGBTQ erotica because customs officials frequently withheld the material that it attempted to import. The Supreme Court of Canada unanimously agreed that the customs officials did indeed target the imports of Little Sisters because of the LGBTQ content, that this treated the LGBTQ communities differently than the heterosexual communities, and that the dignity of the persons seeking to import material was diminished by the differential treatment. Therefore, there was a breach of s. 15. However, the Court did not agree that the discrimination was inherent in the definition of obscenity in the customs legislation; the definition was capable of application to both LGBTQ and heterosexual material without differentiation. The discrimination occurred "at the administrative level in the implementation of the customs legislation".[11] The legislation itself did not offend s. 15, and the remedy was not to strike down the legislation, but to insist on more even-handed and sensitive administration of the legislation.

The traditional definition of marriage, espoused by the common law, is "the voluntary union for life of one man and one woman, to the exclusion of all others".[12] The reference to "one man and one woman" excluded the possibility of same-sex marriage. This led to challenges by same-sex couples who wished to get married. In 2003, the courts in British Columbia, Ontario and Quebec all held that the opposite-sex requirement for marriage constituted discrimination on the ground of sexual orientation.[13] This was invalid as a breach of s. 15, which could not be justified under s. 1. The Attorney General of Canada had supported the traditional definition of marriage in all three cases. After losing the cases, the Government changed its policy. It decided not to appeal the decisions,[14] and, instead, to introduce legislation defining marriage as "the lawful union of *two persons* to the exclusion of all others". The Government directed a reference to the Supreme Court of Canada for an advisory opinion as to whether the new law would be constitutional. In

---

[10] *Little Sisters Book and Art Emporium v. Canada*, [2000] 2 S.C.R. 1120; the discussion of equality is at paras. 108-125 per Binnie J. for majority and para. 165 per Iacobucci J. for minority (agreeing on this issue).

[11] *Little Sisters Book and Art Emporium v. Canada*, [2000] 2 S.C.R. 1120, para. 125.

[12] *Hyde v. Hyde* (1866), L.R. 1 P.&D. 130, 133 per Lord Penzance. In the province of Quebec, the definition was statutory: Federal Law-Civil Law Harmonization Act, No. 1, S.C. 2001, c. 4, s. 5 (applicable only to Quebec).

[13] *EGALE v. Can.* (2003), 225 D.L.R. (4th) 472 (B.C.C.A.); *Halpern v. Can.* (2003), 225 D.L.R. (4th) 529 (Ont. C.A.); *Hendricks v. Que.*, [2002] R.J.Q. 2506 (Que. Sup. Ct.).

[14] An appeal of the *Hendricks v. Que.*, [2002] R.J.Q. 2506 (Que. Sup. Ct.) had been commenced, but it was discontinued by the Attorney General, and the Court of Appeal of Quebec refused to allow another party to pursue the appeal: *Hendricks v. Can.* (2004), 238 D.L.R. (4th) 577 (Que. C.A.).

the *Same-Sex Marriage Reference* (2004),[15] the Court held that Parliament's power over "marriage" in s. 91(26) of the Constitution Act, 1867 extended to the legalization of same-sex marriage.[16] The Court was also asked to determine whether the opposite-sex requirement for marriage was consistent with the Charter of Rights. This question was, of course, the issue that was dropped when no appeals were taken from the three decisions striking down the opposite-sex requirement. The Court refused to answer this question on the ground that it would serve no purpose, since the Government was planning to introduce legislation to eliminate the opposite-sex requirement. The Government did introduce the legislation and it was passed.[17] This made Canada the fourth country (after The Netherlands, Belgium and Spain) to enact a definition of marriage that includes same-sex unions.[18]

While Parliament has the power over "marriage" (s. 91(26)), the provincial Legislatures have the power over "the solemnization of marriage in the province" (s. 92(12)). In providing for solemnization, the provinces are of course bound by the federal definition of marriage. However, in *Re Marriage Commissioners* (2011),[19] Saskatchewan proposed a law allowing "marriage commissioners" (civil officials authorized to perform civil marriages) to refuse to solemnize a marriage that would be contrary to their personal religious beliefs. The province directed a reference to the Saskatchewan Court of Appeal for a ruling on whether the proposed law would be valid. The evidence was that the solemnization of same-sex marriages would be contrary to the personal religious beliefs of some of the marriage commissioners. The evidence also showed that many religious denominations refused to solemnize same-sex marriages, which meant that civil marriage was an important option for same-sex couples. The Court held that the effect of the proposed law would be to raise obstacles to the civil marriage of same-sex couples that did not exist for opposite-sex couples. That was a "negative distinction based on sexual orientation", and one that perpetuated historical discrimination and stereotypes about the lesser worth of same-

[15] *Re Same-Sex Marriage*, [2004] 3 S.C.R. 698.

[16] See ch. 27, The Family, under heading § 27:3, "Formation of marriage".

[17] Civil Marriage Act, S.C. 2005, c. 33.

[18] In the United States, the power over marriage belongs to the state Legislatures, not the federal Congress. By 2015, eleven states and the District of Columbia had enacted laws legalizing same-sex marriage, and in five other states the highest state court had legalized same-sex marriage. In the remaining states, the traditional definition of marriage remained in place. Then came the decision in *Obergefell v. Hodges* (2015), 576 U.S. xxx, when a five-judge majority of the Supreme Court of the United States (opinion of Kennedy J.) held that the traditional definition of marriage was contrary to the Fourteenth Amendment as a deprivation of the "liberty" of same-sex couples without due process of law and a denial to same-sex couples of "equal protection of the laws". Since the Fourteenth Amendment applies to the states, after that decision all states were required to license same-sex marriages in the state and recognize same-sex marriages legally performed outside the state.

[19] *Re Marriage Commissioners* (2011), 327 D.L.R. (4th) 669 (Sask. C.A.). For fuller description, see ch. 42, Freedom of Religion, under heading § 42:11, "Religious marriage".

sex unions.[20] The law offended s. 15 for that reason. The law was not saved by s. 1: the religious freedom of the marriage commissioners had to "yield to the larger public interest" in the "impartial and non-discriminatory" delivery of public services.[21] The Court concluded that the proposed law would be invalid.

§ 55:49 Place of residence

Place of residence is not an analogous ground.[1] It lacks the element of immutability that is common to most of the listed grounds, and which factors heavily into the decision about whether to recognize a new analogous ground.

In *R. v. Turpin* (1989),[2] a provision of the Criminal Code that was applicable only in Alberta gave to a person accused of murder the right to waive trial by jury and elect trial by judge alone. In the other provinces, trial by jury could not be waived. Three accused, who were charged with murder in Ontario and wished to be tried by judge alone, argued that the Code's denial of a trial by judge alone in Ontario was a breach of s. 15, because they would have had that option had they been tried in Alberta. Wilson J. for a unanimous Supreme Court rejected the argument on another ground,[3] but she also held that province of residence was not an analogous ground. However, she added the obscure qualification that perhaps "in some circumstances" a person's province of residence could be "a personal characteristic of the individual or group capable of constituting a ground of discrimination."[4] She did not address the point that province of residence is a matter of personal choice, lacking the characteristic of immutability.

In *Corbiere v. Canada* (1999),[5] members of the Batchewana Indian Band who lived off the band's reserve challenged the provision of the Indian Act that made residence on the reserve a requirement for voting in band elections. The Supreme Court unanimously held that "Aboriginality-residence" was an analogous ground, and that the voting requirement, being based on that ground, was a breach of s. 15. However,

---

[20] *Re Marriage Commissioners* (2011), 327 D.L.R. (4th) 669 (Sask. C.A.), paras. 44-45 per Richards J.A. for the majority, paras.106-108 per Smith J.A. for the concurring minority.

[21] *Re Marriage Commissioners* (2011), 327 D.L.R. (4th) 669 (Sask. C.A.), paras. 98, 100 per Richards J.A. for the majority, para.161 per Smith J.A. for the concurring minority.

[Section 55:49]

[1] Place of residence will be a ground of unconstitutional discrimination under the right to vote in s. 3 where malapportioned electoral districts make an urban vote significantly less effective than a rural vote: ch. 45, Voting, under heading § 45:3, "One person, one vote". See also P.W. Hogg, "Equality as a Charter Value in Constitutional Interpretation" (2003) 20 Supreme Court L.R. (2d) 113.

[2] *R. v. Turpin*, [1989] 1 S.C.R. 1296.

[3] The reasoning is described in § 55:27, "Group disadvantage".

[4] *R. v. Turpin*, [1989] 1 S.C.R. 1296, 1333.

[5] *Corbiere v. Canada*, [1999] 2 S.C.R. 203.

the Court was at pains to make clear that its decision was confined to "off-reserve band member status" and did not apply to residence in general. "The ordinary 'residence' decision faced by the average Canadian should not be confused with the profound decisions Aboriginal band members make to live on or off their reserves, assuming choice is possible."[6] For an aboriginal person, the decision to live off the reserve was often dictated by the inadequate size of the reserve, the lack of housing and job opportunities on the reserve, and the fact that previous amendments to the Indian Act (now reversed) had removed band membership from some Indians and forced them to move off the reserve. Residence off the reserve was therefore in many cases practically immutable in that the contrary decision would involve unacceptable personal cost.[7]

Apart from the special case of Indian reserves, the high level of personal mobility in Canada suggests that the difficulties of changing one's place of residence should not be regarded as so great as to qualify place of residence as an analogous ground.[8] As well, place of residence raises some distinctive considerations in a federal state such as Canada.

Differences in the treatment of individuals that are caused by federalism must be able to be accommodated by the Charter of Rights.[9] It cannot be a breach of s. 15 that the minimum wage is higher in Manitoba than it is in Prince Edward Island, or that nurses have the right to strike in Ontario but not in Alberta. These differences flow from the fact that labour law is a matter coming within property and civil rights in the province, which is one of the topics allocated to the jurisdiction of provincial Legislatures by s. 92 of the Constitution Act, 1867. The federal distribution of powers is a fundamental characteristic of the Constitution of Canada. Differences between provincial laws are the inevitable outcome of ten provincial Legislatures, each exercising extensive legislative authority, each acting independently, and each accountable to a different local population. "There can be no question, then, that unequal treatment which stems solely from the exercise, by provincial legislators, of their legitimate jurisdictional powers cannot be the subject of a s. 15(1) challenge on the basis only that it creates distinctions based on province of residence".[10]

If federalism must be an exception to the guarantee of equality, how far does the exception extend? As a minimum, federalism must preclude an argument that involves comparing the law of one province with the law of another province. As argued in the previous paragraph, that line of argument is inadmissible under s. 15. The same conclusion would

---

[6] *Corbiere v. Canada*, [1999] 2 S.C.R. 203, para. 15; para. 62 is similar.

[7] Compare *Kahkewistahaw First Nation v. Taypotat*, [2015] 2 S.C.R. 548, 2015 SCC 30, para. 26 (on-reserve residence is not an analogous ground).

[8] Contra, Gibson, The Law of the Charter: Equality Rights (1990), 159, emphasizing "the powerful deterrents to migration that so frequently exist in the real world".

[9] See §§ 55:33 to 55:38, "Discrimination permitted by Constitution".

[10] *R. v. S. (S.)*, [1990] 2 S.C.R. 254, 288 per Dickson C.J. (obiter dictum).

seem to follow when the Charter claim involves a comparison between a federal law and a provincial law. Once again, two independent legislative bodies, exercising the jurisdictions conferred on them by the Constitution Act, 1867, responding to different electorates, will inevitably produce different outcomes, and s. 15 ought not to be interpreted as denying such a basic federal fact.[11]

Does s. 15 require that federal laws be uniform across the country? In areas of federal jurisdiction, the federal Parliament has the authority to enact uniform national laws. However, apart from any effect of the equality guarantee, there is no constitutional requirement that federal laws must apply uniformly across the country, and in fact many federal laws do not do so.[12] In *R. v. S.(S.)* (1990),[13] the Supreme Court of Canada considered the question of whether the Parliament of Canada could make distinctions between different provinces without offending the equality guarantee.[14] At issue was a provision of the federal Young Offenders Act which authorized the Attorney General of each province to establish a programme of "alternative measures" to divert young offenders away from the courts. Not only did this provision contemplate that different provinces would establish different programmes, it also permitted a province to establish no programme at all. A young offender in Ontario, where there was no programme, argued that the failure of Ontario to establish a programme, when nine other provinces had done so, was a violation of his equality right under s. 15. This argument was rejected by the Court for reasons not germane to the present topic.

In *S.*, no challenge was actually made to the provisions of the Young Offenders Act that authorized the establishment (or non-establishment) of differing provincial diversion programmes. However, Dickson C.J., for a unanimous Court, went on to discuss the question. After noting that differences between *provincial* laws could never amount to discrimination because of the federal principle,[15] he pointed out that province-based distinctions in *federal* laws could also be "a legitimate means of

---

[11]This issue arose in two cases under the Canadian Bill of Rights, in which the federal Indian Act was compared with the law applicable to non-Indians, which was territorial law in *R. v. Drybones*, [1970] S.C.R. 282 (Indian Act drunkenness offence struck down), and provincial law in *A.G. Can. v. Canard*, [1976] 1 S.C.R. 170 (Indian Act succession rules upheld). The issue was ignored by the majority in *Drybones*, although adverted to by Pigeon J. in dissent; and the issue attracted a variety of opinions in *Canard*.

[12]See ch. 17, Peace, Order, and Good Government, under heading § 17:4, "Definition of national concern". *R. v. Turpin*, [1989] 1 S.C.R. 1296, is an example.

[13]*R. v. S.(S.)*, [1990] 2 S.C.R. 254.

[14]Province-based distinctions in federal laws had been upheld under the equality guarantee of the Canadian Bill of Rights: *R. v. Burnshine*, [1975] 1 S.C.R. 693; *R. v. Cornell*, [1988] 1 S.C.R. 461. However, the *pre-Andrews* cases in provincial courts of appeal had sometimes struck down such distinctions under s. 15: e.g., *R. v. Hamilton* (1986), 57 O.R. (2d) 412 (C.A.); *R. v. Frohman* (1987), 60 O.R. (2d) 125 (C.A.); *Re French in Criminal Proceedings* (1987), 44 D.L.R. (4th) 16 (Sask. C.A.).

[15]*R. v. S. (S.)*, [1990] 2 S.C.R. 254.

forwarding the values of a federal system".[16] This was especially so in the field of criminal justice, where "the balancing of national interests and local concerns has been accomplished by a constitutional structure that both permits and encourages federal-provincial co-operation".[17] He concluded that the diversion-programmes authority in the Young Offenders Act was an appropriate reflection of federal values, allowing as it did the adoption of diversion programmes that were suitable to the particular needs of local communities. Therefore, the distinctions in the Young Offenders Act based on province of residence did not constitute discrimination within s. 15.

In *Haig v. Canada* (1993),[18] an equality challenge was made to the federal referendum that was held to approve the set of constitutional amendments known as the Charlottetown Accord. The referendum was held under the authority of a federal statute, which authorized the federal government (the Governor in Council) to hold a referendum in "one or more provinces". The government held the federal referendum in all provinces (and territories) except for Quebec. The reason for the exclusion of Quebec was that Quebec had enacted its own referendum statute, and the province held a provincial referendum on the same question on the same date. Unfortunately, the dual referendums left a gap in coverage. The qualification for voting in the federal election was residence on voting day in one of the nine provinces and two territories that were covered by the federal referendum. The qualification for voting in the Quebec election was residence in Quebec for six months prior to voting day. The plaintiff in *Haig* moved to Quebec from Ontario two months before voting day. The move disqualified him from the federal franchise and did not qualify him for the Quebec franchise. He challenged the constitutionality of the federal referendum's exclusion of Quebec. L'Heureux-Dubé J., who wrote for the majority of the Supreme Court of Canada, quoted and followed Dickson C.J.'s opinion in *S.* Without examining the reasons that led to the exclusion of Quebec from the federal referendum, she assumed that the decision not to apply the federal referendum law in all of the provinces was a legitimate reflection of "the values of a federal system";[19] she concluded that the decision could not be attacked under s. 15.

The opinions in *S.* and *Haig* do not say that every province-based distinction in a federal law is invulnerable to s. 15 attack. However, the opinions make clear that differences between the provinces do not disappear in fields of federal jurisdiction. Even if province of residence were a personal characteristic that could be the basis of discrimination under s. 15, it seems obvious that distinctions in federal laws based on province

[16]*R. v. S.(S.)*, [1990] 2 S.C.R. 254, 289.

[17]*R. v. S.(S.)*, [1990] 2 S.C.R. 254, 289, 290.

[18]*Haig v. Canada*, [1993] 2 S.C.R. 995. The opinion of the majority was written by L'Heureux-Dubé J. The two concurring opinions of Cory and McLachlin JJ. and the two dissenting opinions of Lamer C.J. and Iacobucci J. did not need to address the equality argument.

[19]*Haig v. Canada*, [1993] 2 S.C.R. 995, 1047.

of residence would usually be accepted as a proper reflection of federal values. Distinctions based on province of residence that are caused by different laws in different provinces will always be accepted as an inevitable outcome of a federal system.

Each province is organized into municipalities, and each municipality has an elected council with extensive by-law making powers delegated to it by the provincial Legislature. The inevitable outcome is that the residents of each municipality are governed by a set of by-laws that regulate their use of land and many other matters somewhat differently from the residents of other municipalities. In this way, each province is like a federal system in miniature.[20] It would be destructive of local self-government to interpret s. 15 as requiring that municipal by-laws must all be uniform. For the same reason, provincial laws that make distinctions between municipalities should not be held in breach of s. 15. In *Siemens v. Manitoba* (2003),[21] for example, a provincial law established a local-option scheme for video lottery gaming in the province. Each municipality was authorized by the law to hold a plebiscite on the banning of video lottery terminals. The provincial law gave effect to any such plebiscite by providing that video lottery gaming was prohibited in any municipality in which the electors had held a plebiscite and approved the ban. The law also singled out the town of Winkler, which had held such a plebiscite before the passage of the enabling law. In that plebiscite, the electors had resolved to request the province to ban video lottery terminals in Winkler. Because the electors of Winkler had already expressed their opinion in a plebiscite, the provincial law directly prohibited video lottery gaming in Winkler. The operators of video lottery terminals in Winkler challenged this prohibition under s. 15. The Supreme Court of Canada (citing *Haig)* doubted that place of residence could be an analogous ground under s. 15, and held that it certainly was not in this case, where the law simply gave effect to the majority will of the residents of the municipality.[22]

§ 55:50 Occupation

Occupation is not an analogous ground.[1] It lacks the element of immutability that is common to most of the listed grounds, and which fac-

[20]The scheme of local government, which of course predates confederation, is contemplated by the Constitution Act, 1867, which, by s. 92(8), confers on the provincial Legislatures the power to make laws in relation to "municipal institutions in the province".

[21]*Siemens v. Manitoba*, [2003] 1 S.C.R. 6. Major J. wrote the opinion of the Court.

[22]*Siemens v. Manitoba*, [2003] 1 S.C.R. 6, paras. 48-49.

[Section 55:50]

[1]In addition to the cases discussed in the following text, see *Municipal Contracting v. IUOE* (1989), 60 O.R. (4th) 323 (N.S.A.D.) (employment in construction industry not an analogous ground); *OPSEU v. National Citizens' Coalition* (1990), 74 O.R. (2d) 260 (C.A.) (earning of employment income not an analogous ground); *Can. v. Taylor* (1991), 81 D.L.R. (4th) 679 (F.C.A.) (employment as a teacher not an analogous ground); *R. v. Généreux*, [1992] 1 S.C.R. 259, 311 (employment in the armed forces not an analogous

tors heavily into the decision about whether to recognize a new analogous ground.

In the *Workers' Compensation Reference* (1989),[2] a challenge was mounted against the provision of the Workers' Compensation Act of Newfoundland that denies to an injured worker the right to sue his or her employer in tort for injuries suffered in the course of employment. The reason for the provision, which exists in every province, is to make the workers' compensation benefits the exclusive source of compensation for work-related injuries. It was argued that the denial of the tort action was a violation of s. 15, because other accident victims, for example, those injured in road accidents, could bring a tort action against the person whose fault caused the injury. The Supreme Court disposed of the case in a single paragraph, the essence of which was that the singling out of work-related accident victims was not based on a listed or analogous ground. The brevity of the reasons is unfortunate. The only way in which an individual could avoid the restrictions imposed by the workers' compensation scheme was by not being employed at all. Since that is not a practical choice for those who lack independent wealth, one could well argue that the status of being employed is immutable (not alterable except on the basis of unacceptable costs). However, the ratio decidendi of the case must be that employment status is not an analogous ground.

Many laws single out particular occupations for special treatment. These laws cannot be attacked on the basis of s. 15, since employment status is not an analogous ground. And it is true that an individual's employment in a particular occupation (as opposed to being employed in general) is often a product of personal choice that lacks the quality of immutability.

In *Delisle v. Canada* (1999),[3] the Supreme Court, in a majority opinion written by Bastarache J., held that the exclusion of members of the Royal Canadian Mounted Police from the federal Public Service Staff Relations Act, which regulates labour relations in the federal public service, was not a breach of s. 15. To be sure, the Act placed the members of the RCMP in a worse position than other federal employees, because the exclusion meant that the RCMP was unable to form a certified trade union with the right to bargain collectively (and strike). But a legislative distinction between occupational groups could not be challenged under s. 15, because occupation was not a "functionally immutable" character-

---

ground, but obiter dictum that special circumstances could change this conclusion); *Baier v. Alta.*, [2007] 2 S.C.R. 673 (employment by school board not an analogous ground).

[2] *Re Workers ' Compensation Act, 1983 (Nfld.)*, [1989] 1 S.C.R. 922; affd. *Nova Scotia v. Martin*, [2003] 2 S.C.R. 504, para. 72.

[3] *Delisle v. Canada*, [1999] 2 S.C.R. 989. Bastarache J. wrote the opinion of the majority with the concurrence of Gonthier, McLachlin and Major JJ. L'Heureux-Dubé J. wrote a separate concurring opinion. Cory and Iacobucci JJ. dissented, holding that the exclusion of the RCMP from the collective bargaining regime was a breach of freedom of association.

istic that could qualify as an analogous ground.[4] The Court also rejected an argument based on the guarantee of freedom of association in s. 2(d) on the ground that the police officers still had their common law right to associate even though they lacked the superior statutory rights of collective bargaining.[5]

In *Dunmore v. Ontario* (2001),[6] the Supreme Court, with Bastarache J. again writing for the majority, reversed itself on the freedom of association argument, and held that the exclusion of agricultural workers from Ontario's Labour Relations Act was a breach of s. 2(d) (and could not be saved under s. 1). But the case was not really a freedom of association case. The agricultural workers in *Dunmore* were making an equality claim. The legislation from which they were excluded did not diminish their common law right to associate (which at that time was all that was guaranteed under s. 2(d)). What the legislation did was to give superior rights to other workers in Ontario. The agricultural workers asked to be treated equally with the workers to whom the Act did apply, and the Court said yes. Bastarache J. said that it was "not necessary" to consider s. 15 of the Charter, because the remedy could be had under s. 2(d).[7] With respect, that was a rather disingenuous statement, because, as Major J. pointed out in dissent, it was obvious on the basis of the prior case law that the agricultural workers would not be able to satisfy the analogous ground requirement that had defeated the police officers in *Delisle*. What the Court was doing in *Dunmore* was importing a Charter value of equality into the right to freedom of association in order to avoid its own insistence that equality claims must be based on listed or analogous grounds. This case allows occupation to be a ground of unconstitutional discrimination by the device of importing an equality value into the guarantee of freedom of association.[8] This device is not available, of course, with a law that deals with occupation in ways that do not implicate freedom of association (or other Charter rights).[9]

---

[4] *Delisle v. Canada*, [1999] 2 S.C.R. 989, para. 44 per Bastarache J. for majority.

[5] This case and the *Dunmore* case, discussed next, are also discussed in ch. 44, Assembly and Association, under heading § 44:4, "Formation of association".

[6] *Dunmore v. Ontario*, [2001] 3 S.C.R. 1016. Bastarache J. wrote the opinion for the majority of seven. L'Heureux-Dubé J. wrote a concurring opinion. Major J. wrote a dissenting opinion.

[7] *Dunmore v. Ontario*, [2001] 3 S.C.R. 1016, para. 2. Of the majority judges, only L'Heureux-Dubé J. faced the issue directly in her concurring opinion, in which she held (para. 170) that occupational status should be accepted as an analogous ground, and that the agricultural workers were entitled to succeed under s. 15 as well as s. 2(d). Major J., dissenting, also faced the issue directly, arguing that s. 15 did not apply in the absence of a listed or analogous ground.

[8] See P.W. Hogg, "Equality as a Charter Value in Constitutional Interpretation" (2003) 20 Supreme Court L.R. (2d) 113 (when the Court imports equality values into other rights, such as freedom of association or the right to vote, it leaves out the requirement of listed or analogous grounds and the requirement of an impairment of human dignity).

[9] After *Dunmore*, the Legislature enacted the Agricultural Employees Protection Act, which continued the exclusion of agricultural workers from the Ontario Labour Re-

In the *Health Services Bargaining* case (2007),[10] British Columbia had enacted an Act that purported to override some of the rights possessed by the province's unionized health care workers under their collective agreements. The Act laid down new rules respecting seniority, layoffs, bumping and contracting out, which were designed to give the hospitals and other health-sector employers more freedom in managing their workforce in order to deliver services more efficiently and rein in the costs of publicly funded health care. The unions successfully attacked the Act as a breach of freedom of association in s. 2(d) of the Charter. The Supreme Court did not import an equality value into s. 2(d), as it had done in *Dunmore* (previous paragraph). Instead, the Court held for the first time that s. 2(d) directly protected the union right of collective bargaining. Because the Act substantially interfered with the terms of the collective agreements (the fruits of past collective bargaining), it was invalid. On this robust interpretation of s. 2(d), it made no difference that the Act singled out health care workers (who were predominantly female). If the Act had been perfectly general (applicable to all workers in the province), it would have been equally unconstitutional. The unions also made an equality argument under s. 15, which was based on the singling out of health care workers, and this was rejected unanimously by the Court. The Court said[11] that the adverse effects of the Act on health care workers "relate essentially to the type of work they do, and not to the persons they are." There was no "differential treatment based on personal characteristics". Once again, occupational status was rejected as an analogous ground.

---

lations Act, but which did enact some protections for the associational rights of agricultural workers. In *Ont. v. Fraser*, [2011] 2 S.C.R. 3, the Supreme Court by a majority upheld the Act on the ground that it satisfied the requirements of s. 2(d). The majority opinion and two concurring opinions all rejected a s. 15 challenge based on occupational status: paras. 116 per McLachlin C.J. and LeBel J, 295 per Rothstein J., 315 per Deschamps J. Abella J., who dissented, holding that s. 2(d) was breached, did not discuss s. 15.

[10] *Health Services and Support—Facilities Subsector Bargaining Assn. v. B.C.*, [2007] 2 S.C.R. 391.

[11] *Health Services and Support—Facilities Subsector Bargaining Assn. v. B.C.*, [2007] 2 S.C.R. 391, para. 165 per McLachlin C.J. and LeBel J. for majority; Deschamps J., who dissented on other issues, agreed (para. 170) on this issue.

Chapter 56

Language

I. LANGUAGE IN CANADA

§ 56:1 Language in Canada

II. DISTRIBUTION OF POWERS OVER LANGUAGE

§ 56:2 Distribution of powers over language

III. LANGUAGE OF CONSTITUTION

§ 56:3 Language of Constitution

IV. LANGUAGE OF STATUTES

§ 56:4 Constitutional requirements
§ 56:5 Quebec's Charter of the French Language
§ 56:6 Manitoba's Official Language Act
§ 56:7 Incorporation by reference
§ 56:8 Delegated legislation

V. LANGUAGE OF COURTS

§ 56:9 Constitutional requirements
§ 56:10 Definition of courts
§ 56:11 Language of process
§ 56:12 Language of proceedings
§ 56:13 Right to interpreter

VI. LANGUAGE OF GOVERNMENT

§ 56:14 Section 16 of Charter
§ 56:15 Section 20 of Charter

VII. LANGUAGE OF COMMERCE

§ 56:16 Language of commerce

VIII. LANGUAGE OF EDUCATION

§ 56:17 Section 93 of Constitution Act, 1867
§ 56:18 Mackell case
§ 56:19 Section 23 of the Charter
§ 56:20 Mother tongue of parent
§ 56:21 Language of instruction of parent in Canada

§ 56:22 Language of instruction of child in Canada
§ 56:23 Where numbers warrant
§ 56:24 Denominational schools
§ 56:25 Supervision of remedial orders

I. LANGUAGE IN CANADA

§ 56:1 Language in Canada

Language[1] has been a controversial issue throughout the history of British North America, and the controversy continues to this day. It could hardly be otherwise in a country settled by two different language groups. Because English-speakers constitute a majority in the country as a whole, and French-speakers constitute a majority in the province of Quebec, it is important to determine the distribution-of-powers question of which level of government has the constitutional authority to legislate in respect of language. Because French-speakers constitute a minority in the country as a whole and in every province except Quebec, and English-speakers constitute a minority in the province of Quebec, it is important to determine whether there is constitutional protection for the language of the minority. While English and French, as the languages of the European founders, have been given special constitutional recognition, it must not be over-looked that these questions are also important for the aboriginal peoples, who were here long before the European "founders",[2] and for those immigrant groups that have arrived since confederation and have continued to use their language of origin.

The scheme of this chapter will be, first, to examine the distribution of powers over language, and, secondly, to examine the constitutional protections for minority languages.

II. DISTRIBUTION OF POWERS OVER LANGUAGE

§ 56:2 Distribution of powers over language

It is a remarkable fact that language is not one of the classes of subjects (or heads of legislative power) which the Constitution Act, 1867 enumerates and distributes to the two levels of government. Of course, language could still be held to be a "matter" coming within one of the classes of subjects which are enumerated. The most likely candidate is "property and civil rights in the province" (s. 92(13)), which would mean that the provincial Legislatures had the legislative power. Or language could be held to be a matter which is outside any of the enumerated classes of subjects and which therefore comes within the peace, order, and good government power (s. 91's opening words); this would mean that the federal Parliament had the legislative power.

[Section 56:1]

[1]See P.W. Hogg, "Constitutional Power over Language" in Law Society of Upper Canada, The Constitution and the Future of Canada (Special Lectures, 1978), 229.

[2]The right to speak aboriginal languages is probably protected by s. 35 of the Constitution Act, 1982, which guarantees aboriginal and treaty rights. See generally ch. 28, Aboriginal Peoples.

It is now clear from the decided cases that neither of these solutions is correct. The cases decide that language is not an independent matter of legislation (or constitutional value). Therefore, there is no single plenary power to enact laws in relation to language. Instead, the power to enact a law affecting language is divided between the two levels of government by reference to criteria other than the impact of the law upon language. On this basis, a law prescribing that a particular language or languages must or may be used in certain situations will be classified for constitutional purposes not as a law in relation to language, but as a law in relation to the institutions or activities that the provision covers.[1]

In *Jones v. Attorney General of New Brunswick* (1974),[2] the Supreme Court of Canada upheld the federal Official Languages Act. The Act purported to make the English and French languages the official languages of Canada "in the institutions of the Parliament and Government of Canada".[3] In a unanimous opinion written by Laskin C.J., the Court held that the law was authorized by federal power over federal governmental and parliamentary institutions (which stemmed from the peace, order, and good government power). Provisions recognizing both languages in federal courts could also be authorized by federal power over federal courts (s. 101), and provisions concerning languages in criminal proceedings in provincial courts could also be authorized by the federal power over criminal procedure (s. 91(27)). In the same case, the Court upheld a section of New Brunswick's Official Languages Act, which provided for the use of both official languages in the courts of New Brunswick; this section was authorized by the provincial power over the administration of justice in the province (s. 92(14)).[4]

It is true that in *Jones* the Court did not have to decide, and expressly left open, the question whether the federal Parliament would have the power "to give official status and equality to English and French throughout Canada and in respect of any operations or activities which are otherwise within provincial competence".[5] This dictum does leave open the possibility that a broader language law might be sustainable on the footing that the subject of language had attained a national

---

[Section 56:2]

[1]This passage in the 2nd edition (1985) of this book was approved by the Supreme Court of Canada in *Devine v. Que.*, [1988] 2 S.C.R. 790, 807-808. See also *R. v. Beaulac*, [1999] 1 S.C.R. 768, para. 14.

[2]*Jones v. Attorney General of New Brunswick*, [1975] 2 S.C.R. 182.

[3]The Act was enacted in 1969; it was repealed and replaced by a new Official Languages Act in 1988.

[4]Some of the provisions of the two Official Languages Acts have now been constitutionalized in ss. 16-20 of the Charter of Rights, which are discussed in §§ 56:14 to 56:15, "Language of government". Amendments to these provisions would have to satisfy the relevant formal constitutional amending procedure in Part V of the Constitution Act, 1982. Raising the possibility that amendments to the federal Official Languages Act may also have to satisfy Part V, see ch. 4, Amendment, under headings § 4:6, "Constitution of Canada", and § 4:16, "Unanimity procedure (s. 41)".

[5]*Jones v. Attorney General of New Brunswick*, [1975] 2 S.C.R. 182, 187.

concern which brought it within the peace, order, and good government power of the federal Parliament. However, since *Jones* was decided, the Court has held that the peace, order, and good government power should be confined to subjects of legislation that are relatively narrow and specific;[6] and it seems likely that the subject of language would be too broad to qualify.[7]

In *Devine v. Quebec* (1988),[8] the Supreme Court of Canada upheld various provisions of Quebec's Charter of the French Language that regulated the language of commerce; they required the use of the French language in public signs, commercial advertising, catalogues, brochures, orders, invoices, receipts and other commercial forms. The Court accepted the view, expressed in an earlier edition of this book, that "for constitutional purposes language is ancillary to the purpose for which it is used, and the language law is for constitutional purposes a law in relation to the institutions or activities to which the law applies".[9] In this case, the challenged provisions were in relation to commerce within the province, which was a matter within the provincial jurisdiction over property and civil rights in the province (s. 92(13)).[10]

If it seems odd that such an important topic as language is not one of the classes of subjects enumerated by the Constitution Act, 1867, and is not even an independent "matter" or constitutional value, it should be noticed that the division of legislative power over language, by denying to either level of government full power over language, constitutes an indirect protection of minority language rights.[11] Of course the protection is quite insufficient, but it is not insignificant. For example, the province of Quebec, in legislating to make French the official language of the province,[12] may be incompetent to apply its law to undertakings within the legislative jurisdiction of the federal Parliament, such as

---

[6]Chapter 17, Peace, Order and Good Government, under heading §§ 17:3 to 17:6, "The national concern branch".

[7]Lederman, Continuing Canadian Constitutional Dilemmas (1981), 298.

[8]*Devine v. Quebec*, [1988] 2 S.C.R. 790.

[9]*Devine v. Quebec*, [1988] 2 S.C.R. 790, 808.

[10]For distribution of powers purposes, there was no difference between those provisions that required the exclusive use of French (prohibiting English), and those that required the nonexclusive use of French (permitting English as well). However, although all the provisions were held to infringe s. 2(b) of the Charter of Rights (freedom of expression), the exclusive requirements were not saved by s. 1, while the non-exclusive requirements were saved by s. 1. The Charter aspect of the case is discussed in § 56:16, "Language of commerce".

[11]This is also true of laws respecting other civil liberties; the impact on civil liberties is normally relegated to an incidental or subordinate position for purposes of constitutional classification: see ch. 34, Civil Liberties, under heading § 34:6, "Distribution of powers".

[12]Quebec's Charter of the French Language, S.Q. 1977, c. 5, which was enacted in 1977 to give effect to the language policy of the Parti Québécois government, is by far the most sweeping legislation on language which has ever been attempted by a province. It makes French "the official language of Quebec"; it provides that in most situations everyone has "a right" to use, or be communicated with, in French; it makes French "the language of the legislature and the courts in Quebec", of the "civil administration", of the

federal governmental agencies, federal Crown corporations, banks, shipping lines, airlines, railways, radio and television stations and other undertakings engaged in interprovincial or international transportation or communication, or otherwise within federal regulatory authority.[13]

I shall now turn to the more direct constitutional protections of minority language rights.

III. LANGUAGE OF CONSTITUTION

§ 56:3 Language of Constitution

The Constitution Act, 1867, like all other constitutional instruments emanating from the United Kingdom before 1982, was enacted in English only.[1] The French version that is to be found in the Appendix to the Revised Statutes of Canada[2] is unofficial.

Section 55 of the Constitution Act, 1982 directs the Minister of Justice to prepare a French version of the English-only parts of the Constitution of Canada, and to put it forward for adoption as an official text by the appropriate amending procedures. Although a French text has been drafted and tabled in Parliament by the Minister of Justice,[3] it has never been introduced into the amendment process. So long as the French version of the Constitution Act, 1867 remains unofficial, any discrepancy between the English and French version would have to be resolved by recourse to the English version, because that is the only authoritative one.

The Canada Act 1982 and the Constitution Act, 1982 were enacted by

---

professions, of work, of commerce and business and of instruction in the schools. All this is laid out in a wealth of detail (there are 232 sections in the Act), including exceptions, transitional provisions and elaborate mechanisms of enforcement by various administrative agencies. The provisions of the Act respecting the Legislature and courts were held to be unconstitutional in *A.-G. Que. v. Blaikie*, [1979] 2 S.C.R. 1016. The provisions respecting access to English-language schools were held to be unconstitutional in *A.-G. Que. v. Que. Protestant School Bds.*, [1984] 2 S.C.R. 66. The provisions respecting the language of commercial signs and advertisements were held to be unconstitutional in *Ford v. Que.*, [1988] 2 S.C.R. 712. For the recent history of language rights in Quebec, see W.Tetley, "Language and Education Rights in Quebec and Canada" (1982) 45 Law and Contemp. Problems 177.

[13]See ch. 15, Judicial Review on Federal Grounds, under heading §§ 15:16 to 15:21, "Interjurisdictional immunity".

[Section 56:3]

[1]The instruments listed in the schedule to the Constitution Act, 1982, which comprise the "Constitution of Canada" (see s. 52(2)), include seven Canadian statutes. These were enacted in both English and French, as required by s. 133 of the Constitution Act, 1867. All the other instruments were enacted or made in English only.

[2]R.S.C. 1985, Appendix II, No. 5; see also Department of Justice, *A Consolidation of the Constitution Acts, 1867 to 1982* (2001).

[3]The Final Report of the French Constitutional Drafting Committee (Department of Justice, Ottawa, 1990) contains a French version of all the parts of the Constitution of Canada that were enacted in English only. The Minister of Justice tabled the report in the House of Commons on December 19, 1990.

the United Kingdom Parliament in both languages.[4] The Charter of Rights, being Part I of the Constitution Act, 1982, is therefore in both languages. Section 57 of the Constitution Act, 1982 provides that the English and French versions of that Act are "equally authoritative", and s. 56 provides that the English and French versions of other parts of the Constitution of Canada that have been enacted in English and French are also "equally authoritative". The rule of equal authority is, of course, the only appropriate one for a bilingual country, but it does not tell us how to resolve discrepancies between the English and French versions.

Since confederation, federal statutes have been enacted in both languages, because that was required by s. 133 of the Constitution Act, 1867.[5] The Courts have held that the English and French versions are equally authoritative,[6] and have developed rules for resolving discrepancies.[7] These are the rules that should be applied to the bilingual texts of the Constitution of Canada.[8] The rule that is most helpful is addressed to the case where one language version is doubtful or ambiguous and the other is clear; in that case, the doubt or ambiguity is resolved by reference to the clear version.[9] This rule is really a species of the more general rule that, where there is divergence between the two language versions, that meaning should be selected that is compatible with both versions.[10] However, the meaning selected must be reasonable in the context of the statute. If one language version gives better effect

---

[4]To be precise, the Canada Act 1982 was enacted in English only, but a French version was appended as Schedule A, and the French version was declared in s. 3 to have "the same authority *in Canada* as the English version". The Constitution Act, 1982 was appended as Schedule B; it consisted of an English and a French version, and both versions were declared by s. 57 to be "equally authoritative". See generally J.P. McEvoy, "The Charter as a Bilingual Instrument" (1986) 64 Can. Bar Rev. 155, arguing that the task of interpretation should always start with a consideration of both language versions of the provision to be interpreted.

[5]The federal requirement is now repeated by s. 18(1) of the Constitution Act, 1982. Section 133 imposes a similar obligation of bilingual enactment on Quebec. Section 23 of the Manitoba Act, 1870 imposes a similar obligation on Manitoba. Section 18(2) of the Constitution Act, 1982 imposes a similar obligation on New Brunswick. The remaining seven provinces are under no constitutional obligation of bilingual enactment. But note *R. v. Mercure*, [1988] 1 S.C.R. 234 (statutory requirement in Saskatchewan); *R. v. Paquette*, [1990] 2 S.C.R. 1103 (statutory requirement in Alberta).

[6]*The King v. Dubois*, [1935] S.C.R. 378.

[7]See Beaupré, Interpreting Bilingual Legislation (2nd ed., 1986); Sullivan and Driedger, Construction of Statutes (4th ed., 2002), ch. 10; Coté, The Interpretation of Legislation in Canada (3rd ed., 2000), 323-332.

[8]See A. Gautron, "French/English Discrepancies in the Charter" (1982) 12 Man L.J. 220; R.M. Beaupré, "Vers l'interpretation d'une constitution bilingue" (1984) 25 Les Cahiers Droit 939; Charles, Cromwell, Jobson, Evidence and the Charter of Rights and Freedoms (1989), 62-66.

[9]*The King v. Dubois*, [1935] S.C.R. 378. This rule has been applied to the Constitution Act, 1982 in *R. v. Conway*, [1989] 1 S.C.R. 1659, 1706-1707; *Mahe v. Alta.*, [1990] 1 S.C.R. 342, 370; *R. v. Schmautz*, [1990] 1 S.C.R. 398, 415-416; *Harvey v. N.B.*, [1996] 2 S.C.R. 876, para. 28.

[10]*Jones and Maheux v. Gamache*, [1969] S.C.R. 119; *R. v. Daoust*, [2004] 1 S.C.R. 217, paras. 26, 29; *Montréal (City) v. Quebec*, [2008] 2 S.C.R. 698, para. 53; *R. v. Poulin*,

to the purpose of the statute, then that version should be selected, even if a narrower meaning would be common to both versions.[11] This last rule would also provide the approach to resolving the rare case of irreconcilable conflict between the two language versions.

IV. LANGUAGE OF STATUTES

§ 56:4 Constitutional requirements

The only explicit guarantee of language rights in the Constitution Act, 1867 is contained in s. 133,[1] which provides as follows:

> **133.**Either the English or the French language may be used by any person in the debates of the Houses of the Parliament of Canada and of the Houses of the Legislature of Quebec; and both those languages shall be used in the respective records and journals of those Houses; and either of those languages may be used by any person or in any pleading or process in or issuing from any Court of Canada established under this Act, and in or from all or any of the Courts of Quebec. The Acts of the Parliament of Canada and of the Legislature of Quebec shall be printed and published in both those languages.

Section 133 permits either English or French to be used in debates in the Houses of the federal Parliament and Quebec Legislature; it requires both English and French to be used in the records and journals of those Houses; and it requires the statutes of the federal Parliament and Quebec Legislature to be printed and published in both languages. (Section 133 also provides that either English or French may be used in any pleading or process in the federal courts and the Quebec courts: this part of s. 133 is discussed in a later section of this chapter.)[2]

Section 133 applies only to the legislative bodies (and courts) of the federal government and of Quebec. It does not apply to the Legislature (and courts) of any province other than Quebec. However, the Manitoba Act, 1870 includes, as s. 23, a provision that provides for the use of English and French in the Legislature (and courts) of Manitoba in terms very similar to s. 133. None of the other provinces that were created or admitted after 1867 had language guarantees written into their constituent instruments or terms of union.[3]

The Charter of Rights, which is Part I of the Constitution Act, 1982,

---

2019 SCC 47, paras. 65-68.

[11] *The Queen v. Compagnie ImmobilièreBCN*, [1979] 1 S.C.R. 865. This rule has been applied to the Constitution Act, 1982 in *R. v. Collins*, [1987] 1 S.C.R. 265, 287; *R. v. Turpin*, [1989] 1 S.C.R. 1296, 1314.

[Section 56:4]

[1] For discussion of s. 133, see Royal Commission on Bilingualism and Biculturalism, Report, Book 1 (1967), 52-55; Bastarache (ed.), Language Rights in Canada (2nd ed., 2003), ch. 2. Magnet, Official Languages of Canada (1995).

[2] §§ 56:9 to 56:13, "Language of courts".

[3] But note *R. v. Mercure*, [1988] 1 S.C.R. 234 (statutory requirement in Saskatchewan); *R. v. Paquette*, [1990] 2 S.C.R. 1103 (statutory requirement in Alberta). The Ca-

includes, as ss. 16 to 23, a variety of language provisions.[4] Sections 17 to 19 virtually duplicate the provisions of s. 133 in their application to the legislative bodies (and courts) of the federal government, although not of Quebec. Curiously, however, the Constitution Act, 1982 does not expressly repeal any part of s. 133. Sections 17 to 19 of the Charter of Rights also apply to New Brunswick, so that New Brunswick is now in a similar position to Quebec and Manitoba (as well as being bound by additional language provisions in the Charter).[5]

Confining ourselves for the moment to the enactment of statutes, the effect of the constitutional provisions that have been described is that the federal Parliament, the Quebec Legislature, the Manitoba Legislature and the New Brunswick Legislature are each subject to a constitutional requirement that their statutes must be "printed and published" in both English and French.[6] The meaning of this requirement has been considered in cases arising out of the attempts by Quebec and Manitoba to enact their statutes in one language only. Those cases are considered next.

---

nadian Bill of Rights and statutory provincial bills of rights also contain no protection for language rights, except that the Canadian Bill of Rights, by s. 2(g), and the Quebec Charter of Human Rights and Freedoms, by s. 36, require an interpreter in court proceedings. An interpreter is also required by the Charter of Rights, s. 14.

[4]For discussion of ss. 16-23 see Beaudoin and Mendes (eds.), The Canadian Charter of Rights and Freedoms (4th ed., 2005), ch. 15 (by J. Woehrling and A. Tremblay), ch. 16 (by M. Power and P. Foucher); Bastarache (ed.), Language Rights in Canada (2nd ed., 2003), chs. 3-5; Canadian Charter of Rights Annotated (Canada Law Book, loose-leaf), annotation to ss. 16-23; the last work includes a bibliography of the relevant literature.

[5]The provisions of s. 133, s. 23 and ss. 17-19 are all entrenched in the sense that they cannot be *diminished* by the unilateral action of any of the legislative bodies to which they apply: Constitution Act, 1982, ss. 41(c), 43(b). This was true even before the enactment of the amending procedures in 1982: *A.G. Que. v. Blaikie*, [1979] 2 S.C.R. 1016. However, the provisions do not prohibit the *expansion* of the guaranteed rights: *Jones v. A.G. N.B.*, [1975] 2 S.C.R. 182; *MacDonald v. City of Montreal*, [1986] 1 S.C.R. 460, 496; see also Constitution Act, 1982, s. 16(3).

[6]In *R. v. Mercure*, [1988] 1 S.C.R. 234, it was held that a pre-confederation statute imposed a requirement of bilingual enactment on the Saskatchewan Legislature, and in *R. v. Paquette*, [1990] 2 S.C.R. 1103, it was held that the same requirement applied to the Alberta Legislature. However, the Court made clear that the requirement could be repealed by the Legislature itself, acting in the correct bilingual manner and form; and each Legislature did in fact repeal the requirement: The Language Act, S.S. 1988, c. L-6.1; Languages Act, S.A. 1988, c. L-7.5. *Mercure* and *Paquette* were affirmed in *Caron v. Alberta*, 2015 SCC 56, in which the majority of the Court rejected the argument that legislative bilingualism had been implicitly guaranteed by the 1870 Order made under s. 146 of the Constitution Act, 1867, which added to Canada the territories from which Alberta and Saskatchewan were later created (in 1905). Ontario has moved in the opposite direction, imposing on itself a requirement starting in 1991 of bilingual enactment: French Language Services Act, R.S.O. 1990, c. F.32, s. 3(2); of course, this requirement could also be repealed by the Legislature, provided it acted in the correct bilingual manner and form.

§ 56:5 Quebec's Charter of the French Language

In *Attorney General of Quebec v. Blaikie* (1979),[1] the Supreme Court of Canada struck down those provisions of Quebec's Charter of the French Language[2] that purported to make French the language of the Legislature. The Act provided that bills were to be drafted and enacted in French only, and that only the French version was to be official, although an English translation was to be printed and published. The Court held that these provisions contravened s. 133. It was not sufficient to produce an unofficial English translation of the statutes. Section 133's requirement that the statutes be "printed and published" in both languages should be interpreted as a requirement of "enactment in both languages",[3] especially in light of the requirement that the "records and journals" of the Legislature should be in both languages. Exactly what would be involved in "enactment" was not spelled out by the Court, but it would certainly involve bilingual texts of all bills and all amendments at all stages of the legislative process.[4]

The decision in *Blaikie* meant, among other things, that all of Quebec's statutes enacted after the passage of Quebec's Charter of the French Language in 1977 were in violation of s. 133.[5] These statutes had been enacted in French only, and were therefore invalid. Fortunately, however, Quebec's Charter had insisted upon the publication of an unofficial English translation, so that the task of translating the statutes into English had been accomplished. The decision in *Blaikie* came down on December 13, 1979. The Quebec Legislature sat overnight to re-enact the statutes in both their French text and their English translation. The enactment of the curative statute was completed the next day.[6] Quebec's prompt and effective remedial action stands in contrast to Manitoba's reaction to a similar problem. The situation in Manitoba is the topic of the next section of this chapter.

[Section 56:5]

[1] *Attorney General of Quebec v. Blaikie*, [1979] 2 S.C.R. 1016. The opinion was rendered by "the Court".

[2] Charter of the French Language, S.Q. 1977, c. 5.

[3] *Attorney General of Quebec v. Blaikie*, [1979] 2 S.C.R. 1016, 1022.

[4] Bills and amendments would also be within the phrase "records and journals", which s. 133 requires to be kept in both languages. The phrase "records and journals", which also appears in s. 23 of the Manitoba Act, 1870 and s. 18 of the Constitution Act, 1982, has never been authoritatively defined, although it was examined by Deschênes C.J. in *Blaikie* at first instance (1978), 85 D.L.R. (3d) 252, 257-260.

[5] The Charter of the French Language itself was in a similar plight, having been enacted in French only.

[6] S.Q. 1979, c. 61.

§ 56:6 Manitoba's Official Language Act

We have already noticed that s. 23 of the Manitoba Act, 1870[1] provides for the use of English and French in the Legislature (and courts) of Manitoba in terms similar to s. 133 of the Constitution Act, 1867.[2] The reason for s. 23, of course, was to guarantee the rights of the French-speaking minority in Manitoba.[3] Its text is so similar to that of s. 133 of the Constitution Act, 1867 that it can be safely assumed that all the points of interpretation of s. 133 that have been discussed in the previous section of this chapter are equally relevant to s. 23.

In 1890, the Manitoba Legislature enacted the Official Language Act.[4] The Act provided that "the English language only" shall be used in the records and journals of the Legislature, and in pleadings and process in the Manitoba courts; the Act also provided that Manitoba statutes "need only be printed and published in the English language". In effect, the Act was an attempt to repeal most of s. 23 of the Manitoba Act. The Act was held to be invalid by county courts in 1892[5] and 1909,[6] but these decisions were not appealed, were not reported, and were completely disregarded by the authorities in Manitoba. In 1976, a third attack was mounted against the Official Language Act, and the Act was again held to be invalid by a county court.[7] The Attorney General of Manitoba announced that: "The Crown does not accept the ruling of the Court with respect to the constitutionality of the Official Language Act"; but he declined to appeal the decision to a higher court.[8] The Legislature and

[Section 56:6]

[1]R.S.C. 1985, Appendix II, No. 8. The Manitoba Act, 1870 is a federal statute which created the province of Manitoba in 1870. It was ratified by the Constitution Act, 1871, R.S.C. 1985, Appendix II, No. 11. It is part of the "Constitution of Canada": Constitution Act, 1982, s. 52(2).

[2]The text of s. 23 is as follows:

23.

Either the English or the French languages may be used by any person in the debates of the Houses of the Legislature, and both those languages shall be used in the respective records and journals of those Houses; and either of those languages may be used by any person, or in any pleading or process, in or issuing from any Court of Canada established under the British North America Act, 1867, or in or from all or any of the Courts of the Province. The Acts of the Legislature shall be printed and published in both those languages.

[3]In 1870, French-speakers were actually in a slight majority in the Red River settlement. The Riel provisional government, rightly fearing an influx of English-speakers, insisted upon s. 23 as one of the terms of provincehood. See W. Tetley, "Language and Education Rights in Quebec and Canada" (1982) 45 Law and Contemp. Problems 177, 180.

[4]S.M. 1890, c. 14.

[5]*Pellant v. Hebert* (1892), reported in 1981 in 12 R.G.D. 242 (Man. Co. Ct.).

[6]*Bertrand v. Dussault* (1909), reported in 1977 in 77 D.L.R. (3d) 458 (Man. Co. Ct.).

[7]*R. v. Forest* (1976), 74 D.L.R. (3d) 704 (Man. Co. Ct.).

[8]In a later case, Monnin J.A. described this as an "arrogant abuse of authority": *Re Forest* (1977), 77 D.L.R. (3d) 445, 458 (Man. C.A.).

Courts of Manitoba continued the unilingual procedures purportedly authorized by the Official Language Act of 1890, as if that Act were valid.

In 1978, the Official Language Act was challenged for the fourth time. This time, the French-speaking plaintiff brought an action in the Manitoba Court of Queen's Bench seeking a declaration that the Act was invalid, and he was fortunate enough to lose at first instance (for lack of standing), thus giving him the carriage of an appeal to the Manitoba Court of Appeal. He succeeded in the Manitoba Court of Appeal, and this time the Attorney General of Manitoba elected to appeal to the Supreme Court of Canada. The Supreme Court of Canada rendered its judgment in *Attorney General of Manitoba v. Forest* (1979)[9] on the same day as it rendered its judgment in *Blaikie.*[10] The Court wrote a brief opinion, essentially adopting its reasoning in *Blaikie* to hold that s. 23 of the Manitoba Act could not be amended by the unilateral action of the Manitoba Legislature; Manitoba's Official Language Act was therefore unconstitutional.

The *Forest* decision had not expressly ruled on the constitutional status of the Manitoba statutes that had been enacted in English only. That ruling came in *Re Manitoba Language Rights* (1985)[11] when the Supreme Court of Canada confirmed that the failure to comply with s. 23's requirement of bilingual enactment resulted in the invalidity of the purported statute. This meant that nearly all of the laws of the province were unconstitutional, because statutes had been enacted in English only from 1890 (when the Official Language Act was enacted) until 1979 (when the *Forest* case was decided), and even since 1979 many statutes had been enacted in English only. In order to save the province from the vacuum of law that would be caused by the Court's finding of wholesale invalidity, the Court declared that the province's statutes were to be "deemed to have temporary force and effect for the minimum period necessary for their translation, re-enactment, printing and publication".[12] This provided a transitional period, the duration of which was later settled with precise dates directed by the Court,[13] during which the existing body of Manitoba laws would remain in force. Future laws, that is, those enacted after the date of the Court's opinion (June 13, 1985), had to comply with s. 23's requirement of bilingual enactment; they did not benefit from the period of temporary validity.[14]

In *Re Manitoba Language Rights*, the Court also considered a two-

---

[9]*Attorney General of Manitoba v. Forest*, [1979] 2 S.C.R. 1032.

[10]*Attorney General of Quebec v. Blaikie*, [1979] 2 S.C.R. 1016.

[11]*Re Manitoba Language Rights*, [1985] 1 S.C.R. 721. The opinion was rendered by "the Court". I disclose that I was one of the counsel for the Attorney General of Canada.

[12]*Re Manitoba Language Rights*, [1985] 1 S.C.R. 721, 782.

[13]*Re Manitoba Language Rights Order No. 1*, [1985] 2 S.C.R. 347 (for most statutes, the deadline was December 31, 1988); *Re Manitoba Language Rights Order No. 2*, [1990] 3 S.C.R. 1417 (extending the period of validity for some instruments); *Re Manitoba Language Rights Order No. 3*, [1992] 1 S.C.R. 212 (clarifying original order and further extending the period of validity).

[14]The aftermath of *Re Manitoba Language Rights* is more fully discussed in ch. 58,

stage procedure for bilingual enactment that had been established by the Manitoba Legislature after the *Forest* decision in order to facilitate compliance with s. 23 of the Manitoba Act. The first stage of the procedure was the enactment of a bill in English only; the second stage was the preparation of a French translation of the bill, which on deposit in the Legislature would have full legal effect. This procedure did not satisfy s. 23, the Court held, because it denied to French-speakers participation in the legislative process. "Simultaneity in the use of both English and French is therefore required throughout the process of enacting bills into law".[15] This conclusion was reinforced by s. 23's requirement that both languages were to be used in the "records and journals" of the Legislature. Therefore, the statute prescribing the two-stage procedure was unconstitutional.

The Manitoba statute prescribing the two-stage procedure provided that in case of conflict the original (English) enactment prevailed over the subsequently deposited (French) translation. This provision was also invalid, because s. 23 implicitly required that both language versions be "equally authoritative",[16] The preference for one language version "renders the non-preferred text legally irrelevant, since it cannot safely be relied upon".[17] Any mechanism that attributed "superior status" to one language version of a statute would violate s. 23.[18]

Section 23 is so similar to s. 133 of the Constitution Act, 1867 and to ss. 17 to 19 of the Charter of Rights that these interpretations of s. 23 would undoubtedly apply to the other provisions.

§ 56:7 Incorporation by reference

Where a statute makes reference to another document, so as to incorporate (or adopt) the document as part of the statute,[1] then the general rule is that, if there is a constitutional requirement that the incorporating statute be in both languages, then the requirement will apply to the incorporated document as well. In *Attorney General of Quebec v. Collier* (1985),[2] two Quebec statutes fixed public sector wages and other terms of employment. They did so by reference to session papers that had been tabled in the Legislature; the details of the wages and other terms of employment were to be found not in the statutes, but

---

Effect of Unconstitutional Law, under heading § 58:9, "Wholesale invalidation of laws".

[15] *Re Manitoba Language Rights*, [1985] 1 S.C.R. 721, 775. Another constitutional flaw was the absence of any requirement of royal assent for the translation: *Re Manitoba Language Rights*, [1985] 1 S.C.R. 721, 777.

[16] *Re Manitoba Language Rights*, [1985] 1 S.C.R. 721, 774.

[17] *Re Manitoba Language Rights*, [1985] 1 S.C.R. 721, 778.

[18] *Re Manitoba Language Rights*, [1985] 1 S.C.R. 721, 778.

[Section 56:7]

[1] Incorporation by reference is discussed in ch. 14, Delegation, under heading §§ 14:12 to 14:14, "Referential legislation".

[2] *Attorney General of Quebec v. Collier* (1985), 23 D.L.R. (4th) 339 (Que. C.A.); affirmed under name *Que. v. Brunet*, [1990] 1 S.C.R. 260.

in the session papers to which the statutes referred. The statutes had been enacted in both French and English, but the session papers were in French only. The Quebec Court of Appeal, in a decision that was affirmed by the Supreme Court of Canada, held that the two statutes were unconstitutional. The session papers were an integral part of the statutes. Since the session papers had been tabled in one language only, the statutes could not be said to have been enacted in both languages as required by s. 133 of the Constitution Act, 1867.[3]

In *Collier*, it was important that the incorporated session papers contained the substance of the legislative scheme. It would have been a clear denial of access by English-speakers to the Legislature and its laws if the substance of a legislative scheme had been allowed to be embodied in a document that was in French only. However, where a statute refers to an extrinsic document that is not essential to the operation of the statute, so that the document is not an "integral part" of the statute, then there is no "true incorporation", and the document would not be subject to the requirement of bilingual texts.[4]

When a statute refers to a document that is essential to the operation of the statute, the general rule is, as noted above, that the document comes under the same language requirements as the statute itself. The Supreme Court of Canada has indicated, however, that this is not an absolute rule. There could be bona fide reasons for exempting the incorporated document from the requirement of bilingual texts. This would be the case where (unlike *Collier)* the incorporated document emanated from a source that was under no obligation of translation, and where (unlike *Collier)* it was not practicable for the legislative body to produce translations.[5]

In *R. v. Massia* (1991),[6] a challenge was brought to the federal Government Property Traffic Regulations, which applied on federal Crown property (such as military bases), and which provided that drivers must observe the law of the province in which the Crown property was situated. The Regulations (and the enabling Act) had been enacted in both languages. The accused, who was convicted under the Regulations of driving a vehicle while his licence was suspended on a miliary base in Ontario, challenged the relevant regulation on the basis that it incorporated by reference a law of Ontario (prohibiting driving while under suspension) that had been enacted in English only. The majority of the Ontario Court of Appeal rejected the challenge. They pointed out that Ontario's prohibition of driving while under suspension had been

---

[3]Followed in *Sinclair v. Que.*, [1992] 1 S.C.R. 212 (statute operated by reference to a unilingual document to be issued in future; held breach of s. 133).

[4]*Re Manitoba Language Rights Order No. 3*, [1992] 1 S.C.R. 212, 228.

[5]*Re Manitoba Language Rights Order No. 3*, [1992] 1 S.C.R. 212, 229-231 (suggesting as examples the incorporation of the legislation of another jurisdiction and the incorporation of safety standards set by a non-governmental body).

[6]*R. v. Massia* (1991), 4 O.R. (3d) 705 (C.A.). The majority opinion was written by Galligan J.A., with the agreement of Brooke J.A.; Doherty J.A. dissented.

enacted by a body that was at the time of enactment[7] under no obligation to produce bilingual texts, and, although the charge was laid under the federal Regulations, the Ontario prohibition was capable of operating of its own force on federal Crown property. They might have added that the sensible scheme of subjecting military personnel to local traffic laws could not be effective if it were necessary to continuously produce translations of the changing bodies of provincial traffic laws.[8]

§ 56:8 Delegated legislation

In *Attorney General of Quebec v. Blaikie* (1979),[1] the Supreme Court of Canada decided that s. 133's requirement that "Acts" be printed and published in both languages applied to delegated legislation as well as to statutes.[2] On this point, the Court simply said that "it would truncate the requirement of s. 133 if account were not taken of the growth of delegated legislation".[3] This brief observation appeared to impose the requirement of bilingual enactment on all kinds of delegated legislation.[4] Quebec immediately applied to the Court for a rehearing to determine whether some kinds of delegated legislation were exempt from s. 133.

In *Attorney General of Quebec v. Blaikie (No. 2)* (1981),[5] the Court qualified the earlier ruling by holding that only regulations made by "the Government" were subject to s. 133. By "the Government" the Court meant the Lieutenant Governor, the Executive Council and Ministers; the Court took notice of the conventions of responsible government as creating "a considerable degree of integration between the Legislature and the Government", so that the enactments of the Government "must be viewed as an extension of the legislative power of the Legislature"

---

[7]The facts arose before the coming into force of s. 3(2) of the French Language Services Act, R.S.O. 1990, c. F.32.

[8]This case was decided before *Re Manitoba Language Rights Order No. 3*, [1992] 1 S.C.R. 212, 228-231, indicated a rather flexible approach to the question of translation of incorporated documents. In light of the later decision, the dissenting opinion of Doherty J.A., who would have held that the incorporation was unconstitutional for breach of the language requirements, is wrong.

[Section 56:8]

[1]*Attorney General of Quebec v. Blaikie*, [1979] 2 S.C.R. 1016.

[2]The same word, "Acts", is used in s. 23 of the Manitoba Act, 1870. The word "statutes" is used in s. 18 of the Charter of Rights; this change in nomenclature would not, in my view, change the interpretation.

[3]*Attorney General of Quebec v. Blaikie*, [1979] 2 S.C.R. 1016, 1027.

[4]In the federal jurisdiction, the Official Languages Act, 1988, by s. 7, requires legislative instruments to be made in both official languages. Because this legislation was only prospective, it was belatedly supplemented by the Legislative Instruments Re-enactment Act, S.C. 2002, c. 20, which saves any legislative instruments that were enacted in only one language before the coming into force in 1988 of s. 7 of the Official Languages Act. If the instrument (although made in only one language) was published in both languages, then the 2002 Act re-enacts the instrument in both languages. If the instrument was published in only the one language in which it was made, the 2002 Act authorizes the Governor in Council to repeal it and re-enact it in both languages.

[5]*Attorney General of Quebec v. Blaikie (No. 2)*, [1981] 1 S.C.R. 312.

and accordingly as being within s. 133.[6] In the same category, the Court held, were regulations which, although made by officials or bodies outside the Government, were subject to the approval of the Government; they too were subject to s. 133.[7] Regulations which were neither made by the Government nor subject to approval by the Government were not subject to s. 133. Also not subject to s. 133 were the by-laws of local municipalities and school boards, even if they were subject to the approval of the Government.[8] Another special category was court rules of practice: these rules, although made by the judges not the Government, were subject to s. 133; and so were the rules of those administrative tribunals whose functions were "quasi-judicial".[9]

In *Re Manitoba Language Rights* (1985),[10] the Supreme Court of Canada made clear that the scope of s. 23 of the Manitoba Act was the same as the scope of s. 133 of the Constitution Act, 1867. This meant that Manitoba was under an obligation to translate and re-enact not only the statutes that had been enacted in English only, but also the categories of delegated legislation that were defined in *Blaikie No. 2.*[11] In due course, the Government of Manitoba returned to the Court for a further clarification of this ruling. Did it include orders in council? An order in council clearly emanated from "the Government", as stipulated in *Blaikie No. 2*, because an order in council is a formal instrument made by the Lieutenant Governor in Council, acting on the "advice" (that is, direction) of the Executive Council (that is, the cabinet). Many regulations are required by their enabling statute to be made by the Lieutenant Governor in Council. Obviously, any order in council that enacted a regulation would be covered by *Blaikie No. 2.* But what of those orders in council that were of an executive rather than a legislative nature, for example, an order appointing a person to an office, or an order authorizing the granting of a contract or permit?

In *Re Manitoba Language Rights Order No. 3* (1992),[12] the Supreme Court of Canada held that s. 23 applied only to "instruments of a legislative nature".[13] An instrument would have the following three characteristics: (1) it would establish a "rule of conduct"; (2) it would

---

[6]*Attorney General of Quebec v. Blaikie (No. 2)*, [1981] 1 S.C.R. 312, 319-321.

[7]*Attorney General of Quebec v. Blaikie (No. 2)*, [1981] 1 S.C.R. 312, 329. However, the Court explained that regulations which were subject to disallowance by the Government, being effective unless and until disallowed, were not subject to s. 133.

[8]*Attorney General of Quebec v. Blaikie (No. 2)*, [1981] 1 S.C.R. 312, 321-326. But compare *Charlebois v. Moncton* (2001), 242 N.B.R. (2d) 259 (N.B.C.A.) (holding that s. 18(2) of the Charter required by-laws of New Brunswick municipalities to be in both English and French).

[9]*Attorney General of Quebec v. Blaikie (No. 2)*, [1981] 1 S.C.R. 312, 330-333.

[10]*Re Manitoba Language Rights*, [1985] 1 S.C.R. 721.

[11]*Re Manitoba Language Rights*, [1985] 1 S.C.R. 721, 744. ("All types of subordinate legislation that in Quebec would be subject to s. 133 of the Constitution Act, 1867, are, in Manitoba, subject to s. 23 of the Manitoba Act, 1870.")

[12]*Re Manitoba Language Rights Order No. 3*, [1992] 1 S.C.R. 212.

[13]*Re Manitoba Language Rights Order No. 3*, [1992] 1 S.C.R. 212, 223.

have the "force of law"; and (3) it would be "of general application rather than directed at specific individuals or situations".[14] The obligation of bilingual enactment applied only to instruments possessing those three characteristics. Of course, "Legislatures will often find it appropriate or desirable to translate instruments that go beyond those criteria",[15] but they would be under no constitutional obligation to do so.

The Court had an opportunity to apply its definition of instruments of a legislative nature in *Sinclair v. Quebec* (1992),[16] where the issue was whether the Government of Quebec, acting under statutory authority, could create a new municipality by the issue of letters patent in the French language only.[17] The Court held that the creation of local government institutions, which would have among other things legal powers over the residents of the municipality, was not like the incorporation of a private company, which would simply have the powers of an individual. In this case, the purpose of s. 133 of making laws accessible in both languages would be violated if the structure and powers of local government institutions could be ascertained only from a document that was not in the English language. The Court held, therefore, that the new municipality had not been validly established.[18]

V. LANGUAGE OF COURTS

§ 56:9 Constitutional requirements

With respect to the courts,[1] s. 133 of the Constitution Act, 1867 requires that either French or English "may be used by any person or in any pleading or process in or issuing from any Court of Canada established under this Act, and in or from all or any of the Courts of Quebec". This gives a choice of either French or English to litigants in the federal courts and the courts of Quebec.[2] Section 23 of the Manitoba

---

[14] *Re Manitoba Language Rights Order No. 3*, [1992] 1 S.C.R. 212, 224-225 (adapting a parliamentary committee's definition of regulation as "a rule of conduct, enacted by a regulation-making authority pursuant to an Act of Parliament, which has the force of law for an undetermined number of persons").

[15] *Re Manitoba Language Rights Order No. 3*, [1992] 1 S.C.R. 212, 224-225.

[16] *Sinclair v. Quebec*, [1992] 1 S.C.R. 579. The judgment was rendered by "the Court".

[17] The Court described the statute that authorized the letters patent as merely "a shell"; the detail of the new municipality was all contained in the letters patent and two other related documents, all three of which were in French only. The Court held that all three documents had to be in both languages.

[18] In deference to the fact that the municipality had actually been functioning for five years, the Court held that the invalid instruments were to have legal effect for one year in order to permit the Legislature of Quebec to take curative action.

[Section 56:9]

[1] On bilingualism in the judicial system, see Bastarache (ed.), Language Rights in Canada (2nd ed., 2003), ch. 3.

[2] The structure of the federal courts and the provincial courts is explained in ch. 7, Courts.

Act, 1870 imposes a similar requirement on the courts of Manitoba.[3] Section 19(2) of the Charter of Rights imposes a similar requirement on the courts of New Brunswick. The courts of the other seven provinces are under no similar constitutional obligation. The language of civil proceedings in the provincial courts is regulated by the provinces under s. 92(14) ("procedure in civil matters");[4] the language of criminal proceedings in the provincial courts is regulated by Parliament under s. 91(27) ("procedure in criminal matters").[5]

Quebec's Charter of the French Language provided that, in the courts of Quebec, French was to be the language of pleading and process, except in certain defined circumstances. Like the other assaults on s. 133 that were mounted by the Quebec language law,[6] this one was repulsed by the Supreme Court of Canada in *Attorney General of Quebec v. Blaikie* (1979).[7] The Court held that it was not sufficient to give litigants the option of using English in defined circumstances only. Section 133 gave to litigants in the courts of Quebec the option of using English in *any* pleading or process.

§ 56:10 Definition of courts

Which courts are covered by s. 133? In *Blaikie*, the Supreme Court of Canada held that the reference to "the Courts of Quebec" included not only s. 96 courts (with federally-appointed judges), and the inferior courts (with provincially appointed judges), but also administrative tribunals established by statute that exercised "adjudicative" functions. The Court said that "it would be overly technical to ignore the modern development of noncurial adjudicative agencies which play so important a role in our society, and to refuse to extend to proceedings before them the guarantee of the right to use either French or English by those subject to their jurisdiction".[1]

---

[3]The text of s. 23 is as follows:

> 23. Either the English or the French languages may be used by any person in the debates of the Houses of the Legislature, and both those languages shall be used in the respective records and journals of those Houses; and either of those languages may be used by any person, or in any pleading or process, in or issuing from any Court of Canada established under the British North America Act, 1867, or in or from all or any of the Courts of the Province. The Acts of the Legislature shall be printed and published in both those languages.

[4]*Conseil scolaire francophone de la Colombie-Britannique v. B.C.*, [2013] 2 S.C.R. 774, 2013 SCC 42, para. 1 (civil proceedings in B.C. required to be in English; documents in French without English translation inadmissible). Of course, a province is free to impose a statutory bilingual requirement, e.g., Courts of Justice Act, R.S.O. 1990, c. C.43, s. 126.

[5]Criminal Code, R.S.C. 1985, c. C-46, ss. 530-533 (bilingual requirement for criminal trials).

[6]§ 56:2 note 12, above.

[7]*Attorney General of Quebec v. Blaikie*, [1979] 2 S.C.R. 1016.

[Section 56:10]

[1]*Attorney General of Quebec v. Blaikie*, [1979] 2 S.C.R. 1016, 1029.

§ 56:11 Language of process

In *MacDonald v. City of Montreal* (1986),[1] an English-speaking Quebecer defended a charge of speeding on the ground that the summons, which included the charge, had been issued by the Quebec court in the French language only. The majority of the Supreme Court of Canada, speaking through Beetz J., held that the unilingual summons did not infringe s. 133.[2] Section 133, by providing that "either" of the two languages may be used in any process issuing from a Quebec court, gave to the issuing court the choice of either the English or the French language. The express provision for choice of language made clear that court process need not be bilingual. Nor was the choice of language by the court to be governed by the wishes of the recipient of court process, which would in any case not necessarily be known to the issuing court. Beetz J. said that s. 133, where it conferred a choice of language, "does not guarantee that the speaker, writer or issuer of proceedings or processes will be understood in the language of his choice by those he is addressing".[3]

In the *MacDonald* case, Wilson J., who dissented, was willing to find by implication in s. 133 a duty in the court to accommodate both English and French speakers. That duty could be discharged by a bilingual summons, or even a French document with some explanation in English; but it was breached by a summons that was wholly in French. Beetz J. for the majority rejected this view, adhering to the more literal interpretation of s. 133 as permitting the court to issue its process in one language only. Beetz J. defended the narrower approach to s. 133 by drawing a distinction between language rights and other human rights. While both types of rights were constitutionally protected, most human rights had a quality of universality, in that they were recognized by all democratic societies; language rights, on the other hand, were "peculiar to Canada":[4]

> They are based on a political compromise rather than on principle and lack the universality, generality and fluidity of basic rights resulting from the rules of natural justice. They are expressed in more precise and less flexible language.

[Section 56:11]

[1]*MacDonald v. City of Montreal*, [1986] 1 S.C.R. 460. Beetz J. wrote the majority opinion with the agreement of four others; Dickson C.J. wrote a short concurring opinion; Wilson J. dissented.

[2]The decision was followed with respect to s. 23 of the Manitoba Act in *Bilodeau v. A.G. Man.*, [1986] 1 S.C.R. 449 (summons issued by Manitoba court in English only; held valid).

[3]*MacDonald v. City of Montreal*, [1986] 1 S.C.R. 460, 496.

[4]*MacDonald v. City of Montreal*, [1986] 1 S.C.R. 460, 500, rejecting the view that the requirements of natural justice should be imported into s. 133; see also 496, where the distinction is also stressed.

This suggestion that language rights should receive a more restrained interpretation than other Charter rights[5] was reiterated and applied in the *Acadiens* case, which is discussed next.

§ 56:12 Language of proceedings

In *Société des Acadiens v. Association of Parents* (1986),[1] Beetz J., again speaking for the majority of the Supreme Court of Canada, repeated that language rights were "based on political compromise"; this distinguished them from legal rights, which "tend to be seminal in nature because they are rooted in principle".[2] That case arose in New Brunswick, where s. 19(2) of the Charter of Rights imposed on the courts language requirements in terms very similar to those of s. 133. The Société des Acadiens claimed that s. 19(2) was breached when an application made by the Society in French to the New Brunswick Court of Appeal was heard by a panel of three judges, one of whom, the Society alleged, was not capable of understanding the French language. The Supreme Court of Canada held unanimously that the Society had not established their allegation that the judge was incompetent in French. However, Beetz J. for the majority held that s. 19(2) did not in any case confer on a French-speaking litigant the right to be heard by a judge who understood French. Following *MacDonald*, he said that, while the litigant had the constitutional right to use either English or French, neither s. 19(2) nor s. 133 conferred any guarantee that the litigant "will be heard or understood, or that he has the right to be heard or understood in the language of his choice".[3] Dickson C.J. and Wilson J. each disagreed with Beetz J. They held that the litigant's right to use either English or French impliedly included the right to be understood in the litigant's language of choice by the judge hearing the case.[4] (Later cases have emphatically rejected Beetz J.'s holdings that language rights

---

[5]The distinction between language rights and other rights has found little favour among commentators: see L. Green, "Are Language Rights Fundamental?" (1987) 25 Osgoode Hall L.J. 639; L. Green and D. Réaume, "Second Class Rights? Principle and Compromise in the Charter" (1990) 13 Dal. L.J. 564. The Supreme Court of Canada has changed its mind on this issue: see *DesRochers v. Can.*, [2009] 1 S.C.R. 194, para. 31; *R. v. Beaulac*, [1999] 1 S.C.R. 798, para. 25; and *Solski v. Que.*, [2005] 1 S.C.R. 201, para. 20.

[Section 56:12]

[1]*Société des Acadiens v. Association of Parents*, [1986] 1 S.C.R. 549. Beetz J. wrote the majority opinion with the agreement of four others. Dickson C.J. and Wilson J. each wrote concurring opinions, disagreeing with Beetz J. that s. 19(2) conferred no right to a judge who understood French, but agreeing with the result on the basis that it had not been established that one of the judges did not understand French.

[2]*Société des Acadiens v. Association of Parents*, [1986] 1 S.C.R. 549, 578.

[3]*Société des Acadiens v. Association of Parents*, [1986] 1 S.C.R. 549, 574-575. The decision was followed with respect to a pre-confederation statutory language right in *R. v. Mercure*, [1988] 1 S.C.R. 234.

[4]This is clearly Dickson C.J.'s view, although he left open the question whether the right could be satisfied by the use of an interpreter or simultaneous translation. Wilson J.'s opinion is less clear, but seems to be the same.

must receive a more restrictive interpretation than other constitutional rights; it is now clear that language rights, like other rights, must receive "a liberal and purposive interpretation".)[5]

The reader by now will have conjured up the image of a unilingual judge presiding impassively over a trial in which the witnesses and their counsel are all speaking in a language that the judge cannot understand! Only Franz Kafka could appreciate such a disturbing possibility.[6] Needless to say, Beetz J. in the *Acadiens* case did not intend such a result. He pointed out that the right to a fair hearing, which was recognized by the common law rules of natural justice, and which was protected in part by ss. 7 to 14 of the Charter, would be offended by a presiding judge's failure to comprehend the evidence or argument. But the fair-hearing right to be heard and understood by a court was not a language right, and it extended to those who spoke or understood neither official language.[7] It had not been breached in this case, because the judge's alleged incompetence in French had not been established as a matter of fact.

§ 56:13 Right to interpreter

The right of a party or witness to an interpreter is expressly dealt with by s. 14 of the Charter of Rights.[1] Section 14 provides:

> A party or witness in any proceedings who does not understand or speak the language in which the proceedings are conducted or who is deaf has the right to the assistance of an interpreter.

Section 14 confers upon a party or witness who does not understand or

---

[5]*DesRochers v. Can.*, [2009] 1 S.C.R. 194, para. 31 per Charron J. for the Court. To the same effect is *R. v. Beaulac*, [1999] 1 S.C.R. 798, para. 25 per Bastarache J. for the majority ("To the extent that [*Acadiens*] stands for restrictive interpretation of language rights, it is to be rejected."); *Solski v. Que.*, [2005] 1 S.C.R. 201, para. 20 ("language rights must be interpreted in a broad and purposive manner"); *Conseil Scolaire Francophone de la Colombie-Britannique v. B.C.*, 2020 SCC 13, paras. 18-19.

[6]The Criminal Code, by s. 530, confers on an accused in a criminal trial the right to a judge, or a judge and jury, "who speak the official language of Canada that is the language of the accused or, if the circumstances warrant, who speak both official languages of Canada". The provision was applied in *R. v. Beaulac*, [1999] 1 S.C.R. 768, where the Supreme Court of Canada held that a French-speaking accused in British Columbia was entitled to a new trial before a judge and jury who spoke both official languages, regardless of whether or not the accused had received a fair trial before a judge and jury who spoke only English. Bastarache J. for the majority said, obiter, paras. 21-25, 41, that the liberal interpretation of the language right and its distinctness from the right to a fair trial were interpretative principles that applied to the constitutional language rights as well.

[7]*Société des Acadiens v. Association of Parents*, [1986] 1 S.C.R. 549, 577

[Section 56:13]

[1]For commentary on s. 14, see Beaudoin and Mendes (eds.), The Canadian Charter of Rights and Freedoms (4th ed., 2005), 910-920 (by Y. Landry and V. Désilets); Canadian Charter of Rights Annotated (Canada Law Book, loose-leaf), annotation to s. 14; the last work includes a bibliography of the relevant literature.

speak the language of the proceeding, or who is deaf,[2] the right to an interpreter. There is a similar right in s. 2(g) of the Canadian Bill of Rights, although deafness is not a qualification under s. 2(g).[3] There is a common law right to an interpreter, which is possessed by any person who cannot speak or understand the language of proceedings where that person's rights may be affected, because the failure to provide interpretation would be a breach of the rules of natural justice.[4] There is also a statutory right to an interpreter, which is possessed by an accused person in a criminal trial, because the Criminal Code requires that an accused person "be present in court during the whole of his trial", and an accused person is not "present" if he or she cannot understand what is going on.[5]

Under s. 14 of the Charter, a party or witness[6] is entitled to an interpreter if the person "does not understand or speak the language in which the proceedings are conducted or who is deaf". It is for the trial judge to determine whether the need for an interpreter has been established, and in case of dispute the person asserting the right would have to establish the need on the balance of probabilities.[7] But it is the duty of the trial judge to take the initiative in supplying an interpreter to a party or witness who needs the help but who through ignorance or timidity does not assert the right.[8]

In *R. v. Tran* (1994),[9] the accused, a native of Vietnam who could not speak or understand English, was provided with a Vietnamese interpreter for a trial that took place in English. For most of the trial, the interpretation followed the normal pattern of "consecutive" interpretation, in which words spoken in English by counsel, witnesses or the judge were immediately followed by a translation of those words. This pattern was broken in the case of a witness called by the defence (who happened to be the interpreter himself). This witness testified in English and then gave a brief summary of his testimony in Vietnamese at

[2]Section 14 was in the October 1980 version of the Charter, but without the words "or who is deaf. These words were added in the April 1981 version.

[3]For discussion of s. 2(g), see Tarnopolsky, The Canadian Bill of Rights (2nd ed., 1975), 277; *R. v. Sadjade*, [1983] 2 S.C.R. 361.

[4]*R. v. Tran*, [1994] 2 S.C.R. 951, 967.

[5]*R. v. Tran*, [1994] 2 S.C.R. 951, 971.

[6]*Cormier v. Fournier* (1986), 29 D.L.R. (4th) 675 (N.B.Q.B.), affirmed (1987) 78 N.B.R. (2d) 406 (C.A.) (s. 14 applies only to a party or witness; it has no application to a lawyer who cannot understand the language of the trial).

[7]*Roy v. Hackett* (1987), 62 O.R. (2d) 365 (Ont. C.A.) (opposing party has the right to challenge a s. 14 application, by means of cross-examination on the applicant's competence in the language of the trial).

[8]*R. v. Tran*, [1994] 2 S.C.R. 951, 979. However the accused must take the initiative to notify the court if *written* translations of the information of the trial are required. Without such a request, s. 14 is satisfied by oral interpretation alone: *R. v. Simard* (1995), 27 O.R. (3d) 116 (Ont. C.A.).

[9]*R. v. Tran*, [1994] 2 S.C.R. 951. The opinion of the Court was written by Lamer C.J.

the end of his direct examination and then again at the end of his cross-examination. The accused was convicted of the offences charged, and he appealed the convictions on the ground that there had been a breach of his s. 14 right to an interpreter. The Supreme Court of Canada held that there had been a breach of s. 14. The Court held that the quality of the interpretation had to meet the standard of "continuity, precision, impartiality, competence and contemporaneousness".[10] In this case, continuity was not observed, because of the break in interpretation during the defence evidence. Precision was not observed, because the little summaries at the end did not convey everything that was said. Contemporaneousness was also not observed, because the interpretation was not contemporaneous with the asking of questions and the giving of answers. (The impartiality and competence of the interpreter were not put in issue). The constitutional standard of interpretation had to be maintained throughout the trial, except at points where the vital interests of the accused were not involved, for example, a discussion of scheduling. Therefore, although the lapse affected only one witness (and that one called by the defence), that was enough to offend s. 14. Nor was it necessary for the accused to show that he had suffered any prejudice in his ability to make full answer and defence; the mere fact that he was unable to follow some of the proceedings in which his vital interests were involved was itself prejudicial. It followed that the accused's s. 14 right had been infringed, and the Court ordered a new trial.

The right to an interpreter was an important element of the reasoning of the Supreme Court in *Mazraani v. Industrial Alliance Insurance* (2018).[11] The case originated in a trial in the Tax Court of Canada in which most of the witnesses were French-speaking. One of the witnesses was unilingual in English and he requested an interpreter. In response, the judge asked the French-speaking witnesses to "make an effort" and testify in English in order to avoid the delay that would be caused by employing an interpreter. The French-speaking witnesses complied with the judge's request and testified in English. When one of the counsel spoke in French, the judge intervened to request that he switch to English. In this fashion, the trial proceeded in English without an interpreter. The case was appealed up to the Supreme Court of Canada. The Court pointed out that the language rights of the witnesses had been breached. The right to speak in either English or French was guaranteed both by s. 133 of the Constitution Act, 1867 and by s. 19(1) of the Charter of Rights and the right to an interpreter was guaranteed by s. 14 of the Charter. It was the duty of the trial judge to do whatever was necessary to ensure that these rights were not breached in the conduct of the trial.[12] Although the trial was conducted in French, an official language, it was also a breach of the language rights to require a witness to speak in a language other than that of the witness's choice in

---

[10] *R. v. Tran*, [1994] 2 S.C.R. 951, 979.

[11] *Mazraani v. Industrial Alliance Insurance*, 2018 SCC 50. Gascon and Côté JJ. wrote the opinion of the nine-judge Court.

[12] *Mazraani v. Industrial Alliance Insurance*, 2018 SCC 50, paras. 3, 28, 32-33.

order to avoid employing an interpreter.[13] And it was also a breach of the language rights for the judge who saw that a party would be testifying or arguing in an official language that a witness for the other party did not understand not to advise that other party of his or her right to an interpreter, even if the retention of an interpreter would cause some delay of the trial.[14] The Supreme Court held that the only remedy for this catalogue of constitutional errors was a new trial, which is what the Court ordered.

Under s. 14, the right to an interpreter applies "in any proceedings", which can be criminal, as in *Tran*, or civil, as in *Mazraani*; and probably also includes proceedings before administrative tribunals as well as courts.[15] Whether the right exists only at the hearing or also applies to an investigatory or even merely preparatory phase of the proceedings will eventually require judicial decision.[16] The interpreter should probably be paid for out of public funds, at least for a party or witness who cannot afford to pay the cost himself.[17]

VI. LANGUAGE OF GOVERNMENT

§ 56:14 Section 16 of Charter

The previous sections of this chapter have addressed the constitutional requirements, in the federal jurisdiction, Quebec, Manitoba and New Brunswick, with respect to the use of the English and French languages in legislative bodies and courts. We have noticed the limited form of bilingualism that is required by s. 133 of the Constitution Act, 1867, s. 23 of the Manitoba Act, 1870 and ss. 16 to 22 of the Charter of Rights. The first two sources, namely s. 133 and s. 23, do not go beyond legislative bodies and courts; they say nothing about government services. But two of the provisions of the Charter of Rights, namely, ss. 16 and 20, do go beyond legislative bodies and courts.[1]

Section 16 of the Charter provides as follows:

---

[13] *Mazraani v. Industrial Alliance Insurance*, 2018 SCC 50, paras. 34.

[14] *Mazraani v. Industrial Alliance Insurance*, 2018 SCC 50, paras. 35.

[15] *Roy v. Hackett* (1987), 62 O.R. (2d) 365 (Ont. C.A.) (arbitration boards are subject to the rules of natural justice, making s. 14 applicable to their proceedings); *R. v. Tran*, [1994] 2 S.C.R. 951, 961 (leaving open the possibility that the provision applies to administrative proceedings).

[16] *R. v. Dennie* (1997), 43 C.R.R. (2d) 144 (Ont. Gen. Div.) (s. 14 does not apply to investigatory processes or to arrests); *R. v. Cornelio* (1998), 58 C.R.R. (2d) 43 (Ont. Gen. Div.) (s. 14 does not require an impartial interpreter to be present at an arrest). Note, however, that in both cases, the court excluded evidence obtained without the use of a proper interpreter, relying on s. 10(b) rights on arrest or detention.

[17] Although most courts do provide interpretation services, rules vary from court to court. The Court in *Mazraani*, para. 30, commented that "the TCC's [Tax Court of Canada's] rules are less clear on this point." Compare the right to counsel in s. 10(b): ch. 50, Rights on Arrest or Detention, under heading § 50:15, "Legal aid".

[Section 56:14]

[1] On bilingualism in government, see Bastarache (ed.), Language Rights in Canada (2nd ed., 2003), ch. 4.

16.(1) English and French are the official languages of Canada and have equality of status and equal rights and privileges as to their use in all institutions of the Parliament and government of Canada.

(2) English and French are the official languages of New Brunswick and have equality of status and equal rights and privileges as to their use in all institutions of the legislature and government of New Brunswick.

(3) Nothing in this Charter limits the authority of Parliament or a legislature to advance the equality of status or use of English and French.

This section makes English and French the "official languages" of Canada and New Brunswick. It is not clear what, if any, practical consequences flow from official status.[2] The section also confers on English or French "equality of status and equal rights and privileges as to their use in all institutions of the Parliament and government of Canada" (subs. (1)), and "in all institutions of the legislature and government of New Brunswick" (subs. (2)).[3] These subsections (1) and (2) of s. 16 are probably not addressed to communications between government and the public, because that topic is addressed by s. 20 (to be considered in the next paragraph). Subsections (1) and (2) of s. 16 may well have the effect, however, of conferring on public servants, in the institutions of the federal Parliament and government and the New Brunswick Legislature and government, the right to use either the English or the French language as the language of work.[4]

Subsection (3) of s. 16 provides that nothing in the Charter "limits the authority of Parliament or a legislature to advance the equality of status or use of English and French". This provision has been described as a "codification"[5] of the existing constitutional rule that authorizes the Parliament and Legislatures to create language rights above and beyond those conferred by the Constitution.[6] In other words, the constitutional language rights are a "minimum not a maximum", and they "can be complemented by federal and provincial legislation".[7] In Ontario, for

---

[2]The issue is inconclusively discussed, obiter, in *Société des Acadiens v. Assn. of Parents*, [1986] 1 S.C.R. 549, 565, 579, 613-621.

[3]The phrase "the Parliament and government of Canada" also appears in s. 32 of the Charter of Rights, which is discussed in ch. 37, Application of Charter, under heading §§ 37:6 to 37:14, "Burden of rights". However, in s. 16 and in s. 20 (discussed next in text) the phrase is preceded by "institutions of, which would give a much narrower scope to "Parliament", although it may not alter the scope of "government".

[4]The issue is discussed in the context of s. 2 of the Official Languages Act in *Assn. des Gens de l'Air du Qué. v. Lang*, [1978] 2 F.C. 371 (Fed. C.A.); *Joyal v. Air Can.*, [1982] C.A. 39 (Que. C.A.).

[5]*Société des Acadiens v. Assn. of Parents*, [1986] 1 S.C.R. 549, 579.

[6]§ 56:4 note 5, above.

[7]*MacDonald v. City of Montreal*, [1986] 1 S.C.R. 460, 496. In *Lalonde v. Ont.* (2002), 56 O.R. (3d) 505, paras. 90-95 (C.A.), it was held that s. 16(3) did not create constitutional rights by rendering irreversible every advance in the status of the French

example, the French Language Services Act[8] guarantees the use of both languages in the proceedings of the Legislative Assembly, in bills, statutes and regulations, and in government services. The last category is broadly defined and was used by the Court of Appeal to set aside a government decision to reduce the functions of the only French-language community hospital in the Ottawa area; the Court also invoked an unwritten constitutional principle of respect for the French-language minority in the province.[9]

§ 56:15 Section 20 of Charter

Section 20 of the Charter of Rights provides as follows:

> **20.**(1) Any member of the public in Canada has the right to communicate with, and to receive available services from, any head or central office of an institution of the Parliament or government of Canada in English or French, and has the same right with respect to any other office of any such institution where
>
> (a) there is a significant demand for communications with and services from that office in such language; or
>
> (b) due to the nature of the office, it is reasonable that communications with and services from that office be available in both English and French.
>
> (2) Any member of the public in New Brunswick has the right to communicate with, and to receive available services from, any office of an institution of the legislature or government of New Brunswick in English or French.

This section imposes an obligation on government to provide bilingual services to the public.[1]

In *DesRochers v. Canada* (2009),[2] the Supreme Court of Canada held that, like other language rights, s. 20 should be given "a liberal and purposive interpretation".[3] This requires that, when s. 20 applies, the principle of equality of both official languages that is guaranteed by s. 16(1) must be respected. It is not just a question of accommodating the minority language speakers: "services of equal quality" in both official

---

language in Ontario.

[8]R.S.O. 1990, c. F.32.

[9]*Lalonde v. Ont.* (2002), 56 O.R. (3d) 505 (C.A.), paras. 168 (French Language Services Act), 187 (unwritten constitutional principle).

[Section 56:15]

[1]The phrase used is "any member of the public", which would probably include a corporation: see ch. 37, Application of Charter, under heading §§ 37:1 to 37:5, "Benefit of rights".

[2]*DesRochers v. Canada*, [2009] 1 S.C.R. 194. Charron J. wrote the opinion of the Court.

[3]*DesRochers v. Canada*, [2009] 1 S.C.R. 194, para. 31.

languages must be provided.[4] In this, as in other contexts, equality means substantive equality not formal equality. What this meant in this case was that a federal program to promote economic development in rural areas did not have to provide identical services or yield identical results to each language community because they had different needs and priorities; but the program had to provide benefits of equal quality to those who sought to access the program. The Court concluded that, although fewer French-speakers than English-speakers were taking advantage of the program, the French-language community was receiving equal benefits from the program.

In the federal jurisdiction, the obligation attaches to any "head or central office" of an institution of the Parliament or government of Canada without qualification. In *Knopf v. Canada* (2007),[5] a member of the public who was an expert on copyright appeared before a standing committee of the House of Commons in the Parliament Buildings in Ottawa and made submissions to the committee on copyright reform. He testified orally in English. Before his appearance, to support his testimony, he had sent four documents that existed in English only to the clerk of the committee, with the request that they be distributed to the members of the committee. The clerk made copies for the members, but the committee determined that they would not be distributed because they were in English only. The applicant claimed that this was a violation of his constitutional right to communicate with an institution of the Parliament "in English or French". The issue went on up to the Federal Court of Appeal, which, surprisingly, held that his constitutional right was satisfied by the committee receiving his oral testimony in English; the right did not extend to the distribution to the committee of supporting documentation in English only. With respect, the refusal to distribute the supporting English documentation to the members of the committee places a burden of translation on the testifying member of the public, which seems to me to be a breach of the right to communicate to the committee in either English or French.[6]

The s. 20 obligation applies to a federal government office that is not a "head or central" office only where either (a) there is a "significant demand" for bilingual services from that office, or (b) due to the "nature of the office", it is "reasonable" that bilingual services be provided by that office. The alternative tests of significant demand and reasonableness are not elaborated by s. 20. Ultimately, it will be for the courts to give meaning to the tests.

In New Brunswick, the obligation to provide bilingual services at-

---

[4] *DesRochers v. Canada*, [2009] 1 S.C.R. 194, para. 3.

[5] *Knopf v. Canada*, [2008] 2 F.C.R. 327 (C.A.).

[6] I am aware of the practice of some parliamentary committees to arrange for the translation of material sent to them in a timely fashion in only one official language. This works well, and is an advantage to the witness, especially for the written text of the witness's remarks. However, if this is not practicable, as it may not be for lengthy or technical documents, the documents should be distributed in whichever official language they were created.

taches to "any office of an institution of the legislature or government of New Brunswick". The obligation is unqualified by standards of significant demand or reasonableness.

The Government of New Brunswick (like that of seven other provinces) has entered into an agreement with the federal police force, the Royal Canadian Mounted Police, under which the RCMP provides provincial police services in the province.[7] The plaintiff in *Société des Acadiens v. Canada* (2008)[8] was a French-speaking resident of New Brunswick who received a speeding ticket from an RCMP officer who spoke to her only in English. She paid the fine, but brought a proceeding for a declaration that, by virtue of subsection (2) of s. 20, she was entitled to receive police services in the French language. The Supreme Court of Canada confirmed that the RCMP was a federal institution that was in all provinces subject to the minimum obligations of subsection (1) of s. 20, whether it was acting as a federal police force or a provincial police force. However, when providing provincial police services under contract to a province, the RCMP was also a provincial institution, which meant that in New Brunswick, when the force was providing provincial police services (as was the case here), the force was subject to the unqualified obligations of subsection (2) of s. 20. Therefore, the plaintiff in New Brunswick was entitled to communications in French from the RCMP officer who gave her the ticket, regardless of the demand for or reasonableness of French-language services.

In the other nine provinces, there is no constitutional obligation to provide government services in both official languages, although some provinces by statute or administrative practice do in fact provide some services in both languages.[9]

VII. LANGUAGE OF COMMERCE

§ 56:16 Language of commerce

None of the *language* rights in the Constitution of Canada protects the use of the English or French language in commercial (or private)

---

[7]See ch. 19, Criminal Justice, under heading § 19:10, "R.C.M.P. policing contracts".

[8]*Société des Acadiens v. Canada*, [2008] 1 S.C.R. 383. Bastarache J. wrote the opinion of the Court.

[9]Quebec may provide the most extensive services in fact to its (English-speaking) linguistic minority. However, by s. 1 of the Charter of the French Language, S.Q. 1977, c. 5, French is declared to be the "official language of Quebec". While some parts of this legislation have been held to be unconstitutional, no doubt has been cast on the validity of s. 1. Apart from New Brunswick, where s. 16(2) of the Charter of Rights and s. 2 of the Official Languages of New Brunswick Act, R.S. N.B. 1973, c. O-1, both make English and French the official languages of the province, none of the other provinces has made statutory provision for an "official" language or languages. Manitoba's (unconstitutional) Official Language Act, 1890, S.M. 1890, c. 14, despite its title, did not provide that English was the official language of Manitoba. Ontario's French Language Services Act, R.S.O. 1990, c. F.32, travels a long way towards official bilingualism, but does not make French (or English) an "official language".

settings.[1] However, statutory language requirements may offend the guarantee of freedom of expression in s. 2(b) of the Charter of Rights.[2] In *Ford v. Quebec* (1988),[3] the Supreme Court of Canada struck down the provisions of Quebec's Charter of the French Language[4] that required commercial signs and advertisements to be in French only. The Court held that freedom of expression included "the freedom to express oneself in the language of one's choice".[5] It followed that the prohibition of the use of any language other than French was a breach of freedom of expression. The Court also held that, while s. 1 would save some laws designed to protect the French language, the total prohibition of other languages on commercial signs and advertisements was a disproportionately severe measure that could not be saved under s. 1. The law was therefore held to be invalid.

In a companion case, *Devine v. Quebec* (1988),[6] the Court held that other provisions of Quebec's Charter of the French Language, which required the non-exclusive use of French in brochures, orders, invoices and other business documents also offended freedom of expression, even though for those documents there was no prohibition of English (or any other language). The Court explained that "freedom consists in the absence of compulsion as well as an absence of restraint".[7] However, the Court held that s. 1 saved the non-exclusive requirements. The provisions were therefore upheld.

The Government of Quebec could not accept the nullification of its sign-language law in the *Ford* decision. The Government caused the Legislature of Quebec to re-enact the prohibition of English on outside commercial signs and advertisements (while allowing bilingual interior signs).[8] The new law was protected from judicial review by a notwithstanding clause, as authorized by s. 33 (the override power) of the Charter of Rights. This use of s. 33 illustrated an important difference between the guarantees of language rights, none of which is subject to override, and the guarantee of freedom of expression, which is subject to override.[9]

[Section 56:16]

[1]The power to regulate the use of language is discussed in § 56:2, "Distribution of powers over language".

[2]See ch. 43, Expression.

[3]*Ford v. Quebec*, [1988] 2 S.C.R. 712. The opinion was rendered by "the Court".

[4]Charter of the French Language, S.Q. 1977, c. 5.

[5]*Ford v. Quebec*, [1988] 2 S.C.R. 712, 748.

[6]*Devine v. Quebec*, [1988] 2 S.C.R. 790. The opinion was rendered by "the Court".

[7]*Devine v. Quebec*, [1988] 2 S.C.R. 790, 813.

[8]An Act to amend the Charter of the French Language, S.Q. 1988, c. 54.

[9]Section 33 permits the override of only ss. 2 and 7-15 of the Charter. This excludes all the language rights of ss. 16-23, as well as s. 133 of the Constitution Act, 1867 and s. 23 of the Manitoba Act, 1870. See ch. 39, Override of Rights.

VIII. LANGUAGE OF EDUCATION

§ 56:17 Section 93 of Constitution Act, 1867

Section 93 of the Constitution Act, 1867 confers upon the provincial Legislatures the power to make laws in relation to education,[1] but the section prohibits the Legislatures from prejudicially affecting rights or privileges with respect to denominational (or separate) schools existing by law at the time of confederation. The section applies to each of the original confederating provinces, namely, Ontario, Quebec, New Brunswick and Nova Scotia; and to British Columbia (admitted in 1871) and Prince Edward Island (1873) as well.[2] Slightly different versions of s. 93 were negotiated upon the creation or admission of the remaining provinces, and these are to be found in the statutes which constituted Manitoba (1870),[3] Alberta (1905)[4] and Saskatchewan (1905)[5] and in the Terms of Union of Newfoundland (1949).[6]

Because s. 93 (and its counterparts) confers upon the provincial Legislatures the power to make laws in relation to education, it follows from the ancillary nature of the power over language that the provincial Legislatures have the power to prescribe the language of instruction in the schools. However, s. 93 prohibits the provincial Legislatures from prejudicially affecting "any right or privilege with respect to denominational schools which any class of persons have by law in the province at the union." If, therefore, a particular language of instruction was a right or privilege of denominational schools in a particular province at the time of confederation (or admission), then the province would be disabled from compelling the denominational schools to instruct in a different language.

§ 56:18 Mackell case

The question whether language rights are guaranteed to the denominational schools of a particular province cannot be answered in the

[Section 56:17]

[1]Education is the topic of the next chapter (ch. 57) of this book.

[2]British Columbia and Prince Edward Island were each admitted by order in council under s. 146 of the Constitution Act, 1867. Each order in council provided that the terms of the Constitution Act, 1867 (including s. 93) were to apply to the newly admitted province: British Columbia Terms of Union, R.S.C. 1985, Appendix II, No. 10, s. 10; Prince Edward Island Terms of Union, R.S.C. 1985, Appendix II, No. 12, second-last unnumbered para. The protections for denominational schools in s. 93 no longer apply to Quebec as the result of Constitution Amendment Proclamation, 1997 (Quebec), Can. Stat. Instruments, SI 97-141.

[3]Manitoba Act, 1870, R.S.C. 1985, Appendix II, No. 8, s. 22.

[4]Alberta Act, R.S.C. 1985, Appendix II, No. 20, s. 17.

[5]Saskatchewan Act, R.S.C. 1985, Appendix II, No. 21, s. 17.

[6]Terms of Union of Newfoundland, s. 17; schedule to Newfoundland Act, R.S.C. 1985, Appendix II, No. 32. This provision has been amended by Constitution Amendment Proclamation, 1998 (Newfoundland Act), Can. Stat. Instruments, SI 98-25, which repealed and replaced an amendment in 1997.

abstract. It will depend upon an analysis of the legal position of the denominational schools in the province at the time of confederation. However, the question has been determined for Ontario, and the determination has implications for the other provinces. In *Ottawa Roman Catholic Separate School Trustees v. Mackell* (1916),[1] the Privy Council held that Ontario had the power to require that English be the language of instruction in hitherto French-speaking Roman Catholic separate schools in the province. Their lordships examined the statute law governing the separate schools in Ontario at the time of confederation, and concluded that the law did not confer upon the separate schools the legal right to use French as the language of instruction. Since no such right existed at confederation, it followed that no such right was preserved by s. 93.

Their lordships in *Mackell* pointed out that s. 93 reserves the rights with respect to denominational schools of a "class of persons", and they held that the "class of persons" in s. 93 meant a "class of persons determined according to religious belief, and not according to race or language".[2] Since the Roman Catholics in Ontario comprised both French-speaking and English-speaking people, the French-speakers could not claim to be a class of persons entitled to rights under s. 93. This part of their lordships' reasoning is obviously unfavourable to the recognition of language rights under s. 93 in any province. But it is wrong to assume that *Mackell* completely precludes the recognition of language rights under s. 93. After defining the "class of persons" referred to in s. 93, their lordships in *Mackell* went on to examine an argument that the French language was guaranteed to the entire class of Roman Catholics by statutory provisions conferring upon the trustees of separate schools the right to *choose* the language of instruction. This argument was rejected on the ground that the statute law of Ontario at the time of confederation did not confer that right on the trustees of the Roman Catholic separate schools. The implication from the discussion of this point is that, if the law at confederation had conferred that right, then s. 93 would have preserved (and entrenched) it, and the province would have been unable to stipulate to the trustees of separate schools the language of instruction in any of their schools.

It seems a fair conclusion from *Mackell* that s. 93 would preserve from legislative change the language of instruction in denominational schools if it could be established that the trustees of those schools had at the time of confederation (or admission) a legal right to choose the language of instruction in their schools. *Mackell* decides that no such right exists in Ontario, and it is reasonably clear that no such right would be held to

---

[Section 56:18]

[1]*Ottawa Roman Catholic Separate School Trustees v. Mackell*, [1917] A.C. 62.

[2]*Ottawa Roman Catholic Separate School Trustees v. Mackell*, [1917] A.C. 62, 69.

exist in New Brunswick, Nova Scotia, Prince Edward Island and British Columbia,[3] but the point is still open in the other provinces.[4]

§ 56:19 Section 23 of the Charter

Minority language educational rights have now been provided for in s. 23 of the Charter.[1] Section 23 provides:

23.(1) Citizens of Canada

(a) whose first language learned and still understood is that of the English or French linguistic minority population of the province in which they reside, or

(b) who have received their primary school instruction in Canada in English or French and reside in a province where the language in which they received that instruction is the language of the English or French linguistic minority population of the province,

have the right to have their children receive primary and secondary school instruction in that language in that province.

(2) Citizens of Canada of whom any child has received or is receiving primary or secondary school instruction in English or French in Canada, have the right to have all their children receive primary and secondary school instruction in the same language.

(3) The right of citizens of Canada under subsections (1) and (2) to have their children receive primary and secondary school instruction in the language of the English or French linguistic minority population of a province

(a) applies wherever in the province the number of children of citizens who have such a right is sufficient to warrant the provision to them out of public funds of minority language instruction; and

(b) includes, where the number of those children so warrants, the right to have them receive that instruction in minority language educational facilities provided out of public funds.

Section 23 confers upon "citizens of Canada" who are members of the

---

[3]Schmeiser, Civil Liberties in Canada (1964), 155-156; Bastarache (ed.), Language Rights in Canada (2nd ed., 2003), ch. 5.

[4]Schmeiser, Civil Liberties in Canada (1964), ch. 4. A decision of Quebec's Superior Court denies the existence of the right in Quebec: *Protestant School Bd. of Montreal v. Min. of Education of Que.* (1976), 83 D.L.R. (3d) 645 (Que. S.C.); appeal dismissed on ground that statute in issue had been repealed: (1978) 83 D.L.R. (3d) 679n (Que. C.A.). Note, however, that the constitutional protections of s. 93 were repealed for Quebec in 1997 as a result of Constitution Amendment Proclamation, 1997 (Quebec), Can. Stat. Instruments, SI 97-141.

[Section 56:19]

[1]For commentary on s. 23, see Beaudoin and Mendes (eds.), The Canadian Charter of Rights and Freedoms (4th ed., 2005), ch. 15 (by J. Woehrling and A. Tremblay), ch. 16 (by M. Power and P. Foucher); Bastarache, note 27, above, chs. 3-5; Canadian Charter of Rights Annotated (Canada Law Book, loose-leaf), annotation to ss. 16-23; the last work includes a bibliography of the relevant literature.

English-speaking minority in Quebec or the French-speaking minority in the other provinces "the right to have their children receive primary and secondary school instruction in [the minority] language in that province." This right,[2] which applies to denominational and non-denominational schools,[3] is possessed by parents[4] who fit into one of the three categories established by s. 23. Those categories are defined by (1) the mother tongue of the parent (s. 23(1)(a)); (2) the language of primary school instruction in Canada of the parent (s. 23(1)(b)); and (3) the language of instruction in Canada of one child of the parent (s. 23(2)). Each of these categories is examined in the text that follows.

The minority language education rights of s. 23 are granted to individual parents who fit one of the three stipulated categories in subsections (1) and (2). But, as subsection (3) makes clear, the right only applies where the numbers of qualifying children warrant, and the facilities and programs to which the parents are entitled vary with the number of qualifying children. These restrictions on the right give to minority language education rights a "unique collective aspect even though the rights are granted to individuals".[5]

The minority language education rights of s. 23 are a "constitutional minimum".[6] This means that provincial legislation which is more restrictive of access to minority-language education than s. 23 will be unconstitutional (unless justified under s. 1). But, subject to the constitutional minimum, the provinces retain their constitutional power to make laws in relation to education (s. 93), and they can enact laws that broaden access to minority language-education. For example, some provinces have granted minority-language school boards the power to admit children to the minority-language school even though their parents are not s. 23 rights holders.[7]

§ 56:20 Mother tongue of parent

The first category of parent entitled to minority language educational rights is defined by the mother tongue of the parent. Paragraph (a) of s. 23(1) applies to citizens "whose first language learned and still

---

[2]This right cannot be made subject to the discretion of school boards: *Re Education Act (Ont.)* (1984), 47 O.R. (2d) 1, 30 (C.A.).

[3]*Re Education Act (Ont.)* (1984), 47 O.R. (2d) 1, 50-51 (C.A.); and see §§ 56:24, "Denominational schools".

[4]The right is conferred upon parents. The section does not require that the children be French-speaking: *Re Education Act (Ont.)* (1984), 47 O.R. (2d) 1, 29 (C.A.).

[5]*Doucet-Boudreau v. Nova Scotia*, [2003] 3 S.C.R. 3, para. 28 per Iacobucci and Arbour JJ. for majority.

[6]*Yukon Francophone School Board v. Yukon*, 2015 SCC 25, para. 70, following *Mahe v. Alberta*, [1990] 1 S.C.R. 342, 379.

[7]*Yukon Francophone School Board v. Yukon*, 2015 SCC 25, paras. 71-73, approving the grants of power. However, the Court decided (para. 74) that Yukon (which had provincial powers over education) had not authorized its Francophone School Board to admit children of non-rights holders to the French-language school in the territory (para. 74).

understood is that of the English or French linguistic minority population of the province[1] in which they reside". For example, in Ontario (or any of the other provinces with English-speaking majorities), a Canadian citizen whose mother tongue ("first language learned and still understood") is French has the right under para. (a) to have his or her children receive primary and secondary school instruction in French. Paragraph (a) will include French-speakers from other parts of Canada and from outside Canada (provided that they have become citizens). It will not include persons whose mother tongue is English or persons whose mother tongue is neither English nor French. The mother tongue criterion would be satisfied by an Ontario parent who could establish (1) that his or her "first language learned" was French and (2) that this language is "still understood". Neither of these stipulations will be easy to apply, and the second (if disputed) seems to require the use of language tests: how else would one establish that a language is "still understood"?

Paragraph (a) is drafted to apply to English-speakers in Quebec as well as to French-speakers elsewhere in Canada. But, by virtue of s. 59 of the Constitution Act, 1982, the paragraph does not apply in Quebec until the legislative assembly or government of Quebec decides to adopt it.[2] This exemption was added in recognition of the fact that Quebec alone of the provinces did not join in the constitutional agreement of November 5, 1981, which accepted (among other things) the terms of the Charter, including s. 23. Since the mother tongue clause would be the most controversial of the minority language educational rights, the decision was made to exempt Quebec from it, until Quebec itself decided that it was willing to be bound by the clause.[3] The effect of the exemption is that English-speaking parents in Quebec have no right to send their children to English-speaking schools, unless they fit into the second or third category of parent recognized by s. 23. For example, a person of English mother tongue, who received her own schooling outside Canada, and who did not already have a child in an English-language school in Canada, would have no right to send her children to an English-language school in Quebec. If and when Quebec opts into the mother tongue clause, that person would become entitled to send her children to an English-language school in Quebec.

[Section 56:20]

[1]Note that the right depends upon membership of the linguistic minority population *of the province*. It does not apply to a person who is a member of the linguistic majority population of the province, even if the person resides in a region of the province where his or her language is in the minority, for example, an English-speaker in northern New Brunswick or northern Ontario.

[2]By An Act respecting the Constitution Act, 1982, S.Q. 1982, c. 21, s. 4, the Quebec Legislature has purported to require that the adoption requires the consent of the Legislature, and not just of the "government", as s. 59 contemplates as an alternative.

[3]Section 59 was not part of the constitutional agreement of November 5, 1981, but was one of the additional points agreed to shortly afterwards by the Prime Minister and the nine agreeing Premiers.

§ 56:21 Language of instruction of parent in Canada

The second category of parent entitled to minority language educational rights is defined by the language of primary school instruction in Canada of the parent. Paragraph (b) of s. 23(1) applies to citizens who have received their primary school instruction in Canada in the minority language of the province where they now reside. Paragraph (b) has become known as the "Canada clause" because, under paragraph (b), Canadian citizens, who move from one province to another, retain the right to have their children educated in the same language as that in which the parent was educated anywhere in Canada. Quebec is not exempted from paragraph (b). Thus, a Canadian citizen who had been educated in English in Nova Scotia, and who moved to Quebec, would have the right under paragraph (b) to send his children to English-language schools in Quebec. Paragraph (b) would not apply to that person in Quebec if he had been educated in Nova Scotia in French (instead of English), or if he had been educated outside Canada.

Quebec's Charter of the French Language, a statute enacted in 1977 to give effect to provincial language policies,[1] limited admission to English-language schools in Quebec to the children of persons who had been educated in English in Quebec. In *Attorney General of Quebec v. Quebec Protestant School Boards* (1984),[2] the Supreme Court of Canada held that this "Quebec clause", which excluded the children of persons who had been educated in English in provinces other than Quebec, was in conflict with the "Canada clause" (s. 23(1)(b)) of the Charter of Rights. Therefore, the Quebec clause had to yield to the Canada clause, and school boards in Quebec were obliged to admit to English-language schools the children of parents who had been educated in English anywhere in Canada.[3]

§ 56:22 Language of instruction of child in Canada

The third category of parent entitled to minority language educational rights is defined by the language of instruction in Canada of one child in the family. Subsection (2) of s. 23 applies to citizens who have a child who has received or is receiving primary or secondary school instruction in English or French in Canada. Such persons have the right to have all their children receive their schooling in the same language. Quebec is not exempted from this clause either. Subsection (2) would include a Quebecer who already had a child in an English-language school in Quebec. It would also include an Albertan who moved to Quebec and

---

[Section 56:21]

[1]Charter of the French Language, S.Q. 1977, c. 5.

[2]*Attorney General of Quebec v. Quebec Protestant School Boards*, [1984] 2 S.C.R. 66. The opinion was rendered by "the Court"

[3]The province's attempt to justify the Quebec clause under s. 1 of the Charter failed, on the ground that the Quebec clause was such a direct denial of the right guaranteed by s. 23(1)(b) that s. 1 had no application: for discussion, see ch. 38, Limitation of Rights, under heading § 38:6, "Limits".

who before the move had a child in an English-language school in Alberta. In the English-speaking provinces, subsection (2) will confer a right to French-language education on any citizen who has, or has had, a child in a French-language school anywhere in Canada. The purpose of s. 23(2) is to encourage mobility within Canada by guaranteeing the continuity of a child's minority language education, and by ensuring that all of the children in the same family can go to the same schools.

Quebec's Charter of the French Language restricted admission to English-language schools in the province by providing that a child who has received or is receiving English-language instruction in Canada (and the child's siblings) is eligible for admission to English-language schools in Quebec only if the English language instruction constituted "the major part" of that child's schooling in Canada. Since s. 23(2) makes no stipulation as to the amount of time spent by the child in English-language programs in Canada, the "major part" restriction appeared to be inconsistent with the s. 23(2) right, which would make the law invalid unless it could be justified as a reasonable limit under s. 1. However, in *Solski v. Quebec* (2005),[1] the Supreme Court of Canada held that the Quebec law was consistent with the s. 23(2) right and upheld the law without resort to s. 1. According to the Court, the "major part" requirement would be inconsistent with s. 23(2) if it called for a "quantitative" measurement of the proportion of time spent by the child in English-language instruction in Canada. (This was how the provision had been applied by the authorities in Quebec.) But the Court held that the requirement should be "read down" to a "qualitative" restriction, which would only require "a significant part, though not necessarily the majority" of the child's instruction to have been in English.[2] Read in this fashion, the Court held that it was consistent with s. 23(2) and was therefore constitutional. With respect, even if "the major part" will bear the meaning of "significant part", it is hard to see why even the latter requirement is not an infringement of s. 23(2), especially in light of the Court's insistence that "language rights must be interpreted in a broad and purposive manner".[3]

In 2002, Quebec amended its Charter of the French Language to provide that instruction in English received in Quebec in an unsubsidized private school was to be disregarded in calculating the major part of that child's schooling. This reflected a concern by the Government of

---

[Section 56:22]

[1]*Solski v. Quebec*, [2005] 1 S.C.R. 201. The unanimous opinion is attributed to "the Court". In two companion cases, the Court rejected an equality challenge to the Quebec law: *Gosselin v. Que.*, [2005] 1 S.C.R. 238, and upheld the jurisdiction of the Administrative Tribunal of Quebec to resolve disputes as to eligibility for admission to English-language schools: *Okwuobi v. Lester B. Pearson School Bd.*, [2005] 1 S.C.R. 257.

[2]*Solski v. Quebec*, [2005] 1 S.C.R. 201, para. 28. The Court went on (paras. 39-48) to list the factors to be taken into account in assessing whether a child's schooling in English constituted a significant part of the child's primary and secondary education in Canada.

[3]*Solski v. Quebec*, [2005] 1 S.C.R. 201, para. 20.

Quebec that the restrictions on admission to English-language public schools were being circumvented by the growth of unsubsidized private schools in Quebec, so called "bridging schools" (écoles passerelles), to which parents would send their children for instruction in English for enough time to qualify them for admission to an English-language public school. In *Nguyen v. Quebec* (2009),[4] the Supreme Court held that the amendment was a limit on the right guaranteed by s. 23(2), and that it could not be justified under s. 1. The Court accepted the importance of the legislative objective, which was to protect and promote the French language in Quebec, and the Court accepted that the amendment was rationally connected to the objective. However, the absolute exclusion of instruction in unsubsidized private schools as a pathway into Quebec's English-language public system was an "excessive" legislative response in relation to "the seriousness of the identified problem"; it was "overly drastic"; and was therefore not a minimum impairment of the right.[5] The Court accordingly declared that the amendments were invalid, although it suspended the declaration of invalidity for a period of one year to enable the province to come up with a more proportionate solution to the bridging-schools problem.[6]

§ 56:23 Where numbers warrant

The right to minority language education that is conferred on the three categories of parents that have just been described is not an absolute right. By virtue of paragraph (3)(a) of s. 23, the right to "instruction" is limited to "wherever in the province the number of children of citizens who have such a right is sufficient to warrant the provision to them out of public funds of minority language instruction". By virtue of paragraph (3)(b) of s. 23, the right "includes, where the number of those children so warrants, the right to have them receive that instruction in minority language educational facilities provided out of public funds".

In *Mahe v. Alberta* (1990),[1] the Supreme Court of Canada, speaking through Dickson C.J., held that the effect of paragraphs (a) and (b) of subsection (3) of s. 23 was to establish a "sliding scale" of entitlement,[2] based on the number of children whose parents qualify under s. 23.[3] At one end of the scale, the number of children might be so small that the

---

[4]*Nguyen v. Quebec*, [2009] 3 S.C.R. 208. LeBel J. wrote the opinion of the Court.

[5]*Nguyen v. Quebec*, [2009] 3 S.C.R. 208, para. 42.

[6]The suspension of the declaration of invalidity would have denied the appellants any immediate remedy, but the Court held (para. 51) that, "despite the suspension", the appelants' claims to admission to English-language public schools were to be immediately granted (in the case of one appellant) or (in the other case) reviewed in light of the (unsuspended) Court's judgment.

[Section 56:23]

[1]*Mahe v. Alberta*, [1990] 1 S.C.R. 342. The opinion of the Court was given by Dickson C.J.

[2]*Mahe v. Alberta*, [1990] 1 S.C.R. 342, 366.

[3]The application of the where-numbers-warrant test cannot be based solely on the numbers of qualified children in a single school district; s. 23(3)(a) uses the phrase

where-numbers-warrant threshold of paragraph (a) would not be crossed, and no programme of minority language instruction would be required. It is arguable, however, that a very small number of minority language students would warrant the provision of bus transportation to a minority language school, if there is one within reasonable driving distance. A somewhat larger number of students would warrant the provision of classroom space and some intensive minority language instruction within a majority language school. A larger number would cross the where-numbers-warrant threshold of paragraph (b), which requires the provision out of public funds of "minority language educational facilities". Those facilities might include part of a school or an entire school. At the high end of the scale, the number of children might be so large that paragraph (b)'s requirement of "minority language educational facilities" would require the establishment of a minority language school board. "The idea of a sliding scale is simply that s. 23 guarantees whatever type and level of rights and services is appropriate in order to provide minority language instruction for the particular number of students involved."[4]

The issue in *Mahe* was the extent of the s. 23 right near the high end of the sliding scale. In Edmonton, there were about 4,000 children whose parents had s. 23 rights, and there was a French-language school in operation with 242 students and space for another 480 students. The sole question was the entitlement of the s. 23 parents to powers of management and control over their children's French-language education. The Court rejected the argument that the phrase "minority language educational facilities" in paragraph (b) of subsection (3) referred only to physical facilities. The phrase did of course include physical facilities, which in this case was satisfied by the provision of Edmonton's French-language school. The phrase also included public funding on a basis at least equivalent to that of the majority's schools, which in this case also seems to have been satisfied.[5] But the phrase extended beyond physical facilities to a degree of management and control that was proportionate to the number of qualifying children.

The degree of management and control that was required by s. 23 could include a minority language school board, but in *Mahe* Dickson C.J. was "not satisfied on the basis of present evidence that the number of students likely to attend Francophone schools in Edmonton is sufficient to mandate the establishment of an independent Francophone school board".[6] However, he concluded that the numbers did warrant a guaranteed number of Francophone representatives on the school board that operated the existing French-language school (and other pro-

---

"wherever in the province", which transcends the territorial limits of school boards: *Mahe v. Alberta*, [1990] 1 S.C.R. 342, 386; *Re Education Act (Ont.)* (1984), 47 O.R. (2d) 1, 33 (C.A.).

[4] *Mahe v. Alberta*, [1990] 1 S.C.R. 342, 366.

[5] *Mahe v. Alberta*, [1990] 1 S.C.R. 342, 378. There was no complaint in the proceedings about the level of funding.

[6] *Mahe v. Alberta*, [1990] 1 S.C.R. 342, 388-389.

grammes of French-language instruction). Those representatives should (subject to provincial regulation) be given exclusive control over the French-language instruction, including the expenditure of funds for that purpose, the appointment of administrators and teachers, and the design of programmes of instruction.

Mahe was followed in *Re Public Schools Act (Man.)* (1993),[7] in which the Supreme Court of Canada struck down Manitoba's legislation respecting French-language schools, because it made no provision for the parents of French-language students to have management and control over French-language education. The Court, speaking through Lamer C.J., estimated that the number of potential French-language students in Manitoba was 5,617 at the minimum, with a possibility that the number was much higher. The Court held that, even on the basis of the low figure, the number warranted the establishment of an independent French language school board in Manitoba under the exclusive management and control of the French-language minority.

In *Arsenault-Cameron v. Prince Edward Island* (2000),[8] the issue was whether the where-numbers-warrant test in s. 23 mandated a French-language school in the community of Summerside, as the French-speaking parents insisted, or whether it was sufficient to provide bus service to an existing French-language school 28 kilometres away, as the provincial Minister of Education insisted. The number of students prepared to enroll in a new French school in Summerside was only 49, and the proposed bus service was less than the average bus journey for English-language students in the province. Nevertheless, the Supreme Court of Canada unanimously sided with the parents in ordering the establishment of a French school in Summerside. The Court held that it was a mistake to work from the known demand for a French-language school, because if a school were to be established demand would likely rise. The relevant number was "somewhere between the known demand and the number of persons who could potentially take advantage of the service".[9] This meant that the relevant number was more than 49, because the number of children who could potentially take advantage of the school was 155. The Court did not fix on a number, but acknowledged that the number of students was likely to be less than 100. The Minister had taken the view that any school with less than 100 students would have difficulty in meeting curriculum requirements as well as providing services such as guidance, music, gym and resource teaching. The Court rejected this approach, saying that "the pedagogical requirements established to address the needs of the majority language students cannot be used to trump cultural and linguistic concerns appropriate for the

---

[7] *Re Public Schools Act (Man.)*, [1993] 1 S.C.R. 839. The opinion of the Court was given by Lamer C.J.

[8] *Arsenault-Cameron v. Prince Edward Island*, [2000] 1 S.C.R. 3. Major and Bastarache JJ. wrote the judgment of the Court.

[9] *Arsenault-Cameron v. Prince Edward Island*, [2000] 1 S.C.R. 3, para. 32.

minority language students".[10] The Court held that the flourishing and preservation of the French-language minority, which was the purpose underlying s. 23 of the Charter, was best pursued by the establishment of a French school in Summerside, and the Court accordingly ordered that the school be established.

In *Association des parents de l'école Rose-des-vents v. British Columbia* (2015),[11] the parents of students at Rose-des-vents (RDV), a French-language elementary school in Vancouver, sued the school board and the province for a declaration that there was a breach of s. 23 on the ground that the educational services provided by RDV were inferior to those provided by English-language schools in the city: it was smaller than the English-language schools, it was overcrowded, and the majority of students did not live within walking distance of the school and had to travel by bus. The Supreme Court granted the declaration. Karakatsanis J., who wrote for the Court, started with the proposition that in this case the where-numbers-warrant test was at the upper end of the sliding scale. In that case, the rights-holders were entitled to "full educational facilities that are distinct from, *and equivalent to*, those found in the schools of the majority language group."[12] Equivalence did not entail identical facilities. On the contrary, "the comparative exercise is contextual and holistic, accounting for not only physical facilities, but also quality of instruction, educational outcomes, extracurricular activities and travel times, to name a few factors."[13] The relevant factors were those that would be taken into account by parents in choosing a school for their children. The decision to be reached was an assessment of "the *substantive equivalence* of the educational experience."[14] The first-instance judge had granted the declaration, and he had taken into account the "factors that influence parental enrollment decisions", which were the correct factors. The judge found that RDV was superior to the English-language schools in quality of instruction and academic outcomes, but not so superior as to offset its inadequate physical facilities, its overcrowding and its long travel times. The Court accepted the judge's findings and affirmed the declaration that there was a failure of equivalence in breach of s. 23. However, the Court also deferred to the judge's refusal to make any finding of fault (as between the school board and the province), and the judge's consequent refusal to grant any positive remedy to the parents. These issues were left for a later phase of the proceedings, but with the hope that the Court's grant of the declaration would cause the school board and province to address the inade-

---

[10] *Arsenault-Cameron v. Prince Edward Island*, [2000] 1 S.C.R. 3, para. 38.

[11] *Association des parents de l'école Rose-des-vents v. British Columbia*, [2015] 2 S.C.R. 139, 2015 SCC 21. Karakatsanis J. wrote the opinion of the Court.

[12] *Association des parents de l'école Rose-des-vents v. British Columbia*, [2015] 2 S.C.R. 139, 2015 SCC 21, para. 29 (emphasis added).

[13] *Association des parents de l'école Rose-des-vents v. British Columbia*, [2015] 2 S.C.R. 139, 2015 SCC 21, para. 39.

[14] *Association des parents de l'école Rose-des-vents v. British Columbia*, [2015] 2 S.C.R. 139, 2015 SCC 21, para. 41 (emphasis in original).

quate facilities at RDV without the need for any more litigation.[15] The Court also made a broader call for provincial governments and minority language school boards to work out their disputes about how best to satisfy s. 23 through negotiation.

This call for negotiation instead of litigation seems to have gone unheeded, at least in British Columbia, as just five years later, in *Conseil Scolaire Francophone de la Colombie-Britannique v. British Columbia* (2020),[16] the Court was asked to consider another major s. 23 case involving the province's French-language education system. The challenge, which once again involved the province's French-language school board and concerned parents, alleged a number of infringements of s. 23 – some involving systemic claims related to how the province funds French-language schools and programs, and others specific claims seeking the improvement of existing schools and the construction of new schools. Clearly concerned about the cost and delays associated with s. 23 claims (10 years had already elapsed since this case began),[17] the Court took the opportunity to clarify the "sliding scale" and "substantive equivalence" analysis under s. 23.

Wagner C.J., who wrote for the majority of the Court, turned first to the sliding scale analysis (which, recall, is used to determine the level of minority language education services required by s. 23, operationalizing the where-numbers-warrant thresholds in s. 23, which are described at the beginning of this section). The Court's decision in *Mahe*, which is discussed earlier, set out two factors to consider in situating a case on the sliding scale: (1) the level of services that is pedagogically appropriate; and (2) the cost of the services.[18] Wagner C.J said that clarification was needed about how to apply these two factors, and with this goal in mind, he set out a three-stage approach that is to be applied in situating a case on the sliding scale. At the first stage, it is necessary to determine the numbers of students involved. This determination is future looking; it requires a long-term projection of how many minority language students will *eventually* use the services (school or program) being claimed. At the second stage, it is necessary to compare the number of students identified at the first stage with the number of students in majority language schools either locally or elsewhere in the province in order to determine whether the services being claimed are appropriate

[15]*Association des parents de l'école Rose-des-vents v. British Columbia*, [2015] 2 S.C.R. 139, 2015 SCC 21, para. 64-67.

[16]*Conseil Scolaire Francophone de la Colombie-Britannique v. British Columbia*, 2020 SCC 13. Wagner C.J. wrote the opinion for the majority of the Court, which was joined by Abella, Moldaver, Karakatsanis, Côté, Martin and Kasirer JJ. Brown and Rowe JJ. wrote a joint opinion dissenting in part. Other aspects of this decision are discussed elsewhere in this book: see ch. 38, Limitation of Rights, under headings § 38:17, "Cost", and § 38.14(g), "Section 23"; and ch. 40, Enforcement of Rights, under heading § 40:19, "Damages".

[17]See e.g. *Conseil Scolaire Francophone de la Colombie-Britannique v. British Columbia*, 2020 SCC 13, paras. 20, 56.

[18]*Conseil Scolaire Francophone de la Colombie-Britannique v. British Columbia*, 2020 SCC 13, para. 52, citing *Mahe v. Alberta*, [1990] 1 S.C.R. 342, 384.

from the standpoint of the two *Mahe* factors (pedagogy and cost). If "comparably sized majority language schools" exist locally or elsewhere in the province, a rebuttable presumption would arise "that the province considers maintaining those . . . schools to be appropriate from the standpoint of pedagogy and cost".[19] However, the province could rebut this presumption by showing that the comparator schools *or* the school being claimed are inappropriate from the standpoint of pedagogy and cost. At the third and final stage of the analysis, it is necessary to determine what level of services is appropriate, by placing the case on the sliding scale. If the number of minority language students is comparable to the numbers of students attending majority language schools, the case falls at the high end of the sliding scale and a separate "homogenous school" will be required by s. 23. However, if the number of students is not comparable, the case falls below the high end of the sliding scale, and a separate homogenous school will not be required. The level of services that will be appropriate in such a case will vary, and might consist of only a few hours of minority language classes (if the case falls at the low end of the sliding scale) or control by the language minority over a portion of the school (if the case falls more in the middle of the sliding scale).[20] Applying this new three-stage approach, Wagner C.J. held that the school board was entitled to eight more homogenous schools that had been denied in the courts below. The trial judge had erred by relying on short-term projections to determine the number of minority language students, and by comparing this number of students only to the numbers in local majority language schools rather than schools across the province.

Wagner C.J. then turned to the substantive equivalence analysis. The *Rose-des-vents* case, which is also discussed earlier in this section, prescribed a standard of substantive equivalence that is to be applied in determining the quality of services that must be provided to minority language students to satisfy s. 23. However, in *Rose-des-vents*, the number of minority language students was comparable to the number of students at majority language schools. In *Conseil scolaire*, the Court had to determine whether – and how – to apply the substantive equivalence standard where the number of minority language students is lower than – and hence not comparable to – the number of students in majority language schools. The trial judge held that, in such cases, a "proportionality test" should be applied: differences in the educational experience of

[19]*Conseil Scolaire Francophone de la Colombie-Britannique v. British Columbia*, 2020 SCC 13, para. 52. Brown and Rowe JJ., dissenting in part, criticized and rejected this presumption: see paras. 193, 215.

[20]Wagner C.J. acknowledged that, if the number of students is not comparable, and the case therefore falls below the high end of the sliding scale, it will not be possible to use a comparative approach in determining where to place the case on the sliding scale. He left the approach to be applied to a future case. However, he did say that, in such cases, deference should be shown to the level of services proposed by minority language school board; and also that cost, one of the two *Mahe* factors, "will rarely be decisive" in determining the appropriate level of services: *Conseil Scolaire Francophone de la Colombie-Britannique v. British Columbia*, 2020 SCC 13, para. 88.

minority language students would be acceptable, unless their educational experience is "meaningfully disproportionate" to the educational experience of majority language students, "based on a local comparison of the global educational experience".[21] Wagner C.J. rejected this proportionality test. He said that "[t]he substantive equivalence test applies everywhere on the sliding scale", because language minorities are entitled to have their children receive substantively equivalent educational experiences everywhere in Canada.[22] However, he added one qualification – the need to "take into account the inherent characteristics of attendance at a small school".[23] He framed the test that is to be applied where minority language schools do not have comparable numbers of students as follows: "whether reasonable parents who are *aware of the inherent characteristics of small schools* would be deterred from sending their children to [a minority language school] because the educational experience there is meaningfully inferior to the experience at available majority language schools".[24] This modified substantive equivalence test is clearly stricter than the trial judge's proportionality test. Wagner C.J. then applied this modified substantive equivalence test to three of the minority language schools at issue in the case. He agreed with the trial judge that the educational experience at one school (in Nelson) did not fall short and said that there was inadequate evidence to draw a conclusion about another school (in Mission). However, he disagreed with the trial judge's conclusion about a third school (in Chilliwack); this school passed muster under the trial judge's proportionality test, but it failed the substantive equivalence test. Wagner C.J. held that none of the infringements of s. 23 that were identified in the case – under either the sliding scale analysis described in the previous paragraph or the substantive equivalence analysis described in this paragraph – were justified under s. 1, because "a very stringent standard" of justification applies in s. 23 cases,[25] and this stringent standard of justification was not satisfied.

---

[21] *Conseil Scolaire Francophone de la Colombie-Britannique v. British Columbia*, 2020 SCC 13, paras. 36, 117.

[22] *Conseil Scolaire Francophone de la Colombie-Britannique v. British Columbia*, 2020 SCC 13, paras. 107, 110. Brown and Rowe JJ., dissenting in part, agreed with Wagner C.J. that the substantive equivalence test should apply broadly; however, they said that problems would result when this approach is combined with the presumption advocated by Wagner C.J. at step two of the sliding scale analysis: para. 244.

[23] *Conseil Scolaire Francophone de la Colombie-Britannique v. British Columbia*, 2020 SCC 13, para. 109. By way of example, Wagner C.J. said that a reasonable parent would understand that, in a small school, there may not be the same number of specialized teachers or the same range of facilities, and that multiple grades may need to be combined into one classroom to attain sufficient numbers of students: para. 114.

[24] *Conseil Scolaire Francophone de la Colombie-Britannique v. British Columbia*, 2020 SCC 13, para. 116 (emphasis in original).

[25] *Conseil Scolaire Francophone de la Colombie-Britannique v. British Columbia*, 2020 SCC 13, para. 151. See further, ch. 38, Limitation of Rights, under heading § 38.14(g), "Section 23".

§ 56:24 Denominational schools

In *Mahe*,[1] most of the s. 23 parents were Roman Catholic separate school supporters, and the French-language school was operated by the separate school board. Under s. 19 of the Charter, nothing in the Charter was to abrogate or derogate from the denominational school rights conferred on separate school supporters by the Constitution of Canada, which in the case of Alberta meant s. 17 of the Alberta Act.[2] This raised the question whether the exclusive powers of management and control that the Court required to be vested in the representatives of the s. 23 parents would derogate from denominational school rights. The Court pointed out that the representatives of the s. 23 parents on the separate school board would also be denominational trustees, so that there was no requirement that the separate school board cede any powers to non-denominational trustees, and there was no interference with the denominational character of the board. The Court took the view that the vesting of exclusive powers of management and control in the s. 23 representatives "amounts to the *regulation* of a non-denominational aspect of education, namely, the language of instruction, a form of regulation which the courts have long held to be valid".[3] Therefore, the Court held that denominational school rights were not prejudiced—they were merely "regulated"[4]—by the vesting of some exclusive powers of management and control in trustees who represented French-speaking parents.

§ 56:25 Supervision of remedial orders

A breach of s. 23, like a breach of any of the other Charter guarantees, may be remedied under s. 24(1) of the Charter.[1] Section 24(1) authorizes a court of competent jurisdiction to award "such remedy as the court considers appropriate and just in the circumstances". In *Doucet-Boudreau v. Nova Scotia* (2003),[2] a superior-court judge in Nova Scotia, acting on the application of French-speaking parents, found that in five districts of the province the numbers of children of French-speaking parents warranted French-language schools. Under the authority of s. 24(1), he ordered that the five schools be built and that programs of

---

[Section 56:24]

[1]*Mahe v. Alberta*, [1990] 1 S.C.R. 342.

[2]Alberta Act, R.S.C. 1985, Appendix II, No. 20, s. 17.

[3]*Mahe v. Alberta*, [1990] 1 S.C.R. 342, 382 (emphasis in original).

[4]On the "regulation" of denominational schools, see ch. 57, Education, under heading § 57:9, "Regulation".

[Section 56:25]

[1]Chapter 40, Enforcement of Rights, under heading §§ 40:11 to 40:25, "Remedy clause".

[2]*Doucet-Boudreau v. Nova Scotia*, [2003] 3 S.C.R. 3. Iacobucci and Arbour JJ. wrote the opinion for the five-judge majority. LeBel and Deschamps JJ. wrote the opinion for the four-judge dissenting minority. The decision is discussed (and criticized) in ch. 40, Enforcement of Rights, under heading § 40:23, "Supervision of court orders".

instruction be developed for each school. He stipulated the dates by which each school should be built and its curriculum developed. And he also decreed that "the Court shall retain jurisdiction to hear reports from [the government] respecting [the government's] compliance with the order". Pursuant to this last provision, the judge held a series of reporting hearings throughout the period of construction of the schools, at which the government was required to file affidavits as to the progress of its work, the parents were permitted to file affidavits of rebuttal, and all deponents were subject to cross-examination. This was the first time that a Canadian court had made provision for judicial supervision of compliance with a s. 24(1) order. The Attorney General of Nova Scotia appealed only the provision for judicial supervision. The Supreme Court of Canada, by a narrow majority of five to four, upheld the provision for judicial supervision. The dissenting minority pointed out that Canada had an unbroken tradition of governmental compliance with s. 24(1) orders, and in the unlikely event of non-compliance the parents could obtain a contempt order. In their view, the supervisory order was inappropriate: in undertaking the supervision of school construction and curriculum development, the court moved outside its traditional adjudicative role and outside its expertise. But the majority of the Court upheld the trial judge's order. They repeated his concerns about the danger of progressive assimilation of the French-speaking majority in the province, and past delays in developing French-language schools. They took the view that the supervisory order was appropriate and just in the circumstances, and upheld it as a valid exercise of s. 24(1).

APPENDICES

Appendix A. Constitution Act, 1867
Appendix B. Canada Act 1982
Appendix C. Constitution Act, 1982
Appendix D. Canadian Bill of Rights
Appendix E. American Bill of Rights
Appendix F. International Covenant on Civil and Political Rights
Appendix G. Optional Protocol to International Covenant on Civil and Political Rights

APPENDIX A
Constitution Act, 1867

U.K., 30 & 31 Victoria, c. 3.

(Consolidated with amendments by the Department of Justice, Canada)[1]

An Act for the Union of Canada, Nova Scotia, and New Brunswick, and the Government thereof; and for Purposes connected therewith

[*29TH MARCH 1867.*]

WHEREAS the Provinces of Canada, Nova Scotia, and New Brunswick have expressed their Desire to be federally united into One Dominion under the Crown of the United Kingdom of Great Britain and Ireland, with a Constitution similar in Principle to that of the United Kingdom:

And whereas such a Union would conduce to the Welfare of the Provinces and promote the Interests of the British Empire:

And whereas on the Establishment of the Union by Authority of Parliament it is expedient, not only that the Constitution of the Legislative Authority in the Dominion be provided for, but also that the Nature of the Executive Government therein be declared:

And whereas it is expedient that Provision be made for the eventual Admission into the Union of other Parts of British North America:[2]

I.—PRELIMINARY

1. **Short title** —This Act may be cited as the *Constitution Act, 1867.*[3]
2. **[Repealed]** —Repealed.[4]

II.—UNION

3. **Declaration of Union** —It shall be lawful for the Queen, by and

---

[1]Source: Department of Justice, Canada, online: http://laws.justice.gc.ca/en/const/c1867_e.html

[2]The enacting clause was repealed by the *Statute Law Revision Act*, 1893, 56-57 Vict., c. 14 (U.K.). It read as follows:

> Be it therefore enacted and declared by the Queen's most Excellent Majesty, by and with the Advice and Consent of the Lords Spiritual and Temporal, and Commons, in this present Parliament assembled, and by the Authority of the same, as follows:

[3]As enacted by the *Constitution Act, 1982*, which came into force on April 17, 1982. The section, as originally enacted, read as follows:

1.

This Act may be cited as The British North America Act, 1867.

[4]Section 2, repealed by the *Statute Law Revision Act, 1893*, 56-57 Vict., c. 14 (U.K.), read as follows:

2.

with the Advice of Her Majesty's Most Honourable Privy Council, to declare by Proclamation that, on and after a Day therein appointed, not being more than Six Months after the passing of this Act, the Provinces of Canada, Nova Scotia, and New Brunswick shall form and be One Dominion under the Name of Canada; and on and after that Day those Three Provinces shall form and be One Dominion under that Name accordingly.[5]

4. Construction of subsequent Provisions of Act —Unless it is otherwise expressed or implied, the Name Canada shall be taken to mean Canada as constituted under this Act.[6]

5. Four Provinces —Canada shall be divided into Four Provinces, named Ontario, Quebec, Nova Scotia, and New Brunswick.[7]

—The Provisions of this Act referring to Her Majesty the Queen extend also to the Heirs and Successors of Her Majesty, Kings and Queens of the United Kingdom of Great Britain and Ireland.

[5]The first day of July, 1867, was fixed by proclamation dated May 22, 1867.

[6]Partially repealed by the *Statute Law Revision Act, 1893*, 56-57 Vict., c. 14 (U.K.). As originally enacted the section read as follows:

4.

The subsequent Provisions of this Act shall, unless it is otherwise expressed or implied, commence and have effect on and after the Union, that is to say, on and after the Day appointed for the Union taking effect in the Queen's Proclamation; and in the same Provisions, unless it is otherwise expressed or implied, the Name Canada shall be taken to mean Canada as constituted under this Act.

[7]Canada now consists of ten provinces (Ontario, Quebec, Nova Scotia, New Brunswick, Manitoba, British Columbia, Prince Edward Island, Alberta, Saskatchewan and Newfoundland) and two territories (the Yukon Territory and the Northwest Territories).

The first territories added to the Union were Rupert's Land and the North-Western Territory, (subsequently designated the Northwest Territories), which were admitted pursuant to section 146 of the *Constitution Act, 1867* and the *Rupert's Land Act, 1868*, 31-32 Vict., c. 105 (U.K.), by the *Rupert's Land and North-Western Territory Order* of June 23, 1870, effective July 15, 1870. Prior to the admission of those territories the Parliament of Canada enacted *An Act for the temporary Government of Rupert's Land and the North-Western Territory when united with Canada* (32-33 Vict., c. 3), and the *Manitoba Act, 1870*, (33 Vict., c. 3), which provided for the formation of the Province of Manitoba.

British Columbia was admitted into the Union pursuant to section 146 of the *Constitution Act, 1867*, by the *British Columbia Terms of Union*, being Order in Council of May 16, 1871, effective July 20, 1871.

Prince Edward Island was admitted pursuant to section 146 of the *Constitution Act, 1867*, by the *Prince Edward Island Terms of Union*, being Order in Council of June 26, 1873, effective July 1, 1873.

On June 29, 1871, the United Kingdom Parliament enacted the *Constitution Act, 1871* (34-35 Vict., c. 28) authorizing the creation of additional provinces out of territories not included in any province. Pursuant to this statute, the Parliament of Canada enacted the *Alberta Act*, (July 20, 1905, 4-5 Edw. VII, c. 3) and the *Saskatchewan Act*, (July 20, 1905, 4-5 Edw. VII, c. 42), providing for the creation of the provinces of Alberta and Saskatchewan, respectively. Both these Acts came into force on Sept. 1, 1905.

Meanwhile, all remaining British possessions and territories in North America and the islands adjacent thereto, except the colony of Newfoundland and its dependencies, were admitted into the Canadian Confederation by the *Adjacent Territories Order*, dated July 31, 1880.

6. Provinces of Ontario and Quebec —The Parts of the Province of Canada (as it exists at the passing of this Act) which formerly constituted respectively the Provinces of Upper Canada and Lower Canada shall be deemed to be severed, and shall form Two separate Provinces. The Part which formerly constituted the Province of Upper Canada shall constitute the Province of Ontario; and the Part which formerly constituted the Province of Lower Canada shall constitute the Province of Quebec.

7. Provinces of Nova Scotia and New Brunswick —The Provinces of Nova Scotia and New Brunswick shall have the same Limits as at the passing of this Act.

8. Decennial Census —In the general Census of the Population of Canada which is hereby required to be taken in the Year One thousand eight hundred and seventy-one, and in every Tenth Year thereafter, the respective Populations of the Four Provinces shall be distinguished.

III.—EXECUTIVE POWER

9. Declaration of Executive Power in the Queen —The Executive Government and Authority of and over Canada is hereby declared to continue and be vested in the Queen.

10. Application of Provisions referring to Governor General —The Provisions of this Act referring to the Governor General extend and apply to the Governor General for the Time being of Canada, or other the Chief Executive Officer or Administrator for the Time being carrying on the Government of Canada on behalf and in the Name of the Queen, by whatever Title he is designated.

11. Constitution of Privy Council for Canada —There shall be a Council to aid and advise in the Government of Canada, to be styled the Queen's Privy Council for Canada; and the Persons who are to be Members of that Council shall be from Time to Time chosen and summoned by the Governor General and sworn in as Privy Councillors, and Members thereof may be from Time to Time removed by the Governor General.

12. All Powers under Acts to be exercised by Governor General with Advice of Privy Council, or alone —All Powers, Authorities, and Functions which under any Act of the Parliament of Great Britain, or of the Parliament of the United Kingdom of Great

---

The Parliament of Canada added portions of the Northwest Territories to the adjoining provinces in 1912 by *The Ontario Boundaries Extension Act*, S.C. 1912, 2 Geo. V, c. 40, *The Quebec Boundaries Extension Act, 1912*, 2 Geo. V, c. 45 and *The Manitoba Boundaries Extension Act, 1912*, 2 Geo. V, c. 32, and further additions were made to Manitoba by *The Manitoba Boundaries Extension Act, 1930*, 20-21 Geo. V, c. 28.

The Yukon Territory was created out of the Northwest Territories in 1898 by *The Yukon Territory Act*, 61 Vict., c. 6, (Canada).

Newfoundland was added on March 31, 1949, by the *Newfoundland Act*, (U.K.), 12-13 Geo. VI, c. 22, which ratified the Terms of Union of Newfoundland with Canada.

Nunavut was created out of the Northwest Territories in 1999 by the *Nunavut Act*, S.C. 1993, c. 28.

Britain and Ireland, or of the Legislature of Upper Canada, Lower Canada, Canada, Nova Scotia, or New Brunswick, are at the Union vested in or exerciseable by the respective Governors or Lieutenant Governors of those Provinces, with the Advice, or with the Advice and Consent, of the respective Executive Councils thereof, or in conjunction with those Councils, or with any Number of Members thereof, or by those Governors or Lieutenant Governors individually, shall, as far as the same continue in existence and capable of being exercised after the Union in relation to the Government of Canada, be vested in and exerciseable by the Governor General, with the Advice or with the Advice and Consent of or in conjunction with the Queen's Privy Council for Canada, or any Members thereof, or by the Governor General individually, as the Case requires, subject nevertheless (except with respect to such as exist under Acts of the Parliament of Great Britain or of the Parliament of the United Kingdom of Great Britain and Ireland) to be abolished or altered by the Parliament of Canada.[8]

13. Application of Provisions referring to Governor General in Council —The Provisions of this Act referring to the Governor General in Council shall be construed as referring to the Governor General acting by and with the Advice of the Queen's Privy Council for Canada.

14. Power to Her Majesty to authorize Governor General to appoint Deputies —It shall be lawful for the Queen, if Her Majesty thinks fit, to authorize the Governor General from Time to Time to appoint any Person or any Persons jointly or severally to be his Deputy or Deputies within any Part or Parts of Canada, and in that Capacity to exercise during the Pleasure of the Governor General such of the Powers, Authorities, and Functions of the Governor General as the Governor General deems it necessary or expedient to assign to him or them, subject to any Limitations or Directions expressed or given by the Queen; but the Appointment of such a Deputy or Deputies shall not affect the Exercise by the Governor General himself of any Power, Authority, or Function.

15. Command of armed Forces to continue to be vested in the Queen —The Command-in-Chief of the Land and Naval Militia, and of all Naval and Military Forces, of and in Canada, is hereby declared to continue and be vested in the Queen.

16. Seat of Government of Canada —Until the Queen otherwise directs, the Seat of Government of Canada shall be Ottawa.

IV.—Legislative Power

17. Constitution of Parliament of Canada —There shall be One Parliament for Canada, consisting of the Queen, an Upper House styled the Senate, and the House of Commons.

---

[8]The restriction against altering or repealing laws enacted by or existing under statutes of the United Kingdom was removed by the *Statute of Westminster*, 1931, 22 Geo. V., c. 4 (U.K.) except in respect of certain constitutional documents.

18. Privileges, etc. of Houses —The privileges, immunities, and powers to be held, enjoyed, and exercised by the Senate and by the House of Commons, and by the members thereof respectively, shall be such as are from time to time defined by Act of the Parliament of Canada, but so that any Act of the Parliament of Canada defining such privileges, immunities, and powers shall not confer any privileges, immunities, or powers exceeding those at the passing of such Act held, enjoyed, and exercised by the Commons House of Parliament of the United Kingdom of Great Britain and Ireland, and by the members thereof.[9]

19. First Session of the Parliament of Canada —The Parliament of Canada shall be called together not later than Six Months after the Union.[10]

20. [Repealed] —Repealed.[11]

The Senate

21. Number of Senators —The Senate shall, subject to the Provisions of this Act, consist of One Hundred and five Members, who shall be styled Senators.[12]

22. Representation of Provinces in Senate —In relation to the

---

[9]Repealed and re-enacted by the *Parliament of Canada Act, 1875*, 38-39 Vict., c. 38 (U.K.). The original section read as follows:

18.

The Privileges, Immunities, and Powers to be held, enjoyed, and exercised by the Senate and by the House of Commons and by the Members thereof respectively shall be such as are from Time to Time defined by Act of the Parliament of Canada, but so that the same shall never exceed those at the passing of this Act held, enjoyed, and exercised by the Commons House of Parliament of the United Kingdom of Great Britain and Ireland and by the Members thereof.

[10]Spent. The first session of the first Parliament began on November 6, 1867.

[11]Section 20, repealed by the *Constitution Act, 1982*, read as follows:

20.

There shall be a Session of the Parliament of Canada once at least in every Year, so that Twelve Months shall not intervene between the last Sitting of the Parliament in one Session and its first sitting in the next Session. **Section 20 has been replaced by section 5 of the** *Constitution Act, 1982*, which provides that there shall be a sitting of Parliament at least once every twelve months.

[12]As amended by the *Constitution Act, 1915*, 5-6 Geo. V, c. 45 (U.K.) and modified by the *Newfoundland Act*, 12-13 Geo. VI, c. 22 (U.K.), the *Constitution Act (No. 2), 1975*, S.C. 1974-75-76, c. 53, and the *Constitution Act, 1999 (Nunavut)*, S.C. 1998, c. 15, Part 2. The original section read as follows:

21.

The Senate shall, subject to the Provisions of this Act, consist of Seventy-two Members, who shall be styled Senators.

The *Manitoba Act, 1870*, added two for Manitoba; the *British Columbia Terms of Union* added three; upon admission of Prince Edward Island four more were provided by section 147 of the *Constitution Act, 1867;* the *Alberta Act* and the *Saskatchewan Act* each added four. The Senate was reconstituted at 96 by the *Constitution Act, 1915.* Six more Senators were added upon union with Newfoundland, and one Senator each was added for the Yukon Territory and the Northwest Territories by the *Constitution Act (No. 2), 1975.* One Senator was added for Nunavut by the *Constitution Act 1999 (Nunavut).*

Constitution of the Senate Canada shall be deemed to consist of *Four* Divisions:

1. Ontario;
2. Quebec;
3. The Maritime Provinces, Nova Scotia and New Brunswick, and Prince Edward Island;
4. The Western Provinces of Manitoba, British Columbia, Saskatchewan, and Alberta;

which Four Divisions shall (subject to the Provisions of this Act) be equally represented in the Senate as follows: Ontario by twenty-four senators; Quebec by twenty-four senators; the Maritime Provinces and Prince Edward Island by twenty-four senators, ten thereof representing Nova Scotia, ten thereof representing New Brunswick, and four thereof representing Prince Edward Island; the Western Provinces by twenty-four senators, six thereof representing Manitoba, six thereof representing British Columbia, six thereof representing Saskatchewan, and six thereof representing Alberta; Newfoundland shall be entitled to be represented in the Senate by six members; the Yukon Territory and the Northwest Territories shall be entitled to be represented in the Senate by one member each.

In the Case of Quebec each of the Twenty-four Senators representing that Province shall be appointed for One of the Twenty-four Electoral Divisions of Lower Canada specified in Schedule A. to Chapter One of the Consolidated Statutes of Canada.[13]

23. Qualifications of Senator —The Qualifications of a Senator shall be as follows:

(1) He shall be of the full age of Thirty Years:

(2) He shall be either a natural-born Subject of the Queen, or a Subject of the Queen naturalized by an Act of the Parliament of Great Britain, or of the Parliament of the United Kingdom of Great Britain and Ireland, or of the Legislature of One of the Provinces of

---

[13]As amended by the *Constitution Act, 1915*, 5-6 Geo. V, c. 45 (U.K.), the *Newfoundland Act*, 12-13 Geo. VI, c. 22 (U.K.), and the *Constitution Act (No. 2), 1975*, S.C. 1974-75-76, c. 53. The original section read as follows:

22.

In relation to the Constitution of the Senate, Canada shall be deemed to consist of Three Divisions:

1. Ontario;
2. Quebec;
3. The Maritime Provinces, Nova Scotia and New Brunswick;

which Three Divisions shall (subject to the Provisions of this Act) be equally represented in the Senate as follows: Ontario by Twenty-four Senators; Quebec by Twenty-four Senators; and the Maritime Provinces by Twenty-four Senators, Twelve thereof representing Nova Scotia, and Twelve thereof representing New Brunswick.

In the case of Quebec each of the Twenty-four Senators representing that Province shall be appointed for One of the Twenty-four Electoral Divisions of Lower Canada specified in Schedule A. to Chapter One of the Consolidated Statutes of Canada.

Upper Canada, Lower Canada, Canada, Nova Scotia, or New Brunswick, before the Union, or of the Parliament of Canada after the Union:

(3) He shall be legally or equitably seised as of Freehold for his own Use and Benefit of Lands or Tenements held in Free and Common Socage, or seised or possessed for his own Use and Benefit of Lands or Tenements held in Franc-alleu or in Roture, within the Province for which he is appointed, of the Value of Four thousand Dollars, over and above all Rents, Dues, Debts, Charges, Mortgages, and Incumbrances due or payable out of or charged on or affecting the same:

(4) His Real and Personal Property shall be together worth Four thousand Dollars over and above his Debts and Liabilities:

(5) He shall be resident in the Province for which he is appointed:

(6) In the Case of Quebec he shall have his Real Property Qualification in the Electoral Division for which he is appointed, or shall be resident in that Division.[14]

24. Summons of Senator —The Governor General shall from Time to Time, in the Queen's Name, by Instrument under the Great Seal of Canada, summon qualified Persons to the Senate; and, subject to the Provisions of this Act, every Person so summoned shall become and be a Member of the Senate and a Senator.

25. [Repealed] —Repealed.[15]

26. Addition of Senators in certain cases —If at any Time on the Recommendation of the Governor General the Queen thinks fit to direct that Four or Eight Members be added to the Senate, the Governor General may by Summons to Four or Eight qualified Persons

[14]Section 44 of the *Constitution Act*, 1999 *(Nunavut)*, S.C. 1998, c. 15, Part 2, provided that, for the purposes of that Part, (which added one Senator for Nunavut) the word "Province" in section 23 of the *Constitution Act, 1867*, has the same meaning as is assigned to the word "province" by section 35 of the *Interpretation Act*, R.S.C. 1985, c. I-21, which provides that the term "province" means "a province of Canada, and includes the Yukon Territory, the Northwest Territories and Nunavut."

Section 2 of the *Constitution Act (No. 2)*, 1975, S.C. 1974-75-76, c. 53 provided that for the purposes of that Act (which added one Senator each for the Yukon Territory and the Northwest Territories) the term "Province" in section 23 of the *Constitution Act*, 1867, has the same meaning as is assigned to the term "province" by section 28 of the *Interpretation Act*, R.S.C. 1970, c. I-23, which provides that the term "province" means "a province of Canada, and includes the Yukon Territory and the Northwest Territories."

[15]Repealed by the *Statute Law Revision Act, 1893*, 56-57 Vict., c. 14 (U.K.). The section read as follows:

25.

Such Persons shall be first summoned to the Senate as the Queen by Warrant under Her Majesty's Royal Sign Manual thinks fit to approve, and their Names shall be inserted in the Queen's Proclamation of Union.

(as the Case may be), representing equally the Four Divisions of Canada, add to the Senate accordingly.[16]

27. Reduction of Senate to normal Number —In case of such Addition being at any Time made, the Governor General shall not summon any Person to the Senate, except on a further like Direction by the Queen on the like Recommendation, to represent one of the Four Divisions until such Division is represented by Twenty-four Senators and no more.[17]

28. Maximum Number of Senators —The Number of Senators shall not at any Time exceed One Hundred and thirteen.[18]

29. Tenure of Place in Senate— (1) Subject to subsection (2), a Senator shall, subject to the provisions of this Act, hold his place in the Senate for life.

(2) Retirement upon attaining age of seventy-five years—A Senator who is summoned to the Senate after the coming into force of this subsection shall, subject to this Act, hold his place in the Senate until he attains the age of seventy-five years.[19]

[Sections 30 to 36 are omitted]

The House of Commons

37. Constitution of House of Commons in Canada —The House of Commons shall, subject to the Provisions of this Act, consist of two hundred and ninety-five members of whom ninety-nine shall be elected for Ontario, seventy-five for Quebec, eleven for Nova Scotia, ten for New Brunswick, fourteen for Manitoba, thirty-two for British Colum-

---

[16]As amended by the *Constitution Act, 1915*, 5-6 Geo. V, c. 45 (U.K.). The original section read as follows:

26.

If at any Time on the Recommendation of the Governor General the Queen thinks fit to direct that Three or Six Members be added to the Senate, the Governor General may by Summons to Three or Six qualified Persons (as the Case may be), representing equally the Three Divisions of Canada, add to the Senate accordingly.

[17]As amended by the *Constitution Act, 1915*, 5-6 Geo. V, c. 45 (U.K.). The original section read as follows:

27.

In case of such Addition being at any Time made the Governor General shall not summon any Person to the Senate except on a further like Direction by the Queen on the like Recommendation, until each of the Three Divisions of Canada is represented by Twenty-four Senators and no more.

[18]As amended by the *Constitution Act, 1915*, 5-6 Geo. V, c. 45 (U.K.), the *Constitution Act (No. 2), 1975*, S.C. 1974-75-76, c. 53, and the *Constitution Act 1999 (Nunavut)*, S.C. 1998, c. 15, Part 2. The original section read as follows:

28.

The Number of Senators shall not at any Time exceed Seventy-eight.

[19]As enacted by the *Constitution Act, 1965*, S.C., 1965, c. 4, which came into force on June 1, 1965. The original section read as follows:

29.

A Senator shall, subject to the Provisions of this Act, hold his Place in the Senate for Life.

bia, four for Prince Edward Island, twenty-six for Alberta, fourteen for Saskatchewan, seven for Newfoundland, one for the Yukon Territory and two for the Northwest Territories.[20]

38. Summoning of House of Commons —The Governor General shall from Time to Time, in the Queen's Name, by Instrument under the Great Seal of Canada, summon and call together the House of Commons.

39. Senators not to sit in House of Commons —A Senator shall not be capable of being elected or of sitting or voting as a Member of the House of Commons.

[Sections 40 to 49 are omitted]

50. Duration of House of Commons —Every House of Commons shall continue for Five Years from the Day of the Return of the Writs for choosing the House (subject to be sooner dissolved by the Governor General), and no longer.[21]

[Section 51 is omitted]

51A. Constitution of House of Commons —Notwithstanding anything in this Act a province shall always be entitled to a number of members in the House of Commons not less than the number of senators representing such province.[22]

52. Increase of Number of House of Commons —The Number of Members of the House of Commons may be from Time to Time increased by the Parliament of Canada, provided the proportionate Representation of the Provinces prescribed by this Act is not thereby disturbed.

Money Votes; Royal Assent

53. Appropriation and Tax Bills —Bills for appropriating any Part of the Public Revenue, or for imposing any Tax or Impost, shall originate in the House of Commons.

54. Recommendation of Money Votes —It shall not be lawful for

---

[20]The figures given here result from the application of section 51, as enacted by the *Constitution Act, 1985 (Representation)*, S.C., 1986, c. 8, Part I, and readjusted pursuant to the *Electoral Boundaries Readjustment Act*, R.S.C. 1985, c. E-3. The original section (which was altered from time to time as the result of the addition of new provinces and changes in population) read as follows:

37.

The House of Commons shall, subject to the Provisions of this Act, consist of one hundred and eighty-one members, of whom Eighty-two shall be elected for Ontario, Sixty-five for Quebec, Nineteen for Nova Scotia, and Fifteen for New Brunswick.

[21]The term of the twelfth Parliament was extended by the *British North America Act, 1916*, 6-7 Geo. V., c. 19 (U.K.), which Act was repealed by the *Statute Law Revision Act, 1927*, 17-18 Geo. V, c. 42 (U.K.). See also subsection 4(1) of the *Constitution Act, 1982*, which provides that no House of Commons shall continue for longer than five years from the date fixed for the return of the writs at a general election of its members, and subsection 4(2) thereof, which provides for continuation of the House of Commons in special circumstances.

[22]As enacted by the *Constitution Act, 1915*, 5-6 Geo. V, c. 45 (U.K.)

the House of Commons to adopt or pass any Vote, Resolution, Address, or Bill for the Appropriation of any Part of the Public Revenue, or of any Tax or Impost, to any Purpose that has not been first recommended to that House by Message of the Governor General in the Session in which such Vote, Resolution, Address, or Bill is proposed.

55. Royal Assent to Bills, etc. —Where a Bill passed by the Houses of the Parliament is presented to the Governor General for the Queen's Assent, he shall declare, according to his Discretion, but subject to the Provisions of this Act and to Her Majesty's Instructions, either that he assents thereto in the Queen's Name, or that he withholds the Queen's Assent, or that he reserves the Bill for the Signification of the Queen's Pleasure.

56. Disallowance by Order in Council of Act assented to by Governor General —Where the Governor General assents to a Bill in the Queen's Name, he shall by the first convenient Opportunity send an authentic Copy of the Act to One of Her Majesty's Principal Secretaries of State, and if the Queen in Council within Two Years after Receipt thereof by the Secretary of State thinks fit to disallow the Act, such Disallowance (with a Certificate of the Secretary of State of the Day on which the Act was received by him) being signified by the Governor General, by Speech or Message to each of the Houses of the Parliament or by Proclamation, shall annul the Act from and after the Day of such Signification.

57. Signification of Queen's Pleasure on Bill reserved —A Bill reserved for the Signification of the Queen's Pleasure shall not have any Force unless and until, within Two Years from the Day on which it was presented to the Governor General for the Queen's Assent, the Governor General signifies, by Speech or Message to each of the Houses of the Parliament or by Proclamation, that it has received the Assent of the Queen in Council.

An Entry of every such Speech, Message, or Proclamation shall be made in the Journal of each House, and a Duplicate thereof duly attested shall be delivered to the proper Officer to be kept among the Records of Canada.

V.—PROVINCIAL CONSTITUTIONS

Executive Power

58. Appointment of Lieutenant Governors of Provinces —For each Province there shall be an Officer, styled the Lieutenant Governor, appointed by the Governor General in Council by Instrument under the Great Seal of Canada.

59. Tenure of Office of Lieutenant Governor —A Lieutenant Governor shall hold Office during the Pleasure of the Governor General; but any Lieutenant Governor appointed after the Commencement of the First Session of the Parliament of Canada shall not be removeable within Five Years from his Appointment, except for Cause assigned, which shall be communicated to him in Writing within One Month after the Order for his Removal is made, and shall be communicated by Message to the Senate and to the House of Commons within One Week thereafter if the Parliament is then sitting, and if not then within One Week after the Commencement of the next Session of the Parliament.

60. Salaries of Lieutenant Governors —The Salaries of the Lieutenant Governors shall be fixed and provided by the Parliament of Canada.[23]

61. Oaths, etc., of Lieutenant Governor —Every Lieutenant Governor shall, before assuming the Duties of his Office, make and subscribe before the Governor General or some Person authorized by him Oaths of Allegiance and Office similar to those taken by the Governor General.

62. Application of provisions referring to Lieutenant Governor —The Provisions of this Act referring to the Lieutenant Governor extend and apply to the Lieutenant Governor for the Time being of each Province, or other the Chief Executive Officer or Administrator for the Time being carrying on the Government of the Province, by whatever Title he is designated.

63. Appointment of Executive Officers for Ontario and Quebec —The Executive Council of Ontario and of Quebec shall be composed of such Persons as the Lieutenant Governor from Time to Time thinks fit, and in the first instance of the following Officers, namely,—the Attorney General, the Secretary and Registrar of the Province, the Treasurer of the Province, the Commissioner of Crown Lands, and the Commissioner of Agriculture and Public Works, with in Quebec the Speaker of the Legislative Council and the Solicitor General.[24]

64. Executive Government of Nova Scotia and New Brunswick —The Constitution of the Executive Authority in each of the Provinces of Nova Scotia and New Brunswick shall, subject to the Provisions of this Act, continue as it exists at the Union until altered under the Authority of this Act.[25]

65. Powers to be exercised by Lieutenant Governor of Ontario or Quebec with Advice, or alone —All Powers, Authorities, and Functions which under any Act of the Parliament of Great Britain, or of the Parliament of the United Kingdom of Great Britain and Ireland, or of the Legislature of Upper Canada, Lower Canada, or Canada, were or are before or at the Union vested in or exerciseable by the respective Governors or Lieutenant Governors of

---

[23]Provided for by the *Salaries Act*, R.S.C. 1985, c. S-3.

[24]Now provided for in Ontario by the *Executive Council Act*, R.S.O. 1990, c. E.25, and in Quebec by the *Executive Power Act*, R.S.Q. 1977, c. E-18.

[25]A similar provision was included in each of the instruments admitting British Columbia, Prince Edward Island, and Newfoundland. The Executive Authorities for Manitoba, Alberta and Saskatchewan were established by the statutes creating those provinces.

those Provinces, with the Advice or with the Advice and Consent of the respective Executive Councils thereof, or in conjunction with those Councils, or with any Number of Members thereof, or by those Governors or Lieutenant Governors individually, shall, as far as the same are capable of being exercised after the Union in relation to the Government of Ontario and Quebec respectively, be vested in and shall or may be exercised by the Lieu-tenant Governor of Ontario and Quebec respectively, with the Advice or with the Advice and Consent of or in conjunction with the respective Executive Councils, or any Members thereof, or by the Lieutenant Governor individually, as the Case requires, subject nevertheless (except with respect to such as exist under Acts of the Parliament of Great Britain, or of the Parliament of the United Kingdom of Great Britain and Ireland,) to be abolished or altered by the respective Legislatures of Ontario and Quebec.[26]

66. Application of Provisions referring to Lieutenant Governor in Council —The Provisions of this Act referring to the Lieutenant Governor in Council shall be construed as referring to the Lieutenant Governor of the Province acting by and with the Advice of the Executive Council thereof.

67. Administration in Absence, etc., of Lieutenant Governor —The Governor General in Council may from Time to Time appoint an Administrator to execute the Office and Functions of Lieutenant Governor during his Absence, Illness, or other Inability.

68. Seats of Provincial Governments —Unless and until the Executive Government of any Province otherwise directs with respect to that Province, the Seats of Government of the Provinces shall be as follows, namely,—of Ontario, the City of Toronto; of Quebec, the City of Quebec; of Nova Scotia, the City of Halifax; and of New Brunswick, the City of Fredericton.

Legislative Power

1.—ONTARIO

69. Legislature for Ontario —There shall be a Legislature for Ontario consisting of the Lieutenant Governor and of One House, styled the Legislative Assembly of Ontario.

[Section 70 is omitted]

2.—QUEBEC

71. Legislature for Quebec —There shall be a Legislature for Quebec consisting of the Lieutenant Governor and of Two Houses, styled the Legislative Council of Quebec and the Legislative Assembly of Quebec.[27]

[Sections 72 to 85 are omitted]

86. Yearly Session of Legislature —There shall be a Session of

[26]The restriction against altering or repealing laws enacted by or existing under statutes of the United Kingdom was removed by the *Statute of Westminster*, 1931, 22 Geo. V., c. 4 (U.K.) except in respect of certain constitutional documents.

[27]The Act respecting the Legislative Council of Quebec, S.Q. 1968, c. 9, provided

the Legislature of Ontario and of that of Quebec once at least in every Year, so that Twelve Months shall not intervene between the last Sitting of the Legislature in each Province in one Session and its first Sitting in the next Session.[28]

[Section 87 is omitted]

4.—Nova Scotia and New Brunswick

88. Constitutions of Legislatures of Nova Scotia and New Brunswick —The Constitution of the Legislature of each of the Provinces of Nova Scotia and New Brunswick shall, subject to the Provisions of this Act, continue as it exists at the Union until altered under the Authority of this Act.[29]

5.—Ontario, Quebec, and Nova Scotia

89. [Repealed] —Repealed.[30]

---

that the Legislature for Quebec shall consist of the Lieutenant Governor and the National Assembly of Quebec, and repealed the provisions of the *Legislature Act*, R.S.Q. 1964, c. 6, relating to the Legislative Council of Quebec. Now covered by the *Legislature Act, R.S.Q. 1977, c. L-1. Sections 72 to 79 following are therefore completely spent.*

[28]See also section 5 of the *Constitution Act, 1982*, which provides that there shall be a sitting of each legislature at least once every twelve months.

[29]Partially repealed by the *Statute Law Revision Act, 1893*, 56-57 Vict., c. 14 (U.K.), which deleted the following concluding words of the original enactment:

> and the House of Assembly of New Brunswick existing at the passing of this Act shall, unless sooner dissolved, continue for the Period for which it was elected.

A similar provision was included in each of the instruments admitting British Columbia, Prince Edward Island and Newfoundland. The Legislatures of Manitoba, Alberta and Saskatchewan were established by the statutes creating those provinces.

See also sections 3 to 5 of the *Constitution Act, 1982*, which prescribe democratic rights applicable to all provinces, and subitem 2(2) of the Schedule to that Act, which sets out the repeal of section 20 of the *Manitoba Act, 1870*. Section 20 of the *Manitoba Act, 1870* has been replaced by section 5 of the *Constitution Act, 1982*.

Section 20 reads as follows:

20.

> There shall be a Session of the Legislature once at least in every year, so that twelve months shall not intervene between the last sitting of the Legislature in one Session and its first sitting in the next Session.

[30]Repealed by the *Statute Law Revision Act, 1893*, 56-57 Vict. c. 14 (U.K.). The section read as follows:

5.—Ontario, Quebec, and Nova Scotia.

89.

> Each of the Lieutenant Governors of Ontario, Quebec and Nova Scotia shall cause Writs to be issued for the First Election of Members of the Legislative Assembly thereof in such Form and by such Person as he thinks fit, and at such Time and addressed to such Returning Officer as the Governor General directs, and so that the First Election of Member of Assembly for any Electoral District or any Subdivision thereof shall be held at the same Time and at the same Places as the Election for a Member to serve in the House of Commons of Canada for that Electoral District.

6.—THE FOUR PROVINCES

90. Application to Legislatures of Provisions respecting Money Votes, etc. —The following Provisions of this Act respecting the Parliament of Canada, namely,—the Provisions relating to Appropriation and Tax Bills, the Recommendation of Money Votes, the Assent to Bills, the Disallowance of Acts, and the Signification of Pleasure on Bills reserved,—shall extend and apply to the Legislatures of the several Provinces as if those Provisions were here re-enacted and made applicable in Terms to the respective Provinces and the Legislatures thereof, with the Substitution of the Lieutenant Governor of the Province for the Governor General, of the Governor General for the Queen and for a Secretary of State, of One Year for Two Years, and of the Province for Canada.

VI.—DISTRIBUTION OF LEGISLATIVE POWERS

Powers of the Parliament

91. Legislative Authority of Parliament of Canada —It shall be lawful for the Queen, by and with the Advice and Consent of the Senate and House of Commons, to make Laws for the Peace, Order, and good Government of Canada, in relation to all Matters not coming within the Classes of Subjects by this Act assigned exclusively to the Legislatures of the Provinces; and for greater Certainty, but not so as to restrict the Generality of the foregoing Terms of this Section, it is hereby declared that (notwithstanding anything in this Act) the exclusive Legislative Authority of the Parliament of Canada extends to all Matters coming within the Classes of Subjects next here inafter enumerated; that is to say,

1. Repealed.[31]

1A. The Public Debt and Property.[32]

2. The Regulation of Trade and Commerce.

---

[31]Class I was added by the *British North America (No. 2) Act, 1949*, 13 Geo. VI, c. 81 (U.K.). That Act and class I were repealed by the *Constitution Act, 1982*. The matters referred to in class I are provided for in subsection 4(2) and Part V of the *Constitution Act, 1982*. As enacted, class I read as follows:

1.

The amendment from time to time of the Constitution of Canada, except as regards matters coming within the classes of subjects by this Act assigned exclusively to the Legislatures of the provinces, or as regards rights or privileges by this or any other Constitutional Act granted or secured to the Legislature or the Government of a province, or to any class of persons with respect to schools or as regards the use of the English or the French language or as regards the requirements that there shall be a session of the Parliament of Canada at least once each year, and that no House of Commons shall continue for more than five years from the day of the return of the Writs for choosing the House: provided, however, that a House of Commons may in time of real or apprehended war, invasion or insurrection be continued by the Parliament of Canada if such continuation is not opposed by the votes of more than one-third of the members of such House.

[32]Re-numbered by the *British North America (No. 2) Act, 1949*.

2A. Unemployment insurance.[33]

3. The raising of Money by any Mode or System of Taxation.

4. The borrowing of Money on the Public Credit.

5. Postal Service.

6. The Census and Statistics.

7. Militia, Military and Naval Service, and Defence.

8. The fixing of and providing for the Salaries and Allowances of Civil and other Officers of the Government of Canada.

9. Beacons, Buoys, Lighthouses, and Sable Island.

10. Navigation and Shipping.

11. Quarantine and the Establishment and Maintenance of Marine Hospitals.

12. Sea Coast and Inland Fisheries.

13. Ferries between a Province and any British or Foreign Country or between Two Provinces.

14. Currency and Coinage.

15. Banking, Incorporation of Banks, and the Issue of Paper Money.

16. Savings Banks.

17. Weights and Measures.

18. Bills of Exchange and Promissory Notes.

19. Interest.

20. Legal Tender.

21. Bankruptcy and Insolvency.

22. Patents of Invention and Discovery.

23. Copyrights.

24. Indians, and Lands reserved for the Indians.

25. Naturalization and Aliens.

26. Marriage and Divorce.

27. The Criminal Law, except the Constitution of Courts of Criminal Jurisdiction, but including the Procedure in Criminal Matters.

28. The Establishment, Maintenance, and Management of Penitentiaries.

29. Such Classes of Subjects as are expressly excepted in the Enumeration of the Classes of Subjects by this Act assigned exclusively to the Legislatures of the Provinces.

And any Matter coming within any of the Classes of Subjects enumerated in this Section shall not be deemed to come within the Class of Matters of a local or private Nature comprised in the

[33]Added by the *Constitution Act, 1940*, 3-4 Geo. VI, c. 36 (U.K.).

App. A CONSTITUTIONAL LAW OF CANADA

ince, are before or after their Execution declared by the Parliament of Canada to be for the general Advantage of Canada or for the Advantage of Two or more of the Provinces.

11. The Incorporation of Companies with Provincial Objects.

12. The Solemnization of Marriage in the Province.

13. Property and Civil Rights in the Province.

14. The Administration of Justice in the Province, including the Constitution, Maintenance, and Organization of Provincial Courts, both of Civil and of Criminal Jurisdiction, and including Procedure in Civil Matters in those Courts.

15. The Imposition of Punishment by Fine, Penalty, or Imprisonment for enforcing any Law of the Province made in relation to any Matter coming within any of the Classes of Subjects enumerated in this Section.

16. Generally all Matters of a merely local or private Nature in the Province.

Non-Renewable Natural Resources, Forestry Resources and Electrical Energy

92A. Laws respecting non-renewable natural resources, forestry resources and electrical energy— (1) In each province, the legislature may exclusively make laws in relation to

(a) exploration for non-renewable natural resources in the province;

(b) development, conservation and management of nonrenewable natural resources and forestry resources in the province, including laws in relation to the rate of primary production therefrom; and

(c) development, conservation and management of sites and facilities in the province for the generation and production of electrical energy.

(2) Export from provinces of resources—In each province, the legislature may make laws in relation to the export from the province to another part of Canada of the primary production from non-renewable natural resources and forestry resources in the province and the production from facilities in the province for the generation of electrical energy, but such laws may not authorize or provide for discrimination in prices or in supplies exported to another part of Canada.

(3) Authority of Parliament—Nothing in subsection (2) derogates from the authority of Parliament to enact laws in relation to the matters referred to in that subsection and, where such a law of Parliament and a law of a province conflict, the law of Parliament prevails to the extent of the conflict.

(4) Taxation of resources—In each province, the legislature may make laws in relation to the raising of money by any mode or system of taxation in respect of

(*a*) non-renewable natural resources and forestry resources in the province and the primary production therefrom, and

(*b*) sites and facilities in the province for the generation of electrical energy and the production therefrom,

whether or not such production is exported in whole or in part from the province, but such laws may not authorize or provide for taxation that differentiates between production exported to another part of Canada and production not exported from the province.

(5) "Primary production"—The expression "primary production" has the meaning assigned by the Sixth Schedule.

(6) Existing powers or rights—Nothing in subsections (1) to (5) derogates from any powers or rights that a legislature or government of a province had immediately before the coming into force of this section.[36]

Education

93. Legislation respecting Education —In and for each Province the Legislature may exclusively make Laws in relation to Education, subject and according to the following Provisions:

(1) Nothing in any such Law shall prejudicially affect any Right or Privilege with respect to Denominational Schools which any Class of Persons have by Law in the Province at the Union:

(2) All the Powers, Privileges, and Duties at the Union by Law conferred and imposed in Upper Canada on the Separate Schools and School Trustees of the Queen's Roman Catholic Subjects shall be and the same are hereby extended to the Dissentient Schools of the Queen's Protestant and Roman Catholic Subjects in Quebec:

(3) Where in any Province a System of Separate or Dissentient Schools exists by Law at the Union or is thereafter established by the Legislature of the Province, an Appeal shall lie to the Governor General in Council from any Act or Decision of any Provincial Authority affecting any Right or Privilege of the Protestant or Roman Catholic Minority of the Queen's Subjects in relation to Education:

(4) In case any such Provincial Law as from Time to Time seems to the Governor General in Council requisite for the due Execution of the Provisions of this Section is not made, or in case any Decision of the Governor General in Council on any Appeal under this Section is not duly executed by the proper Provincial Authority in that Behalf, then and in every such Case, and as far only as the Circumstances of each Case require, the Parliament of Canada may make remedial Laws for the due Execution of the Provisions of this Sec-

[36] Added by the *Constitution Act, 1982*.

tion and of any Decision of the Governor General in Council under this Section.[37]

[37] An alternative was provided for Manitoba by section 22 of the *Manitoba Act, 1870*, 33 Vict., c. 3 (Canada), (confirmed by the *Constitution Act, 1871)*, which reads as follows:

22.

In and for the Province, the said Legislature may exclusively make Laws in relation to Education, subject and according to the following provisions:

(1) Nothing in any such Law shall prejudicially affect any right or privilege with respect to Denominational Schools which any class of persons have by Law or practice in the Province at the Union:

(2) An appeal shall lie to the Governor General in Council from any Act or decision of the Legislature of the Province, or of any Provincial Authority, affecting any right or privilege, of the Protestant or Roman Catholic minority of the Queen's subjects in relation to Education:

(3) In case any such Provincial Law, as from time to time seems to the Governor General in Council requisite for the due execution of the provisions of this section, is not made, or in case any decision of the Governor General in Council on any appeal under this section is not duly executed by the proper Provincial Authority in that behalf, then, and in every such case, and as far only as the circumstances of each case require, the Parliament of Canada may make remedial Laws for the due execution of the provisions of this section, and of any decision of the Governor General in Council under this section.

An alternative was provided for Alberta by section 17 of the *Alberta Act*, 4-5 Edw. VII, c. 3, 1905 (Canada), which reads as follows:

17.

Section 93 of the *Constitution Act, 1867*, shall apply to the said province, with the substitution for paragraph (1) of the said section 93 of the following paragraph:

(1) Nothing in any such law shall prejudicially affect any right or privilege with respect to separate schools which any class of persons have at the date of the passing of this Act, under the terms of chapters 29 and 30 of the Ordinances of the Northwest Territories, passed in the year 1901, or with respect to religious instruction in any public or separate school as provided for in the said ordinances.

2.

In the appropriation by the Legislature or distribution by the Government of the province of any moneys for the support of schools organized and carried on in accordance with the said chapter 29 or any Act passed in amendment thereof, or in substitution therefor, there shall be no discrimination against schools of any class described in the said chapter 29.

3.

Where the expression "by law" is employed in paragraph 3 of the said section 93, it shall be held to mean the law as set out in the said chapters 29 and 30, and where the expression "at the Union" is employed, in the said paragraph 3, it shall be held to mean the date at which this Act comes into force.

An alternative was provided for Saskatchewan by section 17 of the *Saskatchewan Act*, 4-5 Edw. VII, c. 42, 1905 (Canada), which reads as follows:

17.

Section 93 of the *Constitution Act, 1867*, shall apply to the said province, with the substitution for paragraph (1) of the said section 93, of the following paragraph:

(1) Nothing in any such law shall prejudicially affect any right or privilege with respect to separate schools which any class of persons have at the date of the passing of this Act, under the terms of chapters 29 and 30 of the Ordinances of the Northwest Territories, passed in the year 1901, or with respect to religious instruction in any public or separate school as proviced for in the said ordinances.

2.

In the appropriation by the Legislature or distribution by the Government of the province of any moneys for the support of schools organized and carried on in accordance with the said chapter 29, or any Act passed in amendment thereof or in substitution therefor, there shall be no discrimination against schools of any class described in the said chapter 29.

3.

Where the expression "by law" is employed in paragraph (3) of the said section 93, it shall be held to mean the law as set out in the said chapters 29 and 30; and where the expression "at the Union" is employed in the said paragraph (3), it shall be held to mean the date at which this Act comes into force.

An alternative was provided for Newfoundland by Term 17 of the Terms of Union of Newfoundland with Canada (confirmed by the *Newfoundland Act*, 12-13 Geo. VI, c. 22 (U.K.)). Term 17 of the Terms of Union of Newfoundland with Canada, set out in the penultimate paragraph of this footnote, was amended by the *Constitution Amendment, 1998 (Newfoundland Act)*, (see SI/98-25) and now reads as follows:

17.

(1) In lieu of section ninety-three of the *Constitution Act, 1867*, this term shall apply in respect of the Province of Newfoundland.

(2) In and for the Province of Newfoundland, the Legislature shall have exclusive authority to make laws in relation to education, but shall provide for courses in religion that are not specific to a religious denomination.

(3) Religious observances shall be permitted in a school where requested by parents.

Prior to the *Constitution Amendment*, 1998 (*Newfoundland Act*), Term 17 of the Terms of Union of Newfoundland with Canada had been amended by the *Constitution Amendment*, 1997 *(Newfoundland Act)*, (see SI/97-55) to read as follows:

17. In lieu of section ninety-three of the *Constitution Act, 1867*, the following shall apply in respect of the Province of Newfoundland:

In and for the Province of Newfoundland, the Legislature shall have exclusive authority to make laws in relation to education but

(*a*) except as provided in paragraphs (b) and (c), schools established, maintained and operated with public funds shall be denominational schools, and any class of persons having rights under this Term as it read on January 1, 1995 shall continue to have the right to provide for religious education, activities and observances for the children of that class in those schools, and the group of classes that formed one integrated school system by agreement in 1969 may exercise the same rights under this Term as a single class of persons;

(*b*) subject to provincial legislation that is uniformly applicable to all schools specifying conditions for the establishment or continued operation of schools,

(i) any class of persons referred to in paragraph *(a)* shall have the right to have a publicly funded denominational school established, maintained and operated especially for that class, and

(ii) the Legislature may approve the establishment, maintenance and operation of a publicly funded school, whether denominational or non-denominational;

(*c*) where a school is established, maintained and operated pursuant to subparagraph (*b*) (i), the class of persons referred to in that subparagraph shall continue to have the right to provide for religious education, activities and observances and to direct the teaching of aspects of curriculum affecting religious beliefs, student admission policy and the assignment and dismissal of teachers in that school;

(*d*) all schools referred to in paragraphs (*a*) and (*b*) shall receive their share of public funds in accordance with scales determined on a non-discriminatory basis from time to time by the Legislature; and

(*e*) if the classes of persons having rights under this Term so desire, they shall have the right to elect in total not less than two thirds of the members of a school board, and any class so desiring shall have the right to elect the portion of that total that is proportionate to the population of that class in the area under the board's jurisdiction.

93A. Quebec —Paragraphs (1) to (4) of section 93 do not apply to Quebec.[38]

Prior to the *Constitution Amendment, 1997 (Newfoundland Act)*, Term 17 of the Terms of Union of Newfoundland with Canada had been amended by the *Constitution Amendment, 1987 (Newfoundland Act)*, (see SI/88-11) to read as follows:

17.

(1) In lieu of section ninety-three of the *Constitution Act, 1867*, the following term shall apply in respect of the Province of Newfoundland:

In and for the Province of Newfoundland the Legislature shall have exclusive authority to make laws in relation to education, but the Legislature will not have authority to make laws prejudicially affecting any right or privilege with respect to denominational schools, common (amalgamated) schools, or denominational colleges, that any class or classes of persons have by law in Newfoundland at the date of Union, and out of public funds of the Province of Newfoundland, provided for education,

(*a*) all such schools shall receive their share of such funds in accordance with scales determined on a non-discriminatory basis from time to time by the Legislature for all schools then being conducted under authority of the Legislature; and

(*b*) all such colleges shall receive their share of any grant from time to time voted for all colleges then being conducted under authority of the Legislature, such grant being distributed on a non-discriminatory basis.

(2) For the purposes of paragraph one of this Term, the Pentecostal Assemblies of Newfoundland have in Newfoundland all the same rights and privileges with respect to denominational schools and denominational colleges as any other class or classes of persons had by law in Newfoundland at the date of Union, and the words "all such schools" in paragraph (*a*) of paragraph one of this Term and the words "all such colleges" in paragraph (*b*) of paragraph one of this Term include, respectively, the schools and the colleges of the Pentecostal Assemblies of Newfoundland.

Term 17 of the Terms of Union of Newfoundland with Canada (confirmed by the *Newfoundland Act*, 12-13 Geo. VI, c. 22 (U.K.)), which Term provided an alternative for Newfoundland, originally read as follows:

17.

In lieu of section ninety-three of the *Constitution Act, 1867*, the following term shall apply in respect of the Province of Newfoundland:

In and for the Province of Newfoundland the Legislature shall have exclusive authority to make laws in relation to education, but the Legislature will not have authority to make laws prejudicially affecting any right or privilege with respect to denominational schools, common (amalgamated) schools, or denominational colleges, that any class or classes of persons have by law in Newfoundland at the date of Union, and out of public funds of the Province of Newfoundland, provided for education,

(*a*) all such schools shall receive their share of such funds in accordance with scales determined on a non-discriminatory basis from time to time by the Legislature for all schools then being conducted under authority of the Legislature; and

(*b*) all such colleges shall receive their share of any grant from time to time voted for all colleges then being conducted under authority of the Legislature, such grant being distributed on a non-discriminatory basis.

See also sections 23, 29 and 59 of the *Constitution Act, 1982*. Section 23 provides for new minority language educational rights and section 59 permits a delay in respect of the coming into force in Quebec of one aspect of those rights. Section 29 provides that nothing in the *Canadian Charter of Rights and Freedoms* abrogates or derogates from any rights or privileges guaranteed by or under the Constitution of Canada in respect of denominational, separate or dissentient schools.

[38]Added by the *Constitution Amendment, 1997 (Quebec)*. See SI/97-141.

Uniformity of Laws in Ontario, Nova Scotia and New Brunswick

94. Legislation for Uniformity of Laws in Three Provinces —Notwithstanding anything in this Act, the Parliament of Canada may make Provision for the Uniformity of all or any of the Laws relative to Property and Civil Rights in Ontario, Nova Scotia, and New Brunswick, and of the Procedure of all or any of the Courts in those Three Provinces, and from and after the passing of any Act in that Behalf the Power of the Parliament of Canada to make Laws in relation to any Matter comprised in any such Act shall, notwithstanding anything in this Act, be unrestricted; but any Act of the Parliament of Canada making Provision for such Uniformity shall not have effect in any Province unless and until it is adopted and enacted as Law by the Legislature thereof.

Old Age Pensions

94A. Legislation respecting old age pensions and supplementary benefits —The Parliament of Canada may make laws in relation to old age pensions and supplementary benefits, including survivors' and disability benefits irrespective of age, but no such law shall affect the operation of any law present or future of a provincial legislature in relation to any such matter.[39]

Agriculture and Immigration

95. Concurrent Powers of Legislation respecting Agriculture, etc. —In each Province the Legislature may make Laws in relation to Agriculture in the Province, and to Immigration into the Province; and it is hereby declared that the Parliament of Canada may from Time to Time make Laws in relation to Agriculture in all or any of the Provinces, and to Immigration into all or any of the Provinces; and any Law of the Legislature of a Province relative to Agriculture or to Immigration shall have effect in and for the Province as long and as far only as it is not repugnant to any Act of the Parliament of Canada.

VII.—JUDICATURE

96. Appointment of Judges —The Governor General shall appoint the Judges of the Superior, District, and County Courts in each Province, except those of the Courts of Probate in Nova Scotia and New Brunswick.

97. Selection of Judges in Ontario, etc. —Until the Laws relative to Property and Civil Rights in Ontario, Nova Scotia, and New Bruns-

---

[39]Added by the *Constitution Act, 1964*, 12-13 Eliz. II, c. 73 (U.K.). As originally enacted by the *British North America Act, 1951*, 14-15 Geo. VI, c. 32 (U.K.), which was repealed by the *Constitution Act, 1982*, section 94A read as follows:

94A.

It is hereby declared that the Parliament of Canada may from time to time make laws in relation to old age pensions in Canada, but no law made by the Parliament of Canada in relation to old age pensions shall affect the operation of any law present or future of a Provincial Legislature in relation to old age pensions.

wick, and the Procedure of the Courts in those Provinces, are made uniform, the Judges of the Courts of those Provinces appointed by the Governor General shall be selected from the respective Bars of those Provinces.

98. Selection of Judges in Quebec —The Judges of the Courts of Quebec shall be selected from the Bar of that Province.

99. Tenure of office of Judges— (1) Subject to subsection two of this section, the Judges of the Superior Courts shall hold office during good behaviour, but shall be removable by the Governor General on Address of the Senate and House of Commons.

(2) Termination at age 75—A Judge of a Superior Court, whether appointed before or after the coming into force of this section, shall cease to hold office upon attaining the age of seventy-five years, or upon the coming into force of this section if at that time he has already attained that age.[40]

100. Salaries etc., of Judges —The Salaries, Allowances, and Pensions of the Judges of the Superior, District, and County Courts (except the Courts of Probate in Nova Scotia and New Brunswick), and of the Admiralty Courts in Cases where the Judges thereof are for the Time being paid by Salary, shall be fixed and provided by the Parliament of Canada.[41]

101. General Court of Appeal, etc. —The Parliament of Canada may, notwithstanding anything in this Act, from Time to Time provide for the Constitution, Maintenance, and Organization of a General Court of Appeal for Canada, and for the Establishment of any additional Courts for the better Administration of the Laws of Canada.[42]

VIII.—REVENUES; DEBTS; ASSETS; TAXATION

[Sections 102 to 104 are omitted]

105. Salary of Governor General —Unless altered by the Parliament of Canada, the Salary of the Governor General shall be Ten thousand Pounds Sterling Money of the United Kingdom of Great Britain and Ireland, payable out of the Consolidated Revenue Fund of Canada, and the same shall form the Third Charge thereon.[43]

[Sections 106 and 107 are omitted]

108. Transfer of Property in Schedule —The Public Works and

---

[40]Repealed and re-enacted by the *Constitution Act, 1960*, 9 Eliz. II, c. 2 (U.K.), which came into force on March 1, 1961. The original section read as follows:

99.

The Judges of the Superior Courts shall hold Office during good Behaviour, but shall be removable by the Governor General on Address of the Senate and House of Commons.

[41]Now provided for in the *Judges Act*, R.S.C. 1985, c. J-1.

[42]See the *Supreme Court Act*, R.S.C. 1985, c. S-26, the *Federal Court Act*, R.S.C. 1985, c. F-7 and the *Tax Court of Canada Act*, R.S.C. 1985, c. T-2.

[43]Now covered by the *Governor General's Act*, R.S.C. 1985, c. G-9.

Property of each Province, enumerated in the Third Schedule to this Act, shall be the Property of Canada.

109. Property in Lands, Mines, etc. —All Lands, Mines, Minerals, and Royalties belonging to the several Provinces of Canada, Nova Scotia, and New Brunswick at the Union, and all Sums then due or payable for such Lands, Mines, Minerals, or Royalties, shall belong to the several Provinces of Ontario, Quebec, Nova Scotia, and New Brunswick in which the same are situate or arise, subject to any Trusts existing in respect thereof, and to any Interest other than that of the Province in the same.[44]

[Sections 110 to 116 are omitted]

117. Provincial Public Property —The several Provinces shall retain all their respective Public Property not otherwise disposed of in this Act, subject to the Right of Canada to assume any Lands or Public Property required for Fortifications or for the Defence of the Country.

[Sections 118 to 120 are omitted]

121. Canadian Manufactures, etc. —All Articles of the Growth, Produce, or Manufacture of any one of the Provinces shall, from and after the Union, be admitted free into each of the other Provinces.

122. Continuance of Customs and Excise Laws —The Customs and Excise Laws of each Province shall, subject to the Provisions of this Act, continue in force until altered by the Parliament of Canada.[45]

[Sections 123 and 124 are omitted]

125. Exemption of Public Lands, etc. No Lands or Property belonging to Canada or any Province shall be liable to Taxation.

[Section 126 is omitted]

IX.—MISCELLANEOUS PROVISIONS

General

[Sections 127 and 128 are omitted]

129. Continuance of existing Laws, Courts, Officers. etc. —Except as otherwise provided by this Act, all Laws in force in Canada, Nova Scotia, or New Brunswick at the Union, and all Courts of Civil and Criminal Jurisdiction, and all legal Commissions, Powers, and

---

[44]Manitoba, Alberta and Saskatchewan were placed in the same position as the original provinces by the *Constitution Act, 1930*, 20-21 Geo. V, c. 26 (U.K.).

These matters were dealt with in respect of British Columbia by the *British Columbia Terms of Union* and also in part by the *Constitution Act, 1930*.

Newfoundland was also placed in the same position by the *Newfoundland Act*, 12-13 Geo. VI, c. 22 (U.K.).

With respect to Prince Edward Island, see the Schedule to the *Prince Edward Island Terms of Union*.

[45]Spent. Now covered by the *Customs Act*, R.S.C. 1985, c. 1 (2nd Supp.), the *Customs Tariff*, S.C. 1997, c. 36, the *Excise Act*, R.S.C. 1985, c. E-14 and the *Excise Tax Act*, R.S.C. 1985, c. E-15.

Authorities, and all Officers, Judicial, Administrative, and Ministerial, existing therein at the Union, shall continue in Ontario, Quebec, Nova Scotia, and New Brunswick respectively, as if the Union had not been made; subject nevertheless (except with respect to such as are enacted by or exist under Acts of the Parliament of Great Britain or of the Parliament of the United Kingdom of Great Britain and Ireland), to be repealed, abolished, or altered by the Parliament of Canada, or by the Legislature of the respective Province, according to the Authority of the Parliament or of that Legislature under this Act.[46]

[Sections 130 and 131 are omitted]

132. Treaty Obligations —The Parliament and Government of Canada shall have all Powers necessary or proper for performing the Obligations of Canada or of any Province thereof, as Part of the British Empire, towards Foreign Countries, arising under Treaties between the Empire and such Foreign Countries.

133. Use of English and French Languages —Either the English or the French Language may be used by any Person in the Debates of the Houses of the Parliament of Canada and of the Houses of the Legislature of Quebec; and both those Languages shall be used in the respective Records and Journals of those Houses; and either of those Languages may be used by any Person or in any Pleading or Process in or issuing from any Court of Canada established under this Act, and in or from all or any of the Courts of Quebec.

The Acts of the Parliament of Canada and of the Legislature of Quebec shall be printed and published in both those Languages.[47]

---

[46]The restriction against altering or repealing laws enacted by or existing under statutes of the United Kingdom was removed by the *Statute of Westminster*, 1931, 22 Geo. V., c. 4 (U.K.) except in respect of certain constitutional documents. Comprehensive procedures for amending enactments forming part of the Constitution of Canada were provided by Part V of the *Constitution Act, 1982*, (U.K.) 1982, c. 11.

[47]A similar provision was enacted for Manitoba by section 23 of the *Manitoba Act, 1870*, 33 Vict., c. 3 (Canada), (confirmed by the *Constitution Act, 1871).* Section 23 read as follows:

23.

Either the English or the French language may be used by any person in the debates of the Houses of the Legislature, and both these languages shall be used in the respective Records and Journals of those Houses; and either of those languages may be used by any person, or in any Pleading or Process, in or issuing from any Court of Canada established under the British North America Act, 1867, or in or from all or any of the Courts of the Province. The Acts of the Legislature shall be printed and published in both those languages.

Sections 17 to 19 of the *Constitution Act, 1982* restate the language rights set out in section 133 in respect of Parliament and the courts established under the *Constitution Act, 1867*, and also guarantees those rights in respect of the legislature of New Brunswick and the courts of that province.

Section 16 and sections 20, 21 and 23 of the *Constitution Act, 1982* recognize additional language rights in respect of the English and French languages.

Section 22 preserves language rights and privileges of languages other than English and French.

[Sections 134 to 145 are omitted]

XI.—ADMISSION OF OTHER COLONIES

146. Power to admit Newfoundland etc., into the Union —It shall be lawful for the Queen, by and with the Advice of Her Majesty's Most Honourable Privy Council, on Addresses from the Houses of the Parliament of Canada, and from the Houses of the respective Legislatures of the Colonies or Provinces of Newfoundland, Prince Edward Island, and British Columbia, to admit those Colonies or Provinces, or any of them, into the Union, and on Address from the Houses of the Parliament of Canada to admit Rupert's Land and the Northwestern Territory, or either of them, into the Union, on such Terms and Conditions in each Case as are in the Addresses expressed and as the Queen thinks fit to approve, subject to the Provisions of this Act; and the Provisions of any Order in Council in that Behalf shall have effect as if they had been enacted by the Parliament of the United Kingdom of Great Britain and Ireland.[48]

[Section 147 is omitted]

SCHEDULES

[The first and second schedules are omitted]

THE THIRD SCHEDULE

Provincial Public Works and Property to be the Property of Canada

1.Canals, with Lands and Water Power connected therewith.

2.Public Harbours.

3.Lighthouses and Piers, and Sable Island.

4.Steamboats, Dredges, and public Vessels.

5.Rivers and Lake Improvements.

6.Railways and Railway Stocks, Mortgages, and other Debts due by Railway Companies.

7.Military Roads.

8.Custom Houses, Post Offices, and all other Public Buildings, except such as the Government of Canada appropriate for the Use of the Provincial Legislatures and Governments.

9.Property transferred by the Imperial Government, and known as Ordnance Property.

10. Armouries, Drill Sheds, Military Clothing, and Munitions of War, and Lands set apart for general Public Purposes.

---

[48]All territories mentioned in this section are now part of Canada.

[The fourth and fifth schedules are omitted]

THE SIXTH SCHEDULE[49]

Primary Production from Non-Renewable Natural Resources and Forestry Resources

1. For the purposes of section 92A of this Act,

(*a*) production from a non-renewable natural resource is primary production therefrom if

(i) it is in the form in which it exists upon its recovery or severance from its natural state, or

(ii) it is a product resulting from processing or refining the resource, and is not a manufactured product or a product resulting from refining crude oil, refining upgraded heavy crude oil, refining gases or liquids derived from coal or refining a synthetic equivalent of crude oil; and

(*b*) production from a forestry resource is primary production therefrom if it consists of sawlogs, poles, lumber, wood chips, sawdust or any other primary wood product, or wood pulp, and is not a product manufactured from wood.

---

[49] As enacted by the *Constitution Act, 1982.*

APPENDIX B

Canada Act 1982

U.K., 1982, c. 11

An Act to give effect to a request by the Senate and House of Commons of Canada

Whereas Canada has requested and consented to the enactment of an Act of the Parliament of the United Kingdom to give effect to the provisions hereinafter set forth and the Senate and the House of Commons of Canada in Parliament assembled have submitted an address to Her Majesty requesting that Her Majesty may graciously be pleased to cause a Bill to be laid before the Parliament of the United Kingdom for that purpose.

Be it therefore enacted by the Queen's Most Excellent Majesty, by and with the advice and consent of the Lords Spiritual and Temporal, and Commons, in this present Parliament assembled, and by the authority of the same as follows:

1. *Constitution Act, 1982* enacted —*The Constitution Act, 1982* set out in Schedule B to this Act is hereby enacted for and shall have the force of law in Canada and shall come into force as provided in that Act.

2. Termination of power to legislate for Canada —No Act of the Parliament of the United Kingdom passed after the *Constitution Act, 1982* comes into force shall extend to Canada as part of its law.

3. French version —So far as it is not contained in Schedule B, the French version of this Act is set out in Schedule A to this Act and has the same authority in Canada as the English version thereof.

4. Short title —This Act may be cited as the *Canada Act 1982*.

APPENDIX C

Constitution Act, 1982

Schedule B to Canada Act 1982 (U.K.)

(Consolidated with amendments by the Department of Justice, Canada)[1]

PART I

CANADIAN CHARTER OF RIGHTS AND FREEDOMS

Whereas Canada is founded upon principles that recognize the supremacy of God and the rule of law:

Guarantee of Rights and Freedoms

1. Rights and freedoms in Canada —The *Canadian Charter of Rights and Freedoms* guarantees the rights and freedoms set out in it subject only to such reasonable limits prescribed by law as can be demonstrably justified in a free and democratic society.

Fundamental Freedoms

2. Fundamental freedoms —Everyone has the following fundamental freedoms:

(*a*) freedom of conscience and religion;

(*b*) freedom of thought, belief, opinion and expression, including freedom of the press and other media of communication;

(*c*) freedom of peaceful assembly; and

(*d*) freedom of association.

Democratic Rights

3. Democratic rights of citizens —Every citizen of Canada has the right to vote in an election of members of the House of Commons or of a legislative assembly and to be qualified for membership therein.

4. Maximum duration of legislative bodies— (1) No House of Commons and no legislative assembly shall continue for longer than five years from the date fixed for the return of the writs of a general election of its members.[2]

---

[1]Source: Department of Justice, Canada, online: http//laws.justice.gc.ca/en/const/annex_e.html

[2]See section 50 and the footnotes to sections 85 and 88 of the *Constitution Act,*

(2) Continuation in special circumstances—In time of real or apprehended war, invasion or insurrection, a House of Commons may be continued by Parliament and a legislative assembly may be continued by the legislature beyond five years if such continuation is not opposed by the votes of more than one-third of the members of the House of Commons or the legislative assembly, as the case may be.[3]

5. Annual sitting of legislative bodies —There shall be a sitting of Parliament and of each legislature at least once every twelve months.[4]

Mobility Rights

6. Mobility of citizens— (1) Every citizen of Canada has the right to enter, remain in and leave Canada.

(2) Rights to move and gain livelihood—Every citizen of Canada and every person who has the status of a permanent resident of Canada has the right

(*a*) to move to and take up residence in any province; and

(*b*) to pursue the gaining of a livelihood in any province.

(3) Limitation—The rights specified in subsection (2) are subject to

(*a*) any laws or practices of general application in force in a province other than those that discriminate among persons primarily on the basis of province of present or previous residence; and

(*b*) any laws providing for reasonable residency requirements as a qualification for the receipt of publicly provided social services.

(4) Affirmative action programs—Subsections (2) and (3) do not preclude any law, program or activity that has as its object the amelioration in a province of conditions of individuals in that province who are socially or economically disadvantaged if the rate of employment in that province is below the rate of employment in Canada.

Legal Rights

7. Life, liberty and security of person —Everyone has the right to life, liberty and security of the person and the right not to be deprived thereof except in accordance with the principles of fundamental justice.

8. Search or seizure —Everyone has the right to be secure against unreasonable search or seizure.

9. Detention or imprisonment —Everyone has the right not to be arbitrarily detained or imprisoned.

10. Arrest or detention —Everyone has the right on arrest or detention

1867.

[3]Replaces part of Class 1 of section 91 of the *Constitution Act, 1867*, which was repealed as set out in subitem 1(3) of the Schedule to this Act.

[4]See the footnotes to sections 20, 86 and 88 of the *Constitution Act, 1867*.

(*a*) to be informed promptly of the reasons therefor;

(*b*) to retain and instruct counsel without delay and to be informed of that right; and

(*c*) to have the validity of the detention determined by way of *habeas corpus* and to be released if the detention is not lawful.

11. Proceedings in criminal and penal matters —Any person charged with an offence has the right

(*a*) to be informed without unreasonable delay of the specific offence;

(*b*) to be tried within a reasonable time;

(*c*) not to be compelled to be a witness in proceedings against that person in respect of the offence;

(*d*) to be presumed innocent until proven guilty according to law in a fair and public hearing by an independent and impartial tribunal;

(*e*) not to be denied reasonable bail without just cause;

(*f*) except in the case of an offence under military law tried before a military tribunal, to the benefit of trial by jury where the maximum punishment for the offence is imprisonment for five years or a more severe punishment;

(*g*) not to be found guilty on account of any act or omission unless, at the time of the act or omission, it constituted an offence under Canadian or international law or was criminal according to the general principles of law recognized by the community of nations;

(*h*) if finally acquitted of the offence, not to be tried for it again and, if finally found guilty and punished for the offence, not to be tried or punished for it again; and

(*i*) if found guilty of the offence and if the punishment for the offence has been varied between the time of commission and the time of sentencing, to the benefit of the lesser punishment.

12. Treatment or punishment —Everyone has the right not to be subjected to any cruel and unusual treatment or punishment.

13. Self-crimination —A witness who testifies in any proceedings has the right not to have any incriminating evidence so given used to incriminate that witness in any other proceedings, except in a prosecution for perjury or for the giving of contradictory evidence.

14. Interpreter —A party or witness in any proceedings who does not understand or speak the language in which the proceedings are conducted or who is deaf has the right to the assistance of an interpreter.

Equality Rights

15. Equality before and under law and equal protection and benefit of law— (1) Every individual is equal before and under the law and has the right to the equal protection and equal benefit of the law without discrimination and, in particular, without discrimination based on race, national or ethnic origin, colour, religion, sex, age or mental or physical disability.

(2) Affirmative action programs—Subsection (1) does not preclude any law, program or activity that has as its object the amelioration of conditions of disadvantaged individuals or groups including those that are disadvantaged because of race, national or ethnic origin, colour, religion, sex, age or mental or physical disability.[5]

Official Languages of Canada

16. Official languages of Canada— (1) English and French are the official languages of Canada and have equality of status and equal rights and privileges as to their use in all institutions of the Parliament and government of Canada.

(2) Official languages of New Brunswick—English and French are the official languages of New Brunswick and have equality of status and equal rights and privileges as to their use in all institutions of the legislature and government of New Brunswick.

(3) Advancement of status and use—Nothing in this Charter limits the authority of Parliament or a legislature to advance the equality of status or use of English and French.

16.1. English and French linguistic communities in New Brunswick— (1) The English linguistic community and the French linguistic community in New Brunswick have equality of status and equal rights and privileges, including the right to distinct educational institutions and such distinct cultural institutions as are necessary for the preservation and promotion of those communities.

(2) Role of the legislature and government of New Brunswick—The role of the legislature and government of New Brunswick to preserve and promote the status, rights and privileges referred to in subsection (1) is affirmed. (83.1)

17. Proceedings of Parliament— (1) Everyone has the right to use English or French in any debates and other proceedings of Parliament.[6]

(2) Proceedings of New Brunswick legislature—Everyone has the right to use English or French in any debates and other proceedings of the legislature of New Brunswick.[7]

18. Parliamentary statutes and records— (1) The statutes, records and journals of Parliament shall be printed and published in

---

[5]Subsection 32(2) provides that section 15 shall not have effect until three years after section 32 comes into force. Section 32 came into force on April 17, 1982; therefore, section 15 had effect on April 17, 1985. (83.1) Section 16.1 was added by the *Constitution Amendment, 1993 (New Brunswick)*. See SI/93-54.

[6]See section 133 of the *Constitution Act, 1867*, and the footnote thereto.

[7]Section 133 of the *Constitution Act, 1867*.

English and French and both language versions are equally authoritative.[8]

(2) New Brunswick statutes and records—The statutes, records and journals of the legislature of New Brunswick shall be printed and published in English and French and both language versions are equally authoritative.[9]

19. Proceedings in courts established by Parliament— (1) Either English or French may be used by any person in, or in any pleading in or process issuing from, any court established by Parliament.[10]

(2) Proceedings in New Brunswick courts—Either English or French may be used by any person in, or in any pleading in or process issuing from, any court of New Brunswick.[11]

20. Communications by public with federal institutions— (1) Any member of the public in Canada has the right to communicate with, and to receive available services from, any head or central office of an institution of the Parliament or government of Canada in English or French, and has the same right with respect to any other office of any such institution where

(*a*) there is a significant demand for communications with and services from that office in such language; or

(*b*) due to the nature of the office, it is reasonable that communications with and services from that office be available in both English and French.

(2) Communications by public with New Brunswick institutions—Any member of the public in New Brunswick has the right to communicate with, and to receive available services from, any office of an institution of the legislature or government of New Brunswick in English or French.

21. Continuation of existing constitutional provisions —Nothing in sections 16 to 20 abrogates or derogates from any right, privilege or obligation with respect to the English and French languages, or either of them, that exists or is continued by virtue of any other provision of the Constitution of Canada.[12]

22. Rights and privileges preserved —Nothing in sections 16 to 20 abrogates or derogates from any legal or customary right or privilege acquired or enjoyed either before or after the coming into force of this Charter with respect to any language that is not English or French.

---

[8]Section 133 of the *Constitution Act, 1867.*

[9]Section 133 of the *Constitution Act, 1867.*

[10]Section 133 of the *Constitution Act, 1867.*

[11]Section 133 of the *Constitution Act, 1867.*

[12]See, for example, section 133 of the *Constitution Act, 1867*, and the reference to the *Manitoba Act, 1870*, in the footnote thereto.

Minority Language Educational Rights

23. Language of instruction— (1) Citizens of Canada

(*a*) whose first language learned and still understood is that of the English or French linguistic minority population of the province in which they reside, or

(*b*) who have received their primary school instruction in Canada in English or French and reside in a province where the language in which they received that instruction is the language of the English or French linguistic minority population of the province, have the right to have their children receive primary and secondary school instruction in that language in that province.[13]

(2) Continuity of language instruction—Citizens of Canada of whom any child has received or is receiving primary or secondary school instruction in English or French in Canada, have the right to have all their children receive primary and secondary school instruction in the same language.

(3) Application where numbers warrant—The right of citizens of Canada under subsections (1) and (2) to have their children receive primary and secondary school instruction in the language of the English or French linguistic minority population of a province

(*a*) applies wherever in the province the number of children of citizens who have such a right is sufficient to warrant the provision to them out of public funds of minority language instruction; and

(*b*) includes, where the number of those children so warrants, the right to have them receive that instruction in minority language educational facilities provided out of public funds.

Enforcement

24. Enforcement of guaranteed rights and freedoms— (1) Anyone whose rights or freedoms, as guaranteed by this Charter, have been infringed or denied may apply to a court of competent jurisdiction to obtain such remedy as the court considers appropriate and just in the circumstances.

(2) Exclusion of evidence bringing administration of justice into disrepute—Where, in proceedings under subsection (1), a court concludes that evidence was obtained in a manner that infringed or denied any rights or freedoms guaranteed by this Charter, the evidence shall be excluded if it is established that, having regard to all the circumstances, the admission of it in the proceedings would bring the administration of justice into disrepute.

General

25. Aboriginal rights and freedoms not affected by Charter —The guarantee in this Charter of certain rights and freedoms shall not be construed so as to abrogate or derogate from any aboriginal, treaty

[13]Paragraph 23(1)(a) is not in force in respect of Quebec.

or other rights or freedoms that pertain to the aboriginal peoples of Canada including

(*a*) any rights or freedoms that have been recognized by the Royal Proclamation of October 7, 1763; and

(*b*) any rights or freedoms that now exist by way of land claims agreements or may be so acquired.[14]

26. Other rights and freedoms not affected by Charter —The guarantee in this Charter of certain rights and freedoms shall not be construed as denying the existence of any other rights or freedoms that exist in Canada.

27. Multicultural heritage —This Charter shall be interpreted in a manner consistent with the preservation and enhancement of the multicultural heritage of Canadians.

28. Rights guaranteed equally to both sexes —Notwithstanding anything in this Charter, the rights and freedoms referred to in it are guaranteed equally to male and female persons.

29. Rights respecting certain schools preserved —Nothing in this Charter abrogates or derogates from any rights or privileges guaranteed by or under the Constitution of Canada in respect of denominational, separate or dissentient schools.[15]

30. Application to territories and territorial authorities —A reference in this Charter to a Province or to the legislative assembly or legislature of a province shall be deemed to include a reference to the Yukon Territory and the Northwest Territories, or to the appropriate legislative authority thereof, as the case may be.

31. Legislative powers not extended —Nothing in this Charter extends the legislative powers of any body or authority.

Application of Charter

32. Application of Charter— (1) This Charter applies

(*a*) to the Parliament and government of Canada in respect of all matters within the authority of Parliament including all matters relating to the Yukon Territory and Northwest Territories; and

(*b*) to the legislature and government of each province in respect of all matters within the authority of the legislature of each province.

(2) Exception—Notwithstanding subsection (1), section 15 shall not have effect until three years after this section comes into force.

33. Exception where express declaration— (1) Parliament or the legislature of a province may expressly declare in an Act of Parliament or of the legislature, as the case may be, that the Act or a provi-

[14]Paragraph 25(*b*) was repealed and re-enacted by the *Constitution Amendment Proclamation, 1983*. See SI/84-102. *Paragraph 25(*b*) as originally enacted read as follows: "(*b*) any rights or freedoms that may be acquired by the aboriginal peoples of Canada by way of land claims settlement."

[15]See section 93 of the *Constitution Act, 1867*, and the footnote thereto.

sion thereof shall operate notwithstanding a provision included in section 2 or sections 7 to 15 of this Charter.

(2) Operation of exception—An Act or a provision of an Act in respect of which a declaration made under this section is in effect shall have such operation as it would have but for the provision of this Charter referred to in the declaration.

(3) Five year limitation—A declaration made under subsection (1) shall cease to have effect five years after it comes into force or on such earlier date as may be specified in the declaration.

(4) Re-enactment—Parliament or the legislature of a province may re-enact a declaration made under subsection (1).

(5) Five year limitation—Subsection (3) applies in respect of are-enactment made under subsection (4).

Citation

34. Citation —This Part may be cited as the *Canadian Charter of Rights and Freedoms.*

PART II

RIGHTS OF THE ABORIGINAL PEOPLES OF CANADA

35. Recognition of existing aboriginal and treaty rights— (1) The existing aboriginal and treaty rights of the aboriginal peoples of Canada are hereby recognized and affirmed.

(2) Definition of "aboriginal peoples of Canada"—In this Act, "aboriginal peoples of Canada" includes the Indian, Inuit and Métis peoples of Canada.

(3) Land claims agreements—For greater certainty, in subsection (1) "treaty rights" includes rights that now exist by way of land claims agreements or may be so acquired.

(4) Aboriginal and treaty rights are guaranteed equally to both sexes—Notwithstanding any other provision of this Act, the aboriginal and treaty rights referred to in subsection (1) are guaranteed equally to male and female persons.[16]

35.1. Commitment to participation in constitutional conference —The government of Canada and the provincial governments are committed to the principle that, before any amendment is made to Class 24 of section 91 of the "*Constitution Act, 1867*", to section 25 of this Act or to this Part,

(*a*) a constitutional conference that includes in its agenda an item relating to the proposed amendment, composed of the Prime Minister of Canada and the first ministers of the provinces, will be convened by the Prime Minister of Canada; and

[16] Subsections 35(3) and (4) were added by the *Constitution Amendment Proclamation, 1983.* See SI/84-102.

(*b*) the Prime Minister of Canada will invite representatives of the aboriginal peoples of Canada to participate in the discussions on that item.[17]

PART III

EQUALIZATION AND REGIONAL DISPARITIES

36. Commitment to promote equal opportunities— (1) Without altering the legislative authority of Parliament or of the provincial legislatures, or the rights of any of them with respect to the exercise of their legislative authority, Parliament and the legislatures, together with the government of Canada and the provincial governments, are committed to

(*a*) promoting equal opportunities for the well-being of Canadians;

(*b*) furthering economic development to reduce disparity in opportunities; and

(*c*) providing essential public services of reasonable quality to all Canadians.

(2) Commitment respecting public services—Parliament and the government of Canada are committed to the principle of making equalization payments to ensure that provincial governments have sufficient revenues to provide reasonably comparable levels of public services at reasonably comparable levels of taxation.[18]

PART IV

CONSTITUTIONAL CONFERENCE

37.[19]

PART IV.I

CONSTITUTIONAL CONFERENCES

37.1[20]

---

[17]Section 35.1 was added by the *Constitution Amendment Proclamation, 1983.* See SI/84-102.

[18]See the footnotes to sections 114 and 118 of the *Constitution Act, 1867.*

[19]Section 54 provided for the repeal of Part IV one year after Part VII came into force. Part VII came into force on April 17, 1982 thereby repealing Part IV on April 17, 1983. Part IV, as originally enacted, read as follows: 37. (1) A constitutional conference composed of the Prime Minister of Canada and the first ministers of the provinces shall be convened by the Prime Minister of Canada within one year after this Part comes into force.(2) The conference convened under subsection (1) shall have included in its agenda an item respecting constitutional matters that directly affect the aboriginal peoples of Canada, including the identification and definition of the rights of those peoples to be included in the Constitution of Canada, and the Prime Minister of Canada shall invite representatives of those peoples to participate in the discussions on that item.(3) The Prime Minister of Canada shall invite elected representatives of the governments of the Yukon Territory and the Northwest Territories to participate in the discussions on any item on the agenda of the conference convened under subsection (1) that, in the opinion of the Prime Minister, directly affects the Yukon Territory and the Northwest Territories.

[20]Part IV.I, which was added by the *Constitution Amendment Proclamation, 1983* (see SI/84-102), was repealed on April 18, 1987 by section 54.1. Part IV.I, as originally

PART V

PROCEDURE FOR AMENDING CONSTITUTION OF CANADA[21]

38. General procedure for amending Constitution of Canada— (1) An amendment to the Constitution of Canada may be made by proclamation issued by the Governor General under the Great Seal of Canada where so authorized by

(*a*) resolutions of the Senate and House of Commons; and

(*b*) resolutions of the legislative assemblies of at least two-thirds of the provinces that have, in the aggregate, according to the then latest general census, at least fifty per cent of the population of all the provinces.

(2) Majority of members—An amendment made under subsection (1) that derogates from the legislative powers, the proprietary rights or any other rights or privileges of the legislature or government of a province shall require a resolution supported by a majority of the members of each of the Senate, the House of Commons and the legislative assemblies required under subsection (1).

(3) Expression of dissent—An amendment referred to in subsection (2) shall not have effect in a province the legislative assembly of which has expressed its dissent thereto by resolution supported by a majority of its members prior to the issue of the proclamation to which the amendment relates unless that legislative assembly, subsequently, by resolution supported by a majority of its members, revokes its dissent and authorizes the amendment.

(4) Revocation of dissent—A resolution of dissent made for the purposes of subsection (3) may be revoked at any time before or after the issue of the proclamation to which it relates.

39. Restriction on proclamation— (1) A proclamation shall not be issued under subsection 38(1) before the expiration of one year from the adoption of the resolution initiating the amendment proce-

---

enacted, read as follows:37.1 (1) In addition to the conference convened in March 1983, at least two constitutional conferences composed of the Prime Minister of Canada and the first ministers of the provinces shall be convened by the Prime Minister of Canada, the first within three years after April 17, 1982 and the second within five years after that date.(2) Each conference convened under subsection (1) shall have included in its agenda constitutional matters that directly affect the aboriginal peoples of Canada, and the Prime Minister of Canada shall invite representatives of those peoples to participate in the discussions on those matters.(3) The Prime Minister of Canada shall invite elected representatives of the governments of the Yukon Territory and the Northwest Territories to participate in the discussions on any item on the agenda of a conference convened under subsection (1) that, in the opinion of the Prime Minister, directly affects the Yukon Territory and the Northwest Territories.(4) Nothing in this section shall be construed so as to derogate from subsection 35(1).

[21]Prior to the enactment of Part V certain provisions of the Constitution of Canada and the provincial constitutions could be amended pursuant to the *Constitution Act, 1867*. See the footnotes to section 91, Class 1 and section 92, Class 1 thereof, *supra*. Other amendments to the Constitution could only be made by enactment of the Parliament of the United Kingdom.

dure thereunder, unless the legislative assembly of each province has previously adopted a resolution of assent or dissent.

(2) Idem—A proclamation shall not be issued under subsection 38(1) after the expiration of three years from the adoption of the resolution initiating the amendment procedure thereunder.

40. Compensation —Where an amendment is made under subsection 38(1) that transfers provincial legislative powers relating to education or other cultural matters from provincial legislatures to Parliament, Canada shall provide reasonable compensation to any province to which the amendment does not apply.

41. Amendment by unanimous consent —An amendment to the Constitution of Canada in relation to the following matters may be made by proclamation issued by the Governor General under the Great Seal of Canada only where authorized by resolutions of the Senate and House of Commons and of the legislative assembly of each province:

(*a*) the office of the Queen, the Governor General and the Lieutenant Governor of a province;

(*b*) the right of a province to a number of members in the House of Commons not less than the number of Senators by which the province is entitled to be represented at the time this Part comes into force;

(*c*) subject to section 43, the use of the English or the French language;

(*d*) the composition of the Supreme Court of Canada; and

(*e*) an amendment to this Part.

42. Amendment by general procedure— (1) An amendment to the Constitution of Canada in relation to the following matters may be made only in accordance with subsection 38(1):

(*a*) the principle of proportionate representation of the provinces in the House of Commons prescribed by the Constitution of Canada;

(*b*) the powers of the Senate and the method of selecting Senators;

(*c*) the number of members by which a province is entitled to be represented in the Senate and the residence qualifications of Senators;

(*d*) subject to paragraph 41(*d*), the Supreme Court of Canada;

(*e*) the extension of existing provinces into the territories; and

(*f*) notwithstanding any other law or practice, the establishment of new provinces.

(2) Exception—Subsections 38(2) to (4) do not apply in respect of amendments in relation to matters referred to in subsection (1).

43. Amendment of provisions relating to some but not all provinces —An amendment to the Constitution of Canada in relation to any provision that applies to one or more, but not all, provinces, including (*a*) any alteration to boundaries between provinces, and

(*b*) any amendment to any provision that relates to the use of the English or the French language within a province, may be made by proclamation issued by the Governor General under the Great Seal of Canada only where so authorized by resolutions of the Senate and House of Commons and of the legislative assembly of each province to which the amendment applies.

44. Amendments by Parliament —Subject to sections 41 and 42, Parliament may exclusively make laws amending the Constitution of Canada in relation to the executive government of Canada or the Senate and House of Commons.

45. Amendments by provincial legislatures —Subject to section 41, the legislature of each province may exclusively make laws amending the constitution of the province.

46. Initiation of amendment procedures— (1) The procedures for amendment under sections 38, 41, 42 and 43 may be initiated either by the Senate or the House of Commons or by the legislative assembly of a province.

(2) Revocation of authorization—A resolution of assent made for the purposes of this Part may be revoked at any time before the issue of a proclamation authorized by it.

47. Amendments without Senate resolution— (1) An amendment to the Constitution of Canada made by proclamation under section 38, 41, 42 or 43 may be made without a resolution of the Senate authorizing the issue of the proclamation if, within one hundred and eighty days after the adoption by the House of Commons of a resolution authorizing its issue, the Senate has not adopted such a resolution and if, at any time after the expiration of that period, the House of Commons again adopts the resolution.

(2) Computation of period—Any period when Parliament is prorogued or dissolved shall not be counted in computing the one hundred and eighty day period referred to in subsection (1).

48. Advice to issue proclamation——The Queen's Privy Council for Canada shall advise the Governor General to issue a proclamation under this Part forthwith on the adoption of the resolutions required for an amendment made by proclamation under this Part.

49. Constitutional conference —A constitutional conference composed of the Prime Minister of Canada and the first ministers of the provinces shall be convened by the Prime Minister of Canada within fifteen years after this Part comes into force to review the provisions of this Part.

Part VI

Amendment to the Constitution Act, 1867

50.[22]

51.[23]

Part VII

General

52. Primacy of Constitution of Canada— (1) The Constitution of Canada is the supreme law of Canada, and any law that is inconsistent with the provisions of the Constitution is, to the extent of the inconsistency, of no force or effect.

(2) Constitution of Canada—The Constitution of Canada includes

(*a*) the *Canada Act 1982*, including this Act;

(*b*) the Acts and orders referred to in the schedule; and

(*c*) any amendment to any Act or order referred to in paragraph (*a*) or (*b*).

(3) Amendments to Constitution of Canada—Amendments to the Constitution of Canada shall be made only in accordance with the authority contained in the Constitution of Canada.

53. Repeals and new names— (1) The enactments referred to in Column I of the schedule are hereby repealed or amended to the extent indicated in Column II thereof and, unless repealed, shall continue as law in Canada under the names set out in Column III thereof.

(2) Consequential amendments—Every enactment, except the *Canada Act 1982*, that refers to an enactment referred to in the schedule by the name in Column I thereof is hereby amended by substituting for that name the corresponding name in Column III thereof, and any British North America Act not referred to in the schedule may be cited as the *Constitution Act* followed by the year and number, if any, of its enactment.

54. Repeal and consequential amendments—Part IV is repealed on the day that is one year after this Part comes into force and this section may be repealed and this Act renumbered, consequentially upon the repeal of Part IV and this section, by proclamation issued by the Governor General under the Great Seal of Canada.[24]

54.1.

[Repealed][25]

55. French version of Constitution of Canada —A French ver-

---

[22]The amendment is set out in the Consolidation of the *Constitution Act, 1867*, as section 92A thereof.

[23]The amendment is set out in the Consolidation of the *Constitution Act, 1867*, as the Sixth Schedule thereof.

[24]Part VII came into force on April 17, 1982. See SI/82-97.

[25]Section 54.1, which was added by the *Constitution Amendment Proclamation, 1983* (see SI/84-102), provided for the repeal of Part IV.1 and section 54.1 on April 18,

sion of the portions of the Constitution of Canada referred to in the schedule shall be prepared by the Minister of Justice of Canada as expeditiously as possible and, when any portion thereof sufficient to warrant action being taken has been so prepared, it shall be put forward for enactment by proclamation issued by the Governor General under the Great Seal of Canada pursuant to the procedure then applicable to an amendment of the same provisions of the Constitution of Canada.

56. English and French versions of certain constitutional texts —Where any portion of the Constitution of Canada has been or is enacted in English and French or where a French version of any portion of the Constitution is enacted pursuant to section 55, the English and French versions of that portion of the Constitution are equally authoritative.

57. English and French versions of this Act —The English and French versions of this Act are equally authoritative.

58. Commencement —Subject to section 59, this Act shall come into force on a day to be fixed by proclamation issued by the Queen or the Governor General under the Great Seal of Canada.[26]

59. Commencement of paragraph 23(1)(*a*) in respect of Quebec— (1) Paragraph 23(1)(*a*) shall come into force in respect of Quebec on a day to be fixed by proclamation issued by the Queen or the Governor General under the Great Seal of Canada.

(2) Authorization of Quebec—A proclamation under subsection (1) shall be issued only where authorized by the legislative assembly or government of Quebec.[27]

(3) Repeal of this section—This section may be repealed on the day paragraph 23(1)(*a*) comes into force in respect of Quebec and this Act amended and renumbered, consequentially upon the repeal of this section, by proclamation issued by the Queen or the Governor General under the Great Seal of Canada.

60. Short title and citations —This Act may be cited as the *Constitution Act, 1982*, and the Constitution Acts 1867 to 1975 (No. 2) and this Act may be cited together as the *Constitution Acts, 1867 to 1982.*

61. References —A reference to the "*Constitution Acts, 1867 to 1982*" shall be deemed to include a reference to the "*Constitution Amendment Proclamation, 1983*".[28]

1987. Section 54.1, as originally enacted, read as follows: "54.1 Part IV.1 and this section are repealed on April 18, 1987."

[26]The Act, with the exception of paragraph 23(1)(a) in respect of Quebec, came into force on April 17, 1982 by proclamation issued by the Queen. See SI/82-97.

[27]No proclamation has been issued under section 59.

[28]Section 61 was added by the *Constitution Amendment Proclamation, 1983*. See SI/84-102. See also section 3 of the *Constitution Act, 1985 (Representation)*, S.C. 1986, c. 8, Part I and the *Constitution Amendment, 1987 (Newfoundland Act)* SI/88-11.

SCHEDULE
to the
Constitution Act, 1982
Modernization of the Constitution

Item	Column I Act Affected	Column II Amendment	Column III New Name
1.	British North America Act, 1867, 30-31 Vict., c. 3 (U.K.)	(1) Section 1 is repealed and the following substituted therefor: "1. This Act may be cited as the *Constitution Act. 1867.*" (2) Section 20 is repealed. (3) Class 1 of section 91 is repealed. (4) Class 1 of section 92 is repealed.	Constitution Act, 1867
2.	An Act to amend and continue the Act 32-33 Victoria chapter 3; and to establish and provide for the Government of the Province of Manitoba, 1870, 33 Vict., c. 3 (Can.)	(1) The long title is repealed and the following substituted therefor: "*Manitoba Act, 1870.*" (2) Section 20 is repealed.	Manitoba Act, 1870
3.	Order of Her Majesty in Council admitting Rupert's Land and the North-Western Territory into the union, dated the 23rd day of June, 1870		Rupert's Land and Northwestern Territory Order
4.	Order of Her Majesty in Council admitting British Columbia into the Union, dated the 16th day of May, 1871		British Columbia Terms of Union
5.	British North America Act, 1871, 34-35 Vict., c. 28 (U.K.)	Section 1 is repealed and the following substituted therefor: "1. This Act may be cited as the *Constitution Act, 1871.*"	Constitution Act, 1871
6.	Order of Her Majesty in Council admitting Prince Edward Island into the Union, dated the 26th day of June, 1873		Prince Edward Island Terms of Union
7.	Parliament of Canada Act, 1875, 38-39 Vict., c. 38 (U.K.)		Parliament of Canada Act, 1875
8.	Order of Her Majesty in Council admitting all British possessions and Territories in North America and islands adjacent thereto into the Union, dated the 31st day of July, 1880		Adjacent Territories Order

Item	Column I Act Affected	Column II Amendment	Column III New Name
9.	British North America Act, 1886, 49-50 Vict., c. 35 (U.K.)	Section 3 is repealed and the following substituted therefor: "3. This Act may be cited as the *Constitution Act, 1886.*"	Constitution Act, 1886
10.	Canada (Ontario Boundary) Act, 1889, 52-53 Vict., c. 28 (U.K.)		Canada (Ontario Boundary) Act, 1889
11.	Canadian Speaker (Appointment of Deputy) Act, 1895, 2nd Sess., 59 Vict., c. 3 (U.K.)	The Act is repealed.	
12.	The Alberta Act, 1905, 4-5 Edw. VII, c. 3 (Can.)		Alberta Act
13.	The Saskatchewan Act, 1905, 4-5 Edw. VII, c. 42 (Can.)		Saskatchewan Act
14.	British North America Act, 1907, 7 Edw. VII, c. 11 (U.K.)	Section 2 is repealed and the following substituted therefor: "2. This Act may be cited as the *Constitution Act, 1907.*"	Constitution Act, 1907
15.	British North America Act, 1915, 5-6 Geo. V, c. 45 (U.K.)	Section 3 is repealed and the following substituted therefor: "3. This Act may be cited as the *Constitution Act, 1915.*	Constitution Act, 1915
16.	British North America Act, 1930, 20-21 Geo. V, c. 26 (U.K.)	Section 3 is repealed and the following substituted therefor: "3. This Act may be cited as the *Constitution Act, 1930.*"	Constitution Act, 1930
17.	Statute of Westminster, 1931, 22 Geo. V, c. 4 (U.K.)	In so far as they apply to Canada, (*a*) section 4 is repealed; and (*b*) subsection 7(1) is repealed.	Statute of Westminster, 1931
18.	British North America Act, 1940, 3-4 Geo. VI, c. 36 (U.K.)	Section 2 is repealed and the following substituted therefor: "2. This Act may be cited as the *Constitution Act, 1940.*"	Constitution Act, 1940
19.	British North America Act, 1943, 6-7 Geo. VI, c. 30 (U.K.)	The Act is repealed.	
20.	British North America Act, 1946, 9-10 Geo. VI, c. 63 (U.K.)	The Act is repealed.	

Item	Column I Act Affected	Column II Amendment	Column III New Name
21.	British North America Act, 1949, 12-13 Geo. VI, c. 22 (U.K.)	Section 3 is repealed and the following substituted therefor: "3. This Act may be cited as the *Newfoundland Act.*"	Newfoundland Act
22.	British North America (No. 2) Act, 1949, 13 Geo. VI, c. 81 (U.K.)	The Act is repealed.	
23.	British North America Act, 1951, 14-15 Geo. VI, c. 32 (U.K.)	The Act is repealed.	
24.	British North America Act, 1952, 1 Eliz. II, c. 15 (Can.)	The Act is repealed.	
25.	British North America Act, 1960, 9 Eliz. II, c. 2 (U.K.)	Section 2 is repealed and the following substituted therefor: "2. This Act may be cited as the *Constitution Act, 1960.*"	Constitution Act, 1960
26.	British North America Act, 1964, 12-13 Eliz. II, c. 73 (U.K.)	Section 2 is repealed and the following substituted therefor: "2. This Act may be cited as the *Constitution Act*, 1964."	Constitution Act, 1964
27.	British North America Act, 1965, 14 Eliz. II, c. 4, Part I (Can.)	Section 2 is repealed and the following substituted therefor: "2. This Part may be cited as the *Constitution Act, 1965.*"	Constitution Act, 1965
28.	British North America Act, 1974, 23 Eliz. II, c. 13, Part I (Can.)	Section 3, as amended by 25-26 Eliz. II, c. 28, s. 38(1) (Can.), is repealed and the following substituted therefor: "3. This Part may be cited as the *Constitution Act, 1974.*"	Constitution Act, 1974
29.	British North America Act, 1975, 23-24 Eliz. II, c. 28, Part I (Can.)	Section 3, as amended by 25-26 Eliz. II, c. 28, s. 31 (Can.), is repealed and the following substituted therefor: "3. This Part may be cited as the *Constitution Act (No. 1), 1975.*"	Constitution Act (No. 1), 1975
30.	British North America Act (No. 2), 1975, 23-24 Eliz. II, c. 53 (Can.)	Section 3 is repealed and the following substituted therefor: "3. This Act may be cited as the *Constitution Act (No. 2), 1975.*"	Constitution Act (No. 2), 1975

(a) authorize or effect the arbitrary detention, imprisonment or exile of any person;

(b) impose or authorize the imposition of cruel and unusual treatment or punishment;

(c) deprive a person who has been arrested or detained

(i) of the right to be informed promptly of the reason for his arrest or detention,

(ii) of the right to retain and instruct counsel without delay, or

(iii) of the remedy by way of *habeas corpus* for the determination of the validity of his detention and for his release if the detention is not lawful;

(d) authorize a court, tribunal, commission, board or other authority to compel a person to give evidence if he is denied counsel, protection against self crimination or other constitutional safeguards;

(e) deprive a person of the right to a fair hearing in accordance with the principles of fundamental justice for the determination of his rights and obligations;

(f) deprive a person charged with a criminal offence of the right to be presumed innocent until proved guilty according to law in a fair and public hearing by an independent and impartial tribunal, or of the right to reasonable bail without just cause; or

(g) deprive a person of the right to the assistance of an interpreter in any proceedings in which he is involved or in which he is a party or a witness, before a court, commission, board or other tribunal, if he does not understand or speak the language in which such proceedings are conducted.

3. (1) Subject to subsection (2), the Minister of Justice shall, in accordance with such regulations as may be prescribed by the Governor in Council, examine every regulation transmitted to the Clerk of the Privy Council for registration pursuant to the *Statutory Instruments Act* and every Bill introduced in or presented to the House of Commons by a Minister of the Crown, in order to ascertain whether any of the provisions thereof are inconsistent with the purposes and provisions of this Part and he shall report any such inconsistency to the House of Commons at the first convenient opportunity.

(2) A regulation need not be examined in accordance with subsection (1) if prior to being made it was examined as a proposed regulation in accordance with section 3 of the *Statutory Instruments Act* to ensure that it was not inconsistent with the purposes and provisions of this Part.[1]

4.The provisions of this Part shall be known as the *Canadian Bill of Rights.*

PART II

5. (1) Nothing in Part I shall be construed to abrogate or abridge any

[1]Section 3 was repealed and replaced by S.C. 1985, c. 26, s. 105.

human right or fundamental freedom not enumerated therein that may have existed in Canada at the commencement of this Act.

(2) The expression "law of Canada" in Part I means an Act of the Parliament of Canada enacted before or after the coming into force of this Act, any order, rule or regulation thereunder, and any law in force in Canada or in any part of Canada at the commencement of this Act that is subject to be repealed, abolished or altered by the Parliament of Canada.

(3) The provisions of Part I shall be construed as extending only to matters coming within the legislative authority of the Parliament of Canada.

APPENDIX E

American Bill of Rights

AMENDMENTS TO THE CONSTITUTION OF THE UNITED STATES

First Ten Amendments passed by Congress September 25, 1789.

Ratified by three-fourths of the States December 15, 1791.

ARTICLE I

Congress shall make no law respecting an establishment of religion, or prohibiting the free exercise thereof; or abridging the freedom of speech, or of the press; or the right of the people peaceably to assemble, and to petition the government for a redress of grievances.

ARTICLE II

A well regulated militia, being necessary to the security of a free State, the right of the people to keep and bear arms, shall not be infringed.

ARTICLE III

No soldier shall, in time of peace be quartered in any house, without the consent of the owner, nor in time of war, but in a manner to be prescribed by law.

ARTICLE IV

The right of the people to be secure in their persons, houses, papers, and effects, against unreasonable searches and seizures, shall not be violated, and no warrants shall issue, but upon probable cause, supported by oath or affirmation, and particularly describing the place to be searched, and the persons or things to be seized.

ARTICLE V

No person shall be held to answer for a capital, or otherwise infamous crime, unless on a presentment or indictment of a grand jury, except in cases arising in the land or naval forces, or in the militia, when in actual service in time of war or public danger; nor shall any person be subject for the same offense to be twice put in jeopardy of life or limb; nor shall be compelled in any criminal case to be a witness against himself, nor be deprived of life, liberty, or property, without due process of law; nor shall private property be taken for public use without just compensation.

ARTICLE VI

In all criminal prosecutions, the accused shall enjoy the right to a speedy and public trial, by an impartial jury of the State and district wherein the crime shall have been committed, which district shall have been previously ascertained by law, and to be informed of the nature and cause of the accusation; to be confronted with the witnesses against him; to have compulsory process for obtaining witnesses in his favor, and to have the assistance of counsel for his defense.

ARTICLE VII

In suits at common law, where the value in controversy shall exceed twenty dollars, the right of trial by jury shall be preserved, and no fact tried by a jury shall be otherwise reexamined in any court of the United States, than according to the rules of the common law.

ARTICLE VIII

Excessive bail shall not be required, nor excessive fines imposed, nor cruel and unusual punishments inflicted.

ARTICLE IX

The enumeration in the Constitution of certain rights shall not be construed to deny or disparage others retained by the people.

ARTICLE X

The powers not delegated to the United States by the Constitution, nor prohibited by it to the States, are reserved to the States respectively, or to the people.

ARTICLE XIII

Passed by Congress January 31, 1865. Ratified December 6, 1865.

SECTION 1. Neither slavery nor involuntary servitude, except as punishment for crime whereof the party shall have been duly convicted, shall exist within the United States, or any place subject to their jurisdiction.

SECTION 2. Congress shall have power to enforce this article by appropriate legislation.

ARTICLE XIV

Passed by Congress June 13, 1866. Ratified July 9, 1868.

SECTION 1. All persons born or naturalized in the United States, and subject to the jurisdiction thereof, are citizens of the United States and of the State wherein they reside. No State shall make or enforce any law which shall abridge the privileges or immunities of citizens of the United States; nor shall any State deprive any person of life, liberty, or property, without due process of law; nor deny to any person within its jurisdiction the equal protection of the laws. . . .

SECTION 5. The Congress shall have power to enforce, by appropriate legislation, the provisions of this article.

ARTICLE XV

Passed by Congress February 26, 1869. Ratified February 3, 1870.

SECTION 1. The right of citizens of the United States to vote shall not be denied or abridged by the United States or by any State on account of race, color, or previous condition of servitude.

SECTION 2. The Congress shall have power to enforce this article by appropriate legislation.

ARTICLE XIX

Passed by Congress June 4, 1919. Ratified August 18, 1920.

The right of citizens of the United States to vote shall not be denied or abridged by the United States or by any State on account of sex.

The Congress shall have power by appropriate legislation to enforce the provisions of this article.

ARTICLE XXIV

Passed by Congress August 27, 1962. Ratified January 23, 1964.

SECTION 1. The right of citizens of the United States to vote in any primary or other election for President or Vice President, for electors for President or Vice President, or for Senator or Representative in Congress, shall not be denied or abridged by the United States or any State by reason of failure to pay any poll tax or other tax.

SECTION 2. The Congress shall have the power to enforce this article by appropriate legislation.

ARTICLE XXVI

Passed by Congress March 23, 1971. Ratified June 30, 1971.

SECTION 1. The right of citizens of the United States, who are eighteen years of age or older, to vote shall not be denied or abridged by the United States or any State on account of age.

SECTION 2. The Congress shall have the power to enforce this article by appropriate legislation.

ARTICLE XXVII

Passed by Congress September 25, 1789. Ratified May 7, 1992.

No law, varying the compensation for the services of the Senators and Representatives, shall take effect, until an election of Representatives shall have intervened.

APPENDIX F

International Covenant on Civil and Political Rights

THE STATES PARTIES TO THE PRESENT COVENANT,

Considering that, in accordance with the principles proclaimed in the Charter of the United Nations, recognition of the inherent dignity and of the equal and inalienable rights of all members of the human family is the foundation of freedom, justice and peace in the world,

Recognizing that these rights derive from the inherent dignity of the human person,

Recognizing that, in accordance with the Universal Declaration of Human Rights, the ideal of free human beings enjoying civil and political freedom and freedom from fear and want can only be achieved if conditions are created whereby everyone may enjoy his civil and political rights, as well as his economic, social and cultural rights,

Considering the obligations of States under the Charter of the United Nations to promote universal respect for, and observance of, human rights and freedoms,

Realizing that the individual, having duties to other individuals and to the community to which he belongs, is under a responsibility to strive for the promotion and observance of the rights recognized in the present Covenant,

Agree upon the following articles:

PART I

Article 1

1. All peoples have the right of self-determination. By virtue of that right they freely determine their political status and freely pursue their economic, social and cultural development.

2. All peoples may, for their own ends, freely dispose of their natural wealth and resources without prejudice to any obligations arising out of international economic co-operation, based upon the principle of mutual benefit, and international law. In no case may a people be deprived of its own means of subsistence.

3. The States Parties to the present Covenant, including those having responsibility for the administration of Non-Self-Governing and Trust Territories, shall promote the realization of the right of self-determination, and shall respect that right, in conformity with the provisions of the Charter of the United Nations.

PART II

Article 2

1. Each State Party to the present Covenant undertakes to respect and to ensure to all individuals within its territory and subject to its jurisdiction the rights recognized in the present Covenant, without distinction of any kind, such as race, colour, sex, language, religion, political or other opinion, national or social origin, property, birth or other status.

2. Where not already provided for by existing legislative or other measures, each State Party to the present Covenant undertakes to take the necessary steps, in accordance with its constitutional processes and with the provisions of the present Covenant, to adopt such legislative or other measures as may be necessary to give effect to the rights recognized in the present Covenant.

3. Each State Party to the present Covenant undertakes:

(*a*) To ensure that any person whose rights or freedoms as herein recognized are violated shall have an effective remedy, notwithstanding that the violation has been committed by persons acting in an official capacity;

(*b*) To ensure that any person claiming such a remedy shall have his right thereto determined by competent judicial, administrative or legislative authorities, or by any other competent authority provided for by the legal system of the State, and to develop the possibilities of judicial remedy;

(*c*) To ensure that the competent authorities shall enforce such remedies when granted.

Article 3

The States Parties to the present Covenant undertake to ensure the equal right of men and women to the enjoyment of all civil and political rights set forth in the present Covenant.

Article 4

1. In time of public emergency which threatens the life of the nation and the existence of which is officially proclaimed, the States Parties to the present Covenant may take measures derogating from their obligations under the present Covenant to the extent strictly required by the exigencies of the situation, provided that such measures are not inconsistent with their other obligations under international law and do not involve discrimination solely on the ground of race, colour, sex, language, religion or social origin.

2. No derogation from articles 6, 7, 8 (paragraphs 1 and 2), 11, 15, 16 and 18 may be made under this provision.

3. Any State Party to the present Covenant availing itself of the right of derogation shall immediately inform the other States Parties to the present Covenant, through the intermediary of the Secretary-General of

the United Nations, of the provisions from which it has derogated and of the reasons by which it was actuated. A further communication shall be made, through the same intermediary, on the date on which it terminates such derogation.

Article 5

1. Nothing in the present Covenant may be interpreted as implying for any State, group or person any right to engage in any activity or perform any act aimed at the destruction of any of the rights and freedoms recognized herein or at their limitation to a greater extent than is provided for in the present Covenant.

2. There shall be no restriction upon or derogation from any of the fundamental human rights recognized or existing in any State Party to the present Covenant pursuant to law, conventions, regulations or custom on the pretext that the present Covenant does not recognize such rights or that it recognizes them to a lesser extent.

PART III

Article 6

1. Every human being has the inherent right to life. This right shall be protected by law. No one shall be arbitrarily deprived of his life.

2. In countries which have not abolished the death penalty, sentence of death may be imposed only for the most serious crimes in accordance with the law in force at the time of the commission of the crime and not contrary to the provisions of the present Covenant and to the Convention on the Prevention and Punishment of the Crime of Genocide. This penalty can only be carried out pursuant to a final judgement rendered by a competent court.

3. When deprivation of life constitutes the crime of genocide, it is understood that nothing in this article shall authorize any State Party to the present Covenant to derogate in any way from any obligation assumed under the provisions of the Convention on the Prevention and Punishment of the Crime of Genocide.

4. Anyone sentenced to death shall have the right to seek pardon or commutation of the sentence. Amnesty, pardon or commutation of the sentence of death may be granted in all cases.

5. Sentence of death shall not be imposed for crimes committed by persons below eighteen years of age and shall not be carried out on pregnant women.

6. Nothing in this article shall be invoked to delay or to prevent the abolition of capital punishment by any State Party to the present Covenant.

Article 7

No one shall be subjected to torture or to cruel, inhuman or degrading treatment or punishment. In particular, no one shall be subjected without his free consent to medical or scientific experimentation.

Article 8

1. No one shall be held in slavery; slavery and the slave-trade in all their forms shall be prohibited.

2. No one shall be held in servitude.

3. (*a*) No one shall be required to perform forced or compulsory labour;

(*b*) Paragraph 3(*a*) shall not be held to preclude, in countries where imprisonment with hard labour may be imposed as a punishment for a crime, the performance of hard labour in pursuance of a sentence to such punishment by a competent court;

(*c*) For the purpose of this paragraph the term "forced or compulsory labour" shall not include:

- (i) Any work or service, not referred to in sub-paragraph (*b*), normally required of a person who is under detention in consequence of a lawful order of a court, or of a person during conditional release from such detention;
- (ii) Any service of a military character and, in countries where conscientious objection is recognized, any national service required by law of conscientious objectors;
- (iii) Any service exacted in cases of emergency or calamity threatening the life or well-being of the community;
- (iv) Any work or service which forms part of normal civil obligations.

Article 9

1. Everyone has the right to liberty and security of person. No one shall be subjected to arbitrary arrest or detention. No one shall be deprived of his liberty except on such grounds and in accordance with such procedure as are established by law.

2. Anyone who is arrested shall be informed, at the time of arrest, of the reasons for his arrest and shall be promptly informed of any charges against him.

3. Anyone arrested or detained on a criminal charge shall be brought promptly before a judge or other officer authorized by law to exercise judicial power and shall be entitled to trial within a reasonable time or to release. It shall not be the general rule that persons awaiting trial shall be detained in custody, but release may be subject to guarantees to appear for trial, at any other stage of the judicial proceedings, and, should occasion arise, for execution of the judgement.

4. Anyone who is deprived of his liberty by arrest or detention shall be entitled to take proceedings before a court, in order that that court may decide without delay on the lawfulness of his detention and order his release if the detention is not lawful.

5. Anyone who has been the victim of unlawful arrest or detention shall have an enforceable right to compensation.

Article 10

1. All persons deprived of their liberty shall be treated with humanity and with respect for the inherent dignity of the human person.

2. (*a*) Accused persons shall, save in exceptional circumstances, be segregated from convicted persons and shall be subject to separate treatment appropriate to their status as unconvicted persons;

(*b*) Accused juvenile persons shall be separated from adults and brought as speedily as possible for adjudication.

3. The penitentiary system shall comprise treatment of prisoners the essential aim of which shall be their reformation and social rehabilitation. Juvenile offenders shall be segregated from adults and be accorded treatment appropriate to their age and legal status.

Article 11

No one shall be imprisoned merely on the ground of inability to fulfil a contractual obligation.

Article 12

1. Everyone lawfully within the territory of a State shall, within that territory, have the right to liberty of movement and freedom to choose his residence.

2. Everyone shall be free to leave any country, including his own.

3. The above-mentioned rights shall not be subject to any restrictions except those which are provided by law, are necessary to protect national security, public order (*ordre public*), public health or morals or the rights and freedoms of others, and are consistent with the other rights recognized in the present Covenant.

4. No one shall be arbitrarily deprived of the right to enter his own country.

Article 13

An alien lawfully in the territory of a State Party to the present Covenant may be expelled therefrom only in pursuance of a decision reached in accordance with law and shall, except where compelling reasons of national security otherwise require, be allowed to submit the reasons against his expulsion and to have his case reviewed by, and be represented for the purpose before, the competent authority or a person or persons especially designated by the competent authority.

Article 14

1. All persons shall be equal before the courts and tribunals. In the determination of any criminal charge against him, or of his rights and obligations in a suit at law, everyone shall be entitled to a fair and public hearing by a competent, independent and impartial tribunal established by law. The Press and the public may be excluded from all or part of a trial for reasons of morals, public order (*ordre public*) or national security in a democratic society, or when the interest of the private lives of the parties so requires, or to the extent strictly necessary in the opinion of the court in special circumstances where publicity would prejudice the interests of justice; but any judgement rendered in

a criminal case or in a suit at law shall be made public except where the interest of juvenile persons otherwise requires or the proceedings concern matrimonial disputes or the guardianship of children.

2. Everyone charged with a criminal offence shall have the right to be presumed innocent until proved guilty according to law.

3. In the determination of any criminal charge against him, everyone shall be entitled to the following minimum guarantees, in full equality:

(*a*) To be informed promptly and in detail in a language which he understands of the nature and cause of the charge against him;

(*b*) To have adequate time and facilities for the preparation of his defence and to communicate with counsel of his own choosing;

(*c*) To be tried without undue delay;

(*d*) To be tried in his presence, and to defend himself in person or through legal assistance of his own choosing; to be informed, if he does not have legal assistance, of this right; and to have legal assistance assigned to him, in any case where the interests of justice so require, and without payment by him in any such case if he does not have sufficient means to pay for it;

(*e*) To examine, or have examined, the witnesses against him and to obtain the attendance and examination of witnesses on his behalf under the same conditions as witnesses against him;

(*f*) To have the free assistance of an interpreter if he cannot understand or speak the language used in court;

(*g*) Not to be compelled to testify against himself or to confess guilt.

4. In the case of juvenile persons, the procedure shall be such as will take account of their age and the desirability of promoting their rehabilitation.

5. Everyone convicted of a crime shall have the right to his conviction and sentence being reviewed by a higher tribunal according to law.

6. When a person has by a final decision been convicted of a criminal offence and when subsequently his conviction has been reversed or he has been pardoned on the ground that a new or newly discovered fact shows conclusively that there has been a miscarriage of justice, the person who has suffered punishment as a result of such conviction shall be compensated according to law, unless it is proved that the non-disclosure of the unknown fact in time is wholly or partly attributable to him.

7. No one shall be liable to be tried or punished again for an offence for which he has already been finally convicted or acquitted in accordance with the law and penal procedure of each country.

Article 15

1. No one shall be held guilty of any criminal offence on account of any act or omission which did not constitute a criminal offence, under national or international law, at the time when it was committed. Nor shall a heavier penalty be imposed than the one that was applicable at the time when the criminal offence was committed. If, subsequent to the commission of the offence, provision is made by law for the imposition of a lighter penalty, the offender shall benefit thereby.

2. Nothing in this article shall prejudice the trial and punishment of any person for any act or omission which, at the time when it was committed, was criminal according to the general principles of law recognized by the community of nations.

Article 16

Everyone shall have the right to recognition everywhere as a person before the law.

Article 17

1. No one shall be subjected to arbitrary or unlawful interference with his privacy, family, home or correspondence, nor to unlawful attacks on his honour and reputation.

2. Everyone has the right to the protection of the law against such interference or attacks.

Article 18

1. Everyone shall have the right to freedom of thought, conscience and religion. This right shall include freedom to have or to adopt a religion or belief of his choice, and freedom, either individually or in community with others and in public or private, to manifest his religion or belief in worship, observance, practice and teaching.

2. No one shall be subject to coercion which would impair his freedom to have or to adopt a religion or belief of his choice.

3. Freedom to manifest one's religion or beliefs may be subject only to such limitations as are prescribed by law and are necessary to protect public safety, order, health, or morals or the fundamental rights and freedoms of others.

4. The States Parties to the present Covenant undertake to have respect for the liberty of parents and, when applicable, legal guardians to ensure the religious and moral education of their children in conformity with their own convictions.

Article 19

1. Everyone shall have the right to hold opinions without interference.

2. Everyone shall have the right to freedom of expression; this right shall include freedom to seek, receive and impart information and ideas of all kinds, regardless of frontiers, either orally, in writing or in print, in the form of art, or through any other media of his choice.

3. The exercise of the rights provided for in paragraph 2 of this article carries with it special duties and responsibilities. It may therefore be subject to certain restrictions, but these shall only be such as are provided by law and are necessary:

(*a*) For respect of the rights or reputations of others;

(*b*) For the protection of national security or of public order (*ordre public*), or of public health or morals.

Article 20

1. Any propaganda for war shall be prohibited by law.

2. Any advocacy of national, racial or religious hatred that constitutes incitement to discrimination, hostility or violence shall be prohibited by law.

Article 21

The right of peaceful assembly shall be recognized. No restrictions may be placed on the exercise of this right other than those imposed in conformity with the law and which are necessary in a democratic society in the interests of national security or public safety, public order (*ordre public*), the protection of public health or morals or the protection of the rights and freedoms of others.

Article 22

1. Everyone shall have the right to freedom of association with others, including the right to form and join trade unions for the protection of his interests.

2. No restrictions may be placed on the exercise of this right other than those which are prescribed by law and which are necessary in a democratic society in the interests of national security or public safety, public order (*ordre public*), the protection of public health or morals or the protection of the rights and freedoms of others. This article shall not prevent the imposition of lawful restrictions on members of the armed forces and of the police in their exercise of this right.

3. Nothing in this article shall authorize States Parties to the International Labour Organisation Convention of 1948 concerning Freedom of Association and Protection of the Right to Organize to take legislative measures which would prejudice, or to apply the law in such a manner as to prejudice, the guarantees provided for in that Convention.

Article 23

1. The family is the natural and fundamental group unit of society and is entitled to protection by society and the State.

2. The right of men and women of marriageable age to marry and to found a family shall be recognized.

3. No marriage shall be entered into without the free and full consent of the intending spouses.

4. States Parties to the present Covenant shall take appropriate steps to ensure equality of rights and responsibilities of spouses as to marriage, during marriage and at its dissolution. In the case of dissolution, provision shall be made for the necessary protection of any children.

Article 24

1. Every child shall have, without any discrimination as to race, colour, sex, language, religion, national or social origin, property or birth, the

right to such measures of protection as are required by his status as a minor, on the part of his family, society and the State.

2. Every child shall be registered immediately after birth and shall have a name.

3. Every child has the right to acquire a nationality.

Article 25

Every citizen shall have the right and the opportunity, without any of the distinctions mentioned in article 2 and without unreasonable restrictions:

(*a*) To take part in the conduct of public affairs, directly or through freely chosen representatives;

(*b*) To vote and to be elected at genuine periodic elections which shall be by universal and equal suffrage and shall be held by secret ballot, guaranteeing the free expression of the will of the electors;

(*c*) To have access, on general terms of equality, to public service in his country.

Article 26

All persons are equal before the law and are entitled without any discrimination to the equal protection of the law. In this respect, the law shall prohibit any discrimination and guarantee to all persons equal and effective protection against discrimination on any ground such as race, colour, sex, language, religion, political or other opinion, national or social origin, property, birth or other status.

Article 27

In those States in which ethnic, religious or linguistic minorities exist, persons belonging to such minorities shall not be denied the right, in community with the other members of their group, to enjoy their own culture, to profess and practise their own religion, or to use their own language.

PART IV

Article 28

1. There shall be established a Human Rights Committee (hereafter referred to in the present Covenant as the Committee). It shall consist of eighteen members and shall carry out the functions hereinafter provided.

2. The Committee shall be composed of nationals of the States Parties to the present Covenant who shall be persons of high moral character and recognized competence in the field of human rights, consideration being given to the usefulness of the participation of some persons having legal experience.

3. The members of the Committee shall be elected and shall serve in their personal capacity. . . .

APPENDIX G

Optional Protocol to International Covenant on Civil and Political Rights

THE STATES PARTIES TO THE PRESENT PROTOCOL,

Considering that in order further to achieve the purposes of the Covenant on Civil and Political Rights (hereinafter referred to as the Covenant) and the implementation of its provisions it would be appropriate to enable the Human Rights Committee set up in part IV of the Covenant (hereinafter referred to as the Committee) to receive and consider, as provided in the present Protocol, communications from individuals claiming to be victims of violations of any of the rights set forth in the Covenant,

Have agreed as follows:

Article 1

A State Party to the Covenant that becomes a party to the present Protocol recognizes the competence of the Committee to receive and consider communications from individuals subject to its jurisdiction who claim to be victims of a violation by that State Party of any of the rights set forth in the Covenant. No communication shall be received by the Committee if it concerns a State Party to the Covenant which is not a party to the present Protocol.

Article 2

Subject to the provisions of article 1, individuals who claim that any of their rights enumerated in the Covenant have been violated and who have exhausted all available domestic remedies may submit a written communication to the Committee for consideration.

Article 3

The Committee shall consider inadmissible any communication under the present Protocol which is anonymous, or which it considers to be an abuse of the rights of submission of such communications or to be incompatible with the provisions of the Covenant.

Article 4

1. Subject to the provisions of article 3, the Committee shall bring any communications submitted to it under the present Protocol to the attention of the State Party to the present Protocol alleged to be violating any provisions of the Covenant.

2. Within six months, the receiving State shall submit to the Committee written explanations or statements clarifying the matter and the remedy, if any, that may have been taken by that State.

Article 5

1. The Committee shall consider communications received under the present Protocol in the light of all written information made available to it by the individual and by the State Party concerned.

2. The Committee shall not consider any communication from an individual unless it has ascertained that:

(*a*) The same matter is not being examined under another procedure of international investigation or settlement;

(*b*) The individual has exhausted all available domestic remedies. This shall not be the rule where the application of the remedies is unreasonably prolonged.

3. The Committee shall hold closed meetings when examining communications under the present Protocol.

4. The Committee shall forward its views to the State Party concerned and to the individual. . . .

BIBLIOGRAPHY

This bibliography lists only books with substantial direct relevance to Canadian constitutional law. It accordingly includes few English, Australian or American books, despite their occasional citation in the text. Even within its narrow scope, the bibliography makes no claim to completeness. For the reader with a serious interest in constitutional bibliography, the excellent writings of R.C.B. Risk have been conveniently collected in R.C.B. Risk, A History of Canadian Legal Thought: Collected Essays (U. Toronto P., Toronto, 2006).

Abel A.S., Towards a Constitutional Charter for Canada (U. Toronto P., Toronto, 1982)

Advisory Commission on Intergovernmental Relations, In Search of Balance—Canada's Intergovernmental Experience (U.S. Government Printing Office, 1971)

Ajzenstat J. (ed.), Canada's Founding Debates (U. Toronto P., Toronto, 2003)

Allen T. The Right to Property in Commonwealth Constitutions (Cambridge U.P., Cambridge, 2000)

Anisman P. and Linden A.M. (eds.), The Media, the Courts and the Charter (Carswell, Toronto, 1986)

Archibald T.L., Jull K.E. and Roach K.W., Regulatory and Corporate Liability: From Due Diligence to Risk Management (Canada Law Book, Aurora, Ont., 2005, annually supplemented)

Ashley C.A. and Smails R.G.H., Canadian Crown Corporations (Macmillan of Canada, Toronto, 1965)

Atrens J., The Charter and Criminal Procedure (Butterworths, Toronto, 1989)

Aucoin P., Jarvis M.D. and Turnbull L., Democratizing the Constitution: Reforming Responsible Government (Emond Montgomery P., Toronto, 2011)

Bakan J., Just Words: Constitutional Rights and Social Wrongs (U. Toronto P., Toronto, 1997)

Banting K.G. and Simeon R.E.B. (eds.), And No One Cheered (Methuen, Agincourt, Ont., 1983)

Bastarache M. (ed.), Language Rights in Canada (Yvon Blais, Montreal, Que., 2nd ed., 2003)

Bastien R., Federalism and Decentralization: Where Do We Stand (Minister of Supply and Services Canada, Ottawa, 1981)

Bayefsky A.F. (ed.), Canada's Constitution Act, 1982 and Amendments: A Documentary History (McGraw-Hill Ryerson, Toronto, 1989)

Bayefsky A.F., International Human Rights Law (Butterworths, Toronto, 1992)

Bayefsky A.F. and Eberts M. (eds.), Equality Rights and the Canadian Charter of Rights and Freedoms (Carswell, Toronto, 1985)

Beatty D.M., Constitutional Law in Theory and Practice (U. Toronto P., Toronto, 1995)

Beatty D.M., Talking Heads and the Supremes (Carswell, Toronto, 1990)

Beaudoin G.-A. and Mendes E. (eds.), The Canadian Charter of Rights and Freedoms (Butterworths, Toronto, 4th ed., 2005)

Beaudoin G.-A., La Constitution du Canada: institutions, partage des pouvoirs, droits et libertés (Wilson & Lafleur, Montréal, 3rd ed., 2004)

Beaudoin G.-A., Essais sur la Constitution (U. Ottawa P., Ottawa, 1979)

Beaudoin G.-A. (ed.), Your Clients and the Charter—Liberty and Equality (Yvon Blais, Cowansville, Que., 1987)

Beaudoin G.-A. (ed.), The Supreme Court of Canada (Yvon Blais, Cowansville, Que., 1986)

Beaupré R.M., Interpreting Bilingual Legislation in Canada (Carswell, Toronto, 2nd ed., 1986)

Beck J.M., The Government of Nova Scotia (U. Toronto P., Toronto, 1957)
Beck S.M. and Bernier I. (eds.), Canada and the New Constitution (Institute for Research on Public Policy, Montreal, 1983)
Behiels M.D. (ed.), The Meech Lake Primer (U. Ottawa P., Ottawa, 1989)
Bellamy D.J., Pammett J.H. and Rowat D.C. (eds.), The Provincial Political Systems (Methuen, Toronto, 1976)
Benson E.J., The Taxing Power and the Constitution of Canada (Government of Canada Working Paper on the Constitution, Queen's Printer, Ottawa, 1969)
Berger B.L., Law's Religion: Religious Difference and the Claims of Constitutionalism (U. Toronto P., Toronto, 2015)
Berlin M.L. and Pentney W.F., Human Rights and Freedoms in Canada (Butterworths, Toronto, 1987)
Bernier I., International Legal Aspects of Federalism (Longman, London, 1973)
Birch A.H., Federalism, Finance and Social Legislation (Oxford U.P., London, 1955)
Birks S.M., The Survival of the Crown in the Canadian State (LL.M. thesis, Osgoode Hall Law School, York University, Toronto, 1980)
Black E.R., Divided Loyalties: Canadian Concepts of Federalism (McGill-Queens U.P., Montreal, 1975)
Bohémier A., La faillite en droit constitutionnel canadien (P.U. Montréal, Montréal, 1972)
Bourinot J.G., A Manual of the Constitutional History of Canada from the earliest period to 1901 (Copp Clark, Toronto, rev. ed., 1901)
Bourinot J.G., Federal Government in Canada (Johns Hopkins U.P., Baltimore, 1889)
Bourinot J.G., Parliamentary Procedure and Practice (Dawson Bros., Montreal, 2nd ed., 1892)
Boyer J.P., Lawmaking by the People: Referendums and Plebiscites in Canada (Butterworths, Toronto, 1982)
Boyer J.P., Money and Message (Butterworths, Toronto, 1983)
Boyer J.P., Political Rights (Butterworths, Toronto, 1981)
Boyle C.L.M. and others (eds.), Charterwatch: Reflections on Equality (Carswell, Toronto, 1986).
Brodsky G. and Day S., Canadian Charter Equality Rights for Women (Can. Advisory Council on the Status of Women, Ottawa, 1989)
Brossard J., L'accession à la souveraineté et le cas du Québec (P.U. Montréal, Montréal, 1995)
Brossard J., La cour suprême et la constitution (P.U. Montréal, Montréal, 1983)
Brossard J., L'Immigration. Les droits et pouvoirs du Canada et du Québec (P.U. Montréal, Montréal, 1967)
Brossard J., Patry A. and Weiser E., Les pouvoirs extérieurs du Québec (P.U. Montréal, Montréal, 1967)
Browne G.P., Documents on the Confederation of British North America (McClelland & Stewart, Toronto, 1969)
Browne G.P., The Judicial Committee and the British North America Act (U. Toronto P., Toronto, 1967)
Brun H., Tremblay G. and Brouillet E., Droit Constitutionnel (Yvon Blais, Cowansville, Quebec, 5th ed., 2008)
Buchan R.J. and others, Telecommunications Regulation and the Constitution (Institute for Research on Public Policy, Montreal, 1982)
Burns R.M., One Country or Two? (McGill-Queens U.P., Montreal, 1971)
Bushnell, I., The Captive Court: A Study of the Supreme Court of Canada (McGill-Queens U.P., Montreal, 1992)
Byers R.B. and Reford R.W. (eds.), Canada Challenged: The Viability of Confederation (Canadian Institute of International Affairs, Toronto, 1979)
Calvo-Garcia M. and Felstiner W.L.F. (eds.), Federalism (Dykinson, Madrid, 2004)
Cameron E.R., The Canadian Constitution as interpreted by the Judicial Committee of the Privy Council in its Judgments (vol. 1, Butterworths, Winnipeg, 1915; vol. 2, Carswell, Toronto, 1930)

Cameron J. (ed.), The Charter's Impact on the Criminal Justice System (Carswell, Toronto, 1996)

Canadian Bar Association, Committee on the Constitution, Towards a New Canada (Canadian Bar Foundation, Ottawa, 1978)

Canadian Bar Association, Committee on the Supreme Court of Canada, Report (Canadian Bar Foundation, Ottawa, 1987)

Canadian Charter of Rights Annotated (Canada Law Book, Toronto, 1985, loose-leaf)

Charles W.H., Cromwell T.A. and Jobson K., Evidence and the Charter of Rights and Freedoms (Butterworths, Toronto, 1989)

Cheffins R.I. and Johnson P.A., The Revised Canadian Constitution (McGraw-Hill Ryerson, Toronto, 1986)

Cheffins R.I. and Tucker R.N., The Constitutional Process in Canada (McGraw-Hill Ryerson, 2nd ed., 1976)

Chevrette F. and Marx H., Droit Constitutionnel (P.U. Montréal, Montréal, 1982)

Chrétien J., Securing the Canadian Economic Union in the Constitution (Minister of Supply and Services Canada, Ottawa, 1980)

Clement W.H.P., The Law of the Canadian Constitution (Carswell, Toronto, 3rd ed., 1916)

Code M.A., Trial within a Reasonable Time (Carswell, Toronto, 1992)

Conklin W.E., Images of a Constitution (U. Toronto P., Toronto, 1989)

Conklin W.E., In Defence of Fundamental Rights (Sijthoff & Noordhoff, The Netherlands, 1979)

Constantineau A., A Treatise on the De Facto Doctrine (Canada Law Book, Toronto, 1910)

Constitutional Committee of the Quebec Liberal Party, A New Canadian Federation (Quebec Liberal Party, Montreal, 1980)

Cooper-Stephenson K., Charter Damages Claims (Carswell, Toronto, 1990)

Côté P.-A., The Interpretation of Legislation in Canada (Carswell, Toronto, 3rd ed., 2000)

Creighton D., The Road to Confederation (Macmillan of Canada, Toronto, 1964)

Crépeau P.-A. and Macpherson C.B. (eds.), The Future of Canadian Federalism (U. Toronto P., Toronto, 1965)

Cromwell T.A., Locus Standi (Carswell, Toronto, 1986)

Cullen R., Federalism in Action: the Australian and Canadian Offshore Disputes (Federation, Sydney, 1990)

Cyr, H., Canadian Federalism and Treaty Powers (P.I.E. Peter Lang, Brussels, Belgium, 2009)

Davenport P. and Leach R.T. (eds.), Reshaping Confederation (Duke U.P., Durham, N.C., 1984)

Davis L.B.Z., Canadian Constitutional Law Handbook (Canada Law Book, Aurora, Ont., 1985)

Dawson R.M., Constitutional Issues in Canada 1900-1931 (Oxford U.P., London, 1933)

Dawson R.M., The Development of Dominion Status 1900-1936 (F. Cass, London, 1965)

de Mestral A. and others (eds.), The Limitation of Human Rights in Comparative Constitutional Law (Yvon Blais, Cowansville, Que., 1986)

de Smith S.A. and Brazier R., Constitutional and Administrative Law (Penguin, New York, 8th ed., 1998)

Department of Justice, A Consolidation of the Constitution Acts 1867 to 1982 (Canadian Government Publishing, Ottawa, 2001)

Deschênes J., Masters In Their Own House (Canadian Judicial Council, Ottawa, rev. ed., 1981)

Dicey A.V., The Law of the Constitution (St. Martin's Press, New York, 10th ed., 1965, introduction by E.C.S. Wade)

Dodek A., The Canadian Constitution (Dundurn P., Toronto, 2013)

Dodek A. and Sossin L. (eds.), Judicial Independence in Context (Irwin Law, Toronto, 2010)

Donnelly M.S., The Government of Manitoba (U. Toronto P., Toronto, 1963)
Edwards J.Ll.J., The Attorney General, Politics and the Public Interest (Sweet & Maxwell, London, 1984)
Ellis R., Unjust by Design: Canada's Administrative Justice System (UBC Press, Vancouver, 2013)
Evatt H.V., The King and his Dominion Governors (Cheshire, Australia, 2nd ed., 1967, introduction by Z. Cowen)
Evatt H.V., The Royal Prerogative (Law Book Co., Sydney, Australia, 1987, introduction by L. Zines)
Faribault M. and Fowler R.M., Ten to One: The Confederation Wager (McClelland and Stewart, Toronto, 1965)
Favreau G., The Amendment of the Constitution of Canada (Queen's Printer, Ottawa, 1965)
Finkelstein M., The Right to Counsel (Butterworths, Toronto, 1988)
Finkelstein N. and Finkelstein M., Constitutional Rights in the Investigative Process (Butterworths, Toronto, 1991)
Finkelstein N. and Rogers B.M. (eds.), Charter Issues in Civil Cases (Carswell, Toronto, 1988)
Finkelstein N. and Rogers B.M. (eds.), Administrative Tribunals and the Charter (Carswell, Toronto 1990)
Fitzgerald O., Understanding Charter Remedies (Carswell, Toronto, 1994, loose-leaf service)
Flemming R.B., Tournament of Appeals: Granting Judicial Review in Canada (UBC P., Vancouver, 2004)
Fogarty K.H., Equality Rights and their Limitations in the Charter (Carswell, Toronto, 1987)
Forest R.-A. (ed.), L'adhésion du Québec à l'Accord du Lac Meech (Les Editions Thémis, Montréal, Que., 1988)
Forsey, E.A., Freedom and Order (McClelland & Stewart, Toronto, 1974)
Forsey E.A., The Royal Power of Dissolution of Parliament in the British Commonwealth (Oxford U.P., Toronto, 1943; reprinted, 1968)
Foucher P., Constitutional Language Rights of Official-Language Minorities in Canada (Canadian Law Information Council, Ottawa, 1985)
Friedland M.L., A Place Apart: Judicial Independence and Accountability in Canada (Canadian Judicial Council, Ottawa, 1995)
Friedland M.L., Double Jeopardy (Clarendon P., Oxford, 1969)
Funston B.W. and Meehan E., Canadian Constitutional Documents Consolidated (Carswell, Toronto, 1994)
Gérin-Lajoie P., Constitutional Amendment in Canada (U. Toronto P., Toronto, 1950)
Gibbins R. and others (eds.), Meech Lake and Canada: Perspectives from the West (Academic Printing, Edmonton, 1988)
Gibson D., The Law of the Charter: Equality Rights (Carswell, Toronto, 1990)
Gibson D., The Law of the Charter: General Principles (Carswell, Toronto, 1986)
Gilbert C.D., Australian and Canadian Federalism 1867-1984 (Melbourne U.P., Melbourne, 1986)
Gilliland R. (ed.), The Charter at Thirty (Canada Law Book, Toronto, 2012)
Gosselin J. and Laporte G., La Charte canadienne des droits et libertés: les grands énoncés de la Cour suprême (Éditions Yvon Blais, Montreal, 2014)
Gotlieb A.E., Canadian Treaty-Making (Butterworths, Toronto, 1968)
Gotlieb A.E. (ed.), Human Rights, Federalism and Minorities (Canadian Institute of International Affairs, Toronto, 1970)
Grand Council of the Crees, Sovereign Injustice (Grand Council of the Crees, Montreal, 1995)
Greene I., The Charter of Rights (James Lorimer, Toronto, 1989)
Grenier B., La Declaration Canadienne Des Droits, Une loi bien ordinaire? (U. Laval P., Quebec, 1979)

Hassard A.R., Canadian Constitutional History and Law (Carswell, Toronto, 1900)
Hawkins G. (ed.), Concepts of Federalism (Canadian Institute of Public Affairs, Toronto, 1965)
Hazel R. and Paun A (eds.), Making Minority Government Work (Institute for Government, London, 2009)
Heard A.D., Canadian Constitutional Conventions (Oxford U.P., Toronto, 1991)
Henderson J.Y., Treaty Rights in the Constitution of Canada (Carswell, Toronto, 2007)
Hendry J. McL., Memorandum on the Office of Lieutenant-Governor of a Province: its Constitutional Character and Functions (Department of Justice, Ottawa, 1955)
Hiebert J., Charter Conflicts: What is Parliament's Role? (McGill-Queens U.P., 2002)
Hocken T.A. (ed.), Apex of Power (Prentice-Hall of Canada, Scarborough, Ont., 2nd ed., 1977)
Hogg P.W., Canada Act 1982 Annotated (Carswell, Toronto, 1982)
Hogg P.W., Monahan P.J. and Wright W.K., Liability of the Crown (Carswell, Toronto, 4th ed., 2011)
Hogg P.W., Meech Lake Constitutional Accord Annotated (Carswell, Toronto, 1988)
Hopkins E.R., Confederation at the Crossroads (McClelland & Stewart, Toronto, 1968)
Horsman K. and Morley G. (eds.), Government Liability: Law and Practice (Canada Law Book, Aurora, Ont., 2006, annually supplemented)
Howe P. and Russell P.H. (eds.), Judicial Power and Canadian Democracy (McGill-Queen's U.P., Montreal, 2001)
Hurley J.R., Amending Canada's Constitution: History, Processes, Problems and Prospects (Canada Communication Group, Ottawa, 1996)
Hurley J.R., Amending Canada's Constitution (Privy Council Office, Government of Canada, Ottawa, 1996)
Huscroft G. and Brodie I. (eds.), Constitutionalism in the Charter Era (Butterworths, Toronto, 2004)
Hutchinson A.C., Waiting for Coraf: A Critique of Law and Rights (U. Toronto P., Toronto, 1995)
Ip I. and Mintz J.M., Dividing the Spoils: the Federal-Provincial Allocation of Taxing Powers (C.D. Howe Institute, Toronto, 1992)
Irvine W.P., Does Canada Need a New Electoral System? (Institute of Intergovernmental Relations, Queens U., Kingston, Ont., 1979)
Jackson D.M. and Lagassé P. (eds.), Canada and the Crown: Essays on Constitutional Monarchy (McGill-Queens U. P., Montreal, 2013)
Jacomy-Millette A., Treaty Law in Canada (U. Ottawa P., Ottawa, 1975)
Jennings I., Constitutional Laws of the Commonwealth (Clarendon P., Oxford, 3rd ed., 1957)
Jennings I., The Law and the Constitution (U. London P., London, 5th ed., 1959)
Kahana T., The Partnership Model of the Canadian Notwithstanding Mechanism: Failure and Hope (J.S.D. thesis, University of Toronto, 2000)
Kelly J., Governing with the Charter (U.B.C. P.,Vancouver, 2005)
Kelly J.B. and Manfredi C.P., Contested Constitutionalism: Reflections on the Canadian Charter o f Rights and Freedoms (U.B.C. Press, Vancouver, 2009)
Kennedy W.P.M., The Constitution of Canada 1534-1937 (Oxford U.P., London, 2nd ed., 1938)
Kennedy W.P.M., Essays in Constitutional Law (Oxford U.P., London, 1934)
Kennedy W.P.M. and Wells D.C., The Law of the Taxing Power in Canada (U. Toronto P., Toronto, 1931)
Kunz F.A., The Modern Senate of Canada 1925-1963 (U. Toronto P., Toronto, 1965)
Kwavnick D. (ed.), The Tremblay Report (McClelland & Stewart, Toronto, 1973)
La Forest G.V., The Allocation of Taxing Power under the Canadian Constitution (Canadian Tax Foundation, Toronto, 2nd ed., 1981)
La Forest G.V., Disallowance and Reservation of Provincial Legislation (Queen's Printer, Ottawa, 1965)
La Forest G.V., Natural Resources and Public Property under the Canadian Constitution (U. Toronto P., Toronto, 1969)

Lajoie, A., Conceptions autochtones des droits ancestraux au Québec (Les Éditions thémis, Montréal, 2008)

Lajoie A., Expropriation et fédéralisme au Canada (P.U. Montréal, Montréal, 1972)

Lajoie A., Le pouvoir déclaratoire du Parlement (P.U. Montréal, Montréal, 1969)

Lalonde M. and Basford R., The Canadian Constitution and Constitutional Amendment (Federal-Provincial Relations Office, Ottawa, 1978)

Lamontagne M., Le fédéralisme canadien: évolution et problèmes (P.U. Laval, Québec, 1954)

Lang O.E. (ed.), Contemporary Problems of Public Law in Canada (U. Toronto P., Toronto, 1968)

Laskin B., The British Tradition in Canadian Law (Stevens, London, 1969)

Laskin B., Canadian Constitutional Law (Carswell, Toronto, 3rd ed. rev., 1969 by B. Laskin; 4th ed. rev. 1975 by A.S. Abel; 5th ed., 1986 by N. Finkelstein)

Latham R.T.E., The Law and the Commonwealth (Oxford U.P., 1949)

Law Society of Upper Canada, The Constitution and the Future of Canada (Special Lectures, 1978: De Boo, Toronto, 1978)

L'Ecuyer G., La Cour Suprême du Canada et le Partage des Compétences 1949-1978 (Gouvernement du Québec, Ministère des Affaires intergouvernementales, 1978)

Lederman W.R., Continuing Canadian Constitutional Dilemmas (Butterworths, Toronto, 1981)

Lederman W.R. (ed.), The Courts and the Canadian Constitution (McClelland & Stewart, Toronto, 1964)

Lefroy A.H.F., Canadian Constitutional Law (Carswell, Toronto, 1918)

Lefroy A.H.F., Canada's Federal System (Carswell, Toronto, 1913)

Lefroy A.H.F., Leading Cases in Canadian Constitutional Law (Carswell, Toronto, 2nd ed. by R.F. McWilliams, 1920)

Lefroy A.H.F., Legislative Power in Canada (Toronto Law Book Co., Toronto, 1897-8)

Lepofsky M.D., Open Justice (Butterworths, Toronto, 1985)

Livingston W.S., Federalism and Constitutional Change (Clarendon P., Oxford, 1956, reprinted Greenwood, Westport, Conn., 1974)

Livingston W.S. (ed.), Federalism in the Commonwealth (Cassel & Co., London, 1963)

Lokan A.K. and Dassios C.M., Constitutional Litigation in Canada (Carswell, Toronto, 2006) (looseleaf supplemented)

Lordon P. (ed.), Crown Law (Butterworths, Toronto, 1991)

Lower A.R.M. and others, Evolving Canadian Federalism (Duke U.P., Durham, N.C., 1958)

Lyon J.N. and Atkey R.G., Canadian Constitutional Law in a Modern Perspective (U. Toronto P., Toronto, 1970)

MacDonald L.G., A Contemporary Analysis of the Prerogative (LL.M. thesis, Osgoode Hall Law School, York University, Toronto, 1988)

Macdonald R. St. J. and Humphrey J.P. (eds.), The Practice of Freedom (Butterworths, Toronto, 1979)

MacKay R.A., The Unreformed Senate of Canada (McLelland and Stewart, Toronto, rev. ed., 1963)

MacKinnon F., The Crown in Canada (Glenbow-Alberta Institute, McClelland & Stewart West, Calgary, 1976)

MacKinnon F., The Government of Prince Edward Island (U. Toronto P., Toronto, 1951)

MacKinnon V.S., Comparative Federalism (Martinus Nijhoff, The Hague, 1964)

Macklem P., Indigenous Difference and the Constitution of Canada (U. Toronto P., Toronto, 2001)

Magnet J.E., Constitutional Law of Canada (Yvon Blais, Montreal, 7th ed., 1998)

Magnet J.E., Official Languages of Canada (Yvon Blais, Montreal, 1995)

Mahoney K.E. and Martin S.L., Equality and Judicial Neutrality (Carswell, Toronto, 1987)

Mallory J.R., Social Credit and the Federal Power in Canada (U. Toronto P., Toronto 1954; reprinted 1976)

Mallory J.R., The Structure of Canadian Government (Gage, Toronto, rev. ed, 1984)
Mandel M., The Charter of Rights and the Legalization of Politics in Canada (Thompson; rev. ed. 1994)
Manfredi C., Judicial Power and the Charter: Canada and the Paradox of Liberal Constitutionalism (Oxford U.P., Toronto, 2001)
Manning M., Rights, Freedoms and the Courts (Emond-Montgomery, Toronto, 1983)
Marshall G., Constitutional Conventions (Clarendon P., Oxford, 1984)
Marshall G., Constitutional Theory (Clarendon P., Oxford, 1980)
Marshall G., Parliamentary Sovereignty and the Commonwealth (Clarendon P., Oxford, 1957)
Marshall G. and Moodie G.C., Some Problems of the Constitution (Hutchison, London, 4th rev. ed., 1967)
Martin P.J.J., Federalism and International Relations (Dept. of External Affairs, Ottawa, 1968)
McAllister, D.M. and Dodek, A.M. (eds.), The Charter at Twenty (Ontario Bar Assn., Toronto, 2002)
McAllister D.M., Taking the Charter to Court: A Practitioner's Analysis (Carswell, Toronto, 1998)
McConnell W.H., Commentary on the British North America Act (Macmillan of Canada, Toronto, 1977)
McDonald D.C., Legal Rights in the Canadian Charter of Rights and Freedoms (Carswell, Toronto, 2nd ed., 1989)
McKercher W.R., The U.S. Bill of Rights and the Canadian Charter of Rights and Freedoms (Ontario Economic Council, Toronto, 1983)
McLeod R.M. and others, The Canadian Charter of Rights (Carswell, Toronto, 1983, loose-leaf service)
McNairn C.H.H., Governmental and Intergovernmental Immunity in Australia and Canada (U. Toronto P., Toronto, 1977)
McNeil K. Emerging Justice (Native Law Centre, U. of Saskatchewan, 2001)
McRoberts K. and Monahan P.J. (eds.), The Charlottetown Accord, the Referendum and the Future of Canada (U. Toronto P., 1993)
McRuer Report: Royal Commission of Inquiry into Civil Rights, Report (Ontario, 1968-71)
McWhinney E., Canada and the Constitution 1979-1982 (U. Toronto P., Toronto, 1982)
McWhinney E., Constitution-making: Principles, Process, Practice (U. Toronto P., Toronto, 1981)
McWhinney E., Judicial Review (U. Toronto P., Toronto, 4th ed., 1969)
McWhinney E., Quebec and the Constitution 1960-1978 (U. Toronto P., Toronto, 1979)
McWhinney E., Supreme Courts and Judicial Law-making: Constitutional Tribunals and Constitutional Review (Martinus Nijhoff, Dordrecht, The Netherlands, 1985)
McWhinney E., The Governor General and the Prime Ministers (Ronsdale P., Vancouver, 2005)
Meehan E. and others (eds), The 1995 Annotated Charter of Rights and Freedoms (Carswell, Toronto, 1995)
Meekison J.P., Canadian Federalism: Myth or Reality (Methuen, Toronto, 3rd ed., 1977)
Milne D.A., The Canadian Constitution (James Lorimer, Toronto, 2nd ed., 1991)
Monahan, P.J., Constitutional Law (Irwin Law, Toronto, 3rd ed., 2006)
Monahan P.J. and Finkelstein M. (eds.), The Impact of the Charter on the Public Policy Process (York University Centre for Public Law and Public Policy, Toronto, 1993)
Monahan P., Meech Lake: The Inside Story (U. Toronto P., Toronto, 1991)
Monahan P., Politics and the Constitution (Carswell, Toronto, 1987)
Moon R., Freedom of Conscience and Religion (Irwin Law, Toronto, 2014)
Moon R., The Constitutional Protection of Freedom of Expression (U. Toronto P., Toronto, 2000)
Morellato, M. (ed.), Aboriginal Law Since Delgamuukw (Canada Law Book, Aurora, Ont., 2009
Morton F.L. and Knopff R., The Charter Revolution and the Court Party (Broadview Press, Peterborough, Ont., 2000)

Morton F.L. (ed.), Law, Politics and the Judicial Process in Canada (U. Calgary P., Calgary, 3rd ed., 2002)
Morton J.C. and Hutchison S.C., Presumption of Innocence (Carswell, Toronto, 1987)
Munro J.E.C., The Constitution of Canada (Camb. U.P., Cambridge, 1889)
Newcombe E.L., The British North America Acts (King's Printer, Ottawa, 1908)
Newman D.G., The Duty to Consult: New Relationships with Aboriginal Peoples (Purich P., Saskatoon, 2009)
O'Connor Report: Senate of Canada, Parliamentary Counsel, Report Relating to the British North America Act, 1867 (Canada, 1939; reprinted, 1961)
O'Hearn P.J.T., Peace, Order and Good Government (Macmillan of Canada, Toronto, 1964)
Oliver P.C., The Constitution of Independence (Oxford U.P., 2005)
Oliver P., Macklem P. and Des Rosiers N. (eds.), The Oxford Handbook of the Canadian Constitution (Oxford U. P., New York, 2017)
Ollivier M. (ed.), British North America Acts and Selected Statutes 1867-1962 (Queen's Printer, Ottawa, 1962)
Ollivier M. (ed.), The Colonial and Imperial Conferences from 1887 to 1937 (Queen's Printer, Ottawa, 1954)
Olmsted R.A. (ed.), Decisions of the Judicial Committee of the Privy Council relating to the British North America Act and the Canadian Constitution 1867-1954 (Queen's Printer, Ottawa, 1954)
Ontario Advisory Committee on Confederation, The Confederation Challenge (Background Papers and Reports) (Ontario, 1967 (vol. 1), 1970 (vol. 2))
Ontario Advisory Committee on Confederation, First Report (April 1978), Second Report (March 1979) (Ontario, 1978, 1979)
O'Sullivan D.A., A Manual of Government in Canada (Carswell, Toronto, 2nd ed., 1887)
Paciocco D.M., Charter Principles and Proof in Criminal Cases (Carswell, Toronto, 1987)
Patenaude P., La preuve, les techniques modernes et le respect des valeurs fondamentales (Les Editions revue de droit, Sherbrooke, Que., 1990)
Pelletier B., La modification constitutionnelle au Canada (Carswell, 1997)
Peltomaa A., Understanding Unconstitutionality: How a Country Lost its Way (Teja P., Toronto, 2018)
Pépin G., Les tribunaux administratifs et la constitution (P.U. Montréal, Montréal, 1969)
Petter A., The Politics of the Charter: The Illusive Promise of Constitutional Rights (U. Toronto P., Toronto, 2010)
Plaxton C.P. (ed.), Canadian Constitutional Decisions of the Privy Council, 1930 to 1939 (Queen's Printer, Ottawa, 1939)
Pope J., Confederation: Being a Series of Hitherto Unpublished Documents Bearing on the British North America Act (Carswell, Toronto, 1895)
Régimbald G. and Newman D., The Law of the Canadian Constitution (LexisNexis Canada, Toronto, 1st ed., 2013)
Rémillard G., Le Fédéralisme Canadien (Québec/Amérique, Montréal), vol. 1 (1983), vol. 2 (1985)
Richard J.D. and Robertson S.M., The Charter and the Media (Canadian Bar Foundation, Ottawa, 1985)
Riddell W.R., The Canadian Constitution in Form and in Fact (Columbia U.P., New York, 1923)
Riddell W.R., The Constitution of Canada (Yale U.P., New Haven, Conn., 1917)
Risk R.C.B., A History of Canadian Legal Thought: Collected Essays (U. Toronto P., Toronto, 2006)
Roach K., Constitutional Remedies in Canada (Canada Law Book, Toronto, Ont., 2nd ed., 2013, loose-leaf service)
Roach K., The Supreme Court on Trial: Judicial Activism or Democratic Dialogue (Irwin Law, Toronto, 2001)
Romanow R., White J. and Leeson H., Canada . . . Notwithstanding (Carswell/Methuen, Toronto, 1984)

Rowell-Sirois Report: Royal Commission on Dominion-Provincial Relations, Report (Canada, 1940)
Royal Commission on Bilingualism and Biculturalism, Report (Canada, 1967-1970)
Royal Commission of Inquiry into Civil Rights, Report (McRuer Report) (Ontario, 1968-1971)
Royal Commission of Inquiry on Constitutional Problems, Report (Tremblay Report) (Quebec, 1956)
Royal Commission on Dominion-Provincial Relations, Report (Rowell-Sirois Report) (Canada, 1940)
Royal Commission on the Economic Union and Development Prospects for Canada, Report (Macdonald Report) (Canada, 1985)
Russell P.H., Constitutional Odyssey (U. Toronto P., Toronto, 2nd ed., 1993)
Russell P.H., The Judiciary in Canada: The Third Branch of Government (McGraw-Hill Ryerson, Toronto, 1987)
Russell P.H., Knopff R. and Morton F.L., Leading Constitutional Decisions (Carleton U.P., Ottawa, 5th ed., 1989)
Russell P.H., The Supreme Court of Canada as a Bilingual and Bicultural Institution (Documents of the Royal Commission on Bilingualism and Biculturalism, Queen's Printer, Ottawa, 1969)
Russell, P.H., Two Cheers for Minority Government (Emond Montgomery, Toronto, 2008)
Russell, P.H. and L. Sossin (eds.), Parliamentary Democracy in Crisis (U. of Toronto P., Toronto, 2009)
Safarian A.E., Canadian Federalism and Economic Integration (Queen's Printer, Ottawa, 1974)
Salhany R.E., The Origin of Rights (Carswell, Toronto, 1986)
Savoie D.J., Governing from the Centre: The Concentration of Power in Canadian Politics (U. Toronto P., Toronto, 1999)
Saywell, J.T., The Lawmakers: Judicial Power and the Shaping of Canadian Federalism (U. Toronto P., Toronto, 2002)
Saywell J.T., The Office of Lieutenant-Governor (U. Toronto P., Toronto, 1957)
Schabas W.A. and Beaulac S., International Human Rights Law and Canadian Charter Law (Carswell, Toronto, 3rd ed., 2006)
Schindeler F.F., Responsible Government in Ontario (U. Toronto P., Toronto, 1969)
Schmeiser D.A., Civil Liberties in Canada (Oxford U.P., London, 1964)
Schneiderman D. (ed.), Freedom of Expression and the Charter (Carswell, Toronto, 1991)
Schneiderman D. (ed.), Language and the State (Yvon Blais, Montreal, 1991)
Schwartz B., Fathoming Meech Lake (Legal Research Institute of University of Manitoba, Winnipeg, 1987)
Scott F.R., Civil Liberties and Canadian Federalism (U. Toronto P., Toronto, 1959)
Scott F.R., Essays on the Constitution (U. Toronto P., Toronto, 1977)
Scott W.S., The Canadian Constitution Historically Explained (Carswell, Toronto, 1918)
Segall E.J., Originalism as Faith (Cambridge U.P., Cambridge, 2018)
Senate and House of Commons of Canada, Special Joint Committee, Report on the Constitution of Canada (Canada, 1972)
Senate of Canada, Parliamentary Counsel, Report relating to the British North America Act 1867 (O'Connor Report) (Canada, 1939; reprinted, 1961)
Sharp M., Federalism and International Conferences on Education (Dept. of External Affairs, Ottawa, 1968)
Sharpe R.J. (ed.), Charter Litigation (Butterworths, Toronto, 1987)
Sharpe R.J., The Law of Habeas Corpus (Clarendon P., Oxford, 2nd ed., 1989)
Sharpe R.J., Interprovincial Product Liability Litigation (Butterworths, Toronto, 1982)
Sharpe R.J. and Roach K., The Charter of Rights and Freedoms (Irwin Law, Toronto, 4th ed., 2009)
Sherrin C., Objectionable Objectives?: An Analysis of the First Branch of the Oakes Test (D. Jur. thesis Osgoode Hall Law School of York University, 1994)

Simeon R.E.B. (ed.), The Division of Powers and Public Policy (U. Toronto P., Toronto, 1985)
Simeon R.E.B., Federal-Provincial Diplomacy (U. Toronto P., Toronto, 1972)
Simeon R.E.B. (ed.), Must Canada Fail? (McGill-Queen's U.P., Montreal, 1977)
Smiley D.V., Canada in Question (McGraw-Hill Ryerson, Toronto, 3rd ed., 1980)
Smiley D.V., The Canadian Charter of Rights and Freedoms (Ontario Economic Council, Toronto, 1981)
Smiley D.V., The Canadian Political Nationality (Methuen, Toronto, 1967)
Smiley D.V., Conditional Grants and Canadian Federalism (Canadian Tax Foundation, Toronto, 1963)
Smiley D.V., Constitutional Adaptation and Canadian Federalism since 1945 (Document of the Royal Commission on Bilingualism and Biculturalism, Queen's Printer, Ottawa, 1970)
Smiley D.V., The Federal Condition in Canada (McGraw-Hill Ryerson, Toronto, 1987)
Smiley D.V. (ed.), The Rowell-Sirois Report (McClelland and Stewart, Toronto, 1963)
Smith A., The Commerce Power in Canada and the United States (Butterworths, Toronto, 1963)
Smith D.E., Federalism and the Constitution of Canada (U. Toronto P., Toronto, 2010)
Smith D.E., MacKinnon P. and Courtney J.C., Drawing Boundaries: Legislatures, Courts and Electoral Values (Fifth House, Saskatoon, 1992)
Smith, J. (ed.), The Democratic Dilemma: Reforming the Canadian Senate (McGill-Queen's U.P., Kingston, Ont., 2009)
Smith J. and Jackson D.M. (eds.), The Evolving Canadian Crown (McGill-Queens U.P., Montreal, 2012)
Smith L. (ed.), Righting the Balance: Canada's New Equality Rights (Canadian Human Rights Reporter, Saskatoon, 1986)
Snell J.G. and Vaughan F., The Supreme Court of Canada: History of the Institution (Osgoode Society, Toronto, 1985)
Stanley G.F.G., A Short History of the Canadian Constitution (Ryerson, Toronto, 1969)
Songer, D.R., The Transformation of the Supreme Court of Canada: An Empirical Examination (U. of Toronto P., Toronto, 2008)
Sossin L.M., Boundaries of Judicial Review (Carswell, Toronto, 1999)
Stephenson S., From Dialogue to Disagreement in Comparative Rights Constitutionalism (Federation P., Annandale, N.S.W., 2017)
Stewart H., Fundamental Justice: Section 7 of the Canadian Charter of Rights and Freedoms (Irwin Law, Toronto, 2012)
Stratas D., The Charter of Rights in Litigation (Canada Law Book, Toronto, 1990)
Strayer B.L., Canada's Constitutional Revolution (U. Alberta P., Edmonton, 2013)
Strayer B.L., The Canadian Constitution and the Courts (Butterworths, Toronto, 3rd ed., 1988)
Strayer B.L., The Patriation and Legitimacy of the Canadian Constitution (Cronkite Memorial Lectures, College of Law, U. Saskatchewan, 1982)
Stuart D., Charter Justice in Canadian Criminal Law (Carswell, Toronto, 4th ed., 2005)
Sullivan R., Sullivan and Driedger on the Construction of Statutes (Butterworths, Markham, Ont., 4th ed., 2002)
Sunkin M. and Payne S. (eds.), The Nature of the Crown: A Legal and Political Analysis (Oxford U.P., 1999)
Swinton K.E. and Rogerson C.J. (eds.), Competing Constitutional Visions: The Meech Lake Accord (Carswell, Toronto, 1988)
Swinton K.E., The Supreme Court and Canadian Federalism (Carswell, Toronto, 1990)
Tarnopolsky W.S., The Canadian Bill of Rights (McClelland & Stewart, Toronto, 2nd ed., 1975)
Tarnopolsky W.S. (ed.), Discrimination in the Law and the Administration of Justice (Éditions Thémis, Montréal, 1993)
Tarnopolosky W.S. and Pentney W.F., Discrimination and the Law (Carswell, Toronto, 2004, looseleaf, supplemented)

Task Force on Canadian Unity, A Future Together (Pepin-Robarts Report, Minister of Supply and Services Canada, Ottawa, 1979)

Trakman L.E., Reasoning With the Charter (Butterworths, Toronto, 1993)

Travis J., A Law Treatise on the Constitutional Powers of Parliament and of the Local Legislatures under the B.N.A. Act, 1867 (Sun Publishing, Saint John, N.B., 1884)

Trebilcock M.J., Prichard J.R.S., Courchene T.J. and Whalley J. (eds.), Federalism and the Canadian Economic Union (U. Toronto P., Toronto, 1983)

Tremblay A., Les compétences législatives au Canada et les pouvoirs provinciaux en matière de propriété et de droits civils (U. Ottawa P., Ottawa, 1967)

Tremblay A., Droit Constitutionnel—Principes (Les Éditions Thémis, Montréal, 2nd ed., 2000)

Tremblay A., La Réforme de la Constitution au Canada (Les Éditions Thémis, Montréal, 2nd ed., 2000)

Tremblay L.B. and Webber G.C.N., (eds.), The Limitation of Charter Rights: Critical Essays (éditions Thémis, Montreal, 2009)

Tremblay Report: Royal Commission of Inquiry on Constitutional Problems, Report (Quebec, 1956)

Tribe L.H., The Invisible Constitution (Oxford U.P. New York, 2008)

Trudeau P.E., A Canadian Charter of Human Rights (Government of Canada Working Paper on the Constitution, Queen's Printer, Ottawa, 1968)

Trudeau P.E., The Constitution and the People of Canada (Government of Canada Working Paper on the Constitution, Queen's Printer, Ottawa, 1969)

Trudeau P.E., Federalism and the French Canadians (Macmillan of Canada, Toronto, 1968)

Trudeau P.E., Federal-Provincial Grants and the Spending Power of Parliament (Government of Canada Working Paper on the Constitution, Queen's Printer, Ottawa, 1969)

Trudeau P.E., Income Security and Social Services (Government of Canada Working Paper on the Constitution, Queen's Printer, Ottawa, 1969)

Twomey, A., The Veiled Sceptre: Reserve Powers of Heads of State in Westminster Systems (Cambridge U.P., Cambridge, 2018)

Varcoe F.P., The Constitution of Canada (Carswell, Toronto, 2nd ed., 1965)

Verrelli N. (ed.), The Democratic Dilemma: Reforming Canada's Supreme Court (McGill-Queen's U.P., Kingston, Ont., 2013)

Waldron J., The Dignity of Legislation (Cambridge U.P., Cambridge, 1999)

Walker M. (ed.), Canadian Confederation at the Crossroads (Fraser Institute, Vancouver, B.C., 1978)

Ward N., Dawson's The Government of Canada (U. Toronto P., Toronto, 6th ed., 1987)

Watts R.L., Comparing Federal Systems (McGill-Queen's U.P., Montreal, 2nd ed., 1999)

Weiler J.M. and Elliot R.M. (eds.), Litigating the Values of a Nation: The Canadian Charter of Rights and Freedoms (Carswell, Toronto, 1986)

Weiler P.C., In the Last Resort (Carswell Methuen, Toronto, 1974)

Wheare K.C., The Constitutional Structure of the Commonwealth (Clarendon P., Oxford, 1960)

Wheare K.C., Federal Government (Oxford U.P., London, 4th ed., 1963)

Wheare K.C., Modern Constitutions (Oxford U.P., London, 2nd ed., 1966)

Wheare K.C., The Statute of Westminster and Dominion Status (Oxford U.P., London, 5th ed., 1953)

Wheeler G.J., Confederation Law of Canada (Eyre and Spottiswoode, London, 1896)

Whitley S.J., Criminal Justice and the Constitution (Carswell, Toronto, 1989)

Whyte J.D. and Lederman, W.R., Canadian Constitutional Law (Butterworths, Toronto, 3rd ed., 1992)

Wildsmith B.H., Aboriginal Peoples and s. 25 of the Charter (U. of Sask. Native Law Centre, Saskatoon, 1988)

Wintemute R., Sexual Orientation and Human Rights: The United States Constitution, the European Convention, and the Canadian Charter (Clarendon P., Oxford, 1995)

Witkor C.L. and Tanguay G., Constitutions of Canada (Oceana Publications, Dobbs Ferry, N.Y., 1978)

Young R.A., The Secession of Quebec and the Future of Canada (McGill-Queens U.P., Montreal, rev. ed., 1998)

Table of Cases

A.-G. v. A.-G. Ont. (Unemployment Insurance) [1937] A.C. 355—§ 17:7
A.-G. Alta. v. A.-G. Can. (Alta. Bill of Rights) [1947] A.C. 503, 518—§§ 15:14, 15:27
A.-G. Alta. v. A.-G. Can. (Bank Taxation) [1939] A.C. 117—§§ 8:8, 15:5, 15:8, 15:9, 15:11, 15:14, 15:16, 43:2
A.-G. Aust. v. Colonial Sugar Refining Co., [1914] A.C. 237, 252–254—§ 5:9
A.-G. B.C. v. A.-G. Can. (Farmers' Creditors Arrangement) [1937] A.C. 391—§§ 17:7, 17:11
A.-G. B.C. v. A.-G. Can. (Natural Products Marketing) [1937] A.C. 377, 389—§§ 14:10, 14:11, 15:14, 17:7, 17:11, 17:12, 20:2, 20:4
A.-G. B.C. v. A.-G. Can. (Price Spreads) [1937] A.C. 368—§§ 17:7, 17:11, 18:2, 18:11
A.-G. B.C. v. A.-G. Can. (Johnny Walker) [1924] A.C. 222—§ 20:2
A.-G. B.C. v. A.-G. Can. (Employment of Japanese) [1924] A.C. 203—§§ 16:3, 55:1
A.-G. B.C. v. A.-G. Can. (Fishing Rights) [1914] A.C. 153, 162—§ 8:11
A.-G. B.C. v. A.-G. Can. (Natural Products Marketing) [1937] A.C. 377—§ 17:7
A.-G. B.C. v. Can. Trust Co., [1980] 2 S.C.R. 466, 478—§ 15:27
A.-G. B.C. v. E. & N. Ry. Co., [1950] A.C. 87, 110—§ 6:8
A.-G. B.C. v. McDonald Murphy Lumber, [1930] A.C. 357, 363—§ 15:9
A.-G. B.C. v. McKenzie, [1965] S.C.R. 490, 498–499—§ 7:17
A.-G. B.C. v. Smith, [1967] S.C.R. 702, 714—§§ 16:6, 17:4, 18:16
A.-G. Can. v. A.-G. Alta. (Insurance) [1916] 1 A.C. 588—§§ 20:2, 20:4, 21:6, 21:18
A.-G. Can. v. A.-G. Ont. (Unemployment Insurance) [1937] A.C. 355—§§ 14:10, 15:14, 17:1, 17:7, 17:11, 17:12, 20:4, 21:6, 21:10
A.-G. Can. v. A.-G. Ont. (Labour Conventions) [1937] A.C. 326—§§ 8:2, 8:13, 12:2, 15:27, 17:2, 17:7, 17:11, 17:12, 18:13, 21:10, 22:16
A.-G. Can. v. A.-G. Ont. (Indian Annuities) [1897] A.C. 199—§ 28:3
A.-G. Can. v. A.-G. Ont. (Unemployment Insurance), [1937] A.C. 355—§ 17:11
A.-G. Can. v. A.-G. Que. (Bank Deposits) [1947] A.C. 33—§ 15:6
A.-G. Can. v. Boeing Co. (1983), 41 O.R. (2d) 777 (C.A.)—§ 7:11
A.-G. Can. v. Cain, [1906] A.C. 542, 547—§ 14:4
A.-G. Can. v. Canard, [1976] 1 S.C.R. 170, 176—§§ 7:14, 7:20, 28:2, 28:4, 35:3, 37:4
A.-G. Can. v. CN Transportation, [1983] 2 S.C.R. 206, 279–280—§§ 15:7, 15:24
A.-G. Can. v. Hallet & Carey, [1952] A.C. 427, 444—§ 15:8
A.-G. Can. v. Lavell, [1974] S.C.R. 1349—§§ 28:4, 55:1
A.-G. Can. v. Law Society of B.C., [1982] 2 S.C.R. 307, 327—§§ 7:1, 7:2, 7:11, 7:20, 18:11, 21:9
A.-G. Can. v. Nykorak, [1962] S.C.R. 331—§§ 15:24, 17:8
A.-G. Can. v. Public Service Staff Relations Bd., [1977] 2 F.C. 663 (C.A.)—§ 12:10
A.-G. Can. v. St. Hubert Base Teachers' Assn., [1983] 1 S.C.R. 498—§ 21:11
A.-G. Can. and Dupond v. Montreal, [1978] 2 S.C.R. 770—§§ 15:8, 18:15, 18:20, 21:4, 43:3

A.-G. Cwlth. v. The Queen (Boilermakers) (1957) 95 C.L.R. 529—§ 14:5
A.-G. Man. v. A.-G. Can. (Natural Products Marketing) [1937] A.C. 377, 388–389—§ 15:14
A.-G. Man. v. A.-G. Can. (Manitoba Securities) [1929] A.C. 260—§§ 15:17, 21:15, 21:16
A.-G. Man. v. Man. Egg & Poultry Assn., [1971] S.C.R. 689—§§ 15:5, 20:3, 21:14
A.-G. Man. v. Manitoba Egg and Poultry Assn., [1971] S.C.R. 689, 704–705—§ 15:9
A.-G. N.S. v. A.-G. Can. (Nova Scotia Inter-delegation) [1951] S.C.R. 31—§§ 8:3, 14:10, 14:16, 16:10
A.-G. N.S.W. v. Trethowan, [1932] A.C. 526—§ 12:10
A.-G. Ont. v. A.-G. Can. (Privy Council Appeals) [1947] A.C. 127—§§ 8:2, 15:27, 36:19
A.-G. Ont. v. A.-G. Can. (Canada Standard Trade Mark) [1937] A.C. 405—§§ 17:7, 17:11, 18:11, 20:4
A.-G. Ont. v. A.-G. Can. (Judges) [1925] A.C. 750—§ 7:2
A.-G. Ont. v. A.-G. Can. (Reference Appeal) [1912] A.C. 571—§§ 7:15, 8:10, 8:11, 12:2, 12:8
A.-G. Ont. v. A.-G. Can. (Local Prohibition) [1896] A.C. 348, 370—§§ 8:11, 15:7, 17:1, 17:3, 17:7, 20:2
A.-G. Ont. v. A.-G. Can. (Voluntary Assignments) [1894] A.C. 189—§ 15:7
A.-G. Ont. v. A.G. Can. (Local Prohibition) [1896] A.C. 348—§§ 16:5, 17:3
A.-G. Ont. v. Barfried Enterprises, [1963] S.C.R. 570—§§ 15:5, 15:7, 16:7, 21:8, 21:20
A.-G. Ont. v. Canada Temperance Federation, [1946] A.C. 193—§ 17:3
A.-G. Ont. v. Can. Temperance Federation, [1946] A.C. 193—§§ 8:9, 8:13, 17:4, 17:11, 22:13, 22:16
A.-G. Ont. v. Hamilton Street Railway, [1903] A.C. 524—§§ 14:17, 18:12, 18:13
A.-G. Ont. v. Policy-holders of Wentworth Ins. Co., [1969] S.C.R. 779—§ 16:3
A.-G. Ont. v. Policy-holders of Wentworth Insurance Co., [1969] S.C.R. 779—§ 21:7
A.-G. Ont. v. Reale, [1975] 2 S.C.R. 624—§§ 35:3, 35:8
A.-G. Ont. v. Reciprocal Insurers, [1924] A.C. 328—§§ 15:11, 15:14, 18:19, 21:6, 21:18
A.-G. Ont. v. Scott, [1956] S.C.R. 137—§§ 14:12, 14:13
A.-G. Ont. v. Victoria Medical Building, [1960] S.C.R. 32—§ 7:15
A.-G. Ont. v. Winner, [1954] A.C. 541—§§ 14:13, 15:18, 22:2, 22:5, 22:6, 22:11
A.-G. Que. v. Blaikie (No. 2) [1981] 1 S.C.R. 312, 320—§ 1:11
A.-G. Que. v. Blaikie, [1979] 2 S.C.R. 1016, 1029—§§ 15:27, 36:18, 36:19, 56:2
A.-G. Que. v. Farrah, [1978] 2 S.C.R. 638—§§ 7:15, 7:19
A.-G. Que. v. Grondin, [1983] 2 S.C.R. 364—§§ 7:19, 7:20
A.-G. Que. v. Kellogg's Co., [1978] 2 S.C.R. 211—§§ 15:5, 22:18, 22:20, 22:23, 43:3
A.-G. Que. v. Kellogg's Company, [1978] 2 S.C.R. 211—§ 15:24
A.-G. Que v. Lechasseur, [1981] 2 S.C.R. 253, 259—§ 18:16
A.-G. Que. v. Que. Protestant School Bds., [1984] 2 S.C.R. 66—§ 56:2
A.-G. Que. v. Udeco, [1984] 2 S.C.R. 502—§ 7:19
A.-G. Que. and Baillargeon, Re (1978), 97 D.L.R. (3d) 447 (C.A.)—§§ 22:6, 22:11
A.-G. Sash v. A.-G. Can. (Sask. Farm Security) [1949] A.C. 110—§ 15:11
A.-G. Sask. v. A.-G. Can. (Farm Security) [1949] A.C. 110—§ 21:12
A.-G. Sask. v. CPR, [1953] A.C. 594—§ 17:1
A.B. v. Bragg Communications, [2012] 2 S.C.R. 567—§ 43:32

Abbate v. United States (1959), 359 U.S. 187—§ 16:8
Abdelrazik v. Can., [2010] 1 F.C.R. 267 (F.C.)—§ 1:9
Abdelrazik v. Canada, [2010] 1 F.C.R. 267—§§ 37:14, 40:23
Abingdon School District v. Schempp (1963), 374 U.S. 203—§ 42:8
Abington School District v. Schempp (1963), 347 U.S. 203—§ 36:5
Abitibi Power and Paper Co. v. Montreal Trust Co., [1943] A.C. 536—§§ 15:6, 15:8
Abood v. Détruit Bd. of Education (1977), 431 U.S. 209—§ 44:8
Abrams v. United States (1919), 250 U.S. 616, 630—§ 43:7
A.C. v. Manitoba, [2009] 2 S.C.R. 181—§§ 42:6, 47:26, 55:44
Adams v. Adams, [1971] P. 188 (P.D.A. Div.)—§ 5:26
Addy v. The Queen, [1985] 2 F.C. 452 (T.D.)—§ 7:14
Adler v. Ont., [1996] 3 S.C.R. 609—§§ 36:23, 55:28
Adler v. Ontario, [1996] 3 S.C.R. 609—§§ 42:9, 55:35
Adoption Act, Re, [1938] S.C.R. 398—§§ 7:16, 7:17
Aeronautics Reference:, [1952] 1 S.C.R. 292, 303—§ 17:3
A.G. v. De Keyser's Royal Hotel, [1920] A.C. 508 (H.L.)—§ 1:9
A.G. Alta. v. Putnam, [1981] 2 S.C.R. 267—§ 15:19
A.G.B.C. v. Smith, [1967] S.C.R. 702—§ 16:4
A.G. Can. v. A.-G. Alta. (Insurance) [1916] 1 A.C. 588—§ 17:7
A.G. Can. v. A.G. Ont. (Unemployment Insurance) [1937] A.C. 355—§§ 4:20, 6:8
A.G. Can. v. A.G. Ont (Labour Conventions) [1937] A.C. 326, 354—§ 6:8
A.G. Can. v. Canard, [1976] 1 S.C.R. 170—§§ 55:2, 55:34, 55:49
A.G. Can. v. CN Transportation, [1983] 2 S.C.R. 206—§ 20:4
A.G. Can. v. Hallet & Carey, [1952] A.C. 427, 450—§ 34:2
A.G. Can. v. Lavell, [1974] S.C.R. 1349—§§ 28:2, 55:2, 55:8, 55:34, 55:41
A.G. Can. v. Law Society of B.C., [1982] 2 S.C.R. 307, 364—§§ 34:7, 43:3
A.G. Can. v. Pattison (1981), 123 D.L.R. (3d) 111 (Alta. C.A.)—§ 18:15
A.G. Can. v. St.-Hubert Base Teachers' Assn., [1983] 1 S.C.R. 498—§ 15:19
A.G. Can. and Dupond v. Montreal, [1978] 2 S.C.R. 770, 796—§§ 34:7, 44:1, 44:2
Agence Maritime v. Canada Labour Relations Board, [1969] S.C.R. 851—§§ 22:6, 22:12
Agence Maritime v. Can. Labour Relations Bd., [1969] S.C.R. 851—§ 22:1
Agency for Health Care Administration v. Associated Industries of Florida (1996), 678 So. 2d 1239 (S.C.Fla.)—§ 7:3
A.G. Man. v. Forest, [1979] 2 S.C.R. 1032—§ 4:17
A. G. Ont. v. Can. Temperance Federation, [1946] A.C. 193—§ 14:15
A.G. Ont. v. Hamilton Street Ry., [1903] A.C. 524—§ 34:7
A.G. Que. v. Blaikie, [1979] 2 S.C.R. 1016—§§ 4:17, 56:4
A.G. Que. v. Kellogg's Co. of Can., [1978] 2 S.C.R. 211—§ 15:18
A.G. Que. v. Lechasseur, [1981] 2 S.C.R. 253—§ 16:4
A.G. Que. v. Que. Protestant School Bds., [1984] 2 S.C.R. 66—§§ 4:3, 38:6, 38:14
A.G. Que. and Keable v. A.G. Can., [1979] 1 S.C.R. 218—§ 15:19
Agricultural Products Marketing Act, Re, [1979] 1 S.C.R. 42, 74—§ 21:14
Agricultural Products Marketing Act, Re, [1978] 2 S.C.R. 1198—§§ 8:9, 8:11, 8:13, 14:5, 14:11, 14:13, 15:14, 20:3, 21:14
Ahani v. Can. (2002), 58 O.R. (3d) 107 (C.A.)—§§ 36:28, 37:14, 47:38
Ahani v. Canada, [2002] 1 S.C.R. 72—§ 37:14
Ahousaht First Nation v. Can. (2008), 297 D.L.R. (4th) 722, para. 34 (F.C.A.)—§ 40:26

Air Can. v. B.C., [1986] 2 S.C.R. 539—§ 1:9
Air Canada v. B.C., [1986] 2 S.C.R. 539—§§ 7:20, 40:25
Air Canada v. Ont., [1997] 2 S.C.R. 581—§ 20:2
Air Canada v. Ontario, [1997] 2 S.C.R. 581—§§ 15:18, 22:15
Alberta v. Cunningham, 2011 SCC 37—§ 55:32
Alberta v. Hutterian Brethren of Wilson Colony, [2009] 2 S.C.R. 567—§§ 38:22, 42:6
Alberta v. Moloney, [2015] 3 S.C.R. 327, 2015 SCC 51—§§ 16:3, 16:4
Alberta v. United Food and Commercial Workers, [2013] 3 S.C.R. 733, 2013 SCC 62—§ 43:26
Alberta Government Telephones v. CRTC, [1989] 2 S.C.R. 225—§§ 22:4, 22:5, 22:22
Alberta Statutes, Re, [1938] S.C.R. 100—§§ 15:14, 20:4, 43:2, 43:16
Alex Couture v. A.G. Can. (1991), 83 D.L.R. (4th) 577 (Que. C.A.)—§ 18:11
Alex Couture v. Can. (1991), 83 D.L.R. (4th) 477 (Que. C.A.)—§ 44:3
A. (L.L.) v. B. (A.), [1995] 4 S.C.R. 536—§ 47:35
Allen v. Alta., 2015 ABCA 277 (Alta. C.A.)—§§ 32:6, 47:12
Alltrans Express v. B.C., [1988] 1 S.C.R. 897—§ 15:18
also RWDSU v. Dolphin Delivery, [1986] 2 S.C.R. 573, 583-586—§§ 43:7, 43:8
Alta. v. Hutterian Brethren of Wilson Colony, [2009] 2 S.C.R. 567—§§ 38:7, 38:21, 55:22, 55:28, 55:30, 55:40
Alta. v. Moloney, [2015] 3 S.C.R. 327—§ 16:3
Alta. v. United Food and Commercial Workers, [2013] 3 S.C.R. 733—§§ 15:14, 36:16, 38:22, 40:4
Alta. Statutes, Re, [1938] S.C.R. 100—§§ 15:28, 34:7
Amalgamated Society of Engineers v. Adelaide SS. Co. (1920), 28 C.L.R. 129—§ 8:13
Amaratunga v. Northwest Atlantic Fisheries Organization, [2013] 3 S.C.R. 866—§ 47:38
Amax Potash v. Government of Saskatchewan, [1977] 2 S.C.R. 576—§ 40:25
Amax Potash v. Govt. of Sask., [1977] 2 S.C.R. 576—§ 7:20
American Federation of Labour v. Swing (1941), 312 U.S. 321—§ 37:12
Andrews v. Law Society of B.C., [1989] 1 S.C.R. 143—§§ 36:20, 36:21, 38:3, 55:2, 55:6, 55:11, 55:18, 55:19, 55:23, 55:27, 55:28, 55:29
Andrews v. Law Society of B.C. (1986), 27 D.L.R. (4th) 600, 610 (B.C.C.A.)—§ 55:17
Andrews v. Law Society of British Columbia, [1989] 1 S.C.R. 143—§§ 38:12, 38:23, 55:17, 55:19, 55:27, 55:37, 55:46
Angers v. M.N.R., [1957] Ex. C.R. 83—§ 6:8
Antares Shipping Corp. v. The Ship "Capricorn", [1980] 1 S.C.R. 553—§ 22:12
Anti-Inflation Act, Re, [1976] 2 S.C.R. 373, 433—§§ 5:27, 14:16, 15:5, 15:8, 15:9, 17:2, 17:5, 17:6, 17:7, 17:8, 17:10, 17:11, 17:12, 18:6, 20:4, 21:11, 32:1, 34:2
Anti-Inflation Reference, [1976] 2 S.C.R. 373, 424–425—§ 12:8
Anti-Inflation Reference, [1976] S.C.R. 373, 426–427—§ 20:4
Application under s. 83.28 of the Criminal Code, Re, [2004] 2 S.C.R. 248—§§ 7:3, 7:5
Application under s. 82.28 of the Criminal Code, Re, [2004] 2 S.C.R. 248—§ 47:31
Appointment of Senators, Re (1991), 78 D.L.R. (4th) 245 (B.C.C.A.)—§§ 9:3, 9:10
Argentina v. Mellino, [1987] 1 S.C.R. 536, 547—§ 8:13
Aris Steamship Co. v. Associated Metals, [1980] 2 S.C.R. 322—§ 22:12

Arnold v. Ont. (1987), 61 O.R. (2d) 481 (H.C.)—§ 45:2
Arsenault-Cameron v. Prince Edward Island, [2000] 1 S.C.R. 3—§ 56:23
Asbjorn Horgard v. Gibbs/Nortac Industries, [1987] 3 F.C. 544, 559—§ 20:4
Ashcroft v. Free Speech Coalition (2002), 535 U.S. 234—§§ 43:29, 47:24
Assisted Human Reproduction Act, Re, [2010] 3 S.C.R. 457—§§ 5:7, 15:24, 18:2, 18:9, 32:1, 32:2
Assn. des Gens de l'Air du Qué. v. Lang, [1978] 2 F.C. 371 (Fed. C.A.)—§ 56:14
Assn. des parents de l'école Rose-des-vents v. B.C., [2015] 2 S.C.R. 139, 2015 SCC 21—§ 40:23
Associated Press v. Walker (1967), 388 U.S. 130—§ 43:28
Association des parents de l'école Rose-des-vents v. British Columbia, [2015] 2 S.C.R. 139, 2015 SCC 21—§ 56:23
Association of Justice Counsel v. Can., [2017] 2 S.C.R. 456, 2017 SCC 55—§ 47:9
Attorney General of Manitoba v. Forest, [1979] 2 S.C.R. 1032—§ 56:6
Attorney General of Quebec v. Blaikie, [1979] 2 S.C.R. 1016—§§ 56:5, 56:6, 56:8, 56:9, 56:10
Attorney General of Quebec v. Blaikie (No. 2), [1981] 1 S.C.R. 312—§ 56:8
Attorney General of Quebec v. Collier (1985), 23 D.L.R. (4th) 339 (Que. C.A.)—§ 56:7
Attorney General of Quebec v. Ford, [1988] 2 S.C.R. 712—§ 38:14
Attorney General of Quebec v. Quebec Protestant School Boards, [1984] 2 S.C.R. 66—§ 56:21
Aubry v. Editions Vice-Versa, [1998] 1 S.C.R. 591—§ 43:28
Auckland Harbour Bd. v. The King, [1924] A.C. 318 (P.C., N.Z.)—§ 1:9
Australian Consolidated Press v. Uren, [1969] 1 A.C. 590—§ 2:2
Authorson v. Can., [2003] 2 S.C.R. 40—§§ 12:9, 12:10, 35:3, 35:7, 35:8
Authorson v. Can. (2007), 86 O.R. (3d) 321 (C.A.)—§§ 47:13, 55:22
Authorson v. Canada, [2003] 2 S.C.R. 40—§ 47:13
Auton v. B.C., [2004] 3 S.C.R. 657—§ 55:45
Auton v. British Columbia, [2004] 3 S.C.R. 657—§§ 32:5, 55:23

Babcock v. Can., [2002] 3 S.C.R. 3—§§ 7:20, 15:28
Babcock v. Canada, [2002] 3 S.C.R. 3—§ 7:3
Baier v. Alberta, [2007] 2 S.C.R. 673—§ 43:40
Baier v. Alta., [2007] 2 S.C.R. 673—§ 55:50
Bainbridge v. Postmaster-General, [1906] 1 K.B. 178 (C.A.)—§ 9:7
Baker v. Carr (1962), 369 U.S. 186—§§ 36:5, 45:2
Baldy v. Hunter (1898), 64 Davis (171 U.S.) 388, 400, 491—§ 5:26
Bank of Montreal v. Hall, [1990] 1 S.C.R. 121—§§ 16:4, 16:5
Bank of Montreal v. Marcotte, [2014] 2 S.C.R. 725, 2014 SCC 55—§§ 15:18, 15:20, 16:7
Bank of Montreal v. Royal Bank of Can., [1933] S.C.R. 311—§ 7:11
Bank of N.S.W. v. Commonwealth (State Banking) (1948) 76 C.L.R. 1, 368–372—§ 15:14
Bank of Toronto v. Lambe (1887), 12 App. Cas. 575, 587—§§ 12:2, 15:5, 15:6, 15:15, 15:20, 36:13
Banks v. Globe & Mail, [1961] S.C.R. 474—§ 43:28
Bartkus v. Illinois (1959), 359 U.S. 121—§ 16:8
Barton v. Cth. of Aust. (1974), 131 C.L.R. 477—§ 1:9

B.C. v. Can., [1994] 2 S.C.R. 41—§§ 5:4, 22:1, 22:10
B.C. v. Can. (Vancouver Island Ry.), [1994] 2 S.C.R. 41—§ 1:4
B.C. v. Christie, [2007] 1 S.C.R. 873—§§ 15:28, 43:33
B.C. v. Imperial Tobacco, [2005] 2 S.C.R. 473—§ 47:32
B.C. v. Lafarge Canada, [2007] 2 S.C.R. 86—§ 22:12
B.C. v. Phillip Morris International, [2018] 2 S.C.R. 595, 2018 SCC 36—§ 7:3
B.C. v. Provincial Court Judges' Association of British Columbia, 2020 SCC 20—§ 7:11
B.C.E.G.U. v. B.C., [1988] 2 S.C.R. 214—§§ 38:7, 38:31
B.C. Elec. Ry. v. CNR, [1932] S.C.R. 161—§§ 22:1, 22:4, 22:10, 22:11, 22:13
B.C. Elec. Ry. Co. v. CNR, [1932] S.C.R. 161, 169—§ 22:8
B.C. Family Relations Act, Re, [1982] 1 S.C.R. 62—§§ 7:15, 7:16
B.C. Freedom of Information and Privacy Assn. v. B.C., [2017] 1 S.C.R. 93, 2017 SCC 6—§ 38:4
B.C. Freedom of Information and Privacy Association v. British Columbia, [2017] 1 S.C.R. 93, 2017 SCC 6—§ 43:38
BCGEU v. B.C., [1988] 2 S.C.R. 214—§§ 37:11, 37:12, 38:21, 43:26, 43:27
BCGEU v. B.C. (Vancouver Courthouse) [1988] 2 S.C.R. 214—§§ 43:12, 43:14, 43:33, 43:35
B.C. Government Employees' Union v. British Columbia, [1988] 2 S.C.R. 214—§ 36:23
B.C. Legislative Assembly Resolution on Judicial Compensation, Re (1998), 160 D.L.R. (4th) 477 (B.C. C.A.)—§ 7:5
B.C. Motor Vehicle Act, Re, [1985] 2 S.C.R. 486, 509-512—§§ 35:8, 36:5, 36:18, 36:19, 36:20, 36:27, 38:17, 38:25, 38:33, 47:2, 47:9, 47:10, 47:14, 47:38
B.C. Securities Commn. v. Branch, [1995] 2 S.C.R. 3—§§ 47:15, 47:31
B.C. Teachers' Federation, Re (1985), 23 D.L.R. (4th) 161 (B.C. C.A.)—§ 16:1
Beauharnais v. Illinois (1952), 343 U.S. 250—§ 43:27
Beaule v. Corp. of Master Electricians (1969), 10 D.L.R. (3d) 93 (Que. C.A.)—§ 21:9
Beauregard v. Can., [1986] 2 S.C.R. 56, 75—§§ 7:2, 55:2
Becker, Re (1983), 148 D.L.R. (3d) 539 (Alta. C.A.)—§ 47:13
Beckman v. Little Salmon/Carmacks First Nation, [2010] 3 S.C.R. 103—§§ 28:21, 28:26, 28:38, 40:26
Bedard v. Dawson, [1923] S.C.R. 681—§§ 18:15, 18:20, 21:17
Behn v. Moulton Contracting, [2013] 2 S.C.R. 227—§§ 28:38, 28:40
Bell v. A.-G. P.E.I., [1975] 1 S.C.R. 25—§ 16:5
Bell v. A.G.P.E.I., [1975] 1 S.C.R. 25—§ 22:11
Bell Can. v. Que., [1988] 1 S.C.R. 749, 867—§ 15:20
Bell Canada v. Can. Telephone Employees Assn., [2003] 1 S.C.R. 884—§§ 7:9, 35:3, 35:5, 35:7, 35:8, 47:14
Bell Canada v. Quebec, [1988] 1 S.C.R. 749—§§ 15:18, 15:20, 21:11, 22:22
Bell ExpressVu v. Rex, [2002] 2 S.C.R. 559—§§ 36:8, 37:12
Benn v. Moulton Contracting, [2013] 2 S.C.R. 227, 2013 SCC 26—§ 28:38
Benner v. Can., [1997] 1 S.C.R. 358—§ 55:19
Benner v. Canada, [1997] 1 S.C.R. 358—§§ 36:31, 38:18, 40:5, 55:41
Benner v. Can. (No. 2), [1997] 3 S.C.R. 389—§ 40:5
Benton v. Maryland (1969), 395 U.S. 784—§ 16:8
Bernard v. Canada, [2014] 1 S.C.R. 227, 2014 SCC 13—§ 44:8
Bernshine Mobile Maintenance v. CLRB, [1986] 1 F.C. 422 (C.A.)—§§ 22:9, 22:11
Bertrand v. Dussault (1909), reported in 1977 in 77 D.L.R. (3d) 458 (Man. Co. Ct.)—§ 56:6

Bertrand v. Que. (1996), 138 D.L.R. (4th) 481 (Que. S.C.)—§ 5:24
Bertrand v. Que. (1995), 127 D.L.R. (4th) 408 (Que. S.C.)—§ 5:24
Bhatnager v. Can., [1990] 2 S.C.R. 217—§ 9:7
Bhindi, Re (1986), 29 D.L.R. (4th) 47 (B.C.C.A.)—§§ 37:8, 44:8
Bill 30, Re (Ont. Separate School Funding), [1987] 1 S.C.R. 1148—§§ 36:23, 37:7
Bill 30, Re, (Ontario Separate School Funding) [1987] 1 S.C.R. 1148—§§ 42:9, 55:35
Bill 30 (Ont. Separate School Funding), Re, [1987] 1 S.C.R. 1148, 1195—§ 8:13
Bilodeau v. A.G. Man., [1986] 1 S.C.R. 449—§ 56:11
Bisaillon v. Keable, [1983] 2 S.C.R. 60—§§ 7:11, 16:1
Black v. Can. (2001), 54 O.R. (3d) 215 (C.A.)—§ 9:21
Black v. Chrétien (2001), 54 O.R. (3d) 215 (C.A.)—§ 1:9
Black v. Law Society of Alberta, [1989] 1 S.C.R. 591—§ 38:7
Black v. Law Society of Alta., [1989] 1 S.C.R. 591—§§ 37:8, 38:20, 44:3
Blackwoods Beverages, Re (1984), 15 D.L.R. (4th) 231 (Man. C.A.)—§ 40:17
Blainey v. Ontario Hockey Association (1986), 54 O.R. (2d) 513 (C.A.)—§ 55:7
Blainey v. Ont. Hockey Assn. (1986), 54 O.R. (2d) 513 (C.A.)—§ 55:42
Blainey, Re (1986), 54 O.R. (2d) 513 (C.A.)—§ 37:13
Blainey and Ont. Hockey Assn., Re (1986), 54 O.R. (2d) 513 (C.A.)—§ 38:9
Blencoe v. B.C., [2002] 2 S.C.R. 307—§ 47:13
Blencoe v. B.C., [2000] 2 S.C.R. 307—§§ 37:8, 37:11, 38:32
Blencoe v. British Columbia, [2000] 2 S.C.R. 307—§§ 47:9, 47:12
Bliss v. A.G. Can., [1979] 1 S.C.R. 183—§§ 55:2, 55:8, 55:41
Blueberry River Indian Band v. Can., [1995] 4 S.C.R. 344—§§ 28:18, 28:21
Board v. Board, [1919] A.C. 956—§ 7:1
Board of Commerce Act, Re, [1922] 1 A.C. 191—§§ 18:19, 20:2, 20:4
Board of Commerce Act, Re (1920), 60 S.C.R. 456, 507—§ 17:3
Boggs v. The Queen, [1981] 1 S.C.R. 49—§ 18:2
Boivin v. The Queen CMAC-410; (1998) 245 N.R. 341 (Ct. Martial Appeal Court)—§ 7:6
Bonanza Creek Gold Mining Co. v. The King, [1916] 1 A.C. 566—§ 9:3
Borowski v. A.G. Can. (1987), 39 D.L.R. (4th) 731 (Sask. C.A.)—§§ 37:2, 37:3
Borowski v. Can., [1989] 1 S.C.R. 342—§ 37:2
Borowski v. Can., [1989] 1 S.C.R. 342—§ 37:3
Boucher v. The King, [1951] S.C.R. 265—§ 34:2
Boulanger v. Fédération des producteurs d'oeufs (1982), 141 D.L.R. (3d) 72 (Que. C.A.)—§ 20:3
Bou Malhab v. Diffusion Métromédia, [2011] 1 S.C.R. 214—§ 43:28
Bowles v. Bank of England, [1913] 1 Ch. 57—§ 1:9
Bow, McLachlan & Co. v. The Ship "Camosun", [1909] A.C. 597—§ 7:11
Bozanich, Re, [1942] S.C.R. 130—§ 16:3
B.(R.) v. Children's Aid Society, [1995] 1 S.C.R. 315—§§ 42:6, 47:9, 47:11
Branigan, Re (1986), 26 D.L.R. (4th) 268 (Y.T.S.C.)—§ 35:2
Brant Dairy v. Milk Comm. of Ont., [1973] S.C.R. 131, 152–153—§ 8:13
Bribery Commr. v. Ranasinghe, [1965] A.C. 172—§ 12:10
Briére v. Can. Mtge. & Housing Corp., [1986] 2 F.C. 484—§ 7:11
Brink's Canada v. CLRB, [1985] 1 F.C. 898 (T.D.)—§ 7:20
British Coal Corp. v. The King, [1935] A.C. 500, 520—§§ 3:3, 8:2, 15:27, 36:19
British Columbia v. Imperial Tobacco, [2005] 2 S.C.R. 473—§§ 7:3, 15:28
British Columbia v. Lafarge Canada, [2007] 2 S.C.R. 86—§§ 15:18, 16:3, 22:12

British Columbia v. Provincial Court Judges' Association of British Columbia, 2020 SCC 20—§ 7:5
British Columbia Human Rights Tribunal v. Schrenk, [2017] 2 S.C.R. 795—§ 15:8
Broadrick v. Oklahoma (1973), 413 U.S. 601, 611—§ 47:24
Brooks-Bidlake and Whitall v. A.G. B.C., [1923] A.C. 450—§ 6:9
Brooks-Bidlake and Whittall v. A.-G. B.C., [1923] A.C. 450—§ 55:1
Brooks v. Canada Safeway, [1989] 1 S.C.R. 1219, 1243–1250—§ 8:13
Brooks v. Can. Safeway, [1989] 1 S.C.R. 1219—§ 55:41
Brown v. Bd. of Education (1954), 347 U.S. 483—§§ 8:13, 36:5
Brown v. Board of Education (1954), 347 U.S. 483 overruled Plessy v. Ferguson (1896), 163 U.S. 537—§§ 36:18, 55:3
Brown v. Entertainment Merchants Assn. (2011), 564 U.S. xxx—§ 43:10
Brown v. The Queen (1980), 107 D.L.R. (3d) 705 (B.C.C.A.)—§ 28:2
Brownridge v. The Queen, [1972] S.C.R. 926—§§ 35:3, 35:8
Bruker v. Marcovitz, [2007] 3 S.C.R. 607—§§ 34:4, 37:24, 42:7
Budge v. Alta. (1991), 77 D.L.R. (4th) 361 (Alta. C.A.)—§§ 47:13, 47:32
Buhlers v. B.C. (1999), 170 D.L.R. (4th) 344 (B.C.C.A.)—§§ 18:20, 47:9
Buhlers v. Superintendent of Motor Vehicles (B.C.) 1999 BCCA 0114; 119 B.C.A.C. 207 (B.C.C.A.)—§ 18:20
Burlington Airpark v. City of Burlington, 2013 ONSC 6990—§ 22:15
Burmah Oil Co. v. Lord Advocate, [1965] A.C. 75 (H.L.)—§ 1:9
Burns Foods v. A.-G. Man., [1975] 1 S.C.R. 494—§§ 20:3, 21:14
Burwell v. Hobby Lobby Stores (2014), 134 S.Ct. 2751—§§ 37:2, 42:4
Bypass Pipelines, Re (1988), 64 O.R. (2d) 293 (C.A.)—§ 22:11

Caisse populaire Desjardins de l'Est de Drummond v. Can., [2009] 2 S.C.R. 94—§ 7:11
Calder v. A.G.B.C., [1973] S.C.R. 313—§§ 28:18, 28:22, 28:24
Calder v. B.C., [1973] S.C.R. 313—§ 28:21
Caloil v. A.-G. Can., [1971] S.C.R. 543—§§ 20:2, 20:3, 21:13
Cambie Surgeries Corp. v. B.C., 2020 BCSC 1310—§§ 32:6, 47:12
Campbell-Bennett v. Comstock Midwestern, [1954] S.C.R. 207—§§ 14:14, 15:18, 15:20, 22:11
Campbell v. Can. (1988), 49 D.L.R. (4th) 321, 324-327 (B.C.C.A.)—§ 4:16
Campbell v. Canada (1988), 49 D.L.R. (4th) 321 (B.C.C.A.)—§§ 4:14, 4:18
Campbell v. East-West Packers (1982), 143 D.L.R. (3d) 136, 137 (Man. C.A.)—§ 8:6
Campbell v. Hall (1774), 1 Cowp. 204, 98 E.R. 1045—§§ 2:5, 2:6
Can. v. Barnaby, [2015] 2 S.C.R. 563, 2015 SCC 31—§ 37:14
Can. v. Bedford, [2013] 3 S.C.R. 1101, 2013 SCC 72—§§ 8:11, 8:13, 38:25, 43:9, 43:25, 47:24
Can. v. British Columbia Investment Management, 2019 SCC 63—§ 5:27
Can. v. Can., [2011] 2 S.C.R. 306—§ 43:41
Can. v. Can., [1989] 2 S.C.R. 49, 103—§ 12:9
Can. v. Chambre des notaires du Québec, [2016] 1 S.C.R. 336, 2016 SCC 20—§ 40:7
Can. v. Chiarelli, [1992] 1 S.C.R. 711—§ 47:2
Can. v. Craig, [2012] 2 S.C.R. 489—§ 8:13
Can. v. Friends of the Can. Wheat Bd. (2012), 352 D.L.R. (4th) 163 (F.C.A.)—§ 12:10

Can. v. Friends of the Can. Wheat Bd. (2012), D.L.R. (4th) 163 (F.C.A.)—§ 12:10
Can. v. Harkat, [2014] 2 S.C.R. 33—§ 47:38
Can. v. Hislop, [2007] 2 S.C.R. 391—§ 40:4
Can. v. Hislop, [2007] 1 S.C.R. 429—§§ 36:18, 37:3, 38:12, 38:15, 40:4, 55:18
Can. v. JTI-Macdonald Corp., [2007] 2 S.C.R. 610—§§ 18:5, 36:8, 38:9, 38:20, 38:21, 38:22, 47:28
Can. v. Kamel, [2009] 4 F.C.R. 449 (F.C.A.)—§§ 1:9, 38:7, 38:9
Can. v. Khadr, [2010] 1 S.C.R. 44—§§ 1:9, 36:10, 37:14
Can. v. Khadr, [2008] 2 S.C.R. 125—§§ 40:18, 47:38
Can. v. Khadr (2010), 321 D.L.R. (4th) 448 (F.C.A.)—§ 40:18
Can. v. Lameman, [2008] 1 S.C.R. 372—§§ 28:40, 40:25
Can. v. McArthur, [2010] 3 S.C.R. 626—§ 7:20
Can. v. NutraSweet Co. (1990), 32 C.P.R. (3d) 1—§ 18:11
Can. v. PHS Community Services Society, [2011] 3 S.C.R. 134—§§ 15:5, 18:4, 32:2, 47:26
Can. v. Schmidt, [1987] 1 S.C.R. 500—§§ 16:1, 16:8, 37:14, 47:15
Can. v. Taylor, [1990] 3 S.C.R. 892—§§ 38:9, 43:27
Can. v. Taylor (1991), 81 D.L.R. (4th) 679 (F.C.A.)—§ 55:50
Can. v. Vaid, [2005] 1 S.C.R. 667, para. 29(10)—§§ 1:7, 37:7
Can. v. Vavilov, 2019 SCC 65—§§ 7:20, 21:11, 38:32, 40:26
Canada v. Bedford, [2013] 3 S.C.R. 1101, 2013 SCC 72—§§ 8:13, 40:4, 47:12, 47:25, 47:26
Canada v. E.F., 2016 ABCA 155, 34 Alta. L.R. (6th) 1, para. 41 (Alta. C.A.)—§ 40:4
Canada v. Federation of Law Societies, [2015] 1 S.C.R. 401, 2015 SCC 7—§ 40:7
Canada v. Federation of Law Societies, [2015] 1 S.C.R. 401; 2015 SCC 7—§§ 38:26, 40:6, 47:15
Canada v. Harkat, [2014] 2 S.C.R. 33; 2014 SCC 37—§ 47:32
Canada v. Harkat, [2014] 2 S.C.R. 33, 2014 SCC 37—§ 36:9
Canada v. Hislop, [2007] 1 S.C.R. 429—§§ 40:4, 55:48
Canada v. JTI-Macdonald Corp., [2007] 2 S.C.R. 610—§§ 36:9, 43:11, 43:16, 43:23
Canada v. Khadr, [2010] 1 S.C.R. 44—§§ 40:18, 40:19
Canada v. Khadr, [2008] 2 S.C.R. 125—§§ 37:14, 47:34
Canada v. PHS Community Services Society, [2011] 3 S.C.R. 134—§§ 15:21, 32:1, 47:25
Canada v. PHS Community Services Society, [2011] S.C.R. 134—§ 18:4
Canada v. Schmidt, [1987] 1 S.C.R. 500, 522—§ 47:15
Canada v. Taylor, [1990] 3 S.C.R. 892—§ 43:14
Canada v. Vaid, [2005] 1 S.C.R. 667—§ 1:7
Canada v. Vavilov, 2019 SCC 65—§ 7:20
Canada Assistance Plan, Re, [1991] 2 S.C.R. 525—§§ 6:7, 6:8, 12:9, 12:10, 36:12
Canada Assistance Plan (B.C.), Re, [1991] 2 S.C.R. 525, 548-49—§ 5:27
Canada Labour Relations Board v. Paul L'Anglais, [1983] 1 S.C.R. 147—§ 7:20
Canada Mortgage and Housing Corp. v. Iness (2004), 70 O.R. (3d) 148 (C.A.)—§ 6:8
Canada Post Corp. v. Hamilton (2016), 134 O.R. (3d) 502, 2016 ONCA 767—§ 16:3
Canada Post Corp. v. Hamilton (City) (2016) 134 O.R. (3d) 502, 2016 ONCA 767—§ 22:11
Canada Temperance, [1952] 1 S.C.R. 292, 308–309, 311, 318, 328—§§ 17:3, 22:13
Canadian Broadcasting Corp. v. Can., [2011] 1 S.C.R. 65—§ 43:32

Canadian Broadcasting Corp. v. Can., [2011] 1 S.C.R. 19—§§ 38:7, 43:20, 43:32
Canadian Broadcasting Corp. v. Canada, [2011] 1 S.C.R. 19—§ 43:33
Canadian Civil Liberties Association v. Ontario (1990), 71 O.R. (2d) 341 (C.A.)—§ 42:8
Canadian Federation of Students v. Greater Vancouver Transportation Authority,, [2009] 2 S.C.R. 295—§ 38:7
Canadian Foundation for Children,Youth and the Law v. Can., [2004] 1 S.C.R. 76—§ 40:7
Canadian Foundation for Children, Youth and the Law v. Canada, [2004] 1 S.C.R. 76—§§ 40:9, 47:12, 47:15, 47:24, 47:28, 55:21, 55:26, 55:44
Canadian Newspapers Co. v. Attorney General of Canada, [1988] 2 S.C.R. 122—§ 38:21
Canadian Newspapers Co. v. Can., [1988] 1 S.C.R. 122—§ 43:12
Canadian Newspapers Co. v. Canada, [1988] 1 S.C.R. 122—§ 43:32
Canadian Taxpayers Federation v. Ontario (2004), 73 O.R. (3d) 621 (S.C.J.)—§ 12:10
Canadian Western Bank v. Alberta, [2007] 2 S.C.R. 3—§§ 15:18, 16:5, 22:12
Canadian Western Bank v. Alta., [2007] 2 S.C.R. 3—§§ 15:20, 15:21, 22:12, 28:37
Canadian Western Bank v. Alta. v. Alta., [2007] 2 S.C.R. 3—§ 15:20
Can. Assistance Plan, Re, [1991] 2 S.C.R. 525, 545—§§ 8:11, 12:10
Can. (CHRC) v. Can., [2018] 2 S.C.R. 230—§ 7:20
Can. Civil Libs. Assn. v. Ont. (1990), 71 O.R. (2d) 341 (C.A.)—§ 38:15
Can. Disability Rights Council v. The Queen, [1988] 3 F.C. 622 (T.D.)—§ 45:2
Can. Egg Marketing Agency v. Richardson, [1998] 3 S.C.R. 157—§§ 40:14, 44:5
Can. Federation of Agriculture v. A.-G. Que., [1951] 1 A.C. 179—§ 15:14
Can. Federation of Agriculture v. A.-G. Que., [1951] A.C. 179—§§ 17:3, 18:2, 18:3, 20:2, 21:8, 21:12, 34:6
Can. Federation of Agriculture v. A.-G. Que., [1949] S.C.R. 1, 50—§§ 18:2, 18:12
Can. Federation of Agriculture v. A.G. Que., [1951] A.C. 179—§§ 17:7, 17:12
Can. Foundation for Children, Youth and the Law v. Can., [2004] 1 S.C.R. 76—§§ 40:7, 47:28, 55:20, 55:25
Can. Foundation/or Children, Youth and the Law v. Can., [2004] 1 S.C.R. 76—§ 37:12
Can. Indemnity Co. v. A.-G. B.C., [1977] 2 S.C.R. 504—§§ 15:5, 15:17, 21:6, 21:14, 22:23, 22:25
Can. Indemnity Co. v. A.G.B.C., [1977] 2 S.C.R. 504—§ 22:3
Can. Industrial Gas and Oil v. Govt. of Sask., [1978] 2 S.C.R. 545—§§ 20:3, 21:14
Can. Industrial Gas and Oil v. Sask., [1978] 2 S.C.R. 545—§ 4:21
Can. Labour Code, Re, [1987] 2 F.C. 30 (C.A.)—§§ 22:9, 22:11
Can. Labour Relations Bd. v. Paul L'Anglais, [1983] 1 S.C.R. 147—§§ 7:2, 7:11, 7:20
Can. Labour Relations Bd. v. Yellowknife, [1977] 2 S.C.R. 729—§ 21:11
Can. Metal Co., Re (1982), 144 D.L.R. (3d) 124 (Man. Q.B.)—§ 17:3
Cannet Freight Cartage, Re, [1976] 1 F.C. 174 (C.A.)—§§ 22:4, 22:9
Can. Northern Ry. Co. v. Pszenicnzy (1916), 54 S.C.R. 36—§ 18:17
Can. Pioneer Management v. Labour Relations Bd. Sask., [1980] 1 S.C.R. 433—§ 21:7
Can. Saltfish Corp. v. Rasmussen, [1986] 2 F.C. 500 (C.A.)—§ 7:11
Can. Western Bank v. Alta., [2007] 2 S.C.R. 3—§§ 5:7, 15:5, 15:16, 21:6
Cape Breton v. Nova Scotia (2009), 277 N.S.R. (2d) 350 (N.S. C.A.)—§ 6:6

Capital Cities Communications v. CRTC, [1978] 2 S.C.R. 141—§§ 17:6, 22:9, 22:16, 22:17, 22:18, 22:19, 22:20, 43:4
Capital Regional District v. Concerned Citizens of B.C., [1982] 2 S.C.R. 842—§§ 7:19, 7:20
Cardinal v. A.-G. Alta., [1974] S.C.R. 695—§ 28:7
Carltona v. Commrs. of Works, [1943] 2 All E.R. 560 (C.A.)—§ 1:11
Carl Zeiss Stiftung v. Rayner and Keeler (No. 2), [1967] 1 A.C. 853—§ 5:26
Carnation Co. v. Que. Agricultural Marketing Bd., [1968] S.C.R. 238—§§ 15:5, 20:3, 21:8
Carnation Co. v. Quebec Agricultural Marketing Board, [1968] S.C.R. 238—§ 21:14
Caron v. Alberta, 2015 SCC 56—§ 56:4
Caron v. The King, [1924] A.C. 999, 1006—§ 15:21
Carter v. Can., [2015] 1 S.C.R. 331, 2015 SCC 5—§§ 8:13, 15:21, 32:1, 38:25, 40:8, 47:8, 55:45
Carter v. Canada, [2015] 1 S.C.R. 331, 2015 SCC 5—§§ 8:13, 32:2, 40:4, 47:9, 47:12, 47:15, 47:24
Carter v. Carter Coal Co. (1936), 298 U.S. 238, 312–313, 321–322—§ 15:14
Case of Proclamations (1611)12 Co. Rep. 74, 77 E.R. 1352—§ 14:2
Case of Proclamations (1611), 12 Co. Rep. 74, 77 E.R. 1352 (K.B.)—§§ 1:9, 2:4, 34:2
Catholic Children's Aid Society v. S.(T) (1989), 69 O.R. (2d) 189 (C.A.)—§§ 44:3, 55:11
CBC v. Cordeau, [1979] 22 S.C.R. 618, 640—§ 15:15
CBC v. Lessard, [1991] 3 S.C.R. 421—§ 43:18
CBC v. N.B., [1996] 3 S.C.R. 480—§ 38:9
CBC v. N.B., [1991] 3 S.C.R. 459—§ 43:18
CBC v. New Brunswick, [1996] 3 S.C.R. 480—§ 43:33
Central Alta. Dairy Pool v. Alta., [1990] 2 S.C.R. 489—§ 8:13
Central Canada Potash v. Government of Saskatchewan, [1979] 1 S.C.R. 42—§ 21:14
Central Canada Potash v. Govt. of Sask., [1979] 1 S.C.R. 42—§ 40:19
Central Canada Potash Co. v. Government of Saskatchewan, [1979] 1 S.C.R. 42—§ 15:9
Central Can. Potash v. Govt. of Sask., [1979] 1 S.C.R. 42, 75—§§ 12:2, 20:3
Central Can. Potash Co. v. Sask., [1979] 1 S.C.R. 42—§ 4:21
Central Computer Services v. Toronto Dominion Bank (1980), 109 D.L.R. (3d) 660, 662–664 (Man. C.A.)—§ 8:6
Centrale des syndicats du Québec v. Que., [2018] 1 S.C.R. 522—§ 55:32
Centrale des syndicats du Québec v. Quebec, [2018] 1 S.C.R. 522—§§ 55:22, 55:31, 55:42
Central Hudson Gas & Electric Corp. v. Public Service Commn. of N.Y. (1980), 447 U.S. 557, 566—§ 38:1
Central Mortgage and Housing Corp. v. Co-op College Residences (1975), 13 O.R. (2d) 394 (C.A.)—§ 6:8
CFRB, Re, [1973] 3 O.R. 819 (C.A.)—§§ 22:16, 22:17, 22:18, 22:20
Chagnon v. Syndicat de la fonction publique et parapublique du Québec, [2018] 2 S.C.R. 687—§§ 1:7, 4:19, 37:7
Chagnon v. Syndicat de la function publique et parapublique du Québec, [2018] 2 S.C.R. 687—§ 1:7
Chamney v. The Queen, [1975] 2 S.C.R. 151—§§ 20:2, 22:10

Chaoulli v. Que., [2005] 1 S.C.R. 791—§§ 34:4, 36:12, 38:25, 47:8, 47:10
Chaoulli v. Quebec, [2005] 1 S.C.R. 791—§§ 32:6, 47:12, 47:26
Chapman, Re (1984), 46 O.R. (2d) 65 (C.A.)—§ 40:17
Chaput v. Romain, [1955] S.C.R. 834—§ 34:2
Charkaoui v. Can., [2008] 2 S.C.R. 326—§§ 47:32, 47:34, 47:36, 47:38
Charkaoui v. Can., [2007] 1 S.C.R. 350—§§ 7:20, 38:25, 40:4, 40:5, 40:6, 47:9, 47:15, 47:32, 47:38, 55:37
Charkaoui v. Canada, [2007] 1 S.C.R. 350—§§ 36:9, 47:32
Charlebois v. Moncton (2001), 242 N.B.R. (2d) 259 (N.B.C.A.)—§ 56:8
Charlottetown v. Prince Edward Island (1998), 168 D.L.R. (4th) 79 (P.E.I.C.A.)—§ 45:3
Chatterjee v. Ont., [2009] 1 S.C.R. 624—§§ 15:5, 15:8, 16:8
Chatterjee v. Ontario, [2009] 1 S.C.R. 624—§ 18:20
Cherry v. Advocate General for Scotland, [2019] CSOH 70—§ 9:21
Cherry v. Advocate General for Scotland, [2019] CSIH 49—§ 9:21
Chiarelli v. Can., [1992] 1 S.C.R. 711—§§ 47:32, 55:37
Chicago Teachers' Union v. Hudson (1986), 475 U.S. 292—§ 44:8
Chippewas of the Thames First Nation v. Enbridge Pipelines, [2017] 1 S.C.R. 1099, 2017 SCC 41—§§ 28:38, 40:26
Chromiak v. The Queen, [1980] 1 S.C.R. 471—§§ 35:8, 41:11
Chrysler Can. v. Can., [1992] 2 S.C.R. 394, 416—§ 7:19
C.I.B.C. v. Rifou, [1986] 3 F.C. 486, 491, 493—§ 7:14
Citizens' Insurance Co. v. Parsons (1881), 7 App. Cas. 96—§§ 17:2, 20:1, 20:4, 21:2, 21:6
Citizens United v. Federal Election Commn. (2010), 558 U.S. 310—§ 43:38
City of Arlington, Texas v. Federal Communications Commission (2013), 569 U.S. 290, 299—§ 7:20
City of Medicine Hat v. A.G. Can. (1985), 18 D.L.R. (4th) 428 (Alta. C.A.)—§ 15:21
City of Toronto v. Ont., 2018 ONSC 5151 (S.C.J.)—§ 39:2
Clark v. CNR, [1988] 2 S.C.R. 680, 704—§§ 8:13, 15:15, 15:20, 15:21, 18:17
Clarke v. Clarke, [1990] 2 S.C.R. 795—§ 16:5
Clarkson v. The Queen, [1986] 1 S.C.R. 383, 394-395—§§ 37:15, 41:11
Clayton v. Heffron (1960), 105 C.L.R. 215 (H.C. Aust.)—§ 12:10
CLRB v. Paul L'Anglais, [1983] 1 S.C.R. 147, 154—§ 7:20
CLRB v. Yellowknife, [1977] 2 S.C.R. 729—§ 17:1
Clyde River v. Petroleum Geo-Services, [2017] 1 S.C.R. 1069, 2017 SCC 40—§ 28:38
Clyde River (Hamlet) v. Petroleum Geo-Services, [2017] 1 S.C.R. 1069—§ 40:26
CNR v. Commrs. of Public Utilities, [1976] 2 S.C.R. 112—§ 22:1
CNR v. Courtois, [1988] 1 S.C.R. 868—§ 15:18
C.N. Railway v. Can., [2014] 2 S.C.R. 135—§ 15:8
Co-op. Committee on Japanese Canadians v. A.-G. Can., [1947] A.C. 87—§§ 17:3, 17:8, 17:12, 55:1
Cobb & Co. v. Kropp, [1967] 1 A.C. 141—§ 14:4
Cochrane v. Ont. (2008), 92 O.R. (3d) 321 (C.A.)—§§ 47:24, 47:28
Cohen v. California (1971), 403 U.S. 15—§ 43:6
Cole v. Whitfield (1988), 165 C.L.R. 360—§ 8:13
Colonial Coach Lines, Re, [1967] 2 O.R. 25 (H.C.)—§§ 22:11, 22:14
Commission du Salaire Minimum v. Bell Telephone Co., [1966] S.C.R. 767—§§ 15:17, 15:18, 15:20, 16:10, 21:11, 22:22

Committee for Cth. of Can. v. Can., [1991] 1 S.C.R. 139—§§ 38:7, 43:12, 43:30
Committee for Justice and Liberty v. Nat. Energy Bd., [1978] 1 S.C.R. 369, 394—§ 7:5
Commonwealth v. Cigamatic (1962), 108 C.L.R. 372—§ 8:13
Communications, Energy and Paperworkers Union of Canada v. Native Child and Family Services of Toronto, [2010] 2 S.C.R. 737—§ 28:9
Conacher v. Can. (2009), 311 D.L.R. (4th) 678 (F.C.), affd. (2010) 320 D.L.R. (4th) 530 (F.C.A)—§ 9:21
Conacher v. Canada (2010), 320 D.L.R. (4th) 530 (F.C.A.)—§§ 1:14, 9:20
Confédération des syndicats nationaux v. Can., [2008] 3 S.C.R. 511—§ 14:5
Confederation des syndicats nationaux v. Canada, [2008] 3 S.C.R. 511—§§ 14:5, 40:4
Conférence des juges de paix magistrats du Québec v. Quebec, [2016] 2 S.C.R. 116, 2016 SCC 39—§ 7:5
Congrégation des Témoins de Jéhovah v. Lafontaine, [2004] 2 S.C.R. 650—§ 42:6
Conklin & Garrett v. Ont. (1989), 70 O.R. (2d) 713 (Div. Ct.)—§ 22:3
Connolly v. Woolrich (1867), 11 L.C. Jur. 197 (Que. S.C.); affd. (1869) 17 R.J.R.Q. 266 (Que. Q.B.)—§ 2:1
Conseil scolaire francophone de la Colombie-Britannique v. B.C., [2013] 2 S.C.R. 774, 2013 SCC 42—§§ 2:10, 56:9
Conseil scolaire francophone de la Colombie-Britannique v. B.C., 2020 SCC 13—§§ 38:30, 56:12
Conseil scolaire francophone de la Colombie-Britannique v. British Columbia, [2013] 2 S.C.R. 774, 2013 SCC 42—§ 2:3
Conseil scolaire francophone de la Colombie-Britannique v. British Columbia, 2020 SCC 13—§§ 38:17, 40:19, 56:23
Consolidated Fastfrate v. Western Canada Council of Teamsters, [2009] 3 S.C.R. 407—§§ 22:3, 22:4, 22:9
Consortium Developments v. Sarnia, [1998] 3 S.C.R. 3—§ 15:5
Construction Montcalm v. Minimum Wage Comm., [1979] 1 S.C.R. 754—§§ 15:5, 21:11, 22:6, 28:7, 28:9
Construction Montcalm v. Minimum Wage Commission, [1979] 1 S.C.R. 754—§§ 16:5, 22:15
Construction Montcalm v. Minimum Wage Commn., [1979] 1 S.C.R. 754—§§ 15:20, 16:10, 22:9, 22:14
Contrast Taylor v. Can. (2007), 286 D.L.R. (4th) 385 (F.C.A.)—§ 36:31
Cooper v. Can., [1996] 3 S.C.R. 854—§ 40:26
Corbeil, Re (1986), 27 C.C.C. (3d) 245 (Ont. C.A.)—§ 40:24
Corbiere v. Can., [1999] 2 S.C.R. 203—§§ 36:8, 40:8, 55:18, 55:22, 55:39
Corbiere v. Can., [1999] 2 S.C.R. 203—§ 55:47
Corbiere v. Canada, [1999] 2 S.C.R. 203—§§ 28:5, 28:41, 36:10, 40:4, 55:49
Cormier v. Fournier (1986), 29 D.L.R. (4th) 675 (N.B.Q.B.), affirmed (1987) 78 N.B.R. (2d) 406 (C.A.)—§ 56:13
Corp. Professionnelle des Médecins v. Thibault, [1988] 1 S.C.R. 1033—§§ 36:31, 38:4
Coughlin v. Ontario Highway Transport Board, [1968] S.C.R. 569—§ 14:13
Coughlin v. Ont. Highway Transport Bd., [1968] S.C.R. 569—§§ 7:1, 14:11, 14:13, 17:4
Council of Canadians v. Canada (2006), 277 D.L.R. (4th) 527 (Ont. C.A.)—§ 7:19
Council of Canadians with Disabilities v. VIA Rail Canada, [2007] 1 S.C.R. 650—§ 55:7

Council of Civil Service Unions v. Minister for the Civil Service, [1985] A.C. 374 (H.L.)—§ 9:21
Council of Civil Service Unions v. Minr. for Civil Service, [1985] 1 A.C. 374 (H.L.)—§ 1:9
County Courts of B.C., Re (1892), 21 S.C.R. 446—§ 7:2
Court of Québec, Re, 2019 QCCA 1492—§ 7:16
Covington and Lexington Turnpike Road Co. v. Sandford (1896), 164 U.S. 578—§ 37:2
CPR v. A.-G. B.C. (Empress Hotel) [1950] A.C. 122—§§ 17:3, 21:10, 21:11, 22:2, 22:7
CPR v. A.G.B.C. (Empress Hotel) [1950] A.C. 122, 142—§ 22:3
CPR v. Notre Dame de Bonsecours, [1899] A.C. 367—§ 15:18
Craig v. Boren (1976), 429 U.S. 190—§ 55:3
Craton v. Winnipeg School Division No. 1, [1985] 2 S.C.R. 150—§ 37:24
Credit Foncier Franco-Canadien v. Ross, [1937] 3 D.L.R. 365 (Alta. A.D.)—§§ 14:3, 14:5, 14:8
Crevier v. A.-G. Que., [1981] 2 S.C.R. 220—§§ 7:15, 7:16, 7:19, 7:20
Crevier v. Que., [1981] 2 S.C.R. 220—§ 40:19
Criminal Law Amendment Act 1968–69, Re (Breathalyzer) [1970] S.C.R. 777—§ 14:5
Criminal Law Amendment Act, 1968–69, Re, [1970] S.C.R. 777—§§ 14:5, 14:15
Crown Grain Co. v. Day, [1908] A.C. 504—§§ 8:5, 16:4
Cuddy Chicks v. Ont., [1991] 2 S.C.R. 5—§§ 40:13, 40:26
Cuddy Chicks v. Ontario, [1991] 2 S.C.R. 5—§ 40:26
Cunningham v. Canada, [1993] 2 S.C.R. 143—§§ 47:9, 47:15
Cunningham v. Tomey Homma, [1903] A.C. 151—§§ 15:6, 37:4, 45:1, 55:1
Curr v. The Queen, [1972] S.C.R. 889, 896—§§ 35:3, 35:8
Curran v. Grand Trunk Ry. Co. (1898), 25 O.A.R. 407 (Ont. C.A.)—§ 18:17
Currie v. MacDonald (1949), 29 Nfld. & P.E.I.R. 294 (Nfld. C.A.)—§§ 1:10, 2:12
Curtis Publishing Co. v. Butts (1967), 388 U.S. 130—§ 43:28
Cusson v. Quan (2007), 87 O.R. (3d) 241 (C.A.)—§ 43:28

Dagenais v. CBC, [1994] 3 S.C.R. 835—§§ 36:23, 37:12, 38:22, 38:31, 43:12, 43:32, 43:33
Daniels v. Can., [2016] 1 S.C.R. 99, 2016 SCC 12—§ 28:2
Daniels v. White, [1968] S.C.R. 517—§§ 28:6, 28:17
David Polowin Real Estate v. Dominion of Canada General Insurance Co. (2005), 76 O.R. (3d) 161, paras. 126–145 (C.A.)—§ 8:13
De Boers Consolidated Mines v. Howe, [1906] A.C. 455 (H.L.)—§ 37:5
Dehghani v. Can., [1993] 1 S.C.R. 1053, 1076—§ 47:15
Delgamuukw v. B.C., [1997] 3 S.C.R. 1010—§§ 28:9, 28:19, 28:22
Delgamuukw v. British Columbia, [1997] 3 S.C.R. 1010—§§ 28:3, 28:20, 28:21, 28:34
Delisle v. Can., [1999] 2 S.C.R. 989—§ 55:18
Delisle v. Canada, [1999] 2 S.C.R. 989—§§ 44:4, 44:5, 55:50
Derrickson v. Derrickson, [1986] 1 S.C.R. 285—§§ 15:15, 28:9, 28:13, 28:14
Dersch v. Can., [1990] 2 S.C.R. 1505—§ 47:34
De Savoye v. Morguard Investments, [1990] 3 S.C.R. 1077—§ 15:28
Desgagnés Transport v. Wärtsilä Canada, 2019 SCC 58—§§ 15:5, 15:7, 15:9, 15:18, 15:20, 16:1, 16:3, 22:12

DesRochers v. Can., [2009] 1 S.C.R. 194—§§ 56:11, 56:12
DesRochers v. Canada, [2009] 1 S.C.R. 194—§ 56:15
Devine v. Que., [1988] 2 S.C.R. 790—§§ 12:10, 15:14, 18:20, 38:14, 38:20, 43:3, 43:22, 56:2
Devine v. Quebec, [1988] 2 S.C.R. 790—§§ 43:17, 56:2, 56:16
Dick v. The Queen, [1985] 2 S.C.R. 309—§§ 14:14, 16:6, 28:7, 28:8, 28:9, 28:14, 28:15
Dickason v. U. of Alta., [1992] 2 S.C.R. 1003—§ 55:44
Di Iorio v. Montreal Jail Warden, [1978] 1 S.C.R. 152—§ 18:15
Direct Lumber Co. v. Western Plywood Co., [1962] S.C.R. 646, 649—§ 18:18
Disallowance and Reservation of Provincial Legislation, Re, [1938] S.C.R. 71—§ 1:10
Divito v. Can., [2013] 3 S.C.R. 157, 2013 SCC 47—§§ 36:28, 38:17
Dixon v. British Columbia (1989) 60 D.L.R. (4th) 445, 448 (B.C.S.C.)—§ 40:4
Dixon v. British Columbia (1989), 59 D.L.R. (4th) 247 (B.C.S.C.)—§ 40:4
Dixon, Re (1986), 31 D.L.R. (4th) 546, 556-557 (B.C.S.C.)—§§ 1:4, 2:10
Dominion Stores v. The Queen, [1980] 1 S.C.R. 844—§§ 20:3, 20:4
Dominion Trade and Industry Comm. Act, [1936] S.C.R. 379—§ 18:11
Donald v. Hamilton Bd. of Education, [1945] O.R. 518 (C.A.)—§ 42:6
Doré v. Barreau du Québec, [2012] 1 S.C.R. 395—§§ 38:32, 40:26, 42:9
Doucet-Boudreau v. Nova Scotia, [2003] 3 S.C.R. 3—§§ 36:10, 40:16, 40:23, 56:19, 56:25
Doucet-Boudreau v. N.S., [2003] 3 S.C.R. 3—§ 36:19
Douglas v. Tucker, [1952] 1 S.C.R. 275—§ 43:28
Douglas/Kwantlen Faculty Assn. v. Douglas College, [1990] 3 S.C.R. 570—§§ 37:8, 37:10, 37:12, 37:13, 55:6, 55:44
Douglas/Kwantlen Faculty Association v. Douglas College, [1990] 3 S.C.R. 570—§ 40:26
Doyle v. Bell (1884), 11 O.A.R. 326 (C.A.)—§ 18:17
Dr. Bonham's Case (1610), 8 Co. Rep. 113, 118; 77 E.R. 646, 652 (K.B.)—§ 12:1
Dred Scott v. Sandford (1857), 60 U.S. (19 How.) 393—§ 36:5
Du-Lude v. Can. (2000), 192 D.L.R. (4th) 714 (F.C.A.)—§ 40:19
Dubois v. The Queen, [1985] 2 S.C.R. 350—§ 36:31
Duke v. The Queen, [1972] S.C.R. 917, 923—§ 47:14
Dunbar v. A.G. Sask. (1984), 11 D.L.R. (4th) 374 (Sask. Q.B.)—§ 6:9
Dunmore v. Ont., [2001] 3 S.C.R. 1016—§§ 40:5, 55:18
Dunmore v. Ontario, [2001] 3 S.C.R. 1016—§§ 37:7, 37:13, 38:20, 40:4, 44:4, 44:5, 55:50
Dunsmuir v. N.B., [2008] 1 S.C.R. 190—§§ 7:20, 40:26
Dywidag Systems v. Zutphen Bros., [1990] 1 S.C.R. 705—§§ 7:11, 37:2, 37:3, 47:4, 47:10

Eaton v. Brant County Bd. of Ed., [1997] 1 S.C.R. 241—§ 55:19
Eaton v. Brant County Bd. of Education, [1997] 1 S.C.R. 241—§ 38:8
Eaton v. Brant County Board of Education, [1997] 1 S.C.R. 241—§§ 55:24, 55:30, 55:45
Edmonton Journal v. Alberta, [1989] 2 S.C.R. 1326—§ 43:32
Edmonton Journal v. Alta., [1989] 2 S.C.R. 1326—§§ 37:2, 38:20, 43:12, 43:33
Education Act (Ont.), Re (1984), 47 O.R. (2d) 1, 30 (C.A.)—§§ 56:19, 56:23
Edwards v. A.-G. Can., [1930] A.C. 124, 136—§§ 36:18, 36:19, 45:6

Edwards v. A.-G. Can., [1930] A.C. 114, 136—§ 15:27
Edwards v. Aguillard (1987), 482 U.S. 578—§ 42:8
EGALE v. Can. (2003), 225 D.L.R. (4th) 472 (B.C.C.A.)—§§ 55:18, 55:48
Egan v. Can., [1995] 2 S.C.R. 513, 620—§ 40:6
Egan v. Canada, [1995] 2 S.C.R. 513—§§ 55:17, 55:18, 55:19, 55:25, 55:27, 55:48
Egan v. Canada, [1995] 2 S.C.R. 418, 496—§ 55:27
Eldridge v. B.C., [1997] 3 S.C.R. 624—§§ 6:8, 32:1, 32:3, 32:5, 36:19, 36:20, 37:10, 38:4, 40:4, 55:19, 55:25, 55:30, 55:42
Eldridge v. British Columbia, [1997] 3 S.C.R. 624—§§ 32:4, 37:8, 55:6, 55:28, 55:29, 55:45
Electoral Boundaries Commission Act (Alta.), Re (1991), 86 D.L.R. (4th) 447 (Alta. C.A.)—§ 45:3
Elk v. The Queen, [1980] 2 S.C.R. 166—§ 28:17
Ell v. Alberta, [2003] 1 S.C.R. 857—§ 7:5
Ell v. Alta., [2003] 1 S.C.R. 857—§ 7:5
Ellen Street Estates v. Min. of Health, [1934] 1 K.B. 590, 597 (C.A.)—§ 12:9
Employment Division, Department of Human Resources of Oregon v. Smith (1990), 494 U.S. 872—§ 42:4
Employment Division, Dept. of Human Resources of Oregon v. Smith (1990), 494 U.S. 872—§ 42:6
Employment Insurance Act, Re, [2005] 2 S.C.R. 669—§ 15:27
Endean v. B.C, [2016] 2 S.C.R. 163—§ 28:39
Engel v. Vitale (1962), 370 U.S. 421—§§ 36:5, 42:8
Entick v. Carrington (1765), 19 St. Tr. 1030, 95 E.R. 807 (K.B.)—§§ 1:9, 34:2
Entreprises M.G. de Guy Ltée v. Que., [1996] R.J.Q. 258 (Que. C.A.)—§ 47:9
Environmental Management Act, Re (2019), 434 D.L.R. (4th) 213 (B.C.C.A.), affd. 2020 SCC 1—§ 22:11
Epilepsy Can. v. Alta. (1994), 115 D.L.R. (4th) 501 (Alta. C.A.)—§ 43:12
Erie Railroad Co. v. Tompkins (1938), 304 U.S. 64—§ 8:5
Ermineskin Indian Band and Nation v. Can., [2009] 1 S.C.R. 222—§ 28:26
Ermineskin Indian Band and Nation v. Canada, [2009] 1 S.C.R. 222—§§ 28:5, 55:22, 55:26, 55:34
Ernst v. Alberta Energy Regulator, [2017] 1 S.C.R. 3, 2017 SCC 1—§ 40:19
Escobedo v. Illinois (1964), 378 U.S. 478—§ 36:5
Eskimos, Re, [1939] S.C.R. 104—§§ 28:2, 37:4
Esso Standard v. J.W. Enterprises, [1963] S.C.R. 144—§ 21:16
E.T. v. Hamilton-Wentworth District School Board (2017), 140 O.R. (3d) 11—§ 38:32
Eurig Estate, Re, [1998] 2 S.C.R. 565—§§ 4:19, 14:5, 40:4
Ewert v. Canada, [2018] 2 S.C.R. 165—§§ 47:15, 47:24, 47:26, 55:24
Exported Natural Gas Tax, Re, [1982] 1 S.C.R. 1004—§§ 8:9, 15:7, 16:1

Farm Products Marketing Act, Re, [1957] S.C.R. 198—§§ 8:13, 20:1, 21:14
Fawcett v. A.-G. Ont., [1964] S.C.R. 625—§ 18:4
Federation des producteurs v. Pelland, [2005] 1 S.C.R. 292—§§ 14:13, 20:3, 21:14
Felipa v. Can., [2012] 1 F.C.R. 3 (C.A.)—§ 7:14
Felipa v. Minister of Citizenship and Immigration, 2010 FC 89 (Lufty C.J.)—§ 7:14
ference re Dominion Trade and Industry Comm. Act, Re, [1936] S.C.R. 379—§ 18:19

ference re Legislative Jurisdiction over Hours of Labour, Re, [1925] S.C.R. 505—§ 18:13
Ferguson Bus Lines v. ATU, [1990] 2 F.C. 586 (C.A.)—§ 22:11
Field Aviation Co. v. Indust. Relations Bd. (Alta.), [1974] 6 W.W.R. 596 (Alta. A.D.)—§ 22:14
Fielding v. Thomas, [1896] A.C. 600—§§ 1:7, 4:19
50478 Ont., Re (1986), 56 O.R. (2d) 781 (H.C.)—§ 21:11
Figueroa v. Can., [2003] 1 S.C.R. 912—§ 38:17
Figueroa v. Canada, [2003] 1 S.C.R. 912—§§ 40:4, 45:4
Filip v. Waterloo (1992), 98 D.L.R. (4th) 534 (Ont. C.A.)—§ 55:18
Finlay v. Canada, [1986] 2 S.C.R. 607—§ 6:8
Firearms Act, Re, [2000] 1 S.C.R. 783—§§ 15:5, 15:10, 15:13, 18:14, 18:15, 18:19, 21:17
First Nat. Bank of Boston v. Bellotti (1978), 435 U.S. 765—§ 37:2
First Nation of Nacho Nyak Dun v. Yukon, [2017] 2 S.C.R. 576, 2017 SCC 58—§ 28:26
Fitzgerald v. Muldoon, [1976] 2 N.Z.L.R. 615 (N.Z. S.C.)—§ 34:2
Fleming v. Atkinson, [1959] S.C.R. 513—§ 2:2
Fletcher v. Peck (1810), 10 U.S. 87, 135—§ 12:9
Flora v. Ont. (2008), 91 O.R. (3d) 412 (C.A.)—§§ 32:6, 47:12
Forbes v. A.-G. Man., [1937] A.C. 260, 274—§ 16:9
Ford v. Que., [1988] 2 S.C.R. 712—§§ 4:3, 34:4, 35:3, 36:8, 36:19, 38:6, 38:20, 39:2, 39:3, 43:8, 56:2
Ford v. Quebec, [1988] 2 S.C.R. 712—§§ 12:10, 39:2, 39:5, 39:6, 39:7, 43:17, 43:22, 43:24, 56:16
Forest, Re (1977), 77 D.L.R. (3d) 445, 458 (Man. C.A.)—§ 56:6
Forest Industries Flying Tankers, Re (1980), 108 D.L.R. (3d) 686 (B.C. C.A.)—§ 22:15
Fort Frances Pulp and Power Co. v. Man. Free Press Co., [1923] A.C. 695—§§ 17:8, 17:10, 17:12
Fort Massey Realties, Re (1982), 132 D.L.R. (3d) 516 (N.S.C.A.)—§ 7:19
Forum des maires de la Péninsule acadienne v. Can., [2005] 3 S.C.R. 906—§ 8:6
Four B Manufacturing v. United Garment Workers, [1980] 1 S.C.R. 1031—§§ 15:5, 15:20, 21:11, 28:7, 28:9
407 ETR Concession Co. v. Canada, [2015] 3 S.C.R. 397, 2015 SCC 52—§§ 16:3, 16:4
Fowler v. The Queen, [1980] 2 S.C.R. 213, 224, 226—§ 15:24
Francis v. The Queen, [1956] S.C.R. 618—§§ 28:6, 28:16
Frank v. Can., [2019] 1 S.C.R. 3—§§ 38:1, 38:12, 45:2
Frank v. Canada, 2019 SCC 1—§ 45:2
Frank v. The Queen, [1978] 1 S.C.R. 95—§ 28:17
Fraser v. Can., 2020 SCC 28—§§ 38:12, 55:18, 55:32
Fraser v. Canada, 2020 SCC 28—§§ 55:22, 55:28, 55:42
Fraser v. Canada (Attorney General), 2020 SCC 28—§ 55:31
Fraser v. Ont. (2006), 79 O.R. (3d) 219 (S.C.J.)—§ 44:5
Fraser v. Public Service Staff Relations Bd., [1985] 2 S.C.R. 455, 462-463—§ 34:7
Fraser v. Public Service Staff Relations Bd., [1985] 2 S.C.R. 455, 462-463—§ 34:7
Freedom of Informed Choice (Abortions) Act, Re (1985), 25 D.L.R. (4th) 751 (Sask. C.A.)—§ 18:8

French in Criminal Proceedings, Re (1987), 44 D.L.R. (4th) 16 (Sask. C.A.)—§ 55:49
Friends of Oldman River Society v. Can., [1992] 1 S.C.R. 3—§§ 15:15, 17:2, 17:5, 18:6, 32:1
Friends of the Can. Wheat Bd. v. Can. (2008), 373 N.R. 385 (F.C.A.)—§ 12:10
Fulton v. Energy Resources Conservation Bd., [1981] 1 S.C.R. 153, 162, 164—§§ 15:23, 22:11
Furman v. Georgia (19972), 408 U.S. 238—§ 36:5

Gallant v. The King, [1949] 2 D.L.R. 425 (P.E.I. S.C.)—§ 12:10
Gamble, Re, [1988] 2 S.C.R. 595—§ 40:18
Gay Alliance Toward Equality v. Vancouver Sun, [1979] 2 S.C.R. 435, 455—§ 43:4
Gehl v. Can. (2017), 138 O.R. (3d) 52—§ 38:32
General Motors v. City National Leasing, [1989] 1 S.C.R. 641, 670—§§ 15:24, 17:5, 18:11, 18:17, 18:18, 20:2, 20:4, 21:16
Genetic Non-Discrimination Act, Re, 2020 SCC 17—§§ 18:2, 18:10
Gibbons v. Ogden (1824), 9 Wheat. (22 U.S.) 1—§ 22:1
Gideon v. Wainwright (1963), 372 U.S. 335—§ 36:5
Gillespie v. Gillespie (1973), 36 D.L.R. (3d) 421 (N.B. C.A.)—§ 16:3
Global Securities Corp. v. B.C., [2000] 1 S.C.R. 494—§§ 15:24, 21:9, 21:15
Globe & Mail v. Boland, [1960] S.C.R. 203—§ 43:28
Globe and Mail v. Can., [2010] 2 S.C.R. 592—§§ 43:19, 43:32
Godbout v. Longueuil, [1997] 3 S.C.R. 844—§§ 34:4, 37:8, 37:24, 47:9
Gold Seal v. A.-G. Alta. (1921), 62 S.C.R. 424—§ 20:3
Gold Seal v. Alberta (1921), 62 S.C.R. 424—§ 8:13
Gold Seal v. Dom. Express Co. (1921), 62 S.C.R. 424—§ 17:4
Gold Seal v. Dominion Express Co. (1921), 62 S.C.R. 424—§ 14:17
Gold Seal Ltd. v. Dominion Express Co. (1921), 62 S.C.R. 424—§ 20:2
Gonzales v. O Centro Espirita Beneficente Uniao do Vegetal (2006), 546 U.S. 418—§ 42:4
Gonzales v. Raich (2005), 545 U.S. 1—§§ 20:1, 47:15
Good Spirit School Division No. 204 v. Christ The Teacher Roman Catholic Separate School Division No. 212, [2017] 9 W.W.R. 673, 2017 SKQB 109 (Sask. Q.B.)—§ 39:2
Goodwin v. British Columbia, [2015] 3 S.C.R. 250, 2015 SCC 46—§ 18:20
Goodyear Tire and Rubber Co. v. The Queen, [1956] S.C.R. 303—§§ 18:2, 18:11, 18:15, 18:18
Gosselin v. Que., [2005] 1 S.C.R. 238—§§ 55:18, 55:38, 56:22
Gosselin v. Que., [2002] 4 S.C.R. 429, paras. 338-343—§§ 47:2, 47:10, 47:12, 55:20
Gosselin v. Quebec, [2002] 4 S.C.R. 429—§§ 55:21, 55:44
Grand Trunk Ry. v. A.G. Can., [1907] A.C. 65, 68—§ 15:24
Grand Trunk Ry. Co. v. A.-G. Can., [1907] A.C. 65—§ 18:17
Granovsky v. Can., [2000] 1 S.C.R. 2003—§ 55:20
Granovsky v. Canada, [2000] 1 S.C.R. 703—§ 55:45
Grant v. Torstar Corp., [2009] 3 S.C.R. 640—§§ 37:12, 38:31, 43:28
Grassy Narrows First Nation v. Ont., [2014] 2 S.C.R. 447, 2014 SCC 48—§§ 28:22, 28:35, 28:38
Grassy Narrows First Nation v. Ontario, [2014] 2 S.C.R. 447, 2014 SCC 48—§ 28:16

Gratton v. Can., [1994] 2 F.C. 769 (T.D.)—§ 7:3
Gray, Re (1918), 57 S.C.R. 150—§ 14:4
Greater Montreal Protestant School Bd. v. Que., [1989] 1 S.C.R. 377, 401—§ 34:5
Greater New Orleans Broadcasting Assn. v. U.S. (1999), 527 U.S. 173—§§ 43:6, 43:23
Greater Toronto Airports Authority v. Mississauga (2000), 50 O.R. (3d) 641 (C.A.)—§§ 15:18, 22:13, 22:15
Greater Vancouver Transportation Authority v. Canadian Federation of Students, [2009] 2 S.C.R. 295—§§ 38:7, 43:30
Greater Vancouver Transportation Authority v. Can. Federation of Students, [2009] 2 S.C.R. 295—§§ 37:8, 38:7, 40:1, 40:13, 43:40
Greater Vancouver Transportation Authority v. Cdn. Federation of Students, [2009] 2 S.C.R. 295—§ 38:18
Great West Saddlery v. The King, [1921] 2 A.C. 91—§ 15:17
Green v. U.S. (1958), 356 U.S. 165, 195—§ 8:13
Greer v. C.P.R. (1915), 51 S.C.R. 338—§ 18:17
Gregory & Co. v. Imperial Bank, [1960] C.S. 204 (Que. S.C.)—§ 21:15
Gregory & Co. v. Que. Securities Comm., [1961] S.C.R. 584—§ 21:15
Gregory Co. v. Imperial Bank, [1960] C.S. 204 (Que. S.C.)—§ 15:6
Groyned v. City of Rockford (1972), 408 U.S. 104, 108-109—§ 38:9
Grutter v. Bollinger (2003), 539 U.S. 306—§ 55:3
GST, Re, [1992] 3 S.C.R. 445—§ 15:24
GST, Re, [1992] 2 S.C.R. 445, 485-486—§ 8:11
Guergis v. Novak (2012), 112 O.R. (3d) 118 (S.C.J.)—§§ 1:9, 9:21
Guerin v. R., [1984] 2 S.C.R. 335—§ 28:21
Guerin v. The Queen, [1984] 2 S.C.R. 335—§§ 28:18, 28:19, 28:21
Guimond v. Que. [1996] 3 S.C.R. 347—§ 40:19
Gulf Oil Corp. v. Gulf Canada, [1980] 2 S.C.R. 39—§§ 8:8, 8:10

Haida Nation v. B.C., [2004] 3 S.C.R. 511—§§ 28:38, 40:26
Haig v. Can., [1993] 2 S.C.R. 995—§§ 45:2, 55:27
Haig v. Can. (1992), 9 O.R. (3d) 495 (C.A.)—§§ 40:6, 55:48
Haig v. Canada, [1993] 2 S.C.R. 995—§§ 43:39, 43:40, 55:49
Hak v. Que., 2019 QCCS 2989—§ 39:2
Halpern v. Can. (2003), 225 D.L.R. (4th) 529 (Ont. C.A.)—§§ 55:18, 55:48
Hamilton v. Al Fayed, [2000] 2 All E.R. 224 (H.L.)—§ 1:7
Hamilton Harbour Commrs. v. City of Hamilton (1978), 21 O.R. (2d) 459 (Ont. C.A.)—§§ 15:18, 22:12
Harper v. Can., [2004] 1 S.C.R. 827—§§ 22:18, 36:8, 36:9, 38:19, 43:7, 43:12, 47:28
Harper v. Canada, [2004] 1 S.C.R. 827—§§ 43:38, 45:4
Harris v. Min. of Interior, [1952] 2 S.A.L.R. (A.D.) 428—§ 12:10
Harrison v. U.B.C., [1990] 3 S.C.R. 451—§ 55:44
Hartling v. Nova Scotia (2009), 314 D.L.R. (4th) 114 (N.S. C.A.)—§ 55:45
Harvey v. N.B., [1996] 2 S.C.R. 876—§§ 1:7, 37:7, 56:3
Harvey v. New Brunswick, [1996] 2 S.C.R. 876—§§ 37:15, 38:21, 45:6
Hawley v. Bapoo (2005), 76 O.R. (3d) 649 (Ont. S.C.J.)—§ 40:19
Health Services and Support—Facilities Subsector Bargaining Assn. v. B.C., [2007] 2 S.C.R. 391—§§ 1:4, 8:13, 36:28, 38:17, 40:4, 44:4, 44:5, 44:7, 47:10, 55:28, 55:50

Health Services and Support—Facilities Subsector Bargaining Assn. v. B.C., [2007] 2S.C.R. 391—§ 37:8
Hellens v. Densmore, [1957] S.C.R. 768, 784; Re Broddy (1982), 142 D.L.R. (3d) 151, 157 (Alta. C.A.)—§ 16:1
Heller v. Doe (1993), 509 U.S. 312—§ 55:3
Hendricks v. Can. (2004), 238 D.L.R. (4th) 577 (Que. C.A.)—§ 55:48
Hendricks v. Que., [2002] R.J.Q. 2506 (Que. Sup. Ct.)—§ 55:48
Henry v. B.C., [2015] 2 S.C.R. 214, 2015 SCC 24—§ 36:28
Henry v. British Columbia, [2015] 2 S.C.R. 214, 2015 SCC 24—§ 40:19
Henry Birks & Sons v. Montreal, [1955] S.C.R. 799—§§ 14:17, 18:12
Hernandez v. Palmer, [1992] O.J. No. 2648 (Ont. Gen. Div.)—§ 55:45
Hill v. Church of Scientology, [1995] 2 S.C.R. 1130—§§ 36:19, 37:12, 38:20, 38:21, 38:31, 43:3, 43:28
Hislop v. Can. (2009), 95 O.R. (3d) 81 (C.A.)—§§ 16:1, 16:3
Hitzig v. Canada (2003), 231 D.L.R. (4th) 104 (Ont. C.A.), leave to appeal refused (2004) 112 C.R.R. (2d) 376(n) (S.C.C.)—§ 47:15
Hodge v. Canada, [2004] 3 S.C.R. 357—§§ 55:23, 55:47
Hodge v. The Queen (1883), 9 App. Cas. 117—§§ 5:11, 12:2, 14:3, 14:9, 14:10, 14:15, 15:7, 17:3
Hodge v. The Queen (1883) 9 App. Cas. 117, 132—§ 14:4
Hogan v. Newfoundland (2000), 183 D.L.R. (4th) 225 (Nfld. C.A.)—§§ 4:17, 43:38
Hogan v. Nfld. (2000), 183 D.L.R. (4th) 225 (Nfld. C.A.)—§§ 1:4, 4:7
Hogan v. The Queen, [1975] 2 S.C.R. 574, 579—§§ 35:3, 41:2
Home Insurance Co. v. Lindal and Beattie, [1934] S.C.R. 33, 40—§ 16:7
Home Oil Distributors v. A.-G. B.C., [1940] S.C.R. 444—§§ 21:8, 21:14
Hoogbruin, Re (1985), 24 D.L.R. (4th) 718 (B.C.C.A.)—§§ 40:17, 40:18, 45:2
Horn v. Lockhart (1873), 17 Wall. (84 U.S.) 570, 580—§ 5:26
Hours of Labour, Re, [1925] S.C.R. 505—§§ 21:10, 21:11
Hunt v. T & N, [1993] 4 S.C.R. 289—§§ 15:28, 17:1
Hunter v. Southam, [1984] 2 S.C.R. 145—§§ 15:14, 18:11, 36:8, 36:18, 36:19, 36:20, 37:2, 38:26, 40:5, 40:9, 47:14
Husky Oil Operations v. M.N.R., [1995] 3 S.C.R. 453—§§ 16:7, 16:10
Hyde v. Hyde (1866), L.R. 1 P.&D. 130, 133—§ 55:48

Ibralebbe v. The Queen, [1964] A.C. 900, 923—§ 17:1
Idziak v. Can., [1992] 3 S.C.R. 631—§§ 7:5, 47:38
IJ v. Canada, 2016 ONSC 3380—§ 40:4
Illinois v. Krull (1987), 480 U.S. 340—§§ 41:2, 41:11
Illinois v. Rodriguez (1990), 497 U.S. 177—§ 37:19
Illinois Elections Bd. v. Socialist Workers Party (1979), 440 U.S. 173, 188-189—§ 38:21
ILWU v. Can., [1994] 1 S.C.R. 150—§§ 44:5, 47:10
Imrie, Re, [1972] 3 O.R. 275 (H.C.)—§ 21:9
In Auton v. British Columbia, [2004] 3 S.C.R. 657—§ 55:23
Industrial Acceptance Corp. v. The Queen, [1953] 2 S.C.R. 273—§§ 17:6, 18:4, 18:18
Industrial Relations and Disputes Investigation Act, Re (Stevedores Reference) [1955] S.C.R. 529, esp. 535, 566, 582—§§ 15:15, 22:9, 22:12
Industrial Relations and Disputes Investigation Act (Can.), Re, [1955] S.C.R. 529—§§ 21:10, 21:11

Initiative and Referendum Act, Re, [1919] A.C. 935—§§ 4:19, 14:8, 14:9, 15:14, 34:7
Initiative and Referendum Reference (1916), 27 Man. R. 1 (Man. C.A.)—§ 14:9
In New Brunswick v. G. (J.), [1999] 3 S.C.R. 46—§ 38:22
In R. v. Glad Day Bookshops (2004), 70 O.R. (3d) 691 (S.C.J.)—§ 38:8
In R. v. Mills, [1999] 3 S.C.R. 668—§ 36:23
Insurance Act of Can., Re, [1932] A.C. 41—§§ 15:11, 21:6, 21:8, 21:18
Insurance Act of Canada, Re, [1932] A.C. 41—§ 15:14
Interprovincial Cooperatives v. The Queen, [1976] 1 S.C.R. 477—§ 16:1
Irwin Toy v. Que., [1989] 1 S.C.R. 927—§§ 18:5, 18:20, 21:21, 22:18, 22:23, 36:19, 37:2, 38:7, 38:8, 38:21, 43:3, 43:7, 43:8, 43:10, 43:14, 47:4, 47:10, 47:12, 47:13, 47:14
Irwin Toy v. Quebec, [1989] 1 S.C.R. 927, 953—§§ 15:11, 15:18, 16:5, 38:9, 38:12, 43:8, 43:23, 43:30
Irwin Toy Ltd. v. Que., [1989] 1 S.C.R. 927, 968—§ 43:8
Isen v. Simms, [2006] 2 S.C.R. 349—§ 22:12
ITO-International Terminal Operators v. Miida Electronics, [1986] 1 S.C.R. 752—§§ 7:11, 22:12

Jack v. ne Queen, [1980] 1 S.C.R. 294—§ 28:17
Jack v. The Queen, [1980] 1 S.C.R. 294—§ 5:4
Jack and Charlie v. The Queen, [1985] 2 S.C.R. 332, 338—§§ 28:4, 35:2
Jackson v. Ont. (2009), 2 Admin. L.R. (5th) 248 (Ont. C.A.)—§ 14:11
Jameel v. Wall Street Journal, [2007] 1 A.C. 359 (H.L.)—§ 43:28
James Doyle v. Anderson (1990), 71 D.L.R. (4th) 731 (Nfld. C.A.)—§ 40:24
Janssen-Ortho v. Amgen Can. (2005), 256 D.L.R. (4th) 407, paras. 73-78 (Ont. C.A.)—§ 1:7
Jodrey Estate v. Nova Scotia (1978), 29 N.S.R. (2d) 369, 370 (N.S. A.D.)—§ 8:6
Johannesson v. West St. Paul, [1952] 1 S.C.R. 292—§§ 15:5, 17:1, 17:2, 17:3, 17:4, 17:12, 22:13, 22:14, 22:15
John Deere Plow Co. v. Wharton, [1915] A.C. 330—§§ 15:17, 20:4
Johnson v. A.-G. Alta., [1954] S.C.R. 127, 136–138—§§ 16:7, 18:20, 21:17, 34:6
Johnson v. Zerbst (1938), 404 U.S. 458, 464—§ 37:15
Jones v. A.-G. N.B., [1975] 2 S.C.R. 182, 195—§§ 12:2, 17:2
Jones v. A.G. N.B., [1975] 2 S.C.R. 182—§ 56:4
Jones v. Attorney General of New Brunswick, [1975] 2 S.C.R. 182—§ 56:2
Jones v. Bennett, [1969] S.C.R. 277—§ 43:28
Jones v. Edmonton Catholic School Trustees, [1977] S.C.R. 872—§ 7:19
Jones and Maheux v. Gamache, [1969] S.C.R. 119—§ 56:3
Jorgensen v. A.-G. Can., [1971] S.C.R. 725—§ 22:10
Jorgenson v. A.-G. Can., [1971] S.C.R. 725—§§ 20:2, 22:10
Jorgenson v. North Vancouver Magistrates (1959), 28 W.W.R. 265 (B.C.C.A.)—§ 22:14
Joyal v. Air Can., [1982] C.A. 39 (Que. C.A.)—§ 56:14
Judicature Amendment Act, 1970 (No. 4), Re, [1971] 2 O.R. 521 (C.A.)—§ 7:17
Judiciary and Navigation Act, Re (1921), 29 C.L.R. 257—§ 8:10

Kahkewistahaw First Nation v. Taypotat, [2015] 2 S.C.R. 548, 2015 SCC 30—§§ 55:22, 55:28, 55:49
Katz v. United States (1967), 389 U.S. 347—§ 36:18

Kazemi Estate v. Islamic Republic of Iran, [2014] 3 S.C.R. 176, 2014 SCC 62—§§ 35:3, 35:7, 35:8, 37:14, 47:15, 47:38
Keizer v. Hanna, [1978] 2 S.C.R. 342, 347—§ 8:13
Khadr v. Canada (2008), 331 F.T.R. 1 (F.C.)—§ 37:14
Kienapple v. The Queen, [1975] 1 S.C.R. 729—§ 16:8
Kindler v. Can., [1991] 2 S.C.R. 779, 832—§§ 37:14, 47:15
Kindler v. Canada, [1991] 2 S.C.R. 779—§ 37:14
Kingstreet Investments v. N.B., [2007] 1 S.C.R. 3—§ 40:19
Kingstreet Investments v. New Brunswick, [2007] 1 S.C.R. 3—§ 40:25
Kirkbi v. Ritvik Holdings, [2005] 3 S.C.R. 302—§§ 15:24, 18:17, 20:4
Kitkatla Band v. B.C., [2002] 2 S.C.R. 146—§§ 15:5, 15:9, 15:24, 17:5, 28:8
Kitkatla Band v. British Columbia, [2002] 2 S.C.R. 146—§§ 21:19, 28:9
Kleinys, Ex parte (1965), 49 D.L.R. (2d) 225 (B.C. S.C.)—§ 14:16
Knopf v. Canada, [2008] 2 F.C.R. 327 (C.A.)—§ 56:15
Knox Contracting v. Can., [1990] 2 S.C.R. 338, 360—§§ 7:1, 18:1, 18:2
Knox Contracting v. Canada, [1990] 2 S.C.R. 338—§ 40:24
Kootenay and Elk Ry. v. CPR, [1974] S.C.R. 955, 980, 982—§ 22:8
Korematsu v. United States (1944), 323 U.S. 214—§ 55:3
Korponay v. Can., [1982] 1 S.C.R. 41, 49—§ 37:15
Koumoudouros, Re (1984), 45 O.R. (2d) 426 (Div. Ct.)—§ 36:19
Kourtessis v. Minister of National Revenue, [1993] 2 S.C.R. 53—§ 40:24
Kourtessis v. M.N.R., [1993] 2 S.C.R. 53—§§ 7:1, 18:1, 40:24
Krieger v. Law Society of Alberta, [2002] 3 S.C.R. 372—§§ 7:6, 15:7, 21:9, 47:34
Kruger and Manuel v. The Queen, [1978] 1 S.C.R. 104, 110—§§ 28:9, 28:14
Ktunaxa Nation v. British Columbia, [2017] 2 S.C.R. 386, 2017 SCC 54—§ 28:19
Kungl v. Schiefer, [1962] S.C.R. 443, 448—§ 2:2
Kuruma v. The Queen, [1955] A.C. 197 (P.C.)—§ 41:2

Labatt Breweries v. A.-G. Can., [1980] 1 S.C.R. 914—§§ 4:11, 17:4, 18:3, 20:3, 20:4, 34:6
Labour Rels. Bd. (Sask.) v. John East Ironworks, [1949] A.C. 134—§ 7:19
Ladore v. Bennett, [1939] A.C. 468—§ 15:5
Lagiorgia v. Can., [1987] 3 F.C. 28 (C.A.)—§ 40:17
Lake v. Can., [2008] 1 S.C.R. 761—§ 37:14
Lalonde v. Ont. (2002), 56 O.R. (3d) 505 (C.A.)—§§ 15:28, 56:14
Lamb v. Benoit, [1959] S.C.R. 321—§ 34:2
Lamb v. Lamb, [1985] 1 S.C.R. 851—§ 16:9
Lauzon v. The Queen, CMAC-415; (1998) 230 N.R. 272 (Ct. Martial Appeal Court)—§ 7:6
Lavallee v. Alta. (2010), 317 D.L.R. (4th) 373, paras. 26-29 (Alta. C.A.)—§ 47:12
Lavell v. A.-G. Can., [1974] S.C.R. 1349, 1364-1365—§ 35:3
Lavigne v. OPSEU, [1991] 2 S.C.R. 211—§§ 37:8, 37:10, 43:16, 43:38, 44:8
Lavigne v. OPSEU, [1991] 1 S.C.R. 211—§ 37:12
Lavoie v. Can., [2002] 1 S.C.R. 769—§§ 8:3, 55:18, 55:20, 55:31
Lavoie v. Canada, [2002] 1 S.C.R. 769—§§ 55:18, 55:37, 55:46
Lavuie v. Can., [2002] 1 S.C.R. 769—§ 55:31
Law v. Can., [1999] 1 S.C.R. 497—§§ 55:21, 55:32, 55:47
Law v. Canada, [1999] 1 S.C.R. 497—§§ 55:17, 55:20, 55:21, 55:23, 55:25, 55:27, 55:44

Law Society of B.C. v. Mangat, [2001] 3 S.C.R. 113—§§ 15:7, 16:4, 16:5, 21:9
Law Society of British Columbia v. Trinity Western University, [2018] 2 S.C.R. 293—§§ 37:2, 38:32, 42:9
Law Society of Upper Can. v. Skapinker, [1984] 1 S.C.R. 375, 365-366—§ 36:18
Law Society of Upper Can. v. Skapinker, [1984] 1 S.C.R. 357—§ 36:20
Law Society of Upper Can. v. Spakinker, [1984] 1 S.C.R. 357, 370—§ 36:20
Lax Kw'alaams Indian Band v. Can., [2011] 3 S.C.R. 535—§ 28:19
Lehnert v. Ferris Faculty Assn. (1991), 111 S. Ct. 1950—§ 44:8
Leighton v. B.C. (1989), 57 D.L.R. (4th) 657 (B.C.C.A.)—§ 28:8
Letter Carriers' Union v. Can. Union of Postal Wkrs., [1975] 1 S.C.R. 178—§ 21:11
Letter Carriers' Union of Can. v. Can. Union of Postal Wkrs., [1975] 1 S.C.R. 178—§ 21:11
Letter Carriers' Union of Can. v. Can. Union of Postal Workers, [1975] 1 S.C.R. 178—§§ 15:19, 22:9, 22:11
Lévis v. Fraternité des policiers de Lévis, [2007] 1 S.C.R. 591—§ 16:1
Levis v. Tétreault, [2006] 1 S.C.R. 420—§§ 47:16, 47:17, 47:18
Levkoe, Re (1977), 18 O.R. (2d) 265 (Div. Ct.)—§ 21:9
Libman v. Que., [1997] 3 S.C.R. 569—§§ 38:20, 43:7
Libman v. Quebec, [1997] 3 S.C.R. 569—§ 43:38
Lieberman v. The Queen, [1963] S.C.R. 643—§ 18:13
Liquidators of Maritime Bank v. Receiver General of N.B., [1892] A.C. 437—§ 9:3
Liquidators of the Maritime Bank v. Receiver General of N.B., [1892] A.C. 437—§ 5:11
Little Sisters Book & Art Emporium v. Can., [2000] 2 S.C.R. 1120—§§ 36:8, 38:7, 55:28
Little Sisters Book and Art Emporium v. Canada, [2000] 2 S.C.R. 1120—§§ 38:7, 43:13, 43:29, 55:6, 55:18, 55:48
Liversidge v. Anderson, [1942] A.C. 206 (H.L.)—§ 1:11
Lochner v. New York (1905), 198 U.S. 45, 76—§§ 5:21, 8:13, 36:5, 47:10, 47:14
London (City) v. Polewsky (2005), 202 C.C.C. (3d) 257, para. 4 (Ont. C.A.)—§ 47:9
London Drugs v. Red Deer (1988), 52 D.L.R. (4th) 203 (Alta C.A.)—§ 42:5
London Street Tramways Co. v. London County Council, [1898] A.C. 375 (H.L.)—§ 8:13
Lord's Day Alliance v. A.-G. B.C., [1959] S.C.R.497—§ 18:19
Lord's Day Alliance v. A.-G. Man., [1925] A.C. 384—§ 14:17
Lord's Day Alliance of Can. v. A.-G. B.C., [1959] S.C.R. 497—§§ 16:6, 17:4, 34:7
Lord's Day Alliance of Canada v. A.-G. B.C., [1959] S.C.R. 497—§§ 14:17, 18:12
Lorillard Tobacco Co. v. Mass. (2001), 533 U.S. 525—§§ 43:6, 43:23
Lovelace v. Can. (1983), 1 Can. Human Rights Yearbook 305—§ 28:2
Lovelace v. Ont., [2001] 1 S.C.R. 950—§ 55:32
Lovelace v. Ont., [2000] 1 S.C.R. 950—§§ 6:9, 55:39
Lovelace v. Ontario, [2000] 1 S.C.R. 950—§§ 28:5, 28:9, 55:6
Lovibond v. Grand Trunk Ry. Co., [1939] O.R. 305 (Ont. C.A.)—§ 17:11
Lower Mainland Dairy Products v. Crystal Dairy, [1933] A.C. 168—§ 8:13
Lowry and Lepper v. The Queen, [1974] S.C.R. 195—§§ 35:3, 35:8
Loyola High School v. Quebec, [2015] 1 S.C.R. 613, 2015 SCC 12—§§ 36:28, 38:32
Loyola High School v. Quebec, 2015 SCC 12—§ 42:9

Luscar Collieries v. McDonald, [1972] A.C. 925—§ 22:11
Luscar Collieries v. McDonald, [1927] A.C. 925—§ 22:8
Luscher v. Deputy Minr., Revenue Can., [1985] 1 F.C. 85 (C.A.)—§ 38:9
Luscher v. Revenue Can., [1985] 1 F.C. 85 (C.A.)—§§ 43:13, 43:29
Lymburn v. Mayland, [1932] A.C. 318—§§ 15:5, 15:17, 21:15

M. v. H., [1999] 2 S.C.R. 203—§§ 55:18, 55:20
M. v. H., [1999] 2 S.C.R. 3—§§ 36:8, 40:4, 55:47, 55:48
M.(A.) v. Ryan, [1997] 1 S.C.R. 157—§§ 37:12, 47:35
MacBain v. Lederman, [1985] 1 F.C. 856 (C.A.)—§§ 12:10, 34:4, 35:3, 35:5, 35:7, 35:8, 47:13, 47:38
MacDonald v. City of Montreal, [1986] 1 S.C.R. 460, 496—§§ 56:4, 56:11, 56:14
MacDonald v. Vapor Can., [1977] 2 S.C.R. 134—§§ 15:14, 17:10, 20:4
MacDonald v. Vapor Canada, [1977] 2 S.C.R. 134—§§ 18:17, 18:18, 20:4
Mack v. Can. (2002), 60 O.R. (3d) 737 (C.A.)—§ 40:10
Mack v. Canada (2002), 60 O.R. (3d) 737 (C.A.)—§ 36:31
MacKay v. Man., [1989] 2 S.C.R. 357—§ 43:38
MacKay v. Russell (2007), 284 D.L.R. (4th) 528 (N.B. C.A.)—§ 22:12
MacKay v. The Queen, [1980] 2 S.C.R. 370—§ 55:2
MacKeigan v. Hickman, [1989] 2 S.C.R. 796—§ 7:3
Mackin v. N.B., [2002] 1 S.C.R. 405—§§ 15:14, 36:16, 36:22, 40:19
Mackin v. New Brunswick, [2002] 1 S.C.R. 405—§§ 7:5, 7:8, 15:28, 38:28
MacLean v. A.G.N.S. (1987), 35 D.L.R. (4th) 306 (N.S.S.C.)—§§ 1:4, 4:7, 45:6
MacMillan Bloedel, [1995] 4 S.C.R. 725—§ 7:19
MacMillan Bloedel v. Simpson, [1995] 4 S.C.R. 725—§§ 7:15, 7:16, 7:18, 7:19, 7:20
Madzimbamuto v. Lardner-Burke, [1969] 1 A.C. 645 (P.C., So. Rhodesia)—§§ 1:10, 5:26
Mahe v. Alberta, [1990] 1 S.C.R. 342, 379—§§ 56:19, 56:23, 56:24
Mahe v. Alta., [1990] 1 S.C.R. 342, 369—§§ 55:38, 56:3
Man. v. Metropolitan Stores, [1987] 1 S.C.R. 110, 121-125—§ 38:5
M & D Farm v. Man. Agricultural Credit Corp., [1998] 1 S.C.R. 1074—§ 8:5
M & D Farm v. Manitoba Agricultural Credit Corporation, [1999] 2 S.C.R. 961—§ 16:3
Man. Govt. Employees Assn v. Govt. of Man., [1978] 1 S.C.R. 1123—§ 34:2
Manitoba Language Rights, Re, [1985] 1 S.C.R. 721, 746—§§ 3:4, 8:11, 12:10, 14:8, 40:4, 56:6, 56:8
Manitoba Language Rights Order No. 1, Re, [1985] 2 S.C.R. 347—§ 56:6
Manitoba Language Rights Order No. 3, Re, [1992] 1 S.C.R. 212—§§ 56:6, 56:7, 56:8
Manitoba Language Rights Order No. 2, Re, [1990] 3 S.C.R. 1417—§ 56:6
Manitoba Métis Federation v. Can., [2013] 1 S.C.R. 623, 2013 SCC 14—§ 28:40
Man. Language Rights, Re, [1985] 1 S.C.R. 721, 740–743—§ 12:10
Mann v. The Queen, [1966] S.C.R. 238—§§ 15:7, 16:5, 16:7, 18:20, 22:11
Manuel v. A.-G., [1982] 3 W.L.R. 821 (Eng. C.A.)—§ 3:8
Mapp v. Ohio (1961), 367 U.S. 643—§§ 36:5, 41:2
Marbury v. Madison (1803), 5 U.S. (1 Cranch) 137—§§ 5:20, 8:10, 36:4
Margarine Reference, Can. Federation of Agriculture v. A.G. Que., [1951] A.C. 179—§ 38:16
Marine Services International v. Ryan Estate, [2013] 3 S.C.R. 53, 2013 SCC 44—§§ 15:18, 15:20, 16:3, 22:12

Marine Services International Ltd. v. Ryan Estate, [2013] 3 S.C.R. 53—§ 16:1
Marriage Commissioners, Re (2011), 327 D.L.R. (4th) 669 (Sask. C.A.)—§§ 42:11, 55:28, 55:48
Marshall v. The Queen, [1986] 1 F.C. 437, 449—§ 7:11
Martin v. Alta., [2014] 1 S.C.R. 546, 2014 SCC 25—§§ 14:11, 14:13
Martineau v. Matsqui Institution Inmate Disciplinary Bd., [1978] 1 S.C.R. 118—§ 38:7
Martineau & Sons v. Montreal, [1932] A.C. 113, 120—§ 7:2
Massachusetts v. Sheppard (1984), 468 U.S. 981—§ 41:11
Massachusetts Board of Retirement v. Murgia (1976), 427 U.S. 307—§ 55:3
Masse v. Ont. (1996), 134 D.L.R. (4th) 20 (Ont. Div. Ct.)—§ 47:12
Massey-Ferguson Industries v. Govt. of Sask., [1981] 2 S.C.R. 413, 429—§ 7:19
May v. Ferndale Institution, [2005] 3 S.C.R. 809—§ 47:9
Mazraani v. Industrial Alliance Insurance, 2018 SCC 50—§ 56:13
McAteer v. Canada (2014), 121 O.R. (3d) 1, 2014 ONCA 578 (Ont. C.A.)—§ 43:16
McCloy v. New South Wales, [2015] HCA 34—§ 43:38
McCutcheon v. Federal Election Commn. (2014), 572 U.S. xxx—§ 43:38
McEvoy v. A.-G.N.B., [1983] 1 S.C.R. 704—§§ 7:14, 7:15, 7:16, 8:9, 8:11
McIvor v. Can. (2009), 306 D.L.R. (4th) 193 (B.C.C.A.)—§ 28:2
McKay v. Man., [1989] 2 S.C.R. 357—§ 43:16
McKay v. The Queen, [1980] 2 S.C.R. 370, 390—§ 17:8
McKay v. The Queen, [1965] S.C.R. 798—§§ 15:19, 15:20
McKinney v. University of Guelph, [1990] 3 S.C.R. 229—§§ 37:24, 55:7, 55:25, 55:44
McKinney v. U. of Guelph, [1990] 3 S.C.R. 229—§§ 37:8, 37:10, 37:13, 55:27, 55:44
McKinney v. U. of Guelph, [1990] 2 S.C.R. 229, 276-278—§ 55:6
McLean, Ex parte (1930), 43 C.L.R. 472, 483—§ 16:5
McLeod v. Egan, [1975] 1 S.C.R. 517—§ 40:26
McNamara Construction v. The Queen, [1977] 2 S.C.R. 655—§§ 7:11, 8:13
McNamara Construction v. The Queen, [1977] 2 S.C.R. 654, 664—§ 7:11
Medovarski v. Can., [2005] 2 S.C.R. 539—§§ 37:12, 47:9, 55:37
Meredith v. Canada, [2015] 1 S.C.R. 125, 2015 SCC 2—§ 44:5
Miazga v. Kvello Estate, [2009] 3 S.C.R. 339—§ 7:6
Mikisew Cree First Nation v. Can., [2018] 2 S.C.R. 765—§ 28:38
Mikisew Cree First Nation v. Can., [2005] 3 S.C.R. 388—§ 28:26
Mikisew Cree First Nation v. Canada, [2005] 3 S.C.R. 388—§ 28:38
Mi'kmaq of PEI v. PEI, 2019 PECA 26, paras. 42-43 (P.E.I.C.A.)—§ 40:26
Miller v. California (1973), 413 U.S. 15, 24—§ 43:29
Miller and Cockriell v. The Queen, [1977] 2 S.C.R. 680, 686—§ 35:3
Mills v. The Queen, [1986] 1 S.C.R. 863, 971—§§ 40:17, 40:24
Minimum Wage Act, Re (Sask.) [1948] S.C.R. 248—§ 8:8
Minimum Wage Act (Sask.), Re, [1948] S.C.R. 248—§§ 15:19, 15:20, 21:11
Minister of Justice v. Borowski, [1981] 2 S.C.R. 575—§ 40:14
Min. of Finance (B.C.) and Pacific Petroleums, Re (1979), 99 D.L.R. (3d) 491 (B.C. CA.)—§ 16:3
Min. of Home Affairs v. Fisher, [1980] A.C. 319, 328—§ 36:19
Min. of Indian Affairs v. Ranville, [1982] 2 S.C.R. 518, 527—§ 8:13
Min. of Revenue (Ont.) and Hala, Re (1977), 18 O.R. (2d) 88 (Ont. H.C.)—§ 21:18
Miranda v. Arizona (1966), 384 U.S. 436—§ 36:5

Mirhadizadeh v. Ont. (1989), 69 O.R. (2d) 422 (C.A.)—§ 55:18
Miron v. Trudel, [1995] 2 S.C.R. 418—§§ 37:8, 40:6, 55:18, 55:19, 55:24, 55:27, 55:47
Mirun v. Trudel, [1995] 2 S.C.R. 418—§ 55:17
Mississauga v. Peel, [1979] 2 S.C.R. 244—§ 7:19
Mitchell v. Minister of National Revenue, [2001] 1 S.C.R. 911—§ 28:19
Mitchell v. M.N.R., [2001] 1 S.C.R. 911—§ 28:20
Mitchell v. Peguis Indian Band, [1990] 2 S.C.R. 85, 108–109—§ 28:37
Mitchell and the Queen, Re (1983), 42 O.R. (2d) 481 (H.C.)—§ 36:31
MNR v. Creative Shoes, [1972] F.C. 1425, 1428 (C.A.)—§ 8:6
Montreal v. Arcade Amusements, [1985] 1 S.C.R. 368—§ 18:20
Montreal v. Montreal St. Ry., [1912] A.C. 333—§§ 22:1, 22:2, 22:4, 22:8, 22:10, 22:11, 22:13
Montreal v. 2952-136 Que., [2005] 3 S.C.R. 141—§ 38:7
Montreal v. 2952-1366 Que., [2005] 3 S.C.R. 141—§§ 37:12, 40:7, 40:9, 43:7, 43:30
Montréal (City) v. Quebec, [2008] 2 S.C.R. 698—§ 56:3
Moonen v. Film and Literature Board of Review, [2000] 2 N.Z.L.R. 9, 17 (C.A.)—§ 12:1
Moore v. B.C., [2012] 3 S.C.R. 360—§ 55:22
Moore v. Johnson, [1982] 1 S.C.R. 115—§ 16:1
Mooring v. Can., [1996] 1 S.C.R. 75—§ 40:16
Moosehunter v. The Queen, [1981] 1 S.C.R. 282—§§ 5:4, 28:17
Moreau-Bérubé v. N.B., [2002] 1 S.C.R. 249—§ 7:8
Morgan v. A.-G. P.E.I., [1976] 2 S.C.R. 349—§§ 21:18, 55:1
Morgentaler v. The Queen, [1976] 1 S.C.R. 616—§§ 18:8, 18:19
Morguard Investments v. De Savoye, [1990] 3 S.C.R. 1077, 1100—§§ 17:1, 47:13
Morrow v. Zhang (2009), 307 D.L.R. (4th) 678 (Alta. C.A.)—§ 55:45
Morse v. Frederick (2007), 551 U.S. 393—§ 43:6
Motard v. Can., 2019 QCCA 1826 (Que. C.A.)—§§ 3:1, 4:6, 4:16, 9:3
Motard v. Canada, 2019 QCCA 1826 (Que. C.A.), leave to appeal to the S.C.C. denied April 23, 2020—§ 1:4
Moulton Contracting v. B.C. (2015), 381 D.L.R. (4th) 263, 2015 BCCA 89,—§ 28:38
Mounted Police Assn. v. Can., [2015] 1 S.C.R. 3, 2015 SCC 1—§§ 8:13, 40:4, 44:4
Mounted Police Association v. Canada, [2015] 1 S.C.R. 3, 2015 SCC 1—§§ 38:18, 44:5
Mounted Police Association of Ontario v. Can., [2015] 1 S.C.R. 3—§§ 36:19, 36:20
Mouvement laïque québécois v. Saguenay, [2015] 2 S.C.R. 3, 2015 SCC 16—§§ 34:4, 42:3, 42:10
Muldoon v. Can., [1988] 3 F.C. 628 (T.D.)—§ 45:2
Multani v. Commission scolaire Marguerite-Bourgeoys, [2006] 1 S.C.R 256—§§ 38:32, 40:26, 42:6
Multiple Access v. McCutcheon, [1982] 2 S.C.R. 161, 181—§§ 15:7, 15:24, 16:3, 16:5, 16:7, 16:9, 18:17, 21:15, 21:16
Municipal Contracting v. IUOE (1989), 60 O.R. (4th) 323 (N.S.A.D.)—§ 55:50
Munro v. National Capital Comm., [1966] S.C.R. 663—§§ 15:5, 17:1, 17:12, 21:2
Munro v. National Capital Commission, [1966] S.C.R. 663—§§ 17:2, 17:3, 17:4, 17:12
Murphy v. CPR, [1958] S.C.R. 626, 643—§§ 12:2, 20:3, 21:13
Murray Hill Limousine Service v. Batson, [1965] B.R. 788 (Que. C.A.)—§ 22:14
Musqueam Indian Band v. B.C. (2005), 251 D.L.R. (4th) 717 (B.C.C.A.)—§ 28:38

NAACP v. Alabama (1958), 357 U.S. 449—§ 44:3
Nadan v. The King, [1926] A.C. 482—§ 3:3
Nadan v. The Queen, [1926] A.C. 482—§ 8:2
National Bank of Can. v. RCIU, [1984] 1 S.C.R. 269—§ 43:37
National Battlefields Commn. v. CTCUQ, [1990] 2 S.C.R. 838—§ 15:19
National Citizens' Coalition v. A.-G. Can. (1984), 11 D.L.R. (4th) 481 (Alta. Q.B.)—§ 43:38
National Energy Bd. Act, Re, [1988] 2 F.C. 196, 220 (C.A.)—§§ 22:3, 22:4, 22:9, 22:11
National Federation of Independent Businesses v. Sebelius (2012), 567 U.S. 519—§ 6:8
National Federation of Independent Businesses v. Sebelius (2012), 567 U.S. xxx—§ 20:1
National Freight Consultants v. Motor Transport Bd., [1980] 2 S.C.R. 621—§ 14:14
Native Women's Assn. of Can. v. Can., [1994] 3 S.C.R. 627—§ 55:41
Native Women's Assn. of Canada v. Canada, [1994] 3 S.C.R. 627—§ 43:40
Nat. Labour Relations Bd. v. Jones & Laughlin Steel Corp. (1937), 301 U.S. 1—§ 21:10
Natural Parents v. Superintendent of Child Welfare, [1976] 2 S.C.R. 751, 760–761—§§ 15:20, 28:7, 28:9
Natural Parents v. Superintendent of Child Welfare, [1967] 2 S.C.R. 751, 760–761—§ 28:9
Natural Products Marketing Act Reference, [1936] S.C.R. 398, 420—§ 17:3
Ndlwana v. Hofmeyr, [1937] A.D. 229, 237—§ 3:8
Néron v. Chambre des notaires du Québec, [2004] 3 S.C.R. 95—§§ 38:21, 43:3, 43:28
Néron v. Chambres des notaries du Québec, [2004] 3 S.C.R. 95—§ 43:28
Neskonlith Indian Band v. Salmon Arm, 2012 BCCA 379—§ 28:38
New Brunswick v. G.(J.), [1999] 3 S.C.R. 46—§§ 38:17, 38:25, 40:15, 40:17, 47:9, 47:12, 47:32, 47:38
New Brunswick Broadcasting Co. v. Nova Scotia, [1993] 1 S.C.R. 319—§§ 1:4, 1:7, 4:19, 37:7, 43:34
New Brunswick Broadcasting Co. v. N.S., [1993] 1 S.C.R. 319, 393-394—§ 1:7
New Brunswick Broadcasting Co. v. N.S., [1993] 1 S.C.R. 319, 364—§ 1:7
New Brunswick Broadcasting Co. v. N.S, [1993] 1 S.C.R. 319, 396—§§ 1:4, 1:7, 34:7
Newfoundland v. N.A.P.E., [2004] 3 S.C.R. 381—§§ 38:17, 55:31, 55:41
Newfoundland and Labrador v. Uashaunnuat (Innu of Uashat and of Mani-Utenam), 2020 SCC 4—§ 28:39
New State Ice Co. v. Liebmann (1932), 285 U.S. 262, 311—§ 5:8
New York Times v. Sullivan (1963), 376 U.S. 254—§§ 37:12, 43:6, 43:28
Nfld. v. N.A.P.E., [2004] 3 S.C.R. 381—§§ 32:5, 38:4, 55:23, 55:43
Nfld. v. Uashaunnuat (Innu of Uashat and of Mani-Utenam), 2020 SCC 4—§ 7:11
Nfld. Continental Shelf, Re, [1984] S.C.R. 86, 127—§ 17:2
Nfld. Telephone Co. v. Nfld., [1992] 1 S.C.R. 623—§ 7:5
Ng Extradition, Re, [1991] 2 S.C.R. 858—§§ 37:14, 47:15
Nguyen v. Quebec, [2009] 3 S.C.R. 208—§§ 40:4, 56:22
NIL/TU,O Child and Family Services Society v. B.C.G.S.E.U., [2010] 2 S.C.R. 696—§§ 21:11, 28:7, 28:9

North American Co. v. SEC (1946), 327 U.S. 686—§ 20:4
Northern Telecom Can. v. Communications Workers (No. 1), [1980] 1 S.C.R. 115, 132—§ 22:9
Northern Telecom Can. v. Communications Workers of Can., [1983] 1 S.C.R. 733—§§ 7:11, 7:20, 22:9
Nova Scotia v. Martin, [2003] 2 S.C.R. 504—§§ 15:14, 28:9, 32:5, 36:16, 38:17, 40:4, 40:26, 40:28, 55:21, 55:23, 55:45
Nova Scotia v. Phillips (1986), 34 D.L.R. (4th) 633 (N.S.C.A.)—§ 40:6
Nova Scotia v. Walsh, [2002] 4 S.C.R. 325—§§ 55:18, 55:20, 55:21, 55:26, 55:47
Nova Scotia Board of Censors v. McNeil, [1978] 2 S.C.R. 662—§§ 18:19, 43:3
Nowegijick v. The Queen, [1983] 1 S.C.R. 29—§§ 28:2, 28:25, 28:26, 28:34
N.S. v. Judges of the Provincial Court and Family Court of Nova Scotia, 2020 SCC 21—§ 7:5
N.S. Bd. of Censors v. McNeil, [1978] 2 S.C.R. 662—§§ 14:7, 15:13, 15:14, 16:7, 18:15, 18:20, 21:4, 21:8, 21:17, 22:23, 22:25, 36:26
Nuva Scutia v. Walsh, [2002] 4 S.C.R. 325—§ 55:20
nvoi relatif à la réglementation pancanadienne des valeurs mobilières, Re, 2017 QCCA 756—§ 12:9
Nykorak v. A.-G. Can., [1962] S.C.R. 331—§ 18:17

Obergefell v. Hodges (2015), 576 U.S. xxx—§ 55:48
Objection by Que. to Resolution to Amend the Constitution, Re, [1982] 2 S.C.R. 793—§§ 1:11, 1:12, 4:1, 4:2, 8:11
O'Brien v. Allen (1900), 30 S.C.R. 340—§ 22:11
Ocean Port Hotel v. B.C., [2001] 2 S.C.R. 781—§ 15:28
Ocean Port Hotel v. British Columbia, [2001] 2 S.C.R. 781—§ 7:9
O'Donohue v. Canada (2003), 109 C.R.R. (2d) 1 (Ont. S.C.J.), affd. (2005) 137 A.C.W.S. (3d) 1131 (Ont. C.A.)—§ 1:4
O'Donohue v. The Queen (2003), 109 C.R.R. (2d) 1 (Ont. S.C.J.), affd. (2005) 137 A.C.W.S. (3d) 1131 (Ont. C.A.)—§ 1:4
Offshore Mineral Rights of B.C., Re, [1967] S.C.R. 792, 816—§§ 3:1, 17:2, 17:3
O'Grady v. Sparling, [1960] S.C.R. 804—§§ 15:7, 16:5, 16:7, 18:20, 22:11
Oil, Chemical and Atomic Wkrs. v. Imperial, Oil [1963] S.C.R. 584, 600—§ 34:7
Oil, Chemical and Atomic Wkrs. v. Imperial Oil, [1963] S.C.R. 584—§§ 15:5, 21:10
Oil, Chemical and Atomic Workers v. Imperial Oil, [1963] S.C.R. 584—§ 15:20
Oklahoma v. U.S. Civil Service Commn. (1947), 330 U.S. 127—§ 6:8
Okwuobi v. Lester B. Pearson School Bd., [2005] 1 S.C.R. 257—§§ 7:20, 40:26, 56:22
O.N.A. v. Mount Sinai Hospital (2005), 255 D.L.R. (4th) 195 (Ont. C.A.)—§ 55:45
114957 v. Hudson, [2001] 2 S.C.R. 241—§ 16:1
114957 Canada v. Hudson, [2001] 2 S.C.R. 241—§§ 5:7, 16:2, 16:5
Ont. v. Bear Island Foundation, [1991] 2 S.C.R. 570—§§ 28:18, 28:22, 28:24
Ont. v. Bogaerts, 2019 ONCA 876, para. 49 (C.A.)—§ 47:9
Ont. v. Canadian Pacific, [1995] 2 S.C.R. 1031—§ 47:24
Ont. v. Fraser, [2011] 2 S.C.R. 3—§§ 36:19, 36:20, 38:20, 44:4, 55:50
Ont. v. Miracle (2005), 74 O.R. (3d) 161 (C.A.)—§ 43:24
Ont. v. Ont. (2001), 54 O.R. (3d) 595 (C.A.)—§ 37:7
Ont. v. Pembina Exploration, [1989] 1 S.C.R. 206, 215, 217, 225, 226—§§ 7:1, 7:16

Ontario v. Canadian Pacific, [1995] 2 S.C.R. 1031—§ 47:28
Ontario v. Canadian Pacific, [1995] 2 S.C.R. 1031—§§ 47:24, 47:27, 47:28
Ontario v. Canadian Pacific, [1995] 2 S.C.R. 1028—§ 15:18
Ontario v. Canadian Pacific (1993) 13 O.R. (3d) 389 (C.A.)—§ 15:18
Ontario v. Criminal Lawyers' Association, [2010] 1 S.C.R. 815—§ 43:41
Ontario v. Fraser, [2011] 2 S.C.R. 3—§§ 40:9, 44:5
Ontario English Catholic Teachers' Association v. Ontario, [2001] 1 S.C.R. 470—§ 14:5
Ontario Farm Products Marketing Reference, [1957] S.C.R. 198—§ 20:3
Ontario Film and Video Appreciation Society, Re (1984), 45 O.R. (2d) 80 (C.A.)—§ 38:8
Ontario Hydro v. Ontario, [1993] 3 S.C.R. 327—§§ 17:3, 17:4, 17:12, 22:10
Ont. English Catholic Teachers' Assn. v. Ont., [2001] 1 S.C.R. 470—§ 1:15
Ont. Film and Video Appeciation Society and Ont. Bd. of Censors, Re (1984), 45 O.R. (2d) 80 (C.A.)—§ 18:19
Ont. Film and Video Appreciation Soc., Re (1984), 45 O.R. (2d) 80 (C.A.)—§ 36:26
Ont. Film and Video Appreciation Society, Re (1984), 45 O.R.(2d) 80 (C.A.)—§§ 38:7, 43:29
Ont. Film and Video Appreciation Society, Re (1984), 41 O.R. (2d) 583 (C.A.)—§§ 43:12, 43:29
Ont. Human Rights Cummn. v. Simpsons-Sears, [1985] 2 S.C.R. 536—§ 55:30
Ont. Hydro v. Ont., [1993] 3 S.C.R. 327—§§ 21:11, 22:10
Operation Dismantle v. The Queen, [1985] 1 S.C.R. 441—§§ 1:9, 36:12, 37:10, 37:12, 47:2, 47:9
Opitz v. Wrzesnewskyj, [2012] 3 S.C.R. 76—§ 45:5
OPSEU v. National Citizens' Coalition (1990), 74 O.R. (2d) 260 (C.A.)—§ 55:50
OPSEU v. Ont., [1987] 2 S.C.R. 2, 44–45—§§ 1:11, 4:19, 14:9, 15:20, 21:10, 34:7, 45:6
OPSEU v. Ont. (1988), 65 O.R. (2d) 689 (H.C.)—§ 43:36
OPSEU v. Ont., [1987] 2 S.C.R. 2, 57—§ 34:7
OPSEU v. Ontario, [1987] 2 S.C.R. 2—§ 43:36
Orangeville Airport, Re (1976), 11 O.R. (2d) 546 (C.A.)—§ 22:15
Ordon Estate v. Grail, [1998] 3 S.C.R. 437—§§ 15:18, 15:20, 18:17, 22:12
Orphan Well Association v. Grant Thornton, [2019] 1 S.C.R. 150—§§ 16:3, 16:4
Osborne v. Can., [1991] 2 S.C.R. 69—§§ 1:14, 37:12, 38:9, 40:8
Osborne v. Canada, [1991] 2 S.C.R 69—§ 43:36
Ottawa-Carleton Regional Transit Comm., Re (1983), 44 O.R. (2d) 560 (C.A.)—§ 22:11
Ottawa-Carleton Regional Transit Commission, Re (1983), 44 O.R. (2d) 560 (C.A.)—§ 22:6
Ottawa-Carleton Regional Transit Commn., Re (1983), 44 O.R. (2d) 560 (C.A.)—§ 22:5
Ottawa Roman Catholic Separate School Trustees v. Mackell, [1917] A.C. 62—§ 56:18

Pacific Produce Delivery and Warehouses, Re (1974), 44 D.L.R. (3d) 130 (C.A.)—§ 22:6
Pacific Western Airlines v. The Queen, [1980] 1 F.C. 86 (C.A.)—§ 7:11
Pan-Canadian Securities Regulation, Re [2018] 3 S.C.R. 189—§§ 5:27, 12:9

Pan-Canadian Securities Regulation, Re, 2018 SCC 48—§§ 20:4, 21:16
Panama Refining Co. v. Ryan (1935), 293 U.S. 388—§§ 14:5, 14:9
Papp v. Papp, [1970] 1 O.R. 331 (Ont. C.A.)—§§ 7:1, 7:14, 15:5, 15:7, 15:23, 15:24, 18:17
Paquette v. The Queen, [1977] 2 S.C.R. 189, 197—§ 8:13
Parents v. Seattle School Dist. No. 1 (2007), 551 U.S. 701—§ 55:3
P.A.T.A. v. A.-G. Can., [1931] A.C. 310, 326—§§ 8:13, 15:27, 18:2, 18:11, 18:19, 20:2
Patriation Reference (Re Resolution to Amend the Constitution, [1981] 1 S.C.R. 753—§ 4:2
Paul v. B.C., [2003] 2 S.C.R. 585—§§ 7:1, 28:9, 28:18
Paul v. British Columbia, [2003] 2 S.C.R. 585—§§ 28:7, 28:9, 40:26, 40:28
Paul v. Paul, [1986] 1 S.C.R. 306—§ 28:9
Paul v. Virginia (1868), 75 U.S. 168—§ 21:6
Paulette, Re (1973), 42 D.L.R. (3d) 8 (N.W.T. S.C.)—§ 28:24
Payson v. Hubert (1904), 34 S.C.R. 400—§ 1:7
P.(D.) v. S.(C.), [1993] 4 S.C.R. 141—§ 42:6
Pearlman v. Man. Law Society, [1991] 2 S.C.R. 869, 882—§ 47:38
Peel v. Can., [1989] 2 F.C. 562 (C.A.)—§ 7:11
Peel v. Great Atlantic and Pacific Co. (1991), 2 O.R. (3d) 65 (C.A.)—§ 42:5
P.E.I. v. CNR, [1991] 1 F.C. 129 (C.A.)—§ 22:1
P.E.I. Potato Marketing Board v. Willis, [1952] 2 S.C.R. 392—§§ 14:11, 14:13
Pellant v. Hebert (1892), reported in 1981 in 12 R.G.D. 242 (Man. Co. Ct.)—§ 56:6
Penikett v. Can. (1987), 45 D.L.R. (4th) 108 (Y.T.C.A.)—§ 4:7
Pennsylvania v. Nelson (1956), 359 U.S. 497, 501–505—§ 16:5
Pepita and Doukas, Re (1979), 101 D.L.R. (3d) 577 (B.C.C.A.)—§ 7:19
Pepsi-Cola Canada Beverages v. R.W.D.S.U., [2002] 1 S.C.R. 156—§§ 37:12, 43:20, 43:26, 44:4
Peralta v. Ont., [1988] 2 S.C.R. 1045—§ 14:11
Peralta, Re (1985), 49 O.R. (2d) 705 (C.A.)—§ 14:11
Pickin v. British Railways Bd., [1974] A.C. 765 (H.L.)—§ 12:1
Plessy v. Ferguson (1896), 163 U.S. 537—§ 8:13
Ponoka-Calmar Oils v. Wakefield, [1960] A.C. 18—§ 8:2
Potter v. Que., [2001] R.J.Q. 2823 (Que. C.A.)—§ 4:17
Powell v. Apollo Candle Co. (1885), 10 App. Cas. 282—§ 14:4
Powers of Disallowance and Reservation, Re, [1938] S.C.R. 71—§ 5:13
Powers to Levy Rates on Foreign Legations, Re, [1943] S.C.R. 208—§ 36:28
Practice Statement (Judicial Precedent), [1966] 1 W.L.R. 1234—§ 8:13
Prebble v. Television New Zealand Ltd., [1995] 1 A.C. 321 (P.C.)—§ 1:7
Prete v. Ontario (1993), 16 O.R. (3d) 161 (C.A.)—§ 40:25
Pretty v. United Kingdom (2002), 35 E.H.R.R. 1—§§ 47:12, 55:45
Pringle v. Fraser, [1972] S.C.R. 821—§ 7:20
Professional Institute v. Northwest Territories,, [1990] 2 S.C.R. 367, 403—§ 44:7
Professional Institute v. N.W.T., [1990] 2 S.C.R. 367, 402—§§ 44:4, 44:5, 44:6
Prohibition del Roy (1607), 12 Co. Rep. 63, 77 E.R. 1342—§ 1:9
Proposed Legislation Concerning Leased Premises, Re (1978), 89 D.L.R. (3d) 460 (Alta. A.D.)—§ 7:19
Protestant School Bd. of Montreal v. Min. of Education of Que. (1976), 83 D.L.R. (3d) 645 (Que. S.C.); appeal dismissed on ground that statute in issue had been repealed: (1978) 83 D.L.R. (3d) 679n (Que. C.A.)—§ 56:18

Prov. Electoral Boundaries (Sask.), Re, [1991] 2 S.C.R. 158, 180—§§ 36:18, 36:19, 55:18
Prov. Electoral Boundaries (Sask.), Re, [1991] 2 S.C.R. 158—§§ 45:3, 45:4
Provincial Court Judges' Association v. New Brunswick, [2005] 2 S.C.R. 286—§ 7:5
Provincial Electoral Boundaries (Sask.), Re, [1991] 2 S.C.R. 158, 179—§ 4:7
Provincial Secretary of P.E.I. v. Egan, [1941] S.C.R. 396—§§ 16:5, 22:11
Provincial Secretary of Prince Edward Island v. Egan, [1941] S.C.R. 396—§ 18:20
Provincial Secretary P.E.I. v. Egan, [1941] S.C.R. 396—§ 21:4
Prov. Secretary of P.E.I. v. Egan, [1941] S.C.R. 396, 400–403—§ 16:7
PSAC v. Can., [1987] 1 S.C.R. 424—§§ 44:5, 44:7
Public School Boards' Assn. of Alta. v. Alta., [2000] 2 S.C.R. 409—§ 1:15
Public Schools Act (Man.), Re, [1993] 1 S.C.R. 839—§ 56:23
Public Service Bd. v. Dionne, [1978] 2 S.C.R. 191—§ 22:20
Public Service Board v. Dionne, [1978] 2 S.C.R. 191—§§ 22:9, 22:20
Public Service Employees Relations Act, Re, [1987] 1 S.C.R. 313—§§ 44:5, 44:7
Public Utilities Comm. and Victoria Cablevision, Re (1965), 51 D.L.R. (2d) 716 (B.C. C.A.)—§ 22:16
Purdy v. Can. (2003), 230 D.L.R. (4th) 361 (B.C.C.A.)—§ 37:14

Quan v. Cusson, [2009] 3 S.C.R. 712—§ 43:28
Quance v. Thomas A. Ivey & Sons, [1950] O.R. 397 (C.A.)—§ 7:19
Que. v. Alliance du personnel professionnel et technique de la santé et des services sociaux, [2018] 1 S.C.R. 464—§ 38:12
Que. v. Bombardier Inc. (Bombardier Aerospace Training Center), [2015] 2 S.C.R. 789—§ 41:11
Que. v. Brunet, [1990] 1 S.C.R. 260—§ 56:7
Que. v. Can., [2011] 3 S.C.R. 635—§ 16:4
Que. v. Can., [2011] 1 S.C.R. 368—§ 6:8
Que. v. Canadian Owners and Pilots Assn., [2010] 2 S.C.R. 536—§ 15:18
Que. v. Can. (Firearms Sequel), [2015] 1 S.C.R. 693, 2015 SCC 14—§§ 5:27, 12:2, 15:9, 18.14, 18:15
Que. v. Can. Owners and Pilots Assn., [2010] 2 S.C.R. 536—§§ 16:4, 22:13
Que. v. Lacombe, [2010] 2 S.C.R. 453—§§ 15:9, 15:24, 16:1, 22:13
Que. v. Moses, [2010] 1 S.C.R. 557—§§ 5:27, 28:24
Que. v. Nguyen, [2009] 3 S.C.R. 208—§ 38:30
Que. Assn. of Protestant School Bds. v. A.-G. Que. (1982), 140 D.L.R. (3d) 33 (Que. S.C.)—§ 40:15
Quebec v. A, [2013] 1 S.C.R. 61, 2013 SCC 5—§§ 55:22, 55:47
Quebec v. Alliance du personnel professionel et technique de la santé et des services sociaux, [2018] 1 S.C.R. 464—§§ 55:22, 55:31, 55:32, 55:42
Quebec v. Can., [2015] 2 S.C.R. 179, 2015 SCC 22—§§ 8:1, 8:14
Quebec v. Canada (Firearms Sequel), [2015] 1 S.C.R. 693, 2015 SCC 14—§ 18:19
Quebec v. Canadian Owners and Pilots Association, [2010] 2 S.C.R. 536—§§ 15:5, 15:18, 22:12, 22:14, 22:15
Quebec v. Lacombe, [2010] 2 S.C.R. 453—§§ 15:5, 15:18, 22:15
Quebec v. Montreal, [2000] 1 S.C.R. 665—§ 12:10
Quebec v. Moses, [2010] 1 S.C.R. 557—§ 28:26

Quebec Magistrate's Court, Re, [1965] S.C.R. 772—§ 7:16
Quebec North Shore Paper Co. v. Canadian Pacific, [1977] 2 S.C.R. 1054—§ 7:11
Queensland v. Commonwealth (1977), 139 C.L.R. 585, 605 (H.C. Aust.)—§ 8:13
Que. North Shore Paper Co. v. CP, [1977] 2 S.C.R. 1054, 1063, 1065–1066—§§ 7:11, 15:15
Que. Ready Mix v. Rocois Construction, [1989] 1 S.C.R. 695—§ 7:11
Que. Ry. Light and Power Co. v. Beauport, [1945] S.C.R. 16—§ 22:10
Quong-Wing v. The King (1914), 49 S.C.R. 440—§ 55:1

R. v. A., [1990] 1 S.C.R. 995—§ 37:4
R. v. Adams, [1996] 3 S.C.R. 101—§§ 28:19, 28:21, 28:22, 28:33, 28:34
R. v. Advance Cutting & Coring, [2001] 3 S.C.R. 209—§§ 38:21, 44:8
R. v. Ahmad, [2011] 1 S.C.R. 110—§§ 7:16, 7:20, 47:33
R. v. Allen (2005), 257 D.L.R. (4th) 458 (N.S.C.A.)—§ 44:8
R. v. Amway Corp., [1989] 1 S.C.R. 21, 37-40—§ 37:2
R. v. Anderson (1930), 54 C.C.C. 321 (Man. C.A.)—§ 15:19
R. v. Antoine (1983), 41 O.R. (2d) 607, 613 (C.A.)—§ 36:31
R. v. Appleby, [1972] S.C.R. 303—§ 35:8
R. v. Appleby (No. 2) (1976), 76 D.L.R. (3d) 110 (N.B. A.D.)—§ 17:2
R. v. Appulonappa, [2015] 3 S.C.R. 754, 2015 SCC 59—§§ 36:28, 37:4, 47:24
R. v. Appulonappa, [2015] 3 S.C.R. 485, 2015 SCC 59—§ 40:7
R. v. Arkell, [1990] 2 S.C.R. 695—§ 47:19
R. v. Arp, [1998] 3 S.C.R. 339—§ 37:19
R. v. Askov, [1990] 2 S.C.R. 1199—§ 40:4
R. v. Aucoin, [2012] 3 S.C.R. 408—§ 41:11
R. v. Badger, [1996] 1 S.C.R. 771—§§ 28:17, 28:35, 28:37
R. v. Bain, [1992] 1 S.C.R. 91—§§ 7:5, 7:7, 40:4
R. v. Beare, [1988] 2 S.C.R. 387—§ 47:9
R. v. Beatty, [2008] 1 S.C.R. 49—§ 47:18
R. v. Beaulac, [1999] 1 S.C.R. 798—§§ 56:11, 56:12
R. v. Beaulac, [1999] 1 S.C.R. 768—§§ 56:2, 56:12
R. v. Beaulieu, [2010] 1 S.C.R. 248—§ 41:8
R. v. Bellusci, [2012] 2 S.C.R. 509—§ 40:17
R. v. Belnavis, [1997] 3 S.C.R. 341—§ 40:14
R. v. Big M Drug Mart, [1985] 1 S.C.R. 295—§§ 14:17, 15:5, 15:8, 15:14, 15:27, 18:12, 34:7, 35:8, 36:5, 36:14, 36:16, 36:19, 36:20, 36:26, 37:2, 37:3, 38:6, 38:15, 38:16, 40:8, 40:13, 40:14, 42:4, 42:5, 42:6, 42:9, 42:10
R. v. Big M Drug Mart, [1985] 1 S.C.R. 293, 313—§ 37:3
R. v. Biller (1999), 174 D.L.R. (4th) 721, 737 (Sask. C.A.)—§ 47:24
R. v. Bjelland, [2009] 2 S.C.R. 651—§§ 40:21, 47:32, 47:34
R. v. B. (K.G.), [1993] 1 S.C.R. 740—§ 8:13
R. v. Blais, [2003] 2 S.C.R. 236—§§ 15:27, 28:2, 28:17, 28:31
R. v. Borden, [1994] 3 S.C.R. 145—§ 37:19
R. v. Bouchard-Lebrun, [2011] 3 S.C.R. 575—§ 47:23
R. v. Boudreault, [2018] 3 S.C.R. 599—§ 38:29
R. v. Boutilier, [2017] 2 S.C.R. 936—§ 47:24
R. v. Brown, [2002] 2 S.C.R. 185—§§ 47:15, 47:35
R. v. Broyles, [1991] 3 S.C.R. 595—§§ 37:13, 38:7, 41:11, 47:31
R v. Bryan, [2007] 1 S.C.R. 527—§§ 38:4, 38:22, 43:7, 45:4

R. v. Brydges, [1990] 1 S.C.R. 190, 214—§§ 36:28, 40:4
R. v. Buhay, [2003] 1 S.C.R. 631—§§ 37:8, 37:13, 41:11
R. v. Burah (1878), 3 App. Cas. 889—§§ 14:4, 14:16
R. v. Burlingham, [1995] 2 S.C.R. 206—§§ 41:4, 41:6
R. v. Burnshine, [1975] 1 S.C.R. 693—§§ 17:4, 35:3, 35:8, 55:2, 55:49
R. v. Burt, [1988] 1 W.W.R. 385 (Sask. C.A.)—§ 47:9
R. v. Butler, [1992] 1 S.C.R. 452—§§ 36:19, 38:9, 38:16, 38:19, 43:4, 43:13, 43:29, 47:28
R. v. Buzunis (1972), 26 D.L.R. (3d) 502 (Man. C.A.)—§ 21:9
R. v. Malmo-Levine; R. v. Caine, [2003] 3 S.C.R. 571—§ 18:2
R. v. Calder, [1996] 1 S.C.R. 660—§ 41:3
R. v. Campbell (1965), 58 D.L.R. (2d) 673 (S.C.C.)—§§ 18:2, 18:11
R. v. Can. Labour Relations Bd.; Ex parte Federal Elec. Corp. (1964), 44 D.L.R. (2d) 440, 462-463 (Man. Q.B.)—§ 7:14
R. v. Carosella, [1997] 1 S.C.R. 80—§ 47:36
R. v. Catagas (1977), 81 D.L.R. (3d) 396 (Man. C.A.)—§§ 28:6, 34:2
R. v. Cawthorne, [2016] 1 S.C.R. 983, 2016 SCC 32—§§ 7:6, 47:32
R. v. Chaplin, [1995] 1 S.C.R. 727—§ 47:34
R. v. Chaulk, [1990] 3 S.C.R. 1303—§§ 38:17, 47:23
R. v. Chaulk, [1989] 1 S.C.R. 369—§ 8:7
R. v. Chief (1963), 42 D.L.R. (2d) 712, affd. (1964) 44 D.L.R. (2d) 108 (Man. C.A.)—§ 18:20
R. v. CIP, [1992] 1 S.C.R. 843—§ 37:2
R. v. CIP, [1992] S.C.R., 843, 854—§ 47:14
R. v. City of Sault Ste. Marie, [1978] S.C.R. 1299—§§ 47:15, 47:16, 47:18
R. v. Clay, [2003] 3 S.C.R. 735—§ 47:24
R. v. Colarusso, [1994] 1 S.C.R. 20—§§ 37:19, 41:11
R. v. Cole, [2012] 3 S.C.R. 34—§ 37:19
R. v. Collins, [1987] 1 S.C.R. 265, 281—§§ 41:3, 41:5, 41:6, 41:7, 56:3
R. v. Comeau, [2018] 1 S.C.R. 342, 2018 SCC 15—§§ 8:13, 20:2, 20:3
R v. Conception, [2014] 3 S.C.R. 82—§ 47:28
R. v. Conway, [2010] 1 S.C.R. 765—§ 40:16
R. v. Conway, [1989] 1 S.C.R. 1659, 1706-1707—§ 56:3
R. v. Cook, [1998] 2 S.C.R. 597—§§ 37:2, 37:4, 37:14, 41:3
R. v. Cook, [1997] 1 S.C.R. 1113—§ 47:33
R. v. Cooksville Magistrate's Court; ex parte Liquid Cargo Lines, [1965] 1 O.R. 84 (H.C.)—§§ 22:6, 22:11
R. v. Corbett, [1988] 1 S.C.R. 670—§ 47:33
R. v. Cornelio (1998), 58 C.R.R. (2d) 43 (Ont. Gen. Div.)—§ 56:13
R. v. Cornell, [1988] 1 S.C.R. 461—§§ 17:4, 55:49
R. v. Cosman's Furniture (1976), 73 D.L.R. (3d) 312 (Man. C.A.)—§ 18:19
R. v. Côté, [2011] 3 S.C.R. 215—§§ 41:8, 41:9
R. v. Côté, [1996] 3 S.C.R. 139—§§ 2:1, 7:11, 28:19, 28:21, 28:34, 28:35, 28:37
R. v. Côté, [1978] 1 S.C.R. 8, 16—§ 8:6
R. v. Crawford, [1995] 1 S.C.R. 858—§ 47:31
R. v. Creighton, [1993] 3 S.C.R. 3—§§ 47:19, 47:20
R. v. Criminal Injuries Comp. Bd.; Ex parte Lain, [1967] 2 Q.B. 864—§ 1:9
R. v. Crown Zellerbach, [1988] 1 S.C.R. 401, 432—§§ 15:5, 15:26, 17:1, 17:2, 17:3, 17:4, 17:5, 17:6, 17:11, 17:12
R. v. Cularussu, [1994] 1 S.C.R. 20, 78—§ 41:13

R. v. Czuczman (1986), 54 O.R. (2d) 574 (C.A.)—§ 37:15
R. v. Daoust, [2004] 1 S.C.R. 217—§ 56:3
R. v. Darrach, [2000] 2 S.C.R. 443—§ 47:33
R. v. Daviault, [1994] 3 S.C.R. 63—§§ 38:31, 40:9, 47:23
R. v. D.B., [2008] 2 S.C.R. 3—§§ 18:16, 38:25, 47:15
R. v. Debot, [1989] 2 S.C.R. 1140—§ 41:4
R. v. Dell (2005), 256 D.L.R. (4th) 271 (Alta. C.A.)—§§ 37:8, 37:13
R. v. Demers, [2004] 2 S.C.R. 489—§§ 14:18, 18:15, 38:25, 40:4, 40:13, 40:15, 47:24
R. v. Dennie (1997), 43 C.R.R. (2d) 144 (Ont. Gen. Div.)—§ 56:13
R. v. Derriksan (1976), 71 D.L.R. (3d) 159 (S.C.C.)—§ 28:22
R. v. Dersch, [1993] 3 S.C.R. 768—§§ 37:13, 37:19, 38:7
R. v. DeSousa, [1992] 2 S.C.R. 944—§§ 47:19, 47:20
R. v. D. (G.) (1991), 2 O.R. (3d) 498 (C.A.)—§§ 37:16, 37:17
R. v. Dixon, [1998] 1 S.C.R. 244—§ 47:34
R. v. Donnelly (2016), 135 O.R. (3d) 336 (C.A.)—§ 40:22
R. v. Drybones, [1970] S.C.R. 282—§§ 28:4, 35:3, 35:4, 35:5, 35:8, 55:2, 55:34, 55:41, 55:49
R. v. Duarte, [1990] 1 S.C.R. 30—§§ 36:18, 36:20, 41:11
R v. Taillefer; R v. Duguay, [2003] 3 S.C.R. 307—§ 47:34
R. v. Duguay, [1989] 1 S.C.R. 93—§ 41:9
R. v. Durette, [1994] 1 S.C.R. 469—§ 47:34
R. v. Dyment, [1988] 1 S.C.R. 417—§ 41:11
R. v. Edwards, [1996] 1 S.C.R. 128—§ 40:14
R. v. Edwards Books and Art, [1986] 2 S.C.R. 713—§§ 15:8, 18:13, 36:14, 36:15, 38:4, 38:15, 38:18, 38:21, 38:22, 40:8, 42:1, 42:5, 42:8, 47:10
R. v. Egger, [1993] 2 S.C.R. 451—§ 47:34
R. v. Ellis-Don, [1992] 1 S.C.R. 840—§ 47:18
R. v. Ertel (1987), 20 O.A.C. 257 (C.A.)—§ 55:11
R. v. Evans, [1996] 1 S.C.R. 8—§§ 41:11, 41:13
R. v. Fearon, [2014] 3 S.C.R. 621, 2014 SCC 77—§ 41:11
R. v. Feeney, [1997] 2 S.C.R. 13—§§ 40:4, 41:4, 41:11, 41:13
R. v. Feeney (No. 3), [1997] 3 S.C.R. 1008—§ 40:4
R. v. Feeney (No. 2), [1997] 2 S.C.R. 117—§ 40:4
R. v. Ferguson, [2008] 1 S.C.R. 96—§§ 40:8, 40:13, 40:14
R. v. Finlay, [1993] 3 S.C.R. 103—§§ 47:18, 47:19
R. v. Finta, [1994] 1 S.C.R. 701—§§ 47:19, 47:28
R. v. Fitzpatrick, [1995] 4 S.C.R. 154—§ 47:31
R. v. Foreign Secretary; Ex parte Everett, [1989] Q.B. 811 (C.A.)—§ 1:9
R. v. Forest (1976), 74 D.L.R. (3d) 704 (Man. Co. Ct.)—§ 56:6
R. v. Francis, [1988] 1 S.C.R. 1025—§§ 14:14, 16:6, 28:7, 28:14
R. v. Frohman (1987), 60 O.R. (2d) 125 (C.A.)—§ 55:49
R. v. Furtney, [1991] 3 S.C.R. 89—§§ 14:11, 14:14, 15:7, 18:19
R. v. Furtney, [1991] 2 S.C.R. 89, 103—§ 18:20
R. v. Gamble, [1988] 2 S.C.R. 595—§§ 36:31, 47:30
R. v. Gautreau (1978), 88 D.L.R. (3d) 718, 723 (N.B. A.D.)—§§ 16:8, 20:2
R. v. Généreux, [1992] 1 S.C.R. 259—§§ 7:6, 41:11, 47:15, 55:50
R. v. Genest, [1989] 1 S.C.R. 59—§ 41:9
R. v. George, [1966] S.C.R. 267—§§ 28:6, 28:22
R. v. Glad Day Bookshops (2004), 70 O.R. (3d) 691 (S.C.J.)—§§ 43:3, 43:12, 43:29
R. v. Gladstone, [1996] 2 S.C.R. 723—§§ 28:19, 28:22, 28:33, 28:34

R. v. Golden, [2001] 3 S.C.R. 679—§ 37:12
R. v. Goldhart, [1996] 2 S.C.R. 463—§ 41:4
R. v. Gowdy (2016), 135 O.R. (3d) 371 (C.A.)—§ 40:22
R. v. Graham (1991), 1 O.R. (3d) 499 (C.A.)—§ 41:4
R. v. Grant, [2009] 2 S.C.R. 353—§§ 36:19, 36:20, 41:7, 41:8, 41:9, 41:11, 41:12, 41:13
R. v. Grant, [1993] 3 S.C.R. 223—§§ 15:15, 41:4, 41:11
R. v. Graveline, [2006] 1 S.C.R. 609—§ 47:21
R. v. Gray, [1989] 1 W.W.R. 66 (Man. C.A.)—§ 47:9
R. v. Gray (1991), 4 O.R. (3d) 33 (C.A.)—§ 47:31
R. v. Gubbins, [2018] 3 S.C.R. 35—§ 47:35
R. v. Guignard, [2002] 1 S.C.R. 472—§§ 40:4, 43:24
R. v. Hall, [2002] 3 S.C.R. 309—§§ 36:9, 47:29
R. v. Hamill, [1987] 1 S.C.R. 301—§ 41:11
R. v. Hamilton (1986), 57 O.R. (2d) 412 (C.A.)—§ 55:49
R. v. Hape, [2007] 2 S.C.R. 292—§§ 36:28, 37:14
R. v. Harrer, [1995] 3 S.C.R. 562—§ 37:14
R. v. Harrison, [2009] 2 S.C.R. 494—§§ 41:8, 41:11
R. v. Harrold (1971), 19 D.L.R. (3d) 471 (B.C. C.A.)—§ 42:6
R. v. Hauser, [1979] 1 S.C.R. 984, 1026—§ 18:2
R. v. Hayden (1983), 3 D.L.R. (4th) 361 (Man. C.A.)—§§ 28:4, 35:3, 35:8
R. v. Hebert, [1990] 2 S.C.R. 151 205—§ 38:7
R. v. Hebert, [1990] 2 S.C.R. 151—§§ 37:18, 38:7, 41:3, 41:11, 47:31
R. v. Henry, [2005] 3 S.C.R. 609—§§ 8:6, 8:13
R. v. Hess, [1990] 2 S.C.R. 906—§§ 36:5, 38:20, 38:25, 40:5, 47:17, 55:27, 55:41
R. v. Heywood, [1994] 3 S.C.R. 761—§§ 47:9, 47:24
R. v. Hill (1907), 15 O.L.R. 406 (C.A.)—§ 28:7
R. v. Home Secretary; Ex parte Northumbria Police Authority, [1989] Q.B. 26 (C.A.)—§ 1:9
R. v. Horse, [1988] 1 S.C.R. 187—§ 28:17
R. v. Horseman, [1990] 1 S.C.R. 901—§§ 28:17, 28:22
R. v. Howard, [1994] 2 S.C.R. 299—§§ 28:22, 28:33
R. v. Hufsky, [1988] 1 S.C.R. 621—§§ 38:7, 38:8, 38:27
R. v. Hundal, [1993] 1 S.C.R. 867—§§ 47:18, 47:19, 47:20
R. v. Hydro-Québec, [1997] 3 S.C.R. 213—§§ 15:9, 17:5, 18:2, 18:7, 18:19
R. v. Hynes, [2001] 3 S.C.R. 623—§§ 40:16, 40:28
R. v. I. (L.R.), [1993] 4 S.C.R. 504—§ 41:4
R. v. Isaac (1976), 13 N.S.R. (2d) 460 (N.S.A.D.)—§ 28:9
R. v. Jackson, [1993] 4 S.C.R. 573, 587—§ 47:20
R. v. James, [1988] 1 S.C.R. 669—§ 36:31
R. v. Jarvis, [2002] 3 S.C.R. 757—§ 47:31
R. v. Jim (1915), 26 C.C.C. 236 (B.C.S.C.)—§ 28:9
R. v. Johnston (1991), 2 O.R. (3d) 771 (C.A.)—§ 47:31
R. v. Jones, [1994] 2 S.C.R. 229—§ 47:31
R. v. Jones, [1986] 2 S.C.R. 284—§§ 36:15, 38:4, 38:25, 42:9, 47:9
R. v. Jordan, [2016] 1 S.C.R. 631, 2016 SCC 27—§ 8:13
R. v. J.Z.S., [2010] 1 S.C.R. 3—§ 47:32
R. v. Kang-Brown, [2008] 1 S.C.R. 456—§ 41:11
R. v. Kapp, [2008] 2 S.C.R. 484—§ 55:22
R. v. Kapp, [2008] 2 S.C.R. 483—§§ 28:41, 55:20, 55:31, 55:32

R. v. Keegstra, [1990] 3 S.C.R. 697—§§ 36:19, 36:23, 36:27, 38:2, 43:4, 43:7, 43:8, 43:9, 43:10, 43:11, 43:14, 43:27, 43:29
R. v. Keegstra (No. 3), [1996] 1 S.C.R. 458—§ 43:27
R. v. Keegstra (No. 2), [1995] 2 S.C.R. 381—§ 43:27
R. v. Khawaja, [2012] 3 S.C.R. 555—§§ 43:10, 43:16, 47:25
R. v. Khela, [1995] 4 S.C.R. 201—§ 47:34
R. v. Kissick, [1942] 2 W.W.R. 418 (Man. C.A.)—§ 16:8
R. v. Klassen (1959), 20 D.L.R. (2d) 406 (Man. C.A.)—§§ 20:3, 21:13
R. v. Kokesch, [1990] 3 S.C.R. 3—§ 41:9
R. v. Kokopenace, [2015] 2 S.C.R. 398—§ 55:24
R. v. Konechny (1983), 6 D.L.R. (4th) 350 (B.C. C.A.)—§ 36:31
R. v. Kopyto (1987), 62 O.R. (2d) 449 (C.A.)—§§ 37:12, 43:35
R. v. K.R.J., [2016] 1 S.C.R. 906—§§ 38:12, 38:22
R. v. La, [1997] 2 S.C.R. 680—§ 47:36
R. v. Laba, [1994] 3 S.C.R. 965—§ 40:6
R. v. Ladouceur, [1990] 1 S.C.R. 1257—§§ 38:7, 38:8, 38:27
R. v. Latimer, [2001] 1 S.C.R. 3—§ 32:2
R. v. L. (D.O.), [1993] 4 S.C.R. 419—§ 47:32
R v. Le, 2019 SCC 34—§§ 41:9, 41:11
R. v. Lee, [1989] 2 S.C.R. 1384, 1411—§§ 37:15, 37:22, 38:17
R. v. Lefthand (1985), 19 D.L.R. (4th) 720 (Alta. C.A.)—§§ 28:4, 35:3
R. v. Leipert, [1997] 1 S.C.R. 281—§ 47:34
R. v. Lenart (1998), 39 O.R. (3d) 55 (C.A.)—§ 32:1
R. v. Lerke (1986), 25 D.L.R. (4th) 403 (Alta. C.A.)—§§ 37:8, 37:13
R. v. Levkovic, [2013] 2 S.C.R. 204—§ 47:28
R. v. Levogiannis, [1993] 4 S.C.R. 475—§ 47:32
R. v. Liew, [1999] 3 S.C.R. 227—§ 47:31
R. v. Lippé, [1991] 2 S.C.R. 114—§ 7:5
R. v. Lloyd, [2016] 1 S.C.R. 130, 2016 SCC 13—§ 47:25
R. v. Lloyd, 2016 SCC 13—§ 40:29
R. v. Logan, [1990] 2 S.C.R. 731—§§ 36:5, 38:20, 38:25, 47:19, 47:20, 47:31
R. v. L. (S.J.), [2009] 1 S.C.R. 426, paras. 21-23, 89—§ 47:32
R. v. Lucas, [1998] 1 S.C.R. 439—§§ 36:19, 40:5, 43:9, 43:11, 43:14, 43:28
R. v. L.(W.K.), [1991] 1 S.C.R. 1091, 1100—§ 47:15
R. v. Lyons, [1987] 2 S.C.R. 309, 354—§ 47:15
R. v. M. (A.), [2008] 1 S.C.R. 569—§ 41:11
R. v. MacAskill, [1931] S.C.R. 330—§ 47:23
R. v. Malmo-Levine, [2003] 3 S.C.R. 571—§§ 17:6, 18:2, 18:4, 18:19, 47:9, 47:15, 47:25, 55:18
R. v. Man. Lab Bd.; ex parte Invictus (1968), 65 D.L.R. (2d) 517 (Man. Q.B.)—§ 22:11
R. v. Mann, [2004] 3 S.C.R. 59—§ 41:11
R. v. Manninen, [1987] 1 S.C.R. 1233—§ 41:11
R. v. Manning, [2013] 1 S.C.R. 3, 2013 SCC 1—§ 18:18
R. v. Mannion, [1986] 2 S.C.R. 272—§ 38:7
R. v. Marakah, [2017] 2 S.C.R. 608, 2017 SCC 59—§ 41:11
R. v. Marshall, [2005] 2 S.C.R. 220—§§ 28:21, 28:26
R. v. Marshall, [1999] 3 S.C.R. 533—§ 28:26
R. v. Marshall, [1999] 3 S.C.R. 456—§§ 28:26, 28:34, 28:35
R. v. Marshall (No. 2), [1999] 3 S.C.R. 533—§§ 28:34, 28:35

R. v. Martin, [1992] S.C.R. 838—§ 47:18
R. v. Martineau, [1990] 2 S.C.R. 633—§§ 36:5, 38:20, 47:19
R. v. Massia (1991), 4 O.R. (3d) 705 (C.A.)—§ 56:7
R. v. McClure, [2001] 1 S.C.R. 445—§ 47:35
R. v. McNeice, 2013 BCCA 98—§ 37:19
R. v. McNeil, [2009] 1 S.C.R. 66—§§ 47:34, 47:35
R. v. McQuaid, [1998] 1 S.C.R. 285—§ 47:34
R. v. Mellenthin, [1992] 3 S.C.R. 615—§ 37:19
R. v. Mentuck, [2001] 3 S.C.R. 442—§§ 36:23, 43:32, 43:33
R. v. Mercure, [1988] 1 S.C.R. 234—§§ 12:10, 40:4, 56:3, 56:4, 56:12
R. v. Michaud (2015), 127 O.R. (3d) 81; 2015 ONCA 585—§ 38:25
R. v. Miller and Cockriell, [1977] 2 S.C.R. 680, 686—§ 35:3
R. v. Mills, [1999] 3 S.C.R. 669—§ 47:37
R. v. Mills, [1999] 3 S.C.R. 668—§§ 36:9, 47:34, 47:35
R. v. Morales, [1992] 3 S.C.R. 711—§§ 36:9, 47:28, 47:29
R. v. Morgentaler, [1988] 1 S.C.R. 30—§§ 14:17, 15:14, 18:8, 36:5, 40:14, 42:3, 47:9
R. v. Morgentaler (No. 3), [1993] 3 S.C.R. 463, 480—§§ 15:5, 15:11, 18:8
R. v. Morgentaler (No. 2), [1988] 1 S.C.R. 30—§§ 32:2, 32:6, 37:2, 37:13, 38:25, 47:6, 47:12, 47:14
R. v. Morgentaler (No. 2), [1988] 1 S.C.R. 30—§ 37:3
R. v. Moriarity, [2015] 3 S.C.R. 485, 2015 SCC 55—§§ 47:9, 47:24, 55:2
R. v. Morin, [1992] 1 S.C.R. 771, 790—§ 37:21
R. v. Morris, [2006] 2 S.C.R. 915—§§ 28:9, 28:26, 28:37
R. v. Morrison, [2019] 2 S.C.R. 3—§ 47:19
R. v. Naglik, [1993] 3 S.C.R. 122—§§ 47:18, 47:19
R. v. Nasogaluak, [2010] 1 S.C.R. 206—§§ 40:22, 47:12
R. v. Nat Bell Liquors, [1922] 2 A.C. 128—§§ 4:19, 14:8, 14:9
R. v. Nat Bell Liquors Ltd., [1922] 2 A.C. 128, 138—§ 18:20
R. v. National Post, [2010] 1 S.C.R. 477—§§ 37:12, 43:19
R. v. Ndhlovu, [1968] 4 S.A.L.R. 515, 532—§ 5:26
R. v. Nikal, [1996] 1 S.C.R. 1013—§ 28:34
R. v. 974649, [2001] 3 S.C.R. 575—§§ 40:16, 40:20
R. v. Nixon, [2011] 2 S.C.R. 566—§ 47:32
R. v. Noble (1984), 48 O.R. (2d) 643, 667-668 (C.A.)—§ 38:26
R. v. Nova Scotia Pharmaceutical Society, [1992] 2 S.C.R. 606—§§ 47:18, 47:19, 47:24, 47:27, 47:28, 47:29
R. v. N.S., [2012] 3 S.C.R. 726—§§ 36:23, 42:6
R. v. N.S. Pharmaceutical Society, [1992] 2 S.C.R. 606—§ 18:11
R. v. N.T.C. Smokehouse, [1996] 2 S.C.R. 672—§ 28:19
R. v. Nur, [2015] 1 S.C.R. 773—§ 38:29
R. v. Oakes, [1986] 1 S.C.R. 103—§§ 35:8, 36:19, 38:2, 38:3, 38:4, 38:11, 38:13, 38:14, 38:15, 38:18, 38:20, 38:21, 38:22, 55:17
R. v. O'Connor, [1995] 4 S.C.R. 411—§§ 36:9, 36:23, 40:17, 47:9, 47:35, 47:37
R. v. Orbanski, [2005] 2 S.C.R. 3—§ 38:7
R. v. Osmar (2007), 84 O.R. (3d) 321 (C.A.)—§ 47:31
R. v. Pamajewon, [1996] 2 S.C.R. 821—§ 28:20
R. v. Pan, [2001] 2 S.C.R. 344—§ 47:33
R. v. Paquette, [1990] 2 S.C.R. 1103—§§ 12:10, 40:4, 56:3, 56:4
R. v. Parker (2000), 49 O.R. (3d) 481 (C.A.)—§ 47:15
R. v. Parks, [1992] 2 S.C.R. 871—§ 47:21

R. v. Paterson, [2017] 1 S.C.R. 202—§ 41:9
R. v. Pearsall (1977), 80 D.L.R. (3d) 285 (Sask. C.A.)—§ 22:15
R. v. Penno, [1990] 2 S.C.R. 865—§§ 38:25, 47:17
R. v. Plant, [1993] 3 S.C.R. 281—§§ 41:4, 41:11
R. v. Pontes, [1995] 3 S.C.R. 44—§§ 47:9, 47:17
R. v. Pontes, [1991] 3 S.C.R. 154, 219—§ 47:18
R. v. Potvin, [1993] 2 S.C.R. 880, 899, 915—§ 47:15
R. v. Poulin, 2019 SCC 47—§§ 36:20, 56:3
R. v. Powley, [2003] 2 S.C.R. 207—§§ 28:19, 28:31
R. v. Putvin, [1989] 1 S.C.R. 525—§ 47:33
R. v. Rahey, [1987] 1 S.C.R. 598, 639—§ 36:27
R. v. Rahey, [1987] 1 S.C.R. 588—§§ 37:11, 40:16
R. v. Reeves, [2018] 3 S.C.R. 531—§ 37:19
R. v. Regan, [2002] 1 S.C.R. 297—§ 40:17
R. v. Richard, [1996] 3 S.C.R. 525—§ 37:17
R. v. Robart, [1998] 1 S.C.R. 279—§ 47:34
R. v. Robinson, [1996] 1 S.C.R. 683—§§ 8:13, 38:31, 40:9, 47:23
R. v. Rose, [1998] 3 S.C.R. 262—§ 47:33
R. v. Rosenblum (1998), 167 D.L.R. (4th) 639 (B.C.C.A.)—§ 18:18
R. v. Roy, [2012] 2 S.C.R. 60—§ 47:18
R. v. Ruzic, [2001] 1 S.C.R. 687—§ 47:22
R. v. R.V., 2019 SCC 41—§ 47:33
R. v. Sadjade, [1983] 2 S.C.R. 361—§ 56:13
R. v. Safarzadeh-Markhali, [2016] 1 S.C.R. 180, 2016 SCC 14—§§ 38:25, 47:24, 47:25
R. v. Sappier, [2006] 2 S.C.R. 686—§§ 28:19, 28:22
R. v. Schmautz, [1990] 1 S.C.R. 398, 415-416—§ 56:3
R. v. Schmidt (2014), 119 O.R. (3d) 145, para. 44 (C.A.)—§ 47:9
R. v. Schwartz, [1988] 2 S.C.R. 443, 472—§ 38:17
R. v. Sciascia, [2017] 2 S.C.R. 539, 2017 SCC 57—§ 7:1
R. v. Seaboyer, [1991] 2 S.C.R. 577—§§ 40:8, 40:16, 40:28, 41:3, 47:33
R. v. Seaboyer, (1987) 61 O.R. (2d) 290 (C.A.)—§ 40:8
R. v. Secretary of State; Ex parte Bentley, [1994] Q.B. 349 (Div. Ct.)—§ 1:9
R. v. Secretary of State for Transport; Ex parte Factortame, [1990] 2 A.C. 85 (H.L.)—§ 12:1
R. v. Secretary of State for Transport; Ex parte Factortame (No. 2), [1991] 1 A.C. 603 (H.L.)—§ 12:1
R. v. S.(G.), [1990] 2 S.C.R. 294—§ 55:6
R. v. Sharma (2020), 152 O.R. (3d) 209 (C.A.)—§ 55:39
R. v. Sharpe, [2001] 1 S.C.R. 45—§§ 36:19, 38:19, 38:22, 40:6, 40:7, 43:4, 43:7, 43:29
R. v. Sharpe, [2002] B.C.J. No. 610 (QL)—§ 43:29
R. v. Shelley, [1981] 2 S.C.R. 196—§§ 35:3, 35:8
R. v. Sieben, [1987] 1 S.C.R. 295—§ 41:11
R. v. Silveira, [1995] 2 S.C.R. 297—§ 41:10
R. v. Simard (1995), 27 O.R. (3d) 116 (Ont. C.A.)—§ 56:13
R. v. Simmons, [1988] 2 S.C.R. 495—§§ 38:7, 41:11
R. v. Sinclair, [2010] 2 S.C.R. 310—§§ 36:20, 47:31
R. v. Singh, [2007] 3 S.C.R. 405—§§ 37:18, 47:31
R. v. Singh (2013), 118 O.R. (3d) 253 (C.A.)—§ 40:17
R. v. Sioui, [1990] 1 S.C.R. 1025—§§ 28:16, 28:25, 28:26, 28:27, 28:34

R. v. Sit, [1991] 3 S.C.R. 124—§ 47:19
R. v. S.J.L.-G., [2009] 1 S.C.R. 426—§ 18:16
R. v. Skeir (2005), 253 D.L.R. (4th) 221 (N.S. C.A.)—§§ 37:8, 37:13
R. v. Skinner, [1998] 1 S.C.R. 298—§ 47:34
R. v. Skinner, [1990] 1 S.C.R. 1235, 1250-1251—§ 44:3
R. v. Smith, [2015] 2 S.C.R. 602, 2015 SCC 34—§§ 47:9, 47:12, 47:15, 47:26
R. v. Smith, [1998] 1 S.C.R. 291—§ 47:34
R. v. Smith, [1989] 2 S.C.R. 1120—§§ 40:16, 40:17
R. v. Smith, [1987] 1 S.C.R. 1045—§§ 38:29, 40:8, 47:15, 47:19
R. v. Smith, [1972] S.C.R. 359—§ 14:14
R. v. Sobey's Inc. (1998), 172 D.L.R. (4th) 111 (N.S.C.A.)—§ 18:5
R. v Sparrow, [1990] 1 S.C.R. 1075—§§ 28:9, 28:18, 28:19, 28:22, 28:33, 28:34, 28:37
R. v. Spencer, [2014] 2 S.C.R. 212, 2014 SCC 43—§ 41:11
R. v. Spratt (2008), 298 D.L.R. (4th) 317 (B.C. C.A.)—§ 43:20
R. v. Squires (1992), 11 O.R. (3d) 385 (C.A.)—§ 43:33
R. v. S. (R.J.), [1995] 1 S.C.R. 451—§ 47:31
R. v. S.(S), [1990] 2 S.C.R. 254—§§ 14:11, 17:4, 18:16, 55:6, 55:49
R. v. St-Onge Lamoureux, [2012] 3 S.C.R. 187—§ 47:33
R. v. Stevens, [1988] 1 S.C.R. 1153—§ 36:31
R. v. Stillman, [1997] 1 S.C.R. 607—§§ 41:8, 41:11
R. v. Stillman, 2019 SCC 40—§§ 36:20, 36:25, 55:2
R. v. Stinchcombe, [1991] 3 S.C.R. 326—§§ 21:9, 37:14, 40:21, 47:34, 47:37
R. v. Stone, [1999] 2 S.C.R. 290—§§ 38:31, 47:21
R. v. Strachan, [1988] 2 S.C.R. 980—§§ 41:4, 41:10
R. v. Sullivan, [1991] 1 S.C.R. 489—§ 37:2
R. v. Sullivan (2020), 151 O.R. (3d) 353 (C.A.)—§ 47:23
R. v. Sullivan, [1991] 1 S.C.R. 489—§ 37:3
R. v. Sundown, [1999] 1 S.C.R. 393—§§ 28:9, 28:16, 28:26, 28:37
R. v. Sutherland, [1980] 2 S.C.R. 451, 455—§ 28:8
R. v. Sutherland (1990), 96 N.S.R. (2d) 271 (C.A.)—§ 47:9
R. v. Swain, [1991] 1 S.C.R. 993—§ 47:38
R. v. Swain, [1991] 1 S.C.R. 933—§§ 18:15, 37:12, 38:7, 38:25, 38:31, 40:4, 40:9, 47:9, 47:34, 55:6, 55:25
R. v. Swimmer (1971), 17 D.L.R. (3d) 476 (Sask. C.A.)—§ 28:24
R. v. Taillefer, [2003] 3 S.C.R. 307—§ 47:34
R. v. Taylor, [2014] 2 S.C.R. 495, 2014 SCC 50—§ 41:9
R. v. Terry, [1996] 2 S.C.R. 207—§ 37:14
R. v. Therens, [1985] 1 S.C.R. 613, 639—§§ 35:8, 38:7, 41:3, 41:11
R. v. Thomas, [1990] 1 S.C.R. 713—§ 40:25
R. v. Thomas Fuller Construction, [1980] 1 S.C.R. 695, 706—§§ 7:1, 7:11, 15:24
R. v. Thompson, [1990] 2 S.C.R. 1111—§§ 41:3, 41:11
R. v. Thomsen, [1988] 1 S.C.R. 640—§ 38:7
R. v. Tinker, 2017 ONCA 552, paras. 71-82 (C.A.)—§ 47:12
R. v. Tran, [1994] 2 S.C.R. 951, 996—§§ 37:23, 56:13
R. v. Transport Robert (2003), 68 O.R. (3d) 51 (C.A.)—§ 47:17
R. v. Transport Robert (1973) Lteé (2003), 68 O.R. (3d) 51, paras. 17-18 (C.A.)—§§ 47:9, 47:12
R. v. Tremblay, [1987] 2 S.C.R. 435—§ 41:10
R. v. Trimarchi (1987), 63 O.R. (2d) 515 (C.A.)—§ 7:1
R. v. Tse, [2012] 1 S.C.R. 531—§§ 40:4, 47:28

R. v. Turpin, [1989] 1 S.C.R. 1296—§§ 17:4, 37:22, 55:6, 55:27, 55:49, 56:3
R. v. Vaillancourt, [1987] 2 S.C.R. 636—§§ 15:14, 36:5, 38:20, 38:25, 40:5, 47:19
R. v. Van der Peet, [1996] 2 S.C.R. 507—§§ 2:1, 28:19, 28:34
R. v. Vu, [2013] 3 S.C.R. 657, 2013 SCC 60—§ 41:11
R. v. Wason (1890), 17 O.A.R. 221, 250 (C.A.)—§ 18:20
R. v. Westfair Foods (1989), 65 D.L.R. (4th) 56 (Sask. C.A.)—§§ 40:8, 42:5
R. v. Wetmore, [1983] 2 S.C.R. 284—§§ 18:2, 18:3, 18:5
R. v. White, [1999] 2 S.C.R. 417—§§ 40:21, 47:31
R. v. White and Bob (1965), 52 D.L.R. (2d) 481n (S.C.C.)—§ 28:16
R. v. Whiteman (No. 1), [1971] 2 W.W.R. 316 (Sask. Dist. Ct.)—§ 28:4
R. v. Wholesale Travel Group, [1991] 3 S.C.R. 154—§§ 18:11, 40:14, 47:4, 47:18, 47:19
R. v. Wholesale Travel Group Inc., [1991] 3 S.C.R. 154—§ 47:20
R. v. Whyte, [1988] 2 S.C.R. 3—§§ 35:8, 38:21
R. v. Wicksted, [1997] 1 S.C.R. 307—§ 47:36
R. v. Wiggins, [1990] 1 S.C.R. 62—§ 41:11
R. v. Wigglesworth, [1987] 2 S.C.R. 541, 561—§§ 7:9, 16:8, 47:14
R. v. Wiley, [1993] 3 S.C.R. 263—§§ 41:4, 41:11
R. v. Wills (1992), 7 O.R. (3d) 337 (C.A.)—§ 37:19
R. v. Wilson (1980), 119 D.L.R. (3d) 558 (B.C. C.A.)—§§ 14:11, 16:4
R. v. Wise, [1992] 1 S.C.R. 527—§ 41:11
R. v. Wittwer, [2008] 2 S.C.R. 235—§ 41:4
R. v. W. McKenzie Securities Ltd. (1966), 56 D.L.R. (2d) 56 (Man. C.A.)—§ 21:15
R. v. Wong, [1990] 3 S.C.R. 36—§ 41:11
R. v. Zelensky, [1978] 2 S.C.R. 940—§§ 15:24, 15:27, 18:18, 18:20, 40:17
R. v. Zundel, [1992] 2 S.C.R. 731—§§ 38:16, 43:9, 43:11, 43:27
R. v. Zwicker, 2003 NSCA 140, paras. 16-19 (C.A.)—§ 47:9
Rahn v. The Queen, [1985] 1 S.C.R. 659—§ 41:11
Ramsden v. Peterborough, [1993] 2 S.C.R. 1084—§§ 37:8, 38:7, 43:20, 43:30
R.A.V. v. St. Paul (1992), 505 U.S. 377—§ 43:27
Ravndahl v. Sask., [2009] 1 S.C.R. 181—§§ 36:31, 40:25
Ravndahl v. Saskatchewan, [2009] 1 S.C.R. 181—§ 40:25
Reader's Digest Assn. v. A.-G. Can. (1965), 59 D.L.R. (2d) 54 (Que. C.A.)—§ 21:8
Re Anti-Inflation Act, [1976] 2 S.C.R. 373—§ 15:26
Re Assisted Human Reproduction Act, [2010] 3 S.C.R. 457—§ 18:19
Re Assisted Human Reproduction Act, [2010] 3 S.C.R. 457,—§ 18:2
Re B.C. Motor Vehicle Act, [1985] 2 S.C.R. 486, 492—§§ 47:14, 47:15, 47:17
Re Board of Commerce Act, [1922] 1 A.C. 191—§§ 17:7, 17:11, 17:12, 18:2
Re Board of Commerce Act, Board of Commerce, [1922] 1 A.C. 191—§ 18:11
Re CFRB, [1973] 3 O.R. 819, 822—§ 22:16
Re Employment and Social Insurance Act, [1936] S.C.R. 427, 434—§ 6:9
Reference re Legislative Authority of Parliament of Canada, [1980] 1 S.C.R. 54, 72—§ 14:9
Reform Party of Can. v. Can. (1995), 123 D.L.R. (4th) 366 (Alta. C.A.)—§ 43:38
Regents of University of California v. Bakke (1978), 438 U.S. 265—§ 55:3
Regional Municipality of Peel v. MacKenzie, [1982] 2 S.C.R. 9, 18—§§ 15:24, 18:16
Regional Municipality of Peel v. McKenzie, [1982] 2 S.C.R. 9—§§ 15:14, 18:18
Registrar of Motor Vehicles v. Can. American Transfer, [1972] S.C.R. 811—§ 15:18

Regulation and Control of Aeronautics in Can., Re, [1932] A.C. 54—§§ 22:13, 22:16
Regulation and Control of Radio Communication in Can., Re, [1932] A.C. 304—§§ 17:2, 22:2, 22:16, 22:17, 22:19, 22:20
Regulation and Control of Radio Communication in Can., Re, [1932] A.C. 54, 77—§ 22:14
Reilly v. The King, [1934] A.C. 176—§ 8:13
Re Initiative and Referendum Act, [1919] A.C. 935, 945—§ 14:9
Re Manitoba Language Rights, [1985] 1 S.C.R. 721, 752—§ 15:28
Re Man. Keewatinowi Okimakanak v. Man. Hydro-Electric Bd. (1992), 91 D.L.R. (4th) 554, 557 (Man. C.A.)—§ 6:6
Remuneration of Judges, Re, [1997] 3 S.C.R. 3—§§ 1:8, 7:2, 7:3, 7:5, 7:6, 7:8, 7:9, 7:14, 7:20, 15:28, 34:7, 38:28
Remuneration of Judges, Re, [1997] 3 S.C.R. 3—§ 34:7
Remuneration of Judges (No. 2), Re, [1998] 1 S.C.R. 4—§§ 7:5, 8:11
Remuneration of Judges (No. 2), Re, [1998] 1 S.C.R. 3—§ 40:4
Re Objection by Que. to Resolution to Amend the Constitution, [1982] 2 S.C.R. 793—§ 1:13
Republic of Fiji v. Prasad, [2001] FJCA 1 (Fiji C.A.)—§ 5:26
Re Regulation and Control of Aeronautics in Can., [1932] A.C. 54—§ 17:3
Re Regulation and Control of Aeronautics in Can., [1932] A.C. 54—§§ 17:2, 17:3, 17:7
Re Regulation and Control of Radio Communication in Can., [1932] A.C. 304—§§ 8:13, 17:3
Re Secession of Quebec, [1998] 2 S.C.R. 217—§§ 5:24, 5:26
Residential Tenancies Act, Re, [1981] 1 S.C.R. 714—§§ 7:15, 7:16, 7:19, 15:27
Residential Tenancies Act (N.S.), Re, [1996] 1 S.C.R. 186—§ 7:19
Resolution to Amend the Constitution, Re, [1981] 1 S.C.R. 753, 909—§§ 1:10, 1:11, 1:12, 1:14, 3:8, 4:1, 5:13, 8:11
Resolution to Amend the Constitution of Canada, Re, [1981] 1 S.C.R. 753, 790, 794, 797, 799, 801—§ 3:8
R. ex rel. Tolfree v. Clark, [1943] O.R. 501 (C.A.)—§ 4:19
Reynolds v. Sims (1964), 377 U.S. 533—§§ 36:5, 45:2
Reynolds v. Times Newspapers, [2001] 2 A.C. 127 (H.L.)—§ 43:28
Rhine v. The Queen, [1980] 2 S.C.R. 442, 447—§ 7:11
Ricci v. DeStefano (2009), 557 U.S. xxx—§ 55:32
Riel v. The Queen (1885), 10 App. Cas. 675—§ 17:1
Rio Hotel v. N.B., [1987] 2 S.C.R. 59, 65—§§ 15:7, 18:20, 21:4, 43:3
Rio Hotel v. New Brunswick, [1987] 2 S.C.R. 59—§ 16:5
Rio Tinto Alcan v. Carrier Sekani Tribal Council, [2010] 2 S.C.R. 650—§§ 28:38, 40:26
Rizzo & Rizzo Shoes Ltd. (Re.), [1998] 1 S.C.R. 27—§ 15:8
R. (Jackson) v. Attorney General, [2006] 1 A.C. 262 (H.L.)—§§ 12:1, 12:10
RJR-MacDonald v. Can., [1995] 3 S.C.R. 199—§§ 8:3, 16:4, 32:1, 36:8, 36:9, 36:19, 38:18, 38:20, 43:14
RJR-MacDonald v. Canada, [1995] 3 S.C.R. 199—§§ 18:5, 18:19, 38:12, 38:19, 43:16, 43:23
R. (Miller) v. The Prime Minister, [2019] EWHC 2381 (Q.B.)—§ 9:21
R. (Miller) v. The Prime Minister, [2019] UKSC 41, 3 W.L.R. 589—§§ 1:9, 9:21
Roach v. Can., [1994] 2 F.C. 406 (C.A.)—§ 43:16
Roberts v. Can., [1989] 1 S.C.R. 322—§§ 7:11, 28:18

Roberts v. Canada, [1989] 1 S.C.R. 322, 333—§ 7:11
Robertson and Rosetanni v. The Queen, [1963] S.C.R. 651—§§ 34:7, 35:8
Robins v. National Trust Co., [1927] A.C. 515, 519—§§ 2:2, 8:13
Robinson v. Countrywide Factors, [1978] 1 S.C.R. 753—§ 15:7
Robinson v. Countrywide Factors, [1977] 2 S.C.R. 753—§ 16:5
Roche v. Kronheimer (1921), 29 C.L.R. 329—§ 14:5
Rocket v. Royal College of Dental Surgeons, [1990] 2 S.C.R. 232—§§ 36:19, 38:20, 38:22, 40:9, 43:8, 43:14
Rocket v. Royal College of Dental Surgeons, [1990] 1 S.C.R. 232—§ 43:23
Rodriguez v. B.C., [1993] 3 S.C.R. 519—§§ 32:2, 40:8, 55:28
Rodriguez v. British Columbia, [1993] 3 S.C.R. 519—§§ 8:13, 47:12, 47:15, 47:24, 55:45
Roe v. Wade (1973), 410 U.S. 113—§ 36:5
Rogers Communications v. Châteauguay, [2016] 1 S.C.R. 467, 2016 SCC 23—§§ 15:18, 22:22
Romer v. Evans (1996), 517 U.S. 620—§ 55:48
Roncarelli v. Duplessis, [1959] S.C.R. 121—§ 34:2
Rookes v. Barnard, [1964] A.C. 1129 (H.L.)—§ 2:2
Rosen v. Ont. (1996), 131 D.L.R. (4th) 708 (Ont. C.A.)—§ 43:23
Rosenberg v. Can. (1998), 38 O.R. (3d) 577, para. 31 (C.A.)—§§ 38:15, 38:17, 40:6, 55:48
Rosenberg v. Canada (1998), 38 O.R. (3d) 577 (C.A.)—§ 38:12
Ross v. New Brunswick School District No. 15, [1996] 1 S.C.R. 825—§§ 38:19, 38:20, 42:6, 43:14, 43:27
Ross v. New Brunswick School District No. 15, [1995] 1 S.C.R. 827—§ 15:14
Ross v. Registrar of Motor Vehicles, [1975] 1 S.C.R. 5—§§ 16:5, 16:6, 22:11
Ross River Dena Council Band v. Can., [2002] 2 S.C.R. 816—§§ 1:9, 28:3
Roth v. United States (1957), 354 U.S. 476, 484—§ 43:29
Rothman v. The Queen, [1981] 1 S.C.R. 640—§§ 41:3, 41:7, 47:31
Rothmans, Benson & Hedges v. Sask., [2005] 1 S.C.R. 188—§ 14:18
Rothmans, Benson & Hedges v. Saskatchewan, [2005] 1 S.C.R. 188—§ 16:4
Roy v. Hackett (1987), 62 O.R. (2d) 365 (Ont. C.A.)—§ 56:13
Roy v. Plourde, [1943] S.C.R. 262—§ 15:14
Royal Bank of Can. v. LaRue, [1928] A.C. 187—§ 16:3
R. (Privacy International) v. Investigatory Powers Tribunal, [2019] UKSC 22 (U.K.S.C.)—§ 12:1
Ruby v. Can., [2002] 4 S.C.R. 3—§§ 40:7, 43:33, 47:32
Rudolf Wolff & Co. v. Can., [1990] 1 S.C.R. 695—§§ 7:11, 37:3, 55:18
Ruffo v. Conseil de la Magistrature, [1995] 4 S.C.R. 267—§§ 7:5, 47:10, 47:28
Russell v. The Queen (1882), 7 App. Cas. 829—§§ 8:13, 14:15, 17:3, 17:4, 17:6, 17:7, 17:12
RWDSU v. Dolphin Delivery, [1986] 2 S.C.R. 573, 584—§§ 34:7, 37:11, 37:12, 37:13, 38:4, 38:7, 38:31, 43:10, 43:15, 43:26, 43:35
RWDSU v. Dolphin Delivery, [1986] 2 S.C.R. 573, 584—§ 34:7
RWDSU v. Govt. of Sask., [1985] 5 W.W.R. 97 (Sask. C.A.)—§ 39:2
RWDSU v. Sask., [1987] 1 S.C.R. 460—§§ 39:2, 44:5, 44:7

Saanichton Marina v. Tsawout Indian Band (1989), 57 D.L.R. (4th) 161 (B.C.C.A.)—§ 28:16
Sagen v. Vancouver Organizing Committee (2009), 313 D.L.R. (4th) 393 (B.C. C.A.)—§ 37:13

Same-Sex Marriage, Re, [2004] 3 S.C.R. 698—§§ 8:11, 12:2, 15:27, 42:11, 55:18, 55:48
Sask. v. Whatcott, [2013] 1 S.C.R. 467, 2013 SCC 11—§§ 36:23, 40:5
Saskatchewan v. Lemare Lake Logging, [2015] 3 S.C.R. 419, 2015 SCC 53—§§ 16:3, 16:4
Saskatchewan v. Whatcott, [2013] 1 S.C.R. 467, 2013 SCC 11—§§ 38:18, 42:6, 43:27
Saskatchewan Federation of Labour v. Saskatchewan, [2015] 1 S.C.R. 245, 2015 SCC 4—§ 44:5
Sask. Federation of Labour v. Sask., [2015] 1 S.C.R. 246—§§ 15:14, 36:16
Sask. Federation of Labour v. Sask., [2015] 1 S.C.R. 245, 2015 SCC 4—§§ 8:13, 36:28, 38:18, 44:5
Sask. Federation of Labour v. Sask., 2014 SCC 4—§ 40:4
Sask. Fed. of Labour v. Sask., [2015] 1 S.C.R. 245, 2015 SCC 4—§ 8:13
Sask. Power Corp. v. Trans Can. Pipelines, [1979] 1 S.C.R. 297—§§ 22:5, 22:11
Sask. Power Corp. v. TransCan. Pipelines (1988), 56 D.L.R. (4th) 416 (Sask. C.A.)—§ 20:3
Saumur v. City of Que., [1953] 2 S.C.R. 299, 333—§ 43:3
Saumur v. City of Quebec, [1953] 2 S.C.R. 299—§§ 34:7, 42:1, 42:6, 43:2
Saumur v. Que., [1953] 2 S.C.R. 299, 333—§§ 15:5, 15:15, 21:3, 47:27
Saumur v. Quebec, [1953] 2 S.C.R. 299, 333—§§ 14:7, 15:9, 15:26
Sauve v. Can., [2002] 3 S.C.R. 519—§§ 36:9, 38:4, 38:15, 45:2
Sauvé v. Can., [1993] 2 S.C.R. 438—§§ 36:9, 45:2
Sauvé v. Canada, [2002] 3 S.C.R. 519—§ 36:9
Schachter v. Can., [1992] 2 S.C.R. 679, 695-719—§§ 40:2, 40:13
Schachter v. Canada, [1992] 2 S.C.R. 679, 719—§§ 36:10, 40:4, 40:6, 40:9
Schafer v. Can. (1997), 35 O.R. (3d) 1 (C.A.)—§§ 40:4, 55:44
Schechter Poultry Corp. v. U.S.A. (1935), 295 U.S. 494—§§ 14:5, 14:9
Schneider v. The Queen, [1982] 2 S.C.R. 112—§§ 16:5, 17:4, 17:5, 18:4, 21:4, 32:1
Schreiber v. Canada, [1998] 1 S.C.R. 841—§ 37:14
Schwella v. The Queen, [1957] Ex. C.R. 226—§ 7:11
Scott v. A.-G. Can., [1923] 3 W.W.R. 929 (P.C., unreported in A.C.)—§ 7:2
Scott v. Scott (1970), 15 D.L.R. (3d) 374 (N.B.A.D.)—§ 2:1
Scowby v. Glendinning, [1986] 2 S.C.R. 226, 236—§ 12:10
Seafarers' International Union v. Crosbie Offshore Services, [1982] 2 F.C. 855 (C.A.)—§ 22:12
Secession of Quebec, Re, [1998] 2 S.C.R. 217—§§ 1:8, 4:3, 5:24, 5:25, 8:10, 8:11, 15:28, 28:43, 36:12
Secession Reference, [1998] 2 S.C.R. 217—§ 7:15
Securities Act, Re, [2011] 3 S.C.R. 837—§§ 15:7, 15:9, 20:4, 21:15, 21:16
Segura v. United States (1984), 468 U.S. 796—§ 41:2
Seminary of Chi-coutimi v. A.-G. Que., [1973] S.C.R. 681—§ 7:15
Seminary of Chicoutimi v. A.-G. Que., [1973] S.C.R. 681—§ 7:16
Senate Reform, Re, [2014] 1 S.C.R. 704, 2014 SCC 32—§§ 1:4, 4:8, 4:11, 4:14, 4:16, 4:17, 4:18, 9:10, 12:10, 14:9
s. 5(a) of the Dairy Industry Act, Re (Margarine) [1949] S.C.R. 1—§ 15:14
Shannon v. Lower Mainland Dairy Products Board, [1938] A.C. 708—§§ 14:3, 14:5, 21:14
Shelley v. Kraemer (1948), 334 U.S. 1, 19—§ 37:11
Sibbeston v. Can. (1988), 48 D.L.R. (4th) 691 (N.T.C.A.)—§ 4:7
Siemens v. Man., [2003] 1 S.C.R. 6—§§ 14:17, 15:7, 15:13, 18:20, 21:4, 47:10

Siemens v. Manitoba, [2003] 1 S.C.R. 6—§§ 14:15, 55:49
Sierra Club of Can. v. Can., [2002] 2 S.C.R. 522—§ 47:32
Sikyea v. The Queen, [1964] S.C.R. 642—§§ 28:6, 28:22
Silverthorne Lumber Co. v. United States (1920), 251 U.S. 385—§ 41:4
Simon v. The Queen, [1985] 2 S.C.R. 387, 411—§§ 28:9, 28:16, 28:24, 28:25, 28:26, 28:27, 28:34, 28:37
Simpson v. A.-G., [1955] N.Z.L.R. 271 (N.Z. C.A.)—§ 12:10
Sinclair v. Que., [1992] 1 S.C.R. 579—§ 40:4
Sinclair v. Que., [1992] 1 S.C.R. 212—§ 56:7
Sinclair v. Quebec, [1992] 1 S.C.R. 579—§ 56:8
Singbeil v. Hansen (1985), 19 D.L.R. (4th) 48 (B.C.C.A.)—§ 22:12
Singh v. Can. (1991), 3 O.R. (3d) 429 (C.A.)—§§ 9:3, 9:10
Singh v. Minister of Employment and Immigration, [1985] 1 S.C.R. 177—§§ 37:2, 40:9
Singh v. Minr. of Emplmt. and Imm., [1985] 1 S.C.R. 177—§§ 35:3, 35:5, 35:7, 35:8, 38:17, 40:9, 47:5, 47:9, 47:12, 47:13, 47:38
Singh v. Minr. of Emplmt. and Immig., [1985] 1 S.C.R. 177, 202—§ 37:4
Singh v. Minr. of Emplmt. and Immigration, [1985] 1 S.C.R. 177, 224—§ 36:32
Singh v. Minr. of Emplmt. and 1mm., [1985] 1 S.C.R. 177—§ 47:9
Singh v. Minr. of Emplt. and Imm., [1985] 1 S.C.R. 177—§ 34:4
620 Connaught v. Can., [2008] 1 S.C.R. 131—§ 14:5
Skelley and the Queen, Re (1982), 140 D.L.R. (3d) 186 (B.C. C.A.)—§ 18:20
S.L. v. Commission scolaire des Chênes, [2012] 1 S.C.R. 235—§§ 42:6, 42:8, 42:9, 42:10
Slaight Communications v. Davidson, [1989] 1 S.C.R. 1038—§§ 37:8, 37:11, 38:2, 38:7, 38:8, 38:32, 43:16, 43:37
Smith v. The Queen, [1983] 1 S.C.R. 554—§ 28:3
Smith v. The Queen, [1960] S.C.R. 776—§§ 15:7, 16:3, 16:5, 16:7, 18:2, 18:20, 21:15, 21:16
Smith, Kline & French Laboratories v. Can., [1986] 1 F.C. 274 (T.D.)—§ 32:2
Smylie v. The Queen (1900), 27 O.A.R. 172—§ 6:9
Smyth v. Ames (1897), 169 U.S. 466—§ 37:2
Snepp v. United States (1980), 444 U.S. 507—§ 37:24
s. 92(4) of the Vehicles Act 1957 (Sask.), Re, [1958] S.C.R. 608—§§ 16:3, 22:11
Sobeys Stores v. Yeomans, [1989] 1 S.C.R. 238—§ 7:19
Société Asbestos v. Société nationale de l'amiante (1981), 128 D.L.R. (3d) 405 (Que. C.A.)—§ 15:6
Société des Acadiens v. Assn. of Parents, [1986] 1 S.C.R. 549, 565, 579, 613-621—§ 56:14
Société des Acadiens v. Association of Parents, [1986] 1 S.C.R. 549—§ 56:12
Société des Acadiens v. Canada, [2008] 1 S.C.R. 383—§ 56:15
Solski v. Que., [2005] 1 S.C.R. 201—§§ 40:7, 56:11, 56:12
Solski v. Quebec, [2005] 1 S.C.R. 201—§ 56:22
Somerville v. Canada (1996), 136 D.L.R. (4th) 205 (Alta. C.A.)—§ 43:38
Sommers v. Sturdy (1957), 10 D.L.R. (2d) 269 (B.C. C.A.)—§ 15:6
s. 193 and 195.1 of Criminal Code, Re (Prostitution Reference) [1990] 1 S.C.R. 1123—§ 8:13
Southam v. Can., [1990] 3 F.C. 465 (C.A.)—§ 7:11
Southam v. Coulter (1990), 75 O.R. (2d) 1 (C.A.)—§ 43:33
Southam and The Queen (No. 1), Re (1983), 41 O.R. (2d) 113 (C.A.)—§§ 43:12, 43:33

Southam and The Queen (No. 2), Re (1986), 53 O.R. (2d) 663 (C.A.)—§§ 43:12, 43:33
South Dakota v. Dole (1987), 483 U.S. 203—§ 6:8
Spencer v. The Queen, [1985] 2 S.C.R. 278—§ 37:14
Spooner Oils v. Turner Valley Gas Conservation Bd., [1933] S.C.R. 629—§ 21:14
s.16 of Special War Revenue Act, Re, [1942] S.C.R. 429; leave to appeal to the P.C. refused [1943] 4 D.L.R. 657—§ 21:6
ss. 193 and 195.1 of Criminal Code, Re, [1990] 1 S.C.R. 1123—§§ 18:20, 36:19, 38:9, 38:21, 38:25, 43:4, 47:10, 47:28
ss. 193 and 195.1 of Criminal Code, Re (Prostitution Reference) [1990] 1 S.C.R. 1123, 1180—§§ 43:8, 43:9, 43:14, 43:25, 47:9, 47:10, 47:25, 47:27
ss. 193 and 195.1 of Criminal Code, Re (Prostitution Reference) [1990] 1 S.C.R. 1122, 1156—§ 47:28
St. Catherine's Milling and Lumber Co. v. The Queen (1888), 14 App. Cas. 46—§ 28:3
Stelco v. Can., [1990] 1 S.C.R. 617—§§ 18:11, 47:9
Stephens v. The Queen, [1960] S.C.R. 823—§§ 15:7, 16:5, 16:7, 18:20, 22:11
Stevedores Reference, [1955] S.C.R. 529—§§ 15:5, 22:14
Stoffman v. Vancouver General Hospital, [1990] 3 S.C.R. 483—§§ 37:8, 37:10, 37:13, 55:44
Stone v. Graham (1980), 449 U.S. 39—§ 42:8
Stony Plain Indian Reserve, Re (1981), 130 D.L.R. (3d) 636, 652 (Alta. C.A.)—§ 28:9
Stuart v. Bank of Montreal (1909), 41 S.C.R. 516—§ 8:13
s. 293 of the Criminal Code, Re (2011), 28 B.C.L.R. (5th) 96 (B.C. S.C.)—§ 42:6
Sunday Times v. United Kingdom (1979), 2 European Human Rights Reports 245 (Eur. Ct. of Hum. Rts.)—§ 38:7
Sun Indalex Finance v. United Steelworkers, [2013] 1 S.C.R. 271, 2013 SCC 6—§ 16:3
Supreme Court Act, ss. 5 and 6, Re, [2014] 1 S.C.R. 433—§§ 1:2, 1:4, 4:6, 4:14, 4:16, 5:20, 7:14, 8:1, 8:3, 8:4, 8:5, 8:14
Supreme Court of Canada Act, ss. 5 and 6, Re, [2014] 1 S.C.R. 433, 2014 SCC 21—§ 8:6
Suresh v. Can., [2002] 1 S.C.R. 3—§§ 37:2, 38:25, 43:10, 47:9, 47:15, 47:28, 47:38
Suresh v. Canada, [2002] 1 S.C.R. 3—§ 37:14
Surrey Corp. v. Peace Arch Enterprises (1970), 74 W.W.R. 380 (B.C.C.A.)—§ 28:9
Sutcliffe v. Ont. (2004), 69 O.R. (3d) 257 (C.A.)—§ 36:11
Sutherland, Re (1982), 134 D.L.R. (3d) 177 (Man. C.A.)—§ 8:5
Switzman v. Elbling, [1957] S.C.R. 285—§§ 15:11, 21:3, 21:17, 34:6, 34:7, 43:2, 43:7
Symes v. Can., [1993] 4 S.C.R. 695—§ 55:28
Symes v. Canada, [1993] 4 S.C.R. 695—§ 55:42
Syndicat Northcrest v. Amselem, [2004] 2 S.C.R. 551—§§ 34:4, 37:13, 42:6, 42:8
Syndicat Northwest v. Amselem, [2004] 2 S.C.R. 551—§§ 37:24, 42:7

Taku River Tlingit First Nation v. B.C., [2004] 3 S.C.R. 550—§ 28:21
Taku River Tlingit First Nation v. British Columbia, [2004] 3 S.C.R. 550—§ 28:38
Tank Truck Transport, Re, [1960] O.R. 497 (H.C.); affd. without written reasons [1963] 1 O.R. 272 (C.A.)—§§ 22:6, 22:11

Tanudjaja v. Can. (2013), 116 O.R. (3d) 574 (S.C.J.)—§ 47:12
Taylor v. Can. (2007), 286 D.L.R. (4th) 385 (F.C.A.)—§ 47:13
Téléphone Guèvremont v. Quebec, [1994] 1 S.C.R. 878—§ 22:22
Téléphone Guèvremont c. Québec [1994] 1 S.C.R. 878, 879—§ 22:22
Téléphone Guèvremont c. Québec (1992) 99 D.L.R. (4th) 241 (Que. C.A.)—§ 22:22
Tennant v. Union Bank of Can., [1894] A.C. 31—§ 16:4
Teskey v. Can. (2014), 377 D.L.R. (4th) 39 (Ont. C.A.)—§ 1:4
Tessier v. Que., [2012] 2 S.C.R. 3—§§ 21:11, 22:7, 22:9, 22:12
Tessier v. Quebec, [2012] 2 S.C.R. 3—§§ 22:7, 22:9
Tétreault-Gadoury v. Can., [1991] 2 S.C.R. 22—§ 40:26
Tétreault-Gadoury v. Canada, [1991] 2 S.C.R. 22—§§ 40:5, 40:6, 55:44
Texada Mines v. A.-G. B.C., [1960] S.C.R. 713—§§ 15:9, 15:14
Texas v. Johnson (1989), 491 U.S. 397—§ 43:7
Texas v. White (1868), 74 U.S. (7 Wall.) 700, 725—§ 5:24
Texas v. White (1868), 7 Wall. (74 U.S.) 700, 733—§ 5:26
The King v. Hume; Consolidated Distilleries v. Consolidated Exporters Corp., [1930] S.C.R. 531—§ 7:11
The King v. Dubois, [1935] S.C.R. 378—§ 56:3
The King v. Eastern Terminal Elevator Co., [1926] S.C.R. 434—§ 20:4
The King v. Eastern Terminal Elevator Co., [1925] S.C.R. 434—§§ 20:2, 22:10
The King v. Eastern Terminal Elev. Co., [1925] S.C.R. 434, 438—§ 17:7
The Nova Scotia Barristers' Society v. Trinity Western University, 2016 NSCA 59—§ 42:9
The Queen v. Beauregard, [1986] 2 S.C.R. 56, 72—§ 5:13
The Queen v. Compagnie ImmobilièreBCN, [1979] 1 S.C.R. 865—§ 56:3
The Queen v. Hauser, [1979] 1 S.C.R. 984—§§ 17:6, 18:4
The Queen v. Mousseau, [1980] 2 S.C.R. 89—§ 28:17
The Queen v. Sutherland, [1980] 2 S.C.R. 451—§ 28:17
The Queen v. Wetmore, [1983] 2 S.C.R. 284, 296—§ 17:4
The Queen v. Wray, [1971] S.C.R. 272—§ 41:2
The Queen (Alta.) v. Can. Transport Comm., [1978] 1 S.C.R. 61—§ 6:9
The Queen and Van Goal, Re (1987), 36 D.L.R. (4th) 481 (B.C.C.A.)—§ 22:15
The Queen (Can.) v. Sask. Wheat Pool, [1983] 1 S.C.R. 205—§ 18:18
The Queen (Can.) v. The Queen (P.E.I.), [1978] 1 F.C. 533 (C.A.)—§§ 5:4, 22:1
The Queen (Man.) v. Air Can., [1980] 2 S.C.R. 303—§ 15:15
The Queen (Ont.) v. Bd. of Transport Commrs. (Go-Train) [1968] S.C.R. 118—§§ 6:9, 22:5, 22:8, 22:11, 22:14
Therrien, Re, [2001] 2 S.C.R. 3—§§ 7:8, 15:28
The Ship "Sparrows Point" v. Greater Vancouver Water District, [1951] S.C.R. 396—§ 7:11
Thibaudeau v. Can., [1995] 2 S.C.R. 627—§ 55:42
Thibaudeau v. Canada, [1995] 2 S.C.R. 627—§§ 55:24, 55:25
Thomson Newspapers v. Can., [1990] 1 S.C.R. 425—§§ 18:11, 47:4, 47:9
Thomson Newspapers v. Canada, [1990] 1 S.C.R. 425—§ 47:15
Thomson Newspapers Co. v. Can., [1998] 1 S.C.R. 877—§§ 22:18, 38:20, 43:7, 43:12, 43:38
Thomson Newspapers Co. v. Canada, [1998] 1 S.C.R. 877—§§ 43:20, 45:4
Tinker v. Des Moines School District (1969), 393 U.S. 503—§ 43:7
Tiny Roman Catholic Separate School Trustees v. The King, [1928] A.C. 363—§ 8:13

Tiny Separate School Trustees v. The Queen, [1927] S.C.R. 637—§ 8:3
Tomen v. FWTAO (1989), 70 O.R. (2d) 48 (C.A.)—§ 37:8
Tomko v. Labour Relations Board (Nova Scotia), [1977] 1 S.C.R. 112, 120—§ 7:19
Tomko v. Labour Rels. Bd. (N.S.), [1977] 1 S.C.R. 112—§ 7:19
Tooth v. Power, [1891] A.C. 284, 292 (P.C., Aust)—§ 8:13
Toronto v. Bell Telephone Co., [1905] A.C. 52—§§ 15:18, 15:27, 21:11, 22:5, 22:22
Toronto v. Olympia Edward Recreation Club, [1955] S.C.R. 454—§ 7:19
Toronto v. Quickfall (1994), 16 O.R. (3d) 665 (C.A.)—§ 43:30
Toronto v. York, [1938] A.C. 415, 426—§§ 7:2, 7:19, 15:14
Toronto (City) v. Ont. (2018) 142 O.R. (3d) 481, 2018 ONCA 761 (C.A.)—§ 39:2
Toronto (City) v. Ont. (2019), 146 O.R. (3d) 705, 2019 ONCA 732 (C.A.)—§ 39:2
Toronto Electric Commissioners v. Snider, [1925] A.C. 396—§§ 17:3, 17:7, 17:12, 20:2, 21:10, 21:11
Toronto Electric Commissioners v. Snider, [1925] A.C. 394—§ 14:18
Toronto Electric Commrs. v. Snider, [1925] A.C. 396—§§ 18:2, 20:4, 32:2
Toronto Star Newspapers v. Canada, [2010] 1 S.C.R. 722—§ 43:32
Toronto Star Newspapers v. Ontario, [2005] 2 S.C.R. 188—§ 43:32
Total Oilfield Rentals v. Can. (2014), 375 D.L.R. (4th) 433 (Alta.C.A.)—§ 22:7
Town of Summerside and Maritime Electric Co. (No. 2), Re (1983), 3 D.L.R. (4th) 577—§ 22:11
Tranchemontagne v. Ont., [2006] 1 S.C.R. 513—§§ 12:10, 40:26
Tranchemontagne v. Ontario, [2006] 1 S.C.R. 513—§ 40:26
Transport Oil Co. v. Imperial Oil Co., [1935] O.R. 215, 219 (C.A.)—§ 18:18
Trask v. The Queen, [1985] 1 S.C.R. 655—§ 41:11
Tremblay v. Daigle, [1989] 2 S.C.R. 530—§§ 37:2, 37:12, 37:13
Tremblay v. Daigle, [1989] 2 S.C.R. 530—§ 37:3
Trial Lawyers' Association of British Columbia v. B.C., [2014] 3 S.C.R. 31—§ 7:20
Trial Lawyers' Association of British Columbia v. British Columbia, [2014] 3 S.C.R. 31, 2014 SCC 59—§§ 7:18, 15:28, 40:6
Triglav v. Terrasses Jewellers, [1983] 1 S.C.R. 283—§§ 21:7, 22:12
Trinity Western University v. Law Society of Upper Canada, [2018] 2 S.C.R. 453—§§ 38:32, 42:9
Trociuk v. British Columbia, [2003] 1 S.C.R. 835—§§ 40:4, 55:41
Tropwood A.G. v. Sivaco Wire and Nail Co., [1979] S.C.R. 157—§ 22:12
Truchon c. Procureur général du Canada, 2021 QCCS 590—§ 40:4
Truchon c. Procureur général du Canada, 2020 QCCS 4388—§ 40:4
Truchon c. Procureur général du Canada, 2020 QCCS 2019—§ 40:4
Truchon c. Procureur général du Canada, 2020 QCCS 772—§ 40:4
Truchon c. Procureur général du Canada, 2019 QCCS 3792—§§ 40:4, 47:24
Tsilhiqot'n Nation v. B.C., [2014] 2 S.C.R. 257, 2014 SCC 44—§ 28:21
Tsilhqot'in Nation v. B.C., [2014] 2 S.C.R. 257, 2014 SCC 44—§§ 8:13, 28:21, 28:22, 28:38
Tsilhqot'in Nation v. British Columbia, [2014] 2 S.C.R. 257, 2014 SCC 44—§§ 28:9, 28:12, 28:14, 28:16, 28:21, 28:34, 28:37
TurnAround Couriers v. Canadian Union of Postal Workers (2012), 347 D.L.R. (4th) 149 (F.C.A.)—§ 22:11
Turp v. Can. (2012), 415 F.T.R. 192 (F.C.)—§ 1:9
2241906 v. Scugog Township, 2011 ONSC 2337 (Div. Ct.)—§ 22:15

U.C.F.W. v. KMart Canada, [1999] 2 S.C.R. 1083—§§ 38:20, 43:26
U.E.S., Local 298 v. Bibeault, [1988] 2 S.C.R. 1048, 1090—§ 7:20
UFCW v. Kmart Canada, [1999] 2 S.C.R. 1083—§§ 40:4, 43:20
UL Can. v. Que., [2005] 1 S.C.R. 143—§§ 18:3, 21:8, 21:14
UNA v. Alta., [1992] 1 S.C.R. 901, 930—§§ 37:11, 43:35
Underwood McLellan, Re (1979), 103 D.L.R. (3d) 268 (Sask. C.A.)—§ 21:9
Uniacke v. Dickson (1848), 2 N.S.R. 287 (S.C. N.S.)—§ 2:1
Union Colliery v. Bryden, [1899] A.C. 580—§ 55:1
Union Colliery Co. v. Bryden, [1899] A.C. 580, 584–585—§§ 12:2, 14:18, 15:5, 15:23
United Nurses of Alberta v. Alberta, [1992] 1 S.C.R. 901—§§ 47:27, 47:28
United States v. Burns, [2001] 1 S.C.R. 283—§§ 8:13, 37:14, 38:25, 47:15
United States v. Carolene Products Co. (1938), 304 U.S. 144—§ 55:27
United States v. Cobb, [2001] 1 S.C.R. 587—§§ 37:14, 47:32
United States v. Cotroni, [1989] 1 S.C.R. 1469, 1480—§§ 36:19, 38:8, 38:21
United States v. Ferras, [2006] 2 S.C.R. 77—§§ 40:7, 47:32
United States v. Jamieson, [1996] 1 S.C.R. 465—§ 47:15
United States v. Jamiesun, [1996] 1 S.C.R. 465—§ 37:14
United States v. Kwok, [2001] 1 S.C.R. 532—§ 47:32
United States v. Leon (1984), 468 U.S. 897—§ 41:11
United States v. Lopez (1995), 514 U.S. 549—§ 20:1
United States v. Matlock (1974), 415 U.S. 164—§ 37:19
United States v. Morrison (2000), 529 U.S. 598—§ 20:1
United States v. O'Brien (1968), 391 U.S. 367—§ 43:7
United States v. Ross, [1996] 1 S.C.R. 469—§§ 37:14, 38:21, 47:15
United States v. Ross (1994), 119 D.L.R. (4th) 333, 370-371 (B.C.C.A.)—§ 47:15
United States v. Shulman, [2001] 1 S.C.R. 616—§§ 37:14, 47:32
United States v. Tsioubrios, [2001] 1 S.C.R. 613—§§ 37:14, 47:32
United States v. White (1944), 322 U.S. 694, 698—§ 37:2
United States v. Whitley, [1996] 1 S.C.R. 467—§§ 37:14, 38:21, 47:15
United States v. Windsor (2013), 570 U.S. xxx—§ 55:48
United States v. Yang (2001), 56 O.R. (3d) 52 (C.A.)—§ 47:32
United States v. Ziegler (2007), 474 F.3d 1184 (9th Circ.), 1191—§ 37:19
United States Steel v. Can. (2011), 333 D.L.R. (4th) 1 (F.C.A.)—§ 21:18
Upper Churchill Water Rights, Re, [1984] 1 S.C.R. 297—§§ 15:11, 15:17
Upper House, Re, [1980] 1 S.C.R. 54, 60—§§ 4:1, 4:18, 9:10, 12:10, 14:9
Urban Outdoor Trans Adv. Scarborough (2001), 196 D.L.R. (4th) 304 (Ont. C.A.)—§ 43:30
U.S. v. Butler (1936), 297 U.S. 1, 65–66—§ 6:8
U.S. v. Darby (1941), 312 U.S. 100—§ 21:10
U.S. v. South-Eastern Underwriters Assn. (1944), 322 U.S. 533—§ 21:6
U.S. v. Winstar Corp. (1996), 518 U.S. 839, 873—§ 12:9
UTU v. Central Western Ry., [1990] 3 S.C.R. 1112—§§ 22:1, 22:4, 22:8, 22:9, 22:10, 22:11, 22:13

Valente v. The Queen, [1985] 2 S.C.R. 673—§§ 7:3, 7:5, 7:8
Valentine v. Chrestenson (1942), 316 U.S. 52—§ 43:21
Valin v. Langlois (1879), 3 S.C.R. 1, 19—§ 7:1

Valley Rubber Resources v. B.C. (2002), 219 D.L.R. (4th) 1 (B.C. C.A.)—§ 6:9
Van Buren Bridge Co. v. Madawaska (1958), 15 D.L.R. (2d) 763 (N.B. A.D.)—§ 15:6
Vancini, Re (1904), 34 S.C.R. 621—§ 7:1
Vancouver v. Ward, [2010] 2 S.C.R. 28—§§ 40:18, 40:19
Vancouver International Airport v. Lafarge Canada (2011), 331 D.L.R. (4th) 737 (B.C.C.A.)—§§ 15:18, 22:15
Vancouver Sun, Re, [2004] 2 S.C.R. 332—§ 43:33
Vann Media v. Oakville (2008), 311 D.L.R. (4th) 556 (Ont. C.A.)—§ 43:24
Vann Niagara v. Oakville, [2003] 3 S.C.R. 158—§ 43:24
Vann Niagara v. Oakville (2002), 60 O.R. (3d) 1 (C.A.)—§ 43:24
Vapor Canada Ltd. v. MacDonald (1972) 33 D.L.R. (3d) 434, 449—§ 20:4
Varnam v. Can., [1988] 2 F.C. 454 (C.A.)—§ 7:11
Vauxhall Estates v. Liverpool Corp., [1932] 1 K.B. 733, 746 (Div. Ct.)—§ 12:9
Vetrovec v. The Queen, [1982] 1 S.C.R. 811, 830—§ 8:13
Victoria v. Commonwealth (Second Uniform Tax Case) (1957) 99 C.L.R. 575—§ 8:13
Victorian Stevedoring and Gen. Contracting Co. v. Dignan (1931), 46 C.L.R. 73—§§ 14:5, 14:7
Vidéotron v. Industries Microlec, [1992] 2 S.C.R. 1065, 1071, 1079, 1100—§ 37:12
Virginia State Bd. of Pharmacy v. Virginia Citizens Consumer Council (1976), 425 U.S. 748—§§ 43:6, 43:21
Vriend v. Alberta, [1998] 1 S.C.R. 493—§§ 37:7, 37:13, 38:12, 40:6, 55:7, 55:18, 55:28, 55:48
Vriend v. Alta., [1998] 1 S.C.R. 493—§§ 36:8, 37:13, 38:15, 55:19, 55:25, 55:42
Vriend v. Alta. (1996), 132 D.L.R. (4th) 595, 605 (Alta. C.A.)—§ 37:7

Wakeling v. United States of America, [2014] 3 S.C.R. 549—§ 47:28
Walker and Minister of Housing, Re (1983), 41 O.R. (2d) 9 (C.A.)—§ 22:15
Wallace v. Jaffree (1985), 472 U.S. 38—§ 42:8
Walter v. A.-G. Alta., [1969] S.C.R. 383—§§ 15:5, 21:17, 42:6
Walter v. A.G. Alta., [1969] S.C.R. 383—§ 42:1
Ward v. Can., [2002] 1 S.C.R. 569—§§ 18:2, 18:19
Ward v. Canada, [2002] 1 S.C.R. 569—§§ 15:8, 15:10
Ward v. Rock against Racism (1989), 491 U.S. 781, 798-799—§ 43:20
Wartime Leasehold Regulations, Re, [1950] S.C.R. 124—§ 17:3
Wartime Leasehold Regulations Reference, [1950] S.C.R. 124—§§ 17:8, 17:12
Washington v. Glucksberg (1997), 521 U.S. 702—§ 47:12
Waters and Water Powers, Re, [1929] S.C.R. 200—§ 22:12
Weatherall v. Canada, [1993] 2 S.C.R. 872—§§ 55:27, 55:41
Weber v. Ont. Hydro, [1995] 2 S.C.R. 929—§ 40:16
Weir v. Can. (1991), 84 D.L.R. (4th) 39 (C.A.)—§§ 9:3, 9:10
Weisfeld v. Can. (1994), 116 D.L.R. (4th) 232 (Fed. C.A.)—§ 43:34
Wellbridge Holdings v. Greater Winnipeg, [1971] S.C.R. 957—§ 40:19
Wells v. Newfoundland, [1999] 3 S.C.R. 199—§§ 8:13, 9:12, 12:9
Weremchuk, Re (1986), 35 D.L.R. (4th) 278 (B.C.C.A.)—§ 45:2
Westcoast Energy v. Can., [1998] 1 S.C.R. 322—§§ 22:3, 22:11
Westcoast Energy v. Canada, [1998] 1 S.C.R. 322—§ 22:8

West Coast Hotel v. Parrish (1937), 300 U.S. 379—§§ 5:21, 8:13, 36:5
West Coast Hotel Co. v. Parrish (1937), 300 U.S. 379 overruled Lochner v. New York (1905), 198 U.S. 45—§ 36:18
Westendorp v. The Queen, [1983] 1 S.C.R. 43, 46—§§ 15:2, 18:20, 34:6
Western Industrial Contractors v. Sarcee Developments (1979), 98 D.L.R. (3d) 424 (Alta. C.A.)—§ 28:9
West Virginia State Bd. of Education v. Barnette (1943), 319 U.S. 624—§ 43:7
Wewaykum Indian Band v. Can., [2002] 4 S.C.R. 245—§§ 14:14, 28:13, 28:40
Wewaykum Indian Band v. Canada, [2003] 2 S.C.R. 259—§ 8:3
Whitbread v. Walley, [1990] 3 S.C.R. 1273—§§ 18:17, 22:12, 22:14
Whitebear Band Council, Re (1982), 135 D.L.R. (3d) 128 (Sask. C.A.)—§ 28:9
Whiten v. Pilot Insurance Co., [2002] 1 S.C.R. 595—§ 40:19
Whitman v. American Trucking Assns. (2001), 531 U.S. 457—§ 14:5
WIC Radio v. Simpson, [2008] 2 S.C.R. 420—§§ 37:12, 43:28
Williams v. CNR (1976), 75 D.L.R. (3d) 87 (N.S. A.D.)—§ 18:17
Wilson v. Medical Services Commn. (1988), 53 D.L.R. (4th) 171 (B.C.C.A.)—§ 47:10
Windsor v. Canadian Transit Co., [2016] 2 S.C.R. 617, 2016 SCC 54—§ 7:11
Windsor Airline Limousine Service, Re (1980), 30 O.R. (2d) 732 (Div. Ct.)—§ 22:11
Winko v. B.C., [1999] 2 S.C.R. 625—§§ 18:15, 47:27, 55:20, 55:45
Winner v. S.M.T. Eastern, [1951] S.C.R. 889, 919—§ 55:37
Winnipeg Child and Family Services v. K.L.W., [2000] 2 S.C.R. 519—§§ 47:12, 47:32, 47:38
Winnipeg School Division No. 1 v. Craton, [1985] 2 S.C.R. 150, 156—§§ 12:10, 16:1, 55:7
Winterhaven Stables v. Can. (1988), 53 D.L.R. (4th) 413 (Alta. C.A.)—§ 6:8
Wire Rope Industries v. B.C. Marine Shipbuilders, [1981] 1 S.C.R. 363—§ 22:12
Withler v. Can., [2011] 1 S.C.R. 396—§ 55:22
Withler v. Canada, [2011] 1 S.C.R. 396—§§ 55:22, 55:23, 55:28, 55:44
Wittman v. Emmott (1991), 77 D.L.R. (4th) 77 (B.C.C.A.)—§§ 47:13, 47:32
Wong Sun v. United States (1963), 371 U.S. 471—§ 41:4
Wooley v. Maynard (1977), 430 U.S. 705—§ 43:7
Workers ' Compensation Act, 1983 (Nfld.), Re, [1989] 1 S.C.R. 922; affd. Nova Scotia v. Martin, [2003] 2 S.C.R. 504—§ 55:50
Workmen's Comp. Bd. v. CPR, [1920] A.C. 184—§§ 15:5, 15:20
Wyeth v. Levine (2009), 555 U.S. xxx—§ 16:5
Wynberg v. Ont. (2006), 82 O.R. (3d) 561 (C.A.)—§§ 32:5, 55:20, 55:45
Wynberg v. Ont. (2006), 82 O.R. (3d) 561 (C.A.) (leave to appeal to S.C.C. denied April 12, 2007)—§ 55:21
Wynberg v. Ontario (2006), 82 O.R. (3d) 561 (C.A.) (leave to appeal to S.C.C. denied April 12, 2007)—§§ 55:44, 55:45

YMHA Jewish Community Centre v. Brown, [1989] 1 S.C.R. 1532—§§ 6:8, 21:11, 22:3, 22:10
Young v. Blaikie (1822), 1 Nfld. L.R. 277, 283 (S.C. Nfld.)—§§ 2:2, 2:12
Young v. Young, [1993] 4 S.C.R. 3—§§ 37:11, 42:6, 47:28
Young Offenders Act, Re, [1991] 1 S.C.R. 252—§§ 7:1, 7:16, 7:18, 7:19, 7:20
Yukon Election Residency Requirement, Re (1986), 27 D.L.R. (4th) 146 (Y.T. C.A.)—§ 45:2

Yukon Francophone School Board v. Yukon, 2015 SCC 25—§ 56:19

Zundel v. Boudria (1999), 46 O.R. (3d) 410 (C.A.)—§ 43:34
Zylberberg v. Sudbury Bd. of Ed. (1988), 65 O.R. (2d) 641 (C.A.)—§ 38:15
Zylberberg v. Sudbury Board of Education (1988), 65 O.R. (2d) 641 (C.A.)—§ 42:8

Index

ABDICATION OF LEGISLATIVE POWER
See LEGISLATIVE POWER

ABEL A.S.
Matter, on, **15:5**
Uniformity of law, on, **8:5**

ABORIGINAL PEOPLES OF CANADA
See also ABORIGINAL RIGHTS, INDIANS AND INDIAN LANDS
Customary law, **2:1**
Definition of, **28:2, 28:31**
Eskimos (Inuit), **28:2**
Indian, **28:2, 28:4, 28:31, 37:4, 55:1, 55:2, 55:34, 55:39**
Inuit, **28:2**
Metis, **15:27, 28:2, 28:17, 28:19, 28:31, 55:32**
Non-status Indians, **28:2**
Participation at constitutional conferences, **28:28, 28:41, 28:42**
Representation on jury, **51:23**
Rights of
See ABORIGINAL RIGHTS

ABORIGINAL RIGHTS
Aboriginal peoples of Canada
See ABORIGINAL PEOPLES OF CANADA
Aboriginal rights, **28:3, 28:18 to 28:22, 28:33**
Aboriginal title, **28:3, 28:20, 28:21, 28:32**
Administrative tribunal, power to determine, **7:1, 28:9, 28:18, 40:26**
Affirmative action, **55:32**
Common law, at, **28:19**
Consent to infringement, **28:21**
Constitutional protection of, **28:12, 28:28, 28:29 to 28:39, 28:41**
Consultation
by Crown, **28:21, 28:38**
by regulatory agency, **28:38**
Customary law, survival, **2:1, 28:19**
Evidence of, **28:21, 60:8 to 60:13**

ABORIGINAL RIGHTS—Cont'd
Extinguishment of, **28:3, 28:9, 28:14, 28:20 to 28:22, 28:26, 28:29 to 28:39, 28:34, 28:36**
Forestry, **28:19, 28:26, 28:38**
Gaming laws, **28:20**
Heritage property, **15:24, 21:19**
History of, **4:3, 4:20, 28:18, 28:24**
Honour of the Crown, **28:39**
Hunting and fishing, **28:6, 28:9, 28:11, 28:17, 28:19, 28:24, 28:26, 28:31, 28:33 to 28:35, 55:32**
Language, **28:18, 28:19, 56:1**
Metis rights, **28:19, 28:31, 28:39**
Progressive interpretation of treaties, **28:26**
Property, **15:24, 21:19, 28:2, 28:3, 28:9**
Provincial laws, effect of, **28:29 to 28:39**
Quebec secession, effect of, **5:25**
Recognition of, **28:19, 28:34**
Religion, **28:19**
Remedies for breach, **28:39**
Self-government, **4:20, 28:20, 28:42**
Self-help remedies, **28:39**
Sexual equality, **28:2**
Treaty rights, **10:1, 28:6, 28:12, 28:14, 28:16, 28:23 to 28:27, 28:33, 28:35, 28:38**

ABORIGINAL TITLE
See INDIANS AND INDIAN LANDS, NATIVE RIGHTS

ABORTION
Mootness, **59:8**
Standing, **59:5**
United States, in
See AMERICAN BILL OF RIGHTS
Validity of regulation, **15:10, 18:8, 18:18, 32:2, 32:6, 37:12, 47:6, 47:8, 47:12**

ABSOLUTE LIABILITY
See FUNDAMENTAL JUSTICE

ACCESS TO GOVERNMENT
See EXPRESSION

ACT OF SETTLEMENT
Generally, **1:4, 7:3**

ADMINISTRATION OF JUSTICE
Civil procedure
See CIVIL PROCEDURE
Corrections
See CRIMINAL LAW
Courts
See COURTS
Criminal justice, includes, **19:8 to 19:13, 19:15**
Criminal law
See CRIMINAL LAW
Criminal procedure
See CRIMINAL PROCEDURE
Definition, **7:1**
Description of law, **7:1 to 7:20**
Disrepute, bringing into, **42:5 to 42:11**
Extraterritorial restriction
See EXTRATERRITORIAL COMPETENCE
Judges
See JUDGES
Legal profession, **15:7**
Legislative power over, **7:1 to 7:9**
Police
See POLICE
Prosecutions
See CRIMINAL LAW
Unitary character, **5:15, 7:1, 8:5, 16:8**

ADMINISTRATIVE LAW
See JUDICIAL REVIEW OF ADMINISTRATIVE ACTION

ADMINISTRATIVE MONETARY PENALTY
See CRIMINAL LAW

ADMINISTRATIVE TRIBUNAL
Bias
See BIAS
Charter applicable to
See CHARTER OF RIGHTS
Constitutional limitations on establishment, **7:15, 7:19, 7:20**
Constitutional questions, power to decide, **7:1, 7:19, 18:18, 28:9, 28:18, 40:16, 40:26 to 40:29**
Consult with aboriginal people, power to, **28:38, 40:26**

ADMINISTRATIVE TRIBUNAL —Cont'd
Court of competent jurisdiction, as, **40:16, 40:26**
Criminal law power, establishment under, **18:18**
Delay by, **47:9, 47:12**
Fair procedures, **7:1, 47:38**
Independence, **7:8, 7:9, 15:29**
Judicial power, exercise by, **7:15, 7:19, 7:20**
Judicial review
See JUDICIAL REVIEW OF ADMINISTRATIVE ACTION
Language in
See LANGUAGE
Law, power to decide questions of, **40:16, 40:27**
Natural justice
See NATURAL JUSTICE
Privative clause
See PRIVATIVE CLAUSE
Reasons for establishment, **7:19**
Severance of decisions, **15:14, 42:6, 47:16 to 47:18**

ADMINISTRATOR
Governor General, in place of, **9:3**

ADMIRALTY LAW
Generally, **7:11, 22:12**

ADOPTION OF CHILDREN
Generally, **7:16, 7:19**

ADOPTION OF LAWS
Conflict of laws, by, **13:14**
Contract, by, **10:15**
English law
See ENGLISH LAW IN CANADA
French law
See FRENCH LAW IN CANADA
Indian Act, s. 88, **28:13**
Inter-delegation
See INTER-DELEGATION
Statute binding Crown, **10:15, 10:19**

ADVERTISING
See EXPRESSION

ADVISORY OPINION
See REFERENCE

AERONAUTICS
Aerodrome, location, **15:5, 15:18, 22:14, 22:15**
Airport, construction, **15:18**
Economic regulation, **22:14**
Federal power over, **17:2, 22:13 to 22:15**
Interjurisdictional immunity, **22:15**
Labour relations, **21:11**
Local airline, **22:14, 22:20**
Navigational regulation, **22:14**
Provincial regulation, **22:15**
Taxation of aircraft, **13:4, 15:18, 22:15, 31:18**
Vital part, **15:18, 22:15**

AFFIRMATIVE ACTION
See EQUALITY

AGE
See EQUALITY

AGENCY
See ADMINISTRATIVE TRIBUNAL

AGENCY SHOP
See LABOUR RELATIONS

AGRICULTURE
Agricultural workers
See LABOUR RELATIONS
Concurrent power over, **15:25, 26:1**
Property and civil rights, relation to, **29:4**
Scope, **25:7**
Unionization of workers, **35:2, 37:7, 38:20, 44:4**
Zoning of land, **15:5, 15:18, 25:7**

AIR
See AERONAUTICS, EXTRATERRITORIAL COMPETENCE

ALBERTA
Bill of rights
See ALBERTA BILL OF RIGHTS
Creation of province, **1:6, 2:9**
Crown in right of, liability of
See CROWN
Fiscal capacity, **6:6**
Language rights in, **34:1, 58:8**
Natural resources agreement
See NATURAL RESOURCES AGREEMENTS
Reception of law, **2:2 to 2:4, 2:9**
Region, as, **5:6**

ALBERTA—Cont'd
Responsible government, **9:2**
Tax agreements
See TAX AGREEMENTS

ALBERTA ACT
Generally, **1:6, 12:9**

ALBERTA BILL OF RIGHTS
Generally, **1:6, 31:8, 31:9, 36:18 to 36:24**

ALIEN
See CITIZEN, EQUALITY, NATURALIZATION AND ALIENS

ALIMONY
Generally, **27:8**

AMENDMENT OF CONSTITUTION
Aboriginal participation
See ABORIGINAL PEOPLES OF CANADA
Australia, **4:5, 4:21, 5:23**
Charter of Rights
See CHARTER OF RIGHTS
Compensation for opting out, **4:2, 4:12**
Constitution of Canada
See CONSTITUTION OF CANADA
Constitution of the province
See CONSTITUTION OF THE PROVINCE
Culture in relation to, **4:2, 4:12**
Education in relation to, **1:4, 4:2, 4:12**
Federalism in relation to, **5:19, 5:23**
Future amendments, **4:20 to 4:23**
General amending procedure, **4:8 to 4:15, 4:23**
Governor General
in relation to, **4:6, 4:16, 14:8**
proclamation by, **4:9**
History of Part V, **1:2, 4:1 to 4:3**
House of Commons, in relation to, **4:14, 4:16, 4:18**
Imperial Parliament, by, **1:2, 3:4, 3:9**
Initiation of, **4:9, 4:10**
Judicial adaptation
See INTERPRETATION OF CONSTITUTION
Language in relation to, **4:6, 4:16, 4:18, 4:19, 56:3, 56:4 to 56:8**
Lieutenant Governor, in relation to, **4:6, 4:16, 4:19, 5:9, 12:10, 14:8, 14:9**
Ministers, role of, **4:15**

AMENDMENT OF CONSTITUTION —Cont'd
Native rights, affecting, **28:41**
New provinces, establishment, **1:6, 4:14**
Opting out, **1:11, 4:2, 4:9, 4:11, 4:13, 4:22, 4:23, 5:4, 57:2**
Parliament alone, by, **1:4, 1:6, 4:7, 4:18**
Past amendments, **15:27**
Patriation
See PATRIATION
Procedures before, 1982, **1:2, 4:1 to 4:3**
Provinces, role of, **1:12, 4:1 to 4:3, 4:8 to 4:15, 5:6**
Provincial boundaries, in relation to, **4:14**
Provincial Legislature alone, by, **1:7, 4:6, 4:7**
Quebec role of, **1:11, 1:12, 4:3, 4:4 to 4:7, 4:8, 4:15, 4:17, 4:19, 4:20**
Queen, in relation to, **3:1, 4:6, 4:16, 9:24, 12:10**
Regional veto formula, **4:3, 4:8, 4:15**
Revocation of province's assent or dissent, **4:3, 4:11, 4:13**
Royal assent, **4:6, 4:16**
Secession
See SECESSION
Senate
approval dispensable, **4:3, 4:8, 9:10**
in relation to, **4:14, 4:18, 9:6, 9:10, 12:10, 14:9**
Succession to throne, **1:4, 9:3**
Supreme Court of Canada, in relation to, **1:4, 4:6, 4:14, 4:16, 8:1, 8:2, 8:14**
Time limit on ratification, **4:3, 4:9, 4:16, 4:23**
Unanimity procedure, **4:16, 4:23**
United States, **4:5, 5:23**

AMERICAN BILL OF RIGHTS
See also UNITED STATES
Abortion, **36:5, 47:14**
Affirmative action, **55:3, 55:32**
Agency shop arrangement, **44:8**
Assembly, **44:2**
Association, **44:3**
Bail, **51:18**
Compellability of accused, **51:6**
Contraception, **47:14**
Corporations, and, **37:2**
Counsel, right to, **36:5, 50:6, 50:15**

AMERICAN BILL OF RIGHTS—Cont'd
Cruel and unusual punishment, **36:5, 53:1, 53:7**
Death penalty, **53:7**
Defamation, **43:28**
Definition, **12:3, 34:2, 36:5**
Double jeopardy, **16:8, 51:27**
Due process
See DUE PROCESS
Eighth amendment, **36:5, 51:18, 53:1, 53:7**
Enforcement by Congress, **40:31**
Equal protection, **36:5, 37:10, 45:2, 46:3, 55:3, 55:13**
Equal rights amendment, **55:49**
Evidence obtained in violation of, **36:5, 41:2, 41:4, 41:11, 41:13**
Ex post facto laws, **51:26, 51:31**
Federal government, application to, **37:6**
Fifteenth amendment, **36:5, 45:2**
Fifth amendment, **16:8, 36:5, 46:8, 47:2, 47:10, 50:6, 51:6, 51:13, 51:27, 54:1**
First amendment, **36:5, 37:11, 41:2, 41:7, 43:6, 43:28 to 43:30, 44:2, 44:3, 44:8**
Fourteenth amendment, **5:21, 16:8, 36:5, 37:6, 37:10, 46:3, 47:2, 47:10, 47:13, 51:13, 55:3**
Fourth amendment, **48:3, 48:5 to 48:12, 48:17, 49:1**
Information of charge, **51:4**
Innocence presumption of, **51:13**
Interpretation, **36:4 to 36:7**
Japanese Americans case, **38:32**
Jury, **51:13, 51:19, 51:22, 51:23**
Limitation clause, lacks, **38:1, 55:3**
Nineteenth amendment, **45:2**
Ninth amendment, **36:30**
Non-compellability of accused, **51:6**
Override power, lacks, **36:7**
Police caution, **50:6**
Pornography, **43:29**
Privacy, **48:5 to 48:12**
Property protection, **47:13**
Public forum, **43:30**
Public trial, **51:13**
Religion, **42:2, 42:8, 42:9**
Remedy for breach, **40:17**
School desegregation, **36:5**
School prayers, **36:5, 42:8**

AMERICAN BILL OF RIGHTS—Cont'd
Search or seizure, **48:3, 48:5 to 48:12, 48:14, 48:17, 49:1**
Self-incrimination, **37:2, 51:6, 54:1**
Sentencing, **53:4**
Silence, right of, **36:5, 50:6**
Sixth amendment, **36:5, 50:15, 51:13, 51:19, 51:22, 51:23**
Slavery amendments proscribing, **36:5, 37:13**
Speech, **37:5, 43:6, 43:28 to 43:30**
Speedy trial, **52:1**
State action, **37:11, 37:13**
State aid to denominational schools, **42:9**
States application to, **37:6**
Thirteenth amendment, **36:5, 37:6**
Travel right to, **46:2, 46:3**
Twenty-fourth amendment, **45:2**
Twenty-sixth amendment, **45:2**
Vote, right to, **36:5, 45:2**

AMERICAN DECLARATION OF THE RIGHTS AND DUTIES OF MAN
Generally, **36:20**

AMICUS CURIAE
Generally, **59:12, 59:13**

ANCILLARY JURISDICTION
Generally, **7:11**

ANCILLARY POWER
Generally, **15:5, 15:23, 15:24**

ANTI-TRUST
See COMPETITION

ANYONE
Generally, **37:2**

APPEAL
See COURTS

APPLICATION FOR JUDICIAL REVIEW
See REMEDY

APPROPRIATION
Generally, **6:8, 9:16, 10:13, 10:21, 55:16**

ARBITRARINESS
See FUNDAMENTAL JUSTICE

ARBITRARY DETENTION OR IMPRISONMENT
Arbitrary, **49:3 to 49:11**

ARBITRARY DETENTION OR IMPRISONMENT—Cont'd
Arrest
See ARREST
Canadian Bill of Rights, under, **49:1**
Charter under, **49:1 to 49:11**
Cruel and unusual compared, **53:3**
Detention
See DETENTION
Illegal, **49:9**
Procedural standards, **49:10**

ARISTOTLE
Equality, on, **55:10 to 55:12**

ARMED FORCES
Court martial
See MILITARY TRIBUNAL
Disciplinary procedures, **7:6, 51:3**
Dismissal of member, **10:11**
Education, **57:3**
Equal treatment
See EQUALITY
Legislative power over, **17:8**
Loss of services, action for, **15:24, 18:13**
Provincial law, application to, **15:19**
Trial of member
See MILITARY TRIBUNAL

ARREST
Arbitrary
See ARBITRARY DETENTION OR IMPRISONMENT
Citizen's arrest, **37:8, 37:13**
Counsel, right to
See COUNSEL, RIGHT TO
Definition, **50:2, 50:3**
Detention
See DETENTION
Dwelling house in, **40:4, 48:21, 48:22**
Hot pursuit, following, **48:21, 49:3 to 49:8**
Police powers, **49:3 to 49:11, 50:2, 50:3**
Reasons, right to, **50:4**
Search or seizure incident to, **37:12, 48:2, 48:21 to 48:23, 49:3 to 49:8**
Warrant, requirement of, **40:4, 48:21**

ASSEMBLY
Charter protection, **18:19, 44:2, 48:3**
Legislative power over, **18:19, 21:4, 43:3, 44:1**

ASSISTED HUMAN REPRODUCTION
Legislative power over, **5:7, 18:2, 18:9, 18:18, 32:1**

ASSOCIATION
Charter protection, **17:3, 30:10, 37:7, 37:13, 38:20, 44:3 to 44:8**
Legislative power over, **41:1**

ASYMMETRY
See SPECIAL STATUS

ATOMIC ENERGY
Generally, **17:3, 17:4, 22:10, 30:10, 30:30**

ATTORNEY GENERAL
Action against, **10:5**
Independence, **7:6, 47:32**
Intervention in constitutional cases, **59:1, 59:12**
Minister of justice role, **36:11**
Minister of national defence, analogy, **7:6, 47:32**
Notice in constitutional cases, **17:3, 58:3, 59:12**
Police control of
See POLICE
Prosecutions control of
See CRIMINAL LAW
Rule of law, obligation to, **36:11**
Scrutiny of bills, **35:9, 36:11**
Standing in constitutional cases, **59:3, 59:4**

AUSTRALIA
Amendment of constitution, **4:5, 4:23**
Ancillary power, **15:24**
Civil liberties, **31:6, 31:7**
Classification of laws, **15:8**
Commerce clause, **20:1**
Compensation for property taken, **29:8**
Concurrent powers, **15:25**
Cooperative federalism, **6:10**
Criminal law, **5:9, 18:1, 19:15**
Crown liability in tort, **10:12**
Delegation, **14:5, 14:10**
Divorce
See DIVORCE
Double jeopardy, **16:8**
Enumerated powers, **5:9, 15:23, 15:24, 20:1**
External affairs, **11:9**

AUSTRALIA—Cont'd
Extraterritorial competence, **13:3**
Federalism
See FEDERALISM
Financial arrangements, **6:10**
Full faith and credit, **13:11**
Governors of states, appointment, **9:2**
High Court of Australia
advisory opinions, **7:15, 8:10**
precedent in, **2:2, 8:13**
Inconsistent laws, **15:25, 16:1, 16:5**
Inter se questions, **8:2**
Judges, appointment, **7:2**
Judicial review, **5:21**
Labour relations, **21:10**
Legislative scheme, **15:14**
Marriage and divorce, **27:1, 27:4, 27:9**
Member of Commonwealth, **3:1**
Ministry, **9:5**
Paramountcy, **15:25, 16:1, 16:5**
Premier, dismissal, **9:18**
Prime Minister, dismissal, **9:10, 9:18**
Privy Council appeals, **8:2**
Reservation of bills, **9:11**
Residuary power, **5:9, 15:24, 15:25**
Senate, **9:10**
Severance clause, **15:14**
Spending power, **6:8**
Taxation, **31:6, 31:12, 31:24**
Treaties, **11:9, 11:12**
U.K. Parliament, termination of authority, **3:4**

AUTOCHTHONY
Generally, **3:7, 3:8**

AUTOMATISM AS DEFENCE
See FUNDAMENTAL JUSTICE

AUTONOMY
See also CANADA
Generally, **3:3**

AVIATION
See AERONAUTICS

BAIL
Generally, **19:6, 36:9, 43:32, 47:29, 51:18**

BALFOUR DECLARATION
Generally, **2:12, 3:1, 3:2, 4:2, 11:10**

BANKING
Account, situs, **13:5**
Australia, **5:9**
Definition, **15:27, 24:2**
Federal power over, **5:9, 24:1, 46:13**
Incorporation, **23:1 to 23:5, 24:6, 24:7**
Insurance as part of, **15:18, 24:3**
Near-banks, **24:2, 24:3**
Provincial law affecting, **15:5, 15:9, 15:10, 15:18, 15:20, 16:7, 24:3 to 24:5, 29:4**
Taxation of banks, **15:5, 15:9, 15:10, 15:20, 31:18, 31:23**
United States, **5:9**

BANKRUPTCY AND INSOLVENCY
Adjustment of debts, **25:5 to 25:9**
Adjustment of interest, **25:7**
Concurrent powers, **15:7**
Definition, **25:3 to 25:4**
Disclaimer of assets, **16:3**
Fresh-start provision, **16:3, 16:4, 25:3**
Insurance regulation, **21:7**
Legislation, **25:2**
Power over, **25:1, 25:5, 25:6, 25:10**
Priority of debts, **16:10, 25:10 to 25:13**
Property and civil rights, relation to, **15:23, 25:5, 25:6, 25:10 to 25:13**
Receiver appointment of, **16:3, 16:4**
Statutory lien, **25:11**
Statutory set-off, **25:13**
Voluntary assignments, **25:14**

BAR
See PROFESSIONS

BENNETT, PRIME MINISTER R.B
See NEW DEAL

BENTHAM, JEREMY
Natural rights, on, **36:13**
Utilitarianism on, **38:2**

BIAS
Generally, **7:5, 8:3, 8:4, 47:10, 58:6**

BILL OF RIGHTS
See also CIVIL LIBERTIES
Alberta Bill of Rights
See ALBERTA BILL OF RIGHTS
American Bill of Rights
See AMERICAN BILL OF RIGHTS

BILL OF RIGHTS—Cont'd
Bill of Rights, 1688 (Eng.), **1:9, 34:2, 58:8**
Canadian Bill of Rights
See CANADIAN BILL OF RIGHTS
Canadian Charter of Rights and Freedoms
See CHARTER OF RIGHTS
Constitution Act, 1867
European Convention on Human Rights
See EUROPEAN CONVENTION ON HUMAN RIGHTS
explicit bill of rights lacks, **44:2**
implied bill of rights, **12:3, 34:7**
little bill of rights, **12:3, 34:5, 57:1, 57:2**
surreptitious bill of rights, **15:2, 34:7**
International Covenant on Civil and Political Rights
See INTERNATIONAL COVENANT ON CIVIL AND POLITICAL RIGHTS
Magna Carta, 1297 (Eng.), **34:2**
Provincial, **34:4**
Quebec Charter of Rights and Freedoms
See QUEBEC CHARTER OF RIGHTS AND FREEDOMS
Saskatchewan Bill of Rights Act
See SASKATCHEWAN BILL OF RIGHTS ACT
Statutory, **34:4**
United Kingdom lacks, **1:2, 34:2**
Universal Declaration of Human Rights, **35:1**

BLOOD
Collection, **48:5 to 48:12, 48:13**
Transfusion, **42:6, 47:10, 47:26, 55:44**

BODILY SAMPLE
See SEARCH OR SEIZURE

BOUNDARIES OF PROVINCES
Generally, **2:7, 2:9, 13:4, 30:12, 30:13, 30:22**

BOURASSA, PREMIER R.
Generally, **4:3**

BRANDEIS BRIEF
See EVIDENCE

BREATH SAMPLE
See ROADS

BRITISH COLUMBIA
Aboriginal rights in, **28:21**
Admission to Canada, **1:5, 2:10**
Boundaries, **13:4**
Constitution, **1:4, 9.6(d)**
Crown in right of, liability of
See CROWN
Fiscal capacity, **6:6**
History, **2:10**
Offshore, **13:4, 17:2, 30:12**
Reception of law, **2:10**
Region, as, **5:6**
Responsible government, **2:10, 9:2**

BRITISH COLUMBIA TERMS OF UNION
Generally, **2:10**

BRITISH COMMONWEALTH
See COMMONWEALTH

BRITISH EMPIRE
Canada within
See CANADA
Colony within
See COLONY
Commonwealth, evolution to
See COMMONWEALTH
Dominions within
See DOMINION
Treaty-making, **11:2, 11:10 to 11:12**

BROADCASTING
See RADIO, TELEVISION

BURDEN OF PROOF
Charter, breach of
See CHARTER OF RIGHTS
Limitation of rights
See LIMITATION CLAUSE (s. 1)
Presumption of innocence
See PRESUMPTION OF INNOCENCE
Reverse onus clause
See REVERSE ONUS CLAUSE

BY-LAW
See DELEGATED LEGISLATION

BYNG, GOVERNOR GENERAL
See KING, PRIME MINISTER W.L. McK.

CABINET
Collective responsibility, **9:7, 9:16**
Constitution does not mention, **1:2**
Described, **9:5, 9:13**
Minister
See MINISTER
Prime Minister
See PRIME MINISTER
Privy Council (Canada), part of, **9:5**
Secrecy, **7:19, 7:20, 10:5, 10:7, 15:28**
Statutes do not mention, **1:14**
Voting by members, **9:6**

CABINET GOVERNMENT
See RESPONSIBLE GOVERNMENT

CAISSE POPULAIRE
Banking by, **24:3**
Incorporation, **24:6**

CANADA
Confederation
See CONFEDERATION
Constitution of Canada
See CONSTITUTION OF CANADA
Crown in right of, liability of
See CROWN
Definition, **5:5**
Dominion
See DOMINION
Federalism
See FEDERALISM
Independence evolution to, **1:2, 1:9, 3:1 to 3:5**
Member of Commonwealth, **3:1**
Parliament
See FEDERAL PARLIAMENT
Provinces
See PROVINCES
Union
See CONFEDERATION
United Kingdom subordinate to, **3:1 to 3:5**
United province of
See UNITED PROVINCE OF CANADA

CANADA ACT 1982
Citation, **4:1**
French version, **1:3, 56:3**
History, **1:3, 1:11, 3:4, 3:5, 4:1, 4:2**

CANADA ACT 1982—Cont'd
Incorporation of Constitution Act, 1982, **1:3**
Patriation as
See PATRIATION
Termination of U.K. power over Canada, **3:4, 3:8**

CANADA ASSISTANCE PLAN
Generally, **6:5, 6:7, 6:8, 12:9, 33:5**

CANADA EAST
See also LOWER CANADA, QUEBEC, UNITED PROVINCE OF CANADA
Generally, **2:6, 2:7, 5:4**

CANADA HEALTH AND SOCIAL TRANSFER
Generally, **6:5, 6:7, 6:8, 6:10, 33:5**

CANADA PENSION PLAN
Generally, **5:4, 6:7, 14:10, 33:3, 55:44, 55:48, 58:1**

CANADA WEST
See also ONTARIO, UNITED PROVINCE OF CANADA, UPPER CANADA
Generally, **2:6, 2:7, 5:4**

CANADIAN BILL OF RIGHTS
Arbitrary detention, **49:1**
Assembly, **44:2**
Association, **44:3**
Bail, **51:18**
Charter of Rights, relation to
See CHARTER OF RIGHTS
Common law, application to, **35:1**
Companies, application to, **37:3**
Compellability of accused, **51:6**
Constitutional status, **1:2, 1:8, 35:1, 35:4**
Counsel, right to, **50:1, 50:15**
Cruel and unusual punishment, **53:1**
Due process
See DUE PROCESS
Effect, **12:10, 35:3**
Equality before the law, **55:2, 55:14**
Evidence obtained in violation of, **41:2**
Exempting clause, **12:10, 17:9, 35:3, 36:7, 39:8**
Fair hearing, **35:1, 35:7, 47:2, 47:13**
Federal laws, application to, **1:2, 35:1, 35:2, 37:6 to 37:14**

CANADIAN BILL OF RIGHTS—Cont'd
Fundamental justice
See FUNDAMENTAL JUSTICE
History, **1:2, 34:2, 35:1**
Indian Act, **28:2, 28:13 to 28:16, 35:3, 35:4, 55:2, 55:34, 55:39**
Innocence presumption of, **51:13**
Interpretation canon, as, **35:8**
Interpreter, **56:13**
Judicial review under, **35:3**
Jury, **51:19**
Military justice, **55:2, 55:14**
Minister of Justice, duty of scrutiny, **35:1, 35:9, 40:30**
Notwithstanding clause
See exempting clause
Override power
See exempting clause
Pre-confederation laws, application to, **35:1**
Property protection
See PROPERTY
Provincial law, application to, **35:1, 37:6**
Self-incrimination, **51:6, 54:1**
Statutory basis, **1:2, 1:4**
War Measures Act exempted, **35:3**

CANADIAN CHARTER OF RIGHTS AND FREEDOMS
See CHARTER OF RIGHTS

CANADIAN HUMAN RIGHTS COMMISSION
Powers of, **40:27**

CANADIAN PARLIAMENT
See FEDERAL PARLIAMENT

CANALS
Generally, **22:12**

CAPITAL
Foreign investment, **46:12 to 46:15**
Mobility, **46:12 to 46:15**
Power to regulate, **46:12 to 46:15**
Securities regulation
See SECURITIES REGULATION

CAPITAL PUNISHMENT
See DEATH PENALTY

CASE LAW
See COMMON LAW, PRECEDENT

CENSORSHIP
See EXPRESSION

CERTIORARI
Generally, **34:2**

CHARACTERIZATION OF LAWS
See CLASSIFICATION OF LAWS

CHARGED
Generally, **51:2**

CHARGES
See TAXATION

CHARLOTTETOWN ACCORD, 1992
Generally, **1:4, 4:3, 4:6, 4:12, 4:14 to 4:16, 4:20, 4:23, 5:4, 5:13, 5:17, 5:24, 6:7, 6:8, 8:1, 8:14, 9:10, 22:10, 28:20 28:42, 43:40**

CHARTER OF RIGHTS
See also CONSTITUTION ACT 1982
Amendment of, **36:1**
American jurisprudence, relevance, **36:26**
Application to
aboriginal self-government, **28:42**
administrative tribunals, **37:7, 38:31**
amending procedures, **4:7, 37:9**
anyone, **37:2**
citizen, **37:4**
collective agreement, **44:8**
common law, **37:12, 37:13, 43:14, 43:19, 43:26, 43:28, 43:35, 55:6, 55:7**
convention, **1:14**
corporation, **37:1 to 37:5, 37:13, 47:4, 47:10 51:21, 52:3, 59:6**
courts, **37:9**
Crown corporations, **37:10, 37:13**
deceased person, **37:3**
discretion, **38:8, 38:31**
education, **57:14 to 57:18**
everyone, **37:2**
extradition proceedings
See EXTRADITION
federal and provincial governments, **37:10**
federal and provincial laws, **15:2, 35:1, 36:1, 37:6 to 37:8**
foetus, **37:3, 47:8**
foreign governments, **37:10**
hospitals, **37:8, 37:10**

CHARTER OF RIGHTS—Cont'd
Application to—Cont'd
illegal immigrants, **37:4**
individual, **37:3, 55:5**
Legislature, **1:7, 37:7, 37:8**
member of the public, **37:2, 56:15**
municipalities, **37:8, 37:10**
Parliament, **1:7, 37:7, 37:8**
parliamentary privilege, **1:7, 37:7**
permanent resident, **37:5**
person, **37:2, 51:21, 52:3**
prerogative powers, **1:9, 37:10**
private action, **34:3, 37:7, 37:12, 37:13, 42:7, 43:26, 43:30, 44:8, 55:7**
security guards, **37:13**
silence of legislature, **37:7**
statutory interpretation, **37:12**
Benefit of rights, **37:1 to 37:5**
Burden of proof of justification
See LIMITATION CLAUSE (s. 1)
Burden of rights, **37:6 to 37:14**
Canadian Bill of Rights
comparison, **36:1, 36:25**
impact on, **34:4, 35:1, 35:7, 36:1**
Charter values, **37:12**
Commencement, **36:30, 40:10, 40:25**
Conflict between rights, **36:6, 36:23, 42:6, 42:11, 43:32**
Constitutional status, **35:1, 36:1**
Cost of compliance, **38:4, 38:17, 55:41**
Costs for breach of
See COSTS
Damages for breach of
See DAMAGES
Declaration for breach of
See DECLARATION
Dialogue with legislatures, **36:8 to 36:11**
Distinct society, **38:14**
Due process omitted, **36:5**
Emergency measures, **38:32**
Enforcement
by administrative tribunals, **40:26 to 40:29**
by courts, **21:3, 40:1 to 40:25**
by legislatures, **5:20, 40:31**
English-French discrepancies, **36:24**
Evidence exclusion for breach of
See EVIDENCE

CHARTER OF RIGHTS—Cont'd
Evidence obtained in breach of, **40:2, 41:1 to 41:13, 48:1, 48:14, 48:36, 50:16**
Extraterritorial effect, **13:1, 36:27, 37:2, 37:6 to 37:14, 37:10**
Federalism review compared, **36:4 to 36:7, 36:13, 36:25**
Generous interpretation, **36:19**
Hierarchy of rights, **36:22, 36:23**
History
See CONSTITUTION ACT, 1982
Horizontal effect, **37:13**
International jurisprudence, relevance, **36:20, 38:1**
Interpretation, **36:13 to 36:17, 36:18 to 36:24**
Interpretation Acts, application to, **36:15**
Judicial review under
See JUDICIAL REVIEW OF LEGISLATION
Legislative history, admissibility
See LEGISLATIVE HISTORY
Legislative implementation, **36:2, 55:4**
Legislative power not created by, **36:2**
Limitation clause (s. 1)
See LIMITATION CLAUSE (s. 1)
Minister of Justice, scrutiny by, **35:9, 40:30**
National unity, effect on, **36:3**
New grounds of review, **36:4**
Notwithstanding clause
See override power (s. 33)
Opting out
See override power (s. 33)
Override power (s. 33)
description, **1:11, 4:2, 4:3, 12:3, 15:2, 34:2, 36:7, 36:8, 36:19, 39:1 to 39:8**
evaluation, **39:8**
five-year limit, **39:4**
history, **39:2**
judicial review, **39:7**
retroactive effect, **39:6**
rights that may be overridden, **39:3**
specificity of declaration, **39:5**
use by Ontario, **39:2**
Political questions, **36:12, 36:19**
Preamble, **42:10**
Precedent, **36:25**

CHARTER OF RIGHTS—Cont'd
Pre-Charter jurisprudence, relevance, **36:25**
Presumption of constitutionality under, **38:5**
Progressive interpretation, **36:18**
Property not protected
See PROPERTY
Protective function, **37:13**
Public/ private distinction, **37:13**
Purposive interpretation, **36:20, 36:21**
Remedy for breach, **21:3, 36:30, 40:1 to 40:31**
immunity clause, effect of, **40:19**
Retroactive effect, **36:30**
Scope of rights, **36:19**
Severance
See SEVERANCE
State action
See application to
Supremacy of
See CONSTITUTION
Trivial effects, **36:15**
Undeclared rights, **36:31**
Vagueness of concepts, **36:5**
Waiver of rights
See WAIVER
Work, right to, not protected, **47:10**

CHARTER VALUES
Generally, **37:12, 43:19, 43:28**

CHIEF JUSTICE OF CANADA
See also SUPREME COURT OF CANADA
Administrator, as, **9:3**
Appointment, **1:10, 8:3**
Powers, **8:3**

CHILD
Adoption
See ADOPTION OF CHILDREN
Apprehension, **47:12, 47:32**
Best interests of, **42:6, 47:15, 47:26, 55:44**
Corporal punishment of, **47:12, 47:15, 47:24, 47:28, 53:1, 55:44**
Custody
See CUSTODY AND MAINTENANCE
Parental rights, **42:6, 47:10**
Pornography, **38:22, 43:7, 43:29**

CHILD—Cont'd
Welfare, **27:6, 27:7, 28:7 to 28:12, 42:6, 47:10, 48:14**
Young offenders
See YOUNG OFFENDERS

CHOICE OF LAW
See CONFLICT OF LAWS

CINEMA
See FILMS

CITIZEN
Candidate for election, right to be, **45:6**
Corporation as, **26:3, 37:4, 46:3**
Definition, **26:3, 37:4, 46:3**
Discrimination in favour of
See EQUALITY
Entry to Canada
See MOBILITY
Extradition of, **37:14, 46:2**
Legislative power to define, **37:4, 46:3**
Mobility rights of, **26:1, 26:2, 46:1 to 46:6**
Oath of allegiance, **43:16**
Occupational requirement, as, **37.9(a), 46:1 to 46:6**
Passport right to
See MOBILITY
Sex as a qualification, **36:30, 55:41**
Voting rights of, **45:2**

CIVIL LAW
History in Canada, **2:6, 2:7**
Law of Canada, not, **7:11**
Privy Council, appeals to, **8:5**
Supreme Court of Canada, appeals to, **8:5**

CIVIL LIBERTIES
Bill of rights
See BILL OF RIGHTS
Charter of Rights
See CHARTER OF RIGHTS
Civil rights distinguished, **21:3**
Common law protection, **1:2, 1:8, 34:2**
Competitive with other values, **34:1, 36:6**
Constitution Act, 1867, under
See BILL OF RIGHTS
Definition, **21:3, 34:1, 34:6**
Democracy and, **34:2, 36:2**
Discrimination
See EQUALITY

CIVIL LIBERTIES—Cont'd
Education
See EDUCATION
Egalitarian liberties
See EQUALITY
Expression
See EXPRESSION
Federalism as protection, **5:8, 34:6**
Human rights codes
See HUMAN RIGHTS CODES
Judicial independence and, **34:2, 36:2**
Language
See LANGUAGE
Legal, **34:1**
Legal rights
See LEGAL RIGHTS
Matter as, **34:6**
Parliamentary sovereignty and, **34:2, 34:7**
Political, **34:1**
Power over, **42:2, 43:1, 47:1**
Press
See EXPRESSION
Protection of, **36:2**
Religion
See RELIGION
Speech
See EXPRESSION

CIVIL PROCEDURE
Federal power over, **7:1**
Provincial power over, **7:1**

CIVIL REMEDY
Criminal law power, **18:1**
Damages
See DAMAGES
Federal power generally, **18:16**
Property and civil rights, **20:4**
Trade and commerce power, **15:24, 20:4**

CIVIL RIGHTS
Civil liberties
See CIVIL LIBERTIES
Definition, **21:3, 34:6**
United States usage, **21:3**

CIVIL SERVANT
See PUBLIC SERVANT

CLASS ACTIONS
See COURTS

CLASSES OF SUBJECTS
Description, **15:4, 15:22 to 15:30**
Exclusive, **15:23**
Exhaustive, **12:2, 15:26, 17:1**
Mutual modification, **15:23, 20:1**
Progressive interpretation
See INTERPRETATION OF CONSTITUTION

CLASSIFICATION OF LAWS
Charter of Rights review, for, **15:5, 15:14, 36:12, 36:25**
Distribution of powers review, for, **15:4, 15:5 to 15:13**

COKE C.J.
Judicial review, on, **12:1**

COLLECTIVE AGREEMENT
See LABOUR RELATIONS

COLONIAL LAWS VALIDITY ACT
Generally, **3:2 to 3:4, 5:20**

COLONY
Definition, **2:13, 3:1 to 3:5**
Independence evolution to, **10:1, 11:2, 11:10**
Prerogative power over, **2:1, 2:4, 2:5, 2:7**
Reception of law, **2:1 to 2:13**

COLOURABLE LAW
Generally, **15:11, 31:1**

COMBINES
See COMPETITION

COMMERCE
See TRADE AND COMMERCE

COMMON INFORMER
Generally, **18:13**

COMMON LAW
Canadian Bill of Rights, application to
See CANADIAN BILL OF RIGHTS
Charter of Rights, application to
See CHARTER OF RIGHTS
Civil liberties protected by, **1:8, 34:2**
Constitutional status, **1:8**
Contempt of court
See EXPRESSION
Crown
See CROWN
Definition, **7:11**

COMMON LAW—Cont'd
Federal, **7:11**
International law, adoption of, **11:6**
Laws of Canada
See LAWS OF CANADA
Paramountcy, **16:1**
Prerogative power
See PREROGATIVE POWER
Prescribed by law, **38:7 to 38:9**
Reception
See ENGLISH LAW IN CANADA
Retroactive change, **51:26**
Rights
See UNDECLARED RIGHTS
Uniformity, **2:2 to 2:4, 8:5**

COMMON MARKET
Generally, **2:7**

COMMONWEALTH
Agreements between members, **1:13**
British empire, evolution from, **3:1 to 3:3, 5:5**
Colony
See COLONY
Dominion
See DOMINION
Member, **3:1, 4:20, 5:5**
Monarchy and, **4:20, 9:24**
Treaty-making by members, **11:2, 11:10**

COMMUNICATION
See EXPRESSION, TRANSPORTATION AND COMMUNICATION

COMPANY
Bail, no right to, **51:21**
Banks
See BANKING
Business activity regulation of, **23:6**
Canadian Bill of Rights, application to, **37:2**
Charter of Rights, application to
See CHARTER OF RIGHTS
Citizen as
See CITIZEN
Compellability as accused, **51:11**
Compellability of employee, **51:11**
Directing mind, **51:11**
Equality rights lacks, **55:5**
Expropriation of assets
See EXPROPRIATION

COMPANY—Cont'd
Extraprovincial licensing, **23:2, 23:7, 46:6**
Federally-incorporated
provincial laws, application to, **23:6, 23:7 to 23:9**
Federal power to incorporate, **17:2, 17:7, 20:4, 23:1, 23:4**
Functional limit on objects, **6:9, 23:3, 23:4**
Jury trial, right to, **51:21**
Mobility rights, lacks, **46:6, 46:11**
Provincially-incorporated
capacity outside province, **13:7, 23:2, 23:3, 23:9, 37:4, 37:5, 46:6**
federal law, application to, **23:9**
Provincial power to incorporate, **13:7, 17:2, 23:1 to 23:5**
Religion lacks, **59:6**
Section 7 does not apply, **47:4, 47:10, 59:6**
Securities regulation
See SECURITIES REGULATION
Shares situs, **31:19**
Standing
See STANDING
Territorial limits on powers, **23:2, 23:4**
Trial within reasonable time, **52:3**
Trust company
See TRUST COMPANY

COMPELLABILITY OF ACCUSED
See also EVIDENCE, SELF-INCRIMINATION
Generally, **51:6 to 51:12, 54:3**

COMPENSATION
Property expropriated, for, **13:5, 29:8**
Victim of crime, **15:24, 18:13**

COMPETITION
Civil remedy, **18:10, 18:18**
Conspiracy to lessen, **47:18, 47:27, 47:28**
History of regulation, **18:10**
Power to regulate, **17:7, 18:2, 18:10, 18:18, 20:2, 20:4, 46:13**
Preventive aspect, **18:13**
Prosecution of offences, **19:14, 19:15**
Provincial law inconsistency, **16:4**
Tribunal, **18:10**
United States, **18:10**

COMPETITIVE FEDERALISM
Generally, **5:27**

COMPULSORY PURCHASE
See EXPROPRIATION

COMPUTER
See SEARCH OR SEIZURE

CONCURRENT POWERS
Agriculture, **15:25**
Australia
See AUSTRALIA
Custody, **15:7**
Description, **15:25**
Double aspect
See DOUBLE ASPECT
Entertainment, **15:7**
Gaming, **15:7**
Immigration, **15:25**
Inconsistent laws
See PARAMOUNTCY
Insolvency, **15:7**
Interest, **15:7**
Maintenance, **15:7, 27:8**
Natural resources, export of, **15:25, 21:14, 30:30**
Paramountcy
See PARAMOUNTCY
Penal laws, **18:16**
Pensions, **15:25**
Prosecutions, **19:14, 19:15**
Roads, **15:7**
Securities regulation, **15:7**
Taxation, **15:25, 33:1**
Temperance, **15:7**
United States
See UNITED STATES

CONDITIONAL LAW
Generally, **14:15 to 14:17**

CONFEDERATION
See also CANADA
Definition, **5:2**
Financial arrangements, **6:1**
History, **1:2, 2:6, 2:7, 2:8 to 2:12, 5:2, 5:3**
Laws
See PRE-CONFEDERATION LAWS
Public property, **29:1**

CONFESSIONS
See COUNSEL, RIGHT TO, FUNDAMENTAL JUSTICE

CONFLICT OF LAWS
See also INCONSISTENCY, PARAMOUNTCY REPEAL
Choice of law, **13:10, 13:14**
Companies outside incorporating jurisdiction
See COMPANY
Constitutional law and, **13:9 to 13:14**
Custody and maintenance orders, **27:10, 27:11**
Defamation cases, **13:10**
Foreign laws recognition, **8:5, 13:9**
Limitation periods, **13:14**
Paramountcy distinguished, **27:10**
Recognition of foreign judgments, **13:11**

CONSCIENCE
See RELIGION

CONSENT
See WAIVER

CONSTITUTION
Amendment
See AMENDMENT OF CONSTITUTION
Australia
See AUSTRALIA
Canada, **1:1 to 1:10**
See also CONSTITUTION OF CANADA
Definition, **1:1 to 1:4**
Flexible, **5:19, 5:20**
New Zealand
See NEW ZEALAND
Province
See CONSTITUTION OF THE PROVINCE
Rigid, **5:19**
Supreme, **5:19, 5:20, 15:2, 40:1 to 40:10**
United Kingdom
See UNITED KINGDOM
United States
See UNITED STATES
Unwritten principles, **7:5, 7:8, 7:9, 7:14, 15:28, 36:17, 38:28, 56:14**
Writing in, **5:19**

CONSTITUTION ACT, 1867
Amendment
See AMENDMENT OF CONSTITUTION
Bill of rights in
See BILL OF RIGHTS
Colonial origin, **1:2**
French version unofficial, **56:3**
Gaps in, **1:2**
History, **1:2, 2:6, 2:7**
Judicial review under
See JUDICIAL REVIEW OF LEGISLATION
Legislative history
See LEGISLATIVE HISTORY
Patriation
See PATRIATION
Preamble, **1:2, 1:4, 7:5, 7:8, 7:9, 9:3, 15:28, 34:7**
Statute of Westminster, exemption from, **3:3**
Supremacy, **3:3**
Unwritten rules, **1:8, 7:2, 7:3, 7:8, 7:14, 34:7, 47:15**

CONSTITUTION ACT, 1871
Generally, **2:9, 4:14, 7:13**

CONSTITUTION ACT, 1982
Canada Act 1982, incorporation in, **1:3**
Canadian Charter of Rights and Freedoms
See CHARTER OF RIGHTS
Citation, **4:1**
Commencement, **3:4, 4:1**
French version, **56:3**
History, **1:3, 1:11, 3:4, 4:1, 4:2, 36:1, 39:2, 56:20**
Legislative history
See LEGISLATIVE HISTORY
Part V
See AMENDMENT OF CONSTITUTION
Patriation as
See PATRIATION

CONSTITUTIONAL ACT, 1791
Generally, **1:4, 2:6**

CONSTITUTIONAL COURT
Proposal for, **5:22, 8:14**

CONSTITUTIONAL EXEMPTION
See INTERPRETATION OF CONSTITUTION

CONSTITUTIONALISM
See also RULE OF LAW
Generally, **1:1**

CONSTITUTIONALITY, PRESUMPTION OF
Generally, **5.5(h), 5:21, 15:15, 38:5, 60:13**

CONSTITUTIONAL LAW
See also CONSTITUTION OF CANADA
Definition, **1:1**

CONSTITUTIONAL TORT
See REMEDIES

CONSTITUTIONAL VALUE
See MATTER

CONSTITUTION AMENDMENT PROCLAMATION, 1983
Generally, **1:4, 4:23**

CONSTITUTION OF CANADA
Amendment
See AMENDMENT OF CONSTITUTION
Definition, **1:2, 1:4, 1:7, 3:7, 4:6, 4:14, 4:16, 4:18, 36:1, 37:7, 40:1**
Entrenchment, **1:4, 1:6, 4:10, 5:19**
French version, **1:3, 56:3**
Interpretation
See INTERPRETATION OF CONSTITUTION
Patriation
See PATRIATION
Supremacy, **1:4, 1:6, 3:4, 5:19, 5:20, 36:1, 58:1, 59:1**

CONSTITUTION OF THE PROVINCE
Definition of, **4:17, 4:19, 5:25**
Delegation, **14:7**
Power to amend, **4:17, 4:19, 9:19, 12:10**

CONSTITUTION OF UNITED STATES
Amendments to
See AMERICAN BILL OF RIGHTS
Bill of rights
See AMERICAN BILL OF RIGHTS
General
See UNITED STATES

CONTEMPT OF COURT
Charged with offence, **51:2**
Charter application of, **37:12, 51:2**
Compellability of accused, **51:10**
Expression restraint of
See EXPRESSION
Jurisdiction over, **7:16, 7:19**
Tribunal's power to punish, **7:19**
Vagueness, **47:25**

CONTINENTAL SHELF
Generally, **13:4, 32:3**

CONTRACT
Constitutional protection, **1:4, 9:12, 12:9, 29:8**
Crown liability, **10:10**
Debt adjustment
See DEBT ADJUSTMENT
Extraprovincial right
See EXTRATERRITORIAL COMPETENCE
Forum selection clause, effect of, **13:10**
Power to
See SPENDING POWER
Power to regulate
See PROPERTY AND CIVIL RIGHTS

CONTROL TEST
Charter of Rights application, **37:10**
Crown agent, **10:3**

CONVENTION
Caretaker, **9:4, 9:14**
Charter of Rights
See CHARTER OF RIGHTS
Choice of counsel, **50:12, 50:14**
Constitutional status, **1:2, 1:4, 1:10**
Definition, **1:10**
Enforceability, **1:9, 1:10, 8:11**
Fixed election dates, no convention, **1:14, 9:20**
Governor General's powers limited by, **1:10**
Imperial Parliament's powers limited by, **1:10, 3:3, 4:1**
Law relation to, **1:10**
Newfoundland admission, **2:13**
Origin, **1:10**
Provincial role in amendments, **1:10, 4:1**
Queen's powers limited by, **1:10**

CONVENTION—Cont'd
Responsible government
See RESPONSIBLE GOVERNMENT
Treaty
See TREATY
USA, in, **1:10**
Usage contrasted, **1:10**
Writing, **1:10**

CONVEYANCING
See PROPERTY

COOPERATIVE FEDERALISM
Constitutional principle, as, **5:27, 18:18**
Description, **5:27**
Environmental harmonization, **30:32**
Federal-provincial conferences
See FEDERAL-PROVINCIAL CONFERENCES
Federal-provincial financial arrangements
See FINANCIAL ARRANGEMENTS
Federal-provincial inter-delegation
See INTER-DELEGATION
Judicial appointments, **7:2**
Marketing, **20:3**
Shared-cost programmes
See SHARED-COST PROGRAMMES

COPYRIGHT
Generally, **18:16, 20:4**

CORPORATION
See COMPANY

CORRECTIONS
See CRIMINAL LAW

COST
See LIMITATION CLAUSE (s. 1)

COSTS
Advance costs, **50:15, 59:15**
Charter remedy, as, **40:16, 40:20, 47:34, 59:17**
Constitutional cases, in, **59:14 to 59:17**
Crown, against, **59:12, 59:14 to 59:17**
Special costs, **59:16**

COUNSEL, RIGHT TO
Canadian Bill of Rights, under, **50:1, 50:15**
Description, **50:5 to 50:16**
Evidence obtained in breach of, **41:4, 41:8, 41:9, 50:8, 50:16**

COUNSEL, RIGHT TO—Cont'd
Legal aid, **19:6, 36:20, 38:17, 40:4, 47:32, 50:8, 50:15**
No general right, **38:17, 43:33, 50:15**
Plea bargain, **50:14**
Police caution, **40:9, 50:5 to 50:16**
Police questioning, **47:27 to 47:29, 47:31, 50:7, 50:12**
Roadside stops, **50:3**
Search, at time of, **50:3, 50:4**
Silence, right to
See FUNDAMENTAL JUSTICE
Waiver
See WAIVER

COURT MARTIAL
See MILITARY TRIBUNAL

COURT OF COMPETENT JURISDICTION
See REMEDY

COURTS
See also ADMINISTRATION OF JUSTICE, JUDGES, JUDICIAL POWER
Access to
See EXPRESSION
Advisory opinions
See REFERENCE
Amalgamation of county and district, **7:1, 7:17**
Appeal right to, **47:32**
Bias
See BIAS
Charter of Rights, application to
See CHARTER OF RIGHTS
Choice of law, **13:6, 13:9, 13:14**
Civil jurisdiction, **7:1, 13:10, 13:11**
Class actions, **13:10, 13:11**
Constitutional cases
See JUDICIAL REVIEW OF LEGISLATION
Constitutional limits on jurisdiction, **7:15 to 7:20, 13:9 to 13:14, 19:4, 27:14 to 27:17, 43:28**
Contempt of court
See CONTEMPT OF COURT
Core jurisdiction, **7:16, 7:19, 7:20**
Criminal jurisdiction, **7:1, 7:4, 7:11, 7:16, 19:3, 19:17**
Establishment, **7:1 to 7:14**

COURTS—Cont'd
Exchequer Court of Canada
See EXCHEQUER COURT OF CANADA
Extraterritorial competence
See EXTRATERRITORIAL COMPETENCE
Fair trial, **36:9, 47:32**
Family courts, **7:16, 27:14 to 27:17**
Federal Court of Canada
See FEDERAL COURT OF CANADA
Federal courts, **7:1, 7:10 to 7:14, 19:5, 27:15**
Federal questions, **7:1, 7:2, 7:11**
Full faith and credit
See FULL FAITH AND CREDIT
Hearing fees, **7:18, 40:6**
High Court of Australia
See AUSTRALIA
House of Lords
See HOUSE OF LORDS
Independence
See JUDGES
Interpreter, right to, **56:11, 56:13**
Judges
See JUDGES
Judgments, recognition of
See JUDGMENTS RECOGNITION OF
Judicial review of administrative action
See JUDICIAL REVIEW OF ADMINISTRATIVE ACTION
Judicial review of legislation
See JUDICIAL REVIEW OF LEGISLATION
Jury
See TRIAL
Language rights in, **56:3, 56:4, 56:9 to 56:13, 56:14, 56:15**
Law-making by, **58:1**
Martial
See MILITARY TRIBUNAL
Non-judicial functions, **7:15, 7:18**
Precedent
See PRECEDENT
Pre-confederation powers, **13:10**
Preliminary inquiry judge
See PRELIMINARY INQUIRY
Privative clause
See PRIVATIVE CLAUSE

COURTS—Cont'd
Privy Council
See JUDICIAL COMMITTEE OF PRIVY COUNCIL
Procedure
See CIVIL PROCEDURE, CRIMINAL PROCEDURE
Provincial courts, **7:1 to 7:9, 40:28, 40:29**
Remedy
See REMEDY
Reporting of proceedings
See EXPRESSION
Superior courts, **7:1 to 7:9, 7:10 to 7:14, 7:15 to 7:20, 11:6**
Supervision of remedial orders, **36.4(e), 40:23, 56:25**
Supreme Court of Canada
See SUPREME COURT OF CANADA
Supreme Court of United States
See UNITED STATES
Territorial courts, **7:13**
Testimony behind veil, **36:23, 42:6**
Unified criminal court, **7:16, 19:4, 19:5**
Youth courts, **7:16, 7:19**

CREDIT
See BANKING, BANKRUPTCY AND INSOLVENCY, DEBT ADJUSTMENT, INTEREST

CREDITORS' RIGHTS
See BANKING BANKRUPTCY AND INSOLVENCY, DEBT ADJUSTMENT, INTEREST

CREDIT UNION
Banking by, **24:3**
Incorporation, **24:7**

CRIMINAL LAW
Abortion, **15:11, 18:8, 18:18**
Absolute liability
See FUNDAMENTAL JUSTICE
Administrative monetary penalty, **51:3, 59:12**
Assembly, **18:16, 44:1**
Assisted human reproduction
See ASSISTED HUMAN REPRODUCTION
Australia
See AUSTRALIA
Automatism as defence
See FUNDAMENTAL JUSTICE

CRIMINAL LAW—Cont'd
Censorship
See EXPRESSION
Civil remedy, **18:10, 18:16, 18:17**
Compensation of victim, **15:24, 18:17, 40:17**
Competition regulation
See COMPETITION
Conviction review of, **58:4**
Corrections
See Punishment
Courts
See COURTS
Deception, **18:3**
Definition, **15:27, 18:2**
Discrimination, prohibition of, **55:1**
Double jeopardy
See DOUBLE JEOPARDY
Drugs
See FOOD AND DRUGS
Duress as defence
See FUNDAMENTAL JUSTICE
Economic regulation, **18:2**
Environment, **18:7, 18:18, 30:32**
Expression
See EXPRESSION
Federal power over, **5:9, 18:1**
Food
See FOOD AND DRUGS
Forfeiture of goods, **18:17, 18:19, 51:3**
Gambling, **18:18, 18:19, 21:17**
Gun control
See GUNS
Harm principle, **18:2, 47:15, 47:24**
Health
See HEALTH
Innocence presumption of
See INNOCENCE, PRESUMPTION OF
Inquiry into organized crime, **19:8, 19:16**
Insanity
See INSANITY
Insurance regulation, **18:18**
Intoxication as defence
See FUNDAMENTAL JUSTICE
Jurisdiction vesting of, **19:4**
Juvenile delinquency
See YOUNG OFFENDERS
Legal product, advertising of, **18:5, 43:23**
Magistrate's jurisdiction, **19:3 to 19:5**

CRIMINAL LAW—Cont'd
Mens rea requirement
See FUNDAMENTAL JUSTICE
Mental disorder, **18:14, 47:24, 49:3 to 49:8, 55:45**
Murder
See MURDER
Narcotics
See FOOD AND DRUGS
Offence defined, **51:3**
Pardon, **19:17**
Parole, **19:19, 47:9, 47:15, 51:31**
Penal laws, **18:19**
Police
See POLICE
Police informer rule
See EVIDENCE
Pollution, **18:7, 18:18, 30:32**
Prevention of crime, **18:14, 18:19, 48:21**
Probation, **19:20**
Procedure
See CRIMINAL PROCEDURE
Professional responsibility, **15:7, 19:6, 19:14, 47:34**
Prosecution
control by Attorney General, **7:6, 36:11, 47:24**
federal, **17:6, 18:1, 19:15, 20:5**
provincial, **18:1, 18:19, 19:14**
Prostitution, **18:19**
Provincial penal laws, **16:5, 16:8, 18:1, 18:16, 18:19, 19:18**
Public inquiries, **19:16**
Punishment
capital
See DEATH PENALTY
cruel and unusual
See CRUEL AND UNUSUAL PUNISHMENT
delay in sentencing, **52:8**
double
See DOUBLE JEOPARDY
forfeiture of property, **18:13, 18:19**
imprisonment, **18:19**
industrial school, custody in, **51:20**
judicial discretion, **53:4**
powers over, **18:1, 18:19, 19:17, 47:9, 47:15**
pre-sentence custody, **47:24**
Regulation by province, **19:6, 19:14, 21:9**

CRIMINAL LAW—Cont'd
Regulation under, **18:7, 18:18, 19:18, 21:8**
Regulatory offence, **47:16 to 47:18, 51:14, 52:4**
Repeal, power to, **18:14, 18:18**
Restitution to victim, **18:17**
Retroactive
See RETROACTIVE LAWS
Roads
See ROADS
Sentence
See punishment
Speech
See EXPRESSION
Strict liability
See FUNDAMENTAL JUSTICE
Sunday observance
See SUNDAY OBSERVANCE
Tobacco
See FOOD AND DRUGS
True crime, **47:17, 47:18, 51:14, 52:4**
United States
See UNITED STATES
Young offenders
See YOUNG OFFENDERS

CRIMINAL PROCEDURE
Bail
See BAIL
Disclosure to defence, **40:19, 47:34, 47:35**
Double jeopardy
See DOUBLE JEOPARDY
Evidence
See EVIDENCE
Fitness to stand trial, **18:11, 47:24, 51:13**
Full answer and defence
See FUNDAMENTAL JUSTICE
Judicial investigative hearing, **7:5, 43:33, 47:27 to 47:29**
Legal rights
See LEGAL RIGHTS
Power over, **7:1, 18:1, 19:6**
Preservation of property, **48:4**
Presumption of innocence
See INNOCENCE, PRESUMPTION OF
Search or seizure
See SEARCH OR SEIZURE
Trial of indictable offences, **19:4**

CROWN
See also CANADA, PROVINCES, QUEEN
Agent, **10:2 to 10:4, 10:13 to 10:15, 31:24, 37:10**
Attorney General, action against, **10:5**
Bankruptcy claim in, **25:11 to 25:13**
Commercial activity, **31:27**
Common law origin, **1:8**
Contractual liability, **10:10**
Costs against
See COSTS
Criminal liability, **10:4**
Definition, **10:1, 10:16, 10:17, 37:10**
Discovery against, **10:6**
Evidence, power to withhold, **7:3, 7:19, 7:20, 10:5, 10:6 to 10:9, 15:1, 15:28, 47:32, 60:2**
Expropriation of Crown property, **10:21, 29:7**
Extraterritorial capacity, **13:8**
Federal court proceedings, **7:11, 10:5, 55:16**
Fiat for suit, **10:5**
Injunction immunity, **40:16**
Interjurisdictional immunity, **10:16 to 10:21, 28:20**
Legislative power over, **10:13**
Levy taxes may not, **58:6**
Mandamus, immunity, **40:16**
One and indivisible, **10:1, 10:16, 10:17, 10:20**
Prerogative power
See PREROGATIVE POWER
Privilege, evidence, **10:5, 10:6 to 10:9**
Proceedings against, **7:11, 10:5**
Proceedings by, **7:11**
Property
in general
See PUBLIC PROPERTY
recovery of, **10:10**
Public interest immunity, **10:5, 10:6 to 10:9**
Restitution against, **58:7**
Servants
definition, **10:3**
dismissible at pleasure, **10:11**
taxation, liability to pay, **31:22**
tortious liability, **10:12, 34:2, 58:4, 58:6**

CROWN—Cont'd
Special powers and privileges, **10:5**
Spend money may not, **58:6**
Statutes
common law immunity, **10:3, 10:13**
constitutional limitations, **10:18 to 10:21, 29:7, 31:24 to 31:27**
statutory immunity, **10:14**
Succession to throne
See QUEEN
Taxation of Crown property, **31:21 to 31:23, 31:24 to 31:27**
Tortious liability, **58:4**
Unconstitutional taxes, recovery from, **58:7**

CROWN CORPORATION
Charter application to
See CHARTER OF RIGHTS
Crown equivalent to, **10:2 to 10:4, 31:24, 37:10**
Ministerial control, **9:7**

CRUEL AND UNUSUAL PUNISHMENT
Arbitrary detention compared, **53:3**
Corporal punishment of child, **53:1**
Death penalty, **47:15, 53:7**
Described, **53:1 to 53:7**
Extradition
See EXTRADITION
Foreign law, **47:15, 53:3**
Indeterminate sentence, **53:5**
Life imprisonment, **47:19, 53:4**
Minimum sentence, **37:14, 40:8, 40:29, 47:15, 47:25, 53:3, 53:4**
Prison conditions, **53:6**

CULTURE
Amendments relating to, **4:2, 4:12**
Charlottetown Accord proposals, **4:3, 9:6**
Education
See EDUCATION
Expression
See EXPRESSION
Heritage property, **15:24, 21:19, 28:9**
Language
See LANGUAGE
Literature
See LITERATURE
Matter as, **17:5**
Radio
See RADIO

CULTURE—Cont'd
Religion
See RELIGION
Television
See TELEVISION
Theatre
See THEATRE

CUSTODY AND MAINTENANCE
See also DIVORCE, FAMILY, MARRIAGE
Alimony, **27:8**
Concurrent powers, **15:7, 15:24**
Conflicting laws or orders, **16:3, 27:10 to 27:13**
Court jurisdiction over, **7:16**
Fair hearing, **27:6, 38:17, 47:12, 47:32, 50:15**
Federal power, **15:24, 18:16, 27:6, 27:7**
Provincial power, **18:16, 27:6**
Religious instruction of child, **42:6**

CUSTOM
Generally, **1:12**

CUSTOMS DUTY
Aboriginal exemption, **28:19**
Australia, **31:6**
Confederation, **5:9, 6:1**
Customs declaration, disclosure of, **48:5 to 48:12**
Forfeiture of goods not penal, **51:3**
Indirect character, **31:8**
Power to impose, **5:9, 6:2, 20:2, 31:8**
Provinces, between, **31:4, 46:8**
Provincial government liability for, **31:25**
Regulatory effect, **31:25**
Search at border
See SEARCH OR SEIZURE
United States, **31:6**

DAMAGES
Cap on, **55:45**
Charter breach, for, **40:19**
Illegal official action, for, **34:2**
Unconstitutional law, for
See UNCONSTITUTIONAL LAW

DANGEROUS OFFENDER
Generally, **49:3 to 49:8, 51:2, 51:31**

DEAFNESS
See EQUALITY

DEATH PENALTY
Cruel and unusual, **36:5, 53:7**
Deportation to face, **37:14**
Extradition to face, **37:14, 46:2, 47:15, 53:7**
Power to impose, **18:16**

DEBT ADJUSTMENT
Generally, **13:5**

DECLARATION
See also UNCONSTITUTIONAL LAW
Administrative tribunal, power to make, **40:26**
Apprehended infringements of rights, **40:15**
Attorney-General action against, **10:5, 59:1, 59:2**
Constitutional remedy, **40:18, 40:19, 40:25, 59:1, 59:18, 59:19**
Judicial review of administrative action, means of, **34:2**
Limitation period, **40:10, 40:25, 59:18, 59:19**
Standing
See STANDING
Suspended, **40:4, 58:1**

DECLARATORY JUDGMENT
See DECLARATION

DECLARATORY LAW
See RETROACTIVE LAW

DECLARATORY POWER
Generally, **5:9, 5:18, 20:2, 22:1, 22:10, 22.14(b), 30:8**

DE FACTO OFFICER
Generally, **58:6, 58.8(c)**

DEFAMATION
See EXPRESSION

DEFEAT OF GOVERNMENT
Australia, in, **9:10, 9:18**
Dissolution of Parliament
See FEDERAL PARLIAMENT
House of Commons, in, **9:11, 9:14, 9:16, 9:18, 9:20**
Senate in, **9:11**
Snap vote, **9:16**
United Kingdom, **9:16**

DEFENCE
See ARMED FORCES, NATIONAL SECURITY, WAR, WAR MEASURES ACT

DELAY
Charge, in laying, **51:2, 51:4, 52:6**
Informing of specific offence, in, **51:4**
Trial within reasonable time
See TRIAL

DELEGATED LEGISLATION
See also DELEGATION
By-law, **14:1, 55:40**
Charter, application to, **37:8, 38:7**
Language requirements, **56:8**
Policy as, **37:8, 38:7, 40:1**
Power to enact, **14:1, 38:7 to 38:9**
Regulation, **14:1**
Rule, **14:1**

DELEGATION
See also DELEGATED LEGISLATION
Acquiescence by, **14:18**
Australia, **14:5, 14:10**
By provinces, **20:4**
Executive power, of, **14:5**
Federal power to provinces
See INTER-DELEGATION
Initiative and referendum
See INITIATIVE AND REFERENDUM
Judicial power, of, **14:6**
Legislative power, of, **14:5, 14:11**
Power of, **14:1 to 14:18**
Provincial power to Dominion
See INTER-DELEGATION
Taxation power of, **14:5, 31:1**
United Kingdom, **14:2**
United States, **14:5, 14:9**

DELICT
See TORT

DEMOCRACY
See ELECTIONS, EXPRESSION, RESPONSIBLE GOVERNMENT

DEMOCRATIC RIGHTS
See ELECTIONS

DENOMINATIONAL SCHOOLS
See EDUCATION

DEPORTATION
See also EXTRADITION
Citizen, of, **47:9, 55:46**
Cruel and unusual, not, **53:2**
Death penalty, to face, **37:6 to 37:14**
Non-citizen of, **47:9, 47:32, 55:37, 55:46**
Power of
See MOBILITY
Procedure, **47:31**
Refugee, of, **47:9**
Torture, to face, **11:6, 36:20, 37:14, 47:9, 47:15**

DEPUTY MINISTER
Generally, **9:4, 9:7**

DE SMITH, S.A.
Patriation on, **3:8**
Revolution, on, **5:26**

DETENTION
Arbitrary
See ARBITRARY DETENTION OR IMPRISONMENT
Arrest
See ARREST
Counsel right to
See COUNSEL, RIGHT TO
Defined, **41:11, 49:2, 50:2, 50:3**
Insanity, on account of
See INSANITY
Investigative, **48:25, 49:3 to 49:8, 50:2**
Police powers, **49:3 to 49:11, 50:2, 50:3**
Psychological, **49:3 to 49:8, 49:9, 50:2, 50:3**
Reasons right to, **50:4**
Review by habeas corpus
See REMEDY

DEVOLUTION
See also DELEGATION
Generally, **5:3, 5:4, 5:20, 12:1, 14:2**

DIALOGUE
See JUDICIAL REVIEW OF LEGISLATION

DICEY A.V.
Prerogative, on, **1:9**
Rule of law, on, **58:3**
Sovereignty, on, **12:1**

DICKSON, CHIEF JUSTICE R.G.B.
Appointment, **1:12**

DICKSON, CHIEF JUSTICE R.G.B. —Cont'd
Composition of bench, policy, **8:3**

DIEFENBAKER, PRIME MINISTER J.G.
Canadian Bill of Rights, **35:1**

DIRECTORY RULE
Generally, **1:10, 12:10, 14:5, 56:6, 58:9**

DISABILITY MENTAL
See EQUALITY

DISABILITY PHYSICAL
See EQUALITY

DISALLOWANCE
Federal statutes, of, **3:1, 5:13, 9:3, 9:11**
Provincial statutes, of, **3:1, 5:9, 5:13, 9:3, 9:11**

DISCIPLINE OFFENCE AS
Generally, **51:3**

DISCOVERABILITY RULE
See EVIDENCE

DISCRIMINATION
See EQUALITY

DISPENSING POWER
Generally, **1:9, 34:2**

DISPROPORTIONALITY
See FUNDAMENTAL JUSTICE
Suspended declaration of invalidity, **36:10, 40:4**

DISTINCT SOCIETY
See QUEBEC

DISTRIBUTION OF POWERS
See also FEDERALISM, LEGISLATIVE POWER
Classes of subjects
See CLASSES OF SUBJECTS
Executive matches legislative, **1:9**
Federal state, in, **5:1 to 5:7, 5:19, 5:20, 15:1, 17:2**
Gaps in, **12:2, 17:2**
Prerogative powers, **1:9**
Reform of, **4:21**

DIVISION OF POWERS
See DISTRIBUTION OF POWERS

DIVORCE
See also MARRIAGE
Australia, **5:9, 27:1, 27:9**
Corollary relief
See CUSTODY AND MAINTENANCE
History in Canada, **27:1, 27:14 to 27:17**
Power over, **5:9, 27:1, 27:5 to 27:9**
Procedure, **27:5**
Property division, **27:9, 27:16**
Provincial superior courts, **27:16**
Recognition, **27:1**
United States, **5:9, 27:1**

DIXON SIR OWEN
Judicial review on, **5:21**

DOCUMENTS
Compelled production
See SEARCH OR SEIZURE
Crown privilege
See CROWN

DOMINION
See also CANADA
Abandonment of word, **5:5**
Canada, of, **2:12, 3:1, 5:5**
Colony, evolution from, **3:1, 5:5**
Definition, **3:1, 5:5**
Member of Commonwealth, evolution to, **3:1, 5:5**
Newfoundland as, **2:12**

DOMINION-PROVINCIAL CONFERENCES
See FEDERAL-PROVINCIAL CONFERENCES

DOUBLE ASPECT
Generally, **15:7, 15:23, 15:25, 16:1, 16:7, 17:1**

DOUBLE JEOPARDY
Generally, **16:8, 16:9, 51:27 to 51:30**

DRIVER'S LICENCE
See ROADS

DRUGS
See FOOD AND DRUGS

DUE PROCESS
American Bill of Rights, under, **47:2, 47:10, 47:13**

DUE PROCESS—Cont'd
Canadian Bill of Rights, under, **29:8, 35:1, 47:2, 47:13**
Charter, not included in, **36:5, 47:2**
Compensation for property taken, **29:8**
Emancipation of slaves, **36:3, 36:5**
Equal protection included, **55:3**
Extraterritorial restrictions, **13:10, 13:14**
Incorporation of other rights, **16:8, 28:21, 37:6, 47:2, 55:3**
Jury right to, **51:19**
Presumption of innocence, **51:13**
Proof beyond reasonable doubt, **51:13**
Substantive, **5:21, 29:8, 36:5, 47:10, 47:14**
Travel right to, **46:2, 46:3**

DUPLESSIS, PREMIER M.
Generally, **34:2**

DUPLICATION OF LAWS
See DOUBLE ASPECT, PARAMOUNTCY

DURESS AS DEFENCE
See FUNDAMENTAL JUSTICE

DURHAM LORD
Generally, **2:6, 9:2**

DWORKIN RONALD
Rights, on, **38:2**

EDUCATION
Amendments relating to
See AMENDMENT OF CONSTITUTION
Charter, application to, **57:14 to 57:18**
Corporal punishment, **27:2, 40:9, 47:12, 47:15**
Denominational school rights, **5:9, 5:16, 34:5, 40:31, 42:9, 55:35, 56:17, 56:18, 57:1 to 57:13**
Federal power, **57:3 to 57:5**
Indian, **28:2, 57:3**
Language of
See LANGUAGE
Legislative powers over, **42:1, 55:17, 57:1 to 57:13**
Manitoba school question, **5:16**
Private religious schools, **42:9, 55:35, 57:6**
Protected rights and privileges, **57:2, 57:5, 57:6, 57:7 to 57:13**

EDUCATION—Cont'd
Provincial power, **56:19, 57:1, 57:2**
Reduction in funding, **57:12**
Religion in schools, **36:5, 42:8, 42:9, 57:15**
School boards, elections, **43:40, 58:2**
Search of students, **41:11, 48:5 to 48:12, 48:22, 48:27, 57:18**
Separate schools, **57:1 to 57:13**
Students with disabilities, **55:24, 55:30, 55:45, 57:17**

EFFECT OF LAW
Charter of Rights relevance to, **36:13 to 36:17, 36:25**
Distribution of powers, relevance to, **15:9**

ELECTIONS
Absentee voting, **40:17**
Advertising, **15:15, 15:19, 15:20, 43:38, 45:4**
Broadcasting, **22:18**
Candidate, right to be, **37:15, 45:6**
Contested, **45:5**
Expenditures, **15:20, 36:9, 36.11(a), 43:12, 43:38, 45:4**
First-past-the-post, **45:4**
Five-year terms, **9:10, 9:18, 9:19, 45:7**
Fixed dates, **1:14, 9:19, 9:20**
Importance of freedom of, **34:2**
One person, one vote, **40:4, 45:3**
Opinion polls, **38:20, 43:12, 43:18, 45:4**
Political speech
See EXPRESSION
Power over, **9:19, 45:1**
Prisoners voting, **36:9, 45:2**
Public servants' involvement
See PUBLIC SERVANTS
Referendum
See REFERENDUM
Regulation, **43:39, 45:4**
Residence requirement, **43:39, 45:2, 46:4, 55:49**
Voting, **38:6, 45:1 to 45:5**

ELECTRICITY
Consumption as evidence of crime, **48:5 to 48:12**
Export, **30:28**
Nuclear, **17:4, 22:10, 30:10, 30:29, 30:30**
Power over, **30:28**
Taxation, **31:14**

ELECTRICITY—Cont'd
Transmission, **30:28**

ELECTRONIC SURVEILLANCE
See SEARCH OR SEIZURE

EMERGENCY
Charter of Rights and
See CHARTER OF RIGHTS
Emergencies Act, **14:15, 17:8, 17:9**
Extension of legislative bodies, **9:19, 38:32, 45:7**
Legislative power over
See PEACE ORDER, AND GOOD GOVERNMENT
Necessity in, **40:4**
Proof of, **17:10, 60:10, 60:13**
Temporary validity, **40:4**
War Measures Act
See WAR MEASURES ACT

EMIGRATION FROM CANADA
See MOBILITY

EMINENT DOMAIN
See EXPROPRIATION

EMPLOYMENT
See LABOUR RELATIONS

EMPLOYMENT INSURANCE
See UNEMPLOYMENT INSURANCE

ENFORCEMENT
See REMEDY

ENGLAND
See UNITED KINGDOM

ENGLISH LANGUAGE
See LANGUAGE

ENGLISH LAW IN CANADA
History, **2:1 to 2:13**

ENTERTAINMENT
See FILMS, LITERATURE, RADIO, TELEVISION, THEATRE

ENTRENCHMENT
See CONSTITUTION OF CANADA, LEGISLATIVE POWER

ENUMERATED POWERS
Australia
See AUSTRALIA
Canada, **17:1**

ENUMERATED POWERS—Cont'd
United States
See UNITED STATES

ENVIRONMENT
Environment as matter, **17:5, 18:6, 30:31**
Fisheries protection of
See FISHERIES
Pollution as matter&, **17:5, 30:31**
Pollution of river, **13:6**
Power over, **17:4, 17:5, 18:2, 18:6, 18:7, 18:18, 30:20, 30:31 to 30:33**

EQUALITY
Affirmative action, **43:4, 55:3, 55:32**
Age, **33:2, 33:5, 37:24, 40:5, 40:26, 40:27, 55:1 to 55:3, 55:7, 55:18, 55:20 to 55:24, 55:28, 55:44**
Alienage, **21:18, 26:2, 55:1**
American Bill of Rights, under
See AMERICAN BILL OF RIGHTS
Analogous grounds, **55:17, 55:18**
Canadian Bill of Rights, under
See CANADIAN BILL OF RIGHTS
Child's rights
See CHILD
Citizenship, **36:30, 46:4, 47:13, 55:18, 55:37, 55:41, 55:46**
Comparator group, selection of, **55:23**
Confidential records, disclosure, **47:35, 47:36**
Corporations and, **37:2, 55:5**
Deafness, **32:4, 55:28, 55:45**
Delayed application of s.15, **55:4**
Description of law, **55:1 to 55:50**
Disability, **55:24, 55:30, 55:45, 57:17**
Disadvantage, **55:23 to 55:27, 55:32**
Discretion, application to, **55:6**
Discrimination, **55:16 to 55:30**
Distribution of powers over, **34:6, 55:1**
Educational attainment, **55:22**
Employment status, **37:7, 55:18, 55:50**
Extension, remedy of, **40:4 to 40:9**
Father's rights, **55:41 to 55:43**
Formal, **55:10 to 55:12, 55:28 to 55:30, 55:41**
Gender
See sex
Hate propaganda
See EXPRESSION
Human dignity, **55:19 to 55:22**

EQUALITY—Cont'd
Human rights codes
See HUMAN RIGHTS CODES
Indians
See INDIANS AND INDIAN LANDS
Language, **55:18, 55:38**
Limitations on, **55:31**
Marital status, **27:9, 40:6, 55:18, 55:22, 55:24, 55:47**
Mental disability, **55:30, 55:45**
Military status, **55:2**
Municipal by-laws, **55:49**
Occupation, **55:18, 55:50**
Over-inclusive law, **40:8**
Override of rights, **55:43**
Physical disability, **32:4, 33:4, 55:30, 55:45, 57:17**
Race, **(d), (e), 26:2, 27:9, 27:14 to 27:17, 28:4, 36:29, 55:1 to 55:3, 55:34, 55:39**
Reasonable accommodation, **55:30, 55:45**
Region
See residence
Religion, **42:9, 55:18, 55:35, 55:40**
Residence, **21:18, 26:2, 28:5, 28:40, 33:5, 55:18, 55:22, 55:36, 55:49**
Reverse discrimination, **55:32**
Same-sex marriage
See MARRIAGE
Sex, **4:2, 28:2, 38:17, 40:5, 40:6, 43:40, 55:2, 55:3, 55:7, 55:27, 55:31, 55:41 to 55:43, 59:6**
Sexual orientation, **27:3, 27:8, 37:7, 37:13, 38:12, 40:6, 55:18, 55:28 to 55:30, 55:48, 59:5**
Substantive, **55:12, 55:28 to 55:30, 55:42**
Temporal distinction, **55:18**
Under-inclusive law, **38:15, 40:4 to 40:9**
Unwritten constitutional principle, as, **15:28**
Voting
See ELECTIONS
Waiver, **37:24**

EQUALIZATION
Constitutional guarantee of, **6:6, 6:8**
Financial arrangements in, **5:27, 6:6, 6:8**
Grants, **5:27, 6:4 to 6:6, 6:8, 6:10**
Horizontal imbalance, **6:1**

EQUAL PROTECTION
See EQUALITY

ESKIMOS
See ABORIGINAL PEOPLES OF CANADA, INDIANS AND INDIAN LANDS, NATIVE RIGHTS

EUROPEAN CONVENTION ON HUMAN RIGHTS
Charter, relevance to, **36:20, 38:1**
Individual's right to petition, **36:20**
Limitation clauses, **38:1, 38:9**
United Kingdom, application to, **5:20, 12:1**

EUROPEAN COURT OF HUMAN RIGHTS
Generally, **36:20**

EUTHANASIA
See SUICIDE

EVERYONE
Generally, **37:2**

EVIDENCE
Aboriginal cases, in, **28:21, 60:8 to 60:13**
Adjudicative facts, **60:8**
American exclusionary rule, **36:5, 41:2, 41:4, 41:11, 41:13**
Appellate court, in, **60:8, 60:11**
Brandeis brief, **8:12, 52:5, 60:9 to 60:11**
Burden of proof, **38:4, 60:13**
Canada Evidence Act, **7:16, 7:20, 10:7**
Canadian Bill of Rights, obtained in breach of, **41:2**
Charter cases, in, **38:4, 60:13**
Charter obtained in breach of
See CHARTER OF RIGHTS
Compellability of accused
See COMPELLABILITY OF ACCUSED
Confidential records, **36:9, 47:35 to 47:37**
Conscriptive, **41:8, 50:12**
Constitutional cases, in, **60:8 to 60:13**
Constitutional jurisdictional facts, **7:20, 21:11**
Credibility, to impeach, **41:3, 47:31, 51:8, 54:5, 54:8**
Criminal cases, in, **18:2, 19:7**
Crown's power to withhold
See CROWN
Derivative, **47:31, 54:10**
Disclosure by Crown, **40:22, 47:34, 47:37**

EVIDENCE—Cont'd
Disclosure by third parties, **36:4, 36.7(f), 47:35, 47:37, 51:12, 59:10**
Discoverability rule, **41:5, 41:8, 41:13, 54:8**
DNA, **41.8(d), 48:13, 48:21, 48:23, 48:27, 50:12, 51:31**
Emergency finding of, **17:10, 60:10, 60:13**
Exclusion power of, **40:21, 40:22, 41:1 to 41:14**
Extradition cases, in, **47:32**
Illegally obtained, **41:2, 48:27**
Incriminating
See SELF-INCRIMINATION
Informer privilege
See INFORMER PRIVILEGE
Inquest at, **19:7, 51:10**
Insanity, of, **40:6, 51:14, 55:24**
Journalist secret source privilege, **37:12, 43:19**
Judicial notice, **60:8**
Legislative facts, **60:8**
Legislative history
See LEGISLATIVE HISTORY
Litigation privilege, **48:31**
Motion to suppress, **40:17**
Police informer rule, **10:6, 19:7**
Preservation of, **47:36**
Professional secrecy
See SOLICITOR-CLIENT PRIVILEGE
Purpose of statute, as to, **15:8, 60:2**
Rape-shield law, **40:8, 40:28, 41:3, 47:33, 47:34**
Reference in, **8:12, 60:10**
Search for
See SEARCH OR SEIZURE
Seizure of
See SEARCH OR SEIZURE
Sexual activity of complainant, **47:33**
Silence right to
See FUNDAMENTAL JUSTICE
Similar fact, **51:14**
Social-science brief
See Brandeis brief
Solicitor-client privilege, **47:15, 47:35, 48:31**
Standard of proof, **38:4, 60:13**
Trial, in, **60:12**

EVIDENCE—Cont'd
Trick, obtained by, **41:3, 41:7, 47:31**
Unreliable, **41:8**
Witness, compellability, **10:9, 54:3, 54:4**

EXCHEQUER COURT OF CANADA
Generally, **7:1, 7:11**

EXCISE TAX
Generally, **5:9, 6:1, 6:2, 31:8**

EXCLUSIVE POWERS
Generally, **15:7, 15:20, 15:25**

EXECUTIVE COUNCIL
Generally, **9:3, 9:5**

EXECUTIVE FEDERALISM
Generally, **4:2, 5:27**

EXECUTIVE GOVERNMENT OF CANADA
Generally, **14:7**

EXECUTIVE POWER
See also CROWN
Cabinet
See CABINET
Delegation
See DELEGATION
Distribution matches legislative, **9:3, 11:13**
Extraterritorial capacity, **13:8**
Foreign affairs, **11:1**
Governor General
See GOVERNOR GENERAL
Judicial power, relation to, **7:15, 9:12**
Legislative power, relation to, **1:9, 7:15, 9:3, 9:12, 11:13, 18:1, 19:13, 19:15**
Lieutenant Governor
See LIEUTENANT GOVERNOR
Premier
See PREMIER
Prerogative power
See PREROGATIVE POWER
Prime Minister
See PRIME MINISTER
Queen
See QUEEN

EXILE
Generally, **46:2, 49:1**

EXPORT
Generally, **13:5, 21:14**

EX POST FACTO LAW
See RETROACTIVE LAW

EXPRESSION
Access to government, **43:40**
Advertising, **18:5, 38.1(i), 38:9, 38:12, 38:19, 38:20, 43:3, 43:6, 43:13, 43:18, 43:21 to 43:25, 46:10**
Assembly
See ASSEMBLY
Association
See ASSOCIATION
Buses, on, **37:8, 38:18, 43:30, 43:40**
Censorship, **15:9, 21:4, 43:3, 43:12, 43:29**
Commercial expression, **16:4, 43:21 to 43:25**
Compelled expression, **18:5, 43:15**
Conduct as, **43:7, 43:9, 43:10**
Confidentiality agreement, **37:24**
Content neutrality, **43:11, 43:27**
Court
access to, **7:18, 40:6, 43:12, 43:31 to 43:33, 50:15**
contempt of, **43:14, 43:35, 47:24**
reporting of proceedings, **36:23, 43:12, 43:32, 51:18**
Criminal law power over, **43:1 to 43:4**
Defamation, **13:10, 37:12, 43:3, 43:9, 43:11, 43:14, 43:28**
Definition, **43:8 to 43:11**
Democracy and, **43:7**
Description of law, **43:1 to 43:40**
Election expenditures
See ELECTIONS
Election signs
See ELECTIONS
Falsehoods, **38:16, 43:6, 43:9, 43:11, 43:27**
Films, **21:4, 43:3, 43:8, 43:12, 43:29, 46:10**
Government documents, access to, **43:41**
Hate propaganda, **38:16, 38:18, 41:6, 43:9 to 43:11, 43:13, 43:27, 51:14**
Implied bill of rights protection, **34:7**
Informer privilege
See INFORMER PRIVILEGE
Journalist secret source privilege, **37:12, 43:19**
Language requirements
See LANGUAGE

EXPRESSION—Cont'd
Legislative assembly, access to, **1:7, 43:34**
Libel tourism, **13:10**
Limits on, **16:4, 36:6, 40:9, 43:5, 43:6, 43:11**
Local matter, **43:3**
Noise by-law, **40:9, 43:30**
Oath of allegiance, **43:16**
Peace order, and good government power over, **43:1 to 43:4**
Picketing, **37:11, 37:12, 43:12, 43:18, 43:20, 43:26, 44:2**
Political speech, **21:17, 34:7, 43:1, 43:2, 43:7, 43:36, 43:38**
Pornography, **38:9, 38:16, 43:29**
Postering, **37:8, 43:18, 43:30**
Powers over, **43:1 to 43:4**
Press, **43:17, 43:28, 43:31 to 43:33**
Prior restraint on, **43:12**
Private property, **43:30**
Profanity, **43:6**
Public property, **43:12, 43:30**
Radio regulation
See RADIO
Reasons for protection, **43:7**
Religion
See RELIGION
Reputation, **43:9, 43:11, 43:28**
Signs, **43:3, 43:24**
Statutory platform, **43:40**
Television regulation
See TELEVISION
Theatre
See THEATRE
Threats of violence, **43:10**
Time manner and place, **43:18**
Violence as, **43:10**
Voting, **43:39**
Waiver, **37:24**
Warnings on products
See FOOD AND DRUGS
Whistle blower protection, **37:24**

EXPROPRIATION
Compensation, **13:5, 23:7, 23:8, 29.4(d), 29:5, 29:8**
Crown property, **10:21, 29:7**
Disguised, **29:8**
Extraprovincial right, **13:5, 23:8, 29:7, 29:8**

EXPROPRIATION—Cont'd
Federally incorporated company, **13:5, 23:7, 23:8, 29:7, 29:8**
Federally regulated undertaking, **29:5, 29:7**
National capital region, **29:5**
Navigation, **29:5**
Provincial power, **23:7, 23:8, 29:3, 29:6**
Regulation contrasted, **29:8**
Seizure, not a, **48:4**
Work for general advantage of Canada, **22:10, 28:17, 28:18**

EXTENSION, REMEDY OF
Generally, **37:13, 38:20, 40:8**

EXTRADITION
See also DEPORTATION
Charged in Canada, not, **51:2**
Charter of Rights, application to, **37:10, 47:15, 53:3**
Citizen of, **37:14, 46:2**
Cruel and unusual foreign laws, **37:10, 37:14, 46:5, 47:15, 53:3, 53:7**
Double jeopardy plea, **51:28**
Procedure, **37:14, 46:2, 47:32**

EXTRATERRITORIAL COMPETENCE
Administration of justice, **13:6, 13:9 to 13:14**
Australian states, **13:3**
Charter of Rights
See CHARTER OF RIGHTS
Company, **13:7, 23:2**
Contractual rights, **13:5, 13:6, 15:10, 23:8**
Courts, **13:6, 13:9 to 13:14**
Description, **13:1 to 13:14**
Executive power not limited, **13:8**
Extraterritorial Act, **13:2**
Federal Parliament, **3:1, 3:3, 8:2, 13:2**
Interest adjustment and, **25:7**
Location of rights
See SITUS
Marketing, **13:6, 21:22**
Pollution control, **13:6**
Privy Council appeals, abolition, **8:2, 13:2**
Provinces, **10:20, 13:3 to 13:7, 16:1**
Situs
See SITUS
Spending power not limited, **13:8**

EXTRATERRITORIAL COMPETENCE —Cont'd
Statutory interpretation, **13:2**
Taxation
See TAXATION
United Kingdom Parliament, **13:1, 13:2**
United States' states, **13:3**
Workers' compensation, **13:6**

FACTS
See EVIDENCE

FAIR HEARING
Administrative tribunal
See ADMINISTRATIVE TRIBUNAL
Canadian Bill of Rights, s. 2(f), under, **51:13**
Charter of Rights, s. 11(d), under, **51:15**
Due process
See DUE PROCESS
Fundamental justice
See FUNDAMENTAL JUSTICE
Military tribunal
See MILITARY TRIBUNAL
Natural justice
See NATURAL JUSTICE
Trial
See TRIAL

FAMILY
Adoption
See ADOPTION OF CHILDREN
Alimony
See CUSTODY AND MAINTENANCE
Crime and delinquency, **27:2**
Custody
See CUSTODY AND MAINTENANCE
Distribution of powers, **27:1**
Divorce
See DIVORCE
Jurisdiction of courts, **27:14 to 27:17**
Maintenance of children
See CUSTODY AND MAINTENANCE
Maintenance of spouse
See CUSTODY AND MAINTENANCE
Marriage
See MARRIAGE
Power over, **27:1 to 27:17**

FAMILY—Cont'd
Property, **5:8, 15:15, 27:4, 27:9, 27:16**
Punishment of children, **27:2, 40:1 to 40:10**
Same-sex relationships
See MARRIAGE

FARM
Protective legislation, **16:3, 16:4**

FEDERAL COURT OF CANADA
Appeal to Supreme Court of Canada, **8:6**
Appointment of judges, **7:2, 7:14**
Constitutional questions, power to decide, **7:11, 7:20**
Constitutional status, **1:6**
Crown, suits against, **10:5**
Establishment, **7:1, 7:11**
Evidence exclusive jurisdiction to admit, **7:16, 7:20, 10:7, 47:33**
Independence of judges, **7:14**
Intergovernmental disputes, **10:1**
Jurisdiction
See FEDERAL JURISDICTION
Payment of judges, **7:11, 7:14**
Retirement of judges, **7:11, 7:14**

FEDERAL GOVERNMENT
See CABINET, CANADA, DOMINION FEDERAL PARLIAMENT, FEDERALISM, GOVERNOR GENERAL

FEDERAL IMMUNITY
See INTERJURISDICTIONAL IMMUNITY

FEDERALISM
Asymmetry
See SPECIAL STATUS
Australia, **5:9 to 5:18, 15:4, 15:8**
Canada, **5:1 to 5:27, 12:2, 15:1**
Charter of Rights and, **38:21, 55:36, 55:49**
Civil liberties and
See CIVIL LIBERTIES
Constitution
See CONSTITUTION
Cooperative
See COOPERATIVE FEDERALISM
Definition, **5:1 to 5:7, 15:1**

FEDERALISM—Cont'd
Delegation between Dominion and provinces
See INTER-DELEGATION
Distribution of powers
See DISTRIBUTION OF POWERS
Diversity of laws, **38:21, 52.23, 55:18, 55:36**
Executive federalism, **4:2**
Horizontal imbalance, **6:1**
Inconsistent laws
See PARAMOUNTCY
Interstate federalism, **4:22**
Intrastate federalism, **4:22, 9:10**
Judicial review
See JUDICIAL REVIEW OF LEGISLATION
Paramountcy of federal laws
See PARAMOUNTCY
Reasons for, **5:8**
Special status
See SPECIAL STATUS
Treaty problems
See TREATY
United States, **5:1, 5:9 to 5:18, 15:4**
Vertical imbalance, **6:1**

FEDERAL JURISDICTION
Generally, **7:10 to 7:14, 15:15**

FEDERALLY-REGULATED UNDERTAKINGS
See INTERJURISDICTIONAL IMMUNITY

FEDERAL PARLIAMENT
See also PROVINCIAL LEGISLATURE
Annual sessions, **9:4 to 9:7, 9:10, 47:4 to 47:6**
Binding itself, **10:14, 12:9, 12:10**
Cabinet domination, **9:12**
Candidate right to be
See ELECTIONS
Composition, **9:8**
Concurrent powers
See CONCURRENT POWERS
Constitutional amendment role in
See AMENDMENT OF CONSTITUTION
Crown power to bind
See CROWN
Definition of Parliament, **5:5, 12:10, 37:7**

FEDERAL PARLIAMENT—Cont'd
Delegation power of, **14:4**
Description, **9:8 to 9:12, 9:14**
Dissolution, **9:6, 9:14, 9:15, 9:19, 9:20, 45:7**
Elections
See ELECTIONS
Exclusive powers
See EXCLUSIVE POWERS
Extraterritorial competence
See EXTRATERRITORIAL COMPETENCE
Government bills, **12:9**
Governor General
See GOVERNOR GENERAL
House of Commons
See HOUSE OF COMMONS
Imperial statutes, power over, **3:1 to 3:4**
Language rights in, **36.7(g), 56:4, 56:9, 56:14, 56:15**
Law and custom of, **1:8**
Money bill, **9:10, 9:12, 12:9, 14:5**
New powers, proposed, **4:21**
Powers and privileges, **1:7**
Prime Minister
See PRIME MINISTER
Private bills, **9:12**
Private members' bills, **9:12, 12:9**
Procedure review of, **12:10, 47:13**
Prorogation, **9:18, 9:21**
Provinces, power to bind, **10:21**
Residuary power
See RESIDUARY POWER
Royal assent
See ROYAL ASSENT
S. 96, whether bound by, **7.2(f), 7:14, 19:5**
Senate
See SENATE
Speech from the throne, **9:20**
Summon into session, **9:3, 9:6, 9:20**
Treaty
implementation, role in, **11:6 to 11:9**
making role in, **11:5**
Uniform law not necessary, **17:4, 55:49**

FEDERAL-PROVINCIAL CONFERENCES
Amending formula, to review, **4:16**
Description, **4:23, 5:27**

FEDERAL-PROVINCIAL CONFERENCES—Cont'd
Meech Lake Constitutional Accord
See MEECH LAKE CONSTITUTIONAL ACCORD
November 5, 1981, **4:2, 4:12, 36:1, 36:14, 39:2**

FEDERAL-PROVINCIAL DELEGATION
See INTER-DELEGATION

FEDERAL-PROVINCIAL FINANCIAL ARRANGEMENTS
See FINANCIAL ARRANGEMENTS

FERRIES
Generally, **22:12**

FILMS
Censorship
See EXPRESSION
Power over, **22:23**

FINANCIAL ARRANGEMENTS
Confederation, at, **5:9, 5:12, 6:1**
Cooperative, **5:27**
Description, **6:1 to 6:10**
Equalization
See EQUALIZATION
Grants
See GRANTS
Shared-cost programmes
See SHARED-COST PROGRAMMES
Spending power
See SPENDING POWER
Tax agreements
See TAX AGREEMENTS

FINKELSTEIN N.
Reasonable search or seizure, on, **38:26**

FIREARMS
See GUNS

FIRST MINISTERS' CONFERENCES
See FEDERAL-PROVINCIAL CONFERENCES

FISHERIES
Environmental protection, **7(b), 30:1 to 30:33, 30:20, 30:26**
Legislative power over, **29:4, 30:15 to 30:20**

FISHERIES—Cont'd
Marketing of fish, **15:8, 15:10, 18:2, 29:4, 30:15 to 30:20**
Natural resource agreement, **28:17**
Processing of fish, **29:4, 30:27**
Proprietary rights in, **30:22 to 30:25**
Public rights in, **30:16**
Records of catch, disclosure, **47:31**
River obstruction of, **30:19, 30:21**
Transportation of fish, **30:27**

FOOD AND DRUGS
See also HEALTH
Manufacture and sale, **18:3**
Marihuana
criminalization of, **47:15, 47:24, 47:25 55:18**
medical use, **47:26, 59:6**
Narcotics
control of, **15:21, 17:3, 17:6, 18:4, 32:1, 47:15, 47:24, 47:25**
denial of bail, **51:18**
religious use, **42:4**
treatment of addiction, **15:21, 18:4, 21:4, 32:1, 47:25**
Prosecution of offences, **19:15**
Standards, **18:3, 20:3, 20:4, 32:1**
Tobacco advertising, **16:4, 18:5, 38:9 38:12, 38.10(d), 38:19, 38:20, 43:11, 43:13, 43:23**
Tobacco health care costs, **7:3, 15:28**
Warnings on products, **18:5, 43:16**

FOREIGN LAWS
See CONFLICT OF LAWS

FOREIGN OWNERSHIP
See PROPERTY

FORESTRY
See NATURAL RESOURCES

FORFEITURE OF RIGHTS
See WAIVER

FOURTEENTH AMENDMENT
See AMERICAN BILL OF RIGHTS

FRANCHISE
See ELECTIONS

FRAUDULENT PREFERENCES
Generally, **25:15**

FREE TRADE
Provinces, between, **31:4, 46:7 to 46:10, 46:11, 46:12 to 46:15**
United States with, **11:10**

FREIGHT FORWARDING
Jurisdiction over, **22:4**

FRENCH LANGUAGE
See LANGUAGE

FRENCH LAW IN CANADA
Civil law
See CIVIL LAW
History, **2:1 to 2:7**

FULL ANSWER AND DEFENCE
See FUNDAMENTAL JUSTICE

FULL FAITH AND CREDIT
Generally, **13:9, 13:11, 15:28, 27:1**

FULTON-FAVREAU FORMULA
Generally, **4:2, 14:10**

FUNDAMENTAL FREEDOMS
Assembly
See ASSEMBLY
Association
See ASSOCIATION
Expression
See EXPRESSION
Religion
See RELIGION

FUNDAMENTAL JUSTICE
Absolute liability, **40:6, 47:14, 47:15, 47:16 to 47:18, 51:14**
Arbitrariness, **47:24 to 47:26**
Automatism as defence, **38:30, 47:21**
Canadian Bill of Rights, s. 2(e), under, **35:1, 47:2, 47:13**
Charter s. 7, under, **47:1 to 47:38**
Compellability, **51:12**
Confessions, **47:31**
Corporation, no right to, **47:4, 47:10, 59:6**
Counsel, right to
See COUNSEL, RIGHT TO
Definition, **47:14, 47:15**
Deportation, **11:6**
Disproportionality, **47:25**
Due process
See DUE PROCESS
Duress as defence, **47:22**

FUNDAMENTAL JUSTICE—Cont'd
Extradition, **37:14, 46:2, 47:15, 51:2**
Fairness of trial, **27:6, 47:12, 47:32**
Full answer and defence, **36:23, 40:7, 41:3, 47:33 to 47:36, 51:4, 53:3**
Intoxication as defence, **38:30, 47:23**
Limits under s. 1, **38:25, 47:3**
Mens rea requirement, **40:5, 40:6, 47:14, 47:15, 47:16 to 47:18, 47:20, 47:21 to 47:23, 51:14**
Negligence requirement, **47:16 to 47:18, 51:14**
Overbreadth, **47:24, 47:25, 47:27**
Pre-charge delay, **51:4, 52:6**
Privacy, right to
See PRIVACY
Procedural requirements, **40:6, 47:14, 47:32 to 47:37, 49:10**
Property not protected, **47:2, 47:13**
Silence, right to, **37:16, 37:18, 47:15, 47:31, 50:2, 50:3, 50:12, 50:13, 51:8, 51:10, 54:1, 54:3**
Strict liability, **47:16 to 47:18, 51:14**
Substantive justice, includes, **47:14, 47:15, 60:7**
Vagueness, **47:24, 47:27 to 47:29**
Wrong laws, **47:30**

GAMBLING
Generally, **14:15, 14:17, 15:7, 18:18, 18:19, 21:4, 21:17, 28:20, 34:6, 55:49**

GENERAL POWER
See PEACE, ORDER, AND GOOD GOVERNMENT

GIBSON, DALE
Interjurisdictional immunity, on, **15:18**
Peace order, and good government, on, **17:4**

GOODS
See MARKETING, MOBILITY, TRADE AND COMMERCE

GOODS AND SERVICES TAX
Generally, **31:12**

GOVERNMENT
Agent of, **37:7**
Cabinet
See CABINET

GOVERNMENT—Cont'd
Canada, of
See GOVERNMENT OF CANADA
Coalition
See RESPONSIBLE GOVERNMENT
Crown
See CROWN
Defeat
See DEFEAT OF GOVERNMENT
Defined, **37:10, 56:8**
Dialogue within, **36:11**
Liability
See CROWN
Minority
See RESPONSIBLE GOVERNMENT
Municipalities
See MUNICIPALITIES
Province, of
See PROVINCIAL GOVERNMENT
Responsible government
See RESPONSIBLE GOVERNMENT

GOVERNMENTAL IMMUNITY
See CROWN, INTERJURISDICTIONAL IMMUNITY

GOVERNMENT OF CANADA
Charter applicable to, **37:10**
Constitutional amendment in relation to, **4:18**
Definition of, **37:10**
Language in, **34:5, 56:14, 56:15**

GOVERNOR GENERAL
Advice to, **9:16**
Appointment, **1:2, 3:1, 9:3, 9:6**
Cabinet, does not attend, **9:5**
Constitutional amendment
See AMENDMENT OF CONSTITUTION
Conventions limit powers, **1:10, 9:3, 9:4 to 9:7, 9:11**
Delegation to
by Parliament, **14:1**
by Queen, **9:3, 11:2, 11:3, 11:13**
Disallowance of statutes by
See DISALLOWANCE
Education rights appeals, **57:5**
Great Seal, **11:3**
Judges, appoints, **7:2, 9:22**
Judges, removes, **7:3**
King-Byng dispute, **9:19**

GOVERNOR GENERAL—Cont'd
Letters patent constituting office, **1:2, 1:4, 11:2, 11:6**
Lieutenant Governors appoints, **5:9, 5:14, 9:3**
Ministers appoints, **1:9**
Money bills recommends, **9:10, 14:5**
Parliament
dissolves, **9:3, 9:14, 9:19, 9:20**
prorogues, **9:18, 9:20**
summons, **9:3, 9:20**
Personal prerogatives, **1:9, 9:3, 9:4, 9:16 to 9:24**
Prime Minister
appoints, **1:9, 9:3, 9:4, 9:15**
dismisses, **9:14, 9:15**
Reservation of bills
See RESERVATION
Reserve powers, **1:9, 9:3, 9:4, 9:16 to 9:24**
Responsible government
See RESPONSIBLE GOVERNMENT
Royal assent to statutes
See ROYAL ASSENT
Salary, **9:3**
Senators, appoints, **9:3, 9:10, 9:22**
Speech from the throne, **9:20**
Tenure, **1:2, 3:1, 9:3**

GOVERNOR IN COUNCIL
See GOVERNOR GENERAL

GRANTS
See also FINANCIAL ARRANGEMENTS
Abatement compared, **6:4, 6:5**
Conditional, **6:5, 6:7, 6:8, 6:10, 32:2, 33:3**
Equalization
See EQUALIZATION
Shared-cost programmes
See SHARED-COST PROGRAMMES
Statutory subsidies, **5:9, 6:1, 6:8**
Tax rental agreement
See TAX AGREEMENTS

GREAT BRITAIN
See UNITED KINGDOM

GREAT SEAL
Generally, **11:3**

GUNS
Control, **5:27, 18:13, 18:18, 21:17**
Search for, **48:21, 48:24, 48:27, 49:3 to 49:8**

HABEAS CORPUS
See REMEDIES

HALDANE, LORD
Generally, **5:11, 5:21, 17:3, 17:7**

HANSARD
See LEGISLATIVE HISTORY

HARBOURS
Generally, **22:12**

HATE PROPAGANDA
See EXPRESSION

HEAD OF STATE
See also GOVERNOR GENERAL, LIEUTENANT GOVERNOR, QUEEN
Generally, **9:24**

HEADS OF POWER
See CLASSES OF SUBJECTS

HEALTH
Assisted human reproduction
See ASSISTED HUMAN REPRODUCTION
Canada Health Act, **6:7, 6:8, 32:3, 32:4 to 32:6**
Compelled treatment, **42:6, 47:26, 55:44**
Drugs
See FOOD AND DRUGS
Federal power over, **6:8, 15:10, 18:3, 18:5, 18:6, 32:2**
Food
See FOOD AND DRUGS
Hospitals power over
See HOSPITALS
Medical profession, power over, **6:8, 18:6, 32:1**
Mental disorder, **32:1**
Physician-assisted dying, **8:13, 15:21, 32:2, 40:8, 47:8, 47:9, 47:12, 47:15, 47:24, 53:2**
Private health care prohibition, **32:6, 47:8, 47:12, 47:26**
Provincial power over, **6:8, 18:5, 18:6, 32:1, 32:3**

HEALTH—Cont'd
Shared-cost programmes
See SHARED-COST PROGRAMMES
Tobacco
See FOOD AND DRUGS
Waiting times, **32:6, 47:8, 47:12, 47:26**

HEARING
See FAIR HEARING

HIGHWAYS
See ROADS

HOLMES, OLIVER WENDELL
Due process, on, **47:10**
Freedom of speech, on, **43:7**
Judicial review, on, **5:21**

HOMOSEXUALITY
See EQUALITY

HOSPITALS
See also HEALTH
Charter, application to, **37:8, 37:10**
Mandatory retirement in, **55:44**
Marine, **32:1**
Power over, **6:8, 18:6, 32:1**

HOUSE OF COMMONS
See also FEDERAL PARLIAMENT
Candidate right to be
See ELECTIONS
Defeat of government
See DEFEAT OF GOVERNMENT
Description, **9:9**
Dissolution
See FEDERAL PARLIAMENT
Duration, **9:6, 9:15, 9:19, 45:7**
Employees, management of, **1:7**
Money bill
See FEDERAL PARLIAMENT
Reference to Supreme Court, **8:8**
Representation by population, **4:14, 4:16, 4:18, 9:6**
Vote right to
See ELECTIONS

HOUSE OF LORDS
Precedent in, **2:2, 8:13**
Supreme Court of U.K., replacement by, **8:13**
Supreme tribunal to settle English law, **2:2, 8:13**

HUGHES, CHIEF JUSTICE, C.E.
Judicial review, on, **5:21**

HUMAN RIGHTS CODES
Charter, application to, **34:3, 37:7, 37:13, 55:7, 55:32, 55:48**
Description, **34:3, 55:7, 55:42**
Discrimination prohibitions, **55:22**
Power to enact, **34:6, 55:1**
Primacy, **12:10, 40:26, 55:7**

HUMAN RIGHTS COMMITTEE OF UNITED NATIONS
Generally, **11:6, 36:20**

IGNORANCE OF LAW
See MISTAKE OF LAW

IMMIGRATION
See also MOBILITY, NATURALIZATION AND ALIENS
Deportation
See DEPORTATION
Head tax on Chinese immigrants, **36:29**
Immigrants' rights, **47:5, 47:38**
Legal representation, **16:3, 26:2**
Meech Lake proposal, **4:3**
Powers over, **26:1, 26:2, 46:2**
Refugee determination, **26:1, 40:9, 46:3, 47:5**
Security certificate process, **47:9, 47:32, 49:11, 53:5**

IMMUNITY OF INSTRUMENTALITIES
See INTERJURISDICTIONAL IMMUNITY

IMPERIAL CONFERENCES
1930, **1:13, 3:1 to 3:3, 4:1, 9:3, 9:11**
1926, **3:1 to 3:3, 8:2, 9:3, 11:10**

IMPERIAL PARLIAMENT
Abdication of power by
See LEGISLATIVE POWER
Constitutional amendment by
See AMENDMENT OF CONSTITUTION
Power to legislate for Canada, **1:3, 1:13, 3:1 to 3:5**
Power to legislate for dominions, **2:1, 2:5, 2:6, 2:13, 3:1 to 3:5**

IMPERIAL STATUTE
British North America Act
See CONSTITUTION ACT, 1867
Canada applicable in, **1:5, 2:7, 2:13, 3:2**
Canada's ability to alter, **2:13, 3:1 to 3:5**
Colonial Laws Validity Act
See COLONIAL LAWS VALIDITY ACT
Definition, **1:5, 2:13, 3:2**
Repugnancy, **3:1 to 3:4, 5:20**
Statute of Westminster
See STATUTE OF WESTMINSTER

IMPLIED BILL OF RIGHTS
Generally, **12:3, 15:28, 34:7**

IMPORT
Generally, **13:6, 22:23, 22:25, 43:13**

IMPRISONMENT
See ARBITRARY DETENTION OR IMPRISONMENT, CRIMINAL LAW, CRUEL AND UNUSUAL PUNISHMENT, LIBERTY, MURDER, PENITENTIARIES

INCIDENTAL EFFECT
Generally, **15:5, 15:24, 17:1**

INCOME TAX
See TAXATION

INCONSISTENCY
Federal and provincial laws
See PARAMOUNTCY
Same jurisdiction, within
See REPEAL

INCORPORATION OF COMPANY
See COMPANY

INCORPORATION OF LAWS
See ADOPTION OF LAWS

INDEPENDENCE
See CANADA, UNITED STATES

INDETERMINACY
See VAGUE LAW

INDIA
Directive principles of state policy, **6:6**

INDIANS AND INDIAN LANDS
Aboriginal title, **28:3, 28:20, 28:21, 28:32**
Adoption laws, **27:6**

INDIANS AND INDIAN LANDS —Cont'd
Canadian Bill of Rights and, **28:4**
Charter of Rights and, **28:5**
Child welfare, **28:7 to 28:12**
Definitions
See ABORIGINAL PEOPLES OF CANADA
Drunkenness laws, **28:2, 28:4**
Education, **28:2, 57:1, 57:2**
Gaming laws, **28:20**
Heritage property, **15:24, 21:19, 28:9**
Indian Act, s. 88, 14:15, **28:7 to 28:12, 28:13 to 28:16**
Indian lands, ownership, **28:3, 29:4**
Indians discrimination against, **28:2, 55:1, 55:2, 55:34, 55:39**
Investment of band money, **55:22, 55:26, 55:34**
Labour relations, **21:11, 28:7**
Lands reserved for the Indians, **1:9, 28:3, 28:9**
Natural resources agreements and, **28:17**
Power over, **28:1 to 28:6, 28:7 to 28:41**
Prerogative power over reserves, **1:9, 28:3**
Property law, **28:2, 28:3**
Provincial laws applicable to, **15:19, 15:20, 28:7, 28:37**
Retroactive law regarding status, **28:2**
Rights
See NATIVE RIGHTS
Status law, **27:6, 28:2, 55:32**
Treaties affecting, **28:6, 28:21**
Treaties with, **28:1, 28:6, 28:7, 28:13, 28:23 to 28:27, 28:41**
Vote right to, **28:2, 28:5, 28:40, 45:1 to 45:5, 55:18, 55:49**

INDIVIDUAL
Generally, **37:3**

INDUSTRIAL RELATIONS
See LABOUR RELATIONS

INDUSTRY
See BUSINESS

INFLATION
Matter, as, **17:5, 18:6, 30:31**
Wage and price control
See PEACE ORDER, AND GOOD GOVERNMENT

INFORMATION
Counsel, of, right to
See COUNSEL, RIGHT TO
Laying of, **19:6, 51:2**
Reasons for arrest, of, **50:4**
Specific offence, of, **51:4**

INFORMER PRVILEGE
Generally, **43:32**

INITIATIVE AND REFERENDUM
Generally, **4:19, 4:23, 12:10, 14:8, 14:9**

INJUNCTION
See REMEDIES

INNOCENCE, PRESUMPTION OF
Crown's burden of proof, **51:14**
Reverse onus, **38:30, 43:13, 43:29, 47:16 to 47:18, 47:21, 51:14, 51:17**
Waiver, **51:17**

INOPERATIVE LAW
Canadian Bill of Rights, effect of, **35:3, 35:4**
Invalid law contrasted, **16:10, 35:4, 35:5**
Paramountcy, effect of
See PARAMOUNTCY
Repealed law contrasted, **16:10, 35:4, 35:5**

INQUEST
Compellability of testimony, **19:7, 51:10**

INSANITY
Burden of proving, **51:14**
Detention on account of, **18:14, 40:4, 40:9, 47:24, 49:3 to 49:8, 51:13**
Evidence of, **40:6, 51:14, 55:24**

INSOLVENCY
See BANKRUPTCY AND INSOLVENCY

INSURANCE
Bank, offered by, **15:18**
Criminal law power, **15:10, 18:18**
Crown monopoly, **23:7**
Federal attempts to regulate, **17:7, 20:2, 21:6, 21:7**
Marine, **17:7, 20:2, 21:6, 21:7, 22:12**
Power over, **21:5 to 21:7, 40:6**
Reasons for regulation, **21:5**
Taxation, **31:23**

INSURANCE—Cont'd
Unemployment insurance
See UNEMPLOYMENT INSURANCE
United States, **21:6**

INTENTION OF LEGISLATORS
Generally, **15:8, 15:14, 38:16**

INTER-AMERICAN COMMISSION ON HUMAN RIGHTS
Generally, **36:20**

INTER-DELEGATION
Acquiescence by governments, **14:18**
Administrative, **13:7, 14:11, 14:18, 15:10, 46:14**
Adoption of laws, **10:19, 14:12 to 14:14, 14:18**
Conditional laws, **14:15 to 14:17, 14:18**
Description, **14:10 to 14:18**
Fisheries, over, **14:11**
Incorporation by reference, **14:12 to 14:14, 14:18**
Legislative, **12:2, 14:10**
Referential legislation, **14:12 to 14:14, 14:18**

INTEREST
Concurrent powers, **15:7**
Federal power over, **21:8, 21:20**
Property and civil rights, relation to, **15:23**
Provincial attempts to regulate, **15:10, 25:7 to 25:9**

INTERGOVERNMENTAL LIAISON
See COOPERATIVE FEDERALISM

INTERJURISDICTIONAL IMMUNITY
Aeronautics, **22:15**
Bank, **15:18, 24:6**
Crown
See CROWN
Description, **15:16 to 15:21**
Federally-incorporated company, **15:6, 15:17, 23:9**
Federally-regulated undertaking, **15:6, 15:18, 21:11, 29:7, 33:4**
Indians, **28:7 to 28:9, 28:14**
Navigation and shipping, **15:18, 16:3, 22:12, 33:4**
Paramountcy compared, **15:18, 15:21, 16:3, 16:10, 23:9, 25:13**

INTERJURISDICTIONAL IMMUNITY —Cont'd
Provincially-incorporated companies, **15:21, 23:9**
Provincially-regulated undertaking, **15:21, 23:9**
Public property, **29:1**
Taxation, **31:4, 31:21 to 31:23**
United States, **31:24, 31:27**

INTERNATIONAL BRIDGE
Jurisdiction over, **7:11**

INTERNATIONAL COVENANT ON CIVIL AND POLITICAL RIGHTS
Charter relevance to, **36:20**
Counsel right to, **36:20**
Individual's right to petition, **11:7, 36:20**
Limitation clauses, **38:1**
Optional protocol under, **11:7, 36:20**
Property not protected by, **47:13**
Religion freedom of, **41:4**

INTERNATIONAL LAW
Constitutional interpretation and, **36:27**
Human rights, on, **11:6 to 11:9, 36:27**
Internal law and, **11:6 to 11:9, 36:27**
Power to decide, **36:12**
Statutory interpretation and, **11:6 to 11:9, 36:27**
Treaty
See TREATY

INTERPRETATION OF CONSTITUTION
See also STATUTORY INTERPRETATION
Constitutional exemption, **40:2, 40:7 to 40:9, 42:6, 53:4**
English-French discrepancies, **36:24**
Extension remedy of, **37:13**
Originalism, **15:27, 48:5 to 48:12, 60:5**
Progressive interpretation, **15:27, 18:2, 23:6, 24:2, 26:3, 28:26, 36:18, 60:6, 60:7**
Reading down
See READING DOWN
Severance
See SEVERANCE

INTERPRETER, RIGHT TO
Generally, **37:23, 56:13**

INTERPROVINCIAL TRADE
See TRADE AND COMMERCE

INTERPROVINCIAL UNDERTAKING
See INTERJURISDICTIONAL IMMUNITY TRANSPORTATION AND COMMUNICATION

INTERVENER
Amicus curiae compared, **59:12, 59:13**
Attorney General as
See ATTORNEY GENERAL
Private person as, **59:13**
Reference in, **59:13**

INTOXICATION AS DEFENCE
See FUNDAMENTAL JUSTICE

INUIT
See ABORIGINAL PEOPLES OF CANADA, INDIANS AND INDIAN LANDS, NATIVE RIGHTS

INVALID LAW
See UNCONSTITUTIONAL LAW

JEHOVAH'S WITNESSES
Generally, **34:2, 42:6, 47:10, 47:26, 59:14**

JORDAN F.J.E.
Application of Charter to private action, on, **37:13**

JOURNALIST
See EXPRESSION

JUDGES
See also ADMINISTRATION OF JUSTICE, COURTS, JUDICIAL POWER
Appointment, **1:12, 5:9, 5:15, 7:2, 7:14, 7:15, 13:14**
Immunity from suit, **37:11**
Impartiality
See independence
Independence, **1:8, 5:15, 5:21, 7:2 to 7:8, 7:14, 7:17, 15:28, 34:2, 36:2, 36:17, 38:28, 51:16, 58:7**
Investigative role, **7:5, 43:33, 47:31**
Judicial councils, **7:3**
Legislative power over, **7:3**
Non-judicial functions, **7:15**
Payment, **7:2, 7:3, 7:5, 7:8, 7:14, 7:15, 15:28, 38:28**

JUDGES—Cont'd
Qualifications, **5:21, 7:2, 7:14, 7:15**
Removal, **7:3, 7:8, 15:28**
Retirement, **4:20, 7:3, 55:33**
Supernumerary status, **7:5, 7:8, 15:28, 38:28**
Taxation liability to pay, **31:22**
Tenure
See independence
Voting, **45:2**

JUDGMENT, RECOGNITION OF
Generally, **13:9, 13:11**

JUDICIAL BRANCH
See JUDICIAL POWER

JUDICIAL COMMITTEE OF PRIVY COUNCIL
Abolition of appeals, **1:2, 3:1, 8:2**
Advice not judgment, **8:2, 9:5**
Appeals from Australia, **8:2**
Appeals from Canada, **1:2, 3:1, 5:11, 5:20, 8:1, 8:2**
Appeals from New Zealand, **8:2**
Appointment of members, **8:2**
Composition, **8:2**
Dissenting views not disclosed, **8:2, 11:12**
Division of powers, impact on, **17:3, 17:7**
Judicial review, power of, **5:20**
Jurisdiction, **8:2**
Precedent in, **2:2, 8:2, 8:13**
Uniformity of common law, **2:2**

JUDICIAL INTERIM RELEASE
See BAIL

JUDICIAL NOTICE
See EVIDENCE

JUDICIAL POWER
See also ADMINISTRATION OF JUSTICE COURTS, JUDGES
Administrative tribunals, exercise by, **7:19**
Delegation
See DELEGATION
Executive power relation to, **7:15, 9:12**
Legislative power, relation to, **7:15, 9:12**

JUDICIAL REVIEW OF ADMINISTRATIVE ACTION
Appeal contrasted, **7:20**
Common law origin, **34:2**

JUDICIAL REVIEW OF ADMINISTRATIVE ACTION —Cont'd
Constitutional guarantee of, **7:20**
Constitutional issue in, **7:20, 21:11, 40:26**
Constitutional jurisdictional facts, **7:20, 21:11**
Exclusion of
See PRIVATIVE CLAUSE
Federal tribunals, **7:11**
Privative clause
See PRIVATIVE CLAUSE
Remedies to secure, **7:20, 34:2**
Scope of review, **7:20, 40:26**

JUDICIAL REVIEW OF LEGISLATION
Administration of law, **15:9**
Advisory opinions, **59:1**
Alternative grounds, **59:11**
Alternatives to, **5:22**
Ancillary power
See ANCILLARY POWER
Arbitrariness, **47:26**
Arguments for and against, **36:4**
Attorney-General
See ATTORNEY GENERAL
Australia, **5:20 to 5:22**
Canada, **5:20 to 5:22, 12:2 to 12:8**
Canadian Bill of Rights, under, **35:3**
Charter of Rights, under, **5:20, 12:10, 36:1, 36:2, 36:4 to 36:7, 39:7, 40:1 to 40:10, 40:11 to 40:25**
Classification of laws, **15:5 to 15:13**
Colourable law
See COLOURABLE LAW
Constitutional reference
See REFERENCE
Declaration of invalidity, **40:3, 40:29**
Description, **15:1 to 15:30**
Dialogue with legislatures, **36:9, 40:4, 47:37**
Directory rule, **1:10, 12:10, 14:5, 56:6, 58:9**
Discretion of judges, **5:21**
Disproportionality, **47:25**
Double aspect
See DOUBLE ASPECT
Effect of law
See EFFECT OF LAW
Evidence
See EVIDENCE

JUDICIAL REVIEW OF LEGISLATION —Cont'd
Exclusion of
See PRIVATIVE CLAUSE
Federal courts power of, **7:11**
Federalism and Charter compared, **15:2, 36:18, 36:25 to 36:28**
Federalism takes priority over Charter, **15:2, 36:25 to 36:28**
Hansard
See LEGISLATIVE HISTORY
History, **5:20 to 5:22, 12:2 to 12:8**
Interjurisdictional immunity
See INTERJURISDICTIONAL IMMUNITY
Judicial activism, **36:5, 36:14**
Lapse of time irrelevant, **14:18**
Legislative history
See LEGISLATIVE HISTORY
Mandatory rule, **1:10, 12:10, 56:6, 58:9**
Manner and form
See LEGISLATIVE POWER
Moot issue
See MOOT ISSUE
Neutral principles, **5:21, 12:8, 15:11**
New Zealand, not in, **5:20**
Non-justiciable issue, **1:10, 1:12**
Overbreadth, **47:24**
Paramountcy
See PARAMOUNTCY
Policy element, **5:21, 12:8, 15:5, 15:11, 36:5**
Political question
See POLITICAL QUESTION
Presumption of constitutionality, **5:21, 15:12, 38:5, 55:24**
Privative clause
See PRIVATIVE CLAUSE
Procedure, **15:1, 59:1 to 59:13**
Prospective overruling, **58:1**
Purpose of law, **15:8, 36:13, 38:12 to 38:17**
Rational basis test, **17:10, 60:13**
Rationale, **3:4, 5:20, 12:4, 15:1, 40:1, 60:5**
Reading down
See READING DOWN
Ripe issue
See RIPE ISSUE

JUDICIAL REVIEW OF LEGISLATION —Cont'd
Severance
See SEVERANCE
Silence of legislature, **37:7**
Singling out
See SINGLING OUT
Standing
See STANDING
Unconstitutional law, effect of
See UNCONSTITUTIONAL LAW
United Kingdom, not in, **5:20, 12:1**
United States, **5:20**
Vagueness
See VAGUE LAW
Wisdom or efficacy of law, **12:8, 15:10**

JUDICIARY
See COURTS, JUDGES, JUDICIAL POWER

JURY
See TRIAL

JUSTICES OF THE PEACE
Independence, **7:5**
Salaries, **7:5**

JUVENILE DELINQUENCY
See YOUNG OFFENDERS

KING
See CROWN, QUEEN

KING, PRIME MINISTER W.L. MCK
Byng Lord, dispute with, **3:3, 9:18, 9:19, 9:21**
New deal, **17:7**

LABOUR RELATIONS
Agricultural workers, **40:9, 44:5, 55:18**
Airports, on, **15:18**
Arbitrator's powers, **40:16**
Australia, **21:10**
Charter protection, **36:13, 37:7**
Collective agreement, status of, **1:4, 44:5, 55:50**
Collective bargaining, right to, **38:18, 44:5**
History, **21:10**
Hours, **18:12, 21:10**
Nuclear power plant, in, **22:10**
Occupational health and safety, **15:18, 32:1, 32:2**

LABOUR RELATIONS—Cont'd
Parental benefits, **15:27, 33:2**
Pensions
See PENSIONS
Picketing
See EXPRESSION
Police
See POLICE
Power to regulate, **17:7, 20:2, 20:4, 21:10, 21:11, 22:7, 22:10, 24:3, 43:1 to 43:4**
Privacy of employees, **43:26, 44:8**
Provincial laws, immunity from, **15:18, 15:19**
Standards, **11:11, 17:7, 18:6, 21:10, 21:11**
Strike right to, **38:18, 44:5**
Trade union
agency shop, **43:15, 44:8**
bargain collectively right to, **1:4, 40:4, 44:4, 44:5, 44:7, 55:50**
closed shop, **44:8**
form, right to, **37:7, 37:13, 38:20, 44:1 to 44:8**
power to regulate, **44:1**
strike, right to, **44:5, 44:7**
union shop, **44:8**
Unemployment insurance
See UNEMPLOYMENT INSURANCE
United States, **21:10**
Work, right to, **44:8, 46:4, 47:10**

LA FOREST G.V.
Taxation, on, **31:3**

LAND
See PROPERTY

LANDLORD AND TENANT
See PROPERTY

LANGUAGE
Aboriginal peoples, of, **27:6, 56:1**
Administrative tribunals, in, **56:10**
Alberta, in
See ALBERTA
Commerce of, **56:16**
Constitutional amendment in relation to
See AMENDMENT OF CONSTITUTION
Courts in, **56:4 to 56:8, 56:9 to 56:13, 56:14, 56:15**

LANGUAGE—Cont'd
Delegated legislation of, **56:8**
Discrepancies between English and French, **36:24**
Discrimination on basis of, **55:28, 55:38, 56:15**
Education of
remedy for breach, **40:4, 56:22**
under s. 23, **4.11(b), 37:4, 38:6, 40:4, 40:15, 40:23, 56:19 to 56:24**
under s. 93, **55:38, 57:6, 57:16**
Expression as, **43:16, 43:22**
French version of constitution, **56:3**
General discussion, **56:1 to 56:25**
Government of Canada, in
See GOVERNMENT OF CANADA
Incorporated legislation, **14:12**
Incorporation by reference, **56:7**
Interpreter right to, **56:13**
Judicial supervision of remedial order, **40.3(g.1), 40:23, 56:25**
Legislative power over, **17:2, 56:2**
Manitoba, in
See MANITOBA
Matter, as, **56:2**
New Brunswick, in
See NEW BRUNSWICK
Official languages of Canada, **56:2, 56:14**
Parliament of Canada, in
See FEDERAL PARLIAMENT
Police services, **19:10, 56:15**
Proceedings language of, **56:12**
Process language of, **56:11**
Quebec, in
See QUEBEC
Records and journals, **56:5**
Rights can be expanded, **56:4**
Saskatchewan in
See SASKATCHEWAN
Simultaneous enactment in English and French, **56:6**
Statutes of, **12:10, 36:22, 40:9, 56:4 to 56:8, 56:9, 56:15**

LASKIN, CHIEF JUSTICE B.
Appointment, **1:12**
Canadian Bill of Rights, on, **35:3**
Classification, on, **15:4**
Composition of bench, policy, **8:3**
Delegation, on, **14:13, 14:14**
Incorporation power, on, **23:3**

LASKIN, CHIEF JUSTICE B.—Cont'd
Matter, on, **15:5**
Paramountcy on, **16:5**
Privy Council appeals, on, **8:2**

LAURIER PRIME MINISTER W.
Generally, **5:16**

LAW
Overbroad
See OVERBROAD LAW
Policy as, **38:7, 40:1**
Prescribed by law, **38:7 to 38:9**
Reviewable under s. 52(1), **40:1, 40:13**
Vague
See VAGUE LAW

LAW AND CUSTOM OF PARLIAMENT
Generally, **1:6**

LAWS OF CANADA
Generally, **5:5, 7:11, 35:1**

LAWS OF GENERAL APPLICATION
See also SINGLING OUT
Generally, **15:6, 15:20, 28:13 to 28:16, 46:4**

LAWYERS
See PROFESSIONS

LEAGUE OF NATIONS
Generally, **3:1**

LEDERMAN W.R.
Delegation, on, **14:10, 14:11**
Double aspect, on, **15:7**
Incorporation power, on, **23:3**
Legislative purpose, on, **15:8**
Matter, on, **15:5, 15:8**
Patriation, on, **3:9**
Peace, order, and good government, on, **17:1, 17:12**

LEGAL AID
See COUNSEL, RIGHT TO

LEGAL PROFESSION
See PROFESSIONS

LEGAL RIGHTS
Charter protections, **47:1**
Definition, **47:1, 47:10**
Distribution of powers over, **47:1**

LEGISLATIVE ASSEMBLY
See PROVINCIAL LEGISLATURE

LEGISLATIVE BRANCH
See LEGISLATIVE POWER

LEGISLATIVE COUNCIL
Abolition by provinces, **9:10, 12:10**

LEGISLATIVE HISTORY
Constitution Acts of, **36:28, 47:14, 47:15, 60:3 to 60:7**
Definition, **60:1**
Originalism
See INTERPRETATION OF CONSTITUTION
Progressive interpretation
See INTERPRETATION OF CONSTITUTION
Statutes of, **15:8, 38:12, 60:2, 60:8**

LEGISLATIVE POWER
Abdication, **3:4, 3:5, 12:10, 14:4**
Bill of rights limitations
See BILL OF RIGHTS
Binding other governments
See CROWN
Civil liberties and, **34:3, 34:6**
Constitutional restrictions, **12:2 to 12:8**
Delegation
See DELEGATION, INTER-DELEGATION
Executive matches, **9:3, 11:13**
Executive power, relation to, **1:8, 7:15, 9:3, 9:12, 11:13, 18:1, 19:13, 19:15**
Exhaustive distribution, **12:2 to 12:8, 17:1**
Extraterritorial competence
See EXTRATERRITORIAL COMPETENCE
Failure to exercise, effect of, **15:23**
Federal limits
See FEDERALISM, DISTRIBUTION OF POWERS, JUDICIAL REVIEW OF LEGISLATION
Federal Parliament
See FEDERAL PARLIAMENT
Imperial Parliament
See IMPERIAL PARLIAMENT
Judicial power, relation to, **7:15, 9:12**
Language requirements, **12:10, 56:4 to 56:8**

LEGISLATIVE POWER—Cont'd
Manner and form limitations, **5:20, 12:10, 35:5, 39:5**
New Zealand, **12:1**
Parliamentary sovereignty, **3:4, 3:8, 4:15, 10:14, 12:1 to 12:10, 14:9**
Procedural limitations
See manner and form limitations
Proprietary rights contrasted, **28:3, 29:3**
Provincial Legislature
See PROVINCIAL LEGISLATURE
Retroactive law
See RETROACTIVE LAW
Self-imposed limitations, **12:9, 12:10, 14:9, 35:5**
Unwritten restrictions on, **7:5, 7:8, 7:9, 15:28, 38:28, 56:14**

LEGISLATIVE SCHEME
See also INTER-DELEGATION
Generally, **15:14**

LEGISLATIVE UNION
Generally, **5:2**

LEGISLATURE
See FEDERAL PARLIAMENT, PROVINCIAL LEGISLATURE

LEGITIMATE EXPECTATIONS
Generally, **12:9**

LENDING POWER
See SPENDING POWER

LEVESQUE PREMIER R.
Generally, **4:2, 4:3**

LIBERTY
Generally, **36:5, 47:9 to 47:11**

LICENSING
Fees, **6:1, 31:3, 31:15, 31:16**
Regulation by, **31:3, 31:15, 31:16**

LIEUTENANT GOVERNOR
See also GOVERNOR GENERAL
Amendment in relation to
See AMENDMENT OF CONSTITUTION
Appointment, **5:9, 5:14, 9:3, 9:6**
Cabinet, does not attend, **9:6**
Conventions limit powers, **1:10, 5:14**
See also RESPONSIBLE GOVERNMENT

LIEUTENANT GOVERNOR—Cont'd
Delegation to by Legislature, **14:1, 14:8, 14:11**
Initiative and referendum
See INITIATIVE AND REFERENDUM
Personal prerogatives, **1:9, 5:14**
Powers, **9:3**
Representative of Crown, **9:3, 10:1**
Reservation of bills
See RESERVATION OF BILLS
Reserve powers, **1:10, 5:14**
Royal assent to statutes
See ROYAL ASSENT

LIFE
Generally, **47:8**

LIMITATION CLAUSE(s. 1)
American Bill of Rights lacks
See AMERICAN BILL OF RIGHTS
Application to s. 7, **38:25, 47:3, 47:38**
Application to s. 8, **38:26, 48:2**
Application to s. 9, **38:27**
Application to s. 11, **38:28**
Application to s. 12, **38:29**
Application to s. 15, **38:23, 55:19, 55:31**
Burden of proof under, **38:4, 38:11**
Canadian Bill of Rights lacks
See CANADIAN BILL OF RIGHTS
Common law, application to, **38:7 to 38:9, 38:30**
Cost as justification, **38:17, 38:20, 38:22, 38:25, 47:12**
Description, **38:1**
Discretion, **38:8**
Emergency measures, **38:32**
Equality clauses, relation to, **38:23, 55:31**
European Convention on Human Rights, in, **38:1**
Evidence, **38:4**
Federalism and, **38:21**
Free and democratic society, values of, **36:27**
International Covenant on Civil and Political Rights, in, **38:1**
Judicial independence, application to, **36:17, 38:28**
Least drastic means, **38:11, 38:20**
Limits, **38:6, 56:17**
Margin of appreciation, **38:21**

LIMITATION CLAUSE(s. 1)—Cont'd
Override clause, relation to, **39:1**
Policy decision, requires, **36:6**
Prescribed by law, **37:13, 38:4, 38:7 to 38:9, 43:30**
Pressing and substantial concern, **38:14**
Proportionality of law, **38:22, 42:5**
Provincial policies, effect on, **36:3**
Purpose of law, **38:11, 38:12 to 38:17, 38:16, 42:5**
Qualified rights, application to, **38:24 to 38:29**
Rational connection, **38:11, 38:12, 38:18, 38:19**
Rationale, **38:2**
Rights, relationship to, **43:11**
Standard of justification, **38:3, 38:7 to 38:22**
Vagueness, **38:9, 43:29**

LIMITATION OF ACTIONS
Constitutional cases, in, **40:10, 58:8, 59:18, 59:19**
Foreign limitations, effect of, **13:14**
Power over, **15:15**

LIQUOR
See TEMPERANCE

LITIGATION
See EVIDENCE, JUDICIAL REVIEW OF ADMINISTRATIVE ACTION, JUDICIAL REVIEW OF LEGISLATION, REMEDY

LIVELIHOOD
See LABOUR RELATIONS

LIVING TREE METAPHOR
Generally, **15:27, 36:13 to 36:17, 36:18**

LOCAL MATTERS
Assembly, **21:4, 41:1**
By-laws
See DELEGATED LEGISLATION
Film censorship
See EXPRESSION
Health, **18:6, 21:4, 32:1**
Highway regulation, **21:4**
Legislative power over, **15:26, 21:4**
Local option, **14:15, 55:49**
Municipalities
See MUNICIPALITIES
Residuary character, **15:26, 17:1**

LOCAL MATTERS—Cont'd
Social assistance, **33:5**
Trade regulation, **20:1, 21:4**

LOCAL WORKS
See DECLARATORY POWER, TRANSPORTATION AND COMMUNICATION

LOCKE, JOHN
Judicial independence, on, **7:3**

LOCUS STANDI
See STANDING

LONG-ARM STATUTES
Generally, **13:10, 13:11**

LORD'S DAY
See SUNDAY OBSERVANCE

LOWER CANADA
See also CANADA EAST, QUEBEC, UNITED PROVINCE OF CANADA
Generally, **2:6, 2:7, 5:4, 9:2**

LYSYK, K.
Indians, on, **28:2**
Peace order, and good government, on, **17:6**

MACDONALD, SIR JOHN A.
Confederation, on, **5:3**

MAGNA CARTA
Generally, **34:2**

MAINTENANCE
See CUSTODY AND MAINTENANCE

MALLORY, J.R.
Constitutional litigation, on, **59:1**
Judicial review, on, **5:21**

MANDAMUS
See REMEDY

MANDATORY RULE
Generally, **1:10, 12:10, 56:6, 58:9**

MANITOBA
See also MANITOBA ACT, 1870
Boundaries, **2:7, 2:9**
Creation, **1:6, 2:9**
Crown in right of, liability
See CROWN

MANITOBA—Cont'd
Education rights in, **56:17, 57:6**
Invalidity of laws, **15:28, 58:9, 58:10**
Language rights in, **4:16, 4:17, 5:4, 12:10, 14:8, 15:28, 40:4, 56:3, 56:4, 56:6, 58:9 to 58:11, 58:13**
Legislative Council abolition, **9:10, 12:10**
Natural resources agreement
See NATURAL RESOURCES AGREEMENTS
Reception of law, **2:5, 2:9**
Responsible government, **9:2**
School question, **5:16, 57:1, 57:2, 57:6**
Translation of laws, **55:17**
Unilingual laws, validity, **56:6**

MANITOBA ACT, 1870
Generally, **1:6, 2:9, 12:9**

MANNER AND FORM
See LEGISLATIVE POWER

MARGARINE
Generally, **17:7, 17:12, 18:2, 18:3, 20:2, 20:4, 21:8, 34:6**

MARGIN OF APPRECIATION
Generally, **38:21**

MARITIME
See NAVIGATION AND SHIPPING

MARITIME PROVINCES
New Brunswick
See NEW BRUNSWICK
Nova Scotia
See NOVA SCOTIA
Prince Edward Island
See PRINCE EDWARD ISLAND

MARKETING
Agriculture, **29:4**
Cooperative regulation, **20:3, 21:14, 46:14**
Declaratory power, **20:2, 22:10**
Delegation of power, **14:11**
Federal power, **17:7, 20:2 to 20:4, 21:8, 21:12 to 21:14**
Food and drugs
See FOOD AND DRUGS
Free trade between provinces, **13:6, 31:4, 46:8, 46:9**
Levies, **20:3, 31:16**

MARKETING—Cont'd
Margarine
See MARGARINE
Natural resources
See NATURAL RESOURCES
Production controls, **20:3, 21:14, 30:2, 30:18**
Product standards, **20:3, 46:10**
Provincial power
extraterritorial effects, **15:9, 21:14**
in general, **20:2, 20:3, 21:14, 30:2**
Reasons for regulation, **21:12**
Stocks and bonds
See SECURITIES REGULATION
Surplus disposal, **20:3**
United States, **21:13, 21:14**

MARRIAGE
See also FAMILY
Australia, **5:9, 27:1**
Civil union, **27:3**
Divorce
See DIVORCE
Indians effect on status, **28:2**
Judicial separation, **27:5**
Marital status
See EQUALITY
Power over, **5:9, 12:2, 27:1, 27:3, 27:4, 42:1, 55:47**
Property rights in, **27:4, 27:9, 55:18, 55:24, 55:47**
Recognition, **27:1, 27:3**
Same-sex marriage, **8:11, 12:2, 15:27, 27:3, 27:8, 42:11, 55:18, 55:48**
Sexual orientation
See EQUALITY
Solemnization, **15:23, 27:3, 42:11**
United States, **5:9, 27:1**

MARSHALL, G.
Patriation, on, **3:8, 3:9**

MATTER
Competition as, **20:4**
Definition, **15:4, 15:5 to 15:13, 15:14, 36:18, 60:2**
Distinctness, **17:5**
Environment as, **30:31**
Expression as, **43:3**
Health as, **18:6**
Inflation as, **17:5, 20:4**
Labour relations as, **21:11**

MATTER—Cont'd
Language as, **56:2**
New, **17:6**
Pollution as, **20:4, 30:31**
Religion as, **42:1**

MEDICARE
Generally, **5:8**

MEECH LAKE CONSTITUTIONAL ACCORD
Generally, **1:4, 4:3, 4:6, 4:12, 4:15, 4:16, 4:20, 4:23, 5:4, 5:24, 6:7, 6:8, 8:1, 8:14, 9:10, 39:2**

MEETING
See ASSEMBLY

MEMBER OF COMMONWEALTH
See COMMONWEALTH

MEMBER OF THE PUBLIC
Generally, **37:2, 56:15**

MENS REA
See FUNDAMENTAL JUSTICE

MENTAL DISABILITY
See EQUALITY

MENTAL DISORDER
See INSANITY

METIS
See ABORIGINAL PEOPLES OF CANADA, INDIANS AND INDIAN LANDS, NATIVE RIGHTS

MILITARY TRIBUNAL
See also ARMED FORCES
Equality argument, **55:2**
Fair hearing, **7:6**
Independence, **7:6, 58:7**
Jury, no right to, **51:24**
Minister, role of, **7:6, 47:32**
Offence under military law, **47:24, 51:3, 51:24, 55:2, 58:7**

MILL, JOHN STUART
Direct and indirect taxation, on, **31:6**
Freedom of speech, on, **43:7**

MINISTER
Appointment, **1:9, 9:4, 9:6**
Cabinet membership, **9:5**
Deputy minister contrasted, **9:4**

MINISTER—Cont'd
Dismissal, **1:9, 9:4, 9:6, 9:7**
Duties, **9:7**
Member of Parliament, **9:4**
Personal liability, **9:7**
Resignation, **9:7**
Responsibility to Parliament, **9:7**
Role in constitutional amendment, **4:15**
Taxation liable to pay, **31:22**
Testimony power to compel, **10:9, 15:8**

MINISTERIAL RESPONSIBILITY
Generally, **9:7**

MINISTER OF JUSTICE
See also ATTORNEY GENERAL
Extradition, **47:15, 51:2**
Scrutiny of statutes, **36:11, 40:30**

MINORITY LANGUAGE EDUCATIONAL RIGHTS
See EDUCATION

MISTAKE OF LAW
Defence as, **47:16 to 47:18**

MOBILITY
Aboriginal right, **28:19**
Capital, **46:12 to 46:15**
Corporation not entitled to, **37:4, 46:6, 46:11**
Deportation, **17:8, 46:1, 46:2, 47:9, 55:46**
See also DEPORTATION
Description, **46:1 to 46:15**
Emigration, **46:2**
Entry to Canada, **37:14, 40:23, 46:2**
Extradition, **37:14, 46:2**
See also EXTRADITION
Goods, **8:13, 20:3, 28:19, 31:2, 46:7 to 46:10**
Immigration
See IMMIGRATION
International, **26:1, 26:2, 28:19, 46:2**
Interprovincial, **26:1, 26:2, 32:4, 46:3**
Livelihood, **36:14, 46:4, 46:11**
Passport, right to
See PASSPORT
Persons, **46:1 to 46:6, 46:11**
Prisoner in foreign gaol, **46:2**
Services, **46:11**

MONARCHY
See CROWN HEAD OF STATE, QUEEN

MONEY BILL
See FEDERAL PARLIAMENT

MOOT ISSUE
Generally, **1:11, 8:11, 40:23, 43:2, 59:7 to 59:9**

MOVEMENT
See MOBILITY

MOVIES
See FILMS

MULRONEY, PRIME MINISTER M. BRIAN
Generally, **4:3**

MULTI-CULTURALISM
Generally, **42:10, 43:11, 55:35**

MUNDELL, D.W.
Matter, on, **15:5**

MUNICIPALITIES
Charter, application to, **37:8, 37:10**
Duty to consult aboriginal people, **28:38**
Prayer in, **42:10**
Provincial power over, **55:49**
Variations in municipal laws, **55:49**

MURDER
Attempted murder, **47:19, 47:20**
Felony murder, **47:19, 58:4**
Life imprisonment for, **47:19, 53:4**
Mens rea requirement, **47:19, 47:20**
Party to, **47:19**

MUTUAL MODIFICATION
Generally, **15:23, 20:1, 36:23**

NARCOTICS
See FOOD AND DRUGS

NATIONAL SECURITY
Generally, **10:7, 19:12, 36:9, 47:32**

NATIONAL UNITY
Generally, **36:3**

NATIVE RIGHTS
See ABORIGINAL RIGHTS

NATURALIZATION AND ALIENS
Generally, **21:18, 26:2, 26:3, 29:2, 46:3, 55:1**

NATURAL JUSTICE
Generally, **34:2, 47:14, 47:38**

NATURAL LAW
See NATURAL RIGHTS

NATURAL RESOURCES
Aboriginal rights to
See NATIVE RIGHTS
Agreements
See NATURAL RESOURCES AGREEMENTS
Electricity
See ELECTRICITY
Environment
See ENVIRONMENT
Export, **13:5, 21:14, 29:3, 29:8, 30:2, 30:5, 30:30, 31:14**
Fisheries
See FISHERIES
Forestry, **29:3, 30:15 to 30:20, 31:14**
Import, **30:7**
Legislative powers over, **4:20, 4:21, 15:27, 18:2, 30:1 to 30:33**
Marketing
See MARKETING
Offshore minerals, **17:2, 17:3, 30:4 to 30:10**
Oil and gas, **21:14, 30:1, 31:14**
Onshore minerals, **29:3, 30:1 to 30:3**
Pipeline
See PIPELINE
Pollution
See ENVIRONMENT
Production controls
See MARKETING
Proprietary rights over
See PUBLIC PROPERTY
Public property
See PUBLIC PROPERTY
Taxation, **4:21, 15:9, 29:3, 31:1, 31:14**
Territories in, **30:5, 30:16**
Uranium, **17:3, 30:6, 30:10, 30:30**

NATURAL RESOURCES AGREEMENTS
Generally, **28:11, 28:17, 29:2**

NATURAL RIGHTS
Generally, **36:13**

NAVIGATION AND SHIPPING
Expropriation of works, **29:5**
Floating of logs, **30:17**
Labour relations, **21:11**
Local shipping, **22:1, 22:12**
Marine insurance
See INSURANCE
Maritime law, **7:11, 15:19, 15:20, 16:3, 22:12, 33:4**
Pollution of water, **30:32**
Port regulation of land use, **15:18, 22:12**
Power over, **22:1, 22:12**
River obstruction of, **30:17, 30:28**

NECESSITY
Bias, cure for, **58:7**
Justification for usurper's act, **5:27**
No defence to tort action, **34:2**
Parliamentary privilege, test for, **1:7**
Validation of invalid decisions, **7:5, 58:7**
Validation of invalid laws, **5:27, 40:4, 56:6, 58:9**

NEUTRAL PRINCIPLES
See JUDICIAL REVIEW OF LEGISLATION

NEW BRUNSWICK
Confederation, **2:7**
Constitution, **1:4, 1:9, 2:2 to 2:4, 2:7**
Courts, language in, **56:2, 56:9, 56:10**
Crown in right of liability of
See CROWN
Government services, language of, **56:14, 56:15**
History, **2:2 to 2:4**
Legislative Council, abolition of, **9:10, 12:10**
Legislature, language in, **56:4**
Liquor regulation, **8:13, 20:3**
Official languages, **56:14, 56:15**
Reception of law, **2:1, 2:2 to 2:4**
Responsible government, **9:3**

NEW DEAL
Generally, **6:2, 17:7, 17:11, 36:13**

NEWFOUNDLAND
Admission to Canada, **2:12, 5:6**
Change of name, **1:4**

NEWFOUNDLAND—Cont'd
Constitution, **1:4, 2:4**
Crown in right of, liability of
See CROWN
Denominational school rights, **1:4, 4:17**
History, **2:2 to 2:4**
Offshore, **13:4, 17:2, 30:13**
Reception of law, **2:2 to 2:4, 2:12**
Responsible government, **2:12, 9:2**
Terms of union, **1:4, 4:17**

NEWFOUNDLAND ACT
Generally, **1:4, 2:12, 4:17, 56:17**

NEW FRANCE
Generally, **2:6**

NEW ZEALAND
Civil liberties, **31:6, 31:7**
Constitutional amendment, **5:19, 5:20**
Crown liability in tort, **10:12**
Judicial review, absence of, **5:20, 12:1**
Member of Commonwealth, **3:1**
Parliamentary sovereignty, **12:1**
Privy Council appeals, **8:2**
Same-sex marriage, **27:3**
Supreme Court, **8:2, 8:6**
Treaty implementation, **11:7**
U.K. Parliament, termination of authority, **3:4**
Unitary state, **5:19, 5:20, 12:1**

NON-JUSTICIABLE ISSUE
See also POLITICAL QUESTION
Generally, **1:10, 1:12**

NORTHERN IRELAND
Generally, **2:13, 5:1, 5:3, 5:20, 12:1, 14:2**

NORTHWEST TERRITORIES
Admission to Canada, **2:9**
Annexations to provinces, **2:7, 2:9**
Courts, **7:13**
Devolution, **5:3, 14:4**
Federal power over
See TERRITORIES

NOTWITHSTANDING CLAUSE
See CHARTER OF RIGHTS

NOVA SCOTIA
Confederation, **2:7**
Constitution, **1:4, 1:9, 2:1, 2:2 to 2:4, 2:7**

NOVA SCOTIA—Cont'd
Crown in right of, liability of
See CROWN
History, **2:1, 2:2 to 2:4, 2:11**
Legislative Council, abolition, **9:10, 12:10**
Reception of law, **2:1, 2:2 to 2:4, 2:11**
Responsible government, **9:2**
Secession attempt, **5:25**

NUCLEAR POWER
See ATOMIC ENERGY

NULLIFICATION
See UNCONSTITUTIONAL LAW

NUNAVUT
Creation, **2:9**
Devolution, **5:3**
Representation in Parliament, **1:4**

OATH OF ALLEGIANCE
Generally, **43:16**

OCCUPATIONS
See BUSINESS, LABOUR RELATIONS, PROFESSIONS, TRADES

OCCUPIED FIELD
See PARAMOUNTCY

O'CONNOR REPORT
Peace, order, and good government, on, **17:1**

OFFENCE
Definition, **51:3**
Military law, under, **51:3, 51:24**
Penalty change in, **43:28**
Power to create
See CRIMINAL LAW
Regulatory
See CRIMINAL LAW
Retroactive, **51:26**
True crime
See CRIMINAL LAW

OFFICIAL LANGUAGES
See LANGUAGE

OFFSHORE MINERALS
See NATURAL RESOURCES

OIL AND GAS
See NATURAL RESOURCES

ONTARIO
Boundaries, **2:7, 2:9**
Canada West
See CANADA WEST
Confederation, **2:5, 2:6**
Crown in right of, liability
See CROWN
Fiscal capacity, **6:6**
History, **2:5, 2:6**
Language rights in, **12:10**
Reception of law, **2:2 to 2:4, 2:5, 2:6**
Responsible government, **9:2**
Supreme Court of Canada, judges from, **8:3, 8:14**
Tax agreements
See TAX AGREEMENTS
United Province of Canada
See UNITED PROVINCE OF CANADA
Upper Canada
See UPPER CANADA

ONUS OF PROOF
See BURDEN OF PROOF

OPTING OUT
See AMENDMENT OF CONSTITUTION, CHARTER OF RIGHTS, SHARED-COST PROGRAMMES

ORIGINALISM
See INTERPRETATION OF CONSTITUTION

OVERBROAD LAW
Section 1, **38:20, 38:21**
Section 7, **47:24, 47:27**

PARADE
See ASSEMBLY

PARAMOUNTCY
Australia, **15:25, 16:1**
Common law, **16:1**
Conflict of laws distinguished, **27:10**
Covering the field, **16:4, 16:5**
Description of law, **16:1 to 16:10**
Double civil liability, **16:9**
Double criminal liability
See DOUBLE JEOPARDY
Double taxation
See TAXATION
Duplication, **16:5, 16:6, 16:7 to 16:9**

PARAMOUNTCY—Cont'd
Effect of inconsistency, **15:16, 16:10**
Enlargement by Indian Act, **16:5, 28:10, 28:15**
Express contradiction, **16:3, 16:4, 25:15**
Express extension of, **16:6**
Federal systems, in, **5:1, 16:1**
Frustration of federal purpose, **16:4**
Interjurisdictional immunity and
See INTERJURISDICTIONAL IMMUNITY
Judicial review under, **5:20, 16:10**
Maintenance and custody orders, **27:6 to 27:8**
Negative implication, **16:4, 16:5**
Overlap of laws, **16:7 to 16:9**
Pensions, **16:1**
Permissive rules and, **16:4**
Pre-confederation law, **16:1**
Reversed, **16:1**
United States, **15:25, 16:1, 16:5**
Validity contrasted, **15:16, 16:1, 16:8, 16:10**
Waiver of, **14:17, 16:6**

PARDON
See CRIMINAL LAW

PARENS PATRIAE
Generally, **27:11**

PARENT
See CHILD

PARKS
Generally, **15:19, 29:2, 31:16, 43:3**

PARLIAMENT
See FEDERAL PARLIAMENT, IMPERIAL PARLIAMENT, PROVINCIAL LEGISLATURE, UNITED KINGDOM PARLIAMENT

PARLIAMENTARY GOVERNMENT
See RESPONSIBLE GOVERNMENT

PARLIAMENTARY PRIVILEGE
Charter of Rights, application to
See CHARTER OF RIGHTS
Constitutional status, **1:4, 1:7, 37:7**
Definition, **1:7**
Party caucus, composition of, **1:9**

PARLIAMENTARY PROCEDURE
See also FEDERAL PARLIAMENT
Access to legislative Chamber, **1:7, 37:7, 43:34**
Enforceability, **12:10, 14:5**
Law and custom of Parliament, **1:6**
Manner and form contrasted, **12:10**
Parliamentary privilege
See PARLIAMENTARY PRIVILEGE
Royal consent to bill affecting prerogative, **1:9**

PARLIAMENTARY SOVEREIGNTY
See LEGISLATIVE POWER

PAROLE
See CRIMINAL LAW

PASSPORT
Prerogative power to issue, **1:9, 46:2**
Right of citizen, **37:14, 40:23, 46:2**

PATENTS
Generally, **18:16, 20:4, 32:2**

PATRIATION
See also AMENDMENT OF CONSTITUTION
Generally, **3:5, 4:20**

PEACE ORDER, AND GOOD GOVERNMENT
Aeronautics
See AERONAUTICS
Apprehended insurrection, **17:9**
Atomic energy, **17:3, 30:10**
Citizenship, **37:4, 46:3**
Companies incorporation, **17:2, 23:1**
Competition, **17:7**
Delegation, **14:7**
Deportation, **17:8**
Depression not emergency, **17:7, 17:11, 17:12**
Distinctness of matter, **15:5, 15:26, 17:5, 17:12**
Double aspect doctrine, **17:2**
Drugs, **17:3, 17:6, 18:4**
Emergency branch, **17:3, 17:7 to 17:11, 17:12, 21:11**
Expression
See EXPRESSION
Extraterritorial restriction, **13:2**
Gap branch, **17:2, 17:7**

PEACE ORDER, AND GOOD GOVERNMENT—Cont'd
Health, **18:6, 32:2**
Inflation as emergency, **15:26, 17:10, 21:11**
Insurance, **17:9**
Labour relations
See LABOUR RELATIONS
Language, **17:2, 56:2**
Margarine
See MARGARINE
Marketing, **17:7**
National capital region, **17:3, 17:4, 21:2, 29:5**
National concern branch, **17:3 to 17:6, 17:12**
National security
See NATIONAL SECURITY
New deal
See NEW DEAL
New matters, **17:6**
Offshore minerals, **17:2, 17:3**
Pollution, **11:12, 17:3, 18:6, 30:32**
Precedent
See PRECEDENT
Provincial inability test, **17:4**
Radio, **22:16 to 22:18**
Rent control, **17:8, 21:8**
Residuary character, **12:2, 17:1**
Royal assent, **4:16**
Royal style and titles
See QUEEN
Speech
See EXPRESSION
Temperance, **17:3, 17:6, 17:12**
Temporary character of emergency law, **17:11, 17:12**
Treaty implementation, **11:12, 17:2, 17:3, 17:7, 22:13, 22:16**
Trenching, **15:5**
Unemployment insurance, **17:1, 17:7**
Voting qualifications, **45:1**
Wage and price control, **15:26, 17:5, 17:7, 17:10, 21:8**
Wartime legislation
See WAR MEASURES ACT

PENAL LAW
See CRIMINAL LAW

PENDENT JURISDICTION
Generally, **7:11**

PENITENTIARIES
See also CRIMINAL LAW
Australia, **5:9**
Cruel and unusual conditions in, **53:6**
Definition, **19:18**
Power over, **5:9, 18:1, 19:18**
Prisoners voting, **36:9, 45:2**
Prisons, power over, **19:18**
Search of prisoners, **48:22, 55:27, 55:41**
Transfer of prisoners, **46:2, 47:9, 50:17**
United States, **5:9**

PENSIONS
Amendment, **6:7, 14:10, 15:27, 17:7, 33:1, 33:3**
Canada Pension Plan, **5:4, 6:7, 33:3**
Federal-provincial delegation, **14:10, 33:3**
Old age, **4:20, 6:7, 14:10, 15:25, 15:27, 17:7, 33:3**
Power over, **15:25, 33:1, 33:3**
Quebec Pension Plan, **5:4, 6:7, 33:3**
Taxation of, **31:20**

PERMANENT RESIDENT
Generally, **26:1, 37:5, 46:3, 46:4, 51:31**

PER SALTUM APPEALS
Generally, **8:2**

PERSON
Generally, **37:2, 45:6, 51:21**

PHYSICAL DISABILITY
See EQUALITY

PICKETING
See EXPRESSION

PIPELINE
Immunity from provincial law, **15:18**
Power over, **15:18, 22:11, 28:38, 30:3, 30:8**

PITH AND SUBSTANCE
Generally, **13:5, 13:6, 15:4, 15:5, 15:9, 15:14, 15:15, 15:20, 15:25**

PLAIN VIEW
See SEARCH OR SEIZURE

POLICE
See also CRIMINAL LAW

POLICE—Cont'd
Arrest
See ARREST
Caution to suspect, **40:9, 50:5 to 50:16**
Detention
See DETENTION
Disciplinary procedures, **51:3**
Evidence obtained in breach of Charter, **38:12 to 38:17**
Federal power over, **18:1, 19:13**
Private person as agent, **48:17**
Provincial forces, **19:8, 19:9**
Provincial power over, **15:19, 18:1, 19:8**
Questioning of suspect, **47:31, 50:2, 50:7, 50:12, 50:14**
Royal Canadian Mounted Police
collective bargaining, right to, **38:18, 44:5**
federal policing, **19:13**
inquiry into force, **19:16**
language obligations, **19:10, 56:15**
national security policing, **19:10**
provincial policing, **19:10**
provincial power over, **15:19, 19:10**
strike right to, **38:18, 44:5**
territorial policing, **19:11**
union, **44:4**
Schools, in, **41:11, 48:5 to 48:12, 57:18**
Search and seizure
See SEARCH AND SEIZURE
Security guards compared, **37:13**
Sniffer dogs, use of, **41:11, 48:5 to 48:12, 48:14, 48:27, 57:18**
Trickery, **47:31**

POLITICAL PARTIES
Regulation, **45:4**

POLITICAL QUESTION
Generally, **5:21, 8:11, 15:11, 36:8 to 36:11, 36:12**

POLLUTION
See ENVIRONMENT

POLYGAMY
See RELIGION

PORNOGRAPHY
See EXPRESSION, SEARCH AND SEIZURE

PORT
See NAVIGATION AND SHIPPING

POSTAL SERVICE
Generally, **15:19, 22:9, 22:11**
Community mail boxes, **22:11**

PRACTICE
See USAGE

PRAIRIE PROVINCES
Alberta
See ALBERTA
Manitoba
See MANITOBA
Saskatchewan
See SASKATCHEWAN

PREAMBLE
Constitution Act, 1867, of
See CONSTITUTION ACT 1867
Statute, of, **15:8**

PRECEDENT
See also CASE LAW, COMMON LAW, RES JUDICATA
Constitutional cases, **8:13, 36:18**
High Court of Australia, **2:2, 8:13**
House of Lords, **2:2, 8:13**
Privy Council, **2:2, 8:13**
Prospective overruling, **58:1**
Reference cases, **8:13**
Supreme Court of Canada, **2:2, 8:13**
Supreme Court of United States, **2:2, 8:13**

PRE-CONFEDERATION LAWS
Generally, **2:7, 3:2, 3:3, 13:7, 35:1**

PREEMPTION
See PARAMOUNTCY

PRELIMINARY INQUIRY
Charge, power to, **51:4**
Constitutional questions, power to decide, **40:28**
Court of competent jurisdiction, as, **40:16, 40:28**

PREMATURITY
See RIPENESS

PREMIER
See also PRIME MINISTER
Appointment, **9:17**
Death, **9:4, 9:17**

PREMIER—Cont'd
Dismissal, **9:18**
Dissolution power to advise, **45:7**

PREROGATIVE POWER
Charter, application to, **1:9**
Crown's power, **1:8, 1:9, 29:3, 34:2**
Dispensing power, **1:9, 34:2**
Displacement by statute, **1:9, 8:2, 11:5, 29:3**
Federal distribution, **1:9, 9:3, 10:1, 19:17**
Immunity from statute, **10:13**
Indian reserves, **1:9, 28:3**
International affairs, **1:9, 11:2, 11:4**
Judicial Committee of Privy Council, **8:2**
Legislative power over colonies, **1:9, 2:4**
Letters Patent constituting office of Governor General, **1:2, 1:9, 11:2, 11:13**
Pardon, **19:17**
Proprietary right contrasted, **29:3**
Responsible government
See RESPONSIBLE GOVERNMENT
Rights of subject, over, **1:9**
Royal consent to bill affecting prerogative, **1:9**
Suspending power, **1:9, 34:2**

PRESCRIBED BY LAW (s. 1)
See LIMITATION CLAUSE (s. 1)

PRESS
See EXPRESSION

PREVENTIVE LAW
Generally, **17:11, 18:11, 18:16**

PRICE CONTROL
See WAGE AND PRICE CONTROL

PRIMACY CLAUSE
Generally, **12:10, 40:26, 55:7**

PRIME MINISTER
See also PREMIER
Acting or deputy, **9:17**
Appointment, **1:9, 9:4, 9:15, 9:17**
Cabinet
calls meetings, **9:6**
chooses members, **9:5**
defines consensus, **9:6**
presides over, **9:5**
settles agenda, **9:6**

PRIME MINISTER—Cont'd
Chief Justices, recommends appointment, **1:12, 8:3, 9:6**
Constitution does not mention, **1:2**
Death, **9:4, 9:17**
Dismissal, **9:14, 9:15, 9:18**
First ministers' conferences, chairs, **5:27**
Government power to bind, **5:27**
Governor General, recommends appointment of, **9:3, 9:6**
Lieutenant Governor, recommends appointment of, **9:3, 9:6**
Ministers appoints and dismisses, **1:9, 9:4, 9:6**
Parliament
advises dissolution, **9:6, 9:19, 42:3**
advises summoning, **9:6**
President of United States compared, **9:6**
Resignation, **9:4, 9:15, 9:17, 9:18**
Retirement, **9:4, 9:17**
Statutes do not mention, **1:14**

PRINCE EDWARD ISLAND
Constitution, **1:4, 1:9, 2:2 to 2:4, 2:11**
Crown in right of, liability
See CROWN
History, **1:5, 2:1, 2:2 to 2:4, 2:11**
Legislative Council, abolition, **9:10, 12:10**
Reception of law, **2:1, 2:2 to 2:4, 2:11**
Responsible government, **9:2**

PRISONERS
See PENITENTIARIES

PRISONS
See PENITENTIARIES

PRIVACY
Corporation, **48:5 to 48:12**
Employees of
See LABOUR RELATIONS
Liberty element of, **47:10, 47:32 to 47:37**
Litigants of, **43:32**
Search or seizure protection, **48:5 to 48:12**
Witness, of, **36:23, 47:27 to 47:29**

PRIVATE INTERNATIONAL LAW
See CONFLICT OF LAWS

PRIVATIVE CLAUSE
Constitutional limitations on, **7:19, 7:20, 12:2, 40:26, 58:2**
Definition, **7:20**
Interpretation of, **7:20, 34:2**
Notice requirements contrasted, **58:3**
Taxation, barring recovery, **58:7**

PRIVILEGE
See EVIDENCE

PRIVY COUNCIL
Amending procedures, role in, **4:9**
Cabinet active part of, **9:5**
Court, as
See JUDICIAL COMMITTEE OF PRIVY COUNCIL
Establishment, **9:2, 9:5**
Judicial committee
See JUDICIAL COMMITTEE OF PRIVY COUNCIL
Membership, **9:2, 9:5**

PROBATE FEES
See TAXATION

PROBATION
See CRIMINAL LAW

PROCEDURE
See ADMINISTRATION OF JUSTICE, CIVIL PROCEDURE, CRIMINAL PROCEDURE, FUNDAMENTAL JUSTICE, JUDICIAL REVIEW OF LEGISLATION, PARLIAMENTARY PROCEDURE

PRODUCT STANDARDS
See MARKETING

PROFESSIONS
Advertising by
See EXPRESSION
Disciplinary procedures, **38:31, 51:3**
Independence of the bar, **15:28, 38:31, 47:15**
Power over, **15:7, 19:6, 19:14, 21:9**
Solicitor-client privilege
See EVIDENCE

PROGRESSIVE INTERPRETATION
See INTERPRETATION OF CONSTITUTION

PROHIBITION
See REMEDY, TEMPERANCE

PROPERTY
American Bill of Rights protection, **29:8, 47:2, 47:10, 47:13**
Canadian Bill of Rights protection, **29:8, 35:1, 35:7, 47:2, 47:13**
Charter of Rights lack of protection, **13:11, 29:8, 35:7, 47:2, 47:10, 47:13, 48:4**
Divorce, division on, **27:4, 27:9, 27:16**
Expropriation
See EXPROPRIATION
Foreign ownership, **21:18, 46:5**
Forfeiture, **18:17, 18:19, 51:3**
Gun control, **18:13, 18:18, 21:17**
Heritage, **15:24, 21:19, 28:9**
Indian property
See NATIVE RIGHTS
Land use, **15:5, 15:18, 22:15, 25:7**
Location of
See SITUS
Non-resident ownership, **46:5**
Power over, **21:17 to 21:19, 31:9**
Public property
See PUBLIC PROPERTY
Search or seizure
See SEARCH OR SEIZURE
Taxation
See TAXATION
Zoning, **15:5, 15:18, 22:15**

PROPERTY AND CIVIL RIGHTS
Agriculture relation to
See AGRICULTURE
Bankruptcy and insolvency
See BANKRUPTCY AND INSOLVENCY
Builders lien, **15:18**
Business
See BUSINESS
Civil liberties excluded, **21:3**
Civil rights defined, **21:3**
Contracts, **9:12, 12:9, 21:20, 29:8**
Debt adjustment, **21:20**
Definition, **21:2**
Environment
See ENVIRONMENT
Expropriation
See EXPROPRIATION

PROPERTY AND CIVIL RIGHTS —Cont'd
Federal laws affecting, **17:12**
Films
See FILMS
Fisheries, relation to
See FISHERIES
Health, **32:1**
History, **2:6, 5:11, 21:2**
Insurance
See INSURANCE
Interest
See INTEREST
Intraprovincial trade and commerce, **20:2**
Labour relations
See LABOUR RELATIONS
Land use
See PROPERTY
Literature
See LITERATURE
Local trade and commerce, **20:2, 21:4**
Marital
See MARRIAGE
Marketing
See MARKETING
Natural resources
See NATURAL RESOURCES
Pollution
See ENVIRONMENT
Prices
See WAGE AND PRICE CONTROL
Professions
See PROFESSIONS
Property
See PROPERTY
Residuary character, **17:1**
Securities regulation
See SECURITIES REGULATION
Speech
See EXPRESSION
Sunday observance
See SUNDAY OBSERVANCE
Territorial limitation, **21:14, 21:22**
Theatre
See THEATRE
Trade and commerce
See TRADE AND COMMERCE
Trades
See TRADES

PROSECUTION
See CRIMINAL LAW

PROSPECTIVE OVERRULING
See PRECEDENT

PROSTITUTION
Bawdy house, **40:4, 47:12, 47:25**
Charter protection, **43:9, 43:13, 43:25, 47:12, 47:24, 47:25, 47:27 to 47:29, 60:8**
Communicating for sale, **40:4**
Living on avails, **40:4, 47:12, 47:24, 47:25, 51:14**
Power to regulate, **18:19, 40:4**
Standing to sue, **59:5**

PROVINCES
Admission to Canada, **1:5, 2:10 to 2:12**
Airspace, jurisdiction over, **13:4**
Alberta
See ALBERTA
Boundaries, **2:7, 2:9, 4:14, 4:17, 13:4**
British Columbia
See BRITISH COLUMBIA
Confederation, **2:7**
Constitutional amendment, role in
See AMENDMENT OF CONSTITUTION
Constitutions
See CONSTITUTION OF THE PROVINCE
Contract power to, **6:9, 11:13**
Creation, **1:6, 2:9, 4:14**
Crown in right of
See CROWN
Equality, **4:2, 5:1, 5:4, 5:6**
Government
See PROVINCIAL GOVERNMENT
Legislative Councils, abolition, **9:10, 12:10**
Legislatures
See PROVINCIAL LEGISLATURE
Lieutenant Governors
See LIEUTENANT GOVERNOR
Manitoba
See MANITOBA
New Brunswick
See NEW BRUNSWICK
Newfoundland and Labrador
See NEWFOUNDLAND

PROVINCES—Cont'd
Nova Scotia
See NOVA SCOTIA
Offshore jurisdiction over, **13:4**
Ontario
See ONTARIO
Premiers
See PREMIER
Prince Edward Island
See PRINCE EDWARD ISLAND
Public property, distribution
See PUBLIC PROPERTY
Quebec
See QUEBEC
Responsible government
See RESPONSIBLE GOVERNMENT
Revenues
See FINANCIAL ARRANGEMENTS
Saskatchewan
See SASKATCHEWAN
Secede, power to
See SECESSION
Social laboratories, as, **5:8, 5:27**
Special status
See SPECIAL STATUS
Terms of union, enforceable, **5:4**
Territorial limits, **13:4**
Treaty-making power, **11:13, 22:1**

PROVINCIAL GOVERNMENT
Charter applicable to, **37:6, 37:7, 37:10**
Definition of government, **37:10**

PROVINCIAL IMMUNITY
See INTERJURISDICTIONAL IMMUNITY

PROVINCIAL LEGISLATURE
Access to proceedings, **1:7, 37:7, 43:34**
Annual sessions, **9:6, 45:8**
Binding itself, **10:14, 12:9, 12:10, 14:9**
Candidate, right to be
See ELECTIONS
Concurrent powers
See CONCURRENT POWERS
Definition of Legislature, **5:5, 37:7**
Delegation power of, **14:3**
Dissolution, **45:7**
Dominion, power to bind, **10:19**
Duration, **4:19, 9:6, 45:7**

PROVINCIAL LEGISLATURE—Cont'd
Exclusive powers
See EXCLUSIVE POWERS
Extraterritorial competence
See EXTRATERRITORIAL COMPETENCE
Imperial statutes power over, **3:3**
International law, power to violate, **11:6**
Other provinces, power to bind, **10:20**
Powers and privileges, **1:7, 4:19**
Treaty implementation, role in, **11:6, 11:7, 11:11, 11:12**
Upper houses abolished, **9:10, 12:10**
Vote right to
See ELECTIONS

PUBLIC HEARING
See TRIAL

PUBLIC INQUIRY
Generally, **19:16**

PUBLIC LAW
Conquest, effect on, **2:5, 21:2**
Definition, **21:2**

PUBLIC PROPERTY
See also SPENDING POWER
Confederation at, **29:1**
Definition, **29:2**
Expression on
See EXPRESSION
Expropriation
See EXPROPRIATION
Federal power over, **6:8, 29:2, 29:5**
Federal property, application of provincial law, **29:2**
Indian lands
See INDIANS AND INDIAN LANDS
Natural resources agreements
See NATURAL RESOURCES AGREEMENTS
Ownership and legislative power, **28:3, 29:3**
Pollution on, **30:32**
Proprietary right, **29:2, 29:3, 30:1, 30:4, 30:16, 30:17, 30:23, 30:24, 31:15**
Provincial power over, **21:14, 29:2, 30:1**
Royalties, **29:3, 30:1, 30:16, 31:14, 31:15**
Taxation of, **29:3, 31:4, 31:16, 31:21 to 31:23**

PUBLIC SERVANTS
Liability of
See CROWN
Political activity by, **9:7, 15:20, 43:36**

PUNISHMENT
See CRIMINAL LAW, CRUEL AND UNUSUAL PUNISHMENT

PURPOSE OF LAW
Charter of Rights for, **36:13, 36:14**
Distribution of powers, for, **15:8, 36:13**

QUEBEC
Amending procedures, role in
See AMENDMENT OF CONSTITUTION
Amendment, role of
See AMENDMENT OF CONSTITUTION
Bill of rights
See QUEBEC CHARTER OF RIGHTS AND FREEDOMS
Boundaries, **2:7, 2:9**
Canada East
See CANADA EAST
Charlottetown Accord
See CHARLOTTETOWN ACCORD
Civil law, **2:5 to 2:7, 43:28**
Confederation, **2:5, 2:6**
Courts, language in, **56:4, 56:5, 56:9 to 56:13**
Crown in right of liability of
See CROWN
Defamation, **43:28**
Distinct society, **4:3, 4:15, 4:20, 5:4, 38:14**
Education language of (s. 23), **56:5, 56:19 to 56:24**
History, **2:5, 2:6**
House of Commons, representation in, **4:3, 5:4**
International relations, **11:13**
Interpreter, right to, **56:13**
Language guarantees (s. 133), **40:4, 56:4 to 56:16, 58:13**
Language policies, **4:3, 43:16, 43:22, 56:5**
Legislative Council, abolition, **4:19, 9:6, 12:10, 14:9**
Legislature language in, **56:4 to 56:8**

QUEBEC—Cont'd
Lower Canada
See LOWER CANADA
Meech Lake Constitutional Accord
See MEECH LAKE CONSTITUTIONAL ACCORD
Nation, **4:1**
Official language, **56:3, 56:14**
Pension plan
See QUEBEC PENSION PLAN
Responsible government, **9:2**
Right to vote in, **43:39, 45:2, 55:49**
Secession, **4:3, 4:20, 5:24 to 5:26, 15:28**
Shared-cost programmes, opting out, **6:5, 6:7, 6:10**
Sovereignty-association, **4:3, 4:20, 5:4, 5:24**
Special status
See SPECIAL STATUS
Supreme Court of Canada, judges from, **5:4, 8:3, 8:4, 8:14**
Tax agreements
See TAX AGREEMENTS
Treaty-making, **11:13**
United Province of Canada
See UNITED PROVINCE OF CANADA

QUEBEC ACT, 1774
Generally, **1:4, 2:6, 21:2**

QUEBEC CHARTER OF HUMAN RIGHTS AND FREEDOMS
Generally, **1:6, 34:4, 36:7, 39:8, 42:7, 42:10, 47:8, 47:12, 47:26, 56:4**

QUEBEC CHARTER OF THE FRENCH LANGUAGE
Generally, **56:5, 56:21**

QUEBEC PENSION PLAN
Generally, **6:7**

QUEEN
See also CROWN, HEAD OF STATE
Abolition of monarchy, **3:5, 4:16, 4:20, 9:24**
Amendments in relation to
See AMENDMENT OF CONSTITUTION
Canada head of state, **4:20, 9:3**
Commonwealth head of, **3:5, 9:23, 9:24**
Constitution references to, **1:2, 9:3**

QUEEN—Cont'd
Conventions limit powers, **1:10, 9:3**
See also RESPONSIBLE GOVERNMENT
Definition of Queen, **1:4, 9:3**
Disallowance of statutes
See DISALLOWANCE
Executive power, **1:2**
Governor General
appoints, **1:2, 3:1, 9:3**
delegates power to, **9:3, 11:2, 11:3**
Law-making power, lacks, **1:9**
Oath of allegiance to, **43:16**
Personal prerogatives, **1:9**
Royal assent to statutes
See ROYAL ASSENT
Royal style and titles, **3:1, 4:6, 9:3**
Senators role in appointment, **9:3**
Succession to throne, **1:4, 3:1, 9:3**

QUO WARRANTO
See REMEDY

RACE
See EQUALITY

RADIO
Content regulation, **22:18, 43:4**
Local broadcasting, **22:17**
Power over, **22:15, 22:16 to 22:18**
Technical regulation, **22:18**
Television similarity to, **22:16, 22:19**

RAILWAY
Federal power over, **18:16, 22:1, 22:7 to 22:9, 22:11**
Labour relations, **21:11, 22:7**
Local railways, **22:1, 22:2, 22:7 to 22:9, 22:13**
Provincial power over, **15:20, 22:1, 22:11**

RAPE-SHIELD LAW
See EVIDENCE

READING DOWN
Generally, **10:18, 15:15, 15:16, 36:17, 40:2, 40:7**

READING IN
Generally, **37:13, 40:2, 40:4, 40:6, 40:7, 40:9, 47:16 to 47:18**

REASONABLE
Bail
See BAIL
Compensation for opting out of amendments
See AMENDMENT OF CONSTITUTION
Delay in informing of charge
See DELAY
Limits
See LIMITATION CLAUSE (s. 1)
Residency requirement for social services, **46:3**
Search or seizure
See SEARCH OR SEIZURE
Time to be tried within
See TRIAL

RECEPTION
See ENGLISH LAW IN CANADA, FRENCH LAW IN CANADA

RECONSTRUCTION OF INVALID LAW
See also READING IN, SEVERANCE
Generally, **40:6**

RECORDS
See LITERATURE

REFERENCE
Advisory only, **7:15, 8:8, 8:11, 8:13**
Constitutionality, **7:15, 8:10**
Description, **8:8 to 8:12, 40:1**
Discretion not to answer, **1:10, 8:11**
Non-legal questions, of, **1:10, 8:11**
Parties, **59:13**
Proof of facts in, **8:12, 60:10**
Standing, **8:8, 8:9, 59:1**

REFERENDUM
Amendment by, **3:7, 4:23**
Australia for amendment, **4:5, 4:23**
Charlottetown Accord, for approval, **4:3, 4:23**
Conscription for approval, **4:23**
Expenditures, **43:38**
Law-making by
See INITIATIVE AND REFERENDUM
Local option, **14:15**
Newfoundland, for entry, **2:12, 5:25**
Power to impose, **12:10**

REFERENDUM—Cont'd
Prohibition, for approval, **4:23**
Right to vote in, **43:39, 45:2, 55:49**
Scotland, for secession, **5:24**
Sovereignty, for approval (1995), **4:3, 4:20, 5:24, 5:25**
Sovereignty-association for approval (1980), **4:3, 4:20, 5:24, 5:25**
Taxes for approval, **12:10**
Western Australia, for secession, **5:25**

REFERENTIAL LEGISLATION
See INTER-DELEGATION

REFORM OF CONSTITUTION
See also AMENDMENT OF CONSTITUTION, PATRIATION
Generally, **4:20 to 4:23**

REFUGEE
See IMMIGRATION

REGION
Generally, **5:6, 6:10, 8:14, 9:10**

REGIONAL VETO
See AMENDMENT OF CONSTITUTION

RELIGION
Atheism, **42:3, 42:10**
Charter of Rights, **42:2 to 42:9**
Conscience, **41:3**
Corporation lacks, **37:2, 59:6**
Denominational school rights
See EDUCATION
Denominational schools, in, **42:9**
Discrimination on basis of
See EQUALITY
Hate speech, **36:23, 42:6**
Jehovah's Witnesses
See JEHOVAH'S WITNESSES
Municipality, in, **42:10**
Neutrality, public duty of, **42:8, 42:10**
Polygamy, **42:6**
Power over, **42:1**
Public schools, in, **36:5, 42:6, 42:8, 57:15**
Solemnization of marriage, **27:3, 42:11**
Sunday observance
See SUNDAY OBSERVANCE
Testimony behind veil, **36:23, 42:6**
Waiver of right, **37:24, 42:7**

REMEDY
Appeal from s. 24 application, **40:23**
Application for judicial review, **34:2, 40:1, 59:1**
Apprehended infringements of rights, for, **40:15**
Breach of Charter, for, **21:3, 36:29, 40:1 to 40:31**
Breach of Constitution, for, **1:9, 40:1 to 40:31**
Breach of convention, for, **1:9**
Certiorari, **34:2**
Constitutional tort, **40:17**
Costs
See COSTS
Court of competent jurisdiction, **40:2, 40:16**
Damages
See DAMAGES
Declaration
See DECLARATION
Dismissal of charge, **40:17**
Evidence, exclusion of
See EVIDENCE
Extraterritorial effect, **13:10**
Foreign court, issued by
See JUDGMENT, RECOGNITION OF
Habeas corpus, **34:2, 50:17, 53:5**
Illegal official action, for, **34:2**
Injunction, **34:2, 40:1, 40:16, 40:17**
extraterritorial effect, **13:10**
interlocutory, **13:10**
Judges, against, **37:11**
Judicial supervision of compliance, **36.4(e), 40:23, 56:25**
Mandamus, **34:2, 40:16**
Prohibition, **34:2, 40:16**
Prospective, **40:4, 55:48, 58:1**
Quashing conviction, **40:17**
Quo warranto, **34:2, 40:16**
Recovery of invalid tax, **58:8**
Reference
See REFERENCE
Release from custody, **50:17**
Restitution, **18:17, 58:6**
Retroactive, **40:4, 58:1**
Return of seized goods, **40:17**
Section 24(1) described, **40:11 to 40:25**
Standing
See STANDING

REMEDY—Cont'd
Stay of proceedings, **40:16, 40:17, 52:16, 58:2**
Suspended, **40:4, 58:1**
Trial unreasonably delayed, for, **52:16**
Unconstitutional law
See UNCONSTITUTIONAL LAW

REPATRIATION
See PATRIATION

REPEAL
Implied, **12:9, 35:5, 35:6**
Inoperative law contrasted, **16:10**
Manner and form restriction on, **12:10**
Protection from, **12:10**
Revival, **16:10**

REPUGNANCY
See IMPERIAL STATUTE, INCONSISTENCY

REPUTATION
See EXPRESSION

RESERVATION OF BILLS
Federal bills, **3:1, 9:3, 9:11**
Provincial bills, **3:1, 5:14, 9:3, 9:11**

RESIDENT
Corporation as, **37:5**
Discrimination against non-residents, **46:3**
Mobility rights of, **46:3, 46:4**
Occupations restricted to, **46:4**
Permanent resident, **37:5, 46:3**
Property right to hold, **46:5**
Social services, right to, **46:3**
Voting restricted to, **46:4**

RESIDUARY POWER
See also PEACE, ORDER, AND GOOD GOVERNMENT
Australia
See AUSTRALIA
Canada, **5:9, 5:11, 14:9, 15:26, 17:1**
United States
See UNITED STATES

RES JUDICATA
Generally, **8:13, 58:4, 58:5, 58:9**

RESPONSIBLE GOVERNMENT
Cabinet
See CABINET

RESPONSIBLE GOVERNMENT —Cont'd
Canada, **1:2**
Coalition government, **9:9, 9:20**
Conventional basis, **1:2, 1:4, 1:9, 1:10, 5:14, 9:3**
Defeat of government
See DEFEAT OF GOVERNMENT
Description, **9:1 to 9:24**
Elections under, **9:19**
Governor General
See GOVERNOR GENERAL
Head of state, role of
See HEAD OF STATE
History, **1:2, 1:9, 1:10, 2:6, 9:2**
Lieutenant Governor
See LIEUTENANT GOVERNOR
Minister
See MINISTER
Minority government, **9:9, 9:20**
Premier
See PREMIER
Prime Minister
See PRIME MINISTER
Queen
See QUEEN
Separation of powers
See SEPARATION OF POWERS
United States compared, **1:9**
Withdrawal of confidence
See DEFEAT OF GOVERNMENT

RESTITUTION
See REMEDY

RETROACTIVE LAW
Charter of Rights, retroactive effect
See CHARTER OF RIGHTS
Declaratory law, **51:26**
Judicial decision, created by, **58:1**
Statutes, **7:3, 15:28, 28:2, 34:2, 36:5, 36:30, 51:26, 51:31**

RETROSPECTIVE LAW
See RETROACTIVE LAW

REVENUE
See FINANCIAL ARRANGEMENTS, SHARED-COST PROGRAMMES, TAX AGREEMENTS, TAXATION

REVERSE DISCRIMINATION
See EQUALITY

REVERSE ONUS CLAUSE
See INNOCENCE, PRESUMPTION OF

REVOLUTION
See also SECESSION
Generally, **5:26**

RIPE ISSUE
Generally, **8:11, 59:10**

RIVERS
Dam, **30:28**
Fisheries
See FISHERIES
Floating of logs, **30:19, 30:20**
Hydro-electricity
See ELECTRICITY
International or interprovincial, **30:32**
Obstruction, **30:19, 30:21**
Pollution, **30:32**

ROADS
Billboards alongside, **43:24**
Breath sample, demand for, **18:19, 48:30, 50:3, 51:3, 51:9, 51:13, 51:14**
Bus line
See transport regulation
Concurrent powers over, **15:7, 15:25**
Dangerous driving, **47:17, 47:18, 47:20**
Driver's licence
production, **48:18**
religious exemption, **38:22, 42:6, 55:40**
suspension, **16:3 to 16:5, 18:2, 18:16, 47:9, 51:3**
Expression on, **43:3, 43:24**
Federal power over, **15:7**
Inter-delegation, **14:13, 22:5**
Offences, **18:16**
Paramountcy, **16:5**
Power over, **15:24, 18:16, 18:19, 21:4, 22:11**
Random stops by police, **48:22, 49:3 to 49:8, 50:3**
Speed-limiter requirement, **38:25**
Tolls payment of, **16:3, 16:4**
Transport regulation, **14:13, 22:5, 22:7, 22:11, 22:13 to 22:15**
Trucking
See transport regulation
Vehicle search of, **48:26**

ROOSEVELT, PRESIDENT F.D.
Court-packing plan, **36:5**

ROWELL-SIROIS REPORT
Generally, **6:2, 6:3, 6:6**

ROYAL ASSENT
Amendments in relation to
See AMENDMENT OF CONSTITUTION
Disallowance
See DISALLOWANCE
Legislative power over, **4:16**
Procedure, **4:6, 4:16**
Requirement, **1:12, 9:3, 9:11, 12:10, 14:8, 14:9**
Reservation
See RESERVATION OF BILLS
Royal consent to affect prerogative contrasted, **1:9, 9:11**
Royal recommendation for money bill contrasted, **9:11**
Withholding, **1:10, 1:13, 5:14, 9:11**

ROYAL CANADIAN MOUNTED POLICE
See POLICE

ROYAL PREROGATIVE
See PREROGATIVE POWER

ROYAL PROCLAMATION, 1763
Generally, **1:4, 2:6, 28:1, 28:3, 28:21, 28:40**

ROYAL STYLE AND TITLES
See QUEEN

RULE
See DELEGATED LEGISLATION

RULE OF LAW
Generally, **1:1, 7:16, 15:28, 36:11, 40:6, 40:9, 58:4, 58:9, 59:2**

RUPERT'S LAND
Generally, **2:9**

RUSSELL P.H.
Canadian Bill of Rights, on, **35:9**
Judicial independence, on, **7:4**

SASKATCHEWAN
Creation, **1:6, 2:9**
Crown in right of, liability of
See CROWN
Language rights in, **12:10, 40:4, 58:11**

SASKATCHEWAN—Cont'd
Natural resources agreement
See NATURAL RESOURCES AGREEMENTS
Reception of law, **2:2, 2:9**
Responsible government, **9:2**

SASKATCHEWAN ACT
Generally, **1:6, 2:9, 5:4, 12:9, 56:17 to 56:25**

SASKATCHEWAN BILL OF RIGHTS
Generally, **1:6, 34:4**

SASKATCHEWAN HUMAN RIGHTS CODE
Generally, **34:4**

SAVINGS BANKS
See BANKING

SCHOOLS
See EDUCATION

SCOTLAND
Generally, **2:2, 2:13, 5:1, 5:3, 5:20, 5:24, 12:1, 14:2**

SCOTT, S.A.
Initiative and referendum, on, **14:8**

SCOTT F.R.
Crown liability, on, **10:12**
Treaty power, on, **11:12**

SEARCH OR SEIZURE
Abandoned property, **48:15**
Airport, in, **48:5 to 48:12, 48:28, 50:3**
Arrest incident to
See ARREST
Bodily samples, **48:15, 48:21, 48:23, 48:26**
Border at, **48:28, 50:3**
Bus station, in, **41:11, 48:5 to 48:12, 48:28**
Common law powers, **34:2, 48:2, 48:5 to 48:12**
Computer, **41:11, 48:5 to 48:12, 48:15**
shared computer, **48:27**
Consensual, **37:19, 48:35**
Counsel, right to
See COUNSEL RIGHT TO
Description, **48:2 to 48:37**
Documents, production, **37:14, 48:18 to 48:20**

SEARCH OR SEIZURE—Cont'd
Dwellinghouse of, **48:21**
Electricity consumption, **48:5 to 48:12**
Electronic surveillance, **41.8(b), 41:11, 48:16, 48:17**
Evidence admissibility, **41:4, 41:8, 41:9**
Expropriation not seizure, **48:4**
Foreign documents, **37:14, 48:20**
Garbage, **48:15**
Genital swab, **48:23**
Government records, **48:5 to 48:12**
Hospital records, **48:5 to 48:12**
Illegal, **48:34**
Investigative detention, incident to, **48:24, 49:3 to 49:8, 50:2**
Law office, of, **48:31**
Persons, of, **48:4, 48:21, 48:23, 49:1**
Plain view, **48:3, 48:14, 49:3 to 49:8**
Pornography, **48:5 to 48:12**
Press premises, of, **43:17**
Preventative, **48:32**
Prisons, in, **48:22, 55:27, 55:41**
Private person, by, **48:17**
Public buildings, on entry, **48:29**
Reasonable expectation of privacy, **48:5 to 48:12**
Regulatory inspections, **47:31, 48:21 to 48:35**
Rented locker, **48:5 to 48:12**
Return of goods seized, **40:17, 48:37**
Safety (or protective) search, **48:25**
Schools in, **41:11, 48:5 to 48:12, 48:22, 48:27, 50:3**
Search defined, **48:4 to 48:15**
Securing of premises, **41:9**
Security guard, by, **37:13, 48:5 to 48:12**
Seizure defined, **48:4 to 48:15**
Smell as search, **41:9, 48:5 to 48:12, 48:14, 48:21**
Sniff by dog as search, **41:11, 48:5 to 48:12, 48:14, 48:24, 48:27, 48:28, 49:3 to 49:8, 57:18**
Solicitor-client privilege
See EVIDENCE
Strip search, **48:26**
Telephone, **48:4 to 48:15, 48:23**
Text messages, **48:5 to 48:12**
Thermal imaging, by, **48:5 to 48:12, 48:14**
Unreasonable, **48:21 to 48:35**

SEARCH OR SEIZURE—Cont'd
Vehicle, of, **48:26, 49:3 to 49:8**
Warrant, quashing, **40:17**
Warrant, requirement of, **40:6, 48:3, 48:21 to 48:35**
Warrant, sealing order, **43:32**
Wiretap
See electronic surveillance
Writ of assistance, **41:11, 48:3, 48:33**

SECESSION
See also REVOLUTION
Amendment, by, **5:25**
Confederacy's attempt, **5:25**
Nova Scotia's attempt, **5:25**
Power of, **5:24 to 5:26**
Quebec
See QUEBEC
Scotland's attempt, **5:24**
Western Australia's attempt, **5:25**

SECURITIES REGULATION
Cooperative, **5:27, 20:4, 21:16**
National, **20:4, 21:16**
Paramountcy, **16:3, 16:5, 16:7**
Power over, **15:7, 15:24, 18:2, 18:16, 18:19, 20:4, 21:15, 21:16, 23:6, 23:7, 29:4, 46:13**
Provincial disability, **21:15, 23:7**
United States, **21:16**

SECURITY OF THE PERSON
Generally, **47:12, 47:32 to 47:37**

SECURITY SERVICE
Generally, **19:12**

SEIZURE
See SEARCH OR SEIZURE

SELF-INCRIMINATION
See also COMPELLABILITY OF ACCUSED
Generally, **34:2, 34:6, 47:15, 47:31, 48:15, 51:7, 54:1 to 54:11**

SENATE
See also FEDERAL PARLIAMENT
Abolition, **4:16, 12:10, 14:9**
Age qualification, **55:33**
Amendments in relation to
See AMENDMENT OF CONSTITUTION
Appointment of senators, **9:3, 9:10, 9:22**

SENATE—Cont'd
Australia compare, **9:10**
Candidate, right to be, **45:6**
Consultative elections, **4:14, 9:10**
Defeat of government in, **9:7**
Description, **9:10**
Money bill
See FEDERAL PARLIAMENT
Powers, **9:10**
Privileges, **7:11**
Property qualifications, **4:18**
Reference to Supreme Court, **8:8**
Reform, **4:14, 4:22, 9:10**
Representation by region, **2:7, 5:6, 9:10**
Retirement, **55:33**
Term limits, **4:14, 4:18, 9:10**
United States, compare, **9:10**

SENTENCE
See CRIMINAL LAW

SEPARABILITY
See SEVERANCE

SEPARATION
See SECESSION

SEPARATION OF POWERS
Generally, **7:15, 8:10, 9:12, 14:5**

SERVICE EX JURIS
Generally, **13:10, 13:11**

SEVERANCE
See also READING DOWN, READING IN
Consistent from inconsistent laws, **16:7, 16:10**
Valid from invalid laws, **15:14, 36:16, 37:13, 38:18, 40:2, 40:4 to 40:6, 40:9, 42:6, 47:16 to 47:18**

SEX
See EQUALITY

SEXUAL ORIENTATION
See EQUALITY

SHARED-COST PROGRAMMES
Canada Assistance Plan
See CANADA ASSISTANCE PLAN
Canada Health Act
See HEALTH

SHARED-COST PROGRAMMES —Cont'd
Canada Health and Social Transfer
See CANADA HEALTH AND SOCIAL TRANSFER
Canada Pension Plan
See CANADA PENSION PLAN
Conditional grant as contribution, **6:5, 6:7, 6:8**
Description, **6:7, 6:8, 6:10**
Education, **6:5, 6:7, 6:10**
Financial arrangements
See FINANCIAL ARRANGEMENTS
Health services, **6:5, 6:7, 6:8, 6:10, 17:7, 18:6**
Legal aid, **50:15**
Opting out, **6:5, 6:7, 6:8, 6:10**
Policing
See POLICE
Quebec Pension Plan
See QUEBEC PENSION PLAN
Spending power
See SPENDING POWER
Standing to challenge, **36:12**
Tax agreements
See TAX AGREEMENTS
Tax points as contribution, **6:5, 6:10**

SHIPPING
See NAVIGATION AND SHIPPING

SILENCE RIGHT TO
See FUNDAMENTAL JUSTICE

SIMEON R.E.B.
Federalism, on, **15:11**
Federal-provincial diplomacy, on, **5:27**

SINGLING OUT
Generally, **10:20, 15:6, 15:20, 23:7, 23:8, 28:2, 28:8, 28:14, 31:23**

SITUS
Aircraft operations, **31:18**
Bank account, **13:5**
Company shares, **31:20**
Debt, **13:5**
Insurance policy, **31:20**
Rules described, **31:19**

SLATTERY, B.
Independence, on, **3:9**

SMALLWOOD PREMIER J.R.
Generally, **10:9**

SMILEY D.V.
Executive federalism, on, **5:27**

SOCIAL ASSISTANCE
See WELFARE

SOCIAL CREDIT
Banking law, **15:6, 24:4**
Currency law, **24:4**
History, **5:8, 24:4**
Relief of debtors, **21:20**
Trade and commerce law, **20:4**

SOCIAL SECURITY
See HEALTH, PENSIONS, SHARED-COST PROGRAMMES, UNEMPLOYMENT INSURANCE, WELFARE

SOCIAL SERVICES
Residency requirements, **46:3**

SOLEMNIZATION OF MARRIAGE
See MARRIAGE

SOURCES OF LAW
Generally, **1:1 to 1:10**

SOUTH AFRICA
Devolution in, **5:3**

SOUTHERN RHODESIA
Unilateral declaration of independence, **5:26**

SOVEREIGNTY
See LEGISLATIVE POWER, SECESSION

SOVEREIGNTY-ASSOCIATION
See SECESSION

SPECIAL ADVOCATES
Generally, **36:9, 47:32**

SPECIAL STATUS
Generally, **4:2, 4:11, 4:21, 5:1, 5:4**

SPEECH
See EXPRESSION

SPENDING POWER
See also PUBLIC PROPERTY
Appropriation required
See APPROPRIATION

SPENDING POWER—Cont'd
Charlottetown Accord proposal, **4:3, 6:7, 6:8**
Description, **6:8, 28:7 to 28:12, 29:3**
Education, **57:4**
Extraterritorial capacity, **13:8**
Grants
See GRANTS
Health care, **32:2, 32:3**
Income support, **33:1, 33:3, 33:5**
Meech Lake proposal, **4:3, 6:7, 6:8**
Shared-cost programmes
See SHARED-COST PROGRAMMES
Taxation compared, **33:3, 33:5**
United States, **6:8**

SPORTING EVENTS
See THEATRE

STANDING
Attorney General
See ATTORNEY GENERAL
Corporation, **40:14, 47:4, 59:5, 59:6**
Declaration, for, **40:14, 59:2 to 59:6**
Defendant in criminal case, **40:14, 59:6**
Habeas corpus, for, **50:17**
Public interest, **59:5**
Reference
See REFERENCE
Requirement of, **1:10**
Scholars' briefs in U.S., **59:13**
Section 24(1), under, **40:1, 40:14**
Third party, **40:14, 50:17, 59:6**

STARE DECISIS
See PRECEDENT

STATE
See AUSTRALIA, CROWN, UNITED STATES

STATE ACTION
See AMERICAN BILL OF RIGHTS, CHARTER OF RIGHTS

STATUTE
Crown, binding on
See CROWN
Implied repeal
See REPEAL
Inconsistency between
See PARAMOUNTCY, REPEAL

STATUTE—Cont'd
Inoperative
See INOPERATIVE LAW
Interpretation
See STATUTORY INTERPRETATION
Judicial review
See JUDICIAL REVIEW OF LEGISLATION
Language of, **56:4 to 56:8**
Legislative history
See LEGISLATIVE HISTORY
Legislative power
See LEGISLATIVE POWER
Prerogative displacement by
See PREROGATIVE POWER
Repeal
See REPEAL

STATUTE OF WESTMINSTER
Australian constitution, exemption, **3:3**
British North America Act, exemption, **3:3, 3:4, 4:1**
Constitution of Canada, included in, **1:4**
Extraterritorial competence, **8:2, 13:2, 13:3**
History, **3:3, 4:1**
Imperial statutes power to repeal, **3:3, 8:2**
Newfoundland application to, **2:12, 3:3**
New Zealand constitution, exemption, **3:3**
Repugnancy abolition, **3:3, 3:4**
Royal style and titles, **3:1, 9:3**
Succession to throne, **3:1, 9:3**
United Kingdom, limitation of power, **3:3**

STATUTORY INTERPRETATION
See also INTERPRETATION OF CONSTITUTION
Canadian Bill of Rights and, **35:8**
Charter and, **37:12**
Civil libertarian values, **34:2**
Crown and, **10:13 to 10:15, 10:16 to 10:18**
Extraterritorial effect, presumption against, **13:2**
International law and
See INTERNATIONAL LAW
Legislative history
See LEGISLATIVE HISTORY
Manner and form contrasted, **12:10**
Paramountcy and, **16:3**

STATUTORY INTERPRETATION —Cont'd
Presumption of constitutionality, **15:5 to 15:13**
Privative clauses, avoidance by, **7:20, 34:2**
Reading down
See READING DOWN
Retroactive effect, presumption against, **51:26**
Statutory lien, **25:12**
Strict construction, **34:2**

STAY OF PROCEEDINGS
See REMEDY

STERILIZATION
See also INTERJURISDICTIONAL IMMUNITY
Generally, **15:18**

STRICT LIABILITY
See FUNDAMENTAL JUSTICE

SUBORDINATE LEGISLATION
See DELEGATED LEGISLATION

SUBSIDIARITY
Generally, **5:7, 16:2**

SUBSIDIES
See GRANTS

SUCCESSION
See PROPERTY

SUCCESSION TO THRONE
Generally, **3:1**

SUICIDE
Generally, **32:2, 47:12, 47:15, 53:2, 55:45**

SUNDAY OBSERVANCE
Freedom of religion, and, **40:8, 42:4, 42:5**
Inter-delegation, **14:17**
Power over, **14:17, 15:8, 18:11, 18:12, 21:8, 34:7, 42:1**

SUPPLY
See APPROPRIATION

SUPREMACY OF CONSTITUTION
See CONSTITUTION OF CANADA

SUPREME COURT OF CANADA
Abolition of appeal to, **8:5**

SUPREME COURT OF CANADA —Cont'd
Advisory opinions, **8:8 to 8:12**
Amendments affecting
See AMENDMENT OF CONSTITUTION
Appeals to Privy Council, **1:2, 5:15, 8:1, 8:2**
Appointment of judges, **1:12, 4:3, 8:1, 8:3, 8:4, 8:14**
Bias, **8:3, 8:4**
Chief Justice
See CHIEF JUSTICE OF CANADA
Civil law, authority over, **8:5, 8:14**
Composition, **1:12, 4:6, 4:16, 5:6, 5:15, 8:1, 8:3, 8:14**
Constitutional status, **1:4, 4:6, 4:14, 4:16, 8:1, 8:14**
Decision-making process, **8:3**
Establishment, **1:2, 7:10, 8:1**
Judicial review, power of, **5:20 to 5:22**
Jurisdiction, **5:15, 5:22, 7:1, 8:5 to 8:7**
Leave to appeal, **8:5 to 8:7, 58:4**
Opinion-writing practices, **8:5**
Original jurisdiction, **8:10**
Precedent in
See PRECEDENT
Provincial court, acting as, **13:9, 13:11, 13:14**
Provincial laws recognition, **8:5, 13:9**
References to
See REFERENCE
Reform, **4:23, 5:15, 5:22, 8:14**
Specialization within, **5:22, 8:14**
Split decisions, **8:3**
Statutory basis, **1:2, 1:4, 1:6, 5:15, 8:1, 8:14**
Uniformity of law, **5:15, 8:5**

SUPREME COURT OF UNITED KINDGOM
Establishment in 2005, **8:13**
Precedent in, **8:13**

SUSPENDING POWER
Generally, **1:9, 31:6, 31:7**

SWITZERLAND
Constitutional amendment, **4:23**
Federalism in, **5:9**

TAKING
See EXPROPRIATION

TAX AGREEMENTS
See also FINANCIAL ARRANGEMENTS, SHARED COST PROGRAMMES
Generally, **6:2 to 6:4**

TAXATION
Aircraft, **13:4, 15:18, 22:15, 31:18**
Audit powers, **47:31, 48:21 to 48:35**
Australia in
See AUSTRALIA
Banks, of
See BANKING
Business, **31:10**
Carbon tax, **31:14**
Civil penalty, **51:3**
Commercial charges distinguished, **31:15**
Concurrent powers over, **31:1**
Customs
See CUSTOMS DUTY
Death taxes, **6:2, 6:3, 14:5, 31.11(e), 31:13, 31:16, 31:18**
Definition of tax, **31:15, 31:16**
Delegation of power, **14:5, 31:1**
Direct tax
- Australia, **31:6, 31:12**
- definition, **31:6, 31:7**
- history, **6:2**
- power to levy, **5:9, 6:2 31:1**
- United States, **31:6**

Documents seizure, **47:31, 48:18 to 48:20, 48:21 to 48:35**
Double, **16:9, 31:1 to 31:5**
Employment insurance premiums, **14:5, 31:16, 33:2**
Estate tax
See death taxes
Excise
See EXCISE TAX
Export tax, **31:8, 31:14, 31:26**
Expropriation distinguished, **31:25**
Extraterritorial, **13:6, 31:8, 31:13, 31:17 to 31:20**
Federal-provincial sharing
See TAX AGREEMENTS
Freedom of interprovincial trade, **31:4**
Goods and services tax, **31:12**
History, **6:1 to 6:5**

TAXATION—Cont'd
Income tax
direct character, **31:9**
extraterritorial income, **31:18**
history, **6:2 to 6:5**
ministers, officials, judges, on, **31:22**
power to levy, **31:9**
Indirect tax
abortive amendment, **14:10**
definition, **31:6, 31:7**
history, **6:1, 6:2**
power to levy, **5:9, 31:3**
Inheritance tax
See death taxes
Insurance
See INSURANCE
Interjurisdictional immunity
See INTERJURISDICTIONAL IMMUNITY
Legislative authority required, **58:7**
Licence fees
See LICENSING
Marketing levies distinguished, **31:16**
Natural resources
See NATURAL RESOURCES
Persons within province, **31:18**
Pollution discouragement, **30:32**
Powers over, **31:1 to 31:28**
Probate fees, **14:5**
See also death taxes
Property, **31:11, 31:14, 31:19**
Public property
See PUBLIC PROPERTY
Regulatory charge distinguished, **31:11, 31:16, 31:25, 57:12**
Royalties
See NATURAL RESOURCES
Sales tax, **14:10, 15:10, 31:6, 31:12**
Situs of property
See SITUS
Spending power
See SPENDING POWER
Succession duty
See death taxes
Tariffs, **8:13, 20:3**
Transactions, **31:20**
Unconstitutional, recovery of, **31:24 to 31:27, 40:25, 58:6, 58:8, 59:19**
United States, in
See UNITED STATES

TAXATION—Cont'd
Value-added tax, **31:12**

TAX COURT OF CANADA
Generally, **7:12, 7:14**

TAX EXPENDITURES
Generally, **6:8**

TELEPHONE
Connecting systems, **22:22**
Federal power over, **15:18, 15:27, 22:5, 22:22**
Mobile network, **15:18, 22:22**
Provincial power over, **15:18, 22:22**
Search
See SEARCH OR SEIZURE
Wiretap
See SEARCH OR SEIZURE

TELEVISION
Cable television, **22:18, 22:20**
Closed-circuit, **22:20**
Content regulation, **22:18, 22:20, 43:4**
Local broadcasting, **22:20**
Local programmes, **22:20**
Pay television, **22:21**
Power over, **22:15, 22:16, 22:18, 22:19 to 22:21**
Provincial regulation, **15:18, 22:18, 22:20**
Radio similarity to, **22:16, 22:19**

TEMPERANCE
Concurrent powers, **15:7**
Local option, **14:17**
National binge theory, **17:7**
Paramountcy, **16:5**
Power over, **17:3, 17:6, 17:12**

TERMS OF UNION
See PROVINCES

TERRITORIAL LIMIT
See EXTRATERRITORIAL COMPETENCE

TERRITORIAL SEA
Generally, **13:4**

TERRITORIES
Admission to Canada, **1:5, 2:8 to 2:12**
Courts, **7:13**
Devolution of power to, **5:4, 14:4**
Natural resources
See NATURAL RESOURCES

TERRITORIES—Cont'd
Northwest Territories
See NORTHWEST TERRITORIES
Nunavut
See NUNAVUT
Policing, **19:9**
Power over, **2:9, 14:4, 14:7, 17:1, 30:6**
Prairie provinces, creation, **2:9**
Rupert's Land
See RUPERT'S LAND
Yukon Territory
See YUKON TERRITORY

TESTIMONY
See EVIDENCE

THEATRE
Generally, **22:24**

TOBACCO
See FOOD AND DRUGS

TORT
Constitutional torts, **37:13, 40:19**
Crown liability
See CROWN
Crown servant's liability
See CROWN
Defamation
See EXPRESSION
Extraterritorial tort, **13:10, 13:14**
Federal power over, **15:24, 18.9(a), 20:4**
Maritime law, **16:3, 22:12, 33:4**
Provincial power over, **5:7, 21:2**
Unconstitutional act as, **40:19, 58:4**
Workers' compensation
See WORKERS' COMPENSATION

TORTURE
Action for damages for, **35:7, 37:14, 47:15**
Convention against Torture, **36:20**
Cruel and unusual, **53:3**
Deportation to face, **11:6, 36:27, 37:14, 47:15**

TRADE AND COMMERCE
Australian commerce clause contrasted, **20:1**
Capital, mobility
See MOBILITY
Companies, incorporation, **23:1**

TRADE AND COMMERCE—Cont'd
Competition law
See COMPETITION
Customs duty, **20:2, 31:6, 31:25, 46:8**
Description, **20:1 to 20:5**
Export of goods, **13:5, 30:7**
Federal power over, **5:9, 5:11**
Foreign ownership, **46:5**
Freedom of interprovincial trade, **13:6, 31:4, 46:7 to 46:10**
General, **20:1, 20:4**
Importation of goods, **13:6, 20:3, 30:7**
Insurance
See INSURANCE
Interprovincial or international, **20:2**
Intraprovincial
See PROPERTY AND CIVIL RIGHTS
Labour relations
See LABOUR RELATIONS
Local
See PROPERTY AND CIVIL RIGHTS
Margarine
See MARGARINE
Marketing
See MARKETING
Property and civil rights, relation to, **15:23, 20:1, 21:3**
Trade mark, **20:4**
United States commerce clause contrasted, **5:9, 20:1**
United States free trade agreement, **11:12**
Wage and price controls, **20:4**

TRADEMARKS
Generally, **15:24, 18:8, 18:16, 20:4**

TRADE PRACTICES
See COMPETITION

TRADES
Generally, **21:9**

TRADE UNION
See LABOUR RELATIONS

TRAFFIC
See ROADS

TRANSFER PAYMENTS
See GRANTS

TRANSPORTATION AND COMMUNICATION
See also MOBILITY

TRANSPORTATION AND COMMUNICATION—Cont'd
Aeronautics
See AERONAUTICS
Bus line
See ROADS
Delegation of powers, **14:13, 46:9, 46:14**
Education
See EDUCATION
Electricity transmission
See ELECTRICITY
Films
See FILMS
Freight forwarding
See FREIGHT FORWARDING
Interjurisdictional immunity
See INTERJURISDICTIONAL IMMUNITY
Interprovincial works and undertakings, **22:2**
Labour relations, **21:11**
Literature
See LITERATURE
Mixed local and long-distance business, **22:5**
Pipeline
See PIPELINE
Postal service
See POSTAL SERVICE
Power over, **22:1 to 22:25**
Press
See EXPRESSION
Radio
See RADIO
Railway
See RAILWAY
Shipping
See NAVIGATION AND SHIPPING
Telephone
See TELEPHONE
Television
See TELEVISION
Theatre
See THEATRE
Trucking
See ROADS
Undertaking defined, **22:2, 22:10, 22:16**
United States, **22:1**
Work defined, **22:1**

TRANSPORTATION AND COMMUNICATION—Cont'd
Works for general advantage of Canada
See DECLARATORY POWER

TRAVEL
See MOBILITY

TREATMENT
See CRUEL AND UNUSUAL PUNISHMENT

TREATY
Aeronautics
See AERONAUTICS
Australia
See AUSTRALIA
Definition, **11:1**
Dispute resolution, **7:19, 11:6**
Federal state clause, **11:12**
Human rights treaties, **36:20**
Implementation, **11:6 to 11:9, 15:27, 17:2, 17:3, 17:7, 22:13 to 22:15, 22:16, 36:20**
Indians with
See NATIVE RIGHTS
Internal law, effect on, **11:6, 28:7**
North American Free Trade Agreement, **7:19, 11:6**
Power to make, **1:9, 3:1, 11:2, 11:13**
Power to withdraw, **11:5**
Procedure for making, **11:3 to 11:5**
Radio
See RADIO
Ratification, **11:5**
United States
See UNITED STATES
Withdrawal from, **11:5**

TREATY OF PARIS, 1763
Generally, **2:1, 2:6, 2:11**

TREATY OF VERSAILLES, 1919
Generally, **3:1**

TRENCHING
Generally, **15:5, 17:1**

TRIAL
See also FAIR HEARING
Appeal
See COURTS
Dangerous offender application, **51:2**

TRIAL—Cont'd
Evidence
See EVIDENCE
Fairness requirement, **41:8, 47:32 to 47:37, 50:15, 52:7**
Independence of jury, **7:7, 51:16, 51:23, 55:24**
Joint trial of provincial and criminal offences, **7:1**
Jurors selection of, **40:4, 51:23, 55:24**
Jury by, **7:7, 19:4, 37:2, 51:16, 51:19 to 51:25**
Presence of defendant, **37:15**
Public, **37:16, 37:17, 43:33, 51:13**
Reasonable time, within, **36:30, 40:4, 51:5, 52:1 to 52:17**
Testimony behind veil, **42:6, 46.8(f)**
Waiver of delay, **37:16, 37:21, 52:9**
Waiver of jury, **37:15, 37:22, 51:22**

TRUCKING
See ROADS

TRUDEAU, PRIME MINISTER P.E.
Role in 1982 amendments, **1:11, 4:2, 4:3, 36:1**
Spending power, on, **6:8**

TRUST COMPANY
Banking by, **24:3**
Incorporation, **23:4, 23:6, 24:3, 24:7**
Labour relations, **24:3**
Regulation, **23:4, 23:6, 24:3, 24:5**

ULTRA VIRES
See also JUDICIAL REVIEW OF LEGISLATION UNCONSTITUTIONAL LAW
Judicial review, basis of, **5:20, 5:21**

UNCONSTITUTIONAL LAW
Acts done under, **58:3**
Damages for, **40:17, 58:4**
Effect of, **1:10, 15:16, 40:1 to 40:10, 40:19, 40:25, 58:1 to 58:8, 59:18, 59:19**
Exclusion of judicial review
See PRIVATIVE CLAUSE
Judicial review
See JUDICIAL REVIEW OF LEGISLATION
Nullification, **40:1 to 40:10**

UNCONSTITUTIONAL LAW—Cont'd
Reading down
See READING DOWN
Reading in
See READING IN
Severance
See SEVERANCE
Temporary validity, **36:10, 40:2, 40:4, 40:6, 40:9, 58:1, 58:8**

UNDERTAKING
See TRANSPORTATION AND COMMUNICATION

UNEMPLOYMENT INSURANCE
Age-65 bar, **40:5, 55:44**
Delegation of power over, **14:10**
History of power, **33:2**
Job-creation measures, **33:2**
Maternity benefits, **15:27**
Power over, **4:20, 14:10, 17:1, 17:7, 21:6, 21:10, 33:1, 33:2**
Premiums as taxes, **14:5, 31:16, 33:2**

UNIFORMITY OF LAW
Common law, **2:2 to 2:4**
Federal law, **2:7, 2:9, 14:16, 17:4, 55:49**

UNION
See CONFEDERATION, UNITED STATES

UNION ACT, 1840
Generally, **1:4, 2:6**

UNITARY STATE
Generally, **5:1, 5:3, 5:20, 11:7, 12:1**

UNITED KINGDOM
Breaks in legal continuity, **5:26**
Civil liberties, **34:2**
Constitution, **1:2, 5:3, 5:19, 5:20**
Crown in right of liability of
See CROWN
Definition, **2:2, 2:13**
Delegation, **14:2**
Dismissal of Prime Minister, **9:18**
EU, exit from, **11:5**
European Convention on Human Rights, **5:20, 12:1**
Judicial review, **5:20, 12:1**
Parliamentary sovereignty
See UNITED KINGDOM PARLIAMENT

UNITED KINGDOM—Cont'd
Privy Council, **8:2, 9:5**
Responsible government, **9:2**
Treaty-implementation, **11:7**
Unitary state, **3:3, 5:1 to 5:7, 5:19, 5:20**

UNITED KINGDOM PARLIAMENT
See also IMPERIAL PARLIAMENT
Delegation by, **5:1, 5:3, 5:20, 12:1, 14:2**
Extraterritorial competence, **13:1, 13:2**
Manner and form rules, **12:10**
Sovereignty, **12:1**

UNITED NATIONS
Generally, **3:1**

UNITED PROVINCE OF CANADA
Generally, **2:6, 2:7, 5:3, 9:2**

UNITED STATES
Amendment of constitution, **4:5**
Ancillary power, **15:24**
Anti-trust, **18:10**
Articles of confederation, **5:2, 5:26**
Banking, **5:9**
Bill of rights
See AMERICAN BILL OF RIGHTS
Brandeis brief, **8:12, 60:9**
Commerce clause, **5:9, 20:1, 21:6, 21:10, 22:1**
Common law, **2:2, 8:5**
Compensation for property taken, **29:8**
Competition law, **18:10**
Concurrent powers, **15:25**
Congress
enforcement of civil rights, **5:16, 5:20**
regional accommodation, **5:27**
Constitution, **1:2, 3:7, 5:3, 5:26**
Convention in, **1:10**
Cooperative federalism, **6:10**
Criminal law, **5:9, 18:1, 19:15**
Delegation, **14:5, 14:9**
Double jeopardy, **16:8**
Electoral college, **1:10**
Enumerated powers, **15:4, 15:23, 15:24, 20:1**
Equal protection
See AMERICAN BILL OF RIGHTS
Equal rights amendment, **55:43**
Ex post facto laws, **36:5, 51:26, 51:31**
Extraterritorial competence, **13:3, 13:10, 13:11, 13:14**

UNITED STATES—Cont'd
Federal court jurisdiction, **7:11, 8:5, 8:10**
Federalism
See FEDERALISM
Financial arrangements, **6:10**
Free trade with Canada, **11:12**
Full faith and credit, **13:9, 13:11, 27:1**
Inconsistent laws, **15:25, 16:1, 16:5**
Insurance, **21:6**
Interjurisdictional immunity, **31:24, 31:27**
Judges appointment, **7:2, 8:14**
Judicial review, **5:20, 5:21**
Labour relations, **21:10**
Marketing, **21:12 to 21:14**
Marriage and divorce, **5:9, 27:1**
Motion to suppress evidence, **40:17**
National securities regulator, **20:4**
Obscenity, **43:29**
Offshore jurisdiction, **30:11, 30:14**
Overbreadth, **47:24**
Paramountcy, **15:25, 16:1, 16:5**
Parliamentary sovereignty in, **12:9**
Penitentiaries, **5:9**
Police power, **21:1**
President, **9:1, 9:6, 9:12, 14:8**
Religion, freedom of, **42:2, 42:4**
Residuary power, **5:9, 15:24, 15:25**
Responsible government not adopted, **9:2, 9:23**
Retroactive laws, **36:5, 51:26, 51:31**
Same-sex marriage, **55:48, 60:5**
Secession of states
See SECESSION
Securities regulation, **21:15, 21:16**
Senate, **9:10**
Separation of powers, **7:15, 8:10, 9:12**
Severance clause, **15:14**
Spending power, **6:8**
Supremacy clause, **16:1**
Supreme Court of United States
advisory opinions, **7:15, 8:10**
appointment of judges, **8:14**
evidence in, **60:9**
jurisdiction, **8:5, 8:6**
opinion-writing practice, **8:4**
precedent in, **2:2**
scholars' briefs, **59:13**
Taxation, **31:6, 31:27, 33.13(d)**
Territorial competence of states, **13:3, 13:10, 13:11, 13:14**

UNITED STATES—Cont'd
Transportation and communication, **22:1**
Treaty power, **11:5, 11:6, 11:8, 11:12**

UNIVERSAL DECLARATION OF HUMAN RIGHTS
Generally, **35:1**

UNIVERSITIES
See also EDUCATION
Charter application to, **37:10**
Grants to, **6:5**
Mandatory retirement in, **55:44**
Regulation of, **57:1**

UNWRITTEN RULES
See CONSTITUTION, CONVENTION, RESPONSIBLE GOVERNMENT, USAGE

UPPER CANADA
See also CANADA WEST, ONTARIO, UNITED PROVINCE OF CANADA
Generally, **2:6, 2:7, 5:4, 9:2**

UPPER HOUSE
See LEGISLATIVE COUNCIL, SENATE

URANIUM
See NATURAL RESOURCES

USAGE
Generally, **1:12**

UTILITARIANISM
Generally, **38:2**

VAGUE LAW
Federalism, **12:2, 14:7, 15:26**
Section 1, **38:9, 43:29**
Section 7, **47:20, 47:27 to 47:29**

VALIDITY OF LAW
See JUDICIAL REVIEW OF LEGISLATION

VETO
See DISALLOWANCE, RESERVATION OF BILLS, ROYAL ASSENT

VICTORIA CHARTER
Generally, **4:2, 4:15, 5:6**

VITAL PART OF UNDERTAKING
Generally, **15:18**

VOTE
See ELECTIONS

WAGE AND PRICE CONTROL
See PEACE, ORDER, AND GOOD GOVERNMENT

WAIVER
Contract by, **37:24**
Delay in trial, of, **37:16, 37:21, 52:9**
Expression, **37:24**
Forfeiture distinguished, **37:15, 37:17, 37:22**
Mandatory retirement, **37:24**
Paramountcy of, **14:17, 16:6**
Presumption of innocence, of, **37:16, 37:17, 51:17**
Religious practice, **37:24, 42:7**
Rights generally, of, **37:15 to 37:24**
Right to counsel, of, **37:15, 37:20, 50:13**
Right to interpreter, **37:23, 56:13**
Right to jury trial, of, **37:15, 37:16, 37:22, 51:22**
Right to silence, **37:18**
Third-party consent, **37:19, 48:5 to 48:12**
Unreasonable search and seizure, **37:19, 48:5 to 48:12**

WALES
Generally, **2:13, 5:1, 5:3, 5:20, 12:1, 14:2**

WAR
See also EMERGENCY, PEACE, ORDER, AND GOOD GOVERNMENT
Crimes, **47:19, 51:26, 53:7**
Declaration of, **1:9, 3:1**
Extension of legislative bodies, **45:7**
War Measures Act
See WAR MEASURES ACT

WAR MEASURES ACT
Canadian Bill of Rights, exemption from, **35:3**
Charter of Rights, no exemption from, **38:32**
Conditional on proclamation, **14:15**
Delegation in, **14:4**
Deportation under, **17:8**
F.L.Q. crisis, **17:9**
Labour relations under, **21:10, 21:11**
Price control under, **17:8**
Rent control under, **17:8**

WAR MEASURES ACT—Cont'd
Validity, **17:8**

WARREN, CHIEF JUSTICE EARL
Influence, **36:5**

WATER
Boundaries of provinces
See BOUNDARIES OF PROVINCES
Canada Water Act, **30:32**
Continental shelf
See CONTINENTAL SHELF
Fisheries
See FISHERIES
Hydro-electricity
See ELECTRICITY
Natural resources
See NATURAL RESOURCES
Navigation and shipping
See NAVIGATION AND SHIPPING
Pollution
See ENVIRONMENT
Rivers
See RIVERS
Territorial sea
See TERRITORIAL SEA

WATERTIGHT COMPARTMENTS
Generally, **6:8, 11:11, 15:27**

WATSON, LORD
Generally, **5:11, 5:21**

WEGENAST F.W.
Incorporation power, on, **23:3**

WEILER PAUL C.
Power of override, on, **39:8**
Surreptitious bill of rights, on, **15:2**

WEINRIB L.E.
Charter compliance cost of, on, **38:16**

WELFARE
Canada Assistance Plan, **6:7, 6:8, 33:5**
Powers over, **33:5**
Workfare, **33:5, 47:12, 55:32**

WESTERN AUSTRALIA
Secession attempt, **5:25**

WESTERN PROVINCES
Alberta
See ALBERTA

WESTERN PROVINCES—Cont'd
British Columbia
See BRITISH COLUMBIA
Manitoba
See MANITOBA
Regional grievances, **4:20**
Saskatchewan
See SASKATCHEWAN

WHEARE, K.C.
Federalism on, **5:1, 5:9**

WHITLAM PRIME MINISTER G.
Denials of supply to, **9:10, 9:18**
Dismissal, **9:10, 9:18**

WHYTE, J.D.
Security of the person, on, **47:12**

WIRETAP
See SEARCH OR SEIZURE

WITNESS
See EVIDENCE

WORK, RIGHT TO
See LABOUR RELATIONS

WORKERS' COMPENSATION
Chronic pain, **33:4, 55:45**
Federal delegation to provinces, **14:12 to 14:14, 33:4**
Jurisdiction over, **33:4**
Maritime law and, **16:4, 22:12, 33:4**
Railway and, **15:20, 33:4**

WORKS
See also TRANSPORTATION AND COMMUNICATION
Defined, **22:2, 22:10**
For the general advantage of Canada
See DECLARATORY POWER
Local
See LOCAL WORKS

WRIT OF ASSISTANCE
See SEARCH OR SEIZURE

YOUNG OFFENDERS
Generally, **7:16, 7:19, 15:24, 16:4, 18:15, 19:4, 19:13, 27:2, 47:15**

YUKON TERRITORY
Courts, **7:13**
Creation, **2:9**
Devolution, **5:3, 14:4**

YUKON TERRITORY—Cont'd
Federal power over
See TERRITORIES

ZIEGEL, J.S.
Incorporation power, on, **23:3**

ZIMBABWE
Generally, **5:26**

ZONING
See PROPERTY